150   155   160   165   170   175

Guadalcanal   Malaita

S. Cristobal

Sta. Cruz
Is.
(Br.)

10

Cooktown

Cairns

Coral Sea

artle
rere
611

nsville

Vanuatu

15

Great Barrier Reef

Mackay

Chesterfield Is.
(Fr.)

AND

Divide

Mt. Table
Top
823
Mackenzie

Mt. Morgan

Rockhampton

Loyalty
Is.
(Fr.)

New
Caledonia
(Fr.)

20

raka

Bundaberg

Charleville

Maryborough

Warrego

Cunnamulla

Toowoomba   Brisbane

Dirranbandi

Gold Coast

Barwon

PACIFIC   OCEAN

Walgett

Grafton

New England Ra.

25

Bourke

SOUTH

Round Mt.
1615

Tamworth

Dubbo   Cessnock   Maitland

Lord Howe I.
(N.S.W.)

ALES

Bathurst

Newcastle
SYDNEY

Great Divide

Wagga
Wagga

Wollongong

Canberra
AUST. CAP. TERR.

30

bury

Mt. Kosciusko
2230

RIA

Australian
Alps

MELBOURNE

loe   Traralgon

North C.

Tasman   Sea

ss Strait   Flinders I.

35

Launceston

North
Island   Auckland

Hamilton

Ossa
1617   Hobart

New Plymouth

Rotorua

Wanganui

Napier

South East C

Nelson   Palmerston N.

Greymouth   Blenheim

Mt. Cook
3764   Southern Alps

Hutt
Wellington

Christchurch

Invercargill   Timaru

South

40

Stewart I.
S.W. Cape

Dunedin   Island   Chatham Is.

150   155   160   165   170   175   180

COLLINS
AUSTRALIAN
ENCYCLOPEDIA

COLLINS
AUSTRALIAN
ENCYCLOPEDIA

Editor
John Shaw

COLLINS, Sydney

in association with David Bateman Limited

First published 1984 by
William Collins Pty Ltd, Sydney

National Library of Australia
Cataloguing in Publication data:

Shaw, John
  The Collins Australian Encyclopedia

  Includes Index
  ISBN 0 00 217315-8

  1. Australia — Dictionaries and Encyclopedias

994' .003

Produced by David Bateman Ltd

Typeset in Plantin by Graphicraft, Hong Kong
and Typocrafters Ltd, Auckland

Printed by Everbest Printing Co. Ltd, Hong Kong

EDITORIAL STAFF

EDITOR   John H. Shaw MSc, MEd, FRGS

PRINCIPAL AUTHORS   J. Mark Howard MA, DipEd
                          Arthur Woods MA
                          Valma M. Howard MEc
                          Bruce Bluett BA, MEd

CONTRIBUTING AUTHORS   Patricia A. Brown MA (Music), DipLib
                          F. P. Dickson PhD
                          David Ellyard BSc(Hons), MEd
                          Peter Gerdes PhD
                          Tom Harwood
                          Kate F. Inglis BA
                          Robert Irving MArch, ARMTC, FRAIA
                          John P. Kennedy MSc, BSc, MAIAS
                          Patricia M. McDonald BEM, BSc, MEd, FMAA
                          Carmel J. Maguire BA, MA, FLAA
                          Hannah Middleton BA, PhD
                          David Millar MA(Hons)
                          John P. Morgan BE, ASTC, FSASM, FIEAust, MAus IMM, MAIME
                          Philip J. Schofield BSc, PhD
                          Truda M. Straede BSc, PhD
                          Ian Webster MD, BSc, FRACP
                          Patricia Willard BA, MLib, ALAA
                          Margaret Williams BA, PhD
                          Celia Winter-Irving

PUBLISHING DIRECTOR   Michael J. White

PRODUCTION EDITOR   Katherine Sayce BA(Hons)

PRODUCTION MANAGERS   Wendy Canning
                          Janet Bateman

ARTISTS   John Coate Palgrave BSc, IAEZ assisted by
                          Fiona Muat

EDITORIAL CONSULTANTS   Richard Appleton
                          Margaret Forde MA(Hons) Edin

Personal Acknowledgements Many people have assisted in a variety of ways to make the publication of this encyclopedia possible. Among them, particular mention must be made of my colleagues, the principal authors — Mark and Val Howard, Arthur Woods and Bruce Bluett — not only for the extensive writing they did, but for their wise counsel, generous aid and kindly forbearance over a period of almost seven years.

To my personal assistant over many years, Miss Helen Webb, I am deeply grateful for her untiring help; and to my professional colleagues Owen Munn, Christina Keogh, Catherine Marciniak and Richard Jones I express my sincere appreciation for their advice and co-operation in artistic and photographc work.

Picture Acknowledgements The acknowledgements for all black and white photographic material used in this encyclopedia appear alongside the photograph concerned; colour pictures are acknowledged on pages xii–xvi.

CONTENTS

PREFACE

The correct selection of material is very important in the compilation of a one-volume encyclopedia. Decisions about what to include and what not to include played an important part in the early planning of this book and have continued to be significant throughout the whole publication process. The result is a broad, yet representative coverage of topics in almost every field of knowledge: history and geography, literature and drama, politics and government, social and economic matters, theatre and music, native and introduced fauna and flora, sport and films, art and architecture, mineral and rural industries, science and agriculture. Of necessity, some entries are brief, but we hope they are clear and balanced carefully with the longer ones, and provide in one volume a convenient reference for people in all walks of life.

Many authors have contributed within their fields of expertise and it was left largely to them to decide how to treat their subject, thus providing the opportunity for subjective interpretations in some sections. The result is an encyclopedia which we think is lively as well as factual.

Entries are in alphabetical order using common rather than scientific names. (There is a separate glossary of scientific terms.) The index at the back of the book lists broad categories of subjects for readers who may be pursuing particular interests or lines of study.

The illustrations, both colour and monochrome, have been chosen for the practical contribution they make rather than for visual effect.

Biological Entries Within the encyclopedia the arrangement of the entries on plants and animals reflects their hierarchical classification. Information on beetles, for example, will be found under BEETLES, but characteristics which the beetles share with most other insects are discussed under INSECTS. Similarly, the insect entry refers to the ARTHROPODS, the phylum of animals of which the insects form one class. An outline of BIOLOGICAL CLASSIFICATION explains the various levels in the hierarchies for plants and animals.

A compromise has been made in the choice of names. With familiar groups such as KANGAROOS and BEETLES a common name has been used rather than the scientific name (Macropodoidea; Coleoptera) but with less familiar groups, such as the sea slugs, sea urchins and so on, the technical term (ECHINODERMS) has been used with ample cross-referencing. The scientific names of species and plants and animals have been used throughout but always with the most often used common name, when one exists.

The scientific names have been used because of their internationality and because many common names mean different things in different places — even within Australia. Unfortunately, even scientific names do tend to change as the groups to which the organisms belong become better known to science. Thus, unavoidably, some names will have changed by the time the book is published. This is particularly true, for example, of the marine fishes but will scarcely apply, if at all, to the birds. In the entries on birds, some names will be found to be marked thus★. This indicates that the species, genus or family so indicated is endemic to Australia, i.e. the bird(s) concerned is now restricted to Australia as a native animal though it may have had a wider distribution in the past.

Animals vary in size, even within a species. The dimensions given are therefore to be taken only as a guide. Usually a mean is given, but sometimes the maximum is recorded, or the range of a large sample, is provided.

Aborigines/Aboriginal Throughout the encyclopedia, the word 'Aboriginal' has been used adjectivally (for example, Aboriginal housing) or to describe one person (for example, Bennelong was an Aboriginal). The word 'Aborigines' has been used for the plural (for example, six Aborigines).

National Parks The source of the statistics for the areas of National Parks, and for the names of these parks, has been the publication edited by M. D. Hinchey, entitled *Nature Conservation Reserves in Australia (1980)*, Occasional Paper No. 5, published by the Australian National Parks and Wildlife Service, Canberra, 1981.

Just prior to publication of this encyclopedia, a new edition of *Nature Conservation Reserves in Australia (1983)* was published. It shows that a number of changes to our National Parks have been gazetted.

Alphabetical Organisation The alphabetical system used in this encyclopedia is one that considers only the first word of the (bold type) entry heading; only where the first words are identical in two or more entries are succeeding words considered. Thus, **Bank of New South Wales** precedes **Bankcard** and **Australia Party** precedes **Australian Alps.** It should also be noted that all entry headings beginning with **Mc** or **Mac** are treated as if they begin **Mac** and those beginning with **St** as **Saint.** Thus **McPherson Range** precedes **Macquarie Harbour,** and **St Arnaud** follows **sailing** and precedes **salamanders.**

Abbreviations Names of States and Territories are abbreviated as capital letters with no full stops, thus ACT (Australian Capital Territory), NSW (New South Wales), NT (Northern Territory), QLD (Queensland), SA (South Australia), TAS (Tasmania), VIC (Victoria) and WA (Western Australia). However, where the name of a State or Territory is part of a proper name, it is printed in full (for example, New South Wales Corps, not NSW Corps). Compass direction points are given in capital letters without hyphens or full stops (for example, NW, ESE, SSW) except when they immediately precede another abbreviation (for example, north-eastern NSW, not NE NSW) and when they are part of a proper name (for example, South Grafton, Southern Tablelands, not S Grafton, S Tablelands). Other abbreviations used are Mt and Mts (for Mount and Mountains) and Is (for Islands) where these words are not part of a cross-reference *(see below)*, and the standard ones for metric measures, such as mm (millimetres), cm (centimetres), ha (hectares) and ML (megalitres).

Cross-References The system of cross-referencing used throughout the encyclopedia, in order to direct the reader's attention to other relevant entries, is that the titles of other entries are place in small capital letters. Thus, within the entry on Harvey River WA, there is a mention of the Darling Range, which is placed in small capital letters — DARLING RANGE — to indicate that there is an entry on this subject which will give more detailed information. Also, at the end of some articles, there are cross-references listed as a guide to readers; for example, at the end of the entry on Singleton NSW there is a cross-reference written thus: *See also* Maitland; Muswellbrook.

Population Statistics The population figures throughout the encyclopedia for cities, towns and other urban units are statistics of urban centres and bounded localities (not of local government areas, nor of statistical divisions, unless specifically stated). The particular statistics were used because it was felt that they provided more realistic figures to indicate the relative sizes of urban agglomerations. The basic sources for these population data were the series, one for each State and Territory, under the general title *Census of Population and Housing, 30 June 1981 — Persons in Local Government Areas and Urban Centres,* published by the Australian Bureau of Statistics. In general, entries have been included in the encyclopedia for all urban centres with populations of over 2000, but some smaller centres are also included where they have unique features or where it was thought useful to have gazetteer-type entries on those towns.

The tables of population growth figures have been compiled from official publications of the Australian Bureau of Statistics (or of its predecessor, the Commonwealth Bureau of Census and Statistics). The 1981 statistics of State and Territory populations are figures of Estimated Resident Population (Preliminary); these are figures from a new official series of population estimates, compiled according to the place of usual residence of the population, by the Australian Bureau of Statistics; the two basic sources for these data are: *Estimated Resident Population, Australia, States and Territories, 30 June 1981, 1976 and 1971 (Preliminary),* Australian Bureau of Statistics, Catalogue No. 3217.0, Canberra, 31 March 1982; and *Estimated Resident Population by Sex and Age: States and Territories of Australia, June 1971 to June 1981,* Australian Bureau of Statistics, Catalogue No. 3201.0, Canberra, 23 August 1982.

References There are references listed for further reading at the end of many entries in the encyclopedia. These, it is hoped, will guide readers to some sources of more detailed information and encourage further investigation of relevant issues.

Among the general references which readers may find useful (and which have been used in preparing material for the encyclopedia) are: *Year Book Australia,* formerly called the *Official Yearbook of the Commonwealth of Australia,* published by the Bureau of Statistics, Canberra; *Atlas of Australian Resources,* published by the Department of National Development, Canberra; the various State Yearbooks and government statistical publications; and numerous journals and periodicals such as *The Australian Geographer,* published by the Geographical Society of New South Wales, the *Current Affairs Bulletin,* published by the Department of Adult Education, University of Sydney, and *Geo* Magazine, Sydney.

John H. Shaw
Editor

How to use the Encyclopedia

Here are sample entries from the main part of the encyclopedia showing the various aids provided to help the reader make the best possible use of the information.

emu Next to the ostrich, the emu, *Dromaius novaehollandiae* (2m long and 2m tall) of the family Dromaiidae,* is the largest of all BIRDS. It has a large bill, long, dark greyish-brown, down-like feathers and a white ruff; the sparsely feathered face and throat have a pale grey-blue skin. It is a swift-footed, flightless bird, able to run at a speed of about 50 kph; its powerful legs are also used for defence and for

Species endemic to Australia

Measurements quoted are metric

F

Fadden, Sir Arthur William (1895–1973) Politician and Prime Minister. Born in INGHAM in QLD, he worked first in canefields and a sugar mill, then joined the service of the MACKAY Town Council and rose to the position of Town Clerk. Meanwhile, he had been studying accountancy, and in 1918 opened his own business as a public accountant in TOWNSVILLE and BRISBANE. He was a Country Party member of the QLD Legislative Assembly from 1932 to 1935 and of the federal House of Representatives from 1936 to 1958, during which time he held a number of Cabinet posts, most notably that of Treasurer (1940–41, 1949–58). He became leader of the Country Party in the Commonwealth Parliament in 1941, was Prime Minister for about seven weeks after the resignation of Robert MENZIES in 1941, and was deputy Prime Minister from 1949 until his retirement in 1958.
Further reading: Fadden, A. W. *They Called Me Artie.* Jacaranda, Milton QLD, 1969.

States abbreviated to capital letters

Denotes cross-reference to subject covered elsewhere in the encyclopedia

Reader can research subject further by referring to books mentioned; publisher, author and year of publication listed

mushrooms *see* agriculture; fungi

music This article provides an outline of the history of music in Australia.
Aboriginal music Tribal music of the Australian Aborigines had existed for thousands of years in Australia prior to the arrival of Europeans. The early white settlers failed to understand or assess the sacred, semi-sacred and secular music of the Aborigines they encountered, although in the earlier half of the 19th century a few composers did try to come to terms with this music by attempting to assimilate it into western-style songs and choral works. Little further interest was taken until the appearance of John ANTILL's ballet score *Corroboree* in the 1940s, while more recently George DREYFUS has written a *Sextet for Didjeridu and Wind Quintet*. However, the rhythmic complexity of much Australian Aboriginal music is such that it does not blend

Subject covered under another main heading

Sub-headings under main entries

Titles of books, music, etc. in italics

How to use the Subject Index

The subject index at the end of the encyclopedia lists a wide range of general topics such as Arts, History, Natural History, Politics and Politicians, in some cases with sub-headings, e.g., Music, Birds, etc. Under these headings are grouped the encyclopedia entries which relate to them, together with the appropriate page numbers.

By referring to this, and following up the cross-references in the main text, the reader can find all the relevant information for any particular line of research. Numerals in *italics* refer to colour illustrations.

Major articles on a particular topic are indicated by an †.

A sample from the index is shown below.

LIST OF COLOUR PAGES AND MAPS
WITH ACKNOWLEDGEMENTS

xiii

A

abalones *see* gastropods

ABC *see* Australian Broadcasting Corporation

Aborigines The Aborigines have been native to Australia for perhaps longer than 40 000 years. Most of their history during this long period can be deduced only from archaeological findings, from the conclusions of other scientific research, and from their own customs and oral traditions; no written record of them was made before European explorers first visited the continent early in the 17th century. However, research indicates the existence, up to that time, of a society whose life-style had been stable for a very long period, and which was integrated with the natural environment to a remarkable degree. They evidently had a complex and rich culture, a sufficient and healthy diet, a great deal of leisure, habits of co-operation and sharing, and a deep and strong religious life.

Archaeological records The oldest Aboriginal bones yet discovered were found by J.M. Bowler in 1974 at Lake Mungo in southwestern NSW, where erosion had revealed a 30 000-year-old burial; stone tools, freshwater food shells and cooking hearths, 5000 years older, were found in the same area. On the Upper Swan river, near Perth, human occupation also dates from around 38 000 years ago. Sites excavated in northern Australia are younger, but this is probably because the oldest are submerged beneath the Arafura sea. Around 20 000 years ago, during the ice age, sea level was over 120 metres below its present level. It was during this period when Bass Strait was dry land, that Aborigines migrated to Tasmania.

It seems beyond doubt that the Australoid ancestors of the Aborigines came here from South-East Asia, possibly in several migrations. At no period since *Homo sapiens* appeared has Australia had a complete landbridge to Asia (*see* AREA); it is supposed, therefore, that the crossings might have been made by chance drifting on the floating debris of storms, or, more probably, by design on some form of watercraft, as the water crossing was never less than 75km.

Since that distant past the Aborigines had lived in almost complete isolation until European discovery, and consequently appear to have changed little from the ancestral stock. Only in the far N are there traces of outsiders—seasonal visits of Indonesian trepang-fishers and, on the tip of CAPE YORK, some Papuan influence.

Traditional society and culture During their long isolation, there were many changes in environmental conditions, but Aboriginal society proved adaptable and resilient. Although the economy was based upon hunting, collecting and fishing, there were many changes through time and, by 1788, there existed complex regional variants. It is becoming evident that, during the last few thousand years, there was an intensification in the exploitation of available plant and animal resources. These included harvesting and grinding wild grass seeds in arid areas, extensive artificial channels for trapping eels in VIC, and washing toxic material from cycad nuts.

Daily life The main occupation of daily life was the search for food for immediate use, for there was little that could be stored. In poor country in a bad season the work of obtaining food would have been one of ceaseless effort; but death from hunger or thirst was probably a rare fate.

Collecting vegetable foods, insects and small animals was women's work. Various nuts, seeds and roots were powdered or ground to be made into dampers (a type of unleavened bread) but some would have to be soaked overnight in running water to remove toxic substances. Certain vegetable substances not usually eaten were collected for medicinal purposes, including *pituri*, the dried leaves of *Duboisia* which contain small quantities of a drug resembling cocaine and serving as their main stimulant. Along the E coast, the women fished with hook and line in estuarine waters from bark canoes; they cooked and ate some of their catch while fishing—a small fire was made on a bed of sand in the canoe—and the rest was taken back to camp. The Aborigines made no fireproof containers so most cooked food was roasted, or baked in a pit.

Hunting—carried out in strict silence, or using a highly developed sign language—was men's work, although Tasmanian women clubbed seals. With long training and muscular development it was possible, with the aid of a spear-thrower, to launch a spear at 30m per second over a range of 60m or more. Game secured by patient tracking far afield or by fishing with spears, nets or traps would be shared among the people in the camp strictly according to totem and kinship rules.

Another occupation for both sexes was the making or repairing of tools, or the rolling and twisting of bark fibre into cords for such items as bags or netting. Apart from ceremonial occasions, evening was a time for discussion, story-telling and work that could be done by firelight.

Children were breast-fed for about three years and were, to a large extent, dependent upon their mothers for several more. Five-year-olds were already becoming adept at food-gathering, the boys learning to throw miniature spears at small animals, the girls foraging with small digging sticks. Very little clothing was worn, though in the cooler S regions large cloaks made from animal skins were worn.

Fire Tending camp-fires and providing them with fuel was an endless task. Although Aborigines had several ways of making fire through friction, camp-fires were not allowed to go out, and a burning torch of wood or bark was always carried when people were on the move.

The Aborigines also made extensive use of fire as an aid to hunting—partly to keep down the undergrowth and partly to promote the growth of the following season's grass for animals hunted for food. In much of the inland, fire is the only way to keep the impenetrable *Spinifex* grass at bay, permitting the growth of plants providing food for man and animals. Because Australian flora had become adapted to fire long before the arrival of man, and because fuel did not accumulate for many years at a time, the Aborigines' seasonal fires were not disastrous to the environment, though it may have been modified.

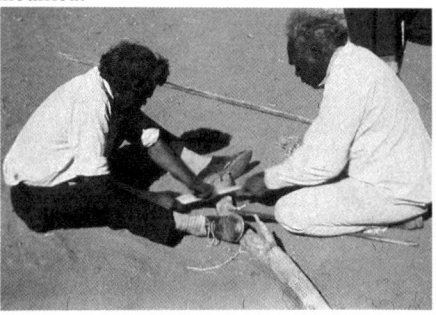
Kimber/Aboriginal Arts & Crafts Sydney

Two old men of the Warlpiri tribe making fire

Social organisation Research indicates the existence by 1788 of about 600 tribes, living in separate territories whose size was largely dependent on productivity. The total population at the time of European settlement may have been at least 300 000, of whom approximately 4000 were in TAS. A tribe might number up to 1 500 or fewer than 500.

The tribe was the largest unit of Aboriginal society and was governed by the elders, none of whom had any formally special position. Any fully initiated member of the tribe who by long experience and wisdom was recognised as worthy could participate in decision making.

It would appear that there was little to encourage or necessitate political confederacies between the largely independent tribes. However, there existed complex reciprocal ceremonial exchange or 'trade' routes, sometimes hundreds of kilometres long, over which gifts were exchanged. For example, red ochre, *pituri* and stone for hatchets circulated over great distances. Movement within these exchange cycles was governed by strict rules. Only in exceptional circumstances, and when his safety was guaranteed by his hosts, would a tribesman venture outside his territory, for beyond it his ancestral spirits could not protect him, and the rest of the world was potentially hostile.

Religious orientation The families of tribesmen moved as the search for food and water dictated, and had no permanent settlements within their own tribal lands; however, within the well-known boundaries of their territory were specific sacred places to which tribal initiates would go periodically to commune with their ancestral spirits and to refresh and strengthen their spiritual life. To these people, voluntary migration to another territory, though it must have happened in the distant past, was unthinkable. The Aboriginal concept of belonging had at least as much religious as material content, and there could be no understanding of the European idea that land is something saleable, that title and possession could be transferred as one might barter a stone hatchet for a boomerang.

Nor did the Aborigines see themselves as the only conscious beings in their environment—for them animals, trees, rocks and water holes all had individual spirits and names, and according to totem any one of these might be descended from the same ancestors as themselves or might even be those remote ancestors.

For such a people, for whom living memory could reach no further back than four generations, history was telescoped so that the very distant past, with its great significance enshrined in the legends of the DREAM TIME, pressed close upon the living. The Aborigine could perceive the dream time figures as vividly present realities with whom he could communicate during rituals.

It would not be correct to say that the Aborigines had a religion in the sense of a organised body of doctrine, although specific items of belief were evident. Rather, the term 'religion' can be said to embrace their laws, mythology, kinship bonds and totems, and was thus pervasive and inseparable from any other aspect of their lives. Their religious practices might be loosely described as a combination of animism, ancestor-worship and fertility cults. Like their largely unstratified social system, their religion worshipped neither a supreme creator nor a hierarchy of gods and godesses. They worshipped the ancestral spirits from whom they were lineal descendants, and who were thus seen as superhuman rather than supernatural, although they were thought to possess enormous powers.

Aboriginal children learn their own language, Bandjalang, an Aboriginal language from northern NSW

Language The study of Aboriginal languages, especially attempts to reconstruct parts of the ancient mother tongue, is specialised, difficult and controversial. There were hundreds of Aboriginal languages, clearly related in structure and presumably having a common origin, though differing greatly in vocabulary. Very little has survived of many of these languages and attempts to connect them with the languages of other countries have been completely unsuccessful; it seems likely that they evolved from very ancient languages that were brought to Australia by the first Aborigines and have long since vanished elsewhere.

Law It was essential to the Aboriginal that he lived in harmony with the spirit world. The law, preserved in the traditions of his tribe and expounded by the elders, prescribed right conduct and the reverent performance of ceremonies; on this depended successful hunting and gathering, abundance of water, good health and fair climate. Times of drought, scarcity and trouble indicated that the spirit world was displeased and that man must make good his shortcomings. The law prescribed the proper behaviour for almost every occasion in life, and even unknowing violation brought its penalty. For wilful breaches, punishment would also come directly from the delinquent's fellow tribesmen, under the authority of the elders. Improper behaviour was against the interests of the community, and the rigid and detailed code of the law permitted none of the easy Western distinction between legality and morality.

Kinship bonds and totem The tribes were subdivided, on the basis of kinship, into various clans. The complex structure of kinship systems within the different tribes evidently served as a means of regulating social conduct, prescribing behaviour for every relationship within the tribe; in default of identifiable blood relationship, some formal relation could always be established. When—rarely—a white man has been admitted to tribal membership he has not only had to be properly initiated but also formally provided with relatives, thus defining, in addition, which tribal woman he could or should marry. For the Aborigines the rules governing marriage were as much concerned with social as with blood relationship.

Totem embodied another kind of relationship—that of a man to his dream time ancestors, carried over the ages by his spirit. A spirit never died, but was reincarnated at the conception of a new child, which would then bear the same totem. This totem could be clearly recognised by various signs, and brought with it certain taboos, preventing the person from hunting or eating animals of the same totem. In practice, such restrictions acted gratuitously like a conservation scheme, preventing the excessive consumption of any one species, though they were probably not intended to serve this purpose.

Fertility The most important power wielded by the ancestral spirits was the control of fertility in all its aspects. Essential in women for propagation of the race, and also in animals and plants for sustaining human life, fertility was vested solely in the female. The father's part in conception was of relatively minor importance: he simply prepared the way for the entry of a spirit into the womb. Consequently, it was essential that ceremonies for natural increase and fertility should be correctly and reverently performed before the mating and growing seasons. The ritual chants and dances of fertility rites were highly traditional, but not unchangeable: expert elders might devise improvements, and sometimes a ceremony that appeared to be particularly effective might be adopted by a neighbouring tribe. An interesting phenomenon of more recent prehistoric times concerns the development of a fertility cult centred on a female spirit, Kunapipi, which was spreading among the tribes, and which in time might conceivably have developed into a distinct mother-goddess religion.

Magic It is often hard to distinguish between religious and magical practices in primitive societies. Although everyone could use magic to some degree, certain men and women in traditional Aboriginal society appeared to enjoy a significant, though informal, status as skilled practitioners in magic. Malice backed by magic was the usual theory of inexplicable misfortune, and victims might seek help from the 'medicine man' in averting the harmful magic.

Craftsmanship and art The Aborigines were among the first people in the world to use ground-edge tools, about 10 000 years before it was thought of in Europe, and were highly skilled at shaping stone implements by chipping and delicate flaking. Some tools were made of bone or shell; most of their tools were for wood-working and their implements were made mainly of wood (for example, spear-throwers, spears, shields, clubs, BOOMERANGS, digging sticks, COOLAMONS). Sheets of bark were also used for shelters (such as GUNYAHS) and canoes. Also well known to the Aborigines was the use of natural resins, loaded with fibrous and other materials, for bonding together the parts of implements; developed only recently in the modern world with synthetic materials, this technique had been practised by the Aborigines for at least 15 000 years.

Aboriginal dancing ritual

It is almost impossible to separate Aboriginal art and craftsmanship from religious and magical practices. Thus artistic expression extended from skilfully worked patterns on the most ordinary implements to symbolic representations of sacred topics carved and painted on sacred objects (such as the TJURINGA). In effect, no implement was insignificant: the maker would often sing a special song as he crafted the implement and painted or carved a design on it to give it dream-time power. Songs, dancing and associated visual arts were inextricably connected, and expressed common themes.

Visual arts were expressed in painting, carving and incising as well as fibrework. In painting, they utilised natural earth pigments such as red and yellow ochres, charcoal and white pipe clay, applying them with chewed twigs, feathers or human hair. For special effects, feathers and down might be incorporated into the designs. Pictures found on the walls of shallow caves, or on sheets of bark, depict animals and what appear to be spirit-beings or ancestral people. For rituals, celebrants painted their bodies in detailed patterns, and added other effects such as feather head-dresses, string girdles and armbands. In some areas, elaborate string constructions called *woniga* were made, to be carried on the shoulders or worn as head-dresses during ceremonies. Other fibrework included feathered twine on *rangga*, carved ceremonial poles of durable hardwood used in E ARNHEM LAND. Bark was folded and tied to make canoes, containers for carrying water, food or babies; and grass was dried and woven into mats, baskets and bags. Rock engravings, laboriously pecked or chiselled into stone surfaces, appear to have had religious or magical significance for their makers, and it seems probable that they were made in ceremonially important places. Many of the representations are now obscure and their original meaning is lost.

The arrival of the Europeans The high value which traditional Aboriginal society placed on co-operation and sharing between its members, and also on a harmonious and reverent relationship with nature, was the opposite of Western individualism and competitiveness; with the added difference between simple and sophisticated cultures, it is not surprising that misunderstandings should have arisen between Europeans and Aborigines from the time of their earliest encounters onwards. Carstenz (1623) seemed puzzled by the hostility of the Aborigines 'in spite of our kindness and fair semblance'; DAMPIER (1688) compared them unfavourably with the African Hottentots, hitherto the most uncivilised people he had seen.

Policy patterns up to 1860 Such attitudes were to predominate when colonies were formally established. However, a different viewpoint informed official attitudes; Captain COOK's observations on the Aborigines (1770) reflect how European sociological thought had been influenced by the concept of the 'Noble Savage', which supposed all primitive peoples to be living a simple, idyllic life, free from the vice, greed and competition of sophi-

sticated societies. In 1788, both Governor PHILLIP and his superiors in London held a similar viewpoint: in setting up a few penal colonies, their policy was simply to make friends and establish peaceful relationships with Aboriginal inhabitants living in the immediate area of the colonies. Besides the inherent contradiction in this policy—that the British assumed right of sovereignty over as much land as they needed—few amongst the common soldiers and settlers shared the official humanitarianism. Although the imperial authorities intended to protect the indigenous population by the strict application of British law, this policy was difficult to enforce: at the frontiers of settlement, Aborigines were virtually dependent upon the restraint of individual pioneers.

Consequently, as settlement expanded beyond the perimeter of the original convict establishments, the Aboriginal way of life was drastically disrupted by the progressive loss of life-sustaining hunting grounds, water holes and ceremonial sites in the coastal areas. Though possibly they were already suffering from infectious diseases contracted through previous chance encounters with Asian and European sailors, as settlement expanded after 1788 new diseases, alcohol and the use of force by settlers and police led to rapid population decline and social dislocation. In TAS, between 1800 and 1830, the Aboriginal population decreased from a probable 4000 to fewer than 500; ultimately, the depopulation there was almost total (*see* BLACK WAR). In VIC, a population estimated at over 10 000 was reduced to 2000 within 30 years of the colony's establishment.

Prolonged (but sporadic and unco-ordinated) resistance to the encroachment of European settlers did lead to the temporary abandonment of grazing and farming ventures in some areas, and on some occasions settlers who took reprisals against Aborigines were punished, military or police action being taken at the same time against the Aborigines to discourage or prevent attack. Nevertheless, such resistance could do no more than delay the expansion of European settlement. By the 1840s the Merino sheep boom was under way, and the discovery of gold in the 1850s led to an enormous increase in the European population and encouraged the development of agriculture. At the same time an unofficial policy of extermination of Aborigines established itself among settlers despite official attitudes.

Protection policies 1850-1940 After 1850, European control of the land was secure, and there was growing recognition of the diminished Aboriginal population as a source of cheap labour. Official policy became concerned primarily with protecting the Aborigines from physical violence, sexual abuse, murder, poverty and malnutrition. Laws were introduced to segregate Aborigines, confining them to reserves and missions run by mission and government officials with extensive powers to control, for example, employment, marriage, education, the supply of alcohol and the transfer of people to and from these areas.

Such control continues today, particularly for Aborigines who live on the geographically and socially isolated 'settlements'; in these areas, the extensive control exercised by the authorities has given the Aborigines little incentive to develop their own power structures or to experience competition or choice, with the result they appear to be submissive and lacking in initiative and individuality.

In recent years, school programmes and vocational training schemes have been developed as an integral part in the use of settlements as a stage in the transition of Aborigines to life in the wider (white) community. It seems, however, that the social and psychological results of living in settlements make it unlikely that most Aborigines will achieve this aim successfully.

The issue of Aboriginal land rights has evoked protest in some unique ways

Contemporary development World War II marked a watershed in black-white relations in Australia, for the ensuing social and political changes in the country and around the world laid the basis for changes in white attitudes and for the development of Aboriginal organisation and political protest. Around the major cities in the S and E the Aborigines had been almost totally exterminated, but further inland a rural population of Aboriginal descent existed by the early decades of the 20th century. In parts of NSW and VIC, organisations of black and white Australians had developed by the 1930s. There were no such organisations in the central and N parts of Australia where most of the Aborigines were either still living in a semi-nomadic hunting-and-collecting society or had only recently emerged from it.

The war with Japan meant that thousands of soldiers were sent N and many white workers were drafted there to build new roads and landing strips. Aborigines were evacuated from coastal areas; some were employed in the expanded beef industry while others were given jobs by the army with equal pay and conditions. (In most cases, this was the first time that Aborigines had received cash wages.) These interracial contacts had a profound effect on the thinking of both black and white; some white people became more aware of the treatment of Aboriginal people, and Aborigines came in contact with white people who were different from managers and stockmen and who showed sympathy and support. In addition, the new employment opportunities and the forced moves helped to break down the old tribal barriers between Aboriginal communities and laid the basis for new, wider links and the development of an Australia-wide national Aboriginal identity.

Up to this time the Aboriginal population in Australia had been getting steadily smaller but more jobs and improved health and hygiene facilities stopped this trend and laid the basis for a new growth in Aboriginal numbers (see Table 1). Life in the N for Aborigines changed decisively at this time in another way too: before the war, over 50 per cent of the Aborigines were still living a semi-nomadic life but by 1965 few remained in the bush away from the government and mission stations. The trend has reversed today, with numerous 'outstations' resettled by groups following mainly traditional ways.

One of the earliest results of the new ideas that were growing among the Aborigines was a strike of pastoral workers in the PILBARA area of north-western WA, the first industrial strike among Aborigines. The size and structure of the striking group has changed over the years but today it has a membership of about 200 and is known as 'Nomads'. Although its members have retained much of their traditional social and religious organisation, they have moved successfully from hunting and gathering to an economy based on subsistence mining. The earliest protest about land rights took place in 1962 at Gove in the Arnhem Land reserve. The YIRRKALA Aborigines sent a bark-painting petition to the federal government strongly objecting to bauxite mining on their traditional land and the desecration and destruction of their sacred sites, pointing out that mining companies would not knock down churches or cathedrals of the white community if there were minerals underneath them. They lost their case before the Supreme Court in Darwin in March 1971. In 1966 Gurindji pastoral workers from cattle stations in the NT went on strike demanding equal pay

with white stockmen. Later they re-occupied an area of their traditional land at Dagu Ragu (Wattie Creek) and stayed there for eight years until they were granted not the land rights they were claiming but a lease of land covering 3 108km² in August 1975. The Gurindji demand became a test case and profoundly influenced Aboriginal ideas and organisation. At first, much of the impetus for the land rights struggle came from the more traditional groups in the N, but groups in the urban and rural areas of the S and E are now also involved and active, and tend to be concerned with 'the power generated by people who seek to identify their own problems and those of the community as a whole, and who strive to take action in all possible forms to solve those problems'. Such actions have included the establishment in 1958 of the Australia-wide, multiracial Federal Council for the Advancement of Aborigines (expanded in 1962 to become the Federal Council for the Advancement of Aborigines and TORRES STRAIT Islanders and renamed the National Aboriginal and Islander Liberation Movement, in 1977) and of the Tribal Councils in 1970.

Table 2

ABORIGINAL POPULATION OF AUSTRALIA: PERCENTAGES OF RURAL AND URBAN DWELLERS (1966-81)

Year	Urban %	Rural %
1966	27.3	72.7
1971	43.5	56.5
1976	58.3	41.7
1981	57.4	42.6

Source: Australian Bureau of Statistics, Canberra.

Current problems

1. Employment. There is a high rate of unemployment among Aborigines throughout Australia and when in employment, they are mainly in unskilled, casual and seasonal work. Employers have made a considerable contribution to this situation for their negative attitudes concerning Aborigines in the labour force are often based on a lack of appreciation of Aboriginal culture. A study

made in the NT shows that where employers provide good conditions, treat their Aboriginal employees as equals and show an understanding of Aboriginal culture, the number of complaints about the value of Aboriginal labour is significantly lower.

There is evidence to suggest that there is relatively greater financial security and employment stability among Aborigines in settled urban areas. This, and the declining job opportunities in the rural sector, has led to increased Aboriginal migration to urban areas (see Table 2).

2. Education. The common practice before World War II was to exclude Aborigines from the State education systems; although this persists in some places, today almost every Aboriginal child is within reach of educational facilities. Although the recent development of bilingual education programmes with community involvement in the NT and of Aboriginal pre-schooling indicates that serious attempts are being made to overcome the social and cultural gap existing between the two communities, the new schemes have had little success because material and social problems outside the schools severely handicap the Aboriginal child at school. Also, the need to educate the white community about Aborigines has not received nearly as much attention.

3. Housing. The very different housing needs of Aborigines throughout the continent and the lack of any comprehensive survey make an accurate overview difficult. Considerable time and money have been spent in recent years to improve Aboriginal housing in quantity and quality but the lack of consultation with the Aborigines themselves (for example, on designs suitable for family sizes, local climate and conditions, and personal tastes) have frustrated these efforts. Most housing for Aborigines is sub-standard. There are almost twice as many people per dwelling and nearly three times as many people per room as other (white) Australians. These figures do not include visitors; Aborigines have difficulty in finding hotel accommodation in many places and so turn for hospitality to their own people, thus making a significant contribution to overcrowding in most Aboriginal houses. When renting is impossible or homes are simply not available, Aborigines build their own from whatever materials are to hand; these shacks are usually on the outskirts of urban areas and the resultant squalor reinforces the whites' belief in Aboriginal 'laziness' or 'dirtiness', justifying the refusal to allow Aborigines into decent houses in the wider community.

4. Health. There are many mutually reinforcing factors which contribute to the very low level of Aboriginal health. Aborigines on reserves and settlements, fringe-dwellers and those in city slums have in common a lack of facilities to maintain cleanliness and health, and insufficient resources, financial or social, to obtain such facilities. Overcrowding puts additional pressures on already sub-standard conditions and contributes to the transmission of infection. Sanitation services tend to be absent and the water supply is often inade-

NUMBER AND DISTRIBUTION OF ABORIGINES IN AUSTRALIA 1788-1981

Year	NSW	VIC	QLD	SA	WA	TAS	NT	TOTAL
1788	40 000	11 500	100 000	10 000	52 000	2 500	35 000	251 000
1901	8 065	521	26 670	3 070	5 261	0	23 363	66 950
1921	6 067	573	15 454	2 741	17 671	0	17 973	60 479
1947	11 660	1 277	16 311	4 296	24 912	214	15 147	73 817
1954	12 386	1 395	18 460	4 972	16 215	93	17 157	70 678
1961	14 859	1 796	19 696	4 884	18 276	38	19 704	79 253
1966	13 709	1 790	19 003	5 505	18 439	55	21 119	79 620
1971	23 349	5 656	24 414	7 140	21 903	575	23 253	106 290
1976	38 457	12 415	31 948	9 940	25 565	2 522	23 535	144 382
1981	34 177	5 283	33 966	9 476	30 749	2 334	28 680	144 665

Note: figures for the ACT are combined with those for NSW.
Source: Australian Bureau of Statistics, Canberra.

quate. Despite the efforts of the Aborigines themselves to improve this situation (the attempts to keep a slum home decent and clean and the setting up of the Aboriginal Medical Services, for example), such conditions inevitably encourage dirt, infection and sickness. Resistance to disease is lowered by poor dietary patterns and malnutrition. This is partly because of poverty and partly because of ignorance of basic dietary needs. Fresh fruit, milk and vegetables are frequently unavailable or too expensive in stores on more isolated stations and settlements.

In Outback areas access to medical services may be difficult, especially for Aborigines with no transport or communications. In fringe camps and urban areas the distance to a doctor and the fares involved may still be a real obstacle to seeking medical advice. A great deal more research and money are needed in the area of Aboriginal health. Equally essential is a far greater involvement of the Aboriginal people themselves, both as patients and as medical personnel, if there is to be any improvement in the situation indicated by the Aboriginal infant mortality figures in Table 3.

Table 3

ABORIGINAL INFANT MORTALITY RATES
(per thousand live births)

Year	In Northern Territory Aboriginal population	In total Australian population
1970	115.1	17.9
1971	142.9	17.3
1972	87.0	16.7
1973	79.7	16.5
1974	55.6	16.1
1975	50.1	14.2
1976	52.8	13.8
1977	74.6	12.5
1978	48.1	12.2
1979	45.0	11.4
1980	36.3	10.7

Source: NT Govt, Dept of Health, Annual Reports 1978-79 and 1980-81.

Current and future issues Aborigines today form a national minority of at least 160 000. Although theoretically equal before the law (with the exception of QLD where the discriminatory Aborigines and Torres Strait Islanders Acts remain), Aborigines cannot be sure that their civil liberties and human rights are guaranteed. There is still, for example, unofficial segregation in housing and schooling, differences in wage-levels and administrative means to restrict Aboriginal movement. Their lives are characterised by disease, malnutrition, insecurity, stress, petty crime, discharge of tensions and frustration in alcoholism and some personal violence, and by their reactions to white society of suspicious hostility and aggression, or of withdrawal into 'apathy' or excessive co-operation with authority. However, the development of a political protest movement among the Aborigines, the land rights cam-

paign and the growth of 'self-help' organisations, such as the Aboriginal Legal and Medical Services, may contribute to the improvement of this situation. Since the 1960s there has been a growing consciousness of and pride in identifying oneself as Aboriginal or black.

There are no easy or quick solutions for Australia's complex race-relations situation. A move towards giving Aborigines communal land rights, including rights to all natural resources on those lands restored, would provide an economic base for regenerating many communities. Considerably more money and research is needed to improve Aboriginal health, housing, education, employment and civil and legal rights. Increased aid and welfare programmes might not succeed if they are not carried out in conjunction with the development of genuine possibilities for choice and decision-making by the Aboriginal people themselves.

Further reading: Berndt, R.M. *Australian Aboriginal Art.* Ure Smith, Sydney, 1964; Rowley, C.D. *The Destruction of Aboriginal Society* and *Outcasts in White Society.* Australian National University Press, Canberra, 1970; Bonner, N. & Sykes, B. *Black Power in Australia.* Heinemann, Melbourne, 1975; Mulvaney, D.J. *The Prehistory of Australia.* Pelican, Melbourne, 1975; Berndt, R.M. *The World of the First Australians.* Ure Smith, Sydney, 1977; Smith, L.R. *The Aboriginal Population of Australia.* Australian National University Press, Canberra, 1980; Kirk, R.L. *Aboriginal Man Adapting.* Clarendon Press, Oxford, 1981; Broome, R. *Aboriginal Australians.* Allen and Unwin, Sydney, 1982; Flood, J. *Archaeology of the Dreamtime.* Collins, Sydney, 1983; Gale, F. (ed.), *We Are Bosses Ourselves.* Australian Institute of Aboriginal Studies, Canberra, 1983.

Abrolhos Islands *see* Houtman Abrolhos

Acacia *see* Mimosaceae

Acanthocephala *see* spiny-headed worms

acclimatisation societies These groups, which flourished for a few years in the middle of the 19th century in Australia and other countries, including the UK, were devoted to the introduction and establishment in their respective countries of alien species of animals and plants. The objects of the acclimatisation society in VIC, for example, included 'the introduction, acclimatization and domestication of all innoxious animals, birds, fishes, insects and vegetables whether useful or ornamental' and the giving of rewards to those 'who may render valuable services to the cause of acclimatization.'

Unfortunately, the activities of these societies were not based upon a knowledge of ecology, and many of the introductions proved disastrous because the animals and plants themselves became pests, or introduced diseases. Animals which were introduced or seriously considered as candidates for acclimatisation in

Australia included house sparrows, the Indian myna, starlings, agoutis, alpacas, elands, mongooses, monkeys, silkworms, secretary birds and various fishes. Those exported from Australia to be introduced into Britain included wallabies, parrots and pigeons. The activities of the acclimatisation societies were stopped in 1871 by the introduction of quarantine regulations by the colonial governments.

See also animals, introduced; Commonwealth Scientific and Industrial Research Organisation *Further reading:* Rolls, E.C. *They All Ran Wild.* Angus & Robertson, Sydney, 1969; Lever, C. *The Naturalised Animals of the British Isles.* Granada, London, 1979.

Achernar *see* astronomy

acorn worms These marine animals form the class Enteropneusta of the phylum Hemichordata—the 'half-chordates'. They have been so called because although there is no true notochord (the elastic rudimentary spinal chord or column of the CHORDATES), it is considered by some zoologists that a branch of the gut which passes into the proboscis is homologous with the notochord. However, it appears that they may be more closely related to animals such as the sea cucumbers (ECHINODERMS) than to the chordates (*see* VERTEBRATES; SEA SQUIRTS, etc).

Not often seen unless deliberately searched for, acorn worms are generally found in shallow marine waters (though there are some deep-water species), where they burrow into sand and mud, which they draw in, sifting out fine particles of food. The body, which may grow to a length between 5cm and almost 2m (as in *Balanoglossus gigas*), is divided into three parts: the proboscis, used for burrowing and foraging, rather than in eating; the collar, where the mouth opens, directly behind the proboscis; and the trunk, which carries several gill pores or slits at the front end, just behind the collar. The long, straight gut extends from the mouth through the trunk, ending in an anus at the end of the body. The sexes are separate. Fertilisation occurs externally, the developing larvae then drifting in the plankton for several weeks.

B. australiensis is a common species of some small, partly sheltered bays in Australia, burrowing in gravelly sand or in mud under stones. *Balanoglossus* species live in 'U'-shaped tubes.

Adams, Arthur Henry (1872-1936) Author. He was born and educated in New Zealand and worked there as a journalist before coming to Australia in 1898. In 1900 he went to China as a war correspondent, and before returning to Australia in 1906 lived in New Zealand and in England. He was editor of the Red Page of the *Bulletin* from 1906 to 1909 and in later years edited *The Lone Hand* and the Sydney *Sun.* Apart from his work as a journalist he wrote prolifically and published several volumes of verse, plays, short stories and novels, including *Three Plays for the Australian Stage* (1910), the novel *Gallahad*

Jones (1914) and *The Collected Verses of Arthur H. Adams* (1913).

Adams, Francis William Lauderdale

(1862-93) Author. Born in Malta and educated in England, he came to Australia in 1884 and during the following few years contributed freely to the *Bulletin* and other Australian journals. He returned to England in 1890 and three years later, in an advanced state of tuberculosis, shot himself. His publications included poems, novels, short stories and a verse drama, but he is best remembered for two volumes of essays, *Australian Essays* (1886) and *The Australians* (1893).

adders, death *see* snakes

Adelaide

SA (population 882 520 in 1981) The capital city of SA and the fourth-largest urban centre in Australia, it is located on the coastal plain on the E shore of ST VINCENT GULF, W of the MOUNT LOFTY RANGES. The central business district of the city is situated on the banks of the TORRENS RIVER, about 8km inland from the coast. The city was named in honour of Queen Adelaide, the consort of King William IV of Britain.

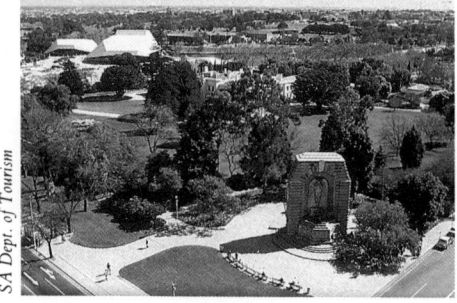

S A Dept. of Tourism

Adelaide

History The gulf coastline in the area where Adelaide now stands was explored by Matthew FLINDERS in 1801-1802, but settlement did not take place until the 1830s, with Captain John HINDMARSH as the first Governor and Colonel William LIGHT as the Surveyor-General. The settlement of SA was inspired by the theory of colonisation advanced by Edward Gibbon WAKEFIELD, based on the principle that land should be sold to new settlers at a 'sufficient' price, such that men of capital would be attracted, together with others who would work for wages. Thus SA became the only Australian colony established by free settlers, no convicts being sent there. Initial settlements were made on KANGAROO ISLAND and at Holdfast Bay (Glenelg) and the selection of the site for the establishment of the city was a matter of considerable controversy in the 1830s. The ultimate choice, on the Torrens, midway between the coast and the fault-scarp of the Mt Lofty Ranges, owes much to the foresight of Colonel Light. He designed the layout of the city core within one square mile, with five garden-like squares, broad streets on a grid plan, and a belt of parkland surrounding the city centre. His plan has been followed since 1840, when Adelaide was officially incor-

porated as a municipality, though the suburban spread has reached far beyond the parkland belt, over the alluvial plains and on to the foothills of the range.

Climate Adelaide experiences mild conditions throughout the year, with warm to hot days in the summer months, and cool, occasionally crisp, winters. The average monthly temperature in January, the hottest month, is 26.7°C; July is the coldest month with an average of 13.9°C. Long hot spells can occur in midsummer. The average annual rainfall is 533mm, with maximum falls in the winter months; May and June receive most rain (69mm and 73mm respectively), January receives least (20mm). On about half the days in winter months rain can be expected (July and August 16 days each), while in summer rain can be expected much less frequently (only on four days in January and February).

Population From the 1830s, the city grew steadily to reach a population of over 160 000 by 1900. It had passed the quarter-million mark by the census of 1921, the half-million mark by the 1961 census, and was over 800 000 by 1971 (*see* Table 1). Similar to other States of Australia, SA has a very high proportion (about 69 per cent) of its population in the metropolitan capital.

Table 1

URBAN GROWTH OF ADELAIDE IN THE TWENTIETH CENTURY

Year	Population	% of State population
1901	162 261	44.7
1911	189 646	46.4
1921	255 375	51.6
1933	312 629	54.0
1954	483 508	60.7
1961	587 957	60.7
1971	809 482	69.0
1976	857 196	68.9
1981	882 520	68.7

Source: Australian Bureau of Statistics, Canberra.

Structure and functions Colonel Light's original plan of the city included a grid street pattern both N and S of the Torrens, with parklands between them, as well as a broad encircling park-belt. He designed the N area as the initial dormitory suburb, and the S as the central business district; this basic planning has left its stamp on the present-day city. The riverside park area contains numerous sporting ovals, golf links, gardens and open recreation areas. Near the heart of the city, the Torrens has been dammed to form LAKE TORRENS, thus providing an aquatic playground in the midst of the inner city parkland. On Montefiore Hill, in a N Adelaide park known appropriately as 'Light's Vision', stands a statue of Colonel Light, commanding a panoramic vista of the city and its suburbs.

The architecture of the inner city includes many attractive 19th-century buildings (over 100 sites have been listed for preservation in S Adelaide alone by the National Trust of SA),

and numerous churches (it is often called 'the city of churches'), along with modern high-rise office blocks and business houses. The main thoroughfare, King William Street, runs N-S, passing through Victoria Square, a park in the city centre. On North Terrace, a major street running E-W, are the main railway station, Parliament House, the public library, Government House, the art gallery, Royal Adelaide Hospital, the university, the museum and the botanic gardens at the E end.

The suburban growth of the city has extended urban development some 20km to the N and S of the inner city, to the coast on the W, and into the hilly areas of the lower Mt Lofty Ranges region to the E. Several large conservation parks are located in these hills to the E and SE of the city, including Morialta (374ha, established in 1913), and Belair (835ha, established in 1891). For about 30km along the gulf coast to the NE, E and SE of the city, there is a stretch of holiday and recreation suburbs; the better-known beaches include Marino, Seacliff, Brighton, Glenelg, Somerton, West Beach, Henley, Semaphore and Largs Bay. PORT ADELAIDE, 24km by road NW of the city, has a container terminal and modern facilities for handling international passenger vessels.

During the early days of settlement, Adelaide's water supply came from the Torrens. As the city grew, this source was supplemented by supplies from reservoirs on other streams draining from the Mt Lofty Ranges (Onkaparinga, South Para and Myponga). Since 1954, a pipeline from MANNUM on the MURRAY RIVER has brought water a distance of 84km from the Murray, across the Mt Lofty Ranges to the metropolitan area.

Adelaide, as the State capital, is the administrative centre for most government departments, as well as the major commercial and financial centre. It has a wide variety of industrial enterprises including motor-body assembly works, engineering and railway workshops, chemical factories, electrical plants, oil refining works, many factories processing rural produce (such as fruit canning) and abattoirs.

Further reading: Davies, J. (ed) 'Culture in Australia: Adelaide's Festival' in *Current Affairs Bulletin.* (vol 33, no 12, 1964); Williams, M. *Adelaide.* Longmans, Melbourne, 1966; Lamshed, M. *Adelaide Sketchbook.* Rigby, Adelaide, 1967; Whitelock, D. *Adelaide 1836-1976: A History of Difference.* University of Queensland Press, Brisbane, 1977.

Adelaide Festival of Arts

This, Australia's most important cultural festival, has been held every two years since 1960. Lasting about three weeks during March, it includes a wide range of exhibitions, recitals and concerts, including popular entertainment such as concerts in jazz, rock and contemporary song. It incorporates Writers' Week, and many community activities are also associated with it. Many internationally famous orchestras, companies and artists have taken part in the Festival. Since the completion of the Adelaide Festival Centre, a performing arts complex, overseas artists now appear at the Centre throughout the year enabling the Festival to concentrate more than before on the commissioning of new works and the encouragement of local companies and performers. Notable world premières have included Sir Robert Helpmann's ballets, *The Display* and *Perisynthyon,* the Patrick White play *Night on Bald Mountain,* the Australian Dance Theatre's *Transfigured Night* and *Stripsody,* and Robin Archer's *Songs from Sideshow Alley.*

Famous writers who have been guests at Festival Writers' Week include Yevgeny Yevtushenko, Anthony Burgess, Allen Ginsberg, John Updike and Nadine Gordimer.

Adelaide River

NT Located in the NW part of the Territory, its headwaters lie about 120km S of Darwin and it flows on a general S-N course for over 150km to Adam Bay on the mangrove-fringed coastline of VAN DIEMEN GULF, some 50km NE of Darwin. Like all rivers in these N parts, it experiences high flows during the wet season (November to March), with a much reduced volume in the dry. The river flats and plain lands in the lower parts of the valley have fertile black soil which has encouraged a number of attempts at commercial cropping: during World War II, a successful vegetable growing venture to provide fresh food for the troops was established; in the 1950s an unsuccessful rice growing venture was undertaken at HUMPTY DOO. The CSIRO Central Plains research station, carrying out investigations on rice growing and cattle grazing, is located here. The small township, also called Adelaide River, is situated where the Stuart Highway and the North Australian Railway cross the river, 116km S of Darwin; the Adelaide River cemetery contains graves of men and women of the armed forces who were killed in the Japanese air raids on Darwin in 1942-43.

Admiral's Cup *see* sailing

Aerial Medical Services *see* Flying Doctor Service

Afghanistan, settlers from *see* Indian subcontinent, settlers from

African box thorn *see* Solanaceae; weeds

Agavaceae *see* Palmae

Agents-General for States

When colonies were established in Australia an agent was maintained in London by each of them to encourage immigration, trade and financial negotiations on its behalf. When the colonies federated in 1901 each State government continued to appoint an Agent-General in London. All State Agents-General work in close co-operation with the High Commissioner for Australia, who is appointed by the federal government.

agriculture

The term 'agriculture' here refers to crop farming; pastoral farming is discussed in the entry on the GRAZING INDUSTRY. Many farms, of course, both grow crops and keep stock.

Development from 1788 Before the coming of the Europeans the Australian Aborigines evidently practised no true form of agriculture, even in the far 'N, where they must have been aware of gardening carried out in the nearest parts of New Guinea. Agriculture was introduced by members of the FIRST FLEET, under the leadership of Captain Arthur PHILLIP, who brought to the infertile sandy and wooded soils of the Sydney area seeds and cuttings of various British, South American and South African plants. The first crops were grown at FARM COVE where Sydney's Royal Botanical Gardens are now sited. The first efforts were beset with difficulties: trees had to be cleared by hand because of the shortage of draught animals; the wheat seed had deteriorated during the long voyage, and the varieties were not suited to local conditions; crops which came to fruition often became infested with fungus diseases (probably rusts) and were often not worth the trouble of harvesting; and hand tools were of poor quality. Though Phillip harvested eight tonnes of wheat and 1.6 tonnes of barley in December 1790, the early settlers often faced starvation, and were largely dependent upon imported supplies. The emancipist James RUSE, who may be called Australia's first farmer, played an important part by demonstrating that a man could support himself and his family by farming.

More land was settled in the following years and until the middle of the 19th century the bias of farming was towards animal husbandry, crop farming being pursued simply to meet local needs. Reasons for this trend included the problems of transporting fresh produce to the coast, overcome in NSW and VIC by the spreading of the railway network in the second half of the 19th century. By contrast, the wool-clip was easily conveyed and readily exported. Moreover, crop farming was labour-intensive and laborious until late 19th-century inventions initiated the mechanisation of ploughing, harvesting and threshing. Cultivation was also limited by climatic conditions and, in many areas, by the scarcity of water and the mineral deficiencies of soils in a continent which has been geologically quiet for millions of years. Such problems have been reduced greatly by the application of scientific research and modern technology in the late 19th and 20th centuries.

Nevertheless, cereals, vegetables and fruit were grown on a substantial scale in certain areas, from the earliest days of settlement. At first TAS, its climate being more similar to that of Britain, proved better suited to cereal growing than NSW, and because transportation by boat was relatively cheap, TAS served as a larder for NSW for a time. When SA took over the role of wheat exporter from about 1850, TAS devoted itself to producing potatoes, oats and peas and later—with the

development of improved shipping methods—top-grade fruit, for the export market. The progressive growth in the extent of cultivation in NSW (interrupted between 1851 and 1855 by the gold rushes) was accelerated by the establishment of the railways. Likewise in VIC, rail transport gave impetus to the expansion of wheat farming so that by 1900 it was Australia's chief grain-producing State. In QLD the climate prevented extensive cereal production, the chief crops there being cotton (which flourished through gaining markets during the American Civil War), and later sugar cane, which largely replaced cotton; both crops used KANAKAS as labourers. In WA, agriculture was slow to start, principally because of the infertility of the soil, and until this century it supplied only local needs.

Technological improvements The technological improvements which have made a substantial contribution to the development of agriculture include the invention of a number of machines. The stump-jump plough designed in 1876 by R.B. Smith of SA was particularly important in bringing areas of MALLEE scrub under cultivation in VIC and SA, as it permitted the ploughing of land from which tree stumps had not been cleared. Grain crops benefited from the invention and development of harvesting machines, which have made harvesting less labour-intensive. The first of these was the Ridley stripper, invented by John RIDLEY in 1843, which stripped off the wheat ears and threshed the grain with revolving beaters. The combine harvester developed in 1884 by Hugh McKAY of SA, an improvement on the stripper in that it was able to bag the threshed grain, was subsequently further improved by Hedley Taylor of NSW into the famous 'Sunshine' harvesters (later manufactured in conjunction with McKay); in 1913 Taylor produced the header harvester, which was able to strip even storm-flattened grain, and in 1924 he developed the first self-propelled harvester.

Since 1947 aeroplanes have been used in agricultural operations, mainly for spreading fertilisers (especially superphosphates), for seeding pastures, for spraying insecticides and herbicides, and for dropping bait for rabbits and other animal pests such as dingoes.

Scientific research This has had a wide application in agricultural development. Early experiments (by Amos HOWARD in SA and Charles PRELL in VIC) in using subterranean clover, which increases the nitrogen content of the soil, led to the radical improvement of arable and pasture lands, in combination with applications of superphosphate and other chemicals to soils deficient in trace elements. New plant varieties, better adapted to local conditions, were also developed—wheat breeding in particular advanced rapidly after William FARRER's pioneering work around the turn of the century in the crossing, selection and fixing of wheat varieties.

Such improvements led to the extension of farming into the more arid areas (where the tapping of ARTESIAN WATER has also been significant in some places), and the intensification of farming in longer-settled areas. State departments of agriculture, agricultural colleges and university departments and the COMMONWEALTH SCIENTIFIC AND INDUSTRIAL RESEARCH ORGANIZATION (CSIRO) have all ensured propagation and encouragement of scientific research in agriculture.

The principal crops are discussed below.

Wheat In terms of tonnage, area and export value, wheat is Australia's most important crop (*see* Table 2). About 11 million hectares of wheat are grown each year for export and domestic consumption, and a further 100 000ha for other purposes, such as fodder. Of the total area under wheat in 1979-80, 37 per cent is in WA, 31 per cent in NSW, 13 per cent in VIC, 13 per cent in SA, seven per cent in QLD and 0.02 per cent in TAS. The highest average yield in tonnes per hectare from 1974 to 1980 was in VIC (1.76), the lowest was in QLD (1.05). Although Australia produces only about three per cent of the world's wheat, it accounts for 10-15 per cent of the world's wheat exports, most of it going to China, Egypt, Iraq, Japan and the USSR (*see* Table 3).

Australian wheat is a 'winter' grain grown in autumn, winter and spring mostly in areas lying between the 954mm and 501mm isohyets. It is important that there is enough rainfall from April to October or from May to November (depending on the district) but in many areas the necessary spring rains are unreliable. Wheat varieties for Australian conditions must be drought resistant, disease resistant and able to mature before the onset of the hot summer weather. The varieties commonly grown in Australia (about 45) are divided into: Prime Australian Hard Wheat (ideal for bread-making; protein content about 12 to 14 per cent); Australian Hard Wheat (protein content about 11 to 13 per cent); Australian Standard White (used for blending and general purposes; protein content about nine to 12 per cent); and Australian Soft Wheat (used for biscuit-making; protein content about eight to 10 per cent). NSW also grows some durum wheat, which has a high gluten content and is used in such products as macaroni.

Before the work of William Farrer, most wheat varieties were of European origin and would have been classified as soft wheat. Yields were low; the average yield in tonnes per hectare in 1860-69 was 0.87 and this dropped to 0.49 in 1890-99, partly because of progressive impoverishment of the soil, rust attacks and the lack of fertilisers. Yields began to rise again early this century with the increasing use of superphosphate and Farrer's introduction in 1901 of Federation, a high-yielding, short-strawed variety which matured so early that it avoided rust and the effects of drought in most years and which remained the leading variety for over 20 years. Farrer's success with Federation and other varieties prompted research into new varieties and by the 1940s the average yield was about 0.88 tonnes per hectare. The difficulty in obtaining superphosphate during World War II and the unsatisfactory rotation techniques which led to soil impoverishment and erosion caused a levelling off of average yields until 1950, after which it became common practice to bring livestock onto wheat farms, thereby allowing the farmer to adopt a rotation system in which pastures containing nitrogen-enhancing legumes and fertilised with superphosphate are used at different times for livestock raising and wheat cultivation. The added attraction of this system is that it gives the farmer more flexibility—emphasis on sheep or beef cattle when they bring good returns, and emphasis on wheat when this is more valuable.

The central marketing authority is the Australian Wheat Board (the only receiver of grain), which guarantees export and domestic prices and arranges the receiving and bulk-handling of the wheat. There are about 1000 reception points and wheat is exported from 19 ports.

Wheat harvesting near Gunnedah, New England NSW

NSW Dept. of Tourism

Oats Grown quite widely in the S States of Australia since the development of suitable varieties, the oat crop (usually grown in temperate zones) is cultivated as a winter cereal, partly for fodder and partly for grain; about three-quarters of the crop is used for human or livestock consumption in Australia. (*See* Table 4).

Barley Climatically the most adaptable of the cereals, barley is grown in all the mainland States and is used for malting and stock feeding, and as a fodder crop. About 90 per cent of the barley grown is of the two-row group of varieties, preferred for malting; the rest are of the six-row varieties. The production of barley has increased fivefold since the early 1950s. (*See* Table 5).

Table 2

WHEAT-GRAIN CROP STATISTICS 1979-84

	1979-80	1980-81	1981-82	1982-83	1983-84
Gross value (grain) $m	2 478.0	1 684	2 660	1 540†	3 136†
Volume of production (grain) '000t	16 188	10 856	16 360*	8 818†	17 250†
Area of crop (grain) '000ha	11 153	11 283	11 885*	11 564†	12 900†
Value of exports (grain and flour) $m	2 190.1	1 752.6	1 735*	1 393†	1 854†
Volume exported (unprepared wheat and grain equivalent of flour) '000t	14 953	10 674.7	10 996*	8 350†	10 300†
Mean yield t/ha	1.45	0.96	1.38*	0.76†	1.34†

Note: * provisional, subject to revision; † estimated.
Source: *Quarterly Review of the Rural Economy,* (vol 5, no 3, Aug 1983), Australian Govt Publishing Service, Canberra.

Table 3

MAJOR IMPORTERS OF AUSTRALIAN WHEAT AND FLOUR 1978-80

Country	1978-79		1979-80*	
	'000t	$ million	'000t	$ million
China	1 438	139.6	3 572	452.9
Egypt	1 213	144.3	1 683	251.1
Indonesia	563	70.5	660	98.2
Iraq	431	57.5	1 201	179.3
Japan	969	117.6	985	147.0
USSR	157	15.3	2 617	432.0
TOTAL	6 824	794.2	14 840	2 178.1
WORLD TOTAL PRODUCTION	236 600		n.a.	

Note: * provisional.
Source: *Year Book Australia.* (no 65, 1981) Australian Govt Publishing Service, Canberra.

Table 4

OATS CROP STATISTICS 1978-83

	1978-79	1980-81	1981-82	1982-83
Area for grain '000ha	1 359	1 093	1 387*	1 340†
Gross value $m	100.5	139*	183*	126†
Volume '000t	1 763	1 128	1 619*	840†
Mean yield t/ha	1.3	1.03	1.17*	0.63†

Note: * provisional; † estimated by the Bureau of Agricultural Economics.
Source: *Quarterly Review of the Rural Economy*. (vol 4, no 4, Nov 1982) Australian Govt Publishing Service, Canberra.

Table 5

BARLEY CROP STATISTICS 1979-84

	1979-80	1980-81	1981-82	1982-83	1983-84
Area for grain '000ha	2 482	2 451	2 685*	2 495†	3 052†
Gross value $m	449.8	381	510*	314†	516†
Export value $m	407.3	340.9	344*	206†	237†
Volume '000t	3 703	2 682	3 450*	1 858†	3 985†
Mean yield t/ha	1.49	1.09	1.28*	0.74†	1.31†

Note: * provisional, subject to revision; † estimated by the Bureau of Agricultural Economics..
Source: *Quarterly Review of the Rural Economy*, (vol 5, no 3, Aug 1983), Australian Govt Publishing Service, Canberra.

Sorghum A summer-grown crop of warm regions, sorghum is cultivated mainly in QLD and northern NSW. Various species are grown, for silage, hay-making or green grazing, and also for grain used as stock feed. Some varieties (broom sorghum or millet) are used for making brooms.

Maize A summer cereal grown mainly in NSW and the ATHERTON TABLELAND, maize is cultivated to provide green fodder and grain for stock. The use of higher-yielding hybrid varieties is becoming common.

Oilseeds Cotton, linseed, peanuts, rapeseed, safflower, sunflower and soybeans are grown in Australia. All yield oils which generally have high proportions of unsaturated fatty acids, making them (in the opinion of some dieticians) more suitable for margarine production than, for example, palm and coconut oils. With the exception of linseed, which gives an industrial oil now largely replaced by synthetic products, oilseed is sold as seed, extracted oil (used for both food and industrial purposes) and protein residue (used for human and livestock consumption).

At present, sunflower accounts for the greatest area of the cultivation. It is a summer-growing annual cultivated mainly in the E States, the crop being used principally for oil. Peanuts (or groundnuts), almost all grown in QLD, provide nuts mainly for eating, the production of oil being a minor use. Soybeans grow best in temperate regions with hot, damp summers (though they are drought-resistant from their flowering onwards), and are cultivated mainly in QLD and NSW. Oilseed exports are substantial, but overseas sales fluctuate markedly. (*See* Table 6).

Cotton Grown for its fibre as well as for oil, the cotton shrub is usually grown as an annual on irrigated land, though some is grown without irrigation in QLD. The main areas of production are the NAMOI RIVER valley and the MACQUARIE RIVER valley in NSW, and in central QLD and the ST GEORGE area, QLD. Attempts were made to cultivate cotton in the ORD RIVER area in WA, but serious insect infestations made it impracticable: despite the application of insecticides at a rate that has been claimed as a world record, various insects and particularly *Heliothis* caterpillars developed high resistance to pesticides and could no longer be controlled. Because of the wide variety of insects that feed upon it in various parts of the world, cotton is sometimes described as the crop most beloved by entomologists.

The initial processing of cotton involves removing the long fibres (lint) from the seed-cotton in ginneries. The short fibres (linters), used for felt-making, surgical cotton and so on, are removed in the oil mills where the kernels are crushed. The protein residue may be used as a livestock feed, and the husks as fuel. A substantial proportion of the crop is exported as raw cotton.

NSW Dept. of Tourism

Rice harvesting at Leeton, Riverina NSW

Rice Australian yields from rice crops are about eight times greater than those of tropical Asian countries. Short-, medium- and long-grain varieties are all produced, being grown under irrigation in the summer in NSW

Table 6

OILSEED CROP STATISTICS (EXCLUDING COTTONSEED AND PEANUTS) 1980-82

	Sunflower seed		Soybeans		Other oil seeds	
	1980-81	1981-82	1980-81	1981-82	1980-81	1981-82
Area '000ha	198	178*	44	41*	52	58*
Gross value $m	34	27	22	20*	9	10*
Volume '000t	139	115*	73.2	77*	32.8	40*

Note: * provisional.
Source: *Quarterly Review of the Rual Economy*. (vol 5, no 3, Aug 3) Australian Govt Publishing Service, Canberra.

(yielding one crop per annum), and in the INGHAM area and on the BURDEKIN delta in QLD, where it is also grown as a winter crop (thus yielding two crops per annum). Summer crops are drilled into the ground or seeded from the air directly into water. Drill-sown crops are flooded and drained alternately until the plants are advanced enough for permanent flooding.

Sugar cane First grown commercially near Brisbane in 1862, sugar cane is now grown from Mossman in northern QLD to the CLARENCE RIVER in NSW, in areas with suitable soils and an annual rainfall of 1000mm or more, or under irrigation. About 6 600 properties in the two States grow cane. Cane is initially grown from setts (cuttings from mature cane), planted mechanically between June and December and maturing in about a year in QLD but in up to two years in NSW. When the crop is cut, new shoots grow from the established root-stock, growing a 'ratoon' crop which may be harvested for three or four successive years before fallowing and the planting of new setts. Australia was the first country to introduce mechanical cultivation of the crop, formerly labour-intensive (using first KANAKA and later European labour); since 1964 the whole industry has been subject to bulk-handling. Thirty-four mills receive cane on a quota system from the growers, and there are six bulk-handling terminals holding almost 1.5 million tonnes. Current long-term contracts and the domestic market ensure sales for about 65 per cent of the product, the remainder of the export sugar entering the free market. Australia is the world's third-largest exporter of raw sugar. The bagasse (fibrous residue left after the extraction of the raw sugar) is used as fuel in the mills. Because cane is so productive in suitable climates, it is thought that it may serve as a source of liquid fuel in the future. (*See* Table 7).

Vegetables CHINESE market gardeners who began growing vegetables commercially during the gold rushes were once responsible for almost all such produce, and a few still continue the tradition (for instance, near BOTANY BAY), but the industry is now largely carried out by people of German, Italian or Yugoslav origin and by native-born Australians. The largest proportion of vegetables produced is grown in VIC, followed in order by NSW, QLD, TAS, SA and WA. Only a very small percentage is grown for export, large quantities being transported to city markets to be sold as fresh produce, and a considerable proportion being grown under contract with food processors for canning and freezing. Important crops are beans, cabbages and brussels sprouts, carrots, cauliflowers, onions, green peas and tomatoes. Also commonly grown are cucumbers, melons and other cucurbits, peppers, sweet corn, turnips, spinach, silver beet and asparagus.

However, the largest hectarage is devoted to potato growing, which has become a highly mechanised industry. Much of the crop is now grown under irrigation in deep, well-fertilised, easily worked soil, usually as a summer crop because of its vulnerability to severe frosts. Potatoes are also very vulnerable to pests and diseases in both field and store, and in particular to virus diseases transmitted by APHIDS. Some such viruses persist in the tubers so that growers in warm districts where aphids are common must buy their seed potatoes from cooler areas, under seed-certification schemes. About a quarter of the entire crop is processed in various ways to produce foodstuffs such as crisps, frozen chips, dehydrated powder, tinned salad and baby foods. Only a few thousand tonnes are exported each year and, indeed, large quantities of processed potatoes are imported.

Hops Grown mainly in TAS and VIC, hops are used for flavouring beer. They grow each year from perennial rootstocks and are trained on trellis wires. After picking, green hops are dried in kilns (called oast houses in England), and bleached with sulphur dioxide.

Mushrooms The bulk of the mushroom crop is grown in NSW. Requiring a temperature of between 4°C and 21°C and a relative humidity of about 80 per cent, mushrooms are usually grown indoors or in old railway tunnels, caves and so on, the mushroom spawn being mixed with compost containing horse manure and the beds later being cased with sterilised soil. Several 'flushes' are gathered each year, 70 per cent being sold fresh and the remainder being processed.

Tobacco A summer-growing annual of tropical and warm temperate regions, most tobacco in Australia is grown under irrigation, mainly at MAREEBA in QLD and MYRTLEFORD in VIC. Almost all Australian tobacco is of the flue-cured variety. Australia produces enough tobacco to meet just over half the market demand, the remainder being imported either unmanufactured or as cigarettes.

Other crops Various other crops grown in Australia include specialist crops, such as ginger, and opium poppies for the pharmaceutical industry.

See also fruit growing; wine industry
Further reading: Year Book of Australia. (various issues) Australian Bureau of Statistics, Canberra; Wheelhouse, F. *Digging Stick to Rotary Hoe.* Cassell, Sydney, 1966; Molnar, I. (ed) *A Manual of Australian Agriculture.* (3rd

Harvesting sugar cane, Ord river irrigation project

Courtesy of A.I.S. Canberra

AUSTRALIAN AGRICULTURE: GENERAL STATISTICS INCLUDING LIVESTOCK INDUSTRIES

	1978-79	1980-81*	1981-82*
Gross value of rural production $m	10 228	11 525	12 450
Farm costs $m	5 768	7 381	8 330
Farm income $	4 460	4 144	4 120
Number of farm establishments	177 220	175 760	n.a.
Income per farm $	25 166	23 578	n.a.
Value of rural exports $m	6 011	8 180	7 930

Note: * provisional; n.a. not available.
Source: *Quarterly Review of the Rural Economy.* (vol 3, no 2, Aug 1981 & vol 4, no 4, Nov 1982) Australian Govt Publishing Service, Canberra.

Table 7

SUGAR CROP STATISTICS 1978-83

	1978-79	1979-80	1980-81	1981-82	1982-83
Area cut for crushing '000ha	252	267	288	316*	319*
Gross value of cut cane $m	396.5	548.2	800	585*	503*
Exports value (sugar) $m	448.2	666.8	1 145.9	716*	588*
Volume '000t					
(a) cane	21 457	21 151	23 976	25 136*	24 909*
(b) sugar	2 902	2 963	3 329	3 434*	3 535*
Mean yield t/ha of sugar cane	85.1	79.2	83.2	79.5*	78.1

Note: * provisional, subject to revision; † estimated by the Bureau of Agricultural Economics.
Source: *Quarterly Review of the Rural Economy,* (vol 5, no 3, Aug 1983), Australian Govt Publishing Service, Canberra.

edn) Heinemann, Melbourne, 1974; Lazenby, A. & Matheson, E.M. (eds) *Australian Field Crops*. (vol 1) Angus & Robertson, Sydney, 1975.

AIF *see* Australian Imperial Force

Air Force, Royal Australian *see* defence

albacores *see* fishes, bony

Albany WA (population 15 222 in 1981) The port and main regional centre for the SW of WA, Albany is located on Princess Royal Harbour, an inlet off KING GEORGE SOUND on the S coast of the State, about 400km by road SE of Perth. It is the terminus of the Great Southern Railway, with several alternative routes to Perth (some now serviced by Westrail buses) and links to numerous towns on the SW such as KATANNING and NARROGIN to the N, and PEMBERTON, BRIDGETOWN and BUNBURY to the NW. Albany was the site of the first British settlement in WA, dating from 1826 when Major Edmund LOCKYER landed and established a foothold, two and a half years before Perth was settled. It developed as a port and business focus, though was somewhat eclipsed by the opening of the FREMANTLE inner harbour in 1897; recent rural development in the hinterland has accelerated its growth. It handles wheat, wool, meat and other rural produce, has oil storage facilities, a superphosphate factory and woollen mills, and is a wool selling centre.

The town has an average annual rainfall of 815mm, concentrated in winter (June, July and August all have averages over 100mm), with dry and sunny summer months. A well-known feature of the summer weather is the 'Albany Doctor', a cool afternoon sea breeze which provides welcome relief from the daytime heat. These ideal climatic conditions, combined with the beaches, the scenic landscapes, the historic features and the opportunities for fishing, surfing, sailing and other aquatic sports, have made the area a popular tourist and holiday resort. At the W of the Sound, on Frenchmans Bay, a whaling station operated until late in the 1970s. Some of the tourist features of the town and district are the Residency building where Lockyer's monument stands, the Old Farm (Strawberry Hill) built in 1831, the Patrick Taylor Museum containing mementos of the colonial days, the Desert Mounted Corps Memorial (brought from Egypt after the Suez crisis in 1956 and re-erected near the summit of Mt Clarence), and the Gap and National Bridge, two spectacular rock formations 16km out of town. Over 20 buildings have been listed for preservation by the National Trust (WA), including several historic homes and churches, the old hospital (1888), the old gaol (1873), the courthouse (1896), the Residency Museum (1850s), the old post office (1868) and the town hall (1888). The town takes its name from the Duke of York and Albany, brother of King George IV. *See also* Swanland

Further reading: Wilson, H.H. *Albany Sketchbook*. Rigby, Adelaide, 1975.

albatrosses *see* sea birds

Albizia *see* Mimosaceae

Albury NSW (population 36 686 in 1981) This city is on the N side of the MURRAY RIVER, 588km by road SW of Sydney, at the junction of the Hume and Riverina Highways. It is a railway centre, 643km from Sydney and some 300km from Melbourne, and was formerly the change point from the NSW gauge to the VIC system until the standard gauge link was made in 1962. At an elevation of 163m above sea level, it has an average annual rainfall of 680mm, July and August being the two months of highest rainfall and the summer months (January through March) receiving the lowest. The city is an important commercial and service centre to a rich agricultural and pastoral district producing a wide range of crops and livestock. It contains numerous secondary industries, including wool processing and clothing factories, sawmills and furniture making, brick works, a honey processing plant, abattoirs, engineering workshops and even a boomerang factory (32km N of the city) where the art of making and throwing boomerangs is demonstrated.

The settlement of the region began as a result of the important overland journey by the explorers HUME and Hovell in 1824. The town, named after a village in Surrey, England, was gazetted in 1839; the first Murray River steamer reached Albury in 1856 and the paddle-wheelers continued to navigate the stream regularly for about three decades, until overtaken by road and rail transport. Albury became a municipality in 1859 and a city in 1946. On the S side of the Murray, 7km away, in VIC, is the city of WODONGA. Plans were made in the 1970s to develop Albury-Wodonga as an inland growth centre with an ultimate population of 300 000 (their combined population in 1981 was 54 830).

The HUME DAM, located 16km upstream on the Murray, forms a vast lake which attracts many tourists and local residents for swimming, fishing and other aquatic sports. At the N end of the lake is a trout hatchery, the first commercial undertaking of its kind in NSW. The National Trust (NSW) has classified several buildings and listed many more for preservation as part of the nation's cultural heritage: a number of hotels, many cottages, the railway station, the courthouse, the town hall, the post office, the Technical College, several churches and a number of other buildings.

Further reading: Carroll, B. *Albury-Wodonga Sketchbook*. Rigby, Adelaide, 1977.

alder flies These INSECTS form the endopterygote order Megaloptera. There are 16 species of alder fly in Australia, in two families, Corydalidae and Sialidae, the latter being represented by only two species, one in TAS and the other in E Australia. They were

formerly classified under the Neuroptera (*see* ANTLIONS, etc.), but they differ from them in several features, notably in that the venation of their wings is less intricate than that of the lacewings. Alder flies live predominantly in temperate regions and are usually found near cold, clear streams (they take their name originally from the alder trees which in Europe commonly grow on the margins of such streams or ponds).

Adult alder flies are between 15mm and 30mm in length. They have long, filamentous antennae and large, bulging eyes. The anterior mouthparts are of the biting and chewing type, though adult alder flies have not been seen feeding. Their bodies are long and slender (elongate) and rather soft, and carry two similar pairs of long, membranous wings. The abdomen carries a pair of small claspers.

The alder fly larvae are long and flattened in shape, and are aquatic predators with strong, well-developed biting mandibles. They have three pairs of thoracic legs, and the abdomen carries filamentous gills. The alder fly pupae are also active animals, similar to beetle pupae.

algae This is the name given to a large, dissimilar group of primitive plants ranging in size from microscopic single-celled organisms to giant seaweeds such as the kelps. They contain chlorophyll, and are thus photosynthetic plants, but the green colouring is often masked by other pigments. The plant body (thallus) is not divided into roots, stems and leaves (though the non-motile seaweeds are 'anchored' by a holdfast) and there is no vascular tissue, so that algae cannot efficiently transport water and food. Consequently, they are mainly aquatic, though some of the small species can live in damp places on land. There are no flowers, fruits or true seeds. Though the term algae is used for all such plants, many modern classifications now place them in two distinct kingdoms: Monera (blue-green algae) and Plantae (eucaryotic algae).

Blue-green algae Extremely primitive organisms, single-celled or filamentous (formed in a linear column of cells), the blue-green algae may be ancestral to other celled organisms. They are procaryotic; that is, the chromosomes are not enclosed within a nucleus delimited by a membrane. The cell also lacks membrane-enclosed mitochondria, plastids and vacuoles (specialised structures within the cell). For this reason they are now usually regarded as constituting the division Cyanophyta, close to the bacteria (division Schizomycophyta) in the kingdom Monera. Biochemically versatile, many species of blue-green algae can fix nitrogen; reproduction, as far as is known, is always asexual. They are found in many kinds of waters, including saline lakes and hot springs; the genus *Nostoc* sometimes occurs in gelatinous masses on damp soils.

Eucaryotic algae The other forms of algae, comprising over 20 000 species, all have chromosomes enclosed in nuclei (hence 'eucaryotic'), and belong to the Plantae. They are classified largely on the basis of colour, which has been found to correspond to other important characteristics such as food-storing materials and the structure of the cell walls. They are divided into five divisions: Pyrrophyta (dinoflagellates); Chrysophyta (diatoms and related algae); the various kinds of seaweed and related forms, Phaeophyta (brown algae); Rhodophyta (red algae); and Chlorophyta (green algae, including desmids). Seaweeds, often massive plants over 100m long, are attached to the seabed by their holdfasts. Red seaweeds are found in deep water along the shores, and are rarely uncovered by the tides; green algae are generally found at higher levels on the shore, and brown seaweeds are generally intermediate. All the eucaryotic divisions are represented in Australia.

1. Division Pyrrophyta. Comprising some 1 100 species worldwide, the dinoflagellates are mobile, single-celled plants with two flagella (serving for locomotion), one situated in a longitudinal groove, the other in an equatorial (encircling) one, but both arising from the same point. The cell wall contains cellulose. Dinoflagellates are important constituents of the phytoplankton, especially in the sea. Some produce a nerve toxin and when they occur in large numbers (a 'red tide') hundreds of thousands of fish may be killed. Sometimes fatally poisonous to humans is the toxin, produced by the genus *Gonyaulax*, which accumulates in the tissues of shell fish. Some dinoflagellates are luminescent, especially when the water is disturbed, as by the passage of a ship.

2. Division Chrysophyta. This group contains about 10 000 species (worldwide) in three classes: Xanthophyceae (yellow-green algae), Chrysophyceae (golden-brown algae) and Bacillariophyceae (diatoms). The diatoms are the most important members of the group and are well represented in freshwater and marine phytoplankton. Unicellular or filamentous, and either bilaterally or radially symmetrical, diatoms use oils rather than starches for food storage. They reproduce by cell division. They have remarkably sculptured, silica-containing cell walls which are very persistent: after death they often accummulate on the floor of the sea to form, eventually, the sedimentary rocks from which diatomaceous earths are obtained.

3. Division Phaeophyta. The brown algae, a diverse group of about 1000 species of seaweeds containing the brown pigment fucoxanthin, offer a variety of commercial uses: the alginates derived from them are valuable as non-toxic compounds which readily form gels, used as thickeners in foods, additives to cosmetics, and so on. Their food-storing materials are chrysolaminarin, oils and mannitol, and the cell walls contain cellulose, pectin and alginic acids. Several species are common in Australian waters. Neptune's necklace, *Hormosira banksii*, a seaweed of the mid-tide zone of rocky coasts, is aptly described by its common name, the round 'beads' being vesicles containing either sperm or eggs. The bull kelp, *Durvillea potatorum*, occurring at the lowest intertidal level on S coasts to about as far N as Sydney, and also on

South American coasts, has a characteristic attachment disc, and the strap-like fronds can attain a length of 7.5m. *Ecklonia*, occurs in the same zones as the bull kelp. Species of *Sargassum* (related to the notorious free-floating weed of the Sargasso Sea) are often abundant at low-tide level.

4. Division Rhodophyta. Comprising about 3000 species, of which about half the world's genera are represented in Australian waters, the red algae contain the red pigment phycoerythrin and the blue pigment phycocyanin. The food-storing material of rhodophytes is a form of starch, and the cell walls contain cellulose, pectins and mucilages such as those yielding the valuable product agar-agar, extensively used in bacteriological research, and in the manufacture of foodstuffs and cosmetics. The colour of 'red' algae is relative to the intensity of light penetrating the habitat: specimens which are red when growing in shaded positions may be bright green when exposed to sunlight. Most red algae, however, grow below the tidal ranges. Most are small plants, often with filamentous fronds. A common seashore species forming slippery mats on rocks close to low-tide level is *Bangia fuscopurpurea*, whose hair-like filaments, only a few centimetres long, are brown rather than red.

Many brown and red seaweeds deposit calcium carbonate in their cell walls but this is carried to the extreme in the coralline seaweeds, which have stony 'foliage'. Among the genera common on the seashore are *Corallina*, *Jania*, *Amphiroa* and *Arthrocardia* (whose fronds often appear to be jointed). Several coralline seaweeds are important in coral-reef building (*see* CORALS) forming the 'cement' which binds the reef together. The most important genera in Australian coral reefs are *Lithophyllum* and *Porolithon*. Unicellular algae often live as symbionts in coral polyps.

5. Division Chlorophyta. The green algae and the desmids (unicellular or colonial algae related to the diatoms but lacking the siliceous cell wall) number some 6 000 species worldwide. Containing large forms as well as many microscopic organisms, the group is believed to be ancestral to the land plants; of the photosynthetic pigments characteristic of higher plants, chlorophytes are the only algae containing chlorophyll *b* as well as chlorophyll *a*. They store food as starch, and their cell walls contain cellulose and pectins. Among the larger forms is the sea lettuce, *Ulva lactuca* (also common in Britain), whose flat fronds, consisting of two layers of cells, may be cooked or eaten as salads. The smaller forms include photosynthetic flagellates akin to members of the Protozoa (some are classed with them), such as the single-celled *Euglena* and the colonial *Volvox* species, both common in freshwater. An interesting and valuable non-motile chlorophyte is the genus *Chlorella*, which can be grown in great quantities in a volume of water with a very small surface area: rich in proteins and B-complex vitamins, it has been tested as a source of food, and as a source of oxygen for space flights.

Further reading: Dakin, W.J., Bennett, I. & Pope, E. *Australian Seashores.* (6th edn) Angus & Robertson, Sydney, 1976; Raven, P.H., Evert, R.F. & Curtis, H. *Biology of Plants.* (2nd edn) Wurth, New York, 1976; Clayton, M.N. & King, R.J. (eds) *Marine Botany: An Australasian Perspective.* Longman-Cheshire London, 1981; Christianson, I.G., Clayton, M.N. & Allender, B.M. (eds) *Seaweeds of Australia.* Reed, Sydney, 1981.

Alice Springs NT (population 18 395 in 1981) To the local folk the town is just 'The Alice', but for most Australians it stands as the symbol of the vast 'Red Centre', the focal point of the arid inland of the continent and an oasis of civilisation in the great central desert. The name dates back to the 1870s when the OVERLAND TELEGRAPH line was being built: the Alice Springs were waterholes, named after the wife of Sir Charles Todd, Postmaster General of SA; the town was originally called Stuart, after the explorer, John McDouall STUART, and it retained this name until 1933. Located on the TODD RIVER, 1 524km S of Darwin along the Stuart Highway, some 1 594km NNW of Adelaide, and 294km N of the SA border, it is the terminus of the railway from SA and since 1929, when the line was built from OODNADATTA, it has been a railhead for the cattle and mining industries of the CENTRE. At an elevation of 545km, the town is situated near Heavitree Gap, a break in the MACDONNELL RANGES. Noted for its dry climate, the town's average yearly rainfall is only 246mm, but this is most unpredictable and unreliable: months may pass with no rain at all, or a heavy thunderstorm may bring brief torrential falls. In winter (April to October), the days are warm, and the evenings are pleasantly, sometimes crisply, cool. In the summer period, days are hot—sometimes scorchingly so, but usually with very little humidity—and the nights are warm.

Alice Springs Camel Cup

The town is linked by jet airlines to the capital cities of the nation. But the FLYING DOCTOR SERVICE base and the School of the Air are reminders that it provides a vital link with the people of the wide Outback regions. It is the tourist focus for visits to some of the scenic grandeur and unique features of the Centre: to the W in the MacDonnell Ranges are Simpson's Gap, STANDLEY CHASM, and Ormiston Gorge; to the E are Emily and Jessie

Gaps, Corroboree Rock, Trephina Gorge and the Valley of the Eagles; to the S along the railway line are the famed Ewaninga Aboriginal rock carvings; to the SW, 149km away, are the Henbury meteorite craters; and further afield, 246km to the SW, lie AYERS ROCK and, 32km beyond it, MOUNT OLGA.

Alligator Rivers NT Three rivers in the NW of the Territory bear this name, distinguished only by a directional prefix, namely the East, South and West Alligator Rivers. All drain into VAN DIEMEN GULF via mangrove-fringed, crocodile-infested estuaries. The East and South rivers have their headwaters in the uplands of ARNHEM LAND and flow for over 300km from this rugged gorge country across the coastal plains to the swampy lowlands. The West Alligator is a shorter coastal stream. Typical of NT rivers, they all experience a high water flow in the wet season (November to March) when their channels spread over a wide expanse of the plains making land travel virtually impossible. The Arnhem Highway branches off the Stuart Highway 35km S of Darwin and crosses the lower reaches of these rivers, extending over 220km to Jabiru near the border of the Arnhem Land Aboriginal Reserve. The rivers were discovered in 1818 by Phillip King, son of Governor KING, and named Alligator by him, though they should, more correctly, have been called 'Crocodile', there being no members of the alligator genus in Australia.

allseed see Caryophyllaceae

ALP see Australian Labor Party

aluminium This metal and its alloys are used in all sectors of the world's economies, principally in transportation, construction, electrical engineering, containers and packaging, consumer durables and mechanical equipment.
Extraction The main source of aluminium is bauxite, an ore composed mainly of aluminium hydroxides and small quantities of numerous other secondary minerals. To be used for the production of aluminium, bauxite should contain less than 10 per cent iron and six per cent silica.

Large-scale production of aluminium became feasible with the simultaneous discovery in 1886 by C.M. Hall, in the USA, and P. Heroult, in France, of an electrolytic process to reduce alumina (aluminium oxide) to metal. In the same year an Austrian, Karl Bayer, invented a chemical process to produce alumina from bauxite. The production of aluminium from bauxite by the Bayer-Hall method comprises two stages: the reduction of bauxite to produce alumina, and the smelting of alumina to make aluminium. This process requires about 4kg of bauxite to produce 1kg of aluminium. Although other processes of extracting aluminium from bauxite and low-grade clays have been developed, the Bayer-Hall method remains the cornerstone of the aluminium industry. Interesting by-products from aluminium production include gallium, a unique metal with potential industrial and atomic uses, and vanadium, which is used as an alloy in the manufacture of hard steels and

as a catalyst in oxidising aniline.
Production in Australia In 1980 Australia produced just over 27 million tonnes of bauxite, accounting for about 29 per cent of the world's total production. Table 1 shows the output figures for the various States and emphasises the marked increase in production during the period 1970-80. The major centres of bauxite production are WEIPA in QLD, GOVE PENINSULA in the NT and in the DARLING RANGE, S of Perth. A small quantity is mined near MOSS VALE in NSW, and there is some intermittent production from Mirboo North in VIC. Aluminium refineries are located at GLADSTONE in QLD, at KWINANA and PINJARRA in WA, and at Gove, and there are aluminium smelters at KURRI KURRI in NSW, at BELL BAY in TAS, and at Point Henry in VIC.
World production The world's aluminium industry is controlled by six integrated firms; they have a direct interest in almost half the world's production and, through 40 private companies, an indirect interest in a further 25 per cent. The remainder of the production capacity is owned by the governments of 24 countries in association with private mining and metallurgical firms. The high capital costs of aluminium-producing facilities make it difficult for new companies to enter the industry. Costs per tonne of annual capacity for new enterprises lie within the following ranges: a bauxite mine $30 to $90; an alumina-producing plant $500 to $800; a primary aluminium plant $1 500 to $2 000; and an aluminium scrap melting installation $200 to $500.

The world production of aluminium in 1980

The Aluminium Industry in Australia

Table 1

PRODUCTION OF BAUXITE IN AUSTRALIA 1970-81
(in tonnes)

State	1970	1973	1976	1979	1981
QLD	5 771 164	8 980 832	8 226 368	9 576 944	8 694 409
NSW	9 896	7 839	3 857	3 289	1 727
VIC	849	—	2 136	3 108	7 104
WA	3 474 440	5 740 532	11 539 150	13 378 637	12 322 355
NT	—	2 866 717	4 521 000	4 621 451	4 415 797
TOTAL	9 256 349	17 595 920	24 292 511	27 583 429	25 441 392

Source: *Australian Mineral Industry Annual Review*, (1970-81), Australian Govt Publishing Service, Canberra.

was 16 051 000 tonnes; with an estimated five per cent annual increase, this figure should reach 73 million tonnes by the end of the century. The known reserves of bauxite are, however, adequate to meet the cumulative world demand beyond AD 2000. Other resources such as clay of the kaolin type, anorthosite and alunite will be used in the future. The primary aluminium brought to the world markets will also be increasingly augmented by a feedback of recovered aluminium scrap (secondary aluminium) introduced into the production cycle.

The historical price stability of aluminium has been an important factor in the high growth rate of the industry. For many years the demand for other major metals has been falling, with the result that the uses of aluminium now exceed that of any other metal except iron. Because aluminium is of significant strategic value, it is in the interests of producing countries to formulate policies ensuring an adequate supply of the metal during periods of international conflict.

Further reading: see under minerals and mining.

ambergris *see* dolphins, etc.

America's Cup *see* sailing

amoeba *see* protozoons

amphibians

The amphibians are VERTEBRATES belonging to the class Amphibia, which contains such animals as the FROGS AND TOADS (order Anura, having about 2000 species worldwide); the lizard-like newts and salamanders (order Caudata, about 300 species, virtually restricted to the N hemisphere); and the legless, burrowing caecilians (order Apoda, about 75 species, tropical animals which do not seem to occur in Australia). The amphibians are of particular interest because of their position in the evolutionary series; they appear to have been the first land vertebrates, and are known from the end of the Devonian period (the 'age of fishes') about 270 million years ago, having apparently evolved from fishes with lungs, and thus being distantly related to the QUEENSLAND LUNG FISH and its allies. The earliest REPTILES have been traced back to one amphibian line which became independent of the water by the development of a shelled, watertight egg. Amphibian classification is by no means standardised, however, there being as yet insufficient fossil material to allow definitive lines to be traced from the modern groups to their Paleozoic ancestors.

Amphibians are cold-blooded animals with soft, glandular skins which make them susceptible to drying out, and thus they need a moist environment. Most species have aquatic larval stages, the shell-less eggs being deposited in water, and the larvae (tadpoles) then metamorphosing into the predatory adults, nearly all of which spend part of their life cycle on land, though usually either in moist debris or in the vicinity of water. Some are wholly aquatic (such as the eel-like sirens and others of the salamander group), and others wholly terrestrial—many Australian frogs lay their eggs on land, the larvae developing within the eggs and emerging as miniature frogs.

Further reading: Cogger, H.G. *Reptiles and Amphibia of Australia.* A.H. & A.W. Reed, Sydney, 1975.

amphioxus *see* lancelets

anabranch

This is probably a uniquely Australian name used to describe a river feature when a stream leaves the main river and rejoins it further downstream. That is, an anabranch is a distributary of a river (the reverse of a tributary) which links up with the river again. Many anabranches are found in Australian inland rivers; for instance, the Great Anabranch of the DARLING, which branches off the river S of MENINDEE, flows for some 480km and joins the MURRAY RIVER below the Darling confluence.

Ancher, Sydney Edward (1904-79)

Architect. The work of Sydney Ancher holds a unique place in the story of Australian architecture, for it was he who first introduced the crisp tight lines of the Bauhaus, and fought public prejudice and bureaucracy in order to have the aesthetics of the Modern Movement accepted.

After obtaining the Sydney Technical College diploma and winning a scholarship, Ancher worked overseas until the mid-1930s. His first Australian house was at Bellevue Hill in 1937 —a severe and ordered composition of white walls, a flat roof, a wide balcony and curved glass, very Continental and stylish.

After five years of war service he returned to private practice and won the coveted Sulman Award with the design of his own house in Gordon. It was not the house he wanted to build, however, for the local council insisted on brick walls where he had intended a steel frame, and on slate or tile (he selected slates) where he had intended a flat roof. Two years later Ancher faced a similar municipal interference when Warringah Council refused a building permit for a large modern flat-roofed house unless the architect made modifications to its appearance. The resentful architect and his client appealed at law. In 1948, in a now famous judgement, Mr Justice Sugerman upheld the architect on the grounds that architectural progress was in the public interest. 'The development of architecture must be impeded', part of the judgement read, 'while any large and important area closes its gates to the unfamiliar in architecture.'

Until 1956, Sydney Ancher's work was the most influential in NSW and though he retired in 1965 his practice continues as Ancher, Mortlock and Woolley. Ancher himself was the recipient in 1975 of the Gold Medal of the Royal Australian Institute of Architects.

Andamooka

SA (population 402 in 1981, though it varies according to the fortunes of the opal prospectors) An opal-mining centre located off the Stuart Highway about 750km N of Adelaide, near the NW shore of LAKE TORRENS, 127km NNE of WOOMERA, Andamooka's opal diggings are spread over a wide area of low undulating hills where visitors, by obtaining a 'Precious Stones Prospecting Permit', can try their luck—providing that they do not trespass on any of the pegged claims of the local prospectors. The town is at an elevation of 76m and has a climatic pattern typical of the semi-arid inland regions, receiving an annual average rainfall of 203mm, though this is unpredictable and variable from year to year. Andamooka is the youngest Australian opal field, discovered in 1930 by two prospectors who had been forced by floods to move to higher ground where, by chance, they found black opals. Regular tourist bus services operate from Adelaide to the town and an airline service brings supplies, mail and visitors.

Further reading: Colahan, J. *Australian Opal Safari.* Rigby, Adelaide, 1973.

Anderson, John (1893-1962)

Philosopher. Born in Lanarkshire, Scotland, he was educated at the University of Glasgow, and lectured at a number of British universities before becoming Challis Professor of Philosophy at the University of Sydney in 1927. His tenure of that position lasted until 1958, and during this long period he exercised a profound influence not only on philosophical thought but on the general intellectual life of Sydney. His readiness to comment on public issues, and perhaps most of all his criticism of religious indoctrination, made him a controversial figure. In view of his great influence it is strange that he himself published no major work. However, most of his writings have been collected and published since his death.

Anderson, Dame Judith (1898-)

Actress. Born in Adelaide as Frances Margaret Anderson, she migrated to the USA in 1918 and soon laid the basis for an outstandingly successful stage career. After touring Australia in 1927, she filled a succession of starring roles in the USA in plays by contemporary playwrights—most notably the title role in *Medea*. In 1948 she received the Donaldson award for 'the most distinguished actress in the American theatre'. She has also had a number of screen successes, including those in *Rebecca, Salome, King's Row, Laura,* and *Cat on a Hot Tin Roof*. Dame Judith visited Australia again in 1955 and 1966. She was appointed DBE in 1960.

anemones, sea *see* coelenterates

Angas, George Fife (1789-1879)

Philanthropist and a founder of SA. He was born at Newcastle upon Tyne, and became wealthy as a shipowner, both in his own right and through inheriting his father's shipping interests. He became interested in plans to found a colony in SA in 1832, when he accepted a position on the committee of the short-lived South Australian Land Co. After the passing of the South Australian Act of 1834, he became a member of the Board of Commissioners set up to promote and control land sales in the proposed colony. However, he resigned from that position after founding the South Australian Co., which bought a large amount of land from the Board. He played a major part in organising the first party of settlers sent to SA by the company.

Mitchell Library

George Fife Angas

In 1838 he gave encouragement and financial assistance to the first large party of German settlers to emigrate to SA, and later helped two more shiploads. In 1840 he purchased a large amount of land in the BAROSSA VALLEY, and in 1843 sent his son, John Howard Angas, to supervise his business interests in the colony. In 1850 he decided to come to SA himself and on his arrival in the following year joined his son at ANGASTON in the Barossa. In the same year he was returned unopposed as a member for the Barossa in the Legislative Council, and in 1857 was elected to membership of the first Legislative Council under responsible government, a position he retained until 1866. In both England and Australia he engaged in many forms of humanitarian and religious activity, and was an office-holder in many philanthropic societies.
Further reading: Price, A.G. *Founders and Pioneers of South Australia.* F.W. Preece & Sons, Adelaide, 1929.

Angaston SA (population 1 753 in 1981) This is a small town in the NE part of the BAROSSA VALLEY, 83km by rail NE of Adelaide. The surrounding rural regions, typical of the valley, produce grapes, stone fruits and vegetables. The town contains wineries, a fruit canning factory and cement works.
Further reading: Chinner, B. *Angaston Sketchbook.* Rigby, Adelaide, 1977.

angelica *see* Umbelliferae

Angiospermae Angiosperms are flowering plants in which the seeds are enclosed within the pistil. They exceed all other vascular plants in range and diversity of the plant body and habitat and are the most recent group of plants to develop on earth, their origins being in the Cretaceous period; they constitute the largest group of modern plants, containing about 250 000 species. The diversity, distribution and relationships of Australia's angiosperms are discussed in the entries entitled FLORA and VEGETATION.

Angiosperms may be woody or herbaceous and include herbs, shrubs, trees, vines, aquatics and epiphytes. They occur in all Australian plant communities; some Australian angiosperms are aquatic, though few occur in the marine environment. Woody angiosperms are used extensively as timber, as fuel, for paper-making and as the source of commercial cork; herbaceous types are important sources of fibres, textiles, drugs and vegetable oils. Both woody and herbaceous angiosperms are major sources of food, with both the reproductive parts (buds, seeds and fruits) and vegetative parts (leaves, stems and roots or tubers) being used.

Angiosperms may be divided into annual or perennial plants. In annual plants the seed germinates, grows, flowers and sets seed within one year or often in very much less time in harsh environments such as deserts, where such annuals are known as ephemerals. All annuals are herbaceous. Perennial plants may be either herbaceous or woody, and may live from two to several hundred years. In many woody perennials flowering and seed setting may be delayed for many years after seed germination.

The angiosperm flower is a specialised region of the plant solely concerned with reproduction. In general, the flower is made up of whorled parts, the outermost, or sepals, forming the calyx; these are often green and leaf-like. The next whorl, often brightly coloured, is the corolla, made up of petals. Neither of these whorls plays any direct part in reproduction but may be important in protecting the developing sexual organs (sepals) and in attracting pollinators (petals). The central whorl is the pistil, the female part of the flower, which is surrounded by the male parts (stamens). Each pistil is made up of a swollen basal portion—the ovary, containing one or more ovules which after fertilisation develop into seeds—and a more or less elongated portion—the style, supporting the stigma which has a specialised surface designed to catch the pollen grains and allow them to germinate. The stamen is made up of a supporting stalk, or filament, and a terminal anther in which pollen grains develop. Pollination may be effected by wind, insects, birds or mammals, and involves transfer of the pollen from the anther to the style. Fertilisation occurs when the nucleus of the pollen grain fuses with that of the ovule, having been carried to this position by the growth of a pollen tube through the tissues of the stigma and style, on which it is parasitic for nutrients.
Classification Flowering plants are classified according to the number and arrangement of flowers on the plant and of parts within the flower. Those plants with identical arrangements are grouped into species, species into genera and genera into families. In this encyclopedia, information on Australian flowering plants is, in most cases, entered under family names (for example, GRAMINEAE—grasses; MYRTACEAE—eucalypts, tea trees, bottle brushes; PROTEACEAE—*Banksia, Grevillea, Hakea;* PAPILIONACEAE—peas; MIMOSACEAE—wattles).

Classification of plants is based on the reproductive structures because these alone remain constant in form. Unlike animals, plants exhibit much variation in form, with the local environment and growth history of individual plants contributing significantly to the shape and size of the mature plant. The flowers of each species, however, remain consistent in structure and arrangement, regardless of the general shape of individuals within a species. In some genera, notably *Acacia* and *Eucalyptus,* the structure of the flower remains remarkably consistent throughout the whole genus; in such cases, the arrangement of the flowers and selected vegetative characteristics (for example, leaf shape and arrangement, bark type) are also used for field recognition of individual species.
See also Appendix 6, Flower Structure and Glossary of Botanical Terms; Caryophyllaceae; Casuarinaceae; Chenopodiaceae; Compositae; Cyperaceae; Epacridaceae; Euphorbiaceae; Haemodoraceae; Liliaceae; Orchidaceae; Palmae; Restionaceae; Rutaceae; Solanaceae; Sterculiaceae; Umbelliferae
Further reading: see Appendix 6, A Bibliography for Plants.

Anglican Church of Australia Until recently this Church was known officially in Australia as the Church of England. This name has therefore been used in this article in describing the Church's historical development. Proceedings for changing the name from 'Church of England in Australia' to 'Anglican Church of Australia' were begun in 1970. However, the change required the passing of legislation by all Australian Parliaments, and this was completed only in 1981.

From the beginning of British settlement in Australia until fairly recently, the majority of settlers have come from England. It is not surprising therefore to find that the Church of England has always had more professed adherents than any other denomination. However, the flood of non-British immigrants since World War II has lowered the proportion of Anglicans in the Australian population from 39.01 per cent in 1947 to 26.1 per cent in 1981. In TAS, which has not attracted its due share of post-war immigration, the proportion of Anglicans is considerably higher than the national average. In SA and VIC, where Methodism in the one and Presbyterianism in the other have been particularly strong, the proportion of Anglicans is below the national average.

Historical development When the colony of NSW was founded the Church of England was the Established Church of its native land and thus it was natural that one of its clergymen should have been appointed as official chaplain. He was Rev. Richard JOHNSON, a member of the evangelical wing of the Church, who had been supported in his application for the position by no less a person than William Wilberforce, the anti-slavery campaigner. He held the colony's first religious service under a tree on 3 February 1788, but did not succeed in opening the first church building until 1793, and was not reimbursed for the cost of it for another four years. A second chaplain, Samuel MARSDEN, arrived in NSW in 1794, and 10 years later the first chaplain in VAN DIEMEN'S LAND, Rev. Robert Knopwood, arrived in Hobart with the party commanded by Lieutenant-Governor David COLLINS.

St. Phillip's Church, Sydney 1810

National Library of Australia

These and other early Anglican chaplains were appointed government officials, but in ecclesiastical matters were subject to the Bishop of London. For some years they were the only ministers of religion in Australia. However, by 1820 there were also Roman Catholic priests and Methodist clergy, and in 1823 the first Presbyterian cleric, John Dunmore LANG, arrived. Nevertheless, for some years efforts were still made to keep the Church of England in a privileged position. Following John BIGGE's enquiry into the state of the colony in 1819-21, the organisation of the Church was strengthened. Thomas Hobbes SCOTT, who had been Bigge's secretary during the enquiry, was appointed Archdeacon, and in 1826 an Act was passed providing for a seventh of the land in the colony to be set aside for the support of the Church and its schools through a Church and School Corporation. However, in a colony which from the start had contained people from all parts of Britain, including many members of each of the main religious denominations, it proved impossible to keep the Church of England in such a favoured position. Opposition to the Church and School Corporation was so strong that it was suspended in 1829 and abolished in 1833. By the latter date Governor BOURKE, who was opposed to the policy of Anglican privilege, was in office. By his Church Act of 1836 State aid was given to the four main denominations—Anglican, Roman Catholic, Presbyterian and Methodist—an arrangement which was not completely abandoned until 1862. Similar schemes were introduced in other colonies, but abandoned at various times

between 1860 and 1890.

Scott was succeeded as Archdeacon by William Grant BROUGHTON, who in 1836 became the first Bishop of Australia. There followed a period of great development for the Church, in spite of the removal of its former privileges. A separate diocese of TAS was created in 1842, and dioceses of Melbourne, Adelaide and NEWCASTLE in 1847, by which time Broughton had been made the first Bishop of Sydney.

As development continued, strong links were retained with the mother country. Until the 20th century all Bishops were English by birth and education, and until 1962 the Church in Australia was considered part of the mother Church in England. In that year, however, it became officially independent as 'The Church of England in Australia'.

The Church today The basic governing unit in the Church is the diocese. This is the area ruled by a bishop and a synod (an assembly of clergy and laymen who represent the churches of the diocese). A diocese is divided into parishes, each under the direction of a clergyman known as a vicar or rector. The dioceses in each mainland State are grouped together as a province, with an Archbishop in charge of the main diocese (that of the capital city). The Bishop of TAS has the whole of that State as his diocese.

St. Ninian's Church, Canberra

Courtesy of A.I.S. Canberra

For Australia as a whole there is a General Synod, consisting, like the diocesan synods, of both clergy and laymen. Its president, chosen from among the Bishops, is known as the Primate of Australia. The General Synod makes laws ('canons') which, if they affect the whole Church, must be accepted by diocesan synods. However, in most matters the dioceses have considerable autonomy.

All Anglicans accept the religious principles laid down in the Book of Common Prayer and the set of beliefs known as the Thirty-nine Articles. However, in Australia, as in other countries, there are differences of opinion among Anglicans, especially over matters of ceremonial, the various schools of thought being commonly referred to as Anglo-Catholic, High Church, Broad or Middle Church, Low Church and Evangelical. In general, Anglo-Catholics, who are not numerous in Australia, are the most strongly in favour of elaborate ceremonial. Evangelicals

favour particularly simple rituals and a lack of ceremonial; they tend too to lay stress on man's sinful condition, and the need for open participation in the experience of redemption through faith. The Sydney Archdiocese has generally been regarded as the centre of the evangelical tradition; however, all schools of thought may be found represented in a particular diocese.

Like the Roman Catholic Church, the Anglican Church has a number of religious orders which require their members to remain celibate. These include the Bush Brotherhoods, which are separate groups of clergy who have agreed to work for a period in sparsely inhabited areas of NSW and QLD. The best-known order for women is the Sisters of the Church, whose members conduct a number of schools. Again like Roman Catholics, Anglicans commonly refer to their clergy as priests. So far all moves to have women accepted into the priesthood in Australia have failed.

In the 19th century the Church conducted many primary, as well as secondary, schools. After the setting up of 'free, compulsory and secular' systems of education and the abolition of State aid for denominational schools, it continued to maintain a number of schools, but with an emphasis on secondary education. Traditionally there have been separate schools for boys and girls, but in recent years a number have become co-educational in their upper forms.

Like other denominations, the Anglican Church has in recent decades expanded the range of its social welfare work. One of the areas in which it has been particularly active is in the provision of housing of various kinds for elderly people in 'retirement villages' and similar institutions.

Further reading: Giles, R.A. *Constitutional History of the Australian Church.* Skeffington, London, 1929; Rowland, E.C. *A Century of the English Church in New South Wales.* Angus & Robertson, Sydney, 1948; Border, R. *Church and State in Australia, 1788-1872.* SPCK, London, 1962.

Angophora *see* Myrtaceae

Angry Penguins *see* Ern Malley Hoax

animals, feral *see* animals, introduced

animals, introduced Many mammals, birds and fishes, and one species of toad, have been introduced accidentally or intentionally into Australia and have established breeding populations in the wild. They become established partly because they may fill an empty niche, and partly because they no longer have to contend with the many parasites, pathogens and predators that troubled them in their countries of origin. In many cases, however, they are successful in habitats that have been modified by man and cannot gain a foothold in completely natural habitats. The introduction of these animals often has disastrous results; for example, the

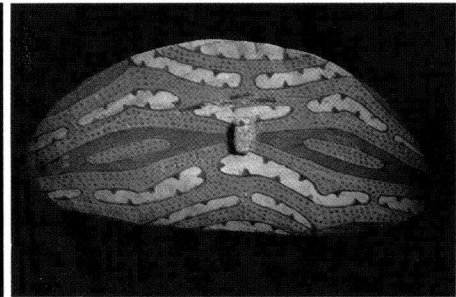

Shields made by the rainforest Aborigines of N QLD (Townsville to Cairns). These large softwood shields were cut from the root buttresses of the Moreton Bay fig tree. Clan symbols were painted on the outer surfaces in earth pigments and charcoal. These shields were found only in the rainforest and were used in conjunction with heavy hardwood swords in close combat

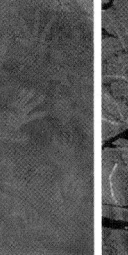

Aboriginal cave painting at Christmas Creek NT   Aboriginal cave painting near Mootwingee NSW   Rock carvings, Mt Chambers Gorge SA

Aboriginal corroboree

Aboriginal dance   Warlpiri man with a perentie goanna

A proclamation issued by Lt-Governor Davey in an effort to explain to the Aborigines the white man's system of justice

Bark painting from Yirrakala NT by Munggerwai, a member of the Dua moiety, of Wuyal, a spiritual ancestor of Djankawu, the Creator of the Dua people. *Story:* After the Djankawu created Wuyal, he sent him travelling round the country. He has a spear thrower, a stone-headed spear and 3 boomerangs. There is a scar on his chest and he is wearing a lap lap made from stringy bark and a special dilly bag around his neck

Bark painting from Caledon Bay, near Yirrkala NT by Bununga, a member of the Yiritja moiety, depicting a symbolic death scene of his mother. *Story:* When someone is dying the dolphins feel this. They come from the sea into shallow water and wait to carry the spirit of the dead person to the spirit land

X-ray style art of the Gunwinggu people who live around Oenpelli NT. The painting shows an emu in X-ray style against a plain red-ochred background. The internal organs are shown clearly

Art from Yirrkala NT. Art style of this region is characterised by a complex pattern of cross-hatching, diamonds, animals and figures

invaders displace the native species by competition or destroy them by predation. The TASMANIAN WOLF and the Tasmanian devil (see NATIVE CATS, etc.) once lived on the mainland but were probably displaced by the DINGO, introduced by the Aborigines; the TAS Aborigines did not have dingoes. Feral domestic cats and the fox have destroyed many small mammals and birds in the areas that they have invaded. It is difficult, however, to determine whether or not a particular native species has disappeared because of an introduced animal or because man has destroyed its habitat.

The following paragraphs list the introduced species that are now established in Australia. Other species such as mongooses have been released from time to time but have not become established.

Mammals
1. Lagomorphs. The two species of lagomorphs now established in Australia are the European rabbit, *Oryctolagus cuniculus* (see RABBITS), and the European hare, *Lepus europaeus*. The latter is larger than the rabbit and lives entirely above ground. It can be a pest of crops and trees.
2. Carnivores. The dingo, *Canis familiaris dingo*, arrived with one of the later waves of Aborigines, probably about 10 000 years ago. It sometimes interbreeds with domestic dogs which can also become feral. The number of feral domestic cats, *Felis catus*, is constantly being replenished by the irresponsible and illegal dumping of unwanted pets in the bush. They have been found in areas as remote as the GIBSON DESERT and the Jardine River in CAPE YORK. Feral cats are generally much larger and far more ferocious than the domestic varieties. The fox, *Vulpes vulpes*, which is now widespread in the S half of the continent, was introduced for hunting. Studies in the Canberra district showed that most of their diet consisted of rabbits, sheep carrion and foetal membranes at lambing time. They are probably a threat to native species.

The black or ship rat

The brown or sewer rat

A. Woods

3. Rodents. The black, ship or roof rat, *Rattus rattus*, the brown or sewer rat, *R. norvegicus*, and the house-mouse, *Mus musculus*, were all early introductions and are now widespread, being found even in the bush. In contrast to European ratios, the black rat is far commoner than the brown (see RODENTS).
4. Deer. Six species, from India, South-East Asia and Europe, are now well established in Australia. They are the axis or chital, *Cervus axis*; the fallow deer, *C. dama*; the red deer, *C. elephas*; the rusa deer, *C. timorensis*; the sambar deer, *C. unicolor*; and the hog deer, *C. porcinus*. All States have herds of at least one species, and none of the species is as troublesome as the introduced deer in New Zealand, where red deer especially have caused severe erosion in alpine areas.
5. Cattle. Within a few weeks of the arrival of the FIRST FLEET the new colony lost most of its seven cows. Seven years later their 60 or so descendants were found at COWPASTURES, 60km from Sydney. Many cows are still feral in remote areas but it is difficult to differentiate between feral and 'domestic' cattle when they are on the open range. Often a brand is the only distinction. On the COBOURG PENINSULA there is a population of the banteng, *Bos javonicus*, a native of Java, Borneo and South-East Asia. They were brought to RAFFLES BAY and PORT ESSINGTON between 1829 and 1840 and became feral when these sites were abandoned. A similar chain of events led to the establishment in the far N of the Indian water buffalo, *Bubalus bubalus*, animals which are ecologically damaging to the wetlands.
6. Sheep and goats. Some sheep, *Ovis aries*, become feral when very large flocks are kept. Goats, *Capra hircus*, were used for milking at mining and railway construction camps, and were often abandoned; they are now feral in a wide range of habitats, and recently it has been found that some carry high-quality Angora wool which may be of value in the future.
7. Camels. The only wild camels in the world, *Camelus dromedarius*, occur in the arid regions of Australia. Camels were invaluable for the opening up of the Centre but were replaced, in the 1920s, by the internal combustion engine. Being well adapted to desert regions, feral camels are found mainly in the Centre.
8. Horses. Feral horses are called brumbies, possibly after an early settler, James (or William) Brumby, who abandoned his horses in 1804. Brumbies were often a pest as they competed with stock for food. Timor ponies (a variety of the horse, *Equus cabellus*) were brought to Raffles Bay, and there is a small population of these attractive animals on the Cobourg Peninsula. Donkeys, *E. asinus*, are still numerous in the interior.
9. Pigs. Many of the wild pigs, *Sus scrofa*, in Australia resemble the wild boars of Europe. Possibly they have reverted to this form after many generations in the wild, but it is also probable that many are descended from pigs imported during the early years of colonisation when few of the modern varieties had been bred. In recent years, feral pigs have become

troublesome in the outer suburbs of large cities such as Sydney. They are dangerous in that they would become an important reservoir of foot-and-mouth disease, and one difficult to eradicate, if the virus were to become established in Australia (see DISEASES, ANIMAL).

Birds Introduced birds have been far less successful than introduced mammals: most of them are confined largely to habitats modified by man.
1. Ostrich, *Struthio camelus*. Large flocks were established in the 19th century for commercial use of the tail feathers. Some still persist near PORT AUGUSTA in SA.
2. Game birds. There are small feral populations of the California quail, *Lophortyx californicus*, (on KING ISLAND); the ringneck pheasant, *Phasianus colchicus*; the peafowl, *Pavo cristatus*; and the jungle fowl, *Gallus gallus* (see PHEASANTS, etc.).
3. Water fowl. White swans, *Cygnus olor*, are well established but have not moved into natural habitats. The mallard or wild duck of Europe, *Anas platyrhynchos*, is widespread and, unfortunately, interbreeds with the native black duck, *A. superciliosa* (see DUCKS, etc.).
4. Pigeons. Feral rock or domestic pigeons, *Columba livia*, are common in most Australian towns, where they are troublesome because of their fouling of buildings and raiding of food stores. The spotted turtle dove, *Streptopelia chinensis*, and the Senegal turtle dove (in WA), *S. senegalensis*, are well established; they belong to a genus which spreads easily throughout the world (see DOVES, etc.).
5. Skylark. This European species, *Alauda arvensis*, was introduced by the VIC ACCLIMATISATION SOCIETY between 1863 and 1874. It is now flourishing in S coastal areas and in TAS.
6. Bulbuls. The red-whiskered bulbul, *Pycnonotus jocosus*, a crested black and red bird, is very common in Sydney where it feeds on fruits, berries and insects. A related species is sometimes seen in Melbourne.
7. Thrushes and blackbirds. Both the European song thrush, *Turdus philomelos*, and the blackbird, *T. merula*, were introduced during the 19th century for their song. The first persists only in Melbourne and southern VIC; the blackbird is widespread in SE Australia and TAS. Unlike most exotic birds the blackbird is at home in some kinds of native bushland, as well as in habitats modified by man (see THRUSHES, etc.).
8. Sparrows. The European house sparrow, *Passer domesticus*, was enthusiastically imported by acclimatisation societies who apparently thought it would eat insects attacking fruit trees. The bird now occurs from TAS to central QLD and central SA, and is still spreading. The closely related tree sparrow, *P. montanus*, occurs in VIC, NSW and possibly TAS (see WEAVERBIRDS).
9. Starlings. The family is represented by two introduced species, the European starling, *Sturnus vulgaris*, and the Indian myna, *Acridotheres tristis*. The latter has often been introduced into new countries for the control

of insects though in Australia it is usually a scavenger in urban areas (see STARLINGS).

10. Finches and grass finches. The true FINCHES would be absent from Australia if it were not for the greenfinch, *Chloris chloris*, and the colourful goldfinch, *Carduelis carduelis*. The latter feeds on the seeds of thistles and other weeds and both species are largely restricted to introduced trees when nesting. The two introduced species of grass finches, the spice finch, *Lonchura punctulata*, and the black-headed mannikin, *L. atricapilla*, probably escaped from aviaries and are now well established.

Amphibians The only introduced amphibian or reptile is the cane toad (see FROGS, etc.) which was introduced to control pests of sugar cane but which has itself become a pest.

Fishes Introduced fishes are often blamed for the decline in native Australian species but European settlers have so drastically modified many Australian rivers by dam and canal-building and the clearing of vegetation that it is doubtful if any fishes, other than introduced ones, could survive in many places. Most exotic fishes were introduced for food or for sport (see FISHES, FRESHWATER). One, the mosquito fish, *Gambusia affinis*, was released for the control of mosquitoes, and a few have escaped from, or have been discarded from, aquarium tanks. The main introduced fishes are: the brown trout, *Salmo trutta*; the rainbow trout, *S. gairdneri*; the roach, *Rutilus rutilus*; the tench, *Tinca tinca*; the crucian carp, *Carassius carassius*; the goldfish, *C. auratus*; the common carp, *Cyprinus carpio*; and the redfin or European perch, *Perca fluviatilis*.

Further reading: Rolls, E.C. *They All Ran Wild*. Angus & Robertson, Sydney, 1969.

animals, venomous A venom is a toxic substance that is injected into the victim; a poison is a toxic substance that is eaten, inhaled or absorbed through the skin. SNAKES are therefore not poisonous though many are venomous. This article discusses venomous Australian animals other than fishes (see FISHES, VENOMOUS). Although there are many extremely venomous animals in Australia and the surrounding seas, deaths are now relatively rare because of the availability of antivenenes for most venoms and the practice of wearing shoes or boots in infested areas. First aid treatment is discussed at the end of this article.

Snakes Each year in Australia there are at least 200 cases of snake-bite which entail the use of antivenenes supplied by the Commonwealth Serum Laboratories (CSL). There are other cases in which no signs of envenomation appear and in which antivenenes are not used. There are five or more snake-bite deaths each year.

The most dangerous snakes in Australia belong to the front-fanged elapid group and to the sea snake group. The most important species according to CSL records are listed in Table 1. The danger posed by any particular species of snake is a function of several factors including the absolute toxicity of the venom, the average yield of venom, the commonness of the snake in its habitat, the distribution of the habitat in relation to the distribution of people, and the aggressiveness of the species. About one half of the bites by venomous snakes in Australia do not lead to sickness; however, a bite from a taipan is almost always fatal unless treated with antivenene and about 45 per cent of untreated bites from tiger snakes would end in death.

Although a bite from a venomous snake may have no ill effects, medical help should be sought immediately. The treatment usually involves intensive care as some patients, particularly those who have been bitten and treated previously, react to the antivenene itself because it contains horse serum.

Arachnids Two species of SPIDERS, one of TICKS and one of SCORPIONS have caused human deaths in Australia. Several other species of spiders are potentially dangerous.

1. Red-back spider. This species, *Latrodectus mactans hasselti*, found in all States, is closely related to, and possibly identical with, the black widow spider of America and the katipo of New Zealand. Only the female is dangerous; the male is too small to be of consequence. The female often makes her web near or in buildings, the outdoor 'privy' being a common site. She is not aggressive and normally bites only when disturbed. The venom contains proteins, and produces pain at the site of action—the junction between muscles and the nerves which activate them. There are at least 230 cases annually which require treatment with antivenene. Although the bite is rarely fatal, only sick people, children and the aged being likely to suffer serious consequences, it does merit medical attention as the symptoms can be uncomfortable and prolonged without treatment.

2. Funnel-web spiders. Bites from funnel-web spiders are always dangerous and sometimes fatal. Two species among the 10 or so known are regarded as very dangerous: the rare tree-dwelling funnel-web, *Atrax formidabilis*, of coastal northern NSW and southern QLD, and the Sydney funnel-web, *A. robustus*, a highly aggressive species probably restricted to an area within 160km of the city. The Sydney species is often common in gardens

SNAKES MOST COMMONLY CAUSING DEATHS IN AUSTRALIA

Species	Mean yield* (dry venom, mg)	Total number of fatal doses for guinea pigs (GP) or mice (M)	Distribution
King brown snake or mulga snake, *Pseudechis australis*	180	3 800 (M)	Throughout, except SE and SW Australia and TAS
Brown Snake (probably 3 species) eastern, *Pseudonaja textilis* western, *P. nuchalis* dugite, *P. affinis*	4	3 800 (M)	Together, throughout except TAS
Copperhead, *Austrelaps superbus*	25	1 250 (GP)	TAS, NSW, VIC, SA (including Kangaroo Is)
Tiger snake, *Notechis ater* and *N. scutatus*	35	14 800 (M)	*N. ater*, south-western WA, southern SA (including Kangaroo Is), TAS, Bass Strait islands; *N. scutatus*, NSW, south-eastern QLD, VIC, south-eatern SA
Red-bellied black snake, *Pseudechis porphyriacus*	37	740 (M)	SA, VIC, NSW, QLD
Death adder, common, *Acanthopis anarcticus* desert, *A. pyrrhus*	40	833 (GP)	Together throughout, except TAS and VIC(?)
Taipan, *Oxyuranus scutellatus*	120	60 600 (M)	Exact distribution in dispute: all coastal QLD, northern NT and possibly northern WA
Sea snake, *Pelamis platurus*	2	87 (GP)	To as far S as Sydney, sometimes further
Fierce snake (small-scaled snake)* *Parademansia microlepidotus*	44	88 000 (M)	Central Australia, not known in detail

Note: * only recently recognised (previously confused with the taipan), the fierce snake may be potentially the most venomous snake in the world.
Sources: Worrell, E. *Reptiles of Australia*, (2nd edn) Angus & Robertson, Sydney, 1970; Sutherland, S.K. *Treatment of Snake-bite in Australia and Papua New Guinea*, Commonwealth Serum Laboratories Reprint, Melbourne, 1977; Sutherland, S.K. *Venomous Creatures of Australia*, Oxford Univesity Press, 1981.

and under houses where it lives in tunnels or natural crevices. Both sexes wander from their burrows, especially after rain. Although the female is larger, the venom of the male is considered to be about five times as toxic. Most bites occur when the spider is disturbed while hiding during the heat of the day, often under clothing or inside shoes.

The venom is particularly toxic to man and monkeys but comparatively harmless to small animals, such as cats and rabbits. Recently, after many years of research, an antivenene has been produced, and is now prepared from rabbits. Experiments showed that it reversed the symptoms of envenomation in monkeys. In January 1981 it rapidly cured an extremely sick 49-year-old man who had been bitten on the foot and in May 1981 it was used successfully on a gravely ill three-year-old boy bitten on the toe. The antivenene is made by the CSL. As the spider injects only a small quantity of venom, only a small quantity of antivenene is needed to counteract it, so the side effects are relatively small. The venom acts very quickly, producing frightening symptoms, so first aid calls for the application of a firm bandage, within seconds if possible, and immobilisation of the limb. Formerly, the use of an arterial tourniquet was recommended but severe symptoms, calling for intensive care, could develop within minutes of its being loosened.

Many bites produce no symptoms at all as the spider apparently fails to inject any venom in many cases. In all fatal cases in which the sex of the spider has been determined, it has proved to be male. About a dozen deaths have occurred since 1925, a remarkably low number considering the large number (probably several hundred thousands) of spiders living in the densely populated Sydney area.

3. Paralysis tick. The paralysis tick, *Ixodes holocyclus*, found only in E Australia, can feed on a wide variety of mammalian hosts including bandicoots, dogs and man. At first these ticks are usually so small (about the size of a pin's head) that they are not noticed but within four days of feeding their size is 400 times greater. While feeding, the tick injects a saliva containing a toxic material which can produce a progressive and sometimes fatal paralysis (by causing failure of the breathing control-centre). It has caused about 20 deaths in NSW in this century. Sometimes it enters orifices of the body, such as the ear or the vagina; one fatal case was caused by a tick attached to the eardrum of a child. Children sometimes show vague symptoms of sickness and muscular weakness as a result of infestations.

4. Scorpions. The Australian species are relatively harmless, only one fatality having been recorded in Australia (an unidentified scorpion killed a baby in WA in 1929). Nevertheless, scorpions should be treated with respect as the stings are painful and can cause illness for several days.

Ants and bees Some people are extremely sensitive to the stings of bees and ants (Hymenoptera; *see* ANTS, etc.). They suffer from anaphylactic shock (an immediate reaction in the smooth muscles of the body after the injection of a protein to which the body has previously been subjected) and should receive appropriate first aid immediately, if the site of the injury allows it, as death can occur within 15 minutes.

Venomous marine invertebrates The venom of several marine invertebrates is extremely toxic, often made more dangerous by the circumstances of the stinging. As most of the skin of a swimmer is exposed to a jellyfish, a large part of the body can be affected and the subsequent shock can lead to the drowning of the victim even when the sting alone would not prove fatal. Also, the victim is often stung at a place which is far from medical help, such as on a coral reef. Visitors to coral reefs should wear stout shoes or boots; thin sand shoes give little protection against, for instance, the spines of the stonefish.

The invertebrates that have caused deaths on Australian or Indo-Pacific coasts are jellyfish (COELENTERATES), octopuses (CEPHALOPODS) and cone shells (GASTROPODS). Many others can produce severe envenomation.

1. Jellyfish. Many earlier records of fatalities due to jellyfish stings placed the blame on the Portuguese men-of-war (bluebottles) but there is no undeniable case of a death resulting from this species. Most, if not all, deaths from jellyfish stings in Indo-Pacific waters can be attributed to cubomedusoids, in particular the sea wasp, *Chironex fleckeri*, a species not described until 1955, and possibly also to the closely related *Chiropsalmus quadrigatus*.

2. Octopuses. There have been one or two deaths from the blue-ringed or spotted octopus, *Hapalochlaena maculosus*, in Australia. The venom works extremely rapidly, and thus a pressure bandage should be applied immediately. Artificial respiration will almost certainly be needed. Bites are most likely to occur on the limbs. Fortunately this species, with its rapid colour changes, is easy to recognise but might prove attractive to children.

3. Cone shells. The various species of cone shells feed either on fishes or marine invertebrates. Some of those which feed on fishes possess a venom that can be dangerous to human beings. The cone shells have a highly modified radula that can be plunged into the victim. The venom apparatus, which emerges from the narrow end, is both strong and flexible and collectors should handle these shells with great care, picking them up between two fingers at the larger end. At least one death resulting from a sting from *Conus geographus* has occurred in Australia, at HAYMAN ISLAND; the victim became paralysed in the legs after about 30 minutes, and became unconscious after about one hour. Artificial respiration may therefore be necessary for people stung by cone shells.

First aid Venomous bites and stings are best avoided. In areas where dangerous snakes and spiders are likely to be met, the following rules should be observed: wear boots or shoes, not 'thongs' or sandals; if possible wear jeans or slacks rather than shorts; always wear thick-soled shoes on coral reefs; never put hands into thick grass or underneath stones or pieces of wood, unless wearing thick gloves; use a torch in snake country at night; do not leave clothing on the floor, especially during the summer when funnel-web and similar spiders are dispersing; check that shoes are empty before putting them on; give snakes the right-of-way—most try to escape from human beings; remember that unnecessary attempts to kill snakes often result in the snake biting its attacker; and do not knowingly antagonise any venomous animal.

The first aid treatment for a bite or sting varies with the kind of venom. If the venom produces only a painful local effect, and does not directly damage a whole body system (such as the circulatory, nervous or respiratory system), allow it to disperse from the site of the bite. If the venom produces generalised effects it should be kept in the region of the bite till medical help is obtained. On no account should the bite be cut into, or a tight tourniquet applied to a limb; both can do more damage than good.

The pressure/immobilisation technique This method was developed by Dr Struan Sutherland (*see* Further reading) and his colleagues of the CSL and is used in those cases in which tourniquets were formerly employed.

It is used for snake bites, bites from funnel-web spiders and similar spiders (but not the red-back spider), cone shells and the blue-ringed octopus, and for ant, bee or wasp stings *when the victim is known to suffer from a severe allergy to these*. Most of these bites or stings are on limbs, and the object is to prevent the venom from being spread from the site to other parts of the body by the blood stream. The patient must be kept as still as possible—do not, for example, try to remove a victim's trousers if the bite is on the leg. Apply a broad bandage to the limb, starting at the site and working up the limb as far as possible; it should be about as tight as a bandage applied to a sprained ankle. If the bite is on the forearm, bandage as far as the elbow. Splint the limb, bandaging the splint to as much of the limb as possible. Place the bitten arm or forearm in a sling. As the patient must move as little as possible it is often better to bring medical help to the patient, rather than making the patient walk out of, for example, rough scrub country. The patient will be suffering from shock and will probably need reassurance. It is worth remembering that not all bites from venomous animals result in illness. Its venom stocks may have been depleted, or only a small amount may have entered the wound.

Formerly, it was recommended that the offending snake should be killed and taken to the hospital for identification so that the correct antivenene (rather than a general antivenene) could be given. Most Australian hospitals now have the equipment to identify the venom type from the tissues of the patient so this dangerous procedure is no longer necessary. It is advisable to bring in the spider in the case of spider bites, taking care not to crush it beyond recognition.

Treatment for other venoms

1. Ants, bees and wasps. Do not use the pressure/immobilisation technique unless the patient is known to suffer from severe allergic reactions to ants, bees or wasps, or unless the reactions are obviously abnormally severe. Iced water inside a plastic bag will give relief when applied to the site.

2. Red-back spider bites. No first aid is needed but get medical help. Iced water (*see* ants, bees and wasps *above*) will give relief.

3. Paralysis ticks. Remove the ticks with half-opened, fine scissors, levering the animal, complete with mouthparts, from the skin. Beware of squashing the tick. The members of a family should carry out mutual inspections for several days after being in tick-infested bush. After the ticks are removed the patient usually begins to recover without incident.

4. Box jellyfish stings. Pour vinegar or *diluted* acetic acid over the tentacles clinging to the body to inactivate the stinging cells; five minutes later the tentacles can be wiped off with a dry cloth or towel. Do not use alcohol or similar fluids (which were recommended till recently) and do not rub the tentacles before applying vinegar, as this will only cause further stinging. Give mouth-to-mouth resuscitation if needed (external cardiac massage may also be necessary) and get professional help as quickly as possible. If the patient is breathing without trouble, take him to a doctor or a hospital directly.

5. Other jellyfish stings. Treat as for box jellyfish stings (*see above*), but usually mouth-to-mouth resuscitation and medical help will not be needed.

6. Stings from fishes, including stonefishes. The main symptoms are local pain and shock. If medical help cannot be obtained immediately the pain can be lessened by bathing the limb in hot water, but avoid scalding the patient. Do not use the pressure/immobilisation method. Mouth-to-mouth resuscitation and/or external cardiac massage may be needed with severe stonefish stings; there is an antivenene for the last.

Further reading: see under coelenterates; snakes. *Also* Keegan, H.L. & Macfarlane, W.V. (eds) *Venomous and Poisonous Animals and Noxious Plants of the Pacific Region.* Pergamon, Oxford, 1963; Cleland, Sir John B. & Southcott, R.V. *Injuries to Man from Marine Invertebrates in the Australian Region.* (Special Report Series, no 12) National Health and Medical Research Council, Canberra, 1965; Halstead, B.W. *Poisonous and Venomous Marine Animals of the World.* (vol 1) United States Govt Printing Office, Washington DC, 1965; Stackhouse, J. *Australia's Venomous Wildlife.* Summit Books, Sydney, 1970; Worrell, E. *Reptiles of Australia.* (2nd edn) Angus & Robertson, Sydney, 1970; Southcott, R.V. *Survey of Injuries to Man by Australian Terrestrial Arthropods.* The author, Mitcham SA, 1973; Sutherland, S.K. 'Treatment of snake-bite in Australia and Papua New Guinea' and 'Treatment of arachnid poisoning in Australia' Commonwealth Serum Labora-

tories Reprint, Melbourne, 1977, revised from *Family Physician.* (April 1966), and *Family Guide to Dangerous Animals and Plants of Australia.* Rigby, Adelaide, 1979, and *Venomous Creatures of Australia: A Field Guide with Notes on First Aid.* Oxford University Press, Melbourne, 1981.

Annear, Harold Desbrowe- *see* Desbrowe-Annear, Harold

annelids The annelids form the invertebrate phylum Annelida, which contains such well-known animals as earthworms and leeches, and also many less familiar aquatic, mainly marine, worms.

Their most striking feature is the division of the body into a series of segments (metameres). Externally, the segments are usually very similar one to another; internally, the segments are separated by thin membranes (septa) which, together with mesenteries, support the almost straight digestive tract.

The annelids have a relatively soft skin covered by a thin, continuous cuticle. Their blood is contained within vessels as it is in the vertebrates, whereas in the ARTHROPODS, also segmented animals, the blood fills the general body cavity. The skin of most annelids contains minute, socketed, protruding bristles (chaetae or setae), made of chitin, a substance also found in the arthropods.

The phylum is divided into three classes, all well represented in Australia: Polychaeta (mainly marine worms); Oligochaeta (earthworms and their allies); and Hirudinea (leeches).

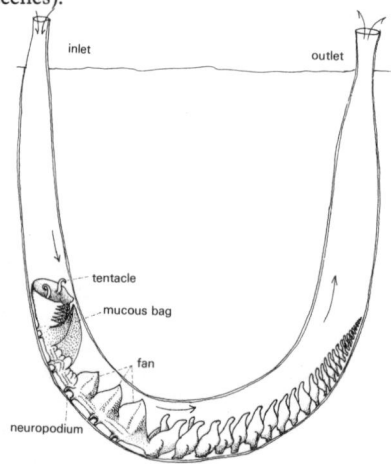

A tube-dwelling worm, *Chaetopterus* species

Polychaetes These annelids are more complex and diverse than are the members of the other two classes (though the oligochaetes are believed to have evolved from the polychaetes or from some kind of worm very similar to them). They have very well-developed heads, well furnished with sense organs, and lateral fleshy outgrowths of the body called parapodia, which carry bundles of chaetae and are well supplied with blood vessels. A typical polychaete has a definite head consisting of a region called the prostomium in front of the mouth, and a peristomium immediately behind it. The head carries the eyes, tentacles,

antennae and sensory palps. The ventral mouth is armed with a pair of chitinous jaws which can be protruded forwards. The larger species can inflict quite a deep wound with these jaws. The fleshy parapodia are carried on each of the segments behind the peristomium; the peristomium also carries parapodia but these have been converted to the two pairs of tentacles. The normal parapodia are each divided into an upper and lower lobe, both supported by chitinous rods. In the free-living, mobile polychaetes the segments behind the head are similar to one another but in those that live in tubes there is often a reduction in the size of the parapodia and a distinct division of the body into regions. Planktonic larvae emerge from the eggs and after floating for some time settle and transform to the adult form.

Polychaetes are divided into two subclasses, Errantia and Sedentaria, both of which have many representatives in Australian waters.

1. Errantia. These carnivorous worms move about freely, usually crawling or swimming, sometimes burrowing.

The family Amphinomidae contains *Eurythoë complanata* (7cm long), occurring throughout the tropical Pacific and in some warm parts as well (for example, the shores of NSW). It is a salmon-pink worm with relatively long chaetae which break off in the skin when the animal is handled; the broken chaetae are best removed with adhesive tape, and ammonia or alcohol will remove the stinging sensation. It is found only under stones.

The family Aphroditidae contains the scale worms, relatively broad polychaetes with scales (elytra) in pairs along the back. *Lepidonotus melanogrammus* (about 4cm), a black-and-white or fawn species, is found under stones at low tide. The genus *Aphrodite*, found in deeper water throughout the world, contains the sea mice. *A. australis* (about 15cm) is covered with iridescent chaetae which resemble fur.

The Nereiidae is a cosmopolitan family of polychaetes that burrow in the mud and sands of estuaries. *Australonereis ehlersi* (about 10cm), which lives in fragile, temporary tubes, ranges from QLD to WA; it can sometimes be forced from its burrow (to be used as bait) by placing an empty tin, open end down, on the sand and then stamping on it to compress air.

The family Eunicidae contains the largest Australian polychaetes. The endemic giant beach-worm, *Onuphis teres* (up to 3m), found in SA, NSW and QLD, lives hidden in the sand where the surf breaks at low tide.

2. Sedentaria. The tube-dwelling polychaetes are highly modified for their sedentary life. They have no jaws or teeth, and they feed on organic material suspended in the water. The body is usually divided into distinct regions, and its front end is often drawn out into tentacles which are used to collect food.

The members of the family Serpulidae, which all secrete small tubes of lime, include *Galeolaria caespitosa* whose white tubes form a conspicuous zone on most of the rocky coasts of VIC and NSW, just above the cunjevoi zone (see SEA SQUIRTS, etc.), below mid-tide level; the tubes are tough, and are between 2cm and 2.5cm long with openings of about 0.25cm in diameter. The prostomium is very small and is concealed by two fleshy lappets from which arise 36 filaments surrounding the mouth, each filament having a fringe of leaflets on each side. The crowns filaments probably serve as gills but their hair-like appendages (cilia) carry food particles down to the mouth. When the worm retracts, the opening is closed by a lid-like organ (operculum). Several other serpulids are found on Australian coasts. *Hydroides norvegica* (up to 38mm), is a common fouling organism of boats.

The family Sabellidae contains the feather duster worm, *Sabellastarte indica* (length 18cm; diameter 2cm), whose feathery tentacles give it the appearance of a feather duster when it expands from its muddy tube. The tentacles are arranged in two spirals with perhaps 140 in each group; the stem of the tentacle is reddish-brown and the side leaflets usually white. The body consists of about 150 abdominal segments and eight thoracic ones.

Most tubes made by polychaetes in the subclass Sedentaria are fixed to the substrate but that of a member of the family Amphictenidae, *Pectinaria antipoda*, is a fragile structure (about 6cm) of sand grains that is carried about by its owner. This worm, in its tube, burrows head first into sand, using two fans of the long, golden chaetae as spades.

The family Chaetopteridae contains the widespread *Chaetopterus* species which show the differentiation of the body into distinct regions more clearly than any other polychaete of the subclass Sedentaria. The worm lives inside a dark green, papery 'U'-shaped tube, constructed in the sand and mud of estuaries and with both of the open ends projecting above the surface. The two end pieces are narrower than the rest of the tube and resemble drinking straws; sea water is drawn into the tube at the head end and expelled at the tail end. The small prostomium carries two eyes. Behind the head there are nine segments with large parapodia and chaetae. The middle section contains five larger segments; the first has a pair of tentacles and the last three carry the fans, used as paddles to maintain the flow of water through the tube. The rest of the body consists of several parapodia-carrying segments that are fairly normal in appearance. *C. variopedatus* (20cm), a common, widespread species, lives permanently within its tube but, for some unknown reason, is phosphorescent.

The family Myzostomidae, which consists of small, disc-shaped annelids with parapodia, is sometimes included in the polychaetes. They live on crinoids, feeding on plankton collected by their hosts.

Very few polychaetes live in freshwater. In Australia they are represented by tiny (1mm) worms, *Stradiodrilus tasmanica* (TAS) and *S. novae-hollandiae* (NSW); other members of this genus are known from QLD. These worms live as parasites in the gill chambers of freshwater crayfish and related crustaceans.

Oligochaetes As their name suggests, these annelids have relatively few chaetae when compared with the polychaetes; they have no parapodia and no head, the mouth being on the lower surface and overhung by the prostomium. The segments are all similar to one another externally, and are well separated by grooves. The body carries a whitish, swollen, glandular area (clitellum) that is important in mating. The well-known earthworms are typical of this class. Oligochaetes are hermaphrodites, unlike the polychaetes in which the sexes are usually separate. After mating the two worms secrete a cocoon around their clitella; they then slide out of the cocoon, leaving the eggs enclosed within.

Almost all oligochaetes are terrestrial or freshwater. They swallow soil and mud from which they extract food particles, bacteria and diatoms, and excrete the soil particles. Those living in soil help to aerate it by their burrowing, and to move nutrients to the surface. Some species also help to recycle the organic contents of leaves and other litter by dragging them below the surface.

1. Terrestrial oligochaetes. Australia has about 100 endemic species of earthworms, most of which belong to the family Megascolecidae, a mainly S hemisphere family which includes the giant earthworms of Australia, believed to be the largest oligochaetes. The Gippsland giant earthworm, *Megascolides australis* (up to 3.7m long; up to 2.5cm in diameter), and *Digaster longmani* (up to 1.7m long; up to 2.5cm in diameter), burrow in rich basaltic soils on the tops of some ridges in the GREAT DIVIDING RANGE; the Gippsland species is found, for example, on the S slopes of the STRZELECKI RANGES and near the Bass River. The squirter worm, *Didymogaster sylvaticus* (about 10cm to 15cm), is a rainforest species of coastal E Australia. When disturbed, this stout, purple worm squirts out fluid from a row of pores; the sprays can reach a height of 60cm.

2. Freshwater oligochaetes. These have been little studied but several families are known to occur in Australia. Some of the worms are very small. The cosmopolitan *Aeolosoma* species of the family Aeolosomatidae, for example, are only 1mm or 2mm long. Some probably occur in Australia. Often they curl up and encyst into coloured spherical bodies. They have cilia on the prostomium, and hair-like chaetae along the body, the mouth cilia working like a vacuum cleaner when feeding. These worms reproduce by budding, and often chains of two or three individuals are found.

The worms of the family Naididae, which also reproduce by budding, have swellings on the tail which serve as gills though most aquatic oligochaetes breathe through the general body surface.

The worms of the family Tubificidae usually have red blood; the body is white and the red blood vessels stand out in contrast. Tubificid worms (about 3cm) live in mud tubes from which their tails project. The commonest genus is the cosmopolitan *Tubifex*, which is common in polluted water, or in deep water where there is little oxygen.

The family Lumbricidae contains several aquatic or semi-aquatic worms (a few centimetres long), probably all introduced and including the genera *Eisenia*, *Eiseniella* and *Helodrilus*.

Some members of the predominantly terrestrial family Enchytraeidae (pot worms) live in freshwater; they are whitish and up to about 2.5cm long.

Hirudinea Leeches are easily distinguished from other annelids by their posterior and anterior suckers. Unlike almost all other worms they have a definite number of segments though these may be divided into sections (annuli) externally. There are usually no chaetae but a clitellum may be present in the breeding season. Australian species range from about 7mm to 20cm. Most leeches live in still or slow-moving freshwater but there are many terrestrial and marine species (the latter appear to have received little attention in Australia). They move by a looping motion which is similar to that of certain moth caterpillars but aquatic species also swim.

1. Freshwater leeches. There are about 13 species of freshwater leeches in Australia, belonging to two suborders and three families. Those of the family Hirudidae have a large mouth armed with teeth. The body is long and thin, the blood is red, and there are five pairs of eyes on the side of the front of the body. The commonest species, *Limnobdella australis*, occurring in all Australian States, is several centimetres long, and yellow in colour with dark brown, longitudinal stripes.

The shorter leeches of the family Glossophoniidae have colourless blood. The mouth is a small pore or oral sucker, mounted on a proboscis. The pale green, blind *Semilagenta hilli*, an endemic species, is roughly pear-shaped in outline. *Glossiphonia australiensis*, a flesh-coloured species with three pairs of eyes near the front of the body, is known from NSW and TAS. The leeches of this family are unusual in that the eggs are not laid within a cocoon but remain attached to the body of the parent, as do the young leeches. *Glossiphonia* species are thought to live entirely on small freshwater gastropods, whereas most leeches are parasites of vertebrates.

The two Australian species of the family

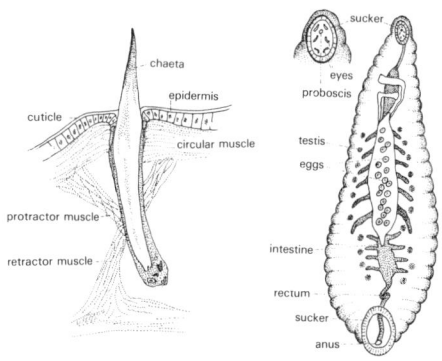

(a) Chaeta of an annelid   (b) Structure of a leech

Erpobdellidae are rare, and have been recorded only from NSW.

2. Terrestrial leeches. In Australia, these are represented by the family Domanibdellidae, the two-jawed leeches. They occur in rainforest areas on the coastal side of the Great Dividing Range from sea level to about 1 500m, in TAS and in coastal forests in the NT; some are found on LORD HOWE ISLAND. They feed on mammals, birds, reptiles and frogs. Their attack causes prolonged bleeding because they inject an anti-coagulating agent into the wound. They can withstand drought in a dried up condition, and can fast for about a year. Most Australian species are between 2cm and 8.5cm long when extended. The back is striped longitudinally in various colours such as yellow, gold and green.
Further reading: Dales, R. *Annelids.* (2nd edn) Hutchinson, London, 1967; McMichael, D.F. (ed) *A Treasury of Australian Wildlife.* Ure Smith, Sydney, 1968; Bennett, I. *The Fringe of the Sea.* (revd edn) Rigby, Adelaide, 1974; Dakin, W.J., Bennett, I. & Pope, E. *Australian Seashores.* (6th edn) Angus & Robertson, Sydney, 1976; Williams, W.D. *Australian Freshwater Life.* (2nd edn) Macmillan Australia, Melbourne, 1980.

Ansett, Sir Reginald Myles (1909-1981)
Company director and aviator. Born in the small town of Inglewood in VIC, he was taken to live in Melbourne in 1914. Not long after leaving school he became interested in aviation, and in 1929 became the 419th Australian to obtain a pilot's licence. His first major business venture, however, was in road transport. Beginning with a passenger service from BALLARAT to MARYBOROUGH, VIC, he built up a network of routes throughout Western VIC. He turned to air transport in 1936, with a service from HAMILTON to Melbourne, which led to the formation of Ansett Airways Ltd. In 1957 he took over Australian National Airways, merging it with Ansett Airways Ltd. to form Ansett Airways of Australia, which then became the major non-government airline in Australia. He later expanded into other areas of transport and tourism and into the ownership and operation of television stations. In 1981, Ansett Transport Industries was taken over by a combination of other companies, but Sir Reginald kept the position of chairman. He was appointed KBE in 1969.

Antarctica
The great southern continent, covering 13 million square kilometres (which is more than one and a half times the area of Australia) differs from other continents in that, because of the vast extent of the Antarctic ice cap and the extreme climatic conditions, extensive permanent settlement is impossible. It has, however, been possible to occupy selected points as meteorological bases and research stations, with facilities especially designed for polar conditions, and regular relief of the personnel manning them, supplies being brought from outside.

In 1959 an international treaty was made whereby it was agreed that no nation would claim sovereignty of the Antarctic continent. It was stated by one writer in 1976 that this treaty had proved to be 'the most successful example of international co-operation in world history'. A number of the countries which signed this agreement operate bases, including the USA, the USSR, the UK, Australia and New Zealand. Australia maintains stations at MAWSON, CASEY and DAVIS, as well as on subantarctic MACQUARIE ISLAND.

Winter quarters on King George V Land of the 1911–14 Australian Antarctic Expedition led by Mawson

Australia's long and active interest in Antarctica dates back to 1907 when Douglas MAWSON and Edgeworth DAVID were members of the Shackleton expedition. Mawson led further expeditions in 1911-14 and 1929-31; in 1933 the Australian Antarctic Territory was created when the former British claims in Antarctica were transferred to Australia. This territory, covering over six million square kilometres, comprises an arc between 160°E and the 45°E meridians of longitude (except for a narrow segment, Adélie Land, a French area). Various sections of this territory are known by different names, such as MacRobertson Land, King George V Land, Kemp Land and Princess Elizabeth Land. Since 1947 the Australian bases have been operated by the Australian National Antarctic Research Expeditions (ANARE) and personnel at these stations have worked in co-operation with scientists from other nations on a variety of investigations and projects on the unique problems of Antarctica. The modern bases stand in marked contrast to the primitive conditions under which the early Antarctic explorers operated. Buildings nowadays are mainly prefabricated structures, with special facilities for the comfort of the personnel, often with sophisticated equipment for their scientific work, and with aircraft and motor vehicles for much of the transport.
Further reading: Mawson, D. *Home of the Blizzard.* Hodder & Stoughton, London, 1938; Cherry-Garrard, A. *The Worst Journey in the World.* Penguin, Harmondsworth, 1948; Swan, R.A. *Australians in the Antarctic.* Melbourne University Press, Melbourne, 1961; Grenfell-Price, A. *The Winning of Australian Antarctica.* Angus & Robertson, Sydney, 1962.

anteater, banded *see* native cats, etc.

anteater, spiny *see* monotreme mammals

antechinus *see* native cats, etc.

Antill, Sir John Henry (1904-)
Composer. Antill is best known for his orchestral score *Corroboree*, a ballet suite which remains probably the first and one of the few distinctively Australian compositions. *Corroboree* was inspired by his boyhood experience of a ceremony of Aboriginal dances at La Perouse, BOTANY BAY, and although the musical idiom bears no resemblance to that of genuine Aboriginal music, it is an outstandingly inventive and exciting score: totally Western in idiom and instrumentation, and paying a remote yet sincere homage to Aboriginal culture, it possesses an unmistakably Australian identity. First performed in 1946, conducted by Sir Eugene Goossens (later conductor of the Sydney Symphony Orchestra), the work was subsequently performed in its orchestral version in the UK and the USA and won international acclaim. It was first performed in Australia as a full-length ballet in 1950.

Interestingly, the rhythmic aggression and tensions exploding in *Corroboree* are conspicuously absent from most of Antill's many other compositions. In this sense *Corroboree* stands like Ayers Rock among soundscapes of the gentler works which precede and follow it. These include operas, ballets and an oratorio; music for films, radio plays and television; overtures, fanfares and pageant music; choral music; solo songs; concertos, a symphony and miscellaneous orchestral and instrumental scores. Like most composers of his generation, Antill was not able to make a living as a composer and some of his earlier occupations include work as a performer and conductor with the Sydney Symphony Orchestra, the Williamson Imperial Opera Company and the Fuller Opera Company. He later joined the AUSTRALIAN BROADCASTING COMMISSION (now corporation) and became its Federal Music Editor. Born in Sydney, he now lives in Cronulla where he continues to compose and to accept conducting invitations. He received an OBE in 1971 and was made a KCMG in 1981.

antlions and lacewings
These make up a rather archaic endopterygote order (Neuroptera) of INSECTS that have remarkably complex veining of the wings. The two pairs of wings are rather similar, and have many cells and branches that fork near the wing margins. Neuropterans have compound eyes but usually no simple eyes (ocelli). The active, predatory larvae have specialised sucking mouthparts: their sickle-shaped maxillae and mandibles fit together to make two hollow tubes. The adults have biting mouthparts and well-developed, many-segmented antennae. Antlions and lacewings feed on other small

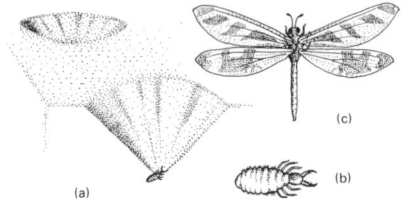

Antlions: (a) larval antlion awaiting prey; (b) enlarged larva; (c) adult animals, destroying many APHIDS and other soft-bodied pests. There are about 400 species in Australia.

The superfamily Myrmeleontoidea contains the antlions, of which there are almost 200 species in Australia. Typical antlion larvae live half-buried in the sand at the bottom of a conical depression. When an ant or some other insect strays over the edge of the pit antlions flick sand at it to accelerate its descent into the larvae's jaws. The larvae of some species of the family Nemopteridae have extremely long necks—often as long as the rest of the body. The adults of the superfamily resemble dragonflies (*see* DAMSELFLIES, etc.); they have speckled wings and relatively long antennae which, in some families, are clubbed. They are mainly nocturnal insects that often come indoors, attracted by the light.

There are eight families of lacewings represented in Australia. The family Coniopterygidae contains tiny, aphid-like, meal-covered lacewings which feed as adults and larvae on aphids and mites on trees. The Ithonidae is a small family, almost endemic, of large, active, moth-like insects which often live in sandy areas; their larvae resemble the grubs of chafer BEETLES. The closely related family Osmylidae (about 28 species) consists of large, broad-winged lacewings with wingspans of up to 55mm; most osmylids are associated with water and many larvae are semi-aquatic. Larval stages of the Sisyridae are unique in that they are parasites of freshwater sponges. The family Mantispidae consists of lacewings that are superficially like MANTIDS; their larvae feed on the egg sacs of spiders. The family Hemerobiidae consists of the brown lacewings, small, delicate insects with rather narrow wings, which fly mainly at night or at dusk and are often attracted to lights. The family Chrysopidae consists of large green lacewings with conspicuous reddish eyes; they are also attracted to lights. The larvae and adults of both brown and green lacewings are active predators which feed on aphids and similar insects. The lacewings of the family Psychopsidae are larger forms with short antennae and broad, often patterned, wings; the larvae live beneath the bark of trees, often *Eucalyptus*, and emerge at night to feed on the insects attracted by the kino ('gum').

ants, bees and wasps These INSECTS belong to an endopterygote order, Hymenoptera, which contains about 110 000 known species (9 000 in Australia) of ants, bees, wasps and allied insects but it is probable that many hundreds of the smaller species await discovery. These small to medium-sized insects (the length ranges from about 0.21mm to about 5cm) occur in most habitats and are important as pollinators and as parasites of harmful insects. In most of the advanced species there is a distinct waist, which lies between the abdomen and the body's mid-region (the apparent thorax); the apparent abdomen is called the gaster. Most hymenopterans have two pairs of membranous

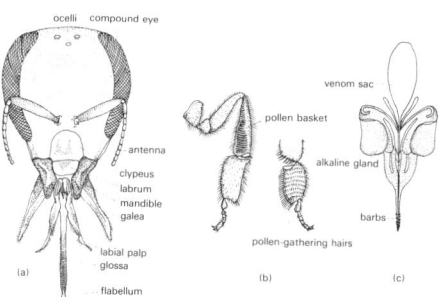

Some parts of a bee: (a) mouthparts; (b) pollen collection and carriage on bee's leg; (c) sting

wings; the hind-wings are smaller than the fore-wings but the two pairs are strongly coupled in flight. An unusual feature of many hymenopterans is that sex is determined by whether or not an egg is fertilised: an unfertilised egg becomes a male, a fertilised egg becomes a female. There are two suborders: Symphyta (sawflies and woodwasps) and Apocrita (ants, bees, wasps and most parasitic species).

Symphyta The members of this suborder (about 166 species in Australia) do not have a distinct waist of the kind described above, and none of them are social insects. The larvae resemble caterpillars but usually have more prolegs (*see* BUTTERFLIES, etc.); they feed on plants and fungi. The introduced woodwasp, *Sirex noctilio*, tunnels into the wood of introduced *Pinus radiata* trees, feeding on a fungus that develops from spores inserted with the egg. This species is coming under BIOLOGICAL CONTROL by introduced parasitic wasps and ROUNDWORMS. The native Eucalyptus sawfly, *Perga affinis,* attacks eucalypt leaves. The female uses her egg-laying organ (ovipositor) to saw slits in leaves or stems into which the eggs are inserted (the ovipositor in all other hymenopterans is used for piercing or stinging). The larvae feed in concerted groups. When disturbed they regurgitate, in unison, an unpleasant sticky fluid—hence their name, spitfire grubs.

Apocrita These insects are traditionally divided into two groups though it cannot be said that the division is clear cut. The two groups are the Parasitica (mainly parasitic wasps) and the Aculeata (mainly stinging species—wasps, bees and ants).

Parasitica. There are about 4 300 known Australian species of these immensely important, tiny to medium-sized wasps. None are social, and most are PARASITES of animals (and sometimes plants) in the larval stage. There are about 36 families, but the identification of parasitic wasps is usually a task for the expert.

Unlike most parasites of animals, the larvae of parasitic wasps eventually destroy their hosts and for this reason they are often called parasitoids rather than parasites. The relationship is more like a drawn-out act of predation than true parasitism for it is usually not in the best interests of a parasite to destroy its host—unless the host species is capable of rapid reproduction, like most insects. Adult parasitic wasps usually feed on nectar and honey dew though the adult females sometimes obtain

protein from the body fluids of the insects which their offspring are to attack. The eggs may be laid on the surface of the host or within its tissues. Usually the larva lives within the host but ectoparasitism also occurs. In many cases only one parasite larva can survive in each host individual. Sometimes, however, groups of larvae can successfully develop in the host, as is the case with *Apanteles glomeratus*, a species which attacks the caterpillars of the small cabbage white butterfly. Its sulphur-yellow cocoons may often be seen festooning the cadaver of the caterpillar.

While some parasitic wasps need a large caterpillar or a woodwasp grub for their successful development, many are parasites of the eggs of other insects or of single APHIDS. The remains of parasitised aphids may often be seen in healthy colonies; they look like empty brown 'mummies' and have a tiny exit hole from which the adult wasp emerges. Parasitic wasps are often themselves parasitised by other parasitic wasps. This hyperparasitism may have interfered with earlier attempts at biological control when natural enemies of a pest were introduced to control it but brought with them parasites of their own.

In many cases the relation between the parasite and its host is highly specific but many parasitic wasps attack a range of hosts, though these are generally of the same type (for example, different aphids or different moth caterpillars). Examples of members of the Parasitica group are the fig insects (family Agaonidae) and the gall wasps (family Cynipidae). Fig insects live in the 'fruits' of FIGS, acting as caprification (ripening) and pollinating agents. For example, if the endemic *Pleistodontes froggatti* is not present in the Moreton Bay fig, the fruits do not mature. The gall wasps form galls or live within galls formed by other species. Although common in America and Europe, only nine species occur in Australia where most plant galls are caused by coccids (*see* BUGS) and other insects.

Aculeata. There are about 4 300 species in Australia of these familiar predatory or vegetarian social wasps, bees and ants. All grades of organisation—from a completely solitary life to the complex social structure of the hive bee—may be found among the insects of this group. Many, especially in the more primitive families, are parasites. In most cases the ovipositor is modified into a stinging organ with associated venom glands. Many of the Parasitica stun their victims with venom, but it is only insects among the Aculeata that can inject venom into human beings.

1. Ants. The superfamily Formicoidae consists of the ants (at least 1 100 species in Australia). All ants are completely social, with a queen and wingless, worker castes (and sometimes also soldiers), though the colonies of some species may consist of only a few hundred individuals. Depending upon the species, a colony may contain one or several queens. There are also, of course, the males needed for mating the virgin queens. Ants may be distinguished from other hymenopterans by the presence of one or two distinct swellings

(nodes) on the waist. Workers and soldiers (when present) are incomplete females, but any fertilised egg has the potential to develop into a virgin queen or a worker; in this, ants resemble bees and TERMITES.

Most ants are omnivores though some are highly specific predators of other ARTHROPODS; many species collect large quantities of seeds. Most Australian species build their nests underground though some nest in wood or plants.

Because of their astronomical numbers ants play an important role in most Australian terrestrial ecosystems (*see* ENVIRONMENT). Among the more interesting groups are the primitive bulldog ants of the subfamily Myrmeciinae which, though once widespread, are now confined to Australia and New Caledonia. These large, ferocious ants have huge mandibles which must get a grip on a victim before the ant can sting. The potent venom consists of a complex mixture of proteins and other substances which is closer to the venoms of the wasps than to the simpler venoms of other ants. Other common ants of the bush are the meat ants (*Iridomyrmex* species) and the sugar ants (*Camponotus* species). Several troublesome species have been introduced. The most important of these is the Argentine ant, *I. humilis*, which, when established, swarms in houses, hospitals and other institutions in search of food. The Argentine ant will take over an area, continuously expanding its network of colonies and driving out every other ant species, including the bulldog ants. Specimens of any small brown or light brown ant which has a distinct, single peg on the waist, and no spines on the thorax, may be an Argentine ant and should be sent to a museum, local authority or State agricultural authority for identification as great efforts are being made to prevent the further spread of the Argentine ant.

2. Bees. The superfamily Apoidea contains six families of bees, all of which are represented in Australia (about 1 656 known species in Australia). Bees may be regarded as basically sphecoid wasps that have taken to feeding their young with pollen and honey rather than with spiders or insects. A useful distinguishing feature of the bees is the branched (plumose) structure of at least some of the body hairs; in the wasps all the hairs are unbranched. These hairs give many bees their characteristic fluffy appearance.

Most bees are solitary insects, and many are tiny—only about 2mm long. The nest of a solitary bee is usually a burrow in the ground, or a cavity in a plant stem, but some use resin or mud to make small nests. The nest consists of a number of cells, each of which contains an egg or larva, and pollen and honey. Though these bees are solitary in the sense that each female tends to her own young without help from other females, the nests often occur in large groups. In the more socially advanced species, the females co-operate in the making and provisioning of a nest, while in the completely social species large colonies are composed of a fertile female (the queen) and infertile females (the workers).

Australia is the headquarters of the largest family, Colletidae (over 800 species in Australia). None are social and, in Australia, none are parasitic. The nests are in burrows in the ground, or in tunnels in twigs, and the cells are lined with a cellophane-like dry saliva.

The family Apidae, which contains the introduced hive bee, *Apis mellifera*, is represented by only 14 species in Australia. The native species belong to the genus *Trigona* and are small, dark-coloured and stingless. They form large colonies similar to those of the hive bee, mostly in the N half of Australia. The family Apidae also contains the cuckoo bees, parasitic species which are relatively rare in Australia. Bumble bees, also in this family, do not occur in Australia, despite several attempts to introduce them as pollinators of clover. They have been established successfully in New Zealand.

3. Wasps. The social wasps belong to the superfamily Vespoidea (about 280 species in Australia). Apart from some of the solitary wasps of the family Masaridae which feed their larvae with pollen, all members of this superfamily raise their grubs on animal food, especially on larval insects. They run parallel to the bees in the graduation of organisation from the solitary forms to the large social groupings of vespid wasps and hornets.

The family Vespidae is represented by only 14 species in Australia but these are often conspicuous insects. The European social wasp, *Vespula germanica*, has become established in TAS and New Zealand, and more recently, on the Australian mainland. Its social organisation is similar to that of the honey bee. These S hemisphere colonies are much larger than the ones formed by this species in England where the workers die off during the winter. The nests are built underground (for example, in tree trunks) and the material used is 'wasp-paper', a substance produced from chewed wood. The commonest Australian vespids, commonly known as paper wasps, belong to the genus *Polistes* (not represented in TAS). These black and yellow wasps have spindle-shaped abdomens. They make a single horizontal comb of cells from 'paper', the whole being attached to a support by a stalk; these are sometimes found in hollow trees and similar sites. Several females share the colony and in Australia at least there is no obvious division into queens and workers.

The largest family of the Vespoidea is the Eumenidae (about 240 species in Australia), commonly known as potter wasps. These are solitary wasps though some species nest in groups. Many species construct the nests from mud; sometimes these nests are built in houses, as is the case with *Abispa* species in QLD.

Also belonging to the superfamily Vespoidea are the spider wasps of the family Pompilidae (121 species in Australia). These species prey on spiders; the adult female either stocks the cells in which she places her eggs with stunned spiders, or lays her eggs in the spider's retreat so that the grub can feed externally on the spider.

Wasps of the superfamily Sphecoidea (442 species in Australia) are also predatory wasps which provision their cells with insect food, such as grasshoppers, for their offspring.

The superfamily Bethyloidea contains the cuckoo wasps of the family Chrysididae, parasitic wasps whose common name derives from the fact that they lay their eggs in the nests of other wasps, and the larvae feed on the host grubs within the cells. Cuckoo wasps are brightly coloured metallic blue, green or red.

The superfamily Scolioidea (about 780 species in Australia) also contains parasitic wasps. Scoliids (family Scoliidae) are large wasps whose females dig into the ground to lay eggs in scarab larvae (*see* BEETLES). Mutillids (family Mutillidae) are called velvet ants because the wingless females are ant-like and covered with short dense hairs; they lay their eggs in the larvae of ground-nesting bees and wasps. Tiphiids (family Tiphiidae) are often large insects with, in most cases, wingless females that can sting viciously; they too parasitise scarab larvae and possibly also mole CRICKETS.

Further reading: Spradbery, J.P. *Wasps.* Sidgwick & Jackson, London, 1973.

Anzac Day

Anzac Day 25 April. The anniversary of the landing of units of the Australian and New Zealand Army Corps on the GALLIPOLI Peninsula on 25 April 1915, Anzac Day is celebrated as a public holiday in all States. In all Australian cities it is traditional on this day to hold a march of those who served in the armed forces, not only at Gallipoli or elsewhere in World War I, but in all wars in which Australia has participated. The word 'Anzac' is based upon the initials of the Australian and New Zealand Army Corps.

Anzus Pact

Anzus Pact Signed on 1 September 1951 and ratified on 29 April 1952, this treaty is a cornerstone of Australia's DEFENCE policy. The negotiations leading to it were initiated by Australia, this move being largely prompted by Australian and New Zealand anxiety regarding the terms of the peace treaty with Japan. The Anzus Pact can, indeed, be regarded partly as a concession by the USA designed to quell fears of a resurgent Japan and to secure Australian and New Zealand support for the peace treaty.

It contains an undertaking by the three signatories to 'consult together when the territorial integrity, political independence or security of any is threatened in the Pacific' and states that: 'Each Party recognises that an armed attack in the Pacific area on any of the Parties would be dangerous to its own peace and safety and declares that it would act to meet the common danger in accordance with its constitutional processes.' It provides for the setting up of a Council consisting of the foreign ministers or their deputies, which held its first meeting in August 1952.

Although the treaty was generally welcomed in Australia, and supported strongly by all major political parties, there was some criticism because the UK had not been given the opportunity to participate, even to the extent of providing an observer at meetings of the council.

Apex Clubs
Apex is a community service organisation for young men between the ages of 18 and 40. It was founded in GEELONG in VIC in 1930 and by 1983 comprised over 18 000 members in about 800 clubs throughout the Commonwealth, organised nationally through the Association of Apex Clubs. The movement has also spread to South-East Asia, where there are about 100 clubs.

Recent national Apex projects have included the 'Help a Kid Make It' campaign, which in 1978-79 raised nearly $1 250 000 to aid the Children's Leukaemia and Cancer Foundation; the $1 000 000 Craniofacial Surgery fund-raising scheme of 1983-84, and a scheme launched by Apex and Woolworths Ltd in 1984, which aims at teaching at least one Australian in 10 the art of cardiovascular resuscitation. Earlier national schemes have included those concerned with Aboriginal welfare, the education and care of spastic children and 'Operation Handclasp', through which over 11 000 migrants were sponsored by Apex.

In addition to its service work, Apex aims at encouraging young men to become proficient at public speaking, debating, chairmanship and management, and each club has extensive social activities for members and their families.

aphids
These small INSECTS form a family, Aphididae (suborder Homoptera), of the order Hemiptera (the true BUGS). There are about 110 species in Australia, but only about 12 are native. The remainder have been introduced from Europe, Asia and North America.

Aphids use their piercing and sucking mouthparts to feed on the sap of a wide variety of trees and plants, and this, combined with their ability to reproduce rapidly and in large numbers, makes them of great economic significance worldwide. They have soft bodies and often membranous wings in the adult stage, but within a species there are usually both winged and wingless adults. The abdomen of many species carries two tube-like projections (cornicles or honey tubes) which release a waxy fluid which helps to protect the aphids from predators. In the case of the grey cabbage aphid, *Brevicoryne brassicae*, the copious wax fouls the host plant (usually cabbage or brussels sprout). Aphids also excrete, but through the anus, a sugary fluid (honeydew). This is rich in carbohydrates because the aphids must absorb large quantities of the sugary sap in order to obtain enough protein; the unneeded sugars are passed out unchanged.

Honeydew is the cause of a symbiotic relationship between some ANTS and aphids, the ants caring for the aphids and in return 'milking' them (by stroking) for the honeydew. However, honeydew coating the surface of a leaf also serves as food for a black fungus growth which interferes with photosynthesis. Despite their parasitism of plants, the main economic importance of aphids is that they are important carriers of viral plant diseases. This is particularly true of the peach-potato aphid, *Myzus persicae*, which because of its catholic tastes, and its tendency to probe one plant after another in search of a suitable home for its numerous progeny, transmits well over a hundred different diseases. Among the natural predators of aphids are ladybird BEETLES and lacewings (*see* ANTLIONS, etc.), but they are also controlled by chemical sprays.

A. Woods
Aphis nereis, one of the many introduced aphids commonly found on ornamental plants

Aphid life cycles are relatively complex. The life cycle varies from species to species, but that of *M. persicae*, which is well established in Australia, serves as an example.

In the cooler parts of Eurasia, where *M. persicae* is native, the winter is spent in the egg stage on peach and nectarine trees, the eggs hatching in the spring. In Australia this winter egg stage is apparently omitted because of the more favourable climate and, as in warmer parts of Europe or in favourable sites (such as mangold clumps), *M. persicae* continues to breed—though at a relatively slower rate—during winter. Several generations will be born on the host trees during the spring. All aphids produced at this stage, and throughout the season till autumn, are parthenogenetic females (reproducing without fertilisation), and are viviparous (producing live young). After a few generations, winged forms migrate to the summer host plants—commonly potatoes and beets, though many species of herbaceous plants are suitable. Throughout the spring and summer, colonies build up on the plants. At this stage, the aphids are generally wingless even when adult, and the sense organs are not as well developed as those of the winged forms. In fact, as much as possible is sacrificed to rapid reproduction, and young within the mother often contain living young themselves. As the plant begins to 'harden off', winged forms develop which migrate to new hosts. At the end of summer, as days grow shorter and the herbaceous host plants begin to die off, winged forms (male and female) again appear in cooler regions. They migrate back to the primary hosts, the peaches and nectarines, where most mate and produce winter eggs. Like *M. persicae*, many species which in Europe typically have a sexual stage breed parthenogenetically all the time in Australia.

apostlebird *see* mudnest builders

apple The early settlers gave the name 'apple' to many trees whose fruits are not related to those of the true apple (*Malus* species, family Rosaceae) of Europe and Asia, which is discussed under FRUIT GROWING The native species include the black apple, or wild plum, *Planchonella australis* (family Ochnaceae), of QLD and NSW. *Planchonella* species have elongated, pointed seeds, and fleshy fruit which may be used to make a jelly. The cocky apple, *Planchonia careya* (family Lecythidaceae), is common in eucalypt forests in parts of QLD. The name 'kangaroo apple' is given to several species of *Solanum* (family SOLANACEAE) whose fruits are said to be edible. Logan apples belong to *Acryonichia*, rainforest trees of QLD and NSW. The native apple, or muntries, is *Kunzea pomifera* (family MYRTACEAE), a prostrate, trailing shrub of sandy deserts in VIC and SA, whose fleshy fruit is edible.
Further reading: Crib, A.B. & Cribb, J.W. *Wild Food in Australia*. Collins, Sydney, 1974.

apple of Peru *see* Solanaceae

apple of Sodom *see* Solanaceae

Arabic-speaking people in Australia
There are no accurate figures for immigrants and their descendants who could be included in the term 'Arabic-speaking people in Australia'. In 1978 the then Commissioner for Community Relations, A.J. Grassby, estimated that 150 000 immigrants and their descendants could be included in this term. However, the overlap in the persons counted in different classifications is somewhat confusing.

The official figures provided by the Department of Immigration and Ethnic Affairs lists the following figures for the period January 1959 to June 1983: immigrants from Lebanon, 51 220; immigrants from the Arab Republic of Egypt, 12 662; and immigrants from Syria, 3 779. These figures do not reveal the number of persons who regard themselves as Assyrians, and another complication is that a bond between many Arabic-speaking people is adherence to the Muslim religion and the figures available do not separate the Christians from the Muslims. The Muslims are united under the Federation of Islamic Councils but the number covered by this organisation would also include people who would not regard themselves as 'Arabic-speaking people'. The Christians are divided between the Maronite Catholic Church and the Antiochan Orthodox Church which has links with the Greek Orthodox Church but conducts part of its services in English.

Many Lebanese have become very prominent in commerce and in NSW the names of Moubarak and the Scarf Brothers are well known. Others have become leaders in the field of government: Louis Fleyfel, who came to Australia in 1949 and became the owner of a number of restaurants, was appointed Consul in VIC and TAS by the Republic of Lebanon in 1969; Alexander Alam became a member of the NSW Legislative Council; and Lord Mayor N. Shehadie of Sydney was the grandson of an early Lebanese settler.

arachnids The Arachnida is a large class of the phylum Arthropoda (ARTHROPODS); it includes such familiar animals as SPIDERS, SCORPIONS, MITES and TICKS and less familiar ones such as PSEUDOSCORPIONS and HARVEST MEN. Arachnids differ from all other arthropods in the shape of the mouthparts. These consist of chelicerae, which are pincer-like jaws (reduced to a fang in the spiders), and pedipalps. The pedipalps are often leg-like but in the case of the scorpions they are huge pincers.

The body is divided into two parts: cephalothorax (head-thorax, or prosoma) and abdomen (or opisthosoma). The cephalothorax carries simple eyes (sometimes absent, but never compound), the chelicerae and the pedipalps, and four pairs of walking legs. There are no antennae. There are sometimes appendages on the abdomen but they are not used for walking. In some mites there are fewer than four pairs of legs.

Most arachnids are carnivorous and şome are parasitic (some mites, and all ticks) but some mites feed on plant saps, stored food, moulds and so on. They imbibe liquid food (for example, the body juices of their prey). Several are venomous. Most are terrestrial but a few are aquatic, and one or two marine. Several species of mites and ticks transmit diseases.
See also parasites; animals, venomous

Arafura Sea A relatively shallow sea, located N of Australia, the Arafura Sea in past geological times formed a land-bridge between Australia and the islands to the N. It is bounded on the E by TORRES STRAIT (separating it from the Coral Sea); the Timor Sea lies to the W, and to the NW a string of Indonesian islands separates it from the Banda Sea; part of the S coast of Irian Jaya gives it its NE bounds.

Ararat VIC (population 8 335 in 1981) A city located in the central W highlands of the State, E of the GRAMPIANS, near the headwaters of the Hopkins River, Ararat is 204km by road and 211km by rail WNW of Melbourne, at the junction of the Western and Pyrenees Highways. It is 90km WNW of BALLARAT and 31km SE of STAWELL. At an elevation of 332m above sea level, it is the centre of a large grain growing and sheep grazing area. It has an average annual rainfall of 616mm, falling throughout the year, but with a maximum in winter and spring; the months May to October receive an average of over 60mm, while January is the driest (31mm average). The nearby hill was named Mt Ararat in 1841 by the first squatter in the district, H.S. Wills, whose journal records that 'like the Ark we rested here.' The town was surveyed in 1858, became a shire

centre in 1864 and in 1950 was proclaimed a city. As well as being a commercial and service centre for the adjacent rural areas, it has a number of secondary industries such as sawmilling and clothing manufacture. More than a dozen buildings in Ararat have been classified by the National Trust (VIC) because of their historic and architectural importance; among these are the former office of the Warden of the Goldfields (1857), Aradale Mental Hospital (1866), the post office (1861), the police courthouse (1866-67), the old wool store (pre-1876) and the shire hall (1871).

Araucaria *see* Gymnospermae

arbitration and conciliation, industrial Of all countries, Australia and New Zealand have made the most ambitious attempts to regulate industrial relations by means of State systems of conciliation and arbitration. Industrial tribunals of various kinds are in operation in each of the Australian States as well as in the federal sphere.
Historical beginnings in the States Although the notion that it is a government's duty to regulate relations between employers and employees had been a topic of public discussion in the 1880s, it was the great strikes early in the following decade that caused positive attempts to put it into practice. Various liberal politicians, appalled by the economic and social effects of the strikes, adopted the view that governments must work out procedures for settling future disputes peacefully. At the same time the trade unions, and the Labor Leagues which were being formed to take political action on their behalf, began to look more favourably on the possibilities of arbitration. The strike weapon having failed so disastrously, the general feeling was that unionists needed to try (in the words of the 1891 NSW Labor Party platform) 'any measure that will secure for the wage-earner a fair and equitable return for his or her labour' and that arbitration might possibly prove to be one such measure.

At first there was considerable difference of opinion among advocates of arbitration on the methods to be used: whether there should be one court to settle all disputes in a particular colony, or separate wages boards for different industries; whether the main stress should be on conciliation—getting the parties together before disputes became open—or on arbitration of disputes as they arose; and whether submission of disputes to arbitration should be voluntary or compulsory.

NSW was the first to take action, setting up a court system by Acts passed in 1892 and 1899. However, it proved ineffectual, being a voluntary system according to which awards could be given only if both parties to a dispute agreed to submit to arbitration.

In the meantime in New Zealand a compulsory system had been introduced in 1894 which provided for the registration of associations of employers and employees. In the event of a dispute between such registered associations, either side could refer the matter

to a court, the resulting award being legally binding. Informed opinion in Australia soon began to consider this a better system than that of NSW. WA and NSW therefore legislated, in 1900 and 1901 respectively, to copy it. The NSW legislation prohibited strikes or lock-outs by registered organisations until each dispute had been brought before a court consisting of a judge, a representative of employers and one of employees. VIC, however, followed a different course. Its Factories and Shops Act of 1896 set up six wages boards, each consisting of equal numbers of employers and employees with an independent chairman. Each board had power to set minimum wages in a particular industry, the industries covered being those in which wages were particularly low and conditions bad. If a worker was paid less than the wage set by a board, he could have recourse to a Court of Industrial Appeals. After 1902 provision was made for extending the system by creating boards for other industries.

The VIC pattern was followed in three other States, wages boards being set up in SA (1906), QLD (1908) and TAS (1910). However, in 1912 QLD added a compulsory court system, eventually dropping its wages boards, while in the same year SA set up a court, but also retained its boards. This is essentially the pattern in the States today.
The Commonwealth enters the field At the national conventions that produced the constitution of the Commonwealth of Australia, it was pointed out by some delegates that many industrial disputes had involved unions with members in more than one colony. They argued that such disputes would in a future federation be handled more satisfactorily by the central government, and succeeded in having included in the list of Commonwealth powers in Section 51 'conciliation and arbitration of industrial disputes extending beyond the limits of any one State'. This was given effect in 1904 by the Conciliation and Arbitration Act, which set up a Commonwealth Arbitration Court whose first president was Mr Justice HIGGINS.

As with other court systems, the setting up of the Commonwealth Arbitration Court encouraged the growth of unionism, for it was only in industries where unions existed that the benefits of court awards could be obtained. It also promoted the federation of unions that had previously existed as separate State organisations, for only unions with members in more than one State could gain Commonwealth awards. Finally, almost from the beginning it set various trends and laid down certain principles which State bodies found it convenient to follow, and it thus more or less dictated the course of industrial conciliation and arbitration throughout Australia. The first such principle was that of the basic wage, laid down by Mr Justice Higgins in the Harvester Case in 1907.
The Harvester judgement This famous judgement arose from the passing of the Excise Tariff Act of 1906 which was part of an attempt to spread the benefit of tariff protec-

tion to employees as well as to manufacturers. Excise duties were levied on domestic production of protected goods, but an employer could gain exemption from such duties if he could demonstrate that he paid 'fair and reasonable wages'. To obtain exemption, H.V. McKay & Co. (*see* Hugh Victor McKAY), manufacturer of agricultural machinery at Sunshine VIC, applied to the Court for a declaration that its wages satisfied this condition. Higgins, faced with the problem of setting criteria for classing wages as fair and reasonable, examined the household budgets of nine families whose breadwinners worked at the McKay factory. After seeing what they spent on clothes, food, rent and other essential living expenses, he declared that seven shillings a day, or 42 shillings a week, was the minimum that would meet 'the normal needs of the average employee, regarded as a human being living in a civilised community'. It would enable such a person to maintain a family of about five at a reasonable standard of comfort, and was also fair and reasonable in view of the wages paid by Australian employers in general. He therefore prescribed it for unskilled workers, with extra payments—up to another three shillings a day—for various grades of skilled workers. These extra payments became known as 'margins'.

Main developments, 1907-61 For many years after 1907 the general tendency was for the principles of the Harvester award to be applied to each new case by both Commonwealth and State tribunals. This became easier in 1912, when the Commonwealth Statistician began publishing the first cost-of-living index. From the following year this was used by the Commonwealth Court to work out the 'Harvester equivalent'—that is, the wage which had the same purchasing power as that of the Harvester wage in 1907. In 1921 the practice was begun of making automatic cost-of-living adjustments to the basic wage every three months. Court hearings were therefore concerned mainly with setting margins for skill and with hours and working conditions.

In theory the cost of living was by far the main consideration in setting wage levels until 1934. In that year the Commonwealth Court restored a 10 per cent cut in wages that had been made three years previously, during the economic depression. At the same time it announced that wages would in future be set according to two main criteria, namely the 'cost of living', or 'needs' consideration, as before, and the 'capacity to pay' principle. In applying the latter the Court would consider both the general profit levels in industry and the extent to which wage increases could be given without harm to the national economy. In later years, therefore, various 'prosperity loadings' were added to wages, the most notable being an increase of £1 in the male basic wage in 1950. In 1953 the automatic quarterly adjustments were discontinued, the basic wage being thereafter considered yearly. With some variations the State wage-fixing authorities followed the Commonwealth lead in these matters.

In 1956 the tasks of conciliation and arbitration were transferred to the new Commonwealth Conciliation and Arbitration Commission, while the Commonwealth Industrial Court was set up to enforce awards. The Commission's judgement in the 1961 Basic Wage Enquiry was particularly important, since it decided that the capacity of the economy to pay would in future be the main consideration in wage-fixing.

Equal pay for women Until recently women's wages in most jobs were lower than those of men doing the same work; but in 1966 the Conciliation and Arbitration Commission accepted the general principle of paying the same rates to women performing the same work as men, or work of a like nature. However, this principle was difficult to apply in jobs where the work force was entirely, or almost entirely, female. In 1972, therefore, the Commission ruled that wages should in future be set on a 'work value' basis, without discrimination on the basis of sex. In general the same principle has been adopted in State legislation.

The concept of the total wage A major change in methods of wage fixation came in 1967 when the splitting of each wage rate into the basic wage and a margin for skill was abandoned in favour of the concept of the total wage. Since then the rate for each job has simply been stated as a single rate, not as the basic wage plus a margin. However, the Commission also sets a minimum wage for adult males, and has made this fully applicable to adult females since 1975. Minimum rates for adults are also prescribed in all States.

Conditions of employment Besides wages, awards specify certain conditions of work. The wages prescribed are for a normal-length working week (ranging from 40 hours in some industries to 35 in others), with each day's work being done in daylight hours. Hours worked in excess of the standard working week, or on evening or night shifts, or on Saturday afternoons, Sundays or public holidays, are paid at higher than the standard rate. Paid annual leave, long service leave and sick leave are also provided for, in some cases by awards, in others under State legislation.

Some awards specify preference in employment to members of trade unions, while some prescribe the period of notice that must be given before an employee may be dismissed, and place other limitations on the employer's right to stand employees down.

Minimum standards of working conditions are prescribed mainly by State legislation, but partly by State and federal industrial awards. They include conditions regarding premises construction, cleanliness, space per worker, ventilation, temperature, drainage and safety equipment. Workers' compensation schemes covering injuries sustained at or arising in the course of employment are prescribed by State legislation, each Act placing liability on employers and requiring them to insure against it.

Wage indexation 1975-81, and the 1983 wage freeze The adoption by the Commis-

sion of a system of wage indexation in 1975 brought considerable change to the whole Australian economic system. The step was taken in response to the high inflation rates of the preceding three years. On the one side the unions were demanding that real wages be maintained by the reintroduction of the quarterly adjustments abandoned in 1953; on the other, employers and the federal government were putting forward the view that the country's economic troubles could not be handled unless the rate of increase in wages was controlled. In March 1975 the Commission increased award wages by 3.6 per cent—the increase in the CONSUMER PRICE INDEX (CPI) for the preceding quarter. But it made clear that future increases would not be granted automatically. In 1978 it was decided to conduct hearings at intervals of six months instead of three months.

Scene during the rail strike 1979

John Fairfax & Sons Ltd

Under indexation the Commission granted an increase each quarter- or half-year, except on one occasion when the increase in the CPI was less than one per cent. In most cases, however, not all workers received an increase in line with the full rise in the CPI, since the Commission used various methods of 'partial indexation'. At the same time many groups won considerable increases in addition to full or partial indexation. By mid-1979, when there was a wave of strikes, the indexation system was under heavy attack as having failed to preserve either the purchasing power of all wages, or industrial peace, and for having distorted established wage relativities. It was abandoned in July 1981. Late in 1982, following the Commonwealth government's imposition of a wage freeze on public service wages and salaries for 12 months, the Commission announced that it would, with certain limited exceptions, freeze award wages for the first half of 1983, after which it would review the situation.

State governments and tribunals also applied a freeze, but in some cases they too made it subject to review after six months. The wage freeze ended in September 1983, when the Commonwealth Arbitration Commission awarded a general increase of 4.3%, on condition that each union undertook not to claim (except in very exceptional circumstances) any increases outside those given by the Commission in national wage cases, for the following two years.

The Commonwealth system today The two main Commonwealth bodies are those set up in 1956, namely the Commonwealth Conciliation and Arbitration Commission and the Commonwealth Industrial Court. Separate bodies have been set up for particular groups of employees. Wages, hours of work and other employment conditions of Commonwealth government employees are regulated by the Public Service Arbitrator and deputy Public Service Arbitrators. The Flight Crew Officers' Industrial Tribunal deals with industrial disputes involving pilots, navigators and flight engineers of aircraft. The Coal Industry Tribunal considers interstate disputes and NSW disputes in the coal mining industry.

The Commission consists of a President, Deputy Presidents and Commissioners. Most of the cases coming before it are heard by individual members, but some matters, including standard hours, national wage cases, equal pay principles, the minimum wage for adults, paid annual leave and long service leave, are decided by a Full Bench, which consists of at least three members, of whom at least two are Presidential members. Appeals are also heard by a Full Bench.

State tribunals The principal State tribunals are as follows.

NSW: Industrial Commisson, Public Service Board.
VIC: Industrial Relations Commission, Public Service Board, Teachers Tribunal, Police Service Board.
QLD: Industrial Conciliation and Arbitration Commission.
SA: Industrial Commission, Public Service Arbitrator, Teachers Salaries Board.
WA: Industrial Commission, Coal Industry Tribunal, Public Service Arbitrator, Railway Classification Board, Government School Teachers Tribunal.
TAS: Industrial Boards, Public Service Board, Public Service Arbitrator.

Most States also have wages boards, conciliation committees or other bodies for particular industries. Further details are provided in State Year Books.
See also trade unions; employers' associations
Further reading: Foenander, O. de R. *Industrial Conciliation and Arbitration in Australia.* Law Book Co., Sydney, 1959 and *Recent Developments in Australian Industrial Regulation.* Law Book Co., Sydney, 1970; Walker, K.F. *Australian Industrial Relations Systems.* (2nd edn) Harvard University Press, Cambridge, Mass., 1970; Portus, J.H. *Australian Compulsory Arbitration, 1900-1970.* Hicks Smith & Sons, Sydney, 1971.

archery A sport which has experienced fluctuating popularity in its brief history in Australia, archery was introduced in the mid-19th century. London-born publican and painter Wilbraham F.E. Liardet was one of the earliest pioneers of the sport and at a meeting held in his hotel in October 1840, he promised to supply the necessary equipment for those who wanted to try the sport. The interest that Liardet inspired waned after 1880 and was not rekindled until the late 1920s and 1930s when many new clubs came into existence, only to cease functioning during World War II. After the war the sport experienced another revival in all States. In 1948 the establishment of a controlling body, the Archery Association of Australia, provided for the conducting of championships annually in rotation in the various States. 'Mail tournaments' are also held annually, clubs contesting events on their own ranges, then mailing the results to the Association for judging.

Archibald Prize In terms of the bequest of the influential journalist J.F. Archibald (1856-1919), co-founder and editor of the *Bulletin* and donor of the Archibald Fountain in Hyde Park, Sydney, the trustees of the Art Gallery of New South Wales have awarded annually since 1921 a prize for a portrait of any 'man or woman distinguished in art, letters, science or politics', painted in the year preceding the award by any artist resident in Australia or New Zealand. The prize represents a tenth of the profits of Archibald's estate. *See* Appendix 3.

The awarding of the prize has been controversial in some years. In 1933, the prize, awarded for Charles Wheeler's *Ambrose Pratt,* was withdrawn because, according to the Solicitor-General, the winner had painted from a photograph, not from life, and therefore had not fulfilled the requirements of the will. In 1944 the prize became the centre of a legal case which dominated the Australian newspapers for several days. Two competitors with traditional views on painting challenged the award made by the trustees in 1943 to William DOBELL for his portrait of the artist Joshua Smith. This case was heard before Mr Justice Roper in the NSW Supreme Court, but the plaintiffs' claim—that the painting was a caricature rather than a portrait and therefore ineligible—was not upheld. In 1953, students demonstrated against the awarding of the prize for the seventh time to William DARGIE.

In 1975, John Bloomfield was awarded the prize for his portrait of the film producer, Tim Burstall. His subsequent statement at a Press interview that he had worked from photographs, and that Burstall had not sat for him, aroused considerable interest. The trustees, in order to clear the air, and concerned that this admission might throw their decision into doubt, referred the matter to the State Attorney-General's Office, who ruled that working exclusively from photographs violated the intention of the Archibald Trust. The trustees therefore had no alternative but to withdraw the award. Although portrait painting has, since the 1960s, been of limited interest to most artists worldwide, the Archibald Prize has continued to command the interest of the Sydney public. The combination of portraits of contemporary people, the occasional uproar resulting upon the judges' decisions and the strong media interest have all combined to give the award a high profile in the public's imagination.

architecture Buildings reflect man's need to provide shelters for his activities and to endow those shelters with functional and aesthetic qualities, according to the values, technology and physical and mental resources of his society. In Australia, there have been three fairly distinct phases of architectural styles: the colonial period, 1780 to about 1850, which was strongly influenced by British Georgian architecture; the latter half of the 19th century, during which Victorian architectural styles predominated; and 20th-century Australian architecture, which reflects European and American tastes and technology.

Aboriginal shelters As hunters and foragers, the Aborigines lived in caves or built huts and windbreaks which, depending on the nature of the campsite, were usually arranged in a row or a semi-circle. Early descriptions of these shelters tended to be superficial. In 1788 in Sydney, Watkin Tench, an officer who came to NSW with the FIRST FLEET and whose accounts provide a valuable record of the early years of settlement, wrote: 'Than these huts nothing more rude in construction, or deficient in conveniency, can be imagined. They consist only of pieces of bark laid together . . . open at one end, and very low, though long enough for a man to lie at full length.' Recent studies indicate that the Aborigines built a considerable variety of shelters to satisfy their needs. The basic hut, which according to locality was called a *gunyah* (NSW), a *mia-mia* (VIC and WA), an *oompi* (QLD) or a *wurley* (SA), ranged from 'tents', made of poles and sheets of bark, and structures of mulga-wood and leaves, built in the shape of a half-cylinder, to comparatively elaborate stone-under-thatch huts, one of which was recorded in QLD in 1906.

There were also many forms of symbolic monuments, as well as special rock alignments. A site designated for initiation ceremonies in central Australia, recorded in 1894, had an axial arrangement of screens, mounds, poles and paths; focusing attention on the apse-like space where the initiations were carried out, the plan of this site makes an interesting comparison with the layout of a Christian church. In northern NSW a series of ceremonial stone circles, reminiscent of Stonehenge, were discovered recently.

British background The early white settlers in Australia did not develop a distinctive style of architecture (as other colonists had done in, for example, the Americas and South Africa); their designs were in the main an accurate though usually simplified, reflection of the Georgian styles popular in Britain in the late 18th and early 19th century. In Georgian society in Britain, while most people lived in the meanest of hovels, the wealthy few built town houses and country mansions of great beauty. The town houses in cities such as London, Bath and Exeter were grouped together, sometimes making whole streets of terraces; each house was well proportioned and had a simple exterior design, compatible with its neighbours, giving the terraces an overall effect of orderliness. The typical country house was also simple in design but larger, having as its focal point a central doorway and usually featuring a hipped roof and fine, delicate doorcases, fanlights, pediments and plinths. Landscapes were contrived to complement the ordered Classicism of these buildings; landscape designers, such as Lancelot 'Capability' Brown, provided the beautiful settings which made Georgian country homes memorable.

Georgian buildings were characterised by the warm colour and fine texture of the brickwork, by the detailed attention given to joinery, and by the use of crown-glass sash windows. The old casting process, which produced small, thick pieces of glass, was replaced by the technique of glass-blowing, whereby a bubble of molten glass blown in the end of a pipe was flattened into a large, thin disc or crown; this crown was annealed and cut into rectangular panes. In windows, these panes were set into pairs of timber sashes so as to slide vertically in frames.

The underlying theme of Georgian architecture was Palladianism, a style developed by a 16th-century Italian, Andrea Palladio, and revived in England in the 18th century. Buildings were strictly ordered, restrained and distinctively symmetrical, usually featuring a double-storeyed central block linked to single-storeyed wings. There were many successive variations of the Palladian theme. The first was the Regency style, popularised in London by John Nash and characterised by such features as parapets, porticoes, balconies and pilasters. The next variation was a revival, called Gothick to distinguish it from genuine Gothic; buildings were often asymmetrical in form and medieval imitations, such as pointed doors and windows, appeared. This was followed by a period during which architects favoured Grecian styles, and finally by a period of Baroque Revival characterised by robust buildings with curved facades.

Regency style Camden Park House, Menangle NSW designed by John Verge. Probably the first Australian slate roof.

The colonial period During the early years of settlement in Australia, only a minority of Georgian buildings were designed by architects. The rest were 'vernacular' buildings (that is, improvised or primitive work in the traditional style) designed and built by convict builders or amateurs using local materials. The frames for military buildings and convicts' huts were made of timber from she-oak trees, pit-sawn into posts and beams by convicts. The wall panels between the posts consisted of horizontal logs of cabbage-palm or of interwoven *Acacia* twigs. The cracks between the posts and the cabbage-palm panels were plastered with clay, whereas the basket-weave panels, called 'wattles' in England (hence the name 'wattle' for Australian *Acacia* trees), were plastered on both sides with 'daub', a mixture of clay and dung, and then white-washed. Many of the early houses in the Georgian vernacular, particularly those in the hotter and wetter areas of Australia, featured the verandahs common in other colonies; as conditions improved, bricks and stone were used more frequently, the mortar being made from burnt oyster shells mixed with sand or loam.

In the early years, bricks and glass were reserved for government buildings or those built for wealthy settlers. The bricks were made at Sydney's Brickfield Hill, but, until about 1850, crown-glass had to be imported from England. During the first two decades about 200 buildings were erected. Two of them heralded the Industrial Revolution in Australia—a prefabricated temporary house for Governor PHILLIP, made in London from timber and canvas, and the 'portable' hospital, which came on the second fleet in 602 parts, including a copper-panelled roof. Phillip's permanent house, designed and built by James Bloodsworth, a convict brickmaker who was appointed Superintendent of Buildings, was the first two-storeyed structure; it was built in 1788-89 in what is now Bridge Street, Sydney, and was a simplified but confident version of the British Georgian style. In 1983 its foundations were unearthed, and the NSW government announced its intention to preserve them.

Under the guidance of Governor MACQUARIE, who was dubbed the 'Building Governor', a large building programme got under way with the services of trained architects such as Daniel Mathew and Henry Kitchen, (free settlers), John Watts (a designer of military buildings) and Francis GREENWAY. Public buildings conceived on a grand scale were erected in the HAWKESBURY towns, in Liverpool, CAMPBELLTOWN, Hobart and BATHURST. Sydney was transformed from a camp into a town; streets were named and widened and churches, courts, pubs, houses and a new hospital were built. Examples of buildings during this period which illustrate the Palladian theme of late 18th-century Britain are the courthouse at WINDSOR, built by Francis Greenway, and Old Government House, PARRAMATTA, as enlarged by John Watts.

Macquarie's building programme paved the way for the rich architectural growth of the following two decades. Sydney, for the first time, boasted shops, hotels, terrace houses, theatres and bathrooms. VAN DIEMEN'S LAND came alive with a programme of public buildings after its separation from NSW. Perth, Brisbane, Melbourne and a host of smaller towns were designed according to Governor DARLING's town planning regulations in 1829; these regulations controlled allotment sizes, building lines and footpaths and stipulated that street patterns should always be straight-lined with main streets 30m wide and secondary streets 24m wide. The layout of Adelaide, conceived in 1837 by Colonel William LIGHT, is a fine example of a Georgian town.

All the above-mentioned style variations of Georgian architecture were reflected in the buildings in these towns. The Regency style was adopted for the courthouse at RICHMOND in TAS, designed in 1825 by David Lambe, and for Elizabeth Bay House, designed by John VERGE in 1832. The facade of Mac's Hotel in Franklin Street, Melbourne, is also in the Regency style. The Gothick style was applied particularly to churches, such as Holy Trinity in North Terrace, Adelaide. Among the most competent designers during the Greek Revival was Mortimer LEWIS, who designed the Darlinghurst courthouse in 1832 in the Doric style. Other examples of the Grecian style are St George's Church in Hobart, designed by John Lee Archer (Colonial Architect in the 1830s) and James BLACKBURN, and the Baptist Church in Collins Street, Melbourne, designed by Joseph Reed. Representative of the Baroque Revival is the Congregational Church in Pitt Street, Sydney; it was built in 1841 by John Bibb after the style of many English Palladian churches and it features Ionic columns of two different sizes.

Terrace houses in Surry Hills NSW built about 1880

The Victorian era The architecture of this period, in both Britain and Australia, was characterised by a mixture of ornate and often vulgar style excesses. Earlier styles, in particular Gothic and Classical Renaissance, but also Oriental, Egyptian, Byzantine and Baroque, were revived and adapted to suit new functions. Church design switched from rational Georgian to sentimental Gothic; banks were built in stolidly Classical styles; large buildings often featured the ponderous arches and heavy walls of the Romanesque style; and most buildings were dressed up in intricate cast-iron work and given a coat of elaborate stucco decoration.

The strongest characteristic of Victorian building was its exploration of new technical resources. Cast iron was perhaps the most obvious of these and it had many uses—posts, balustrades and street furniture, to name a few. Extensive use was made in Australia of corrugated galvanised iron, a cheap, light-weight and durable material; in the inland areas it was used for walls and roofs, and in curved shapes, for water tanks and verandahs. In the cities, many tall buildings were built after the introduction of the elevator. Concrete appeared but its use was not really developed until the 20th century. Building processes were transformed by new mediums such as steam-powered saws and lathes. Mechanised brick-making produced stronger and harder bricks and made easy the production of moulded bricks, which in turn promoted more fancifully decorated buildings. Other innovations that affected Victorian architecture included plate glass and interlocking roof tiles.

In Australia, the Victorian era coincided with the greatest journeys of exploration, the opening up of the hinterland, the gold rushes, the development of trade and transport, self-government for the States, the autonomy of municipalities and a growing national wealth. Life became more complex and new buildings were needed to house new activities: compulsory education led to a great increase in school buildings; railways promoted the need for stations and hotels; rural expansion gave rise to the need for banks, warehouses, shearing sheds and wool stores; with the introduction of local government, countless town halls were built; city growth caused a boom in retail trading and in buildings such as department stores.

Australia's heritage of Victorian architecture is illustrious. Good examples of the Romanesque are the National Mutual Building in Sydney, designed by a New York architect, Edward Raht, and the Queen Victoria Building in Sydney, designed by George McRae when he was City Architect of Sydney. Melbourne's Treasury Building, designed by John Clark in 1862, is probably Australia's finest Classical Renaissance building, while the Mitchell Building at the University of Adelaide, designed by E.J. Woods in 1879, is an excellent example of the Gothic style. Three buildings which illustrate the Victorian obsession with elaborate stucco work for the exteriors of their buildings and lush, decorative paint work for the interiors are LAUNCESTON Town Hall, Melbourne's Block Arcade and Her Majesty's Opera House in Brisbane.

The four outstanding architects of Australia's Victorian era are Edmund BLACKET, William WARDELL, Joseph REED and James BARNET. Blacket worked mainly in NSW, and designed such buildings as the University of Sydney (Gothic); Wardell designed many important buildings in Melbourne and Sydney, such as the E.S. & A. Bank in Melbourne (Venetian) and the New South Wales Club in Sydney (Renaissance); a great number of Melbourne's buildings were designed by Reed and include the Public Library (Roman), the Exhibition Building (Florentine) and Scots Church (Gothic); and the enormous output of Barnet, NSW's longest-serving Colonial Architect, included the Post Office in Sydney (Classical), many courthouses and the Garden Palace (1879), the first international exhibition venue in the S hemisphere.

Vernacular buildings flourished, particularly in the rural areas. Spurred by necessity and often using great ingenuity, squatters and diggers built huts, barns and shearing sheds of corrugated iron and of local materials, making particular use of stringybark. The bark was prised from the tree with an axe, dried and flattened over a fire, and tied to the timber frame of the building with wire or raw-hide; the roof bark was held down by a system of purlins and outriggers straddling the ridge and tied or pegged together. Roofs were often thatched with wheat straw. A very common walling material was mud; a new system was developed whereby saplings were nailed at short intervals to the inside and outside of wall posts and the space between them filled with mud. Where the earth was clayey enough, pisé and adobé walls were built. A vernacular technique that was perhaps uniquely Australian, produced many beautiful buildings and made use of big gum trees, was slab-walling, whereby large split eucalypt slabs were fitted into grooves in wall-plates at top and bottom. Another vernacular type worth mentioning is the so-called 'Queensland style', in which timber houses were raised above the ground on stumps (for better termite control and cool air circulation), wall frames were boarded internally but left exposed outside (more economical and faster evening cooling), and beams were handsomely spaced and decorated.

In the cities and towns, vernacular work ranged from crude to attractive and efficient buildings. Small versions of such stylish terraces as, for instance, Royal Terrace in Melbourne or Milton Terrace in Sydney, were built in great numbers as a result of land speculation and the availability of such standard components as doors, windows, precast decoration, verandah posts and factory-made staircases.

Architecture since 1900 The beginning of the 20th century in Australia saw a recovery from the depression of the mid-1890s, during which little building had been done, and the emergence of the Federation style which, for the first time, took account of the Australian climate and lifestyle. This style was applied particularly to private homes at a time when the emphasis was shifting from terrace houses to suburbs of single-storeyed detached or semi-detached 'villas'. The Federation style had several components. Firstly, it was reminiscent of the English 'Queen Anne' style: houses were predominantly red—red brick, red Marseilles terra-cotta roof tiles and red-painted woodwork—and their roofs displayed gables, towers and bays. It also incorporated a kind of ornamentation called art nouveau (a far cry from the revolutionary art form of that name in Europe), which rejected historical forms and favoured those derived from nature, such as sinuous curves and tendrilled plants. The third component was the Edwardian style, based on Classical design and featuring bulbous columns and heavy window frames. Outstanding examples of Federation houses include those designed by Robin Dods in Brisbane and by Robert HADDON and Harold DESBROWE-ANNEAR in Melbourne.

World War I brought a halt to the building programme, as did the Depression and World War II, but in the intervening years building went on apace and began to show signs of a strong American influence. Films produced in Hollywood made Australians aware of the similarities between the Australian and Californian coasts, which led to the introduction of the Californian Bungalow and Spanish Mission styles. At first built in timber, with outdoor rooms and wide, low-pitched roofs, the Bungalow style became popular with speculators and soon spread throughout the continent. Some of the finest examples may be seen in Adelaide. The Spanish Mission style, which displayed arches, coloured wall and floor tiles, window grilles and rough white stucco, drew attention to the virtues of courtyards, arcades and pergolas. The most outstanding architect of this period was Walter Burley GRIFFIN, who had arrived shortly before World War I to supervise the construction of his prize-winning design for Canberra.

The technological advances of the early 20th century were reflected in Australian buildings. Among some of the far-reaching innovations were the brick cavity wall, brick veneer construction and the use of fibrous plaster. In the 1930s, metal windows, stainless steel, kitchen units and built-in cupboards appeared; among the first architects to use these were Roy GROUNDS and Sydney ANCHER. In the commercial and industrial fields, rolled steel sections for framed buildings virtually eliminated the load-bearing wall, making tall structures quicker and thus more economical to build; ready-mixed concrete, pioneered in Australia, was used extensively; electric elevators replaced the slow hydraulic lifts; and structural glass and chromium-plated elements gave buildings the sleek and shiny 'international' look.

This house on stilts at Clermont is a good example of Queensland style architecture

Technology pervaded architecture to an even greater extent after World War II. As arbitrary height limitations were removed, commercial buildings in the cities grew higher, not only to gain prestige but to maximise the use of costly land. In such buildings, weight-reduction and modular co-ordination were used to lower construction costs. SYDNEY OPERA HOUSE, designed by Joern Utzon and arguably Australia's only contribution to world architecture, expanded the knowledge of materials, design, quality, and construction management. The use of reinforced concrete, both cast-in-place and pre-cast, made possible the very fast construction of Australia Square, designed by Harry SEIDLER in the 1960s and the first project in Australia wherein an area was redeveloped by amalgamating many small land holdings into one.

The search for a truly Australian house-style resumed after a period of post-war austerity. Robin BOYD, by writing as well as designing, popularised and sought to improve architecture in the community. In Melbourne, Roy Grounds explored the qualities of light, shade and geometry: he designed circular and triangular houses and made much use of pergolas. At Turramurra, Harry Seidler built his first house, a sophisticated example of the International style. In Brisbane, architects such as Hayes and Scott designed distinctive houses in a revived form of the Queensland style. The most consistent attempt to design a truly Australian house-style began with the work of the 'Sydney School' in the 1950s. The strongest qualities of this style are the harmony of the building with its site, the expression of protection and stability, and emphasis on space, light and view. But it is the particular means used that are interesting: richness of texture, achieved by rugged clinker bricks or rough bricks painted white; timber used off-the-saw, inside as well as out; raw off-the-form concrete; and angled roof lines covered with heavy-textured tiles. Houses by Peter Johnson, Don Gazzard and Ken Woolley are among many that achieve these qualities and which represent a richer, warmer, more aesthetically pleasing architecture which is particularly 20th century and thoroughly Australian.
Further reading: Freeland, J.M., Cox, P. & Stacey, W. *Rude Timber Buildings in Australia.* Thames & Hudson, 1969; Freeland, J.M. *Architecture in Australia, A History.* Penguin Books, Ringwood, 1972; Herman, M. *The Early Australian Architects and Their Work.* Angus & Robertson, Sydney, 1973; Oliver, P. (ed) *Shelter, Sign and Symbol.* Barrie & Jenkins, London, 1975; Lewis, M. *Victorian Primitive.* Greenhouse Publications, Carlton, 1977.

Ardrossan SA (population 961 in 1981) This is a small port on the ST VINCENT GULF coast of YORKE PENINSULA, NW across the gulf from Adelaide. It handles the export of wheat and barley from the rural regions of the peninsula, as well as the export of dolomite and salt. Richard Bowyer Smith, a resident of Ardrossan, invented the 'Vixen' stump-jump plough, and in 1880 opened a factory for the production of ploughs. The factory was forced to close down in the Depression of the 1930s, but is commemorated by a restored plough, located at a lookout on the cliffs at the E end of the town's main street. The town was named by Governor Fergusson after Ardrossan in Ayrshire, Scotland.

area The area of Australia is 7 682 300km²; WA is the largest State (2 525 500km²) and TAS the smallest (67 800km²). It is only about 6000 years since the shores of the continent

took on the contours which, to a greater or lesser extent, they have retained to the present; for most of the past 120 000 years the sea has been low enough for TAS and New Guinea to be joined to Australia, and for the GULF OF CARPENTARIA and most of the Timor and the ARAFURA Seas to be dry land. But as the last Ice Age receded, the waters, rising approximately 100m, separated the continent from New Guinea and TAS, and reduced the area of the continent by about a third.

In 1973 the Division of National Mapping of the Department of Natural Resources computed the respective areas of the States and Territories and the length of the coastline by a system which involved the manual 'digitising' of these features using the map sheets of the 1:250 000 series of Australia. The use of these maps meant that only features of a size measurable on that scale could be considered. About 60 000 points were digitised at an approximate spacing of 0.5km; these points were joined by chords which were used as the basis for computer calculations. This work required the making of many decisions on questions such as the precise location of the coastline (at approximate high-water mark); the position of the shoreline on mangrove coasts (assumed to be on the landward side); and how far into river estuaries is considered to be coastline.

argonauts *see* cephalopods

SA Dept. of Tourism

Arkaroola sanctuary and reserve

Arkaroola SA The Arkaroola-Mt Painter sanctuary and historic reserve lies some 600km N of Adelaide in the N FLINDERS RANGES, covering an area of 61 000ha. Though the sanctuary is located in the arid region NW of LAKE FROME, two motels, a camping area and modern facilities have been constructed there to cater for travellers visiting the far N Flinders region.

Armidale NSW (population 18 923 in 1981) A city on the NEW ENGLAND Plateau at an elevation of 995m above sea level, Armidale is the principal business and commercial centre of the plateau; it is situated on the New England Highway 564km by road and 579km by rail N of Sydney, and linked to Sydney and to Brisbane by regular air services (its airport is claimed to be the highest in Australia). It experiences mild to warm summer conditions, but the winters are cold with regular daily frosts and occasional snow. The mean annual rainfall is 795mm, falls occurring throughout the year, but with a slight concentration in the summer months from December to February. The city is situated on the gently sloping valley and hills adjacent to Dumaresq Creek (not to be confused with the DUMARESQ RIVER in QLD/NSW), a headwater tributary of the MACLEAY RIVER which rises in the New England Range near Guyra to the N, and flows generally E to the Pacific. Just W of Armidale lies the main watershed dividing the streams flowing E from those which flow in a general NW direction to the GWYDIR RIVER. The surrounding rural district is a rich grazing and farming area noted for the production of high-grade wool and for a number of fine-wool studs. Beef cattle raising is also important to the district, together with orcharding (mainly of stone fruits) and potato growing. Timber-getting is a significant activity in the nearby forest areas and there are sawmills and a plywood factory in the city.

The land around the present site of Armidale was settled in the 1830s by the pioneer squatter William Dumaresq, after whom the creek and the local shire are named. A Scottish Commissioner for Crown Lands who came to the area late in the 1830s named the city after his family estate in Scotland. The town was officially gazetted in 1849, proclaimed a municipality in 1863 and a city in 1885.

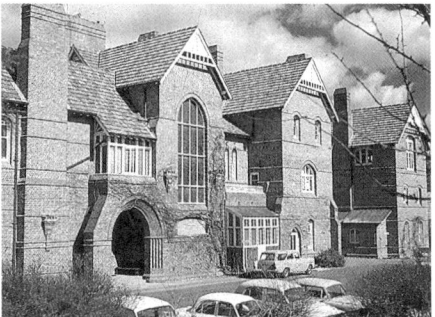

J.H. Shaw

'Booloominbah' building at the University of New England, Armidale NSW

Armidale is well known as an educational and ecclesiastical centre. On the NW edge of the city is the University of New England (originally established in 1938 as a College of the University of Sydney, it became an autonomous university in 1953); the College of Advanced Education (constructed in 1929 and formerly called the Armidale Teachers' College) is located on a knoll to the S of the main business centre — it once housed the famed Howard Hinton art collection, which included many noted paintings by Australian artists; in 1983 the collection was transferred to a special new building in Armidale, the New England Regional Art Museum. The city has a technical college and several State and private schools (The Armidale School, De La Salle College, St Ursula's College and New England Girls' School). It also has two cathedrals: St Peter's (Anglican, dating from 1875; the tower was built in 1937–38) and St Mary's (Roman Catholic, opened in 1912); both have been classified by the National Trust (NSW) as essential parts of the cultural heritage. Many other buildings in Armidale have been similarly classified by the Trust (the courthouse; the Lands Office; the Imperial Hotel; the Rural Bank; The Armidale School; 'Booloominbah' and 'Trevenna' buildings at the university; and the building in the central city area which houses the Folk Musuem).

To the E of Armidale along the scarplands of the plateau there is much rugged and scenically attractive country where the headwater streams of the Macleay cascade over the escarpments in spectacular waterfalls, then flow through sheer gorges.

The New England National Park, covering 23 554ha, is located some 70km E on the Armidale-GRAFTON road; within the park are vast stretches of forest wilderness, and from Point Lookout the panoramic view of the dissected scarps and valleys of the upper Macleay extends on a clear day to the Pacific coast. The Apsley Gorge National Park (6 630ha), lying SE beyond Walcha, includes spectacular gorges and waterfalls.
See also New England
Further reading: Thorpe, E. The New England Plateau. Longmans, Melbourne, 1957; Drummond, D.H. A University is Born. Angus & Robertson, Sydney, 1959; Armidale: 100 Years of Local Government, 1863-1963. Armidale City Council, 1963.

Army, the see defence

Arnhem Land NT Named after the
Dutch ship Arnhem which sailed along the coast in 1623, this vast tract of tropical land extends over much of the N and NE section of the NT. It is an Aboriginal reserve, covering an area of 96 089km². Stretching from GOVE PENINSULA on the NE coast to COBOURG PENINSULA at its NW extent, it includes the off-shore islands (ELCHO ISLAND and GROOTE EYLANDT, amongst others), and stretches along the entire W shore of the GULF OF CARPENTARIA, as far as the ROPER RIVER, and along most of the N coastline on the ARAFURA SEA. It is the largest Aboriginal reserve in Australia and is closed to non-Aboriginals, except with the special permission of a council of Aboriginal residents. Some tourist safaris are allowed into the reserve and, until recent decades, the only white settlements were mission stations, such as YIRRKALA on Gove Peninsula. However, the discovery of rich mineral ores, such as the manganese at Groote Eylandt, the bauxite at Gove and the uranium at NABARLEK, have led to agreements with the Aboriginal people for the mining of these

deposits. At the 1981 census, the East Arnhem Statistical Subdivision had a population of 10 429. The average yearly rainfall along the coastal areas is about 1 300mm (Elcho Is, 1 329mm; Yirrkala on Gove, 1 315mm), while the highlands inland receive up to 1 500mm. The rainfall pattern is typical of N Australia, the rain being concentrated in the summer months, the long dry season lasting from May to October. The W and SW parts of the reserve consist of rugged dissected highlands rising to over 300m above sea level, with steep scarps cut by deep gorges. The major river systems of the N part of the Territory have their headwaters in this highland area. The Katherine River rises in the SW corner, the South and East ALLIGATOR RIVERS rise along the W fringes; the Mann, Blyth and Goyder Rivers flow from the upland zone N to the Arafura coastline; and the Koolatong, Walker and Rose Rivers drain E to the Gulf of Carpentaria.

Aroona Valley SA Lying N of WILPENA
POUND in the FLINDERS RANGES, this strikingly scenic valley was made known through the paintings of Hans HEYSEN; the W border of the valley is called Heysen Range. The name Aroona comes from an Aboriginal word meaning 'flowing water'. Two other features located some 80km NNW of Aroona Valley bear the same name: Mt Aroona (elevation 427m), and Aroona Dam, a reservoir constructed in 1956 to supply LEIGH CREEK.

arrow worms The arrow worms form a
small phylum, Chaetognatha, of carnivorous marine animals. From their embryology it is considered that they belong to the group of phyla which includes the SEA SQUIRTS and the ECHINODERMS. They are from a few mm to 10cm in length, the body being shaped like a feathered dart. The head carries grasping spines and eyes, and there are usually one or two pairs of lateral fins and a tail fin.

art galleries see museums

artesian water This is a form of under-
ground water, stored in porous rock formations (aquifers) and confined between two impermeable rock strata. Artesian water is under hydraulic pressure sufficient to force it to the surface when the aquifer is penetrated by a bore; if the pressure is insufficient to bring the water right up to the surface, it is called subartesian water, and pumps may be used to raise it. Artesian and sub-artesian water thus occurs in special geological basin formations or trough-shaped structures in which there is a sequence of rock strata, containing both porous layers (usually sandstone or conglomerate or limestone) and impermeable layers (usually shale or similar fine-grained sedimentary rocks). Some of the artesian formations are closed basins in which the rock strata are folded upward around the basin rim so that the water cannot escape from them, except by way of wells bored through the upper rock layers; others are open artesian

basins in which the water flows through the porous rock formations from a highland intake zone to a natural outlet at a lower level. The name 'artesian' comes from the Artois Province in France where such a basin formation is found.

Australia has vast areas, especially in the dry inland regions, that are underlain by artesian basins. Water from such basins has made it possible to establish pastoral activities in these arid regions. The principal use of artesian water is for livestock, as the supplies of water from the basins are generally too limited to support irrigation schemes and also, in most instances, the waters are too impure for plant growth. This impurity is caused by mineral salts, such as sodium carbonate, potassium carbonate and sodium chloride, which make the water mildly alkaline. It is usually unfit for human consumption, but may be used for other domestic purposes. In some cases, the artesian water is at high temperatures when it reaches the surface, due to the depth from which it comes and the pressure under which it is stored.

The Great Artesian Basin is the largest in Australia, and one of the world's largest, covering over 1.7 million square kilometres in QLD, NSW, SA and NT. It is a typical basin structure, comprising a saucer-shaped formation with the E rim higher than the other parts; the main aquifers outcrop along this E rim in the GREAT DIVIDING RANGE of QLD and NSW, where rainfall is quite high; they form the intake zone for the artesian basin and the water passes through the aquifer to the arid W areas where it comes to the surface in natural spring outlets. But man-made bores have been much more important than the springs; the first, sunk in 1878 near BOURKE in NSW to a depth of 44m, was so successful that it encouraged further searching for artesian water. In subsequent years many hundreds of bores were sunk, and even though some bores ceased to flow and others dried up, the basin has continued to be a major source of livestock water for the sheep and cattle grazing industries. In the 1970s there were about 3000 flowing bores (artesian) and some 20 000 which yielded water but required pumping (sub-artesian), ranging in depth from under 60m to over 1 800m, the majority of them being less than 1000m deep.

Other major artesian basins in Australia are the Canning Basin in WA (474 000km²), the Murray Basin in NSW, VIC and SA (300 000km²), the Eucla Basin in SA and WA (180 000km²) and the Georgina-Daly Basin in QLD and NT (450 000km²).

Arthrophyta The phylum Arthrophyta
contains vascular plants which were common in Carboniferous times. The only living genus, Equisetum, does not occur in Australia, except as an introduced ornamental; some species are WEEDS in other parts of the world. Commonly known as horsetails or scouring rushes, these plants are rush-like, often tall, perennial herbs with a stiff whorled branch arrangement and hollow, jointed stems that, in

A re-creation of James Pugh's house in the Black Ridge goldfields

Australia's first Government House in Sydney in the Palladian style

Cadman's Cottage at Sydney Cove today

A fine Federation style house built about 1910 at Eaglemont in Melbourne

A Californian-style bungalow

Harbourside houses in Sydney

Parliament House, Adelaide

The old QLD State Parliament House

Sydney Opera House

'The Block' in Melbourne exuberantly stuccoed in the Baroque manner

King George Tower in Sydney

The Grace Building in Sydney, built in 1910, exemplifies the early skyscraper

See also architecture

Tobacco growing

Sorghum harvesting

Sugar cane harvesting

Wheat harvesting

Cotton harvesting

Pineapple farming

Sunflower field

See also agriculture

some species, bear terminal spore cones.
See also Appendix 5, Flower Structure and Glossary of Botanical Terms
Further reading: see Appendix 6, A Bibliography for Plants.

arthropods This group of invertebrates is the largest phylum in the Animal Kingdom. It contains the following classes, all of which are represented in Australia: Arachnida (ARACHNIDS—SPIDERS, MITES, TICKS and SCORPIONS); Crustacea (CRUSTACEANS—including crabs, prawns, slaters and barnacles); Insecta (the INSECTS); Diplopoda (the MILLIPEDES); Chilopoda (the CENTIPEDES); Pauropoda (PAUROPODS); Symphyla (SYMPHYLIDS); Pycnogonida (SEA SPIDERS); Collembola (SPRINGTAILS); Diplura (DIPLURANS); Protura (PROTURANS); and Trilobita (the TRILOBITES, now extinct). The Arthropoda has been an immensely successful group, and examples are found in all habitats, marine, freshwater and terrestrial.

Arthropods are characterised by an exoskeleton (outer skeleton) consisting of jointed plates forming a cuticle which supports the body and protects the internal organs. Being rigid, the exoskeleton prevents growth, so it is periodically cast (ecdysis), the animal then rapidly increasing in size before the new cuticle hardens. During this period, the arthropod is vulnerable to its enemies (and sometimes to its brethren).

The body is divided into a series of segments, usually grouped as head, thorax and abdomen. Several of the segments carry the jointed appendages to which the phylum owes its name (*arthron*, joint; *podos*, foot). The appendages include antennae, mouthparts and legs, and project from the body as tubular structures made from sections of the exoskeleton.

Respiration in the aquatic arthropods, other than adult insects, is by external gills which extract dissolved oxygen from the water, but in colonising the land (possible because the exoskeleton can become waterproof) arthropods developed means of breathing air. Thus very small arthropods (some mites, for example) can respire through their thin cuticle; larger terrestrial insects and mites breathe through spiracles (openings on the surface of the body) which lead to a branching network of narrow tubes (tracheae and tracheoles); these tubes lead to every cell in the body. In spiders, the spiracle leads to 'book' lungs; oxygen passes into the 'pages' of a booklike structure to reach the tissue within. They may also have some tracheae. The network of tracheae makes it unnecessary for the blood of arthropods to carry oxygen, and there is in fact no system of enclosed veins, arteries and capillaries. Instead, the blood fills the main body cavity, surrounding the viscera.
Further reading: Buchsbaum, R. *Animals Without Backbones.* (2 vols) Penguin Books, Harmondsworth UK, 1951.

Arthur, Sir George (1784-1854) Lieutenant-Governor of TAS. Born in Plymouth, he joined the army in 1804 and saw active service in a number of campaigns during the Napoleonic Wars. He was appointed Lieutenant-Governor of VAN DIEMEN'S LAND in 1823, arriving in Hobart in 1824. In the following year the island was proclaimed a separate colony, but Arthur's rank remained only that of Lieutenant-Governor.

He was determined to make the penal system work effectively, mainly by a system of punishments and rewards. He did not favour flogging as a punishment, but made extensive use of chain gangs and opened a special penal settlement for hardened criminals at PORT ARTHUR. The chief reward was the ticket of leave for good conduct, the granting of which was put on a more systematic basis. A second problem of concern to him was that of bushranging. By vigorous pursuit measures he cut down the bushrangers' numbers greatly, and by strict supervision of convicts he cut down the opportunities for the more desperate among them to escape and take up an outlaw's life. In dealing with the third of TAS's major problems, that of the Aborigines, he failed to find a satisfactory solution. At first he relied on a policy of friendliness and of even-handed justice in conflicts between settlers and Aborigines. Then he turned to a policy of segregation, culminating in 1830 in an effort to drive all the remaining Aborigines into the TASMAN PENINSULA—a bizarre incident commonly known as the BLACK WAR. Finally, he encouraged men such as John BATMAN and George ROBINSON to visit the Aborigines and persuade them to put themselves under government protection. This was done successfully, and the last survivors of the race—only about 200—were sent to FLINDERS ISLAND. There, however, they rapidly decreased in numbers.

Sir George Arthur

An intensely religious man, Arthur devoted great attention to raising the colony's moral tone, encouraging the work of clergymen of all denominations, and assisting in the founding of a number of schools. He also conducted a vigorous campaign of public works. There is no doubt of his sincerity, devotion to duty and great administrative ability. On the other hand he was strongly authoritarian in attitude and was firmly opposed to the introduction of trial by jury, to all proposals for a popular assembly and to freedom of the Press. Following his recall from TAS in 1836 he filled the positions of Lieutenant-Governor of Upper Canada (1837-41) and Governor of Bombay (1842-46). His portrait is in the Mitchell Library.
Further reading: Levy, M.C.I. *Governor George Arthur: A Colonial Benevolent Despot.* Georgian House, Melbourne, 1953; Forsyth, W.D. *Governor Arthur's Convict System.* (2nd edn) Longmans, London, 1970.

Arthur Range TAS Located in the central S of the State, this range extends 32km on a NW-SE alignment, forming the watershed between the HUON RIVER basin and the basins of the Old and Crossing Rivers which drain into PORT DAVEY on the SW coast. At the NW end of the range is Mt Hayes (elevation 1 118m), while at the SE end stands FEDERATION PEAK (1 224m).

Arthur River TAS Located in the far NW region of the State, the Arthur River rises in the rugged mountain ranges near WARATAH and flows for about 160km, first N, then NW and finally W to the coast at Gardiner Point. Its main tributaries are the Rapid and Frankland Rivers from the S. The upper reaches of the basin contain much wilderness country, heavily forested, which was deeply dissected and glaciated during the Great Ice Age. The middle reaches have some major areas of State forests, while the lower parts of the valley and the coastal plain are used for livestock grazing.

Arthurs Lake TAS Located in the CENTRAL PLATEAU region of the State about 125km NW of Hobart, it lies SE of the GREAT LAKE to which it has been artifically connected: a dam constructed in 1963 on the W side, increasing the capacity of the lake to 423 000ML, raised the water level and thereby enabled the diversion into the Great Lake. Its waters thus contribute to the vast hydro-electricity generating schemes of the central highlands. Situated in a sparsely populated area NE of the Lakes Highway, Arthurs Lake is a popular tourist and fishing resort in summer. Some books and maps refer to it as Arthurs Lake*s*, though it is in fact a single body of water.

artichokes *see* Compositae

Arts Council of Australia This is an independent, non-government organisation founded shortly after the end of World War II to foster public appreciation of the arts. It should not be confused with the AUSTRALIA COUNCIL (formerly entitled the Australian Council for the Arts), which is a government statutory authority.

The main functions of the Arts Council are to arrange professional performances of music, drama, opera, dance and puppetry, and exhibitions of art and crafts, in country areas, and to conduct weekend and vacation 'schools'.

Many of its performances and exhibitions are held in schools. It is organised on a federal basis, with a Division in each State and Territory. Each Division is based on local branches in country centres.

aschelminths Several groups of invertebrate animals, regarded as phyla in this encyclopedia, are collected together as classes by some zoologists and placed in the phylum Aschelminthes. They have in common the mode of formation of the main body cavity. The group includes Nematoda (ROUNDWORMS), Nematomorpha (HAIRWORMS), Rotifera (ROTIFERS) and Gastrotricha (GASTROTRICHS).

ash This is the name given to various *Eucalyptus* species (*see* MYRTACEAE).

Ashburton River WA Located in the NW of the State, with headwater tributaries in the Collier and Ophathalmia Ranges, the Ashburton River flows for over 600km in a general NW direction through steep-sided gorges, then meanders through extensive flood plains to a swampy estuary on the Indian Ocean coast about 20km SW of ONSLOW. Since much of the river course traverses areas of low rainfall, it flows intermittently and sections of the streambed are often dry, or contain merely a series of pools, especially in the spring and early summer months before the rains of the wet season arrive.

Ashes, The *see* cricket

Ashton, Julian Rossi (1851-1942) Artist. Born in the UK, Ashton arrived in Melbourne in 1878 to be an illustrator for the *Illustrated Australian News*, having studied at the West London School of Art and the Académie Julien, Paris. He was important in the history of Australian painting for practising the painting of landscape in the open rather than from sketches in the studio (then a common practice). His Sydney Art School, founded in 1896, had a long and influential history, though his demand that all students should have access to life-drawing classes caused some opposition in prudish society. Ashton became a champion in Sydney for Australian painters, as Tom ROBERTS had been in Melbourne. As a trustee of the National Gallery of New South Wales he advocated the purchase of several works of the HEIDELBERG SCHOOL when such confidence in Australian painting was not shared by the guardians of public galleries. He supported the New South Wales Society of Artists, which was more sympathetic to the work and aspirations of talented younger artists than the 'establishment' Art Society of New South Wales. The New South Wales Society of Artists Travelling Scholarship was established in 1889 through his enthusiasm. He also helped to organise the first exhibition of Australian art to be sent overseas, to London's Grafton Gallery. He was made a CBE in 1930.

ASIO *see* Australian Security Intelligence Organization

Askin, Sir Robert William (1909-81) Premier of NSW. Born and educated in Sydney, he worked as a bank officer, and also served in the AIF (1941-45). His political career began in 1950, when he stood successfully as the Liberal candidate for the Sydney suburban seat of Collaroy in the NSW Legislative Assembly. After only four years he was elected deputy leader of the Liberal Party, and in 1959 became leader. At that time the party had been in opposition in NSW for 18 years and morale was low among its members, but Askin brought new vigour to the leadership and in the 1965 elections had the satisfaction of seeing Labor defeated. He formed a Liberal/Country Party coalition government, and held the positions of Premier and Treasurer until early in 1975, when he retired and was succeeded as Liberal leader and Premier by T.L. Lewis.

Asparagus *see* Liliaceae

Aster *see* Compositae

Astley, William *see* Warung, Price

astronomy It is very appropriate that the Australian flag carries the image of a group of stars, the stars of the Southern Cross. The skies over Australia are a magnificent sight after dark, even to the unaided eye, and Australian astronomers have been active in the study of the southern heavens since the early days of European settlement.

Step out of doors on a clear night and gaze up at the southern sky. If city lights and air pollution do not spoil the view, the sight is unparalleled and a few minutes a night spent with the aid of a star chart will soon make you as familiar with the night sky as with the layout of your suburb.

The Southern Cross is a good place to begin. Depending on the time of night and the month of the year, the Cross may be high in the sky or upside-down close to the horizon. Running through the Cross is the filmy band of light known as the Milky Way, which runs right around the sky. It marks the edge of our galaxy, the immense whirlpool of stars in which our sun resides. The centre of our galaxy, full of fascination for astronomers, lies about 30 000 light-years away beyond the stars of the constellation Sagittarius. The constellation passes directly overhead in Australia, making this continent one of the best places from which to observe the heart of the Milky Way.

Grouped around the Southern Cross are many things of interest. Hard by the Cross is a dark patch known as the Coal Sack, formed by a huge cloud of dust floating in space and cutting off the light from the Milky Way. On the same side of the Cross are the two bright stars known, for obvious reasons, as the Pointers. The brighter of these is actually a group of three stars very close together, one of which is the closest star to the sun and the earth. It lies a mere four light-years away.

A line drawn through the long axis of the Cross leads to the bright star Achernar. Halfway between the Cross and Achernar lies the S pole of the sky, a point around which the heavens seem to turn as the night wears on and the year advances. It is also a very good way to find S on the horizon. If the stars are shining you should always be able to find your way.

Forming a lopsided square with the S pole and Achernar are two wispy patches of light, the Clouds of Magellan. They are a beautiful sight with the naked eye and even a small telescope reveals that they are in fact immense clusters of stars like our sun, lying outside our own Milky Way galaxy. Not far away is the brilliant blue-white star Canopus, the second-brightest in the whole night sky. Canopus and the other splendid bodies we have discussed are really our own stars, for when viewed from southern Australia, they never set.

The discovery of the E coast of Australia is linked with the stars. Throughout the 17th and 18th centuries major advances in astronomical observation and time-keeping had made long sea voyages less hazardous. The passage of the planet Venus across the face of the sun provided an opportunity to advance knowledge even further and the British Admiralty dispatched Captain James COOK in the *Endeavour* to the S Pacific to observe this rare event. That task successfully completed, Cook voyaged S and W to fulfill what was most likely his major mission, probing unknown seas for the Great South Land.

Observation of the stars guided the FIRST FLEET to these shores and as early as 1789 a naval officer called Dawes was exploring the sky from an observatory in Sydney, looking for a predicted comet.

Telescope inside the Siding Spring Observatory near Coonabarabran NSW

Courtesy of A.I.S. Canberra

A great step forward was taken in 1821 when Governor Thomas BRISBANE, a keen astro-

ASTRONOMY **39**

nomer, built a small observatory at Government House in PARRAMATTA. Brisbane was excited at the prospect of probing an area of the sky unknown to astronomers in Europe and he staffed and equipped the observatory at his own expense. He and his two assistants made a number of valuable discoveries and published the *Parramatta Catalogue* of stars in 1828. He also set up a network of stations to keep weather records. The work of the Parramatta Observatory was so impressive that the colonial government purchased the telescopes when Brisbane returned to England and the observatory continued to operate until 1848 under the men who had worked with Brisbane.

The present Sydney Observatory was set up in 1856 on Observatory Hill in the heart of the city and despite growing interference from city lights and air pollution it has operated from the site ever since. Observatories in other colonies followed, often more concerned with the gathering of weather information than with studying the stars. Of these only the Perth Observatory, founded in 1896, remains active today.

For a time Melbourne was the centre of astronomy in Australia. This followed the erection there of the first large telescope built in this country, a 1.27m reflector known as the Great Melbourne Telescope. This telescope was an acknowledgement of the importance of studying the southern skies with a powerful instrument, comparable with those in the N hemisphere, though the telescope in Melbourne, erected at a cost of £5 000, did not ever fulfill its promise. When the Melbourne Observatory finally closed in 1944, the telescope was rebuilt at Mt Stromlo.

Today the major centre for optical astronomy in this country is the Mt Stromlo Observatory in Canberra. Founded in 1924, it concentrated on studies of the sun until Dr Richard Woolley, later Astronomer Royal, became its director in the 1930s. Under Woolley and his successors the observatory rapidly acquired an international reputation and a number of major telescopes, some of which were erected on a new site at SIDING SPRING MOUNTAIN near COONABARABRAN in NSW. This site provided astronomers with clear dark skies most nights of the year, essential conditions for observation of faint distant stars and galaxies.

Australia still lacked a really big sophisticated telescope to rival the modern giants in Europe and North America. In 1967 work was begun on the Anglo-Australian Telescope, a joint venture of the Australian and British governments costing $15 million. It was built at Siding Spring Mt and like all big modern telescopes is a reflector; that is, it gathers light with a large mirror rather than a lens. The main mirror in this case is 3.75m in diameter and at the time of its official opening by Prince Charles in 1973 the telescope was the largest in the S hemisphere and the second-largest in the world.

One of the first big achievements of the telescope was the discovery of flashes of light coming from the Vela pulsar, the remains of a star that exploded about 10 000 years ago in a region of the sky not far from the Southern Cross.

One of the reasons for the building of a really large telescope in Australia was the need to confirm some of the startling new discoveries being made in the totally new field of astronomy that has grown up since the last war, the science of radio astronomy. Radio telescopes explore the cosmos by detecting and analysing radio signals transmitted by stars and galaxies, just as traditional telescopes gather light.

Australia has been very prominent in this new field and has some of the world's best radio astronomers. Most of the early research was done at the Radiophysics Laboratory of the CSIRO in Sydney, which had been established at the start of World War II as a secret laboratory for the development of radar sets. Being part of the CSIRO, the laboratory was not disbanded at the end of the war, as were those of radar groups overseas. Scientists here turned their expertise to a multitude of peacetime tasks, including rain-making and the development of navigational aids for aircraft.

Just before the war, radio waves coming from the Milky Way were discovered, while during the war radio signals from the sun had sometimes jammed radar sets. After the war, scientists at the Radiophysics Laboratory under the leadership of Dr Joseph Powsey and Dr Edward Bowen were soon leading the world in many aspects of the study of these cosmic and solar radio disturbances. They discovered that intense radio waves were given out by sunspots, and that the Crab Nebula, the remains of an exploding star seen by the Chinese astronomers in 1054, was a powerful radio-wave transmitter. Some of the earliest surveys of the distribution of stars and galaxies giving off radio waves were done in Australia and this added greatly to our understanding of the cosmos. Many of the early observations were done with old radar sets or with cheap, simple radio telescopes designed and built by

the scientists themselves. These included the early versions of the famous Mills Cross, an instrument based on the interferometer, having two long intersecting rows of antennae stretching across a flat surface, used to locate the source of waves emanating from the cosmos; and receivers that picked up radio waves from the sun on a number of frequencies at the same time.

It soon became clear that progress in radio astronomy, as in astronomy using light, depended on having larger and more expensive telescopes able to pick up fainter signals. In the late 1950s funds were obtained from several foundations in the USA enabling the building of a big radio telescope at PARKES in NSW. The dish of the telescope was 64m in diameter and the instrument worked so well that it became the model for a number of dishes built by the USA space agency, NASA, for tracking spacecraft. The Parkes dish itself was used to communicate with spacecraft during the Apollo series of flights to the moon.

One of the early discoveries made using the Parkes dish was the identification in 1960 of the first known 'quasar' (quasi-stellar object). These puzzling objects have since proved to be the most distant sources of energy in the universe. Thousands of millions of light-years away at the edge of the cosmos, they are pouring out light and radio waves at an unbelievable rate.

Australian radio astronomers are continuing to make major discoveries about the sun using, among other instruments, a unique piece of equipment known as a 'radioheliograph', designed and built in Australia. This produces 'radio pictures' of the sun and is an excellent way of studying the huge explosions that occur regularly on the sun's surface, producing streams of particles that influence conditions on earth. In recent years they have successfully joined the hunt for chemical compounds floating in space, in clouds of gas and dust where stars are forming. These compounds are located and identified by picking up their

Mt. Stromio Observatory, Canberra ACT

NSW Dept. of Tourism

distinctive radio signals. Many of these compounds are organic, that is, they are associated on earth with living things, and their existence is an important clue to the origin of life. The most fruitful place to search for these compounds is at the heart of the Milky Way, and radio telescopes in Australia are very well placed for this work.

Working together, optical and radio astronomers at Australian observatories have found out much about the structure of the Milky Way and other galaxies like it. In this way the secrets of the Magellanic Clouds have been exposed.

Courtesy of A.I.S. Canberra

Space tracking station

Over the years, many radio astronomers from the CSIRO group have moved to other institutions, both in Australia and overseas, spreading their expertise. A major group has grown up at Sydney University, operating the world's largest Mills Cross, near Canberra. Techniques developed for radio astronomy found a new application with the development by CSIRO scientists of INTERSCAN, a new microwave landing system for aircraft. This was adopted in 1978 for worldwide use by all countries belonging to the International Civil Aviation Organisation.

Modern astronomy depends heavily on large and expensive pieces of hardware like the telescopes at Parkes and at Siding Spring, and on elaborate detectors and computers to analyse the light and radio signals. But there is still a place for the amateur working with a simple telescope in his spare time. Amateur astronomy is well developed in Australia, drawing inspiration from people like the 19th-century astronomer John Tebbutt who laboured alone with modest instruments for 50 years at his private observatory at Windsor in NSW. His contribution was at least equal to that of astronomers working with government patronage and far more powerful equipment.

Casting the net even wider, it is possible for people with no more equipment than the naked eye to participate in the adventure of astronomy simply by going out of doors and looking up. With our clear skies and heavens throbbing with light there is perhaps no better place to join in, than in Australia.

Atherton Tableland QLD Forming

part of the GREAT DIVIDING RANGE, the Atherton Tableland is a plateau region lying W of the BELLENDEN KER RANGE in the NE of the State, inland from CAIRNS and INNISFAIL. The tableland covers an area of some 80km², with an elevation varying between 600m and 900m above sea level. Much of its surface consists of basalt lava poured out in relatively recent geological times and there are numerous extinct volcanic cones in the region, some now occupied by crater lakes such as Lakes Eacham and Barrine.

The main urban centres on the plateau are MAREEBA (population 6 309 in 1981) and Atherton (population 4 196) on the Kennedy Highway. The BARRON RIVER has its headwaters in the tablelands and flows on a general N course beyond Atherton and Mareeba; the W section of the plateau is the catchment area for a number of headwater tributaries of the MITCHELL RIVER, which drains NW to the GULF OF CARPENTARIA. The region is well known for its tobacco production, particularly around the Mareeba-Dimboola area where irrigation released from the Tinaroo Falls Dam on the upper Barron is used to produce leaf of a high quality. Dairying, maize cultivation, vegetable growing and forestry are also important industries in the region. The yearly rainfall is about 900mm, falling mainly in the summer months with a markedly dry season from May to September. Though it is situated within the tropics at latitude 17°S, temperatures are mild throughout the year due to the elevation, and this, combined with the scenic beauty of the region, has made it a popular tourist area. There are several national parks: the Lake Eacham (490ha) and Lake Barrine (491ha) Parks, both located E of Atherton, are surrounded by rainforest and noted for their bird life, for animals such as the muskrat kangaroo and the carpet python, and for many varieties of butterflies; the Crater (Mt Hypipamee) National Park (364ha), 20km S of Atherton, includes areas of rainforest and eucalypt forest with fine examples of staghorn and elkhorn ferns; E of Mareeba the Davies Creek National Park (486ha) preserves an area of eucalypt forest noted for its fine displays of wild flowers, growing on a granite outcrop where the creek tumbles into a deep valley over a 100m waterfall.

athletics This is a blanket term used to cover a variety of competitive sporting activities. These activities are divided broadly into two sections: track and field. Track events range from sprints over 100m to marathons over 42km, and include hurdle races, walking races and relays; field events include high jump, long jump, triple jump (formerly hop, step and jump), pole vault, shot putt, discus, javelin, hammer throw and pentathlon and decathlon events. While Australians have had some outstanding international successes in track events, successes in field events have been rare.

The first athletic organisation in Australia, the Sydney Amateur Athletic Club, was formed in 1872. Several other clubs in the Sydney area came into being shortly afterwards, and at a meeting of these clubs in 1887 the New South Wales Amateur Athletics Association (NSWAAA) was formed. Other States were quick to follow this example, VIC forming an association in 1891, QLD in 1895, TAS in 1902 and SA and WA in 1905. The national controlling body of athletics in Australia is the Amateur Athletics Union of Australia (AAU of A) which although founded in 1897 has existed in its present form only since 1927. Women athletes in Australia formed their own union in 1932, the Australian Women's Amateur Athletic Union (AWAAU).

Athletes In international athletics, Australian men have done best in middle-distance and distance events. In the 1896 Olympic Games, Edwin Flack won gold medals in the 800m and 1500m events. After Flack's success it was more than half a century before another runner talented enough to win international acclaim came on the scene. The athlete was John LANDY of Melbourne who became in 1954 only the second man in the world to run one mile in under four minutes. He was

Courtesy of A.I.S. Canberra

Golden Girls' Marlene Mathews (left) and Betty Cuthbert in a sprint event, Sydney 1960 followed by Herb ELLIOTT who established world records for the 1500m and the mile and won the gold medal for the 1500m in the 1960 Olympic Games. In a two-year period he ran 17 sub-four-minute miles. In the mid-1960s the spotlight fell on Ron CLARKE who in 1965 in 16 races smashed 11 world records. During his career Clarke set 18 world records over distances from one mile to 20 000m—no other athlete before or since has set more. Surprisingly, Clarke never won an Olympic gold medal. In the late 1960s the little-known Ralph Doubell surprised the international athletic world by winning the 800m at the 1968 Olympic Games in Olympic record time. By a series of victories between 1981 and 1983, Robert de CASTELLA established himself as the world's leading marathon runner.

Australian women in contrast have an excellent record in races over shorter distances, mainly 100m and 200m, with outstanding athletes such as Decima Norman, Shirley STRICKLAND, Marjorie JACKSON, Marlene Mathews, Betty CUTHBERT and Raelene Boyle winning gold medals in Olympic and Commonwealth Games. Maureen Caird of Australia became the youngest track and field champion in Olympic history in 1968 when, at 17, she won the 80m hurdles final.

In field events in Olympic Games, Australia has never had much success, with only two gold medals up to 1980. A.W. Winter won the hop, step and jump event in the 1924 Olympics and J.L. Winter won a gold medal in the high jump in 1948. The only field event in which Australia won a medal at the 1980 Olympics was the 400m men's sprint in which Richard Mitchell gained second place. One of the outstanding women athletes in field events was Katrina Gibb who unexpectedly scored a win in the high jump at the 1978 Commonwealth Games, clearing 1.93m. In field events at the 1982 Brisbane Commonwealth Games, Australia won nine gold medals, nine silver and four bronze. Among the nine gold wins, those of Debbie Flintoff in the 400m hurdles, Raymond Boyd in the pole vault, Gary Honey in the long jump and Suzanne Howland in the javelin throw, all set new Commonwealth Games records.

Professional running events were widely popular in the period 1870-1910 with meetings attracting large crowds, particularly throughout VIC. Even in the isolated WA gold-mining town of KALGOORLIE a meeting at which Arthur Postle (the 'Crimson Flash') raced Irishman R.B. Day over 75, 130 and 300 yards in 1906 drew a crowd estimated to be in excess of 15 000. Betting was a popular feature of professional running at the time and runners who were successful could expect to win large sums of money from side wagers in addition to prize money. The sport now attracts public interest only on the day when the richest prize for any foot-race in the world goes to the winner of the 120m Stawell Gift, in VIC.

atomic energy Substantial Australian involvement in the field of atomic or nuclear energy began in 1953, with the establishment of the Australian Atomic Energy Commission. The AAEC's research establishment at Lucas Heights on the SW outskirts of Sydney houses Australia's only nuclear reactors. These are used for research into reactor physics and the effects of radiation on materials, rather than for power production. In the 1960s, plans were carried out for the construction of an electricity-generating reactor on Commonwealth territory at JERVIS BAY on the S coast of NSW. Site works were begun but the project was discontinued in 1970, the reason given for the halt being that electricity from the reactor would be more expensive than electricity from coal.

In the 1950s Australia co-operated with the British government in a series of nuclear weapons tests, first on the MONTE BELLO ISLANDS, off the NW coast and later at two sites in the SA desert, Emu Field and Maralinga. Australia itself has never possessed nuclear weapons and is a signatory to the Nuclear Non-Proliferation Treaty, by which it is bound not to construct such weapons.

Australia is well supplied with URANIUM, the 'fuel' of nuclear reactors, possessing in its rich deposits in the NT about a fifth of the non-communist world's easily accessible supplies. There are no immediate plans for the construction of power reactors in Australia, though some could be in operation in the 1990s, WA being the most likely site.

Research and development into atomic energy is a significant consumer of scientific manpower. The Atomic Energy Commission has an annual budget of about $30 million and a staff of 2000. Research into nuclear physics is carried out in a number of universities, notably the Australian National University and the University of Melbourne.

atropine *see* Solanaceae

Augusta WA (population 588 in 1981) A small town located on the W side of Hardy Inlet (the BLACKWOOD RIVER estuary), N of CAPE LEEUWIN, Augusta is the S terminus of the Bussel Highway, 301km S of Perth. Dairying and cattle and sheep grazing are the main rural industries, with fishing in both the river and the adjacent sea, and timber-getting in the vast areas of jarrah, karri and pine forest of the region. The town was established in the 1830s following the exploratory journey of Lieutenant J.S. Roe, and was named in honour of Princess Augusta, the second daughter of King George III. There are limestone caves in the district; the best-known and most spectacular is Jewel Cave, 8km N of the town. The Scott National Park (3 273ha), located 6km NE of Augusta, includes stretches of jarrah and karri forest.

aurora australis Commonly called the 'southern lights', though 'southern dawn' would be a better translation, these are spectacular shimmering lights often seen in the sky close to the South Pole but occasionally glimpsed from S regions of Australia. A similar phenomenon in the N hemisphere is called the *aurora borealis*. The auroral displays are often likened to moving draperies, usually of a white or pale green colour but sometimes showing flashes of stronger colours along the lower edge. The cause of aurorae has puzzled thinkers since Aristotle. We now know that aurorae have their origins in outbursts in the sun which release great clouds of charged particles, protons and electrons. These then become entangled in electric and magnetic fields around the earth, gaining enough energy to cause the thin upper atmosphere to glow in much the same manner as the gas in a fluorescent light tube.

Austral, Florence (1894-1968) Singer. She was born Florence Wilson in Richmond VIC and studied at the Melbourne University Conservatorium, the London School of Opera, and in New York. After adopting the professional name Florence Austral in 1921, the following year she made her debut at Covent Garden with the British National Opera Company as Brunnhilde in *The Valkyrie*, and subsequently sang Brunnhilde in the complete cycle of *The Ring* at Covent Garden and at the Berlin State Opera House. Successful on both the operatic stage and the concert platform, Florence Austral appeared frequently at the Albert Hall and at Queen's Hall, London, with the BBC Orchestra, conducted by Sir Henry Wood, and with the London Symphony Orchestra. In 1925 she married the flautist John Amadio. After World War II she returned to Australia, and from 1952 until 1959 she taught at NEWCASTLE Conservatorium. She died in Newcastle.

Australasia This name has been used at different times to denote various areas. It seems to have been employed from the early days of exploration in the SW Pacific Ocean to describe lands which were believed to exist S of Asia. Later, it was applied to Australia and the islands in the adjacent region, including New Guinea and even the islands of Melanesia and Polynesia. In more recent times, it has been used to denote Australia and New Zealand, though it is not widely used and is found currently only in the names of organisations and business firms which have interests in both countries.

Australia The name comes from the phrase *terra australis* (southern land), which was used long before the continent was discovered to indicate a land which it was presumed would exist in the S hemisphere to 'balance' the large continental masses in the N half of the world. As European explorers, particularly the Dutch from the East Indies (now Indonesia), reached the Australian coastline in the 17th century, the W section of the continent was called NEW HOLLAND. Then, when the British established settlements in the E, this section was called New South Wales. It was not until the early 19th century, when it had been confirmed that these two sections were in fact parts of the same land mass, that

Comparative size of Australia with Europe

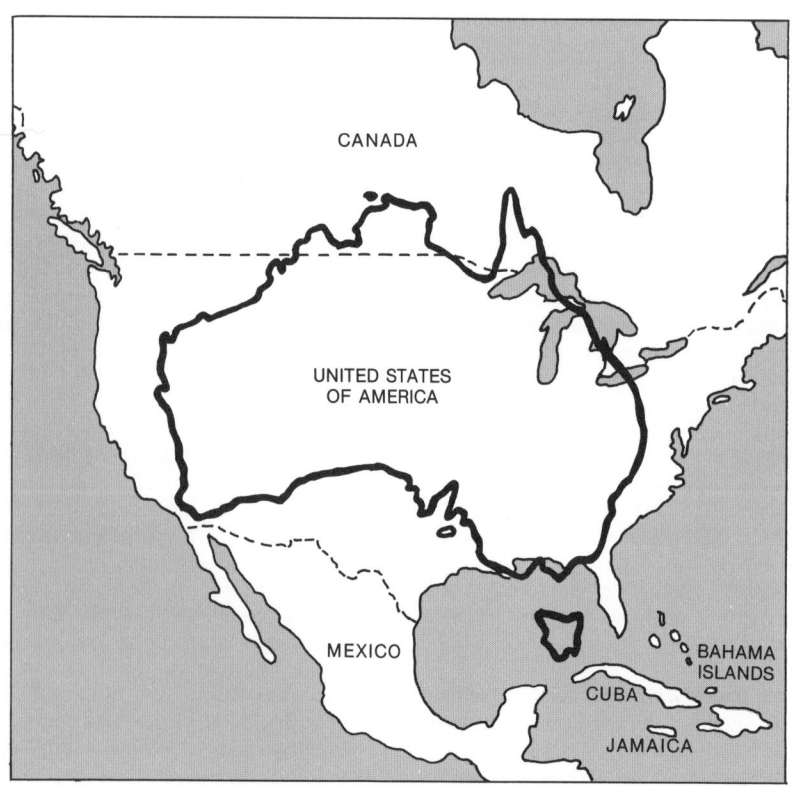

Comparative size of Australia with North America

the explorer Matthew FLINDERS suggested that the name Australia be adopted.
See also area

Australia Council This statutory authority is the federal government's cultural adviser for the funding of the arts. It is the successor to the Australian Council for the Arts (not to be confused with the ARTS COUNCIL OF AUSTRALIA) formed in 1968 mainly to promote the interests of the performing arts and so to supplement the work of the Commonwealth Literary Fund, the Commonwealth Art Advisory Board and Commonwealth Aid to Composers. In 1973 the Australia Council was founded to take over the work of all these organisations, and two years later, under the Australia Council Act, it was made a statutory authority, free from direct ministerial control.

Boards of the Council The Council's main aims are to raise and maintain high standards in the arts, to allow and encourage more people to become involved in the arts, and to make Australians and people in other countries more aware of Australia's artistic heritage and achievements. It provides financial assistance and frames policies through eight boards, which advise it with regard to their respective art forms. These boards are: the Aboriginal Arts Board, which aims at the revival and preservation of Aboriginal culture; the Community Arts Board, which is concerned with projects such as arts centres, workshops and festivals that involve more than one art form; the Crafts Board, which gives assistance to individuals and organisations concerned with the making of traditional handmade objects and also those designed for mass production; the Design Arts Board, the Literature Board, which supports all forms of creative writing by making direct grants to writers and by supporting various writers' organisations, festivals and functions; the Music Board, which makes grants to individuals and organisations both to assist the development of music (including opera) in Australia, and to promote Australian music and musicians overseas; the Theatre Board, which is concerned with developing a high quality of writing, performing and production in drama, dance, poetry and mime; and the Visual Arts Board, which makes direct grants to individuals and organisations and administers such programmes as the commissioning and public exhibition of works of art. There was also a Board for film, radio and television, but in 1976 its responsibilities were transferred to the Australian Film Commission (*see* FILM).

Public Lending Right For some years the Council made payments in respect of PUBLIC LENDING RIGHT, administration of which was carried out by a standing committee which included representatives of various interested groups and public bodies. Since October 1980, however, all responsibilities for the Public Lending Right scheme have been transferred to the Department of Home Affairs.

Australia Day 26 January. This national holiday commemorates the landing of Governor PHILLIP at SYDNEY COVE in 1788. It is held on 26 January if that date falls on a Monday, but otherwise on the following Monday. Although Phillip reached BOTANY BAY—previously chosen as the site for settlement—on 18 January, he decided almost immediately that it was not suitable. After rapid exploration of nearby PORT JACKSON, he selected SYDNEY COVE, brought the fleet there, and on 26 January officially proclaimed the foundation of the colony of New South Wales.

Australia Party A political party which began as the Liberal Reform Group. It first contested a federal general election under that name in November 1966, its main policy being to protest against the VIETNAM WAR. Its organisation was a spontaneous reaction in support of a letter to the then President of the USA, Lyndon B. Johnson, placed as an advertisement in the *Sydney Morning Herald*, in which Gordon Barton, a prominent Sydney businessman, expressed his private opposition to involvement in the Vietnam War by both Australia and the USA.

In 1967 this organisation became the Australian Reform Movement and it contested the Senate elections of 1967 under that name. In 1969 it became the Australia Party and Senator Turnbull, an independent Senator for TAS, joined it. In the 1969 federal general election Gordon Barton and Senator Turnbull undertook a national campaign with disappointing results. Senator Turnbull resigned from the party in March 1970.

The Australia Party came nearest to electoral success at the 1970 Senate elections, when its NSW team—Diana Ward, Gordon Barton and George Black—polled 5.4 per cent of the vote. Although many members left the party in 1977 to join the AUSTRALIAN DEMOCRATS, it continued to field candidates, albeit unsuccessfully. Apart from its opposition to involvement in the Vietnam War, the Australia Party has been firmly committed to its interpretation of 'participatory democracy', which it has demonstrated by publishing the journal *Reform*, in which members debate questions of party policy and decision-making.

In 1983 the Australia Party policies indicated that it was strongly in favour of changing the structure of government from a constitutional monarchy to a republic; it supported the anti-uranium lobby; wanted an unaligned foreign policy; advocated decentralised government; and, while supporting free enterprise, it believed in the introduction of worker participation to prevent confrontation in industrial relations.
Further reading: Cole, K. 'The Australia Party: an historical perspective' in Lucy, R. (ed) *The Pieces of Politics*. Macmillan, South Melbourne, 1975.

Australian Alps This name is used for the highest section of the GREAT DIVIDING RANGE, located in south-eastern NSW and

eastern VIC. It extends from about Kiandra in NSW, S across the State border, into the GIPPSLAND region where it is called the Victorian Alps. Much of the upper parts of the Alps are snow-covered during winter and numerous ski resorts have been developed in both States. The main peaks are KOSCIUSKO (2 230m, the highest in Australia) and Mt Townsend (2 209m, adjacent to Kosciusko) in NSW; and MOUNT BOGONG (1 986m) and MOUNT FEATHERTOP (1 922m) in VIC. The area is the source of some of the major rivers in the SE of the continent: the MURRAY and MURRUMBIDGEE which flow inland, and the SNOWY, TAMBO and MITCHELL which drain to the S coast. The area is also the site of the SNOWY MOUNTAINS SCHEME, a major engineering project for the generation of hydro-electricity and the provision of irrigation water.

Skiing in the Australian Alps

Australian Broadcasting Corporation In 1983 this organisation was set up as the successor to the Australian Broadcasting Commission. It provides a national radio and television BROADCASTING service, and is also a major concert entrepreneur and a publisher. It is a statutory authority, financed mainly through a direct annual grant from the federal government. In general, it is independent of programme control by the government of the day. However the Minister for Communications has the power to direct the Corporation, 'in the national interest', to broadcast or televise certain information, or not to do so. When the Minister does give such direction, he must inform each House of parliament within seven sitting days. The ABC must report any such direction or request in its annual report.

History The Corporation's predecessor was set up under the Australian Broadcasting Commission Act of 1932, which in effect provided for the nationalisation of radio stations known as 'A Class' stations. Since 1924 these had been financed from listeners' licence fees, and were run by the Australian Broadcasting Company, with facilities being provided by the federal Postmaster-General's Department. The Act required the Commission to 'provide and broadcast adequate and comprehensive programmes, and to take, in the interests of the community, all such measures as, in the opinion of the Commission, are conducive to the full development of suitable broadcast

programmes'. Half of the radio-set licence fee paid by owners was to be allocated to the ABC, which was not allowed to broadcast advertisements. Sir Charles Lloyd Jones was appointed first chairman, and H.P. Williams general manager. Operations began on 1 July 1932, with the following stations: 2FC and 2BL in Sydney, 3AR and 3LO in Melbourne, 4QG in Brisbane, 5CL in Adelaide, 6WF in Perth, 7ZL in Hobart, and the regionals 2NC NEWCASTLE, 2CO ALBURY, 4RK ROCKHAMPTON and 5CK PORT PIRIE. By the end of the year regular national programme relays had been started between Brisbane, Sydney, Melbourne and Adelaide and during the following year a relay link with Perth was also established.

Within a few years the Commission's activities had become extremely varied. Its role as concert entrepreneur arose from its acceptance in 1933 of the financial responsibility for all concerts arranged by it for broadcasting, this step being followed three years later by the establishment of studio orchestras in all States and the beginning of subscription concerts. In 1939 a federal Department of Publications and the overseas short-wave service, Radio Australia, were established. Meanwhile, educational broadcasts had also become very important, a Department of Youth Education having been founded in 1937 and a National Children's Session begun in 1939.

The Commission after 1942 In 1942 a new Broadcasting Act, based in the report of the Joint Parliamentary enquiry on Broadcasting, confirmed the ABC's independence by confirming that the Commission should have unqualified power to decide when and in what circumstances political speeches should be broadcast, and stipulating that any direction from the Minister in relation to broadcasting should be mentioned in the annual report. After World War II the ABC's activities were further expanded by its establishment of a symphony orchestra in each State capital, by its undertaking the broadcasting of proceedings of the federal Parliament, by the foundation of its own independent news service, and by entry into television broadcasting. Television channels ABN-2 Sydney and ABV-2 Melbourne opened in November 1956, and by the end of 1963 channels were operating in the other State capitals, Canberra and nine non-metropolitan locations.

Later initiatives included entry into colour television broadcasting in 1975, the establishment in the same year of 2JJ Sydney (a 24-hour radio station broadcasting popular music) and of 3ZZ Melbourne (an access radio station, which, however, ceased broadcasting in 1977 because of lack of funds), and entry into FM broadcasting in 1976. Meanwhile in 1967 the number of commissioners had been increased to nine, and in 1977 was raised to 11. In 1976 the Report of the Enquiry into the Australian Broadcasting System, conducted by F.J. Green, reinforced the independence of the Commission.

The Dix Report A major restructuring of the

ABC was recommended in 1981 in the report of a committee, chaired by a Sydney businessman, Alex Dix. In the following year the government announced the acceptance of a number of Dix recommendations, in particular: that the Commission be replaced by a Corporation, free from Public Service Board control and with a nine-member Board of Control appointed by the government; that the Board of Directors appoint a Managing Director to act as chief executive, and an ABC Advisory Council to represent the community: that the Corporation have a formal charter defining its role and responsibilities. Two important recommendations of the Dix Committee—namely, that the ABC's musical activities be curtailed and the symphony orchestras entrusted to a new body, Music Australia, and that corporate sponsorship be allowed for some programmes—were not accepted.

The Corporation The Australian Broadcasting Act of May 1983 provided for the Corporation to come into being on 1 July of that year. Shortly afterwards, Mr Kenneth Myer, AC, DSC, of Melbourne, was appointed as Chairman. At its inception the Corporation was providing radio programmes for the domestic and overseas services through a total of 133 stations. Television programmes were available through 270 channels (including translator stations), being within reach of over 99 per cent of the population.

In radio there were two main medium-wave services—Radio 1, which offered popular and light music, news, entertainment, sport, public affairs and other spoken-word programmes; and Radio 2, which concentrated on serious music, drama, features, and other cultural and educational programmes. These extended to all capital cities and to Newcastle, some programmes being relayed from Sydney and Melbourne and others originating locally. Listeners in Canberra, the State capitals and 17 other population centres also had the choice of a 24-hour-a-day FM network in stereo. One ABC-FM station—Sydney 2JJJ-FM—broadcast mainly rock music.

Rural listeners, and those in most country towns, were catered for mainly by Radio 3, which carried items from Radio 1 and Radio 2, as well as local news and specialised features such as 'The Country Hour' and 'National Farm Report'. There were also six short-wave stations to provide programmes to the inland areas where reception of medium-wave transmission is unsatisfactory.

For overseas listeners Radio Australia broadcasts in English for 24 hours a day, and for shorter periods in a number of other languages, including Indonesian, Standard Chinese, Cantonese, Vietnamese, Japanese, French, Thai and Neo-Melanesian.

Australian Broadcasting Tribunal

This Commonwealth statutory body came into being on 1 January 1977, with responsibility for some of the functions of the former Australian Broadcasting Control Board. Broadly, its function is to supervise all non-technical aspects of the operation of commercial radio and television BROADCASTING stations. It is empowered to grant, renew, suspend or revoke licences, and to determine programme and advertising standards. It is required to conduct public enquiries into the granting and renewal of licences, the setting of standards for broadcasting practices, and into alleged breaches of licence conditions. The public nature of its hearings provides incidentally a useful forum for expressions of public opinion on broadcasting standards. Thus at its first hearings on the renewal of television station licences, late in 1978, representatives of a wide spectrum of interest groups—including students' groups, women's organisations, trade unions, religious organisations and ethnic groups—appeared to put forward points of view.

Australian Capital Territory

(ACT) In the 1890s, the question of the location of the national capital was a matter of considerable controversy. Under the Commonwealth Constitution Act of 1900 the issue was partly resolved in these terms: 'The seat of Government of the Commonwealth shall be determined by the Parliament, and shall be within territory which shall have been granted to or acquired by the Commonwealth ... and shall be in the State of New South Wales, and be distant not less than one hundred miles from Sydney. Such territory shall contain an area of not less than one hundred square miles ...' But this still left the exact location of the national capital and the territory adjoining it in question. Many sites were investigated and the final choice of the 'Yass-Canberry' district, made in 1909, was ratified by a Commonwealth Act (Seat of Government Acceptance Act) and a corresponding NSW Act (Seat of Government Surrender Act). The former Act was proclaimed on 1 January 1911, and thereby the ACT was created as a separate political entity, located in the MONARO district of the SOUTHERN TABLELANDS of NSW, and within which the nation's capital, Canberra, was to be established. An additional area at JERVIS BAY on the S coast was also transferred to the Commonwealth in 1915 for development as a port.

The landforms of the ACT comprise a series of ridges and valleys with a general N-S alignment. The MURRUMBIDGEE RIVER flows through the Territory in a S-N direction and several of its tributaries (Cotter, Paddy's, Gudgenby and Naas Rivers) follow a similar S-N course. The MOLONGLO RIVER, also a tributary of the Murrumbidgee, enters the ACT at the E border and flows W, cutting across the main hill-and-ridge grain of the country. Scrivener Dam on the Molonglo was completed in 1963 to form Lake Burley Griffin as a central feature of Canberra's planned development. The Bimberi-Franklin-Brindabella Ranges form the W border of the Territory, with peaks in the SW rising to over 1 800m (Mt Bimberi 1 913m, Mt Gingera 1 857m) and others in the W somewhat lower (Mt Franklin 1 646m, Mt Brindabella 1 356m). The higher sections of these ranges are partly snow-clad during winter and some have been developed as ski resorts. Canberra is located in the N part of the Territory on the plains of the Molonglo Valley at a general elevation of 580m, and the suburbs extend on the adjacent hill lands which rise to over 800m. The Barton and Federal Highways in the N of the Territory link Canberra with YASS and GOULBURN respectively. The Monaro Highway follows a N-S route, generally parallel to the Murrumbidgee, beyond the E boundary of the Territory in NSW, to COOMA. The main rural activity in the ACT is sheep grazing though there is dairying and vegetable cultivation on some of the river alluvials near Canberra. Much of the rugged range-country in the W and SW remains timbered with the lower slopes partly cleared for grazing. The total population of the ACT at the 1976 census was 197 622 (including 687 at Jervis Bay) and of this, Canberra accounted for 196 583, indicating the sparse rural population and the dominance of the urban development of the national capital city. At the 1981 census the population of the ACT had grown to 227 255 (estimated resident population) with over 219 000 in Canberra.

See also Queanbeyan

Further reading: King, H.W.H. *Land Classification and Utilization in the Australian Capital Territory—A Preliminary Survey.* Commonwealth Govt Printer, Canberra, 1946; White, H.L. (ed) *Canberra: A Nation's Capital.* Angus & Robertson, Sydney, 1954; Shaw, J.H. & Kirkwood, F.G. *Landscape Studies.* Longmans, Croydon VIC, 1969.

Cotter Dam on a tributary of the Murrumbidgee river in the ACT

Australian Copyright Council

This organisation was formed in Sydney, in 1968, on the initiative of the Australian Society of Authors. It is incorporated as a company and consists of representatives of a number of constituent organisations whose members include holders of COPYRIGHT. The Council receives affiliation fees from the constituent organisations and a grant from the AUSTRALIA COUNCIL. Its interest is in the whole field of copyright, with regard to which it carries out research, makes representations, and gives free advice to interested persons and organisations. It also publishes a periodical bulletin on copyright matters.

Australian Council of Churches

Constituted in 1946, this inter-Church organisation had in 1983 13 member Churches, namely: the ANGLICAN CHURCH OF AUSTRALIA, the UNITING CHURCH IN AUSTRALIA, Churches of Christ, the SALVATION ARMY, the Society of Friends, the Greek, Antiochan, Armenian, Romanian, Serbian, Syrian and Coptic ORTHODOX CHURCHES, and the Assyrian Church of the East. The BAPTIST, LUTHERAN and ROMAN CATHOLIC Churches send observers to its proceedings. The PRESBYTERIAN CHURCH of Australia, formerly a member, withdrew in 1979.

The Council is officially stated to exist in order to seek the unity of Christ's followers; to further the renewal of His Church; to serve the member Churches by encouraging and stimulating their mission of evangelisation and service; and to facilitate a more effective Christian presence in the nation and the world. It has a Council or Committee in each State, and national headquarters in Sydney, and is associated with the World Council of Churches. In recent years, in addition to its purely religious activities, it has been concerned with a wide range of issues, such as racism, the place of minority ethnic groups in Australia, Aboriginal welfare, the mining and export of uranium, international disarmament, financial aid to developing countries, refugee problems and international affairs in general. Perhaps inevitably, its actions with regard to some of these matters have been controversial.

Australian Council of Trade Unions

As its name indicates, this is the national co-ordinating body of the Australian trade union movement. The various metropolitan Labor Councils (entitled Trades and Labor Councils, or Trade Hall Councils in some States) constitute its State branches.

Historical development During and after World War I there were moves for industrial unions (each covering all the workers in a particular industry) to replace the many craft unions, and a campaign was waged by the Industrial Workers of the World, and others, for 'One Big Union'. Such moves failed, however, largely because they aroused the opposition of the leaders of many of the existing unions. One reason for the success of the ACTU lies in its having been built upon the structure of unions and their co-ordinating bodies in each State.

Set up at a congress of trade unions convened by the Melbourne Trades Hall Council in 1927, the ACTU's constitution conferred on it 'power to take hold of and handle every dispute likely to extend beyond the province of any one State'. Its executive was to consist of a president, two vice-presidents and a secretary (all elected at biennial congresses by delegates of affiliated unions), and two representatives of each Labor Council. In 1957, however, the composition of the executive was changed to include only one representative of each Labor Council, and also one representative of each of six industrial groupings among

The 1979 ACTU Congress in session

affiliated unions. Subsequent restructurings have enlarged it to 26 members, of whom 13 are representatives of industrial groupings.

For many years the ACTU was weakened by the failure of the trade union movement in the WA and of the Australian Workers' Union (Australia's largest union) to affiliate; and also by the fact that its affiliated unions included few of the 'white collar' type. Other sources of weakness have been political and ideological differences among leaders of its affiliated unions and the unwillingness of many of them to surrender the control of industrial disputes to it. However, during the presidencies of A.E. Monk (1949-69) and Bob HAWKE (1969-80) it gained greatly in power and prestige due as much to the effective leadership and ability of these two men as to such factors as the constitutional changes mentioned above; the participation since 1962 of the WA union movement; the affiliation of the AWU in 1967; the Australian Council of Salaried and Professional Associations merger (1979); and the subsequent merger of the Council of Commonwealth Public Service Organisations in 1981.

Under the presidency of Bob Hawke, the ACTU embarked on various business ventures, such as ownership of a Melbourne retail store, establishment of ACTU Jetset Travel Service, and the foundation of the ACTU-Solo chain of petrol-retailing outlets. It also showed a strong tendency to take action on public issues, in calling for a boycott of French goods at times when France has exploded nuclear bombs in the Pacific; in organising opposition to the visit of a South African Rugby team; and in trying to achieve a common union policy on environmental issues, notably the mining and export of uranium ore.

Its role today, as is generally accepted, is to act as the voice of the trade union movement. With a combined membership of over two million in its affiliated unions, the ACTU is consulted on industrial matters by State governments and is responsible for submitting to the Commonwealth government the names of persons suitable for selection as delegates for Australian workers to the International Labour Organisation. It is affiliated with the International Confederation of Free Trade Unions, and pays particular attention to maintaining contact with the Asian Regional

Organisation of that body. The growth of its financial resources has enabled it to employ research officers and industrial advocates and so to offer valuable services to its affiliated unions. It conducts a programme of trade union education, including the National School of Industrial and Labor Studies, held annually in Canberra; courses organised on a State basis for shop stewards, job delegates and union officials; and a number of postal courses.

Whenever the Commonwealth Arbitration Commission (*see* ARBITRATION, etc.) hears cases affecting all employees under its awards —such as wage indexation hearings—the ACTU advocate plays a leading role, and is regarded as speaking with authority on behalf of trade unionists in general. The ACTU also frequently intervenes in industrial disputes, especially those which involve interruptions to essential public services, and which therefore affect a wide section of the community and tend to lower public esteem for the trade union movement. Its official policy regarding industrial disputes is that any affiliated organisation is obliged to notify it of a dispute before taking strike action. The ACTU Disputes Committee then meets union representatives in order to work out the course of action to be taken. Many strikes, however, take place without this process being followed.

Further reading: Turner, I. *In Union is Strength: A History of Trade Unions in Australia, 1788-1974.* Nelson, West Melbourne, 1976; Hagan, J. *The ACTU: A Short History.* Reed, Sydney, 1977.

Australian crawl *see* swimming, etc.

Australian Democrats

This political party was formed in May 1977 by the Hon. (now Senator) Donald Chipp, formerly a parliamentary member of the Liberal Party and for a time a Cabinet Minister. Some of the members of two small political parties—the AUSTRALIA PARTY and the Liberal Movement—joined the new party and a National Steering Committee was set up under the chairmanship of Chipp to organise the branches throughout Australia for the new organisation. New detailed policies were gradually developed on many aspects of Australian life.

The Australian Democrats want to avoid being tied to any particular sector of the community and to concentrate on current issues as they arise. They have developed policies for the major political, social and economic issues which have become prominent during the 1960s and 1970s, such as conservation of natural resources, unemployment, inflation, industrial relations, uranium and the energy problems, individual rights and ethnic affairs. Their policies are also concerned with traditional fields such as social services, health, education, agriculture and decentralisation.

The Australian Democrats faced the electorate for the first time in September 1977 when Robin Milhouse was elected to the State Legislature in SA and the party polled 13 per cent of valid votes cast in the electorates contested. In the Greensborough VIC by-election of November 1977, the party received 18.3 per cent of the primary vote, and its preference votes helped determine the final result. In the same month the party contested the general election in QLD and secured 12 per cent of votes in seats contested and up to 20 per cent of valid votes in city and suburban seats. In the Senate elections of December 1977 two Democrats—Colin Mason for NSW and Don Chipp for VIC—were elected. Also in December, 1977 the SA State Government appointed Janine Haines to fill a casual Senate vacancy. Three years later, in October 1980 Janine Haines (SA) was re-elected and Dr Michael Macklin (QLD) and John Siddons (VIC) were elected to the Senate. This made a total of five Senators and gave the Australian Democrats the balance of power in the Upper House. In March, 1983 John Siddons lost his seat but Jack Evans (WA) was elected to the Senate, so the party still held the balance of power in the Senate with five senators and represented five States.

Don Chipp stated that the main aim of the Australian Democrats would be to ensure that the government did not break its election promises. The party made a major innovation in Australian government in 1982 when it introduced two Bills in the Senate which were passed. Never before had a political party holding the balance of power scored such a success.

Australian Film and Television School *see* film

Australian Film Commission *see* film

Australian Film Institute *see* film

Australian Imperial Force This title was given to the volunteer military force raised for overseas service in each of the world wars. However, in common speech and indeed in most written references, these forces are referred to by the initial letters rather than by the full title. The force raised during the war of 1939-45 is referred to as 'the second AIF' in cases where the speaker or writer wishes to distinguish it from that of 1914-18.
See also World War I; World War II

Australian Inland Mission In 1911, the Rev. John FLYNN, a newly ordained Presbyterian minister, was sent to Beltana in northern SA, and not long afterwards was asked to report to his Church on the needs of the people of the thinly inhabited areas of central and N Australia. Following his report, in 1912 the Church set up the Australian Inland Mission with Flynn as its first organiser and superintendent. Its first bases were established soon afterwards at OODNADATTA in SA, PINE CREEK in NT and PORT HEDLAND in WA.

Throughout its history the Mission has catered for the educational, social and medical, as well as the spiritual needs of the Outback people, establishing nursing and educational hostels, pre-school kindergartens, homes for the elderly, and travelling community health services as well as churches. Its most widely publicised achievement has been the launching of the FLYING DOCTOR SERVICE. This was the brainchild of Flynn himself, but its implementation was made possible only by the work of Alf Traeger, an Adelaide electrical engineer and radio 'ham', who with Flynn's encouragement devised a light transceiver radio, worked by means of pedals like those of a bicycle. This gave people in isolated stations a means not only of contacting the aerial medical service, but also of communicating with their neighbours, and it later made possible the establishing of 'schools of the air'. The Mission established the first Aerial Medical Service base at CLONCURRY in 1928. However, the costs of running a number of such bases proved to be beyond resources, and they now form part of the government-funded Royal Flying Doctor Service of Australia.

Courtesy of A.I.S. Canberra

A pupil taking a 'School of the Air' lesson

In 1977, when many Presbyterians joined with Methodists and Congregationalists to form the UNITING CHURCH IN AUSTRALIA, most of the assets of the Mission were transferred to the new Church. However, the Presbyterian Church of Australia has continued its own Australian Inland Mission activities on a modified scale.

Australian Institute of Sport The Australian Institute of Sport was incorporated under the Australian Capital Territory Companies Ordinance on 24 September, 1980 and functions as a public company limited by guarantee. The Federal Minister for Sport, Recreation and Tourism appoints a board of directors and the board appoints the members of the company. The Institute began operations in January, 1981 as the principal tenant of the National Sports Centre in the Canberra suburb of Bruce.

At the end of 1983 it was providing opportunities for people in the late teenage group who win full or part scholarships in one of eight different sports — basketball, gymnastics, netball, soccer, swimming, tennis, track and field or weight lifting. A full scholarship covers full board, travel and educational allowances.

Most of the Institute's financial support comes from the Federal Government but a co-ordinator of marketing and promotions has been appointed to solicit funds from the private sector through sponsorship.

The AIS is designed to produce high performance — or, as some critics claim, to function as a gold medal factory. It is predicted that its efforts will be reflected in the performance of Australians in international competitions by the turn of the century and in the wider Australian sporting community when the AIS graduates move out and undertake coaching.

Australian Labor Party The Australian Labor Party (ALP) was founded mainly by the trade union movement for the benefit of the working class. It has had a continuous history from 1891 although its present name was not adopted uniformly throughout Australia until 1918. It has been the largest single political party in Australia and has been firmly committed to using the economic powers of the government to bring about social and economic changes in the community, to eliminate poverty and to create a more equal society. Its periods in office, both State and federal, have been marked by important reforms which have in most cases not been reversed by its opponents.

Early notable victories for Labor were in 1891 when NSW Labor won 37 seats out of a total of 141 seats in the Legislative Assembly, and in 1893 when QLD Labor won 16 seats out of a total of 72 seats in the Legislative Assembly and SA Labor won 10 seats out of a total of 54 seats in the House of Assembly. At the first federal general election in 1901 Labor won 16 seats in the House of Representatives and eight in the Senate. During the 94 years between 1889 and 1983 the ALP formed the government in State Parliaments as follows: in TAS for a total of 54 years; in NSW and WA for a total of 42 years; in QLD for a total of 39 years; in SA for a total of 22 years; and in VIC for a total of nine years. In the 83 years since federation the ALP formed the government in the federal Parliament for a total of 19½ years. In 1983 the ALP held office in the federal Parliament and in the NSW, VIC, WA and SA Parliaments.

The most notable aspects of the ALP are its connections with the trade union movement, its methods of organisation and discipline, its history of splits and quarrels and its policies and achievements.

Trade union connections The trade unions were responsible for founding the ALP and they are its most reliable source of funds. Trade unions are affiliated with the State parties and send delegates to the State conferences; all the ALP 'safe' seats are trade union strongholds. For some years Bob HAWKE was both president of the AUSTRALIAN COUNCIL OF TRADE UNIONS (ACTU) and president of the ALP. In 1980 he was elected MHR for Wills and became the ALP's 'shadow minister for industrial relations, employment and youth affairs'. On 8 February 1983 he became the parliamentary leader of the ALP and on 11 March 1983 Prime Minister of Australia.

Organisation The ALP consists of six State parties two Territory parties and a Federal Executive. Each State or Territory party is organised as a pyramid, the base being the local branches. These send delegates to the supreme State body, the State Conference, which meets once every two years to decide State policy and elect a State Council. The latter runs the State party between conferences, controlling finance, affiliations, constituency organisation and propaganda.

Each State sends six representatives to the Federal Conference, which also meets every two years, to determine party policy, rules and constitutional matters. Its decisions are binding on all other ALP organisations. Under new rules adopted in 1981 the Federal Conference will consist of approximately 100 members. These include the party leader and deputy leader in the Senate and House of Representatives, the parliamentary leaders in the States and the NT, and a representative of Australian Young Labor. The remainder are to represent the party organisation in each State and Territory, the numbers being decided in accordance with the number of federal electorates in each. A minimum of 25 per cent of the representatives from each State and Territory must be women. The Conference meets in public sessions for about a week to consider and make decisions on reports prepared by special policy-committees and on motions submitted by the State parties, by federal trade unions, by the federal women's organisation within the ALP, and by the federal parliamentary Labor Party. A Federal Executive is appointed which is responsible for the administration of the party between Federal Conferences and for interpreting policy.

The ALP is the only major Australian political party in which, theoretically, the ultimate decision-making power or policy of the party is set by the organisation and not exclusively by the parliamentary representatives of the party, and in which all decision-making is carried on in public view rather than in secret.

Discipline The ALP maintains rigid discipline over endorsed candidates who stand for election, and also over those who are elected to Parliament, by the introduction of three main innovations: the candidate's pledge; caucus control in Parliament; and the subjection of the parliamentary representatives to a general policy, determined and revised from time to time (in the case of federal Labor parliamentarians, by the Federal Conference of the party, and by the respective State Conference in the case of State Labor parliamentarians).

Splits and quarrels The ALP's long history has been marred by splits and quarrels which have weakened it and have kept it in Opposition in the federal Parliament for most of the time since federation. On two occasions its leaders have left the party to join with their former opponents and create new anti-Labor parties, leaving the weakened ALP to struggle for many years to regain its strength. On a third occasion the dissenters formed a rival Labor Party on their own, managing to undermine the parent party for more than a decade. The splits were 1892 and 1895 in NSW

Nat. Sec. Aus. Labor Party

John Curtin House, Canberra, national headquarters of the Australian Labor Party

over fiscal policy; 1905-1908 in QLD over enforced discipline; 1916-17, an Australia-wide split over the issue of conscription; a three-way split over policy differences in the 1930s, between the federal Labor and the NSW State Labor parliamentarians, and within the federal Labor itself over the correct way to cope with Depression; and finally, in 1955, a split concerned with the party's attitude towards Communism and the activities within the party of members of the Catholic Social Movement.

Personalities who became involved in these splits and quarrels are discussed elsewhere (*see* Dr Herbert Vere EVATT, William Arthur HOLMAN, William Morris HUGHES, John Thomas LANG, Joseph Aloysius LYONS, James Henry SCULLIN and Edward Granville THEODORE).

Policy and achievements The three distinguishing characteristics of the ALP policy throughout its history have been its emphasis on increased economic and social equality, on further government intervention and participation in economic life, and on a more independent foreign policy. The policies have never been confined to matters of concern only to trade unions, although they have included legislation for compensation for industrial accidents, for unemployment insurance and for industrial arbitration, all of which were trade union objectives. Even in its early years the party attempted to appeal to other sections of the community by proposing legislation for closer settlement, for the right to mine on private property, for electoral reforms, old-age pensions and the extension of State education. Nor is the tag 'socialist' entirely justified when an analysis is made of the ALP's policy and performance. It is true that a significant section of the ALP has always favoured the public ownership of at least the major industries, but the party as a whole has never strongly supported comprehensive socialism; moreover, the party has been forced to recognise that the Commonwealth Constitution prevents extensive nationalisation. However, the ALP does try to exert some control over the policy and practices of private enterprise through control of monopolies, through taxation, and by government spending. Its taxation policies do tend to take more from the rich and redistribute it to the poor. When Labor formed the government during the period 1941-49 in the federal Parliament, social service legislation was passed covering widows' pensions, sickness and unemployment benefits, funeral benefits and hospital and pharmaceutical benefits, and legal provision was made for a national health service. An unsuccessful attempt was made to nationalise the banks, and this later led to greater controls being introduced over the banks by anti-Labor governments. During the long record of the NSW Labor Party, in power 1941-65, NSW led all the other States in the introduction of industrial legislation and in arbitration awards favouring wage and salary earners, such as the 40-hour week, long-service leave and three weeks' annual leave.

Between 1969 and 1971 the party platform was rewritten to lay stress on current problems relating to urban affairs, pollution, civil liberties, State aid, health, social welfare and industrial relations. In defence it advocates minimum commitment of armed forces outside Australia, emphasising instead the defensive role of aid, diplomacy and trade. In foreign affairs the party has tended to lay more emphasis than its opponents on action through the United Nations Organisation, and less on defensive alliances.

From 1978, under the leadership of William HAYDEN, the party paid greater attention to questions of economic management. In January 1982 he outlined Labor's strategy based on three pillars: economic and social reform with priority given to housing interest rates, health insurance, school funding, taxation and ownership of Australian resources; consitutional and legal reform by a referendum proposing limits to the power of the Senate and a proposal that the federal government have exclusive authority over all industrial relations; and parliamentary reform which would give the public freedom of information generally and access to information on the financial interests of MPs. On 3 February 1983 Hayden resigned as parliamentary leader of the party and on the same day the Prime Minister asked the Governor-General to dissolve both Houses of Parliament. Bob Hawke was unanimously elected leader on 8 February 1983 and won the election held on 5 March with the slogan 'Bring Australia together' and the promise to introduce a price-incomes policy. On 11 April 1983 Hawke called an Economic Summit—a conference of 100 representatives from business, the unions and government to discuss the economic policies of the government in order to arrive at a consensus on the direction economic policy would take.

See also political history; Appendix 2, Government of Australia
Further reading: Rawson, D.W. *Labor in Vain?* Longmans, Croydon VIC, 1966; Solomon, D. *Australia's Government and Parliament.* Nelson, West Melbourne, 1976; Loveday, P., Martin, A.W. & Parker, R.S. *The Emergence of the Australian Party System.* Hale & Iremonger, Sydney, 1977; North, J. & Weller, P. *Labor—Directions for the Eighties.* Ian Novak Publishing Co., Sydney, 1980.

Australian Press Council

This is a voluntary organisation founded in July 1976 by the Australian Journalists' Association and three newspaper proprietors' and managers' associations, namely the Australian Newspaper Council, the Australian Provincial Press Association and the Regional Dailies of Australia Ltd. It consists of persons nominated by those bodies, a chairman who must be a person otherwise unconnected with the Press, and three other members of the public, also otherwise unconnected with the Press and appointed on the nomination of the chairman.

The objects of the Council are defined in its Articles of Constitution as follows: to maintain the character of the Australian Press in accordance with the highest journalistic standards and to preserve its established freedom; to consider, investigate and deal with complaints about the conduct of the Press and the conduct of persons and organisations towards the press; to keep under review developments likely to restrict the supply by and to the Press of information of public interest and importance; to report publicly on developments in Press ownership and control and to publish statistical information about them; to make representations concerning the freedom of the Press on appropriate occasions to governments, public inquiries and other organisations in Australia and abroad; to publish reports recording the Council's work; to review from time to time developments in the Press and factors affecting them; and to exchange information with other Press Councils.

As with its British counterpart and a number of similar bodies in overseas countries, the Australian Press Council has powers of restriction or punishment. In accordance with the recommendation of a British Royal Commission in 1949, it adheres to the principle that its only sanction should be publicity.

Australian Red Cross Society

The principles of the organisation now known as the Red Cross were conceived by a Swiss, Jean Henri Dunant, on the battlefield of Solferino in Italy in 1859. From 1863 the movement spread rapidly to many countries, but the first move to establish it in Australia was not made until October 1913, when a meeting of interested people was held in Sydney. Nothing more was done until the outbreak of war in 1914, when Lady Helen Munro Ferguson cabled the British Red Cross Society, asking permission to form an Australian branch of the Society. Consent was given, recognition by the federal government obtained and the branch established within about a week of the declaration of war. In 1927 the Australian Red Cross Society became independent and was recognised as such by the International Committee of the Red Cross. It was incorporated by Royal Charter in 1941.

The work of the Society in caring for the wounded and providing comforts for troops in wartime is well known, as is its Blood Transfusion Service. However, the public image tends to be of a 'blood bank and war relief' service, with perhaps some notion of work for refugees and for the victims of natural disasters. Such a picture does not do justice to the range of welfare work undertaken by the Red Cross today. Besides providing blood for about 150 000 people each year in NSW alone, it provides food, clothing and shelter to those in need and lends crutches, wheelchairs and other medical equipment to patients being nursed at home. Social workers of the Red Cross Welfare Service interview people who need such services as family counselling, disaster relief, migrant services or family daycare. Skills are taught to the disabled, visits made to the homebound, training given in first aid and home nursing, and many aged and infirm people are cared for in Red Cross hospitals and homes. Considerable overseas aid is also given. The Society receives most of its revenue from donations, bequests, appeals and other fund-raising activities undertaken by the members of its many branches, and by school children, through Red Cross Youth.

Australian Rules

This is the popular name accorded to Australian National Football. Invented in the 19th century, the game has grown in popularity to become Australia's most popular spectator sport. No other sport can boast such huge crowds as those attracted to the last game of the annual Melbourne club competition, the Grand Final, which regularly draws crowds in excess of 100 000, the record being 121 696 at the match between Carlton and Collingwood in 1970. It is by far the most popular code of football in all States except QLD and NSW. More interest is generated by inter-club competitions in each capital city than by inter-State competition, which has generally been dominated by VIC.

Internationally, there have been club competitions in South Africa, New Zealand and Scotland (where in the early 1900s there were 10 clubs in the Clyde ship-building area and 17 clubs in Glasgow). World War I took its toll on international interest, however, and the game gradually lost its following overseas.

The objective of the game, which fields 18 men in each side, is to kick the ball between two of the four upright posts at either end of the field. A kick between the centre pair is worth six points (a goal); through either of the outside pairs, one point (a behind). The oval ball can be kicked or punched in any direction but never thrown. If a player runs while carrying the ball he must bounce it every 10m; if he catches a kicked ball on the full—that is, before it bounces—he has the option of a free kick. Called a mark, this leads to spectacular leaping, especially near the goals, since a free kick near the goals gives a side its best scoring opportunity. The game is divided into four 25-minute quarters, the teams changing ends for each quarter. There is no standard prescription governing the size of the oval field, but in general it is between 135m and 185m in length, and between 110m and 155m wide.

Devised in 1858 by cricketers Thomas Wentworth Wills and Henry Harrison, Australian Rules football was originally intended as a form of football which would provide cricketers with healthy exercise during the off-season. Dismissing Rugby and soccer as being inadequate for their purpose, Wills and Harrison thought up a new form of football which incorporated what they considered were the more admirable aspects of all known codes, but with particular emphasis on running and ball-handling. To give a demonstration of the new game, two teams were recruited, from Scotch College and Melbourne Grammar School, the first side scoring two goals to be the winner. The teams met on 7 August 1858, playing over a huge area; the fact that the two sets of goal posts were more than a kilometre apart kept goals to a minimum. Nightfall stopped play after Scotch had scored only one goal, so the game was resumed on 21 August and yet again on 4 September; but as neither team scored the necessary two goals the game was declared a draw.

Victoria The game quickly gained popular support in VIC, and by the turn of the century was firmly established as that State's most popular sport. Then, as now, there were two controlling bodies: the Victorian Football Association (VFA, formed in 1877), and the Victorian Football League (VFL, a break-away from the VFA, established in 1896).
South Australia In SA the first recorded game was played in 1860, between two teams of the newly formed Adelaide Football Club. As in VIC the new game quickly established itself as a major sporting attraction. Today, the South Australian National Football League controls a flourishing competition between 10 teams.
Western Australia In WA the first match was played in 1883 between fellow members of a team named Swans, but the real establishment of the game came two years later when four teams formed the West Australian Football Association. As in VIC and SA, the game was a great success, and since the turn of the century has been unrivalled as the State's

major sporting attraction.

Tasmania The first Australian Rules football games, under the official rules of the Tasmanian Football Association (TFA), were played in Hobart in 1879. By the early 1900s, as in the other S States, the game had eclipsed all other football codes; its dominance has not been seriously threatened since that time. Today, play is regulated by three controlling bodies: in the S, around Hobart, by the Tasmanian Football League (which took over from the TFA in 1906), and in the N by the Northern Tasmanian Football Association (founded in 1886) and the North-Western Football Union (founded in 1910).

Queensland and New South Wales Australian Rules football does not receive the same popular support in these States as in the S States. Though played since 1866 in QLD and since 1880 in NSW, the game has never gained supremacy in the public favour. In NSW, competition died out in 1898 because of the low standard of play and the lack of public interest. Although in 1902 a group of enthusiasts convened a meeting to revive the game, introducing in the following year a six-club competition under the control of the NSW Australian National Football League, the game has never replaced the two established Rugby codes and now also encounters competition from soccer, which is gaining in popularity. However in 1982 a VFL club, South Melbourne, made Sydney its headquarters, and changed its name to the Sydney Swans. In QLD the game has been injected with new vigour since the 1950s: in the Brisbane area, the number of teams playing increased from 214 in 1958 to 361 in 1963, and the game has been introduced into many Brisbane high schools. But even such notable gains have not carried Australian Rules beyond third place in the popular rating of football codes in QLD.

Medals A feature of Australian Rules is the award of a medal to the most outstanding player of the year. As only one medal is awarded annually in each State, the medals have come to represent a footballer's crowning achievement. The first such medal was awarded in SA in 1898, by W.A. Magarey. In 1921 WA introduced its Sandover Medal, and in 1924 VIC's Brownlow Medal—now the most famous medal—was awarded for the first time. These three are the most highly esteemed medals, but it is still a considerable achievement for a footballer to win the William Leitch Medal (TAS), the J.A. Grogan Medal (QLD) or the Phelan Medal (NSW). *See* Appendix 12.
See also Barassi, R., Cazaly, R.
Further reading: Pollard, J. (ed) *High Mark.*

K.G. Murray, Sydney, 1967; Main, J. *Australian Rules Football.* Lansdowne Press, Melbourne, 1974.

Australian Rules football Grand Final

Australian Security Intelligence Organization Established by the CHIFLEY government in March 1949, with Mr Justice Reed as its first Director-General, the first legislation to refer specifically to ASIO was the Australian Security Intelligence Organization Act of 1956, which placed ASIO on a statutory basis and gave security of employment to its members. Its basic function, which applied only to affairs within Australia, was 'to obtain, correlate and evaluate intelligence relevant to security and, at the discretion of the Director-General, to communicate any such intelligence to such persons, and in such manner, as the Director-General considers to be in the interests of security'. It was not designed as an enforcement agency, the Act stating in particular that 'it is not a function of the organization to carry out or enforce measures for security within a Department of State or authority of the Commonwealth.'

A particularly controversial incident relating to ASIO occurred in March 1973, when Senator Lionel Murphy, Attorney-General in the newly formed WHITLAM government, claimed that he had not been given complete information with regard to the operations of extremist right-wing Croatian organisations in Australia, and took the step of going with Commonwealth Police to the ASIO headquarters in Melbourne and carrying out a search for documents relating to the issue. In the following year the government appointed Mr Justice Hope as Royal Commissioner to enquire into the operations of Australia's intelligence services. His report, issued in October 1977, led to the passing of the Australian Security Intelligence Act in 1979 which redefined ASIO's powers in various respects. In May 1983 Mr Justice Hope was appointed to conduct a further enquiry into the operation of the intelligence service.

FIELD AND PLAYER POSITIONS IN AUSTRALIAN RULES

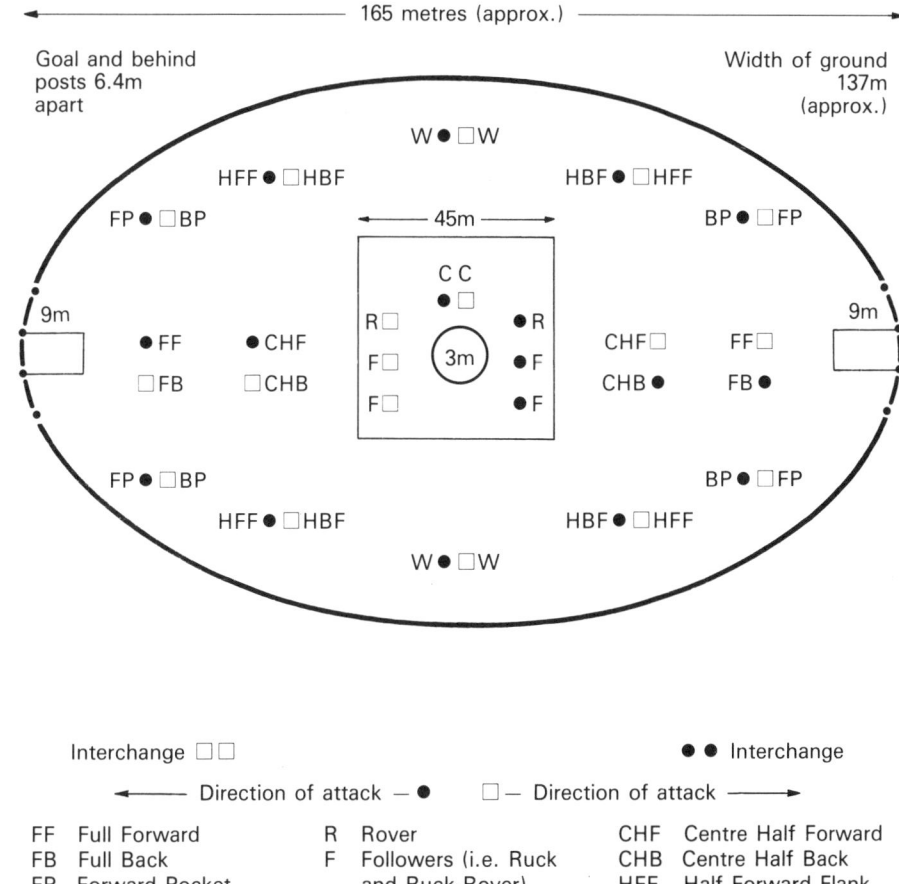

FF	Full Forward	R	Rover	CHF	Centre Half Forward
FB	Full Back	F	Followers (i.e. Ruck and Ruck-Rover)	CHB	Centre Half Back
FP	Forward Pocket			HFF	Half Forward Flank
BP	Back Pocket	W	Wing	HBF	Half Back Flank

Australind WA (population 1 681 in 1981) A small township on the shore of Leschenault Inlet, just N of the Collie River estuary, Australind lies 11km by road NE of BUNBURY and some 164km S of Perth. It is a holiday resort, providing summer visitors with fishing, swimming and aquatic sports. The town takes its name from an unsuccessful settlement attempt in 1841, when the Western Australia Land Co. subdivided a large land grant into lots of 100 acres (40.5ha) and sold them in London to prospective settlers. The National Trust (WA) has listed two homes in Australind—Upton House (1847) and Henton Cottage (1840s)—and St Nicholas' Anglican Church (1860) for preservation as part of the national cultural heritage.

australwinks *see* gastropods

aviation *see* transport

Avoca Beach NSW This is a holiday resort on the central coast, some 16km SE of GOSFORD, where there are good surfing beaches, and opportunities for swimming, boating and fishing in nearby lagoons. Though there are still some 'weekend' residences, and the town experiences an influx of tourists in summer, the area is increasingly becoming a retirement centre for people from Sydney and a dormitory settlement for those working in the Gosford district. The surrounding areas produce poultry, vegetables and fruit.

avocet *see* waders

Avon River VIC Located in GIPPSLAND, it rises near Mt Wellington about 170km ENE of Melbourne, flows S and SE for over 100km, and drains into LAKE WELLINGTON on its N shore. Water is diverted from the Avon to augment supplies to the MACALISTER irrigation scheme for pasture and fodder crop cultivation in the MAFFRA-SALE areas. It was named in 1840 after the Scottish Avon River.

Avon Valley WA The upper section of the SWAN RIVER is called the Avon. It rises to the W of the DARLING RANGE about 180km SE of Perth, flows in a general NW Direction beyond NORTHAM, then changes direction in a giant loop to flow SW and W to reach the Indian Ocean at FREMANTLE. In its middle section, the Avon-Swan cuts across the Darling Range for some 30km in a gorge with numerous rapids. The Avon Valley is one of the pioneer rural areas of WA and is a productive agricultural and pastoral region, with wheat growing and sheep grazing as the main farming pursuits.
Further reading: Wilson, H.H. *Avon Valley Sketchbook*. Rigby, Adelaide, 1977.

Ayers Rock NT This massive rock, with the Aboriginal name Uluru, is probably the best known and most widely publicised landscape feature of the CENTRE. It doubtless deserves to be, since it is the world's largest monolith ('single stone'), technically called an inselberg, meaning that the hard rock (conglomerate) of which it is composed, stands stark above the surrounding plain of softer rock which has been eroded away over long periods of geological time. Ayers Rock is 8.8km in circumference, 3.6km long and 2.5km wide, rising 348m above the surrounding ground level and 867m above sea level. It is located 426km by the road SW of ALICE SPRINGS within the Uluru National Park which covers 132 538ha and includes MOUNT OLGA 32km to the W. The region is arid, with temperatures that rise to 44°C and fall below zero; the average yearly rainfall is only 262mm, but this is highly variable from year to year and long drought spells are not uncommon. 'The Rock' and 'The Olgas' are important in the mythological beliefs and the ritual life of the Aborigines of the Yankuntjatjara and Pitjantjatjara tribes, and caves in the Rock contain Aboriginal paintings. There is motel accommodation, and regular tourist trips are available either by road or by plane. Visitors can climb to the top of the Rock though some may find it a steep trip. The Rock was named in 1873 after the then Premier of SA.

Ayr QLD (population 8 787 in 1981) The twin towns of Ayr and Home Hill are located respectively on the N and S sides of the BURDEKIN RIVER estuary, in the NE coastal belt of the State, about 1 400km by road NNW of Brisbane and 88km SE of TOWNSVILLE. The two towns are some 11km apart, linked by a long bridge (over 1000m) across the Burdekin, and both are business and service centres to a rural hinterland noted for its diversity of products. Sugar cane is the main crop of the adjacent rural lands, but rice, maize, potatoes, tobacco and different types of beans are also grown and cattle grazing is important in the district's economy. There are four sugar crushing mills in the area and the raw sugar is sent to the bulk terminal at Townsville for export. A unique feature of the Burdekin delta is the availability of large supplies of underground water which are used for crop and pasture irrigation.

Azalea *see* Epacridaceae

B

babblers, logrunners, quail-thrushes and whipbirds These BIRDS belong to the family Timaliidae, mainly an Old World family of varied PASSERINE BIRDS.

Babblers are noisy, dark brownish-grey birds, with white 'eyebrows' and broad black, white-tipped tails. Their habit of moving around in small compact groups on the ground or in bushes, feeding on insects and seeds, is similar to that of the apostlebird (*see* MUDNEST BUILDERS), with the result that the grey-crowned babbler is often mistakenly called the apostlebird. The four species of babblers found in mainland Australia (none occur in TAS) build large dome-shaped nests of twigs and rootlets, lined with grass and fur; the nests have a spout-like top entrance and are usually placed on the outer or topmost branches of trees. The grey-crowned babbler, *Pomatostomus temporalis* (23cm to 26cm long), found in woodlands throughout VIC, NSW and QLD and in most of the NT and northern WA, has a grey streak on its whitish crown and a long, curved bill. The chestnut-crowned babbler, *P. ruficeps*★ (22cm), is a bird of creek-side timber and saltbush areas of western NSW, north-western VIC, eastern SA and south-western QLD. The white-browed babbler, *P. superciliosus*★ (20cm), found throughout the S half of the continent in dry country, has a white throat and a dull white breast, whereas the Hall babbler, *P. halli*★ (18cm), of the woodland areas of central QLD has a white throat and a black breast.

Chestnut-crowned babbler

The two species of logrunners found in Australia live on rainforest floors where they scratch for grubs and insects amongst fallen leaves and debris; they use their spine-like tail feathers as a prop when shifting leaf mould with their large feet. Their platform-shaped nests, composed of sticks and partly hooded with interwoven twigs sometimes covered with moss, are usually placed on the ground. The southern logrunner, *Orthonyx temminckii* (18cm to 20cm), dark mottled brown above and white below, occurs in north-eastern NSW and south-eastern QLD. The northern logrunner, *O. spaldingi*★ (25cm to 27cm), has a plain blackish back and is found in north-eastern QLD.

Quail-thrushes are shy, solitary ground birds which, when disturbed, rise quickly into the air making a whirring sound with their short wings, fly a short distance and then seek cover in shrubs or trees. They are well camouflaged birds, generally speckled brown or greyish-brown above and lighter below; the males have black and white markings on the face and breast. Their eggs are laid under bushes in shallow depressions in the

★Species, genus or family is endemic to Australia (see Preface)

ground, lined with bark, twigs and grass. The spotted quail-thrush, *Cinclosoma punctatum** (27cm to 30cm), occurs in dry forests and woodlands in south-eastern QLD, eastern NSW and most of VIC and TAS; the chestnut quail-thrush, *C. castanotum** (20cm to 23cm), is found in the dry woodlands and heaths of most of southern Australia; and the cinnamon quail-thrush, *C. cinnamomeum** (20cm), frequents the semi-desert scrublands of central Australia, extending to the coast of WA.

The whipbirds are more often heard than seen for they are birds of dense thicket and have a loud call; the whistle of the eastern species often ends with a whip-like crack. They are ground birds which feed on insects. The eastern whipbird, *Psophodes olivaceus** (25cm to 28cm), is olive-green above, lighter below, with a black head, throat and crest and, in the adult, a white throat patch; the long tail is tipped with white. Found in north-eastern QLD and on the E coast, this species places its loosely made nests of twigs and rootlets near the ground in thick undergrowth. The colouring of the western whip-bird, *P. nigrogularis** (23cm), is similar, but there is less black on the head and throat. The harsh, grating call of this species may be heard in the low dense thickets of south-western WA and south-central SA. The eggs are laid in cup-shaped nests of twigs, bark and grass, usually placed near the ground in thick vegetation. The similarly shaped but light brown wedgebill, *P. cristatus** (20cm), a bird with an incessant harsh, squeaky call, lives on or near the ground in semi-arid country, mainly in central Australia. It places its cup-shaped nest of twigs in thick scrubby bushes.

Babesia *see* parasites, livestock; protozoons; ticks

baby's breath *see* Caryophyllaceae

Bacchus Marsh VIC (population 6 222 in 1981) A town on the Western Highway 53km by road from Melbourne, and 61km by road E of BALLARAT, on the Werribee River, it is a service and commercial centre for an orcharding, dairying and vegetable growing area, supplying fresh foods to the Melbourne metropolitan market. It is also a railway town, 51km from Melbourne on the route to Ballarat. Named after Captain W.H. Bacchus who settled in the valley in 1838, the town became important in the 1850s as a river-crossing point on the route to the goldfields. Several buildings have been listed for preservation by the National Trust (VIC); among these are the courthouse, the old blacksmith's shop, the Manor (Bacchus' home), 'Millbank' homestead and the Mechanics Institute.

back-swimmers *see* bugs

badminton This game has never achieved widespread popularity as a sport in Australia, although most Australians at some time in their lives have played a similar game, shuttle-cock, at the picnic ground, on the beach or in the backyards of their homes. Introduced into Australia in the early 1900s with the establishment of a small club in Perth WA, badminton did not gain any following at all in other Australian States until the 1930s. In 1935 the Australian Badminton Association was formed and in the following year became affiliated with the International Badminton Federation.

Annual interstate carnivals are held in each State in rotation, the winner being awarded the Ede-Clendinnen Shield. Individual national championships are played during the second week of the carnival.

Internationally, Australia competes in the World Championships in the Australasian zone. Men compete for the Thomas Cup while women compete for the Uber Cup.

Bairnsdale VIC (population 9 457 in 1981) Located at the junction of the Princes and Omeo Highways, on the MITCHELL RIVER in E GIPPSLAND, 283km by road E of Melbourne and 5km upstream from LAKE KING, Bairnsdale is the service and commercial hub of the Lakes area. Situated on the alluvial flats of the coastal plain at an elevation of only 14m above sea level, it experiences a mild climate with warm to hot summers and cool winters. The average annual rainfall is 696mm, spread throughout the year, December being the wettest month (68mm average) and August the driest (49mm). The rural hinterland is important for sheep grazing, dairying, timber production and the farming of maize, oil seeds and fodder crops. The Gippsland Lakes area is a major holiday resort during summer. The town's name comes from the property of an early Scottish settler, Archibald McLeod, who named his station in 1844 after Bairnsdale village on the Isle of Skye.

Baker, Reginald Leslie 'Snowy' (1884-1953) All-round sportsman. Born in the Sydney suburb of Darlinghurst, Baker first began winning sporting events at school and by the age of 15 was playing Rugby Union for NSW; at 16 he was playing for Australia against England. In 1905 he became amateur middleweight boxing champion of Australasia. From 1903 to 1906 his water-polo team took the State title four times. But these were only three of the sports at which Baker was to excel. In all, he won distinction in 29 different sports which ranged from fencing, ground acrobatics, steeplechasing and polo to yachting and rowing. Youthfully vigorous and energetic all his life, he not only participated in sport but also promoted it. He bought Sydney Stadium in 1909 and promoted and refereed fights there; he built Melbourne Stadium and acquired another stadium in Brisbane. Attracted to films, in 1920 he left for the USA where he was soon to star in 'he-man' films. Later he was to become polo coach to Will Rogers and equestrian coach to such film stars as Rudolf Valentino, Shirley Temple and Elizabeth Taylor. A personable and highly talented sportsman, Baker spent the rest of his life in the USA, where he gained more popularity than he had ever been accorded in his home country.

Balaklava SA (population 1 306 in 1981) A country town located on the N fringe of the Adelaide Plains, it is 108km by rail N of Adelaide and 70km by road NNW of GAWLER. It is a commercial and service centre for a productive wheat growing and livestock grazing region.

baleen *see* dolphins, etc.

Ballarat VIC (population 62 640 in 1981) The third-largest urban centre in VIC (after Melbourne and GEELONG) and located 114km by road WNW of Melbourne in rolling hill country S of the GREAT DIVIDING RANGE, Ballarat lies near the headwaters of the Yarrowee River at an elevation of 460m above sea level. As well as being a major market and commercial centre for a productive agricultural and pastoral region, Ballarat is an industrial city with a variety of manufacturing enterprises. It is also a transport focus of road and rail routes: the Midland, Western, Glenelg and North-Western Highways meet at the city, and it has rail links S to Geelong and N to MARYBOROUGH and is on the main interstate railway (Melbourne-Adelaide). The district was settled by graziers in the late 1830s, but it was the discovery of gold in 1851 that made it a boom town. The township was surveyed in 1852, the original plans laying the foundation for the fine central area, the boulevards, parks and gardens which today give the city its distinctive atmosphere. The name was at first spelt 'Ballaarat', coming from the Aboriginal *balla* (elbow) and meaning 'resting one's elbow'. By 1854 it had a population of 27 000, and by the 1870s one of 48 000. The town became a municipality in 1855, a borough in 1863 and was proclaimed a city in 1870.

Ballarat is famous in Australian history because it was there, in 1854, that the EUREKA STOCKADE took place. The event is commemorated at Montrose Cottage (a restored home typical of those built by miners of the 1860s) with a display of colonial military uniforms and a collection of period arms, and also at the Eureka Stockade Memorial where a diorama provides visitors with a graphic portrayal of the incident. The Sovereign Hill Historical Park, opened in 1970, is a major tourist attraction which features about 40 buildings selected to depict the life and style of the gold-rush period. It contains a replica of Ballarat's main street, typical alluvial diggings, a deep-lead gold mine and a historical museum. Among other tourist attractions of the city is Lake Wendouree bordering the botanical gardens, open for boating, fishing, swimming and yachting; it was the venue for rowing events in the Melbourne Olympic Games in 1956. The city's annual Begonia Festival takes place in the botanical gardens, where the Adam Lindsay GORDON memorial cottage may also be seen. On the N face of Mt

Warrenheip, 8km E of the city, is another popular tourist attraction, Kryal Castle, resembling a medieval structure complete with moat and drawbridge, dungeon, torture chamber, tavern and banquet hall.

Further reading: Ballarat Historical Park Association *Sovereign Hill and Historical Ballarat*. Rigby, Adelaide, 1976.

ballet Prior to the 1960s ballet was not readily accepted by the Australian public. Its early history was beset by lack of public support and the absence of financial subsidy from the government; interest in ballet was kept alive only by the dedication and enthusiasm of the dancers and a small group of supporters. Budding choreographers and soloists were easily attracted overseas to become members of prestigious international ballet companies based in Europe. However, with the formation in the early 1960s of The Australian Ballet under the direction of Dame Peggy VAN PRAAGH and Sir Robert HELPMANN, ballet in Australia became injected with a new vigour. Ballets became identifiably Australian with Australian themes and with choreography, music and set-design all by Australians, some of whom, like Sir Robert Helpmann, had previously achieved international acclaim. The 1970s saw the evolution of a vibrant mode of dancing combining elements of both classical and modern ballet in a style which was uniquely representative of Australia and which gained The Australian Ballet a high reputation in the aesthetically selective world of ballet.

History Australia was given its first taste of well-performed classical ballet in 1913, when the Danish ballerina, Adeline Genée, toured with a company from the Imperial Russian Ballet. But it was not until the late 1920s, after two visits by Anna Pavlova, that ballet began to become firmly established in Australia. Pavlova made her first visit in 1926, with a company of 42, and performed 17 ballets, including *The Dying Swan*. This tour was so successful that she returned for an equally successful tour in 1929. These visits provided the impetus for Australian classical ballet, and following the 1929 tour, Mischa Burlakov, in association with Louise Lightfoot, formed the first Australian Ballet.

The 1930s were formative years for ballet in Australia, and a number of leading companies visited Australia at this time. Of particular importance was Colonel de Basil's Ballets Russes de Monte Carlo. De Basil controlled two companies, both of which toured Australia during the 1930s, and he himself visited with a company in 1938. Australian students of ballet often took lessons from leading members of these companies, gaining experience by working backstage or appearing as extras, and were able to see the performance of top dancers of the day.

When the company of the 1938 tour left, one of the soloists, Edouard Borovansky, stayed to become one of the formative influences of Australian ballet. Borovansky opened a ballet school in 1940 in Melbourne and in 1942 established the Borovansky Ballet which presented its first professional season in 1943. Over the following two decades his company was one of the pioneer forces in ballet in Australia, although frequently in financial difficulties and often on the verge of bankruptcy. After Borovansky's death in 1959, the company formed the nucleus of The Australian Ballet.

Scene from 'The Merry Widow'

The Australian Ballet In 1961 the Australian Ballet Foundation was formed; it conducted nationwide auditions for dancers for a new national company, resulting in the formation of The Australian Ballet with Peggy van Praagh (later Dame) as Artistic Director. The new company attracted artistes such as Garth Welch, Marilyn Jones and Kathleen Gorham back to home shores from overseas successes for its first season, which began in Sydney on 2 November 1962. The company performed *Swan Lake* (in full), *Coppélia* and *Les Sylphides*, and even in this first season an Australian identity was being sought with the inclusion in the programme of Rex Reid's *Melbourne Cup*. Two years later, Robert Helpmann, who had been the principal male dancer with the Sadler's Wells Ballet Company from 1935 to 1950, created the first all-Australian ballet. Using the Australian lyrebird as a theme and based on its colourful and visually exciting mating dance, the ballet was titled *The Display*. The music was composed by Malcolm WILLIAMSON, the décor created by Sidney NOLAN, and the choreography by Helpmann. These were the first clear indications that Australia had something to offer which was original in concept, vigorous in performance and uniquely Australian.

In 1965, as part of its first overseas tour, the company visited 12 countries and gave performances at the Baalbeck Festival, at the Paris International Festival, and at the Commonwealth Arts Festival. Ballets performed included Helpmann's *Yugen* (a lyrical ballet he had created for the company based on a Japanese folk tale) and *Elektra* (a ballet based on the ancient Greek legend which he had originally created for the Royal Ballet) and Reid's *Melbourne Cup*. Helpmann became joint director in the same year and choreographed *Sun Music* (music by Peter SCULTHORPE) in 1968, and *Perisynthion* (music by Williamson) in 1974, before retiring in 1976 after producing the company's biggest hit, *The Merry Widow*.

During the 1970s, subsidisation by the federal government enabled the company to provide continuous employment for its dancers. This resulted not only in more highly trained and disciplined dancers but also in the retention by the company of its principal soloists who in previous years had been forced to pursue their ballet careers overseas. One of the consequences of this for Australian ballet was demonstrated in 1973 when Marilyn Rowe and Kelvin Coe won medals in the Moscow International Ballet Competitions, where they were the first Australians to compete.

In the 1980s, the company is firmly established as a significant influence in world ballet,

The Australian Ballet

and the enthusiastic energy of the previous three decades is reflected in the development of a style whose emergent elements, while still based in classical traditions, are identifiably Australian.

Ballina NSW (population 9 735 in 1981) A small seaside town at the mouth of the RICHMOND RIVER on the NORTH COAST, Ballina is a holiday and tourist centre offering stretches of surfing beach, facilities for aquatic sports, and ocean and river fishing. It is also the location of shipbuilding yards and of a fish canning factory, and the surrounding district, comprising the delta and dune lands of the Richmond, is a productive dairying and mixed farming area.

Balmain, William (1762-1803) Pioneer surgeon. Probably the most competent doctor in the early years of the colony of NSW, he arrived with the FIRST FLEET as an assistant surgeon. In September 1790 he used his skill to extract from Governor PHILLIP the spear thrown by an Aboriginal in an incident at Manly Cove. After serving on NORFOLK ISLAND for four years, in 1795 he became principal surgeon at Sydney. Among the three land grants made to him was one of 550 acres in an area now incorporated in Sydney as the suburb of Balmain.

Balonne River QLD The CONDAMINE RIVER, beyond the township of Surat, becomes the Balonne. Located in the SE of the State, where the rainfall pattern has a marked summer concentration with a drier period in the winter and spring, the stream flows seasonally and can flood in wet years. Upstream from ST GEORGE, the Maranoa River joins the Balonne as a right-bank tributary; downstream from St George, the Balonne divides to form ANABRANCHES (the Culgoa River being the major one) and thence flows S across the NSW/QLD border to join the DARLING RIVER system. The main rural activity in the valley is sheep grazing, beef cattle being fattened on the alluvial lands adjacent to streams. About 20km upstream from St George the Beadmore Dam at the Maranoa-Balonne confluence, completed in 1972, has a capacity of 101 000ML, and serves to regulate river flow and to provide water for crop and pasture irrigation.

Balranald NSW (population 1 442 in 1981) A small town on the lower MURRUMBIDGEE RIVER near its junction with the MURRAY RIVER, Balranald is located on the Sturt Highway (871km by road from Sydney) and on the VIC rail system (438km from Melbourne via SEYMOUR and ECHUCA). At an elevation of 61m above sea level, it is set in the midst of semi-arid plain country devoted to sheep grazing, and receives an annual average rainfall of only 317mm, uniformly spread throughout the year, with droughts a common feature. In the later decades of the 19th century it was a river port for paddle-wheel steamers.

Balson, Ralph (1890-1964) Artist. Born in Botherhampton, Dorset, England, Balson came to Australia in 1913. As well as attending evening classes at Julian ASHTON's Sydney Art School, he received much stimulation at the art school of Grace CROWLEY and Rah FIZELLE—located at 215c George Street, Sydney, and established by them to teach a more modern approach in art—where he made many friends. He began to experiment with pure form and design, moving steadily to geometric abstracts. His systematic reading introduced him to the ideas of modern European artists; he was particularly impressed by ideas reflected in Mondrian's *Plastic Art and Pure Art*. In 1940 Balson held the first one-man exhibition of abstract art in Australia, at the Modern Art Centre, Margaret Street, Sydney. It was not until 1961 that Balson travelled overseas, a trip which only served to reinforce his progress towards completely abstract Expressionism.

Bancks, James Charles (1889-1952) Cartoonist. Born in Sydney, he practised drawing in his spare time for some years after leaving school, but later had lessons from Datillo Rubbo and Julian ASHTON. His first cartoon was published in 1911, and within a few years he had become a full-time artist. His fame rests on his creation of Ginger Meggs, hero of the comic strip series of the same name. This harum-scarum, adventurous boy, constantly in trouble but adept at working his way out of it, first appeared in 1921 as Ginger Smith, a minor character in the comic strip *Us Fellers*. In the following year he was given the name Meggs, and rapidly became Australia's best known boy character. For 30 years the comic strip *Ginger Meggs* appeared regularly in the *Sunday Sun*. It was also published at various times in other Australian newspapers and books, in the UK, USA, and (with French and Spanish dialogue) in Montreal and Buenos Aires. After Bancks' death it was continued in other papers, and today appears in the Sydney *Sun Herald* with the acknowledgment 'created by Bancks'.

Bancroft, Joseph (1836-94) Medical scientist and physician. Born in England, Bancroft established a practice in Brisbane in 1864 but devoted much of his time to research, being first to investigate the Aboriginal drug plant *pituri*. He experimented on wheat rusts and the hybridisation of crop plants, and was a leading authority on tick paralysis and leprosy, but he is best known for his work on filariasis (elephantiasis) which was then common in N Australia. He discovered the adult filarial Nematoda (ROUNDWORMS) in a Chinese patient in 1877. This work led to research on the transmission of disease by MOSQUITOES.

His son, Thomas Lane Bancroft (1860-1933), also born in England, carried out research on the QUEENSLAND LUNG FISH, on protozoan parasites of Australian animals, and on hookworms; he showed how hookworms enter the human body (though this was also done

independently in Egypt in 1896 by Artur Looss), and in 1905 demonstrated that the mosquito *Aedes aegypti* is a carrier of dengue fever. Thomas Bancroft's daughter Josephine carried out research on cattle TICKS and sheep BLOWFLIES.

bandicoots These animals belong to the families Peramelidae and Thylacomyidae. Australasian bandicoots are MARSUPIALS though the common name was originally given to a large Indian rodent. They have syndactyl hind feet like KANGAROOS but they belong to a separate order (Polyprotodonta) in which there are at least three pairs of incisor teeth in the lower jaw. All bandicoots have long noses but in some species the nose is comparatively short. For convenience they are therefore often placed in four groups, namely: the short-nosed bandicoots, the long-nosed bandicoots, the pig-footed bandicoot (probably extinct) and the rabbit-eared bandicoots. All are digging, terrestrial animals which live on such things as grubs and slugs, scraped from soil litter.

The rabbit-eared bandicoot

Advertiser Newspapers Ltd

The short-nosed bandicoot, *Isoodon obesulus* (head and body 36cm long; tail 13cm long), a solitary, nocturnal species, has harsh, rather spiny fur which is easily detached. The snout is relatively short and pointed, and the ears are short and rounded. Its colour is a grizzled greyish- or yellowish-brown above and yellowish-white below. It is a widespread species, being found wherever there is good ground cover in coastal areas from southern NSW to south-eastern SA, TAS, CAPE YORK, and south-western WA. The short-nosed bandicoots make flattened heaps of sticks and rubbish as nests into which they burrow.

The long-nosed bandicoots are represented in Australia by two genera but one of these, *Echymipera*, is known only from a single specimen found in dense rainforest in Cape York. Four species belong to the other genus, *Perameles*. The long-nosed bandicoots are not as robustly built as the short-nosed species, and their ears are longer. The fur is rather coarse. They are solitary animals, except when mating, and nocturnal, and their food consists mainly of invertebrates but berries are also eaten. The common long-nosed bandicoot, *P. nasuta* (head and body 41cm; tail 13cm), of coastal E Australia, lives in forests and woodlands of various kinds, including rainforest. It is grey or greyish-brown with white on the legs, but the body is unbarred. Gunn's bandicoot, or the striped bandicoot, *P. gunnii*, of TAS and southern VIC, is similar but has distinct bars on the hindquarters. It lives in woodland and open country with ground cover. The presence of long-nosed bandicoots can often be detected by the characteristic conical pits which they dig when searching for prey.

The rabbit-eared bandicoots (family Thylacomyidae) are the most attractive of the bandicoots for the soft hair is long and silky, and the tail is black and white. They are mainly desert animals which escape the heat by digging spiral burrows from 1m to 2m long. They seem to have suffered in competition with the rabbits introduced into many areas.
Further reading: see under marsupials.

bandy-bandy *see* snakes

Banfield, Edward James (1852-1923) Naturalist and author. Born in Liverpool, England, he was brought to Australia as a boy by his father, who became proprietor of a newspaper in ARARAT in VIC. He worked as a journalist in Ararat, Melbourne, Sydney and TOWNSVILLE in QLD, but in 1897 leased a portion of DUNK ISLAND, living there with his wife for the remainder of his life. He wrote a number of books and many articles, concerned mainly with the scenery and natural life of the island and its surroundings, the most notable of the books being *The Confessions of a Beachcomber* (1908).

bangalay *see* mahogany; Myrtaceae

Bangladesh, settlers from *see* Indian subcontinent, settlers from

Bank of New South Wales This, the first bank in Australia, was founded with the encouragement of Governor MACQUARIE in 1817, but operates today under a new name. When he assumed office at the beginning of 1810, Macquarie noticed the acute shortage of cash and credit in the colony. Wages were often paid in kind, while business transactions were commonly conducted by means of local promissory notes (called 'currency' by the colonists) or even by barter. In March 1810 the Governor wrote to the Colonial Secretary suggesting that he found a government bank on the lines of the Government Loan Bank of the Cape of Good Hope. The proposal was rejected, but in 1816 Macquarie's legal adviser, deputy Judge Advocate John Wylde, expressed the opinion that the granting of a charter of incorporation to a non-government bank would be in order. Consequently, in November that year 14 prominent citizens were invited to a meeting in Wylde's chambers, and passed resolutions in favour of the setting up of a 'public colonial bank', with initial capital of not less than £20 000 in shares of £100. In the following February a meeting

of subscribers adopted a set of rules and regulations, chose the name 'Bank of New South Wales', and appointed a board of directors. The bank opened for business in April, with authority to issue notes ranging in value from 2s.6d. to £5. The initial charter, issued in March, was later declared invalid by the British government, but was re-issued with amendments in 1823. In 1850 the bank was reconstituted and incorporated under an Act of the Legislative Council.

In 1981, following a merger with another major trading bank, the Commercial Bank of Australia, the directors proposed a change of name to Westpac Banking Corporation, in order to indicate that the bank operates extensively throughout the whole Western Pacific area, and is not confined to NSW, or even to Australia. The new title was approved at a shareholders' meeting in January 1982 and came into effect later that year.

Bankcard This credit card system was established in 1974 by the major Australian banks. By early 1983 there were 11 trading and savings banks participating and over two million of their customers were Bankcard holders. The number of outlets in all Australian States and New Zealand to accept Bankcard was at that time approximately 122 000.

banking At federation in 1901 the Commonwealth Parliament was given power, under Section 51 (xiii) of the Constitution, to legislate with respect to 'banking other than State banking, also State banking extending beyond the limits of the State concerned, the incorporation of banks, and the issue of paper money'. Until the 1950s banks dominated the finance market, but as they have come more and more under the control of the Commonwealth government, other institutions have evolved and have avoided the same degree of control. Also, in recent years the banks have tended to extend their functions. In the field of consumer credit a number of them have either acquired holdings in existing finance companies, or have established such companies as subsidiaries. They have also co-operated in establishing the credit card system known as BANKCARD.

Main features of banking The Australian banking system has followed the pattern set in England and Scotland, and is predominantly privately owned and competitive. Commercial banking is carried on by the government-owned Commonwealth Trading Bank, three major private trading banks and seven minor trading banks. The major banks have widespread networks of branches extending throughout Australia. This is in strong contrast with the position in the USA, where banking is carried on by thousands of local institutions, each operating in a limited territory.

Early in 1984, the major private trading banks were the Australian and New Zealand Banking Group, the National Commercial

Banking Corporation of Australia (incorporating the former National Bank of Australasia and the Commercial Banking Company of Sydney) and Westpac Banking Corporation (incorporating the former BANK OF NEW SOUTH WALES and the Commercial Bank of Australia). The minor trading banks include the Australian Bank, the Bank of Queensland Ltd, the Bank of New Zealand, the Banque Nationale de Paris, the State Bank of New South Wales, the State Bank of South Australia, and the Rural and Industries Bank of Western Australia (Rural Department).

Until 1956 only government-owned savings banks operated, including the Commonwealth Savings Bank, two trustee savings banks in TAS and State-owned banks in VIC, SA and WA. Between 1956 and 1962, however, all the major private trading banks established subsidiary savings-bank companies. The Bank of New Zealand Savings Bank Ltd was also granted authority to conduct savings-bank business in Australia in 1972.

History of banking In 1817 Governor MACQUARIE granted a charter to the first Australian bank, the Bank of New South Wales. By 1841 there were 18 banks operating, three of which had been formed in London, and the rest in Australia. The gold rushes of the 1850s encouraged the establishment of eight 'gold banks', and between 1863 and 1873 another 12 banks were founded. Not all these banks survived, but during the land boom of the 1880s a further 13 commenced business. They lent freely but not always wisely: during the depression of the 1890s many borrowers were unable to repay their loans and a number of banks crashed, only 10 surviving to the end of the century.

The Commonwealth government entered the banking field in 1911, when it established the Commonwealth Bank as a competitive trading bank. However, between that year and 1945 the Commonwealth Bank became increasingly responsible for central banking functions, and by the Commonwealth Bank Act of 1945 the Commonwealth Parliament legislated to constitute it formally as a central bank. The need for effective regulatory control of finance through banks was given further recognition by the Banking Act of 1959, which applies to all banks operating in Australia except State banks trading in their own States. It provides a uniform legal framework for regulating the banking system; safeguards depositors from loss; provides for the co-ordination of banking policies under the direction of the Reserve Bank; controls bank interest rates and the volume of credit in circulation; and mobilises and provides machinery for control of the foreign exchange and the gold resources of the Australian economy.

Other legislation in the same year (the Reserve Bank Act of 1959 and the Commonwealth Banks Act of 1959) effected a reallocation of the functions of the former Commonwealth Bank of Australia. The former provided for the constitution and management of the Reserve Bank of Australia (which took over the central banking function), for the administration of the Banking Act of 1959, and for the management of the issue of Australian notes. The latter made provision for the constitution and management of a group of Commonwealth Banks: the Commonwealth Banking Corporation, the Commonwealth Trading Bank of Australia, the Commonwealth Savings Bank of Australia and the Commonwealth Development Bank of Australia.

Reserve Bank of Australia While competition is basic to the Australian banking system, the Reserve Bank of Australia nevertheless has regulatory powers which it is required to use in ways that, in the opinion of its Board, will best contribute to the stability of the currency of Australia, the maintenance of full employment in Australia and the economic prosperity and welfare of the people of Australia. Its policy is determined by a Board consisting of the Governor, Deputy Governor, the Secretary to the Treasury and seven other members appointed by the Governor-General. In the event of disagreement between the government and the Board, the Governor-General, acting with the advice of the Executive Council, may determine the policy to be adopted by the Bank.

Development banks The Commonwealth Development Bank of Australia is authorised to provide assistance for the development of worthwhile enterprises in the fields of primary and secondary industry which would otherwise be unable to obtain necessary finance on reasonable and suitable terms and conditions.

The Australian Resources Development Bank was established in 1967, capital being provided by the major trading banks. Its basic objective is to assist Australian enterprises to participate more fully in the development of the nation's resources. It provides finance for major development projects, obtaining funds by accepting deposits and by borrowing on the Australian and overseas capital markets.

Merchant banks Foreign banks have not been allowed to become licensed under the Banking Act, apart from two which have been established in Australia for a long time. However, a number of large international banks have joined with Australian financial institutions to form merchant or investment banks. These cannot issue cheque books to customers or grant overdrafts to individuals, but operate in the money market, lend money to companies in very large minimum parcels, advise companies on takeovers, and manage share investments for superannuation funds. For the smaller investor they have introduced cash management trusts.

The Campbell Report In 1979 the Australian government set up the Campbell Committee of Enquiry to examine the overall efficiency of the financial system and to report on the operations of government regulations affecting it. The Committee's report, presented late in 1981, included a general recommendation for a lessening of regulations. This implied the removal of government controls over interest rates charge by banks, the amount lent by them and the direction of lending; increased freedom for foreign banks to operate in Australia; and increased opportunities for building societies, credit unions and similar institutions to compete with banks. Other aspects of the report dealt with such matters as taxation, superannuation, foreign exchange rates and the removal of restrictions on the transfer of money into and out of Australia.

Banks, Donald Oscar (1923-80)

Composer. Don Banks was born in South Melbourne. Having lived with music throughout his childhood (his father was a professional jazz musician), it is not surprising that he later joined various jazz groups, including that of Roger and Graeme Bell. After service during the war he began a diploma course at the University of Melbourne Conservatorium.

In 1950 he left for England and worked as secretary to Edward Clark, who had assisted progressive musicians since the 1920s as the ISCM's first secretary, head of music at the BBC, and chairman of the London Contemporary Music Centre. Banks' next major influence in composition came through his studies with the inspiring teachers Matyas Seiber and Milton Babbitt. During this time, his *Duo for Violin and 'Cello* and his *Divertimento for Flute and String Trio* were performed at an ISCM concert.

Composition studies in Italy followed. In October 1952 he was awarded an Italian government scholarship and studied composition and orchestration with Luigi Dallapiccola. He also represented Australia at the ISCM festival in Salzburg that year. In 1956 he returned to Italy to study with Lugi Nono. In the early 1950s, with Margaret Sutherland, he established the Australian Musical Association in London, which proved to be the principal platform for Australian composers and performers in Europe for many years. He received many commissions in Britain and Europe, taught composition privately, and was Music Director at the Goldsmith's College, University of London, from 1969 to 1971. He also composed music for feature films and television series.

He returned to live permanently in Australia in 1972, and spent some years in Canberra, first as a Creative Arts Fellow at the Australian National University, and later as head of composition and electronic music at the Canberra School of Music (1973-78). He was appointed head of the School of Composition at the New South Wales State Conservatorium of Music in 1978 and was still in that post when he died in 1980. His list of published compositions is both impressive and extensive, and includes chamber music, vocal, orchestral, jazz and electronic music.

Further reading: Murdoch, J. *Australia's Contemporary Composers.* Macmillan, Melbourne, 1972; Bracanin, P. 'Don Banks' in Callaway, F. & Tunley, D. (eds) *Australian Composition in the Twentieth Century.* Oxford University Press, Melbourne, 1978.

Banks, Sir Joseph (1743-1820)

Naturalist. Born in London, he was educated at Harrow, Eton and Oxford, developing a strong interest in botany, and in 1766 becoming a Fellow of the Royal Society. Meanwhile his father had died, leaving him the family estate in Lincolnshire and a considerable fortune. He accompanied COOK on the latter's first great voyage (1769-71), meeting his own expenses and those of Dr Daniel SOLANDER, the naturalist H.D. Sporing, two artists and four servants, as well as providing a great amount of equipment. According to Solander, Banks' expenses for the voyage totalled £10 000. After the voyage his reputation for knowledge of the earth and its resources grew steadily. He became President of the Royal Society in 1778 and in the following year, giving evidence before a parliamentary committee, he recommended BOTANY BAY as the best possible site for a convict settlement. After the foundation of Sydney in 1788 he kept up a close interest in the colony, and was frequently consulted by the Colonial Office regarding its affairs. It was only after 1810 that his influence on developments in NSW began to wane.

In the meantime his reputation for scientific knowledge and general wisdom became immense, gaining him the name of 'father of Australia'. He encouraged and often financed the expeditions of explorers and naturalists (including, in Australia, Alan CUNNINGHAM and George CALEY) to many parts of the world, and amassed at his home a remarkable natural history museum and library. He was consulted by George III regarding the development of Kew Gardens, and during the reign introduced several thousand new species of exotic plants to England. In addition to these activities, he was a member of a great number of clubs, societies and committees. Although he published little himself, he encouraged and helped the work of many other scientists. The Sydney suburb of Bankstown, Cape Banks (the N head of Botany Bay), the plant genus *Banksia* and a number of plant species are named after him.

Further reading: Mackaness, G. *Sir Joseph Banks: His Relations with Australia.* Angus & Robertson, Sydney, 1938; Cameron, H.C. *Sir Joseph Banks.* Batchworth Press, London, 1952; Beaglehole, J.C. *The Endeavour Journal of Joseph Banks, 1768-1771.* (2 vols) Angus & Robertson, Sydney, 1962.

Banksia *see* honeysuckle; Proteaceae

Bannon, John Charles (1943-)

Politician. At Adelaide University he was prominent in student politics, and in 1969, shortly after graduating in arts and law, he stood unsuccessfully for selection as a Labor candidate for the Senate. He then became an industrial officer for the Australian Workers Union, and later served as special adviser to Clyde Cameron, a Minister in the WHITLAM federal Cabinet. He entered the SA House of Assembly in 1977 by winning the seat of Ross Smith, became a member of Cabinet in the following year, and after the defeat of his party in the 1979 election replaced Desmond Corcoran as its leader. He became Premier after a narrow win by the Australian Labor Party in the election of November 1982. He is widely regarded as being in a new style of post-Whitlam Labor leaders, such as Neville WRAN and John CAIN, avoiding flamboyance and concentrating on management skills to win and retain office.

Baptist Churches

In the 1981 census, about 1.3 per cent of Australians were identified as Baptist in religion, making them the sixth-largest Christian denomination. However, in Australia as elsewhere, there is, strictly speaking, no 'Baptist Church' in the sense of a denomination whose central organisation has jurisdiction over the whole body of members. Rather there are autonomous Baptist Churches, which are linked together in Unions in order to co-operate in such matters as social welfare, missionary, publishing and educational work.

National Library of Australia

Sketch of the Baptist Chapel in Bathurst St, Sydney, 1847

Baptist Churches originated among English Independents (or Congregationalists) in the early 17th century. They belong to the evangelical tradition, stressing reliance on the gospels and belief in man's need for spiritual rebirth and redemption through faith. They recognise the individual's right to interpret the Bible for himself, and refrain from imposing a formal creed on their members; and they have always insisted on separation between Church and State. Their services, which follow no set form, are marked by emotional fervour and individual profession of faith. They practise baptism by complete immersion, and reject infant baptism, insisting that those being baptised should be old enough to make the ceremony an act of convinced belief.

History in Australia The Baptists were slower to become established in Australia than a number of other Christian denominations. The first service was held in Sydney in 1831 by the Rev. John McKaeg, who in either the same or the following year performed the first baptisms, in Woolloomooloo Bay. The first church was built in 1836 in Bathurst Street, from where, 101 years later, the congregation moved to the present Central Baptist Church in George Street. In TAS the first minister, the Rev. Henry Dowling, arrived in 1834, and Churches were formed in both Hobart and

LAUNCESTON in the following year. Churches were first formed in other colonies as follows: SA 1838, VIC (then the PORT PHILLIP District) 1842, QLD (then the MORETON BAY District) 1855, and WA 1894.

John Shaw

Central Baptist Church, Sydney

Unions between Churches in the various colonies were formed from the 1860s, but some congregations of 'strict' or 'particular' Baptists—strict adherents of the Calvinistic doctrine of predestination—have not joined these. Although the State Unions joined to form the Baptist Union of Australia in 1926 they have retained their autonomy. They are active in social welfare work and, considering the number of Baptists in Australia, have been very heavily engaged in missionary activities, both among Aborigines and abroad.

Further reading: van Sommers, T. 'The Baptists' in *Religions in Australia*. Rigby, Adelaide, 1966; Bollen, J.D. *Australian Baptists: A Religious Minority*. Baptist Historical Society, London, 1975.

Barassi, Ronald Dale

(1936-) AUSTRALIAN RULES footballer and coach. Barassi started his very successful career playing for Melbourne in the Victorian Football League but it was as a coach that he was to become outstandingly successful. He played 204 games for Melbourne and captained the team for several years before leaving the club in 1965 to become captain/coach of the Carlton team. Injury soon forced him to retire from playing, but as coach he lifted Carlton to win in 1968, their first premiership for 20 years, and to repeat their win two years later. He then retired, but in 1973 was persuaded to become coach of North Melbourne, the team at the very bottom of the VFL ladder the year before. Under his coaching they won premierships in 1975 and 1977, and were runners-up in 1974, 1976 and 1978. In 1981 he returned as coach to his old club, Melbourne, but by 1983, while he had improved the team's performance, it had not yet reached a place in the finals. Possessed of a fierce and single-minded will to win, Barassi, known as 'Mr Football', was the first man to be made a life member of the VFL, having coached 300 games.

barbers *see* fishes, bony

Barcaldine

QLD (population 1 432 in 1981) A small service town located on a

tributary of the BARCOO RIVER in the central W of the State, Barcaldine is 1 095km by road NW of Brisbane, 589km W of ROCKHAMPTON and 108km E of LONGREACH at the junction of the Capricorn and Landsborough Highways. It is also a rail town on a line running W from Rockhampton to WINTON.

Barcoo River

QLD One of the upper streams which joins with the Thomson River to form COOPER'S CREEK, it is located in the SW of the State, and flows intermittently for about 550km from its headwaters NE of BARCALDINE, in a general SW direction, through a region of low and unreliable rainfall. There is a marked seasonal pattern in the rainfall, a high proportion of rain falling in the summer months and a dry period extending through the winter and spring. As a result, there is distinct variation in river flow at different times of the year; because of variability in the amount of rain received from year to year, there can be severe flooding over wide stretches of the plain during a wet year.

bardick *see* snakes

Barkly Tableland

NT/QLD Though the name 'Barkly Tableland' is applied to various different areas, it is generally used for the plateau region in the NE of the NT lying S of the GULF OF CARPENTARIA and extending across the State border into QLD. The W limit is usually accepted as being E of the Stuart Highway between NEWCASTLE WATERS and DALY WATERS and it stretches for some 500km to Camooweal in QLD. The N-S extent varies between 160km and 200km. The scarplands (facing and generally parallel to the coast of the Gulf of Carpentaria) lie about 160km inland, where the highest parts reach over 300m elevation, and form a distinct, though much dissected, limit to the NW extent of the plateau. Numerous water courses rise on the uplands of the plateau and cross this scarpland zone to the coastal plains, flowing generally NNE to mangrove-fringed estuaries on the gulf. The largest of these is the McARTHUR RIVER; others are (in the NT) the Towns, Cox, Limmen, Robinson and Calvert Rivers, and (in QLD) the Nicholson River, but most flow only during the wet season, persisting merely as a string of waterholes in the dry. To the S and W, the tableland slopes gently to merge into arid plains, and the streams draining S and SW across the plateau show as rivers only during the wet season; the lakes into which most of them flow are usually dry saltpans for many months each year.

The rainfall pattern on the tableland is typical of these N parts, with a two-cycle climatic rhythm of a hot wet summer season and a milder dry season. At Brunette Downs the average yearly rainfall is only 385mm, most of which falls between December and March, little falling in the rest of the year. Much of the tableland is grassland; the grass grows rapidly in the wet season to become a carpet of tussocks, often growing to a metre

high; but as the rains end these apparently lush pastures deteriorate and become dry and coarse and have little pasture value. Thus the seasonal nature of the rainfall, the long dry months, and the scarcity of the grasses in this period pose problems for the cattle grazing industry, the main activity of the tableland. Underground water at depths between 90m and 150m can be pumped from bores over most of the tableland (see ARTESIAN WATER), and these form the mainstay for livestock supplies in the dry season. Grazing properties are large, and use open-range methods with few fences. The Barkly Statistical Subdivision of the NT had a population of 6 322 at the 1981 census. In former days drovers 'walked' the cattle from the Barkly region to railheads in QLD or to the CHANNEL COUNTRY of south-western QLD for fattening, but today road-trains are more commonly used. The Barkly Highway, linking the Stuart Highway (from 26km N of TENNANT CREEK) to MOUNT ISA, is one of the main cattle routes.
Further reading: Shaw, J.H. & Kirkwood, F.G. 'From jungles to snowlands' in *The Savanna Lands of Northern Australia*. Shakespeare Head, Sydney, 1957; Bayne, M. *The Barkly Tableland*. Longmans, Melbourne, 1967.

QLD Nat. Parks/Wildlife Service

Exposed rocks on the east side of Barkly Tableland

Barklya A small to medium-size rainforest tree, *Barklya syringifolia* (family PAPILIONACEAE) of northern NSW and QLD, it has long, terminal racemes of orange-yellow flowers, and rounded or heart-shaped leaves. It can be grown as a garden tree.

barley *see* agriculture; Gramineae

Barmera SA (population 2 014 in 1981) This town and irrigation area is situated at Lake Bonney, 40km SW of RENMARK, on the flood plain N of the MURRAY RIVER. The lake is located within a major meander loop of the river, 218km by road and 377km by rail NE of Adelaide. The town is the service centre for a productive rural area of vineyards and orchards, developed as an irrigated 'Soldier Settlement' scheme after World War I. The town name is derived from the Aboriginal *Barmeedjie*, the name of the tribe that occupied the region.

barnacles *see* crustaceans

Barnard Eldershaw, M. The pen-name M. Barnard Eldershaw has been used for a work of literary criticism, five novels and three historical works written jointly by Marjorie Faith BARNARD and Flora ELDERSHAW.

Barnard, Marjorie Faith (1897-) Historian, novelist and short-story writer. Born and educated in Sydney, she worked as a librarian at the State Library of New South Wales, at the Sydney Technical College and for the CSIRO. The main body of her work has been written in collaboration with Flora ELDERSHAW under the joint pen name of M. Barnard Eldershaw. She has also published in her own name *The Persimmon Tree and Other Stories* (1944), sensitively written stories which deal mainly with the emotional life of women; the historical works *Macquarie's World* (1941), *Sydney: The Story of a City* (1956), and *A History of Australia* (1959) and a work of criticism, *Miles Franklin* (1965).
See also literature
Further reading: Rorabacker, L.E. *Marjorie Barnard and M. Barnard Eldershaw.* Twayne, New York, 1973.

Barnet, James Johnstone (1827-1904) Architect. As Colonial Architect for 25 years in NSW, James Barnet had an important influence on Australian architecture. Born in Arbroath, Scotland, and trained in building and architecture in London, he came to Sydney at the end of 1854. He was made Clerk of Works at the University of Sydney, at that time under construction to the design of Edmund BLACKET, and in 1865 became Colonial Architect, holding the position until 1890. In this office he controlled an enormous output of building and engineering work during the years of Australia's greatest expansion. In 1879 he was responsible for the design and erection of the Sydney International Exhibition building, a mammoth temporary structure in the Botanical Gardens. Its final cost was £184 570, nearly four times that of the estimate, but it was a very successful and popular building. The Garden Palace, as it was called, was burnt down a few years after the exhibition. In 1866 the building of the General Post Office, in what is now Martin Place, commenced. It is a powerful Italian Renaissance composition whose tall tower was the most important landmark in Sydney before the skyscraper age. The design called for Pyrmont sandstone blocks of the largest size ever handled, and for novel fire-proof concrete vaulting. Its decorative carvings portraying arts, sciences and customs—one of which includes a portrait of Barnet—were much criticised as 'grotesque', but they survive today as a sample of robust Victoriana.
Barnet's buildings appeared all over NSW as well as in the capital. There were 130 court-houses, of which those of BATHURST and GOULBURN are among the finest; 169 post-and-telegraph offices, 155 police stations, 110 lock-ups and 20 lighthouses, and a great many defence structures. It is significant that most of Barnet's designs were based on Renaissance themes, but two of his most interesting were the Gothic-styled Mortuary Stations, one at

Redfern and one at Rookwood Cemetery, which allowed funeral corteges to go from the city to the cemetery by train. The Rookwood Station was dismantled a few years ago and re-erected as All Saints' Church at Ainslie, Canberra.
In Sydney dozens of buildings still testify to the quality of James Barnet's endeavours. Ill-tempered censure of him in 1890, following charges of inefficiency and insubordination, was a regrettable end to his distinguished career.
Further reading: Pike, D. (ed) *Australian Dictionary of Biography.* (vol 3) Melbourne University Press, Melbourne, 1969.

Barossa Valley SA Located some 60km NE of Adelaide in the MOUNT LOFTY RANGES, this valley, drained by the North Para River, is one of Australia's major wine producing regions. The valley, named by Colonel William LIGHT after the Battle of Barossa, Spain, in which he fought, forms the division between the N and S section of the Mt Lofty Ranges. The North Para River rises in the ranges, flows through the valley on a NNE-SSW route, is joined by the South Para River at GAWLER and flows across the Adelaide plain, as the Gawler River, to drain into ST VINCENT GULF.
In the 1840s the first Lutheran settlers from Silesia (S Germany) settled in the Barossa Valley, where wheat farming and sheep grazing were the main occupations. But between 1847 and 1851 three large vineyards were established: by Gramp at Orlando, Smith at Yalumba, and Seppelt at Seppeltsfield. They were not the first grape growers in the valley, but the large wineries they established encouraged rapid development of grape growing. The area experiences a mild winter climate, warm dry summer conditions and an average yearly rainfall of about 500mm, concentrated mainly in the winter months. Though the soils of the area are not rich they suit grape growing, as does the climate. The descendants of many of the early Lutheran families still live in the valley and the annual Barossa Vintage Festival retains a distinctively German flavour. Along with grape growing, other farming pursuits include market gardening, poultry raising, pig breeding, orcharding and sheep grazing. The main towns of the valley are NURIOOTPA, TANUNDA and ANGASTON.
Further reading: Slessor, K. *The Grapes are Growing: The Story of Australian Wine.* O. Ziegler, Sydney, 1965; Thiele, C. *Barossa Valley Sketchbook.* Rigby, Adelaide, 1968.

barracoutas *see* fishes, bony

barracudas *see* fishes, bony

barramundi *see* fisheries; fishes, bony; fishes, freshwater

Barrington Tops NSW This basalt-capped plateau at the S end of the MOUNT ROYAL RANGE forms part of the catchment area for two river systems draining to the Pacific coast: the HUNTER RIVER to the S and the MANNING RIVER to the N. It is an area which has been greatly dissected by river valleys and hence contains much rugged terrain, with spectacular waterfalls and attractive scenery. Many parts of the plateau are clad in forests of eucalypts and dense semi-tropical vegetation. Native animals and birds are abundant—kangaroos, wallabies, wombats, lyrebirds, brush turkeys and eagles can be seen in their natural habitat in the remoter parts of the plateau. It is a popular bushwalking region, and offers trout fishing for stream anglers. The highest parts of the plateau reach 1 586m above sea level, with a number of minor peaks over 1 500m. The Barrington Tops National Park covers an area of 16 325ha on the N escarpment of the Hunter Valley. Access to the area is usually via DUNGOG, thence by road up the Williams River valley to Barrington House; from there on, the visitor must use rough tracks, either on foot or by four-wheel-drive vehicle. There is an alternative access route from GLOUCESTER to the E section of the plateau, called Gloucester Tops. Heavy rain and snowfalls on the plateau are not uncommon, and sudden weather changes can occur. Because of these unpredictable conditions, bushwalkers are requested to notify the ranger in charge of the park about their journey plans. During periods of heavy rain, roads may be cut at fords, or made impassable by falling trees.

Barron River QLD Located in the NE of the State, it rises in the S part of the ATHERTON TABLELAND and flows in a general N direction beyond MAREEBA, then turns E, plunges 250m from the uplands to the coastal plain, and crosses the narrow alluvial flats to an estuary on Trinity Bay, about 10km N of CAIRNS. The Tinaroo Falls Dam on the upper river NE of Atherton was completed in 1955 and has a 45m-high wall and a storage capacity of 407 000ML, harnessing the waters of the Barron for irrigation of the tobacco lands downstream and for power generation at the Barron Falls hydro-electricity station. The main urban centres within the river basin are Mareeba (population 6 309 in 1981) and Atherton (4 196 in 1981). The yearly rainfall over the valley is about 900mm, falling mainly in the summer months, with a dry period in winter and spring. The Kennedy Highway follows the valley on a N-S route for some 30km and then, from Mareeba, it goes E and NE to join the coastal Bruce Highway 13km N of Cairns. The Gillies Highway goes E from Atherton down the E face of the tableland to GORDONVALE on the Bruce Highway.

Barrow Island WA Located some 50km off the NW coast of the State, 96km N of ONSLOW, Barrow Is is geologically part of the CARNARVON Basin and is the site of one of Australia's richest oilfields. It has an area of over 200km²; at a latitude of 21°S, it experiences high temperatures throughout the year, with cyclones a rather common feature.

It has a low annual rainfall of 431mm, the months of highest rainfall being May (90mm average) and June (84mm). Oil was discovered on the island in 1964 by West Australian Petroleum Ltd (WAPET). The oilfield came into production in 1967 (making it the first commercial field in WA) and in 1970 accounted for 26 per cent of the nation's total crude oil output. Because of shallow water adjacent to the island, a 10km-long pipeline was built to carry the oil to a loading jetty. Though production declined after 1972, the field had produced a total of 172 million barrels of crude oil (one barrel = 159 litres) and 2.6 million cubic metres of natural gas by December 1980, and it was estimated then to have oil reserves of 82 million barrels and gas reserves of 10.8 million cubic metres.

Barton, Sir Edmund (1849-1920) First Prime Minister of Australia. Born in the Sydney suburb of Glebe, he graduated MA from the University of Sydney in 1870, was called to the Bar in the following year, and became a QC in 1889. He was elected to the Parliament of NSW in 1879 and later filled the positions of Speaker of the Legislative Assembly and Attorney-General.

Following Sir Henry PARKES' Tenterfield speech of 1889 he became such an enthusiastic supporter of the federation movement that in 1892 Parkes, nearing the end of his own political career, asked him to take over its leadership. He was a delegate to both federal conventions, being chosen as 'leader of the convention' and chairman of the constitutional committee in that of 1897-98. He also led the delegation which went to London in 1900 to discuss the Commonwealth Bill with members of the British Cabinet. By this time his importance in the federation movement was such that when the Governor-General, Lord Hopetoun, made the mistake of offering the position of first Prime Minister to Sir William LYNE, so few leading politicians were willing

Courtesy of A.I.S. Canberra

Sir Edmund Barton

to serve under the latter that Hopetoun was forced to realise his error and send for Barton.

The years of his prime ministership were occupied mainly with organising the Public Service and High Court, establishing a Commonwealth Defence Force, and legislating to prevent non-European immigration and to provide for the repatriation of KANAKAS to their islands. Then in 1903, in debt and worried about the effects of the strain of office on his health, he accepted a position on the bench of the High Court, where he served until his death.
Further reading: Rutledge, M. *Edmund Barton*, Oxford University Press, 1974.

Barwick, Sir Garfield Edward John (1903-) Chief Justice of Australia. Born and educated in Sydney, he was admitted to the NSW Bar in 1927 and took silk in 1941. He practised with great distinction in all jurisdictions, before turning to politics and winning the federal seat of Parramatta in 1958. He was Attorney-General in LIBERAL/COUNTRY PARTY governments from 1958 to 1964 and also Minister for External Affairs from 1961 to 1964. After resigning from parliament in 1964 he served as Chief Justice of Australia until 1981. During this time he took a keen interest in the building of the High Court building in Canberra, and exercised an influence on its design. Throughout his career he took an active part in the work of a great number of professional and public bodies, being, for example President at various times of the NSW Bar Association, the Law Council of Australia, the Australian Institute of International Affairs and the Australian Conservation Foundation. He was created Knight in 1953 and GCMG in 1964; in the latter year he was also appointed Privy Councillor.

Barwon Heads VIC (combined population of Barwon Heads and OCEAN GROVE 6 776 in 1981) A seaside holiday resort situated on the W side of the BARWON RIVER estuary, it is 24km by road SE of GEELONG. On the opposite side of the river estuary is the twin town of Ocean Grove. The two resort centres are popular with holiday-makers from Melbourne and Geelong, providing opportunities for good swimming, fishing, surfing and boating. There has been a great deal of urban and commercial development in the area in recent decades.

Barwon River NSW/QLD Part of the Barwon-DARLING river system, this stream forms a section of the border between NSW and QLD. The upper section of this system is called the MACINTYRE RIVER; downstream it changes its name to Barwon, and then, beyond the GWYDIR RIVER confluence, it is called, somewhat confusingly, 'Barwon or Darling'. The main towns along the river are Mungindi (on the State's border), Collarenebri, WALGETT, Brewarrina and BOURKE (where the river is called the Darling). Thus it flows through the dry NW plains region in a meandering course with numerous BILLA- BONGS and ANABRANCHES, but can be subject to flooding, when much of the adjacent plains are covered in vast sheets of slow-moving muddy water. The catchment area feeding the MacIntyre River receives an average yearly rainfall of 800mm; downstream, the average yearly rainfall at Walgett is 474mm and at Brewarrina 410mm. The name Barwon comes from an Aboriginal word meaning 'a great, wide river' or 'a river of muddy water'.

Barwon River VIC This stream rises in the OTWAY RANGES SW of Melbourne, descending to the coastal plain to flow through some fertile agricultural and pastoral country. It passes through the city of GEELONG, further downstream spreads its waters to become the swampy expanse of Lake Connewarre, and then, after a course of some 120km, enters the sea on the BASS STRAIT coastline, W of PORT PHILLIP BAY. At its mouth are the twin resort centres BARWON HEADS and OCEAN GROVE.

baseball In Australia, this sport does not attract the spectator following that it claims in America and Japan, where top players attain pop-star status. Still, the game is played with vigour and lively interest, attracting a growing band of supporters in all States.

First played in Australia in 1856 by American gold miners, the game did not arouse significant interest until 1888, when two American teams toured Australia. This tour encouraged the establishment of several Australian teams and a series of inter-colonial matches was played in 1889. An Australian team toured America unsuccessfully in 1897.

In 1914 a tour by the New York Giants and the Chicago White Sox, who played a series of exhibition games throughout the country, revitalised interest in the sport. And in 1926, a match between an American naval team from a visiting fleet and a NSW team attracted a crowd of 15 000 spectators.

The year 1933 saw the formation of the Australian Baseball Council whose function was to control the activities of the State associations, and in the following year an interstate carnival was introduced. At this carnival, which since that time has been held annually, States competed for the Claxton Shield, a trophy donated by a patron of the SA association. Internationally, Australia partici- pates in biennial matches organised by the Baseball Federation of Asia of which Australia has been a member nation since 1971 and an Australian Team toured America in 1976.

Baseball is now played at all levels from school through an expanding junior division to senior grades.

basic wage see arbitration and conciliation, industrial

basketball was introduced as a men's game in the late 1920s and became popular in the 1950s when American professional teams, the Harlem Globetrotters and the Boston Whirl-

winds, toured Australia. It should not be confused with NETBALL, a similar game which has different rules but was known until 1970 as women's basketball.

Associations were nevertheless formed in some States in the 1930s, leading to the establishment in 1939 of the Amateur Basket- ball Union of Australia (re-named Australian Basketball Federation in 1979). The outbreak of World War II curtailed the activities of these organisations, but in 1946 the game was placed on a firm administrative base with the formation of associations in all States and the re-organisation of the national union. This led to interstate championships, the first of which was held in Sydney in September 1946. These championships were held until 1979 when a National League comprising the top 16 clubs replaced them.

Since the 1960s there have been significant improvements in available facilities and coaching techniques. The result has been a substantial improvement in the standard of play, indicated by Australia's performance in Olympic competition—though unplaced in the 1968 Olympics, Australia finished in ninth place in 1976 and in seventh place in 1980. In the 1982 World Championships in Colombia the Australian men's team came fifth, Ian Davies being the top scorer among all countries.

Women's basketball has rapidly won inter- national recognition and Australian teams rank among the best in the world. A VIC team visited the USA in 1975, winning all 16 games played against top teams there, and in 1976 a NSW team had similar success, remaining undefeated throughout its tour of the USA. Women's basketball was introduced into the Olympic Games for the first time in 1976 and the Australian women were eager to show their prowess in the game, but were dis- appointed by a decision made by the Australian Olympic Federation Justification Committee which refused permission for the team to compete in the Olympic Qualification Tourn- ament. In 1978 they won the world champion- ship held in Korea.

In the early 1980s over 300 000 basketball players (of whom 200 000 were registered) throughout Australia were participating in competitions at all levels from school through community to senior grades; it appears that the sport has a growing prestige, and that it is becoming firmly established throughout Australia.

bass see fishes, bony; fishes, poisonous and venomous

Bass, George (1771-?1803) Explorer. Born in Lincolnshire, Bass was trained as a surgeon and apothecary, and later became a naval sur- geon. He arrived in Sydney on the *Reliance* in 1795 with Matthew FLINDERS, who held the position of master's mate and with whom he had become friendly. In the *Tom Thumb*, a tiny craft with an eight-foot keel which Bass had brought on the *Reliance*, the two men

George Bass

explored BOTANY BAY and George's River in 1795 and Port Hacking and the ILLAWARRA coastline in the following year. Also in 1796, he made an unsuccessful attempt to cross the BLUE MOUNTAINS, and in 1797-98 made an epic voyage in a whaleboat along the SE coast as far as WESTERN PORT BAY. This led him to believe that there must be a strait (now named after him) between TAS and the mainland. Flinders had been unable to accompany him on this voyage, but in 1798-99 the two friends sailed through BASS STRAIT and around TAS in the sloop *Norfolk*.

Later in 1799 Bass left the *Reliance*, having been declared physically unfit for his duties. He went to England, married, and in 1801 made a trading voyage to Sydney in the *Venus*. This was not a success financially, so he made a trip to islands in the S Pacific to procure salt pork for the colony. In 1803 he sailed on a trading voyage to Chile but was never heard of again. Despite a rumour that he was arrested in South America, convicted of smuggling and sent to labour in a silver mine, his fate must be considered a mystery.

Further reading: Bowden, K.M. *George Bass.* Oxford University Press, Melbourne, 1952.

Bassia see Chenopodiaceae

Bass Strait Lying between the Australian mainland and the island State of TAS, this stretch of water is 130km across at its narrowest extent and 250km at its widest. The FURNEAUX ISLANDS lie at the E end of the Strait; KING ISLAND lies at the W end. It was named after the explorer George BASS who, with Matthew FLINDERS in 1798, proved that

Courtesy of A.I.S. Canberra

Platform in oil and gas field, Bass Strait

the Strait existed and thus settled the question (unresolved in the early days of British colonial settlement on the mainland) of whether or not TAS was joined to the mainland. In fact, TAS was once connected to the mainland; in the Great Ice Age of the Pleistocene epoch, the sea level was lower and Bass Strait was almost dry, but when the ice melted and the sea level rose again, the Strait was flooded, separating TAS from the mainland. Islands within the Strait are remnants indicating the links between the TAS highlands and the Eastern Highlands of the mainland. Today, the Strait has become nationally important because of the discoveries of petroleum and natural gas in rocks in the area offshore from GIPPSLAND. The first discovery, in 1965, was the Barracouta field, 24km off the Gippsland coast, containing both gas and oil; it came into production in 1969. The Marlin field, a gas field discovered 48km offshore in 1966, came into production in 1970, and the Halibut and Kingfish fields, located about 80km offshore, both discovered in 1967, were brought into production in 1970 and 1971 respectively. Kingfish proved to be one of the world's major oil fields. Almost two-thirds of Australia's oil supply in the mid-1970s came from the Gippsland Basin. The development of two more fields, Mackerel and Tuna, was underway by 1978, and the Cobia field is currently under development as a commercial oilfield. Other small discoveries in the Strait were Snapper, Flounder and Fortescue fields, and production from the region reached a peak of about 450 000 barrels per day in 1980; it dropped to 380 000 in 1981 (largely because of industrial disputes), and it was predicted in late 1982 that, unless major new fields are discovered, Australia can expect its level of self-sufficiency to decline in the late 1980s.

Batchelor NT A small mining town on the North Australian Railway, 100km by road S of Darwin, Batchelor was an airforce base during World War II, but was developed in the 1950s to house mine workers at the RUM JUNGLE uranium field, located 6km N.

Batemans Bay NSW (population 4 911 in 1981) A town and coastal inlet on the S coast of the State, it is 282km by road S of Sydney on the Princes Highway. The area is a popular tourist centre with facilities for boating, fishing and other aquatic sports. The town is also a commercial and service centre for the rural hinterland where timber, fish, oysters and vegetables are produced, and where dairying is the major grazing activity. The inlet on which the town stands was named by James COOK in 1770 after Captain Bateman of HMS *Northumberland*.

Bates, Dame Daisy *née* O'Dwyer Hunt (1863-1951) Social worker among the Aborigines. Born in Tipperary, Ireland, she came to Australia for health reasons in 1884, and married John Bates. In 1894 she went to England, where she obtained a post on the literary staff of the *Review of Reviews*, but returned to Australia in 1899, having been commissioned by *The Times* to investigate allegations of maltreatment of Aborigines. Not long afterwards her husband died, and she acquired a large property in WA. She lived there for a while, but had by then developed a consuming interest in the life of the Aborigines. She accepted commissions from the governments of WA and SA to investigate welfare problems among them, and for more than 30 years she lived with them, most notably at Ooldea, on the NULLARBOR PLAIN, where she stayed from 1919 to 1935. She wrote voluminous notes on the culture and welfare problems of Aborigines, and published her views in *The Passing of the Aborigines* (1938). She recorded there her belief that the race was doomed to die out, and that Western education, or most other forms of contact with Western civilisation, would not be to the advantage of its members. During her lifetime she aroused various reactions, some people regarding her as a rather comic eccentric and others as the fount of all wisdom on Aboriginal affairs. There can be no doubt of her deep concern for the people among whom she lived for so long, nor of the affection which many of them felt for 'Kabbarli' (grandmother), as they called her. However, her belief in the inevitable 'passing' of the race was certainly mistaken, and she is commonly regarded today as having played a part in delaying the adoption of more constructive, forward-looking policies on Aboriginal affairs.
Further reading: Salter, E. *Daisy Bates, the Great White Queen of the Never-Never.* Angus & Robertson, Sydney, 1971; Hill, E. *Kabbarli: A Personal Memoir of Daisy Bates.* Angus & Robertson, Cremorne NSW, 1973.

Bathurst NSW (population 19 640 in 1981) A city in the central W region of the State, it is located at the junction of the Great Western and Mitchell Highways and on the main W railway, 213km by road and 240km by rail W of Sydney. It is situated on the MACQUARIE RIVER and was named by Governor Lachlan MACQUARIE in 1815 in honour of Earl Bathurst, then Secretary of State for the Colonies. It was gazetted as a town in 1833, and became a booming centre in the gold-rush days of the 1850s when fields such as Ophir, Hill End and Sofala flourished; it was proclaimed a borough in 1862 and a city

NSW Dept. of Tourism

'Woolstone' Bathurst built during convict days

in 1885. At an altitude of 675m above sea level, it experiences warm to hot summer conditions, with cool to cold winters and occasional snow on the surrounding hill lands. The average annual rainfall is 639mm, spread uniformly over all seasons.

It is the commercial and business focus for a productive rural region where sheep and cattle are grazed, wheat and oats are grown and fruit and vegetables are cultivated; lucerne is grown on river flats and timber is produced from the nearby forests. Among the varied secondary industries in the city are food processing and canning, rubber works, furniture-making, flour mills, engineering, a freezing works, and brick and pipe making. A major tourist attraction during the Easter and October weekends is the Mt Panorama racing circuit where car and motor-cycle events are held. Also over the October weekend, the Carillon City Festival (so called because of the carillon bells in the central square of the city) is held, with art and craft exhibitions, street carnivals and special sporting fixtures. Other tourist attractions in the city and district are: the Sir Joseph BANKS Nature Reserve located on Mt Panorama, comprising 41ha of bushland with kangaroos,

NSW Dept. of Tourism

Courthouse, Bathurst, built during convict days

wallabies and koala bears; Ben CHIFLEY cottage, the modest home of the renowned Labor politician who was Prime Minister of Australia from 1945 to 1949; 'Gold Diggings' at Karingal village (on Mt Panorama) with an authentic re-creation of mining in the gold-rush days; Abercrombie House, 8km NW on the Ophir road, a historic mansion in the baronial style of the 1870s; and a folk museum, an art gallery and a handicrafts centre.

The whole of the central grid section of the city has been classified by the National Trust (NSW) for preservation as an essential part of the nation's historic and cultural heritage; this includes many houses and terraced cottages, several parks, the civic centre zone, the buildings of the Technical College Annexe, the courthouse and the post office, St Stanislaus College, the Bank of New South Wales and numerous church buildings. In addition, the Trust has listed a large number of sites and buildings which should be preserved, thereby indicating their historical and architectural significance. Bathurst is an important educational centre with many State and private schools and colleges (including St Stanislaus College, The Scots School and All Saints College), a technical college and the Mitchell College of Advanced Education (formerly Bathurst Teachers' College). There are a number of State government offices in the city, including the headquarters of the Mapping Authority.

Further reading: Greaves, B. *The Story of Bathurst.* Angus & Robertson, Sydney, 1961; *Bathurst, New South Wales: Carillon City of the Central West.* Bathurst City Council, 1972; Webb, J. & Pile, S. *Bathurst Sketchbook.* Rigby, Adelaide, 1975; *National Trust Register.* The National Trust of Australia (NSW), Sydney, 1978.

Bathurst Island NT (population 1 032 in 1981) An Aboriginal reserve off the NW coast of the Territory, it is separated from the mainland by Clarence Strait and from MELVILLE ISLAND by the narrow Apsley Strait. It has an area of 2 072km² and the main settlement, Ngulu, on the SE coast, is a Roman Catholic mission where timber-getting and sawmilling have been developed. The island was charted in 1819 by Phillip King, son of Governor KING, and named in honour of the British Secretary of State for the Colonies. Much of the coastline along the NW and NE shores is deeply indented by mangrove-fringed swampy inlets.

Batman, John (1801-39) Pioneer and co-founder of Melbourne. The son of a convict, he was born in PARRAMATTA but in 1821 went to live in TAS, where he established himself as a grazier. He also won fame for capturing the bushranger Matthew BRADY, and for persuading a number of Aborigines to place themselves under the protection of the government.

A PORTRAIT OF BATMAN

In 1827 he applied for a grant of land on the mainland, at WESTERN PORT BAY, but was refused. Then his attention was directed to PORT PHILLIP BAY, and late in 1834, with Joseph GELLIBRAND and others, he founded the Port Phillip Association. In 1835 he sailed to Port Phillip in the schooner *Rebecca*, examined the lower reaches of the YARRA, noted the present site of Melbourne as 'the place for a village', and decided to settle there. He had brought with him two deeds of conveyance, on which he persuaded several Aborigines to 'make their mark'. By this alleged 'treaty', the Aborigines of the district granted to Batman about 200 000ha of land around the site of Melbourne, and a further 40 000ha near the site of GEELONG. In return, Batman gave them various trade goods, and undertook to make further payments each year.

After returning to TAS, Batman brought his wife and seven daughters to Port Phillip, and settled on Batman's Hill. By that time, however, a group of settlers organised by J. P. Fawkner had come across from TAS and established themselves a little further upstream. Whether Batman or Fawkner should be considered the actual founder of Melbourne is therefore a matter of controversy. The 'treaty' had in the meantime been declared void by Governor BOURKE. Batman hoped that he might nevertheless be given some financial reward for his pioneering work, but not long after settling in Melbourne he became ill, and died only three years later, without any such official recognition having been granted.

Further reading: Bonwick, J. *John Batman the Founder of Victoria.* (2nd edn) Ferguson & Moore, Melbourne, 1868; Latham, M. *John Batman.* Oxford University Press, Melbourne, 1962.

bats (which include the animals known as flying foxes) Bats are the only mammals capable of sustained flight. They compose an order (Chiroptera) of EUTHERIAN MAMMALS with about 1000 species in the world. The Chiroptera is thus the largest mammalian order apart from the Rodentia (RODENTS) and about a seventh of all mammals are bats. There is some doubt about the number of species in Australia, but it probably exceeds 55. Most species feed on insects, the remainder feed on fruit, blossom and nectar.

Bats are nocturnal or crepuscular (active at twilight), and usually spend the day in caves, under culverts, inside buildings or within crevices, though some of the fruit bats sleep hanging from the branches of trees. They are rarely seen and most people are unaware of how common bats are in many districts.

There are two suborders, both with representatives in Australia. The Megachiroptera contains the (usually) large fruit bats and flying foxes, and the Microchiroptera the generally smaller bats. Many of the latter are insect-eaters.

Megachiroptera Most members of this group have a claw on the second digit as well as on the first digit; in Australia the only exception is the bare-backed fruit bat, *Dobsonia moluccense*, of CAPE YORK. The tail is very short or absent, except in one non-Australian species. Many species are called flying foxes, on account of their dog-like faces. The only family in this suborder is Pteropodidae, which is confined to the tropics and subtropics of the Old World and Australasia. The Australian representatives fall into two groups: typical flying foxes and other blossom-eating bats.

1. There are four species of Australian flying foxes, all of the genus *Pteropus*. They feed mainly on blossoms during most of the year but also eat fruit (such as wild figs and cultivated fruit). The males are larger and more brightly coloured than the females. In summer flying foxes collect in large groups and form 'camps', usually in the trees of rainforests and mangroves. These summer camps contain both sexes, and the young are born soon after the camps are formed. Some summer camps have been occupied for over 80 years. During the winter, the large camps break up as there is not enough food within a night's flying range to maintain the large numbers.

The black fox, *P. alecto*, and the spectacled fox, *P. conspicillatus*, are the largest, with wingspans of 1.2m or more. The black fox, dark in colour and usually having a reddish or

Tube-nosed fruit bat

yellowish mantle, ranges from north-eastern NSW to the KIMBERLEYS and the coast of WA. The spectacled fox, also dark, with a yellowish mantle and yellow around the eyes, is found in rainforest in north-eastern QLD.

2. There are four species of blossom-eating bats in Australia. The largest, the bare-backed fruit bat is exceptional in that it roosts in caves and mines. The forearm is about 15cm long (forearm length is a commonly used index of bat size as, unlike the wingspan, it can be measured accurately). The Queensland tube-nosed fruit bat, *Nyctimene robinsoni*, found in Cape York and eastern QLD, has protruding, tubular nostrils.

The other two members of the family are small and are easily confused with some of the microchiropteran bats but they can be distinguished by the claw on the second digit. The northern blossom bat, *Macroglossus lagochilus*, is found in northern WA, QLD and northern NT. The very similar Queensland blossom bat, *Syconycteris australis*, light fawn to reddish, occurs in eastern QLD and northern NSW near rainforest and swamp areas, and has a brush-tongue similar to that of the honey POSSUMS.

Microchiroptera Most of these bats are small and none has a claw on the second digit. Although a few roost in tree branches, most congregate in caves, mine-tunnels and buildings, under culverts and inside hollow trees. In some caves bats are so numerous that their droppings accumulate on the floor forming a thick layer of guano from which large quantities of ammonia are given off. Microchiropteran bats use echolocation to detect prey and obstacles; their high-pitched (usually ultrasonic) squeaks reflect off objects within range, enabling them to judge the distance, direction, size and nature of an object. This ability is clearly of great importance for bats flying in pitch-dark caves but it is also valuable in hunting the insects on which many of them prey. The face and the ears are often highly modified to increase the accuracy and discrimination of this faculty. The ears are often large, and are usually equipped with a large tragus which increases the accuracy of the biaural hearing. Eyes are usually of little importance though, despite the proverb, no bat is blind; however, many insects can detect the ultrasonic sounds and avoid capture; some even produce their own trains of ultrasonic signals which either advertise that they are distasteful or jam the bat's echolocation apparatus. Of the 16 families in this suborder, five are represented in Australia.

1. The Megadermatidae, an Old World family of false vampire bats, is represented by the ghost bat, *Macroderma gigas* (wingspan 50cm), a large carnivore with large ears which are joined above the head, a prominent nose flap (*see* Rhinolophidae *below*), large, keen eyes and no tail. The fur is usually ashy-grey above and white below, and the wing membranes are pale. Until recently, ghost bats were thought to be rare but it is now known that they are common in Australia N of 29°S. They roost in small groups in rock crevices and caves, and feed at night on small mammals, reptiles, frogs, birds and other bats.

2. The Emballonuridae consists of the sheath-tailed bats of which there are seven Australian species, all in the genus *Taphozous*. The tail is enclosed in a sheath which penetrates through the tail membrane and sticks up above, and the snout is long and fox-like. These active bats feed on high-flying, large insects. The most widespread is the yellow- or white-bellied sheath-tail bat, *T. flaviventris*, a black-backed species found over much of the mainland.

Yellow-bellied or white-bellied sheath-tailed bat

Courtesy of A.I.S. Canberra

3. The horseshoe bats, Rhinolophidae, are so called because of their grotesque nose flaps which, in Australia, are more developed in this group than in any other. The nose flap consists of three main parts: a large, horseshoe-shaped lower section, a central piece round the nostrils and a third flap on the forehead. Horseshoe bats live in small colonies, roosting in hollow trees, caves and buildings.

The eastern horseshoe bat, *Rhinolophus megaphyllus* (forearm less than 5cm), found in E Australia mainly in coastal areas, varies in colour from mouse-grey to reddish; the upper part of the nose flap is triangular. The large-eared horseshoe bat, *R. philippinensis*, which occurs from TOWNSVILLE to Cape York, is larger, with relatively longer ears and a rounded projection on the upper flap. The four species of *Hipposideros* horseshoe bats, restricted to N Australia, usually roost in caves and mine tunnels, the orange horseshoe bat, *R. aurantius*, found in the N Kimberleys and northern NT, lives in hot, very humid caves; there is a very large colony at KATHERINE in the NT which contains many thousands of bats during the wet season.

4. The mastiff bats, Molossidae, found in nearly all tropical and temperate regions, are so called because of the heavy wrinkling of the lips and the square muzzle in many species. Mastiff bats fly swiftly, often above water, feeding on flying insects. There are five species in Australia, most parts of the country having at least one representative. They belong to the genera *Tadarida*, *Mormopterus* and *Chaerophon*, and have conspicuous, rather rodent-like tails and strong limbs. Some scurry actively on the ground; this is particularly true of the largest species, the white-striped bat, *T. australis*, found in southern WA, SA, southern QLD, NSW and VIC; it roosts in hollow trees.

5. The bats belonging to the largest family, Vespertilionidae (275 species), may be called typical bats and are found throughout the world in a wide variety of habitats. In Australia there are about 28 species.

The long-eared bats (subfamily Nyctophilinae) stand apart from the others of this family. The ears are joined above the head, and there are well-marked nose flaps. There are probably six Australian species, all belonging to the genus *Nyctophilus*. The greater long-eared bat, *N. timoriensis*, and the long-eared bat, *N. geoffroyi*, have wide ranges. The former lives in dry, open woodlands inland, from QLD to VIC, and the latter is found throughout Australia and TAS, apart from Cape York.

The rest of the family is divided into three subfamilies, all containing small bats, usually with short ears, short, blunt faces and the tails enclosed in tail membranes. It is often necessary to examine the skulls in detail to distinguish some of these bats. Some species are very common: colonies of the bent-wing bat, *Miniopterus schreibersii*, an E Australian species, sometimes contain over 18 000 individuals.

The subfamily Kerivoulinae has only one Australian species, *Phoniscus papuensis*, the golden-lipped bat, found from CAIRNS QLD to southern NSW.

The subfamily Kerivoulinae has only one Australian species, *Phoniscus papuensis*, which has been collected on only three occasions, each in QLD.

The two species of the subfamily Miniopterinae are the bent-wing bat and the little bent-wing, *M. australis*. The last joint of the third digit is very long and has to be folded between the second digit and the forearm when the bat is at rest. The tail is very long, sometimes longer than the head and body together. The bent-wing bat occurs E of the GREAT DIVIDING RANGE from northern QLD to south-eastern SA and is also found in north-western NT and the W Kimberleys. It roosts in caves, mines and sometimes houses (for example, in the cellar of Elizabeth House, Sydney). The little bent-wing is found in north-eastern NSW and QLD, east of the Great Dividing Range.

Most of the family belong to the subfamily Vespertioninae. The large-footed myotis, *M. adversus*, is common in E Australia and northern NT where it lives in caves and the roofs of houses. It is a small greyish-brown bat with a long muzzle and a long heel support for the tail membrane. The little bat, *Eptesicus pumilus*, the only Australian member of its genus is one of the most common bats in Australia; this very small species has dark fur, the hairs being grey at the base but brown at the tips, and it roosts in caves, hollow trees, buildings and the nests of martins.

The number of Australian species of the genus *Nycticeius* is uncertain but is probably five. Known as broad-nosed bats they are small or medium-sized bats which live in trees and sometimes in roofs of buildings. The greater broad-nosed bat, *N. rueppellii*, a brown species found in eastern NSW and south-eastern QLD, is one of the first bats to start hunting after sunset. The little broad-nosed bat, *N. greyi*, which occurs throughout the mainland, lives in trees and sometimes in caves. The Hughendon broad-nosed bat, *N. influatus*, a medium-sized species, is found in central QLD; little is known of its habits.

The bats of the genus *Chalinolobus* are endemic to the Australian region; there are probably five species. These small, dark brown bats have fleshy lobes at the corner of the mouth and glandular swellings on the muzzle; they live in small colonies in caves and sometimes in trees. Two examples of this genus are Gould's wattled bat, *C. gouldii*, a dark-mantled species found throughout Australia, and the chocolate bat, *C. morio*, found in the S of the continent and in TAS.

The genus *Pipistrellus* is a cosmopolitan group with two species recorded in Australia. The great pipistrelle, *P. tasmaniensis*, lives in hollow trees and caves and occurs from south-eastern QLD to TAS and in WA; the Papuan pipistrelle, *P. tenuis*, Australia's smallest bat, occurs in Cape York where it roosts in roofs of houses.

Further reading: Ratcliffe, F. *Flying Fox and Drifting Sand*. Angus & Robertson, Sydney, 1963; Ride, W.D.L. *A Guide to the Native Mammals of Australia*. Oxford University Press, Melbourne, 1970; Hall, L.S. & Richards, G.C. *Bats of Eastern Australia*. (Queensland Museum booklet, no 12) Brisbane, 1979; Strahan, R. (ed.) *The Australian Museum Complete Book of Australian Mammals*. Angus & Robertson, Sydney, 1983

Baudin, Nicolas (1750?-1803) French navigator and naturalist. Baudin is remembered in Australian history for his voyage of 1800-1803, undertaken on behalf of the Institut de France with the vessels *Le Géographe* and *Le Naturaliste*. The object of this expedition was an ambitious one—to survey all sections of the Australian coastline which were still undiscovered by Europeans. Had Baudin been luckier and more energetic, he might have accomplished a large part of this task, and so have anticipated a great deal of the work of FLINDERS. However, he was hampered by sickness among his crews and showed himself to be, at best, a mediocre navigator and leader of men.

On reaching the W coast of Australia, he surveyed part of it, sailed to Timor, and after a long delay went around CAPE LEEUWIN to TAS, before beginning to survey the S coast of the mainland from WESTERN PORT BAY westwards. He did not know that Lieutenants GRANT and MURRAY between them had already explored the coast as far W as Cape Banks, near the present border of VIC and SA. He believed, therefore, that he was the first European to see a very large part of the S coast, though he was in fact the discoverer only of the stretch from Cape Banks to ENCOUNTER BAY, near the mouth of the MURRAY RIVER, where he met Flinders. Baudin died in Mauritius on the return

National Library of Australia

Nicholas Baudin

voyage. Meanwhile Governor KING, who feared that the expedition might lead to the founding of a French settlement in TAS, had decided to confirm British rights to the island by colonising it.

Further reading: Cornell, C. (trans) *The Journal of Post Captain Nicolas Baudin*. Libraries Board of South Australia, Adelaide, 1974.

Bauer, Ferdinand (1760-1826) Botanical artist. Born in Austria, Bauer was the botanical draughtsman on Matthew FLINDERS' expedition in the *Investigator* to Australia in 1801.

bauxite *see* aluminium

Baylebridge, William (1883-1942) Poet. Originally named Charles William Blocksidge, he was born and educated in Brisbane, went to London in 1908 and after extensive travels returned to Australia in 1919. His early poems possessed little literary merit, and he seems to have realised this, for after the publication of his first two volumes, *Songs of the South* (1908) and *Australia to England and Other Verses* (1909), he withdrew them from circulation. Between 1910 and 1918 he published a number of volumes, but privately, and in small editions. The uneven quality of his work, his failure to publicise it sufficiently, and his refusal to allow his poems to be included in anthologies prevented him from gaining wide public acceptance or critical praise. However, the publication of a volume of love sonnets, *Love Redeemed* (1934), and of a selection of his poems under the title *This Vital Flesh* (1939), established him as a poet of some note. He left part of his estate to establish the Grace Leven Poetry Prize for the best volume of poetry published in each calendar year by an author 'writing as an Australian'.

beach curlew *see* waders

Beaconsfield TAS (population 14 150 in 1981) A town on the W side of the TAMAR RIVER estuary on the N coastal plains, it is 40km NW along the West Tamar Highway from LAUNCESTON. The history of the town dates from 1804 when Colonel William PATERSON explored the district and established a settlement there (initially called York Town). The discovery of gold in 1869 led to a mushroom growth of the town. Its prosperity during the gold-mining period is reflected in the big brick buildings with Romanesque arches, erected in 1904 at the pithead of the Tasmanian Gold Mine; they still dominate the townscape and have been listed for preservation by the National Trust (TAS). The town is now a commercial and service centre for a productive dairying and orcharding district.

bean, black A rainforest tree, *Castanospermum australe* (family PAPILIONACEAE), of northern NSW and QLD, its timber is used in cabinet work. It is also known as the Moreton Bay chestnut.

Bean, Charles Edwin Woodrow (1879-1968) Journalist, editor and author. Born in BATHURST in NSW, he attended school both there and in England, graduated in arts and law from the University of Oxford and was called to the Bar, but in 1908 turned from the law to journalism. From 1914 to 1919 he was war correspondent with the AIF, and at the end of the war was appointed Official War Historian. In this position he wrote six volumes of the *Official History of Australia in the War of 1914-18* and edited the whole 12-volume work, which soon won an international reputation for the brilliance of its reporting and its high value as both a general and a military history. He also played an important part in the establishing and development of the Australian War Memorial museum and archives in Canberra. His other published works include two books dealing with life and conditions of the inland of Australia, *On the Wool Track* (1910) and *Dreadnought of the Darling* (1911); a book of essays, *In Your Hands, Australians* (1918); and a history of independent schools in Australia, *Here, My Son* (1950).

Further reading: Inglis, K.S. *C.E.W. Bean, Australian Historian*. Queensland University Press, St Lucia QLD, 1970.

beans *see* Papilionaceae

bear animalcules *see* water bears

beardie *see* fishes, bony

Beaudesert QLD (population 3 780 in 1981) A business and service town W of TAMBORINE MOUNTAIN in the LOGAN RIVER valley, it is situated on the Mt Lindesay Highway, 68km S of Brisbane. It is the administrative headquarters of the Beaudesert Shire, a productive region of dairying, beef cattle grazing and crop farming. At an elevation of 46m above sea level, it experiences a mild climate, with an average yearly rainfall of 937mm, concentrated in the summer months. There are some interesting old homesteads in the area dating from the early days of settlement, and Pioneer Cottage, established by the local historical society, gives a picture of life in bygone days. The NATIONAL TRUST (QLD) has listed All Saints Memorial Church and the old Beaudesert post office for preservation.

Beaurepaire, Sir Frank (1891-1956)

Swimmer and industrialist. Sir Frank was born in Melbourne. As a swimmer, he showed outstanding ability at an early age and in 1907 won every freestyle event he entered from 440 yards to one mile. His swimming career lasted an unusually long period and he represented Australia in three Olympic Games—1908, 1920 and 1924. He came third in the 1500m freestyle event in all three Olympics, his time in the 1924 Olympics being his best ever. In the 1908 Games he also won a silver medal in the 400m freestyle, and in the 1920 and 1924 Games he was a member of the men's 800m relay team which came second on both occasions. In swimming competitions in Europe in 1910 he was the dominant competitor, winning all 48 of the events he entered. During his swimming career he broke 14 world records.

Sir Frank established the Beaurepaire Tyre Service in 1922, a business which expanded to produce a variety of rubber products marketed under the trade name of 'Olympic'. He was elected Lord Mayor of Melbourne in 1940, having served as a member of the Melbourne City Council since 1928. He received his knighthood in 1942. Dedicated throughout his life to sport, as a member of the VIC Legislative Council from 1942 to 1951 he strove successfully to have Melbourne chosen as the venue for the 1956 Olympic Games, but Sir Frank died on 19 May 1956, before the Games began.

Beauty Point

TAS (population 998 in 1981) A small town located on the W shore of the TAMAR RIVER estuary, 6km N of BEACONSFIELD and 48km NW of LAUNCESTON, Beauty Point is situated on the West Tamar Highway and is important as a deep-water harbour for overseas shipping.

bêche-de-mer *see* sea cucumbers

Becke, George Lewis 'Louis' (1855-1913)

Short-story writer and novelist. Born in PORT MACQUARIE in NSW, he was sent to San Francisco at the age of 14 to learn trading and then spent several years at sea before returning to Australia in 1874 to work as a miner on the PALMER RIVER field in northern QLD. He was soon off to sea again, sailing to many parts of the Pacific and working for a time as supercargo for 'Bully' Hayes, the notorious recruiter of KANAKAS. He lived in Sydney from 1892 to 1896, then went to London and did not return until about two years before his

death. Altogether, he published more than a score of novels and collections of short-stories, nearly all related to life in the Pacific. His first story with a Pacific island setting was published in the *Bulletin* in 1893 and his first volume of them, *By Reef and Palm*, appeared in the following year. His writing is not marked by any notable skill in characterisation or psychological analysis, but his dramatic plots and vivid descriptions brought him great popular success.

Further reading: Day, A.G. *Louis Becke.* Twayne, New York, 1966.

John Fairfax & Sons

Sir Frank Beaurepaire

beech, southern

Trees and shrubs of the genus *Nothofagus* are commonly known as southern beeches, and are usually evergreen, though some species are deciduous. *Nothofagus* is the only genus in the S hemisphere which represents the Fagaceae (the family of oaks and true beech trees), and is of great interest to bio-geographers because its distribution in the southernmost and colder parts of South America and Australasia (including highland New Guinea and New Caledonia, E Australia, TAS and New Zealand) is strong evidence in support of the theory of CONTINENTAL DRIFT, which regards all these areas as parts of the old GONDWANALAND supercontinent.

The Australian or negrohead beech, *N. moorei*, an evergreen with large, glossy leaves up to 7.5cm in length, grows to a height of 45m. It grows at altitudes over 1 200m in the McPHERSON RANGE in QLD and on mountain slopes in coastal NSW, where it was once abundant in the GREAT DIVIDING RANGE. The Tasmanian beech, *N. cunninghami*, is a bulky evergreen occurring in moist valleys in the W mountains of TAS and in some parts of VIC. It grows up to 60m in height and 12m in girth, and the leaves are small and more or less diamond-shaped, attached by very short, downy leaf-stalks. Its timber, known as red myrtle, is valued in furniture making. The

tanglefoot, *N. gunni*, is a small, deciduous tree or shrub of alpine TAS.

Beechworth

VIC (population 3 154 in 1981) The historic town of Beechworth nestles in the Victorian Alps at an elevation of 55m above sea level, 272km by road NE of Melbourne and 37km E of WANGARATTA off the Hume Highway. Located in rocky hill-country to the N of the OVENS RIVER valley, the town grew from a goldfield discovered in 1852, and many fine buildings from the 1850s have been restored; over 30 have been classified or recorded by the National Trust (VIC). During the 1870s Beechworth was closely associated with the KELLY gang of bushrangers. Gold was mined commercially until 1920 and even today can be panned in local creeks. The town was named by a government surveyor in 1853 after his birthplace in Leicestershire, England. There are several museums in the town and much of historic interest, as well as such attractions as the Golden Hills trout farm (about 2km out of town), scenic views from massive granite hilltops, and several lakes and streams for fishermen.

bee-eaters *see* rainbow bird

beef cattle industry

Cattle are widely distributed throughout Australia. The population increased dramatically in the early 1970s, reaching a peak of 33.4 million in March 1976. In terms of stock equivalents, biomass, and country commanded for grazing or pasture consumed, cattle are the dominant animal species in Australia. Approximately 90 per cent of the cattle are beef types, with the remainder being for production of milk and cream. In 1980, 39.3 per cent of the cattle were in QLD, 21.7 per cent in NSW, 17.1 per cent in VIC, 8.1 per cent in WA, 4.3 per cent in SA, 6.7 per cent in the NT and 2.6 per cent in TAS.

Australia has only approximately 4.5 per cent of the world's beef cattle and produces a similar proportion of beef and veal. However, she exports more beef and veal than any other country, usually supplying between 20 and 24 per cent of the commodity entering the world trade, and exporting to over 40 countries. The main importer from Australia is the USA, but Japan, Canada and the Middle East countries also take substantial quantities; in some years, the USSR and the E European countries are a significant market. In the five years ending 1981, Australia exported 55.4 per cent of the total production of beef and veal (carcase weight).

Veal A very small amount of the total of both production and exports consists of veal. Veal is the meat derived from young calves, almost all of which originate in the dairy industry. For export grading as veal there is no maximum dressed carcase weight, providing the following characteristics, indicative of veal, are present: distinct separation of the sacral vertebrae; only slight signs of ossification of the cartilaginous tips of the spinous processes

CATTLE NUMBERS IN AUSTRALIA 1955-81
(in millions)

Period		NSW	VIC	QLD	SA	WA	TAS	NT	TOTAL
Average	1955	3.6	2.3	6.8	0.5	0.9	0.3	1.0	15.4
over 5	1960	3.8	2.6	7.2	0.6	1.0	0.4	1.1	16.7
years	1965	4.5	3.2	7.2	0.7	1.2	0.4	1.1	18.3
ending	1970	4.6	3.8	7.3	0.8	1.4	0.6	1.1	19.6
31 March	1975	7.8	5.6	9.6	1.6	2.2	0.8	1.3	28.9
	1980	7.5	4.8	11.1	1.4	2.3	0.7	1.7	29.5
As at	1969	4.8	3.9	7.7	0.9	1.5	0.6	1.2	20.6
31 March	1970	5.7	4.5	7.5	1.0	1.7	0.6	1.2	22.2
	1971	6.5	5.1	7.9	1.2	1.8	0.7	1.2	24.4
	1972	7.4	5.5	9.0	1.5	2.0	0.8	1.2	27.4
	1973	7.9	5.5	9.8	1.6	2.2	0.9	1.2	29.1
	1974	8.5	5.8	10.3	1.7	2.3	0.9	1.3	30.8
	1975	8.9	6.2	10.9	1.9	2.5	0.9	1.4	32.8
	1976	9.1	5.9	11.3	1.9	2.7	0.9	1.6	33.4
	1977	8.3	5.1	11.5	1.6	2.5	0.8	1.7	31.5
	1978	7.5	4.6	11.4	1.3	2.2	0.7	1.6	29.3
	1979	6.5	4.1	10.8	1.1	2.1	0.7	1.8	27.1
	1980	6.1	4.3	10.3	1.1	2.1	0.6	1.7	26.2
	1981	5.4	4.3	9.7	1.1	2.0	0.7	1.7	25.2

Source: Australian Bureau of Statistics, Canberra.

Courtesy of A.I.S. Canberra

Hereford cattle at Moree NSW

of the sacral vertebrae; no ossification of the cartilaginous tips of the spinous processes of the lumbar and thoracic vertebrae; only a slight tendency of flatness; and some redness of the ribs. Minimum carcase weights for 1st and 2nd Quality export grades of veal are 22.6kg, and 19kg for 3rd Quality. Boneless veal is derived from carcases of animals not less than 14 days old when slaughtered and yielding a boneless full side of 4.5kg minimum weight. In the five years ending June 1981 the average carcase weight of calves slaughtered was 38kg, compared with an average carcase weight of 203kg for cattle slaughtered in the same period.

Breeds Before European settlement there were no · cattle in Australia. The present population consists of British and European breeds (*Bos taurus*), Zebu breeds (*Bos indicus*), breeds derived from these, and crossbred cattle.

In southern Australia (NSW, VIC, TAS, SA and south-western WA) British breeds predominate, with Herefords comprising approximately 50 per cent of the population and Shorthorns and Angus each making up about 10 per cent of the population. The remainder consist of other British breeds such as Devons, Red Polls, Galloways, Lincoln Reds and South Devons; the Australian breed, Murray Greys (derived from Angus and Shorthorn); European breeds such as Charolais, Simmental, Limousin, Chianina, Maine Anjou and Friesian; and crosses between these breeds. Small numbers of Zebu-cross cattle also are represented in this region.

In N Australia the cattle population consists of Herefords, Shorthorns and crosses between these breeds and with the Zebu. The only Zebu breeds which have been introduced in significant numbers have been the Santa Gertrudis (derived from Brahman and Short-

horn) and the Brahman. The Zebu introductions have been used to combine the resistance to cattle ticks and tolerance of hot weather with the meat-producing ability and quieter temperament of British breeds. Breeds which have been established include Braford (three parts Brahman, five parts Hereford), Brangus (three parts Brahman, five parts Angus) and Droughtmaster (three to four parts Brahman, four to five parts Shorthorn with some Hereford). At ROCKHAMPTON in QLD, the CSIRO has developed the Belmont Red (four parts Africander, two parts Hereford, two parts Shorthorn) through an intensive selection programme.

Systems of production Grazing properties conduct four main production and fattening systems with beef cattle. There is no standard classification for the various types of slaughter cattle but the systems can be described as follows.

1. Breeding and fattening vealers. Vealers are defined in this system as cattle of either sex between six and 12 months of age with a carcase weight of 90kg to 180kg. The meat produced is beef rather than veal, and is consumed on the domestic market.

2. Breeding and fattening male cattle older than 12 months. Most cattle are slaughtered between one and three years of age with carcase weights ranging from 170kg to 300kg. As a generalisation, the older the animal the lower the proportion of the carcase that is likely to be consumed in Australia.

3. Breeding and selling store cattle. This refers to cattle, usually males, between one and two years old, which require further fattening, and possibly growing, before slaughter.

4. Purchasing and fattening store cattle. This system depends on the former for the supply of cattle, which are fattened and turned off (*see below*) for slaughter generally within a 12-month period.

In some cases more than one system is in operation on the same property. Another activity on some properties is the breeding of bulls from a stud herd. All systems operate in all States, except in the NT where vealers are not bred. Breeding and selling fat cattle, either vealers or older cattle, is the most common activity in all States, except in the NT where

CATTLE POPULATION, MEAT PRODUCTION AND PRODUCTION PER HEAD FOR AUSTRALIA AND SELECTED COUNTRIES: AVERAGE FOR FIVE YEARS ENDING 1979

Country	Million head of cattle & buffalo	Beef & veal production ('000t)	Average annual production per head (kg)
Australia	31	1 929	62.9
USA	122	11 165	91.6
USSR	111	6 285	56.6
Argentina	59	2 886	48.9
Brazil	99	2 170	21.9
Mexico	29	988	34.1
Colombia	25	536	21.4
France	24	1 798	74.9
Germany, F.R.	15	1 370	93.8
UK	14	1 068	77.4
South Africa	10	432	41.2
New Zealand	9	553	59.5

Source: Australian Bureau of Statistics, Canberra.

breeding of store cattle is an important enterprise. Approximately 20 per cent of properties which carry beef cattle rely on cattle as the only activity on the property; consequently, most beef cattle are run in conjunction with sheep, dairy cattle or crops.

Lot feeding In Australia small numbers of cattle are fattened in a dry lot feeding system which involves the restraint of the cattle in yards for some months while all their nutritional requirements are provided by grain and hay. The Bureau of Agricultural Economics (BAE) estimated that five per cent of all cattle slaughtered in 1973-74 had been finished in a feedlot; however, the proportion is often much smaller when prices and demand for feedlot beef are low. Generally, the demand for this type of beef comes from only one segment of the Japanese market. Lot feeding is a departure from the traditional reliance on pasture for finishing cattle. However, as cattle spend only about three months in the lot, a high proportion of the carcase weight of lot fattened cattle results from growth while grazing prior to entry into the lot.

Feedlots range in size from one-time capacity of only a few hundred head to over 5000 head. Most smaller lots are run by individual producers on a seasonal or opportunistic basis and are often integrated with the production of grazing cattle and/or grain growing on the property. Larger lots frequently have arrangements with related business interests and in some cases are joint ventures with Japanese meat traders.

Levels of production Productivity can be estimated by branding, mortality and turn-off (*see* table previous page) percentages, and by the production of meat per head of cattle population.

Branding percentage refers to the number of calves mustered for branding during the year as a percentage of cows in the breeding herd. There is wide variation over different regions of Australia, with averages of around 50 per cent and less being obtained in the NT, the KIMBERLEYS of WA and far N and western QLD and SA, compared to averages of over 80 per cent in the S coastal regions of QLD, VIC, SA and WA.

Mortality represents the annual losses of all classes of stock after branding and tends to be inversely related to branding percentages.

Turn-off refers to the number of cattle sold annually as a percentage of the number on the property. The lowest turn-offs (10 to 20 per cent) are recorded in regions with low branding percentages and high mortality.

Production of meat per head of cattle depends on turn-off, age and level of nutrition prior to slaughter. The average weight of beef and veal produced in Australia per head of cattle population was 62.9 per year for the five years ended 1979. According to this measure of productivity, Australia produces less than North America and Europe, about the same as New Zealand and more than other countries. *See also* diseases, animal and livestock; grazing industry.

Further reading: Alexander, G. & Williams, O. *The Pastoral Industries of Australia*. Sydney University Press, Sydney, 1973; Yeates, N.T.M. & Schmidt, P.J. *Beef Cattle Production*. Butterworths, Sydney, 1974; Cole, V.G. *Beef Production Guide*. The Graziers' Association of New South Wales, Sydney, 1975.

beefsteak plant *see* Euphorbiaceae

bee-keeping and honey production

The honey bee, *Apis mellifera* (*see* ANTS, etc.) is not native to Australia. The Rev. Samuel MARSDEN had two colonies in 1810 but lost both in a wet season. The first successful colonies were imported in 1822 from Britain and since then the stocks have been improved by strains from Italy, Yugoslavia and America; fortunately, a proposal to bring African bees to improve the vigour was not followed up for this could have led, as it did in Brazil, to the establishment of a ferocious and dangerous feral population. Queens are still imported, accompanied by supporting workers for the journey, but only under strict quarantine, so as to prevent the entry of various diseases and parasites such as the Isle of Wight disease (*see* MITES). Most of the bees belong to the Italian, Carniolan and Caucasian varieties. Two interesting extant populations are: on KANGAROO ISLAND a population of the Italian Ligurian bee, which has disappeared almost everywhere else; and in TAS a population of the original black bee from Europe.

Most of the honey produced in Australia is derived from eucalypts (family MYRTACEAE) so that Australian honeys have their own unique flavours. About a quarter comes from ground plants and from Salvation Jane (also known as Paterson's Curse) which is regarded as a weed by many graziers (*see* WEEDS). As blossoms appear at different times in different parts of the country bee-keepers must move their hives frequently to follow the blossom. Because eucalypts flower only once every two or three years, the success of a bee-keeper depends upon his ability to forecast when a given area will produce its blossom. Beeswax is an important by-product by the industry.

The Australian Honey Board supervises research, controls honey exports and promotes the product within Australia. All beehives are registered. In 1978-79 there were 2 201 bee-keepers in Australia, compared with 5 926 in 1972-73. There were, however, almost as many hives (total number 528 000 and 501 000 respectively; productive hives, 395 000 and 369 000). The total quantity produced in 1978-79 was 18 300 tonnes, with a gross value of $14 111 000. In addition, 349 tonnes of beeswax, worth $1 213 000, were produced. Exports consisted of 7 400 tonnes of honey, worth $6 164 000, and 194 tonnes of beeswax, worth $743 000. As an exporter of honey, Australia ranks fourth in the world.

Further reading: Langridge, D.F., Rufford-Sharp, J. & Freeman, W.A. *Bee-Keeping in Victoria*. Government Printer, Melbourne, 1964.

Beenleigh QLD (population 7 839 in 1981) A satellite town of Brisbane, it is located just off the Pacific Highway, 37km S of the city centre. It is situated in the LOGAN RIVER valley, where sugar cane cultivation and dairy farming are the principal rural activities; other primary pursuits in the district are fruit growing, fishing and beef cattle grazing. The town is noted for its rum distillery. The name Beenleigh was given to the area by pioneer settlers who called it after their family estate in Devonshire, England.

bees *see* ants, etc.; bee-keeping, etc.

beetles Contained in an endopterygote, order (Coleoptera) of INSECTS, beetles form by far the largest order in the animal kingdom, containing about 280 000 known species in the world, of which about 20 000 occur in Australia.

Most adult beetles have two pairs of wings though only the hind pair is membranous and used for flying. The fore-wings (elytra) are hardened protective cases for the folded hindwings and, usually, the abdomen. When folded back the elytra meet in a straight line along the insect's back. In some beetles the elytra are fused together and may also be partly fused with abdominal segments. Beetles have typical biting mouthparts with strong mandibles. The larvae have well-developed heads, usually hardened. A few larvae (mainly those of weevils and their relatives) are legless but most have well-developed thoracic legs and, rarely, abdominal prolegs. The shape varies from the grub-like weevil larvae to the long-legged, active, predatory larvae of the ground beetles. In some parasitic species the form of the larvae differs greatly from stage to stage.

Beetles and their larvae are found in all kinds of habitats and display a great variety of life histories. It is difficult to generalise but probably the majority live rather concealed lives in the soil, litter, under bark and so on, though many, such as the ladybirds and leaf beetles, are often conspicuous on foliage.

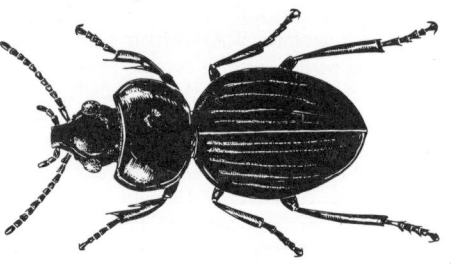

Typical ground beetle

There are more than 106 beetle families in Australia but only the largest, the economically important and the bizarre are discussed below. There are four suborders; two (Archostemata and Myxophaga) are represented by only eight species and are not mentioned further.

Adephaga The members of this suborder (about 1 900 species in Australia) are distin-

guished by the hind coxae (the basal segments of the hind-legs), which are immovably fused to the underside of the thorax and which divide completely the basal plate of the first visible abdominal segment. Apart from the family Carabidae, all these beetles are aquatic.
Ground beetles The Carabidae (over 1 600 species in Australia) contains the ground beetles, which vary in size from small to large and are usually of dark metallic colours. Although active, they rarely fly and are often found sheltering beneath bark or stones during the day. All are predators though some occasionally feed on plants. The long-legged, elongated larvae, which have well-developed, segmented 'tails' (cerci), also prey on other insects. About one half of the Australian species are ground-dwellers; the remainder are equally divided between arboreal species and those associated with the banks of creeks, ponds and swamps. The bombardier beetle, *Pheropsophus verticalis*, is a common though atypical species, readily recognised by its black elytra marked with four yellow spots. When disturbed it puffs out a corrosive mixture of oxygen gas and quinones produced by the sudden mixing of hydrogen peroxide with other chemicals. The release is heard as a distinct popping noise.
Water beetles The best-known family of aquatic beetles is the Dytiscidae (about 200 species in Australia), found in both running and stagnant freshwater. The adults are smooth and boat-shaped; they gather a supply of air at the surface and carry it between the elytra and the abdomen. The larvae, also aquatic, periodically come to the surface for air, but the pupae rest in cells in damp soil near the water. Both the adults and the larvae are fierce predators.
Whirligig beetles The family Gyrinidae (about 28 species in Australia) contains the whirligig beetles, which are similar in shape to the Dytiscidae but stay mainly on the surface, swimming rapidly, often in circles. The eye is completely divided, having a lower section below the surface, and an upper section above it.
Polyphaga This suborder (over 17 000 species in Australia) is distinguished from the Adephaga by the free coxa of the third leg, and by the non-division of the first abdominal segment.
Rove beetles The family Staphylinidae (about 650 species in Australia) contains the rove beetles, elongated species with short elytra which leave most of the abdomen exposed. They range from tiny to moderate in size, and because many are so inconspicuous there are probably a considerable number awaiting discovery. Most are predators or carrion-feeders but some are parasites of mammals and insect pupae. Several species live within ant or termite nests; other species are found in seaweed on the shore. The common whiplash rove beetle, *Paederus cruenticollis*, a river-bank species, blisters the skin.
Chafer beetles The family Scarabaeidae (about

2 100 species in Australia) contains the chafer beetles, stout, small to medium-sized beetles with strong spiny legs well suited to digging. The terminal segments of the antennae are plates whose arrangement resembles the fingers of a hand. The larvae of many scarabs are the root-feeding curl bugs well known to gardeners. The group includes the various Christmas beetles (*Anoplognathus* species) and the lawn scarab, *Sericethis geminata*, of the E States. The adults of these beetles frequently defoliate native trees. The larvae of many other scarabs are dung-feeders but the native species are usually adapted only to the relatively small pellets of marsupials. Until recently there were few or no dung beetles in

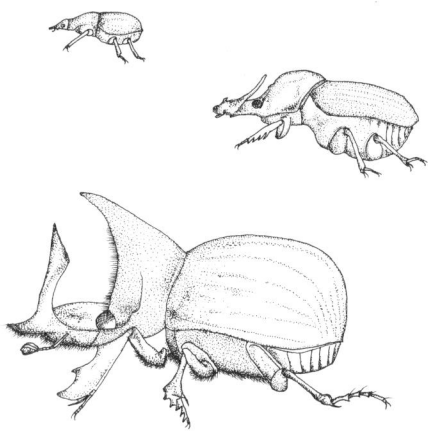

Three species of dung beetles

Australia that could recycle the larger dung-pats produced by cattle, which consequently lay on the pastures for many months, thus preventing the full use of the grazing, and serving as breeding sites for the bushfly and the BUFFALO FLY, as well as various parasitic ROUNDWORMS. The CSIRO has imported several species of dung beetles from Africa and Hawaii to fill this niche and has plans to establish several more in future.

The Scarabaeidae belong to the superfamily Scarabaeoidea, which also contains the bizarre rhinoceros beetle, *Xylotrupes gideon*, whose males have horns projecting from the head and thorax; the larger the specimen, the larger the relative size of the horns.
Stag beetles The family Lucanidae (about 75 species in Australia), which also belongs to the Scarabaeoidea, contains the stag beetles. The males have enlarged mandibles, but these are not so disproportionate as those of the European stag beetle.
Jewel beetles The family Buprestidae (about 800 species in Australia) contains the jewel beetles, which are particularly common in the tropics. The name is appropriate, for these elongated oval beetles are usually brightly coloured. The legless larvae tunnel in wood and tree roots but the adults visit the blossoms of many native plants.
Click beetles The family Elateridae (over 600 species in Australia) contains the click beetles. Some species come indoors at night and dis-turb householders by the clicks they make as

they right themselves after landing on their backs. A small peg beneath the thorax fits into a cavity and when it is suddenly released the body is rapidly flexed, producing the charac-teristic sound. The adult beetles are generally drably coloured and elongated. The larvae of some species are carnivorous, but others, such as the wireworm larvae, feed on the roots of grass, cereals and potatoes.
"Fireflies" The family Lampyridae (16 species in Australia) contains the so-called fireflies. The luminescent organs are found on the abdomens of the adults of both sexes; the eggs, larvae and pupae also have a diffuse lumino-sity. The larvae feed on snails.
Carpet and allied beetles The family Dermestidae (about 90 species in Australia, including several introduced species) contains small, oval beetles, the adults of which often feed on flowers. The larvae, however, feed on dry animal matter with a high protein content and are common in carcases, skins and hides, preserved meats, cheeses and the nests of bees, birds and mammals. Nests often prove to be the foci of domestic infestations. The family includes the carpet beetles, whose larvae, known as 'woolly bears', are frequent pests of carpets, blankets and other woollen goods. Another familiar dermestid is the museum beetle, *Anthrenus museorum*, so called because it often destroys museum collections; it is sometimes used by taxidermists to remove residual flesh and gristle from museum skeletons.
Furniture beetles The family Anobiidae (about 100 species in Australia) consists of reddish or dark brown beetles whose larvae are usually wood-borers. The head of the adult beetle cannot be seen from above as it is hidden by the overhanging thorax. The family contains the now cosmopolitan furniture beetle ('wood worm'), *Anobium punctatum*, which is well established in Australia. Despite common belief and frequent reports the infamous deathwatch beetle does not occur in Australia.
Powder-post beetles The family Lyctidae (five species in Australia) includes the introduced powder-post beetles (*Lyctus* species). The dust produced by their larvae is as fine as talcum powder, whereas that of the wood worm is gritty to the touch.
Ladybirds The family Coccinellidae (about 260 species in Australia) contains the familiar ladybird beetles. These range from tiny to small insects and many are brightly coloured and adorned with spots. Many are carnivorous in the larval and adult stages, feeding on aphids, scale insects, white flies and mites, but a few species skeletonise the leaves of cucurbits and solanaceous plants. Several of the carnivores have been used in BIOLOGICAL CONTROL campaigns.
Flour and allied beetles The family Tenebrionidae (about 1 200 species in Australia) is a diverse group of small to medium-sized brown beetles with a hard cuticle. In the field they are usually found in rather dry habitats but many introduced

species are pests of stored products. The flour beetles (*Tribolium* species) are, for example, cosmopolitan pests of flour in stores and mills, and are also widely used in laboratories as experimental animals.

Longhorn beetles The family Cerambycidae (about 1 040 species in Australia) contains small to large beetles which are easily recognised by their elongated bodies and extremely long antennae; they are commonly known as longhorn beetles. The adults feed on pollen but the larvae are wood-borers; one group of longhorn beetles in Australia attacks figs. Abroad, structural timber is often damaged by the European house-borer, *Hylotrupes bajulus*; this beetle is not yet established in Australia though it is sometimes intercepted by quarantine officials.

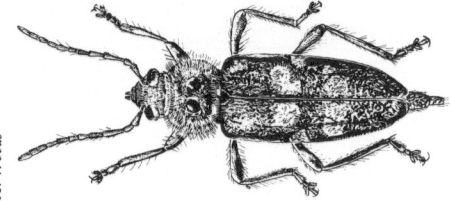

European house borer *Hylotrupes bajulus*

Leaf and flea beetles The family Chrysomelidae (about 2 100 species in Australia) contains the leaf beetles which attack native and introduced plants. Most species have oval, domed bodies, and many are brightly coloured. Some could be confused with ladybirds but are distinguished by their having four tarsal segments (ladybirds have three). The flea beetles are small species with greatly thickened hind femora; they are excellent jumpers. The tortoise beetles, which are largely tropical in distribution, are circular in outline.

Weevils The family Curculionidae (60 000 species; about 4000 in Australia) contains the weevils and is by far the largest family in the Animal Kingdom, even outnumbering the vertebrates. Weevils are easily recognised by the snout, a prolongation of the head which carries the mouthparts right at the tip, and the antennae, which are usually elbowed, on the sides. The body is more or less cylindrical and bears hard elytra which often enclose most of the abdomen. The larvae burrow inside their food and are rarely seen; they are legless and curled. The well-known diamond weevil of Sydney, *Chrysolopus spectabilis*, a species with

Fig longhorn *Dihammus vastator*

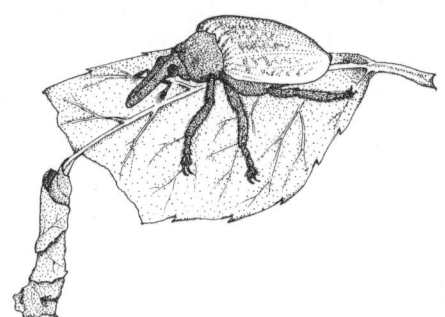

Leaf-rolling weevil; the eggs are laid in the rolled leaf

brilliant green and blue scales, was one of the first insects to be discovered by Sir Joseph BANKS at Botany Bay. Its larvae tunnel in wattles. The family also contains many species of economic importance, such as the *Sitophilus* species (the cosmopolitan granary and rice weevils), which are important pests of stored grain; the larvae develop within the kernels. The flightless, parthenogenetic white-fringed weevil from the Argentine, *Graphognathus leucoloma*, is now a serious agricultural pest in Australia, while the large, dark banana weevil, *Cosmopolites sordidus*, is a serious pest of the fruit in the E States.

beets *see* Chenopodiaceae

Bega NSW (population 4 384 in 1981) A small town in the dairying region of the far S coast, 433km S of Sydney on the Princes Highway, Bega is located where the Bemboka and Brogo Rivers join to form the Bega River, some 16km inland from the coast. Situated on the narrow coastal plain between the E scarp of the SOUTHERN TABLELANDS and the ocean, at an elevation of only 13m above sea level, Bega experiences warm summers and cool winters, with an average annual rainfall of 871mm. Despite its relatively small size, the town is an important commercial and service centre for a rich agricultural and pastoral district where dairying is the major rural activity. It is noted for cheese production; other industries include sawmills, engineering works and brick, tile and furniture production. The name Bega comes from an Aboriginal word meaning either 'a large camping ground' or 'a beautiful place'. The National Trust (NSW) has listed a number of buildings in the town for preservation, including the courthouse, the Red Cross centre, the Historical Society Museum (formerly the police station) and St John's Anglican Church. The adjacent coastal areas are popular holiday resorts. The Kameruka Estate, 35km SW of Bega, a model dairy farm over a century old, is a popular tourist attraction.

Bell, George Henry Frederick (1878-1966) Artist. Born in Kew VIC, Bell studied at the National Gallery School in Paris from 1904 to 1906, had work hung in the Royal Academy in London, and was an official war artist with the 4th Division of the AIF. Returning to Australia in 1920, he became an

art critic on the Melbourne *Sun News Pictorial*, and in 1922 started his own art school. Up to this point, his background had been faultless, and he could easily have become a respected member of 'the establishment'; but unlike his Edwardian colleagues, Bell began to reject academic realism with enthusiasm and missionary fervour.

This tendency was reinforced when he travelled to Europe in 1934-35, where the work of notable recent artists, particularly that of Cézanne, influenced him profoundly. His rejection of his former 'traditional' style and his embracing of another vision had the effect of a bomb-blast on the art circles of VIC. A counter-attack was led by Robert Gordon MENZIES, then Attorney-General and later Prime Minister, who hoped to head off the increasing influence of Bell and his friends and colleagues, William FRATER and Arnold SHORE, by establishing an Academy of Australian Art, complete with a Royal Charter. But by 1943, the attempt to discipline the moderns had failed, in no little part because of Bell's controversial leadership of the forces of experimentation, and the establishment by him of the Contemporary Art Society in 1938. Bell's influence as a teacher and controversialist was enormous, and much more important than his own painting. His pupils, many of considerable talent, included Sir Russell DRYSDALE, Sali HERMAN and David Strachan, all of whom later left the heated discussion of Melbourne for what was then the quieter, less politically minded art world of Sydney. Although a strong critic of the forces of conservatism in art, Bell did not represent the radical wing of the contemporary art movement in Australia. The patrons and champions of that were John Reed and his wife, who encouraged and purchased the work of Sydney NOLAN, John PERCEVAL, Albert TUCKER and Arthur BOYD. But as a symbol for change, Bell was a force to reckon with.

Bell Bay TAS Located on the E shore of the TAMAR RIVER estuary in the central N coastal plains, Bell Bay is 49km NNW of LAUNCESTON along the East Tamar Highway and 6km SE of GEORGE TOWN. The bay has become a major port and industrial centre since the establishment of an aluminium works (now Comalco) in 1949. Other major industrial installations include those of the Vacuum Oil Co. and Temco (a subsidiary of BHP); cool stores to handle frozen goods; and a large woodchip plant. It is also the site of TAS's first thermal electricity plant, which has two oil-fired generating sets each of 120MW—the first came into operation in 1971, and the second in 1974. Berthing facilities for tankers provide for the discharge of oil direct into the storage tanks of the power station.

bellbird *see* thickheads

Bellenden Ker Range QLD A granite range located in the NE of the State between CAIRNS and INNISFAIL, it lies W of the Bruce

Highway about 15km inland from the Coral Sea coast. It stretches on a NNW-SSE alignment, generally parallel to the coastline, for about 40km S from the town of GORDONVALE, and includes QLD's two highest peaks, MOUNT BARTLE FRERE (near the S end; 1 657m in elevation) and Mt Bellenden Ker (in the N; 1 561m). The Musgrave River has its headwaters to the W of the range, then swings around the N limit of the mountains at Gordonvale, and skirts the E side in a narrow valley W of the Malbon Thompson Range, flowing to a swampy mangrove-fringed estuary at Mutchero Inlet. The Bellenden Ker National Park, covering 31 000ha on the E slopes of the range, includes numerous waterfalls (notably Josephine Falls at the S end) and streams flowing through dense upland rainforest.

Ben Lomond TAS A major skiing resort, this mountain lies in the NE region of the State, 61km SE of LAUNCESTON. Though called a mountain, it more closely resembles a plateau as its flat top extends for about 12km between Legges Tor (the highest point, 1 572m elevation) near the NW edge and Stacks Bluff (1 527m) at the S end. The surface is capped by a dark grey igneous rock (dolerite); steep cliffs form the boundaries and numerous waterfalls tumble from the plateau surface over the scarps. During the Great Ice Age the upper areas were glaciated and there is evidence of this in landscape features such as lakes, moraine deposits and armchair-shaped depressions called cirques (the largest is Grant Cirque to the SW). The plateau is included within the Ben Lomond National Park, declared in 1952, covering 16 526ha. The upland parts and the W side of the park are the headwater zones for tributaries of the North and South ESK RIVERS which join to form the TAMAR RIVER.

Benalla VIC (population 8 151 in 1981) Located at the junction of the Hume and Midland Highways, 195km by road NE of Melbourne and 40km SW of WANGARATTA, Benalla is a service centre to a productive rural region growing wheat, flax, barley and potatoes, with sheep and cattle grazing, dairying and pig raising. The city is situated on the Broken River, a tributary of the GOULBURN RIVER, at an elevation of 170m above sea level. The district was first settled in the 1840s; the shire of Benalla, proclaimed in 1869, was created a borough in 1948 and became a city in 1965. It receives a yearly rainfall of 670mm spread throughout the year, but with heavier falls in winter; June is the wettest month (77mm average), February the driest (37mm). As well as being a commercial and business centre, it has a number of industrial enterprises such as clothing manufacture, timber milling and railway workshops. The small town of GLENROWAN, where the bushranger Ned KELLY made his last stand, is located 24km NE. The Kelly Museum in Benalla, which depicts the times and activities of the gang, is an interesting

tourist feature. The town takes its name from an Aboriginal word meaning 'big waterholes'.
Further reading: Carroll, B. *Kelly Country Sketchbook.* Rigby, Adelaide, 1972.

Benaud, Richard 'Richie' (1930-) Cricketer. Benaud was born in Penrith NSW. Modest and unassuming throughout his career, he was one of the finest all-round cricketers ever known in Australia. He started playing first-class cricket in 1948-49 and soon gained a name for being a fine leg-break and googly (off-break bowled with a leg-break action) bowler, and as a batsman with an aggressive driving stroke. He appeared in Test cricket for the first time in the 1951-52 series against the West Indies but it was not until Australia met the West Indies again in 1955 that he began to make his presence felt by scoring a sparkling century in just 78 minutes, going on to score 121. In the latter part of the 1950s, he reached top form as a bowler and in the 1957-58 series against South Africa took 106 wickets for an average of 19.4. Benaud assumed the captaincy of Australia in the 1958-59 series against England, and in the Tests of this series took 31 wickets, for an average of 18.33—more wickets than any other bowler on either side. In 63 Tests (28 as captain) he took 248 wickets and scored 2 201 runs in addition to taking 65 catches. Australia never lost a Test series under the leadership of this dedicated, capable and at times forceful captain, able to inspire his team to optimum performance. Although retiring from competitive cricket in 1964, he remained actively involved in the game as a writer and radio and television commentator.

National Library of Australia

Richie Benaud in action

Bendigo VIC (population 52 739 in 1981) The fourth-largest city in VIC, set in rolling hill country between the fertile valleys of the LODDON and CAMPASPE Rivers, Bendigo is 150km by road and 162km by rail NNE of Melbourne. It is a modern commercial and service centre, and a focus of transport routes, making it the gateway to the rich N pastoral lands of the State: the Calder Highway passes through the city; the Loddon Valley Highway goes N from the city to KERANG; the McIvor Highway leads E beyond the EPPALOCK RESERVOIR; and the Midland Highway goes NE along the Campaspe Valley. At an elevation of 225m, it experiences a mild climate, with warm to hot summer days and cool frosty winters, and an average annual rainfall of 546mm; rain falls throughout the year, the

heaviest falls being in winter and spring (June average 61mm, December-January 33mm).

Once called Sandhurst, but changed officially in 1891 to Bendigo (after a local shepherd, nicknamed 'Bendigo' after the English pugilist Abednego William Thompson), the city grew from a rich goldfield discovered in 1851; the site of the first discovery is marked by a monument near the Golden Square fire-brigade station in the city. It became a municipality in 1855, a borough in 1863 and a city in 1871. Many famous gold mines—including Central Nell Gwynne, Ironbank, Hercules and North and South Deborah—made the city's name as a gold centre. Mining had ceased by 1954, but poppet-heads, scarred land and many historic buildings remain as relics of the gold era. The Central Deborah Mine, just off the Calder Highway, has been restored and is open to visitors.

Today, as well as its business and service functions, the city has a variety of secondary industries: an armaments factory, food and fruit processing, engineering workshops, and clothing and knitwear manufacture. Located SE of Bendigo on the upper Campaspe is Lake Eppalock, from which the city receives part of its water supply by a 26km-long pipeline; it is also a popular recreation area for aquatic sports. There are numerous tourist attractions and many historic buildings in the area: the 'talking trains', which run on a 3km-long track of the now defunct tramway system from the Central Deborah Mine to the Chinese joss house (built in the 1860s) at Emu Point, are a museum in themselves, and the route they follow introduces the visitor to much of the city's historic past. Six kilometres NE of the city is the Bendigo Pottery, founded in 1857 by a Scottish potter who migrated to Australia in search of gold. Over 30 buildings and sites in the city have been listed for preservation by the National Trust (VIC); among these are several hotels, banks, churches and homes, as well as such unique features as the Chinese funeral oven and the hitching posts at the city cemetery.

Benjamin, Arthur Leslie (1893-1960) Composer. Benjamin was born in Sydney and after studying at the Royal College of Music, London, he returned to Australia and from 1919 to 1921 was Professor of Pianoforte at the Conservatorium of Music, Sydney. He then went back to the Royal College of Music where he taught intermittently between 1925 and 1953. One of his most outstanding students there was the young Benjamin Britten. By virtue of his temperament and his eclecticism, Arthur Benjamin was best equipped to contribute to music through opera composition, and his operas include *The Devil Take Her* (1931), *Prima Donna* (1933), *A Tale of Two Cities* (1951) and *Tartuffe* (1959). He was one of the pioneers of film music in Britain, and also wrote *Mañana* (1956), the first opera for British television. Other works include *Pastoral Fantasia, Jamaican Rumba, Symphony No. 1* and a concerto for harmonica and orchestra.

Bennelong (?-1813) Bennelong was an Aboriginal captured, with a fellow-tribesman named Colbee, on Governor PHILLIP's orders in November 1789. Phillip, wishing to see the effect of European civilisation on Aborigines, and hoping to use the two captives as a means of spreading civilisation to others, had them brought to Government House in Sydney. Colbee soon escaped, but Bennelong lived there for about a year, and later lived nearby in a hut which had been built for him at the place which became known as Bennelong Point (site of the modern SYDNEY OPERA HOUSE). When Phillip left NSW in December 1792, Bennelong and an Aboriginal youth named Yemmerrawannie sailed with him. The latter died in England, but Bennelong survived, was presented to King George III, and returned to the colony with Governor HUNTER in 1795. Although he declared himself ready to spread peace and enlightenment among his people, he proved quite unequal to the task, becoming a drunkard and losing the respect of both the settlers and the Aborigines, and was eventually killed in the course of a tribal fight.

Bennelong

Bennett, Henry Gordon (1887-1962) Soldier. Born and educated in Melbourne, he served during World War I at Gallipoli and on the Western Front, rose to the rank of Brigadier-General, and was decorated with the DSO and Montenegrin Order of Danilo. During the inter-war years he engaged in business and also commanded the 2nd Division in the Australian Military Forces. In 1941-42, as a Lieutenant-General, he commanded the 8th Division in Malaya. Nearly the whole of this Division became prisoners of war after the fall of Singapore, but Bennett managed to escape and return to Australia. He argued that it was important for him to pass on the knowledge he had gained in fighting against the Japanese. However his escape made him a controversial figure, and he did not receive

another combat command. He resigned from the army in 1944, and in the same year published *Why Singapore Fell*. He was created CMG in 1915 and CB in 1916.

Bent, Andrew (1790-1851) Pioneer printer and publisher. Born in London, Bent was apprenticed as a printer and was sentenced to death in 1810 for burglary, the sentence being commuted to transportation for life. In 1812 he arrived in Hobart, where he was employed by George Clark, the government printer, and when the latter was dismissed, he succeeded him in that post. In 1816 he began publishing the *Hobart Town Gazette* (later the *Hobart Town Gazette and Van Diemen's Land Advertiser*), and in 1818 he printed the first book to be published in TAS, a life of Michael HOWE, the bushranger. In 1825 criticisms of Lieutenant-Governor ARTHUR's administration, made in editorials and a series of letters by 'A Colonist', were used as the basis of a successful libel action against him, and he was sentenced to a term of imprisonment. He later began publication of the *Colonial Times*, but after the passing of an Act requiring newspapers to be licensed, he declined to apply for a licence for it, though he kept the *Colonial Times* in circulation for some time longer by reducing it to advertisements. After the British government had disallowed the Licensing Act, he published *Bent's News and Tasmanian Threepenny Register*. In 1838 he moved to Sydney, but suffered misfortune in business and died in poverty in the Sydney Benevolent Asylum. He is remembered as a printer of considerable talent, as well as a champion of freedom of the Press.
Further reading: Woodberry, J. *Andrew Bent and the Freedom of the Press in Van Diemen's Land*. Fuller's Bookshop, Hobart, 1972.

Bent, Ellis (1783-1815) Judge-Advocate of NSW. In 1809, having practised as a barrister for four years in England, he accepted the position of Judge-Advocate, being the first qualified barrister to come to NSW. He travelled to the colony with Governor MACQUARIE, with whom he had cordial relations until 1813, when he became involved in bitter quarrels with Macquarie regarding his status and rights. With Macquarie's support, he had proposed reforms in the colony's legal system, these including the setting up of a Supreme Court and the introduction of trial by jury. The latter suggestion was not accepted, but in 1814 a new charter of justice, which provided for a Supreme Court, was brought into operation. He had hoped to be made Judge of this court, but the position was given to his brother Jeffrey Hart BENT. He continued to criticise Macquarie fiercely, and supported his brother in his disputes with the Governor. Macquarie's complaints about Ellis Bent's conduct finally led the Colonial Office to decide that his appointment should be terminated, but he died before the letter of

Paddle wheeler on the Murray River at Berri

dismissal reached Sydney.
Further reading: Currey, C.H. *The Brothers Bent*. Sydney University Press, Sydney, 1968.

Bent, Jeffrey Hart (1780-1852) First judge of the NSW Supreme Court. After practising as a barrister in England for eight years, he came to NSW in 1814 as Judge of the Supreme Court set up under the revised charter of justice, being authorised to hear criminal cases and also civil cases where the amount at issue was in excess of £50. However, as the result of disputes with Governor MACQUARIE, he heard no cases during his three years in the colony. Ex-convict attorneys had in the past been allowed to practise in the courts, and the Governor wanted this arrangement to apply also to the Supreme Court. He was supported in this stand by the two magistrates, Riley and Broughton, whom he appointed to sit with Bent, but was bitterly opposed by Bent, who wanted to delay the court's opening until the arrival of two free attorneys who had been persuaded to come to the colony by the Colonial Office. Macquarie insisted on his opening the court, but quarrels on the Bench between Bent and the two magistrates led to its being closed again pending appeal to the Colonial Office. In the interim, he kept up a stream of complaints against the Governor regarding alleged insults and lack of respect. Notice of his recall arrived in April 1816, but he took the view that his commission was not actually terminated until the arrival of his successor. He remained therefore to plague Macquarie until May 1817, and even after reaching England kept up a campaign of complaints and defamation against him. He subsequently filled positions as Chief Justice in Grenada, St Lucia and British Guiana. In Guiana he was involved in a quarrel with the Governor which was similar in some ways to that with Macquarie. This resulted in his suspension for three years, but his case was finally upheld by the Privy Council.
Further reading: see under Bent, Ellis.

Bergner, Vladimir Jossif 'Josl' (1920-) Artist. Born in Vienna, Bergner graduated as a teacher of traditional Hebrew art in Warsaw, and at 17 came to Australia to avoid the holocaust. His work at this time shows his anger at Nazi policies in particular, and at social injustice in general. His works, moody and dark in tone, had a great influence in Melbourne in the 1940s, where the growing social concern of many young artists was increasingly portrayed in an Expressionist manner. His series on the Warsaw ghetto, with their implied criticism of Russian inactivity, resulted in his expulsion from the Communist Party and, ironically, in his being branded a fascist. He left Australia for Israel in 1947.

Berri SA (population 3 419 in 1981) A town and irrigation settlement on the MURRAY RIVER, downstream from RENMARK, it is located 233km by road and 362km by rail NE of Adelaide. At an elevation of 31m above sea level, it experiences a mild semi-arid climate, with a low annual rainfall of 269mm, evenly spread throughout the year. It is the service centre for a productive rural area of vineyards and orchards, irrigated with water pumped from the Murray. The town was originally known as Berri Berri, from the Aboriginal name for a bush which grows in the region.

Berry, Sir Graham (1822-1904) Radical politician, advocate of protection, and Premier of VIC. Born in London, he emigrated to VIC in 1852, set up as a storekeeper and wine-and-spirit merchant in South Yarra, and in 1854 was on one of the juries that acquitted miners captured at the EUREKA STOCKADE. He was elected to the Legislative Assembly in 1860 and by the mid-1870s was acknowledged as the leader of radical forces in Parliament. He was also the leading parliamentary advocate of protection, and in 1871, as Treasurer in Charles Gavan DUFFY's Ministry, introduced the first strongly protectionist tariff. He was Premier for three terms, totalling about four years, and in 1877 was involved in a bitter dispute between the Legislative Assembly and the Legislative Council. In the hope of getting through the Council a Bill providing for the payment of Members of Parliament, he 'tacked' it on to an Appropriation Bill. When the Council rejected this, he retaliated by persuading the Governor, Sir George Ferguson BOWEN, to dismiss over 200 of the top public servants, on the grounds that the government did not have the funds to continue paying their salaries. The day on which this was done, 9 January 1878, became known as 'BLACK WEDNESDAY'. The crisis was solved by a compromise, the Council agreeing to the payment of Members of Parliament until 1880. Its chief effects were to enable Berry to get rid of many of his political opponents in the higher ranks of the public service (many of those dismissed never being re-appointed), and to strengthen the demand for reform of the Upper House. In 1881 the Council's membership was increased, its electoral term shortened and the voting qualifications lowered. Berry left Parliament in 1886 to take up the position of Agent-General for VIC in London. He was again a member of the Legislative Assembly from 1892 to 1897, but was not as prominent as he had been previously.

Further reading: Turner, H.G. *A History of the Colony of Victoria.* (vol 2) Longmans Green, London, 1904; Deakin, A. *The Crisis in Victorian Politics, 1879-1881.* Melbourne University Press, Melbourne, 1957.

bettongs *see* kangaroos, etc.

BHP *see* Broken Hill Proprietary Company Limited

Bigge, John Thomas (1780-1843) King's Commissioner. He was Chief Justice of Trinidad when in 1819 Lord Bathurst, the Colonial Secretary, appointed him as Commissioner to enquire into conditions in the colony of NSW. He was also empowered to recommend to Governor MACQUARIE any immediate changes in the administration of the colony which he thought desirable, and the latter was instructed to adopt them promptly, or, in the event of his taking the 'weighty responsibility' of not doing so, to report immediately on his reasons. The Governor, against whom there had been complaints of autocratic behaviour, resented the sending of Bigge, and quarrelled repeatedly with him. The Commissioner, on his side, criticised Macquarie's public works programme and his policy towards emancipists (ex-convicts), and spent a great deal of his time in the company of those critical of the Governor, such as John MACARTHUR. He left early in 1821 and later in the year Macquarie resigned, obviously feeling that he had been unfairly criticised. Bigge issued three reports: *Report of the Commissioner of Enquiry into the State of the Colony of New South Wales* (1822), *On the Judicial Establishments of New South Wales and Van Diemen's Land* (1823); and *On the State of Agriculture and Trade in the Colony of New South Wales* (1823). He saw the future of the colony as lying mainly with men of capital, who would make it self-supporting by their success in growing wool. Such people should be encouraged by being given land and assigned convict labour, but free settlers without capital, and convicts on the expiry of their sentences, should not be given free land grants. Convicts should still be sent to the colony, he advocated, but their treatment should be more consistent, so as to make transportation a more effective deterrent. While he did not specifically recommend the setting up of a Legislative Council to assist the Governor, nevertheless his comments on the situation in NSW were a factor in causing the British government to do so in 1823.
Further reading: Ritchie, J.D. *Punishment and Profit.* Heinemann, Melbourne, 1970.

bilby *see* bandicoots

billabong This uniquely Australian word is used to describe a river feature where a meander loop has become cut off from the main stream, thus forming a curved lagoon or lake which may be reconnected to the stream in flood times. The word may not always be used in this strict sense and was not originally

used for this particular feature of rivers. In other countries, this feature is termed an ox-bow lake or a mort lake. The name billabong comes from two Aboriginal words, *billa*, meaning 'a pool or stretch of water', and *bong*, meaning 'dead'. The word has been given permanence and prominence in Australian language through the song WALTZING MATILDA.

billiards and snooker Australia has produced many outstanding billiards players, the most notable being Walter LINDRUM who dominated the sport during his lifetime. In 1932, before the baulk line rules was introduced, he made a record break of 4 137.

The first billiards saloon in Australia was established by Thomas Spencer in 1851 but because all the equipment for the game had to be imported, the game did not start to flourish until Henry Upton Alcock (who had learnt to make billiard tables in London) opened a small factory in Melbourne in 1853. As the equipment became more readily available, interest in the game became more widespread. Alcock, to increase the sale of his locally manufactured tables, promoted the game by arranging tours by top-class English players, such as John Roberts. During his visit in 1864 Roberts played against Frederick W. Lindrum, who had come to Australia in 1838 as a migrant. To everyone's surprise, Lindrum won the game; the Lindrum family went on to dominate the sport over four generations. A notable amateur billiards players was Robert Marshall of WA, the foremost player in national and international events from 1936 to 1969.

Snooker was developed in India in 1875 by members of the British Army and was introduced into Australia by Army personnel. The then manager of the billiard room at the Australia Hotel in Sydney, Frank Smith, did much to increase the popularity of the game and his son, Frank Smith, became the leading

Courtesy of A.I.S. Canberra

Japanese billiards champion with Eddie Charlton in Melbourne exponent of the game until the 1930s. During the 1930s in Australia, and throughout the world from 1946 until the mid-1950s, Horace Lindrum, nephew of Walter Lindrum, dominated the game, and was acknowledged as the greatest snooker player of all time. In 1983 the position of top snooker player in Australia was held by Eddie CHARLTON, who has won a number of State, Australian and international titles. The outstanding talent Charlton brought to the snooker table led to a revival of interest in the game in Australia where it had been experiencing a 20-year slump.

Biloela QLD (population 4 643 in 1981) The principal town of the CALLIDE VALLEY, Biloela is located at the junction of the Dawson and Burnett Highways, 592km NNW of Brisbane, 145km SSW of ROCKHAMPTON and 122km SW of GLADSTONE. The town's name comes from an Aboriginal word for 'white cockatoo'. It is a business and service centre for a productive rural hinterland growing cotton, safflower, grain and lucerne. Grazing is also important in the area and biloela buffel grass, a specially developed strain, has proved successful as fodder for beef cattle, sheep and dairy herds. At an elevation of 174m above sea level the town has an average annual rainfall of 699mm; though all months receive some rain, there is marked concentration in the summer, and a drier period during autumn and winter. ARTESIAN WATER, as well as supplies from the Callide Dam, is used to irrigate crops and pastures during this dry season and in periods of drought. Open-cut coal mines in the Callide Valley provide fuel for power generation from the Calcap power station, which supplies electricity to the district and to the Rockhampton and BLACKWATER areas. Coal is also railed to Gladstone for export overseas. There is a cotton gin and a meatworks in the town.

bindi-eye This daisy-like flower, *Calotis cuneiflora* (family COMPOSITAE), is found in dry areas of central and E Australia. The flowers are either white or blue and yellow, and the fruit is a prickly burr.

biological classification With the exception of viruses, all living organisms are placed in one or other of five kingdoms: Monera (bacteria and blue-green algae); Protista (many single-celled organisms and their close relatives, such as advanced algae); Fungi; Plantae (the higher plants, from mosses to flowering plants); and Animalia. Each kingdom is subdivided, on a hierarchical system, as follows: phyla (singular, phylum) or divisions (the latter being used by botanists); classes; orders; families; genera (singular, genus); and species (*see* Figure 1). The levels or taxa (singular, taxon) listed are the obligatory ones but others, such as sub-phylum, are used for convenience to deal with very large groups. As far as possible, modern classifications indicate evolutionary relation-ships.

The binomial or scientific name of an organism consists of two parts: the name of the genus and the name of the species within the genus. The HOUSE FLY, for example, is the species *domestica* in the genus *Musca,* and its scientific name is therefore *Musca domestica*; the genus *Musca* also contains certain closely related flies, such as the bushfly, *Musca vetustissima.* The complete classification of the house fly, with obligatory levels, is thus: kingdom Animalia, phylum Arthropoda, class Insecta, order Diptera, family Muscidae, genus *Musca*, species *domestica*. The scientific names of animals and plants, unlike their common names, are internationally recognised, and the rules of naming and classification are governed by strictly kept, internationally agreed regulations. As knowledge increases and evolutionary histories are unravelled classifications tend to change. For example, a species may be shifted to a new genus, or an order may be split into two or more new orders.

Some terms used to describe distributions A native or indigenous species is one that occurs in a particular area, and has evolved or arrived there without man's help. An endemic species is one that is at present restricted to a particular region as a native species. Thus the LYREBIRDS are endemic to Australia. The term is also applied to diseases

but in a different sense: an endemic disease is one that persists in a particular region but is not, at the time in question, in an epidemic phase. An introduced species is one that has been brought by man to an area, accidentally or intentionally, and has become established. Some introduced species are feral: that is, they are descendants of domesticated animals but now live and reproduce in the wild without man's control (*see* ANIMALS, INTRODUCED). Cosmopolitan is a term used loosely to describe a widely distributed species, usually found on all continents, with the probable exception of Antarctica. For example, the house mouse is now described as a cosmopolitan species, although it is not yet found on every land mass in the world.

biological control This term refers to various PEST CONTROL methods that do not involve the use of insecticides, weedkillers and so on (chemical control). It has been defined as the introduction of living material, other than resistant varieties of plants and animals, into the pest's environment in order to destroy the pest, or to lessen the damage that it causes. Classical biological control is the introduction of the natural enemies of the pest (parasites, pathogens and predators). These may be either 'inoculated' into the environment and allowed to multiply, year after year, at the pest's expense, or released in large numbers or quantities (the inundation technique) so that they act as living insecticides. In the second case, the persistence of the agent in the years that follow is regarded as a bonus rather than as a goal. Generally, classical biological control is most effective when used against introduced pests, which are often successful mainly because they have left behind their natural enemies in their country of origin. In Australia nearly all INSECTS and MITES which are serious pests, and most of the WEEDS, are introduced species.

The concept of biological control goes back to antiquity but the first successful, large-scale application concerned an Australian insect introduced accidentally into California on young wattle trees. This insect, the cottony-cushion scale, *Icerya purchasi*, attacks native shrubs and some introduced plants in Australia but, because of native natural enemies, is rarely a pest. In California, however, it turned to *Citrus* and nearly ruined the Californian industry. It was quickly controlled by the descendants of a few hundred Australian lady-bird BEETLES, *Rodolia cardinalis*, and an Australian parasitic fly.

In the 1920s, Australia was the scene of a most spectacular case of biological control—the control of the PRICKLY PEAR and pest pear cacti by the South American moth *Cactoblastis cactorum*. In QLD and NSW, 24 million hectares were infested by prickly and pest pear cacti and by other *Opuntia* species, and the area was increasing by about 400 000ha annually, making the land useless and uneconomical to clear, mechanically or chemically. Biologists were sent before and just after

Figure 1

HIERARCHICAL CLASSIFICATION OF THE ANIMAL KINGDOM

KINGDOM		Animalia	
PHYLA	Echinodermata	Arthropoda	Chordata
CLASSES	Arachnida	Insecta	Crustacea etc.
ORDERS	Coleoptera (beetles)	Diptera	Lepidoptera etc.
FAMILIES	Culcidae (mosquitoes)	Muscidae	Calliphoridae etc. (blowflies)
GENERA	*Stomoxys*	*Musca*	*Fannia* etc.
SPECIES	*sorbens*	*domestica*	*vetustissima* etc.

World War I to the Americas (all cacti except one are native to the Americas) and to other countries where cacti had become a problem. The various expeditions sent back 52 different kinds of insects and one mite for further study; after tests to ensure that they would not attack any useful plants, several of these were released. Four moth species, three beetles, two heteropteran BUGS and eight scale insects (of the cochineal group) became established for at least a few years but the effects of most of them were eclipsed by those of *C. cactorum* which was released in 1926. Millions of the eggs, which were conveniently laid in sticks on the pads of the cacti, were distributed in NSW and QLD in the following year or two and within a few years pest pear and prickly pear were no longer important pests in QLD, although they persisted in the cooler parts of NSW where the moth did not flourish as well as in QLD.

Several other weeds have been at least partly controlled in this way in Australia. St John's wort, *Hypericum perforatum*, a troublesome perennial which contains a poison that makes the skin of livestock sensitive to sunlight, is attacked by two leaf beetles which have reduced the infestations both here and in the USA. The most important weed affecting wheat, skeleton weed, *Chondrilla juncea* (family COMPOSITAE), is under attack from rust (a specific fungal disease), a gall midge and a gall mite. Unfortunately, the rust attacks only one of the three forms of the weed occurring in Australia; however, this is by far the most important variety and the biological control of the weed has been the most spectacular success since the prickly pear campaign. Research is under way on the biological control of, among other weeds, WATER HYACINTH, the toxic ragwort, and Paterson's Curse. The proposed release of natural enemies of Paterson's curse has been held up by the courts because some graziers and many bee-keepers regard it not as a weed but as an invaluable plant; indeed, in some areas it is called Salvation Jane.

In Australia several insects have been controlled, completely or partially, by introduced parasitic or predatory insects. One example is the South American green vegetable bug, *Nezara viridula*.

Insect diseases, especially FUNGI and viruses, are also promising control agents. In America, the spotted alfalfa aphid, *Therioaphis maculata*, has been controlled in various ways, including the use of a fungal disease, and it is possible that this may be used in Australia now that these APHIDS have become established here. A virus disease is now attacking the potato tuber moth, *Phthorimaea operculella*, which is a serious pest of the tubers both in the ground and in store. Allied to these methods is the use of a dead, crystalline material obtained from the microbe, *Bacillus thuringiensis*, for the control of the caterpillars of BUTTERFLIES AND MOTHS; this is now available commercially.

Vertebrates are sometimes used as control agents. The Indian myna (*see* STARLINGS), and the cane toad (*see* AMPHIBIANS) were originally introduced to kill pests, and cats were released in the bush to kill RABBITS. These are examples of biological control that turned sour. An interesting Australian example of biological control is the use of introduced scarab beetles to dispose of the droppings of cattle.

Biological control is an excellent method, when it works. There are few, if any, bad side effects except when an obviously unsuitable agent, such as the cane toad, is introduced. It does, however, need a large amount of research and exploration in order to set it in motion and therefore must be carried out at a national or State level. Once it is started it is self-perpetuating and is thus, in the long run, far cheaper than chemical control with its recurrent costs. However, it is difficult to find out how often biological control is successful for failures are not always reported. Of those that can be counted as successful in the world, about a third were completely successful in the sense that no further measures needed to be taken to control the pest.

There is no doubt about the economic success of the prickly pear and skeleton weed campaigns but recent studies have shown that the return on some biological control research in Australia has not been as great as was popularly supposed. Marsden and his colleagues (*see below*) studied several projects carried out by the COMMONWEALTH SCIENTIFIC AND INDUSTRIAL RESEARCH ORGANIZATION (CSIRO) Division of Entomology, and expressed their findings in terms of benefit/cost ratios at various discount rates. At a five per cent discount rate (the most favourable one quoted) the benefit/cost ratios for the three most successful projects were: 751.74 for blowfly control with the organophosphate insecticide diazinon; 192.16 for skeleton weed control; and 58.83 for orchard mite control. The first was concerned with the more efficient use of the insecticide rather than with biological control, and the last with the integration of chemical and biological control methods. At the other extreme, however, is the work on the biological control of subterranean clover stunt virus (ratio, 0.22) and fruit fly control (1.20). The work on the virus is probably not worth pursuing but some of the others listed by Marsden and his colleagues may produce favourable ratios (for example, the work on scarab beetles attacking trees in some rural districts where only grazing management has been taken into account so far, and where the as yet untried control of the beetles by pathogens may produce good results).

The sterile male technique and genetic control are allied to biological control. They are also known as autocidal techniques because the pest species is used to control itself. In the sterile male technique, millions of the males are made sterile by irradiation or by chemicals and released to compete with the wild males for mates. Though sterile, the released males must be otherwise sexually competitive with the wild males which they must outnumber. Most of the matings are then abortive, and the wild population falls. Yet more males are released as the population falls till eventually, with luck, it is eradicated. This method has been very successful with the screwworm fly, an ectoparasite of cattle, in southern USA. It has been considered for the control of the sheep BLOWFLIES in Australia but because of their wide distribution it would be far too expensive.

Genetic control involves changing the genetic constitution of the pest population in such a way that its numbers are reduced. At first sight this would seem to be an impossible task as it is flying in the face of natural selection but it might be possible to introduce, for example, a gene that is harmful only at high temperatures. This might be pushed into the population by continual releases during the cool season. The CSIRO is at present investigating the use of chromosomal translocations for the control of sheep blowflies in Australia. A chromosomal translocation is the interchange of segments between two chromosomes. In flies that are homozygous for the translocation, sperm and egg production are normal but in flies that are heterozygous there are difficulties in the production of the sex cells and their fertility is greatly reduced. Nevertheless, some of the cells carrying translocated chromosomes are passed on to the next generation. Homozygous flies are being bred in the laboratory and will be released to mate with wild type males and females in the field. Calculations show that this technique, allied with other methods, could be used to control blowflies economically.

Other autocidal methods include the use of pheromones, chemicals produced by one individual which influence the behaviour or physiology of its fellows. Some female moths, for example, release a chemical which induces males to seek them out for mating. It may be possible to use these, or chemical analogues, to attract the males to traps where they can be killed or made sterile, or, alternatively, if the chemicals are cheap enough they can be used to saturate the environment so that the males no longer respond to the females' attractions. So far, however, pheromones have been used mainly for monitoring an area for the presence of the pests.

There are several other useful or potentially useful methods of autocidal control. Descriptions of these will be found in the references below.

see also myxomatosis

Further reading: Desbach, P. *Biological Control by Natural Enemies*. Cambridge University Press, Cambridge, 1974; Woods, A. *Pest Control: A Survey*. McGraw-Hill, UK, 1974; Marsden, J.S., Martin, G.E., Parham, D.J., Ridsill Smith, T.J. & Johnston, B.G. *Returns on Australian Agricultural Research*. Industries Assistance Commission/CSIRO Division of Entomology, Australian Govt Publishing Service, Canberra, 1980.

birds These feathered, warm-blooded, egg-laying VERTEBRATES belong to the class Aves. There are between 8000 and 9000 species of birds in the world, almost 750 of which are found in Australia and her adjacent waters. About 368 Australian species are endemic and 125 are non-breeding visitors, mainly WADERS and SEA BIRDS which breed in the N hemisphere. There are about 20 established introduced species.

About 83 families are represented in Australia (the number depends upon the opinion of the classifier; here, mainly Macdonald's classification is followed—*see below*). The following families are endemic: Dromaiidae* (the EMU), Menuridae* (LYREBIRDS), Atrichornithidae* (SCRUB-BIRDS) and Ephthianuridae* (Australian CHATS). Several other families are typically Australian/New Guinean, because all or most of their species occur in the region. The first category includes the families Paradisaeidae (BIRDS OF PARADISE), Ptilonorhynchidae (BOWERBIRDS) and Cracticidae (BUTCHERBIRDS, MAGPIES AND CURRAWONGS); the second includes the families Meliphagidae (HONEYEATERS) and Maluridae (FAIRY-WRENS, EMUWRENS AND GRASS-WRENS). Surprisingly, some families are absent as indigenous species, the most notable examples being the woodpeckers (Picidae), the true finches (Fringillidae) and the flamingoes (Phoenicopleridae), though the last are known as fossils.

Birds are found in almost every kind of habitat in every part of Australia. Many are well adapted to arid environments and most of these are nomadic, moving to food and water supplies as necessary. Many birds of the arid and semi-arid regions breed only after rain has fallen. A surprisingly large proportion of Australian birds show complex social behaviour in which groups of birds, such as kookaburras (*see* KINGFISHERS), raise their young communally. Similarly, several Australian birds (bowerbirds; lyrebirds) have special 'arenas' on which the males display during courtship. The MOUND BIRDS are well represented by three species in Australia; these are birds which use some source of heat other than body-heat to incubate their eggs. Regular migratory movements are not as marked a feature of the Australian birds (other than waders) as they are of those in North America and Europe; most breed in Australia, though some migrate during the non-breeding season to, for example, New Guinea or the Philippines.

Until recently, it was believed that Australia had been colonised from South-East Asia, some species having arrived so late in the evolutionary time scale (that is, during the later Holocene epoch) that they are more or less identical to their Old World relatives; at the other extreme, it was said of those birds that have been in Australia a long time and have evolved greatly, that their 'affinities are shrouded in obscurity' (for example, emus, FROGMOUTHS, some PARROT groups, scrub-birds, bowerbirds and butcherbirds). In the light of recent acceptance of the theory of CONTINENTAL DRIFT and of the former existence of the GONDWANALAND land mass, theories concerning the origin and structure of the Australian bird fauna have changed. More attractive now is the theory put forward by Dr D.L. Serventy (*see* Macdonald *below*) that several groups entered from the S—for example, the emu, the CASSOWARY, and possibly the pied goose, the mound birds, lyrebirds, scrub-birds, parrots and some PASSERINE BIRDS.

In this encyclopedia, the various groups of birds are considered mainly in families, the most familiar common names being used as headings. In the various articles on birds, details are given on the structure of nests. It must be stressed, however, that nests containing eggs must not be approached as this may make the hen desert her brood.

The distribution of many species in Australia is imperfectly known, and the ranges given in this encyclopedia should be taken as rough guides only. The COMMONWEALTH SCIENTIFIC AND INDUSTRIAL RESEARCH ORGANIZATION (CSIRO), working with a small army of professional and amateur ornithologists, recently completed an Australia-wide survey of all species, using computer-retrieval methods, and planned to begin publishing the results in 1983. This will be the most comprehensive survey of its kind for any continent or large land mass.

Further reading: There are now many books on Australian birds. The texts followed mainly in this publication are: Slater, P. *A Field Guide to Australian Birds: Non-Passerines.* Rigby, Adelaide, 1970 and *A Field Guide to Australian Birds: Passerines.* Rigby, Adelaide, 1974; Macdonald, J.D. *Birds of Australia.* A.H. & A.W. Reed, Sydney, 1973 and *Understanding Australian Birds.* (2nd edn) A.H. & A.W. Reed, Sydney, 1982; Frith, H.J. (ed) *The Reader's Digest Book of Australian Birds.* (revd edn) Reader's Digest Services Pty Ltd, Surry Hills, 1979.

birds, introduced *see* animals, introduced

birds of paradise These BIRDS are closely allied to BOWERBIRDS and belong to the family Paradisaeidae, which contains 43 species of PASSERINE BIRDS restricted to Australia and New Guinea. The four Australian species—the manucode and three species of riflebirds—live in rainforest and are highly decorative, though their colouring is subdued compared with the many-plumed species of New Guinea. Most birds of paradise perform elaborate courtship displays on the bare, horizontal branches of trees.

The manucode, *Phonygammus keraudrenii* (30cm long), an iridescent black bird with red eyes, may be distinguished from the glossy STARLINGS and the DRONGO by its broad, rounded tail. The iridescence is green, and there are long, lance-like feathers on the neck.

Species, genus or family is endemic to Australia (see Preface)

It is a solitary bird which frequents fruit and berry trees in N CAPE YORK, feeding on fruit and insects. The call is a trumpet-like squawk. The open, shallow nests of vine-tendrils and plant-stems are usually placed high in a tree, often close to the nests of black BUTCHER BIRDS.

The riflebirds have long, down-curved bills. The males are black, with iridescent purplish-green on the throat and head, while the females are browner. The magnificent riflebird, *Ptiloris magnificus* (30cm), also known as the Prince Albert riflebird, is found at the tip of Cape York. Like other riflebirds, it feeds on insects and fruit. The open, saucer-shaped nests of leaves and vine-tendrils are built in tangled foliage. The Victoria riflebird, *P. victoriae** (24cm), is found in north-eastern QLD. The eggs are laid in saucer-shaped nests of dead leaves and rootlets, sometimes decorated with snakeskin. Further S, in south-eastern QLD and north-eastern NSW, is the paradise riflebird, *P. paradiseus** (28cm), a rarer species. The nest is shallow and bowl-shaped, made of leaves and vine-tendrils and often decorated around the rim with snakeskin; it is placed at the top of tall, bushy trees.

birds of prey These BIRDS belong to the order Falconiformes which contains diurnal birds of prey, such as eagles and hawks, but excludes nocturnal predators, such as OWLS. They are powerful birds with strong claws and hooked bills; the plumage is generally brown and, unusually for birds, the females are mostly larger than the males.

Three families are represented in Australia. The Accipitridae consists of eagles, kites, buzzards and hawks, all of which soar and glide while watching for prey; their wings are usually broad and are either rounded at the tips or have feathers spread out like fingers. The Falconidae contains the falcons; they have narrow, pointed, swept-back wings, and make short but vigorous and swift flights in pursuit of prey. The only species in the family Pandionidae is the osprey; it has broad, rounded wings, and dives into the water from a great height to catch fish.

Three species of eagles are found in Australia. The white-breasted sea-eagle, *Haliaeetus leucogaster* (75cm to 1m long; wingspan 2m to 2.3m), a close relative of the American bald eagle, is a grey and white species whose legs are bare of feathers, unlike those of true eagles. It ranges from India to

Osprey *Pandion haliaetus*

W Polynesia, and is found throughout the coastal areas of Australia, and also along some of the larger inland rivers, feeding on fish and most animals, living or dead. These birds build large nests of sticks in tall trees or on projecting rock ledges, and may use them for several years in succession.

The wedge-tailed eagle, *Aquila audax* (1m to 1.2m long; wingspan about 2.5m), is brown when young and almost completely black when mature; it may be recognised in flight by the upswept 'fingered' wings and the long wedge-shaped tail. Found throughout Australia in timbered country and plains, it is the fourth-largest eagle in the world. The speed of its flight in pursuit of its prey is astounding, and it seldom misses its intended victim. The nests, sometimes over 2m in diameter, are composed of sticks lined with bark and leaves, and are usually placed in a good lookout position in a large tree.

Wedge-tailed eagles make an elaborate and spectacular courtship flight. Usually two eggs are laid and both hatch, but only one chick survives. The young birds wander for two or three years before reaching maturity, finding a mate and establishing a territory, which can vary in size from about 1000ha to 3000ha. Prey is caught either by a plummeting dive or by pursuit. The diet has changed since European settlement, rabbits now forming the greatest part. Wallabies, and sometimes even fully grown red kangaroos and euros, are also important, as are reptiles, corvid birds, foxes, feral cats and possums. Several authorities consider that predation on lambs is not of economic importance as many of the lambs eaten are sickly or dead when taken.

The little eagle, *Hieraaetus morphnoides* (length 53cm; wingspan 1.5m), which preys heavily on immature rabbits, is a solitary forest and woodland bird found throughout mainland Australia. It is either mainly dark brown or has a buff head and neck, a dark brown back and a white breast and belly. The legs are feathered, and the crest on the head is distinctive when raised. The bluish-white eggs, spotted with brown, are laid in large nests of sticks placed high up in trees or in the abandoned nests of other birds, such as CROWS.

There are several species of kites in Australia. These medium-sized birds have weak, unfeathered legs and long, broad wings with prominent fingering. They have a soaring or hovering flight, and many of them are scavengers. A widespread species in Australia and the Old World is the black kite, *Milvus migrans* (length 56cm; forked tail 28cm). It is a dark brown species which holds its wings flat in flight. These birds are often seen near garbage tips, meatworks and homesteads scavenging for food, but they also eat small mammals, reptiles and grasshoppers. Their small, flat nests of sticks, lined with soft materials such as fur, are placed in the high branches of trees and are used for several successive years; the eggs are white, spotted and streaked with brown.

A rarer though fairly widespread species is the square-tailed kite, *Lophoictinia* * *isura* (51cm to 56cm), a solitary predator with brownish-black and cinnamon plumage and a white face. It hawks for insects round the tree canopy or over clearings, and builds large nests of sticks high in the horizontal forks or branches of the tree canopy.

The black-shouldered kite, *Elanus notatus* * (35cm), is a fairly common, mainly coastal species found on the mainland. It is grey and white with black shoulders, and is most often seen sitting on poles or dead trees or hovering with dangling legs over farmlands. This nomadic bird feeds on mice, lizards and insects, and lays its eggs in platform-shaped nests of sticks. It is very similar to the rarer letter-winged kite, *E. scriptus* * (35cm), though the latter may be distinguished by the black streaks on the underwing which together form a broken 'W'. Found mainly in open and lightly timbered inland areas, these birds hunt their prey, mainly rats, at night or in the early morning. The eggs are laid in platform-shaped nests composed of thin sticks and lined with fur.

The whistling kite, *Haliastur sphenurus* (up to 58cm), is a widespread tree living species with a light-coloured head, a greyish-brown body and a long, narrow tail. It is a scavenger which feeds mainly on the ground, taking carrion, sick animals and insects. It builds its large, flat nests of sticks on the horizontal branches of tall trees. Belonging to the same genus is the Brahminy kite, *H. indus* (48cm), a widespread coastal species with a reddish back and tail and a white head. Its diet includes carrion, fish, crabs and sea-snakes. The nests of these birds are placed near the top of trees in the vicinity of estuaries and swamps and are large structures made of sticks, often lined with strips of seaweed.

The black-breasted buzzard or kite, *Hamirostra* * *melanosternon* (58cm), a rare species with a slow, wheeling flight, is not closely related to the Old World buzzards. The colouring of these birds varies from mainly black to mainly brown, but their tails are always grey. Their food includes EMU and BUSTARD eggs, which they break by gripping a stone in their talons and dropping it on the eggs. The large flat nests are composed of sticks and placed in trees.

The group of birds referred to as hawks includes harriers, goshawks, and a sparrowhawk; it also contains the crested hawk, *Aviceda subcristata* (35cm to 40cm), easily recognised by its short black crest and the bold brown bars on its white belly; it is mainly dark grey above. It lives in thick woodland, especially in E Australia, feeding on insects in the foliage. When in flight, it sometimes indulges in a spectacular tumbling display. The loosely made nests of green twigs are placed in the high branches of tall trees.

Harriers are hawks with long tails, long wings and long, thin legs. They have facial discs which give them an owl-like appearance.

Species, genus or family is endemic to Australia (see Preface)

Crested hawk *Aviceda Subcristata*

When in search of prey—birds and small mammals—they glide lazily over open country, but they do not hover. The more common of the two species found in Australia is the swamp harrier, *Circus approximans* (56cm), a square-tailed bird, mostly dark brown above and white with brown streaks below. It lays its eggs in loosely constructed nests of reed stalks and twigs, well hidden among long rushes. The spotted harrier, *C. assimilis* (60cm), which frequents dry plains, is mainly grey with a reddish-brown face and a brown-and-white speckled breast. Its bulky nest, made of sticks and lined with leaves, is placed in trees and bushes.

The goshawks and the sparrowhawk have long, powerful yellow legs, long tails, broad, rounded wings and fierce yellow or red eyes. Their flight is characterised by short, vigorous flaps interspersed with long glides and sudden, swift flights to capture their prey—birds and other small animals such as rabbits and reptiles. The brown goshawk, *Accipiter fasciatus* (up to 50cm), and the collared sparrowhawk, *A. cirrhocephalus* (30cm to 38cm), look alike; both have barred breasts in the adult stage but the former has a rounded tail, whereas the latter is square-tailed. Both species are common and are found throughout Australia, in open and timbered areas. The flat nests, built in tall trees, are made of sticks or twigs and lined with green leaves. A much rarer species is the red goshawk, *Erythriotri-orchis* * *radiatus* (50cm), found in N and E Australia in open forests and woodland. The eggs are laid in large nests of sticks set in tall trees.

All species of the family Falconidae belong to the cosmopolitan genus *Falco*. They fly swiftly, most of them relying on their speed and diving ability to catch their prey, which is killed with the talons. A rare, dark species of the plains and open forest throughout the mainland is the black falcon, *F. subniger* * (up to 50cm), which has long thigh feathers and is notable for its ability to stay on the wing for long periods. Usually a solitary bird, it is sometimes seen in the company of black kites. It feeds on birds and carrion, and usually lays its eggs in the abandoned nests of crows and other species of hawks. The grey falcon, *F. hypoleucos* * (up to 40cm), is a widespread though uncommon species. Bluish-grey above, white below and with a distinctive black 'moustache', it frequents dry, open and lightly timbered areas; its loud, chicken-like call is also heard in mountain ranges. Grey falcons feed on small birds and other animals, and lay their eggs in large nests placed near the top of trees and composed of loosely assembled sticks lined with soft materials. The little falcon, *F. longipennis* (up to 35cm) is a fairly common species found throughout the mainland and TAS in open country and thin woodland. This strong, bold bird is bluish-grey above, reddish below, and has black on the head and face; the colouring is more subdued on little falcons found in arid regions. Its food, birds and insects, is caught in flight. Although they sometimes build their own nests, these birds usually re-line deserted nests.

A very common falcon found in open country throughout Australia is the Nankeen kestrel, *F. cenchroides* (up to 36cm), a reddish-brown species, pale below and with a barred tail—the male has a single bar and a grey head, the female has several bars and a brown head. The eggs are usually laid in caves, hollows or suitable old nests. The kestrel is particularly common in cultivated areas, where it is of great importance in keeping down the population of mice and insects. To catch its prey, it hovers, then swoops down to seize its victims on the ground; sometimes it swoops from a tree or pole. The brown falcon, *F. berigora* (up to 50cm), has a similar way of hunting its prey of birds and insects, especially grasshoppers. It is a very common species, found throughout Australia. The colouring varies widely; the upperparts may range from blackish-brown to reddish-brown, and the underparts from dusky brown to white. The eggs are usually laid in the deserted nests of other species of hawks.

The peregrine falcon, *F. peregrinus* (up to 45cm), is a cosmopolitan species which is fairly common in Australia, especially in high country, though it has declined in many other countries as a result of modern agricultural methods and of shooting to protect carrier pigeons during World War II. It has a greyish-blue plumage, a black cap and a strikingly barred grey and black abdomen. It kills its prey by delivering a blow with the hind claw while swooping swiftly; because the victims are large birds, such as ducks, this species has been popular with falconers. The nesting sites, used for several successive years, are usually on projecting ledges of rocky cliffs.

The osprey, *Pandion haliaetus* (length 50cm to 60cm; wingspan 1.75m), also called the fish hawk, is fairly common and of cosmopolitan distribution. It has brown upperparts, white underparts, a white head and a black tail; a black streak runs through the eye, forming a 'necklace' on the front. Ospreys frequent coastal areas and the lower reaches of large rivers, feeding entirely on fish which they catch by diving into the water feet first and gripping the prey in their talons. They usually build their large, bulky nests, of sticks lined with seaweed, in trees or on rocks overlooking the sea.

Birdsville Track SA/QLD This notorious road, about 520km long, crosses STURT'S STONY DESERT in the arid NE of SA, joining the small QLD township of Birdsville to the railhead at MAREE in SA. The explorer Charles STURT in 1845 said this incredibly inhospitable, barren and harsh region was 'a country such as I firmly believe has no parallel on earth's surface'. The Track became a major cattle-droving route from the 1880s, linking the inland with the railway and thence with seaport outlets. Cattle herds from the rich CHANNEL COUNTRY of south-western QLD were mustered at Birdsville (12km across the SA border), then driven down the Track to Maree on the Central Australian Railway line. The problems of these droving trips became legendary: scorchingly high temperatures, stinging sand storms, floods in periods of unexpected rain, cattle dying from exhaustion and lack of fodder; but for the artesian bores established by the government at 40km intervals, these treks would have been impossible in drought years. Though in recent years the road has been improved and is generally passable to most types of vehicles, warnings such as those quoted below are published by motoring associations for would-be travellers along the Track:

The journey should not be undertaken by the inexperienced motorist ... drive with the utmost concentration at all times ... the vehicle must be in first class condition and fully equipped for all emergencies ... the danger of travel in this isolated area is underscored heavily by the deaths which have occurred in recent years due to mechanical failure or heat exhaustion.

bishop birds *see* weaverbirds

bitterns, herons and egrets These BIRDS belong to a cosmopolitan family, Ardeidae, which consists of two distinct groups—one containing the bitterns, the other the herons and egrets. There are four species of bitterns in Australia (one recorded only once) and 11 species of herons and egrets.

Bitterns are secretive, well camouflaged birds which frequent reed beds fringing rivers, lakes and swamps; partly nocturnal, they are solitary and tend to stay in the depths of dense reed beds, seldom being seen during the day. When disturbed, they freeze, their necks out-stretched and their long beaks pointing upwards. The eyes are placed so that they continue to look directly forward when the bird freezes. Their loudly booming call can be heard at a great distance, and may be a reason for the Aboriginal belief in the BUNYIP. Like herons and egrets, they fly with the neck folded so that the head is tucked against the body.

The common brown bittern, *Botaurus poici-loptilus* (1m long), is streaked with dark and light brown. It is found in SE and SW Australia and in TAS, and feeds on water animals such as frogs and crayfish. The eggs are laid in platform-shaped nests of trampled reeds, and are usually found in the dense parts of swamps. The little bittern, *Ixobrychus minutus* (30cm), found in SE and SW Australia, is a very shy species. The male has a black crown, black back and a mottled dark-and-light brown breast; the female's colouring is generally browner. Its open nests, composed of water plants, are usually placed among the reeds just above the surface of the water. The black bittern, *I. flavicollis* (60cm), sooty-black with a black and buff neck and bare yellow skin on the face, may be common in various coastal areas of W, N and E Australia. It lays eggs in platform-shaped nests of sticks, usually built on a branch overhanging water.

Herons and egrets (excepting the cattle egret) are almost always found near water. They are completely or largely white, and the egrets have distinctive, decorative breeding plumes (aigrettes) once popular with milliners. Four of the five egrets represented in Australia are true egrets, belonging to the genus *Egretta*; their eggs are laid in platform-shaped nests of sticks built in trees or bushes at the water's edge.

The reef heron, *E. sacra* (60cm), found in all coastal areas except the Bight, is a white species often seen stalking among the rocks at low tide or perched on a rock, its hunched attitude giving it a dejected appearance. It feeds on marine animals, such as fish and crustaceans. A rarer species is the little egret, *E. garzetta* (56cm to 60cm), a nomadic bird which is mainly white with black legs, a yellow head and plumes on the breast and back; it is usually found in the coastal swamps and waters of N Australia. The plumed egret, *E. intermedia* (56cm to 60cm), a white bird with back and breast plumes and a green face, is also found mainly in the N in coastal areas and near inland rivers, lakes and swamps. The much larger white egret, *E. alba* (1m), is found near water throughout Australia and is often seen silently wading in pursuit of its prey of frogs, fish and aquatic insects.

One of the most notable species introduced into Australia is the cattle egret, *Ardeola (Bubulcus) ibis* (46cm), a species which is becoming more widespread. It was probably first introduced by a group of farmers in WA in 1933 to combat the cattle-tick. A hunched, completely white bird whose head and breast plumes become bright orange during the breeding season, it is usually seen taking insects disturbed by cattle. The eggs are laid in saucer-shaped nests of sticks built in trees in swamp areas.

Among the herons found in Australia there is only one representative of night herons, the widespread Nankeen night heron, *Nycticorax caledonicus* (60cm). It has a black nape, a white breast, a chestnut back and two white head plumes. It fishes for yabbies, frogs, water insects and molluscs in swamps, rivers and quiet sea inlets, and may even be seen in city suburbs. The nests, loosely constructed plat-

P. Muchenberg (N.P.I.A.W.)

Black bittern, *Ixobrychus flavicollis*

forms of sticks, are built on the horizontal branches of trees standing in or near water.

Another common, though solitary, species is the mangrove heron, *Butorides striatus* (about 40cm). Its plumage is either dark greenish-grey above and light grey below or reddish-brown above and brownish-grey below, and it inhabits the mangroves and mudflats of the N coastal area from WA to NSW. The pale bluish-green eggs are laid in scanty, platform-shaped nests of sticks which are usually placed in a mangrove tree growing in or near water.

The common pied heron, *Hydranassa picata* (45cm), a black bird with long breeding plumes and a white throat and neck, occurs in swamps and grasslands in N Australia. Its bluish-green eggs are laid in slightly concave nests of sticks and twigs, usually built in mangrove trees.

All other species of herons in Australia belong to the cosmopolitan genus *Ardea*. The white-necked heron, *A. pacifica** (75cm), a freshwater bird common throughout the mainland and TAS, has a black body, a white head and neck, a slender bill and, during the breeding season, hackled feathers on the back and foreneck. A shy, wary bird, it favours areas where it has a clear view of its surroundings, and feeds on water animals such as frogs and small reptiles. Its nests, usually placed in dead trees in swampy or flooded lands, are bulky, platform-shaped structures of sticks, and its eggs are green. The white-faced heron, *A. novaehollandiae* (60cm), also seasonally hackled, is often seen wading in shallow waters throughout the mainland and TAS. It is a grey bird which, when disturbed, utters a loud croaking call and takes off in a laboured manner. The nests, platform-shaped and composed of sticks, are sometimes built well away from water; the eggs are pale bluish-green. A much rarer species is the great-billed heron, *A. sumatrana* (1.5m), a large, dark bird of the N coast. It too has an

ungainly flight when disturbed. Its diet consists of marine animals and its flat, bulky nests of sticks are usually built in a mangrove tree; the eggs are light bluish-green.

bivalve molluscs The bivalves form the second-largest class (Pelecypoda or Lamellibranchia) of the MOLLUSCS, and include such species as oysters, scallops and cockles. The shell of a bivalve is composed of two sections or valves, usually roughly oval in shape and equal in size. The two valves are hinged dorsally by a ligament which may lie inside or outside the shell. Lateral movement is prevented by interlocking teeth near the oldest part of the shell, the umbo, which is dorsal. Adductor muscles keep the two valves together; when they relax, the ligament opens the valves. In most bivalves there are two large adductor muscles but in some, such as the oysters, there is only one.

There is no head; the body consists of a hatchet-shaped foot (this is the meaning of the name Pelecypoda) and a visceral mass. The mantle lines the inside of the shell and there is a large mantle cavity between the mantle and the rest of the body. Sometimes small particles such as grains of sand get between the mantle and the shell, and the bivalve responds to this irritation by covering the intrusion with smooth layers of nacre, producing a pearl. Virtually all kinds of bivalves can produce pearls, though the best are produced by pearl oysters.

Most bivalves burrow in soft mud or sand, and the body is laterally compressed to facilitate the tunelling. The foot pushes forward then expands by filling with blood, giving it a good grip on the substrate so that it can draw the rest of the animal after it. A few bivalve molluscs swim, but many, such as oysters and mussels, are sessile. Oysters become fixed by fusing one shell with the substrate; mussels used byssal threads (tufts of filaments of

tanned protein) for attachment.

The gills lie in the mantle cavity. There is one gill on each side but usually they are folded so that it appears that there are several gills. They are used, of course, for respiration but in most bivalves the gills are also food-collecting devices. Tiny food particles carried by the stream of water entering to bathe the gills are trapped by cilia (microscopic hair-like structures) on the gill plates, and carried to the mouth. A few primitive bivalves feed by proboscises which gather up food particles from the surroundings and a few are carnivores which feed on small crustaceans, but none has a radula (file-like structure used to scrape off food particles and draw them into the mouth); indeed, none has a head in which to house a radula. In most bivalves, the sexes are separate.

All bivalves are aquatic and most are marine. Though some families contain both marine and freshwater species the two groups are treated separately here.

Marine bivalves The classification of marine bivalves is difficult. Some authorities base it on the nature of the hinge, others on the form of the gills. All appear to agree, however, that there is a primitive group called the Protobranchia (treated here as a subclass) and a more advanced group, the Lamellibranchia. It is the subdivision of the latter group which causes difficulty, and here only families, not the orders to which they belong, will be mentioned.

In the Protobranchia, the gills are not folded and are not used for feeding; palps (feelers) extended as proboscises are used to collect food. The small number of Australian species belong to three families: Solemyidae (date shells); Nuculidae (nut shells); and Nuculanidae (beaked cockles). A common example is the Austral solemya or date shell, *Solemya australis* (length 5cm; width 2.5cm), which has a brittle, dark-brown shell without hinge-teeth, and is found burrowing in sand or mud on S coasts.

The Lamellibranchia is a much larger group, with about 47 families represented in Australian waters.

1. The family Arcidae contains one of the best-known bivalves of Australia, *Anadara trapesia* (up to 7.5cm long), commonly known as the Sydney cockle though it ranges from QLD to VIC and TAS, and is not a true cockle. It occurs in the sands and muds of tidal flats, and was once collected in huge quantities by the Aborigines. The shell is very thick, white and trapeziform in shape, and is usually covered by a brown periostracum (the outermost layer of a mollusc shell). There are about 26 ribs. The hinge-line is straight with an unbroken series of teeth. This bivalve formerly occurred in SA but it is now represented there only by fossils. The family contains many other species, including *Barbatia pistachia*, which has complex eyes along the mantle edge and lives under stones on rocky shores or in holes in honeycombed rocks, and the jingle shell, *Anomia descripta*, an attractive beach bivalve

which occurs in NSW. The translucent shell of the latter species is often bright orange, but white or silvery-peach specimens are also common; the lower valve is flattened and usually has a hole through which the animal attaches itself to the substrate by byssal threads.

2. The family Pectinidae contains the scallops, which would be recognised even by those who have never visited the seashore for the shell is often used as a plate, an ashtray, or a trade mark. Scallops are common offshore where they swim by rapidly opening and closing their shells, pushing themselves along by a kind of jet propulsion. The animal itself is often orange or scarlet in colour, and there are numerous eyes at the base of the mantle.

Most scallop fishing in Australia takes place at the D'ENTRECASTEAUX CHANNEL, SE of TAS, though there is local collection elsewhere. The part of the scallop which is eaten is the 'eye', which is really the large, single adductor muscle. Three species are usually dredged in TAS: the commercial or king scallop, *Notovola meridionalis* (the largest; up to 15cm long), an orange to purplish-brown scallop; the Tasmanian queen scallop, *Equichlamys bifrons*, a lilac species, magenta-purple inside; and the doughboy or prickly scallop, *Chlamys asperrimus*, a species with tiny scales.

3. The family Ostreidae contains the oysters, which are very variable in shape because they are attached to objects and are often crowded together. Different species are found in most coastal areas of the world, wherever there are clean, hard surfaces on which the spat (spawn) can settle. Oysters are attached by the left valve to such objects as mangrove trunks, rocks or wharf pilings; this valve is concave so that it can contain the body, while the upper valve is more or less flat. There is only one adductor muscle, and the foot in the adult is greatly reduced as the animal is sessile.

The commercial oyster of SA, the common mud or PORT LINCOLN oyster, *Ostrea sinuata* (up to 15cm in diameter), attaches itself to a support when young but later breaks away and drops to the sea floor, from which it is often dredged. The commercial rock oyster of NSW and southern QLD, *Crassostrea commercialis*, ranges from northern QLD to VIC; its irregular shell is purple on the outside and white inside. The two species differ greatly in their mode of reproduction: the rock oyster releases eggs and sperm into the water where fertilisation takes place, whereas in the mud oyster the young develop for a time within the parent. The rock oyster is an example of those species which change sex, sometimes more than once, during their lives.

The rock oyster is cultivated in oyster leases in many estuaries in NSW and southern QLD. The waters of the estuaries are rich in food particles, but it is also possible that the lower salinity promotes their growth. The oyster farmers lay down various objects such as mangrove sticks, stones, tiles and concrete structures, collectively called cunch, for the spat to settle on. Within a couple of days of

Commercial oyster, *Crassostrea commercialis*

settling the young larvae have developed a tiny shell, and three to five years later they reach a marketable size. Oysters in farms and growing wild are attacked by several predators, including various GASTROPODS and starfish (*see* SEA STARS). They are also parasitised. In 1978 oyster farms near Sydney lost a large part of their market as a result of gastric sicknesses caused by the eating of oysters which had apparently been contaminated by a virus, but since the introduction of new regulations the farmers have regained much of their market.

There are about nine other species of common oysters in Australian waters, and a few species have been introduced in attempts to improve the local fisheries. The value of the production of edible molluscs—mostly oysters —in 1975-76 was, for Australia, just over $20 million.

(Several other bivalves are called oysters, although they are not closely related to the family Ostreidae. The family Spondylidae contains the often beautifully coloured thorny oysters, such as the northern thorny oyster, *Spondulus ducalis*, which is common on the GREAT BARRIER REEF and in much of the Indo-Pacific; it is pink on the outside with brown lines, and bluish-white or yellow on the inside, and is attached to rocks at the end of the right valve. The family Vulsellidae contains the appropriately named hammer oysters, species which live in sand, anchored by their byssal threads, and the sponge-finger shells, such as *Vulsella spongiarum* which lives within living sponges.)

4. The family Pteriidae contains the true pearl shells from which PEARLS are obtained; these species are noted for the pearly, iridescent nacre of the innermost layer of the shell. The pearl-shell industry of Australia extends from BROOME to CAIRNS. The species *Pinctada maxima* is used for pearl culture. The value of the pearl-shell industry in 1975-76 was $260 000.

5. The family Mytilidae contains the mussels. The shells are oval or elongated and dark yellow to purplish-black in colour. They are fastened to the substrate, and often to each other, by byssal threads, and can move when necessary by attaching a thread at some distance then moving along 'hand over hand' to the new position. The edible mussel of southern Australia, *Mytilus planulatus*, closely resembles the edible mussels of Europe. Generally, mussels are among the most

productive of sea animals and research is being carried out in Australia to find the best way to farm them; in some experiments the mussels are grown successfully on thick ropes hanging from rafts.

6. The family Cardiidae contains the heart cockles, heart-shaped edible molluscs which are also neglected in Australia. The southern heart cockle, *Cardium racketti*, ranges round the S coasts and is most common on sheltered beaches.

7. The family Donacidae contains the wedge shells, such as the pipi, *Plebidonax deltoides* (width 5cm), which is still used as food or bait and was once popular with the Aborigines; it may be the commonest bivalve of the E coasts. It is mauve or pale pink in colour, has faintly coloured radii, conspicuous concentric rings, and the inside of the shell is violet.

8. The family Tridacnidae contains the clams, the largest of living shells. Most of the species are found in warmer seas, particularly among coral reefs. Some of the smaller species bore into the coral but the larger forms, having lost their byssal threads while young, merely rest on the bottom. Like many of the corals among which they live, clams have photosynthetic unicellular algae within their bodies, under the lobes of the mantle edges. It has been suggested that the large clams have been able to attain their gigantic size because of this association.

The giant clam, *Tridacna gigas*, is found throughout the warmer Indo-Pacific Ocean and is common on the Great Barrier Reef. A pair of shells from Sumatra weighed 230kg and one of the valves was 1.4m long. Because of their size and the great weight of water that must be displaced, the open valves can be closed only very slowly, and therefore the stories of divers being caught by 'man-eating clams' are almost certainly all fictional; furthermore, the mantle is vividly coloured and very easy to see. The commonest boring clam, *T. croca* (about 10cm long), is also found throughout the Indo-Pacific.

Giant clam, *Tridacna gigas*

9. The family Pholadidae contains some of the boring bivalves, such as the common *Barnea* species which normally tunnel into hard clay or soft rock. The two thin valves of the shell are not linked by a ligament and do not completely enclose the animal. Despite their fragility the shells are used for boring, the adductor and foot muscles supplying the power. The bivalve lives permanently within

the burrow, communicating with the sea water by its siphons. A relative newcomer to the Sydney region is *Martesia striata*, which burrows into wood; it is widespread in the Pacific, and has been a great pest at Panama. 10. The family Teredinidae contains the remainder of the boring bivalves, such as the infamous shipworms (called cobras in Australia), the best-known genus of which is *Teredo*; other genera in Australian waters include *Noroteredo* and *Bankia*. It is probable that these animals have been inadvertently spread by man in the timbers of wooden ships; they are very damaging to any timber that remains in water for too long. Although this bivalve tunnels in wood, it must remain in contact with the surrounding water, which it does by the constant elongation of the siphons so that it eventually grows to perhaps 1m long, but remains only 2cm thick. The valves are relatively tiny. The mantle produces two other calcareous plates, the pallets, which are used to close off the tunnel at the siphon end when necessary. For most of its length a fully grown teredo is simply a hollow tube. The tunnel it makes is often lined with lime, and the entrance hole of the tunnel is very narrow because the animal begins tunnelling when it is very small; often there is little indication from the outside of the severe damage within. These bivalves feed on small organisms in the water, brought in through the siphons, but they probably also obtain some nutrients from the wood.

Freshwater bivalves Three families occur in Australia: Hydriidae (the freshwater mussels); Sphaeriidae (pea-shell mussels); and Corbiculidae (orb-shell mussels). The Hydriidae (5cm to 20cm long) are confined to Australia and South America; the Sphaeriidae (about 1.2cm long) are cosmopolitan; and the Corbiculidae (about 1.25cm long), though widespread, are represented by only one genus in Australia, *Corbiculina*. The sperm of freshwater mussels is carried into the female through the siphon. The eggs are fertilised on the gills and develop into the glochidium larvae, which are then released and are parasitic for a time on the gills of freshwater fish. Most freshwater bivalves live in shallow, unpolluted water, on fairly stable silt or mud bottoms, and some of them can survive for years out of the water.
Further reading: see under molluscs. *Also* Caras, R. *Dangerous to Man.* Penguin Books, Harmondsworth, 1978.

Bjelke-Petersen, Johannes (1911-) Premier of QLD. The son of a Danish immigrant who became a Lutheran pastor, he was born in Dannevirke, New Zealand, but in 1913 was taken by his parents to QLD, where his father took up land near the town of KINGAROY. He left school at the age of 13 to work on the family farm, which he later acquired and still owns. He entered the QLD Legislative Assembly as a member of the Country Party in 1947, but did not attain Cabinet rank until 1963, when he was

Premier's Dept. QLD

The Hon. J. Bjelke-Petersen

appointed Minister for Works and Housing. In 1968 he was elected deputy leader of the Country Party in QLD (since renamed the NATIONAL PARTY). Later in the same year, shortly after the death of Premier C.J.A. Pizzey, he became party leader and Premier. Bjelke-Petersen has shown himself to be without doubt the most conservative of all State Premiers of his time. He has been criticised by many for his curtailment of the right to carry out street demonstrations in Brisbane, for his Aboriginal policies and for the failure to remedy an unequal electoral distribution. However, he has also shown himself to be a master at judging the mood of the electorate, and has won wide support for his success in developing QLD's resources and his championing of States' rights.

Black War This name is often applied to the whole history of conflict between British settlers and Aborigines in TAS (then known as VAN DIEMEN'S LAND). It includes the ludicrously unsuccessful attempt by Lieutenant-Governor ARTHUR in 1830 to drive all the surviving Aborigines in the E part of the island onto the TASMAN PENINSULA.
Further reading: Turnbull, C. *Black War.* Cheshire, Melbourne, 1948.

Black Wednesday 9 January 1878. This is the popular name for the day when over 200 of VIC's top public servants were dismissed, following the rejection by the Legislative Council of an Appropriations Bill, introduced by Sir Graham BERRY with the design of curbing the powers of the Legislative Council.

blackberry *see* weeds

blackbirding This was the colloquial term for the recruiting of Pacific islanders (commonly known as KANAKAS), mainly for work in the QLD sugar industry, in the late 19th century.

blackboys *see* Palmae

Blackburn, James (1803-54) Architect and engineer. Transported for life after forging a cheque, Blackburn arrived in Hobart as a convict in 1833. In VAN DIEMEN'S LAND he showed his abilities in many phases of the island's development, particularly in road and bridge design. He was pardoned in 1841 and began a private practice as an architect and contractor, in partnership with James Thomson. One of his early designs was for Hobart's Government House, though this was never completed. Another Blackburn project unrealised at that time was a water supply for Hobart. The buildings designed by Blackburn in TAS display his competence in a wide range of Georgian tastes. His masterpiece in the Gothic mode was Holy Trinity Church, Hobart, a forerunner of the full Gothic Revival. He was a leading exponent of the Grecian style, as can be seen in his designs for Lady Franklin Museum, and the tower and vestries of St George's, Battery Point. St George's has the only Greek Revival storied steeple of Australian colonial architectural. However, Blackburn's unique contribution to Georgian architecture in Australia was his use of Romanesque motifs, as at St Mark's Church at Pontville and St Matthew's, Glenorchy, both designed in 1839.

In 1849 Blackburn sailed with his family to Melbourne and set up as an engineer and architect. He designed St Stephen's Church at Richmond and several other distinctive buildings, but his most notable memorial in VIC is his concept for supplying Melbourne with water from the Yan Yean Reservoir, a plan which was realised after his death.

Although a large number of James Blackburn's designs and ideas were never realised, he was one of TAS's most advanced and original architects and one of the greatest engineers in Australia at that time.

blackbutt *Eucalyptus pilularis* (family MYRTACEAE) is a large timber tree of NSW and QLD. It has white flowers, and the leaves narrow to a point at the tip (lanceolate); the bark is scaly or fibrous at the base and smooth and mottled grey above. The name is also sometimes applied to other eucalypts, such as *E. patens* in WA.

Blacket, Edmund Thomas (1817-83) Architect. One of the greatest architects of 19th-century Australia, Blacket migrated to Sydney in 1842 and was employed first as Inspector of Buildings for the Church of England; within a year he had designed a church in the Gothic Revival style (the first All Saints', SINGLETON) and a Georgian house (for Dr Ross in Sydney). These two styles, Gothic and Classical, were to mark all his subsequent architecture, though he favoured Gothic.

Appointed Diocesan Architect, he designed many churches during his first decade in Australia: Christ Church St Lawrence, St

A. Healy

St. Andrew's Cathedral, Sydney, an example of
Blacket's work

Philip's and the Cathedral of St Andrew in Sydney, St Mark's at Darling Point, and many others, all in the Gothic idiom. The second phase of his career began when he succeeded Mortimer LEWIS as Colonial Architect in 1849. One of his mildly Classical public-building designs from this period is the Watch House at Balmain. In 1854 he resigned to accept the invitation of the Senate of the University of Sydney to design its first buildings. The Great Hall of the university, completed in 1857, is generally considered to be the finest example of the Gothic Revival style in Australia.

From this time Blacket's practice and reputation grew, and his commissions included schools, colleges, banks, hospitals, commercial buildings and houses, as well as numerous churches, which remained his favourite projects. One of his largest churches was St Thomas's, North Sydney (1881), while St Stephen's at Newton (1874; it includes some of the earliest structural ironwork in its design) is one of his best. St John's Glebe (1868) is more Romanesque than Gothic—an example of the influence of his associate John Horbury Hunt. Blacket's later Classical buildings included Palmer Street Presbyterian Church, Woolloomooloo, which completely covers and still enhances its small inner-city site; and the impressive wool store built opposite the wharves at Circular Quay for Thomas Sutcliffe Mort, completed in 1867, which is now replaced by a skyscraper.

At the time of Edmund Blacket's death he was in partnership with his son Cyril and the firm was working on a score of buildings, one of which was St George's Cathedral in Perth. Afterwards Cyril was joined by his brother Arthur; the practice continued into the 20th century. A shy man, Blacket was conservative,

a traditionalist rather than an innovator, but his impact on Australian building was tremendous. The designer of 58 churches, he was been called 'the Christopher Wren of Australia'.
Further reading: Herman, M. *The Blackets.* Angus & Robertson, Sydney, 1963.

Blackfellow's bread *see* fungi

blackfish *see* dolphins, etc.; fishes, bony; fishes, freshwater

Blackheath NSW (population 3 026 in 1981) This town is in the BLUE MOUNTAINS region, on the Western Highway, 118km W of Sydney and 11km by road from KATOOMBA. Blackheath was so named by Governor MAC-QUARIE, in 1815, because of its wild and black appearance. It is a popular holiday resort, though it is increasingly becoming an urban centre of permanent, rather than vacation, residence. Typical of the Blue Mts, the district surrounding Blackheath has a majestic scenery of steep sandstone cliffs, sheer gorges, water-falls and bushland. A Rhododendron Festival, held annually in November, attracts many visitors to Blackheath.

Blackman, Charles Raymond (1928-) Artist. Born in Sydney, Blackman studied at the East Sydney Technical College, and worked as an artist for the Sydney *Sun* before settling in Melbourne, which was a base for his extensive travels in the bush. In the 1950s his two exhibitions, entitled 'School-girls', showed many characteristics that were to become hallmarks of his style—the silhouette, the static quality of his homely subject matter, and the melancholy but tender participants. Blackman's work is focussed on the warmth of human relationships—on his wife, almost blind, and his children. This preoccupation has virtually never changed, although his work has shown an increasing richness of colour, as recorded by his London exhibition of 1961, a venture made possible by his winning of the Rubenstein Scholarship, the Dyason Endowment (administered by the Art Gallery of New South Wales), and the Crouch Prize at BALLARAT. Although widely known for his sensitive but non-erotic figure paintings of young girls and children, Black-man has painted a number of landscapes, which are typically melancholy, moonlit and empty of human activity.

black nightshade *see* weeds

Blackwater QLD (population 5 434 in 1981) A town on the Capricorn Highway 73km E of EMERALD and 190km by road inland from ROCKHAMPTON, on a tributary of the MACKENZIE RIVER, Blackwater is the centre of a beef cattle grazing region. Two major developments in recent years have markedly affected its progress: coal mining and the Brigalow land settlement project. At

Blackwater Coal Mine, 24km S of the town, coking coal is extracted by mechanised open-cut methods for export to Japan; visitors can view the operation of the huge drag-lines and the loading facilities. The land development scheme consists of a vast project of clearing more than 400 000ha of brigalow scrub (*see* MIMOSACEAE) and forest land for conversion into pastures for cattle fattening, and into arable land for wheat, sorghum and safflower. On the Mackenzie River, Bedford Weir (completed in 1968) provides water for Blackwater and the mine, and for livestock on rural properties along the pipeline route.

blackwood *see* forestry; Mimosaceae

Blackwood River WA Located in the far SW of the State, the headwater streams of the Blackwood rise over a wide tract of country in the plateau, including the NARROGIN, WAGIN and KATANNING areas. Many of the streams in the plateau section are non-perennial, usually flowing only during the wet winter season. The river flows in a general SW direction over a course of some 300km, and in its lower section turns sharply to flow S to its estuary, Hardy Inlet, entering Flinders Bay on the S coast, E of CAPE LEEUWIN. Inland, the rural areas of the catchment basin are used mainly for sheep grazing and grain growing; further downstream around BRIDGETOWN orcharding is important, and on the alluvial soils of the flood plain, dairying is a major rural activity. Forestry and beef cattle grazing are important in the hinterland. The small town of AUGUSTA is located on the W side of the estuary. The river is crossed by numerous roads: the Albany Highway (running between Perth and ALBANY) cuts across the upper river basin on a N-S route; the South Western Highway from BUNBURY crosses the river at Bridgetown; the Bussel Highway links Augusta to BUSSELTON; the Brockman Highway cuts across the lower valley at Alexandra Bridge. The river passes through the Scott National Park (3 273ha), located 6km NE of Augusta and including stretches of jarrah and karri forests, and the Leeuwin-Naturaliste National Park (13 239ha), which includes rugged coastline and forest lands N and E of the cape.

Blair Athol QLD This is a coal-mining township located NW of Clermont off the Gregory Highway, 1 048km by road NW of Brisbane, about 120km NNW of EMERALD and 280km SW along the Peak Downs Highway from MACKAY. The bituminous coal seams of the area, claimed as Australia's largest deposits of black coal, are unusually thick (up to 24m) and relatively close to the surface (the upper seam is only 18m below ground level). They are mined by mechanical open-cut methods.

Blake Prize This prize for religious art is awarded annually to the winner of a competition for a religious painting, drawing or sculpture. It was established in 1949 by a Sydney committee drawn from most of the mainstream Christian Churches and aimed to strengthen the connection between art and the Church by encouraging religious art. The competition is open to any person resident in Australia or to any Australian citizen resident overseas; it was initially sponsored by the retail trading firm of Mark Foys. The value of the prize in 1980 was $1000, given by the Commonwealth Banking Corporation; the artistic works submitted for the competition are usually exhibited at the bank's branch in Martin Place, Sydney. The prize takes its name from William Blake, the English painter whose work most successfully combined religious and artistic content. See Appendix 3.

Blamey, Sir Thomas Albert (1884-1951)
Soldier, and first Australian Field Marshal. Born near WAGGA WAGGA, Blamey became a probationer teacher in 1899 and four years later joined the service of the Education Department of WA. For a time he considered joining the Methodist ministry, but in 1906 decided to aim for a career in the army, and having passed the competitive examination was commissioned as lieutenant. Five years later he was admitted to the Imperial Staff College at Quetta, India, where he remained until 1913. With the ANZAC forces he landed at GALLIPOLI on 25 April 1915, remaining there for most of the time until evacuation, and in the later part of the war was Chief of Staff to General MONASH in France. In 1925 he retired from the regular army to become Chief Commissioner of Police in VIC, but continued to serve in the militia. His police career ended with his resignation in 1936 after he had been criticised in the report of a Royal Commission for concealing facts relating to the shooting of a senior police officer.

General Sir Thomas Blamey

Soon after the outbreak of war in 1939 he was appointed General Officer Commanding, 1st Australian Corps. He later commanded the AUSTRALIAN IMPERIAL FORCE (AIF) in the Middle East and the Anzac Corps in Greece, and became deputy Commander-in-Chief in the Middle East. After returning to Australia in March 1942 he became Commander-in-Chief, Australian Military Forces, and Commander, Allied Land Forces, under General MacArthur (who was Supreme Commander of the South-West Pacific area). In late 1942 and early 1943, when Japanese forces were being driven back along the Kokoda Trail, he commanded in the field in Papua New Guinea. He retired from the army in November 1945 and was created Field Marshal in 1950.

Further reading: Hetherington, J. *Blamey, Controversial Soldier.* Australian War Memorial, Canberra, 1973 and *Thomas Blamey.* Oxford University Press, Melbourne, 1974.

Blattodea *see* cockroaches

Blaxland, Gregory (1788-1853)
Pioneer grazier and explorer. Born in Kent, England, he came to NSW as a free settler in 1806 and acquired land at South Creek, near the site of modern St Mary's, where he raised cattle and sheep. Having difficulty in obtaining as much land as he wanted, he decided that his best chance of prosperity lay in the discovery of a route to new country beyond the BLUE MOUNTAINS. In 1813, when drought had made the problem of expansion more urgent, he, William LAWSON and William Charles WENTWORTH succeeded in finding a route most of the way across the mountain barrier. After their work had been followed up and the W plains reached, Governor MACQUARIE made large land grants there to the three explorers, but Blaxland did not settle there. He lived for many years at Brush Farm, near Dundas, and later at North PARRAMATTA, where he ended his life by hanging himself.
See also exploration by land

Blayney NSW (population 2 694 in 1981)
A small country town in the central-W of the State, it is on the railway line between BATHURST and ORANGE, and on the Mid-Western Highway, 249km by road W of Sydney. At an elevation of 862m above sea level, it receives an average annual rainfall of 768mm, spread fairly evenly throughout the year. The surrounding rural district produces wool and wheat, fat lambs and pigs, fruit and vegetables. The town has gained a reputation for its cold winter winds, perhaps partly because so many travellers have waited for trains there on winter nights.

bleeding heart *see* Euphorbiaceae

blennies *see* fishes, bony

Bligh, William (1754-1817)
Governor of NSW. Involved as he was in a famous naval mutiny and a military rebellion, Bligh is one of the most controversial characters associated with early Australian history. Born in Plymouth, he joined the British Navy in 1770 and when only 21 was appointed master of the *Resolution* under Captain COOK. In 1787 he was given command of the *Bounty*, with the task of bringing breadfruit trees from Tahiti to the West Indies. On the return voyage Fletcher Christian, acting Lieutenant, led a successful mutiny and cast adrift Bligh and 18 loyal members of the crew in an open boat less than 9m long. With only five days' rations, and without navigating instruments, Bligh sailed nearly 6000km to Timor, in what was possibly the greatest small-boat voyage in history. A court martial cleared him of blame for the loss of his ship, and in 1791 he was put in charge of another expedition to Tahiti, and succeeded in bringing back breadfruit trees. In 1801 he was made a Fellow of the Royal Society, and in the same year was personally congratulated by Nelson for his courage in the Battle of Copenhagen.

He obtained the governorship of NSW on the recommendation of Sir Joseph BANKS. For some years before the appointment, affairs in the colony had been dominated by officers of the garrison regiment, the NEW SOUTH WALES CORPS, who had successfully resisted the efforts of Bligh's predecessors, HUNTER and KING, to curb their privileges and trading activities. Bligh's instructions urged him particularly to curb their trading in rum. He did so with vigour and naturally incurred the officers' hostility. Among many of the other settlers, however, especially small farmers on the HAWKESBURY, he earned gratitude for his efforts to break the officers' trading monopolies and for the aid he gave to those in need.

The leader of the anti-Bligh faction was an ex-officer, John MACARTHUR, with whom the Governor had a series of quarrels and legal disputes. Following the arrest of Macarthur in December 1807, Bligh's opponents persuaded the commander of the New South Wales Corps, Major JOHNSTON, to depose him—an incident commonly referred to as the RUM REBELLION. He was kept under arrest for more than a year, then released on condition that he sail to England on the *Porpoise*. However, on boarding the vessel he sailed to Hobart, where he still was when his successor, MACQUARIE, reached Australia at the end of 1809. He then returned to Sydney, gathered witnesses in his favour, and sailed to England to give evidence at Johnston's court martial. The court rejected the claim that he had been so autocratic as to justify Johnston's action. Nevertheless, the wording of the verdict, and the fact that Johnston was merely cashiered as punishment, could be interpreted as implying some criticism of Bligh. Subsequently, he was promoted to Rear-Admiral and finally Vice-Admiral, but was never again given a position of active command.

NSW Govt. Printer

Governor William Bligh

His character has been subjected to various interpretations, but its salient points seem clear. He was a man of courage and determination and a navigator of outstanding skill. His faults did not include the brutality which has come to form part of the popular image of him, but consisted mainly of impatience, lack of tact, poor judgement in dealing with people, and an ungovernable temper and tongue.
Further reading: Mackaness, G. *The Life of Vice-Admiral William Bligh, RN, FRS.* Angus & Robertson, Sydney, 1951; Evatt, H.V. *Rum Rebellion.* Angus & Robertson, Cremorne NSW, 1975.

bloodroot *see* Haemodoraceae

bloodwoods *see* Myrtaceae

bloodworms *see* flies

blowflies These FLIES belong to the family Calliphoridae, of the order Diptera, and are represented by about 135 species in Australia. Most are stout, moderately large flies. The adults are attracted by moisture and feed on nectar and honeydew, but the females feed on the liquids of decaying organic matter in order to obtain the protein needed for their eggs. The larvae breed in earthworms (ANNELIDS), in carrion or ectoparasitically on vertebrates.

The various species which breed in earthworms are called cluster flies (Polleniinae) because they often cluster together in large numbers in dark places during the winter, some species coming indoors and assembling in the same spot, year after year.

A few species of blowflies have modified the carrion-breeding habit so that they now attack living animals. Such blowflies are called primary blowflies because they initiate the strike. For example, the sheep blowfly, *Lucilia cuprina*, the most important species in Australia, introduced earlier this century, probably from South Africa or India, lays her eggs on various parts of the sheep's body

where the skin has been 'scalded' by moisture such as rain or urine; the larvae first feed on discharge from the scalded area but as they grow they turn to the animal's tissues. The fully fed larvae fall to the ground where they pupate. *Lucilia* will also breed in carrion but suffer greatly from competition with other species living there. Some native species which are primary blowflies include *Calliphora auger* (SE Australia), the lesser brown blowfly, *C. nociva* (W regions and dry inland), and the brown blowfly, *C. albifrontalis* (WA). In WA the sheep blowfly is responsible for about 80 per cent of the primary strikes, the lesser brown blowfly for about five per cent, and the brown blowfly for the rest; the first occurs in WA throughout the year, the second from spring to early winter, and the third in late winter and spring.

After the initial strike, the wound becomes attractive as an egg-laying site for other kinds of blowflies, the secondary species. In Australia the commonest secondary blowfly is the native *Chrysomya rufifacies*, a species with 'hairy maggots' which attack both the animal and the maggots of the primary flies. When the animal is dead or dying, tertiary blowflies may infest the wound.

Chemical control is still the main method of protecting sheep against blowfly strikes (*see* GRAZING INDUSTRY) but it has been bedevilled by the development of resistance to organophosphates and organochlorines. Surveys in 1962 and 1972 suggested that sheep blowflies cost Australia about $20 million annually. An estimate made in 1979 for the year 1975-76 indicated that the national cost (in the values of that time) was about $44 million. In 1979, a new type of compound, with the trade name Vetrazin, was introduced: this interferes with the orderly development of the maggots.
See also biological control

VIC Dept. of Agriculture

Side view of a blowfly

blubbers *see* coelenterates

bluebell This descriptive flower name is applied to several species of plants in Australia. Among them are three species of the genus *Sollya* (family Pittosporaceae), found only in WA, which are shrubs with clusters of deep blue flowers. The plants known as Australian bluebells are herbs with solitary blue flowers borne on long stems, and are species of the cosmopolitan genus *Wahlenbergia* (family Campanulaceae), represented in all States and overseas.

bluebottles *see* coelenterates

blue bush *see* Chenopodiaceae; vegetation

Blue Lake SA The largest and best-known of the crater lakes within extinct volcanic cones in the MOUNT GAMBIER district of the SE part of the State, Blue Lake is so named because of the striking colour of its waters in summer. Covering an area of 70ha, the lake is 80m deep and is encircled by the sheer walls of the volcanic crater rising 80m above the water level. It is the source of Mt Gambier's domestic water supply and, with other lakes of the area (Valley Lake, Leg of Mutton Lake and Brownes Lake), is a popular tourist attraction.

Blue Mountains NSW This region of renowned scenic beauty is part of the GREAT DIVIDING RANGE of E Australia. It is located W of Sydney in NSW and, though called mountains, the region is really a plateau extending 160km N-S and between 60km and 100km E-W. The best-known and largest urban centre of the Blue Mts is KATOOMBA, 106km W of Sydney at an elevation of 1 020m. The general elevation varies between 600m and 1 100m, rising gradually from E to W. The E edge of the plateau is formed by a distinct scarp, some 55km inland from Sydney, adjacent to the NEPEAN RIVER.

When viewed from a distance, the Blue Mts exhibit two distinct features—first, a strikingly even surface, typical of a level plateau skyline, and secondly, a marked blue haze from which their name is derived. On top of the plateau there are a number of basalt-capped hills, rising like minor knobs above the surface, such as Mt Tomar (1000m), Mt Wilson (998m) and Mt King George (1 058m). The plateau is thus nowhere very high, yet it is exceedingly rugged, for it has been dissected by a multitude of deep valleys of the Grose and Cox Rivers.

Steep scarps and sheer valley sides made this plateau a barrier to the expansion of settlement in the first 20 years of Sydney's history. This was because the British method of crossing mountains was to ascend through the valleys; but those in the Blue Mts lead to massive cliffs often over 200m high. The first crossing was made in 1813 by three explorers, BLAXLAND, LAWSON and WENTWORTH. They kept to the higher ground, avoided the valleys and followed the ridge forming the divide between the Cox and Grose Rivers. The present main road and railway across the plateau follow the general route taken by these explorers.

The main rocks of the plateau are sedimentary. The upper surface is sandstone, with a softer, more easily eroded shale beneath. It is the sandstone which gives the region its distinctive landscape features and is responsible for the scenic grandeur of the area. The sedimentary rocks were originally deposited horizontally (Triassic in geological age); then the whole area was uplifted gently and slowly

A. Healy

Grose Valley in the Blue Mountains

so that the sediments were left more or less horizontal over the whole plateau. Any views of the cliffs along the valleys, or of features such as the Three Sisters, clearly show the level bedding of the sandstone. Along the E edge the rocks were tilted and warped to give a distinct monoclinal (single-fold) scarp. Since the uplift, rivers have carved out valleys giving spectacularly rugged terrain, with narrow gorges in the E where the sandstone is thicker, and broad canyons in the central and W parts where the valleys reach through the sandstone to the softer shales beneath. As these shales have been worn away, the sandstone above has collapsed to give sheer cliffs; the process still continues and rock-slides occasionally occur. Over the cliffs tumble many waterfalls, such as Leura Cascades, the Katoomba Falls and dozens of others. The broad canyons also provide striking views, seen from vantage points such as Govetts Leap and Echo Point. Along the edges of canyons stand jagged pieces of sandstone, producing features such as Orphan Rock and the Three Sisters.

Until about the time of World War II, the Blue Mts region was mainly a tourist area where Sydney dwellers spent their annual vacations, or where the more affluent among them had holiday houses for their weekend leisure. This tourist function has continued to the present, but as car ownership has become more common and transport more rapid, the region has increasingly become a commuter area for people who live in the mountain towns and work in Sydney or in the outer W suburbs of the city. The electrification of the railway to Katoomba in 1957 reinforced this trend; the journey to the city can be made in under two hours.
Further reading: Shaw, J.H. *The Face of Our Earth.* Shakespeare Head, Sydney, 1958; Taylor, G. *Sydneyside Scenery and How it Came About.* Angus & Robertson, Sydney, 1970; White, U. & Bechervaise, J. *Blue Mountains Sketchbook.* Rigby, Adelaide, 1971; Morrison, R. *Blue Mountains in Colour.* Rigby, Adelaide, 1973.

blue streak *see* fishes, bony

Boake, Barcroft Henry Thomas

(1866-92) Poet. He was born in Sydney and after leaving school worked as a surveyor in the MONARO district and as a boundary-rider and drover in western NSW. Dissatisfied with his work as a surveyor and depressed by family misfortunes, he ended his life by hanging himself with the lash of his stockwhip. During the last few years of his life he had a number of poems published in the *Bulletin* and some years later a collection of his work, *Where the Dead Men Lie and Other Poems* (1897), appeared. In general his style is rough and uncultivated, and little of his verse has literary merit. Nevertheless, the power of the one poem by which he is still well remembered, *Where the Dead Men Lie*, and the sense of atmosphere which its lines convey, suggest that if he had lived he might have become a poet of considerable worth.
Further reading: Semmler, C. *Barcroft Boake: Poet of the Stockwhip.* Lansdowne, Melbourne, 1965.

Boat People

In the late 1970s the term 'Boat People' was applied to refugees from Vietnam who managed to sail away from their homeland. By June 1982, 57 boats carrying 2 135 refugees had arrived in N Australia. Although the refugees who came on the boats had no authorisation, nearly all of them were finally allowed to remain in Australia as permanent residents under the special provisions for refugees contained in the government's immigration guidelines.

It is interesting to reflect that Australia was first colonised by 'boat people'—the Aborigines —who crossed 100km of water perhaps as many as 50 000 years ago, coming from more or less the same direction as the Vietnamese Boat People.

bockadam *see* snakes

Boer War

Events in South Africa in 1899, leading up to the Boer War of 1899-1902 between Britain and the Republics of the Transvaal and Orange Free State, were followed closely in Australia. Even before the outbreak of hostilities in October, some Australian governments had pledged armed support for Britain, and immediately after the invasion of the Cape Colony by the Boers, recruiting of volunteer infantry and 'mounted bushmen' began. Although by that time federation had been agreed to and the birth of the Commonwealth was only a few months away, the first contingents were organised separately by the various colonial governments. However, not long after their arrival in South Africa some of the men from VIC, SA, WA and TAS were combined to form the Australian Regiment. After federation the Commonwealth government began recruiting, and early in 1902 the first battalion of the Australian Commonwealth Horse was dispatched. A total of over 16 000 men sailed to South Africa and about the same number of

Australian War Memorial

Boer War trooper, SA

horses were sent. Australian troops won a high reputation for courage and for their ready adaptability to South African conditions. Casualties among them totalled about 1 400, including 518 dead. Six Australians were awarded the Victoria Cross.

In general, public opinion in Australia supported Britain enthusiastically, although some prominent people, including Professor G. Arnold Wood of Sydney University, criticised her strongly. The general support sprang not only from feelings of loyalty to the mother country and the Crown, but also from commercial and strategic considerations—as noted by Edmund BARTON, addressing the House of Representatives, when he said that if Britain ever lost control of the Suez Canal, the route around the Cape of Good Hope would once again be of vital importance to Australia.
Further reading: South African War, 1899-1902. Australian War Memorial, Canberra, 1974; Sutton, R. (ed) *A Boer War Chronicle.* New South Wales Military Historical Society, Ryde NSW, 1974; Wallace, R.L. *The Australians at the Boer War.* Australian War Memorial, Canberra, 1976.

Bogan River

NSW This is an inland stream rising on the W slopes of the GREAT DIVIDING RANGE NE of PARKES and flowing for over 720km in a general NW direction across the plains to join the BARWON RIVER upstream from BOURKE. The headwater tributaries rise in hilly country, where the average yearly rainfall is about 570mm, and sheep grazing and wheat farming dominate the rural landscape. The Newell Highway crosses this headwater area between Parkes and Peak Hill. Further downstream, beyond NYNGAN, it flows much more slowly, with many meander loops, BILLABONGS and ANABRANCHES; because the rainfall here is lower (Nyngan 425mm average) and less reliable, the river flow is seasonal, and sheep raising for wool becomes the main rural pursuit. The Mitchell Highway crosses the middle-Bogan at Nyngan and the long straight stretch of railway from Nyngan to Bourke crosses the plains SW of the river. The name Bogan comes from an Aboriginal word meaning 'birthplace of the tribal headman'. On the W bank of the river, 18km NE of the small town of Tottenham, is the burial site of Richard Cunningham (brother of the botanist Allan CUNNINGHAM), a member of Major MITCHELL's exploration party who died there in 1835 when the group was crossing the Bogan Plains.

Bogong High Plains VIC An undulating plateau lying between 1 400m and 1 800m above sea level, this area forms the headwater catchment of the KIEWA and MITTA MITTA Rivers. It includes MOUNT BOGONG and the small township of Bogong, and is part of the Victorian Alps. A section of the High Plains falls within the catchment of the Kiewa hydro-electricity scheme and is a sanctuary where shooting is prohibited and where plants may not be picked or removed; a track for walkers crosses the High Plains, linking MOUNT HOTHAM (1 862m), Mt Cope (1 837m) and Mt Nelse (1 882m), and continuing N to Mt Bogong; snow-covered in winter, the High Plains have a number of ski resorts. Although there are access roads to some parts of the High Plains, vehicles may not leave the main roads as damage to flora and soils may result.

The plateau was formerly an area of summer grazing for beef cattle brought from the lower-lying areas in the valleys, but grazing is no longer permitted because it poses a threat to the plant ecology and can lead to excessive soil erosion. The name Bogong comes from the Aboriginal word for a large moth; the High Plains were once a favourite venue for Aborigines who visited them seasonally to roast and feast on the large numbers of these moths.

Boldrewood, Rolf (1826-1915) Novelist. This was the pen-name used by Thomas Alexander Browne. Born in England, he was brought to Australia at the age of four. His father established a sheep station in the PORT PHILLIP District, and in 1844 he himself took up land at Port Fairy, where he remained until 1856. He then visited England, and after his return farmed unsuccessfully in the RIVERINA area of NSW. In 1871 he obtained a

Rolf Boldrewood (Thomas Browne)

Courtesy of A.I.S. Canberra

position as police magistrate and goldfields commissioner at Gulgong NSW, and later held similar posts at DUBBO and ALBURY. It was from his experiences in these positions that he gathered much of the material for his novels.

From 1866 he contributed articles and serial stories to English and, to a lesser extent, Australian magazines, and in 1878 one of his serials was published as a novel, *Ups and Downs: A Story of Australian Life*. Between then and 1905 he published more than a dozen novels, but his fame rests almost entirely on *Robbery Under Arms* (first published as a serial 1882-83). The story, narrated by a character named Dick Marston as he ends his 12-year gaol term, tells of his bushranging exploits under the leadership of Captain Starlight. It is frankly cautionary, warning Australian youth of the consequences of turning to a life of crime. Like his other novels it lacks emotional depth, but its simple style, well-constructed plot and air of romantic adventure brought it great success. Of his other novels the most highly regarded is *The Miner's Right* (1890).
See also literature
Further reading: Moore, T.I. *Rolf Boldrewood.* Oxford University Press, Melbourne, 1968.

Bolte, Sir Henry Edward (1908-) Premier of VIC. Born in BALLARAT in VIC, he became a farmer in 1934, but enlisted in the army in 1940 and served as a gunnery instructor in Puckapunyal Camp. In 1947 he stood successfully as a Liberal candidate for the VIC Legislative Assembly, and six years later became leader of the party. At that time the VIC division of the Liberal Party (known temporarily as the Liberal and Country Party) was suffering from internal disagreement. However, largely owing to Bolte's astute leadership, the party was successful in the elections of 1955. He was Premier from that year until 1972. Throughout his record term in office he showed himself to be an extremely shrewd political tactician and judge of public opinion, leading the Liberals to victory in five successive elections, and winning a reputation as an outspoken 'States-righter'. He was appointed KCMG in 1966 and GCMG in 1972.
Further reading: Blazey, P. *Bolte: A Political Biography.* Jacaranda, Milton QLD, 1972.

Bomaderry NSW (combined population of Bomaderry and NOWRA, 17 855 in 1981) A small town in the ILLAWARRA region on the S coast, about 160km by road S of Sydney, Bomaderry is located on the N bank of the SHOALHAVEN RIVER about 14km from its mouth. On the S side of the river is the twin town of Nowra. Bomaderry is the rail terminus of the S coast line and travellers to places further S on the coast take bus transport from this point.

Bombay duck *see* fishes, bony

Bond, Alan (1938-) Company director and yachtsman. Born in London, he was brought to Western Australia by his parents in 1951. After leaving school, he began work as a signwriter, but soon established himself as a real estate agent, and later branched out into several other areas of business. Today he is chairman of the board of the Bond Corporation, a holding company with interests in brewing (Swan Brewery), energy, retailing (including the Waltons Bond chain of stores), land development and mining. Early in his career he became actively engaged in ocean yacht racing, and in 1970 became interested in 12-metre yachts, and particularly in the America's Cup race, which had been won by the New York Yacht Club since 1851. During the next 13 years syndicates headed by him issued four America's Cup challenges, all with yachts designed or co-designed by Ben Lexcen. His *Southern Cross* (1974) and *Australia* (1977) lost 4-0 to *Courageous*; in 1980 a rebuilt *Australia* went down 4-I to *Freedom*; then in 1983 *Australia II* after being down 2-0 to *Liberty*, won the challenge series 4-3. The Cup therefore passed into the keeping of the Royal Perth Yacht Club, and the next challenge series will be held in Australia.

boneseed *see* Compositae; weeds

Bongaree QLD (population 4 789 in 1981) The principal town of BRIBIE ISLAND, Bongaree is situated on the SW of the island, at the N extent of DECEPTION BAY and at the S end of Pumicestone Channel, which separates the island from the mainland. Some 23km E of CABOOLTURE and about 70km by road N of Brisbane, it is a major holiday and tourist resort.

bonito *see* fishes, bony

Bonner, Neville Thomas (1922-) Senator, and the first Aboriginal to be elected to any Parliament in Australia. Born at Tweed Heads NSW, he was educated at BEAUDESERT State School in south-eastern QLD and became a carpenter with the Moreton Shire Council. He also became active in the Liberal Party, holding a number of branch offices and eventually attaining membership of its State Executive. He was elected a Senator for QLD in 1971. For the 1983 general election he was placed only third on the Liberal Party's list of Senate candidates. This caused him to resign his party membership and stand as an independent. However, although he polled strongly, he did not gain re-election. Soon afterwards he was appointed a founding Director of the AUSTRALIAN BROADCASTING CORPORATION. Although attracting less attention than some more radical Aboriginal leaders, he has been active as a spokesman for his race and as a member of many organisations concerned with Aboriginal and general social welfare.

Chestnut quail-thrush, *Cinclosoma castanotum*

Noisy scrub-bird, *Atrichornis clamosus*

Male zebra finch, *Poephila guttata*

Spangled drongo, *Dicrurus bracteatus*

Crimson chat, *Ephthianura tricolor*

Victoria riflebird, *Ptiloris paradiseus* (*P. victoriae*) (*see* BIRD OF PARADISE)

See also under separate entries

*Species, genus or family is endemic to Australia (see Preface)

Spinifexbird, *Eremiornis carteri*

Laughing kookaburra, *Dacelo gigas* (*see* KING FISHERS)

Fairy martin, *Petrochelidon ariel* (*see* SWALLOWS)

Golden whistler, *Pachycephala pectoralis* (*see* THICKHEADS)

Blue wren, *Malurus cyaneus* (*see* FAIRY WRENS)

Spotted bowerbird, *Chlamydera maculata*

See also under separate entries

★Species, genus or family is endemic to Australia (see Preface)

Senator Neville Bonner, the first Aboriginal Senator

Bonynge, Richard (1930-) Opera conductor. Bonynge studied at the New South Wales State Conservatorium of Music before going to London for further training and study as a pianist and conductor. He married Australian soprano Joan SUTHERLAND in 1954, and thus began their extraordinarily fruitful musical partnership. Apart from his conducting of Miss Sutherland's operatic performances and his fine work as an accompanist, Richard Bonynge is perhaps best known for his discovery and performances of lesser known operas of the 19th-century repertory, many of which he has recorded with Miss Sutherland for Decca. In 1976 he was appointed Musical Director of the Australian Opera. He made his conducting début at Covent Garden in 1964 and in addition to a wide variety of operatic conducting engagements throughout the world, he has also

Richard Bonynge

worked as Artistic Director of Vancouver Opera Association. He was made a CBE in 1977.

boobies *see* sea birds

boobook *see* owls

Booby Island QLD A small island located at the W end of TORRES STRAIT, it is the site of the most northerly Australian lighthouse. It takes its name from the gannets (boobies) which nest there. In the days of sailing ships, a cavern on the island was used to store emergency supplies for mariners in distress.

booklice These INSECTS belong to a small exopterygote order (Psocoptera), which is represented in Australia by about 120 species. The name 'booklice' is misleading as most are found in natural habitats; it is preferable to use the alternative common name, psocids. They are small, inconspicuous insects, usually overlooked by the layman. The relatively large mobile head carries biting and chewing mouthparts and long filiform antennae (that is, with the segments alike and resembling narrow cylinders). The two pairs of wings, when present, are membranous and held in a roof-like position above the abdomen when at rest. There are no cerci ('tails') on the abdomen.

Psocids live in a wide range of habitats: on foliage, on or under bark, in leaf-litter, under stones, in houses and in stored grain and sugar. Some introduced psocids (for example, *Liposcelis* species) can become numerous indoors if the conditions are damp, and they are often found emerging from encyclopedias which have not been opened for some time. Some species live communally under webs which, in the case of the *Archipsocus* species, may be very large. Psocids feed on unicellular ALGAE, small pieces of FUNGI and LICHENS, and scraps of dead animal and plant material.

boomerang This is the name used for a throwing-stick by a tribe which lived near the Georges River NSW. One of the traditional hunting weapons of the Australian Aborigines, the boomerang has attracted much interest and curiosity by its unique design and aerodynamic properties, which make it spin round in the air during flight. Despite popular belief, however, not all boomerangs come back, even when they leave the hands of an expert. Returning boomerangs were not known, for example, to the Aborigines of SA and northwards, and indeed no boomerangs at all were made by some people from the Western Desert, nor by Aborigines from CAPE YORK, ARNHEM LAND and the coastal KIMBERLEYS. However, although a similar weapon has been known in certain other primitive societies, the returning boomerang is believed to be a purely Australian invention.

A returning boomerang is usually 30cm to 75cm long, sharply bent or deeply curved with, often, one face flat and the other convex.

Its circling flight is caused by the contra-twist of the two halves. Returning boomerangs were used more for sport than for serious matters, but sometimes they were employed to scare birds into nets. The non-returning boomerang, longer and heavier, and with a shallower curve, was thrown or used as a club for killing game or in fighting. Sometimes it was thrown so that it bounced along the ground, end over end. Besides hunting and fighting, boomerangs were also used as digging-sticks, and as clapping sticks in ceremonies (*see* CORROBOREE). Wooden remains found at Wyrie SA, and reported in 1975, may have been been fragments of a returning boomerang. They were about 10 200 years old.

In modern competitive sport the boomerang has been recognised as offering sportsmen two challenges. The first is to throw it on its teardrop-shaped flight path so that at the apex of its curve it is furthest from the thrower. The record for this challenge is held by Bob Burwell who winged his boomerang on a huge arc which measured 111m at its furthest point. The second challenge is to throw the boomerang so that it returns closest to the point from which it was thrown. Yoshi Kimura—now resident in Japan—set an unbeatable record for accuracy when his boomerang returned to land at the exact spot from which he had thrown it.

The Boomerang Association of Australia was officially recognised in 1978 by the Confederation of Australian Sport. It holds official boomerang competitions, including an annual national championship.

Boonah QLD (population 1 874 in 1981) A small country town located in the Fassifern Valley, it is 42km E of BEAUDESERT and 87km by road SW of Brisbane, in the upland country between the Cunningham and Mt Lindesay Highways.

bootlace worms *see* ribbon worms

Bordertown SA (population 2 138 in 1981) Located in the SE of the State 19km W of the VIC/SA border, the town is on the Dukes Highway 285km by road and 294km by rail SE of Adelaide. It was planned in 1852, intended to provide an escort depot for the transport of gold from VIC to Adelaide. At an elevation of 82m above sea level, it experiences a mild climate, with an average annual rainfall of 541mm, concentrated mainly in winter (August average 76mm). It is a service centre for a productive hinterland where the principal rural pursuits are wheat growing, forestry and livestock grazing.

Boronia *see* Rutaceae

Borroloola NT (population 420 in 1981) Often called 'the end of the line', it is a small town in the NE of the Territory on the McARTHUR RIVER about 80km inland from the GULF OF CARPENTARIA. It is the terminus of the Carpentaria Highway.

National Library of Australia

The police station at Borroloola in the 1890's

Botany Bay NSW This coastal inlet S of Sydney is where the British explorer Captain COOK first landed in 1770. It was originally named Stingray Harbour, because of the abundance of the fish, but Cook later changed the name to Botany Bay in recognition of the unique plant collection made in the vicinity by Joseph BANKS. In 1788, the FIRST FLEET came to the bay to establish a penal colony, but Governor PHILLIP decided it was unsuitable: the waters of the bay were so shallow that his sailing vessels had to anchor opposite the entrance and so were exposed to easterly winds; moreover, the water supply was inadequate, the soils were sandy and some of the foreshores were swampy, which Phillip considered would be unhealthy. He therefore transferred the site of settlement to PORT JACKSON, some 9km N.

Today, most of the foreshores of the bay are occupied by the residential suburbs and industrial areas of metropolitan Sydney. The Sydney (Kingsford Smith) Airport, serving both domestic and international aircraft, is located on the NW shore of the bay, the longest runway projecting into the bay on reclaimed land. At Kurnell on the SE shore there is an oil refinery, close to Cook's landing place. The two headlands at the entrance of the bay are historic reserves—the tip of the N headland is called Cape Banks, and on the S one an obelisk commemorates Cook's landing. Until comparatively recently Botany Bay was not an important seaport. However the opening of the Kurnell oil refinery in 1955 has brought a steady stream of tankers to the bay, and since the late 1970s Port Botany, on the northern shore, has been developed as a site for container terminals and bulk chemical facilities. Today, therefore, Botany Bay is a major cargo port. However a proposal to build a coal loader there has been rejected by the NSW government.
Further reading: Birth of a Port. Maritime Services Board of New South Wales, Sydney, 1970; Anderson, D.J. (ed) *The Botany Bay Project: A Handbook of the Botany Bay Region.* Botany Bay Project Committee, Sydney, 1973; Butlin, N.G. (ed) *The Impact of Botany Bay.* Australian National University, Canberra, 1976.

Bothwell TAS (population 356 in 1981) A small service town located 74km NW of Hobart on the Lakes Highway, it is the administrative centre of the Bothwell municipality. Situated on the Clyde River, a N tributary of the DERWENT RIVER, and at an elevation of 350m, it is the focus of the surrounding pastoral district and a popular base for fishing in the lakes of the CENTRAL PLATEAU.

bottle brushes see Myrtaceae

bottle tree see Sterculiaceae

Boulder WA (combined population of Boulder and KALGOORLIE 19 848 in 1981) A gold-mining town which began as a tent-town in the 1890s when the Great Boulder Mine was discovered on the Golden Mile, 5km S of Kalgoorlie, Boulder is now part of the municipality of Kalgoorlie. In the early days, miners found the daily trek from Kalgoorlie to the Great Boulder Mine too long, so they established a campsite nearer the mine. This became Boulder township, which grew with the mining prosperity of the area, and at one stage, according to one old verse, there were 'six pubs to the bloomin' acre'. The town was laid out officially in 1897, with the famous 'Boulder Rock' area as its business section. As in all goldfield towns, water was a major problem; until Boulder was connected to the GOLDFIELDS WATER SUPPLY scheme in 1903, residents got their supply from nearby Lake Charlotte by distilling the salty water. Several buildings in the town have been listed for preservation by the National Trust (WA) including the former post office (1898), Albion Hotel (1898), the Central School (1899), the Masonic hall (1901) and the town hall (1908).

Bourke NSW (population 3 326 in 1981) A town on the banks of the DARLING RIVER, 786km by road NW of Sydney, it is often called the 'Gateway to the Real Outback'. It is located on the Mitchell Highway and is the terminus of one of the main railway routes into the NW plains (825km by rail from Sydney). At an elevation of 107m above sea level, it is the largest town in an extensive sheep and cattle grazing region stretching across the inland plains of the far NW part of the State. Grazing properties in the district are large, and over 50 000 bales of wool are despatched annually from Bourke for the city wool sales. It has a climate typical of inland areas, with very hot summer conditions, but warm days and crisp evenings in the cooler months from June to August. The average yearly rainfall is a low 346mm, with a concentration in summer, but the amount received varies considerably from year to year and long droughts are a feature of the region. In contrast with these dry conditions, floods can occur covering vast stretches of the plain for long periods with slow-moving muddy waters.

The town has many links with the early history of Australia; the explorers STURT, MITCHELL and OXLEY all passed close by the site of the present township and three of the town's streets bear their names. It was Mitchell who built Fort Bourke Stockade (named after Governor Richard BOURKE) in 1835 as a storage depot protected from attack by Aborigines. In the early days of settlement, paddle-wheel steamers travelled up the Darling River as far as Bourke, and COBB & CO. coaches served the town and much of the surrounding district. A bridge built across the river in 1883 at North Bourke has a lift-up span designed to allow river steamers to pass. Downstream (3km from the town) is a weir on the Darling constructed in 1897, which provides the town's water supply; incorporated with the weir is a lock used by the paddle-wheelers in bygone days. The present town is a busy commercial centre, with a major abattoir on its outskirts where some 250 000 sheep and 30 000 cattle are slaughtered each year. Bourke is also noted for the high quality of the citrus fruit grown N of the town adjacent to the river.

Bourke, Sir Richard (1777-1855) Governor of NSW. Born in Ireland, in his youth he came under the influence of his distant relative, Edmund Burke, the orator and statesman. Although he had qualified as a barrister, he joined the army in 1798, saw active service in a number of campaigns, and by 1821 was a major-general. From 1826 to 1828 he was Lieutenant-Governor of the Eastern District of Cape Colony and for part of that time acting Governor of the whole colony.

SIR RICHARD BOURKE.
Governor New South Wales, 1831-1837.

His years as Governor of NSW (1831-37) were very important in the colony's development, and his achievements were considerable. In the year of his arrival the practice of granting land was ended, and a system of transferring Crown lands by auction with a minimum price of five shillings an acre was introduced. This was part of the general policy of consolidating settlement. However, Bourke persuaded the British government to agree to two notable departures from this policy. In 1836 he was allowed to deal with the squatting problem by introducing a licensing system, whereby each squatter gained legal right to the use of his run by paying a yearly fee of £10. In the same year he obtained approval for the official opening up of settlement of the PORT PHILLIP District, where BATMAN and others had settled already without permission. He introduced State aid for all religious denominations, subsidising both the salaries of clergy and the building of churches, and tried unsuccessfully to introduce a system of 'national' schools on the Irish model. He co-operated very well with his Legislative Council, and advocated as a further reform the setting up of a Council of 36 members, 24 of whom would be elected. This was done under his successor, GIPPS, in 1842. He also extended trial by jury, by having it introduced in criminal cases. *Further reading:* Shaw, A.G.L. *Heroes and Villains in History: Governors Darling and Bourke in New South Wales.* Sydney University Press, Sydney, 1966; King, H. *Richard Bourke.* Oxford University Press, Melbourne, 1977.

Bowen QLD (population 7 336 in 1981) A port and service town on the E coast of the State, it is 1 273km by road along the Bruce Highway NNW of Brisbane, about 190km NW of MACKAY and 200km from TOWNSVILLE. It is situated on Port Denison, a sheltered natural harbour on the NW side of Edgecumbe Bay, with Gloucester Is to the E across the wide bay entrance. The rural environs of Bowen are noted for the production of tomatoes, tropical fruits (especially mangoes) and beef cattle. It experiences a tropical climate with high temperatures throughout the year and an average annual rainfall of 1 020mm; the precipitation is concentrated in the summer months, January being the wettest (253mm average), September the driest (16mm). There are several nearby seaside beaches: Horseshoe Bay, Rose Bay and Queen's Beach. Salt is produced at two plants by solar evaporation; there is a meatworks at Merinda, 6km W, and a coke-making plant treating coal brought from COLLINSVILLE. The development of the town as a port has been somewhat eclipsed by the expansion of shipping facilities in recent decades at Mackay and Townsville.

Bowen, Sir George Ferguson (1821-99) First Governor of QLD and later Governor of VIC. A classical scholar, he had been president of the Ionian University at Corfu and Political Secretary to the government of the Ionian Islands before coming as Governor to QLD in 1859. There he arranged for the first elections in 1860, encouraged exploration, took a close interest in education, and advocated the introduction of Indian labour for the sugar industry. In 1868 he went to New Zealand as Governor, and in 1873 to VIC. In the latter colony he had to deal with a constitutional crisis arising fom disagreement between the two Houses of Parliament. His support of Sir Graham BERRY's action in dis-

missing public servants as a counter to the Legislative Council's blocking of an Appropriation Bill was widely criticised as being politically partisan, and led to his recall. He was later Governor in turn of Mauritius, Hong Kong and Malta. The QLD town of BOWEN is named after him, and a QLD river and town after his first wife, Diamantina Roma.

Sir George Bowen

Bowen, John (1780-1827) Founder of Hobart. Born in Devon, he joined the British Navy at the age of 14 and was a lieutenant by the time he came to Sydney in 1803. Soon after his arrival, Governor KING entrusted him with the task of founding a settlement in TAS. He landed at RISDON COVE on the DERWENT RIVER in September 1803, with a party of 49 including convicts, members of the NEW SOUTH WALES CORPS and a few free settlers. In accordance with the Governor's instructions he named the settlement Hobart, after Lord Hobart, the Colonial Secretary. Early in 1804 he sailed to Sydney to ask for transfer to active naval service, and by the time he returned David COLLINS had arrived as Lieutenant-Governor and had chosen a new site for Hobart. Bowen handed over command to him, left again for Sydney in August and returned to England early in the following year. He is commemorated by a monument at Risdon Cove.
Further reading: Giblin, R.W. *The Early History of Tasmania.* (vol 1) Methuen, London, 1928.

bowerbirds These PASSERINE BIRDS belong to a small family, Ptilonorhynchidae, which contains 18 species (nine occurring in Australia, seven of them endemic); they are believed to be closely related to BIRDS OF PARADISE. All male bowerbirds, apart from the catbirds, clear arenas in which they perform their courtship displays; within the arena, most species build a bower of sticks which they decorate with small coloured objects such as flower petals, shells and, nowadays, litter. These arenas are, of course, quite distinct from the nests. The colour of the decoration tends to be consistent for any parti-

cular species. These BIRDS are skilled at mimicking the songs of their neighbours, and all species feed on fruit and insects.

The stage-maker or tooth-billed bowerbird, *Scenopoeetes* ⋆ *dentirostris* (23cm long), which frequents the mountain rainforest areas of E CAPE YORK, is a robust bird with brown plumage, streaked underparts and a notched bill. It does not build a bower, but clears an arena which is decorated daily with fresh green leaves, symmetrically placed and always turned upside-down. The nests of these birds are usually built in thick foliage, often at considerable heights, and are delicate, saucer-shaped structures made of thin sticks. Another species restricted to rainforest areas of Cape York (usually above 90m) is the golden bowerbird, *Prionodura* ⋆ *newtoniana* (23cm to 26cm). Its large bowers are pyramids of sticks built around two adjacent saplings and decorated with white objects. The male is a beautiful brown and golden-yellow bird while the female is dull brown and grey; the male displays around a bare stick in the cleared area between the two structures. Golden bowerbirds favour trees in dense forest for their cup-shaped nests of leaves, twigs and moss. The regent bowerbird, *Sericulus chrysocephalus* ⋆ (23cm to 28cm), occurs further S in south-eastern QLD and north-eastern NSW. The black and orange male builds an avenue-bower sparsely decorated with snail shells, leaves and berries. The eggs are laid in saucer-shaped nests composed of twigs and usually placed in thick foliage.

The satin bowerbird, *Ptilonorhynchus* ⋆ *violaceus* (27cm to 33cm), builds a similar bower, but it is usually more highly decorated, with blue and yellowish-green objects. The male has violet-black plumage and gleaming blue eyes, ringed with red; the female is olive-green. Found in the rainforest areas from VIC to eastern QLD, these birds build shallow nests of thin twigs and leaves.

There are three species of bowerbirds which do not inhabit rainforest; all belong to the genus *Chlamydera*. The spotted bowerbird, *C. maculata* ⋆ (27cm to 31cm), a blackish-brown bird with lighter brown spots and a lilac patch on the nape, is found in various habitats, from arid savanna to woodland, in western WA and E and central Australia. Its avenue-bower of twigs and grass is decorated with bleached shells and bones. The saucer-shaped nests of twigs are built in tall, leafy trees. The similar great bowerbird, *C. nuchalis* ⋆ (30cm to 33cm), which frequents woodland and forest areas in northern WA, NT and QLD, adorns its bower with a variety of objects, such as bleached coral, bones and snail shells. It lays eggs in a nest similar to that of the spotted bowerbird. The fawn-breasted bowerbirds, *C. cerviniventris* (23cm), are restricted to low-lying woodlands, paper-bark thickets and mangrove swamps in Cape York. They decorate their avenue-bowers with green objects, particularly berries. Their eggs are laid in saucer-shaped

⋆Species, genus or family is endemic to Australia (see Preface)

Mitchell Library

nests composed of twigs and bark and placed in tall trees.

Two species of catbird occur in Australia, both belonging to the genus *Ailuroedus*. So called because their song resembles the mewing of a cat, they are plump rainforest birds with stout bills; their plumage is mostly green. The green catbird, *A. crassirostris** (33cm), found in south-eastern QLD and eastern NSW, is occasionally seen with regent and satin bowerbirds. Its eggs are laid in bowl-shaped nests of interwoven twigs and plant stems, lined with leaves and moss; the nests are usually placed at the top of low bushy trees. The spotted catbird, *A. melanotis* (23cm), restricted to the E Cape York area, has greyish-brown spots on its black head and face. The nest and eggs resemble those of the green catbird.

Further reading: Marshall, A.J. *Bower Birds.* Oxford University Press, Oxford, 1954.

Bowral NSW (population 6 862 in 1981) A town near the N edge of the SOUTHERN TABLELANDS, it is 129km by road SW of Sydney, just off the Hume Highway. At an elevation of 674m above sea level, it experiences a pleasantly mild climate, with an average yearly rainfall of 925mm, and has long been a popular holiday resort, especially for those wishing to escape the summer heat of Sydney. It is on the main S railway line between Sydney and Melbourne (133km by train from Sydney) in a verdant countryside of dairy and mixed farms, where many business and professional people from the metropolis have country homes. The adjacent dissected scarplands of the plateau provide attractive scenery of gorges and waterfalls such as the Fitzroy and Belmore Falls.

box barks *see* Myrtaceae

box, brush *see* forestry; Myrtaceae

box thorn *see* weeds

boxing Until recently, one could walk into any hotel in Australia and expect boxing to feature as a major topic of conversation, but the current shortage of Australian world-champion boxers and the growing popularity of other spectator sports has tended to reduce interest in boxing.
In the early days of settlement, fights were contested with bare knuckles. In such contests, which could be long and torrid battles, the fight ended when one of the contestants was either knocked out or thrown to the ground. The earliest recorded bare-knuckle contest, in which John Berringer defeated Charles Lifton, took place in 1814 at Sydney racecourse (now Hyde Park). Probably the best-known fighter of the bare-knuckle era was Laurence (Larry) Foley of Sydney. After his retirement from fighting he opened a boxing arena at the back of the White Horse Hotel in Sydney where he trained young boxers and promoted the sport.

Two famous fighters trained by Foley were Albert Griffiths ('Young Griffo') and Paddy Slavin.

Bare-knuckle fighting was banned in 1884 following the death of Melbourne boxer Alex Agar after he was knocked out by James Lawson of Sydney. Consequently, in the first Australian heavyweight title, held in the same year, contestants Peter Jackson and Bill Farnan both wore gloves and followed a form of Queensberry Rules. Farnan was the victor. The following 20 years proved a boom time for boxing, legendary figures such as Albert Griffiths and Les DARCY coming to the fore in this period.

Boxing experienced a rather dismal period in the 1920s but bounced back during the Depression of the 1930s. Stadiums sprang up all over Australian cities—at one time there were 11 stadiums in operation, all featuring weekly fights. During World War II, like many other sports, boxing experienced a slump, but interest was revived with the emergence of the idolised Vic Patrick, a southpaw who held the Australian lightweight and welterweight titles during the mid-1940s. Another popular fighter in the 1940s was Dave Sands, one of a family of six boxers; by the age of 26 (when he died in a motor accident, in 1952) he held the Empire middleweight title, the Australasian light-heavyweight title and three Australian titles.
Sydney Stadium In the early 1900s, as promoters booked outstanding fighters from overseas, professional boxing became better organised and more popular. As a result of this increased popularity, sports-promoter Hugh D. McIntosh built Sydney Stadium in 1908 to provide a suitable venue for boxing championships. The first fight to take place there was between Peter Felix and Sid Russell and was refereed by Tommy Burns, the Canadian world heavyweight champion, on 21 August 1908. McIntosh had previously arranged a world-title fight between Tommy Burns and Australia's Bill Squires and this took place three days later, Squires being knocked out in the 13th round. The contest proved an enormous financial success for McIntosh, and in December 1908, he offered Burns £6000 to defend his title against Jack Johnson, the first negro to try for a world heavyweight title. Johnson was declared the winner after police stopped the fight in the 14th round. Several other big fights promoted at Sydney Stadium by McIntosh included such notable imports as champions Bob Fitzsimmons and Sam Langford. However, of the many championship fights staged at Sydney Stadium, only four were universally recognised as world championships. They were: Squires v Burns (1908), Burns v Johnson (1908), Sandro Mazzinghi v Ralph Dupas (1963), and Johnny FAMECHON v 'Fighting' Harada (1969). The stadium was pulled down in the 1970s to make way for the Eastern Suburbs Railway.
Australian world champions include southpaw bantamweight Jimmy CARRUTHERS, the first Australian to win a universally recognised world title (against South African

Vic Toweel, 1952); Aboriginal Lionel ROSE who defeated 'Fighting' Harada in Tokyo to become the world bantamweight champion in 1968; Johnny Famechon, who took out the world featherweight title in 1969 when he defeated José Legra in London; Rocky Mattioli, who won the world junior middle-weight title in 1977, and held it until 1979.
Professional boxing is now almost entirely controlled by the Australian Boxing Federation (formed in 1967), which has branches in five States. Moves to set up a government-controlled Boxing Commission were abandoned following investigations into boxing by the Australian government in 1973-74.
Amateur boxing is controlled by the Amateur Boxing and Wrestling Union (formed in 1924), which organises championships in all divisions of boxing.
Internationally, Australians have performed well in the COMMONWEALTH GAMES, and boast five gold-medal winners up to 1980; no Olympic gold medals have yet been won by Australians. At the 1982 Commonwealth Games held in Brisbane, Australia won one silver medal and four bronze medals.
See also Baker, R.L.

Boyd, Arthur Merric Bloomfield (1920-) Artist. Born in Murrumbeena VIC, Boyd's early art training came from his family environment. Arthur Boyd, the landscape painter, was his grandfather, and his father was W.M. Boyd, the potter. His mother, Doris Gough, herself a painter, created a warm atmosphere in their home, where religion and art were combined. By 1941, Boyd had worked through a series of landscape paintings, and was converted to creating works full of rich colour, applied free-hand and with a palette knife, depicting the grotesque. These paintings, interrupted by a three-year stint in the army, were vehicles for poetic and psychological fantasies sited in the decaying inner suburbs of Melbourne and of St Kilda's beach and parks. But there is another side to Boyd besides the world of human fears, conflicts and fantasies. After his marriage, his paintings of northern VIC and the WIMMERA district were carefree, colourful and gentle. From the late 1940s onwards, his interest in the surrealism and religion was fuelled by an increasing fascination with Bruegel and Bosch, resulting in a series of religious works, including the murals (1928) at the Grange at Harkaway. A visit to central Australia aroused him to the plight of Aborigines and half-castes, and resulted in his immensely powerful series *Love, Marriage and Death of a Half-Caste.* A subsequent retrospective exhibition at Whitechapel (London) further established his position and saw the beginning of a new series of paintings, in which he explored the world of love and sex, appearing to ask the question 'where does innocence end and experience (or guilt) begin?' Boyd has frequently enjoyed returning to ceramics, the most dramatic being his work in the 1950s, which was often religious in its content. He has also established himself as a

*Species, genus or family is endemic to Australia (see Preface)

master of etching and drypoint since the 1960s.

Boyd, Benjamin (?1800-51) Entrepreneur.
Born in London, he became a stockbroker and shipowner, and in the late 1830s became interested in the prospects for profitable investment in Australia. In 1839 he founded the Royal Bank of Australia and in 1842 emigrated to Sydney. By investing the bank's capital and his own in pastoral properties, mainly in the MONARO and PORT PHILLIP districts, he became one of the largest landowners in Australia. He also engaged in many shipping enterprises, and at TWOFOLD BAY built the township of Boydtown as a port and whaling station. In 1847 he imported about 200 Pacific islanders to work on his properties, but they adapted poorly to the climate and were unsuited to pastoral work. Their employment was also strongly opposed by humanitarians and free workers, and within a year he had returned most of them to their homes. At about this time it became clear that he had overreached himself financially: his bank failed in 1849, as did most of his other ventures. In that year, he sailed to California in his ship *Wanderer*, hoping to retrieve his fortunes on the goldfields. However, he found little gold and in 1851 sailed back towards Australia. Reaching the Solomon Islands, he went ashore and was never seen again. He is thought to have been killed by islanders.

Boyd, Martin à Beckett (1893-1972)
Novelist. A member of a long-established VIC family, he was related to a number of artists and architects, including the painter Arthur BOYD and the architect and author Robin BOYD. Born in Lucerne, Switzerland, he was brought to VIC in infancy and educated in Melbourne. However, after serving in the British Army and the Royal Flying Corps during World War I, he returned to Australia for only two brief periods. Of his novels, three were written under the name Martin MILLS and a dozen others under his own name. These include *Lucinda Brayford* (1946), *The Cardboard Crown* (1952), *A Difficult Young Man* (1955), *Outbreak of Love* (1957) and *When Blackbirds Sing* (1962). He also published a volume of poetry, *Retrospect* (1920), and two autobiographical works, *A Single Flame* (1939) and *Days of My Life* (1965).

Boyd, Robin Gerard Penleigh
(1919-71) Architect, probably better known as a prolific architectural writer and critic. Robin Boyd was born into a family of distinguished Melbourne artists, and trained in architecture at Melbourne Technical College, completing his course in 1946 after service in World War II. He began his critical writing as editor of *Smudges*, a student broadsheet, and his architectural work began with the design of his own house in Camberwell, a simple and beautiful building nestling in a secluded site.

In several partnerships, especially with Roy GROUNDS and Frederick Romberg, he de-

John Fairfax & Sons Ltd

Robin Boyd with one of the exhibits at Expo '70

signed many notable buildings in Australia and overseas, including the Australian pavilions in the Montreal 'Expo '67' and the Osaka 'Expo '70'. Within tightly disciplined formal restraints Boyd's work was highly innovative, demonstrated in the corrugated concrete vaults at Jordanville Supermarket, and in his own house in South Yarra, with its large roof supported by tensile steel cables. He did much to bring architecture to public attention, particularly by founding and directing the first 'Small Homes Service', run jointly by the Royal Victorian Institute of Architects and the Melbourne *Age*. It was a service offering advice, news and design facilities for home builders who would otherwise not have access to architects' skills. He lectured overseas as well as throughout Australia, and produced a television series on architectural design.

Apart from his buildings it is Robin Boyd's books that will ensure him a place in posterity. They include *Victorian Modern* (1947), a short history of architecture in VIC; *Australia's Home* (1961), where the same theme is broadened to include builders and users; and *The Australian Ugliness* (1961), a critical look at the urban environment. He wrote two important books on world architecture: *The Puzzle of Architecture* (1965) and *New Directions in Japanese Architecture* (1968). His *The Great Australian Dream* was published posthumously in 1972. Robin Boyd was one of the most admired and respected architects of his generation, and in 1969 he was awarded the Gold Medal of the Royal Australian Institute of Architects.

Boydtown see Eden; Twofold Bay

Boyer TAS
Located 6km E of NEW NORFOLK, Boyer is the site of a major newsprint mill on the DERWENT RIVER. Established in 1941, it was claimed to be the world's first plant to produce newsprint from hardwoods, and uses the timber from forests to the W of New Norfolk. The mill employs some 1 500 people and supplies about 40 per cent of Australia's newsprint requirements. Barges carry the newsprint downstream to Hobart for export.

Boyer, Sir Richard James Fildes
'Dick' (1891-1961) Pastoralist and chairman of the then AUSTRALIAN BROADCASTING COMMISSION (ABC). He was born at TAREE in NSW. He took his MA at the University of Sydney in 1913, joined the AIF in the following year, and saw active service at GALLIPOLI and on the Western Front. After the war he took up land near CHARLEVILLE in QLD, and in later years became prominent in primary producers' organisations, being at various times president of the United Graziers' Association of Queensland and of the Graziers' Federal Council of Australia. He also became interested in the use of radio broadcasting for educational purposes, and in 1940 was appointed a member of the ABC. He became chairman in 1945 and retained that position until his death. During his term as chairman, television broadcasting was begun, and the ABC's symphony orchestras were greatly expanded. Each year the ABC invites a prominent Australian to speak on major social, scientific or cultural issues in a series of radio talks known as the Boyer Lectures, as a memorial to Sir Richard.
Further reading: Bolton, G.C. *Dick Boyer, an Australian Humanist*. Australian National University Press, Canberra, 1967.

Brabham, Sir John Arthur 'Jack'
(1926-) Racing driver, designer and manufacturer. Born in Hurstville NSW, Brabham started his racing career in 1947, driving a midget car that he and a friend had built. In 1955, after several successes in Australia, he decided to try his luck overseas where he did well, winning many European races. In 1959 he won the world championship for the first time, the British Automobile Racing Club's (BARC) gold medal and the Driver of the Year award. He retained his world championship title in the following year. In 1966 he and his cars were the dominant force in Formula Two racing in Europe. In that year he won the world championship a third time (the first driver to win the title in a car which carried his name, a Repco-Brabham); he also won his second BARC gold medal, was again Driver of the Year, and won the Constructors championship. He was made an OBE in the same year. In 1967 he became the first person to have won the BARC gold medal three times; he won the Constructors championship for the second time, and was voted Australian of the Year.

Factors contributing to Brabham's success included a deep and specialised knowledge of mechanical engineering with respect to cars, a calm temperament and a love of racing. Today he devotes most of his time to his diverse business interests which include the design and manufacture of motor accessories and parts, aviation and the manufacture of luxury motor-cruisers.

bracelet honey myrtle see Myrtaceae

Brachiopoda see lamp shells

Brack, Cecil John (1920-) Artist.
Born in Melbourne, Brack studied at the

Melbourne National Gallery School, served with the AIF during World War II, and from 1963 taught at the Gallery School where he later became principal, doing a great deal to enhance the school's standards and status. Until recently, his painting was distinguished by strident, bitter colours, a precise arrangement of forms and space, and a preference for figurative subjects. His early paintings—such as *Collins Street, 5pm* (1956), now in the National Gallery of Victoria—had a pessimistic and detached view of Melbourne life. This social criticism, with its description of the alienating influences of the city upon its suburban inmates, was obvious in the 1950s and 1960s. It was replaced by a brief foray into a more abstract style in the early 1960s. Since then, his work has not shown an obvious preoccupation with social comment, and now seems concerned rather with the more subjective matters of how we perceive the world around us, showing a warmer range of colours and a manipulation of the traditional rules of perspective.

bracken *see* Pteridophyta

Bradfield, John Job Crew (1867-1943)

Engineer. Born in Ipswich QLD, he studied engineering at the University of Sydney, graduating BE in 1889. After working briefly with the Queensland Railways he was appointed principal engineer of design in the NSW Department of Public Works. He graduated ME in 1896 and DScEng in 1924. The latter degree, the first doctorate in engineering awarded by the University of Sydney, was awarded for a thesis on Sydney's proposed electric and underground railways and harbour bridge. These projects were completed during the following several years, and his harbour bridge design in particular won him international fame. The highway approaches to the bridge were named after him.

Bradman, Sir Donald George (1908-)

Cricketer. Born in the NSW country town of COOTAMUNDRA, Bradman, from an early age, set his mind on playing cricket well. To this end he was willing to spend many lonely hours as a youngster hitting a golf ball with a cricket stump to sharpen his batting skills. His success can be gauged from the the the fact that before he was 20 years old he held the world record for an individual first-class score: 452 not out, scored in just 415 minutes, for NSW in a match against QLD. But this was only the first of a string of records that were to fall to the determined and resolute Bradman. His remarkable Test average of a record 99.94 runs per match, compiled in 80 Test innings, has not been superseded, or even threatened, by any other player. He amassed runs quickly and spectacularly (28 067 in first-class cricket), and is holder of the records for the fastest triple century in Test cricket, for the fastest double century in Anglo-Australian Tests, and for the most boundaries hit in one day of an

Sir Donald Bradman in action

Anglo-Australian Test. He captained Australia from 1936 to 1948, during which time Australia never lost a series played against England. His exceptionally competitive spirit and ruthless dedication took him to the highest peaks of cricketing achievement and assured him a permanent place in world cricketing history.

Brady, Matthew (1799-1826)

Bushranger. Convicted for stealing food in 1820, Brady was transported to TAS and was at first assigned to a free settler. However, he quickly gained a reputation for insubordination, was flogged on a number of occasions and was sent to the special penal settlement at MACQUARIE HARBOUR, from which he escaped by boat with several companions in 1824. The escapees formed a bushranging gang which soon gathered other recruits and at one time had a membership of about 30. Their most daring exploit was to capture the town of SORELL and lock up the soldiers who had been sent there to hunt them down. By 1826, the strong measures taken by Lieutenant-Governor ARTHUR had been successful in eliminating the gang. Brady himself was captured by a party under the leadership of John BATMAN and hanged in Hobart in May 1826. Although he had terrorised a large part of the colony for two years, he had gained the reputation of avoiding unnecessary violence.
Further reading: von Stieglitz, K.R. *Matthew Brady.* Fuller's Bookshop, Hobart, 1964.

Braidwood

NSW (population 944 in 1981) A small township 290km by road SSW from Sydney, located near the E edge of the SOUTHERN TABLELANDS, it is situated on Jillamatong Creek, an upper tributary of the SHOALHAVEN RIVER, at an elevation of 657m above sea level. The town is named after a pioneer settler, Dr Thomas Braidwood Wilson, who was granted land there in 1833. The name of the creek, Jillamatong, is also given to a prominent hilly dome nearby, and comes from an Aboriginal word meaning 'a large isolated mountain'. The early history of Braidwood is linked with the gold-mining days and the bushranger times of the latter half of the 19th century. Gold discoveries in the district, at places such as Araluen, Major's Creek and Jemaicumbene, caused a mushroom growth of the town; it developed as a service centre for the upper Shoalhaven region and became a typical mining-boom town with numerous pubs, and connected by stagecoach to GOULBURN, QUEANBEYAN and COOMA. Gangs of bushrangers operated along the coaching routes; in 1865 the HALL gang 'stuck up and robbed the Braidwood mail 12 miles from Goulburn'. With the passing of the gold-boom days, the town declined, though some mining is still practised in the district. The surrounding rural areas produce beef cattle, fat lambs, wool and timber; the distillation of eucalypt oil from the leaves of native trees is a local subsidiary industry. Some historic homes and buildings have been preserved and the NATIONAL TRUST (NSW) has classified the

Tamar River from Brady's Lookout

whole of the central part of the town, as well as several public buildings and cottages in the town and district, as being of such historical and architectural significance that they must be conserved as part of the cultural heritage.

Brampton Island QLD One of the CUMBERLAND group of coral-fringed islands, it is located at the S end of the Whitsunday group. It is a hilly and wooded island of 464ha and although it is a national park, tourist accommodation is available, with facilities for fishing, coral viewing and aquatic sports. Access is by launch or plane from MACKAY, about 40km away.

Brand, Sir David (1912–79) Premier of WA. Born in Dongara WA, he served in the AIF from 1939 to 1942, entered politics as Member of the Legislative Assembly for Greenough in 1945, and became a member of D.R. McLarty's Liberal/Country Party Cabinet as Minister for Works and Water Supplies in 1950. Three years later Labor gained office, and in 1957 Brand became leader of the Liberal Party and of the Opposition. Following the Labor defeat of 1959 he became Premier, remaining in office until 1971, when he again became leader of the Opposition. He retired from the Liberal Party leadership in 1972, being succeeded by Charles COURT.

Branxton NSW (combined population of Branxton and GRETA 2 849 in 1981) This town is in the HUNTER RIVER valley, situated on the New England Highway adjacent to the town of Greta, between MAITLAND and SINGLETON, and on the railway route through the valley, 222km by rail N of Sydney. Coal mining began in this area in the 1860s and is still a significant industry; in the adjoining rural district there is dairying, fodder crop farming, fruit growing and viticulture. Statistically, Branxton is part of the city of Greater CESSNOCK.

bream *see* fisheries; fishes, bony

Brennan, Christopher John (1870-1932) Poet and scholar. Born in Sydney, he took an MA in philosophy, with Honours, at the University of Sydney in 1892, read classics at Berlin University for two years, and in 1895 was employed at the Sydney Public Library. After lecturing for some time to evening classes at Sydney University, he gained a full-time position there as lecturer in French and German in 1909. In 1921 he was made Associate Professor of German and Comparative Literature, but four years later was dismissed from this position because of his unconventional style of life and publication of the grounds on which his wife had brought an action for legal separation from him. From that time he lived in near-poverty, dependent on limited earnings from coaching and a small pension, and on help from friends.

His poetry, which was heavily influenced by

Premier's Dept. QLD
View from the walking track on Brampton Island

the German Romantics and French Symbolists, has not had great popular appeal. However, its craftsmanship and intellectual and emotional depth have won him general acceptance among critics as a major literary figure. His most important published work was *Poems 1913*.
Further reading: McAuley, J.P. *C.J. Brennan.* Oxford University Press, Melbourne, 1963.

Brent of Bin Bin Novelist. This was the pen-name used by Miles FRANKLIN for six of her novels, namely *Up the Country* (1928), *Ten Creeks Run* (1930), *Back to Bool Bool* (1931), *Prelude to Waking* (1950), *Cockatoos* (1954) and *Gentlemen at Gyang Gyang* (1956). The identity of the author of these novels was suspected for some time but not confirmed until Miles Franklin's private papers were made public in 1966, 12 years after her death.

Bribie Island QLD (population 4 789 in 1981) This coastal island in the SE of the State is located at the N end of MORETON BAY, adjacent to DECEPTION BAY, and separated from the mainland by a narrow stretch of water called Pumicestone Channel. The island, which is about 30km N-S, and about 8km at its widest point, is a major tourist and holiday resort, linked to the mainland by a bridge near its SW end. The principal town of the island is BONGAREE, located at the SW end, 23km by road E of CABOOLTURE and about 70km N of Brisbane. The ocean side of the island has a fine surfing beach, while the calm coastal side of Pumicestone Channel provides safe swimming sites and a special area reserved for water skiing. There is good fishing all around the island.

bridge This is a card game, derived from whist, in which (usually) two couples compete for the highest number of points. Competitive bridge requires considerable intellectual skill. Since the emergence of Contract Bridge as an organised game in Australia in the early 1930s, representative teams have had a number of successes in international contests. Australia's first win in international competition was in 1951 when she took first, third and fourth places in a world Par-Point championship. Australia also won first-place honours in the first world Bidding Contest in 1953. The Australian open team won the Far East Championship in 1968 and 1970; the women's

team won the Far East Championship in 1973, 1974, 1975 and 1977. On a national level, the game is controlled by the Australian Bridge Federation; national championships are held annually, participants competing in teams, pairs, mixed pairs and individual events.

Bridgetown WA (population 1 521 in 1981) A small inland service town on the BLACKWOOD RIVER in the far SW of the State, it is 282km by rail S of Perth, 97km SE of BUNBURY and 37km N of MANJIMUP. Bridgetown is an important orcharding centre, especially for apples.

brigalow *see* Mimosaceae

Bright VIC (population 1 545 in 1981) A tourist centre in the upper OVENS RIVER valley near MOUNT BUFFALO, 312km by road NE of Melbourne, Bright is the rail terminus of a branch line off the main Melbourne-Sydney route. At an elevation of 310m above sea level it experiences mild summers and cold winters, and has a high yearly precipitation (1 264mm) spread throughout the year; January has the lowest rainfall (62mm average) and August has the highest (160mm). Tourism, timber and tobacco are the basis of the town's economy. Originally a goldfield dating from the 1850s, it was named in 1862 by one of the early mining prospectors after John Bright, British agitator and political writer. The National Trust (VIC) has listed several buildings for preservation including the courthouse, the log lock-up, the powder magazine and the railway station.

Brisbane QLD (population 942 836 in 1981) The State capital and third-largest city in Australia, it is situated on the riverine plains and adjacent hills on both sides of the Brisbane River in the SE corner of the State. The centre of the city is some 20km inland from the mouth of the river on MORETON BAY.
Settlement Though James COOK and Matthew FLINDERS both sailed along the QLD coast, the discovery of the Brisbane River was left to the surveyor, John OXLEY, who explored the lower reaches of the stream in 1823-24. His purpose was simple and direct: to locate a suitable site for the establishment of a maximum security prison for convicts too intransigent for Sydney to restrain. His first choice was N of the estuary, on a peninsula facing the N part of Moreton Bay, where REDCLIFFE is now located. However, in his investigations of the lower river he noted a better site, some 32km upstream from the mouth. After the original settlement had been established in 1824, it was moved to this new site, on the N bank of the river overlooking a major meander loop. The original name given to the settlement was 'Edinglassie' but in 1834 this was changed to Brisbane, in honour of Sir Thomas BRISBANE, then Governor of NSW.
The environs The nucleus of the city was thus located at the head of the delta of the Brisbane River at a point where the river cuts

through a gap in the coastal range. The broad meander sweeps—with adjacent alluvial flats, stream terraces, some steep ridges of resistance rocks and nearby hilly country—have proved to be a setting of considerable natural beauty for the development of the metropolis. The D'Aguilar Range lies to the W and NW of the city; Mt Coot-tha, reaching an elevation of 286m above sea level and only 8km from the city centre, is an outlier of this range, dominating the W suburbs and providing panoramic vistas of the city, particularly dramatic at night. To the SE is Mt Gravatt (elevation 194m), just 10km from the city centre, which similarly provides scenic views.

The Brisbane River rises in the Brisbane Range, E of KINGAROY, and flows in an ESE direction, receiving the Stanley River as its major left-bank tributary and several others from the Main Range as right-bank tributaries, such as Lockyer Creek and the Brewer River. North of IPSWICH, the Brisbane River changes direction from its general ESE course, flows ENE cutting across the coastal ranges and thence through the city to its estuary on Moreton Bay.

City growth Relics of the convict era of Brisbane's early days still remain, not only in the stories about its commandant, Captain Patrick LOGAN, and in records of harsh discipline and suffering among its prisoners, but also in the old Windmill standing on Wickham Terrace and the Government Stores and Commissariat at North Quay. Free settlement began with land sales in 1842, but this was a time of economic depression and so initial growth was slow. In 1846, when the first newspaper, the *Moreton Bay Courier*, was established the population numbered less than 400. The initial sites of settlement were in the area of the present central business district and in Fortitude Valley. The arrival of Scottish artisans in 1849, sponsored by the Presbyterian clergyman John Dunmore LANG, provided a stimulus to growth. But squatters who had already settled in the DARLING DOWNS and other rural areas of south-eastern QLD advocated that Ipswich should become the capital city and Cleveland the port. However, Brisbane was the choice and it officially became a municipality in 1859, a few months before the QLD colony was separated from NSW. By 1880, the population had reached over 40 000, settlement had spread across the river to South Brisbane and Kangaroo Point, and the town was beginning to function as a farming and processing centre for sugar growing lands to the SE. Though a rudimentary network of roads was constructed, linking it to rural townships in the region, the capital relied on its river connections in the early stage of its urban development. The first bridge was built across the river in 1865, but was destroyed by flood in 1869, rebuilt in 1874, and again swept away in 1893. Lower-lying parts of the city are still subject to floods; the most recent disaster was in 1974.

Population By the turn of the century, Brisbane had over 100 000 people and contained

Aerial view of Brisbane

Premier's Dept. QLD

about one quarter of the State's population. By the 1920s it had doubled and after World War II it reached half a million. At the 1976 census, it had grown to almost 900 000 and accounted for about 44 per cent of the total QLD population.

Climate Located at a latitutde of 27°30′S, Brisbane experiences a typically sub-tropical climate, with hot summer conditions and mild winters. In January and February, the two hottest months, the average maximum daily temperature is 28.9°C, while in July, the coolest month, it is 20.4°C. The average yearly rainfall is 1 164mm, spread over all months, but with a concentration in the summer; January is the wettest month (166mm average), August the driest (47mm), and 52 per cent of the year's total rainfall occurs in the four months from December to March.

URBAN GROWTH OF BRISBANE IN THE TWENTIETH CENTURY

Year	Population	% of State population
1901	119 428	24.0
1911	139 480	23.0
1921	209 946	27.8
1933	299 782	31.6
1954	502 320	38.1
1961	612 550	41.0
1971	818 423	44.8
1976	892 987	43.8
1981	942 836	40.2

Source: Australian Bureau of Statistics, Canberra.

Metropolitan development The physical growth of the city in the 20th century has been closely linked with the pattern of the transport routes. Local railway services played an early part in suburban expansion, but the construction of a network of electric tramway routes had a marked effect on suburbanisation during this century. From 1962 the trams were replaced by bus services and in 1969 the railways of the city were converted from steam to diesel operation. Bridging the Brisbane River has occupied planners since the city's beginnings; in 1969 the old Victorian Bridge was replaced and in 1973 the Captain Cook Bridge linked the Riverside Expressway to the SE Freeway. The well-known City Hall Clock, once the highest landmark (92m), is now dwarfed by tall office blocks and these indicate the wide array of commercial, governmental, cultural and industrial functions of the city. The rapid population growth in recent decades has led to the outward spread of suburbs, including bayside developments along the coast and almost continuous urban areas along the road and rail routes to Ipswich. This urban spread, combined with increasing traffic congestion in the inner city, has been influential in the establishment of numerous suburban retail shopping centres. The city contains a variety of industrial enterprises including engineering works, food processing plants, a shipyard, motor-vehicle assembly works, a fertiliser plant, an oil refinery and factories producing electrical goods, agricultural machinery and building materials. The port and many of the heavy industrial enterprises are located downstream from the city centre where there are facilities for handling cargoes from large ships and a container berth at Hamilton wharf.

Many parkland areas have been preserved

within the city and suburbs. Mt Coot-tha Forest Park (1 379ha) is a mountain reserve, an oasis of tall eucalypts, native shrubs and varied birdlife, in the inner suburban area; the Botanic Gardens (20ha) are adjacent to the Brisbane River, close by Parliament House and the University of Queensland; Victoria Park (74ha), near the Royal Brisbane hospital, contains golf links and several sports grounds; Queen's Gardens (between George and Williams Streets, near the public library) was a cathedral site until 1904; and other notable reserves are New Farm Park (renowned for its rose, jacaranda and poinciana displays), Albert Park, Newstead Park, the Oasis Tourist Gardens, Lone Pine Sanctuary, and Bunya Park Wild Life Sanctuary. The city is also distinguished for its cathedrals and churches; for numerous museums and galleries; for its two universities (the University of Queensland at St Lucia, and Griffith University in the suburb of Nathan); for its variety of entertainment and sporting facilities; for its many historical buildings; and for the scenic hinterland both inland and along the coast, including such areas as the GLASSHOUSE MOUNTAINS, TAMBOURINE MOUNTAIN, the GOLD COAST and the SUNSHINE COAST.

Further reading: Davies, J. (ed) 'Brisbane' in *Current Affairs Bulletin*. (vol 34, no 6, August 1964); Newell, P. *Brisbane Sketchbook*. Rigby, Adelaide, 1967; Wood, P. & Philpott, M. (eds) *Brisbane and its River*. Department of Geography, University of Queensland (for Australia and New Zealand Association for the Advancement of Science), Brisbane, 1971.

Brisbane, Sir Thomas Makdougall

(1773-1860) Governor of NSW. Born in Ayrshire, Scotland, he joined the army as an ensign in 1789 and pursued a distinguished military career, including active service in the Peninsular War and the American War of 1812-14. He also developed a very active interest in astronomy, which he continued in NSW, where he set up an observatory at PARRAMATTA. As Governor (1821-25) he aimed at consolidation of settlement rather than expansion. In an effort to encourage genuine settlers and to deter speculators, he reorganised the Crown lands policy by restricting free grants and beginning the practice of selling a certain amount of Crown land. In accordance with BIGGE's recommendations, he systematised the administration of the convict system, and as a deterrent to crime reopened the special penal settlement at NORFOLK ISLAND and also established a new one at MORETON BAY, which later grew into the city of Brisbane. However, he was opposed to the wide use of corporal punishment. During his term of office the colony received its first Legislative Council, and a Supreme Court whose Chief Justice had the power to block any Act of the Governor and Council if he considered it to be incompatible with the laws of England.

After leaving NSW, he continued his work in

State Library of NSW

Governor Brisbane

astronomy, achieving distinction in this field, being awarded the gold medal of the Astronomical Society and receiving a number of honorary degrees. He was made a baronet in 1836 and was promoted to General in 1841.
Further reading: Brisbane, T.M. *Reminiscences of General Sir Thomas Makdougall Brisbane*. T. Constable, Edinburgh, 1860; Teale, R. *Thomas Brisbane*. Oxford University Press, Melbourne, 1971.

Brisbane Water

NSW This is a N arm of BROKEN BAY, located about 80km by road N of Sydney. It is a shallow, sheltered inlet, with many tourist and holiday centres along the foreshores and on the coastal beaches nearby. It is well known as a fishing area and for aquatic sports such as sailing, water skiing, swimming and surfing. GOSFORD lies near the N end of the Water and WOY WOY is on its W shore; some popular beaches on the coast are Ettalong, Pearl Beach and Ocean Beach.

Early in the history of British settlement in Australia, this stretch of Broken Bay was explored by Governor PHILLIP and was originally given the name North-East Arm, being changed in 1825 to Brisbane Water in honour of Governor BRISBANE. The first settler in the region was James Webb who was given a land grant of 40ha in 1823 by Governor MACQUARIE. Access to the area in those days was either by coastal vessel or overland from Sydney, taking a ferry across Broken Bay from Barrenjoey. When the bridge across the HAWKESBURY RIVER was completed in 1889, the Brisbane Water region was linked to Sydney by the railway, electrified in 1960; many residents of the region now commute daily by train or car to Sydney.

The Brisbane Water National Park (over 8 294ha) lies SW of the inlet, providing some panoramic vistas of the sandstone cliffs along the Hawkesbury River. The Bouddi National Park (1 148ha) is located on the coast 16km

along the scenic drive from Gosford. In recent decades there has been much residential development in some of the townships around the Water. The construction of the Rip Bridge (opened in 1974) across the narrowest part of the inlet between Booker Bay and Daley's Point was an important stimulus to residential growth for it provided a much shorter road route to areas where access had formerly been less direct. Settlements such as St Hubert's Is, Green Point and Copocobana were developed and others, including Empire Bay, Kincumber and AVOCA BEACH, felt the impact of better road connections. Gosford, the main commerical centre of the district, experienced considerable residential expansion in the 1970s, particularly towards the N at Wyoming and Narara.

bristlebirds *see* warblers, etc.

bristletails

These primitive wingless INSECTS are contained in an apterygote order, Thysanura; the common name is derived from the two or three bristle-like appendages at the tip of the body. The bodies (5mm to 20mm long) are more or less spindle-shaped, though slightly flattened, and are usually covered by scales. Bristletails moult several times a year, and sometimes live for seven years. Some species are vegetarian but most are omnivorous; several species in Australia are introduced, cosmopolitan household pests which frequently bite small holes in wallpaper, fabrics and book covers. There are about 23 species in Australia, including the introduced forms.

A worldwide species is the silverfish, *Lepisma saccharina*, so called because of its agile, twisting movements and its silvery appearance.

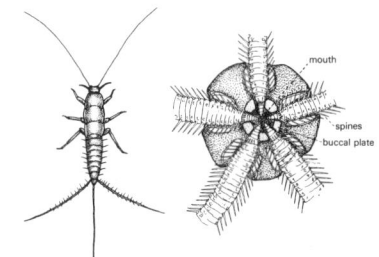

(a) A silverfish   (b) Oral surface of a brittle star

brittle stars

These ECHINODERMS belong to the class Ophiuroidea. They superficially resemble SEA STARS, but can be distinguished from them by the abrupt way in which the arms (usually five) arise from the central disc. The arms are mobile, and can be twisted in a snake-like fashion; in some, the basket stars, the arms are branched. Each arm consists of a number of 'joints', each of which carries spines and consists of four plates; there are no arm grooves and the tube feet arise between the joints. The arms of a brittle star, like the tail of many lizards, are deliberately snapped when grasped. The mouth, on the lower or oral surface, is surrounded by plates which serve as jaws. The sieve plate, which in most species has only one pore, is on the oral surface. Brittle stars are very active and can scuttle along the sea bed very quickly. They feed on small dead or living animals and detritus on the sea bed. They break for reproduction, though they also reproduce sexually. Some, such as the common Australian *Ophionereis schayeri*, are luminescent.

Most brittle stars are small though the arms are relatively long. One of the larger species, *Ophiocoma pulchra*, common under stones at low water-levels on southern Australian rocky coasts, is uniformly very dark red or purple (most species have lighter cross bands on the arms) and its relatively short arms carry long, smooth spines. Brittle stars are also common at greater depths; sometimes there may be about one hundred per square metre.

Further reading: see under sea stars.

broadcasting In both radio and television broadcasting Australia has a dual system, consisting of a national service and a commercial service. The former is provided by a Commonwealth government statutory authority, the AUSTRALIAN BROADCASTING CORPORATION (ABC), which is financed mainly through a direct government grant and gains no revenue from advertising. The latter is provided by stations which operate under licences granted by the government on the advice of the AUSTRALIAN BROADCASTING TRIBUNAL, and which obtain most of their revenue from advertising. All broadcasting operates under the provisions of the Broadcasting and Television Act.

Establishment of radio services In Australia, as in other countries, many experiments in the use of radio (or wireless) were carried out following the success of Guglielmo Marconi in sending a message across the Atlantic in 1901. In 1905 the Commonwealth Parliament passed a Wireless Telegraphy Act. As the name of the Act indicates, radio was used at this stage only for the sending of messages, mainly by Morse code. The direct broadcasting of sounds (radio telephony) took longer to achieve. In 1918 Mr (later Sir) Ernest FISK, in the Sydney suburb of Wahroonga, received the first radio-telephone transmission from Britain, and in the following year the Act of 1905 was amended to include 'wireless telephony'.

By the early 1920s the invention and improvement of the radio valve had made public broadcasting a practical proposition. In 1922 in the UK the British Broadcasting Company (later to become the British Broadcasting Corporation) was founded, and in the same year Amalgamated Wireless (Australasia) Ltd applied to the Postmaster-General for permission to begin broadcasting commercially. In 1923 the first two stations, 2SB (later 2BL) and 2FC, both in Sydney, started broadcasting. At first a 'sealed set' system was used, each set being adjusted and sealed so that it could receive broadcasts from only one station, to which the owner paid a fee. However, this arrangement was abandoned in the following year, when radio stations were divided into two classes. 'A Class' stations were to be financed by means of a listener's licence fee, paid by all owners of radio sets, regardless of what stations they favoured. 'B Class' stations were allowed to accept paid advertising, and were expected to receive most of their revenue from this source. The first 'B Class' station to become licensed was 2UE Sydney, in January 1925.

In 1928 the Commonwealth government decided that all 'A Class' stations should be combined into one national service, the Postmaster-General's Department providing the necessary technical facilities. The Australian Broadcasting Company tendered successfully for the service, and in 1929 began taking over 'A Class' stations as their licences expired. Two years later, however, the SCULLIN government decided that Australia's national service should be run by a statutory authority, as in the UK. The LYONS government followed up this plan, and in 1932 set up the Australian Broadcasting Commission (now Corporation).

Developments in radio since 1932 The dual system begun in 1932 has become permanent, but the method of financing the national service has changed: in 1974 the listeners' licence fee was abolished, the ABC having been financed since then by a direct government grant. Both national and commercial stations have multiplied; the ABC has more than 130 radio stations for its domestic services, as well as several transmitters for its overseas broadcasts through Radio Australia, which broadcasts for overseas listeners in English, Indonesian, standard Chinese, Cantonese, Vietnamese, Japanese, French, Thai and neo-Melanesian. There is no clear dividing line between the types of programmes offered by the national and commercial services, but in general the former tends to concentrate more on 'serious' programmes that often have minority appeal, such as classical music, lectures and talks, and also on service programmes such as those for schools and primary producers, while the latter has a more 'popular' bias.

The advent of television in 1956 had an adverse effect on radio, but the growing use of radios in cars and as portable transistors, together with the introduction of new types of programmes such as 'phone-in' sessions, has helped to restore its popularity. The introduction in 1974 of FM (frequency modulation) broadcasts, which give reproduction of a very high quality, has also been of great benefit to some listeners, particularly devotees of classical music.

Television During the 1930s experiments in television transmission were carried out in Australia, the most notable being in Brisbane. Interest was greatly stimulated by the beginning of broadcasts in the UK in 1936 and in the USA in 1939, but with the outbreak of World War II all work on the new medium in Australia was discontinued. Towards the end of the war a parliamentary committee recommended that preparations be made for the introduction of television in the fairly near future. In 1948 the Australian Broadcasting Control Board was set up, its functions including the provision of television services and the control of technical standards and programme quality in television as well as radio. However, the MENZIES administration which came into office late in 1949 delayed further moves, mainly on economic grounds, and it was only in 1954, after a Royal Commission had reported in favour of the gradual introduction of television services, that a firm decision to proceed was made. The ABC was appointed the authority for a national television service, and in the following year the Control Board began hearing applications for commercial licences. In September 1956 TCN9 Sydney began the first regular service.

Extension of television services From late 1956 television was gradually extended in a number of carefully planned stages, first in Melbourne and Sydney, then in other State capitals, and in a number of later stages to Canberra and non-metropolitan cities and towns. By the early 1970s black-and-white television had been brought within the reach of about 98 per cent of the population. In the meantime the Broadcasting Control Board had carried out an investigation into colour systems and had chosen the PAL (phase alternation line) system, developed originally in West Germany and used in Britain and many other parts of Europe. Colour television broadcasts began in 1975.

By 1983 there were 50 commercial television stations in Australia, while ABC services were available through more than 80 transmitters. Naturally, the choice of programmes is greatest in the large cities, Sydney, Melbourne, Brisbane and Adelaide each having services on four channels and Perth on three. Television has given rise to more public controversy than has radio. Among the issues involved have been the high proportion of imported programmes shown; the lack of educational broadcasts of a high quality; the use of the VHF (very high frequency) band, which gives limited scope for increasing the number of channels in the capital cities and which therefore hinders the opening of special educational, community and access stations; and the concentration of the control of commercial stations in the hands of a relatively small number of proprietors.

An inquiry into broadcasting was commissioned by the Commonwealth government in 1976. Conducted under the chairmanship of F.J. Green, Secretary of the Postal and Telecommunications Department, the inquiry presented its report (commonly termed the Green Report) in November that year, leading to a decision by the government to split the powers formerly exercised by the Australian Broadcasting Control Board between a new Australian Broadcasting Tribunal and the Postal and Telecommunications Department. The Tribunal's main functions are to issue, renew and revoke the licences of commercial broadcasters and to hold public enquiries into broadcasting issues. The Department is responsible for the planning of broadcasting services.

Ethnic broadcasting Broadcasting in languages other than English, for audiences within Australia, has been a comparatively recent development. Ethnic radio, begun in 1975, is at present run by the Special Broadcasting Service, a statutory body set up in 1977. It broadcasts in more than 40 languages from 2EA in Sydney and 3EA in Melbourne. Ethnic television, also controlled by the Special Broadcasting Service, was launched on a permanent basis in the same two cities in October 1980.

Broken Bay NSW Forming the estuary of the HAWKESBURY RIVER some 25km due N of Sydney, Broken Bay is a drowned valley, appropriately named from the steep, rugged foreshores and broken outline, like Sydney Harbour, typical of a ria formation, and hence having deep water up to the shoreline in most places. The bay is divided into three distinct branches, BRISBANE WATER on the N, Pitt Water on the S, and the central section where the Hawkesbury River enters. The N peninsula at the entrance of the bay is named Box Head, and that to the S is Barrenjoey. Midway between these heads, almost like a guardian, stands Mt Eliot, better known as Lion Is because its shape resembles a crouching lion.

Pitt Water, the arm nearer to Sydney, has steep hilly land along much of the foreshore and provides good shelter for yachts and power boats. Though parts of its W shore have been preserved as a national park, and so have remained heavily wooded, much of the area is now occupied by urban residential development. Places on Brisbane Water, such as WOY WOY, Ettalong, Davistown and Umina, have long been holiday resorts for Sydney dwellers. The area is also a popular retirement place for city people because of its mild climate, quiet pace of life, plentiful fishing, good beaches, and abundant sunshine. However, in recent decades it has increasingly become a commuter zone for people working in metropolitan Sydney.

Broken Hill NSW (population 26 913 in 1981) Though often called 'The Silver City', a more appropriate title might be 'The Lead-Zinc City', for it has been the mining of these ores over 90 years that has dominated the life of this city in the arid W region of the State. Located 1 170km by road W of Sydney at the junction of the Silver City and Barrier Highways, at an elevation of 300m above sea level, it receives an average annual rainfall of only 241mm and can experience long drought spells which, in former days, led to serious water-supply problems. Summer conditions are hot, with daily maximum temperatures frequently reaching above 35°C, though the low humidity tends to make these times less uncomfortable than might be expected. Winter days are sunny and mild, with crisply cool evenings.

Diesel loco hauling slag pots

The city is a rail centre on the Indian Pacific route, 1 125km W of Sydney and some 56km from the SA border. The rail route continues to PORT PIRIE in SA, where some ores are taken for smelting; this rail line was formerly a narrow-gauge track, but is now standardised. The city has many commercial connections with SA and keeps to SA Time rather than Eastern Time.

The Broken Hill area was discovered and named by the explorer Charles STURT in 1844 when he was seeking a route N from SA across the continent. He observed a 'broken hill', forming a break in the ridges of the Barrier Range, rising above the W plains. Since the area was then in the throes of a drought, Sturt noted in his diary that it was one of the most desolate regions he had ever seen. Following Sturt came the graziers, with their sheep herds; but because of the low rainfall and the poor pasturage, it was then and still is sparse grazing country, the best of it carrying one sheep to about 4ha, and the poorest supporting only one sheep to 6ha or 8ha. The sheep property which covered the present-day site of the city was Mt Gipps Station, and it was German-born boundary rider Charles Rasp, from this station, who discovered a mineral outcrop in 1883 which he believed to be tin oxide. He pegged a claim and sent samples of the outcrop to Adelaide to be assayed. The rocks proved to contain a little silver, but a later shaft yielded rich deposits and it was only a few years before the desolate area became a boom town of tents and shacks. Rasp, with some friends, formed the BROKEN HILL PROPRIETARY COMPANY LIMITED which, though it ceased operations in Broken Hill in 1939, has developed into a major national industrial enterprise.

The mineral ores are nowadays controlled and worked by three major companies — North Broken Hill, the Zinc Corporation and New

Broken Hill. A fourth company, Minerals Mining and Metallurgy, extracts ore from mines formerly closed. The area has proved to be one of the world's main deposits of lead-silver-zinc ores and the fortunes of the city are tied to the mining industry. Many of the streets have been appropriately named: Crystal, Mica, Argent, Nickel, Carbon, Sulphide, Slag and Oxide. From the early days, water supplies proved a problem and it was only in 1952 with the construction of a pipeline from MENINDEE on the DARLING RIVER that the city had an assured supply; this was further improved when the Menindee Lakes scheme was completed in 1968. Since 1939, the major base of the Royal FLYING DOCTOR SERVICE has been at Broken Hill and the radio network of this service is used for broadcasting lessons of the School of the Air to children on isolated properties. The National Trust (NSW) has listed many buildings in Broken Hill for preservation as part of the nation's historic and cultural heritage, including the post office (1891), the town hall (c1890), the police station (c1890), the technical college and the museum (1901), the courthouse (1889), the Caledonian Hotel (c1900), the Catholic Cathedral of the Sacred Heart (1903), and the Sulphide Street railway station (1895).

Further reading: Curtis, I.S. *The History of Broken Hill: Its Rise and Progress.* Frearson's Printing House, Adelaide, 1908; Shaw, J.H. 'Broken Hill—A Mining Oasis' in *Man and His World.* Shakespeare Head Press, Sydney, 1956; Blainey, G. *The Rise of Broken Hill.* Macmillan, Melbourne, 1968.

Broken Hill Proprietary Company Limited For long the largest of Australian companies, BHP has also now become one of its most diversified. It was incorporated in VIC in 1885 to work silver-lead-zinc deposits at BROKEN HILL, but early in the 20th century, as its reserves there began to dwindle, the directors felt that it was impera-

Open pit manganese mining

BHP

Continuous casting machine run-out bed

tive to find a new major field of operations. A decision to enter the iron and steel industry was made in 1911 and the NEWCASTLE works opened in 1915. Twenty years later the acquisition of Australian Iron and Steel Ltd, whose main works are at PORT KEMBLA, gave BHP a monopoly of basic iron and steel making in Australia. The opening of a blast furnace at WHYALLA in 1941 and of a merchant bar-mill at KWINANA in 1956 led to the development of integrated iron and steel works at both of those places as well. Meanwhile the company's Broken Hill mine had been closed, in 1939.

Diversification of the company's activities was at first concerned mainly with the iron and steel industry. From the beginning of its entry into that industry the company obtained the necessary iron ore from leases which it had held since the 1890s in the Iron Knob-IRON MONARCH area (SA). In the 1920s it acquired coal mining and shipping interests, in 1941 opened a shipyard at Whyalla (closed down in 1977), and in 1950 began mining iron ore for the Port Kembla works at YAMPI SOUND. More recent diversification has been on a wider and larger scale. A joint venture begun in 1964 with Esso Exploration and Production, Australia, Ltd, led to the discovery and development of Australia's first major oil and gas field in BASS STRAIT, and in 1976 saw the acquisition of an interest in a venture covering the development of oil and gas discoveries on the North West Shelf (WA). It has also been a major participant in manganese mining at GROOTE EYLANDT and in the MOUNT NEWMAN iron ore project, and has interests in bauxite and coal mining and export, in various steel-consuming companies, in cement mixing, brick making, chemicals, petrochemicals and plastics.

brolga *see* cranes

Bronhill, June (1929-) Soprano. Born
June Gough, she changed her name after winning the Sydney *Sun* Aria competition in 1950; the name is a contraction of BROKEN HILL, her home city, which raised a considerable sum of money to send her to England for further study in 1952. Two years later she made her début at Sadler's Wells, where she won recognition as Adèle in *Die Fledermaus*, Gilda in *Rigoletto* and Norina in *Don Pasquale*. Her Covent Garden début took

place in 1959 in the title role of *Lucia di Lammermoor*, for which her coloratura voice was well suited.

She enjoyed enormous success in the title role of *The Merry Widow*, produced in 1958 by Sadler's Wells; she sang this role in more than 200 performances during two London engagements in 1958 and 1960 and during a provincial tour in the same period. Despite her undoubted success as an opera singer, she was persuaded by the producer Garnet Carroll to return to Australia in 1962 to sing the lead in the Rodgers and Hammerstein musical, *The Sound of Music*. This had long runs in Sydney and Melbourne, and June Bronhill was as popular in this production as she had been in *The Cunning Little Vixen* and *La Vie Parisienne* in London. After returning to England in 1964 she was to have another great success in the musical *Robert and Elizabeth*, with musical score by an Australian, Ron Grainer. In 1975 she returned to Australia to sing Gilda in the Australian Opera's production of *Rigoletto* in Sydney Opera House. June Bronhill was made an OBE in 1977. She lives in Sydney.

Courtesy of A.I.S. Canberra

Singer June Bronhill meets Prince Charles in Sydney

bronzewings *see* doves, etc.

Brookes, Sir Norman Everard
(1877-1968) Tennis player. Born in Melbourne, and receiving his first tennis racquet at the age of five, Brookes, a left-handed player, was to be rated by the great American player William Tilden as 'the greatest tennis player and the tennis genius of all time', making his mark initially as a player and in later life as an administrator. A slow developer by modern standards, he was 30 before he won his first international tournament in 1907. This was at Wimbledon where he won not only the singles title, but also the doubles and the mixed doubles titles, and ably supported by Anthony Wilding of New Zealand won Australasia's first Davis Cup. Brookes and Wilding formed a redoubtable combination that was to retain the Davis Cup for Australasia from 1907 to 1911. The tournament was not held in 1910 simply because no country felt strong enough to even issue a challenge to this pair. Brookes won his first Australian singles title in 1911 and took the Wimbledon title again in 1914—his first attempt since winning seven years previously. It was said of him that his strong

temper—in his youth almost an obsession to have his own way—was steeled with maturity into a fierce determination to win which never left him. In 1924, partnered by J.O. Anderson, he won the Australian doubles championship at the age of 47. After retiring from professional tennis, he transferred his considerable capabilities to tennis administration, and was president of the Lawn Tennis Association of Australia from 1926 to 1955. He also founded the Australian branch of the International Lawn Tennis Federation in 1951. He was knighted in 1939.

Broome WA (population 3 666 in 1981)
Located on Roebuck Bay on the NW coast of the State, Broome is some 2 300km from Perth via the North West Coastal Highway. Named after the then Governor of WA, the town was established in 1883 as a port for the W KIMBERLEYS, and has been an important telegraph substation since 1889, when a submarine cable from Java reached Broome. However, its chief importance has been as the focus of a vast pearling industry which flourished from the 1890s until the early decades of the 20th century. Many of modern Broome's residents are of Asian descent, their forebears having been among the many Japanese divers employed in the pearling industry.

Subject, like most ports on the NW coast, to a difference of as much as 9m between high and low tidal levels, Broome has a 600m-long deep-water jetty jutting out into the bay. The town has a tropical climate, with an average annual rainfall of 541mm, concentrated in the very hot summer months (January and February both average 150mm), and a marked dry season from July to November. The production of mother-of-pearl and cultured pearls is still an important industry, and cattle are raised in the surrounding district, beef products being processed at a meatworks in the town.

Broughton, William Grant (1788-
1853) First Anglican Bishop in Australia. Born in Westminister, he became a King's Scholar at the King's School, Canterbury, and won an exhibition to Cambridge University, where he intended to study for the Anglican ministry. However, the death of his father caused him to take a position as clerk with the East India Co. in 1807, and he did not go to Cambridge until a legacy from a relative in 1814 gave him a measure of financial independence. He was ordained in 1818 and 10 years later accepted an appointment as Archdeacon of NSW in succession to Thomas Hobbes SCOTT. He reached Sydney in September 1829, and immediately became a member of the Legislative and Executive Councils. In 1835, while on a visit to England, he was nominated for the newly created position of Bishop of Australia, was consecrated early in 1836 at Lambeth Palace and installed at St James', Sydney, in June of the same year.

Bishop William Broughton

Before long his huge see was divided: by 1847 there were bishoprics of TAS, Melbourne, Adelaide and Newcastle, and his title was Bishop of Sydney. He not only welcomed this development, but contributed £500 a year from his salary to help establish new sees. In 1852 he went to England to obtain advice on the question of drawing up a constitution for the Church of England in Australia, but became ill suddenly and died there. He is buried in Canterbury Cathedral.

Broughton was widely respected for his sincerity and piety. His interest in education led to the foundation of the King's School at PARRAMATTA in 1832, and he was responsible for the building of many new churches, for the foundation of a school of divinity in Sydney and for beginning the construction of St Andrew's Cathedral. However, he was intolerant of other denominations, being particularly fearful of the influence of Irish Catholicism in the colonies; he fought to retain the privileged position of the Church of England, and so became engaged in sectarian controversy on a number of issues. Thus he opposed BOURKE's scheme for founding schools on the lines of the Irish 'national' system, and protested against the creation of the Roman Catholic Archbishopric of Sydney in 1843.

Further reading: Whittington, F. T. *William Grant Broughton, Bishop of Australia.* Angus & Robertson, Sydney, 1936.

Brown, Robert (1773-1858) Botanist.
Born in Scotland, Brown trained as a physician, and had served for four years as ensign and assistant surgeon in the British Army before coming to the notice of Sir Joseph BANKS in 1798. On Banks' recommendation, Brown joined Matthew FLINDERS as a naturalist on the *Investigator* in 1801. Between 1801 and 1803 he collected 8 400 species of plants, about 2000 of which were new to science. His findings on this expedition were published in 1810 as *Prodromus Florae Novae Hollandiae.* He was subsequently librarian to Banks, and was later Keeper of Botany at the British Museum (1827-58). While studying the fertilisation of plants in this period, he recognised the nuclei of plant cells and discovered 'classical' Brownian movement (the erratic motion of

small particles, such as pollen grains, in fluids), a concept expounded in his treatise, *A Brief Account of Microscopical Observations* (1828).

Browne, Thomas Alexander see Boldrewood, Rolf

Brownlee, John Donald Mackenzie (1900-69) Baritone. John Brownlee was probably Dame Nellie MELBA's most famous protégé. Born in GEELONG, he enjoyed both singing and acting from early childhood, his father being a fine singer and one of his uncles being a well-known Shakespearian actor. He studied in Paris, and his début in *Thaïs* at the Paris Opera in 1927 established his reputation as an artist of international stature. He was awarded a permanent contract with the Paris Opera and later one for the international seasons at Covent Garden. He appeared also at other leading opera houses in Europe and in South America, and his reputation as a fine interpreter of Mozart made him a regular particpant in the Glyndebourne Festivals. There, as at the Metropolitan Opera House, his interpretation of the roles of Don Giovanni and Papageno won special recognition. His repertoire was large, and ranged from Golaud in Debussy's *Pelléas et Mélisande* to Scarpia in Puccini's *Tosca*. He taught at the Manhattan School of Music from 1953, assuming the distinguished position of director there in 1956. Though he returned to Australia several times to make professional appearances (including his visit in 1928 at the request of Dame Nellie Melba), he did not again live in Australia.

Bruce, Stanley Melbourne Viscount Bruce of Melbourne (1883-1967) Prime Minister. Born in Melbourne, he went to England in 1902 to attend Trinity College, Cambridge, and did not return to Australia for 15 years. He was called to the Bar in 1907, practised in London, and also filled the position of chairman of the London board of his family's warehouse company. Having enlisted in a British regiment early in World War I, he served at GALLIPOLI, won the MC and the Croix de Guerre, and after being wounded twice was invalided out of the army. Returning to Australia, he won a seat in the House of Representatives in 1918 and three years later entered the Cabinet of William HUGHES as Treasurer. Fortune then not merely smiled on him, but could almost be said to have forced him into the prime ministership. After the 1922 elections the Nationalists depended on the support of the newly formed Country Party, which Hughes despised, and whose leader, Dr Earle PAGE, refused to serve under him. To many influential Nationalists it appeared imperative to replace Hughes, and Bruce, in spite of his lack of political experience, was chosen to succeed him. In spite of a certain electoral disadvantage, springing from the fact that in speech, manner and dress he appeared to many to be English rather than Australian, he

Stanley Melbourne (later Lord) Bruce

remained Prime Minister, at the head of the Nationalist/Country Party coalition ministries, until 1929. These Bruce-Page ministries, following the slogan 'men, money and markets', presided over a period of high immigration and rapid economic growth, and were also responsible for such important steps as the placing of Commonwealth-State financial relationships on a new basis through the setting up of the LOAN COUNCIL, and the promotion of applied scientific research by the foundation of the body now known as the COMMONWEALTH SCIENTIFIC AND INDUSTRIAL RESEARCH ORGANIZATION (CSIRO).

In 1929, as the nation's economic conditions deteriorated and the government's popularity declined, Bruce incurred a further loss of public support by proposing changes to the industrial arbitration system, and in the elections of that year not only was the government defeated, but he himself lost his seat in Parliament. However, he continued to serve his nation with distinction for many years. Re-elected in 1931, he was sent to London as Resident Minister in the following year, and after resigning from Parliament in 1933 served as Australian High Commissioner in London, continuously until 1945. He also represented the Australian government on the British War Cabinet and the Pacific War Cabinet, and was the first Chancellor of the Australian National University, from 1951 to 1961. On the international scene he was chairman of the preparatory commission for the establishment of the Food and Agriculture Organisation. When created Viscount Bruce of Melbourne in 1947 he became the first Australian to enter the House of Lords.

Further reading: Edwards, C. *Bruce of Melbourne: Man of Two Worlds.* Heinemann, London, 1965.

brumbies *see* animals, introduced

Bruny Island TAS (population 390 in 1981) Located in the SE of the State between STORM BAY and D'ENTRECASTEAUX CHANNEL, the island was discovered by Abel TASMAN, who in 1642 sheltered there

but did not land. Bruny Is figured prominently in the early exploration of the southern seas; Captain COOK visited it in 1777, Captain BLIGH in 1788 and again in 1792, and the French admiral, Bruni D'Entrecasteaux, surveyed the channel to the W in 1792 and gave the island his Christian name. Bruny is almost two distinct islands, connected by an isthmus 5km long and about 50m wide. Signs on the road along this narrow isthmus connecting N and S Bruny warn motorists to watch out for penguins, as the birds often waddle with comic dignity across the roadway at dusk. A vehicular ferry service links the mainland (from Kettering, 34km S of Hobart) to the island (at Barnes Bay on the N). The rural activities on the island are fruit growing, dairying, timber-getting and sheep grazing. Bligh Museum, at Adventure Bay, records the history of the island.

brush cherry *see* Myrtaceae

Bryophyta Bryophytes, or mosses, are widespread in rainy or humid places, but rarer in the arid zone. Only a few species are adapted to survive long droughts, though many can withstand temporary desiccation. The individual moss plant consists of a slender leafy axis, either erect or prostrate, and may have slender multicellular absorptive rhizoids. Mosses rarely occur as individuals, but form extensive colonies on moist soil, rocks or wood. The largest mosses are native to the S hemisphere (for example, those in the genera *Dawsonia* and *Polytrichum*, both represented in Australia, may exceed 30cm and 18cm in length respectively).

Mosses produce airborne spores which are able to withstand drying out; upon reaching a suitable habitat the spores germinate, forming a prostrate filamentous system (protonema), which subsequently buds to produce the leafy shoots. In common with liverworts (phylum HEPATOPHYTA) these plants are haploid, and upon reaching sexual maturity produce either eggs or mobile sperm. Under dewy conditions the sperm are able to swim to the eggs and fertilisation takes place; a capsule is formed within which spores are produced; these then disperse and germinate to form new plants. Asexual reproduction from fragments of rhizoids, stems and leaves occurs with ease, a characteristic shared also by liverworts.

The moss FLORA of Australia is rich and diverse. The species occurring in TAS and in moist parts of VIC have close affinities with those of New Zealand, while those of the drier regions of VIC, SA and WA have a greater affinity with those in South Africa. Mosses in tropical QLD are more closely related to those of New Guinea and the Malaysian region.

Although mosses form a conspicuous element of closed forest communities and are important soil-binding colonisers of bare, moist soil such as stream banks, only one genus, *Sphagnum* (peat moss), has any real economic importance. Peat moss is widely used as a soil conditioner, either to make soils more acid and/or to improve their water-holding characteristics. In the latter case it is the pulverised remains of dead plants which are used, particularly for growing plants in containers. Although *Sphagnum* grows in Australia most supplies are imported, particularly from Germany, where it is taken from peat bogs. *Sphagnum* is an interesting moss in that it can hold a very large amount of water. Because of its ability to take up run-off from heavy downpours or snow, and subsequently to release the water slowly into streams, *Sphagnum* bogs in the alpine catchments of Australia, though limited in extent, are important in regulating stream flow. Both peat mining and cattle are excluded from such areas as part of water resource management.
See also Appendix 5, Flower Structure and Glossary of Botanical Terms
Further reading: see Appendix 6, A Bibliography for Plants.

Bryozoa *see* ectoprocts

bubble shells *see* gastropods

Buccaneer Archipelago WA This is a group of small islands located off the indented coast of the W KIMBERLEYS, between King Sound and Collier Bay, in the far NW of the State. The area is dotted with reefs which, with the large tidal range and the fast tidal race in many of the channels, create hazards for ships. Many of the reefs and the low-lying islands are exposed only at low tide. The archipelago was discovered by William DAMPIER in 1688; it was charted and named by the cartographer Phillip Parker King (during his voyages between 1817 and 1822) to commemorate Dampier, the buccaneer mariner.

buckjumping *see* roughriding

Buckley, William (1780-1856) Convict. Transported to Australia for the crime of having received stolen goods, Buckley was a member of the party brought by David COLLINS to PORT PHILLIP BAY in 1803. There he escaped, and lived with the Aborigines until July 1835, when a group of settlers led by John BATMAN found him. For a while he acted as interpreter between the white settlers and the Aborigines, but was not very effective in the role. He was given a free pardon and in 1837 went to TAS, where he lived on a small pension. The colloquial phrase 'Buckley's chance', meaning a very slim chance, arose from his story.
Further reading: Bonwick, J. *William Buckley, the Wild White Man and his Port Phillip Black Friends.* G. Nichols, Melbourne, 1856; Pyke, W.T. *The Story of William Buckley.* E.W. Cole, Melbourne, 1889.

Buderim QLD (population 4 016 in 1981) A country town and tourist resort in the SUNSHINE COAST region, it is located 3km off the Bruce Highway, 8km inland from MAROO- CHYDORE and 100km by road N of Brisbane. It is situated in an area of rich red volcanic soils, between the Blackall Range and the coast, where there is a wide variety of crops: avocado pears, citrus fruits, vegetables, strawberries and ginger (the town boasts the only ginger-processing factory in Australia). The name Buderim comes from an Aboriginal word meaning 'honeysuckle'.

budgerigar *see* parrots, etc.

Budgewoi NSW (population of the township and adjacent urban areas 25 468 in 1981) A tourist area on the central coast some 120km N of Sydney, Budgewoi is a popular holiday resort comprising a township (which lies on the narrow isthmus separating Budgewoi Lake from Munmorah Lake), the two lakes and the area surrounding them as far as the N shore of TUGGERAH LAKE. Urban centres nearby include Toukley, Norah Head, Buff Point and Gorokan.

buffalo fly A small grey bloodsucking fly, *Haematobia exigua* (4mm long), the buffalo fly attacks cattle in vast numbers, slowing down the rate of fattening and reducing milk production. Bulls are more troubled by these FLIES than are cows, and British breeds are more susceptible than Brahman breeds. Buffalo fly invaded Australia at PORT ESSINGTON in the NT in 1838, having been brought in, it is thought, with buffaloes from Timor. The pest is now widespread in the wetter parts of N Australia, from PORT HEDLAND to BUNDABERG.

bugs, Balmain and Moreton Bay
see crustaceans

bugs These belong to the Hemiptera, an order of INSECTS known to entomologists as the 'true bugs' and including such familiar insects as APHIDS, bedbugs, CICADAS and mealy bugs. There are almost 4000 known species in Australia. True bugs range in size from 1mm to about 90mm. Apart from some non-feeding adults, all have piercing and sucking mouthparts. With very few exceptions bugs extract blood, plant-sap and other fluids for food, the maxillae and mandibles of the mouthparts interlocking to form a double-channelled beak, with one channel drawing food and the other injecting saliva. Apart from some wingless specimens, all bugs have two pairs of wings. The nymphs almost always resemble wingless adults. Many bugs are of economic or medical significance. The Hemiptera is one of the most important insect orders as many of the members attack crops, often transmitting serious virus diseases (*see* DISEASES, PLANT). A few attack man and animals but in Australia at least they are not important as disease spreaders. Some bugs are useful predators of pests such as MITES.

The order is divided into two suborders:

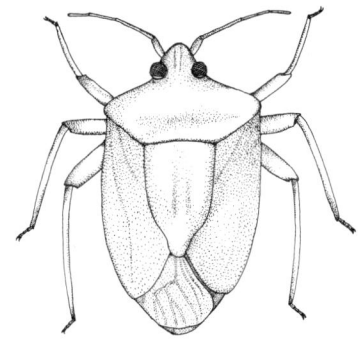

A shield or stink bug

Homoptera (terrestrial plant-feeders); and Heteroptera (which contains predatory and aquatic bugs as well as terrestrial plant-feeders).

Homoptera In this suborder the fore-wings, when present, are of a uniform texture, either entirely membranous or entirely thickened. The two pairs are usually folded in a tent-like fashion. Most homopterans produce large quantities of honeydew, an excretory liquid rich in carbohydrates. This is eagerly sought by ants which will sometimes husband the producers. There are about 2000 homopteran species in Australia, divided into 39 families. Homopterans are divided into two series, Auchenorrhyncha and Sternorrhyncha.

Auchenorrhyncha contains bugs which have very short antennae, ending in a bristle, and the mouthparts clearly arise from the head. There are four superfamilies.
1. The Fulgoroidea contains the Delphacidae, a family of small bugs most of which feed on grasses to which they often transmit virus diseases—for example, the Fiji disease which affects sugar cane. The Fulgaridae, the lantern flies, are medium to large bugs, sometimes brightly coloured and usually found in the tropics. Some have elongated snouts which were once thought to be luminous.
2. The Cercopoidea contains the plant-hoppers, such as the familiar spittle bugs and froghoppers. Many of the nymphs in this superfamily develop in a protective froth on plants which is produced by blowing air through anal secretions.
3. The Cicadoidea contains only the cicadas and the similar family Tettigarctidae.
4. The Cicadelloidea is a large group of varied leaf-hoppers. Most Australian species feed on trees, whereas elsewhere herbs are the usual hosts. Among them are the members of the family Membracidae, which have a greatly enlarged pronotum (upper part of first thoracic segment), often grotesquely shaped; many membracids resemble thorns.

Sternorrhyncha contains bugs in which the antennae are relatively well developed, and the mouthparts appear to rise between the bases of the legs. Many species are fairly inactive and, in the case of certain adult females, completely immobile. A few of the most important superfamilies and families are mentioned here.
1. The Psyllidae is a large family of small leaf-hoppers that resemble tiny cicadas with long antennae. They include the lerps whose nymphs produce a white woolly material once relished by the Aborigines. The lerp insect, *Cardiaspina*, often defoliates, and sometimes kills, eucalypts.
2. The superfamily Aphidoidea contains the aphids and several closely related families.
3. The members of the family Aleyrodidae are tiny, winged, moth-like bugs covered with a white, waxy secretion, hence their common name of white flies. Some introduced species are serious pests of plants such as citrus and vegetables.
4. The Coccoidea contains several families of scale insects and mealy bugs in which the adult females are sessile plant-suckers with reduced legs and sense organs, and the adult males are usually winged. The native cottony-cushion scale, *Icerya purchasi*, feeds on wattles but has become a pest of citrus. In the 1880s it became a serious problem in California until it was controlled by a ladybird beetle, *Rodolia cardinalis*, and a parasitic fly from Australia. This was the first successful large-scale use of BIOLOGICAL CONTROL. Several species of scale insects and mealy bugs have been introduced into Australia and have become serious pests of fruit and trees. In some cases irritation of the plant tissue by the parasite causes outgrowths (galls) to develop on the host plant.

Heteroptera In the bugs of this suborder the bases of the fore-wings are thicker than, and differ in texture from, the apices, and the wings are usually folded flat over the body. There are 48 known families in Australia. Heteropterans may be divided into two clearly distinguished groups, the Gymnocerata and the Cryptocerata.

The Gymnocerata have long antennae and are contained in 10 superfamilies, the most important of which are mentioned here.
1. The Cimicoidea is named after the family Cimicidae, which is represented by the introduced bedbug, *Cimex lectularius*. This flattened, wingless bug can creep into small crevices in walls and furniture and emerge during the night to feed on the blood of its sleeping victim. It is still surprisingly common, especially in cities, and there was a recent infestation in a residential college in Sydney. The related family Anthocoridae contains small dark bugs which feed on insects and their eggs. The Miridae is a large family (about 100 known species in Australia) of usually green and brown, fragile bugs that feed on plant-sap or other insects. A few live on sundew plants in WA where they feed on trapped insects.
2. The Tingoidea is a group of lace-winged, plant-feeding bugs which includes the azalea lace-wing bugs, *Stephanitis queenslandensis* and *S. pyrioides*, and various American species that have been introduced for the control of LANTANA.
3. The Reduvoidea contains the assassin bugs, all predators with long stabbing beaks and sometimes predatory fore-legs. Many of the 244 species found in Australia are brightly coloured, especially when nymphs. Abroad, many suck mammalian blood and some even spread diseases, such as Chaga's disease which is related to African sleeping sickness. Recently a member of the bloodsucking group, *Triatoma*, has been found in QLD.
4. The superfamily Pentatomoidea (in Australia, about 460 species in 10 families) contains the shield bugs (family Pentatomidae), so called because of their shape; these are also known as stink bugs because of the foul smell they release when disturbed. A common example is the green vegetable bug, *Nezara viridula*, a shiny green bug which was introduced from South America. Several pentatomids feed on other insects, including caterpillars and bedbugs. The related family Tessaratomidae contains the familiar bronze orange bug, *Musgraveia sulciventris*, a native pest of citrus.
5. All members of the superfamily Gerroidea live on the surface of water, feeding on dead or living animals. They differ from the rest of the Gymnocerata in that they have long spindly legs and an ability to skate rapidly over the surface. Many of the remaining Gymnocerata live below the surface, though with few exceptions they must come to the surface to collect air.

The remaining families belong to the Cryptocerata; all species within this group are aquatic and have tiny antennae that are not visible from above.
1. The Notonectidae contains the backswimmers which scull along upside-down, using their long hind-legs as oars. The other legs are used to seize prey. The saliva is toxic and they can bite painfully.
2. The Nepidae contains predatory but sluggish species, usually called water scorpions, probably because of the long tail-breathing siphon which is mistaken for a sting.
3. The Belostomatidae are the giant water bugs, some of which measure 70mm. Their stout front legs are raptorial. Normally they prey on small fish, tadpoles and large insects but their extremely toxic saliva causes severe pain in human beings, hence their common name 'toe-biters'. A South-East Asian species was once the source of a flavouring for curries.
4. The Corixidae, unlike the other members of the Cryptocerata, are mainly vegetarian. Their front legs scoop up material from the bottom of ponds for the algae contained within it. These water boatmen are superficially like the notonectids but they swim the 'right-way up'.

bulbuls see animals, introduced

Bulletin, the Founded in 1880 by John Hayes and J.F. Archibald (whose bequest established the ARCHIBALD PRIZE), this weekly publication played an important part in the development of Australian literature and in the growth of Australian nationalism. Under the editorship of Archibald, with Alfred STEPHENS as literary editor, and W.H. Traill and William Macleod (in succession) as managers, the newspaper was by the 1890s the most widely read and influential literary magazine in Australian publishing history.

Up to the time of its foundation, the writings of Australian authors had, almost without exception, reflected English attitudes and writing styles. But the *Bulletin* published, on its literary Red Page, many distinctively Australian writers, including Henry LAWSON, Andrew Barton PATERSON and Tom COLLINS. Moreover, the increased opportunity for publication provided by the *Bulletin,* and the encouragement and advice given by Stephens, served to increase the general output of good writing within Australia.

With regard to political, economic and social matters, the *Bulletin* favoured republican government, the severing of all ties with Britain, the introduction of land tax, the complete secularisation of public education and the protection of Australian industries. It was outspoken in its criticism of the royal family, opposed to any form of imperial federation, and was against Asian immigration. However, in spite of its republican leanings, it supported Australian participation in World War I.

After Stephens left in 1906 the *Bulletin*'s literary influence declined, and from the 1920s it moved away from political radicalism towards conservatism. It is still widely read today, but concentrates on financial affairs and on topical matters of political and social interest; in format, style and outlook it bears little resemblance to the original newspaper.

Bulloo River QLD An intermittent stream located in the arid SW corner of the State, its headwaters rise N of QUILPIE in the N part of the GREY RANGE, over 1000km W of Brisbane. It flows in a general NNE-SSW direction, broadly parallel to the Grey Range, over a course some 500km long, ending in Lake Bulloo swamps, an area of internal drainage. Small urban centres within the valley include Adavale, Quilpie and Thargomindah. The N parts of the river basin are used for sheep grazing and some of the S parts are good for cattle fattening. Rainfall over the area is low and is concentrated mainly in the summer months; consequently, river flooding is common in wet years.

bull-roarer A flat piece of wood traditionally used in some Aboriginal ceremonies, it is about 20cm to 30cm by about 100cm to 130cm in size, and is often attached to a string. Bull-roarers are swung around, producing a roaring sound, to warn uninitiated men and women away from a sacred site or ceremony. They also had sacred and symbolic significance for the Aborigines who owned them. *See also* tjuringa

bullrouts *see* fishes, bony; fishes, poisonous and venomous

bulrushes Also known as cumbungi, bulrushes are reed-like perennial plants of the family *Typhaceae*. They grow in shallow water, and may reach a height of between 1m and 3m. The plants are monoecious (having both male and female flowers on the same plant). Native species of bulrushes include *Typha orientalis, T. angustifolia* and *T. muelleri*, and there is also an introduced species, the European great reedmace, *T. latifolia*. Bulrushes often grow as weeds in irrigation canals.

Bunbury WA (population 21 749 in 1981) Located on Leschenault Inlet at the N end of GEOGRAPHE BAY, some 175km S of Perth, Bunbury is a major port and commercial centre serving the SW of the State. Named after Lieutenant Bunbury who explored the region in 1836, it was once a whaling port, and has long been the outlet for exporting timber from the hardwood forests of the hinterland. The harbour breakwater, which greatly improved the safety of the port, was constructed in 1903; the port now has facilities for the bulk handling of oil and wheat. Secondary industries in the town include a woollen mill, a superphosphate plant, and mineral sandmining, which has become important in recent years. Bunbury receives a yearly rainfall of 881mm, concentrated mainly in the cool winter season (June average 186mm); in the hot, dry summer months the town is a popular tourist and holiday resort offering good fishing, swimming, boating and sailing, and a variety of sporting facilities.

Bundaberg QLD (population 32 560 in 1981) A city on the lower reaches of the BURNETT RIVER, some 12km upstream from its mouth, it is the centre of a prosperous sugar cane growing area. At an elevation of only 14m above sea level and at a latitude of 26°S, it experiences warm to hot conditions throughout the year, with a high average annual rainfall of 1 159mm; rain occurs in all months, but summer is the period of heaviest falls; January is the wettest month (221mm average), while August is the driest (32mm). During the dry season, the cane crops are irrigated with underground water from an aquifer which covers 500km^2 of the coastal plain and is estimated to have a storage capacity of 2 700 000ML. The city is located on the Isis Highway, 393km NNW of Brisbane (about 50km off the Bruce Highway) and 113km by road N of MARYBOROUGH. Sugar dominates the economic life of the city; there are five crushing mills in the district, a sugar manufacturing plant (Millaquin Mill) in the city and ancillary industries such as rum-making and the production of methylated spirits and in-

Memorial to aviator Bert Hinkler who was born in Bundaberg

Premier's Dept. QLD

dustrial alcohol. There are regular tours for visitors to inspect the crushing of the cane and other processes. At the mouth of the Burnett River is a huge sugar export terminal, also open for inspection by tourists. The city is noted for engineering works producing cane-growing equipment and harvesting machinery. Among the tourist attractions of the city are the memorial in Buss Park to Bert HINKLER; 'Birra Barra' homestead, which has a collection of farm implements from the pioneering days; the Dream Time Reptile Reserve (4km S of the city); Avocado Grove tourist gardens; Langbecker's rose nursery; and the Hummock (10km E), a 96m-high extinct volcano which is the only hill in the district. Several buildings in the city have been listed for preservation by the National Trust (QLD) including the School of Arts, the water tower, the Soldier's Memorial and the post office.

Bunny, Rupert Charles Wulsten (1864-1947) Artist. Born at St Kilda VIC, Bunny pursued some studies in architecture and engineering at the University of Melbourne before studying art, first at the Melbourne National Gallery School, and then at Calderon's in London and with J.P. Laurens in Paris. Fascinated by French colour and light, especially in the Provence landscape, he remained in France most of his life. He exhibited regularly at the Old Salon in Paris, and a number of his works were bought for the Luxembourg Collection and various public galleries in France. The wide respect he gained in France was indicated by the offer to him of a post at the Gobelin Tapestry works. Bunny worked through several themes: mythological subjects; scenes of everyday life which show a gently idealised feminine grace and charm; and, after World War I, the sunny landscapes of Provence. The impact on Europe of the spectacular Ballets Russes, organised by Diaghilev and with sets by such artists as Picasso, Braque and Matisse, is reflected in Bunny's post-war works with brilliant colouring and dramatic silhouetting. After the death of his wife, Léanne Morel, he returned to Australia, and died in South Yarra, almost unknown.

Bunny's work is marked by scrupulous composition, whether in his large, salon-subject paintings such as *Summer* (in the Art Gallery of New South Wales), or in his intimate Provencal paintings. His work shows a progressive paring down to essentials during his career; his earlier grand scenes, bordering on the monumental and heavy, gave way to work in which no brush stroke was wasted in gaining maximum effect. As a colourist, Bunny was an enthusiast, exploring different effects at various times.

Bunya Range QLD A section of the GREAT DIVIDING RANGE in south-eastern QLD, it forms the watershed between streams flowing inland to the CONDAMINE RIVER system and those draining E into either the

Small marbled scorpion, *Lychas marmoreus* (*see* SCORPIONS)

Yellow-winged locust, *Gastrimargus musicus* (*see* CRICKETS)

Mole cricket, *Gryllotalpa* species (*see* CRICKETS)

Common dragonfly, *Aeshna brevistyla* (*see* DAMSELFLIES)

Diamond weevil, *Chrysolophus spectabilis* (*see* BEETLES)

Praying mantis, *Archimantis latistyla* (*see* MANTIDS)

Jewel beetle, *Melobasis cuprifera* (*see* BEETLES)

Nymphal stage of a bronze orange bug, *Musgraveia sulciventris* (*see* BUGS)

Adult stage of a bronze orange bug (*see* BUGS)

Falconer's land snail, *Hedlyella falconer* (*see* SLUGS AND SNAILS)

Native snail, *Helicarion* species (*see* SLUGS AND SNAILS)

Stick insect a mantid species (*see* STICK INSECT)

Blue triangle butterfly, *Graphium sarpedon*

Orchard butterfly, *Papilio aegeus*

Common brown butterfly (male), *Heteronympha merope*

Caper white butterfly, *Anaphaeis java*

Monarch butterfly, *Danaus plexippus*

Common jezebel butterfly, *Delias nigricans*

Imperial white butterfly, *Delias harpalyce*

See also BUTTERFLIES

Bunya Mountains, National Park

QLD Nat. Parks/Wildlife

Brisbane River or the BURNETT RIVER systems. The range, separated from the MAIN RANGE (lying to the S) by a gap E of TOOWOOMBA, extends N, becoming lower and less rugged. The highest points in the range are Mt Kiangarow (1 135m) and Mt Mowbullen (1 101m). The Bunya Mts National Park, located 48km NE of DALBY, covering 11 700ha, is noted for its areas of rainforest, open-forest country and grassy patches (known locally as 'balds').

bunyip This is a monstrous legendary animal said to live in swamps and greatly feared by the Aborigines. The first European report—an account of a terrible roar from a bed of reeds—was provided in 1801 by a party of French explorers from the *Géographe* who were working along the SWAN RIVER in WA. Other Europeans who have claimed to have seen or heard a creature which may be a bunyip include William BUCKLEY (at Lake Modewarre); Hamilton HUME (at Lake Bathurst in 1821), who said that it resembled a 'manatee or a hippopotamus'; a BATHURST grazier, E.S. Hall (1821); a surveyor, MacBrien (near Bathurst, 1823); and Stocqueler, a naturalist (on the MURRAY RIVER, 1857). Some reports described the bunyip as having a human face and feet pointing backwards; a similar creature, the 'moalgewanke' of LAKE ALEXANDRINA in SA, was said by the Rev. George Taplin in 1879 to be a peculiar merman with a red wig. Such accounts of bunyips have been attributed to the sighting of seals on a rare foray upriver and their roaring to the booming call of bitterns.

Other animals, as yet unknown to science, are reported from time to time in Australia. The 'yowie', a creature similar to the 'abominable snowman' or 'bigfoot', is said to live in the mountains of the SE. There have been several reports in QLD of a large, striped marsupial tiger: the late Ion IDRIESS described two encounters, in one of which the animal killed his staghound.
Further reading: Heuvelmans, B. *On the Track of Unknown Animals.* Paladin, London, 1970; Costello, P. *In Search of Lake Monsters.* Garnstone Press, London, 1974; Bord, J. & Bord, C. *Alien Animals.* Granada, London, 1980.

Burdekin River QLD A major river of the E coast, draining a catchment basin of about 130 000km², the Burdekin rises in the Seaview Ranges only 60km inland from INGHAM and flows for over 720km on a circuitous course to an estuary on the Pacific coast downstream from AYR. From its headwaters, it flows first in a SW direction, receiving the Clarke River (which rises in the Gregory Ranges) as a tributary; it then follows a SE course, generally parallel to the coast, and W of the Coane, Hervey and Roby Ranges; thence it turns sharply to flow NE, cuts through the Leichhardt Range in a gorge section, and finally crosses the coastal plain, forming a broad delta. It has the Belyardo-Mistake-Suttor river system as a tributary from the S, and the Bowen from the SE. Over most of the middle and upper sections of the valley beef cattle grazing is the main rural activity. The coastal lowlands and the delta are dominated by cane growing, but rice, maize, tobacco and vegetables are also cultivated. The delta region is a source of underground water supplies used for irrigating crops and pastures, though in recent years there has been considerable concern that the high rate of utilisation may cause the intrusion of seawater into the water source. A scheme has been established since 1965 to recharge this by diverting the Burdekin flow and pumping water from the river into a series of natural and artificial channels, so as to maintain the level of the underground water and prevent the invasion of seawater.

Burke, Brian (1947-) Premier of WA. Born and educated in Perth, he joined the AUSTRALIAN LABOR PARTY at the age of 16, and before entering Parliament worked as a newspaper journalist and then as a television news reporter. He won election to the Legislative Assembly in 1973 for the metropolitan seat of Balcatta by a margin of only 30 votes, but now holds the seat of Balga. He became Leader of the Opposition in September 1981, and after a sweeping Labor victory in the general election of February 1983 succeeded the Liberal, R.J. O'CONNOR, as Premier. He is regarded as a moderate, aiming at gradual social reform and possessing an outlook generally similar to those of other current Labor Premiers, Neville WRAN, John CAIN and John BANNON.

Burke, Robert O'Hara (1821-61) Explorer. Born in Ireland, he served in the Austrian Army and the Irish Mounted Constabulary before coming to Australia and joining the Victorian Police Force in 1853. In 1860, while serving as Superintendent of Police in the CASTLEMAINE district, he was chosen as leader of an exploratory expedition, organised by a committee of Melbourne citizens, with the aim of making the first crossing of the continent from S to N. The story of this expedition is recorded more fully in the entry on EXPLORATION BY LAND. Although four members of the expedition, Burke, Wills, King and Gray, reached the waters of the GULF OF CARPENTARIA, all of this party except King died on on the return journey. In retrospect it is easy to see that Burke was a bad choice as leader of such an expedition, since he had had no previous experience of the Australian interior and was both quarrelsome and impatient. Although the expedition was magnificently equipped, he frittered away most of its resources. Not only did loss of life result, but very little scientific observation was carried out, although the organising committee had intended this to be an integral part of the expedition's work.
Further reading: Wills, W. *A Successful Exploration through the Interior of Australia.* Richard Bentley, London, 1863; Clune, F. *Dig.* (new edn) Angus & Robertson, Sydney, 1971; Moorehead, A. *Cooper's Creek.* Macmillan, South Melbourne, 1977.

Robert O'Hara Burke

Mitchell Library

Burketown QLD (population 210 in 1981) This small township in the remote GULF COUNTRY is located in the NW of the State on the Albert River, a distributary of the GREGORY RIVER, about 30km inland from the SE coast of the GULF OF CARPENTARIA.

Burnet, Sir (Frank) Macfarlane (1899-) Physician, virologist and joint winner of the Nobel Prize for medicine. Born in TRARALGON in VIC, Burnet began his life-long career in medical research after taking his medical degree at the University of Melbourne in 1923. He held a research fellowship at the Lister Institute of Preventive Medicine in London (1926-27), and returned to London in the 1930s to further his research into viral diseases; except for these two short periods overseas, his entire professional career was spent at the Walter and Eliza Hall Institute at the University of Melbourne, of which he was director from 1944 to 1965, at the same time being Professor of Experimental Medicine at the University of Melbourne.

Much of Burnet's research up to 1957 was concerned with the activity of viruses and the diseases they cause. He was the first to isolate the influenza virus in Australia during an outbreak of the disease in 1935, and two years later he established that there was more than one strain of influenza virus, a discovery of great importance in the search for an influenza vaccine. He also did valuable work on the Murray Valley fever (encephalitis) virus, and his work on the poliomyelitis virus helped towards the development of the Salk anti-polio vaccine. By the mid-1950s many of the principal questions relating to virus diseases had been answered and Burnet turned his attention to a field in which he had been interested for a number of years: the 'immune system', that is, the way in which the human body mobilises its defences against invading organisms which cause disease. Burnet's discoveries in this field were of such importance that he was awarded the Nobel Prize for medicine in 1960, sharing the prize with the distinguished British immunologist Sir Peter Medawar.

Burnet's work on the immune system led him to believe that there was a tendency for the system to become less efficient as the body ages. This, coupled with his own advancing age, drew him to study the process of growing old, about which he has written much in recent years. Many honours have been awarded to him, including a KBE, the Order of Merit, the Fellowship of the Royal Society and the Copley Medal of that society.

Burnett River QLD Rising in the Burnett Range about 100km NW of BUNDABERG in the SE of the State, the Burnett drains to the E coast, flowing for over 320km on a circuitous course first S and SSW to Mundubbera, then E to Gayndah, and finally NE to an estuary on the Pacific Ocean about 12km downstream from Bundaberg. Some of the N and W headwater streams rise in the Dawes and Auburn Ranges, while S tributaries, such as the Boyne River and Barambah Creek, rise in the section of the GREAT DIVIDING RANGE between DALBY and KINGAROY. The catchment basin of the whole river system, covering over 32 000km², is thus shaped like a large lopsided mushroom, with the narrow stalk at the coast and the major extension to the inland S and SW. This S section of the basin, where the towns of Wondai, Murgon, Goomeri and Nanango are located, is a region of rich volcanic soils, supporting beef cattle grazing and dairying as the major rural activities. In the lower reaches of the valley and along the coastal plain, sugar cane plantations dominate the farming scene. Waruma Dam on the Nagoa River, an upper tributary of the Burnett, was completed in 1969 and has a capacity of 194 000ML; it is a storage reservoir designed to stabilise river flow and supply irrigation water for crops and pastures in the lower valley.

Burnie TAS (population 20 368 in 1981) An important rail centre and shipping port in the NW coastal region, Burnie (incorporating nearby Somerset) is the fourth-largest city in TAS (after Hobart, LAUNCESTON and DEVONPORT). It is located on Emu Bay below the steep slopes of Montello Heights, 49km W of Devonport along the Bass Highway and 150km from Launceston. Burnie experiences a mild climate, typical of the N coastal plains, with an average yearly rainfall of 1 005mm

concentrated mainly in the winter months; July is the month of highest rainfall (135mm average), January the lowest (38mm). Though the city functions as the major service centre for the rich surrounding farmlands, noted for the production of potatoes and cereal crops, fat lambs, beef cattle and timber, its growth has been influenced by manufacturing developments. The giant industrial enterprise is the Associated Pulp and Paper Mills which, with its two subsidiaries, employs over 2 500 people. In addition to the production of paper, there is a plywood mill at Somerset (6km W of Burnie), Australian Titan Products Ltd at Heybridge (10km E), and at Wivenhoe (4km E) the North West Acid plant which produces sulphuric acid from pyrites mined at ROSEBERY and QUEENSTOWN. Burnie is also the headquarters of the privately owned Emu Bay Railway which brings minerals from Rosebery and MOUNT LYELL for processing and export. The city takes its name from one of the directors of the Van Dieman's Land Co. which was granted the original land concessions in the area.

Burra SA (population 1 222 in 1981) A small town in the N section of the MOUNT LOFTY RANGES, on the main road between Adelaide and BROKEN HILL, Burra is 156km N of Adelaide. It is one of Australia's oldest mining settlements—copper was first discovered in 1845 and mining brought a boom growth to the area; by 1877, when mining ceased, the town had a population of about 5000. In recent years, the mining of low-grade copper ores by open-cut methods has been established.

burramys see possums, etc.

burrawong see Gymnospermae

Burrendong Dam NSW A storage reservoir on the MACQUARIE RIVER, near its junction with the Cudgegong, some 30km SE of WELLINGTON, it has a storage capacity of 1 680ML, collecting drainage from a catchment area of 13 866m². The dam supplies water for irrigation and livestock in the middle and lower Macquarie Valley, where the average annual rainfall is low (Wellington 614mm, DUBBO 584mm), and where dry spells are not uncommon; it also plays an important role in flood mitigation by permitting controlled release of water when the river is high. The dam, completed in 1967, is a rolled-earth-core structure supported by outer zones of gravel and rock.

Burrinjuck Dam NSW Located on the MURRUMBIDGEE RIVER, 60km by road SW of YASS, Burrinjuck was the State's first large dam, designed as a key part of the major conservation and irrigation scheme. Construction commenced in 1907 and water was being stored by 1912, though the dam was not completed until after World War I. In 1938 it was decided to strengthen and enlarge the dam, but World War II intervened and this work

was not finished until 1957. The dam now has a storage capacity of 1 026 000ML, collected from a catchment area of 12 953km²; the main wall is 79m high and the length of the crest is 233m; the lake formed by the dam has a surface area of 5 500ha. Water is stored mainly during winter and spring, and released during the drier period from September to April for irrigation of crops and pastures (in the Coleambally, HAY and MURRUMBIDGEE IRRIGATION AREAS), for livestock watering, and for urban supplies to towns along the valley. Set in picturesque bushland the dam is the centre of a recreation and tourist area offering fishing, swimming and other aquatic sports, and bush-walking. The name of the dam is taken from the Aboriginal word meaning 'a rugged-topped or precipitous mountain'.

burrs see Compositae

bush curlews see waders

bushfires These are serious hazards in forested areas in the S regions of the continent and in the interior grassland areas when long dry spells prevail. Although some of the outbreaks are caused by natural phenomena, particularly lightning, many bushfires are the result of such carelessness as the failure to extinguish a camp fire or the thoughtless dropping of a match or cigarette butt. The damage caused by bushfires is often quite extensive, including stands of forest timber, grassland pastures, crops, livestock, houses, fences and farming equipment, which may amount to many millions of dollars. It is not uncommon for bushfires to claim human lives; in a BLUE MOUNTAINS fire in 1968-69, six people died and over 160 buildings were destroyed; in February 1977, a fire which swept across the SA border into the WESTERN DISTRICT of VIC caused five deaths and the loss of about three million sheep; in 1966-67, in a particularly disastrous fire near Hobart, 62 people were killed and 1 400 homes were destroyed. In 1983, fires in VIC and SA, which, ironically, broke out on Ash Wednesday, caused more than 70 deaths.

Much has been done to prevent and control bushfires. The danger is widely publicised and people are urged to take every precaution against starting fires, and in times of high risk, bans are placed on the lighting of fires in the open. Volunteer fire brigades in rural areas are trained and equipped to face emergencies; fire-breaks are cleared in forest areas and on many grazing and farming properties, excess growth of bush and grassland is also cleared during the cooler season (often by controlled burning); fire-spotting towers, with radio or other communication facilities, keep a watch on potentially dangerous areas in times of high risk. The most hazardous time of the year is summer, especially when hot and dry conditions are combined with high winds. Since this is also the holiday season when many people—especially city dwellers—visit rural areas, the dangers become acute, and consequently part

Firetower in the Pilliga Scrub at Baradine in the Orana Region NSW

of the programme of fire-prevention attempts to impress upon travellers in country regions that one careless act can lead to a disastrous outbreak of fire.

See also conservation; vegetation

bushfly *see* house fly

bushrangers From at least the early 19th century, this name was applied to robbers, especially highway robbers, who operated from the bush (thinly settled, undeveloped country). The earliest recorded use of the term seems to have been in the *Sydney Gazette* of 17 February 1805, where it was reported that a cart had been stopped on the road to the HAWKESBURY RIVER 'by three men whose appearance sanctioned the suspicion of their being bushrangers'. Four years later the deposed Governor BLIGH, while on the *Porpoise* (anchored in the DERWENT RIVER), wrote of 'a set of Free Booters (Bushrangers as they are called)', and claimed that 'about Sixty, and some of them well armed, are now in the Woods.'

During the convict period—that is, until the 1850s—nearly all bushrangers were escaped CONVICTS. TAS, which received the greater proportion of hardened criminals, was the first part of Australia to be seriously troubled by bushrangers. Though Governor MACQUARIE kept urging Lieutenant-Governor DAVEY to use more vigour in suppressing them, he raised strong objections when in 1815 Davey tried to deal with them by placing the whole island under martial law. At this stage the most notorious of the 'Bandittis or Ruffians', or 'Atrocious Miscreants', as Davey called them, was the gang led by Michael HOWE. Davey's successor, SORELL, succeeded in hunting down most members of this group, and after Howe's death in 1818 there was a short lull in bushranging. However, after the opening of a special penal settlement at MACQUARIE HARBOUR it became more serious than ever. It was difficult for convicts to escape from Macquarie Harbour and reach the settled districts, but those who succeeded in

doing so made very resourceful bushrangers, among whom Matthew BRADY, who was captured and hanged in 1826, was the most notorious. Within a few years of his death vigorous measures by Lieutenant-Governor ARTHUR had practically eliminated bushranging from the island, and it was never again a great problem there. Although Martin CASH attracted widespread attention in the 1840s, he presented a far less serious threat to the peace of the island than earlier bushrangers had done.

On the mainland, bushranging began within two years of the founding of the colony, with the escape of John ('Black') Caesar, a negro convict who escaped and took to the bush in 1789. It was only after Governor HUNTER had offered a reward of five gallons of rum for his capture, dead or alive, that he was run down and shot dead in 1796. But the problem of bushranging did not reach proportions comparable to those in TAS until settlement began to spread beyond the BLUE MOUNTAINS after 1815. Thereafter it flourished, and by 1830 the situation was so serious that police were given power to arrest suspects without a warrant and, if provided with a general search warrant, to enter, or even break into, any house. Particularly notorious about this time was 'Bold Jack Donohoe' (celebrated in the folk song of that title), who survived a number of encounters with police, but was eventually shot dead by a party of troopers near CAMPBELLTOWN in 1836. Most brutal of all was the maniac ex-convict John Lynch, who operated mainly in the Berrima district. Before being hanged in 1841 he confessed to murdering nine people with an axe, but claimed that he did so by divine guidance. Another bushranger of note was William Westwood, nicknamed 'Jacky Jacky'.

The abolition of transportation to E Australia in 1852 soon made bushranging by escaped convicts a thing of the past. At the same time the gold rushes provided a new motive and greater opportunities for highway robbery, since there were many more travellers and large amounts of gold were being transported by road. Many robberies occurred on the roads between Melbourne and the goldfields during the 1850s (the height of the gold rushes); as far as can be ascertained they were carried out largely by ex-convicts from TAS, though no particular individuals or gangs working from hideouts in the bush—and therefore justifying the name 'bushranger'—stood out prominently.

The second great period of bushranging covers the 1860s and 1870s, and the famous bushrangers of the time operated predominantly in NSW. This was the era of free-born bushrangers, generally from the poorer classes and often of ex-convict parentage, who shared with the escaped convicts of an earlier time an attitude of hostility towards the police, the rich and authority in general.

The two most notorious bushrangers of the 1860s were Frank GARDINER, who operated in the central slopes and tablelands of NSW, and

Ben HALL, who took over the remnants of Gardiner's gang in 1863 and of all bushrangers was probably the best organiser. Others in the same decade were Frederick WARD ('Captain Thunderbolt'), who operated mainly in NEW ENGLAND, Thomas and John Clarke of Araluen, who were hanged in 1867, and Daniel ('Mad Dog') Morgan, one of the few loners, who operated from 1862 to 1864 in the RIVERINA and MONARO districts of NSW, winning an unenviable reputation for brutality before being ambushed and shot in VIC in 1865 as he was leaving a station near WANGARATTA which he had robbed.

The 1870s produced the most famous of all bushrangers, Ned KELLY. Kelly's career, marked by a number of particularly daring raids, was short; he formed his gang in 1878 and was captured, after a spectacular battle with police at GLENROWAN in VIC, only two years later. Also notorious in this decade was Andrew George Scott ('Captain Moonlight'), who had taken to the bush with a gang of five others in 1879, after serving an 11-year gaol sentence for bank robbery. A brilliant confidence trickster, he posed as a lay preacher as a cover for his activities; but his career, too, was brief, for he was captured near WAGGA WAGGA in NSW in 1880 and hanged in the same year.

Popular attitudes towards bushrangers, almost from the beginning, had inclined towards admiration of the alleged daring and courage of bushrangers, a tendency reflected in songs such as 'The Wild Colonial Boy' and 'Bold Jack Donohoe'. By the 1860s, many of the poorer settlers, resentful of the police, willingly provided food, shelter and information for criminals such as Frank Gardiner and Ben Hall; the effectiveness with which they provided bushrangers with information about police movements gave rise to the term 'bush telegraph'. Another phrase, 'as game as Ned Kelly', indicates the awe with which that robber was regarded, and the dramatic nature of his exploits and final defeat has been widely featured in Australian literature and art. All told, however, it seems doubtful that popular admiration for bushrangers in Australia has been stronger than the same tendency in other countries to glamourise certain types of criminals.

Further reading: White, C. *A History of Australian Bushranging*. NSW Bookstall Co., Sydney, 1921; Joy, W. & Prior, T. *The Bushrangers*. Shakespeare Head Press, Sydney, 1963; Prior, T., Wannan, B. & Nunn, H. *Plundering Sons: A Pictorial History of Australian Bushranging*. Lansdowne Press, Melbourne, 1966; Mendham, R. *The Dictionary of Australian Bushranging*. Hawthorn Press, Melbourne, 1975.

bushwalking A form of recreation which can be enjoyed in all States, bushwalking is most popular in NSW, VIC and TAS, where the variety of land and scenery offer stimulating and refreshing exercise. Though established as an organised recreational activity since the formation in the 1890s of bushwalking clubs (such as the Warrangamba Club in NSW and the Melbourne Walking and Touring Club in VIC), it was not until after World War II that bushwalking became a widely popular pastime, due in part to the development of lightweight gear. By the early 1980s there were more than 8000 active registered members in approximately 70 clubs throughout Australia. These clubs, and some church and community groups such as the Scout Association of Australia, include more serious-minded bushwalkers who, with the aid of map and compass, enjoy pursuing a course through rugged and occasionally hazardous country far from the beaten track. However, there are numerous Australians who enjoy a quiet walk through bush country during the weekend or on holidays. Such bushwalkers usually head for the nearest national park where well-marked trails, taking between one and eight hours to complete, feature a variety of scenic attractions.

Busselton WA (population 6 463 in 1981) A coastal town on GEOGRAPHE BAY, 239km S of Perth, Busselton is one of the earliest sites of settlement in WA, and was named in 1837 after the Bussells, a pioneering family. It is a service and commercial centre, a timber port, and increasingly important as a holiday and tourist centre. Like most of south-western WA, it experiences a mild climate with hot and mostly dry summer days, ideal for surfing, fishing, sailing and other aquatic sports. The average yearly rainfall of 838mm falls mainly in winter (June average 180mm). About 20 buildings in the town have been listed by the National Trust (WA) for preservation, among them many old homes such as Newton House (1850s), Bovell's Cottage (1860s), Villa Carlotta (1897), Fairlawn (1839) and Yarre Mia (*c*1899), and the Ship Hotel, several churches and the courthouse (1860; formerly a police station and gaol).
Further reading: Vines, F. *Bunbury and Busselton Sketchbook*, Rigby, Adelaide, 1975.

bustard Also known as the plain turkey, this large, stately bird, *Ardeotis* (*Eupodotis*) *australis*★ (about 1.3m long), belongs to the family Otididae. It is grey and brown, with a black cap sometimes standing out as a crest, and has long legs and a long neck. The male has a striking courtship display in which it utters a low, hollow-sounding roar, inflates the two throat pouches and expands the tail feathers into a turkey-like fan. Bustards tend to move singly or in small flocks, and they are found generally in open country where they feed on insects and plant material. One or two camouflaged eggs are laid on the ground.

Bustards were common throughout Australia until the arrival of the early settlers, who killed them for food. This, coupled with a low rate of reproduction, the destruction of their natural habitat, and predation by introduced animals such as foxes, greatly reduced their numbers. They occur throughout Australia but are now comparatively rare in SE and SW Australia.
See also birds

butcherbirds, magpies and currawongs Bold-natured and fine singers, these are probably the best-known Australian BIRDS, after the kookaburra, (*see* KINGFISHERS). Generally pied or black, and CROW-like in appearance, they are PASSERINE BIRDS belonging to the family Cracticidae, which contains 10 species, nine of which are represented in Australia.

Butcherbirds are smaller than magpies and currawongs, and have hooked bills and short legs. Their habit of taking animal prey—small mammals and insects—and wedging it in a tree notch or impaling it on a spike in order to dismember it, resembles that of the European shrike. They often swoop down on intruders who appear to pose a threat to their eggs or prey. The pied or black-throated butcherbird, *Cracticus nigrogularis*★ (32cm to 35cm long), is found in woodlands and parks throughout the mainland, except in the extreme S and on the tip of CAPE YORK. The opening notes of one version of its clear, flute-like song have been compared to the beginning of Beethoven's *Fifth Symphony*. The eggs are laid in shallow, cup-shaped nests of sticks placed in the vertical forks of trees. The grey butcherbird, *C. torquatus*★ (28cm to 32cm), identified by its white underparts and grey back, has a harsher song than that of the pied species and is found in most types of woodland and forest throughout Australia (except in N Cape York). It is possibly just a lighter-coloured version of the black-backed butcherbird, *C. mentalis* (25cm), which has a similar but weaker song and is found only in N Cape York. Both species build their shallow, cup-shaped nests of sticks and twigs in the forked branches of trees. Also occurring in Cape York, as well as in northern QLD and the NT, is the black butcherbird, *C. quoyi* (32cm to 36cm). A handsome bird, it has a deep, bubbling call and feeds mainly on crustaceans and insects. While the adult is completely black, the immature bird is either black or cinnamon brown. The open, cup-shaped nests of sticks and twigs are built in high forked branches of trees.

Magpies, like butcherbirds, have black-tipped bills, but the hook is less obvious and the legs are longer. They feed mainly on the

Black-backed magpie, *Gymnorhina tibicen*

Courtesy of A.I.S. Canberra

ground, digging up grubs and beetles or catching grasshoppers. There is some doubt about the separation of magpies into species because the black-backed magpie, *Gymnorhina tibicen* (36cm to 40cm), and the white-backed magpie, *G. hypoleuca*★ (36cm to 40cm), sometimes interbreed in the regions of overlap. There are probably three species: the white-backed magpie of SA, southern NT, VIC and TAS, the black-backed magpie, occurring over most of the mainland except the S and SW parts, and the more gregarious western magpie, *G. dorsalis*★ (36cm to 40cm), of SW Australia. All three species inhabit woodlands, forests and parks, and have one of the most joyous bird-songs in Australia. Owing to the problems caused in the past by the magpies' liking for building nests on telegraph poles, the authorities in some parts of Australia provide special receptacles for the birds' use.

The two currawongs—the pied currawong, *Strepera graculina*★ (45cm), and the grey currawong, *S. versicolor*★ (50cm)—are the largest birds in the family Cracticidae. The common name derives from the resounding call of the smaller bird, which is dull black in colour, with some white on the wings and tail, and has a slightly hooked black bill. It is an omnivorous bird, known to raid poultry farms and orchards, and is found in forests and in clumps of trees, often in suburbs in E Australia and TAS. The TAS form is sometimes regarded as a separate species, the black currawong, *S. fuliginosa* (45cm). The grey currawong is found in southern Australia and TAS; it is browner or greyer than other currawongs, and is variable enough for different forms to be regarded by some authorities as different species. Its call can be said to resemble the clinks of a blacksmith's hammer. Like the pied currawong, it builds bowl-shaped nests of sticks and twigs, lined with grass, in tree forks.

Butlers Gorge TAS This is a section of the upper DERWENT RIVER, 138km NW of Hobart, where the gorge topography and the steep drop from the highlands have been utilised for the generation of hydro-electricity as part of the vast power scheme on the Derwent. Upstream from the gorge is LAKE KING WILLIAM, artificially created by the construction of Clark Dam (wall 67m high) and fed from LAKE ST CLAIR via a section of the Derwent. The Butlers Gorge power station at the foot of Clark Dam, commissioned in 1951, has an installed capacity of 12 200kW. After generating power at this station, the water passes through a series of canals and pipelines to other stations, such as TARRALEAH, TUNGATINAH, LIAPOOTAH and WAYATINAH, where it is used for further power generation.

buttercups These familiar yellow flowers belong to the genus *Ranunculus* (family Ranunculaceae), and are found in many parts of the world. Australia has about 35 native species, and some introduced species as well.

★Species, genus or family is endemic to Australia (see Preface)

The common or native buttercup, *R. lappaceus*, a perennial with divided leaves and long stalks, is found in all States. The river buttercup, *R. rivularis*, grows in swampy regions in all States except WA.

butterflies and moths Butterflies and moths are contained in the order Lepidoptera, one of the largest and most studied endopterygote orders of INSECTS and popular with amateur entomologists and small boys because of the colour of many of the specimens. There are over 11 220 species, divided into about 75 families; the classification depends largely upon the wing venation which is often obscured by the scales which cover the wings and body of most lepidopterans. For this reason most collectors usually identify specimens by comparison with coloured plates.

There is no real scientific difference between butterflies and moths but the following generalisations apply to most:

	Butterflies	Moths
Antennae	Clubbed at tip	Not clubbed at tip
Activity	Day-flying	Night-flying
Colour	Usually bright	Often dull
Wing at rest	Held vertically	Folded over body

Most lepidopterans have mouthparts in the form of a long tube formed from the maxillae. When at rest this is coiled beneath the head and resembles the shape of a watch spring; it is uncoiled to suck up nectar, water and, sometimes, fluid from decaying animal and vegetable matter. The larvae are the familiar caterpillars. A few species in the most primitive families are predators, but most caterpillars feed on living plant tissues. Caterpillars have typical biting mouthparts, three pairs of jointed thoracic legs, and up to five pairs of unjointed abdominal prolegs.

Lepidopterans are divided into four suborders, but about 98 per cent of them belong to the Ditrysia, which is distinguished technically by the presence of two genital openings in the female. The lepidopterans of the suborder Monotrysia have one or two genital openings, and include the family Hepialidae (109 species) which, although cosmopolitan, has its headquarters in Australia. This family contains the swift-moths, medium to very

Monarch butterfly feeding, *Danaus plexippus*

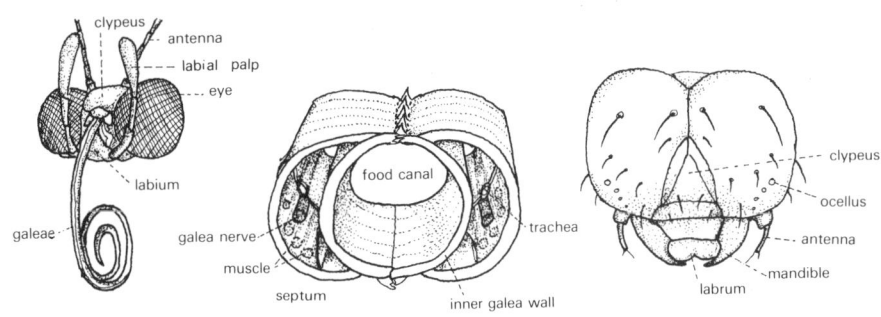
(a) The head of a butterfly, a section through the proboscis of a butterfly and the head capsule of a caterpillar

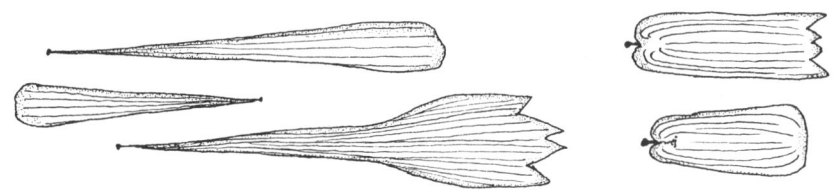
(b) Some scales from the fore-wing of a butterfly

large insects with long, oval wings. The larvae of many species tunnel within the stems of shrubs and trees, often feeding on the bark as it grows again round the tunnel entrance; some burrow in the soil, feeding on roots or emerging at night to eat adjacent plants. This group includes a number of pasture pests such as the grass-grubs (*Onchopera* species).

The remaining superfamilies and families that are considered here all belong to the Ditrysia.
1. The true butterflies belong to the superfamily Papilionoidea (about 250 species in Australia). One of the most conspicuous species is the monarch or wanderer butterfly, *Danaus plexippus*, a North American species which makes long distance migrations on that continent. It apparently introduced itself into Australia in the 1870s after its food plants became established. Its movements are being studied by the staff of the Australian Museum in Sydney but its Australian migrations are not as spectacular as those in North America. Another common introduced species is the small cabbage white butterfly, *Pieris rapae*, a European species which arrived in Australia, probably from New Zealand, in the 1940s. The larvae of some of the 'blues' (family Lycaenidae; about 124 species in Australia) live in ant nests where they feed on larvae and pupae. The ants are attracted to the caterpillars by the secretions that they produce. The family Papilionidae (about 18 species in Australia) contains several striking swallowtail species, two of which attack citrus in the caterpillar stage. The larger species, *Papilio aegeus*, has markedly different males and females. The beautiful birdwing butterflies which are common in the N parts of the continent also belong to this family.
2. The family Cossidae (99 species in Australia) contains the goat moths, such as *Xyleutes boisduvali* which, with a wingspan of 230mm

in the female, is one of Australia's largest insects. A related species is the original witchety grub, *X. leucomochla*, of the Aborigines; the caterpillar feeds on the roots of inland acacias. The larvae of this family are wood-borers.
3. The family Tortricidae (about 800 species in Australia) contains generally small moths with long fringes on the wings. The larvae either tunnel into plants, or spin two leaves together and feed within the shelter thus created. Among the tunnellers is the notorious codling moth, *Cydia (Laspeyresia) pomonella*, a widespread pest which is the cause of 'maggoty' apples, and among the leaf feeders is the native light brown apple tortrix moth, *Epiphyas postvittana*, which has been introduced into Britain, New Zealand and Hawaii.
4. The family Pyralidae (about 1 090 Australian species) are medium to large moths, commonly known as web-worm moths. The wings, which are fringed, are more or less triangular in shape. The caterpillars of many species feed beneath shelters of silk but the

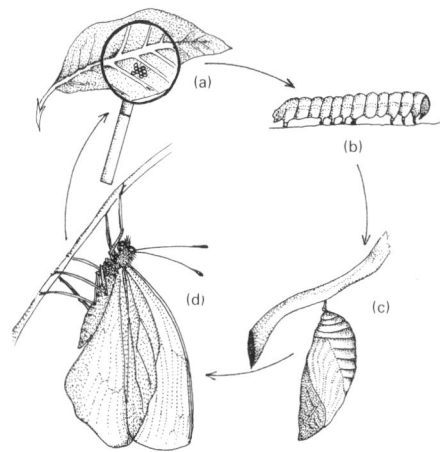
Stages in the development of a butterfly: (a) eggs; (b) caterpillar (larva); (c) pupa; (d) adult

larvae of the immensely important *Cactoblastis cactorum* tunnel in the pads of the PRICKLY PEAR. The family also contains several pests, such as the wax moths, *Achroia grisella* and *Galleria mellonella*, which infest the combs of honey bees. (The clothes moths and the house moths, all pests of fabrics, belong to two other families, the Tineidae—about 150 species in Australia—and the Oecophoridae—over 2 400 species in Australia.)

5. The family Geometridae (about 1 200 species in Australia) are the looper moths. Both the family name ('Earth measurers') and the common name refer to the way the larvae walk: there is a large gap between the thoracic legs and the abdominal legs, so the caterpillar loops as it walks, a mode of progression made famous by Danny Kaye's song 'Inch-worm' in the film *Hans Christian Andersen*. Many of the caterpillars mimic twigs and stick out, motionless, from a branch when disturbed. Adult geometrids often come to light and can be recognised by the way they spread out and flatten the wings against the wall on which they rest.

6. The family Saturniidae (13 species in Australia) is probably best known by the gum emperor moth, *Antheraea eucalypti*, whose larvae feed on *Eucalyptus*. The tough pupal case is covered with irritant fibres. The large brown adult has a conspicuous eye mark on each wing (a common feature in the family) which may deter predatory birds when suddenly exposed.

7. The family Sphingidae (about 58 species in Australia) contains the hawk moths. Many of these very swift, powerful moths are widespread in the world. Several species hover like hummingbirds while feeding at flowers. Many of the caterpillars have a conspicuous spine on the tail but this is lacking in the large double-headed hawk moth, *Coequosa triangularis*, of QLD. In place of the spine there is a swelling of the anal claspers (the last pair of prolegs) which come to resemble a second head. It feeds on native plants of the PROTEACEAE. A common species which is found as far S as Sydney is the dark green *Cizara ardeniae*.

8. The family Noctuidae (about 1 140 species in Australia) contains mostly dull-coloured, medium-sized moths which are very difficult to tell apart. The larvae feed on foliage or flowers of plants, and many are important pests. Often the larvae spend the day in the soil, and emerge at night to feed on plants. These so-called cutworms often work their way down a row of seedlings, girdling one plant after another. Some are known as army worms because they move through a crop in great numbers, like an army advancing. There are several species of *Heliothis*, native and introduced, whose larvae tunnel into the developing buds or fruits of cotton, linseed and tomatoes. The level of insecticide resistance in some species has greatly obstructed the growing of cotton in parts of Australia. The family also contains the remarkable bogong moth (an Aboriginal name), *Agrotis infusa*. The larvae are cutworms which develop mainly during the winter on the slopes and plains

The Emperor gum moth, *Antheraea euealypti*, expanding and drying its wings immediately after emergence

A. Woods

to the W of the GREAT DIVIDING RANGE. In some years large numbers of the adults are blown to coastal cities such as Sydney, where they tend to be attracted by lights. Many, however, migrate to caves and crevices in the SNOWY MOUNTAINS and other parts of the Great Dividing Range and aestivate (the summer-time equivalent of hibernation) in huge masses. Formerly, these sites were visited by local Aborigines for bogong feasts.

9. The family Agaristidae (37 species in Australia) is closely related to the Noctuidae and contains the day-flying, black, yellow and red vine moth, *Agarista agricola*. The banded black and white caterpillars feed on several native vines and on the introduced grape vine and Virginia creeper, which they often defoliate.

See also insects, introduced

Further reading: Common, I.F.B. *Australian Moths.* Jacaranda, Brisbane, 1963 and *Australian Butterflies.* Jacaranda, Brisbane, 1964; D'Abrera, B. *Moths of Australia.* Lansdowne, Melbourne, 1974; Hadlington, P.W. *A Guide to Pest Control in Australia.* (3rd edn) New South Wales University Press, Sydney, 1979; Flood, J. *The Moth Hunters; Aboriginal Prehistory of the Australian Alps.* Aust. Inst. Aboriginal Studies, Canberra, 1980; Common, I.F.B. & Waterhouse, D.F. *Butterflies of Australia.* (2nd edn) Angus & Robertson, Sydney, 1981.

Butterley, Nigel Henry (1935-)

Composer. Butterley was one of the group of young Australian composers who came to prominence in the 1960s. Early influences on his musical development included the music of English composers such as Vaughan Williams, and in 1962 a turning point in his own development came as a result of studies with Priaulx Rainier in London. His style stands out from Australian composition as being individual and intensely personal. The sources of his inspiration are often to be found in architecture (for example *Laudes*), and poetry (for example, his *Meditations of Thomas Traherne*; 1968). In 1966 he won the international Italia Prize for a musical work for radio broadcast, *In the Head the Fire*. Other works include his *Violin Concerto* (1970), *Exploration for Piano and Orchestra* (1970), *Letter from Hardy's Bay* (for piano, 1971) and *Fire in the*

Heavens (for orchestra, 1973). After working for many years as a producer and programme-planner in the ABC music department, he became a lecturer in contemporary music at NEWCASTLE Conservatorium of Music in 1973.

Further reading: Swale, D. 'Nigel Butterley' in Callaway, F. & Tunley, D. (eds) *Australian Composition in the Twentieth Century.* Oxford University Press, Melbourne, 1978.

button grass *see* Cyperaceae

button quails and the plain wanderer

These BIRDS belong to the family Turnicidae. Button quails resemble true quails in appearance and habits (*see* PHEASANTS, etc.), but they are actually closely related to CRANES. They have only three toes, whereas true quails have four. The females are larger and more distinctively marked than the males. The nests are shallow depressions in the ground, lined and sometimes canopied over with grass, and the male tends the eggs and rears the young. There are seven Australian species, six endemic. Among the largest is the painted quail, *Turnix varia** (18cm to 20cm long), which has a mottled chestnut back and buff underparts. It frequents open forest and clearings in coastal areas from northern QLD to VIC, and in south-western WA. The most widespread of the genus is the little quail, *T. velox** (13cm to 15cm), a nomadic bird, reddish-brown with white underparts, found in most of Australia's grassland areas.

Painted quail, *Turnix varia*

The unique plain wanderer, *Pedionomus** *torquatus* (15cm to 18cm), is sometimes placed in a separate family, Pedionomidae. It has four toes and, when alarmed, has a more upright stance than the quails. It is brown above, spotted below, and has a black collar with white spots. It is a shy bird which rarely flies; when running rapidly over the ground it tends to raise itself on its toes. The plain wanderer is now a rare and declining species which feeds on seeds and insects and inhabits open country, mainly in the SE.

Further reading: Frith, H.J. *Wildlife Conservation.* Angus & Robertson, Sydney, 1973.

Buvelot, Abram Louis (1814-88)

Artist. Born in Morges, Switzerland, Buvelot arrived in Melbourne during its gold-boom period, in 1865. As a youth, he had pursued art studies in Lausanne, and had studied land-

Species, genus or family is endemic to Australia (see Preface)

scape painting in Paris for a few months before emigrating in 1834 to work on his uncle's coffee plantation in Brazil, where he continued to paint. Returning to Switzerland in 1852, he taught drawing for nine years at Neuchâtel, eventually emigrating to Australia to escape the winter cold. In Melbourne he set up a photographic studio to establish himself financially, and assisted by the income from the French language lessons given by his wife he was able to exhibit from 1866 until 1882, when failing sight interrupted his work. He died in Melbourne.

His work in Australia was influenced by the Barbizon school of French painters; like them, he rejected the romanticised subject-treatment and large canvasses favoured by many contemporary painters in Europe, preferring natural, everyday rural views. His paintings of settled rural scenes around Melbourne, frequently painted in the soft light of a late-afternoon summer sun, are somewhat reminiscent of the work of his French contemporary, Camille Corot (a forerunner of the Impressionist movement), and moved a Melbourne commentator to state, 'What the work of M. Corot is to France, that of M. Buvelot is to Australia', a comment which is perhaps extravagant, but not altogether unwarranted.

Buzo, Alexander John (1944-) Playwright. Born in Sydney, he was educated in ARMIDALE in NSW and in Geneva, and pursued studies in arts at the University of New South Wales. He gained early theatrical experience at the New Theatre in Sydney, where his first play, *The Revolt*, was the subject of a workshop in 1967. In 1968 *Norm and Ahmed* was staged by the Old Tote Theatre Company in Sydney, followed by *Rooted* and *The Front Room Boys* (1969). His more recent plays include *Macquarie* (1971), *Coralie Lansdowne Says No* (1973), *Martello Towers* (1976) and *Makassar Reef* (1978). In 1969 he was co-author of the screen-play for the film *Ned Kelly* (starring Mick Jagger), and for a time was resident playwright of the Melbourne Theatre Company. He now lives in Sydney.
Further reading: Rees, L. *A History of Australian Drama.* (vol 2) Angus & Robertson, Sydney, 1978.

buzzard *see* birds of prey

Byrne, Samuel (1883-1977) Artist. Born at BAROSSA in SA, this former silver miner began painting when he was 73 years old, using the BROKEN HILL area as his inspiration. His paintings frequently portray the life of Broken Hill, typically in a panoramic format. Simple and technically untutored, his work nevertheless has a strong and compelling quality that arrests attention.

Byron Bay NSW (population 3 183 in 1981) A town on the NORTH COAST, it is 6km E of the Pacific Highway, 839km by road and 883km by rail N of Sydney. It is on a branch railway line, which leaves the main N line at CASINO, passing through LISMORE in the mid-RICHMOND RIVER valley, continuing in a NE direction to Byron Bay, from where it goes N to its terminus at MURWILLUMBAH. The town has a large butter and dairy food processing factory, a rutile (a dioxide used in colouring glass and porcelain) processing plant and a whale-oil factory. It was formerly a leading port for the export of timber and rural produce from the region, but in recent decades shipping has declined. Cape Byron (the most easterly point on the Australian coast) and the lighthouse rising from its steep cliffs are well-known landmarks of the Byron Bay district. The cape was noted and named by Captain COOK on his voyage along the E coast in 1770. The surfing beaches of the nearby coastal zone attract many summer tourists.

by-the-wind sailor *see* coelenterates

C

Cabinet government The type of Cabinet government practised in Australia is modelled on that of Great Britain. It is government by a committee of Ministers, presided over by a chief, or Prime, Minister, or in the case of the states, by a Premier. Its members must also be Members of Parliament.

The terms 'Minister' and 'Cabinet' are derived from British practice, 'Minister' is Latin for servant, Ministers originally having been royal servants who advised the king on state matters, and saw that the laws were enforced. The word 'Cabinet' was applied to meetings between the king and his advisers (or Ministers) held in the royal private apartment (or cabinet); use of the word was common by the late 17th century.

The powers of Cabinet have been extended over time and now cover every sphere of government, so that Cabinet is responsible for all government policies and programmes. Cabinet decides the programmes to be presented to Parliament for approval, controls finance, arranges the timetables of the two Houses of Parliament and exercises potential supervision over and co-ordination of every department of administration.

Cabinet must present its programmes and policies to Parliament, because Parliament is the only institution which can pass laws and make the supply of money available to the government. Thus Cabinet must have the support of the majority of Members of Parliament, or its programmes and policies will be defeated and no money voted to carry them out. With the development of major political parties in Australia, her Cabinet is now chosen from the political party which holds the majority of Members in the Lower House (or House of Representatives). If no one party commands a majority of Members then a coalition is formed by two political parties to give a majority of Members. Ministers are responsible to the Lower House and although they can be chosen from elected Members of either House of Parliament, most of the Ministers are chosen from the Lower House, and only a few from the Senate, or Upper House.

Until 1956 all Ministers in the federal Parliament were also members of Cabinet, but since then some Prime Ministers have selected a small group of Ministers to form a Cabinet. Some Ministries, because of their nature and importance, will have Cabinet rank in every government; the Prime Minister, for example, is always head of Cabinet, and several other Ministries such as the Treasury, Foreign Affairs and Trade will always be included, while others, such as Education and Science, Health, and Environment, if included, might indicate that these areas of government activity are especially important in a government's programme, or that the Minister given responsibility for this matter is considered by the Prime Minister (and by his colleagues) as being especially valuable in the process of making vital government decisions. When Cabinet does not include all Ministries there is justifiable interest in announcements showing where the line is drawn between Cabinet and the rest of the Ministry.
Further reading: Encel, S. *Cabinet Government in Australia.* Melbourne University Press, Melbourne, 1962; Atkins, R. & Graycar, A. *Governing Australia.* Wiley, Sydney, 1972; Forell, C.R. *How We Are Governed.* Cheshire, Melbourne, 1978.

Caboolture QLD (population 6 451 in 1981) A town in the SUNSHINE COAST region of the State, situated on the Caboolture River which flows into DECEPTION BAY, it is 49km by road N of Brisbane. It is a rapidly developing urban centre in a productive rural district where dairying is the principal activity, and where sawmilling, fruit growing, beef cattle grazing and tobacco farming are also found. About 25km E from the town is BRIBIE ISLAND separated from the mainland by the quiet waters of Pumicestone Channel. The name Caboolture comes from an Aboriginal word meaning 'carpet snake'.

cachalot *see* dolphins, etc.

caddis flies These comprise a cosmopolitan order (Trichoptera) of moth-like endopterygote INSECTS. About 260 species occur in Australia, divided into two suborders containing 19 families. Caddis flies have hairy wings and bodies, which sometimes carry scales, but they differ from moths, to which they are related, in the reduced mouthparts

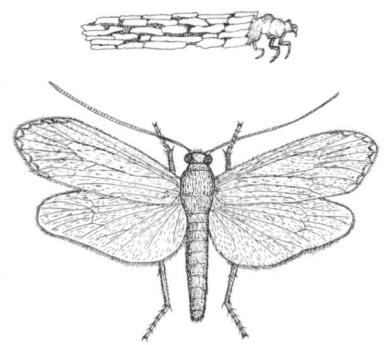

(above) emerging caddis fly larva
(below) adult caddis fly

and the venation of the wings. All caddis flies are associated with water, and the larvae, many of which resemble caterpillars, are all aquatic and have only one pair of abdominal prolegs. The larvae are usually omnivores; the adults may sometimes drink liquids or nectar. Caddis fly larvae are important food items for fish. Many of the larvae live within portable cases which they construct from silk to which they add fragments of sand, pieces of plant material and so on; the construction of the case is characteristic of the particular species, some making cases of silk only, and the members of four families not making a case at all. The larvae of the family Hydropsychidae construct a net at the entrance. One species, *Philanisus plebeius*, breeds in saltwater pools in S Australia and New Zealand, while another lives in lakes which are three times saltier than the sea.

Cadman, John (?-1848) Convict and Superintendent of Government Boats. Born in England, he came to Sydney in 1798 after being sentenced to transportation for life on a charge of horse-stealing. Granted a conditional pardon in 1814 and a free pardon in 1821, he became Superintendent of Government Boats at Sydney (1827-45). For the last three years of his life he was a publican at the Steam Packet Hotel, George Street, PARRAMATTA.

Although his historical importance is negligible, he is widely remembered because he occupied from 1816 and 1845 the building in George Street known as Cadman's Cottage, built in 1815 or 1816, now the oldest house in Sydney. Used by the Water Police from 1847 to 1965, it has since been restored and forms part of the Sydney Cove Maritime Museum. It is open to public inspection.
Further reading: Provis, J.S. & Johnson, K.A. *Cadman's Cottage: The Life and Times of John Cadman in Colonial Sydney, 1798-1848.* The authors, Sydney, 1972.

Caesalpinaceae *see* Papilionaceae

Cahill, John Joseph (1891-1959) Premier of NSW. He was born in the Sydney suburb of Redfern, became a fitter with the NSW Department of Railways and in 1925 was elected to the Legislative Assembly, remaining a Member, except for the years 1932-35, until his death. He held a number of portfolios in Labor administrations from 1941 onwards, and was Premier from 1952 to 1959. A sincere, modest man, he lacked brilliance, but was a sound administrator and a skilful conciliator. Among the many public works which were begun during his premiership were the Cahill Expressway (built to ease traffic congestion at the S end of the SYDNEY HARBOUR BRIDGE) and the SYDNEY OPERA HOUSE.

Cain, John (1931-) Premier of VIC. Born in Melbourne, he graduated LLB from Melbourne University and before to his entry into Parliament conducted a suburban law practice. He also took an active part in the work of professional organisations, being a member of the Council of the Law Institute of Victoria (1967-76), president of the Institute (1972-73), and a part-time member of the Law Reform Commission of Australia (1975-77).

His father, also John Cain, was leader of the AUSTRALIAN LABOR PARTY (ALP) in the VIC Parliament and was Premier on three occasions. Following his father's death in 1957, the younger John Cain hoped to gain his seat in the Legislative Assembly, but failed to secure Labor selection, and did not succeed in entering Parliament until 1976. However, he then rose to prominence quickly, becoming Opposition leader in September 1981. After the victory of the ALP in the elections of April 1982, he became the first Labor Premier of VIC since his father's loss of the position 27 years previously.

Cairn Curran Dam VIC The largest storage reservoir on the LODDON RIVER, located downstream from Newstead in the central N of the State, it has a capacity of 148 800ML. The reservoir, which gathers water from a catchment area of $1\,593km^2$, provides an assured supply for the irrigation of farmlands along the river and to the W sector of the GOULBURN RIVER irrigation system, supplementing waters from the WARANGA RESERVOIR and the Western Main Channel. The outlet works at Cairn Curran incorporate a small hydro-electricity station.

Cairns QLD (population 48 557 in 1981) The most northerly city in QLD, it is located on the Bruce Highway 1 856km by road NNW of Brisbane and 370km N along the highway from TOWNSVILLE. It is situated on the W shore of Trinity Bay and was originally established in 1875 on a swampy mangrove area to serve as the outlet for the Hodgkinson gold mines and later for the Herbertson tin fields. It is now a major commercial centre in the midst of productive sugar cane country, and on the waterfront there is a bulk sugar terminal for handling the exports of the industry. The cane harvesting season usually extends from June to December when four crushing mills in the region are busy processing the crop. The city (latitude 17°S) has a tropical climate with a high yearly rainfall of 2 001mm, concentrated mainly in the summer and early autumn seasons; March is the month of highest rainfall (464mm average) and more than 80 per cent of the yearly total falls between December and April. Along with its business and port activities, tourism is an important industry in the city. Abundant sunshine and superb displays of tropical shrubs and flowers; opportunities for deep-sea big-game fishing; launch and air tours of the GREAT BARRIER REEF and coral island resorts such as GREEN ISLAND; interesting features inland such as the ATHERTON TABLELAND with its crater lakes and the BARRON RIVER gorge with its hydro-electricity plant: all make the city a tourist mecca for people from the S States of Australia as well as for visitors from overseas.
Further reading: Watling, P. *Cairns and District Sketchbook.* Rigby, Adelaide, 1976.

Caley, George (1770-1829) Botanist and minor explorer. Born in Yorkshire, he developed an interest in botany in his youth, and in 1795 obtained a position as gardener at Kew Gardens through the patronage of Sir Joseph BANKS. Five years later Banks sent him as a botanical collector to NSW, where he was made superintendent of the botanical gardens at PARRAMATTA. He carried out minor explorations in the foothills of the BLUE MOUNTAINS, and in 1804 made an attempt at crossing them. He also accompanied James GRANT on a voyage to WESTERN PORT BAY in 1801, and later explored the Picton district. Meanwhile he had sent many botanical specimens to Banks and had also made collections of mammals and birds. In 1810 he returned to England where he spent the rest of his life except for the years 1816-22, when he was superintendent of the botanical gardens at St Vincent in the West Indies. Although his standing as a scientist was not high, he laid the ground for further study of Australian fauna and flora. A genus of orchids and several plant species are named after him.

Callaway, Frank Adams (1919-) Musician. Born in Timaru, New Zealand, and appointed Professor of Music at the University of Western Australia in 1959, he has contributed much to Australian life as a music administrator and educator: among the many national and international committees on which he has served are the International Society for Music Education (as a board member since 1958, president 1968-72, and treasurer since 1972), and various Australian UNESCO committees. Largely responsible for the founding of the Australian Society for Music Education and its national president from 1966 to 1971, he founded and has continued to edit two important music journals, the *Australian Journal of Music Education* and *Studies in Music*, both initiated in 1967 to serve the varied educational and musicological needs of the country. He was made an OBE (1970) and a CMG (1975) for his services to music.

Callide Valley QLD Callide Creek, a right-bank tributary of the DAWSON RIVER, rises in the Calliope Range SE of GLADSTONE, and joins the main stream near BILOELA. The rural lands of the valley produce cotton, sorghum and wheat, but the area is more noted for its coal production. The Callide seam, originally discovered in 1890, averages 15m thick and has been mined since 1944 by open-cut mechanised methods. Some of the coal is used in the Calcap power station which supplies electricity to Biloela, as well as to the ROCKHAMPTON and BLACKWATER districts; some coal is railed to Gladstone for export. Underground water is tapped to irrigate crops and pasture lands along the valley, but because of the heavy demand for water supplies, an artificial recharge system has been constructed to replenish the underground storage. This consists of three weirs (two in existence since 1972, the third completed in 1977), together with a dam on Callide Creek completed in 1965, with a maximum capacity of 576 000ML; the dam not only helps in giving a more assured irrigation supply, but also meets the needs of the thermal power station and provides a recreation area for aquatic sports.

Callistemon *see* Myrtaceae

Callitris *see* Gymnospermae

Caloundra QLD (population 16 758 in 1981) A beach resort on the SUNSHINE COAST, located at the N end of Pumicestone Channel which separates BRIBIE ISLAND from the mainland, it is 100km by road N of Brisbane. Lying 11km E of the Bruce Highway, it has an average annual rainfall of 1 569mm; the wettest month is March (222mm average), the driest is September (57mm). It is a popular tourist resort, with surf beaches, estuary swimming, fishing and other aquatic sports. Among the local attractions for visitors are cruises on the *Pumicestone Paddler* into the quiet waters of the channel, the *Endeavour Replica* (a two-thirds size reproduction of Captain COOK's ship), a military museum containing a collection of World War II vehicles, and a unique display of exhibits made of matches, called 'World of Matchcraft'. The name Caloundra is taken from an Aboriginal word meaning 'beautiful headland'.

Caloundra beach

Arthur Augustus Calwell

National Library of Australia

Calwell, Arthur Augustus (1896-1973) Labor parliamentary leader. Born in West Melbourne, he joined the VIC Public Services as a clerk in 1913, became secretary of his local AUSTRALIAN LABOR PARTY (ALP) branch in the following year, and was elected president of the VIC branch of the Labor Party in 1931. He also became prominent in Roman Catholic lay activities. He held the seat of Melbourne in the House of Representatives from 1940 to 1972, and was Minister for Information from 1943 to 1949, Minister for Immigration from 1945 to 1949, and leader of the ALP and of the Opposition from 1960 to 1967. Most would consider that his most effective work was done as the architect of Australia's immigration programme in the immediate post-war years.

Following the split in the Labor Party in 1955, he proved to be one of the most relentless opponents of the 'industrial groupers' and the DEMOCRATIC LABOR PARTY, although that party drew its main support from his co-religionists. Ironically, although he was created a Papal Knight in 1963, there was strong antagonism between him and the Roman Catholic Archbishop of Melbourne, Dr MANNIX. Although his harsh voice and manner were electoral handicaps, he came close to becoming in Prime Minister at the 1961 elections when the Liberal/Country Party coalition won a majority of only one in the House of Representatives. However, in 1963 and 1966, when he campaigned strongly against Australian participation in the VIETNAM WAR, Labor was soundly beaten, and he resigned the party leadership shortly after the 1966 results were announced.
Further reading: Calwell, A.A. *Be Just and Fear Not.* Hawthorn Press, VIC, 1972.

Camballin WA This small township is located on the alluvial flood-plain of the lower FITZROY RIVER in the far N of the State, SE of DERBY between the Great Northern Highway and the Fitzroy. At an elevation of only 45m above sea level, it experiences a tropical climate, with hot, wet summers.

Cambridge, Ada (1844-1926) Novelist. Born in England, she came to Australia in

1870 with her husband, an Anglican clergyman, lived in several VIC country towns and then from 1893 to 1909 in the Melbourne suburb of Williamstown. After her husband's death in 1909 she visited England, but returned to spend the rest of her life in Melbourne. Her writings include three volumes of poetry, two books of reminiscences and a collection of short stories, but she is best remembered for her novels. Eighteen of these, ranging in time from *My Guardian: A Story of the Fen Country* (1878) to *The Making of Rachel Rowe* (1914), were published in book form and six others appeared as magazine serials. She wrote mainly for the English market, most of her stories picturing the social environment of the colonial middle class (which was really more English than Australian) and not treating the local setting in depth. Of all her works those with the greatest literary value are probably *A Marked Man* (1891) and *Not All in Vain* (1893).

Camden NSW (population 8 999 in 1981) This town is located 60km SW of Sydney on the Hume Highway. At an elevation of 68m above sea level, it is situated adjacent to and on the W side of the NEPEAN RIVER, in a region of low, gently undulating hills, which form a SW extension of the Sydney Plain.

Camden has many connections with the early history of settlement in Australia. In 1795 two convicts discovered a herd of wild cattle in the area; these were descendants of livestock that had strayed from Sydney. The district was thus originally named the COWPASTURES. In 1805 John MACARTHUR was granted 2000ha of land in the area and he called one of his farms Camden Park after Lord Camden, then British Secretary of State for the Colonies. This farm, located some 5km SE of the present town, was where Macarthur conducted the sheep breeding experiments which were so important in founding the nation's sheep grazing industry; he also established fruit growing and vine cultivation in this area. The district is still important for many types of rural production: dairying, orcharding, fat lamb raising, beef cattle, pigs, poultry, vineyards and horse breeding. The town has two interesting museums: the Camden Historical Museum which includes a special section featuring John Macarthur, and the Camden Museum of Aviation located in a hangar at the local airport. The National Trust (NSW) has classified several buildings in Camden for preservation as part of the cultural heritage; among these are the CBC Bank, and St John's Anglican Church together with its rectory, stables and church grounds. The town is now a satellite of Sydney and many residents are daily commuters to the metropolitan area. Plans have been made to develop it, together with CAMPBELLTOWN and Appin, as a major urban centre in the future.

Camden Haven NSW (population 3 161 in 1981) An inlet and a holiday resort on the mid-NORTH COAST of the State, it is 396km by road NNE of Sydney, lying E of the Pacific Highway, SSW of PORT MACQUARIE and SE of WAUCHOPE. The Camden Haven area, comprising the urban settlements of Laurieton, North Haven and Dumbogan, is a popular coastal resort, particularly during the summer vacation. The area offers the visitor opportunities for swimming, boating and fishing, as well as fine coastal and bushland scenery.

camels *see* animals, introduced

Campaspe River

VIC Located in the central part of the State, it is a tributary of the MURRAY RIVER, rising in the mid-section of the GREAT DIVIDING RANGE near MOUNT MACEDON about 70km NW of Melbourne. It flows for some 240km in a general N direction across the N plains, joining the Murray near ECHUCA. The headwaters rise in steeply dissected country with peaks rising to over 1 000m elevation (Mt Macedon 1 011m), where high rainfall can bring seasonal flooding. The rainfall declines progressively downstream.

The waters of the Campaspe have been controlled for irrigation and urban supplies by a number of structures. The largest of these is EPPALOCK RESERVOIR (built 1960-62) located about 30km SE of BENDIGO, with a storage capacity of 311 900ML. Waters of the reservoir are utilised downstream for irrigating orchards, crop land, and pastures, as well as to provide part of Bendigo's domestic supplies. On the Coliban River, one of the upper tributaries of the Campaspe, dams control river flow; the earliest of these was Malmsbury Dam, constructed in 1865, with a capacity of 17 760ML and a catchment area of 290km^2. In conjunction with other dams on the Coliban River—Lauriston Dam (19 620ML capacity) and Upper Coliban Dam (31 700ML)—Malmsbury provides domestic water for Bendigo, CASTLEMAINE and other towns, and irrigation supplies for orchards and pastures. The Calder Highway crosses the Campaspe at Kyneton; the Northern Highway passes along the valley on a general S-N route and joins the Murray Valley Highway W of Echuca. The Campaspe was named by the explorer Major (later Sir) Thomas MITCHELL in 1836, after Campaspe, a mistress of Alexander the Great.

Campbell, Robert

(1769-1846) Pioneer merchant, pastoralist and philanthropist. Born in Greenock, Scotland, he went to Calcutta in 1798 to join his brother in the merchant firm of Campbell, Clarke & Co. In 1800 he moved to Sydney and began the construction of warehouses and a wharf on the W side of SYDNEY COVE. He very quickly won a reputation for fair dealing and during the following several years became the colony's leading merchant, a pastoralist, and a major promoter of the sealing industry.

Governor BLIGH, whose attempts at reform he supported strongly, made him collector of taxes and customs, and manager of the convict

Robert Campbell

National Library of Australia

and orphan funds. It is not surprising therefore that after deposing Bligh in January 1808, Colonel JOHNSTON dismissed Campbell from these positions and even arrested him and his business partner and brother-in-law, John Palmer, and kept them imprisoned for a time. Governor MACQUARIE reinstated him, but after a few months persuaded him to resign on the grounds that it was not fitting for him to be responsible for levying taxes on his business rivals. Shortly afterwards he went to England as a witness at the court martial of Johnston. In the meantime his business affairs had suffered such interruptions that in 1815 the firm of Campbell & Co. went into liquidation. However, he re-established himself in 1820 and prospered once more as a commission agent, merchant and shipowner.

He was an original shareholder of the BANK OF NEW SOUTH WALES, founded in 1817, and a co-founder of Australia's first savings bank, in 1819. He was active in the affairs of the Presbyterian Church, the Church of England and the London Missionary Society, and contributed generously to the building of a number of churches. He was one of the first settlers in the Argyle County, in what is now the Canberra district. His property, named 'Duntroon', remained in the possession of his family until 1910, when it was purchased by the Commonwealth government as a site for a military academy. He was also a member of the Legislative Council of NSW from 1825 to 1843.
Further reading: Steven, M. *Merchant Campbell 1769-1846*. Melbourne University Press, Melbourne, 1965.

Campbell Town

TAS (population 879 in 1981) This small historic settlement is located 134km N of Hobart along the Midland Highway, 68km S of LAUNCESTON and 10km N of ROSS. It is in the MIDLANDS region at an elevation of 183m above sea level, on the Elizabeth River, an upper tributary of the South ESK system. It was named by Governor MACQUARIE in 1821 after his wife's maiden name, and was originally established as one of a series of garrison towns between Hobart and Launceston. It is now a service centre for a productive farming and grazing district. It is of considerable historic interest.

Campbelltown

NSW (population 91 494 in 1981) This city is located 60km by road and 51km by rail SW of Sydney on the main S railway. It is set in undulating hills between the valleys of the NEPEAN and Georges Rivers where the SW extension of the Sydney Plain merges into the Woronora Plateau. The area played an important role in the early settlement of Australia. Surgeon George BASS explored it in 1795 and Governor MACQUARIE, visiting the district in 1810, named it 'Airds' after his wife's family estate in Scotland; by the following year over 100 settlers were farming there. Macquarie again visited the locality in 1820 when he formally founded the town and named it 'in honour of Mrs Macquarie's maiden name'. Wheat growing was one of the early local farming activities, and James RUSE built the first grist mill there —it still stands today as a relic of the convict colony. A number of colonial homes also still stand in Campbelltown, and many pioneers, among them Ruse, are buried in the grounds of historic St Peter's Church (opened in 1823). Though wheat cultivation did not survive in the district because of rust problems, it has remained an important rural region, having orchards, poultry farms, and dairies which supply milk to the Sydney metropolis. In the Sydney Region Outline Plan adopted by the State government in 1968, Campbelltown was designated as a growth centre planned to become a major satellite of Sydney with a residential population of over 300 000. But parts of the town and district still retain a flavour of the 19th century; many colonial homes and other buildings have been listed by the National Trust (NSW) for preservation as part of the cultural heritage. Among them are 'Denfield' (1830s), 'Glenavon' (c1840), and 'Glenlee' (c1824); St Peter's Anglican Church (1823), and St John's Catholic Church (1825-41) which is now a convent school.
See also Camden; Macarthur, John
Further reading: The New Cities of Campbelltown, Camden, Appin: Structure Plan. State Planning Authority of New South Wales, Sydney, 1973; Bayley, W.A. *History of Campbelltown, New South Wales.* Campbelltown City Council, 1974.

Camperdown

VIC (population 3 545 in 1981) This town is on the Princes Highway 195km by road and 198km by rail WSW of Melbourne, and 69km ENE of WARRNAMBOOL in the rich farming and grazing lands of the WESTERN DISTRICT. At an elevation of 165m above sea level it is situated at the foot of Mt Leura, an extinct volcanic crater. It is a commercial and service centre, with a flour mill and a large dairy factory. There are several lakes nearby (among them Lake Bullen Merri and Lake Colongulac) which provide fine aquatic recreation areas. It experiences a mild climate, with an average annual rainfall of 777mm, concentrated in winter and spring. The locality was named in 1854 after Admiral Duncan, Earl of Camperdown; it became a borough in 1952 and was proclaimed a town in

1959. Over a dozen buildings in the area have been listed by the National Trust (VIC) for their historic and architectural importance, including several colonial homesteads, two churches, the shire hall (1885) and the courthouse (c1886).

campion *see* Caryophyllaceae

Canberra (population 219 331 in 1981) The national capital of Australia, it is located in the NE of the ACT some 304km SW of Sydney by road, 324km by rail and 237km by air; from Melbourne it is 717km by road via ALBURY. The city is situated on the plains and hill land adjacent to the MOLONGLO RIVER, a tributary of the MURRUMBIDGEE RIVER. The general elevation of the plain is 580m above sea level and the hills rise to over 800m.
Climate Canberra experiences warm to hot summers, and cool to cold winter conditions. In January, the hottest month, the average maximum temperature is 27.5°C, while in July, which normally has the lowest temperatures, the average minimum is just below zero. The average yearly rainfall is 633mm, fairly evenly spread throughout the year, with some light snowfalls in winter.
A planned city It was a rather common joke, some years ago, to refer to Canberra as 'the largest illuminated paddock in Australia' or as 'the bush capital', or even as 'several suburbs in search of a city'. Some, however, who took a pride in the city's growth and development, called it 'the garden city of the Commonwealth' or 'the front window of the nation'. However, it seems that many a visitor has ended his stay there in a state of mild confusion, particularly about finding his way through the apparent maze of circular streets and curving avenues. Nevertheless, Canberra is unique among the cities of Australia, not only because it is the national political centre, but also because the city plan was designed in its entirety before the city came into existence, and because it has the fastest-growing population of any city in the nation.

The need for a national capital arose only when the Australian colonies decided to join together as a federation; at the time there were some who thought that the capital should be established either in Melbourne or in Sydney, but in the end the opinions of those who advocated the establishment of a new and quite separate centre won through. So when federation became a reality in 1901, the following provision was included in the Constitution Act:

The seat of Government of the Commonwealth shall be determined by the Parliament, and shall be within territory which shall have been granted to or acquired by the Commonwealth, and shall be vested in and belong to the Commonwealth, and shall be in the State of New South Wales, and be distant not less than one hundred miles from Sydney.

Academy of Science, Canberra

NSW Dept. of Tourism

Site selection Over a period of nine years (1899-1908) two Royal Commissions were held, parliamentary committees conducted investigations, and many possible sites were examined. Many towns in NSW, ranging from ORANGE and BATHURST in the central W region, to Albury and TUMUT in the S, put forward their claims. Finally it was decided in 1909 that the 'Yass-Canberry' region was to be the general location; the precise site was selected by Scrivener, a surveyor, and a geological survey was made by Griffith TAYLOR. The countryside at that time was sparsely settled grazing land. In 1911 the ACT, comprising an area of 2 538km², was transferred from NSW to the Commonwealth and thus became a separate political entity.
The plan A worldwide competition was conducted by the Commonwealth government shortly after this. Competitors were supplied with a contoured map of the area and paintings of the environs. The Royal Institute of British Architects boycotted the competition because of an objection to a lay member of the judging panel, King O'Malley. Despite their boycott, 137 entries were received, the winning plan being submitted by the American, Walter Burley GRIFFIN, a landscape architect from Chicago.

In setting out his city on virgin land, Griffin aimed to blend the pattern of streets and buildings in harmony with the landscape features, planning a garden city with many open spaces and tree-lined boulevards. The low knolls rising above the Molonglo Plain were designated as the sites of major public buildings. The road pattern was one of concentric circles and arcs linked by radial routes; a chain of ornamental lakes along the Molonglo Valley was designed as a unifying feature in the centre of the city.

Genesis and growth Although Griffin came to Canberra in 1913 to supervise the construction of the city, times were difficult during World War I and little building was carried out before 1920. In the following decade, however, good progress was made in shaping the city and in May 1927 the federal Parliament House was officially opened by the Duke of York (later King George VI). But the Depression years of the late 1920s and early 1930s had serious effects on the whole Australian economy and Canberra was no exception. City growth almost ceased during this period; it was not until the late 1930s that construction again got under way. Progress was halted once more in 1939 by the onset of World War II, but when the war ended building was resumed and the city has since grown at a rapid rate, particularly over recent decades, as population statistics show (*see* Table 1).

Table 1

URBAN GROWTH OF CANBERRA 1921–81

Year	Population
1921	1 150
1925	3 500
1935	7 700
1947*	15 156
1954*	28 277
1961*	56 449
1965	85 690
1973	167 190
1976*	196 517
1981*	219 331

Note: * indicates census years; other figures are estimates or population counts.
Source: Australian Bureau of Statistics, Canberra.

116 CANE TOAD

In the planned development of the city careful attention has been paid to its aesthetic aspects, and much of the original concept of Griffin's design has been preserved. Over two million trees, both exotic and indigenous, have been planted, and large areas have been devoted to playing fields, gardens and public parks. The establishment in 1957 of the National Capital Development Commission ensured that while the spirit of Griffin's plan was retained adequate modifications could be made to cope with changing conditions. The Griffin concept of a central lake came to fruition in 1963 with the building of Scrivener Dam across the Molonglo River, the flooding of the lower alluvial plain land and the naming of Lake Burley Griffin.

As more government departments moved their head offices to the national capital, extensions to the city were planned in the form of new towns, better adapted to the needs of a car-owning population. The first of these was Woden, begun in 1962 and located 10km SW of the city; others are Belconnen (10km to the NW) and Tuggeranong (18km to the S). These newer sub-centres are separated from the main city focus by ridges, hills and open land, but connected by major expressways. Feeder road, cul-de-sacs and pedestrian areas have been included in these new suburban developments. Many of the suburbs are named after former Prime Ministers, but more recently some Aboriginal names have been used.

Many important buildings and monuments dominate the scenery of Canberra. Parliament House, though it is still 'temporary' accommodation for the House of Representatives and the Senate, lies on the S border of the lake. The Australian War Memorial on the lower slopes of Mt Ainslie, N of the lake, houses a major collection of paintings, models, relics and records of Australia's participation in various theatres of war. Crossing Lake Burley Griffin are the impressive Kings Avenue and Commonwealth Bridges. The 79m-high metal shaft of the Australian-American War Memorial with its superimposed eagle commemorates the contribution made by the people of the USA to the defence of Australia in World War II. The Academy of Science building is of unconventional design, its copper-covered concrete dome, 46m in diameter, resting on arches set in a ring-shaped pool. The Carillon and Water Jet, a gift from the UK government to mark Canberra's 50th Jubilee, is situated on Aspen Is in the lake. Other main buildings and institutions include the National Library, the Australian National University (established in 1946), the High Court of Australia building, the Australian National Gallery, the Prime Minister's Lodge, 'Yarralumla (the residence of the Governor-General), the Australian Institute of Anatomy, Duntroon Royal Military College, Mt Stromlo Observatory and the headquarters of overseas diplomatic representatives.

The responsibilities of civic administration, carried out by the Department of the Capital Territory, include the provision of public transport, tourist services, welfare and fire protection, motor-vehicle registration, management of government-owned houses and flats, parks and gardens, building construction, rural leases, forest plantations and the city's general community services. The planning and development of the city is the function of the National Capital Development Commission.

A meeting place for many national and international conferences, Canberra has also become an important tourist centre, and attracts over one million visitors each year. Like New Delhi in India, Washington in the USA, and Brazilia, Canberra has been established as a seat of government, the national capital and the focus of political administration, and consequently a high proportion of its workforce is employed in the public service; but in recent years it has developed increasingly as a commercial, financial, educational and general business centre.
Further reading: White, H.L. (ed) *Canberra: A Nation's Capital*. Angus & Robertson, Sydney, 1954; Wilson, J.L.J. (ed) 'Canberra: 1959' in *Current Affairs Bulletin*. (vol 24, no 13, 1959); White, U. & Luck, P. *Canberra Sketchbook*. Rigby, Adelaide, 1968; *Tomorrow's Canberra*. National Capital Development Commission, Canberra, 1970; Roberts, R. *Canberra in Colour*. Rigby, Adelaide, 1970; Mullins, B. & Baglin, D. *Canberra on the Monaro*. Reed, Sydney, 1977.

cane toad *see* frogs, etc.

Canning Basin *see* artesian water

canoeing As a competitive sport, canoeing does not arouse a great deal of public interest in Australia although there are a number of rivers, lakes, sheltered bays and harbours suitable for racing. The sport is thought to have been introduced first in VIC in the early 1900s, the first canoes being imported from Canada. Canoeing was included in the Olympic Games for the first time in Melbourne in 1956, and Australians Walter Brown and Dennis Green won a bronze medal in the two-seater kayak event over 10 000m. In 1980 at Moscow, J. Sunegi won the silver medal for the 1 500m men's kayak. To coordinate the activities of the canoe clubs throughout Australia (35 in the early 1980s), the Australian Canoe Federation was established in 1949, and it has since been active in promoting canoeing both as a competitive sport and as a pleasurable recreation.

cape gooseberry *see* Solanaceae

Cape Howe NSW/VIC This coastal headland on the SE of the continent is the border point between NSW and VIC. It was initially fixed as a dividing point when the PORT PHILLIP District was created in 1842 and was defined by an Imperial Act in the words '. . . the boundary of the District of Port Phillip on the North and North-East shall be a straight line drawn from Cape Howe to the nearest Source of the River Murray.' The line boundary was adopted when VIC was made a separate colony in 1851 and a definitive point on the cape was fixed following an on-site meeting between surveyors of NSW and VIC the point was marked and named Conference Point.

cape ivy *see* Compositae; weeds

Cape Leeuwin WA Located at the extreme SW point of the State, it is a rocky peninsula to the W of Flinders Bay, forming the dividing point between the Southern and Indian Oceans, and named after the Dutch ship *Leeuwin* (meaning 'lioness') which passed this point in 1622. The lighthouse on the cape, built of local limestone, was started in 1895; it is a meteorological station and its records show an average annual rainfall of 994mm, winter being the rainy period (July, with an average of 185mm, is the wettest month). During the building of the lighthouse, a spring was tapped to provide fresh water for the workers and a wooden water wheel constructed; the wheel remains as a tourist attraction, though it is slowly being turned to stone by the calcifying action of the water. The wheel and the lighthouse have been listed for preservation by the National Trust (WA). The Leeuwin-Naturaliste National Park covers 13 239ha of rugged coastline and forest lands in the N and E of the cape.

Cape Nelson VIC Located 10km SW of PORTLAND, this headland divides Portland Bay from DISCOVERY BAY, on the far W coast of the State. It was named by Lieutenant James GRANT in 1800 after his ship, the *Lady Nelson*. The headland is comprised of several rocky peninsulas: Cape Duquesne and Cape Bridgewater on the W, Cape Nelson in the middle, and Cape Grant, Point Danger and Black Nose Point on the E.

cape pigeons *see* sea birds

cape weed *see* Compositae; weeds

Cape York QLD The northernmost point of mainland Australia, only about 150km from Papua New Guinea, Cape York is at the tip of a peninsula extending S from the cape for some 800km beyond the GILBERT RIVER, the S limit usually being defined by a line drawn from CAIRNS to NORMANTON. The cape was named in 1770 by Captain COOK when he discovered it during his journey N along the E coast of the peninsula; although Dutch navigators had explored the W coast of the peninsula in the 17th century, they had not discovered the cape. Down the E side of the peninsula extends the GREAT DIVIDING RANGE, its highest points rising to over 800m above sea level. Different sections of the range have individual names: in the far N the Richardson Range; further S the Tozer, Sir William Thompson, Table, Geike and McIlwraith Ranges. The W part of the peninsula consists of vast alluvial lowlands across which rivers—including the Wenlock, Archer and Holroyd Rivers in the N, and the MITCHELL

The northernmost point of Cape York QLD

and the Gilbert to the S—drain into the GULF OF CARPENTARIA.

Much of the N part of the peninsula is inhospitable country, rugged and largely uninhabited; the W sections are sparsely populated, occupied mainly by large beef grazing properties. WEIPA, on the NW shore of the peninsula, is an important bauxite mining and export centre. Along parts of the SE coastal zone there is sugar cane farming, and inland in the S parts beef cattle and grain production are important in the rural economy. There is a marked contrast between the coastal landscapes along the E and W shores: the E coast consists of a series of rocky headlands and smoothly curved bays, with longer beaches where major rivers enter the sea; the W coast lacks the solid-rock outcrops and consists of long, gently curving beaches backed by parallel sand ridges. The coral formations also offer a contrast: on the W coast there is very little coral, while along the E the GREAT BARRIER REEF boasts an abundance of coral.

Capricorn Coast QLD
This is a string of holiday resorts along a 47km stretch of the E coast of the State, lying E and NE of ROCKHAMPTON. YEPPOON, situated on Keppel Bay, is the largest of the resorts and is known for its annual September Pineapple Festival. Other resort centres are Cooee Bay, Bosslyn Bay, Causeway Lake and Emu Park. The KEPPEL ISLES lie 13km off the coast. At Emu Park is the unique modern artistic structure called the 'Singing Ship' which commemorates the discovery of Keppel Bay by Captain James COOK in 1770.

Capricorn Group QLD
Part of the GREAT BARRIER REEF, this island group consists of typical sandy islets built on coral platforms with fringing coral reefs. Located near the S extremity of the Barrier Reef, the group lies astride the Tropic of Capricorn about 140km ESE of ROCKHAMPTON and 80km NE of GLADSTONE. The best-known island of the group is HERON ISLAND; others are One Tree Is, Erksine Is, Wreck Is and Wilson Is; there are also several reefs, including the Wistari, Sykes and Irving Reefs. The greater part of Heron Is (12ha) and the Heron-Wistari Reefs (9 700ha) are a marine national park.

To the SE of the Capricorn Group, about 110km E of Gladstone, is the Bunker Group, comprising three islands: Lady Musgrave Is (20ha), Hoskyn Is (8ha) and Fairfax Is (16ha).

They are also typical coral islets with surrounding reefs, and are important sea-bird nesting sites. They form the Bunker Group National Park. Lady Elliott Is, located about 50km SE of the Bunker Group, is the southernmost extent of the Barrier Reef.

capsicum *see* Solanaceae

caraway *see* Umbelliferae

Carnarvon
WA (population 5 053 in 1981) Located 983km by road NNW of Perth and 483km NNW of GERALDTON on the NW Coastal Highway, where the estuary of the GASCOYNE RIVER enters SHARK BAY, the town was named in the 1880s after the then British Secretary of State, Lord Carnarvon. It is the service centre for an extensive sheep and cattle grazing hinterland and an important communications centre; on Brown Range just outside the town the Overseas Telecommunications earth-station, with a 29.5m antenna dish, receives television and other signals relayed by satellite, and 6km beyond the town is the USA Apollo space-tracking station. The region is a low-rainfall area, receiving an average of 232mm yearly, falling mainly in the winter months (June, the wettest month, 50mm average), with very hot and markedly dry summers (February, the hottest month, 32°C average maximum; December, the driest month, 1mm average). Little wonder that under these semi-arid conditions, the bed of the Gascoyne River is dry most of the year. Underground water, flowing beneath the dry river bed, has been utilised for the irrigation of some 800ha, which produce bananas, pawpaws, citrus fruits, pineapples, melons and vegetables. After World War II, Carnarvon was the site of a whaling station for some 15 years, but it ceased operation in 1963 when Australia agreed to an international embargo on the killing of hump-backed whales; the plant was converted to a processing works for treating prawns.

QLD Nat. Parks/Wildlife

Carnarvon Gorge, National Park

Carnarvon Range QLD
A part of the GREAT DIVIDING RANGE located about 400km inland from MARYBOROUGH and 150km N of ROMA, it forms the watershed between the headwaters of the DAWSON RIVER system and streams draining inland to the Maranoa and Warrego Rivers. The range is over 150km long and rises to more than 900m above sea level in some spectacular sandstone outcrops, much dissected by stream valleys and containing numerous Aboriginal cave paintings.

carnations *see* Caryophyllaceae

carnivorous plants *see* parasitic plants

carrots *see* Umbelliferae

Carruthers, James William 'Jimmy'
(1929-) Boxer. Born in the Sydney suburb of Paddington, Carruthers was to become the first Australian to win a universally recognised world boxing title. A sandy-haired southpaw bantamweight, he won the Australian bantamweight championship as an amateur in 1947 and represented Australia in the 1948 Olympic Games. Turning professional in 1950, he won the Australian bantamweight title from Elley Bennett in the following year. Then on 15 November 1952 he burst onto the international boxing stage when he knocked out previously unbeaten Vic Toweel in the first round of their world-title bout in Johannesburg, South Africa. This win made him the sporting hero of the day and when he fought American Pappy Gault in his second defence of the world title in 1953, the bout attracted to the Sydney Sports Ground the largest crowd ever to watch a boxing contest in Australia—32 500. In Bangkok in 1954 he fought his third successful defence, against Chamrern Songkitrat, in a bout which was fought in an open-air arena during a typhoon with both boxers fighting barefoot to try to gain some purchase on the wet canvas. Following this fight he announced his retirement and became the first world champion from any division to retire without having lost or drawn a professional bout. Seven years later in 1961 during a comeback he was defeated for the first time. A rapid puncher noted for his speed and courage, Carruthers' record included 13 knockout wins and eight wins on points. His only four losses occurred during his unsuccessful comeback attempt in 1961.

cartooning
In little more than a hundred years, Australia has developed a strong tradition of black and white cartooning. The number of excellent cartoonists that Australia has produced is disproportionately high for its population but there is still no plausible explanation as to why that should be so. In fact, in recent times it has been suggested that Australia's quality exports are opera singers and cartoonists. However, that has not always been the case. In the first years of the Australian colonies, there were few cartoons, and fewer cartoonists. Freedom of speech, and of the press, was not encouraged by the early military Governors. The few surviving cartoons are crude, and reflect the opinions of various factions in colonial society. Cartooning, in a modern sense, did not commence until 1855 with the founding of the *Melbourne Punch,* which was modelled on the English *Punch.* The *Melbourne Punch* was followed by similar illustrated magazines in the other colonies. In general, these magazines catered for a conservative, middle class population, and did not reflect the growth of Australian idealism and nationalism. The humour was essentially a

transposition to the colonies of the current English joke drawings, with long laboured captions about servants, country bumpkins, etc. But it was the *Bulletin* which revolutionised Australian cartooning, and in doing so gave rise to the popularisation of national images which survive to this day. The *Bulletin* was founded in 1880, and the first 'Bulletin' cartoonist was an American, Livingston Hopkins (1846-1927), known professionally as 'Hop'. His black and white drawing influenced later *Bulletin* artists, and helped to establish a distinctive *Bulletin* style. Hop produced illustrated jokes about characters such as the clergy and the cocky farmer, and commented on pre-Federation politics.

In 1886 English-born Phil MAY (1864-1903) joined the *Bulletin*. May quickly established himself as an outstanding comic artist. His favourite themes were Sydney low-life characters of the time, especially the larrikin element. May simplified the joke caption and, together with Hopkins, laid the foundations of the irreverence for politics, the Monarchy and the Church, which has now become a dominant feature of the *Bulletin*. He left the *Bulletin* staff in 1888, but his style influenced many subsequent comic artists. Outstanding contributors in the next two decades included George Ashton, Tom Durkin, Frank Mahoney and George LAMBERT. The cartoons of the 1890's consolidated the romantic concept of the bush, but without the Aborigine as the 'noble savage'. This was also a time of encouragement for artists and writers to establish a national identity, free of British interference. The cartoons reflected other major issues including the White Australia policy and the rise of trade unionism. Norman LINDSAY (1879-1969) joined the *Bulletin* in 1901 and within a short time his talent was widely recognised. His comic themes were those of the bush, characters from the Sydney back streets, and animals, as in The Magic Pudding which he both wrote and illustrated. The other major *Bulletin* cartoonists of the time were Will DYSON (1880-1938) who later gained considerable recognition in Britain, and David Low (1891-1963). New Zealand born, Low joined the *Bulletin* in 1911. Although he also drew joke cartoons pertaining to the First World War and to urban subjects, Low is best remembered for his political caricatures, particularly those of Prime Minister Billy Hughes. He was offered a position in England where he subsequently established himself in the forefront of European newspaper cartoonists. He was knighted in 1962.

The *Bulletin* era, from its founding to the end of World War 1, was the first great period in Australian cartooning. The second great period was brought about by *Smith's Weekly,* founded in 1919. 'Smith's', as it was known, fostered the Digger attitude and character. Many of its first cartoonists were ex-soldiers themselves, and their humour was that of the archetypal laconic Aussie. This form of humour was popular during the dark days of the Depression and the Second World War. The 'Bluey and Curly' comic strip drawn by Alex Gurney, gained a wide following for its humour and lack of pretension. The other notable soldier comic strip, 'Wally and the Major', was drawn by Stan Cross. Cross had been responsible for the first established Australian comic strip, 'The Potts', which appeared initially in *Smith's Weekly.* The strip was later drawn by Jim Russell.

Comic papers or comic supplements to newspapers were introduced in the 1920's. *Sunbeams* was the first comic supplement (1921) and here Ginger Meggs, created by Jim BANCKS, made his first appearance as a minor character in 'Us Fellers'. The 'Ginger Meggs' title was introduced later. The strip appeared continuously for more than thirty years. Other similar strips were created, including 'Fatty Finn' by Syd Nicholls.

During the late 1940s and early 1950s, the general standard of cartooning declined. The composition of the Australian population was changing, and with the increased trend to urbanisation, the bush-based, male-oriented humour was now regarded as unacceptably unsophisticated. However, no indigenous humour of the new social attitudes had yet developed, leaving an effective vacuum. This situation changed in the 1960s with the emergence of satirical cartooning which was critical of growing urban attitudes and the consumer society. Prominent cartoonists included architect, George Molnar, whose cool, calculated line punctured the vantities and conformities of the contemporary environment, and the brutally graphic Martin Sharp, mocking the hypocrisy of Australian society. Sharp's work first came to the notice of the public when he he and the editors of the satirical magazine 'Oz' were charged under the Obscene Publications Act.

A major influence from this time is the work of Bruce Petty, whose work appeared in the *Australian* in 1965. Petty is widely regarded as one of the world's finest cartoonists, and as the most committed and intellectual of contemporary Australian cartoonists. He has produced a dazzling array of books and films, and in 1977 won an Academy Award for his film *Leisure.* His style has influenced a whole generation of younger cartoonists, including Peter Nicholson, Patrick Cook and Ron Tandberg; unnecessary detail is eliminated from the drawing to provide an image and caption that is devastating in its impact. Larry Pickering provided a pungent daily comment on contemporary politics. The late 1970s and early 1980s has seen a boom in cartooning, with a group of new cartoonists with a wide variety of individual styles. They include Michael Leunig, Victoria Roberts, Peter Nicholson, John Spooner, David Bromley and Ward O'Neill.

While contemporary cartooning has taken off in several different directions, there remains a core of highly talented, more traditional humorous cartoonists, including Les Tanner, whose work has spanned several decades and who created the Henry Bolte image; Benier, Paul Rigby and Pat Oliphant. A Pulitzer prize winner, Oliphant has lived in the USA for the last decade. His style has subsequently influenced contemporary American political cartoonists.

Outside the range of political cartoonists are comic artists not easily categorised. These include Eric Jolliffe, whose Aboriginal series, 'Witchetty's Tribe', with its juxtaposed Western values, has been very popular, and Emile Mercier, whose zany humour is forever remembered for its incidental details, particularly gravy cans. There are many other cartoonists, working in both the recognized media and in the underground media. The diversity of styles is assurance that Australian cartooning will maintain its vigour in the future, and that the strong tradition will be sustained.

cartrut shell *see* gastropods

Caryophyllaceae This is a dicotyledonous family of flowering plants with about 80 genera containing 2000 species. Most of these are native to the temperate N hemisphere, but many have become WEEDS throughout the world, including Australia.

Catchfly, *Silene anglica,* a roadside weed Sydney region

Members of the family Caryophyllaceae are annual or perennial herbs with opposite leaves and often swollen stem joints. The flowers are regular and bisexual, with four or five sepals surrounding the same number of petals. There are up to 10 stamens and a superior ovary formed by up to five carpels; these are usually fully united so that the ovary consists of a single chamber, but the styles, each bearing a stigma, remain separate. In most species the ovary develops into a capsule containing many seeds which are shed when the fruit dries out and the sections of its wall separate at the apex.

The best-known garden plants in this family are baby's breath (*Gypsophila* species) and the carnations and pinks (*Dianthus* species). Weeds include chickweed (*Cerastium* and *Stellaria* species), allseed, *Polycarpon tetraphyllum,* and corn spurrey, *Spergula arvensis.* Most of the weeds are annuals of European origin and occur mainly in the cooler parts of Australia. Native species include pearlwort (*Sagina* species) and sand spurrey (*Spergularia* species), which occur on coastal sand dunes and in the arid inland, and starwort (*Stellaria* species), which often grows in swamps and other moist habitats.

See also Angiospermae; Appendix 5, Flower Structure and Glossary of Botanical Terms
Further reading: see Appendix 6, A Bibliography for Plants.

Lord Casey
Courtesy of A.I.S. Canberra

Casey, Richard Gardiner Lord Casey (1890-1976) Politician and Governor-General. Born in Brisbane, he was educated at Melbourne and Cambridge Universities, served in the AIF from 1914 to 1919 and then worked as a professional engineer. Between 1924 and 1931 he was Australian political liaison officer in London. Then he returned to Australia and as a United Australia Party candidate won election to the House of Representatives for the seat of Corio in VIC in 1931.

In 1940 he was appointed Australian Minister to the USA and not long afterwards became a member of the British War Cabinet as Minister of State for the UK in the Middle East. From 1944 to 1946 he was Governor of Bengal. He then returned to Australia, was re-elected to the House of Representatives in 1949, and during the following 11 years held a number of Cabinet positions, most notably that of Minister for External Affairs from 1951 until his retirement in 1960. In this position he showed a keen realisation of the importance to Australia of the newly independent nations to the N. He served as Governor-General from 1965 to 1969, and in 1966 was created Baron Casey of Berwick and of the City of Westminster, this being the first life-peerage given outside the UK.
Further reading: Casey, R.G. *Personal Experience, 1939-1946.* Constable, London, 1962; Millar, T.B. (ed) *Australian Foreign Minister: The Diaries of R.G. Casey.* Collins, London, 1972.

Casey A meteorological and research station in ANTARCTICA, operated by the Australian National Antarctic Research Expeditions (ANARE), it is located on the coast of Wilkes Land at latitude 66°17′S. It was established in 1969 to replace WILKES Station (an American base which had been transferred to Australian administration) and was named after Lord CASEY, a former Governor-General of Australia.

Cash, Martin (1808-77) Bushranger. Born in County Wexford, Ireland, he was sentenced to seven years' transportation in 1827 on a charge of housebreaking which arose from an incident in which he fired through the window of a house and wounded a man who was his rival in a love affair. After serving his sentence in NSW, in 1837 he went to TAS, but a few years later incurred another seven-year sentence for receiving stolen goods. He proceeded to escape from custody three times, on the final occasion swimming with two companions across an allegedly shark-infested inlet at EAGLEHAWK NECK, near PORT ARTHUR. A few years of very active bush-ranging followed, but he was captured after a chase in which he shot and mortally wounded a policeman. Although he was condemned to death for this offence, the sentence was finally commuted to life imprisonment.

On this occasion he was sent to NORFOLK ISLAND, where he won such a reputation as a model prisoner that before the prison was closed down in 1854 he was allowed to marry and was given a ticket of leave. He returned to TAS, worked for a time in the Domain Gardens, and having gained a conditional pardon in 1856 went to New Zealand. Back in TAS four years later, he became a farmer at GLENORCHY, where he lived for the rest of his life.
Further reading: Clune, F. *Martin Cash.* Angus & Robertson, Sydney, 1955.

Casino NSW (population 9 741 in 1981) This town is on the RICHMOND RIVER in the NORTH COAST region of the State. Located on the Bruxner Highway, 30km by road WSW of LISMORE on the route from the North Coast to the NEW ENGLAND Plateau, it is also a rail junction (805km N of Sydney) where the main line N to Brisbane meets the branch line through Lismore. In the surrounding rural regions beef and dairy cattle are raised and fodder crops are grown, and on the hill lands timber-getting is a major industry. The homestead and adjoining buildings on Dyraaba Station, 20km NW of Casino, have been classified by the National Trust (NSW) for preservation as part of the cultural heritage.

cassava *see* Euphorbiaceae

cassowary A large rainforest bird of the family Casuariidae, the cassowary, *Casuarius casuarius*, is endemic to NE Australia and New Guinea. It has a deep and booming call which may be heard at a considerable distance. It is distinguished by a large yellow and black casque (a bony protuberance which extends above the front of the head, protecting the head), which, in combination with its powerful legs, enables it to move rapidly through dense vegetation. The adult male, which grows to about 1.5m long and tall, is black; the immatures are brown. The wings are rudimentary and carry bare, quill-like feathers—another feature suiting it to the dense vegetation it inhabits. The head and neck are bare, coloured blue, black and red, with red wattles. The cassowary does not build a nest; the light-green eggs are laid during July and August on a rough clearing scratched on the forest floor. The male incubates and rears the young. The diet of the cassowary is mainly soft fruit, seeds and other vegetable matter.

Cassythaceae *see* parasitic plants

Casterton VIC (population 1 945 in 1981) This small country town is located on the Glenelg Highway where it crosses the GLENELG RIVER, 354km by road W of Melbourne and about 60km from the SA border. It is also the railway terminus of a branch line off the HAMILTON-PORTLAND route, 394km by rail from Melbourne. The town is situated at an elevation of 53m above sea level and receives an average yearly rainfall of 679mm, with the major concentration in the winter months. The town is a service centre for a productive rural region where there is dairying, fat lamb production, mixed farming, sheep grazing and pig raising. It was named after Casterton in Westmoreland, England.

Castle Hill Rising This is the name given to a revolt of Irish convicts which began at Castle Hill, not very far from PARRAMATTA, on 4 March 1804. It was suppressed by troops of the NEW SOUTH WALES CORPS the following day at a place which became known for a time as Vinegar Hill (after the place in Ireland where the rebellion of 1798 had been crushed), but which is now part of the suburb of Rouse Hill. For some time before, there had been rumours of an impending rebellion among the Irish convicts, who included a far higher proportion transported for political offences than did those from England and Scotland, and who had a reputation for insubordination. When the revolt finally did come it was poorly planned. The day was a Sunday, and the leaders, Philip Cunningham and William Johnston, seem to have spent the day going around Castle Hill urging their fellows to join them. At about eight o'clock in the evening some 200 gathered, seized what arms they could, and marched towards Parramatta. Later, however, they turned W, intending to reach the HAWKESBURY and gather more recruits before attacking Parramatta and Sydney.

News of the event reached Sydney towards midnight, whereupon Governor KING called out the New South Wales Corps and hurried towards Parramatta, calling on Major George JOHNSTON, commander of the Corps, on his way. Major Johnston himself reached Parramatta early in the morning, and with a force of 25 soldiers and a handful of civilian volunteers rode in pursuit of the rebels, whose numbers were now probably about 400. When he came within sight of them he sent an Irish priest, Father James Dixon, to negotiate with them, but they refused to listen. Then Major Johnston himself, accompanied by Thomas Laycock, quartermaster of the Corps, rode forward and asked to speak to the leaders. When Cunningham and William Johnston approached, they were asked what they wanted, and are reported to have answered, 'death or liberty'. Thereupon the officers drew their pistols and firing broke out on both sides. The convicts, poorly organised and armed, proved no match for their opponents and soon fled, leaving nine of their number dead and several others mortally wounded. Cunningham was captured alive and promptly hanged without trial. Subsequently eight other rebels were publicly hanged, nine were flogged, each receiving between 200 and 500 lashes, and 50 were sent to Coal River (renamed NEWCASTLE at about that time).

Castlemaine VIC (population 7 584 in 1981) Located at the junction of the Calder and Pyrenees Highways, 117km by road NW of Melbourne, and 42km S of BENDIGO, on a tributary of the LODDON RIVER, it is a market and service centre for a productive dairying and sheep grazing region. It was once a famous gold-mining town and in those prosperous days was known as Forest Creek Diggings. Gold was first discovered there in 1851 and it proved to be an exceptionally rich field which attracted a population of 30 000. The settlement was officially gazetted in 1851, became a borough in 1855 (named after Castlemaine in Ireland) and was proclaimed a town in 1950. It is a rail centre, at a distance of 125km from Melbourne, linked W to MARYBOROUGH, N to Bendigo, with a branch line 18km to Maldon. At an elevation of 281m above sea level, it experiences warm summer conditions and cool winters, with an average yearly rainfall of 624mm, spread over all months. The National Trust (VIC) has classified 20 buildings in the town and recorded another seven, indicating its historical importance; among these are the Bank of New South Wales (1855), Frendale Manor (1853), the former courthouse (1850s), the gaol (1861), Christ Church (1854) and several homes and public buildings.

Castlereagh River NSW This inland stream drains into the BARWON-DARLING system. It rises in the WARRUMBUNGLE RANGE, some 600km NW of Sydney, flowing through COONABARABRAN before making a semi-circular loop to GILGANDRA; from there it flows generally NW past COONAMBLE to join the MACQUARIE RIVER above its confluence with the Darling. The Castlereagh was discovered in 1818 by a member of John OXLEY's expedition and was named after Lord Castlereagh, then British Secretary of State for the Colonies. The upper reaches of the river have an annual rainfall of over 720mm and are mainly wheat and sheep country, with some timber-getting in cypress pine forest areas. Further downstream, where the river meanders through broad plains with numerous ANABRANCHES, the rainfall is lower (Coonamble 597mm) and sheep grazing dominates the rural scene. The Oxley Highway traverses the upper sections of the river basin on a general NE-SW route, crossing the river at both Coonabarabran and Gilgandra. The Castlereagh Highway starts at Gilgandra and extends N along the river valley through Coonamble to WALGETT (a distance of 212km). The Newell Highway, from the S parts of the State, enters the Castlereagh basin from DUBBO and extends to Gilgandra.

castor oil plant *see* Euphorbiaceae

Casuarinaceae This dicotyledonous family of flowering plants is represented by only one genus, *Casuarina*, distributed throughout the Australian and Malaysian regions; in Australia it occurs predominantly in heaths, woodlands and open forests, from the coast to the arid interior. All *Casuarina* species are wiry branched shrubs or trees. The most curious features of this genus are the jointed branchlets (often called 'needles' because they superficially resemble pine needles) and the apparent absence of leaves. Leaves are in fact present; they are fused to the stems and only the tips are visible as a whorl of 'teeth' at each node on the branch, similar to those on the unrelated horsetail (phylum ARTHROPHYTA). Male and female flowers are borne separately, either on the same plant (monoecious) or on separate plants (dioecious). Male flowers are borne in cylindrical spikes usually at the tips of branchlets; each flower consists of a single stamen, two small leaves (bracts) and two smaller scale-like leaves (bracteoles). Male flowers are often borne in such abundance that the crowns of the plants become brown to gold in colour, and clouds of pollen are emitted in dry conditions. The female flowers have no petals; they occur in globular or ovoid spikes at the end of very short lateral branches, often arising from quite mature wood; each flower has two long stigmas, two ovules and woody bracteoles, and, when mature, becomes woody and cone-like. The seeds are usually winged, and may be retained in the cones for many years; the cones open and shed seed when detached from the parent plant, or may be opened on the plant by forest fire. This long storage of seeds by *Casuarina* is a characteristic shared by some members of two of Australia's largest families, PROTEACEAE and MYRTACEAE, and may be considered an adaptation to frequent forest fires and/or the infrequency of suitable conditions for seedling establishment.

Casuarina species are excellent landscape subjects and many are now cultivated for parks and gardens. Large species include the forest oak, *C. torulosa*, for dry sites, the swamp oak, *C. glauca*, for damp sites, especially near the coast, and the river oak, *C. cunninghamiana*, for damp freshwater sites. Attractive small species for the coast and inland include the drooping she-oak, *C. stricta*, and the black she-oak, *C. littoralis*. Shrubby species include *C. distyla* and *C. nana*.

See also Angiospermae; Appendix 5, Flower Structure and Glossary of Botanical Terms

Further reading: see Appendix 6, A Bibliography for Plants.

cat, tiger *see* native cats, etc.

Catagunya TAS A dam and power station on the DERWENT RIVER upstream from the small township of Ouse, it is located 89km NW of Hobart on the Tarraleah Highway. The dam (completed in 1962, storage capacity 12 300ML) and the generating station associated with it form part of the vast hydro-electricity system of the upper Derwent Valley in the CENTRAL PLATEAU. This system comprises 10 power stations, six dams on the main Derwent and several on its tributaries. Upstream from Catagunya is the WAYATINAH Dam and power station (where the water is utilised for hydro-electricity generation before passing on to Catagunya) which was commissioned in 1962 and has an installed capacity of 48 000kW. The name Catagunya comes from a Tasmanian Aboriginal word for 'black swan'.

catbirds *see* bowerbirds

catchfly *see* Caryophyllaceae

cats, feral *see* animals, introduced

cats, native *see* native cats, etc.

cattle *see* beef cattle industry; dairy cattle industry; grazing industry

caustic bush *Sarcostemma australe*, also called caustic vine, is a native shrub with cylindrical branches and leaves. It belongs to the Asclepiadaceae, a family which contains several poisonous plants with a milky latex. The caustic bush is a widespread weed in dry regions. Some spurges (family EUPHORBIACEAE) are also called caustic weeds.

Cavill family Swimmers. The Cavill family, who migrated to Australia in 1879, have a unique position in Australian swimming history. Members of the family have been credited with developing the swimming stroke known as the Australian crawl, and they used the stroke with outstanding success in long-distance and competitive swimming. In addition, as swimming coaches they introduced Americans to the new stroke, which has been the internationally accepted competitive stroke in all freestyle events ever since.

Frederick Cavill (1839-1927) was born in London. He became an apprentice in the royal yacht *Fairy*. While still resident in England, he won the English national 500 yards swimming title in 1862. He made two attempts to swim the English Channel, in 1876 and 1877, failing by only a few metres in the latter attempt. When he arrived in Australia he set up a floating swimming pool in Sydney Harbour and, styling himself 'Professor', set out to teach swimming.

Ernest Cavill (dates unknown) was the eldest son of Frederick Cavill. He won his first NSW championships, over 1000 yards, at the age of 15 and went on to become the world champion for distances ranging from 500 to 1000 yards.

Charles Cavill (1871-97) gained international fame in 1896 when he became the first man to swim the Golden Gate crossing in San Francisco. He drowned at the age of 26 while giving a demonstration of underwater swimming in California.

Percy **Cavill** (1875-1940) was a consistent winner of State and national titles between 1895 and 1898; in 1897 he also won two world championship titles, for 440 yards and for the marathon swimming distance of five miles. Like Charles, he went to the USA where he took up coaching.

Arthur **Cavill** (1877-1914) was NSW amateur champion over 500 and 1000 yards in 1895, and Australian professional champion over 220 yards in 1898. Like his brothers before him, he went to the USA where he established himself both as a coach and as a long-distance swimmer. Emulating his brother Charles he successfully swam the Golden Gate crossing; but he died from exposure following another long-distance swim, across Seattle Harbour.

Sydney **Cavill** (1880-1945), amateur champion of NSW at 16, also went to the USA and it is thought that he was the first coach to teach the Australian crawl in that country. He also originated the butterfly stroke.

Richard **Cavill** (1884-1938), the youngest of Cavill's six sons, was thought to be the first man to use the crawl rather than the trudgeon stroke in competition swimming. He was to use it with outstanding success, winning 18 Australian and 22 NSW championships, and becoming the first man to break one minute for the 100 yards.

Fredda **Cavill** (1878-1961), one of Cavill's several daughters, although not a swimming champion herself, was the mother of Dick Eve, gold medal winner for diving at the Paris Olympic Games in 1924.

Cawley, Evonne Fay *née* Goolagong (1951-) Tennis player. Born in the NSW country town of Barellan, of part-Aboriginal parents, Evonne was to become the first tennis player of Aboriginal descent to represent Australia or to compete at Wimbledon. She began playing tennis at the age of seven, was spotted by her coach (later guardian), Vic Edwards, at the age of nine and won 43 Junior State and Interstate titles before her first overseas tour in 1970 at the age of 18. On this tour she played in 21 Open tournaments, winning no fewer than eight of them. In the following year she again toured and this time captured the French singles title and the most highly prized title of all, the Wimbledon singles title, beating three-times Wimbledon singles winner Margaret COURT 6-4, 6-1 in just 63 minutes in the final. A tireless worker and dedicated to perfecting her game, she also won the Australian doubles title in 1971, 1974 and 1975, the Australian singles title in 1974, 1975, 1976 and 1978, and won all her Federation Cup matches of 1970 and 1972-74. In 1972 she was made an MBE for her services to sport. Following a withdrawal from competitive tennis to have her first child, she returned with renewed vigour to win the Wimbledon title again in 1980.

cayenne pepper *see* Solanaceae

Australian tennis star Evonne Goolagong (Cawley)

Courtesy of A.I.S. Canberra

Cazaly, Roy (1893-1963) Footballer. Born in Melbourne, Cazaly started his Australian Rules football career at the age of 11, playing for his school, the Albert Park State School. When he was 15 years old he joined the St Kilda Club and it was not long before he became a spectator attraction because of his ability to take high marks (in Australian Rules when a player catches the ball he is entitled to a free kick—this is called taking a mark and often leads to spectacular leaping during a game). The catch phrase 'Up there, Cazaly!' was adopted by St Kilda supporters to encourage him to leap higher and the phrase eventually became part of the language used by spectators to encourage any Australian Rules footballer to take high marks. Cazaly played senior football in Melbourne for many years before transferring to Hobart, where he remained actively involved in the sport until he was 58.

cedar Two species of trees highly valued for their timber are known in Australia as cedar. Both belong to the Meliaceae, the family containing the true mahogany.

The red cedar, *Toona australis*, a rainforest species, grows to a height of between 15m and 46m. It has spreading branches, compound leaves and large panicles of sweet-smelling white-to-pink flowers. The timber is highly esteemed for cabinet work and boat-building, but is now scarce. It grows in coastal areas from ULLADULLA in NSW to northern QLD. Cedar-getting was a major industry in the ILLAWARRA district and the RICHMOND Valley, and in other parts of NSW and QLD, from about 1820 to about 1900. White cedar, *Melia azedarach* var. *australica*, also occurs in coastal NSW and QLD. In natural habitats (rainforest) it is tall and straight but when planted as a specimen tree it has a spreading habit. The foliage is green and glossy and the flowers, in erect terminal panicles, are lilac. The open-grained timber is used for interior woodwork.

Ceduna SA (population 2 794 in 1981) This small town at the NW corner of EYRE PENINSULA is located on the Eyre Highway 782km from Adelaide and some 435km NW of PORT LINCOLN. Its twin town, Thevenard, is a fishing centre and port for the shipping of wheat, wool and gypsum produced in the region. Ceduna has an average annual rainfall of 321mm, concentrated in the winter months. The town takes its name from the Aboriginal word meaning 'to sit down and rest'.

celery *see* Umbelliferae

centipedes These ARTHROPODS comprise the class Chilopoda, which was formerly grouped with the MILLIPEDES, PAUROPODS and SYMPHYLIDS in the class Myriapoda. There are from 3000 to 4000 described species in the world of which 76 species are known in Australia.

Centipedes are elongated, predatory animals, usually found in soil, leaf-litter, and so on. The body is flattened from top to bottom and has between 15 and 177 body segments, depending upon the species. The largest, a Brazilian species, is about 25cm long, but many are very small. The largest Australian species are about 10cm long.

Each of the trunk segments, apart from the last two, carries a single pair of legs ending in a sharp claw. The last pair of legs point backwards and upwards, and they are sensory, defensive and offensive. The legs of the first segment, the maxillipeds, are used for feeding and each carries a strong venom-claw. The venom of some of the largest centipedes can be painful, but is rarely dangerous to man. The head carries a pair of long antennae, groups of simple eyes (though some centipedes are blind), a pair of mandibles and two pairs of maxillae. They differ from the other myriapods in the position of the genital opening, which is near the tail. Centipedes breathe by tracheae opening through spiracles on the trunk segments.

The class is divided into two subclasses, Anamorpha and Epimorpha.

Anamorpha Centipedes of this subclass have 18 body segments and 15 pairs of legs but spiracles on not more than seven segments. Three orders occur in Australia.

1. Craterostigmorpha. This order contains only one species, *Craterostigmus tasmanianus*, which is known only from Australia and New

Scolopendromorph centipede

A. Woods

Zealand. It is a small centipede that lives in dead wood where it feeds on other small animals.

2. Scutigeromorpha. This order contains distinctive centipedes with very long legs and antennae. The spiracles are single and are situated on the mid-dorsal line. They are swift runners which quickly shed legs when attacked. Sometimes they cause alarm when they come indoors, but they are in fact beneficial, feeding on household insects.

3. Lithiobiomorpha. The centipedes of the Lithiobiomorpha are small, ground-living animals most easily recognised by their 15 pairs of legs and alternating large and small tergal plates along the dorsal surface of the trunk.

Epimorpha The better-known subclass, it contains two orders.

1. Scolopendromorpha. This order contains the largest centipedes. There are 21 or 23 leg-bearing segments, the tergal plates are more or less equal in size, and the antennae each have 17 to 30 segments. The 14 species of the family Cryptopodidae are all blind whereas the 22 forms in the family Scolopendridae have eyes. The thick-bodied, yellowish *Scolopendra morsitans* is probably the most familiar of the Australian centipedes.

2. Geophilomorpha. This order contains the so-called thread centipedes. These have from 31 to 177 leg-bearing segments. The legs are short and the antennae have 14 segments. They are unusual among centipedes in being accomplished tunnellers.

Central Plateau TAS One of the main landform regions of the island, it is located, as its name implies, in the central part of the State. Varying in elevation between 600m and 1 100m above sea level, it is composed of horizontal or gently dipping sedimentary rocks which have been considerably injected with igneous rock (dolerite from the Jurassic period) to such an extent that this now forms the dominant surface rock. The structure and landscape features of the plateau have been further affected during the geological history of the region by considerable block-faulting to produce step-like features, especially evident in the steep scarps forming the N and NE boundaries, called the GREAT WESTERN TIERS. Another major element which has contributed to the shaping of the plateau landscapes is the glaciation of the region during the most recent Great Ice Age, when hollows were gouged in the surface, and with the retreat of the ice, moraine deposits were left blocking valleys and damming these hollows, so that there are now about 4000 lakes on the plateau. The largest of these are GREAT LAKE, ARTHURS LAKE, LAKE SORELL and LAKE ECHO; many of these natural lakes have been artifically enlarged by dams and their waters are utilised for generation of hydro-electricity, as part of the vast power schemes of the central highlands. The highest parts of the plateau are in the N where several peaks of the Great Western Tiers rise to over 1 100m (Mt Franklin,

Millers Bluff, Drys Bluff, Ironstone Mt). The DERWENT RIVER and its tributaries drain the main part of the plateau in a general S and SE direction; the upper reaches of the MERSEY RIVER rise in the NW section of the plateau; and some tributaries of the TAMAR RIVER system have their headwaters in the NE section of the plateau. The Lakes Highway crosses the region in a general N-S direction and provides access to many of the dams and power stations of the hydro-electricity schemes, and also to the streams and lakes with their abundant fishing opportunities, the winter ski resorts of the highlands, and the rugged scenic grandeur which attracts many summer tourists. To the W of the plateau lies a higher mountain area which includes numerous peaks over 1 400m high, such as CRADLE MOUNTAIN (1 545m) and MOUNT OSSA (1 617m, the State's highest peak).

Centre, the This is a general term applied to the vast semi-arid and arid interior of the continent where ALICE SPRINGS is the best-known town. Much of the area is occupied by deserts, such as the SIMPSON and STURT'S STONY Deserts; there are several rocky ranges, such as the MUSGRAVE and MACDONNELL Ranges, and some large monoliths, such as AYERS ROCK and MOUNT OLGA, which rise sheer above the surrounding landscape. Parts of the area have been set aside as Aboriginal reserves and others are occupied by extensive cattle stations. In recent times, the Centre has increasingly become a tourist attraction and much has been done to promote tourism and to provide facilities for visitors.

cephalopods The class Cephalopoda contains octopuses, squids, cuttlefishes and the nautilus. Only the octopuses live commonly at the seashore, though all are marine.

The cephalopods are certainly the most advanced MOLLUSCS, and possibly the most advanced invertebrates. They have relatively large brains and complex behaviour. The class also includes the largest of all invertebrates. One of the largest specimens ever captured, the squid *Architeuthis* of the N Atlantic, was 16.76m in length, including the 10.66m-long tentacles. It was believed to weigh two tonnes. The remains of one cast on the beach in Florida in 1896 was believed to have come from an animal between six and seven tonnes in weight. It is probable that some of these giant oceanic squids are the basis of some stories of sea serpents. Octopuses, despite legend, are never very large. The largest known species has a body length of only 30cm, though the slender arms are much longer.

Very few cephalopods have an external shell, most either lacking one completely or having a small internal one. The body, which is bilaterally symmetrical, is divided into a head (carrying complex sense organs and the mantle), and the tentacles or legs (which are homologous with the foot of other molluscs). The tentacles carry suckers which work on the vacuum principle, or other attachment struc-

tures such as hooks. The mantle cavity forms a pouch into which water is drawn for respiration. A funnel which can be closed by a press-stud mechanism allows water to be forced from the mantle cavity, pushing the animal through the water. The cephalopods thus used jet-propulsion and the press-stud device long before man invented them. The tentacles are also used in swimming, and by the octopuses for walking and climbing underwater.

The mouth is at the base of the tentacles, and is furnished with a radula and a horny, parrot-like beak. All cephalopods are carnivorous, and most can move swiftly in pursuit of prey. The beak-like jaws are used for biting and tearing. In squids and octopuses two pairs of salivary glands empty into the mouth cavity. In some octopuses this saliva is extremely venomous.

Most cephalopods have an ink gland opening into the mantle cavity. When pursued the animal releases a quantity of ink (sepia) to cover its escape. It is often said that the animal disappears 'in a smoke screen', but it has recently been suggested that the ink, which for a time forms a separate mass roughly the size of the animal, deludes the pursuer into thinking that the ink is the prey. The ink was formerly extracted and used as writing ink.

One of the most remarkable features of the cephalopods is the eye, which very closely resembles the eye of a vertebrate in its structure. It is, in fact, superior in one respect: that in the cephalopods the light does not have to pass through a layer of nerve processes before reaching the sensitive surface of the retina. The resemblance between the octopus eye and the mammalian eye is regarded as an excellent example of the result of convergent evolution, in which two quite unrelated organisms evolve similar structures from quite different origins to solve similar problems. The cephalopod needs an excellent eye for hunting.

There are about 400 known living species of cephalopods in the world. Many of them live in the open ocean, often at considerable depths, and can be collected only be special methods, so it is not possible to say how many occur near Australia. There are more than 10 000 different fossil species known, including ammonites and nautiloids, so the group is obviously past its peak. The living forms fall into two subclasses: Tetrabranchia (or Nautiloidea), and Dibranchia (or Coeoidea).

Tetrabranchia These cephalopods have, as the name suggests, four gills (in two pairs). They also possess an external shell. Many extinct forms are known, but the only survivors belong to the genus *Nautilus*, which has a coiled shell. The shell of the pearly nautilus, *N. pompilius*, which is sometimes washed ashore empty on E beaches, is a beautiful and greatly prized curio. It is coiled and chambered, and about 15cm to 29cm in diameter. The colour is pearly-white, with brown bands. The animal itself lives in the last chamber that is made. The shell is filled with gas so that the animal can float just above the sea bed where it appears to scavenge on dead fishes, crabs, and

so on. There are many tentacles, each enclosed in a leathery sheath until extended. The eye is far simpler than those of other cephalopods as it lacks the lens and cornea. The shell can be closed off by a shield on the top of the head.
Dibranchia These molluscs have one pair of gills and the shell is either absent or internal. Many members of their subclass which live in the open ocean have luminous light-organs. Most, possibly all, species can change colour extremely rapidly as they pass over different backgrounds. The various colour pigments occur in special cells; when necessary, the pigment migrates to fill the whole cell, producing the colour-transformation. The whole process is under direct nervous control. There are two living orders.

1. Decapoda. This order contains the squids and the cuttles. They have two long tentacles and eight shorter, sessile arms. The body is more or less elongated and carries side extensions (fins) which are used in slow swimming.

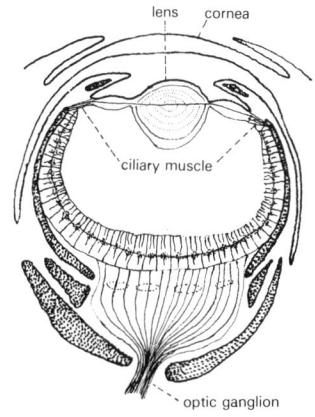

A section through the eye of a cuttlefish

The cuttlefishes (family Sepiidae) contain a shield-shaped internal shell of calcareous material whereas the squids have a horny, pen-shaped internal shell. The shells are often cast up among shore debris and give some indication of the squid and cuttlefish species living in the adjacent seas. Cuttlefish shells were formerly used in medicine, for feeding to birds (because of their calcium content) and as casting moulds in the jewellery trade. The cuttlefishes are distinguished from squids by their relatively broad bodies, roughly oval in shape, with narrow fins running the full length of the sides. The arms and the tentacles have suckers but never hooks. The fourth left arm in males is modified (hectacotylised) near the base for the transfer of sperm (the sexes are separate in all cephalopods). Fishes are caught by the tentacular arms which draw the prey towards the head where it is embraced by the shorter arms and killed with the beak. Judging from the cast-up shells, several species live in Australian waters.

The family Onychoteuthidae consists of the clawed squids, which occur in all oceans. Hooks replace some of the arm suckers and the tentacles have clawed clubs. They are fast-swimming species with streamlined bodies.

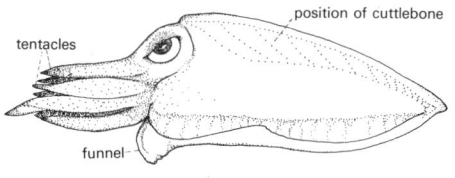

A cuttlefish

The calamaries, family Omnastrephidae, are important culinary squids in the Mediterranean, and some are sold as food in Australia. They are sometimes called sea arrows or flying squids because they leap from the water when pursuing fishes. The arms carry suckers: two rows on the arms and four on the tentacles, the rings of the suckers being toothed. They are often attracted by lights. Though they range greatly in size, they are uniform in appearance. Gould's calamary or squid, *Notodarus gouldi*, is a common southern-waters species which may reach a length of 60cm, including arms. Another common southern species is the long-finned calamary, *Sepioteuthis australis*, which is somewhat cuttle-like in shape. It is a good table squid and is also used as bait.

The dumpling squids, family Sepiolidae, are small animals with short, rounded bodies and rounded fins set near the middle of the body. A few live in Australian waters and some are found near the shore. A few have luminous organs near the ink sac. Pigmy squids (family Idiosephiidae) have longer bodies than the dumpling squids and the fins are terminal.

A common shell on Australian seashores at certain times is the ram's horn shell. It is a small curled shell in the shape of a ram's horn, divided into chambers, and translucent when held up to the light. Only two living specimens of the animal which produces the shell have been reported from Australia, and virtually all that is known about its owner is from deep-sea sampling in the Atlantic. The shell, which belongs to a small squid *Spirula spirula*, is internal, a small part of it reportedly being exposed at the tail end. The shell gives buoyancy to the squid, whose body is cylindrical, with two small tail fins between which there is a light organ.

2. Octopoda. This order contains the octopuses, which are the only cephalopods common on the seashore. It also contains the argonauts or paper nautili, pelagic animals whose 'shells' are sometimes cast ashore. Octopods have eight legs and globular bodies without fins. Often the arms are webbed, like the feet of a duck.

The octopuses favour shallow water where they can scuttle along the rocky bottom, which offers crevices for cover during the day. Their food consists mainly of molluscs and crustaceans. Several octopus species occur in Australian waters. A common species in the Sydney region is *Octopus cyaneus*, which can be from 60cm to 90cm in length though most specimens are much smaller. The blue-ringed octopus, *Hapalochlaena maculosa*, is a much smaller species whose total length is not usually more than 10cm. This species is fortunately recognised at once by its colour,

yellow-ochre with patches of brown and rings of brilliant blue which intensify when the animal is goaded; it can deliver a fatal bite, the saliva being extremely venomous. There has been at least one human death resulting from bites of this octopus—at Camp Cove, Sydney, in 1967. Another death resulted from the bite of a close relative of the species, *O. lunulata*, at Darwin in 1954 (for first aid treatment see ANIMALS, VENOMOUS).

Four species of the pelagic argonaut are known from Australian waters. The female is much larger than the male, and her dorsal arms are expanded into very broad membranes. These secrete a delicate shell of lime and hold it round the animal. Later she lays a mass of eggs inside the shell which takes up so much space that the mother is forced out.
See also animals, venomous
Further reading: see under molluscs. *Also* Stackhouse, J. *Australia's Venomous Wildlife*. Paul Hamlyn, Sydney, 1970; Sutherland, S.K. *Venomous Creatures of Australia: A Field Guide with Notes on First Aid*. Oxford University Press, Melbourne, 1981.

CER (Closer Economic Relations)
see New Zealand; Economic Relations.

cereals *see* agriculture

Cessnock NSW This city is located in the HUNTER RIVER valley, some 40km inland from NEWCASTLE and 25km by road SW of MAITLAND. Combined with the adjacent township of Bellbird, Cessnock had a population of 16 916 in 1981, but when linked with other small settlements in the area, such as KURRI KURRI, WESTON, BRANXTON and GRETA, the city of Greater Cessnock comprised over 38 000 people.

Coal was known in the Cessnock area from the middle of the 19th century, but the discovery of the rich Greta-Maitland coal measures in the 1880s led to the development of coal mining as the major activity of the region. Though the mining industry has declined in recent years, it remains an important part of the economy. The surrounding rural districts include much fertile farming land with dairying, cattle raising and fodder-crop cultivation as the main activities. Also in the Cessnock district are some of the Hunter Valley vineyards, particularly at Pokolbin, which produce the fine wines for which the valley is renowned. Among the secondary industries of the city are pottery and brick making, timber milling and clothing manufacture.
Further reading: Walker, A. *Coaltown: A Social Survey of Cessnock*. Melbourne University Press, Melbourne, 1945; Bloomfield, W.A.G. *Cessnock 1826-1954: A History of the Cessnock District*. Eagle Press, Cessnock, 1954.

Chaetognatha *see* arrow worms

Chaffey brothers Irrigation pioneers. George (1848-1932) and William (1856-1926)

Chaffey were born in California, where they became involved in a number of irrigation schemes. In 1885, Alfred DEAKIN met George Chaffey in California, and was so impressed by his work that he suggested that he might come to VIC. He did so in the following year and reached an agreement with the VIC government whereby he and his brother would be granted land in proportion to the capital they invested in improving it by irrigation. A company formed by the two brothers irrigated and sold large areas of the land at MILDURA, and they were so encouraged by their success that they began a second irrigation settlement at RENMARK in SA. By 1890 there were 3000 settlers in the Mildura district, but the Chaffeys were unable to weather the depression of the following years and in 1895 had to wind up their affairs. The report of a subsequent Royal Commission stated that the main cause of failure at Mildura had been bad management of Chaffey Bros Ltd, but it seems arguable that the terms of the agreement with the VIC government were insufficiently generous for the company to have had good prospects for success under the conditions encountered. At no stage was doubt cast on the honesty or sincerity of the brothers. After the crash George vindicated his earlier reputation for business ability by returning to California and engaging very successfully in a number of irrigation projects. William stayed in Mildura, where he became Mayor and was prominent in various local associations.

Further reading: Alexander, J.A. *The Life of George Chaffey.* Macmillan, Melbourne, 1928.

Chambers Pillar

NT This sandstone monolith, rising some 34m above the surrounding terrain, is located in the S part of the Territory between the Stuart Highway and the route of the central Australian railway. It is on the Maryvale pastoral station, about 130km N of the NT/SA border, 130km S of ALICE SPRINGS and just N of the FINKE RIVER. This striking outcrop was discovered by the explorer John McDouall STUART in 1860 and named by him in honour of one of his patrons. The area was declared a national reserve in 1970.

Channel Country

QLD A region in the arid SW of the State, it is so named because of the multitude of river channels which cross the broad plains. The main streams in the region are the BULLOO, DIAMANTINA, GEORGINA and Mulligan Rivers and COOPER'S CREEK, all of which flow towards lakes of internal drainage. The Bulloo River flows into Lake Bulloo, just N of the QLD/NSW border, and the other streams flow into LAKE EYRE. All the rivers are intermittent, since the region is one of low and unreliable rainfall; and since rain is concentrated mainly in the summer season, this is the time of high river flow—at other seasons there may be little evidence of the streams and the landscape is furrowed by silt-laden channels. Only in occasional years of heavy rain do the streams reach the lakes; at

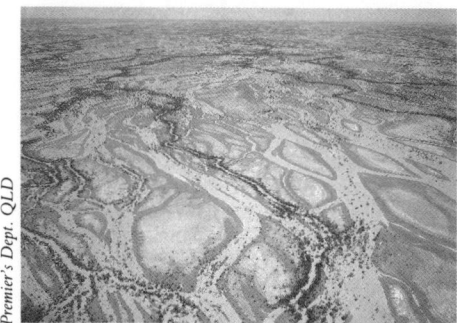
Premier's Dept. QLD

Floodwaters of Cooper's Creek near Windora, spread over 30 miles, show clearly the channel effect

these times many of the channels overflow and join with the waters of adjacent streams, covering the area in vast sheets of slow-moving muddy water. After good rains the countryside changes from its typically dry, brown appearance to one of lush green grasses and shrubs, when it becomes fine land for cattle fattening.

In 1860 the explorers BURKE and Wills were the first Europeans to set foot in the Channel Country. Following their expedition came the pioneer settlers with their livestock herds. But the region has remained a difficult land because of the unpredictable seasons and the variable rainfall. Cattle grazing has remained the dominant rural activity, though in recent decades the district has become both a breeding and a fattening area.

Chappell, Gregory Stephen

(1948-) Cricketer. Born in Adelaide, a grandson of Australian Test captain Victor Richardson and brother of Australian Test captain Ian CHAPPELL, he was to continue the family tradition of captaining Australia's Test side. In the 1973-74 season, following an apprenticeship in his home State of SA and a two-year stint with the English county side, Somerset, he became State captain for QLD and on the retirement of his brother Ian from the Australian captaincy in 1975 he assumed the reins for Australia. Almost the opposite of his militant and aggressive brother Ian, the quiet and sometimes introverted Greg started his captaincy with a flourish, scoring centuries in both innings against the West Indies in Brisbane in 1975. Described as a copybook batsman with a classical upright stance at the wicket, in the 1970s he was ranked as one of the three best batsmen in the world (the other two being West Indian Vivian Richards and South African Barry Richards). In 1977 he transferred his allegiance to World Series Cricket where he continued to display his superior batting skills. He then returned to official cricket, and maintained his reputation as one of the world's leading batsmen. In Australia in the 1982-83 season he led Australia to victory in a Test series against England, so regaining the Ashes. By the end of that season he had scored 6 430 runs in 78 Tests, at an average of 54.03 per innings.

Chappell, Ian Michael

(1943-) Cricketer. Born in Adelaide, a grandson of Australian Test captain Victor Richardson,

Chappell rose rapidly through the cricketing ranks, from playing Sheffield Shield for SA in 1961-62 to become one of the most controversial Australian captains during the 1970s. He led Australia in 30 Tests, a record number for an Australian captain, and during his captaincy Australia had 15 victories, 10 draws and five losses, but never lost a series. A militant leader, the clashes he had with umpires, State selectors, and the Australian Cricket Board kept him continually in the public eye; but these often bitter disputes did not affect his skills on the cricket field. He relinquished the captaincy in 1975, being succeeded by his brother, Greg. When World Series Cricket was formed in 1977, in keeping with his often anti-establishment stand, Ian Chappell was one of the first players to join the breakaway movement. After WSC players had been allowed to rejoin traditional cricket, he played again in Tests, but retired after the 1981 series in England. During his career he played in 76 Tests, scoring 5 345 runs at an average of 42.42. An outstanding fieldsman, he took 105 catches in Tests.

Charleville

QLD (population 3 523 in 1981) Located at the junction of the Mitchell and Warrego Highways, 766km by road WNW of Brisbane, it is a service and transport centre for an extensive pastoral region in the SW of the State. At an elevation of 304m above sea level on the Warrego River, it is a railway town on a line W from Brisbane extending S to CUNNAMULLA; just S of the town a branch line goes to QUILPIE. The surrounding plain country is sheep grazing land in the heart of the 'mulga' region, where the more densely stocked downlands to the E give way to drier scrub country. The average annual rainfall is 515mm, with the maximum concentration in the summer season; January has the highest rainfall (78mm average), June the lowest (19mm). The town is the administrative centre for the Murweh Shire which includes the townships of Augathella to the N and Morven to the E (shire population 5 585 in 1976).

The history of Charleville is fused with the early struggles of pastoral settlement and the development of transport links. The explorer Edmund KENNEDY passed near the present town site in 1847; a township grew at the Warrego River crossing and by the 1880s it had several hotels and even its own brewery (it

A flock of sheep being driven to Charleville railway station in the 1920s

is indeed a thirsty Outback centre). Even before the railway reached Charleville in 1888, it was a busy frontier town of bullock waggons carrying wool and the COBB & CO. coaches which served the outlying stations. It was the site of a Cobb & Co. coach building factory; the building is now used as a motor-vehicle showroom. The town is a centre for the Royal FLYING DOCTOR SERVICE and a transmitting point for the School of the Air which brings education to children on isolated properties of the region. There is a pastoral research laboratory which undertakes investigations into animal management and native pastures. The town's reticulated water supply comes from bores which tap the artesian reserves 400m to 1000m below ground level. A monument 191km NW marks the spot where the pioneer aviators Sir Ross and Sir Keith SMITH landed for repairs on their historic flight from London to Sydney. The winter cattle sales and the annual 'Booga Woongaroo' festival are popular tourist attractions.

Charlton, Andrew 'Boy' (1907-75)

Swimmer. Born in Sydney, Charlton had an unusual swimming style, making great use of his powerful arms but doing little work with his legs. At the age of 14 he won a 440 yards Open race in 5 minutes 45 seconds. In 1923, at the age of 15, he swam 880 yards in 11 minutes 5.2 seconds to set a new world record. His consistent wins, usually featuring exciting fast finishes, soon made him the popular sporting hero of the time, so much so that Arne Borg, then European swimming champion, was invited to Sydney to race against him. Over 10 000 people crammed into the Domain Baths to watch Charlton defeat Borg over three distances: 220, 440 and 880 yards. Charlton, Borg and Johnny Weismuller (of 'Tarzan'-movie fame) were the three best-known swimmers of the day and all three met in the 1924 Olympic Games in Paris. In the 440m freestyle event, Charlton won the bronze medal behind Weismuller and Borg; but in the 1500m event he eclipsed all, winning the gold medal in world-record time from Borg and Frank BEAUREPAIRE, also of Australia. He won two silver medals in the 1928 Olympic Games but failed to gain a place in the 1932 Games after which he retired.

Charlton, Edward Francis 'Eddie'

(1929–) Snooker player. Born at Merewether NSW, he was first introduced to snooker as a nine-year-old in his grandfather's billiards saloon, where he had to stand on a fruit box in order to hit the balls. A successful amateur billiards and snooker player, he turned professional in 1960; it was not until the mid-1960s that he began to win State and national titles, but once he started winning he became unbeatable. He won the NSW championship in 1964, the Australian championship in 1966, and has dominated the national snooker scene ever since. Internationally, Charlton has also had considerable success, winning the World Open champion-

ship in 1968 and holding it ever since. But perhaps his best-known successes have been on the BBC television series 'Pot Black'. In 1972 he became the first Australian to be invited to play in 'Pot Black', and he celebrated by winning the series. Strongly self-disciplined and willing to spend countless hours in practice to perfect his game, he has at one time or another defeated every prominent snooker player in the world over the last 20 years.

Charters Towers QLD (population

6 823 in 1981) A city in the BURDEKIN RIVER valley, it is 135km SE of TOWNSVILLE along the Flinders Highway and some 1 400km by road NW of Brisbane. It is a rail centre on the line from Townsville to CLONCURRY and MOUNT ISA. Gold discoveries in the 1870s made it a boom mining town and it became QLD's richest gold-producing area. Mining lasted until the early part of this century and even though mullock heaps and old gold-workings can still be seen outside the city, it is nowadays a commercial and service centre for a pastoral region. At an elevation of 306m above sea level, it has an average annual rainfall of 650mm which falls mainly in the summer months. The city is noted for its educational institutions, particularly the boarding schools, which draw students from a wide region. There is much of historic interest in the city and the National Trust (QLD) has listed more than a dozen buildings for preservation including the stock exchange (which has been restored), the post office, the courthouse and the Venus Gold Battery.

chats These small, brightly coloured

PASSERINE BIRDS belong to the family Ephthianuridae*. The five species found in Australia are often seen hurrying over the ground in pursuit of insects, particularly in areas of low bush, long grass and samphire swamps; some species catch large insects, fix them in tree forks and then tear them apart as BUTCHERBIRDS do.

The white-faced or white-fronted chat, *Ephthianura* * *albifrons* (11cm long), also known as the tang on account of its metallic call, is found in the S half of Australia. It is mainly greyish-brown above and white below with a broad black band on the breast, and it often feigns injury if it suspects that its eggs or nestlings are threatened. Like all members of this genus, it builds cup-shaped nests of grass and fibres in low bushes or tussocks. The widespread crimson chat, *E.* * *tricolor* (10cm to 11cm), so called because of its crimson crown (male only), rump and belly, sometimes moves in large nomadic flocks. The orange chat, *E.* * *aurifrons* (11cm), and the yellow chat, *E.* * *crocea* (11cm to 12cm), are both fairly widespread in swamp and saltbush areas, particularly inland. Both species are mainly orange or yellow with a light brown back; the male orange chat has a black mask, while the male yellow chat has a black breast band.

The arid, stony plains of central Australia are

the home of the desert or gibber chat, *Ashbyia* * *lovensis* (12cm), a fawn and yellow bird which spends most of its time on the ground; when it flies, it rises swiftly, like a LARK, and then dives rapidly uttering a sharp 'whit-whit' sound. The eggs are laid in saucer-shaped nests of dried vegetation placed in depressions in the ground or in the shelter of large stones. *See also* birds

Chauvel, Charles Edward (1897-

1959) Film director and producer. Born in Warwick, QLD, he did stunt-riding for 'Snowy' BAKER in the years 1920-21, and founded his own film company in 1923. The most successful films made by him, in partnership with his wife, Elsa, were *In the Wake of the Bounty* (1933), which started Errol Flynn on his career, *Forty Thousand Horsemen* (1941), which dealt with the deeds of the Australian Light Horse in the Middle East in World War I, *Rats of Tobruk* (1944), *Sons of Matthew* (1949) and *Jedda* (1955) a colour film dealing with Aboriginal life.

cheese tree *see* Euphorbiaceae

Chenopodiaceae This is a dicotyledon-

ous family of flowering plants with about 102 genera and 1 400 species of worldwide distribution but occurring primarily in maritime regions and the saline habitats of steppes and semi-deserts or as weeds of cultivated ground. Chenopods are annual or perennial herbs or small shrubs. The leaves are simple, usually alternate and often succulent. Flowers are unisexual, mostly regular, and sessile or arranged in clusters. The perianth is herbaceous and usually consists of a single five-segmented joined whorl. Stamens are opposite and equal in number to perianth segments, or solitary. The superior ovary contains one ovule; there may be one to three styles and two to three stigmas. The fruit is a nut (usually surrounded by the perianth, which in some cases enlarges, becoming succulent or remaining dry) or a single-seeded berry.

The family is very important in the semi-arid regions of Australia, being the most common plant of the low shrubland VEGETATION of the S part of the continent. Saltbushes (*Atriplex* and *Rhagodia* species), cotton bush and blue bush (*Kochia* species) are valuable fodder plants which in many areas have almost been eliminated by overgrazing, generally leaving thorny-fruited, unpalatable chenopods (*Bassia* species) as the dominant cover. Extensive areas of marine salt-flats in the S parts of Australia are also dominated by chenopods, particularly the glassworts or samphires (*Arthrocnemum* and *Salicornia* species), which have leafless succulent stems resembling strings of beads, and the seablites (*Suaeda* species), which have succulent leaves. The family Chenopodiaceae also contains a number of food plants, including red beet, sugar beet and mangel-wurzel, which are all cultivars of *Beta vulgaris*; spinach, *Spinacia*

Species, genus or family is endemic to Australia (see Preface)

oleracea; and *Chenopodium quinoa*, cultivated in the tropical highlands of South America and Mexico for grain which is either baked into bread or fermented to yield chica. Prominent among species classed as WEEDS are the goosefoots (*Chenopodium* species), many of which are annuals and have a mealy-white leaf surface.

See also Angiospermae; Appendix 5, Flower Structure and Glossary of Botanical Terms
Further reading: see Appendix 6, A Bibliography for Plants.

cherry, brush *see* Myrtaceae

cherry, native *see* parasitic plants

chess This conventional and ancient game finds a place in the wide range of sports and games enjoyed by Australians, and matches are played in both national and international competitions. Chess, however, in common with all competitive pursuits in Australia had to overcome the problem of distance—not only from the major centres of competition in the N hemisphere, but also between Australian capital cities. Although the Australian Chess Club was founded in 1840 in Sydney, it was not until 1868 that chess players' ingenuity found a solution in the telegraph, and matches were played between colonies first by means of the telegraphic system and, as technology improved, by teletype and telephone. In the 1940s international matches were played by wireless with the co-operation of the Overseas Telecommunications Commission. The expense of playing by telephone or wireless led to the introduction of correspondence chess, which became widely popular throughout Australia. The first World Correspondence Chess championships were held in 1953; out of 78 competitors representing 23 countries, the event was won by Australian C.J.S. Purdy. Australia was the second nation (after the USSR) to have three grandmasters in correspondence chess: L. Endzelins, R. Arlauskas and C.J.S. Purdy.
National championships are represented by three events: the Australian Chess championship has been held biennially since its inauguration in Melbourne in 1885; the Australian Open, started in 1971, is also held every other year, alternating with the Australian Chess championships; and the first Australian Women's Chess championship was held in 1966.

Today, chess has a healthy following in Australia with a greater interest being shown in the game at the school and junior levels, ensuring a continuing supply of competitive players for the senior grades for some years to come.

chestnut, Moreton Bay *see* bean, black; Papilionaceae

Chevalier, Nicholas (1828-1904) Artist. Born in Russia, son of a Swiss overseer of a princely estate, Chevalier studied painting in Lausanne and Rome, and architecture in Munich, before becoming a lithographic illustrator in London, occasionally having his works hung in the Royal Academy. He arrived in Melbourne in 1855, where he became cartoonist for the *Melbourne Punch*. A great traveller and a genial clubman, Chevalier visited New Zealand in 1867, and accompanied the Duke of Edinburgh on a world tour on HMS *Galatea*, before settling in London in 1871, where he died. As the London adviser to the Trustees of the National Art Gallery of New South Wales, he was instrumental in having Ford Maddox Brown's *Chaucer at the Court of Edward III* purchased for the State collection. Chevalier's own romanticised landscapes, in oils and water colours, are typified by mountains and nestling lakes, executed in a style and colouring that owes little to his Australian experience but much to contemporary European Romanticism.

chickweed *see* Caryophyllaceae

Chifley, Joseph Benedict 'Ben' (1885-1951) Prime Minister. Born and educated in the BATHURST district of NSW, he joined the NSW Railways in 1902 and rose to the position of engine driver. He took part in the anti-conscription campaign of 1916-17 and the railway strike of 1917, and was dismissed after the collapse of the strike. He entered the House of Representatives as Member for Macquarie in 1928, and three years later became Minister for Defence in the Labor administration of James SCULLIN. He had by this time emerged as one of the strongest opponents within the Labor movement of John LANG, Premier of NSW, and in the 1931 elections, when 'federal Labor' and 'Lang Labor' fielded rival candidates, he was one of the many federal candidates defeated. In 1935-36 he was a member of the Royal Commission on Banking and Monetary Reform, and submitted a minority report in which he advocated the nationalisation of banking. He regained the seat of Macquarie in 1940, and when Labor regained office under John CURTIN in the following year he was appointed Treasurer. He was also Minister for Post-War Reconstruction from 1942 to 1945, and Prime Minister from shortly after Curtin's death in 1945 until Labor's electoral defeat in 1949.

J.B. (Ben) Chifley

A man of considerable charm, unaffected manner and remarkably simple tastes, who as Prime Minister continued to live frugally in a private hotel while the Lodge, the Prime Minister's official residence, remained empty, Chifley won wide respect for his integrity, intelligence and capacity for hard work. Despite his lack of formal education, he developed a deep understanding of financial matters and was widely regarded as a particularly able Treasurer. His government's achievements included the beginning of the greatest immigration programme in the nation's history, the foundation of the SNOWY MOUNTAINS Hydro-Electric Authority and of Trans-Australia Airlines, and the nationalisation of Qantas and of overseas telecommunications. He also attempted to nationalise domestic airlines and the private trading banks, but on each occasion the High Court declared the enabling legislation unconstitutional. From a Labor point of view his most controversial act was the crushing of a coal miners' strike in 1949 by means which included the use of troops as labour in mines.
Further reading: Bennett, S. *J.B. Chifley.* Oxford University Press, Melbourne, 1961; Crisp, L.F. *Ben Chifley: A Biography.* Longmans, Melbourne, 1961.

chiggers *see* mites

Childe, Vere Gordon (1892-1957) Prehistorian. Childe was born in Sydney, and studied at Sydney and Oxford Universities. From 1919 to 1921 he was the Private Secretary to the Premier of NSW. After travelling in the Balkans, Greece and central Europe he became librarian to the Royal Anthropological Institute. From 1927 to 1946 he was Professor of Prehistoric Archaeology at Edinburgh University. From 1946 to 1957, when he returned to Australia, he served as the Director of the Institute of Archaeology in the University of London. He died in October 1957 after falling from a cliff at BLACKHEATH in the BLUE MOUNTAINS NSW.

Childe was an authority on early societies of Europe and the Middle East. Among his notable 'digs' was the excavation of the Neolithic village of Skara Brae in the Orkneys. His work is the foundation of knowledge of the Neolithic in Europe though his chronology has been modified by more recent studies. He also popularised archaeology and prehistory, and among his many popular works is *The Prehistory of European Society* (1958).

chillies *see* Solanaceae

chimaeras *see* sharks, etc.

Chinchilla QLD (population 3 092 in 1981) An inland country town located on the Warrego Highway, in the N section of the DARLING DOWNS, it is 301km by road NW of Brisbane and 86km NW of DALBY. It is also a railway town on the route from Brisbane to ROMA, CHARLEVILLE and QUILPIE. At an elevation of 302m above sea level, it is a commercial and service centre for a rural district where sheep and cattle grazing, dairying and forestry are the main activities. The town name comes from an Aboriginal word meaning 'cypress pine trees'.

Chinese in Australia

The 1981 census revealed that 25 883 persons resident in Australia had been born in China. C.A. Price, a leading authority on multicultural affairs, in a study on the ethnic origins of the Australian population based on an eight-generation analysis, estimated the total Chinese component to be equivalent to 383 000 persons in 1978. Although the Chinese have a rich heritage of language and culture, they have been unable to share it with the Australian community because of attitudes which developed towards them as a people during the second half of the 19th century. However, since the abolition of the last remnants of the 'White Australia Policy' in 1973, recognition has been given to the contribution made by Chinese migrants to Australia and a new awareness has emerged of the value of Chinese culture and tradition to the future Australian community.

History of Chinese migration In the many centuries of Chinese history it is quite likely that wandering junks from China established contact with the Australian continent long before British settlement; but the first Chinese settlers came to Australia in 1848 when there was a serious shortage of cheap labour in NSW due to the end of convict transportation in 1840. Employers brought unskilled Chinese labourers to Australia on a contract basis. Some reports claim employers promised them £6 per year and two suits of clothing, others claim the pay was £12 or £24 a year. Many Chinese worked as shepherds on the great sheep runs, some became farm hands and others became waterside workers. It is reported that one QLD squatter employed 40 Chinese at a time, and many thousands of acres were cleared by Chinese workers. Indeed, Chinese labourers cleared the bush and paved the way for farming to begin in much the same way as bulldozers do in modern times. The experiment of bringing Chinese labourers to NSW was a great success and many other colonies also recruited Chinese labour. In 1850 it was recorded that the Chinese were regarded as being temperate, frugal, hardworking, law-abiding and most desirable citizens.

Then came the discovery of gold in VIC in 1851. Large numbers of Chinese workers left their jobs and walked enormous distances overland to join the gold rush. In addition, many thousands more arrived from China in search of gold. In 1854 there were 2 341 Chinese in VIC and by 1858 this figure had increased to 42 000. Indeed, in 1858 15 per cent of the entire male population of VIC was Chinese and the Chinese language became a second language of commerce in many VIC and NSW country towns, with streets and shops carrying bilingual signs. The farmers and graziers were made hostile by the loss of cheap labour; the European miners were made hostile by the success of the Chinese in their search for gold; and the news that half-a-million pounds in gold had been shipped from Melbourne to China acted as a catalyst to unite public opinion against the Chinese, fostering attitudes which lasted many years. Although the basis of the opposition was economic, it was soon converted into racial conflict of the worst kind. The Chinese were now regarded as a sinister element in the community, and a number of riots occurred at various goldfields. The first occurred at the Buckland River goldfield in north-eastern VIC, where a group of white miners attacked the Chinese camps and burned down their tents and shanties, chasing them into the bush. Many Chinese died as a result of this attack, but the public feeling against the Chinese was so strong that the leaders of the raid were found not guilty. Riots also broke out at Lambing Flat in NSW in 1860 (see LAMBING FLAT RIOTS). The hostility towards the Chinese as a people was intensified by widely read journals such as *Punch*, the *Bulletin* and the *Worker*. These journals and other media built up a myth of 'the Yellow Peril' and developed this theme by predictions of the disasters which would follow if the arrival of 'hordes of gully-raking, rice-devouring, pig-tailed chinkies' was allowed to continue. The fear produced by this sort of propaganda resulted in the passing of legislation preventing the entry of Chinese into Australia (see IMMIGRATION RESTRICTIONS). The majority of the Chinese men who had come to Australia in search of gold returned to their homeland because they had family and clan obligations there. Some remained, but at federation the doors were shut against further Chinese settlement in Australia.

Chinese contribution to Australia's development Chinese citizens have made material contributions to the progress of Australia and they have typically been useful and law-abiding citizens. Their contribution to the development of farmland has been discussed above. Those who remained in Australia after federation developed trade with China, and they controlled nearly all of Australia's import and export trade with their homeland. In addition, about half of all the cooks in country towns and a quarter of all station cooks in Australia were Chinese. Others became market gardeners and the *Cairns Post* in 1887 reported that 'the Chinese farmer and fruit grower of the North may almost be regarded as the father of agriculture in the CAIRNS district.' Cairns became completely dependent upon the Chinese for fruit and vegetables. The Chinese also pioneered the sugar industry and established the Hop Wah sugar mill in 1886; they began growing rice in 1887 and built a rice mill in the same period; they pioneered the growing and export of bananas: there can be no doubt that they made a major contribution to Cairns' early prosperity. Other Chinese engaged in cabinet making until the development of factories with modern machinery drove them out, and they also introduced the Chinese laundries.

Many Chinese have become successful members of the medical, legal and other professions—particularly in teaching at tertiary level. Some have become involved with the Australian community as leaders, notable examples being Harry Chan, who was Mayor of Darwin and a member of the NT Legislative Council, and David Wang who became a member of the Melbourne City Council.

Chinese heritage The Chinese in Australia have kept alive their language and broadcasts in Standard Chinese and Cantonese are now made through Radio Australia. Chinese societies are reviving. Chinese newsletters are being printed and Chinese restaurants have increased in numbers. Dixon Street in Sydney has become the heart of the Chinese ethnic community with Chinese lanterns, oriental-style neons, and shops selling dried fish, sesame seed, *Chrysanthemum* tonic, woks (Chinese frying pans), marinated ducks, and the abacus. It is also the centre for the celebration of the Chinese New Year when the colourful Chinese dragon parades the street. The NSW State government has hopes of developing the Dixon Street centre as a tourist attraction similar to the Chinatowns found in many major cities of the world.

Further reading: Huck, A. *The Chinese in Australia*. Longman, Melbourne, 1968; Choi, C.Y. *Chinese Migration and Settlement in Australia*. Sydney University Press, Sydney, 1975; Price, C.A. *Australian Immigration, A Bibliography and Digest*. Australian National University Press, Canberra, 1981.

Chisholm, Alexander Hugh

(1890-1977) Journalist, author and naturalist. Born in VIC, he worked on several Australian newspapers, and was editor of *Who's Who in Australia* (1947) and editor-in-chief of the 10-volume *Australian Encyclopaedia* published in 1958. He was a prolific writer and reviewer of books on natural history (particularly on birds) and on other subjects; amongst his titles are a biography (1976) of the popular poet C.J. DENNIS; *Strange Journey: The Adventures of Ludwig Leichhardt and John Gilbert* (3rd edn, 1973); and an anthology of Australian nature writing, *Land of Wonder* (1971).

Chisholm, Caroline

(1808-77) Philanthropist. She was born in Northampton, England, into a family with a strong tradition of charitable work. After marrying Captain Archibald Chisholm, an officer in the forces of the East India Co., she went with him to Madras in India, where she founded a Female School of Industry for the Daughters of European Soldiers. In 1838, when her husband was on sick leave, she came with him and their two sons to NSW and remained there when he returned to active service in 1840. By that time she had become seriously concerned about the difficulties being faced by many immigrants, especially single women.

Caroline Chisholm

Mitchell Library

Through a direct approach to Governor GIPPS and his wife in 1841, she obtained permission to open a Female Immigrants' Home in a disused barracks building near Circular Quay. She quickly realised that her best way of finding employment for immigrant girls was to send them inland. She herself accompanied large parties of these girls, as far afield as YASS, GUNDAGAI, BATHURST and PORT MACQUARIE. During this period, she also turned her attention to the problem of placing men and their families on the land. In six years, her efforts helped considerably to relieve the congestion of the Sydney area and to supply country districts with necessary labour, 11 000 persons passing through her care.

In 1845 her husband retired, and in the following year the family returned to England where she and her husband set up an office in London to promote and assist emigration to NSW.

Following the outbreak of the Crimean War in 1854 it became difficult to charter ships, and Caroline Chisholm returned with the last boatload to Australia in that year. Having toured the goldfields to get to know the social conditions of the mining communities, she then devoted herself to providing wayside shelters for people travelling to the gold diggings. Later she moved to Sydney, where she founded a girls' school at Newtown, and where her husband rejoined her.

They finally returned in 1866 to England, where she was granted a civil list pension of £100 per annum. By that time she was in ill health, and found it necessary to cease devoting herself to public charitable causes.
Further reading: Kiddle, M. *Caroline Chisholm.* Discovery Press, Penrith NSW, 1972.

chitons The chitons or coat-of-mail shells form a small class, Amphineura, of the MOLLUSCS. About 180 species are known from Australia. These herbivorous marine molluscs are flattened and usually slow-moving, and cling to smooth rocks, scraping algae and other plant food from the rocks by means of the file-like radula. They are easily distinguished from all other molluscs by the shell which consists of a row of eight overlapping plates. The body extends out from the plates as a fleshy margin called the girdle. The head is greatly reduced but otherwise these bilaterally symmetrical organisms are very similar to the presumed ancestral mollusc. They show the basic structure described in the entry on molluscs.

Most chitons are rather drab in colour. The largest Australian species reach a length of about 20cm—for example, *Acanthozostera gemmata*, a species found in N waters, and distinguished by a spiny girdle. Most species, however, are much smaller.
Further reading: see under molluscs.

chordates The Chordata is a phylum of animals containing the VERTEBRATES (subphylum Vertebrata) and several groups of small invertebrate animals in the subphyla Urochordata (SEA SQUIRTS, etc.) and Acrania (or Cephalochordata; LANCELETS, amphioxus). The common characteristics of the chordates are discussed in the entry on vertebrates.

chough *see* mudnest builders

Christmas bells *see* Liliaceae

Christmas bush This small tree or shrub, *Ceratopetalum gummiferum* (family Cunoniaceae), is widespread in gullies, open forests and heaths and is often grown as an ornamental. The shiny green leaves are compound, having three leaflets; the petals of the white flowers carry tiny horns, and after flowering the sepals turn red.

Closely related to the Christmas bush is the coachwood, or scented satinwood, *C. apetalum*, a very important timber tree in NSW. It can grow to a height of 30m with a trunk diameter of 1m, and the pale pink wood has a wide variety of uses. The coachwood is found in rainforests and gullies. Its flowers lack petals, but the sepals turn a reddish-purple.

In VIC, *Prostanthera lasianthos* (family Lamiaceae), a bushy shrub with white and purple flowers, also goes by the name of Christmas bush, although other members of its genus are called mint bushes.

Christmas Island An Australian territory in the Indian Ocean, it is located about 2 600km NW of FREMANTLE and 300km S of the Indonesian island of Java. The island is an important source of phosphate, and the mining and export of the deposits are the only commercial activities there. A Dutch sea captain named the uninhabited island in 1643, probably because he sighted it on Christmas Day. It was claimed by Britain in 1888 and three years later a settlement was established at Flying Fish Cove by George Clunies Ross, whose descendants are still there. A mining company was formed in 1897 and operated until 1948 when its assets were acquired by the Australian and New Zealand governments. In 1958 the island became an Australian territory.

Chrysanthemum *see* Compositae

chuditch *see* native cats, etc.

Church of England *see* Anglican Church of Australia

Churchill VIC (population 4 798 in 1981) A town in the LATROBE RIVER valley, it is located on the Midland Highway, 11km SSE of MORWELL, and some 160km ESE of Melbourne. The town is a modern planned urban centre, built in the 1960s to house workers who were associated with the construction of the Hazelwood power station, and now for maintenance workers of the State Electricity Commission. It was named after the British statesman Sir Winston Churchill (1874-1965).

Churchill Fellowships *see* Winston Churchill Memorial Trust

churinga *see* tjuringa

cicada birds *see* cuckoo-shrikes, etc.

cicadas These large BUGS make up the family Cicadidae, which is represented by almost 200 species in Australia. They are commonly, and quite wrongly, called locusts. They are sucking insects, and have three simple eyes (ocelli) between the compound eyes, and two pairs of uniform, membranous wings.

The eggs are laid on trees from which the young nymphs drop to burrow into the ground where they suck sap from the roots. This nymphal stage may last several years. In the USA the periodical cicada, *Magicicada septendecim*, is know to have a life spanning 13 or 17 years. Though cicadas in Australia also occur in great abundance in some years (the summer of 1978-79 was noteworthy, in the Sydney region at least), the phenomenon is not as clear-cut as in the USA, though further analysis may reveal patterns.

Cicadas are noted for the shrill sounds made by the males. Traditionally, the chorus begins in SE Australia just before Melbourne Cup day (early November). The noise can be deafening and maddening to human listeners but the ears of the cicada males have an enviable adaptation: the ear drums, which lie near the sound-producing membranes at the base of the abdomen, are automatically slackened as soon as the membranes begin to vibrate.

Green Monday, *Cyclochila australasiae*

Cicadas, of course, are keenly hunted by small boys and some have acquired common names: double drummer, *Thopha saccata*; green Monday, *Cyclochila australasiae*; bladder cicada, *Cytosoma saundersi*, a night 'singer'; and floury miller, *Abricta curvicosta*. The largest genus is *Cicadetta*.
Further reading: Hughes, R.D. *Living Insects.* Collins, Sydney, 1974; McKeown, K.C. *Insect Wonders of Australia.* Angus & Robertson, Sydney, 1974.

Cineraria *see* Compositae

Cinesound *see* film

cisticola *see* warblers, etc.

Citizen Military Forces This title was used until recently for the main reserve troops of the Defence Force. Such troops, who have part-time training obligations, are now known as the Army Reserve (ARES).

citizenship The Australian Citizenship Act (1948) provides for the acquiring of citizenship: by birth in Australia; by descent, in the case of birth abroad to Australian parents; or by grant of citizenship to people who have lived in Australia for at least three years, are of good character, have an adequate knowledge of English, understand the responsibilities and privileges of citizenship, and declare that they intend to reside permanently in Australia. Matters related to nationality and citizenship are the responsibility of the Department of Immigration and Ethnic Affairs. The term 'naturalisation' is no longer used in the granting of citizenship.

citrus *see* fruit growing; Rutaceae

clams *see* bivalve molluscs

Clare SA (population 2 381 in 1981) A small town, founded in 1842 and named after County Clare in Ireland, it is located on the Main North Highway to the FLINDERS RANGES, 135km N of Adelaide, in a picturesque wooded valley of the northern MOUNT LOFTY RANGES. At an elevation of 398m above sea level, it receives an average yearly rainfall of 632mm, concentrated in the winter months (July average, the highest, 81mm; March average, the lowest, 24mm). The Clare Valley is famed for its wine production, and also for dairy produce, wool and cereals. With its many historic 19th-century buildings, the town has an old-world charm, and attracts many visitors in the summer months. Also within the district are several other buildings of historic interest, such as 'Wolta Wolta' homestead (3km W) and Martindale Hall at Mintaro (20km SE), now used as a conference centre for Adelaide University. The National Trust (SA) has listed over 20 buildings in the town for preservation, and a museum housed in the old police station and courthouse preserves much of the district's early history. The poet C.J. DENNIS—the 'sentimental bloke'—was born at Auburn, 28km S of Clare.

Claremont TAS A suburb of GLENORCHY, 12km N of Hobart, it is the home of the Cadbury-Schweppes organisation in Australia. The factory, which covers 100ha, is situated on a peninsula in the DERWENT RIVER, where confectionery production commenced in 1922; some 1 300 people are now employed there. The factory specialises in the manufacture of block chocolate and boxed assorted confectionery, and visits to it are popular with tourists.

Clarence River NSW The largest coastal river in the N of the State, it is located between the RICHMOND Valley to the N and the Bellinger and MACLEAY river systems to the S. It drains a catchment area of over 22 500km^2, which reaches 140km inland from the Pacific coast to the GREAT DIVIDING RANGE, and extends over a distance of 400km from the McPHERSON RANGE in the N to the DORRIGO Plateau and other ranges which form the S rim of the basin. Among the tributaries which make up the Clarence system are the Nymboida, Guy Fawkes, Mann and Orara Rivers from the S and SW, and the Timbarry, Boonoo Boonoo and Cataract Rivers from the W and NW. The upper parts of the Clarence Basin include much dissected and rugged country, often heavily forested, quite remote and sparsely populated. The Gibraltar Range National Park in the mid-W part of the basin comprises a wilderness area of 17 273ha with deep gorges, spectacular waterfalls and granite rock formations which were of rich mythological significance to the Aborigines of the area. Downstream from these upper catchment areas, the tributaries converge with the main river in a narrow steep-sided gorge. Beyond the gorge section of the Clarence, the valley widens and the river meanders in wide loops across a broad coastal plain to the sea.

The main urban centres in the Clarence Valley are GRAFTON (population 17 000 in 1981), MACLEAN (2 589), Yamba (2 528) and Iluka (1 359). Ulmarra is a small town (population 395) in the closely settled lower valley of the Clarence; the Ulmarra Shire, which covers the adjacent rural areas, had a population of 3 872 at the 1981 census. The Pacific Highway crosses the valley from S to N, the Gwydir Highway runs from Grafton, generally in an E-W direction, to GLEN INNES on the NEW ENGLAND Plateau, and the Bruxner Highway traverses the upper valley, crossing the river at Tabulam, and providing another route from the coast to the tablelands. The main NORTH COAST railway also passes through the lower valley on a N-S route, crossing the river at Grafton.

In the upper valley, timber-getting is important and sawmills dot the landscape. On the Nymboida River there is a small hydroelectricity generating station. On the middle

Beef grazing country in the upper Clarence Valley

parts of the valley, beef cattle grazing, fodder crop cultivation (on the alluvial flats), dairying and pig raising are important. On the wide expanses of the lower river plains, dairying and sugar cane growing are the main farming activities. There is a sugar mill on Harwood Is downstream from Maclean. While the upland areas can experience cold weather conditions, the lower parts of the valley have a subtropical climate with warm humid summers and mild dry winters. Heavy rainfall in the summer months is the usual pattern and if this occurs over the catchment area, serious river-flooding of both farmlands and towns can occur. Along the river and the adjacent coastal zone, there are numerous holiday and tourist sites: Yamba, Iluka, Broom's Head, Wooli and Minnie Water. It has long been the hope of many people that Iluka would develop into a major port, but so far this has not occurred. The annual Family Fishing Festival at Yamba attracts many competitors. The Yuraygir National Park (13 055), located along the coastal zone E of Grafton and S of Yamba, includes beaches and rocky headlands, woodlands and reed swamps, dry heath and dune forest, and provides a sanctuary for many birds, including honeyeaters, pelicans, black swans, emus and brolgas.

Clark, Charles Manning Hope (1915-) Historian, Emeritus Professor of the Australian National University. Born and educated in Melbourne he taught in schools in England and Victoria for several years and lectured in Political Science and History at Melbourne University before being appointed Professor of Australian History at the School of General Studies, Australian National University, in 1949. His publications include short stories, works of literary criticism, selections of historical documents, a short history of Australia and a volume of occasional writings and speeches. However his fame rests mainly on his monumental *A History of Australia*, of which five volumes, covering the years 1788-1915, had appeared by 1981. In this work he takes a new approach to his topic, enquiring particularly into the ideals and faiths by which the nation's builders have been motivated. It has been widely hailed as a work of literature as well as of historical scholarship.

Clarke, Marcus Andrew Hislop (1846-81) Journalist and author. Born in

London, he came to Melbourne in 1863, worked briefly in a bank and then on a sheep station in the WIMMERA district, and while in the latter position began writing sketches for the *Australian Magazine*. In 1867 he joined the literary staff of the *Argus* and at later periods was sub-librarian at the Melbourne Public Library and owner and editor of the *Colonial Monthly* magazine. However, he was too unstable in temperament to persevere at routine work, and for most of his adult life worked as a free-lance journalist. In 1869 the *Australian Journal* commissioned him to write a novel about the convict days, and the result, the highly melodramatic *His Natural Life* ran as a serial between 1870 and 1872. It appeared as a book in 1874. Modern editions have been entitled *For the Term of His Natural Life*.

Clarke wrote four other novels, some plays and pantomimes, and volumes of essays, sketches and short stories, but he is remembered today almost solely for his first novel. Although it is based on a close study of historical records and written with all the skill of a brilliant journalist, its literary merit is marred by a plot based on a series of improbabilities and by over-drawn characters.

See also literature
Further reading: Elliott, B.R. *Marcus Clarke*. Oxford University Press, Melbourne, 1969.

Clarke, Ronald William (1937-) Middle-distance runner. Born in Melbourne, Clarke was a talented mile runner as a junior, and was to become one of the greatest middle-distance runners the world has known. He first gave notice of his potential as a distance runner when he broke the world junior mile record in 1956. In the same year he was chosen as the final carrier of the flame which lit the Olympic torch to open the 1956 Games in Melbourne. A courageous and ruthless runner, by 1965 he held world records for three, six and 10 miles, 5000m, 10 000m and 20 000m and the one-hour distance of 12 miles, 1 006 yards, 1 foot and 10 inches. By 1973, eight years later, he had added the two-mile record and still held the three- and six-mile records. Characterised by modesty, humility and absolute dedication, during his career he broke 18 world records from one mile to 20 000m—no other athlete before or since has broken as many world records.

Cleary, Jon Stephen (1917-) Popular novelist. Born in Sydney, he served in the second AIF as a gunner in the Middle East and as a member of the Military History Section in New Guinea. Shortly after the war he published *These Small Glories* (1946), a collection of short stories of war service, and *You Can't See Around Corners* (1948), a novel with a wartime setting. He has since published several other novels, of which *The Sundowners* (1952), is the best known. He writes in a simple, laconic style which shows the influences of Graham Greene and Ernest Hemingway.

Clift, Charmian *see* Johnston, George Henry

climate *see* weather, etc.

Cloncurry QLD (population 1 961 in 1981) A railhead and service town in the NW of the State, it is located on Cloncurry Creek, a tributary of the FLINDERS RIVER, 1 721km by road NW of Brisbane and 124km E of MOUNT ISA. It was a copper-mining centre from the 1860s, but has now been overshadowed by the growth of Mt Isa. It is on the rail route running inland from TOWNSVILLE, and is the main railway point for cattle from the GULF COUNTRY. At an elevation of 189m above sea level, it experiences a hot tropical climate, with an average yearly rainfall of 470mm which is concentrated in the summer months.

Premier's Dept. QLD

The Council Chambers in Cloncurry

Clouds of Magellan *see* astronomy

clover *see* Papilionaceae

club mosses *see* fossils; Microphyllyta

Clune, Francis Patrick 'Frank' (1893-1971) Author. He was born in Sydney and after leaving primary school worked in a variety of jobs in many parts of the world, served in the United States Cavalry and the Canadian Mounted Police, joined the AIF, and was wounded at GALLIPOLI. His first book, the autobiographical *Try Anything Once*, did not appear until 1933, but he then proceeded to turn out more than 60 titles, dealing mainly with biographical and descriptive themes related to Australia and with accounts of his travels overseas. They included *Dig* (1937), *The Red Heart* (1944), *Wild Colonial Boys* (1948), and one work of fiction, *Ben Hall the Bushranger* (1947). Although his work lacks literary value, he has been very widely read.

cluster flies *see* blowflies

CMF *see* Citizen Military Forces

coachwood *see* Christmas bush

coal A combustible sedimentary rock, coal was formed many millions of years ago from the accumulation of plant material. The oldest coal deposits were formed about 350 million years before the present era, but the time of greatest formation was during the Carboniferous period, about 225 million years ago.

Classification Coals are classified either in order of rank or according to grade. Rank is determined by the amount of alteration and compaction to which the coal has been subjected; as the rank increases so does the amount of fixed carbon, with moisture and volatile matter decreasing. The main classes of coal, based on increasing rank, are lignite, sub-bituminous, bituminous and anthracite. Lignite, which is used mainly in the production of electricity, is a soft, brown and distinctly woody coal; sub-bituminous coal is black and contains little or no woody texture; the most abundant form is bituminous coal, which is commonly used for industrial purposes—it is black and often banded, with layers of bright coal or vitrain alternating with dull bands; and anthracite, used extensively as a domestic fuel, is a hard coal with a brilliant black colour. The grade of coal is described by either proximate or ultimate analyses. Proximate analyses involve the determination of moisture, ash, volatile matter and fixed carbon, whereas the ultimate analyses of coal indicate the content of ash, carbon, hydrogen, sulphur, nitrogen and oxygen. The heating value of coal is expressed in British thermal units (Btu), kilocalories (kcal) or kilojoules (kj); it is an important factor and varies with each type or variety.

Almost half the world's coal output is consumed by static power stations for the production of electricity, with 25 per cent used in all aspects of iron and steel manufacture and the remainder in industry as a source of heat and power. The volatile constituents released when coal is carbonised to make coke include ammonia, light oils and coal tar. These yield numerous products such as phenols, cresols, naphthalene, benzene, drugs, nylon, explosives, fertiliser and insecticides. Certain types of fly ash are produced when coal is burned and may be used in the manufacture of bricks. Strategically, coal is essential for the production of electric power and metals which might be required for national defence.

Production The building of railroads gave great impetus to the growth of the coal industry throughout the world: not only could coal be transported cheaply, but the railroads themselves were important consumers of the product. Railways also fostered the growth of energy-consuming industries and encouraged the expansion of the IRON AND STEEL INDUSTRY, resulting in the close interlocking of the coal-mining, transportation and smelting industries.

In 1982, Australia produced just over 99.4 million tonnes of black coal, making it the world's ninth-largest producer. Of this, about 42 million tonnes were exported, mainly to Japan. The principal producing States are NSW and QLD, which together account for 95 per cent of Australia's output.

There was a marked expansion in coal production in QLD in the 1970s. The main centres of production in this State are in the BOWEN, IPSWICH and MARYBOROUGH regions;

Table 1

AUSTRALIAN BLACK COAL PRODUCTION 1970-81
(× '000t)

State	1970	1978	1979	1980	1981
QLD	10 124	34 461	37 508	37 579	45 026
NSW	35 900	50 679	50 888	50 720	60 749
TAS	114	224	237	234	346
SA	1 856	1 585	1 674	1 719	1 577
WA	1 217	2 404	2 735	3 154	3 247
TOTAL	49 211	87 353	93 042	93 406	110 945

Source: *Australian Mineral Industry Annual Review.* (1970-81) Australian Govt Publishing Service, Canberra.

within these vast areas are numerous mining sites such as COLLINSVILLE, MOURA, BLACK-WATER, PEAK DOWNS, CALLIDE VALLEY, Saraji, GOONYELLA and BLAIR ATHOL. Some 89 per cent of QLD's total production in 1980 was from open-cut mining. In NSW, the main production area is the Sydney Basin with the NEWCASTLE-MAITLAND coal belt located on the N boundary, the WOLLONGONG-Bulli region in the S, the LITHGOW-Lidsdale mining area lying to the W and the Burragorang Valley district located inland on the S boundary of the basin. The bulk of NSW coal comes from underground mines, with only 27 per cent from open-cut operations. In WA, sub-bituminous coal is produced at the COLLIE coalfield, about 220km SSE of Perth. In SA, coal is produced at the LEIGH CREEK open-cut mine, but there are at least 15 other areas in SA which contain identifiable coal measures, most of which have been found in the course of drilling or sinking for underground water supplies. In TAS, limited production of coal is obtained from fields located SE of LAUNCESTON, though coal has been recorded from many other localities. VIC is the only State which produces brown coal (lignite). The major deposits are in the LATROBE RIVER valley, at YALLOURN and MORWELL. Other coal measures exist at BACCHUS MARSH and Altona; WONTHAGGI was the only locality in VIC which produced black coal, but the mine was closed in 1968.

Reserves In 1974 it was estimated that world reserves of hard coal were nearly 80 per cent of the total, unexploited reserves of 12 599 billion tonnes. The reserves of hard coals, which include all coals of higher rank than lignite, were estimated at 9 933 billion tonnes, while those of brown coal and lignite were calculated at 2 666 billion tonnes. Australia is considered to have 218.9 billion tonnes of coal and lignite resources available.

The time/price relationship for lignite and bituminous coal from 1970 to 2000 indicates that the basic value of coal will change very little; the price may be affected by inflationary influences and shortages of other fuels. In the year 2000 demand for all coals will be 5 300 million tonnes, representing an average annual increase of two per cent.

Further reading: see under minerals and mining.

coastline *see* area

coat-of-mail shells *see* chitons

coats of arms, Australian and State *see* flags, etc.

Cobar NSW (population 3 581 in 1981) A town on the Barrier Highway, 718km by road NW of Sydney, and 132km W of NYNGAN, Cobar is the rail terminus of a branch line from Nyngan, and is 622km by train from Sydney via the route across the GREAT DIVIDING RANGE to ORANGE, DUBBO, Trangie and Nyngan. At an elevation of 174m above sea level, it has a climate typical of the inland plains, with very hot summer conditions, warm winter days, but crisply cool evenings in the winter months. The average yearly rainfall is 425mm, the summer period (December to March) receiving the highest falls. The rainfall, however, is extremely variable from year to year and droughts are not uncommon. The surrounding rural region, with large station properties, is an extensive grazing area. However, it has not been rural produce which has made Cobar so well known, but mining activities, for it is the site of one of the largest copper mining operations in Australia. Copper was first discovered here in 1869 and intermittent mining—depending mainly on world copper prices—has continued since then. The Pastoral, Mining and Technological Museum, overlooking the original open-cut mine in the town, has displays depicting the history of the district; and 'The Stele', an upright slab

NSW Dept. of Tourism

Aboriginal cave paintings at Wuttagoona Sation, Cobar NSW

bearing sculptured designs portraying the history of copper in Cobar, was unveiled in 1969 during the celebrations marking the centenary of copper mining. Visitors can tour the CSA mine, located NW of the town, which produces copper and copper-zinc ores. The Mt Grenfell Aboriginal cave paintings, depicting human figures, birds, animals and linear patterns, are located 40km W of Cobar along the Barrier Highway.

Cobb & Co. This, the most famous of Australian coaching companies, was founded in Melbourne in 1853 by Freeman Cobb and three other Americans. The first route was from the city of Melbourne to Sandridge (Port Melbourne), but services to the goldfields were soon added. By 1859, when the company was acquired by James Rutherford and five partners, railways were beginning to offer competition on routes around Melbourne, and three years later its headquarters were moved to BATHURST in NSW. In the 1860s it began services in QLD, and by the following decade was harnessing over 6000 horses a day in the three E colonies combined. At the same time, however, it was being forced to concentrate increasingly on the thinly inhabited areas as the railways absorbed the traffic near the capital cities. This trend was accompanied by

Courtesy of A.I.S. Canberra

Cobb & Co. coach

diversification as the company began to engage in pastoral, shipping and railway construction activities and in iron making at the Eskbank works in LITHGOW. In 1881 the QLD section became a separate company, and kept running coaches until 1924. The last coach to run, on the Yeulba-Surat route, is now in the Queensland Museum, Brisbane. Among others which have been preserved are those in the Power House Museum and at Vaucluse House, Sydney, and those in the National Museum, Melbourne.

Further reading: Austin, K.A. *The Lights of Cobb & Co.* Rigby, Adelaide, 1967.

cobblers peg *see* Compositae; weeds

Cobourg Peninsula NT Located at the NW extremity of the Territory, the peninsula extends about 100km on a WNW-ESE alignment from the ARNHEM LAND Aboriginal Reserve to its W tip, Cape Don. To the N is the ARAFURA SEA and to the S is VAN DIEMEN GULF. The N coast is indented by numerous bays, and two of these, RAFFLES BAY and PORT ESSINGTON, were sites of unsuccessful early white settlements. CROKER ISLAND lies off the N coast at the E end. The peninsula is a wildlife sanctuary and a flora and fauna reserve.

cobra *see* bivalve molluscs

Cobram VIC (population 3 817 in 1981) This country town is on the Murray Valley Highway in the central N of the State. Located NNE of SHEPPARTON and down-river from YARRAWONGA, it is 250km by rail from Melbourne. It is a commercial and service town for a productive rural region, where citrus fruits and wine grapes are grown under irrigation, where dairying is a major industry, and where sheep and beef cattle are grazed. The district was first settled in 1834 when John Kennedy Hume, a brother of the explorer Hamilton HUME, took up land there. With the coming of the railway in 1887 the town developed, and as irrigation schemes were established, the rural productivity of the district increased. After World War II, there was some closer settlement in the area and in 1949 the Murray-Goulburn Co-operative, one of the nation's largest dairying companies, was started by ex-servicemen settlers. The town takes its name from an Aboriginal word which means 'head' or 'head station'.

cockatiel *see* parrots, etc.

Cockatoo Island WA This is one of the many islands of YAMPI SOUND, located between the BUCCANEER ARCHIPELAGO and the W KIMBERLEYS coast, in the far NW of the State. The island consists of a vast mass of high-grade iron ore which has been mined since 1950 by BHP. The open-cut mining operations are highly mechanised and special wharf facilities have been constructed to cope with the big tidal range (as much as 10m between high and low tide) experienced in the Sound. By 1976, however, the ore reserves above sea level on Cockatoo Is were almost exhausted, and the feasibility of recovering material below sea level was investigated. The inquiry indicated that mining could continue, and early in 1981, ore near sea level was extracted and there were plans to extend to about 10m below this level. The other iron ore island in the Sound, KOOLAN ISLAND, lies just E of Cockatoo.

cockatoos *see* parrots, etc.

Cockburn Sound WA A section of the Indian Ocean coastal waters S of FREMANTLE, it stretches for some 28km to Cape Peron, with Garden Is and several reefs on the W forming a sheltered deep-water inlet. It has been developed in recent decades as a main part of the Fremantle outer harbour, especially serving the KWINANA industrial expansion.

cockles *see* bivalve molluscs

cockroaches These form an ancient order (Blattodea) of easily recognised exopterygote INSECTS; about 450 species occur in Australia. Cockroaches are flattened insects with long legs adapted for running. The pronotum (the top part of the first thoracic segment) is a large shield covering the head, which carries large compound eyes, long, many-segmented antennae and strong biting and chewing mouthparts. The fore-wings, when present, are thickened tegmina (wing coverings) which protect the membranous hind-wings; the abdomen carries a pair of segmented 'tails' (cerci). The eggs of cockroaches are laid in two rows in small purses called oothecae. These may be carried by the female for some time after completion, or they may be deposited in a hidden place as soon as they are full. The nymphs of cockroaches resemble the adults and are found in similar habitats. Most species are, in fact, gregarious, and all stages may be found together. Development is usually slow, especially in the larger species, and some may live for several years.

A. Woods

The introduced German cockroach, the most common domestic species in Australia

Most cockroaches are nocturnal insects which live in concealed places such as under bark, in leaf-litter and in rotting wood. Although most favour damp habitats, some species are found in arid areas of Australia. Little is known about what the Australian native species eat but it is probable that most of them are omnivores, though some are known to live on rotting wood.

Australia, like most other countries, has two kinds of cockroach: cosmopolitan species which live close to man and are familiar to householders; and native species, often lumped together as 'bush cockroaches' which live in natural habitats.

There are about nine cosmopolitan species in Australia, the best known of which are the so-called American cockroach, *Periplaneta americana*, the German cockroach, *Blatella germanica*, and the Australian cockroach, *P. australasiae*. The geographical names are misleading: though these three species are now so widespread that their countries of origin are obscure, the two *Periplaneta* species (about 40mm long), for example, probably evolved in Africa. The *Periplaneta* species invade and infest neglected premises, but they are not as common in houses as the much smaller and much faster breeding *B. germanica*. *P. americana* is, however, a common denizen of sewers and garbage tips, and is also a common pest of ships; Captain BLIGH tried to rid one of his commands of the pest with boiling water. The so-called common cockroach, *Blatta orientalis*, a flightless species which is confined to the S half of Australia, is apparently relatively uncommon, while *Supella supellectilium*, a species which began its world expansion this century, is becoming more common. Though domestic cockroaches spoil some food by eating it they foul more with faeces and with their characteristic odour; they also damage such items as book covers, papers and fabrics. They are mechanical carriers of microorganisms and viruses.

The bush cockroaches are represented by four families in Australia—Blattidae, Polyphagidae, Blatellidae and Blaberidae—none of which is restricted to Australia. Few bush cockroaches come indoors though one species, *Shawella couloniana*, could possibly establish populations there. Many bush cockroaches, unlike the drab brown domestic species, are attractively coloured.

See also insects, introduced; pests

Cocos Islands (population 569 in 1981) Since 1955, this group of islands in the Indian Ocean has been an Australian territory. The group consists of 27 coral islands, located 2 770km NW of Perth and almost 4 000km W of Darwin, in two separate atolls: the S atoll includes several low islands (including West Is and Home Is, where the main population lives), lying in a horseshoe shape around a central lagoon; the N atoll, 24km from the main group, is called North Keeling Is. The whole group is commonly known as the Cocos (Keeling) Islands.

The islands were settled by John Clunies Ross, who became known as the 'King of the Cocos' in the late 1820s; he brought labourers of Malay origin, mainly from Java, to develop coconut plantations on the island. The descendants of the Malay people still live on Home Is, while the administration headquarters is on West Is. Charles DARWIN visited the islands in 1836 on HMS *Beagle* and based his theory of coral-reef formation on the observations he made there. In 1857 the islands became part of the British Empire and in 1886 Queen Victoria made a grant in perpetuity of all land in the group to the Clunies Ross family. In 1901 a cable station was established there as part of the communication system across the Indian Ocean linking Australia to Europe. Early in World War I, the islands attained fame when the German cruiser *Emden* was defeated and grounded on North Keeling Is. During World War II, the Cocos were developed as an air base which, in the post-war years, became an important link in civilian airways services from Australia to South Africa. Coconuts remain the territory's basic product. An Administrator, appointed by the Governor-General, and responsible to the Minister for Home Affairs, is the senior government representative in the Territory. In 1979 the Commonwealth purchased the Clunies-Ross interests, except for the family home and its grounds; in the same year a representative form of local government was established.

cods *see* fisheries; fishes, bony

coelenterates The phylum Coelenterata (or Cnidaria) contains simple invertebrate, aquatic animals including the jellyfish, the coral animals, sea anemones, many small encrusting organisms related to the *Hydra*, and the siphonophores (colonial, floating forms such as the Portuguese man-o'-war, or bluebottle). Although the group is predominantly marine there are some freshwater forms. The phylum is divided into three classes (Hydrozoa, Scyphozoa and Anthozoa) in which there are about 9000 species, up to a third of them occurring in Australian waters.

There are two basic body patterns among coelenterates: the tube-shaped polyp, with the mouth, surrounded by tentacles, at the top end (for example, *Hydra*); and the medusa, usually an umbrella-shaped form with the tentacles surrounding the rim, and with the mouth (except in the Rhizostomeae, *see below*) hanging centrally from the underside (for example, jellyfish species). The terms Coelenterata and Cnidaria indicate the distinguishing characteristics of the phylum: arranged around a large hollow gut opening from the mouth (which serves both ingestion and excretion), coelenterates are radially symmetrical, without either front or rear end; in addition, the tentacles (and in some medusa species the upper surface as well) are well supplied with stinging cells (nematocysts or cnidoblasts) used in defence or for immobilising prey, though they are not always venomous. The common name for some medusa forms, jellyfish, derives from the watery, jelly-like matter lying between the cells of the ectoderm on the outside and those of the endoderm lining the gut. There is no heart or circulatory system, nutrients distributing by diffusion and (in some coelenterates) by a network of canals extending from the digestive cavity. The nervous system is a simple network of fibres. All coelenterates are carnivorous.

Coelenterates may reproduce by budding new individuals, and sexually; in the latter case fertilisation occurs after eggs and spermatozoa are released into the water, the egg developing into a small, worm-shaped, ciliated planula larva which floats in the plankton for some time before becoming a new adult.

Hydrozoa This class includes the various species of *Hydra* and many similar but more complex tiny forms called hydroids which are often colonial. Often mistaken for seaweed, the colonies are extremely common on seashores,

wharf pilings, rocks and as fouling organisms on boats. They are divided into two groups: in the first the entire colony is protected by transparent sheathing of a material called chitin; in the second the sheath covers only the stalks, leaving the polyps and hydranths free. Whereas the buds of *Hydra* break away as the new individual matures, those of the various colonial hydroids remain attached by an elaborate system of hollow stalks linking the guts of all the individual polyps of the colony. Polyps in a colony are specialists: some are gastrozooids, catching food with their tentacles and digesting it; some are protective dactylozooids; and some (called gonophores) are concerned with reproduction, budding off small medusae which float away, later to reproduce sexually. The planula larvae thus produced settle after a brief period of planktonic existence and develop into new colonies.

The stinging hydroid, *Lytocarpus philippinus*

Also in this class is the order Siphonophora, containing free-floating colonial forms usually buoyed up by a gas-secreting individual. Below the gas float hang the feeding, reproductive and defensive individuals, the last having tentacles. The most notorious species in Australian waters are the Portuguese men-o'-war (bluebottles), which, though well-known stingers of surfers, have probably not been responsible for many deaths. The Pacific species, *Physalia utriculus*, has a smaller float and shorter fishing tentacles than the Atlantic species, *P. physalis*. The by-the-wind sailor, *Velella*, much smaller than the bluebottle, has a small vertical sail on a flat oval plate containing gas-filled tubes; on the underside there is only one feeding individual, its large mouth in the centre of the colony. The nematocysts of this small blue siphonophore are harmless

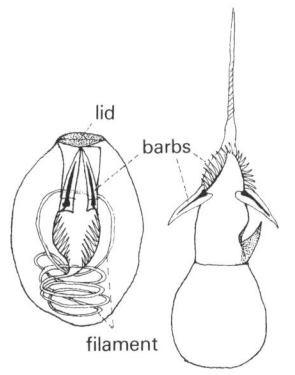

Nematocyst cell of a *Hydra* species showing undischarged and discharged barbs

lid

barbs

filament

to man. The float is set like a sail, allowing the colony to move at an angle to the wind when blown. As some siphonophores are 'left-handed' and others 'right-handed', only part of a group will be stranded by strong winds, the others being blown away from the shore. Another species sometimes cast ashore in Australia is the small, flat, circular and sail-less *Porpita pacifica*.

Scyphozoa This class contains the 'true' jellyfish, the large medusa being the dominant type of the class. The polyp stage, when it occurs, is represented by a small larval form which buds off, transversely, tiny immature medusae called ephyrae. Three orders of Scyphozoa are known from Australian waters: Charybdeida (Cubomedusae), Semaeostomae and Rhizostomae. The cup of the medusa may be shallow, like a plate, almost hemispherical, or cube-shaped, like a box. The sexes are separate, the gonads, one in each quarter, usually visible from above. The mouth is the opening of a four-sided structure, the manubrium, which hangs centrally from the underside. The tentacles (numbering from four to several hundreds, and well armed with nematocysts) hang from the lappetted rim. On the undersurface near the rim are muscles whose contractions force water out of the bell, 'jet-propelling' the animal upwards or horizontally. Much of the interior of the bell is taken up by the digestive cavity but there are also canals for transporting digested food about the body.

1. The order Charybdeida or Cubomedusae, an Indo-Pacific group of box jellies, contains some of the most dangerous of venomous animals (*see* ANIMALS, VENOMOUS), euphemistically called sea wasps. The venom is both highly toxic and extremely rapid in action, posing a danger heightened by the fact that the jellyfish swarm in tropical shallows during the hottest season when bathing is most popular. Furthermore, their transparency makes them almost invisible in the water. More than 70 people have been killed by box jellies since 1900 in N Australia. Military operations in the Pacific during World War II stimulated research into the problems of jellyfish stings, but it was not until 1955 that the most venomous species, *Chironex fleckeri*, was described. With a bell usually 'slightly larger than a man's head' and often slightly blue in colour, the species has 15 long tentacles at each corner of the cube. Its food consists largely of crustaceans. During the dry season it apparently occurs out to sea, entering the shallows during the wet season. Another important species, slightly smaller and with about seven tentacles at each corner, is *Chiropsalmus quadrigatus*. Though there are other cubomedusoids in the Australian region, Cleland, Southcott and Sutherland (*see below*) believe that these two are most likely to deliver fatal stings.

2. The order Semaeostomae, represented by several jellyfish in Australian waters, includes the saucer jellyfish, *Aurelia aurita*, which occurs in all seas throughout the world. The bell is round and fairly shallow, almost colourless apart from the four violet crescents (the gonads) around the centre. Four wide tentacles

hang from the square mouth, and many hang from the rim, which has eight lappets. This species is harmless to man; indeed, a bathful of them was used as a cure for rheumatism in Germany's East Frisian Islands in the 19th century. Two members of the order that do sting come seasonally into coastal waters: the luminescent mauve stinger or blubber, *Pelagia noctiluca* (diameter 8cm to 10cm), has 'warts', or batteries of nematocysts, on the umbrella and on the eight tentacles; the sea blubber or hairy stinger, *Cyanea capillata*, a pink, reddish-brown or yellow species with many large tentacles, can reach a diameter of 1.2m.

3. Jellyfish of the order Rhizostomae lack marginal tentacles, and the 'mouth' consists of a large number of small pores on the branches of the much-divided oral tentacles. They feed on micro-organisms drawn in by currents of water. The common *Catostylus mosaicus*, readily noticed because of its opaqueness, is probably the jellyfish most commonly seen in Australian waters: blue in the open ocean, in the estuaries and lagoons it is usually yellowish because of the presence of large numbers of symbiotic algae in the tissues. This species can reach a diameter of 45cm.

Anthozoa This is the largest coelenterate class (about 6000 species in the world) and contains the familiar sea anemones and CORALS. Anthozoans are polyps and have no medusoid stage. Their distinguishing feature is the stomach, divided into numerous compartments by longitudinal partitions, called septa, which often carry nematocysts. A further characteristic of the group is the secretion by many species of a skeleton of calcium carbonate, a feature most marked in the reef-building corals. There are two distinct subclasses: Zoantharia (sea anemones and true corals) and Alcyonaria (sea pens, organ-pipe corals, sea fans, and so on).

1. Zoantharia. The tentacles of the sea anemones and true corals are simple (rarely branching), and like the septa occur in multiples of six.

The order Actiniaria (sea anemones) contains over 1000 species, possibly 100 of which occur in Australian waters. Though common on the seashore, they include some of the deepest-living of all animals, being found at a depth of 9000m. Solitary animals with a thick,

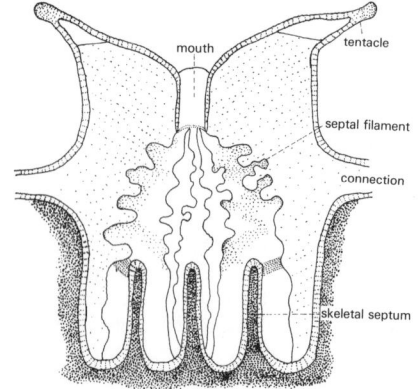

Section through a coral polyp

muscular body wall, most are firmly attached to the substrate (though able to move by gliding or somersaulting); some are free-floating, and a few live half-buried in sand or silt. The largest species grow to a diameter of about 30cm. The tentacles carry stinging and clinging nematocysts. They will eat most kinds of animals including fishes, though some fishes (*see* FISHES, BONY) and shrimps live safely within their tentacles. They reproduce sexually, by budding, or by cleaving into two. An easily recognised shore species is the small red Waratah anemone, *Actinia tenebrosa*, whose tentacles are lighter in colour than the rest of the body.

The true corals (various orders) are very similar to the anemones, but are colonial and secrete limestone skeletons.

2. Alcyonaria. Members of this subclass flourish in warm waters, especially on coral reefs. Often colonial, the species vary greatly in shape. The polyps are in a jelly-like mass into which they can contract, and which is supported by a network of limestone spicules (horny rods). Often uncovered by the tide, the polyps expand when the water returns.

In the organ-pipe corals, *Tubipora musica* (order Stolonifera), of the GREAT BARRIER REEF, the calcareous spicules fuse, forming a brick-red skeleton around the green polyps.

In the soft corals (order Alcyonacea) the bases of the polyps are fused in a mass, the spicules scattered within the tissues. Various species occur in the Great Barrier Reef; among them, the greenish or brownish convoluted masses of *Sarcophyton trocheliophorum* colonies often cover large areas of the reef. The luminescent *Cavernularia obesa* occurs in southern estuaries.

The gorgonians or horny corals (order Gorgonacea) include the rare precious coral of the Mediterranean, and are often brightly coloured in reds, yellows and browns. The skeletons of each colony, composed of horny material called gorgonin, arise from a single thick base connected to the substrate. The sea whip species have skeletons either unbranched (as in *Junceella*) or with relatively few branches (as in some of the family Ellisellidae); but the many branches of the sea fans interlace to form a lattice, often fan-shaped. Several genera of sea fans are found on the Great Barrier Reef. Unlike the soft corals which live in intertidal parts of the reefs, the gorgonians are found in deep water on the edge of the reefs, where the currents are strong.

Sea pens (order Pennatulacea) live in sandy areas with their swollen bases deeply embedded in the sand. The colony consists of one main polyp forming the central axis, with many small polyps at the side, the shape thus resembling an old-fashioned quill pen. Sea pens are more common in cold and temperate waters than in tropical seas.

Further reading: Hardy, Sir Alistair C. *The Open Sea, its Natural History.* Collins, London, 1956; Cleland, Sir John B. & Southcott, R.V. *Injuries to Man from Marine Invertebrates in the Australian Region.* (Special Report Series no 12) National Health & Medical

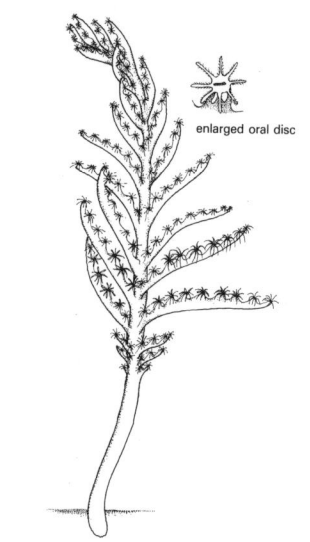

enlarged oral disc

A sea pen showing an enlarged oral disc

Research Council, Canberra, 1965; Stackhouse, J. *Australia's Venomous Wildlife.* Hamlyn, Sydney, 1970; Bennett, I. *The Fringe of the Sea.* (revd edn) Rigby, Adelaide, 1974; Dakin, W.J., Bennett, I. & Pope, E. *Australian Seashores.* (6th edn) Angus & Robertson, Sydney, 1976; Deas, W. *Corals of the Great Barrier Reef.* Ure Smith, Sydney, 1976; Sutherland, S.K. *Venomous Creatures of Australia: A Field Guide with Notes on First Aid.* Oxford University Press, Melbourne, 1981.

coelocanth This is a deep-water fish (*see* FISHES, BONY) belonging to a group thought to be extinct 90 million years ago, until its discovery in 1938 in the Indian Ocean in deep water near Madagascar. Since then other specimens have been caught near the Comoro Islands. The coelocanth, *Latimeria chalumnae*, belongs to the order Crossopterygii in the subclass Sarcopterygii (tassel-finned fishes); the Crossopterygii contained fish thought to be close to the ancestors of the AMPHIBIANS, and thus to all the land VERTEBRATES. The subclass also contains the order Dipnoi which includes the QUEENSLAND LUNG FISH and its American and African allies. Coelocanths have not yet been found on the Australian side of the Indian Ocean though it is possible that they occur in deep water off the continental shelf.

Coffs Harbour NSW (population 16 018 in 1981) A seaside town on the mid-NORTH COAST of the State, it is located on the Pacific Highway and the main N railway line, 584km by road and 608km by rail N of Sydney. The town really consists of two small urban centres: one is situated on the Pacific Highway; the other, called Jetty Town, about 2km E, is clustered around the railway station and the long wharf that juts out 600m into the man-made harbour. Coffs Harbour is a minor cargo port, handling timber and other produce from the adjacent rural region. Dairying and banana growing are the main farming pursuits on the alluvial coastal belt and nearby hill land. The district experiences mild temperatures throughout the year, with abundant summer sunshine, even though the months of heaviest rain are from January to March. The average yearly rainfall at Coffs Harbour is 1 759mm.

The region is a popular tourist resort and provides varied accommodation, diverse sporting facilities and opportunities for aquatic sports. It is scenically an attractive area. Coastal holiday resorts, such as SAWTELL to the S and Woolgoolga to the N, as well as small beach sites such as Arrawarra, Red Rock, Wooli and Mullaway, attract large numbers of visitors. The Yuraygir National Park (13 055ha) is located along the coastal zone N of Coffs Harbour and can be reached by several branch roads off the Pacific Highway; it contains a number of interesting landscape features: beaches and headlands, sand dunes and lagoons, and a tombolo (tied-island) at Station Creek headland.

Cohuna VIC (population 2 178 in 1981) This small country town is located on the Murray Valley Highway, 32km E of KERANG, 64km NW of ECHUCA, and 266km by road NNW of Melbourne. It is also a rail terminus of a branch line, off the route to Echuca, 298km by rail from Melbourne. The town is a service centre for a productive irrigation district, watered from the MURRAY RIVER by canal from the Yarrawonga Weir storage. The area is important for dairying, fodder crop cultivation and livestock grazing: the town has a large cheese factory. There have been some important discoveries of Aboriginal fossils in the district, including the 'Cohuna skull'.

Colac VIC (population 10 587 in 1981) A city located in the WESTERN DISTRICT on the Princes Highway, it is 150km by road SW of Melbourne, 76km from GEELONG and 45km E of CAMPERDOWN. It is situated on the S shores of Lake Colac, a shallow freshwater lake covering 40km² which serves as an aquatic playground for local residents and visitors. At an elevation of 134m above sea level it experiences a mild climate throughout the year with an average annual rainfall of 721mm, concentrated in winter and spring. The city is a market and commercial centre for a productive farming and grazing region noted for dairying, vegetables (especially potatoes and onions), oats, barley and flax. It has a number of secondary industries: clothing, butter making, flax processing, brick making and engineering. It is also a rail centre on the S route to WARRNAMBOOL, 153km from Melbourne. LAKE CORANGAMITE, the largest lake in VIC, lies NW of the city and there are numerous smaller lakes, mostly in volcanic craters, to the N. The district was settled by pastoralists in the late 1840s; the shire was proclaimed in 1864; it became a borough in 1938, a town in 1948 and a city in 1960. It takes its name from an Aboriginal word which means either 'a rosella parrot' or 'a freshwater lake'. The National Trust (VIC) has listed 10 buildings for preservation including the former National

Bank (1885-86), the shire hall and the post office (1876).

Coleoptera see beetles

Colleges of Advanced Education
see Appendix 4, Higher Educational Institutions; education

Collie WA (population 7 667 in 1981) The only commercial coalfield in WA is located in the middle section of the Collie River basin, with the town of Collie as its urban centre. It is about 200km SSE of Perth and 60km inland from BUNBURY. The town and river were named in honour of Alexander Collie who explored much of the SW of the State and was the first Government Resident at ALBANY from 1831 to 1833. At an elevation of 190m above sea level, the town is set in the midst of extensive jarrah forests and sheep grazing farms. The coal, mined since 1889, is near the surface and is extracted by open-cut methods; visitors can inspect the operations of the Muja Mine. Wellington Dam on the Collie River, downstream from the town, was originally constructed in 1933 to supply water to the Collie Irrigation District on the coastal plains E of Bunbury; between 1949 and 1956 a 129km pipeline was built from the dam to NARROGIN to provide water for towns and farms along the Great Southern Railway.

Collins, Dale (1897-1956) Journalist and author. He was born in Sydney, but was taken to TAS by his parents early in life and then from the age of 14 worked as a journalist in Melbourne. In 1922 he went with a wealthy American on a world cruise in the motor-yacht *Speejacks*, and in the following year published his first book, *Sea Tracks of the Speejacks Round the World*. For the following 25 years he lived in London, and during that time wrote many short stories for English and American magazines, and a number of novels, most of which were based on shipboard life or had Pacific island settings. They included *Ordeal* (1924), *The Haven* (1925) and *The Sentimentalists* (1927). His published works also include plays, books for children and two volumes of reminiscences. He returned to Australia in 1948, spending the rest of his life in Melbourne.

Collins, David (1756-1810) First Lieutenant-Governor of TAS (then VAN DIEMEN'S LAND). Born in London, he served in the British Marines from the age of 14, served in the American War of Independence, and rose to the rank of Captain. Appointed as the first Judge-Advocate of NSW, he arrived with the FIRST FLEET in 1788, stayed in Sydney until 1796 and then returned to England, where he wrote *An Account of the English Colony in New South Wales*, a work containing much valuable information not hitherto recorded. In 1802, on the recommendation of Governor KING, it was decided to found a convict settlement at PORT PHILLIP BAY, in order to forestall any possible French

plans to colonise southern Australia. Collins was appointed Lieutenant-Governor and arrived at Port Phillip with about 300 convicts and a few free settlers in October 1803. He made the mistake of landing on the sandy SE shore of the bay, near modern Sorrento; he failed to make a thorough search for better land, but decided that the district was unsuitable for settlement, and after a few months obtained King's permission to move to TAS. Reaching the DERWENT RIVER in February 1804 he chose the site of Hobart, where Lieutenant BOWEN's small party at RISDON COVE later joined him.

During his term in office conditions in Hobart were difficult. He had to rely on Sydney for supplies and on a number of occasions was forced to reduce food rations. Settlers charged with crimes too serious to be dealt with in a magistrate's court had to be sent to Sydney for trial, and all despatches from Britain came through Sydney. In 1809 the deposed Governor BLIGH appeared in the *Porpoise*. Having been released by his captors, he was hoping for Collins' help in regaining control in Sydney. Collins received him with respect, but declined to give him the support he expected. On hearing that a new Governor, Lachlan MACQUARIE, had reached Sydney,

David Collins

Mitchell Library

Bligh departed, and a few months later Collins died unexpectedly. St David's Cathedral, where he is buried, was later named in his honour. During his long term of office he had come under considerable criticism for lack of energy, wastefulness and loose morals. However, he evidently enjoyed the support and goodwill of the colonists over whom he was in authority; and he was undoubtedly a cultured and humane man, with a cheerful disposition which he maintained in spite of many setbacks.
Further reading: Giblin, R.W. *The Early History of Tasmania.* (vol I) Methuen, London, 1928; Rienits, R. *David Collins.* Oxford University Press, Melbourne, 1969.

Collins, Tom (1843-1912) Author. This was the pen-name used by Joseph Furphy. Born at Yering (now known as Yarra Glen) VIC, he lived at later stages of his boyhood at Kangaroo Ground and KYNETON. In adult life he worked as a threshing contractor, farmer and bullock driver, and in an iron foundry owned by his brother in SHEPPARTON. His major work, *Such Is Life* (1903), when first submitted to Alfred STEPHENS of the *Bulletin*, was very long; Stephens pruned it heavily and the material omitted from it was later incorporated in *Rigby's Romance*, which ran as a serial in the *Barrier Daily Truth* newspaper in 1904-1905 and was published in abridged form as a book in 1921, and in *The Buln-Buln and the Brolga* (1948). He also wrote a number of short stories for the *Bulletin*, and a quantity of verse which was collected and edited by Kate Baker and published under the title *This Poems of Joseph Furphy* (1916).

Such Is Life is set in northern VIC and in the RIVERINA district of NSW and is presented in the guise of a series of extracts from the pocket diaries of the narrator. Although classed as a novel, it has no connecting plot, but consists of loosely linked anecdotes and rambling reminiscences on a wide range of human affairs. The author himself described it with these words: 'temper: democratic; bias: offensively Australian'.

See also literature
Further reading: Franklin, M. & Baker, K. *Joseph Furphy: The Legend of a Man and His Book.* Angus & Robertson, Sydney, 1944.

Collinsville (population 2 756 in 1981) A coal-mining centre located in the Bowen River valley, between the Clarke and Leichhardt Ranges, it is 85km SW of BOWEN and some 1 360km by road NNW of Brisbane. Mechanised open-cut and underground mining is carried out in the Collinsville-Scottsdale region, the coal then being railed to the Bowen coking plant. The Collinsville thermal power plant, one of the State's largest, uses local coal; the power station receives its water supplies from Eungella Dam on the Broken River, a headwater tributary of the BURDEKIN RIVER system. Collinsville is also a cattle selling centre and the railhead for grazing properties in the district.

Colombo Plan This scheme was initiated in 1950, following a meeting of Commonwealth of Nations ministers in Colombo, at which Sir Percy SPENDER of Australia suggested the starting of a co-operative scheme for helping in the economic development of Commonwealth members and dependent territories is South and South-East Asia. A Consultative Committee, consisting of representatives of Australia, Canada, Ceylon (now Sri Lanka), India, Pakistan, New Zealand and the UK, met in Sydney in May 1950, and requested that six-year development programmes be submitted by the Asian members and for British dependent territories. At a second meeting in London in September such programmes were submitted by India, Pakistan, Ceylon, Malaya, Singapore, North Borneo (now Sabah) and Sarawak, and were used as a basis for planning towards economic co-operation between these states, and for the giving of aid in the form of grants, loans and technical advice and training by the developed nations.

Scene from the opening parade of the 1982 Commonwealth Games in Brisbane

Premier's Dept. QLD

The plan soon spread beyond the limits of the Commonwealth of Nations. The USA and Japan joined as donor nations in 1951 and 1954 respectively, and by the latter date most countries of South-East Asia had joined as recipient members. At present the Consultative Committee meets yearly and a Council for Technical Co-operation meets several times a year in Colombo. A small permanent organisation, the Colombo Plan Bureau, is maintained in Colombo. Australia's financial contribution up to mid-1975 totalled $A359 million, excluding aid given through the Plan to Papua New Guinea. By that date she had also, as part of the Plan, sent over 4000 technical experts to Asian countries and given training to over 15 000 students and others.

comb jellies *see* ctenophores

common reed *see* Gramineae

Commonwealth Film Censorship Board *see* film

Commonwealth Film Unit *see* film

Commonwealth Games (formerly known as the British Empire and Commonwealth Games) The Commonwealth Games follow the Olympic model in that only amateur athletes may compete, and that, like the Olympic Games, they are held every fourth year (midway between Olympics). The first Games of this sort were held in 1911, when athletes from Australasia, Britain, Canada and South Africa competed in a 'Festival of Empire' which was part of the celebrations to mark the coronation of King George V. There was a break of 19 years before the next Games were held in 1930 in Hamilton, Canada. These were the first British Empire Games, later renamed Commonwealth Games, which have since been

held regularly every four years, except during World War II. The Games were held for the first time in Australia in 1938, in Sydney, as part of the celebrations for Australia's 150th Anniversary. Of the Games held up to 1982, Australia has been overall winner of five of them. At the 1982 Games held in Brisbane, the UK headed the list of medal winners, with a total of 108 medals (38 gold, 38 silver and 32 bronze); Australia was second with 107 medals (39 gold, 39 silver and 29 bronze). Of the 39 gold medals won by Australians, 13 were in swimming events, nine were in athletics and seven were in shooting events. A list of Australian gold medallists is given in Appendix 9, Australian Gold Medallists in Commonwealth Games.

Commonwealth Scientific and Industrial Research Organization (CSIRO) The CSIRO is Australia's leading scientific research institution. Funded in the main by direct grant from the Commonwealth government, the CSIRO, in 1981-82, employed some 7 400 scientists and support-staff in laboratories scattered all over the country. Although the CSIRO is active in some fields of pure research such as radio astronomy, its main task has been to support Australian primary and secondary industry.

The origins of the CSIRO date back to 1916 when Prime Minister W.M. HUGHES initiated the formation of an Institute for Science and Industry to work on the problems besetting Australian primary industry. Although this body eventually failed through lack of finance and political support, something of value was achieved in this initial period, including the first moves towards the eradication of the PRICKLY PEAR, a pest on valuable grazing lands since its introduction in the mid-19th century (*see* BIOLOGICAL CONTROL). Ten years later the political climate was more conducive to success. Australia's role as a supplier of raw materials made improvements in the efficiency of primary industry vital. Attempts to revive the dying Institute, together with a report on the state of research in Australia compiled by a British expert, Sir Frank Heath, resulted in the establishment of the Council for Scientific and Industrial Research (CSIR) in 1926, the foundation continuing under this name until 1940.

Much of the early success of the CSIR in working on problems affecting agricultural and pastoral industries was a consequence of the support given to the fledgling organisation by Prime Minister S.M. BRUCE, and of the high quality of the men chosen to lead it. George Julius, a prominent Sydney businessman and consulting engineer, was its first chairman; Dr David Rivett left a highly valued post as Professor of Chemistry at the University of Melbourne to become Chief Executive Officer; and the third member of the Executive was the distinguished agricultural scientist Professor A.E.V. Richardson. Work of great value was done in the 1920s, and included research into virus diseases in tobacco and pleuro-pneumonia in cattle; an attack on the problems of transporting fruit and chilled meat to British markets; and studies on the propagation of radio waves, a matter of vital concern if Australia's vast distances were to be bridged by telecommunications.

In the mid-1930s, the problems of secondary industry were taken up, with the establishment of a National Standards Laboratory, a Division of Industrial Chemistry and an Aeronautical Laboratory. This work gained rapidly in importance with the approach of World War II and the CSIR played a major part in the war effort with research in many fields, including scientific study of lubricants and bearings, work on the preservation of foodstuffs to be transported into battle zones, and the development of radar.

In the immediate post-war period, the CSIR experienced some difficulty in making a transition back to a peace-time role. The problems were aggravated by the untimely retirement and death of Julius at the end of the war, differences of opinion over the importance of secret defence work in the research programme and allegations that the CSIR was employing known communists.

By 1949, all secret work had ceased and legislation had been passed setting up a new body (CSIRO) to take over the tasks of the CSIR. Rivett retired soon afterwards. CSIRO chairmen in recent years have been Sir Ian Clunies Ross (1949-59), Sir Frederick White (1959-70), Sir Robert Price (1970-77), V.D. Burgmann (1977-78) and Dr J.P. Wild (1978-).

The CSIRO's contribution to the growth of knowledge and the development of technology has been of great benefit to Australian industry. Some of the highlights of research within the CSIRO in the 1960s and 1970s were: the extension of expertise gained in wartime radar development into new fields, including radio astronomy, cloud physics and rain-making; the development of landing aids for aircraft (including the highly successful INTERSCAN system, adopted for worldwide use by the International Civil Aviation Organisation); research into the use of the virus disease MYXOMATOSIS to control rabbits; a series of developments in textile processing such as shrink-proofing, moth-proofing and the 'Siroset' permanent pleating process that greatly enhanced the reputation of wool and increased its competitiveness against synthetic fibres; work on biological control, the use of natural predators and parasites to control plant and insect pests; and the development of such devices as the Atomic Absorption Spectrophotometer, the self-twist spinning machine and the 'Sirotherm' water purifier, which have earned many millions of dollars in sales and royalties. There are very few areas of agriculture that have not benefited from such studies; fundamental research has been done on the nature of soils, on land use and management, pastures and animal husbandry, and major contributions have been made to the industrial and environmental problems of mining industries.

The first major enquiry into the CSIRO was conducted in 1976, shortly after the 50th anniversary of the founding of CSIR, and it was found to be functioning well, needing only a few administrative changes to prepare it for many more years of service to Australian industry and the Australian people.
Further reading: Surprise and Enterprise: Fifty Years of Science in Australia. CSIRO, Melbourne, 1976.

Communism in Australia

In 1983 the three most prominent Marxist organisations in Australia were the Communist Party of Australia, the Socialist Party of Australia and the Socialist Workers' Party. Smaller Marxist groups included the International Socialists, the Socialist Labour League, the Spartacist League of Australia and New Zealand and the Communist Party of Australia (Marxist-Leninist).

The original Communist Party of Australia was founded on 30 October 1920 by 25 socialists inspired by the Russian revolution of 1917 and encouraged by the Bolshevik Consul in Australia. The early policy of the Communist Party was to gain support in the trade union movement by joining the AUSTRALIAN LABOR PARTY (ALP), the aim being gradually to replace the latter body. In 1922 the Communist Party affiliated itself to the Communist International (Comintern) and made itself formally subordinate to the Moscow-based Comintern with the intention of carrying out the mission of this organisation to change the world by predicted world revolution. The ALP became alarmed, terminated its co-operation with the Communist Party, and declared that no Communist could join the ALP.

In order to make the Communist Party a highly centralised body which could demand unswerving loyalty from its followers, a number of Australians were trained in Moscow and by 1933 the Moscow-trained personnel took over the leadership of the Communist Party of Australia. These men, J.B. Miles, L.L. Sharkey and R. Dixon, remodelled the party structure along the Moscow lines and insisted that the leaders' orders must be followed without dissent. Political committees were established to lead factory units and all members declared loyalty to the Party Secretary (J.B. Miles, 1931-48, and L.L. Sharkey, 1948-65).

The association with Moscow was a great disadvantage to acceptance of the Communist Party in Australia because the ideas and policies initiated in Moscow were of no relevance to the local situation, and indeed were recognised as a great hindrance to Australia during the Depression. Australia's recovery from the Depression depended on foreign investment, a policy strongly denounced by the Communist Party, following the Moscow lines. In effect, their denunciation channelled workers into the ALP rather than into the Communist Party. The Communist Party tried to counter this trend by announcing its willingness to co-operate with the ALP but unfortunately for the Communists, Moscow signed a non-aggression pact with Nazi Germany and this ended the Labor Party co-operation; indeed, between 1940 and 1942 the Communist Party was banned under wartime emergency powers, being regarded as a menace to Australia and the agent of a foreign power.

The revival of the Communist Party as a socially acceptable organisation occurred in 1945 when the USSR entered World War II on the Allies' side. It was then that a Communist-endorsed candidate, Fred Paterson, was elected to the QLD State Parliament. Although the Communist Party has endorsed candidates at both federal and State elections since 1920, Fred Paterson has been their only candidate elected.

Trade unions While the Communist Party has never been a power in government, it has had a powerful influence on trade unions, an influence at its height between 1948 and 1966. In 1948 more than 300 trade union leaders were also members of the Communist Party. The ALP responded to the Communist challenge in the trade union movement by establishing Industrial Groups, which were also supported by the Catholic Social Movement (*see* ROMAN CATHOLIC CHURCH). At the height of its power the Communist Party almost gained complete control of the AUSTRALIAN COUNCIL OF TRADE UNIONS (ACTU) and in 1965 there were more than 620 Communists holding key positions in the trade union movement. By the 1970s this figure was reduced to approximately 200 Communist members who were now split up into three different and mutually hostile groups.

Divisions The first major split in the Communist Party of Australia occurred in 1963 when E.F. Hill announced his support for the Chinese Communist Party and his opposition to the Moscow line. He formed the Communist Party of Australia (Marxist-Leninist) which was based in VIC and supported by a few VIC trade unions and militant action at VIC universities.

In 1968 the Communist Party of Australia denounced the crushing of Czechoslovakia by the USSR and this tended to reduce the Moscow influence of the party. After this break with Moscow the party displayed friendship with the Italian, Yugoslavian and Romanian Communist Parties—all with a world reputation for being anti-Moscow. These anti-Moscow policies led to a second split in the original party. This occurred on 5 December 1971 when many top trade union officials, including Pat Clancy, the only Communist on the ACTU executive, left the party and formed the Moscow-oriented Socialist Party of Australia.

Since 1968 the original Communist Party of Australia has tried to adopt a more democratic party structure and new policies. The activities of one of its members, Jack Mundey, has received a great deal of publicity and found new followers among both workers and students.

Although the Socialist Party of Australia has survived into the 1980s it too has had its internal conflicts. A recent one between its president, Pat Clancy, and the chairman of its Central Committee, Jack McPhillips, led to the resignation of some Greek party members and some members of the Seamen's Union. The party is still closely focused on Moscow and runs competitions with prizes being a trip for two to the Soviet Union. Its policy is strongly anti-USA, it advocates the removal of the USA military bases from Australian soil and it wants to end USA alliances.

The Socialist Workers Party was formed in January, 1972. It traces its political origin from the dispute within world communism, and claims to follow the policies of Trotsky as the political heir to Lenin rather than the policies of Stalin. The Party regards Cuba as providing an example of the sort of government and society it would like to see operating in Australia.

In 1983 the publications of the various Communist groups were: Communist Party of Australia—*Tribune*, a weekly newspaper, and *Australian Left Review*, a journal; Socialist Party Australia—*The Socialist* and *Youth Voice*, fortnightly newspapers, and *Australian Marxist Review*, a journal; Socialist Workers' Party—*Direct Action* and *Resistance*, weekly newspapers, and *Socialist Worker*, a journal; Socialist Labour League—*Workers' News*, a twice-weekly newspaper; and the Spartacist League of Australia and New Zealand—*Australian Spartacist*, a weekly newspaper. The Communist Party of Australia (Marxist-Leninist) has published the *Vanguard* and the *Australian Communist*.
Further reading: Davidson, A. *The Communist Party of Australia: A Short History.* Hoover Institution Press, Stanford, 1969; Taft, M. 'Communism in Australia' and Wells, F. 'The Communist Parties of Australia' in Mayer, H. & Nelson, H. (eds) *Australian Politics.*

Cheshire, Melbourne 1973; Costar, B.J. '. . . and then there were three: the 1971 split in the Communist Party of Australia' in Lucy, R. (ed) *The Pieces of Politics.* Macmillan, South Melbourne, 1975; O'Brien, G. 'Revolution . . . they're working on it on the fringe' in *Sydney Morning Herald*, 15 November 1982.

Compositae This is the largest family of flowering plants in the world, with some 1000 genera containing 20 000 species of herbs, shrubs and trees distributed throughout the world. The Compositae (also called the daisy family) includes a large number of ornamental plants, such as *Aster, Zinnia, Dahlia, Cosmos, Tagetes* (marigold), *Chrysanthemum* and *Cineraria*. It also contains many edible and economically important plants, including endive, *Cichorium endivia*; lettuce, *Lactuca sativa*; artichoke, *Cynara scolymus*; Jerusalem artichoke, *Helianthus tuberosus*; and sunflower, *H. annuus.* A natural insecticide, pyrethrum, is made from the crushed flower heads of *Chrysanthemum cinerariae-folium.* Large shrubby species include *Olearia, Cassinea* and *Bedfordia.* Smaller shrubs include species of *Olearia, Vittadinia, Calocephalus* and *Senecio.* By far the largest number of genera are perennial or annual herbs, and include *Sonchus, Taraxacum, Hypochoeris, Crepis, Centaurea, Cirsium, Senecio, Cotula, Achillea, Lagenophera* and *Erigeron.* Among all the horticultural Compositae introduced from other countries, a place has now been found for native members of the family, particularly members of *Helichrysum* and *Helipterum*, known as everlasting or paper daisies because of their ability to last indefinitely as dried flowers.

The leaves of the Compositae plants are usually alternate, sometimes opposite, and often basal; they are simple or compound, and have no stipules. The inflorescence is either a solitary head, in several heads or in corymbs and panicles. Each head is surrounded by one or more rows of bracts which are green or coloured, papery or fleshy, and sometimes have spines. The flowers are bisexual or unisexual. The calyx is either represented by a pappus or is absent; the pappus may consist of fine bristles, hairs, scales, barbs, horns or spines. Each head is composed of many florets; those in the centre may be tubular disc florets, while the outer florets, which extend from the centre, are strap-shaped ray florets which may be sometimes bent back. There are five stamens, joined round the style. The single-seeded ovary has two styles and two stigmas; the fruit is dry, with a hard outer covering.

Members of the family Compositae are widespread in temperate Australian plant communities, such as woodlands and open forests, but are particularly abundant in sub-alpine communities and in the short-lived FLORA of the arid regions. Many species fulfill the same role in natural communties as WEEDS do in agricultural ecosystems, in that they are excellent, fast colonisers of disturbed ground. Their abundant seed production and varied

Boneseed, *Chrysanthemoides monilifera*

dispersal mechanisms and their long viability in the soil contribute to this colonising ability, and combine with dormancy mechanisms to enable them to survive in unpredictable or highly variable environments, such as arid or alpine regions. The short-lived herbs which bloom in the desert after rain include a large number of Compositae.

Compositae are also well adapted to become weeds. Many species which have been introduced into Australia, usually accidentally, are now common weeds, both of agricultural and natural communities. Dandelions (*Taraxacum* and *Hypochoeris* species), cobblers peg (*Bidens* species) and cudweed (*Gnaphalium* species) are familiar examples; skeleton weed, *Chondrilla juncea*, was one of the worst weed threats ever posed to Australia's wheat farms, and ragwort, *Senecio jacobea*, now widespread in TAS, is poisonous to stock. Boneseed or bitou bush, *Chrysanthemoides monilifera*, now a serious weed of coastal communities in E Australia, was purposefully introduced to stabilise dunes after they had been mined for mineral sands; it is distributed by birds as it has a fleshy fruit (drupe), unlike all the dry-fruited Australian species.
See also Angiospermae; Appendix 5, Flower Structure and Glossary of Botanical Terms
Further reading: see Appendix 6, A Bibliography for Plants.

Condamine River QLD Located in the SE of the State, the Condamine rises on the W slopes of the GREAT DIVIDING RANGE and flows first in a NW direction across the DARLING DOWNS, then makes a great arc to flow W and SW, changes its name to become the BALONNE RIVER, and thence joins the DARLING RIVER system in NSW. The upper tributaries have their headwaters in the MAIN and BUNYA Ranges, E and SE of WARWICK, where the yearly rainfall exceeds 1000mm. Since the annual pattern of rain shows a marked summer concentration, the Condamine is liable to flood during the wet season and to flow only intermittently in its lower reaches during the drier months of the year. The Leslie Dam on Sandy Creek, about 8km above its confluence with the Condamine, was completed in 1965; it has a storage capacity of 107 310ML and provides irrigation for crops including lucerne, cotton, maize, wheat and sorghum, as well as for pasture lands along the riverine flats downstream. The main river flows for some 700km, numerous non-perennial streams contributing to its flow in the middle and lower sections. The main urban centres within the valley are Warwick, DALBY and ROMA. The Warrego Highway cuts across the basin from TOOWOOMBA to beyond Roma; the Moonie Highway traverses it on a NE-SW route from Dalby; the Cunningham Highway crosses the upper reaches at Warwick.

Conder, Charles (1868-1909) Artist. Born in London, Conder arrived in Australia as an adolescent in 1884. He started his working life as a surveyor, but began painting almost simultaneously, attending night classes at the Royal Art Society's School in Sydney. His first success came when he was 20, when the Art Gallery of New South Wales purchased his work, *Departure of the SS 'Orient'*, which drew attention to his relaxed and competent skills. The influences of both Julian ASHTON and Girolamo NERLI show in his work, with its mild flirtation with Impressionism. Moving to Melbourne in 1888, he joined Tom ROBERTS, Frederick McCUBBIN and Arthur STREETON at the Box Hill camp, as well as sharing Roberts' studio and painting with him at Mentone. His work at this stage showed a greater interest in brightness and light. By the time he left Australia in 1890 to study in Europe, Conder was beginning to become interested in symbolism and the flowing lines of art nouveau. In Europe he soon became known as one of the European aesthetes, enjoying the company of Toulouse Lautrec, Max Beerbohm, J.M. Whistler, Aubrey Beardsley, William Rothenstein and Oscar Wilde. Although he achieved recognition as an associate of the Société Nationale des Beaux Arts in 1893, and his work was widely acclaimed in Europe during his life, he is not considered to have produced any significant work in this period. His most interesting work was done in Australia. He died at Virginia Water near London.

Condobolin NSW (population 3 355 in 1981) A country town in the central-W region of the State, it is located on the Lachlan River, 473km by road WNW of Sydney and 106km W of PARKES. It is situated on the Lachlan Valley Way and on the main W railway route to BROKEN HILL, at an elevation of 189m above sea level. The average annual rainfall of 439mm falls fairly evenly throughout the year. The district is noted for the production of wool, wheat, cattle and pigs. The town name comes from an Aboriginal word meaning 'hop rush'.

cone shells *see* gastropods

conesticks *see* Proteaceae

Confederation of Australian Industry *see* employers' associations

Congregational Church Congregationalists were originally known as Independents, because in Britain in the sixteenth century they founded independent congregations in protest against what they saw as the over-centralised government of other Churches. From 1798 a number of their clergymen held occasional services in Sydney, but it was 1833 before a chapel was built there and a continuing congregation established under the Rev. William Jarrett. In the meantime the Rev. Frederick Miller had established a congregation in Hobart in 1830. By the mid-1850s there were congregations in all Australian colonies and in the Moreton Bay District (later QLD).

Since Congregationalists believe in the complete separation of church and state, they refused to accept government grants for the support of their ministers or the building of their chapels. They also supported the establishment of national systems of education. They have never comprised a large portion of the Australian population, but have exerted an influence out of proportion to their numbers. They have tended to be active in public affairs, and in professions such as politics and journalism which exercise an influence on public opinion. They have been notable too for enlightened biblical scholarship and criticism, and in the twentieth century have been among the leaders in moves for interdenominational union. In 1977 most Congregationalists merged with METHODISTS and PRESBYTERIANS to form the UNITING CHURCH IN AUSTRALIA. In the census of the preceding year, 53 455 Australians had been identified as Congregationalists.

conifers *see* forestry; fossils; Gymnospermae

conscription Military conscription has been a highly controversial issue at two stages of Australian history, namely 1916-17 and 1965-72. In each case the matter at issue was conscription for active service outside Australia and its territories. Compulsory military training in time of peace for the purpose of building up a reserve of trained men, as introduced in 1910, and conscription in time of war for service within Australia and its territories, as authorised by the Defence Acts of 1903 and 1904, and practised on a large scale during World War II, has not aroused widespread opposition.

World War I The attempts of Prime Minister William HUGHES to introduce conscription for overseas service in 1916 and 1917, and the split in the AUSTRALIAN LABOR PARTY (ALP) caused by this move, are described in the biographical article on Hughes and in the entry on POLITICAL HISTORY. The case for conscription rested on the belief that the Australian divisions on the Western Front should be kept up to full strength, so ensuring that Australia would continue to maintain her share of the Allies' war effort. Opposition to conscription derived from a number of factors, including a general objection to the principle of compulsion and a belief that the very creditable performance of the AUSTRALIAN IMPERIAL FORCE (AIF) was largely the result of its being an entirely voluntary force. A decline in real wages caused many Labor supporters to believe that the working class was contributing an undue share towards the war effort, and should not have to bear the extra burden of compulsory service; many Irish Australians, for whom Archbishop MANNIX was a very effective spokesman, were bitter at the failure of Britain to grant home rule to Ireland, and therefore begrudged support; many parents were unwilling for their sons to experience the horrors of the Western Front unless through an act of free choice; and farmers objected to losing more of their labour force. The outcome was a very even division of public opinion, the referendum voting figures being 1 087 557 for and 1 160 033 against conscription in 1916 and 1 015 159 for and 1 181 747 against in 1917.

World War II In the earlier stages of World War II, only troops of the volunteer AIF were sent to the Middle East, but conscripts of the militia took part in the fighting in the territories of Papua and New Guinea. Then, as land operations against the Japanese moved further N, the question of whether the militia should be used beyond Australia's territories became a strongly debated issue, especially in the ALP. However, at the 1942 Federal Conference of the party, Prime Minister CURTIN obtained backing for the sending of conscripts to 'other territories in the South-West Pacific associated with the defence of Australia'. In the following year the Defence Act was amended accordingly, to allow conscription for service within a specified zone extending as far N as the equator.

Conscription by ballot Compulsory military training lapsed after the end of the war, but was reintroduced on a limited basis by the National Service Act of 1951. This provided

THUMBS DOWN!

A pro-conscription cartoon

An anti-conscription poster, 1916

for training courses of a maximum duration of six months, for 18-year-olds, and did not arouse very strong public opposition. However, in 1965 a new scheme was introduced, with the object not only of creating a trained reserve, but also of building up the strength of the Australian Regular Army. Registration of 20-year-olds was compulsory, and men were selected from the registers by a type of ballot based on dates of birth. Subject to health and other suitability tests, they were conscripted into the army for two years, with the obligation of serving overseas if required. Service in the part-time CITIZEN MILITARY FORCES (CMF) was accepted as an alternative.

Opposition to this scheme mounted from 1966, when national servicemen were first sent to Vietnam. The ALP and many other organisations and individuals campaigned against it, and as the scale of military operations in Vietnam increased there were many protest demonstrations. Many young men refused to register, or to report for service when selected, and some were gaoled as a consequence. On this occasion the traditional objections to conscription were bolstered by the belief among many Australians that their country's participation in the VIETNAM WAR was unjustified. Among the first acts of the WHITLAM government, elected in December 1972, were the release of national servicemen from the army and the repeal of the National Service Act. No form of compulsory military training or service has since been introduced.
Further reading: Forward, R. & Reece, B. *Conscription in Australia.* Queensland University Press, St Lucia QLD, 1968; Main, J.M. (ed) *Conscription: The Australian Debate, 1901-70.* Cassell Australia, North Melbourne VIC, 1970.

conservation The conservation of natural resources may be described as the wise use of resources, using those that are exhaustible with due regard to the needs of future generations, and ensuring that potentially renewable resources are renewed. This article deals mainly with the conservation of animal resources and VEGETATION; other aspects of conservation are dealt with in the entries on AGRICULTURE, IRRIGATION and ENVIRONMENT.

Vegetation conservation has two not always compatible aspects; economic conservation aims at the maximum *sustained* production of selected foods and fibres; nature conservation aims to preserve natural communities of associated plants, animals and other organisms, without primary consideration for their economic value. Yet there are sound economic reasons for the conservation of such communities. The first is to maintain standards of native vegetation against which change can be measured: such reference points are important in the reclamation of marginal areas, such as certain unproductive areas in western NSW now being restored by the reintroduction of saltbushes. A second reason is the necessity to preserve as many natural communities as pos-

sible for ecological study leading to a greater understanding of natural ecosystems.

Although there are more than 12 000 known native species of vascular plants in Australia, about 85 per cent of them endemic, many species remain to be discovered. Of 25 common species of trees found by botanists in the 1960s in a small area of QLD rainforest that was being cleared, three were unknown to science. It is possible that some species will have disappeared, and that others will be threatened with extinction, before we have learnt of their existence or their potentialities. Besides their intrinsic individual value, natural plant communities may serve important practical uses: they may be regarded as a huge genetic bank from which new material can be drawn to improve existing cultivars; previously uncultivated species may be found useful as food (the only native Australian plant to be thus adopted, so far, is the macadamia nut); many plants may yield chemicals—421 previously unknown biologically active compounds were discovered in an examination of 4000 native plants by the Australian Phytochemical Survey (1969), at least one of which showed some promise for the treatment of leukaemia.

Development and BUSHFIRES pose the most significant threat to existing plant communities. On the whole, the Australian FLORA (individual varieties of plants present in any given region) does not appear to have changed greatly apart from the establishment of several hundred exotic species, but it is impossible to say how many species have disappeared since European colonisation; moreover, it is clear that many species have a much smaller range now, because of the encroachment of agriculture, forestry and urbanisation. As opposed to the flora, Australian vegetation (plant life in general) has undergone extensive change. In the arid and semi-arid zone, great tracts of spinifex hummock grassland and saltbush country, which evolved beside native grazers without sharp hooves, have suffered severely from the selective grazing of domestic stock and the depredations of feral camels and rabbits. Elsewhere, natural communities exist only in patches, and exploited country is also deteriorating: thousands of hectares of open woodland show little or no regeneration, and even the younger trees are suffering from dieback apparently caused by chafer beetles, which have reproduced freely as a result of partial clearing.

Clearly the reservation of large areas as NATIONAL PARKS and floral reserves representing all the major types of natural vegetation in the continent is of great importance.
Animal conservation is of course interdependent with that of vegetation, and is important for similar reasons. It requires an accurate knowledge of the existing FAUNA, and of the past status of the various species. Since no species is immortal, eventual extinction being probable even without the influence of man, some species were probably declining when Europeans came to Australia; possibly these will disappear despite conservation

efforts. Other species, now restricted to small areas because of the destruction of their habitats, are more viable, and are likely to respond better to conservation attempts.

Yet little is known about the biology and ecology of most Australian wildlife, and the records of the past and present distribution and status of species are limited—some animals are known only from one or two specimens collected during the 19th century or earlier in this century, notably the broad-faced rat kangaroo, *Potorous platyops* (represented in collections by only eight specimens taken between 1842 and 1875), and the desert hare wallaby, *Lagorchestes asomatus* (known only from a single skull collected in the NT in 1932). Some animals thought to be extinct have been rediscovered by recent expeditions (for example, the night PARROT, *Geopsittacus occidentalis*, in 1979, and the parma wallaby, *Macropus parma*, in several places since the 1960s). Evidently the recorded distribution of many animals in Australia reflects the sparse distribution of trained field zoologists rather than the actual distribution of the animals. Many of the animals being small, nocturnal, arboreal and cryptically coloured, they are rarely seen by the casual observer.

Though surprisingly few species of vertebrates have disappeared since the arrival of Europeans, many must be considered to be in peril, and many have far smaller ranges than before. Many of the smaller marsupials have become rare, and are now restricted to a few offshore islands of small colonies in wildlife sanctuaries. The numbat, *Myrmecobius fasciatus*, once found throughout southern Australia, now survives only in the Wandoo forests of south-western WA, which unfortunately cover shallow bauxite deposits. As numbats live in hollow logs, it is probable that the burning-off of ground rubbish to prevent forest fires has led to their decline.

Nevertheless, many species of wildlife have apparently benefited from the same conditions. Judging from the journals of early explorers, very few of the large kangaroos were seen in some areas where large mobs are now common; the increase is due to the clearing of forest and woodland and the provision of water and improved pasture for stock. During the drought of 1979-83, red kangaroos were decidedly pests in some areas. Again, seed-eating birds (notably the galah, *Eolophus roseicapilla*) thrive on cultivated crops, and the fruit-eating brush-tailed possum is now common in some large cities, often living in the roofs of suburban houses.
Conservation techniques today aim at the provision of reserves where conditions allow native plants and animals to maintain their normal roles in that ecosystem, protected from development and from invasion by exotic organisms (such as feral cats, goats and pigs) which would destroy them or their habitats, and thence, their ecosystems. Reserves must also be large enough to be self-perpetuating, to be able to regenerate and for organisms from another section to re-invade, for instance, an

area burnt out by a bushfire.

Yet reserves pose their own problems: they do not accommodate migratory and nomadic animals (such as fruit-eating pigeons), which would require areas too vast; they must usually compromise the need for protection with the legitimate wishes of the public to visit them; they invariably require some management (if only the destruction of exotic organisms), which in itself may have important long-term ecological effects; and frequently, sites suitable for reserves (such as the coastal wetlands needed by inland waterfowl during prolonged droughts) are favoured for development by business interests.

Government agencies take responsibility for conservation through both the individual States and the Commonwealth. Although there is unfortunately little money available for studies to fill the gaps in our knowledge, the Commonwealth has set up the Australian Biological Resources Interim Council to channel funds for research on the taxonomy and ecology of Australian fauna and flora; and centres are being established for the storage and retrieval of biological resources data on a national basis. The Commonwealth also provides the services of various divisions of the CSIRO, and it exercises some influence by its ability to control the export of organisms or their products.

Conservation within each State is the responsibility of its government, and so there is considerable variety in administration from State to State: in some cases conservation is the function of a separate department, in others it falls under an area such as agriculture which may have conflicting interests, or it may be combined with the administration of national parks and reserves. The Council of Conservation Ministers, advised by various committees on flora and fauna, co-ordinates the activities of the States; such means of collaboration are potentially useful for the conservation of nomadic or migratory species.

Numerous conservation societies and organisations, of which the best known is the Australian Conservation Council, are open to public membership.

See also Appendix 7, Animals Extinct or Rare since 1788
Further reading: Webb, L.J., Whitelock, D. & Brereton, J. le Gay *The Last of Lands: Conservation in Australia.* Jacaranda, Milton QLD, 1969; Martin, A. *Pollution and Conservation in Australia.* Lansdowne, Melbourne, 1971; *Wildlife Conservation: Report from the House of Representatives Select Committee.* Australian Govt. Publishing Service, Canberra, 1972; Routley, R. & Routley, V. *The Fight for the Forests.* Research School of Social Sciences Australian National University, Canberra, 1973; Costin, A.B. & Frith, H.J. (eds) *Conservation.* Penguin Books, Ringwood VIC, 1974; Frith, H.J. *Waterfowl in Australia.* (2nd edn) Reed, Sydney, 1977; Tyler, M.J. (ed) *The Status of Endangered Australasian Wildlife: Proceedings of the Centenary Symposium of the Royal Zoological Society of South Australia.* RZS of SA Inc., Adelaide, 1979.

Constitution of Australia *see* government of Australia

Consumer Price Index Since the early years of this century, the Commonwealth Statistician has collected information regarding the retail prices of food and groceries and average rentals of houses, and since 1923 prices of a more extensive range of goods and services have been included. Such statistics have been used, according to a number of different systems, to measure variations in the cost of living for an average family. The current system, the Consumer Price Index, was first published in 1960. It measures quarterly changes in the price of a set of goods and services which account for the bulk of expenditure by the families of metropolitan wage and salary earners. The term 'indexation' is used for any procedure of adjusting salaries and wages or pensions in accordance with the CPI.

continental drift The land masses of the world have not always occupied their modern positions on the surface of the earth; once they were all united in a vast supercontinent called Pangaea, which about 200 million years ago divided into two to become: Laurasia, consisting of modern North America and Eurasia to the N, and GONDWANALAND, containing the remaining land masses, to the S. They were, however, still linked in the area that was to become the Straits of Gibraltar. Eventually the two smaller supercontinents themselves fragmented and slowly drifted (at rates of a few centimetres each year) to their present positions. The continents are, however, still on the move and the outline above describes, apparently, the latest cycle in a series of formations and disruptions of supercontinents.

The theory of continental drift was first advanced to help explain the distribution of various groups of plants and animals, the correspondence of the coasts of Africa and South America and the great similarity in sequences of rock strata at places now separated by vast stretches of ocean. Geologists were, however, reluctant to accept the theory for there was no known mechanism for the movement of large continents over the surface of the globe. But during the past 30 years much more evidence has been collected, and the reality of continental drift has been generally accepted.

The outer shell of the earth is divided into several large plates and many small ones. These are moved individually on the semi-fluid layer beneath. At some places (oceanic troughs), one plate is diving beneath its neighbour. At other places along the boundaries of plates (the mid-oceanic ridges), semi-molten material rises to the surface, pushing the old ocean bed apart and forming a new oceanic floor as it solidifies. At yet other places, such as the San Andreas Fault in California and in parts of New Zealand, one plate slides jerkily by its neighbour, causing earthquakes as it does so.

The plates consist of an area of oceanic floor composed of dense rocks, with rafts of lighter rocks, the continents, floating upon them. When two continents come together one does not slide beneath the other. Instead they collide, throwing up huge mountain chains such as the Himalayas as they do so. Eventually the two continents grind to a relative halt. Australia stands on the large Indo-Australian plate which is being renewed at ridges to the S and the W. Its oceanic troughs are the Java, the New Hebrides, the Kermadec-Tonga and the Macquarie Trenches. India, once part of Gondwanaland, has collided with the Laurasian/Eurasian land mass, throwing up the Himalayas. The spread of the ocean floors outwards from the mid-oceanic ridges has been demonstrated by the patterns of magnetisation in the rocks on each side of the ridges, and by the comparative youth of the oceanic floors.

The new science of 'plate tectonics' (the study of the structure and behaviour of the plates) has helped to explain the nature and distribution of volcanoes and earthquakes. Australia is fortunate in that it is far from the boundaries of its plate and is thus tectonically stable.

See also geology
Further reading: Calder, N. *Restless Earth.* Angus & Robertson, Sydney, 1972; Raven, P.H. 'An introduction to continental drift' in *Australian Natural History.* (vol 17, no 8, 1972); Wilson, J.T. (ed) *Continents Adrift: Readings from Scientific American.* W.H. Freeman, San Francisco, 1973; Colbert, E.H. *Wandering Lands and Animals.* Hutchinson, London, 1974.

convicts In Britain during the 18th and early 19th centuries, one of the most common criminal penalties was transportation to the colonies. Not only was it prescribed for a large number of offences, but many of those condemned to death for what would today be considered minor offences later had their sentences commuted to transportation. For many years most transported felons were taken to the American colonies, where settlers paid to acquire their services for the term of their sentences. However, after the outbreak of the American War of Independence it became impracticable to send convicts W across the Atlantic. Consequently, the government, now pressed for prison space, placed many of them in disused ships (known as hulks) anchored in rivers and harbours; but it proved difficult to preserve the health of prisoners there and to prevent them from escaping. In 1786 the government announced that the problem would be solved by the foundation of a penal colony in NSW. Whether there were other motives for establishing this colony is a matter of debate, but the only one given in the first announcement by Lord Sydney, the Home Secretary, was the need to dispose of convicts. In January 1788 the FIRST FLEET, with over 700 convicts on board, arrived at BOTANY BAY. During the following 80 years over 160 000 were sent, most of them to NSW (which during the convict era included the areas now forming VIC and QLD) and to TAS (then known as VAN DIEMEN'S LAND and until

1825 also part of NSW). A much smaller number was sent to WA leaving SA as the only colony to receive no convicts at all.

Types of convicts The convicts included some educated men, such as the architect Francis GREENWAY, and Doctors William REDFERN and D'Arcy WENTWORTH. This educated minority included a number of political prisoners, among them the SCOTTISH MARTYRS, transported for advocating parliamentary reform. A much larger category of political prisoners consisted of Irishmen who had either taken part in, or expressed support for, rebellions such as that of 1798. The convicts also included some who had taken part in riots as a protest against poverty and unemployment; there were, for instance, a few hundred Luddites, who had smashed factory machines, and several hundred farm labourers who had participated in riots in 1830 and 1831.

Research into the backgrounds of the convicts shows, however, that all the categories so far mentioned accounted for only a minority. The majority of the convicts came from the poorer classes in the cities. They were mostly habitual criminals, who had been used to gaining a livelihood largely by stealing, cheating and begging; it was for various forms of theft that most of them were transported. In judging their character, however, it is well to remember that these were times of social and economic change in Britain, and were marked by a great deal of unemployment and insecurity. It is therefore no exaggeration to say that most of those transported to Australia were victims of bad social conditions.

The treatment of convicts varied greatly according to place and time, and other circumstances. During Governor PHILLIP's term of office all convicts were in government service, some on government farms, others in construction work or other forms of manual labour, and a minority in positions such as those of clerks, messengers and even constables. Their hours of work generally ended at three o'clock in the afternoon, after which they were free to work for themselves. They were not usually confined, and many had to find their own accommodation; indeed it was not until Governor MACQUARIE's Hyde Park Barracks were completed in 1819 that the authorities were able to provide accommodation for practically all convicts in government service in Sydney.

In 1793 permission was given for assigning convicts to free settlers as labourers or servants, and in later years an increasing proportion of the convict population was used in this way. Masters of assigned convicts were required to give them clothes and rations according to government requirements, and often provided extras, such as tea, tobacco or even nominal wages. Standards of treatment, as might be expected, varied greatly according to the temperament of the masters and the attitudes and standards of behaviour of the convicts. Some assigned servants were treated generously and leniently, others brutally. For those who were lazy, disobedient or insolent, the lash was always waiting, and all too often a complaint by a master was regarded by the local magistrate as proof of guilt.

A convict who behaved well had a good chance of receiving, before the full term of his sentence, a ticket of leave, which allowed him to work for himself on certain conditions, including that of reporting to the police regularly. He might even obtain a conditional pardon, which gave him freedom on condition that he did not return to Britain. Such concessions were sometimes given soon after a convict's arrival. A convict whose sentence had expired was officially known as an expiree, while those who had been given freedom before the full term had expired were called

emancipists. In common speech, however, the tendency was for all ex-convicts to be called emancipists. Until the early 1820s ex-convicts were encouraged to settle on the land, being given grants of land as well as tools, stock and provisions for some time. Very few of them succeeded as farmers, although quite a few became rich in other ways.

By Governor Macquarie's time there were many complaints that the treatment of convicts was so lenient that transportation was not effective as a deterrent from crime. Justice John BIGGE, sent as a commissioner of enquiry in 1819, accepted this view, and his recommendations were important in helping to make the whole system more severe from the early 1820s. From that time ex-convicts were no longer given land grants, and greater use was made of chain gangs and special penal settlements, or 'places of secondary punishment', for prisoners who were considered hardened, or who committed fresh crimes after coming to Australia. The most notorious special penal settlements were those at MACQUARIE HARBOUR and PORT ARTHUR in TAS, and at NORFOLK ISLAND. Convicts in such places, and also those in chain gangs, were kept under rigid discipline and in many cases were treated with the most extreme brutality.

The abolition of transportation Criticism of the convict system mounted in both Australia and Britain during the 1830s. In that decade great numbers of working-class people were brought to the colonies under schemes of assisted immigration, and these tended to view convicts as competitors, the cheapness of whose services kept wages down. Most emancipists too, having experienced discrimination both as convicts and ex-convicts, wanted to see transportation brought to an end. In Britain some critics were revolted by the brutality with which many convicts were treated; others still claimed that on the whole the system was too lenient.

A Select Committee of the House of Commons, having examined the whole question very thoroughly in 1837-38, concluded that transportation was not effective as a deterrent, since most criminals expected to become prosperous in Australia and it was singularly ineffective in reforming criminals. It noted the inequalities in the treatment meted out to convicts and referred to the two categories as 'those who are prosperous and those who are miserable, the drawers of prizes and the drawers of blanks in this strange lottery'. In short, it argued that the amount of suffering undergone by each particular convict depended largely on sheer luck. As for the economic effects, the prosperity of the colonies had certainly been built partly on the benefits of cheap convict labour, but that stage was now past. The committee therefore recommended that transportation to NSW and the settled portions of TAS should be ended as soon as possible. This recommendation was partly accepted in 1840, when transportation to the mainland of NSW was abolished. However, it was continued to Norfolk Is and TAS,

Convicts in Sydney about 1830

the latter receiving almost 4000 convicts each year for several years afterwards, with disastrous social and economic effects.

On the mainland the decision was welcomed by most settlers, but brought disappointment to many employers, especially the owners of large pastoral properties, who had come to depend on the cheap labour of convicts. Influenced by their views, the British government resumed transportation in 1844, though the system was modified, and operated on a small scale. At first, convicts who had served part of a sentence in Britain were sent to NSW on conditional pardons. Then, from 1846, it was decided to send them on tickets of leave. These steps, however, were met with protests in Sydney and Melbourne. In 1850 an Anti-Transportation Association was formed, and early in 1851 the Australasian League for the Abolition of Transportation co-ordinated the activities of this and other anti-transportation organisations in Hobart, LAUNCESTON, Melbourne, GEELONG and Sydney. In TAS particularly, public protest reached a crescendo in that year. Then came the final argument against transportation—the gold rushes. In 1852 therefore the British government announced the abandonment of transportation to the whole of E Australia. As the British Colonial Secretary explained in a despatch at the time, it seemed pointless 'to convey offenders, at the public expense . . . to the immediate vicinity of those very goldfields which thousands of honest labourers are in vain striving to reach'.

Meanwhile in WA the situation was very different. There was a labour shortage, and the pastoralists, like those in the E, wanted cheap convict labour. As there were no large working-class or middle-class groups to oppose transportation there, the British government sent convicts to WA from 1850 to 1868; the number, however, was very small in comparison with the numbers formerly sent to the E colonies.
Further reading: Shaw, A.G.L. *Convicts and the Colonies*. Faber, London, 1966; Robson, L.L. *The Convict Settlers of Australia*. Melbourne University Press, Melbourne, 1970; Tate, J.E. *Convicts*. Jacaranda, Milton QLD, 1970; Bateson, C. *The Convict Ships, 1787-1868*. Reed, Sydney, 1974.

Convolvulaceae *see* parasitic plants

Coober Pedy SA (population 2 078 in 1981) This opal-mining settlement is in the arid centre of the State, 931km NW of Adelaide on the Stuart Highway and some 220km W of LAKE EYRE. Located at an elevation of 213m in the barren Stuart Range, the town has an average annual rainfall of only 139mm, with excessively hot temperatures reaching over 40°C in the summer months. The opal field was discovered in 1911, but new finds in the 1960s brought an influx of miners to the town. Originally known as the Stuart Range Opal Field, the town later was given its Aboriginal name, meaning 'hole in

the ground'; this name was apt because in the early mining days all dwellings were dugouts excavated in the hillsides. Nowadays, many miners and their families still live in underground dugouts, but the main town has a modern motel, shops and other service facilities characteristic of an ordinary country town. Tourist buses regularly bring visitors to Coober Pedy and there is an air service linking it to Adelaide.
Further reading: Colahan, J. *Australian Opal Safari*. Rigby, Adelaide, 1973.

Cook, James (1728-79) Navigator and chart-maker. The son of a Yorkshire farmer, he was apprenticed at the age of 18 to a coal shipper of Whitby, and served on colliers and in the Baltic trade before joining the Navy in 1775. During the Seven Years' War he did important work in charting the St Lawrence River in preparation for Wolfe's successful attack on Quebec in 1757. Later he won favourable attention for chart-making work in Newfoundland, and for writing a paper, published by the Royal Society, entitled *An Observation of an Eclipse of the Sun at the Island of Newfoundland*. These achievements must obviously have been influential in gaining him the command, in 1768, of an expedition, organised by the Admiralty at the request of the Royal Society, to take scientists to Tahiti to observe the transit of Venus across the face of the sun. His instructions were that he should then explore the South Pacific, to see if there was an undiscovered continent there. He sailed around Cape Horn to Tahiti, and when the observation was completed continued to New Zealand, where he spent six months charting the coastline.

Cook then decided to sail W to VAN DIEMEN'S LAND (TAS), to see if it was joined to NEW HOLLAND (as the Australian mainland, named by Dutch explorers, was then known) and to explore the E coast of the latter. However, unfavourable winds drove the *Endeavour* further to the N than he had wished, and landfall was made near the SE corner of the mainland. The southernmost point in sight was named Point Hicks after the lieutenant who had sighted land. Sailing N, Cook looked for a favourable landing place, but did not find one until reaching BOTANY BAY, so named because of the great number of new botanical specimens gathered there by Sir Joseph BANKS and Dr SOLANDER, the botanists accompanying the expedition. A week was spent at Botany Bay. Shortly after leaving it, Cook noted the entrance to an inlet which he named PORT JACKSON (the modern Sydney Harbour). A few weeks later the *Endeavour* entered the passage between the GREAT BARRIER REEF and the mainland. Recognising the dangers of these waters, Cook took great precautions, but nevertheless nearly lost his ship when it ran onto a submerged coral reef at night. Repairs were carried out on the mainland, on the bank of a river which Cook named the Endeavour, close to the site of modern COOKTOWN. Continuing N, Cook rounded CAPE YORK and

James Cook
National Library of Australia

landed on a small island which he named Possession Is. Here he claimed in the name of King George III the whole of 'New South Wales', as he named that part of Australia discovered by him. His assessment of its quality was realistic. Without exaggerating its fertility, he noted that it was far superior to the land viewed by DAMPIER, and that it could be made to produce immense quantities of food. In describing the Aborigines, he showed an awareness of the links between their way of life and the natural environment that was in marked contrast to the attitude of earlier European observers. He returned to England by way of TORRES STRAIT, Batavia (now Djakarta) and the Cape of Good Hope, reaching home in 1771.

On his second voyage of exploration, 1772-75, he sailed in the *Resolution*, accompanied by the *Adventure*. From the Cape of Good Hope he went S beyond the Antarctic Circle and then to New Zealand. He spent most of 1773 exploring the S Pacific, visiting New Zealand again, and on his way back to England (via Cape Horn) crossing the Antarctic Circle twice again, thus completely disproving the myth of a Great South Land, and becoming the first person to circumnavigate the world from W to E, and the first to sight the Antarctic ice barrier. On a third voyage (1776-79), again in the *Resolution*, he discovered the Hawaiian islands, explored the coasts of British Columbia and part of Alaska, passed through Bering Strait and across the Arctic Circle in search of a Northwest Passage, and then returned to Hawaii. There, in the course of a dispute regarding the theft of his ship's cutter, he was attacked and killed.

Cook's three remarkable voyages won him fame as one of the greatest navigators and hydrographers in the history of exploration, and also earned him a great respect for the quality of his scientific observations and for his unprecedented success in keeping his crews free from scurvy. A cottage in which his parents, but probably not Cook himself, lived, can be seen in the Fitzroy Gardens, Melbourne; built originally at Great Ayton in

Yorkshire, it was dismantled and shipped to Australia in 1934 after Sir Russell Grimwade had acquired and presented it to the VIC government. Various relics of his voyages, including one of the cannons from the *Endeavour*, are displayed in a museum at Kurnell, close to the spot where he landed on the shore of Botany Bay; other relics may be seen in the James Cook Museum at Cooktown.

Further reading: Beaglehole, J.C. (ed) *The Exploration of the Pacific*. A. & C. Black, London, 1934 and *The Journals of Captain Cook*. Cambridge University Press, London, 1955; Rienits, R. & Rienits, T. *The Voyage of Captain Cook*. Paul Hamlyn, London, 1968.

Cook, Sir Joseph (1860-1947) Prime Minister. Born in Staffordshire, England, he worked in coal mines from the age of nine, emigrating in 1885 to NSW, where he became a coal miner at LITHGOW. He entered the Legislative Assembly as a Labor member in 1891, but left the Labor Party three years later, being unwilling to accept its insistence that members be bound by caucus decisions. In 1901 he was elected to the federal House of Representatives as a free trader. By 1909, when the free trade and protectionist groups in Parliament joined to form the anti-Labor 'Fusion' group (soon afterward entitled the Liberal Party), he was leader of the free traders. He became deputy to Alfred DEAKIN, and when Deakin's health collapsed in 1913, Cook succeeded him as leader, in preference to Sir John FORREST.

Following the Liberal victory in the elections of May 1913, Cook became Prime Minister. However, his party did not control the Senate and it had a majority of only one in the House of Representatives. In the following year he applied successfully to the Governor-General for a double dissolution, only to see Labor win a comfortable majority in both Houses. He remained leader of the Opposition until 1917, attended the Paris Peace Conference in 1919, and was High Commissioner in London from 1921 to 1927. Although he possessed no great gifts of eloquence, imagination, or even of political skill, his career is interesting in that it illustrates the steps by which the modern alignment of Australian political parties evolved.

Cooktown QLD (population 913 in 1981) This town is situated at the mouth of the Endeavour River in the far NE of the State, where James COOK in 1770 beached his ship the *Endeavour* for repairs on his epic journey along the E coast of the continent. The town was established in 1873 to serve the inland goldfields on the PALMER RIVER; it developed into a prosperous and notoriously riotous mining camp with 64 hotels and a main street 3km long, but the decline of the boom days saw the demise of the town. In recent years it has become a minor tourist centre, and is the access point to the LIZARD ISLAND resort in the GREAT BARRIER REEF. The James Cook Museum in the town has a display of historical items including a copy of Cook's log and one of the *Endeavour*'s cannons, recovered from the sea bed after two centuries. Annually in June, the town presents a re-enactment of Cook's landing.

coolabah *Eucalyptus microtheca* (family MYRTACEAE), an inland tree of Australia, is famous throughout the English-speaking world because of its mention in WALTZING MATILDA. It is found in all States except VIC and TAS, growing along water courses or in depressions in very dry areas, where it is an indication of the presence of water near the surface. The tree has a very spreading habit, and reaches a height of between 12m and 21m. The rough bark is usually thick and tough, and the timber extremely hard and termite-resistant.

coolamon This is a shallow bowl of wood, hollowed out for carrying water, grass seeds and so on, traditionally used by Aborigines. Being light it is far more suitable for nomadic people than pottery containers (which were not made by the Aborigines). The word is Aboriginal in origin.

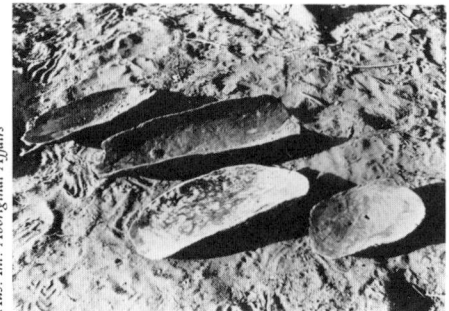

Aus. Int. Aboriginal Affairs

Four different shaped coolamon on a natural surface

Coolangatta QLD The southernmost settlement of the GOLD COAST and twin town of Tweed Heads which lies across the QLD/NSW border, it is part of the City of the Gold Coast (population 135 437 in 1981), which has been extensively developed as a major tourist area. Among its attractions are Yesteryear World (a collection of veteran and vintage vehicles) and Natureland Zoological Gardens. Flights along the coastline and hinterland are provided from Coolangatta airport. Coolangatta area was named after a schooner wrecked off the coast in 1846, but the name actually comes from the local Aboriginal language and means 'beautiful lookout'.

Coolgardie WA (population 891 in 1981) A mining ghost town, it is located 37km SW of KALGOORLIE in the arid inland of the State. Gold was discovered here in 1892 and though the area experienced several boom times when the town is claimed to have had 26 hotels and a population of 15 000, the gold did not last. The National Trust (WA) has listed over 40 buildings in the town for preservation and has declared the whole area within the present townsite boundary to be an Historic Town.

Cooma NSW (population 7 978 in 1981) A town on the MONARO Plateau, it is 425km by road SSW of Sydney, located at the junction of the Monaro and Snowy Mts Highways in the hilly headwater country of the MURRUM-BIDGEE RIVER. It is a rail centre on a branch line from GOULBURN, off the main S route, 432km by rail from Sydney. At an elevation of 811m above sea level, it experiences warm to hot summer conditions, cold winters with frequent frosts, and an annual average rainfall of 558mm spread throughout the year, but with a spring and summer maximum. It is a service centre to a pastoral district noted for merino wool, fat lambs and beef cattle. But more important than this function is its role as a gateway to the KOSCIUSKO National Park and the SNOWY MOUNTAINS SCHEME. The name Cooma comes from the Aboriginal word meaning either 'big lake' or 'open country'.

This rolling hill country of the SOUTHERN TABLELANDS was explored and settled by graziers in the 1820s. In 1849 an official survey for a village site was made and after gold was discovered at Kiandra in 1859, it became a boom town. In 1879 it became a municipality and remained a quietly developing rural centre until 1949 when it experienced another boom as the headquarters of the Snowy Mts Authority, charged with building the massive hydro-electricity scheme. The National Trust (NSW) has listed many buildings in the town for preservation: the courthouse, the Royal Hotel, St Paul's Anglican Church, St Patrick's Catholic Church, the Raglan Art Gallery and several cottages. Among the town's other tourist attractions are the Traveller's Rest Museum located in an old hotel of the gold-rush days, the Aviation Pioneer's Memorial erected in memory of the commercial airliner *Southern Cloud* which disappeared in 1931 on a regular flight from Sydney to Melbourne (the wreckage being found only in 1958), and the 'Man from Snowy River', a statue of the legendary hero of Banjo PATERSON's poem.

Coombs, Herbert Cole 'Nugget' (1906-) Economist. Born in Kalamunda WA, he graduated from the University of Western Australia and the London School of Economics, and in 1935 joined the Commonwealth Bank as an assistant economist. In 1939 he joined the Treasury in Canberra, and was responsible for setting up food-rationing in Australia during World War II. He was Director-General of Post-War Reconstruction, 1943-49, and became Governor of the Commonwealth Bank in 1949, and chairman of the Bank Board two years later. In 1959, when the Reserve Bank and the Commonwealth Banking Corporation were made separate, he continued as chairman of the former, filling this position until his retirement in 1968. In later years he was an economic adviser to Prime Ministers McMAHON and WHITLAM. Of all government economic advisers over the whole post-war period, he has probably been the most influential, and has also been notable for his interest in and influence on the arts, Aboriginal affairs and environmental issues. He was a key figure in the establishment of the Australian Elizabethan Theatre Trust, of which he was chairman from 1954 to 1968, and since the latter date has been at various times Chancellor of the Australian National University, chairman of the Council for Aboriginal Affairs, and chairman of the Australian Council for the Arts (predecessor of the present AUSTRALIA COUNCIL).

Coonabarabran NSW (population of the town 3 001, and of the shire 7 287, in 1981) Situated in the NW plains near the intersection of the Newell and Oxley Highways, 580km by road NW of Sydney, it is a rail terminus for two lines from Sydney, one (via DUBBO) covering a distance of 625km, the other (via MUDGEE) a shorter route of 508km. At an elevation of 509m above sea level, it experiences hot summer conditions and in winter the days are warm but evenings can be quite cool. The average yearly rainfall is 730mm, with the highest falls in the two summer months, January and February. The town is located on the CASTLEREAGH RIVER, near its source, and takes its name from an Aboriginal word meaning 'an inquisitive person'.

Forming a broad arc round the E, N and W of the town is the WARRUMBUNGLE RANGE. Rising abruptly from the surrounding plain, the range provides spectacular scenery, consisting of a cluster of ancient volcanic peaks, some rising to 1 200m in height. The Warrumbungle National Park located 24km W of the town covers an area of 19 456ha, and includes much of this mountain grandeur. The Siding Spring Observatory, just outside the national park on top of SIDING SPRING MOUNTAIN, has become a focal point of international scientific interest; its major instrument, completed in 1974, is one of the most sophisticated and finely adjusted optical telescopes in the world. Five optical telescopes are in operation and an educational exhibition on astronomy, 'Exploring the Universe', is on display. Located N of the Warrumbungle Range 44km NW of Coonabarabran is the Pilliga Scrub Forest, the centre of a cypress pine logging industry. The name 'Pilliga' is derived from an Aboriginal word meaning 'swamp oak'.

Coonamble NSW (population 3 090 in 1981) A country town situated on the CASTLE-REAGH RIVER in the NW plains region of the State, it is 576km by road NW of Sydney. The town is located on the Castlereagh Highway, about midway between GILGANDRA and WALGETT, at an elevation of 180m above sea level. The average annual rainfall of 497mm occurs throughout the year, with no distinctly seasonal distribution. The town is a service and social centre for a rich pastoral area where beef cattle, fat lambs, wool and wheat are the main products. The town's water supply comes from artesian sources; among the tourist attractions of the district is the Yowie Bore, located 20km N of Coonamble; it is over 716m deep and the ARTESIAN WATER flowing from it (at a rate of 650 000 litres per day) is

hot, averaging 40°C. Coonamble takes its name from an Aboriginal word meaning 'plenty of dirt' or 'bullock dung'.

Cooper's Creek QLD/SA The joining of the Thomson and BARCOO Rivers forms Cooper's Creek (sometimes called Cooper Creek), which flows across the SW corner of QLD on a general NNE-SSW course, then changes direction to flow W across the QLD/SA border to LAKE EYRE. It is an intermittent stream in a region of low and unreliable rainfall, and even though it has a course of some 800km, only in exceptionally wet years will it reach the lake. It is one of the main streams of the CHANNEL COUNTRY where, in good years, the land is fine cattle-fattening country.

Coorong SA This is a narrow, shallow, saline coastal lagoon which extends from the MURRAY RIVER mouth on ENCOUNTER BAY for about 145km along the SE coast. It is bounded along the coastline by the long, narrow ridge of sand dunes which form the Younghusband Peninsula. The lagoon waters and the peninsula, covering an area of 37 186ha, were established as a national park in 1966, thus providing a wildlife sanctuary for wombats and many species of water birds. The Coorong Game Reserve, established in 1968 in the central section of the region, covers 6 884ha and provides a breeding ground for pelicans and other birds. The name Coorong comes from an Aboriginal word meaning 'the neck' or 'narrows'.
Further reading: Thiele, C. *Coorong*. Rigby, Adelaide, 1972.

coot *see* rails, etc.

Cootamundra NSW (population 6 540 in 1981) A town in the SW slopes region of the State, 406km by road WSW of Sydney, on the Olympic Highway, it is on the Sydney-Melbourne railway line (426km from Sydney) and is a major junction for lines SE to TUMUT and NW to TEMORA. At an elevation of 330m above sea level, it experiences hot summer months, cool frosty winters and an average annual rainfall of 616mm, uniformly spread throughout the year. The district was settled by pastoralists in the 1830s and a village was officially established in 1861, becoming a municipality in 1884. The town's name (originally Cootamundry) comes from an Aboriginal word with several meanings— 'swamp', 'low-lying place', or 'turtles'. The district produces wool, wheat, fat lambs and beef cattle; the town is an important stock selling centre and hosts one of the State's largest sheep shows. Secondary industries include an abattoir, brick works, a furniture factory, concrete and fibrous plaster works. The National Trust (NSW) has listed several buildings in Cootamundra for preservation— the post office, three banks, the courthouse and the railway station.

'The Burke and Wills tree at Cooper's Creek' by Arthur Esam

National Library of Australia

Copeton Dam NSW On the GWYDIR RIVER in the NW slopes region, 35km by road SE of INVERELL, it has a storage capacity of 1 364 000ML, collecting drainage from a catchment area of 5 360km². The dam supplies water for domestic, stock and irrigation purposes lower downstream in the Gwydir Valley. Because of the relatively low and variable rainfall of the region, investigations were made as early as the 1930s into the possibilities of dam construction and water conservation on the Gwydir River. However, it was not until 1968 that work commenced on construction, the final storages being completed in 1976. The dam comprises an earth-and-rockfill embankment 113m high and, 800m to the N, a spillway controlled by nine radial gates. The lake formed by the dam has a maximum depth of 104m and is also used for a variety of aquatic sports. There is a recreation area of 260ha on the S shore of the lake.

copper This metal has been used by man for at least 6000 years and has been one of the important materials in the advances of tools, weapons, ornaments, industry and technology. The use of copper and simple copper alloys marked the transition from the Stone Age to the Metal Age or, more specifically, the Bronze Age. The growth of the copper industry closely mirrored that of mechanisation during the Industrial Revolution; similarly, the development of electricity production and transportation has been closely linked with the copper industry.

Because of its corrosion resistance, the uses of copper extend from the electrical to the construction industry and include the manufacture of products where a high heat transfer is necessary. It also has a wide application in the transport industry; miscellaneous uses include the manufacture of chemicals, pigments, jewellery, coinage and decorative items. Bronze (copper and tin) and brass (copper and zinc) also have many uses.

Extraction The main copper ores are chalcopyrite (CuFeS$_2$) and chalcocite (Cu$_2$S), with others of lesser importance being bornite, cuprite and malachite. The extraction of copper involves concentration, mainly by flotation methods; roasting to eliminate sulphur and certain impurities; smelting with either sand or lime to form blister copper; and, finally, refining by electrolysis.

The by-products and co-products of copper mining are gold, silver, molybdenum, nickel, platinum, selenium, tellurium, paladium, arsenic, rhenium and sulphur together with base metals such as iron, lead and zinc. Some of the products are separated from copper minerals by selective flotation whilst others are recovered from anode sludges at refineries.
Production The USA has been the leading copper producer since 1883, followed by the USSR, Chile, Canada, Zambia and Zaire, in that order. Australia achieved self-sufficiency in copper in the early 1950s, when the copper lodes of MOUNT ISA were brought into production. In 1980, the mine production of copper in Australia amounted to 243 545 tonnes, or about three per cent of the total world production. Outputs of the various States for the period 1970-80 are shown in Table 1. The principal centres of production are Mt Isa and MOUNT MORGAN in QLD; BROKEN HILL, COBAR and near GOULBURN in NSW; MOUNT LYELL and ROSEBERRY in TAS; BURRA, Kanmantoo and Mt Gunson in SA; and TENNANT CREEK in the NT. In WA, copper is derived from nickel concentrates, which are mined in the KALGOORLIE district and smelted at KWINANA.
The industry The copper industry is capital-intensive and requires almost $5000 per tonne per year of new capacity for all facilities, from mining to refining. The distribution of direct operation-cost components in terms of percentage of the price of copper have been established as 15 per cent for mining, 25 per cent for freight, smelting and refining, 25 per cent for beneficiation (treating for smelting) and 35 per cent for exploration, development, taxes, marketing, general overheads and profit.
Further reading: see under minerals and mining.

copperhead *see* snakes

Coppin, George Selth (1819-1906)
Actor, entrepreneur and politician. Born in Sussex, the son of an actor and manager, George Coppin grew up in the midst of show business, helping in his father's theatre, and playing violin solos as a child. As a musician and low comedian, he worked in London and the counties until 1842, when he left England for Sydney where he and his first wife, Maria Burroughs, were engaged for the Royal Victoria Theatre. He performed in Hobart in 1845, and in 1846 went to Adelaide. There he lost his money in speculation on copper; but at the beginning of the gold rushes he moved to Melbourne and by the mid-1850s had several theatres there, including his famous 'Iron Pot', a prefabricated theatre imported from Manchester. Retiring from the stage in 1858, he was a Member of the VIC Legislative Council

Table 1

MINE PRODUCTION OF COPPER IN AUSTRALIA 1970-81
(× '000t)

State	1970	1978	1979	1980	1981
QLD	107 279	152 701	173 706	174 606	147 225
NSW	15 184	14 258	18 540	19 080	18 474
TAS	23 934	23 908	22 591	23 018	22 402
SA	1 529	12 631	13 651	11 755	19 886
WA	3 353	4 782	3 383	3 112	5 784
NT	6 465	3 381	5 739	11 974	17 568
TOTAL	157 790*	222 111	237 610	243 545	231 339

Note: * includes 46 tonnes produced in VIC.
Source; *Australian Mineral Industry Annual Review.* (1970-80) Australian Govt Publishing Service, Canberra.

until 1862. He retained his theatrical interests, however, and returned to acting and promoting in 1863; notable among the artists he brought over during this period were J.C. WILLIAMSON and his wife (in 1874). From 1874 he served terms of office in both the Legislative Council and the Legislative Assembly. He made his final stage appearance in 1881.
Further reading: Bagot, A. *Coppin the Great: Father of Australian Theatre.* Melbourne University Press, Melbourne, 1965.

copyright The power to make laws with regard to copyright is vested in the Commonwealth Parliament by Section 51 (xviii) of the Constitution. The first legislation under this power was the Copyright Act of 1912, which adopted for Australia the British Copyright Act of the previous year, and so gained recognition for Australian copyrights throughout the British Empire, including the self-governing Dominions. Still wider recognition was gained when Australia joined the Berne Union system of international copyright.

A new Copyright Act was passed in 1968. Its essential provisions follow earlier legislation, so that in most cases copyrights which existed before its enactment remained in force. However, it introduced certain new features which enabled Australia to become a party to the Universal Copyright Convention, which had been negotiated under the auspices of UNESCO in 1952 and has particularly wide coverage, including the USA and USSR, neither of which is a party to the Berne Union.
Features of Australian copyright Although some essential features of Australian copyright law are given here, it must be stressed that the substance and interpretation of such law are complex matters, and that for people directly involved in question of copyright it may be necessary to obtain further information and advice.

The Copyright Act (1968-73) provides for copyright in two kinds of subject matter, namely 'works' and 'subject matter other than works'. The former category is defined as 'a literary, dramatic, musical or artistic work'. Copyright gives the 'maker' of such a work—

that is, the author, playwright, composer or artist—the sole right to reproduce, publish, perform in public, broadcast or adapt the work, for a specific period (usually the lifetime of the maker plus 50 years). However, the law applies only when the 'maker' is a 'qualified person', namely 'an Australian citizen, an Australian protected person, or a person resident in Australia'.

'Subject matter other than works' includes sound recordings, cinematograph films, television broadcasts, sound broadcasts, and published editions of works. For these the ownership of copyright is as follows: for sound recordings, the maker; for television and sound broadcasts, the Australian Broadcasting Commission, licence holder of the relevant station, or 'prescribed person', as the case may be; for films, the producer; and for published editions of works, the publisher.

Copyright applies to unpublished works, being provided from the act of composition—that is, from the time an idea is reduced to writing or some other 'material form'. If, however, a work is made by someone in the course of his employment by another person, then that other person is, in general, the first owner of the copyright. Whether this is the case or not, the first owner is empowered to assign or licence the copyright to others. An author, for example, may assign the copyright of his work to a publisher under terms and conditions specified in his contract. Copyright is infringed when an unauthorised person 'does in Australia, or authorises in Australia the doing of' any act which only the owner has the right to do—that is, reproduces, publishes, performs in public, broadcasts, or adapts the work or a 'substantial part' of it.

A particularly debatable issue has been the right of students or others to make copies of works, or parts of works, with photocopying machines in public or educational libraries. The Copyright Amendment Act of 1980 deals particularly with this matter. Among other provisions, it establishes a statutory licence system whereby educational institutions may make multiple copies of the whole or part of periodical articles and of works. In general, records must be kept of the copying, and

owners have the right to claim payment.
See also Australian Copyright Council

Coral Sea, Battle of the 7-8 May
1942. Following their attack on Pearl Harbour in 1941, the Japanese had gained control of nearly the whole of South-East Asia by March 1942, and had established bases close to Australia on the N coast of the New Guinea mainland and in New Britain and New Ireland. To guard their Pacific conquests against counter-attack, they planned next to occupy Port Moresby, New Caledonia, Fiji, Samoa, Midway and the Aleutians. On 4 May an invasion force consisting of transports, two aircraft carriers and escorting cruisers and destroyers, left Rabaul with the object of capturing Port Moresby. However, the Allies had learnt of the move through intercepted radio messages, and a force consisting of the carriers *Lexington* and *Yorktown*, eight cruisers (including the Australian vessels *Australia* and *Hobart*) and 11 destroyers, was sent to intercept the enemy fleet in the Coral Sea. The battle was the first in which opposing fleets attacked by means of carrier-based aircraft, without coming within range of each other's guns. On the Allied side, Australian and American aircraft from land bases in QLD also took part.

The Allied force lost the naval tanker *Neosho* and the destroyer *Sims* during the battle, and suffered damage to both carriers, the *Lexington* later sinking. The Japanese, who lost the carrier *Shoko* and suffered damage to the carrier *Shokaku*, won a tactical victory. However, the fact that they felt compelled to call off the invasion, the transports returning to Rabaul and the warships to Truk, meant that they had suffered a strategic defeat. Although the forces engaged were smaller than at Midway in the following month, the Battle of the Coral Sea attracted perhaps even more attention in Australia, since it prevented the Japanese from establishing a major base less than 400km from the QLD coast. Ceremonies are held each year in Australian cities to celebrate the anniversary of the battle, serving as a reminder of Australian-American co-operation in WORLD WAR II.

coral tree *see* Papilionaceae

corals The true corals are invertebrate marine animals closely related to the sea anemones. They form a subclass, Zoantharia, of the class Anthozoa in the phylum Coelenterata (COELENTERATES). Although a number of coelenterates are often called corals, the true corals—including all the reef-building corals—are zoantharians.

Almost all true corals are colonial, the individuals (polyps) being interconnected by a thin living 'skin'. The coral polyp resembles that of a sea anemone, but it is usually smaller, and it secretes limestone to form a small cup-like structure (corallite) in which it lives. Corals feed at night, using the tentacles surrounding the mouth at the free end of the polyp to capture prey. Stinging cells (nematocysts) in the

tentacles paralyse or immobilise the prey, which consists of small marine animals. Corals may reproduce by budding (the new polyp growing out as an extension of the 'parent', and remaining attached), or sexually, usually by cross-fertilisation after eggs and sperm are released into the water. In this case a planula larva develops and floats in the water until it settles to found a new colony. Because the polyps in a colony continuously secrete limestone, the colony expands constantly, the shape it takes varying according to the species. Some typical forms are: branch-like, rounded and boulder-like, leaf-like and table-like; some encrust the reef, and a few lie unattached on the seabed.

The reef-building (or zoantharian) corals are found only in tropical marine waters, and can only flourish under certain conditions: a fall in salinity in the surrounding waters can kill coral, and so reefs do not occur at the mouths of rivers and streams; again, the water level must remain reasonably constant, as the polyps die if exposed to air for too long, yet the water must be in movement to bring the polyps their food, and must not contain much sediment, which would smother the polyps. Most zoantharian corals have unicellular plants, zooxanthellae, living symbiotically within their tissues. Corals of this kind are described as hermatypic (needing warmth and sunlight), and will not flourish if the water temperature lies outside the 20°C–30°C range (limiting the distribution of reefs to tropical regions); and because their symbiotic plant guests need light, corals grow well only in shallow water, at a depth between 2m and 13m. This is well illustrated in the GREAT BARRIER REEF, which displays its greatest diversity of species among the corals of the warmer sections. Although zoantharian corals can survive without zooxanthellae, both gain by the relationship.

A typical coral reef is not constructed by the corals working alone. Coelenterates such as some hydrozoans contribute their limestone skeletons, and ALGAE play a very important part. Calcareous algae are particularly common on the windward side of a reef. They secrete a limestone that cements the debris together, giving the surface of the reef a brown, pink or purple tinge. There are several genera of these plants, including *Lithothamnium* and *Lithophyllum*.

The Great Barrier Reef contains some 350 species of true corals (representing about 60 genera). The most common genus is probably *Acropora*, which includes the plate corals and knobby corals, and the well-known staghorn corals, typical colonies of which can grow to a diameter of several metres. Several of the large solitary polyps belong to the family Fungiidae, notable among them being the mushroom corals (*Fungia* species) which resemble mushrooms except that the 'mushroom gills' are on the upper surface; well-grown specimens are from 5cm to 20cm in diameter, and lie free on the reef surface. Other genera common on the Barrier Reef are *Favites*, the honeycomb corals, which are boulder-shaped and grow to

about 20cm across; and *Leptoria* and *Platygyra*, the brain corals, aptly named from the convolutions on the surface of their rounded masses, resembling those on a human brain. Most living corals are brown but many are brightly coloured: blue, green, red and orange corals are common.

Fragile species of staghorn coral, *Acropora*, that inhabits the deeper waters of the Great Barrier Reef

Among the natural predators to which corals are susceptible, the large crown of thorns starfish (ECHINODERMS) has been a source of considerable concern of conservationists in recent years: increasing dramatically in numbers in the 1960s and 1970s, it has denuded many Indo-Pacific coral reefs—including some in the Barrier Reef—of living polyps. Although reasons for the population explosion of the starfish are not clear, some biologists have blamed pollution, and others the removal by divers of the natural predators of the starfish. However, evidence indicates that the crown-of-thorns starfish increases its numbers periodically, independently of human activity. It is probable that the starfish had passed their peak by 1979, and that the attacked reefs will recover.
Further reading: Deas, W. & Domm, S. *Corals of the Great Barrier Reef*. Ure Smith, Sydney, 1976.

cordyline *see* Palmae

corellas *see* parrots, etc.

coriander *see* Umbelliferae

Corio Bay VIC The westernmost section of PORT PHILLIP BAY, it extends about 8km N-S and 6km E-W; on its SW shores stands the city of GEELONG. The port facilities of the city fringe the bay shoreline: the oil refinery pier to the N, and the huge bulk-wheat pier further S, as well as Rippleside, Cunningham and Yarra Piers and several wharves for handling the shipping trade. Numerous industrial establishments are located adjacent to the bay: the Shell Oil Refinery, the International Harvester Co., the Ford Motor Works, woollen mills, a phosphate fertiliser factory and freezing works; and on Point Henry, at the SE of the bay, is the Alcoa aluminium smelting plant. Hovell's Creek drains into an estuary at the N of the bay, and the BARWON RIVER skirts it to the SW. To the SE of the bay, near Geelong Botanic Gardens, is eastern Beach, a popular recreation and holiday area in the summer months. The Bellarine Highway,

along the S shores of the bay, leads to numerous bayside and ocean beach resorts of the Bellarine Peninsula, such as Clifton Springs, QUEENSCLIFF, Point Lonsdale and Barwon Heads. About 24km N of Corio Bay are the steep rocky hills of the You Yangs, whose highest point, Flinders Peak (climbed by explorer Matthew FLINDERS in 1802) rises 352m above sea level.

cormorants These aquatic fishing BIRDS belong to the family Phalacrocoracidae and are related to the pelican group (*see* SEA BIRDS). Although they are popularly linked with the sea, many frequent inland waters as well. They feed on fish and crustaceans by diving from their perches or by pursuing their prey under water, and are able to stay submerged for about 30 seconds. Their webbed feet are set

Little pied cormorant drying its wings

well back on the body. Strangely, their plumage is easily soaked, and so they spend long periods with outstretched wings, drying their feathers.

There are five Australian species, all common. The black cormorant, *Phalacrocorax carbo* (75cm to 1m long), is a widespread, mainly inland species with a crest, an entirely black plumage and orange skin on the face. It is usually seen on sandbanks and mudflats, or perching on rocks and debris in streams. The eggs are laid in flat nests of the sticks and twigs which are built on the horizontal branches of trees or on rocky ledges overlooking rivers. The similar little black cormorant, *P. sulcirostris* (60cm), is usually seen in flocks and is found throughout Australia. It builds a platform-shaped nest of sticks, lined with bark.

The black-faced cormorant, *P. fuscescens** (60cm), is a white-bellied species which frequents the S coasts and TAS. Its flat nest of seaweed and flotsam is often placed on a rock ledge. The yellow-faced cormorant, *P. varius* (75cm), frequents coastal areas and inland waters, but is absent from TAS. It is white below and black above, with black thighs and orange skin on the face. Its nests of sticks, are built in trees, low bushes or on the ground. A familiar species on inland waters, often seen in association with wading birds, is the little pied cormorant, *P. melanoleucos* (60cm). Its platform nests of sticks and green bark are often seen near the water's edge on the branches of trees.

Species, genus or family is endemic to Australia (see Preface)

Corner Inlet VIC A coastal bay some 180km SE of Melbourne, it is bounded on the S and SE by WILSON'S PROMONTORY, on the W by the low Sandy Yanakie Isthmus (which connects the promontory to the mainland), and on the N by an indented coastline with several beach resorts, lying S of the South Gippsland Highway. The inlet covers an area of about 450km², with an E-W extent of some 25km and a maximum distance N-S of about 25km. The shallow entrance to the inlet is on the E side, almost closed by low-lying sandy islands, particularly Snake and Little Snake Islands. There are several islands within the inlet: Doughboy Is off the isthmus shore, and Granite and Benson Islands off the coast of the promontory. The inlet was discovered and named by the explorer George BASS in 1798.

Cornforth, John Warcup (1917-) Scientist and Nobel Prize winner. Cornforth was born in Australia but has done most of his research in Britain. Though handicapped by deafness, he undertook work on the shapes of molecules involved in living systems which was of such importance that he shared the Nobel Prize for chemistry in 1975.

corn spurry *see* Caryophyllaceae

Corowa NSW (population 3 390 in 1981) A country town downstream from ALBURY on the MURRAY RIVER, Corowa is situated on the Riverina Highway, 646km by road SW of Sydney. Its twin town on the VIC side of the Murray is Wahgunyah. At an elevation of 125m above sea level, it receives an average yearly rainfall of 536mm, spread fairly uniformly throughout the year; June is the wettest month (58mm average), January the driest (36mm). The surrounding rural district produces wool and fat lambs, wheat and other cereals, and wine grapes. The town name comes from an Aboriginal word for a pine tree from which gum was obtained for fixing spear heads to shafts.

Correa *see* Rutaceae

corroboree This is a secular Aboriginal ceremony, usually combining singing, dancing, clapping, DIDJERIDU music (in some areas) and percussion. The theme is usually based on everyday incidents of the present or the past— animal behaviour, European behaviour and objects, tribal misdemeanours, and so on.

Cosme This was the name given to a utopian socialist settlement founded in Paraguay in 1894 by a breakaway group from the New Australia settlement.
See also Lane, William

Cosmos *see* Compositae

cotton *see* agriculture

cotton bush *see* Chenopodiaceae

cottony-cushion scale *see* biological control

coucals *see* cuckoos, etc.

country music Australian country music has come virtually full circle, while continuing to evolve and develop.

Its origins were with the early CONVICTS, particularly the Irish, who employed their traditional folk styles to express their sorrows and frustrations in song. Gradually, settlers took the music with them to the bush where they found new subjects for songs in their experiences with bushrangers, drovers, shearers and miners.

The songs, with their Australian flavour and concern for the underdog, proved popular even in the cities, but it wasn't until after the depression of the 1930's that singing what became known as country songs could be seen as a professional activity.

Robert Lane, a New Zealander, born in 1916, arrived in Australia in 1932 and, as Tex Morton, became one of the country's best-known performers. Tex started recording in Sydney in 1936 and travelled widely. During the forties and fifties, he toured the United States and Canada with a show that featured Tex as a hypnotist, sharp-shooter and memory expert as well as a singer who beat Bing Crosby in a popularity contest. Into the seventies, Tex Morton moved from recording to acting. He died in Sydney in 1983.

If Tex Morton was the father of Australian country, then the King is undoubtedly Slim Dusty, real name David Gordon Kirkpatrick, born in Kempsey, New South Wales in 1927.

When D. G. Kirkpatrick was about ten years old he was at a local dance where he heard an Aborigine sing 'The Drunkard's Child'. Over the next twelve months or so, he adopted the stage name 'Slim Dusty' and when he was twelve he wrote his first song, 'The Way the Cowboy Died'. In November 1946 Slim had his first recording session and for the next eleven years he recorded and toured regularly.

In 1958, rock'n'roll was well and truly in its ascendancy and it was widely recognised that a hillbilly song had no hope of making the pop charts in the cities. However, Slim Dusty's recording of 'The Pub With No Beer' by Gordon Parsons changed that idea by reaching Number 1 Australia-wide and Number 3 in the UK. Until recently, it was the biggest-selling Australian recorded single ever.

1970 saw Slim Dusty awarded the MBE for his services to entertainment, then seven years later he celebrated his fiftieth birthday with his fiftieth gold record. Already the biggest selling totally Australian artist, Slim Dusty continues to record and is about to feature in a movie of his life story.

The songs of Tex Morton, Slim Dusty and their contemporaries, Buddy Williams, Gordon Parsons and Smoky Dawson, who starred in a radio drama series and made international headlines by losing his kangaroo in New York) were usually full of sadness and misery, but this was balanced by the emergence of Queenslander, Chad Morgan.

Chad, with his protuding teeth came on the scene with the autobiographical 'Sheik of Scrubby Creek', and went on to tell us about the joys of chasing sorts, cane cutting, boozing, gambling, and handling women. His songs were occasionally bawdy, usually cheeky, and always hilarious. Chad continues to perform and record, poking fun, like a musical Groucho Marx, at all aspects of life.

In spite of the efforts of these seasoned performers, country music has remained a vague mystery to the younger generation, particularly in the cities, where traditional country, with rare exceptions, was unable to receive airplay on radio stations.

This situation has changed with the arrival of 'redneck' bands who are playing a modernised form of country, based on the style of Texas-based bands in America. Artists such as Saltbush, Moose Malone, Buckskin, Grand Junction and Colin Millington have tended to change the shape and sound of Australian Country Music, bringing it to, and having it received enthusiastically by city audiences.

Yet, Australian country began in bush ballads and left the cities in that form for the bush where it acquired an identity of its own. Some two hundred years later, the bush ballads are also returning to the cities. The Bushwackers, Cobbers, Bullamakanka, are all bands whose musical roots are in the traditional Irish style but whose lyrics are distinctly Australian. Bushdancing is becoming increasingly popular across Australia, and these bands and others like them are reaping the benefits and bringing the music back home.

Country music in Australia is now being promoted more than at any time in the past. Every January is Country Music Month on radio, and Tamworth, NSW, calling itself country music capital, rounds out the month by playing host to the Australian Country Music Awards. Metropolitan radio is gradually programming an increasing amount of country music and various newspapers have regular columns on country music.

Country Party *see* National Party of Australia

coursers *see* pratincoles, etc.

coursing *see* greyhound racing, etc.

Court, Sir Charles Walter Michael (1911-) Premier of WA. Born in England, he was educated in Perth WA, became a chartered accountant there, and from 1940 to 1946 served in the AIF. Elected to the Legislative Assembly of WA in 1953, he reached Cabinet rank six years later as Minister for Railways and for Industrial Development and the North-West. In the election of 1971 the Liberal/Country Party coalition was defeated, and in the following year Court became leader of the Liberal Party and therefore of the parliamentary Opposition. When the coalition

The Hon. Sir Charles Court

parties returned to power in 1974, he became Premier. In that position he concentrated on the mineral and industrial development of his State, and also came to be regarded, after BJELKE-PETERSEN of QLD, as the most vigorous defender of States' rights among the Premiers. He resigned from Parliament in January 1982 and was succeeded as Premier by Raymond James O'CONNOR.

Court, Margaret (1942-) Tennis player. Born in the NSW border town of ALBURY, she began tennis as a left-hander but for fear of being thought odd changed to a right-handed style. Unaffected by the change she went on to win 29 major world titles. Noted for her power in all facets of the game, she won her first Australian championship in 1960. This was the start of a domination of Australian tennis which is not likely ever to be equalled—of the 14 Australian championships played from 1960 to 1973 she won 11. And her domination was not confined to Australia. During the same period she won Wimbledon three times, the US title five times, and the French title four times. Plagued by recurrent and rebellious bouts of nervousness before major matches, she had often to gain mastery over herself before settling down to master her opponent. In 1970 she became the second woman in the world to win the 'Grand Slam'— that is, the Australian, French, US and Wimbledon titles in the same year.

Covell, Roger (1931-) Musician. Born in Sydney, and educated at the Universities of Queensland and New South Wales, Roger Covell became music and drama critic for the Brisbane *Courier Mail* after working in London in the theatre, for the Festival of Britain and for the BBC. In 1960 he was appointed chief music and drama critic for the *Sydney Morning Herald*, and it is in this capacity that he has become well known for his writings on music, including some on Australian MUSICAL COMPOSITION AND COMPOSERS in the late 1960s. He has published *Australia's Music: Themes of a New Society* (1967), has edited one of Australia's earliest musical plays, Edward

GEOGHEGAN's *The Currency Lass* (1976), has edited and translated a number of Italian operas and has contributed articles on music to books, journals and reference works.

In 1966 he was appointed foundation Head of the Music Department at the University of New South Wales, became Associate Professor in 1974 and was awarded his Ph.D in 1977. Other contributions include work for music education (he has been national president of the Australian Society for Music Education since 1978), lecturing and performing, and serving on in various committees (he has been a member of the AUSTRALIA COUNCIL since 1978). He is Musical Director of the University of New South Wales Opera which he founded in 1968 and with which he has introduced many early, modern and Australian operas to Australian audiences.

Cowen, Sir Zelman (1919-) Lawyer, academic and Governor-General. Born in the Melbourne suburb of St Kilda, he was educated at Scotch College, Melbourne, at Melbourne University and at New and Oriel Colleges, Oxford. He was a Rhodes Scholar for VIC in 1940 and was first called to the Bar at Gray's Inn, London, in 1947. He was a member of the Royal Australian Naval Volunteer Reserve from 1941 to 1945, and after the war held the positions of Fellow and Tutor at Oriel College (1947-50), Professor of Public Law and Dean of the Faculty of Law at Melbourne University (1951-66), Vice-Chancellor of the University of New England (1967-70), and Vice-Chancellor of the University of Queensland (1970-77). He was appointed Governor-General, in succession to Sir John KERR, in 1977. In July 1982 he took up the position of Provost of Oriel College, Oxford, and was succeeded as Governor-General by Sir Ninian STEPHEN.

Sir Zelman Cowen

Cowpastures NSW This name was given to river flats on the NEPEAN RIVER, near the present town of CAMDEN, because a herd of cattle, descendants of some which had strayed from Sydney soon after the first settlement, were discovered there some years later. In 1804 the Colonial Secretary Lord Camden granted John MACARTHUR permission to select 10 000 acres in the district. In gratitude Macarthur named his estate there Camden Park, and the name CAMDEN was given to the town which grew up nearby.

Cowper, Sir Charles (1807-75) Premier of NSW. Born in Dryford in Lancashire, England, he was brought to Sydney in 1809, when his father was appointed assistant chaplain of NSW. In 1826 he became secretary of the Church and School Land Corporation. During the following few years he acquired large areas of land, partly by grant and partly by purchase, and when the Corporation was abolished in 1833 he did not seek another public position, but devoted himself to farming and sheep breeding.

At the colony's first elections in 1844 he became a Member of the Legislative Council for the County of Cumberland. At this stage of his life he was moderately conservative in his views, and was best known for his support of the claims of the Church of England to be regarded as the colony's established Church. He resigned his seat in 1850, but in the following year was elected for the seat of Durham. By this time he had become much more liberal in his views. He was prominent in the movement against the renewal of transportation in any form, and in 1851 became president of the Anti-Transportation League.

In the first elections for the NSW Parliament in 1856 he was returned for the seat of Sydney and immediately became leader of the Liberal Opposition group. As Member at various times for Sydney, East Sydney and Liverpool Plains, he remained in the Legislative Assembly for most of the period up to 1870, and was Premier on five occasions for a total of nearly five years. The most notable pieces of legislation which he introduced or with which he was closely associated were the Act establishing manhood suffrage and the secret ballot, Sir John ROBERTSON's Land Act of 1861, the Act abolishing State grants to religious bodies in 1862, and the Real Property Act of the same year, which introduced the TORRENS system of land titles. Following his resignation from Parliament in 1870 he was Agent-General for NSW in London until his death.

Cowra NSW (population 7 900 in 1981) A town in the central W slopes region of the State, on the banks of the LACHLAN RIVER, it is located at the junction of the Mid-Western Highway and the Olympic Way 320km by road W of Sydney. It is on a link railway line and can be reached either via BLAYNEY (366km by train from Sydney to Cowra) or via HARDEN (a longer route, 491km). At an elevation of 298m above sea level, situated in the midst of gently rolling hill land, it experiences hot summer conditions, mild winters with frequent frosts, and has an average annual rainfall of 612mm, spread uniformly throughout the year. The town serves as the business and market centre for a fertile rural district producing fat lambs, wool, wheat and cattle, with intensive farming on the alluvial flats growing lucerne, asparagus and a variety of vegetables,

which are processed and canned in a local factory. Other secondary industries in the town include a wool processing plant, an abattoir and freezing works, a gravel works producing ornamental pebbles, light engineering workshops, and brick and tile factories. The name of the town comes from the Aboriginal word meaning 'a rocky place'.

The area was settled by pastoralists early in the 19th century, following the explorations of George EVANS in 1815. The town was gazetted in 1849 and became a municipality in 1888. During World War II, there was a Japanese prisoner-of-war camp at Cowra and in August 1944 the prisoners staged a suicidal break for freedom in which four Australian soldiers and 247 Japanese died, many of the Japanese committing suicide. A war cemetery 5km N of the town containing their graves is landscaped in traditional Japanese style; it was officially opened in 1964 and many Japanese visitors to Australia now travel to Cowra to see the cemetery. An agricultural research station and experimental farm established in 1903 is located N of the town. It was here that William FARRER worked on the development of rust-resistant wheat and bred several valuable varieties. Nearby, there is also a soil conservation research station which undertakes investigations into various aspects of soil conservation and erosion control. The WYANGALA DAM on the Lachlan, 48km upstream from Cowra, stores water for irrigation and livestock supplies further downstream. The National Trust (NSW) has listed several buildings in Cowra for preservation, including the Australian Hotel, the courthouse and the ANZ Bank.

cowries *see* gastropods

CPI *see* Consumer Price Index

crab grass *see* Gramineae; weeds

crabs *see* crustaceans

Cradle Mountain TAS Located in the NW of the State, in a region of rugged mountain peaks, deep glaciated valleys, steep-sided gorges, wild open moorland and alpine heath, Cradle Mt forms part of the ranges dividing the headwaters of the FORTH RIVER (flowing N to BASS STRAIT) and the upper tributaries of the PIEMAN RIVER. Rising 1 545m above sea level, the mountain is in the N part of the Cradle Mt-LAKE ST CLAIR National Park which covers 126 205ha and includes the State's highest peak, MOUNT OSSA (1 617m). The average annual precipitation at Cradle Valley is 2 774mm, the highest falls being in winter (July average 320mm) but heavy falls occur throughout the year (February 135mm). Much of the precipitation in winter is snow, subjecting the road into the N part of the national park to ice and snow conditions for several months. Until relatively recently, access to this area was limited to surveyors and a few intrepid bushmen; it was only in 1941 that a road was built to the vicinity of Cradle Mt. Since then it has become a popular bush-

Cradle Mountain TAS

walking area, but bushwalkers are warned that the 'risk of death from exposure is an ever-present hazard', since there are no fast means of communication with civilisation in an emergency and the unpredictable climate may subject them to muddy conditions, heavy rain and snowfalls, even in summer months. The track from Cradle Mt to Lake St Clair (about 84km) is a favourite journey; it usually takes four to five days, though many attractions along the route and numerous side-tracks to spectacular scenic features often extend the time beyond this. Shelter huts are available at intervals approximately a day's walk apart, but in summer months, these often prove too few for the numbers of walkers, and tents must be used to accommodate the overflow. At its S end, the track skirts Lake St Clair for 18km, passing between the lake shore and MOUNT OLYMPUS.

Crafers-Bridgewater SA (population 9 764 in 1981) Located SE of Adelaide on the Princes Highway, about 20km from the city centre, these two towns, with two others, Aldgate and Stirling, form a ribbon of urban development along the highway. The four urban centres have developed in recent years as residential areas for people who commute daily to work in Adelaide. The surrounding rural district, a major wheat growing area in the 1850s, is now intensively farmed to produce fruit and vegetables for the city market. Stirling, at an elevation of 496m above sea level, has an average annual rainfall of 1 121mm, making it one of the wettest places in SA.

Craigieburn VIC (population 4 293 in 1981) A small country town located on the central N railway route to SEYMOUR, it is located 24km by road and 26km by rail N of Melbourne. It is thought to have been named by a group of Scottish settlers who occupied the district as sheep farmers before the 1850s, after the estate of Craigieburn in the County of Dumfries in Scotland.

crakes *see* rails, etc.

Crampton, Bruce Sidney (1935-) Golfer. Crampton was born in Sydney. After becoming assistant professional at the Beverley

Park course he had only one major success in Australia, the Australian Open in 1956, before leaving for the USA where he was to be outstandingly successful. A consistent winner on the fiercely competitive USA circuit, winning 15 tournaments, in 1973 he became the fifth golfer ever to have won more than US$1 million in prize-money in the USA. In 1975 his earnings topped the US$100 000 mark for the eighth successive year. Despite his not having won any of the four major championships, although he was second on four occasions (in the US Open and US Masters in 1972, and in the US PGA championships in 1973 and 1975) he was unchallenged as Australia's greatest golfer of the 1970s.

Cranbourne VIC (population 9 396 in 1981) A country town on the Gippsland Highway, it is 50km SE of Melbourne, 16km SE of DANDENONG and some 14km from the N shore of WESTERN PORT BAY. Dairying is the main rural activity in the district; some gravel quarrying is also done, and there are light engineering and building industries. The town was first surveyed in 1856 and was probably named after Cranbourne in Berkshire, England.

cranes These stork-like terrestrial BIRDS belong to the family Gruidae and are famous for their dancing displays. The brolga, *Grus rubicunda** (about 1.1m long)—also called the native companion—grows to about 1m in height and can have a wingspan of 2m. The plumage is grey and the head, set on a long neck, is partly naked and red; the beak is 15cm long. The brolga lives in grasslands, farmlands and by the swampy margins of lakes where it feeds on insects and plants. One or two light-coloured, mottled eggs are laid in a large nest in swampy ground. A gregarious bird, the brolga is very common in the N, but much rarer in the S. Recently, the very similar sarus crane, *G. antigone* (1.2m), has been discovered in northern QLD, often living with the brolga with which it may have been confused in the past. It is distinguished by a more extensive area of naked red skin.

Brolga, *Grus rubicunda*

Crapp, Lorraine (1939-) Swimmer. Born in BATHURST in NSW, Lorraine Crapp learnt to swim at the age of five, and eventually became, in the period 1954-56, outstandingly successful, at one time holding world records for 100m, 200m, 400m and 800m, and 220,

440 and 880 yards. The first woman to break five minutes for the 440 yards, her first taste of gold came at the Commonwealth Games in Vancouver (1954) where she won the 110 yards and 440 yards freestyle events. Two years later she again struck gold at the Melbourne Olympic Games where she won the 400m freestyle and was a member of the victorious 4 × 100m relay team. At the same Games she had to settle for silver in the 100m freestyle event in which she was narrowly defeated by arch rival Dawn FRASER. She was chosen to represent Australia at the Commonwealth Games in 1958, again winning a gold medal in the 4 × 100 yards relay. Quiet and unassuming but a tenacious competitor, she retired after the Rome Olympics (1960) where she won a silver medal in the 4 × 100m relay.

Crawford, John Herbert 'Jack' (1908-) Tennis player. Born in the NSW country town of Urangeline, Crawford was introduced to tennis on a rough-hewn country court with a makeshift net made of twine, but he was to become the most acclaimed player of the 1930s. Australian junior champion from 1926 to 1929, Crawford gained international prominence in 1933. In that year he won the Australian singles title, became the first Australian to win the French singles title, won the Wimbledon singles (defeating American Ellsworth Vines before a crowd of 18 000, in what is still spoken of as possibly the greatest-ever Wimbledon final), and narrowly missed his chance to win the 'Grand Slam', losing to Fred Perry in the US singles final. Other wins included the NSW State championship (seven successive times), the Australian singles (successively 1931-33 and in 1935), the Australian doubles with Harry HOPMAN in 1929 and 1930, and the French and Wimbledon doubles with Adrian QUIST in 1935. An impressive and stylish player with a fluid and powerful forehand, Crawford also played for the Davis Cup, representing Australia in as many as nine Cup teams.

crayfish *see* crustaceans

Cressy TAS (population 640 in 1981) A town in the N part of the MIDLANDS region, it is located some 38km by road SSW of LAUNCESTON. At an elevation of 152m, it receives an average annual rainfall of 647mm, July being the month of highest rainfall. Sheep grazing for both wool and fat lambs is the major rural activity, with some cereal and pulse crops, a little beef cattle grazing and dairying. Until the 1930s, wheat and other farm crops dominated the rural scene, but depleted soil fertility and trace-element deficiencies caused the change to grazing. In 1971, the first and so far the only large-scale TAS irrigation project was established in this area. Named the Cressy-LONGFORD Irrigation District, it covers an area of about 9000ha and its source of water supply is from the tailrace of the POATINA hydro-electricity station (part of the GREAT LAKE power scheme).

Creswick VIC (population 2 036 in 1981) This small country town is located on the Midland Highway, 132km by road and 137km by rail NW of Melbourne, and 18km by road N of BALLARAT. The town takes its name from the Creswick family, who were pioneer settlers in the area in the 1840s. In 1852 it was the scene of an important gold strike and it experienced the subsequent rush of hopeful prospectors seeking their fortunes. Nowadays, however, the major activities are grazing, farming and timber-getting. The Victorian Forests Commission has established extensive pine plantations in the area; it is also the site of the Victorian School of Forestry and the State Nursery.

Crib Point VIC (population 2 083 in 1981) A small coastal town on the E shore of the MORNINGTON PENINSULA (that is, on the W shore of WESTERN PORT BAY, opposite French Is), it is 73km by rail SE of Melbourne. There is a major oil refinery on Crib Point near the town. The name comes from a 'crib' or hut, built by local fishermen in the early days of settlement.

cricket is extremely popular throughout Australia; in 1983 the Australian Cricket Board calculated that over 400 000 people were playing it. Only international matches, however, attract very large numbers of spectators. For Test matches (international matches normally played over five days) the record attendance on any one day is 90 800, on the second day of a Test against the West Indies in 1961; for one-day, limited-over international matches the record is 86 133, in a match against the West Indies in 1984. Both were set at the Melbourne Cricket Ground, and both are world as well as Australian records. **The first organised match** in Australia, arranged by the officers of HMS *Calcutta*, was played on the site of present-day Hyde Park, Sydney, in 1803. In 1826 a group of military regiments in NSW formed the Military Club, and the civilian Australian Club was formed later the same year to provide competition for the soldiers. In VIC the first club to be formed (1838) was the Melbourne Cricket Club.

In the early days cricket was as much entertainment as sport, so it was natural that Adelaide's first match, promoted by a publican in 1839, should be part of a programme featuring exhibitions of foot-running, juggling and climbing the greasy pole. In those days, fine, carefully positioned modern pitches were unknown. Dr W.G. Grace, captaining a touring English side in 1873-74, inspected the ground before play in STAWELL in VIC; asking where the wicket was, he received the remarkable reply, 'You're standing on it.' But such conditions evidently did not dull the enthusiasm of the early Australians. By the turn of the century all States had well-organised club competitions. WA was a late-comer in this regard, regular club competitions not starting in Perth until 1900—Melbourne (since 1860), Sydney (1871),

*Species, genus or family is endemic to Australia (see Preface)

Adelaide (1873) and Brisbane (1876) were by then well established in club competition.

Interstate competition was established on a regular basis with the inauguration of the Sheffield Shield in 1892, but sporadic inter-colonial matches date back to the summer of 1850-51, when VIC played TAS in LAUNCE-STON. The Sheffield Shield, prize of the annual interstate competition, is a silver trophy 115cm × 75cm which dates from the visit of an English side sponsored by Lord Sheffield and captained by Dr W.G. Grace in 1891–2. Although the Australians regained 'the Ashes' at that time, Lord Sheffield was so delighted by the reception his team received in Australia that he presented £150 sterling, 'for the better-ment of Australian cricket', to the Australian Cricket Council. In the following 33 years, NSW, VIC and SA competed for the shield, QLD becoming a competitor in 1926, WA in 1947 and TAS in 1977. NSW holds the highest record of wins (37 times to the end of the 1982-83 season), followed by VIC (24 times) and SA (12 times); but WA's perform-ance is outstanding, six of her total of seven wins having been made in the 13 seasons between 1967-68 and 1979-80.

Test cricket International cricket began in 1861 when a Melbourne catering firm spon-sored the tour of an English team under the captaincy of H.H. Stephenson. Although at first Stephenson's objections to fielding his 11-man team against the VIC side of 22 led to the reduction of the VIC team to 18 men, the Australians proved no match for the English batsmen and after the first game in Melbourne (attended by a crowd variously estimated at between 25 000 and 40 000), the Englishmen agreed to play for the rest of the tour against 22-man sides.

AUSTRALIA'S INTERNATIONAL CRICKET RECORD (up till January 1984)

Opponent	Won	Lost	Tied	Drawn
England	95	83		73
India	20	8		11
New Zealand	8	2		5
Pakistan	11	9		8
South Africa	29	11		13
West Indies	26	13	1	12
Sri Lanka	1			

But it is the English tour of 1876-77 which is regarded as the first Anglo-Australian Test. When the English visitors, all professionals, lost their first three matches to Australian teams, it was thought that Australia might dare to better England at eleven-a-side cricket, and a national team was duly selected to play the English side in Melbourne before they left Australia. Australia beat England by 45 runs. Coincidentally, the centenary Anglo-Australian Test played on the same grounds (Melbourne Cricket Ground, originally 'Richmond Paddock') in 1977 again saw Australia defeat England by a margin of 45 runs.

International cricket match

Courtesy of A.I.S. Canberra

Spurred by the Melbourne victory of 1877, a team of 13 Australian cricketers embarked on a tour of England in the following year. Although an all-Aboriginal side had toured England in 1868, this was the first represen-tative side to tour overseas. The highlight of their tour was a match against the Marylebone Cricket Club at Lord's, and to the astonish-ment of all England, the MCC side was dis-missed for 33 runs in its first innings and 19 in its second. However, in the first Test played on English soil two years later, the Australians were soundly defeated, avoiding an innings defeat only by the superlative batting of their captain Murdoch, who top-scored for the match with 153 not out.

The Ashes Murdoch led another side to England in 1882, and in matches preparatory to the Test to be played in late August, the side showed strength in both batting and bowling which caused serious concern to the selectors of the English side. The two sides met on Kennington Oval on 28 and 29 August. Australia batted first, amassing only a miserable 63 to which England replied with 101. Australia's second innings gave them a lead of only 84 when England began her now historic second innings. Frederick SPOFFORTH, 'the Demon', spurred on by anger at what the Australians considered the unsportsmanlike behaviour of Dr Grace (who, concealing the ball behind his beard, had unexpectedly whipped off the bails while Australian batsman Jones was advancing down the wicket to pat down some rough spots) was determined that the English would not get the 85 they needed to win. At 70 for seven wickets (six taken by Spofforth) an 'awful silence' enveloped the ground; several men fainted with the tension, and when Spofforth took yet another wicket making it 75 for eight, one spectator dropped dead. The final English wicket fell for 77 to the victorious Australians, who shouldered Spofforth from the ground. The following morning the *Sporting Times* published, in memoriam, this notice:

In Affectionate Remembrance of
English Cricket
Which died at the Oval 29th August, 1882
Deeply lamented by a large circle of
sorrowing friends and acquaintances.
R.I.P.
N.B. The body will be cremated and the ashes
taken
to Australia

And thus 'the Ashes' came into being, al-though at the time nothing was symbolically burned to create ashes. But during the 1883 series a bail was ceremoniously cremated, the burned remains placed in an urn and the Ashes presented to the English captain. Although the Ashes now rest permanently at Lord's, Test series between the two countries have since been contested for the symbolic ownership of the Ashes. At the close of the 1983-84 season after over 100 years of Anglo-Australian Test cricket the record stood at 95 victories to Australia against 83 to England, with 73 Tests drawn.

Against other cricketing nations Australia again records more wins than losses. Competi-tion with South Africa began in 1902 when a team returning from England stopped off there and won this first match. Test cricket has not been played with South Africa since the 1969-70 season because of the difficulties posed by the South African commitment to the policy of *apartheid*. Australia's first inter-national match with the West Indies was played in 1930-31 in Australia, and the first Test with New Zealand was played in Wellington in 1946; India first visited Australia in 1947-48, and Australia toured Pakistan for the first time in 1956.

World Series Cricket (WSC) came into being in the 1977-78 season after the Sydney television magnate Kerry Packer announced that he had signed on most of the world's top cricketers to play in a series of Super Tests between Australia and the best team the rest of the world could produce. Before the Series began the original two teams had grown to four: two Australian teams, a World XI includ-ing players from England, Pakistan and South Africa, and a West Indies team. Although the first year of the Series was an undoubted success, drawing increasingly large crowds to watch these teams vie for rich rewards, this introduction to cricket of professionalism on a large, organised scale, with its emphasis on sport entertainment provided for spectators and television viewers by full-time professional players, engendered a good deal of bad blood in the cricket world. The ruling cricketing bodies of most nations initially banned all WSC players from representing their countries in traditional Test matches. Some nations gradually relaxed this uncompromising stand; but the 1978 Australian side touring the West Indies contained no WSC players. In 1979 a compromise was reached between WSC and the cricket establishment, by which WSC players were welcomed back to the official fold.

In more than a century of participation in international cricket, the Australians can be claimed to have injected new life into it. Bowlers such as Spofforth and TURNER ('the Terror') were held in awe by English batsmen; at the turn of the century TRUMPER enthralled spectators by his effortless power; and the 1930s and 1940s brought the domination of the inimitable scorer, BRADMAN. After World War II, such sportsmen as Lindwall, MILLER,

Ocean beach surf crab, *Ovalipes australiensis*

Mangrove crab, *Sesarma erythrodactyla*

Red-eyed rock crab, *Eriphia sebana*

Freshwater crab, *Paratelphusa transversa*

Ghost crab, *Ocypode cordimana*

Shore crab, *Plagusia glabra*

Horn-eyed ghost crab, *Ocypode ceratophthalma*

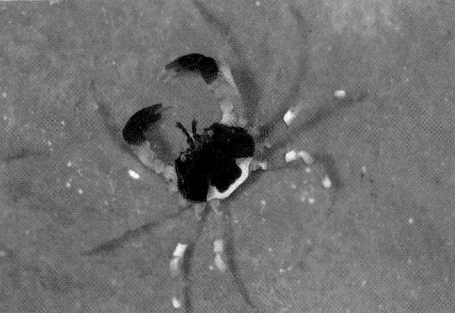
Spider crab, *Halicarcinus ovatus*

Freshwater crayfish, *Cherax destructor*

Freshwater crayfish, *Euastacus spinifera*

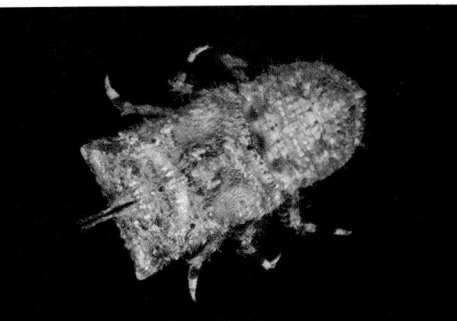
Flapjack cray, *Scyllarus demani*

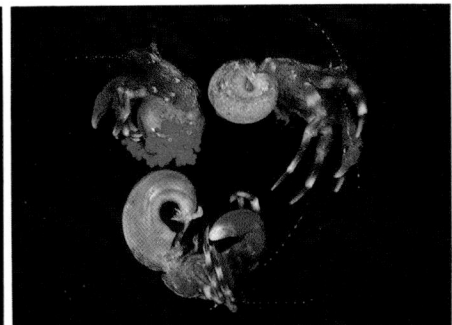
Hermit crabs *Pagurus lacertosus* out of shells

See also CRUSTACEANS

King prawn, *Penaeus plebejus*

Freshwater crayfish, *Euastacus australasiensis*

Intertidal shrimp, *Alope orientalis*

Rock pool shrimp, *Palaemon serenus*

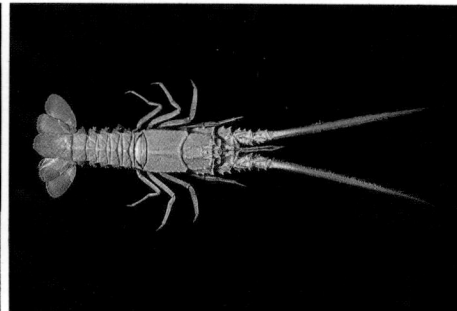

Barking lobster, *Linnpartus trigonus*

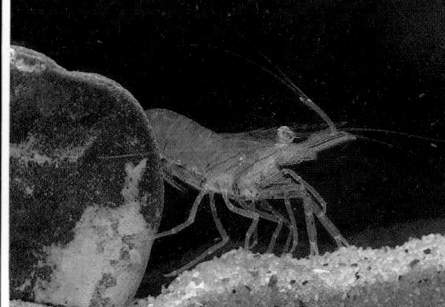

Rock pool shrimp, *Palaemon litoreus*

Barnacles

Goose-necked barnacles washed ashore

Pelagic barnacles

Pill bug, *Zuzara venosa*

Balmain bug, *Ibacus* species

Amphipod, *Ceradocus rubromaculatus*

See also CRUSTACEANS

Hasset, BENAUD, the CHAPPELL brothers, Jeff Thompson, Rodney MARSH and Dennis LILLEE have excited spectators and kept Australia near, and often at, the top of the international cricketing ladder. *See* Appendix 13.

See also Gregory family; Macartney, C.G.; Marsh, R.W.; McCabe, S.; Noble, M.A.

Further reading: Whitington, R.S. *An Illustrated History of Australian Cricket.* Lansdowne Press, Melbourne, 1972.

crickets and grasshoppers

These exopterygote INSECTS belong to the order Orthoptera (about 2000 known Australian species), which also contains the LOCUSTS. The Orthoptera is an order of great importance because of the destructive plant feeding of many of its members. Orthopterans have biting and chewing mouthparts, their hind-legs are usually adapted for jumping, their fore-wings are thickened and straight and their large membranous hind-wings fold like a fan when at rest. The top part of the first thoracic segment (the pronotum) extends downwards as lobes.

Many orthopterans are famous for the shrill, jarring song (stridulation) which is produced by rubbing two specialised areas of the body together. The structure and position of the ears and stridulatory organs vary from group to group. It is often the males that are the best performers. The songs, of course, are used in mating, and the 'melody' is almost always highly specific, serving to lessen the chances that two individuals will attempt cross-mating between species. In many cases the song is a more reliable method of distinguishing between species than studying the colour and form of the insects. Studies on some overseas crickets have shown that the frequency of the trills is closely related to the temperature which the investigator could estimate to within 1 °C by counting the trills.

Mountain Katydid, *Acripeza reticulata*

Many species live in exposed positions on foliage or on the ground; such species are either camouflaged or brightly coloured to indicate to potential predators that they are distasteful. The female mountain katydid, *Acripeza reticulata*, raises her fore-wings suddenly when disturbed, exposing a banded abdomen of vivid red, blue and black, and, standing on the tips of her feet, she sways from side to side. If the interference is continued the thin, yellow cuticle between her thorax and head balloons out. The female lacks the large hind-wings used for flying but her mate, a slim, dark-coloured typical grasshopper, has normal hind-wings. The yellow-winged locust, *Gastrimargus musicus*, has a brown-banded patch of yellow on the hind-wing which is very conspicuous when the insect is flying. As soon as it lands the wings are folded and the yellow disappears—and the locust seems to do so also. Many other species live in crevices, under stones and in rotting wood, emerging only occasionally. Some are found only in caves, and a few are entirely subterranean.

When captured many orthopterans kick with the hind-legs which often have spines, and vomit their crop contents onto the attacker. Some, such as the king crickets, have mouth-parts that can pierce human skin.

The order is divided into two suborders, the Ensifera (mainly crickets) and the Caelifera (mainly grasshoppers).

Ensifera This suborder contains crickets and long-horned grasshoppers, including katydids. These insects have long antennae with well over 30 segments. The stridulatory organs, when present, are on the wings; the ears, when present, are on the legs. Normally only the males produce the song. The egg-laying organ (ovipositor) of the female is sword-like.

The superfamily Grylloidea contains the true crickets (at least 700 species in Australia). Typical examples are usually pale, drab or black omnivores which hide during the day; some are common in and around buildings. They prefer humid habitats and are often common in fermenting garbage dumps. Some gryllids (tree crickets) attack plants and place their eggs in slits in the plant tissues. The family Gryllotalpidae contains the mole crickets, large insects which live in permanent burrows in the soil, though they can fly. They often stridulate at the entrances of their burrows after rain. The legs are modified for digging and superficially resemble those of the mole. Some are minor pests of, for example, potato tubers, and are often found by gardeners. The female mole cricket is one of the few insects which broods its eggs and which cares for its young for a time after hatching. The nursery is a deep residential burrow dug by the female in the spring.

The superfamily Gryllacridoidea (about 160 species in Australia) contains the cave and king crickets. Several are restricted to caves; others hide during the day in burrows or rotting wood and emerge at night to feed on plants, or on other insects and spiders.

The superfamily Tettigonoidea (about 320 species in Australia) contains the katydids and other long-horned grasshoppers. The katydids are so called because their song sounds like 'Katy did, Katy didn't'. The members of this superfamily usually feed exposed on foliage but most species are well camouflaged.

Caelifera This suborder contains the short-horned grasshoppers (about 900 species in Australia). The antennae of these insects have fewer than 30 segments and are always shorter than the body. Sound is produced by rubbing the spiny legs against the wings; the ears,

Short-horned grasshopper, *Petasida ephippigera*

when present, are on the first segment of the abdomen.

The superfamily Acridoidea contains the largest family, Acrididae (about 600 species in Australia). These are the familiar grasshoppers and locusts (locusts are simply grasshoppers that have the ability in certain conditions to form large destructive swarms).

The superfamily Tetrigoidea contains the Tetrigidae, small grasshoppers whose thorax extends over the abdomen as a cover. Known as grouse-locusts, they are usually found on sand or soil in damp places; many species can swim and may stay under water for some time. They feed on algae and organic matter in mud.

The superfamily Tridactyloidea contains the family Tridacylidae; these are the pigmy mole crickets, small, usually smooth and black species which make galleries in sandy lake shores. Also contained in this superfamily is the family Cylindrachetidae, a small family of insects, superficially like mole crickets, which burrow in sand. They have an interesting distribution: five species in Australia, one in New Guinea and one in Patagonia.

crinoids *see* sea lilies

croakers *see* fishes, bony

crocodiles

These large carnivorous REPTILES belong to the order Crocodylia, which is divided into three families: Alligatoridae (true alligators and caimans); Crocodylidae (true crocodiles); and Gavialidae (gavial, one species only). There are 21 species in eight genera; two known species, both true crocodiles, occur in Australia. One, the inoffensive freshwater or Johnstone's crocodile, *Crocodylus johnstoni*, is endemic; the estuarine, or salt water species, *C. porosus*, ranges from India to China, and also occurs in Malaysia and New Guinea.

The crocodiles are the closest living relatives of the dinosaurs and the birds. They are known from the Triassic period, 195 to 225 million years ago, but modern types first appeared in the Cretaceous period, 65 to 135 million years ago.

Crocodiles have webbed feet; the hind legs are longer than the front legs, and this indicates that they are descended from bipedal (two-footed), terrestrial ancestors. In the water the crocodile pushes itself along with its powerful, laterally-flattened tail, and the bones of the backbone are modified to allow a fish-like movement of the body. The back is covered with horny plates (scutes), roughly rectangular in shape. Beneath these are strong, bony, dermal plates. The scutes of the belly are small, and the dermal plates are not so prominent, at least in true alligators and the true crocodiles. Because the bony plates are absent on the belly, the skin is attractive to manufacturers of hand-bags, shoes and the like.

The nostrils and the eyes are high on the head so that the crocodile can see and breathe while the rest of the body is submerged. The mouth is separated from the breathing channel, and the crocodile can thus swallow prey beneath the water. The heart is divided into four chambers, like those of birds and mammals.

Prey is often killed by being dragged underwater and drowned. Large prey, not necessarily dead, is often dismembered, the crocodile gripping a limb then rolling and twirling the prey around. Newly hatched crocodiles live on small insects, fish fry and other small animals, but their prey becomes larger as they grow. The eggs, which sometimes number 100, are buried in simple pits on the shore, or in masses of rotting vegetation. The mother stays in the vicinity, and when the hatching young start to squeak, she uncovers the brood.

The Australian estuarine crocodile occurs from the KIMBERLEYS region to MARY-BOROUGH in QLD. Though it is mainly an animal of brackish waters and the sea, it is sometimes found living in freshwater. Crocodiles are frequently met swimming far from the shore and at least one has been recorded in Fiji. They can reach a length of 7m but specimens longer than 5m are uncommon, largely because the older and larger individuals are killed by hunters. The back is grey, brown or almost black, with darker mottlings, and the underparts are whitish. The snout is relatively short and blunt when compared with that of a freshwater crocodile. The saltwater crocodile is a nocturnal animal feeding on mammals, birds, reptiles, fish and crustaceans. The female lays about 60 eggs during the wet and the early dry seasons (October to May) in a nest of leaf-mould, high on the bank, protected by scrub. The eggs hatch in three to five months and the young stay with the mother for three or four days before dispersing.

Courtesy of A.I.S. Canberra

Estuarine or salt-water crocodile, *Crocodylus porosus*

Biologists do not agree about the danger of saltwater crocodiles to man. There have been few European deaths in Australia but un-reported Aboriginal deaths may have been more common. Caras (*see below*) records the fate of 1000 Japanese soldiers who were trapped in a Burmese mangrove swamp in February 1945. Only 20 soldiers survived the gunfire and the attacks by the numerous salt-water crocodiles. It can at least be said that the saltwater crocodile is the only Australian animal, apart from sharks, that would consider a human being as a possible meal.

There is no doubt that the freshwater crocodile, *C. johnstoni*, is harmless to man, except when wounded. It is a timid animal and tries to hide when disturbed. It is found in freshwater in the far N, from the FITZROY RIVER in WA to north-eastern QLD. The snout is smooth, long and slender, unlike the snout of the saltwater species which is short, broad and granular. This species grows to about 3m and in colour is grey to olive-brown above and whitish below. It appears to feed mainly on frogs, small fish, large crustaceans, insects and spiders. The female lays her eggs (about 20) in a hollow which she digs in a sandbank near the water, in August and September, and they hatch in November/December, before the sandbank is flooded. The populations of both certified species have fallen dramatically since World War II because of commercial hunting, but crocodiles are now protected. In November 1979 a population of dwarf crocodiles, all of 1m long or less, was discovered in a remote part of N Australia. They resembled small freshwater crocodiles but may prove to be a new species.

Further reading: Cogger, H.G. *Reptiles and Amphibia of Australia*. A.H. & A.W. Reed, Sydney, 1975; Worrell, E. *Reptiles of Australia*. (2nd edn) Angus & Robertson, Sydney, 1970; Caras, R. *Dangerous to Man*. Penguin Books, Harmondsworth, 1975.

Croker Island NT Lying off the NE shore of COBOURG PENINSULA and separated from it by Brown Strait, this long, narrow island (over 80km N-S extent and less than 10km wide) is the site of a UNITING CHURCH mission which has encouraged Aboriginal development of tropical fruit and vegetable growing. The main settlement, located on the E of the island, is Minjilong. The island has a hot tropical climate, typical of these N parts, with an average annual rainfall of 1 343mm, concentrated in the period between November and March.

Crookwell NSW (population 2 063 in 1981) A small country town in the headwaters of the LACHLAN RIVER catchment area, it is about 50km NW of GOULBURN and 260km by road SW of Sydney. It is a service and commercial centre for a rich rural district producing wool, grain crops, beef cattle, fat lambs, dairy produce, potatoes, apples, pears and cherries. At an elevation of 887m above sea level, it has an average annual rainfall of 869mm, spread throughout the year, but with a concentration in the winter season. An annual rodeo is held at Crookwell over the Labour Day weekend in October, and at Tuena, a village nearby, a Gold Rush Festival is held each year over Easter.

croquet Introduced into Australia by English settlers in the late 1860s, croquet was considered a game for men until the start of World War I when, with many men away fighting, the women took sufficient interest to keep the game alive during the war years. Croquet was revived as a game for men after World War II through the efforts of two English settlers, Major Robert Tingey and Colonel A. Edward Saalfield, the latter convincing people that croquet was not just a game for the meek and elderly but that it required skill, precision and intelligence.

Within Australia the game has been controlled by the Australian Croquet Council since 1950. Australian Open championships are held annually, the winner from each State being awarded the Australian Gold Medal, and the gold medallists then competing for a silver medal donated by the English Croquet Association. In international matches held every four years, Australia, Britain and New Zealand compete for the MacRobertson Shield.

Croton *see* Euphorbiaceae

Crowea *see* Rutaceae

Crowley, Grace Adela (1890-) Artist. Born in Cobbadah NSW, she went to Julian ASHTON's classes while she attended boarding school in Sydney. She became a full-time student at Ashton's school in 1915, and later taught there for four years, leaving in 1923. She studied in Paris at Colarossi's and the Académie of André Lhote, returning in 1930 to Australia, where she became one of a group of modern artists which included Frank and Margel Hinder, Roy DE MAISTRE, Rah FIZELLE, Ralph BALSON, Roland WAKELIN and Grace Cossington SMITH. She assisted at Dorrit Black's Modern Art Centre, and between 1932 and 1937 co-operated with Rah Fizelle in establishing an art school at 215c George Street. Her influence in the cubist-constructivist trend in avant-garde painting circles in Sydney was significant, and she was associated with several exhibitions which were important in the history of the 'modern' movement in Sydney, namely, 'A Group of Seven' (Macquarie Galleries, 1930), 'Exhibiton 1' (David Jones', 1939), 'Constructive Paintings' (Macquarie Galleries, 1944) and 'Abstract' (David Jones', 1948), and with two 'abstract' exhibitions at Macquarie Galleries, 'Abstract Compositions' (1951) and 'Abstractions' (1954).

crown of thorns *see* corals; Euphorbiaceae; sea stars

crows and ravens The one hundred PASSERINE members of the family Corvidae

Little crow, *Corvus bennettii*

P. Klapste (N.P.I.A.W.)

are believed to represent the peak of avian evolution. They are adaptable, intelligent BIRDS with well-organised social relationships. The plumage is black, with concealed whites and greys. These birds are omnivores; most feed on carrion, young birds and insects, and some kill lambs and sickly sheep. Until recently, it was believed that there were only three Australian species, but now there are five known species, all belonging to the genus *Corvus*. It is very difficult to distinguish some of these species, and it has been suggested that as the differences are quantitative rather than qualitative, a computer would be needed for accurate identification. No attempt is made here to show how they can be distinguished.

The crow, *Corvus cecilae** (48cm to 55cm long), is a solitary or gregarious species, though it seldom forms large flocks. It is found mainly in mountain ranges, forests and woodlands in tropical N Australia, extending S to the N parts of NSW, SA and WA. Like most other Australian representatives of this family, it builds large, open and sometimes deep nests of twigs and sticks, lined with grass and wool and placed in tall trees.

The little crow, *C. bennettii** (45cm to 52cm), is sometimes found in large flocks, often with the little raven, and frequents areas of dry scrub throughout the Australian interior and western WA. Its call-note, which resembles the word 'car' repeated six times, is a familiar sound in small towns, particularly in WA. The eggs are greenish-grey, with brown markings.

The raven, *C. coronoides** (50cm to 56cm), is a wary, solitary bird, occasionally found in flocks of up to about 30 birds. During the day, it prefers open country, but returns to woodland areas at night. It is found in SE Australia, inland QLD, SW Australia and southern SA. The nests of sticks, bark and hair are built in the forked branches of tall trees. The habits of the little raven, *C. mellori** (40cm to 45cm), resemble those of the raven, but it is far less widespread, being found only in SE Australia, and it tends to keep to lower levels in trees. The only raven found in TAS and on FLINDERS ISLAND is the forest raven, *C. tasmanicus** (50cm to 60cm), a solitary or gregarious bird which forms flocks up to 100 strong and frequents thick woodlands, beaches or open country.

Species, genus or family is endemic to Australia (see Preface)

Further reading: Rowley, I. *Bird Life*. Collins, Sydney, 1974.

crow's ash Also called Australian teak, the crow's ash, *Flindersia australis* (family RUTACEAE), is a large, bushy tree found in NSW and QLD, particularly in rainforest, and also in mixed softwood forests and scrub. It is a durable timber, used for various purposes in building. The genus *Flindersia* contains several large trees yielding valuable timber, and is characterised by large, usually pinnate, glossy leaves dotted with oil glands which give off a pungent odour. Among other members of the genus, the Queensland maple, *F. brayleyana*, is considered to be a particularly fine cabinet timber, and the leopard wood, *F. maculosa*, recognised by its mottled bark, has simple leaves which are valuable feed for stock.

crow's foot grass *see* Gramineae; weeds

crustaceans The Crustacea is a class of the phylum Arthropoda (ARTHROPODS) containing the crabs, lobsters, barnacles and slaters, and a host of related animals. Most crustaceans are marine, though there are freshwater and land species; and although most are free-living, some are sedentary and others parasitic. The class, now usually divided into eight subclasses (Cephalocarida, Mystacocarida, Branchiopoda, Ostracoda, Copepoda, Branchiura, Cirripedia, Malacostraca), contains some 26 000 species, several thousand of them occurring in Australia and adjacent waters.

Members of the Crustacea can be identified by the appendages on the head, and often have a horny shell fold (carapace) covering the thorax and sometime also projecting forward (a rostrum) to protect the head. The entire cuticle (or exoskeleton) usually contains calcium carbonate and other calcium salts, which reinforce it. A feature peculiar to the crustaceans is the presence of two pairs of sensory appendages (antennules and antennae) on the head. Three other pairs of appendages on the head handle food (mandibles; first and second maxillae), and the head carries a pair of compound eyes, which may be on stalks. The trunk segments vary greatly from group to group: in most living forms a thorax and an abdomen can be distinguished, different groups of segments being specialised for various tasks, but in some existing primitive forms there is little such differentiation, except in the last segment (the telson), which carries the anus. The number of trunk segments varies, and each may carry a pair of appendages, which in crustaceans are typically biramous (having two branches, in contrast to the uniramous limbs of INSECTS), and which may be used in locomotion, grasping food, creating food currents, and carrying eggs. The breathing gills, too, are usually processes carried on the appendages. The sexes are generally separate, though reproduction may be parthenogenetic (the young developing from unfertilised eggs) in some species.

The newly hatched young of freshwater species may closely resemble miniature adults, but marine species often emerge as a tiny nauplius larva, unsegmented, and roughly oval in shape, with a single median eye at the front of the head and three pairs of appendages (the antennae, antennules and mandibles) used for swimming in the plankton. The nauplius larva may pass through a further stage (the zoea) before reaching the adult stage.

The food value of crustaceans to man is overshadowed by their importance to other animals. The copepods and similar small species that breed so abundantly in the sea provide the entire diet of some whales and many fish.

Subclasses Cephalocarida and Mystacocarida Only a few small species, none of which is known in Australia, belong to each of these groups.

Subclass Branchiopoda This group contains three orders, all of which occur in Australia. Mainly freshwater species, but also found in the sea and in saline lakes, branchiopods have leaf-like appendages used in swimming and collecting food (mainly micro-organisms), and which carry gills. Branchiopod antennules are small and the telson carries a pair of long 'tails' (cercopods).

1. The order Anostraca contains the small, delicate fairy shrimps and brine shrimps, which have stalked eyes and lack a carapace, the elongated trunk consisting of about 20 seg-

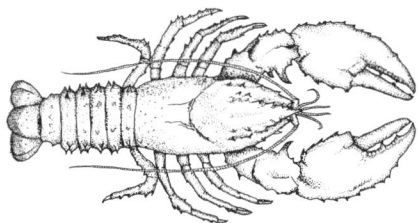

Freshwater crayfish, *Euastacus armatus*

ments. Found in freshwater in all mainland States, they generally have a local distribution, and nearly all are believed to be endemic. The eggs can withstand desiccation, which may in fact be necessary to their development. The brine shrimp, *Artemia salina*, is cosmopolitan. Its desiccated eggs are often supplied by dealers in aquarium fishes.

2. The order Notostraca has only two known Australian species, *Triops australiensis*, found in the N two-thirds of the continent, and *Lepidurus apus viridus*, found in the SW, the SE and in TAS. Called tadpole shrimps, they actually look more like miniature king crabs, having a large, shield-shaped carapace. They live in ephemeral waters, but their occurrence is sporadic, probably because the eggs, light and easily carried long distances by the wind, must dry out thoroughly before development can be completed.

3. The order Diplostraca has two suborders, Conchostraca (the clam shrimps) and Cladocera (the water fleas); in both groups there is lateral compression of the body. The clam shrimps, named from the dorsally hinged bivalve carapace which encloses the body, may

grow to about 2.5cm long, the surface often showing growth lines. The large antennae, which can be protruded from the shell, are used for swimming. Of 20 species known in Australia, all but one appear to be endemic. In the water fleas, found throughout Australia in fresh and saline water, and in the sea, the carapace envelops the trunk, leaving the head free. They may be from 0.25mm to 6mm long. No external segmentation is evident and there are only five or six pairs of trunk appendages; the large antennae assist the animal's jerky movements. Five families are represented in Australia, containing over 70 known species, of which some are extremely common, and important in the diet of other organisms.

Subclass Ostracoda This group contains some 80 Australian species common in inland and marine waters, usually just above muddy and silty bottoms. Sometimes called mussel or seed shrimps, ostracods resemble clam shrimps, though they are generally smaller. The large head and small, unsegmented trunk are enclosed in a calcified and hinged carapace, the valves of which can be tightly closed by muscles. True growth lines in the carapace are absent, though 'sculpturing' may be seen. There are rarely more than two trunk appendages, which may be modified for various purposes, or may serve as legs, used in conjunction with the antennae for swimming, climbing or jumping. Most ostracods are free-living, feeding on micro-organisms and detritus, but some are scavengers or predators, and a few are parasitic.

Subclass Copepoda Members of this group, numbering some 4 500 species worldwide, have no carapace. Free-living or parasitic, they are predominantly marine, though there are many freshwater species; a few terrestrial species are found in damp leaf-litter. The free-living marine copepods, being extremely abundant, are key organisms in ocean food webs. Most free-living species are small (rarely more than a few millimetres long) and similar in form, the cylindrical or pear-shaped body having a well-defined head fused with one or two of the thoracic segments, which carry appendages. Instead of compound eyes, there is a compact median group of three simple eyes (ocelli). The abdomen is of variable length; the telson carries a pair of long tail filaments (caudal rami). Females may carry a pair of egg-sacs on the abdomen. Among parasitic copepods there is often considerable modification in form, particularly among endoparasites, which usually absorb food through the skin. Parasitic copepods attack most kinds of marine animals, and there are also freshwater forms.

Subclass Branchiura Flattened parasites found on the skin or in the gill chambers of marine and freshwater fish, branchiurans have a large, shield-like carapace and compound eyes. Of some 75 species represented in Australia, several (such as the fish-louse, *Argulus* species, a pest in aquaria) appear to be exotic.

Subclass Cirripedia The barnacles, of which there are about 800 species in the

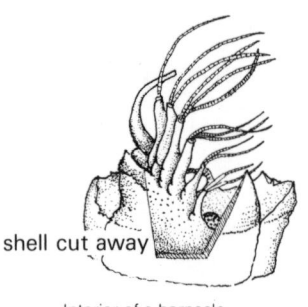

shell cut away

Interior of a barnacle

world, are mostly free-living, though a large number are parasitic and some are commensal on whales and other marine organisms. The adult barnacle (once described as 'a little shrimp-like animal standing on its head in a limestone house and kicking food into its mouth') is either stalked (as in goose barnacles, which are often cast ashore on driftwood) or sessile. Barnacles are mostly hermaphrodite, usually reproducing by cross-fertilisation. The egg generally hatches first as a nauplius larva, transforming into a cypris larva before settling and cementing itself onto a hard substratum to pass into the adult stage. The adult carapace is covered with several calcareous plates, an opening at the top allowing the thoracic legs through to collect food. Different species of barnacles characterise various seashore zones, massing on surfaces which may be relatively exposed by the tides or never exposed, the maximum size of individuals varying according to the degree of crowding and predominating local conditions.

Barnacles common along Australian shores include the large, rather flattened and many-plated surf-barnacle, *Catophragmus polymeris*

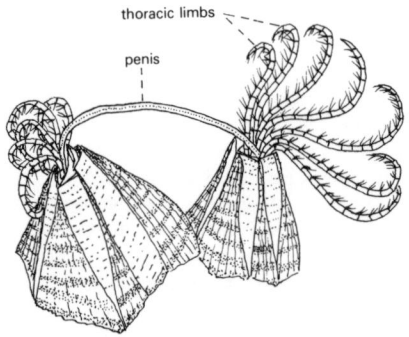

thoracic limbs

penis

Cross fertilisation between acorn barnacles, *Balanus* species

(SE Australia); the pink four-plated *Tetraclita rosea* and the less evident *T. purpurescens*; the small *Chthamalus antennatus*; and the large *Balanus nigrescens*, almost black externally, but caerulean blue just inside the opening. *Chamaesipho columna*, probably the most numerous species, often completely covers rocks between the mid- and high-tide marks. Parasitic barnacles may live within the body cavities of other animals (such as ECHINO-DERMS), absorbing food through their skin, or they may attach themselves to marine turtles or whales, most of the shell lying below the host's skin. Members of the order Rhizoce-phala show extreme parasitism, forming a

tumour-like bag on the ventral surface of the decapod crustaceans.

Subclass Malacostraca including crabs, crayfish, lobsters and slaters, this large group contains about 75 per cent of all crustaceans and all the largest forms. The subclass is commonly divided into two series with five superorders: series Leptostraca, superorder Leptostraca; series Eumalacostraca, super-orders Syncarida, Hoplocarida, Peracarida and Eucarida. Typical malacostracans have bira-mous first and second antennae, a trunk of eight thoracic and six abdominal segments (each carrying a pair of appendages) and a tail fan, often used for propulsion, formed by the telson and the flattened two branches (uropods) of the last abdominal segment. Thoracic appendages carry gills, and may serve as legs or be modified for feeding (maxillipeds). A carapace generally covers the thorax. The first five pairs of abdominal appendages (pleopods) may serve for locomotion, creating respiratory currents, and carrying eggs (or in males, for mating).

1. Superorder Leptostraca. Containing under 10 species in one order, Nebaliacea, members of this group have a conspicuous carapace and seven abdominal segments. The cosmopolitan shrimp-like *Nebalia* species live in coastal sea-weed and bottom-mud.

2. Superorder Syncarida. Only one order, Anaspidacea, is known in Australia. Usually found on the bottom in shallow waters in TAS and VIC, they grow to about 5cm long. They lack a carapace, and there is little or no differentiation between thoracic appendages, but the tail fan is well developed. Members of the family Anaspididae (species *Paranaspides lacustris*, *Anaspides spinulae* and *A. tasmaniae*) have stalked eyes, but those of the family Koo-mungidae (species *Micraspides calmani* and *Koonunga cursor*) are sessile or absent. All are restricted to TAS apart from *K. cursor* which has also been found in VIC.

3. Superorder Hoplocarida. Contained in one order, Stomatapoda, the mantis shrimps are fierce nocturnal predators which may grow to 30cm long. With an elongated flattened trunk, a short, shield-like carapace, long first antennae and large, stalked eyes, they are distinguished by a pair of large and powerful raptorial (prey catching) limbs on the second thoracic segment. Common species are the mantis shrimp, or prawn killer, *Squilla raphidea*, found in QLD and the smaller *S. laevis*, found in the Sydney region.

4. Superorder Peracarida. With some 9000 species worldwide, this group is notable for the female's brood pouch, formed between the thoracic segments. The many orders include marine, freshwater and terrestrial forms.

The order Mysidacea contains the mysid or opossum shrimps found in all oceans, and im-portant as food to many marine animals. Often transparent, they swim hanging vertically in the water.

The order Cumacea, mainly marine, is known from about 160 species in Australia. Small, but carrying a large carapace almost

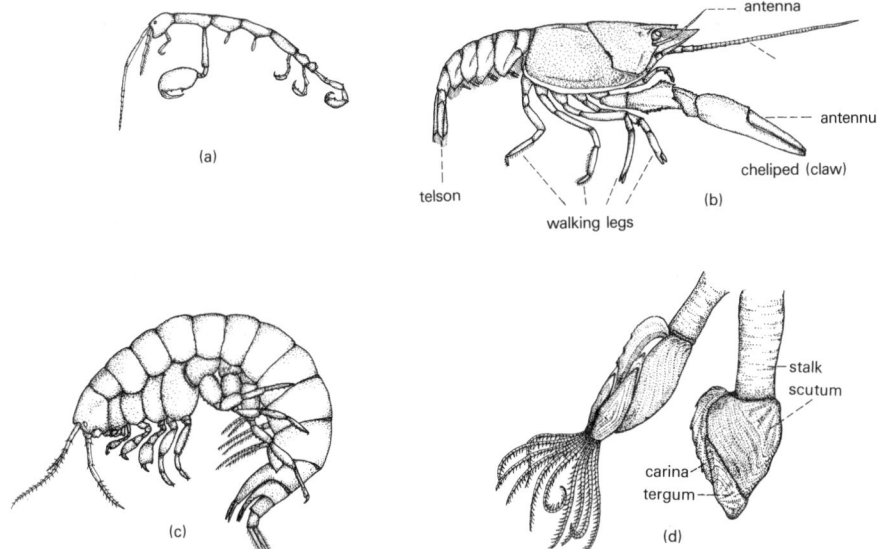

(a) an amphipod, *Caprella* species; (b) a beach hopper (c) a typical crayfish; (d) goose barnacles

enveloping the thorax, cumaceans burrow for small organisms, often rising to the surface at night.

The order Tanaidacea comprises some 250 species of tiny, flattened crustaceans which live in tubes in mud or in cracks in rocks and pilings. They have a carapace, but otherwise resemble isopods.

The order Isopoda, predominantly marine, but also freshwater and terrestrial, represents the second-largest crustacean order, having some 4000 species worldwide. Secretive animals rarely seen, isopods are generally drab-coloured, flattened and lack a carapace. The shield-shaped head carries rather long second antennae and sessile eyes; the first pair of thoracic appendages are maxillipeds, but the rest are used for crawling. Two important pests of this order are the marine gribble (*Limnoria* species), a tiny but extremely destructive pest of jetty timbers, and the pill bugs (*Sphaeroma* species), which often infest wooden supports in oyster leases. Many of the scavenging terrestrial woodlice found in suburban gardens (such as *Porcellio scaber*) are introduced. Fish lice (not to be confused with the *Argulus* fish-lice mentioned earlier) are parasites of marine and freshwater fish; they attach themselves to the gills, or burrow into their hosts; those attacking invertebrates may become greatly modified. Of the numerous freshwater isopods in Australia, the most common are members of the suborder Phreatoicidea, unusual among isopods in being nearly cylindrical, or laterally flattened. They are also found in logs in damp forests and slightly saline artesian bores.

The order Amphipoda has marine, freshwater and terrestrial forms, and contains scavengers (such as sand-hoppers, *Talorchestia* species, common on beaches, and some terrestrial forms inhabiting damp leaf-litter), predators (such as skeleton shrimps, or caprellids, which feed on such animals as small colonial hydroids), a wood-boring species, *Chelura tere-*

brans (sometimes a serious pest), and some parasites. Amphipods are shrimp-like in being laterally flattened, but their eyes are sessile and they lack a carapace. The first two pairs of thoracic appendages (gnathopods) are adapted for clinging, and can be markedly prehensile.

5. Superorder Eucarida. Containing in two orders most of the large and economically important crustaceans, this group is distinguished by a well-developed carapace fused with all the thoracic segments, and stalked eyes. There is no brood chamber.

The order Euphausiacea contains the shrimplike, luminescent KRILL (2.5cm to 5cm long), found in vast shoals in the open sea, and extremely important in the diet of whales and whale sharks. Particularly notable is the red *Euphausia superba*, which feeds near the surface in Antarctic regions.

The order Decapoda, with some 8 500 species, represents approximately one third of all crustaceans. The two suborders of this group, the swimming Natantia (true shrimps and prawns) and the crawling Reptantia (crabs, lobsters and crayfish) are predominantly marine, but include freshwater and terrestrial forms. Of the five pairs of thoracic appendages (hence 'decapod'), the first three are modified as maxillipeds, the first pair generally being larger and chelate (having pincers); the remaining two serve as legs. The thorax and the head are fused, and the carapace, overhanging

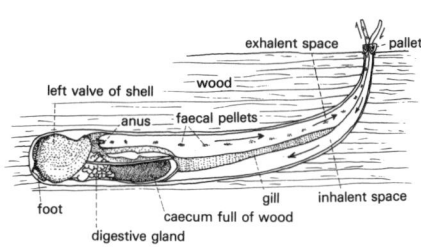

A wood-boring crustacean, *Teledo* species

the sides of the thorax, encloses the gills in a pair of branchial chambers.

Shrimps and prawns are generally laterally flattened and have well-developed abdomens. The carapace projects forward as a conspicuous rostrum over the head. There are three sections—Penaeidea, Caridea and Stenopodidea—differentiated by the respective types and numbers of chelae borne by the anterior thoracic appendages.

The Penaeidea, containing most of the commercially valuable prawns (*see* FISHERIES; PRAWN FISHERIES) includes the greasy-back or greentail, *Metapennaeus benettae*, which breeds in coastal lakes and inlets; and the school prawn, *M. macleayi*, the king prawn, *Penaeus plebejus*, and the banana prawn, *P. merguiensis*, all marine breeders.

Carid shrimps, represented by at least 15 families in Australia, include the well-known snapping or pistol prawns (family Alpheidae). In the family Palaemonidae, a common rockpool species is *Palaemon serenus*, an almost transparent shrimp with red markings; the family also contains about 19 freshwater species, but little is known of their biology. Of the freshwater family Atyidae, about 15 species, generally small and transparent, are known in Australia. Some live in subterranean water.

The only family of the Stenopodidea, Stenopodidae, typically brilliantly coloured and having conspicuously large chelate third legs, includes the striking scarlet-and-white porcelain, or banded, shrimp, *Stenopus hispidus* (10cm long), a cleaner shrimp picking small parasites from the skin of fish in shallow coral pools.

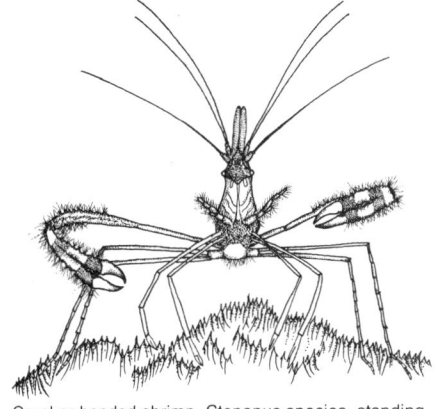

Coral or banded shrimp, *Stenopus* species, standing on coral

The suborder Reptantia is divided into three sections: Macrura (lobsters and crayfish), Anomura (hermit crabs) and Brachyura (true crabs). In members of this suborder the body tends to be flattened from top to bottom, and the heavy first pair of appendages usually bears large chelae; the rostrum is small or absent, and the first abdominal segment is smaller than the rest.

Lobsters and crayfish are characterised by a long abdomen terminating in a large tail fan. In Australia the term 'lobster' applies only to members of the family Palinuridae (which in the N hemisphere are known as spiny lobsters, or langoustes). They lack the large chelae characteristic of the foreign homarid lobsters, and have a roughly cylindrical body, a spiny cuticle, and long, whip-like antennae. Besides commercial lobsters (*Jasus novaehollandiae*, found in the NE, *J. verreauxi*, found in the SE, and *Panulirus cygnus* of WA), several brightly coloured species inhabit tropical waters. In the family Scyllaridae, the Balmain bug, or flapjack, *Scyllarus demani*, and the Moreton Bay bug, *Thenus orientalis* (about 25cm long), are sometimes trawled from deep water; though unattractively squat, flattened, burrowing animals with broad, plate-like antennae, they are nevertheless edible. Freshwater crayfish in Australia, sometimes known as yabbies, belong to the family Parasticidae. Of some 90 species, ranging from 2.5cm, most are aquatic, though able to move over land. Some live in damp soils in pastures, lawns or orchards, many burrowing several metres down during dry periods. There is now some commercial interest in rearing crayfish as food.

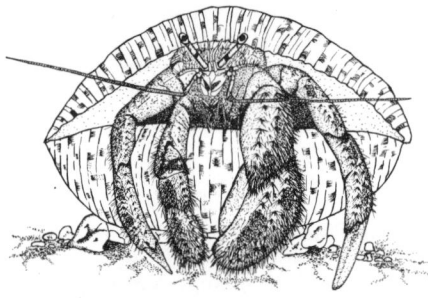

A hermit crab

Hermit crabs protect their soft, asymmetrical abdomens by enclosing them in the empty shells of other molluscs, periodically casting their skins and seeking new shells as they grow. When fully withdrawn into an adopted shell, the hermit blocks the entrance with its large claw.

The true crabs, of which there are some 700 species in 23 families in Australia, may be divided into four subsections: Gymnopleura, Dromiacea, Oxystomata and Brachygnatha. In all true crabs the abdomen is reduced and tucked into a groove below the carapace; the first pair of appendages are strong chelipeds, but the third pair is never chelate. Marine species (accounting for the majority) pass through several planktonic larval stages.

The Gymnopleura subsection contains the deep-water, burrowing frog crabs (family Raninidae), which have paddle-like appendages adapted for burrowing.

The Dromiacea subsection contains the sponge crabs (family Dromiidae), which carry a mass of living sponge or other organisms, secured over the body by the upward-bent hind appendages. Dromiids have direct development, without larval stages.

Members of the Oxystomata subsection are characterised by a triangular mouth-frame and include the box and dawn crabs (family Calappidae). The former, of tropical and sub-tropical occurrence, are notable for the large, flat pincers, fitting in front of the carapace to conceal the face; the latter (*Matuta* species), of tropical distribution, are notable for the spine projecting outward on each side of the shell, and limbs flattened for swimming and burrowing.

The Brachygnatha subsection contains most true crabs; members of this group are characterised by the quadrangular mouth-frame and are divided into two superfamilies, Oxyrhyncha and Brachyrhyncha.

Oxyrhynchans generally have a triangular carapace, the sharp front end usually projecting forward as a rostrum, or a pair of spines; many species have particularly long legs, and cover themselves with pieces of seaweed, and so on, as camouflage. The group includes deep-water species, notably the spider crabs (family Majidae).

Brachyrhynchans, comprising most of the world's crabs, have a circular, oval or square carapace, the rostrum being small or absent. Eight families are considered here: Xanthidae, Portunidae, Grapsidae, Ocypodidae, Mictyridae, Pinnotheridae, Potamidae (or Potamonidae) and Hymenosomatidae.

The Xanthidae, which have rounded carapaces, include the deep-water giant Tasmanian crab, *Pseudocarcinus gigas*, found off southern Australia; sometimes over 35cm in body width and 14kg in weight, it is smaller only than the Japanese spider crab (family Majidae), the world's largest crustacean.

The Portunidae are swimming crabs and have paddle-shaped terminal joints on the last appendages. This family includes the widespread Indo-Pacific blue swimming crab, or sand crab, *Portunus pelagicus*, and the mangrove crab, or mud crab, *Scylla serrata*, both table delicacies.

The Grapsidae, containing most of the common shore crabs, have roughly quadrangular shells and broad fronts. Common on rocky shores is the widespread *Leptograpsus variegatus*, with distinctive lines on the carapace and large purple and white chelae. *Sesarma* species, are found in tropical and sub-tropical mangrove swamps and estuarine mud.

The Ocypodidae contains several groups which have long eyestalks and are particularly interesting for their chelae. The amphibious fiddler crabs (*Uca* species) live in burrows between the tides, mainly on muddy shores and near mangrove swamps, in tropical and sub-tropical areas. One of the male's nippers, brightly coloured and twice as long as the body width, is used in courtship display and in fighting. The semaphore crab, *Heleocius cordiformis*, living in similar habitats and common in muddy estuaries round Sydney, is distinguished by the purple back and large, cream-coloured pincers, also used in display. *Macrophthalmus carnimanus*, occurring in mudflats, has particularly long eyestalks and a carapace about 2.5cm wide but less than half as long. The sandy-coloured ghost crabs (*Ocypode* species), which have almost square shells, leave their burrows (above the tides) at night, to go to the water. The sand-bubbler

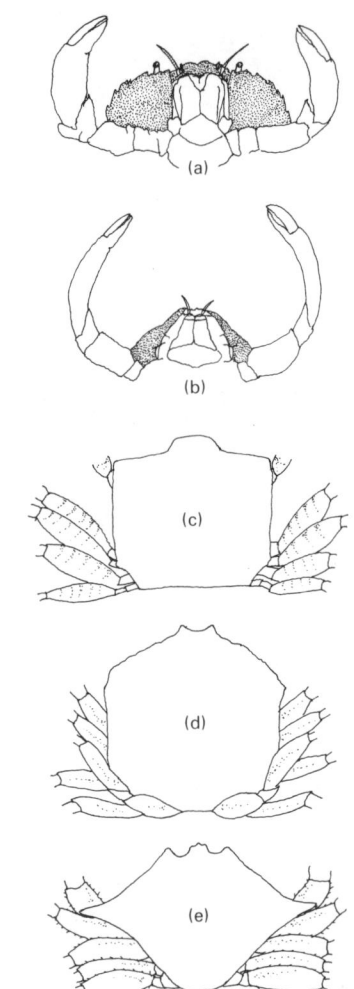

Shapes of crab mouth frames and carapaces: (a) box-shaped mouth frame; (b) triangular mouth frame; (c) ghost crab carapace; (d) sponge crab carapace; (e) dawn crab carapace

crab, *Scopimera inflata*, deposits little pellets of sand in lines radiating from its burrow.

The Mictyridae contains the soldier crabs (*Mictyris* species), numerous on Australian estuarine sand-flats. With almost spherical, bluish bodies carried on stilt-like legs, and sensitive mouthparts, they separate tiny food particles from the sand, leaving the remains as small pellets on the surface. They disappear when disturbed, burrowing swiftly into the wet sand.

The widespread Potamidae contains the six Australian species of the freshwater genus *Paratelphusa*. Most common is *P. transversa* (about 5cm wide), found in a broad diagonal band from the NW coast to QLD and NSW, but reaching the coast only in northern QLD (though not found in CAPE YORK). It inhabits long burrows in the banks of creeks, swamps and dams, plugging the entrance with earth during drought periods; the eggs hatch to miniature crabs which are carried about for several days by the female.

The Hymenosomatidae, though predominantly marine, contains the round-bodied 'freshwater' species, *Halicarcinus lacustris*,

which occurs in slightly saline lakes in SE Australia and TAS, on LORD HOWE and NORFOLK ISLANDS, and in New Zealand.
Further reading: Schmitt, W.L. *Crustaceans.* David & Charles, Newton Abbott UK, 1973; Dakin, W.J., Bennett, I. & Pope, E. *Australian Seashores.* (6th edn) Angus & Robertson, Sydney, 1976; Olszewski, P. *A Salute to the Humble Yabby.* Angus & Robertson, Sydney, 1980; Williams, W.D. *Australian Freshwater Life.* (2nd edn) Macmillan, Melbourne, 1980.

Crystal Brook SA (population 1 240 in 1981) A country town in the mid-N of the State, situated on a stream of the same name, it is 29km SE of PORT PIRIE and 50km SW of JAMESTOWN. It is a railway town, linked to Adelaide by a number of routes. Crystal Brook is a service centre for a grain growing, sheep grazing and dairying district. The stream was discovered and named by the explorer Edward John EYRE in 1840.

CSIRO *see* Commonwealth Scientific and Industrial Research Organization

CSR Limited This company, one of the oldest and largest in Australia, was for long associated solely with the sugar industry, but in recent times has undergone major diversification. Founded as an unlimited partnership in 1855, the Colonial Sugar Refining Co. engaged at first only in sugar-cane growing, milling and refining in QLD and northern NSW. However, in 1857 it opened a refinery and distillery in Melbourne, later established other refineries in capital cities and in 1882-83 extended its activities to Fiji and New Zealand. It was incorporated as the Colonial Sugar Refining Co. Ltd. in 1887 and formally adopted its present name in 1973.

Substantial diversification of the company's activities began when it set up factories for the manufacture of wallboards, plaster and asbestos products during World War II. It established CSR Chemicals in 1948, subsequently acquired additional shareholdings in various building products and cement, and entered the pastoral industry by acquiring Australian Estates Co. Ltd. Perhaps the most striking aspect of its diversification in recent years, however, has been its entry into the minerals industry by such steps as participation in the MOUNT NEWMAN iron ore joint venture and in the GOVE PENINSULA bauxite and alumina joint venture; the acquisition of tin-mining interests in Indonesia, of the mining companies AAR and Thiess, and of natural gas producer and explorer, Delhi. Activities are now conducted through five main operating divisions, namely the Sugar Division, the Building Materials Division, the Aluminium Minerals and Chemicals Division, the Coal Division and the Oil and Gas Division.

ctenophores The phylum Ctenophora, which includes comb jellies, sea walnuts and sea gooseberries, is a group of small planktonic marine animals once thought to belong to the jellyfish phylum, the COELENTERATES. They

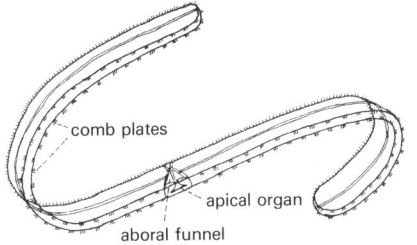
Venus' girdle, *Cestum* species

do not, however, possess the stinging cells (nematocysts) characteristic of the coelenterates, though they do carry sticky cells on their tentacles. As in the coelenterates much of the body's bulk consists of a jelly-like material, and there is no anus—merely a mouth at one end. They also resemble the coelenterates in being radially symmetrical.

The body is usually roughly spherical in shape, and carries two tentacles. There are eight rows of transversely placed 'comb plates' running along the body. Each comb plate is composed of minute 'hairs' (cilia) which are fused at the base but free at the ends, giving them a comb-like appearance under the microscope. The cilia beat in a synchronised way, moving the animal along. Many ctenophores are luminescent, and as the waves of movement pass along a row of comb plates there are rainbow flashes of iridescent colours. They feed on small planktonic animals caught by the tentacles.

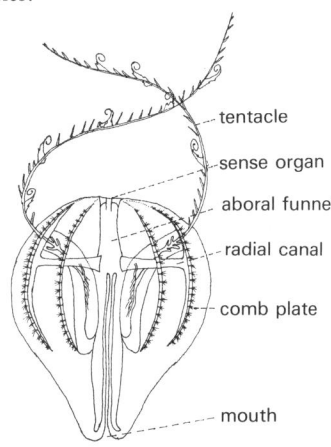
Internal structure of a sea gooseberry

There are about 80 species in the world, and several species occur abundantly in Australian coastal waters though their transparency makes them difficult to see, and their fragility, difficult to catch and examine. Two common species are the small sea gooseberries *Pleurobrachia pileus* and *Bolinopsis chuni*. Venus' girdle is a form with an expanded body that has been aptly compared to a celluloid belt. It belongs to the genus *Cestum.*

cuckoos and coucals These BIRDS belong to the family Cuculidae. Of the 12 species of cuckoos in Australia, the nine species classed as common are discussed below. There is one species of coucal in Australia.

Although they share the name with their European cousin, none of the Australian cuckoos calls 'cuckoo'. They do, however, share with it the parasitic habit of laying eggs in the nests of foster-parent species. The fledgling cuckoo destroys its nestmates. Another peculiar feature of many cuckoos is their passion for hairy caterpillars. Cuckoos are generally long, slender, insectivorous birds with long tails, zygodactylous feet (two toes pointing forwards, two backwards) and fairly stout bills. The colour is usually brown and grey, and the underparts are barred, but immature cuckoos may resemble the host species.

The koel, *Eudynamys scolopacea*

The pallid cuckoo, *Cuculus pallidus** (30cm long), is a migratory bird, occurring in woodland throughout Australia, and has no bars on the underparts. The eggs are flesh-coloured, sometimes with a few dark spots; the foster-parents are usually builders of open nests. The fantailed cuckoo, *Cacomantis pyrrophanus* (25cm), a blue-grey and brown, broad-tailed species, is found in forest and woodland areas of the E and SW. Its eggs are usually laid in domed nests near the ground. Its yellow eyering distinguishes it from the similar brush cuckoo, *C. variolosus* (23cm), a N and E species inhabiting wet forests and mangroves. It breeds in Australia, parasitising species with open, cup-shaped nests, and migrates to New Guinea. The eggs are white, with brown spots.

The little bronze cuckoo, *Chrysococcyx malayanus* (15cm), is uniformly glossy bronze-green on the back and inhabits the forests and mangroves of N Australia. It usually lays eggs in the nests of certain WARBLER species, as does the golden bronze cuckoo, *C. lucidus* (18cm). This latter species has a barred face and purple-bronze on the crown and neck. It inhabits forests and woodlands in the W and the E, including TAS, and is particularly useful in keeping down the numbers of harmful caterpillars. The genus also includes the widespread Horsfield bronze cuckoo, *C. basalis** (18cm), which migrates to Malaysia. Its piercing, mournful, whistle-like call can often be heard at night. The pink, red-spotted eggs are usually laid in domed nests near the ground.

The koel, *Eudynamys scolopacea* (40cm), is a widespread breeding visitor to the forest country of N and E Australia from the islands N of the continent. The male has red eyes and a glossy black plumage, while the female

**Species, genus or family is endemic to Australia (see Preface)*

is brown with white speckles. Like most cuckoos, this species is often chased by other birds, particularly those which serve as foster-parents, such as large HONEYEATERS. The channelbill cuckoo, *Scythrops novaehollandiae* (50cm), is easily recognised by its massive bill (6cm) which has a deep groove along the side of the upper part. It is a breeding visitor to the forests and woodlands of most of N and E Australia, and usually lays its eggs in the nests of currawongs (see BUTCHERBIRDS) and CROWS.

Unlike cuckoos, coucals are not parasitic. The pheasant coucal, *Centropus phasianinus* (60cm, including tail about 30cm), is a black and brown bird which lives in thickets in swamps and other damp areas from WA northwards and eastwards to NSW. It is a shy, largely terrestrial bird whose call is a series of loud booming notes. Like cuckoos, it feeds on insects, but supplements this diet with small animals such as frogs. The white eggs are laid in nests on or near the ground; the nests are made of rushes, and grass is pulled over the top to form a hood.

cuckoo-shrikes and trillers These BIRDS belong to an Old World and Australasian family (Campephagidae) of PASSERINE BIRDS. Cuckoo-shrikes are neither CUCKOOS nor shrikes. Although some do resemble certain cuckoos in appearance, they do not have barred tails like the cuckoos; like the European shrikes they have notched, hooked bills, but they do not have the shrikes' habit of impaling their prey on thorns and twigs.

The ground cuckoo-shrike, *Pteropodocys* maxima* (length 36cm; forked tail 20cm), is pale grey above with black wings and tail and black bars on the white underparts. It is a ground-dwelling species with a pigeon-like walk, and is found in open, inland areas throughout the mainland. It moves rapidly over the ground feeding on insects and when in flight utters a rippling call-note. The eggs are laid in scanty saucer-shaped nests composed of twigs, grass and rootlets interwoven with soft materials such as fur.

The genus *Coracina* includes four species found in Australia; all have mainly grey plumage with some black about the head. The most widespread is the black-faced cuckoo-shrike, *C. novaehollandiae* (length 33cm; rounded tail 15cm), a partly nomadic species found in woodlands, suburban areas and orchards throughout Australia. It always shuffles and adjusts its wings when alighting. The food consists of insects and their larvae, berries and seeds. Like all other species in this genus, its small, saucer-shaped nests of twigs and bark are bound with cobwebs and built in the high branches of trees. The most uncommon species in this genus is the cicada bird, *C. tenuirostris* (25cm long), a breeding migrant from New Guinea to the E coast and N Australia. It takes its name from its cicada-like call, and possibly from its habit of feeding on foliage insects in forests and mangroves. The male is dark blue-grey and has a white patch

Species, genus or family is endemic to Australia (see Preface)

on the underwing; the female is brownish with darker bars below.

Trillers are smaller birds with pointed wings and fine songs. The males are mainly pied, the females are brown. Both species—the white-winged triller, *Lalage sueurii* (18cm), and the pied triller, *L. leucomela* (19cm)—are common within their ranges. The white-winged triller is a breeding visitor, plentiful in some years, scarce in others, and frequents woodlands, parks and gardens throughout Australia. It takes insects from the leaves of trees and on the ground. The pied triller is a sedentary species which inhabits the mangroves and wet forests of the coastal areas of QLD, northern NT and north-eastern WA. It feeds on insects, particularly caterpillars, and fruit. Both species build small, shallow nests of twigs and grasses, bound with cobweb.

cudweed see Compositae

Cumberland Islands QLD This is the name given to a group of about 100 islands lying N of MACKAY and S of the WHITSUNDAY PASSAGE, about 30km off the E coast, separated from the mainland by Hillsborough Channel, and lying between the outer section of the GREAT BARRIER REEF and the mainland coast. The group stretches over a distance of some 60km, on a general NW-SE alignment, parallel to the coast. The N cluster of islands, called the Sir James Smith Group, located 55km N of Mackay, consists of rocky and precipitous islands, covered by low eucalypt forest; 11 of them have been set aside as a national park, ranging in size from Anvil Is (3ha) to Goldsmith Is (648ha). Brampton Is (464ha) is also a national park and has been developed as a tourist resort, with access by launch or plane from Mackay.

cumbungi see bulrushes

Cummings, James Bartholomew 'Bart' (1927-) Horse trainer. Born in Adelaide, and introduced to HORSE RACING as a strapper for his trainer father, Cummings was to become one of Australia's most successful horse trainers. Leaving his father to branch out on his own in 1953, by 1983 he had trained more than 2000 winners. He is best known for his successes in the richest race on the Australian racing calendar, the Melbourne Cup, a race in which he has been outstandingly successful since 1965. He is the only trainer to have won three successive Melbourne Cups (1965-67) and the only trainer to have won seven Melbourne Cups (1965-67, 1974, 1975, 1977, 1979). But perhaps the record which best indicates his dominance of this race is his having trained the quinella—that is, first and second, on four occasions (1965, 1966, 1974, 1975). Modest and unassuming, in sharp contrast to his arch rival, the extrovert Tommy SMITH, Cummings has developed a deep understanding of horses and a successful training method which have made him one of the top two trainers in Australia.

cunjevoi see sea squirts

Cunnamulla QLD (population 1 627 in 1981) Located at the junction of the Mitchell and Balonne Highways, 823km by road W of Brisbane and 208km S of CHARLEVILLE, it is the main centre of the Paroo Shire in the SW of the State. At an elevation of 188m above sea level, situated on the Warrego River, it is a rail terminus on a branch line from Brisbane via ROMA and Charleville, and a service and distribution centre for an extensive pastoral area in the vast semi-arid Outback. It has an average annual rainfall of 363mm, concentrated mainly in the summer months. Wool growing is the main industry of the region and, in good seasons, the town becomes the biggest wool-loading centre on the QLD railway network. The grazing of beef cattle and angora goats is also important. The Warrego River and the Paroo (to the W) are noted for cod and perch fishing; in good seasons, wild duck are plentiful. The district has a varied bird life: brolgas, pelicans, galahs, black swans, bowerbirds and even seagulls. The Yowah opal field lies about 145km W of Cunnamulla. An annual festival of opals is held in the town each August.

Cunningham, Allan (1791-1839) Explorer and botanist. Born in Surrey, he became interested in botany at an early age. In 1814, when assistant to the manager of Kew Gardens, he obtained a position as a plant collector in an expedition to Brazil. In 1816, shortly after returning from the successful expedition, he came to NSW, and in the following year accompanied OXLEY on the latter's attempt to trace the LACHLAN RIVER. For nearly five years after this, Cunningham was attached to hydrographic survey expeditions, and made plant collections at various places on the W and N coasts, on islands of the GREAT BARRIER REEF and in TAS. In later years he also carried out botanical work in New Zealand and on NORFOLK ISLAND.

In 1823 he discovered a route through 'Pandora's Pass' from the MUDGEE district to the Liverpool Plains, which gave settlers direct access from BATHURST to the HUNTER RIVER valley; two years later his further exploration in the latter area influenced the mainstream of

ALLAN CUNNINGHAM.

Mitchell Library

pastoral expansion to flow in that direction. He gave added impetus to the spread of settlement northwards in 1827, when he led an expedition from the Hunter Valley to the DARLING DOWNS. In the following year he attempted to reach the Darling Downs from MORETON BAY, but without success.

Having returned to England in 1831 to catalogue the collection of plants he had sent there, he came back to Sydney in 1837 as Colonial Botanist, a position he resigned shortly afterwards as it prevented him from further collecting. He died in Sydney of tuberculosis. His manuscripts and many of his botanical specimens are preserved at Kew Gardens.
Further reading: McMinn, W.G. *Allen Cunningham, Botanist and Explorer.* Melbourne University Press, Melbourne, 1970.

curl grub *see* beetles

curlews *see* waders

currant, native *see* parasitic plants

currawongs *see* butcherbirds, etc.

currency In the early years of British settlement coins of many types were in circulation, the first distinctively Australian currency being that issued by Governor MACQUARIE in 1812. In an attempt to keep coinage within the colony, Macquarie obtained a large supply of Spanish dollars and had a disc punched out of the centre of each. This portion, known as a 'dump', was given a value within the colony of one shilling and threepence, and the outer portion, or 'holey dollar', was valued at five shillings. Before long, however, British currency became sufficiently plentiful to make such devices unnecessary. The first Australian banknotes were issued by the BANK OF NEW SOUTH WALES founded in 1817, but coins were not minted until a branch of the Royal Mint was established in Sydney in 1855. Other branches were established in Melbourne in 1872 and Perth in 1899.

At the time of federation in 1901 the currency in the various colonies consisted of coinage of the UK, notes issued by a number of banks, and QLD Treasury notes, which had superseded bank notes in that colony at the time of the financial crash in 1893. The federal Constitution vests the control of currency, coinage and legal tender, and the issue of paper money, in the Commonwealth, but Australian currency was not issued until 1910, being then based on the British unit of the pound (£), divided into 20 shillings of 12 pence each. The Australian pound retained parity with the British pound sterling until the beginning of the Depression of 1930. There was then a general depreciation in its value until in December 1931 it was stabilised at the rate of £125 Australian to £100 sterling.

A decimal system of currency was introduced in February 1966, its major unit being the dollar ($), this being equal to 10 shillings in the former currency, and the minor unit, the cent, being one-hundredth of the dollar. At present notes are issued by the Reserve Bank in denominations of $2, $5, $10, $50 and $100, but may be issued in any other denomination that the Treasurer determines. Decimal coinage consists of 1-cent and 2-cent pieces (bronze); 5-cent, 10-cent 20-cent and 50-cent pieces (cupro-nickel); and a $1 piece (aluminium-bronze).

Curtin, John Joseph (1885-1945) Prime Minister. Born in CRESWICK in VIC, he left school at the age of 12, began work in a printing shop and later worked as a journalist. He first came to public attention as a leading opponent of CONSCRIPTION in 1916-17, and then moved to WA, where he edited the *West Australian Worker* from 1917 to 1928. He stood successfully as a Labor candidate for the FREMANTLE seat in the House of Representatives in 1928, and while he did not attain Cabinet rank after Labor's 1929 victory, he achieved some prominence in the party as an opponent both of Jack LANG's policies and of the deflationary, wage-cutting approach to the Depression (which Prime Minister SCULLIN finally accepted in the shape of the Premiers' Plan). Defeated in the 1931 elections, he won back his seat in 1934, and to the surprise of many commentators was elected leader of the Labor Party in the following year. For several years after this he worked tirelessly and successfully to reunify the party and restore its public image.

After the outbreak of war in 1939 Labor refused an offer to join in a national government, but Curtin consented to become a member of an inter-party War Advisory Council. In the 1940 elections Labor came close to victory, and in October in the following year, when two independents announced that thenceforth they would give general support to Labor, he was asked by the Governor-General to form a government. In 1943 he led Labor to a comfortable electoral victory, and remained Prime Minister until his death in July 1945.

His two most notable acts as Prime Minister were his public acceptance of the fact that Australian security had come to depend more on help from the USA than from the UK, and his persuasion of his party to drop its traditional anti-conscriptionist stand, to the extent of allowing conscripts to fight anywhere in a defined area of the S Pacific. The former of these acts was followed up by his support of the American General Douglas MacArthur as Supreme Commander in the SW Pacific, and by clashes with Churchill when the latter wished the 6th and 7th Divisions, returning from the Middle East, to be diverted to Burma. With regard to the war effort in general, he worked tirelessly to place the national economy on a wartime footing. Manpower controls, rationing and the curtailment of many types of production were imposed on a scale that would have been hard to envisage only a few years previously. Curtin's sincerity and devotion to duty were invaluable in winning support for these measures, and there

Courtesy of A.I.S. Canberra
John Joseph Curtin

is no doubt that his death was hastened by the weight of his workload and by the cares of office during years of unprecedented national emergency.
See also political history
Further reading: Beazely, K.E. *John Curtin: An Atypical Labor Leader.* Australian National University Press, Canberra, 1971; Ross, L. *John Curtin: A Biography.* Macmillan, South Melbourne, 1977.

Curtis Island QLD Located off the E coast, between ROCKHAMPTON and GLADSTONE, with Keppel Bay to the N and Port Curtis to the S, it is separated from the mainland by a narrow channel bordered by mangrove mud flats. The Tropic of Capricorn passes through the N part of the island and the S part of the island shelters Port Curtis on which Gladstone stands. It is about 40km long on its NW-SE axis and 20km at its widest E-W section, consisting of low wooded hills, with some cattle grazing. Cape Capricorn at the NE of the island is where James COOK entered the tropics on his journey along the E coast of the continent in 1770. About 70km to the E is HERON ISLAND, situated in the CAPRICORN GROUP.

cuscuses *see* possums, etc.

cushion plant *see* Caryophyllaceae

Cuthbert, Betty (1938-) Athlete. Born in Sydney, she was attracted to running as a child, but it was not until she met June Ferguson, her physical education teacher at secondary school, that she started to train seriously. In 1956 at the Melbourne Olympics she realised her potential, winning three gold medals, for the 100m, 200m, and 4 × 100m relay respectively. After missing the 1960 Rome Olympics owing to a torn hamstring muscle, she announced her retirement from competitive running. But after 18 months away from the track she decided on a comeback which resulted in her selection for Australia at the 1964 Tokyo Olympics where she won yet another gold medal in the 400m.

One of the finest women sprinters Australia has produced, she held 16 world records during her career. Her dedication and will to win, coupled with an engaging appearance and innate modesty, endeared her to Australians to whom she was affectionately known as the 'Golden Girl'.

cuttlefish *see* cephalopods

cycads *see* fossils; Gymnospermae

cycling Cycling is both a competitive sport and a popular recreation. As a competitive sport it attracts cyclists eager to pit their speed and endurance against each other, and Australians both amateur and professional have been particularly successful in international events. As a recreation, cycling has experienced a boom period since about 1970, and in the early 1980s more Australians own bicycles than ever before.

Early days Bicycles were introduced into Australia in the late 1860s. The bicycles of that era—heavy wooden machines with cast-iron bearings—were aptly known as boneshakers, and they featured in the first cycle race in Australia in 1869 organised by the Boneshaker Club of Melbourne. In 1875 a bicycle was designed with a tubular frame, wire spokes and solid rubber tyres which because of its frail-looking wheels was at first not readily accepted but soon proved its superior qualities. With the introduction of pneumatic tyres in 1890 came the first boom in cycling. Such was the popularity of cycling in Melbourne with its wide and level roads that the municipality of Melbourne proclaimed a law to protect pedestrians. The law required cyclists to sound a bell continuously, but this generated so much noise that the law was soon abolished.

Competitive racing Following the first boneshaker race of 1869, bicycle races became regular events, though mostly as features at athletic meetings. In 1880, however, the first meeting consisting solely of bicycle races was organised by the Melbourne Bicycle Club. During the 1890s and early 1900s attendances at races were the best ever experienced in Australia and the prize-money offered was among the highest in the world, attracting many overseas cyclists. One of these was American Arthur Zimmerman who in 1895 competed with top NSW rider Joe Megron, 65 000 spectators paying approximately £14 000 to watch the contest.

Australian professionals benefited greatly from the increased competition and a number of them went overseas where they were conspicuously successful. Among these was Alf Grenda who, with Walter Demara of the USA, won the world tandem championship in 1912. Another Australian, Alf Goullet, set the world record for the unpaced flying mile at Salt Lake City in 1912 and became a well-known track star in the USA. Bob SPEARS won many Commonwealth championships before winning the title of all-round champion of the USA in 1918.

Courtesy of A.I.S. Canberra

Russell Mockridge with Lionel Cox after winning the 2 000m gold medal at the 1952 Olympics

Olympic participation Australia first sent cycling representatives to the Olympic Games at Antwerp in 1920, and Australia has been represented at every Olympic Games since. The first Australian to win an Olympic gold medal in cycling was E.L. Gray, who won the 1000m time-trial at Los Angeles Games in 1932. Twenty years later at the Helsinki Olympic Games in 1952 Russell MOCKRIDGE set a new Olympic record of 1 minute 11 seconds in winning the same event. Partnered by L. Cox, he also won a gold medal in the tandem event. In the 1956 Melbourne Olympic Games Ian Brown and Tony Marchant won the 2000m tandem gold medal.

Current popularity The emergence of many good young cyclists in the 1970s coincided with a boom in the popularity of cycling as a recreation. Bicycle sales have rocketed, bicycle-hire shops have mushroomed near large city and suburban parks which are thronged with families of cyclists on weekends, and most cities have built or are building cycleways. Such an expanding interest in cycling has also led to increased attendances at major velodromes throughout Australia.

Top riders who have been part of this resurgence include Gordon Johnson of Melbourne who won the 1970 world championship in England directly after turning professional; Danny Clark of TAS, winner of a Commonwealth Games silver medal in 1970, an Olympic silver in 1972, winner with Don Allen of the Ghent six-day race in France in 1976 (a win which prompted one critic to comment: 'It was like a French cricket team beating Australia') and winner of the Kierin Championship of the World in 1980 and 1981; John NICHOLSON of Melbourne who as an amateur won gold medals in the 1970 and 1974 Commonwealth Games, a silver medal at the 1972 Olympics and, as a professional, the world sprint title in 1975 and 1976; and Gary Sutton, winner of the 1980 50km Points Score Championship of the World. In the 1982 Commonwealth Games, gold medals were won by Michael Turter (Individual Pursuit), Gary West, Michael Turter, Kevin Nichols and Michael Grenda (Team Pursuit), Kenrick

Tucker (1 000m Sprint) and Kevin Nichols (10 miles).
See also Opperman, Sir Hubert.

Cymbidium *see* Orchidaceae

Cyperaceae This is a large family of monocotyledonous flowering plants with 90 genera containing some 4 100 species of worldwide distribution. The Cyperaceae are often confused with grasses (family GRAMINEAE), but they occupy damper areas and have a narrower ecological range. Two very large genera, *Carex* (which is mainly temperate) and *Cyperus* (which is mainly tropical) are both well represented in Australia and account for most of the distribution.

Members of the family Cyperaceae are grass-like herbs, usually with solid, stiff stems. Leaves are at the base of the stems, with closed sheaths or reduced to sheathing scales. The small spikes on the end of the stems contain minute flowers and are not enclosed by bracts. The flowers are bisexual or unisexual, each containing a pistil and two or three stamens; the ovary contains a single ovule, and the style is divided into two or three filiform branches. The fruit is a small nut, flattened or triangular.

The best-known member of the family Cyperaceae is papyrus, *Cyperus papyrus*, a native of Egypt, and used by the Ancient Egyptians to make paper. This plant is now widely grown as an ornamental in large ponds and waterlogged soils. Nut grass, *C. rotundus*, is a serious WEED in tropical and warm temperate gardens in Australia. Swamp vegetation derives its typical grass-like appearance from members of this family, particularly species of *Baumea*, *Schoenus*, *Scirpus* and *Cyperus*. The slender plumes of the *Lepidosperma* and *Gahnia* species, both found in swamps and layered woodlands, are prized for dry arrangements, as is button grass, *Gymnoschoenus sphaerocephalus*, found extensively in sedgelands in TAS. Old man's whiskers (*Caustis* species) has delightful curly green plumes, much prized as florists' greenery, so much so that it is now totally protected in NSW.

Short-lived members of the family Cyperaceae also play an important role in ecological succession, being amongst the first species to occupy areas where the vegetation has been destroyed by fire. This is due to both vegetative characteristics such as rhizomes, which are undamaged by fire and hence able to reshoot immediately after a burn, and to the vast amounts of long-lived seed which is stored in the soil, and which is stimulated to germinate by the steaming effect of the fire.
See also Angiospermae; Appendix 5, Flower Structure and Glossary of Botanical Terms
Further reading: see Appendix 6, A Bibliography for Plants.

cypress *see* Gymnospermae

D

daddy-longlegs *see* harvestmen; spiders

Dahlia *see* Compositae

dairy cattle industry Dairying in Australia tends to be confined to the coastal regions, including a small area SW of Perth in WA, the N coast of TAS and a coastal strip extending from Adelaide in SA, through VIC, NSW and QLD up to the ATHERTON TABLE-LAND. The only inland region of consequence is in northern VIC where irrigation is used to ensure pasture growth. In all regions cows graze on pasture throughout the year, although during periods of low pasture production the diet may be supplemented with fodder crops, hay, silage and concentrated feeds such as grain and prepared meals. There is widespread cultivation of improved pastures based on the application of fertilisers and the sowing of grasses and legumes.

Dairy cattle numbers declined in Australia between 1960 and 1980; in 1980 there were approximately 3.1 million cows, heifers and heifer calves in dairy herds. Over the same period was a substantial decline in the number of dairy farms, from approximately 120 000 to less than 20 000. This change occurred through the movement of small farmers out of the industry. Total milk production reached a peak level in 1969-70 owing to increases in productivity per cow but between 1970 and 1980 the continued decline in the cattle population was reflected in a decline in total milk production.

Approximately 72 per cent of the milk produced is processed into butter, cheese, condensed milk, skim-milk powder, full-cream milk powder, casein, infant and invalids' food and health beverages made essentially of milk. Butter is the single most important processed item, utilising almost half of the milk produced. Although total milk production declined in the 1970s, domestic consumption of both fluid milk and butter also declined, leaving approximately 22 per cent of the production of dairy products available for export in 1980-81.

Japan, the largest single export outlet for dairy products, imports cheese, casein, skim-milk powder and, in some years, butter. The USA and Canada are substantial importers occasionally but are not regular outlets for significant quantities of Australian dairy produce. Latin America, Mexico and Peru import skim-milk powder, and Venezuela has become a significant importer of whole-milk

powder. Australia has entered into joint-venture arrangements for the operation of milk-reconstituting plants in the Philippines, Thailand and Indonesia; consequently, these countries import substantial quantities of skim-milk powder. Taiwan, Malaysia and the Philippines are the principal Asian markets for whole-milk powder.

Whole-milk production and distribution is almost entirely controlled by various State milk authorities which effectively maintain a continuity of supplies to their respective cities. The authorities also enforce standards of quality and hygiene. Production is controlled by quotas and contracts in all States except SA. Contractors are paid for the quota of whole milk at a volume rate determined by the authorities, while milk produced in excess of

Dairying land of the lower Clarence Valley NSW

quota allocations is bought for manufacturing at a much lower price. In SA all milk is purchased on a butterfat basis, farmers initially receiving a basic price based on the value of milk used for cheese making. The price of whole milk is determined by the Metropolitan Milk Equalisation Agreement Committee and wholesalers pay to the Committee the difference between the wholesale price and the basic price. These contributions are subsequently equalised among all licensed dairymen as a 'city milk bonus', irrespective of the use made of each individual supplier's milk. This equalisation scheme acts as an incentive in months of low total production as these are the months with the highest bonus.

Breeds of dairy cattle The Jersey, the Friesian and the Australian Illawarra Shorthorn (AIS) are the most common breeds. The AIS was developed in the ILLAWARRA district in NSW between 1870 and 1890. The basic stock, milking Shorthorns, were crossed with Ayrshires and Devons to produce large cattle with high milk yields. The breed has now

A dairy cooperative in the lower Clarence Valley NSW

spread through NSW to QLD and WA but it is not widely used in VIC. Small numbers of Ayrshire, Guernsey, Dairy Shorthorn and Red Poll cattle are also used for milk production.

A new breed, the Australian Milking Zebu (AMZ), has been developed by the CSIRO through a breeding project which began in 1956. The objective was to develop a breed of dairy cattle which would be better adapted than European breeds to tropical and sub-tropical regions. The breed has been derived from cross-breeding Sahiwals and Jerseys and appears to be resistant to cattle ticks and to thrive on sub-tropical coasts. Despite the handicap of low production in the Sahiwal parent breed, milk yields of AMZ cows are equal, and in some cases superior, to European cattle producing under similar conditions. *See also* diseases, livestock; grazing industry

daisies *see* Compositae

Dalby QLD (population 8 784 in 1981) A commercial and service town at the junction of the Moonie, Warrego and Bunya Highways, it is 215km WNW of Brisbane and 84km NW of TOOWOOMBA, situated on Myall Creek, a tributary of the CONDAMINE RIVER. At an elevation of 342m above sea level, in the N part of the DARLING DOWNS, it is a rail centre on the Brisbane-CHARLEVILLE line, with branch routes NE to Bell, NW to Jandowae and W to Glenmorgan. The surrounding downs country is a productive wheat growing and beef cattle grazing region, which has an average annual rainfall of 673mm, concentrated mainly in summer with lower falls in winter and spring. The large wheat silos, which tower above the town and the livestock saleyards, symbolise its rural servicing functions. Lake Broadwater, 32km to the SW in the BUNYA RANGE, is a popular picnic and aquatic sporting area. The Bunya Mts National Park, located 48km NE of the town and covering 11 700ha of the GREAT DIVIDING RANGE, is noted for its varied vegetation, which includes rainforest, open forest and grassy stretches; the park contains several species of wallabies, as well as possums, snakes and a varied bird life, notably of parrots, bowerbirds and brush turkeys; the highest points in the park are Mt Kiangarow (1 135m) and Mt Mowbullan (1 101m). Dalby has many reminders of the early days of exploration and the town museum depicts some features from these pioneering times; its main street is named after explorer Allan CUNNINGHAM; it was from 'Jimbout' homestead, 24km N, that the explorer Ludwig LEICHHARDT set out on his last trek (the building has been listed by the QLD National Trust as part of the national heritage); a cairn at Patrick Leslie Bridge records the fact that it was at Dalby that the insect *Cactoblastis*, which so effectively combated the prickly pear infestation, was first released in 1925. The annual rodeo held in mid-September is a time of festivity and a popular tourist attraction.

Daley, Victor James William Patrick (1858-1905) Poet. Born in Ireland, he was taken as a boy to England by his mother, emigrated to Australia in 1878, lived for a while in Adelaide, and after drifting back and forth between Melbourne and Sydney settled down in the latter city for the last seven years of his life. He supported himself by free-lance journalism, contributing prose and verse to the *Bulletin* in particular, and became well known in bohemian circles in Sydney. Most of his poems are to be found in *At Dawn and Dusk* (1898), *Wine and Roses* (1911) and *Creeve Roe* (1947). Of romantic quality, the best of them are considered to have great charm but lack emotional or intellectual depth. Although he was in sympathy with radical social and political movements of his time, this is not reflected in his poetry.

dalgyte *see* bandicoots

Daly River NT Located in the NW of the Territory, the headwaters of the Daly are formed by the Katherine and King Rivers. Below their confluence, the river takes the name Daly and flows in a general NW direction some 320km to its estuary at Anson Bay on JOSEPH BONAPARTE GULF about 115km SW of Darwin. The main right-bank tributary is the Fergusson River; those from the S are the Flora and Fish Rivers, and Bradshaw and Muldiva Creeks. The Daly River local government area, covering 38 632km², contained only 1 830 people at the 1981 census. The Daly River police station, a small settlement located some 70km inland from the coast, receives an annual rainfall of 1 484mm, concentrated in the wet season from November to March. Owing to the long dry season and to the unreliability of the rainfall, the Daly River area has proved difficult country to settle and is principally occupied by large cattle stations, owned mostly by companies which hold properties for fattening elsewhere; the growing of sorghum for fodder has become important in recent years. Overland access to the cattle area is by roads branching off the Stuart Highway between KATHERINE and ADELAIDE RIVER. To the S of the Daly River estuary, stretching along the coastline of Joseph Bonaparte Gulf, are the Daly River wildlife sanctuary (covering 258 933ha) and the Daly River Aboriginal Reserve (13 468km²).

Daly Waters NT This small town is situated near the junction of the Stuart and Carpentaria Highways, 620km SE of Darwin, where the explorer John McDouall STUART carved his initials on a tree in 1862 and where a staging post was established in 1872 for the building of the OVERLAND TELEGRAPH. Located near the headwaters of the King River (one of the sources of the DALY RIVER) at an elevation of 210m, it receives an annual rainfall of only 589mm with considerable variability from year to year and an ever-present possibility of long drought periods.

Dampier WA (population 2 471 in 1981) This is a new iron ore port, built since 1965 on King Bay by Hamersley Iron Ltd to handle the pelletising and loading of ore which is transported 294km by rail from MOUNT TOM PRICE. The town is just off the North West Coastal Highway, situated 64km W of ROEBOURNE and 20km W of KARRATHA, and is about 1 530km by road N of Perth. Modern, and with air-conditioned buildings and up-to-date shopping facilities, Dampier takes its water supply from a local desalination plant and from the Maitland River, 24km distant. Visitors can arrange to inspect the ore treatment works and the port facilities; the annual 'FeNaCl Festival' is held in August.

Dampier, Alfred (*c*1847-1908) Actor and manager. Born in London, he began a career as a barrister, but turned to acting and for a time was in the Manchester Theatre Royal Company headed by Henry Irving. In 1873 he was invited to Australia where, in about 1876, he formed his own company. A Shakespearean by choice, he is remembered today chiefly for his staging of several notable Australian melodramas, including a dramatisation of *For the Term of His Natural Life* (1886), *Marvellous Melbourne* (1889), and—in particular—*Robbery Under Arms* (1890), based on the novel by Rolf BOLDREWOOD. Dampier's wife, the actress Katherine Russell, and his two daughters, Lily and Rose, were also members of his company. Dampier's career declined after the turn of the century. He died in Sydney.
Further reading: Rees, L. *The Making of Australian Drama*. Angus & Robertson, Sydney, 1973.

Dampier Land WA A low-lying triangular peninsula at the W end of the KIMBERLEYS in the NW of the State, it is located between Roebuck Bay on the SW, and King Sound on the NE, with Cape Leveque at its N tip. The area is named after the buccaneer mariner, William DAMPIER. It is poor scrub country, which experiences a tropical climate, with hot wet summers and a markedly dry period in the cooler months. Cape Leveque has an average annual rainfall of 718mm, most of which falls in the four months between December and March; the highest rainfall is in February (187mm average). The dry season occurs between April and November. Most of the peninsula is an Aboriginal reserve, with mission stations at Lombardina (in the far N) and Beagle Bay (on the NW coast).

Dampier, William (*c*1652-1715) Adventurer and navigator. He was born in Somerset, England, but little is known of his early life. Having gone to sea as a young man, he engaged in various trading and privateering ventures, particularly in the West Indies, before coming to the South Seas and joining the crew of the buccaneer ship *Cygnet*. In 1688, looking for a quiet place where the ship could be careened and overhauled in safety, the *Cygnet*'s captain brought her to the NW coast of Australia, near the site of the modern port of DAMPIER. While the ship was being overhauled, Dampier observed the land and its people closely.

Soon afterwards, he left the *Cygnet*, returned to England and wrote *A New Voyage Round the World*, which won him considerable fame. In it he described that part of Australia which he had visited as barren and its people as the most primitive in the world. Nevertheless, he wanted to explore other parts of Australia, and persuaded the Admiralty to give him the command of the *Roebuck*, in which he proposed to sail around Cape Horn to the E coast of Australia. He sailed in 1699, but owing to a late start decided to go by way of the Cape of Good Hope instead of via Cape Horn. He came to the Australian coast near SHARK BAY, on the W coast, sailed along part of the W and N coasts, and then went N of New Guinea and discovered the islands of New Britain and New Ireland before the poor condition of his ship forced him to turn for home. By a mixture of ill luck and bad judgment, he had failed to become the first European to explore the E coast of Australia.
Further reading: Shipman, J.C. *William Dampier, Seaman-Scientist*. The University Libraries of Kansas & Lawrence, Kansas, 1962; Lloyd, C. *William Dampier*. Faber & Faber, London, 1966.

damselflies and dragonflies These INSECTS belong to an exopterygote order (Odonata) which is represented in Australia by about 283 species. Both the adults and nymphs are carnivores, the nymphs below the water surface, the adults while on the wing. Some Australian dragonfly species are closely allied to South American species.

Damselflies (suborder Zygoptera) are medium-size insects which hold their membranous, richly veined wings vertically while at rest, and have large compound eyes, placed at the sides of the head. They are rarely found far from water; they often form large swarms over water and occasionally undertake long-distance mass migrations. Dragonflies (suborder Anisoptera) are larger insects; their wings are held horizontally, at right-angles to the body when at rest, and the large compound eyes occupy most of the head. They often stray far from water. Male dragonflies often patrol well-defined territories and will drive off any intruders of their own or other species.

Damselflies and dragonflies have a unique mating pattern. The male transfers sperm to special pouches at the front of the abdomen, and then grasps the female around the neck or the thorax with his anal (tail) claspers. The pair then usually fly in tandem for some time before the female curls her abdomen so that the sperm can be transferred from the male's pouches. The eggs are laid, often with the male still in attendance, either in slits in water plants just below the surface or in the water itself. The lower lip (labium) of the nymph is modified into a hinged organ with hooks (the so-called face mask) that can be projected forwards to capture prey. The nymphal life may last from a few weeks (in species that breed in temporary waters) to several years.

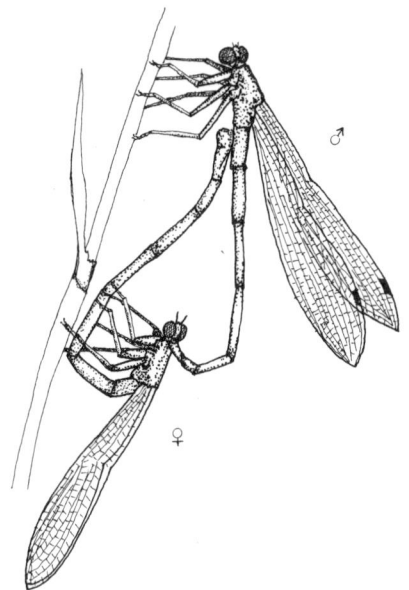

Mating damselflies

dandelions *see* Compositae; weeds

Dandenong Ranges VIC Located only 40km E of Melbourne, these ranges have long been a popular and attractive recreation area for metropolitan residents. The Ferntree Gully National Park, located 35km E of the city and only 1km from the Upper Ferntree Gully railway station, covers 459ha of densely forested country with lush tree ferns in the gullies. Despite serious bushfires in 1962, 1968 and 1983, and the large numbers of picnickers and walkers who visit the area, there is still a varied bird life of over 100 species in the park. The summit of Mt Dandenong, the highest point in the ranges (634m above sea level), provides scenic vistas of the surrounding valleys and hilly lands. Also on Mt Dandenong is the William Ricketts sanctuary, where the work of this unusual artist—sculptures depicting Aboriginal people—may be seen. Among the other attractions of the ranges are: Sherbrooke Forest, famed for its lyrebirds; the rhododendron and azalea gardens; the tulip displays in springtime; the cherry and berry-fruit orchards around Monbulk, Olinda and Sassafras; and the 20km ride from Belgrave to Emerald and back on *Puffing Billy*, a vintage narrow-gauge steam train. On the SW slopes of the ranges the city of Dandenong (population 54 962 in 1981), now part of the Melbourne city area, is a major industrial centre with a wide range of manufacturing enterprises including the General Motors vehicle plant, engineering works, food processing factories and glass works.
Further reading: Hayes, J. *Dandenongs Sketchbook.* Rigby, Adelaide, 1970.

daphne, native *see* wax flowers

Darcy, James Leslie 'Les' (1895-1917) Boxer. Born at Stradbroke, NSW, Darcy contested his first public fight at the age of 15. Apprenticed to a MAITLAND blacksmith at the age of 15, the heavy work at the forge quickly built up his chest and arm muscles, while at home he undertook dancing lessons to improve his footwork. His fame in the ring spread quickly and he had his first fight at Sydney Stadium in 1914. In the following year he won both the Australian middleweight title and the Australian heavyweight title and gave every indication of being in the world-championship class. The world middleweight title was vacant in 1915; Darcy defeated a leading contender, Eddie McGoorty, twice in 1915, and former middleweight champion, George Chip, in 1916.

In September 1914 Darcy had been rejected for enlistment in the Army on the grounds that he was under age. By October 1916 he had received a tempting offer for a series of quick fights in the USA. However, World War I was going badly for the Allied forces in 1916; when Darcy stated his case to the Australian government, sought permission to spend six months in the USA and offered to leave a bond to guarantee his return and enlistment for military service, his offer was refused. He stowed away on an American freighter bound for the USA, but was branded as a 'slacker' by the Governor of New York, and victimised by an American newspaper campaign accusing him of cowardice and desertion from military service. He succumbed to an attack of pneumonia following a tonsil operation, and died in Memphis. In all, Darcy had had 44 fights for 40 wins, 20 by knockout; and although he did not win a world title, he is considered to have been one of the most brilliant and talented boxers in international boxing history.

dargawarra *see* rodents

Dargie, Sir William Alexander (1912-) Portraitist. Born in Melbourne, Dargie trained at the Melbourne Technical School, where he was influenced by the tradition of tonal Impressionism associated with Bernard Hall. He was an official war artist with the AIF from 1939 to 1945, and then head of the National Gallery School, Melbourne, from 1946 to 1953. His adoption of a conservative view in painting won him the patronage of Prime Minister MENZIES, who for a time hoped to establish an academy patterned on the Royal Academy, London, with Dargie as a leading member. Winning the ARCHIBALD PRIZE eight times between 1941 and 1956, and receiving three commissions to paint members of the Royal Family, he became established as Australia's best-known society portraitist. He was made an OBE in 1959 and a CBE in 1969, and in 1970 was knighted.

Dark, Eleanor (1901-) Novelist. The daughter of short-story writer and poet Dowell O'Reilly, Eleanor Dark was born and educated in Sydney and during the 1930s established

herself as one of Australia's leading novelists with *Slow Dawning* (1932), *Prelude to Christopher* (1934), *Return to Coolami* (1936), *Sun Across the Sky* (1937) and *Waterway* (1938). These were essentially studies of personal psychological conflict, although *Waterway*, with its backward glances at Australian history, indicated a new direction of her interest which became fully revealed in the historical novel *The Timeless Land* (1941), which was based on the foundation and early years of Sydney and was particularly effective in its treatment of the Aborigines. Its theme was continued in *Storm of Time* (1948) and *No Barrier* (1953), the three works between them giving a picture of the first half-century of the history of NSW. Another novel of this period of her work was *The Little Company* (1945), which has a more recent setting, dealing with social problems at the time of World War II. *See also* literature
Further reading: Day, A.G. *Eleanor Dark.* Twayne, Boston, 1976.

Darling Downs QLD Called the 'Granary of QLD', this region in the SE of the State covers an area of 72 520km², lying W of the GREAT DIVIDING RANGE at an elevation of between 350m and 600m above sea level. No other area of comparable size in QLD is so richly endowed with wide stretches of fertile soil derived from volcanic rocks. The landforms of the region consist of the highland ranges in the E (MAIN and BUNYA Ranges), falling in the W to a zone of hilly undulating country, and merging further W into broad alluvial plains. The CONDAMINE RIVER and its tributaries (Myall, Oakley, Hodgson, Cooranga and Canaga Creeks) drain the Downs in a general NW direction before the stream makes a great arc to flow W then SW. The inland location of the region gives it comparatively hot summer conditions; winter days are warm but nights in July can be frosty. The annual rainfall at WARWICK in the S of the Downs is 644mm, at TOOWOOMBA the average is 955mm and at DALBY, further N, it is 693mm. There is a distinctly seasonal pattern in the rainfall, with a concentration in summer and a drier period during winter and spring. About half the annual rainfall comes in the four months between November and February.

Rural production in the region is rich and varied: crops include wheat, barley, maize, sorghum, millet, soya beans, linseed and cotton; livestock include sheep, beef cattle, dairy herds and horses (particularly notable are the bloodstock studs). Strip-cropping is a widely adopted farming method in the area, and gives the landscape a variegated pattern of crop lands interspersed with bands of newly turned soil. The Downs are crossed by the New England and Burnett Highways on a N-S route, by the Warrego Highway on a SE-NW route, and by the Moonie-Bunya Highway on a SW-NE route. The Downs were discovered by the explorer Allan CUNNINGHAM in 1827 and were first settled in 1840 by Patrick Leslie at a site near Warwick. It was from the Downs that Ludwig LEICHHARDT set out in 1848 on his ill-fated expedition. The main urban centre of the region is Toowoomba; other service and commercial centres are Warwick, Dalby and KINGAROY.

Further reading: Greenwood, R.H. *The Darling Downs.* Longmans, London, 1957; Newell, P. *Darling Downs Sketchbook.* Rigby, Adelaide, 1973.

Darling, Sir Ralph (1775-1858)

Governor of NSW. He joined the British Army as an ensign in 1793, had risen to the rank of major-general by 1813, and from 1819 to 1823 served as military commandant in Mauritius. Appointed Governor of NSW in 1824, he reached Sydney late in 1825. An able and conscientious administrator, he reorganised the civil service of NSW, considerably increased colonial revenue without raising taxes, and instituted monetary reforms involving the phasing out of the colony's dollar currency. He also introduced the Ripon Land Regulations of 1831, by which a system of sale-by-auction replaced that of land grants; and applied the policy of keeping settlement concentrated by trying to confine it to the NINETEEN COUNTIES. In accordance with instructions based on the recommendations of John BIGGE, he reorganised the treatment of convicts, assigning as many as possible to settlers, and making great use of chain gangs and special penal settlements for those who were judged unruly. In exploration, he was responsible for sending STURT and CUNNINGHAM on important expeditions.

National Library of Australia

Governor Darling

In spite of his considerable achievements, Darling could be considered the wrong man to have been put in charge of NSW at that particular time, for he tried to apply to it standards typical of military discipline at the very time when the first small steps were being taken towards self-government and the demand for civil liberties was growing. His authoritarian manner and policies involved him in considerable conflict, particularly with regard to freedom of the Press. (For this issue, *see* NEWSPAPERS). He left Australia in 1831. Ten years later he was knighted and promoted to general.

Further reading: Shaw, A.G.L. *Heroes and Villains in History: Governors Darling and Bourke in New South Wales.* Sydney University Press, Sydney, 1966 and *Ralph Darling.* Oxford University Press, Melbourne, 1971.

Darling Range

WA Located between 20km and 30km inland from the SW coast of the State, and running parallel to the coast, this range is really the escarpment of the great inland plateau. The range extends N-S over a distance of about 300km from MOORA (190km by road N of Perth) to DONNYBROOK (212km by road S of Perth); it rises sharply from the coastal plain to an even skyline, typical of a plateau landscape, between 250m and 300m high, with the highest point, Mt Cook, reaching to just over 580m. Many rivers which rise on the plateau, such as the Collie, HARVEY and the AVON-SWAN Rivers, have carved steep gorges where they cut across the range before descending to the coastal plain and flowing into the Indian Ocean. The rainfall of the range, particularly in the S parts, is quite high (yearly averages are often above 1 200mm) and dams have been constructed on many of the streams to provide storage for urban supplies, for irrigation schemes along the coastal plain, and for the GOLDFIELDS WATER SUPPLY scheme. Among these are MUNDARING RESERVOIR on the Helena River (a tributary of the Swan), completed in 1902; the Harvey Dam (built in 1916 and enlarged in 1931) and the Stirling Dam (1948), both on the Harvey River; and Wellington Dam (1933) on the Collie River. In recent years the range has become important as a source of bauxite, which is railed to a treatment plant at PINJARRA and to the alumina refinery at KWINANA.

Darling River

NSW An inland system which traverses the W plains of the State in a NE-SW direction, the Darling River, with its tributaries, drains a vast area of some 650 000km², including much of southern QLD and western NSW. The headwater streams of the system drain from the slopes of the GREAT DIVIDING RANGE; the main tributaries rising in QLD are the CONDAMINE and Maranoa (which join to become the BALONNE), the Moonie and DUMARESQ (part of which forms the State border), and the Warrego and Paroo (which flow intermittently in the arid interior). The tributaries rising in NSW are the MACINTYRE (part of which forms the State border), GWYDIR, NAMOI, CASTLEREAGH, MACQUARIE and BOGAN Rivers. The stream has several names along its course: part of the upper reaches are called Dumaresq; it then becomes the BARWON, and further downstream is known as the 'Barwon or Darling'; and finally, from its confluence with the Culgoa River about 48km upstream from BOURKE, it becomes the Darling for the remainder of its course until it joins the MURRAY RIVER near Wentworth. Since the major part of its 1 900km course is across plains of the arid interior, it is a slow, meandering stream with many BILLABONGS and ANABRANCHES; in flood times, the plains are covered by great sheets of slow-moving water which often linger for months. One big anabranch, Talywalka Creek, leaves the Darling's left bank upstream from WILCANNIA and rejoins it some 400km downstream near MENINDEE. Another one, called the Great Anabranch, leaves the Darling S of Menindee, flows for some 480km, and joins the Murray downstream from Wentworth.

The discovery and exploration of the Darling River by white settlers began with the journey of Allan CUNNINGHAM in 1827 when he traversed the upper tributaries from the Condamine to the Namoi. Then in 1835 Thomas MITCHELL explored some 500km of the river as far downstream as Menindee, and in 1844 Charles STURT travelled upstream from the Murray-Darling junction to Menindee. Following these exploratory journeys, the rivers became important for transport; paddle-wheel steamers with barges brought in supplies and carried out the wool bales from the 1850s until early in this century. Bourke was the furthermost point upstream that the river traffic reached. The river trips were often hazardous, for the streamers could be stranded for months when the river was low, and the river trade was progressively eclipsed by road and rail transport. Dams have been built on several tributaries of the Darling (for example, COPETON DAM on the Gwydir, KEEPIT on the Namoi and BURRENDONG on the Macquarie); weirs have been constructed along the main stream to stabilise and regulate flow (four weirs upstream and three downstream from Bourke); and the Menindee Lakes storage scheme (the main weir of which was completed in 1960) has provided an important water conservation system for irrigation and for livestock and domestic supplies in the lower reaches of the river. In 1952, a pipeline 110km long was constructed from the Darling near Menindee to BROKEN HILL; the Menindee Lakes scheme has added an element of greater reliability to this pipeline supply.

Darrell, Edward Price George

(*c*1850-1921) Actor and playwright. Born in England, the son of a hotel-keeper, Darrell left home when he was a teenager and found his way to the New Zealand goldfields where he became a singer and actor. He later moved to Melbourne, and in 1877 founded the Dramatic Company for the Production of Australian Plays. Thereafter he performed in a succession of his own sensation-melodramas about Anglo-Australian life which enjoyed popularity until the end of the century. *The Sunny South* (1883) is his most famous play, but *Transported for Life* (1877), *Back from the Grave* (1878), *The Squatter* (1885), *The New Rush* (1886) and *The Double Event* (1893) were also regularly staged by his company. His last play was *The Land of Gold* (1907). He apparently committed suicide, leaving a message to say that he was 'going on a long voyage'; his body was found on Dee Why Beach, Sydney.

Further reading: Darrell, G. *The Sunny South.* Currency Press, Sydney, 1975; Irvin, E.

Gentleman George, King of Melodrama. University of Queensland Press, St Lucia, 1980.

darter Belonging to the family Anhingidae, the darter, *Anhinga rufa* (1m long), is a large black diving bird (the female has white underparts) which is related to the CORMORANTS. Also called the snake-bird on account of its long 'G'-shaped neck and tiny head, it has a long, pointed, hookless beak. It is a shy bird which frequents deep pools and secluded inland waters, particularly swamps, throughout the Australian mainland, feeding on aquatic animals; when swimming, it sinks so that only its neck and head are visible. Its nests are placed in trees in or near water.

Darter, *Anhinga rufa*

Dartmouth Dam VIC The largest storage reservoir in VIC, with a capacity of 3 700 000ML, the dam is located in a 'V'-shaped gorge of the MITTA MITTA RIVER, a tributary of the MURRAY. It is an earth-and-rockfill structure, 180m high, and forms part of the Murray River water conservation scheme. It drains a catchment area of 3 600km² and is designed to increase the seasonal capacity of the scheme and regulate river flow. The construction of the dam, commenced in 1972 and completed in 1979, was a joint venture between the three States (VIC, NSW and SA) and the Australian government; water from the reservoir is controlled by the River Murray Commission. A 150MW hydro-electricity power station and a regulating pondage weir are also part of the Dartmouth development, under the control of the State Electricity Commission of VIC. At a site 4km downstream from the dam, the new township of Dartmouth has been designed as the administrative and residential centre of the Dartmouth development scheme.

Darwin NT (population 56 482 in 1981) The largest urban centre, the administrative capital and the main port of the Territory, it is located on the NW coast on a peninsula bounded on the W by Fannie Bay and on the E by Francis Bay, though growth in recent decades has extended the urban settlement beyond the limits of the peninsula. The coastal inlet on which the city is situated, called Port

Darwin, was discovered in 1839 by Lieutenant Stokes of HMS *Beagle* and was named after the British scientist Charles DARWIN, who had been with the ship on a previous voyage. Prior to Stokes' discovery, a number of attempts had been made to establish settlements in different locations in the NT (for example, in 1824 at PORT ESSINGTON and in 1827 at RAFFLES BAY, both on COBOURG PENINSULA), but none of these had been successful, mainly because of supply problems and the difficulties imposed by the climate. In 1863 the British Imperial government placed the NT under the control of the SA government, which in 1869 sent Surveyor-General George Goyder to the NT to establish a settlement; his first base was at Adam Bay, about 48km E of Darwin, and from there he looked for a site for permanent settlement. His recommendation was Port Darwin, where the city now stands. The town was first named Palmerston, after the British Prime Minister, and it was not until 1911 when the federal government took over control of the NT that the name was officially changed to Darwin.

The progress of the city since its establishment in 1869 has been characterised by short periods of rapid growth followed by long years of relatively little development. The discovery of gold between Darwin and PINE CREEK in 1871 brought a sudden growth in the population; the building of the OVERLAND TELEGRAPH (1870-72) gave the town further impetus; rich gold finds in the Pine Creek area in 1873 brought new settlers and many Chinese were recruited in Singapore to alleviate the acute labour shortage in Darwin; and the construction of the Darwin-Pine Creek railway in 1889 and the establishment of meatworks in 1917 led to further short-term growth.

World War II brought many changes: from 1942 to 1945 the Territory was placed under army administration; the Stuart Highway was built as a vital supply link between Darwin and the ALICE SPRINGS railhead; and the Barkly Highway was constructed to provide a link to the SE. The Japanese air raids of 1942 and 1943 caused severe damage to many old buildings, and replacements were erected; in addition, the port facilities were upgraded, air services were improved, and the Manton Dam, 68km from Darwin, was built to provide greater and more reliable urban water supplies. After the war many servicemen, construction workers and road builders stayed to make their homes in the Territory.

In the following decades there was a period of rapid expansion, assisted by faster and more dependable transport for the cartage of food and building supplies. The discovery of uranium at RUM JUNGLE in the late 1940s, and further big finds in the ALLIGATOR RIVERS area, added to this growth. Aviation also played a vital role in development, with the upgrading of the airport to international standards. Further contributions to development have been provided through improved facilities for handling cattle, the expansion of the fishing industry, the improvement of the

port, and the development of tourism.

Early on Christmas Day 1974 cyclone 'Tracy' hit the city. The catastrophe devastated many homes, businesses and public buildings throughout the city, disrupted communications and necessitated the evacuation of over half the population. The magnitude of this disaster and the extent of the destruction brought a response from people throughout the nation, who liberally contributed to appeals for assistance. Out of the debris left by 'Tracy' a new Darwin emerged in the late 1970s, with modern buildings, high-rise terrace blocks, up-to-date tourist facilities and new residential developments, designed so that in future the city should be able to withstand a similar natural disaster.

Destruction caused by cyclone 'Tracy' in December 1975 at Darwin

Darwin experiences a two-season climate—the 'wet' and the 'dry'. The wet season extends from November to March, when the rains and high humidity transform Darwin into a colourful and verdant tropical city. The dry season is characterised by clear skies and hot days, and although this is the cooler part of the year, night temperatures rarely fall below 15°C. The average annual rainfall is 1 813mm, of which 1 612mm falls between November and March; February has the highest rainfall (430mm average).

Darwin, Charles Robert (1809-82) Scientist. A great English naturalist and the first biologist to put forward a comprehensive theory of evolution by natural selection, Darwin visited Australia in 1836 on board HMS *Beagle*. He travelled from Sydney to BATHURST and in TAS, but did not see the site of Darwin, the city which was later named after him. Some of his Australian observations are incorporated in *The Origin of Species* (1859) and he gives an account of his visit in *The Voyage of the Beagle* (1839). His grandfather Erasmus Darwin, who was given to expounding his scientific theories in verse, forecast the construction of the SYDNEY

HARBOUR BRIDGE in one of his poems.
Further reading: Marshall, A.J. *Darwin and Huxley in Australia.* Hodder & Stoughton, Sydney, 1970.

National Library of Australia

Charles Darwin aged 30, a painting by George Richmond R.A.

date palm *see* Palmae

Davey, John Andrew 'Jack' (1910-59) Radio entertainer. He was born in Auckland, New Zealand, and after having some success there as a stage and radio singer, moved to Sydney. In 1934 he was engaged as a singer by 2GB, the radio station with which he was mainly associated for the remainder of his career. He soon turned to announcing and compering, became renowned for his quick wit and friendly manner, and for about 20 years was probably the best-known figure in Australian broadcasting. His greatest success was in compering radio quiz shows such as 'Give it a Go'; however he was not notably successful in adapting to television.

Davey, Thomas (1758-1823) Lieutenant-Governor of TAS. Born at Tiverton in Devon, he was commissioned as a second lieutenant in the Royal Marines in 1778, came to NSW with the FIRST FLEET, and returned to England in 1792. In 1810, on hearing of the death of David COLLINS, Lieutenant-Governor at Hobart, he applied for the vacancy and was appointed Lieutenant-Governor of the whole of TAS. However, he did not arrive in Hobart until February 1813. From the outset his superior, Governor MACQUARIE, was repelled by what he described as the 'frivolity and low buffoonery in his manners', and regarded him as quite unfit for his position. In his defence it can be said that when he arrived the TAS settlements were very poorly organised and badly equipped, and that during his four years in command he did improve their material condition somewhat. Nevertheless, it must be admitted that he lacked skill as an administrator, and that his conviviality, open association with convict women and remarkable informality in dress and manner—all of which contributed to his nickname 'mad Tom' —weakened his authority. Macquarie succeeded in having him relieved of his post in 1816, and he handed over to William SORELL in the following year. He then went to Sydney, was given land grants totalling over 3000ha, and in 1818 returned to TAS as a settler. However, he was notably unsuccessful as a farmer and in managing his financial affairs. He died intestate, leaving an estate of only about £20.
Further reading: West, J. *The History of Tasmania.* (vol 1) Henry Dowling, Launceston, 1852; Giblin, R.W. *The Early History of Tasmania.* (vol 1) Methuen, London, 1928.

David, Sir Tannatt William Edgeworth (1858-1934) Geologist and Antarctic explorer. Born near Cardiff, Wales, he graduated from Oxford University and came to Australia in 1882 as the assistant geological surveyor with the NSW Department of Mines. His work in this position included a study of the alluvial tin deposits near Emmaville in the NEW ENGLAND region of northern NSW, and an investigation of the GRETA coal measures in the lower HUNTER RIVER valley. In 1891 he was appointed to the post of Professor of Geology and Physical Geography at the University of Sydney. In 1907 he joined the Shackleton expedition to ANTARCTICA, where he led the ascent of Mt Erebus in 1908 and made the epic journey to the magnetic South Pole. In 1910 he was made a CMG and in 1920 a KBE. He resigned his professorial position at the university in 1924 so as to devote his time to writing a book on the geology of Australia. However, at the time of his death the book was incomplete and it was subsequently finished by one of his academic colleagues, Dr W.R. Browne, and published in 1950. David's outstanding scientific contributions were internationally recognised and he was awarded many scholarly honours.

Davis This is an Australian base in ANTARCTICA, located at latitude 68°35'S in the Vestfold Hills area of the Ingrid Christensen coast. It was established by the Australian National Antarctic Research Expeditions (ANARE) in 1957 (closed temporarily in 1965-69), and was named after John King Davis, a navigator who was a member of Antarctic expeditions early this century.

Davis, Arthur Hoey *see* Rudd, Steele

Davis Cup *see* tennis

Dawson, Peter (1882-1961) Bass-baritone. The son of a Scottish seaman who settled in Adelaide, Dawson went to Britain in 1902 and studied first in Glasgow, and then with Sir Charles Santley in London. He later toured W England with Madame Albani, and visited Australia with Amy Castles' company. His first operatic appearance at Covent Garden was in 1909, and in 1910 he became principal baritone for Chappell's ballad concerts.

Dawson was best known for his singing of ballads and he reached large and varied audiences through the medium of gramophone records, making his first recording for the Edison-Bell Phonograph Co. in 1904. In 1906 Dawson performed as a singing comedian under the name of Hector Grant, and later recorded a number of Scottish songs under that name. He sang under several pseudonyms, keeping his own name for opera, oratorio and ballad singing. He also composed many songs under the name of J.P. McCall. On his retirement he lived permanently in Australia. He died at Harbord NSW.

Dawson River QLD Located in the SE of the State, it rises in a section of the GREAT DIVIDING RANGE known as the CARNARVON RANGE, and flows for over 600km, first NE, then generally N to join with the MACKENZIE RIVER and form the FITZROY RIVER. Towns along the river are Taroom (population 688 in 1981), Theodore (643), MOURA (2 871) and Baralaba (367), while BILOELA (4 643) is located in the valley of a right-bank tributary. The Dawson Highway from GLADSTONE goes through Biloela and crosses the river on an E-W route at Moura; the Leichhardt Highway from the S passes through Taroom and Theodore, then meets the Dawson Highway E of Moura. Since the 1920s, the waters of the river have been used for irrigation by the construction of a series of weirs (Theodore, Orange Creek, Moura and Binda) and this scheme was further developed by the completion in 1971 of the Glebe Weir (17 220ML capacity), 32km E of Taroom, and the Neville Hewitt Weir (12 600ML capacity) near Baralaba. The irrigation water is used for growing cotton, sorghum and wheat, and for watering pastures for cattle grazing. Coal is mined by open-cut methods at Moura and railed to Gladstone for overseas export.

Daydream Island QLD A coral-fringed island in the inner 'lagoon' of the GREAT BARRIER REEF, it is located NE of PROSERPINE and W of the WHITSUNDAY PASSAGE, between the MOLLE ISLANDS and the mainland coast. Now a tourist centre, it is the smallest of the island resorts in the region, and can be reached by launch from Shute Harbour or by helicopter from MACKAY.

Daylesford VIC (population 2 883 in 1981) A small town on the N side of the GREAT DIVIDING RANGE near the headwaters of the LODDON RIVER, it is 111km by road and 121km by rail NW of Melbourne and 45km NE of BALLARAT along the Midland Highway. It was founded in the 1850s as a goldfields town, known as Jim Crow Diggings, and was later named Daylesford after the home of Warren Hastings in Worcester, England. It is now a popular tourist resort, famed for its mineral springs.

Koala, *Phascolarctus cinereus* (*see* KOALA)

Dingo *Canis familiaris dingo* (*see* DINGO)

Squirrel glider, *Petaurus norfolcensis*
(*see* POSSUMS AND GLIDERS)

Tasmanian devil, *Sarcophilus harrisii*
(*see* NATIVE CATS)

Tiger cat or spotted-tail quoll, *Dasyurus maculatus* (*see* NATIVE CATS)

Rabbit-eared bandicoot or bilby, *Macrotis lagotis*
(*see* BANDICOOTS)

Emu, *Dromaius novaehollandiae* (*see* EMU)

Common wombat, *Vombatus ursinus* (*see* WOMBAT)

Grey kangaroo *Macropus giganteus* (*see* KANGAROO)

Saddled butterfly fish, *Chaetodon ephippium*

Knight fish, *Cleidopus gloriamaris*

Sergeant baker (male), *Aulopus purpurissatus*

Blue spotted coral cod, *Cephalopholis miniatus*

Flute mouth or trumpet fish, *Aulostoma chinensis*

Adult blue angelfish, *Pomacanthus semicirculatus*

See also FISHES, BONY

daylight saving This is a system of varying the standard times of the TIME ZONES of Australia during the summer months by putting clocks forward by one hour. The effect of this clock change is to push the 'regular' day forward by one hour, thereby giving an extension of daylight hours into the early evening. This system was started during World War I, and was revived during World War II and again in the 1970s, though it has been a matter of some disagreement between the States and not all States have accepted it. At present, it is used in NSW, ACT, VIC, TAS and SA, but not in QLD, NT and WA. The supporters of daylight saving claim that it increases the hours available for leisure activities at the end of the day and also reduces the consumption of electricity for lighting. However, those opposed to the idea claim that it creates problems for shift workers and for farmers whose daily routine is disrupted by the time change.

de Castella, Robert (1957-) Marathon runner. Born and educated in Melbourne, he began to attain success as an athlete towards the end of his school years, under the coaching of Pat Clohessy, who still coaches him. At first he concentrated on middle distance running, but then turned to the marathon, and in his first race, in 1979, won the VIC championship. His rise to international fame was then rapid. In 1981 at the Fukuoka marathon in Japan he ran the second-fastest time ever recorded—and the fastest ever on an out-and-back course. In the following year he scored a convincing win in the Brisbane COMMONWEALTH GAMES, and in 1983 won the Rotterdam marathon and the world championship at Helsinki.

De Grey River WA Located in the NW region of the State, it rises in the Robertson Range (the Oakover River is the main headwater stream), flows first N then NW for over 500km to a mud-lined estuary on the Indian Ocean, NE of PORT HEDLAND. It flows only intermittently, mainly after the summer rains, and many stretches of the stream bed are dry for long periods.

de Maistre, Leroy Leveson Laurent Joseph 'Roy' (1894-1968) Artist. Born at BOWRAL in NSW, the son of a wealthy grazier with wide social connections, de Maistre developed an early interest in music and painting. At the age of 17 he went to the Sydney Conservatorium to study violin and viola, and also attended art classes at Dattilo Rubbo's and Julian ASHTON's. De Maistre was impressed by the experimentation in neo-Impressionism being undertaken at Rubbo's by Norah Simpson, the Australian painter who had returned to Sydney for two years (1913-15), bringing with her reports and reproductions of the work of Gauguin, Cézanne and Van Gogh. While in hospital recovering from tuberculosis, he became interested in the relationship of theory of music and colour schemes. The result was an exhibition in 1919

of such works as *The Boat Sheds in Violet Red Key*. Four years later he visited Europe and on his return became a leader in the Contemporary Group, a modernist movement in Sydney. From 1930 until his death he lived in London and during this period his work became high-tonal, linear, abstract and, after his conversion to Roman Catholicism, dominated by religious themes. He was made a CBE in 1962.

Deakin, Alfred (1856-1919) Architect of federation and Prime Minister. Born in the Melbourne suburb of Fitzroy, he studied law, but found himself more attracted to journalism and in early manhood became associated with David Syme, proprietor of the Melbourne *Age* and one of the leading advocates of protectionist policies. His interest in journalism persisted after he had entered politics, and for 13 years he continued to contribute anonymous articles on the Australian political scene to the London *Morning Post*, keeping them up even after he had become Prime Minister. He also maintained throughout his career a deep interest in literature, philosophy and other intellectual subjects.

Alfred Deakin

He entered the VIC Legislative Assembly in 1879, held a number of portfolios in various ministries between 1883 and 1900, and won attention by his presentation of an Australian viewpoint on Pacific affairs at the 1887 Colonial Conference in London, and by his untiring advocacy of a federation of the colonies.

Elected to the first Commonwealth Parliament, he became Attorney-General in Edmund BARTON's Ministry, and after the latter had moved to the High Court bench in 1903 Deakin succeeded him as Prime Minister and leader of the protectionist party. His first Ministry lasted only seven months and was chiefly notable for the passing of Defence Acts providing for voluntary enlistment in time of peace and giving the Governor-General power in time of war to call on all males between the ages of 18 and 60 for the defence of Australia. During his second Ministry (1905-1908) he moved his party's emphasis to social and industrial legislation, establishing the Commonwealth Court of Conciliation and Arbitration

and bringing the Commonwealth Parliament into the field of social services by introducing age and invalid pensions.

By 1908 the middle ground which Deakin had held in federal politics was becoming difficult to maintain. Although he disliked the organisation of the Labor Party, his views on social reform made him more sympathetic to its aims than to those of the conservatives in the free trade party. Nevertheless, Labor, on whose support he had depended to stay in office, had been gaining strength and was anxious to govern in its own right. The two non-Labor groups were therefore driven together, and in 1909 joined to form the 'Fusion' or Liberal Party. For a year Deakin was again Prime Minister, but with 'all of my enemies since federation' among his supporters. During this time he was successful in winning British acceptance of the idea that Australia should have her own navy, and made plans for the founding of military and naval academies. After the Labor victory of 1910 he became leader of the Opposition, but in 1913, after a tragic mental collapse, retired from Parliament.

Deakin is generally regarded as one of the most distinguished Australian Prime Ministers, but is criticised by some historians as an opportunist who accepted at various times the support of politicians from one end of the political spectrum to the other in order to stay in power.
Further reading: Murdoch, W.L.F. *Alfred Deaken: A Sketch.* Constable, London, 1923; la Nauze, J.A. *Alfred Deakin: A Biography.* (2 vols) Melbourne University Press, Melbourne, 1965 and *Alfred Deakin.* Melbourne University Press, Melbourne, 1968.

Deane, John Phillip (1796-1849) Musician. Born in London, he became organist at St David's Church, Hobart, in 1826. He moved to Sydney in 1836, and with his daughter established one of the first music teaching studios. For many years he was a leading figure in the musical scene of Sydney. His son, John Deane, was conductor for the Sydney Philharmonic Society and also was active in the city's musical circles as a violinist.

death adder *see* snakes

Deception Bay QLD (population 3 857 in 1981) This popular holiday resort is situated in the SE of the State, between BRIBIE ISLAND and REDCLIFFE, some 15km SSE of CABOOLTURE, and about 40km N of Brisbane. It offers sheltered and safe swimming areas, good fishing, and opportunities for boating and other aquatic sports.

deer *see* animals, introduced

defence This article discusses the history of Australia's defence policies and forces, and the current strength and organisation of the defence force. Further information on the part played by Australian servicemen in major wars is provided in the entries on the BOER WAR,

GALLIPOLI, KOREAN WAR, VIETNAM WAR, WORLD WAR I and WORLD WAR II.

History of defence policy and organisation When the British colonies in Australia attained self-government, their overall defence remained the responsibility of the Imperial government in London. However, they were encouraged to organise and control their own local military forces, especially after 1862, when the House of Commons passed a resolution that 'Colonies exercising the right of self-government ought to undertake the main responsibility of providing their own internal order and security, and ought to assist in their own external defence.' In accordance with this principle the last British troops were withdrawn from Australia in 1870.

The federal Constitution of 1901 made defence an exclusive Commonwealth power, and so the small military and naval forces of the six former colonies were amalgamated under the control of a Commonwealth Department of Defence. The Defence Acts of 1903-1904 set up a Defence Council, to deal with general policy, and separate Naval and Military Boards. In 1920, after the government had decided to maintain a separate air force, an Air Board was also created.

General defence policy continued to be closely linked with the British Imperial defence system. Nevertheless, Australia's view of her defence needs had come to differ in some respects from Britain's view. Since the 1880s, Australian politicians had expressed concern about the spread of non-British colonies in the Pacific and the danger of attack from them, and about the growing strength of Japan. When Britain signed a defence treaty with Japan in 1902, many Australians feared that this might cause her to rely too heavily on Japan, instead of maintaining a sufficiently strong naval force in the Pacific. Fear of Japan became stronger in the 1930s, and when war broke out in 1939, although Australia sent forces to aid Britain, she also introduced conscription for home defence, a step which had not been considered necessary in World War I.

The outbreak of war in the Pacific in December 1941 marked a turning point in Australia's defence policy. Britain and Australia were not able to prevent the Japanese from driving S; only the USA could do so and therefore links with the USA began to replace those with Britain. Australians in the South-West Pacific Area served under an American Supreme Commander, General Douglas MacArthur, and defence policy has ever since been based on friendship with the USA. The ANZUS PACT of 1952 has come to be regarded as a cornerstone of Australian defence.

The post-war process of decolonisation in Asia, the spread of Communism there, and the memory of the threat of attack during World War II have also led Australia to join various security arrangements in South-East Asia. In 1948 she participated in the ANZAM agreement for joint military planning with Britain and New Zealand, in 1954 she joined the SOUTH-EAST ASIA TREATY ORGANISATION

(SEATO), and in 1971, when the bulk of the British forces in Asia were withdrawn, she entered on the Five-Power Defence Arrangement with Britain, New Zealand, Malaysia and Singapore. Australian forces have been deployed in Asia on a number of occasions since 1945. In 1946 units of all three armed services were sent to Japan as part of the British Commonwealth Occupation Force (BCOF). In 1949 units of the Royal Australian Air Force (RAAF) were sent to Singapore, and later both ground forces and RAAF units were used against Communist insurgents in Malaya. Australian forces participated in the Korean War and on a much smaller scale in the defence of the newly formed Federation of Malaysia during the period of its 'confrontation' with Indonesia. Between 1962 and 1972, Australian forces served in Vietnam.

Changes in organisation during recent years have been aimed at co-ordinating the activities of the three services more effectively. Early in World War II, Departments of the Navy, Army and Air Force had been set up in addition to the Department of Defence. Following the report of the Morshead Committee on defence organisation in 1957, the authority of the Minister for Defence to formulate and apply a unified defence programme was extended. However, the Committee's recommendation that the three service departments be re-absorbed into the Department of Defence was not carried out until 1976. This amalgamation is still in force but in 1982 a Department of Defence Support, concerned essentially with the supply of goods and services for defence purposes, and similar therefore to the pre-1975 Department of Supply, was created.

Defence Public Relations, Aus.

Graduation ceremony, Royal Military College, Duntroon

History of naval defence Since Australia consists of islands, its defence needs, from the beginning, were seen mainly in terms of naval protection. Fears of attack flared up on a number of occasions, particularly during the Crimean War (1854-56) when, although the colonies were not authorised to maintain their own navies, NSW and VIC each acquired an armed sloop, named *Spitfire* and *Victoria* respectively. In 1859 the British government gave in to pleas from the colonies for stronger naval protection by forming the Imperial Squadron of the Royal Navy in Australia. At first, the vessels assigned to this force were old and far from formidable. However, the squadron's strength was increased after the Colonial Conference of 1887, at which the

colonies agreed to subsidise it, and further increased after the Imperial Conference of 1902, at which the new Commonwealth government promised to pay a much larger subsidy.

Meanwhile, the Colonial Naval Defence Act of 1865 had given the colonies authority to provide, maintain and man their own vessels of war, and the four E mainland colonies had proceeded to do so on a small scale. VIC's best-known vessel of war was the monitor *Cerberus*, SA's only sea-going warship was *Protector*, which was loaned to the British Admiralty for service in China during the Boxer Rebellion; QLD's largest vessels were the the gunboats *Gayundah* and *Paluma*; and NSW, secure in the knowledge that Sydney was the base for the Australian Squadron of the Royal Navy, bought only two torpedo boats.

By 1900 opinion in Australia was hardening in favour of the establishment of a strong separate Australian Navy, and at the Imperial Defence Conference of 1909 it was agreed that Australia and Canada should form their own navies, over which they would exercise full control, subject only to the provision that in time of war they would operate as an integral part of the Royal Navy. Meanwhile, Prime Minister FISHER had ordered the building of two destroyers, *Parramatta* and *Yarra*, which reached Australia in 1910. In July 1911 King George V granted the title 'Royal Australian Navy' to the Commonwealth Naval Forces, and in 1912 a third destroyer, *Warrego*, was commissioned. In the following year all Royal Naval Establishments in Australia were transferred to Commonwealth control, a Naval College was opened at GEELONG, and the main Australian fleet, consisting of the battle-cruiser *Australia*, the cruisers *Melbourne* and *Sydney* and the destroyers *Parramatta*, *Warrego* and *Yarra*, entered Sydney Harbour. Under construction at the same time were the cruiser *Brisbane*, and the destroyers *Huon*, *Torrens* and *Swan*, the submarines *AE1* and *AE2*, a depot ship and a fleet oiler.

The RAN's first task after the outbreak of war in 1914 was the capture of German New Guinea, during which operation the *AE1* disappeared with all hands off New Britain. *AE2* was lost in 1915 when she was forced to scuttle in the Sea of Marmara, her crew becoming prisoners of war in Turkey. These two submarines were the only losses during the war. Although RAN ships served in British waters, the North Atlantic, the Mediterranean and the Far East, only once was one of them engaged in action—the cruiser *Sydney* destroyed the German raider *Emden* in November 1914 at the COCOS ISLANDS.

The post-war years brought a considerable reduction in naval strength. HMAS *Australia* was towed to sea and scuttled in 1924, and the *Sydney* and *Melbourne* scrapped a few years later. However, as the international situation worsened after Hitler's accession to power in Germany there was some expansion, and by 1939 the RAN possessed the heavy cruisers *Australia* and *Canberra* and the light cruisers *Hobart*, *Perth* and *Adelaide* (all of these except the last-mentioned having been constructed during the 1930s), five destroyers and three sloops.

HMAS *Perth*, *Supply* and *Vampire*

About 5000 men were serving in the RAN in 1939; by 1945 this figure had reached over 39 000 (including 2 617 in the Women's Royal Australian Naval Service and 57 nursing sisters). Its ships served in all the main theatres of war and were engaged in action on many occasions. Losses included the cruisers *Sydney*, *Perth* and *Canberra*, the destroyers *Waterhen*, *Nestor* and *Voyager*, the sloops *Yarra* and *Parramatta*, three minesweepers and 22 other miscellaneous vessels.

Shortly after the end of the war the Fleet Air Arm was established, the fleet carrier *Sydney* being acquired in 1948 and the *Melbourne* in 1955. It was hoped to maintain two carriers permanently but because of lack of manpower and finance, when HMAS *Sydney* was converted to a troop carrier no replacement was made. Both *Melbourne* and *Sydney* have since been decommissioned. Since 1945, Australian ships have participated in the wars in Korea and Vietnam. Details of the present strength of the RAN are given below.

History of the Australian Army For the first several years of federation the main defence responsibility of the Commonwealth government was the Army. The small forces of the former colonies were taken over in 1901, and the Defence Acts of 1903-1904 set up an organisational structure, made provision for voluntary enlistment in peace-time, and authorised the Governor-General to conscript males between the ages of 18 and 60 for service within Australia in time of war. In 1908 compulsory military training was authorised and in 1909 a Defence Act provided for the establishment of the Royal Military College at Duntroon, and of factories for the manufacture of war supplies. In 1911, following a visit and report by Lord Kitchener, compulsory military training was extended.

When war broke out in 1914 the Australian government, fully supported by public opinion, was determined to send troops to the aid of Britain. However, since it had no regular army, a special volunteer force, known as the AUSTRALIAN IMPERIAL FORCE (AIF) was raised, and saw action in the Middle East and on the Western Front. After the war the men of the AIF were discharged, and in 1920 a committee recommended that Australia should again maintain a citizen army, with a nucleus of permanent staff. This plan was adopted,

with compulsory military training being retained in a modified form.

The Depression years brought further reductions and economies. The SCULLIN government abolished compulsory military training, and reduced the strength of the militia from 48 000 to 35 000 men. However, as the economic situation improved and the threat of war in Europe increased in the late 1930s, expansion again took place. In November 1938 Prime Minister LYONS announced a programme which involved increasing the strength of the militia to 70 000, establishing a Command and Staff College (later the Australian Staff College), building up stocks of military materials and raising for the first time a small regular field force.

Australian infantry in action

By 1939 the strength of the Army had reached 82 800, of which 80 000 were members of the militia. Within a few weeks of the outbreak of war Prime Minister MENZIES had announced that a volunteer force would be raised for service overseas. Lieutenant-General (later Field Marshal) Sir Thomas BLAMEY was appointed to command this second AIF, and by late 1940 four divisions had been formed. The 6th and 7th Divisions by that time were in the Middle East, the nucleus of the 9th was in Britain, and the 8th was in training in Australia. Meanwhile, in view of the uncertain situation in the Pacific, service in the militia, had been made compulsory. During the whole war enlistments in the AIF totalled over 460 000 and in the militia over 224 000.

After the end of the war the government decided to return to a policy of voluntary enlistment, but felt that Australia could no longer afford to depend almost entirely on citizen forces. It planned therefore to maintain an Australian Regular Army (ARA) of 17 000 men, and 50 000 in the CITIZEN MILITARY FORCES(militia), and in 1949 amended the Defence Act to authorise the raising of regular infantry troops in peacetime. The Liberal/Country Party government which came into office late in 1949 soon departed from the principle of completely voluntary enlistment. Alarmed by developments in Asia and the Pacific — particularly the Korean War, Communist insurgency in Malaya and the intensification of war in Vietnam — it introduced a compulsory system of National Service training in 1951 (*see* CONSCRIPTION).

Australian troops have been deployed overseas on several occasions since 1945. In 1946 an infantry brigade group was sent to Japan as

part of the BCOF. From 1948 the BCOF consisted solely of Australians, the last of whom were withdrawn in 1951. Three battalions participated in the Korean War, a battalion was sent to Malaya as part of the British Commonwealth Far East Strategic Reserve in 1955, and a force which finally reached a strength of three battalions fought in the Vietnam War.

Beach landing during a combined training exercise

History of air defence The beginning of military aviation in Australia was marked by the decision in 1912 to establish an Australian Flying Corps (AFC), and by the opening of a Central Flying School at Point Cook VIC in 1913. During World War I many Australian airmen, some trained in Australia and others overseas, served either in the Royal Flying Corps or the AFC. The first to be sent from Australia went to Mesopotamia (modern Iraq) in 1915, the officers being given commissions in the Royal Flying Crops. The first complete squadron, No. 1 Squadron, AFC, was sent to Egypt in 1916, and served in the campaign against the Turks in Palestine and Syria. Three other squadrons were later sent to England and saw action on the Western Front.

The AFC had operated under Army command, but in 1919 the government decided form a separate Australian Air Force. Late in 1920 an Air Board was constituted and in March 1921 the Australian Air Force came into being, the prefix 'Royal' being added several months later. During the following few years bases were established at Laverton VIC and RICHMOND in NSW, and an experimental station was established at Randwick, a Sydney suburb. By 1939 bases had been set up also at Pearce WA, Brisbane and Darwin. In the meantime, local production of war planes had been made possible by the establishment of an Australian branch of de Havilland Aircraft in 1927 and of the Commonwealth Aircraft Corporation in 1936. By September 1939 the RAAF had a total of 246 aircraft, manned by 310 officers and 3 179 airmen.

On the outbreak of war the Australian government at first proposed to send an expeditionary air force of several squadrons to Britain. However, this plan was superseded by the launching of the Empire Air Training Scheme, under which airmen in various parts of the British Commonwealth and Empire received elementary training in their own countries and advanced training mainly in Canada. Consequently, most of the Australian aircrew in operational squadrons in Britain and the Middle East were integrated into RAF squadrons, only about a third remaining in separate RAAF squadrons. After the Japanese attack on Pearl Harbour had made the Pacific the main area for Australia's war effort, the RAAF operated there as a separate force under the overall command of an American, General George C. Kinney, Commander Allied Air Forces, South-West Pacific Area. Before the end of the war the RAAF had reached a strength of 183 000 men and women.

Defence Public Relations, Aus.

RAAF P3B Orion

In the period since 1945 the main RAAF commitments overseas have been as follows: three fighter squadrons formed part of the occupation force in Japan; one fighter and one transport squadron participated in the Korean War; a fighter wing was stationed in the Mediterranean from 1952 to 1955; transport, fighter, bomber and construction squadrons have been sent since 1950 to the Singapore-Malaysia area, most being based at Butterworth, near Penang, in West Malaysia; and at times between 1964 and 1971 one squadron of Caribou transport aircraft, one of Iriquois helicopters and one bomber squadron served in Vietnam. Details of the present strength of the RAAF are given below.

The Defence Force today Although the three armed services have kept their separate identities, they are now known collectively as the Defence Force, the organisation of which is based on the realisation that under modern conditions most armed operations are certain to be joint affairs in which two or all three of the services are involved.

Under the Constitution the Governor-General is nominal Commander-in-Chief of the armed forces, acting on the advice of his Ministers. The Minister for Defence has the general responsibility for the control and administration of the Defence Force. Under him are the Secretary of the Department of Defence, who advises him on defence policy and the use of defence resources, and the Chief of Defence Force Staff, who exercises general supervision of the Defence Force. Below the latter are the Chief of Naval Staff, the Chief of General Staff and the Chief of Air Staff, who are the officers commanding the Navy, Army and Air Force respectively. The Minister for Defence, the Minister for Defence Support, the four commanding officers and the Secretary of each of the two Departments constitute the Council of Defence.

Early in 1984 the total strength of the Permanent Defence Force was over 72 000, including 5000 women. The strength of the Navy was about 17 000, the Army 33 000 and the Air Force 22 000. Reserve Forces with part-time training obligations totalled about 36 000, most of whom were in the Army Reserve (ARES). About 15 000 civilians were employed in the Defence Force.

The RAN today is comparable with the navies of other middle powers. Ships of the RAN (early in 1984) include the guided-missile destroyers *Perth, Hobart* and *Brisbane*; the destroyer escorts *Yarra, Parramatta, Stuart, Derwent, Swan* and *Torrens*; the guided-missile frigates *Adelaide, Canberra* and *Sydney*; the Oberon Class submarines *Oxley, Otway, Onslow, Ovens, Orion* and *Otama*; the minesweeper *Ibis* and minehunter *Curlew*; the training ship *Jervis Bay*; and 15 patrol boats, the amphibious heavy lift-ship *Tobruk*, six heavy landing craft and nine support ships of various kinds. The Fleet Air Arm has in its training squadrons Iriquois and Wessex helicopters, as well as Macchi, Skyhawk and Tracker aircraft. Former flagship of the fleet, the aircraft carrier *Melbourne* (20 000 tonnes) which was equipped with Skyhawk and Tracker fixed-wing aircraft and Sea-King helicopters, was decommissioned in 1982. HMAS *Melbourne* was the Fleet Air Arm's only carrier; HMAS *Sydney*, after being used as a training vessel and troop carrier, was decommissioned in 1973. The HAWKE government does not intend to replace *Melbourne* with another carrier. However, it intends the Fleet Air Arm to have an expanded, and very important, helicopter role. The RAN Staff College, located at HMAS *Penguin* in Balmoral NSW, prepares officers of Lieutenant and Lieutenant Commander rank for command and staff appointments. The Royal Australian Naval College at JERVIS BAY, HMAS *Creswell*, is the training centre for officers; HMAS *Nirimba* at Quaker's Hill, NSW is a naval school for apprentices; HMAS *Leeuwin* at FREMANTLE in WA is the junior recruit training establishment; and HMAS *Cerberus* at WESTERN PORT BAY in VIC is the main training establishment for adult-entry sailors. After initial training, further branch and category training is given in other schools. Some specialist training courses are conducted in the UK and USA.

Defence Public Relations, Aus.

RAN destroyer escort HMAS *Torrens*

The present structure of the Army is the result of several reorganisations which have taken place since the 1950s, particularly the reorganisation in 1973 which involved the

rationalisation of senior command and control systems, replacing the old geographic commands, based on State and Territorial boundaries, by three functional commands—Field Force Command, Training Command and Logistic Command—with military districts in each State and Territory. All combat units come under Field Force Command, based in Sydney. Training Command, controlling all Army training centres with the exception of the Royal Military College, Duntroon (under the command of the Chief of the General Staff), also has its headquarters in Sydney. Logistic Command, based in Melbourne, is responsible for transport, supply, catering and repair. In 1974 a review of the CMF, now known as the Army Reserve (ARES), arranged for it to operate under the same functional command structure as the ARA and for its members to train and operate alongside professional soldiers of the ARA. The Army has a number of training establishments, of which the following are the most important. The Australian Staff College at QUEENSCLIFF in VIC trains selected officers for appointment in all branches of the staff and prepares them to assume, after experience, command and higher staff appointments. The Royal Military College at Duntroon ACT offers four-year and five-year courses of military and academic studies to provide officers for the Army. The Officer Cadet School at Portsea VIC provides a 44-week course for serving members of the ARA, the ARES and civilians, leading to appointment as second lieutenants in the ARA. The Women's Royal Australian Army Corps School at Mosman NSW provides basic training, the training of officer cadets, and the training of junior non-commissioned officers. The Land Warfare Centre at Canungra QLD provides training in tactics and administration, prepares senior non-commissioned officers for commissions and gives sub-unit and individual training in battle skills. The Army Apprentices School at Balcombe VIC trains youths as skilled tradesmen for the Regular Army.

The RAAF is controlled and administered by the Chief of Air Staff through two Commands: Operational Command, responsible for the command of operational units and the conduct of their operations in Australia; and Support Command, responsible for training and the supply and maintenance of equipment. In actual air operations there are five elements—the Strike/Reconnaissance Force, Tactical Fighter Force, Air Transport Force, Tactical Air Support Force and the Maritime Force. The Strike/Reconnaissance Force is equipped with two squadrons of F111 aircraft, based at Amberley QLD. The RAAF's fighter plane is the Mirage, which can fly at more than twice the speed of sound at an altitude of 9km. One Mirage squadron is based at Butterworth in Malaysia, one at DARWIN, and a third at Williamtown, NSW. Transport aircraft include Hercules, Caribou, HS-748, Mystere 20, Boeing 707 and BAC-111. For Army support there are two squadrons of Iriquois and one of Chinook helicopters. Maritime squadrons are one of Orion P3B aircraft and one of Orion P3C.

Training aircraft include the Macchi, the Hawker Siddeley 748 and the CT4 Air-trainer. Late in 1981 it was decided to order the McDonnell Douglas F18 fighter as a replacement for the Mirage.

RAAF F-111 strike aircraft

The RAAF Staff College at Fairbairn ACT provides staff training and higher service education to selected senior officers. The RAAF Academy, an affiliated college of the University of Melbourne, provides a three-year course leading to a Bachelor of Science degree, after which graduates undertake a basic aircrew training course, and a first-year course for cadets in the Engineer Branch, who then attend the University of Sydney and graduate with a Bachelor of Aeronautical Engineering degree. The Engineering Cadet scheme provides education for degree or diploma status in various branches of engineering. Cadets selected for Equipment Branch duties undertake a course leading to a Bachelor of Business Studies degree from the Darling Downs Institute of Advanced Education at TOOWOOMBA in QLD. Training for officers is also provided by the Officers' Initial Training Course at the Officers' Training School, Point Cook VIC. Major ground training schools are the School of Radio at Laverton VIC and the School of Technical Training at WAGGA WAGGA in NSW. Basic flying training is provided at Point Cook VIC and Pearce WA, and basic training in navigation at East Sale VIC.

In 1980 it was decided that the tertiary education officer cadets from all of the three armed services should be concentrated in one institution. To be known as the Australian Defence Force Academy, this will be built beside the existing Royal Military College at Duntroon. However, plans to give it the status of a separate university were dropped, and it is expected that it will be a college of the University of New South Wales. The existing college at Jervis Bay and the RAAF college at Point Cook are to be used for non-university training of their own officer cadets, but the Army's present non-university establishment at Portsea will be transferred to Duntroon.

Other bodies for which the Department of Defence is responsible include the Natural Disasters Organisation (NDO), which took over the functions of the former Directorate of Civil Defence, and the Defence Science and Technology Organisation (DSTO), which engages in research, development and evaluation activities in most physical sciences and in some fields of engineering which are relevant to defence.

Further reading: Millar, T.B. *Australia's Defence.* (2nd edn) Melbourne University Press, Melbourne, 1969 and *Australia in Peace and War: External Relations 1788-1977.* Australian National University Press, Canberra, 1978; Firkins, P.C. *The Australians in Nine Wars.* Pan, London, 1973 and *Of Nautilus and Eagles: History of the Royal Australian Navy.* Cassell, Stanmore NSW, 1975; Department of Defence *Defence Report.* (annually), *Army, the First 200 Years.* 1976, *Air Force Today.* 1977, *Australian Naval History.* 1977 and *Navy Today.* 1978, Australian Govt Publishing Service, Canberra.

Deloraine TAS (population 1 923 in 1981) Located in the central N part of the State, it is the focus of a rich agricultural area, set amidst undulating countryside at an elevation of 274m above sea level; it lies at the foot of the GREAT WESTERN TIERS, and is divided into two by the Meander River, a tributary of the South ESK. Situated at the junction of the Bass and Lake Highways, it is 210km by road

NNW of Hobart via the Lake Highway, 51km SE of DEVONPORT along the Bass Highway, and 40km N of the N section of GREAT LAKE. It experiences mild summer conditions and crisply cool winters, and receives an average annual rainfall of 1 162mm, concentrated mainly in the cooler months. The farmlands are devoted to dairying, pig raising, fat lamb production, beef cattle grazing and fodder cropping. The town has a large butter factory. Deloraine was named by the surveyor Thomas Scott from the poem 'The Lay of the Last Minstrel' by Sir Walter Scott. Settlement dates from the 1830s and the town has much historic charm, with over 30 buildings designated for preservation by the National Trust (TAS).

Democratic Labor Party The Democratic Labor Party (DLP) was formed on an Australia-wide basis in August 1957 with R. Joshua as Federal President and J.T. Kane as Federal Secretary. This organisation linked together the various splinter groups which had split from the AUSTRALIAN LABOR PARTY (ALP) during 1955; the QLD splinter group did not link up with the others until 1962.

The underlying reasons for the split in the ALP were associated with leadership, organisation and policy. Conflict over these issues had existed for some years prior to the actual breakaway, but were brought to a head by opposition to Communism. In 1946 the ALP had set out to combat the influence of the Communist Party in trade unions by the establishment of 'Industrial Groups'. Roman Catholics were active in the Industrial Groups, many of them also being members of a Church organisation, the Catholic Social Movement, generally referred to as 'the Movement', the leader and strategist of which was Bartholomew SANTAMARIA. While the combination of the anti-Communist forces was most effective in winning trade unions away from Communist control, a majority of ALP members felt that the party was being too greatly influenced and controlled by 'the Movement'. So in 1955 the ALP abolished the Industrial Groups and came into conflict with

Rocket testing – anti-aircraft missiles

A cartoon of 1958. Liberal leader, Menzies, looks on while Democratic Labor Party and Australian Labor Party are locked in battle

their supporters, many of whom eventually left the party in all States.

The existence of the DLP led to a fairly emotional controversy on whether or not it was a Church party, while its electoral role was very complex indeed. It certainly gained a large proportion of its votes from Roman Catholics, and by allocating its preferences to the Liberal Party it helped to keep the ALP out of office in the federal government until 1972. Thus it was referred to as a 'veto party', which meant that although it could not achieve its objectives directly it could exert pressure on other parties through its control of preferences. The DLP was not successful in having any member elected to the House of Representatives, but it did manage to have five Senators elected at the height of its power. When the ALP was returned to office in 1972 the DLP was reduced to a very weak position and after 1975 had no representation in the Senate. In 1978 it was proposed to wind up the party. However, it remained active in VIC where DLP candidates were endorsed for the 1980 and 1983 federal general elections, but none was elected.

Further reading: Duffy, P. 'The Democratic Labor Party' in Mayer, H. (ed) *Australian Politics.* F.W. Cheshire, Melbourne, 1966; Strangman, D. 'The DLP: the unchartered area' in Lucy, R. (ed) *The Pieces of Politics.* Macmillan, South Melbourne, 1975; Theophanous, A.C. *Australian Democracy in Crisis.* Oxford University Press, Melbourne, 1980.

Denham WA (population 402 in 1981) Situated on the W side of Peron Peninsula, which divides SHARK BAY into two sections, this small township was formerly a pearling port. Today its significance hinges on the freezing, processing and exporting of the lobsters and fish which abound in the adjacent waters and which make it a haven for fishing enthusiasts. The mixture of Malays, Chinese and Europeans in the town's original population is reflected among its present-day residents.

Deniliquin NSW (population 7 354 in 1981) A town in the RIVERINA, it is located at the junction of the Cobb and Riverina Highways, 778km SW of Sydney. Though in NSW, it is on the VIC railway system, 306km by train N of Melbourne, the terminus of a line crossing the MURRAY RIVER at ECHUCA. The town is situated on the EDWARDS RIVER, a major ANABRANCH of the Murray at an elevation of 91m above sea level, in semi-arid country which receives an average annual rainfall of only 410mm. The district is important for sheep grazing, and has some quite famous Merino studs. It is also the main business and service centre for large irrigated areas (Berriquin, Deniboota, Denimein and WAKOOL) which produce rice, fat lambs, cattle, wool, wheat, tobacco, vegetables and dairy produce. Secondary industries in the town include rice mills, brick works, timber mills, a seed processing factory and steel fabrication works.

The name Deniliquin comes from the Aboriginal leader of the local tribe. The National Trust (NSW) has classified several buildings in the town because of their historical and architectural significance, including the town hall, the courthouse, the council offices, some shops and the former Globe Hotel. Among the interesting features of the town and district are the CSIRO regional laboratory (concerned with the use of arid land), Boonoke station (a well-known Merino stud, 24km NE of the town), Denilakoon Exhibition (which includes an extensive collection of Aboriginal artifacts), the rice-growers' co-operative mill, Lawson syphon (carrying water from the Murray, beneath the Edwards and into irrigation channels), and the Peppin Merino Stud Memorial (the bronze statue of a ram, located 40km N of Deniliquin, commemorating the Peppin family who bred this important strain of Merino sheep).

Further reading: Shaw, J.H. *The Effects of Irrigation Development in the Social Growth of Deniliquin.* Deniliquin and District Education Committee, Deniliquin, 1951; *Deniliquin: Basic Information.* Deniliquin Chamber of Commerce, Deniliquin, 1970.

Dennis, Clarence Michael James (1876-1938) Poet and journalist. Born in Auburn SA, he worked in Adelaide in a solicitor's office and as a journalist, but in 1906 moved to Toolangi VIC, where he lived for the remainder of his life. Although he was on the staff of the Melbourne *Herald* for a time, he lived mainly by free-lance writing and the proceeds from his many volumes of light verse. His first volume, *Backblock Ballads and Other Verses* (1913), attracted little notice, but *The Songs of a Sentimental Bloke* (1915), which contained romantic verse-stories concerning a larrikin, Bill, and his girlfriend, Doreen, related humorously in broad vernacular, was immensely popular, as were *The Australaise: A Marching Song* (1915) and *The Moods of Ginger Mick* (1916). Of his many other volumes of

C.J. Dennis about 1920

Mitchell Library

light verse the best-known is *The Glugs of Gosh* (1917). Although his sentimentality may be considered excessive, the humour, wit and air of warm humanity that pervade his verse entitle him to a place in the history of Australian literature.

Further reading: Chisholm, A.H. *The Making of a Sentimental Bloke.* (2nd edn) Melbourne University Press, Melbourne, 1963 and *C.J. Dennis, His Remarkable Career.* Angus & Robertson, Sydney, 1976.

D'Entrecasteaux Channel TAS Named by the French Admiral, Bruni d'Entrecasteaux, who surveyed it in 1792, this channel is located in the SE of the State, between the main coast and BRUNY ISLAND, and is the centre of the famed scallop industry of TAS. The HUON RIVER enters the channel.

Depression of the 1930s *see* economic history

Derby WA (population 2 933 in 1981) Located on King Sound near the mouth of the FITZROY RIVER in the NW of the State, some 2 530km NNE of Perth via the Great Northern Highway and 234km by road NE of BROOME, Derby is the administrative centre for the W KIMBERLEYS. It is the principal port and commercial centre for the cattle grazing lands of the region and has a modern plant for processing frozen meat. Like most ports on the NW coast, it experiences a big tidal range (as much as 11m between high and low tides) and hence a long jetty juts out from the shore to berth freighters. The town has a tropical climate, with very hot summer conditions, and an average annual rainfall of 621mm; summer is the rainy season (January average, 175mm; February, 151mm) with a marked dry period from July to November. The town is a centre for the FLYING DOCTOR SERVICE whose radio network is also used by the School of the Air for teaching children in remote areas.

Dermaptera *see* earwigs

Derwent River TAS The major river in the SE part of the State, it rises in the CENTRAL PLATEAU and flows from LAKE ST CLAIR and LAKE KING WILLIAM in a general SE direction to STORM BAY over a course of about 190km. The upper reaches of the Derwent have been extensively developed for generation of hydro-electric power. The main tributaries from the N are the Nive, the Dee, the OUSE, the Clyde and the Jordan; those from the SW are the Florentine, the Plenty and the Styx. The CRADLE MOUNTAIN—Lake St Clair National Park, covering a vast area of 126 205ha, includes the headwaters of the Derwent; it also contains many lakes of glacial origin (Lake St Clair is the largest) and numerous peaks rising to over 1 400m high. The MOUNT FIELD National Park, covering 16 257ha, located in the SW of the Derwent catchment basin, contains much rugged country, glaciated during the Great Ice Age, with sheer-sided valleys, waterfalls, lakes and moraine deposits; the Lake Dobson area within the park, 98km from Hobart by road, is a popular skiing resort in winter.

In the lower reaches of the Derwent, the valley broadens and the alluvial deposits provide rich farming lands centred on NEW NORFOLK. This is Australia's greatest hop growing region, apple and pear orcharding also being important. Further downstream are important industrial enterprises such as the BOYER newsprint mills and the electrolytic zinc refinery at RISDON COVE. Hobart lies on the deep-water estuary of the lower Derwent, 20km from its mouth.

The Lyell Highway follows the main Derwent Valley from New Norfolk to Ouse, then traverses the valleys of the Dee and Nive Rivers, and crosses the Derwent at the town of Derwent Bridge between Lakes King William and St Clair. The Tarraleah Highway runs from Ouse along the main valley into the upland forested areas where the dams and power stations of the hydro-electricity schemes can be visited (for example, Catagunya, Wayatinah and Tungatinah dams and power stations; Liapootah, Tarraleah and Butler Gorge generating stations).

The first explorer to enter the Derwent was Bruni d'Entrecasteaux who sailed upstream for 32km in 1792. In 1803 the first British settlement was made at Risdon Cove on the E bank of the river by Lietuenant BOWEN's party of 49 people, which included 24 convicts. A year later Governor COLLINS moved the settlement to the present site of Hobart on the W bank of the river.

Desbrowe-Annear, Harold (1866-1933) Architect. A native of BENDIGO in VIC, Desbrowe-Annear was the first Functionalist architect in Australia. He strove for an architecture appropriate to what he called 'a new country, far from the medieval examples of the northern world'. He believed that this would come from an understanding of the 'climate that is only definable as Australian'. His projects were very varied. One of the largest was Church Street Bridge, built in 1924 over the YARRA RIVER at Richmond. Stage sets, a shire hall, a museum, telegraph stations and a beach kiosk indicate the range of his work, but his houses are his most significant contribution to Australian architecture.

His early domestic work of the 1890s was eclectic and romantic, but in the planning of his own house at the Eyrie, Eaglemont, in 1902, he was highly innovative. It is simple but commodious, without passages or corridors but with vast doors sliding into cavities, a fully glazed living-room wall which opens onto a shaded balcony overlooking a fine view, and much built-in furniture. It was the first 'open-planned' house in Australia. He later designed two matching adjacent houses, and the three survive intact.

'Real architects have always been and must be inventors—in mechanics, in form, in tone and in colour', he once told students. He in-vented a counter-balanced, vertically sliding window that disappeared into the wall, trailing a fly-screen into place after it; he devised chimneys which incorporated built-in warm-air ducts for room ventilation; and he developed an early type of flush-panelled door.

To Desbrowe-Annear, architecture grew logically from an understanding of its function. He wrote: 'The importation of ideas from other countries cannot help us; they must be our own, born of our own necessities, our own climates, and our own methods of pursuing health and happiness.'
Further reading: Boyd, R. *Australia's Home.* Melbourne University Press, Melbourne, 1952.

Devils Marbles NT On both sides of the Stuart Highway, 96km S of TENNANT CREEK and 9km N of the small settlement of Wauchope, lies the Devils Marbles conservation reserve, covering 1 828ha and containing a collection of gigantic rounded granite boulders some of which are balanced precariously on top of each other. The 'Marbles' have been fashioned from the basic granite rock which splits into blocks along joint planes; under the arid environmental conditions of the area, where temperature extremes between day and night can be quite marked, the natural weathering processes have gradually rounded the blocks to produce spherical boulders, up to 3m in diameter, which are scattered in heaps across a wide shallow valley.

devil's twine *see* parasitic plants

Devlin, Bruce William (1937-) Golfer. Born in ARMIDALE in NSW, Devlin first came to the notice of the Australian golfing world in 1958 when he won the New South Wales Amateur championship and rose rapidly from there to rank second among Australian golfers in the early 1970s. An outstanding amateur, he won the Australian Amateur Championship in 1959, and in the following year, while still a amateur, he won the Australian Open championship—a tournament open to both professionals and amateurs. He turned professional in 1961 and between 1962 and 1970 won a number of tournaments in Australia and overseas, including the Carling World Golf championship in 1966, the Australian PGA title in 1969 and 1970, and, also in 1970, the Bob Hope Classic and the Cleveland Open in America, and the Alcan Tournament in Ireland. In the same year, 1970, Devlin teamed up with David GRAHAM to win the World Cup (formerly the Canada Cup) for Australia. Devlin was well liked, both by the spectators and by fellow players, for his easy-going temperament which remained even no matter how he was playing.

Devonport TAS (population 21 424 in 1981) The third-largest city in TAS (after Hobart and LAUNCESTON), it is located on the MERSEY RIVER, 49km E of BURNIE and 101km NW of Launceston along the Bass Highway. The city spreads on both sides of the Mersey and was once two separate towns (Formby on the W bank and Torquay on the E) which were merged in 1890 to form Devonport. Although it originally developed as a commercial and service centre for a rich agricultural and orcharding district, and still functions in this role, its growth in recent years has been because of industrial expansion and of the increasing development of its port activities, for it is the TAS terminal for passenger and cargo vessels linking the island State with the mainland. Among its secondary industries are textile mills, food processing factories, carpet manufacturing, can making, meat processing and metal fabrication works. It experiences the mild climate typical of the N coast, with an average annual rainfall of 924mm, concentrated mainly in the winter months. Scenically, the region has many attractions for tourists and visitors: the rural areas of the lower Mersey are one of TAS's main apple growing districts; potato cultivation is also important, together with dairying, beef cattle raising and fodder crop growing; along the coast and in the inland streams there is good fishing; Mersey Bluff, a promontory at the river mouth which shelters the port estuary, is a popular picnic area and caravan park.

Diamantina River QLD/SA Rising in the arid SW of QLD, its headwaters lie in the Selwyn Range SE of CLONCURRY and NW of WINTON. It is an intermittent stream, with a course over 800km long, flowing in a general NE-SW direction beyond Birdsville and across the QLD/SA border to LAKE EYRE. Since it is located in a region of low and variable rainfall, it reaches the lake only in exceptionally wet years. It is one of the streams of the CHANNEL COUNTRY, which in good seasons is fine for cattle fattening. In its lower reaches, near Lake Eyre, the river is called the Warburton.

diatoms *see* algae

dibbler *see* native cats, etc.

Dickerson, Robert (1924-) Artist. Born in Hurstville NSW, Dickerson had no formal art training. He was a factory worker and, as 'Bobby Moody', a professional boxer, before joining the RAAF in World War II. He began painting systematically in 1950 and became well known for his images of various emotions—the negative ones of fear, isolation, emptiness and non-communication. His people are not recognisable personalities, but symbols, which on the canvas are linked by empty spaces and hostile colours.

didjeridu The best-known musical instrument of the Australian Aborigines, the didjeridu was traditionally used only in N Australia, especially in the ARNHEM LAND area. It is classified as an aerophone; the wood, usually just over 1m long, has often been hollowed out first by termites. The didjeridu

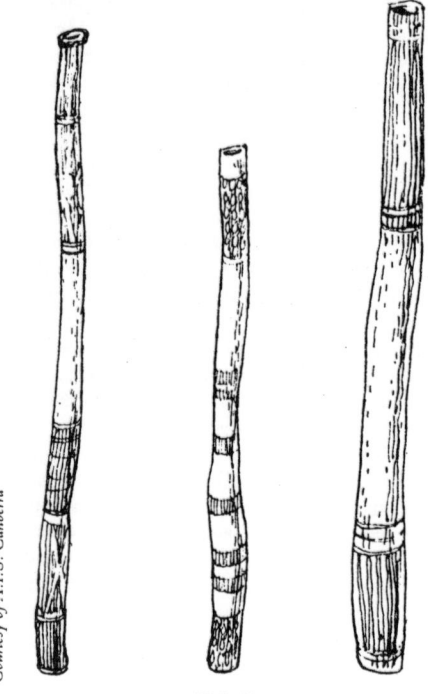

Courtesy of A.I.S. Canberra

Didjeridu

is not primarily a melodic instrument, having as it does only a fundamental note and an overtone, usually a tenth higher. Rather, it serves as a percussive and rhythmic instrument, and was always used in combination with singing and dancing.

digger This popular term was first used to refer to those digging for alluvial gold in the 1850s. During World War I it became the most common nickname for the Australian soldier, and has retained this meaning.

dill see Umbelliferae

dillybag This is an Aboriginal bag made of grasses, fur, hair or fibres twisted into cords. The original Aboriginal name was *dhilla*; the second part of the name was added by the European settlers.

dingo The dingo or warrigal, *Canis familiaris dingo*, was the only member of the mammalian order Carnivora in Australia before European colonisation, though it has been suggested that there may have been some feral cats, introduced, presumably, by Asian visitors to the N. In one sense the dingo is not a native mammal for it was introduced about 10 000 years ago by one of the later groups of Aborigines. The TAS Aborigines did not possess dingoes.

The dingo is close to the line which led from the first domesticated dogs, almost certainly derived from wolves, to the modern dogs but there is controversy about the identity of its closest relatives. The colour of pure-bred dingoes varies but a typical specimen is tawny yellow above with paler underparts and usually with white on the tail-tip and paws. The ears are erect and the general shape is wolf-like; a typical dingo is about 1.85m long, 35cm of that being contributed by the tail. Dingoes in the wild carry their tail at a droop but pet dingoes often hold them erect, exposing the anus, in the manner of domestic dogs but unlike wolves. The dingo differs from a domestic dog in various small ways: the feet, for example, are relatively large, the teeth are bigger and the last carnassial (shearing) tooth is relatively larger than the others; and dingoes never bark, they howl, though doubt has been thrown on this blanket statement recently.

Dingoes interbreed with domestic dogs. Some authors have argued that this rarely, if ever, occurs in the wild but recent research by the CSIRO shows that it is a common occurrence and that there are very few, if any, purebred dingoes left in the Eastern Highlands. Pure-bred dingoes mate between April and June (a little earlier in the N). The gestation period is about 63 days (the same as that of the domestic dog), and the average litter is five. At other times of the year both sexes are virtually infertile but as a result of interbreeding with domestic dogs some 'dingo' populations now breed at various times of the year. Consequently, some of the resulting packs (of which about 75 per cent are hybrid and include some feral domestic dogs, at least in the Eastern Highlands) are larger and more permanent than the normal dingo group, and, consequently, more troublesome. Pure-bred dingoes are, in fact, usually solitary but they sometimes hunt in groups of two or three. Grouping often takes place at breeding time when non-mating adults help to raise the pups, or in times of stress when small game is scarce and the animals must take larger prey. In the CSIRO studies in the Centre and in GIPPSLAND, it was found that rabbits were the main food, supplemented by small native mammals and some carrion (such as drought-killed cattle). Dingoes will also kill sheep, and long stretches of fences have been erected to keep them out of pastoral country.

Aborigines brought dingo pups into camp to rear but the adult camp dogs were left to fend for themselves and usually left the camp when old enough. Some recent studies suggest that the Aborigines did not use the dogs for hunting. An anthropologist living with the Jankuntjara of the Everard Ranges found that the group had 84 dogs in the camp, mainly of European origin. The net gain in meat from the activities of the dogs for a whole year was only 64kg, most of the kills being made when the dogs went with the women.

Courtesy of A.I.S. Canberra

Dingo

In the CSIRO studies it was found that dingoes do not travel long distances. Of 100 radio-marked and released dingoes 75 were found within 6.5km, and the greatest distance travelled from the release point, within 15 months, was 34km.

Dingoes are often destroyed by shooting, trapping and poisoning because of the threat they pose to livestock. When the destruction has been thorough it has sometimes been followed by increases in the number of other animals, such as rabbits; in NEW ENGLAND there have been troublesome increases in the number of wallabies after dingo baiting, and in western QLD feral pigs have become greater pests.

Dingoes still occur throughout most of Australia, apart from the densely populated districts, but the proportion of pure-bred animals is falling constantly. There is now a movement for popularising dingoes (or, as breeders prefer to call them, Australian native dogs) as pets.
Further reading: Newsome, A.E., Best, L.W. & Green, B. 'The dingo' in *Australian Meat Research Committee Reviews*. (no 14, October 1973).

dinoflagellates see algae

dinosaurs see fossils

diplurans These INSECT-like ARTHROPODS belong to the class Diplura, which was formerly included in the insects. There are about 32 species known in Australia. They are eyeless and six-legged, and usually live in damp soil under stones, logs and so on. The largest are the EARWIG-like species of the genus *Heterojapyx* (50mm long) which use their forceps (cerci) on the end of the abdomen to catch prey; in some species cerci are segmented. Most, however, are small (5mm or less), pale, soft-skinned creatures and live on vegetable matter. Sometimes some species are found in ant or termite nests but these are probably casual visitors rather than true guests of the social insects.

diprotodon see fossils

Diptera see flies

Dirk Hartog Island WA This island, named after the Dutch explorer, forms part of the island-arc boundary of SHARK BAY on the mid-N coast of the State. It is an elongated island, aligned NW-SE, about 50km long and less than 10km wide at its broadest section, with limestone cliffs on its seaward coast and sand dunes on the bay shoreline. The N tip is called Cape Inscription and it was here in 1616 that Dirk HARTOG left the famed pewter plate as a record of his landing. West Point on Dirk Hartog Is is the most westerly point of Australia.

discovery Naturally, any estimate as to how long ago Australia was first discovered

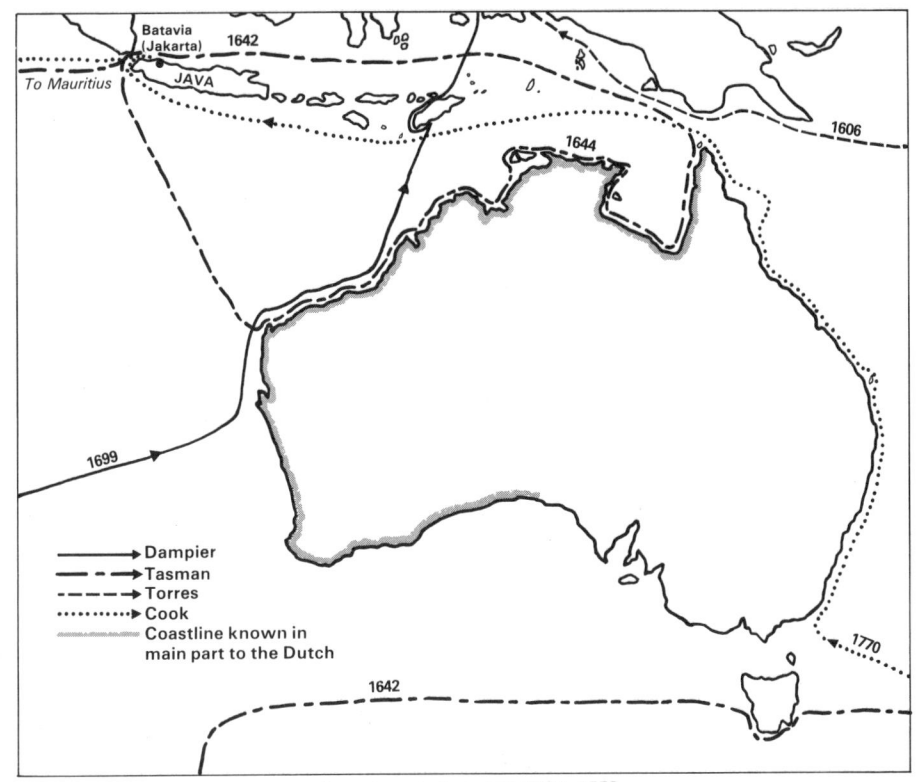

Some important voyages 1606–1770

of trade. The Portuguese, sailing around the Cape of Good Hope, followed routes which took them far to the NW of Australia. Magellan, coming by way of South America, passed far to the NE.

Dutch discoveries Only with the coming of the Dutch to the East Indies did the situation change, for from their bases there they sent a number of expeditions S in search of new trading prospects. Thus in 1605 Captain JANSZ was sent in the *Duyfken* to explore the New Guinea coast and, as mentioned above, early in 1606 came to part of Australia. Later in the same year, by a remarkable coincidence, the Spaniard TORRES, having come all the way from Peru, sailed through the strait that now bears his name. It is unlikely that he saw the coast of Australia, and although the Dutch soon learned about his voyage, they were not sure how far S of New Guinea he had sailed, and their maps for many years showed New Guinea as being joined to Cape York.

The chance of further Dutch discoveries was greatly increased in 1613 when captains of the East India Co. were instructed to sail about 6000km W from the Cape of Good Hope before turning N to Java. A number of ships following this route came within sight of the coast of Australia, either because their captains mistimed the turn N, or because storms drove them too far to the E. The first was the *Eendracht*, which came to SHARK BAY in 1616. Its captain, Dirk HARTOG, landed on the island named after him and left as a memorial of his visit a pewter plate with an inscription scratched on it, nailed to a tree. In 1618 the *Zeewolf* and the *Mauritius* sighted the W coast, and the latter, which had on board Willem Jansz, landed a party in the Exmouth Gulf area. In 1619 the *Dordrecht* and the *Amsterdam*, both under the command of Frederick de Houtman, came to the coast near the present site of BUNBURY; their commander gave the name

and settled by human beings must be very tentative, but it is significant that in recent decades archaeologists have tended to estimate a much earlier period than was previously believed. Even in the 1950s estimates of 20 000 years or less were common, but today it is generally believed that Australia has been inhabited for more than 40 000 years. It is generally presumed that the first discoverers and settlers came by way of South-East Asia at a time when there were land bridges between TAS, the Australian mainland and New Guinea, and when the sea passages between New Guinea, the Indonesian islands and the Asian mainland were much narrower than they are today. Nevertheless, the first arrivals must have possessed, as D.J. Mulvaney puts it, 'seaworthy water craft and the capacity to cross empty sea horizons'. They may have been the first people anywhere to make sea voyages of such distances.

The possible arrival of other pre-European discoverers is even more deeply shrouded in uncertainty. Praus from Macassar and other parts of Indonesia were visiting N Australia in considerable numbers in search of TREPANG by the early 19th century, but when the first of such contacts may have occurred is uncertain. Pre-European visits by Arab traders and by Chinese have also been suggested, but are unproven.

Lateness of European discovery Even on the question of European discovery, there is a slight degree of uncertainty. Sixteenth-century maps such as that of Mercator in 1569 show a great S continent, the coastline S of Java and New Guinea showing a superficial resemblance to that of N Australia. It has been

suggested that this indicates the likelihood of Portuguese visits. However, there is no firm evidence of Europeans sighting the Australian coast until the Dutch ship *Duyfken* sailed down the W coast of CAPE YORK in 1606.

In any case, Australia was the last of the inhabited continents to be discovered by Europeans. The reasons for this are clear if one considers the aim of European explorers in the late 15th and early 16th centuries—to reach South and South-East Asia for purposes

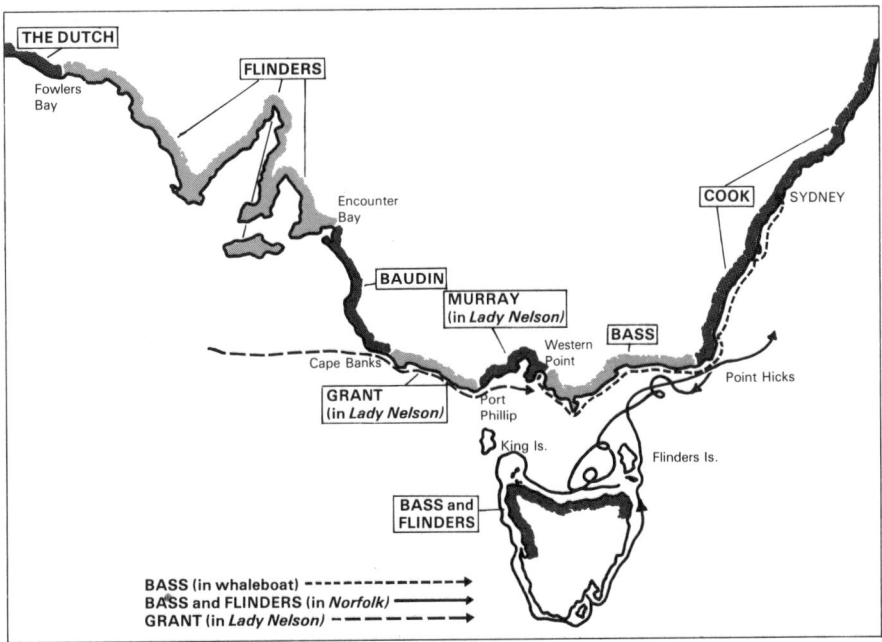

Exploration of Bass Strait and the south-east mainland coast

HOUTMAN ABROLHOS to a group of shoals and low islands further N. In 1622 the *Leeuwin* reached the cape named after it at the SW corner of the continent, and in 1627 the *Gulden Seepaart* was blown past CAPE LEEU-WIN and sailed along the S coast beyond the head of the GREAT AUSTRALIAN BIGHT. In 1629 Pelsaert's *Batavia* was wrecked on the Abrolhos islands, and the captain and a group of survivors, making towards Java in a long-boat, had a close view of a long stretch of coastline, as well as landing a number of times. In the meantime, in 1623, the *Pera* and *Arnhem* had been sent to the N coast, and their captains had charted parts of the GULF OF CARPENTARIA and ARNHEM LAND, but had failed to find Torres' sea passage into the Pacific.

The greatest Dutch explorer in Australian waters was undoubtedly Abel TASMAN, who was sent in 1642 by Anthony VAN DIEMEN, Governor of the Netherlands East Indies, to solve the mystery of the fabled Great South Land, which, Tasman's instructions stated, must surely contain excellent prospects for trade. Following these instructions, Tasman took his two ships, the *Heemskerk* and the *Zeehaen*, from Batavia to Mauritius, S beyond the 40° latitude and then E. This brought him to the W coast of TAS, which he named VAN DIEMEN'S LAND. After sailing around the S coast he sent a landing party ashore at Blackman's Bay, and continued E to become the discoverer of New Zealand. There he charted most of the W coast, but unfavourable winds prevented him from proving the existence of a strait between the two main islands, and a clash with a Maori war canoe, in which four Dutch sailors were killed, deterred him from landing. Two years later van Diemen sent him to the N coast of Australia, with instructions to seek a passage into the Pacific between Australia and New Guinea or S of Arnhem Land, which was thought to be an island. Unfavourable winds and the fear of shoals prevented him from penetrating TORRES STRAIT, but he sailed right along the N coast, charting most of the parts hitherto unknown to the Dutch, and showing that all their previous discoveries in W and N Australia were parts of one continent, to which he gave the name NEW HOLLAND.

By this time, then, the Dutch had knowledge of half of the Australian coastline, but as they had found not the slightest prospect of trade they had no incentive to explore further. Moreover, even if they had been looking for sites for settlement, the parts of Australia they had seen, being mostly barren, would not have tempted them very strongly. After Tasman's time, therefore, Dutch visits were few and far between. The most notable was that of Willem de Vlamingh, sent in 1696 to look for traces of a ship which had disappeared two years previously. He landed on an island which he named ROTTNEST ISLAND (spelt 'Rottenest' by him), explored the SWAN RIVER and noted with amazement its black swans, landed on DIRK HARTOG ISLAND, and found Hartog's

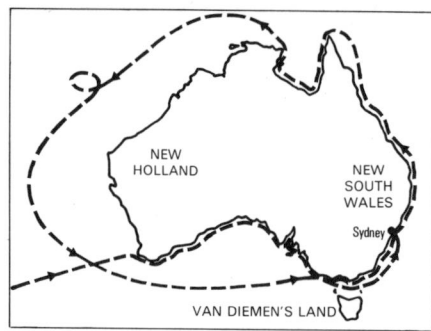

Matthew Flinders' circumnavigation of Australia in *Investigator* 1801–1803

pewter plate, which he took with him, replacing it with one of his own.

British discoveries The section of the coastline undiscovered by the Dutch, the hinterland of which contains most of Australia's fertile land, and where most of its population is now clustered, was discovered almost entirely by British explorers. DAMPIER visited the N coast in 1688 and again in 1699, but added nothing of importance to existing knowledge. In 1770 COOK in the *Endeavour*, after leading a scientific expedition to Tahiti and then charting the whole coastline of New Zealand, decided to return to England by way of the E coast of New Holland. His intention was to examine Van Diemen's Land first, but he was driven too far N by strong winds, and landed near the SE corner of the mainland. He proceeded to chart most of the E coast, which he named New South Wales, and where he made three landings—at BOTANY BAY, where he spent a week; at the Endeavour River, where his ship was repaired after running onto a section of the GREAT BARRIER REEF; and at Possession Is, where he claimed NSW in the name of King George III. This most important discovery led to the foundation of the British colony of NSW in 1788.

At this point it is worth noting that the discovery of the E coast, the key to settlement, had been delayed by a remarkable series of errors and mischances. Had not Torres, as he approached Australia, changed his course and passed through Torres Strait instead of sailing to the QLD coast, had not Jansz, Tasman and the captains of the *Pera* and *Arnhem* all failed to pass through Torres Strait from the W, or

had not Dampier changed his mind and sailed via the Cape of Good Hope instead of Cape Horn in 1699, then the whole of the E coast would not have been left for Cook to discover, and the history of the continent might have followed a very different course.

Exploration after the founding of Sydney After the foundation of Sydney two young naval officers, George BASS and Matthew FLINDERS, explored a large part of what was still unknown. In 1797-98 Bass made an epic voyage from Sydney to WESTERN PORT BAY in a whaleboat less than 9m long, thus becoming the first European to see the coast from Cook's landfall to Western Port Bay, and showing the likelihood of the existence of what was later called BASS STRAIT. In 1798-99 Bass and Flinders sailed the 25-tonne *Norfolk* through Bass Strait and around TAS. Bass took no further part in Australian exploration, but Flinders' ambition was to complete the work of surveying the whole coastline, and on returning to England he obtained the patronage of Sir Joseph BANKS for this project. He was given command of the *Investigator*, and left England in 1801. Reaching the Australian coast near Cape Leeuwin, he sailed along the S coast, being the first to survey the section from Fowler's Bay, which was the furthest point reached by the Dutch, to ENCOUNTER BAY, where he met the Frenchman, BAUDIN, sailing W. Baudin had become the first to survey the coast from Cape Banks, a little W of the present VIC/SA border, to the point where he met Flinders. Further E Lieutenant GRANT, in the *Lady Nelson*, had in 1800 surveyed from Cape Banks to Cape Otway, and in 1802 Lieutenant MURRAY had entered PORT PHILLIP BAY and surveyed the nearby coast between Western Port Bay and Cape Otway.

From Encounter Bay Flinders went to Sydney, and after a short stay there surveyed uncharted sections of the E coast, the Gulf of Carpentaria and Arnhem Land. However, he was hampered by the unseaworthy condition of the *Investigator*. After a call at Timor for repairs, he completed the circumnavigation of the continent and returned to Sydney without carrying out a survey of the NW and W coasts. Nevertheless, by the end of his voyage the basic work of exploring the Australian coastline could be regarded as complete. Only comparatively minor details were left for

HMS Endeavour being repaired at Endeavour River

hydrographic surveyors to fill in later.
See also exploration by land
Further reading: Heeres, J.E. *The Part Borne by the Dutch in the Discovery of Australia, 1606-1765.* E.J. Brill, Leiden, 1899; Scott, Sir Ernest *Australian Discovery.* (vol 1) Dent, London, 1929 (reprinted Johnson Reprint Corp., New York, 1966); Wood, G.A. *The Discovery of Australia.* (revd edn by Beaglehole, J.C.) Macmillan, South Melbourne, 1969.

Discovery Bay VIC/SA A broad curving bay on the W coast of VIC, extending along the SE coast of SA, it stretches for about 80km from Cape Bridgewater in VIC (20km W of PORTLAND) to Port Macdonnell in SA. Much of the coastline is dominated by sand dunes, with shallow lagoons behind them. In the mid-section of the bay is the GLENELG RIVER estuary with the town of Nelson on its E shore. The bay was discovered and named by the explorer Thomas MITCHELL in 1836.

diseases, livestock Because of its relative isolation and strict quarantine regulations, Australia is free from many of the bacterial and viral diseases that attack livestock in other countries. There have been three phases in the movement of livestock in Australia. At first there were virtually no restrictions as settlers built up the numbers and the quality of their livestock. This period culminated in the activities of the ACCLIMATISATION SOCIETIES which sought to naturalise as many exotic species as possible. In 1871 their activities were curtailed and animal quarantine was introduced. The quarantine regulations became more and more stringent, until by the end of World War II there were virtually no imports of stock except from New Zealand. The most recent period started with increased knowledge of exotic diseases and better means of detecting them, and with the establishment of offshore stations where animals could be safely quarantined. Breeders realised that the domestic animals needed an infusion of new genes for many of the Australian breeds of livestock are based on remarkably few founder animals. This relaxation of the ban on imports has been hampered by the fear of the introduction of the virus of bluetongue (*see below*).

The failure of many diseases to arrive during the first phase can be attributed to the long sea voyages from Europe and the Cape of Good Hope. Any animals suffering from acute diseases did not survive the journey though there was a danger of diseases arriving with cattle and horses being brought into N settlements from Indonesia. The activities of the acclimatisation societies possibly led to the establishment of some exotic parasites and pathogens (disease-producing agents).
Tick fever This is a protozoal disease transmitted by the cattle tick, *Boophilus microplus* (see PROTOZOONS; TICKS). It was estimated that the tick cost Australia $41 927 000 in 1972-73 both by its direct damage and as

vector of disease. The tick and the disease were probably introduced from Djakarta in 1872; the first outbreak was at Glencoe NT in 1880. Ticks were carried over much of the N but strict quarantine is preventing their spread within NSW from a small N area of the State.

The organisms that cause the fever are *Babesia argentina, B. bigemina* and *Anaplasma marginale.* The first is the commonest and most pathogenic. *Babesia* invades the red blood cells. Each individual grows and splits into two cells which rupture the blood cell and escape to invade others. When *Babesia* organisms are taken up by the adult female tick they invade the gut cells where they multiply. Some enter the egg; later they develop in the larva and eventually find their way to the maturing tick's salivary glands from which, after further multiplication, they enter the cow's blood stream. The fever is caused by the rapid multiplication of the parasite in the host animal. Red-stained urine is a common feature of the disease. Some animals recover, returning to normal after about a week, but the parasites persist in the animal with periodic fluctuations in the numbers. Outbreaks are most severe shortly after the tick and the parasites enter a new geographical area. After the initial outbreak the mortality rate falls.

Young cattle are far less susceptible than adults and having once been attacked they are immune to further infestations. Zebu and Zebu-cross European cattle breeds are far more resistant to tick attack than are pure European breeds. Furthermore, a milking Zebu-cross has been developed which should be valuable in the campaign against tick fever. Vaccines have also been widely used. One of the difficulties in tick control is the widespread resistance of the ticks to many of the commonly used pesticides.

Virus diseases Classical bluetongue and foot-and-mouth disease have not yet occurred in Australian livestock but various less serious virus diseases are present, such as scabby mouth, which affects sheep, and ephemeral fever, bovine malignant catarrh and para-influenza, which affect cattle. The peculiar disease scrapie was once introduced with Suffolk sheep but it has been eradicated. Pseudo-cowpox is extremely common and has been seen in almost every herd at one time or another; it sometimes causes nodules or lesions on the hands of milkers, and may be responsible for scabby mouth in sheep.

Ephemeral fever is a disease that can suddenly attack a herd of cattle (bringing fever and the occasional death) then disappear within a few days. It was first recorded in Australia in 1936 when an epizootic (animal epidemic) moved quickly through southern Australia after first appearing in the NT. Several epizootics have occurred since. Between epizootics the disease probably persists, in a milder form, in the NT. Research into the subject (epidemiology) suggests that the virus is spread by insects, possibly *Anopheles* MOSQUITOES.

Bovine malignant catarrh is almost always fatal but rare; it is sporadic and kills only one

or two animals in any herd. In Africa, cattle acquire the disease from wildebeeste; cow-to-cow transmission is rare. The disease appeared in Australia in the 1950s and had spread to all mainland States, except VIC and the NT, by the 1970s.

Swine influenza is apparently absent though it is suspected from time to time. The disease is complex because it is caused by a specific myxo virus 'Type A' which acts together with the bacterium *Haemophilus influenza suis.* The latter is common in Australia and causes, in the absence of the virus, Glasser's disease of swine. The 1918 human influenza epidemic was caused by the swine influenza virus. It is believed that during or after the epidemic the virus became localised in pigs in the USA.

Swine fever or hog cholera is a very infectious, often fatal, virus disease. Epizootics occurred in 1927, 1928, 1943 and 1961; the last was caused by a relatively mild strain. The disease is spread easily by contaminated pork products.

Bacterial diseases Livestock suffer from several diseases caused by species of *Clostridium;* many of these are soil organisms that may have been present before European colonisation. Horses are particularly susceptible to to tetanus, which is caused by *C. tetani.* The related black disease, which is often associated with LIVER FLUKE of sheep, is caused by *C. novyi.*

Anthrax is one of the most serious bacterial diseases of cattle and other livestock. It is caused by *Bacillus anthracis* which may persist in the spore stage as a latent infection. In acute cases the bacteria multiply in the blood stream producing a high fever, collapse and death. Human beings can be easily infected during a post mortem or, as occurred during the 1970s, when slaughtering animals at an abattoir. Dead animals that have been confirmed as anthrax victims must be thoroughly burned on the spot to prevent the spread of the extremely resistant spores, and the surrounding soil must be thoroughly treated with chloride of lime. The disease has been in Australia since about 1847, having probably arrived as spores in contaminated hay.

Species of *Salmonella* cause typhoid-like diseases of sheep (ovine salmonellosis, sheep paratyphoid) which can kill their victims within a day. Species of *Brucella* attack cattle, sheep, horses and pigs (brucellosis) and can be transmitted to human beings (*see* DISEASES AND EPIDEMICS, HUMAN). In livestock they cause sterility, abortion and other disorders. Since 1969 the Commonwealth has been carrying out a campaign against bovine brucellosis involving vaccination and the slaughter of positive reactors. The presence of brucellosis in an area can lead to difficulties in exporting beef.

Bovine tuberculosis is caused by the organism that is responsible for human tuberculosis, *Mycobacterium tuberculosis;* human beings can be infected from cattle, the commonest route of infection being through unpasteurised milk. The disease was once widespread in Australian cattle—in the 1940s about half the cows in the Brisbane area were tuberculous—but since then the disease has been almost eliminated by stringent testing and the slaughtering of infected beasts.

Threatening exotic diseases There are certain diseases of livestock which threaten the Australian livestock industry but which are not, at the moment, present in Australia. The establishment of any one of these would be catastrophic for Australia. It would call for the wholesale slaughter of many farm animals, and would prevent the export of produce to other countries that are free from the disease concerned. Some of these diseases could be introduced into Australia by people ignoring the quarantine regulations which, though efficient, are not unduly strict. The following briefly describes the most important of these diseases.

Vesicular diseases include in their symptoms a blistering of the mouth and sometimes other parts of the body. Examples of such diseases are foot-and-mouth disease (FMD), vesicular stomatitis (VS) and vesicular exanthema of swine (VES). The most important and threatening is FMD which is present in all continents apart from America N of Panama and Australia. New Zealand is free from the disease. There are outbreaks from time to time in Britain.

The animals susceptible to FMD include cattle, sheep, goats, pigs and deer. Despite its notoriety it is rarely a killing disease but it cuts production of meat, wool and milk drastically, and makes about one quarter of the pregnant animals abort. It is extremely contagious and the virus can persist for very long periods in meat and meat products. In 1978 the Commonwealth Department of Health estimated that if FMD entered Australia it would cost, in lost exports and direct losses, $600 million each year. An outbreak of a disease suspected of being FMD at a piggery in TAS in 1979 resulted in the immediate slaughter and burning of all the pigs and cattle, and the burning of the buildings which housed them. Export of animals or animal products from TAS was banned for several days until it was decided that the disease was not one of the vesicular diseases.

The virus is most likely to enter Australia in smuggled meats or meat products (European sausages being the most probable vehicle); in 1977-78 nearly seven tonnes of material of plant or animal origin were confiscated at Sydney airport alone by quarantine officials. Feral pigs in Australia would probably become an ineradicable reservoir of the disease if it became established.

Bluetongue disease of sheep (BT) was first described in South Africa in 1876 but it has since spread to many other countries. The main symptom of the classical form of the disease in sheep is a severe mouth ulceration with a discoloration of the tongue. Many, if not most, of the infected animals die within a few days. The virus is spread by tiny biting FLIES belonging to the genus *Culicoides* and research has shown that many of the representatives of the genus that are native to Australia

could spread the disease. The virus also infects cattle in which it produces no signs of the disease so that cattle in the N of Australia could act as a symptomless reservoir of the disease for months before it spread to sheep. Though no clinical cases of BT have been seen in Australian sheep, antibodies to the virus have been detected in sheep in various parts of the country. There are, however, at least 20 known forms of the virus which differ in the severity and symptoms of the disease that they cause. If the disease did appear in its clinical, virulent form all ungulates in an area of 250km^2 would be slaughtered, and livestock movements banned for a radius of about 160km.

Newcastle disease is a virus disease of poultry, and probably also of many other birds, including native Australian species. A mild form appears to occur in some Australian birds which may give immunity to the severe form which is common in Asia. The virus could be imported with eggs, smuggled aviary birds and even feathers.

The greatest threat at present is not a disease but a fly, the Old World screw worm fly, *Chrysomya bezziana*, which is common in Papua New Guinea (see BIOLOGICAL CONTROL). It is a parasite of warm-blooded animals, including man. In 1978 it was estimated that it would cost the livestock industries alone more than $100 million each year if the fly became established in Australia.

There are certain other diseases which are considered to be threatening. They include African swine fever, swine fever, trichinosis (a ROUNDWORM parasite of man, acquired from pig meats), sheep pox, African horse sickness and Aujeszky's disease (pseudorabies), all of which are carried in animal products, and equine viral encephalomyelitis and Rift Valley fever (both with insect vectors which could enter with aircraft).

Further reading: Hudson, J.R. 'The threat presented by exotic diseases to Australian livestock' in *Australian Veterinary Journal.* (vol 38, April, 1962); Erasmus, B.J. 'Bluetongue in sheep and goats' in *Australian Veterinary Journal.* (vol 51, April 1975); Hungerford, T.C. *Diseases of Livestock.* (8th edn) McGraw-Hill, Sydney, 1975; Pierce, A.E. 'An historical review of animal movements, exotic diseases and quarantine in New Zealand and Australia' in *New Zealand Veterinary Journal.* (vol 23, no 7, July 1975); Spradbow, P.B. 'Viral infections and viral diseases of cattle in Australia' in *Australian Meat Research Council Reviews.* (no 22, April 1975); 'Monitoring insect-borne viruses' in *Rural Research.* (no 96, September 1977); French, E.L. & Geering, W.A. (eds) *Exotic Diseases of Animals: A Manual for Diagnosis.* (2nd edn) Australian Govt Publishing Service, Canberra, 1978.

diseases, plant The main agents that cause plant diseases are nutrient deficiencies, and pathogenic organisms such as viruses, bacteria, FUNGI, and eelworms (nematodes; see ROUNDWORMS). Hundreds of pathogens (agents causing disease) have been introduced

into Australia since the first seed crops came to the colony and although many of these have become established, the continent has so far avoided some important ones, partly because of effective plant quarantine regulations. However, many new diseases, or established pathogens attacking new host plants, are recorded each year. One of the most spectacular examples was the destructive rust species of poplar trees, *Melampsora larici-populina*, which first appeared near Sydney in 1973.

Plant disease was largely responsible for the food shortages that the early colonies experienced. Lieutenant-Governor COLLINS was the first to record a disease of wheat in Australia when he reported in 1795 that a crop of bearded wheat grown at Petersham Hill (where Sydney University now stands) had not been worth the labour of sowing. In 1804 Governor KING reported to London that the wheat crop had suffered greatly from rusts and smuts. Ten major rust outbreaks occurred between 1799 and 1889; they led to Australia's pioneering work in the study of the disease and the breading of resistant varieties (see AGRICULTURE).

Stem rust of wheat, *Puccinia graminis tritici*, has been known in Australia since 1803, and may have been present even earlier. In the N hemisphere it is a two-host species, one part of the life cycle occurring on the shrub barberry, *Berberis vulgaris*, and the other on wheat; both host plants are infected by wind-borne spores. Barberry is very common in Australia, so it is believed that the life cycle of the rust fungus is truncated. Since it is unlikely that Australian crops could have been infected by spores blown from overseas or that viable spores would have been imported with seed grain, it is possible that the rust occurred on native grasses before the arrival of the Europeans.

Oat plants attacked by a rust disease, probably crown rust

Take-all is a disease of wheat caused by the fungus *Gaeumannomyces graminis* which encrusts the roots and bases of plants with black growths. Yields of infected crops may be reduced by up to three-quarters. It is most severe when wheat is grown in the same soil in successive years, and thus it is controlled by crop rotation. If susceptible crops are grown in succession for long enough, however, the importance of the disease declines, probably because antagonistic organisms build up in the soil.

Smut, bunt and ergot attack the flowers and grain of cereals. Loose smut of wheat, *Ustilago nuda*, replaces the flowers with a mass of brown spores. These spores germinate to produce mycelium which invades the seeds of other wheat plants; when these affected seeds are sown, they produce infected plants. Bunt diseases (*Tilletia* species), attack the grain and replace the interior with a mass of spores. Affected seeds look normal from the outside but when crushed they release the spores which can contaminate healthy seeds. Fungicidal seed dressings effectively control the disease. Ergots are the sclerotia (hard masses of fungal mycelium) of various species of *Claviceps* which replace the grain in infected heads of rye, wheat and other grasses. One species is a common parasite of *Paspalum* grass. Ergots can contaminate grain when it is milled, and ergot in rye bread often caused mass poisoning in medieval Europe, but with modern milling technology this is extremely rare. Ergots contain toxic alkaloids, some of which are closely related to LSD and can cause hallucinations. Human ergot poisoning is very rare in Australia but livestock is sometimes affected.

Fungal diseases of fruit are especially troublesome because of the difficulty in selling blemished fruit. Black spot or apple scab, *Venturia inaequalis*, is one of the most important diseases of apple; a closely related species attacks pears. The fungus overwinters in fallen leaves and twigs, and the spores infect fruit and leaves in the spring. Dark corky spots develop on the fruit and leaves, and severely infected fruit becomes distorted and splits. Growers are forced by market demands to use several fungicidal sprays during the growing season. Powdery mildew of apple and pear, *Podosphaera leucotricha*, is a dry-weather parasite which forms a mycelium on the foliage, overwinters in the dormant buds, and gradually weakens the tree. Another powdery mildew, *Uncinula necator*, attacks grape vines, as does the downy mildew, *Plasmopara viticola*. An epidemic of this species in France led to the discovery of Bordeaux Mixture, still one of the most effective sprays against leaf-infecting fungi.

In potatoes, virus diseases are of particular concern because the crop is grown vegetatively from tubers. Virus infections persist in the tubers from generation to generation, leading to a decline in the yield. Many plant viruses are spread by INSECTS, particularly APHIDS. Plant viruses are rarely lethal to their hosts,

A cabbage leaf attacked by downy mildew

A. Woods

but may reduce yields drastically. Many interfere with the development of chlorophyll in the leaves, resulting in the common symptoms of mottled or yellowed foliage. No chemicals can be used to cure a plant of a viral infection, but insecticides can often prevent their spread. Some viruses, such as fanleaf of grapevine, are transmitted by soil-dwelling nematodes but their spread is very slow. Several are passed on mechanically, for example by the grafting knife, and some are seed-transmitted.

Bacterial diseases of plants are less common but one, *Pseudomonas tonelliana*, is conspicuous in SE Australia; this disease galls the flower buds of oleander bushes so that few flowers are produced, and these are marred with brown patches. Bacterial canker of tomatoes, *Corynebacterium michiganense*, is a widespread disease in many countries, including Australia.

Most plant-parasitic nematodes attack the roots of plants but a few, such as the *Chrysanthemum* eelworm, *Aphelenchoides ritzemabosi*, live in the foliage. Some soil nematodes are more or less permanent inhabitants of the roots, penetrating deep within the tissues; but others, the ectoparasites, feed only on the surface by inserting their mouthparts to suck out fluids.

In warm parts of the world, including much of warm and temperate Australia, the rootknot nematodes (*Meloidogyne* species) are of great importance and attack a very wide range of plants. The female nematodes become permanently lodged in the root of the host and cause swelling of the surrounding tissues so that root nodules are formed. The males spend only their larval stages in the root. The nodules interfere with the flow of water and sap through the root, and so reduce the growth of the host. Root-cyst nematodes have a similar life cycle, the females forming swollen cysts containing eggs which protrude from the host root. These cysts remain viable for many years so that long rotations are needed between susceptible crops. The beet cyst nematode, *Heterodera schachtii*, and the cereal cyst nematode, *H. avenae*, are well established in Australia but as yet the potato root nematodes (*Globodera* species) have not been found. In many parts of the world they are regarded as the worst pests of potatoes as they are hard to detect before an infestation is well advanced.

None of the pathogens that have been introduced into Australia has severely damaged native vegetation, with one possible exception.

This is the fungus *Phytophthora cinnamomi*, which is widespread outside Australia and was not recorded in the natural vegetation before the middle of this century, but by its distribution may be native to at least parts of E Australia. The fungus attacks the roots of a very wide variety of plants; if the damage is severe the plant dies, apparently from drought as it cannot absorb enough water from the soil. The susceptible host species are mostly trees and shrubs, including many MYRTACEAE, PROTEACEAE, PAPILIONACEAE and EPACRIDACEAE which are important components of the forests of southern Australia. The most severe damage has been to the forests of jarrah, *Eucalyptus marginata*, in WA where 3 600ha or more of this valuable timber tree were being lost each year during the 1970s. The fungus was spread in soil clinging to vehicles and forestry machinery and in the water run-off resulting from the construction of roads and fire trails.

Many plant pathogens, unlike *Phytophthora cinnamomi*, are highly host-specific and could be considered as BIOLOGICAL CONTROL agents for WEEDS. The rust *Puccinia chondrillina*, for example, is used in the control of skeleton weed; it was released at nine sites in 1971 and is now established throughout the range of the weed.

Further reading: Large, E.C. *The Advance of the Fungi*. Jonathan Cape, London, 1940; Carefoot, G.L. & Sprott, E.R. *Famine on the Wind: Plant Diseases and Human History*. Angus & Robertson, Sydney, 1969; Walker, J.C. *Plant Pathology*. (3rd edn) Tate McGraw-Hill, Bombay, 1969; Fish, S. 'The history of plant pathology in Australia' in *Annual Review of Phytopathology*. (vol 71, 1971); Newhook, F.J. & Podger, F.D. 'The role of *Phytophthora cinnamomi* in Australian and New Zealand forests' in *Annual Review of Phytopathology*. (vol 13, 1973); Morschel, J.R. *Plant Diseases Recorded in Australia and Overseas: Part 1 Vegetable Crops*. Australian Govt Publishing Service, Canberra, 1975.

diseases and epidemics, human

This article discusses only those diseases of man in Australia that are caused by parasites or pathogens (agents causing disease); in other words, infectious rather than degenerative diseases.

Diseases before European contact Two diseases from which the Aborigines almost certainly suffered before European colonisation were yaws and trachoma, which may have been brought by an original group of Aborigines or by visitors from islands to the N.

Yaws causes sores in the soft parts of the body and sometimes deformation of the bones producing, for example, the so called sabre tibia or 'boomerang leg'. The causal organism is a spirochaete, *Treponema pertenue*, very closely related to the one that causes venereal syphilis, *T. pallidum*; the microbe usually enters through a cut or abrasion and forms a primary sore at the site. The two organisms cannot be distinguished by electron microscopy and they react similarly in blood tests. Yaws is not, however, a venereal disease but is one that is associated with poor hygienic conditions. Some of the symptoms of yaws resemble those of syphilis and the two diseases were often confused by early workers. Syphilis probably did not occur among Aborigines in the NT before 1939 but the control of yaws, using the highly efficient penicillin treatment, has made the spread of syphilis more likely. Syphilis was introduced into Australia by the Europeans and also probably by pre-European visitors.

Trachoma or sandy blight is an eye disease caused by a Rickettsial type of organism, *Chlamydia trachomatis*, which is spread by flies, water, infected clothing and towels, and by contact. It is an ancient scourge of man, being mentioned in the *Ebers Papyrus* (c1500 BC) and still affects many of the people of the world: in 1972 it was estimated that over 20 million people were blind as a result of infection. The incidence of the disease is still high among Aborigines. (*see below*).

Diseases in the first settlement at Sydney
David COLLINS and other early settlers remarked upon the healthy climate at PORT JACKSON and on the absence of diseases associated with warm climates. However, three epidemics occurred between 1788 and 1792. Some deaths were due to poor nutrition and tuberculosis of long standing (for example, the death of Forby Sutherland, the first Englishman buried in Australia). Only 32 'First Fleeters' died on the journey, but the second fleet lost 260 convicts from scurvy, dysentery and 'fever'; and the third fleet lost 218. The first epidemic (January to June, 1788) involved dysentery and scurvy, the second July and August, 1790 scurvy, dysentery and probably typhus and typhoid. After the arrival of the third fleet there was a third epidemic, lasting about one year, and many healthy people succumbed rapidly and died at Rose Hill and Sydney; in this epidemic, dysentery was probably the main disease.

Diseases (viral and Rickettsial) after European colonisation
1. Smallpox. A smallpox epidemic at PORT JACKSON in 1789 caused the death of many Aborigines but only one settler. As it is improbable that all the colonists were immune as a result of earlier attacks, some authorities have suggested that the disease was not smallpox, but a form of chickenpox to which the Aborigines were very susceptible; others suggest that the smallpox had been introduced not by the Europeans but by the Indonesian trepangers on the N coasts. Whatever the disease was, it spread rapidly among the Aborigines of SE Australia and, according to some writers, throughout the continent, persisting until 1845. The Europeans of Australia did not escape smallpox completely. An outbreak in 1884 led to the first Australian Health Conference, at which the question of quarantine was discussed. By 1983 smallpox had been completely eradicated throughout the world (except in laboratory culture).
2. Measles. In *The Voyage of the Beagle* (1839) Charles DARWIN attributed the decline of the Aboriginal population partly to measles because of the often fatal effect on people who had not been previously exposed to it. In 1865 half the Aborigines in the YORK district of WA died from the disease. The last serious outbreak in 1965-66 affected about 2000 Aborigines. Measles among European children in Australia is usually a mild disease, but there can be serious complications.
3. Arboviruses. The word 'arboviruses' is a contraction of 'arthropod-borne viruses', and refers to such diseases as yellow fever, dengue fever and Murray Valley encephalitis (MVE). It is a characteristic of these viruses that they develop in both the ARTHROPOD host and in a VERTEBRATE; many of them affect the central nervous system of the vertebrate host but most of the 200 kinds of arboviruses so far discovered (several in Australia) produce insignificant symptoms in the vertebrate and have

been called 'viruses in search of a disease'. Some arboviruses persist in a reservoir of animals, spilling over into the human population from time to time. The classic example is yellow fever which has not occurred in Australia, though the insect vector, *Aedes aegypti*, is common. The most important example in Australia is MVE, which causes a fever and affects the central nervous system. Although often a very mild disease it sometimes causes death. The reservoir of MVE occurs among waterfowl from which it is spread, after periods of flooding in the inland, by MOSQUITOES, particularly *Culex annulirostris*. The disease was probably first observed in 1917 and 1918 when several cases were fatal in western NSW and northern VIC; it was then known as Australian X-disease. It broke out again in the early 1950s, coinciding with the spread of MYXOMATOSIS. The public assumed that the two diseases had been caused by the same micro-organisms, but to prove that this was not so Sir Macfarlane BURNET Sir Ian Clunies Ross and Dr F.J. Fenner injected themselves with the myxoma virus and suffered no ill effects.

MVE is probably native to Australia and New Guinea but dengue fever (breakbone fever, dandy fever) is almost certainly introduced. Although extremely painful, dengue fever is rarely fatal and does not have permanent after effects. The occasional epidemics in Australia probably originate from travellers returning from South-East Asia. The disease is believed to be confined to man and the vectors (disease-carriers) mainly *Aedes aegypti*.

Recent studies have shown that Aborigines and some Europeans in northern QLD are often involved in epidemics caused by other arboviruses, such as the Ross River virus which is believed to be responsible for epidemic polyarthritis. It may be even more widely distributed and is arousing the interest of epidemiologists in the S States.
4. Rabies. The only countries now free from rabies are Australia, New Zealand, Britain, Ireland, Norway, Sweden, Hawaii and Japan; rabies is at present spreading through Europe, mainly in foxes. Earlier this century a rabid dog was intercepted at a port in QLD and in TAS in the 19th century rabies caused one or two human deaths. Rabies is a terrible death; once the symptoms appear little can be done for the patient. Strict quarantine regulations have prevented the entry of the disease into Australia and it is criminal for anybody to try to evade them. Vampire and insectivorous BATS are vectors of the disease, and it is possible, therefore, that migratory bats could bring rabies into N Australia.
5. Poliomyelitis. This disease has been important in the past in both Aboriginal and European communities. Before 1955, more than 90 per cent of Aboriginal children in the NT under the age of five showed serological evidence of past infections of type II poliomyelitis; most of these infections would have been so mild that they may not even have been noticed. Since the widespread immunisation of

Table 1

COMMON CONDITIONS AMONG ABORIGINES AND NON-ABORIGINES IN WESTERN AUSTRALIA AND THE NORTHERN TERRITORY IN 1976 (rates per thousand)

Conditions	Aboriginal	Non-Aboriginal	Ratio
Infective and parasitic			
WA	95	8	12:1
NT	18	4	4.5:1
Respiratory system			
WA	137	22	6:1
NT	30	17	2:1
Skin and subcutaneous tissue			
WA	38	6	6:1
NT		n.a.	
Total			
WA	270	36	8:1
NT (incomplete)	48	21	2:1

Note: n.a. not available.
Source: House of Representatives Standing Committee on Aboriginal Affairs *Aboriginal Health*. Australian Govt Publishing Service, Canberra.

Australians the disease has almost disappeared.

6. Influenza. This disease is often dismissed as relatively unimportant but it has been responsible for the greatest of all known human plagues—the 'Spanish influenza' pandemic of 1918-19 which affected half of the world's population and led to the death of over 20 million people. Troops returning from the war brought it to Australia, and for a time it was confined to the quarantine camps. When it did eventually escape, the resulting epidemic was not as severe as that in Europe and a smaller proportion of cases were fatal; the disease was most severe among young adults. There are two main types of influenza, A and B, each with several subtypes, and new forms are constantly appearing. An attack or vaccine against one type does not provide immunity from the others, and thus it is possible to have two separate influenza attacks within a few weeks.

7. Q fever. This is caused by a Rickettsial organism, *Coxiella burnetii*, named after its discoverer, Sir Macfarlane Burnet. The 'Q' stands for 'query'. The disease is associated mainly with people in the cattle industry and is rarely fatal; in NSW about 10 per cent of abattoir workers carry antibodies in their blood. Q fever is a typical zoonosis (that is, a disease of animals which man can acquire). There is evidence that marsupials of various kinds can be infected, and that the disease is carried by TICKS to cattle, sheep and goats, but not to humans; man is infected by the inhalation of particles of dried fluids from infected, slaughtered animals. Q fever was first noted in Australia in 1934 when men from a Brisbane abattoir developed a severe fever that bore some resemblance to typhoid.

8. Hepatitis. This is a virus disease which affects the liver. The two forms—infectious hepatitis (IH; virus hepatitis A) and serum hepatitis (SH; virus hepatitis B)—differ mainly in their modes of transmission. IH is spread from person to person by contagion, and by food or water contaminated with faecal matter, an outbreak among New Zealand and Australian soldiers at El Alamein in 1942 strongly implicated flies as carriers of the disease. SH, sometimes transmitted when vaccines containing human serum are administered, was first recognised in 1938 in a group of patients who had received a measles convalescent serum; it may also be transmitted among drug addicts who share unsterilised hypodermic needles. The two viruses are not identical but the clinical syndromes are the same. IH is commoner among children and adolescents but affects older people more severely; there appears to be no correlation between age and infection with SH. The incubation period of IH is about 25 days, of SH about 100. The fever associated with SH is mild or absent but may be high in IH.

Hepatitis may be congenital. In 1965 it was shown that there was a 250 per cent increase in the births of children with Down's syndrome (Mongolism) about every five years in Australia and later it was found that the increase occurred about nine months after the last epidemic of IH. The number of cases of hepa-

titis notified in Australia in 1979 were: IH, 1 897; SH 785. Together they were the most common notifiable disease in that year, after gonorrhoea.

9. Typhus. There are several forms of typhus, the most serious being louse-borne typhus which is spread by human body LICE and is associated with natural disasters and wars when people are forced to live in wretched conditions. It has not been recorded in Australia for many years. The causal organism of louse-borne typhus (classic typhus) is *Rickettsia prowazekii*; the name immortalises two men who died of typhus while studying the disease. Many authorities believe that it has developed from the murine typhus organism *R. typhi*, which is transmitted from rodent to rodent by FLEAS, lice and biting midges (*see* FLIES). Murine typhus sometimes attacks man (one case was notified in Australia in 1976) but the disease is far less severe than classic typhus. Typhus and typhoid were not differentiated clinically until 1837 so early records of outbreaks can be difficult to interpret.

Aids In 1983 two men died from AIDS—acquired immune deficiency syndrome—in VIC. This disease, which had been first reported only a year or two previously, may be caused by viruses similar to those involved in some forms of leukaemia. The patient loses his ability to recruit his physiological defences against various infections, and the fatality rate is high. The incidence is greatest among homosexuals in the USA, and among Haitians. Recently it has been suggested that many of the Haitian victims were also homosexuals. Both the Australian victims are thought to have acquired the disease in the USA.

Diseases (bacterial) after European colonisation

1. Typhoid. This is an enteric fever caused by *Salmonella* organisms spread by polluted drinking water or contaminated food. It is the classic carrier disease in which people, completely free from symptoms, harbour vast numbers of the organism which they innocently pass on to other people. There were severe outbreaks in the VIC goldfields in the 1850s and at COOLGARDIE between 1892 and 1895; in 1905 it caused 630 deaths in Australia and in 1907, 564. It is now an uncommon disease in Australia, with only about 20 cases noted each year. In 1977, when there were 59 cases, 41 of these were in Melbourne and were probably associated with a small outbreak stemming from an English immigrant, an innocent carrier, who was working in a Melbourne sandwich bar. There was another small outbreak, caused by infected take-away chicken, in 1983.

2. Salmonella. Some species of *Salmonella*, related to, but distinct from, the causal organisms of typhoid, infect various animals. These sometimes contaminate food and can cause severe food poisoning with diarrhoea and gastroenteritis. In August 1981 contaminated salamis, and possibly other small-goods, caused several cases with at least one death in Australia.

3. Tuberculosis. Pulmonary tuberculosis was an important disease among the first European settlers in Australia. Aboriginal people were more susceptible to it than the Europeans, although a study in 1950 showed that the Aborigines of the KIMBERLEYS and PORT HEDLAND areas had only 15 cases among 3 209 people, a lower incidence than that among the Europeans. In the 1960s, however, it was estimated that the new active rate among Aborigines in NSW was about one in a thousand, about three times higher than the European rate. It was found that Aborigines in closer contact with Europeans, such as nurses and servants, were more likely to contract tuberculosis than those with less contact.

The incidence of tuberculosis has declined because of new methods of treatment and the active campaigns of the federal government. The measures taken to eliminate tuberculosis include intermittent mass radiographic examination, BCG immunisation and the prevention of active cases entering Australia as immigrants. The government pays all people who have contracted the disease a pension so that they may give up work during the treatment. The number of cases notified in 1979 was 1 612 but there is no indication of the proportion of these cases involving Aborigines. The House of Representatives 1979 Report on Aboriginal Health showed that in the NT the disease was still chronic among older Aborigines but the number of notifications declined from 28 in 1976 to 11 in 1977 (non-Aboriginals: 17 to nine). The report also showed that in WA in 1976 the incidence of the disease among Aborigines was half the 1971 figure but three times greater than the overall incidence for the State, and between 1971 and 1976 the number of Aboriginal notifications was 51.

4. Leprosy. Also called Hansen's disease, this is caused by a microbe closely allied to that of tuberculosis, *Mycobacterium leprae*. It was probably brought here by Chinese and KANAKAS during the 19th century. Studies in 1976 showed that in the NT and WA Aborigines were the commonest victims whereas the disease attacked all races in QLD. Though endemic only in the N it was recorded in a few Aborigines who had never left NSW. In the NT in 1976 there were 710 Aboriginal cases, 40 non-Aboriginal and 67 unreviewed cases. Despite the small number of leprosy patients in Australia compared with the numbers 30 years earlier (a total of 59 patients in 1979) the disease is still dreaded because of its deforming effects when neglected. Leprosy victims were separated from their families for many years and there was a social stigma associated with the disease. Leprosy is not a highly infectious disease; the infection rate of spouses of sufferers is less than 10 per cent. It is now successfully treated with long-acting, injectable preparations.

5. Plague. Bubonic plague, caused by *Yerwinia (Pasteurella) pestis*, is a zoonosis that is usually dependent upon a reservoir of susceptible wild rodents in which the disease persists. Outbreaks occur when the disease is transferred by

fleas to commensal rodents which, in turn, pass it on to man. There is no such reservoir among wild rodents in Australia though the usual commensal rodent concerned, the ship rat, *Rattus rattus*, is common. The most important flea vector, the oriental rat flea, *Xenopsylla cheopis*, is relatively uncommon. When the plague occurred in Australia at the beginning of this century it was almost certainly the result of infected black rats coming ashore; the epidemic was insignificant (compared with the pandemic of the time in other parts of the world), causing about 150 deaths in 1900 and between 10 and 50 annually from 1901 to 1906. Most were in the Rocks area of Sydney, much of which was subsequently bought by compulsory purchase by the NSW government. There was a second brief episode of plague in Australia in Sydney and Brisbane in 1921-22, stemming from infected rats coming ashore in fodder carried by the SS *Wyreema*. In Sydney there were 35 cases with 10 deaths; in Brisbane 59 cases and 28 deaths. Some other QLD ports also reported cases.

Once plague is established in a human population it can change to the pneumonic form which is transmitted directly. This was apparently unimportant in the Australian outbreaks. Australia has played an important part in the study of the causes of plague. The role of fleas as vectors of the disease had been proposed by the Frenchman, Simond, but it was an English-born Medical Officer of Health in Sydney, John Ashburton THOMPSON, who proved that they did indeed transmit the disease from rats to human beings.

6. Cholera. This has not been recorded as a transmitted disease in Australia but there have been a few recent 'scares' caused by returning travellers who have been in contact with the disease. The most recent pandemic, which began in Asia in 1961, differs from earlier ones in that the causal organism, *Vibrio cholerae*, is of a new type, the El Tor vibrio, which because it can be carried for some time without the victim displaying symptoms is difficult to exclude by quarantine. Its transmission is unlikely because it is a disease which results from drinking water contaminated by infected sewage. However, there were two non-fatal cases in NSW in 1981, involving an elderly couple who had not been out of Australia for some years.

7. Leptospirosis. This is a typical zoonosis, usually acquired by people in contact with infected animals and caused by spirochaete bacteria belonging to the genus *Leptospira*. Some infect dogs and livestock, others are found in wild hosts such as RODENTS and BANDICOOTS. Man is usually affected by these organisms when they have been excreted in urine. One form of leptospirosis, Weil's disease, is acquired from rats; another form, caught from dogs, was first observed in NSW in 1951 and has since been found in a few separate Sydney suburbs. The symptoms often resemble those of influenza; later symptoms may include conjunctivitis, jaundice, haemoglobinuria (red urine) and, in severe cases, meningitis and paralysis. There

were 66 notified identified cases in Australia in 1979, but this is probably an underestimate because of incorrect diagnosis of influenza.

8. Brucellosis. This fever is a disease of goats, cattle and pigs, caused by *Brucella* bacteria, which man acquires either by direct contact or by drinking infected milk. Most cases of human brucellosis are mild and almost symptomless but there are also acute forms. The latter usually disappear spontaneously after two or three months. Brucellosis often causes abortion in cattle but seldom in humans. There is a vigorous campaign to eliminate the disease from Australian cattle, and the disease should be eradicated within a few years. There were 58 notified human cases in Australia in 1979. Human brucellosis is mainly an occupational disease (affecting meat workers, for example) but it has been suggested that it was the cause of Beethoven's deafness and death.

9. Venereal diseases. Syphilis and gonorrhoea, caused by *Treponema pallidum* and *Neisseria gonorrhoea*, are common and increasing in advanced countries, including Australia, largely, it is said, because of the freedom brought by contraceptive pills. The diseases were probably introduced into Australia by Europeans though they may have entered by the N route as well. Because there is no good serological test for gonorrhoea, no reliable figures are available for the incidence of the disease in Australia; this ignorance is aggravated by the reluctance of sufferers from venereal diseases to report their condition. Nevertheless, gonorrhoea heads the list of notifiable diseases; in 1972 there were 11 037 cases (54 per cent) and in 1979 11 647 cases (54 per cent). There were 1 217 cases of syphilis in 1972 (6 per cent, fourth-commonest) and in 1979, 3 165 cases (14.4 per cent, third-commonest, after gonorrhoea and hepatitis). The 1979 House of Representatives Report on Aboriginal Health pointed out that although there was little statistical evidence of the prevalence of venereal diseases, gonorrhoea had probably remained fairly constant in the NT over the last few years but syphilis had increased markedly.

Other bacterial and viral diseases The once-common childhood diseases such as diphtheria and whooping cough are now far less troublesome. There are continuing immunisation programmes against poliomyelitis, measles, rubella, diphtheria, tetanus and whooping cough. Rubella (German measles) immunisation is limited to girls and women in their reproductive years because the disease during early pregnancy can lead to congenital defects such as blindness (30 to 35 per cent risk).

Diseases caused by animal parasites

1. Malaria. This disease is rarely transmitted in Australia, most of the few cases each year (389 notified in 1979) probably being contracted overseas. Some vectors, various species of *Anopheles* mosquitoes, occur in Australia, but without a sufficiently large reservoir of the disease in the human population outbreaks are unlikely. The last endemic focus of the

disease, among Aborigines at the ROPER RIVER in the NT, was eliminated in 1962 with the help of drugs.

2. Amoebic dysentery. The causal organism of this disease is *Entamoeba histolytica* (see PROTOZOONS). The 'adult' lives in the large intestine where it is commonly harmless but in certain conditions it stops feeding on bacteria and food material and turns to the cells of the gut, forming ulcers. Some move with the blood to the liver.

The disease is associated with poor hygienic conditions. In 1970 the infestation rates in Aboriginal settlements and missions in QLD varied from 46 per cent to nil.

3. Filariasis. This disease, a common symptom of which is elephantiasis, results from infestations of ROUNDWORMS (nematodes) transmitted by mosquitoes. The part played by nematodes was demonstrated by Joseph BANCROFT in Brisbane in 1876. Though the disease once occurred in N Australia, Australian cases now originate overseas.

4. Ascariasis. This disease results from the infestation of the cosmopolitan nematode, *Ascaris lumbricoides*, one of the largest of all roundworms (females up to 410mm long). The adults can block the small intestine when numerous. A female can produce 200 000 eggs a day; the eggs are remarkably resistant and in damp soil they can remain viable for years. Infestations are most likely to occur among people forced to live in unhygienic conditions; in 1954, 46.5 per cent of the Aboriginal children in some reserves in NSW were infested but the incidence has since been greatly reduced by medical treatment.

5. Hookworms. These nematodes include the so-called New World hookworm, *Necator americanus*, and the Old World species, *Ancylostoma duodenale*, both still common in the warmer parts of Australia where they were probably introduced by Chinese and Kanaka workers during the 19th century. During the 1920s the Australian Hookworm Campaign was more or less successful among Europeans and Chinese in N Australia but not among the Aborigines. Hookworms penetrate the body through the skin and find their way to the intestinal tissues, causing anaemia when the infestations are heavy. Other symptons include cycles of diarrhoea and constipation, and retardation of growth, sexual maturity and mental powers. Some other nematodes attack man, as it were, in error. They search his tissues for an organ suitable for further development and in doing so can cause considerable harm. The so-called cutaneous larva migrans is caused by certain dog nematodes; the disorders are commonly known by the descriptive names of creeping eruption, sand itch and so on. Visceral larva migrans is more serious for the foreign nematodes invade deeper tissues and have caused blindness or death. Other common nematode infestations are caused by whipworms (*Trichuris* species) and pinworm or threadworm, *Enterobius vermicularis*. The latter is common among school children who often re-infest themselves by swallowing eggs laid by the females which

issue from the anus during the night; their movements cause intense itching.

Diseases among rural Aborigines Owing to the poor hygienic conditions in which many rural Aborigines are forced to live, the incidence of certain diseases is higher among these people than among the white population of Australia. This is exemplified in Table 1, which is based on one published in the 1979 House of Representatives Report on Aboriginal Health. The diseases concerned have already been discussed in the previous sections.

In the first report of the National Population Inquiry the Aboriginal life expectancy rate in 1976 was calculated to be 50 years, compared with 69.3 years for the male population of Australia as a whole. However, the recommendations of the House of Representatives for the provision of clean and adequate water supplies, sewerage facilities and housing in all Aboriginal communities should, if followed, greatly improve living conditions, thereby helping to reduce the high incidence of disease.

Trachoma is the outstanding disease among rural Aborigines. A national programme which began in 1975, aided by over 70 opthamologists who gave their services free, entailed the examination of about 100 000 people, 61 700 of them Aboriginal. Trachoma was detected in 38.3 per cent of the Aborigines; in central Australia 77 per cent were infected; 1.4 per cent of all Aborigines were blind in both eyes, and 2.3 per cent in one. About 25 000 needed treatment, and about 1 400 needed surgery. Most of the surgery cases had been completed by 1982.

Quarantine The Quarantine Act of 1908 is administered by the Commonwealth Department of Health and contains three sections: human quarantine; animal quarantine; and plant quarantine. These regulations concern movements into the country but can be applied to interstate movements. The function of the human quarantine section is to detect quarantinable diseases in passengers entering the country (in particular, cholera, yellow fever, plague and typhus) and to maintain and keep open at all times quarantine stations at major ports. People suffering from other infectious diseases such as chickenpox and mumps are directed to medical centres for treatment. Some passengers may need valid international certificates of vaccination before they are allowed free entry into Australia. The requirements vary from time to time and with the area from which the traveller comes to Australia. All passengers have to state where they intend to stay in Australia so that they can be traced if disease is found to be present among their fellow passengers.

Notifiable diseases Cases of the following diseases in Australia must be reported (usually by the doctor in charge) to the medical authorities. The numbers in parenthesis are the numbers of cases reported in Australia in the first 40 weeks of 1982: brucellosis (58); cholera (0); diphtheria (1); gonorrhoea (9 807); leprosy (24); hepatitis, infective (905); hepatitis, serum (619); HYDATID (9); leptospirosis (84); malaria (384); ornithosis (psittacosis, etc.) (8); poliomyelitis (0); salmonella (1 594); syphilis (2 516); tetanus (10); tuberculosis (1 046); typhoid fever (19); typhus (all forms) (2); anthrax, cholera, plague, smallpox, yellow fever (0).

See also diseases, livestock; mites; parasites, human; parasites, livestock

Further reading: Cumpston, J.H.L. *The History of Smallpox in Australia, 1788-1908, Commonwealth of Australia Quarantine Service.* (no 3) Govt Printer, Melbourne, 1914; Lapage, G. *Animals Parasitic in Man.* Penguin Books, Harmondsworth, 1957; Burnet, Sir Macfarlane *Changing Patterns: An Atypical Autobiography.* Heinemann, London, 1968; Abbie, A.A. *The Original Australians.* A.H. & A.W. Reed, Sydney, 1969; Ewers, W.J. & Jeffrey, W.T. *Parasites of Man in Niugini.* Jacaranda Press, Brisbane, 1971; Burnet, Sir Macfarlane & White, D.O. *Natural History of Infectious Diseases.* (4th edn) Cambridge University Press, London, 1972; Moodie, P.M. *Aboriginal Health.* Australian National University Press, Canberra, 1973; Gandevia, B. & Cobley, J. 'Mortality at Sydney Cove, 1788-1792' in *Australian and New Zealand Journal of Medicine.* (1974); Snow, K.R. *Insects and Disease.* Routledge & Kegan Paul, London, 1974; Blainey, G. *Triumph of the Nomads.* Macmillan, Melbourne and Sydney, 1975; Hungerford, T.C. *Diseases of Livestock.* (8th edn) McGraw-Hill, Sydney, 1975; Woods, A. 'Global Diseases' in *Current Affairs Bulletin.* (vol 53, no 4, 1976); *Year Book Australia 1977-78.* Australian Bureau of Statistics, Canberra, 1978; *Aboriginal Health: Report from the House of Representatives Standing Committee on Aboriginal Affairs.* Australian Govt Publishing Service, Canberra, 1979; Hennessy, W.B. (ed) *Lay Course in Tropical Medicine* (2nd edn) Commonwealth Department of Health and School of Public Health and Tropical Medicine, University of Sydney, Australian Govt Publishing Service, Canberra, 1980; Stevenson, W.J. & Hughes, K.L. *Synopsis of Zoonoses in Australia.* Commonwealth Department of Health, Australian Govt Publishing Service, Canberra, 1980; Broughton, C.R. *A Coast Chronicle: The History of Prince Henry Hospital 1881-1981.* (2nd edn) Knudsen, Sydney, 1981.

dispersal of plants *see* weeds

diving *see* swimming, etc.

Dixon, Sir Owen (1886-1972) Jurist. Born and educated in Melbourne, he was called to the Bar in 1910 and appointed KC in 1922. Generally considered to be the foremost constitutional authority and greatest advocate of his time, he was appointed a Justice of the High Court of Australia in 1929. Following the outbreak of war in the Pacific in 1941, he served as Australian Minister in Washington, then resumed his position on the High Court in 1944, and was Chief Justice from 1952 until his resignation in 1964. His international standing was shown in 1950 by his appointment by the Security Council of the United Nations to mediate in the Kashmir dispute between India and Pakistan. He became a Privy Councillor in 1951, and was appointed KCMG (1941) and GCMG (1954).

Dobell, Sir William (1899-1970) Artist. Born in NEWCASTLE in NSW, Dobell came to Sydney and attended evening art lessons at Julian ASHTON's. In 1929, a Society of Artists' Travelling Scholarship took him to the Slade School in London; while there he also had private drawing lessons from Sir William Orpen. He exhibited with the Royal Academy, the New English Art Club and the London Group. In 1936, he began painting a series of portraits of people in the South Kensington area—charladies, restaurant waiters and the like—which he treated with witty insight and technical elan. His return to Australia in 1939 resulted in an expansiveness in his work. The tones became richer and wider, the canvasses larger, the style more expressive and the techniques more various. Examples of his work at this time are *The Billy Boy* (1943), now in the Australian War Memorial, *Portrait of a Strapper* (1941), now in the Newcastle Regional Art Gallery, and *The Cypriot* (1940), now in the Queensland Art Gallery.

In 1943 Dobell was awarded the ARCHIBALD PRIZE for the portrait of a fellow artist, Joshua Smith. The verdict resulted in a cry of outrage, resulting in a heated clash between the conservatives and the moderns that went as far as the Supreme Court of NSW, where two members of the Royal Art Society attempted, unsuccessfully, to have the award set aside. A modest and diffident person, Dobell was upset by the stress of the trial, and the subsequent awards of the WYNNE PRIZE and the Archibald Prize in 1948 and 1959 respectively and the commission in 1960 by *Time* magazine to paint a portrait of the Prime Minister, Robert MENZIES, did little to restore his equanimity. As the embattled hero of the modern movement, a role he disliked, and as a portraitist who broke the crust of predictability that had surmounted this art form for several decades, Dobell attracted support of almost religious fervour. It embarrassed and inhibited him, and he sought seclusion at WANGI WANGI in NSW where he remained for the rest of his life, working on landscapes of the area and some portraits. His New Guinea series, the result of visits to that country in 1949 and 1950, allowed his fascination for colour to find an outlet in exotic miniature works. The Art Gallery of New South Wales honoured him with a retrospective exhibition in 1964.

dodders *see* parasitic plants

dogfishes *see* sharks, etc.

dogs Australians keep most of the varieties of dogs that are to be found in Europe and North America—probably more than 100 different breeds. In 1980 the five most popular breeds were said to be the German shepherd, the cocker spaniel, the Australian silky terrier, the chihuahua and the collie but fashions change in dogs as in clothes. Dogs do not always see eye to eye with dog-breeders and owners about the most suitable mating partners and, consequently, cross-breeds are far commoner than any particular variety. The Royal Agricultural Societies of the States keep the registers of purebreeds.

Four varieties can be claimed as Australian in origin. The Australian terrier, a sporting dog, is a short-legged breed with a long head, erect ears, and a harsh hair of medium length. The body hair is usually blue or silver-grey and the legs tan, the height is about 25cm. The Australian or Sydney silky terrier is a trifle smaller with flatter, longer and silkier hair, blue or silver-blue and tan in colour. It is classed among the toy varieties.

The harsh conditions of the more arid parts of Australia led to the belief that British cattle and sheep dogs would be unsuitable and, consequently, two important breeds of working dog, the kelpie and the Australian cattle dog, were developed. Both breeds have comparatively short hair, unlike many of the British working dogs. The Australian cattle dog originated in crosses between a pair of merles (blue-mottled, smooth-haired Scotch collies) and dingoes. Later the breed was improved by the introduction of dalmatian (giving the breed its characteristic blue speckles) and black-and-tan kelpie genes. It has been falsely claimed that this is the only pure-bred cattle dog in the world but the Welsh corgi has been used for this purpose for centuries. The kelpies are descended from a bitch of that name which itself was probably derived from black-and-tan, smooth-haired Scotch collies. Some authorities believe that the modern kelpie also carries dingo genes, and some have suggested that the fox had a part in its development though this is biologically most unlikely. A kelpie dog is about 46 to 51cm high, and a bitch is a little smaller.

Dollarbird, *Eurystomus orientalis*

dollarbird This species is the only Australian representative of the Old World and

Australian family Coraciidae, which contains the rollers, so called because of their swooping and rolling flight. The dollarbird, *Eurystomus orientalis* (30cm long), is related to KINGFISHERS and the RAINBOW BIRD, and is so named because of the round white patch seen on each wing when in flight. It is dark brown and violet, with a red bill, and sits for long periods on the dead branches of tall trees from which it darts out to catch flying insects. Towards sunset, it remains on the wing for long periods, uttering harsh, discordant notes. It breeds in Australian woodlands in the N and E, but migrates to New Guinea and nearby islands when not breeding. It lays its white eggs in a hole in a dead tree, usually at great heights.

dolphins and whales Belonging to the order *Cetacea,* these animals are perfectly adapted for an aquatic life. They are warmblooded EUTHERIAN MAMMALS which must, like their terrestrial cousins, breath air and suckle their young. They have lost their hindlimbs, apart from some remnants embedded in muscle. They propel themselves with their strong, horizontal, boneless tail-flukes, using their flipper-like fore-limbs for steering. Some also have dorsal fins for stability.

Whales and dolphins (dolphins are, in fact, small, toothed whales) have lost virtually all the hair which covered their terrestrial ancestors; hair is represented by a few tactile bristles near to the mouth. The insulation of the body is taken over by the blubber, deposits of fat beneath the skin which also help to streamline the body and which serve as food reserves.

Cetaceans often dive to great depths for long periods. They have various physiological adaptations to help them to do so, such as the storage of relatively large quantities of oxygen in their muscle and blood, but the most important adaptation is the stopping of the flow of blood to all tissues, apart from the brain and the heart muscle, during a dive. The other tissues build up an 'oxygen-debt' which is repaid as soon as the animal surfaces. Unlike a scuba diver they use only the air that they take down with them and consequently avoid the risk of the 'bends' or caisson sickness which develops when nitrogen, dissolved in the blood under high pressures at great depths, bubbles out again as the diver rises. During a dive the breathing passage is sealed off from the mouth by the tightly fitting epiglottis (the fleshy flap at the base of the tongue). The nostrils (blow holes) are also closed during a dive. Sperm whales can dive to depths of over 1000m and stay below for up to 75 minutes.

Most whales have functional eyes but the sense of sight cannot be important for animals that often swim where little or no light penetrates. The sense of sound, however, is of supreme importance, and whales use a sonar system similar to the echolocation system of BATS. Dolphins click audibly but their calls also have an ultrasonic component ranging from 20KHz to 200KHz. Whales also communicate with sound. Water is such a good

conductor that it is believed that some whales can hear each other over hundreds of kilometres. Whales' ears are merely slits at the opening of the auditory canal.

Some authorities have claimed that dolphins are as intelligent as man but although there is little solid evidence for this belief dolphins do readily learn tricks and even, it seems, invent games for themselves. There are several records of wild dolphins associating with human beings. One at Opononi Beach, New Zealand, would play ball with surfers and even allow small children to ride on her back. Dolphins are often reported helping sick members of their schools, pushing them to the surface to allow them to breathe.

As whales are seldom seen it is difficult to be certain about the number of species occurring in any particular region. Some whales are known only from rare beached specimens. Although the oceans are interconnected there are still barriers to the universal distribution of marine animals. Thus the belugas, narwhals and grey whales are restricted, as far as is known, to the N hemisphere, but it is possible that a rare straggler could reach Australian waters. A recent estimate of the number of Australian species is 45.

All the families, and some of the species, which occur in the Australian region or are likely to turn up there are listed below; they are divided into two suborders, one containing the toothed whales, the other containing the whalebone whales.

Toothed whales These whales, of the suborder Odontoceti, are the only ones with teeth, though in many species the teeth do not erupt. None of them, however, has baleen (whalebone), which is characteristic of the other suborder. Toothed whales have the nostrils joined to form a single blow-hole. Many have a conspicuous swelling (melon), containing oil and fat, above the upper jaw and in front of the skull; this probably serves as an acoustic lens in echolocation.

1. The family Ziphiidae (about 18 species) contains the beaked whales, small to medium-sized whales, usually slender in shape. Several members of the largest genus, *Mesoplodon*, have been recorded near Australia where they feed, like all beaked whales, on squid. All species have a single pair of teeth in the lower jaw, the position varying from species to species. The southern bottle-nosed whale, *Hyperoodon planifrons* (10m), found in S hemisphere oceans, has a very conspicuous melon. Another species found in Australian waters is the universally distributed Cuvier's whale, *Ziphius cavirostris* (5m to 8.5m), a species in which the males have a pair of teeth at the tip of the lower jaw. The largest beaked whales belong to genus *Berardius* from the Pacific; the S species, Arnoux's beaked whale, *B. arnouxi*, can grow to 12m in length.

2. The family Physeteridae contains two species of sperm whale: the sperm whale or cachalot, *Physeter catodon* (8.5m to 20m), and the much rarer pygmy sperm whale, *Kogia breviceps* (2m to 4m). Both occur in all oceans and are similar in shape; little is known of the

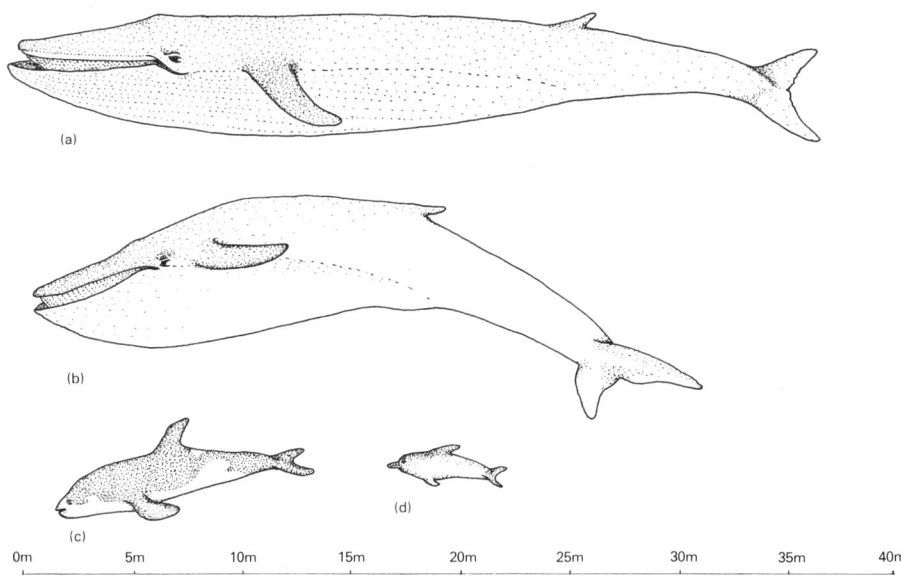

0m 5m 10m 15m 20m 25m 30m 35m 40m

Some cetaceans: (a) blue whale; (b) finback/rorqual; (c) killer whale; (d) bottlenose dolphin

biology of the latter species. The sperm whale was the victim of the first large-scale whaling industry. Its huge, barrel-like head accounts for about a third of its length, much of this bulk being composed of the enlarged melon which contains the spermaceti, a clear liquid which sets to a wax when cooled. Sometimes the gut contains ambergris which was once prized for making perfumes. The sperm whale has about 50 large teeth in its lower jaw, and is blue-grey in colour. There is no dorsal fin but there is a row of tubercles on the back. The food consists mainly of deep-sea squid and cuttlefish. Sperm whales swim at about 16kph and congregate in schools of about 20 bulls and cows. Mating bulls collect a harem of cows; the gestation period is 10 to 20 months and the 4m-long calf grows very quickly, nourished on very rich milk. In 1977 it was estimated that there may be 500 000 sperm whales left but the numbers have fallen greatly in the N Pacific where hunting is concentrated.

3. The family Stenidae contains estuarine and freshwater dolphins. Like the dolphins of the family Delphinidae (*see below*) they have beaks, but in the family Stenidae the beak is ill-defined. The local species, the speckled or (in QLD) white dolphin, *Sousa lentiginosa* (2.4m), is uniformly light in colour.

4. The family Delphinidae contains the remaining dolphins and is divided into several subfamilies. The most familiar species is the cosmopolitan bottle-nosed dolphin, *Tursiops truncatus* (3m to 3.5m), which has recently been intensively studied, with most attention being paid to its communication by sound. It has a short, stout beak, a relatively stout body, a hooked dorsal fin and broad flippers. The back and tail are black or dark-grey and the underparts are lighter in colour. It is mainly a coastal species, living in small schools.

The cosmopolitan common dolphin or saddle-back, *Delphinus delphis* (2m), found in southern Australian waters, is the dolphin of

classical writers and artists. It forms large schools (up to 100 individuals) and is found further from the coasts than the bottle-nosed species. Like all dolphins, it has numerous sharp teeth, well adapted to catching and holding its prey (small surface fish, particularly pilchards and other herring-like species). The gestation period is about 12 months. When giving birth the female often has another female in attendance; the calf is almost always born tail first. The colour of the common dolphin is variable but the back is usually dark brown, the underparts white, and the flanks streaked with yellowish-grey. The beak is very narrow, the dorsal fin is well developed, and the body is slim compared with that of the bottle-nosed species.

Dolphins occurring in Australian waters which are closely related to the common dolphin are: the dusky dolphin or Gray's dolphin, *Lagenorhynchus obscurus* (1.5m to 3m), dark grey above and lighter below; the Electra dolphin, *Peponocephala electra* (1.5m to 3m), which has a tiny beak, white lips and a black body; the extremely rare Fraser's dolphin, *Lagonodelphis hosei* (2.4m), dark above and pinkish below, with a short beak and a low, triangular dorsal fin; and the spinner dolphins (*Stenella* species), some of which can complete two or more barrel rolls when they leap from the water.

The following species belong to other subfamilies of the Delphinidae: the right whale dolphin, *Lissodelphis peroni* (1.5m to 2.4m), black and white, with no dorsal fin, found in S sea; and the Irrawaddy River dolphin, *Orcaella brevirostris* (2.5m to 3m), called after the river where it was first discovered, and occurring from TOWNSVILLE to the TORRES STRAIT— the snout is very short with each jaw containing 12 to 19 teeth.

The Irrawaddy River dolphin belongs to the subfamily Orcinae which also contains species that are so large that they are usually called

whales. The killer whale, *Orcinus orca* (bulls up to 9m), also known as the grampus, is found in all oceans. It has a long, scythe-like dorsal fin (2m long in the male), long flippers (2m long in the male) and a distinctively marked black and white body. Killer whales are ferocious mammals that hunt in packs of about 40 individuals, preying on other dolphins and whales, seals, penguins, squid and fishes; it is the only member of the order that feeds on warm-blooded vertebrates. It is believed by many that killer whales attack man, but there is very little evidence to support this. However, because they are large, predatory animals, they should be treated with respect. There are persistent stories that three packs of killer whales co-operated with whalers at TWOFOLD BAY, driving the prey to their human colleagues in return for scraps (*see* WHALING). The false killer whale, *Pseudorca crassidens* (up to 5.8m), resembles the killer whale but the flippers are relatively small. Both species are sometimes stranded on Australian shores.

The pilot whale or 'blackfish', *Globicephala melaena* (8.2m), is black apart from some paler areas on the throat and underparts. The head is very rounded and the dorsal fin long and low. This species is found throughout the world. When large schools come near to land in the Faeroes most of the inhabitants of Torshavn turn out to drive the whales on to the shore for slaughtering ('grinds'). In 1981 a large school was stranded on the coast of NSW.

Common dolphin, *Delphinus delphis*

G.W. Johnstone (N.P.I.A.W.)

Whalebone or baleen whales The 12 or 13 species of whalebone whales belong to the suborder Mysteceti. Teeth are found only in the foetus where they are vestigial and unused. In place of teeth there are cross sheets of baleen (keratin) which are frayed to comb out the tiny plankton on which these huge animals feed. There are two nostrils. This suborder contains three families.

1. The family Eschrichtidae contains a single species, the Californian grey whale, *Eschrichtius robustus* (13m), which is now found only in the N Pacific.

2. The family Balaenidae contains the right whales, which lack dorsal fins; these were the whales caught in the early days of whaling. The

southern right whale, *Eubalaena australis* (up to 18m), was the most important catch in the early days of Australian and New Zealand whaling; it is a slow swimmer and is now rare. The baleen is 2m long. The head is bowed because of the high arching of the upper jaw; this distinguishes the species from all others found in Australian waters. It also lacks the furrows on the throat that are characteristic of many baleen whales. In 1983, for the first time in 80 years, the species appeared off the Australian coast. A group of females wintered with their calves in VIC. It is estimated that fewer than 5000 survive. The pygmy whale, *Caperea marginata* (6m), though placed in the family Balaenidae, has a dorsal fin, but no throat furrows. It is rarely seen but it sometimes gets stranded on S coasts of Australia.

3. The family Balaenopteridae includes the two largest animals that have ever existed, as far as is known: the blue whale, *Balaenoptera musculus*, and the common rorqual or fin whale, *B. physalus* (25m), both found in all oceans, and in Australian waters.

The blue whale has an average length of 29m. The largest ever landed, according to the *Guinness Book of Records* (1974) was 33.58m long (South Georgia, *c*1912). A pregnant female could weigh as much as 35 adult male African elephants. The body is bluish-grey with some pale mottlings but yellow diatoms often grown on the underparts, hence the alternative name, the sulphur-bottom. As in all the finned whales the throat is furrowed for expansion (80 to 100 furrows); the small dorsal fin is set well back. It has been estimated that the blue whale eats about four tonnes of KRILL daily. Suckling whales also have large appetites, consuming on average about a half tonne of milk daily. Reproducing whales migrate N from their Antarctic feeding grounds in late summer. The gestation period is about one year, and calves (7m at birth) are born every second year. The life span is about 20 years. Blue whales are retiring mammals which live in small groups and normally travel at between 10 and 20kph. It is believed that two or three centuries ago there were over 200 000 blue whales. Now there are less than 5000—in 60 years of Antarctic whaling about 350 000 have been killed. Despite attempts to preserve the blue whale it is probable that it will become extinct.

The common rorqual or finback is slimmer than the blue whale, and has about 85 throat furrows. The upperparts are dark grey and the underparts white but the head is asymmetrically coloured: the right half of the lower jaw is white, the left half grey; inside the mouth and on the tongue this pigmentation is reversed. These whales usually form larger schools than do blue whales; they swim at about 20kph, migrating from Arctic or Antarctic waters to warmer regions for breeding. There are probably 80 000 to 90 000 left.

The smallest whale in the family Balaenopteridae is the little piked whale, *B. acutorostrata* (8m to 10.5m), a rare species also known as the minke whale and found in most waters,

including the Black Sea. This species lives in schools which may contain hundreds of individuals. A fast swimmer, it sometimes plays around ships. Its diet contains a large proportion of fish although, like other whalebone whales, it has baleen for filtering out organisms from the sea.

The sei whale, *B. borealis* (up to 18m), lives in both hemispheres, feeding in polar waters and returning to warmer waters for breeding. It is a relatively slender whale with a long, pointed snout, a large dorsal fin and short flippers. The back is blue-grey and the belly white. There are 32 to 60 throat furrows. There are no records of strandings on Australian coasts but this whale occurs in New Zealand waters, and probably therefore also in Australian seas. It is estimated that the world population has been halved by whalers to about 100 000; hunting of these whales has increased with the decrease in the numbers of the other whales.

The humpback whale, *Megaptera novaeangliae* (11m to 16m), has large amounts of blubber beneath the dorsal fin which gives the humpbacked appearance. This is accentuated by the way in which the whale arches its back when diving. This plump species is black above and pale below with some black markings. The pectoral fins are about one third the length of the body and scalloped on the leading edge. The head and fins have many lumps and tubercles on their surfaces. There are only 14 to 30 throat furrows. This species is now protected as there are only about 4000 individuals left. It is thought that there are 11 distinct populations, four in the N hemisphere, and seven in the S hemisphere. They live in small, slow-moving schools and feed in polar seas from which they migrate along fixed routes to breed in tropical regions near coasts. After World War II most Australian whaling concentrated on this species as they migrated along the E and W coasts. Between 1949 and 1962, 33 532 were caught in Australian waters. In 1949 there were about 25 000 migrating along Australian coasts; when whaling ended in 1962 there were about 1100. It was also the chief species in the early whaling at Twofold Bay NSW. The humpback whale is a noisy species—its 'songs' sometimes last up to 30 minutes and each individual repeats its own repertoire. It is also an apparently playful species which sometimes leaps right out of the water.

Further reading: Lyneborg, L. *Mammals in Colour*. Blandford, London, 1971; Matthews, L.H. *The Life of Mammals*. Universe Books, New York, 1971; Martin, R.M. *Mammals of the Oceans*. Hutchinson, Richmond VIC, 1977; Caras, J. *Dangerous to Man*. Penguin Books, Harmondsworth, 1978. R. Hughes et al. *Australian Natural History* Vol. 21, No. 2, 1983. The Australian Museum, Sydney

donkey vote This refers to the method adopted by people who are compelled to vote at elections in Australia but who make no effort to consider candidates, political parties or policy issues in a rational manner. These

people comply with the compulsory voting law by writing 1, 2, 3, 4, 5, (and so on, as required) straight down the ballot paper. Donkey-voting gives an advantage to the candidates whose names appear at the top of the ballot paper. The electoral system is an important mechanism for legitimising the government of the nation (or State) and it is based on the assumption that each individual will vote in a rational and informed way. The law can compel a citizen to vote and thus recognise his or her personal responsibility towards the community's affairs but the law cannot force the least interested of voters to make a reasoned choice.

Further reading: MacKerras, M. 'Preferences and donkeys' in *Politics*. (vol V, no 1, May 1970); Emy, H.V. *The Politics of Australian Democracy*. Macmillan, Melbourne, 1974.

Donnybrook WA (population 1 197 in 1981) A small town at the foot of the DARLING RANGE in the SW of the State, it is 212km by road S of Perth and 40km SE of BUNBURY. At an elevation of 63m above sea level, about 24km inland from the Indian Ocean coast on the Preston River, it has a mild climate with an average annual rainfall of 1 019mm, concentrated in the winter months; June is the wettest (208mm average) and January the driest (11mm). Apple orcharding is important in the adjacent rural areas and the region is noted for its fine building sandstone.

dories *see* fishes, bony

Dorrigo NSW (population 1 192 in 1981) A small town in the NORTH COAST region of the State, 592km by road N of Sydney, it is situated 730m above sea level on the N side of the Dorrigo Plateau, overlooking the Bellinger Valley. Dairying, beef cattle raising and potato growing are major rural pursuits, with much timber-getting and sawmilling in the forest areas. Trout fishing is a popular activity in the local streams. Situated 4km E of Dorrigo township, on the road to Bellingen, is the Dorrigo National Park, covering 3 909ha and including some densely vegetated rainforest with sassafras, red cedar and coachwood trees, and myriads of colourful orchids in spring. This area is one of the last remnants of the rainforest which once clothed much of the N coastal region. The abundant bird life within the park includes lyrebirds, brush turkeys and bowerbirds. Among the mammals in the park are swamp wallabies, tiger cats, and brush-tailed and gliding possums.

dotterels *see* waders

doves and pigeons These BIRDS belong to the family Columbidae; of the 26 species found in Australia, three are introduced. There is no real distinction between doves and pigeons. Most resemble the common introduced pigeons and turtle doves of the cities in that they have short legs and soft bills with a large basal cere carrying the nostrils; in some species the colouring is a subdued hue, such as dove grey, while in others it is brilliant and iridescent. The take-off flight is noisy, and the call-note of most species is a cooing sound. These birds feed on fruits, berries and seeds, though some eat only seeds while others may supplement their diet with insects. All species are common, save for the flock and banded pigeons whose status is not known; the native species of these birds are currently being studied by the CSIRO.

The family Columbidae is divided into 12 genera. The cosmopolitan genus *Columba* contains the introduced domestic pigeon, *C. livia* (33cm long), and the white-headed pigeon, *C. leucomela*★ (38cm to 41cm). Most domestic pigeons are feral, and are great pests in many coastal urban areas and around farms. They are very variable in colour. Their white eggs are laid in holes and caves or in the crevices of buildings. The white-headed species, which has white underparts and an iridescent black back (the female differs slightly in that the breast is greyish-brown with pink iridescence), is a woodland and forest bird found in the E coastal areas. Its nests are loosely constructed platforms of twigs and are placed on the low branches of trees.

The genus *Streptopelia* contains the turtle doves, a group of Old World pigeons which spreads easily. The two introduced species—the Senegal turtle dove, *S. senegalensis* (25 cm), which has a pinkish head, and the spotted dove, *S. chinensis* (28cm), which has a bluish-grey head—are common in urban localities. Introduced towards the end of the 19th century, many of these hardy birds escaped or were released from captivity and subsequently colonised south-western WA, in the case of the former, and TAS, E Australia and parts of WA, in the case of the latter. Both species make scanty nests of sticks placed on buildings or in shrubs.

The only Australian species in the genus *Macropygia* is the brown pigeon, *M. phasianella* (40cm), which has a pink patch on the breast (male only) and a long tail which is sometimes used as a prop when climbing. It lives in E coastal rainforests and builds its nests—often bulky structures of twigs and leaves—on the lower horizontal branches of trees.

The bronzewing group of pigeons are divided into three genera. All the species within this group have a patch of iridescent colour on the wings, although in the case of the rock pigeons the patch is inconspicuous. The genus *Phaps* contains three species. The common bronzewing, *P. chalcoptera*★ (30cm), a plump brown bird with grey underparts, lives in dry woodland and open country throughout Australia, apart from CAPE YORK. It forms flocks out of the breeding season and, like most pigeons of the arid and semi-arid zones, congregates in vast numbers for drinking. Its platform-shaped nests are made of sticks and placed in trees or bushes or on the ground. The similar, though slightly more stocky, brush bronzewing, *P. elegans*★ (28cm), inhabits woodlands

Diamond dove, *Geopelia cuneata*

H & J Beste (N.P.I.A.W.)

and heathlands, especially near the coast of SW and SE Australia and TAS. This bird spends most of its time on the ground, over which it runs rapidly; its nest is usually placed on the ground, under a bush. The third species in this genus is the flock pigeon, *P. histrionica*★ (28cm), an inland bird found in the N half of the continent in open country. The male has a distinctive black and white pattern on the face, and a chestnut back; the colouring of the female is more subdued. These birds congregate in large flocks, but the numbers fluctuate widely. Their eggs are laid in a shallow depression in the ground, in the shelter of a bush.

The most arboreal species among the bronzewings is the crested pigeon, *Ocyphaps lophotes*★ (30cm), a mainly grey bird with a long, thin black crest. These birds are never far from water and are found throughout Australia, apart from the coastal areas of the SE, SW, NE and N. They build scanty, platform-shaped nests of sticks.

The six bronzewings of the genus *Petrophassa* fall into three pairs, with the two species in each pair being very similar in appearance and ecology. All these birds are terrestrial, and lay their eggs in shallow depressions in the ground. The plumed pigeon, *P. plumifera*★ (20cm), and the red-plumed pigeon, *P. ferruginea*★ (20cm), have black and cinnamon-coloured plumage, long thin crests and black, white and reddish faces; the plumed pigeon can be distinguished by its white belly. These species are found mainly in inland areas, in open country with stony hills and outcrops, the former in western WA and the latter more to the E, in central Australia and the NT. The squatter pigeon, *P. scripta*★ (28cm), and the partridge pigeon, *P. smithii*★ (25cm), are plumper than the plumed species. They are brown, with white below the wings, and whereas the squatter pigeon has a pied face and throat and a dark eye patch, the partridge pigeon has a mostly brown face, a white throat

and a yellow or red eye patch. These birds frequent open woodland areas, the former in northern NSW and the eastern QLD, the latter in northern WA and the NT. The darkest species in this genus are the rock pigeons which inhabit the rocky hills of the far N. The white-quilled rock pigeon, *P. albipennis*★ (30cm), which has a white patch that can be seen when the wings are open, and the chestnut-quilled rock pigeon, *P. rufipennis*★ (30cm), are shy birds which hide among the rocks, their dark brown colouring providing an effective camouflage.

A genus which is closely related to the bronzewing group, *Chalcophaps*, is represented in Australia by the green-winged pigeon, *C. indica* (25cm to 28cm). This species is one of the emerald doves; plump and short-tailed, its body is brown and its back and wings are iridescent glossy green. It ranges from India to New Caledonia, and is found in the forests of the NT and E Australia. This usually fearless bird builds well-constructed flat nests of sticks and twigs.

The three species of ground-feeding doves contained in the genus *Geopelia* are long-tailed, slender birds that look rather like turtle doves. The bar-shouldered dove, *G. humeralis* (28cm), is mostly brown with white underparts, a grey head and breast and a reddish-brown scalloped neck. Found in the E and N of Australia, it is one of the few birds in the continent which inhabits both coastal mangroves and thick inland woodlands. The nests, placed in low bushes or small trees, are platform-shaped structures of twigs and grass. The peaceful dove, *G. striata* (23cm), is greyish in colouring with some dark bars on the body. It is found in woodlands and savannas in all the mainland States, and is often seen near settlements. It builds flat, frail nests of thin twigs. Also seen near settlements is the diamond dove, *G. cuneata*★ (20cm), a white-speckled greyish-brown species which inhabits savanna, often in small flocks, in all States except VIC and TAS. Its frail nests of thin twigs are placed in low bushes and trees or on the ground.

One of the Australia's largest pigeons is the wonga pigeon, *Leucosarcia* melanoleuca* (38cm). Because of their large size and tasty flesh, these birds were killed in great numbers before being protected. Found in the E, from central coastal QLD to VIC, these distinctive forest birds have a dark grey plumage, adorned with a white 'necklace'. Their flat, open nests of twigs are placed high in trees.

The genus *Ptilinopus* contains the fruit pigeons, all Australasian birds which frequent mangroves and forests; in Australia they occur mainly in the N and E. They are either brightly coloured or mainly darkly iridescent and white. The purple-crowned pigeon, *P. superbus* (23cm), is a plump bird with white underparts and mainly bright green upperparts; the male has a purple cap and a dark purple band on the breast. It ranges from Cape York to north-eastern NSW. Like the red-crowned pigeon, *P. regina* (23cm), it is often difficult to see because its plumage blends with the foliage of the trees it frequents. The red-crowned pigeon, found in the NT and NE Australia, is also green above, but both sexes have a red crown and a yellowish-orange belly. Both species build small, platform-shaped nests of twigs high up in trees and bushes. The wompoo pigeon, *P. magnificus* (38cm to 50cm), is a fig-loving species found in coastal rainforest areas from Cape York to NSW. It has a white head, a purple and yellow breast and belly, and green wings and tail. It uses twigs and vine-tendrils to build its large, flat nests. Another white-headed, fig-loving species in this genus is the banded pigeon, *P. alligator** (33cm to 36cm), so called because of the black band on its grey breast; the wings and tail are black also. Known in Australia from only the W escarpment of ARNHEM LAND, it lives on wooded rocky ridges.

An unmistakable Australian species is the topknot pigeon, *Lopholaimus* antarcticus* (45cm), a large bird which often forms immense flocks and travels great distances in search of fruit and berries. Its plumage is grey, its tail black with a white band and its round, distinctive crest is black and brown. Occurring mainly in forest canopy from Cape York to eastern VIC, the topknot pigeon lays in platform-shaped nests, made of thick twigs and usually placed at great heights in tall trees.

The Torres Strait pigeon, *Ducula spilorrhoa* (38cm), is one of the imperial pigeons of which there are many species in New Guinea. Also called the nutmeg pigeon because it feeds mainly on nutmegs, it is a white bird with black at the tips of its wings and tail. It lives in dense mangroves and woodlands on the coast and coastal islands of north-western QLD and the NT, but makes frequent flights across the Strait. Its substantial nests consist of twigs and branches laid across each other. The Torres Strait pigeon is believed to have been the first Australian non-marine animal reported by a European—Diego de Prado of the Luis Vaez de TORRES expediton.

Further reading: Whitely, G.P. *Early History of Australian Zoology.* Royal Zoological Society of NSW, Sydney, 1970.

dragonets *see* fishes, bony

dragonflies *see* damselflies, etc.

dragons *see* lizards

drama Although Australia has had its share of lively theatrical activity since convict days, locally written drama formed only a small part of this until fairly recently. The earliest theatre licence in 1832 permitted only English plays, and proven overseas successes continued to be preferred, particularly by the J.C. WILLIAMSON 'Firm' which for over a century held a near-monopoly of Australian commercial theatre. However, the growth of subsidised theatres from the 1950s, and their encouragement of playwrights, led to a 'new wave' of successful dramatists in the late 1960s, and to a much more representative number of Australian plays in the contemporary theatre.

Early plays The earliest play known to have been written in Australia (or, more accurately, on a homeward sea voyage) is David Burn's *The Bushrangers* (1828), performed in Edinburgh in 1829, and based on the life of the TAS bushranger Matthew BRADY. Another early play was Henry Melville's *The Bushrangers; or, Norwood Vale* (1834-35), reputedly the first play written, published and staged in Australia. Other early plays, such as Evan Henry Thomas' *The Bandit of the Rhine*, staged at LAUNCESTON in 1835, are now lost to us. Relatively few local plays were staged until the 1840s; in NSW the theatre licence granted to Barnett LEVEY in 1832 stipulated that only those plays which had been licensed for performance in London could be performed.

Headquarters of the National Institute of Dramatic Art, University of NSW

Colonial drama From the 1840s onwards a number of plays, written mainly for the Royal Victoria Theatre in Sydney, were licensed by the NSW Colonial Secretary, and copies are retained in the NSW Archives. Only a handful of these are about Australian subjects, largely because of the Colonial Secretary's prejudice against local comment on what was still a penal settlement. Most are verse or prose quasi-tragedies with historical subjects. Notable among them are the convict Edward GEOGHE-

GAN's *The Hibernian Father* (1844), which caused a stir in the Sydney Press because of accusations of plagiarism, and *The Currency Lass; or, My Native Girl* (1843), a celebration in song-and-dance of the lively Australian heroine. *Life in Sydney; or, The Ran Dan Club* (1843), a new settler's view of the high and low spots of Sydney, was submitted anonymously and refused a licence on the grounds that it contained some libellous references. Another play of the period is *Jemmy Green in Australia* (?1845), reputedly by a convict James Tucker, a charming comedy of a settler's introduction to colonial sharp practices.

Pantomime The goldfields theatres staged locally written sketches such as *The Stage-struck Digger*, performed at BALLARAT in 1854; these survive only in playbills and reviews. But the new spirit of prosperity caused by the gold rush was also reflected in pantomimes such as *The House that Jack Built; or, The Loves, Laughs, Laments and Labours of Jack Melbourne and Little Victoria* (1869), which celebrated Melbourne's and Sydney's 'arrival' as centres of affluence and respectability. Pantomimes with local references were written till well after the turn of the century, and managed to get away with satirical, even libellous, material which would not have been tolerated in other forms of theatre. An exception was Marcus Clarke's adaptation *The Happy Land*, which was withdrawn from the Melbourne Academy of Music in 1880 when the Chief Secretary threatened withdrawal of the theatre's licence.

Melodrama From the 1870s onwards melodramas were written on Australian themes, favourite subjects being convicts, emigration, the gold rush and bushranging. *The Sunny South* (1883) by George DARRELL is concerned with the adventures of an English aristocrat who repairs his family fortunes on the goldfields, in spite of the perils of bushranging and other colonial skulduggery. Alfred DAMPIER also staged Australian melodramas, the most famous being his adaptation of Rolf BOLDREWOOD's novel *Robbery Under Arms* in 1890. After 1900 Bland Holt and William Anderson produced melodramas which depicted the hardships and homely virtue of life 'on the land', among them *The Breaking of the Drought* (1902), *The Squatter's Daughter* (1907), and the stage version of Steele RUDD's *On Our Selection* in 1912. Melodramas in this tradition were written until the 1920s, and the Dad and Dave characters survived in film and radio productions for several decades longer.

The 'little theatre' movement Early this century a 'little theatre' movement emerged, devoted to encouraging serious Australian drama. Leon Brodzky's Australian Theatre Society was founded in 1904, and William Moore held annual Drama Nights at the Turn Verein Hall in East Melbourne from 1910 to 1912, at which the earliest works of Louis ESSON, regarded as Australia's first serious dramatist, were performed. Gregan McMAHON's Melbourne Repertory Theatre produced Esson's first full-length play, a political comedy entitled *The Time is Not Yet Ripe*, in

1912. But the first co-ordinated movement to develop an Australian drama came from Esson's own group, the Pioneer Players.

Esson and his literary friends, Vance and Nettie PALMER and Stewart Macky, founded the Pioneer Players in 1922 to perform plays which would explore Australian 'life and problems', and which would foster and enrich a national consciousness. The Players were led by the actor George Dawe, their first production being Esson's *The Battler* (also entitled *Diggers' Rest*). The group presented works by such playwrights as Esson, Macky, Palmer and Furnley MAURICE before disbanding in 1924 through lack of funds, although it re-formed briefly in 1926 to present Esson's *The Bride of Gospel Place*.

The Pioneer Players illustrated the difficulties the little theatres had in presenting Australian plays from the 1920s to the 1950s. In contrast to the glossy productions of overseas comedy and musical successes by the commercial theatres, they were presenting untried works by little known authors in converted halls, with semi-trained actors and low budgets. However, small theatres, such as May Hollinworth's Metropolitan Theatre, Carrie Tennant's Community Playhouse, the Independent Theatre in Sydney, St Martin's (the Little Theatre) in Melbourne, and the New Theatre branches, staged works by playwrights such as Oriel Gray, Mona Brand, George Landen Dann and Betty Roland, and kept Australia drama alive between the wars.

Many of the plays, in particular Betty Roland's *The Touch of Silk* (1928) and Henrietta Drake-Brockman's *Men Without Wives* (1938), depicted the harsh life of the Outback and the tensions placed on personal relationships through drought and isolation. Katharine Susannah PRICHARD's *Brumby Innes* (1927) dramatised the relationship between white men and black women in the Outback, perhaps too outspokenly for its time (it was not staged until 1972). *Rusty Bugles* by Sumner Locke-Elliott, a comedy-drama about soldiers stationed at a remote ordnance depot in the NT during the war, was produced at the Independent Theatre in 1948 and gained publicity when the police objected to some of its lively colloquialisms. Douglas STEWART's *Ned Kelly*, staged at the Union Theatre, Melbourne in 1947, is a powerful verse drama about the famous Australian bushranger. In spite of the number of plays written and performed, Australian playwrights were still not widely known outside the little theatres and the medium of radio at this time.

'The Doll' and its successors Not until the formation of the Elizabethan Theatre Trust in 1954 was the need to encourage Australian drama through subsidy accepted. The Trust Players toured a number of Australian plays in the 1950s, including a revival of *Ned Kelly* in 1956, with the expatriate Leo McKern in the title role. The most notable success was *Summer of the Seventeenth Doll*, first staged at the Union Theatre, Melbourne in 1955, and later taken by the Trust around Australia and to London and New York. *The Doll* is a realis-

Scene from 'Summer of the Seventeenth Doll' staged by the Melbourne Theatre Company

tic and well-made play showing the decline of a long-standing relationship between two QLD cane-cutters and the Melbourne girls with whom they spend the annual 'lay-off'. The familiarity of its characters, setting and colourful idiom had immediate impact, but the play has lasting appeal as a poignant study of physically active and uncomplicated people who cannot adjust to growing older. (Its author, Ray Lawler, has recently completed a trilogy which was staged by the Melbourne Theatre Company in 1977 and shows the relationship in earlier and happier years.) *The Doll* was followed by a number of plays showing facets of Australian working-class life and exploiting the raciness of Australian speech. The best-known of them are Richard Beynon's *The Shifting Heart* (1957), a drama about an Italian immigrant family in Melbourne, Peter Kenna's *The Slaughter of St Teresa's Day* (1959), set in the Sydney underworld, and Alan Seymour's *The One Day of the Year* (1960), showing the generation gap and class tensions in an ex-serviceman's family over the celebration of Anzac Day.

The most important playwright of the 1960s was Patrick WHITE; four of his plays were staged between 1961 and 1964—*The Ham Funeral* (1961), *The Season at Sarsaparilla* (1962), *A Cheery Soul* (1963) and *Night on Bald Mountain* (1964). They were a landmark in Australian drama in their use of anti-realistic theatrical devices such as split sets and heightened language—a marked contrast to the rather grim realism of most drama since Esson. A number of plays of the 1960s were written by novelists, poets and painters who turned to the theatre in the new climate of interest in Australian plays: Hal PORTER's *Eden House* (1969), Rodney Milgate's *A Refined Look at Existence* (1966), Dorothy Hewett's *This Old Man Comes Rolling Home* (1968), Thomas KENEALLY's *Halloran's Little Boat* and *Childermas* (both 1968). Several of these were staged by the Old Tote Theatre Company in

Sydney, in its seasons of Australian plays, or in the small Jane Street Theatre, also in Sydney, which was set up to try out new plays and had a striking success in 1969 with *The Legend of King O'Malley*, scripted from workshop improvisation by Michael Boddy and Bob Ellis. This vaudeville-style documentary about the politician O'MALLEY was toured around Australia, and helped to generate a renewed interest in fostering Australian drama.

The 'alternative' theatres A 'new wave' in drama began in the late 1960s with the small La Mama Theatre in Melbourne, which gave workshop production to new plays. The Australian Performing Group, based at the Pram Factory in Melbourne, and the Nimrod Theatre, in Sydney, also fostered a number of new playwrights, the Pram Factory in particular having its own 'stable' of writers who collaborated with actors in group-devised shows such as *Marvellous Melbourne* (1970), a knockabout vaudeville history of Melbourne in the 1890s. Other plays with historical subjects and broad music-hall treatment were staged at the Pram Factory and the Nimrod Theatre, including Ron Blair's *Flash Jim Vaux* (1971) and Barry Oakley's *The Feet of Daniel Mannix* (1971).

Recent playwrights Perhaps the best known of the recent playwrights is David WILLIAMSON, an astute and amusing observer of Australian social behaviour, particularly in close-knit domestic or work situations. Alex BUZO also uses the comedy of manners in confined social groups, while Jim McNeil depicts the claustrophobic world of prison with similar precise observation and insight in plays such as *The Old Familiar Juice* (1972) and *How Does Your Garden Grow* (1974).

Scene from 'On Our Selection' staged by the Fortune Theatre Company at the Playhouse in Canberra

Other playwrights have used a more rumbustious cartoon style reminiscent of vaudeville to develop historical themes and explore Australian myths. Jack HIBBERD writes of folk heroes such as Nellie MELBA and Les DARCY; his best-known play is the wedding play *Dimboola* (1969), where the people in the audience become the 'guests'. John Romeril in *The Floating World* (1974) and Dorothy Hewett in such plays as *The Chapel Perilous* (1971) and *The Tatty Hollow Story* (1974) also make use of larger-than-life cartoon-style figures, songs, and broad theatrical effects to explore their characters' states of mind. The more recent playwrights, such as Louis Nowra, David Allen, Mil Perrin, Tim

Gooding, Steve J. Spears (*The Elocution of Benjamin Franklin*) and Stephen Sewell seem to be working more in this flamboyant style than in the social realism of earlier writers, and are also less concerned with obviously Australian themes. If the playwrights of the 1950s and 1960s could be said to be exploring facets of Australian society and character, it seems that the preoccupations of contemporary playwrights are wider and less localised.

Encouragement of playwrights At the Australian National Playwrights Conference, held each year in Canberra, at least six new scripts submitted for consideration are workshopped, and several of these have gone on to professional production. The Literature Board of the AUSTRALIA COUNCIL has awarded grants to established playwrights, and theatre companies have commissioned new scripts.
Further reading: Kippax, H.G. 'Drama' in Davies, A.F. & Encel, S. (eds) *Australian Society*. Cheshire, Melbourne, 1970; Brisbane, K. 'Australian drama' in Dutton, G. (ed) *The Literature of Australia*. Penguin Books, Melbourne, 1976; Rees, L. *A History of Australian Drama*. (2 vols) Angus & Robertson, Sydney, 1978; Palmer, J. (ed) *Contemporary Australian Playwrights*. Adelaide University Union Press, Adelaide, 1979; Fitzpatrick, P. *After 'The Doll'*. Edward Arnold, Melbourne, 1979; Irvin, E. *Australian Melodrama*. Hale & Iremonger, Sydney, 1981.

dream time Also called the dreaming, this refers to an Aboriginal mythical time during which the Aborigines' ancestors were active and establishing the world as the Aborigines know it today. Every Aboriginal should have a dream time; without it his life has no meaning, for the social and spiritual meaning of his existence is inextricably tied to his ancestral past. This past can be re-enacted by sacred ceremonies but in a sense the re-enactment is itself a part of the dream time, and is indicative of the rich spiritual life of the Aborigines. Dream time is symbolised for the Aborigines by their TJURINGAS.
Further reading: Elkin, A.P. *The Australian Aborigines*. (4th edn) Angus & Robertson, Sydney, 1974.

Dreyfus, George (1928-) Composer. Dreyfus has emerged as one of the most consistent and active of the generation of composers who chose to pursue careers almost entirely within Australia. He was born in Wuppertal, Germany, and arrived in Australia in 1939 when his family was forced to migrate from Europe. His style owes certain qualities, such as its unfailing craftsmanship, to aspects of Austro-Germanic tradition, but his music has an overriding clarity and wit which is his very own. Perhaps his early years as a bassoonist with the Melbourne Symphony Orchestra helped develop his agile compositions for wind instruments, prominent in his recent *Symphonie Concertante* and in many of his earlier works.

Dreyfus is a composer who defies any attempts at categorisation. His works cover a wide spectrum of vocal and instrumental forces (he has even written a *Sextet* for DIDJERIDU and wind instruments). As well as his two symphonies and his orchestral, chamber, vocal and choral works, he has written operas, of which *Garni Sands*, performed by the University of New South Wales Opera in 1972 under the musical direction of the composer, was the first full-length Australian opera to be performed in the country for more than half a century. It has since been performed in New York, again under the composer's direction. Dreyfus has also a long list of film scores to his credit and in recent years has reached a very wide Australian audience through his highly successful music for the acclaimed television series 'Rush' and 'Power Without Glory'.
Further reading: Covell, R. *Australia's Music: Themes of a New Society*. Sun Books, Melbourne, 1967; Dobson, E. 'George Dreyfus' in Callaway, F. & Tunley, D. (eds) *Australian Composition in the Twentieth Century*. Oxford University Press, Melbourne, 1978.

drongo The spangled drongo, *Dicrurus bracteatus**** (28cm to 30cm long), is the only Australian representative of the family Dicruridae, a group of strongly territorial PASSERINE BIRDS with distinctive fishtail-shaped tails, robust bills and bristles on the mouth. Found in forests and mangroves in coastal N and E Australia (common in the N but rare in the S), the spangled drongo has a shiny black plumage, with iridescent blue-green spots on the head, neck and breast. It feeds on insects, often caught on the wing, and builds saucer-shaped nests of tendrils and fibre on slender horizontal branches; the eggs are pale pink, with red and purple spots.
See also birds

droughts *see* weather and climate

Drouin VIC (population 3 492 in 1981) A country town on the Princes Highway and on the railway route through GIPPSLAND, 92km by rail ESE of Melbourne, it is located 7km along the highway W of WARRAGUL and is a service centre for a rich dairying and farming district. The town has a large milk processing factory, timber mills, engineering works and a weaving mill. Originally called Whisky Creek, the name Drouin probably came from an Aboriginal word meaning 'north wind'.

drug plants *see* Compositae; Solanaceae; Umbelliferae

drummers *see* fishes, bony

drum sticks *see* Proteaceae

dry sclerophyll forest *see* vegetation

Drysdale River WA It rises near MOUNT HANN in the KIMBERLEYS region and flows generally N for over 400km to a swampy,

mangrove-fringed estuary on the E side of Napier-Broome Bay on the far N coast of the State. The rainfall pattern over the whole river basin is one of a wet summer season followed by a markedly dry cooler period, so that the river floods in the rainy months and flows only intermittently in the dry season. The Drysdale River Mission Station, established by the Catholic Church to work among the Aborigines, is located W of the river near the S section of the bay. The Drysdale River National Park covers 435 591ha of rugged country, much of it inaccessible, in the middle section of the valley.

Drysdale, Sir (George) Russell (1912-81) Artist. Born in Sussex, England, Drysdale settled in VIC on a grazing property with his parents in 1924. Although he had intended to farm, he was redirected by the intervention of Sir Daryl Lindsay, who, on being shown Drysdale's drawings, urged him to study art seriously. Between 1931 and 1939 he attended the school run by George BELL and Arthur SHORE in Melbourne, the Grosvenor School in London and La Grande Chaumiere in Paris. An eye defect made it impossible for him to serve in the armed forces during World War II, while his dislike of the art squabbles in Melbourne led him to move to Sydney, where he settled in 1940. It was here, between 1944 and 1960, that his work began to assert its own personal characteristics. His illustrations for the *Sydney Morning Herald's* coverage of the 1944 drought gave him the opportunity to express his own vision. In complete contrast to the followers of STREETON and HEYSEN, who depicted Australia as a tranquil arcadia of rolling grazing properties and stands of gum trees in impressive settings, Drysdale painted the 'other' Australia—the land of drought, burnt trees, marginal farming land, heat, isolation and the stoic acceptance of this environment by its human inhabitants. The rich colours, the theatrical placement of the elements of each scene, the obvious concern for traditional painting and drawing skills, and the ominous silence that permeates his Outback scenes were all factors that appealed to Australians very strongly. Drysdale later worked in N and central Australia, where he rediscovered the Aborigines as a subject for painting, portraying them with sympathy and lonely dignity—not since Oscar Tristrom (1856-1918) had depicted the QLD Aborigines had these people been shown such respect by a painter.

Dubbo NSW (population 23 986 in 1981) A city on the E bank of the MACQUARIE RIVER, it is 419km NW by road from Sydney at the junction of the Mitchell and Newell Highways. It is an important railway focus (462km by rail from Sydney) connected by two lines S to ORANGE, a line N to COONAMBLE, a line NE to COONABARABRAN and Gwabegar, and a line W to Narromine and thence on to NYNGAN, COBAR and BOURKE. At an elevation of 264m above sea level, it is in a region where the W

*Species, genus or family is endemic to Australia (see Preface)

Wheatfields between Dubbo and Narromine

slopes of the GREAT DIVIDING RANGE merge into the W plains region of the State. The name Dubbo comes from an Aboriginal word meaning 'a cap' or 'head covering'. Founded as a town in 1849, it became a municipality in 1872 and was proclaimed a city in 1966. The climate is typical of inland towns, with hot summer days, warm sunny winter days and crisply cool evenings in the winter months. The average annual rainfall is 584mm, fairly evenly distributed throughout the year, but liable to vary from year to year, with dry spells not uncommon. In wet seasons the Macquarie River may flood, inundating the farmlands on the adjoining river flats. The city serves as the business and commercial centre for a productive rural region, with wheat and wool growing, fat lamb and cattle raising, and fruit and vegetable growing on the alluvial flats. The Dubbo stock markets, 4km N of the city, are second-largest in the State, after Sydney's Homebush saleyards. There are numerous secondary industries in the city—a textile mill, engineering works, a flour mill, brick and fibrous plaster works, an abattoir, sawmills, a stock feed plant, an airline engineering workshop, and factories for concrete pipes and blocks.

Dubbo is also the regional centre for many wholesale distributors, a major depot for bulk supplies of petrol and oil, the divisional headquarters of some government agencies and an extensive RAAF depot. The city takes pride in its War Memorial Civic Hall, its Victoria Park (18ha) which has a wide variety of sporting facilities, and its Pioneer Museum. The Old Dubbo Gaol, officially opened in 1974 for visitors, and the Western Plains Zoo, 5km SW of the city, are popular tourist attractions. The National Trust (NSW) has listed many buildings in Dubbo and classified others (the courthouse and the land board office) to be preserved as part of the cultural heritage of the nation.

Duboisia see Solanaceae

Duchess QLD A small mining centre in the NW of the State, located in the Selwyn Range, it is about 100km SSE of MOUNT ISA and 127km by road SW of CLONCURRY. It is on the rail line from TOWNSVILLE to Mt Isa. Copper is mined in the area, but more recently phosphate mining has become important.

duck-billed platypus see monotreme mammals

ducks, geese and swans These familiar, web-footed water birds belong to the family Anatidae; most have large bills, stout bodies and long necks, and many are important game birds. The Australian fauna is small but unusual, and of the 23 species represented two are introduced. A few of these species eat water animals, but most are vegetarian and either wet feeders, gathering their food under water, or dry feeders which feed on land. The breeding of waterfowl depends upon water and rainfall. In the S, breeding is in late winter or spring; in the N it is in late summer and autumn; and in the dry interior, breeding is erratic, occurring after a rise in water levels. Waterfowl often move in great numbers, particularly to drought refuges on the coasts, but true migration is doubtful. Many species are highly nomadic.

The family Anatidae is divided into three sections: the first contains the unique pied or magpie goose, the second comprises swans, true geese and tree or whistle ducks, and the third group contains typical ducks.

The pied goose, *Anseranas* * *semipalmata* (75cm long), is a black and white, goose-shaped bird with partly webbed feet and a distinctive bony knob on the head. It frequents the swamps, lakes and rivers of N Australia, but its numbers are declining. These birds have been known to lay as many as 14 eggs; their nests, flat and sometimes bulky structures of swamp vegetation, are placed among reeds in shallow water.

The waterfowl in the second group are characterised by the similarity of the male and female plumage. The Cape Barren goose, *Cereopsis* * *novaehollandiae* (1m), and the freckled duck, *Sticonetta* * *naevosa* (56cm), are unique species which are usually included in this group. The former is a grey and black bird which resembles true geese in its habit of feeding, in flocks, on pastures. It is restricted to coastal islands and some parts of the mainland coasts in the S (some have been introduced into New Zealand), and rarely takes to water. The world population of these birds is small, but may be increasing. Their large, flat nests of grass and plants are placed on the ground. The freckled duck is an uncommon and unique bird which has a typical duck shape; the plumage is dark, speckled with white. Found in the freshwater swamps of the S, these birds usually conceal their shallow, cup-shaped nests of sticks and twigs in herbage growing in or near water.

The black swan, *Cygnus atratus* * (body 60cm; head and neck 45cm), a widespread species in WA and E Australia which breeds freely in gardens and parks, favours small islands of reeds as sites for its large, open nests of twigs and water plants. The similarly sized white mute swan, *C. olor*, an introduced species, is confined largely to ornamental waters.

There are two species of the pan-tropical whistle ducks in Australia: the widespread grass whistle duck, *Dendrocygna eytoni* * (43cm), and the water whistle duck, *D. arcuata* (46cm), found mainly in the N. These birds have short, stumpy bodies, long necks and legs, an upright stance, and plumes on the flanks; the plumage is brown above and reddish-yellow below, and the face and neck are buff-brown. Both species lay eggs in a slight hollow in the ground, lined with dry grass.

The common feature of the typical ducks which comprise the third group is that the males and females differ in appearance, though when the males go into 'eclipse' each year they closely resemble the females. However, in the case of two species in this group—the mountain shelduck, *Tadorna tadornoides* * (60cm), and the Burdekin shelduck, *T. radjah* (50cm)—there are only minor sex differences. Predominantly brown, the mountain shelduck has white, green and chestnut patches on its wings and a white collar at the base of the neck. Found in coastal areas in W and southern Australia, this shy bird is generally seen far from the shoreline of shallow swamps and lakes; like the Burdekin shelduck, it lays white eggs in a hole in a tree. The Burdekin shelduck, which frequents suitable habitats in N Australia, is mostly white, with brown and white wings and a brown crescent on the breast.

Most of the typical dabbling 'up-ending' ducks belong to the widespread genus *Anas*. The very common black duck, *A. superciliosa* (50cm), is found throughout the continent; its plumage is mottled brown, with white and black streaks on the face. The nests are built either near water, in reeds or grass, or some distance away from water in a field or the hollow stump of a tree. The black duck commonly interbreeds with the introduced European mallard, *A. platyrhynchos* (56cm), a familiar bird in town parks; the drake has a glossy black and purple head, a white collar and a greyish body, while the female is browner.

The four other *Anas* species found in Australia are: the widespread grey teal, *A. gibberifrons* (40cm); the chestnut teal, *A. castanea* * (43cm), a green-headed species found mostly in the S half of the continent; the shoveler, *A. rhynchotis* (51cm), which frequents most suitable areas of Australia except the far N; and the garganey, *A. querquedula* (38cm), a rare non-breeding visitor. The teals are often seen in each other's company, and both species nest near water in the hollow of a tree, in tall grass or on the ground. The shoveler, a very wary bird which makes a strange humming noise with its wings when flushed, has a long beak, expanded at the tip; the drake is mainly blackish-brown with a blue-grey face and neck. These birds usually nest near water in a grass-lined hollow in the ground. The male garganey has a sharply contrasting brown breast and white belly and dark brown plumage on the face and neck. The northern shoveler, *A. clypeata*, has been recorded only once.

Black swan, *Cygnus atratus*

The unique pink-eared duck, *Malacorhynchus* * *membranaceus* (40cm), is a very common species which may be recognised by the pink patch behind the eye. This extremely nomadic and widespread bird sifts micro-organisms and plankton from the water with the aid of hairlike fringes on the bill. It nests in bushes or holes in trees.

A widespread species whose numbers are apparently declining is the white-eyed duck, *Aythya australis* * (51cm), a shy, stout-bodied, mainly brown, diving bird usually seen on wide stretches of fresh water. The male is dark reddish-brown above and has a white ring around the eye; the colouring of the female is paler.

There are several species of perching ducks in Australia, all of which lay white eggs in tree nests. The wood duck or maned goose, *Chenonetta* * *jubata* (48cm), found throughout Australia, is mainly brownish-grey with a brown head and a mane-like extension of the neck feathers. It feeds terrestrially on green plants and is one of the few ducks to have benefited from agriculture. The goose-shaped green pygmy goose, *Nettapus pulchellus* (33cm), of NW and NE Australia, is a dark glossy-green bird with a white face patch. It is a diving bird which lives in large, permanent tropical lakes and lagoons with thick vegetation. It is similar in shape to the white pygmy goose, *N. coromandelianus* (35cm), also known as the white-headed cotton teal; the male is glossy green above and white below, with a distinctive green band around the base of the neck, while the female is mostly dark brown above. This species does not dive, but has a curious jerking movement of the head and neck.

Black duck, *Anas superciliosa*, a common species in city parks

A common diving species which frequents the well-vegetated rivers and permanent lakes of inland SW and SE Australia is the bluebilled duck, *Oxyura australis* * (40cm). It is a stiff-tailed bird, and the male has a blue beak and mainly chestnut plumage while the female is dull grey-brown. The nests are bulky, cupshaped structures made of reeds and quillfeathers.

The musk duck, *Biziura* * *lobata* (male 65cm; female 56cm), is also a stiff-tailed diving species. Found throughout Australia in permanent waters, swamps and estuaries, musk ducks have a blackish-brown plumage; the male has a conspicuous lobe beneath the bill and, when breeding, emits a musky odour. Their bulky, cup-shaped nests are built among reeds.

Further reading: Frith, H.J. *Wildlife Conservation*. Angus & Robertson, Sydney, 1973 and *Waterfowl in Australia*. (2nd edn) Reed, Sydney, 1977.

Duffy, Sir Charles Gavan (1816-1903)

Irish patriot and Premier of VIC. Born in Monaghan, Ireland, he became deeply involved in the Irish nationalist movement, founded the weekly journal *Nation*, and in 1848 was tried for treason but acquitted. In 1852 he was elected to the House of Commons, but became disillusioned by the lack of unity among its Irish members and after three years

resigned and emigrated to Melbourne.

Elected to the VIC Legislative Assembly in 1856, he remained a member, except for a few years' absence abroad, until his retirement in 1880. He was a member of Cabinet in each of John O'SHANASSY's three Ministries, Premier from June 1871 to June 1872 and Speaker during his last three years in Parliament. The legislation he introduced included the Act of 1856 abolishing property qualifications for Members of the Legislative Assembly, and the Land Act of 1862, which was designed to promote closer settlement by enabling farmers to select land from pastoral leases, but, like similar measures in VIC and elsewhere, was not very effective.

Several members of his family were also prominent in public affairs. Of his sons the eldest, John Gavan Duffy, held a number of Cabinet posts in the VIC governments between 1880 and 1899; Sir Frank Gavan Duffy was Chief Justice of Australia from 1930 to 1936; and Charles Gavan Duffy was Clerk of the House of Representatives from 1901 to 1917 and Clerk of the Senate from 1917 to 1920. His grandson, Sir Charles Gavan Duffy, was a Justice of the Supreme Court of VIC from 1933 to 1961.

dugite *see* snakes

dugong *see* sea cows

Dumaresq River

A tributary of the BARWON-DARLING system, the Dumaresq rises just N of the NSW/QLD border in the hilly granite country adjacent to STANTHORPE, which is about 800m above sea level and receives an annual rainfall of over 750mm. The Dumaresq flows inland from the GREAT DIVIDING RANGE, forms the State border for 130km and then joins the MACINTYRE RIVER, which changes its name further downstream to the Barwon. The river was named in 1827 by the explorer Allan CUNNINGHAM after the Dumaresq family, pioneer settlers in NEW ENGLAND.

Tobacco harvesting in the Dumaresq valley along the QLD/NSW border

Dumbleyung

WA (population 274 in 1981) A small inland township, it is located 267km SE of Perth, 40km E of WAGIN off the Great Southern Highway and 53km NE of KATANNING. The surrounding rural region is dominated by wheat farming. In 1964, Dumbleyung made world headlines when Sir Donald Campbell broke the world water-speed record on Lake Dumbleyung. The town name comes from the corruption of the Aboriginal name for the lake.

dun see mayflies, etc.

dunes see vegetation

Dungog NSW (population 2 126 in 1981) This country town is situated on the Williams River, a tributary of the HUNTER RIVER, 270km NNE of Sydney and some 70km by road N of NEWCASTLE. It is a service centre to a productive rural hinterland where dairying, beef cattle grazing and timber-getting are the main activities. At an elevation of 61m above sea level, it has an average annual rainfall of 1 020mm, concentrated mainly in the summer months. The name Dungog comes from an Aboriginal word meaning 'clear hills'.

Dunk Island QLD A granitic coral-fringed island made famous by the author Edward BANFIELD who settled there at the turn of the century and whose works, such as *The Confessions of a Beachcomber* (1908), depict the natural history of the island. Although it has become a modern tourist resort, it retains much of the tranquility and romance he knew. It is located off the NE coast of the State, E of Tully, and N of HINCHINBROOK ISLAND in the waterway between the GREAT BARRIER REEF and the mainland coast. It can be reached by launch from Clump Point (NE of Tully) or by plane from TOWNSVILLE.

dunnart see native cats, etc.

Dunstan, Sir Albert Arthur (1882-1950) Premier of VIC. Born in the WIMMERA district of VIC he worked as a farmer in both QLD and VIC before being elected to the VIC Legislative Assembly in 1920. As a member of the newly formed Country Party of Australia, he argued against the policy of automatically supporting the Nationalists, and proposed that support be given to, or accepted from, whichever of the two main parties was the more willing to give concessions in line with Country Party objectives. He joined Sir Stanley Argyle's Cabinet in 1932, became leader of the Country Party in the following year, and in 1935 formed the State's first Country Party government, with Labor support. He remained Premier until Labor withdrew its support in September 1943, but after a Labor Ministry had been in office for a mere five days he became Premier once more, this time at the head of a Country/United Australia Party coalition. In 1945 he lost office and resigned from the leadership of his party, but later served as Minister for Health in T.T. Hollway's coalition government.

Dunstan, Donald Allan (1926-) Premier of SA. Born in Fiji, of Australian parents, Dunstan was educated at St Peter's College, Adelaide, and the University of Adelaide. After graduating with a bachelor's

Donald Dunstan in 1974
Premier's Dept SA

degree in law, he practised as a solicitor, and entered politics in 1953 when he stood successfully as Labor candidate for the seat of Norwood in the House of Assembly. He was Attorney-General and Minister for Aboriginal Affairs and Social Welfare from 1965 to 1967, and then succeeded to the leadership of the Labor Party and became Premier, Attorney-General and Minister for Housing. After the Labor defeat in 1968 he was Leader of the Opposition until 1970, when Labor won the elections and Dunstan became Premier and Minister for Development and Mines.

In this position, he continued the policies of industrial development carried on for many years by Sir Thomas PLAYFORD, and introduced legislation for a wide range of reforms in such areas as consumer protection, legal aid, Aboriginal welfare and the controversial field of abortion laws. His personal style, polished but in some respects unconventional, helped to maintain his popularity, and he succeeded in keeping Labor in office in SA at a time when support for it in the federal sphere had declined sharply. However, in 1979 his health deteriorated rapidly, and in April that year he resigned from Parliament, being succeeded by J.D. Corcoran.

Durack family A family of Irish origin, its members opened up large areas of cattle country in western QLD and the KIMBERLEYS of WA. John ('Darby') Durack reached Australia about 1849 and settled near GOULBURN. His brother Patrick died soon after coming to Australia in 1853, but two of the latter's sons, Patrick and Michael, later established Thylungra cattle station on COOPER'S CREEK in western QLD and other members of the family followed them there. In 1883 several of the Duracks and their relatives took thousands of cattle from Thylungra and nearby properties and made an epic overland journey to the ORD RIVER in the Kimberleys, which they reached in 1885. Mary Durack (Mrs H.C. Miller, *b*1913) has given a vivid account of the family's achievements and adventures in her book *Kings in Grass Castles* (1959).

Durack, Fanny (1889–1956) Swimmer. Born in Sydney and teaching herself to swim at Wylie's Baths, near Coogee NSW, Fanny Durack was to become the first Australian woman to win an Olympic gold medal. She won the gold medal in the 100m freestyle event at the 1912 Stockholm Olympic Games, the first Olympic Games in which women were allowed to compete; Mina Wylie with whom Fanny Durack had trained, won the silver medal in the same event. Fanny Durack went on to break 11 world records and at one stage of her career she held every women's freestyle record. Had women's swimming events been held in Games prior to 1912, she would undoubtedly have won more medals, but by 1912 she was already 20 years old and, by swimming standards, past her peak.

Durack River WA Located in the KIMBERLEYS in the far N of the State, it rises in the rugged central plateau and flows for some 240km, partly through deep sandstone gorges, first N then NE to a swampy mangrove-fringed estuary on the W arm of Cambridge Gulf, near WYNDHAM. Because the climate of the basin is distinctly seasonal, with wet summer months and a markedly dry winter period, the river flow varies considerably throughout the year; floods are a regular feature of the rainy season and intermittent flow is characteristic of the dry period. Cattle grazing on large properties is the dominant rural activity of the region. The river is named after the DURACK FAMILY, one of the pioneer grazing families.

Dutch in Australia The 1981 census revealed that 96 044 persons resident in Australia had been born in the Netherlands. C.A. Price, a leading authority on multicultural affairs, in a study of the ethnic origins of the Australian population based on an eight-generation analysis, estimated the total Dutch component to be equivalent to 219 000 persons in 1978.
Dutch influence in Australia The discovery of Australia by Dutch navigators in the 17th century (*see* DISCOVERY) explains why so many places on the Australian coastline carry Dutch names, and why the whole continent was named NEW HOLLAND, a name which dropped out of use only after British settlement began. The Dutch made no attempt to colonise New Holland themselves. Indeed, at the time of federation there were only 594 Dutch-born people in Australia and this number had increased to only 2 174 by 1947. The majority of the Dutch settlers have arrived from the Netherlands since the end of World War II and from Indonesia since 1949, when that country gained independence.
Contributions of Dutch settlers The Dutch have built up a reputation for hard work, efficiency and economic independence. Some have established their own businesses and others have found employment in skilled trades, particularly in the building and printing industries. People of Dutch ancestry coming from Indonesia included servicemen, traders and administrators.
Pattern of settlement Although the general

impression is that the Dutch have become integrated into Australian society to a greater degree than most ethnic groups, and that they are reasonably dispersed throughout the community, small Dutch communities have developed which are usually based on regional origins or on similar religious persuasion. The best-known groups in VIC live at MOE and on the outskirts of Melbourne in Ferntree Gully and Springvale. In NSW they are found at BOWRAL and MOSS VALE and on the outskirts of Sydney at Dural, Hornsby Heights, WINDSOR, Bankstown and in the Sutherland Shire area.

Dutch heritage Windmills, clogs and tulips are symbolic of links with the Netherlands and Dutch families sometimes erect model windmills in their gardens and have plants growing in clogs. Tulip Festivals are held annually at Bowral. The Dutch community is one of only two large ethnic groups in Australia who do not hold after-school or weekend language classes for their children to teach them their native language and cultural background. While they are prepared to accept the English language for means of communication they retain links with their national heritage in cultural societies such as the Dutch Folk Dance Group which performs in Sydney and in some large provincial centres. They also organise social clubs, clubs for playing klavergas (a Dutch card game), societies for Dutch pensioners, Dutch soccer clubs, Dutch credit co-operatives and Dutch benevolent organisations. The Boomerang Club and Jokers Club are organisations which hold carnival-type functions similar to those held traditionally in the Netherlands. Members of the Dutch community have also founded a 'retirement village', Juliana Village, at Miranda in the Sutherland Shire of Sydney. A bilingual newspaper, the *Dutch-Australian*, has been published weekly since 1951.

Notable Dutchmen in Australia Men and women of Dutch descent who have contributed to development in Australia include: Dr Rudy de Iongh, born in Indonesia of Dutch parents, now senior lecturer in Indonesian at the University of Sydney; William Lodewyk Browther, Premier of TAS in 1878; Jessie Catherin Couvreur, novelist; and Henry Benedictus van Raalte, painter and etcher who founded the School of Art in Perth.
Further reading: Price, C.A. *Australian Immigration, A Bibliography and Digest*. Australian National University Press, Canberra, 1981.

Dutton, Geoffrey Piers Henry (1922-) Author and literary critic. Born in KAPUNDA in SA, he graduated BA from Magdalen College, Oxford, attained the rank of flight lieutenant in the Royal Australian Air Force in World War II, and has since then established himself as one of the most versatile of contemporary Australian writers. His published works include the novel, *Andy* (1968); the anthologies *Night Flight and Sunrise* (1944), *Poems Soft and Loud* (1967), *Findings and Keepings: Selected Poems, 1939-69* (1970) and *A Body of Words* (1978); and biographies

of William LIGHT, Edward John EYRE and Ernest GILES, entitled respectively *Founder of a City* (1960), *The Hero as Murderer* (1967) and *Australia's Last Explorer* (1970). He has also been editor or co-editor of a number of works, including *Australian Writers and Their Work* (1962) and *Australia and the Monarchy* (1966), and has been co-translator of works by the Russian poet Yevtushenko.

Dyson, William Henry (1880-1938) Artist. Born at Alfredton, near BALLARAT in VIC, he attended art classes in MELBOURNE and spent most of his working life as a black and white artist for magazines and newspapers in Adelaide, Melbourne, London and Sydney. During World War I he was appointed an official Australian war artist, much of his best work appeared in *Australia at War* (1918). During the interwar period he held exhibitions in London and New York. His reputation rests mainly on his cartoons, which marked him as the most effective Australian satiric artist of his time. He is represented in the Australian National Gallery, the national galleries of Melbourne and Sydney, and in the Victoria and Albert Museum, London.

E

Eaglehawk Neck TAS But for this narrow isthmus, only a few hundred metres wide, TASMAN PENINSULA would have been an island. Traversed by the Arthur Highway, it is located 95km by road E of Hobart and joins Forestier and Tasman Peninsulas. In the colonial convict days of TAS between 1830 and 1877, when PORT ARTHUR was a penal settlement, the Neck was the site of a military guard and savage hounds were tethered at short intervals across the isthmus. The system proved highly effective for few prisoners ever escaped. The Neck is now a base for game fishing from charter boats. In the nearby district are several unique coastal formations such as the Tesselated Pavement, the Blowhole, Devil's Kitchen and Tasman's Arch.

eagles *see* birds of prey

ear shells *see* gastropods

earthquakes *see* geology

earthworms *see* annelids

earwigs These INSECTS belong to a relatively small exopterygote order, Dermaptera, represented by about 60 species in Australia. Their elongated bodies carry a pair of strong forceps, used for defence and for capturing prey, on the end of the abdomen. The thickened fore-wings (tegmina) are small and

protect the almost semicircular membranous hind-wings. Earwigs can fly but are rarely seen doing so. The mouthparts are of the biting and chewing type. These nocturnal, omnivorous insects lead hidden lives in ground litter, under logs and bark, and so on. When at rest they try to bring their bodies into close contact with their surroundings, a habit which may account for the general belief that they invade the human ear. Mating, in which it possible that the forceps are used, follows a short courtship display by the male. The eggs, which may not be laid for several months after mating, are deposited in a small burrow where the female remains on guard, now and then turning the eggs until they hatch. Later she becomes cannibalistic and the nymphs have to begin to fend for themselves.

All known species in Australia belong to the suborder Forficulina and are contained in five families. The largest family is the Labiduridae, which contains the largest of all earwigs, *Titanolabis colossea* (up to 5.5cm long), found in rainforest and wet sclerophyll bush in E Australia. The cosmopolitan introduced European earwig, *Forficula auricularia*, is the species most often seen in Australia, particularly in and near houses. It is possible, however, that one of the other two suborders, the Arixeniina, also occurs in Australia, for in Malaysia, Indonesia and the Philippines they are parasites of bats, related species of which occur in New Guinea and near Cape York. These parasites are wingless, almost blind, hairy earwigs with rod-like forceps.

Eastern Highlands *see* Great Dividing Range

Eaton WA (population 2 226 in 1981) A town in the coastal section of SWANLAND, it is 170km by road S of Perth and 5km NE of BUNBURY, situated near the mouth of the Collie River where it enters Leschenault Inlet. Though the area was taken up by pioneer settlers in the 1840s, it was not until 1957 that the town was gazetted. It is located in a popular resort region where there has been some urban development in recent years.

Eccles, Sir John Carew (1903-) Neurophysiologist. Born in Australia, Sir John studied at Melbourne University and, as a Rhodes scholar, at Oxford. He worked with Sherington at Oxford, returned to Australia in 1937, and after working there and in New Zealand, shared with Hodgkin and Huxley the Nobel Prize in medicine and physiology in 1963. His best-known work has been on the chemical transmission of nervous impulses, and in particular on the transmission of the impulse across the gaps—the synapses—between successive links in a nervous chain. He left Australia in 1966 to work at the Institute for Biomedical Research in Chicago.

echidnas *see* monotreme mammals

echinoderms The Echinodermata is a large, entirely marine phylum of animals containing about 5 300 known species, many of which occur on Australian coasts. The name means 'spiny skinned', and the phylum contains such familiar animals as SEA STARS (starfish), BRITTLE STARS, SEA URCHINS, SEA CUCUMBERS and SEA LILIES AND FEATHER STARS.

Structure The adults are radially symmetrical, usually on a fivefold basis, and in all but the last two groups mentioned above they sit on the sea bed with the mouth downwards and the anus upwards. The lower surface is thus called the oral surface, the upper one, the aboral surface. The larvae, however, are bilaterally symmetrical and their structure has led zoologists to link them with the CHORDATES.

There is an endoskeleton of plates (reduced to spicules in the sea cucumbers) covered by the skin which carries spines and tubercles. The most characteristic feature of the phylum, however, is the water-vascular system which probably first evolved as a method of feeding but now also used for locomotion. If a sea star is watched in an aquarium it will be seen that hundreds of small moving tubes, each equipped with a sucker, protrude from grooves in the lower surfaces of the arms; these link with a system of internal canals within the body, and the canals themselves link with a structure called the stone canal which opens to the surrounding sea water by a small perforated plate—the sieve plate or madreporite—near the anus. The movement of the tube feet is controlled by hydrostatic pressure, and they work in co-ordinated groups to move the animal or to open the shells of bivalves. In addition, they are used in respiration and sensory perception.

Echinoderms have no well-developed circulatory or excretory system, and although there is an alimentary canal, digested foodstuffs are generally distributed by movement through the fluid-filled space which represents most of the inside of the animal.

Reproduction The sexes are separate in the echinoderms. In sexual reproduction numerous eggs are spawned into the water, where they are fertilised by spermatozoa shed by the males. Most echinoderms can reproduce by fission. A starfish torn into two pieces will usually regenerate into two complete animals.

Echuca

Echuca VIC (population 7 946 in 1981) Located on the S bank of the middle MURRAY RIVER at its confluence with the CAMPASPE RIVER, and at the junction of the Northern, Murray Valley and Cobb (NSW) Highways, 208km by road N of Melbourne, 94km NNE of BENDIGO and 72km NW of SHEPPARTON, Echuca is the twin town to the small settlement of Moama on the N side of the Murray in NSW. At an elevation of 96m above sea level, it receives an average annual rainfall of only 436mm, spread throughout the year, but with the highest rainfall in winter (June average, 45mm) and much drier conditions in summer (all three summer months average 29mm each).

Echuca has all the romance and atmosphere of the old riverboat days on the Murray. The town was founded in 1853 by a pioneer settler, Henry Hopwood, and was first known as Hopwood's Ferry. The name Echuca was taken from an Aboriginal word meaning 'the meeting of the waters'. It is the closest point on the Murray to Melbourne and when the railway reached it in 1864 the town became a booming river port; by the 1880s it was one of VIC's biggest ports (second only to Melbourne) for riverboats carrying wool, timber and wheat, but the development of railways into the RIVERINA eclipsed the river trade and the town declined. It experienced a new lease of life when the GOULBURN RIVER irrigation scheme was constructed and it has become a service and commercial centre for a productive hinterland of irrigated farms on the alluvial plains of the Murray Valley. It is also a tourist centre, with cruises along the Murray on the paddle-steamer *Canberra* and houseboats for hire. In 1969, the National Trust (VIC) declared the old port site an historic area; in addition, the Trust has listed numerous structures in the town for preservation, such as the bridge across the Murray, the customs house, the courthouse, the flour mills, the police station, the town hall and the pumping station. An aquatic reserve of 7ha has been established along the river banks and features species of birds and fish indigenous to the area.

Further reading: Blyth, I. *Echuca Sketchbook.* Rigby, Adelaide, 1978.

economic history

economic history Prior to 1788 the Australian natural environment was subjected to only those forms of economic development practised by nomadic hunters and food gatherers. Since that date, however, European settlers have developed the country's enormous resources to produce for themselves one of the highest material standards of living in the world. How wisely this has been done is in some respects a matter of vigorous current debate.

Foundations, 1788-1821 In founding a penal settlement in NSW, the British authorities seem to have given little thought to its long-term economic development. The immediate aim was to make it self-sufficient in food, and for this purpose a mixed system of public and private farming was proposed, the latter being practised mainly by ex-convicts on small properties. Convict labour was to be used on government farms and for constructing public works; as convicts became free they were to be given land, stock and equipment, as well as government rations during their first year of freedom. In fact, few emancipists succeeded in making a living from farming. Just after Governor PHILLIP's departure, however, permission arrived for the granting of land to officers of the NEW SOUTH WALES CORPS and for the assigning of convicts to them as servants. Many officers became farmers, and since they had capital and the opportunity to manipulate the market, they acquired large properties and prospered. This led to the establishment of larger properties and a decline in government farming. By 1804 there were about 600 farmers in the colony, 37 of them (nearly all officers) owning about 40 per cent of the land under cultivation. Several years later government farming was abandoned altogether.

Meanwhile, other colonists had become involved in WHALING and SEALING, and by the early years of the 19th century these industries were bringing in considerable profits, supplying NSW and TAS with their best source of export income until the late 1820s. However, those engaged in these industries had to contend with strong foreign competition and with restrictions imposed by British protectionist policies, and subsequently the depletion of the whale and seal population reduced the importance of the two industries. For a time sandalwood, obtained in the Pacific islands and sold in China, also provided considerable profits, but supplies became seriously depleted by about 1810.

The colony's greatest need was to develop a staple export commodity, and this was finally provided by the SHEEP AND WOOL industry. By 1805 John MACARTHUR had shown that fine wool could be produced profitably even in the coastal area, and when settlement spread into more suitable country beyond the BLUE MOUNTAINS the colony's flocks increased rapidly. However, the wheat industry flourished only in TAS, which by 1819 was exporting half its harvest to the mainland.

The pastoral age, 1821-51 It was in this period that a capitalist economy began to dominate Australian development, the keys to its operation being the industrial revolution in the UK, with its demand for raw materials, and the existence in Australia of vast areas of land eminently suitable for the production of fine wool. Another factor of importance was J.T. BIGGE's report on the colony's progress, which accepted the argument that prosperity could best be secured through the activities of men of capital, using cheap convict and ex-convict labour on large properties.

Wool exports rose from 900 000kg in 1830 to over 18 million kilograms in 1850, by which time Australia had become the UK's main supplier. This expansion was achieved despite an official policy of keeping settlement concentrated. In 1829 Governor DARLING prohibited settlement outside the NINETEEN COUNTIES and in 1831 free land grants were abolished in favour of the sale of Crown lands by auction. But many graziers ignored such regulations, spreading far and wide over the inland (see SQUATTERS), and because the economy depended on the wool they produced, in 1836 they gained the right to occupancy of their land by a system of annual licences, and in 1847 secured long leases, except in settled districts. In the meantime, they had survived the major depression of 1842-45, during which the price of sheep had dropped.

During the pastoral boom free settlers began arriving in unprecedented numbers. Most of them, however, settled in urban areas, working in building and construction and the many industries associated with the wool trade. Thus the trend to urbanisation, stemming from the dependence of the first settlers on government and on sea communications, was strengthened.

During this period three new colonies—WA, SA and the Port Phillip District (later the colony of VIC)—were founded as the result of free enterprise rather than government initiative. The Port Phillip District followed the general line of development described above, except that because it was settled only shortly before the abolition of transportation to E Australia, convict labour played a very small part in its growth. WA failed to prosper until long after the pastoral age. SA was less dependent on wool than NSW, and in the 1840s developed an export trade in wheat; its COPPER mines produced Australia's first important mineral exports. TAS also differed from NSW in that, like SA, it produced a surplus of wheat. Its intake of population was also different in that it received a higher proportion of convicts, especially after the abolition of transportation to the mainland in 1840. During the whole of the pastoral age the island colony received three convicts for each free settler.

The gold rush and the 'long boom', 1851-90 The GOLD rush marked a turning point in Australia's development. By 1861 it had caused a threefold increase in the combined non-Aboriginal population of the colonies (from 437 000 to 1 168 000) and a sevenfold increase in that of VIC, while the wealth which it produced directly is indicated by the output of gold—over 50 million ounces (1 400 000kg) between 1851 and 1871. The gold rush led to a diversification of the economy and an increase in skilled manpower.

Although gold mining had passed its peak before the end of the 1850s, the succeeding three decades were marked by continuing high rates of immigration. Total net immigration was nearly 750 000 and the population again trebled. The economic growth rate was such that the period 1860-90 is often referred to as the 'long boom', during which the increase in population maintained the high demand for goods and services generated by the gold rush, secondary and tertiary industries assumed greater importance than previously, MANUFACTURING increased and the trend towards urbanisation grew. Mining was given fresh impetus by discoveries of gold in QLD and TAS and of SILVER in NSW.

Meanwhile, AGRICULTURE had undergone a technological revolution, based mainly on fencing and water conservation and financed largely by investment capital from Britain. This resulted in more intensive use of the land and in decreased dependence on labour. The numbers of sheep increased from 21 million in 1861 to 80 million in 1880, and wool was reinstated as the country's most important product. The wheat industry continued to expand in SA and VIC, but was slower to develop in NSW, which continued to depend partly on imports until the 1890s. Towards the end of the period, the CHAFFEY BROTHERS launched Australia's first two large irrigation

settlements in VIC and SA.

Government encouragement of economic expansion included extensive railway construction. In NSW this was financed mainly from the sale of Crown lands, but VIC, smaller in area, tried to compensate for the lower revenue from land sales by raising tariffs higher than those of the other colonies. In this she was also motivated by desire to encourage manufacturing, thereby using the skilled labour made surplus by the decline mining. The period was also marked by efforts through legislation to 'unlock the land'— breaking up large properties and giving opportunies for small farmers to become established —but this had very limited success. When closer settlement was achieved, it resulted more from favourable economic conditions than from legislation.

Depression, recovery and war, 1890-1918 Various underlying elements of weakness in the economy during the 1870s and 1880s, such as a general fall in wool prices and a tendency to ill-judged investment, contributed to the depression of the 1890s. The prelude occurred late in 1888, when the Melbourne land boom collapsed, causing unemployment, bankruptcies and a drop in building. In 1890 external factors contributed strongly, a financial crisis in Britain causing a decrease in the supply of investment capital. Public works were curtailed, unemployment soared and by 1891 the country was in the grip of a general depression. In 1893 there was a general banking crisis. Meanwhile, there was a series of major strikes, lasting from 1890 to 1894. Then, as the economy was beginning to recover, primary producers were afflicted by drought between 1895 and 1902. By the latter year the sheep population, which had reached 106 million in 1891, was down to half that figure.

Many factors contributed to recovery from the depression. One was a revival in gold mining, particularly in VIC and NSW. Another was the advent of refrigerated shipping which gave a boost to meat exporters and, with the spread of railways, promoted the DAIRY CATTLE INDUSTRY, which by 1910 became a major export earner. In QLD, Commonwealth protection gave the sugar industry a secure future in spite of the phasing out of KANAKA labour. Most striking of all the developments in the rural sector of the economy, however, was the great expansion of the wheat industry, particularly in NSW and WA. The wool industry was slow in recovering, although by 1914 sheep numbers had reached 90 million and, because of better breeding and the use of mechanical shears, the total clip was well above that in 1891. Overall, by 1914 the rural sector was marked by greater diversity than before, and the growth of non-pastoral rural industries had led to closer settlement. Manufacturing also revived after 1901, under the stimulus of a moderately protectionist Commonwealth tariff.

Further restructuring of the economy took place during World War I. The vast responsibilities undertaken by the Commonwealth government changed the balance of power

between it and the States in its favour—a trend which has continued ever since. The war also led to some expansion of manufacturing and to the local smelting and refining of base metals. Finally, the real beginning of a viable IRON AND STEEL INDUSTRY was made in 1915, when the BROKEN HILL PROPRIETARY COMPANY LIMITED opened its NEWCASTLE works.

The Depression of the early 1930s affected Australia severely, causing a fall of over 25 per cent in the GNP between 1928 and 1932, an increase in unemployment to over 28 per cent of the workforce, many bankruptcies, the selling of their properties by many primary producers and the virtual cessation of immigration. For some time before the Depression various adverse external forces had contributed to weaknesses in the Australian economy. One weakness was over-dependence on exports of wool and wheat, which accounted for about three-quarters of total export income; between 1928 and 1932 world prices of both commodities fell by more than 50 per cent. Another weakness lay in massive government borrowing to finance settlement schemes and public works, and to cover the excess of imports over exports. Although by 1927-28 most States were cutting back on their borrowing, by then it was too late, and in November 1929 crisis point was reached as Australia began to find difficulty in borrowing enough to pay its interest bills and redeem maturing loans. The SCULLIN government had come into office in October on a policy of expanding social services and public works. Its treasurer, Edward THEODORE, favoured inflationary methods of dealing with the Depression, but the government lacked sufficient power over the Commonwealth Bank to go as far as it wanted in this direction, and was further hampered by the Opposition's control of the Senate. Initially, Scullin tried to cope by small economies in government spending and by raising tariffs and taxes. However, as the Depression deepened he agreed to a suggestion from the Bank of England that it send a representative, Sir Otto Niemeyer, to conduct an enquiry into Australia's financial situation. At a Premier's Conference in May-June 1931 he had to agree to the 'Premiers' Plan', which incorporated the type of deflationary policy recommended by Niemeyer. Further economies were made in public spending, taxation was again increased, interest rates lowered and the Australian pound devalued by 20 per cent in relation to sterling. Subsequently, the Commonwealth Arbitration Court lowered the basic wage by 10 per cent, thus bringing about a general lowering of wages.

Slow improvement took place after 1933, based on a recovery in wool prices, increased prosperity in the mining industry, a return to pre-Depression levels in building and the achievement of higher than pre-Depression output in manufacturing.

Between the wars The first few years after 1918 were marked by the difficulties of post-war adjustment, but the period 1920-28 was one of optimistic development. Population

BHP

Tapping the first iron from No 1 blast furnace, Newcastle 1915

increase was fostered mainly by agreements with Britain, over 260 000 settlers, 80 per cent of whom received government assistance, arriving from Britain between 1921 and 1930. State governments pursued schemes of closer settlement but many of these were not soundly based financially, and the proportion of rural settlers who cultivated their holdings successfully was very low. Money for immigration, irrigation, closer settlement schemes, railway construction and other public works was obtained by extensive borrowing, giving the Commonwealth a major opportunity to establish financial dominance over the States. In 1923 the LOAN COUNCIL was established, on a voluntary basis, to co-ordinate loan-raising, and in 1927 was made a permanent institution. In 1928 a constitutional amendment gave the Commonwealth the power to assume responsibility for State debts and, since the States had only one vote each on the Loan Council as against two and a casting vote for the Commonwealth, their independence was substantially reduced.

The 1920s were marked also by increased tariff protection, aimed mainly at the manufacturing industry, in which there was now a new emphasis on the production of iron and steel, motor car bodies and components, electrical goods, chemicals and textiles. In the cities there was great activity in home building, street widening, slum clearance, establishment of bus services, extension of tramways, construction of electricity power stations, and in Melbourne and Sydney the electrification of

suburban railways. There was a great increase in ownership of homes, motor cars and household appliances. Economic activity was also stimulated by the establishment of radio broadcasting stations and the growing popularity of motion pictures. Employment figures showed a great increase in the proportion of the workforce engaged in tertiary industries. Finally, as regards markets Australia remained heavily dependent on exports of primary products, especially wool and wheat, to the UK, with minerals declining in importance.

World War II and its aftermath, 1945-72
During World War II, Australia was cut off from her traditional sources of imported manufactures to a greater degree than in 1914-18. This led to greater total output and a wider range of products in the manufacturing industry, including the production of aeroplanes, ships and munitions, and considerable expansion in the electrical, chemical, metallurgical, machine tool and engineering industries. As in World War I, the great responsibilities assumed by the Commonwealth government increased its financial dominance over the States, in some respects permanently. Particularly important was the taking over by the Commonwealth in 1942 of the whole field of income tax, a step which has ever since made the States dependent on Commonwealth grants for a very high proportion of their revenue.

The period from 1945 to the early 1970s was one of prosperity and full employment. Development was stimulated by a massive

immigration programme and by heavy domestic and foreign investment. GNP per head increased by an average of about two per cent a year for the whole period, rising to over three per cent in the late 1960s, which compared favourably with countries such as the USA, UK and New Zealand, but well below the growth rates in Japan and most W European countries.

Initially, prosperity was based mainly on high prices for primary products—wheat and wool prices rose to unprecedented heights in the Korean War boom of 1950-51. Manufacturers and builders also experienced a boom as they strove to catch up with the backlog caused by wartime restrictions. Certain developments during this period were continuation of old trends, such as the further growth of manufacturing, the tendency for primary industries to use more scientific methods and so become less labour-intensive, and the employment of a higher proportion of the workforce in tertiary industries. Within these general trends, however, there were new features. In manufacturing there was particularly strong development of types of production typical of advanced industrial economies, with a greater portion of output coming from the iron industries; steel output increased fivefold between 1945 and 1971. In motor manufacturing, vehicles built mainly from Australian-made components captured the bulk of the market; General Motors-Holden, Ford Australia and Chrysler Australia were the most successful, but by the early 1970s they were under strong threat from Japanese manufacturers. Meanwhile, by the late 1960s most primary industries were in grave difficulties, caused basically by over-supply on world markets and, in the case of wool, by competition from synthetics. All primary producers were adversely affected by the loss of markets in the European Economic Community.

Prime Minister Chifley inspects the first Holden to come off the assembly line

Among developments which were not continuations of earlier trends two were outstanding, namely the discovery and exploitation of minerals (*see* MINERALS, etc.) and a striking change in the pattern of overseas trade. Asia had become more important than Europe, and Japan had replaced the UK as Australia's main trading partner, being in particular the largest buyer of her wool and minerals. Most imports came from the USA, the UK and Japan.

One last point to note is the importance in post-war developments of overseas capital, which was now less in the form of government borrowing and more in direct investment by overseas companies. This trend was particularly noticeable in the motor car manufacturing industry, where all manufacturers were branches or subsidiaries of overseas companies, and in the mining of newly found mineral resources such as the IRON ORE of the PILBARA, bauxite (the source of ALUMINIUM) at WEIPA and GOVE and PETROLEUM in BASS STRAIT.

In summary, the period 1945-70 can be seen as one of remarkable economic stability and growth, during which the average person's control over goods and services rose by about half. Over the whole period unemployment averaged below 1.5 per cent of the workforce, and even after the deflationary budget of 1951 it rose to only about two per cent. Inflation showed more variation. In the immediate post-war years shortages of many goods, rises in export prices and a high level of investment produced a burst of inflation that reached an annual rate of over 21 per cent during the Korean War boom. However, the spiral was then quickly checked and for nearly 20 years inflation averaged only about 3.5 per cent.

By 1972 there were signs that the period of relative stability was ending. The pressure of trends in the world's major industrial nations —a drop in international trade and rises in inflation and unemployment—were being felt in Australia. Unemployment had reached two per cent, higher than seemed acceptable at the time.

At the same time there was growing criticism of the pattern of development. Advocates of economic growth pointed out that the Australian rate in the 1950s and 1960s had been well below that of most industrialised nations, and that exports of some primary products were maintained only by charging the Australian consumer higher than export prices. Others expressed concern about environmental and social factors, such as increased pollution, the devastation of natural bushland, the 'suburban sprawl' in the capital cities, and the effect of the high population growth rate on public services. Economic nationalists also criticised the degree of foreign ownership of manufacturing and mining ventures, and called for a drive to 'buy back the farm'.

Developments since 1972 The Labor government which took office in 1972 was committed to many new initiatives in areas such as education, public health, Aboriginal affairs and urban and regional planning. Although it was evident that this programme would be difficult to implement in view of the worsening economic situation throughout the industrialised world, the government pressed ahead, incurring increased expenditure in the public sector, restricting the inflow of foreign capital, and trying to stimulate the economy by revaluing the Australian dollar and making an 'across the board' tariff cut of 25 per cent during its first year in office. At the same time,

trade unions pressed more vigorously and successfully for wage increases, particularly in 1974, when average earnings rose by 26 per cent. Meanwhile, the rural sector slipped further into recession, particularly after the UK joined the European Economic Community in 1973. The mining sector alone flourished, with exports still rising, but even here pessimists pointed out that oil exploration had practically ceased, and that at some point during the 1980s Australia might well be faced with a huge annual bill for imported petroleum products that could cancel out any likely gains from increased export of coal and metal ores. This general slackening of economic growth was accompanied by rises in inflation and unemployment. Australia's annual inflation rate reached 17 per cent in 1974, and by 1975 over four per cent of the workforce was unemployed.

The responsibility for the economic troubles of these years became the subject of bitter political debate. Prime Minister WHITLAM argued that they were mainly the result of overseas pressure, and that all industrialised nations were experiencing similar difficulties. The Opposition stressed the fact that the inflation rate was above the average for countries belonging to the Organisation for Economic Co-operation and Development (OECD) in general and for Australia's main trading partners in particular. It argued, too, that since Australia was almost self-sufficient in petroleum products, she had been spared the inflationary effects of the dramatic rise in world petroleum prices in 1973-74, and should therefore have been more successful than other countries in handling inflation. The sweeping Liberal/Country Party victory in the elections of December 1975 indicated that most Australians had come to accept the anti-Labor view.

The FRASER government adhered to the view that its central task was to reduce inflation, and that the reduction of unemployment was dependent on success in this primary aim. It curbed the rate of growth in public expenditure, consistently argued in favour of wage restraint in its submissions to the Commonwealth Conciliation and Arbitration Commission, allowed interest rates to rise and, in general, followed restrictive monetary policies.

These measures reduced inflation from an annual rate of 14 per cent at the end of 1975 to 8.2 per cent early in 1978. However, it later rose, reaching 11 per cent for the calendar year 1982. Meanwhile, unemployment had risen, and by February 1983 746 000 persons (10.7 per cent of the workforce) were unemployed.

The 1980s commenced with bright prospects and expectations of economic growth as a result of expansion in energy and resource-based industries. However, a number of factors undermined these expectations, and a domestic recession which began in late 1981 deepened during 1982. In March 1983 the Labor Party returned to office under the leadership of R.J. ('Bob') HAWKE, pledged to promote growth, cut unemployment and achieve wage restraint by means of a prices-

incomes accord with the AUSTRALIAN COUNCIL OF TRADE UNIONS. However the prospect of an unexpectedly large budget deficit for 1983-84 immediately placed limits on the extent to which the new government might be able to follow its desired expansionary policy. In April Mr. Hawke held a National Economic Summit conference, whose members included representatives of governments, employers and trade unions. This was followed by the setting up of an Economic Planning Advisory Council, the purpose of which is to offer the government independent community-based advice on economic policy.

Further reading: Griffin, J. (ed) *Essays in the Economic History of Australia.* (2nd edn) Cheshire, Melbourne, 1970; Boehm, E.A. *Twentieth Century Economic Development in Australia.* Longman, Melbourne, 1971; Shaw, A.G.L. *The Economic Development of Australia.* (6th edn) Longman, Melbourne, 1973; Sinclair, W.A. *The Process of Economic Development in Australia.* Cheshire, Melbourne, 1976.

ectoprocts Most species in the phylum Ectoprocta are marine animals, and were formerly grouped with the ENTOPROCTS in the phylum Bryozoa (sea mosses). Zoologists no longer regard this as a natural classification, and the ectoprocts are now placed in a phylum of their own. Their embryology suggests that they are close to the phyla containing SEA STARS and SEA SQUIRTS AND THEIR ALLIES.

The phylum contains about 4000 species but they are little studied; about 50 are freshwater species, some of which are gelatinous. Almost all are colonial and encrusting, a whole colony looking like a growth of moss. The individual animals are only about 0.5mm long, and each is partly enclosed in a tiny non-living box or vase. In some marine forms the box can be closed by a lid. Most marine forms have a covering of calcium carbonate. The food-catching structure (lophophore) is a circular or horseshoe-shaped fold of the body with tentacles which carry tiny hair-like appendages (cilia). The lophophore encloses the mouth, and planktonic food is carried in by a current of water propelled by the cilia.

Among the marine forms *Bugula* is one of the commonest genera in Australian waters. Many of these species have highly modified individuals that, under a microscope, look like birds' heads; each 'head' has a snapping beak, which may be defensive. *Watersipora cucullata* is a common species in rock pools, particularly in the Sydney area. It forms crescent-shaped blue-black encrustations on rocks. Over 100 other species have been found in and near Sydney.

Further reading: Dakin, W.J., Bennett, I. & Pope, E. *Australian Seashores.* (6th edn) Angus & Robertson, Sydney, 1976; Williams, W.D. *Australian Freshwater Life.* (2nd edn) Macmillan, Melbourne, 1980.

Eden NSW (population 3 107 in 1981) A small town on the far S coast plain, 494km S of Sydney on the Pacific Highway, it is located on the shores of TWOFOLD BAY. Its leading tourist attraction is fishing, both for the rod-and-line coastal fisherman and the off-shore big-game angler. Commercial trawl-and-line fishing is important and the town has freezing, canning and packing facilities. Eden's whaling museum, which contains the skeleton of Tom the killer whale (famed for his part in herding giant whales towards the harpooners), recalls the whaling days. On the S shore of the bay, 11km from Eden, is the interesting 'ghost town' of Boydtown, founded in 1843 by the colourful financier-adventurer Ben BOYD. Today it consists only of a church (in ruins), a tower (intended as a lighthouse) and the Sea Horse Inn (which is now a tourist hotel). Also at Eden is the Harris-Daishowa woodchip mill which processes logs from nearby forests for export to Japan. The Mt Imlay National Park, covers 3 764ha of heavily forested country, lying 32km SW of Eden. The Ben Boyd National Park (9 421ha) comprises two coastal sections, N and S of Eden; the N section includes the prominent rock features known as Haycock Point and the Pinnacles, while the S section covers a stretch of heath and woodland, where kangaroos, wallabies and a wide variety of birds (including sea-eagles, yellow-tailed black cockatoos and lyrebirds) are common.

education Under the Constitution, power with regard to State education remains with the State Parliaments, but there is no constitutional barrier against the Commonwealth government making grants to the States for educational purposes, or arranging to assume responsibility for some areas of State education. In recent years it has followed these courses and now plays a very important role in the provision of educational services.

This article discusses education in Australia generally. It does not attempt to give a separate account of education in each State, but in some parts makes particular reference to NSW as an example of general trends. Supplementary information on tertiary education is provided in Appendix 4, Higher Education Institutions.

Early history In late 18th-century Britain, the education of children was not regarded as the responsibility of government. Although this attitude was transferred in part to Australia, the granting of public assistance to education and the founding of schools under government control came about earlier than in Britain. This was in keeping with the general trend in newly founded colonies—and penal colonies in particular—for governments to take on wide responsibilities. Moreover, since local government institutions did not exist at first, and were very slow to develop, the administration of public education tended to be more highly centralised than in Britain and most other countries.

In 1793 the Rev. Richard JOHNSON opened a school. It was subsidised by the Society for the Promotion of the Gospel in Foreign Parts, which within a few years was giving aid to six schools in the colony. Government aid began in 1800, when Governor KING began imposing certain customs duties in order to obtain money for the running of a Girls' Orphan School. Similar aid was later extended to denominational schools. Most of these belonged to the Church of England, which, through the Church and School Act of 1826, was given about a seventh of the land in the colony for the support of its activities, including its school system. The strong opposition to this Act, however, led to its suspension in 1829 and its withdrawal in 1833.

By the 1830s there was considerable opposition to the continuation of a denominational system of schooling. Governor BOURKE suggested the introduction of a system on the lines of the National Schools in Ireland, but vested interests were able to delay such a move until the 1844 report by a Select Committee of the Legislative Council which showed that while in some areas there were no schools, in others there were too many, and that about half of the colony's children between the ages of four and 14 were receiving no education at all. These findings led to the establishment in 1848 of a Board of National Education to found and control schools which would be open to pupils of all denominations, and to provide religious instruction in beliefs held in common by all Christians; instruction in the beliefs of each particular denomination was to be left to the clergy. Aid was still given to denominational schools, but a growing number of people, including the Presbyterian clergyman, Dr John Dunmore LANG, felt that public funds should not be used to support religious institutions, schools included.

The tower block, NSW Institute of Technology, Sydney

'Free, compulsory and secular' education The gold rush, the subsequent separation of VIC and QLD and the attainment of self-government by the five E colonies heralded a new social and political environment in which the dual system of education was soon swept away. The process of change was similar in all six colonies, the view being finally accepted by most Australians that all children should receive primary education; that this could be achieved only if governments introduced a system of 'free, compulsory and secular' education ('secular' being understood as including general religious instruction, but not instruction in the teachings of particular denominations); and that parents wishing their children to be educated outside this system should do so at their own expense.

In NSW, these aims were achieved in two stages. First, the New South Wales Public Schools Act of 1866, introduced by Mr (later Sir) Henry PARKES, set up a Council of Education with much wider powers than those held by the Board of National Education. It had authority to grant aid to denominational schools, but under various restrictions as to the number of pupils, the condition of the buildings, and the proximity of public schools to those requesting aid; also, these schools had to follow the same course of instruction as that prescribed for public schools, and to be open to inspection.

Secondly, the Public Instruction Act of 1880 abolished grants to denominational schools, set up a Department of Public Instruction (later renamed the Department of Education) under the control of a Minister of the Crown, made school attendance compulsory for children between the ages of six and 14, provided for the establishment of public secondary as well as primary schools, and made allowance for clergymen to visit public schools for up to one hour per day to give religious instruction to children whose parents wished it. However, this Act did not make public education completely free, and fees continued to be charged until 1906.

Developments in NSW were paralleled in the other colonies, Acts similar to that of 1880 being passed in VIC in 1872, QLD and SA in 1875, TAS in 1885 and WA in 1893.

Non-government schools since the 1880s Despite the withdrawal of State aid, non-government schools continued to play a major role in Australian education. The Roman Catholic Church continued to build schools to which all members of the Church were urged to send their children, and since the great majority did so, Roman Catholic schools were soon catering for nearly a fifth of the nation's school pupils. The other Churches continued to maintain schools, with an emphasis on secondary education. They did not build enough schools to cater for all children of their respective congregations, but made use of the provisions for clergymen to give religious instruction in public schools. Some undenominational schools continued to operate, or were founded after the 1880s.

Australians generally refer to non-government schools as 'private schools' or, particularly for those which are not Roman Catholic, as 'independent schools'. Most have 'College' or 'Grammar School' as part of their official titles, but neither of these terms refers to a particular class of school. In some capital cities

Table 1

SCHOOL ENROLMENTS 1982

| States and Territories | Government Schools | Non-government schools | | | | ALL SCHOOLS |
		Anglican	Roman Catholic	Other	Total	
NSW	782 080	17 360	199 863	27 784	245 007	1 027 087
VIC	584 780	22 973	166 731	37 499	227 203	811 983
QLD	367 860	6 915	82 734	14 839	104 488	472 348
SA	207 940	4 234	30 417	11 321	45 972	253 912
WA	208 340	5 403	38 104	8 031	51 538	259 878
TAS	69 140	1 873	10 479	2 974	15 326	84 466
NT	23 800	–	3 789	583	4 372	28 172
ACT	39 010	2 344	14 890	542	17 776	56 786
AUSTRALIA	2 282 950	61 102	547 007	103 573	711 682	2 994 632

Source: *Government Schools, Australia 1982*, & *Non-Government Schools Australia 1982*, Australian Bureau of Statistics, Catalogue Nos. 4215, 4216, Commonwealth Govt Printer, Canberra, 24 June & 2 Aug 1983.

a few of the older or more prestigious private schools refer to themselves as the Great Public Schools.

Renewal of State aid for non-government schools For several decades the principle that State aid should not be given to non-government schools was maintained. By the early 1960s, however, the climate of public opinion was changing. The rise in education costs was causing a lowering of standards in accommodation, staffing and equipment in many of the less affluent private schools. The argument was increasingly used that these schools would either fall further behind or would be unable to cater for such a high proportion of the nation's children, in which case government schools would have to cope with increased numbers. At the same time, political considerations began to favour a change of policy. While the Australian Labor Party (ALP) was strongly opposed to State aid, the Democratic Labor Party (DLP), whose support was needed by the Liberal/Country Party government in office at the time, was strongly in favour. Moreover, the proportion of Roman Catholic voters, whose Church had never ceased demanding State aid for its schools, was increasing.

The federal government led the way in breaking from the traditional principle. It had already given indirect aid by allowing income tax deductions for school fees and other educational expenses, and for donations to school building funds. Then in 1964 it began giving grants for buildings and equipment used for science teaching in both government and private secondary schools. Soon afterwards direct per capita grants were given to private schools and also general education grants to the States. By the late 1960s the States had begun making per capita grants to private schools. By the time the ALP gained office in Canberra in December 1972, it had abandoned outright opposition to State aid, but was critical of the fact that such aid was being given to the wealthiest private schools as well as to the least affluent. The WHITLAM government therefore instructed its Schools Commission to classify schools according to need, and

graduated its aid accordingly. This general principle has been followed by the FRASER and HAWKE governments. However there has been considerable disagreement regarding the amount of aid to be given to particular schools.

Developments in primary education In the late 19th and early 20th centuries the main stress in public education was on primary schools. A common curriculum was prescribed in each State, with emphasis on the teaching of literacy and numeracy. Teaching methods were based largely on rote learning and constant drilling in basic facts and skills; there was little scope for real self-expression, discipline was severe and corporal punishment was used freely.

Primary school pupils

Courtesy of A.I.S. Canberra

Today the scene is very different. School buildings are more attractive and better equipped with teaching aids; average class sizes have decreased; corporal punishment is seldom used; and teaching methods have become less formal, with many schools being organised on 'open classroom' principles whereby children spend a large part of their time working individually or in small groups, rather than being instructed by teachers in full class groups. Very recently there has been a strong trend towards allowing each school to frame its own curriculum, within very broad guidelines laid down by the central authority.

These liberalising trends have caused much controversy. Defenders of traditional methods claim that primary schools are failing to train children in the basic skills necessary for them to function effectively in the community; and that young children cannot make effective use of the degree of freedom which many schools

give them. Defenders of the new trends claim that basic skills are being imparted at least as effectively as in the past, and that the opportunities which children are given for decision-making, discussion and creative self-expression will equip them well for effective citizenship.

Attendance is compulsory from the age of six, but most children enroll at the age of five, the non-compulsory year generally being referred to as Kindergarten or Preparatory. Compulsory years have in the past been called Grade 1, Grade 2 and so on, the final year being Grade 6 or Grade 7, according to the State, but in many schools they are now called Year 1, Year 2 and so on, with the years of secondary schooling continuing this numbering system.

Most government primary school classes are co-educational. Those for children up to the age of eight are commonly known as Infants' classes, and organised into an Infants' Department. Some schools 'stream' the children—that is, divide those in each year into classes according to their abilities. Others have 'parallel' classes—that is, classes encompassing the whole range of abilities.

Developments in secondary education In the later part of the 19th century the new Departments of Education began providing for secondary education in two ways. The first was to add junior secondary classes to some of the primary schools. The second was to found separate high schools; however, these remained few in number for many years, and in 1911 contained a total of only about 6000 pupils. From then on, although the number of schools and pupils increased markedly, the general pattern was to allow only a minority of pupils, selected by an entrance examination, to enter academic high schools which offered courses leading to university matriculation. Other secondary pupils were either put into classes attached to primary schools, or went to schools known by titles such as Junior Secondary School or Domestic Science School, which concentrated on practical subjects such as woodwork, metalwork, bookkeeping, cooking and needlework. In the cities, boys and girls were generally enrolled in separate schools.

Small towns usually had a Central School, which included primary and junior secondary classes, while large towns usually had one comprehensive, co-educational high school.

The period after World War II brought even greater changes to secondary schools than to primary. The raising of the school-leaving age (to 16 in TAS; to 15 in the other States), the increasing numbers of pupils staying at school beyond the legally required age, and the rapid rise in population combined to caused an enormous increase in secondary enrolments.

There have also been organisational and curriculum changes. In general, the pattern of comprehensive, co-educational high schools has been widely adopted, and even where selective high schools still exist they tend to be less selective than formerly. (A notable exception to this trend is in VIC, where secondary technical schools have been retained.) The number of years of secondary schooling has been increased to six (except in QLD, where it is five, but where pupils enter high school at a slightly higher age than elsewhere), so that the average age of students sitting for examinations at the end of secondary school is now about 18. This has brought a demand in some quarters for the setting up of Senior High Schools to cater only for students in the last two years of schooling. However, only TAS and the ACT have taken this step.

Teaching methods have become more varied and pupil-centred activities more common. Extra-curricular activities have become more prominent, cultural subjects such as art and music are given more attention, but the study of foreign languages and the classics has declined greatly. Schools have been given more freedom to plan syllabuses for junior secondary classes. In senior years the existence of a final examination has caused the retention of centrally imposed syllabuses, but there is greater freedom in the choice of courses and in the topics within each course. These liberalising tendencies have become the subject of much debate.

Finally, it should be noted that many high schools, besides offering a wide range of normal subjects, provide special opportunities for the study of agriculture; and the Conservatorium High School in Sydney caters for pupils of high musical talent.

Public examinations The systems by which secondary school students have been assessed have varied so much from time to time and from State to State that a detailed description of them would be impossible here. In general, however, the pattern which emerged during the first few decades of this century included two external public examinations. The first, held at the stage which pupils would normally reach at about the legal school-leaving age, was generally called the Intermediate Certificate. The second, held a year or two later, was for a Leaving Certificate or Senior Certificate. The rigidity of this pattern has been broken down in recent decades. By the early 1980s, public examinations at the end of junior secondary schooling had been abolished. In VIC, SA and

the NT no certificate was awarded; in the other States the certificates being awarded were based on school assessments, various moderating procedures being used in attempts to maintain common standards.

At the end of the final year of secondary education, certificates were still issued in all States and Territories. In QLD and the ACT they were based entirely on school assessments, with the use of complex moderating techniques in order to maintain common standards. Elsewhere public examinations were still held at this level, with assessments playing a part in the award of marks. The title Higher School Certificate was most commonly used.

Pre-school education This has been left almost entirely to voluntary and private individuals. Between 1896 and 1912 a Kindergarten Union or similar organisation was founded in each State and several Kindergarten Teachers' Colleges (KTCs) were established. The State governments at various times, and the Commonwealth from the late 1930s, provided some aid to these bodies and to the federal Australian Pre-School Associations formed by the State bodies in 1938. However, only since the late 1960s has such aid become significant. In 1968 the Commonwealth began making capital grants to KTCs and by 1976 they had become Colleges of Advanced Education (CAEs), fully funded by the Commonwealth. Since 1974 the Commonwealth has provided large sums for grants to approved pre-school centres, and State governments have also contributed considerable sums. However, no co-ordinated plan for the development of child-care and pre-school centres has yet been framed.

Education of children in remote areas Since Australia is the most thinly inhabited of the continents, the education of children living in remote areas has presented a major challenge. Many attend independent boarding schools, some are housed in Department of Education hostels in towns where there are high schools, and others are brought long

distances by bus each day to small primary schools. Other methods of instruction include: correspondence schools, maintained by the State Department of Education; and 'schools of the air', which supplement the correspondence courses by means of radio. The latter are associated with the FLYING DOCTOR SERVICE, whose transceivers are used for some hours each day for educational purposes.

Technical and further education The tendency to establish separate schools for those children who, it was thought, would benefit most from the study of technical subjects still exists in VIC, but elsewhere the trend has been towards comprehensive schools which offer a wide range of technical subjects to those who wish to select them.

At the tertiary level, technical colleges began to be established in the late 19th century, grew steadily in numbers, and have experienced rapid growth since World War II. They differ from universities and CAEs in that they accept students who have not completed secondary schooling. However, besides providing training for a great number of apprentices and others who wish to work in skilled manual occupations, they offer many other courses, some of which can be undertaken only by students who have gained a Higher School Certificate or equivalent qualification. Formerly, these included many high-level technological courses leading to the award of diplomas comparable in status to university degrees. A recent trend has been, however, to transfer these to the new institutes of technology.

Technical colleges play a vital role in education, and have a total enrolment greater than that of universities and CAEs combined. Their importance has been recognised since the late 1960s by greatly increased grants from the Commonwealth government, to supplement expenditure on them by the States. In 1975 a Technical and Further Education Commission was appointed to advise the Minister for Education; its functions were taken over in 1977 by the new Tertiary Educa-

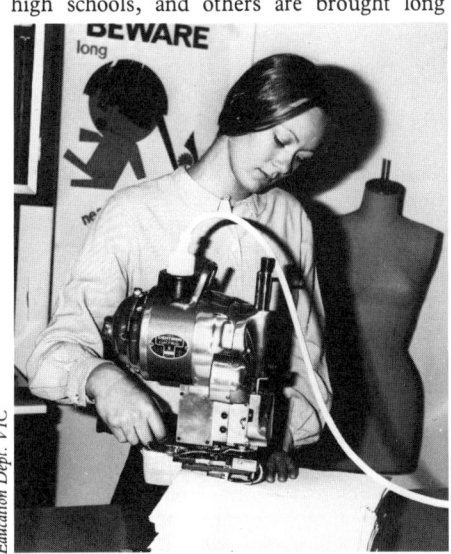

Education Dept. VIC

A Clothing Studies Certificate student at Whitehorse Technical College

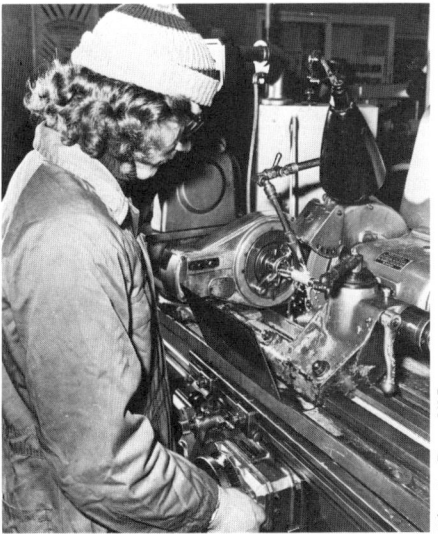

Education Dept. VIC

A Machines and Materials Studies student at Swinburne Technical College

tion Commission.

Agricultural education Although courses in agriculture are offered in many high schools, agricultural education is generally considered more suitable for post-school study. The first systematic courses in agriculture were given in agricultural colleges founded in the late 19th century; these provided practical training for prospective farmers and graziers and tertiary-level courses for people seeking technical positions in the public service or in industries providing services to primary producers. Ten of Australia's universities also developed degree courses in agriculture and some offered graduate diploma Agricultural Extension courses.

The setting up of CAEs since the late 1960s has affected a number of the older agricultural colleges in that they have become, or been absorbed by, CAEs. Several of the more recently established colleges, however, have confined themselves to certificate courses intended for persons going on the land.

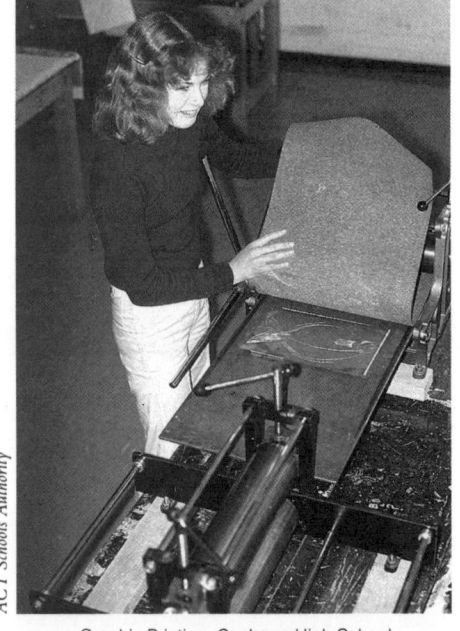

ACT Schools Authority

Graphic Printing, Canberra High School

Teacher education When government education systems were first set up, teachers were trained mainly by the pupil-teacher method, whereby selected students aged between 13 and 17 were placed in schools and gave lessons under the guidance of experienced teachers. After some years those who did best in a competitive examination received a one-year scholarship to a teacher training college, while the others were appointed as teachers without further training. In the early 20th century this system was gradually replaced by full-time pre-service training, most primary school teachers attending teachers' colleges, at first for a one-year and later for a two-year course, and most secondary school teachers gaining university degrees followed by a one-year Diploma in Teaching course.

By the late 1960s most teachers colleges were beginning to extend their minimum courses to three years, and the subsequent creation of

Sydney University

CAEs brought further changes. All former State teachers' colleges and most private ones are now either CAEs in their own right or have become Schools of Education in multi-purpose CAEs. They are now better financed than their predecessors and many of them award degrees as well as diplomas. However, the universities still educate a high proportion of secondary teachers.

Universities Australia's first six universities were in the colonial and State capitals, being opened in the following order: Sydney University 1852, Melbourne University 1855, Adelaide University 1876, University of Tasmania 1889, University of Queensland 1909 and University of Western Australia 1911. No more were founded until after World War II, although some of the metropolitan universities opened university colleges in other locations. After the war there was a remarkable expansion, the number of universities being trebled and total enrolments increasing from 14 500 in 1939 to 167 000 in 1982.

Commonwealth involvement in education

1. Universities. The growth of universities contributed greatly to direct Commonwealth involvement in education. The system prior to World War II, whereby universities depended on endowments, fees and grants from the State governments, changed during the war when the Commonwealth government began to subsidise those activities considered vital to the war effort. This was followed by the establishment of Commonwealth scholarships and by the Commonwealth undertaking to pay the fees and living expenses of ex-servicemen attending universities and colleges. The combined result of these schemes was that the Commonwealth was soon contributing signifi-

cantly, by way of fees, to the universities' running expenses. A more direct step towards Commonwealth involvement in education was the establishment in Canberra in 1946 of the Australian National University. In 1951 the Commonwealth began making matching grants to the States to help maintain their universities. In 1959, two years after receiving the report of an enquiry held under the chairmanship of Sir Keith (later Lord) Murray, it set up a Universities Commission and increased the size of its grants considerably. In 1974 the Whitlam government assumed financial responsibility for all universities and CAEs but insisted that course fees be abolished.

Armidale College of Advanced Education (formerly the Teachers' College)

2. Colleges of Advanced Education. The greatest growth area in tertiary education since the mid-1960s has been that of CAEs, a term which applies to many types of institutions, all of which are, however, more strongly vocationally-oriented than universities. In 1964 the Commonwealth government received the report of a committee, under the chairmanship of Sir Leslie Martin, appointed to enquire into tertiary education. Following the recommendations of this report, in 1965 the government began making grants to

CAEs; teachers' colleges did not receive these grants until the mid-1970s, when they were removed from the control of the State Departments of Education and gathered under the CAE umbrella. In 1982 there were 68 CAEs, with a total enrolment of 165 000.

3. *General*. The role of the Commonwealth government in the giving of aid to private schools has been mentioned above. From 1964 it has also made grants to the States specifically for educational purposes, and these, combined with aid to private schools and the expenses of universities and CAEs, have made the funding of education a major responsibility of the central government. In allocating money for education, the government receives advice from the Schools Commission and the Tertiary Education Commission, the latter having been set up in 1977 to combine the functions of the former Universities Commission, the Commission on Advanced Education and the Technical and Further Education Commission.

Further reading: Fogarty, R. *Catholic Education in Australia, 1806-1950.* (2 vols) Melbourne University Press, Melbourne, 1959; Barcan, A. *A Short History of Education in New South Wales.* Martindale, Sydney, 1965; Austin, A.G. *Australian Education, 1788-1900.* (3rd edn) Pitman, Carlton VIC, 1972; Cleverley, J. & Lawry, J. (eds) *Australian Education in the Twentieth Century.* Longman, Camberwell VIC, 1972; Jones, P.E. *Education in Australia.* Nelson, Melbourne, 1974.

Edwards River NSW A large ANAB-RANCH of the MURRAY RIVER located in the RIVERINA region, it leaves the main stream between Tocumwal and ECHUCA (at a point 48km upstream from Echuca) and rejoins it downstream from SWAN HILL. It thus follows a vast looping course, first N, then turning WNW just before DENILIQUIN; this section of the Murray Valley is part of the semi-arid inland plains where the rivers have meandering courses and form many anabranches. The Yanco-Billabong Creek system is one such anabranch which connects the MURRUM-BIDGEE RIVER to the Edwards and thence to the Murray. The Edwards itself splits into numerous additional anabranches, the largest of which is the WAKOOL RIVER. There has been much irrigation development in this region: to the N and NE of Deniliquin are the Berriquin and Denimein Irrigation Districts (325 800ha and 59 500ha respectively), supplied with water via the Mulwala Canal from YARRAWONGA WEIR on the Murray; to the SW of Deniliquin is the Deniboota Irrigation District (136 800ha); and 25km downstream from Deniliquin, the Stevens Weir on the Edwards diverts water for the Wakool Irrigation District (covering 204 000ha and including the Tullokool Irrigation District) where rice and other cereals, oil seeds and fodder crops, fat lamb raising and dairying are important.

eels *see* fishes, bony; fishes, poisonous and venomous

eelworms *see* roundworms

eggplant *see* Solanaceae

eggs-and-bacon *see* Papilionaceae

egrets *see* bitterns, etc.

Eighty Mile Beach WA This great arc of barren sand dune coast and salty marshland, facing the Indian Ocean in the NW of the State, is traversed by the Great Northern Highway along the route between PORT HEDLAND and BROOME. The coastal zone is a W extension of the GREAT SANDY DESERT and is a desolate arid stretch of country with sparse livestock grazing. The average annual rainfall at Mandora Homestead (about 300km ENE of Port Hedland) is only 319mm, concentrated mainly in summer, with a marked dry season from April to November.

Eildon Reservoir VIC Located on the upper GOULBURN RIVER, the original weir to store water for irrigation was constructed between 1915 and 1927, modified in the 1930s (when it was called Sugarloaf Reservoir) and much enlarged in the 1950s. The main Eildon embankment is 79m high and 983m long, and Lake Eildon, formed by the dam, has a shoreline of 482km and a capacity of 3 390 000ML, making it the second-largest reservoir in VIC (DARTMOUTH DAM is the biggest). Water released from the reservoir flows down to the Goulburn Weir where it is diverted E into a major channel (supplying farms in the Goulburn Valley region) and W into a second major channel leading to WARANGA RESERVOIR and thence to the CAMPASPE, LODDON and WIMMERA-MALLEE irrigation systems. It is thus one of the most important reservoirs in Australia, supplying water to more than 145 000ha. Although constructed primarily for irrigation purposes, it also has hydro-electricity generating turbines with a capacity of 120 000kW. Many parts of Lake Eildon provide aquatic recreation areas for yachting, water skiing and fishing. The small township of Eildon (population 737 in 1981), situated on timbered slopes below the main dam wall, was originally built in the early 1950s to house construction employees and is now a tourist centre, 137km by road from Melbourne. Along the W side of Lake Eildon is Fraser National Park, covering 3 750ha, established in 1957. Grey kangaroos are common in the park and the varied bird life includes wedge-tailed eagles, wood ducks and gang-gang cockatoos.

Elcho Island NT Located off the NE coast of ARNHEM LAND, E of the Glyde River estuary, this low narrow island is about 48km long, on a SW-NE alignment, and forms part of an island chain which stretches into the ARAFURA SEA with the WESSEL ISLANDS at its NE tip. It is part of the Arnhem Land Aboriginal Reserve and is thus closed to non-Aborigines, except with special permission. There is a Methodist mission on the island

which has developed tropical fruit growing and rice farming. Cutting of cypress pine timber is also of some significance. The main settlement, Galawinku (population 1 279 in 1981), and the airport are on the SW of the island.

Eldershaw, Flora Sydney Patricia (1897-1956) Author. Born in Sydney, she was educated in WAGGA WAGGA in NSW and at the University of Sydney, and worked as secretary of the Sydney University Women's Union and as a teacher. She wrote literary criticism and historical articles under her own name, and in collaboration with Marjorie BARNARD, under the pen-name M. BARNARD ELDERSHAW, published a work of criticism, *Essays in Australian Fiction* (1938), three historical works, including *Phillip of Australia* (1938), and the novels *A House is Built* (1929), *Green Memory* (1931), *The Glasshouse* (1936), *Plaque With Laurel* (1937) and *Tomorrow and Tomorrow* (1947). Of the novels the first and last are the most notable. *A House is Built*, which with Katharine PRICHARD's *Coonardoo* (1929) won the *Bulletin*'s first novel competition, deals with the fortunes of a naval quartermaster-turned-businessman and his family in the early days of Sydney. *Tomorrow and Tomorrow* deals with events from the Depression to World War II and with a vision of Australia in the future. She was president of the Fellowship of Australian Writers from 1935 to 1943 and a member of the Commonwealth Literary Fund Advisory Board from 1939 to 1953.

Further reading: Rorabacker, L.E. *Marjorie Barnard and M. Barnard Eldershaw.* Twayne, New York, 1973.

elections Government in Australia is made legitimate through the electoral system. At each election, the government has to account for its actions, and the electors have the opportunity to choose an alternative government if they wish. Elections for federal and State Parliaments must be held at least every three years. A federal and State election cannot be held at the same time. All Australian citizens and British subjects aged 18 years and over are required by law to register as voters provided they have been living in Australia for more than six months. Migrants from other countries can obtain full citizen rights, including the right to vote, when they become naturalised.

Each State in Australia is divided by geographical boundaries into electorates and each elector is registered in a particular electorate. The geographical boundaries within each State will vary for federal, State and local government elections. Variations in the geographical boundaries may become necessary as a result of changes in population distribution, with one electorate losing population and another experiencing a rapid expansion in population. This may result from natural increase or from the movements of people into and out of the area.

While the Australian system of elections has

been based on the principle of 'one person one vote', it has not been successful in the adoption of the principle 'one vote one value'. The Constitution guarantees a minimum of five seats for each State in the House of Representatives, yet TAS's population would not entitle it to five MHRs and so technically TAS is over-represented compared with the mainland States. All States have equal representation in the Senate and thus the votes of people in the smaller States are worth more than a vote of a person in one of the larger (in terms of population) States. Because rural electorates have always had a smaller number of people than metropolitan electorates, they have a weighted advantage. Finally, there have been some glaring examples of electoral boundaries being unfairly distorted by a gerrymander. The term 'gerrymander' comes from the name of an allegedly unscrupulous American politician, Governor Elbridge Gerry of Massachusetts who, in 1812, had the electoral map of his State redrawn so that he had a considerable advantage. The shape of one district in his State resembled a salamander and since then the term 'gerrymander' has been applied to deliberate distortions of electoral boundaries which favour the political party in office at the time the boundaries were redrawn.

All elections for the Lower Houses in mainland States, for the TAS Legislative Council, and for the federal House of Representatives are based on PREFERENTIAL VOTING and the single-member constituencies. In the Legislative Councils of WA and VIC there are two members for each electoral province or constituency; however, only one of these retires before each general election. Systems of PROPORTIONAL REPRESENTATION, with multi-member constituencies, are used for the federal Senate, the TAS House of Assembly and the Legislative Councils of NSW and SA.

Voting is compulsory in all federal and State elections and in most local government elections. Compulsory voting has had the effect of forcing the least interested of voters to the polls to record their choice of candidate and has resulted in the development of the DONKEY VOTE.

If a person is ill or infirm or for any other reason is unable to vote at a polling booth on election day, that person can apply to the returning officer before the polling day and arrangements will be made for a postal vote. People absent from their homes may vote at any other booth in their State and people travelling overseas can arrange to vote at any Australian Embassy.

electric fish *see* sharks, etc.

electricity supply As a developed nation, Australia ranks high in the world in the consumption of energy per head of population; and about one-third of all the primary energy she consumes is used for the production of electricity.

Sources of electricity Australia has abundant reserves of coal, but has generally low rainfall

CONSUMPTION OF ELECTRICITY, 1981–82 (MILLIONS OF KILOWATT HOURS), AND KILOWATT HOURS PER CAPITA.

	Residential	Commercial, Industrial	Traction	Public lighting	Total	kWh per capita
NSW	12 620	17 303	489	208	30 619	5 885
VIC	7 847	11 965	280	170	20 261	5 122
QLD	4 459	6 432	20	72	10 983	4 759
SA	2 661	3 528	2	51	6 243	4 755
WA	1 832	3 085	—	46	4 963	3 768
TAS	1 662	5 743	—	16	7 381	17 145
ACT	844	678	—	32	1 554	6 928
NT	164	379	—	—	543	4 470

Tasmania's high consumption, relative to its population, is mainly due to the presence of several large electro-chemical industries.

ELECTRICAL ENERGY PRODUCED FROM VARIOUS RESOURCES (%) 1981–82

	NSW	VIC	QLD	TAS	SA	WA	NT	TOTAL
Black Coal	32.8	—	12.7	—	1.5	5.7	—	52.7
Brown Coal	—	21.1	—	—	—	—	—	21.1
Oil	0.3	0.4	0.2	0.4	0.1	0.4	0.7	2.5
Gas	0.1	3.7	0.03	—	6.0	—	—	9.8
Hydro	4.3	1.0	0.7	7.9	—	—	—	13.9
TOTAL	37.5	26.2	13.6	8.3	7.6	6.1	0.7	100.0

Output of the Snowy Scheme has been allocated to NSW and VIC, and the ACT hydro figure included in that for NSW.

and limited areas of highlands. Consequently she relies for electricity mainly on coal-fired thermal stations. Hydro-electricity plays only a minor role. It is confined almost entirely to the E States, and in particular to TAS and the area of the SNOWY MOUNTAINS SCHEME. A certain amount of the latter's output is reserved for the use in the ACT; the remainder being divided between NSW and VIC on a two-thirds/one-third basis. Other sources which play a minor role are oil and natural gas.

Historical development The first power stations were built in the late nineteenth century, most of them by municipal authorities, but some by independent companies. To take NSW as an example, in 1888 TAMWORTH became the first town in Australia, and indeed the first in the Southern Hemisphere, to light its streets with electricity. Before the end of the century several other towns and the Sydney municipality of Redfern had followed suit, and a few small independent companies had begun generating electricity in parts of Sydney. In 1899 the Department of Railways opened a power station at Ultimo, to supply electric trams, and in 1904 the Sydney Municipal Council opened a station at Pyrmont.

The growth of electrical services was slow up to World War I, the chief uses of electricity being for lighting (where it gradually displaced gas) and for electric trams. However the 1920s brought a great diversification of use, and a great increase in generating capacity. Factories made greater use of electric power, electric home appliances came into wider use, electric tram services were extended, and Sydney and Melbourne electrified their suburban railway

systems.

In the inter-war years there came a tendency for each State to set up one central statutory authority for the generation of electricity. TAS had set up a Hydro-Electric Department in 1914, and replaced this with a Hydro-Electric Commission in 1929-30. VIC and QLD each set up a State Electricity Commission in 1921 and 1938 respectively (although the QLD authority was for many years a controlling, not a generating body), and the other States set up central authorities either during or shortly after World War II. These statutory authorities gradually took over municipal and company power stations and linked most of their distribution networks to central grids.

Generation and transmission today In NSW the generating authority is the Electricity Commission of NSW, which sells electricity in bulk to distributing authorities (known as County Councils, and each covering a group of shire and/or municipal councils), to the government railways and to certain large consumers. Its thermal power stations are mainly built on coal fields. In 1983 the largest of them was Vales Point, on the shore of LAKE MACQUARIE (2195MW). However the Earring station, when completed, is expected to have a capacity of 2640MW.

In VIC, generation depends mainly on the brown coal deposits of the LATROBE VALLEY, but there are hydro-electric stations in the mountainous NE of the State. The State Electricity Commission of VIC sells part of its output direct to consumers, and part in bulk to metropolitan municipalities for distribution. Its largest station, Hazlewood (1600MW) will be surpassed when Loy Yang A (2000MW) is completed.

The State Electricity Commission of QLD is responsible for nearly all generation and for main transmission in that State, and sells in bulk to distributing boards. Its largest station, at GLADSTONE (1650MW), will be approached in size by that at Tarong (1400MW) when the latter is completed.

The Electricity Trust of SA uses two main fuels—natural gas from the Gidgealpa-Moomba field, and sub-bituminous coal from LEIGH CREEK. Its largest station is Torrens Island B (800MW). In WA the main generating authority is the State Energy Commission of WA. Its largest station is at KWINANA (880MW), but this will be surpassed when the Muja station reaches its planned capacity of 1040MW. In TAS the only thermal station is the oil-fired one at Bell Bay (240MW), and the largest hydro-electric station is POATINA (300MW). The shape of future development has been thrown into doubt by the action of the HAWKE federal government in legislating to prevent the damming of the lower GORDON RIVER.

The requirements of the ACT Electricity Authority are provided by power from the Snowy Mountains Scheme and the Electricity Commission of NSW. The NT Electricity Commission's largest power station is that at Stokes Hill, in DARWIN (141MW). The Commission also operates a considerable number of diesel stations.
Further reading: Electricity Supply Association of Australia. *The Electricity Supply Industry in Australia.* Yearly, 1946 to date.

elephant snail *see* gastropods

Elizabeth SA (population 122 200 in 1981) This city, 27km NNE of Adelaide, was named in honour of Queen Elizabeth II and was planned on the coastal plain as a new industrial town in 1954. The General Motors-Holden factory is located on the outskirts of the city. Some of the residents of Elizabeth commute to Adelaide, while others are employed at the Weapons Research establishment in Salisbury.

elkhorns *see* Pteridophyta

Elkin, Adolphus Peter (1891-1979) Anthropologist. Born in NSW, he carried out the first systematic anthropological survey of Australian Aborigines (1927-31). He wrote several books and many articles on the Aborigines, the best-known being *Australian Aborigines: How to Understand Them* (1938) and *Aboriginal Men of High Degree* (1944).

Elliott, Herbert James 'Herb' (1938-) Athlete. Born in Perth WA, Elliott is regarded as the most competitive runner over a mile and 1500m that Australia has produced. He was undefeated over both these distances as a senior runner. In 1958 he burst into the international limelight by winning two gold medals at the Commonwealth Games

in Cardiff (for the mile and half mile), breaking the world mile record at Dublin and breaking the world 1500m record at Gothenburg in Sweden. Elliott's regular training programme included an exhausting run over a course which wound up and down dunes covered with loose sand. This tough course was part of a programme established by his coach Percy Cerutty. Elliott broke the four-minute mile on 17 occasions. He retired in 1960 after winning the 1 500m Olympic gold medal in Rome in record time.

Elsey NT This is a cattle station on the upper ROPER RIVER, 35km E of the Stuart Highway and 138km by road SE of KATHERINE. The name 'Elsey' was made famous by the authoress Mrs Aeneas GUNN in her book *We of the Never Never* (1908). In 1902 she came as a bride to the Old Elsey Homestead and wrote of her experiences. The original homestead was demolished in 1906 and a new one built 32km away near the Roper River, but a cairn at the old site and a cemetery containing the graves of some of the characters featured in the book are located just off the Stuart Highway 114km S of Katherine.

emancipists *see* convicts

Embioptera *see* web-spinners

Emerald QLD (population 4 628 in 1981) Located on the Nogoa River, a tributary of the MACKENZIE RIVER, in the central highlands region of the State, it is a commercial and service town for a productive grain growing and livestock grazing district, and for an irrigation area developed in the 1970s. At an elevation of 175m above sea level, it is situated at the junction of the Capricorn and Gregory Highways, 921km NW of Brisbane and 263km inland from ROCKHAMPTON. It is also a rail junction on the Rockhampton-WINTON line, with branches N to BLAIR ATHOL and S to Springsure. Rich gemstone deposits, first found a century ago, were once Emerald's sole means of livelihood, but now they account for only a small part of the area's prosperity, though some of the nearby fields (such as Sapphire, Rubyvale, Tomahawk Creek, The Willows and Glenalva) are popular tourist attractions. Whether the town was named after the gems is a matter of local debate. Cattle breeding and fattening is a major activity of the area, though sheep grazing and the production of prime lambs have been developed recently. Crops include lucerne and pastures for stock fodder, wheat, sorghum, maize, cotton and safflower. There is a modern processing plant in the town, crushing the safflower seeds for oil extraction. A pastoral college for training in agriculture and grazing is located 6km E of the town on the Capricorn Highway. Though the average annual rainfall is 631mm, it is concentrated mainly in the summer months, with a dry season during winter and spring; it is variable from year to year and drought can seriously

affect the rural industries. The Emerald irrigation scheme was designed to conserve water and ensure a stable supply for crops and pastures, as well as to provide water for the coal mining areas in the BLACKWATER and Saraji regions. The central feature of the scheme is the Fairbairn Dam on the Nogoa River, SW of Emerald, with a storage capacity of 1 440 000ML. Completed in 1972, it drains a catchment area of 16 320km^2, and provides annually 101 000ML of irrigation water by gravitation through channels to over 1 600ha of irrigable land. The Fairbairn Dam also supplements Emerald's water supply.

Emerald VIC (population 2 857 in 1981) This small country town is located in farming and grazing land, 51km by rail E of Melbourne. In 1858 it was the scene of a major gold rush, though it was not until the 1880s that it developed as a township. It was originally called Main Range, but the name was later changed to Emerald, probably after an early prospector, Jack Emerald, who was murdered there. Some people, however, have claimed that it was so named because emeralds were found in the district.

Emerson, Roy Stanley (1936-) Tennis player. Born at KINGAROY in QLD he became a leading amateur tennis player. His best years came after 1961. From 1961 to 1967 inclusive he was defeated only once in the Australian singles title (in 1962), he won the French singles twice (1963 and 1967), the US singles twice (1961 and 1964), and the Wimbledon title twice (1964 and 1965). During the same period he set a record for the greatest number of singles victories (11) in Davis Cup challenge rounds. When LAVER turned professional in 1962, Emerson became number one amateur in the world, a position he held until he too turned professional in 1967.

Empire Games *see* Commonwealth Games

employers' associations As in the case of trade unions, the advent of industrial conciliation and arbitration systems, combined with various economic considerations, has brought about a strong growth of employers' associations since the late 19th century. At present there are over 500 such associations, varying greatly in size, scope and organisational structure. Most of them are quite small and are affiliated with larger associations at State and national levels.

The larger associations fall into several types. Most numerous are those which are confined to a particular industry or to a very few closely associated industries. Examples are the Association of Employers of Waterside Labour, Australian Woolgrowers' and Graziers' Council, Australian Retailers' Association, Master Builders' Federation of Australia and, particularly important because of its wide coverage and the central position of its members' activities in the manufacturing sector, the Metal Trades Industry Association. Such national bodies usually consist of affiliated State organisations, and serve the function of formulating policies on matters of national concern. Secondly, there are many State organisations which cover either a group of industries or aim at co-ordinating the policies of all employers' associations. These include the Queensland Confederation of Industry, the Chamber of Manufactures of New South Wales, the Victorian Chamber of Manufactures, the Tasmanian Chamber of Industries, the Chamber of Commerce and Industry (SA) Inc., the Western Australian Chamber of Manufactures Inc., the Chamber of Industries (NT) Inc., and the Employers' Federations of NSW, VIC, SA and the ACT. Chambers of Commerce are not included because they are service organisations rather than employers' associations; moreover, they are organised at district, city and regional level rather than at State level. Finally, at the broadest level of all, there is the Confederation of Australian Industry (CAI), which was formed in 1977 as a national 'umbrella' organisation, and with which all the associations mentioned in the two classifications above are affiliated.

Historical development Employers' associations grew rapidly in the last two decades of the 19th century, partly as a counter to the growth of trade unionism and the power of the new industrial unions, such as the Australian Shearers' Union and the Amalgamated Miners' Association. By the end of the century there were also various co-ordinating associations in the colonies, and some of these had begun to hold intercolonial conferences. After federation the movement towards co-ordination at the national level grew stronger. Thus in 1903 the Associated Chambers of Manufacturers (ACMA) was formed, and in the following year, a conference of State Employers' Federations formed the Central Council of Employers of Australia.

The ACMA's activities developed and widened as manufacturing became more important in the Australian economy, especially in the period after World War II. It provided its affiliated associations with information on current and expected economic conditions, prepared submissions for the federal government and carried out studies on matters such as external trade and international trade agreements, taxation, trends in production, employment, consumer demand and the pattern of imports and exports; and in conjunction with the BANK OF NEW SOUTH WALES it began issuing a quarterly survey of industrial trends.

Meanwhile, the name of the Central Council of Employers of Australia had been changed in 1942 to the Australian Council of Employers' Federations (ACEF). Its main fields of operation were industrial relations and providing its members with services concerning arbitration and industrial regulations. It aimed at bringing about closer co-operation between employers throughout Australia, and was mainly responsible for the formation in 1946 of the National Employers' Association, a

loose organisation composed of over 30 nation-wide employers' associations and two single companies—Qantas and the BROKEN HILL PROPRIETARY COMPANY LIMITED. In 1961 this body, which consisted only of its member organisations and had no permanent staff of its own, formalised its operations to some extent by setting up a National Employers' Policy Committee and a National Employers' Industrial Committee, serviced by ACEF staff. However, the feeling was growing that employers' associations needed a more formal national organisation, and in the 1970s this was brought into being by two steps. First, in 1972, the ACMA and ACEF formed a Central Industrial Secretariat. Then in December 1977 they merged to form the CAI. Meanwhile, similar mergers had taken place in two States, with the formation of the Queensland Confederation of Industry and the Tasmanian Chamber of Industries.

The Confederation of Australian Industry The objectives of the CAI, as defined in its Memorandum and Articles of Association, include the following: to promote industry, trade and commerce in Australia and its Territories; to promote unity of purpose and of action in all matters relating to employers and to promote and foster their general welfare in the interests of Australian industry, trade and commerce generally; to safeguard the interests of employers throughout Australia and its Territories by promoting or opposing by lawful means legislation or other measures affecting or likely to affect employers and Australian industry, trade and commerce generally; to appear as far as the law allows in any Court or before any Tribunal, Commission, Committee or Inquiry whether industrial or otherwise to represent and protect employers as a body or individually; to improve the relations of employers with their employees; and to discuss and consider matters affecting employers, industry, trade and commerce; and to collect and disseminate such information relating thereto as may be of use to employers, industry, governments and the public.

Twelve State employers' associations comprised the foundation membership of the CAI, and within a few months nearly 30 other State and national bodies had become members. The CAI contains two operational wings— The National Employers' Industrial Council, which determines the policy of the CAI in respect of all matters concerning industrial relations, and the National Trade and Industry Council, which determines policy in respect of all matters concerning trade, industry and commerce. Each member association may elect to be represented on either or both of these Councils. Each Council elects annually a Committee consisting of 10 of its members to implement the policy of the CAI in the area of responsibility of that Council. A Board of Directors is responsible for administration, management of funds and property and co-ordination of policy matters determined by the two Councils.

See also arbitration and conciliation, industrial

Emu, *Dromaius novaehollandiae*

emu Next to the ostrich, the emu, *Dromaius novaehollandiae* (2m long and 2m tall) of the family Dromaiidae*, is the largest of all BIRDS. It has a large bill, long, dark greyish-brown down-like feathers and a white ruff; the sparsely feathered face and throat have a pale grey-blue skin. It is a swift-footed, flightless bird, able to run at a speed of about 50kph; its powerful legs are also used for defence and for swimming. Emus were once plentifully distributed throughout Australia, but settlement has driven them into sparsely populated open country where they are either sedentary or nomadic, depending on water supplies; unlike the related CASSOWARY, they tend to avoid forested areas.

Although emus are omnivorous, feeding on grasses, fruits, vegetable matter and insects such as caterpillars and grasshoppers, they suffer severely in times of drought. This, and the fact that many pastoralists consider them a pest because they break fences, has reduced their numbers and they are now found only on the Australian mainland. The nests are rough circles of stones or sticks, placed on the ground. Emus breed from April to November, laying six to 11 large, dark green eggs; the male cares for the eggs and the young. The chicks hatch after about eight weeks and are greyish-white with broad black stripes. The emu is featured on the Australian coat of arms.

emu bushes The several species of emu bush belong to the widespread genus *Eremophila* (family Myoporaceae), which contains about 100 species. They are shrubs or small trees with moderately large tubular flowers of various colours. The fruit is a drupe which falls from the plant. One common species often grown in gardens is the spotted emu bush, *E. maculata*, of E Australia; it has long, lanceolate leaves and spotted reddish or yellow flowers.

emuwrens see fairy-wrens, etc.

Encounter Bay SA Located on the S coast of the FLEURIEU PENINSULA near the mouth of the MURRAY RIVER, it was named in honour of the meeting here in 1802 between the ships of the French navigator, Nicholas BAUDIN, and the English explorer, Matthew FLINDERS. It became a whaling and sealing port but is now a holiday and recreation area with VICTOR HARBOUR as the main town.

endives *see* Compositae

energy minerals and energy policy *see* minerals, etc.

entoprocts The small phylum Entoprocta consists mainly of marine, encrusting animals which were once included with the ECTO-PROCTS in the phylum Bryozoa (sea mosses). It is now known that the way in which the body cavity is formed is profoundly different in the two groups (technically, the entoprocts have a pseudocoelom, the ectoprocts a true coelom). The only freshwater genus, *Urnatella*, has not been found in Australia. Marine species are seaweed-like, colonial animals that cling to rocks, weeds, shells, crabs, sponges and so on. They are small—each individual is only a few millimetres long—and they sweep minute particles into their mouths with the aid of minute hair-like appendages (cilia) on a crown of tentacles.
Further reading: see under ectoprocts.

Entrance, The NSW A tourist resort and retirement centre on the central coast, 108km by road N of Sydney, it is located where TUGGERAH LAKES have an entrance through the coastal dunes to the sea. There are numerous holiday centres clustered around the area, both on the coast (Bateau Bay, Toowoon Bay) and the lakeside (Long Jetty, Berkeley Vale, Tumbi Umbi); at the 1981 census, the urban area (including these smaller settlements) had a population of 37 881. The district has a mild climate, abundant summer sunshine and opportunities for fishing, swimming, surfing and other aquatic sports.

Clearing areas of natural vegetation in QLD

environment To a biologist the environment of an organism consists of all the entities which affect its existence. Some of these are non-living components (climate, soil, topography, water), while others are living organisms, including other members of the same population. It is thus common to refer to the 'physical environment' (non-living components) and the 'biological (or biotic) environment' (the living ones).

The concept of environment is often widened by other professions, such as sociologists, economists and architects, when they speak of the 'cultural environment' or of the human or man-made or built environment (*see* NATIONAL TRUST; HERITAGE CONSERVATION LEGIS-LATION).

It seems that the Australian Aborigines, as hunter-gatherers, had less effect on the Australian environment than the Europeans with their farming, forestry, engineering, buildings and alien animals, though the Aborigines wrought many changes with fire and may have killed off some of the larger marsupials.
See also animals (introduced); biological control; conservation; forestry; insects (introduced); irrigation; Murray River; national parks; pest control; rabbits.

Epacridaceae This mainly Australian family of dicotyledonous flowering plants contains about 30 genera and 400 species generally known as heaths. Epacrids are closely allied to the predominantly tropical and temperate family, Ericaceae, whose members are also known as heaths. (The family Ericaceae, which includes heather, *Calluna vulgaris*, is poorly represented in Australia, and is best known by snowberries, which belong to the native genus *Gaultheria*, and the many introduced species of *Erica*, *Azalea* and *Rhododendron*; some species of *Erica*, notably *E. lusitanica*, have become naturalised, particularly in TAS, where they occasionally become serious WEEDS.)

Members of the family Epacridaceae are ever-green shrubs, usually small and rarely tree-like. The leathery leaves are simple and alternate, with parallel longitudinal veins, and are hard and rigid, often with rigid tips. The flowers are solitary or in spikes or racemes, and are axillary or terminal. Each flower is surrounded by many overlapping bracts which merge into the calyx. The flowers are regular and usually bisexual. The ovary is superior with one to 10 locules usually surrounded at the base by a disc which secretes nectar. The four to five sepals are persistent, and either partly fused or free. There are four to five petals which are usually fused into a tube which has spreading lobes or which splits transversally from a persistent base. In most species the four to five stamens are attached to the petals; the anthers are single-celled at maturity. The stigma is small and simple, and the fruit occurs as a drupe or a capsule.

Epacrids occur in a wide range of temperate plant communities, including sedgeland (swamps), heath, woodland and open and closed forest. Many species are small-leafed shrubs which are popular garden plants; they belong to such familiar genera as *Sprengelia* (swamp heath), *Leucopogon* (bearded heath) and *Epacris*, which includes such heaths as *E. impressa*, in which the flower colour varies from white to pink to crimson, and *E. longi-*

Coral heath, *Epacris microphylla*

flora, which has pendant, crimson, bell-shaped flowers tipped with white. Most epacrids are odourless but *Woolsia pungens*, a handsome grass-green shrub, has aromatic white flowers. The family also contains a number of prostrate shrubs, such as pine heath and cranberry heath (*Astroloma* species), honey pots and ground berry (*Acrotriche* species) and urn heath (*Melichrus* species). Tall small-leafed shrubs include daphne heath (*Brachyloma* species) and broom heath (*Monotoca* species).

Large-leafed shrubs of the family Epacridaceae include members of the *Dracophyllum* and *Richea* genera. *Richea* is a particularly interesting endemic Australian genus, represented by nine species in TAS and one in VIC; the leaves are crowded and overlapping, and give the larger members of the genus an appearance similar to some palms. The largest species is the giant grass tree, *R. pandanifolia*, which occurs in S closed forests; it grows to 12m tall and has leaves up to 1.5m long.

The most curious member of the family is *Wittsteinia vacciniacea*, which is endemic to VIC. This rather soft, broad, glossy-leafed shrub forms dense mats in S closed forests, and is unique in that it has an inferior ovary, and for a long time was considered to be a member of the Ericaceae.
See also Angiospermae; Appendix 5, Flower Structure and Glossary of Botanical Terms
Further reading: see Appendix 6, A Bibliography for Plants.

Ephemeroptera *see* mayflies

Eppalock Reservoir VIC Located on the CAMPASPE RIVER, a tributary of the MURRAY RIVER, about 30km SE of BENDIGO, it is an earth-and-rockfill structure built in 1960-62. With a capacity of 311 900ML, it is the largest storage reservoir on the Campaspe and is designed to control seasonal flooding of the river and to store water for irrigation and urban supplies. The dam has a maximum height of 45m and a catchment area of 2 124km². Waters of the reservoir are released downstream by the Campaspe Weir to irrigate farmlands on the riverine plains of the lower stream S of ROCHESTER. At periods of peak demand for irrigation, water is pumped into the GOULBURN irrigation system to augment supplies in the WARANGA Western Channel. Water from the Eppalock Reservoir is also conveyed through a 26km-long pipeline to supply Bendigo; a unique feature of this supply system is that three turbo-pump units are activated by water released from the reservoir to the river for irrigation supplies. Lake Eppalock is a popular recreation area for aquatic sports. The name appears to be of Scottish origin, but probably came from the Greek word *epi* meaning 'upon' or 'at that location'.

Erica *see* Epacridaceae

Ericaceae *see* Epacridaceae

Eriostemon *see* Rutaceae

Ern Malley Hoax This, the most famous literary hoax in Australian history, was perpetrated in 1943 by the two Sydney poets, James McAULEY and Harold Stewart. Repelled by what they saw as the irrationally uncritical pursuit of modernism practised by the Adelaide literary magazine *Angry Penguins*, they concocted a number of poems allegedly written by one Ern Malley and discovered after his untimely death by his sister, Ethel. These pieces, they later claimed, were composed in the course of a single afternoon, mainly by opening various reference books at random and stringing together passages from them in a style reminiscent of modernist poems published in *Angry Penguins*. Two of the poems were then sent to the magazine's editor, Max Harris, with a covering letter from 'Ethel', who gave a Sydney address. Harris replied, and was supplied with a collection of poems and prose aphorisms entitled *The Darkening Ecliptic*. All were published in *Angry Penguins*, and hailed as the work of a poet 'of tremendous power'. When the hoax was revealed in mid-1944, Harris took the stand that McAuley and Stewart, by using the style which they had set out to ridicule, had in fact produced poetry of merit.
Further reading: Mandle, W.F. 'Angry Penguins and the poet's vision of Australia' in *Going It Alone*. Penguin, Ringwood VIC, 1977.

Esk Rivers TAS The two rivers, the North Esk and the South Esk, join at LAUNCESTON to become the TAMAR RIVER which drains N into BASS STRAIT. Both streams are located in the N-central part of the State, both have some of their headwater streams in the BEN LOMOND National Park highlands at elevations of over 1 300m, and both drain generally W across the N MIDLANDS region. The North Esk lies to the N, nearer Bass Strait, and its main tributary, the St Patrick River, makes a great arc to the N and W of Mt Barrow (1 413m high) before joining the North Esk about 20km SE of Launceston. The South Esk, over its course of some 240km, curves around the Ben Lomond Plateau from its source, then flows generally NW, roughly parallel to a section of the Midland Highway N of CAMPBELL TOWN, makes a series of meander loops E of LONGFORD, and then flows N to Launceston. The Nile and Ben Lomond Rivers are two right-bank tributaries of the South Esk; another major tributary is the Macquarie River which drains from the E coast highlands past the town of ROSS; other tributaries, such as the Lake and Meander Rivers, rise in the CENTRAL PLATEAU, cut through the GREAT WESTERN TIERS, and drop to the N coastal plain to join the South Esk. The Trevallyn Dam (dam wall 33m high), completed in 1955 on the South Esk near Launceston, is a link in the vast GREAT LAKE hydro-electricity scheme: water from the plateau is used to generate power at POATINA, then conveyed into the Lake River and, with the South Esk and its other tributaries, contributes to the Trevallyn Dam; it then flows through a 3km-long tunnel to the Trevallyn power station, which has an installed generating capacity of 80 000kW and is located on the W bank of the Tamar, 5km from Launceston.

Esperance WA (population 6 375 in 1981) A port and resort town on the S coast of the State, it is situated on Esperance Bay, 409km by rail S of KALGOORLIE and 1 066km from Perth. The bay was named by the French explorer Bruni d'Entrecasteaux after one of his ships, *L'Esperance*, when he sheltered there in 1792 in the calm water protected on the SW by Dempster Head. It was a whaling port until the development of the goldfields to the N in the 1890s, when it became a port and a holiday haven for the mining population and the wheat and wool farming communities of the hinterland. Its many scenic attractions have made it a popular resort centre. The town has an average annual rainfall of 675mm, concentrated mainly in winter.
The plains, inland from the coast, are quite well watered but have a natural vegetation cover of low scrub, much like semi-desert country. For many decades, attempts to grow crops and cultivate pastures had been unsuccessful and the land supported only sparse sheep grazing, but in 1949 an agricultural research station was established to investigate the reasons for this anomaly and it was found that superphosphate and various trace elements (copper, zinc and molybdenum) could greatly enhance the soil's fertility. Since the 1960s there has been considerable land development in the region, not all of it successful. Some Americans (the best known is Art Linkletter) have invested in this agricultural and pastoral development scheme, which has concentrated on beef cattle, sheep grazing, cereals and fodder crops.

Esson, Thomas Louis Buvelot (1879-1943) Journalist and playwright. Born in Edinburgh, Esson came to Australia as a child and was brought up in Melbourne in an artistic environment. In 1905 he visited the Abbey Theatre, Dublin, whose playwrights, particularly Yeats, encouraged him to found a similar national theatre in Australia. His earliest plays were staged by William Moore in 1910-12, and his first full-length play, *The Time is Not Yet Ripe*, was produced by Gregan McMAHON in 1912. Living in London after World War I, Esson wrote *The Drovers*, perhaps his best-known play, before returning to Australia to help found the Pioneer Players in 1922. However, the group, which was set up to stage Australian plays, lasted only four years. A noted wit and raconteur in private, Esson tended to show a rather gaunt and melancholy strain in his plays, particularly in *Shipwreck*, *Mother and Son* and *The Bride of Gospel Place*. Disappointed in his attempt to create an Australian drama he returned to journalism and lived in Sydney until his death. *Further reading:* Rees, L. *The Making of Australian Drama*. Angus & Robertson, Sydney, 1973.

ethnic groups in Australia C.A. Price, a leading authority on multicultural affairs, in a study on the ethnic origins of the Australian population based on an eight-generation analysis, estimated the total English component to be equivalent to 6 471 400 persons or 45.37% of the total population in 1978. The Scottish component was estimated to be 1 747 661 persons or 12.25% and the Welsh 198 700 persons or 1.39%. Thus the total British component was 59.01%. No separate entry has been provided for the English, Scottish or Welsh ethnic groups because together they have provided the mainstream of Australian culture, including the English language, literature, historical knowledge, political and legal institutions and many of our social customs. In the nineteenth century further ethnic variety was added by the Irish, German and Chinese immigrants and in the second half of the twentieth century the percentage of other ethnic groups in Australia has increased. The historical origin of these groups and their contribution to our way of life is recorded in separate entries. *See* Arabic-speaking people in Australia; Boat People; Chinese in Australia; Dutch in Australia; Germans in Australia; Greeks in Australia; Irish in Australia; Indian sub-continent, settlers from; Italians in Australia; Japanese in Australia; Jews in Australia; Maltese in Australia; Spanish-speaking people in Australia; Vietnamese refugees in Australia; Yugoslavs in Australia

Eucalyptus *see* Myrtaceae

Eucla WA This small isolated hamlet is on the EYRE HIGHWAY in the SE corner of the State, S of the transcontinental railway line, near the WA/SA border. At an elevation of 87km above sea level, it lies in the S part of the NULLARBOR PLAIN in an arid region which receives an average annual rainfall of only 254mm. It was formerly a telegraph station on the line between Perth and Adelaide. The

Eucla Basin is the name applied to the artesian basin which underlies the Nullarbor region, from which highly mineralised bore water is obtained.

Eucla Basin *see* artesian water

Eucumbene River NSW A tributary of the SNOWY RIVER in the SW part of the Monaro Plateau of the SOUTHERN TABLE-LANDS in south-eastern NSW, it rises in rugged range country SW of the ACT in the KOSCIUSKO area and flows S to join the Snowy at Lake Jindabyne. The construction of a major dam on the Eucumbene has given the river prominence in recent decades; with a capacity of 4 800ML, the dam forms the key storage reservoir of the SNOWY MOUNTAINS SCHEME. Lake Eucumbene and Lake Jinda-byne are popular summertime tourist attrac-tions for trout fishing and aquatic sports. The Gaden trout hatchery near JINDABYNE, 60km from COOMA, breeds fingerlings for release into the lakes and streams of the region.

Euphorbiaceae This dicotyledonous family of flowering plants contains 280 genera and 7000 species; most occur in tropical regions but a few herbaceous genera, particu-larly *Euphorbia*, grow in temperate latitudes.

Members of the family Euphorbiaceae are trees, shrubs or herbs. Most species have simple leaves, either alternate or opposite, but a few have no leaves. Many species have stipules. The flowers are unisexual and rarely have petals; there are four to six sepals and one to many stamens. The ovary is superior and usually has three locules, each containing one or two ovules; the styles are free or joined at the base and are often branched. The fruit, which occurs as a capsule and may be succu-lent, splits at maturity into mericarps, leaving a persistent axis.

The family Euphorbiaceae contains a number of economically important plants, including: two rubber-producing species, *Hevea brasilien-sis* and *Manihot glaziovii*; cassava, *M. esculenta*; and the castor oil plant, *Ricinus communis*. A number of species, such as those in the genus *Toxicodendron*, are extremely poisonous or, like the castor oil plant, contain small quantities of poisonous substances.

The most familiar species of the family Euphorbiaceae are either WEEDS, such as petty spurge, *Euphorbia peplus*, or colourful culti-vated plants, including: poinsettia, *E. pulcher-rima*; croton, *Codiaeum variegatum*; beefsteak plant, *Acalypha wilkesiana*; and crown of thorns, *E. milii*. The latter is almost leafless and armed with strong thorns. Some entirely leafless species, such as the gorgon's head, *E. caputmedusae*, are succulent cactus-like plants.

Australian members of the family include a number of trees and shrubs, concentrated mainly in N closed forest, but extending into tall open forest and woodland. The cheese tree, *Glochidion fernandii*, is common in closed forest and coastal gullies around Sydney, and bleeding heart, *Omolanthus populifolius*, with

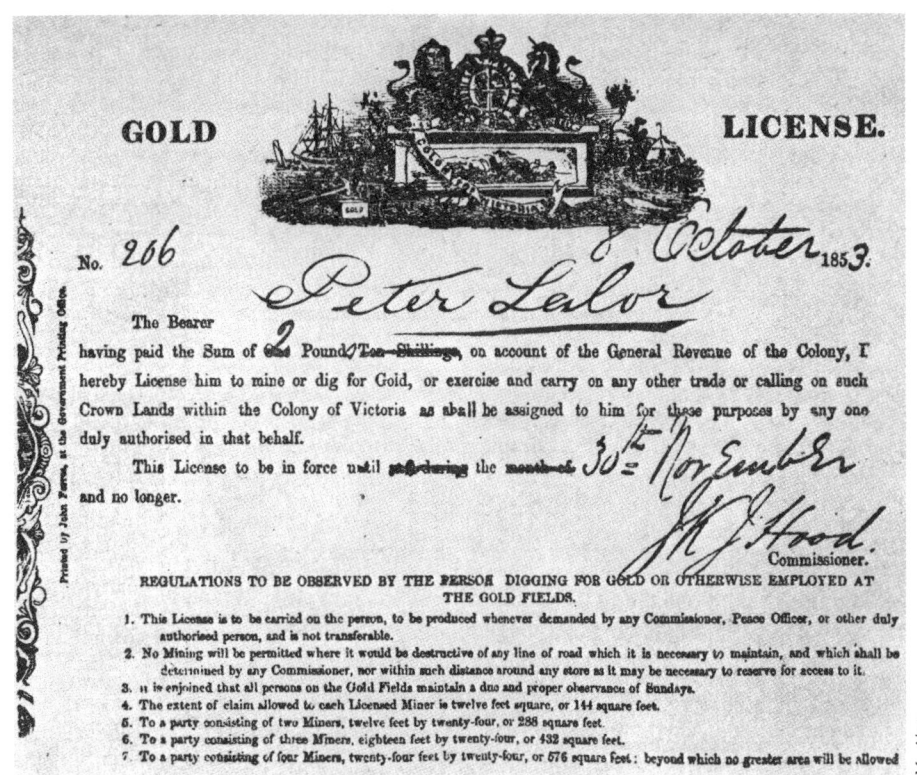

Gold licence 1853

M. Akers

its scattering of brilliant scarlet leaves amongst the green, has found a place as a cultivated species.
See also Angiospermae; Appendix 5, Flower Structure and Glossary of Botanical Terms
Further reading: see Appendix 6, A Biblio-graphy for Plants.

Eureka Stockade This was the site of an armed insurrection at BALLARAT on the VIC goldfields in 1854.
Causes of discontent The basic cause of the incident was resentment against the licence fee of 30 shillings a month which each miner was required to pay. This licence system had been adopted by the governments of NSW and VIC to meet the enormous administrative costs arising from the gold rushes. At first, when average earnings per miner were high, it did not seem an unreasonable burden. Even at this stage, however, the miners who made a great deal of money were in a minority, and as the number of diggers increased and most deposits of easily won surface gold were exhausted, average earnings fell sharply, and as the incomes decreased, resentment against the fee became stronger. Ill feeling was also caused by the methods used to collect the fee. In VIC, licences were checked by a special force of armed police, many of whom were ex-convicts. Sometimes they organised 'digger hunts', raiding a section of the diggings and asking every miner to produce his licence. Those who could not produce them immediately were taken into custody, sometimes being chained to logs or trees until the 'hunt' was over and they could be taken before a magistrate. The penalty for failing to produce one's licence was

£5. Political grievances, especially lack of voting rights, also played a part. The franchise was based on property qualifications, and most miners, because they were newcomers and moved from field to field, did not own property.

Ill feeling came to a head when a miner named James Scobie was murdered near the Eureka Hotel in Ballarat. His fellow miners believed that the publican, an ex-convict named Bentley, who was friendly with a number of police officers, was guilty. Bentley was charged with the crime, but a magistrate dismissed the charge. This was seen as another, and particularly flagrant, act of official injustice towards miners. A mob stormed the hotel and burned it, and the Ballarat Reform League was formed to press for the abolition of the licence fee and for other reforms.
The insurrection and its consequences Although Bentley was re-arrested and sub-sequently convicted, feelings continued to rise. The police continued to hold licence inspec-tions, but the miners held meetings at which hundreds of them burned their licences. The League came increasingly under the domina-tion of extremists, and finally about 500 men, under the leadership of an Irishman, Peter LALOR, took up arms, constructed a stockade in the Eureka district of Ballarat, and pro-claimed a 'Republic of Victoria'. The revolt was quickly crushed. Early on the morning of Sunday 3 December, when only about 150 miners were in the stockade, a force of about 300 soldiers and police attacked and captured it after a 15-minute battle. Six of the attackers were killed. There is disagreement about the exact death toll among the miners, but Lalor

put it at 22. Lalor escaped but 13 other miners were captured and charged with sedition. However, it soon became clear that, while general public opinion in the colony did not approve of the rebellion, there was such widespread sympathy with the miners regarding their grievances that it would probably be impossible to obtain convictions against any of the rebels. The charge against one of them was withdrawn and the other 12 were brought to trial but acquitted. No action was taken against Lalor when he emerged from hiding.

Although the insurrection had been crushed so easily, the most important demands of the Ballarat Reform League were granted soon afterwards. In 1855 the miner's licence was replaced with a document called a Miner's Right, costing only £1 a year and entitling the holder to the vote. Two years later manhood suffrage was granted for elections of the Legislative Assembly. To what extent the Eureka incident had been instrumental in securing these reforms, and how important it is in Australian history, are matters of debate among historians.

See also gold discoveries
Further reading: Currey, C.H. *The Irish at Eureka.* Angus & Robertson, Sydney, 1954; *Historical Studies: Eureka Supplement.* (2nd edn) Melbourne University Press, Melbourne, 1965; Carboni, R. *The Eureka Story.* Melbourne University Press, Melbourne, 1969.

Euroa VIC (population 2 641 in 1981) This country town is on the Hume Highway and on the Melbourne-Sydney railway route, 151km by rail NNE of Melbourne, and 44km SW of BENALLA. At an elevation of 175m above sea level, it receives an average annual rainfall of 649mm, and is a service centre for the adjacent sheep grazing areas. In December 1878 the Ned KELLY gang of bushrangers held up the bank in Euroa and robbed it of £2000. The town's name may be derived from either of two Aboriginal words: *yera-o* meaning 'joyful' or *eurawa* meaning 'push' or 'thrust'.

euros *see* kangaroos, etc.

eutherian mammals This group of MAMMALS belongs to the subclass Eutheria, which contains such familiar animals as man, rabbits, mice, dogs, lions and deer. They are sometimes called placental mammals but this term is misleading as some MARSUPIALS have placentas. Eutherians differ from the MONOTREME MAMMALS and marsupials in that they produce young at an advanced stage of development. In some cases the young are able to run within a few hours of birth.

Eutherians are found in all continents and most land masses, with the exception of some remote oceanic islands. They are also found in all oceans. The subclass is divided into several orders, the following of which contain native Australian species, or species within her adjacent seas: Carnivora (DINGO); Cetacea (DOLPHINS AND WHALES); Chiroptera (BATS AND FLYING FOXES); Pinnipedia (SEALS);

Primates (Man); Rodentia (RODENTS); and Sirenia (SEA COWS).

Many of the species are endemic to Australia or to Australia and New Guinea, though they belong to widespread families. The bats and rodents, or their ancestors, entered Australia in several waves by 'island hopping' along the chain from South-East Asia. The bats would have found no difficulty in crossing water gaps; the rodents, being small mammals, would have floated across on floating debris. The dingo came to Australia with one of the later migrations of Aborigines who would have used boats or rafts.

Further reading: see under monotreme mammals; marsupials. *Also* Simpson, G.G. *The Geography of Evolution.* Chilton Books, Philadelphia & New York, 1965. Strahan, R. *The Australian Museum Complete Book of Australian Mammals.* Angus and Robertson, Sydney, 1983.

Evans, George William (1780-1852) Explorer. Born in Warwick, England, Evans learned the elements of surveying during his apprenticeship to an engineer and architect. He reached Sydney from the Cape of Good Hope in 1802, gained the position of acting Surveyor-General in 1803 and in the following year discovered and explored the lower reaches of the WARRAGAMBA RIVER. In 1805 Governor KING dismissed him 'for fraud', but the details of the accusation are not known.

After several years of farming near the HAWKESBURY RIVER, he was appointed assistant surveyor at PORT DALRYMPLE in TAS in 1809 but for the following nine years his services were used chiefly on the mainland. In November 1813 Governor MACQUARIE sent him to follow up the exploration of BLAXLAND, LAWSON and WENTWORTH in the BLUE MOUNTAINS. Although these three men are commonly credited with crossing the Blue Mts, it was Evans who first made a complete crossing and reached the W plains. On this journey he discovered the MACQUARIE RIVER and proceeded past the present site of BATHURST. In 1814 Macquarie sent him to Hobart, and gave him a grant of 400ha there, but several months later recalled him to act as guide for the Governor's official tour of the Bathurst Plains. In May 1815, Evans set out from the newly founded town of Bathurst, discovered the LACHLAN RIVER near the site of COWRA, and followed it for some distance.

In 1817 and 1818 he was again summoned from Hobart, but on each occasion only as second-in-command to OXLEY in the expeditions along the Lachlan and Macquarie Rivers. Otherwise he was fully occupied with his duties in TAS until his retirement in 1825, an event which was clouded by a serious dispute with Lieutenant-Governor ARTHUR. Apart from his work in surveying and exploring, he possessed some skill as an artist, and during the 1830s was the art teacher at the King's School; several of his paintings are in the Dixson Library, Sydney.

See also exploration by land

Dr. H.V. Evatt

Mitchell Library

Further reading: Weatherburn, A.K. *George William Evans, Explorer.* Angus & Robertson, Sydney, 1966.

Evatt, Herbert Vere (1894-1965) Jurist and Labor political leader. Born in East Maitland NSW, Dr Evatt had a brilliant academic career at the University of Sydney, was called to the Bar in 1918 and became a KC in 1929. In the meantime he had entered politics by standing successfully in 1925 as a Labor candidate for the Balmain seat in the NSW Legislative Assembly, but in 1930 he resigned in order to become the youngest-ever Justice of the High Court of Australia. He returned to politics in 1940 as a member of the House of Representatives, and when John CURTIN became Prime Minister in the following year Evatt was made Attorney-General and Minister for External Affairs—portfolios which he retained until Labor's defeat in 1949. During this period he attracted international attention, particularly through his participation in the San Francisco Conference of the UN in 1945, at which he came to be regarded as a leading spokesman for the smaller nations. He was also president of the General Assembly of the UN in 1948-49.

In 1951, on the death of Ben CHIFLEY, he became leader of the Australian Labor Party (ALP) and of the federal Opposition. However, in spite of his intellectual brilliance, he failed to revive the party's fortunes. His brusque manner and lack of skill as an orator were considerable handicaps, and his appearances as counsel in the High Court appeal against the Communist Party Dissolution Act in 1951 and the PETROV ENQUIRY in 1954 were considered by many to be tactical errors. After the Petrov enquiry, his accusations against the activities within the ALP of members of the Roman Catholic Social Movement precipitated the split which culminated in the foundation of the DEMOCRATIC LABOR PARTY. He left politics in 1960 to become Chief Justice of the Supreme Court of NSW, but retired from that position two years later on account of ill health. During his career, Evatt published a number of books, including *The King and His*

Dominion Governors (1936), *Rum Rebellion* (1938) and a biography of William HOLMAN entitled *Australian Labour Leader* (1940). *Further reading:* Dalziel, A. *Evatt the Enigma.* Lansdowne Press, Melbourne, 1967.

eventing *see* show-jumping, etc.

everlastings *see* Compositae

Exmouth WA (population 2 583 in 1981) A modern town established in 1967 on the NORTH WEST CAPE, it is 1 428km by road NNW of Perth and 371km off the North West Coastal Highway. It was founded as a support town to the Harold E. Holt communications station, operated by the US Navy as part of its world network. The navy base is a restricted area (over 10km²) but its 13 soaring towers (each taller than the Eiffel Tower, the tallest being almost 396m high) and its deep-water pier can be viewed from Lighthouse Hill. Nearby is the Cape Range No 2 oil well, which struck oil in non-commercial quantities and is now sealed. The town is named after Exmouth Gulf, a shallow inlet E of the cape, important for prawn fisheries and as a base for game-fishing vessels. The 'Exmo-Gamex' festival is held in September-October each year. The town experiences hot conditions throughout the year, with high summer temperatures, an average annual rainfall of only 325mm and a dry season in spring and early summer. The Cape Range National Park, covering 50 581ha in the central and W parts of the cape, is noted for its gorges, caves, Aboriginal paintings and wildlife.

exploration by land This article discusses only the exploration of the Australian mainland (for the exploration of TAS, *see* TASMANIA; for sea exploration *see* DISCOVERY).
Stage 1: 1788-1830 For the first few years in the history of NSW the main aim of exploration was to find enough good farming land to make the colony self-sufficient in food. Within a few years the search had resulted in the exploration of the whole Sydney Plain, but further progress inland was for many years blocked by the BLUE MOUNTAINS. The difficulty of crossing these mountains was not the result of their height, but of their formation. They consist of a plateau dissected by deep gorges, most of which are fringed with precipices. Early explorers made the mistake of following the river valleys, only to find themselves confronted with cliffs too high and sheer for them to climb. The solution was found by Gregory BLAXLAND, Lieutenant William LAWSON and William Charles WENTWORTH who in 1813, accompanied by four convicts, followed the plan of keeping to the ridges that form the watershed between the WARRAGAMBA and Grose Rivers. They went as far as Mt Blaxland, from where it seemed evident that the remainder of the way was comparatively easy going. Shortly after their return, George EVANS was sent by Governor MACQUARIE to follow up their work, went as

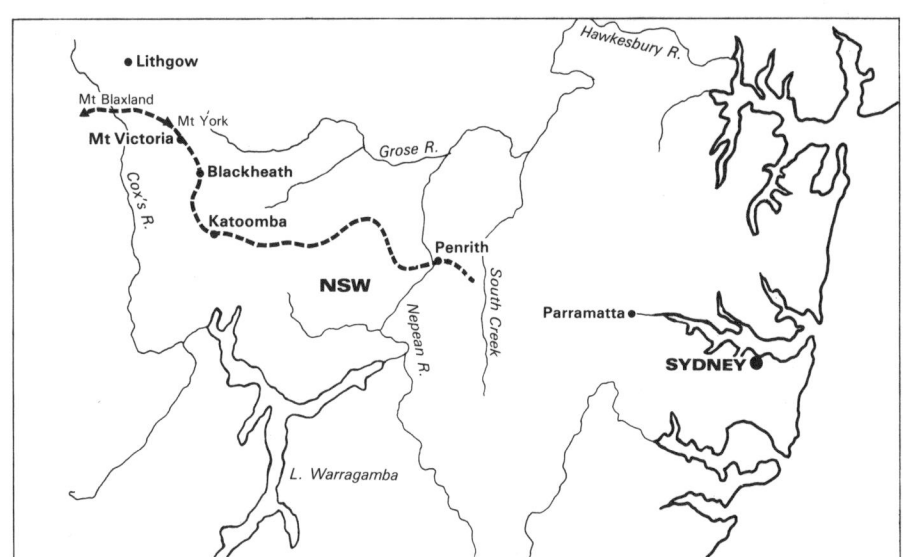

The route of Blaxland, Lawson and Wentworth (modern towns and the man-made Lake Warragamba included)

far as the site of BATHURST and discovered the MACQUARIE RIVER.

During the remainder of the period up to 1830 there were many minor feats of exploration in the area around Sydney that eventually became known as the NINETEEN COUNTIES, but on the larger scale, exploration was concerned mainly with the problem of the W rivers. In 1815 Evans discovered the LACHLAN RIVER, and in 1817 John OXLEY followed it until it became lost in swamps. In the following year Oxley set out along the Macquarie, but again finished in 'an ocean of reeds'. He then turned E, reaching the sea at PORT MACQUARIE and on the way crossing the CASTLEREAGH, Peel and Namoi Rivers, all flowing inland. The problem became more complex with the journey of Hamilton HUME and William Hovell in 1824-25. They set out from Hume's property near Gunning, which was then the limit of settlement SW from Sydney, with the aim of reaching WESTERN PORT BAY, but actually reached the sea at CORIO BAY. On the way they crossed the MURRUMBIDGEE, the Tumut, the MURRAY (which they called the Hume) and a number of the Murray's S tributaries, such as the MITTA MITTA, OVENS and GOULBURN Rivers. Another journey of major importance was made in 1827 by Allan CUNNINGHAM, who led an expedition from the HUNTER RIVER to the DARLING DOWNS, in what is now southern QLD, and discovered the pass, now named Cunningham's Gap, leading from the Downs to the MORETON BAY district. On the way he crossed the GWYDIR, DUMARESQ and CONDAMINE RIVERS, all flowing inland.

The expeditions made by Hume, Hovell and Cunningham were important in opening the way for the spread of the squatting movement, but they merely deepened the mystery of the W rivers. Since navigators such as FLINDERS had observed no large estuaries on the S coast, there was wide support for the idea, first put forward by Oxley, that the rivers flowed into an inland sea. This theory was disproved by

Charles STURT. In 1828, a drought year, Sturt followed the Macquarie until it ran dry, discovered the DARLING RIVER and saw where the Castlereagh joined it. This led him to conclude, correctly, that all the N rivers flowed to the Darling. In 1829-30 he went by boat down the Murrumbidgee to the Murray and followed the latter all the way to its unobtrusive entrance to the sea across the shoals of ENCOUNTER BAY. He presumed that the Murray was the same river as that which Hume had named after himself, and that the large river joining the Murray from the N was the Darling, so concluding that all the inland rivers formed part of one large Murray-Darling system.
Stage 2: 1831-42 By the end of this stage the whole of SE Australia, the SW corner and an area to the N of Adelaide beyond LAKE TORRENS had been penetrated. Explorers had also journeyed along the shores of the GREAT AUSTRALIAN BIGHT and the W coast, but without penetrating more than a few miles inland.

In the SE the most important explorer was Major Thomas MITCHELL, who completed the work of Sturt and confirmed his theory about the W rivers. In 1831 Mitchell followed a number of N rivers and decided that they must join the Darling. In 1835 he traced the Darling downstream far beyond the point reached by Sturt. In 1836 he went down the Lachlan, Murrumbidgee and Murray Rivers to the Murray-Darling junction and followed the latter N until he had to admit that it was indeed the Darling. Finally, he ascended the Murray to the site of modern SWAN HILL, went S across what is now the W part of VIC, met the HENTY brothers at Portland Bay, and returned to Sydney across northern VIC. Few Australian journeys of exploration have been as important as this in opening up new territory to settlement. Working on a smaller scale than Mitchell, Angus Macmillan in a series of expeditions from the MONARO district between 1839 and 1841 crossed the GREAT DIVIDING RANGE into E GIPPSLAND. The

Polish explorer STRZELECKI also journeyed into Gippsland in 1840, after exploring the district around KOSCIUSKO, which he named after a famous Polish patriot.

In SA the outstanding explorer was Edward John EYRE, who led three expeditions between 1839 and 1841. On the first he explored the FLINDERS RANGES and discovered Lake Torrens. On the second he sailed to PORT LINCOLN and explored parts of EYRE PENINSULA. In 1840 he went N again, passed Lake Torrens and saw a S arm of LAKE EYRE, but found the whole area extremely barren. From the hill which he named Mt Hopeless he turned back and decided to lead his party W. After resting at Port Lincoln he went to Fowler's Bay, and then continued along the shore of the Great Australian Bight accompanied only by three Aborigines and Baxter, his overseer. Two months later two of the Aborigines killed Baxter and left with most of the stores. Eyre and the remaining Aboriginal, a boy known as Wylie, struggled on. They were fortunate in obtaining supplies from a French whaling vessel at Rossiter Bay, near the site of ESPERANCE, and finally reached ALBANY. Their journey, while it added little to knowledge of Australia, was certainly one of the greatest feats of endurance in the history of its exploration.

In WA the main features of the SW corner were discovered by Captain Thomas Bannister, W.H. Bunbury and the colony's first Surveyor-General, J.S. Roe. George GREY explored the Hanover Bay area in the NW in 1837; two years later, having been taken by ship to SHARK BAY, he was forced by the loss of his stores to return to Perth by land almost immediately, but in the course of his journey added considerably to knowledge of the W coast. Sections of N Australia were also explored during this period by John WICKHAM, commander of the *Beagle*, and by J.L. Stokes, who succeeded him in command in 1841. They had been sent to survey parts of the coast missed by Flinders, but Stokes went beyond mere naval survey work, leading parties many miles inland in a number of places.

Stage 3: 1842-58 This was a period of great progress, at the end of which the only large unexplored areas were the driest parts of the continent in central, W and NW Australia. The greatest progress of all was in the NE and far N, where in 1844-45 Ludwig LEICHHARDT travelled from the Darling Downs to PORT ESSINGTON. A particularly tragic expedition was that led by Edmund KENNEDY along the E coast of CAPE YORK in 1848. His party was landed at Rockingham Bay, about half way between modern CAIRNS and COOKTOWN, with the intention of travelling to Cape York, where a ship was to pick them up. Towards the end of the journey, however, illness, lack of food, and an accident in which one man shot himself led Kennedy to leave eight men at Weymouth Bay and another three at Shelbourne Bay, while he and an Aboriginal boy went on. Six of the men at Weymouth Bay eventually died of starvation and illness, and

the three at Shelbourne Bay were killed by Aborigines, as was Kennedy himself. The Aboriginal boy, known only by the nickname 'Jacky Jacky', was wounded but managed to reach the ship, which then sailed to the rescue of the other two survivors. A third expedition of importance in the far N and NE was that of Sir Augustus GREGORY in 1855-56, from a point on the coast not far from modern Darwin to Port Curtis, on the QLD coast.

In exploration towards central Australia the important figures were Sturt, Mitchell, Kennedy and Gregory. In 1844-45 Sturt tried to reach the centre of the continent by following the Murray and Darling to the site of MENINDEE and then striking NW. He passed close to the site of modern BROKEN HILL, and was then trapped by drought at a place which he called Rocky Glen. When rain came at last he continued N to COOPER'S CREEK and across STURT'S STONY DESERT, but failed in attempts to cross the great sand ridges of the SIMPSON DESERT. Further to the E Mitchell discovered the BARCOO RIVER and Kennedy followed it far enough to show that it was probably only the upper reaches of Cooper's Creek. Shortly after this Leichhardt disappeared while trying to cross the continent from E to W, and in 1858 Gregory, looking for traces of Leichhardt's expedition, travelled down the Barcoo and Cooper's Creek and on to Adelaide, thus providing fresh knowledge of the forbidding country to the E of Lake Eyre and Lake Torrens.

Stage 4: 1858-76 The early 1860s were marked by rival attempts to make the first crossing of the continent from S to N. In 1860 an expedition led by Robert O'Hara BURKE set out from Melbourne with this objective. Financed by public subscription, it included 18 men and was lavishly equipped. However, owing to Burke's inexperience and poor leadership, and to the pressure by the organising committee to make haste, most of this manpower and equipment was wasted. After reaching Menindee, Burke pushed on with an advance party to Cooper's Creek, and after five weeks there waiting in vain for the main party to catch up, divided his forces again. With his second-in-command, W.J. Wills, and two men named Gray and King, he pushed on to the GULF OF CARPENTARIA, leaving William Brahe in charge at Cooper's Creek. The four reached the waters of the Gulf, but on the return journey Gray died. The others reached Cooper's Creek in a state of exhaustion, only to find that Brahe had abandoned the depot just seven hours earlier. The sequel was that Burke and Wills died not far from the abandoned depot, while King, who had been helped by Aborigines, was rescued by a search party three months later.

Meanwhile, in 1860 John McDouall STUART had set out from Adelaide and had reached the geographical centre of the continent, where he gave the name Central Mount Sturt to a hill which was later renamed Central Mount Stuart. He continued a little further N but turned back at a place he called Attack Creek,

the site of an attack on his party by Aborigines. On a second attempt he reached the site of NEWCASTLE WATERS, and on a third attempt in 1862 succeeded in reaching the N coast near the site of Darwin.

Following these expeditions and one by F.T. Gregory in the PILBARA district of WA in 1861, there was little left to explore except the E half of WA. In 1872 the completion of the OVERLAND TELEGRAPH from Darwin to Adelaide made penetration of this region much easier. In 1873 P.E. Warburton crossed from the line near ALICE SPRINGS to the NW coast at ROEBURNE. In the following year John FORREST, who had won attention by crossing the NULLARBOR PLAIN from W to E in 1870, made a journey from GERALDTON to Peake telegraph station in the N of SA. In 1875-76 Ernest GILES made a double crossing—from Beltana, near Lake Torrens, to Perth and then, by a more N route, back to Peake. By this time the main problems of Australia geography had been solved, and the exploration of the remaining patches of territory was comparatively easy.

Further reading: Favenc, E. *The History of Australian Exploration.* Turner & Henderson, Sydney, 1888 and *The Explorers of Australia.* Whitcombe & Tombs, Christchurch, 1908; Fitzpatrick, K. *Australian Explorers.* Oxford University Press, London, 1958; Scott, Sir Ernest *Australian Discovery.* (vol 2) Dent, London, 1929 (reprinted Johnson Reprint Corp., New York, 1966); Feeken, E.H.J., Feeken, G.E.E. & Spate, O.K.H. *The Discovery and Exploration of Australia.* Nelson, Sydney, 1970.

external affairs *see* foreign relations

Eyre, Edward John (1815-1901) Explorer. Born in Bedfordshire, England, he arrived in Sydney in 1833 and after various farming and droving ventures, including overland trips with sheep and cattle to Adelaide, settled in the latter city in 1839. His explorations in the LAKE TORRENS area and EYRE

Edward John Eyre

PENINSULA, and his epic journey around the GREAT AUSTRALIAN BIGHT are recounted in the entry on EXPLORATION BY LAND. After these journeys he served for a short time as magistrate and protector of Aborigines at Moorundie on the MURRAY RIVER.

Eyre left Australia in 1844 and later filled positions as Lieutenant-Governor in New Zealand and at St Vincent in the West Indies, as acting Governor in the Leeward Islands, and as acting Governor and, subsequently, Governor-in-Chief of Jamaica. In 1865 he was responsible for suppressing Negro riots in Jamaica and was widely accused of brutality. He was relieved of his governorship and recalled to England, where many of the country's leading intellectuals became involved either in attempts to have him brought to trial, or in defending him. A Royal Commission finally cleared him of serious guilt, but found that he had acted with 'unnecessary rigour'. This ending to his career was in strong contrast to his record in Australia, where he had won a reputation for sympathy towards, and skill in dealing with, the Aborigines.

Further reading: Uren, M. *Edward John Eyre.* Oxford University Press, Melbourne, 1964; Dutton, G. *The Hero as Murderer.* Collins, Sydney, 1967.

Eyre Highway

WA/SA This 1 900km-long road, linking PORT AUGUSTA and COOLGARDIE, is the route across the NULLABOR PLAIN, a journey which has become increasingly popular in recent years as the quality of the surface has been improved. It passes through arid, sparsely populated regions in both SA and WA, with only isolated hamlets, such as EUCLA, dotted at intervals along the route. The general direction of the highway is E-W, but at NORSEMAN it changes to a N-S route for 186km to Coolgardie, where it joins the Great Western Highway to Perth.

Eyre Peninsula

SA A triangular-shaped peninsula, lying between SPENCER GULF to the E and the GREAT AUSTRALIAN BIGHT to the W, it extends N-S for about 280km from the GAWLER RANGES in the N to its SE tip at Cape Catastrophe. The first white man to see the peninsula was the Dutchman, Pieter Nuyts, in 1627; he charted much of the coastline of the Great South Land and his maps were used by Matthew FLINDERS when he explored the coast in 1802. In 1839 Edward John EYRE explored much of the peninsula, which was named in his honour by Governor GAWLER. The region is now an important sheep, wheat and barley producing area, and the MIDDLEBACK RANGES in the NE of the peninsula are a major source of iron ore. The ports of WHYALLA and PORT AUGUSTA are located in the NE near the head of Spencer Gulf, and PORT LINCOLN is located near the SE tip of the peninsula. The Lincoln Highway skirts the E coast, the Flinders Highway follows the W coast, and the EYRE HIGHWAY crosses the mid-N of the peninsula on an E-W route. The

Lincoln National Park, dedicated in 1962 and comprising 17 083ha, covers the SE tip of the peninsula and several offshore islands; the park includes Cape Catastrophe, so named by Flinders in 1802 because eight members of his crew were drowned there when their cutter overturned; eight of the offshore islands bear the names of the seamen who lost their lives. Coffin Bay Peninsula, covering about 29 000ha at the SW tip of YORKE PENINSULA, was acquired by the SA government in 1975 for the creation of the Coffin Bay National Park.

F

Fadden, Sir Arthur William

(1895-1973) Politician and Prime Minister. Born in INGHAM in QLD, he worked first in canefields and a sugar mill, then joined the service of the MACKAY Town Council and rose to the position of Town Clerk. Meanwhile, he had been studying accountancy, and in 1918 opened his own business as a public accountant in TOWNSVILLE and Brisbane. He was a Country Party member of the QLD Legislative Assembly from 1932 to 1935 and of the federal House of Representatives from 1936 to 1958, during which time he held a number of Cabinet posts, most notably that of Treasurer (1940-41, 1949-58). He became leader of the Country Party in the Commonwealth Parliament in 1941, was Prime Minister for about seven weeks after the resignation of Robert MENZIES in 1941, and was deputy Prime Minister from 1949 until his retirement in 1958.

Further reading: Fadden, A.W. *They Called Me Artie.* Jacaranda, Milton QLD, 1969.

Fairfax, John

(1804-77) Newspaper proprietor. Born in Warwick, England, he worked as a printer, bookseller, newsagent and part-owner of two newspapers before bringing his mother, wife and three children to Sydney in 1838. He found work as a journalist and a librarian, and in 1841, in partnership with Charles Kemp, bought the *Sydney Herald*; it was renamed *Sydney Morning Herald* in the following year and was soon firmly established as the colony's leading newspaper. In 1853 Fairfax bought out Charles Kemp and three years later, after his sons Charles and James had become partners, the family company became known as John Fairfax and Sons. The Fairfax family still holds a major interest in the company, and the *Sydney Morning Herald* remains one of Australia's most influential newspapers.

Fairweather, Ian

(1891-1974) Artist. Born near Stirling in Scotland, Fairweather's

early career in forestry ended with the outbreak of World War I, during which he served with the Scots Greys and spent a considerable time as a prisoner of war. His interest in painting was aroused by a Dutch artist with whom he stayed while recuperating from imprisonment. After studying at the Hague Academy and at the Slade School, London, he led a nomadic life, living in Canada, Hong Kong, China, Korea, India and Java. In 1934 he arrived in Melbourne where he became accepted by the avant-garde painters; William FRATER set him up with a studio and arranged commissions, but he soon grew weary of city life and began travelling again as an itinerant painter. He served as a captain in the British Army in India during World War II and returned to Australia as an invalid. Until his death he lived in Melbourne, Darwin and BRIBIE ISLAND. Fairweather was never a 'popular' painter—his work appeals to those who have a knowledge of art history and some experience of the techniques of painting. His enthusiasm for Chinese art, especially calligraphy, led to increasingly linear and abstract work which included nuances from his varied past—Christianity, primitive mythology, and memories from his many travels.

Black-backed wren, *Malurus melanotus* (male)

A. Woods

fairy-wrens, emuwrens and grasswrens

These PASSERINE BIRDS belong to the family Maluridae. There is some doubt about the total number of species in Australia, but there are at least 24, all endemic. They are not related to the true WRENS of Europe, but their stance is similar and they often raise their very long tails in a wren-like manner. Although some of the fairy-wrens visit gardens in small flocks, most species are shy birds given to skulking in the undergrowth.

The fairy-wrens, about 13 species, belong to the genus *Malurus**, which is represented in most parts of the country. Generally measuring 11cm to 15cm long, with tails about 6cm long, most fairy-wrens have brown plumage which, in the case of the male, becomes mostly bright blue or violet during the breeding season. Most species are fairly common within their ranges. Their nests, usually placed in tussocks and bushes, are domed, with a side entrance, and made of grass and fibres bound with cobweb. One species often seen in gardens in E Australia is the blue wren, *M.* * *cyaneus* (13cm), a white-bellied species with dark

Species, genus or family is endemic to Australia (see Preface)

shoulders which hops and flits energetically on the ground or among low bushes, searching for insects.

Emuwrens, so called because their long, filamentous tail feathers resemble those of the EMU, are small birds, about 8cm long, which keep very close to the ground, moving more like mice than birds. These exclusively Australian birds are mainly light brown, with black streaks above, and the males are distinguished by their bright blue throats. The southern emuwren, *Stipiturus* * *malachurus*, is found in wet heathland and swamps in SE and SW Australia; the rufous emuwren, *S.* * *ruficeps* lives in porcupine grass in central and W Australia; and the mallee emuwren, *S.* * *mallee*, occurs in the mallee country bordering the MURRAY RIVER. Their well-concealed, loosely made nests resemble those of the fairy-wrens.

Grasswrens are secretive birds which scuttle rapidly over the ground in Australia's arid regions. They resemble fairy-wrens, but their brown plumage is streaked with white and sometimes patched with black. Their open or partly domed nests of grass are hidden in bushes near the ground. Because of their secretive habits and remote habitats, little is known of their biology or status. There are about eight species, all belonging to the genus *Amytornis**, and some, such as the thick-billed grasswren, *A.* * *textilis* (15cm to 18cm), of WA, may be quite common. The Eyrean grasswren, *A.* * *goyderi* (14cm), a white-throated species with a black moustache, is probably very rare and occurs only in a small area of cane grass near LAKE EYRE; it was discovered in 1874 and not seen again until 1961. The grey grasswren, *A.* * *barbatus* (18cm), was unknown before 1967 and seems to be restricted to a small area in the far NW of NSW.

falcons *see* birds of prey

Falls Creek

VIC This winter skiing centre and summer holiday resort is located in a natural sheltered bowl in the heart of the BOGONG HIGH PLAINS, SSE from MOUNT BEAUTY, NE from MOUNT HOTHAM, E of MOUNT FEATHERTOP and S of MOUNT BOGONG. Although the potential of the snowfields in the Falls Creek area had been recognised in the 1920s, it was not until 1946 that the first ski lodge was established. Today there are over 20 commercial lodges and a considerable selection of luxury flats for rent; the village has about 3000 beds overall. By road the approach to the resort is via WANGARATTA and MYRTLEFORD, thence either through Happy Valley (a journey of 377km from Melbourne) or via BRIGHT (4km shorter, but including 13km of winding road over Towong Gap).

Famechon, Johnny

(1945-) Boxer. Born in France and brought to Australia by his family when he was five, Famechon was to become only the third Australian to hold a universally recognised world boxing title (the other two were Jimmy CARRUTHERS and Lionel ROSE). Turning professional in 1961,

An old alpine hut at Falls Creek

VIC Govt Travel Authority

he lost only one bout in his first 22 fights, culminating with a win over Ollie Taylor on 18 September 1964 for the Australian featherweight title. He successfully defended this title three times before winning the British Empire featherweight title on 24 November 1967. On 21 January 1969 in London he took the World featherweight title from Jose Legra, and successfully defended this title on two occasions before succumbing to Mexican Vicente Saldivar in Rome on 9 May 1970. Extremely fast on his feet and capable of thrilling fans with his brilliance in boxing skill and evasion, Famechon lost only five of his 67 professional bouts.

fan flowers

These plants (*Scaevola* species) belong to the mainly Australian family Goodeniaceae. There are about 70 endemic species represented in all States, particularly in WA. Some species are common shore plants in Australia and overseas. Fan flowers are shrubs or scramblers, with blue, purple or pink flowers, the five petals of which are arranged asymmetrically, like a fan.

Hairy fan flower, *Scaevola ramosissima*

D. Greig

fantails *see* flycatchers, etc.

Farm Cove

NSW A small bay on the S shore of PORT JACKSON, near the central business district of Sydney, it was so named because it was the site of the first attempts at farming in the colony in 1788. On the E side of the cove is Bennelong Point where the SYDNEY OPERA HOUSE stands; the foreshores of the cove are occupied by the Sydney Botanic Gardens.

Farrer, William James

(1845-1906) Agricultural scientist. The portrait of Farrer, Australia's most famous wheat breeder, appears on the Australian $2 note. Farrer was born in England and having studied at Cambridge he emigrated to Australia. After various government surveying posts he eventually settled on his own property, near modern Canberra, and began his work on breeding wheats suitable for Australian conditions and resistant to rusts and other diseases. For 20 years he carried out 200 to 400 crosses annually, his most famous variety being Federation, the main wheat in Australia for many years. His work laid the foundations of the modern Australian wheat industry.
See also agriculture; diseases, plant

fauna

Fauna is the collective name for the animals of a particular region or time. The animal kingdom is divided into several major groups called phyla (singular, phylum), and these are further subdivided by a hierarchical system which reflects, as far as possible, the evolutionary relationships of the animals. Each of these taxonomic groups is called a taxon. The obligatory taxa in the hierarchy may be illustrated by the HOUSE FLY, *Musca domestica*: kingdom Animalia; phylum Arthropoda; class Insecta; order Diptera; family Muscidae; genus *Musca*; species *domestica*. Other optional levels, such as suborder and subfamily, can be added for convenience (*see* BIOLOGICAL CLASSIFICATION).

Many taxonomists argue that the only 'real' taxonomic level is that of the species. With bisexually reproducing organisms two organisms (of the opposite sex) belong to the same

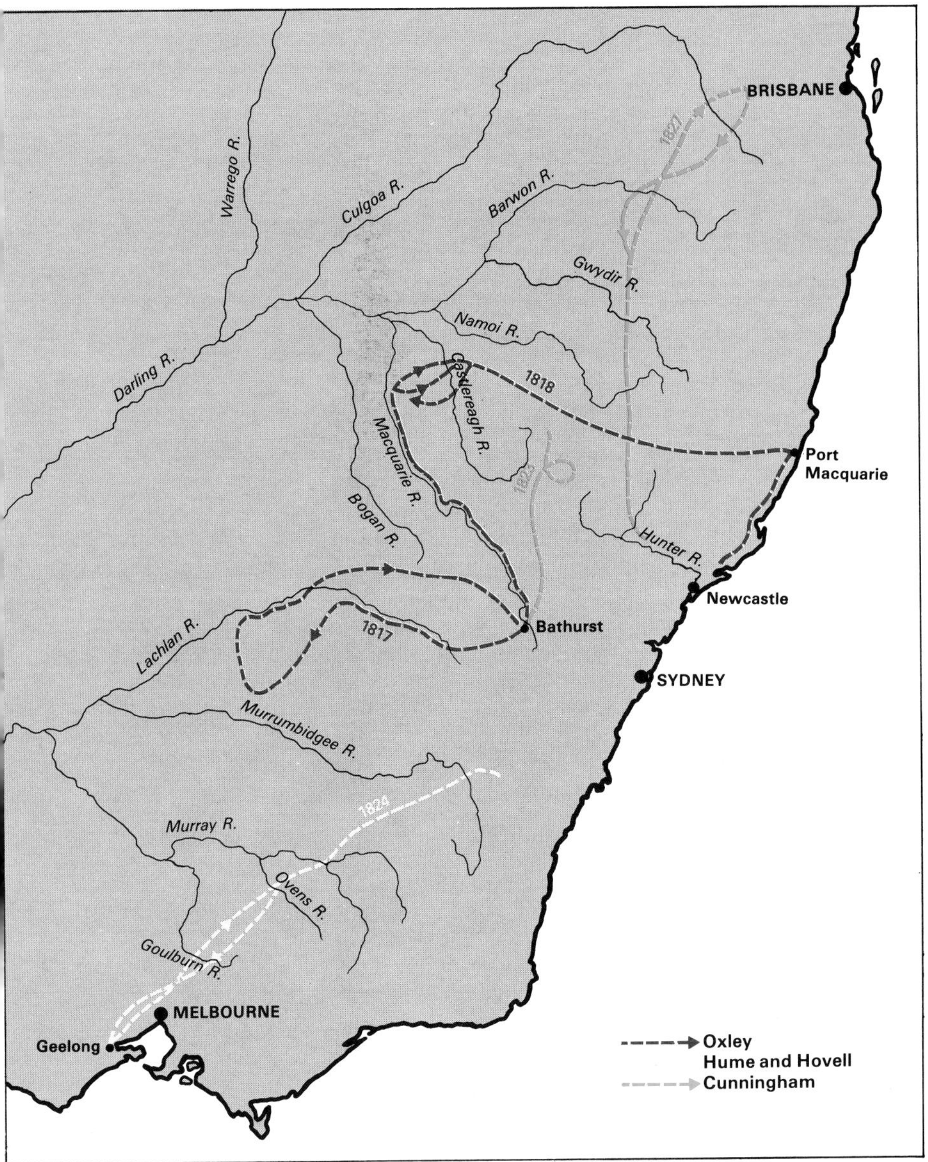

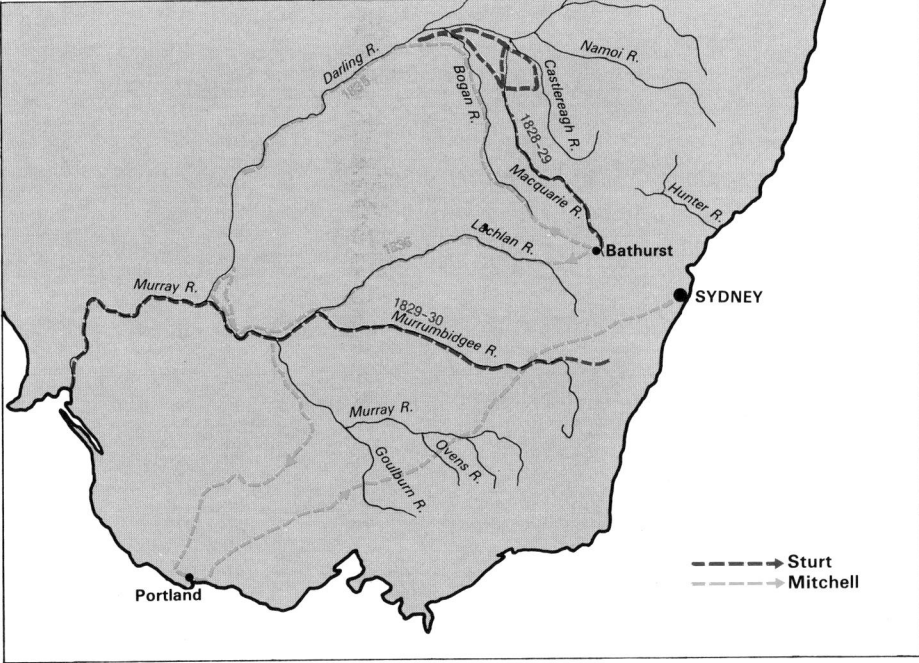

Exploration of SE Australia to 1827. As each of the expeditions of Oxley, Hume and Hovell, and Cunningham was completed, the mystery of the western rivers merely deepened

The solving of the mystery of the W rivers by Sturt and Mitchell. Although Sturt is credited with solving the mystery of the western rivers, his solution was not then completely proven. Mitchell, seeking to prove Sturt wrong, filled in the gaps and proved him to be right

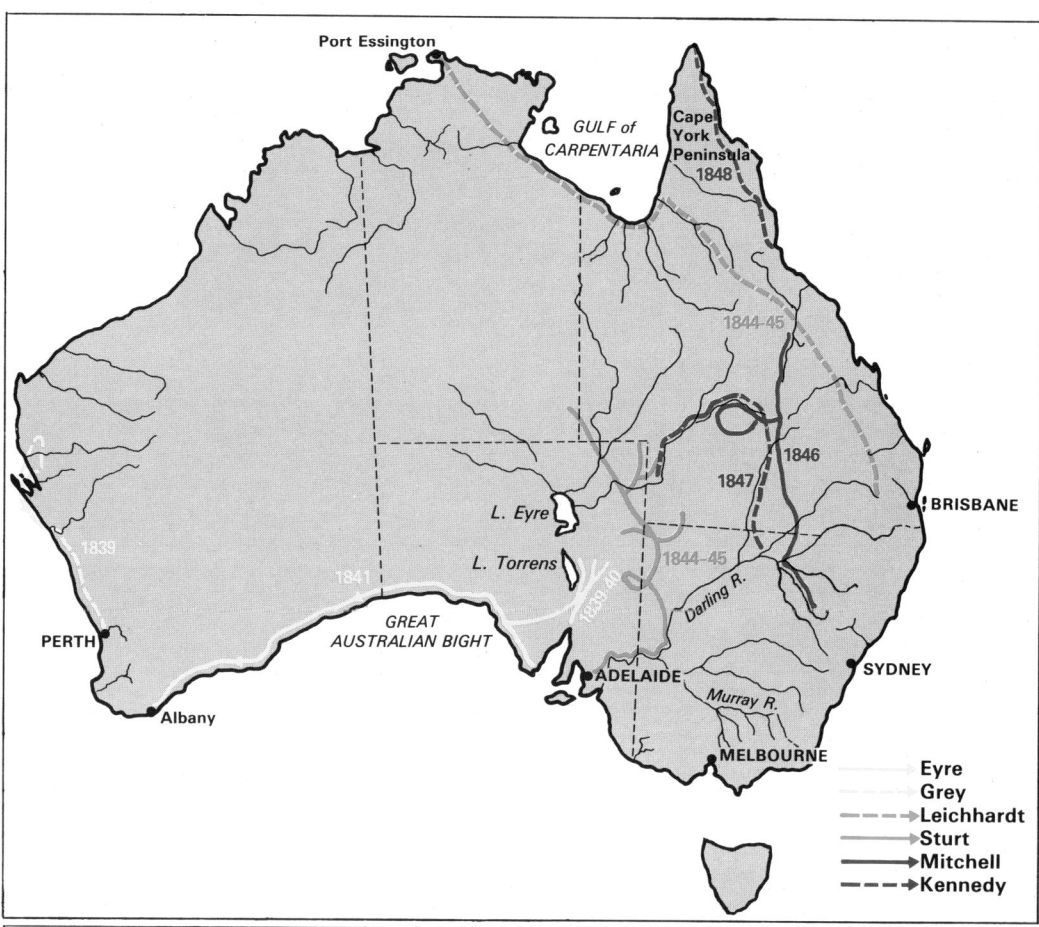

Principal journeys of exploration
1839–1848. At the end of this period,
the only large unexplored areas were
the arid interior and north-west of the
continent

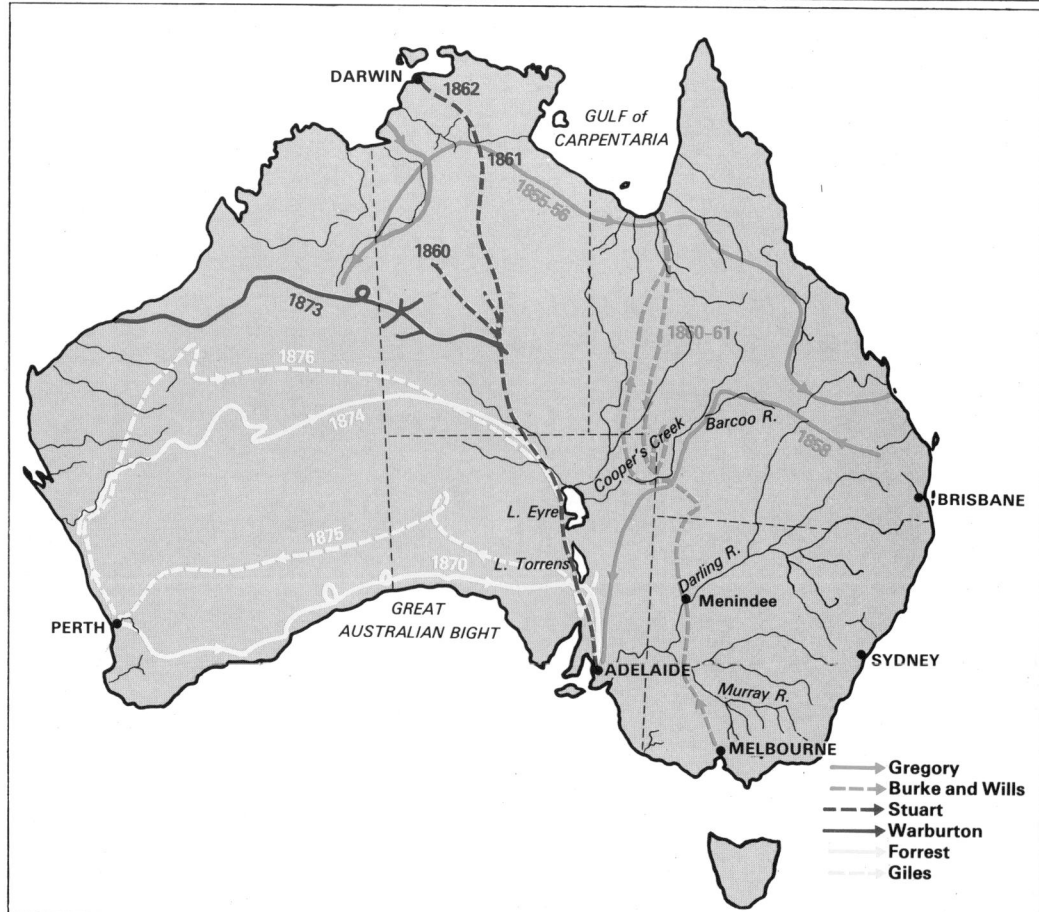

Principal journeys of exploration
1855–1876. By 1876 the main
problems of exploration had been
solved

species if they can mate and produce fertile offspring. All other taxa depend to a certain extent on the opinions of the experts in a particular field, and these opinions often differ. Classifications, therefore, tend to vary from time to time, and from authority to authority, and thus tend to change. There are, however, internationally accepted rules relating to biological nomenclature and, furthermore, scientific names such as *Musca domestica* are recognised by biologists everywhere, whereas the name 'house fly', or its equivalent in other languages, may well refer to quite different kinds of animals in different countries, or even in different parts of a single country.

The Australian fauna is strikingly different from that of other continents. It consists of native (indigenous) species and species introduced accidentally or intentionally by man (*see* ANIMALS, INTRODUCED) which have established wild, breeding populations. Feral species are those which were originally domesticated and which have become wild and self-sustaining (for example, the camel in Australia). The native species of Australia include a large proportion which are endemic; that is, they do not occur outside the continent though they may have done so in the past. Because of Australia's long isolation from other land masses, apart from New Guinea, many higher taxa are endemic to Australia (for example, the Vombatidae, a family of the WOMBATS) or to Australia and New Guinea (for example, the subclass Prototheria, the egg-laying MAMMALS).

Australia and New Guinea, and several of the adjacent islands, lie within the Australasian biogeographical realm. Its W margin follows what is known as Wallace's line, which traces channels of deep water that separate Bali and Lombok, and Celebes and Borneo. Though Wallace's line is no longer regarded as a sharp faunistic boundary it is true that typically Australian freshwater and terrestrial animals are rare to the W of this line, while EUTHERIAN MAMMALS, other than man, rodents and bats, are rare to the E of it. This biogeographical barrier has been effective against most large mammals and freshwater fish since the Australian-New Guinea land mass approached Asia at the end of the Cretaceous period (*see* CONTINENTAL DRIFT).

Excluding introduced species, parasites of widely spread animals and species that can be spread passively by currents of air and water over immense distances, the Australian fauna can be divided into four elements as far as origins are concerned.

1. An autochthonous group of higher taxa of forms which are believed to have evolved in Australia. Little is known generally of their relationships and ancestry.

2. An archaic element of forms such as the QUEENSLAND LUNG FISH which have changed little since Palaeozoic or Mesozoic times and which were once found over much of the world. The lung fish and its allies survive, as relict populations, in Australia, Africa and South America.

3. The Southern (Antarctic) element which

consists of forms whose ancestors existed on the former supercontinent of GONDWANALAND and which consequently entered Australia from the S. Such forms are recognised by their close relationship to species which exist in one or more of the other Gondwanaland land masses: southern Africa, Madagascar, South America and New Zealand. There are many examples among the invertebrates, while vertebrate examples include the EMU and CASSOWARY (related to the ostrich and the rhea), the MARSUPIALS (disputed by some zoologists), leptodactylid FROGS and side-neck turtles.

4. The Northern element which consists of forms derived from species which entered from the N along the chain of islands from the Asian mainland. Aboriginal man, the RODENTS, the BATS and most of the BIRDS entered Australia by this route.

All the major phyla are represented in Australia or in adjacent waters, and they are discussed under their respective headings. Knowledge of many phyla is incomplete and many species, including some vertebrates, still await discovery and description.

Further reading: Mackerras, I.M. 'Composition and distribution of the fauna' in *The Insects of Australia*. CSIRO & Melbourne University Press, Melbourne, 1970; Keast, A. *Evolution, Mammals and Southern Continents*. State University of New York Press, New York, 1972; Serventy, D.L. 'Origin and structure of the Australian bird fauna' in Macdonald, J.D. *Birds of Australia*. A.H. & A.W. Reed, Sydney, 1973.

Fawkner, John Pascoe (1792-1869) Co-founder of Melbourne. He was born in London, and in 1804 came with his family to Hobart, his father having been transported there for receiving stolen goods. In 1814 he himself received a three years' sentence, which he served at NEWCASTLE, for helping some convicts to escape. Returning to Van Diemen's Land, he established himself at Launceston, founded the *Launceston Advertiser*, and practised as an unqualified advocate in the lower courts. In 1835, not long after John BATMAN had claimed to have purchased large areas of land from the Aborigines at PORT PHILLIP BAY, Fawkner sent a schooner there with a party of settlers. They landed on the banks of the Yarra a little upstream from the site chosen by Batman for his settlement, and closer to the present Melbourne city centre, and could therefore be considered the true founders of Melbourne. Fawkner joined them a few months later. Subsequently he became a hotel and store owner, founded two newspapers in Melbourne and one in Geelong, and was a member of the Melbourne Town Council for a few years and of the Legislative Council of Victoria from 1851 to 1869. The suburb (formerly village) of Pascoe Vale is named after him.

feather stars *see* sea lilies, etc.

Federal Council of Australasia *see* political history

federation *see* political history

Federation Peak TAS At an elevation of 1 244m above sea level, this mountain is located at the SE end of the ARTHUR RANGE, which lies in the central-S of the State. This range forms the watershed between tributaries of the HUON RIVER and the headwaters of the Old River and the Crossing River which drain into PORT DAVEY on the SW coast.

fencing This sport involves the use of swords (the foil, the épée or the sabre) for attack and defence, the aim being to touch a target area on the opponent's body and to avoid being touched. Fencing has a long history in Australia, with occasional matches taking place as early as the 18th century. Albert Schulch, formerly a member of the German Army, was the first to offer formal fencing instruction, giving private lessons in Sydney from the early 1900s. One of Schulch's first students was Alfred E. Finckh who gave up his watch making business when he was over 40 to enroll as a medical student at Sydney University, where he took up fencing to keep fit. During the following 40 years Finckh did much to promote fencing in Australia as an amateur sport, and he was instrumental in establishing the first Amateur Fencing Club in 1910. Interest in fencing declined during and after World War I and it was not until the mid-1940s that the State fencing associations combined to form the Australian Amateur Fencing Federation.

Australian fencers compete in many international events, including those incorporated in the Commonwealth Games. Two of the better-known Australian fencers are John Fethers and Ivan Lund, who apart from winning many Australian championships have done well overseas. Fethers won silver medals in the 1950 and 1954 Commonwealth Games, while Lund won gold medals in the 1954 and 1962 Commonwealth Games. In 1982 Gregor Benko of VIC showed himself to be an outstanding performer by winning a gold medal at the épée championship in Paris and by coming second at foil in the commonwealth championships in England.

fennel *see* Umbelliferae

feral animals *see* animals, introduced

feral cats *see* animals, introduced

ferns *see* Pteridophyta

fernwren *see* warblers, etc.

Ferrier, James (1915-) Golfer. Born in Manly NSW, Ferrier started playing golf at the age of nine and developed into Australia's leading amateur golfer for the period 1931-39, regularly defeating the top professionals of the day in Open tournaments. In 1931, at the age of 16, he won his first major amateur title, the New South Wales Amateur championship; he won this title again in 1934, 1937 and 1938. He won the New South Wales Close championship (renamed the New South Wales Open in 1958) for four years in succession, 1935-38, sweeping aside all comers, amateur and professional. He was Australian Amateur champion in 1935, 1936, 1938 and 1939 and while still an amateur won the most prestigious event on the Australian professional circuit, the Australian Open, in 1938 and 1939. In 1940 he went to the USA and turned professional, and in 1947 became the first Australian to win one of the world's four major championships when he took out the American PGA title. In all, he won 18 tournaments in the USA, in addition to two Canadian Opens.

fiddlers *see* sharks, etc.

fieldwren *see* warblers, etc.

fig, blue *see* quandong

figbirds *see* orioles, etc.

figs Species of fig trees (genus *Ficus*; family Moraceae) occur in most tropical and subtropical parts of the world and in some warm temperate regions also. Several large species are found in rainforests in Australia, particularly in the N. The fruits of all the native figs are edible, and many were used as food by the Aborigines, but most are far inferior to those of the cultivated fig, *F. carica*, an introduced Eurasian species. The flowers of the fig grow inside the developing fruit where they are fertilised by minute wasps (Agaontidae, *see* ANTS, etc.) which, in general, develop within the fruit. The genus includes strangler figs which begin life as a seed lodged in a crevice of another tree; in time, roots from the fig reach the ground and eventually the original tree is enveloped and subsequently dies and decays.

Many fig trees are massive, with thick trunks buttressed by the roots. The familiar Moreton Bay fig, *F. macrophylla*, occurs in rainforests in N coastal NSW and QLD but grows commonly in cities such as Sydney; the large leaves (23cm long; 10cm wide), glossy green above and brown below, form a dense foliage which makes the fig a valuable shade tree. A similar species is the rusty leaved or Port Jackson fig, *F. rubiginosa*, which has smaller, rounder, rust-coloured leaves, covered with hairs on the underside. The sandpaper fig, *F. coronata*, has very rough leaves which were used by the Aborigines to smooth their wooden weapons.

filarial worm *see* roundworms

film Australian film production has had a chequered history. Financially, one of its more successful periods was from 1906 to World War I but, partly because of the subsequent rapid expansion of American production and distribution, Australian producers found it

A scene from 'The Sentimental Bloke' 1915

increasingly difficult during the rest of the silent era to raise finance and obtain satisfactory releases. During the 1930s, sound films were made by several companies, one of which produced a series of features which was successful mainly because their distribution was guaranteed by one of Australia's main theatrical chains.

Feature film production between 1940 and 1970 was intermittent, most of the larger budget films being financed by overseas companies and most productions being financially unsuccessful. Only since the early 1970s has local feature film production increased again, mainly due to government investment through the Australian Film Development Corporation (AFDC) and the Australian Film Commission (AFC); at present, more feature films (in current AFC terminology, 'feature film' means any film over 60 minutes) and shorts (under 60 minutes) are produced and released than ever before. Apart from these films many completely independently produced films are made each year.

Early history, 1896-1918 Australian film production began, like that in other countries, as a result of the Lumière brothers' first public showing of films on 28 December 1895 in Paris. A travelling French cinematographer, Marius Sestier, and an Australian photographer, Walter Barnett, opened Australia's first cinema in Sydney in September 1896. Australia's first film show, however, took place in the Melbourne Opera House in August 1896 when some short films were screened by the illusionist Carl Hertz. Sestier began by filming items of local interest, such as the Horse Artillery at drill, the films usually being about 50 seconds long; his film of Melbourne Cup Day, 1896, was his most successful and is the oldest Australian film

kept by the National Film Archive. After Sestier's departure from Australia in 1897 most films were imported from France, the UK and the USA and were usually screened as 'chasers' at the end of more traditional entertainment shows.

The first well-equipped film unit was attached to the Limelight Department of the Salvation Army. Realising the potentially powerful impact of visual presentations, Herbert Booth, son of the Army's founder, and J.H. Perry presented a show in 1900 entitled *Soldiers of the Cross* which combined film sequences with slides; the films have been lost, but most of the slides and the original music score are in the National Film Archive. In 1901, valuable scientific and anthropological films were made by Sir Walter Baldwin SPENCER of his expedition through central and N Australia; Spencer also managed with an Edison cylinder to catch location sound.

Feature film production began with the first adaptation of the feats of Ned KELLY's gang, namely *The Story of the Kelly Gang* (1906) made by J. and N. Tait. This is the oldest Australian feature film of which any part is known to survive. (Two sequences were discovered in 1979 in Melbourne and have been restored by the National Film Archive in Canberra.) The success of this film encouraged some exhibitors to produce their own films and some of the busiest exhibitors, such as Cousens Spencer, T.J. West and J.D. Williams, became the busiest producers. G. and A. Cornwell made *Eureka Stockade* (1907) and Charles MacMahon directed *Robbery Under Arms* (1907) and *For the Term of His Natural Life* (1908). In 1908 the first permanent buildings for motion pictures were erected and in 1909 J.D. Williams introduced the first continuous picture show, running from 11 a.m. to 11 p.m.

Film production was now becoming established, most films being adapted from novels, plays and poems and usually featuring such popular topics as the adventures of bush-rangers, convicts and squatters.

A significant personality in the Australian film industry between 1906 and 1914 was Cousens Spencer, who employed the Higgins brothers, highly qualified cameramen, and hired the actor Raymond Longford and the best-known actress of the silent era, Lottie Lyell. His rival, T.J. West, introduced the newsreel in 1911 and made it a regular feature of the programme.

In the most productive years of the silent era, 1911-13, 98 feature films were produced, among them Longford's *The Romantic Story of Margaret Catchpole* (1911) featuring Lottie Lyell.

Although the Australian cinema had expanded quickly, it was difficult for the indigenous product to keep pace in quantity and quality with foreign films. Local audiences preferred American films, which were superior in quality and more entertaining, resulting in the decline of local production and the growth of exhibition and distribution. West Pictures, Amalgamated Pictures and Spencer's Theatrescope Co. merged in 1911 to form Union Theatres which, with its production and distribution arm, Australasian Films, was the largest film company in the country. Hoyts Theatres, founded in 1908 in Melbourne, soon expanded to Melbourne suburbs and then to Sydney. By 1921, there were about 800 picture theatres (114 in Sydney); several 'palace-like' cinemas, with a seating capacity of up to 3 500 people, were being planned.

The crisis, 1918-27 After the war some producers disappeared from the scene, including Spencer who sold his business in 1918 and left for Canada. Many of the new producers began to use stage actors and stories from stage productions. James WILLIAMSON used Fred Niblo, later a film director in Hollywood, in his film, *Officer 666* (1916). Beaumont Smith, a former journalist, began to develop a comedy series about Dad Rudd and his son, including *The Hayseeds Backblocks Show* (1917) and *The Hayseeds Come to Town* (1917). E.J. Carroll discovered 'Snowy' BAKER, a versatile Australian athlete who could perform any stunt needed in an action-packed Outback drama such as *The Man From Kangaroo* (1920). Franklyn Barrett's first film, *A Blue Gum Romance* (1913), was outshone by his later films *Australia's Peril* (1917) and *The Breaking of the Drought* (1920). Raymond Longford's film, *The Sentimental Bloke* (1919) based on C.J. DENNIS' poem of the same name, was the masterpiece of Australian silent cinema and one of the best films ever made in the country. The excellent casting of Lottie Lyell as Doreen, Arthur Tauchert as the Kid and Gilbert Emery as Ginger Mick, the impressive location photography by Arthur Higgins and the use of Dennis' verse contributed to the film's success. This film was an overwhelming success in the UK, the USA and Canada.

Among the pioneer documentarists was Captain Frank HURLEY whose work took him from the Antarctic—*Home of the Blizzard* (1913), *In the Grip of the Polar Ice* (1917) and *Endurance* (1933)—to the Outback—*Into Australia's Unknown* (1915)—and to Papua New Guinea—*With the Headhunters of Unknown Papua* (1923). Hurley's *Pearls and Savages* (1921) was a considerable success in the UK and the USA.

Although by 1920 the annual attendance figures had reached 67.5 million, very few Australian films made a profit. Beaumont Smith made enough money with his comedies to keep him in regular production with films such as *The Adventures of Algy* (1925). The McDonagh sisters began their productions with *Those Who Love* (1926) but produced only three more films before closing down in 1932. The last major film of the silent era was Australasian Films' *For the Term of His Natural Life* (1927).

By this time, the Australian film industry had reached crisis point. Like most other nations, Australia was swamped with feature films from the major film producing countries, particularly the USA. Large cinema chains, in particular Union Theatres and Hoyts, began to dominate the scene but even they had to accept American big business rules, some of which were outlawed in the USA in 1930 but remained in force for some time in Australia. Such practices included 'block-booking', whereby an exhibitor was forced to book a whole package of films of which only a few would be commercially promising, and 'blind-booking', whereby exhibitors and distributors had to book films they had never seen.

Royal Commission, 1927 In response to the demand of three groups (the Empire Loyalist, which wanted protection for British films in Australia, the Australian Motion Pictures Producers Association, which fought against the big theatre chains, and various women's organisations, which were campaigning for more rigorous censorship) a Royal Commission investigated the film industry in 1927-28. However its recommendations, which included the setting up of a Board of Censors, an increase in the tariff on imported films, and the setting of an Empire quota, were doomed to failure. The report was not debated in the Commonwealth Parliament and the States were not willing to concede their rights to the Commonwealth as required by 31 of the recommendations.

A fight for survival, 1927-65 The introduction of sound (the first commercial sound film appeared in 1927 in the USA) ensured the continued dominance of American products, and only financially successful exhibitors, who could afford to convert cinemas to sound, survived the change, while the independent local producer almost disappeared.

The first 'talking film' was made in Australia on the occasion of the arrival of the Duke of York in Sydney in 1927. The first sound feature film (and also Australia's first film musical) was *Showgirl's Luck* (1930) by Norman Dawn. Most Australian films in the 1930s were produced by Cinesound, a subsidiary of Greater Union Theatres ('Greater' had been added in 1928), at the Bondi Junction studio and were distributed by Australasian Films. This closed circuit system at least guaranteed the films a local release. Cinesound's success was largely attributable to Ken G. Hall, a former public relations man with Union Theatres, who made 16 commercially successful films for the organisation. By efficient use of studio facilities and outdoor locations, Hall's films were of a consistent

A scene from 'Breaking of the Drought' 1920

competitive quality. His first film, *On Our Selection* (1932), introduced the famous stage actor Bert Bailey to the screen; it was followed by *The Squatter's Daughter* (1933). Hall discovered other local talents, such as Peter Finch, who made his film début in *The Silence of Dean Maitland* (1934), and Roy RENE, who starred as 'Mo' in *Strike Me Lucky* (1934); he also employed well-known but fading overseas stars, such as Helen Twelvetrees, who starred in his film *Thoroughbred* (1936). Hall's studios were equipped with the best modern facilities available and he introduced sophisticated sound equipment, back projection, model work and the stunning studio effects seen in *Orphan of the Wilderness* (1936) and *Tall Timbers* (1937).

The Efftee studios, opened in Melbourne in 1931 by Frank W. Thring and supported by the Fox Film Corporation and Hoyts, had by 1935 produced 10 low-budget feature films, including *A Co-respondence Course* (1931), *Diggers* (1931) and *The Haunted Barn* (1931); the last-mentioned was one of the first Australian films to run into trouble with a censor who thought that the wailing of the wind might frighten children. Thring's musical, *His Royal Highness* (1932), which established George Wallace as a screen comedian, and proved most successful, whereas his version of *The Sentimental Bloke* (1932) was not. His last production, *Clara Gibbings* (1934), was allowed only limited release. The studio closed when Thring died in 1936.

One of Australia's greatest directors during this period was Charles CHAUVEL, who, after working for a while in Hollywood in a minor capacity, had returned to Australia in 1923. His first two films, *Moth of Moonbi* (1926) and *Greenhide* (1926), were financed with whatever money he could find and both ran into distribution trouble. His first sound film, *In the Wake of the Bounty* (1933), introduced Errol Flynn to the screen. A film which became a worldwide success and which played an important role in terms of propaganda in the early years of the war was Chauvel's *Forty Thousand Horsemen* (1940), in which Chips Rafferty established his future career. During the war, Chauvel directed four short propaganda films. His next feature film, *The Rats of Tobruk* (1944) did not live up to his former success. His later films, *Sons of Matthew* (1949) and *Jedda* (1954), portrayed his romantic vision of Australia.

In 1934 a second enquiry into the Australian film industry had begun, the aim being to investigate the possibilities of introducing a workable quota system. Australian producers wanted a change from an Empire quota to an Australian quota, but the British government and American companies opposed any form of quota, leading to rifts between the various States and making Commonwealth legislation impossible.

With the cessation of feature film production by Cinesound, the local film industry began to decline again. Regular production occurred only at the two major newsreel companies, Cinesound and Fox Movietone. Some top cameramen were employed by the Department of Information and joined the Australian forces as war photographers and cameramen, but few documentaries of World War II were made; among the most spectacular were *Advance into Libya* (1941) by Frank Hurley and the Academy Award-winning *Kokoda Front Line* (1942) by Damien Parer.

In 1946, Stanley Hawes took over the direction of the Commonwealth Film Unit which, under various names, had always provided a solid basis for documentary and informational film making. It could rely on Australia's best documentarists, such as Hawes himself, whose *School In The Mailbox* (1946) received an Oscar nomination, and John Heyer, who made *Native Earth* (1946), *The Valley is Ours* (1948) and the successful *Back of Beyond* (1954). Ken G. Hall's last feature film, *Smithy* (1945), was produced by Columbia Pictures, thus setting a new pattern whereby American and British companies began to make films in Australia. Ealing Studios made *The Overlanders* (1946), and *Eureka Stockade* (1949), both directed by Harry Watt, and sent Ralph Smart to make *Bitter Springs* (1950). Twentieth Century-Fox sent Lewis Milestone to direct *Kangaroo* (1951), a financial disaster, partly because it was full of predictable cliches. Other foreign productions of this period include *Robbery Under Arms* (1957) directed by Jack Lee for the Rank Organisation, *Summer of the Seventeenth Doll* (1959) produced and directed by Leslie Norman for United Artists, *On the Beach* (1959) by Stanley Kramer, and *The Sundowners* (1960) directed by Fred Zinneman and produced by Warner Brothers. Apart from *The Sundowners*, none of these films showed any interest in the Australian way of life; Australia merely served as an exotic background.

The few local productions attempted include Cecil Holmes' moderately successful bushranger film, *Captain Thunderbolt* (1953) and an interesting trilogy, *Three in One* (1956). In 1953, actor Chips Rafferty and the documentarist Lee Robinson made *The Phantom Stockman* (1953), *King of the Coral Sea* (1954), which gave Rod Taylor his first screen role, and *Walk Into Paradise* (1956). Between the filming of *The Sundowners* and *They're a Weird Mob* (1965), directed by Michael Powell, no feature film was produced in Australia.

Attempts at a recovery, 1965-74 The introduction of television in 1956 helped the local film industry by keeping small production firms busy making commercials. Production of television commercials is the only area of Australian film making which has been completely protected from foreign competition. Whilst the AUSTRALIAN BROADCASTING CORPORATION (ABC) maintains its own production units to produce filmed television drama, the commercial stations have few such units and rely mainly on packagers to produce programme material. Because a third of the television audience is under 18, drama programmes are most important in volume and in impact, occupying nearly half the transmission time of all metropolitan commercial stations; however, only 15 per cent of all drama televised in Australia is produced in the country. In 1963, by which time the local film industry had almost ceased production, the Senate Select Committee on the 'Encouragement of Australian Production for Television' pointed out the need to protect an industry with a strong cultural element. In 1967, the Commonwealth government directed the Australian Council for the Arts 'to advise the Government on initiatives to help Australian film makers'. In May 1969, the Council recommended that there should be a policy of protection and that this should be investigated by the Tariff Board or some specially constituted body; the Council also recommended that a National Film and Television School, an Australian Film and Television Development Corporation and an Experimental Film and Television Fund be established immediately. All these recommendations were implemented. The Australian Film Commission Act of 1975 established the AFC, the most powerful body in Australia concerned with film production and one which set the industry going again. Its functions are 'to encourage, whether by the provision of financial assistance or otherwise, the making, promotion, distribution and exhibition of Australian films ... to make, promote, distribute any films ... (and) to encourage the proper keeping of films in archives in Australia.'

This period also saw the development of a strong independent movement. Prominent in this movement were: Tim Burstall who had made the successful children's film, *The Prize* (1960), and went on to make *Two Thousand Weeks* (1969), a full-length, low-cost feature film of a technically high standard; Giorgio Mangiamele, who directed *Clay* (1964) and *99 Per Cent* (1966); Brian Davies and James Wilson, who made *The Pudding Thieves* (1967); the Melbourne University Film Society, which made *The Girl Friends* (1968) and *Hey Al Baby* (1968); and Albie Thoms, David Perry and Andrew Read, who formed Ubu Films in 1965, the first company to take experimental film seriously.

Phillip Adams wrote, produced, directed and photographed *Jack and Jill: A Postscript* (1970); though highly praised throughout the country, the film failed commercially. John B. Murray's *The Naked Bunyip* (1970) fared only slightly better. In 1971 a major breakthrough happened: Tim Burstall's film adaptation of David WILLIAMSON's play *Stork*, was a success; it hit the market at the right time with the right topic. This was followed by the financially successful productions *The Adventures of Barry McKenzie* (1972), directed by Bruce Beresford, and *Libido* (1973), a quartet of stories, produced by Tim Burstall and directed by John B. Murray, Tim Burstall, Fred Schepisi and David Baker. Burstall's *Alvin Purple* (1973) was among the first Australian feature films screened by one of the larger cinema chains, Village Theatres. This group had begun operations in 1954 with a drive-in cinema. The novelty proved to be successful and the company expanded steadily, a third of its shares being bought by the Greater Union Organisation in the early 1960s. Its distribution arm, Roadshow, also handles Warner Brothers distribution. In spite of the AFDC's and later the AFC's direct support of film production, distribution of Australian films was still a major problem. *27A* (1973), directed by Esben Storm and one of the first local films to attempt serious social criticism, had to rely on festivals and on a small independent distribution company.

On the way to success, 1974-82 This period began with a number of notable productions including: Tom Cowan's *Promised Woman* (1974), one of the first Australian films to involve some ethnic aspects; Tim Burstall's *Petersen* (1974), worked from an original script by David Williamson; Peter Weir's *The Cars That Ate Paris* (1974); and Michael Thornhill's *Between Wars* (1974). By 1975, the new Australian feature film industry began to show confidence in its ability and its future; the 26 feature films made that year included several top box-office money spinners, such as Peter Weir's *Picnic at Hanging Rock*. The topics ranged from 'sexploitation' (*The True Story of Eskimo Nell* by Richard Franklin; *Australia After Dark* by John Lamond) to history (*Sunday Too Far Away* by Ken Hannam), to crime and mystery (*Inn of the Damned* by Terry Bourke; *End Play* by Tim Burstall) and contemporary issues (*Pure S...* by Bert Deling).

Greg Rowe and David Gulpilil in a scene from 'Storm Boy'

Jimmie Blacksmith played by Tommy Lewis in 'The Chant of Jimmie Blacksmith'

This pattern has since repeated itself. The past features prominently in many Australian films, including *Mad Dog Morgan* (1976) by Phillipe Mora, *Eliza Fraser* (1976) by Tim Burstall, *Caddie* (1976) by Don Crombie, *The Getting of Wisdom* (1977) by Bruce Beresford, *The Mango Tree* (1977) by Kevin Dobson, *The Picture Show Man* (1977) by John Power, *The Irishman* (1978) by Don Crombie, *The Chant of Jimmie Blacksmith* (1978) by Fred Schepisi, *Newsfront* (1978) by Phil Noyce, *My Brilliant Career* (1979) by Gillian Armstrong, *Breaker Morant* (1980) by Bruce Beresford, *Manganinnie* (1980) by John Honey and *Gallipoli* (1981)

by Peter Weir. Crime and mystery feature in *Summer of Secrets* (1976) by Jim Sharman, *Summerfield* (1977) by Ken Hannam, *The Last Wave* (1977) by Peter Weir, *Weekend of Shadows* (1978) by Tom Jeffrey, *Patrick* (1978) by Richard Franklin, *The Night, The Prowler* (1978) by Jim Sharman, *The Money Movers* (1978) by Bruce Beresford, *Harlequin* (1979) by Simon Wincer, and *Chain Reaction* (1979) by Ian Barry. A number of film makers attempt to look at contemporary society and its problems; such films include *High Rolling* (1977) by Igor Auzins, *Inside Looking Out* (1977) by Paul Cox, *The Devil's Playground* (1976) by Fred Schepisi, *FJ Holden* (1977) by Michael Thornhill, *Mouth to Mouth* (1978) by John Duigan, *The Odd Angry Shot* (1978) by Tom Jeffrey, *In Search of Arms* (1978) by Esben Storm, *Cathy's Child* (1978) by Donald Crombie, *Stir* (1979) by Stephen Wallace, *Hard Knocks* (1979) by Don McLennan, *The Club* (1980), Beresford's adaptation of yet another successful play by David Williamson, and *Puberty Blues* (1981), also directed by Beresford. Films on surfing have proven to be a quiet but steady industry; since 1960 over 30 have been made, among them *Crystal Voyager* (1973) by George Greenough and *Rolling Home* (1974) by Paul Witzig. Locally made children's films which have been successful overseas include *Let the Balloon Go* (1975) by Oliver Howes, *Ride a Wild Pony* (1975) by Don Chaffey, *Storm Boy* (1976) by Henri Safran, *Blue Fin* (1978) by Carl Schultz, and the animated films *Dot and the Kangaroo* (1977) and *The Little Convict* (1979), both made by Yoram Gross. Another animation film, *Leisure* (1976) by Bruce Petty, won an Academy Award in 1977. The tradition of high-quality documentary film making is

carried on by Tom Haydon whose most recent film, *The Last Tasmanian* (1978), was a multinational co-production.

Production by foreign firms and the import of foreign directors and stars has continued, but few such productions have had any success. Michael Powell directed *Age of Consent* (1969) for Columbia; Tony Richardson directed *Ned Kelly* (1970) for United Artists; Canadian Ted Kotcheff directed *Wake in Fright* (1971); and Brian Trenchard-Smith made *The Man from Hong Kong* (1975). Two feature films shot in Australia by Japanese companies are *Moepu Tairiku* (*The Blazing Continent*) (1968) directed by Sogoru Nishimura and *Koya No Toseinin* (*The Drifting Avenger*) (1968) made by Junya Sato. Luigi Zampa directed an Italian feature in Australia, *Bello Onesto Emigrato Australia Sposerebbe Compaesan Illibata* (*The Girl in Australia*) (1971) and Tony Williams directed the first Australia-New Zealand co-production of a feature length film, *Solo* (1978). In 1978, the new wave of Australian film production was set to enter a period of consolidation. Production standards had reached high levels and there was no lack of ideas; funding, however, remained a continuous problem. In order to attract more private investors, the federal government decided to amend the Commonwealth Income Tax Assessment Act, making investments in Australian feature films tax-deductible by 100 per cent over two years. Unfortunately, this Act has been changed many times since 1978, thus becoming largely responsible for the irregular production output over the following years.

During 1979, 20 Australian feature films were released and 27 were in production. The most notable successes were George Miller's

Mad Max, which had been shot on a medium budget and over the years became the highest-earning Australian film, and Gillian Armstrong's *My Brilliant Career*, which was selected for the Cannes Film Festival where it received wide acclaim. Joint ventures such as *The Earthling* and *Blue Lagoon*, both produced mainly with American money, raised once more a problem which has plagued the industry for many years and is still not solved: the terms and conditions relating to the employment of local and foreign actors (and occasionally technicians). At present, Actors' Equity (a union which started in 1939 and has about 10 000 members, of whom 6000 are actors) has to approve of every foreign actor participating in an Australian production. It maintains that there is enough talent in the country to sustain the industry, but producers claim that in order to survive in the international market, foreign stars have to be included in locally made films. As a result of this dispute, a new group, Screen Actors Guild of Australia, was formed in 1983. It attacks Equity's stand as old-fashioned and claims that Australian actors will find work overseas only if reciprocal rights are granted.

In 1980 14 films were released, among them Bruce Beresford's *Breaker Morant* (which won Jack Thompson the award for Best Supporting Actor at Cannes), *The Club* (an adaptation of yet another David Williamson play), Don McLennan's *Hard Knocks* (an uncompromising look at contemporary life in a city) and John Honey's *Manganinnie* (a story about a lone TAS Aboriginal woman). Because of the ongoing confusion about the handling of tax incentives, only 11 productions were begun in 1980, less than half the number in 1977. However, towards the end of the year, the government agreed to the most generous tax concessions, allowing a 150 per cent write-off of investment over a one-year period plus tax exemption from profits to some degree. This financial boost was badly needed since technical costs and wages had jumped dramatically in the preceding few years.

In 1981, 19 features were released, the best one of which was Peter Weir's *Gallipoli*. George Miller produced and directed a sequel to his first success, *Mad Max II*, and Richard Franklin finished *Roadgames*.

A record number of 49 features came on the market in 1982. *Far East*, directed by John Duigan with two of Australia's top stars, Brian

Shooting a scene for 'Breaker Morant'

Brown and Helen Morse, *The Man from Snowy River*, based on 'Banjo' Paterson's classic epic poem, *The Year of Living Dangerously* by Peter Weir with Mel Gibson, and *We of the Never Never* based on yet another Australian classic by Mrs Aeneas GUNN and directed by Igor Auzins, were among the most successful films of the year.

With growing costs on one side and a steady loss of revenue for the government on the other, as well as an audience which is increasingly difficult to please because 'Australianess' alone is no longer attractive, the industry by the end of 1982 once again faced an uncertain future. Locally produced films held up to a 30 per cent share of the box office (in 1980 it was only seven per cent) and production companies with considerable assets were ready to invest at a scale never seen before in the country: Rupert Murdoch and Robert Stigwood formed Associated R & R Productions, Frank Packer teamed up with film and advertising expert Phillip Adams, and entrepreneur Michael Edgley joined Hoyts to invest and promote Australian films on a large scale.

In order for the industry to become commercially viable, and independent of direct or indirect government subsidies, many problems still have to be solved: containment of rising production costs, the role of overseas actors, a final wording of the conditions pertaining to tax concessions, new crew safety regulations, and many others. As far as styles are concerned, there has been a strong trend away from historical and nostalgic dramas to contemporary themes, comedies and even musicals. This is a clear indication of the great creative potential among scriptwriters. Contemporary, non-escapist topics tend to attract only a selective though highly motivated audience, but since production costs are rising steadily, larger audiences must be tapped and a trend to more escapist and/or exploitative films seems almost inevitable. The original thinkers among the film makers are seriously endangered. Since 1970 the Australian film industry has been working at establishing a satisfactory relationship with its local audience and at conquering overseas markets. The reputation and trust gained were worth the efforts. Today, the creative energy in Australia is greater than ever before but film making is also business; the quality of the compromise between the creative desire to make the best possible film and the financial limitations imposed upon its production will determine the survival of Australian film production.

Government film funding organisations
Since the 1970s several government organisations have been established to encourage the making, promotion, distribution and broadcasting of Australian programmes. In some cases they also make, promote and distribute programmes that deal with matters of national or State interest, as well as programmes made for government Departments and authorities.

The Australian Film Commission (AFC) is an independent statutory authority established under the Australian Film Act 1975. One of its five branches is Film Australia, which has a modern studio complex, including complete production facilities, at Lindfield NSW.

The South Australian Film Corporation, established in 1972, is a statutory body charged with the responsibility of developing a film industry in SA. Film Victoria was set up in 1982 to replace the 1972 Victorian Film Corporation. The NSW Film Corporation, Queensland Film Corporation and Tasmanian Film Corporation, were all established in 1977. The last-mentioned was sold to private enterprise in 1983, but continues to function under the same name. The Western Australian Film Council, formed in 1979, gives priority in its funding to projects which use Western Australian actors, writers, technicians and production personnel, and have AFC investment.

A high proportion of the most successful and highly regarded Australian films made in recent years have received funding or other help from these bodies.

Film organisations
1. The Australian Film Institute. This is an independent, non-profit making national cultural organisation, formed in 1958 with the principal aim of encouraging the development of the art of film in the country. The AFI is involved in publishing, is curator of a museum and runs three cinemas (in Melbourne, Sydney and Hobart). It organises the yearly presentation of the Australian Film Awards which are intended to stimulate the Australian film production and to call public attention to the latest achievements of the nation's film industry.
2. The National Library of Australia. This organisation incorporates three sections which are relevant to film: the National Film Lending Collection; the Film Study Collection, and the National Film Archive. The National Film Archive preserves the widest possible range of Australian film and television productions. It has a collection of over 29 000 titles, almost a quarter of a million film stills, 30 000 posters and 3000 scripts. The Archive is keen to recover 'lost' films and transfer them before they deteriorate.
3. The Australian Film and Television School. Established by an Act of Parliament in 1973 to serve the needs of the industry and education in film and television, it is an independent statutory authority with the status of a college of advanced education. The AFTVS officially opened in 1975 in North Ryde NSW, its first director being Professor Jarzy Toeplitz.
4. Sydney Filmmakers' Co-operative. Founded in 1966, it is concerned with providing alternative services for film makers. It is open to all film makers and people active in the production of film. It is a non-profit organisation and members are encouraged in formulating policies.

Film festivals The first Australian film festival took place in January 1952, in Olinda VIC. The Melbourne Film Festival has taken place regularly each year since then; the

Sydney Film Festival has taken place since 1954. These are the two major festivals, showing over 60 feature films and many more shorts once a year over a two-week period. Such festivals are the only occasion for the public to get acquainted with the most important current developments in the film industry throughout the world. Most of the films can be shown uncensored and come with sub-titles so as to preserve as much as possible of their artistic integrity. Other festivals, running on an irregular pattern, are those in Perth (since 1952), Hobart (since 1956), Adelaide (since 1959) and Brisbane (since 1966).

The Commonwealth Film Censorship Board This full-time statutory body was established in 1917. Its functions are: to register films under Commonwealth legislation; to classify them under the various State legislations; to act as agents of the Australian Broadcasting Control Board with regard to imported television films; and to examine advertising in relation to imported films and Australian films as required.

The idea behind the classification system is to inform the public of the nature of a film, taking into account both merit and context. Present classifications are: 'G' (For General Exhibition; all ages; family entertainment); 'NRC' (Not Recommended for Children under 12; plot, theme or treatment offends against concepts of 'G'); 'M' (Mature Audiences, 15 years and over; the film may deal with essentially adult content, but the treatment is more discreet than 'R'); and 'R' (Restricted; persons between two and 18 years of age will not be admitted, for the film deals with adult themes often treated in an overt and explicit way). Only 'R' is a legally enforceable classification; the others are merely advisory.

Further reading: Hall, K.G. *Directed by Ken G. Hall.* Lansdowne Press, Melbourne, 1977; Bertrand, I. *Film Censorship in Australia.* St Lucia, 1978; Thoms, A. *Polemics For a New Cinema.* Wild & Woolley, Sydney, 1978; Murray, S. (ed) *The New Australian Cinema.* Thomas Nelson, Melbourne, 1980; Pike, A. & Cooper, R. *Australian Film 1900-1977.* Oxford University Press, Melbourne, 1980; Tulloch, J. *Legends on the Screen.* Woollahra, 1981 and *Australian Cinema, Industry, Narrative and Meaning.* North Sydney, 1982; *Australian Motion Picture Yearbook,* Thomas Nelson, Melbourne.
Films: Forgotten Cinema (1966), produced and directed by Anthony Buckley; *The Pictures That Moved* (1969), Commonwealth Film Unit; *A Passionate Industry* (1973), Film Australia; *Now You're Talking* (1979), Film Australia.

filmy ferns *see* Pteridophyta

finback *see* dolphins, etc.

finches These non-Australian PASSERINE BIRDS belong to the family Fringillidae and should not be confused with the GRASS FINCHES. They have been introduced into

Greenfinch, *Chloris chloris*

Australia and New Zealand, with much greater success in the latter country.

The two introduced fringillid finches in Australia are the goldfinch, *Carduelis carduelis* (12cm long), a red-masked bird with white, black and gold plumage, and the greenfinch, *Chloris chloris* (15cm), which is mostly green but has a yellow rump and yellow and black markings on the wings. The small and pretty goldfinch is a common sight in parks and gardens in SE Australia and TAS, whereas the larger, more robust greenfinch is an uncommon species found mainly in the woodland areas of VIC. Both species feed on seeds, thistle seeds being favoured by the goldfinch. Their cup-shaped nests are built in trees.
See also animals, introduced

Fingal TAS (population 424 in 1981) A small town in the NE of the State, it is situated on a tributary of the South ESK RIVER between BEN LOMOND and the NE coast, 21km W of the Tasman Highway. The district was settled in the 1820s and the first payable gold in TAS was found in 1852 at 'The Nook', near Fingal. The town is also a coal-mining centre, though production is declining and forestry schemes have been developed to provide work for displaced miners. The National Trust (TAS) has classified numerous buildings in the town and district, including two churches (St Peter's and St Joseph's), the Fingal Hotel, old stables, a former flour mill, a school building and several cottages.

Finke River NT Rising in the MAC-DONNELL RANGES in the S part of the Territory, the Finke follows a general SE course for over 600km flowing across the NT/SA border towards LAKE EYRE; it flows only in wet years and seldom reaches the lake. The headwaters of the Finke lie W of ALICE SPRINGS and the upper streams have cut gaps through the ridges of the MacDonnells; the most famous of these is STANDLEY CHASM (48km W of Alice Springs), but there are numerous others, not quite so accessible nor perhaps so spectacular, such as Ormiston, Serpentine and Ellery Gorges. The Finke Gorge National Park (covering 45 856ha) includes a section of gorge country over 60km long on the main stream. The Finke was discovered and named in 1860 by the explorer John McDouall STUART, who wrote: 'I christened it after William Finke, my

sincere and tried friend, and one of my liberal supporters in the explorations I have had the honour to lead.'

Finley NSW (population 2 193 in 1981) A country town in the RIVERINA region, it is located at the junction of the Newell and Riverina Highways, some 60km E of DENILI-QUIN, and 742km by rail SW of Sydney. Like several towns in this region on NSW side of the MURRAY RIVER, Finley is also linked to the VIC railway network. At an elevation of 107m above sea level, the town receives an average annual rainfall of 411mm; May is the wettest month (53mm average), February is the driest (11mm). Finley is a commercial and service centre for the Berriquin Irrigation District which produces wheat and beef cattle, wool and fat lambs, pigs and dairy produce.

fir *see* Gymnospermae

fire, effect on plants *see* bushfires; Mimosaceae; Myrtaceae; Papilionaceae; Proteaceae; Restionaceae; vegetation

firebrat *see* bristletails

fireflies *see* beetles; flies

First Fleet This name refers to the fleet which brought the first British settlers to NSW in 1788. It included two warships— HMS *Sirius*, about 520 tonnes, commanded by Governor PHILLIP with John HUNTER as second captain, and the 170-tonne sloop *Supply.* The remaining vessels, all chartered merchantmen, were the transports *Alexander, Charlotte, Friendship, Lady Penrhyn, Prince of Wales* and *Scarborough* and the supply ships *Borrowdale, Fishburn* and *Golden Grove.* The total tonnage of the fleet was probably just under 4000.

Between them, these 11 vessels carried about 1 500 people. Accounts differ as to the exact numbers, but the most likely figures at the time of sailing were 443 seamen; 586 male and 192 female convicts, and 13 children of convicts; four companies of marines totalling 211 men, with 27 wives and 19 children; and the Governor, his staff and some civilian officials, a total of 20. Among those who were to become well known in the colony's history, besides Phillip and Hunter, were the chaplain, the Rev. Richard JOHNSON, Judge-Advocate David COLLINS, Lieutenant Watkin Tench, author of a *Narrative of the Expedition to Botany Bay* (1789) and *A Complete Account of the Settlement at Port Jackson in New South Wales* (1793), Lieutenant Philip Gidley KING, Lieutenant George JOHNSTON and Lieutenant Thomas DAVEY. Major Robert Ross was Lieutenant-Governor and commander of the marines.

The food carried was expected to be enough not only for the voyage but for the first two years of settlement. It included great quantities of salt pork and beef, flour, biscuits, oatmeal, cheese and butter, and was supplemented with fresh fruit, vegetables and meat at each port of call. Sheep, pigs, goats and poultry were carried in pens on the decks of some vessels, and more livestock, including cattle and horses, was taken on board at Cape Town. Many kinds of plants and seeds were bought at Rio de Janeiro and Cape Town.

Almost as soon as he was appointed, Governor Phillip began supervising the victualling and other aspects of preparation in the closest detail, addressing a stream of complaints and requests to the responsible authorities. This zeal in preparation, backed up by the firm application of health precautions and the high quality of the rations issued on the voyage, was no doubt largely responsible for the fact that only 23 people died on the actual voyage, a figure which by the standards of the late 18th century was very satisfactory.

Ships of the First Fleet in Sydney Cove in August 1788 as sketched by Lieutenant Bradley of *Sirius*

After being assembled at Spithead, near Portsmouth, the fleet waited for two months before sailing in May 1787. Its ports of call were Teneriffe in the Canary Islands, Rio de Janeiro and Cape Town. Shortly after leaving Cape Town, Phillip transferred to the *Supply*, the fastest sailer in the fleet, in the hope that he would arrive at BOTANY BAY well before the transports and thus have time to select the exact site of the settlement and make preparations for landing the convicts. However, his date of arrival at Botany Bay, 18 January, proved to be only two days earlier than that of the last of the transports. As is explained in his biography, he soon decided that Botany Bay was unsuitable, and took the fleet to nearby PORT JACKSON. After the foundation of the colony the *Charlotte*, *Lady Penrhyn* and *Scarborough*, which were under charter to the East India Co., sailed to China to load tea, while the other transports and store ships returned to England. Phillip retained the services of the two naval vessels.
Further reading: Bateson, C. *The Convict Ships*. Reed, Sydney, 1974.

Fisher, Andrew (1862-1928)

Prime Minister. Born in Ayrshire, Scotland, he worked in the Scottish coal mines as a boy, migrated to QLD in 1885 and worked again as a miner, in the GYMPIE and Burrum fields. He was a Labor member of the QLD Legislative Assembly from 1893 to 1896 and from 1899 to 1901, after which he was elected to the first House of Representatives and in 1907 became leader of the Labor Party. He was Prime Minister on three occasions (1908-1909, 1910-13 and 1914-15) and from 1916 to 1921 was the Australian High Commissioner in London.

Although lacking in brilliance, he played an important role in the rise of the AUSTRALIAN LABOR PARTY. Respected by supporters and opponents alike as a man of integrity and dignity, he gave Labor the image of a moderate reformist party, and widened its electoral appeal to the point where it had prospects of attracting a majority of votes. He also judged correctly when the time was ripe for his party to aim at gaining power in its own right instead of merely holding the balance of power between two other parties.
Further reading: Makin, N.J.O. *Federal Labor Leaders*. Union Printing, Sydney, 1961.

fisheries

This article discusses commercial fishing for true fishes, such as scaled fish and sharks; PRAWN FISHERIES, OYSTER CULTURE, PEARLS AND PEARLING, WHALING and SEALING are discussed under their own headings. Many of the fishes mentioned here are described briefly in the entries on: FISHES; FISHES, BONY; FISHES, FRESHWATER; and SHARKS AND RAYS.

About 2000 species of fishes occur in Australian marine and fresh waters but only about 40 are fished commercially to any significant degree (*see* Table 1). Most commercial fisheries are in southern Australia. The total production of fish landed in Australia is between 55 000 and 66 000 tonnes a year; in the 1978-79 period the annual average haul was 63 395 tonnes. The fisheries also provide average annual yields of about 32 000 tonnes of CRUSTACEANS and about 27 000 tonnes of edible MOLLUSCS (such as cultivated oysters, octopuses, abalones and squids). One reason for the comparatively low yields of the Australian scale fish industry (in Peru; it is about eight million tonnes per annum; in Japan, about seven million tonnes) is that Australian waters lack the vast shoals composed of single species that are characteristic of colder waters, such as the N Pacific and N Atlantic Oceans; in these regions fish can be caught in bulk and need little sorting after capture. In warmer waters, such as those surrounding most of Australia, small areas contain many different species and although some species do form shoals these are relatively small.

Early history of commercial fishing in Australia

Sir Joseph BANKS commented on the 'great plenty of fish' at BOTANY BAY when he was urging the British government to establish a penal colony there. The FIRST FLEET accordingly included small boats and fishing equipment among its stores. William Bryant, transported for smuggling and one of the very few on the First Fleet with any experience of commercial fishing, was appointed Master Fisherman by Captain PHILLIP. He and his helpers provided a reasonable quantity of fish from PORT JACKSON in the early days but the yields soon decreased, partly because of the poor quality of the gear, and partly because,

unknown to the colonists, the fish migrated along the coast during winter. After Bryant, his family and seven convicts absconded to Timor in a small open boat in 1791, there was little fishing in Australia for many years; the first legislation did not come till 1865 when the NSW government introduced controls on net sizes and other matters.

Throughout the 19th century, commercial fishing was hampered by the lack of knowledge about the habits of the local fishes, and the difficulties of transporting fish without ice in a warm climate, and therefore most fishing was carried out in estuaries and along ocean beaches, supplying only local markets. By the end of the century the extensions of the railways and the manufacture of ice enabled Sydney and other large cities to be supplied from farther afield.

In 1908 the Commonwealth government appointed the Norwegian Harold Dannevig as the first Commonwealth Director of Fisheries and then supplied him with the *Endeavour*, a 40m-long research vessel. Until 1914, when Dannevig and his ship were lost in a storm, promising surveys were made of the fisheries on the continental shelf stretching from southern QLD to near FREMANTLE in WA, and excellent potential trawling grounds were discovered S of PORT STEPHENS NSW and in the GREAT AUSTRALIAN BIGHT. In 1914 the NSW government bought three North Sea trawlers to work out of Sydney and later added four locally built boats. The fishing proved good but the profits were low until private businesses took over and increased the size of the fleet. In 1936 a smaller, more economical vessel, the Danish seiner, was added to the fishing fleets.

Modern fishing in Australia

Commercial marine fishing may be divided into three classes: estuarine fisheries in tidal waters, coastal lagoons and lakes, and along beaches and bays; pelagic fisheries, which take surface fish in the open ocean; and demersal fisheries, exploiting the bottom layers of the sea.

The estuarine fisheries produce mullet, such as the common mullet, *Mugil cephalus*, bream, such as the black bream, *Acanthopagrus butcheri*, and yellow-fin bream, *A. australis*, and, in N waters, the giant perch or barramundi, *Lates calcifer*. Among the important pelagic fish are Australian salmon, *Arripis trutta* (used mainly for canning), southern bluefin tuna, *Thunnus maccoyii*, snook, *Leionura atun*, Spanish mackerel, *Scomberomorus commersoni*, and herring-like fishes such as the pilchard, *Sardinops neopilchardus* and the anchovy, *Engraulis australis*. Commercially important demersal fish include snapper, *Chrysophrys auratus*, whitings (family Sillaginidae) and the rock-cods (*Epinephelus* species) of N waters. Trawling in the VIC and NSW waters produces flathead such as the tiger flathead, *Neoplatycephalus richardsoni*, morwong, *Nemadactylus macropterus*, and John Dory, *Zeus faber*. The market for school sharks, *Galeorhinus australis*, and gummy sharks, *Mustelus antarcticus*, fell drastically in 1972-73

Table 1

FISH PRODUCTION 1977-78
(tonnes live weight)

	NSW	VIC	QLD	SA	WA	TAS	NT	AUSTRALIA
Tuna	5 227	15	24	4 992	1 801	45	—	12 153
Mullet	3 041	196	1 557	170	1 003	3	3	5 973
A. Salmon	467	228	—	1 056	770	611	—	3 133
Snapper	790	192	153	334	536	—	—	2 006
Morwong	1 058	255	1	—	18	20	—	1 352
Flathead	1 060	610	83	7	33	112	—	1 905
Shark	1 453	2 792	20	1 022	803	1 710	1	7 801
Mackerel	113	28	1 087	—	94	—	15	1 337
Bream (including Tarwhine)	338	178	274	12	32	—	—	835
Ruff	—	8	—	386	754	—	—	1 148
Whiting	261	671	354	613	271	2	—	2 171
Leatherjacket	231	4	—	7	17	—	—	260
All other species	8 329	4 031	2 144	1 452	2 919	602	1 432	20 907
TOTAL	22 419	9 209	5 697	10 051	9 051	3 105	1 451	60 981
VALUE ($'000)	16 731	11 580	6 067	7 329	5 705	2 438*	1 900	51 751*

Note: * including seaweed, TAS.
Source: *Australian Fisheries*. March 1979.

because of mercury pollution in the former species. The market for gummy shark has since partly recovered.

Despite the early work of the *Endeavour* in the Great Australian Bight before World War I, little large-scale fishing was carried out there for many years. Recently large freezer trawlers have begun to work in the area.

Freshwater fishing concentrates on Murray cod, *Maccullochella macquariensis*, golden perch, *Plectroplites ambiguus*, and eels, *Anguilla australis*.

Fishing techniques Commercial fishermen catch scale fish either in nets or on lines with hooks. Seine netting, used in shallow waters, is a method by which a long net is suspended between the floating cork-line and the lead-line with its weights. The net is concave, and sometimes has a bag in the middle or to one side into which the trapped fish are forced as it is drawn through the water and the area enclosed diminishes; a beach seine is arranged in a semicircle, and then drawn into the shore or onto a sandbank, or even up to another net. The success of seine netting depends upon the bottom being reasonably smooth so that it comes into close contact with the lead-line, blocking off the escape of the fish below.

A related technique, gill netting, uses a net in which the fish become entangled as they try to force their way through the mesh. The gill net may be used as a set net (usually in estuaries) with the ends anchored, or as a drift net which moves along with the tide, attached to boats or buoys.

Demersal fish can be caught by trawling (dragging a bag-like net behind the boat). Originally, the trawl net was held open by a beam but as the nets became larger the beam became too heavy and unwieldy, and was replaced by otter boards at each side of the net, attached to the boat by lines; the shape of the otter boards is such that when the trawl is pulled they are forced apart by the water pressure. The top of a trawl net is supported by the upper or head rope, which is attached to floats, and the lower edge is kept down by weights on the foot rope. In the Vigneron-Dahl trawl net the otter boards are not fastened to the net itself, but to long lines which run from the wings. In recent years mid-water trawling, which allows the skipper to make full use of his echo-sounding equipment to locate shoals, has become a common practice.

Commercial fishermen rarely use fishing rods or poles but the exception is the rod fishing for tuna in inshore waters in southern Australia. A more common method of catching tuna is long line fishing, whereby lines of hooks are set, either attached to a series of buoys or floats, or with one end fastened to an anchor and the other to the vessel. Shorter long lines are used for shark fishing in SE Australia. Technical advances which have aided fishermen in recent years include the use of aircraft for spotting (especially tuna), and of echo-sounding and echolocation gear, and navigation aid from satellites.

Further reading: see under fishes, bony; sharks and rays. *Also: Australian Fisheries.* (monthly) Australian Govt Publishing Service, Canberra; Thomson, J.M. *Fish of the Ocean and Shore.* Collins, Sydney, 1974.

fishes The aquatic VERTEBRATES commonly called fishes belong to several distinct and not closely related groups. All living fishes are CHORDATES. The phylum Chordata (the vertebrates, and the SEA SQUIRTS AND THEIR ALLIES) contains the subphyla Acrania (small animals without a skull, but with a stiffening rod—a notochord—which is replaced in higher forms by a backbone) and Craniata (vertebrates with a skull enclosing the brain).

The subphylum Acrania contains the class Amphioxi, to which LANCELETS belong.

The subphylum Craniata is divided into two superclasses, Agnatha (vertebrates with skulls but without jaws and without paired limbs) and Gnathostomata (vertebrates with jaws, a skull and paired limbs, though these are lost in some forms such as snakes). The superclass Agnatha contains the class Cyclostomata (LAMPREYS AND HAGFISHES). The superclass Gnathostomata contains the class Chondrichthyes (SHARKS AND RAYS) in which the skeleton consists of cartilage, at least in modern forms, and the gill openings are not covered with a bony plate; the class Holocephali (ghost sharks), in which the skeleton consists of cartilage but the single gill opening on each side is covered by a flap; and the class Osteichthyes (the true fishes; *see* FISHES, BONY; FISHES, FRESHWATER), in which the skeleton consists largely of bone and in most cases a bony plate (the operculum) covers the gill openings.

All the classes mentioned are found in Australian waters. The lancelets, small marine, bottom-living animals, 5cm or less in length, would not be regarded as fishes by many people. In the sharks, rays, ghost sharks and bony fishes the limbs are normally represented by two pairs of paired fins: the pectoral fins, associated with the shoulder girdle, and the pelvic or ventral fins with the pelvic girdle. There are also unpaired fins: dorsal, tail or caudal and anal. The sharks and rays and the bony fishes occur in marine and brackish waters and in freshwaters, but the ghost sharks are entirely marine.

The common names of Australian fishes are confusing. The early European settlers named many fishes after species that they knew in Europe, although the Australian animals were completely unrelated to their European namesakes; European sailors named local fishes after fishes that they had seen in other parts of

the world; and sometimes Aboriginal names were adopted. At least three different kinds of fish are called barramundi, an Aboriginal name which refers to large scales. The common names of many commercially important species are not even consistent from State to State, despite conferences and decisions of fishery authorities. The term 'cod', for example, is applied to several fishes in different families and orders, though the true cod order is relatively unimportant in the Australian area. *See also* fisheries; Queensland lung fish
Further reading: Whitley, G.P. 'An outline classification of Australian fishes' and 'The common names of fishes' in McMichael, D.F. (ed) *A Treasury of Australian Wildlife.* Ure Smith, Sydney, 1968; Pollard, J. (ed) *Australian and New Zealand Fishing.* Paul Hamlyn, London & Sydney, 1969; Pulley, K. *Marine Fishes of Australian Waters.* Lansdowne Press, Melbourne, 1974; Scott, T.D., Glover, C.J.M. & Southcott, R.V. *The Marine and Freshwater Fishes of South Australia.* (2nd edn) Govt Printer, Adelaide, 1974; Thomson, J.M. *Fish of the Ocean and Shore.* Collins, Sydney, 1974 and *A Field Guide to the Common Sea and Estuary Fishes of non-Tropical Australia.* Collins, Sydney, 1977; Burton, M. & Burton, R. *Encyclopaedia of Fish.* Octopus, London, 1975; Carcasson, R.H. *A Field Guide to the Reef Fishes of Tropical Australia and the Indo-Pacific Region.* Collins, Sydney, 1977; Grant, E.M. *Guide to Fishes.* Department of Harbours and Marine, Brisbane, 1978.

fishes, bony Most modern FISHES (class Osteichthyes) have bony skeletons in contrast to the cartilaginous skeletons of the SHARKS AND RAYS or elasmobranchs. They also differ in having a bony plate (the operculum) covering the gills, and in most cases by the possession of scales and a swim bladder. Fertilisation is almost always external.

The class is divided into two subclasses: Actinopterygii (ray-finned fishes) and Sarcopterygii (Choanichthyes, lobe- or tassel-finned fishes). The latter contains the QUEENSLAND LUNG FISH and its American and African allies (order Dipnoi) and the COELOCANTH (order Crossopterygii).

The ray-finned fishes are subdivided into three superorders, only one of which, the Teleosteii, is represented in the region. There are about 20 000 species of teleost fishes in the world with about 2000 species in Australian waters. The classification of teleost fishes is far from settled and, furthermore, some widespread fishes have been named several times independently by different authorities. Consequently, some species may be given more than one scientific name here. In general, the names used follow the references in the bibliography under the entry on FISHES. Several of the families have both freshwater and marine members but for convenience the first are considered in a separate entry (*see* FISHES, FRESHWATER); this article therefore discusses only marine ray-finned fishes.

The marine teleosts fill a remarkable range of niches. Many species produce millions of eggs

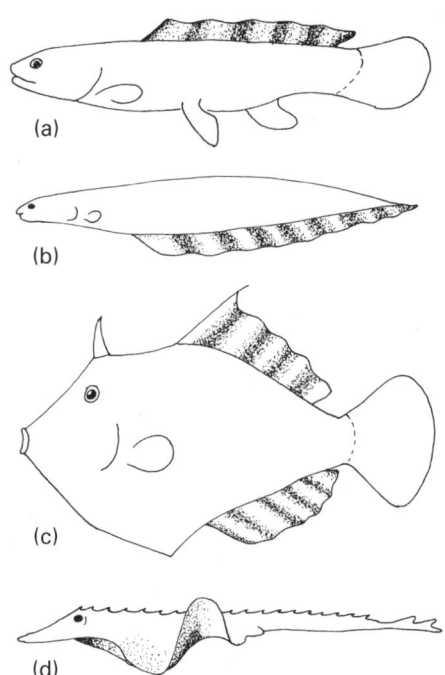

Swimming modes among fish that use their median or pectoral fins for propulsion: (a) Amiiform; (b) Gymnotiform; (c) Balniform; (d) Rajiform

but very few survive to become adult, reproducing fishes. Only the most important orders are covered here. They include the groups with fishes that are important in commercial fisheries or angling and groups with unusual or bizarre forms. In general only coastal species are considered but a few oceanic and deep-sea forms that are sometimes brought to shore either by fishermen or by storms are mentioned.

In the following sections, the more primitive orders are discussed first.

Order Clupeiformes (Isospondyli): herrings and their allies This is a large order of fishes with soft-rayed fins that lack spines. There is usually only a single dorsal fin set about halfway along the body. The two ventral fins are set in the front two-thirds of the body. Typically, the fishes of this order are migratory, schooling species, usually feeding on plankton. The family Clupeidae contains the typical herrings which are small shoaling fishes, long in form and somewhat flattened from side to side. They lack the lateral line (a line of sense organs down the side of the fish). The pilchard, *Sardinops neopilchardus* (up to 23cm long), is the commonest Australian clupeid and is found in all States. Other fishes of the order are the anchovy, *Engraulis australis* (15cm), the silver-side, *Argentina elongata* (18cm), and the ox-eye herring or tarpon, *Megalops cyprinoides* (1.5m).

Order Myctophiformes: grinners, lantern fishes, Sergeant Baker and Bombay ducks These are mainly small fishes with fins that lack spines. There is usually a small fatty (adipose) dorsal fin behind the larger anterior one. Some species, the lantern fishes, are herring-shaped, but carry light organs or

photophores on their bodies. Most are deep-sea fishes but some are taken in shallow waters. Lizard fishes or grinners are, in contrast, small bottom-dwellers in shallow waters where they often bury themselves in sand in wait for prey. Bombay ducks are medium-sized translucent fishes of muddy estuaries. The glassy Bombay duck, *Harpadon translucens* (70cm), is often caught in the MARY RIVER in QLD. The Sergeant Baker, *Aulopus purpurissatus* (30cm), is a crimson-mottled, wide-mouthed fish of rocky reefs in E Australia.

Order Siluroidiformes: catfishes Catfishes are carnivores which feed on the bottom. They have sensitive barbels around the mouth and a naked, slimy skin. The Plotosidae is an Indo-Pacific, predominantly marine family which contains the eel-tailed catfishes. The body is pointed at the tail end, and the unforked tail fin reaches more than halfway along the body, both above and below. The estuarine catfishes (family Tachysuridae) have forked tails and a lateral line.

All catfishes have sharp pectoral and dorsal spines covered with poisonous slime and should be handled carefully. Many species are, however, good food.

Order Anguilliformes (Apodes): eels This is an order of snake-shaped fishes with more than 350 species in about 27 families. Most are scaleless or have minute scales, often deeply embedded in the skin. They can be distinguished from sea SNAKES by the presence of fins. The larvae are transparent, ribbon-like animals, called Leptocephalus, which live in the sea, even when the adults are freshwater. Eels are not venomous but their bites often inject pathogenic bacteria. Some of the larger moray eels can be dangerous as they will bite limbs that intrude into their territory.

Snake-eels (family Ophichthyidae) have sharply pointed tails, and burrow into the sand or mud. Many boldly patterned species live in coral reefs. Moray or reef eels (family Muraenidae) are predominantly tropical fishes which lurk in holes and crevices in coral in wait for passing prey. The head is short and blunt, and well armed with strong, sharp teeth. Many are dark in colour, but some, such as the black and yellow zebra moray, *Echidna zebra* (1.2m), are strikingly patterned. The pied black-blotched moray, *Gymnothorax favagineus* (1.8m), is one of the larger, potentially dangerous species.

Pike-eels (family Muraenesocidae) are strong eels, round in section at the front but somewhat flattened from side to side in the tail region. The teeth are large and sharp, and the head is shaped like that of a pike. Pike-eels are often very difficult to subdue in a small boat.

Conger-eels (family Leptocephalidae) are large eels similar to morays, but generally duller in colour and with pectoral fins.

Order Synbranchiformes: one-gilled eels These small, rock-pool eels have only one gill opening below the head, whereas the true eels have two gill openings, one on each side of the head.

Order Beloniformes: garfishes, long toms and flying fishes These are silvery, often long fish which live near the surface. The single dorsal fin, and pectoral fins, which are often quite large, are high on the body. Long toms (family Belonidae) are long, thin, predatory fishes with both jaws forming a long beak, well furnished with sharp teeth; the eyes are large, and the bones greenish.

The garfishes or half-beaks (family Hemirhamphidae) are similar to long toms but only the lower jaw projects as the beak. The teeth are small and absent from the beak; garfishes feed on plant material near the surface. All are small (less than 50cm) but are important commercial fishes. Many species occur in Australian coastal water.

Garfishes and long toms often skitter across the surface of the sea. This habit is carried to the extreme in the flying fishes (family Exocoetidae) which use their expanded pectoral fins as planes to give them more lift. They lack the beaks of their allies. Though they are mainly tropical, some flying fishes extend as far S as VIC and NSW. They fly to escape from predators such as the dolphin fishes; flights can reach a length of 50m. One of the larger Australian species is the black-tipped flying fish, *Cypselurus furcatus* (35cm), found in all warm seas. The common flying fish, *Exocoetus volitans*, is slightly smaller but has more rays in the anal fin.

Order Gadiformes: codfishes The true cods belong to this order. They are long-bodied fishes with small scales. The spineless dorsal fin is divided into two or three parts, and the chin usually has a barbel. Most of these fishes are found in rather deep water. None is longer than 50cm. In the family Moridae (or Eretmophoridae) the dorsal fin is in two or three parts which are close together. The beardie or ling, *Lotella callarias* (50cm), and the bearded rock cod, *Physiculus barbatus* (43cm), which occur in shallow S waters, both have two dorsal fins.

Order Lampridiformes: oarfishes Oarfishes are long, ribbon-shaped fishes of the open oceans. The oarfish or king of the herrings, *Regalecus pacificus* (to 5m), is a silvery species with a crimson to pink 'crest'.

Order Pleuronectiformes: flatfishes This is a large cosmopolitan family of often commercially important bottom-living fishes with asymmetrical bodies. The larvae are bilaterally symmetrical but in the adult both eyes are on one side of the head, usually the right, and the body is flat. The upper surface is cryptically coloured, and the undersurface white. Many species can change colour to blend with their backgrounds. The paired fins are either asymmetrical or represented only on the upper side. Flatfishes are carnivores, feeding on crustaceans and so on.

The Queensland halibut, *Psettodes erumei* (60cm), belongs to the toothed flounders (family Psettodidae). It can be left- or right-handed and unlike other flatfishes swims in a vertical position. The left-handed flounders (family Bothidae) include several small or

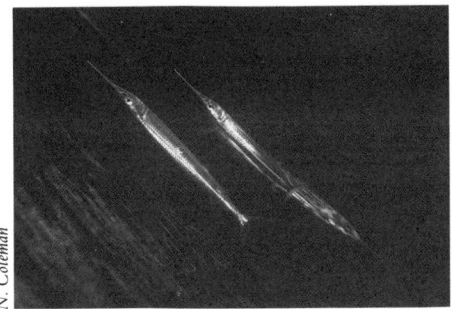

Eastern sea garfish, *Hyporhamphus australis*

medium flatfishes with mottled coloration and a tail fin separate from the dorsal and anal fins. One of the commonest and larger, economically important species is the large-toothed flounder, *Pseudorhombus arsius* (33cm), of QLD, NSW and WA. In the right-handed flounders (family Pleuronectidae), found mainly in cooler Australian seas and including many of the N hemisphere food fishes, the right pectoral and ventral fins are larger than the left. The widespread long-snouted flounder, *Ammotretis rostratus* (25cm), is the most important table flatfish in Australia. Soles (family Soleidae) have the dorsal fin extending on to the head and are right-handed. Several species are common. Tongue soles (family Cynoglossidae) are small, extremely flattened left-handed fishes with a hooked snout and the tail end of the body tapering to a sharp point. They are too small to be of value.

Order Beryciformes: knight fishes and squirrel fishes There are several families, some confined to deep seas.

The knight fishes (family Monocentridae), popular aquarium species, have a few large scales which are joined to form a body armour. They are also known as pineapple or pine-cone fishes because of their shape and texture. There are light organs on the chin.

The squirrel or soldier fishes (family Holocentridae), typical carnivores of the coral reefs, are small, large-eyed, nocturnal fishes which spend the day in crevices in the coral. There are spines in the dorsal and anal fins, and on the gill covers; the scales are serrated.

Red snappers (family Berycidae) are reddish, deep-water fishes with deeply forked tails. The nannygai, *Centroberyx affinis* (46cm), is a deep-bodied, short, large-eyed species that is trawled on the E continental shelf.

Order Zeiformes: dories Dories (family Zeidae) are short, deep fishes, flattened from side to side. The mouth can be protruded well forward to catch prey. The eyes are large. Many species, such as the John Dory, *Zeus faber* (to 60cm), have a black spot on the side; this S species is highly prized on the table. Most dories are deep-water fishes.

Order Syngnathiformes: pipefishes and sea horses This is a large order of peculiar fishes all of which have a small, toothless mouth at the end of a tubular snout. The body is protected by a sheath of bony rings or plates, but there are no true scales. They have one or two dorsal fins. The young fishes develop from

eggs placed by the female in a brood pouch on the belly of the male, near the tail.

Pipefishes (family Syngnathidae) generally have long bodies enclosed in bony rings. The very small fins lack spines; the caudal fin may be absent, and there are no ventral fins. They often hook themselves with their prehensile tails to eel grass (*Zostera*). In this vertical position they are difficult to see. Pipefishes feed on small animals which they suck in through the mouth. Sea horses belong to the same family and can be regarded as stout pipefishes with the head bent at an angle to the body so that they assume the shape of the knight in a chess set. Neither pipefishes nor sea horses are good swimmers and they rely heavily on camouflage for security. This is carried to the extreme in the peculiarly

Sea horse, *Hippocampus* species

Australian leafy and weedy sea-dragons, *Phycodurus eques* (30cm), of SA and WA, and *Phyllopteryx taeniolatus* (46cm), from NSW to WA, which have large leafy outgrowths. The common or White's sea horse, *Hippocampus whitei* (21cm), which ranges from SA to QLD, is of the more familiar shape.

Flute mouths or trumpet fishes (family Aulostomatidae) are long snouted fishes with spines on the back, and with the second dorsal and anal fin set well back.

Order Pegasiformes: sea moths or dragon fishes These are small warm-sea fishes with wing-like pectoral fins and reduced ventral fins. They have toothless mouths overhung with a bony process (the rostrum); the trunk and head are enclosed in bony rings. They live in shallow weed beds.

Order Mugiliformes: mullets, barracudas and sea pikes This is a large and important order of small to large fishes, variable in form. They have two dorsal fins which are well separated, and ventral fins placed well back; the front dorsal fin is spiny. The body is often long and narrow and the scales are moderate to large.

Barracudas and sea pikes (family Sphyraenidae) are large, swift predators, sometimes gregarious, which are found in warm seas. The tail is forked. The large mouth has large, formidable fangs and the lower jaw is longer than the upper one. The barracuda, *Agrioposphyraena (Sphyraena) barracuda* (2.4m), found in all warm oceans, especially near coral reefs, is greyish-blue and silvery, with dark, indistinct cross bars. There are over 30 records of this species attacking human beings in various parts of the world.

Mullets (family Mugilidae) are long fishes with broad, flattened heads. There is no lateral line; the small mouth has minute teeth which are sometimes completely absent. The sea mullet, *Mugil cephalus* (to 69cm), olive above and silvery below, is an extremely important commercial fish, accounting for about half the catch in QLD and NSW. Found in all Australian States, and in temperate and warm waters, it can be distinguished from other Australian mullets by the fatty eyelid.

Sea mullets are estuarine fishes that often enter freshwater. They wander in search of the small algae and diatoms which they suck from the bottom, mixed with mud which they spit out. They spawn at sea during the winter. They mature at the end of the third year.

Order Polynemiformes: threadfins These are fishes of muddy estuaries which have long sensory filaments at the front of the pectoral fins because of the poor visibility. Their fins otherwise resemble those of mullets. Two large species are commercially important in QLD and the N: the Burnett salmon, *Polydactylus sheridani*, and the colonial or Cooktown salmon, *Eleutheronema tetradactylum*.

Order Perciformes: perch-like fishes This is by far the largest order of fishes with perhaps 8000 species in the world. Though many are similar in shape to the European perch or redfin, an introduced species in Australia, the order is very diverse and it is difficult to point to any characteristics common to all. There are usually two dorsal fins and these are often united. The ventral fins often have one spine followed by five, but never more than six, soft rays. The most important suborders are considered here.

1. Suborder Scomboidei: mackerels, tunas and their allies. These are streamlined, predatory fishes and include most of the game fishes. The two dorsal fins are separate, the first with spines, but there is also a series of little fins between the tail and the second dorsal fin, and a similar series beneath the body. The base of the tail is narrow and keeled on the sides. The teeth are small and pointed.

The true mackerels are medium-sized fishes belonging to the genus *Scomber* (family Scombridae). The slimy mackerel, *S. australicus* (36cm), is found in all States and is very common in the S seas. The wahoo, *Acanthocybium solandri* (to 2m), an outstanding game fish of coral reefs in the Indo-Pacific and tropical Atlantic, is dark blue above and silvery below with many cobalt-blue vertical bars. The first dorsal fin is long and rectangular for most of its length. It is the only member of its family, Acanthocybiidae. Spanish mackerels (family Scomberomoridae) are medium-sized or large schooling fishes which feed on fishes in coastal waters; when taking small fishes such as anchovies the larger species often dash into the shoals with the mouths wide and sieve out the smaller fishes with the gill-rakers. The narrow-barred Spanish mackerel, *Scomberomorus (Sybium) commersoni* (to 2.3m), is the most important fish, after mullet, in QLD commercial catches.

The tunas, tunnies and bonitos (family Thunnidae) are robust, compact school fishes of warm waters. The base of the tail is very narrow and the tail fin sickle-shaped. There are several species in the Australian area, some of great economic importance, but the yellowfin tuna, *Neothunnus macropterus* (*Thunnus albacares*) (to about 2m), is one of the commoner and more colourful species. The albacore, *Thunnus alalunga* (76cm), considered the best tuna for the table, is a dark blue and silver species which ranges from WA to NSW. Skipjacks or frigate-mackerels (family Katsuwonidae) are warm-seas migratory, schooling fishes similar to tunas but lacking scales except behind the head. The skipjack, *Katsuwonus pelamis* (about 60cm), forms immense shoals off TAS and NSW.

The marlins and sailfishes (family Istiophoridae) are large game fishes with the upper jaw extended to a long offensive bill or sword. The body is very deep behind the head, and the tail fin is divided into two distinct sections. The Pacific sailfish, *Istiophorus orientalis* (*I. albicans*) (3.2m), has an immense, sail-like anterior dorsal fin which is sometimes seen above the water as the fish rests. The black marlin, *Istiompax marlina* (4.6m), a steel blue or purplish fish, is the most important game fish in the GREAT BARRIER REEF. The swordfish, *Xiphias gladius* (4.6m), of the family Xiphiidae, sometimes spears small boats.

2. Suborder Trichiuroidei: barracoutas and frost fishes. These fishes are not related to the barracudas. Most are very long fishes, flattened from side to side. The tail may either taper to a fine thread, or may be forked. The mouth has sharp, pointed teeth and the scales, when present, are small. The barracouta or snoek, *Leionura (Thyrsites) atun* (1.4m), of the family Gempylidae, is a steely blue and silver, elongated fish with small, easily detached scales.

3. Suborder Percoidei: dolphin fishes, trevallies and their allies. This is a very large suborder with many families. The dolphin fish, *Coryphaena hippurus* (1.8m), of the family Coryphaenidae, is a long, compressed predatory fish whose body tapers towards the tail. The greenish dorsal fin, high at the front, runs the full length of the body. The yellow tail fin is deeply forked. The body is iridescent, blue to green above and gold below. This widely distributed game fish of warm seas feeds largely on schools of flying fishes.

The Carangidae is a large family containing the trevally and other important fishes. The skipjack trevally, *Usacaranx georgianus* (76cm), of WA and SA, is a deep blue and silver, deep-bodied fish, rather perch-like, with a black spot on the operculum. The base of the tail is narrow. There are many other closely related fishes of various colours in the region.

The tailor, *Pomatomus saltator* (*P. saltatrix*) (1.2m), of the family Pomatomidae, is a fast-swimming predator often sought by surf fishermen. The dark blue and silver body is elongated and compressed. The first dorsal fin is composed of short, rather weak spines.

The family Mullidae contains the red mullets or goatfishes. The blue-spotted goatfish, *Upeneichthys porosus* (33cm), is a widespread example with large fins and long barbels on the chin for bottom feeding. The general colour is reddish and there are blue lines on the snout and spots on the belly.

The cardinal fishes and siphon fishes compose a large family, Apogonidae, of coral fishes. In most species the male carries the eggs and young in his mouth. They are small fishes with oblong bodies, usually brightly coloured, and have large mouths with protruding lower jaws. There are two dorsal fins, the first spiny.

The family Latidae (or Centropomidae) contains the barramundi or giant perch, *Lates calcarifer* (1.8m), a well-known table fish; it is both freshwater and marine, and occurs in QLD and extends to Sri Lanka, Melanesia and the Persian Gulf. (The name barramundi is also applied to an unrelated freshwater fish of the genus *Scleropages*; both have large scales.) *L. calcarifer* has a raised back and a pointed head. The spiny dorsal fin is triangular, the anal, second dorsal and tail fins are rounded. The colour is greenish-grey and silver (freshwater specimens are often darker) and the eye is pink.

The Serranidae is a large family of predatory fishes such as rock-cods, coral-cods and groupers. There are two distinct groups: Epinephelinae and Anthiinae. The first are solitary, highly territorial fishes of coral reefs which usually live on the bottom, lurking in holes waiting for passing prey. The fairy cod or coronation trout *Variola louti* (75cm), is a beautiful common coral fish, with a half-moon-shaped tail. The colour is variable but the fish is often vermilion or orange with red spots, and with bright yellow fringes on the fins. The coral trout, *Plectropoma maculatum* (95cm), is a similar fish but with a squarer tail. The Queensland grouper or groper, *Promicrops (Epinephelus) lanceolatus*, is the largest bony fish in Australian waters (with the possible exception of the ocean sun fish). In the Persian Gulf they reach a length of 3.6m but Australian specimens are smaller. The adults are greenish-brown or dark grey. Gropers have a reputation for being dangerous to man but there seems to be little evidence for this. They are certainly not dangerous in the way that man-eating sharks are but they are large fishes with a large appetite and could snap at anything that appears to be edible.

The anthiines are quite different in appearance and behaviour from the epinephelines. They include the butterfly perches and barbers, small, brightly coloured fishes which swim in small schools consisting of, apparently, a male

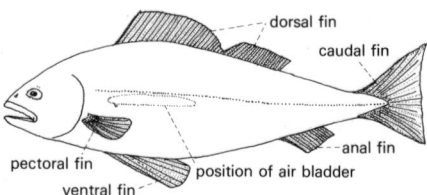

A teleost fish showing position of air bladder and lateral line

W. Gladstone

Painted sweetlips, *Plectorhynchus pictus*, common throughout the coral reefs of Australia

and his harem, and possibly some young males as well.

The family Lutjanidae contains a large number of species some of which are called sea-perches, hussars, bass and snappers. The Lutjanidae is composed of active carnivores found in all warm oceans. Most form small schools on the bottom and feed on small fishes and crustaceans. They are found in a range of habitats such as coral reefs, mangroves and rock pools. They are important in the tropics as food fishes. Most are long, compressed fishes. There are scales on the cheeks and operculum. The single dorsal fin and the anal fin are spiny. Many belong to the genus *Lutjanus*.

The fusiliers and banana fishes are relatives of the *Lutjanus* group. They are brightly coloured fishes which form very large schools, usually near rocks and coral. The sweetlips and thick-lipped grunters form yet another sub-family of the Lutjanidae. They are restricted to Indo-Pacific coral reefs. The young are far more colourful than the adults. The lips are thick and fleshy. The painted sweetlips, *Plectorhynchus pictus* (45cm), is called the morwong in QLD where it is also known as the mother-in-law fish. It is grey with black spots that vary in intensity. The final subfamily contains the emperors, pig-faced breams, naked-headed snappers and scavengers. The head and cheeks are more or less scaleless but there are scales on the operculum. The body is deep, the head pointed and the mouth small.

Silver bream, sea-bream and porgies (family Sparidae), often also called snappers, are large-scaled fishes with enlarged molar teeth for crushing crustaceans. They are deep-bodied fishes with scaly cheeks and operculum, red or silvery in colour. The snapper of the S States is *Chrysophrys auratus* (80cm or more), which is pink with bluish spots when adult, though the colour varies with age. The snapper is

Roman-nosed and many old specimens develop a hump on the back and a bulge on the nose. There are six species of bream in Australian waters: black bream, *Acanthopagrus butcheri* (WA to TAS); yellow-fin bream, *A. australis*; Japanese bream, *A. latus* (tropical WA and NT); pikey bream, *A. berda* (QLD to Darwin); hump-headed bream, *A. palmaris* (north-western WA); and silver bream or tarwhine, *Rhabdosargus sarba* (all States). All are medium-sized fishes (40cm to 70cm).

The family Sciaenidae contains the drummers and jewfishes. The name drummer or croaker refers to the loud drumming noises that these fishes can produce under water, a useful ability in muddy sites. Fierce predators of sandy shores, they are robust in build and rather oblong in shape. The dorsal fin is continuous, but deeply notched. The mulloway or jewfish, *Johnius* (*Sciaena*) *antarctica* (1.8m or more), a good table fish when of moderate size, is a greyish-green fish above, and silver-grey below; the inside of the mouth is bright orange. It ranges from QLD to TAS and SA. The teraglin, *Atractoscion aequidens* (1.2m), is distinguished from the similar jewfish by its concave tail fin.

The whitings (family Sillaginidae) are so called because they resemble the completely unrelated whiting of Europe. Australian whitings are elongated fishes with two dorsal fins (strictly speaking, one deeply notched) and a long anal fin. They have a spine on the operculum; the snouts are long and conical for rooting out small animals from the sand.

Batfishes (family Platacidae or part of the family Ephippidae) are extremely thin fishes with deep bodies which live in shallow water among weeds, *Zostera* or coral in the Indo-Pacific. The young look like dead leaves; when disturbed they sink slowly into the weeds. Scats and butterfishes (family Scatophagidae) are again of a similar shape but the dorsal spines are conspicuous.

The Chaetodontidae is a very large family of deep-bodied fishes that invariably appear in films of coral reefs. They are the angel and butterfly fishes that are popular aquarium subjects. Usually white, orange and yellow with black patches, and often a black stripe through the eye, they have a small head and mouth, sometimes on a prolonged snout, armed with very small teeth with which they feed on small invertebrates. *Chaetodon* is one of the larger genera; the saddled butterfly fish, *C. ephippium* (30cm), is an example. It has a shiny black patch on the back (the saddle) with a broad band of white below, and red and blue stripes behind. The rest of the body is greenish-blue striped longitudinally with bright purplish-blue. The cheek, throat and ventral fins are yellow, and there is a vertical black stripe through the eye. It is common in the Great Barrier Reef.

The family Girellidae contains the black-fishes, heavily built weed-eating fishes. The luderick, *Girella tricuspidata* (to 70cm), is a popular fish with anglers and occurs in all States. It has 12 narrow bars on its back.

The family Toxotidae consists of the unique archer fishes which shoot down insects by spitting water at them. They live in fresh and brackish water, mangroves and river mouths in the central Indo-Pacific; there are two marine species, *Toxotes jaculator* (25cm) and *T. chartareus* (30cm), in N Australia.

The anemone fishes or clown fishes (family Amphiprionidae) are popular photographic subjects as they often live within the tentacles of sea anemones in shallow waters and coral reefs. They secrete a mucus which protects them from the stings of their hosts. They usually occur in small groups, the number depending upon the size of the particular anemone. They gain protection from the host which, presumably, gets scraps of food in return. Anemone fishes are also called clown fishes.

The Pomacentridae is a family of fishes closely related to the anemone fishes, but the scales are larger. Commonly known as damselfishes and sergeant majors, they are small, active, warm-sea fishes, often brightly coloured. They usually live in small schools in coral. The damselfishes have a scaly operculum. They are perch-like in shape. Sergeant majors are similar but the operculum is smooth. Most belong to the strangely named genus *Abudefduf*. Members of this family are popular aquarium fishes.

The wrasses and their allies, rainbow fishes, tusk fishes, pig and hog fishes, belong to the cosmopolitan Labridae, a very large family of variable fishes, often difficult to identify. Most have teeth for crushing molluscs but they eat weeds as well. The lips are thick and fleshy, and the scales large and smooth. The single dorsal fin has a large spiny section. There are about 500 known species in the world, some important as food fishes. Many wrasses make weed-nests for raising their eggs and young. Most are solitary and active during the day. One of the most unusual species is the sling-jaw or telescope fish, *Epibulus insidiator* (32cm), a coral-reef wrasse, which can shoot out its jaws rapidly like the mask of a dragon-fly nymph to catch prey. The family also contains the cleaner wrasse or blue streak, *Labroides dimidiatus* (10cm), one of the many fishes that relieve other fishes of their parasites. They keep to well-defined stations, usually by a piece of coral, and, with complete immunity, work over the body and even in the mouth and gills of much larger fishes. Members of other families also act as barber fishes and often their colour pattern resembles that of the cleaner wrasse.

The parrot fishes (family Scaridae) are colourful reef fishes, medium to large in size, so called because their teeth are fused into a beak for crushing coral and shell fishes. Most are edible but are sometimes poisonous. One of the commonest and largest species in QLD is the blue-barred orange parrot fish, *Scarus ghobban* (1m).

The morwongs (family Cheilodactylidae) are percoid carnivores of cooler waters. The tail is forked and the long lower rays of the pectoral fins are used as feelers. The dorsal fin is sharply notched and clearly divided into a spiny front section and a lower hind section. The jackass fish, *Nemadactylus macropterus* (60cm), is a light bluish and silver species with a black band across the nape of the neck, often trawled, from WA to TAS and NSW. The morwong of QLD and NSW, *N. morwong*, resembles the jackass fish but has no bar on the neck.

The weevers or grubfishes belong to the family Parapercidae. They are small, elongated, cylindrical, carnivorous fishes well armed with dorsal and opercular spines that can cause painful wounds. The eyes are large and near the top of the head. Most are too small to eat.

The Arripidae is a very small family but it contains the well-known Australian salmon which, however, is unrelated to the true salmons. In New Zealand this species, *Arripis trutta* (90cm), is known as kahawai. The forms from SW Australia are larger than those from the SE. They also differ in the gills. The W variety tends to feed on small fishes, and that of the E on plankton, especially krill. Both forms are migratory and use the TAS region as the nursery area. After spawning they return to their feeding grounds. During these migrations Australian salmon are often caught by beach seine netters, mainly for canning. The body of the salmon is similar to that of the true salmon in shape, but the fins differ. The ruff or tommy rough, *A. georgianus* (40cm), is a similar fish, but with a rougher skin.

4. Suborder Blennioidei: blennies. Blennies are small coastal fishes of all warm areas and many temperate ones. Some live in brackish water and freshwater. The largest family, Blennidae (about 200 species in the Indo-Pacific) contains small, active carnivorous fishes of shallow waters, among rocks and corals. Many live in rock pools where they hide under stones or in weed.

The true blennies have normal teeth, firmly fixed to the jaws. In contrast, the other sub-family, the skippers or rockhoppers, contains fishes with weak, movable teeth which are attached to the lips. The common blenny, *Pictiblennius tasmanianus* (13cm), is very common on shallow coasts and in rock pools from WA to VIC and TAS. The head is large and the dorsal fin long. The scaleless body is olive green with several broken, darker bars. The oyster blenny, *Cyneichthyes (Petroscirtes) anolius* (9cm), the larger individuals of which have a crest on the head, above a small mouth, guards its eggs inside empty oyster shells. The skippers or rockhoppers include several species which leave the water to skip over the surface of mud and rocks, but in Australia such amphibious fishes are more likely to be gobies. Weedfishes (family Clinidae) have two dorsal fins, often partly joined, the first consisting of only three spines, and the second of many rays and spines. These small, cryptically coloured fishes live in shallow, weedy water and give birth to living young. There is usually a tentacle over the eye. The Tripterygidae is composed of small blennies with three dorsal fins. The jumping joey, *Lepidoblennius haplodactylus*, of QLD and NSW, and the jumping blenny, *L. marmoratus*, of SA and WA, frequently sun themselves on rocks, leaping back into the water when disturbed.

5. Suborder Ophidoidei: messmate fishes and their allies. This suborder contains the pearl-fishes or messmates (family Carapidae) which are slender coral fishes that shelter inside sea stars, sea cucumbers or oysters which they enter tail first.

6. Suborder Callionymoidei: mandarin fishes and dragonets. These are small, bottom-living coastal fishes of all warm oceans. They spend much time partly concealed in the sand. The scaleless body is long and almost cylindrical. The head is flat but bug-eyed. The gill opening is only a small, rounded pore on each side. The fins are usually very large, and the colouring is often bizarre.

7. Suborder Siganoidei: spinefeet and rabbit fishes. These are economically important food fishes in the tropics and several species occur in QLD. They are medium-sized, slimy, oval herbivores which feed on weeds in small shoals. They have a spiny dorsal fin which can give painful wounds. When disturbed they go for cover, sometimes uncomfortably under the intruder's foot.

8. Suborder Acanthuroidei: surgeon fishes and their allies. These are small or medium-sized herbivores, usually in coral reefs. The sub-order now contains the Moorish idol, *Zanclus canescens* (*Z. cornutus*) (20cm) of the family Zanclidae, which was once thought to be a chaetodontid. This is a popular and well-known aquarium fish. The body is deep with a pronounced snout. The dorsal fin, which is largely white, has a long white streamer. The body is white and yellow with two black, broad, vertical bands. There is a black band on the tail fin and some red on the snout.

Surgeon fishes (family Acanthuridae) take their name from the bony scalpels which they carry on each side of the tail base. These knives can be retracted. Unicorn fishes are similar but their knives are fixed. Old males often have a horn above the snout. In general, acanthurids are deep-bodied or oval fishes, flattened from side to side. They scrape algae off rocks and coral, usually in shallow water. There are about 60 species in the Indo-Pacific.

9. Suborder Gobioidei: gobies and gudgeons. This is a cosmopolitan suborder of small carnivorous fishes some of which occur in brackish water and freshwater. The true gobies (family Gobiidae) include the smallest known vertebrate: the freshwater *Pandaka pygmaea*, from the Philippines, which rarely exceeds 12mm. Most gobies are cryptically coloured bottom-living species in shallows, coral reefs and estuaries but some of the coral species are brightly coloured.

There are two dorsal fins, the first with weak spines. The tail fin is separate. The ventral fins are joined on the inner margin and in many species are modified to form a sucker. The Gobiidae is the largest family of fishes and is poorly known scientifically. One of the commonest southern Australian gobies is the sculptured goby, *Callogobius mucosus* (9cm), a brown species with each scale with a dark border. It lives in rock pools and shallow water from WA to NSW. One of the smaller Australian species is the red-headed goby, *Paragobiodon echinocephalus* (38mm), of QLD. In QLD the mud-hopper or mud-skipper, *Periophthalmus koelreuteri* (15cm), family Periophthalmidae is also common. The eyes are on turrets, and the pectoral fins are muscular and almost limb-like. These amphibious fishes skip on the surface of the mud where they catch small insects. The great mud-hopper, *P. barbarus* (30cm), occurs in NW Australia and QLD.

Gudgeons are small fishes (family Eleotridae) related to the gobies but with the pectoral fins free from each other. They often occur in dense schools over clumps of coral but several species occur in cool waters. Several are brackish or freshwater species.

10. Suborder Cottoidei: mail-cheeked fishes. These are small or medium-sized carnivorous fishes of very varied form. They have in common, however, a bony stay across the cheek which in some cases is elaborated into an armour for the whole head. Sometimes this is covered with thick skin. Usually with large mouths, they are bottom-dwelling, sedentary solitary fishes. A few are freshwater, and the group is cosmopolitan. Many have venomous spines which can be very dangerous. They are often grotesquely shaped and brilliant in colour.

Flatheads (family Platycephalidae) are extremely flattened, wide-mouthed fishes which lie almost completely buried in sand waiting for prey. Several species are trawled and are familiar on the markets. There are two dorsal fins with a small spine in front of the first. The anal fin is long. The best-known edible species is probably the tiger flathead, *Neoplaty-cephalus macrodon* (36cm), a golden brown, blue-spotted species of NSW and VIC.

Gurnards (family Triglidae) are unmistakable fishes with bony-plated heads and a blunt face. The body tapers to the tail. The pectoral fins are very large and the first few rays are separate and stiffened to serve as props and probes. Most are red.

In the flying gurnards (family Dactylopteridae) the enlargement of the pectoral fins is carried to extremes. Though they are mainly bottom-living fishes they can make short glides above the surface of the water.

The family Scorpaenidae, which includes stingfishes, scorpionfishes, lionfishes and dragonfishes, contains some of the most venomous of sea animals. They have spiny, armoured heads and extremely well-developed fin spines. The fins are often very feathery which helps to camouflage these solitary, bottom-living, sluggish fishes. The butterfly cod or red firefish, *Pterois volitans* (38cm), which occurs in coral reefs in QLD, is well known as it is often kept in large aquaria. The fins are very long and feathery and the body is striped vertically with cream, yellow and reddish colours. There are several other closely related butterfly cods. Another widespread coral and weed scorpaenid is the false stonefish, *Scorpaenopsis gibbosa* (*S. diabolus*) (30cm). Mottled red-brown with patches of other hues, this cryptically coloured fish has relatively short fins but strong dorsal spines. The head and the body, and sometimes the fins, have fleshy, green outgrowths. False stonefishes live in deeper water on the rims of coral reefs, from the Great Barrier Reef to past the TORRES STRAIT. The bullrout, *Notesthes robusta* (27cm), and the fortescue, *Centropogon australis* (13cm), are similar cryptically coloured fishes with relatively short fins. The faces are spiny and warty. The bullrout is an estuarine and freshwater species of QLD and

NSW; the fortescue occurs from QLD to TAS.

The family with the most dangerous venomous fishes is the Synanceiidae. Fishes of this family lurk motionless in the mud, among weeds, in coral and so on. Their extremely venomous spines have grooves leading to venom sacs; they can inject a very powerful nerve toxin which can be fatal. They are the ugliest of fishes with large heads and wide mouths; the head is grooved and ridged and the body is scaleless but warty. In general these fishes are so well camouflaged and indisposed to move that they are easily trodden upon. The horrid stonefish, *Synanceia horrida*, can reach a length of 60cm but 30cm is more usual. When at rest the dorsal spines are flat and the fish resembles a piece of old coral or rock. When disturbed it raises its spines. This species ranges from north-western WA to northern NSW, along the N coasts; it also occurs in the East Indies, the Philippines, China and India. The estuarine stonefish, *S. trachynis*, of QLD and Melanesia, is very similar. The related bearded ghoul, *Inimicus barbatus* (*I. dactylus*) (22cm), a brown fish with many dermal outgrowths, including several on the chin, occurs in estuaries in QLD. The goblin fishes, such as *Glyptauchen panduratus* (15cm), a red species found on S coasts, have bulging eyes, mounted on bosses.

Order Echeneiformes or Discocephali: remoras This order contains a single family, Echeneidae, of about 12 species, found in all warm seas. The body is long and narrow. The first dorsal fin is modified into a sucker with which the fish attaches itself to sharks, other large fishes, turtles and so on. They feed on food scraps, faeces and possibly ectoparasites of the hosts. The slender suckerfish or remora, *Echeneis naucrates*, known as the pilot fish in QLD, is about 90cm long. It attaches itself to sharks, and is used for catching turtles in the Torres Strait.

Order Tetrodontiformes or Plectognathi: leatherjackets, toados, angler fishes and their allies This is a diverse order of fishes most of which live solitary lives in tropical waters. The bones of the operculum are reduced, and the mouths and gill openings are small. The ventral fins are rudimentary or virtually absent. Some of these fishes are extremely poisonous and should never be eaten. Some others, on the other hand, are important commercial edible fishes. There are three suborders.

1. Suborder Balistoidei: tripod fishes, horn-fishes, leatherjackets and triggerfishes. These are deep fishes, flattened somewhat from side to side, with two dorsal fins. The first dorsal fin consists of one to six spines, the first of which is by far the longest. It can be locked in an erect position.

Leatherjackets and filefishes (family Aluteridae) are small or medium-sized, sluggish herbivores. They have a single dorsal spine, usually above the eye, and no ventral fins; the scales are very small but they give the skin a rough texture. The family is represented in all warm and temperate seas but most of the 50 or so species are found in the Indo-Pacific. The flesh of most species is bitter but some are sold in the markets. The Chinaman leatherjacket, *Nelusetta ayraudi* (50cm), one of the commercial species, occurs in QLD, NSW, SA and WA. The snout is long so that the small eye is almost a third of the way from the terminal mouth to the base of the tail.

Triggerfishes (family Balistidae) are fishes of coral and weeds. They resemble leatherjackets in their shape but the dorsal fin consists of three spines, the first of which can be locked into position by the second. The scales are large, forming a protective armour. Most triggerfishes are poisonous.

2. Suborder Ostracioidei: boxfishes and cowfishes. These fishes (family Ostraciidae) occur in tropical shallow waters and coral reefs. They are small herbivores with a hard carapace of bony plates which serves as an armour. In most species the carapace is open behind to allow movement of the tail, and there are openings for the eyes, fins and mouth. The fins are small and without spines. Some have spines above the eye which account for the name cowfish.

3. Suborder Tetrodontoidei: porcupine fishes, puffers, toadfishes and ocean sunfishes. Many of these fishes are extremely poisonous because they contain the substance tetraodontoxin. It is reported that it was used as a spear toxin in Polynesia. Despite their toxicity puffer fishes, as *fugu*, are considered a great delicacy in Japan. Specially trained chefs prepare the dish in licensed restaurants, carefully removing the poisonous parts (gonads, liver and so on) without contaminating the rest of the flesh. Nevertheless, people often die from *fugu* poisoning.

Porcupine fishes or spiny puffers (family Diodontidae) are rounded fishes with spines, found in all warm seas. When alarmed they blow up like a football and the spines become

Horrid stonefish, *Synanceia horrida*

erect. They usually live in shallow water among weeds or coral.

Tobies or sharp-nosed puffers (family Canthigasteridae) differ from other members of the suborder in having only a single nostril, a sharp snout and very short gill openings; they have rough skins and no scales. They do not puff their bodies up to the same extent as other puffers.

The fishes generally called toados in Australia belong to two families, Lagocephalidae and Tetraodontidae (Tetrodontidae), which differ mainly in the structure of the nostrils and skull. The first has two nostrils on each side, the second only one. The giant toadfish, *Gastrophysus scleratus* (75cm), is found in coastal waters from Africa to Polynesia. It is a greenish species with dark brown spots, a silver line the length of the body, and massive teeth. This species nearly killed Captain COOK and two of his companions at New Caledonia in 1774. The banded toado, *G. pleurostictus* (15cm), is common in estuaries in QLD and N Australia. The common toado, *Sphoeroides hamiltoni* (13cm), a brown and white, black-spotted fish, is found in coastal waters and coastal streams of Australia and New Zealand.

The suborder also includes the ocean sunfishes (family Molidae), large, round fish (*Mola mola* reaches 3m in length and a half tonne in weight) which are sometimes cast ashore.

Order Xenopterygii: clingfishes This order consists of a single family (Gobiesocidae) of fishes in which the skin of the belly (not the fins) is modified to form a large sucker with which the fish clings to rocks. They are found in all temperate seas.

Order Batrachoidiformes: frogfishes This is a small order of bottom-dwelling fishes with wide mouths and flattened, broad heads that give them a frog-like appearance. When taken from the water, they croak, and the young are tadpole-like. These small fishes, which bury themselves in mud or hide in weeds, have venomous dorsal spines. The scales are absent or covered with thick slime. At least two species occur in QLD.

Order Lophiiformes: anglerfishes and monkfishes These are bottom-dwelling fishes of varied form most of which live in deep water. One suborder, Antennarioidei, contains one family of shallow coastal waters, the Antennariidae, the fishing frogfishes. Like all anglerfishes the first dorsal spine carries a lure which often wriggles like a worm. This attracts other fishes to within reach of the large mouth. They are usually found motionless on the bottom, or moving slowly with the help of their muscular, elbowed pectoral fins though some species float in weed. The body is scaleless and flattened. The skin is flabby and loose. The sargassum fish, *Histrio histrio* (12cm) is a form that floats in weed. There are many fleshy appendages for camouflage.
See also fishes, poisonous and venomous
Further reading: see under fishes.

fishes, freshwater Among the native freshwater fishes of Australia there are only three species which have not come from the sea in relatively recent geological time. With these exceptions, all the groups are predominantly marine and most of the typically freshwater groups, such as the carps, are represented only by introduced species. The three exceptions are the QUEENSLAND LUNG FISH and the bony-tongued barramundis, *Scleropages jardini* and *S. leichhardti*. The reason for this odd selection of native fish probably lies in the drought ridden Australian climate and the temporary nature of many of her inland waters.

About 230 species have been recorded in Australian freshwaters. Of these, 49 are really marine fishes which sometimes enter rivers, 16 (though there may be even more with recent releases of aquarium fish) are introduced species and about 20 are freshwater species which enter estuaries or the sea at some definite stage during their life, such as the reproductive period. This article includes the LAMPREYS, SHARKS AND RAYS and bony fishes (see FISHES, BONY) which fall into the above categories. In this entry, the families with only freshwater representatives in Australia are discussed.

The reproductive behaviour of those that breed in freshwater is of interest for it shows adaptations for survival in ephemeral, stagnant (oxygen-deficient) water that is often turbid as well. Lake (*see below*) lists the following adaptations: a small number of large eggs are incubated in the mouth (buccal incubation); the male carries the eggs on a special hook on the head (the nursery fish, *Kurtus gulliveri*); the parents fan the eggs which are inside nests in shallow water (eel-tail catfishes); the eggs are scattered over plants on which they stick, and the parents sometimes fan the eggs (Queensland lung fish and some others); the eggs are planktonic and hatch very quickly (*Plectoplites ambiguus*). Several species lay only after floods when the water spreads over the surrounding land.

Lampreys: class Agnatha Three species are found in freshwater: the wide-mouthed lamprey, *Geotria australis*, the short-headed lamprey, *Mordacia mordax*, the freshwater lamprey, *M. praecox*.

Sharks and rays: class Chondrichthyes Two whaler sharks (family Carcharhinidae) often enter freshwater. They are the river whaler shark, *Carcharinus leucas* (3m), and the Swan River whaler, *C. mckaii* (1m), of WA which enters rivers to produce its living young.

At least three sawfishes (*Pristis* species; family Pristidae) occur in freshwater but two are mainly marine. The freshwater sawfish, *P. microdon* (5m), occurs in N Australia.

Bony fishes: class Osteichthyes There are two subclasses, namely the Sarcopterygii (which contains the Queensland lung fish), and the Actinopterygii (to which most fishes belong).

1. The herrings and their allies (order Clupei-

formes). These fishes are mainly marine, but a few in the family Clupeidae enter rivers; but the *Fluvialosa* species, of which there are about five, are completely freshwater. With the exception of the Perth herring, *F. vlaminghi*, they are called bony breams. There are probably three species of Australian smelt (family Retropinnidae) in Australia, belonging to the genus *Retropinna*. The first dorsal fin is well back on the body and the second is a small fatty (adipose) fin. The Australian smelt, *R. semoni* (8cm), occurs in E Australia and is abundant in the Murray. Smelts spawn in freshwater. In TAS and New Zealand they make up, with certain other fishes, 'whitebait'.

The bony-tongued fishes (family Osteoglossidae) contains eight living species which are the remnant of a once much larger group which can be traced back for 50 million years. They now occur in NE South America, equatorial Africa, South-East Asia and N Australia. Two species occur in Australia, both called barramundis, a name which leads to confusion with a largely marine unrelated species, *Lates calcarifer*. The spotted barramundi, *Scleropages leichhardti* (90cm), occurs only in the FITZROY river system in QLD. The fish has large scales, long narrow pectoral fins, small ventral fins and anal and dorsal fins set well back. The lower jaw is set at a steep angle and there are two barbels on the chin. The body is dark olive-green and silvery with red or orange spots. The female carries the eggs and the newly hatched fish in her mouth. This species feeds mainly at the surface, insects forming the bulk of the food. It will also eat small fish and frogs. The northern spotted barramundi, *S. jardini* (90cm), is reported to feed at the bottom and in midwater, largely on crustaceans. This species occurs in some rivers draining into the GULF OF CARPENTARIA and Timor Sea, and also in New Guinea and West Irian. It resembles the southern species but the red marks are crescent-shaped.

The family Galaxiidae is placed sometimes among the herrings, and sometimes in an order of its own, Galaxiiformes. There are several common names but the term 'galaxias' is becoming accepted. There are about 26 species in Australia. Some species are restricted to one or two rivers. The native trout or common galaxia, *Galaxias maculatus* (15cm), is one of the commonest and most widespread species, being found in coastal streams in SA, VIC, NSW, TAS and southern QLD. The adults live in the upper reaches and migrate downstream to spawn. The eggs are laid on the first spring tide and are left high and almost dry on rushes and reeds. By the following spring tide, about 14 days later, they have developed to the hatching stage. The common galaxias is a long, slender, scaleless fish with a single dorsal fin set well back. The colour is pale green or yellowish-green with fine, black spots on the upperparts. All the other species appear to spawn in freshwater. The family is restricted to the S hemisphere.

2. The true salmons and their allies (order

Relief guard arriving at a prison hulk at Deptford, England, by E. Tucker, in the Rex Nan Kivell Collection, National Library of Australia

Troops of the New South Wales Corps fire on the Castle Hill rebels, watercolour by an unknown artist, from the Rex Nan Kivell Collection, National Library of Australia

The arrest of Governor Bligh as his enemies reported it, a painting from the National Library of Australia

'Attacking the Mail' by S.T. Gill 1854, from the Australian Sketch Book, in the National Library of Australia

First Commissioner Hardy collecting licences, and diggers evading him. Watercolour by G. Lacy, in the Rex Nan Kivell Collection, National Library of Australia

Australian Gold Diggings, an oil painting by an unknown artist, in the Rex Nan Kivell Collection, National Library of Australia

John McDouall Stuart plants the Union flag at the centre of the Continent in 1860, painted by J. McFarlane
See also PAINTING AND PAINTERS

The Battle of Eureka Stockade 1854, watercolour by J.B. Henderson, in the Mitchell Library

The Kapunda Copper Mine in the 1840s. Lithograph by George French Angas, in the Rex Nan Kivell Collection, National Library of Australia

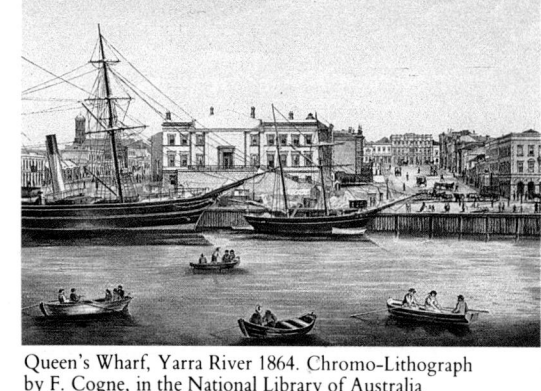

Queen's Wharf, Yarra River 1864. Chromo-Lithograph by F. Cogne, in the National Library of Australia

Hindley St, Adelaide, from the corner of King William St in the 1850s by S.T. Gill, in the Rex Nan Kivell Collection, National Library of Australia

The Entrance to Port Jackson and part of Sydney, 1823, aquatint by Major James Taylor, in the Rex Nan Kivell Collection, National Library of Australia

Hobart Town from Kangaroo Point, Tasmania, tinted lithograph by Eugene von Guerard about 1855, in the National Library of Australia

Perth 1847 by Horace Sampson, in the Art Gallery of Western Australia

Botany Bay

Painting of Brisbane in 1855 by Thomas Baines, in the National Library of Australia

See also PAINTING AND PAINTERS

Salmoniformes). Some authorities consider that the order contains only one family, the Salmonidae, none of which were found S of the equator till taken there by man. Members of this family all lay their eggs in freshwater but some spend much of their adult lives at sea, ascending rivers to spawn, after which they usually die. This is true of the salmon group but trout species often spawn many times. They are carnivorous fishes with the second dorsal fin being small and fatty. The following species have been introduced into Australia and have become established: the brown trout, *Salmo trutta*; the rainbow trout, *S. gairdneri*; and the brook trout, *Salvelinus fontinalis*. The Atlantic salmon, *Salmo salar*, has been introduced into Australian rivers in the past. In recent years attempts have been made to establish salmon in landlocked waters such as the Burrinjuck Dam and Lake Jindabyne but it is not yet known if the experiment was successful. There are now bans on the importation of salmonid fishes because of the danger of the introduction of the serious whirling disease. It appeared in New Zealand, in the 1970s. The quinnat salmon, *Onchorynchus tschwawytscha*, a North American species, is only half established: so far its populations (in VIC) are maintained only by continual restocking.

Brown trout and rainbow trout have many self-maintaining populations but some States run hatcheries to provide eggs and fingerlings to maintain populations where fishing and predation is heavy. There are also commercial trout farms (for example, in the SNOWY MOUNTAINS) to provide trout for the table. Trout prefer cold water, and spawn during the colder months in cool, gravelly reaches of rivers. They are consequently restricted to the upper parts of rivers (for example, above 600m in the NSW tablelands) except where dams cool the lower reaches. In their homelands (Eurasia and North America respectively) some varieties run down to the sea but this occurs in Australia in only southern VIC and TAS, regions where the lower reaches are cool enough for the fishes to survive.

Brown trout and rainbow trout are both variable in colour but though both are spotted it is only in the rainbow trout that many spots extend on to the tail fin. In general trout in Australia (and New Zealand) are larger than in Europe. The rainbow trout has reached a length of 77.5cm (7.9kg) in TAS and the brown trout attains at least 90cm (14.1kg). Both species occur in all States except QLD. Trout feed mainly on insects and crustaceans, but large fishes will eat smaller fishes such as the galaxias. The brook trout is a North American species that has been successfully introduced this century into SA, TAS and NSW. The shape is similar to those of the brown and rainbow trouts, but the mouth is longer.

Some authorities place the family Aplochitonidae in this order though the family is composed of two native fishes—the Australian grayling, *Prototroctes maraena* (30cm), which occurs in coastal streams of southern NSW, VIC and TAS, and the Derwent whitebait, *Lovettia sealii* (7cm), of N and eastern TAS. Both are shaped like trouts. The first is considered to be in danger of extinction, and the second has become rarer since European colonisation.

3. The catfishes (order Siluroidiformes). There are two groups of catfishes with freshwater representatives in Australia. The fork-tailed catfishes (family Ariidae) have two freshwater species (some authorities regard them as four), mainly in N rivers.

The eel-tailed catfishes (family Plotosidae) contains estuarine and freshwater species. The largest Australian genus is *Neosilurus* which contains about eight species that are often called tandans. The desert catfish of SA and the NT, (*Neosilurus* species; 12cm), is often abundant in artesian bore water and spring water.

4. The freshwater eels (order Anguilliformes). There are four species in Australia, all of which spawn in the sea, often migrating for long distances. The pelagic eggs hatch to the leaf-like leptocephalus larvae. Ocean currents bring them to the river mouths which they ascend as juvenile eels or elvers. They spend many years in freshwater before making their one and only descent to the sea. The short-finned eel, *Anguilla australis* (90cm), occurs in SE Australia and TAS and has been introduced into WA. The long-finned eel, *A. reinhardti* (1m or more), is an E coast species, the Pacific eel, *A. obscura* (60cm), a QLD species, and the northern eel, *A. bicolor* (60cm), a species which occurs in N and NW Australia; these three species are probably endemic.

5. The one-gilled eels (order Synbranchiformes). Two species of these eels, one introduced, have been reported from Australia.

6. The half beaks (order Beloniformes). The three species of half beaks that are recorded from freshwater are essentially marine fish, but there is a freshwater long tom, *Strongylura kreffti* (75cm). This species is found in N rivers but its breeding habits are not known.

7. Rainbow fishes, silversides and mullets (order Mugiliformes). About 14 species of rainbow fishes (family Melanotaeniidae) are listed, eight of them belonging to the genus *Nematocentrus*. They are small fishes (7cm to 18cm), restricted to the Australian region and, as their common names (rainbow fishes, jewelfishes, freshwater sunfishes) suggest, they are colourful. The body is deep and of the two dorsal fins the first is the smaller though taller.

There are 12 freshwater species of silversides (family Antherinidae), though one is mainly marine. The two commonest genera are *Pseudomugil* (four species, blue eyes) and *Craterocephalus* (six species, freshwater hardyheads).

Several of the marine mullets (family Mugilidae) spend time in freshwater but one or two species, such as the freshwater mullet, *Trachystoma petardi* (80cm), of E Australia, may be regarded as primarily freshwater fishes.

8. Flatfishes (order Pleuronectiformes). A few flatfishes, all soles (family Soleidae) are found in freshwater but they are apparently rare and very local in distribution.

9. Pipefishes (order Syngnathiformes). Two species often enter rivers of northern NSW and southern QLD.

10. The Burnett salmon, *Polydactylus sheridani* (1.2m) (order Polynemiformes). Though an estuarine species, the Burnett salmon often enters rivers.

11. Blackfishes (order Gadopsiformes). The family Gadopsidae contains only two species and is restricted to Australian freshwaters. Unfortunately they are becoming rare. The river blackfish, *Gadopsis marmoratus* (35cm), of the smaller tributaries of the Murray-Darling, is an elongated, rounded carnivorous fish with a rather large mouth. There is a single long dorsal fin, taller at the back than at the front. The ventral fins consist of only two rays each. The body is covered with small scales. The colour is brownish with irregular darker blotches. They are also known as slipperies or slimies. The Tasmanian blackfish, *G. tasmanicus*, is larger.

12. The perch-like fishes (order Perciformes). This order is the largest among the fishes and, many are found in Australian freshwaters. Of these the majority are essentially marine and only a few of these will be mentioned in passing.

The suborder Kurtoidei contains one family, Kurtidae, with one species, the nursery fish, *Kurtus gulliveri* (60cm), in Australia, from the Norman River in QLD to the Cambridge Gulf WA. The fish is fairly deep-bodied and appears to be scaleless. The male has a hook on the forehead to which the female attaches a group of large eggs, attached by a filament.

The suborder Percoidei takes its name from the perch or English redfin, *Perca fluviatilis*.

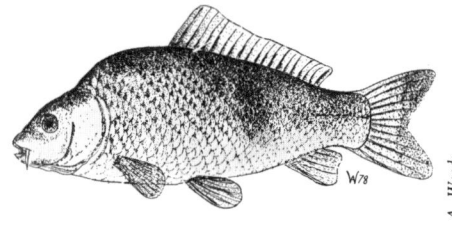

Common carp, *Cyprinus carpio*

The family to which it belongs, the Percidae, is native to the N hemisphere. It cannot survive in rapid streams or at temperatures above 31°C and its most northerly occurrence is near GLEN INNES in NSW. It occurs at present in the Murray-Darling system, WA and TAS. The perch is a deep-bodied, robust fish which reaches a length of 50cm. There are two dorsal fins, the first consisting of strong spines. The mouth is large. The body is greenish-brown or yellow with several vertical, darker stripes. The dorsal fin is dark but the others are red. Perch compete with several native fishes that occur in slow-moving, rather weedy sections of large rivers, and they may also eat their eggs. Fry feed on plankton, adults on crustaceans, insects and other small fishes. They often form shoals. They are sought by anglers and are good table fish.

The cardinal fishes belong to the family Apogonidae, a mainly marine family apart from four species which occur in freshwater though two of these are really sea fishes. The mouth almighty, *Glossamia aprion*, is a perch-shaped whitish-brown fish of E, N and NW coastal streams and rivers. This species grows to about 20cm and is one of the better-known mouth-breeder species. The male incubates the eggs for some time without feeding. They are known also as flabbies, stinkers, soldier fishes and Queensland mouth-breeders.

Seven species of flagtails or mountain perches (family Kuhliidae) live in freshwater though one is a marine species. The jungle perch, *Kuhlia rupestris* (45cm), lives in torrential rivers of eastern QLD and some of the adjacent islands.

The family Latidae (or Centropomidae) has several important freshwater species including the giant perch or silver barramundi, *Lates calcarifer*, which is also marine. Most of the other freshwater members of the family are small (up to 8cm) and are known as perchlets and chanda perches.

The basses (family Serranidae) include such well-known freshwater fishes as the Murray cod and the Australian bass. The Murray cod, *Maccullochella macquariensis*, is Australia's largest bony freshwater fish, reaching a length of 1.8m and a weight of 90kg. It is an elongated thick fish with a slightly concave dorsal profile. The mouth is large but the eye is small. The dorsal fin is continuous with the front part with strong spines that are shorter than the soft rays behind. The large tail fin is rounded. The scales are very small and the colour is usually yellowish-green with dark green or blue mottlings, but with the sides yellowish and the underparts white or dirty white. Murray cods are carnivores, feeding on fishes and crayfishes, but rabbits, birds and rodents are also recorded from their stomachs. They spawn during floods when the water temperature is about 20°C, laying between 20 000 and 50 000 eggs which are attached to firm surfaces. They are common in the Murray-Darling system, and in the headwaters of the RICHMOND and CLARENCE Rivers in NSW. They have been introduced successfully into other waters. The similar but smaller trout cod, *M. mitchelli* (to 16kg), is found in the upper reaches of the Murray (rarely) and its S tributaries. The Macquarie perch, *Macquaria australasica* (43cm), is a perch-shaped fish, dark blue-grey or brown above, yellow below, with yellow pectoral fins and pink and black-margined ventral fins. It lives in the Murray-Darling system but is becoming rarer because of siltation. It is also found in NSW coastal streams and dams where it has probably been introduced. The golden perch, callop or yellowbelly, *Plectroplites ambiguus* (76cm), is the most widespread of the edible freshwater fishes, occurring in all States except TAS. The colour is olive-green and the sides and underparts are golden. Callops live in warmer,

sluggish rivers and are induced to spawn by rising water levels when the temperature is above 23°C. Their eggs are unusual in that they are planktonic. The Australian bass, *Percaletes novemaculeatus* (to about 3.5kg), and the similar estuary perch, *P. colonorum*, probably both spawn in brackish water. Some authorities regard them as one species.

The family Lutjanidae contains one species, the mangrove jack, *Lutjanus argentimaculatus* (90cm), a strong-toothed species which will enter freshwater. It ranges from northern NSW to northern WA.

The Theraponidae is a small percoid family of shallow marine and freshwater fishes with about 18 true freshwater species which are commonly known as terapon perches and grunters. The silver perch, *Bidyanus bidyanus* (41cm), a silver, brown-dotted fish with small scales, lays planktonic eggs. It is common in the Murray-Darling. The Barcoo grunter, *Scortum barcoo* (14cm), is an example of a species with a very restricted distribution, as far as is known. It has apparently been found only once, in COOPER'S CREEK.

The Sparidae (breams or porgies), the Gerridae (silver biddies) and the Sciaenidae (jewfishes) are all essentially marine families but each has a few species which often enter freshwater.

The family Toxotidae (archer fishes) has been discussed with the marine fishes. There are three Australian species. Two can certainly be classed as freshwater species but it is not certain that the archer fish of north-eastern QLD, *Toxotes jaculator*, enters freshwaters. *T. chatareus* (to 25cm), on the other hand, is common hundreds of kilometres along the GREGORY RIVER which flows into the Gulf of Carpentaria. The primitive archer fish, *Protoxetes lorentzi* (14cm), is found in the NT and West Irian, and may be ancestral to the other species.

Two representatives of the Scatophagidae (butterfly fishes) often enter freshwater, especially when young, and in the summer.

The final percoid family, the Bovichthyidae (marble fishes), is represented by one species, the congolli, *Pseudaphritis urvilli* (36cm), which is believed to migrate into rivers from the BASS STRAIT. It is a dark blue and silvery species with a somewhat compressed body, two separate dorsal fins, and a long anal fin. It is a general feeder which can be transferred from freshwater to saltwater quickly with no ill effects. Its closest relatives are found near the Antarctic.

The suborder Gobioidei contains the Gobiidae the largest family of fishes; at least 28 freshwater species occur in Australia. They are all small fishes, rarely more than 30cm long (some only 2cm or 3cm long), and are known as gobies, gudgeons and sleepers. There are about 19 genera. The desert or Central Australian goby, *Chalamydogobius eremius* (6cm), is restricted to the Lake Eyre drainage system where it depends upon waters coming from artesian bores and springs.

The suborder Cottoidei contains the Scor-

paenidae, a family of marine, often venomous fishes which can cause severe pain, which often enters freshwaters. The bullrout, *Notesthes robusta* (27cm), is common in some coastal streams and rivers of the E coast of Australia. Similarly, an extremely poisonous fish, the common toado, *Sphoeroides hamiltoni* (15cm), is often encountered in freshwater in SE and SW Australia.

13. The remaining freshwater fishes belong to the order Cyprinodontiformes, which has no native fishes in the region. The live bearers (family Poeciliidae) are viviparous (that is, they produce living young). The females have a brood pouch from which the young are expelled. One, the mosquito fish or gambusia, *Gambusia affinis* (5cm), is an American species which has been distributed widely in Australia and elsewhere for the control of mosquito larvae. Its effectiveness in Australia is doubtful. They are very prolific. The guppy, *Poecilia reticulata*, and swordtails (*Xiphophorus* species) are established in some areas, especially in QLD, where they have been thrown out by aquarium keepers. It is probable that other freshwater aquarium species are also established in various parts of Australia.

The carp family, Cyprinidae, has five well-established species, all introduced, in Australia. They are fishes of mainly still or slow-moving waters. The goldfish, *Carassius auratus* (36cm), is widespread in the S half of the country. Though domestic goldfishes are often highly coloured and of bizarre shapes the feral fish revert to the rather dull-coloured ancestral type after a generation or two. They are usually golden or dark green above, and silvery below. The closely related crucian carp, *C. carassius* (45cm), is a fish that thrives in very weedy waters. It is hardy, and can withstand low oxygen conditions and pollution. The European carp, *Cyprinus carpio* (1m), is a moderately deep fish with large scales and a protrusible mouth which, unlike the *Carassius* carps, bears barbels. It is found in SA, VIC and NSW and in most places is now regarded as a pest which should be exterminated, partly because it is prolific and partly because it is believed to foul the water by rooting among water plants. The tench, *Tinca tinca* (36cm), is an elongated, strongly built fish, olive or olive brown in colour. The tench is a sluggish fish of muddy backwaters.

European perch or redfin, *Perca fluviatilis*

The roach, *Rutilus rutilus* (25cm), is one of the commonest coarse fishes in canals, rivers and lakes in Britain, schooling near to vegetation. In Australia, however, it is at present restricted to the YARRA RIVER in VIC and to a few scattered places in the Murray.

Further reading: see under fishes. *Also* Lake, J.S. *Freshwater Fishes and Rivers of Australia.* Nelson (Australia), Melbourne, 1971; McDowall, R.M. (ed) *Freshwater Fishes of South-Eastern Australia.* Reed, Sydney, 1980.

fishes, poisonous and venomous

Many Indo-Pacific fishes, including several in Australian waters, are venomous or poisonous. Here, venomous animals are those that inject their poison into the victim while poisonous animals are those that produce toxic effects when eaten. Venoms are toxic materials that are almost always produced by the animal itself, for offence or defence, whereas poisons are sometimes produced by the animal and sometimes acquired by the animal in its food. It follows that certain species of fishes are not poisonous at all times or in all places. Here we exclude those fishes that become poisonous because they have consumed man-made pollutants (such as certain mercury compounds).

Venomous sharks and rays A few species of SHARKS are reported to be venomous. The Port Jackson shark, *Heterodontus portusjacksoni*, has two dorsal spines whose venom can cause local pain, numbness and muscle weakness for a few hours. Some squalid sharks may have similar effects. Several species of rays have spines on their tails which can be driven into a limb if the animal is trodden upon. The spine is often large and barbed so that the wound itself may be severe, even without the venom. There have been a few fatalities, particularly when the barb entered the chest.

Venomous bony fishes The descriptions and classifications of most of these fishes will be found in the entry on FISHES, BONY. Unless otherwise stated the fishes mentioned here are marine.

The scorpion fishes and butterfly cods (family Scorpaenidae) are often beautifully coloured and often have venomous spines. The venom is released from the tissues when the skin of the spine is broken. The firefish or butterfly cod, *Pterois volitans*, is the best known though other members of its genus and related genera are just as dangerous. The sting is very painful and the pain can persist for months. There are systemic effects and sometimes oxygen must be given. Necrosis of the tissues in the area of the sting is common. This species has been found as far S as Sydney. The fortescue, *Centropogon australis*, is often netted in weedy waters and even small specimens sting painfully. The bullrout, *Notesthes robusta*, is often met in freshwater streams and in estuaries. It is often trodden upon among weeds and stones. The sting is very painful: it is reported that children stung can become 'greatly disturbed ... even maniacal'. Other dangerous scorpaenids include the cobbler, *Gymnapistes marmoratus*, the ocellated wasp fish, *Hypodytes carinatus*, the false stonefish, *Scorpaenopsis gibbosa*, the gurnard perch, *Neosebastes pandus*, thetis fishes (*Neobastes* species), the marbled rock cod, *Sebastapistes bynoensis*, and the red rock cod, *Ruboralga argastulorum*.

Stonefish (*Synanceia* species) lie motionless and well camouflaged in warm, shallow waters. They are difficult to discern even in an aquarium when it is known that the fish is there. *It is essential, therefore, to wear stout shoes or boots when wading in water where stonefish are likely to occur.* Sandshoes and sandals give little or no protection. The sting causes immediate and unbearable pain and death results often not from the direct effects of the venom but by the incapacitated victim drowning. Stonefish can stay alive for several hours after being taken from the water. During this time they are dangerous. Even stranded, dead specimens may retain enough venom to be very dangerous. This is the only group of venomous fishes for which an antivenene is available.

Catfish (order Siluroidiformes) are covered with a toxic slime, and have sharp spines in their dorsal and pectoral fins. Their venom can cause pain and tissue damage. Most venomous fishes can be picked up 'safely' by their pectoral fins. Catfish cannot. Some species occur in freshwater.

The following fishes have been recorded as injecting venom in the Australian region, but the effects are slight compared with those of the stonefish and the scorpaenids: the red gurnard, *Chelidonichthys kumu* (family Triglidae); the old wife, *Enoplus armatus*, (Enoplosidae); stargazers (Uranoscopidae); velvet fishes (Aploactidae); red velvet fish (Gnathanacanthidae); butter fishes (Scatophagidae); and spinefeet (Siganidae).

Treatment for fish envenomation Severe stings by scorpaenids, stonefish and stingrays demand urgent medical attention. With stingray wounds the damage may be so great that first-aid measures consist of removing the barb and stemming the flow of blood. With other stings the old methods of cutting open the wound, rubbing in potassium permanganate and other chemicals should be ignored. Fish venoms are sensitive to heat and bathing the affected part in water as hot as the patient can bear will give relief; a car radiator can often provide hot water. Cold packs are not as effective. Treatment for shock (warm clothing, warm drinks, reassurance) is often necessary.

Ciguatera poisoning Many fish become poisonous because of the food that they have eaten. The word 'ciguatera' stems from the Spanish name for a marine snail in the West Indies, 'cigua', which was believed to be the source of the toxin. It is now thought that the source is in some reef plant, possibly a primitive seaweed or alga. The toxin is passed along the food chain from herbivorous fish to carnivores, but without affecting the fish. Its chemical nature is not known.

The symptoms of ciguatera poisoning vary. Sometimes they are severe: it is recorded that 1 500 men from a British Naval expedition to Mauritius died in 1748. The death rate is usually about 10 per cent but recovery may take a long time. Typically, the first symptoms are a tingling of the lips, tongue and throat, followed by numbness in these organs. Other parts of the body may show the same symptoms. The illness usually starts some hours after eating the fish. More severe symptoms include gastro-intestinal disorders, cramps, pain in the teeth and jaws, muscular weakness and inco-ordination, pallor, blueness of the skin, exhaustion and insomnia. There may also be muscular paralysis, particularly of the eye muscles, and muscular pain (there is no muscular pain in tetrodotoxic poisoning; *see below*). Sweating is a very common symptom.

More than 300 species of fish have been recorded as causing the illness at one time or another, many of them normally important food fishes. Southcott (*see below*) stresses that any intestinal distress experienced after eating tropical reef fish should be suspected as possible ciguatoxic poisoning. He lists the following as among the most important fishes: basses (family Lutjanidae); narrow-banded or Spanish mackerel, *Cybium commersoni*; and moray eel, *Gymnothorax undulatus*.

Tetrodotoxic fishes As the fishes that cause this type of poisoning are well known (toados, puffer fishes and so on; order Tetrodontiformes), this type of poisoning is easily avoided—except in Japan where certain restaurants specialise in the preparation of *fugu* from this group of fishes. Most of the poisonous species occur in the family Tetraodontidae, all of which should be regarded as potentially fatal meals. The toxin, the structure of which is known, occurs mainly in the skin, gonads, liver and intestines, and the fishes are most poisonous before and during the reproductive period.

No antidote is known for this poisoning and treatment consists of attempting to alleviate the symptoms. The main symptom is respiratory paralysis; artificial respiration until the patient can be admitted to a well-equipped hospital is obviously the most important part of first-aid. Many medical authorities advise against attempting to make the patient sick as this is dangerous where respiratory paralysis occurs.

Further reading: see under fishes. *Also* Stackhouse, J. *Australia's Venomous Wildlife.* Summit Books, Sydney, 1970; Southcott, R.V. *Australian Venomous and Poisonous Fishes.* R.V. Southcott, Mitcham SA, 1975; Caras, J. *Dangerous to Man.* Penguin Books, Harmondsworth, 1978.

fishing

More Australians are attracted by fishing than by any other leisure-time activity or sport.

As 75 per cent of Australians live within 50km of the sea, most leisure-time fishing is saltwater fishing. For the keen saltwater fisherman there are abundant beaches for surf fishing of tailor, whiting, flathead and salmon. Larger fish such as mulloway (known as 'jewies' and sometimes weighing as much as 45kg) and sharks are also caught occasionally by beach fishermen. Another popular form of saltwater fishing is estuary fishing. Estuaries include tidal stretches of rivers, tidal lakes and the numerous bays, inlets and harbours which characterise the Australian coastline. The most popular estuary fish include bream, flathead, whiting, tailor and blackfish. The most consistently successful estuary fishermen fish from boats, although good catches are sometimes made from jetties and less frequently from the shore. Another form of saltwater fishing is rock fishing, less popular because of the danger of being washed off the rocks by an unexpected large wave. Fish most sought after by rock fishermen include bream, snapper, tailor and kingfish, and reef fish such as rock blackfish, red morwong, groper and mulloway.

The most exciting of all saltwater fishing is game fishing. In Australian waters there are 11 species of shark and 24 species of fish which are classed as game, and these range from the relatively small but fiery yellowfin tuna, sailfish, barracuda and yellow-tail kingfish to the fierce and tenacious mako shark and the marlin, many of which weigh over 500kg. CAIRNS has become the world's most important game-fishing centre.

Freshwater fishing takes place in the abundant river systems, lakes, dams and streams throughout the country. While many species of perch and Murray cod are sought by freshwater anglers, it is the cunning and wily trout which provides the best sport for freshwater fishermen. The best trout fishing is in the cold-water streams, dams and lakes of the SE States, particularly in Lakes Eucumbene and Jindabyne in the SNOWY MOUNTAINS and in LAKE PEDDER in TAS.

Courtesy of A.I.S. Canberra
Trout fishing in a Tasmanian mountain stream

fish lice *see* crustaceans

FitzGerald, Robert David (1902-) Poet. Born and educated in Sydney, FitzGerald became a surveyor, worked for five years in Fiji and, during World War II, did surveying work for the construction of new airfields. Considered by many to be one of the most outstanding of modern Australian poets, he has won a number of literary awards, including the Grace Leven Prize (*see* William BAYLEBRIDGE) three times. His writing is essentially intellectual, being concerned mainly with analysis of character and with speculation on the ultimate nature and meaning of life; it features little description of nature and is not greatly concerned with social issues. His published works include *The Greater Apollo* (1927), *To Meet the Sun* (1929), *Moonlight Acre* (1938), *Heemskirk Shoals* (1948), *Between Two Tides* (1952), *This Night's Orbit* (1953), *The Wind at Your Door* (1953), the anthologies

Forty Years' Poems (1965) and *Product: Later Verses by Robert D. FitzGerald* (1977).
See also literature
Further reading: Day, A.G. *Robert D. Fitz-Gerald.* Twayne, New York, 1974.

J.H. Shaw
Pineapple farming in the lower Fitzroy valley near Rockhampton QLD

Fitzroy River QLD A perennial E coast river formed by the confluence of the MACKENZIE and DAWSON Rivers in the SE of State, it has a circuitous and considerably meandering course, flowing E, then N, then E again, and finally SE to reach a swampy and mangrove-fringed estuary on Keppel Bay, 80km downstream from ROCKHAMPTON. It is the largest of the E coastal rivers of QLD, with a catchment basin of 138 500km^2. The farmlands in the lower valley are intensively cultivated with pineapples, tropical fruits and pastures for dairy herds, beef cattle and stud horses. Major reforestation projects have been developed in the steep parts of the valley. The Capricorn Highway runs WSW from Rockhampton across the valley, the Burnett Highway goes SW from Rockhampton through MOUNT MORGAN, and the Bruce Highway crosses the lower valley plains on a SE-NW route.

Fitzroy River WA Located in the far N of the State, with its headwater tributaries in the Durack Range, it flows for over 550km first SW, then W and NW to a mangrove-fringed estuary on the W arm of King Sound, SW of DERBY. The small township of Fitzroy Crossing is located where the Great Northern Highway crosses the river, 273km by road ESE of Derby. About 19km upstream from the township are the spectacular limestone cliffs of Giekie Gorge, now part of a national park covering 3 136ha on both sides of the river. At CAMBALLIN, located on the flood plain of the lower reaches, irrigated rice and pastures have been developed since the late 1950s. The whole basin of the Fitzroy experiences a markedly seasonal climate, with heavy rains in summer and a very dry season for seven months from April to October. Fitzroy Crossing has an average annual rainfall of 525mm, of which 369mm fall in December, January and February. The flow of the river and of its main tributary, the Margaret, thus varies greatly throughout the year; during the wet season there is widespread flooding on the alluvial flats.

Fizelle, Rah (1891-1964) Artist. Born in GOULBURN in NSW, Fizelle served in the

armed forces during World War I, after which he studied painting at Sydney Teachers College and at Julian ASHTON's until 1926. In the following year he went to Europe and his studies in London at Regent Street Polytechnic and the Westminster Art School introduced him to Cubism and Futurism. After his return to Sydney in 1930, he and Grace CROWLEY established an art school which lasted until 1937 and which was dedicated to experimentation in painting and to a study of European trends. Although Fizelle's work was highly derivative, following European trends, and had a tentative quality, it was important as a genuine and conscientious attempt to come to grips with overseas ideas, and to assist others in breaking away from the predictable pattern into which much Australian painting had sunk.

flags and coats of arms The flags of the Commonwealth of Australia and its six States all feature the Union Flag (commonly called the Union Jack), so commemorating Australia's historic links with Britain. However, the national and State coats of arms and the emblems on the flags of the States are of local derivation.

Description and history of Australia's flags The Australian national flag is based on the British Blue Ensign, a blue flag with the Union Jack in the upper quarter of the hoist (that is, near the staff). It features also the stars of the Southern Cross and, below the Union Jack, the large seven-pointed Commonwealth Star (a point for each of the six States and one for all the Commonwealth Territories). The State flags consist of the Blue Ensign with the emblem or badge of the particular State on the fly (that is, on the half of the flag away from the staff). The NT's flag, flown for the first time on 1 July 1978 to mark the granting of self-government, incorporates the three official Territory colours—black, white and ochre—and a stylised representation of the Territory's floral emblem, Sturt's desert rose, with a seven-pointed star in the centre to represent the six States and the NT. In a black panel on the left are the stars of the Southern Cross.

The historical development of Australian flags has in most respects followed logically from the fact that the Commonwealth was formed as a federation of six British colonies, and from its situation in the S hemisphere, where the most conspicuous constellation in the night sky is the Southern Cross. In particular, it has been influenced by the Colonial Naval Defence Act, passed by the Imperial Parliament in 1865, which authorised the establishment of naval defence forces by the colonies, and specified that colonial vessels of war should wear a Blue Ensign 'with the seal or badge of the colony in the fly thereof'. After a considerable delay in most cases, such flags were finally adopted by all the Australian colonies or States, not merely for vessels of war but for general use.

VIC led the way when in 1870 a proclamation by the Governor directed that the badge of the colony should be 'five white stars, representing the constellation of the Southern Cross', and a flag consisting of a Blue Ensign with this badge in the fly was hoisted on the colony's warship, *Nelson*. This flag was in fact very similar to that used by the Anti-Transportation League of the 1850s. In 1877 both the badge and flag were amended by the addition, above the stars of the Southern Cross, of an Imperial Crown—a fitting symbol for a colony named after the Queen.

In the meantime, in 1876, three other colonies had adopted similar flags, each with a badge in the fly of a Blue Ensign. NSW used as its badge a golden lion on a red St George's Cross, with a star at each extremity of the cross. TAS chose a red lion in a white circle. QLD settled on a blue Maltese Cross with a crown in the centre. Of these details, the majority have obvious reference to Britain or the sovereign, but QLD's choice of a Maltese Cross has never been satisfactorily explained. WA and SA took a different course by choosing birds for their badges. For WA this was the black swan, which had been used as a badge since early colonial days. It is not certain when it was first used on a flag, but it is interesting to note that it was customary to have it facing towards the dexter (right) until 1953, when it was decided to make it more correct heraldically by having it swim towards the sinister (left). In SA, as early as 1872, government ships had used a Blue Ensign with the stars of the Southern Cross in the fly, but the flag, using the State badge of the piping shrike or white-backed magpie, was not officially proclaimed until 1904. It is interesting to note that the flag of the NT, designed long after the colonial period, has departed from tradition, and does not reflect past British rule.

The national flag was chosen in 1901, after a government-sponsored competition which attracted over 38 000 entries. As one might have expected, some of these were decidedly bizarre. In one, for example, the joining of the colonies in federation was symbolised by a six-tailed kangaroo, while another design featured an overturned corrugated-iron water tank with a Union Jack painted on the bottom. Many others, as was also to be expected, were similar to the flags of the States, with the addition of an emblem to symbolise federation. The prize-money was shared among five entries of this type, which were almost identical, and the official flag was based on them, with only minor variations. Originally, the large star symbolising federation had six points, one for each State. The seventh point, for Commonwealth territories, was added in 1908.

Description of Australia's coats of arms The coats of arms of the Commonwealth and States are used to authenticate documents, and for other official purposes. In the UK the right to such arms is granted by the sovereign, through officers of the royal household at the College of Arms in England, by warrant of the Earl Marshal, or through the office of the Lord Lyon King-of-Arms in Scotland. In Australia there is no strict law on the matter, nor has any case dealing with the 'right to

arms' as such ever come before an Australian court. Nevertheless, as one would expect, Australian governments have followed British tradition.

The dates on which the arms of each State were granted, and the meaning of the motto when in Latin, are listed here. Commonwealth: 19 September 1912, to replace earlier arms granted on 7 May 1908; QLD: 29 April 1893, motto 'Bold and Faithful'; NSW: 11 October 1906, motto 'Newly risen, how bright thou shinest'; VIC: 6 June 1910; TAS: 21 May 1917, motto 'Productivity and Fidelity'; SA: 20 November 1936, the centenary of foundation; WA: 17 March 1969.

In each coat of arms the significance of the details is fairly obvious. Thus the arms of the Commonwealth contain the badges of the six States enclosed in an ermine border signifying the bond of federation. In most cases the arms of the States feature important products. For example, those of SA have three garbs (wheat-sheaves), a reminder that the State's prosperity was originally based on the wheat industry.

The supporters (figures at either side of the shield) are in most cases Australian animals. However, the choice of a lion and a kangaroo in the case of NSW is an obvious reference to the bonds between the State and Britain. Some arms also have crests featuring plants associated with the State. For example, those of QLD have two sugar canes and those of WA two kangaroo paw flowers. It will be noticed that the arms of QLD, the only ones granted before 1901, have no supporters. Traditionally, in English heraldry the use of supporters has been confined to the royal family and certain other families and institutions of importance. Their inclusion in the case of the Commonwealth and five States illustrates the higher regard paid to Australia after federation.

Further reading: Cayley, F. *Beneath the Southern Cross: The Story of Australia in Flags.* Reed, Sydney, 1980; Low, C. *A Roll of Australian Arms.* Rigby, Adelaide, 1971.

flame tree *see* Sterculiaceae

flannel flower *see* Umbelliferae

flatheads *see* fisheries; fishes, bony

flatworms These worms belong to a large phylum, Platyhelminthes, which contains about 6000 species, many of which occur in Australia. The common name describes the free-living forms and the parasitic FLUKES exactly, and the parasitic TAPEWORMS less aptly. Most of the members of the phylum are parasites and as a result are often highly modified. Furthermore, some pass through two or even three different kinds of hosts during their life cycle, each kind of host harbouring different stages of the parasite; these stages are usually very unlike the sexually reproducing stage of the adult. The phylum is of great economic and medical importance because it contains the LIVER FLUKE, which affects sheep and cattle, the HYDATID CYST TAPEWORM, which affects man

and sheep, and the beef and pork tapeworms. Though many species are native to Australia most have been introduced.

The phylum is divided into three classes: the Turbellaria, composed of free-living flatworms; the Trematoda, which contains the flukes; and the Cestoda, which contains the tapeworms. The following brief description deals with the turbellarians; flukes and tapeworms are described under their own headings.

The typical free-living flatworm is flattened from top to bottom and bilaterally symmetrical. The shape is usually roughly oval though the head may be more or less triangular. There is often a pair of very simple eyes in the head which can judge the direction from which light comes, but, lacking a lens, cannot form an image. There is only one opening (the mouth) to the usually much branched digestive system; in many species the pharynx, the first part of the digestive system, can be pushed out to surround the food and bathe it in digestive juices. In the most primitive forms, the acoels, which are usually about 2mm long, the mouth simply opens into a mass of loosely packed cells (acoels). The nervous and excretory systems are very simple, but the reproductive systems are complicated and the animals are hermaphrodites. One important feature distinguishes these forms from the more advanced animals: they do not posses a coelom (an internal space surrounding the viscera).

Flatworms move along slowly with a gliding motion by means of minute 'hairs' (cilia) on the underside. They feed on a variety of food, including dead animals and tiny living ones. Most flatworms are aquatic but the shovel-headed garden worm, *Bipalium kewense*, probably introduced, is sometimes found in damp places in Australian gardens. The extremely common terrestrial blue planarian worm, *Geoplana caerulea*, is certainly a native. It can be found widely throughout Australia, and can be uncovered by lifting stones or rotting wood after heavy rain. This species is about 65mm long and has a longitudinal white stripe. Many genera of freshwater turbellarians are known in Australia. The turbellarians of the seashore are often more spectacular than their freshwater allies. *Callioplana marginata*, for example, is velvety black with bands of orange and white. Less spectacular is the oyster wafer, *Notoplana marginata*, a brown species which creeps into the shell of an oyster and damages the flesh.

Further reading: Buchsbaum, R. *Animals without Backbones.* (vol 1) Penguin Books, Harmondsworth, 1951; Bennett, I. *The Fringe of the Sea.* (revd edn) Rigby, Adelaide, 1974; Dakin, W.J., Bennett, I. & Pope, E. *Australian Seashores.* (6th edn) Angus & Robertson, Sydney, 1976; Williams, W.D. *Australian Freshwater Life.* (2nd edn) Macmillan, Melbourne, 1980.

fleas These wingless endopterygote INSECTS with piercing and sucking mouthparts comprise the order Siphonaptera. Fleas are PARASITES of birds and mammals; some species are very specific in their choice of hosts, others have more catholic tastes, but the food is always blood. The adults range in size from about 1mm to 6mm, and the bodies are flattened from side to side so that they can slip easily between hairs or feathers. The numerous spines and combs of bristles which cover the bodies make their removal from the host's body difficult, but as the spines all point backwards they do not impede the insect's movements. The hind-legs are greatly enlarged for jumping.

The legless and worm-like larvae resemble a long fly maggot, and are usually found in the debris of the host's nest or lair where they feed on scraps. Unlike the adults, they do not suck blood; however, it appears that the remains of blood in the faeces of the adults is important for their nutrition. The pupa is in a thin, silken cocoon which is often encrusted with sand. Fleas may remain in the pupal stage for many months and then emerge in response to vibrations. This is the reason why flea attacks are often experienced when long-deserted houses are first re-entered.

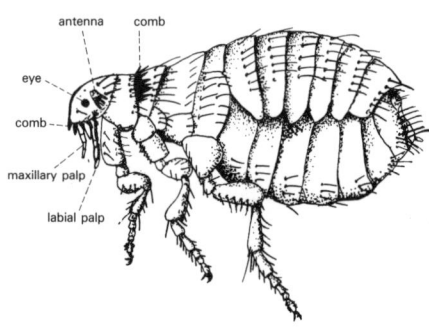

A dog flea, *Ctenocephalides canis*

Like most other blood-sucking insects, fleas can transmit diseases. The most important transmitter of bubonic plague is the Oriental rat flea, *Xenopsylla cheopis*, which carries the bacillus from dying rats to man; this species has been introduced into Australia but fortunately there are no endemic foci of the disease. Various fleas can transmit murine typhus which sometimes breaks out in rural towns, but this disease is far less serious than louse-borne typhus. The European rabbit flea, *Spilopsyllus cuniculi*, has been introduced because it is a vector of MYXOMATOSIS. Dog and cat fleas, *Ctenocephalides canis* and *Ct. felis*, are intermediate hosts of the dog TAPEWORMS, *Dipylidium caninum*, which sometimes infest children.

Most Australian fleas infest mammals. A few are found on petrels and penguins, and two introduced species and one endemic species occur on land birds. There are several introduced fleas that attack mammals, including man, and there are many endemic species on native mammals. In all there are about 70 species in Australia, divided among nine families.

The family Pulicidae contains the Oriental rat flea and the human flea, *Pulex irritans*, a

species which thrives in warm sandy areas. Also contained in this family are the dog flea, *Ctenocephalides canis*, the cat flea, *Ct. felis*, and *Echidnophaga gallinacea*, all introduced species which infest cats and dogs; the last-mentioned also infests poultry and is a typical sticktight flea which buries its mouthparts so firmly that it cannot be brushed off. There are several native members of the genus *Echidnophaga* which attack native mammals in a similar way. *See also* diseases and epidemics, human
Further reading: Roberts, F.H.S. *Insects affecting Livestock*. Angus & Robertson, Sydney, 1952; Busvine, J.R. *Insects and Hygiene*. (2nd edn) Methuen, London, 1966 and *Insects, Hygiene and History*. Athlone Press, London, 1976; Dunnet, G.M. & Mardon, D.K. 'A monograph of Australian fleas (Siphonaptera)' in *Australian Journal of Zoology*. (Supplement 30, 1974).

fleas, water *see* crustaceans

Fleurieu Peninsula SA This peninsula's NW shores are washed by the waters of ST VINCENT GULF, those to the SE by ENCOUNTER BAY, and it is separated from KANGAROO ISLAND by a strait called Backstairs Passage. The peninsula was named by the French explorer Nicholas BAUDIN, after the Comte de Fleurieu, a navigator who gave financial support to Baudin's Australian explorations. The SW extension of the MOUNT LOFTY RANGES forms a hilly central core of the peninsula. On the coast there are many beaches and tourist centres which have become popular holiday resorts. The SW tip of the peninsula is Cape Jervis. VICTOR HARBOUR is located on the S coast overlooking Encounter Bay. The rural lands of the peninsula produce grapes (for example, at McLaren Vale in the NW), wheat, stone fruits, fodder crops, wool, fat lambs, timber and dairy products.

flies The advanced and varied endopterygote order of INSECTS, Diptera, contains over 150 000 species of flies (about 6 800 in Australia, belonging to about 86 families). The order is of great economic, veterinary and medical significance, though most of the species are not pests.

Most adult dipterans are aerial, though some are wingless. Winged dipterans have only one pair of flying wings; the hind-wings are modified into drumstick-shaped structures (the halteres) which control the fly's stability during flight, working on the same principle of stability as a ship's gyroscope. The mouthparts of the adult are basically of the sucking type but there is great variation in the order. MOSQUITOES, for example, have piercing and sucking mouthparts whereas those of the HOUSE FLY and its closest relatives are of the sponge type. The head is relatively large, extremely mobile, and carries large compound eyes.

The larvae lack true thoracic legs though they may have unjointed false legs. Only some of the primitive families, such as the Culicidae

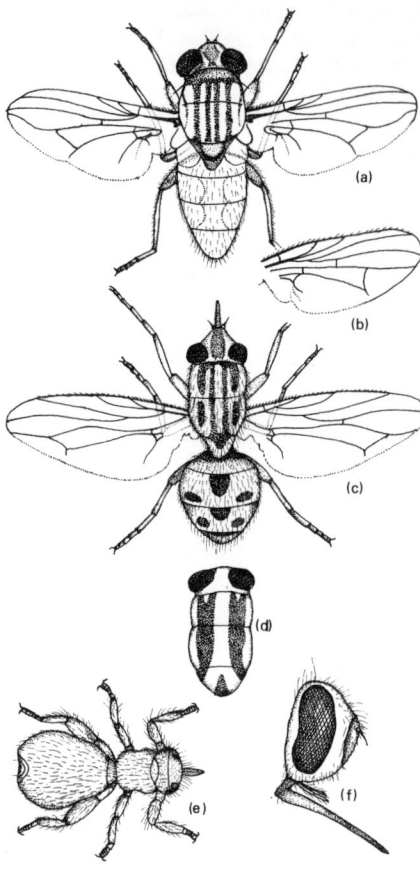

Houseflies and related species: (a) housefly; (b) wing of the lesser housefly; (c) stable fly; (d) head and thorax of bushfly; (e) sheep ked; (f) side of stable fly head

(mosquitoes) have well-developed larval heads. At the other extreme, the larvae of advanced flies such as the house fly are typical maggots with a vestigial head and greatly modified mouthparts, and they retain the last larval skin as a hard shell for the pupa within. The larvae of dipterans are usually found in damp or wet habitats such as rotting vegetation, or in plant or animal tissues; many are aquatic.

There are two suborders, Nematocera and Brachycera. There are two divisions in the latter: Orthorrhapha and Cyclorrhapha.
Nematocera Most species in this suborder are delicate, gnat-like flies which are closest to the ancestral Diptera. The antennae are multi-segmented and often drooping. The adults often form mating swarms consisting mostly of males. There are about 2000 Australian species in 15 families, seven of which are described below.
1. The family Tipulidae (about 700 species in Australia) contains the crane flies, delicate, small to large flies with long, dangling, fragile legs; they are common in damp, shady places. The larvae, which generally have leathery skins, are aquatic or live in wet soil or rotting vegetable matter.
2. The family Psychodidae (about 95 species in Australia) contains tiny, hairy flies, often with scales; they resemble small moths. The adults do not usually feed but the *Phlebotomus* species (rare in Australia) suck blood and abroad they spread serious diseases such as sand fly fever.

3. The family Culicidae (about 228 species in Australia) contains the mosquitoes.

4. The family Chironomidae (about 180 species in Australia) is closely related to the Culicidae; it contains non-biting midges whose larvae breed in water. Some which live in stagnant water are coloured red by haemoglobin (and are known as bloodworms). The adults often swarm over water.

5. The family Ceratopoginidae (197 species in Australia) contains the biting midges known in Australia as sand flies. Almost all of these minute flies suck blood. The larvae are usually aquatic and the adults are most troublesome in tidal areas with brackish water.

6. The family Simuliidae (34 species in Australia) contains the black flies, aggressive bloodsucking, hump-backed flies whose larvae live in clear running water. Abroad, they spread various diseases but in Australia they are not dangerous.

7. The family Mycetophilidae (222 species in Australia) contains the species known as fungus gnats, though not all live in fungi. The larvae of the *Arachnocampa* species (glow worms) are luminescent predatory maggots which catch other insects in hanging, sticky threads.

Brachycera The members of this suborder have relatively short antennae.

In the Orthorrhapha division the antennae of the adults are diverse but always shorter than the head and thorax, and usually consist of three segments, the last segment being longest. This division contains about 2000 species in Australia in 15 families.

1. The family Tabanidae (about 240 species in Australia) contains the familiar biting, horse flies. Tabanids are stocky, bristleless flies with large, often iridescent eyes. The females have stout, dagger-like mouthparts which inflict a painful bite to which many people are allergic. Males usually feed on flowers and plant juices.

2. The family Asilidae (about 380 species in Australia) contains the robber flies, small to very large, bristly flies which feed on other insects. The largest Australian flies belong to this family (*Phellus* and *Blepharotes* species; their wing-spans measure up to 75mm).

The Cyclorrhapha division contains those species which would be identified by the layman as flies—that is, many of them have a shape very similar to that of the house fly. The antennae are tri-segmented with a bristle (the arista) arising from the third segment. The larvae are headless maggots. There are about 2 900 species in Australia, in 53 families.

1. The family Syrphidae (about 170 species in Australia) contains the hover flies, usually small, wasp-like flies seen hovering near flowers which they exploit for pollen and which they often serve to pollinate. Many species have larvae which feed on APHIDS but some larvae, such as those of the narcissus flies, are pests. The common drone flies (*Eristalis* species) are remarkable mimics of bees; their larvae live in stagnant, oxygen-poor water, breathing through a spiracle on the end of their telescopic tails. Drone flies sometimes

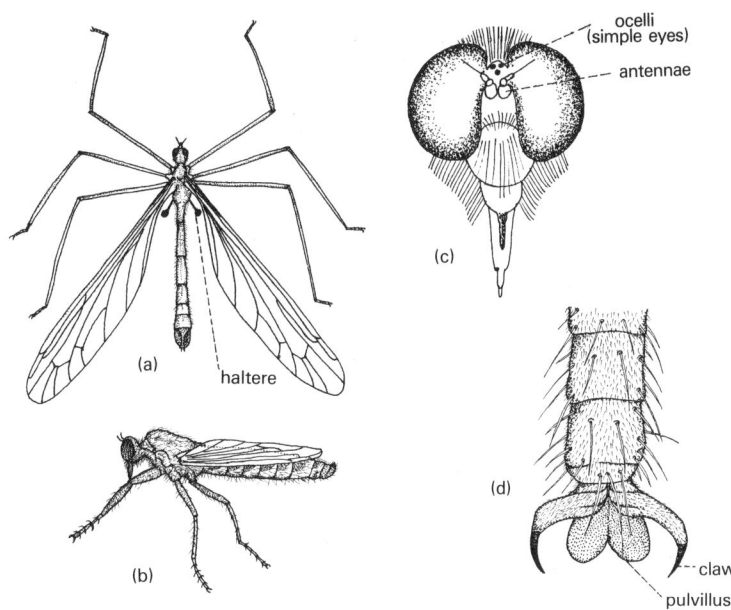

(a) a crane fly; (b) a robber fly; (c) enlarged front view of robber fly head; (d) leg of a typical fly

breed in animal carcases, giving rise to the old belief that bees can be bred from a dead lion. Some larvae live in ant nests.

2. The family Tephritidae (about 130 species in Australia) contains the familiar Queensland and Mediterranean fruit flies, as well as many allied species. The introduced Medfly, *Ceratitis capitata*, was once common in the E States but it seems to have been displaced by the native Queensland fruit fly, *Dacus tryoni*, which has apparently extended its range. The maggots of both species attack a wide range of cultivated and wild fruits. In WA, the Medfly is still an important pest, but *D. tryoni* has so far been excluded by strict quarantine.

3. The family Drosophilidae (about 70 species in Australia) contains species also known as fruit flies, but as these flies are attracted to fermenting and fermented fruits and liquids the name vinegar flies is preferred. These small, red-eyed flies are the animals most used in experimental genetics.

The remaining families discussed here are all in the house fly superfamily.

4. The family Gasterophilidae (three introduced species in Australia) contains the bot flies, which are represented in Australia by three introduced species whose spiky larvae all live in the stomachs of horses.

5. The family Oestridae (two species in Australia) contains the sheep bot fly, the larvae of which live in the nasal passages of sheep; when mature the maggot is sneezed out. Sometimes the female, in error, deposits the larvae on a human face and they then try to develop within the eye.

6. The family Calliphoridae (135 species in Australia) contains the BLOWFLIES.

7. The family Muscidae (about 200 species in Australia) includes two important species—the house fly and the bushfly.

8. The family Sarcophagidae (66 species in Australia) contains the flesh flies which are so closely related to the blowflies that they are often included in that family. Almost all are

viviparous, laying maggots, rather than eggs, on carrion, meat and decomposing organic matter.

9. The family Tachinidae (about 520 species in Australia) contains species ranging from a few millimetres to 35mm. The stout-bodied, rather bristly adults are found in most habitats. The larvae, almost without exception, are internal parasites of other insects, especially the caterpillars of BUTTERFLIES AND MOTHS. Many species have been used in BIOLOGICAL CONTROL.

10. The family Hippoboscidae (30 species in Australia) contains the louse flies, wallaby flies and keds, highly modified bloodsucking ecto-parasites of birds and mammals. Most are winged but the widespread sheep ked or 'tick' has useless vestigial wings.

11. The family Streblidae (seven species in Australia) is a small family of bloodsucking bat parasites.

12. The family Nyceribiidae (16 species in Australia) contains spider-like, wingless species which are also bloodsucking bat parasites.

See also insects, introduced; pests
Further reading: Oldroyd, H. *The Natural History of Flies*. Norton, New York, 1964; Greenberg, B. *Flies and Disease*. (2 vols) Princeton University Press, New Jersey, 1973.

Flinders Island TAS The largest of the FURNEAUX ISLANDS, situated at the E end of BASS STRAIT, it was named after the explorer Matthew FLINDERS, who charted the island group. Although the area was used as a sealing ground for many years in the late 18th and early 19th century, it was not until the 1830s that the island was first settled when remnants of the Tasmanian Aboriginal race were brought to live in the area now known as Settlement Point on the W coast. The original name for this point was Wybalenna meaning 'blackman's houses' or 'man sit down here'. The attempt to protect the Tasmanian Aborigines failed and a few years later the settlement was abandoned. The first white settler, George Boyes, arrived in 1888 and at Palana in the N of the island built a home called 'The Hermitage' which has been listed for preservation by the National Trust (TAS). Development was slow until 1911 when a minor land boom attracted settlers from VIC and mainland TAS. A further surge of development followed World War II when the War Service Land Settlement scheme brought ex-servicemen to the island, mainly for mixed livestock farming. At Pats River on the W side the average annual rainfall is 778mm with the highest falls in autumn and winter (May average 89mm, July 90mm). The Mt Strzelecki National Park (4 215ha) is located on the SW of the island where the Strzelecki Peaks reach 750m elevation. The main industries are grazing (fat lambs, wool and beef cattle), catching mutton birds, abalone fishing and the production of scallops. The civic centre of the island is Whitemark on the W coast where the council chambers, agricultural offices, hospital and main business premises are located. The airport is situated at Pats River, 5km from Whitemark. On the E coast, the mast of the ship *City of Foochow* can still be seen where she was wrecked in 1877.

Flinders, Matthew (1774-1814) Navigator and hydrographer. Born in Lincolnshire, he joined the British Navy in 1789. Two years later he served under Captain BLIGH on his second voyage to Tahiti and in 1795 came to Sydney on the *Reliance*. Almost immediately after arrival he and George BASS surveyed BOTANY BAY and George's River, and in the following year they explored Port Hacking and the ILLAWARRA coastline S of Sydney. Flinders was unable to join Bass on the latter's 1797 voyage into BASS STRAIT as far as WESTERN PORT BAY, but in 1798-99 the two men sailed through Bass Strait and around TAS in the *Norfolk*.

Matthew Flinders

Flinders' ambition was to complete the work of surveying the whole Australian coastline.

His voyage of circumnavigation of 1801-1803 is described in the entry on DISCOVERY. Although he did not achieve as much as he had hoped, his work on this expedition gained him the reputation of being one of the greatest hydrographers of his own or any previous age. After circumnavigating Australia, he attempted to return to England on the *Porpoise* in 1803, but was wrecked off the coast of what is now QLD. He returned to Sydney in a ship's boat and later set off again, this time on the *Cumberland*, but on his arrival at the French island of Mauritius was detained there by Governor Decaen for over six years. Released at last in 1810, he reached England but was too ill to finish his survey of the Australian coastline. His book (*see below*) was published on the day before he died.

Further reading: Scott, Sir Ernest *The Life of Captain Matthew Flinders*. Angus & Robertson, Sydney, 1914; Flinders, M. *A Voyage to Terra Australis*. Reprinted by the Libraries Board of South Australia, Adelaide, 1966; Hill, E. *My Love Must Wait: The Story of Matthew Flinders*. Lloyd O'Neil, Hawthorn VIC, 1971.

Flinders Ranges SA These ranges were named in honour of the explorer Matthew FLINDERS and are the most extensive highland region in SA, over 400km long on a general N-S alignment stretching N from the latitude of PORT PIRIE and PETERBOROUGH to the arid areas between LAKE TORRENS and LAKE FROME. The ranges are a N continuation of the MOUNT LOFTY RANGES and consist of ancient sediments which have been folded, faulted and uplifted; the sheer scarps, deep valleys and precipitous gorges give the region a spectacular scenic beauty and it has become a tourist mecca in recent years. The colourful landscapes and the striking grandeur of the ranges have been portrayed in paintings by the artist Sir Hans HEYSEN.

The S parts of the ranges were seen by Flinders in 1802; he named Mt Brown, a peak on the W edge of the ranges (located 19km inland from PORT AUGUSTA), after Robert BROWN, the naturalist aboard his ship *Investigator*. The S Flinders Ranges have peaks over 900m high (Mt Brown 961m, Mt Remarkable 963m); the N sections are higher, with peaks over 1 100m high (Mt Aleck 1 128m, St Marys Peak 1 189m). The early explorations of the ranges took place in the 1840s and squatters settled the region during the following decades, but the aridity, the unreliability of the climate and the hostility of the Aborigines posed great problems for these early settlers and in many parts of the ranges there are deserted ruins which bear testimony to the difficulties of living in this environment. The main rural activities are wool growing and cattle grazing; in the S there is also wheat farming and fruit growing. Many mineral deposits occur in the ranges and these have been mined intermittently: copper in the Mt Painter area and many other locations; talc at Mt Fitton; magnesite in the Weetootla Gorge;

Flinders Ranges

silver-lead in the Mt Painter region; and barytes at Bunker Hill. Coal was first found at LEIGH CREEK in 1888 and although early exploration proved disappointing, detailed investigations during World War II revealed large deposits which, since 1941, have been mined by open-cut methods.

Three major national parks lie within the Flinders Ranges: Mt Remarkable National Park in the S ranges, covering 8 648ha and including Mambray Creek and Alligator Gorge; the Flinders Ranges National Park, covering 78 426ha and including WILPENA POUND, ORAPARINNA, AROONA VALLEY and St Marys Peak (the highest in the ranges); and Gammon Ranges National Park, covering 15 538ha and located in the N ranges between Leigh Creek and Lake Frome. Further to the NE from Gammon Ranges National Park is the Arkaroola-Mt Painter flora and fauna sanctuary and the Paralana hot springs.

Further reading: Osterstock, A. *Time: In the Flinders Ranges*. The author, Adelaide, 1971; Mincham, H. *The Story of the Flinders Ranges*. Rigby, Adelaide, 1977; *Touring the Flinders Ranges*. Royal Automobile Association of South Australia, Adelaide, 1978.

Flinders River QLD Located in the N of the State, it rises on the W slopes of the GREAT DIVIDING RANGE, NE of HUGHENDEN, and flows in a great arc for 840km to an estuary at the SE corner of the GULF OF CARPENTARIA. Its main left-bank tributary is the Cloncurry River and the main right-bank one is the Saxby River. While the upper sections of the river basin have an average annual rainfall of only 500mm (Hughenden 487mm), the lower sections receive over 900mm, but this is concentrated mainly in the summer months with a long dry spell during the cooler season; hence the river experiences floods in the wet months and may cease to flow during the dry season. In the lowland tract, the Flinders and its tributaries wind across the plains in meander loops, forming ANABRANCHES which link it to the Norman River during times of

high flow. Sheep grazing is the principal rural pursuit in the upper basin, while beef cattle grazing dominates the lower sections.

flora The flora of Australia is extremely rich in both living and fossil plants. The living flora is dominated by seed plants (Spermatophyta), with flowering plants (ANGIOSPERMAE) providing the most conspicuous elements of the vegetation; GYMNOSPERMAE are relatively poorly represented, though cycads and conifers are locally abundant in some vegetation types.

The flora of the world is divided into a number of regions on the basis of the Spermatophyta flora; the flora of Australia is sufficiently distinct for it to be designated as the 'Australian Region'. The only place at which the Australian Region is at present in close contact with another floristic region, the Malaysian Region, is in the NE through New Guinea. In the remote geological past it appears that there was close contact with other areas, those of particular interest being South America, Madagascar, New Caledonia and New Zealand. The flora of the Australian Region, whilst distinct from that of the rest of the world, is not uniformly distributed within the Region, and a number of zones can be defined.

Floristic zones The Australian land mass has no topographical features of major importance, though the GREAT DIVIDING RANGE of E Australia appears to form a definite plant migration route. Consequently, climatic features to a large extent dictate the present delineation of the main floristic zones. The continent is crossed from E to W by the Tropic of Capricorn, and is therefore markedly affected by a high pressure desert area in these latitudes. There are two major rainfall systems, summer rainfall of monsoonal origin in the N, and winter rainfall in the S from the passing of Antarctic low pressure systems. On this basis the continent can be divided into three main climatic-floristic zones: Tropical, Temperate and Eremaean. The boundaries are not always sharp between these zones because of climatic overlaps combined with topographic variation and the varying ecological ranges of individual species occurring within each main zone.

The Tropical Zone is characterised by a dry monsoonal climate. The flora of this zone is rich in both Malaysian elements and Australian endemics.

The Temperate Zone has a cool to warm temperature or subtropical climate, in which precipitation occurs mainly in winter but in the E and SE sections it may be evenly distributed throughout the year. Australian and Antarctic elements dominate the flora of this zone.

The MacPherson-Macleay Overlap occurs between the Temperate Zone and Tropical Zone. Here, differentiation occurs between tropical elements, usually found in the moister habitats of the gullies and on the upper parts of the E slopes of the ranges, whilst temperate elements are best developed on the more open habitats of the plains and tablelands.

The Eremaean Zone occupies the whole of arid Australia, and is characterised by extreme variability of rainfall both annually and seasonally. The zone is crossed by the junction between winter and summer rainfall zones, but this boundary is obscured by local topographic variation. The origin of the flora of the Eremaean Zone appears to be complex, but consists of elements which may be originally temperate or tropical coastal types which have been joined by temperate and tropical recruits from adjacent zones.

Three interzones are also recognisable, each being dependent on local conditions. Interzone 1 has a dry climate and contains intermingled elements of sand heath and arid tolerant genera. Interzone 2 is markedly affected by the flood plain system of the upper DARLING and LACHLAN Rivers; temperate elements follow the better-watered habitats but Eremaean elements become increasingly well represented from E to W in drier habitats. Interzone 3 is also markedly affected by intersecting river systems, largely through soil differences and the presence of deep alluvium.

Family distribution Excluding gymnosperms, the Spermatophyta flora includes genera from 188 families. Ten families, including five monotypic families, are restricted to the Australian Region, and six families (Eupomatiaceae, Pittosporaceae, Stackhousiaceae, Epacridaceae, Myoporaceae, Goodeniaceae) have their main centres of development within the Australian Region but are not wholly restricted to it. A third important group of families is that within which the relatively high number of endemic genera indicates a long history within the Australian Region (GRAMINEAE, CYPERACEAE, LILIACEAE, Amaryllidaceae, PROTEACEAE, Santalaceae, Saxifragaceae, Cunoniaceae, Leguminosae, RUTACEAE, MYRTACEAE, Verbenaceae and COMPOSITAE); these families include several which give the Australian bush its immediately recognisable character, notably the Myrtaceae, which contains eucalypts, tea trees, bottle brushes and paperbarks, and Proteaceae, which includes *Banksia* and *Grevillea*.

Individual families and genera frequently occur in more than one zone within Australia. However, no less than 20 families are limited to the Tropical Zone and, apart from two endemic families, are also well represented in the Malaysian Region. Migration to the S has undoubtedly taken place; evidence for migration of Australian elements to the N is provided by the presence in New Guinea of Australian genera such as *Callitris*, *Banksia* and *Eucalyptus*, and the presence in Malaysia of *Eucalyptus*, *Stackhousia*, *Stylidium* and *Styphelia*. In contrast, relatively few families which are temperate in their occurrence are represented only in the Temperate Zone.

Endemic genera for each major zone when calculated as a percentage of totals for each zone are as follows: Temperate Zone 46.6 per cent (30.8 per cent of which are restricted to south-western WA); Tropical Zone 14 per cent; and Eremaean Zone 47.1 per cent. In general, the Temperate Zone flora seems to represent an older group, or at least includes a higher proportion of the descendants of the early migrants and of the early Australian endemics, than does the Tropical Zone.

Floristic elements The Australian flora is generally considered to consist of three main elements: the Australian, the Antarctic and the Malaysian.

The Antarctic element of the Australian flora today includes a number of S hemisphere conifer genera (several endemic to TAS), as well as *Araucaria* and *Nothofagus*, which both extend into the Malaysian Region. The importance of these and associated genera is very much reduced today, compared with their past distribution. It is these genera which are shared by other S hemisphere land masses (New Zealand, New Caledonia, South America, Antarctic Peninsula, South Africa and Madagascar) as living and/or fossil floras; observation of their distribution was one of the original spurs to the development of the concept of CONTINENTAL DRIFT.

The Australian element is considered to include families and genera which appear to have a major centre of development in the Australian Region. These include MIMOSACEAE, Myrtaceae and some genera of the Proteaceae. Although these families occur in other floristic regions, there appears to have been a marked expansion with species proliferation since the retraction of Antarctic flora at the end of the Tertiary period, generally considered to coincide with a general increase in the aridity of southern Australia.

The Malaysian element of the flora, best developed today in the Tropical Zone, includes elements both of recent origin (same species as in Malaysia) and relics of past more extensive tropical climates in N Australia. Both are probably due to periodic land connections between Australia and New Guinea, the latest being due to lowering of sea level during glacial periods of the Pleistocene era.

See also Arthrophyta; Bryophyta; Caryophyllaceae; Casuarinaceae; Chenopodiaceae; Epacridaceae; Euphorbiaceae; Haemodoraceae; Hepatophyta; Microphyllyta; Orchidaceae; Palmae; Papilionaceae; parasitic plants; Pteridophyta; Restionaceae; saprophytic plants; Solanaceae; Sterculiaceae; Umbelliferae; vegetation; weeds

Further reading: see Appendix 6, A Bibliography for Plants.

Florey, Sir Howard Walter (1898-1968) Scientist and Nobel Prize winner. Though born and educated in Adelaide, Florey spent virtually all his working life in England; he was Professor of Pathology at the University of Oxford from 1935 to 1962. In the immediate post-war years he was one of a group of Australian-born academics living in England who advised the government on the foundation of the Australian National University; another member of this group was Sir Mark OLIPHANT.

The research most closely associated with Florey's name concerns penicillin. In 1929 the Scottish scientist Alexander Fleming, working at St Mary's Hospital in London, found that something produced by the common mould *Penicillium* killed bacteria. Ten years later in Oxford, Florey and his co-worker Ernest Chain isolated the active ingredient in the mould, called penicillin by Fleming, and showed that it protected mice in the laboratory against many common infectious diseases. Intense effort made possible by wartime conditions led to penicillin being widely available for the treatment of injuries suffered in theatres of war; many thousands of lives were saved through the consequent reduction in the infection of wounds. For their work on penicillin Fleming, Florey and Chain shared the Nobel Prize for medicine in 1945. Florey received many awards and honours; in 1960 he became president of the Royal Society, and a medical research institute at the University of Melbourne has been named after him.

flounders see fishes, bony

flowering plants see Angiospermae

flowerpeckers These PASSERINE BIRDS belong to the family Dicaeidae, which ranges from India to Australia. It contains the mistletoe bird and eight species of pardalotes.

The mistletoe bird, *Dicaeum hirundinaceum* (10cm long), found in woodland throughout the mainland, feeds mainly on berries, particularly mistletoe. The male has an iridescent blue-black head, a red throat and breast, some red under the tail and a white belly with a black streak; the female has a grey back and a creamy-white breast. The nests, made of cobweb and plant down, look like a baby's bootie and are suspended from the outer branches of trees.

The pardalotes, unique to Australia, are small, dumpy, short-tailed birds with stout bills and often brilliant coloration. They take insects from foliage and sometimes from flowers. All species lay white eggs, some in grass-lined tree hollows, others in nests of grass and bark placed in tunnels in the ground. Though all belong to the same genus, they may be divided into two groups: the spotted pardalotes, which have white spots scattered on the wings and sometimes on the head, and the streaked pardalotes, which have white streaks on the wings and sometimes on the head. The former group contains the spotted pardalote, *Pardalotes* punctatus* (9cm), found in forests and woodlands in VIC, TAS, eastern NSW, QLD and south-western WA; the yellow-rumped pardalote, *P.* xanthopygus* (9cm), found mainly in the dry woodlands of the coastal areas of southern WA and SA; the forty-spotted pardalote, *P.* quadragintus* (9cm), which frequents the forest canopies of the TAS mainland and KING ISLAND; and the red-browed pardalote, *P.* rubricatus* (9cm), which lives in trees and shrubs near watercourses in central WA, northern SA, western QLD, north-western NSW and most of the NT. The streaked pardalotes include the yellow-tipped species, *P.* striatus* (10cm), of

Sir Howard Florey

National Library of Australia

the dry forest and woodland areas of SE Australia; the almost identical red-tipped species, *P.* ornatus* (10cm), found in the same range but not in TAS; the striated pardalote, *P.* substriatus* (10cm), which frequents woodlands throughout most of the mainland; and the black-headed pardalote, *P. melanocephalus* (10cm), a dry woodland species of N and NE Australia.
See also birds

flukes These leaf-shaped PARASITES of animals belong to the class Trematoda, which is contained in the phylum Platyhelminthes (FLATWORMS). Many species have extremely complex life cycles; some, the Monogenea, need only one kind of host to complete their life cycle, but the others, the Digenea, need two to four.

Monogenetic flukes are mainly ectoparasites living on the skin or gills of their hosts, or within cavities, such as those of the nose, mouth and bladder, which open to the exterior. A few parasitise invertebrates such as octopuses, squids and crustaceans, but most attack vertebrates, especially fishes and amphibians. Superficially, they resemble free-living flatworms but they have developed suckers and hooks to cling to the tissues of their hosts. Digenic flukes are, almost without exception, endoparasites that live within their hosts. One of the hosts is almost always a mollusc, while the final host (in which the adult flukes live) is almost always a vertebrate. These flukes have a sucker surrounding the mouth, and usually a second one on the ventral surface, but no hooks.

Adult flukes are sexually reproducing hermaphrodites. The larvae reproduce parthenogenetically, building up very large numbers because the chance of any one individual surviving and completing its life cycle is extremely small. A fluke's life cycle usually consists of the following stages.
1. A miracidium larva hatches from the eggs which the vertebrate host passes out with its droppings or urine. This is a minute, ciliated animal which must enter the tissues of a particular species of host (usually a mollusc) to survive.
2. The miracidium develops into a sporocyst, a small, bag-like larva, which, internally,

usually buds off the redia, the next larval stage.
3. The rediae usually live within the liver of the mollusc. They produce the next stage, the cercaria.
4. The cercaria is a minute, tadpole-shaped larva, sometimes with a forked tail, which escapes into the water or on to vegetation. It sometimes bores into the tissues of the next host, or encysts in a tough skin which protects it from drying out, and which is eaten by the final host. This final encysted stage is called the metacercaria, and is considered to be a juvenile adult. Cercariae in bathing pools are sometimes the cause of 'bather's itch' when they try, unsuccessfully, to penetrate the skin of the wrong host, man.

Most of the important species of flukes are absent from, or very rare in, Australia, but with the recent trade in exotic fishes, especially from Asia, they could be introduced. The consignments of fishes often contain the water snails that are necessary for the particular life cycles. The number of fishes that have been imported each year rose from about 280 000 in 1963-64 to more than 8 300 000 in 1973-74 and has remained steady since. With them have come at least two potentially dangerous snails, a species of *Thiara* and *Limnaea columella*, a host of the LIVER FLUKE of sheep, cattle and man; both species are established in the wild. In 1983 the quarantine regulations regarding fishes were made more stringent. Many species of flukes infest native Australian vertebates, and several are introduced parasites of domestic animals.
Further reading: Rothschild, M. & Clay, T. *Fleas, Flukes and Cuckoos: A Study of Bird Parasites.* Collins, London, 1952; Lapage, G. *Animals Parasitic in Man.* Penguin Books, Harmondsworth, 1957; Wright, C.A. *Flukes and Snails.* George Allen & Unwin, London, 1971.

flute mouths see fishes, bony

flycatchers, robins, fantails and the willie wagtail These PASSERINE BIRDS are divided into two families—Muscicapidae, which contains the robins, the fantails, the willie wagtail and four species of flycatchers, and Monarchidae, which contains 12 species of flycatchers.

The muscicapids are small, distinctly patterned, insect-eating BIRDS whose ability to catch their prey on the wing is usually fairly inefficient. The gape of the beak is often wide, and the catching area is extended by the stiff bristles around the beak. There are 23 Australian muscicapids, 13 of which are endemic.

The flycatchers contained in the genus *Microeca* normally perch on low branches and dart out to catch flying insects. The most common are the brown flycatcher, *M. leucophaea** (12cm to 13cm long), also called the Jacky Winter, which occurs in open timbered country in most of the mainland except central WA, and the lemon-breasted flycatcher, *M. flavigaster* (11cm to 12cm), which frequents the

Species, genus or family is endemic to Australia (see Preface)

mangroves and forests of N Australia. The former is greyish-brown above and white below, and has a characteristic slow wagging of the tail from side to side; the latter is mainly yellowish-olive and pale yellow below. Both species lay eggs in saucer-shaped nests of grass, hair and bark placed in high, horizontal tree forks.

Most of the male robins contained in the genus *Petroica* have red breasts, while the females have light brown or buff breasts, apart from the female scarlet robin, *P. multicolor* (13cm to 14cm), of SE and SW Australia, whose grey-brown breast is tinged with red. The most widespread species is the red-capped robin, *P. goodenovii★* (11cm to 12cm), which occurs throughout the mainland apart from the NE; it is a black and white species with a red breast and a red patch on the forehead. Like the scarlet robin, it builds cup-shaped nests of grass, lined with cobweb and usually placed low down in trees. The other species contained in this genus are the flame robin, *P. phoenicia★* (13cm to 14cm), a red-throated species common in TAS but less common on the mainland; the rose robin, *P. rosea★* (12cm), found in SE forests; the hooded robin, *P. cucullata★* (14cm to 17cm), a black and white (male) or grey and white (female) bird found on most of the mainland apart from the NE; and the dusky robin, *P. vittata★* (16cm to 17cm), in TAS.

Courtesy of A.I.S. Canberra

Broad-billed flycatcher, *Myiagra ruficollis*, common in northern mangroves

The only species in the genus *Peneoenanthe* is the mangrove robin, *P. pulverulenta* (16cm), a dark grey bird with white underparts which feeds in low branches and on the ground in the coastal mangroves of N Australia. Its cup-shaped nests of bark are bound with cobweb and decorated with bark and lichen. Another species without red on the breast is the grey-headed robin, *Heteromyias cinereifrons★* (17cm), which frequents the rainforests of north-eastern QLD. Often seen near forest roads darting amongst low branches, this bird builds its cup-shaped nests of twigs and fibres in bushes or small palms.

The robins belonging to the genus *Poecilodryas* are very similar, with white patterns on the face and wing, and a white tip to the tail. The two Australian species frequent the wet forests of N Australia. The white-browed robin, *P. superciliosa★* (15cm), olive brown above and white below, and the buff-sided

robin, *P. cerviniventris★* (15cm), similar but with a grey breast and a black crown and face patch, both build cup-shaped nests of leaves and fibres in horizontal tree forks.

The genus *Eopsaltria* includes four yellow-bellied species and the white-breasted species, *E. georgina★* (13cm to 14cm), of SW Australia. All species build cup-shaped nests of grass and bark, bound with cobweb and lined with fibres and leaves; the nests are generally placed low down in trees and bushes. The eastern yellow robin, *E. australis★* (13cm to 14cm), which has bright yellow underparts and a grey back, occurs in SE and E Australia, while the similar western yellow robin, *E. griseogularis★* (13cm to 14cm), occurs in SW Australia and southern SA. Both species live on or near the ground in dry forests and woodlands, and often alight sideways on tree trunks. The pale-yellow robin, *E. capito★* (12cm to 14cm), and the white-faced robin, *E. leucops* (14cm), both greenish above, frequent the coastal rain-forests of E Australia.

There are four species of fantails in Australia, all belonging to the genus *Rhipidura*. They have relatively long tails, which are spread out like a fan and wagged from side to side, possibly to flush out the insects on which they feed. They are restless birds, with a fluttering flight when catching their prey on the wing. The grey fantail, *R. fuliginosa* (15cm), found in forests, woodlands and mangroves through-out Australia, the northern fantail, *R. rufiventris* (15cm), which occurs in open forests in N Australia, and the white-eyebrowed willie wagtail, *R. leucophrys* (20cm) which lives in the forest and desert margins throughout the mainland and is a familiar bird in parks and gardens, are mainly black or grey and white birds; the rufous fantail, *R. rufifrons* (length 15cm; tail 9cm), of coastal N, E and SE Australia, is mainly brown and reddish-brown above with a white breast. The willie wagtail uses grass, bark or fibre to make its nests; the bark and cobweb nests of the other fantails are shaped like an inverted pear.

The 12 Australian species which belong to the Old World family Monarchidae have bristles around the mouth and a wide gape, and most live in rainforests. The genus *Myiagra* contains five species. The male leaden flycatcher, *M. rubecula* (15cm), of N, E and SE Australia, is bluish-grey above, with glossy blue-green on the head, throat and upper breast, black wings and a white belly; the female is paler and lacks the greenish gloss. The satin flycatcher, *M. cyanoleuca★* (15cm), of E and SE Australia, resembles the male leaden flycatcher, while the broad-billed species, *M. ruficollis* (15cm), of coastal N Australia, is very similar to the female leaden flycatcher. All three species place their cup-shaped nests of bark strips, bound with cobweb and decorated with lichen, in trees, sometimes overhanging water. The shining flycatcher, *M. alecko* (18cm), found in mangrove and swamp areas of N and NE Australia, has similar breeding habits. The male is completely black, while the female is mainly chestnut. The restless flycatcher, *M.*

inquieta★ (18cm to 20cm), black above and white below, lives in open forests and woodlands in SW Australia and in a broad band from northern WA through northern NT and eastern QLD to south-western SA. This species hovers when catching insects; its eggs are laid in nests of bark and grass, bound with cobweb and decorated with lichen, and usually built on the high outer branches of trees.

The monarch flycatchers, of the genus *Monarcha*, rarely catch insects on the wing. Of the four Australian species one—the white-eared flycatcher, *M. leucotis* (14cm), of eastern QLD—is pied; the pearly-winged flycatcher, *M. melanopsis★* (18cm), the spectacled fly-catcher, *M. trivirgata* (15cm), and the rare black-winged flycatcher, *M. frater* (18cm), are grey and reddish birds with a black mask, and all occur in coastal NE and E Australia. Monarch flycatchers use bark, moss, fibres and cobweb to build their cup-shaped nests.

The genus *Arses* contains two similar species which are restricted to the rainforests of north-eastern QLD—the pied flycatcher, *A. kaupi★* (15cm), black above with a white collar, and white below with a black band, and the frill-necked flycatcher, *A. lorealis★* (15cm), which lacks the black breast band. Their loosely woven cup-shaped nests of twigs and tendrils are suspended from thin branches. The only species in the genus *Machaerirhynchus* is the boat-billed flycatcher, *M. flaviventer* (12cm), of north-eastern QLD, a dark, yellow-breasted species with a long yellow eyebrow and a very broad, flat, black bill. It is an active bird whose saucer-shaped nests of bark, bound with cobweb, are built fairly high in tree forks.

Flying Doctor Service This is the popular term used to cover all aerial medical services in Australia. The first of such services was established by the Rev. John FLYNN, director of the AUSTRALIAN INLAND MISSION. In time, however, the service became too large for this organisation to support, and thus the Flying Doctor Service of Australia, a non-denominational voluntary organisation financed by contributions, subscriptions and government grants, was formed to carry on the work. The use of the prefix 'Royal' was authorised in 1955. The RFDS operates in the NT and all States except VIC; it maintains 14 bases from which it provides medical services to large areas of sparsely populated country and operates a radio network which keeps it in constant touch with homesteads, missions and hospitals. In cases of emergency a doctor may be flown to the patient within a few hours, or the patient may be flown to hospital; in other cases the doctor may diagnose the patient's condition by radio consultation and prescribe treatment from the standard medical chest which each outpost possesses.

In addition to the RFDS, a number of other aerial medical services are operated by government departments, the most important of these being the Northern Territory Aerial Medical Service, based in Darwin. The radio networks of the aerial medical services are also used to provide facilities for EDUCATION and postal services in the Outback.

flying foxes *see* bats

Flynn, John (1880-1951) Presbyterian minister and founder of the FLYING DOCTOR SERVICE. Born at Moliagul VIC, he was a teacher with the VIC Department of Education from 1898 to 1902. He then began studying for the Presbyterian ministry and after ordination was appointed to Beltana SA. In 1912 he was commissioned to report to his Church on the needs of the people of the NT and central Australia, as a result of which he was placed in charge of the newly formed AUSTRALIAN INLAND MISSION in 1913. He had become deeply concerned about the lack of medical facilities in the Outback, and for some years concentrated on the establishment of nursing hostels in the inland. In 1917, however, in his magazine the *Inlander*, he first broached the idea of aerial medical services. The greatest technical obstacle to such a project was the lack of a wireless transceiver suitable for use over long distances and in locations without electricity. Finally, however, a suitable set, powered by foot pedals, was developed by an Adelaide electrical engineer, Alf Traegar. By 1928 public subscriptions and a grant from the Commonwealth government had provided Flynn with enough money to establish, on a trial basis, an Australian Inland Mission Aerial Medical Service based at CLONCURRY in QLD. This later developed into the Royal Flying Doctor Service of Australia. Flynn's work, particularly in the field of aerial medical services, attracted attention overseas and throughout Australia. He was appointed OBE, received an honorary degree from McGill University, Toronto, and was Moderator-General of the Presbyterian Church of Australia from 1939 to 1942. His grave near ALICE SPRINGS is marked by a monument and a small national reserve; and the John Flynn Memorial Church in Alice Springs commemorates his achievements.
Further reading: McPheat, W.S. *John Flynn, Apostle of the Inland.* Oxford University Press, Melbourne, 1965; Idriess, I. *Flynn of the Inland.* (new edn) Angus & Robertson, London, 1976.

football *see* Australian Rules, rugby, soccer.

Forbes NSW (population 8 029 in 1981) A town in the central W slopes region of the State, it is located on the Newell Highway and on a branch railway from PARKES on the main W line, 478km by rail and 386km by road from Sydney. It is situated on the LACHLAN RIVER, 239m above sea level, and is the market and commercial centre for a rich rural district producing wool, fat lambs, wheat, beef cattle, poultry, dairy products, wine grapes, pigs, lucerne and fruit. It is an important stock selling centre and has an abattoir and freezing plant, a flour mill, a reinforced-concrete factory and timber works. The town is the district headquarters of the Land Board, the Pastures Protection Board and Forbes Shire (population of the shire 10 993 in 1981). Downstream on the Lachlan from Forbes, the Jemalong Weir diverts water from the river for irrigation and livestock supply in the Jemalong and Wyldes Plains Irrigation Districts. The region experiences hot summer conditions and mild winters, with an average annual rainfall of 526mm, uniformly distributed throughout the year. In times of heavy rain over the Lachlan catchment, the river sometimes breaks its banks, flooding the town and the farmlands on the alluvial flats.

In 1817, the explorer John OXLEY reached the site where the town now stands. It was settled as a grazing area in the early days and in the 1860s it became a booming gold town; it was proclaimed a municipality in 1870, named after Sir Francis FORBES, Chief Justice of NSW in the 1820s. Among the tourist features of the town are a historical museum with relics of the bushranging days, the Lachlan vintage village containing a re-creation of the gold-rush era, and the Sandhills vineyard located 3km E of the town. The National Trust (NSW) has listed several buildings in Forbes and has classified the post office and town hall as essential parts of the national heritage.

Forbes, Sir Francis (1784-1841) Chief Justice of NSW. He was born in Bermuda, studied law in London, and in 1811 returned to Bermuda as Attorney-General. From 1816 to 1822 he was Chief Justice of the Supreme Court of Newfoundland, and in 1823, when on leave in England, was consulted on many details of the New South Wales Judicature Act. This led to his appointment as first Chief Justice of the Supreme Court set up under that Act. This position was one of considerable power: before any proposed ordinance of the Governor and his Legislative Council could be

Sir Francis Forbes

put into effect, the Chief Justice had to certify that it was 'consistent with the laws of England, so far as the circumstances of the colony will permit'. Although Forbes disapproved of this section of the Act, he used his power of veto on two occasions to prevent Governor DARLING from curbing the freedom of the Press. He also used the provisions of the Act to introduce trial by jury in certain civil cases, and was mainly responsible for the drafting of the Act of 1828, which abolished the Chief Justice's power of veto but limited the Governor's powers by increasing the size of the Legislative Council and giving it the power to override the Governor's wishes, and which also opened the way for the introduction of trial by jury in criminal cases.
Further reading: Currey, C.H. *Sir Francis Forbes.* Angus & Robertson, Sydney, 1968.

Forde, Francis Michael (1890-1983) Labor politician and Prime Minister. Educated in TOOWOOMBA in QLD, he became a teacher and then an electrical engineer, served in the QLD Legislative Assembly from 1917 to 1922 and from 1955 to 1957, and in the federal House of Representatives from 1922 to 1946. He held Cabinet posts under SCULLIN, CURTIN and CHIFLEY, and was deputy leader of the Opposition from 1932 to 1941 and deputy Prime Minister from 1941 to 1945. After Curtin's death in July 1945 Forde was caretaker Prime Minister for a week, until Chifley was elected Labor leader and therefore became Prime Minister. He was an Australian delegate to the UN conference in San Francisco in 1945 and High Commissioner to Canada from 1946 to 1953.

foreign relations The evolution of Australia's foreign policy has been influenced by four major factors. The first is her geographical position. She is far from the countries from which her culture and the bulk of her population have been drawn, and which until recently provided her with most of her trading links. However, she is comparatively close to Asia, and has become increasingly aware of the possible threat from there and from the Pacific area in general. Secondly, the smallness of her population, especially in relation to her size, gives her no prospect of resisting attack by a major power without the aid of powerful friends. Thirdly, from being absolutely dependent on the UK, she became independent by a series of gradual steps and assumed the responsibility for managing her own external relations. Finally, from about the middle of the 19th century geopolitical developments throughout the world, but especially in Asia and the Pacific, have drawn her attention away from Europe and towards her own more immediate environment, so leading her at last to develop a truly national foreign policy.

From 1788 to 1914 At first the British colonies in Australia relied totally on the UK for their DEFENCE and their relationships with foreign countries.

Mitchell Library

Even when the E colonies gained responsible government in the 1850s, the UK retained overall responsibility for defence, and full control over foreign affairs. However, during the following half-century the outside world began pressing in, as it were, on Australia, forcing her leaders not only to take more note of it, but also to develop views of Australia's interests that were not fully appreciated in the UK. The entry of large numbers of Chinese gold-seekers, particularly into VIC in the 1850s and into QLD in the 1870s, brought fear of the 'yellow peril', and some of the legislation which was introduced by colonial Parliaments (*see* IMMIGRATION RESTRICTION) displeased the British government. Australians were anxious to keep Asians out, by whatever means were necessary; the UK wished to avoid giving offence to Asian governments, or to Asian subjects of Her Majesty.

The founding of foreign colonies in the Pacific also alarmed Australians. In 1853 France took possession of New Caledonia and 10 years later founded a penal colony there. Escaped convicts occasionally reached Australia, serving as reminders that the UK's traditional enemy held bases close by. In later years France gained a foothold in the New Hebrides; the USA gained Hawaii, the Philippines and part of Samoa; and Germany took possession of Nauru, part of Samoa and NE New Guinea. Meanwhile, Russia, although she did not acquire colonies in the Pacific, was strengthening her Pacific provinces and her fleet based on Vladivostok. These developments aroused Australian fears to an extent that seemed unjustified to British officials and politicians, and it was with some reluctance that the UK yielded to colonial promptings and established control over Fiji and Papua.

While these divergences between British and Australian views of foreign affairs were taking place, Australia's relationship with the UK was changing, in practice if not in strict constitutional theory. In 1870 the last British troops were withdrawn, so that the colonies had to undertake some of the burden of their own defence. More importantly, by the end of the century Britain had begun a policy of consulting her self-governing colonies, in Australia and elsewhere, on defence and other matters of common interest. The first instance of this was in 1887, when the premiers of Canada, New Zealand, Cape Colony and the Australian colonies were in London for the celebration of Queen Victoria's Golden Jubilee, and Lord Salisbury, the British Prime Minister, took the opportunity to hold a Colonial Conference. A second was held at the time of the Queen's Diamond Jubilee in 1897 and a third, at which the newly federated Australia was represented by Edmund BARTON, in 1902. Others, known by the title Imperial Conferences, took place in 1907 and 1911, and a special Imperial Defence Conference was held in 1909.

At these meetings it became clear that the views of some Australian politicians on foreign affairs and defence differed in certain respects

THE ANGLO-JAP ALLIANCE.
"Britain will consult the Overseas Dominions before renewing the Anglo-Japanese Alliance" – *Cable*
"You don't mind me being friendly with this little lady, do you, my son?"
"No – but you ain't going to give her the run of the house, Dad?"

The Bulletin

This *Bulletin* of 1920 illustrates Australia's development of independent views on foreign affairs, at least in the Pacific

from those of British leaders. For example, on various occasions Australian representatives spoke vehemently about the dangers posed by French occupation of the New Hebrides, pressed for the strengthening of the Empire's naval forces in the Pacific, and showed uneasiness about the Anglo-Japanese Treaty of 1902, which they felt might cause the UK to rely too heavily on Japan, instead of herself maintaining a sufficiently strong force in the Pacific.

World War I and II Various events during and immediately after World War I illustrated the fact that although no formal change had taken place in imperial relations, the relationship between the UK and Australia had become more like that between partners than between parent and child, or master and servant. Moreover, while Australia followed Britain's lead without question in 1914, it became clear at the peace conference that she had her own particular national interests to pursue.

Australia, like other Dominions, was represented on the Imperial War Cabinet in the closing years of the war, sent representatives to the peace conference, was a signatory of the Treaty of Versailles, and became a member of the League of Nations. She was also entrusted with a mandate in New Guinea. At the peace conference, Prime Minister HUGHES, far from merely reflecting the British point of view, spoke out loudly on behalf of what he considered to be Australia's interests.

In the post-war years there was pressure, mainly from South Africa and Canada, to have the relationship between Britain and her Dominions redefined, and at the Imperial Conference of 1926 a committee was appointed, under the chairmanship of Lord Balfour, to look into the matter. Its report stated that the UK and the self-governing Dominions were 'autonomous communities within the British Empire, equal in status, in no way subordinate one to another in any aspect of their domestic or external affairs, though united by a common allegiance to the Crown and freely associated as members of the British Commonwealth of Nations'. The principles of this declaration were given legal force in 1931 by the Statute of Westminster, by which the British Parliament acknowledged that Canada, Australia, the Union (now the Republic of) South Africa, New Zealand, Newfoundland (now a province of Canada) and the Irish Free State (now the Republic of Ireland) were completely independent. Strangely, Australia did not appear very interested in these formalities, and her Parliament did not formally adopt the Statute of Westminster until 1942. Moreover, during the 1930s Australia still seemed quite content to let the British Foreign Office handle her diplomatic relations with foreign countries. It is true that in 1935 an Australian Department of External Affairs, with its own ministerial head, was set up, but its staff remained very small and the decade ended without Australia having appointed a single diplomatic representative to a foreign (in the sense of non-British) nation.

Effects of the Pacific war The gradual process by which Australia has developed an independent foreign policy was accelerated by the outbreak of war in the Pacific. The Japanese expansion to the S made it abundantly clear that Australia could no longer afford to depend on the Royal Navy for protection. Even before the Japanese had captured Singapore with ease, Prime Minister CURTIN had expressed what all Australians instinctively felt in these words of his New Year's message: 'I make it quite clear that Australia looks to America.' And after Japan had been defeated, mainly by American might, and the victor had decided to allow her a lenient peace treaty, Australia and New Zealand felt it imperative to secure a guarantee of future American protection through the ANZUS PACT.

Since then the foreign policy of every major Australian political party has been based on belief in the necessity of an American alliance. Labor and Liberal/National Country Party governments have differed as to whether Australia should support particular American initiatives (as in the VIETNAM WAR) and as to how far to go in allowing the USA to maintain defence facilities in Australia. However, the necessity of an American alliance and the importance of Pacific and Asian issues in Australian foreign policy are accepted by both parties.

Effects of the decline of colonialism in Asia The most obvious influences on the course of Australian foreign policy since 1945 have been the spread of nationalism and Communism in Asia. The former has involved the gaining of independence by many former colonies comparatively close to Australia, and containing between them about a quarter of the human race. The mere tasks of assessing the impact of independence movements on Australia's interests, framing policies towards the newly independent nations and establishing diplomatic relations with them have been formidable. In addition, difficult decisions have had to be taken on specific issues, especially with regard to events in Malaysia, Indonesia and Vietnam.

Australia was closely involved in the progress of Indonesia towards independence. In general,

the CHIFLEY government sympathised with the nationalists. After the first Dutch 'police action', Australia and India raised the matter in the UN Security Council, and Australia was later nominated by Indonesia as a member of the UN Committee of Good Offices which arranged a ceasefire and paved the way for the granting of independence in December 1949. In subsequent years, however, Indonesian policies on a number of issues were to cause grave concern in Australia. The first such issue concerned West New Guinea (West Irian), which had been left under Dutch administration by the Hague agreement of 1949. Australia supported the Dutch contention that the people of the disputed territory should be given the opportunity to decide their own future, and strongly condemned Indonesia when in 1961-62 she threatened to use force and actually landed small contingents of troops in New Guinea. However, she accepted the subsequent agreement that the administration should be transferred to Indonesia, but that an 'act of self-determination' should be organised before the end of 1969 to allow the people of West New Guinea to decide their future. Although the way the 'act of self-determination' was finally carried out was widely criticised in Australia, the government did not openly challenge the result.

Even more worrying to Australia was Indonesia's bitter opposition to the formation of the Federation of Malaysia in 1963. Australia supported the formation of the new federation and sent military aid to it, including minesweepers of the Royal Australian Navy (RAN) and military engineers.

More recently, Australia has been critical of the circumstances under which East Timor was incorporated into Indonesia. In 1975, when Portugal lost effective control, Prime Minister WHITLAM called for the people of East Timor to be given the right of self-determination. However, he also referred to the possibility that the territory might not be viable as an independent nation, and seems to have made the decision that Australia could do little to influence the course of events and should not put her friendship with Indonesia at risk over the matter. After the Indonesian takeover, Whitlam's successor, FRASER, and the new Minister for Foreign Affairs, PEACOCK, spoke very critically of this action. However, they too made it clear that they did not wish the matter to impair the generally good relationship between Australia and Indonesia, and their government subsequently gave formal recognition to Indonesian control of East Timor. When the ALP returned to power under Mr. HAWKE in March, 1983, it was deeply divided on this issue.

Effects of the spread of Communism in Asia The spread of Communism in Asia resulted in deep divisions of opinion between the major Australian political parties. The Liberal/Country Party government which came into office in December 1949 saw it in the context of the Cold War in general and regarded it as a major threat to Australian security. In accordance with this view,

Australia supported the UN effort in the KOREAN WAR, sent units of the Royal Australian Air Force (RAAF) to Malaya in 1950 to help counter a Communist insurgency there, and in 1955 sent ground troops also, joined the SOUTH-EAST ASIA TREATY ORGANISATION (SEATO) in 1954, refused to recognise the People's Republic of China and voted against its being represented in the UN, and supported the USA in the Vietnam War.

The Australian Labor Party, while declaring its opposition to Communism and giving full support to Australian participation in the Korean War, questioned the wisdom of sending troops to Malaya, advocated from 1955 the recognition of the People's Republic of China and its admission to the UN, and above all bitterly opposed American and Australian involvement in Vietnam. After gaining office late in 1972, it promptly recognised the People's Republic of China and opened diplomatic relations with it, and withdrew the remaining Australian military advisers from Vietnam.

Other post-war developments Only in the post-war period has Australia taken over the task of managing her own diplomatic relations throughout the world. Her first legations outside the Commonwealth of Nations were opened only in 1940, in Washington and Tokyo, but today the Department of Foreign Affairs has more than 80 overseas diplomatic missions and consular posts.

Activities concerned with the UN have featured prominently in Australia's foreign affairs. She was active in the foundation of the organisation, the leader of her delegation at the San Francisco Conference of 1945, EVATT, being prominent there as a spokesman for the smaller nations and later becoming president of the General Assembly for the 1948-49 session. She has been a member of the Security Council for three terms and has been active in the work of the special agencies.

The diversification of Australia's trade, her increased preoccupation with Asian affairs and her dependence on the USA as an ally have meant inevitably that Britain and the Commonwealth of Nations have become less important to her than they were formerly. Moreover, as membership of the Commonwealth widened, Australia found herself not in full accord with the aims of some Asian and African members, to whom she appeared to be lukewarm towards their hopes for a rapid end to colonialism and in disapproval of minority regimes such as that in South Africa. However, from the 1960s she became more openly sympathetic towards their hopes, this change of attitude becoming much more marked during the years of the Whitlam government. After the return to power of the Liberal/National Country Party coalition in 1975, Australia continued to support UN policies in southern Africa and Prime Minister Fraser was outspoken in his condemnation of *apartheid*.

In spite of the lessened importance of the Commonwealth of Nations to her, Australia has remained an active member. In 1950 she took a leading part in the launching of the

COLOMBO PLAN, which was initially confined to Commonwealth members. In recent years she has shown an interest in the possibilities of forming Commonwealth regional associations and in 1978 was host to the Commonwealth Heads of Government Regional Meeting (CHOGRM), which was attended by delegates from Bangladesh, Fiji, India, Malaysia, Nauru, New Zealand, New Guinea, Singapore, Sri Lanka, Tonga and Western Samoa, as well as Australia. This was the largest regional meeting yet organised within the Commonwealth of Nations. In 1981 she was host to a general Commonwealth Heads of Government Meeting (CHOGM).

In view of the circumstances of the Pacific war of 1941-45, Australia's relations with Japan have naturally been a matter of major importance ever since. Fear of a renewal of Japan's militarist policies has not been entirely extinguished. However, the remarkable growth of trade between Australia and Japan has meant that trade relations have now become the main area of concern. A trade treaty was signed between the two countries in 1957 and renewed in 1963, and a more general Treaty of Friendship and Co-operation signed in 1976.

In general, economic matters have tended to become predominant in Australia's foreign policy since the mid-1970s. In view of the worldwide economic recession, and of her own position as a trading nation, and because of particular pressures such as requests by members of the Association of South-East Asian Nations (ASEAN) that she lower her tariffs on various manufactured goods, she has begun to pay increased attention to broad global economic issues, such as the revival of international trade and the economic relationships between the developed and developing nations, as well as to her own economic relationships with particular countries and blocs. She has become a strong supporter of the idea of a Common Fund to provide buffer stocks of agricultural and other commodities and so lessen price fluctuations in raw materials on the export of which she and many developing countries rely. She has also paid close attention to the Multi-lateral Trade Negotiations, formally begun at a meeting of about 100 nations in Tokyo in 1973 with the aim of reducing tariff barriers and other obstacles to the flow of world trade. Her particular concern here has been to have both agricultural products and manufactured goods included in the process of tariff reform. In short, in the course of pursuing her own economic interests, Australia has become increasingly aware of the economic interdependence of the world's nations, and has framed her policies accordingly.

Further reading: Greenwood, G. & Harper, N. *Australia in World Affairs.* (4 vols) Cheshire, Melbourne, 1957-74; Watt, Sir Alan *The Evolution of Australian Foreign Policy 1938-1965.* Cheshire, Melbourne, 1967; Millar, T.B. *Australia's Foreign Policy.* Angus & Robertson, Sydney, 1968 and *Australia in Peace and War: External Relations 1788-1977.*

Australian National University Press, Canberra, 1978.

forest, closed *see* vegetation

forest, open *see* vegetation

forest oak *see* Casuarinaceae

forestry The first settlers in E Australia believed that they had come to a well-forested land in which there would be no shortage of TIMBER. The area of forest in Australia is, however, relatively small. Using the Bureau of Statistics' definition of forest as that land with plantations and native forest 'with an existing or potential mature height of 20m or more, and cypress pine forest in commercial use regardless of height' the estimated area of forest is 42 million hectares (5.5 per cent), distributed as shown as Table 1, and confined mainly to districts with growing periods of nine months or more each year.

Of this area 98 per cent is natural forest, 93 per cent of which is dominated by eucalypts (MYRTACEAE). There are thus enough hardwood supplies to satisfy general construction and many other needs, and to provide some forest materials for export, but softwoods are in short supply. Table 2 summarises the production of timber and timber products in 1975-82. In 1979-80 the provisional approximate values (in thousands of dollars) of imported forest products were: crude wood and timber, including wood waste, charcoal, wood in the rough or roughly squared and railway or tramway sleepers, 1 262; sawn timber, simply worked (a) coniferous, 99 794 (b) non-coniferous, 53 823; timber, planed, grooved, etc. (a) coniferous, 21 690 (b) non-coniferous, 17 331.

In drier inland areas there are wooded areas which do not fall under the above definition of forest but which, nevertheless, provide local stations and settlements with their needs for fuel and general construction. Many of these inland timbers are extremely resistant to decay and attack by termites.

In volume the following species are the most important native timber trees: MESSMATE stringybark, *Eucalyptus obliqua* (TAS, NSW, VIC, SA; used in general construction); jarrah, *E. marginata* (WA; fire- and termite-resistant species which occur in relatively pure stands); alpine ASH, *E. delegatensis* (TAS, NSW, VIC); BLACKBUTT, *E. pilularis* (NSW, QLD; in QLD known as grey blackbutt); MOUNTAIN ASH, *E. regnans* (TAS, VIC; this species and the alpine ash are used for general construction and also for pulping paper and hardboard); cypress pine, *Callitris glauca* (VIC, NSW, QLD; a fine textured softwood with attractive figuring which is very useful for building construction in termite-infested areas); spotted gum, *E. maculata* (QLD, NSW; a good, hard, shock-resistant wood used for general framing and construction work); TALLOW WOOD, *E. microcorys* (NSW, QLD; heavy construction timber); red gum, *E. camadulensis* (NSW, VIC, SA, QLD, WA; used for heavy, durable constructional work); hoop pine, *Araucaria cunninghamii* (NSW, QLD; softwood used for internal work, plywood and so on); and karri, *E. diversicolor* (WA; used for heavy constructions, veneer and plywood). All the above species, apart from cypress pine and red gum, come from forests with growing periods of more than nine months each year.

There are several species, especially in rainforest, which are valued for cabinet work and special purposes. They include: red CEDAR, *Toona australis* (NSW, QLD; one of the first exports from Australia but now largely worked out); rose MAHOGANY or rosewood, *Dysoxylum fraseranum* (NSW, QLD; coastal brush forest); Queensland maple, *Flindersia brayleyana* (north-eastern QLD); northern SILKY OAK, *Cardwellia sublimis* (northern QLD in coastal brush forest); satinay or FRASER ISLAND turpentine, *Syncarpia hillii* (Fraser Is QLD; used for furniture and tool handles); Queensland walnut, *Endiandra palmerstoni* (QLD in coastal tablelands; high electrical resistance); brush box, *Tristania conferta* (NSW, QLD; best Australian timber for wharf and bridge decking); and blackwood, *Acacia melanoxylon* (TAS, VIC, NSW; valuable for cabinet work and shop and office fittings).

Woodchipping In recent years large areas of forests have been clearfelled, denuding the land of all or most of the trees. The larger logs are removed to be used for sawn timber, and most of the remains are taken to mills to be reduced to woodchips; the waste from the sawmills is also chipped. Much of the material is exported to be made into pulp and other products.

The process of clearfelling has been attacked by environmentalists but forestry services claim that the effect is similar to that of BUSHFIRES in that it allows regeneration of the forest, and is less harmful than a fire in that it is selective and is less damaging to wildlife, and reduces the risk of fires. Woodchipping is an economical way of using forest resources, particularly in those areas where the better trees have already been removed by selective felling during the past century. Other arguments in favour of woodchipping are that it provides employment in areas with few alternative industries and that it uses up the wastes (about 40 per cent of each log) from the sawmills. The arguments against woodchipping are discussed below.

Plantations In 1982 there were about 820 000ha of land (1.7 per cent of the forest land in Australia) planted with exotic and native conifers and hardwoods (*see* Table 3). The conifers were planted to reduce the quantity of softwoods that are imported. The native conifers used are hoop pine and other members of the genus *Araucaria*; these plantations are virtually resticted to QLD (42 848ha) and NSW (1 488ha). The exotic conifers are mainly species of *Pinus*. The exotic hardwoods are varieties of poplar (*Populus* species) which are fast-growing trees used for match making.

Table 1

FOREST AREAS IN AUSTRALIA, JUNE 1982
('000ha)

	NSW	VIC	QLD	SA	WA	TAS	NT	ACT	TOTAL
NATIVE FORESTS									
Rainforest	253	—	1 074	—	—	472	38	—	1 873
*Eucalyptus**	13 189	4 095	4 634	—	2 991	2 347	—	51	28 117
Paper bark	—	—	4 078	—	—	—	2 450	—	6 528
Cypress pine	1 908	6	1 685	—	—	—	778	—	4 377
PLANTATIONS	203	188	175	98	73	64	4	14	819
TOTAL	15 553	5 098	11 646	98	3 064	2 883	3 270	65	41 678
PERCENTAGE	37.3	12.2	27.9	0.2	7.4	6.9	7.8	0.2	

Note: *Eucalyptus* forest are graded I, II and III in decreasing order of productivity. The percentage of the three grades for Australia are: I, 9.2; II, 48.9; III, 41.9.
Source: *Australian Forest Resources 1982*. Dept of Primary Industry, Forestry Branch, Canberra.

Unfortunately, poplars are threatened by introduced rust fungus diseases (*see* DISEASES, PLANT).

The first trial plantings of conifers (*P. radiata*) were made in 1870-80 in SA, which has little native forest. Large-scale plantings, which began after World War I with financial help from Britain, were carried out in order to encourage emigration to Australia. There were difficulties in establishing exotic pines in some parts of Australia between 1920 and 1930 because of the absence of the necessary symbiotic soil fungi (mycorrhiza), but this problem was overcome by spreading suitably infected soil in forestry nurseries.

In Australia *Pinus* species have been attacked, for example, by the *Sirex* woodwasp from Europe but this threat has been greatly reduced by the introduction of parasitic wasps and nematodes which attack it (*see* BIOLOGICAL CONTROL). Certain introduced bark beetles are also causing some damage in some plantations. The rust diseases of poplars will prove more difficult to control but there may be success with resistant varieties of the trees.

Under the Softwood Forestry Agreement Acts of 1967, 1972 and 1976 the Commonwealth loaned the States about $55 600 000 towards the establishment of about 100 000ha of plantations above the levels of State plantings. The Softwood Forestry Agreement Act of 1978 provided assistance to the States during the five-year period 1977-78 to 1981-82 for the maintenance of these plantations. The Commonwealth government has also agreed to assist TAS financially with the improvement of native forests and with the establishment of *Eucalyptus* plantations on marginal land.

Multiple use of native forests Because most of the forest land of Australia is in the area of densest settlement, there are demands that this land should be put to additional uses, such as recreation, watershed protection, shelter for livestock and the conservation of wildlife. However, the use of a forest as a timber source (and especially as a source of woodchips) is to a large extent incompatible with these other uses. To a forester who is concerned only with producing timber, the ideal forest consists of large areas of stands of even-aged specimens of

Table 2

VOLUME OF TIMBER AND CERTAIN TIMBER PRODUCTS IN AUSTRALIA 1975-82

	1975-76	1976-77	1977-78	1978-79	1981-82
Undressed sawntimber grown in Australia ('000 cu m)					
Broadleaved	2 372	2 312	2 129	2 128	1 976
Coniferous	856	1 945	927	982	1 181
Woodchips, green weight, hardwood ('000t)	2 603	3 623	3 668	3 800	3 821
Plywood ('000 sq m of 1mm thick)	70 936	76 517	84 681	87 249	89 126
Particle board, resin bonded (000s cu m)	460	496	517	531	647
Wood pulp (tonnes)	555 017	599 680	626 370	646 617	673 449
Paper (tonnes)					
Newsprint	206 228	206 590	207 621	208 143	307 183
Other	536 074	586 487	604 784	655 305	697 040
Paperboard, including strawboard (tonnes)	379 942	430 711	415 290	448 700	453 804

Source: *Year Book Australia, 1979*. (no 63), *Year Book Australia, 1980*. (no 64) and *Year Book Australia, 1981*. (no 65).
* exported.

Table 3

AREA OF PLANTATIONS, CLASSIFIED BY SPECIES, IN 1982
(in hectares*)

Species	States and Territories	Area
CONIFEROUS		
Pinus radiata (radiata pine)	All except NT	551 200
P. pinaster (maritime pine)	SA, WA, VIC	32 600
P. elliottii (slash pine)	NSW, QLD, WA	101 300
P. caribaea (Caribbean pine)	NSW, QLD, NT	26 500
Araucaria species (bunya and hoop pines)	NSW, QLD	44 300
Other conifers	All	21 300
TOTAL		777 200
BROADLEAVED		
Eucalyptus species	All States	39 100
Populus species	NSW, VIC	2 500
Others	VIC, QLD	700
TOTAL		42 300
GRAND TOTAL		819 500

Note: * areas rounded to nearest 100ha.
Source: *Australian Forest Resources 1982* Dept Primary Industry Forestry Branch, Canberra.

Table 4

AREA OF PLANTATIONS, CLASSIFIED BY OWNERSHIP, IN 1979 (in hectares*)

	Public	Private
Coniferous	549 300	228 000
Broadleaved	19 700	22 600
TOTAL	569 000	250 600

Note: * areas rounded to nearest 100ha.
Source: *Australian Forest Resources 1982* Dept Primary Industry Forestry Branch, Canberra.

a single species, all relatively young and healthy; furthermore, the forest floor must be clear of litter so as to minimise the chances of destructive fires. Clearfelling and replanting would be the ideal way to achieve such a forest but the usual practice is to fell selectively to remove the less economically desirable species and to get rid of the overmature specimens so that the desirable trees have more room in which to grow. Selective felling reduces the number of fruit-bearing trees and trees with hollows and holes, thereby causing species of birds and animals which nest in tree hollows or in tree stumps to disappear. Clearfelling, however, is far more destructive than selective felling. In one study 69 per cent of all vertebrate species disappeared from a clearfelled area though a few of them were found later in the coniferous forest which replaced the native forest. Mountain possums, greater gliders and hole-nesting birds were the most seriously affected; many of these animals probably migrated to untouched forest but there they would be in competition with well-established residents.

When regrowth occurs the habitat favours other kinds of species, in particular ground-feeding birds. If relatively small areas are clearfelled it is probable that the number of species will increase, for a uniform, dense forest does not support organisms which need open spaces or ecotones (border areas between ecosystems, such as the edge of a woodland). The unfelled areas must be large enough, however, to support viable populations of those organisms that depend upon them. It has been estimated, for example, that a population of a relatively abundant species such as the greater glider would need an area of at least 6000ha to survive, and populations of rarer species perhaps 20 000ha.

Conservationists also believe that too little consideration has been given to other possible effects of clearfelling for woodchips. There are, for example, the dangers of soil erosion, an increase in salinity in streams and creeks, and the possible destruction of unique plant associations. Furthermore, there is no doubt that a clearfelled area is ugly.

If a clearfelled area is replanted with native species or allowed to regenerate, then, given time, it will be recolonised by at least some of the original animals. Fewer of these will, however, colonise plantations of exotic coni-

Table 5

AREA OF PLANTATIONS, CLASSIFIED BY STATES, IN 1982 (in hectares*)

	Coniferous	Broadleaved	Total
NSW	193 700	9 500	203 200
VIC	174 200	13 600	187 800
QLD	171 900	3 400	175 300
SA	96 900	900	97 800
WA	64 800	8 400	73 200
TAS	57 100	6 600	63 700
NT	4 300	—	4 300
ACT	14 400	—	14 400

Note: * areas rounded to nearest 100ha.
Source: *Australian Forest Resources 1982* Dept Primary Industry, Forestry Branch, Canberra.

fers; brush-tailed, mountain and ring-tailed possums can, if necessary, live in pine forests but the greater, feather-tailed and sugar gliders cannot.

Fire is used as a tool of forestry management but as many forest organisms in Australia are adapted to bushfires this technique may not be as harmful as it might appear at first sight. Natural bushfires are, however, infrequent whereas controlled fires occur at fairly regular and short intervals and may not, therefore, have the same ecological effects as the natural fires.

Administration and research Much of the forest land in Australia is Crown land under the control of the various States. The States employ about 17 900 people for general management of the forests but the harvesting, which is now highly mechanised, is carried out largely by contractors. The Australian Forestry Council, set up in 1964, consists of the State and federal Ministers responsible for forestry. One of its first measures was to encourage the extension of plantings of exotic conifers.

The Commonwealth established the Forestry and Timber Bureau which has an advisory and research role, but much of the scientific research is now carried out by the CSIRO, the States and various universities. There are two divisions of forestry research; the first concerns silviculture, plant pathology and so on and the second concerns the use of forest products.

See also conservation; environment; vegetation
Further reading: Hall, N., Johnston, R.D. & Chippendale, G.M. *Forest Trees of Australia.* Forestry and Timber Bureau, Canberra, 1970; Routley, R. & Routley, V. *The Fight for the Forests: The Takeover of Australian Forests for Pines, Wood Chips and Intensive Forestry.* Research School of Social Sciences, Australian National University, Canberra, 1973; *Multiple Use of Forest Resources.* Forestry and Timber Bureau, Australian Govt Publishing Service, Canberra, 1975; *Report of the Forestry and Wood-Based Industries Development Conference 1974.* Australian Govt Publishing Service, Canberra, 1975; 'Case for and against wood-chipping' in *Australian Forestry.* (no 2, vol 40, 1977); *Woodchips and the Environment: Supplementary Report of the Senate Standing*

Committee of Science and the Environment. Australian Govt Publishing Service, Canberra, 1978; McIlroy, J.C. 'The effects of forestry practices on wildlife in Australia; a review' in *Australian Forestry.* (no 2, vol 41, 1978); 'The export potential of Australian forest products' in *Quarterly Review of the Rural Economy.* (no 3, vol 1, 1979).

Forrest, Sir John (1847-1918) Politician, explorer and First Baron of Bunbury. Born at Preston Point WA, he became that colony's most prominent statesman and the first person born in Australia to be raised to the peerage. After leaving Bishop Hale's School in Perth, he entered the colony's Survey Department and eventually rose to the position of Commissioner of Crown Lands and Surveyor-General in 1883. By that time he had also won a reputation as an explorer, based mainly on three journeys: in 1869 he travelled NW from Perth to well beyond Lake Barlee; in 1870 he went from Perth to Adelaide around the GREAT AUSTRALIAN BIGHT; and in 1874 he crossed the W half of the continent from GERALDTON and the MURCHISON RIVER to the OVERLAND TELEGRAPH. Although his expeditions did not make discoveries of great importance, they were notable as feats of endurance.

Sir John Forrest

In 1890, when responsible government was granted, he became Premier and Colonial Treasurer, positions which he held until 1901. Thus he guided WA through its period of greatest development. He represented WA at meetings of the Federal Council during the 1890s and took part in both federal conventions, in which he was particularly concerned with protecting the rights of the less populous colonies. He had many reservations about federation, and this heightened his unpopularity on the goldfields, where pro-federation feeling was strong and where he was seen as the champion of conservative vested interests. In 1901 he was elected to represent the Swan electorate in the first Commonwealth Parliament. In spite of his conservative views and his fears of protectionist tariff policies, he supported BARTON and was in both his and DEAKIN's Cabinets. He held a variety of portfolios at various times, and was for a few months in 1907 acting Prime Minister. He played an important part in the formation of the LIBERAL PARTY OF AUSTRALIA in 1909, and in 1913, to his great disappointment, was defeated by Sir Joseph COOK by only one vote in a contest for leadership of the party. As the Liberals won the election of that year, Forrest had failed to become Prime Minister by the narrowest of margins. He died at sea and was buried in Sierra Leone, but his body was later brought to WA for reinterment.

Further reading: Rawson, G. *Desert Journeys.* Cape, London, 1948; Crowley, F.K. *Forrest, 1847-1918.* Queensland University Press, St Lucia, 1971.

Forster NSW (combined population of Forster and TUNCURRY 9 260 in 1981) A country town on the lower N coast of the State, it is 333km by road N of Sydney, lying E of the Pacific Highway and SE of TAREE. It is located at the coastal entrance to Wallis Lake, with a twin town, Tuncurry, on the opposite side of the lake entrance. The two towns were linked in 1959 by a pre-stressed concrete bridge. Fishing, boating and swimming in the lake, as well as surfing along the coastal beaches, make Forster a popular holiday resort, especially during the summer vacation. In addition to aquatic sports, there are several tourist attractions including a vintage car museum, an art-and-craft centre, the 'Green Cathedral' (an open-air church on the shores of Wallis Lake, 13km S of Forster), and a horse-riding school.

Forster, Johann Reinhold (1729-98) Naturalist. Born near Danzig in Poland, Forster migrated to England in 1766. In 1772 he and his son, Georg Adam Forster, took part in Captain James COOK's second voyage to the Pacific. Forster senior quarrelled with Cook during the voyage. Father and son published accounts of their voyages, including *Characteres Generum Plantarum* (1776) which described the plants collected during the voyage with Cook. They left England in 1778 and subsequently both held Chairs in German universities.

Fortescue River WA Located in the NW of the State, with its headwaters in the Robertson and Ophthalmia Ranges, it flows for over 600km in a general NW direction along the N side of the HAMERSLEY RANGE through a rift valley, then meanders across a broad flood-plain to a mangrove-lined swampy estuary on the Indian Ocean coast some 130km NE of ONSLOW. Since much of its course lies in regions of low rainfall, the river flow is intermittent and sections of the stream bed are seasonally dry. The Hamersley Range

National Park, covering 590 176ha and lying S of WITTENOOM in the middle section of the river, includes spectacular mountain, gorge and waterfall scenery. To the N of this national park is MOUNT TOM PRICE and to the SE is MOUNT NEWMAN. The Chichester Range National Park lies further downstream; it covers 150 609ha and includes beautiful scenery and Aboriginal rock carvings.

fortescues *see* fishes, bony; fishes, poisonous and venomous

Forth River TAS Located in the central-N of the State, it rises in the rugged terrain of the CRADLE MOUNTAIN LAKE ST CLAIR National Park and flows on a general N course to its estuary on BASS STRAIT between DEVONPORT and ULVERSTONE. The steep drop from the central highlands, where the altitude of the catchment basin is over 1 100m, to the N coastal plains has been utilised in the MERSEY-Forth hydro-electricity scheme. The scheme, begun in 1963 and completed in 1973, consists of seven power stations, seven large dams and three major tunnels, as well as associated penstocks, canals and flumes. On the Forth River, there are five of these power stations, namely (coming downstream): Lemonthyme (commissioned in 1969, with an installed capacity of 51 000kW); Wilmot (1970, 30 600kW); Cethana (1971, 85 000kW); Devils Gate (1969, 60 000kW); and Paloona (1972, 28 000kW). All power stations of the scheme are designed for fully automatic operation, remotely controlled from a centre near Sheffield, 30km S of Devonport.

fossil man About 20 years ago it was believed that the Aborigines had been in Australia for only a few thousand years. Now anthropologists and archaeologists are talking in terms of 30 000, perhaps even 50 000, years. The last figure is based on indirect evidence, namely a change in the FLORA (as indicated by pollen studies) near LAKE GEORGE in NSW about 50 000 years ago. These studies indicated an increase in the number of fires resulting either from a drier climate or the presence of man, or, perhaps, from both.

The oldest positive dating is that of a site with lakeside ovens and man-transported shells at Lake Mungo NSW. The date was 32 750 ± 1 250 BP where BP ('before present') means before 1950. The radiocarbon method does not allow a dating with absolute precision but the limits (31 500 to 34 000 years in this case) indicate a range within which the true age falls with reasonable probability. At Keilor VIC, quartzite tools have been found with an age of probably 26 000 to 36 000 years, but possibly as great as 45 000 years. Lake Mungo also yielded a cremation burial, dated at 24 710 ± c1 200 BP, making it the earliest known cremation burial in the world. The ritual of the burial included the smashing and reburning of the bones.

It should be pointed out that these dates are not necessarily the dates of the first occupation of the Australian continent. Firstly, they are

from sites in the S of the continent, whereas the first Aborigines entered from the N. Secondly, the evidence of earlier occupations may have been eroded away, not yet found or covered by the seas which rose at the end of the Ice Ages. Although the seas were lower then, it has been estimated that even if the people came to Australia from Asia by the route with the shortest sea journeys (through Bali, Flores and Timor) they would have had to make sea crossings of between 19km and 87km. They could thus claim to be the earliest known marine sailors.

The Talgai skull

The discovery of fossil remains of man in Australia was, until recently, uncommon, and in some cases it has not been possible to date the remains, or even to be sure of the exact site or soil level where the bones were originally found. Because it is not always possible to get a date from the remains directly (for example when the bones are heavily mineralised), dating is based on the matrix in which the fossil is found. This is not always reliable as the body may have been buried in an earlier stratum.

Some authorities claim that all the remains found so far fall within the range shown in the dimensions and shapes of the bones in modern Aborigines. The Talgai skull, found in 1866 near WARWICK in QLD, was badly smashed and heavily mineralised and the site where it was found was rediscovered only with great difficulty. All that can now be said of its age is that it is at least 14 000 to 16 000 years old. It has a flat, receding frontal vault and is markedly prognathous (having projecting jaws); the palate and teeth are large. Although these features are all indications of 'primitiveness' they still fall within the modern range. The Cohuna skull, discovered in a swamp near the MURRAY RIVER in 1925, has not been positively dated but may be older than the Talgai skull. The Mossgiel skeleton, found in the RIVERINA in NSW in 1960, consists of most of the skull and about three-quarters of the rest of the skeleton. It is at least 4 800 years old; some estimates suggest it is 11 000 years old. The Mossgiel and Cohuna crania show archaic features similar to those of

Talgai man.

With the exception of the Kow Swamp people (*see below*), the remaining known fossils resemble modern Aborigines in all essential features. The best-worked specimens are the Green Gully bones, found in 1965 near the Keilor site. The grave contained a strange mixture of two skeletons, a male and a female, with no duplication of any bone; the cranium was female, but resembled the Keilor (male) skull morphologically. A radiocarbon date on collagen remains of the Green Gully bones was 6 460 ± 190 BP. The Keilor skull, discovered in 1940 has been dated by radiocarbon examination of the skull and thighbone at about 13 000 BP. Other skeletons and skeletal remains, apart from some fragments near Lake Nitchie NSW (15 300 BP—not to be confused with the Lake Nitchie skeleton, 6 820 BP) and a second cremated skeleton at Lake Mungo, are all less than 10 000 years old on present evidence.

Kow Swamp VIC yielded numerous skeletons between 1968 and 1973. The skeletons were buried between 9 500 and 13 000 BP but although they are therefore relatively modern in time, they are archaic in morphology. The skulls are large and prognathic, with sloping brows and large eyebrow ridges. The backs of the crania are, however, well rounded and modern in most respects though the bones are rather thick; the jaws and teeth are large. In many ways, therefore, these skulls show persistence of *Homo erectus* traits though *H. erectus* flourished hundreds of thousands of years ago. The Kow Swamp people could not have been the ancestors of the modern Aborigines, for people of modern type were living at the same time and in the same general area as the Kow Swamp people. Furthermore, it seems that the Lake Mungo people were essentially the same as modern Aborigines in their morphology. It is not known which of the two groups came first to Australia, but it is tempting to suggest that those with the more archaic features came before the more modern people, and that this happened 50 000 or more years ago.

After decades of being a backwater of archaeological and prehistory research, Australia has now become an important centre for these disciplines. The Aborigines, however, are objecting to the scientific examination of the remains of their ancestors and of the Kow Swamp people, an issue which has led Mulvaney (*see below*) to point out that the remains are treated with respect, and that the methods of research followed are universal.

Further reading: Abbie, A.A. *The Original Australians*. A.H. & A.W. Reed, Sydney, 1969; Mulvaney, D.J. & Golson, J. (eds) *Aboriginal Man and Environment in Australia*. Australian National University Press, Canberra, 1971; Golson, J. 'The remarkable history of Indo-Pacific man', in *Search*. (vol 3, January/February 1972); Blainey, G. *Triumph of the Nomads: A History of Ancient Australia*. Macmillan, South Melbourne, 1975; Mulvaney, D.J. *The Prehistory of Australia*. (revd edn) Penguin Books, Harmondsworth, 1975; White, P.J. & O'Connell, J.F. 'Australian prehistory: new aspects of antiquity' in *Science*. (USA, vol 203, 5 January 1979).

fossils The remains or traces of organisms preserved in rocks are called fossils. The solidified footprint of a dinosaur that stepped in a muddy patch millions of years ago, for example, is as much a fossil as its petrified bones.

Fossilisation of an organism is rare and selective. The organism must die and be covered by deposits before it decays completely. Parts of the body, usually the bones or a shell, are slowly or partly replaced by minerals; alternatively, the organism may decay leaving a space that is filled by minerals to produce a cast. Sometimes the remains are preserved in the rock with little or no change. Organisms with hard parts, living in still water or on land where sand or soil drifts, are more likely to be fossilised than soft-bodied organisms or organisms living in woodlands. Even if an organism becomes a fossil it is not necessarily preserved forever for the rock in which it is embedded may be eroded away or subjected to heat or great pressure.

Fossils are the only direct evidence of life in past ages, and a good series of fossils can show the evolutionary changes that have occurred in a particular group. They are also good indicators of the age of the rocks in which they are found, especially when they belong to a cosmopolitan species. Many of the smaller organisms are associated with oil-bearing rocks and are thus of great value to geologists as indicators. Some fossils help geologists and biogeographers to trace the former connections of the modern continents. This article mentions some fossils that are peculiar to Australia, some that are very well represented and some that are important in establishing the nature of CONTINENTAL DRIFT.

Plants, fungi and bacteria Apart from the plants that make up the coal measures, plant fossils are rare compared with those of MOLLUSCS and VERTEBRATES because plant remains decay quickly unless oxygen is excluded. After the colonisation of the land, spore, pollen and seeds become significant and are now an important field of study for palaeontologists.

1. Precambrian. The oldest-known Australian fossils are bacteria in the Archaean rocks of the Yilgarn or Western Australian shield, some of which are over 2 700 million years old. ALGAE (including blue-green algae) and possibly also FUNGI are known from other Precambrian rocks which are about 800 to 1000 million years old. In some places they form limestone masses with a crenelated structure. Algal genera found include *Collenia, Conophyton, Newlandia* and *Osagia*.

2. Devonian. The fossil remains of Australia's earliest land plants are found in some Devonian rocks which were originally thought to belong to the Silurian. The first discoveries were made at Mt Pleasant, 145km NE of Melbourne, but similar floras have since been found elsewhere in VIC, and in TAS and NSW. Some of these early plants were classed with the Psilophytales, an extinct order, and some with the club mosses (*see* MICROPHYLLYTA). Upper Devonian rocks contain the fossils of other club mosses or scale trees, such as *Leptophloeum australe*, which are easily recognised by the scale-like pattern of the leaf scars.

3. Carboniferous. Though this is the period of the coal measures in the N hemisphere, it yields only scattered plant fossils in Australia. Fossils of *Lepidodendron*, an important genus in the N hemisphere, and the horsetail (*Calamites* species; *see* ARTHROPHYTA) are found in early Carboniferous rocks in Australia; horsetails no longer survive as native plants in Australia. Middle Carboniferous rocks yield the fossils of the primitive ferns (*see* PTERIDOPHYTA) of the genera *Rhacopteris* and *Cariopteris*.

4. Permian. This is the period of the GONDWANALAND coal measures. Club mosses had become relatively rare but members of the extinct order Cordaitales, a group probably ancestral to cycads and conifers (*see* GYMNOSPERMAE) had become common. The fossilised plants of the widespread and important genus *Glossopteris*, which probably grew in cooler regions and had typically tongue-shaped leaves, have also been found in rocks in several Gondwanaland land masses. The exact classification of *Glossopteris* is unclear. Horsetails and ferns, including tree ferns, were also important during this period.

5. Triassic. In this period the *Glossopteris* flora was replaced by one dominated by cycad-like trees (*Dicroidium* species), ferns and seed ferns (for example, *Thinnfeldia* species), horsetails (*Phyllotheca* species) and in some places large CEDAR-like trees (*Cedroxylon* species) which may have been an ancestor of some modern Australian conifers. Later in the Triassic, ginkgo-like trees (*Baiera* species), related to the surviving maidenhair tree of Japan, appeared.

6. Jurassic. In this period the cycads became important. They included members of the genus *Podozamites* and possibly also of the genera *Taeniopteris* and *Otozamites*. Ferns were common and conifers were also well represented.

7. Cretaceous. In this period many of the plant types of the Jurassic survived, the prominent groups being the cycads, the ginkgos and the conifers. The pine forests which occurred in many places contained species closely related to the hoop pine and the celery-top pine. Of great interest, however, is the appearance during this period of the flowering plants (ANGIOSPERMAE).

8. Tertiary. Though the fossil remains of angiosperms are common in the rocks of this period they are often difficult to identify; wood and leaves were often preserved but flowers, on which classification depends, are rare as fossils. A dominant group of this period and one used as evidence of continental drift was the genus of the southern beeches, *Nothofagus* (*see* BEECHES, SOUTHERN). Some coal measures, such as those of the LATROBE RIVER valley, were laid down during the Tertiary.

9. Quaternary. The main changes in the flora during this period were as a result of increasing aridity but no good fossil floras have yet been found.

Invertebrates Many Australian invertebrate fossils are identical or closely related to forms found in other parts of the world. This is not surprising because many of them are the remains of marine animals.

1. Precambrian. There are very few animal fossils in Precambrian rocks. Various explanations have been given for this scarcity, including the probable soft-bodied nature of the early animals, the possible chemical characteristics of the sea and the fact that such old rocks as the Precambrian had a greater chance of being metamorphosed than rocks laid down in later periods. A remarkable Precambrian marine fauna, discovered in 1947 at Ediacara SA, included WORMS, jellyfish and sea pens (*see* COELENTERATES), soft CORALS and ARTHROPODS, and several forms which cannot yet be placed in any known group. Some were as large as 50cm long and it is believed that they were all feeders on organic debris.

2. Cambrian. By the beginning of the Cambrian most of the major phyla had appeared; by the end of the period the only major phylum that had not appeared was the Chordata (CHORDATES).

The first reef-building animals, the Archaeocyatha, appeared early in this period and persisted for about 30 million years. Their classification is a matter of controversy: some authors place them among the SPONGES (Porifera), and some put them in a phylum of their own. They are hollow, double-walled cylinders or cones standing on their points.

The Cambrian also saw the first known appearance of SEA LILIES (Echinodermata) and LAMP SHELLS (Brachiopoda); a few brachiopods still exist, including one species of the genus *Ligula* which has changed little from the primitive Cambrian brachiopods. Univalve molluscs (*see* GASTROPODS) and true worms (ANNELIDS) also made their appearance during this period; some Cambrian rocks contain fossilised bryozoa (*see* ECTOPROCTS; ENDOPROCTS).

The dominant animals of the Cambrian seas were the TRILOBITES, which did not become extinct till the end of the Palaeozoic. There are over 600 known Australian Cambrian trilobites, though not all have been described. They show such a diversity that the group must have existed long before the beginning of the Cambrian.

3. Ordovician. This period saw the beginnings of the reef-building corals (in E Australia), the CEPHALOPODS and BIVALVE MOLLUSCS, but the most characteristic Ordovician fossils are the graptolites, peculiar animals now recognised as being related to the chordates; their remains resemble pencil scribblings on the rock surface, hence their name, which means 'stone writing'. Graptolites were colonial animals living in a branching, chitinous exoskeleton; most floated on the sea surface. Australian rocks show the most nearly complete series so far found in the world. The

group arose during the Cambrian and became extinct during the Carboniferous.

4. Silurian. Silurian fossils, very common in some parts of E Australia, resemble those of the Ordovician. Sea lilies were very common, their remains sometimes forming limestones (for example, at Rockley NSW). Remains of SEA STARS and sea scorpions (Eurypterids) have been found in Australian Silurian rocks (for example, near Melbourne), and trilobites were still common (for example, near YASS) in this period. Massive coral reef building took place in the Silurian, the reefs probably being formed in conditions similar to those in which they are built today.

5. Devonian. This is the period in which the plants consolidated their invasion of the land, opening the way to colonisation by animals. The marine fauna included a series of ammonoid cephalopods in WA which resemble closely those of Eurasia during the same period; in fact, many of the marine animals (such as brachiopods, ostracods and crustaceans) were shared with Eurasia during the Devonian. Brachiopods and corals were abundant, the trilobites were declining and the graptolites disappeared.

6. Carboniferous. Most of the major groups were still present in this period but by at least the later part of it the affinities with Europe had been lost, and there are many indications that at this time Australia was in a relatively cold part of the world. Corals were less important but crinoids and brachiopods were still abundant; trilobites were becoming scarcer.

7. Permian. The marine fauna during this period contained many molluscs. There are no Permian coral reefs in Australia, though single corals existed. Bryozoans, however, were common, as were sea lilies and sea stars, and the brachiopods reached their peak in numbers and diversity. Bivalve molluscs became more varied than the gastropods.

It seems that a wide variety of insects were common in the Permian; many have been found in the upper coal measures of the NEWCASTLE district in NSW. These include BUGS (Hemiptera), BOOKLICE (Psocoptera), ANTLIONS AND LACEWINGS (Neuroptera), BEETLES (Coleoptera), CADDIS FLIES (Trichoptera), SCORPION FLIES (Mecoptera) and some probable ancestors of FLIES (Diptera). Insects of the COCKROACH (Blattodea) group of orders are, strangely, missing apart from one species of STONEFLY (Plectoptera).

8. Triassic. Insect fossils have been found in several places in Triassic rocks in Australia. Some of the wings found at Brookvale, Sydney, a world-famous site, show the pigmentation pattern. The assemblage of insect fossils varies from site to site, cockroaches, for example, being dominant among insects found at Mt Crosby QLD and beetles being most numerous at the site at Denmark Hill QLD. Many insect species of this period were much larger than any living now. Brookvale also yielded specimens of a crustacean (*Anaspides* species) thought to be extinct till rediscovered in TAS mountain lakes in 1906.

Triassic marine deposits in Australia are not

widespread but those found show that the early Triassic fauna of Australia was related to that in other parts of the world. Brachiopods were declining and molluscs, especially cephalopods, were becoming more important; ammonoid cephalopods were particularly common.

9. Jurassic. The only marine Jurassic formations in Australia are found in WA, with a good site near GERALDTON. These sites indicate the importance during this period of molluscs, ostracods, ammonites, and belemnites. One of the most interesting mollusc fossils (*Trigonia* species), a bivalve with a more-or-less triangular outline and a complex hinge, was thought to be extinct till found in Sydney Harbour.

10. Cretaceous. The sea covered much of the continent in this period and the climate was relatively cool in the S and E. In the Great Artesian Basin there are rich fossil deposits of ammonites, belemnites, gastropods, molluscs and ECHINODERMS. Different kinds of fossilised ammonites are to be found in the Cretaceous chalks of W and NW Australia where Foraminifera (PROTOZOONS) made up much of the chalk deposits.

The end of the Cretaceous saw the sudden disappearance of many groups of organisms, including the ammonites and the belemnites, and changes in the composition of other groups, such as the Foraminifera.

11. Tertiary. The marine invertebrate fauna of the Tertiary was similar to that of today, though with different species and often different genera. Foraminifera were very common, some of them (for example, *Nummulites* species) reaching a diameter of between 1cm and 2cm.

Vertebrates Vertebrates are generally rare as fossils compared with, for example, bivalve molluscs and brachiopods.

1. Ordovician. The rocks of this period contain the ostracoderms, the earliest vertebrate fossils. These small, jawless, fish-like animals whose well-armoured bodies are covered with bone are related to the modern LAMPREYS. They have been found in sandstones in the Amadeus Basin NT and are probably the oldest vertebrates yet discovered in the S hemisphere. There is strong evidence that ostracoderms lived in freshwater where they strained organic material from the mud. They persisted into the Devonian.

2. Silurian. Though ostracoderms have been found in Silurian deposits in the N hemisphere, none are known of this age in Australia.

3. Devonian. This period is popularly known as the 'age of fishes'. True jawed fishes had become common by the Devonian though they were quite different from most living now (*see* FISHES, BONY). Several rich deposits, found since the mid-1950s, are still being studied.

Lower Devonian deposits near Wee Jasper NSW and Buchan VIC yielded the fossils of the earliest relatives of the QUEENSLAND LUNG FISH and relatives of the COELOCANTH. The deposits also yielded fossilised arthrodires which belonged to the placoderm group—

jawed fishes with heavy plating on the surface. The arthrodires had a joint or hinge between the bony head shield and the ring of armour behind it; bony plates served as jaws and teeth and the fish probably opened and closed its mouth by raising its head.

Middle Devonian freshwater deposits in western NSW have produced various arthrodires (*Wuttagoonaspis* species and others) and acanthodians, small fishes called 'spiny sharks' though unrelated to the true SHARKS.

Upper Devonian freshwater deposits in the KIMBERLEYS in WA and in the NT, VIC and NSW indicate that the commonest fish were antiarchs, a group of placoderms with jointed fins. Some of the deposits also contained early crossopterygians known as rhipidistians. Shark-like fishes are known from the Devonian in other parts of the world but not, so far, in Australia.

The Devonian saw the development of the first land vertebrates, primitive AMPHIBIANS somewhat similar in shape to massive newts. Their footprints have been discovered in Devonian rocks at the Genoa River in VIC, and an amphibian jaw, of the labyrinthodont *Metarygnathus*—claimed to be the oldest record in the world of a four-footed animal —has been found at FORBES in NSW.

4. Carboniferous. A few deposits of Carboniferous vertebrates—all fishes—have been found in Australia. The groups represented are the palaeoniscids (ray-finned fishes with thick, ganoid scales, represented today by the sturgeons and their allies), acanthodians, lung fishes and crossopterygians.

5. Permian. A few fossilised fishes, mainly ganoids, have been found in the Newcastle coal measures, and a few sites in WA have yielded the remains of small sharks. Also found in the Newcastle coal measures were fossilised labyrinthodont amphibians.

6. Triassic. The Australian Triassic is far richer in vertebrate remains than the Permian. Most of the fishes are freshwater species though at St Peters, Sydney, it is probable that the water was sometimes brackish, sometimes fresh. The fossilised fishes found there included ganoids and a 1.5m-long shark. There are several other sites in the Sydney Basin (for example, at GOSFORD) and a rich deposit was also found on the banks of the DERWENT RIVER at Hobart shortly after the collapse of some sections of the Tasman Bridge in 1975.

Fossilised Murray cod, 20 million years old

Australian Triassic sites, such as the Sydney Basin, the Fitzroy Trough SW of the Kimberleys, the Blina Shale WA, the Perth Basin and the BOWEN Basin QLD have yielded a variety of fossilised amphibians and the remains of several Triassic REPTILES. Until the 1980s, however, there were no traces of mammal-like reptiles. Recently a part of the upper jaw of an undoubted mammal-like reptile, probably the dicynodon *Kannemeyeria* that occurred on other Gondwanaland landmasses, was found in early Triassic rocks (240 to 220 million years old) in south-eastern QLD. It was a stocky, short-legged herbivore.

In 1891 the remains of a palaeopod, *Agrosaurus*, were brought from somewhere on the NE coast of Australia, presumably from Triassic deposits. Palaeopods belong to one of the two dinosaur groups and have some features in common with the huge, herbivorous sauropods, and some with the carnivorous theropods (*see below*, under Jurassic).

The fossilised remains of thecodonts, which were ancestral to the dinosaurs, have been found in the Bowen Basin and in TAS. The thecodonts found so far are all Proterosuchians—sprawling, crocodile-like predators. The skulls of small, LIZARD-like cotylosaurs, a group which is probably ancestral to the turtles and the remains of eosuchians, ancestral to lizards and snakes, were also found in the Bowen Basin.

7. Jurassic. This, with the following Cretaceous, was the age of the dinosaurs but at least two labyrinthodonts, *Austropelor* and the 'Kolane amphibian', survived into the Jurassic in QLD. Australia has therefore yielded the first and the last known labyrinthodonts.

There are two groups of dinosaurs, the Saurischia ('lizard-hips') and the Ornithischia ('bird-hips') which are distinguished by their pelvic girdles. The Saurischia includes the palaeopods, the huge, quadripedal, herbivorous sauropods, and the bipedal, carnivorous theropods. In the Ornithischia are bipedal ornithopods and heavily armoured forms such as ankylosaurs; all were herbivores. The remains of a large sauropod, *Rhaetosaurus* (c. 12m long and 3.7m tall), were excavated near ROMA, QLD in the 1920s.

8. Cretaceous. During this time much of the continent was covered by the sea in which lived various marine reptiles. The skulls and partial skeletons of ichthyosaurs, fish-shaped reptiles up to 7m long, have been found in QLD, and parts of plesiosaurs, long-necked, short-bodied 'sea-monsters' such as *Cimiliosaurus* and *Woolungasaurus*, have been unearthed in QLD, NSW, WA and SA. Four or five kinds of pliosaurs, (short-necked relatives of plesiosaurs) are known, the most spectacular being the 13m long *Kronosaurus queenslandicus*. Many specimens of a marine turtle, *Notochelene*, are known from QLD.

Various fragments of saurischian dinosaurs have been discovered in Australian Cretaceous deposits, including the vertebrae of a giant sauropod, *Austrosaurus*. Until recently, however, there was no sure evidence of the carnivorous theropods but since 1980 Flan-

nery and Rich have reported foot fragments of *Allosaurus* in Cretaceous rocks near INVERLOCH, VIC. *Allosaurus* dinosaurs were up to 10m long and 4m tall. Two other forms have been found at LIGHTNING RIDGE, NSW —*Rapator* and *Kakuru*. The second was about the size of a heron.

The remains of an ornithopod related to the bipedal herbivore *Iguanodon* of the N hemisphere have been excavated in QLD and named *Muttaburrasaurus*. The 7m long dinosaur had a unique inflated hollow bony roof over the snout; its function is not known. In VIC, fragments of at least two kinds of ornithischian dinosaurs close to *Hypsilophodon* or *Dryosaurus* dinosaurs of other parts of the world have been found. These remains, and those of the *Allosaurus* were, however, in rocks 10 to 40 million years younger than any rocks in which such fossils have been found in other countries, which suggests that Australia was a refuge for forms that had become extinct elsewhere. A small ankylosaur, *Minmi*, was found near Roma, QLD. Flying reptiles were also unknown in the Australian fossil record before 1979 when the remains of a small marine fish-eating pterosaur, (wingspan about 2m) were excavated in western QLD.

There are, besides the remains of the animals themselves, other traces of Jurassic and Cretaceous reptiles. Dinosaur tracks, for example, are common and at WINTON, QLD there are thousands of individual prints which tell of a drama that occurred more than 65 million years ago. A group of more than 130 small theropods and ornithopods at a water hole were disturbed by a large theropod, and fled, superimposing their tracks over some of his—or hers. None of the forms in the cast have yet been found as skeletal remains.

Deposits at Koonwarra VIC have yielded a rich fauna of fishes, including several ray-finned species, a lung fish, *Ceratodus*, and several insect larvae. Of particular interest, however, were five bird feathers and two specimens of FLEAS of a kind believed to parasitise mammals. This is the first evidence, indirect though it is, of BIRDS and MAMMALS in Australia. The fossil feathers are the oldest known bird remains in the world, apart from those of *Archaeopteryx*.

9. Tertiary and Recent. In the early Tertiary the freshwater fauna included various fishes, CROCODILES and turtles (*see* TORTOISES, etc.), while the marine fauna in S parts of Australia included sharks, rays, PENGUINS and squalodont whales (*see* DOLPHINS, etc.). Some of the later reptiles, such as the varanid lizard (*Megalania* species; over 6m long), were large compared with modern species.

From the later Oligocene the birds begin to appear in the fossil record. Among the first were penguins but marine and aquatic birds in general are well represented. This is not surprising as they lived in habitats where fossilisation was likely, unlike song birds which live in woodland areas. Flamingos, now unknown in Australia, were common. The most notable birds were the huge carnivorous Dromorthinidae which were endemic to Australia. They were emu-like (though not now regarded as being closely related to the emus) and had large, almost hoof-like feet. They included the largest known bird, *Genyornis stirtoni* (*c.* 3m or more tall, and 500kg). Four genera and six species are known from the mid-Tertiary and the group survived till at least 26 000 BP. It may be, therefore, that dromorthinids were the legendary 'mihirung paringmal' dreaded by the Aborigines.

Despite the above-mentioned fleas found in Cretaceous deposits, mammals put in a late appearance in the Australian fossil deposits. Marsupial fossils are known from Cretaceous deposits in North America and it is presumed that the MARSUPIALS reached Australia by a S route, through Antarctica, soon after they arose in the Americas. The oldest-known Australian marsupial fossils (about 23 million years old; very late Oligocene or early Miocene) were excavated in about 1866 at Geilston Bay on the N shore of the Derwent estuary, TAS. At least three different kinds of mammals appear to be represented among these fossils, all belonging to the order Diprotodonta. Two of them resembled POSSUMS; one should probably be placed in the Phalangeridae, the other in the Burramyidae. The third, a larger animal, resembles a member of the extinct family Diprotodontidae, namely *Ngapakaldia*, of later Miocene deposits. Early Miocene deposits at Fossil Bluff TAS yielded *Wynyardia bassiana*, about 21.4 million years old. The diversity of these four mammals indicates that the marsupials had radiated considerably from the original invaders of the continent and this suggests that they arrived long before the Oligocene, possibly in the Cretaceous (as the fleas at Koonwarra suggest).

Between 1838, the year in which the first Australian fossil mammals were described, and 1977, 137 species were discovered; half were described before 1900 and 40 per cent after 1954. Australian mammalian palaeontology is clearly blooming after half a century of comparative neglect and it is probable that many more species will be discovered in the near future.

Families of mammals that are represented by fossils before the Recent period

1. Dasyuridae. Members of this family, which contains NATIVE CATS AND THEIR ALLIES, are known from mid-Miocene deposits, such as those at Ngapakadi SA. One species, *Ankotarinja burnei*, shows features intermediate between those of the dasyurids and the Didelphidae, the family (unknown in Australia) which contains the Virginia opossum and several other American marsupials. It is not, however, old enough to be ancestral to the Dasyuridae as a whole.
2. Thylacinidae. A tooth of a thylacine and an animal very similar to the modern thylacine (TASMANIAN WOLF), namely *Thylacinus potens*, have been discovered in late-Miocene deposits in SA and the NT respectively. The modern thylacine was found on the mainland till it disappeared at about the time that the DINGO invaded the continent.

3. Phascolarctidae. This family contains the KOALA, apparently a remnant of a once much larger, more diverse family. The family's known fossil history stretches back to several mid-Miocene deposits in SA.
4. Peramelidae and Thylaromidae. These families contain the BANDICOOTS, fossils of which have been found in mid-Miocene deposits at Kutjamarpu SA and indicate that they were very similar to the modern forms. The fossils of rabbit-eared bandicoots have been found in mid-Pliocene deposits in SA.
5. Vombatidae. This family contains the WOMBATS. At least two wombat genera, *Phascolonus* and *Rhizophascolonus*, existed in the Tertiary. *P. gigas*, a Pleistocene form which may also have occurred earlier, was about the size of a large pig and thus is an example of the group of extinct marsupials that were much larger than their living relatives.
6. Diprotodonoidea or Diprotodontidae. This extinct superfamily or family (opinions vary) consisted of two separate groups of diprotodonts which probably should be recognised as full families: Palorchestidae and Diprotodontidae.

The Geilston Bay fauna contained a member of the group which was probably a palorchestid, and which was smaller than the later forms. The skulls of palorchestids found in mid-Miocene and Pleistocene deposits suggest that these animals had a tapir-like small trunk, and were possibly browsers on vegetation.

Diprotodontids, of which there were many kinds and which persisted from the Miocene to the Pleistocene, were also browsers. The family contains the largest of all marsupials, *Diprotodon optatum*, a wombat-shaped animal about 3m long and 2m tall. Large diprotodonts lived side by side with the early Aborigines who, some authors believe, exterminated them.

Courtesy of A.I.S. Canberra

Skeleton parts of the diprotodon

7. Phalangeridae. The earliest phalangers date from the late Oligocene.
8. Petauridae. This family includes the early Pliocene *Pseudokoala*.

9. Thylacoleonidae. This extinct family of marsupial lions is best known from *Thylacoleo*, a leopard-sized predator with remarkable shearing teeth, which lived from the lower Pliocene to the Pleistocene. The earliest definite members of the family (*Wakaleo* species) lived in middle to late Miocene times.
10. Macropodidae and Potoiridae. The members of this group, KANGAROOS AND WALLABIES, were relatively late on the scene. They diversified mainly during the Pliocene and Pleistocene but potoroo-like forms are known from the Miocene. The earliest macropodines (the large kangaroo and wallaby group) may be represented by teeth from the mid-Miocene deposits in SA, and at least two species have been found in the late Miocene deposits at Alcoota NT. The kangaroos and wallabies were not the dominant marsupials during the Miocene and they probably became important only with the spread of grasslands. Some of the later kangaroos were much larger than the modern forms. *Sthenurus* and *Procoptodon*, which survived into the Pleistocene, were tall, short-skulled, massively built animals which browsed on the foliage of trees. Important sites for these and other giant marsupials include Lake Callabonna in SA and the caves at WELLINGTON in NSW.
11. Chiroptera. The oldest placental mammal (*see* EUTHERIAN MAMMALS) fossil known from Australia is a BAT, represented by a tooth in the mid-Miocene deposits at Ngapakaldi SA.
12. Cetacea. The only other Tertiary placentals known from Australia are whales, though it is possible some seal fossils are also Tertiary.
13. Muridae. This family contains the RODENTS, the earliest known remains of which come from early Pliocene deposits from northeastern QLD and early to middle Pliocene deposits at Chinchilla, south-east QLD. The latter belong to the pseudomyine rodents which are endemic to Australia and New Guinea.
14. Families of the order Monotremata. Australian rocks have so far given no indication of the ancestry of MONOTREMES which almost certainly arose in the region. The living forms do not possess teeth when adults so it is difficult to relate them to any extinct group of mammals. The remains of one Tertiary platypus, *Obdurodon insignis*, dated as mid-Miocene, give little idea of the animal. The Pleistocene fossils of echidnas and the platypus are very similar to modern forms.

See also fossil man; geology

Further reading: Romer, A.S. *The Procession of Life.* The World Publishing Co., Cleveland & New York, 1968; Colbert, E.H. *Evolution of the Vertebrates.* (2nd edn) Wiley, New York, 1969; Laseron, C. *Ancient Australia.* (2nd edn) Angus & Robertson, Sydney, 1969; Fletcher, H.O. 'Fossils of the Sydney district' in *The Natural History of Sydney.* Australian Museum, Sydney, 1972; Waldman, M. 'The fossil lake-fauna of Koonwarra, Victoria' in *Australian Natural History.* (vol 17, no 10, 1973); Stahl, B.J. *Vertebrate History: Problems in Evolution.* McGraw-Hill, New York, 1974;

Black, R.M. *The Observer's Book of Fossils.* Warne, London, 1977; Archer, M. & Bartholomai, A. 'Tertiary animals of Australia: a synoptic review' in *Alcheringa.* (vol 2, 1978); Flannery, T.F. & Rich, T.H. 'Dinosaur digging in Victoria' in *Australian Natural History.* (no 6, vol 20, 1981); Rich, P.V. and Thompson, E.M. (eds.). *The Fossil Vertebrate Record of Australasia,* 1st revision. Monash University, Melbourne, 1983; Quirk, S. and Archer, U. (eds.), P. Schouten (illustrator) *Prehistoric Animals of Australia.* Australian Museum, Sydney, 1983.

fowl, mallee *see* mound birds

fowl, scrub *see* mound birds

fox *see* animals, introduced

Fox, Emanuel Phillips (1869-1915)

Artist. Born in Melbourne, the son of a Melbourne photographer, Fox studied at the National Gallery School and in Paris. He returned to Australia in 1890 with a good knowledge of Impressionism, then the avant-garde painting movement in Paris, and attempted to establish the Melbourne School of Art with his friend, Tudor St George Tucker. The school was dedicated to more progressive painting attitudes but its existence was short-lived. In 1902 Fox returned to Europe, where he married Ethel Carrick, a Slade School student. Periods in Paris, Tahiti, England, Spain and Algeria were followed by visits to Australia in 1908 and 1912. Fox absorbed the teachings of the French Impressionists more wholeheartedly than his contemporaries, bringing to Australian artists ideas and methods which were typical of the Impressionist movement, such as unstudied compositions and the portrayal of groups of people doing ordinary things. His masterpiece, *The Art Students* (1895), is a marvellous depiction of two of his pupils at work, and has the distinction of being amongst the great Australian paintings in the collection of the Art Gallery of New South Wales. Fox was one of the few Australian artists of his period whose work had a quality that took it out of the provincial atmosphere into which the artist was born.

Frances Creek

NT An iron ore mining site, it is about 25km N of PINE CREEK in the headwater catchment of the Mary River which flows N to VAN DIEMEN GULF. The mine commenced operations in 1967 and the ore is carried from the mine along a branch rail link to the North Australian Railway at Pine Creek.

Franklin River *see* Gordon River

Franklin, Sir John (1786-1847)

Lieutenant-Governor of TAS and Arctic explorer. Born in Lincolnshire, England, he joined the British Navy at the age of 14, fought in the Battles of Copenhagen and Trafalgar, and between these two engagements sailed with Matthew FLINDERS on his circumnavigation of Australia in the *Investigator.* Between 1819 and 1827 Franklin led two very important exploration expeditions in the far N of Canada.

Franklin was appointed Lieutenant-Governor of TAS in 1836, arriving there early in the following year. At the time, the colony was passing through a difficult transition stage, and was the scene of bitter faction fighting. Many settlers hoped that the departure of the authoritarian Lieutenant-Governor ARTHUR would herald an increase in self-government, but the abolition of transportation to NSW in 1840 resulted in an increase in the number of convicts sent to TAS, and removed all hopes of immediate political progress. At the same time, against the advice of Franklin, the practice of assigning convicts to settlers was abandoned, and so he was faced with the task of reorganising the whole convict system. Despite the fact that Franklin's policies in dealing with these problems were conscientious and well meaning, he suffered considerable criticism. Liberals attacked him for not siding openly with them against the 'Arthur faction'—the officials whom he had inherited from Arthur's regime. On the other hand, a number of leading officials undermined his work, and one of them, John Montagu, whom he dismissed from the post of Colonial Secretary, was largely responsible for having him recalled to England in 1843.

His second wife, Lady Jane Franklin, had accompanied him to Tasmania, and had taken an active part in the intellectual life of the colony, establishing a museum and founding a society which later became the Royal Society of Tasmania. In 1845 Franklin led an Arctic expedition in the *Erebus,* but his vessel was trapped in pack-ice and he died within sight of the Northwest Passage which explorers had sought for so long, and of which he is officially recognised as the discoverer.

Further reading: Fitzpatrick, K. *Sir John Franklin in Tasmania 1837-1843.* Melbourne University Press, Melbourne, 1949.

Franklin, Stella Maria Sarah Miles (1879-1954)

Novelist. Born at Talbingo, in the MONARO district of southern NSW, Miles Franklin won critical acclaim at an early age with the satirical novel *My Brilliant Career* (1901). Disturbed, however, by the belief of some of her friends and relatives that they had been caricatured in this work, she left Australia not long after its publication, engaged in social work in Chicago for 12 years and later lived in England. She returned to Australia in 1927 and lived in Sydney for the rest of her life. Six of her novels were written under the name BRENT OF BIN BIN. Works published under her own name include *Some Everyday Folk and Dawn* (1909), which features feminist ideas, *Old Blastus of Bandicoot* (1931), *Bring the Monkey* (1933), *All That Swagger* (1936), *My Career Goes Bung* (1946) and *Sydney Royal* (1947), a story for children. *Pioneers on Parade* (1939) was written in col-

Miles Franklin from the photograph by Henry Dorner, Goulburn 1902

laboration with Dymphna Cusack, and *Joseph Furphy: The Legend of a Man and His Book* (1944) in collaboration with Kate Baker. Her most notable novel is undoubtedly *All That Swagger* which, like most of the Brent of Bin Bin novels, is set in the Monaro district and deals with the fortunes of a pioneer family.
See also literature
Further reading: Barnard, M. *Miles Franklin.* (revd edn) Hill of Content, Melbourne, 1967.

Fraser, Dawn (1937-)

Swimmer. Born in Sydney, she was introduced to swimming as a five-year-old by her elder brother Don and was to become the greatest woman swimmer the world has ever known. Possessed of an intense will to win, she created swimming history by winning the 100m gold medal in three successive Olympics—Melbourne 1956, Rome 1960 and Tokyo 1964. In her determination to win and to win well she managed to subdue her sometimes rebellious nature and submit to a gruelling programme which included swimming seven or eight miles each day, sometimes with her legs tied together and sometimes towing an open petrol drum through the water. In the swimming pool she could erase the effects of her latest difference of opinion with the swimming authorities, or even of sickness, and focus solely on winning. And this she did with considerable authority, setting along the way some 40 world records and making history by being the first woman to break the minute barrier for the 100m. A film of her life, entitled *Dawn!,* was released in 1978.

Fraser Island

QLD A long sandy island, also called Great Sandy Is, located off the SE coast of the State, E of MARYBOROUGH, it is separated from the mainland at its S end by a narrow channel, called Great Sandy Strait, and at its N end by the wide stretch of HERVEY BAY. Fraser Is stretches for 123km N-S, and varies in width E-W from five to about 25km, with contrasting landscapes ranging from rainforests and mangrove swamps to sand dunes, long surf beaches, lagoons and numerous inland freshwater lakes. Timber-getting on the island has been a major industry since the 1860s; logs go by barge to processing mills at Maryborough. There are State forest areas in the S part of the island, some planted with pines. The N section of the island is a national park, called Great Sandy National Park covering 52 400ha of eucalypt woodland, heath, lakes and swamps. In 1975, despite opposition by conservationists, approval was given by the Federal Government for the mining of sands on the island. However, the controversy was so sharp within government ranks, that a commission of enquiry was set up to examine the environmental impact of this mining. As a result of the commission's report, the government banned the export of mineral sands from Fraser Island and mining ceased in late 1976. There are several resort centres on the island, such as Orchid Beach, Eurong Beach, Happy Valley and Dilli Villi, but tourism is still in its infancy and a vacation there is for the adventurous holidaymaker. A number of ferry and air services operate from the mainland, though the flight times depend on the tides because the aeroplanes land on the beach. Except for a 20km stretch of bitumen road in the far S of the island, a four-wheel drive vehicle is essential for travel. The most E point of the island, Indian Head, was so named by Captain James COOK in 1770 because its shape resembled an Aboriginal and in those days Aborigines were called Indians. The island is named after a sea captain who was wrecked on a reef near ROCKHAMPTON, made his way S by longboat and reached the island in 1836. All the members of his party, except his wife, were murdered by Aborigines.

Fraser, (John) Malcolm (1930-)

Prime Minister. Born in Melbourne, Malcolm Fraser was educated at Melbourne Grammar School and Magdalen College, Oxford, from which he graduated MA. He then took over his father's grazing property, Nareen, near HAMILTON in western VIC, and in 1955 stood successfully as Liberal candidate for the seat of Wannon in the House of Representatives. Despite his obvious ambition and ability he remained a backbencher for 11 years, after which he held the portfolios of the Army (1966-68), Education and Science (1968-69) and Defence (1969-71). His resignation from Cabinet in 1971, on the grounds of Prime Minister GORTON's alleged lack of trust in him, caused the crisis which shortly afterwards resulted in the replacement of Gorton by William McMAHON, under whom Fraser again became Minister for Education and Science.

After the Labor victory in December 1972, the leadership of the Liberal Party was gained by B.M. Snedden. However, during the following few years support for Snedden dwindled, and in March 1975 Fraser was elected in his place. Several months later he brought about a constitutional crisis by deciding to use the Opposition's control of the Senate to defer consideration of two Appropriation Bills (see Sir John KERR). This led to the dismissal of the WHITLAM government, the appointment of Fraser as caretaker Prime Minister, and the sweeping Liberal/National Country Party victory in the elections of December 1975. As Prime Minister he concentrated his attention on the state of the economy, keeping as his main aim the lowering of the inflation rate by measures which included reductions in government expenditure and efforts to minimise wage increases. Many critics called for a modification of this policy, particularly in view of the rising level of unemployment. Nevertheless, he won another convincing victory in the election of December 1977. In December 1980 he again led the coalition to victory in the House of Representatives, albeit with a reduced majority. However, he failed to preserve for it an outright majority in the Senate, where it became dependent on the support of the AUSTRALIAN DEMOCRATS. Following the coalition's defeat in the general election of March 1983, Fraser was succeeded as Prime Minister by Bob HAWKE. At the same time he resigned the leadership of the Liberal Party, being succeeded by Andrew PEACOCK, and a few weeks later resigned from Parliament.

Dept Administrative Services

The Rt. Hon. J.M. Fraser

Fraser, Neale Andrew (1933-)

Tennis player. Born in Melbourne, this dedicated and talented sportsman was to achieve success not only as a player but also as the non-playing captain/coach of the Australian Davis Cup team. Rocketing to international status as a member of the Australian Davis Cup team which won the Cup for four years in succession, 1959-62, Fraser was also carving a more personal niche in tennis history by winning the most sought-after international titles. He won the French singles in 1958 and 1960, the prestigious US singles in 1959 and 1960 and the highly prized Wimbledon singles in 1960. In addition, he teamed up with Roy EMERSON to win the Wimbledon doubles title in 1959 and 1961. He retired from active competition in 1962 but in 1970 he became active once again as the non-playing captain/coach of the Australian Davis Cup team. In this capacity he was also successful, guiding Australia to victory in 1973, 1977 and 1983. In 1974 he was appointed MBE for his services to tennis.

Frater, William 'Jock' (1890-1974)

Artist. Born at Ochiltree in Scotland, Frater studied at the Glasgow Art School while serving his articles as an apprentice in a stained-glass firm, Brooks Robinson. He visited Melbourne in 1910 and returned to live there permanently in 1914. At Brooks Robinson, he had met Arnold SHORE, with whom he became involved in the movement to promote modern art in Melbourne, later forming a threesome with George BELL. He was inspired by the first colour reproductions to be seen in Australia of the works of such artists as Cézanne, van Gogh, Gauguin, Picasso and Chagall, many of which were sold at Gino Nibbi's Melbourne bookshop, a well-known meeting place for artists. Frater became a devotee of Cézanne, and, with George Bell, formed the Contemporary Group, which held its first exhibition in 1932 and which did much to make the post-Impressionist movement a real force in the Melbourne art community.

The Fremantle Museum and Arts Centre, originally built as an asylum in the 1860's, is a fine example of Colonial Gothic architecture

Fremantle

WA (combined population of Fremantle city and the town of East Fremantle 30 060 in 1981) The major port of WA, built at the mouth of the SWAN RIVER, some 17km by road from Perth city centre, it is now part of the Perth metropolitan area. The port consists of an inner harbour, designed originally by Charles O'CONNOR (whose bronze statue stands on Victoria Quay, overlooking the harbour), and a much larger outer harbour, bounded by ROTTNEST ISLAND to the W and including COCKBURN SOUND to the S. The urban area contains many secondary industries and in the 1970s there was rapid industrial and residential growth associated with the development of KWINANA. Fremantle was first settled in 1829 and named in honour of Captain Charles Fremantle who landed near the Swan estuary and took formal possession of the W coast of the continent for Britain in that year. It was a whaling centre until the 1850s and is still WA's chief fishing port. Until the 1890s ships had to anchor at a deep-water jetty which had been constructed from Anglesea Point near Arthur Head, but this was an unprotected berth exposed to S and W winds. O'Connor's plan for harbour development in the river

mouth, though it raised considerable controversy, was started in 1892 and laid the basis for the subsequent port expansion. Today, Fremantle handles passenger vessels and freighters as well as containers and bulk cargoes. The main imports include oil, steel and phosphates, while the main exports are refined oil, wheat and wool. Over 130 buildings in Fremantle have been listed for preservation by the National Trust (WA), including several churches, homes, a flour mill, bond stores, hotels, banks, the police barracks, the customs house, the railway station and the post office.
Further reading: Ward, K. *Fremantle Sketchbook.* Rigby, Adelaide, 1974.

French, Leonard William (1928-)
Artist. Born in Brunswick VIC, he studied at the Melbourne Technical College, and later visited London, Dublin and Amsterdam. His early apprenticeship to a signwriter encouraged him to think in terms of mural painting, and before he was 20 years old he had completed two murals for the Congregational Church, Melbourne. His early reading of Homer inspired his *Iliad* series of the 1950s and his *Odyssey* series of the mid-1950s. Painting in series became his hallmark. *The Seven Days of Creation* (1968-69) was followed by the *Tongues of Fire,* inspired by the 16th-century martyr Richard Campion. Then in 1971 came *Man on a Raft,* followed by *Death of a Revolution* (1974-76), *Journey Series* (1976) and *Fire and Rain* (1974-78).

French's painting has several elements that are immediately recognisable. He shows a recurring interest in the hero, who, dedicated to duty, pits himself against forces that threaten to overwhelm him; his is always the hero of universal significance, not any specific hero of Australian history or myth. French's work is full of solid, static geometric shapes, frequently enamelled and gold-leafed in an elaborate richness reminiscent of Byzantine mosaics or Celtic enamels. His angular and hard-edged painting has enabled him to adapt easily to stained-glass work, as his windows in the National Library, Canberra, the National Gallery's Great Hall, Melbourne, and Monash University attest. His success as an artist has received much public recognition: he won a Harkness Scholarship in 1964, was made an OBE, and received an honorary D. Litt. from Monash University.

Frenchmans Cap
TAS A white quartzite dome rising to an elevation of 1 443m, it is a mecca for rock climbers. Located in the rugged W of the State, between LAKE ST CLAIR and MACQUARIE HARBOUR, and S of the Lyell Highway, it is the dominant feature of the Frenchmans Cap National Park which covers 13 000ha of rugged wilderness country dotted with lakes of glacial origin. Access to the park is from the Lyell Highway, a journey of 200km from Hobart and 54km from QUEENSTOWN, but those planning a trip along the walking tracks of the park are advised by the State National Parks and Wildlife Service that

'it is primarily a wilderness area and should not be tackled by inexperienced bushwalkers.' The mountain has a 300m-high face on the E side presenting a challenge to the venturesome climber. The Cap is snow-covered in winter; however, the colour of the rock is so near to white that there is little difference in its appearance throughout the year. The naming of Frenchmans Cap is a mystery; it was certainly known by that name as early as 1826 and the generally accepted explanation is that it was so named because it bore 'some resemblance to the shape of that article of dress which invariably adorns the head of a French cook'.

Freycinet Peninsula
TAS Located on the mid-E coast, lying E of GREAT OYSTER BAY adjoining the town of Coles Bay, this peninsula has been a national park since 1916. It was named by Captain BAUDIN in 1802 after the cartographer in his crew. The coastline is much indented by deep bays with precipitous headlands and sandy beaches. It is connected to the mainland by two parallel sand spits separated by lagoons and marshes. The Freycinet Peninsula National Park, which includes Schouten Is to the S, covers 10 010ha and is noted for its red granite outcrops and superb coastal scenery, especially at Wineglass Bay. The highest point on the peninsula is Mt Freycinet, 620m high.

friarbirds *see* honeyeaters

Friend, Donald Stuart Leslie (1915-)
Artist. Born in Sydney, he studied at Dattilo Rubbo's School in Sydney and at the Royal Art Society School and Westminster School in London. This was followed by two years in Nigeria, acting as adviser to the Chief of Ikeri, before returning to Australia in 1941 where he trained as a gunner for war service. After World War II, he continued to move around, living in BATHURST, Sydney, Colombo, Bali and the TORRES STRAIT. A very fine draughtsman, frequently using pen and ink over wash, and competent in the use of colour, Friend's stylish depictions of the human figure attracted an immediate and popular following. His sympathy for the male figure and his enthusiasm for the non-European, unrestricted by the indulgences of the consumer society or the repressions of middle-class conventionality, has produced work of great charm and vitality.

frigate birds *see* sea birds

froghoppers *see* bugs

frogmouths, nightjars and the owl nightjar
These BIRDS belong to the order Caprimulgiformes, which is made up of three families of nocturnal birds. All have broad bills, surrounded by bristles in most species, and feed on insects and, in some cases, possibly also on small vertebrate animals; they have a mottled brown and grey plumage which acts as an effective camouflage.

The family Podargidae contains the frogmouths, grotesque birds whose extremely wide gape enables them to capture insects easily, which they normally take on the ground. When disturbed while roosting in a tree during the day, they freeze, and cannot be distinguished, except with great difficulty, from the tree itself. Nor can the three Australian species be distinguished easily from each other, although they appear to have different distributions. They occur in forests and woodlands. The tawny frogmouth, *Podargus strigoides** (38cm to 40cm long), is found throughout the continent. Its nests are platforms of twigs, loosely arranged and usually lined with green leaves, and placed in tree forks or on tree stumps. The Papuan frogmouth, *P. papuensis* (48cm to 56cm), and the marbled frogmouth, *P. ocellatus* (33cm to 38cm), occur in CAPE YORK, and some authorities suggest that the latter species also occurs in northern NSW. Both species place their platform nests of sticks and twigs on the horizontal branches of trees or in tree forks.

Nightjars are cryptically coloured birds, with pointed wings and long barred tails, which belong to the family Caprimulgidae. The gape is wide for catching insects on the wing. They usually roost on the ground, but when in a tree they lie along the branch. At night they are more often heard than seen, making gobbling sounds. They are not found in TAS. The white-tailed nightjar, *Caprimulgus macrurus* (length 25cm; tail 12cm to 15cm), belongs to an Old World group of nightjars. It has broad white patches on the tips of the outer tail feathers and long bristles at the edge of the mouth; it occurs in the wet forests and woodlands in coastal areas of QLD and the NT. The eggs are deposited on bare ground.

The spotted nightjar, *Eurostopodus guttatus** (length 30cm; tail 15cm to 18cm), and the white-throated nightjar, *E. mystacalis* (35cm), lack the hair fringes around the beak. The former has a white bar, made up of large spots, on the wing, and light grey, black and brown plumage. It occurs in dry woodland throughout most of Australia, except in the E coastal regions where it is replaced by the white-throated species. The latter is an uncommon species, with a blackish plumage and a white patch on the side of the throat, and inhabits heavily timbered country. Both species hawk for flying insects in the evening or at night, and prefer areas with much ground litter.

The owlet nightjar, *Aegotheles cristatus* (23cm), belongs to the family Aegothelidae. It resembles a small owl but can be distinguished by a broad, square, long, barred tail. This widespread species catches insects on the wing and lays its white eggs in tree hollows lined with leaves.

frogs and toads
These VERTEBRATES form the order Anura, which belongs to the class Amphibia (AMPHIBIANS). Of some 2000 species worldwide, about 136 are known in Australia, though there are undoubtedly several more species awaiting discovery, particularly in the N tropical area. All known

Species, genus or family is endemic to Australia (see Preface)

Australian anurans are frogs as opposed to toads (that is, members of the family Bufonidae) with one exception—the introduced cane toad.

The classification of frogs is difficult and subject to constant revision (this article follows Cogger's classification, *see below*). It is especially difficult to determine the family that a frog belongs to other than by identifying the species of the frog, and from that determining the family. It can be said, however, that any frog found outside CAPE YORK or northernmost NT is either a hylid or leptodactylid. The reverse rule does not apply. The only other possibility is that the frog is really a specimen of the cane toad. Five families have been distinguished in Australia: Leptodactylidae (the 'southern frogs'); Hylidae (the tree frogs, and others); Microphylidae; Ranidae (the true frogs); and Bufonidae (the true toads).

Leptodactylidae This is the largest Australian family, with 19 genera and about 82 species; leptodactylids are called the 'southern frogs' because they occur only in the S hemisphere. They are distinguished from the Hylidae by various skeletal characteristics and by the toes, which have either no discs or only very small ones; and, unlike hylids, they are found only rarely in trees.

The largest genus, *Crinia*, contains 12 species, examples of which may be found in every part of the continent except the arid regions. Many of the species are so alike that they can be distinguished only by the mating calls of the males. The members of this genus are small frogs which are terrestrial as adults. The only one that has a common name, the common eastern froglet, *C. (Ranidella) signifera* (3cm long), is very variable in both skin colour and texture and may be found in almost every habitat in SE Australia and TAS; it breeds in slow-moving creeks and a variety of other kinds of waters.

The genus *Assa* contains the pouched or marsupial frog, *A. darlingtoni* (3cm). In its breeding behaviour, this species resembles sea horses rather than kangaroos for it is the male that has brood pouches (on the flanks) in which the tadpoles develop. The male frog squirms into the middle of the mass of frog spawn and the emerging tadpoles wriggle across his body to enter the pouches. The frogs live in leaf-litter, under logs and so on in *Nothofagus* forests (*see* BEECHES, SOUTHERN) and rainforests in a small area on the QLD/NSW border.

The genus *Rheobatrachus* contains *R. silus* (4cm), a species which has an even more remarkable form of parental care in that the tadpoles develop within the stomach of the female; it is thought that the female swallows the eggs soon after laying them. This species is known only from Kondalilla, near Montville in south-eastern QLD.

The genus *Pseudophryne* contains 10 species commonly known as toadlets. These small, short-limbed species have black and white underparts, and several have brightly coloured patterns on the back. Representatives are found in all States except the NT. The most striking member of the genus is the corroboree frog, *P. corroboree* (3cm); its back is bright yellow or greenish-yellow with shiny, black, longitudinal stripes—presumably a warning coloration. Many *Pseudophryne* frogs lay their eggs on land that is damp for only short periods. The tadpoles develop within the egg to the stage at which they are ready to emerge, and then wait for the next heavy rain before leaving the eggs.

The four species of frogs contained in the genus *Taudactylus* are, compared to the *Pseudophryne* frogs, very aquatic. Known as torrent frogs, they live in mountain streams in QLD.

Waterholding frog, *Cyclorana platycephalus*

Mantis Wildlife Films

Two genera, *Notaden* and *Cyclorana*, contain frogs which live in arid or semi-arid areas, burrowing to avoid the heat and emerging only during and after rain; good examples are the crucifix frog or toad, *N. bennetti* (5cm), and the water-holding frog, *C. platycephalus* (6cm). Like the three other members of its genus, the crucifix frog is a globular species with a warty skin and short limbs. It is yellowish, with a cross of black and reddish warts on the back; it lives in black-soil flood-plains and mallee, mainly in inland NSW, and breeds in temporary pools. The water-holding frog, which ranges right across central Australia, burrows deeply after rain, and makes a waterproofed chamber which fills with water; its bladder also stores water. This species breeds in temporary pools, claypans and creeks.

The 11 frogs of the genus *Limnodynastes*, mainly drably coloured species with strong bodies and powerful limbs, are called marsh frogs, although some are found in dry areas. They lay their eggs in a mass of foam that resembles a detergent raft, whipped up by special flanges on some of the female's digits. Several are also called banjo frogs because of the nature of their calls; the western banjo frog, *L. dorsalis* (7cm), has the alternative name of pobblebonk, for the same reason. The spotted grass frog, *L. tasmaniensis* (4cm), has the greatest range, being found in a variety of habitats from TAS to CAPE YORK. It is mainly white below and light brown to olive green with dark blotches above, with a lighter stripe running along the backbone and a darker band through the eye to the shoulder.

The genus *Myobatrachus* contains a remarkable species, *M. gouldii* (6cm), which is confined to SW Australia. It is known as the turtle frog from its shape, which is so unusual that it is often taken for a shell-less baby turtle. It is a burrowing species that feeds on termites.

The genus *Mixophyes* contains some of Australia's largest frogs. These strong terrestrial frogs have webbed feet and powerful, barred limbs, and live in *Nothofagus* forests and rainforests in E Australia. The giant barred frog, *M. iteratus* (11.5cm), ranges from the BUNYA RANGE of QLD to WOLLONGONG in NSW.

Hylidae This widespread family of frogs contains about 46 Australian species. Belonging to two genera, hylids are commonly known as tree frogs because many of them climb efficiently with the aid of large rounded, often adhesive, discs on the fingers and toes; some, however, have only small discs and are terrestrial, long-limbed animals. Arboreal species tend to have fairly flat bodies and are able to press themselves close to the surface. All hylids are believed to breed in water and most species are found near the coasts in comparatively wet regions, especially in the N and E, though a few range into arid regions.

The genus *Nyctimystes* contains three species, all of which live in Cape York, for the genus is really a New Guinea group. They have large, dark eyes with vertical, elliptical pupils and a network of fine, pigmented lines on the lower eyelid.

The very diverse genus *Litoria* contains 43 species, which are distinguished from the *Nyctimystes* species by the horizontal pupil and the absence of the network on the lower eyelid. One of the best-known species, the green-and-golden bell frog, *L. aurea* (8.5cm), has well-webbed feet but comparatively small discs; whitish below and olive to bright green with large blotches of brown above, it has blue or blue-green thighs. Found in eastern VIC and in E and south-eastern NSW, usually in or very near permanent water, it is a greedy, cannibalistic species.

The green tree frog, *L. caerulea* (10cm), is the most widespread of the genus, ranging from north-western WA to NSW, in coastal areas and in the dry interior. It lives in many different kinds of habitats including man-made structures such as toilets, water tanks and windmills, and often spends the dry season in hollow trees; it breeds in temporary marshes. The upperparts are bright green, often with white spots, and the toe and finger discs are large.

The giant tree frog, *L. infrafrenata* (about 11cm), a generally brown or bright green species, lives in a variety of habitats, including houses and sheds, in E Cape York and New Guinea. In contrast, the northern dwarf tree frog, *L. bicolor* (3cm), is small enough to shelter in the leaf axil of *Pandanus* palms in the dry season.

Microhylidae Although this family is widespread in the warmer parts of the world there are only six species in Australia, and these are believed to be comparatively recent immigrant species (or derivatives of such species) from New Guinea. As the name suggests, many microhylids resemble very small tree frogs, some measuring less than 1cm long. The toes are webbed, and the toe and finger discs, when present, are truncated. They are found only in tropical and subtropical forests, typically at high altitudes. All Australian and New Guinean species that have been studied lay their eggs on land and there is no free-living tadpole stage.

There are two Australian genera in this family: *Cophixalus* (three species) and *Sphenophryne* (three species).

Ranidae Although true frogs are found throughout the world, the family does not really belong to Australia because the single species, the wood frog, *Rana daemelii* (8cm), is a comparatively recent immigrant from New Guinea and occurs only on Cape York.

Bufonidae Although the early settlers called many Australian frogs toads or toadlets because of their warty skin, there is only one true (that is, bufonid) toad in Australia, the cane toad, *Bufo marinus* (up to 23cm). Introduced into QLD cane fields in 1935 to control beetles attacking cane, the cane toad is a stoutly built animal which is native to Central and South America. It seems to have had little effect on the pests that it was supposed to control and is now being considered as a candidate for BIOLOGICAL CONTROL itself. In QLD and New Guinea it can reach a density of one per square metre in gardens. It will attack bees and is toxic to dogs and cats. It makes a revolting mess on the road when run over by a car—a common occurrence. It breeds in still or slow-moving waters, both temporary and permanent, and is highly prolific—a female can lay 40 000 eggs a year. There is probably only one thing that can be said in its favour: it has replaced native frogs in laboratories for teaching and research. Its main distribution is in coastal areas of QLD and northernmost NSW. However, it now reaches LISMORE in NSW, has reached MT ISA in QLD, and is established in the NT. Its spread is due partly to its own powers of locomotion and partly, not doubt to its occurrence in schools' and children's collections.
Further reading: Cogger, H.G. *Reptiles and Amphibia of Australia.* A.H. & A.W. Reed, Sydney, 1975; Tyler, M.J. *Frogs.* Collins, Sydney, 1976.

fruit growing With a climate ranging from tropical to temperate, Australia produces a wide variety of fruit. The most important are apples, pears, stone fruits, berry fruits, citrus, bananas, pineapples and grapes.

Apples and pears Captain PHILLIP brought apple and pear trees with the FIRST FLEET and Captain BLIGH planted apple trees in TAS in 1788. Commercial apple and pear growing began in TAS in the 1840s. Australian production has fallen recently with the loss of traditional European markets. In 1982-83 it was estimated that there were 5 025 000 bearing apple trees and 1 500 000 pear trees in Australia. The numbers had declined steadily from 1974-75 when there were 5 897 000 and over 2 005 000 respectively. In 1965-66 the volume of apples exported was 159 000 tonnes

Table 1

VALUE OF FRUIT EXPORTS
($ mill)

	1978-79	1979-80	1980-81	1981-82*	1982-83*
Apples, fresh	15.6	20.1	15.3	19	14
Pears, fresh	15.7	18.3	19.9	14	16
Pears, canned	17.2	20.0	20.6	14	14
Peaches, canned	12.2	19.3	16.0	15	18
Apricots, canned	0.8	1.5	1.3	1	1
Citrus, fresh	7.9	15.1	12.1	12	16
Pineapples, canned	1.2	3.1	3.5	4	2
Dried vine fruit	46.5	54.6	75.1	45	50

Note : * provisional.
Source : *Quarterly Review of the Rural Economy.* (vol 3, no 2, Aug 1981 and vol 4, no 4, Nov 1982) Australian Govt Publishing Service, Canberra.

Table 2

VOLUME OF FRUIT EXPORTS
('000t)

	1978-79	1979-80	1980-81	1981-82*	1982-83*
Apples, fresh	44.1	53.1	38.9	48	30
Pears, fresh	32.0	32.7	36.0	23	25
Pears, canned	34.5	36.6	36.4	24	26
Peaches, canned	24.9	34.9	26.4	25	31
Apricots, canned	1.5	2.4	1.8	1	1
Citrus, fresh	26.3	44.2	34.2	30	34
Pineapples, canned	1.9	4.3	5.4	5	2
Dried vine fruit	47.2	41.3	51.8	39	58

Note : * provisional.
Source : *Quarterly Review of the Rural Economy.* (vol 5, no 2, Aug 1983) Australian Govt Publishing Service, Canberra.

Table 3

VOLUME OF FRUIT PRODUCTION
('000t)

	1978-79	1979-80	1980-81	1981-82*	1982-83
Apples	334.9	298.8	306.9	295	300
Pears	135.0†	124.3	145.6	110	125
Peaches	64.8	71.5	79.2	65	55
Apricots	31.0	26.4	30.6	27	35
Citrus	455.0†	488.0	537.0	477	495
Bananas	113.1	125.1	124.3	130	150
Pineapples	105.1	123.3	123.3	126	94
Grapes (all purposes)	766.5	919.2	743.4	963	806
Dried vine fruit	61.3†	97.8	61.2	100	80

Note : * provisional.
Source : *Quarterly Review of the Rural Economy.* (vol 5, no 2, Aug 1983) Australian Govt Publishing Service, Canberra.

and of fresh pears 42 600 tonnes. The 1981-82 export volumes (provisional figures) were 48 000 tonnes and 23 000 tonnes respectively. Canned pear exports have continued to decline (1963-64, 55 700 tonnes; 1977-78, 30 000 tonnes; 1981-82, 24 000 tonnes—provisional figures).

Apples grow best in the high rainfall areas of southern Australia (TAS, VIC, SA near Adelaide and south-western WA). They are also grown commercially in parts of NSW and QLD but only at altitudes of over 900m. TAS

now grows about a quarter of the crop, though 30 years ago it grew half of it.

Many varieties are grown. Some ripen earlier than others. Gravenstein is ready in January, while Cox's Orange Pippin (grown mainly in TAS) ripens in February. Other varieties ripen roughly in this order: Jonathon and Delicious in early March, Granny Smith (a variety originating in Australia; *see* SMITH, Maria Ann) and Rome Beauty in late March and Democrat in mid-April. The harvested apples are sold or exported soon after harvest, or placed in cold storage. Some varieties, such as Granny Smith, are particularly good 'keepers', and others are good for juicing and cider making. Pears are grown in roughly the same areas as apples, and much of the pear crop is canned.

Stone fruits The chief stone fruits are peaches and apricots. In 1982–83 there were approximately 1 120 000 peach trees in Australia and 610 000 apricot trees. Other stone fruits grown are plums, cherries and nectarines. All are grown mainly in the SE but some are also produced in the cooler parts of WA and QLD. Much of the produce is canned, dried or jammed, but a considerable amount is sold as fresh either through city markets or at the farm gate.

The varieties are selected according to local conditions and the destination of the produce. Several varieties, such as the Trevatt apricot, which is used for canning, are Australian in origin. Varieties of clingstone peach such as Golden Queen. also supply the canneries. Large canneries are found in the GOULBURN RIVER area of VIC, the MURRUMBIDGEE IRRIGATION AREAS in NSW, and the MURRAY RIVER valley irrigation areas in SA. Prunes are produced mainly near YOUNG and GRIFFITH in NSW and dried apricots and peaches in SA.

Berry fruits Several kinds of berry fruits are produced for dessert purposes and for canning and jamming. The main cultivars are raspberries, black currants, loganberries, gooseberries and strawberries. Most of the berry fruits are grown in TAS. There has been an overall decline since World War II because of rising production costs and declining export markets. In 1975-76 the total area in Australia devoted to berry and small fruits was 684ha whereas in 1949-50 it had reached 2 429ha. Recently, however, there has been an increase in blackcurrant plantings because of the growing popularity of the juice.

Citrus Oranges, lemons and limes have been grown in Australia since the early days of settlement at SYDNEY COVE. Fortunately, areas near Sydney, Brisbane, Perth and Adelaide all proved to be suitable for these fruits. VIC began to grow citrus with the introduction of irrigation, and many citrus groves have since been established near MILDURA and RED CLIFFS in VIC, RENMARK in SA, and LEETON and GRIFFITH in NSW.

About 80 per cent of the citrus fruits grown in Australia are oranges (Valencias about 67 per cent, navels about 33 per cent); the remainder are lemons (eight per cent), mandarins (seven per cent) and grapefruit (five per cent). In all there were about six million citrus trees in Australian in 1983-84; most citrus fruit is sold fresh, but in recent years a large quantity has been juiced.

Bananas Despite the fact that QLD is sometimes known as the 'Banana State', the bulk of the crop (about 80 per cent) is grown in NSW. Banana plants begin to bear fruit when they are about one year old; the bearing area (about 8000ha in 1983-84) is thus smaller than the area planted. Most of the holdings are only three or four hectares in extent.

Orchards at Narromine, Orana Region NSW

Table 4

AVERAGE YIELDS

	1978-79	1979-80	1980-81	1981-82*	1982-83*
Apples, kg/tree	67	56	58	58	60
Pears, kg/tree	94	86	72	72	83
Peaches, kg/tree	52	57	51	51	45
Citrus, kg/tree	80	84	80	80	83
Bananas, t/ha	16.4	17.9	16.3	16.3	18.8
Pineapples, t/ha	26.9	30.1	31.5	31.5	23.5
Grapes, t/ha	11.6	14.1	15	15	12.6

Note: * provisional.
Source: *Quarterly Review of the Rural Economy*. (vol 5, no 2, Aug 1983 and vol 4, no 4, Nov 1982) Australian Govt Publishing Service, Canberra.

The banana plant is not a tree but a giant herb with the stem (corm) below the ground. The apparent stem (pseudo-stem) consists of leaf bases tightly pressed together. Another botanical curiosity of the cultivated banana is that it is seedless: propagation is by suckers which are grown from the stem. Each plant bears only one bunch which is harvested green. Almost all the crop is consumed in Australia. Bananas are prone to diseases, including the virus disease bunchy top, spread by APHIDS, and they are attacked by insect pests, notably the introduced banana weevil borer which, in view of its widespread distribution, has the apt scientific name *Cosmopolites sordidus*.

Pineapples The fruit of the pineapple is the swollen stem which carries the flowers. The plant is propagated usually from suckers and matures after 18 to 24 months, after which it continues to produce fruit for several years. In Australia most pineapples are grown in QLD, and the bearing area is steady at about 4000ha. Part of the crop is fresh and part canned.

Grapes Dessert grapes are discussed in the

entry on the WINE INDUSTRY.

Other fruits Small quantities of tropical fruits, such as mangoes and avocados, are grown in N Australia.

Dried fruit industry Australia is one of the largest producers of dried fruit and a large part of the crop from some areas is preserved in this way. Most dried vine fruits (sultanas, raisins and currants) are produced under irrigation in the Murray Valley, with the industry centred on SUNRAYSIA. Some of the sultana and raisin grapes are, however, diverted to the wine industry for blending. The fruit is dried on racks or hessian trays in the sun. Sultanas and raisins are dipped in preservative before drying. Small quantities of apricots, nectarines, peaches and pears are also dried. Overseas sales of dried fruits are controlled by the Australian Dried Fruits Control Board.
Further reading: Quarterly Review of the Rural Economy. (no 3, vol 1, August 1983).

fuchsia, native This name is given to various heath species belonging to the genus *Epacris* (family EPACRIDACEAE) because of a superficial similarity between the flowers of these species and those of the true fuchsias. *E. longiflora*, for example, has crowded, sharply pointed leaves, and long, tube-shaped, white and red flowers. The red-flowered *Grevillea wilsonii* of WA (family PROTEACEAE) is also called the native fuchsia.

fungi

Fungi are often thought of erroneously as plants, but because they cannot photosynthesise and must derive their food from dead or living organic matter they are best placed in a separate group. Some scientists place them in a kingdom of their own, the Fungi; others prefer a division, the Mycophyta. They differ from the Bacteria (with which they are placed in some classifications) in being eucaryotic (that is, their chromosomes are contained within a nucleus).

The typical fungal body consists of fine threads (hyphae) which collectively are known as the mycelium. The hyphae ramify through the substance upon which the fungus feeds. From time to time the mycelium produces fruiting bodies (the familiar mushrooms in one case) which release spores. The classification of the fungi is based upon the form of the fruiting body and upon the often complex methods of reproduction. Unfortunately, there are many fungi in which the fruiting body is either undiscovered or absent. These fungi are placed in a 'rag-bag' group, the Fungi Imperfecti. From time to time a member of this group is associated with a fruiting body with the result that the fungus is given, for a short time at least, two names.

Many of the smaller fungi are more or less cosmopolitan and a large proportion of these occur in Australia. Many are plant PARASITES and their occurrence depends upon the distribution of their hosts. Some are discussed in the entry on plant diseases (*see* DISEASES, PLANT). Fungi are divided into four classes: Myxomycetes, Phycomycetes, Ascomycetes and Basidiomycetes.

Myxomycetes This class of fungi contains the slime moulds. Slime moulds begin life as a single cell in which nucleus divides many times but without a corresponding division of the cytoplasm. The process of division finally produces the plasmodium, a mass of protoplasm with many nuclei but no dividing cell walls; the plasmodium flows over rotting vegetation, engulfing bacteria and food particles. In dry conditions it may become hardened or it may produce fruiting bodies which release spores. Some slime moulds, such as those found on forest floors, feed as separate individuals which, when mature, assemble in their thousands to form a slug-like plasmodium which then produces a fruiting body.

Phycomycetes This class consists of filamentous fungi with cell walls consisting of chitin or cellulose, or both. The hyphae are usually long and branched, often forming a dense mycelium, but frequently lacking cross walls. The spores are produced on the tips of the hyphae. A typical example is *Rhizopus stolonifer*, a common black mould on bread.

Members of the genera *Entomophthora* and *Empusa* are important parasites of insects, some of which have been used for BIOLOGICAL CONTROL of spotted alfalfa aphids in the USA, and which may be used similarly in Australia.

Ascomycetes This very large and diversified class of fungi contains the yeasts and many multicellular forms. Apart from the yeasts, the ascomycetes have a well-developed mycelium consisting of branched hyphae with cross walls. The spores (ascospores) are characteristically produced within a specialised mother cell (ascus). Normally, the cell division occurs in such a way that the ascus finally contains eight ascospores.

The class contains about 35 000 known species, many of them of great economic importance. They include the *Penicillium* moulds from which the first antibiotics were obtained, yeasts which are important in fermentation processes and destructive powdery mildews which attack plants.

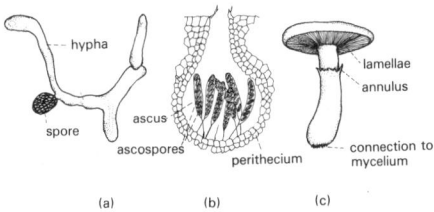

Diagram of a fungi showing: (a) a germinating spore (enlarged); (b) a perithecium containing asci; (c) a mushroom or basidiocarp

Basidiomycetes This class contains most of the large fungi (about 2000 species in Australia) with which the layman is familiar—such as edible mushrooms, toadstools, agarics and bracket fungi—but also many much smaller forms, including some of the most serious diseases of plants. The characteristic feature of this class is the production of the principal spores (basidiospores) on the outside of the mother cell (basidium). Normally, each basidium gives rise to four spores; in the group containing the rusts, however, the basidia occur in chains, sometimes with cross walls, so that many spores are carried. In the larger, more advanced basidiomycetes the large fruiting body has gills which carry and protect the basidia. In the bracket fungi, which grow as shelf-like structures from wood, the basidia are packed inside tiny pores through which the spores escape.

Edible fungi Most large fungi are probably edible but some are extremely poisonous. Furthermore, some species may be harmless to one person but toxic to another, while other species are toxic when taken with alcohol. There is only one rule when it comes to identifying edible fungi, namely, that there is no rule. Each species must be positively identified and in some cases this may be done only by a microscopic examination of the spores. A further difficulty is that many species have not yet been named with certainty in Australia though they may be known by a name applied to a very similar (and, no doubt, often identical) European or North American species.

The following are some of the fungi that have been listed as edible, but as the descriptions given here are brief the reader should not risk his life upon them. Unless otherwise indicated they are all basidiomycetes.

1. Field mushroom; *Agaricus campestris*, and related species. These are similar to the cultivated mushroom, *A. bisporus*, (*see* AGRICULTURE) which rarely grows wild. The cap is white and usually silky. Young specimens have a ring upon the stalk which later disappears. The gills are at first bright pink but later become dark brown. Field mushrooms usually grow singly in grass, generally appearing after rain. They are found in all States.

2. Horse mushroom, *A. arvensis*. Larger than the field mushrooms, this species has a cap that can grow to a diameter of 20cm. The cap is white and silky at first, turning slightly yellow later. The ring round the stem persists and is usually two-layered. The gills are first dirty white, then greyish-pink (but not bright pink) and finally reddish-brown to black. This mushroom is most common in grass and grass cuttings in temperate districts.

3. Ink caps (*Coprinus* species). Many of these fungi grow on dung, including cattle and horse dung. Their common name refers to the progressive collapse of the edges of the cap into a shiny black ink-like substance as the fungus ages. When the fungus is young the cap is close to the stem and almost cylindrical in shape, but it later expands upwards and outwards. A large species, *C. comatus*, which grows to a height of 30cm, is usually found in grass. Ink caps are among the fungi that should not be taken with alcohol.

4. Parasol mushroom, *Macrolepiota* (*Lepiota*) *procera*. This large distinctive mushroom, which grows to a height of about 30cm, is commonly featured in illustrations for children's fairy-tales. The gills are persistently white. The brown flakes on the white cap distinguish this species from the inedible *M. dolichaula*. The white and brown stem has a felt-like texture and a ring which can be moved up and down. The cap breaks off the stem easily and cleanly. The parasol mushroom is found in E States in grass after rain.

5. Puffballs (*Lycoperdon* and *Calvatia* species). When mature, these round to pear-shaped fungi contain millions of dark spores which escape through a pore or after the collapse of the fruiting body. In Australia, puffballs vary in diameter from a few millimetres to 35mm. They may be eaten while they are still white and firm inside. Puffballs are found in all States, in a variety of habitats.

6. Blackfellow's bread, *Polyporus mylittae*. This woodland and forest fungus forms a hard, tuber-like mass (the sclerotium) beneath the soil. The fruiting body which sometimes emerges from the soil has pores instead of gills.

7. Coral fungi (*Ramaria* (*Clavaria*) species). These species have a branched, coral-like form. Most are probably edible but some species in Europe are known to cause sickness and vomiting in some people.

8. Morel, *Morchella esculenta* (Ascomycetes). The morel is one of the most esteemed fungi in Europe and North America but it appears to be rare in Australia. The ochre-coloured cap is roughly conical in shape and its base adheres to the stout stem; its surface is criss-crossed with ridges. The genus is represented by several species in Australia and is reported from all States. Morels should not be eaten with alcohol.

9. Truffles, *Elderia arenivaga*, and other species (Ascomycetes). Truffles grow underground, usually in damp places. European species are highly valued by gourmets but little is known of the Australian species.

An unidentified coral fungus growing on a tree trunk

A. Woods

Poisonous mushrooms and other fungi

1. Iodoform mushroom, *Agaricus xanthodermus*. This mushroom is similar in shape and appearance to the horse mushroom but has a relatively longer stem. The disinfectant-like smell of this species becomes obvious when the mushroom is kept in a closed container for some time.

2. Fly agaric, *Amanita muscaria*. This familiar 'toadstool', easily recognised by its red cap with white spots, is often featured in fairy-tale illustrations. It contains a dangerous hallucinogen which was once used by Siberian tribes for religious rituals. Its common name relates to its use as an insecticide: small pieces were crushed in a saucer of milk to attract and kill flies. It is usually found in coniferous woodland and is almost certainly an introduced species in Australia. All members of the genus *Amanita* have white gills. The stem arises from a cup-like structure at the ground surface, and the fungus emerges from a rubbery 'egg' which later bursts to form the cup. The most notorious member of the genus, the death cap, *A. phalloides*, which grows in temperate parts of the N hemisphere has not yet been found in Australia. The symptoms of poisoning are delayed and very often fatal. Other species of the genus occur in Australia and, as in Europe, some *may* be edible.

3. *Macrolepiota dolichaula*. Closely related to the edible parasol mushroom this species causes sickness in some people. It is known to occur in QLD and NSW.

4. *Lepiota* (*Chlorophyllum*) *molybdites*. This species is also related to the parasol mushroom but may be distinguished from it by the non-felted stem and, in older individuals, the green to grey-green gills.

5. Gold top or hysteria toadstool, *Psilocybe cubensis*. This species is a member of a dangerous, hallucinogenic group of mushrooms which once were used for religious rituals in South and Central America. It contains the hallucinogen psilocybin, and has a yellow-staining cap. The hysteria toadstool could be confused with *Agaricus* species but it usually grows in small clumps on dung, whereas the *Agaricus* mushrooms are relatively solitary. It occurs in QLD and NSW.

Fairy rings Some species of mushrooms, such as the horse mushroom, colonise a piece of ground and exhaust the soil of its nutrients. The mycelium then expands outwards so that when the fruiting bodies appear they are arranged in the form of a ring. The size of the fairy ring indicates its age, in some cases several centuries old.

Luminous fungi Several fungi are luminous. The whole fruiting body of *Pleurotus lampas*, for example, glows, and several basidiomycetes which attack wood have hyphae which produce a cold light.

Parasitic fungi The members of the genus *Cordyceps* (Basidiomycetes) are parasites of insects, usually larvae, and sometimes of other fungi. The mycelium eventually replaces the internal tissues of the insect and the fruiting body emerges, usually from just behind the head. Australia is said to possess the largest species, *C. taylori*; the fruiting body and its branching stem (sporophore) can be 30cm long. This fungus attacks soil larvae in the mountains of VIC. *Cordyceps* fungi are highly valued in Chinese medicine.

Further reading: Large, E.C. *The Advance of the Fungi*. Jonathan Cape, London, 1940; Cribb, A.B. & Cribb, J.W. *Wild Food in Australia*. Collins, Sydney, 1974; Wood, A. *Australian Mushrooms and Toadstools*. NSW University Press Ltd, Sydney, 1980.

fungus gnats *see* flies

Furneaux Islands TAS Located at the E end of BASS STRAIT, off the NE coast of the State, this group of islands, of which FLINDERS ISLAND is the largest, was named by James COOK after one of his captains, Tobias Furneaux. Matthew FLINDERS charted the islands and it is presumed that he named some in the group. Cape Barren Is, lying S of Flinders Is, is the home of the well-known Cape Barren geese. Babel Is, off the E coast of Flinders, is one of the main areas for catching mutton birds. Clarke Is, the most S of the group, is used for sheep and cattle grazing. On the shores of Vansittart Is, between Flinders and Cape Barren Islands, is the hull of the barque *Farsund*, wrecked in 1912.

Furphy, Joseph *see* Collins, Tom

fusiliers *see* fishes, bony

Fysh, Sir Hudson (1859-1974) Pioneer aviator. Born in LAUNCESTON, TAS, he served during World War I in the Light Horse and then in the Australian Flying Corps, and was awarded the DFC. In 1920 he and P. McGuiness, also formerly a member of the AFC, founded Queensland and Northern Territory Aerial Services Ltd. (QANTAS), of which Fysh became managing director in 1923. It was largely at his instigation that in 1934 Qantas embarked on overseas operations through the formation, in conjunction with British Empire Airways, of Qantas Empire Airways Ltd. When the Commonwealth government took over this company in 1947, Fysh stayed on as managing director, and was later chairman. He was appointed KBE in 1953 and retired in 1966.

G

gabba *see* slugs, etc.

Gair, Vincent Clair (1902-80) Politician and Ambassador. Born and educated in the QLD provincial city of ROCKHAMPTON, he worked as a public servant before winning election to the QLD Legislative Assembly in 1932. From 1942 to 1952 he held various portfolios in Labor Ministries, and was then Premier and Chief Secretary for five years. When a split occurred in the AUSTRALIAN LABOR PARTY in 1955, leading to the formation of the Anti-Communist Labor Party (later the DEMOCRATIC LABOR PARTY), Gair was at first able to preserve the unity of the QLD branch. However, in 1957 he and other right-wing members of that branch were expelled and formed the Queensland Labor Party, which later amalgamated with the DLP.

Gair lost his parliamentary seat in the 1960 elections, but four years later gained election to the Senate, and from 1965 to 1973 was parliamentary leader of the DLP. His political career then came to an end under remarkable circumstances. In October 1973 he lost the party leadership to Senator F. McManus, and early in the following year was offered the position of Ambassador to the Republic of Ireland. Prime Minister WHITLAM's motive in making this offer was quite obviously to increase Labor's chances of gaining an extra Senate seat and so achieving control of that House. The outcome was that the leader of the Opposition, B.M. Snedden, believing that public opinion would be turned against Labor by this piece of opportunism, was emboldened to block supply in the Senate. However, Whitlam used the opportunity to obtain a double dissolution, and in the elections of May

1974 his government was returned, although with a reduced majority. Gair accepted the position of Ambassador, was expelled from the DLP, and early in 1976 was recalled from Dublin by the incoming Liberal Prime Minister, Malcolm FRASER.

galah *see* parrots, etc.

galaxias *see* fishes, freshwater

gallinules *see* rails, etc.

Gallipoli The Allied attack on the Gallipoli Peninsula during World War I holds a special place in Australian history. The participation of Australian troops, with distinction, in this important and highly publicised campaign aroused such admiration in their homeland that the date of their first landing, 25 April, is still celebrated each year as ANZAC DAY.

Location of the Gallipoli campaign

Aims of the campaign The basic aim of the campaign was to enable Allied naval forces to sail through the Dardanelles into the Sea of Marmara, from where an attack might then be launched on the Turkish capital, Constantinople (Istanbul). At the very least this would divert some of Turkey's military effort from the Caucasus front, and so take pressure off the Russians there. In addition, the Allies might force a passage through the Bosporus into the Black Sea, and so open up a supply route to Russia, which was desperately short of equipment. Conceivably, they might even force Turkey out of the war. The main architect of the plan, Winston Churchill, hoped at first that a naval attack would be sufficient to open the Dardanelles, but when an Anglo-French fleet attempted this in March 1915 it suffered heavy casualties. It became evident that it would be necessary for troops to land on the Gallipoli Peninsula, gain possession of the heights behind the Turkish forts at the Narrows (the entrance to the Dardanelles) and put them out of action. The force selected to perform this task included men of the Australian and New Zealand Army Corps (ANZAC), who had been training in Egypt, as well as British, French and Indian troops.

The landing at Anzac Cove Unfortunately, the Turks, warned by the naval attack and by signs of military preparations, were expecting a landing. Under the leadership of a German, General Liman von Sanders, they had entrenched themselves strongly on the peninsula, and were able to put up a strong resistance

when the attack came. The Anzacs were doubly unfortunate in that their landing craft drifted in the dark past the beach initially chosen, so that when they went ashore just after dawn it was in the little bay later called Anzac Cove, which had only a narrow beach, backed by a 100m-high hill. Despite heavy rifle and artillery fire they gained the crest of the hill and beat off a number of counter-attacks. By the end of that day, 25 April 1915, 16 000 men had been landed, but the Anzacs had penetrated only half a mile inland, far short of their first day's objective—Hill 971 on the mountain mass known as Sari Bair—and had suffered 2000 casualties.

Australian troops on the beach at Gallipoli

Failure and evacuation The success of the operation was considered to depend so heavily on a quick gaining of high ground that after the first day consideration was given to withdrawing the Anzacs and sending them to reinforce the British, who had landed further S at Cape Helles, also against strong Turkish resistance. However, General Ian Hamilton, commander of the Allied forces, decided that this was impracticable, and instructed the Anzacs to dig in and hold on. This they did, in a complex series of trenches and dug-outs, overlooked by Turkish snipers and artillery and with the enemy trenches so close in places that hand-bombs could be thrown between the opposing forces. In August a plan for breaking the stalemate was tried, with the Anzacs attacking the Turkish line at Lone Pine, while the British made a landing at Suvla Bay and attacked Sari Bair from the other side. Both attacks failed. At Lone Pine 2000 Australians died and seven were awarded Victoria Crosses. The campaign then reverted to trench warfare, punctuated by minor attacks and counter-attacks, under the most difficult conditions.

In December the Allied forces were evacuated. The withdrawal, unlike the landing, was planned with the utmost secrecy and caught the Turks by surprise; not one life was lost. Casualties for the whole campaign included over 33 000 dead, of whom 8 587 were Australians.
Further reading: The Anzac Book: Written and Illustrated in Gallipoli by the Men of Anzac. Cassell, London, 1916 (reprinted Sun Books, South Melbourne, 1975); Moorehead, A. *Gallipoli.* (new edn) Macmillan, South Melbourne, 1976.

gambling It is often claimed that Australians are, per capita, the heaviest gamblers in the world. It is certainly true that

gambling opportunities abound in Australia. In almost every city suburb and in most country towns there is a government-controlled off-course betting agency, the TAB (*see* TOTALIZATORS), a newsagent selling lottery tickets and soccer pools coupons or some version of a numbers game usually called Lotto, and possibly an illegal starting-price (SP) bookmaker in the local hotel. In NSW and the ACT, the same suburb or town may also have a club whose financial viability depends on poker machines. In TAS, casinos have been legal since 1973; they are also legal in the NT, and it is expected that they will be made legal in NSW the ACT, SA and QLD some time in the 1980s.

Poker machines These sophisticated gambling machines, which pay dividends to players lucky enough to gain winning combinations in the pay-out window, were first legalised in 1956, in NSW. Since then they have become the mainstay of the registered clubs in NSW (over 1500 clubs) which rely heavily on the machines for a major part of their income. Although the machines—or 'one-armed bandits', as disgruntled players call them —usually accept only five-cent, 10-cent or 20-cent coins, massive amounts of money are put through them. The NSW government was quick to realise the contribution poker machines could make to State coffers, and by 1979 it was extracting $100 million annually in the form of supplementary taxes from money put through the machines. Frequently blamed for causing financial hardship in the families of addicted players, they have attracted a great deal of adverse criticism, and moves to legalise them in States other than NSW have met with great opposition.

Racing Just as the mainstay of the NSW club industry is the poker machine player, the mainstay of the Australian racing industry is the punter. Without the punter, HORSE RACING, TROTTING and GREYHOUND RACING AND COURSING would collapse. The punter pays an admission fee to enter the race track, financially supports on-course bookmakers, is a generous contributor to the State Treasuries in the form of betting taxes, and since the introduction of the TAB in the 1960s has seen a proportion of the TAB's profits compulsorily returned to the racing industry to increase prize money for races and improve race track facilities.

Other forms of gambling
1. Lotteries. These have been a popular form of gambling since 1881 when George Adams introduced a sweepstake for the 1881 Sydney Cup to his Sydney Tattersall's Hotel patrons. The sweepstake developed into Tattersall's (or Tatt's) lottery, and although based in TAS from 1896 to 1954 and in VIC since then, Tatt's has become the best-known lottery in Australia. All States run public lotteries, the proceeds of which help finance hospitals and some charities.

2. Tattslotto. Following the highly successful introduction of the numbers game Tattslotto in VIC in 1972, which in the late 1970s was

contributing $150 million annually to that State's Treasury, similar numbers games were introduced into WA, SA and NSW.

3. Soccer pools. These were originally based on the results of the English and Scottish soccer competitions. Later they were made year-round by the addition of Australian soccer results during the N hemisphere off-season.

4. Bingo or housie-housie. This is a popular money-raising and gambling game for sporting clubs in those States where poker machines are not legal and for some churches.

5. Casinos. Although a number of illegal casinos were thought to exist in the larger capital cities in the early 1980s, they were legal only in the NT and TAS. With unknown amounts being gambled illegally—either with SP bookmakers or in illegal casinos—it is not possible to make accurate assessments of the amount gambled annually by Australians. However, reliable estimates placed the annual total at approximately $6000 million in the early 1980s.

See also two-up

Game, Sir Philip Woolcott (1876–1961) Governor of NSW. Born at Streatham in Surrey, England, he served in the British army in the BOER WAR and WORLD WAR I. After receiving the DSO in 1915, he moved to the Royal Flying Corps, of which he became Chief of Staff. He was appointed CB (1919), KCB (1924) and GBE (1929), and in 1930 became Governor of NSW. Two years later he found himself involved in a political crisis, and, as related in the entry on J.T. LANG, finally dismissed the latter from his position as Premier of NSW, on the grounds that Lang had acted unconstitutionally. Game left Australia in 1935 and served in London as Commissioner of the Metropolitan Police for the next 10 years. He received the further honours KCMG (1935), GCVO (1937) and GCB (1945).

gannets *see* sea birds

Gardiner, Francis 'Frank' (1830-1903?) Bushranger. Born near GOULBURN, the son of a settler named Christie and a servant girl named Clarke, he adopted the surname Gardiner from an employer, but at times used Christie and Clarke as aliases. In contrast with the escaped convicts who constituted the majority of bushrangers in earlier times, he gained the support of many people in the district where he operated and was invested by them with some of the glamour often attributed to English highwaymen. After being twice convicted of horse stealing, in 1861 he took to highway robbery. After a brush with the police, in which he shot at and wounded Sergeant John Middleton, he organised a bushranging gang based in the Weddin Mts, south of FORBES. Near Eugowra Rocks in June 1862, he and his gang had their greatest success when they held up a coach, escorted by police, carrying gold and banknotes to the

value of £14 000. Shortly after this Gardiner went to QLD, but was traced and arrested in 1864. He was acquitted on a charge of shooting Sergeant Middleton with intent to kill, but received a cumulative sentence of 32 years on other charges. Many people thought that this was vindictively harsh, and in 1874, following the presentation of a widely supported public petition, Governor Sir Hercules Robinson ordered Gardiner's release, on condition that he left the colony. This action became the subject of a bitter public controversy, which culminated in the fall of the PARKES government. After receiving his pardon, Gardiner left Australia altogether, and not long afterwards settled in San Francisco.

garganey *see* ducks, etc.

Garran, Sir Robert Randolph (1867-1957) Barrister and public servant. Son of an editor of the *Sydney Morning Herald*, he was born in Sydney and graduated from the University of Sydney in 1888. He was called to the Bar in 1890, but during the following decade devoted a great deal of his time to furthering the cause of federation. In 1897 he published *The Coming Commonwealth* and in the same year was secretary to the drafting committee of the National Convention in Adelaide. There he met John QUICK, with whom he wrote the *Annotated Copy of the Australian Constitution* (1901).

In January 1901 Garran became a foundation member of the Commonwealth Public Service, as secretary of the Attorney-General's Department, and in 1916 became the first occupant of the newly created position of Solicitor-General. In 1918 he accompanied Prime Minister HUGHES to the Imperial War Conference and in the following year went with him to the Paris Peace Conference. By the time he retired in 1932 he had been the chief legal adviser to 11 Attorneys-General, and had been without any doubt the outstanding member of the Commonwealth Public Service during the first three decades of its existence.

Garran's wide intellectual and cultural interests and his spirit of public service were reflected in the variety of his activities after retirement. He joined in the work of many cultural and community associations, including the Australian League of Nations Union, of which he was for many years the national president, the All Nations Club in Sydney, of which he was a founder, and Rotary International. He also played an important role in the foundation of the Canberra University College and later of the Australian National University. Shortly before his death he finished writing his memoirs, entitled *Prosper the Commonwealth* (published posthumously 1958).

Gascoyne River WA Located in the mid-NW of the State, with headwater streams draining from the Robinson and Collier Ranges, it flows in a generally W direction for over 800km, reaching the sea at CARNARVON

on SHARK BAY. Much of its course is through semi-arid areas of low rainfall and hence its flow is sporadic with parts of the river bed seasonally dry, though cyclonic weather conditions can bring heavy rainfall and river flooding. The main tributary is the Lyons River from the N, which joins the river at the township of Gascoyne Junction. The alluvial flats of the lower reaches have been developed by irrigation and produce bananas and vegetables.

gastropods The Gastropoda is the largest class of the MOLLUSCS. Gastropods are also called univalve molluscs because the shell is a single unit. The group contains the only molluscs to have colonised the land, but most gastropods are marine (a few are PARASITES) and some are freshwater species.

Most gastropods are recognised as such by their coiled shells, though some have lost the shell, and others have simple conical ones. The shell contains the visceral mass. The well-developed head (with tentacles) and the muscular foot can often be withdrawn into the shell which may then be sealed off by a plate (the operculum) which some gastropods carry on the foot. This prevents the drying-out of the animal when it is exposed to the air and sun. The shell normally consists of a number of whorls spiralling round a central axis (columella). In some, the spiral is clockwise and in others, anti-clockwise; the difference is important in identification. The smallest or apical whorl (the protoconch) is laid down by the larva and the rest are added as the animal grows.

During the larval development the visceral hump is rotated through 180° so that the mantle cavity (fleshy lining of the shell's outer wall), with the gills, anus and openings of the excretory system, come to lie near the head. The purpose of this rotation (torsion) is unknown though many explanations have been offered. The process often involves the loss of one or other of certain paired organs, such as kidneys, gills and auricles of the heart. Gastropods feed by means of a file-like structure (radula) which scrapes off food particles and draws them into the mouth. The mouth-parts may be highly modified in such forms as venomous cone shells.

There are more than 35 000 living gastropod species and at least 15 000 fossils. As there are probably over 4000 species in Australia and the adjacent seas, only a few of the more important families are mentioned here; the size of each species is included in parentheses when known and unless otherwise stated refers to length. The class is divided into three subclasses: the subclasses Prosobranchia and Opisthobranchia contain marine gastropods; the subclass Pulmonata is composed mainly of freshwater and terrestrial species, which are described in the entry on SLUGS AND SNAILS.
Prosobranchia This subclass contains many of the marine gastropods of the seashore, coral reefs and coastal seas, where they are generally found on hard substrates; some are freshwater

species and most, if not all, are herbivores. These gastropods are gill-bearing snails with the mantle cavity at the front of the body. Usually the animal can withdraw completely into its shell. There are three orders, each with several families.

1. Archaeogastropoda. This order consists of primitive forms which have all kept two kidneys, two gills and two auricles. The shell is coiled in at least the larval stages but in some, such as the limpets, the adult shell has become symmetrical. Some species have slits or holes in the shell so that waste products from the mantle cavity can be flushed away.

The families Patellidae and Acmaeidae contain the true limpets. These species move around slowly but usually return to the same spot after feeding, their shells fitting exactly into the surface grooves. *Cellana tramosericata* (Patellidae), one of the commonest species throughout Australia, reaches a diameter of about 2.5cm and is recognised by the alternate light and dark radial lines.

The family Fissurellidae contains the false limpets. These species have a small slit in the shell which lines up with the anus beneath. As the shell grows the slit may become a central hole, as in the keyhole limpets. The family also contains the elephant snails (*Scutus* species), in which the small, notched, rather flattened white shell is almost obscured by the large velvety-black body. There are two conspicuous tentacles which sway from side to side. The length of the body can be about 15cm.

The family Haliotidae contains the ear-shells or mutton fish. In these species one large whorl of the shell predominates, and there is a series of exit holes. The family includes the abalones (*Haliotis* species), night-feeding herbivores which are valued for their flesh and for the inner pearly nacreous layer which is worked into ornaments ('sea-opals'). The various species range from about 2cm to 20cm in length.

The family Trochidae contains the top-shells, so-called because their shape resembles that of the child's toy. Trochids are common throughout the world and the *Austrocochlea* species are among the commonest rocky mid-shore snails in Australia. The family Turbanidae contains the closely related and appropriately named turban shells. The shells are heavy and the opening is almost circular.

The family Neritidae contains the black periwinkle, *Melanerita atramentosa* (up to 2.5cm in diameter), one of the commonest seashore molluscs, often found in association with *Austrocochlea* species. It is easily recognised by its matt black shell.

2. Mesogastropoda. This is the largest order of the Gastropoda and contains snails with only one auricle, kidney and gill; some have an operculum and many have a proboscis. Most species are marine but a few are freshwater snails.

The family Littorinidae contains the true periwinkles. Two common Australian species are: *Nodolittorina pyramidalis*, grey-shelled

A tiny blue periwinkle, *Melarapha unifasciata*

with many small nodules (tubercles), which lives higher above the tide than any other seashore animal, being common several metres from the sea; and *Melarapha unifasciata* (1cm in diameter), a tiny purplish-blue winkle which clusters on rocks, especially in crevices. *Bembicium* species are larger; *B. nanum* (1.2cm in diameter), with alternating stripes of brown and white, resembles *Austrocochlea* species in pattern but not in shape.

The family Potamidae contains the well-known Sydney whelk, *Pyrazus ebeninus* (about 10cm), which is not a true whelk and is found in mud-flats and mangrove swamps throughout E Australia, being one of the commonest species in Aboriginal middens.

The family Janthinidae (or Ianthinidae) contain snails which float in the open sea, producing a stable froth from the foot which serves as a float and feeding on planktonic animals. Their shells, which are very light and are violet-blue when fresh, are often cast ashore.

The family Cypraeidae contains the cowries, well-known gastropods found mainly in tropical waters. The early whorls are obscured by the final large whorl, and the opening is long, narrow and toothed. The shells are often beautifully coloured and highly polished. When the animal is alive, folds of the mantle are extended and more or less cover the shell. Cowries have been used for ornament and, in many Pacific islands, as money.

The family Cymatiidae contains the triton shells which are familiar in classical sculptures of Neptune. They are massively built shells and are unusual in that the outer layer of the shell (the periostracum) persists in the adult. In many tritons this outer layer is rather soft and reddish or fawn, but in the hairy oyster-borer, *Monoplex australiasiae* (5cm to 10cm), an estuarine species that is often a pest of oyster leases, the periostracum is in the form of long, hairy processes. The tritons contain some of the largest univalve molluscs, including *Charonia tritonis* (about 46cm), a tropical species, the shell of which is often used as a trumpet in the Pacific region.

3. Neogastropoda. In this order the shell usually has a canal for a siphon which carries water into the mantle cavity. These species, some of which are venomous, are predatory animals with a proboscis and a radula with only a few large teeth in each row.

The family Buccinidae contains the whelks, a

cosmopolitan family of often moderately large gastropods. The shells are relatively tall and the siphon canal is conspicuous.

The family Nassidae (or Nassariidae) contains the similar dog whelks, such as the common *Nassarius particeps* (2.5cm) which ranges from rocky shores to estuarine flats and is a scavenger and predator. This species has a whelk-like shell which is marked with wavy yellow-ochre lines.

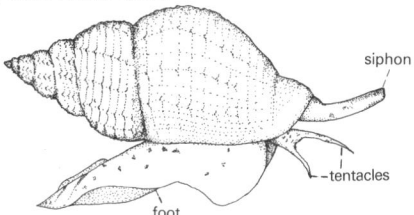

A whelk showing foot, tentacles and siphonal tube

The family Conidae contains the cone shells, mainly tropical gastropods, several species of which are common on the GREAT BARRIER REEF. The shells are often intricately patterned and are popular with collectors. In 1971 a collector paid £1 350 at Sotheby's in London for one of the four known specimens of *Conus bengalensis*, and in 1964 $2000 was paid for a Glory of the Sea, *C. gloriamaris*, a species found on the coasts of several islands N of Australia. The last whorl of the shell is the largest and it envelopes the others. The opening is very long and narrow. The teeth of the radula are on a proboscis which can be pushed out extremely rapidly. Although relatively few in number, the teeth are large, hollow and barbed, and are used to inject venom which appears to act like curare. Some of those that attack fish are lethal to man. At least three QLD species, *C. geographus* (12cm), *C. cattus* (5cm) and *C. tulipa* (7cm), are regarded as potentially lethal, and one of them, *C. geographus*, has caused one known death in Australia.

The family Thaididae contains a few familiar species such as the cartrut shell, *Dicathais orbita* (about 5cm to 7.5cm in diameter), and the mulberry shell or oyster-borer, *Morula marginalba* (2.5cm), which ranges from QLD to VIC in a variety of habitats, preys on bivalve molluscs, boring holes through the shells with its radula. The shell is covered with rows of dark nodules which give it the appearance of a mulberry or a hand-grenade.

The family Muricidae contains the murex gastropods (some are called Venus comb shells). The shells of many of these species have long spines though these are uncommon among the cold-water species. For example, the common *Agnewia tritoniformis* (2.5cm), which occurs on rocky coasts at low-water mark, is shaped like a small triton.

The family Mitridae contains the mitre shells, long awl-shaped species, the most colourful of which are tropical.

The family Volutidae contains species popular with collectors because of their often beautiful colours and high polish. Volutes are carnivores that live in sand, burrowing with the aid of their long, often large, muscular foot. The largest is the golden-yellow baler shell, *Melo amphora* (56cm), which was once used by Aborigines for bailing out dug-out canoes.

Opisthobranchia This subclass contains marine hermaphrodite gastropods which show various degrees of twisting and of reduction of the mantle cavity. They have only one kidney and auricle and the shell is often reduced or absent. Some of the most beautiful of all animals belong to this subclass, but they are often extremely difficult to preserve. The classification varies from one authority to another; the most commonly used classification divides the subclass into three orders.

1. Tectibranchia. All the members of this order have a shell but it may be small and covered by the mantle. There is only one true gill. Some species have become bilaterally symmetrical by detorsion. In the bubble shells the fragile shell is obvious and resembles those of the Prosobranchia, but the soft parts are so large that they cannot be withdrawn completely into the shell. The rose-petal bubble shell, *Hydatina physis* (5cm in diameter), has a rose-pink body, edged with iridescent blue, and the shell has thin dark lines on a light background. This gastropod is seasonal in appearance, but occurs in a variety of habitats from NSW to WA.

The family Aplysiidae contains the sea hares, large gastropods with small thin shells that are almost completely obscured. There are two pairs of tentacles whose shape accounts for the common name of these animals. In the common genus *Aplysia*, the very long foot has a pair of side extensions (parapodia) which some species use for swimming. Sea hares are herbivores which appear sporadically on the Australian coasts. When disturbed, sea hares often discharge a purple inky fluid for cover.

2. Pteropoda. This order consists of the sea butterflies—shelled or shell-less gastropods which swim, with the aid of large parapodia, in the open sea. They are carnivores.

3. Nudibranchia. This order contains the sea slugs, the most beautiful of the molluscs and possibly the most beautiful of all marine animals. The name means 'naked gills', but true gills, shell and mantle cavity are all absent. Sea slugs respire through the general body surface, though secondary gills (cerata) often occur near the anus. The body is bilaterally symmetrical. There are two pairs of tentacles; the second pair (rhinophores) have a ringed appearance. Sea slugs range from 1mm to about 30cm in length, and they may be found in many different habitats. Some are herbivores and some feed on sedentary marine

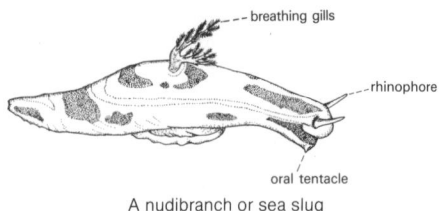

A nudibranch or sea slug

animals. Many of them are markedly seasonal in their appearance on the shore. Apart from the commonest species they are difficult to identify.

The red and blue sea slug, *Glossodoris bennetti* (about 5cm), is one of the most outstandingly coloured animals among a group of creatures famed for their gaudiness. This nudibranch of the lower tidal levels of rocky shores in NSW has a blue body with many red spots and with a bright orange-yellow margin. The rhinophores are red and white and the secondary gills are white. The black-edged sea slug, *Casella atromarginata* (5cm), found in QLD and NSW, has a creamy or greenish body with a black border; the rhinophores and the gills are also black.

The spectacular blue and silver sea slug, *Glaucus atlanticus* (5cm), is an open-sea animal of tropical and sub-tropical regions. Specimens are often blown onto Australian shores but they are so fragile that they are rarely found undamaged. The body has three pairs of multi-branched extensions arising from the sides. This species creeps upside-down on the surface film of the calm ocean, feeding on siphonophores such as *Velella* (*see* COELENTERATES).

Some nudibranchs have evolved a unique defence mechanism: although they feed on coelenterates, they are unharmed by the stinging cells (nematocysts) which pass through the nudibranch to settle in special surface cells, giving the 'thief' protection against its predators; nudibranchs also frequently exude toxic substances into the surrounding water for protection.

Pulmonata The gastropods of this subclass have no gills; the inside of the mantle cavity is well supplied with blood vessels and is therefore used like a lung. Pulmonates have only one kidney and auricle but though they show torsion the concentrated nervous system is symmetrical. There is usually a shell but there is no operculum. All are hermaphrodite, and only a few are marine.

The Pulmonata contains two orders: the Stylommatophora, terrestrial snails which have two pairs of tentacles with eyes at the tip of the second pair; and the Basommatophora, mainly freshwater snails in which there is only one pair of tentacles, and the eyes are at the base.

Among the marine forms, the members of the family Siphonariidae look remarkably like true limpets, but the shells are flattened on the right side, and there is a distinct groove running down the inside of the shell.

The members of the family Onchidiidae are true sea slugs in the sense that they are the shell-less marine gastropods that are most closely related to the land slugs. *Onchidium* species are widespread, and some are very common in mangroves.

See also animals, venomous

Further reading: see under molluscs. *Also* Cleland, Sir John & Southcott, R.V. *Injuries to Man from Marine Invertebrates in the Australian Region.* (National Health and Medical Research Council Special Report, series no 12)

Govt Printer, Canberra, 1965; Sutherland, S.K. *Venomous Creatures of Australia: A Field Guide with Notes on First Aid.* Oxford University Press, Melbourne, 1981.

gastrotrichs These aquatic, microscopic animals form a group which is sometimes regarded as a phylum (Gastrotricha) and sometimes as a class of the ASCHELMINTHS. Gastrotrichs have flattened bodies with hair-like

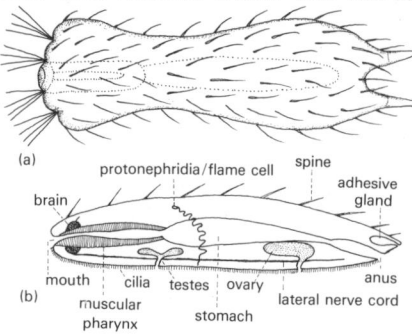

A gastrotrich, *Chaetonotus* species: (a) dorsal view; (b) lateral view

appendages (cilia) and spines on the upper surface. The tail end is usually forked. There are adhesive tubes—sometimes over most of the body, sometimes only on the tail forks—with which they cling to surfaces. Most of the Australian species are freshwater animals. Gastrotrichs feed on micro-organisms and detritus. They are related to the ROTIFERS and ROUNDWORMS.

Further reading: Williams, W.D. *Australian Freshwater Life.* (2nd edn) Macmillan, Melbourne, 1980.

Gatton QLD (population 4 190 in 1981) A country town, situated on Lockyer Creek, it is 92km W of Brisbane along the Warrego Highway, 57km W of IPSWICH and 38km E of TOOWOOMBA. Serving a productive mixed farming and grazing district noted for potato growing, Gatton is the site of the Queensland Agricultural College. It has an average annual rainfall of 912mm, which is concentrated mainly in the summer season. The town was probably named after Gatton in Roxburghshire, Scotland.

Gawler SA (population 9 433 in 1981) This town is located at the W edge of the MOUNT LOFTY RANGES, 42km by road N of Adelaide, where the North and South Para Rivers join to form the Gawler River. The town is the gateway to the BAROSSA VALLEY and is a main road and rail focus. The town site, selected by William LIGHT and laid out in 1839, was named after George GAWLER, second Governor of SA. During the latter decades of the 19th century it was an important industrial centre with several foundries and engineering workshops, but nowadays—increasingly influenced by the urban spread of Adelaide—it is becoming a dormitory town for workers in the city. Over 20 buildings have been classified (and a similar number listed) by the National Trust (SA) for preservation.

Further reading: Auhl, I. *Gawler Sketchbook* Rigby, Adelaide, 1973.

Gawler, George (1795-1869) Governor of SA. He joined the British Army as an ensign in 1810, served in the Peninsular War and at Waterloo, and by 1834 was a lieutenant-colonel. In 1838 he was appointed Governor of SA. He was also made Resident Commissioner for Crown Lands since his predecessor, HINDMARSH, and the first Resident Commissioner, J.H. Fisher, had quarrelled over the line of division between their powers and responsibilities.

On arrival in the colony Gawler found that land surveys had not been able to keep up with demand, and that many of those who had managed to buy land were holding it for resale instead of employing labour to develop it. Unemployment was therefore high. To cope with this situation, he embarked on an ambitious programme of public works. In doing so he went far beyond the limits of authorised expenditure, bridging the gap by issuing bills, to the extent of over £200 000, payable by the Commissioners in London. Late in 1840 the Commissioners referred the whole matter to the Colonial Office, with the result that Gawler was recalled and George GREY appointed in his place. Grey was very critical of Gawler, and this helped to establish the official belief that the latter had mismanaged the colony and that Grey's sound management was mainly responsible for setting it on the road to prosperity. Such an over-simplified judgement is unfair to Gawler. Faced with a difficult situation he had acted as he thought best and in doing so had equipped the colony with the public buildings, wharves and roads necessary for its later prosperity. The funds available to him were certainly insufficient, and the extent to which he exceeded them could be partly blamed on the Commissioners, who failed to give him firm guidance. He must be credited, too, with the speeding up of surveys and the settlement of thousands of settlers on the land, thus helping to make possible the bumper harvest of 1841, which gave the colony its first prospects of self-sufficiency. He also organised the police force and took a keen interest in the founding of schools and in charitable work. He was, however, rightly criticised for the summary punitive measures taken against Aborigines who had killed survivors from the ship *Maria* in 1840.
Further reading: Price, A.G. *Founders and Pioneers of South Australia.* F.W. Preece & Sons, Adelaide, 1929.

Gawler Ranges SA This series of low hills extends in a general E-W direction across the N part of EYRE PENINSULA for about 160km. The ranges are highest in the W section where Mt Bluff reaches an elevation of 475m. They were named by the explorer Edward John EYRE in honour of Governor GAWLER. The region has an average annual rainfall under 300mm and is semi-arid country which supports sparse vegetation used for sheep and cattle grazing on large properties. In the E parts of the ranges are the MIDDLEBACK RANGES, famed for their rich iron ore deposits.

Gayndah QLD (population 1 708 in 1981) A small town on the Burnett Highway in the SE of the State, 344km NNW of Brisbane, located inland from MARYBOROUGH (about 170km by road via the Isis Highway) and SE of BUNDABERG (165km by road via Childers). Situated on the Burnett River, it was founded in 1848 and is thus one of QLD's oldest towns. It has an average annual rainfall of 786mm, concentrated mainly in the summer months. The town is a service centre for a productive rural region where citrus fruit growing is the major industry; the orchards have modern irrigation equipment and are highly mechanised; the co-operative fruit packing shed in the town can be inspected by visitors. An Orange Festival is held every second year over the Queen's Birthday weekend in June. Other farming activities in the district include dairying, fodder crop cultivation and grain growing; there are several well-known cattle studs in the area.

geckos *see* lizards

geebung *see* Proteaceae

Geelong VIC (population 125 269 in 1981) The second-largest city in VIC, and an important port and industrial centre, it is situated on the shores of CORIO BAY, 74km by road SW of Melbourne. It is on the Princes Highway and is a focus of several other major routes: the Midland Highway to BALLARAT, the Hamilton Highway and the Bellarine Highway SE to QUEENSCLIFF. It is also a major rail junction with lines linking it to Melbourne (73km), to Ballarat, to WARRNAMBOOL and to other centres in the WESTERN DISTRICT such as HAMILTON and PORTLAND. The area was discovered in 1824 by the explorer Hamilton HUME, who noted that the Aboriginal word for the district was *jillong*. In 1837 Governor BOURKE named the settlement from this word which appears to have several possible meanings: 'a swampy plain' or 'place of the cliff' or 'white sea bird'. Geelong was incorporated as a town in 1847 and during the gold rush of the 1850s it was a major disembarkation port for fortune-seekers on their way to the goldfields. It developed as the main outlet for the rural produce of the rich Western District of the State and was proclaimed a city in 1910.

The initial site of the urban nucleus was between the bay shore and the BARWON RIVER valley, but with its large and expanding population and large influx of migrants, particularly since World War II, it has spread along the bay foreshore. Industrially, it is a most important city, boasting numerous major manufacturing enterprises. Across Corio Bay at Point Henry is the extensive aluminium smelting plant of Alcoa, using alumina brought from WA. The city is an important wool selling centre, and the huge bulk wheat terminal is one of the largest and most modern in the world. Education has long been an important function of the city; the famed Anglican school, Geelong Grammar, was

Little Malop Street in Geelong, 1866

National Library of Australia

established in 1854 and the city is the site of the youngest university in VIC, Deakin University. There are many tourist attractions in the city and district: the Memorial Art Gallery and the Balmoral Galleries; Balyang bird sanctuary on the banks of the Barwon River; Belmont Common railway (a narrow-gauge line established by the Geelong Steam Preservation Society); Eastern Beach (a summer-time mecca for residents and visitors); Queen's Park; Ceres Lookout (8km SW of the city); and the You Yangs (a rocky range 24km N) with Flinders Peak rising to a height of 352m. There are many historic features in Geelong and the National Trust (VIC) has listed about 90 buildings (of which over 60 have been classified).
Further reading: Blake, L.J. *Geelong Sketchbook.* Rigby, Adelaide, 1971.

geese *see* ducks, etc.

Geeveston TAS (population 860 in 1981) A small town on the Huon Highway in the SE of the State, 60km SW of Hobart and 22km SW of HUONVILLE, and situated just inland from the W foreshore of the HUON RIVER estuary, it is the administrative headquarters of Esperance municipality (population 3 190 in 1981). The town takes its name from William Geeves, a British settler who took up the first selection in the district in 1842. The average annual rainfall is 878mm, May being the month of highest falls. This part of the lower Huon Valley was one of the early apple growing centres of TAS. It is also important for timber production and in 1962 the Australian Paper Mills established a pulp mill at Hospital Bay, 3km from Geeveston, producing pelletised pulp which is shipped to Sydney for final processing into paper. Geeveston is the gateway to the HARTZ MOUNTAINS National Park; a 24km branch road off the highway leads to Waratah Lookout in the NE section of the park.

Gellibrand, Joseph Tice (1786-1837) Attorney-General of TAS. Born in London, he studied law, and in 1823 was appointed Attorney-General of TAS. Following a dispute with Governor ARTHUR and accusations of unprofessional conduct he was dismissed from that position in 1826, but established a successful practice as a barrister. He became one of the leaders of the Port Phillip Association and is generally considered to have drawn up the documents which John BATMAN used to make his 'treaty' with the Aborigines. In 1836 he made a journey on foot from WESTERN PORT BAY to Melbourne and the GEELONG district, but during a second journey along the BARWON RIVER in 1837 he and his companion, George Hesse, were killed by Aborigines.

Geoghegan, Edward

Playwright. Geoghegan arrived in Australia on 25 January 1840 on the convict ship *Middlesex*, transported from his native Ireland for obtaining goods or papers under false pretences. A former medical student, he was employed as a dispenser in the Medical Department at Cockatoo Island, with a shore leave pass. He became a copyist at the Royal Victoria Theatre in Sydney, and was befriended by the actor Francis Nesbitt. Geoghegan wrote several plays for the Royal Victoria, anonymously, since no convict was permitted to engage in theatrical activities. *The Currency Lass* was staged in 1843, followed in 1844 by *The Hibernian Father*, which caused a minor furore when letters in Sydney newspapers alleged it had been plagiarised from an Irish play, *The Warden of Galway*, staged in Dublin some years earlier. Geoghegan also claimed authorship, in a letter to the Colonial Secretary in 1852, of six other plays. Though not Australia's first dramatist, Geoghegan was among the earliest playwrights to produce a substantial body of dramatic writing in Australia.
Further reading: Rees, L. *The Making of Australian Drama*. Angus & Robertson, Sydney, 1973.

Geographe Bay

WA A broad gulf on the SW coast of the State, it curves E from Cape Naturaliste then N for about 50km to BUNBURY. It was named by the French explorer Nicholas BAUDIN in 1801.

geology

Australia is an ancient land. Some of the oldest rocks in the world are exposed in the SW part of WA; they were formed at least one and a half billion years ago and have remained unchanged for perhaps 700 million years. In recent times the continent has enjoyed a quiet life, geologically speaking; there are now no active volcanoes and little evidence of earthquakes. The massive forces that are still at work within the earth's crust elsewhere, building the great mountain ranges of the world, have not been felt in Australia for many years and many an ancient mountain has been laid low by the ceaseless erosion of wind and water. As a result, Australia is a flat country by world standards, and the continent's tallest mountains would be mere foothills elsewhere, a fact which has a profound effect on the weather and climate.

The age and layout of the rocks close to the surface show that Australia may be divided into three main geological areas. The first comprises the ancient rocks of the W and NW, which form a plateau covering much of WA and which occur also in isolated outcrops else-

where. The second area comprises the younger 'mountains' of the E, stretching from northern QLD into TAS, with a separate uplift in SA. Lastly, there is the low-lying land from the GULF OF CARPENTARIA to the coast of SA, covered largely by artesian basins formed when the sea invaded these regions (*see* ARTESIAN WATER). Of Australia's total land AREA (7 682 300km²), some three million square kilometres are taken up with what remains of the ancient W plateau, about one million by the E upland and the GREAT DIVIDING RANGE, and the rest by the central lowlands, including the NULLARBOR PLAIN and sedimentary basins along the coast. To unravel the geological history of Australia in order to discover why the landscape is as it is, it is necessary to read the record of the rocks, determine their ages, and seek in their composition and structure clues as to how and from what they were formed. The later chapters of this history can be written without much difficulty but any record of the origins of Australia has been largely destroyed by the forces that constantly erode, rebuild and alter the rocks that are the only witnesses of these ancient events.

Recent studies of rocks and sediments gathered from the beds of the oceans surrounding Australia by the deep-sea drilling ship *Glomar Challenger* have revealed the striking fact that Australia was once joined with South America, Africa and Antarctica in a supercontinent called GONDWANALAND. This also included India and some regions of crust now covered by oceans. Forces from deep within the earth split Gondwanaland up into a number of pieces or tectonic plates which began to move apart very slowly, opening up the oceans that now run between them. Australia and its surrounding oceans are currently being carried N by the movement of a plate which broke away from the Antarctica plate about 50 million years ago. This plate also carries India and most of the bed of the Indian Ocean.

The major zones of earthquake and volcanic activity and the regions where mountain ranges such as the Himalayas are being raised are found where these plates rub or scrape against each other, or where the edge of one plate is being pushed up or down by another. The boundary of the Australian-Indian plate runs through New Zealand, N to Tonga and then W, through the highlands of New Guinea, and through Indonesia. To the W and S of Australia the Indian and Southern Oceans continue to widen. Australia sits wholly within the plate, well away from the margin. Consequently, the continent is free from active volcanoes, major earthquakes and significant mountain building.

The recorded history of Australia begins with the earliest-known rocks, which lie in the region called the Western Australian Shield, a large plateau, or series of plateaus, rising now to about 500m high. Most of this land has not been under water for 700 million years and it contains rocks which are at least 1 500 million years old, some perhaps twice that age. Some

Warrumbungle Spires, Orana region of NSW

of these ancient rocks are now covered by the sea or by younger rocks, but others are still exposed in the SW corner of WA, a region geologists call Yilgarnia. The W edge of Yilgarnia forms the DARLING RANGE, visible from Perth, and to the E it stretches at least as far as the MUSGRAVE RANGES, SW of ALICE SPRINGS.

Slightly younger but still very ancient rocks border the remains of Yilgarnia to the N and E. To the N lies Nullagine, part of which forms the HAMERSLEY RANGE, now much dissected by rivers. Further N still, separated from Nullagine by a low-lying desert region formed by an invasion of the seas, lies Stuartiana, which underlies the KIMBERLEYS. Hundreds of millions of years ago, these ancient lands were all that existed of Australia, the rest of the modern continent developing later. In times when the seas covered much of the present area of the continent, these regions would have appeared as islands.

Rocks in these areas have been subjected over long periods to intense heat and pressure from forces within the earth. This has altered the appearance and properties of the rocks which were once mostly sandstone. This process can also concentrate minerals scattered through the rocks into deposits of metals and metal ores rich enough to be exploited. One such metal is gold and the gold mines of KALGOORLIE lie in Yilgarnia; in Nullagine there are the iron ore and asbestos deposits of the PILBARA. Other deposits that can be formed in this way include the ores of copper, lead, silver and zinc. It is significant that rocks more than 600 million years old have been uplifted and exposed by natural forces in two places in the E half of the country—around BROKEN HILL and on the E side of the BARKLY TABLELAND near MOUNT ISA. Both of these areas now support major mines extracting non-ferrous metals.

The three mountains to the N of the Musgrave Ranges are among the more striking of the ancient geological formations. These begin with the astounding collection of monoliths known as MOUNT OLGA, rising sheer and smooth to over 500m above the barren plains and separated by deep chasms filled with semi-tropical scrub. To the E are the better-known AYERS ROCK, a single rounded monolith rising to over 300m above the plain, and the 300m-high flat-topped MOUNT CONNER. All of these mountains are composed of ancient sedimentary rocks, mostly sandstones and conglomerates, which were once perhaps part of Yilgarnia. Certainly, like the MACDONNELL RANGES to the N, they are but the remnant stubs of once mighty ranges.

In general, the uplands of the W were very much higher than they are now. They were worn down by erosion and this produced silt, sand and fragments of rock which were carried by rivers and dumped on the bed of the ocean that lay to the S and E. This process went on for millions of years and under the weight of the accumulating sediments the floor of the ocean sank to form a vast trough, known technically as a geosyncline, holding beds of sediment thousands of metres thick. Gradually the weight of over-lying sediments squeezed out the water and hardened the sand, silt and rock fragments into sandstone, shale and conglomerate. Out of these beds of rock have been formed the Great Dividing Range and the other uplands of the E. The rocks were first lifted above sea level and folded into mountains about 200 million years ago. Erosion began at once and a cycle of wearing down and uplift then set in, finally producing the complex pattern of the E highlands which stretch in a discontinuous belt, about 400km wide and of varying elevation, from QLD to TAS. The last small-scale mountain building seems to have been about 12 million years ago when the BLUE MOUNTAINS, W of Sydney, and the SNOWY MOUNTAINS, on the NSW/VIC border, were uplifted.

Between the Eastern Highlands and the older lands of the W lie the central lowlands, occupying much of western QLD, NSW and VIC, and parts of SA. These were formed mainly from the beds of seas and lakes that ran from the N coast to the S coast some 150 million years ago. Beds of sandstone laid down at this time have made possible the pastoral industry in the semi-arid interior, since they now serve as artesian and sub-artesian basins holding reserves of water. There are some 20 separate basins beneath the surface or immediately offshore, including the Great Artesian Basin that underlies the arid region to the N of LAKE EYRE. In some of these basins the remains of marine life have been converted by natural processes to crude oil and natural gas. These include the GIPPSLAND Basin in BASS STRAIT, the BOWEN Basin near ROMA in QLD and the COOPER'S CREEK Basin in north-eastern SA.

At other times various sections of the coastline have been submerged, forming sedimentary basins of particular interest. About 200 million years ago the Sydney area lay beneath a salt swamp. The sediments in that swamp contained plant materials which, under the action of pressure, have become the extensive deposits of black coal that now underlie the city. Deposits of black and brown coal elsewhere were formed in a similar manner. Much more recently the sea invaded the land SE of Yilgarnia. Microscopic creatures with shells of calcium carbonate flourished; when they died, their shells piled up on the floor of the sea to form thick layers of limestone which, now uplifted and eroded by ground water, contain the fascinating limestone caves beneath the Nullarbor Plain. These caves, and others scattered over the continent, are decorated with stalactites and stalagmites formed drop by drop from evaporating lime-rich ground water.

Limestone also forms the major part of the GREAT BARRIER REEF, one of the world's finest collections of coral reefs. This complex structure was formed over a long period and in a variety of circumstances. Hugging the edge of the continental shelf, it is the work of countless tiny polyps, animals who fashion shelters of limestone for themselves. After the polyps die, individual corals and fragments are bound together into solid rock by other lime-bearing organisms, including certain seaweeds.

The events that build and wear away mountains or which lay down beds of coal and limestone are so slow as to be imperceptible. There have on the other hand been much more rapid and violent geological events in Australia's past, such as the outpouring of lava and ash by volcanoes. The existence of ancient, long-dormant volcanoes can be deduced from the presence of basalt, formed when the molten rock or lava from a volcano cooled and hardened, or from the rich red soil produced when these rocks are weathered. In the W, volcanoes were active a billion years ago; beds of volcanic rock 1000m thick can be found near the Kimberleys.

In the E, the activity has been much more recent but irregular in time and space. In some places the rocks formed by the cooling of molten material within the volcano have proved very resistant to erosion. While the surrounding rocks have been weathered away, the more resistant rocks have remained, producing such spectacular formations as Mt Warning near MURWILLUMBAH, the GLASS-HOUSE MOUNTAINS of QLD and the WAR-RUMBUNGLE RANGE in NSW. Flows of lava were common along the E coast, forming pockets of rich soil which in some places support rainforest, or remain largely uneroded to form the distinctive rounded hills common in parts of the Great Dividing Range. The most recent volcanic activity was in western VIC. It ceased only about 15 000 years ago, leaving a plain covered in basalt and ash to a depth of 100m and littered with dozens of old volcanic craters.

Although Australia is free from major earthquakes, there are stresses and strains from time to time within the crust. These lead to small but sometimes significant earthquakes, such as the one which caused millions of dollars worth of damage in Adelaide in 1954 and another which levelled the small town of Meckering in WA in 1968. The regions most prone to earthquakes include the SIMPSON DESERT, the area of the FLINDERS RANGES and some scattered locations in the E.

Natural processes, continuously at work, produce deposits of minerals which man has found of use. The evaporation of shallow seas and lakes has formed beds of salt and gypsum; the weathering of beds of clay in the hot wet regions in the N has built up extensive deposits of bauxite, the ore of aluminium; along the E shore certain compounds, washed from long-eroded mountains, have been concentrated by the action of the waves into the layers of mineral sands that underlie many beaches and which are a source of such metals as titanium.

Although the ages of mountain building and volcanic outpouring are now long past, the face of Australia continues to change. The forces of erosion—wind, waves and running water—are still at work. The Barrier Reef continues to grow. Even the familiar coastline is of recent origin; it is the result of the rise in the level of the sea that followed the end of the last Great Ice Age, little more than 10 000 years ago. Before that time much of the continental shelf was dry land and the mainland was joined above the water line to New Guinea and TAS.

See also mining and minerals

Further reading: Laseron, C.F. *The Face of Australia.* Angus & Robertson, Sydney, 1954; Taylor, G. *Sydneyside Scenery.* Angus & Robertson, Sydney, 1958; Branagan, D. & Packham, G. *Field Geology of New South Wales.* Science Press, Sydney, 1967.

George Town TAS (population 5 592 in 1981) Located in the N coastal plains region, on the E shore of PORT DALRYMPLE (which is formed by the estuary of the TAMAR RIVER where it flows into BASS STRAIT), George Town is 51km from LAUNCESTON along the East Tamar Highway. It is the administrative headquarters of the municipality (population 6 633) and the residential centre for the Comalco BELL BAY aluminium works. Port Dalrymple and the Tamar estuary were explored early in the 1800s, and the first permanent settlement was made in 1811. The town was named by Governor MACQUARIE in honour of King George III. It has a mild climate typical of the N coast, with an average annual rainfall of 865mm, spread throughout the year, but with a concentration in autumn and winter; August is the month of highest rainfall (115mm average), March the lowest (36mm).

Georgina River NT/QLD The headwaters of this stream are located in the BARKLY TABLELAND and it flows intermittently for over 1 100km in S and SE directions through arid western QLD and across the QLD/SA border to LAKE EYRE. Since it traverses a region of low and variable rainfall, it is only in exceptionally wet years that it reaches the lake. Among the headwater tributaries are the Burke and Hamilton Rivers which rise in the

Selwyn Range S of CLONCURRY. Below the confluence with the Hamilton, the Georgina changes its name to Eyre Creek, and runs through the CHANNEL COUNTRY, where there is good cattle fattening in wet years.

Geraldton

Geraldton WA (population 20 895 in 1981) Located 427km by road and 503km by rail NNW of Perth, it is the key port and administrative centre for the mid-W region of WA. Situated on Champion Bay, the town boasts an average of eight hours sunshine per day, all year round; known as the 'sun city', it is a mecca for tourists seeking the beaches and surf along the Indian Ocean coastline. The town has an average annual rainfall of 477mm, concentrated mainly in the winter months (June average 119mm, December 5mm). The first white visitors to the area were Dutch sailors marooned on the coast and the victims of shipwrecks in the 17th century, but the first recorded visit by an Englishman was made in 1822 by Captain Phillip Parker King. It was not until 1849 that the town site was surveyed and named Gerald Town after the Governor of the colony, Sir Charles Fitzgerald.

Its original function was as an export centre for copper, gold and lead mined in the region. It remains an important trading centre today, exporting produce of the hinterland—wheat (the main agricultural product of the area), wool, rock lobsters (a major export item to the USA), barley, vegetables (particularly tomatoes) and iron ore mined at Koolanooka. The town is growing rapidly: between 1971 and 1976 its population grew from 15 457 to 18 773; by 1981 it increased to over 20 000, indicative of its role as a business and service focus for a prosperous rural region which produces about a fifth of the State's grain, as well as wool, fat lambs, pigs and beef cattle.

A maritime museum in the town records the early days of Dutch exploration and the many shipwrecks on nearby reefs. A gem and mineral museum illustrates the significance of mining in the town's economy. The National Trust (WA) has listed several buildings in the town for preservation, including the prison (formerly the district hospital, built in 1887), the Cultural Trust Library (formerly the railway station and mechanics institute, 1879), the post office (1893), several churches and the Mission to Seamen (1861). During World War II, Geraldton was a major army camp and a base for American submarines and flying boats.

Further reading: Wilson, H.H. *Geraldton Sketchbook.* Rigby, Adelaide, 1975.

Germans in Australia

Germans in Australia The 1981 census revealed that 110 758 persons resident in Australia had been born in Germany. C.A. Price, a leading authority on multicultural affairs, in a study of the ethnic origins of the Australian population, based on an eight-generation analysis, estimated that the total German component was equivalent to 581 200 persons in 1978. Germans were the first ethnic minority to form a cultural community in Australia, and they also formed the first religious settlement. They built picturesque villages grouped around their Lutheran churches, held vintage festivals, established German-speaking schools and developed a thriving and convivial club life. The annual BAROSSA VALLEY vintage festival is celebrated in the German tradition.

South Australia Two years after free settlers from the UK founded the colony of SA, the first major influx of German migrants occurred (1838-39) with the arrival of about 500 Lutherans from Klemzig in Prussian Silesia, seeking asylum from religious persecution. They were helped financially by George Fife ANGAS and 200 of them were settled on the TORRENS RIVER a few kilometres from Adelaide on land initially leased at a nominal rental from Angas. This settlement was named Klemzig; the other 300 settled at Hahndorf. The new colonists supplied Adelaide with vegetables and dairy produce.

Other German settlers followed and together they played a most important part in the development of SA. They grew farm and garden produce, participated in the wool industry, exported grain, advanced fruit growing and developed the wine industry. The German community grew most of the grapes and contributed their specialised knowledge and labour to the wine industry while priests from Silesia produced altar wines from a vineyard they established in the CLARE district in the 1840s. The Orlando vineyard was established by J. Gramp in 1847 and other German names—Seppelt, Sobels, Buring, Gottlieb and Hoffman—have all been associated with the wine industry in the Barossa Valley, which is identified particularly with the German ethnic minority.

Dancing at the Schuetzenfest, Hahndorf SA

Victoria German settlement in VIC started in 1845 and Lutheran communities were established mainly in the districts surrounding HAMILTON and HORSHAM. The principal contributions of the German settlers were the creation of a wine industry and the opening up of wheat growing districts in the WIMMERA-MALLEE region. In the 1920s and 1930s German expertise also made a significant contribution to the establishment of the coal-briquette industry at YALLOURN.

Queensland German farmers played a large part in the development of dairying, wheat growing, viticulture and general agriculture in the DARLING DOWNS and the S parts of the State, while in the central and N coastal areas they engaged extensively in the sugar industry.

Lutheran congregations included IPSWICH, TOOWOOMBA, MACKAY, BUNDABERG and KINGAROY.

New South Wales For the most part Germans migrating to NSW have been rapidly absorbed into the rest of the population and Lutheranism has never been as strong in this State as it has been in SA and QLD, although congregations were established in ALBURY and the RIVERINA. In the early years of the colony individual German migrants, rather than communities of German settlers, exercised considerable influence in the colony's development. It was a German surveyor, Baron August Theodore Henry Alt, who laid out the first settlements at SYDNEY COVE and PARRAMATTA for Governor PHILLIP. In 1791 one of the earliest vineyards in Australia was developed by another German, Philip Schaffer, who planted vines provided by Governor Phillip on a grant of 57ha on the Parramatta River. The gold rushes after 1850 brought large numbers of Germans to NSW, both from overseas and from other Australian colonies, but they did not establish permanent ethnic communities.

The effect of the two World Wars During World War I people suspected of having German ancestry suffered economic discrimination, internment and social ostracism. For six years it was not possible to hold religious synods or pastors' conferences. In QLD eight pastors were interned and after the war two were deported. Public pressure led the SA government to take over 50 or more German-speaking schools but this ultimately had the effect of hastening the integration of children born in Australia of German parents. The publication of German-language newspapers was banned and more than 40 German names of towns were replaced with British names: Hahndorf (Hahn's Village) became Ambleside, Blumberg became Birdwood, Kaiserstuhl became Mt Kitchener and Lobethal (Valley of Praise) became Tweedvale. However, in 1935 the German place-names were restored.

After 1928 the Nazi Party in Germany and its associated organisations began to propagate the more aggressive pan-Germanic theory that blood overrides nationality and that the German race was destined to conquer the world. It directed a campaign to gain support from German communities established in SA. Several hundred Australian-born citizens closely identified themselves with the Nazi Party and became a potential Fifth Column during World War II. However, it is estimated that of 26 000 persons of German origin in SA in 1939, 19 000 were completely assimilated while about 7 000 were pro-German and only about 1000 were pro-Nazi. Another effect of the Nazi campaign was that some of the most creative and artistic settlers who came to Australia were the German-speaking Jewish refugees who fled from the persecution of Nazi anti-Semitic policy in Germany during the 1930s. Many of these people have contributed to Australia's musical and artistic life.

The German heritage Other Australians have for many years been able to enjoy the

German heritage because German has been taught as a language in many secondary schools in addition to the ethnic schools maintained by some German communities. The universities have provided Chairs in German and the Goethe Institute helps to maintain the quality of teaching of the language and culture in Australia by its professional support for teachers and its generous scholarships enabling Australians to study in Germany. The embassy of the German Federal Republic has also given support to the German language school movement, and in recent years Professor Michael Clyne of Monash University has pioneered a vigorous experiment of teaching German in primary schools. The ethnic radio groups in both Sydney and Melbourne have contributed to spreading the German heritage, and Australia has two newspapers printed in German: *Neue Welt* ('New World'; Melbourne) and *Die Wolche* ('The Week'; Sydney). It is in fact in the cultural field that German immigrants have contributed most to the enrichment of Australian life; and particularly in the field of music.

Contributors in music The first national anthem competition in 1860 was won by Karl Linger with his music for 'The Song of Australia'. Walter Andreas Dullo, who left Germany in the 1930s, is a founder of MUSICA VIVA AUSTRALIA, one of the world's largest chamber music societies. Australia has also had the benefit of the skills and talents of modern composers Felix WERDER and George DREYFUS; of conductors Henry Krips and Walter Stiasny; of Stefan Haag, formerly a member of the Vienna Boys' Choir; of Werner Baer, a composer-pianist who became Music Development Officer of the Australian Broadcasting Commission; of Charles J. Berg, formerly president of Musica Viva and a chairman of the Australian Opera Company.

Other notable Germans in Australia These include Hans HEYSEN, the well-known landscape artist; Bernhard Holtermann, who found the world's largest specimen of reef gold at HILL END in NSW, in 1872; Ludwig LEICHHARDT, the well-known explorer; Conrad MARTENS, landscape artist; Baron Ferdinand VON MUELLER, botanist; William Rucker, Melbourne's first banker and a pioneer of the overseas shipping trade; Walter Schobel, one of the founders of Radio Ethnic Australia; Gottlieb Schuler, editor of the Melbourne *Age*; and Friedrich Vern, Peter LALOR's first lieutenant at the EUREKA STOCKADE.

Further reading: Price, C.A. *German Settlers in South Australia*. Melbourne University Press, Melbourne, 1945; Borrie, W.D. *Italians and Germans in Australia*. F.W. Cheshire, Melbourne, 1954; Vondra, J. *German Speaking Settlers in Australia*. Cavalier Press, Melbourne, 1981; Price, C.A. *Australian Immigration, A Bibliography and Digest*. Australian National University Press, Canberra, 1979.

giant grass tree *see* Epacridaceae

giant panda *see* slugs, etc.

gibber This is an Aboriginal word meaning 'stone', which has been adopted as the name for rock pebbles and small boulders spread over the surface of some inland arid regions of Australia. These rock fragments, composed of quartz and ironstone, have been worn smooth by the abrasive action of wind-blown sand, so that some desert travellers have described them as glistening like mirrors in the sun. The terms 'gibber plains' and 'gibber country' are used to describe extensive areas where these pebbles and boulders occur in western NSW, in N parts of SA, and in the E arid areas of WA. STURT'S STONY DESERT is typical gibber country. It is commonly found that it is easier to negotiate this type of desert in a motor vehicle, than it is to travel through sand-dune desert areas.

Gibbs, May (*c*1875-1969) Writer and illustrator of children's stories. Born in England, she was brought by her family to WA in 1879 and educated there and at art schools in England. Her fairy-stories and illustrations were aimed at imparting to children her own love for the Australian bush and its wild creatures. They include *The Gumnut Babies* (1916), *Snugglepot and Cuddlepie* (1918) and other stories based on the adventures of fairy-like gumnut flowers. A comic strip 'Bib and Bub', based on her characters, ran for many years in Sydney newspapers.

Gibson Desert WA A vast stretch of arid country, consisting of sand-dunes and GIBBER plains, the Gibson Desert is located in the mid-interior of the State, between the WARBURTON RANGE to the S and the GREAT SANDY DESERT to the N. It is a particularly barren and inhospitable area which few Europeans had ever penetrated until the 1960s when tracks marked out for the recovery of rockets launched at WOOMERA made access possible for four-wheel-drive vehicles. The explorer Ernest GILES crossed the desert from E to W in 1874 under most difficult conditions and named it after a member of his party who died on the journey.

Gidgealpa SA This natural gas field, discovered in 1963, is located in the NE of the State near the QLD/NSW/SA border, on the S edge of STURT'S STONY DESERT. The gas from Gidgealpa and from the MOOMBA field, in the same region, is transported by a 780km-long pipeline to Adelaide where it is used mainly for electricity generation. This pipeline came into operation in 1969. In 1974 work commenced on another major pipeline to convey gas from these fields 1 300km across NSW to Sydney; it was completed and came into operation in late 1976. The name Gidgealpa probably comes from a corruption of the Aboriginal word *kiljalpa*, meaning 'to stand in the shade of a grey rain cloud'.

gidgee This name is given to a grey-foliaged wattle, *Acacia cambagei* (family MIMOSACEAE), which grows in dry, inland Australia. When wet, the foliage smells offensively, hence the alternative name of stinking wattle. The hard timber is termite resistant and is used for fencing.

Gilbert, John (?-1845) Naturalist and explorer. Born in England, he arrived in Australia in 1838 with John GOULD, by whom he had been engaged as a zoological assistant. His work contributed greatly to the comprehensiveness of Gould's books on Australian birds. Between 1839 and 1844 he travelled extensively in WA, and to PORT ESSINGTON and HOUTMAN ABROLHOS, building up a significant collection of specimens of birds and mammals, many of which were unknown to science. In 1844, at the DARLING DOWNS, he joined Ludwig LEICHHARDT's overland expedition to Port Essington as second-in-command. He was killed by Aborigines at MITCHELL RIVER in QLD. The diary he kept during the expedition contains much valuable scientific and historical information and is now in the Mitchell Library in Sydney. Gilbert Range QLD and GILBERT RIVER are named after him.

Gilbert River QLD Located in the far N of the State, it rises on the W slopes of the GREAT DIVIDING RANGE, N of HUGHENDEN, and flows in a general NW course for more than 500km across the S part of CAPE YORK to a mud-fringed estuary on the E shore of the GULF OF CARPENTARIA. Its main tributary is the Einasleigh River which has a course of over 400km and joins the Gilbert on its right bank, about 160km from the mouth. The whole of the river basin is in a region of high rainfall (above 1000mm yearly), but the rain falls mainly in the summer months and there is a marked dry period during the cooler season; hence the river floods in the wet months, inundating the adjacent alluvial lowlands, and ceases to flow during the dry season. The area is scrub country, with beef cattle grazing as the main rural activity. In the lowland tract, the river has a great many meander loops, and divides to form ANABRANCHES, some of which link it to adjacent rivers, such as the Staaten to the N, during flood times.

Giles, Ernest (1835-97) Explorer. He was born in Bristol and in 1851 went to SA, to join his parents who had emigrated while he was still at school. As an explorer he is remembered for a number of inland expeditions, which were more remarkable for their length and difficulty than for the value of his discoveries. In 1872 he went W from the FINKE RIVER in northern SA and discovered LAKE AMADEUS, and in the following year explored further in the same general area. However, his major work was done in 1875-76 when, setting out from Beltana in SA, he went around the S end of LAKE TORRENS and across the NULLARBOR PLAIN to Perth. He returned by a N route, not far S of the Tropic of Capricorn for most of the way, from GERALDTON to Peake telegraph station in the far N of SA. These journeys, which passed through some of the most in-

Ernest Giles

hospitable country in Australia, were remarkable feats of endurance.
Further reading: Green, L. *Ernest Giles.* Melbourne University Press, Melbourne, 1963; Dutton, G. *Australia's Last Explorer: Ernest Giles.* Rigby, Adelaide, 1974.

Gilgandra NSW (population 2 700 in 1981) This country town lies in the NW plains region of the State, at the junction of the Oxley and Newell Highways and the starting point of the Castlereagh Highway, 77km E of WARREN, 66km N of DUBBO and 485km NW of Sydney. It is situated on the CASTLEREAGH RIVER at an elevation of 280m above sea level and has an average annual rainfall of 584mm, spread fairly evenly throughout the year. The major rural activities in the district are wheat growing and sheep grazing, but there is also some beef cattle grazing, pig raising and timber-getting. Gilgandra has been called 'the town of windmills' because for many years the residents used windmills to pump ARTESIAN WATER from the rocks of the basin on which the town was built. The town name comes from an Aboriginal word meaning 'long waterhole'.

Gill, Samuel Thomas (1818-80) Artist. Born in Somerset, Gill arrived in Adelaide in 1839 with his parents. He had some success sketching modest portraits and rural scenes and travelled as the artist with an expedition into the arid mid-N regions of SA. Later he joined the gold rush to VIC, where he became known for a series of sketches of the goldfields, which were published between 1852 and 1868. They were extremely popular, having a primitive gusto that his later lithographic publications of the environs of Sydney and Melbourne lacked. A self-taught artist, his work depended upon his irreverent and sardonic wit to lift it from the banal to the intriguing. He died in 1880, a broken-down alcoholic found on the steps of Melbourne's post office, a victim of the drug whose effects on goldfield life he had so accurately portrayed about 30 years previously.

Gilmore, Dame Mary Jean *née* Cameron (1865-1962) Poet. Born near GOULBURN in NSW, she became a teacher, involved herself in trade union and socialist movements, and in 1895 joined William LANE's socialist

venture, NEW AUSTRALIA, in Paraguay. There she married William Gilmore, one of the foundation members. After the collapse of the settlement in 1899 she taught English in Paraguay for a time, returned to Australia in 1902, lived for 10 years in CASTERTON in VIC, and then spent the rest of her life in Sydney. She published several volumes of poetry, including *Marri'd and Other Verses* (1910), *The Passionate Heart* (1918), *The Tilted Cart* (1925), *Battlefields* (1939), *The Disinherited* (1941) and *Fourteen Men* (1954), and two volumes of autobiographical reflections, *Old Days: Old Ways* (1934) and *More Recollections* (1935). The warm humanity of her reflective verse has won her a very high place among Australian poets, in spite of the lack of precision in thought and expression in some of her writing. She was made a DBE in 1937 for services to literature. Throughout her life she was prominent also in campaigning on issues of Aboriginal and general social welfare. Her protrait by William DOBELL hangs in the Art Gallery of New South Wales.
Further reading: Lawson, S. *Mary Gilmore.* Oxford University Press, Melbourne, 1966.

Gipps, Sir George (1791-1847) Governor of NSW. Born in Kent, he joined the Royal Engineers in 1809, saw active service in the Peninsular War and later served in the West Indies. He came to NSW as Governor early in 1838. At that time the government was faced with many problems. The population was growing rapidly and a desire for self-government developing strongly. The squatters, having gained the legal right to the use of their runs through BOURKE's annual licence system, were pressing their claims for security of tenure; they were also spreading further inland, with disastrous effects on the Aborigines. The expected abolition of transportation had produced among some squatters a desire to import cheap non-European labour, and this appeared likely to become a very contentious issue. Finally, there was considerable disagreement over the future of education.

On the whole Gipps dealt with such problems logically and justly, but in doing so was widely and fiercely criticised. A few months after his arrival, 28 Aborigines were murdered at Myall Creek in retaliation for an alleged 'outrage'. Gipps' insistence that the seven white men responsible should be brought to trial without favour resulted in their being hanged and in his being subjected to a great deal of abuse. In education he personally favoured the foundation of 'national' schools, but decided to continue the existing State-supported denominational system because he judged the weight of public opinion to favour such a course. In land policy he proposed in 1844 to give the squatter security of tenure if he would buy 320 acres (about 130ha) of his run at £1 an acre every eight years. However, this reasonable arrangement was bitterly opposed by the pastoralists and, in 1847, the year after Gipps left NSW, they were granted long leases on terms which made it very difficult for future colonial

governments to promote closer settlement.
Further reading: Barker, S.J. 'The Governorship of Sir George Gipps' in *Journal of the Royal Australian Historical Society.* (vol 16, parts 3 & 4, 1930); Roberts, S.H. *The Squatting Age in Australia, 1835-47.* (2nd edn) Melbourne University Press, Melbourne, 1964.

Gippsland VIC This region in the SE of the State extends from WESTERN PORT BAY to the NSW border. Large stretches of the region are rugged, dissected, forested uplands of the GREAT DIVIDING RANGE which are sparsely settled, while the lower-lying sections along the river valleys and coastal plains are the areas of population concentration. The region is drained by numerous rivers: the SNOWY RIVER in the E; the TAMBO RIVER, the Nicholson River, the MACALISTER RIVER (and its main tributary, the AVON RIVER) and the MITCHELL RIVER which have general N-S courses from the uplands to the Gippsland lakes (LAKE KING); the THOMSON-LATROBE river system draining into LAKE WELLINGTON; and the Tarwin River in the SW of the region with its estuary in Venus Bay, E of WONTHAGGI. In the central part of the Gippsland coast is the NINETY MILE BEACH; at the southernmost point is WILSON'S PROMONTORY and in the SW section are the STRZELECKI RANGES. The main urban centres are MOE-YALLOURN, MORWELL, TRARALGON, SALE, BAIRNSDALE, WARRAGUL, WONTHAGGI and MAFFRA.

Gippsland is crossed from E to W by the Princes Highway which traverses the coastal plains in the E and then follows the Latrobe Valley; the South Gippsland Highway makes a loop from Sale S of the Strzelecki Ranges, while the Bass Highway skirts the E shore of Western Port Bay. The State railway system

Typical Gippsland countryside

serves the S part of the region: a line extends E to ORBOST (372km from Melbourne) with a number of branch lines and a line goes SE to YARRAM (220km from Melbourne) with a branch to Wonthaggi. Rainfall over the region is generally high, and is distributed throughout the year. The highland receives yearly totals in excess of 1 200mm. Elsewhere the average annual rainfall is lower: Warragul, 1 051mm; Yallourn, 910mm; Orbost, 839mm; Sale, 629mm; and Bairnsdale, 696mm.

The Macalister River irrigation scheme, with GLENMAGGIE DAM as its main storage, has been developed to provide water for pastures and crops in the Maffra-Sale area. The economy of the Latrobe Valley is dominated by open-cut mining of the brown coal deposits and the associated power-generation plants, briquette factories and other manufacturing industries. The major rural activities of the region are dairying and beef cattle grazing, with cultivation of crops such as oats and flax, some orcharding and vegetable growing, and timber-getting in the uplands. There are 14 national parks in the region, the largest being Wilson's Promontory National Park (49 000ha), Gippsland Lakes Coastal Park (15 550ha), Holey Plains National Park located SW of Sale (10 450ha) and Croajingolong National Park in the E (86 000ha). The Gippsland region was discovered in 1838 by Angus McMillan who named it Australia Caledonia after his native Scotland, but the explorer STRZELECKI, who traversed the region in 1840, named it in honour of Sir George GIPPS, then governor of NSW, and this name was officially adopted.
Further reading: Wilson, J.L.J. (ed) 'Gippsland' in *Current Affairs Bulletin.* (vol 16, no 12, September 1955); McIntyre, A.J. *Gippsland.* Longmans, London, 1958; Austin, K.A. *Gippsland Sketchbook.* Rigby, Adelaide, 1975.

Girl Guides Association of Australia

The Girl Guides movement began in Australia in 1910. In 1926 the six State Associations agreed to form a Federal Council, which later became the Girl Guides Association of Australia. Two years later Australia became a foundation member of the World Association of Girl Guides and Girl Scouts. Australian membership is about 90 000.

The general objective of Guiding is to provide girls with opportunities for self-development through challenging and enjoyable activities, study courses and community service. Members are divided into four age groups, namely Brownie Guides (seven to 11), Guides (10½ to 14½), Ranger Guides (14-18) and Rangers (18-25). The method used is based initially on the patrol system, with the emphasis on small-group learning and practical activities. Training in skills and crafts and participation in outdoor activities is aimed at making the Guide an all-round person, self-reliant and self-disciplined, with a desire to use her knowledge and skills in the service of others. Activities are arranged in an eight-point programme which is designed to give each girl opportunities to develop her mind, creative ability, character, enjoyment of the outdoors, relationships with others, readiness and ability to serve others, physical fitness and homecraft skills. Adult leaders, known as Guiders, go through a programme of training after which they receive a Warrant. The Association co-operates with many other organisations, including the SCOUT ASSOCIATION OF AUSTRALIA. However, it and the Scout Association are completely separate bodies.

Gladstone

Gladstone QLD (population 22 083 in 1981) This city, port and industrial centre on the E coast of the State, 559km by road NNW of Brisbane and 135km SE of ROCKHAMPTON, experienced a period of boom growth in the 1960s. Located on Port Curtis, it was established in 1847 and named in honour of the then British Prime Minister, who envisaged it as the capital of the new colony of QLD. However, these plans were changed by the succeeding British government and Brisbane was selected as the site of the colony's capital. But Gladstone grew as a commercial and service centre for its grain growing and cattle grazing hinterland and for the gold and copper mines in the region, even though its progress was less spectacular than its N competitor, Rockhampton. The 1960s brought a new era of prosperity: in 1961 the port was developed as the exporting centre for coal to Japan from the MOURA field in the DAWSON RIVER valley and bulk coal-loading facilities now handle these exports as well as coal from the CALLIDE VALLEY; additional grain-handling facilities were installed, a rail link to Moura was constructed, and in 1967 an alumina plant, using bauxite shipped from WEIPA, was established (by 1973 it had become the world's biggest alumina plant); a thermal power station using Callide and Moura coal was built; and a sulphuric acid plant using pyrites from MOUNT MORGAN was established.

All these industrial and port developments, together with other secondary industries based on rural production such as meat works and dairy factories, accelerated the city's growth and it is now the State's biggest tonnage port. The harbour is a deep-water sound, sheltered by CURTIS ISLAND, and the city is flanked by two rivers—to the NW is the Calliope and to the S is the Boyne, which is the source of the city's water supply. Quoin Is, within Port Curtis, is a rugged and heavily wooded recreation and holiday centre, linked to the city by a launch service. There are panoramic vistas of the city and harbour from Auckland and Radar Hills, two vantage points on a sign-posted tourist drive around the city. The surrounding rural district produces beef cattle, grain and cotton; in the Yarwun area, to the NW, paw-paws are grown commercially. Gladstone is the embarkation point for HERON ISLAND, reached by launch or helicopter.

Glanville-Hicks, Peggy

Glanville-Hicks, Peggy (1912-) Composer. Born in Melbourne, she began composition lessons with Fritz Hart at the age of 15. She won an open scholarship to the Royal College of Music in 1931, where she studied with Vaughan Williams (composition), Arthur Benjamin (piano), Constant Lambert and Sir Malcolm Sargent (conducting). At the 1938 International Society for Contemporary Music (ISCM) Festival held in London she was the first Australian composer to be represented when Sir Adrian Boult conducted two movements from her *Choral Suite*.

From 1942 to 1959 Miss Glanville-Hicks lived in the USA and became an American citizen. During this period she composed the bulk of her large output, which placed her firmly as a composer of international status. She also worked as a critic on the New York *Herald Tribune* and wrote many reviews and articles for such journals as the *Musical Quarterly*, *Juilliard Review* and *Musical America*. These gained her a reputation as one of the most perceptive writers on contemporary music in the USA.

Outstanding among her many compositions are her opera scores, of which *The Transposed Heads*, premiered in Louisville in 1954, was her first major work to be performed in Australia. This occurred in 1970 in Sydney, when Roger COVELL directed the performance by University of New South Wales Opera in the composer's presence. Her three-act opera *Nausicaa* was presented at the 1961 Athens Festival with great success.

Peggy Glanville-Hicks was an early pioneer in the use of non-European musical elements, especially those of Asia. After her long stay in the USA and, later, in Greece, she joined the small but important group of composers who have returned to Australia as permanent residents. She lives in Sydney and continues to be an active apologist for the cause of composition in Australia.
Further reading: Murdoch, J. *Australia's Contemporary Composers.* Macmillan, Melbourne, 1972.

Glasshouse Mountains

Glasshouse Mountains QLD Located in the SE of the State, at the S approach to the SUNSHINE COAST and adjacent to the Bruce Highway, about 70km N of Brisbane, these mountains comprise a group of 11 peaks rising sheer from the coastal plain. They are volcanic plugs—giant cores of long-extinct volcanoes, made of hard rocks (rhyolite and trachyte) whose outer cones have been eroded away exposing the monoliths. The highest of the peaks is Mt Beerwah (556m elevation). Four of the mountains have been reserved as national parks: Mt Tibrogargan (in an area of 291ha), Mt Beerwah (245ha), Mt Coonowrin (113ha) and Mt Ngungun (49ha). The mountains were sighted and named by James COOK on his voyage along the E coast of the continent in 1770; it is thought that he gave them the name Glasshouse because their smooth rock surfaces reflected the sun, as if made of glass.

glasswort see Chenopodiaceae

Gleeson, James Timothy (1915-)

Artist. Born in Sydney, he studied art at the East Sydney Technical College and in the USA. Gleeson began experimenting with surrealist paintings in the late 1930s, exhibiting his first work in this style in 1939 at the Contemporary Art Sociey Exhibition, Sydney. The arrival in the same year of Salvador Dali's surrealist work, *L'Homme Fleur*, as part of Sir Keith Murdoch's *Melbourne Herald* exhibition of modern French and British painting, raised a great deal of interest—an interest which became something of a running battle between older, conservative opinion, and youthful, progressive enthusiasm. It nevertheless brought surrealism before the public eye, and confirmed Gleeson in his interest. This now became something of a crusade, for which he wrote and lectured enthusiastically. Although others, notably Albert TUCKER, Eric Thake, Arthur BOYD, Russell DRYSDALE and Sydney NOLAN, have all experimented with surrealism, none has made it so much his personal trademark as Gleeson. A Trustee of the National Gallery, Canberra, Gleeson has also established a reputation as one of the most perceptive art critics in the country.

Glen Innes NSW (population 6 052 in 1981)

A town in the NEW ENGLAND region, it is situated · at the intersection of the New England and Gwydir Highways, and on the N tablelands railway, 665km by road and 681km by rail N of Sydney. At an elevation of 1 073m above sea level, the town has warm summer conditions, but the winters are cold with frequent frosts and occasional heavy snow. The average annual rainfall is 840mm, concentrated mainly in the summer months, from November to February. The town is located just W of the main watershed between streams which flow E to the Pacific (the headwater tributaries of the Nymboida River which flows into the CLARENCE) and those flowing N and W to the MACINTYRE RIVER and on into the DARLING RIVER. The surrounding rural district is important for sheep and cattle raising, mixed farming, dairying, crop cultivation (particularly of maize, oats and vegetables on the better volcanic soils), and some orcharding. There are several forestry reserves in the district and many of the streams provide good seasonal trout fishing. Much of the region contains minerals of commercial value, but they occur in small and widely scattered deposits; tin mining has become important, and other minerals known to occur include bismuth, antimony, copper and arsenic. Gem fossicking, particularly for sapphires, is a popular pastime for both residents and visitors. There are three Crown land sapphire fossicking areas in the district.

The town takes its name from an early settler, Major Archibald Clune Innes, who also bestowed the many Scottish place-names in the district. In 1851 the initial survey for the township was made, and in 1872 it was proclaimed a municipal area. The Land of the Beardies History House and Museum contains

Grey Street in Glen Innes in the 1920's

a collection of relics from the past and depicts life as it was in Glen Innes more than a century ago. The National Trust (NSW) has listed a number of buildings in the town and has classified the town hall, Williams Club Hotel and Grand Central Hotel for preservation as part of the cultural heritage. The town has a number of secondary industries: a butter factory and bacon processing works, a plant for quick-freezing of vegetables, brickyards, cement-pipe works, a tannery and timber mills. An agricultural research station established in 1902, located 8km NW of the town, and the Shannon Vale Nutritional Station situated 15km ENE of the town, are both concerned with research on livestock and agricultural conditions in New England.

There are some unique natural landscape features in the district—the Balancing Rock, 12km S of the town on the highway, consists of a 4m-high pear-shaped granite tor sitting precariously on a bed of flat rock; the Mushroom Rock, 49km SE of Glen Innes near the town of Backwater, consists of three large rocks finely balanced in the shape of a mushroom. The Gibraltar Range National Park, covering 17 273ha, located 68km E of the town, includes some striking granite rock formations, deep gorges and spectacular waterfalls where streams plunge from the plateau heights on their way to the coastal rivers. The Guy Fawkes National Park, located S of the Gwydir Highway, is a rugged, inaccessible wilderness area of 27 763ha covering similar gorge and waterfall country of the Guy Fawkes, Aberfoyle and other tributary rivers of the Clarence system. The Rose Festival, held annually in November at Glen Innes, is a popular attraction for district residents and visitors.

Glenbawn Dam NSW

Located on the HUNTER RIVER, it is an earth-and-rockfill structure, with a storage capacity of 350 000 ML, situated 11km upstream from Aberdeen and 14km SE of SCONE. The dam supplies water for domestic, stock and irrigation purposes lower downstream, and provides an assured water supply to towns on the Hunter such as Aberdeen, MUSWELLBROOK, Denman and SINGLETON. Though the site for the structure was selected in 1939, it was not until after World War II that construction commenced; the main wall was completed in 1957. Average

annual rainfall in the Hunter Valley varies from 1 520mm in the NE section to 530mm in the central part, but most of the valley receives less than 890mm yearly. Consequently, the farming areas of the valley are liable to suffer the ravages of drought, and agriculture is hazardous without irrigation; the importance of Glenbawn Dam in this respect was clearly demonstrated in the exceptionally dry period from 1964 to 1967. In the year 1976-77, the area of irrigated land utilising Glenbawn water was over 15 500ha. Furthermore, in years of unusually heavy rainfall on the catchment ranges of the valley, the Hunter is liable to flood, causing damage to farmlands on the alluvial flats and inundating river towns. The dam has been designed to reduce the incidence and severity of these floods. The lake held back by the dam wall covers an area of 1 214ha, extending into the foothills of the MOUNT ROYAL RANGE and it is noted for its scenic beauty as well as for swimming, fishing and other aquatic sports.

Glenelg River VIC

Located in the SW corner of the State, it rises in the GRAMPIANS between HAMILTON and STAWELL and flows generally W then S for about 460km, passing through a wide rocky gorge in its lower reaches with cliffs up to 46m high, to an estuary on DISCOVERY BAY near the VIC/SA border. The small fishing resort of Nelson is located on the E side of the estuary. The main tributary of the Glenelg is the Wannon River, which also rises in the Grampians, flows first S, parallel to the Serra Range, then in a series of loops generally W to join the main stream just S of CASTERTON. On the upper reaches of the Glenelg is the ROCKLANDS DAM, a concrete structure 28m high, completed in 1953, with a storage capacity of 335 500ML; it is the major storage for the WIMMERA-MALLEE domestic and livestock water supply scheme which serves the low-rainfall regions of north-western VIC. The Lower Glenelg National Park, 27 300ha of bush and heathland, includes the 65km-long gorge section of the river, as well as the Bulley Ranges, Princess Margaret Rose limestone caves, the river lookout at Jones Ridge, and the Kentbruck Heath, an area of swampy heathland and dry ridges to the E of the river. Discovery Bay Coastal Park covers 8 450ha of ocean beach, sand dunes, lagoons and swamps, and stretches along a coastal strip from PORTLAND to the SA border. The Glenelg was discovered and named by the explorer Major Thomas MITCHELL in 1836 in honour of the then Colonial Secretary, Lord Glenelg.

Glenmaggie Dam VIC

Constructed on the MACALISTER RIVER in GIPPSLAND, it has a capacity of 190 300ML and is fed by streams from a catchment area covering 1 891km². It is located upstream from and NW of MAFFRA and SALE. Water stored in the reservoir is used for the irrigation of pastures for beef and dairy cattle in the Macalister River Irrigation District, first settled as an irrigation project in

National Library of Australia

1926. Following World War II, the dam was enlarged and additional areas were supplied with irrigation water as a War Service Land Settlement scheme.

Glenorchy TAS (population 41 910 in 1981). Often referred to as the sister-city of Hobart, Glenorchy lies to the N of and adjacent to the State capital, covering a number of suburbs (including Moonah, Claremont, Collinsvale, Rosetta, Montrose and Austins Ferry). It forms an extension of Hobart's metropolitan development, but it is a city in its own right and dates from the earliest days of the colony when Governor MACQUARIE named it Glenorchy because the countryside reminded him of the Glenorchy district of Argyll in Scotland. The city includes some of the State's major industrial enterprises, such as the Electrolytic Zinc Co.'s Risdon works, the Cadbury-Schweppes factory at CLAREMONT, and the Derwent Park factory of Universal Textiles. Historical buildings are scattered throughout the city; about 15 have been classified, and many more listed, by the National Trust (TAS) for preservation as part of the nation's cultural heritage. These include the Black Snake Inn and the Watch House at Granton, the home 'Lowestoft' at Berriedale, 'Summerholme' and Pitt Farm at Moonah, several churches and numerous cottages.

Glenrowan VIC (population 200 in 1981) A small township established where the Hume Highway and the interstate railway route between Melbourne and Sydney pass through a gap in the Warly Ranges, Glenrowan is 219km by road NE of Melbourne, 16km SW of WANGARATTA and 24km NE of BENALLA. Its claim to fame is that it was here that bushranger Ned KELLY made his last stand in 1880.

gliders see possums, etc.

gliding This sport has experienced increased popularity in Australia since World War II. According to devotees, soaring through the sky in a glider can be exhilarating and mentally stimulating, and these attributes plus the sense of freedom have attracted an increasing number of Australians to the sport.

Gliders are wide-winged motorless aircraft

An AWS 19 Standard Class sailplane over the Murray River in SA

which are usually towed aloft behind conventional light aircraft to altitudes of about 600m and then released. The glider pilot waits until he feels a sudden updraught (a thermal current) beneath his glider before releasing the tow line. On release he circles within the thermal, rising with the air current to altitudes of between 1 500m and 1 800m, depending on the lift of the thermal and his own skill—experienced pilots can gain lifts up to 4 500m or more from a good current (the highest recorded is about 13 700m). The pilot then uses the height to glide across the country, looking for another thermal to gain lift if he descends too near the ground.

Before World War II there were a few clubs flying home-made wooden gliders. However, since the formation in 1949 of the Gliding Federation of Australia the sport has boomed, particularly in the 1970s. In 1970-71 there were fewer than 2 500 registered glider pilots, but by 1982 this figure had almost doubled to 4 500 pilots flying some 900 gliders with 106 clubs. In 1981 Australian glider pilots logged 73 000 hours. Glider pilot deaths average only two a year.

State and national championships are held annually, with the national titles tending to be dominated in the 1970s by Malcolm Jinks and German-born Ingo RENNER. By 1978 Jinks had won a record 10 national titles and in 1976 Renner had the distinction of being the first and only Australian world champion when he won the World Standard Class title in Finland; by early 1983 Renner held 11 national titles.

Glossopteris see fossils

Gloucester NSW (population 2 484 in 1981) A country town situated on the Gloucester River, a tributary of the MANNING RIVER, it is located inland from TAREE, 291km by road NNE of Sydney. It is a service centre and railway town on the NORTH COAST line, 309km by rail from Sydney, where cattle grazing, dairying, fodder crop cultivation and timber-getting are the main local primary industries. There is a large milk processing factory in the town and several timber mills in the district.

Glover, John (1767-1849) Artist. Born near Leicester, England, the son of a farmer, Glover aspired to be a painter from an early age. He belonged to the increasing number of Englishmen who searched the landscape for romantic and picturesque subjects for their paintings. A mediocre, if prolific, English artist, his attempt to become a member of the Royal Academy was never taken seriously. He did have some influence, however, as an organiser and practitioner—he helped to establish water-colouring as as reputable medium for serious artists at the turn of the 19th century through his presidency of the Society of Painters in Watercolour. In 1831 Glover emigrated to TAS with his family. He acquired a land grant in northern TAS, which was then

enjoying a boom as the granary for the mainland.

In Australia, Glover was released from the expectations of English painting and from his preoccupation with the work of the French painter, Claude Lorraine. His work improved greatly. Although his technique is sometimes unsatisfactory on scrutiny, he painted with commendable skill. He captured the bright light and open space of Australia, and the way the scribbly distant bush does not merge into a uniform area of colour. Accordingly, his paintings foreshadow the work of Fred WILLIAMS. Glover's marvellously sinuous gumtrees have a confidence not equalled until those depicted by Hans HEYSEN. After his death at Patterdale TAS, his work in Australia sank into oblivion, but it has been rediscovered recently.

glow worms see flies

goannas see lizards

gobies see fishes, bony; fishes, freshwater

gold This metal has been treasured since ancient times for its permanence and lustre, and its uses pre-date the period of written history. The search for the metal stimulated world exploration and trade for centuries; gold rushes, involving mass migrations of people, took place in California (1848), Australia (1851), South Africa (1886) and the Yukon (1896).

Half the world's stock of gold is stored by governments and has been largely immobilised by agreements between major industrial countries. Traditionally, gold has been used as the basis of monetary systems and as an exchange standard. Because of the increasing demand from industry and from investors who hoard gold as a hedge against inflation, the price climbed from US$35 per troy ounce in 1968 to over US$200 a decade later, representing an increase in price of over 600 per cent. The 1980 price was over US$600 an ounce. Such a sharp rise has had a profound effect upon the economics of gold production and also upon the real value of many national currencies.

Industrial uses include the manufacture of jewellery and decorative articles; electronic components and circuits; alloys and specialised compounds for industry and medicine.

Extraction There are two types of gold deposits, placer and lode. In the former the metal, concentrated in unconsolidated river gravels and sands, is extracted by any one of the heavy mineral separation techniques, the most simple of which is hand panning. In the lode deposits the rock is crushed and the gold obtained by heavy mineral separation methods, cyanidisation or by using mercury to form an amalgam. In all cases the metal is refined to form bullion of nearly 100 per cent purity. The by-products and co-products from gold mining include the platinum-group metals and, in South Africa, a significant amount of uranium.

Table 1

MINE PRODUCTION OF GOLD IN AUSTRALIA 1970-81
(kilograms*)

State	1970	1978	1979	1980	1981
QLD	2 589	607	515	675	1 510
NSW	325	422	471	573	587
VIC	253	12	23	36	75
TAS	1 335	1 892	1 747	1 311	1 950
SA	16	1	6	16	32
WA	10 898	13 332	11 582	11 233	11 724
NT	3 865	3 876	4 221	3 191	2 495
TOTAL	19 281	20 142	18 565	17 035	18 373

Note : *1kg = 32.151 troy ounces.
Source : *Australian Mineral Industry Annual Review.* (1970-81) Australian Govt Publishing Service, Canberra.

Production The early mining was shallow and was concerned with the exploration of alluvial gold, but this soon progressed to more difficult mining of vein-type lodes. Alluvial gold now accounts for only one per cent of the total world production, with approximately 60 per cent derived from lodes and the remainder as a co-product of copper and other base-metal production. Australian gold mining began in about 1849 as an offshoot of the California gold rush. The mine production of gold in Australia in 1980 amounted to 17 035kg, or 1.8 per cent of the world's total. Production figures from the various States are shown in Table 1. In WA the principal gold-mining centre is the KALGOORLIE-NORSEMAN area; in the NT gold is a co-product of copper and bismuth mining in the TENNANT CREEK district; in TAS the base-metal mines produce little gold; in QLD production is from the MOUNT MORGAN area; and in NSW some gold is produced from the BROKEN HILL lead-zinc ores which are refined at PORT PIRIE in SA.

The industry The world's gold resources indicate a reserve of approximately 1.3 billion troy ounces of which 60 per cent is in South Africa and an estimated 15 per cent in the USSR. These reserves are adequate to supply the future demands but inadequate to permit additions to existing gold stocks for international exchange and monetary reserves without creating a shortage. There are several substitutes for gold but, to date, there has been little or no research to establish an alloy which might be more suitable for international exchange or jewellery. It is estimated that by the year 2000 the global demand for primary gold will have increased by 2.4 per cent to 64 700 000 troy ounces. The time/price relationship for gold from 1968 to 2000, based on constant 1968 dollars, indicates that there will be a rise in price.
Further reading: see under minerals and mining.

Gold Coast QLD (population 135 437 in 1981) One of the best-known resort areas of the State, it stretches for 32km along the SE coast from Southport to COOLANGATTA and

consists of a chain of beaches which have been extensively developed to cater for tourists. The whole region is officially classified as the 'City of the Gold Coast', the largest urban centre in QLD after Brisbane. In recent times, especially since the 1950s, the area has been the scene of rapid expansion with the erection of luxury hotels, towering apartment blocks, canal housing estates, retail shopping centres, restaurants, nightclubs, wildlife reserves, sporting facilities, museums and miniature zoos—in fact, almost anything with tourist appeal. This growth is reflected in both the influx of holiday-makers and numbers of permanent residents: the city claims a visitor population of three million people a year and the increase in residents is indicated by the growth from 69 120 in 1971 to over 94 000 in 1976 and over 135 000 in 1981.

The main resort centres (from N to S) are Southport (Main Beach), Surfers Paradise, Northcliffe, Broadbeach, Mermaid Beach, Miami, Burleigh Heads, Tallebudgera Creek, Palm Beach, Currumbin, Tugun, Bilinga, and the twin towns of Coolangatta and Tweed Heads which lie astride the QLD/NSW border. Southport is the administrative centre of the city and the major commercial focus. Among the numerous attractions of the area, apart from surfing, swimming, fishing and other aquatic sports, are the Currumbin bird sanctuary (with the twice-daily feeding of the coloured lorikeets); Sea World (located out of Southport at The Spit, featuring dolphins, underwater shark-feeding and water skiing displays); launch and paddle-boat cruises along the Nerang River; the Surfers Paradise international motor-racing circuit; a model railway exhibition at Nobby Hill; a replica of Captain COOK's ship *Endeavour*, and Burleigh Heads National Park and Fauna Reserve.

gold discoveries Gold discoveries have not only had important effects on Australia's economic development, but have provided some of the most colourful episodes in the history of the continent. The discoveries during the 1850s in VIC and during the 1890s

in WA were the most remarkable but there were many others of importance in all the States except SA.

Early discoveries Small amounts of gold were found in the BATHURST district of NSW as early as 1823, and during the following quarter-century many more small finds were made there and elsewhere, including those in 1839 by the explorer, STRZELECKI, and those in 1841 by a gifted amateur geologist, the Rev. W.B. Clarke. Until the 1850s, however, the discoverers did not widely publicise their finds. Moreover, the authorities were not in favour of their doing so, for fear of the effects which a rush might have on the convict population. Thus Governor GIPPS, when shown some pieces of gold by the Rev. Clarke, is reported to have said, 'Put it away, Mr Clarke, or we shall all have our throats cut.'

The rushes of the 1850s The best-remembered name in the history of Australian gold discoveries is that of Edward HARGRAVES. Some historians have argued that he has been wrongly described as an important discoverer, since he found only an extremely small amount of gold dust. However, the size of his personal discoveries was not related to the importance of his achievement. Having found specks of gold in the Bathurst district in February 1851, he was so successful in publicising the fact, as well as the discoveries of his associates, John Lister and the Toms brothers, that he started a gold rush, and, as he had hoped, gained large government rewards for doing so. By the end of 1851 over 5000 men had taken out gold-mining licences in NSW and a rush had taken place to what became known as the Ophir field, around the place where Hargraves had found his traces. This stimulated the search for gold in other localities, especially in VIC, which became a separate colony in 1851. By the end of that year discoveries had been made there that eclipsed those of NSW, and a large part of the population of Melbourne and GEELONG had flocked to the diggings. Tens of thousands came from the other colonies also, and in 1852 the rush from overseas began. In September 1852 alone, 19 000 people disembarked at Melbourne, and the influx continued at such a rate that in the decade 1851-61 VIC's population rose from 97 000 to 539 000 (the increase being greater than the total population of Australia at the beginning of the decade).

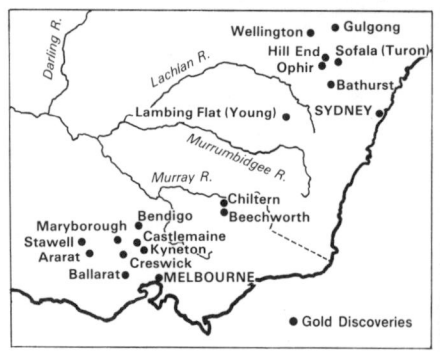

Chief goldfields in NSW and VIC in the 1850s and 1860s

The largest VIC fields were at BALLARAT and BENDIGO, but many others such as CASTLEMAINE, MARYBOROUGH, ST ARNAUD, BEECHWORTH, ARARAT, Chiltern, Clunes, CRESWICK, STAWELL and Walhalla were important too. In NSW the Ophir and nearby Turon fields were the greatest centres throughout most of the 1850s with HILL END, Gulgong and Lambing Flat (the site of the present town of YOUNG) becoming prominent later. Since most of the fields contained great quantities of alluvial gold, often very close to the surface, there were many stories of spectacular finds. A digger at Louisa Creek in NSW claimed to have washed more than a kilogram of gold from a single dishful of soil, four men at Mt Alexander in VIC reported finding about 7kg in four days, and a Ballarat miner was said to have found in a single day gold worth £1 800.

Life on the goldfields Towns sprang up on the goldfields—first forests of tents, then slab huts, and after several years solidly built public and commercial buildings. In general the fields were orderly, and this was all the more remarkable because of the difficulty which the authorities had in recruiting policemen in sufficient numbers and of suitable quality to cope with the great influx of population. In VIC, where many policemen, like members of other occupations, turned to gold digging, the government had to recruit many TAS ex-convicts whose methods of dealing with the miners were a cause of considerable discontent.

Two causes of friction marred the general standard of law and order. The first was resentment against the method used in the early 1850s in both VIC and NSW to raise revenue for the costs of government administration on the fields. In both colonies miners were required to pay a fee of 30 shillings a month to obtain a licence to dig for gold. For the first year or two, when average earnings were high, this fee did not represent a great burden, but as the number of diggers increased and the richest deposits of easily won gold were worked out, it became a hardship. Resentment against this fee and the methods used to collect it, combined with other grievances, led to the EUREKA STOCKADE revolt in Ballarat in 1854. The second cause of grievance was the presence of many CHINESE on the diggings; racial intolerance and fears of economic competition combined to cause a number of anti-Chinese riots.

Most of the gold found during the first few years was alluvial, and was won by self-employed miners working singly or in teams on claims measuring 12 feet (nearly 4m) square per man. Since the gold was usually in or near creek beds, it could be separated from other materials by washing the soil in a 'cradle' and then in a dish. As the alluvial gold was worked out, the era of reef mining by companies began and most miners became employees.

Effects of the rushes The economic effects of the gold discoveries of the 1850s are described in the entry on ECONOMIC HISTORY,

Arrival of the first gold escort at the Treasury in Sydney, 1851

and will be mentioned only briefly here. The rushes were the main factor in raising the population of Australia from 437 000 in 1851 to 1 700 000 in 1871, and the wealth flowing from them is indicated by the fact that in the same 20-year period over 50 million ounces (about 142 tonnes) of gold was mined. Besides providing capital for public works and services and for private investment, the rushes gave a stimulus to manufacturing, agriculture and, above all, to building and construction. In general they led to a diversification of the Australian economy, which nevertheless remained heavily dependent on the wool industry. Politically, the rushes are considered to have had some effect in hastening the British government's decision to allow internal self-government in the E colonies, and to have contributed to the democratic nature of parliamentary institutions in those colonies. Lastly, they provided the final argument against the transportation of convicts to E Australia.

Discoveries after the 1850s After the VIC finds of the 1850s, by far the most important were those in WA at COOLGARDIE in 1892 and at KALGOORLIE in the following year. The Kalgoorlie-Coolgardie field soon became Australia's major producer, and remained so until recently. Gold has been found also in a great number of other places, including the following: Mt Margaret and the Murchison field in WA; CHARTERS TOWERS, GYMPIE, MOUNT MORGAN and the PALMER RIVER field in QLD; PINE CREEK and TENNANT CREEK in the NT; and BEACONSFIELD, MOUNT LYELL and MATHINNA in TAS. SA is the only State to have had no discoveries of importance.

Famous nuggets Gold discovered in Australia included many nuggets of remarkable size. The largest found in VIC were: 'Welcome Stranger' (71kg, Moliagul, 1869), 'Welcome' (68kg, Ballarat, 1858), 'Blanche Barkley'

(54kg, Kingover, 1857), 'Precious' (53kg, Rheola, 1871), 'Canadian' (41kg, Ballarat, 1853), 'Lady Hotham' (36kg, Ballarat, 1854), 'Sarah Sands' (34kg, Ballarat, 1853) and 'Viscount Canterbury' (34kg, Rheola, 1870). In NSW two remarkable masses of gold, mixed with impurities and not strictly classifiable as nuggets, were 'Holtermann's Nugget', which was found at Hill End in 1872 and contained 93kg of gold, and 'Kerr's Hundredweight', which was found at the Turon field in 1851 and contained 39kg of gold. The largest nugget found in WA was the 'Golden Eagle' (35kg, Larkinville, 1931), and the largest in QLD the 'Curtis Nugget' (28kg, Gympie, 1870).

Further reading: Barrett, C. (ed) *Gold in Australia.* Cassell, Melbourne, 1951; Keesing, N. (ed) *Gold Fever.* Angus & Robertson, Sydney, 1967 and *History of the Australian Gold Rushes.* Angus & Robertson, London, 1976; Blainey, G. *The Rush That Never Ended.* (2nd edn) Melbourne University Press, Melbourne, 1969; Flett, J. *The History of Gold Discoveries in Victoria.* Hawthorn Press, Melbourne, 1970; Gilbert, P.F. *Gold.* Jacaranda, Milton, 1970.

goldfields water supply WA In the 1890s gold was discovered at COOLGARDIE, KALGOORLIE and BOULDER, and the development of the rich Golden Mile led to rapid population growth. But these goldfields were located in an area of low and uncertain rainfall and hence water supply was an ever-present problem in the early days. At Boulder, supplies were obtained by boiling and condensing saline waters from nearby Lake Charlotte; brackish underground water was used elsewhere. But water shortages caused typhoid outbreaks on the goldfields and it was evident that sufficiently large and reliable supplies were unavailable locally. A scheme was proposed

whereby water would be pumped through pipelines from the DARLING RANGE, using MUNDARING RESERVOIR as the main storage dam. Though the scheme met with considerable opposition and caused the suicide of the chief engineer, Charles O'CONNOR, it proved to be a major feat of engineering planning. Construction commenced in 1898; by 1902 the weir at Mundaring was built, and by 1903 the 554km-long pipeline to Kalgoorlie was completed. Since then several major alterations and enlargements have been made to the scheme and it is now known as the Goldfields and Agricultural Water Supply Scheme, since many rural towns and farming areas now receive water supplied from extensions of branch lines off the main pipeline. The original scheme provided for eight steam-driven pumping stations but there are now 18 pumping stations, with more powerful machinery, along the main conduit.
Further reading: Landford-Smith, T. 'Water supply in the agricultural areas of Western Australia' in *The Australian Geographer.* (vol 5, no 6, 1947); *Water Supplies and Irrigation.* Public Works Department, Perth, 1975.

goldfinch *see* finches

golf One of the more popular participatory sports in Australia, golf is played in all States throughout the year. In proportion to its population, Australia has more public golf courses than any other nation in the world and the game's popularity may be further gauged from the fact that although there are some 67 courses in the metropolitan area of Sydney alone, the competition to play golf on a Sunday is so intense during the summer months that on many courses golfers start queueing on the first tee at 4 a.m.
History Golf was first played in Australia in the 1820s in TAS, on cleared farmland which was to become the present-day Ratho golf course, about 75km from Hobart. On the mainland, the honour of introducing golf to Australians is generally accorded to James Graham who emigrated from Scotland in the 1840s and whose luggage included golf clubs and a supply of 1840-style golf balls—feathers tightly packed into a leather casing. Graham was among those who formed Australia's first golf club, which played on Falstaff Gardens in the heart of Melbourne until the gold-rush days. In NSW it was not until 1855 that John Dunsmore, another Scot, is recorded as playing that State's first golf on a site near the present Concord Club. In SA in 1869 two Scotsmen— the then Governor, Sir James Fergusson, and David Murray—engaged a former green-keeper from Scotland to lay out a nine-hole course in Adelaide. Golf was first played in QLD by yet another Scottish pair—in 1880 two Scots named Ivory cleared some land on their Eidsvold cattle station and played a few holes.

It was during the 1890s that golf came of age with the establishment throughout the country of permanent courses administered by or-ganised groups of club members and, with the establishment in 1896 of the Newlands Golf Club in TAS, all States could boast at least one golf club. The first still-existing club was the Australian Golf Club, formed in NSW in 1882, followed by the Brisbane Golf Club (1890), the Melbourne Golf Club (1891), the Adelaide Golf Club (1892) and the Perth Golf Club (1895). The game was put on an even more solid basis with the formation in 1898 of the Australian Golf Union, which since that date has instituted, managed and controlled all national championships, both amateur and professional.

Golf during the 19th century and for most of the first half of the 20th century was considered a hobby for the rich. But since World War II this attitude has been changing and golf is now considered a weekend pastime and sport available to anyone. In the early 1980s there were more than 250 000 registered male golfers in Australia and some 1 230 golf courses. In addition, there were more than 100 000 women golfers, or 'associates' as they are more usually called. Professional golf is well established in Australia with most courses supporting a full-time professional who operates the golf course shop and who gives lessons to club members. There is also a large number of professionals not attached to any one course who tour the country following the tournament circuit. Golfers from this latter group often seek success internationally on the Far East and European circuits where prize-money is more attractive, and a select few try their skills on the enormously rich American circuit. Joe Kirkwood was the first to put Australia's name in the international golfing records. After wins in the Australian and New Zealand Opens of 1920 he sought further victories overseas where his significant success in the following years included winning the Canadian Open (twice), the Texas Open (once) and gaining third place in the British Open. Jim FERRIER was the next Australian to make a mark internationally. In 1947, by winning the American PGA title, he became the first Australian to win one of the world's four major championships. While Ferrier was touring the North American continent, in Australia Peter THOMSON was preparing himself for an attack on another of the world's four major championships, the British Open. Thomson was to come first in this most exacting test of golfing skill an astonishing five times in the period 1954-65. In the 1960s and 1970s, prize-money for the world's major tournaments began to increase rapidly and this attracted an increasing number of talented and dedicated young Australian golfers overseas. A few, such as Kel NAGLE, Greg Norman, David GRAHAM and Graham MARSH, carved their names indelibly in international records. In the 1970s, the outstanding success was Bruce CRAMPTON who in 1973 became only the fifth golfer to have won more than $1 million on the American circuit. Towards the end of the decade, this success was capped by David Graham who in 1979 won the US PGA title and in 1981 won the US Open to become the first Australian to win this prestigious tournament.
Further reading: Smith, T. *The Complete Book of Australian Golf.* Jack Pollard Pty Ltd, Sydney, 1975.

Gondwanaland This supercontinent was created about 200 million years ago by the splitting of an even larger land mass, Pangaea, into Laurasia in the N (consisting of modern North America and Eurasia, apart from the Indian sub-continent) and Gondwanaland in the S. Gondwanaland consisted of Antarctica, South America, Africa, Madagascar, Australia, New Guinea, New Zealand and the Indian sub-continent. Geologists are not in complete agreement about the timetable for the rupture of Gondwanaland and the movements, by CONTINENTAL DRIFT mechanisms, of the various modern land masses to their present positions. The outline of the theory proposed by P.H. Raven in 1972 follows.

Africa and South America separated from each other about 110 million years ago, the S Atlantic appearing slowly between them. Africa separated from Antarctica about 90 million years ago, New Zealand about 80 million years ago, India about 65 million years ago and, finally, Australia about 45 million years ago. South America is still virtually linked to Antarctica through the Scotia Arc. When Australia, Antarctica and South America were still connected, Antarctica was evidently further N than it is now for all three continents had forests of *Nothofagus*, PROTEACEAE and southern GYMNOSPERMAE. Antarctica also had a reptilian fauna, including some mammal-like reptiles that have been found as FOSSILS in South Africa, India and South America. This is further evidence of the former broad connections between these land masses.

After its separation from Antarctica, Australia moved N, carrying with it New Guinea, then submerged, and moving through more temperate and well-watered latitudes than those in which it is now situated. During 45 million years the continent has travelled through about 15° of latitude. Recent measurements suggest a velocity of 10cm a year.

The former existence of Gondwanaland neatly explains many otherwise puzzling features of the distribution of animals and plants, particularly those that are restricted to South America and Australia, or to Australia, South America and New Zealand. Marsupials are restricted, for example, to South America and Australasia apart from a few recent immigrants into North America. The fossil plant *Glossopteris* and the modern *Nothofagus*, or southern beeches, also have a Gondwanaland distribution. Other examples are mentioned in the discussions of various groups of animals and plants.
See also geology; parrots; Queensland lung fish
Further reading: see under continental drift.

Goodeniaceae *see* fan flowers

Good Neighbour Councils The Good Neighbour Movement was formed in December 1949 as a Commonwealth government inspired and funded development aimed at bringing community organisations together in order to help migrants. It resulted in the foundation of Good Neighbour Councils in each State and internal Territory. Their activities, as expressed in their Charter, included: welcoming new arrivals and assisting them to settle smoothly and rapidly into the Australian community; acting as advisers to the government on matters of migrant integration; encouraging the establishment and involvement of appropriate community services and organisations in meeting the needs of migrants; and providing direct assistance to migrants where existing services were not readily available.

In 1978 a committee which had been investigating the whole question of migrant services and programmes, under the chairmanship of F. Galbally, concluded its work. Its report, while acknowledging the valuable work done by Good Neighbour Councils, recommended a restructuring of migrant services in ways which would make such voluntary bodies unnecessary. The government accepted these recommendations, and during the following few years the Good Neighbour Councils were therefore phased out.

Goolwa SA (population 1 624 in 1981) This small town is located on the right bank of the lower MURRAY RIVER, 114km by rail SSE of Adelaide and 18km E of VICTOR HARBOUR. It is a service centre for a dairying and fodder crop growing region on the alluvial flats. At this part of its course, near the mouth, the Murray divides into a number of channels with sandy islands between them; five barrages have been built across these channels to prevent tidal salt water inflow during periods when the river is low. The Goolwa Barrage, the largest of these structures, is 633m long and is located downstream from the town, joining the right bank to Hindmarsh Is. The name Goolwa is an Aboriginal word meaning 'elbow'.

Goolwa Barrage at the Murray mouth

Goondiwindi QLD (population 3 576 in 1981) One of the principal crossing points on the QLD/NSW border, it is a commercial and social centre for a vast pastoral district which is increasingly turning to agriculture. Located on the MACINTYRE RIVER, it is a focal point of road transport, 375km by road SW of Brisbane at the intersection of the Cunningham High-

way, the Bruxner Highway (from NSW) and the Barwon Highway (from the W). At an elevation of 216m above sea level, it has an average annual rainfall of 614mm, spread throughout the year but with a concentration in summer. Situated on the great inland artesian basin, much of the sheep and cattle grazing industry of the district depends upon this supply of underground water. The town is a cattle selling centre and the venue for the Australian sheep dog trials. It has a pastoral veterinary centre, established by the University of Queensland, where all final year veterinary students spend some time on field work. The annual Australian Gold Cup for polo is a major event which attracts international players. The town began as a grazing centre following the discovery of the MacIntyre River by the explorer Allan CUNNINGHAM in 1827, and took its name (originally Gundawinda) from an Aboriginal word meaning 'resting place of birds'.

Goonyella QLD An open-cut coal mine, it is located in the central E part of the State, some 214km by road SE of MACKAY, 37km off the Peak Downs Highway, in the headwater tributary area of the Isaacs River, which drains into the MACKENZIE-FITZROY river system. It is connected by rail to Hay Point on the E coast, between Mackay and SARINA, where there are coal loading facilities for overseas shipment. The Goonyella coalfield was opened in 1971 and was part of a major development scheme which involved the establishment of a new town (Moranbah, 24km SE of the mine), and the construction of a coal treatment plant and port facilities.

gooseberries, sea *see* ctenophores

goosefoot *see* Chenopodiaceae

Gordon, Adam Lindsay (1833-70) Poet. Born in the Azores and educated in England, he was sent to Australia by his parents in 1853 because of his restless behaviour. He served for two years in the South Australian Mounted Police, but then resigned and devoted himself mainly to horse-breaking and steeplechase riding. He won election to the SA House of Assembly, but resigned after about a year. While living at 'Dingley Dell', a cottage near Port MacDonnell in south-eastern SA, he began contributing poems—mostly ballads dealing with horse-riding in one form or another—to various periodicals. He later lived at MOUNT GAMBIER, BALLARAT and Melbourne, and in 1867 published a volume of poems, *Sea Spray and Smoke Drift*. Following the death of his only child, Annie, various financial failures and a number of riding accidents, he became increasingly depressed, and only two days after the publication of *Bush Ballads and Galloping Rhymes* (1870) shot himself dead on the beach at the Melbourne suburb of Brighton. After his death his poems, with their stress on physical activity and the cult of the horse, became extremely

popular and many collections of them were published. There is a statue of him in Spring Street, Melbourne, and a bust in Westminster Abbey.

See also literature
Further reading: Elliott, B. *Adam Lindsay Gordon*. Sun Books, Melbourne, 1973.

Gordon River TAS Located in the rugged mountain region in the W of the State, it rises in the King William Range (SW of LAKE KING WILLIAM) and flows for some 200km to MACQUARIE HARBOUR on the W coast. Its main tributaries are the Denison and Franklin from the N, and the Serpentine and Olga from the S. Its upper reaches have been dammed as part of a major hydro-electricity scheme. A 140m-high concrete arch dam on the Gordon, above its junction with the Serpentine, has created Lake Gordon which covers 272km². The Serpentine Dam,

Gordon Dam

Dept of Tourism, Tasmania

upstream from its junction with the Gordon River, together with two other dams (Edgar and Scotts Peak Dams) has created LAKE PEDDER, covering 242km². Water from Lake Pedder flows by canal into Lake Gordon and thence by a 137m shaft to the underground Gordon power station, which was commissioned in 1977 and has an installed capacity of 288 000kW. Proposals to develop the hydro-electricity potential of the lower section of the Gordon have been particularly controversial; in a State referendum on this issue in 1981, Tasmanians were given the choice of two alternative proposals: a dam on the Gordon-below-Franklin or a dam on the Gordon-above-Olga. Although a narrow majority of voters favoured the Gordon-below-Franklin scheme, there was a high informal vote, with many people indicating that they were opposed to any dam construction on the lower Gordon. However, early in 1982 the TAS government decided to proceed with the Gordon-below-Franklin project and preliminary construction began despite much opposition from conservation groups. With the election to power in 1983 of a federal Labor government, pledged to stop the dam construction, a political-legal confrontation between the TAS and federal governments ensued. The matter was brought before the High Court and in mid-1983 the Court found in favour of the federal government; this ruling thus barred the construction of the Franklin Dam.

Gordonvale QLD (population 2 375 in 1981) This small rural town is in the coastal NE of the State, 24km S of CAIRNS, 64km NNW of INNISFAIL and 1 830km by road from Brisbane. It is situated in the Mulgrave River valley with the Isley Hills to the W, the BELLENDEN KER RANGE to the S, and the Malbon Thompson Range to the E. The principal farming activity in the district is sugar cane growing and one of the State's leading mills, established in 1893, is located there. The settlement was initially called Mulgrave, then it became Nelson, and finally in 1912 it was named Gordonvale after John Gordon, a pioneer settler of the area.

gorgon's head *see* Euphorbiaceae

Gorton, Sir John Grey (1911-) Prime Minister. Born in Melbourne, he was educated at Geelong Grammar School and the University of Oxford, from which he graduated MA. He then worked as an irrigation farmer, served as a fighter pilot in the RAAF from 1940 to 1944, attained the rank of flight lieutenant and was seriously wounded. He served as a Liberal Senator for VIC from 1949 to 1968 and during the last 10 years of this period held a number of Cabinet posts. On the death of Harold HOLT in 1968 he was elected leader of the Liberal Party and therefore succeeded Holt as Prime Minister, this being the first time that a Senator had gained that position. Shortly afterwards he moved to the Lower House. During the following three years he drew increasing attention to himself

Courtesy of A.I.S. Canberra

Sir John Gorton

through his informal behaviour. Some saw this as refreshing, but many members of his own party considered that he was lacking in dignity. He also incurred loss of support because he was an avowed centralist, and appeared to some government members and to State Premiers of all parties to pay insufficient attention to State rights. In May 1971, after a public clash with his Minister for Defence, Malcolm FRASER, he called for a vote of confidence in his leadership at a party meeting. The result was a tied vote, whereupon he declined to use his casting vote to keep himself in office, and resigned. He then served as Minister for Defence under his successor, William McMAHON, but controversy over a series of newspaper articles written by him and entitled 'I did it my way' led to his dismissal in August 1971. He later resigned from the Liberal Party and in the 1975 elections stood unsuccessfully as an independent candidate for the Senate for the ACT.

Gosford NSW (population of the BRISBANE WATER urban area, which includes Gosford City and adjacent urban settlements, 71 969 in 1981) Located 85km by road N of Sydney on the N shore of the Brisbane Water, Gosford is the chief trading centre for the coastal settlements of the district, which include numerous tourist resorts and farming areas. It is situated on the main N railway line connecting Sydney with NEWCASTLE; this rail link to Sydney was electrified in 1960, with the result that the journey of 80km now takes about 1½ hours and many Gosford residents are daily commuters to the metropolitan capital. Road travel between Gosford and Sydney was greatly facilitated by the opening of a freeway in the 1960s, covering 24km of the journey. Today, Gosford is the site of the administrative headquarters of Gosford City local government area (population 94 341). The plans for Gosford town were made in 1839 under the direction of Governor GIPPS, who named it probably after the English town of Gosford in Oxfordshire.

The rural activities of the Gosford region include citrus and passion-fruit orcharding, vegetable growing, poultry farming, timber cutting, and, in recent years, horse breeding. Within the town are food processing factories and secondary industries concerned with fruit packing, brick and pipe making, and felt and fibrous plaster manufacture. The local sandstone, quarried in the region, is much valued as a building material.

In common with the whole central NSW coast, Gosford experiences a mild climate; winter frosts are rare and there is abundant sunshine throughout the year. With coastal and lakeside attractions nearby, it has become the focus of a tourist playground and an important retirement region. Many Sydney residents have weekend and holiday cottages in the smaller centres such as WOY WOY, Point Clare, Umina and Ettalong where there is good fishing and where facilities for aquatic

sports are readily available. Tourist attractions in the area include Old Sydney Town (a recreation of Sydney as it was in 1810, 9km W of Gosford on the main highway), a reptile park displaying examples of Australian reptiles, and the cottage where the poet Henry KENDALL lived in the 1870s, now a folk museum. The Central Coast League's Club, with membership of over 25 000, is located in Gosford and provides entertainment and a wide variety of leisure facilities for residents and visitors.
See also Broken Bay; Hawkesbury River
Further reading: Swancott, C. *The Brisbane Water Story, Part 1: Gosford.* Ironmonger, Gosford, 1953 and *Gosford and the Henry Kendall Country.* Central Coast Printery, Gosford, 1966; Brennan, F.E. *A History of Gosford.* Wyong Shire Historical Society, Wyong, 1970; Taylor, G. *Sydneyside Scenery and How It Came About.* Angus & Robertson, Sydney, 1970.

goshawks *see* birds of prey

Goulburn NSW (population 21 750 in 1981) This city is in the NE of the SOUTHERN TABLELANDS region of the State, on the Hume Highway 211km by road SW of Sydney, located at the junction of the WOLLONDILLY and Mulwaree Rivers, tributaries of the NEPEAN-HAWKESBURY system, at an elevation of 632m above sea level on the E side of the watershed of the GREAT DIVIDING RANGE. It is a rail junction where a branch line S to COOMA leaves the main S railway route, a distance of 222km by train from Sydney. The town experiences warm summers with occasionally very hot days, cold winters with frequent frosts and infrequent light snow, and an average annual rainfall of 712mm uniformly spread throughout the year. It is an important commercial and service focus for a productive mixed farming, wool growing and beef cattle raising district. It is a major livestock and wool marketing centre, with an abattoir, textile mills, engineering workshops and a shoe factory. The city is noted for its educational institutions, which include St Patrick's College and the Goulburn College of Advanced Education (formerly the Teacher's College). Among the tourist attractions are a museum of steam engines, Riversdale (once a coaching inn, restored in the style of the 1840s), St Clair Historical Exhibition, and 'Garroorigong' (a homestead built in 1857). The Bungonia recreation area, 24km E of the city, which comprises an extensive stretch of plateau country deeply dissected by gorges and contains limestone caves, is a popular caving and bushwalking area. The Goulburn district was explored in the early decades of the 19th century, was settled in the 1820s and contains a large number of historical buildings which have been listed for preservation by the National Trust (NSW). Among the classified buildings are the town hall (built in 1887), the post office (1881-97), St Saviour's Anglican Cathedral (1874), the courthouse (1849), Mul-

left: Sulphur-crested cockatoo, *Cacatua galerita*
 (*see* PARROTS)
centre: Alexandra parrot, *Polytelis alexandrae*
 (*see* PARROTS)
right: Rainbow lorikeet, *Trichoglossus haematodus*
 (*T. moluccanus*) (*see* PARROTS)

Wompoo pigeon, *Ptilinopus magnificus* (*see* DOVES)

Blue bonnet parrots, *Northiella haematogaster* (*see* PARROTS)

Purple-crowned pigeon, *Ptilinopus superbus* (*see* DOVES)

Spinifex pigeon, *Petrophassa plumifera* (*see* DOVES)

Hoary-headed grebe, *Podiceps poliocephalus* (*see* GREBES)

White egret, *Egretta alba* (*see* BITTERNS)

Royal albatross, *Diomedea epomophora* (*see* SEA BIRDS)

Pied oystercatchers, *Haematopus longirostris* (*H. ostralegus*) (*see* WADERS)

White-necked heron, *Ardea pacifica* (*see* BITTERNS)

Australian pelicans, *Pelicanus conspicillatus* (*see* SEA BIRDS)

Australian dotterel, *Peltohyas australis* (*see* WADERS)

Swamphen, *Porphyrio porphyrio* (*see* RAILS)

waree Hotel (*c*1845), Southern Railway Hotel (*c*1850), the police station (1888) and a number of rural homesteads in the district.

Goulburn River
VIC Located in the mid-N of the State, it is a tributary of the MURRAY RIVER. Its headwaters rise on the N side of the GREAT DIVIDING RANGE in the rugged timbered country about 130km NE of Melbourne where the highest peaks rise to over 1 800m above sea level. The waters of these headwater streams are collected by the EILDON RESERVOIR, the main storage point for the vast Goulburn Valley irrigation scheme. The river course beyond the small township of Eildon goes generally WNW to SEYMOUR, then N to SHEPPARTON, and thence again WNW to join the Murray at a point about 12km upstream from ECHUCA. The general pattern of flow thus makes a giant 'S'-shape, but the details of its course show a multitude of minor meanders. The main tributary of the Goulburn is the Broken River which rises near MOUNT BULLER and flows generally N then W to join the main stream at Shepparton. The rainfall over the river basin is highest in the upper sections and declines downstream: at Woods Point (685m elevation above the Eildon Reservoir) the yearly rainfall is 1 485mm; at Alexandra (208m elevation, W of Eildon) the yearly total is 707mm; at Seymour (142m elevation) it is 596mm; Shepparton (113m elevation) receives 509mm; and Echuca (96m elevation) has a yearly average of 436mm.

Some of the flow from the headwaters of the Goulburn catchment is diverted to provide part of metropolitan Melbourne's water supply, but much more important is the extensive use of the waters for irrigation and for livestock supplies on the N riverine plains, making it one of the nation's major irrigation projects. In addition to the Eildon Reservoir, on the upper Goulburn, the waters of the Broken River have been harnessed by the Nillahcootie Dam, located 37km S of BENALLA, with a capacity of 39 790ML, and by the off-river artificial Lake Mokoan, built in 1970 with a storage capacity of 364 800ML. Also on the Goulburn itself is the Goulburn Weir which is located downstream from Seymour and diverts water either NE into the East Goulburn Main Channel (whence it goes into canals and to farm properties) or NW to WARANGA RESERVOIR. From this storage basin, the third-largest in VIC, located about 20km SW of Shepparton, water is transferred W via the Waranga Western Main Channel, supplying a network of canals and linking with the CAMPASPE, LODDON and WIMMERA-MALLEE irrigation schemes to the W and NW.

Gould, John
(1804-81) British ornithologist and author of books on birds and mammals. Born in Dorset, England, Gould was appointed as taxidermist of the Zoological Society of London when he was 23. In 1832 he published *A Century of Birds from the Himalayan Mountains*, for which he provided many of the sketches; the paintings for this book and

A painting of rosehill parakeets from Gould

National Library of Australia

later works were done by his wife, Elizabeth (1804-41) and after her death he employed various artists including the famous 'nonsense' writer Edward Lear. In 1837 he completed *Birds of Europe* (five volumes); at the same time he produced 10 plates for a work on Australian birds but these were not published immediately. In 1838 Gould and his wife came to Australia to gather more material and with John GILBERT visited TAS, NSW and SA. His book *The Birds of Australia* (seven volumes) was completed in 1848; a supplementary volume was produced in 1869. He also published *Mammals of Australia* (three volumes, 1845-63) and *Handbook to the Birds of Australia* (two volumes, 1863). The long-established Gould League, a conservation society for children, was named in his honour.

Gould, Shane Elizabeth
(1957–) Swimmer. Born in Brisbane, she began to attract attention in 1968 when she swam 100m in the fastest time ever recorded by an Australian 12-year-old. From then until she retired she was the dominant force in Australian and international swimming, seemingly breaking records at will. In one two-year period from April 1970 to January 1972 she broke 11 world records for distances from 100m to 1500m. At the age of 15, a poll of world swimming magazines voted her the best woman swimmer in the world after she had established new world records for the 100m, 200m, 400m and 1500m freestyle distances. In the 1972 Olympic Games, she was entered for 12 events covering a period of nine days, a physically and mentally demanding programme for so young a competitor; but she proved her outstanding ability by winning the 200m individual medley, the 200m and 400m freestyle events (setting world and Olympic records in each), coming second in the 800m freestyle and third in the 100m freestyle—the best one-woman performance in the history of the Olympic Games. She retired from swimming at the age of 17, after the 1973 Belgrade world swimming championships, because she felt that the gruelling and time-consuming training sessions necessary to remain in world-class swimming were interfering with her private and social life.

Gove Peninsula
NT Located at the NE extremity of ARNHEM LAND Aboriginal Reserve, the peninsula contains one of Australia's major bauxite deposits. These are situated 27km inland within the tribal territory of the YIRRKALA people and hence, prior to the commencement of mining operations in 1972, there was controversy over the exploitation of the deposits. Agreement was reached whereby mining royalties are paid into a trust fund for the benefit of the Aborigines. The Yirrkala Methodist Mission station (population 543 in 1981) near the NE coast of the peninsula is where almost all the Aborigines of the area now reside and was, until the mining developments of the 1970s, the only permanent link with them. The Yirrkala have a rich traditional life dating back many thousands of years and from time to time they return to their sacred and ceremonial areas throughout Arnhem Land, and make visits to their relatives at ELCHO ISLAND to the W and GROOTE EYLANDT to the S.

Miners and their families live in a new town called Nhulunbuy (population 4 138 in 1981), which is at the foot of Mt Saunders and overlooks a natural lake S of Cape Wirrawawoi. The ore is brought from the inland mine to Dundas Point, W of the town, on the natural harbour of Melville Bay, which can accommodate ships up to 9m draft; there the ore is stockpiled for shipment overseas or treated at the alumina reduction plant. Melville Bay was noted by Matthew FLINDERS on his voyage along this coast in 1803 as the finest bay in the GULF OF CARPENTARIA. Nhulunbuy, receives an average annual rainfall of 1 362mm, with a marked seasonal concentration in the summer months (January average 275mm, February 281mm), and a dry period, typical of these areas, from June to October.

government of Australia
Australia is ruled as a constitutional monarchy, the reigning British monarch being the formal Head of State and the nominal Head of Government. However, the monarch does not suggest laws but rules according to the Commonwealth Constitution and with the consent of Parliament. Since 1975 there has been a growing lobby to change the form of government to that of a republic but supporters of this policy are still in a minority.

Commonwealth and State Constitutions The Commonwealth of Australia Constitution provides for a federal form of government, the power to govern being divided between seven independent Parliaments. Australian government is described as a parliamentary democracy because the people elect representatives to a Parliament where all laws are made on the principle of majority decision with the preservation of minorities' rights to criticise government policy and publicise their points of view.

The federal or Commonwealth Parliament sits at Canberra in the ACT and State Parliaments sit at Sydney, Melbourne, Adelaide, Brisbane, Hobart and Perth. Before 1901 the States were British colonies; their development as parliamentary democracies is discussed in the entry on POLITICAL HISTORY. The British Parliament legally created Constitutions for each colony, giving each one a Parliament with the power to make laws on any matter necessary for the peace, welfare and good government of the peoples living within the established boundaries of the colony. These Constitutions were simple documents which did not impose many restrictions on the power of the colonial legislatures and in most respects they could be amended freely by statutes passed by the relevant colonial Parliament. However, any major change in these governmental arrangements had to be legalised by another British Act of Parliament and thus it was necessary for the British Parliament to pass the Commonwealth of Australia Constitution Act in 1900 to establish a federal system of government.

The establishment of the federation meant that the former colonies became known as States; they retained their former names and boundaries, with the exception of NSW which gave up some of its territory to form the new ACT where the federal Parliament was to be established.

Serious limitations were placed on the power of the State legislatures by the new provisions, and they could no longer make laws on all matters as some powers previously held by the colonies were now transferred to the federal Parliament. These 'exclusive powers' are listed in Section 51 of the Constitution, and include: postal, telegraphic and telephonic services; quarantine; census and statistics; currency; coinage and legal tender; weights and measures; naturalisation and aliens; external affairs; customs and excise; and defence (only the federal government can declare war, make treaties and have an army). In addition to exclusive powers, Section 51 lists a number of matters over which the federal Parliament and the State Parliaments can share law-making powers. Examples of these concurrent powers are banking, insurance, taxation, and conciliation and arbitration. However, Section 109 of the Constitution provides for the supremacy of laws passed by the federal Parliament over the laws passed by State Parliaments in the event of any conflicting laws.

A number of subjects not listed in the Constitution either under 'exclusive powers' or 'concurrent powers' include internal law and order (police, courts, prisons); public utilities such as power, water, road and rail transport; and education and local government. Any such matters not itemised in the Constitution are known as 'residual powers' and can be exercised by the State Parliaments.

Changing the Constitution The Constitution was established by an Act of the British Parliament but it can be changed only with the consent of the Australian people, given in a referendum. Section 128 indicates the method to be followed. Three steps are necessary, the first being that the proposed amendment must be passed by both Houses of Parliament, or twice by the House of Representatives if the Senate does not pass the amendment. Then the proposal must be the subject of a referendum in which the electors vote 'yes' or 'no'. The proposal is approved if a majority of the electors voting in at least four of the six States vote 'yes' and if this represents a majority of the electorate.

Since 1901, 33 Bills have secured the support of absolute majorities in both the House of Representatives and the Senate and have been submitted to the electors at a referendum, but only seven subject matters of proposed change have been approved by the electorate: Senate elections in 1906; State debts in 1909 and 1928; Social Services in 1946; Commonwealth legislation for Aborigines in 1967; the filling of Senate vacancies in 1977; and the granting of voting rights to the people of the ACT and the NT in 1977. In the 1977 referendum the retiring age for federal judges (not a Constitutional matter) was fixed. It is not unusual to hold referendums for making decisions of national importance. For example, two referendums were held to gain approval for CONSCRIPTION for overseas military service during World War I. Both failed to get the electorate's approval.

The High Court Section 71 of the Constitution vested the judicial power of the Commonwealth in a federal Supreme Court, to be called the High Court of Australia. Legal disputes between the federal and State governments are normally settled in this Court. In addition to handling most Constitutional cases the High Court of Australia also acts as a national court of appeal. Because many sections of the Constitution are vague, more than one interpretation can be given to them, so decisions of the High Court have had very important effects on federal-State relations. The High Court does not give advice on the legality of government legislation or proposed legislation, and will only give an interpretation when a specific case is brought before it. However, if it does interpret federal legislation as being outside the boundaries drawn by the Constitution, its decision is final and this gives it considerable power. A permanent building for the High Court, of great architectural interest, was opened by the Queen in Canberra on 26 May 1980.

Governor-General The Governor-General is appointed by the British monarch as its representative in Australia and thus as the formal Head of State. From 1901 to 1926 the Governor-General was appointed on the advice of the British government but in 1926 and 1930 Imperial Conferences decided that Governors-General in British Dominions would act on the advice of local Ministers rather than that of British Ministers, and that the British monarch would appoint them on the advice of local Ministers rather than that of British Ministers. Until the 1960s it was usual for distinguished

The Prime Minister's Lodge, Canberra

Englishmen to be appointed to this position, the exceptions being Sir Isaac ISAACS (1931-36) and Sir William McKELL (1947-53). However, since the appointment of Australian Lord CASEY (1965-69) all subsequent Governors-General have been notable Australians.

The powers of the Governor-General are by convention to be exercised on the advice of the Ministers of the federal government, although, under the Constitution, the Governor-General has the supreme executive power as representative of the monarch. The existence of reserve powers mentioned in the Constitution which enable the Governor-General to dismiss an elected government in a constitutional crisis—for example, if that government is refused supply by the Senate as occurred in 1975—has been the subject of political controversy. The crisis of 1975 is mentioned in the entries on political history and Sir John KERR, and was important in bringing together people in Australia who believed that the form of government should be changed to that of a republic.

The Federal Executive Council Section 62 of the Constitution establishes a Federal Executive Council to advise the Governor-General in the governing of the Commonwealth of Australia. This Council does not take any part in the formulation of government policy and its main work is to put before the Governor-General all official documents that require his assent or signature, to explain their significance to him, and to obtain his approval. In practice, all Ministers are members of the Federal Executive Council and although the Governor-General can appoint other people as members of the Council, he can only do so on the advice of his Ministers. Throughout its existence no person other than a Minister has been appointed to this Council. In theory, all Ministers may attend meetings of the Council but in practice only two or three Ministers do so.

The House of Representatives and the Senate The federal Parliament consists of the House of Representatives and the Senate, convoked in the presence of the British monarch represented by the Governor-General. The British monarch (or the Governor-General) takes part in the opening session of Parliament only when the 'Speech from the Throne' is read by the one participating. This speech in fact is written by the Prime Minister and sets out the general policy the government will follow for that session of Parliament.

Although all Bills passed by Parliament must be signed by the British monarch or the Governor-General in order to become Acts and Statutes (and thereby, the laws of the land), the real work of Parliament as a lawmaker is done by the House of Representatives and the Senate.

Both Houses of the federal Parliament are elected by the people of Australia (the total electorate, including all citizens who have reached the age of 18). For the House of Representatives, Australia is divided into electorates. The actual number of people comprising an electorate will depend on population movements. A representative is elected for each electorate, the number of representatives from each State depending on its actual population, with the provision that no State is to have fewer than five representatives. In addition, since 1922 one Member has always been elected to represent the NT and since 1949 two Members have been elected to represent the ACT. Table 1 shows the number of representatives from each State and the two Territories following the 1983 general election. In 1983 six women, all Labor candidates, were elected to the House of Representatives and 13 to the Senate—five Labor, six Liberal, one National Party and one Australian Democrat.

Table 1

DISTRIBUTION OF ELECTORATES AT THE 1983 ELECTION

State	Number of electorates each returning one representative
NSW	43
VIC	33
QLD	19
SA	11
WA	11
TAS	5
ACT	2
NT	1
TOTAL	125

The Senate was modelled upon the USA Senate and equal representation for each State is provided regardless of population. In 1983 there were 10 Senators for each of the six States, two for the ACT and two for the NT, making a total of 64. The original reason for electing equal numbers for each State was to counteract any attempt by the Lower House, the House of Representatives (elected on the basis of population distribution), to pass laws which might favour the more populous States. The Senate can impede legislation passed by the House of Representatives but in return the leader of the House of Representatives can be granted a double dissolution, which means an election must be held for both Houses. If after the dissolution the Senate still fails to pass the legislation, a joint sitting is provided for, at which the decision of the House of Representatives is most likely to prevail because it is

twice the size, in numbers, of the Senate. The Senate is not able to initiate or amend money Bills, but can reject them if it is prepared to take the consequences of dissolution; it may also request alterations in them.

Voting for federal elections has been compulsory since 1913 and at general elections voters elect Members for a period of three years; however, the Prime Minister may decide to dissolve Parliament before its three-year term is over. When a Member resigns or dies, his constituents elect a new Member at a by-election for the House of Representatives. In the case of a Senator the State government nominates a replacement and since the 1977 referendum the new Senator must be of the same political persuasion as the deceased or resigning Senator.

Parliamentary procedure The procedure followed in Australian Parliaments is similar to that of the British Parliament. The standing orders (a set pattern of procedure), the privileges of Members as individuals and the control of the House of Representatives and the Senate over Members is similar to that used in the British House of Commons.

When Parliament is sitting, petitions from electors are presented to Parliament and these are important in indicating the demands of sections of the public. At question time Members direct questions to Ministers. Sometimes the questions seek information, sometimes they act as criticism of government policy or administration, and some questions, nicknamed 'Dorothy Dixers', are arranged to enable the Minister to give an answer which will publicise his department or explain some point at issue. Questions can be written, requiring a written answer, in which case they are referred to as being 'on notice'; or they may be verbal, requiring a verbal response, in which case they are referred to as being 'without notice'.

After question time, Ministers make statements on current matters of policy and if some matter of public importance occurs a Member may move that the House adjourn in order that the matter may be discussed. After this, Bills are argued through their various stages. There are four stages in the passing of legislation. The first reading of a Bill (or proposed law) is not debated and serves to provide Members with a printed copy of the relevant

Parliament House, Canberra, opened by HRH Duke of York (late King George VI) on 9th May 1927

NSW Dept of Tourism

Bill; it is during the second reading that the general principles of the Bill are discussed; then a committee is formed to consider every clause and this is followed by a third reading at which amendments are debated. When a Bill has passed all stages in the House of Representatives it is sent on to the Senate because both Houses must give their assent to a Bill before it becomes law.

The Executive Whereas Parliament is the legislature or law-making body, the Executive is responsible for administering the laws. The federal Executive is chosen from members of the House of Representatives and the Senate. When the results of a parliamentary election are known, the Governor-General commissions the leader of the largest political party in the House of Representatives to form a Government. If no one political party has sufficient members elected to form a government on its own a coalition government may be formed. The leader of the government is called the PRIME MINISTER OF AUSTRALIA. Ministers are selected from the governing political party—the method of selection varies according to which party is in power—but the Prime Minister recommends to the Governor-General the names of representatives and Senators who are to be commissioned as Ministers of the Crown. The Prime Minister allocates portfolios to his Ministers (who in 1983 numbered 27). CABINET GOVERNMENT is government by a committee of Ministers—sometimes a selection of Ministers make up the Cabinet and sometimes all Ministers are included in the Cabinet. Cabinet forms a link between the executive and legislative functions of the government in Australia—there is no complete separation of powers as occurs in the USA.

State governments Five of the six State Parliaments have two Houses, QLD having only one. The five Upper Houses are called Legislative Councils; the Lower Houses are called the Legislative Assembly in NSW, VIC, QLD and WA and the House of Assembly in SA and TAS. A State Governor (*see* GOVERNORS, STATE) represents the British monarch and formally heads each State government, but actual power is in the hands of the Premier and his Cabinet Ministers. Because the original law in all States was inherited from Britain there is a certain amount of uniformity of the laws in all of them but differences in detail have crept in over the years and in 1961 a Conference of Attorneys-General was introduced to attempt to promote uniform statutes in important fields of law.

All elections for the Lower House are based on universal suffrage, compulsory voting and secret ballot. Elections are held every three or four years. All elections for the Upper Houses are also based on universal suffrage but the terms of office are different. In 1978 the NT was given wide powers of self-government but it has not yet become a State.

Federal-State co-operation Only a few sections in the Commonwealth Constitution envisage co-operation—Section 51 (xxiv) concerning justice, Section 51 (xxxiv) concerning railways and Section 120 concerning prisons. However, the number of concurrent powers has produced many areas for federal-State co-operation, the most important being in immigration, agriculture, health and the marketing of primary products. In addition, developments since federation—which were not predictable and under the present structure of the Constitution would be a 'residual' matter and therefore purely of State concern—necessitate co-operation with the federal government. Examples are civil aviation and the exploration and development of offshore oil and gas.

Techniques of co-operation have included formal and informal councils and conferences, agreements, and exchange of officers and information. Examples of these are the PREMIERS' CONFERENCE, the Australian LOAN COUNCIL, the Australian Agricultural Council, the National Health and Medical Research Council, the Snowy Mts Council, the River Murray Commission, the Australian Tourist Commission, the Joint Coal Board, the Australian Apprenticeship Advisory Committee, the Australian Education Council, the Australian Transport Advisory Council, the National Consultative Committee on Nuclear Energy and the Australian Environment Council. This is not an exhaustive list but it does indicate the wide area over which there is co-operation between the various governments in Australia in an attempt to gain uniformity, although the reason for the existence of State governments is that a federal structure of government allows for variety and difference to meet local requirements. It should be pointed out that the existence of co-operation between the federal and State governments has not meant in practice that duplication and unnecessary overlapping of activities are always eliminated.

Local government in Australia A system of local government exists in each State in Australia with similar powers and responsibilities. There are differences in titles used, and in terms of office, but in each State the local councils are created by an Act of the State Parliament and they are controlled in a fairly detailed way by a State Department of Local Government. Although some local councils have shown leadership in community efforts, in general local government councillors have power to make and carry out by-laws on such matters as construction and maintenance of roads, streets and street lighting, bridges, water, sewerage and drainage systems, health, protection of food supplies, garbage and sanitary services, slaughtering, the supervision of buildings and the registration of dogs. Some local councils may also provide transport facilities, electricity, gas, hospitals, charitable institutions, recreation grounds, parks, baths, libraries and museums.

The first elected municipal council in Australia was created in Adelaide in 1840; Sydney and Melbourne followed with local councils in 1842, Perth established a Town Trust in the same year, Hobart in 1852 and Brisbane in 1859. However, the establishment of a general system of local government took a long time because the community was unenthusiastic about the cost involved and, since federation, local government systems have in the main been set up by State governments without popular support.

In addition to the six State systems, there are three local councils in the NT but in the ACT federal government agencies substitute for local government councils. Local government is financed by levying rates on property owners and from State and federal grants.
See also Appendix 2, Government of Australia; elections; public service administration
Further reading: Atkins, R. & Graycar, A. *Governing Australia.* John Wiley & Sons, Australasia Pty Ltd, Sydney, 1972; Forell, C.R. *How We Are Governed.* Cheshire, Melbourne, 1978; Sawer, G. *Australian Government Today.* Melbourne University Press, Melbourne 1973; Spann, R.N. *Government Administration in Australia.* George Allen & Unwin, North Sydney, 1979.

Governor-General *see* government of Australia

Governors, State Governors of the States are formally appointed by the reigning British monarch on the advice of the British Secretary for Foreign and Commonwealth Affairs, and they represent the British government as well as the monarch personally. State Premiers are closely consulted by the British government, but the British government no longer presumes to control the Governors.

Grafton NSW (population 17 000 in 1981) A city on the CLARENCE RIVER in the NORTH COAST region, 77km upstream from the river estuary, it is situated on the Pacific Highway, and on the main North Coast railway, 673km by road and 696km by rail N of Sydney, and some 290km by rail S of Brisbane. It is the largest urban centre in the Clarence Valley and functions as the commercial and business centre for a rich grazing and farming district. The main rural pursuits in the area are dairying, lucerne and maize growing, sugar cane cultivation, beef cattle raising and pig breeding. Grafton experiences a sub-tropical climate throughout the year, with warm humid summers and mild dry winters. The average annual rainfall is 1 029mm, with a concentration in the summer months. The Clarence River separates the main city business district and residential area from the urban centre of South Grafton. In times of high river, the lower parts of the city and the nearby low-lying river flats experience flooding. The city contains a wide variety of secondary industries: sawmills, a plywood factory, a brewery, sheet metal works, roofing-tile and fibrous plaster works, and plants processing local rural produce. On Harwood Is, downstream beyond MACLEAN, there is a sugar mill. Along the river and in the nearby coastal areas are several popular tourist resorts which attract large numbers of summer visitors. Among these resorts are Yamba, Iluka, Red Cliff, The Broadwater, Wooli and Broom's Head.

The lower Clarence Valley was settled by cedar-cutters in the late 1830s and so lucrative was the trade in timber that little survives of the former forests. The town was named after the Duke of Grafton, a British peer; it became a municipality in 1859 and was proclaimed a city in 1885. For many years, the river was a barrier to the completion of the railway line to Sydney. The rail came as far as South Grafton, but it was only in 1932, with the building of a double-deck bridge (railway below and road above) across the river, that the main part of the city was linked to the rail route. Citizens of the city are proud of the broad tree-lined streets, many planted with jacarandas, flame trees, silky oaks and bauhinias. Each year, during the first week of November, when the jacarandas are in full bloom, the city holds a floral festival called, of course, the Jacaranda Festival.

Graham, David (1946-) Golfer. Born in WINDSOR in NSW, Graham has proved himself to be one of the finest golfers in the world. He was not widely known when chosen to play for Australia with Bruce DEVLIN in the 1970 World Cup in Buenos Aires, and many critics questioned his selection. However, he justified his selection convincingly with some magnificent rounds of golf leading to an Australian win. He had a highly successful year in 1976 when his fierce will to win brought him the Japanese Chunichi Crowns title, the Piccadilly World Match Play championship, the Westchester Classic and the American Golf Classic. In 1979 he won the coveted US PGA title, one of the world's four major championships, and in 1981 he

David Graham

capped this with a win in yet another of the four major tournaments, the highly prized US Open, to become the first Australian to win this tournament. In 1982 he won the Lancome tournament in France.

grain *see* Chenopodiaceae; Gramineae

Grainger, Percy Aldridge (1882-1961)

Composer and pianist. Percy Grainger is arguably the greatest composer Australia has produced. The variety and fertility of his ideas and the breadth of his concepts as to what constitutes music began to be appreciated more widely only after his death.

Grainger was born in Melbourne, where he commenced his musical studies. He began advanced studies in Germany at the age of 13, counting the influential Busoni amongst his teachers. His friendship in 1906 with the Norwegian composer Grieg inspired him to begin collecting and notating English folk songs, the influence of which is expressed in much of his work. He took up American citizenship after settling in the USA in 1914, becoming head of the music department at New York University in 1932.

Although he returned to Australia only for occasional tours and visits, he always stressed his own awareness of himself as a composer of Australian music, and in 1935 built a museum to house his work, bequeathing it to Melbourne University, in whose grounds it stands, and to Australia at large. Today the Grainger Museum, due to the work and guidance of its curator, Kay Dreyfus, in cataloguing, identifying and displaying its treasures, provides scholars and visitors with a wide range of Grainger's own work—from original manuscripts and correspondence with leading composers of his day, to his now fully restored 'free music machine'.

For a long time Grainger's reputation as a composer rested largely on a handful of popular piano works (such as *Country Gardens*), and on other short works which (according to his concept of 'elastic scoring') could be played by almost any size of instrumental ensemble. However, the full extent of his view of music is evident from the range of his musical works and from the musical innovations which he employed to expand his soundscapes beyond what he increasingly saw as the limiting confines of European musical language. In international terms he takes a place in 20th-century music among the truly innovative and original minds.

Further reading: Covell, R. *Australia's Music: Themes of a New Society.* Sun Books, Melbourne, 1967; Balough, T. (ed) *A Complete Catalogue of the Works of Percy Grainger.* (Music Monograph 2) University of Western Australia, Perth, 1975; Bird, J. *Percy Grainger.* Elek, London, 1976; Hopkins, J. 'Percy Grainger' in Callaway, F. & Tunley, D. (eds) *Australian Composition in the Twentieth Century.* Oxford University Press, Melbourne, 1978; Dreyfus, K. (compiler) *Percy Grainger's Music Collection.* (vol 1) Melbourne University Press, Melbourne, 1978.

Gramineae This is one of the largest plant families in the world, containing some 600 genera and 7 500 species. The Gramineae is a monocotyledonous family of flowering plants generally known as grasses, which have cosmopolitan distribution and are the dominant element in vegetation over great areas of the world. The Gramineae is of outstanding economic importance both directly and indirectly as a human food source, and selected genera are amongst the oldest of domesticated plants. Long-term breeding and selection and more recently controlled hybridisation of some genera have provided the staple carbohydrate diet of most civilisations. These staple food grains include maize, *Zea mays*, rice, *Oryza sativa*, wheat, *Triticum aestivum*, millet, *Sorghum* species, rye, *Secale cereale*, oats, *Avena sativa*, and barley, *Hordeum vulgare*. All these grains are grown worldwide and are under cultivation in Australia today, though the basic grain of Australian cuisine is still wheat.

Besides supplying food directly to man, members of the Gramineae (including waste from grain crops, specially cultivated crops and wild grasses) provide basic fodder crops for meat animals. Man's utilisation of grasses in this manner pre-dates grain domestication; hunting and gathering societies, both past and present, have thus been indirectly dependent on the Gramineae for food. Such societies appear to have exercised some range-management practices (such as regular burning off) in an effort to improve the palatability of grasses for herbivores and to increase the area of grassland, often at the expense of woodlands and forests.

The members of the Gramineae are annual or perennial herbs. Most are tufted, and very few are amphibious or aquatic. The plants may have upright or prostrate stems, or both. The upright (aerial) stem is usually hollow, except at the joints (nodes); the prostrate stems (stolons) and the subterranean stems (rhizomes) may root at the nodes and give rise to separate plants. The leaves are solitary at each node with the basal part sheathing the stem, and a free, parallel-veined blade above. The junction between sheath and blade is marked by a ligule, a fringe of hairs, or a membrane.

The small flowers have no sepals or petals and are located between two bracts, the lemma and the palea; the flower unit is known as a spikelet, and may be stalked or sessile (without stalks). The spikelets are arranged in inflorescences, such as spikes, racemes, panicles, or irregular clusters. The flowers are usually bisexual, and have one ovary, two styles and two feathery stigmas; in some the perianth is represented by one to three lodicules, in others it is absent. There are usually three stamens; these are adapted for wind-pollination and have long filaments and free-swinging anthers which protrude when the plant is in flower. The mature fruit is a grain (caryopsis) and is

Porcupine grass, *Triodia scariosa*

D. Grieg

enclosed within the two bracts; it contains oil, starch and protein.

Some of the best-known and most widespread temperate native grasses are spear grass (*Stipa* species), wallaby grass (*Danthonia* species) and kangaroo grass (*Themeda* species). A conspicuous element of lowland freshwater swamps and streams is the plume-like cosmopolitan common reed, *Phragmites communis*. Coastal sand-binding grasses include the introduced marram grass, *Ammophila arenaria*, and the native *Spinifex* (*S. hirstus*) which has separate male and female flowers; the female flowers form a bristly globular head (diameter 20cm) which falls off at maturity and is blown along the sands by the wind. Much of the arid zone of N Australia is dominated by porcupine grass (*Triodia* species); another tropical native grass is Mitchell grass, *Astrebla lappacea*, which grows on limestone clay soils in NSW and QLD.

Many grasses have been introduced into Australia intentionally as crops, ornamentals or turf, whilst a large number of others have come in accidentally. WEEDS have been derived from all these groups, many capable not only of being a threat to agricultural activities, but also of offering serious competition to native plants in natural communities, particularly after disturbances such as fire. The common lawn grass kikuyu, *Pennesitum clandestinum*, is a most aggressive invader of bushland around warm coastal urban areas, and twitch or English couch, *Agropyron repens*, is equally troublesome in cooler climates.

Whilst typical European fodder grasses, such as perennial rye grass, *Lolium perenne*, have been very successful as pasture grasses in the cool S parts and the warm temperate parts of Australia, satisfactory pasture grasses for subtropical and tropical Australia have come from a wide variety of sources. Amongst the most useful of these is buffel grass, *Cenchrus ciliaris*, a native of tropical Africa, Indonesia and India; Guinea grass, *Panicum maximum*, from Africa; kikuyu, from Kenya; green panic, *Panicum maximum* var *trichoglume*, from arid India and Arabia; Rhodes grass, *Chloris gayana*, from E Africa; and *Setaria*, *S. anceps*, from S Africa. Mitchell grass is also of value as a pasture species in the downs country of NSW and QLD.

See also Appendix 5, Flower Structure and Glossary of Botanical Terms
Further reading: see Appendix 6, A Bibliography for Plants.

Grampians VIC Located in western VIC, these ranges were discovered and named by the explorer Major Thomas MITCHELL in 1836; he gave them this name because they reminded him of the Grampians in his native Scotland. They consist of a series of roughly parallel ranges on a general N-S alignment, stretching E-W for about 50km and N-S for some 90km, and are composed of tilted sandstone beds which rise gently on the W and fall away steeply on the E. The range lies W of ARARAT, SSE of HORSHAM, and NE of HAMILTON. At the E end of the Grampians is the Mt William Range, which lies E of the Wannon River; Mt William is the highest point in western VIC, rising to 1 167m above sea level. On the W of the Wannon, parallel to the Mt William Range, is the Serra Range stretching from Mt Abrupt (829m) in the S to Hall's Gap, N of which it becomes the Mt Difficult Range, though structurally it is a continuation of the same formation. Still further W is the Victoria Range and then, W again beyond ROCKLANDS DAM on the GLENELG RIVER, is the Black Range.

VIC Govt Tourist Authority

Valley overlooking Lake Bellfield at Hall's Gap in the Grampians, VIC

The tourist centre of the Grampians is Hall's Gap, where the spring-time display of wild flowers is renowned and where there is access to several main lookout sites with panoramic views of Mt Rosea to the S, Mt Victory 10km to the E, and Mt Difficult to the N. The State forests of the ranges cover 200 000ha and, although only a fraction of this is of commercial value, it is preserved as a water catchment zone and as a protected area for native flora and fauna, as well as for bushwalking enthusiasts. Kangaroos, wallabies and koalas are common in the ranges and there is a variety of birds including currawongs, kookaburras and emus. There are numerous gorges, lakes and waterfalls which add to the scenic attraction of the area. The Henty Highway on a N-S route traverses the country to the W of the Victoria Range and there are two attractive valley drives: one along the Wannon Valley skirting the rugged E scarp of the Serra Range, and the other along the Victoria Valley, in which the Glenelg River rises. In addition to the Rocklands Dam, the Grampians contain numerous storage sites for the WIMMERA-MALLEE domestic and livestock supply scheme. The first of these, Lake Wartook (capacity 29 360ML), was constructed in 1887; the most recent is Lake Bellfield (78 540ML), completed in 1966.

Further reading: Bechervase, J. *Grampians Sketchbook.* Rigby, Adelaide, 1971.

grampus *see* dolphins, etc.

Granite Belt QLD A region in the SE of the State centred on STANTHORPE, it is really a continuation of the NEW ENGLAND Plateau of northern NSW across the border into QLD. It was a tin-mining area from the 1870s until the turn of the century and is now noted for its orchards and vineyards. Apples, pears, peaches and plums are grown widely throughout the region and wine making is an important industry. Granitic rocks dominate the landscape, with massive tors, stark outcrops and steep peaks. In the Girraween National Park, which covers 11 300ha in the border ranges, there are many unique landscape features formed from the granite; these include the Eye of the Needle, Castle Rock, the Sphinx, Turtle Rock and the Aztec Temple. The highest point in the park is Mt Norman (1 267m elevation), the ascent of which is recommended only to those who have rock climbing experience.

Grant, Hector *see* Dawson, Peter

Grant, James (1772-1833) Navigator. As a naval lieutenant, he was given command in 1799 of the *Lady Nelson*, a small vessel intended for use in coastal exploration, on her voyage from England to NSW. Following instructions, he sailed by way of the newly discovered BASS STRAIT, and became the first to survey the S coastline from Cape Banks, not far W of the present border between VIC and SA, to Cape Otway. In 1801 he was sent to explore the coastline from WESTERN PORT BAY to Cape Otway, but bad weather prevented him from proceeding past Western Port Bay. Later in the same year he took a surveying party to the HUNTER RIVER and before the end of the year returned to England.

Granville NSW A western suburb of Sydney on the main railway route to PARRAMATTA, on 18 January 1977 it was the site of Australia's worst railway disaster. A peak-hour morning train travelling E towards the city left the rails, collided with a stanchion supporting an overhead bridge, causing the bridge to collapse on the train carriages passing beneath; 83 people were killed and over 210 injured.

grass finches These PASSERINE BIRDS belong to the family Estrildidae and are quite distinct from the finches (Fringillidae) of the Old World. There are 19 estrildid finches in Australia. Many of them are brilliantly coloured and compete with parrots for the favours of the aviarist. They are small BIRDS, with short, sharp, thick bills; they feed mainly on grass seeds and, when breeding, on insects.

The commonest and most widespread species is the zebra finch, *Poephila guttata* (9cm long), which occurs throughout Australia, except in forests. The male has a chestnut ear patch and chestnut flanks with white spots; the rump and upper tail coverts are barred black and white, hence the name, and there are horizontal bars on the throat and part of the neck. The female is more subdued in her colouring. It is said that the zebra finch is being displaced in some areas by the introduced spice finch, *Lonchura punctulata* (10cm). Other species belonging to the genus *Poephila* are the doublebar finch, *P. bichenovii** (11cm), brownish-grey above and white below with two black bars, found in N and E Australia; the masked finch, *P. personata** (12cm), a mainly pinkish-brown species with a pointed black tail, found in N Australia; the black-throated finch, *P. cincta** (10cm), which is mainly brown with a black band on the rump and a short, rounded tail, and occurs in NE and E Australia; and the very similar long-tailed finch, *P. acuticauda** (10cm), of N Australia.

The finches belonging to the genus *Lonchura* are sometimes called mannikins. The spice finch, a brown-faced introduced species with a boldly marked grey and white breast, is found near Sydney and coastal QLD. A second introduced species, the black-headed mannikin, *L. atricapilla* (10cm), may also be established near Sydney. The three native species in this genus occur in the N. The pictorella finch, *L. pectoralis** (11cm), found in grassland and dry savanna, is mainly grey above with a black face and throat and white markings on its purplish-buff underparts. The chestnut-breasted finch, *L. castaneothorax** (10cm), mainly brown above with a black face mask and a white belly, is very similar to the yellow-rumped finch, *L. flaviprymna** (10cm), except that the latter species has a creamy-buff face and breast. Both species occur in swamp areas.

Perhaps the most attractive member of this family is the Gouldian finch, *Chloebia*gouldiae* (14cm), found in the savanna areas of N Australia. The breast is lilac, the belly yellow, the rump blue and the back green; the colour of the head varies from mainly crimson or yellow to black edged with dark blue. This species has been bred extensively in aviaries.

The only species in the genus *Aegintha** is the red-browed finch, *A.* temporalis* (12cm), which frequents the mangroves and forests of coastal E and SE Australia (but not TAS). The genus *Emblema** contains three firetails, all with a crimson rump, and the painted finch. The red-eared firetail, *E.* oculata* (12cm), an uncommon forest species of south-western WA, is a mainly black and brown bird with a red ear patch and large white spots on the underparts; the beautiful firetail, *E.* bella* (12cm), an uncommon species of SE Australia, found in woodlands and heaths, has barred black and white underparts, a red rump and olive brown upperparts; and the common diamond firetail, *E.* guttata* (11cm), found in the woodlands of southern QLD, NSW, VIC and south-eastern SA, has a grey head, a buff back and a black band on the white breast. The painted finch, *E.* picta* (10cm), lives in areas

Species, genus or family is endemic to Australia (see Preface)

of porcupine grass in a broad band from WA to W central QLD; the head and rump are scarlet and the black underparts are spotted with white.

The genus *Neochmia* contains the crimson finch, *N. phaeton* (14cm), a long-tailed crimson and grey species, and the star finch, *N. ruficauda*★ (12cm), a red-masked species with a yellow belly adorned with white spots, both found in N Australia. The only species in the genus *Erythrura* is the blue-faced finch, *E. trichroa* (12cm), a mainly green bird with a red rump and a blue face which frequents the edges of mangroves and rainforest in NE CAPE YORK. The plum-headed finch, *Aidemosyne*★ *modesta* (11cm), is found in thick vegetation along river margins ranging from central QLD to central NSW.
Further reading: Immelman, K. *Australian Finches in Bush and Aviary.* (revd edn) Angus & Robertson, Sydney, 1967.

grass trees *see* Palmae

grassbirds *see* warblers, etc.

grasses *see* Gramineae

grass-grubs *see* butterflies, etc.

grasshoppers *see* crickets, etc.

grassland *see* vegetation

grasswrens *see* fairy-wrens, etc.

Gray, Robin Trevor (1940-   ) Premier of TAS. He was born and educated in Melbourne, and became involved in Liberal Party affairs while a student at Melbourne University. After graduating from that university as a Bachelor of Agricultural Science, and also gaining a Diploma of Agriculture from Dookie Agricultural College, he worked as a teacher for a short time, but then became an agricultural consultant, first at COLAC in VIC and then at LAUNCESTON in TAS.

He entered the TAS Parliament in 1976 as a Member of the House of Assembly for Wilmot, and in 1981 became leader of the Liberal Party and therefore of the Opposition. Following the election of May 1982, in which the Liberals scored a convincing victory, he replaced Labor's Harold Holgate as Premier. As explained in the entry on TASMANIA, the politics of the island State have recently been deeply affected by the plan to build a hydro-electric power station on the GORDON RIVER. Immediately after the election results were announced, Gray declared his intention to push ahead with the plan. However the HAWKE federal government legislated against it, and subsequently won a High Court appeal on the matter.

grayling *see* fishes, freshwater

grazing industry In 1981 there were 175 760 farm establishments in Australia of

A rural scene at Mudgee in the Orana region NSW

NSW Dept of Tourism

which approximately 64 per cent were concerned with the production of sheep and/or beef cattle. Of these establishments, 28.7 per cent carried more than 500 sheep, 33 per cent carried more than 50 beef cattle and 15 per cent carried more than 200 sheep and 50 beef cattle. The establishments which carry sheep are distributed widely throughout the country but there is even wider distribution of cattle because Australian sheep are less well adapted than cattle to areas where the climate is hot and humid. Both sheep and cattle spend the whole year out-of-doors without provision of artificial shelter, and they normally obtain all of their feed from pasture. In some instances, most commonly during winter in southern Australia and during drought, pasture may be supplemented with grain, hay or silage. Crops such as oats also may be grazed for short periods during the year, and crop residues left after harvest are eaten by sheep and cattle.

In regions with sufficient rainfall, pastures have been improved for livestock production by the application of fertilisers and the sowing of grasses and legumes. Fertilisers, particularly superphosphate, have been the most widely used, but the supply of other major and minor elements has been necessary for success in some regions. The sowing of legumes, principally subterranean clover, *Trifolium subterraneum*, white clover, *T. repens*, and lucerne, *Medicago sativa*, in temperate regions and various tropical legumes, has been a feature of improvement. Legumes are important for their capacity to increase the levels of nitrogen in the soil through fixation of atmospheric nitrogen (achieved by rhizobia which infect the roots of the plants); adequate levels of nitrogen are necessary for growth of grasses such as rye grasses (*Lolium* species), *Phalaris aquatica* and cocksfoot, *Dactylis glomerata*, which are sown in pasture-improvement pro-

grammes. These programmes have permitted substantial increases in productivity and it is claimed that the use of fertilised, leguminous pastures is the greatest factor of favourable environmental change in Australian agriculture since the arrival of white settlers.

The Bureau of Agricultural Economics (BAE) has conducted surveys of the SHEEP AND WOOL industry since 1952 and of the BEEF CATTLE INDUSTRY since 1962. For survey purposes grazing properties have been divided into three geographical zones.
1. The high-rainfall zone consists of TAS and a narrow zone lying along the mainland coast stretching from N of CAIRNS in QLD to Adelaide, and from ALBANY in WA to just N of Perth. In 1980-81 this zone carried 37 per cent of the sheep and 41 per cent of the cattle in Australia. The average farm size was 830ha in 1981 but there was a wide range in size. Few cereals are grown, oats being more important than wheat, but there is a high proportion of improved pastures. Almost half the grazing properties are located in this zone with 60 per cent of these being in NSW and VIC.
2. The wheat-sheep zone merges inland with the pastoral zone and towards the coast with the high-rainfall zone. It carried 51 per cent of the sheep population and 25 per cent of the cattle in 1980-81 and contained over 90 per cent of the area under wheat. Livestock production is frequently combined with cereal cropping and this versatility of output increases adaptability to market conditions as well as allowing the conservation of soil fertility through rotation of pastures and crops. In 1981, 52 per cent of the grazing properties were in this zone, with NSW having the largest share (41 per cent).
3. The pastoral zone occupies the remainder of the area and is used for livestock production. It is by far the largest of the zones, comprising

the arid and semi-arid regions of NSW, QLD, SA, WA and the entire NT. In 1980-81 it carried 12 per cent of the sheep and 33 per cent of the cattle. In the N and centre of the continent the properties carry cattle only, but in other parts of the zone, properties running sheep only or sheep and cattle are found. Because of the aridity, the area of improved pasture or crops is negligible. The largest sheep flocks and cattle herds in Australia are carried in this zone owing to the relatively low forage productivity and the need for extensive livestock farming. The average area of grazing properties varies widely between the States, the largest being in the NT (average 433-444 × 10^3ha) and the smallest in NSW (average 11-125 × 10^3ha). Only about nine per cent of the grazing properties are located in the pastoral zone and the majority (54 per cent) of these are in QLD.
See also dairy cattle industry; diseases, livestock

Great Artesian Basin *see* artesian water

Great Australian Bight
Commonly called 'the Bight', it is the major indentation on the S coast of the continent. It extends for a distance of over 1 100km from Cape Pasley (located E of ESPERANCE) in WA to West Point (the S tip of EYRE PENINSULA) in SA, and is renowned for wild storms and heavy seas. The only safe anchorage in the whole stretch of the Bight is at STREAKY BAY in SA. Much of the coastline consists of steep cliffs, over 70m high, which are the borderlands of the NULLARBOR PLAIN. The first European known to have sailed the waters of the Bight was the Dutchman, Peter Nuijts, in 1627; the coastline was surveyed by Matthew FLINDERS in 1802.

Great Barrier Reef
QLD The largest coral structure in the world, often claimed as one of nature's wonders, it stretches for over 2000km off the NE coast of the continent. It includes some 700 islands, encloses an area of over 200 000km², and extends from Bramble Cay (latitude 9°8'S) off the S coast of Papua New Guinea, to Lady Elliott Is (latitude 24°8'S), about 155km ESE of GLADSTONE. It consists of a chain of coral reefs built on a comparatively shallow submarine platform which is wider at its S end and gradually narrows towards the N extremity. The term 'outer reef' (or 'outer barrier') refers to the actively growing wall of coral furthest from the mainland; between this outer reef and the mainland coast is a shallow lagoon-channel dotted with numerous islands. The seaward edge of the outer reef, often pounded by heavy surf, is marked by a steep slope of living coral, built on a mass of dead coral; at low tide the coral is exposed, stretching up to 800m wide, sloping gently to the lagoon. The lagoon, between the outer reef and the mainland coast, is widest in the S and narrows towards the N: at MACKAY (latitude 21°S) it is about 160km wide, at TOWNSVILLE (19°S) 80km, at CAIRNS (17°S) 30km, and at Cape Melville (12°S) the reef is only 11km from the coast. N of Cairns,

the outer reef forms an almost continuous unbroken stretch of coral but S of Cairns it is interrupted in places by stretches of water separating sections of the reef, such as the Capricorn Channel, lying between the Bunker-CAPRICORN GROUP of islands and Swain Reefs. The great number of islands, fringing reefs and patches of coral in the channel between the outer reef and the coastline of QLD makes navigation of these waters rather hazardous, as Captain COOK found on his exploratory voyage in 1770.

The islands of the Great Barrier Reef are of two main types: the 'low islands' and the 'high or continental islands'. The former are coral cays, such as GREEN ISLAND off Cairns and HERON ISLAND in the Capricorn Group, formed by the accumulation of sand and coral debris on the leeward side of a reef with their longer axes at right-angles to the prevailing SE winds. This type of island is usually low lying, has a fringing reef, is unstable in its early development and may vary quite quickly both in shape and size under changing conditions, such as a severe storm; but, as sand accumulates on it and dunes are formed, it develops a vegetational cover and becomes more stable. The 'high or continental islands', as their name implies, were formerly part of the continental mass, remnants of the QLD coastal ranges, and have been cut off from the mainland by changes in sea level. These are located in the channel between the outer reef and the coastline; some lie quite close to the coast and rise steeply from the water; most have fringing coral reefs and are thickly vegetated; and the shorelines of some are sandy beaches while others are bordered by mangrove swamps. A number of the better-known island tourist resorts are of this type, such as HAYMAN, South MOLLE, LINDEMAN, DUNK and BRAMPTON Islands.

Several theories have been proposed to explain why the continental shelf bordering the QLD coast has provided ideal conditions for the growth of coral and the formation of the barrier reef. It is well known that corals can survive only in clear, salty, moving and relatively shallow waters where the temperatures do not fall below 20°C. The generally accepted explanation is related to subsidence; that is, the reef developed originally on the continental shelf where suitable conditions prevailed and, as the shelf has progressively subsided, the coral reef has grown upwards. Since there is evidence along the QLD coast of subsidence in such features as drowned river estuaries and numerous isolated offshore islands, this theory would appear to explain the origin of the reef.

There are some 350 species of corals on the reef, coloured by algae living in them. The living polyps extract calcium carbonate from seawater and so form the coral structure around their bodies. When a colony dies, the coral which is left bleaches white. During recent years there has been much concern about the damage caused to corals by the 'crown of thorns' SEA STAR. Also there has been considerable controversy about the possible damage which might be caused to the

Aerial view of part of the Great Barrier Reef

reef by offshore drilling for oil, by dredging for minerals in the region, by sewage effluent and by tourist development.
See also Cumberland Islands; Curtis Is; Daydream Is; Hinchinbrook Is; Lizard Is; Magnetic Is; Whitsunday Passage
Further reading: Roughley, T.C. *Wonders of the Great Barrier Reef.* Angus & Robertson, Sydney, 1943; Gillett, K. & McNeill, F. *The Great Barrier Reef and Adjacent Islands.* Corel Crest, Sydney, 1959; Dakin, W.J. *The Great Barrier Reef and Some Mention of Other Australian Coral Reefs.* (revd edn) Ure Smith, Sydney, 1963; Clare, P. *The Struggle for the Great Barrier Reef.* Collins, London, 1971.

Great Dividing Range
This is the name commonly used for the extensive highland area in the E part of the continent, though it is now more frequently termed the Eastern Highlands or simply the Great Divide. It stretches from CAPE YORK in northern QLD, along the E side of that State, through eastern NSW and into VIC as far W as the GRAMPIANS. It runs generally parallel to the coast and varies in width from about 160km to over 300km. In some parts, the range lies quite close to the E seaboard, such as southern NSW where the coastal plain is less than 1km wide; in other places, such as in southern QLD, the range lies more than 250km inland. It consists of a series of hilly lands, plateaus and high plains country, often deeply dissected by steep gorges and canyons. The highest point is MOUNT KOSCIUSKO (2 230m), in south-eastern NSW. There is a great variety of rock types of all geological ages within the range: some of the older rocks have been strongly folded; in places there are intrusions of granite and other igneous rocks; some areas have been warped and uplifted; and in others there has been block-faulting associated with the formation of the highlands. The steepest slopes are usually along the E scarplands, where many spectacular waterfalls have been formed as rivers plunge from the uplands to the coastal plains. On the inland side of the range, the terrain is generally less rugged and consists of gently sloping hilly country, often referred to as the 'slopes' (for example, the Western slopes of NSW).

Many different names are used for the various parts of the highlands. Sometimes they are called ranges, such as the Richardson Range and the Geike Range in Cape York, the BUNYA RANGE in south-eastern QLD and the

McPHERSON RANGE which forms part of the State border between QLD and NSW; other sections are termed mountains, such as the BLUE MOUNTAINS and the SNOWY MOUNTAINS in NSW and the Bowen Mts and the Barry Mts in VIC; and some parts are called plateaus or tablelands, such as the ATHERTON TABLELAND in QLD, the NEW ENGLAND Plateau in northern NSW, and the SOUTHERN TABLELANDS of NSW.

As the name Great Divide implies, the range forms the watershed in the E part of the continent between rivers which drain towards the coast and those which flow inland. The coastal rivers are usually short with steep gradients in their upper courses, while the inland streams are longer, flow across the broad interior plains with gentle gradients, and are often intermittent. In northern QLD, the main coastal streams are the BARRON, TULLY and HERBERT Rivers; the major inland ones are the MITCHELL and GILBERT which flow W to the GULF OF CARPENTARIA. Further S in QLD are the BURDEKIN, the MACKENZIE-DAWSON, the BRISBANE and the LOGAN, flowing to the E coastline, while the BARCOO, BULLOO and CONDAMINE-BALONNE drain inland. In NSW, the TWEED, RICHMOND, CLARENCE, HUNTER, HAWKESBURY and SHOALHAVEN Rivers flow E to the Pacific seaboard, while the BARWON-DARLING, CASTLEREAGH, MACQUARIE, BOGAN and MURRUMBIDGEE-LACHLAN form the vast inland drainage system. In VIC, the SNOWY, TAMBO, MITCHELL and THOMSON-LATROBE Rivers flow from the highlands to the BASS STRAIT coast, while the MITTA MITTA, OVENS, GOULBURN, CAMPASPE and LODDON Rivers are tributaries of the MURRAY.

Great Keppel Island *see* Keppel Isles

Great Lake
TAS The largest natural freshwater lake in Australia, it is located in the CENTRAL PLATEAU region of the State and is skirted on the S and W shores by the Lake Highway. The S part of Great Lake is about 130km NW of Hobart and the N part is 37km S of DELORAINE. The lake extends about 25km from N to S and varies in its E-W extent between 5km and 8km. Some of the earliest hydro-electricity developments in TAS were located in the S parts of the lake region, first at WADDAMANNA where generation started in 1916, and later at SHANNON RIVER power station, constructed in 1934. These have now been largely superseded by vast hydro-electricity developments to the NE of Great Lake, particularly the POATINA underground power station. The lake is situated in a shallow depression at an elevation of 1000m; its capacity was increased in 1967 by the construction of Miena Dam at the S end, giving it a capacity of 2 309 000ML. The water level is also raised and stabilised by additional supplies diverted into it from the OUSE RIVER and ARTHUR LAKE. The surrounding areas are used for summer livestock grazing and the region, though sparsely settled, is a popular tourist and fishing centre.

Great Oyster Bay
TAS An inlet on the mid-E coast, it extends over 20km N-S, with FREYCINET PENINSULA and Schouten Is lying at its SE boundary, the town of Coles Bay on the NE shore and Swansea on the NW of the bay. The N limit of the bay is Nine Mile Beach, behind which there are extensive lagoons.

Great Sandy Desert
WA A vast stretch of arid country, consisting mostly of sand hills and, in the central portion, stony desert, it occupies the inland part of the PILBARA in the NW of the State, between the KIMBERLEYS region to the N and the GIBSON DESERT to the S. It is a particularly inhospitable area, first crossed from E to W by P.E. Warburton in 1873.

Great Victoria Desert
WA/SA Located N of the NULLARBOR PLAIN and S of the WARBURTON RANGE, in the SE inland part of the State, it consists of a vast stretch of parallel sand dunes. Barren and inhospitable country, it has been made accessible since the 1960s to four-wheel-drive vehicles by the tracks marked for the recovery of rockets launched from the WOOMERA range.

Great Western Tiers
TAS These steep cliffs, rising to over 1 220m above sea level, form the NE escarpment of the CENTRAL PLATEAU region, towering above the MIDLANDS and the central section of the N coastal plain. Several major rivers, such as the FORTH, the MERSEY and the W tributaries of the South ESK, rise on the Central Plateau and cross the Western Tiers on their course to BASS STRAIT. The sheer drop of the Tiers has been utilised for the production of hydro-electricity in the Forth-Mersey and the Great Lake-Esk River schemes. The Lake Highway crosses the Tiers just N of Great Lake.

grebes
These aquatic (fresh and salt water) BIRDS belong to the family Podicepididae. They have partially webbed feet, set well back, very small tails and small rounded wings; because they are almost incapable of walking on land, they seldom leave the water, except to fly or to climb on to their nests, which are rafts of floating vegetation.

There are three species in Australia: the widespread little grebe, *Podiceps novaehollandiae* (23cm long), with a white face patch; the hoary-

Courtesy of A.I.S. Canberra

Little grebe or dabchick, *Podiceps novaehollandiae*

Species, genus or family is endemic to Australia (see Preface)

headed grebe, *P. poliocephalus** (28cm to 30cm), which is more common in the S half of Australia and is dark grey-brown above (greyer when not breeding), white and buff below, and has fine white streaks on the head; and the crested grebe, *P. cristatus* (43cm), an uncommon E and SE species which is similar in colouring to the little grebe but is distinguished by its conspicuous black crest (when breeding) and the black and rufous ruff on its long neck. The crested grebe is justly renowned for its elaborate and beautiful courtship display.

Greeks in Australia
Greek migrants have made a very big impact on the Australian community. They have enriched Australia's culture, contributed to the leadership of the nation and brought with them vitality and enthusiasm in all activities. In the primary industries members of the Greek community have provided expertise in the dried-fruit industry, in cotton growing, tobacco production and commercial fishing. Many have established their own businesses in fish retailing, catering and milk bars, and they have provided thousands of doctors, lawyers, teachers, artists, graziers, academics and chemists (there are an estimated 350 Greek chemists in the E States of Australia). In addition, they have contributed to the labour force in various types of manufacturing industries, engineering workshops and the building industry.

The 1981 census revealed that 146 625 persons resident in Australia had been born in Greece. C.A. Price, a leading authority on multicultural affairs, in a study of the ethnic origins of the Australian population based on an eight-generation analysis, estimated the total Greek component to be equivalent to 336 000 persons in 1978.

Greek migration before 1947 The gold rushes in VIC in the 1850s brought the first Greek migrants to Australia and it is thought that the very first were seamen who jumped ship to make their fortunes at the diggings. Andreas Lekatsas from Ithake is recorded as the first of these Greeks to jump ship; he stayed in Australia for 20 years. The first Greek to work his passage to Sydney on a sailing ship was Athanasios Comino from Kithira. He arrived in the early 1870s and after working at the Old Balmain Collieries ran a fish and chip business in Oxford Street, Sydney. His success in this business, which he later expanded to restaurants and oyster leases, encouraged many of his fellow countrymen to migrate, and at one time it appeared that all the cafes in NSW country towns were run by Kithirian Greeks.

Between 1916 and 1920 the federal government banned the entry of Greeks because of the fear that they would take over jobs vacated by Australians who were recruited to fight in World War I. In 1924 a quota system allowed no more than 1 200 sponsored Greeks to migrate to Australia each year. The original Greek migrants established themselves mainly in the catering trade, agricultural pursuits and fishing, and then sponsored friends or relatives to join them. Greek migration has tended to operate along chains of migration from the original community in Greece to its transplanted counterpart in Australia.

Migration since 1947 The Greek community has been one of the fastest growing of all ethnic groups in Australia and 90 per cent of it has migrated since the end of World War II. The post-war migrants were largely unskilled or semi-skilled workers with little formal education and they came mainly from the rural areas of the Greek mainland and from the Greek islands. The Australian government provided assistance in 1952 but these chains of migration in the 1950s led to the factory process-line where Greeks were prepared to do the heaviest and dirtiest jobs, welcomed overtime and weekend work and sometimes worked at a second job in order to save money.

Greek communities More Greeks have settled in Melbourne than in any other city outside Greece. They have concentrated in the older and poorer inner-city districts of Fitzroy, Collingwood and Richmond. Other Greek communities have been established in Prahan, Port Melbourne, Brunswick, Northcote and Preston as well as in Footscray, South Caulfield and Oakleigh.

In Sydney, Greek communities have concentrated in the older industrial suburbs of Central Sydney, South Sydney, Marrickville and Botany. Smaller communities are located at Bankstown, Ashfield, Burwood and North Strathfield. Small groups are also found in the E suburbs and around PARRAMATTA.

Before 1947, rural Greek settlements were established in the cotton growing district near BILOELA in central QLD, the fishing village of Thevenard in SA and in the horticultural districts near MILDURA and Werribee in VIC, RENMARK SA and MANJIMUP WA. Since 1947, chain migration has extended the Greek settlements at Mildura, Werribee, Renmark and SHEPPARTON.

Greek heritage Strong unifying influences have been exercised in Greek communities because ethnicity, kinship, regional ties and religion reinforce one another. The Greek Orthodox Church has survived transplantation from the homeland to Australia to a much greater extent than most ethnic religious denominations. One small section of this Church has split from the main body to form the Independent Greek Orthodox Church of Australia, but neither the established Greek Orthodox Church nor the Greek government will recognise any marriage performed by this breakaway group—indeed they do not accept the Independent Greek Orthodox Church at all (*see* ORTHODOX CHURCHES).

In all Greek ethnic settlements one Orthodox church has been established and is responsible for running the community's old peoples' homes and nursing homes. Ethnic community centres have been established, ethnic shopping centres have evolved supported by associated business services, and all these developments have led to the growth of the Greek population in each area.

Social clubs are very important to the Greeks in Australia. Regional brotherhoods become community foci and there are Kithirian Clubs, Kastellorizian Brotherhoods, Spartan Brotherhoods, Macedonian Community Associations, the Athenian Society, the New Hellas Club, Kerkirian Brotherhoods and so on.

The Greeks in Australia are anxious to preserve their language and culture. In 1975 courses in Greek were offered in only two universities in NSW and one in VIC and at two Colleges of Advanced Education in NSW, one in VIC and one in SA. The Greek communities have established their own part-time schools to teach their native language and selected aspects of their native culture, particularly history, literature, music and dance.

The Greek communities have a flourishing press which is widely read and well supported by advertisers. There are at least 10 Greek newspapers published in Australia, including the *Greek National Tribune* (Sydney), *Neos Kosmos* (Melbourne), *Neo Patris* (Sydney) and the *Hellenic Herald* (Sydney).

Notable Greeks in Australia Diamantina Roma, daughter of Count and Countess Roma, of Corfu, became the first wife of Sir George BOWEN, the first Governor of QLD, who had spent many years in Greece. Lady Bowen played a prominent role in the social life of the colony and was also an active worker for charity; several geographic names were bestowed in her honour, including those of the town of ROMA in QLD, Roma Street in Brisbane and the DIAMANTINA RIVER.

Other notable Greeks in Australia have included: George Andronicus, coffee merchant; Dr Michael Anthony, clinical neurologist at the Prince Henry Hospital and lecturer at the University of New South Wales; Dr Manuel Aroney, Associate Professor of Chemistry, University of Sydney; Wolfgang Gardamatis, artist; Sir Arthur George, prominent in soccer; Stame George, Head of the Bio-Physics Department at Sydney's Royal North Shore Hospital; Senator George Georges; Dr Archivedes Kalakerinos, health advisor to the National Aboriginal Congress; Sir Nicholas Lourandos, a grazier in the RIVERINA district who endowed the Chair of Modern Greek at the University of Sydney; Sir John Morris, Chief Justice of TAS; Peter Morris, MHR for Shortland; Michael Paspallis, a former mayor of Darwin; George Polites, Director-General of the National Employers' Industrial Council; and Tony Rafty, cartoonist. Finally, in considering the Greek community one must not forget Colonel Alec Sheppard, publisher, who has been made an 'honorary Greek'.

Further reading: Buckland, D. 'Greeks in Australia' in *Current Affairs Bulletin.* (vol 50, no 6, November 1973); Price, C.A. (ed) *Greeks in Australia.* Australian National University Press, Canberra, 1975; Burnley, I.H. *The Social Environment.* McGraw-Hill Book Co., Sydney, 1976; 'The Australian Family, Part 3—The Greeks' in the *Bulletin.* (vol 98, 17 July, 1976); Bowen, M. (ed) *Australia 2000: The Ethnic Impact.* University of New England Publishing Unit, Armidale NSW, 1977; Vondra, J. *Hellas Australia.* Wide Scope International, Camberwell VIC, 1979; Price, C.A.

Australian Immigration, A Bibliography and Digest. Australian National University Press, Canberra, 1979.

Greek Orthodox Church *see* Orthodox Churches

greenfinch *see* finches

greenfly *see* aphids

Green Island QLD A coral cay of the GREAT BARRIER REEF, 27km NE of CAIRNS and 13ha in area, it has been developed as a tourist resort and is noted for its underwater coral observatory. Formed of sand and coral debris, thickly timbered and fringed with reefs, the island is accessible by launch, aeroplane and hydroplane from Cairns. Most of the island and all of the surrounding reefs have been designated as a marine park, covering 3000ha.

Aerial view of Green Island QLD

Courtesy of A.I.S. Canberra

greenshank *see* waders

Greenway, Francis Howard (1777-1837) Architect. Born near Bristol, he practised as an architect in that city and at Bath, and in 1812 was sentenced to death for forging part of a building contract. The sentence was commuted to transportation for 14 years and he arrived in Sydney in February 1814, was given a ticket of leave almost immediately, and before the end of the year had opened a practice. Governor MACQUARIE, who was delighted to have the services of a trained architect, used Greenway at first as an unpaid adviser, and then in 1816 appointed him as civil architect and assistant engineer. His design for his first major work, the Macquarie Lighthouse at South Head, PORT JACKSON, pleased the Governor so much that in 1818 Greenway was granted a conditional pardon and in the following year an absolute pardon. In later years he designed some 40 buildings, of which the most notable still standing are St Matthew's Church at WINDSOR, St Luke's at Liverpool, St James' in Queen's Square, Sydney (somewhat altered from his original design), the convict barracks in Queen's Square (now being restored for use as a museum), Liverpool Hospital (now a Technical College), the courthouse at Windsor, the Supreme Court in King Street, Sydney, and the central structure of the Conservatorium of Music, Sydney, which was designed as the stables of a proposed new Government House.

St Matthew's Church, Windsor NSW, designed by
Francis Greenway

Greenway's unquestionable talent as an architect would have had little scope for expression
but for Macquarie's patronage, for he had little
skill either in managing business affairs or in
dealing with people, and gained few private
commissions during his years in the colony.
Arrogant and temperamental, and with the
effrontery to persist in claiming large fees for
work which he had performed while on a
government salary, he tried even Macquarie's
patience and was dismissed by Governor BRIS-
BANE late in 1822. He did no architectural
work of importance during the remainder of
his life, and died in comparative poverty.
Further reading: Barnard, M. *Australia's First
Architect: Francis Greenway.* Longman, Croydon VIC, 1961; Herman, M. *Francis Greenway.* Oxford University Press, Melbourne,
1964 and *The Early Australian Architects and
Their Work.* (2nd edn) Angus & Robertson,
Sydney, 1970; Ellis, M.H. *Francis Greenway,
His Life and Times.* (revd edn) Angus &
Robertson, Cremorne NSW, 1973.

Greer, Germaine (1939-) Writer and
feminist. Born in Melbourne, she graduated
BA from Melbourne University, MA from the
University of Sydney, and later won a scholarship to Cambridge University, where she was
awarded a PhD. While a lecturer at Warwick
University between 1964 and 1972, she wrote
extensively for intellectual and popular
magazines, and in 1970 published the controversial and extremely successful *The Female
Eunuch*, which immediately made her a
leading figure in the women's liberation movement. Since then she has written many articles
for the Press, has made numerous television
and lecture appearances and in 1979 published
*The Obstacle Race: The Fortunes of Women
Painters and Their Work.*

Gregory, Sir Augustus Charles
(1819-1905) Surveyor and explorer. Born in
Nottingham, he was brought to WA by his
parents in 1829, and in 1841 obtained a posi-
tion with the government Survey Office there.
His reputation as an explorer rests mainly on
three expeditions: from Perth to the Mur-
chison district in 1848; from the NT to Port
Curtis in QLD in 1855-56; and from central
QLD down the BARCOO RIVER and thence to
Adelaide in 1858 (*see* EXPLORATION BY LAND).
In 1859 he was appointed Surveyor-General of
the new State of QLD.
Further reading: Gregory, A.C. & Gregory,
F.T. *Journals of Australian Explorations.*
Libraries Board of South Australia, Adelaide,
1969.

Gregory family Cricketers. The name
Gregory is firmly ensconced in Australian
cricketing history, as is evidenced by the fact
that the road which leads into the main gates
of the Sydney Cricket Ground is named after
Ned (Edward J.) Gregory who played in the
first Test match against England in 1877 and
who was the first curator of the sports ground
which later became the Sydney Cricket
Ground. Ned was one of the seven sons of
Edward William Gregory who came to Australia in 1813 and who started playing in NSW
club cricket in 1826. Five of his seven sons—
Walter, Ned, David, Charles and Arthur—
became cricketers of national and international
fame. David also played in the 1877 Test
against England as Australia's first Test
captain, and he led Australia on the first
cricket tour of England in 1878.
Sydney Edward Gregory (1870-1929), son
of Ned Gregory, made his first Test appearance for Australia in 1891-92 and played in 58
Test matches in a career which lasted until
1912. In his 58 Test appearances he amassed
2 282 runs for an average of 24.53.
Jack Morrison Gregory (1895-1973), son of
Charles S. Gregory, first played for Australia
in Test cricket against England in 1920 and
was considered the best all-rounder of the
1920s. In the 1921-22 series against South
Africa, he made the fastest century in Test
match cricket, taking only 70 minutes to knock
up his 100. In the 24 Tests in which he
appeared for Australia he scored 1 146 runs
for an average of 36.96 and took 85 wickets for
an average of 31.15 runs per wicket.

Gregory River QLD Located in the far
NW of the State, it rises in the BARKLY TABLE-
LAND, flows E then N for over 200km, joins
the Nicholson River and enters an estuary on
the SE shore of the GULF OF CARPENTARIA. In
its lower section, it has a meandering course
and divides to form ANABRANCHES. The Albert
River, on which BURKETOWN is located, is a
distributary in the delta section of the Gregory
River. Beef cattle grazing on extensive properties is the main rural activity throughout
the whole basin.

grenadier weavers *see* weaverbirds

Grenfell NSW (population 2 070 in 1981)
This country town is on the Mid-Western
Highway, 375km by road WSW of Sydney
and 58km W of COWRA. It is located in the W
slopes region, at an elevation of 384m above
sea level, and receives an average annual rainfall of 635mm spread fairly evenly throughout
all seasons. The town owes its origin to the
discovery of gold in the district in 1866 and it
was in a tent on the Grenfell diggings that the
poet Henry LAWSON was born in 1867. A
monument marking this site now stands in the
recreation reserve called Lawson Park, and the
Lawson Festival is held annually in the town.
The surrounding district produces wheat,
wool, fat lambs, fruit and dairy produce. The
town was named after J.G. Grenfell, a gold
commissioner in the area, who was shot by
bushrangers.

Greta NSW (combined population of Greta
and BRANXTON 2 849 in 1981) This coal-
mining town is in the HUNTER RIVER valley,
on the New England Highway, adjacent to the
town of Branxton, located between MAITLAND
and SINGLETON, about 220km N of Sydney.
The village site for Greta was surveyed in
1842 and named, it is thought, after a river
in Cumberland, England. The coal deposits
extending NW from CESSNOCK to MUSWELL-
BROOK, which were located by the geologist
Edgeworth DAVID in 1886, are called the
Greta coal measures.

Grevillea *see* Proteaceae

Grey, Sir George (1812-98) Explorer,
Governor and politician. Born in Lisbon, he
joined the British Army in 1830, but soon
became more interested in exploration and
theories of colonisation than in routine military
duties. In 1836 he offered to lead an exploration expedition in WA, and in 1837-38 explored the Hanover Bay area in the NW of
that colony. In 1839 he led another expedition,
but after being taken by sea to SHARK BAY lost
most of his supplies and had to return to Perth,
partly in open boats and partly on foot. He
was then appointed magistrate at KING GEORGE
SOUND but returned to England in the following year. During his few years in WA he had
made a study of Aboriginal culture and had
written a *Vocabulary of the Dialects Spoken by
the Aboriginal Races of South-Western Australia*
(1839).
In October 1840, when the authorities in
Britain came to realise the extent to which
Governor GAWLER had exceeded his authorised
expenditure in SA, Grey was appointed his
successor. He arrived in Adelaide in May
1841, and immediately imposed a policy of
financial restraint. During the following four
years the number of people settled on the land
increased spectacularly, the wheat industry
boomed and the colony ceased to be dependent
on British grants. At the same time the Governor found time to make a worthwhile study of
native fauna and took a close interest in
Aboriginal welfare.

Sir George Grey

National Library of Australia

He left SA in 1845 and became Lieutenant-Governor of New Zealand. There he ended the First Maori War and, by his conciliation of the Maoris and study of their culture, laid the ground for improved race relations. He was Governor of Cape Colony (South Africa) from 1854 to 1860, and was then sent back to New Zealand as Governor for seven years. He later became a member of the House of Commons at Westminster, afterwards returning to New Zealand as a settler; he became a member of the House of Representatives there in 1875 and was Premier from 1877 to 1879. He represented New Zealand at the federal convention in 1891, and in 1894 was made a member of the Privy Council.
Further reading: Collier, J. *Sir George Grey, High Commissioner and Premier.* Whitcombe & Tombs, Christchurch, 1909; Rutherford, J. *Sir George Grey, KCB, 1812-1898: A Study in Colonial Government.* Cassell, London, 1961.

Grey Range QLD This range of low hills, located in the SW of the State, extends on a NE-SW axis for about 500km, forming the divide between the lower section of the BULLOO RIVER and the intermittent streams of the COOPER'S CREEK system which drain towards LAKE EYRE in SA. It lies within the E part of the CHANNEL COUNTRY in an arid region of low and variable rainfall, where beef cattle grazing on large properties is the main rural activity. Since the 1870s, gold and opals have been mined in various parts of the region.

greyhound racing and coursing

Since the introduction during the 1960s of the Totalizator Agency Board (TAB), which controls all off-course betting and a large part of on-course betting, greyhound racing has become a boom sport in Australia. All capital cities have at least one and usually two tracks where greyhound races are regularly held. Race distances vary, but at a typical track such as Harold Park in Sydney a 10-race programme most often consists of seven sprint races (457m) and three distance races (732m). Bookmakers have been a part of greyhound racing since its inception, offering odds as to

the chances of each dog, but their business is now slowly giving way to betting through TOTALIZATORS. At the most recently completed capital city track, in Perth WA, there are no bookmakers and all betting is done through the totalizator.

Greyhounds were brought to Australia with the FIRST FLEET in 1788 as hunting dogs, and in the early days of the colony played an important part in the hunt for food which in those times required the skill, speed and strength of the greyhound. Greyhounds, as well as the cross between them and Scottish deerhounds which became known as kangaroo dogs, were used to hunt kangaroos. This developed into the sport of coursing in which the dogs chased, and killed if they caught, a live animal. The first public coursing meeting in Australia was held at Naracoorte SA in 1867, the live quarry being a small species of wallaby. Hares were imported into Australia for the first time in 1873 and in the same year they were used as the lure in the first course meeting to be held in VIC. In NSW the sport was sufficiently well established by 1876 to warrant the formation of the New South Wales Coursing Club. But standards began to change and live-hare coursing came to be regarded as a blood sport and inhumane. Coursing was eventually replaced in the 1930s with greyhound racing, in which the dogs chase a mechanical lure, usually a metal device covered with a hare skin and pulled in front of the dogs to attract their attention and make them give chase.

Mechanical-lure (or tin-hare) racing was introduced into Australia from America on 28 May 1927, when the first meeting was held at Epping Raceway (now Harold Park). The NSW government's reaction was to ban night greyhound racing and betting on mechanical-hare racing, but to permit the continuation of live-hare racing. When the tin hare was introduced in VIC in 1928 the VIC government banned betting on mechanical-lure racing on the pretext that it was cruel to make the dogs chase something they could not catch but, as in NSW, live-hare racing was allowed to continue. Eventually, however, live-hare racing was outlawed and the mechanical lure was accepted in all States, although VIC took until 1955 and SA until 1968 to legalise the tin hare.

Greyhound racing attracts a strong and consistent following sufficient, for example, to keep 46 registered greyhound tracks operating in NSW alone, where there is racing on most days of the week except Sunday. Off-course betting on greyhound racing is popular in all States, and in 1980-81 in NSW $124 732 522 was wagered.
Further reading: Agostini, M.G. *The Greyhound in Australia.* Cheshire, Melbourne, 1969.

gribbles *see* crustaceans

Griffin, Walter Burley (1876-1937) Architect and landscape architect. A product of the 'prairie school' and an associate of Frank Lloyd Wright (who initiated the prairie

school movement by building low-lying 'prairie houses' between 1895 and 1910, mainly in the Chicago area), Walter Burley Griffin graduated in architecture from the University of Illinois. He came to Australia in 1913 after winning the first prize in a worldwide competition for the design of Australia's new capital city Canberra. His association with the initial development of Canberra was not a happy one. Though his was a brilliant plan and he was made Federal Capital Director of Design and Construction, there was much political backbiting and controversy. The start of World War I made things even more difficult, and Griffin was forced from his position as director in 1920 without seeing much progress in the work.

Around the time of the Canberra involvement, Griffin and his wife practised in Melbourne where, among other buildings, they designed Newman College and the Capitol Theatre. The strongly textured college and the fantastic theatre were the talk of Australia for years—and may still be enjoyed today, for both are well maintained.

Newman College, University of Melbourne, designed by Walter Burley Griffin

From 1924 the Griffins worked in Sydney. On a bushland promontory in Middle Harbour they created Castlecrag, a suburb where the streets follow the contours of the land and the houses designed by the Griffins merge naturally into their setting. Griffin's versatility is further seen in his designs for municipal garbage incinerators in NSW, QLD and SA. One survives at Willoughby NSW and another at IPSWICH in QLD.

Although at times they experienced extreme frustration in the course of their career in Australia, the Griffins produced some innovative and interesting architecture in Australia. In 1936 they went to India to begin new work, but Walter Griffin contracted peritonitis there and died in the following year.
Further reading: Johnson, D.L. *The Architecture of Walter Burley Griffin.* Macmillan, Melbourne, 1977.

Griffith NSW (population 13 185 in 1981) The largest town of the MURRUMBIDGEE IRRIGATION AREAS in the RIVERINA region of the State, Griffith is 647km by road WSW of Sydney. It is a railhead connected to LEETON and TEMORA, and thence to the main S line, and can be reached by two routes—one via Temora (a journey of 637km from Sydney) and the other via Yanco (658km). At an elevation of 128m above sea level, Griffith has an annual average rainfall of only 411mm, but irrigation water has converted it into a rich agricultural region. The town was designed as a market and service centre in 1914 by Walter Burley GRIFFIN and was named after Arthur Griffith, State Minister for Public Works. The irrigated lands around the town produce a wide variety of fruit crops (citrus, stone and vine), rice, vegetables, cotton, fat lambs, wheat and wool. Secondary industries include fruit and vegetable processing and packing, juice production, wineries, a cannery, rice mills, a distillery, engineering and brick works. The CSIRO irrigation research station, located 5km S of the town, undertakes studies on soil, water and plant relationships. Among the tourist attractions of the area are the Pioneer Park Museum with buildings in the 1880s style; Lake Wyangan (8km NW) which offers opportunities for swimming, fishing and other aquatic sports; the co-operative rice mill; Cocoparra National Park (25km NE, covering 8 356ha); and several wineries (such as Orlando, McWilliams, Miranda, Calamia, Calabria, San Bernadino) where visitors may inspect the operations and taste the produce.

Griffith, Sir Samuel Walker (1845-1920)

Statesman and first Chief Justice of the High Court of Australia. He was born in Wales, the son of a Congregational minister who emigrated to Australia in 1854. After a brilliant academic career at the University of Sydney, he joined his family in Brisbane, and was called to the QLD Bar in 1867. His political career began in 1871, when he gained the East Moreton seat in the Legislative Assembly. He attained ministerial office in 1874 as Attorney-General, and was Premier from 1883 to 1888 and from 1890 to 1893. In 1893 he was appointed Chief Justice of the QLD Supreme Court. During his parliamentary career he had been responsible for introducing a great amount of important legislation (including the 1875 Bill for free, secular and compulsory education), was a leading opponent of the importation of KANAKA labour, and played an important part in establishing the British administration in Papua.

Sir Samuel Griffith

Griffith was one of the most influential figures in the movement for federation. He supported the move by PARKES for a federal Parliament, represented QLD at the federal conference of 1890 and was vice-president of the convention of 1891, at which he played the main part in drafting the Constitution. After his appointment as Chief Justice of QLD in 1893 he considered it imperative to refrain from political involvement in the federation movement, but in 1900 he went to Britain as a delegate to see the Constitution Bill through the Imperial Parliament. When the High Court of Australia was set up in 1903, he was the logical choice for Chief Justice, a position which he filled until 1919.
Further reading: Forward, R.K. *Samuel Griffith.* Oxford University Press, Melbourne, 1964.

Griffiths, Albert 'Young Griffo' (1871-1927)

Lightweight boxer. He was born in Sofala NSW and raised in the Rocks area of Sydney. Beginning his brilliant boxing career as a young street-fighter, Griffiths was trained by the bare-knuckle champion Larry Foley, and in 1889 became Australian featherweight champion when he defeated 'Nipper' Peakes. In 1890 he became world featherweight champion by defeating 'Torpedo' Bill Murphy, but his title was not recognised outside Australia. In a career lasting from 1886 to 1911, Griffiths lost only nine out of 166 fights.

grinners *see* fishes, bony

Stockpile of manganese at Groote Eylandt's port facilities

Groote Eylandt NT

(population 2 230 in 1981) Named by the Dutch explorer Abel TASMAN in 1644, this island lies off the E coast of ARNHEM LAND in the GULF OF CARPENTARIA and contains the largest deposit of manganese in Australia. The island is about 2 630km², with a N-S extent of 65km. It is part of the Arnhem Land Aboriginal Reserve and before mining of the ore commenced in 1966 considerable negotiations were undertaken to reach agreement concerning conditions related to the operations. The ore is won by open-cut methods and is loaded at Milner Bay on the W coast. The main town is Alyangula (population 1 181) on the W coast; the airport is 15km to the S at Angurugu. Orcharding (tropical and

citrus fruits) and cattle grazing are the main rural activities on the island.

gropers *see* fishes, bony

Grose, Francis (1754-1814)

Lieutenant-Governor of NSW. Born in Croydon, England, he entered the British Army as an ensign in 1775, saw active service in the American War of Independence, and was twice wounded. In 1789 he was commissioned to raise the regiment which became known as the NEW SOUTH WALES CORPS, and in 1792 came to Sydney as its commander and the colony's Lieutenant-Governor. By the time Governor PHILLIP sailed for England in December, leaving Grose as acting Governor, the latter had become convinced that if the colony was to become prosperous quickly more scope must be allowed for private enterprise. He therefore welcomed the arrival in 1793 of a despatch authorising the granting of land to officers. Not only did he proceed to give grants of about 100 acres (40ha) to officers who wanted to farm, but he exceeded his instructions by assigning to each officer 10 convicts, who were provisioned at government expense. He also encouraged officers to engage in trade.

In defence of Grose it can be pointed out that he granted land freely to civil officials, emancipists and the few free settlers who arrived during his term of office, as well as to officers. Moreover, his policies were largely responsible for the spread of settlement to the HAWKESBURY area and for the speed with which the colony became self-sufficient in food. Nevertheless, he was responsible for the officers gaining such a position of privilege that Governors HUNTER, KING and BLIGH had to struggle, with limited success, to lessen their power and force them to concentrate more on their military duties.

Grose resigned in May 1794 on the grounds of ill health and sailed for England in December, leaving the colony under the command of Captain William PATERSON. He later served in England, Ireland and Gibraltar, rose to the rank of major-general, and later of brigadier, and twice applied for the post of Governor of NSW. Grose River and the Grose Valley in the BLUE MOUNTAINS are named after him.
Further reading: Ellis, M.H. *John Macarthur.* Angus & Robertson, Cremorne NSW, 1973.

ground berry *see* Epacridaceae

groundnuts *see* agriculture; Papilionaceae

Grounds, Sir Roy Burman (1905-81)

Architect. He was born and educated in VIC. After serving an architectural apprenticeship he travelled in Europe and designed film sets in Hollywood. From 1933, in partnership with Geoffrey Mewton, he designed a range of beautifully simple buildings which, by fitting the Australian climate and way of life, were like modern versions of early colonial buildings. One such group was Ranelagh on the MORNINGTON PENINSULA, in which openness, verandahs, pergolas and good proportion re-appeared as elements of Australian domestic architecture. In 1940 Grounds designed Clendon, a block of eight bachelor flats in Toorak, Melbourne, which are even more simply geometric than Ranelagh. With tiny compact kitchens and tightly planned bed-sitting-rooms, Clendon was probably the most influential domestic building of the decade. After World War II Grounds joined forces with Federick Romberg and Robin BOYD, and this partnership continued until 1963.

Roy Grounds' design for the Melbourne Arts Centre in 1968

Robert Irving

Grounds' essays in unusual plan-forms cul-minated with the design of his own house in Toorak—a square plan pierced by a circular central courtyard—which won the Architec-ture Award of the Royal Victorian Institute of Architects in 1954; the Academy of Science Headquarters in Canberra—circular and domed—which won the Sulman Award in 1951; and the Lutheran Church in Canberra—a cubic form with a square central spire. In 1965 he was appointed architect for the Vic-torian Arts Centre. This vast and controversial scheme consists of a large triple-courtyarded Art Gallery, a triangular Art School, and a dominating, trumpet-shaped tower complex containing halls and restaurants.

Grounds' austere, geometric architecture—the antithesis of his mercurial personality—has won him a sure place in Australian architec-ture. He was knighted in 1968 and received the Gold Medal of the Royal Australian In-stitute of Architects in the same year.
Further reading: Boyd, R. *Australia's Home.* Pelican, 1968.

groupers *see* fishes, bony

grouse-locusts *see* crickets, etc.

Gruner, Elioth (1882-1939) Artist. Born in Gisborne, New Zealand, Gruner came to Australia as a child and studied at Julian ASHTON's in Sydney. A painter of landscape, he introduced a cautious fascination for light

into his works which gave them a mild indi-viduality when compared with his contem-poraries. His work, although popular in his time, has none of the bite of the early period of the HEIDELBERG SCHOOL. Gruner had strong promoters, such as Norman LINDSAY, who lavished praise on his work. His themes of pastoral and farmyard tranquility, caught in misty morning light, made him, with Hans HEYSEN, the most sought after landscape painter of the inter-war period.

grunters *see* fishes, bony

gudgeons *see* fishes, bony

guinea flowers These plants belong to the genus *Hibbertia* (family Dilleniaceae). They are found throughout Australia but are particularly well represented in WA. Guinea flowers are shrubby plants or climbers; the flowers are yellow or orange and have five petals. A scrambling species, *H. scandens*, found in NSW and QLD, has bright yellow flowers (about 2.5cm in diameter) and fleshy, oval leaves.

Gulf Country QLD/NT The lowlands around the GULF OF CARPENTARIA are com-monly called the Gulf Country. The region consists of alluvial plains with many swampy and mangrove-fringed stretches of coastline. It experiences a hot climate throughout the year with rainfall concentrated in the summer months and a markedly dry period for the remainder of the year. The rivers which drain into the gulf thus have a distinctly seasonal pattern of flow, flooding in summer and often becoming a string of pools in the dry season. The main streams on the E shore of the gulf are the MITCHELL and the GILBERT Rivers which rise in the GREAT DIVIDING RANGE and have long meandering courses, with numer-ous ANABRANCHES, across the plains. The FLINDERS and LEICHHARDT Rivers have their headwaters in the Selwyn Range in central western QLD and flow to estuaries at the SE of the gulf. Numerous streams drain to the S and SW shore of the gulf from the BARKLY TABLELAND, such as the Limmen, McArthur, Robinson and Calvert Rivers. The ROPER RIVER in NT has an estuary on Limmen Bight at the SW of the gulf. The main rural activity over the whole region is beef cattle grazing; properties are large and there are many prob-lems related to fodder and water supplies, disease control in the herd, and transportation, though the construction of beef-roads in recent years has assisted the movement of livestock. The region is sparsely populated: in the whole of the NW statistical division (excluding MOUNT ISA city and CLONCURRY local govern-ment area), there were less than 11 000 people at the 1981 census; the only three urban centres with more than 200 residents in 1981 were NORMANTON (926), KARUMBA (670) and BURKETOWN (210).

Gulf of Carpentaria This large inlet on the N coast of the continent was explored by

Dutch navigators more than three centuries ago and was named after the then Governor of the Dutch East Indies, Pierre Carpentier. The gulf is over 500km wide, between ARNHEM LAND on the W and CAPE YORK on the E, and extends for more than 650km S to the shores of the GULF COUNTRY. There are numerous islands near the coastline: GROOTE EYLANDT, off the W shore, is part of the Arnhem Land Aboriginal Reserve; the Sir Edward Pellew Islands lie off the SW shore; and the WEL-LESLEY ISLANDS are located in the SE of the gulf. In recent times, fishing and prawning industries have been developed in the gulf and KARUMBA has become the main port and pro-cessing centre for gulf shipping. WEIPA, a major bauxite mining and exporting town, lies on the NE coast of the gulf.

gulls *see* sea birds

gummy shark *see* fisheries; sharks, etc.

gums *see* Myrtaceae

Gundagai NSW (population of the town 2 308 in 1981; and the shire 4 221) A town in the W slopes district of the State, 403km by road SW of Sydney, it is located on the MURRUMBIDGEE RIVER, at an elevation of 225m above sea level, on the Hume Highway. It is a rail centre on a branch line off the main S route from COOTAMUNDRA, a distance of 481km from Sydney, in the midst of a produc-tive rural district of sheep and cattle properties, dairy farms, wheat and maize crops, lucerne on river flats, asparagus fields and vegetable crops. The town has an average annual rainfall of 716mm, December and January being the months of heaviest falls; it experiences hot summer conditions and cool frosty winters. The district was settled by pastoralists in the 1830s and a village developed as a service focus on the river, but disastrous floods in 1852 indicated the unsuitability of this site and a new town was developed on higher ground. Gold was discovered in the area and numerous small mines were once worked; many a hope-ful fossicker still hunts near Gundagai for riches.

The Dog on a Tuckerbox Monument near Gundagai

The town's name comes from an Aboriginal word which appears to have a number of inter-pretations: 'going upstream' or 'sinews' or 'to cut the back of the knee with a tomahawk'. The bronze statue of the 'Dog on the Tuckerbox', located N of the town on the Hume Highway, gives expression to a well-known aspect of Australian folklore—the close relationship between man and dog in the pioneering days—which was depicted in the ballad 'Nine Miles from Gundagai', written by the poet and traveller Jack MOSES. The tourist attractions of the town and district include the marble cathedral-in-miniature, the Gabriel Photographic Gallery, a historical museum, canoe trips on the river and the opportunity to visit an asparagus farm. The National Trust (NSW) has listed a number of structures in Gundagai for preservation, including the courthouse, Family Hotel, St John's Anglican Church and the bridge across the Murrumbidgee.

Gunn, Mrs Aeneas (Jeannie Taylor)
(1870-1961) Author. Born in Melbourne in 1901 she married Aeneas Gunn, the manager of Elsey cattle station on the ROPER RIVER in the NT. Early in the following year she went to live at the Elscy station, but after her husband's death in 1903 returned to Melbourne. Her books, *The Little Black Princess* (1905) and *We of the Never Never* (1908), were slow in winning acceptance, but after several years became extremely popular. The first is the story of an Aboriginal girl, and the second is based on her own experiences and her general impressions of life in the NT. She was made on OBE in 1938 for her social work in Melbourne during World War I.

Gunnedah NSW (population 8 909 in
1981) A town in the NW of the State, Gunnedah is located where the Oxley Highway crosses the NAMOI RIVER, 76km W of TAMWORTH and 475km by road N of Sydney. It is on a branch rail route off the main N tablelands line, from WERRIS CREEK to WALGETT. At an elevation of 267m above sea level, it experiences hot summer conditions and mild winters. The average annual rainfall is 599mm, with a concentration in spring and summer; January is the month of the highest rainfall (66mm average). The town's name comes from the Aboriginal word meaning 'place of white stone'. It is the service centre for a productive rural region which contains some of the finest stock fattening country in the State, with lucerne and other crops being grown on the alluvial river flats. A large stock market and wheat centre, it has a flour mill, wheat silos, an abattoir and sawmills. There is a soil conservation and research station 6km S of the town. In 1978, the State Minister for Mines and Energy announced that an important coal discovery had been made in the Gunnedah Basin, W of Werris Creek, and that, although more drilling was required to assess the full extent and quality of the coal seams, it was a discovery of major significance. *See also* Keepit Dam

gunyah Also known as a *humpy* or a *mia mia*, this is a roughly constructed Aboriginal shelter, often little more than a windbreak, made of boughs and bark.

gurnards *see* fishes, bony

Gwydir River NSW This important tri-
butary of the BARWON-DARLING system flows from the main watershed of the GREAT DIVIDING RANGE across the NW slopes and plains region of the State to join the Barwon River near Collarenebri. The headwaters are formed by numerous creeks which rise on the W of the NEW ENGLAND Plateau in an area of hilly country stretching from around Uralla N to beyond ARMIDALE and Guyra; this area is between 1000m and 1 300m above sea level and receives an average annual rainfall of over 800mm. From the headwater zone, the Gwydir and its upper tributaries flow 670km W and NW past the towns of Bundarra and Bingara, across a stretch of open plain country to MOREE and then on W to join the Darling. In this section, the river flow is slow and meandering, with numerous ANABRANCHES, non-perennial in dry times but readily flooded in times of high rainfall over the catchment area. The COPETON DAM on the Gwydir, located E of Bingara and 35km SE of INVERELL, has been constructed to store water from the headwater streams and release it as required for irrigation, stock and domestic supplies further downstream. Much of this region is underlain by ARTESIAN WATER which is utilised for stock supplies. The name Gwydir was given to the river by the botanist and explorer Allan CUNNINGHAM in 1827 in honour of a British peer, Lord Gwydir.

Gymnospermae The Gymnospermae are seed-bearing plants which may be woody trees, shrubs or vines and include such familiar examples as pines, spruces, firs, cypresses and cycads. They are distinguished from the other major groups of seed-bearing plants, ANGIOSPERMAE, by the fact that the seeds are borne naked, usually on the surface of cone scales.

In most gymnosperms the pollen cones (male) and the seed cones (female) are borne on the same tree. The microspores produced within the pollen cones develop into abundant pollen grains, which are shed and transferred to the seed cones. The transfer of pollen (pollination) is generally affected by wind in gymnosperms. The pollen of some conifers is produced so abundantly that a yellow cloud may be seen on warm sunny days at pollination time in any large stand of conifers. In the seed cones, the pollen grains come into contact with the immature seeds (ovules); the central portion of each ovule (megasporangium) remains on the mature plant until fertilisation has taken place and a seed developed.

The Gymnospermae are generally divided into four main groups—the Cycadophyta, Ginkgophyta, Coniferophyta and Gnetophyta. The Ginkgophyta contains only one species, the maidenhair tree, *Ginkgo biloba*, which is native to China, though commonly planted as an ornamental tree in Australia. The Gnetophyta contains three curious genera, *Ephedra*, *Gnetum* and *Welwitschia*, each of which is limited in distribution and does not occur in Australia. The Cycadophyta (cycads) is represented in Australia by the genus *Cycas* and by the burrawong (*Macrozamia* species). *Macrozamia* plants are stocky palm-like plants, often making up a large part of E coast woodland and open forest communities. Male and female plants are separate, and pollen or seeds are produced from terminal cones. Female cones may be up to 0.5m long, and the seeds are brightly coloured (orange or red) at maturity. *Macrozamia* kernels were prized as food by the Aborigines, but as they are highly poisonous when fresh, a complex method of preparation involving both heating and soaking is necessary to make them edible.

The Coniferophyta contains by far the greatest number of gymnosperms, and is particularly well represented in the cool temperate and highland areas of the N hemisphere. The families of this group which are represented in Australia are listed below.

Gentlemen of the First Fleet try to make conversation with frightened Sydney aborigines as they take cover in a gunyah of gum branches

Hunter's Journal 1791

1. Pinaceae. This family is represented only by introduced species, especially the Monterey pine, *Pinus radiata*, which is planted extensively for softwood production, whilst other species are planted as ornamentals.

2. Araucariaceae. This family occurs in the tropical regions of the S hemisphere and contains some of Australia's most impressive trees, many of which occur naturally as emergents from the closed forest canopy. Species include bunya pine, *Araucaria bidwillii*, hoop pine, *A. cunninghamii*, Norfolk Is pine, *A. heterophylla*, and Queensland kauri, *Agathis rhomboidalis*. Norfolk Is pine is also planted widely, especially along beach fronts, as it is resistant to salt spray, and will grow successfully as far S as TAS in such frost free situations. Both genera produce excellent quality softwood and useful resin, with that of *Agathis* (especially fossilised) being utilised in the production of linoleum and varnish; the seeds of the *Araucaria* species are edible.

3. Podocarpaceae. Members of this family are confined mainly to mountain forests in the warm temperate to tropical regions of the S hemisphere, and are represented in Australia by a few species of the genera *Podocarpus*, *Phyllocladus*, *Pherosphaera*, *Microcachrys* and *Dacrydium*. With the exception of the Huon pine, *Dacrydium franklinii*, most species are small shrubs to small trees; *Microcachrys* and *Pherosphaera* are both endemic Australian genera. The Huon pine is prized for cabinet work, and for its long-lasting qualities in sea water.

4. Taxodiaceae. This family is represented in the S hemisphere by a single endemic TAS genus, *Athrotaxis*, of which the best-known species is a large tree, the King Billy pine, *Athrotaxis selaginoides*. This species has light coloured, lightweight timber which produces a ringing note when struck, and is locally prized for cabinet work.

5. Cupressaceae. This family is represented in Australia by the subfamily Callitroideae, to which the familiar cypress pine (*Callitris* species) belongs. Unlike the majority of Australia's other conifer species, the genus *Callitris* contains a number of species which are adapted to semi-arid low-rainfall regions. *Callitris* species form the basis of the arid-zone forestry industry, as all species yield a dense fragrant wood, with distinct heart and sapwood colours, which works well, takes a high polish and is termite-resistant. For these reasons it is prized as a flooring timber in Australia. Many of the most popularly cultivated conifers also belong to the Cupressaceae, but come from the subfamily Cupressoideae, the many cultivars of the Monterey cypress, *Cupressus macrocarpa*, being the most common. Many cultivars differ so markedly from the wild plant that it is difficult to believe that they belong to the same species. However, natural spores may be seen occasionally on cultivated specimens, and it is from these that the many cultivars have been vegetatively propagated.

See also Appendix 5, Flower Structure and Glossary of Botanical Terms; flora; vegetation

Further reading: see Appendix 6, A Bibliography for Plants.

Gympie QLD (population with Gympie South, 11 504 in 1981) This commercial and service city is located on the MARY RIVER, 182km N of Brisbane on the Bruce Highway and 92km S of MARYBOROUGH. At an elevation of 94m above sea level, it is surrounded by rich agricultural land where dairying and the growing of tropical fruit (especially pineapples) are the main activities. It has a high average annual rainfall of 1 161mm, occurring throughout the year but with maximum falls in summer (January and February averages, 173mm) and the lowest rainfall in August (41mm). The origins of Gympie go back to gold discoveries in 1869 which led to a mining boom and the nucleus of urban settlement. The goldfield proved to be rich in both alluvial and reef gold and brought wealth to the town. Though mining continued for over 60 years and hopeful fossickers still try their luck, the prosperity of the city is now based on farming, orcharding, timber and dairying. Relics of the mining days have been preserved in the city as a legacy of the golden years and the National Trust (QLD) has classified a number of historical buildings including the former post office, the courthouse and Andrew FISHER's cottage, which houses the mining museum.

H

Haddon, Robert Joseph (1866-1929) Architect. An Englishman trained in London, Haddon came to Australia when he was 25. He moved about the S States and became assistant architect in the Department of Public Works in Perth; in 1900 he settled in Melbourne.

Of all the architects and designers in Australia who were caught up in the art nouveau craze, only Haddon stands out, for to him the style was more than mere surface ornament. He delighted in designing and crafting the most minute parts of his buildings—roof gutter brackets, door handles, locks and knockers, leaded glass windows—combining the spindly curves of art nouveau with Australian motifs such as flowers and trees. An idiosyncratic early design was his own house, 'Anselm', in Glenferrie Street, Caulfield. But in the plan of this house, the deeper significance of Haddon's architecture may be seen, for it is a remarkably compact yet free-flowing arrangement of informal living spaces. In his larger buildings Haddon's facade designs were highly distinctive; his most famous was the fourth Victoria Building in Collins Street, Melbourne, where a simple flat front was embel-

lished with two large green terracotta lions' heads. His churches, such as St Stephen's in BALAKLAVA, are austere blends of Gothic and art nouveau, while his Swinburne Technical College building is as plain as a giant brick box.

Haddon's greatest influence was in education. He was head of the architectural school at Melbourne Technical College, and preached the concept of design totality to his students. His precepts were enshrined in his book *Australian Domestic Architecture* (1908). Since 1929 the Robert and Ada Haddon Travelling Scholarship has been awarded biennially to the most eligible graduate in architecture in VIC. *Further reading:* Boyd, R. *Victorian Modern.* Architectural Students' Society of the Royal Victorian Institute of Architects, Melbourne, 1947.

Haemodoraceae This small family of monocotyledonous flowering plants is represented only in the S Hemisphere, being found in South America, South Africa and Australia. Members of the Haemodoraceae are perennial or annual herbs which form tussocks; some species have rhizomes, others have rounded tubers with fibrous roots. The stiff flowering stems are surmounted by panicles or corymbs of tubular flowers; these flowers are often hairy. The leaves on the stem are small (or absent), while those which form a sheath at the base of the stem are usually sword-shaped.

The most outstanding characteristic of the Australian members lies in the unusual range of colours displayed by the flowers. Bloodroot (*Haemodorum* species) has black to reddish-black flowers, whilst kangaroo paws (*Anigosanthos* species) may have blue-green or yellow flowers or the red and green flowers of WA's floral emblem, *A. manglesii*. Kangaroo paws are widely cultivated, and though many species are temperamental, vigorous clumps of species such as *A. flavidus* are easy to establish and maintain.

See also Angiospermae; Appendix 5, Flower Structure and Glossary of Botanical Terms *Further reading: see* Appendix 6, A Bibliography for Plants.

hagfishes *see* lampreys, etc.

hairworms These extremely elongated ASCHELMINTHS belong to the class Nematomorpha. The adults are so long and narrow (sometimes reaching a length of 30cm or more) that it was once firmly believed that they developed from horse hairs that had fallen into water, hence their alternative name of horsehair worms. The sexes are separate. The adults live in water or damp soil and lay eggs from which emerge larvae that enter insects and crustaceans found in such habitats. The larvae develop within the host's blood space till they are almost complete adults, and emerge from the host when it is in or near water. The commonest hosts are beetles, cockroaches, crickets and grasshoppers. About six genera are known from Australian freshwaters.

Further reading: Williams, W.D. *Australian*

(left) Lebanese-Australians (*see* ARABIC-SPEAKING PEOPLE), (right) Germans in costume (*see* BAROSSA VALLEY), and (middle) Chilean-Australians (*see* SPANISH-SPEAKING PEOPLE) dance at the Shell National Folkloric Festival in Sydney

Members of the Greek community in traditional dress in Melbourne (*see* GREEKS IN AUSTRALIA)

Indian-Australians at the Shell National Folkloric Festival in Sydney (*see* INDIAN SUB-CONTINENT SETTLERS)

Yugoslav-Australians at the Shell National Folkloric Festival in Sydney (*see* YUGOSLAVS IN AUSTRALIA)

Irish-Australians at the Shell National Folkloric Festival in Sydney (*see* IRISH IN AUSTRALIA)

Eleven-armed sea star, *Coscinasterias calamaria* (*see* SEA STARS)

Crown of thorns, *Acanthaster planci* (*see* SEA STARS)

Waratah anemone, *Actinia tenebrosa* (*see* COELENTERATES)

Blue-ringed octopus, *Hapalochlaena maculosa* (*see* CEPHALODS)

Basket star, *Crinoidea* species, on coral (*see* SEA LILIES)

Various species of coral on the Great Barrier Reef (*see* GREAT BARRIER REEF)

Freshwater Life. (2nd edn) Macmillan, Melbourne, 1980.

Hakea *see* Proteaceae

half-beaks *see* fishes, bony

halibut, Queensland *see* fishes, bony

Hall, Benjamin 'Ben' (1837-65) Bushranger. Like Ned KELLY, he was believed by many of his contemporaries, rightly or wrongly, to have been driven to the life of a bushranger by police harassment. Born of ex-convict parents near Murrurundi NSW, in his youth he leased a small pastoral property in the FORBES district and seems to have been hard-working and law-abiding for several years. However, he then began to associate with members of Frank GARDINER's gang, and in 1862 was arrested and tried for highway robbery. He was acquitted, but on returning to his property found that his wife had left him, taking with her their son. Very soon afterwards he was detained again by the police, on suspicion of highway robbery. This time he was not brought to trial, but during his detention his home was burned down and most of his stock killed or scattered.

Shortly after this he took permanently to a bushranger's life. Gardiner had gone to QLD in the hope of escaping arrest for the Eugowra Rocks robbery, so Hall took over the leadership of the remnants of Gardiner's gang and during the following two years organised a series of particularly daring raids and hold-ups. His planning of these showed him to be perhaps the best organiser among all Australian bushrangers. In particular he made sure that his men were mounted on horses of top quality —often stolen racehorses—so that they could outdistance the police if necessary. His daring and his alleged sense of humour and courtesy to women also gained him considerable support among the poorer settlers, making it all the more difficult for the police to catch him.

Such deeds as these were a major factor in causing the government to pass in 1865 the Felons' Apprehension Act, which allowed bushrangers to be declared outlaws and shot on sight, and prescribed heavy penalties for those aiding them. With a price of £1000 on his head, Hall now found it difficult to gain help from his sympathisers. In May 1865 he was ambushed in the bush not far from Forbes and shot dead.
Further reading: Clune, Frank. *Ben Hall the Bushranger.* (new edn) Angus & Robertson, Sydney, 1969.

Hall's Creek WA (population 966 in 1981) This small inland township is located on the Great Northern Highway in the far N of the State, 568km by road ESE of DERBY and 375km S of WYNDHAM. It was established as a gold-mining town in the 1880s on Hall's Creek, a headwater tributary of the ORD RIVER, but was later moved to another site 14km away where there was a water supply. Both the town and the

creek were named after one of the early gold miners. The town functions now as a highway service centre in a sparsely settled region. The climate is typically tropical, with high summer temperatures; the average annual rainfall of 469mm is concentrated in the summer season.

Hamer, Sir Rupert James (1916-) Premier of VIC. Born and educated in Melbourne, he was admitted as a solicitor in 1940. As a member of the AIF from 1939 to 1945 he served in Tobruk, at El Alamein and in New Guinea and Normandy; he was also commanding officer of the VIC Scottish Regiment in the CMF from 1954 to 1958. His political career began in 1958 when he was elected for the seat of Kew in the VIC Legislative Council, but in 1971 he moved to the Legislative Assembly as Member for Kew. He held the portfolios of Immigration (1962-64) and Local Government (1964-71) before becoming Chief Secretary and deputy Premier in 1971. On the retirement of Sir Henry BOLTE in the following year he became Premier, Treasurer and Minister of the Arts. Widely respected for his administrative ability and balanced views, he filled the position of Premier in a less flamboyant style than that of his predecessor. Dissension within the parliamentary Liberal Party led to his resignation as Premier in 1981. He was succeeded by Lindsay Thompson, and was knighted in 1982.

Premier's Dept VIC

Sir Rupert Hamer

Hamersley Range WA Located in the PILBARA region in the NW of the State, the range contains one of the world's largest deposits of iron ore. Running SE-NW for about 460km, it is the most elevated part of the broad and deeply dissected Hamersley Plateau, lying S of the FORTESCUE RIVER and forming the headwater catchment for many tributaries of the ASHBURTON RIVER. Along the NE boundary of the range a fault scarp provides a sheer descent to the Fortescue Valley. Several

peaks within the range rise to above 1000m; Mt Meharry and Mt Bruce, the two highest, are both over 1 230m high. The region is one of low rainfall, high summer temperatures and sparse population. Until iron ore mining began in the 1960s, the main town of the region was WITTENOOM, but new towns have been built close to the mines at MOUNT NEWMAN, MOUNT TOM PRICE and ROBE RIVER. The Hamersley Range National Park (590 176ha) is a major tourist attraction; it includes spectacular mountain, plateau and gorge scenery and vast expanses of wilderness country.

National Parks Authority WA

Hamersley Range National Park

Hamilton VIC (population 9 749 in 1981) This city is in the WESTERN DISTRICT of the State, at the junction of the Henty and Glenelg Highways, 291km by road W of Melbourne, 84km NNE of PORTLAND and 318km by rail from Melbourne. It is a business and marketing centre for a rich dairying and grazing region which produces some of the nation's finest wool. At an elevation of 187m above sea level, it has a mild climate with an average annual rainfall of 692mm spread throughout the year but with a maximum in winter and spring. Following the explorations of Major Thomas MITCHELL in 1836, settlement of the region began the following year. It was originally known as The Grange but in 1851 the name Hamilton was given to it by the surveyor who laid out the township. The city is renowned for its churches; several of them have been listed for preservation by the National Trust (VIC), as have a number of historic homesteads. The Mt Eccles National Park is located 42km S of Hamilton; it covers an area of 400ha around the ancient volcanic crater of Mt Eccles which contains the tranquil expanse of Lake Surprise.

Hammond, Dame Joan Hood (1912-) Soprano. Born in Christchurch, New Zealand, she came to live in Sydney at an early age. She played violin with the Sydney Philharmonic Orchestra while still a student at the Conservatorium, but when an arm injury ended her career as a violinst, a fund sponsored by Lady Gowrie, wife of the then Governor-General, enabled her to study singing abroad. She appeared in the *Messiah* in London in 1938 and in opera in Vienna in 1939. During World War II she was a volunteer ambulance driver. After the war her success as a singer was immediate, and she became one of Britain's best-loved sopranos. She sang leading roles in over 30 operas, made many world tours (visiting Australia in 1946 and 1949) and worthily upheld the tradition established by Nellie MELBA and Florence AUSTRAL until heart trouble forced her to retire in 1965. She was awarded the Coronation Medal and made an OBE in 1953, and a CBE in 1963. For her services to music she was made a CMG in 1972 and DBE in 1974. Her book, *A Voice, A Life*, appeared in 1970, and she has continued to teach and to play an active part in the musical and operatic activities of the country since her return to Melbourne.

Hancock, Langley George 'Lang'

(1909-). Mining industrialist and pastoralist. Born in Perth, of a family with pastoral interests, he undertook his first mining venture at Wittenoom Gorge WA, where he had discovered asbestos deposits. However his main operations have been in the iron-ore industry. A pioneer in the use of aircraft for prospecting, he has been largely responsible for the development of deposits in the PILBARA region of WA. He first discovered iron ore while flying at low level in the Hamersley Range, and after establishing claims to extensive deposits, made a royalty agreement with Rio Tinto Mining Co. of Australia (now Conzinc Rio Tinto of Australia) in 1959. Since 1938 the federal government, believing that Australia's reserves were comparatively limited, had forbidden the export of iron ore, but the knowledge that WA contained some of the largest deposits in the world caused the lifting of this ban in 1960. Lang Hancock can therefore be credited with playing a major role in Australia's emergence as a major iron-ore exporter.

Harden

NSW (combined population of Harden and MURRUMBURRAH 2 070 in 1981) This railway junction town is located in the SW slopes region, 381km by rail SW of Sydney, about 30km by road S of YOUNG and some 70km NW of YASS. Harden and Murrumburrah are adjacent twin towns on Murrimboola Creek, an upper tributary of the MURRUMBIDGEE RIVER system. At an elevation of 416m above sea level, Harden has an average annual rainfall of 607mm, spread fairly evenly throughout the year. The surrounding rural regions are noted for dairying, fat lamb raising, wool production and wheat farming. The town was named after a railway surveyor.

Hardy, Francis Joseph 'Frank'

(1917-) Novelist and short-story writer. Born in Southern Cross, near WARRNAMBOOL in VIC, he worked in various occupations, including those of road construction worker and seaman, joined the Communist Party in 1939, served in the Army from 1941 to 1946, and turned to writing towards the end of the war. His first novel, *Power Without Glory* (1950), which features corruption in financial and political circles in VIC over more than half a century, resulted in an unsuccessful action for criminal libel against him on the grounds that the central character in the book

was recognisably a well-known financier. Hardy's autobiographical work, *The Hard Way* (1963), deals particularly with the writing of *Power Without Glory* and the subsequent libel action. Other works by Hardy include *The Four-Legged Lottery* (1958), a story of dishonesty and corruption associated with horse racing, *The Yarns of Billy Borker* (1965), *The Unlucky Australians* (1968), which deals with strikes by Aboriginal stockmen in the NT, *The Outcasts of Foolgarah* (1971), *But the Dead Are Many* (1975), *Who Shot George Kirkland* (1981), and *The Obsession of Oscar Oswald* (1983). *Power Without Glory* was a television serial in 1976.

Hardy, Sir James Gilbert (1932-)

Yachtsman. Born in SA into a family of yachtsmen, it was not long before Hardy too became keen on sailing. He began sailing at the age of 10 and by 13 was building his own boats, the first a Cadet which he called *Nocroo*. Another boat, called *Noctoo*, which he built for a friend, won the Stonehaven Cup. When at 19 he passed the age limit for sailing Cadets, he built a Twelve Square Metre Sharpie and, with this boat and others in the same class, became a top-class competitor, winning the Australian championship in 1959. His next boats were 505s in which he won the SA championship in 1961. In 1962, after completing his accountancy examinations, he moved to Sydney to become the resident director of the family wine-merchant business, Thomas Hardy & Sons.

It was not long before he was once again involved in the sailing scene, this time in the Flying Dutchman class, winning the NSW championship in 1963 and the Australian championship in 1964. In 1966 he had his greatest victory when he won the world 505 championship. In the 1970s Hardy moved into the heavyweight division of international yacht racing, the Twelve Metre class, skippering *Gretel II* in 1970, *Southern Cross* in 1974 and *Australia* in 1980 in challenges for yachting's greatest prize, the America's Cup. Although unsuccessful in these challenges, in *Gretel II* Hardy crossed the line first in two of the first four races (although he lost one on a protest) and in so doing displayed the cool, yet tough, temperament and the superb tactical skills which have made him so notable on the Australian yachting scene. He was knighted in 1981.

Hargrave, Lawrence (1850-1915)

Aeronautical pioneer. Born in Greenwich, England, he came to Sydney in 1865. In the 1870s he took part in explorations in Papua and then obtained a position as an assistant observer at the Sydney Observatory. He retired in 1883 and devoted the rest of his life to research, especially on aeronautical problems. He made many model aeroplanes, invented a rotary engine driven by compressed air, and in 1892 made the discovery that curved wing surfaces gave better lift than flat surfaces. In the following few years he concentrated on experiments with kites, discovering important

principles about their behaviour that could be applied to aeroplane flight. In 1894 he was lifted about 5m into the air by four box-kites fixed together.

Lawrence Hargrave

NSW Govt Printer

The extent of Hargrave's influence on aeroplane design is difficult to determine. The Wright brothers claimed that they did not owe anything to his discoveries, but he is believed to have had influence in Europe, particularly in Germany where a number of his models were sent in 1910. One of his box-kites and nine monoplane models may be seen today in the Museum of Applied Arts and Sciences in Sydney. The models sent to Germany are now in the Munich Museum.

Further reading: Shaw, W.H. 'Lawrence Hargrave, aviation pioneer: an evaluation' in *A Century of Scientific Progress: The Centenary Volume of the Royal Society of New South Wales.* The Society, Sydney, 1968.

Hargraves, Edward Hammond

(1816-91) Gold-rush promoter. He was born in England, settled in NSW in 1834, and in

'Gold washing at Summerhill Creek' by George French Angas. This scene is near the site of Hargraves' discovery

National Library of Australia

1849 was among those who went from NSW to the Californian gold rush. He was unsuccessful in California but, reflecting on the fact that traces of gold had been found in NSW, decided to return and search there in the hope that he might find gold in payable quantitites and gain a government reward. In February 1851, with a youth named John Lister as guide, he found a very small quantity of gold near BATHURST. He had no success in further searches, but after his return to Sydney, further discoveries were made by Lister and his friends William, James and Henry Tom, all of whom had been taught to use the pan and cradle by Hargraves. Hargraves then so effectively publicised the existence of gold in the district that a rush started. He eventually received rewards of £10 000 from the government of NSW and over £2000 from the government of VIC. He became a Commissioner of Crown Lands, was presented to Queen Victoria and on retirement was given a pension of £250 a year.

harriers *see* birds of prey

Harris, Rolf (1930-) Entertainer and artist.

Born in Perth, Rolf Harris was Australian junior backstroke champion at 15 and an art teacher at 21, before becoming an internationally acclaimed entertainer. Moving to England in 1952, he enrolled in art school, the general plan being to pay his way by doing club and cabaret work at night. He made his television début in England in 1954 as a cartoonist-storyteller and in 1956 was selected to exhibit at the Royal Academy of Art. With time, the scales began to tilt in favour of the entertainment side of his career and in 1960 he recorded the internationally successful song 'Tie Me Kangaroo Down, Sport'. This was the first of a number of highly original recordings, often of Australian origin (such as 'Sun Arise' based on an Aboriginal chant put to words by Harris and well-known naturalist Harry Butler), often humorous (such as 'The Court of King Caractacus' and 'I'm Jake the Peg') and occasionally poignant (such as 'Two Little Boys', the story of two brothers who as adults found themselves on opposite sides in the American Civil War). 'Two Little Boys' was outstandingly successful, with worldwide sales in excess of one million. Noted for introducing to popular entertainment the wobble board (a thin sheet of board held between the hands and shaken or wobbled to produce a rhythmic wind sound) and the Aboriginal wind instrument the DIDJERIDU, he was made an MBE in 1971 and an OBE in 1979 for his services to the performing arts.

Hart, Kevin Charles 'Pro' (1928–) Artist.

Born at BROKEN HILL, he spent his early life on the family sheep property near MENINDEE NSW and showed early enthusiasm for and talent in painting and drawing. He continued to practise his artistic skills through his youth and during his days as a miner. It was while working in the mines that he began to paint seriously, and in 1960 was discovered by an ADELAIDE dealer, Kim Bonython. At the resultant exhibition, which was most popular and great financial success, Hart laid the foundations for a reputation which within a decade was Australia-wide. He was awarded the MBE in 1976 for his services to art. His work, based mainly on the region in and around Broken Hill is instantly recognisable for its bright colours and vivacious humans and animals, painted in an effective primitive style. In recent years, Hart has experimented widely in various techniques and approaches. He illustrated two books on the *Poems of Henry Lawson* and two on the *Poems of Banjo Paterson*. He is the owner of a large and catholic collection of paintings by Australian artists.

Hartigan, Patrick Joseph (1879-1952)

Priest and author. Born in YASS in NSW, he was educated in GOULBURN and Sydney and in 1903 was ordained as a Roman Catholic priest. For more than half of his working life he was a parish priest of NARRANDERA, a rural town in NSW, and while there wrote, under the name John O'Brien, a number of bush ballads depicting the life of Irish settlers. A collection of these, *Around the Boree Log* (1921), had great popular success, and poems from this anthology were for many years almost standard reading in Roman Catholic schools.

Hartley NSW

A small settlement located at the western side of the BLUE MTS, adjacent to the Great Western Highway, 134km by road from Sydney, some 25km NW of KATOOMBA and 10km SE of LITHGOW. It is situated in Hartley Valley which drains into the Cox's River, and thence into the NEPEAN-HAWKESBURY RIVER system. The district was first settled by Europeans in 1819 and, in early colonial days, it was an important rest point for travellers after the journey across the range. Some of the buildings from this period are still standing and in 1972 part of the town was proclaimed an Historic Site. Many buildings have been classified by the National Trust (NSW) including Collits Inn at Hartley Vale (built *c*. 1823), the Court House (the oldest in NSW, built in 1837), St Bernards Catholic Church and Presbytery (1842), the Anglican Church of St John the Evangelist (1858-59, Edmund BLACKET was the architect), 'Rosedale' (formerly the Victoria Inn, 1839) and the former Royal Hotel (1846).

Hartog, Dirk (or Dirck) Dutch seaman of the early 17th century.

(His surname sometimes appears as 'Hatich'). He was almost certainly the first European to land on the W coast of Australia and, apart from the crew of the small ship *Duyfken* captained by Willem JANSZ in 1603, he was the first to see any part of Australia. However, very little is known of his life. Early in 1616 he left Holland in command of the ship *Eendracht*, bound for Java. Until a few years before that date Dutch captains sailing to the E had followed routes that did not bring them close to Australia, but in 1611 a captain named Brouwer had pioneered a new route: from the Cape of Good Hope he had allowed the prevailing westerlies to blow him about 6000km due W and then had used the trade winds to sail approximately NE to Java. He had made such good time that in 1613 all captains of the Dutch East India Co. were told to follow his example.

It was only a matter of time before some of them went a little further E than Brouwer had done and came to the coast of Australia. The first to do so was Hartog, who arrived at SHARK BAY on 25 October 1616, landed on the island named after him, and nailed to a tree trunk a pewter plate with an inscription on it. It was discovered in 1697 by another Dutch captain, Willem de Vlamingh, who substituted one of his own for it. Now on display in the Rijksmuseum, Amsterdam, Hartog's inscription reads: '1616. On 25th October there arrived here the ship *Eendracht* from Amsterdam. Supercargo Gils Miebais of Liege. Skipper Dirk Hatichs of Amsterdam. She sailed again on the 27th of the month.'

Rijksmuseum

Dirk Hartog's pewter plate now in the Rijksmuseum, Amsterdam

Hartog evidently reported his discovery in Holland, but his own log of the event has been lost. Contemporary maps of the W coast refer to this point as 'Dirck Hartog's Ree' (roadstead); it was supposed that it might lie close to the fabled 'Marco Polo's Beach' where there was easy access to the oriental riches of gold and spices. Although Dutch seamen continued to explore the coasts of Australia until 1647, discovering extensive stretches of the N, W and S coasts, they were primarily in search of trading prospects, and so little came of discoveries of parts of NEW HOLLAND such as Hartog's.

Further reading: Heeres, J.E. *The Part Borne by the Dutch in the Discovery of Australia.* E.J. Brill, Leiden, 1899: Wood, G.A. *The Discovery of Australia.* (revd by Beaglehole, J.C.) Macmillan, South Melbourne, 1958; Copley, R. *Hartog and Tasman.* (Great People in Australian History Series) Longmans, Melbourne, 1965.

Hartz Mountains TAS

This range lies in the S of the State between the Picton and Arve Rivers (both tributaries of the HUON RIVER), some 80km SW of Hobart. The N section of the range lies within the Hartz Mountains National Park (6 470ha), established in 1952 and varying in elevation from 160m to Hartz Peak at 1 255m above sea level, most of the area comprising high alpine moorland dotted with lakes of glacial origin. Access to Waratah Lookout in the NE of the park is by a branch road off the Huon Highway from GEEVESTON. The axis of the range lies N-S, extending about 45km, with Hartz Peak in the N, Adamsons Peak (1 226m) in the central part, and Mt Laperouse (1 158m) and Flinders Peak (1 250m) in the S section. The SE slopes of the range form the headwater catchment for several small streams flowing E to the D'EN-TRECASTEAUX CHANNEL and to the SE coast, such as the Esperance and Lune Rivers.

harvesters *see* agriculture

harvestmen These ARACHNIDS belong to the order Opiliones or Phalangida which contains about 3 400 species. About 60 species, in the two suborders Laniatores and Palpatores, are represented in Australia. In Britain they are usually called daddy-longlegs but in Australia this would lead to confusion with *Pholcus,* a genus of SPIDERS.

Although harvestmen resemble spiders at first sight, a number of features clearly distinguish them: there is no waist (pedicel), the cephalothorax and abdomen being broadly joined; the chelicerae (anterior appendages) are of the pincer type, not the single fangs of spiders; and silk is not produced. The pedipalps (the second pair of anterior appendages, with sensory functions), though leg-like, are usually much shorter than the true legs. In the Laniatores, which is the larger group, each of the strong pedipalps is equipped with a large claw, and the legs are also clawed, the two pairs of posterior legs having two or three claws. In the Palpatores, however, the pedipalps are weak, and each of the legs bears only a single claw. In many species of harvestmen, the two outward-facing eyes are set on either side of a turret (tubercle) on the back.

Harvestmen are scavengers on dead animals, and predators of small arthropods. Though many of them are of moderate size they are inconspicuous, living in thick vegetation, debris and so on.
Further reading: see under scorpions.

Harvey WA (population 2 479 in 1981) A small town on the South Western Highway, 138km S of Perth and 47km by road NNE of BUNBURY. Situated on the HARVEY RIVER in the coastal plain region of SWANLAND, it was the site of WA's first irrigation scheme and is still the service town for the Harvey Irrigation District, where dairying, fruit growing and market gardening are the main rural activities. The town is the administrative centre of the Harvey Shire which covers an area of 1 766km² and had a population of 8 027 at the 1981 census.

Harvey River WA Located in the SW of the State, with headwaters E of the DARLING RANGE, it flows for about 60km, first SW cutting across the plateau escarpment, then NW across the coastal plain to a long narrow estuary, which is an arm of Peel Inlet on the Indian Ocean coastline. A flood and drainage channel has been constructed from near the town of HARVEY W across the plain to the sea. The first irrigation scheme in WA was established on the plains adjacent to the lower river in 1916 when the Harvey Dam was built on the upper river to store water for release during the dry summer months. The original dam had a capacity of 2 280ML, enlarged in 1931 to 7 900ML; irrigation water was supplied to about 7000ha of farming lands on the plain. Citrus fruit was at first the main irrigated produce, but it proved unsuccessful and dairying, with improved pasture cultivation, has become the major agricultural activity. Additional water was made available to the Harvey Irrigation District in 1948 when the Stirling Dam, with a capacity of 5 470ML, was built in the headwaters, upstream from Harvey Dam; supplies were further augmented in 1963 when Logue Brook Dam, with a capacity of 2 430ML, was constructed.

Hasluck, Sir Paul Meernaa Caedwalla (1905-) Politician and Governor-General. Born in FREMANTLE in WA, he began work as a member of the literary staff of the *West Australian* in 1922. He later graduated MA from the University of Western Australia and from 1939 to 1940 was a part-time lecturer in history at the university. From 1941 to 1947 he served in the Department of External Affairs (now Foreign Affairs), then returned to the university as a reader in history. In 1949 he was elected to the House of Representatives. During 20 years in the federal Parliament he held the portfolios of Territories (1951-63), Defence (1963-64) and External Affairs (1964-69). His intellectual and administrative abilities won him wide respect and, in spite of his aloofness of manner and unwillingness to canvass for support, made him a strong contender of the leadership of the Liberal Party, and therefore for the position of Prime Minister, after the death of Harold HOLT in 1967.

Courtesy of A.I.S. Canberra

Sir Paul Hasluck

His most valuable work was probably done as Minister for Territories, although in that position he was criticised for having misjudged the speed with which the Territory of Papua and New Guinea should move towards independence, and therefore for having underestimated the need for the training of indigenous people who could take over the administration of that country. In 1969 he was appointed Governor-General, a position he retained until 1974. His publications include two volumes of the official history of Australia in World War II, *The Government and the People, 1939-1945* (1970), and the autobiographical *Mucking About* (1970).

Hastings VIC (population 5 632 in 1981) This town is located on the W shore of WESTERN PORT BAY, NNW of CRIB POINT, 65km by rail SSE of Melbourne. It is a commercial and service centre situated in the midst of the Westernport heavy industrial area. The township was originally named King's Creek, but was renamed in the 1860s, either after the town of the same name in Sussex, England, or after the Marquis of Hastings, once Governor-General of India.

Hastings River NSW One of the smaller river valleys in the mid-N coast of the State, the Hastings River is located between the MANNING RIVER to the S and the MACLEAY RIVER to the N. It drains from the E scarp of the GREAT DIVIDING RANGE about 160km inland and flows in a general E direction, entering the sea at PORT MACQUARIE. The Pacific Highway cuts across the valley in a N-S direction and the Oxley Highway traverses it E-W from the coast up the valley to the NEW ENGLAND Plateau. The NORTH COAST railway crosses the lower valley on a N-S route, with WAUCHOPE, situated on the river 21km inland from the coast, as the main rail centre. The two main towns of the valley are Port Macquarie and Wauchope. Dairying, with associated fodder crop cultivation on the alluvial flats and the lower valley slopes, is the principal farming activity. Timber-getting is important on the hill land of the upper valley, and in the rugged ranges to the W are some of the biggest timber stands on this section of the coast. The Werrikimbe National Park (14 253ha) is located in the upper valley 100km W of Wauchope; it contains large stands of rainforests, tall eucalypt forests, waterfalls and the deep gorge of the Hastings. During wet seasons, the farms on the river flats are sometimes inundated by flood waters. Port Macquarie, at the river mouth, is a popular tourist resort and holiday centre and has fine coastal beaches nearby for surfing; large stretches of water are available for aquatic sports both within the estuary and on coastal lagoons, such as Lake Innes, Queen's Lake and Watson Taylor Lake, located S of Port Macquarie between the Pacific Highway and the coast.

Hawke, Robert James Lee 'Bob' (1929-) Prime Minister. Born in BORDERTOWN in SA, he was taken to WA in his boyhood; he was educated at Perth Modern School, and at the University of Western

Australia from which he graduated BA and LLB. Having won a Rhodes Scholarship in 1952, he gained the degree of B. Litt. at Oxford and in 1956 won a research scholarship to the Australian National University, where he began working for his doctorate in the field of industrial relations. However, before the completion of his thesis he accepted the offer of a position as research officer and industrial advocate for the AUSTRALIAN COUNCIL OF TRADE UNIONS (ACTU). During the following few years he achieved national prominence through his brilliant advocacy before the Commonwealth Arbitration Commission. In 1970 he was elected president of the ACTU and from 1973 to 1978 was also president of the Australian Labor Party (ALP). In these roles he has become one of the best-known public figures in Australia.

R.J. ('Bob') Hawke with his wife, Hazel

As president of the ACTU Hawke was notable for involving the union movement in business undertakings, including a large Melbourne department store, a travel agency and a chain of petrol stations. In 1971, a major manufacturer declined to supply the ACTU store with goods without restrictions on their minimum retail price. By the threat of industrial action, Mr. Hawke not only forced the manufacturer to abandon this stand, but also forced the federal government to hasten the introduction of legislation prohibiting such 'retail price maintenance'. In industrial relations, Hawke tended to become a mediator, called in whenever an industrial stoppage was causing serious dislocation to the economy. He showed keen awareness of the damage done by many strikes to Labor's industrial and political image, and showed great skill in negotiating compromise settlements. In 1980 he resigned from the presidency of the ACTU and won election to the federal House of Representatives.

In February 1983, following the resignation from the parliamentary leadership of the ALP by W.G. HAYDEN, he was chosen to succeed him in that position. In the following month he led his party to a convincing victory in a general election, and so became Prime Minister. His election campaign was based on

promises to follow a more expansionary economic policy than that of the preceding government; to introduce a prices and incomes policy; and to aim at promoting a spirit of national reconciliation. Shortly after the election a National Economic Summit conference, including representatives of governments, employers and trade unions, was held. This was followed by the setting up of an Economic Planning Advisory Council, designed to offer the government independent community-based advice on economic policy. However the prospect of an unexpectedly large budget deficit for 1983-84 immediately cast doubts on the ability of Mr. Hawke's government to follow as expansionary a policy as it had intended.

See also arbitration and conciliation, industrial

Hawker SA (population 351 in 1981) A small town in the FLINDERS RANGES, it is 374km by road N of Adelaide and 109km NE of PORT AUGUSTA. At an elevation of 315m above sea level, it has a mild climate with an average annual rainfall of 301mm, though the rain is unreliable and droughts are experienced. The town is used by some tourists as a 'base camp' for visiting the sights of the Flinders Ranges, such as WILPENA POUND, AROONA VALLEY and ORAPARINNA. The Hawker region was settled by pastoralists and wheat farmers in the 1860s, but farming was abandoned because of droughts and the area is now dominated by large-scale grazing.

Hawkesbury River NSW The lower section of the NEPEAN-WARRAGAMBA river system, which rises to the W and SW of Sydney, is called the Hawkesbury River. The name should be applied only to that part of the main river downstream from the junction of the Grose and Nepean Rivers. Beyond this junction it flows first in a general NE direction and then, where the Macdonald River joins it on the left bank (from the N side) at Wisemans Ferry, it changes to a general SE flow and enters the saltwater tidal estuary of BROKEN BAY. The Nepean-Hawkesbury thus makes a semi-elliptical arc around Sydney with a radius of between 50km and 90km. The Hawkesbury River region was the site of some of the earliest rural settlements in Australia. In 1794 Major GROSE, the acting Governor, stated he had 'settled on the banks of the Hawkesbury, 22 settlers who seemed pleased with their farms'. This was near the present town of WINDSOR. The district is still important for citrus fruit and vegetable production for the metropolitan market, and more recently, for production of turf grass. Oysters cultivated in the lower reaches of the river and around the shores of Broken Bay are renowned throughout the nation.

Scenically, the Hawkesbury is one of Australia's finest rivers. Anthony Trollope wrote that 'the Hawkesbury has neither castles nor islands, nor has it bright, clear water like the Rhine, but the headlands are higher and the

Forested sandstone country of the lower Hawkesbury river, NSW

bluffs are bolder, and the turns and manoeuvres of the course, which the waters have made for themselves, are grander, and, to me, more enchanting than those of the European river.' Much of the middle and lower reaches of the river are important recreation areas for fishing and other aquatic sports, especially water skiing. The Dharug National Park (14 230ha) is a rugged sandstone wilderness on the N side of the lower Hawkesbury, located downstream from Wisemans Ferry between the old N road and Mangrove Creek. Access to the park is either from Sydney via Wisemans Ferry or from GOSFORD through Central Mangrove. This limited road access and the natural barrier of the imposing sandstone bluffs have combined to preserve the area in a natural state, despite its close proximity to the Sydney metropolitan area. Parts of the park have a close forest cover of eucalypts and angophoras; in other parts there is a profusion of native flowering plants; there is a wide variety of birds such as magpies, kookaburras, currawongs, lyrebirds, whipbirds and bowerbirds; and the animal population includes wallaroos, wombats, possums and bandicoots.

Further reading: Hurley, F. *Sydney: A Camera Study* (2nd edn) Angus & Robertson, Sydney, 1958; Clarke, A.N. *Historic Sydney and New South Wales.* The Central Press, Sydney, 1968; Bowd, D.G. *Macquarie Country: A History of the Hawkesbury.* Cheshire, Melbourne, 1969; White, U. & Cayley, F. *Hawkesbury River Sketchbook.* Rigby, Adelaide, 1970.

hawks *see* birds of prey

Hay NSW (population 2 957 in 1981) This small town is located on the N side of the MURRUMBIDGEE RIVER, 736km by road WSW of Sydney, at the junction of the Cobb and Mid-Western Highways, and across the river from their junction with the Sturt Highway. It is the centre for an extensive wool producing region where there are many well-known studs. Though it is a semi-arid area with an average annual rainfall of only 360mm (and this is quite variable from year to year), water from the Murrumbidgee provides irrigation for local properties. Hay is a rail terminus of a branch line off the main S route (753km by rail from Sydney). Following the epic journey of Charles STURT in 1829-30 along the MURRAY and Murrumbidgee Rivers (a plaque in Hay commemorates this), pastoralists settled in this region and in 1859 the town was officially gazetted and named after the local parliamentary member, Sir John Hay. In 1872 it became a municipality and in 1965 it became the headquarters of the shire (population 3 948 in 1981). In the days of river traffic, until the early years of this century, Hay was a river port where paddle-wheelers called to collect the wool bales. The old gaol, built in 1879-80, is now a museum containing relics of the early days of settlement such as a century-old Cobb & Co. coach, and has been listed for preservation by the National Trust (NSW).

Hayden, William George 'Bill'

(1933-) Politician. Born in Brisbane, he was a police constable from 1953 until 1961, when he won election to the House of Representatives for the seat of Oxley, which is based on the mining and industrial city of IPSWICH. By the time Labor ended its 23-year spell in opposition in December 1972, Hayden had become one of the best-known members of the Shadow Cabinet; he had also by that time, through part-time study, graduated B. Econ. from the University of Queensland. As Minister for Social Security in the WHITLAM government he played a major role in the introduction of the Medibank health insurance scheme. In June 1975 he was made Treasurer, and a few months later brought down a budget which was generally considered to be more realistic, in view of the nation's economic troubles, than those of the preceding few years. After Labor's defeat in the elections of December 1975 he resisted suggestions that he contest the position of its parliamentary leader, but when Whitlam resigned the leadership after the further defeat of December 1977, Hayden was elected to succeed him. Under his leadership the ALP came fairly close to victory in the general election of December 1980. Nevertheless, in February 1983, in view of increasing support among his colleagues for Bob HAWKE, he resigned the leadership in the latter's favour, thus preserving party unity and helping to ensure a Labor victory in the election of the following month. He then became Minister for Foreign Affairs in Hawke's Cabinet.

Nat. Secretariat Aus. Labor Party

W.G. Hayden

Hayman Island

QLD This island resort, the most northerly of the islands in the WHITSUNDAY PASSAGE, lies N of MACKAY and NE of PROSERPINE. It has been extensively developed as a tourist centre and can accommodate more than 500 visitors. It can be reached by launch from Shute Harbour, by helicopter from Mackay and Proserpine, or by air-launch from Mackay via the Whitsunday airstrip. A small railway takes visitors from the wharf and helicopter pad along the beach to the resort centre. It is hilly and densely forested, with a fringing coral reef. Launch cruises are available to adjacent islands and to the outer section of the GREAT BARRIER REEF.

Hazelbrook

NSW (combined population of Hazelbrook and LAWSON 6 323 in 1981) This town is located in the BLUE MOUNTAINS, on the Western Highway and on the railway route through the mountains, adjacent to and E of Lawson, about 90km from Sydney. The surrounding area contains many scenic features, which have made it a popular holiday resort, though it is increasingly becoming a town of permanent, rather than vacation, residents, many of whom commute daily to jobs in metropolitan Sydney.

Healesville

VIC (population 4 526 in 1981) A popular holiday resort about 60km NE of Melbourne, it is located in picturesque mountain country at the junction of Watts River and Grace Burn. Besides the natural beauty of forests and waterfalls, there are numerous other attractive features in the district, such as the Sir Colin Mackenzie wildlife sanctuary, the Maroondah Reservoir on Watts Creek, and the bushland setting of Coranderrk and Badger Weirs. As well as holiday visitors, the area attracts many daytrippers from Melbourne. The town was named after Sir Richard Heales, a parliamentarian and former Premier of VIC.

health

The cost of providing health and medical services in Australia more than doubled between 1975 and 1979, and has continued to escalate—in 1982 health expenditure was estimated to be equal to 7.5 per cent of the Gross Domestic Product, higher than that in any previous year. The federal government has made many attempts to alter the balance between the proportion of the doctor's bill paid by government or insurance funds, and the proportion paid solely by patients. The public debate about these changes has made everyone acutely aware that illness is costly. Australia's large city hospitals may have as many as 1000 in-patients and employ up to 4000 full-time staff members, and may run budgets higher than the health budgets of many developing countries. About 90 per cent of State government health expenditure goes to hospitals, and five per cent of the Australian work force is employed in health services, mostly in hospitals or similar institutions.

There is evidence of a heavy community load of chronic sickness: about one in four Australians have one or more chronic conditions.

Almost half of these people are severely restricted in their daily living, and some surveys show that one in five people are psychologically impaired to a significant degree. The burden of these chronic conditions falls heavily on the aged, but a substantial proportion occurs earlier in life. The life style of many Australians places their health at risk: one in 10 men drink enough alcohol to damage their health physically; 30 to 50 per cent of the population smoke cigarettes; obesity is prevalent; many mothers give their small children pain-relieving and sedative drugs unnecessarily; and between 20 and 30 per cent of adolescent children regularly drink alcohol and many more are smokers. It is estimated that four per cent of deaths in Australia are due to alcohol intake and a higher percentage to cigarette smoking. Poverty is another cause of poor health for a certain proportion of the population: the 1976 Poverty Inquiry showed that 10 per cent of Australians are very poor, and a further five per cent are relatively poor. The findings of the Inquiry indicated that the health needs of many groups in Australia were not being adequately met. Aboriginal children have four times the chance of dying in their first year than other Australian children, and in the cities children born into disadvantaged suburbs die at two or three times the rate of those born to parents in wealthier suburbs.

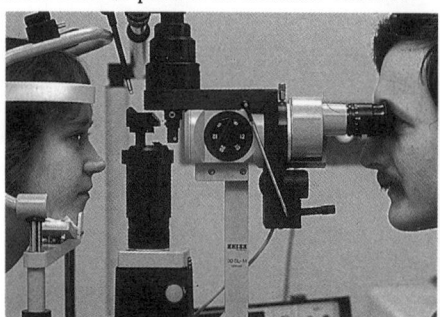

Equipment for laser eye surgery at Flinders University SA

In other respects it could be said that community health has improved during the past century—towards the end of the 19th century, common causes of death included diarrhoea, enteric infections (such as typhoid), tuberculosis, violence, and some other categories no longer recognised as causes of death, such as atrophy, exhaustion, debility and old age. But although the important diseases of that time are now rarely to be found, the list today registers conditions not recognised or understood 100 years ago. Improved standards of living, nutrition and sanitation have nevertheless had a profound effect in reducing the death rates for most Australian children apart from Aboriginal children and those of other disadvantaged groups. Maternal deaths from childbirth have also fallen with the introduction of preventive medical care during pregnancy, improved treatment of infection and methods to control and rectify blood loss. Consequently, a child born into an average Australian family today has 10 times the chance of surviving his first year than he

Table 1

GROUPS OF DISABLING CONDITIONS IN AUSTRALIA IN 1981
(per 1000 population)

Musculoskeletal disease	43.4
Hearing loss	36.3
Circulatory disease	25.6
Mental disorders (other than mental retardation)	20.9
Sight loss	13.3
Nervous system disease	12.6
Respiratory disease	11.3
Mental retardation, mental degeneration	7.6
All other conditions	29.3

Note: 8.6 per cent of the total population are handicapped by a disabling condition.
Source: *Handicapped persons, Australia, 1981*. Australian Bureau of Statistics.

Table 3

MAJOR CAUSES OF DEATH IN AUSTRALIA IN 1981

	Males %	Females %
Coronary heart disease	31	26
Cancer	23	21
Cerebrovascular disease	9	17
Respiratory	8	5
Other forms of heart disease	4	6
Motor vehicle accidents	4	2
Other accidents	3	2
Other causes	18	21
TOTAL	100	100

Source: Australian Bureau of Statistics, Canberra.

Table 4

NUMBERS OF HEALTH PERSONNEL IN 1978

Nurses	112 600
Doctors	25 810
Ambulance officers	7 400
Pharmacists	5 850
Dentists	5 400
Other dental personnel	8 500
Physiotherapists	5 450
Laboratory technologists	3 100
Optical personnel	2 380
Radiographers	2 200
Health surveyors	2 010
Pediatrists	1 470
Natural therapists	1 390
Health administrators	1 330
Occupational therapists	1 310
Other	37 435
TOTAL	223 635

Source: Australian Bureau of Statistics and Commonwealth Department of Health.

Table 2

COMMON CAUSES OF DEATH IN 1861 AND 1981

New South Wales (1861)	Australia (1981)
Violent deaths	Coronary heart disease
Debility	Cancer
Convulsions	Stroke
Diarrhoea	Accidents
Old age	Other heart diseases
Consumption	Bronchitis and related conditions
Dysentery	Pneumonia
Pneumonia	Suicide
Quinsy	Hypertension

Source: Health Commission of New South Wales and Australian Bureau of Statistics.

medical practice for freed citizens excluded from the Colonial Medical Service. Although the first Public Health Act (1848) in Britain was not to be followed in Australian States until 50 years later, there was a strong desire to avoid the conditions found in the work-houses of 19th-century England, and medical practitioners were amongst the leaders of movements committed to the social changes necessary to improved community welfare.

Links between the British and Australian health services in the 20th century have remained strong. Many Australian doctors and nurses have had training and professional experience in the UK, and professional organisations such as the Royal Colleges maintain close contact with their British counterparts. Since World War II, however, demands for health services in developed countries have produced different administrative responses to health-service delivery. In Australia the health care system is now a mixture of public health services and a private system which is subsidised by government and voluntary health-insurance organisations. Government automatically provides public health services where a substantial public risk exists—for instance, in immunisation and quarantine against infectious diseases, the detection and control of tuberculosis, and the control of standards in food preparation and of environmental pollution.

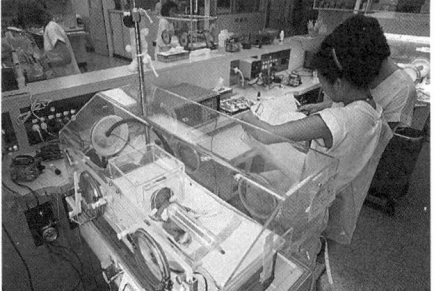

Neo-natal intensive care unit

Medical care has become both more effective and more expensive with newer drugs such as antibiotics, safer surgical procedures and improved diagnostic accuracy. Since World

would have had 100 years ago. He can expect to live for more than 70 years, and is more likely to die from a condition arising from his life style than from the infections and conditions associated with an impoverished society. Infectious diseases are rarely the principal cause of death in Australia, whereas in developing countries 70 per cent of deaths are so caused. Road accidents are an important rising cause of death in young people, although Australia's accident rate relative to the extent of vehicle usage is not as high as in some other countries.

Health services in Australia have developed from the Colonial Medical Service hospital system, from the civilian hospitals established through voluntary and benevolent subscriptions, and from the establishment of private

War II the provision of various special pharmaceutical, medical and hospital schemes, leading to the subsidising of private health insurance funds, and, more recently, to the setting up of universal insurance schemes such as the short-lived Medibank and the current Medicare, has opened up a major field of responsibility for the federal government (*see* social services). It also has other responsibilities—for example, for quarantine, for the development of national policies on health (through the National Health and Medical Research Council), and for the funding of biomedical research.

State governments are concerned with providing health services and maintaining the standards of health care. All registered health professions are controlled by State Acts and all hospitals and long-stay institutions (apart from Repatriation Hospitals) are subject to State legislation. Public hospitals are the principal providers of treatment for acute conditions, and some are also teaching hospitals associated with university medical schools; they are responsible to State governments through boards appointed by the Governor or by election from subscribers. Private hospitals and nursing homes are run by charitable organisations or private groups for profit, and in both cases the patients are subsidised by the federal government. Australia has more nursing-home beds per capita than any other country; in NSW there are approximately 25 000 nursing-home beds—almost as many as the total number of hospital beds (approximately 32 000).

Nearly all mental health institutions are run by State governments. Since the 1950s mental health services have adopted an 'open door' policy and emphasised community mental health services rather than institutional care. Psychiatric units are now being established in general hospitals to break down the barriers which exist between general medical and psychiatric services and to reduce the stigma associated with mental illness. Although the 'open door' policy and the movement towards providing community mental health facilities has reduced the number of people spending extended periods in psychiatric hospitals, the need for further development in this area has been recognised.

Health personnel constitute a rising proportion of the total Australian workforce (3.4 per cent in 1978). Most are employed by public authorities, but a substantial number work in the private sector, including medical practitioners (general and specialist), dentists, optometrists and pharmacists—all representing male-dominated professions. A notable recent trend is the rising proportion of doctors in salaried practice. To ensure high standards, in terms both of qualification and of practice and ethics, most of the health professions are registered in each State. With technological and administrative development, new paramedical disciplines (such as occupational therapy, dietetics and psychology) are now becoming established and seeking registration.

In most cases the patient's first consultant is the general practitioner, who deals with the early stages of illness and arranges for any further treatment by specialists or in hospital. The Medical Benefits System is arranged so that reimbursement of costs at secondary and tertiary levels of medical care depends on agreed referral by general practitioners, virtually all of whom are in private practice. Specialists may consult in both private medical and hospital practice, and in public hospitals; in private practice their patients are referred by general practitioners; in the public sector they attend the patients of the hospital. Hospital treatment is supervised by specialists who either visit or are employed full-time by the hospital. Nurses are the largest professional group in health services, numbering almost 144 000 in 1978. They are employed mainly in hospitals and health care institutions.

Training programmes for health personnel multiplied in the 1970s, facilities for the senior professions being provided by universities, those for nursing and paramedical services being provided by nursing schools and Colleges of Advanced Education.

By 1980, the administration of health services in most Australian States had been transferred from hospital and public health departments to statutory commissions incorporating regional hospital administration, mental health and community health services. Major factors affecting the success of these commissions in the 1980s are the control of costs in hospitals, the promotion of community-based health programmes and the involvement of the medical profession in these initiatives.

See also diseases and epidemics, human
Further reading: Dewdney, J.H.C. *Australian Health Services.* John Wiley & Sons, Australasia, Sydney, 1972; Gordon, D. *Health, Sickness and Society.* University of Queensland Press, St Lucia, 1976; Martin, Rev. G.S. 'Commission of Inquiry into poverty, third main report' in *Social/Medical Aspects of Poverty in Australia.* Australian Govt Publishing Service, Canberra, March 1976; McQueen, H. *Social Sketches of Australia 1888-1975.* Penguin Books, Ringwood, 1978; Walpole, R. (ed) *Community Health in Australia.* Penguin Books, Ringwood, 1979.

Heard Island This is an Australian Antarctic Territory and is located some 4 600km SW of FREMANTLE and 1 300km N of the Antarctic Circle, approximately midway between Australia and South Africa, at latitude 53°S. A scientific research station was established on the island in 1947, but was closed in 1955 (when the MAWSON station was established) and is now uninhabited, though Australian parties to ANTARCTICA occasionally call there. The island is about 40km long and 20km wide; it is volcanic, with the highest point, Mt Mawson, rising to an elevation of over 2 740m. The name Heard comes from an American sea captain who visited the island in 1853, though it had been discovered earlier by British sealers. The rocky McDonald Islands, also Australian territory, are nearby.

heart urchins *see* sea urchins

heartworm *see* roundworms

heath *see* Epacridaceae; vegetation

heather *see* Epacridaceae

heathwrens *see* warblers, etc.

Heidelberg School This was the name adopted by a group of painters who came to dominate Australian art for 30 years spanning the late 19th and early 20th centuries. Led by Tom ROBERTS, the group included Frederick McCUBBIN, Louis Abrahams, Arthur STREETON, Charles CONDER and Walter Withers. The distinctive feature of their painting was its Impressionistic style, introduced by Roberts who felt French Impressionism offered a firm basis for the development of a truly Australian art. Between 1885 and 1890, the group met at a series of painting camps in the bush: first at Box Hill VIC, in 1886 at Mentone, at Eaglemont near the suburb of Heidelberg during 1889 and 1890, and later in 1890 at Chartersville. The painters also earned additional income by offering tuition to students, mostly women, who participated in these camps. The group first gained significant public attention at their Impressionism Exhibition in 1889 in Melbourne (at Buxton's Gallery, Swanston Street). An original challenge to the accepted style of painting, which was highly finished and favoured dark tones, the exhibition displayed 183 Impressionistic landscapes executed on cedar cigar-box lids (provided cheaply by Abrahams' father, who owned a cigar-importing business). Although the free-brush style, the high-keyed tones and bright colours of these paintings at first evoked a tide of public protest, they established a new direction in Australian art.

Heinze, Sir Bernard Thomas (1894-82) Musician. One of the most active and influential Australian musicians, Sir Bernard Heinze will be remembered as a conductor, teacher and music administrator. He was born at SHEPPARTON in VIC and graduated MA from the University of Melbourne. He continued his musical studies in London at the Royal College of Music (1911-14), and later in Berlin and Paris. In 1924 he returned to Australia and joined the staff of the University of Melbourne, where in the following year he was appointed Ormond Professor of Music. At this time he founded the Melbourne String Quartet and 'Young People's Concerts', an idea which he was to develop later into the well-known Youth Concert Series of the Australian Broadcasting Commission (ABC). From 1933 to 1956 he conducted the Victorian Symphony Orchestra, and in 1928 was appointed conductor for life of the Melbourne Philharmonic Society.

When the Australian Broadcasting Company was established in 1929 Sir Bernard was invited to act as music advisor, and in 1934 was appointed in the same capacity to the ABC. Among many distinctions for his services to music are his Fellowship of the Royal College of Music (1931), the award of Officier de la Couronne Belgium (1938), and his knighthood of 1949. In 1955 he resigned from the Ormond Chair of Music to take up the directorship of the NSW State Conservatorium of Music in Sydney, which he held until 1966. Sir Bernard was the first Chairman of Commonwealth Assistance to Australian Composers and also of the Music Advisory Committee of the Australian Council for the Arts (now known as the AUSTRALIA COUNCIL). He was named Australian of the Year in 1974.

Sir Robert Helpmann as an ugly sister in 'Cinderella'

Helpmann, Sir Robert Murray

(1909-) Actor, dancer, director and choreographer. Born at MOUNT GAMBIER in SA, he began ballet training at the age of six, and as a young man toured Australia and New Zealand as a student with Pavlova. He became a principal dancer in J.C. WILLIAMSON's musicals before leaving for England in 1933, where he joined the then Vic-Wells Ballet as a student, and then the Sadler's Wells Ballet (now the Royal Ballet) as a dancer. His acting début in England was as Oberon in *A Midsummer Night's Dream* at the Old Vic in 1937, and he has since played numerous Shakespearean roles at Stratford-on-Avon and the Old Vic, touring Australia in 1955 with Katharine Hepburn in *The Merchant of Venice*, and with the Old Vic tour of 1961. Sir Robert has worked as a choreographer and director at the Royal Opera House, Covent Garden, and in Australia he directed his own ballet *Yugen* for the ADELAIDE FESTIVAL in 1965. From 1965 to 1976 he was Joint Artistic Director with Peggy VAN PRAAGH of The Australian Ballet, and was director of the 1970 Adelaide Festival. He was made a CBE in 1964, and knighted in 1968.

Further reading: Salter, E. *Helpmann: The Authorised Biography.* Angus & Robertson, Brighton, Sussex, 1978.

Hemichordata *see* acorn worms

Hemiptera *see* bugs

hemlock *see* Umbelliferae

Henricks, Jon (1935–) Swimmer. Learning to dog-paddle at the age of seven in a waterhole near the NSW country town of Gulgong, Henricks was to become one of Australia's finest and fastest sprint swimmers. He began winning races at the age of 12 and by 1953, at the age of 18, he had become the fastest swimmer Australia had ever produced and had established Australian records for 100, 110, 200 and 220 yards. He represented Australia at the 1954 Commonwealth Games where he won gold medals in the 110 yards freestyle, the 4 × 220 yards relay and the 3 × 110 yards medley relay. His adherence to a gruelling training programme continued to pay dividends and at the 1956 Olympic Games he won the 100m freestyle and was a member of the victorious men's 4 × 200m relay team. Following his retirement from competitive swimming after the 1956 Olympics, he moved to the USA to take up a business career.

Henty family Pioneers. Thomas Henty (1775-1839) and his sons, James, Charles, William, Edward, Stephen, John and Francis, were between them closely associated with the early history of WA, TAS and VIC as squatters, merchants, shipowners, whalers and politicians. In 1829 James, Stephen and John came to the SWAN RIVER settlement (Perth), but soon decided that the prospects for farming were not good there and moved to LAUNCESTON in TAS, where Thomas, his wife Elizabeth, the other sons and their sister Jane eventually settled also. Finding it difficult to buy enough good land for successful farming in TAS, and failing in an appeal for a land grant to compensate for the grant which they had given up in WA, members of the family twice petitioned the British government for permission to settle on the opposite shore of BASS STRAIT. In November 1834, while awaiting an answer to the second petition, Edward took up land at Portland Bay where Francis joined him a month later and Stephen and John in 1836. Besides farming there, the brothers also engaged in whaling and took up more land on the Wannon River. Their presence on the mainland was not widely known, and in 1836 Major MITCHELL, on a journey of exploration, was surprised to find them at Portland Bay.

After the founding of Melbourne and Governor BOURKE's decision to authorise settlement there, the Hentys hoped to be given title to the land they had occupied. Their claim was not accepted, and when the town of PORTLAND was officially established they were evicted. However, in 1849, after long negotiations, they were allowed to buy land on favourable terms, and were given compensation for the losses to their improvements. Of the brothers who had not moved to Portland in 1834-36,

Charles and William were elected to the first TAS Parliament and the latter was also Colonial Secretary for several years, while James became bankrupt in TAS in 1846, and after some years in England settled in Melbourne where he prospered and where he became a member of the VIC Legislative Council.

The meeting of Major Mitchell and Edward Henty at Portland Bay by John Macfarlane

Hepatophyta Commonly known as liverworts because some species resemble the shape of a liver, these small, moss-like, non-flowering land plants grow in moist situations, such as damp trunks or damp soil; a few genera are aquatic. Liverworts lack the vessels which conduct food and water, and the absence of this vascular tissue probably accounts for their small size. Some species have flat, dichotomously branching plant-bodies and are thalloid (without leaves or a distinct axis); others are foliate (with leaves).

Thalloid liverworts obtain nutrients and moisture through the root-hairs (rhizoids) which fulfill the functions of roots and which anchor them to damp soil and rocks. At the reproductive stage, special upright organs develop which produce either eggs or mobile sperm. The mobile sperm swim to the egg through a film of water on the plant. The cell produced by this union (a zygote) develops into a sporophyte. The fertile cells (spore mother cells) within the sporophyte produce spores which are haploid (having a single set of chromosomes); the haploid spores are dispersed by the wind and develop into new plants. A common genus of thalloid liverworts, *Riccia*, is often found on moist stream banks; the genera *Marchantia* and *Lunularia* are common on burnt ground and may be WEEDS in shadehouses.

The life cycle of foliate liverworts is essentially the same as that of the thalloid species. In both groups there are some species in which a new plant is produced from the branches which separate from the main plant body. Three rows of leaves grow on the main stem of a foliate liverwort; the lower row often differs in size and shape from the upper two rows; the leaves have no midribs. These leafy stems often grow in dense mats, which help to retain water, which is also obtained through the rhizoids which grow from the undersurface of the plant. Leafy liverworts occur on damp tree bark, stones and soil and are in general

confined to closed forest, particularly in southern Australia, and to the environs of streams. Some genera, such as *Plagiochila*, *Schistochilia*, *Frullania*, *Chiloscyphus* and *Lophocolia*, grow in a lace-like pattern which contributes to the 'mossy' appearance of the vegetation on many river banks.
See also Appendix 5, Flower Structure and Glossary of Botanical Terms
Further reading: see Appendix 6, A Bibliography for Plants.

A liverwort, *Marchantia*

Herbert, (Alfred Francis) Xavier

(1901-) Author. Born in north-western WA, he was educated at FREMANTLE, Perth and Melbourne. After graduating in pharmacy from Melbourne University he worked for a time as a hospital pharmacist, and then travelled widely in N Australia working as a stockman, pearl-diver and miner. He was Superintendent of Aborigines in Darwin from 1935 to 1936 and served in the AIF in World War II. He has written numerous short stories and an autobiography, *Disturbing Element* (1963), but is best known for two monumental novels—*Capricornia* (1938) and *Poor Fellow, My Country* (1975). The first of these is set in a country called Capricornia, which is obviously the 'top end' of the NT and deals with the treatment of the native people by Europeans and the difficulties faced by half-castes in their attempt to gain social acceptance amongst Europeans. The second novel, 850 000 words in length, is also set mainly in N Australia; it deals with a wide sweep of Australian history, and reveals Herbert's views on a wide range of national issues, from the destruction of Aboriginal society to the control of Australian resources by overseas interests.
Further reading: Heseltine, H. *Xavier Herbert*. Oxford University Press, Melbourne, 1973.

Herbert River

QLD This perennial stream, in the NE of the State, rises on the E slopes of the GREAT DIVIDING RANGE, about 90km inland from INNISFAIL near MOUNT GARNET, with headwater tributaries rising near Herberton, SW of Artherton. It flows for some 250km, first S, then E and SE beyond INGHAM to an estuary near the S of HINCHINBROOK ISLAND. Much of the upper basin consists of rugged forested country interspersed with beef cattle grazing lands; the mid-valley is dense rainforest, with numerous waterfalls where the streams descend from the uplands; the lowlands are intensively culti-

vated, especially for sugar cane. The basin is in a region of high rainfall, which is concentrated mainly in the summer months and hence seasonal flooding is a feature of the river regime. The Kennedy Highway traverses the N and NW of the basin, and the Bruce Highway crosses the river on the coastal plain near Ingham. There are several national parks in the mid-section of the basin featuring gorge scenery and waterfalls; the best-known of these is Wallaman Falls Park (602ha), located 48km W of Ingham, where the Herbert River falls sheer for 305m, making Wallaman Falls one of the highest single-drop waterfalls in Australia.

Herbicides in Vietnam

During the war in Vietnam, between January 1962 and February 1971, about 1.45 million ha of forest and crops were sprayed with herbicides, to kill vegetation and make it easier to see enemy movements. Some of the herbicides (in particular, Agent Orange) contained 2,4,5-T which itself contained, as a contaminant, the extremely toxic, TCDD. It is estimated that about 165kg of the dioxin were deposited in this period during the war. Dioxin is directly toxic, but it is also believed to be a carcinogen (causing cancer) and a teratogen (causing birth defects when women are exposed during pregnancy). Its most common symptom is a disfiguring skin condition called chloracne.

Since the war many veterans in Australia and the USA have attributed birth defects in their children and certain illnesses in themselves such as neuroses, to their war-time exposure and are trying to obtain compensation from their governments. In 1982 the Australian Senate Standing Committee on Science and the Environment concluded, in their First Report that 'at present' (i.e., 1981) there was no evidence that the defects and diseases attributed to herbicide exposure during the war are due to this though they conceded that new evidence may be found in the future. A Royal Commission began to investigate the claims in 1983.
See also: Pest Control
Further reading: Hay, Alistair, 'It kills weeds, but what about people?', *New Scientist*, 15 July, 1982, and *The Chemical Scythe*. Plenum, New York, 1982; Senate Standing Committee on Science and the Environment, *Pesticides and the Health of Australian Vietnam Veterans. First Report*. Australian Government Publishing Service, Canberra, 1982.

heritage conservation legislation

In recent years, people have become much more aware that the ENVIRONMENT, whether natural or man-made, may be altered or damaged by their actions. This is particularly so in large-scale operations. Open-cut coal mining can completely change a local landscape, whilst an inner-city housing development can destroy familiar surroundings. The argument about such environmental change begins when man's desire to exploit and improve his situation has to be tempered by his wish to keep what already exists. This

balancing of old and new components of the environment is the basis of heritage conservation.

Many State governments have now introduced legislation to protect Australia's heritage. Much of this legislation uses the term 'national estate', which the Australian Heritage Commission Act (1975) describes as '... components of the natural environment of Australia or the cultural environment of Australia, that have aesthetic, historic, scientific or social significance or other special value for future generations as well as for the present community'.

The Heritage Commission, centred in Canberra, is required to advise government upon and encourage interest, understanding, research and education in, national estate matters. It also has the responsibility of identifying places comprising the national estate, by producing a register of them. The Commission has no control over such nominated places unless they are owned by the Commonwealth. The register is thus only an alerting device to all levels of government and the public.

State government legislation is a different matter. In VIC the Historic Buildings Preservation Council was formed under the Historic Buildings Act (1974), which provides not only for the creation of a register of historic buildings, but also prohibits the demolition, removal or alteration of a place on the register without approval from the Historic Buildings Council. The New South Wales Heritage Act (1977) resulted in the appointment of the Heritage Council. The Council can enforce conservation orders, give emergency protection, offer financial assistance, and influence local government procedures in order to safeguard 'buildings, works, relics and places of ... significance for the State'. The other States also have, or are in a process of developing, similar legislation to protect both the natural and the man-made environment.

Herman, Sali

(1898-) Artist. Born in Zurich, Herman showed an early interest in drawing. As a child, having set out to live with an uncle in London, he was so attracted by the art world in Paris that he stayed there for two years, earning a living as a baker's cart boy and in a munitions factory. On his return to Zurich, he began art lessons at the Zurich Technical School and at Max Reinhardt's. With a young family to support, he became an art dealer, and found little time for painting during the following 15 years. A refugee from the impending Jewish holocaust, Herman arrived in Australia in 1937. He studied art at George BELL's school in Melbourne, where he took a stand in the painting community for modernist ideas. In 1939, he moved to Sydney, where he continued to champion the modernist cause. During World War II, he contributed to the war effort by painting camouflage, and in 1945 became a war artist, painting pictures of the Pacific campaign. In 1944, he had won the WYNNE PRIZE for his painting *McElhone Stairs*; the award caused a sensation because of the nonconformist technique and subject—an urban view rather than the traditional scene of gum trees and sheep—of the painting. Coming a year after the DOBELL lawsuit, the award made him a modernist hero, and established his most popular art subject: the Victorian terraces of Sydney's 1880 housing boom. Herman's work expresses enthusiasm for texture and form, its distinctive style being typified by his use of glazes, scrambling and scrapping of the underpainting. He was awarded the OBE in 1971 and CMG in 1982.

Hermannsburg
NT (population 541 in 1981) Located on the FINKE RIVER, 128km by road WSW of ALICE SPRINGS, it is the site of an Aboriginal mission station established by Lutheran pastors from SA in the 1870s. The area, known as Missionaries Plains, is between the MACDONNELL RANGES to the N and the James Range to the S. Though the mission station developed cattle grazing and vegetable growing, and some of the pastors (particularly Pastor Strehlow, in the decades at the turn of the century) studied the language and mythology of the Aranda Aborigines, it has been the artistic ability of many of the Aborigines which has made the mission so well known. It was here that Albert NAMATJIRA, an Aranda, was born; his discovery by the SA painter Rex Batterbee led to the establishment of a watercolour school where the artistic skills of the local people are fostered; paintings and craft work are now produced for sale to visitors to Hermannsburg and are sent to market elsewhere. Road access is from Alice Springs via the Larapinta Drive; there are regular bus tours to Hermannsburg and PALM VALLEY, 15km to the S.

Heron Island
QLD This island is in the CAPRICORN GROUP and lies astride the Tropic of Capricorn, off the E coast, about 70km E of CURTIS ISLAND, 80km NE of GLADSTONE and 140km E of ROCKHAMPTON. It is a small coral cay, with a sandy beach coastline surrounded by a fringing reef exposed at low tide. As the tourist brochures claim, it is a 'paradise for skin-divers'; the goal of such underwater adventures is the 'Big Bommie', a massive coral formation which abounds with sea life. Accessible from Gladstone by launch or helicopter, Heron Is is a popular tourist and holiday resort which offers swimming in the tropical waters, inshore and deep-sea fishing, launch cruising, snorkelling and coral viewing from glass-bottomed boats. The island is a haven for sea birds, including herons; grey and noddy terns nest there and wedge-tailed mutton birds migrate from Siberia between October and May to burrow in the sand and nest. It is also the site of a protected turtle hatchery where, from October to January, the turtles clamber ashore, bury their eggs and then return to the sea, leaving the hatchlings to break through the sand and scamper to the water eight to 10 weeks later. The greater part of Heron Is (12ha), together with the Heron-Wistari reefs (9 700ha) to the W, have been classified as a marine national park. There is a marine bio-

logical station on the island concerned with the ecology of the island, the reef and the surrounding waters.

Heron Island, a coral cay at the southern end of the Great Barrier Reef

herons *see* bitterns, etc.

herrings *see* fisheries; fishes, bony

Hervey Bay
QLD Situated on the SE coast of the State, between the N end of FRASER ISLAND and the mainland coast, this bay consists of a line of beach resorts where the tropical climate, varied scenery, fishing and other aquatic sports attract many holiday-makers. The main resorts are Pialba, Scarness, Torquay and Urangan. At the S end of the bay, at the port of MARYBOROUGH (34km NE of the city itself), is the Urangan Pier, over 1km long, where tankers discharge petroleum products. At the NW end of the bay is the estuary of the BURNETT RIVER and, about 15km inland from the coast, the city of BUNDABERG. The E shoreline of the bay is formed by the curve of Platypus Bay on Fraser Is.

Heysen, Sir Hans
(1877-1968) Artist. Born in Hamburg, Heysen came to SA with his family when he was seven years old. He received his first art training under Archibald Collins, James Ashton and H.P. Gill in Adelaide, and then, from 1899 to 1903, studied in Paris at the Académie Julien, Colarossi's and Ecole des Beaux Arts. In 1904 he returned to Adelaide, where he painted *The Coming Home* and *Mystic Morn*, selling them to the Sydney and Adelaide Art Galleries, respectively. He moved to Hahndorf in 1908, and in 1926 began painting in the FLINDERS RANGES, a practice which became a regular feature of his life until 1933. He was made a trustee of the National Gallery of South Australia in 1940, and was knighted in 1959. Heysen is famous for his SA landscapes, which usually feature the gum tree as an object of dramatic beauty, or the Flinders Ranges, laid bare to show their basic structure. His remark, 'The Sun—its light and warmth—is my religion', indicates his love of light and his enthusiasm for robust colour, which are hallmarks of his work.

Hibberd, John Charles
'Jack' (1940-) Playwright. Brought up in BENDIGO in VIC he studied medicine at Melbourne University, where his first play, *White With Wire Wheels*, was performed in 1967. This was followed by his programme of one-act plays, collectively entitled *Brainrot* and performed at

La Mama in Melbourne the same year. In 1969 *Dimboola*, in which members of the audience become 'guests' at a country wedding breakfast, was performed at La Mama and subsequently became an international success. For some years he was a resident writer for the Australian Performing Group in Carlton, Melbourne, co-writing *Marvellous Melbourne* (1970) and directing his one-man play *A Stretch of the Imagination* twice in 1972. His more recent plays include *A Toast to Melba*, *The Les Darcy Show* and a version of Nikolai Gogol's short story 'The Overcoat'. He has also written and translated poetry. He lives in Melbourne. *Further reading:* Rees, L. *A History of Australian Drama.* (vol 2) Angus & Robertson, Sydney, 1978; Fitzpatrick, P. *After the Doll.* Edward Arnold, Melbourne, 1979.

Hibiscus
This familiar genus of shrubs belongs to the mallow family, Malvaceae. About 30 species are indigenous to Australia and are found mainly in tropical regions throughout the continent (but not in TAS). The bell-shaped flower, usually red, pink, yellow or white, has five large petals and the stamens project as a long tube surrounding the style. Aborigines used to chew the strong fine fibre of *H. heterophyllus* before making it into DILLYBAGS, and they used both the edible roots and the bark fibre (suitable for making nets and fishing line) of the cotton tree, *H. tiliaceus*. Besides the indigenous species, several exotic species are cultivated in gardens.

Henry Bournes Higgins

Higgins, Henry Bournes
(1851-1929) Politician and judge. He migrated from Ireland to VIC with his family in 1870, graduated in arts and law from Melbourne University, and was elected to the VIC Legislative Assembly in 1894. After playing an active part in the proceedings of the national convention of 1897-98, he was elected to the House of Representatives in 1901 and, although not a

member of the Labor Party, was Attorney-General in John WATSON'S short-lived ministry in 1904. In 1906 he was appointed a Justice of the High Court and also president of the Commonwealth Court of Conciliation and Arbitration. In the latter role he established the basic principles on which industrial arbitration was to operate for many years. In particular, in the Harvester Case of 1907, he established the concept of the basic wage. He resigned his position as president of the Commonwealth Court of Conciliation and Arbitration in 1922.
See also arbitration and conciliation, industrial
Further reading: Palmer, N. *Henry Bournes Higgins.* Harrap, London, 1931.

High Commissioners All Heads of Diplomatic Missions representing one member of the Commonwealth of Nations in another Commonwealth country are called High Commissioners; a High Commissioner is equivalent in status to the position of Ambassador.

High Court of Australia *see* government of Australia

Hilder, Jesse Jewhurst (1881-1916) Artist. Born at TOOWOOMBA in QLD, Hilder moved to Sydney where he studied at Julian ASHTON's School. He became fascinated with water-colour as a medium, and stayed with the medium, despite its then low esteem amongst painters and the public. His work, influenced by the French painter, Corot, established him as the first competent water-colourist in Australia since Conrad MARTENS, and he enjoyed a brief popularity with the public. He died in Hornsby, Sydney, of tuberculosis, after a short life plagued by ill health and poverty.

Hill, Alfred Francis (1870-1960) Composer. Often regarded as a father-figure in the history of Australian composition, Hill was born in Melbourne and lived with his family in Wellington, New Zealand, until at the age of 15 he went to study at the Leipzig Conservatorium. A gifted violinist, he took the Helbig Prize on his graduation from the Conservatorium. After his return to New Zealand in 1891, he became conductor of the Wellington Orchestral Society. He returned to Australia in 1897, and became a founder of the New South Wales State Conservatorium of Music in Sydney, being appointed its first Professor of Harmony, Counterpoint and Composition, as well as deputy conductor. He opened his own school of music in 1935.

Like many fellow Australians at that time, including Percy GRAINGER and Henry Handel RICHARDSON, Hill's creative studies had been furthered by a sojourn in Europe, and his compositions reflect the romantic style of the late 19th century. The range of his composition is wide: he wrote symphonies, choral works, chamber music, operas and dozens of miniature works for keyboard, voice, string ensemble groups and small orchestras. His Leipzig training equipped him with an assured technical facility, and enthusiasm for Celtic, Maori and Australian Aboriginal musical folklore, which inspired such works as his Maori opera, *Tapu.* Not only because such sources of inspiration signified an alternative to the traditions of imported Victoriana, but also because his work established new standards in technical accomplishment and professionalism, Hill can be regarded as an innovator in Australian music and his work as establishing a significant advance in Australian musical composition at the start of the 20th century.
Further reading: McCredie, A.D. 'Alfred Hill (1870-1960): some backgrounds and perspectives for an historical edition' in *Miscellanea Musicologica III,* Adelaide, 1968.

Hill, Ernestine (1899-1972) Journalist and author. Born Ernestine Hemmings in ROCKHAMPTON in QLD, she began writing poetry as a girl and in 1916 published *Peter Pan Land and Other Poems.* Her reputation, however, rests on a number of descriptive works and one novel. The former, based on very extensive travelling in the Outback, include *The Great Australian Loneliness* (1937), *Water Into Gold* (1937), *Australia, Land of Contrasts* (1943), *Flying Doctor Calling* (1947) and *The Territory* (1951). The novel, *My Love Must Wait* (1941), based on the life of the explorer Matthew FLINDERS, was the result of careful research but is open to criticism for its sentimentality. *Kabbarli* (1972), containing a personal tribute to Daisy BATES, was published shortly after the author's death.

Hill End NSW Located in the hilly TURON RIVER valley, 80km NNW of BATHURST and 70km S of MUDGEE, this small town was a boom town of the gold-mining era of the 1870s, when it had more than 50 hotels and a population of over 20 000. But the boom was short-lived and a decade later Hill End was virtually a ghost town. Today, although some gold mining is still carried on, the economy of the district is based mainly on mixed farming. Because of the significance of the town in bygone days, it has been dedicated as an official historic site, many of the original buildings having been renovated and restored, and it has become a major tourist attraction. Visitors can not only gain an insight into past life on the goldfields, but can also try their luck at gold panning. The National Trust (NSW) has classified the entire town site for preservation as part of the nation's heritage.

Hinchinbrook Island QLD Located 172km N of TOWNSVILLE and NE of INGHAM, it has an area of 39 350ha, extending some 32km N-S and being about 25km at its widest point E-W. It consists of rugged terrain, with Mt Bowen (1 113m elevation) as the highest point. It rises sharply from the sea along its W coast where it faces Hinchinbrook Channel which separates it from the mainland. Several attempts were made to settle the island from the 1870s, but all were short-lived; it was declared a national park in 1932, and is said to be the world's largest island national park. Unlike many other tropical islands off the QLD coast, Hinchinbrook Is has not been developed as a tourist resort, though it can be reached by boat from Cardwell and there are facilities for visitors.

Hindmarsh, Sir John (?-1860) Governor of SA. He joined the British Navy in 1793, took part in the Battles of the Nile and Trafalgar, and in general had a distinguished naval career. Hearing in 1835 that Colonel Charles Napier had resigned from his appointment as Governor of the proposed colony of SA, Hindmarsh applied successfully to the Colonial Office for the position. His character, however, was hardly suited to such a post. An impulsive, imperious man, he quarrelled with the colonisation commissioners even before leaving London. When he arrived in SA he found that William LIGHT, the Surveyor-General, had already chosen the site of the capital. Hindmarsh would have preferred PORT LINCOLN or a site near the mouth of the Murray River, and even when he came to accept Light's general choice of area, he argued with him that the town centre should be closer to the sea. He became embroiled in arguments with Light over this question, and on other issues quarrelled bitterly with J.H. Fisher, the Resident Commissioner, and with Robert Gouger, the Colonial Secretary.

Governor Hindmarsh

Meanwhile, the colony failed to develop as planned, largely because the supply of surveyed land could not keep up with demand, and those who were fortunate enough to acquire land tended to re-sell it for profit rather than develop it. Hindmarsh can hardly be blamed for this failure in early development, for it sprang more from faults in the planning of the colony than from his administration. Nevertheless, it is worth noting that he himself made considerable profits from speculation in land. Following his dismissal of Gouger from the Council of Government he was recalled in July 1838. He was later appointed Lieutenant-Governor of Heligoland, was knighted in 1851 and made Rear-Admiral in 1856.

Further reading: Price, A.G. *Founders and Pioneers of South Australia.* F.W. Preece & Sons, Adelaide, 1929.

Hinkler, Herbert John Louis 'Bert'

(1892-1933) Aviator. Born in BUNDABERG in QLD, he became interested in aviation as a boy, and at the age of 19 built a glider in which he reached a height of about 9m. After seeing the American, 'Wizard' Stone, fly in a Bleriot aircraft at Brisbane, he obtained a position as his mechanic and toured New Zealand with him. In 1913 he gained a position as a mechanic at the Sopwith Aeroplane Works in England, and after the outbreak of war in 1914 joined the Royal Naval Air Service, in which he served in turn as mechanic, gunner and pilot. After the war he worked for A.V. Roe, makers of Avro aeroplanes, flew an Avro 'Baby' from England to Rome and back, then brought it to Australia by ship and flew it non-stop from Sydney to Bundaberg. His ambition, however, was to fly solo from England to Australia. Returning to England, he obtained work with A.V. Roe once more and in 1927 flew an Avro Avian from London to Riga. In the following year, again in an Avian, he attained fame and a certain degree of fortune by flying from England to Darwin in a little under 16 days— 12 days less than the time taken by the SMITH BROTHERS, which up to that time had not been bettered.

A further proof of his skill came in 1931, when he flew solo in a Puss Moth from New York to London by way of Jamaica, Brazil and West Africa. Meanwhile, his England-Australia record had been broken, and by 1932 was down to 8 days 20 hours. In January 1933 he set out in the Puss Moth in an attempt to regain the record, but crashed in the Appen-

nines, where his body was found when the snows melted three months later. His Avro 'Baby' and Avro Avian are displayed in the Brisbane Museum.
Further reading: Mackenzie, R.D. *Solo: The Bert Hinkler Story.* Jacaranda, Brisbane, 1962.

Hiscoe, Kenneth Jackman (1938-)

Squash player. Born in Sydney, Ken Hiscoe won the Australian Amateur championship seven times (successively from 1960 to 1967, except in 1965), the New South Wales Amateur title seven times and the New South Wales Open title six times. The year 1963 was his best year as an amateur when he became the first Australian ever to win the British Amateur title, generally considered to be the world championship. Hiscoe turned professional in 1971 and since then has travelled worldwide, playing and coaching. Talented in areas other than squash, Hiscoe also played rugby and was an active member of the Bondi Surf Club.

Hispanic settlers in Australia *see* Spanish-speaking people in Australia

history The history of Australia is treated in Appendix 1, Australian History in Dates, and in the entries on DISCOVERY, ECONOMIC HISTORY, EXPLORATION BY LAND and POLITICAL HISTORY. Other important entries which include major historical sections are those on the six States of the Commonwealth, the NORTHERN TERRITORY and PAPUA NEW GUINEA; those on various ethnic groups; and also the entries on ABORIGINES, BROADCASTING, DEFENCE, EDUCATION, FOREIGN RELATIONS, IMMIGRATION, IMMIGRATION RESTRICTION, and ARBITRATION AND CONCILIATION, INDUS-

TRIAL. In addition, there are many shorter entries on particular periods and episodes. Most historical entries contain references to relevant biographies. General histories of Australia are listed below; specialised works are mentioned at the end of the main historical entries.
Further reading: Clark, C.M.H. *A History of Australia.* (5 vols) Melbourne University Press, Melbourne, 1962-78 and *A Short History of Australia.* (new edn) Heinemann, London, 1969; Blackmore, W.H., Cotter, R.E. & Elliott, M.J. *Landmarks: A History of Australia to the Present Day.* (2nd edn) Macmillan, South Melbourne, 1977; Crowley, F. (ed) *A New History of Australia.* Heinemann, Melbourne, 1974; Howard, J.M. & Howard, V.M. *This Century of Change.* Shakespeare Head Press, Sydney, 1975; Ward, R. *Australia: A Short History.* (new edn) Ure Smith, Sydney, 1975; Alexander, F. *Australia Since Federation.* (3rd edn) Nelson, West Melbourne, 1976; Howard Mark. *Shaping a New Nation.* Longman Cheshire, Melbourne 1984.

Hoad, Lewis Alan (1934-)

Tennis player. Born in Sydney. Hoad burst into the headlines in 1953 when as a 19-year-old it fell to him and Ken ROSEWALL (also a 19-year-old), together known as the 'tennis twins', to defend the Davis Cup against America. Their fight back from 2-1 down after three rubbers to a 3-2 victory with both players winning their tension-packed second singles matches made heroes of them both. Hoad represented Australia in Davis Cup matches from 1953 to 1956, and three of those four years were winning years for Australia. His best year was 1956 when, in addition to winning the Australian and Wimbledon doubles titles (both with Rosewall) he also won the Australian, Wimbledon and French singles titles. In the following year he again won the coveted Wimbledon singles title and then turned professional for the biggest guarantee that had ever been paid to an amateur sportsman— £280 000. A powerful player noted for his strong serve and top-spin backhand passing shots and for his ability to raise his game when the occasion demanded it, Hoad retired to live in Spain in 1967.

Hobart TAS (population 128 603 in 1981) This is the capital city and major port of the island State of TAS and Australia's tenth-largest city. Located in the SE of the State on the DERWENT RIVER, 20km upstream from the Iron Pot lighthouse at the river entrance, it is Australia's second-oldest city, founded 16 years after Sydney, and named in honour of Lord Hobart, British Secretary of State for the Colonies when the settlement was established in 1804. Proclaimed a city in 1842, Hobart has grown from a town with a population of 262 (in 1804) to over 128 000 in the 1980s.
History The initial white settlement in TAS was made in 1803 when Lieutenant John BOWEN was sent by Governor KING from BOTANY BAY to VAN DIEMEN'S LAND. He selected a site at RISDON COVE on the E bank of the

Hinkler and his Avro Avian 1928

Derwent, 8km upstream from the present site of the city centre, for his party of 49 persons, including 24 convicts. In the meantime, however, the British government had despatched an expedition under Captain David COLLINS to establish a settlement on BASS STRAIT: in October 1803 Collins landed at PORT PHILLIP BAY near the present site of Sorrento, but could find neither good land nor a suitable water supply there, so he abandoned the settlement and decided to move to the Derwent. He reached Risdon Cove in February 1804, but considered it unsuitable mainly because it lacked a natural water supply. He therefore ordered the removal of the settlement to Sullivan's Cove (now the Port of Hobart) and named it Hobart Town. The present-day town hall in Macquarie Street stands on the site where Collins founded the city in 1804. It remained 'Hobart Town' until the name was officially changed in 1881. In the decades following settlement, it grew rapidly into a busy port town, well known to sailors and merchants all over the world. This early period also saw the erection of many of Hobart's gracious Georgian buildings, some of which survive today; the National Trust (TAS) has classified more than 90 buildings in the city as being historically and architecturally significant. The suburb of Battery Point, Hobart's first residential area, located less than 2km from the present central business core of the city, has been preserved as a unique sample of housing dating back 150 years and more. The waterfront, particularly Salamanca Place, recalls the days when Hobart was a great whaling port, a ship building town and a shelter for sailing vessels from all corners of the world.

URBAN GROWTH OF HOBART IN THE TWENTIETH CENTURY

Year	Population	% of State population
1901	34 626	20.1
1911	39 937	21.9
1921	52 361	24.5
1933	60 406	26.5
1954	95 206	30.8
1961	115 932	33.1
1971	129 928	33.3
1976	131 524	32.3
1981	128 603	30.1

Source: Australian Bureau of Statistics, Canberra.

City site The city centre nestles between MOUNT WELLINGTON to the W (1 271m above sea level) and the Derwent River. The suburban development has spread along the W bank of the river for about 20km, confined in the SW by the Mt Nelson Range. In recent decades the E shores of the river have also seen considerable urban expansion. Until the late 1930s, when a concrete floating bridge was built across the Derwent, these E areas were linked to Hobart by ferry services. The opening of the Tasman Bridge in 1964 led to increased urban development on the E shores, and the

importance of the bridge as a transport link was clearly demonstrated by the disruption of traffic flow when, in 1975, a vessel collided with supporting pylons, causing the collapse of some sections of the bridge. The Derwent provides a deep-water natural harbour where ships can berth very near the city centre, and the river shoreline is broken by a succession of bays and headlands which form a setting of considerable scenic beauty.

Climate Hobart experiences warm to hot summer conditions and cool to cold winters. The average monthly temperature in January, the hottest month, is 17°C; July, the coldest month, has an average of 8°C. Long hot spells can occur in summer, often with little relief even in the evenings, and the prolonged heat can cause marked desiccation of vegetation on the nearby hills. Such conditions can make the area like a tinderbox ready to be sparked into disastrous bushfires; in February 1967 an extensive fire swept down the Derwent Valley and along the slopes of Mt Wellington, causing over 60 deaths and destroying houses, factories and farmlands.

The average annual rainfall in Hobart is 622mm, spread throughout the year; October and November receive most rain (an average of 60mm and 61mm respectively), February (41mm) receives least. During winter, Mt Wellington is often snow-capped; it receives a higher precipitation (790mm) than the city and its temperatures are considerably below those of the urban areas.

Historic cottages at Battery Point, Hobart TAS

Notable features Many of the tourist brochures on Hobart talk of the 'picturesque old-world charm' of the city. This is certainly one of its attractive features, but it is also a major commercial and service centre, a financial and business focus, an educational and cultural centre, as well as the chief port of the State. Among its tourist attractions is Battery Point, which includes St David's Park and its historic cemetery, the old colonial homestead 'Narryna' with its folk museum, The Slips where boat building started as early as 1830, and Arthur's Circus with its quaint collection of colonial cottages. Hobart has always been closely linked with sailors and so it is fitting that it should be the destination of the famous Sydney-Hobart yacht race, the venue for the annual Royal Hobart Regatta (the largest aquatic event in the S hemisphere), the port where Japanese boats fishing in the Southern Ocean call, and the starting point for Antarctic expeditions. Among its other tourist attrac-

St. George's Church, Hobart

tions are the Allport Library and Museum of Fine Art, the Cat and Fiddle Arcade, the University of Tasmania in the suburb of Sandy Bay, the Friends School run by Quakers, and, for those who may wish to try their luck at gambling, the Wrest Point Hotel, home of Australia's first casino. At Taroona, 11km S of Hobart, the Shot Tower, built in 1870 to make shot for firearms, provides panoramic views of the Derwent River estuary.
See also New Norfolk; Port Arthur
Further reading: Adam-Smith, P. *Hobart Sketchbook*. Rigby, Adelaide 1968; Woodberry, J. *Historic Hobart Sketchbook*. Rigby, Adelaide 1976 and *Battery Point Sketchbook*. Rigby, Adelaide, 1978.

hockey There are a number of sports at which Australians excel in international competition but which receive little acclaim within Australia. Until recently, hockey was one such sport. Some of Australia's best players had heroic status in other countries, such as in Pakistan and India, and yet were virtually unknown to the Australian public. The 1970s have seen this position change dramatically, particularly since the 1976 Olympic Games in Montreal where prior to the Games Australia was the gold-medal favourite.

SA was the first State to organise the sport and has Australia's oldest existing club, founded in 1905. Hockey started in NSW later the same year and in VIC in 1906. Other States were much slower in taking up the sport seriously (QLD 1921, TAS 1934). The Australian Hockey Association was established in Melbourne in 1925.

Women took up the game in its very early days in Australia and the All-Australian Women's Hockey Association was formed in 1910. In fact, prior to the 1950s the game was considered more a women's game and attracted little interest as a masculine sport. The change came in 1956 when the first Australian team to perform at Olympic level finished fifth out of the 16 competing nations. A bronze medal at the Tokyo Olympics in 1964 followed by a

Hockey semi-final Australia vs India at the 1968 Mexico Olympics

silver medal at Mexico City in 1968 set the stage for unprecedented growth in the 1970s. In that decade, Olympic successes continued with a silver medal at Montreal in 1976; registered senior men players more than doubled to 20 000 with junior members adding a further 45 000; and the game enjoyed increased spectator appeal and media coverage. Although not represented at the 1980 Moscow Olympics, in 1981 Australia had its first major international success with a win in the Four Nations Tournament.

Holden, Sir Edward Wheewall
(1885-1947) Motor car manufacturer. Born in Adelaide, he graduated BSc from the University of Adelaide in 1905 and then joined his father in the family leather business, established by his grandfather, James Alexander Holden, in 1856. In 1917, because of the federal government's restrictions on the import of motor bodies, he saw the opportunity for manufacturing them in Adelaide, and so Holden's Motor Body Builders was established. In 1923 a new factory was opened in the suburb of Woodville, and within a few years this had become the largest body-building works in the British Empire. In 1931 General Motors Australia merged with the Holden organisation to form General Motors-Holden's Ltd, which in 1948 began production of the Holden, the first car to be mass-produced in Australia. Sir William was a Member of the Legislative Council from 1935 to 1947. He was knighted in 1946.

holey dollar *see* currency

Holman, William Arthur (1871-1934)
Premier of NSW. Born in London, he was brought to Australia in 1888 by his parents, who were actors. He soon became involved in the Labor movement, and in 1898 was elected to the NSW Legislative Assembly. He also began studying law at about this time, and in 1903 was called to the Bar. From the beginning of his political career he was a defender of States' rights. In his maiden speech in Parliament he opposed the Federal Constitution Bill, and in 1911 and 1913 he opposed referendum proposals to increase the power of the Commonwealth in various matters relating to trade, commerce, labour and employment, although they had been put forward by a Labor federal government.

In 1910 he was appointed Attorney-General and Minister for Justice, and in 1913 became Premier. When Prime Minister HUGHES put forward proposals for military conscription in 1916, Holman supported him strongly, and as a consequence was expelled from the Labor Party. Like Hughes, however, he was able to remain in office with the combined support of other ex-Laborites and of the Liberals, and when these two groups joined to form the Nationalist Party he became its leader in NSW. He led the Nationalists to victory in a general election in 1917, but lost his seat three years later. He then devoted himself mainly to his legal practice until 1931, when he was elected as a United Australia Party candidate to the House of Representatives. He died a few months before the 1934 election.

Further reading: Evatt, H.V. *Australian Labour Leader: The Story of W.A. Holman and the Labour Movement.* Angus & Robertson, Sydney, 1940.

Holt, Harold Edward (1908-67)
Prime Minister of Australia. Although born in Sydney, he was educated in Melbourne and after graduating in law from Melbourne University in 1930 practised in that city as a solicitor until his entry into the House of Representatives in 1935. Four years later he became a Minister in the MENZIES government. In 1940 he enlisted in the AIF, but after five months was recalled to the Cabinet, and in subsequent years held various portfolios under Prime Ministers FADDEN and Menzies, most notably that of Treasurer, 1958-66. He succeeded Menzies as Prime Minister on the latter's retirement in 1966.

Holt lacked the oratorical powers and forceful personality of his predecessor, but was widely respected for his sincerity and administrative competence. His greatest, and most controversial, impact was perhaps in the field of foreign affairs, where he showed a greater interest in Asian affairs than Menzies had done, and firmly followed up the latter's decision to commit Australian troops to the VIETNAM WAR. His Vietnam War policy and his close friendship with President Lyndon Johnson, as expressed in his saying, 'All the way with LBJ', brought charges from his opponents that Australian foreign policy involved slavish imitation of the USA. In general, his position as Prime Minister was made difficult by the fact that his predecessor had dominated the political scene for more than two decades. It was perhaps inevitable that signs of disunity began to appear in the Liberal Party and the government coalition after Menzies' retirement, but Holt did not have the opportunity to show whether he could have handled these in the long term, for in December 1967 he was drowned in heavy surf near Portsea VIC.

Harold Edward Holt

Home Hill QLD (population 3 138 in 1981)
Located in the NE coastal belt of the State, it is the twin town to AYR, 1 394km by road N of Brisbane, and about 100km SE of TOWNSVILLE. Situated in the BURDEKIN RIVER delta region, Ayr lies N of the river and Home Hill to the S; 11km apart, the towns are linked by a long bridge (over 1000m) across the Burdekin. Sugar cane, grown under irrigation, is the principal crop in the adjacent rural

areas; other crops include fruit, vegetables, maize, rice, tobacco and cotton. A unique feature of the delta region is the availability of large supplies of underground water, which is pumped to the surface and used for crop and pasture irrigation. The name Home Hill was given to the town in honour of Colonel Home who served in the Crimean War.

honey myrtles see paperbarks

honey pots see Epacridaceae

honeyeaters These PASSERINE BIRDS belong to the family Meliphagidae which contains about 170 species, of which 70 occur in Australia (54 endemic). The family is so variable that some biologists believe that it really consists of BIRDS of different origins linked by their similarities in feeding on nectar. All honeyeaters have brush-tongues as an aid to nectar gathering, and the beaks are down-curved and pointed. In Australia and New Guinea they are closely linked, biologically, to eucalypts which provide the birds with much of their food and which, in turn, are often pollinated by the honeyeaters. Nectar is not their only food: insects, fruit and fruit juices are important, and some eat berries such as mistletoes. Only a few examples of honeyeaters, drawn from the main groups, are mentioned here.

The brown honeyeater, *Lichmera indistincta* (12cm to 15cm long), is a common, widespread example of long-billed species. The sexes are alike but the male is larger; the upperparts are dull brown to olive brown, the underparts buff, and there is a patch of yellow behind the eye. The brown honeyeater is found in the NT, most of WA and QLD, northern SA and north-eastern NSW in habitats ranging from mangroves to gardens. It is a restless bird, solitary or in flocks, that sometimes catches flying insects.

The black honeyeater, *Certhionyx niger*★ (12cm), is a long-beaked, long-winged bird which frequents arid savanna over most of inland Australia. The male is black above and mainly white below, and the female is light brown. The red-headed honeyeater, *Myzomela erythrocephala*, and the scarlet honeyeater, *M. sanguinolenta* (both 10cm to 11cm), are colourful birds which frequent mangroves and, in the case of the latter, coastal forest and savanna woodland, in the N and E respectively. The melodious, tinkling call of the male scarlet honeyeater can often be heard at midday in summer, when most other birds are silent.

The genus *Meliphaga*, the 'typical honeyeaters', contains about 24 Australian species (20 endemic). Represented in most parts of the country, from inland deserts to rainforests, they range in size from 15cm to 20cm. Most are greenish-olive above and whitish, greyish-olive or yellow below; some have streaked underparts. Usually there are patches of yellow on the throat and chin. In the helmeted honeyeater, *M. cassidix*★ (21cm), yellow feathers form a tuft or 'helmet' above the beak. This

rare bird, found near creeks in a few places in southern VIC, will often attack other birds entering its territory. The white-eared honeyeater, *M. leucotis* (20cm to 22cm), a mainly yellowish-green species which lacks the yellow patches on the throat and chin, is common in some woodlands in SW and SE Australia, and in parts of QLD.

Melithreptus honeyeaters are conveniently called white-naped honeyeaters: all but one— the black-headed species, *M. affinis*★ (14cm), of TAS—have a white crescent on the nape. The plumage is greenish-olive to yellow above, whitish below, and black or brown on the head; there is a patch of bare skin above the eye. The call of white-naped honeyeaters alternates between a single whistle and a cheerful chattering sound. The brown-headed honeyeater, *M. brevirostris*★ (14cm), is a fairly common nomadic species of southern Australia, living in open forest, scrub and gardens and feeding mainly on insects. The closely related blue-faced honeyeater, *Entomyzon cyanotis* (25cm to 30cm), is a very large white-naped species with bare blue skin around the eye. It is found in open forest in the N part of the NT, the N and E parts of QLD and most of NSW.

The friarbirds belong to the genus *Philemon* and are represented by six species in Australia. All are drab brown in colour and have bare patches of blackish skin on the face, but the head of the noisy friarbird or leatherhead, *P. corniculatus* (31cm to 36cm), is completely bare. In most species there are knobs on the base of the upper mandible, though not in the little friarbird, *P. citreogularis* (25cm to 28cm), which is found in N and E Australia. In the helmeted friarbird, *P. novaeguineae* (35cm), of north-eastern QLD, the knob is a long ridge. All the friarbirds have loud calls; part of the call of the noisy friarbird sounds like 'four o'clock', while the repetitive call-note of the helmeted friarbird resembles 'poor devil, poor devil'.

Tasmanian yellow wattlebird, *Anthochaera paradoxa*

The white-fronted honeyeater, *Phylidonyris albifrons*★ (18cm), has a thin, down-curved beak and black, white and yellow plumage. There is a patch of white in front of the eye on the black head, and another behind the eye. The belly is white with black streaks. This active bird darts amongst foliage in search of nectar and insects and is well adapted to arid woodland and scrub. Like many arid-zone birds, it is highly nomadic.

The large regent honeyeater, *Xanthomyza*★

(*Zanthomiza*★) *phrygia* (22cm), is an aggressive, handsome species, mottled and scalloped with black and yellow. Apart from the black head, the warts on the face and the long, down-curved bill, it has a parrot-like appearance. It is fairly common in open forests and woodlands in SE Australia, and its call is rich and bell-like, similar to that of bell miners.

The miners of the genus *Manorina*★ may be named after the Indian myna, a quite unrelated STARLING which also has a bare patch of yellow skin behind the eye. They have yellow birds and yellow legs. All the miners are noisy but the bell-like notes of the greenish bell miner, *M.*★ *melanophrys* (18cm), of SE Australia, are distinctive and attractive. It is found in dry sclerophyll forest and feeds mainly on insects such as lerps on the underside of leaves. The noisy miner, *M.*★ *melanocephala* (28cm), has a wide range of notes, most of them not particularly attractive. Found in most of E Australia and TAS, it frequents the foliage of trees in woodlands and parks. Its general colour is greyish. Flocks of noisy miners are well known for their habit of mobbing predatory birds such as hawks. There are two other species in this genus in Australia—the black-eared miner, *M.*★ *melanotis* (26cm to 28cm), which inhabits open forest and mallee country, and the widespread white-rumped miner, *M.*★ *flavigula* (26cm to 28cm) a relatively tame bird often seen in parks and gardens in coastal NE and NW Australia.

There are two species of spinebills (genus *Acanthorhynchus*★) represented in Australia— *A.*★ *tenuirostris* (length 12cm to 15cm; bill 2.5cm) in the E, and *A.*★ *superciliosus* (14cm) in the SW. Both are long, thin-billed birds, greyish in colour with black, white and chestnut on the head, throat and nape. The first occurs in a wide range of habitats from heathlands to rainforests and gardens, the second in woodlands. The call of the E species is a quick succession of shrill, musical notes.

The wattlebirds and the spiny-cheeked honeyeater make up the genus *Anthochaera* which contains four species. Only two have visible wattles hanging from the face—the red wattlebird, *A.*★ *carunculata* (length 32cm to 35cm; tail 16cm), a loud-voiced species with a red wattle and a yellow belly found in the woodlands and parks in southern Australia, and the closely related but much larger Tasmanian yellow wattlebird, *A.*★ *paradoxa* (40cm to 45cm), a bird whose call has been likened to the sound of someone vomiting. The dark, olive brown little wattlebird, *A.*★ *chrysoptera* (27cm to 30cm), of SW and SE Australia has no wattles, despite its name. The widespread spiny-cheeked honeyeater, *A.*★ *rufogularis* (24cm to 26cm), which occurs in various habitats from woodlands to desert scrublands, takes its name from the bristle-like white band of feathers on its neck. It is a streaked bird with a plain buff throat and a black-tipped pink bill. Like the wattlebirds, it feeds on insects, fruit and honey.

Further reading: Officer, H.R. *Australian Honeyeaters.* Bird Observer's Club, Mel-

★Species, genus or family is endemic to Australia (see Preface)

bourne, 1964; Rowley, I. *Bird Life*. Collins, Sydney, 1974.

honeysuckle Strictly, the name honeysuckle applies to shrubs and climbers of the genus *Lonicera* (family Caprifoliaceae), but in Australia certain species of *Banksia* and *Lambertia* (both of the family PROTEACEAE) are known as honeysuckle because of their nectar-producing flower spikes. Aborigines obtained a sugary drink by soaking in water the flowers of the red honeysuckle, *B. serrata*, a rough-barked tree with yellow-grey flowers and tough, serrated leaves found in the E states and in TAS. The only E representative of *Lambertia*, the mountain devil, *L. formosa*, is sometimes known as honeyflower. The other members of *Lambertia* are found in WA, notably the many-flowered honeysuckle, *L. multiflora*, a shrub with narrow leaves and green or yellow flowers.

hookworms *see* parasites, livestock; roundworms

Hope, Alec Derwent (1907-) Poet. Born in COOMA in NSW, he attended the Universities of Sydney and Oxford, taught in schools, at Sydney Teachers' College and at Melbourne University, and from 1951 to 1968 was Professor of English at Canberra University College and the Australian National University. He has published many volumes of poetry, including *The Wandering Islands* (1955), *Poems* (1960), *Collected Poems* (1966), *New Poems, 1965-9* (1970), *Dunciad Minor* (1970), *Selected Poems, 1930–71* (1975), *A Book of Answers* (1978), *The Drifting Continent* (1979) and *Antechinus* (1981); two collections of essays, *The Cave and the Spring* (1965) and *Native Companions* (1974); and works of literary criticism, including *A Midsummer Eve's Dream* (1970), *The Pack of Autolycus* (1978) and *The New Cratylus* (1979).
His poetry, noted for its satiric wit and outstanding for its precise expression, displays both an air of disillusionment with human nature and feelings of genuine compassion. He is acknowledged as one of Australia's leading poets, has won a number of literary awards, and was appointed OBE in 1972.

Hope, Louis (1817-94) Pioneer of the sugar industry. The seventh son of the fourth Earl of Hopetoun, he emigrated to NSW in 1843, and in 1848 moved to the MORETON BAY district, in what is now south-eastern QLD. During the following few years he acquired several properties there. In 1862 he began a sugar plantation on his Cleveland property, built a mill, and in 1865 became the first person to employ a large number of KANAKAS in the canefields. In 1875 he sold the mill, and in 1882, having sold all his Australian properties, he returned to England. Although not the first to plant sugar cane in Australia, he is rightly regarded as the founder of the sugar industry, since he was the first to produce large amounts of sugar and to mill it.

Hopkins, John Raymond (1927-) Musician. Born in Yorkshire, Hopkins worked as a professional conductor in England, Scotland and New Zealand before coming to Australia. As Director of Music for the Australian Broadcasting Commission from 1963 to 1973, he established the 'Prom' series in Sydney and Melbourne and championed Australian musical composition through commissions and performances. He was also responsible for the formation of the National Training Orchestra for young musicians, and has taken an active part in the country's national music camps and in the activities of the Australian Youth Orchestra. He was made an OBE in 1970, and since 1973 has been Dean of the School of Music at the Victorian College of the Arts in Melbourne.

Hopman, Henry Christian 'Harry' (1906-) Tennis player. Born in Sydney, Hopman was an outstanding junior player who became a key figure in the resurgence of Australia as the dominant force in world tennis in the 1950s and 1960s in his role as nonplaying captain of the Australian Davis Cup team. He played in the Davis Cup team for Australia in the challenge rounds of 1928, 1930 and 1932 and was non-playing captain in 1938; his first success was in 1939 when, as playing captain, he led Australia to its first Davis Cup win—Australia's previous wins had been in partnershp with New Zealand, as Australasia. World War II interrupted Davis Cup tennis and it was not until 1950 that he was selected as non-playing captain and coach of the Australian team, a position he held until 1968. A shrewd and wily captain—nicknamed 'the Fox'—he steered Australia to a record 15 Davis Cup successes during this 19-year period. His skilful guidance in preparing his players both physically and mentally kept them and Australia at the top of international tennis for two decades.

hops *see* agriculture

Horne, Donald Richmond (1921-) Author. Born in Sydney, he attended the University of Sydney and Canberra University College, served in the AIF (1942-44) and after a short time as a cadet diplomat took up journalism. He was editor of the *Bulletin* for several years (1961-62, 1967-72), but then turned to academic pursuits as a Research Fellow, and later Associate Professor, in political science at the University of New South Wales. As an author he first became well known through his thought-provoking analysis of Australian society in *The Lucky Country* (1964). Disillusionment resulting from the dismissal of the WHITLAM government in 1975, combined to some extent with his republican views, led to the writing of *Death of the Lucky Country* (1976) and *His Excellency's Pleasure: A Satire* (1977), and his co-editing of *Change the Rules: Towards a Democratic Constitution* (1977). His other published works include an examination of contemporary English society

entitled *God is an Englishman* (1967), the autobiographical *The Education of Young Donald* (1975) and works of historical and social analysis, namely *The Next Australia* (1970), *The Australian People* (1972), *Money Made Us* (1976), *Right Way—Don't Go Back* (1978), *In Search of Billy Hughes* (1979) and *Winner Take All* (1981).

horsehair worms *see* hairworms

horse racing Often referred to as the sport of kings, horse racing has a long history in Australia. Horses arrived with the FIRST FLEET and picnic races began soon afterwards. With the establishment of racing clubs in the mid-1800s horse racing began to develop into what is now as much an industry as a sport. The size and extent of horse racing, as a sporting enterprise, is indicated by the following statistics for metropolitan Sydney. In the financial year 1981-82 the Australian Jockey Club (AJC) had 60 race days in Sydney where over 6 000 horses raced for prize-money of about $5.2 million; in addition, the Sydney Turf Club (STC), over the same period, conducted 524 races on 63 race days in Sydney, with prize-money of about $5.3 million. As well as these metropolitan racing activities, there were dozens of racing events in country districts throughout NSW. More than 25 000 people are involved with horse racing as an industry, from those who breed and prepare the horses (breeders, owners, trainers, veterinarians, jockeys, blacksmiths, stable hands) to those who organise the races (administrators, stewards, handicappers, racecourse workers), and the bookmakers and totalizator workers.
History The roots of horse racing in Australia can be found in the use of horses in hunting and for military purposes. In the early years, hunting was both a sport and a necessity, and a hunt was always a good opportunity for an owner to display his horse's speed and stamina. The racehorse Petrel, which won many races in VIC and TAS in the late 1840s and at one stage was considered the champion of VIC, was a stock horse whose speed was first noticed on an emu hunt. On the other hand, the military forces needed horses to draw supply and armament wagons and to provide transport for officers. It is no surprise, therefore, that the first official race meeting in Australia, held in October 1810 in Hyde Park, Sydney, was organised by officers of Governor MACQUARIE's visiting 73rd Regiment.
New South Wales Race meetings continued at Hyde Park until March 1814 when the 73rd Regiment transferred to Ceylon taking with it the racecourse committee. Official support for the sport diminished and in 1821 Governor BRISBANE banned the sport. However, the ban was short-lived and on St Patrick's Day 1825 an officially recognised meeting was held near Bellevue Hill; horse racing in NSW has flourished ever since.
From 1842 to 1859 the AJC held its meetings at a course in Homebush. In 1860 the AJC moved to Randwick, its present home. Three years later the Crown granted the course to the

AJC for an annual rental of one black peppercorn, after which the Club developed into an influential racing body, playing a major role in securing uniform rules, licensing trainers and jockeys, and appointing stewards. The other major NSW racing club, the STC established in 1943, organises races on the Rosehill and Canterbury racecourses.

Victoria Melbourne's first official races were held in March 1838 on a course marked out for the occasion near Batman's Hill. Flemington racecourse, which has become synonymous with racing in VIC and in particular with the Melbourne Cup, opened in March 1840.

The Victorian Racing Club (VRC), formed in 1864, from an amalgamation of Victoria Turf Club and the Victoria Jockey Club, has become one of the world's outstanding racing clubs, second only in Australia to the AJC. The Victorian Amateur Turf Club (VATC) staged its first meeting near BALLARAT in 1876 and in 1879 conducted the first Caulfield Cup, which has developed into one of the major events on the VIC racing calendar.

Dallas Handicap (won by McCabe, centre horse, ridden by Brent Thompson)

The Herald, Melbourne

Queensland The first recorded meeting in QLD was held at Cooper's Plains in 1843. The Queensland Turf Club (QTC), QLD's major racing club, was founded in 1863 and staged its first meeting at Eagle Farm in 1865. The other principal racing club, the Brisbane Amateur Turf Club (BATC), was founded in 1923 and organises races on the Albion Park and Doomben racecourses.

South Australia The first meeting in SA took place in Adelaide in January 1838 on a course marked out in front of the house of James Hurtle Fisher, a prominent owner and breeder. The major SA racing club, the South Australian Jockey Club (SAJC), was established in 1856; its main racecourse is Morphettville. The Adelaide Racing Club (ARC) challenged the leadership of the SAJC in the early 1880s but in 1884 conceded supremacy; today it organises racing on the Victoria Park course.

Western Australia The first organised race meeting in WA was in 1833 between ponies which had been shipped in from Timor. Thoroughbred horses first raced in 1836. Control of racing in WA is vested in the Western Australian Turf Club (WATC), formed in 1852.

Tasmania The first organised meeting in TAS was held at New Town, near Hobart, in 1814. The major racing club, the Tasmanian Racing Club (TRC), was established in 1874 and controls racing on the Elwick course in Hobart. The Tasmanian Turf Club (TTC) was established in 1871, and controls racing on LAUNCESTON's Mowbray course.

Melbourne Cup The publicity caused by the discovery of gold in the 1850s, particularly in VIC, resulted in the growth of Melbourne's population from 20 000 in 1850 to 140 000 by 1860. The immense wealth won from the goldfields of Ballarat and BENDIGO often found its way on to the racecourse. It was against this background that in 1861 the first Melbourne Cup was staged by the Victoria Turf Club (VTC). The race was won by six lengths by Archer, a horse which had been walked from BRAIDWOOD near Canberra to Melbourne (about 880km) a month before the Cup. His win by eight lengths in 1862 was even more impressive and, until 1969, when Rain Lover won the Cup for the second successive year, Archer was the only horse to have won the gruelling race two years in a row. In 1864 the control of the Melbourne Cup was taken over by the VRC, which has successfully established the Cup as the richest racing event in Australia and one of the more important spring social events. *See* Appendix 10.

A bookmaker lays the odds at Royal Randwick

Courtesy of A.I.S. Canberra

Betting Gambling on the outcome of a horse race began in a minor way with private wagers between officers of the 73rd Regiment and between settlers who were racing their horses but it was not until 1882, with the arrival of the Englishman Robert Standish Sievier, that bookmaking as we know it began. He set the style for a succession of colourful and flamboyant bookmakers, standing on raised platforms shouting the odds they were willing to offer on each horse in a race. Betting is now big business—in 1975, when betting turnover tax was three per cent, the Waterhouse family

of four bookmakers paid more than $2 250 000 into government revenue through turnover tax, and in 1981-82 the TAB turnover on horse racing in NSW alone exceeded $1 150 million.

Horses Some racehorses have been so outstandingly successful that they have become legendary. Carbine, bred in New Zealand in 1885, was one such horse. He raced 33 times for 23 wins and was unplaced only once—because he went lame. Phar Lap, another New Zealand-bred racehorse, popularly considered 'The World's Greatest Horse' in the early 1930s, won 37 races from 51 starts. The weight of his heart—6.36kg, compared with 2.72kg for an average stock horse—has given rise to the epithet 'a heart as big as Phar Lap's' for someone who exhibits stamina and courage. A third champion was Tulloch, also New Zealand-bred. Racing in the late 1950s at the end of his three-year-old season, he had won 15 times from 21 starts. Not long afterwards, he suffered a stomach ailment which took him out of racing for two years. On resuming racing he became the first racehorse in Australia to win more than £100 000 in prize-money. Tulloch's stake winnings were dwarfed in the 1970s: on 11 November 1978 Family of Man became the first racehorse in Australia to have won more than $500 000 in prize-money and by February 1983 Manikato had raced 44 times for 28 wins, six second placings and just over $1 048 000 prize-money.

Jockeys Australian jockeys were among the first in the world to experiment with the crouched riding style in which the rider sits well forward on the horse's shoulders. Called the 'Tod Sloan Crouch' after the American jockey who used the style with considerable success, the style was almost simultaneously and certainly independently pioneered in Australia by top jockeys Tot Flood and James Barden in the late 1800s. Other top jockeys have been Jim Pike (of Phar Lap fame), Darby MUNRO (rider of three Melbourne Cup winners), Scobie Breasley (outstandingly successful in England where he rode more than 100 winners in every year from 1955 to 1968), George MOORE (considered by many to be Australia's greatest jockey ever) and Roy Higgins (who in 1976-77 won the VIC Jockeys' Premiership a record 10th time).

Trainers The success of two trainers since World War II has completely overshadowed all previous training feats. The two trainers are Tommy SMITH (who in 1981-82 won his 30th successive Sydney Trainers' Premiership) and Bart CUMMINGS (who in 1974 became the first Australian trainer to win more than $1 million in prize-money).

See also Appendix 10, Melbourne Cup Winners
Further reading: Pollard, J. *The Pictorial History of Australian Horse Racing.* Paul Hamlyn, Sydney, 1971.

horses *see* animals, introduced

horsetails *see* Arthrophyta; fossils

Horsham VIC (population 12 034 in 1981) This city is located NW of the GRAMPIANS at the junction of the Wimmera, Henty and Western Highways, on the Wimmera River. At an elevation of 138m above sea level, it is 301km by road NW of Melbourne and 66km NW of STAWELL, and is also a station on the interstate railway route (Melbourne-Adelaide), 327km from Melbourne. Horsham is an important commercial and service centre, a transport focus, and the marketing city for a productive agricultural and pastoral hinterland; it is commonly called the 'capital of the WIMMERA'. As well as its business and service functions, the city has several rural-based industries such as flour milling, butter making, meat freezing and farm machinery. The Longerenong Agricultural College lies NE of the city. The climate is mild, with hot summers and cool winters and an average rainfall of 449mm which occurs throughout the year but is concentrated in winter and spring. The city was named in 1841 by the first settler in the district, J.M. Darlot, after the birthplace of the poet Shelley in Sussex, England. It became a borough in 1882, a town in 1932 and was proclaimed a city in 1949.

Hotham, Sir Charles (1806-55) Governor of VIC. Born in Suffolk, he joined the British Navy as a boy and pursued a very distinguished naval career. He gained some diplomatic experience in the Navy in negotiating a commercial treaty with Paraguay. Appointed Lieutenant-Governor of VIC in December 1853, he arrived in the colony in June 1854. However, despite his previous achievements, he is generally considered to have proved unequal to the tasks that confronted him there. VIC was on the verge of attaining responsible government, and in such circumstances his authoritarian manner, his failure to call regular meetings of the Executive Council, and his tendency to dictate to it when it was called, were particularly unfortunate.

He was also faced with a crisis on the goldfields. The miners had a number of grievances, of which the most serious were concerned with the licence fee of 30 shillings a month and the methods used by the police in their efforts to collect it. Hotham failed to keep himself sufficiently well informed on the situation and failed to give sufficient weight to the opinions of the goldfields commissioners. He had the good sense to appoint a Royal Commission to report on the miners' grievances, but in the meantime relied on force rather than conciliation, and insisted that the police collect the fee rigorously. Although the situation was admittedly a very difficult one, Hotham's handling of it must be considered to have contributed to the EUREKA STOCKADE rebellion.

house fly This entry deals with the familiar house fly, *Musca domestica*—a member of the order Diptera (FLIES)—and its close relatives which are often mistaken by the public for house flies.

The house fly was probably introduced to Australia by the first European settlers as it is scarcely ever found far from buildings. It is now cosmopolitan and its area of origin is unknown, but there are several distinct varieties in the world. The maggots develop in decaying organic matter and the adults feed upon various foods which they liquefy by secreting saliva upon the material. They then sponge up the liquid with their mouthparts. Because house flies frequent all kinds of decaying organic matter they are important carriers of disease organisms and viruses both on the surface of their bodies and within their guts. They are probably more serious as disease carriers in tropical regions because the varieties present there have a greater tendency to frequent latrines.

House fly, *Musca domestica*

Not all flies seen in a house are true house flies. The lesser house fly, *Fannia canicularis*, for example, often comes indoors and is sometimes taken to be a house fly that has not yet reached its adult size. It may be distinguished from the true house fly by its wing venation, by the way it holds the wings when at rest (parallel and partly overlapping, not diverging) and by its habit of flying underneath a suspended object such as a light, making sudden and apparently erratic turns. The lesser house fly breeds in decaying organic matter, particularly in poultry droppings. It does not pose as serious a health problem as the true house fly.

Another close relative of the true house fly is the Australian bushfly, *M. vetustissima*, a common outdoor fly which, despite the name, sometimes occurs in large numbers in Australian cities. It has been suggested that it came to Australia on the backs of early Aboriginal immigrants. It breeds in faeces and dung, and moves into the S parts of Australia during the summer. It is notorious for its habit of congregating around the mouth and eyes of man and his domestic animals in search of the exudations on which it feeds. It will also congregate around wounds. It does not, however, bite. The bushfly rarely comes indoors, and then only when the temperatures are very high. It may be distinguished from the house fly by the pattern on its thorax and abdomen. It carries diseases such as trachoma (*see* DISEASES AND EPIDEMICS, HUMAN). The attentions of bushflies are reported prominently in the journals of early visitors such as DAMPIER. The cosmopolitan biting stable fly, *Stomoxys calcitrans*, often comes indoors though it also bites its victims out of doors. It resembles a house fly in appearance but the biting proboscis is stiff and projects forwards.

house-mouse *see* animals, introduced

House of Representatives *see* government of Australia

Houtman Abrolhos WA This is the name given to the group of uninhabited islands with coral-islet outriders, located 64km W of GERALDTON and separated from the coastline by Geelvink Channel. The islands, strung N-S over about 90km, are in three subgroups: Walabi Group in the N, Easter Group in the middle and Pelsart Group to the S. The name Houtman Abrolhos was bestowed by the Dutch merchant and explorer Frederick de Houtman in 1619 and appears on a Dutch chart of 1622; *abrolhos* (a Portuguese word) means 'look out!' or 'watch out!', and the need for this warning has been borne out by the numerous shipwrecks there. The S group is named after the Dutchman François Pelsaert whose ship *Batavia* was wrecked there in 1629; in his book *Island of Angry Ghosts* (1966) H. Edwards tells the story of the discovery of this wreck in 1963.

Hovea *see* Papilionaceae

Hovell, William Hilton *see* Hume, Hamilton

Howard, Amos William (1843-1930) Nurseryman. Born in England, Howard emigrated to SA in 1876. Near his nursery he discovered a previously unnoticed alien plant, subterranean clover, *Trifolium subterraneum*. Realising its potential as a pasture legume that would increase the nitrogen content of soils, he grew crops from the seeds, and promoted the species until it was widely accepted in Australia. Subterranean clover flourishes under a wide variety of climatic and soil conditions, but it is important as a pasture plant only in Australia, where it has been invaluable in the development of the grazing industry.
See also agriculture

Howe, Michael (1787-1818) Bushranger. Born in Yorkshire, England, he was sentenced to seven years' transportation for highway robbery in 1811. Arriving in TAS in the following year he soon joined a band of bushrangers led by John Whitehead and said to number about 30. In 1814 he and Whitehead took advantage of Lieutenant-Governor DAVEY's offer of an amnesty for bushrangers who gave themselves up. However, in 1815 they both took to the bush again. Not long afterwards Whitehead disappeared and Howe took over leadership of the gang. He delighted in calling himself 'Governor of the Woods' or 'Governor of the Ranges', and wrote insulting letters to Davey as if he were the latter's equal, but by the time Davey's successor, SORELL, arrived in 1817, Howe was hard pressed and his followers were losing trust in him. By the end of the year he had left the gang and had written to Sorell offering to give information against his former accomplices in return for a pardon. Sorell accepted his surrender.

However, the only 'information' that Howe offered was the allegation that Rev. Robert Knopwood, the chaplain of the colony, had acted as an agent for the bushrangers. He took to the bush again, and in 1818 he was ambushed by a soldier and stock-keeper and battered to death. A brutal man, with a fierce hatred of all authority, he had aroused little sympathy or trust even among his fellow bushrangers.

Further reading: Wells, T. *Michael Howe, the Last and Worst of the Bushrangers.* (new edn) Folio Society, London, 1977.

Hudson, Sir William (1896-1978)

Engineer. Born in New Zealand, he graduated in engineering from London University, and then served for three years with the British Army in France. Subsequently he worked on dams and hydroelectric schemes in New Zealand, NSW and Scotland, and then become chief engineer of Sydney's Metropolitan Water Sewerage and Drainage Board. However he is chiefly remembered for his work between 1949 and 1967 as Commissioner for the Snowy Mountains Hydro-Electric Authority (*see* SNOWY MOUNTAINS SCHEME). He was created KBE in 1955 and elected FRS in 1964.

Courtesy of A.I.S. Canberra

Sir William Hudson

Hughenden QLD (population 1 657 in 1981)

This small business and service town is located in the central N of the State, on the Flinders Highway, 1 463km by road NW of Brisbane and 246km SW of CHARTERS TOWERS. Situated on the upper FLINDERS RIVER at an elevation of 325m above sea level, in the midst of the black-soil plains, it has an average annual rainfall of 487mm, which occurs mainly in summer, with a markedly dry season in the cooler months. It is a rail centre on the line from TOWNSVILLE to CLONCURRY and MOUNT ISA, with a link line SW to WINTON. The district is noted for sheep and cattle grazing and for grain farming, especially sorghum.

Hughes, William Morris 'Billy' (1862-1952)

Prime Minister. One of the most notable and controversial of Australia's Prime Ministers, he was prominent in public life for over half a century, leading first the Labor Party and then the chief parties opposing it. Noted for his resourcefulness, assertive leadership, strident nationalism, relentlessness in political combat, colourful and often vitriolic language and general wit and vigour in debate, he aroused perhaps stronger feelings of both admiration and antagonism than any other politician in Australian history.

Born in London of Welsh parents, he emigrated to QLD in 1884 and worked in a variety of city and country jobs there and in NSW before settling in the Sydney suburb of Balmain, and opening a shop there which specialised in the sale of second-hand books and the mending of umbrellas. He had by that time become very active in socialist organisations and in trade union circles, and in 1894 stood successfully as a Labor candidate for the NSW Legislative Assembly. In 1901 he moved to the federal House of Representatives. In the meantime he had been studying law and in 1903 was admitted to the Bar. After serving as Minister for External Affairs in WATSON's brief Ministry in 1904, he was Attorney-General in the FISHER Ministries of 1908-1909, 1910-13 and 1914-15, and then succeeded Fisher as Prime Minister. However, in spite of his success within the Labor Party and his strong influence on its development, his domineering personality was ill-suited to its caucus system, and his attempt to introduce military conscription in spite of the opposition of most Labor members led to his expulsion from the party in November 1916. Nevertheless, with the support of other ex-Labor members and of the Liberals, he was able to remain Prime Minister, and after these two groups had united to form the Nationalist Party he led it to victory in the elections of 1917 and 1919. He attended meetings of the Imperial War Cabinet in the closing stages of the war, and at the Paris peace conference obtained a special 'C class' mandate for Australia to administer New Guinea, resisted Japanese efforts to have a declaration of racial equality inserted in the Covenant of the League of Nations and demonstrated a remarkable knack of infuriating President Woodrow Wilson of the USA.

His political career after his departure from the ALP continued to be stormy. Many former Liberals in the Nationalist ranks chafed under his leadership, but had to endure it as long as the party remained victorious. However, in the 1922 elections the Nationalists and Labor won an equal number of seats in the House of Representatives, with the newly formed Country Party, which Hughes regarded with open contempt, holding the balance of power. This situation led to his replacement in 1923 by Stanley BRUCE, who formed a coalition with the Country Party. Hughes had his revenge in 1929, when his opposition to Bruce's proposed legislation on industrial arbitration brought the government down. This led to his expulsion from the Nationalist Party, but in 1931 he

William Morris Hughes during his period as Prime Minister

joined its successor, the United Australia Party, subsequently held a number of portfolios in UAP ministries, and in 1939 was only narrowly defeated by Robert MENZIES for its leadership. Nevertheless, his failure in 1944 to obey a party directive to withdraw from the all-party Advisory War Council led to his expulsion from the UAP. In 1945 he accepted Menzies' invitation to join the new Liberal Party, and remained in it until his death.

Further reading: Whyte, W.F. *William Morris Hughes: His Life and Times.* Angus & Robertson, Sydney, 1957; Fitzhardinge, L.F. *William Morris Hughes: A Political Biography.* (2 vols.) Angus & Robertson, Sydney, 1964-79.

Hume Dam VIC

Located on the MURRAY RIVER just below the confluence with the MITTA MITTA RIVER, 16km upstream from ALBURY on the NSW/VIC border, Hume Dam was completed in 1936 and named after the explorer Hamilton HUME. In 1961 it was enlarged to give a total storage capacity of 3 035 000ML; this increase necessitated moving the site of the township of TALLANGATTA, now located on the Murray Valley Highway SE of Albury. The dam (often referred to as the Hume Weir) is part of the total scheme for conserving and controlling the Murray waters for irrigation of crops and pastures, for livestock supplies in the arid lands downstream and for domestic supplies in towns and on farm properties along the river.

Hume Dam on the Murray river

Hume, Hamilton (1797-1873) Explorer.

The son of a superintendent of convicts, he was born at PARRAMATTA. Between 1814 and 1821 he was a member of several exploration expeditions in the Berrima, GOULBURN and YASS districts and on the S coast of NSW. He is best remembered for his 1824-25 expedition in partnership with W.H. Hovell, from his property near Gunning in NSW to CORIO BAY. He was later involved in bitter arguments with Hovell regarding their error in thinking they had reached the sea at WESTERN PORT BAY. In 1828 he accompanied Charles STURT on the latter's expedition to the DARLING RIVER, and was of great assistance to his leader because of his skill in dealing with the Aborigines. He spent the latter part of his life at Yass, where he was appointed magistrate. The Hume Highway, linking Sydney and Melbourne, and the HUME DAM arc named after him.
See also exploration by land
Further reading: Bland, W. (ed) *Journey of Discovery to Port Phillip, New South Wales.* A. Hill, Sydney, 1831; Prest, J. *Hamilton Hume and William Hovell.* Oxford University Press, Melbourne, 1963.

Humphries, John Barry (1934-)

Actor and author. Born in Melbourne and educated at Melbourne Grammar School and the University of Melbourne, Barry Humphries was to become well known in Australia and Britain as the creator and presenter of satirical one-man shows. The first of these, *A Nice Night's Entertainment*, was produced in 1962 followed by *Excuse I* (1965), *Just a Show* (1968), *A Load of Old Stuff* (1971), *At Least You Can Say You've Seen It* (1974), *Isn't It Pathetic At His Age* (1977) and *An Evening's Intercourse with Barry Humphries* (1981). In these he parodied many Australian behaviour patterns and personality types, creating the famous comic caricature of Melbourne suburbia, Mrs (later Dame) Edna Everage, and the globe-trotting international representative of Australia, Sir Les Patterson. One of his other popular creations, Barry McKenzie, featured in a comic strip in the British satirical magazine *Private Eye* from 1963 to 1974, and in 1972 Humphries wrote and acted in the film *The Adventures of Barry McKenzie.* A sequel, *Barry McKenzie Holds His Own*, was produced in 1974. Noted for his attention to detail in the dress, make-up and expressions of his characters, Humphries experiments constantly with punch lines, tirelessly honing them to the comic perfection he seeks. His most noteworthy achievement is that in spite of rapidly changing attitudes, customs and traditions, he manages not only to maintain topicality with his satire but to increase in popularity. Humphries has also published several books, including *Dame Edna's Coffee Table Book* (1976). He now lives in London.
Further reading: West, J. *Theatre in Australia.* Cassell, Sydney, 1978.

Humpty Doo NT

Located on the alluvial flats of the lower ADELAIDE RIVER 73km by road SE of Darwin, this was the site of a large-scale rice growing venture in the 1950s which proved unsuccessful. During World War II an area of fertile black soil along the Adelaide was used for vegetable growing to provide fresh food for the troops, and subsequent investigations and experiments showed that the enviroment was suited to irrigated rice cultivation. The venture, launched in 1954 as a highly mechanised scheme with joint Australian-American backing, initially gave good yields, but a variety of factors caused it to fail. Some of these were practical errors such as the design and levelling of the rice growing bays to control the irrigation; others were unforeseen elements of the habitat, particularly the unreliability of the climatic conditions and the crop devastation wrought by wild buffalo, geese and rats. The scheme ceased operating in 1960.

Hunt, Geoffrey Brian (1948-)

Squash champion. Born in Melbourne, Hunt was a talented tennis player before turning to squash and becoming the world's leading squash player. In 1965 he won his first Australian Amateur men's championship, the youngest player ever to do so. While in the junior and amateur ranks, he amassed an impressive string of Australian and international titles, including the first three International Amateur championships (1967, 1969 and 1971) and the British Amateur men's title (1970) and the British Open (1969). He turned professional in 1971 and began a relentless drive to success. In 1975 he was ranked number one in the world and in the following year he won every major title in the world, including the first combined World and British Open, to make his tally 406 wins from 424 matches since turning professional. In 1977 he again won the World Open title and in 1978 he won his fifth British Open along with the Australian, New Zealand, Canadian and South African Opens. A consistent winner of the British Open, in 1981 he won the title for a record-breaking eighth time. A dedicated perfectionist capable of unequalled control of speed and placement of the ball, in 1981 Hunt was ranked the world's number one squash player for the seventh consecutive year, and was voted athlete of the year by the Australian Confederation of Sport. In 1972 he was made an MBE for his services to sport. In 1982 he retired, owing to recurring trouble in a back injury.

Hunt, John Horbury (1838-1904)

Architect. Like Walter Burley GRIFFIN, Hunt is an example of the pervasive influence of America in Australia. Born in St. John, New Brunswick, Canada, he was trained as a building tradesman. Deciding to become an architect, he moved to Boston, Massachusetts, when he was 18 years old, and served a six-year apprenticeship with Edward Cabot, a leading architect there. At the outbreak of the Civil War Hunt left for India, but on his stopover in Sydney in 1863, he was so impressed with the opportunities offered by the prosperity of the gold rush that he decided to stay.

After six years in the office of Edmund BLACKET, Horbury Hunt began his own practice. He was in fact such a vivid and eccentric character that others found him difficult to work with; he was energetic, hard-working, intense and quick-tempered. He was also a small man, who designed his own clothes, including high-heeled boots to add to his height. He had special pockets for his drawing instruments, and his bell-topper hat had a hidden compartment for drawing paper. He even rode a bicycle equipped with a collapsible drawing board and an ink reservoir.

Hunt kept up to date by prodigious reading, and had the largest library of architectural books in Australia. His technical skills, his great love of craftsmanship, and his background of North American building tradition helped to make his architecture distinctive.

About half of Hunt's buildings were churches —each one a very personal interpretation of a Mediaeval style. He designed a wonderful array of parish churches, typified by St. John's, BRANXTON, NSW (1878) and St. Luke's, Dapto (1880). His three great NSW cathedrals—St. Peter's ARMIDALE (1871), Christ Church, GRAFTON (1874) and Christ Church, NEWCASTLE (1885, and only recently finished)—earned him a reputation as "that great juggler of brickwork". The enormous, powerful brick entrance arch of Grafton Cathedral is unique. On the other hand, his Chapel of the Convent of the Sacred Heart at Rose Bay, Sydney, has a sandstone multi-curved vault—the first of its kind in Australia.

The most audacious of Hunt's houses were built in the shingle style, i.e. with walls as well as roofs shingled, like the Spurling House at Brighton, VIC (1888). Some, however, were large brick compositions, like romantic castles: one is Camelot, at Narellan, NSW, which has an incredible roofscape of cones, gables, ventilators and chimneys. All the residences Hunt designed expressed the richness of natural materials—particularly well-wrought timber.

Hunt designed Australia's first department store, for Farmer & Company, in Sydney in 1873. He also claimed to have introduced the "sawtooth" roof, for daylighting the wool display floor at T.S. Mort's warehouse at Circular Quay, Sydney, in 1866. Both of these historic structures have now vanished.

John Horbury Hunt was a foundation member of the Institute of Architects of NSW, and became its President. His clients were among the wealthiest in the land. Yet he died a lonely and solitary pauper. He was buried in a grave prepared many years before—along with the remains of his wife, his dogs, his cats, his pony and his gander.

Hunter, John (1737-1821)

Governor of NSW. He was born at Leith, Scotland, began studying for the Presbyterian ministry, but in 1754 decided to join the British Navy, in which he engaged in active service in many parts of the world. In 1786 he was appointed second captain of the *Sirius* in the fleet which was to take convicts to BOTANY BAY (Governor PHILLIP being first captain). After arrival in NSW he took the *Sirius* to Cape Town for supplies and in the course of this errand circumnavigated the globe from W to E, mainly in near-Antarctic latitudes. In 1790 the *Sirius* was wrecked at NORFOLK ISLAND. Two years later he appeared before a court martial in England for the loss of his ship, but was exonerated.

In 1793 Hunter applied successfully for the position of Governor of NSW but did not reach Sydney until September 1795. By that time the officers of the NEW SOUTH WALES CORPS had become the colony's chief farmers and had also succeeded in dominating its trade, including that in 'rum', as the colonists called all alcoholic spirits. In accordance with his instructions, Hunter tried to cut down their privileges, to control the rum trade and to restore government farming, but with little success. Persistent complaints by officers and others led to his recall, and in September 1800 he was succeeded by Philip Gidley KING. It is worth noting that during his years in Australia he had taken a keen interest in local fauna and flora, and had been responsible for sending the first lyrebird and platypus specimens to Britain.

Mitchell Library

Governor Hunter

The degree of blame to be attached to Hunter for his failure is a matter of debate. It may be argued that the officers' position was so strong that no Governor could have coped successfully with the situation and that Hunter did not receive prompt and consistent support from the home authorities. On the other hand, he himself was inconsistent in his policies, showed himself a poor judge of character and may be considered to have lacked patience and determination. After recall he continued to serve in the Navy, and attained the rank of Vice-Admiral in 1810. A collection of his drawings forms part of the Rex Nan Kivell collection in the Australian National Library, Canberra.
Further reading: Bladen, F.M. 'Notes on the life of John Hunter' in *Journal of the Royal*

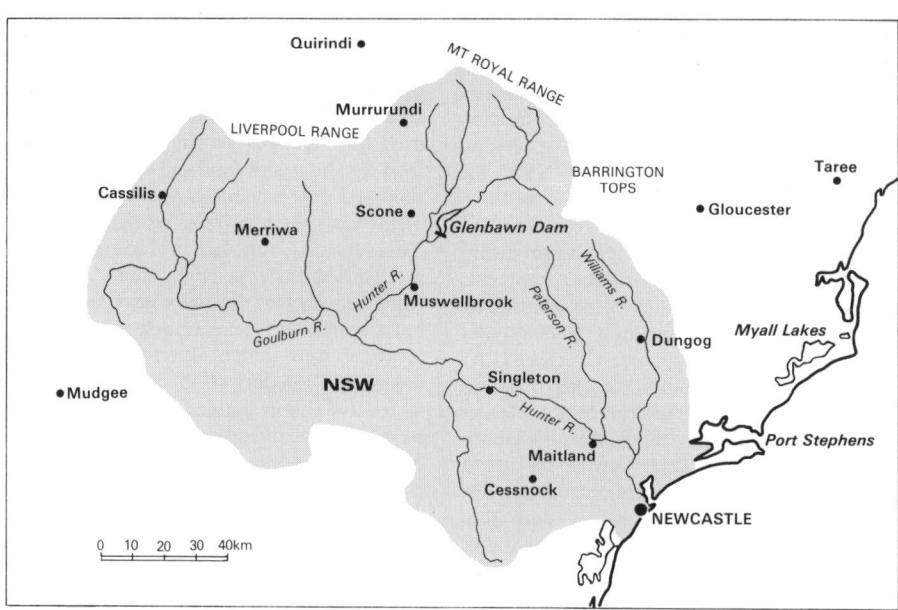

The Hunter Valley NSW

Australian Historical Society. (vol 1, 1901); Wood, G.A. 'Governor Hunter' in *Journal of the Royal Australian Historical Society.* (vol 14, 1928).

Hunter River NSW This major coastal river system flows into the sea at NEWCASTLE, some 170km N of Sydney. The valley occupied by the Hunter and its tributaries forms the longest in E-W extent, covers the largest area and includes the most extensive tracts of alluvial plains of any of the coastal rivers of NSW. The valley is a well-defined topographic unit, comprising a natural drainage basin situated between the N and central coastal areas of the State. Its urban focus is the city of Newcastle, behind which it extends inland for 195km with an average width of 120km, thus covering a total area of about 23 400km^2.

The Hunter River rises in the rugged, heavily forested highlands of MOUNT ROYAL RANGE, which forms part of the N rim of the valley basin, rising to heights of over 1 500m in the vicinity of BARRINGTON TOPS. From this source, the river flows in a general SW direction past MUSWELLBROOK; near Denman it makes a marked elbow turn where it is joined from the W by the GOULBURN RIVER; and then it flows SE past SINGLETON and MAITLAND to the estuary at Newcastle. Except for the Goulburn River in the W and

Owen Munn

Vineyards in the Hunter Valley NSW

Wollombi Brook in the S, the Hunter's main tributaries, the largest of which are the Williams and Paterson Rivers, drain from the N side of the valley. This has given a markedly one-sided drainage pattern which produces periodic flooding, often causing widespread damage to farming lands and urban areas in the lower parts of the valley when heavy rains occur in the highlands. A flood-mitigation scheme has been designed to control the river flow: the GLENBAWN DAM, located 11km upstream from Aberdeen and completed in 1958, was the first of the planned structures and the LOSTOCK DAM on the Paterson River, about 58km from Maitland, was completed in 1971. These dams have been designed to ensure a more even river flow and to provide irrigation water for farmers along the river flats.

There is a wide variety of rural activities in the valley. In the upper Hunter and Goulburn Valley regions grazing of sheep, cattle and horses is important, with fodder crop cultivation on the riverine silts and wheat growing in a few areas, such as near Merriwa. In the ranges and highlands bordering the valley, timber-getting is a significant industry. Along the river flats of the lower Hunter and its tributaries, dairying with associated fodder crop growing, particularly lucerne, is the chief rural activity; others are vegetable growing, orcharding, pig raising and poultry farming. Vineyards are important at a number of centres in the lower Hunter Valley—in the Muswellbrook district (Dalwood and Wybong) and on the lower slopes between CESSNOCK and Singleton, particularly in the vicinity of Pokolbin. The quality wines produced here are widely recognised and inspection tours of the vineyards and wineries are a regular tourist attraction.

Coal mining is a distinctive feature of the lower Hunter Valley. It has provided the basis not only for the mining industry itself but also for the vast industrial complex which has developed in the region. Coal outcrops were discovered in the cliffs near Newcastle in 1797 and an early convict settlement in the area was primarily concerned with mining. This Newcastle seam formed the basis of the original industry and collieries were located in several nearby centres which are now absorbed in the residential expansion of Newcastle city, such as Waratah, Lambton and Wallsend. The discovery by Sir Edgeworth DAVID of the GRETA-Maitland seam was a major step in the expansion of the coal-mining industry of the valley. It led to the development of mines in the Maitland-Cessnock area in the late 1880s, when production from seams elsewhere in the valley was declining. Coal mining, both open-cut and underground, remains an important part of the Hunter Valley economy and the Joint Coal Board, in its Statistical Year Book, *Black Coal in Australia: 1980-81*, listed 48 coal-producing mines located in the Hunter region; a third of these were open-cut mines. A unique feature in the upper valley is Burning Mt, at Wingen, a village located on the New England Highway 20km N of SCONE. The burning, with smoke usually issuing from cracks in the soil, is caused by the slow combustion of a coal seam beneath the surface rocks; the mountain (really a modest hill) can be reached by following a 2km-long walking track E of the highway.

Further reading: Tweedie, A. *The Hunter Valley.* Longmans, Melbourne, 1956; Wilson, J.L.J. (ed) 'The Hunter Valley' in *Current Affairs Bulletin.* (vol 20, no 2, May 1957); *The Hunter Valley Region.* Hunter Valley Research Foundation, Newcastle, 1968; *Hunter 2000: Conservation of Lands and Buildings of Natural, Historical, Scenic or Recreational Value in the Hunter Region.* The National Trust of Australia (NSW), Sydney, 1972; Mullins, B. & Baglin, D. *Australia's Hunter River Valley.* Reed, Sydney, 1977.

Huon River TAS Located in the S part of the State, it rises in the mountain regions near MOUNT ANNE (1 425m high) and Mt Eliza (1 289m), flows first S, then mainly E until near HUONVILLE where it takes a SSE course into D'ENTRECASTEAUX CHANNEL. The main N tributary is the Weld River, and those from the S are the Cracroft, Picton and Arve Rivers. The HARTZ MOUNTAINS National Park, covering 6 470ha in the middle reaches of the Picton Basin, includes much rugged country with peaks, frequently snow-clad, rising to over 1 300m high (Mt Picton 1 328m). The lower Huon Valley, famous for its production of apples and pears, is the focus of orcharding in TAS. The main urban centres are Huonville, through which the river flows, and Cygnet (municipal population 2 100 in 1981) which is located on a bay of the estuary. The Huon was discovered by the French admiral Bruni d'Entrecasteaux in 1792 and named by him after Captain Huon de Kermadec, his second-in-command. In the early days of settlement, a valuable softwood was discovered in the district, and was called Huon pine. There is still some grown there, but the main stands are now located near the GORDON RIVER on the W coast of TAS.

Huonville TAS (population of Huonville-Ranelagh urban area 1 347 in 1981). Situated on the lower HUON RIVER in the SW of the State, this town lies 37km SW of Hobart along the Huon Highway and 48km via the expressway. The centre of the apple industry, it is a prosperous commercial town encircled by orchards, many of which have been cultivated by the same families for over a century. It is the administrative centre of the Huon municipality (population 4 880 in 1981). The district is closely settled, and though apple and pear orchards dominate the landscape there are also sawmills and a pulp mill at Port Huon, which has a deep-water port developed to accommodate ships carrying fruit and timber.

Hurley, James Francis 'Frank' (1890-1962) Photographer, pioneer pilot and author. Born in Sydney, he became a professional photographer in 1909, and in the following few years was official photographer to the Australian Antarctic Expedition (1911-13) led by MAWSON and to the Imperial Trans-Antarctic Expedition (1914-16). These experiences provided material for the two documentary films he made subsequently, *The Home of the Blizzard* (1913) and *In the Grip of Polar Ice* (1917). In 1917-18 he was official photographer to the Australian Imperial Force (AIF). From 1922, flying his own light aircraft, he travelled extensively in New Guinea and the TORRES STRAIT islands to make documentary films. He served as official photographer for the British, Australian and New Zealand Antarctic Research Expedition in 1929-31, and as official war photographer during World War II. He was cameraman for a number of films, and published several photographic books, including *Sydney: A Camera Study* (1948), *Sydney from the Sky* (1952), *Tasmania: A Story of 150 Years* (1953), *Western Australia: A Camera Study* (1953) and *Australia: A Camera Study* (1955). Since his death, *Australia's Wildflowers* (1958), written with Barbara Mullins, has been reprinted twice, and a new edition of *Shackleton's Argonauts* (1948) was published in 1977. For his services in the Antarctic he was awarded the Polar Service Medal and made an OBE.

hussars *see* fishes, bony

Hutcheson, Ernest (1871-1951) Pianist and teacher. Born in Melbourne, Hutcheson is an outstanding example of an extraordinarily talented musician who was to pursue a distinguished career almost entirely outside Australia. He toured within Australia as a child pianist and at the age of 14 entered the Leipzig Conservatory; after a tour of Australia when he was 19 he returned to Germany and resumed his studies in Welmar. From 1898 to 1900 he taught piano at the Stern Conservatory in Berlin, and was successful also as a pianist and conductor.

In 1900 Hutcheson went to the USA (of which he became a citizen) and was appointed chief pianoforte teacher at the Peabody Conservatory in Baltimore. He resigned in 1912 to enable himself to devote more time to concerts, in which he was highly successful. In 1914 he settled in New York City. There he became Dean of the Juilliard Graduate School in 1927 and Dean of the Undergraduate School in 1933. He held both these posts until 1937 when he became President of the Juilliard School of Music, a position he held until his resignation in 1945. As well as writing about many aspects of music, he also composed many works, including concertos, film music and chamber music.

Huxley, Thomas Henry (1825-95) Zoologist. Born in England, Huxley visited Australia in 1847 during the course of his service as assistant surgeon on HMS *Rattlesnake*. In Sydney he met Henrietta Heathorn, who later travelled to England to marry him. He pursued a brilliant career as a zoologist and was amongst the first to give ardent public support to Charles DARWIN's *Origin of the Species* (1859); he was often called 'Darwin's Bulldog' because of his spirited and effective defence of Darwin against attackers such as 'Soapy Sam' Wilberforce, Bishop of Oxford. *Further reading: see* Darwin, Charles Robert.

hydatid cyst tapeworm The most dangerous TAPEWORM in Australia and one which is common in many sheep-raising countries is the hydatid cyst tapeworm, *Echinococcus granulosus*. It is the larval stage of this tapeworm which produces hydatic disease (echinococcosis). The adult normally lives in the intestines of dogs and dingoes but it is so small that it does little harm to its hosts. The eggs pass out with the dog's faeces and are eaten by sheep or wallabies; sometimes the eggs cling to the dog's fur and may be picked up on the fingers of human beings who stroke the dog. Within the sheep, wallabies and human beings the eggs develop into the hydatid cyst, a large fluid-filled bag which buds off, internally, many daughter cysts with embryonic tapeworm heads. If the mother cyst bursts, for example during surgery, the daughter cysts may establish in other parts of the body.

In man the liver, lungs and abdominal cavity are the commonest sites of development of the cysts. The body encases the cyst within fibrous tissue. Often, the cyst grows to the size of an orange; one with a volume said to be 57 litres was taken from an Australian woman. Dogs and dingoes become infested when they eat sheep or wallabies containing the cysts. Station dogs usually acquire the tapeworm when fed with uncooked offal after a sheep is slaughtered.

In 1961 TAS had the highest human incidence of hydatid cyst infestations among all the English-speaking regions of the world—9.29:100 000. Only Dalmatia, Uruguay, Sardinia and Cyprus had higher rates. In 1964, TAS mounted a large-scale publicity campaign and introduced the compulsory examination and treatment of dogs, the

banning of feeding uncooked offal to dogs and the prosecution of owners of dogs in which the tapeworms persisted. In 1964, 11.3 per cent of examined dogs were infested; by 1973-74 the percentage was only 0.67. Human surgical cases in TAS dropped from about one a week to nine in a year. On the mainland, however, hydatid cyst incidence remains steady and may even be increasing. Worming the dogs is useful, but only if they are then denied access to uncooked sheep remains. Worming is valuable when a country dog is brought to the city. The existence of a dingo-wallaby hydatid cyst cycle on the mainland may make eradication impossible for it is not known if this intermeshes with the dog-sheep cycle.
See also diseases and epidemics, human; disease, livestock

Hymenoptera *see* ants, etc.

I

ibises and spoonbills These marsh BIRDS belong to the family Threskiornithidae. There are three species of ibises in Australia; all have long, drooping bills which are used for probing for food. The diet consists of small aquatic organisms and terrestrial animals, such as crayfish and grasshoppers. The white ibis, *Threskiornis molucca* (75cm long), whose head and neck are bare and black, is found near water throughout Australia. It is a useful bird which destroys insect pests. The white eggs are laid on aquatic herbage which has been flattened to form a platform. The straw-necked ibis, *T. spinicollis* * (75cm), which is mainly black above and white below, has straw-like yellow plumes on the throat; it, too, attacks injurious insects. The nests and eggs of this widespread, nomadic species resemble those of the white ibis. The glossy ibis, *Plegadis falcinellus* (56cm), is a cosmopolitan bird, rarer in the S than in the N. Its plumage is dark reddish-brown, tinged with green. It lays dark greenish-blue eggs in platform-shaped nests of twigs and leaves which are placed in bushes and trees in or near water.

Spoonbills have long, straight, spoon-shaped bills which are used to sift small organisms from the water; they also feed on small aquatic animals and insects. Both Australian species—the royal spoonbill, *Platalea regia* (75cm), and the yellow-billed spoonbill, *P. flavipes* * (about 1m)—are white birds which are plumed in the breeding season; in the former, the bill and legs are black, while in the latter they are yellow. Found near water throughout most of Australia, particularly in swampy areas, these birds are often seen stalking in the shallows in search of food, sweeping their bills from side

A. Woods

White ibis, *Threskiornis molucca*

to side on the surface of the water. The royal spoonbill builds its platform-shaped nests of reeds and twigs in swamp vegetation or in trees. The nests of the yellow-billed species are made of trampled vegetation and placed in bushes or trees growing in water.

ice skating Until the advent of artificial ice rinks in the early 1900s, Australians were denied the pleasure of ice skating. The warm climate and the lack of large areas of natural ice meant that Australians could not take up ice skating in their own country. In 1904 several businessmen formed a syndicate to establish an artificial ice rink in SA, the Adelaide Glaciarium. Scotsman Dunbar Poole, a world famous ice-skating promoter, was invited to Australia by the syndicate to help promote the venture. Other glaciariums were built by the same syndicate in Melbourne in 1906 and in Sydney in 1907, and the latter was managed by Poole for the following 25 years. Training is difficult, especially in speed skating, as skaters have only a very limited amount of time allocated to them by the ice rinks for training purposes, however, in the 1977 world championships, Jim Lynch won the 1000m and 1500m events to become the fastest man on ice. In speed skating between 1981 and 1983, Michael Richmand and Colin Coates have scored a number of successes in international competitions in Europe. In the final meeting of the European Four-Town Tour in January 1983, Richmond was first overall.

Idriess, Ion Llewellyn (1890-1979) Author. Born in Sydney, he was educated there and at the BROKEN HILL School of Mines, worked as an opal miner at LIGHTNING RIDGE, served in the AIF during World War I, and later travelled widely in N and inland Australia, New Guinea and the Pacific. He published a great number of narrative and descriptive works which are vigorously written and show great knowledge of the scenes of his travels.

They include *Madman's Island* (1927), *Lasseter's Last Ride* (1931), *Flynn of the Inland* (1932), *The Desert Column* (1932), *Drums of Mer* (1933), *Man Tracks* (1935), *The Cattle King* (1936), *Headhunters of the Coral Sea* (1940), *In Crocodile Land* (1946) and *The Wild White Man of Badu* (1950).

Illawarra NSW This is a coastal region in the S of the State extending from near Stanwell Park S to the SHOALHAVEN RIVER. Much of the N part is occupied by the city of WOLLONGONG and the industrial centre of PORT KEMBLA. It is bordered on the W by the scarplands of the SOUTHERN TABLELANDS which rise sheer in some places to over 500m above sea level. Coal outcrops occur along the scarp and these have provided the basis for the mining and the metalliferous manufacturing industries of the region. Along the Pacific coastline are many fine surfing beaches alternating with rocky headlands. The rural areas of the coastal plain are devoted mainly to dairying, fodder crops and vegetable growing. Most of the milk produced on the farms is transported as whole milk for urban consumption, but there are still some butter factories in a few towns, including Albion Park, Jamberoo and Gerringong. The well-known breed of dairy cattle, the Illawarra Shorthorn, was developed in this district. In the early years of the 19th century, cedar-getting was an important activity, but most of the forests, except on the steeper scarplands, have long since disappeared.

NSW Dept of Tourism

Hampden Bridge in Kangaroo Valley, Illawarra region

Lake Illawarra is a coastal lagoon formed by coastal sand dunes blocking the former estuaries of small rivers. There is a narrow exit through the dunes to the sea near Shellharbour. The suburban growth of Wollongong in recent decades has extended around the lake shores. The waters of the lake are used at the Tallawarra power station located on the W shore. The name Illawarra comes from an Aboriginal word and has several meanings: 'a pleasant place by the sea', 'a white clay hill' or 'a high place near the sea'. Attractive surfing beaches, such as those at Austinmere, Thirroul, Bulli, Corrimal, Bellambi and Towradgi, and the lake provide a popular venue for aquatic sports.

Further reading: Mathieson, R.S. *Illawarra and the South Coast Region.* Longmans, Melbourne, 1960; Beale, E. *Illawarra Sketchbook.* Rigby, Adelaide, 1976.

Illawarra flame *see* Sterculiaceae

immigration Although Australia has been inhabited for more than 40 000 years, about 200 years ago it contained only a few hundred thousand Aborigines. It is evident therefore that most Australians of today are either immigrants or the descendants of immigrants who arrived comparatively recently. For about 40 years after the arrival of the first European settlers in 1788 most immigrants were convicts. Then free settlers began to outnumber convict arrivals and by 1868 had replaced them altogether. For a very long time the great majority of the free settlers, like the convicts, came from Britain. Since 1947, however, a dramatic change has occurred, for settlers arriving from Britain have been outnumbered by those from other parts of Europe. Since about 1966 there has been another significant change in the pattern, with a steady increase in the number of Asians being admitted.

Convicts and free settlers, 1788-1901 Of the people who arrived with Governor PHILLIP in 1788, over 700 were convicts. They were not compelled by law to remain in Australia after they had served their sentences, but since employment opportunities were better for them in Australia, and since most of them lacked the means to return even if they had wished to, nearly all of them became permanent settlers. Of the other people on the FIRST FLEET—marines, civil officials and a few servants and dependants—the great majority returned to Britain after their terms of duty had finished.

For many years little was done to encourage the immigration of free settlers, and very few came. Although the number increased after the end of the long wars with France in 1815, the total for the period 1788-1830 was only about 14 000 compared with 63 000 convict arrivals. In the 1830s, however, the situation changed. By that time it was commonly believed that Britain had a surplus population and Edward Gibbon WAKEFIELD's proposal that the proceeds from the sale of colonial land should be used to bring settlers from the mother country had been accepted by many influential people. In NSW it was decided in 1832 to use part of the receipts from land sales to pay for the passage of working-class people from Britain, and in 1835 this was supplemented by a bounty system, whereby employers were encouraged to select migrants and received payment for each approved person who landed. These schemes, and similar ones in other colonies, were so successful that by 1850 the total number of free settlers who had arrived since 1788 had reached 187 000, compared with 146 000 convict arrivals. By that time, too, Australia had received its first fairly large non-British ethnic group, Germans, most of whom had settled in SA.

The gold rushes of the 1850s brought an influx of people such as Australia had never experienced before. However, most of those who came at their own expense went to the goldfields, so that there were still labour shortages in the cities and on farms and pastoral

Scenes on an immigrant ship in the 1840s

National Library of Australia

properties. Assisted immigration schemes were therefore kept up, and brought more settlers to Australia than ever before. From 1860 to 1890 immigration continued at a generally high level, although it fluctuated greatly according to economic conditions. In the early 1890s the E colonies were struck by a severe economic depression, and from 1895 to 1902 this was compounded by the longest and most severe drought on record. Immigration almost ceased, and in 1892-93 and 1898-1900 departures from Australia exceeded arrivals.

British predominance continues 1901-47 The Australian Constitution which came into effect in 1901 gave the Commonwealth Parliament power to legislate with regard to immigration, but it was not given exclusive power and, until 1920, the States continued to play the leading role in attracting and selecting immigrants. The Commonwealth was concerned mainly with legislating (*see* IMMIGRATION RESTRICTION) in order to exclude some categories of immigrants, particularly those of non-European racial descent, but it also encouraged the States to revive their assisted passage schemes from 1906 onwards. Between that date and 1914, 140 000 assisted settlers

came to Australia.

When immigration revived in 1919, the Commonwealth took over the task of recruiting settlers, while the States continued to help them find accommodation and employment. At that time the British government was anxious to encourage emigration to the Dominions, and between 1921 and 1929, under the Empire Settlement Scheme, about 200 000 assisted British migrants came to Australia. About half as many again came from Britain and elsewhere without government financial assistance. During the Depression of the early 1930s, assisted immigration almost ceased, and for a few years Australia again suffered a net outflow of migrants. In 1938, when the economy was recovering, the Empire Settlement Scheme was renewed, but after a year was brought to a halt by the outbreak of war in Europe.

A feature of immigration during the inter-war period was the rise in the number of non-British arrivals. The imposition of restrictions on immigration to the USA in the early 1920s diverted many S European migrants to Australia, and immigration from Germany and E Europe was also important. Many of the settlers from the latter areas were Jews, migrating because of persecution in Poland during the 1920s and Nazi persecution in the 1930s. At the Evian Conference of 1938 Australia agreed to accept 15 000 refugees from Nazi Germany and its satellites, but only about half that number had arrived by the time war broke out. Although non-British settlers were not numerous enough to make a very great change in the ethnic composition of the Australian population, their arrival marked the beginning of a trend which was to become stronger after the end of World War II.

From 1947 to 1950 Following the end of the World War II, Australia launched the most ambitious and successful immigration programme in her history. The clearest motive for this was the 'populate or perish' line of argument, which had been used at various times in the more distant past, but was now emphasised by the fact that for the first time in Australia's history enemy bombs had landed on her soil and that the possibility of enemy invasion had loomed over her. It was in fact a double argument—Australia needed a larger population in order to be able to defend herself, and if she did not populate her 'empty spaces', others would attempt to do so.

Immigration was also seen as being necessary on grounds of economic development. During the war the production of many goods had been curtailed or even suspended, so that there was an enormous backlog to be made up. Immigration, it was argued, would provide the necessary labour and would also increase the size of the local market, so helping manufacturers to achieve 'economies of scale'. Also, immigration was advocated on humanitarian grounds, particularly with regard to 'displaced persons' who had left their native countries during the war and for various reasons could not, or would not, return.

In 1945, even before the war had ended, the Commonwealth government set up, for the first time, a Department of Immigration, with Arthur CALWELL as its Minister. Its planning was based on the achieving of an annual increase of two per cent in the Australian population. Because natural increase was expected to amount to about one per cent, an immigration programme was needed which would add another one per cent. It was expected that, as in the past, the majority of immigrants necessary for achieving this target would be obtained from the UK. In 1946 the United Kingdom-Australia Assisted Passage Migration Agreement was signed, but when British migration did not produce the expected numbers, agreements regarding the provision of assisted passages were signed also with Malta (1948), the Netherlands (1951), Italy (1951) and West Germany (1952). In 1951 Australia became a foundation member of the Intergovernmental Committee for European Migration, which was formed with the object of providing various forms of assistance for migrants from Europe.

In the meantime, Australia had accepted very large numbers of 'displaced persons'. In 1947 there were still about 1 600 000 such refugees

in camps in Europe, a high proportion of them being former citizens of Latvia, Estonia and Lithuania—countries which had been absorbed by the USSR, and to which the refugees were unwilling to return, because they did not wish to live under Communist rule, because they were known opponents of Communism who could not safely return, or simply because they had been uprooted from their homes and former associations and wished to make a fresh start in life. In collaboration with the International Refugee Organisation, Australia had by 1951 accepted and provided assistance for over 170 000 settlers under the Displaced Persons Scheme. Such people had to agree to accept employment specified by the government for their first two years in Australia, and many fulfilled this obligation by engaging in labouring work unpopular among other Australians.

The 1950s and 1960s These two decades were marked by important changes in the ethnic background of new settlers. Favourable economic conditions in Britain in the 1950s led to a slackening of British migrants, and the ending of the Displaced Persons Scheme, in conjunction with the spread of Communism in the late 1940s, lowered the number from E Europe. On the other hand, the intake included many Dutch, Germans and Yugoslavs, as well as about 14 000 White Russians from China. The most remarkable change, however, was a very great increase in the number of S Europeans, especially Italians and Greeks. Compared with settlers from other areas, there were fewer assisted migrants, professional people and highly skilled workers in this group. Therefore, in addition to having a language barrier to overcome, they faced greater than average difficulties in establishing themselves financially in their new country. Understandably, their settlement pattern was marked by a great amount of 'chain migration'—that is, by new arrivals settling in districts where they already had friends or relatives, who would give them moral and material support. As a consequence of such chain migration, there are now heavy concentrations of particular ethnic groups, especially of Italians and Greeks, in certain suburbs of Australian cities.

Spanish and Greek women landing in Melbourne in the 1960s

In the 1960s there were further significant changes. Economic troubles in the UK caused the number of British migrants to rise sharply, but a wave of prosperity in the European Economic Community, founded by the 1957

A British family disembarking at Adelaide in the 1960s

Treaty of Rome, brought a lowering in the numbers from N and S Europe, with the exception of Greece. Australia therefore had to look to new fields; she signed agreements with Turkey (1967) and Yugoslavia (1970), and accepted an increased number of settlers from Lebanon and parts of South America. Following the 1966 easing of restrictions on the immigration of people of non-European descent, significant numbers of Asians began to arrive.

Since 1970 By 1970 Australia had received well over three million new settlers since the end of World War II. The magnitude of this movement, as well as the ethnic pattern of immigration, is indicated by figures from the census of 1971, which showed that only 80 per cent of Australian residents had been born here. British-born residents accounted for a little over eight per cent and other foreign-born residents for about 12 per cent. The 1970s marked a turning point in a number of ways. From 1972 Australia, like other advanced countries, experienced economic difficulties featuring high levels of inflation and unemployment. Immigration levels fell dramatically in the early 1970s, from 170 000 settlers in 1970-71 to 52 000 in 1975-76. Since then they have increased somewhat, reaching 118 000 in 1981-82, but seem unlikely to reach the levels of the 1960s for a considerable time. During the 1970s and early 1980s the rate of natural increase also dropped. At present there seems no possibility of Australia's population increasing during the remainder of this century at anything like the rate of the 1950s and 1960s. Whether the government should aim at increasing the immigration rate is a matter of public debate.

Present admission policy People who want to migrate to Australia to live there permanently should apply for a resident entry visa at one of the Australian government offices overseas. An Australian who wishes to sponsor a relative should apply to the office of the Department of Immigration and Ethnic Affairs in the State in which the sponsor lives.

The system of selecting migrants has undergone a number of changes in recent years. In 1979 a 'points system' known as NUMAS (numerical multi-factor assessment system) was introduced. Under this system, eligibility was judged in most cases by the allotment of points for both economic and personal factors, such as occupational demand, level of education, competence in English, ability to communicate in the proposed employment, and initiative, self-reliance and independence. In October 1981, following the report of a Committee of Review on Migrant Assessment, it was officially announced that a new system would be introduced on 19 April 1982. This provides for each applicant to be considered in one of five eligibility categories.

The first is family migration (broadly equivalent to the previous 'family reunion') which requires sponsorship by an Australian resident, and may under certain conditions include fiancés or fiancées as well as relatives.

The second category, labour shortage and business migration, is for people whose occupations are in demand, or who have been nominated by an employer, or who propose to establish enterprises in Australia.

The third category, independent migration, is for a limited number of applicants who are not eligible to apply under other categories, but who possess outstanding characteristics which would make them of obvious gain to Australia.

The fourth category covers refugees and special humanitarian programmes.

The fifth category, special eligibility, covers New Zealand citizens, 'patrials' (a child or grandchild of a person born in Australia) and self-supporting retirees.

Prospective migrants are advised to make careful study of the criteria used for selection in the category in which they intend to apply. It should be noted too that in 1981 the government ceased offering assisted passages, except for refugees and other special cases.

Further reading: Phillips, P.D. & Wood, G.L. (eds) *The Peopling of Australia.* (new edn) Macmillan, Melbourne, 1930; Eggleston, F.W. *et al* (eds) *The Peopling of Australia (Further Studies).* Melbourne University Press, Melbourne, 1933; Australian Population and Immigration Council *Immigration Policies and Australia's Population: A Green Paper.* Australian Govt Publishing Service, Canberra, 1977; Department of Immigration and Ethnic Affairs *Australian Immigration: Quarterly Statistical Summary* and *Australian Immigration: Consolidated Statistics.* (annually) Australian Govt Publishing Service, Canberra.

immigration restriction

Racially, Australia has one of the most uniform populations in the world, approximately 97 per cent of its people being of European descent. This is a result, firstly of the devastating effects of European settlement on the Aboriginal population, and secondly of the application for many years of policies of immigration restriction against non-Europeans. These policies, based partly on racist attitudes but partly also on economic and social arguments, have been abandoned only recently. Restrictions were also placed on S Europeans in the late 1920s and the 1930s, in the form of national quotas, and in requirements that settlers possess either a certain amount of capital or a guarantee of employment. However, these had little effect, and were of very slight impor-

'The Chinese invasion of North Queensland'. This newspaper illustration of 1877 wildly exaggerates the real situation but does show accurately Australian fear of unlimited Asian immigration

National Library of Australia

tance compared with restrictions against non-Europeans.

The colonial period As the number of convicts in NSW began to decrease in the late 1830s, moves were made to introduce cheap non-European labour. In 1839 a number of Indians arrived, and in the 1840s Pacific islanders were brought in by Ben BOYD, and Chinese by Captain Robert TOWNS and others. However, the total number of non-Europeans entering the Australian colonies up to 1850 would not have exceeded a few thousand.

The situation changed dramatically during the 1850s, when great numbers of gold seekers came from S China. Their presence aroused hostility and led to a number of anti-Chinese riots. In 1855, therefore, the government of VIC tried to reduce the number entering the colony by an Act which imposed an entry tax of £10 on each Chinese immigrant, and forbade ships to carry more than one Chinese for each 10 tons of the registered tonnage. This measure had little effect, for Chinese now landed mostly in SA or NSW, and then made their way to VIC overland. In 1857 another Act was passed imposing a residence tax of £4 a year on each Chinese, but their numbers continued to grow, until by 1859 there were well over 40 000 of them in VIC.

In 1857 SA passed legislation similar to that of 1855 in VIC, and in 1861, after the LAMBING FLAT riots, NSW did likewise. From that time the number of Chinese entering E Australia decreased sharply, and by 1867 all three colonies had repealed their legislation, which had been thought of as temporary.

The matter cropped up again in the 1870s, when Chinese flocked to the QLD goldfields, particularly to the PALMER RIVER fields, where by 1877 they numbered over 17 000 and formed the great majority of the population. An immigration restriction Act designed to limit their number was passed in the following year. However, by this time the Premiers were coming to realise that matters of immigration restriction could be handled satisfactorily only by means of intercolonial co-operation. Conferences held in 1881 and 1888 were followed

by the passing of fairly uniform legislation in the various Australian colonies.

Motives for restrictive legislation The opposition to non-European immigration was undoubtedly based largely on racist attitudes. Relevant Australian historical documents bristle with unfavourable references to Chinese, such as 'expression of cunning and deceit', 'unmeaning features and shambling gait' and 'practice of the most hideous immorality'.

Other motives, however, were also important. A basic economic argument, used on numerous occasions, was that Asians and other non-Europeans, being used to low material living standards, would work for low wages and under bad conditions, thereby undermining the living standards of Australian workers. Fears that Asians would not become assimilated, that their presence in large numbers would produce racial strife similar to that in the USA, that they would not understand the parliamentary system of government, and that their presence might result in a decrease in immigration from Britain, were also expressed frequently.

Exclusion by dictation test methods Towards the end of the 19th century the whole question became complicated through the arrival of many Pacific islanders as indentured labourers. As explained in the entries on KANAKAS and QUEENSLAND, most of these worked in the QLD canefields. However, their presence there made the colonial governments consider widening their legislation to exclude not merely Chinese, but all non-Europeans. At an intercolonial conference in 1896 it was recommended that restrictions should be applied to 'all coloured persons'. However, the UK objected to such legislation as being 'contrary to the general conceptions of equality which have been the guiding principles of British rule throughout the Empire'. A protest was also made by Japan, which did not consider that it 'should be spoken of in formal documents ... as if Japan were on the same level as the Chinese and other less advanced populations of Asia'.

At an Imperial Conference in 1897 Joseph Chamberlain, the British Colonial Secretary, praised the Natal dictation test method, whereby a prospective immigrant considered to be undesirable on racial or other grounds was simply given a dictation test in a language with which he was unfamiliar. The virtue of this was that there was no need to name particular countries in immigration legislation.

Commonwealth legislation After federation all parties agreed that there was need for Commonwealth legislation to replace that of the colonial Parliaments, so as to ensure the continuation of a 'White Australia' policy (a phrase which had become common in everyday speech, but which was never officially used). This was done in 1901 by the Immigration Restriction Act, which gave the government power to make any prospective immigrant submit to a dictation test of 50 words in any European language. The Act made no mention of the races or types of people to be excluded, but everyone took it for granted that the test would be used to prevent non-European immigration, as well as to exclude the occasional European who was considered as undesirable.

In 1905 the Act was amended to allow the use of any language in the dictation test. However, the test was not used very often, for Australia's opposition to non-European immigrants became well known and therefore very few applied for permission to enter. Whenever the dictation test was given, the authorities took care to choose a language with which the applicant was unfamiliar.

Changes after World War II The years since the end of World War II have seen the traditional 'White Australia' policy at first modified and then formally abandoned. Factors contributing to this development have been various circumstances relating to the war itself, the post-war granting of independence to colonies, the close links which Australia has formed with Asian nations, and a general worldwide reaction against racial discrimination.

Arthur CALWELL, Minister for Immigration in the post-war Labor government, applied the traditional exclusion policy rigidly, but the Liberal/Country Party government that took office in 1949 soon began to modify it slightly. A number of Asians under threat of deportation were allowed to stay, and permits to reside in Australia for a limited period were given more freely. By the late 1950s, however, associations such as the Immigration Reform Group and the New South Wales Society for Immigration Reform had been formed to work for much wider changes. They argued that the traditional grounds of opposition to non-European immigration no longer applied strongly enough to justify total exclusion. They pointed out that most Asians wishing to settle in Australia were well educated and possessed skills which would enable them to find employment in Australia. Moreover, at a time when many British colonies were becoming independent, with Parliaments and legal systems modelled on those of Britain, it was hard to maintain that non-Europeans were incapable of participating in the political process in Australia.

In 1958 the dictation test method of exclusion was abandoned, and a new Immigration Act simply gave the government power to grant or withhold entry permits as it wished. In the following year, the Minister for Immigration, A.R. Downer, defined the categories of non-Europeans whom the government accepted as eligible for permanent admission as follows: first, those who had married Australians, and all children of such marriages; secondly, those who had lived in Australia on temporary permits for 15 years; thirdly, 'distinguished and highly qualified' people.

Further changes since 1959 In the 1960s the process of change continued. In particular, the third category mentioned by Downer in his 1959 statement was widened to include practically anyone who had skills that would ensure employment in Australia, and in 1966 the period of temporary residence required before permanent status was granted was lowered to five years. In the same year, the government announced that: 'Application for entry by well-qualified people wishing to settle in Australia will be considered on the basis of their suitability as settlers, their ability to integrate readily and their possession of qualifications which are in fact positively useful to Australia.' However, it sounded a cautious note by adding: 'The number of (non-European) people entering—though limited relative to our total population—will be somewhat greater than previously, but . . . the basic aims of preserving a homogeneous population will be maintained.'

In 1972 the Australian Labor Party (ALP) came into power after 23 years in opposition in the Commonwealth Parliament. By that time it too had rejected the old exclusionist policy. The basis of its new immigration policy, adopted in 1971, included 'the avoidance of discrimination on any grounds of race, or colour of skin, or nationality'. However, it also advocated 'the avoidance of the difficult social and economic problems which may follow from an influx of people having different standards of living, traditions and culture'.

The Labor government lowered the period of residence required before a migrant could gain citizenship (a term preferred to 'naturalisation') to three years, took a liberal attitude in accepting Asian refugees, and stopped recording details about the racial background of settlers, classifying them only by former countries of residence and citizenship. Subsequent changes in the rules for admission have aimed at continuing the avoidance of discrimination on the grounds of race, colour, nationality or ethnic origin.

The present situation Since 1976 about 25 per cent of new settlers arriving in Australia have been from Asia. The majority of these can be presumed to be of non-European descent, as can some of those entering from Africa, South and Central America and Oceania. The numbers involved have not been large enough to alter greatly the racial balance of the population, but they reflect a change of attitude which would have been hard to forecast only a few decades ago.

This change has been strongly opposed by a number of small organisations. Moreover it appears that a considerable number of Australians fear that the admission of non-Europeans at the present rate could in time cause serious inter-racial tension. Very few, however, would want to see a return to a policy of complete, or almost complete, exclusion.

See also Vietnamese refugees in Australia
Further reading: Yarwood, A.T. *Asian Migration to Australia: The Background to Exclusion, 1896-1923.* Melbourne University Press, Melbourne, 1964; Palfreeman, A.C. *The Administration of the White Australia Policy.* Melbourne University Press, Melbourne, 1967; Willard, M. *History of the White Australia Policy.* Oxford University Press, Melbourne, 1967; Australian Population and Immigration Council *Immigration Policies and Australia's Population.* (annually) Australian Govt Publishing Service, Canberra.

Indian myna *see* animals, introduced; starlings

Indian sub-continent, settlers from
The 1981 census revealed that 62 141 persons resident in Australia had been born in the Indian sub-continent—991 in Bangladesh; 41 657 in India; 2 527 in Pakistan and 16 966 in Sri Lanka. A native from Sri Lanka was on the FIRST FLEET and settlers from India, Pakistan, Bangladesh and Sri Lanka have been coming to Australia since the early 19th century, when small groups of Indians were brought to NSW to work. Although by 1839 the Indian government had prohibited emigration from its territories, small numbers of Indian immigrants continued to come to Australia throughout the 1840s and 1850s to work as labourers on farms and sugar plantations, and the Indian hawker, with his heavily laden pack-horse, penetrated the remotest parts of Australia, bringing isolated settlers clothing and a few luxuries at a reasonable price and giving credit whenever it was desired.

The first Afghans were brought to Australia in 1860 by a VIC settler named Landells, who had participated in the first Afghan-British War (the term 'Afghan' was used in Australia to describe all the Pathans—tribes of SE Afghanistan and NW Pakistan). These men were camel drivers and they took part in the relief expeditions sent to find the missing explorer BURKE. Subsequently, more Afghans were brought out under contract to various pastoralists and after their discharge (mainly in the 1890s) a small number settled in inland Australia and set up their own camel-breeding and camel-carrying enterprises. In 1901 there were more than 600 Indians and Afghans in the camel areas of the Outback.

From the 1870s to the 1930s the Afghans, using camels, horses and bullocks, helped to pioneer Australia. They engaged in exploration, rescue operations and tracking with the police, laying railways and telegraph lines, setting up water pumps and bores, carrying supplies to and wool from pastoral stations, erecting fences and carrying mail. They clung to their traditional way of life and set up 'Ghan towns' outside the main towns. Australia's first mosques were set up in Adelaide and Perth and Mullahs were present in the main camps in the Outback, where they were influential in maintaining order and preventing feuds. The camel trade came to an end after the 1930s and the Afghan population rapidly decreased. Approximately 3000 Afghan camel men came and went between 1860 and 1930; those who stayed became farmers and storekeepers.

Indian community The best-known Indian community in Australia is a group (numbering 300) which has been established for many years in the Woolgoolga district of northern NSW. Most members of this group belong to the Sikh religion and they have built two Sikh temples in the area. They are mostly banana growers but recently many of the younger members have entered the professions.

Population figures In 1901 7 700 persons gave India as their birthplace. In the 1950s migration from India increased and by 1954 there were approximately 12 000 Indian-born people in Australia; this number rose in the following 10 years to nearly 16 000. The 1976 census showed that 37 586 persons in Australia were born in India and 1 797 in Pakistan. NSW, VIC and WA have become the main centres for these settlers with about 8000 in each State capital, followed by SA and QLD with about 2000 each. Most Pakistanis chose NSW, followed by VIC, WA and QLD.

Contribution of post-war migrants The migrants from the Indian sub-continent since World War II have included medical practitioners, university lecturers, engineers and school teachers. These migrants have produced the highest level of professionally qualified people of all the ethnic groups in Australia.

Notable migrants from the Indian subcontinent Notable migrants have included Dr D.P. Singhal, Professor of History since 1969 at the University of Queensland, and R. Vasudeva, Head of the Mathematics Department, Royal Melbourne Institute of Technology. Professor Dharmasoka Laksir Jayasuriya, Professor of Social Work at the University of Western Australia, is perhaps the most well-known migrant from Sri Lanka. He was appointed to the National Community Relations Committee in 1973 and, in the same year, became a member of the Western Australia Migrant Task Force.

industrial arbitration and conciliation
see arbitration and conciliation, industrial

Industries Assistance Commission
This is a statutory authority set up in 1973 in place of the Tariff Board. Its function is to advise the Commonwealth government on the assistance which should be given to domestic industries. The Minister may refer any primary, secondary or tertiary industry to the Commission for enquiry and report, and in the case of any proposed variation in long-term assistance to a primary or secondary industry he is obliged to do so before action is taken by the government. In certain cases the Commission also has the right to initiate enquiries. Besides holding enquiries and issuing reports on specific industries and issues, it is required to report annually on its operations and on the general structure of assistance to industry.

Ingamells, Reginald Charles 'Rex'
see Jindyworobaks *under* literature

Ingham QLD (population 5 598 in 1981) Located on the Bruce Highway, in the NE coastal region of the State, 1 769km by road NNW of Brisbane and 116km NW of TOWNSVILLE, it is a commerical and service town for a sugar producing district. It is situated on the S bank of the HERBERT RIVER, at an elevation of only 14m above sea level, 30km upstream from the mouth, in the midst of canefields, against a backdrop of heavily timbered mountain scenery. The district also produces beef cattle, maize, tobacco and cabinet timbers. It experiences a tropical climate (latitude 19°S), with an average annual rainfall of 2 150mm, concentrated in the summer months. The cane is crushed at two mills just outside the town (Macknade and Victoria mills) and raw sugar and molasses are shipped in bulk from the port of Lucinda, located about 20km NE. The district has many scenic attractions: Mt Fox (875m elevation), an extinct volcanic cone known locally as 'big brother', is located in the Seaview Range 58km SW of the town; 48km W of Ingham is the Wallaman Falls National Park (602ha), where the waterfall on a tributary of the Herbert River is one of the highest single-drop falls (305m) in Australia; the Jourama Falls National Park (1 070ha) is located 35km S of the town; Orpheus Is National Park (1 368ha), one of the Palm Group of coral-fringed islands, is a resort off the E coast, accessible by launch from Dungeness; HINCHINBROOK ISLAND National Park (39 350ha) lies NE of Ingham and the beach resorts along the adjacent coast include Taylors Beach and Forrest Beach. Charter flights over the impressive gorges of the Herbert Valley operate from Ingham.

ink caps see fungi

Innisfail QLD (population 7 933 in 1981) A commercial and service town on the Bruce Highway in the NE coastal region of the State, 1 769km NNW of Brisbane and 87km S of CAIRNS, it is situated on the alluvial plains, at the junction of the North and South Johnstone Rivers, about 8km from the coast in the midst of sugar cane lands. Whilst sugar production forms the basis of the local economy, banana growing, beef cattle grazing, fishing in the rivers and along the coast and timber-getting in the nearby rainforests are also important activities. There are three cane crushing mills in the area (Mourilyan, Coondi and South Johnstone) and the raw sugar is exported by bulk handling operations at Mourilyan Harbour, 10km SE. Tea growing is a relatively new industry, located at Nerada, 35km W; the tea gardens are open for inspection and there are conducted tours of the factory. There is an experimental sugar station at South Johnstone, also open to visitors.

Innisfail has long been a cosmopolitan centre and this is reflected in such features as the Chinese joss house and the cane-cutter statue, erected by the Italian community to honour pioneers of the sugar industry. The Spanish Castle in Paronella Tropical Park is a popular recreation and tourist spot. There are several national parks in the region: the BELLENDEN KER National Park (31 000ha), located NNW of the town, includes stretches of dense rainforest and QLD's two highest mountains, MOUNT BARTLE FRERE (1 612m elevation) and Mt Bellenden Ker (1 561m); the Eubenangee Swamp National Park (1 520ha) comprises a vast area of swampland fringed by rainforest on basaltic soils, N of the town; the Moresby Range National Park (244ha) at Etty Bay, noted for its stands of fan palms and its abundant waterfowl, and the Mt Maria National Park (3 430ha), with its precipitous mountain and its panoramic coastal views, both lie along the coast E of the town.

insecticides and other pesticides
see environment; pest control

insectivorous plants see parasitic plants

insects About three-quarters of the described species of animals in the world are insects; the Insecta (or Hexapoda) is thus by far the largest class in the animal kingdom. It is, nevertheless, possible that only about a third of the insects that exist have been described scientifically and that there may well be about three million different species alive today. An English scientist, C.B. Williams, has estimated that the total number of individual insects alive at any one moment is about one million million million. There are between 55 000 and 56 000 *known* species in Australia; this may be compared with the approximately 89 000 known in America N of Mexico, though it should be remembered that the American and Canadian faunas have been studied over a longer period and more intensively.

Insects are ARTHROPODS. The body, in the adult stage at least, is clearly divided into three parts: head, thorax and abdomen. There are three pairs of legs on the thorax (one pair on each thoracic segment) and usually two pairs of wings, one on the second segment and one on the third. Any invertebrate animal with wings is an insect though not all insects are winged. The head carries a pair of feelers (antennae), the mouthparts, a pair of compound eyes, and often one or more simple eyes (ocelli) as well. The mouthparts consist of an upper lip (labrum), a pair of jaws (mandibles), a pair of accessory jaws (maxillae) and a lower lip (labium); the maxillae and the labium carry sense organs (palps). In the earliest insects the mouthparts were used for biting and chewing, and these kinds of mouthparts are still found in insects such as COCKROACHES and LOCUSTS. It should be noted that the mouthparts work from side to side, not up and down as is the case with human jaws. The insects have been a very successful group and virtually every possible kind of food is now eaten by one or more insect species. Consequently, the mouthparts of many insects have become modified, by evolution, for piercing and sucking blood, sap or other organic fluids (BUGS; MOSQUITOES), for lapping and sucking (HOUSE FLY), and for various other tasks. The form of the mouthparts is important in insect classification.

Life cycles Most insects begin life as eggs laid by the females (although some insects produce living young); from the eggs hatch nymphs or larvae. The development of the nymph is known as direct metamorphosis, while that of the larva is known as indirect metamorphosis.

Nymphs resemble the adults in their general shape, but are smaller, wingless and sexually immature. They often live in the same places as the adults, eating the same kind of food. Nymphs develop into the adult stages by a series of moults (ecdyses), and the wings, if any, develop as external buds; a stage between two moults is known as an instar (first instar, second instar and so on).

Larvae (such as maggots and caterpillars) do not resemble the adults; they exploit habitats that differ from those of their parents, thus avoiding competition and serving to exploit the total environment more efficiently. After a series of moults the larvae pass into a third stage, the pupa, during which the body is completely reorganised to produce the adult form.

Importance While most insects have little direct effect upon human affairs, many have become pests, attacking crops or livestock, or spreading diseases such as malaria, yellow fever, filariasis and bluetongue (in sheep). On the other hand, almost all flowering plants (ANGIOSPERMAE), with the important exception of grasses, cereals and similar groups, depend upon various insects for pollination. Insects are the source of certain goods such as shellac, cochineal and honey. Many insects have been used in the BIOLOGICAL CONTROL of other organisms when these have become pests.

Classification The classification of insects is being revised constantly but the scheme commonly used is to divide the class into two subclasses: Apterygota and Pterygota.

The Apterygota contains those insects that are primitively wingless—that is, none of the ancestors had wings. There are two orders: Archaeognatha (three species in Australia), a group of small, secretive soil insects with three 'tails'; and Thysanura (BRISTLETAILS). Until recently certain six-legged, wingless arthropods—SPRINGTAILS, DIPLURANS and PROTURANS—were included among the insects but these are now placed in separate classes of their own.

The Pterygota contains most of the modern insects. The adults may be winged or wingless, but if wingless they are descended from winged ancestors (for example, FLEAS). The Pterygota

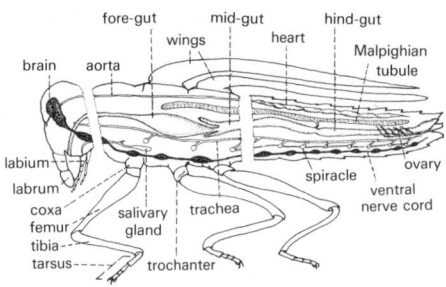

A basic insect showing division of head, thorax and abdomen and some of the internal organs

is divided into two divisions, Exopterygota and Endopterygota.

1. Exopterygota. These are the insects with direct metamorphosis, whose young are called nymphs. The wings, when present, develop externally in buds. The division contains the following orders: Ephemeroptera (MAYFLIES); Odonata (DAMSELFLIES AND DRAGONFLIES); Plecoptera (STONEFLIES); Grylloblattodea (cold-mountain insects, unknown in Australia); Orthoptera (CRICKETS AND GRASSHOPPERS and locusts); Isoptera (TERMITES); Mantodea (MANTIDS); Zoraptera (unknown in Australia); Phasmatodea (STICK INSECTS and leaf insects); Dermaptera (EARWIGS); Embioptera (WEB-SPINNERS); Psocoptera (BOOKLICE); Phthiraptera (LICE); Hemiptera (BUGS); and Thysanoptera (THRIPS).

2. Endopterygota. These are the insects with indirect metamorphosis, whose young are larvae. Most insects belong to this division. The wings, when present, develop inside the pupa. The division contains the following orders: Neuroptera (ANTLIONS AND LACEWINGS); Mecoptera (SCORPION FLIES); Megaloptera (ALDER FLIES); Lepidoptera (BUTTERFLIES AND MOTHS); Trichoptera (CADDIS FLIES); Diptera (FLIES); Siphonaptera (FLEAS); Hymenoptera (ANTS, BEES AND WASPS); Coleoptera (BEETLES); and STREPSIPTERANS. The largest Australian orders, with their approximate numbers of known species, are: Coleoptera, 19 200; Lepidoptera, 11 200; Hymenoptera, 8 800; Diptera, 6 800; Hemiptera, 3 700; and Orthoptera, 2 200.

Biology There are various possible reasons for the great diversity mentioned in the last

A. Woods

Privet hawk moth caterpillar, *Psilogramma nenephron*

section. The insects are the only animals, apart from the VERTEBRATES and certain other arthropods such as SPIDERS, that have successfully colonised the land. They have been able to do so because of their efficient external skeleton which gives them support, mobility and excellent waterproofing. On the land they found many niches that they were able to fill without competition from other kinds of animals. When the flowering plants appeared and diversified there was a parallel great burst of evolution among the insects. As small animals they have been able to use small habitats, such as a clod of dung or the inside of a seed, which other land animals could not use. They have not colonised the deep sea but they can be found virtually everywhere else, following many different life styles—plant-eating, feeding on decaying organic matter, parasitising other animals, or, as predators, capturing and eating their fellow insects.

See also diseases, human; diseases, livestock; insects, introduced

Further reading: Wigglesworth, V.B. *The Life of Insects.* Mentor Books, New York, 1968; CSIRO *The Insects of Australia.* Melbourne University Press, Melbourne, 1970 and *The Insects of Australia: Supplement 1974.* Melbourne University Press, Melbourne, 1974; Hughes, R.D. *Living Insects.* Collins, Sydney, 1974.

insects, introduced Several hundred, possibly thousands, of INSECTS have been introduced accidentally or intentionally into Australia, and have become established. They include useful species, such as the honey bee and BIOLOGICAL CONTROL agents from the orders Hymenoptera, Coleoptera and Diptera, but also many species that have become pests of crops, stored products and houses. Introduced species are often successful because they are introduced without their normal complement of natural enemies and diseases. It is probable that nearly all the most serious pests in Australia are introduced species. Examples of introduced insects may be found in almost all the major orders of insects. A few examples are listed below:

Blattodea (COCKROACHES) All the domestic species, such as *Blatella germanica, Periplaneta americana* and *P. australasiae;*

Psocoptera (BOOKLICE) *Liposcelis* species;

Phthiraptera (LICE) Almost all the species which attack man and his domestic animals;

Hemiptera (BUGS) Almost all APHIDS and many of the leaf-hoppers and scale insects which attack crops, such as the green vegetable bug, *Nezara viridula,* and the bed bug, *Cimex lectularius;*

Thysanoptera (THRIPS) Several species, including the cosmopolitan *Thrips tabaci* which attacks a wide range of plants;

Coleoptera (BEETLES) Almost all the species which infest stored grains and other materials —such as the flour beetles (*Tribolium* species), the grain weevils (*Sitophilus* species), the furniture beetle, *Anobium punctatum,* and the powder-post beetle, *Lyctus brunneus*—and

various plant pests, such as the banana weevil, *Cosmopolites sordidus*;
Siphonaptera (FLEAS) Most of the species which affect man and his domestic animals, such as the human flea, *Pulex irritans*, the dog flea, *Ctenocephalides canis*, the cat flea, *Ct. felis*, and the poultry flea, *Echidnophaga gallinacea*; Diptera (FLIES) Many species including various MOSQUITOES, (such as the yellow-fever mosquito, *Aedes aegypti*), the primary sheep BLOW-FLIES, *Lucilia cuprina* and *L. sericata*, and the HOUSE FLY, *Musca domestica*, and certain of its allies, such as the bushfly, *M. vetustissima*; Lepidoptera (BUTTERFLIES AND MOTHS) Various domestic and stored-product moths (such as the Indian meal moth, *Plodia interpunctella*, and the Mediterranean flour moth, *Anagasta kuhniella*), some agricultural pests (including the cabbage white butterfly, *Pieris rapae*, and the cotton bollworm, *Heliothis armigera*) and the valuable *Cactoblastis cactorum*, introduced for the biological control of prickly-pears.
Hymenoptera (ANTS, BEES AND WASPS) A wide variety of harmful insects (including the Sirex woodwasp, *Sirex noctilio*, the European wasp, *Vespula (Paravespula) germanica*, the Argentine ant, *Iridomyrmex humilis*, and the black house ant, *Technomyrmex albipes*), and several valuable species (such as the honey bee and parasitic wasps for biological control).

international relations *see* foreign relations

Interscan This is a new type of blind landing system for aircraft which was devised by scientists at the Division of Radiophysics of the CSIRO and adopted by the International Civil Aviation Authority in 1978 for worldwide implementation in aircraft and landing fields up to the year 2000. Developed with the aid of USA authorities, Interscan involves a scanning beam technique using microwaves and has many advantages over the Instrument Landing System used previously. Interscan makes use of techniques developed for studies in radio astronomy.

Inverell NSW (population 9 734 in 1981) A town in the NW slopes region, Inverell is located where the Gwydir Highway crosses the MACINTYRE RIVER, 69km W of GLEN INNES. It is 622km by road from Sydney, but by rail via a branch line from NARRABRI, and a further branch from MOREE, it is 820km from Sydney. At an elevation 583m above sea level, it is the centre of a rich wheat growing area, with a wide variety of other crops including oats, maize, barley, sorghum and linseed; sheep and cattle grazing, dairying and orcharding are also important. The average annual rainfall is 765mm, with a concentration in the spring and summer period from October to March. In addition to rural produce, Inverell district possesses rich and varied mineral resources—tin, sapphires, zircons and diamonds. There is a fossicking reserve about 19km NE of the town along the Nullamanna road where visitors

can try their luck searching for sapphires. At Tingha, 24km SE of Inverell, tin was discovered in 1871 and is still won by dredging from a nearby creek.
A number of buildings in Inverell and surrounding districts have been listed by the National Trust (NSW) as being important parts of the national heritage; the best-known is Inverell Homestead, about 6km N of the town on the road to Ashford; others in the town are the courthouse, the council chambers, the Masonic Temple and the Anglican Church. A pioneer village, with authentic buildings representative of the decades from the 1840s to the 1920s, has been constructed 2km SE of the town as a tourist attraction. The COPETON DAM on the GWYDIR RIVER, some 35km by road SE of Inverell, designed to provide irrigation water for farmlands downstream and to control the river flow, was completed in 1976.

Investigator Strait SA This channel lies between YORKE PENINSULA and KANGAROO ISLAND and is about 40km wide. It was named by the explorer Matthew FLINDERS after his ship the *Investigator*.

Ipswich QLD (population 72 310 in 1981) This city is on the Bremer River, 16km above its confluence with the Brisbane River; it is 40km by road WSW of Brisbane and is now part of the metropolis. It is a commercial and service centre for the farming and dairying districts of the LOCKYER, Fassifern and Brisbane River valleys; it is also a coal-mining centre and an important industrial city, with a wide range of manufacturing enterprises, including the State's largest railway workshop, a woollen mill, steel fabrication works, plywood and chipboard factories, a dairy processing plant, foundries and engineering workshops. The settlement of the area dates from 1827 when Patrick LOGAN established a lime kiln there, using convict labour. The lime was taken by boat along the Bremer and Brisbane Rivers for construction work in Brisbane. The original name for the settlement, Limestone, was changed by Governor George GIPPS in 1843 to Ipswich, after the English town of the same name in Suffolk. It developed as a river port for the sheep lands and farming areas of the DARLING DOWNS and the coastal valleys. A rail link to Brisbane was completed in 1865 and Ipswich is now a major rail junction with lines W to TOOWOOMBA and to the farming areas N and S. It is also an important focus of road transport routes, where the Warrego, Cunningham and Burnett Highways converge. The National Trust (QLD) has classified more than a dozen buildings in the district for preservation; these include the Rhondda colliery, Ipswich Grammar School, the courthouse and the Walter Burley GRIFFIN incinerator.
Further reading: Burger, A. *Ipswich Sketchbook.* Rigby, Adelaide, 1976.

Irish in Australia The 1981 census revealed that 67 738 persons resident in Australia had been born in Ireland—21 958 in

Northern Ireland and 45 780 in the Republic of Ireland. C.A. Price, a leading authority on multicultural affairs, in a study of the ethnic origins of the Australian population based on an eight-generation analysis, estimated that the total Irish component was equivalent to 2 527 100 persons in 1978. The Irish in Australia have had their greatest influence in the development of the country's social, political and educational institutions. They have also made an impact on Australian cultural life by sharing with others their sense of humour and love of music.
Early Irish convicts Irish convicts were transported to Australia in the early fleets of convict ships. Many were political prisoners who had participated in the Irish rebellions of 1798, 1801, 1802 and 1804, and some of these were transported to NSW without being given a trial, fair or otherwise. The authorities kept them apart from other convicts by setting up special camps for them because they were regarded as 'trouble-makers', but these camps provided the opportunity for the Irish to react in strength when promises that they would be granted amnesty were disregarded. In 1804 they organised the CASTLE HILL RISING, which only reinforced the traditional attitude that the Irish were trouble-makers and not desirable as immigrants, although the early political prisoners included Henry Fulton, a Church of England clergyman, James Meehan, who became deputy Surveyor-General in NSW, two Roman Catholic priests—Father Harold and Father O'Neil—and Michael Dwyer, who became Chief Constable of the PARRAMATTA district. Many of the educated Irish rebels later settled as landowners in the Bankstown area in Sydney, which became known as Irishtown.
In 1848 members of the Young Ireland Party were transported to TAS after taking part in an insurrection and in 1867 approximately 60 Fenians (named after the legendary warrior of Ancient Ireland, Fianna) were transported to WA. In Hobart in 1850 Patrick O'Donohoe started publishing the *Irish Exile* which argued for social justice.
The Irish campaign for social, educational and political justice The Irish, Celtic by race and most of them Roman Catholic by religion, had for centuries been regarded by people of Anglo-Saxon origin as inferior and had reacted with a lack of respect for power and a distrust of the law. Thus it is not surprising that in Australia the Irish campaigned for their interpretation of justice. In VIC, Sir John O'SHANASSY and the Roman Catholic bishops set up a pressure group in an attempt to gain their objectives, particularly State aid for their schools. The campaign suffered a setback in 1868 when a deranged Irishman tried to kill the Duke of Edinburgh. This deed aroused new resentment against the Irish, causing Sir Henry PARKES, for instance, to state that the Irish were not true Australian colonists and reinforcing his belief that it was necessary to maintain an English majority and a dominant Protestant influence in the colony. These attitudes were reflected in Parkes' education and immigration policies. His government's Edu-

cation Bill of 1880 withdrew all public support for denominational schools and made education 'Free, Compulsory and Secular', thus isolating the Irish-Catholic group completely and starting a new round of conflict. Most of the members of this group aligned themselves with the Australian Labor Movement and this alignment continued until the 1950s when many Roman Catholic supporters left the AUSTRALIAN LABOR PARTY to form the DEMO-CRATIC LABOR PARTY.

Patterns of settlement As a matter of historical fact, approximately half of Australia's Irish population were given equal opportunities because they lived in rural districts where they acquired land and became reasonably prosperous. The life-style of the rural Irish is preserved in short stories, poems and novels. The other half of the Irish population tended to be unskilled or semi-skilled labourers who clustered in the inner suburbs close to their place of work or near to transport. In earlier years the Irish Catholics tended to gather in districts such as Collingwood in Melbourne and Surry Hills in Sydney while the Protestant Irish settled in Woolloomooloo, Sydney; today, however, they are spread throughout the community.

Societies and organisations The Irish have been very active in forming societies and organisations and these tended to become the base for much sectarian conflict. St Patrick societies for the S Irish and Orangemen's groups for the N Irish were established as early as the 1840s, and St Patrick's Day (17 March) and the Battle of the Boyne (12 July) are still celebrated by many Irish Catholics and Irish Protestants respectively. The most important organisations now are the Irish National Association, based in Sydney, which acts as the headquarters for S Irish societies in Australia and New Zealand, and the Loyal Orange Institution of Australia which performs a similar function for Protestant Ulstermen. There are also Gaelic Athletics Clubs, an Irish Information Centre and branches of *Comhaltas Ceoltoiri Eireann* (a Gaelic term for a gathering of Irish musicians).

Irish heritage Apart from the Irish impact on Australia's political development and the struggle to gain State aid for Roman Catholic schools which has resulted in State aid for all denominational private schools, the Irish have made many other contributions to the Australian way of life. Irish music and dancing have been preserved, with State and national championships being held every year. Gaelic dances and concerts are held regularly, and Irish pipe bands, with pipers dressed in green jackets, traditional saffron-coloured kilts, and feathered bonnets like those worn in Limerick in 1573, are a common sight in processions. Gaelic football is one of the ancestors of AUSTRALIAN RULES football.

Notable Irish people in Australia In the political field people of Irish birth or descent include former State Governors Sir Richard BOURKE, Sir Richard MacDonnell and Sir George BOWEN, and Members of Parliaments William Charles WENTWORTH, Sir James

MARTIN, Peter LALOR, Sir Robert TORRENS, Sir George KINGSTON and the Hon. Margaret Guilfoyle. Roman Catholics who combined religion and politics included Dean John McEnroe, Cardinal P.F. Moran and Archbishop Daniel MANNIX. In the field of poetry notable figures include Bernard O'DOWD, Roderic Quinn, Christopher BRENNAN, Victor DALEY, Clarence James DENNIS and John O'Brien (Patrick HARTIGAN); and in theatre W.S. Lyster, James WILLIAMSON, Dion Boucicault and Eugenie Duggan. Professor Patrick O'Farrell, of the School of History of the University of New South Wales, is writing a two-volume history of the Irish in Australia, and Margaret Coffey has occasional Irish programmes on ethnic radio in Melbourne. Notable benefactors have included Samuel McCaughey and Sir J. Winthrop Hackett. Also among well-known men of Irish ancestry in Australian history are the bushrangers Ned KELLY and Ben HALL.
Further reading: Price, C.A. *Australian Immigration, A Bibliography and Digest.* Australian National University Press, Canberra, 1981.

iron and steel industry The Australian iron and steel industry, when viewed in the world context, is relatively small, producing annually between seven and eight million tonnes of both pig iron and steel, accounting for 1.1 per cent of total world steel and 1.4 per cent of world pig iron production (in 1980). However, in terms of the national economy, the industry is most important, as it not only supplies the total local market for pig iron and all but a small fraction of local steel needs, thereby making Australia almost self-sufficient in these commodities, but it also exports considerable quantities abroad. The statistics of production and exports are shown in Table 1. The total value of exports of iron and steel products in 1980 was $585 million. The major markets for Australian pig iron in 1980 were China (44.8 per cent of total exports), Taiwan (12.7 per cent), USA (8.8 per cent) and Japan (8.0 per cent).

The industry in Australia is dominated by one company—the BROKEN HILL PROPRIETARY COMPANY LIMITED (BHP)—a giant enterprise which, with its subsidiaries, employs over 56 000 workers and is Australia's biggest non-

government enterprise. Industrial plans and mining operations include integrated steel works at PORT KEMBLA and NEWCASTLE in NSW and at WHYALLA in SA; iron making and steel rolling activities at KWINANA in WA; a steel rolling mill at GEELONG in VIC; fabrication works at Sydney, Melbourne, Brisbane, Hobart, BELL BAY and Darwin; coal mines adjacent to the steel plants at Newcastle and Port Kembla, and near BLACKWATER and EMERALD in QLD; iron ore mines in the MIDDLE-BACK RANGES in SA and at KOOL-YANOBBING, YAMPI SOUND and MOUNT NEWMAN in WA; and limestone quarries at Marulan in NSW and at Coffin Bay, Rapid Bay and ARDROSSAN in SA.

The beginnings of the iron and steel industry in Australia date from the latter half of the 19th century when several attempts were made to establish iron smelting. The most important of these was at MITTAGONG in NSW where the building of a blast furnace began in 1848; for the following 30 years iron smelting was carried on intermittently at this plant but production costs were too high to compete with imported goods and it ceased production in 1877.

Another iron smelting operation of significance was established at LITHGOW in NSW; the Eskbank Iron Works Co. was formed in 1874 and two years later its Lithgow blast furnace came into production; although the enterprise faced several financial crises, it continued, with some changes in its structure and operations, for 60 years. During World War I and the subsequent building boom, the Lithgow works expanded to meet a rising demand for iron and steel products and gained a reputation for quality goods. In the 1920s the Lithgow plant consisted of two blast furnaces, three steel furnaces and separate mills for bar, rail and billet production. But high wages and freight costs remained basic problems and the local Lithgow coal proved unsuitable for the furnaces. It thus became necessary for the industry to be relocated at a coastal site where water transport could be used and where coal was available nearby. Port Kembla on the southern NSW coalfields was chosen as the new site, a new company called Australian Iron and Steel Ltd (AIS) was formed and construction began in 1927. As Port Kembla grew, so Lithgow declined: in 1928 pro-

Table 1

AUSTRALIAN PRODUCTION AND EXPORTS OF PIG IRON AND STEEL ('000t)

	1970	1973	1976	1978	1979	1980
Pig iron						
production	6 148	7 658	7 417	7 337	7 811	6 959
exports	310	853	698	685	643	515
Crude steel						
production	6 822	7 862	7 774	7 589	8 125	7 594
exports	226	771	1 538	1 007	611	306

Source: *Australian Mineral Industry Annual Review.* (1970-80) Australian Govt Publishing Service, Canberra.

duction of pig iron ceased and in 1931 the Lithgow mills were demolished.

It was also during the early decades of this century that BHP came into prominence in the iron and steel industry. The company was originally formed in 1885 to mine the rich silver-lead-zinc ores at BROKEN HILL in western NSW. As a natural outgrowth from these mining operations, the company established smelting works at PORT PIRIE on the E shore of SPENCER GULF in SA and, in order to operate this smelting plant, it needed an iron-stone flux. Thus BHP acquired the vast iron ore deposits in the Middleback Ranges, some 50km inland from the W shore of Spencer Gulf, and in the early years of this century turned its attention from mining and smelting ores to steel making. In 1911 the company decided to establish an iron and steel works at Newcastle at the mouth of the HUNTER RIVER in NSW, where good quality coking coal was available nearby and where the tidal estuary was suitable for the development of wharves and other port facilities to handle the ore shipments from SA and other cargoes. The growth of the company since those early days, even though it faced some serious financial crises and was given tariff protection in the 1920s, has been little short of spectacular.

The Depression of the 1930s had a marked impact on both Newcastle and Port Kembla but, although production was sharply reduced, the industry survived. Then in 1935 came a development of far-reaching importance: a merger was made between BHP and AIS which set the stage for an extensive programme of expansion and development of the industry. The output of steel products was increased substantially during World War II and, although the immediate post-war years saw a slowing down of Australian industrial development, the decades from 1950 on, as indicated in Table 2, showed a striking pattern of expansion.

Two major centres—Newcastle and Port Kembla—continue to dominate the industry. Both have integrated steel works producing a wide range of products, both are situated adjacent to coalfields, both are on tidewater locations, and both are surrounded by a com-

Courtesy of A.I.S. Canberra

Steel works at Port Kembla

plex of ancillary industries. Until 1953, Newcastle was the leading production centre, but since that year, Port Kembla has produced more pig iron and, since 1954, has surpassed Newcastle in steel production.

The development of Whyalla from the 1940s, when it was a shipping port for iron ore, made it the first example in Australia of an iron and steel plant away from a coalfield location. A marked feature of the expansion of the industry in recent decades has been the development at Kwinana, on a site S of Perth, to meet WA's increasing need for steel products.

See also manufacturing

Further reading: Wilson, J.L.J. (ed) 'Australian Steel' in *Current Affairs Bulletin.* (vol 12, no 9, August 1953); Hunter, A. (ed) *The Economics of Australian Industry—Studies in Environment and Structure.* Melbourne University Press, Melbourne, 1963; Shaw, J.H. & Emery, J.S. *Cities and Industries.* Jacaranda Press, Milton QLD, 1968; 'BHP in Australia', 'Outlook' (booklets) and *Annual Report.* BHP Co. Ltd, Melbourne, 1979.

ironbarks *see* Myrtaceae

Iron Monarch SA Located in the MIDDLE-BACK RANGES, some 54km NW of WHY-ALLA, this hill is the current main source of iron ore in the region. The ore is quarried by open-cut bench methods and transported to Whyalla where it is either used in the local iron and steel works or loaded for shipment.

iron ore The process of smelting iron ore was first developed in the Middle East in about 2700 BC but iron did not become commonly

used until nearly 1000 years later. The slow spread of iron making across Europe was ultimately accelerated by the Roman conquests, and was introduced into Australia and the Americas by European explorers. True steel, a carbon-iron alloy containing trace amounts of other elements, was unknown before the early 18th century. Iron and steel are ideal construction materials and have a virtually unlimited use in the modern world. They are used in the construction, automobile, railroad and ship-building industries and are worked, pressed, rolled or moulded into the thousands of items of daily use. Iron is an important constituent of haemoglobin, the pigment of red blood cells, and is thus essential for all vertebrates and many invertebrates.

Production The chief ores are hematite, limonite, magnetite and siderite. Pig iron, the material from which most iron and steel products are made, is produced by heating together iron ore, coke and limestone in a blast furnace.

In 1980, Australia produced 95.5 million tonnes of iron ore (10.8 per cent of the world production), of which some 80 million tonnes was exported. The production of ore in the various States is shown in Table 1. WA produced just over 94 per cent of Australia's iron ore in 1980, the main centres being in the PILBARA region—the HAMERSLEY mines (at MOUNT TOM PRICE and Paraburdoo), MOUNT NEWMAN mine (at Mt Whaleback), ROBE RIVER mine and the MOUNT GOLDSWORTHY mines (at Mt Goldsworthy, Shay Gap and Sunrise Hill). There are smaller though important sources of ore at YAMPI SOUND (KOOLAN and COCKATOO ISLANDS) and at KOOLYANOBBING. The production of iron ore in SA is centred on the MIDDLEBACK RANGES (IRON MONARCH, Iron Knob, Iron Baron and Iron Prince); in the NT at FRANCES CREEK; and in TAS at SAVAGE RIVER.

The principal market for ore exports is Japan, which in 1980 purchased 72 per cent of exported ore and iron ore pellets. The main exporting centres are DAMPIER, Cape Lambert, PORT HEDLAND and Koolan Is in WA. The 16.5 per cent of Australian iron ore production which is utilised within Australia forms the basic raw material for the nation's IRON AND STEEL INDUSTRY, with major plants at PORT KEMBLA and NEWCASTLE in NSW, at WHY-ALLA in SA and at KWINANA in WA.

Table 2

AUSTRALIAN PRODUCTION OF PIG IRON AND STEEL 1930-80 ('000t)

Year	Pig Iron	Steel
1930	315	321
1940	1 246	1 336
1950	1 098	1 241
1960	2 660	3 577
1970	6 148	6 822
1975	7 475	7 843
1978	7 337	7 589
1979	7 811	8 125
1980	6 959	7 594

Source: *Australian Mineral Industry Annual Review* (1970-80). Australian Govt Publishing Service, Canberra.

Table 1

IRON ORE PRODUCTION IN AUSTRALIA 1970-81 (× '000t)

State	1970	1978	1979	1980	1981
TAS	1 949	2 093	2 212	2 132	2 234
SA	7 706	2 376	2 623	2 498	2 456
WA	40 326	78 665	86 882	90 904	79 971
NT	1 208	—	—	—	—
TOTAL	51 189	83 134	91 717	95 534	84 661

Source: *Australian Mineral Industry Annual Review.* (1970-81) Australian Govt Publishing Service, Canberra.

BHP

Surge piles seen from the top of the plant building, Newman iron ore mine

The total known world resources of iron ore are probably in the range of 750 to 850 billion tonnes, of which 215 billion are considered recoverable at present. This is probably adequate to supply the estimated demand into the 22nd century. A forecast of world requirements for iron ore indicates an annual growth rate of three per cent to a demand of 1.1 billion tonnes in the year 2000. The time/price relationship for iron ore, in terms of the constant 1968 dollar, shows a slight rise in price between 1980 and 2000. This suggests that iron should not be replaced by other materials on the score of pricing and that the technology involved in producing iron and steel from the ore will need to improve to ward off competition from other materials.
Further reading: see under minerals and mining.

ironwood The name ironwood has been bestowed on several trees from different families because of the toughness of the timber. *Acacia estrophiolata* (family MIMOSACEAE), found in the centre of the continent, is an example.

irrigation Over much of the Australian continent, rainfall is low and periods of drought are common. In many regions there is a marked seasonal concentration of the rainfall and hence the flow of rivers is variable throughout the year. These environmental difficulties have posed problems since the early days of rural development and have emphasised the need to store water for both domestic and farm use. Some early settlers, whose properties included stream frontages, constructed small weirs and dams to ensure water supplies for their livestock and to divert water for the irrigation of crops and grazing lands. These private river diversions were small-scale operations, but the idea that such procedures could be applied on a more extensive scale required little imagination, since it had been successfully employed for centuries by ancient civilisations in, for example, Egypt amd Mesopotamia.

In the latter part of the 19th century, two factors spurred the development of irrigation in Australia: drought and the work of Alfred DEAKIN. During the 1870s and early 1880s a series of damaging droughts, particularly in VIC, made rural settlers increasingly conscious of the need for water conservation. The VIC government passed a number of Acts in the 1870s under which a series of private irrigation trusts were established, but these were still

small enterprises, lacking the capital and the expertise to work effectively, and in some cases the developments were undertaken in country unsuited to irrigation. It was at this time that the impact of the politician, Alfred Deakin, became significant; he forcefully advocated the great possibilities of irrigation, visited places overseas where irrigated farming had been successful, and invited the CHAFFEY BROTHERS to come to Australia from California to select land suitable for irrigation. As a result of this, the Chaffeys started the irrigation settlements at MILDURA in VIC and RENMARK in SA in 1887. In the same year, the Wartook Dam was constructed in the GRAMPIANS of western VIC; this was the first step in the development of the WIMMERA-MALLEE water-supply scheme which now includes 10 main storage points and over 16 000km of channels.

The decades around the turn of the century saw the beginnings of several major irrigation developments. In 1900 Mr. (later Sir) Samuel McCaughey started his crop irrigation experiments at YANCO on the MURRUMBIDGEE RIVER

and these led eventually to the construction of BURRINJUCK DAM and the development of the MURRUMBIDGEE IRRIGATION AREAS. In WA, the construction of the GOLDFIELDS WATER SUPPLY scheme commenced in 1898 and MUNDARING RESERVOIR was completed in 1902; though this scheme was designed primarily to provide water for KALGOORLIE, it was subsequently expanded and extended to supply water to many rural towns and farming areas. Also in WA, the irrigation scheme on the plains of SWANLAND was started with the building of the dam on the HARVEY RIVER in 1916.

In the same era, discussions between the three States (NSW, VIC and SA) and the Commonwealth government about co-ordinated development of the MURRAY RIVER waters led to the establishment of the River Murray Commission in 1917 and the subsequent construction of the HUME DAM on the upper Murray, Lake Victoria storage point near the SA border, YARRAWONGA and TORRUMBARRY Weirs, several other weirs and locks on the Murray

Table 1

MAJOR RESERVOIRS STORING WATER FOR IRRIGATION

Dam	Year completed (enlarged)	Location	Capacity ('000ML)
NSW:			
Eucumbene	1958	Eucumbene River, a Snowy tributary	4 807
Hume	1936 (1961)	Murray River, on NSW/VIC border	3 035
Menindee Lakes	1960	Darling River, near Menindee	1 794
Burrendong	1967	Macquarie River, near Wellington	1 680
Blowering	1968	Tumut River	1 628
Copeton	1976	Gwydir River	1 364
Wyangala	1936 (1971)	Lachlan River	1 220
Burrinjuck	1927 (1956)	Murrumbidgee River	1 026
Lake Victoria	1928	Murray River, near SA border	680
Keepit	1960	Namoi River, near Gunnedah	426
Glenbawn	1958	Hunter River, near Scone	360
VIC:			
Dartmouth	1979	Mitta Mitta River	3 700
Eildon	1927 (1955)	Upper Goulburn River	3 390
Waranga	1905 (1917, 1926)	Near Rushworth	411
Mokoan	1971	Near Benalla	365
Rocklands	1953	Glenelg River	336
Eppalock	1964	Campaspe River	312
Glenmaggie	1927 (1958)	Macalister River	190
QLD:			
Fairbairn	1972	Nogoa River, a Mackenzie tributary	1 440
Fred Haigh	1975	Kolan River, near Gin Gin	586
Ross River	1974	Near Townsville	417
Tinaroo Falls	1958	Barron River	407
Glenlyon	1977	Pine Creek, near Stanthorpe	254
Wuruma	1968	Nogo River, near Eidsvold	194
Koombooloomba	1961 (1965)	Tully River	201
WA:			
Lake Argyle	1971	Ord River, near Wyndham	5 658
Wellington	1933 (1944, 1960)	Collie River	185

Note: some of the dams listed here serve several purposes: hydro-electricity generation, irrigation storage, flood control, urban supplies and livestock watering; those designed solely for the purpose of hydro-electricity generation (for example, Jindabyne and Tantangara Dams in NSW) and those designed solely for urban supplies (for example, Warragamba Dam in NSW, Upper Yarra Dam in VIC and Serpentine Dam in WA) have not been included in this table.
Source: Publications of the Queensland Irrigation and Water Supply Commission; New South Wales Water Resources Commission: The State Rivers and Water Supply Commission of Victoria: Public Works Department, Western Australia.

and five barrages across the river mouth in SA. During the same period, several major irrigation developments were undertaken in VIC: the State Rivers and Water Supply Commission was set up in 1905 to take over the former irrigation trusts, the WARANGA RESERVOIR was completed in 1910 (enlarged in 1936), the EILDON RESERVOIR on the GOULBURN RIVER was built between 1915 and 1927 (modified in 1930 and again in the 1950s), several other storage points were constructed as part of the Wimmera-Mallee project, and the MACALISTER RIVER irrigation district near MAFFRA in GIPPSLAND was first settled in 1926. The development of irrigated farming and orcharding in northern VIC by the later expansion of the Goulburn Valley scheme and the construction of channels linking it to the LODDON and CAMPASPE schemes made this section of VIC Australia's largest irrigation area. The SNOWY MOUNTAINS SCHEME, constructed after World War II, made more irrigation water available in inland regions by the diversion of the SNOWY RIVER into the Murray and Murrumbidgee. An agreement between NSW and QLD came into effect in 1947 for the control and use of the waters of the MACINTYRE RIVER and its tributaries, which form part of the interstate boundary; under this agreement, the Glenlyon Dam on Pike Creek was completed in 1977.

The major dams storing water for irrigation are listed in Table 1. The main irrigation schemes in the States are listed below.

Victoria In the Goulburn-Campaspe-Loddon scheme the principal storage points are the Eildon and Waranga Reservoirs; products from the irrigation district include fruits, wool, fat lambs and dairy produce. In the Murray scheme water is diverted from the Murray by the Yarrawonga and Torrumbarry Weirs, carried by gravitational flow in channels and canals, and used for irrigation of dairy farms, orchards, vineyards, market gardens and on grazing properties for raising lambs and beef cattle. The Mildura scheme and other schemes in that section of the Murray are supplied by pumping water from the river for the irrigation of vineyards and citrus orchards. The Southern scheme, located in the Maffra, Heyfield and SALE districts, is mainly for the irrigation of dairying lands; the reservoir for the scheme is GLENMAGGIE DAM on the Macalister River. The Wimmera-Mallee scheme, with storages in the Grampians, provides water for livestock and urban purposes, as well as for irrigated pastures and cereals.

New South Wales Most of the larger irrigation schemes are concentrated along the Murray and Murrumbidgee. There are nine main irrigation areas in the region: Yanco, Mirrool (these two are commonly called the Murrumbidgee Irrigation Areas), Coomealla, Curlwaa, Hay, Tullakool, Buronga, Mallee Cliffs and Coleambally. Smaller areas are: along the LACHLAN RIVER (a tributary of the Murrumbidgee), served by WYANGALA DAM, Lake Cargelligo and Lake Brewster; the HUNTER RIVER valley, served by GLENBAWN

DAM; on the NAMOI RIVER, using underground water as well as that from KEEPIT DAM; the lower DARLING RIVER, served by the MENINDEE lakes storage system; on the MACQUARIE RIVER, with BURRENDONG DAM as the storage point; and along the GWYDIR RIVER valley, served by COPETON DAM. Also in NSW there are extensive irrigation 'districts' (as distinct from 'areas'), particularly along the Murray, where water is available for livestock and domestic supplies, together with some limited irrigation of pastures and crops.

Queensland The greater part of the area irrigated in QLD is by individual private pumping plants which take supplies from streams or underground sources, rather than from channel systems with large headwater reservoirs, as in other States. There are, however, some irrigation areas where water supply is reticulated by gravitational channels: in the DAWSON RIVER valley for cotton and grain crops; in the BURDEKIN RIVER area for the irrigation of sugar cane, rice and seed crops; in the MAREEBAH district for tobacco growing; in the ST GEORGE district along the BALONNE RIVER for the cultivation of cotton, soya beans and cereals; and in the BUNDABERG area for irrigation of sugar cane crops.

A dethridge wheel used to measure irrigation water flow

South Australia The major irrigation areas in SA are concentrated along the Murray, using water pumped from the river for citrus, and stone and vine fruit cultivation. Irrigation developments along the Murray include the Renmark, BARMERA, LOXTON, BERRI and WAIKERIE irrigation areas. On the lower Murray, reclaimed swamp land is irrigated for intensive dairying. In other parts of the State, notably on the N Adelaide Plains and the Padthaway district of the SE, considerable areas are irrigated from underground sources for market gardening and for pastures, seed crops and vines in the SE.

Western Australia Along the coastal plain S of Perth, irrigation has been developed in the Harvey, Waroona, Collie and Preston Valley districts for dairying, stock raising and vegetable growing, using water from dams in the DARLING RANGE. Since the 1930s, CARNARVON has been a centre of irrigated tropical agriculture, producing bananas, citrus fruits and vegetables, and utilising underground water near the mouth of the GASCOYNE RIVER. The ORD RIVER scheme in the KIMBERLEYS, developed in recent years, is the major irrigation project of the State. It has been designed to

irrigate an area of 72 000ha in WA and the NT. In 1971, the dam on the Ord River was completed; cotton was initially the principal crop, but serious problems were encountered in its cultivation; subsequently, other crops including rice, oil seeds and grain sorghum have been grown with limited success, and some irrigated pastures for cattle fattening have been developed.

Two major problems, concerning irrigation developments, have emerged in recent years: the first is an economic one, the second is a physical environmental one. The economic problem has been centred on cost/benefit studies of irrigation projects which have shown that the capital investment and other costs of these schemes have been exceedingly high in relation to the benefits which have accrued. The second problem is concerned with increasing salinity in many irrigated areas, which has made the top soils too salty for crop, orchard or pasture cultivation. This remains a serious issue, especially in arid regions, such as the middle Murray, where large areas have been affected by high salinity. Methods to combat it, such as deep drainage systems to carry off excess irrigation water, have been tried with some success.

Isaacs, Sir Isaac Alfred (1855-1948) Governor-General. Sir Isaac was the first Australian-born Governor-General of the Commonwealth. The son of a Jewish tailor who had migrated to Australia from London, he was born in Melbourne and educated at State schools in the VIC towns of Yakandandah and BEECHWORTH. After working as a pupil-teacher in the latter town, he was appointed a clerk in the Crown Law Department in Melbourne, won a scholarship to Melbourne University, graduated brilliantly in law and became prominent at the Bar. Elected to the Legislative Assembly in 1892, he became Solicitor-General in a succession of Liberal Ministries. He was a delegate to the federal convention of 1897-98, putting a comparatively radical point of view. In 1901 he became a member of the first Commonwealth Parliament.

Isaacs' political views were similar in many respects to those of the Labor Party, but he was too strong an individualist to have submitted to its caucus system. He became Attorney-General under DEAKIN, and in 1906 was appointed to the bench of the High Court, where he and Henry Bournes HIGGINS tended towards a more liberal interpretation of Commonwealth powers than had been shown during the preceding few years of the Court's existence. He remained on the bench until his appointment as Governor-General, becoming Chief Justice during his final year. Prime Minister SCULLIN's nomination of Isaacs as Governor-General was controversial since Isaacs had been active in party politics; many people, indeed, felt that no Australian-born person of sufficient eminence to be considered for the position would be able both to rise above the turmoil of party politics and to convince the public that he was so doing. However, while attending the Imperial Conference in London in 1930, Scullin was able to persuade King George V to accept the nomination, and Isaacs served with distinction as Governor-General until 1936.

Further reading: Cowen, Z. *Isaac Isaacs.* Oxford University Press, Melbourne, 1967.

Isle of Wight disease *see* mites

Isoptera *see* termites

Italians in Australia

The 1981 census revealed that 275 883 persons resident in Australia had been born in Italy. C.A. Price, a leading authority on multicultural affairs, in a study of ethnic origins of the Australian population based on an eight-generation analysis, estimated the total Italian component to be equivalent to 595 300 persons in 1978. Their ethnic culture is well preserved by the strength of old traditions and family relationships. The Italian family is an extremely strong unit and is much wider than the Australian marital family in that it includes uncles, aunts, cousins and their families. Prior to 1870 the area of Italy consisted of a network of small States, sometimes quite independent of each other, and most Italian migrants have never had a 'national feeling' about Italy, but identify with the village from whence they came. In Australia, the Italian community is divided into regional groups which compete with one another and this fragmentation reduces its potential strength and influence in the Australian community at large. The family bond reinforced by regional bonds forms the basis for chain migration.

Chain migration This term refers to the system whereby individual sponsors help relatives and friends from their village or region in Italy to emigrate to Australia. Well-established chains have resulted in many hundreds of persons migrating from one region in Italy to settle in the same district as the sponsors in Australia and this has resulted in the concentration of immigrant Italian communities in large cities as well as in selected rural areas. In contrast to chain migration, affluent individuals who finance their own travel tend to disperse through the community.

Immigration before 1900 The early Italian migrants to Australia were mostly political exiles or adventurers, some of whom returned to Italy. Giuseppe Garibaldi, the Italian liberator, came to Australia to visit them in 1853; his son, Ricciotti Garibaldi, lived in Melbourne from 1877 to 1881, and his grandson, Giuseppe Garibaldi, who was born in Melbourne in 1879, returned to Italy and became a brigadier-general in the Italian Army in World War I.

A small group of Italians settled in WA in 1846 and the gold rushes of the 1850s brought quite a number to NSW and VIC. Italians tended to settle in different parts of the colony but during the 1880s a group of 400 Italian farmers took up land between the RICHMOND and CLARENCE Rivers in northern NSW to form the first Italian community, called 'New Italy', and there they grew grapes and vegetables and engaged in timber-felling. In 1890 a small group of Italians from Piedmont and Lombardy formed an ethnic community in the Wide Bay district in QLD. The QLD government provided assisted passages for several hundred agricultural labourers to work as cane-cutters. Many of these Italian labourers subsequently managed to acquire farms and thus encouraged the further migration of Italians, and so another Italian community was formed.

Immigration between 1900 and 1947 The number of Italians migrating to Australia in this period was not large; they paid their own way to Australia and then sponsored their families and friends in the early pattern of chain migration. The majority of these people lived in the rural areas.

Immigration since 1947 The post-war influx of Italians came from the S or from poorer areas of N cities. A large number were given assisted passages and they came to find work, economic security and opportunities for their children. The post-war migrants have concentrated in the major cities and current census data indicate that the vast majority of Italians now live in Melbourne, Sydney, Brisbane, Perth and Adelaide, where they tend to be lower-paid, semi-skilled or unskilled workers and live in poorer, inner suburbs and middle-distant suburbs. Italians tend to settle close to their fellow countrymen and desire easy access to shops, cafes and clubs run by their compatriots. There are doctors, lawyers and other professional people among first- and second-generation Italian migrants and many Italians own small factories, craft enterprises, concreting businesses, shops and restaurants. Some have founded large companies such as Transfield Engineering, Pioneer Concrete and the switchmaking firm, Electric Power Transmission.

Settlement in rural areas While most Italian immigrants have settled in towns, there are significant groups who have settled in the cane growing districts of northern QLD, in the MURRUMBIDGEE IRRIGATION AREAS of NSW, in the OVENS RIVER valley in VIC, in mining areas such as KALGOORLIE and in fishing areas such as FREMANTLE in WA.

In the GRIFFITH-LEETON area in NSW, the Italians grow either citrus and stone fruits or vegetables. The majority came from Treviso province of N Italy by means of chain migration. Those who have not engaged in primary production have become tradesmen and businessmen in the towns of Griffith, Leeton and WANGARATTA. Elderly Italian farmers tend to retire to the towns and leave the farming to the younger members of the family.

More than 90% of the Italians who have settled in QLD have come from Sicily and from the N regions of Piedmont, Lombardy and Veneto. In the N part of the State they engage in cane farming and in the S they grow fruit or tobacco. In the Ovens Valley the Italians are mostly tobacco farmers. In all areas Italian farm owners prefer to employ Italian labourers.

Italian immigrants disembarking at Melbourne

Italian heritage The contribution of Italian culture is obvious from the wide variety of food and wine of Italian origin in delicatessens and restaurants, the Italian clothes and fine Italian leathergoods and accessories appearing in boutiques, and television programmes such as 'Variety Italian Style'. The Italians have long contributed to the performing arts in Australia and the Italian tenor Lamberto Furlan and his wife Beryl (soprano) are members of the Australian Opera Company. The Transfield Art Prize was funded by companies owned by Italians who had become naturalised Australians and was awarded annually from 1960 to 1971. In 1973 it was replaced by an international art exhibition to be held every second year in Sydney. Melbourne has an Italian Institute of Culture, and the Dante Alighieri Society has branches in all States and aims to bring Italian culture and language to Australians and keep migrants in touch with their own traditions. Since 1969 the Italian government has provided funds to set up schools so that children of Italian parentage will be able to speak, read and write in Florentine Italian and this has encouraged Australian State Departments of Education to hold classes in Italian on Saturday mornings. Only a few Australian secondary schools teach the Italian language as a subject. There are at least six Italian periodicals published in Australia, including *La Fiamma*, founded in 1947 and published twice a week, and *Il Globo*, founded in 1961 and published weekly. Sporting and social clubs encourage contact between Italians and Australians.

Matraville in Sydney was named after James Mario Matra who had been with James COOK when he first explored the E coast of Australia and who first proposed in London that a settlement be made in NSW. Matra's proposed settlement was not for convicts but to accommodate Empire loyalists dispossessed by the loss of the American colonies. There is some doubt whether Matra was in fact Italian, but Italians claim him as a countryman and also as the real father of Australia.

Other notable Italians in Australia These include Raffaello Carboni, Peter LALOR's lieutenant at the EUREKA STOCKADE; Captain Francisco Nicola Rossi, Superintendent of Police in NSW in 1825; Dr Thomas Henry Fiaschi, honorary surgeon at Sydney Hospital, president of the NSW section of the British Medical Association, director of the first Australian hospital in the BOER WAR and a

developer of vineyards on the HAWKESBURY and at MUDGEE; Peter Baracchi, government astronomer of VIC; Carlo Catani, who as chief engineer of the VIC Public Works Department developed the St. Kilda waterfront and extended the Botanic Gardens; Ettore Checci, who did exploratory work on the upper MURRAY RIVER system; artist A. Dattilo Rubbo, who ran one of the leading art schools in Sydney; Alberto Zelman, founder of the first permanent symphony orchestra in Melbourne; Jerome Carandini, operatic conductor and musician; Fred Schepisi, producer of Australian films; Sir Raphael Cilento, an authority on tropical diseases; Jim Bayutti, Qantas director, the first 'New Australian' to be offered such a government appointment; Dr Paolo Totaro, chairman of the NSW Ethnic Affairs Commission; and Frank Pangallo, NSW Ethnic Affairs Commissioner. On the political scene the Italian groups in Australia are identified with Tony Luchetti, former journalist and MHR; Dr Dick Klugman, former medical practitioner and MHR; the Hon. Frank Calabro, NSW MLC; and the Hon. George Paciullo, NSW MLA and Parliamentary Secretary on Ethnic Affairs.
Further reading: Pyke, N.O.P. 'An Outline History of Italian Immigration into Australia' in *Australian Quarterly.* (vol 20, September 1948); Price, C.A. *Southern Europeans in Australia.* Oxford University Press, Melbourne, 1963; Barzini, L. *The Italians.* Penguin Books, London, 1968; Price, C.A. *Australian Immigration, A Bibliography and Digest.* Australian National University Press, Canberra, 1981.

J

jabiru There are 17 species of storks in the world, belonging to the family Ciconiidae, but only one occurs in Australia. Known as the jabiru, *Xenorhynchus asiaticus* (length and height 1.2m; legs 60cm; bill 30cm), this usually uncommon species has long, bright red legs, black and white plumage and a massive black bill. It ranges from India and South-East Asia to N and E Australia, where it frequents coastal and inland waters, feeding on fish and small aquatic animals and insects. Generally sedentary, though sometimes nomadic, the jabiru builds its nests high up in trees; the nests are large collections of sticks and twigs, lined with grass and bark.

jacana *see* waders

jackeroo This is an Australian term for a young man employed on a sheep or cattle grazing property. He works with the station hands, somewhat like an apprentice, learning the various jobs involved in handling the livestock and in running the property. The origin of the name is uncertain, though perhaps it came from the phrase 'Jack Raw', applied by other employees on the property to a lad who was new and inexperienced at livestock work. During World War II, when many young male rural workers were in the armed forces, the term 'jillaroo' was applied to young females who took farming jobs in rural areas.

Jackson, Marjorie (1931-) Athlete. She was born in the NSW country town of COFFS HARBOUR and moved to the NSW coal-mining town of LITHGOW as a child. In 1952, she became the first Australian woman to win an Olympic gold medal in athletics. She won the 100m sprint, equalling the world record, and the 200m, setting a new world record. Australians gave the 'Lithgow Flier', a remarkable homecoming: she was provided with a police escort for the 240km-long journey from Sydney to Lithgow; a song was written to commemorate her achievements, and she flew to Melbourne in a plane named specially the *Lithgow Flier*, for a triumphal tour. In the 1954 Commonwealth Games she again won the 100m and 200m events, but at the 1956 Olympics, she won only bronze medals in these two events. In 1953 she married Peter Nelson, who had represented Australia in cycling at the 1952 Olympic Games.

Jamestown SA (population 1 384 in 1981) This country town is located in the mid-N of the State, 66km inland from PORT PIRIE and 50km NE of CRYSTAL BROOK. It is a railway town, linked to Adelaide by a number of routes. At an elevation of 453m above sea level, Jamestown is a service centre for a district where grain growing, cattle grazing, timber-getting and sheep raising are the primary pursuits. The town was named after the James family, who were pioneer settlers in the area.

Jansz, Willem (*c*1570-?) Dutch colonial official and explorer. As related in the entry on DISCOVERY, in 1606 Jansz sailed the small ship *Duyfken* along the W coast of CAPE YORK Peninsula, as far S as Cape Keerweer (Turn Again) near the modern mining town of WEIPA. As far as is known he and his crew were the first Europeans to see part of the Australian coastline. However, the voyage had no important results. Jansz later commanded other Dutch vessels, and in 1618 landed briefly on the coast of WA in the Exmouth Gulf region. In the following year he became a member of the Council of the Indies, and from 1623 to 1627 he served as Governor of Banda, but very little is known of the remainder of his life.

Japanese in Australia The 1981 census revealed that 8 060 persons resident in Australia had been born in Japan; the majority were living in NSW. In 1983 it was estimated that there were another 20 000 temporary residents in Australia who were staying for varying periods of time. The city of Sydney has the largest Japanese community and 70 large Japanese firms, including Mitsui, Mitsubishi, C. Itoh and Shoji Sumitomo.

The first recorded Japanese settler to come to Australia was Rikinosuke Sakagawa, an acrobat, who arrived in 1871. He married an Australian, became a citizen and a landowner and performed in a circus which travelled throughout QLD for 46 years. For some 110 years there have been Japanese pearl divers working in the fields off WA. In 1880 the QLD government brought a group of Japanese pearl divers to work at THURSDAY ISLAND; by 1896 there were 720 Japanese migrants working there and another 1000 working in the canefields in QLD. However, the Japanese government maintained a very tight rein on emigration to Australia and in 1897 prohibited emigration to QLD for pearling and later prohibited emigration to any part of QLD. After 1901 the federal immigration policy restricted Japanese immigration and there were only small communities of Japanese residing in QLD, the NT and WA. Since the end of World War II, when 600 war brides came to Australia, the number of permanent residents has increased. The post-war Japanese migrants were mainly academics, research officers, teachers and librarians.

Much of the technology associated with Australia's major ship-building industry in WHYALLA in SA has come from the Japanese. The importance of Japan to Australia is also illustrated by the existence of the Japanese Society of Sydney, *Nihonjinkai*, and of Japanese restaurants in Australian cities, the establishment of a school for children of Japanese who are temporary residents and the increase in business and tourist links. The Japanese broadcasting corporation, NHK, has been established in Sydney and this enables direct broadcasts to Japan through the Japanese networks.

jarrah *see* forestry

jazz Despite its remoteness from the American origins of jazz, Australia has produced noteworthy jazz musicians. One of the earliest was Frank Coughlan, a trombone and trumpet player from Glen Innes NSW, who featured on the first professional jazz record made in Australia, 'Milenburg Joys' (1925).

Notable early bands include Graeme Bell's Dixieland Band (later named the Australian Jazz Band and later again the All Stars) and the Port Jackson Jazz Band. In 1957 Ray Price left the Port Jackson Jazz Band to form, with Bob Barnard and Dick Hughes, his own trio (later quartet). These three names remain prominent in Australian jazz.

Other musicians of note, some in traditional jazz, some in modern, include Col Noland, Graeme Lyall, John McCarthy, Errol Buddle, Bryce Rohde and Don Burrows. Among bands, the Daly-Wilson Big Band and Galapagos Duck are of particular note.

Jazz has a firm following in Australia, which unlike that of popular music is drawn from all age groups. It is played regularly on radio, particularly by the ABC, and many restaurants and hotels present jazz bands live to attract patrons.

jellies, comb *see* ctenophores

jellyfish *see* coelenterates

Jenolan Caves NSW This series of limestone caves SW of the BLUE MOUNTAINS, 182km W of Sydney and 77km from KATOOMBA, contains many fine examples of underground limestone formations. There is some uncertainty about the discovery of the caves: one story is that, in the 1830s, the caves were used as a hideout by a bushranger named McKeown, who robbed travellers along the Western Road; in 1838, one of his victims, James Whalan, set out to capture him and duly did so, after tracking him into the hitherto unexplored Jenolan area. Whalan thus discovered the caves, investigated some of them and until 1867 acted as an honorary guide. In 1865 the area was declared a reserve; in 1894 the cave system was illuminated by electricity and in 1898 Caves House was built to provide accommodation for visitors. The caves remain a major tourist attraction, and an area of 2430ha surrounding the site is a flora and fauna reserve. The name Jenolan was taken from the Aboriginal name for a mountain in the district.

Jerilderie NSW (population 1 075 in 1981) A small town on the Newell Highway, 653km SW of Sydney (via WAGGA WAGGA), 108km SW of NARRANDERA, and 93km NE of DENILIQUIN (via the Riverina Highway). Situated on Billabong Creek, which drains into the MURRAY RIVER system, it is surrounded by sparsely settled flat plains of the western RIVERINA region, where the principal rural activity is sheep grazing for wool; there are several prominent sheep studs in the district. The town is the administrative centre of the Jerilderie Shire, which covers an area of 3 400km^2 and, at the census of 1981, had a population of only 2 404. Perhaps Jerilderie's greatest claim to fame is that the bushranger Ned KELLY and his gang raided the township in 1879 and robbed the bank. The old telegraph office, where the gang cut the wires, is now occupied by the local Historical Society.

Jervis Bay NSW An inlet on the S coast, located SE of NOWRA, Jervis Bay is some 190km from Sydney. A portion of the bay and the adjoining lands were acquired in 1915 by the Commonwealth from the State of NSW and thereby became part of the ACT. Initially, it was planned that this should become a port for Canberra, but the development has been confined to the establishment of a naval college (HMAS *Creswell*) and some navy in-

The Lucas Cave Exhibition Chamber in the Jenolan Caves, central western region of NSW

NSW Dept of Tourism

stallations. The bay is a popular holiday area, with Huskisson on the W shore as the main tourist centre. The S and W parts of the Territory have been declared a nature reserve (4 420ha) so as to preserve the heathlands and forests of the coastal zone. S of the bay are the popular resorts of St George's Basin and Sussex Inlet.

Jews in Australia The 1981 census revealed that 62 126 persons resident in Australia were identified as Hebrew in religion, that is, followers of Judaism. C.A. Price, a leading authority on multicultural affairs, in a study of the ethnic origins of the Australian population based on an eight-generation analysis, estimated the total Jewish component to be equivalent to 120 000 persons in 1978. Jews in Australia are a unique minority group because they are fused together by a memory that reaches back through the centuries to the events of their Hebrew Bible. The majority of Australians are Christians. The Jews in Australia have come from a variety of cultural backgrounds and countries; in many of the countries of origin anti-Semitism was common. There has never been any particular discrimination against Jews in Australia at an official level and since the introduction of responsible government Jews have always had the right to vote and many have been elected to the various Parliaments. However, there has been some disquiet felt among the Jewish community because of anti-Israeli propaganda.

History of Jewish migration About 1000 Jews of British origin were transported to Australia as convicts, including eight, and possibly more, on the FIRST FLEET in 1788. One of the first arrivals, Esther Abrahams, who was transported for seven years because she was alleged to have stolen a small piece

of black lace, married Lieutenant-Colonel George JOHNSTON, who later was Lieutenant-Governor of the colony. Another Jew on the First Fleet, John Harris, became Australia's first policeman. Many of the transported Jews became successful businessmen, a few could be regarded as disreputable personalities and one became a bushranger, the only Jewish bushranger on record. Known as 'Teddy the Jewboy', he terrorised the HUNTER RIVER valley until he was captured and hanged.

The composition of Australian Jewry began to change from being predominantly Anglo-Saxon with the gold rushes in the 1850s when there was massive immigration of German and Austrian Jews. Russian and Polish Jews arrived in the 1880s and 1890s as a result of persecutions and again following the 1905 Russian revolution. Jewish welfare organisations estimate that more than 38 600 Jews migrated to Australia between 1938 and 1971. This number included Jews who escaped from Hitler's persecution before the beginning of World War II; displaced persons mostly of Polish origin, with some German and Austrian Jews after the war; Jews escaping from the Communist take-over in Czechoslovakia and the Hungarian uprising in 1956; Egyptian Jews after the Suez crisis; and English Jews from South Africa and the USA following racial troubles in those two countries.

Contribution of Jews to the development of Australia The contribution of Jews to the development of Australia is obvious from the selected list below of notable Jews in Australia. In addition, there are many Jews with the status of professor in the various universities; they are well represented in all the professions but particularly in medicine and law. Jews who migrated from the European continent introduced continental delicatessen shops, restaurants and espresso cafes. They also created many new industries in the textile and fur trade, they have participated in development and business companies and there have been many mayors and senior public servants. Jewish publications in Australia include the *Journal and Proceedings of the Australian Jewish Historical Society* (twice yearly), the *Bridge* (quarterly), the *Australian Jewish News* (weekly in Melbourne) and the *Australian Jewish Times* (weekly in Sydney).

Notable Jews in Australia include:
Art: Judy Cassab, Cedric Emanuel, Ruth Faerber, Maxmilian Feuerring, E. Phillips FOX, Sali HERMAN, Desiderius ORBAN, Joe Rose and Lori Sachs.
Defence: Sir John MONASH, who became Supreme Commander of the Australian forces in France, and Major-General Paul A. Cullen.
Government: It is not possible to list all Jews who have been elected to the various Parliaments in Australia but Saul Samuel, one of the first Jewish magistrates, was the first Jew elected to the NSW Legislative Council in 1854 and was elected to the NSW Legislative Assembly in 1859. After many years as a Minister of the Crown he was Agent-General for NSW in London and on his retirement was created a baronet. Lionel Samson was the first Jew nominated to the WA Legislative Council in 1849. Sir Isaac Alfred ISAACS was the first Australian-born Governor-General and Sir Zelman COWEN was Governor-General from 1977 to 1982.
Literature: Nancy Keesing, David Martin and Judah Waten.
Music: Werner Baer, Arthur BENJAMIN, George DREYFUS, Sir Charles MACKERRAS, Isaac Nathan, Larry Sitsky and Felix WERDER.
Further reading: Price, C.A. *Australian Immigration, A Bibliography and Digest.* Australian National University Press, Canberra, 1981.

Jindabyne NSW (population 1 602 in 1981) This small town in the SNOWY MOUNTAINS region is about 480km SW of Sydney and some 60km SW of COOMA on the Alpine Way. It is located on the shores of Lake Jindabyne, which was created when a dam forming part of the SNOWY MOUNTAINS SCHEME was constructed; the lake submerged the original town site and a new town has been built to replace it. The town is a small service centre for a sheep and cattle grazing district, but more importantly it is a gateway town to the KOSCIUSKO National Park, noted for winter skiing, trout fishing in summer, bushwalking, horse riding and touring through the highlands, and for opportunities to visit the dams and power stations of the hydroelectricity scheme.

Jindyworobaks *see* literature

John Dory *see* fishes, bony

Johnson, Richard (1753-1827) Clergyman. Born near Hull in Yorkshire, he attended Cambridge University and was ordained in 1784. Appointed as chaplain of NSW, he arrived on the FIRST FLEET and on 3 February 1788 celebrated the first service in the colony in the shade of a large tree. He received little encouragement from Governor PHILLIP and was treated with outright hostility by Major GROSE, who acted as Governor after Phillip's departure and who disapproved of the chaplain's evangelical outlook. It was not until August 1793 that Johnson managed to complete the building of a church. Even then he had to pay for it himself, but four years later Governor HUNTER reimbursed him. Johnson devoted himself conscientiously, even if not very successfully, to his religious duties, and also found time to engage in farming, growing a great variety of vegetables and fruit, as well as wheat, oats and barley, on his Brickfield Hill plot and his 140ha farm at Canterbury Vale (modern Canterbury). He returned to England in 1800. His church had been destroyed by fire two years previously.
Further reading: Bonwick, J. *Australia's First Preacher.* Sampson Low, London, 1898; Rainey, W.H. *The Real Richard Johnson.* S. John Bacon, Melbourne, 1949.

Johnston, George (1764-1823) Soldier and farmer. Born in Annandale, Scotland, he was commissioned second lieutenant in the marines in 1776 and sailed to NSW with the FIRST FLEET. In 1790, when the first units of the NEW SOUTH WALES CORPS arrived to replace the garrison of marines, Governor PHILLIP appointed Johnston to raise a company for the Corps from the ranks of the marines. In 1804, by which time he had reached the rank of major, he led the troops which suppressed the CASTLE HILL RISING, and when Lieutenant-Colonel William PATERSON was sent to found a settlement at PORT DALRYMPLE in TAS later in that year, Johnston became commanding officer of the New South Wales Corps in Sydney. Following his deposition of Governor BLIGH in January 1808 (*see* RUM REBELLION) he acted as Governor until the arrival in Sydney in July 1808 of a superior officer, Lieutenant-Colonel Joseph Foveaux. Foveaux in turn was superseded in January 1809 by Paterson, who had returned from Port Dalrymple and who insisted that both Johnston and Bligh should sail for England, where the conflict between them could be judged. Johnston, accompanied by John MACARTHUR, sailed in March 1809. At the subsequent court martial he was found guilty of mutiny, but the court obviously realised that he had been forced to act in very difficult circumstances, for his only punishment was that of being dismissed from the Army. In 1813 he returned to the colony and lived as a farmer and grazier at his property, Annandale (after which the Sydney suburb is named) until his death.
Further reading: Evatt, H.V. *Rum Rebellion.* Angus & Robertson, Cremorne NSW, 1975.

Johnston, George Henry (1912-70) Author and journalist. Born in Melbourne, he became a cadet reporter with the *Argus* newspaper and later a war correspondent. From 1954 to 1964 he and his family lived on the Greek island of Hydra, where he contracted tuberculosis. He and his wife, Charmian Clift, wrote the novels *High Valley* (1948), *The Big Chariot* (1953) and *The Sponge Divers* (1955). His reputation is based mainly on three semi-autobiographical novels which he wrote on his own—*My Brother Jack* (1964), *Clean Straw for Nothing* (1969) and *A Cartload of Clay* which, although unfinished, was published in the year after his death. *My Brother Jack*, which is set in Melbourne during the years of the author's youth and early manhood, is held in particularly high regard for the effectiveness of its characterisation and social analysis.

Joseph Bonaparte Gulf NT/WA This broad coastal inlet off the Timor Sea stretches 130km from Pearce Point NT to Cape Dussejour WA. Within the gulf there are numerous swampy mangrove-fringed river estuaries; the two major ones are Queen's Channel (the VICTORIA RIVER estuary) and Cambridge Gulf (into which the ORD RIVER drains). The E shore is occupied by the DALY RIVER Aboriginal Reserve. The gulf was discovered and named in 1803 by the French explorer, Nicholas BAUDIN.

Joyce, Eileen (1912-) Pianist. Born in ZEEHAN in TAS, Eileen Joyce became a legendary personality in her own lifetime. Her father, a miner, returned to WA where her teachers, recognising her musical talent, arranged tuition for her at the Loreto Convent in Perth. Percy GRAINGER considered her 'the most transcendentally gifted child' he had ever heard. Another distinguished visitor, Wilhelm Backhaus, recommended that she study at the Leipzig Conservatorium, which a public subscription enabled her to do. She made her début in 1931, performed regularly for the BBC, toured Australia in 1936 and played with the London Philharmonic Orchestra in blitzed areas during World War II. The story of her childhood, *Prelude* (by C.H. Abrahall), appeared in 1947, and a film version, *Wherever She Goes*, followed in 1950. She toured Australia again in 1948, toured South Africa in 1950, South America in 1952, the USSR in 1961 and India in the following year. She also provided many sound-tracks for films and performed on harpsichord at a time prior to the great revival of interest in that instrument. She reappeared with the Royal Philharmonic Orchestra in 1967, became an honorary Doctor of Music (Cantab.) in 1971, and in 1979 was awarded an honorary Doctorate of Music by the University of Western Australia, an institution with which she has kept close ties while continuing to live in London.

judo Originally an oriental martial art and only recently considered a sport, judo did not find ready acceptance in Australia until after World War II, although the first club was claimed to have been established in 1928 by Dr A.J. Ross. Newcomers to Australia who had practised the art in their native lands,

Five times Australian judo champion, S. Hendy, in training

visitors from Japan and ex-servicemen who had seen judo during the occupation of Japan were the people responsible for creating an interest in the sport in Australia. Although Australians are not rated high in world-class judo, they have performed well in international competitions considering the short time the sport has been practised in the country. The highest attainable grade in judo is 12th dan—the highest rank held by Australians is 5th dan. Competitors from Australia have taken part in Olympic judo events and have won medals in other international competitions. Sue Hendy became the most noted Australian exponent of the sport when she won a gold medal in the 1978 judo world championships. At the women's world championships in December 1982, Suzanne Williams gained a silver medal in the under 56kg category and Christina Boyd a bronze medal in the under 48kg.

Junee NSW (population 3 993 in 1981) A town in the SW slopes region of the State on the Olympic Highway 459km by road SW of Sydney, Junee is set in gently rolling hill country amidst streams draining into the MURRUMBIDGEE RIVER. It is a rail centre on the main S route to Melbourne, 483km from Sydney, and a junction point from which a branch line goes W to NARRANDERA and beyond. At an elevation of 301m above sea level, it experiences hot summer conditions, cool frosty winters and an average annual rainfall of 533mm spread uniformly throughout the year. The rural area produces wool, fat lambs, wheat and poultry; the town has large railway locomotive workshops and is a major depot and egg pulping centre for the New South Wales Egg Marketing Board. The name Junee comes from an Aboriginal word meaning either 'frog' or 'speak to me'. The town was gazetted officially in 1863 (originally named Jewnee), experienced a gold-mining boom from the late 1860s to about 1880, was

proclaimed a municipality in 1886 and developed as a railway junction and service centre. Several buildings in the town have been listed for preservation by the National Trust (NSW), including the post office, the railway station and workshops, four hotels (Commercial, Junee, Loftus and Broadway) and, 2km W of the town, the restored homestead 'Monte Cristo' which was built in 1884 and contains a collection of carriages and early farm machinery.

K

Kadina SA (population 2 943 in 1981) This small town is located in the NW of the YORKE PENINSULA, about 10km inland from the SPENCER GULF coast and 150km by road NW of Adelaide. At an elevation of 44m above sea level, it has an average annual rainfall of 396mm, with a concentration of rain in the winter months. The town is a service centre for a productive grazing and grain growing district. Between 1860 and 1923 Kadina, together with MOONTA and WALLAROO, was the focus of a flourishing copper mining and smelting industry. The discovery of the copper ore brought a flood of immigrants in the 1860s, many from Cornwall in England, and the Cornish flavour remains in the area. Every two years, a Cornish festival called a Kerewek Lowender is held in May; centred on the three towns, it recalls the life style of the Cornish miners, with fairs and feasting, music and dancing. Numerous buildings in the town, dating from the 1860s, have been listed for preservation by the National Trust (SA). The name Kadina comes from the Aboriginal word meaning 'lizard plain'.

Kakadu NT This is a national park, located about 220km E of Darwin, between the S and E ALLIGATOR RIVERS. It is composed of tidal flats, estuaries, lagoons, mangroves and, further inland, blacksoil plains, grasslands and paperbark country. In the E is the long sandstone escarpment of ARNHEM LAND with its river gorges. The park has abundant wildlife, particularly wildfowl and the introduced buffalo. It also contains outstanding collections of Aboriginal rock art, with mythological figures, x-ray depictions of animals and the TASMANIAN WOLF or tiger which disappeared from the mainland thousands of years ago. Some of the paintings are believed to be more than 20 000 years old, including perhaps the world's oldest surviving graphic art-work. The land traditionally belongs to the Aborigines who, in 1978, leased it to the Director of

National Parks and Wildlife for management; the original area of the park (Stage I) covered over 6 000km^2, but in 1983 this was more than doubled (Stage II). There are regular tourist excursions into Kakadu from Darwin; access roads are good, as they were initially built to service uranium camps at Jabiluka, NABARLEK and other sites.

Kalbarri WA (population 820 in 1981) Situated on the estuary of the MURCHISON RIVER where it flows into the Indian Ocean, 164km N of GERALDTON and 661km by road N of Perth, Kalbarri is a popular holiday resort, famed for its fishing, picturesque scenery and springtime display of wild flowers. It has a mild climate with an average annual rainfall of 416mm, concentrated in the winter months and a markedly dry summer season. The Kalbarri National Park (186 076ha) includes the spectacular gorge country of the Murchison, stretching 80km along the river.

Kalgoorlie WA (combined population of Kalgoorlie and BOULDER 19 848 in 1981) Located in the arid inland of the State, 604km by road and 657km by rail, ENE of Perth and about 400km N of ESPERANCE, Kalgoorlie has been called the 'Queen City of the Golden Mile'. Gold is still produced from the mines and in the past decade has been supplemented by nickel from the nearby KAMBALDA area. The riches of Kalgoorlie were discovered in 1893 by an Irishman, Paddy Hannan, who is reputed to have picked up a stone to throw at a crow, near where one of the town's main thoroughfares is now located, and found that it was a gold nugget. The Hannan Memorial and Hannan's Tree are reminders of the initial discovery which caused a rush of miners from the nearby camp of COOLGARDIE. Many of the gold-rush centres in the region became ghost towns but further discovery of vast rich ores at the Golden Mile, claimed as the richest square mile in the world, located 5km S, assured Kalgoorlie of permanence. By 1896 a railway had connected it to Perth and by 1903 the GOLDFIELDS WATER SUPPLY scheme brought supplies by a 563km-long pipeline from MUNDARING RESERVOIR. In 1927 a rail link was built to Esperance, a port and resort centre on the S coast. Despite the low rainfall (252mm annual average) the surrounding countryside has a large sheep population. Over 20 structures in the town have been listed for preservation by the National Trust (WA), including several churches, the School of Mines, Hannan's statue, the town hall and council chambers, and the Golden Mile Historical Museum (formerly the British Arms Hotel). A special tourist attraction is the Hainault Tourist Mine, originally formed in 1898, located along Boulder Rock Road, where visitors can descend in a cage and see the mining operations.
Further reading: Casey, G. & Mayman, T. *The Mile that Midas Touched.* Rigby, Adelaide, 1964; Lockwood, K. *West Australian Goldfields Sketchbook.* Rigby, Adelaide, 1970.

Kambalda WA (population 4 463 in 1981) This nickel-mining town is located in the arid inland of the State, about 60km SE of KAL-GOORLIE and over 700km by road E of Perth. Gold was discovered here in 1897 and Kambalda flourished as a gold-mining centre until 1906. Then it was virtually abandoned until 1966 when the Western Mining Corporation began nickel-mining operations. It has again become a flourishing centre with a treatment plant on the shores of Lake Lefroy.

Kanakas This name was applied to Pacific Islanders who were recruited to work in Australia—mostly in the QLD sugar industry between 1864 and 1904. Altogether about 57 000 of them came to Australia. The process of recruiting them was commonly known as BLACKBIRDING. The primary motive for recruiting them was economic, their labour costing only about a quarter as much as that of European workers, but the common belief that Europeans were physically incapable of performing heavy outdoor manual labour in the tropics was also cited as a reason.

Grounds of opposition Opposition to the use of Kanaka labour was voiced almost from the start. It was based mainly on economic and humanitarian grounds, backed by the racial prejudice commonly displayed by Europeans to all non-Europeans at the time. White workers feared that the competition of cheap non-European labour would have a bad effect on wage rates and working conditions and, by spreading into other areas of employment besides tropical canefields, would reduce job opportunities. Humanitarian arguments, used particularly by missionaries in the Pacific islands as well as by liberals in Australia, were based on claims that recruitment was often

accompanied by violence or deceit, and that the whole system was little better than slavery.

After the first few years, three-year contracts became common, and guarantees of repatriation at the end of that time were generally included. In theory, all recruits were volunteers, who understood the terms on which they were engaged, but it soon became apparent that some were kidnapped by force, while others had little or no understanding of what the contract involved. In a number of cases islanders who had been recruited by force or deception rose against their captors during the voyage and were shot down.

Attempts at regulation In 1868 the QLD government tried to eliminate abuses by the Polynesian Labourers Act, which laid down minimum wages and rations, required each recruiter to be licensed and to lodge a bond as a guarantee that he would not take islanders against their will, and forbade the landing of Kanakas by a recruiter until they had been inspected by a government agent. However, it soon became apparent that the provisions of the Act were often being evaded. QLD had no power to police the trade at the recruiting end, and even the Pacific Islanders Protection Act of 1875, passed by the British Parliament, was ineffective, since recruiting was sometimes carried out by foreign ships and on islands that were not British colonies or protectorates.

Maltreatment of Kanakas after being brought to Australia also aroused strong criticism. Legislation passed in 1880 laid down that they were not to be employed except in tropical or sub-tropical agriculture and tried to improve their rations, medical services and general working conditions. However, in 1900 the death rate among them was still more than three times as high as for the whole QLD population.

The conviction of the crew of the *Hopeful* for the kidnapping and murder of Kanakas in 1885 led to the holding of a Royal Commission, the report of which was so critical that legislation was passed forbidding recruiting after 1890. The application of this prohibition produced such adverse effects on the sugar industry that in 1892 the government decided that a further period was needed for the industry to adapt itself to the use of white labour, and the legislation was revoked.

Commonwealth action By the 1890s it had become clear that the sugar industry could not survive without Kanaka labour unless it was given a protected market throughout Australia. After federation the Commonwealth government acted promptly to give it such protection. The Pacific Islands Labourers Act of 1901 laid down that recruitment of islanders was to cease in March 1904, and that any islanders still in Australia by the end of 1906 were to be repatriated. The government was anxious to carry out repatriation humanely; this aim was expressed by Alfred DEAKIN: 'The Commonwealth Government will so provide that whenever the closing scenes in the kanaka employment . . . arrive, they shall be accompanied by none of the cruelties and barbarities with which it was initiated.'

A Royal Commission appointed early in 1906 reported that repatriation would be inhumane in some cases. Further legislation was therefore passed exempting islanders who had first come to Australia before October 1879, or who had been there continuously for more than 20 years, any who owned land freehold, and any whom the authorities considered could not be repatriated without danger to their lives or the lives of their families. The number finally repatriated was 3 642. In the meantime, the sugar industry had been preserved by a combination of tariff protection and payment of a bounty on sugar produced by white labour only.

See also immigration restriction
Further reading: Willard, M. *History of the White Australia Policy.* Oxford University Press, Melbourne, 1967; Yarwood, A.T. *Attitudes to Non-European Immigration.* Cassell Australia, Melbourne, 1968; Docker, E.W. *The Blackbirders.* Angus & Robertson, Sydney, 1970.

kangaroo apple *see* apple; Solanaceae

Kangaroo Island SA This large island (4 308km²) lies S of ST VINCENT GULF and is separated from YORKE PENINSULA by INVESTI-GATOR STRAIT and from FLEURIEU PENINSULA by the narrow stretch of water called Backstairs Passage. The island has an E-W extent of 148km, and from N to S is 55km at its widest part. It was discovered by the British explorer Matthew FLINDERS in 1802 and so named by him because he saw many kangaroos there and killed some to provide fresh meat for his crew. Shortly after Flinders reached the island, the French explorer Nicholas BAUDIN arrived, circumnavigated the island and gave French

Kanakas working in a canefield

names to several landscape features; these names still exist (for example, Cape du Couedie on the SW of the island, Vivonne Bay on the S coast and D'Estree Bay on the SE). During the years between its discovery and formal settlement, the island was inhabited by a motley collection of escaped convicts, ships' deserters, whalers and sealers. In 1836, the first official settlement was established at Nepean Bay on the NE coast, where KINGSCOTE now stands.

Geologically, the island is a continuation of the MOUNT LOFTY RANGES separated from the SW tip of Fleurieu Peninsula by a narrow strait. Though the soils of the island are generally poor, they have been made productive by the use of fertilisers, and the rural economy is based on sheep grazing and grain farming. After World War II, a major War Service Land Settlement scheme was developed. Tourism is also important to the island economy. The island can be reached from the mainland by air and sea, with a vehicular ferry from PORT ADELAIDE to Kingscote, and offers the visitor a variety of spectacular scenery, including rugged coastlines and sweeping beaches, as well as opportunities for game fishing, aquatic sports and visits to areas of natural bushland and limestone caves. Seal Bay on the S coast, about 60km from Kingscote, is a conservation park for the protection of sea lions and other native fauna. At the W end of the island is Flinders Chase, a large national park established in 1919, covering 59 003ha and including a stretch of wilderness country. Several houses on the island, together with the Cape Borda lighthouse (on the NW tip), a school and the Kingscote mulberry tree (planted in 1836) have been listed for preservation by the National Trust (SA).
Further reading: Newnham, W.H. *Kangaroo Island Sketchbook.* Rigby, Adelaide, 1975; Osterstock, A. *The Story of Kangaroo Island.* The author, Adelaide, 1975.

kangaroo paws *see* Haemodoraceae

kangaroos and wallabies These herbivorous MARSUPIALS belong to the superfamily Macropodoidea (order Diprotodonta), a well-known and successful group which is restricted to Australia and New Guinea. The pouch opens forwards, the hind-limbs are longer than the fore-limbs, and the strong and muscular tail is used as a prop when the animal is sitting or moving slowly, and as a balancer when the animal is bounding along at speed. The hind-limbs of all species, apart from the musk rat-kangaroo, *Hypsiprymnodon moschatus*, lack the innermost hind-toe, or first toe. The second and third toes are small and bound together as one (syndactyly) with the two closely set claws being used as a comb for grooming the fur. The strongly clawed fourth toe is the longest, and the fifth toe is small.

The teeth are highly specialised for grazing. There are only two incisor teeth in the lower jaw and these oppose three pairs in the upper jaw. The digestive system shows many similarities to that of ruminant placental

mammals (EUTHERIAN MAMMALS) such as cattle. The stomach is divided into four clearly distinguishable sections; one section contains a large quantity of cellulose-digesting bacteria and protozoa.

The large kangaroos and the large and medium-sized wallabies These belong to the family Macropodidae. The large kangaroos are those in which the foot length (not counting the claws) is greater than 25.4cm.
1. The large kangaroos. The red kangaroo, *Macropus rufus* (head and body 93cm to 140cm long; tail 71cm to 100cm long; the largest living marsupial), also known as the plains kangaroo or marloo, and the female as the blue doe or flyer, is a rather slender species with the snout naked between the nostrils. Adults have a blue and white patch at the side of the muzzle. Both sexes have bluish-grey heads but the body of the male is often reddish, and that of the female bluish-grey with white below; the base of the tail is grey and the tip lighter (the colour is variable). The fur is velvety in texture. Red kangaroos occur in most of arid and semi-arid Australia, mainly in open grassland where they usually feed on grasses and herbs at dusk. They are gregarious animals, forming loosely knit mobs of up to 100 individuals.

The grey kangaroos have quite recently been recognised as two distinct species: the eastern or great grey kangaroo, *Macropus giganteus*, also known as the forester, and the western grey kangaroo, *M. fuliginosus*, also known as the black-faced, mallee or sooty kangaroo. They are as large as the red kangaroo, and live in forests and woodland, especially those with adjacent clearings for grazing at dusk. The eastern species has a silvery grey coat but the western species is greyish-brown to chocolate. The fur is short and woolly, and the snout finely hairy. Like the red kangaroo they are gregarious, forming groups of from five to 20 individuals. The eastern grey is found from E and central QLD to VIC and in TAS. The western grey overlaps to some extent in south-western NSW and nearby VIC; it also occurs in SA, on KANGAROO ISLAND, and in southern WA.
M. robustus (59cm to 109cm; 55cm to 90cm) is a species which varies somewhat in size and colour. Four subspecies are recognised at present. The eastern wallaroo, *M. r. robustus*, ranges from north-eastern VIC to CAPE YORK, in rocky hills, stony slopes and escarpments—the typical habitats for the species. The euro, *M. r. erubescens*, also known as the hill kangaroo or the biggada, occurs W of the eastern wallaroo, in the NT and in all States except VIC and TAS. The northern wallaroo, *M. r. woodwardi*, is found in the far N, from the W shore of the GULF OF CARPENTARIA to WA. The Barrow Is wallaroo, *M. r. isabellinus*, is restricted to BARROW ISLAND. Wallaroos and euros are more sedentary than the greys and reds, and rarely stray far from supplies of food and water in their home ranges, except after rain when there may be some migration. They live in small groups, lying among the rocks during

the day, and grazing during the night in flat, open areas. They are large, with a thickset, robust build. The snout is naked and the fur is thick and coarse. The hands and feet are black. In the E the males are dark grey and the females bluish-grey, but further W more red appears in the colouring; in WA both sexes are reddish. The males in any district are, however, darker than the females.

Far less is known about the apparently common antilopine wallaroo, *M. antilopinus* (106cm; 82cm), which lives on plains and broad valleys with open woodland in northern WA, the NT and Cape York. It resembles *M. robustus* but has less black on the tip of the tail. The black wallaroo, *M. bernardus*, occurs in ARNHEM LAND and is of similar size to *M. robustus* of which it was once thought to be a variety.
2. The larger wallabies. This group contains some *Macropus* and *Wallabia* species with head and body lengths from about 80cm to 1.3m and with foot lengths from 16.5cm to 25.4cm. These wallabies are small versions of the large kangaroos and live in dense forests, woodlands or riverside scrub. Unlike the larger kangaroos of open country, in general they have suffered from development, though some do well where patches of timber have been left. Certain of the species have flourished in New Zealand.

The agile or sandy wallaby, *M. agilis* (80cm; 77cm; female distinctly smaller than the male), is a common well-built species found in river country in N coastal districts, from the KIMBERLEYS to S of ROCKHAMPTON. It feeds on grassy plains or savanna, and shelters during the day in woodland. It is sandy coloured, with some hair on the snout and with a white hip stripe; it is usually seen in groups of up to 50 animals.

The red-necked wallaby, *M. rufogriseus* (82cm; 80cm), ranges along the coasts, and in some inland areas, from northern QLD to south-eastern SA; there is a separate group in TAS and on some BASS STRAIT islands. This common but usually solitary species lives in most kinds of forests, apart from rainforest, with dense undergrowth, and emerges to feed at night in clearings and pastures. The snout is naked, the ears are long and the body colour is greyish-fawn but whiter below. There is some white on the cheek, and the shoulders and rump are reddish.

The scrub or black-striped wallaby, *M. dorsalis* (153cm; 77cm), favours thickets and other dense vegetation (rainforest, lantana, brigalow scrub and so on) from Rockhampton QLD to northern NSW. It is commoner in QLD than NSW, but little is known of its biology. It is a slender species with a naked snout, a grey body with reddish shoulders, a black stripe along the spine and a white stripe on the hip. It is gregarious, forming groups of up to six, but secretive.

The pretty-faced or whiptail wallaby, *M. parryi* (92cm; 94cm), is a common slender species with a long thin tail. The head and body are grey and the underparts greyish-white. The name 'pretty-faced' refers to the

Courtesy of A.I.S. Canberra

The pretty-faced or whip-tail wallaby

distinct white facial stripe. The snout is naked. It is found in coastal ranges from Cape York QLD to Stroud NSW. It usually feeds on introduced grasses in pasture, in mobs of up to about 15 animals.

The western brush wallaby or black-gloved wallaby, *M. irma* (78cm; 74cm), is a slender species which is bluish-grey in colour with lighter underparts and has a yellow cheek stripe and partly hairy nostrils. It is common in dry sclerophyll forests in SW Australia. It is closely related to a species which is almost certainly extinct, the toolache (pronounced as three syllables), *M. greyi* (81cm; 73cm). The toolache had a naked snout and a greyish-fawn body with faint grey bands on the rump, and lived in open woodland in small areas of SA.

The swamp wallaby, *W. bicolor* (76cm; 70cm), ranges from Cape York to south-western VIC, mainly E of the GREAT DIVIDING RANGE, but also W in southern QLD and northern NSW. It is an open forest species, preferring habitats with very dense undergrowth, moist gullies and seasonal swamps, but inland it is found also in dry scrubs. It is one of the wallabies that has suffered from forest clearance though it is still common in places. It is a stocky, solitary macropodid, reddish-grey above and reddish-orange below. The tail is dark grey at the base, and black on the distal half. The snout is naked.

The small wallabies and pademelons This group contains macropodids in the genera *Macropus, Setonix* and *Thylogale* with a foot length of less than 15.25cm. The tammar wallaby, *M. eugenii* (61cm; 41cm), also known as the dama wallaby or the scrub wallaby in SA, is a slender, bare-snouted, grizzled grey species living in dense thickets in dry sclerophyll forests. It occurs in south-western WA (including HOUTMAN ABROLHOS and the RECHERCHE ACHIPELAGO), and in southernmost SA and on Kangaroo Is; on the mainland it occurs only in small scattered colonies, but is more secure on some of the islands. It is

possible that this was the first Australian macropodid (and possibly the first Australian marsupial) to be described by a European—the Dutchman François Pelsaert who was shipwrecked on Houtman Abrolhos in 1629. It is well adapted to arid conditions and can, it is said, drink sea water.

The parma wallaby, *M. parma* (48cm; 53cm), was though to be extinct until recently; and only 12 specimens were known from museums. In 1965, however, it was established that it survived, in company with certain other species, on Kawau Is, near Auckland, New Zealand, having been introduced there by Sir George GREY, a former Governor of SA. Since its rediscovery, colonies have been established in several Australian institutions with the eventual goal of re-establishing the species in the wild. Since its return to Australia it has been found that it had not, after all, become extinct; small populations have been found in the area of GOSFORD and in forests in northeastern NSW, but it must still be counted as a rare animal. It resembles the scrub wallaby but is smaller and has a less marked dorsal stripe. It was formerly recorded from the ILLAWARA district and DORRIGO in NSW. It frequents rainforest and scrub.

The quokka, *Setonix brachyurus* (49cm; 29cm) is a small, cat-sized wallaby with a short, tapering tail and short, round ears. The colour is brownish-grey and grey. It was the first marsupial to be studied intensively by biologists (for example, delayed embryological development was first observed among the marsupials in this species). The quokka was formerly common in swampy thickets in SW Australia but it is now rare on the mainland. It is, however, common on ROTTNEST ISLAND and Bald Is WA, where it lives in rather more arid conditions than do mainlanders. Rottnest Is was so named in 1696 by the Dutch explorer Willem de Vlamingh who mistook the quokkas for rats.

Pademelons are small, comparatively short-

tailed wallabies, and live in rainforests and other wet forests in E Australia. There are four species (one is restricted to New Guinea). The red-necked pademelon, *T. thetis* (52cm; 43cm), has reddish shoulders and neck and is found in eastern QLD and eastern NSW. The red-legged pademelon, *T. stigmatica* (49cm; 44cm), is generally brown with red on the face and on the leg above the heel. It also occurs commonly in eastern NSW and eastern QLD. The Tasmanian pademelon or red-bellied wallaby, *T. billardierii* (63cm; 42cm), is found in south-eastern VIC, TAS and on the Bass Strait islands. It appears to be safe at present in TAS but is very rare or extinct on the mainland.

The nail-tailed wallabies These wallabies have a small, dark, horny nail on the tip of the tail, and rather unusual dentition. There are three species but only the northern nail-tail or karrabul, *Onychogalea unguifera* (about 1.2m), is common. It ranges from BROOME in WA to NORMANTON in QLD.

The hare-wallabies These small wallabies were so called because, like the European hare, they make nests under bushes and tussocks of grass and when flushed make off at high speed. They were formerly common on the mainland but now survive mainly on offshore islands. They are small, solitary animals, apart from the gregarious banded hare-wallaby or munning, *Lagostrophus fasciatus* (43cm; 37cm), a cat-sized, dark greyish animal of low scrubs and heathland in SW Australia. It is now restricted to Bernier and Dorre Islands in SHARK BAY but has been re-introduced on to DIRK HARTOG ISLAND.

The eastern or brown hare-wallaby, *Lagorchestes leporides* (45cm; 32cm) has not been collected since 1890 and is almost certainly extinct. It occurred in western NSW and in the MURRAY RIVER district of SA. The similarly sized spectacled hare-wallaby, *L. conspicillatus*, has, like all members of its genus, an eye-ring but in this species it is a conspicuous orange feature. It is said to be still common at two ends of its former range which stretched across N Australia. It occurs on Barrow Is. The rufous hare-wallaby or wurrup, *L. hirsutus* (33cm; 38cm), has an orange eye-ring and orange hair on the hind-quarters. It was formerly widely distributed in the *Spinifex* grasslands in the Centre, but now occurs only on Bernier and Dorre Islands and in the TANAMI DESERT wildlife sanctuary in the NT.

The rock-wallabies Populations of rock-wallabies occur in many scattered areas of Australia. In general, they are solitary or gregarious, nocturnal animals. They are noted for their agility when leaping on cliff faces and among rocks. The feet have rough, thick pads, fringed with hairs to give a good grip on the rocks which are often worn smooth by the animals. The long cylindrical tail with its long hair and tuft at the end is an excellent balancer.

There is doubt about the number of species but in 1983 Strahan (see *further reading*) recognised ten, all but one belonging to *Petrogale*. The black-footed rock-wallaby, *P. lateralis*, has several races which vary in size

(45cm to 55cm; 48cm to 60cm). It is found in WA, and central Australia and in western QLD where a distinct form, the purple-necked rock-wallaby, represents the species, and is a common road victim. The brush-tailed rock-wallaby, *P. penicillata*, is an abundant species in eastern Australia where it is the counterpart of *P. lateralis* with which it was formerly confused. Approximately as large as the black-footed species, it has a distinctive long tail that is brushed at the end. The unadorned rock-wallaby, *P. ornata*, also till recently confused with the preceding species, occurs in eastern QLD, but further north than the brush-tailed wallaby. Further north still, in Cape York, is the similar, but longer-tailed, Godman's rock-wallaby, *P. godmani*. It may be giving ground to a variety of the unadorned species which is expanding its range northwards. Rothschild's rock-wallaby, *P. rothschildii*, somewhat larger than the earlier species, occurs in the HAMERSLEY RANGE area of WA, and on some of the islands of the DAMPIER ARCHIPELAGO. The yellow-footed rock-wallaby, *P. xanthopus* (48cm to 65cm; 57 cm to 60cm) has suffered from its possession of a brightly coloured, attractive pelt. Its most distinctive feature is the irregular barring on the tail. It is still common in parts of the FLINDERS RANGES, SA and also occurs in western NSW and QLD. The Proserpine rock-wallaby, *P. persephone*, first described in 1982, though known by local naturalists for several years, is found in only two small areas near Proserpine, QLD though once it was more widespread. It may have been displaced by the unadorned species. The short-eared rock-wallaby, *P. brachyotis*, is still abundant in parts of its range in north-eastern WA and northern NT. It is variable in size but, on the average, somewhat smaller than the earlier species. The final two species, the warabi, *P. burbidgei,* and the narbalek, *Peradorcas concinna*, are both much smaller than the other rock-wallabies, and were both formerly confused as a single species, the little rock-wallaby, *P. concinna*. The warabi (30cm) to 35cm; 26cm to 29cm) is the smallest known macropodid, and is restricted to rugged parts of the KIMBERLEYS, WA, where its range overlaps with that of the narbalek which is slightly heavier. It occurs in the Kimberleys and adjacent parts of the NT and QLD, and near the western coast and islands of the GULF OF CARPENTARIA.

Recent cytological work has shown that the various *Petrogale* species have different numbers of chromosomes (22, 18 or 16); these and other genetic studies have helped to clarify the systematics of the genus.

The tree-kangaroos Most live in New Guinea but two species occur in NE Cape York in mountain rainforest. In general, they resemble wallabies but the arms are comparatively well-developed and the hind-feet relatively short and broad. The tails are very long but not prehensile. As their name suggests, tree-kangaroos spend most of their time in trees but often come to ground. Lumholtz's tree-kangaroo, *Dendrolagus lumholtzi* (56cm;

67cm), a greyish species, occurs S of the Daintree River QLD, and the similarly sized Bennett's tree-kangaroo, *D. bennettianus* (65cm; 94cm), a brownish species, is found N of that river. Both appear to be secure in reserves.

Rat-kangaroos, bettongs and potoroos These belong to the family Potoroidae and are grouped into five genera. One of these, *Hypsiprymnodon*, is often placed in a separate subfamily for the sole representative, the musk rat-kangaroo, *H. moschatus* (23cm; 15cm), has features that place it between the kangaroos and the possums. It is a rat-like animal with fore-limbs and hind-limbs of approximately equal length. The hind-limb has five toes and the tail is tapering, naked and scaly. The colour is reddish-brown above and greyish-brown below. The musk rat-kangaroo is a solitary terrestrial animal that runs on all fours. It lives in rainforest in north-eastern QLD where it feeds on insects, tubers and other plant material from the ground litter. It is reported to be plentiful though its range has been reduced.

Bettongia is the largest genus of the subfamily. The brush-tailed bettong or rat-kangaroo, *B. penicillata* (33cm; 31cm), also known as the woylie, is a greyish-brown and white, solitary, nocturnal animal with a face more like that of a rat than a wallaby. The ears are short, the snout is naked, and the prehensile tail has a black tuft at the end. The tail is used to carry nesting material. The hind-legs resemble those of wallabies and kangaroos as they are longer than the fore-limbs and are used for bounding. This species lived in sclerophyll woodland in QLD, SW Australia, southern SA, north-western VIC and central NSW; it is believed to be extinct, except in WA and QLD. The eastern bettong or Tasmanian rat-kangaroo, *B. gaimardi*, is similar but the tip of the tail is white. Its range is south-eastern QLD, coastal NSW, southern VIC and TAS, but it survives probably only in TAS. The other species, also similar in size and colouring to the brush-tailed bettong, is the boodie or burrowing bettong, *B. lesueur* (40cm; 30cm), a very rare burrowing species of SA, south-western NSW, the NT and some islands. It is known to survive only on Barrow, Bernier, Dorre

Tree kangaroo

and Boodie Islands. The rufous bettong, *Aepyprymnus rufescens* (39cm; 36cm), is a coarse-haired, long-eared animal with a non-prehensile tail. It lives in open woodland in E Australia and is still common in QLD. The last of this group, the desert rat-kangaroo, *Caloprymnus campestris* (27cm; 32cm) is a long-eared, light-coloured marsupial that lives in sandridge flats and stony plains near the point where the borders of QLD, SA and the NT meet. It has not been seen since 1935 but may survive in the Centre.

The potoroos live in dense tussocks and grasses in forests, woodlands and heaths in areas of high rainfall. They are completely nocturnal. Till comparatively recently they were thought to be rare but are now known to be widely distributed in suitable habitats in SE Australia and TAS and also to occur on some Bass Strait islands. Cytological studies have shown that the three to five surviving species that were once recognised should now be regarded as one, *Potorous tridactylus*, though recently a new, large species, the long-footed potoroo, *P. longipes* has been collected in E GIPPSLAND. The potoroo or long-nosed rat-kangaroo, *P. tridactylus* (41cm; 23cm), is a short, round-eared animal with relatively short hind-feet and a tapering, prehensile tail. Its colour is dark greyish-brown and greyish-white, and the nose is pointed and naked on the snout and above. It is a solitary animal which digs up roots and tubers. The differences between the forms from various areas are sufficient for them to be regarded as subspecies (though not as species, as formerly).

The rat-kangaroos are largely vegetarian but the musk rat-kangaroo and the bettongs are also partly carnivorous.

Culling of kangaroos Journals of early explorers have prompted the suggestion that the large kangaroos (greys and reds) are now more common as a result of the clearing of bush and woodland. Though this has been disputed there is no doubt that several of the smaller species have become rare, or have disappeared, as a result of the destruction of their habitats. (APPENDIX 7). It is also true that large kangaroos, when numerous, can become pests in farming areas, especially during droughts when the range of food plants used by the kangaroos and the livestock overlaps, and when the kangaroos tend to move into farmlands. In these circumstances the farmer or grazier may consider it necessary to reduce their numbers. The management of kangaroos varies from State to State but typically the landowner obtains permission from the wildlife authorities, and is allowed to kill a proportion so that the population as a whole is not endangered. No doubt, however, some illegal shooting occurs and it is not known how this affects the national management. The populations are monitored, however, by the wildlife authorities and the large kangaroos are in no apparent danger. Nevertheless conservation groups have opposed the destruction of any large kangaroos. They have been particularly vociferous in the USA where, from time to time, and to the great amazement of many Australian biologists, the grey and red kangaroos are placed on the endangered species list so that no kangaroo products can be imported into the USA. Consequently any kangaroos that have to be destroyed were simply wasted. Unfortunately the same enthusiasm has not been shown for the smaller marsupials which are in much greater danger.

Further reading: Troughton, E. *Furred Animals of Australia.* (9th edn, abridged) Angus & Robertson, Sydney, 1973; Tyndale-Biscoe, H. *Life of Marsupials.* Arnold, London, 1973; Burbidge, A.A. (ed) *The Status of Kangaroos and Wallabies in Australia.* Australian Govt Publishing Service, Canberra, 1977; Dawson, T.J. 'Kangaroos' in *Scientific American.* (vol 237, no 2, August 1977); Tyler, M.J. (ed) *The Status of Endangered Australian Wildlife.* Royal Zoological Society SA, Adelaide, 1978; Strahan, R. (ed.). *The Australian Museum Complete Book of Australian Mammals.* Angus & Robertson, Sydney, 1983.

Kapunda SA (population 1 340 in 1981) This small town is located in the N MOUNT LOFTY RANGES, 73km by road NNE of Adelaide. At an elevation of 244m above sea level, it experiences a mild climate with an average annual rainfall of 496mm, concentrated mainly in the winter months. It is a service centre for a wheat growing and sheep grazing region. It was the site of SA's first copper mine (1884-88). The town takes its name from an Aboriginal word meaning 'a rocky waterhole'.

karate The word means 'empty hand' and is, as the translation indicates, an art of weaponless combat. Although unarmed combat has been practised throughout many parts of the world for many centuries, the accepted name for the sport originated on the island of Okinawa, Japan, early in the 17th century. The island was invaded and a total ban on weapons imposed, so the islanders developed an undetectable and potentially lethal weapon —the empty hand.

Karate was taken up in Australia by a few men who had read of or seen the sport abroad, particularly servicemen serving in the occupation forces in Japan following World War II. On their return to Australia they taught themselves the art with the aid of textbooks and tuition given by Japanese visitors. Since the 1950s many thousands of Australians have been attracted to karate both as an art—with the emphasis on mental and physical self-discipline—and as a sport—with the emphasis on self-defence or unarmed combat, and karate is now widely taught throughout Australia. A few Australians have been outstandingly successful, among them the Hungarian-born Australian Joe Meissner who, in 1972, became the first non-Japanese to win a world championship when he defeated competitors from Japan, Brazil and West Germany.

Karratha WA (population 8 341 in 1981) A new town built in 1970 in the W part of the PILBARA region on the shores on Nickol Bay on the Indian Ocean coast, Karratha is about 1 550km by road N of Perth off the North West Coastal Highway. It is located 40km W of ROEBOURNE, 20km E of DAMPIER, and is the government administrative centre for the mining and shipping operations of the region. Its name is taken from an Aboriginal word meaning 'good country'.

karri *see* forestry

Karumba QLD (population 670 in 1981) A small fishing port in the GULF COUNTRY of the far NW of the State, it is situated at the mouth of the Norman River downstream from NORMANTON. It is the landfall for ships in the GULF OF CARPENTARIA and the centre of an important prawn fishing and processing industry.

Katanning WA (population 4 413 in 1981) An inland town on the Great Southern Highway, 282km SE of Perth, Katanning is the service and commercial centre for a productive agricultural and pastoral region. It is also a major rail junction on the Great Southern Railway, 340km via YORK and NARROGIN from Perth, at an elevation of 312mm above sea level, on the S part of the inland plateau where wheat growing and sheep grazing are the main rural industries. It has an annual average rainfall of 490mm, concentrated mainly in winter.

Katherine NT (population 3 737 in 1981) A town in the N part of the Territory, it is located on the Stuart Highway, 348km SE of Darwin and 102km SE of PINE CREEK where the Victoria Highway from the W meets the Stuart Highway. It is situated on the Katherine River, the main headwater tributary of the DALY RIVER, at an elevation of 107m above sea level where the highway and the N Australian railway cross the river. The average annual rainfall is 952mm which falls in the hot wet season from October to March, with a marked dry period for the rest of the year. The explorer John McDouall STUART gave the river its name in 1862 in honour of the daughter of his patron, James Chambers, a South Australian pastoralist. During World War II, on the alluvial soils adjacent to the Katherine River, vegetable growing was developed to provide fresh supplies for the troops and this formed the basis for the CSIRO research station located just S of the town, which carries out investigations on tropical crops. The Katherine area today is still a pioneering frontier, but developments since the 1960s have led to the town's growth: in 1963 the Northmeat Export Abattoirs commenced operation; the town has become a regional base for major road construction work; and tourism has been developed, centred mainly on the Katherine Gorge National Park some 30km E—there are regular cruises along

the river to see the giant cliffs of the gorge, reaching 60m high. Other tourist attractions in the region are the Cutta Cutta limestone caves (25km S), 'Springvale' homestead built in 1878 (13km W, the second-oldest station in the NT) where visitors can see an Aboriginal corroboree dance, the Edith Falls (82km N), and the site of the old 'Elsey' homestead (114km S) where Mrs Aeneas GUNN, authoress of *We of the Never Never* (1908), came as a bride in 1902 and wrote of her experiences as a pioneer in this difficult land.

Katoomba NSW (combined population of Katoomba and WENTWORTH FALLS 13 942 in 1981) The best-known and largest urban centre in the BLUE MOUNTAINS, it is located on the Great Western Highway, 106km W by road from Sydney, at an elevation of over 1000m above sea level. The main W railway from Sydney across the highlands to the inland parts of the State passes through Katoomba.

The cable car across a deep canyon in the Blue Mountains NSW

These transport routes, both road and rail, follow the general track of the first British explorers who crossed the Blue Mts in 1813. The district is one of famed scenic beauty due to the deep valley dissection of the sandstone-capped plateau. The Jamison Valley which can be viewed from Echo Point near Katoomba is a classical example, with the Three Sisters standing as jagged rock remnants on the valley edge. Rockfalls from the cliffs into the valleys occur occasionally. A superb vista of these valley and cliff features can be obtained from the Scenic Railway and the Scenic Skyway; the railway provides a trip, on a track 415m long, from the plateau top to the Jamison Valley 230m below and the skyway provides an aerial cable-car trip from one cliff top to another with the valley 275m below. Numerous waterfalls, such as the Bridal Veil, Katoomba Falls and Leura Cascades, near the neighbouring town of Leura, spill over the valley cliffs. It is from these waterfalls that Katoomba takes its name, for the Aboriginal word means 'water tumbling over a hill'.

The area experiences a mild climate with warm to hot summers, foggy cool winters and occasional snowfalls. The average annual rainfall is 1 405mm. Bushfires are a summer-time hazard of the district, for some areas of natural vegetation have been preserved as a national park and in other parts, even adjacent to residential areas, native bush remains.

Though tourism is still an important feature of Katoomba's activities, it has in recent decades, with better road connections to Sydney and with the electrification of the railway in 1957, become increasingly a commuter zone for people working in the metropolitan area. Until World War II, it was a tourist mecca for people on their annual vacations, but now it tends to have much more day-tour traffic. Also, it has become, together with nearby Leura, a centre for residential conferences and conventions. It is the administrative headquarters for the City of the Blue Mts, which was formed in 1947 by linking together many of the urban centres strung along the main transport route through the region, so as to co-ordinate services and development. The city had a population of 55 871 at the 1981 census. *See also* Nepean River; Wentworth, William Charles

Further reading: Taylor, G. *Sydneyside Scenery and How It Came About.* Angus & Robertson, Sydney, 1970; White, U. & Bechervaise, J. *Blue Mountains Sketchbook.* Rigby, Adelaide, 1971.

katydids *see* crickets, *etc.*

kauri *see* Gymnospermae

keds *see* flies

keelback *see* snakes

Keepit Dam NSW This dam is located on the NAMOI RIVER a short distance above its confluence with the Peel River, 56km NW of TAMWORTH and 39km by road NE from GUNNEDAH. It has a storage capacity of 425 600ML, a wall 55m high, with a crest length of 533m, and a catchment area of 5700m². The origin of the word Keepit is uncertain, though it is not an Aboriginal word and its first known use was in 1837 as the name of a station property in the area. The construction of the dam was interrupted by World War II; work commenced again in 1946 and the dam was completed in 1960. The storage provided by Keepit Dam was originally intended to replace, in part, the diminishing flow from artesian bores which were used to supply stock water over a wide area. However, experimental investigations on cotton growing using irrigation in the early 1960s proved so successful that this crop is now of major importance in the Namoi Valley. The lake created by the dam, covering 4 370ha, is now a major recreation area for swimming, sailing, water skiing and angling. Though the dam was not specifically designed for flood mitigation, it is possible, by controlling the release of water, to provide a measure of flood protection to areas downstream. A hydro-electricity system has been installed to generate power as waters are released.
See also Wee Waa

Keith SA (population 1 147 in 1981) This country town in the SE of the State is 249km by rail SE of Adelaide. It is located on Duke's Highway, 45km by road NW of BORDERTOWN, and is a service centre for the surrounding farming and grazing district. At an elevation of 31m above sea level, it receives an average annual rainfall of 471mm, concentrated mainly in the winter season.

Kellerman, Annette Marie Sarah (1886-1975) Swimmer. Born in Sydney, she took up swimming as a therapeutic exercise after poliomyelitis had left her with partially crippled legs. Annette started her long and colourful career by winning the 100 yards event in the NSW swimming championships in 1902. She moved to England in 1904 with her father and started gaining publicity almost immediately because of her 'daring' one-piece bathing costume. While in the USA in 1910 she was arrested for 'indecent exposure' because of the costume she elected to wear. Interviewed later in life she said that she believed that her greatest achievement was the part she played in freeing women from uncomfortable and impractical bathing attire.

Kellerman's most remarkable feats in the water were marked by endurance and stamina. She attempted the crossing of the English Channel three times, her best effort coming in her final attempt when she remained in the water for 10½ hours, creating a women's record which remained unbroken for 17 years. In 1906, she competed in a 12km men's race on the River Seine, defeating all but two of the men. She went to the USA in 1907 where she gave demonstrations and exhibitions of swimming and diving, became a successful vaudeville star and appeared in several films. Not only a great swimmer (the first woman swimmer to gain any acclaim), she was also an author; her books include *How to Swim* (1919), *Physical Beauty: How to Keep It* (1919) and *Fairy Tales of the South Seas* (1926). In 1952 a film of her life, entitled *The Million Dollar Mermaid*, was released. She died in Southport QLD.

Kelly, Edward 'Ned' (1855-80) Bushranger. As in the case of most bushrangers of his time, members of Kelly's family had been convicts. His father had been transported from Ireland for stealing two pigs, and after serving his sentence in TAS had rented a farm at Wallen, about 40km N of Melbourne where Ned was born. His mother, Ellen Kelly, was also Irish, and although she had never been a convict she and her relatives were bitterly anti-English and anti-police. From Wallen the family moved to another small town, Avenel, where, when Ned was 11, his father died. Not long afterwards, Ellen Kelly took her children to a property near BENALLA. By the time Ned was 16 he had served a six-month gaol term for assault and indecent behaviour and had received a three-year sentence for receiving a mare which he knew to be stolen and for resisting arrest.

In 1877 a Constable Fitzpatrick went to the Kelly house to arrest Dan, one of Ned's

A contemporary sketch of Ned Kelly's armour

National Library of Australia

brothers, on a charge of horse stealing, and a struggle took place during which Fitzpatrick was wounded in the wrist. Although Ned denied having been on the scene, he and Dan went into hiding in the Wombat Ranges, where they were joined by two friends, Joe Byrne and Steve Hart. In October 1878 four policemen encountered the gang at Stringybark Creek and Ned shot three of them dead. He and his companions were then declared outlaws and rewards were put on their heads. They carried out two particularly daring bank robberies, one at EUROA VIC, and the other at JERILDERIE NSW, where they locked up two policemen, herded most of the population into the bar of the hotel, and dressed in police uniforms to rob the bank.

Back in the Wombat Ranges, they learned that Aaron Sherritt, a friend of Joe Byrne, had turned police informer, whereupon Byrne shot him dead in the doorway of his home, even though a guard of four policemen was inside. On the following day the four outlaws gathered in the township of GLENROWAN. They forced railway workers to tear up a section of track in order to derail a train which was bringing a detachment of police from Melbourne and herded the town's population of about 60 people into the parlour of the Glenrowan Inn.

However, the police were warned, and laid siege to the hotel. Joe Byrne was mortally wounded by a stray bullet and Ned, emerging with the top half of his body encased in armour made for him by a blacksmith, was shot in the legs and captured. In the early hours of the morning the police set fire to the hotel and later found the bodies of Joe Byrne, Dan Kelly and Steve Hart in the ashes.

In October 1880 Ned was tried for the murder of one of the police at Stringybark Creek, and was hanged in Melbourne Gaol on 11 November. The claim that he had been driven to a life of crime by police harassment is hardly supported by the facts, but has nevertheless gained wide credence. His career was sufficiently dramatic to have provided inspiration for a great deal of literature, drama and art, most notably Douglas STEWART's play *Ned Kelly* and a series of paintings by Sydney NOLAN.

Further reading: Jennings, M.J. *Ned Kelly: The Legend and the Man.* Hill of Content, Melbourne, 1968; Farwell, G.M. *What a Life!* Cheshire, Melbourne, 1970; Keesing, Nancy (ed.) *The Kelly Gang.* Ure Smith, Sydney, 1975; Brierley, A.G. *An Illustrated History of The Kelly Gang*, Melbourne University Press, 1978.

Kempsey NSW (population 9 034 in 1981)
A town on the MACLEAY RIVER in the mid-NORTH COAST region, Kempsey is about 20km inland from the ocean shore and 37km upstream from the river estuary. It is situated on the Pacific Highway, 465km by road N of Sydney, and on the main North Coast railway line, 504km by train from Sydney. It is the largest urban centre in the Macleay Valley and functions as the commercial and business focus for the surrounding rural region. The Kempsey Shire had a population of 19 578 in 1981. The main farming activity of the district is dairying on the rich alluvial flats; lucerne and maize are cultivated, and pig raising and beef cattle grazing are widely practised. Kempsey experiences a mild climate throughout the year, with an average annual rainfall of 1 213mm and a concentration of rain in the summer and early autumn months. The river flats and parts of the town itself are subject to flooding in times of high river. The town has factories for butter and cheese making, milk processing and bacon curing, as well as sawmills, brick and pipe works, and furniture and veneer making. The adjacent coastal zone is a popular tourist area; some of the well-known holiday centres are Crescent Head, Hat Head and South West Rocks. The historic Trial Bay Gaol and the Beranghi Folk Museum are popular tourist attractions.

Settlement of the Macleay Valley began in the 1830s, with timber cutting, particularly of cedar, as the main activity. Over subsequent decades this valuable timber was logged extensively, almost to extinction. In the pioneering days of settlement, contact with Sydney was by sea. The town of West Kempsey was surveyed in 1856 and incorporated as a borough

in 1886. The town was named after the Valley of Kempsey in Worcestershire, England.

Kendall, Henry (1839-82) Poet. Born near ULLADULLA, on the S coast of NSW, he went to sea as a cabin boy for two years, and later worked at various times as a shop assistant, a solicitor's clerk and a public servant. However, he seemed to find it difficult to apply his mind to routine work, lived in poverty for much of his life, lapsed into drunkenness for some years, and at one stage suffered a severe

John Fairfax & Sons Ltd

Henry Kendall's cottage in Gosford where he lived in the 1870s

nervous breakdown. He began contributing verse to Sydney periodicals in 1857 and published three anthologies, *Poems and Songs* (1862), *Leaves from Australian Forests* (1869) and *Songs from the Mountains* (1880). The last of these was very popular, and since his death many anthologies of his poems have been published. His popularity has rested mainly on his descriptive powers, his sense of atmosphere and the musical quality of his verse, particularly his use of rhythm to create effects such as that of thundering hooves in *The Song of the Cattle Hunters* or the flowing effects in *Bell-Birds*.

Further reading: Kramer, L.J. & Hope, A.D. *Henry Kendall*, Sun Books, Melbourne, 1973; Wilde, W.H. *Henry Kendall*. Twayne, Boston, 1976.

Keneally, Thomas Michael (1935-) Novelist. Born in Sydney, he began training for the Roman Catholic priesthood, but did not proceed to ordination. His novels *The Place at Whitton* (1964) and *The Fear* (1965) won favourable attention, but it was *Bring Larks and Heroes* (1967), set in the early years of settlement in Sydney, that established him as one of Australia's leading novelists. Later works include *The Survivor* (1969), *Three Cheers for the Paraclete* (1968), *A Dutiful Daughter* (1971), *The Chant of Jimmie Blacksmith* (1972), which was filmed in 1978, *Blood Red, Sister Rose* (1974), which was based on the life of Joan of Arc, *Gossip from the Forest* (1976), which deals with the circumstances leading up to the signing of the Armistice in 1918, *Season in Purgatory* (1976), *A Victim of the Aurora* (1977), *Passenger* (1978), *Confederates* (1979), *The Cut-Rate Kingdom* (1980), and *Schindler's Ark*, winner of the Booker Prize in 1982. The themes of his novels are

commonly concerned with questions of wrongdoing and its consequences.

Kennedy, Edmund Besley Court (1818-48) Explorer. He was born on Guernsey, one of the Channel Islands, and after training as a surveyor came to Sydney in 1840. In 1845 he was chosen by Sir Thomas MITCHELL as second-in-command of the expedition which explored parts of what is now central QLD and discovered the BARCOO RIVER. Mitchell thought that this stream might flow all the way to the N coast, and might in fact be the upper course of the VICTORIA RIVER. In 1847 Kennedy was sent to see if this was so, but by following the Barcoo nearly to the border of SA he showed that it was probably no more than an upper arm of COOPER'S CREEK, named by Charles STURT in 1845. In the following year he was sent to explore the E coast of CAPE YORK Peninsula, but, as related in the entry on EXPLORATION BY LAND, the expedition turned out to be the most tragic in the history of Australian exploration—only three of its 13 members survived and Kennedy himself was speared to death by Aborigines.

Further reading: Beale, E. *Kennedy of Cape York.* Rigby, Adelaide, 1970.

Kenny, Elizabeth (1886-1952) Nurse. Born at Warialda, NSW, she became a bush nurse in QLD, and developed a method of dealing with poliomyelitis (infantile paralysis) by treating the affected limbs as for muscle spasm, rather than by the traditional method of immobilising them by splinting. This brought considerable opposition from members of the medical profession, and in 1938 a Royal Commission reported against her ideas. Nevertheless the QLD government supported her, and in 1940 helped her to go to the USA, where her methods received wide acceptance, including the approval of the medical committee of the National Foundation for Infantile Paralysis.

Further reading: Thomas, Henry, *Sister Kenny.* Putnam, New York, 1958.

Mitchell Library

Henry Kendall

Keppel Isles QLD This island group lies 13km off the CAPRICORN COAST, NE of ROCKHAMPTON and N of Keppel Bay, with sandy beach coastlines and fringing coral reefs. The main island, Great Keppel (1 400ha), is a major tourist resort, accessible by plane from Rockhampton, or by launch or hydrofoil from Rosslyn Bay, near YEPPOON. The group was discovered and named by James COOK in 1770 in honour of Admiral Keppel, who later became First Lord of the British Admiralty. Cook's discovery is now commemorated by the 'Singing Ship', located at Emu Park on the Capricorn Coast; it is a structure with fluted tubes which catch the wind and make musical sounds. The resort centre on Great Keppel is at Fisherman's Beach, on the W shore, where there are facilities for water skiing, snorkelling, fishing, coral viewing from glass-bottomed boats, and other recreational activities. The island terrain is steeply hilly and heavily wooded. Eleven islands in the group comprise a national park; the smallest of these is 8ha in area, the largest is North Keppel which covers 580ha.

Kerang VIC (population 4 049 in 1981) Located on the lower LODDON RIVER at the junction of the Murray Valley and Loddon Valley Highways, 280km by road and 289km by rail NW of Melbourne and 60km SE of SWAN HILL, it is a small market and service centre for a productive agricultural and pastoral area of irrigated farms which produce vines, citrus, cattle, sheep, cereals and oilseeds. At an elevation of 78m above sea level, situated on the riverine plains of the mid-MURRAY RIVER basin, it experiences a mild climate with an annual average rainfall of 367mm, spread throughout all months but with a maximum in winter and spring. The Kerang Lakes are the nesting grounds for large colonies of ibises, and the area is ranked by ornithologists as one of the most prolific breeding grounds in the world for these birds. The name Kerang comes from an Aboriginal word for an edible root vegetable.

Kerr, Sir John Robert (1914-   ) Jurist and Governor-General. Born in the Sydney suburb of Balmain, he studied law at the University of Sydney, graduated with distinction in 1936 and was called to the Bar two years later. During World War II he served in the Directorate of Research and Civil Affairs, a body which gathered information and formulated options for government action in both domestic and foreign policy areas, and after the conclusion of the war he played a key role in the establishment of the Australian School of Pacific Administration and of the South Pacific Commission. In 1948 he returned to legal practice and in 1972 was appointed Chief Justice of the Supreme Court of NSW. Two years later, on the nomination of the Labor government led by Gough WHITLAM, he was appointed Governor-General, and late in 1975 became involved in the most serious constitutional crisis in Australian history.

Sir John Kerr

The crisis arose from the decision of the Liberal leader, Malcolm FRASER, to use the Opposition's numbers in the Senate to deny supply to the Whitlam government, and so force it to a general election. Since there was a possibility that some Opposition Senators would refuse to vote for outright rejection of any Money Bill, the lesser course was taken of moving that consideration of two Appropriation Bills be deferred. Whitlam, whose party had won a majority in the House of Representatives in the general election of May 1974, argued that his government was entitled to a full three-year term, and that in this crisis, as in all other circumstances, the Governor-General was bound to act in accordance with the advice of his Ministers. However, Sir John finally accepted the view that a Prime Minister who cannot obtain supply must either resign or advise the Governor-General to hold an election, and that the Governor-General has reserve powers enabling him to dismiss a Prime Minister who refuses to follow one or the other of these courses. On 11 November he interviewed Whitlam, and having ascertained that the latter was not willing to advise an election, immediately dismissed him and appointed Fraser caretaker Prime Minister pending an election for both Houses. The election, held on 13 December, resulted in a crushing defeat for Labor.

Among Labor supporters, feeling against Sir John continued to run high after the election, causing many demonstrations and boycotts. Late in 1977 he resigned, and accepted a position as Australian Ambassador to UNESCO, but this appointment was denounced so fiercely by his critics that he resigned before taking up his duties fully.

Kiama NSW (population 7 716 in 1981) A town in the ILLAWARRA region, on the S coast, Kiama is located on the Princes Highway and on the S coast railway, 119km from Sydney. In the 19th century it was a port for the export of cedar from nearby forest regions, but it is now a small commercial centre serving a flourishing rural region of dairy farms, fodder crops and vegetable growing. A well-known tourist attraction is the 'Blowhole', discovered by George BASS in 1797; it is a unique geological feature on the rocky headland near the town where the sea swell sends a vertical column of spray up the 'hole'. About 15km inland from Kiama are the scarplands of the SOUTHERN TABLELANDS where the Minnamurra Falls (plunging 50m into a deep gorge) and an attractive area of subtropical rainforest are located.

Kidman, Sir Sidney (1857-1935) Pastoralist. Born in Adelaide, he left home at the age of 13 with a one-eyed horse named Cyclops, and with five shillings in his pocket. After working for a while on stations near the site of BROKEN HILL and in the MENINDEE district, he bought a bullock team, opened a store in COBAR and began to trade extensively in horses and cattle. In 1880 he bought Owen Springs station, south-west of ALICE SPRINGS, and in later years acquired many other properties in various parts of the Outback, becoming one of the largest landowners in Australian history. According to some estimates, he was finally owner or part-owner of about 170 000 square kilometres of land.
Further reading: Idriess, Ion L. *The Cattle King.* Angus and Robertson, Sydney, 1936.

Kiewa River VIC Located in the NE of the State, it is a tributary of the MURRAY RIVER. Its headwaters rise near MOUNT BOGONG, and it flows for 185km in a general NNW direction to join the Murray, upstream from ALBURY-WODONGA. The upper sections of the valley are snow-covered in winter and are heavily timbered. The average annual rainfall in the area of the headwaters is over 1 800mm, while downstream it is 700mm. This high rainfall, combined with the steep gradient of the stream, has been used to develop VIC's largest hydro-electricity generating scheme, with a capacity of 184 000kW, harnessing water from a catchment of 303km². The Rocky Valley Reservoir at 1 615m elevation on the BOGONG HIGH PLAINS is the main storage for the scheme and penstocks carry water down the slopes of Mt McKay (part of the scarp of the Bogong High Plains) to generate power. The water flows progressively through three power stations (McKay Creek, Clover and West Kiewa), falling 1 250m to the regulating pondage at MOUNT BEAUTY. Two of the stations (McKay Creek and West Kiewa) are deep underground. The townships of Mt Beauty and Bogong were established in the late 1940s by the State Electricity Commission as centres for the construction works of the scheme, which was completed in 1958. An alpine village at Falls Creek, 1 585m elevation on the edge of the Bogong High Plains, is a popular ski resort.

kikuyu grass *see* Gramineae; weeds

Courtesy of A.I.S. Canberra

left: The blowhole at Kiama NSW (*see* KIAMA)
centre: Jenolan Caves NSW (*see* JENOLAN CAVES)
right: Kangaroo Island (*see* KANGAROO ISLAND)

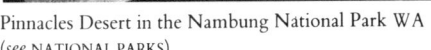

Pinnacles Desert in the Nambung National Park WA
(*see* NATIONAL PARKS)

The Olgas NT (*see* MOUNT OLGA)

The Three Sisters near Katoomba NSW (*see* GEOLOGY)

Ayers Rock NT (*see* AYERS ROCK)

Granite tors and balancing rocks on the New England
plateau NSW (*see* TENTERFIELD)

Glasshouse Mountains QLD
(*see* GLASSHOUSE MOUNTAINS)

Aerial view of the The Kimberleys WA
(*see* KIMBERLEYS)

Devils Marbles NT (*see* DEVILS MARBLES)

Flinders Ranges SA (*see* GEOLOGY)

Left: Spotted emu bush, *Eremophila maculata*
  (*see* EMU BUSHES)
centre: Kangaroo apple, *Solanum laciniatum*
  (*see* SOLANACEAE)
right: Native pigface, *Carpobrotus rossii* (*see* PIGFACE)

Trigger plant, *Stylidium graminifolium*
(*see* TRIGGER PLANT)

Sydney wattle, *Acacia longifolia* (*see* MIMOSACEAE)

Ledun boronia, *Boronia ledifolia* (*see* RUTACEAE)

Shrubby platysace, *Platysace lanceolata (see*
UMBELLIFERAE)

Spiked wax flowers, *Eriostemon spicatus* (*see* WAX
FLOWERS)

Flannel flowers, *Actinotus helianthi* (*see* UMBELLIFERAE)

Kimberleys WA (population 17 970 in 1981) The Kimberley region in the far N of the State, usually called the Kimberleys, is an official statistical division comprising four shires (HALL'S CREEK, West Kimberley, BROOME and WYNDHAM-East Kimberley) covering a total area of over 421 000km². It was named in honour of the Earl of Kimberley who was the British Secretary of State for the Colonies from 1880 to 1882. The region includes the ORD, FITZROY, DURACK and DRYSDALE Rivers and along the indented coastline are the three port towns of the N: Wyndham, DERBY and Broome. The Great Northern Highway traverses the Kimberleys from Broome E to Hall's Creek thence N to Wyndham, a total road distance of almost 1 200km. The landforms of the region consist of a vast plateau much dissected by river gorges, bounded by steep fault ranges on the E (the Durack Range) and SW (the King Leopold Range). The area around the Ord is usually referred to as the East Kimberley and that around the Fitzroy as the West Kimberley. The whole region has a tropical climate, with a hot wet summer season and a somewhat cooler and markedly dry winter period. For many months of the year almost absolute drought conditions are experienced. The summer rains come as tropical storms, with occasional cyclones. The amount of rain received is generally higher near the coast and lower inland. There are four national parks in the Kimberleys: Drysdale River National Park (435 591ha) in the N; Windjana Gorge National Park (2 134ha), 144km E of Derby on the upper Lennard River; Tunnel Creek National Park (91ha), 182km by road E of Derby; and the spectacular Geikie Gorge National Park (3 136ha) on the Fitzroy River.

Hidden Valley in the Kimberley region of WA

The Kimberleys were settled after the journey through the region by Sir John FORREST in 1879. Sheep graziers came from the S parts of WA and cattle herds were driven overland from QLD and NSW. Some of the famous treks lasted several years and are associated with pioneers such as the DURACK FAMILY, the Penton family and the Buchanan family. Gold discoveries at Hall's Creek in 1885 led to an influx of people and although the rush was short-lived it led to the development of Wyndham as a port. Vast grazing properties, raising cattle and sheep, still dominate the rural activity of the region, though the irrigation developments in the lower Ord Valley during

recent decades give promise of more intensive rural occupation. The region suffers, however, from its isolation and the great distances to markets for its products; although the Great Northern Highway and better air and sea services have alleviated this to some extent, much of the Kimberleys still has the flavour of the 'great Outback' of the continent.

Further reading: Idriess, I.L. *One Wet Season.* Angus & Robertson, Sydney, 1949; Durack, M. *Kings in Grass Castles.* Constable, London, 1959; Wilson, J.L.J. (ed) 'Kimberley' in *Current Affairs Bulletin.* (vol 28, no 11, 1961); Hill, E. *The Great Australian Loneliness.* Angus & Robertson, Sydney, 1963.

King George Sound WA This coastal inlet on the S shore of the State was discovered and named by the explorer George Vancouver in 1791. It is a well-sheltered magnificent harbour with ALBANY located on the inner section, Princess Royal Harbour. On Frenchmans Bay, at the W of the Sound, Australia's only whaling station operated until the late 1970s. During World War I the ships carrying the ANZAC troops to GALLIPOLI assembled in the Sound before they sailed on their ill-fated voyage; erected on Mt Clarence, overlooking the Sound, is a monument commemorating this event. In March each year the Albany Open Yacht race takes place from Perth to Albany around the notoriously treacherous CAPE LEEUWIN. The Torndirrup National Park at the W of the Sound covers 3 868ha and includes much rugged coastline and scenic features such as the Gap, the Blowholes and the Natural Bridge.

King Island TAS (population 2 710 in 1981) Situated at the W end of BASS STRAIT, off the NW tip of TAS, the island extends for 65km N-S and 27km E-W at its widest point, with a total area of 126 000ha. About half the island has been cleared for farming and livestock grazing, the rest being natural bushland. The island was named in 1801 in honour of Governor KING of NSW. In the early days of the century it gained a world-wide reputation among hunters for its great numbers of seals and sea elephants (the latter are now almost extinct). Gold and tin were mined in 1905, and scheelite (tungsten) was discovered in 1911. Mining continues to play an important role in the island's economy (the level of activity being dictated by world prices). The town of Grassy on the SE coast is the centre of the King Is Scheelite Co.'s mining operations. Currie on the W coast (population 861 in 1976) is the municipal and main commercial centre. The wild storms experienced in this region are evidenced by the 57 wrecks around the island's coastline.

King, Philip Gidley (1758-1808) Governor of NSW. He was born in Launceston, Cornwall, entered the British Navy in 1770, and served as second lieutenant on the *Sirius*

on the voyage of the FIRST FLEET to NSW. A month after the foundation of Sydney, Phillip sent him to found to settlement on NORFOLK ISLAND. He remained there as superintendent and commandant until 1790, and served there again from 1791 to 1796, this time with the rank of Lieutenant-Governor. Then he went on sick leave to England, and in November 1799 sailed once more for NSW, bearing with him Governor HUNTER's letter of recall, and his own appointment as Governor. He assumed office in September 1800.

Governor Philip Gidley King

National Library of Australia

He had more success than Hunter in reducing the privileges of the officers of the NEW SOUTH WALES CORPS and breaking their near-monopoly in trade. He reduced the number of convict servants assigned to them, forbade their trading in rum, maintained Hunter's practice of selling necessary commodities at fixed prices from the public stores, decreed that the government should have first right to purchase goods from incoming merchant ships, and tried to ensure that no individual purchased any more than 20 per cent of the remainder. To curb the rum trade he reduced the amount of spirits entering the colony, issued regulations forbidding the keeping of spirits in private houses in large quantities or moving them from place to place without permission, and tried to insist that liquor was retailed only in licensed houses. Events of note during his term of office include the resettlement in 1804 of NEWCASTLE (temporarily occupied from 1801 to 1802), the establishment of settlements in TAS at RISDON COVE and PORT DALRYMPLE in 1803 and 1804 respectively, the establishment of a short-lived colony at PORT PHILLIP under David COLLINS in 1803 and its transfer to Hobart in the following year, and the suppression of the CASTLE HILL RISING in 1804. Ill health and friction with officers of the Corps led King to resign in 1806.

Further reading: Mackaness, G. *Admiral Arthur Phillip.* Angus & Robertson, Sydney, 1937; Bassett, M. *The Governor's Lady.* Oxford University Press, London, 1940.

King River TAS Located in the rugged W mountain region, it rises in the W coastal ranges near Eldon Peak (1 439m elevation), flows first to the E of QUEENSTOWN, then turns sharply to flow W into the NE section of MACQUARIE HARBOUR near STRAHAN. Some of the highest rainfalls recorded in TAS (over 3000mm yearly) occur in the area around the upper King River.

Kingaroy QLD (population 5 134 in 1981) Famed as the peanut growing centre of Australia, it is located on the Bunya Highway 224km by road NW of Brisbane, 116km NE of DALBY and 141km by road SW of GYMPIE. At an elevation of 430m above sea level, it is situated in the upper catchment area of the S tributaries of the BURNETT RIVER near the watershed between the Burnett and Brisbane River systems. Towering peanut silos dominate the townscape, reflecting the importance of this rural industry in the town's economy. Dairying and beef cattle grazing are also important on the red volcanic soils of the district and there is a butter factory in the town. Sorghum and maize are grown as winter crops, and wheat in summer. The average annual rainfall is 777mm, concentrated mainly in the summer months. The BUNYA RANGE, with peaks rising to over 1 100m, lies to the SW of the town and forms part of the GREAT DIVIDING RANGE. The Bunya Mts National Park (11 700ha), some 68km SW of Kingaroy, is noted for its scenic landscapes, rainforest vegetation and unique grassland patches.

kingfishers The kingfisher family, Alcedinidae, includes the kookaburras. Kingfishers are large-headed BIRDS, with a large bill, a short neck, short rounded wings and short legs; some of the toes are fused together (in some species a toe is missing). Despite their name, most kingfishers feed on insects, and some may never see a fish. They nest in holes excavated in vertical banks or in termite mounds.

The kookaburras belong to the genus *Dacelo*, which is represented in Papua New Guinea and Australia. Their plumage is fairly dull, but there are some patches of blue on the rump and the shoulders. The kookaburra, *D. gigas** (38cm to 40cm long), is renowned for its raucous laughter. This arboreal bird frequents the dry forests and savanna of E Australia, and has been introduced into the SW and TAS; it feeds on the ground on insects, food scraps and small animals, including snakes. Recent studies show that small groups of up to about five adults maintain territories; of these, one pair mates and the others, of both sexes, help to incubate the eggs and raise the young. The blue-winged kookaburra, *D. leachii* (35cm to 38cm), is a N species which ranges from WA to the QLD/NSW border, in open forest and savanna woodlands. The blue patches are brighter than those on the E species; in the male most of the tail is blue while in the female it is brown with dark blue bars. This species feeds on insects and small animals and sometimes on fish.

The genus *Ceyx* contains two Australian species of kingfishers—the azure kingfisher, *C. azureus* (18cm), which fishes in the inland waters and coastal creeks of N and E Australia, and the little kingfisher, *C. pusillus* (11cm), found in the mangroves and swamps of CAPE YORK and the NT. They are very similar, but the azure species is reddish below and violet-blue above, while the uncommon little kingfisher is white below.

Courtesy of A.I.S. Canberra

The azure kingfisher, *ceyx azureus*

The genus *Halcyon* is widely represented in the Old World. The five species in Australia live in forests and woodlands, including mangroves, and their diet consists mainly of terrestrial and aquatic insects. The forest kingfisher, *H. macleayii* (20cm), of coastal N and E Australia, has a violet-blue crown, a pale blue rump, a white collar and a large white patch in front of the eye. The yellow-billed kingfisher, *H. torotoro* (18cm), a brown and black species with green on the shoulders, rump and tail, lives on the edge of rainforests in N Cape York. A more widespread species is the red-backed kingfisher, *H. pyrrhopygia** (20cm to 23cm), a mainly green bird with a white neck; it frequents dry woodlands and savanna throughout the mainland. A similar species is the sacred kingfisher, *H. sancta* (20cm), found in forests and woodlands throughout Australia; it is distinguished from the red-backed species by its blue rump. The mangrove kingfisher, *H. chloris* (23cm to 25cm), similar to the sacred kingfisher but with a white patch in front of the eye; it is always in or near mangroves and never far from the shore. It feeds in the littoral zone along the N coast from CARNARVON to northern NSW.

A breeding visitor to NE Cape York from New Guinea is the white-tailed kingfisher, *Tanysiptera sylvia* (30cm), easily distinguished by its long, central, white tail feathers.

Kingscote SA (population 1 236 in 1981) The largest town on KANGAROO ISLAND, situated on Nepean Bay in the NE of the island, it is linked to the mainland by both sea and air. At an elevation of 31m above sea level, it has a mild climate, with summer conditions ideal for holiday visitors, since the rainfall (491mm annual average) is concentrated mainly in the winter months (July, the highest, 79mm average). The town was the site of the first official settlement on the island in 1836 and was originally called Angas, then later Queenscliffe; its present name honours Henry Kingscote, a director of the South Australia

Land Co. which established the settlement. It is now a service centre for the grazing and farming communities of the island and the main focus of tourism.

King's Cross NSW An inner suburb of Sydney, located to the E of the central business district and focussed on a number of street intersections (hence the name 'Cross'), it is regarded by some people as the 'heart of Sydney's night life'. It lies adjacent to some of the city's exclusive inner E suburbs, such as Potts Point and Elizabeth Bay, and adjoins other poorer suburbs such as Darlinghurst and Woolloomooloo. The Cross, as it is commonly called, is noted for its cosmopolitan life, with modern hotels, apartment blocks, numerous nightclubs and restaurants, as well as sex shops, illegal gambling houses and massage parlours.

El Alamein fountain, King's Cross, Sydney

Kingsford Smith, Sir Charles Edward (1897-1935) Aviator. Born in Brisbane, he joined the AIF in World War I as soon as he turned 18, but later transferred to the Royal Flying Corps and fought as a pilot in France. After the war he tried to make a living in England, America and Australia by taking people for 'joy rides', by stunt flying and as an air taxi and aerial mail service pilot. However, his ambition was to become a trailblazing aviator, and in particular to become the first person to fly across the Pacific. In order to attract publicity and so gain funds for a trans-Pacific flight, in 1927 he and his friend Charles Ulm flew around Australia in a Bristol plane, by way of Sydney, Adelaide, Perth, Darwin and Brisbane, reducing the record for such a flight from 22 days to a little over 10. He then went to the USA and with the backing of a millionaire, Captain G. Alan Hancock, obtained a three-engined Fokker monoplane. In May 1928, with Ulm as co-pilot, and Americans Harry Lyon and Jim Warner as navigator and radio operator respectively, he made history by flying from San Francisco to Brisbane with stops at Hawaii and Fiji.

The enthusiasm with which his success was acclaimed in Australia can be judged by the

*Species, genus or family is endemic to Australia (see Preface)

Courtesy of A.I.S. Canberra

Kingsford Smith's *Southern Cross*

fact that when he brought his plane, *Southern Cross*, to Sydney, he was welcomed at the airport by a crowd of 300 000. Later in 1928 he flew *Southern Cross* to New Zealand and back, and in 1929-30 took it to England, across the Atlantic and on to California. In 1930 he set a solo England-Australia record of 9 days 22¼ hours in *Southern Cross Junior*, and in 1933 lowered this to 7 days 4¾ hours in *Miss Southern Cross*. In 1934, with P.G. Taylor, he made the first crossing of the Pacific from Australia to the USA. In the following year, with a co-pilot, he tried to regain the England-Australia record, but his plane, *Lady Southern Cross*, disappeared off the coast of Burma. Kingsford Smith Airport in Sydney is named after him and his most famous plane, *Southern Cross*, is preserved at Brisbane Airport.

Kingsley, Henry (1830-76)

Author. The brother of the better-known English novelist Charles Kingsley, he spent the years 1853-57 in Australia, working as a gold digger, station hand, drover, and mounted policeman. While staying on a property in western VIC he began writing the three-volume novel, *The Recollections of Geoffry Hamlyn*, which was published in London in 1859. It deals with life on a sheep station in the squatting age, before the beginning of the gold rushes, and is notable for its lively style and its vigorous description of such incidents as a fight with bushrangers, a kangaroo hunt and a bushfire. Although it over-romanticises the setting and over-dramatises many of the incidents in the story, it remains a landmark in the history of Australia literature. Of the author's other novels and short stories most have little or no reference to Australia.

Kingston TAS

(population 8 556 in 1981) Located 13km S of Hobart on the Channel Highway and linked to Hobart by expressway (a journey of 11km), the town is the administrative centre of the Kingsborough municipality. It is a popular tourist and holiday centre, noted for swimming, sailing and other aquatic sports, as well as for its scenic landscapes and panoramic views of the beach foreshores along the lower DERWENT RIVER. Increasingly, it is becoming a commuter residential area for people working in Hobart. The town is situated inland from the foreshores, at an elevation of 23m above sea level; it receives an average annual rainfall of 671mm, fairly evenly spread throughout the

year. Summer temperatures are pleasantly warm, but winters can be crisply cold. Kingston was once named Browns River after a noted Scottish botanist, Robert BROWN, who accompanied Governor COLLINS when the area was discovered in 1804.

Kingston, Charles Cameron (1850-1908)

Politician. Born in Adelaide, he was admitted to the SA Bar in 1873 and established a very successful practice. He turned to politics in 1881 and from that year until 1901 was Member for West Adelaide in the House of Assembly. He was Attorney-General and Chief Secretary for various periods, and as Liberal leader was Premier from 1893 to 1899. During these years he succeeded in extending the franchise to women, in passing important factory and industrial conciliation legislation and in establishing a State bank.

An ardent supporter of federation, he played an important part in the convention of 1891 and was president of the convention of 1897-98. In January 1901 he was chosen by BARTON as Minister of Trade and Customs, and in the first elections for the federal Parliament was elected member for Adelaide. He introduced the first Commonwealth tariff, which was mildly protectionist, but later resigned from Cabinet because of lack of support for his proposed Bill dealing with industrial arbitration and conciliation. Many expected that he would later become Prime Minister, but his health was failing and although he remained in Parliament until his death he played a less active part in politics after resigning from Cabinet.

Further reading: Turner, H.G. *First Decade of the Australian Commonwealth.* Heritage Publications, Melbourne, 1975.

Kingston South East SA

(population 1 325 in 1981) This town and port is situated on Lacepede Bay on the SE coast of the State, 290km by road SE of Adelaide. The town is a tourist centre, with fishing and aquatic sports for visitors on the lakes and coastal lagoons nearby. It is also a service centre for the adjacent farming and grazing areas. The French explorer, Nicholas BAUDIN discovered and named Lacepede Bay in 1802. In the 1840s the district was known as Maria Creek and later as Port Caroline; the township was established in 1858 and was named after Sir George Strickland Kingston, parliamentarian and assistant surveyor to Colonel LIGHT. The name was subsequently expanded to Kingston South East to avoid confusion with a settlement of the same name on the MURRAY RIVER, W of RENMARK in SA.

kites *see* birds of prey

koala

The koala, *Phascolarctus cinereus* (80cm long), belongs to the family Phascolarctidae (order Diprotodonta); it is a familiar, large tail-less MARSUPIAL found in E Australia. It formerly occurred in SA and has been reintroduced into WA. The fur is grey and greyish-white below. All 20 toes, apart from

NSW Dept of Tourism

Koala, *Phascolarctus cinereus*

the first on the hind-foot, carry sharp claws much used in climbing. The first and second toes of the front foot can oppose the others; in the hind-foot the second and third toes are united (syndactyly).

Koalas leave their trees only rarely, and then merely to cross to another one. Despite their arboreal habits their pouches open backwards, like those of WOMBATS. During the day they usually rest sitting upright in the crotch of a tree. They feed at night, sometimes in small groups, on only a small number of species of *Eucalyptus*, but there must be some variety. (According to one authority, they will also take leaves of mistletoe and other trees.) The range varies with the region. In VIC, for example, the most important species are listed as manna gum, *E. viminalis*, messmate, *E. obliqua*, swamp gum, *E. ovata*, peppermint, *E. radiata*, and mahogany, *E. botryoides*. To cope with this leafy diet the koala is reported to have a 2m-long appendix. It rarely drinks water but often eats soil which may account for the common occurrence of the fungal disease cryptococcosis among koalas.

Koalas were formerly common but the destruction of their habitat (dry sclerophyll forest and woodland) has been partly responsible for the decline in their numbers. They have also suffered from outbreaks of disease and from heavy hunting by man, though now, of course, they are strictly protected. In 1927 the QLD government registered 10 000 trappers, and 600 000 koalas were killed within a few months. Koalas mature fairly slowly, usually in the third or fourth year, and it is believed that a female can produce one young a year. After it leaves the pouch it is carried on the mother's back for some time. Despite its fairly slow rate of reproduction it seems to be reestablishing itself in several places. In 1980 some zoologists suggested that there may be an overpopulation of koalas in some areas, and that this has resulted in the outbreak of disease and the infertility of some females.

Further reading: see under kangaroos, etc. *Also* Bergin, T.J. (ed) *The Koala.* Zoological Parks Board, Sydney, 1978.

koel *see* cuckoos, etc.

Kokoda Trail *see* World War II

Konrads, Ilsa (1944-) Swimmer.

She was born in Latvia and came to Australia with her family, which included her brother, John KONRADS, in 1949. Ilsa was a great swimmer against the clock, breaking world records for distances over 800m and 1500m and 880 yards and 1650 yards in 1959, and 440 yards in 1960. She broke records set by Dawn FRASER but had great difficulty in beating her in races in which they both competed because Ilsa seemed to lack the killer instinct necessary to win consistently against other top class swimmers. One of the reasons for her great speed has been attributed to the fact that she practised with her brother and other men swimmers and so was competing against men's times rather than women's. When Ilsa retired from swimming, she turned to journalism and became the editor of a teenage fashion magazine.

Konrads, John (1942-) Swimmer.

He was born in Latvia and came to Australia with his family, which included his sister Ilsa KONRADS, in 1949. In 1959 he became only the second man in Australian history to win every freestyle title—110, 220, 440, 880 and 1650 yards—contested at the Australian championships. In fact, during the period 1958-61 he broke every world record from 200m to 1500m and from 220 yards to 1650 yards. He was self-disciplined, enthusiastic and a hard worker, and by the end of the 1960 Australian swimming championships had broken 24 world records. He represented Australia in the 1960 Olympic Games and took the gold medal in the 1500m freestyle, a bronze in the 400m and a bronze as a member of the 4 × 200m relay team.

kookaburras *see* kingfishers

Open-cut iron more mine on Koolan Island

WA Dept of Tourism

Koolan Island WA

This is one of the many islands of YAMPI SOUND located between the BUCCANEER ARCHIPELAGO and the indented coastline of the W KIMBERLEYS region, in the far NW of the State. The island contains high-grade iron ore deposits which have been mined since 1965 by the BROKEN HILL PROPRIETARY COMPANY LIMITED by open-cut highly mechanised operations. The name of the island comes from an Aboriginal word, probably meaning 'man'. The other iron ore island in the Sound, COCKATOO ISLAND, lies just W of Koolan.

Koolyanobbing WA (population 277 in 1981)

This small but important iron ore mining township is located 457km by rail inland from Perth, and 52km NE of SOUTHERN CROSS in the semi-arid interior of the State. The high-grade ore deposits are mined by the BROKEN HILL PROPRIETARY COMPANY LIMITED and taken by rail to KWINANA.

Korean War

In June 1950 the UN Commission on Korea reported that Communist-ruled North Korea had invaded South Korea. The Security Council thereupon called for a cease-fire and for the withdrawal of the N forces beyond the 38th parallel, which formed the border. After this appeal had been ignored by North Korea, that country was condemned as an aggressor and UN member states were requested to send aid to South Korea. By that time the USA had already sent forces, and after the UN appeal 15 other nations, including Australia, did so. Although throughout the war the great majority of troops assisting South Korea were American, the combined forces of all 16 nations fought under the UN flag, and South Korea also put her forces under the UN supreme command.

Australian support was particularly prompt; she was the first nation, apart from the USA, to commit forces to the defence of South Korea. On 29 June, only four days after the outbreak of hostilities, Prime Minister MENZIES announced that the destroyer *Bataan* and the frigate *Shoalhaven*, which were in Japanese waters, would be made available to the UN command, and on 2 July No. 77 Squadron of the RAAF, which had been in Japan as part of the Commonwealth Occupation Force, began operational service.

Ground troops took longer to organise, but in September the 3rd Battalion, Royal Australian Regiment, arrived from Japan, where it had been part of the British Commonwealth Brigade in the occupation forces. By that time the North Korean Army, having initially overrun almost the whole of South Korea, had been driven back across the border. Australian troops saw their first action at Yongyu, N of Pyonyang, the Korean capital, and took part in the further N advance of the UN forces.

Following the entry of the Chinese into the war in November 1951, the UN forces were driven well back into South Korea, but then staged a counter-offensive and advanced N again to a line approximating to the 38th parallel. Meanwhile, the Australian forces, including the 1st and later the 2nd Battalion, Royal Australian Regiment, as well as the 3rd, had been made part of the British Commonwealth Division. By the time an armistice was signed in July 1953 Australian casualties totalled over 1 300, including 252 killed in action. The RAAF's contribution to the war included No. 30 Transport Unit as well as No. 77 Squadron. Ships of the RAN which participated included the aircraft-carrier *Sydney*, the destroyers *Anzac, Tobruk, Bataan* and *Warramunga*, and the frigates *Murchison, Shoalhaven, Condamine* and *Culgoa.*

The main economic effect of the war on Australia was that strong American demand for wool pushed the price up to record levels, the unexpectedly high inflow of export earnings being a major factor in causing a burst of inflation in the early 1950s. Australian participation in the war did not bring a division of public and political opinion such as was to occur with regard to the VIETNAM WAR in the 1960s. The Australian Labor Party (ALP) accepted the UN view that North Korea was a clear aggressor; any misgivings that occurred later were with regard to the UN decision to pursue the North Koreans into their own territory, and the effect of this in bringing China into the war, rather than the initial decision to send help to South Korea. However, the occurrence of the War increased Australian fears of Communist expansion in Asia and of subversion within Australia. Thus it might be considered to have strengthened the hold on government of the Liberal/Country Party coalition, and to have helped develop within the ALP the division of attitudes regarding Communism which culminated in the split of 1955 and the subsequent formation of the Democratic Labor Party. It may also have been a major factor in the Menzies government's decision to attempt to ban the Communist Party—an attempt which was finally defeated by an adverse vote in a referendum in September 1951. Finally, it doubtless helped to win public acceptance for the reintroduction in 1951 of national service. (see CONSCRIPTION)

Further reading: Bartlett, N. (ed) *With the Australians in Korea.* (3rd edn) Australian War Memorial, Canberra, 1960.

Korumburra VIC (population 2 798 in 1981)

This country town is on the South Gippsland Highway and on the railway route through the region, 112km by rail SW of Melbourne. At an elevation of 227m above sea level, the town is set in the scenic hill country of the W STRZELECKI RANGES, where dairying, livestock grazing, fodder crop cultivation and vegetable growing are the principal rural activities. The town name comes from an Aboriginal word meaning 'blowfly', 'fly' or 'maggot'.

Kosciusko NSW

The highest mountain peak in Australia (2 230m), Kosciusko is situated in the SNOWY MOUNTAINS, 525km by road SW of Sydney. It was named by the explorer STRZELECKI when he ascended the range in 1840 because of the resemblance it bore to the tomb in Krakow of the Polish patriot Tadeusz Kosciuszko, though there is some controversy as to whether Strzelecki ascended the peak now known as Kosciusko.

Snowfields in the Snowy Mts of the Kosciusko region

There are several peaks in the vicinity (Twynam, Townsend, Carruthers) which rise above the general level of the surrounding landscape. The whole area was subjected to glaciation during the Great Ice Age and the evidence of this can be found in features such as the valley sections, the moraine deposits and the lakes (Blue, Albina, Cootapatamba, Club). The area is a winter snowfield and a summer attraction for trout fishing and bushwalking (though the mountain is above the tree line and the vegetation consists of shrubs, grasses and wild flowers). The Kosciusko National Park covers 629 708ha of this upland country; though there is a road to the summit, there is no private access for vehicles and a shuttle operates in summer holiday periods. *Further reading:* Shaw, J.H. 'Which—Kosciusko or Townsend?' in *The Australian Geographer.* (vol V, no 8, March 1950); Rawson, G. *The Count: A Life of Sir Edmund Strzelecki.* Heinemann, London, 1953.

kowari *see* native cats, etc.

krill This name was originally applied by Norwegian whalers to the shrimp-like CRUSTACEANS which are extremely abundant in polar seas where they provide the whalebone whales (*see* DOLPHINS, etc.) with the bulk of their food. They belong to the order Euphausiacea; a common species in the krill assemblage of the deeper waters of the Indian Ocean is *Thysanopoda cornuta.* Krill shrimps vary in size, with some species measuring about 40mm long. They are transparent but have red spots which are photo-luminescent. They form swarms which have been known to reach a density of 500 000 individuals per cubic metre.

kultarr *see* native cats, etc.

Kununurra WA (population 2 081 in 1981) This new town was specially constructed in the 1960s as the administrative and residential centre for the ORD RIVER irrigation project. Located in the far N of the State, 106km by road SE of WYNDHAM, the town site lies E of the river at the foot of Kelly's Knob, and is flanked to the S by Lake Kununurra which has been created by the construction of a diversion dam on the Ord (at a natural quartzite sill in the river bed called Bandicoot Bar) as a part of the irrigation scheme. At an elevation of 46m above sea level, the area

experiences a typically tropical climate with high temperatures throughout the year, an average annual rainfall of 787mm concentrated in the summer months (January and February, 197mm and 198mm respectively), and a markedly dry season from April to October. The town has been designed for tropical living with modern amenities and recreation facilities. During the winter months it is a popular tourist centre and conducted tours are available to the dams, cotton farms, irrigation areas, the research station, Aboriginal rock paintings and nearby scenic attractions.

Kununurra diversion dam

Kunzea *see* Myrtaceae

kurrajong *see* Sterculiaceae

Kurri Kurri NSW (combined population of Kurri Kurri and WESTON 12 794 in 1981) A town on the lower HUNTER RIVER valley coalfields, Kurri Kurri is adjacent to Weston and is 180km N of Sydney, 16km SW of MAITLAND and 13km by road E of CESSNOCK. Coal mining commenced here in the early years of this century and has remained an important part of the local economy, though an aluminium smelter which commenced operations in 1969 is a major industry; in the adjacent rural region there is dairying, orcharding, fodder crop growing and timber-getting. The town name comes from an Aboriginal term meaning 'man', 'the first man' or 'the first person'. Statistically, the urban centre of Kurri Kurri is part of the city of Greater Cessnock.

Kwinana WA (population 12 355 in 1981) This coastal industrial town is located on COCKBURN SOUND, 19km S of Perth. It has been specially developed in recent decades as an industrial centre and since the 1950s numerous major enterprises have been established, including an oil refinery, steel rolling mills, a blast furance, a nickel refinery, an alumina treatment plant and a power station. New residential areas with modern amenities and facilities, E of the industrial area on the limestone ridge, have been constructed to accommodate employees. The name Kwinana was taken from a freighter wrecked along the coast early this century, but the name originally came from an Aboriginal word meaning 'a young woman'.

Kyabram VIC (population 5 413 in 1981) A small town in the central N irrigation areas

of the State, Kyabram is located between the GOULBURN and CAMPASPE Rivers and between the Midland and Murray Valley Highways, 200km by road N of Melbourne, 40km NW of SHEPPARTON and 40km SE of ECHUCA. It is a market and business centre for the adjacent irrigated farmlands which produce citrus, stone fruits and vegetables, and which raise sheep and beef and dairy cattle. The town's name is taken from an Aboriginal word meaning 'thick forest'.

Kyneton VIC (population 3 815 in 1981) A country town in the central highlands region of the State, Kyneton is situated on the CAMPASPE RIVER, 35km by road SE of CASTLEMAIN. It is located on the Calder Highway and on the railway route from Melbourne to BENDIGO, 92km by rail NW of Melbourne. At an elevation of 509m above sea level, it has an average annual rainfall of 751mm. The surrounding rural district includes areas of fertile basalt soils and is noted for sheep and cattle grazing and dairying, and produces wheat, oats and potatoes. The area was first settled in the 1830s and the original grazing property was called Kineton after the English village near Stratford-on-Avon; later it became known as Kynetown, taken from the old English word 'kyne' meaning 'cow'; it later took its present spelling and the Shire of Kyneton was proclaimed in 1865.

Kyogle NSW (population 3 070 in 1981) A small country town in the NORTH COAST region of the State, Kyogle is situated on the RICHMOND RIVER, 796km by road N of Sydney, located N of CASINO and NW of LISMORE. At an elevation of 60m above sea level, it is a service centre for a productive rural region where dairying and beef cattle grazing are the main activities. Timber-getting is important in the surrounding forested hilly country; there are sawmills in the district and a veneer factory in the town. The name Kyogle comes from an Aboriginal word meaning 'scrub turkey'.

Labor Party, Australian *see* Australian Labor Party

lace bark, Queensland *see* Sterculiaceae

lacewings *see* antlions, etc.

Lachlan River NSW An inland stream, the chief tributary of the MURRUMBIDGEE RIVER, thus draining into the MURRAY-DARLING system, it rises in the SOUTHERN

TABLELANDS, near the small town of Collector, SW of GOULBURN, in hilly sheep country where the annual rainfall exceeds 700mm. The main headwater tributaries are the Boorowa, Crookwell and Abercrombie Rivers which flow in a general NW direction. At the confluence of the Lachlan and Abercrombie is WYANGALA DAM, a major reservoir 48km upstream from COWRA, storing water for irrigation and livestock supply. Downstream from COWRA the Lachlan is joined by the Belubula River on the right bank at Goolagong. On the upper part of the Belubula River, 6km from the township of Carcoar, is the Carcoar Dam; with a storage capacity of 35 800ML, it was constructed in 1970 to conserve water for irrigation and to stabilise the Lachlan flow. Beyond its confluence with the Belubula, the Lachlan continues through the towns of FORBES, CONDOBOLIN, Hillston and Booligal on a slow, meandering course across broad plain lands in a great arc, first NW then W and SW, with multitudes of BILLABONGS and ANABRANCHES. The countryside becomes increasingly arid, and sheep grazing dominates the rural scene.

Over its course of some 1 500km, the Lachlan thus flows from the Southern Tablelands through the SW slopes and across the SW plains. Several weirs have been constructed on the Lachlan (for example, Jemalong Weir below Forbes, and Willandra, Hillston and Booligal Weirs further downstream) to stabilise river flow, to lessen flood effects and to provide water for livestock, domestic use and some irrigation. Several highways traverse the Lachlan River valley: the Mid-Western Highway crosses the river at Cowra and continues W through GRENFELL and on to WEST WYALONG; the Olympic Way crosses it on a N-S route through Cowra; the Newell Highway crosses it on a NE-SW route through Forbes; the Cobb Highway on a N-S route crosses it at Booligal; and the Lachlan Valley Way follows the arc of the river to the Cobb Highway junction. During years of heavy rainfall, much of the low-lying area of the Lachlan River valley is subject to flooding, and the towns can be inundated, though the various structures built on the river, particularly Wyangala Dam, have done much to reduce the severity of these floods. The river was first explored by John OXLEY in 1817 and named by him in honour of Governor Lachlan MACQUARIE. The Willandra National Park (19 386ha), located 65km from Hillston, was established in 1975. It comprises a stretch of plain country with low sand ridges, where it is anticipated the natural vegetation associations will regenerate after a century of sheep grazing. The park has large populations of kangaroos and emus.
Further reading: Clune, *Rolling Down the Lachlan*. Angus & Robertson, Sydney, 1944.

lacrosse This game is the national sport of Canada and is thought to have been introduced into that country by early Norse settlers from Iceland. It is said that a French cleric, visiting Canada to convert the natives to Christianity, likened the stick used in the game to a bishop's crosier and called the sport *la crosse*. The playing stick nowadays has a net at one end and the aim of the game is to carry, bat or throw the ball through the opponent's goal as many times as possible and to prevent one's opponents from scoring. Lacrosse was introduced into Australia in the early 1870s by a Canadian, L.L. Mount, who brought some sticks to VIC, and the game is still more popular in that State than in any other. Australian teams have performed consistently well in international championships and in 1967 finished second to the USA in the world championships. Australia's most successful player to date has been Brian Griffin of WA who was rated the world's greatest player by the Americans in the 1967 world championships.

ladybirds *see* beetles

Lake Albacutya VIC Located in the WIMMERA region of western VIC about 40km W of Hopetown and just NW of Jeparit, it is a lake of internal drainage which receives water from the Wimmera River via LAKE HINDMARSH and Outlet Creek in wet seasons. The area is one of low and uncertain rainfall (Jeparit has an average annual rainfall of only 367mm) and the lake is frequently dry. The name comes from an Aboriginal word meaning 'place of bitter quandongs' (a small native fruit). The Wyperfeld National Park, the largest national park in VIC (100 000ha), lies about 10km N of the lake and includes stretches of mallee country, with linear and crescent-shaped sand dunes and numerous lake beds (Lake Brambuck is the largest) which in wet seasons contain water. Bird life in the park includes emus and mallee fowls.

Lake Alexandrina SA Located at the mouth of the MURRAY RIVER, this broad, shallow lake extends about 38km E-W and its longest N-S distance is approximately 25km, though it stretches S beyond this to the slit islands at the river mouth. To the SE of Lake Alexandrina, and adjoining it, is Lake Albert. Formerly it was also joined to the COORONG, but five barrages, joining the islands across the Murray (Goolwa, Mundoo, Boundary Creek, Ewe Is and Tauwitchere), have been constructed to prevent salty water from coming into the lake and up to the Murray in times of low river flow. The lake was named by the explorer Charles STURT in 1830 in honour of Princess Alexandrina (who later became Queen Victoria).

Lake Amadeus NT Located in the remote SW corner of the Territory, this dazzlingly white expanse of salty mud flats lies within a vast elongated trough bounded on the N by the MACDONNELL RANGES, on the SW by the Petermann Range and on the S by the MUSGRAVE RANGES. The lake is elongated (about 120km) on a NW-SE axis, is quite narrow (from a few kilometres to over 20km wide) and is surrounded by vast areas of sand hills. AYERS ROCK lies about 50km S of the E section of the lake. Curtin Springs, a station on the road to Ayers Rock, SE of the lake and within the same vast depression, is at an elevation of 488m above sea level; it receives an average annual rainfall of only 293mm, but long dry spells can occur and the amount of rain is quite variable from year to year. The Lake Amadeus basin is composed of sedimentary rocks and in 1964 drilling showed that there was natural gas and some oil, though commercial development has not yet been undertaken. The lake was discovered by the explorer Ernest GILES in 1872 and named in honour of the King of Spain.

Lake Cargelligo NSW (population 1 240 in 1981) A small town on the shores of a lake of the same name in the W plains, it is just S of the LACHLAN RIVER, 568km by road W of Sydney. It is a rail centre, the terminus of a branch line off the main S route from COOTAMUNDRA through TEMORA, 666km by rail from Sydney. At an elevation of 169m above sea level, it experiences hot summer conditions, mild but frosty winters, and an average annual rainfall of only 423mm with a slight concentration of rain in winter. However, the amount of rain received is variable from year to year and droughts are not unknown. The town is a service centre and railhead for a rich grazing and wheat growing district. The lake is now an integral part of the Lachlan water conservation scheme, providing recreation for fishing, boating and swimming, as well as a sanctuary for a wide variety of bird life—black swans, pelicans, wild ducks and geese.

Lake Corangamite VIC The largest natural lake in VIC, it is located in the WESTERN DISTRICT, N of the Princes Highway, between COLAC and CAMPERDOWN, some 80km W of GEELONG and 170km WSW of Melbourne. Although located inland it is a salt lake and is relatively shallow with an average depth of only 2m. It has a shoreline of almost 160km; prior to 1956, the lake level would rise during times of heavy rainfall and flood the adjacent low-lying farmlands, but a channel was constructed, linking it to the BARWON RIVER, to carry away excess water. Unlike many of the lakes in the Western District, it is not located in a dormant volcanic crater, but is situated in a depression on the plain. The lake takes its name from an Aboriginal word meaning 'bitter (salty) water'.

Lake Echo TAS Located on the Dee River, a tributary of the DERWENT RIVER, at an elevation of 845m in the CENTRAL PLATEAU region about 130km NW of Hobart, between the Marlborough and Lake Highways, the lake extends N-S for some 11km and is pear-shaped, being wider in the N (over 6km) and narrowing to less than 3km in the S. The storage capacity of the lake has been increased by the construction of a dam and the intake is supplemented by water diverted from the OUSE RIVER. The waters are utilised for hydro-electricity generation at the Lake Echo power station which has an installed capacity of 32 400kW and is part of the integrated hydro-electricity system of the highlands. After being used at this power station, the waters are then diverted to the TUNGATINAH system of the Nive River for further power generation.

Lake Eyre SA The largest salt lake in Australia, located in the arid mid-N of the State, about 600km NNW of Adelaide, it comprises two lakes (Lake Eyre and Lake Eyre South), linked by Goyder Channel, together covering an area of 9 300km² and forming a vast internal drainage system. The N lake is the larger, with a N-S extent of 130km and an E-W extent of 100km. The region is one of low and irregular rainfall, with an average annual total of less than 130mm; the lake is rarely filled and only in the occasional times of high rainfall do the streams in the region reach the lake. The main river systems which drain towards the lake are Cooper's and Warburton Creeks from the CHANNEL COUNTRY in the NE, and the Macumba and Neales Rivers from the NW. The lake bed, sloping from N to S, where it is 12m below sea level, is composed of salt so solid in parts that heavy vehicles can be driven across it. This vast area has also been used in attempts to break land-speed records (Donald CAMPBELL in 1964). The lake was discovered by the explorer Edward EYRE in 1840 and subsequently was named in his honour. To the E of the lake the BIRDSVILLE TRACK leads to QLD, and the railway from PORT AUGUSTA to ALICE SPRINGS skirts the S of the lake and then passes W of it. The SIMPSON DESERT and STURT'S STONY DESERT lie N and NE of the lake and the vast expanse of the WOOMERA rocket-testing range is located to the W and SW.

Lake Frome SA Located NE of the FLINDERS RANGES, this pear-shaped salt lake extends about 100km N-S and is 50km wide at its S end. It is an internal drainage basin and since it is situated in an arid region of low rainfall, only rarely is it filled. It was named in honour of E.C. Frome, the SA Surveyor-General who succeeded Colonel William LIGHT.

Lake Gairdner SA A large salt lake, generally dry, it is located S of the Stuart Highway and the transcontinental railway line, SW of LAKE TORRENS, about 100km NW of PORT AUGUSTA, and S of the WOOMERA rocket range. It is an elongated lake on a NNW-SSE axis over 150km long and about 40km wide. It is an internal drainage basin, and since it is situated in an arid region of low and irregular rainfall, only rarely is it filled. It was named in honour of Gordon Gairdner, the senior clerk in the Australian section of the British Colonial Office.

Lake George NSW Located in the SOUTHERN TABLELANDS adjacent to the Federal Highway between GOULBURN and Canberra, this lake occupies a basin of internal drainage, about 24km long N-S and some 10km wide E-W. Periodically, the lake becomes dry and is used for sheep grazing. When there is a series of rainy years, the lake refills to a depth over 7m. There is a steep scarp along the W side of the lake, formed when the basin subsided due to the faulting and movement of the crustal rocks in past geological times.

Lake Hindmarsh VIC Located in the WIMMERA region of western VIC, about 40km N of Dimboola and 40km NW of WARRACKNABEAL, it is a lake of internal drainage into which the Wimmera River flows. Islands within the lake are noted as pelican breeding grounds. It was discovered and named by the explorer Edward John EYRE in 1838 after the Governor of SA. The size of the lake varies with the seasons; in wet times it may cover 130km², but in drought times it shrinks considerably and may even dry up during prolonged dry periods. LAKE ALBACUTYA lies about 15km N and the two are linked by a stream channel during wet times.

Lake Illawarra *see* Illawarra

Lake King VIC Located in the E section of the GIPPSLAND lakes region, it is a shallow lagoon into which the MITCHELL and TAMBO Rivers drain from the N, forming long silt jetties where they enter it. The lake lies SE of BAIRNSDALE and W of LAKES ENTRANCE, some 300km by road E of Melbourne. It is a popular holiday and tourist resort in the summer months. It was named in 1840 by the explorer Count STRZELECKI after Phillip Parker King, son of Governor KING.

Lake King William TAS An artificial lake, 13km long, in the CENTRAL PLATEAU region, it is about 160km NW of Hobart and was formed as a result of the construction of Clark Dam on the DERWENT RIVER. LAKE ST CLAIR lies 6km N of it, and the two lakes are linked by the Derwent. The Lyell Highway passes between the two lakes and crosses the river at the small town of Derwent Bridge. Both lakes form part of the major hydro-electricity power scheme of the upper Derwent and its tributaries. Water is released from the S end of Lake King William, generates power in BUTLERS GORGE station and is then diverted E via the Tarraleah Canal into the gorge of the Nive River where it is again used for power generation at the TARRALEAH and TUNGATINAH power stations.

Lake Macquarie NSW A coastal lake S of NEWCASTLE, covering an area of 104km², with 174km of winding foreshores, it is claimed as the largest seaboard lake in Australia. The main N railway line runs to the W of the lake and the Pacific Highway skirts the E foreshores. The lake is really an extensive coastal lagoon formed by the accumulation of sand deposits as bars and dunes along the coastal zone. These deposits blocked a series of river estuaries which existed in earlier geological time, and now only a narrow 90m-wide channel through the sand bars remains, connecting the lake to the sea.

The proximity of Lake Macquarie to Newcastle (the N parts of the lake are within 20km of the city) makes it a popular weekend resort for city residents and many substantial homes have been built around its shores. It is also a popular tourist region, particularly for summer vacations, with facilities for fishing, swimming, sailing, riding and many other sports. The three largest tourist centres on the lake are Belmont (on the E shore), Swansea (at the lake entrance) and Toronto (on the W shore), all connected to Newcastle by rail and road. In recent decades these and other lakeside towns have increasingly become residential satellites for commuters to Newcastle. Belmont, 20km S of Newcastle, on the Pacific Highway where it passes along the E shore of the lake, is the headquarters of the Lake Macquarie Yacht Club, one of the largest in the State; the club's annual regatta over the Easter holidays attracts an impressive fleet of local and visiting craft. Boolaroo, a lakeside town on the NW foreshore 16km from Newcastle, is the site of the Sulphide Corporation Cockle Creek works, which smelt lead and zinc and manufacture acids and fertilisers. Toronto is the commercial focus and resort centre for the W section of the lake. Many other small towns are dotted around the foreshores, such as Speers Point, Warner's Bay, Arcadia Vale, Rathmines and WANGI WANGI. The population of the Lake Macquarie Municipality, with its offices at Speers Point, was over 147 000 at the 1981 census. Coal is mined at a number of places adjacent to the lake, such as Belmont and Awaba. Two electricity power stations, located near Wangi township on the W shore and Vales Point at the S end of the lake, form part of the New South Wales Electricity Commission's interconnected generating system. An island in the lake, Pulbah Is, is a wildlife sanctuary. *See also* Hunter River

Lake Macquarie in the Hunter Region NSW

NSW Dept of Tourism

Lake Pedder TAS Located in the rugged SW region of the State on the Serpentine River, a tributary of the GORDON RIVER which flows into MACQUARIE HARBOUR on the W coast, the lake lies in wilderness country, SE of QUEENSTOWN and S of the Lyell Highway, which was extensively glaciated during the Great Ice Age.

Access to the lake is by a branch road off the Lyell Highway via Maydena, a journey of about 160km by road from Hobart. The former natural Lake Pedder was a moraine-dammed lake in a glacial valley, but the present lake, covering a vast area of 242km², has been created by the construction of three dams to form major storage points for the Gordon River hydro-electricity scheme. At the NW end of the lake is the Serpentine Dam (wall 38m high), at the SE end are Scotts Peak Dam (43m) and Edgar Dam (17m). This development was bitterly opposed by conservationists but the lake has proved to be a mecca for anglers and a popular venue of aquatic sports. Lake Pedder lies in the N section of the South West National Park which covers 403 240ha of wilderness country stretching S of the Wilmot and Frankland Ranges with peaks rising to over 1000m (Mt Sprent 1 059m, Double Peak 1 060m); at the SE end of the lake are Mt Eliza (1 289m) and MOUNT ANNE (1 425m).

Lake Reeve VIC A long narrow coastal lagoon extending for about 65km, it is generally parallel to and inland from the sand ridge which forms the NINETY MILE BEACH in the GIPPSLAND region. Part of the lake and the beach are included in the Gippsland Lakes Coastal Park (15 550ha) where aquatic bird life abounds and where there are stretches of wilderness sand dune country. The lake was named after an explorer and pioneer, John Reeve, who settled on Snake Ridge run on the LATROBE RIVER in 1842.

Lake St Clair TAS Located at the S end of the CRADLE MOUNTAIN-Lake St Clair National Park in the central W region of the State, 173km via the Lyell Highway from Hobart, it is Australia's deepest lake, reaching

over 200m in depth. It is a long (17.5km in a NW-SE direction) and relatively narrow lake (average width about 2km), 737m above sea level, with the steep-sloping flat-topped MOUNT OLYMPUS on the SW shore rising to 1 447m and Mt Ida on the NE side rising to 1 253m. To the N of the lake several peaks rise to over 1 400m (Mt Gould 1 491m, Mt Geryon 1 509m, Walled Mt 1 410m, The Acropolis 1 471m, Mt Manfred 1 402m). The valley occupied by the lake was shaped by glacial ice during the Great Ice Age and moraine material, deposited when the ice melted, dams the lake at its SE end. The headwater tributaries of the DERWENT RIVER flow into the lake, which is used as a natural storage point for hydro-electricity generation. As its SE extremity, the lake is linked, by a section of the Derwent River, to the artifical LAKE KING WILLIAM, about 6km further S. The small village of Derwent Bridge is located on the river where the Lyell Highway passes between these two lakes. The average annual rainfall at Lake St Clair is 1 514mm, with the highest falls in the winter months and the lowest amounts in summer. Much of the winter precipitation falls as snow, and roads in the area are subject to snow and ice conditions during this season.

Lake Sorrell TAS Located in the E section of the CENTRAL PLATEAU region, between the Midland and Lake Highways, SE of ARTHURS LAKE and GREAT LAKE and some 110km N of Hobart, it is a shallow lake covering about 50km² and drained by some of the N tributaries of the DERWENT RIVER. It is a sparsely settled area and is a summer fishing resort, separated from Lake Crescent to the S by a narrow isthmus on which the small township of Interlaken is situated.

Lake Torrens SA A large salt lake lying between SPENCER GULF and LAKE EYRE, on a N-S alignment, it is over 200km long and up to about 40km wide. It is a lake of internal drainage, second in size to Lake Eyre, situated in a rift valley W of the FLINDERS RANGES and in recent geological times it was part of a large N-S depression which was linked to Spencer Gulf. The lake bed is some 34m above sea level and only rarely, in times of occasional heavy rain, is it filled. Parts of the surface are bogs, others are covered by layers of salt. The central Australian railway from PORT AUGUSTA to ALICE SPRINGS passes E of the lake and the Stuart Highway skirts the SW shore. The WOOMERA rocket-testing range lies W and NW of the lake.

Lake Tyrell VIC Located in the Mallee (see WIMMERA-MALLEE) region in the NW of the State, some 70km W of SWAN HILL, N of Sea Lake township and SE of Ouyen, adjacent to the Calder Highway, 365km NW of Melbourne, it is a salt-encrusted expanse which contains water in rainy seasons. It is a lake of internal drainage into which Tyrell Creek occasionally flows. Salt is produced from the lake and the adjacent areas are important for wheat growing. The lake was named by the explorer Edward John EYRE in 1838 from the Aboriginal word *derrel* meaning 'sky' or 'space above'.

Lake Victoria VIC One of the GIPPSLAND lakes lying between LAKE WELLINGTON to the W and LAKE KING to the E, this long, narrow and shallow lagoon is a popular summer holiday area. It is joined by the narrow McLennans Strait to Lake Wellington, and is separated from LAKE REEVE by a long isthmus running generally parallel to the sand ridge formation of the NINETY MILE BEACH. The Lakes National Park (2 380ha) covers the NE section of the isthmus, where aquatic bird life is prolific and animal life includes wallabies, kangaroos, possums and emus.

Lake Wellington VIC One of the GIPPSLAND lakes into which the LATROBE and AVON Rivers drain, it is located E of SALE and inland from the NINETY MILE BEACH. It is a shallow (under 4m deep) oval-shaped lake, the innermost of the lakes system, connected to LAKE VICTORIA by McLennans Strait, and is a popular tourist and holiday resort. It was named after the Duke of Wellington in 1840.

Lakes Entrance VIC (population 3 414 in 1981) The major commercial fishing port and resort centre of the GIPPSLAND lakes region, it is located on the Princes Highway 319km by road E of Melbourne, 36km E of BAIRNSDALE and 64km W of ORBOST. This region is one of VIC's most popular tourist centres and in the summer months there is an influx of visitors for fishing, swimming, boating and other aquatic sports on the lakes and adjacent coastal beaches. The 'entrance' is an artificial channel cut through the coastal dune belt, kept clear by tidal scour, connecting the

Dept of Tourism TAS

Lake St Clair with Mt Olympus in the background

lakes (WELLINGTON, KING, VICTORIA and REEVE) with the open sea. Lakes Entrance is one of Australia's busiest fishing centres, with a large trawl fishing fleet; scallops and prawns are also important marine products and visitors can watch the scallops being processed at the dockside plant.

Lakes Entrance in Gippsland

Lalor, Peter (1827-89) Leader of the Eureka rebellion. He was born in Ireland into a family that had a long history of resistance to English rule. After being educated as a civil engineer, he came to VIC in 1852 and worked for a while on the Melbourne-GEELONG railway before going to the Ovens goldfield and from there to BALLARAT. He became prominent in the Ballarat Reform League and on 30 November 1854 was elected leader of those miners who were advocating an act of rebellion. It was under his direction that the EUREKA STOCKADE was built and the Republic of Victoria declared. When troops and police stormed the stockade Lalor was wounded in the left arm, but he managed to escape and to go into hiding. Shortly afterwards his left arm had to be amputated at the shoulder. A reward of £200 was placed on his head, but withdrawn after the captured Eureka rebels had been brought to trial and acquitted.

Peter Lalor

In the meantime a public subscription fund had raised on his behalf a sum sufficient for the purchase of over 60ha of land near Ballarat. He emerged from hiding to buy it, and in November 1855 stood successfully for the seat of Ballarat in elections for the Legislative Council. After the advent of responsible government in the following year he became a member of the Legislative Assembly, and remained in Parliament for 27 years (1856-71; 1875-87), holding at various times the portfolios of Postmaster-General and Minister of Trade and Customs. In 1880 he was appointed Speaker of the House. Ironically, the rebel leader of Eureka was inclined towards conservatism as a parliamentarian. It seems that his stand in 1854 had been based not on any comprehensive plan for social reform but on a general hatred of injustice. When he resigned his seat in 1887 on the grounds of ill health, Parliament voted him a grant of £4000 as recognition of his service to the public.
Further reading: Turnbull, C. *Eureka: The Story of Peter Lalor*. Hawthorn Press, Melbourne, 1946; Currey, C.H. *The Irish at Eureka*. Angus & Robertson, Sydney, 1954.

Lambert, George Washington (1873-1930) Artist. Born in St Petersburg, Russia, of American parentage, his father was a railway engineer who died before his son was born. After a brief sojourn in Germany and England, Lambert's family emigrated to Australia in 1887 and lived on a farm near Nevertire NSW. While a station hand, he became a graphic artist for the *Bulletin*; his confident and incisive drawing earned money and favourable comment. He then moved to Sydney and attended evening classes with Julian ASHTON, who came to regard him as his prize pupil. Lambert's *Across the Black Soil Plains* (1899), now in the Art Gallery of New South Wales, projected him into the public eye as a painter and the award of the Society of Artists' Travelling Scholarship in 1900 gained him entry into Colarossi's and the Atelier Delécluse in Paris. He turned his back on the Impressionists' use of colour, preferring the English love of tone. Lambert was also impressed by the work of such artists as Van Dyck and Sir William Orpen. Lambert returned to Sydney in 1921, where his work and his energetic and magnetic personality attracted much attention. His success as an artist increased his reputation, especially as he depicted war with craftsmanship and unquestioning patriotism. His portraits were in great demand; one of the best-known is *Miss Thea Proctor* (1902), now in the Art Gallery of New South Wales. He died at Cobbity NSW. One son, Constant, became a composer and the other, Maurice, a sculptor.

Lambing Flat Riots During the gold rushes of the 1850s and 1860s, many CHINESE came to the diggings and a number of anti-Chinese riots occurred. A series of these took place at the Lambing Flat field (now the town of YOUNG) in NSW, and in 1861 the situation became so serious that a detachment of 130 soldiers and an artillery squad were sent to the field, arriving early in March. They were recalled in May, but on 30 June a major riot occurred in which white miners drove the Chinese from the field with considerable violence. Two weeks later the arrest of three alleged leaders of the anti-Chinese riot produced fresh violence, culminating in a gun battle, a charge by mounted police with drawn swords and the death of one miner. Troops were again sent to the field and 13 miners were arrested. However, a court at GOULBURN found only one of the arrested men guilty.

Lamington Plateau QLD Located in the SE of the State, it lies N of and adjacent to the McPHERSON RANGE, with which it is geologically linked. A basalt-capped plateau, rugged and much dissected, it is the headwater zone of the Albert and Coomera Rivers and the tributaries of the LOGAN RIVER. The Lamington National Park covers 20 200ha of rainforest, eucalypt forest and heathland, with peaks rising to over 1 100m and innumerable waterfalls; there are several walking tracks through the park, but the wilderness area in the S is recommended only for experienced walkers. There are two resort centres in the plateau: O'Reilly's Green Mts Guest House located on the W summit of the park, noted for its bird life, and Binna Burra Lodge at the NE rim of the park set on the crest of a spectacular bluff. The township of Lamington lies to the W of the park, with Beechmont to the NE, and Canungra to the N.

lampreys and hagfishes These eel-shaped, primitive aquatic VERTEBRATES are CHORDATES (subphylum Craniata, superclass Agnatha, class Cyclostomata). They have naked scaleless skins but no jaws and no paired fins. They have a skull and a skeleton including a backbone, but these are made of cartilage, not bone. The mouth is a circular sucker with horny, rasping teeth. There are seven circular gill openings on either side of the lamprey's body, while the hagfish has five to 15 pairs of gills which either share an opening on either side or open separately on the surface depending on the family. The nostril is single and on top of the head in lampreys and at the tip of the snout in hagfishes. Hagfishes also have barbels round the mouth and are completely marine, while lampreys spend part of their lives in freshwater.

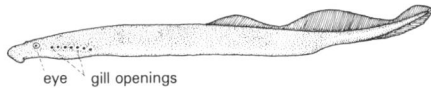

eye   gill openings

A lamprey, showing an eye and seven gill openings

Lampreys ascend rivers, make a nest of stones on the river bed and after laying eggs, they die. The resulting larvae, the ammocoetes, are blind and toothless and feed on organic debris in the mud. After metamorphosing into adults they move into the sea and begin an externally parasitic life feeding on other fish. Hagfishes are hermaphrodites as adults, but an individual is either a male or a female at any one time. Their diet consists of dead fish, molluscs and so on and they burrow into their prey, consuming it from the inside. Because hagfishes secrete large amounts of slime they are sometimes known as slime eels.

There are about 40 species of hagfishes and lampreys in the world, all of which live in cold and temperate waters. There are three known species of lampreys in Australia—the pouched or wide-mouthed lamprey, *Geotria australis* (51cm long), which has large fringes of skin around the mouth, and the narrow-mouthed lamprey, *Mordacia mordax* (56cm) which does not have such flaps. The pouched lamprey is black or brown above, and light below, and is found in freshwater streams in southern WA, SA, VIC and TAS. The narrow-mouthed lamprey is thinner, and is bluish-grey above and silvery below. It occurs in SA, VIC, NSW and TAS. The third species, *M. praecox* (10.2cm to 17.2cm), similar to the narrow-mouthed lamprey, is now recognised and is unusual in that it is entirely freshwater and lacks a parasitic stage. Until recently there were no known hagfishes in Australian waters but now the common New Zealand species, *Eptatretus cirrhatus* (61cm), is known to occur.

lamp shells This is the common name for the marine invertebrates which belong to the phylum Brachiopoda, so called because they look like early Roman oil lamps. Although members of this phylum superficially resemble BIVALVE MOLLUSCS they are quite unrelated. The valves of the shell are above and below the body (not on each side, as in molluscs), and one is larger than the other; the valves are bilaterally symmetrical. Lamp shells first appeared in the Cambrian period and peaked in the Ordovician period, but to date their evolutionary development is little understood. There are about 260 living species, but more than 30 000 fossil species have been described. Most are small (average 2.5cm in length or width) and oval. Most species prefer to live in the shallow, quiet, protected waters of the continental shelves; most are attached to the sea bed but some species burrow. Lamp shells feed by opening the shell which allows the minute hair-like appendages (cilia) attached to the lophophore (a feeding structure, similar to that of ECTOPROCTS, that filters food from sea water) to bring food, in the form of minute organisms, to the mouth.

lancelets Also known as amphioxus, these small, fish-like animals are CHORDATES and belong to the subphylum Acrania or Cephalochordata (*see* FISHES and VERTEBRATES). They lack a skull and limbs but do have a stiffening rod (the notochord) running for most of the length of the back. The body muscles are clearly segmented. Lancelets feed by drawing in water through the mouth as they lie half-buried in the sand, trapping the food particles in a string of mucus which is swallowed, and passing the filtered water out through the gill slits. The deepwater lancelet, *Bathyamphioxus australis* (25mm long), is found in the GREAT AUSTRALIAN BIGHT at depths of 65m to 185m. The southern lancelet, *Paramphioxus bassanus*

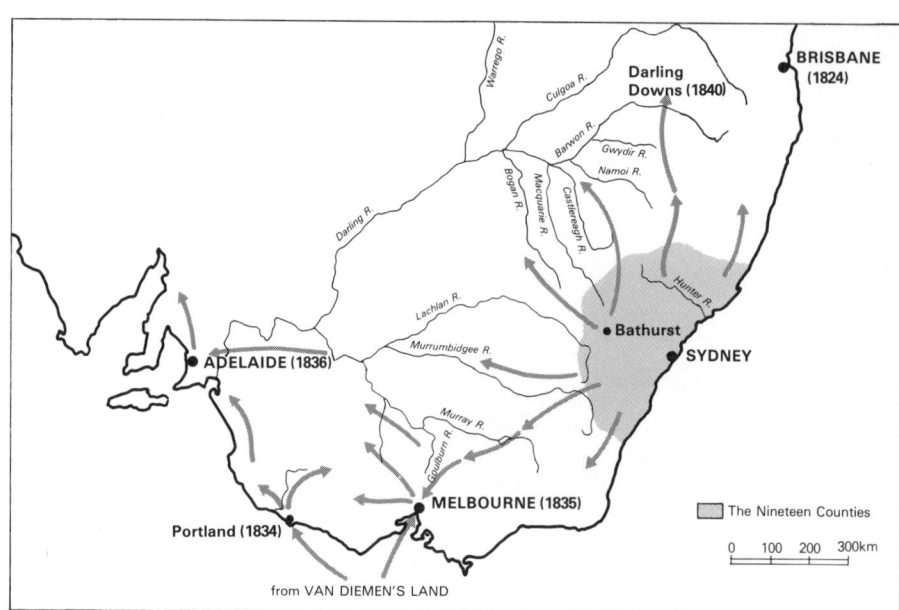

Extension of settlement on the SE mainland of Australia during the squatting period

(50mm), is found in shallower water off SA, VIC and NSW.

land mullet *see* lizards

land settlement and tenure The present forms of land tenure in the States and Territories of Australia are largely a reflection of those adopted in the past to advance European settlement of a vast and sparsely populated continent. From the beginning settlement policy was based on the principle, enforced in England since the time of William the Conqueror, that all land belonged initially to the Crown. In keeping with the general spirit of colonialism, no thought was given to any rights which the Aborigines might consider they had over the land.

Land grants For some time after the foundation of Sydney the only method by which settlers could acquire ownership of Crown land was by means of grants and orders from the Crown. In practice this meant that the Governor made the land grants, subject to the approval of the authorities in Britain. The first person to be given such a grant was the ex-convict James RUSE, in 1789.

Land sales By the mid-1820s concern was being expressed at the readiness with which land was being given away. In 1825 Governor BRISBANE introduced regulations under which Crown lands could be sold by private tender at a minimum price of five shillings an acre. While some land was disposed of by this method, land grants continued, and by 1831 the total area granted in NSW alone since 1789 had reached nearly four million acres (about 1 600 000ha). However, by that time many people in government circles had been influenced by Edward Gibbon WAKEFIELD's theory that land in colonies should be sold at a fairly high price and that settlement should not be allowed to spread too widely. In 1831 orders known as the Ripon Regulations were issued;

these stated that Crown lands were to be disposed of only by public auction, at a minimum price of five shillings an acre (a figure raised to 12 shillings in 1839 and to 20 shillings in 1842). Meanwhile, in 1829 Governor DARLING, in an attempt to keep the colonists within a fairly small area, had decreed that settlement was not to take place on the mainland of NSW outside the area known as the NINETEEN COUNTIES.

Pastoral licences and leases During the 1830s the spread of the wool industry brought about great changes in the settlement needs of the colony, and subsequently in government policy. Wool production became the main source of wealth, and men known as SQUATTERS simply ignored the regulations and pastured their sheep on Crown lands beyond the Nineteen Counties. Governor BOURKE saw that the colony's prosperity depended largely upon these people, and in 1836 he introduced a system whereby each squatter could keep the use of his 'run' by paying an annual licence fee.

The squatters gained a further victory in 1847 when a system of leases was introduced. NSW was divided into settled, intermediate and unsettled areas. In the first category, leases were limited to one year; in the other two they could be for eight years and 14 years respectively. The pastoralist holding a lease had the right to buy all or part of his land at a fixed price of one pound an acre.

Land regulations in WA and SA The colonies which are now the States of TAS, VIC and QLD were originally parts of NSW, and until they became self-governing in the 1850s were subject to land regulations similar or identical to those of the mother colony. Only in WA and SA were there great differences. In the former, founded in 1829, the first settlers were given large grants of land in proportion to the capital which they brought to the colony, with extra amounts for those who brought labourers with them. In 1832 this system was abolished in favour of sale by auction with a minimum price of five shillings an acre. In SA, which was founded in 1836 in accordance with the general principles of Wakefield, a Board of Commissioners was empowered to sell land, by auction or otherwise, at not less than 12 shillings an acre. This provision led to a closer pattern of settlement than that in the other colonies. SA was also notable for the introduction in 1858 of a new land titles system, developed by Sir Robert TORRENS and later adopted in the other Australian colonies.

'Unlocking the land' By the 1860s the colonies' land settlement needs had changed again. There were now many more people wishing to take up land, but most of the first-class agricultural land in E Australia was accounted for by large pastoral leases. In order to 'unlock the land' and facilitate the growth of a farming population side by side with the pastoral tenants, Sir John ROBERTSON of NSW adopted the principle of 'free selection before survey'. His Lands and Occupation Act of 1861 allowed selectors to purchase, for one pound an acre, any block of Crown land from 40 acres to 320 acres (16ha to 129ha) in area, whether it formed part of a lease or not. However, this Act and similar legislation passed to support it in NSW and the other colonies over a period of 30 years were not very successful. The squatters managed to find ways of evading the laws, and in any case the opportunities for gaining a living from small farms were not as common as the legislators imagined.

The introduction of land taxes on large estates at various times from 1884 (SA) to 1910 (the Commonwealth) and 1915 (QLD) was also designed to encourage closer settlement, but probably had little effect. In many cases where large properties were subdivided in order to avoid or lessen the impact of such taxes, they were merely split up among members of the former owners' families. When, closer settlement did come about, mainly from the 1890s onwards, it was chiefly because economic conditions were favourable. The development of new strains of wheat, improvements in farm equipment, the spread of the railways and the advent of fast, refrigerated steamships were all important factors which favoured the development of closely settled farming communities in certain districts. Resumption or repurchase of the land by the Crown for subdivision into small farms also played a part, especially after each World War when it was used to provide farms for ex-soldiers. Soldier settlement schemes, however, had a disappointing success rate, many of the settlers finally abandoning their land because of the lack of skill, the smallness of the blocks or other unfavourable economic circumstances.

Recent trends and the present situation Since World War II the trend towards closer settlement has to some extent been reversed. Many smaller properties, most notably in the dairying industry, have proved to be uneconomic under modern conditions, while the loss of traditional markets in the UK and on the Continent because of agricultural policies of the European Economic Community has told heavily against some forms of intensive farming, such as fruit growing. In many cases governments have therefore taken steps to encourage the amalgamation of small holdings into larger, more economic units. Efforts at urban decentralisation, through the setting up of 'growth centres' at such locations as ALBURY-WODONGA on the NSW/VIC border, have caused the question of land tenure to be given considerable attention in recent years. In 1973 a Commission of Enquiry into Land Tenure recommended that in such centres only residential land should be sold in fee simple (that is, into absolute ownership), and that in all other categories of land use (commercial/industrial, community, public and rural/primary) it should be leased.

Current statistics on land tenure are given in each issue of the *Year Book of Australia*. In brief, land which has been alienated (transferred from the Crown to private ownership) totals only about 15 per cent of the total area of Australia. In all States, Crown lands may be disposed of by unconditional purchase at public auction or by various other forms of conditional or unconditional purchase. In the NT very little land has been alienated, except for areas subject to Aboriginal land rights. In the ACT land tenure is subject to the Seat of Government (Administration) Act of 1910, which allows Crown lands to be leased but not sold or otherwise disposed of. Land which had been alienated before the Act came into force has been largely resumed for the development of the Canberra city area. About another 13 per cent of Australia consists of Crown lands reserved for public purposes—roads, park and recreation reserves, water frontages, forest and timber reserves, national parks and Aboriginal reserves. Most of the remainder of the country is occupied under various forms of lease or licence. About a fifth of the whole country, mainly in arid areas, is still unoccupied.

Aboriginal land rights A major change during recent years has been the granting to Aborigines of land rights over considerable areas of the NT and SA. Following the report of the Woodward Royal Commission of 1972-74, the federal government passed the Aboriginal Land Rights (Northern Territory) Act 1976-78. This provided for the granting to traditional Aboriginal groups of inalienable freehold title to former reserve lands, and laid down a procedure by which Aborigines could lay claim to other areas of unalienated Crown land on the grounds of strong traditional links. The titles of such land are held by Aboriginal Land Trusts and administered by Aboriginal Land Councils. SA has provided similar rights over large areas in the N of that State by the Pitjantjatjara Land Rights Bill 1979, and by an agreement between the government and Aboriginal representatives in 1980 regarding the exact areas to be granted. Land rights legislation was also passed in NSW in 1983, but has been criticised by many Aborigines as being too limited in its scope. Aboriginal groups hope for the extension of these rights and the granting of similar rights in other States.

Further reading: Roberts, S.H. *History of Australian Land Settlement*. Melbourne University Press, Melbourne, 1924; *Report of the Commission of Inquiry into Land Tenures*. Australian Govt Publishing Service, Canberra, 1973.

Landy, John Michael (1930-) Athlete. Born in Melbourne, Landy was the first athlete to undergo the rigorous and demanding training programme developed by Percy Cerutty, a well-known athletics trainer. In early 1954, Roger Bannister of England ran the mile in 3 minutes 59.4 seconds at Oxford. In June 1954, Landy was competing in championships in Turku, Finland, when he set a new world record for the mile and reduced Bannister's time by 1.7 seconds, just 46 days after the Englishman had set his record. Landy thus became the first Australian and the second man in the world to break the four-minute mile. In the same year he also broke the world record for 1500m, running the distance in 3 minutes 41.8 seconds. In the 1954 Commonwealth Games, Landy and Bannister met in the one-mile event; the race was won by Bannister. Landy had sustained an injury requiring four stitches in his foot the night before the race but had told no one because it might have seemed that he was making excuses for his defeat. A modest, considerate and dedicated athlete, Landy retired from international competitive running after winning the bronze medal for the 1500m at the Melbourne Olympic Games in 1956.

Lane, William (1861-1917) Journalist and utopian socialist. Born in Bristol, England, he emigrated to Canada at the age of 16 and worked there and in the USA as a journalist. He settled in Brisbane in 1885, again worked as a journalist, and became deeply involved in the trade union movement. He helped to found two socialist newspapers, the *Boomerang* (1887) and the *Worker* (1890), using them to popularise the ideas of socialists and reformers such as Edward Bellamy and Henry George, to promote the Labor movement and to oppose non-European immigration. However, after the failure of the maritime and pastoral strikes of 1890-91 he became despondent about the prospects of grafting socialism onto established societies, and turned to the founding of new settlements on utopian socialist lines. In 1893 he founded the New Australia Co-operative Settlement Association, and two years later led a party of 220 to found a socialist settlement in Paraguay, where he obtained a grant of land from the government. The settlement, called New Australia, was soon racked by dissension, and in 1894 Lane left it, with a party of 63, to found another settlement, Cosme. It too failed to prosper, its membership dwindled, and Lane withdrew from it in 1899. In the meantime New Australia had lost its socialist character: in 1897 its inhabitants divided their assets and established private ownership of property. The remaining settlers at Cosme did likewise

in 1909. The economic and social causes of the failure of both experiments were complex, and to some extent a matter for debate, but Lane's dictatorial behaviour and his racism, which prevented any attempt to equalise the numbers of the sexes through intermarriage with the surrounding population, must be included among them. After leaving Paraguay he was briefly editor of the Labor newspaper, the *Australian Worker*, in Sydney, but his imperialist sentiments, and particularly his support for Britain in the Boer War, placed him in conflict with general feeling in the Labor movement. Before the end of 1900 he migrated to New Zealand, where he joined the staff of the conservative *New Zealand Herald*, of which he was editor from 1913 until his death. In the later years of his life he became increasingly conservative and strongly imperialist.
Further reading: Ross, L. *William Lane and the Australian Labor Movement*. Forward Press, Sydney, 1937; Souter, G. *A Peculiar People: The Australians in Paraguay*. Angus & Robertson, Sydney, 1968.

Lang, John Dunmore (1799-1878)

Presbyterian clergyman, politician and writer. Born in Greenock, Scotland, he was educated for the ministry at Glasgow University and ordained in 1822. Arriving in NSW in the following year, he became the colony's first Presbyterian minister. He remained minister of Scots Church from its completion in 1826 until his death, in spite of his official deposition by the Synod from 1842 to 1863. In 1872 he became Moderator of the General Assembly of the Presbyterian Church in NSW. A man of strong convictions, remarkably outspoken and a master of vituperation, he was involved throughout his career in disputes within the Presbyterian community, in sectarian controversies and in political conflict. His interest in education led him to found the Australian College in 1832, but it closed down in 1854. He served on the Legislative Council as member for PORT PHILLIP BAY from 1843 to 1847 and for MORETON BAY from 1854 to 1856 and was a vigorous advocate of the separation of these two districts from NSW. He was a strong opponent of transportation, being elected to the Legislative Council in 1850 on an anti-transportation platform, and was also an avowed republican. After the granting of responsible government to NSW Lang was a member of the Legislative Assembly from 1859 to 1869 and strongly supported extension of the franchise. Although in his early years in NSW he had obtained Treasury aid for the building of his church and for his salary, in his later years he came to oppose State aid to religion. Of his many published works, the most widely read was the *Historical and Statistical Account of New South Wales*, which was first published in 1834 and ran to four editions. Throughout his career he worked energetically in promoting emigration to Australia.
Further reading: Gilchrist, A. (ed) *John Dunmore Lang*. (2 vols) Jedgarm Publications, Melbourne, 1951.

Lang, John Thomas (1876-1975)

Premier of NSW. Lang was perhaps the most controversial politician in Australian history. He was born in Sydney and after leaving primary school worked in a number of different jobs before setting up as an estate agent in the W suburb of Auburn. Elected to the Legislative Assembly of NSW in 1913, he became parliamentary leader of the Labor Party 10 years later and served as Premier for two terms, 1925-27 and 1930-32. His first Ministry was notable for a wide range of important achievements, including the setting up of the New South Wales Industrial Commission and the Government Insurance Office, the introduction of a compulsory 44-hour working week, the extension of Workers' Compensation and the introduction of widows' pensions and a family endowment scheme. However, his plan for coping with the Depression during his second term of office helped to cause dissension and confusion within the Labor Party and the nation, and led to his dismissal by the Governor, Sir Phillip GAME.

Lang's plan, which was put forward as an alternative to Edward THEODORE's inflationary approach and the government's deflationary policy (the Premiers' Plan'), rested on three points. The first was that payment of interest by Australian governments to British bond holders should be deferred until Britain gave to her Australian debtors concessions in line with those extended by the USA to its British debtors. The second was that interest on public loans raised within Australia should be reduced to three per cent. The third, generally regarded by economists as meaningless, was that Australia should adopt a currency 'based upon the wealth of Australia, and to be called the "goods standard"'. His remarkable powers as a popular speaker secured fervid support for these proposals among a large section of the population, but opposition was equally impassioned, and helped to bring about the formation of the right-wing paramilitary NEW GUARD movement, whose members proposed to help the police if there was a breakdown of law and order. Feelings rose to fever pitch in March 1931 when Lang repudiated interest payments due on State government loans raised in

John Dunmore Lang

John Thomas Lang

Courtesy of A.I.S. Canberra

London. The federal government of James SCULLIN paid the amounts due and then began legal proceedings to recover them from NSW. Also in March a special federal conference of the Labor Party expelled the whole NSW branch and set up a new organisation there. However, a 'Lang Labor' group of seven federal Members of Parliament continued to back Lang, and in November voted with the Opposition to bring down Scullin's government. In January 1932 NSW again defaulted on interest payments, but the LYONS government obtained legislation which gave the Commonwealth the power to collect money from a defaulting State, and when Lang tried to circumvent this he was dismissed for acting unconstitutionally. Labor was defeated in the subsequent election, and the incoming government paid the outstanding amounts of interest.

The feud between 'Lang Labor' and 'federal Labor' continued until the NSW branch of the party was reunited under William McKELL in 1939. Lang was again expelled from the party in 1943, but retained sufficient local support to win election to the House of Representatives in 1946 as an Independent. He lost his seat in 1949, was readmitted to the Labor Party in 1971 and continued to work vigorously as editor of his weekly newspaper, the *Century*, almost up to the time of his death.
Further reading: Foott, B. *The Dismissal of a Premier: The Phillip Game Papers*. Morgan, Sydney, 1968; Lang, J.T. *The Turbulent Years*. Alpha, Sydney, 1970.

lantana This notorious shrubby WEED, *Lantana camara*, belongs to the family Verbenaceae and is of tropical South American origin. It can grow to 3m tall and is extremely common in coastal areas of E Australia, especially N of Sydney. The flower is yellow or orange, turning red, and the aromatic leaves are rough and oval. It often grows in gullies and on banks, making chemical control difficult as its removal could lead to severe erosion. Various insects have been introduced for its BIOLOGICAL CONTROL.

Mitchell Library

lantern flies *see* bugs

La Pérouse, Jean-François de Galaup, Comte de (1741-88) Navigator.

He entered the Guardes des Marines at the age of 15 and during the rest of his life served in the French Navy with distinction, the most notable episode of his career being his action against the British in Hudson Bay in 1782. He also developed a deep interest in oceanography and in 1785 was chosen to command an exploration expedition in the Pacific, with supplementary instructions to survey the N, W and S coasts of NEW HOLLAND. With the merchant ships *La Boussole* and *L'Astrolabe* he sailed around Cape Horn to Chile, the Sandwich Islands and Alaska, surveyed the North American coastline as far S as Monterey, crossed the Pacific to Macau, visited the Philippines, Formosa, and other places as far N as Kamchatka, and then came S to Samoa. There the captain of *L'Astrolabe* and 11 of his men were killed and 20 others wounded when islanders attacked a landing party which had been obtaining water. La Pérouse then sailed to BOTANY BAY, which he judged would be a safe place where he could put together the parts of two boats which he had brought from Europe. He entered the bay on 26 January 1788 just after most of Governor PHILLIP's fleet had sailed for PORT JACKSON. He stayed until 10 March, making a camp on the N shore, and maintaining good relations with the British settlers, a number of whose officers visited him. After leaving Botany Bay he and his men were not seen by Europeans again. Their fate was a mystery until 1828, when Dumont d'Urville, a French explorer, found relics of their ships near Vanikoro in the Santa Cruz Islands, and from these and the islanders' accounts, it was concluded that both vessels had been wrecked there not long after leaving NSW. A suburb of Sydney on the N shore of Botany Bay, where La Pérouse made his camp, has been named after him.
Further reading: Scott, Sir Ernest *Laperouse*. Angus & Robertson, Sydney, 1912; Maine, R. *Laperouse*. Sagittaire, Paris, 1946.

Lara VIC (population 4 231 in 1981) A

town on the railway route between Melbourne and GEELONG, Lara is 57km by rail SW of Melbourne and 16km NNE of Geelong. The surrounding rural district consists of arable and grazing lands, with several sheep and cattle studs. Lime-burning has been an important local industry from the early days of settlement and is still carried on. The town name comes from an Aboriginal word meaning 'stone' or 'building of stones'.

larapinta *see* native cats, etc.

larks These ground-nesting PASSERINE BIRDS belong to the family Alaudidae which contains 75 species, most of which occur in Africa. There is one Australian species—the bushlark, *Mirafra javanica* (13cm long)—and one introduced species—the skylark, *Alauda arvensis*

(18cm). Both species feed on insects and seeds, and are mostly dark brown above and light brown below, with dark speckles on the throat; the skylark has a small crest. Although mainly terrestrial, these birds are known for their sustained song during erratic, soaring flights.

The bushlark has benefited from settlement and is common in grasslands and paddocks throughout the mainland, apart from southern WA and western SA. The skylark is well established at several places in SE Australia near the capital cities.

Bushlark, *Mirafra javanica*

Larrimah NT A small settlement on the

Stuart Highway, Larrimah is 528km by road SW of Darwin and 92km N of DALY WATERS. It is also a station near the S end of the N Australian railway and, though the rail line extends just beyond it to Birdum, Larrimah is the exchange point for road-rail transport. At an elevation of 184m, it has a climate typical of the N inland regions with an average annual rainfall of 731mm, concentrated mainly in the hot summer season (especially from December to March) and with a long dry period in the cooler months.

Lasseter's Reef Although this gold reef

has never been located, it created considerable interest and a mild outbreak of gold fever in the 1930s. Lance Harold Bell Lasseter claimed to have found an extensive and rich gold reef somewhere between the RAWLINSON and Petermann Ranges near the NT/WA border and a group of Sydney speculators who became interested in the prospect formed a company and sent an expedition in 1930, with Lasseter as the guide, in an attempt to locate the reef. But they failed to find the fabled gold; the party abandoned the search but Lasseter remained in the area and was never seen alive again. In 1931 a body, presumed to be Lasseter's, was found in the Petermann Ranges. Other expeditions, including one in 1971, have tried to locate the reef and although nothing matching Lasseter's claim has been located, it has been shown that there are some gold-bearing rocks in the Petermann Ranges along with lead, zinc and silver.
Further reading: Idriess, I. *Lasseter's Last Ride*. Angus & Robertson, Sydney, 1931; Blakeley, F. *Dream Millions—New Light on Lasseter's Lost Reef*. Angus & Robertson, Sydney, 1972.

La Trobe, Charles Joseph (1801-75)

Superintendent of the PORT PHILLIP District and Lieutenant-Governor of VIC. Although

the TAS town, the VIC river and the Melbourne street named after him are spelled 'Latrobe', he used the form 'La Trobe' consistently. He was born in London, and in early manhood travelled widely on foot in Switzerland, Austria and North America. He wrote four books about these travels, and also showed some talent as an amateur musician, artist and naturalist. In 1837 he was sent to the West Indies by the Colonial Office to make a survey of Negro education, on which he issued a series of very highly regarded reports.

As Superintendent of the Port Phillip District (1839-51) he had to deal with the financial difficulties resulting from the rapid growth of the population, and with the popular demand for separation from NSW. Although he favoured separation and made this clear in his despatches, he came under very strong attack in the Press and elsewhere for not advocating it more vigorously. After separation had been achieved and his position had been raised to that of Lieutenant-Governor (a post which he held from 1851 to 1854), his main problems were in dealing with the effects of the gold rushes which began in the same year. To raise money for the administration of the goldfields and for the public works that were made necessary by the rushes, he favoured an export tax on gold, but accepted the majority vote of the Legislative Council in favour of a licence fee to be levied on each miner. Among his achievements in the development of the colony were the foundation of the Botanic Gardens, the reservation of land for the Fitzroy Gardens, and support for the foundation of Melbourne University, the Royal Melbourne Hospital and the Melbourne Public Library.

Charles Joseph La Trobe

Latrobe TAS (population 2 401 in 1981) A

town on the MERSEY RIVER in the N coastal plains region, Latrobe is 9km SE of DEVONPORT on the Bass Highway. It is the administrative headquaters of the municipality (population 5 600) and a service centre for the rich farming, dairying and orcharding areas of the lower Mersey. The area was settled in the 1830s and the town was named after Charles Joseph LA TROBE. Since the 1890s, bicycle racing has been a prominent activity in the town and nowadays the annual Latrobe Wheel Race held at Christmas is one of the biggest cycling carnivals in Australia.

Latrobe River VIC Named after the first Lieutenant-Governor of the State, Charles Joseph LA TROBE, the Latrobe River in central GIPPSLAND has its headwaters in the steep, forested S scarplands of the GREAT DIVIDING RANGE about 75km E of Melbourne. It flows for over 250km, firstly SE, then E beyond the brown-coal mining centre of YALLOURN through rich dairying country to a delta on LAKE WELLINGTON, whence its waters pass via the Gippsland lakes and LAKES ENTRANCE into BASS STRAIT. Some of its N tributaries (for examples, THOMSON, Tyers and Tanjit Rivers) rise in the vicinity of MOUNT BAW BAW (elevation 1 654km), while the S tributaries (for example, Morwell River, Narracan, Jeeralong and Flynns Creeks) rise in the STRZELECKI RANGES and flow in general N courses to join the main stream. The principal urban areas in the valley are MOE, MORWELL and TRARALGON. The Princes Highway traverses the lower and middle sections of the valley on an E-W route; the Grand Ridge road follows the crest of the Strzelecki Ranges for 132km along the S rim of the Latrobe River basin. Dairying is the major rural activity throughout much of the valley, with some beef cattle and sheep grazing. A feature of the pastoral industries is the widespread development of improved pastures. Relatively small areas are under crops; oats are grown for haymaking and there is some orcharding, vegetable cultivation and flax growing. Forestry is important on the uplands of the basin, producing sawn timber and supplying the raw material for the MARYVALE paper industry. The economy of the middle valley is dominated by the open-cut mines on the vast brown-coal deposits, one of the world's largest sources of such coal. Highly mechanised methods of extraction and transportation are used on the fields at Yallourn and Morwell, where large electricity generating plants and briquette factories have been developed since the 1920s. The State's largest power station is at Hazelwood, located S of Morwell.

Launceston TAS (population 64 555 in 1981) The second-largest city of TAS, it is located 202km N of Hobart where the North and South ESK RIVERS join to form the TAMAR estuary and flow into BASS STRAIT. The city is situated in the wide valleys formed by these rivers, at an elevation of only 8m above sea level, about 55km inland from the coast, with steep and rugged mountains to the E (Mt Barrow 1 413m) and SE (BEN LOMOND 1 573m). It is at the junction of the Midland and Bass Highways, and where the East and West Tamar Highways meet from either side of the estuary. It is often called the 'Garden

City' because of its long-established and outstanding public and private gardens. It experiences a mild climate with warm summers and crisply cool winters; the average annual rainfall is 683mm with the highest falls in winter (June average 98mm) and the lowest in March (29mm) and November (28mm). The city is the major commercial, financial, educational and cultural centre for northern TAS. It is also important industrially, with several textile factories, flour mills and engineering works. The surrounding rural areas of the MIDLANDS and the N plains are noted for orcharding, dairying and vegetable growing, and Launceston functions as the export centre for these products. To the NW of the city, 5km along the West Tamar Highway is the Trevallyn hydro-electricity power station; commissioned in 1955, with an installed capacity of 80 000kW, the station is part of the GREAT LAKES power scheme, utilising water from the lakes and streams of the CENTRAL PLATEAU.

The history of Launceston and the Tamar Valley dates back to 1798 when BASS and FLINDERS named the river estuary PORT DALRYMPLE. The city was founded in 1805 by Colonel William PATERSON and was originally named Patersonia, but shortly after was changed to Launceston in honour of Governor KING's birthplace in Cornwall, England. There are many buildings of historical and architectural importance in the city and the National Trust (TAS) has classified over 100 for preservation, including churches, educational establishments, public and government buildings, banks and numerous old mansions and cottages.

Lauderdale TAS (population 2 117 in 1981) This seaside town and holiday resort centre is located on the E shore of the lower DERWENT RIVER, some 20km by road SE of Hobart. It is situated on a narrow isthmus between Ralphs Bay on the W and Frederick Henry Bay on the E. In the 1920s, the construction of a canal across the narrow isthmus was commenced, so as to provide a short route for small craft between the bays, but it silted up as it was being built and could not be reopened.

laurel, camphor see sassafras

Laver, Rodney George (1938-) Tennis player. His first game of tennis was played on an ant-bed tennis court built by his father on the family farm at ROCKHAMPTON in QLD. From such inauspicious beginnings the slight, freckle-faced youth came to be known all over the world as the 'Rockhampton Rocket' and in 1972 became the first tennis player to have earned $1 million in prize-money. His impressive list of achievements gained on the international tennis circuit were capped in 1962 when he won the world's four major singles titles—the Australian, French, USA and Wimbledon—the Grand Slam of tennis. He turned professional late in 1962 and was thus ineligible to defend these titles. In 1969, the rules were changed and professionals were

admitted to the world's major championships. Laver celebrated by winning the four titles again to become the first and only player ever to win the Grand Slam twice.

Rod Laver in action

law The law is a control by means of which order, peace and justice may be established and maintained in private and public affairs. To understand the development and structure of the Australian legal system it is necessary to delve into English legal history since much of the Australian system of law was inherited from or modelled on the English system.

Development of the legal system Up to the 11th century in England each local Anglo-Saxon community had its own unwritten customs for settling conflicts and each district had its own courts where freemen acted as judges. After the Norman Conquest in 1066 the King appointed the judges; they presided over special courts in London and also began to travel about the country to hear cases in local courts. These judges collected all the local unwritten rules and customs and used them as a single set of principles by which legal decisions were made. They became known as Common Law. In the Middle Ages it was found that Common Law had no remedy for certain types of cases. To meet this need, Courts of Chancery were established under the jurisdiction of the Chancellor, the 'keeper of the King's conscience'. Judges in these courts based their decisions on a sense of fair play and natural justice rather than on strict legal rules. This branch of civil law became known as Equity. When the King and his council of advisers decided on a new law it was issued in a written form and these written laws became known as Statute Law. By the 17th century Parliament had become the chief law-making body in England and it continued to change and add Statute Laws.

Equity, Common Law and Statute Law were inherited by the Australian colonies from England, but when the colonies were granted self-government they changed some of the

Figure 1

THE STATE COURT SYSTEM IN AUSTRALIA

STATE SUPREME COURT
Unlimited Jurisdiction
One in each State and Territory

SUPERIOR COURTS	STATE COURT OF APPEAL Civil Jurisdiction	STATE COURT OF CRIMINAL APPEAL
INTERMEDIATE COURTS	STATE CIVIL JURISDICTION	STATE CRIMINAL AND SPECIAL JURISDICTION
	NSW District Courts VIC County Courts QLD District Courts SA Local Courts in full jurisdiction WA District Courts	NSW District Courts VIC County Courts QLD District Courts SA District Criminal Courts WA Courts of Session
MAGISTRATES' COURTS	STATE COURTS OF SUMMARY JURISDICTION All States have Coroners' Courts and Children's Courts In addition: NSW Local Courts VIC Magistrates' Courts QLD Magistrates' Courts SA Local Courts WA Local Courts TAS Courts of Request; General Sessions; Petty Sessions	

Note: all States have the right of appeal from the State Supreme Court to the High Court in Australia.

Statute Laws and included others of their own making. Statute Laws passed by the Parliament in one colony applied only to that colony, until the formation of the federation in 1901, when Statute Laws enacted by the federal Parliament applied to all the States. However, each State Parliament could still continue to enact its own Statute Law in accordance with the division of power between the federal and State Parliaments laid down by the Commonwealth Constitution of Australia. Sometimes the federal or State Parliaments would enact a general law and leave the details to be worked out by public servants in Departments or other government agencies. This is known as delegated legislation or Administrative law.

Law courts The Australian judicial system has been modelled on the English system and has a graduated series of tribunals which rise in importance from courts of petty sessions through intermediate courts, superior courts, and finally to the High Court of Australia (the state and federal governments agreed to abolish appeals from state Supreme Courts to the Judicial Committee of the Privy Council in England on 25 June, 1982). General tribunals deal with civil and criminal cases and special tribunals have been set up to handle cases of bankruptcy, industrial law and workers' compensation.

1. State courts. The court system in each State evolved during its colonial era and while each State system is divided into superior, intermediate and inferior courts, the titles given to courts covering similar jurisdictions are different. Superior courts can deal with any matter whatsoever; intermediate courts can try cases in Equity; and inferior courts, Australia's lowest courts, including magistrates' courts, coroners' courts and children's courts, can deal only with a specific subject given to them by statute (*see* Figure 1).

2. Federal courts. These include the High Court of Australia (established 1903), the Family Court of Australia (established 1976) and the Federal Court of Australia (established 1976). The High Court has three main functions. It decides questions of validity of federal laws under the division of power between the federal and State governments as laid down in the Constitution—in other words, it interprets the Constitution. It is also a court of appeal from decisions of State courts. Finally, the High Court tends to unify the law throughout Australia, for its decisions are binding in all States. The ACT and the NT have their own systems of federal courts.

3. Special courts and tribunals. Special courts and tribunals have been set up to help to administer particular functions of government by both the federal and the State governments. They have the power to decide certain kinds of disputes—for example, an industrial commission is set up to settle industrial disputes and regulate conditions in industry. The composition, powers and procedures vary greatly and depend on the statute creating the special court or tribunal. Judges, magistrates, practising lawyers or laymen may serve on it, and the law courts can review its findings if the proceedings are found to be irregular in law. Federal tribunals that have been established cover a variety of subjects. They include: the Coal Industry Tribunal, the Commonwealth Conciliation and Arbitration Commission, the Literature Censorship Board, the Repatriation Commission, the Superannuation Board, the Tariff Board, the Taxation Board of Review, and the War Pensions Entitlement Tribunal.

Trial by jury Trial by jury is an integral part of the structure of superior and intermediate courts. Inferior courts can convict without trial by jury but there are provisions for appeals to higher courts composed of judge and jury. A jury can determine only questions of fact and assess compensatory damages. Only a judge can decide questions of law and inflict punishment.

The legal profession In NSW and QLD the English tradition of dividing the legal profession into two main classes, barristers and solicitors, has been followed closely. A barrister will conduct a case in court and give learned opinions on difficult questions of law while a solicitor will attend to the numerous legal problems of clients. Any person who wishes to take legal proceedings will consult a solicitor who may then brief a barrister to appear in court. In the rest of Australia every qualified lawyer is entitled by law to practise as both barrister and solicitor. However, some of them specialise in court appearances, so that in practice the division between barristers and solicitors does still exist to some extent, especially in VIC. Eminent barristers are appointed Queen's Counsel (QC) and this honour entitles them to charge higher fees. It also means that they can appear in court only if accompanied by a counsel who is not a QC.

The number of judges appointed to the High Court is determined by the federal government. They are appointed by the federal government and hold office until they are 70 years old. State judges are appointed by the State government on the advice of the Attorney-General. They are selected from senior and distinguished barristers, and are appointed for life or until they reach a fixed retiring age. Justices of the Peace are appointed by the State Governor to perform minor judicial work. Stipendiary magistrates are professionally trained and receive a salary. The State Governor appoints magistrates and they are selected usually from public servants (in 1983 this process was under review).

Lawn bowls Australia's climate allows bowls to be played all year round and this may explain why Australia has over half the bowlers in the world. In a survey conducted by the Australian Bureau of Statistics in 1975, it was revealed that lawn bowls is the fifth-most popular participatory sport in Australia. In 1983 there were an estimated 400 000 men and women bowlers playing out of approximately 2000 clubs.

The earliest recorded game of bowls in Australia took place on New Year's Day 1845 at Sandy Bay TAS. The match was between T. Burgess and F. Lipscombe at the latter's English-style inn, Beach Tavern, where the amenities included a bowling green. In the same year the first green in NSW was laid down. Like so many of the early bowling greens, this too was laid in the grounds of an inn—the Woolpack Inn, Leichhardt—and by 1895 all States could boast at least one green. The game gradually established itself and by 1903 each State had formed a State Bowling Association. In 1911 the Australian Bowling Council, which controls the game throughout Australia, came into being.

International competition In 1899, in London, the Imperial Bowling Association was formed and one of its functions was to arrange a match between England and Australia. In 1901 Australia sent a team of 30 bowlers who played 23 matches against England, winning the series 11-10 (one match was tied and one unfinished). The official return visit did not take place until 1925 when a team from Britain toured Australia, the visitors winning 22-17 of the 41 decided matches. Australia has competed in the bowling section of the Commonwealth Games since 1934, but with only minor success. At the first world bowls championships, which were held in Sydney in 1966, Australia won the pairs and the triples titles.

Women's bowls The first women's club in Australia, the Rainsford Bowling Club at Glenferrie, Melbourne, came into being in 1898. The Albert Park Ladies' Bowling Club, formed in 1899, changed its name to the South Melbourne Cricket Club Ladies' Bowling Club in 1907 and is the oldest existing women's bowling club in the world. Australia also has the oldest women's bowling association in the world, the Victorian Ladies' Bowling Association, which was formed in 1907. In 1947 the Australian Women's Bowling Council was formed to control the game throughout Australia.

Courtesy of A.I.S. Canberra

Lawn bowls is played by men and women throughout Australia

lawn scarab *see* beetles

Lawrence, Marjorie Florence
(1908-1979) Soprano. She was born at Deans Marsh VIC and won the *Sun Aria* competition at GEELONG in 1928. John BROWNLEE, then visiting Australia, encouraged her to study overseas, and after a début at Monte Carlo in 1932 and appearances in Paris during 1933, she joined the Metropolitan Opera Company, New York. She was a marvellously vocal Brunnhilde in Wagner's tetralogy *Der Ring des Nibelungen* and made operatic history by insisting on leaping upon her horse and dashing into the flames on stage as Wagner had originally intended. She visited Australia on concert tour in 1939, and in 1941, while performing in Mexico, she was struck down by poliomyelitis. By December 1942 she had made the first of many famous wheelchair appearances at the Metropolitan. She also became famous for her wheelchair concerts for troops in the SW Pacific in 1944 and in Britain and Europe in 1945. Her life story, *Interrupted Melody*, was published in 1949, and a film version appeared in 1955. She married Dr Thomas King in 1941 and held the positions of Professor of Voice

and Opera Workshop at Southern Illinois University, and Professor of Voice, University of Arkansas, from 1974. She was awarded the Legion d'Honneur and appointed CBE for her services to music.

Lawson NSW (combined population of Lawson and HAZELBROOK 6 323 in 1981) A town in the BLUE MOUNTAINS region, on the Western Highway and on the railway line through the mountains, Lawson is located between WENTWORTH FALLS and Hazelbrook, 95km by rail from Sydney. It is a popular holiday resort, though it is increasingly becoming an urban centre of permanent, rather than vacation, residents, many of whom commute daily to jobs in Sydney. The Lawson district contains many scenic features typical of the Blue Mts region: bushland trails, sandstone valleys and attractive waterfalls. The town was named in honour of the pioneer explorer, William LAWSON, who was with the first party to cross the Blue Mts, in 1813.

Lawson, Henry Archibald (1867-
1922) Short-story writer and poet. Perhaps one of the most widely acclaimed Australian writers, Lawson was born in a tent on the GRENFELL goldfield in NSW, where his Norwegian-born father was part-owner of a claim. He grew up on a selection at Eurunderie, near MUDGEE, to which the family moved when he was six months old. His schooling did not go beyond elementary level, and he was hampered by his loss of hearing which began at the age of nine and was complete by the time he was 14. However, he received a deep love of reading from his mother, Louisa, with whom he lived for some years in Sydney after she and his father separated in 1883. He later lived briefly in WA and QLD, travelled in the Outback, worked in New Zealand for two short periods, and spent the years 1900-1902 in London with his wife and two young children. After his return from England he and his wife separated, and the remainder of his life was a sad period of alcoholism and illness, punctuated by spells in gaol for failure to pay alimony. He died in poverty.

The sadness of Lawson's life seems to have sharpened his sympathy for others undergoing hardship. His poems and short stories depict the nobility and humour to be found in ordinary people, and the courage with which many of them face the hardships of life, whether in the harsh environment of the bush or in city slums. His sympathy for his fellows and his desire for a better life for the common man found expression in the doctrine of 'mateship'. His first poem, 'Song of the Republic', was published in the *Bulletin* in 1887, and the first of his short stories, 'His Father's Mate', in the same journal in the following year. Lawson's principal works are collections of stories or poems and include *In the Days When the World was Wide* (1896), *While the Billy Boils* (1896), *Verses Popular and Humorous* (1900), *On the Track and Over the Sliprails* (1900), *The Country I Come From* (1901), *Joe Wilson and His Mates* (1901), *Children of the Bush* (1902),

When I Was King and Other Verses (1905), *The Rising of the Court* (1910), and *My Army, O My Army!* (1915).
See also literature
Further reading: Roderick, C. (ed) *Henry Lawson Criticism, 1894-1971.* Angus & Robertson, Sydney, 1972; Murray-Smith, S. *Henry Lawson.* Oxford University Press, Melbourne, 1973; Prout, D. *Henry Lawson, the Grey Dreamer.* Rigby, Adelaide, 1973; Clark, C.M.H. *In Search of Henry Lawson.* Macmillan, Melbourne, 1978.

Lawson, William (1774-1850) Explorer.
Born near London, he came to Sydney as an ensign in the NEW SOUTH WALES CORPS in 1800, served for some years on NORFOLK ISLAND and in 1808 was appointed commandant at NEWCASTLE. After Governor MACQUARIE's arrival he went to England, but returned in 1811 as a lieutenant in the New South Wales Veterans Company. In 1813, with Gregory BLAXLAND and William WENTWORTH, he won fame for discovering a route across the BLUE MOUNTAINS. He was Commander at BATHURST from 1819 to 1824, during which time he made three minor journeys of exploration in the Bathurst and MUDGEE districts. He then retired to his property in Prospect NSW. From 1843 to 1850 he was an elected member of the Legislative Council. *See also* exploration by land

lead This metal was used in a number of ancient civilisations—the Hanging Gardens of Babylon were floored with soldered sheets of lead and in Ancient Egypt lead pipes were used. The Romans referred to lead as *plumbum*, hence the words 'plumber' and 'plumbing'.

Lead is a useful and essential metal to all industrial countries and ranks after aluminium, copper and zinc in its application to industry. Its major uses are in transport—in storage batteries and as an anti-knock additive to petrol; in the construction industry—for sound- and vibration-proofing and radiation shielding; in the electrical industry—for cable sheathing and solder; and in the chemical industry—for lead-based paints and insecticides and as an additive to glass, porcelain and enamel. It is used also in the manufacture of ammunition, brass alloys, type metal and many other components.

Extraction Most lead is mined as the mineral galena (PbS), with cerussite and anglesite constituting minor ores. After concentration, the lead ore is roasted to reduce the sulphur content and then smelted in either a blast furnace or a reverberatory furnace to form impure lead bullion. This is subsequently refined. Scrap lead, derived mainly from old storage batteries, solder and type metal, is generally processed in separate plants. The by-products and co-products of lead mining are usually zinc and silver; in the more complex ores copper, gold and fluorspar may be recovered along with antimony, bismuth, tellurium and sulphur.

Production In 1980, the Australian mine

Pneumatophores (breathing roots) of *Avicennia* mangroves (*see* VEGETATION)

Palm Valley NT (*see* PALM VALLEY)

Dense moss mat (*Bryophyta*) covering bare sandstone surface (*see* BRYOPHYTA)

Closed heath on old sand dunes, Royal National Park, Sydney (*see* VEGETATION)

Blackboys along the Swanland coastal plain WA

Arid lands near Woomera SA (*see* WOOMERA)

Seasonal pan in the Simpson Desert QLD (*see* SIMPSON DESERT)

Saltbush country, Nullarbor Plain WA (*see* CHENOPODIACEAE)

Low eucalypt woodland on Arnhem Land escarpment NT (*see* VEGETATION)

Mallee eucalypt, *Eucalyptus obtusiflora*, regenerating after fire (*see* MYRTACEAE)

Plains extend over large areas of The Centre

Cabbage tree palm, *Livistona australis* (*see* PALMAE)

Myrtle beech, *Nothofagus cunninghami* (*see* MYRTLE)

Mountain ash, *Eucalyptus regnans* (*see* MOUNTAIN ASH)

Christmas bush, *Ceratopetalum gummiferum*
(*see* CHRISTMAS BUSH)

Sydney blue gum, *Eucalyptus saligna*
(*see* MYRTACEAE)

Swamp oak, *Casuarina glauca*
(*see* CASUARINACEAE)

Kurrajong, *Brachychiton populneum*
(*see* STERCULIACEAE)

Typical rainforest in the Atherton Tableland (*see* VEGETATION)

Table 1

MINE PRODUCTION OF LEAD IN AUSTRALIA 1970-80 (tonnes)

State	1970	1978	1979	1980	1981
QLD	162 939	146 928	155 021	141 293	141 529
NSW	279 209	230 574	244 357	240 668	221 045
TAS	13 912	22 754	22 160	15 511	25 527
SA	4	24	12	8	8
WA	163	—	—	—	—
NT	517	11	31	11	13
TOTAL	456 744	400 291	421 581	397 491	388 122

Source: *Australian Mineral Industry Annual Review.* (1970-81) Australian Govt Publishing Service, Canberra.

production of lead ore contained 397 491 tonnes of metal, making Australia the world's third-largest mine producer (10.6 per cent of world production) and the sixth-largest producer of refined lead (4.7 per cent). Lead is mined at BROKEN HILL in NSW, ROSEBERY in TAS and MOUNT ISA in QLD. Production figures for the various States are presented in Table 1, which also shows the substantial decrease in production between 1970 and 1978, a rise in 1979 and a further decline in 1980. Smelting and refining is carried out at Mt Isa and TOWNSVILLE in QLD, Cockle Creek and PORT KEMBLA in NSW and PORT PIRIE in SA.

The industry The five leading producing countries of mine lead in 1980 were the USA, the USSR, Australia, Canada and Peru, which between them accounted for 56 per cent of total world production. There are only four fully integrated mining and smelting companies operating in Australia; seven or eight individual mines provide the current production of lead with a further five prospects under active consideration (there are 31 individual mines in the USA).

The most pressing economic factors concerning the lead industry are associated with air pollution, waste disposal and land utilisation; in addition, many substitutes can be found for the more important uses of lead—for example, cadmium, mercury, nickel, silver, iron and zinc in storage batteries, titanium and zinc in paints, and plastics as a covering for electric cables. The costs of establishing new mines and smelters are high. The capital estimates of a mine range from $5000 to $10 000 per tonne produced per day, with those of establishing a smelter substantially higher. Mining costs vary between $20 to $40 per tonne while the operating costs for a lead-zinc flotation plant range from $3 to $5 a tonne.

Further reading: See under minerals and mining.

leaf-hoppers *see* bugs

leaf insects *see* stick insects

leatherjackets *see* fishes, bony

leeches *see* annelids

Leeton NSW (population 6 498 in 1981) A town in the RIVERINA region, 615km by road SW of Sydney, Leeton is located N of the MURRUMBIDGEE RIVER in the SW section of the irrigation areas. It is a railway junction on lines going E to NARRANDERA, W to HAY and N to GRIFFITH and can be reached by two rail routes—one from JUNEE via Yanco (610km from Sydney) and the other from COOTA-MUNDRA via Griffith (685km from Sydney). At an elevation of 140m above sea level, it receives an annual rainfall of only 432mm spread uniformly throughout all seasons, but irrigation water has made it a rich rural centre. It was designed as a market and service town when the MURRUMBIDGEE IRRIGATION AREAS were developed and the district produces rice and a range of fruit crops (apricots, peaches, citrus and grapes) and vegetables. It has a large co-operative fruit cannery (December to March is the main canning season), a rice-growers co-operative mill, a plant for fruit packing and processing, juice extraction works, and steel fabrication and machinery manufacturing workshops. The Leeton Agricultural Research Station, 10km from the town, carries out research on irrigation pastures, sheep and cattle. The town is the headquarters of the Rice Marketing Board which controls the milling and packing of the crop. The town was named after C.A. Lee who was State Minister for Works when the irrigation areas were developed. The small town of Yanco (population 415 in 1981) lies 6km S of Leeton and it was here that Sir Samuel McCaughey carried out the early experiments in irrigation farming which largely spurred the development of the area; the family mansion is now the Yanco Agricultural High School.

Spray irrigation at Leeton NSW

NSW Dept of Tourism

Legacy This organisation aims to help widows and children of deceased ex-servicemen who served Australia overseas in World War I, World War II, Malaysia, Korea and Vietnam, whether or not death occurred during military action or as a result of war injuries. Also eligible are the families, resident in Australia, of ex-servicemen migrants who served with the Commonwealth of Nations forces. Legacy was founded by Major-General Sir John Gellibrand as the Remembrance Club in March 1923 in Hobart. Its aim at first was to help ex-servicemen re-establish themselves in civilian life. However, a Melbourne offshoot founded by Sir Stanley Savige in September 1923 adopted the name Legacy, and after holding a picnic for 120 war widows and their children in 1925 turned the movement towards its present objective. Today there are 49 Legacy Clubs in Australia and one in London.

Each member of Legacy, known as a Legatee, has a number of families in his care and acts as an adviser to them. He ensures that each family has access to Legacy facilities and knows about other sources of aid, such as social welfare and repatriation benefits. There are many forms of assistance given directly by Legacy. In cases where repatriation benefits do not apply, and sometimes even when they do, financial assistance, food and clothing may be given and immediate assistance is always available to widows in the period just after their husbands' death. Counselling and tutorial help, as well as financial aid, are provided for students. Classes are held in many cultural and recreational activities for girls and boys. Help is given in training widows and children for employment and in finding employment for them. Holidays are provided at a number of sites. In Sydney, Legacy operates a home for children and also a large house for 25 widows. Legacy receives no government subsidy; its funds come from donations and from various activities such as an annual Button Day.

Leguminosae *see* Papilionaceae

Leichhardt, (Friedrich Wilhelm) Ludwig (1813-48) Explorer. Although Lud-

Ludwig Leichhardt

Mitchell Library

wig Leichhardt's journey of 1844-45 was of major importance, he is remembered more for the mystery of his final disappearance than for his achievements. Born in Prussia, he came to Sydney in 1842, and almost immediately became interested in the exploration of N Australia. Setting out from the DARLING DOWNS in 1844 he made a 5000km journey to PORT ESSINGTON (near modern Darwin). His next aim was to cross the continent from E to W. He left the Darling Downs late in 1846 in an attempt to do this, but went only about 800km along his 1844 route before being forced to turn back. Early in 1848 he set out once more, from a point near the present town of ROMA, but he and his six companions were never seen by Europeans again, nor in spite of many searches, have their remains or any of their equipment ever been found.
See also exploration by land
Further reading: Chisholm, A.H. *Strange New World.* (2nd edn) Angus & Robertson, Sydney, 1955 (republished as *Strange Journey.* Rigby, Adelaide, 1973); Webster, E.M. *Whirlwinds in the Plain*, Melbourne University Press, 1980.

Leichhardt River QLD Located in the GULF COUNTRY, it rises in the Selwyn Range, SW of CLONCURRY, and flows in a general N course for 320km to an estuary in the SE corner of the GULF OF CARPENTARIA. Its main right-bank tributary is the Alexandra River and the major left-bank ones are Fiery and Gunpowder Creeks. The mining town of MOUNT ISA is located on the upper reaches of the Leichhardt. Since the catchment basin is a region of summer rains, with a distinct dry period for at least five months, the river flow is markedly seasonal. Beef cattle grazing is the principal rural activity.

Leigh Creek SA (population 1 635 in 1981) This small settlement is the site of the only significant coalfield in SA. It is located in the arid mid-N of the State, with an average annual rainfall of only 205mm, at an elevation of 194m above sea level, about 540km N of Adelaide and 270km NNE of PORT AUGUSTA, on the central Australian railway between the N FLINDERS RANGES and LAKE TORRENS. The coal mines, opened in 1943 to augment coal supplies during World War II, are worked by open-cut methods and are operated by the State Electricity Trust. Most of the coal is taken by rail to Port Augusta where it is used for electricity generation.

lentils *see* Papilionaceae

Leongatha VIC (population 3 736 in 1981) This country town is on the South Gippsland Highway on the railway route through the region, 127km by rail SW of Melbourne. At an elevation of 83m above sea level, the town is set in the scenic hill country of the W STRZE-LECKI RANGES, where dairying and livestock grazing are the main rural activities. Local secondary industries include the processing of dairy products, clothing manufacture and engineering works. The town name comes

from an Aboriginal word meaning 'teeth'.

leopard wood *see* crow's ash

Leopold VIC (population 2 945 in 1981) A small town located N of Lake Connewarre on the Bellarine Peninsular, Leopold is 11km SE of GEELONG and 85km by road from Melbourne. It is situated on the Bellarine Highway in the midst of rural lands which provide produce to the Melbourne metropolitan market. During recent times there has been much urban and commercial development. The town was originally named Kensington, but in 1892 was changed to Leopold after Queen Victoria's son, the Duke of Albany.

Lepidoptera *see* butterflies, etc.

lerps *see* bugs

letter stick Ranging from a few centimetres long to about 30cm long, letter sticks were carried by Aboriginal messengers. The marks carved on the stick served as a passport when passing through foreign territory and possibly also served as an aid to the memory.

lettuces *see* Compositae

Levey, Barnett (1798-1837) Merchant and theatre manager. Levey is credited with establishing the first professional theatre in Australia, in the building known as the Colchester Warehouse in George Street, Sydney. This odd complex, built by his brother Solomon, included a hotel, assembly rooms, a warehouse and mill, and, eventually, a theatre. In 1826 Levey arranged concerts in the Freemasons Tavern in George Street, performing comic songs himself; and in 1829 he obtained

a licence to conduct 'At Home' concerts in the assembly rooms of his hotel. However, he had antagonised Governor DARLING on business matters, and his persistent applications for a theatre licence met with no success until the arrival of Governor BOURKE. The licence Levey obtained in 1832 stipulated that only plays licensed for production in London might be performed. Levey's company gave its opening performance on Boxing Night 1832 in the assembly rooms, and the theatre itself, the Royal, was completed in 1833. The company was not without disharmony, which resulted in Levey's temporarily handing over the management in 1835. After his death the theatre was run by his wife Sarah, until it was destroyed by fire in 1840.
Further reading: Irvin, E. *Theatre Comes to Australia.* University of Queensland Press, St Lucia, 1971.

Lewis, Mortimer William (1796-1879) Architect. The leading designer in the Greek Revival idiom in Australia, Mortimer Lewis was also proficient in the Gothic Revival style, gaining early recognition as an eclectic architect. He was born in London and came to Australia in 1830 as assistant to the Surveyor-General, Thomas MITCHELL, and surveyed the GREAT DIVIDING RANGE, W of Sydney. Mitchell made him Colonial Architect in 1835 and Lewis held this post during 15 years of busy government building. His first building still stands, though altered, as part of Gladesville Hospital in Sydney. He then designed the courthouses at Hartley, Berrima and—perhaps his best-known—Darlinghurst, a beautifully detailed building reminiscent of ancient Greece. He designed gaols, watch-houses, police station and numerous other public buildings in many parts of the colony, includ-

Government House, Sydney NSW, constructed under the supervision of Mortimer Lewis

ing Melbourne. With engineer George Burney, Lewis designed the semi-circular quay, known as Circular Quay, on the S shore of SYDNEY COVE. Opposite that, he built the customs house, which has since been greatly enlarged. Lewis' work in the Gothic style began with the supervision of the construction in Sydney of the new Government House, which was designed in London by Edward Blore. He designed the Church of St John's at CAMDEN, in 1849, and another 12 Gothic Revival churches. Lewis popularised the application of Gothic forms to residential design, and several of his houses survive. Among them is 'Richmond Villa', which was built in 1849 and overlooked the Domain; it was recently moved stone by stone and re-erected in Kent Street, Sydney, at the base of Observatory Hill. During his work on Sydney's first museum, when cost estimates went awry, Lewis was accused of neglect and the misappropriation of materials and, after an official enquiry in 1849, he resigned.
Further reading: Herman, M. *The Early Australian Architects and Their Work.* Angus & Robertson, Sydney, 1954.

Liapootah

TAS A dam and power station on the Nive River just above its junction with the DERWENT RIVER, it forms part of the vast hydro-electricity scheme in the upper Derwent Valley in the CENTRAL PLATEAU. The concrete gravity dam (40m-high wall) receives water from the TARRALEAH and TUNGATINAH power stations, located upstream, and this is then conveyed by a tunnel 7km long from the dam to the Liapootah power station which has an installed capacity of 83 700kW and was commissioned in 1960. The name Liapootah comes from a TAS Aboriginal word meaning 'creek'.

Liberal Party of Australia

The largest political party in Australia professing support for private enterprise and opposition to socialism is the Liberal Party. It was founded in 1944 when Sir Robert Gordon MENZIES convened the Canberra Conference of 18 political and semi-political organisations which had similar non-Labor objectives. One of the organisations which merged with the new political party was the UNITED AUSTRALIA PARTY (UAP). The present Liberal Party of Australia is unique in its organisation in that it emerged at a time of strength in the ranks of the AUSTRALIAN LABOR PARTY (ALP) and has not included in its membership expelled Labor parliamentarians, whereas its predecessors were closely linked with the absorption of ex-Labor parliamentarians when there was a split in the membership of the ALP.

The roots of the Liberal Party can be traced to the political tradition of the Fusion Liberal Party (1909-16) which professed conservative anti-socialist policies. During World War I the issue of conscription split the ALP and those parliamentarians who left or were expelled from the ALP joined the Fusion Liberal Party to form the Nationalist Party (1917-31). This party in turn lost its identity when the ALP split again during the Depression over policy issues and the Nationalist Party, joined by ex-ALP parliamentarians, was renamed the United Australia Party (1931-44). Thus the present Liberal Party is fundamentally different in origin from its predecessors, and has a stronger basis for its organisation.

Organisation The organisation of the Liberal Party is a confederation. Each State in Australia has its own State Liberal Party with branches in each electorate. The branches send delegates to a State Council and the State Council sends eight delegates to a Federal Council which meets once a year to determine the federal platform of the party. However, the platform is written in generalisations, and policy-making power is concentrated in the hands of the parliamentary leader. As long as the Liberal Party wins elections the Federal Council does not assert its right to advise or instruct the parliamentary leader on policy matters, but when the Liberals have lost an election (either State or federal) the relevant organisational wing has insisted on its right to determine party policy and party strategy. At all other times the organisational wings concentrate on fund-raising, electioneering, pre-selection of parliamentary candidates and the extent to which Liberals are to engage in electoral contests with the NATIONAL PARTY—its coalition partner in government.

The Federal Council includes the eight delegates from each State (the majority of whom must not be parliamentarians), the federal parliamentary leader, his deputy and the leader in the Senate. A representative from each State, the three senior office holders, the chairperson for the Federal Women's Committee and for the Federal Young Liberals, and the federal parliamentary leader form a Federal Executive which is responsible for the party's affairs in between Federal Council meetings.

Policies and performance The Liberal Party claims to support private enterprise, the creation of wealth rather than its distribution, the rule of law, loyalty to the Crown, parliamentary traditions, decentralisation of power, the value of personal freedom and individual initiative. It is opposed to socialism and Communism.

It might be claimed that during its long control of federal government (1949-72; 1975-83), in some respects the party's performance has not supported its alleged policy. Private enterprise has been brought more and more under government control and has become dominated by government economic decisions. Also, Liberal federal governments have tended to increase central control rather than increase decentralisation. In other areas its policy and performance are more co-ordinated. It is very strongly opposed to Communism at home and abroad and in 1951 it attempted to ban the Communist Party of Australia. In this it was unsuccessful because the people of Australia refused to support the relevant legislation at a referendum.

In foreign affairs the Liberal Party stresses the value of alliances with traditional friends—USA and UK—and it has allowed the establishment of USA and UK bases in Australia as well as having committed Australian troops to support action in Asia taken by both the USA and the UK. In finance it has encouraged the inflow of large amounts of overseas capital to develop Australia's resources and this has caused great concern as to the effect this will have on Australia's ownership of her basic resources.
See also political history; political parties
Further reading: West, K. *The Australian Liberal Party.* Longmans, Croydon VIC, 1968; Hazlehurst, C. (ed) *Australian Conservatism, Essays in Twentieth Century Political History.* Australian National University Press, Canberra, 1979.

libraries. Australia's aboriginal people enjoyed a rich oral tradition in their tribal groups. Though they had no written languages as such, they left records in cave paintings and rock drawings. Unlocking of these memories is a task which still occupies scholars.

Australia's first white settlers had survival concerns which took precedence over intellectual pursuits but, even so, by 1826 there were citizens in Sydney with wealth and leisure enough to found the Australian Subscription Library, which is usually regarded as Australia's first library. Financial difficulties led to its sales in 1869 to the colonial government and so began, as the Free Public Library of Sydney, what is now the State Library of New South Wales. Today's State Library of Victoria began as the Melbourne Public Library in 1856. It was largely the creation of Sir Redmond Barry, better known as the judge who tried Ned Kelly. Gold discoveries from the 1850s brought prosperity and population to the colonies, which gave impetus to the variously called Mechanics Institutes and Schools of Arts which burgeoned in towns as well as cities. Whitelock says these institutions 'dominated, represented almost, Australian adult education for most of the nineteenth century'. Borrowing from their libraries was available only to subscribers but the reading rooms were open to all. Nearly all attracted government subsidy, though with increasing difficulty as towards the turn of the century billiards became more important features than books.

The early twentieth century witnessed dramatic development of what is now the State Library of New South Wales through the outstanding management of H. C. L. Anderson and outstanding generosity of its benefactor David Scott Mitchell who gave to the Library his great collection of Australiana.

The National Library of Australia was born in the bosom of the new Commonwealth Parliament in 1901, though it was not legitimized under that name or effectively separated from the Parliamentary Library until the National Library Act of 1960. In general, the development of research libraries, including university libraries, was slow. When the post World War II boom in tertiary student numbers took place, the State libraries had to bear most of the burden until federal funding was injected into the universities from the late 1950s.

By the 1930s some Australian librarians were acutely aware of the deficiencies in public

Courtesy of A.I.S. Canberra

Australian National Library, Canberra ACT

library services and, with the help of the Australian Council for Education Research, Carnegie Corporation sponsorship was obtained for a survey by a distinguished US librarian, Ralph Munn. With an Australian colleague he produced the Munn-Pitt report in 1935, which pointed to serious deficiencies in all Australian libraries except those of the Parliaments. The report gave impetus to the Free Library Movement which was founded by Geoffrey Remington, a Sydney solicitor, and vigorously pursued by him and John Metcalfe, then deputy and later to become principal librarian of the Public (now State) Library of New South Wales. The Movement was strongest in NSW but also influenced individuals in other States, and despite the disruption of World War II, by 1946 most of the Australian States had passed legislation enabling local government authorities to set up public library services and entitling them to State government subsidy if they did so. Broadly two patterns of public library services have developed since. In the more populous States, NSW and VIC, services are decentralized under the control of local government authorities individually or in regional groupings. In WA and TAS, by contrast, public library services are highly centralized with State subsidy being provided in the form of books and services through State Library Boards.

Though school libraries were also severely criticized by Munn-Pitt in 1935, more than a quarter of a century passed before their importance in the educational process was recognized. Again a US authority, Sara Fenwick, was imported on the initiative of the Library Association of Australia to survey the situation. Her report was well publicized and quickly followed up by the Association's *Standards and Objectives for School Libraries*. The School Libraries Section of the Association was formed and

immediately directed attention to improvements in the educational opportunities for school librarians. Intensive lobbying by the Library Association of Australia, the Australian Advisory Council on Bibliographical Services, the Australian Library Promotion Council (then known as the Australia Library Week Council), and the Australian School Library Association achieved from 1968 millions of dollars from the Federal Government which were used mainly in the construction of library buildings in government and non-government secondary schools. In the same year, the Commonwealth Secondary Schools Library Committee was established to advise the Federal Government and it drew up *Standards for Secondary School Libraries*. In 1974, one year after its establishment, the Schools Commission set up a Primary Schools Library Committee. In 1975 the Secondary and Primary Schools Committees were merged as the Commission's School Libraries Committee and existing standards were replaced by *Books and Beyond: Guidelines for Library Resource Facilities and Services,* originally published in 1977 and revised in 1979. Since the coming of the Schools Commission, Federal funding has not been confined to capital works and State educational authorities have continued to make substantial contributions to school libraries. A jointly funded computerized cataloguing service for schools, the Australian Schools Cataloguing Information Service (ASCIS) has been set up to provide services from 1984. Resource provision fluctuates with Australia's political and economic fortunes, but the nation's school libraries have been transformed by the work of the pioneering lobbyists of the 1960s such as Andrew Fabinyi and Margaret Trask, of the school library services sections in the State education authorities, of the Schools Commission, and of the

school librarians individually and in their professional associations.

Modern Australian school libraries emphasize the provision of learning resources in all media. This emphasis is part of the outcome of the educational philosophy of individualized learning as distinct from mass teaching based on text books. The philosophy is also reflected in the libraries of many of the Colleges of Advanced Education set up in Australia from the late 1960s, and in the libraries of colleges in the Technical and Further Education sector. Hence many libraries in Australian schools and colleges are referred to as media centres or resource centres. Another important change is in the relationship of school libraries to public libraries. Once dependent on neighboring public libraries to eke out their meagre resources, school library authorities have in recent years frequently been the prime movers in formation of the so-called joint use of school/community libraries. The concept is not new but the challenge of making optimum use of publicly-funded libraries has been taken up and in various forms such libraries have been set up in many parts of Australia in the past decade. Most common in small non-urban communities, they are also to be found in urban settings and a custom-designed school/community library has on occasions been part of the planning of new urban communities such as that at Minto in NSW.

Public libraries in Australia still lack Federal funding which has proved such a boon to university, college and school libraries, despite the strong recommendations to this effect of the 1976 report of the Committee of Inquiry into Public Libraries which was set up by the Federal Government. Despite their lack of access to funds from the most affluent level of government, many pubic libraries offer services tailored to the needs of their communities. Like other Australian libraries they increasingly use computer technology to try to reduce costs of operations and to provide enhanced services.

The combination of computer and telecommunications technologies has transformed the range and scope of services which libraries can offer. The so-called database services make possible access to the world's literature on all subjects from keyboards at terminals in special, academic, State and some public libraries. These services were pioneered as batch services in Australia in the early 1970s by the National Library and the Commonwealth Scientific and Industrial Research Organization (CSIRO). Online facilities were provided by CSIRO from 1973 on its own network, CSIRONET, and services were made available to its own members and a limited number of outside users. The National Library also moved quickly into online services and in 1977 worked with ACI Limited, an Australian company which already had a nationwide computer network, to set up the Australian Information Network (AUSINET) of which ACI became sole proprietor in 1981. AUSINET offers a range of Australian databases, including the National Library's major bibliographical files, such as Australian National Bibliography.

In this period of vigorous innovation in the 1970s, the National Library also introduced the Australian MARC Record Service (MRS) through which other libraries can obtain cataloguing records in machine readable form. This development was an essential ingredient in the formation of the regional library networks which grew up from the late 1970s, the best known of which are Technilib, which serves public libraries in VIC, CLANN in NSW whose members include college, special, public and university lbiraries, and CAVAL which serves academic libraries in VIC. The National Library's major initiative of the early 1980s has been the introduction of the Australian Bibliographic Network (BN), an online system to which many Australian libraries, mainly research libraries, contribute and from which they derive cataloguing data, and which acts as an online union catalogue of the libraries' holdings.

Technological developments continue apace, and a great variety of hardware and software to support library systems is commercialy available in Australia. On the broader national front, communications are becoming plentiful rather than scarce resources with the domestic satellite program and enhancements to terrestrial systems. Australia will soon have a public videotex system through Telecom and cable television systems are certain to be developed later. Librarians' excitement at these developments has to be tempered with economic and social realities. The Library Association of Australia stands firmly for free public access to information services and has taken an active role in lobbying for freedom of information legislation. Librarians are also involved in the dilemma of providing access to information and at the same time copyright protection for authors and publishers in the face of proliferating copying technologies.

State Library of NSW

D.S. Mitchell, M.A., whose collection formed the basis of the Mitchell Library

The turmoil of the times is reflected in the changing curricula of the schools of librarianship in universities and colleges and in the moves by many schools into the wider discipline of information science. Continuing education has also become essential for the practitioners of librarianship. The mission of libraries remains the collection, care and making accessible of the records of Australia's and the world's history and current concerns. Fulfilment of this mission demands perhaps different but not greater skills than those displayed by librarians in building the collections and services and creating the cooperative arrangements which make libraries a rich part of Australia's heritage and an important base on which to build the nation's future.

Further reading: Biskup, P. and Goodman, M. *Australian Libraries. 3rd ed.* London, Bingley, 1982; Bryan, H. and Greenwood, G. eds. *Design for Diversity: Library Services for Higher Education in Australia.* St Lucia, Queensland, University of Queensland Press, 1977; *Committee of Inquiry into Public Libraries. Public Libraries in Australia, Report of the Committee of Inquiry into Public Libraries.* Canberra, Australian Government Publishing Service, 1976; Fenwick, S.I. *School and Children's Libraries in Australia: A Report to the Children's Libraries Section of the Library Association of Australia.* Melbourne, Cheshire for the Library Association of Australia, 1966; Munn, R. and Pitt, E.R. *Australian Libraries: A Survey of Conditions and Suggestions for their Improvement.* Melbourne, Australian Council for Education Research, 1935; *School/Community Libraries in Australia. Report to the Commonwealth Schools Commission.* Canberra, 1983; Vincent, I. *The Campaign for Public Libraries in New South Wales, 1929-1950.* Libri V.31(4), 1981, 271–93; Whitelock, D. *The Great Tradition: A History of Adult Education in Australia.* St Lucia, Queensland, University of Queensland Press, 1974.

lice These wingless, exopterygote INSECTS belong to the order Phthiraptera of which there are about 250 known species in Australia. Several of these have been introduced with domestic stock and man. Lice are small, flattened insects with large claws for clinging to feathers or hairs. They spend their entire lives as parasites on the surfaces of mammals or birds. Two suborders are represented in Australia, the Mallophaga and the Anoplura.

Lice transfer to new host individuals on contact. The human body and head louse (*see* PARASITES, HUMAN) can be transferred with clothing, and some biting lice, which are, in general, more active, may disperse to new hosts by hitch-hiking on flies such as mosquitoes. This phenomenon is called phoresy. Lice hatch from eggs (nits) cemented to hairs, feathers or clothing fibres. The nymphs closely resemble the adults.

Lice harm their hosts by their direct attacks and also by transmitting diseases such as human typhus (*see* DISEASES AND EPIDEMICS, HUMAN). Most species are specific to their hosts and die within a few hours of being taken from them. Some are also restricted in the area of the body that they infest (for example, the face louse and the foot louse of sheep).

Mallophaga The Mallophaga consists of the biting lice or bird lice which have biting and chewing mouthparts. Most parasitise birds but several live on mammals. They feed on fragments of hair, feathers and skin, and, to some extent, blood and sebaceous products. Birds, monotremes (platypus and spiny anteater), marsupials and bats are believed not to be parasitised by sucking lice, therefore most native lice of Australia belong to the Mallophaga. Most are endemic species found on endemic hosts. The family Boopiidae is almost confined to the marsupials but one of the 35 known species has recently transferred to dogs. This species, *Heterodoxus spiniger*, has subsequently been carried to Africa, Asia and the Americas. The remaining 160 or so native species belong to two widespread families that attack birds. The Trichodectidae is represented by six biting lice that have been introduced and which attack cattle, sheep, goats, horses, dogs, dingoes and cats.

J.H. Shaw

Suburban libraries, supported by local government, are common throughout Australia

Anoplura The Anoplura are the sucking lice, parasites with piercing and sucking mouthparts, which live on the blood of mammals. Many of the 20 or so Australian species are introduced; only six found on native rodents are native species. The Pediculidae is a small family of sucking lice restricted to primate hosts.

See also parasites, livestock
Further reading: Busvine, J.R. *Insects and Hygiene* (2nd edn) Methuen, London, 1966 and *Insects, Hygiene and History*. Athlone Press, London, 1976.

lichens These are primitive plants which are difficult to place in any tidy classification because each one consists of two quite different kinds of organism, namely a fungus and an alga (*see* FUNGI; ALGAE) living in intimate association, the algal cells lying within a meshwork of fungus. Presumably both derive benefit from the association. The fungus is usually an ascomycete, and the alga is either one of the blue-green algae or a green algal species (Chlorophyta).

Lichens reproduce either by breaking off into small pieces or by producing light specialised bodies (soredia) which consist of algal cells surrounded by fungal hyphae. They grow in exposed positions such as on the bark of trees and on bare rock or soil. Some are crustaceous (forming an encrustation on a surface); others are foliose (leafy), and still others are fruticose (branching, dendroid or coral-like). Lichens grow slowly, are intolerant of pollution and are resistant to cold and to low humidity. They are found throughout the world; the reindeer 'moss' of the Arctic, upon which Lapps feed their herds, is really a lichen. Tree-dwelling forms are common in Australia: *Strigula elegans* of QLD, for example, grows on the leaves of evergreen forest trees. The branching *Cladonia*

Bright orange lichen on rocks in the Bay of Fires TAS

macilenta, a species with red fructifications, grows on rotting logs, while *Thysanothecium hyalinum* colonises the charred wood of trees burned in bushfires. Species of *Verrucaria* and *Lichina* are common on sea coast rocks. Lichens are usually the first plants to colonise bare rocks, laval flows and so on, and by doing so they prepare the habitat for colonisation by higher plants.

Light, William (1786-1839) Founder of Adelaide. Born in Malaya, he was educated in England, served in the British Navy from 1799 to 1802, joined the British Army in 1808 and served throughout the Peninsular War. He left the army in 1821, but served briefly in the Spanish army in 1823. In 1836 he was appointed Surveyor-General of the proposed colony of SA, with full authority to decide on the location of the first settlement. Sailing in the brig *Rapid*, he reached SA in August of that year, rejected KANGAROO ISLAND, ENCOUNTER BAY and PORT LINCOLN, and chose the site of Adelaide. In spite of later objections by Hindmarsh and officials of the South Australia Co., he kept firmly to this decision. However, he found that he had insufficient staff and equipment to carry out surveys at the speed expected by the board of commissioners controlling land sales and in mid-1838, when his request for extra staff was refused and he was ordered to change his surveying methods to speed up the work, he resigned. By this time he was in ill health and, although he joined a surveying partnership, he was unable to do much work. His most enduring monument is the city plan of Adelaide which was far in advance of its time.
Further reading: Dutton, G. *Founder of a City*. Rigby, Adelaide, 1971.

Lightning Ridge NSW (population 1 112 in 1981) This opal mining centre is located 74km N of WALGETT on the Castlereagh Highway, in the NW plains region, some 770km NW of Sydney. This opal field is the most prolific known source of the rare black opals. The town is quite small but the influx of tourists and fossickers often swells the population considerably, particularly in August at the time of the annual Opal Festival. Opals were first discovered at the ridge in the 1880s, but commercial mining did not start until early this century, and it has only been in recent years that the settlement has changed from a mining camp into a town with modern air-conditioned shops, motels, an artesian bore swimming pool, a caravan park, service stations, a racecourse and recreation facilities.
Further reading: Colahan, J. *Australian Opal Safari*. Rigby, Adelaide, 1973.

Lichen, *Usnea* species

Lichen, *Cladonia* species

'Light's Vision' a statue of Adelaide's founder

lignite *see* coal

Liliaceae This is a large family of monocotyledonous flowering plants belonging to the order Liliales, with some 200 genera and over 3000 species, well distributed throughout the world's temperate and tropical regions. With the closely related Amaryllidaceae and Agavaceae, this family contains a large number of popular plants which have been cultivated over a long period of time; some, such as tulips, narcissus and liliums, have been extensively hybridised and hundreds of cultivars selected. Whilst the Australian members may not all be particularly striking, the members of the genus

Gymea lily, *Doranthes excelsa* Agavaceae

Blandfordia are all worthy of attention (for example, Christmas bells, *B. grandiflora*, is widely cultivated).

All members of the Liliaceae are herbs or shrubby climbers, often with bulbs. The flowers are usually bisexual, regular and arranged in racemes, panicles, or corymbose umbels. The perianth consists of six parts, arranged in two whorls, the segments of which are either free or joined, and usually petaloid, or at least with one whorl coloured. There are six stamens either free or joined to the perianth. The ovary is superior and consists of three parts (or loculi) with more than one ovule per loculus; the style is either divided into three or is whole (entire). The fruit is usually a dry capsule, a fleshy berry or a schizocarp.

Some of the better-known Australian genera include flax lilies (*Dianella* species), chocolate and vanilla lilies (*Dichopogon* and *Arthropodium* species), the fringe lilies (*Thysanotus* species) and early Nancy, *Anguillaria dioica*. These are all herbaceous perennials which display their flowers for a brief season, usually in spring, and are common in woodlands, heaths or grasslands. Some of the more woody and/or climbing members include sarsaparilla (*Smilax* species), *Ripogonum*, the wombat berry (*Eustrephus* species) and the scrambling lily (*Geitonoplesium* species). All these form permanent evergreen plants, and occur in moist habitats such as shaded gullies in tall open forest, or as part of the understorey in closed forest.

An introduced genus, *Asparagus*, contains the popular asparagus ferns and the edible asparagus, but one member, *A. sprengeri* has become a serious WEED in sheltered moist situations in the urban areas of the warmer parts of Australia.
See also Angiospermae; Appendix 5, Flower Structure and Glossary of Botanical Terms
Further reading: see Appendix 6, A Bibliography for Plants.

Lillee, Dennis Keith (1949-) Cricketer. As a fast bowler he has been outstanding not only for his tremendous speed, but for his ability to gain advantage from variations in pace, swing and length. He first played for WA in 1969-70, and in the same season was a member of the Australian team which toured New Zealand. He reached a peak in 1972, when he took 31 wickets in five Tests in England. However he broke down with a back injury during a later tour of the West Indies, and after six weeks in plaster underwent a long period of recovery. He returned to Test cricket in the 1974-75 season, taking 25 wickets against England. By the end of the 1982-83 season he had taken a total of 335 wickets in 65 Tests, this being a Test record among players of all countries. Throughout his career he has also been a useful tail-end batsman.

Dennis Lillee

lilly pilly *see* Myrtaceae

limpets *see* gastropods

Lindeman Island QLD This tropical island resort lies near the S end of the WHITSUNDAY PASSAGE, off the E coast of the State, N of MACKAY and E of PROSERPINE, between Shaw Is and the mainland coast. It has been developed extensively since the 1920s as a tourist centre, and in 1982 had accommodation for 362 guests. It can be reached by launch from Shute Harbour or by air from Mackay. It is a coral-fringed island, hilly and densely forested, which provides a range of recreational activities and opportunities for launch cruises to the outer section of the GREAT BARRIER REEF. Lindeman Is and Little Lindeman Is, which cover an area of 605ha, are part of the Whitsunday Passage Islands National Park.

Lindrum, Walter Albert (1898-1960) Billiards player. Born in the WA goldfields town of KALGOORLIE, Lindrum began playing billiards at an early age on the table his father had installed in the family hotel at Kalgoorlie.

But this table was often busy and the young Walter could not have the continued access he wanted. Instead of complaining to his father (who had been Australian billiards champion himself), the eight-year-old boy began taking his cue to BOULDER, four miles away, to obtain his daily practice. Thus began a daunting practice schedule of eight hours a day, seven days a week, which was to take him to world mastery. From 1914 to 1950 he established 57 world records and made more than 800 breaks of beyond 1000. These included his finest achievement—the still unbeaten world record break of 4 137 which he scored in London on 19 and 20 January 1932. In the same year he became world champion by defeating Joe Davis. Determined to gain control over himself as well as over the billiard balls, he succeeded to such an extent that the English authorities altered two rules and instituted one new one in an effort to curb the Australian's domination of the game. Even though the rule changes were aimed specifically at Lindrum's style of play, he simply changed his style and continued to make breaks of 1000 and more, almost at will. Retiring as undefeated champion of the world in 1950, he died of a heart attact 10 years later.

Lindsay, Norman Alfred William

(1879-1969) Artist and writer. Born at CRESWICK in VIC, Lindsay was a highly competent art student who became a household name as a result of his black-and-white illustrations and cartoons in the *Bulletin*. He had great enthusiasm and single-minded tenacity. He read avidly, particularly the Greek and Roman classics and the works of Rabelais, Boccaccio, Byron, Rosetti and Swinburne. He admired the paintings of Rubens and Delacroix and was influenced by the teachings of the German philosopher Nietzsche. He built model boats, wrote children's books—including *The Magic Pudding* (1918), which became a national institution—moulded concrete sculptures, wrote poetry, and indulged in polemical writing. After living as a young man in Melbourne amongst a group of artists, he married and moved to Lavender Bay, Sydney, and later to Springwood in the BLUE MOUNTAINS. Lindsay became well known for his controversial views on art, religion and literature: he denounced Christianity as a subverter of freedom and creativity; he painted strutting female nudes; he etched prints, such as *Pollice Verso* (1904) and the *Crucified Venus* (1912), which were anticlerical and anti-religious; and after World War II, he made strident attacks upon the works of such writers as Ezra Pound, T.S. Eliot and James Joyce, and such painters as Cézanne, Van Gogh, Gauguin and Picasso. Lindsay's house at Springwood is now a National Trust (NSW) property and, with its paintings, etchings, models and statuary, is open to the public.

ling *see* fishes, bony

lion, marsupial *see* fossils

Lions Clubs These are community service clubs, the first of which was founded by Melvin Jones in Chicago in 1917. The first Australian club was formed at LISMORE in NSW in 1947, and by 1982 there were in the multiple District of Australia and Papua New Guinea 1 274 clubs with a total membership of nearly 36 000.

Membership of Lions Clubs is confined to men, but associated with them are partner organisations called Lionesses and Leos, the former being for women who wish to be associated with the humanitarian work of the clubs, and the latter being open to young people of both sexes under the age of 25. Each club as an individual unit pursues its own programme of activities in the local community, but also participates in combined projects on a wider scale. Joint projects in Australia have included the setting up of a public relief foundation which has provided help for the victims of many natural disasters. In the health and welfare fields achievements include the establishment of the Lions National Opthalmic Research Unit at the Melbourne Eye Hospital, a renal research unit in Brisbane, and university Chairs of Opthalmology in SA and WA, as well as the making of a number of medical research grants by the NSW Save Sight Foundation. Another major project has been the establishment of the Licola Village in VIC for under-privileged young people.

Lismore NSW (population 24 035 in 1981) The largest city in the NORTH COAST region, Lismore is situated on the N arm of the RICHMOND RIVER, 105km by water, but only 28km by road, from the mouth. It is the main commercial and business focus of the Richmond Valley and is surrounded by fertile grazing and farming country. Beef and dairy cattle are bred, crops such as maize and sorghum are cultivated, and sugar cane farms and banana plantations are common in the district. The Richmond Valley is the major dairying region of the State and one of the most densely populated rural regions of Australia. Lismore is 836km by rail, 808km by road, N of Sydney, and located on the Bruxner Highway which links the North Coast with the NEW ENGLAND Plateau. The climate is sub-tropical, with hot humid summer days and mild winter temperatures. The average annual rainfall is 1 349mm and although rain occurs in all months, the period from January to April receives the highest monthly falls. Summer and early autumn is thus the time when the river is likely to flood, causing considerable damage to the low-lying rural regions and even inundating the main business area of the city in particularly rainy years.

The lower Richmond Valley was settled in the 1820s when much of the land was densely timbered. The area was originally called 'The Big Scrub' and cedar-getting was the major occupation. Such were the rewards from this that only remnants of the once superb subtropical forest remain. The name Lismore was given by one of the pioneer settlers to his property, so called after the island of Lismore

in Loch Linnhe in Scotland. The village was officially gazetted in 1856, proclaimed as a municipal district in 1879 and became a city in 1946. In the early days, the town was a river port for timber and other rural products, but siltation of the river, combined with competition by more efficient road and rail transport, eclipsed the river-boat trade. Rail connection with Sydney was not made until 1932, when the bridge across the CLARENCE RIVER at GRAFTON (the valley to the S of the Richmond) was completed. Lismore has a number of secondary industries; Norco, one of the nation's largest manufacturers of dairy products, has its chief factory there, and there are engineering works, a clothing factory, sawmills and steel fabrication works. The Northern Rivers College of Advanced Education, formerly called the Teachers' College, is located in Lismore. Along the coastline E of the city are many resort centres, such as Evan's Head, BALLINA, BYRON BAY and Lennox Head. Many buildings in Lismore have been listed by the National Trust (NSW) and some, such as the post office in the main street and St Carthage's Catholic Cathedral, have been classified for preservation as part of the cultural heritage.

literature This article is concerned with the creative literary works (mostly poetry and fiction) written by people who were either born-and-bred Australians or who lived in the country for some considerable time. Works written by short-term visitors to the country are mentioned only when they are based on the author's Australian experiences. Biographical, historical, descriptive or discursive forms of writing and essays are mentioned only briefly and dramatic works are discussed in the entry on DRAMA.

Verse 1788-1900 Almost from the time that the colony of NSW was founded, folk ballads and songs began to circulate orally, and many were later written down. Although some have literary value, it is difficult to classify them as Australian literature, since their authorship is unknown and many may not have been written in Australia. 'True Patriots All', long believed to have been written by a convict, George Barrington, and spoken as the prologue to the first play produced in Sydney, is now believed to have been written by an Englishman who at no time visited Australia. In the case of 'The Convict's Tour of Hell', composed by a convict, Frank McNamara ('Frank the Poet'), it is uncertain whether any of the several written versions of it are in his exact words.

The first pieces of verse of known authorship seem to be the commemorative odes written by an emancipated convict, Michael Massey Robinson, from 1810 onwards and published in the *Sydney Gazette*. The first volume of verse published in Australia was *First Fruits of Australian Poetry* (1819) by Barron Field, Judge of the Supreme Court and a friend of Charles Lamb; and the first poem by a native-born Australian was William WENTWORTH's 'Australasia' which was placed second in the competition for the Chancellor's Prize at Cambridge University in 1822. However, the real beginning of Australian poetry is probably the work of Charles Harpur, born at WINDSOR in NSW in 1813, whose 'Midsummer Noon in the Australian Forest' and 'The Creek of the Four Graves' are still fairly widely known.

The first Australian poet to achieve wide and lasting popularity was Henry KENDALL, whose descriptive pieces such as 'Bell-Birds' and 'September in Australia' gained him a reputation as a poet of the Australian landscape and showed clearly the influence of English poets such as Tennyson. Adam Lindsay GORDON was more of a narrative poet than Kendall, but was also influenced by English models, particularly the work of Swinburne.

Henry Lawson, a photograph taken about 1890 (Mitchell Library Sydney)

Other poets of the later 19th century include Barcroft BOAKE, James Brunton Stephens and Victor DALEY, but their work was overshadowed by the emergence in the 1890s of the bush ballad as an Australian literary form. Two leading exponents of this form were Andrew ('Banjo') PATERSON and Henry LAWSON; their work was closely linked with the rise of Australian nationalism, and was well publicised by the nationalistic magazine, the *Bulletin*. While both wrote about Australian bush life, Lawson spoke for the common man and depicted the harsher aspects of life, whereas Paterson displayed a somewhat patrician attitude and painted a more romantic picture.

Prose 1788-1900 The early prose works written in the colony, or as a result of experiences there, were accounts of its foundation and progress, such as *A Complete Account of the Settlement at Port Jackson in New South Wales* (1793) by Lieutenant Watkin Tench, and *An Account of the English Colony in New South Wales* (1798-1802) by David COLLINS, the colony's first Judge-Advocate. Fiction was slow to appear, and when it did was in the shape of novels with melodramatic plots interspersed with observations on convict life and Austra-

lian society in general. The first was *Quintus Servinton* (1830-31) by a convict, Henry SAVERY. It was followed by *Ralph Rashleigh*, probably written by James Tucker in the 1840s but not published in complete form until 1952, Charles Rowcroft's *Tales of the Colonies* (1843) and Alexander Harris' *Settlers and Convicts* (1847) and *The Emigrant Family* (1849).

The second half of the century brought novels of greater worth from Henry KINGSLEY, Marcus CLARKE and Thomas Alexander Browne (Rolf BOLDREWOOD). Kingsley's *The Recollections of Geoffrey Hamlyn* (1859) concerns the life of upper-class squatters. Clarke's *For the Term of His Natural Life*, which first appeared as a serial in 1870-72, deals with the more brutal aspects of the convict system and is based on a wide study of historical documents. Boldrewood wrote prolifically, but is remembered mainly for one novel, *Robbery Under Arms*, which first appeared as a serial (1882-83) and is supposedly narrated by a young man who has been gaoled for bushranging offences. The period also produced a number of women novelists. Caroline Leakey wrote *The Broad Arrow* (1859) which describes convict life in VAN DIEMEN'S LAND. Catherine Helen SPENCE wrote *Clara Morrison* (1854) and other novels which give a more realistic picture of colonial life than any earlier fiction. Ada CAMBRIDGE and Mrs Campbell PRAED published their first romantic novels in 1878 and 1880 respectively.

During the 1890s the greatest achievements in fiction were in the short story. Previously, few stories of value had been published apart from the collection *Botany Bay* (1859) by John Lang, but in 1892 William Astley (Price WARUNG) published the first of several volumes of stories based on his study of convict records, and Francis ADAMS published the collection *Australian Life*. Edward Dyson wrote of miners and factory hands, publishing the collection *Below and on Top* in 1898. George Lewis BECKE published his first Pacific islands story in 1893 and a collection of them, *By Reef and Palm*, in 1894. Barbara Baynton wrote several stories depicting the harsh realities of bush life, a collection of them appearing as *Bush Studies* (1902).

Most of the prose writers of the period, like the poets, owed a great deal to the *Bulletin*—not only for the opportunity to have their work published in it, but also for the encouragement and advice received from its literary editor, Alfred STEPHENS. This was particularly true in the case of Henry Lawson, whose stories—generally very short 'yarns', colloquial in style and dealing predominantly with bush life—were the type of material most favoured by the *Bulletin*. Lawson's best-known stories, such as 'The Drover's Wife' and 'The Loaded Dog', seem likely to retain their popularity indefinitely.

There were few literary and critical essays of note before the 1890s. Australia's first novelist, Henry Savery, is commonly regarded also as the first essayist, by virtue of 30 articles which he contributed to the Hobart *Colonial Times* in 1829 and which were published in 1830 in

book form under the title *The Hermit of Van Diemen's Land*. Francis Adams' collection, *Australian Essays* (1886), is also worth noting. In literary criticism the main works were *Fiction Fields of Australia* (1856) by Francis Sinnett, *Australian Literature* (1864) by William Walker and *The Poets and Prose Writers of New South Wales* (1866) by George Barton. Around the turn of the century Alfred Stephens established himself as Australia's first notable literary critic, a volume of his articles being published in 1904 as *The Red Pagan*.

Poetry 1900-40 This period produced a wide range of Australian literature, showing considerable variety in themes, influences, outlook and style. While Paterson and Lawson continued to write popular ballads, Christopher BRENNAN searched for self-fulfilment in poetry, much of which cannot be fully understood without some knowledge of his philosophy of aesthetics and of the influence on him of the French Symbolists. Far apart from these poets is Hugh McCRAE, whose lyrics deal largely with a world of myths and legends. In the first decade of the century Williams BAYLEBRIDGE published two small volumes but he attracted little attention until the publication of his sonnet sequence *Love Redeemed* (1934). Similarly Frank Wilmot (Furnley MAURICE) began publication fairly early in the century, but did not produce his best work, *Melbourne Odes*, until 1934. However, Dame Mary GILMORE's first volume, *Marri'd and Other Verses* (1910), established her as a major poet.

Christopher Brennan, a photograph about 1893 in the Mitchell Library Sydney

Other notable poets of this period include John Shaw NEILSON, Bernard O'DOWD and Clarence DENNIS (better known as C.J. Dennis). Neilson published some lyrics in newspapers in the 1890s, but wrote mainly in the 20th century. O'Dowd, whose first volume, *Dawnward?*, appeared in 1903, believed that all poetry should deal with important social questions. Dennis attained immense popular success with *Songs of a Sentimental Bloke* (1915) and *The Moods of Ginger Mick* (1916).

In the 1920s and 1930s two major poets were Kenneth SLESSOR and Robert FITZGERALD, whose first collections appeared in 1926 and 1927 respectively. Slessor at first favoured poems of fantasy and romance, but most of his best-known poems are products of a later period. A number of them, including 'Captain Dobbin', 'Five Visions of Captain Cook' and 'Five Bells', are concerned with the sea; the last-mentioned, an elegy for a friend drowned in Sydney Harbour, is widely considered his best poem. FitzGerald too showed an early tendency towards fantasy, but is essentially a philosophical writer.

Fiction 1900-40 The first notable novel, unmistakenly Australian in style and outlook, was *Such Is Life* (1903) by Joseph Furphy (Tom COLLINS). It contains a wealth of observations on many aspects of Australian life, and of life in general, appended to a disconnected narrative presented in the guise of a series of extracts from the diaries of a RIVERINA bullock-driver. In 1908 Ethel Robertson (Henry Handel RICHARDSON) published her first work, *Maurice Guest*, but did not attain fame until the publication of *The Fortunes of Richard Mahony* (1917-29).

Ethel Florence Robertson (Henry Handel Richardson)
A photograph by Elliott & Fry, London, about 1940

Mitchell Library

Other notable novelists of this period include Louis Stone, William Gosse Hay, Stella Maria Miles FRANKLIN (BRENT OF BIN BIN), Katharine PRICHARD, M. BARNARD ELDERSHAW (Flora ELDERSHAW and Marjorie BARNARD, writing in collaboration), Eleanor DARK, Leonard MANN, Brian PENTON, Vance PALMER, Norman LINDSAY, Kylie TENNANT, Kenneth 'Seaforth' Mackenzie, Christina STEAD, Frank Dalby Davison and Xavier HERBERT. Stone's best-known novel, *Jonah* (1911), tells of the reformation of a leader of a street gang. Hay wrote several historical novels, notably *The Escape of the Notorious Sir William Heans* (1919), a story of convict days in TAS. The best-known of Miles Franklin's novels, published under her own name, is *All That Swagger* (1936), a family saga which spans a century, from the time when Danny Delacy migrated from Ireland to settle on the upper

MURRUMBIDGEE RIVER. Prichard's novels are set in WA and include *Working Bullocks* (1926), *Coonardoo* (1929) and a goldfields trilogy published in the 1940s.

Of the six novels published by M. Barnard Eldershaw, the most highly regarded is *A House Is Built* (1929). During the 1930s Eleanor Dark wrote several novels concerned primarily with personal psychological conflict. Leonard Mann's *Flesh in Armour* (1932) is based on the experiences of Australian soldiers in World War I. Vance Palmer, perhaps the best-known novelist of the 1930s, wrote about ordinary people and the ordinariness of most lives. Norman Lindsay, better known as an artist, published several novels including the autobiographical *Redheap* (1930) and *Saturdee* (1933). Kylie Tennant published *Tiburon* in 1935, but was to produce most of her work after 1940. 'Seaforth' Mackenzie's first and probably best novel, *The Young Desire It* (1935), deals with life in a boys' boarding school. Christina Stead established an international reputation with *Seven Poor Men of Sydney* (1935). Davison first attracted wide attention with the classic study of animal life, *Man-Shy* (1931). Xavier Herbert published his first mammoth masterpiece, *Capricornia*, in 1938.

The 1920s and 1930s also produced many notable short stories by such novelists as Vance Palmer, Marjorie Barnard and Katharine Prichard. Frank Dalby Davison's stories of the lives of small farmers, such as those in the collection *The Woman at the Mill* (1940), are perhaps of greater merit than his few novels.

Literary movements and magazines The late 1930s and early 1940s were marked by the emergence of two opposed literary movements and by the foundation of a number of literary magazines. The Jindyworobak Club, founded in Adelaide in the late 1930s by Rex INGAMELLS, published over 30 anthologies which favoured literary themes that were 'vitally Australian', including some drawn from Aboriginal culture; while the magazine *Angry Penguins* (1940-46), also founded in Adelaide, was, according to its editor and proprietor, Max Harris, 'aggressively modernist'. *Angry Penguins* also produced a counter-reaction, one expression of which was seen in the ERN MALLEY HOAX of 1943. Two other literary magazines which appeared at this time and are still published are *Southerly*, founded in 1939 by the Sydney branch of the English Association, and *Meanjin Papers*, founded in Brisbane in 1940, but renamed *Meanjin* in 1947 and *Meanjin Quarterly* in 1960.

Poetry since 1940 Judith WRIGHT, Douglas STEWART, James McAULEY and Alec HOPE have been the outstanding poets since 1940; other talented poets include Vincent Buckley, David Campbell, Jack Davis, Bruce Dawe, Geoffrey DUTTON, Rosemary Dobson, Kevin Gilbert, Rodney Hall, Evan Jones, Geoffrey Lehmann, David Malouf, John Manifold, Leonard MANN, Les Murray, Roland Robinson, Thomas W. Shapcott, Harold Stewart, Randolph STOW, John Thompson, Kath WALKER, Chris Wallace-Crabbe and

Judith Wright

Francis Webb.

Judith Wright's work shows sensitivity and technical proficiency; her sense of history and awareness of landscape are clearly apparent in her poetry. Douglas Stewart is perhaps Australia's most versatile poet, having written fantasy, comic poems, nature poems, sonnets, ballads and verse plays. His best-known work is the radio play *Fire on the Snow* (1941), which deals with the tragedy of Scott's Antarctic expedition. James McAuley's verse forms are marked by classical order, and his poems, ranging from brief lyrics to the book-length reflective narrative *Captain Quiros* (1964), are aimed largely at drawing man back to the resources of a more stable age. Alec Hope, the most notable satirist among Australian poets, favours themes about the artificiality of modern life, loneliness and the inability of human beings to communicate fully with one another. His verse features a great deal of sexual imagery.

Fiction since 1940 In the 1940s the short story flourished particularly strongly. Gavin Casey, most of whose best writing was set in the KALGOORLIE area, published the collections *It's Harder For Girls* (1942) and *Birds of a Feather* (1943). Dal STIVENS and Alan MARSHALL concentrated on stories with country settings. Other notable collections of short stories include Margaret Trist's *What Else Is There?* (1946), Don Edwards' *High Hill at Midnight* (1944) and Brian James' stories of rural life in *Cockabundy Bridge* (1946). Novelists who continued to publish collections of short stories also included Marjorie Barnard with *The Persimmon Tree* (1943) and Katharine Prichard with *Potch and Colour* (1944). Collections appearing in the 1950s and 1960s, when attention had swung back to the novel, included *Alien Son* (1952), a set of studies of a Jewish boy and his immigrant family, by Judah Waten; *The Man in the Silo* (1955) and *The Village Hampden* (1958) by E.O. Schlunke; *A*

Bachelor's Children (1962), by Hal PORTER; and *Twenty-Three* (1962), containing realistic stories based on the lives of working-class people, by John Morrison.

By this time Eleanor Dark had begun writing historical fiction. *The Timeless Land* (1941), based on thorough historical research, gives a picture of early British settlement in Australia and of its impact on the lives of the Aborigines. This theme is continued in *Storm of Time* (1948) and *No Barriers* (1954), and the three books constitute an impressive attempt to link early colonial history with Australian nationalism. Martin BOYD, whose pre-war writing had attracted little attention, established himself in the front rank of Australian novelists with *Lucinda Brayford* (1946) and the sequence *The Cardboard Crown* (1952), *A Difficult Young Man* (1955), *Outbreak of Love* (1957) and *When Blackbirds Sing* (1962). Katharine Prichard conveyed a Marxist view of the history of the goldfields of WA in the sequence *The Roaring Nineties* (1946), *Golden Miles* (1948) and *Winged Seeds* (1950). Kylie Tennant followed up the success of *Tiburon* with *The Battlers* (1941) and other works. Xavier Herbert published two more mammoth works—*Soldiers' Women* (1961), set in a wartime coastal city obviously modelled on Sydney, and *Poor Fellow, My Country* (1975). Other established authors who continued to publish novels included Vance Palmer, 'Seaforth' Mackenzie and Leonard Mann. Novels based on the experiences of Australian servicemen in World War II included Lawson Glassop's *We Were the Rats* (1944), Eric Lambert's *Twenty Thousand Thieves* (1951) and *The Veterans* (1954) and T.A. Hungerford's *The Ridge and the River* (1952).

Several notable novelists have established their reputations wholly or mainly since the 1950s. Randolph Stow's works, such as *To the Islands* (1958), show great ability in the evocation of landscape and in linking this with the emotional experiences of his characters. Christopher Koch won favourable attention with *The Boys in the Island* (1958), which deals with the inner world of an imaginative boy, *Across the Sea Wall* (1965), and *The Year of Living Dangerously* (1978), set in Indonesia. Hal Porter's *A Handful of Pennies* (1958), set in Japan during the Allied occupation, and *The Tilted Cross* (1961), set in TAS in convict days, are notable for their characterisation of eccentrics and for their flamboyant style. Frank HARDY attracted attention with *Power Without Glory* (1950), an exposé of alleged political and financial corruption, written from a Marxist viewpoint and containing remarkably detailed documentation. A left-wing viewpoint is also expressed in *Time of Conflict* (1961) and other works by Judah Waten.

New dimensions have been added to Australian fiction by Patrick WHITE, winner of the 1973 Nobel Prize for literature, whose international reputation as a major novelist was first established with *The Tree of Man* (1955). The author who has established himself most recently as a major novelist is Thomas KENEALLY, who skilfully recreated the atmosphere

of early Sydney in his third novel *Bring Larks and Heroes* (1967).

Works of merit by other novelists include *The Catherine Wheel* (1961) and others by Elizabeth Harrower; *The Young Wife* (1962) by Hungarian-born David Martin; *The Girl with a Monkey* (1958) and later works by Thea Astley; *The Wild Grapes* (1963) and other works by Barbara Jefferis; *A Wild Ass of a Man* (1967), *Let's Hear It for Prendergast* (1970) and *A Salute to the Great McCarthy* (1970) by Barry Oakley; *The Unknown Industrial Prisoner* (1971), *The Glass Canoe* (1976) and other works by David Ireland; the 'discontinuous narratives', such as *The Electrical Experience* (1974), of Frank Moorhouse; David Malouf's *An Imaginary Life* (1978) and *Fly Away Peter Venus* (1980); Gabrielle Lord's *Fortress* (1980); Murray Ball's *Homesickness* (1980); Ian Moffit's *The Retreat of Radiance* (1982) and *The Colour Man* (1983).

In popular fiction a number of authors have achieved high qualities of craftsmanship. These include D'Arcy NILAND, Ruth PARK, Jon CLEARY, Olaf Ruhen and John O'Grady (Nino Culotta). Outstanding popular successes have been Colleen McCULLOUGH's *The Thorn Birds* (1977) and *An Indecent Obsession* (1981). The most widely read Australia novelist has been Morris WEST, whose successive best-sellers from *The Devil's Advocate* (1959) to *The World is Made of Glass* (1983) are notable for their introduction of moral and religious themes into popular literature.

Other prose works Of all major forms of prose writing the personal essay is one which has developed least strongly in Australia, and even the best-known essayist, Walter MURDOCH, cannot be considered a major literary figure. However, articles and longer works in the field of literary criticism have abounded, and have often reached a high standard (*see* bibliographies *below* and in entries on individual authors).

With reference to discursive or descriptive writing, much of the latter has been of very high standard, the outstanding example perhaps being C.M.H. (Manning) CLARK's *History of Australia*, of which five volumes have been published since 1962. Apart from its academic value, this monumental work has been widely acclaimed for its literary merit. Other examples are the works of social and cultural analysis by Donald HORNE and J.D. Pringle and the writings of Cyril PEARL who has treated social history with sparkling wit.

Further reading: Miller, E.M. & Macartney, F. *Australian Literature.* (revd edn) Angus & Robertson, Sydney, 1956; Green, H.M. *A History of Australian Literature.* (2 vols) Angus & Robertson, Sydney, 1961; Johnston, G. *Annals of Australian Literature.* Oxford University Press, Melbourne, 1970; Kramer, Leonie *Oxford History of Australian Literature.* Oxford University Press, Melbourne, 1981.

Lithgow NSW (population 12 791 in 1981) A city in the central tablelands region, W of

The war memorial at Lithgow, typical of memorials in many country towns

the BLUE MOUNTAINS, it is located on the Great Western Highway, 147km by road W of Sydney. It is also on the main W railway, 156km from Sydney, just E of the Wallerawang junction where a branch line goes to MUDGEE. The railway between Sydney and Lithgow is electrified. At an elevation of 920m above sea level, Lithgow is situated in a valley at the foot of the steep W escarpment of the Blue Mts. It experiences warm to hot summer conditions and moderately cold winters with frequent frosts and occasional snow; it has an average annual rainfall of 900mm and though rain is experienced in all months there is a concentration in the summer season. The city is an important coal-mining and industrial centre, though most mines near Lithgow are worked out now and production is mainly in the Wallerawang-Lidsdale area, 16km NW. Settlement of the region commenced in the early 1820s after the crossing of the Blue Mts in 1813 and it was named after William Lithgow, Auditor-General of NSW. In 1869 the railway finally reached the city; this led to the opening of several coal mines and in the subsequent decade there was rapid industrial growth. In 1875 a major step was taken with the establishment of an iron works and blast furnace; this plant was transferred to PORT KEMBLA in 1928. The Zig Zag steam railway, begun in 1866 and completed in 1869, enabled trains to descend the steep W face of the Blue Mts by three viaducts and two tunnels cut through the sandstone; in 1910 it was replaced by the present system of tunnels and the Zig Zag fell into disrepair; however, in 1974, a tourist rail system was developed and it is now possible to take a train trip over this breathtaking stretch of railway track. Among other tourist attractions are Hassan's Walls Lookout, 5km S of the city, where there are sweeping views of the cliffs and valleys of the Blue Mts. The Blue Mts National Park, covering 208 756ha of plateau and gorge country, lies E of the city. The National Trust (NSW) has listed and classified a number of buildings in the city including the Lithgow Valley pottery kiln, the courthouse, the iron works blast furnace site, De La Salle College, the Hermitage colliery site and 'Eskbank', a sandstone home built in 1841 by Thomas Brown, the discoverer of the Lithgow coal seam.

See also iron and steel industry

Further reading: Paridaens, *I. Lithgow and Hartley Valley Sketchbook.* Rigby, Adelaide, 1978.

Little Desert VIC So named by the 1870 pioneer settlers, who found the soils unsuitable for crops, this stretch of semi-arid country in the WIMMERA region of western VIC, extending from the SA border to near Dimboola, S of the Western Highway, is not really desert country. The annual rainfall is about 400mm (NHILL, on the Western Highway, has 423mm) and in recent decades research by soil scientists of the CSIRO showed that, with the addition of trace elements (copper, zinc and molybdenum) and nitrogenous fertilisers, it could be utilised for wool growing, fat lamb raising and beef cattle production. The Little Desert National Park, covering 35 300ha of heathland and mallee scrub, lies SW of Dimboola and W of the Wimmera River; the park contains a variety of animal and bird life—kangaroos, possums, parrots and currawongs—but is especially noted for the unique mallee fowls.

liver fluke This is a serious FLUKE parasite found in many countries, which infests sheep and cattle and, sometimes, human beings. The larval stages are passed in a small water snail of the genus *Lymnaea* which commonly occurs on swampy ground. In Europe the species is usually *L. truncatula* but in Australia the main carrier is the native *L. tomentosa*. Recently a second species, *L. columella*, has been introduced, probably with a consignment of aquarium fishes.

The liver fluke is known as *Fasciola hepatica* and the disease that it causes is technically fascioliasis. The sheep or cow swallows the encysted immature fluke (cercaria) and for a time the young fluke wanders about the liver, damaging it. If the numbers are high the animal suffers from acute fluke disease which is often aggravated by attacks of black disease, caused by a soil-dwelling bacterium, *Clostridium novyi*. The adult flukes live in the bile ducts of the liver; large numbers cause the chronic disease. Sheep become anaemic and fluid collects in the abdominal cavities and in the skin below the jaws (bottle jaw). The 30mm-long adult flukes are hermaphrodites that lay eggs which pass out with the faeces. A mildly infested sheep can drop as many as 500 000 eggs a day, and a badly infested one, several million eggs.

In 1969, surveys showed that about 40 million sheep and five million cattle were on pastures in Australia that were potentially endemic for the disease. The disease is controlled by treating the sheep with drugs, by controlling the snails or destroying their

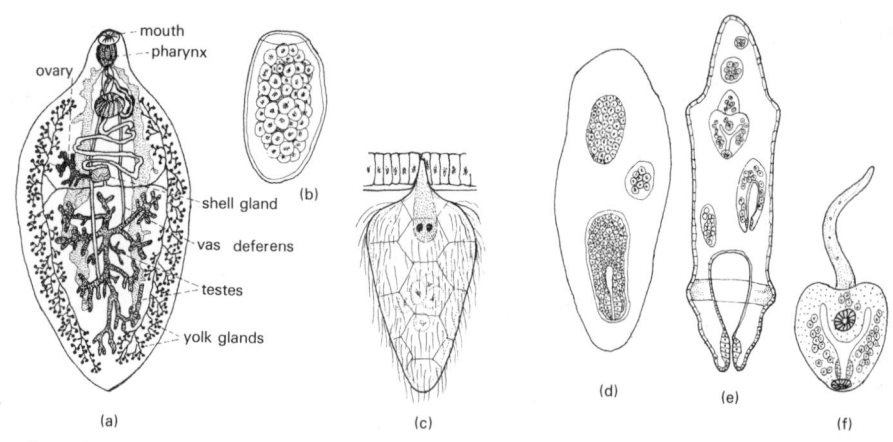

Stages in the life of a liver fluke: (a) adult showing complex internal organs; (b) eggs; (c) Minute miracidium penetrating the skin of the snail; (d) sporocysts containing developing rediae; (e) the redia which reproduces asexually within the snail, eventually producing the cercaria; (f) the cercaria which is swallowed by sheep

habitats, and by grazing management. In the last-mentioned method sheep are moved to clean pasture from time to time, to reduce the number of necessary drug treatments. Unfortunately, some native mammals such as wombats can become infested and spread the fluke to clean pastures. The fluke has attacked people in Europe and Australia; this usually resulted from eating wild watercress carrying the cercaria. In Australia it is, so far, restricted to eastern Australia.

liverworts *see* Hepatophyta

Lizard Island QLD An island tourist resort in the N section of the GREAT BARRIER REEF, 96km N of COOKTOWN, it is claimed as the only resort of the outer reef. It is noted not only for its beaches and coral displays, but also for opportunities to fish for big game. It was here that Prince Charles spent a few days in 1979. It is a small resort, having accommodation in 1982 for about 30 people, and with access from Cooktown by launch or by air. The island was discovered in 1770 by James COOK, and so named because, when he landed there, it was recorded that 'we saw no other animals but lizards'.

lizards The common name for any member of the VERTEBRATE suborder Lacertilia (order Squamata), lizards are REPTILES closely allied to SNAKES but usually distinguished by external ear openings, movable eyelids, the possession of legs, a tail which is longer than the body and usually with an unforked tongue. Furthermore, lizards have a lower jaw which is firmly attached to the skull whereas in snakes the lower jaw is loosely attached by elastic ligaments.

Most lizards are carnivorous, with insects forming a large part of the diet, but some are also herbivorous. In Australia they range in size from about 7cm to about 2.5m. No Australian lizard is venomous (the only venomous lizards are the Gila monster of the USA and its relatives in Mexico), though the bites of some may introduce harmful bacteria. Most reproduce by laying eggs.

There are five families of lizards represented in Australia: the Gekkonidae (the geckos); Pygopodidae (the legless lizards); Agamidae (the dragons); Varanidae (the goannas or monitors); and Scincidae (the skinks). The classification and nomenclature of lizards used here follows Cogger (*see below*). The identification of lizards is difficult as the colour is often variable; length is also an unreliable guide as lizards continue to grow as they age and many species carry a regenerated tail which is usually shorter than the original. Most lizards have planes of weakness in their tails so that when these are seized by a predator they snap off. Biologists therefore use the snout-to-vent length as a more reliable measurement and this is the one that appears in parentheses below.

Gekkonidae Geckos are small carnivorous, usually large-eyed lizards with conical scales that do not overlap so that the body is usually soft. The eyelid is immovable and the eye is protected by a transparent 'spectacle' which is cast when the lizard sloughs its skin. Geckos use their tongues to keep their eyes clean. They are nocturnal and in the daylight their pupils are reduced to narrow, vertical slits or a series of tiny holes. All Australian geckos have an external ear opening. Many geckos have pads on the toes which give them a purchase on smooth surfaces or even ceilings. Some frequent houses in the N, some are terrestrial, and some arboreal. There are about 60 species (16 genera) of geckos which occur throughout Australia (except TAS) and most are endemic. They are widespread in warm parts of the world.

The genus *Diplodactylus* contains about 21 species in Australia. The spiny-tailed gecko, *D. ciliaris* (8.5cm) is a distinctive species with a tail with rows of small spines; it lives in N and central Australia in trees and desert *Spinifex*. When disturbed it exudes a viscous fluid from the tail.

The genus *Gehyra* contains the northern dtella or house gecko, *G. australis* (8cm). Although it frequents houses in the N, waiting for insects attracted by light, its natural habitat is in woodlands, forests, caves and overhangs. In some N towns it is being displaced by the Asian house gecko, *Hemidactylus frenatus* (6cm), an introduced species. Both species have pads on the digits.

The genus *Heterontia* contains the Bynoe's gecko, *H. binoei* (5cm), found throughout Australia, apart from the more humid SW and SE. This common terrestrial gecko, variable in colour, but usually with light blotches on the back, forages in the open and shelters under litter and in crevices during the day.

The genus *Nephrurus* (about 6.5cm to 10cm) is represented by six species in Australia, all with broad short tails ending in knobs. Knob-tailed geckos usually live in burrows which they usurp or dig themselves. Most live in arid N and central Australia.

The genus *Oedura* contains the often highly coloured velvet geckos (nine species in Australia). One or other of the species can be found in most areas. Lesueur's velvet gecko, *O. lesueurii* (8cm), a coastal species of NSW and southern QLD, is dark in colour with a somewhat flattened tail and is usually found in rocky areas, caves and crevices.

The genus *Phyllodactylus* (two species in Australia) contains *P. guentheri* (8cm), a small gecko with retractible claws which lives only on rock faces on LORD HOWE and NORFOLK Islands, and some of the adjacent small islets. This species suffers severely from predation by rats on the main islands. Its mainland relative, the marbled gecko, *P. marmoratus* (7cm), of southern (but not SE) Australia, is an arboreal species.

The genus *Phyllurus* contains the leaf-tailed geckos (three species in Australia), found on the E coast. One, the northern leaf-tailed gecko, *P. cornutus* (16cm), is a widespread arboreal species. Found in rain and beech forests, it is one of Australia's largest geckos, reaching a total length of 25cm, and only its original tail is spiky.

The only member of the genus *Rhynchoedura* is the beaked gecko, *R. ornata* (5cm), which is widespread in the arid interior. It has a small plain beak and is reddish-brown with white spots.

The genus *Underwoodisaurus* (two species in Australia), contains the thick-tailed gecko, *U. milii* (8cm), widespread in the S in a wide range of habitats. It is dark with many small yellow or white spots.

Pygopodidae This family contains about 30 species found only in Australia and New Guinea. These snake-like lizards have no fore-limbs and the hind-limbs are represented by scaly flaps near the vent. They are closely related to geckos and thus have immovable eyelids; a few species have an external ear opening. Most are insectivorous but some also eat lizards. The most widespread species are probably Burton's snake lizard, *Lialis burtonis* (25cm), having small leg flaps, variable colouring and found throughout Australia and New Guinea; the common scaly-foot, *Pygopus lepidopodus* (23cm) a diurnal lizard with large leg flaps and variable colouring found in many different kinds of habitats in southern Australia, from SHARK BAY to south-eastern QLD; and the hooded scaly-foot, *P. nigriceps* (18cm), which is nocturnal and has a more N distribution, though it reaches the S coast in SA and WA.

Agamidae Commonly known as dragons, the members of this large family of lizards are found in Africa, Asia and Australasia, with about 50 species in Australia but only one in TAS. Agamids are large, diurnal, terrestrial (though some are arboreal), carnivorous or insectivorous (though some are herbivorous) lizards and some have elaborate courtship displays. Many can run on their hind-legs, such as the jacky lizard, *Amphibolurus muricatus* (10cm), and several have adapted to Australia's arid conditions. They have movable eyelids, external eardrums (except the genus *Tympanocryptis*) and a thick fleshy tongue with a notched tip; the scales do not overlap and are fragmented on the head, and very often the dorsal surfaces are covered in ridges (keels).

The largest Australian genus is the endemic *Amphibolurus* with 26 diverse species. One of the commonest species in the E half of Australia (though not TAS) is the bearded dragon or jew lizard, *A. barbatus* (25cm); the tail reaches about 33cm in length. This semi-arboreal insectivorous species varies from a light grey or brown to reddish-brown or almost black, but the adults are easily recognised by the beard or pouch which carries a border of long spiny scales. There is another series of spines across the throat. The pouch is inflated when the animal is molested and at the same time it puffs up its body with air. The mountain dragon, *A. diemensis* (6cm to 7cm), occurs mainly in the upland areas of SE Australia and TAS. It can reach a total length of about 20cm, two-thirds of which is the tail. The jacky lizard, occurring in the dry sclerophyll forests and the rocky ridges of the SE, is a grey or brown species above, with some darker mottlings, and greyish below, with a bright yellow mouth and tongue. It has a series of vertebral crests consisting of spines and its tail can reach a length of 20cm.

The genus *Chlamydosaurus* has only one member, the frilled lizard, *C. kingii* (22cm), which has a large, loose frill which is pushed out with great effect when the lizard is alarmed. The tail grows to about 44cm long and the colour varies from grey to orange-brown or black above, and whitish or yellowish below. It is an arboreal species frequenting the dry areas in the N of the continent and New Guinea.

The genus *Moloch* contains only one species, the mountain or thorny devil, *M. horridus* (9cm); the body is covered with conical, thorny processes and there is a spiny nuchal swelling and a spine above each eye. Despite its ferocious appearance this lizard lives on ants. It occurs in QLD, SA, WA and the NT.

The genus *Physignathus* includes the eastern water dragon, *P. lesueurii* (20cm), of E Australia which lives in the branches of trees above water; when disturbed it will drop into the water. Its strongly keeled tail measures up to 50cm and it feeds on insects, frogs, small land vertebrates and berries.

Varanidae Commonly called goannas or monitor lizards this family of about 30 species (about 19 species in Australia) is found in Africa, Asia and throughout Australia but not in TAS. The largest of all lizards, the Komodo dragon of Indonesia, *Varanus komodoensis*, which ranges in length from 2m to 3m, belongs to this family. The Australian name 'goanna' is probably derived from iguana, though iguanas are not closely related to varanids, and do not occur in Australia. Monitors range in size from a total length of 20cm (the short-tailed goanna or monitor, *V. brevicauda*), to about 2.5m (the perentie, *V. giganteus*, though this length is exceptional). Apart from size and body pattern, all monitors are very much alike. They are voracious, carnivorous lizards with slender, flicking forked tongues, strong limbs, a long neck and tail and scales which do not overlap. Most are good climbers and all can swim well (some are semi-aquatic). Goannas will often run on their hind-legs though they are faster on all four. Their diet includes carrion, rabbits, lizards and sometimes snakes. One species has been used for the attempted BIOLOGICAL CONTROL of rats in some Pacific islands.

The average total length of the perentie is 1.6m, of which about 90cm is tail. A terrestrial lizard, living in deep crevices and burrows in rocky country from the central coast of WA to western QLD, this species forages in sandy desert and claypans, and will climb trees. It is brown, with large cream or yellow spots which tend to form rows, and the tail is compressed from side to side, almost from the base. The lace monitor, *V. varius*, is one of the commonest arboreal lizards. It can reach a total length of 2m and is found in E Australia, from CAPE YORK to south-eastern SA. It is blue-black in colour with bands of yellow dots, but the patterning is variable. The eggs are laid in burrows in termite nests. Gould's goanna or sand monitor, *V. gouldii*, reaches a total length of 1.6m and is one of the most widespread of the goannas. It is very variable in colouring and pattern, and is found throughout Australia apart from some parts of the SE, but it avoids wet habitats. It is a terrestrial, burrow-dwelling species. In contrast, the mangrove monitor, *V. indicus*, which can grow to a total length of 1m, is confined, in Australia, to the far N of the NT and NE Cape York where it lives in mangroves and rainforest, feeding on insects, fishes, reptiles, birds and mammals, in and near water. It is dark coloured with specks of cream and yellow. Two other aquatic species live in the extreme N: Merten's water monitor, *V. mertensi*, (1m), and Mitchell's water monitor, *V. mitchelli*, (60cm). The smallest monitor is the short-tailed species, *V. brevicauda*, which reaches about 20cm in total length. It is a light-coloured species, with darker flecks, and lives in sandy deserts, in *Spinifex* or ground litter, in northern WA and the central E parts of the NT.

Scincidae With about 190 species of skinks in 20 genera, this is the largest reptilian family in Australia. Most skinks are small—the largest Australian species is the land mullet, *Egernia major* (30cm), which can reach 75cm—and have large, symmetrical scales on the head. They are very varied: some are legless; many are diurnal, whilst others are nocturnal; most species have smooth, overlapping scales but a few which live in rock crevices are spiny so that they are difficult to extract from their retreats; while most skinks have movable eyelids, in some species the eye is covered by a transparent scale; and although most species produce eggs, some give birth to living young and some even have a well developed placenta.

The genus *Anomalopus* contains nine species (none of which is widely distributed) of small to medium-sized, smooth-scaled, burrowing skinks. The limbs are either greatly reduced or completely absent and the ear opening is hidden, apart from a small depression.

The genus *Carlia* contains small, terrestrial skinks with four 'fingers' and five toes. There are 20 species, mainly scattered about the N half of the continent with none in SA and TAS, and only one reaching VIC. The eye is covered by a transparent disc in all but one species, *C. burnettii* (3cm). Most *Carlia* species are diurnal and bask in the sun; some are brightly coloured and are called jewelled skinks.

The genus *Cryptoblepharus* contains only two species in Australia, one of which, the arboreal wall lizard, *C. boutonii* (4cm), is said to be the most widely distributed lizard in the world, being found in a variety of habitats on all continents, except Antarctica, and on many oceanic islands. The appearance of the wall lizard varies with location but it is usually silvery-grey or brown above. The other Australian species, *C. litoralis* (5.5cm), is confined to the E coast of Cape York and to New Guinea.

The genus *Ctenotus*, with about 42 species, is the largest Australian skink genus. They are medium-sized diurnal lizards with long stripes on the back and flanks. The lower eyelid is scaly and movable. Nearly all are terrestrial and many are well adapted to desert conditions. All have small but conspicuous lobes in front of the ear, and long slender limbs with five digits. The copper-tailed skink, *C. taeniolatus* (8cm) is insectivorous; it is striped and has a bright orange or red tail. It ranges from Cape York to northern VIC, in a wide variety of habitats but usually in rocky localities. The members of this genus all lay eggs.

The genus *Egernia* contains 22 species in Australia, all of which produce living young. They are medium-sized to large lizards with well-developed limbs and moderately long but thick and tapering tails; some have rough scales. Most are diurnal but some desert-dwelling species are nocturnal or are active at twilight and dawn. Cunningham's skink, *E. cunninghami* (15cm), which grows to a total length of about 30cm, is a largely vegetarian, gregarious, rock-dwelling species of SE Australia and SA (not TAS). The land mullet reaches a total length of about 66cm, making it Australia's largest skink. Found in south-eastern QLD and north-eastern NSW in rain-forests and wet sclerophyll forests, it is a shiny, very dark lizard with white, yellow or orange underparts. It is very shy and swift, and shelters in hollow logs or burrows and feeds on insects, snails, small mammals and berries.

The genus *Hemiergis* contains eight species

in Australia, all of which are burrowing lizards found mainly in southern Australia. They are small and slender and have short legs. The lower eyelid is movable and has a transparent disc but the ear opening is usually absent.

The genus *Leiolopisma* is confined to S and E Australia, TAS, New Zealand and Lord Howe Is. They are small or medium-sized diurnal lizards, with smooth scales and conspicuous ear openings and long limbs which nearly always meet or overlap when pressed across the abdomen or thorax. The weasel skink, *L. mustelina* (4.5cm), grows to a total length of 13.5cm and is found in SE Australia. It is a relatively short-limbed insectivorous species that is usually found under wood or rocks; it is common in suburban gardens and in the wild it occurs in wet and dry sclerophyll forest and heathlands and is pale fawn to brown in colour with some stripes and white to lemon-yellow underparts. The Lord Howe Is skink, *L. lichenigera* (8cm), which grows to a total length of 16cm, is now uncommon on the main island but occurs on adjacent islands and Balls Pyramid.

The genus *Morethia* contains six small, diurnal, terrestrial species with immovable lower eyelids. The most striking species is the fire-tailed skink, *M. taeniopluera* (3.5cm), which occurs in the dry and arid areas of N Australia.

The genus *Pseudemoia* contains only two species, one a montane lizard, *P. spenceri* (5.5cm), in SE Australia, the other, *P. palfreymani* (5.5cm), confined to Pedra Branca, a small bare islet, 28km SSE of South East Cape, TAS.

The genus *Sphenomorphus*, which contains about 19 species in Australia, is a variable group—several species are water skinks and some are known as sand swimmers from their snake-like movement when they burrow into sand. All species have five digits but in some the limbs are short; the scales are usually smooth but in some they are rough; and the lower eyelids are movable and scaly. The narrow-banded sand swimmer, *S. fasciolatus* (8cm), is a nocturnal lizard which varies greatly in colour and is found in arid and dry sandy or loamy areas, from the coast of northern WA to the coasts of the NT and central QLD. The Alpine water skink, *S. koskiuskoi* (8cm) is confined to the KOSKIUSKO district. The eastern water skink, *S. quoyii* (10cm), is found in coastal QLD and NSW and along the DARLING RIVER system.

The genus *Tiliqua*, possibly the best-known genus in Australia, contains the blue-tongued lizards, so called because several of the species have vivid blue tongues and mouth interiors which they display when molested. They also hiss, and have an unfounded reputation for being venomous. All species are medium-sized or large skinks with relatively short limbs, each with five digits. The lower eyelid is movable. There are four rather bulky species with the common name 'blue-tongued': the eastern, *T. scincoides* (30cm), with a tail length of between 15cm and 23cm and ranging from northern WA through QLD to SA; the wes-

tern, *T. occipitalis* (30cm), with a tail length of 12cm to 16.5cm, found from southern WA to SA, the southern NT, northern VIC and western NSW; the blotched, *T. nigrolutea* (25cm), with a tail length of 10cm to 12.5cm, found in SE Australia and TAS; and the Centralian, *T. multifasciata* (30cm), tail length 12cm to 16.5cm, found in the interior. Blue-tongued lizards produce living young and feed on animal and plant food. The pink-tongued skink, *T. gerrardi* (20cm), has a tail length of between 22cm and 28cm and lives in rainforest in coastal QLD and northern NSW.

The only member of the genus *Trachydosaurus* is the shingle-back, *T. rugosus* (25cm), which has a tail length of 5cm to 6.25cm. It cannot be confused with any other Australian lizard because the scales on the short tail and upper surfaces of the body are greatly enlarged, giving it a fir-cone appearance. It is a slow, diurnal lizard which forages on carrion, various animals and plant material. It is found in most of southern Australia except for the E coasts and mountains, and TAS.

Further reading: Worrell, E. *Reptiles of Australia.* (2nd edn) Angus & Robertson, Sydney, 1970; Cogger, H.G. *Reptiles and Amphibians of Australia.* A.H. & A.W. Reed, Sydney, 1975; Gow, G.F. & Swanson, S. *Snakes and Lizards of Australia.* Angus & Robertson, Sydney, 1977.

Loan Council This body was set up by the Commonwealth and States in 1924 to co-ordinate their borrowing both in Australia and overseas. After an amendment to the Constitution it was made permanent in 1927. At its meetings the Commonwealth has two votes and a casting vote and each State one vote.

Lobethal SA (population 1 522 in 1981) This small service town is situated in the MOUNT LOFTY RANGES, 35km E of Adelaide. It has woollen mills based originally on local sheep grazing properties. It was founded by German Lutheran settlers and given the name Lobethal, which means 'valley of praise'. During World War I, when anti-German feelings ran high, the name was changed to Tweedvale (because of the woollen mills), but was changed back to Lobethal in 1935. The National Trust (SA) has classified two buildings in the town for preservation: Lobethal College (built in 1845) and St John's Lutheran Church (1843-47).

lobsters *see* crustaceans

local government *see* government of Australia

Lockyer, Edmund (1784-1860) Soldier. Born in Devon, he joined the British Army as an ensign in 1803 and served mainly in India and Ceylon before coming to Sydney, with the rank of major, in 1825. In August of that year Governor BRISBANE sent him to explore the Brisbane River, which he ascended in a small boat for about 250km. In the following March he was instructed to found a settlement at KING

GEORGE SOUND, in SW Australia. He landed there on Christmas Day, with a party of 23 soldiers and 20 convicts and returned to Sydney in the following April, leaving the settlement under the command of Captain Wakefield. He resigned his commission later in 1827 and subsequently became an important landowner. He also held a number of public positions, including that of police magistrate at PARRAMATTA. The Sydney suburb of Ermington is named after his house. The settlement which he founded at King George Sound became the town of ALBANY.

Lockyer Valley QLD Lockyer Creek is a tributary of the Brisbane River, rising on the E slopes of the GREAT DIVIDING RANGE near TOOWOOMBA; it flows in a meandering E course and joins the main stream at a point about 25km NW of IPSWICH and 40km inland from Brisbane. The main urban centre in the Lockyer Valley is GATTON, 92km by road W of Brisbane. The valley is a region of rich alluvial soils, with supplies of underground water used to irrigate crops and pastures. The rural lands are intensively utilised for dairying, fodder crop cultivation and vegetable growing for the Brisbane market. In recent times, however, there has been an increasing demand for water for irrigation and to meet this the Atkinson Dam was constructed across the outlet of a natural depression (Atkinson Lagoon) adjacent to the river course; the construction, completed in 1970, has created a lake with a surface area of 567ha and a capacity of 31 330ML.

locusts These are short-horned grasshoppers which belong to the family Acrididae of the order Orthoptera (*see* CRICKETS, etc.). There are about 600 known members of the family in Australia but only four are classed as locusts. Locusts differ from other short-horned grasshoppers in their behaviour and population dynamics. They are the species which form, from time to time, huge migratory swarms which can cause great damage to crops and pastures.

Various kinds of locusts live in many of the warmer parts of the world. A typical locust has two distinct forms, the solitary phase and the gregarious phase. The solitary phase insect is usually greenish or otherwise cryptically coloured, though the wings, when in use, may be brightly coloured; the gregarious phase, on the other hand, is often marked with contrasting colours such as blacks and yellows. The relative dimensions of the body are also different. When the nymphs grow in an uncrowded environment they develop into solitary forms but when the population density is high, so that the nymphs constantly encounter others of their kind, gregarious forms predominate. Eventually the gregarious nymphs begin to come together in groups or bands and start to migrate from the area. Locusts generally have outbreak areas which are peculiar to each species. The environment of inland Australia provides the locust with the right proportion of vegetation and bare land and the right soil type and climate. The species persists in these areas but the swarms move out when food becomes short.

The most important locust in Australia is the Australian plague locust, *Chortoicetes terminifera*, of the SE parts of the continent. Females may be greenish (solitary) or brown, while the males are always dark in colour. There is often a lighter dorsal strip. The species may be distinguished from other short-horned grasshoppers by the dark spots on the tips of the transparent wings, and the scarlet and cream hind femora (thighs). The female is about 3.8cm long, and the male is a little smaller. Egg pods (each containing 30 to 40 eggs) are laid in bare or scalded patches of soil which range from a few square metres in extent to several hundred square metres. There may be as many as 100 egg pods in one tenth of a square metre. When population densities are high the females will use other oviposition (egg-laying) sites such as fallowed paddocks. In northern NSW the eggs begin to hatch in most years in September, and a few weeks later further S and E. The development time is usually 10 to 12 weeks.

During an outbreak locusts destroy between two and four per cent of vulnerable crops within an infested area and in pasture land their ravages may be considered to be roughly equal to increasing the stocking rate by 10 per cent. Severe outbreaks during the past 50 years have occurred in 1933-34, 1946-47, 1953-54, 1973-74 and 1979. The outbreak in 1973-74 was so severe that the Russian newspaper *Pravda* reported (with some exaggeration) that people in Adelaide were being forced to stay indoors by the swarms of insects; the outbreak in 1979 was judged to be probably the worst this century, if not the worst since European occupation.

Success in the control of locusts depends upon the destruction of the swarms, with persistent insecticides, while they are still in the hopper (nymphal) stage, before they can take to the wing. The control of locusts is under the direction of the State Departments of Agriculture. Interstate co-operation is organised through the Australian Plague Locust Commission which was formed in 1975 by the governments of SA, VIC, QLD, NSW and the federal government.

In the tropical parts of Australia there are three species which sometimes form damaging swarms, namely the yellow-winged locust, *Gastrimargus musicus*, the spur-throated locust, *Austracris guttolosa* and the migratory locust, *Locusta migratoria*. It is possible that farming in the more arid parts of southern Australia has increased the severity of locust outbreaks: overgrazing could have produced the bare patches of soil in which the females lay their eggs.

Further reading: The Old Testament. Exdous ch 10, v 12-15; Williams, C.B. *Insect Migration*. Collins, London, 1958; Uvarov, Sir Basil *Locusts and Grasshoppers*. Cambridge University Press, London, 1966; Ricard, M. *The Mystery of Animal Migration*. Paladin, London, 1969; Huges, R.D. *Living Insects*. Collins,

Sydney, 1974; Carlisle, D.B. 'Locusts' in de Beer, Sir Gavin *et al* (eds) *Encyclopaedia of the Animal World*. (vol 12) Bay Books, Sydney, 1977; Baker, G.L. 'Outbreak of the Australian plague locust' in *Agricultural Gazette of New South Wales* (vol 90, no 4, August 1979).

Loddon River VIC Located in the central N of the State, W of the CAMPASPE RIVER, the Loddon is a tributary of the MURRAY RIVER, rising in the mid-section of the GREAT DIVIDING RANGE, N of BALLARAT. It flows for over 380km on a general NW and N course across the N plains, joining first an ANABRANCH, then the Murray at SWAN HILL. The headwaters rise in dissected hilly country where the average annual rainfall is over 800mm but declines progressively downstream. The Loddon has been dammed at several places for irrigation and for livestock and domestic supplies. The largest storage is CAIRN CURRAN DAM, located in the headwater region downstream from Newstead, with a capacity of 148 800ML, a catchment area of 1 593km^2 and a dam embankment 44m high. It provides an assured supply to irrigated properties along the river, and supplements the W sector of the GOULBURN irrigation scheme. Also in the headwater region is Tullaroop Dam; the wall is a 41m-high earth-and-rockfill structure and the dam has a capacity of 74 140ML which serves irrigation developments in N-central VIC and provides the urban supplies for MARYBOROUGH city. Other storages in the Loddon Valley are the Laanecoorie Reservoir (built originally in 1891 and enlarged in 1909, capacity 7 780ML), Kerang Lakes (72 600ML), Lake Boga (36 570ML) and Newlyn-Hepburns (6 240ML). The Pyrenees Highway cuts E-W across the upper valley, the Calder Highway crosses the river at Bridgetown, and the Loddon Valley Highway from BENDIGO follows the lower river to Kerang where it meets the Murray Valley Highway. The Loddon was discovered and named in 1836 by the explorer Thomas MITCHELL after the river of the same name in Berkshire, England.

Logan, Patrick (1791-1830) Soldier and colonial administrator. Born in Scotland, he joined the army as an ensign in 1810, served in the Peninsular War and the American War of 1812, and came to NSW as a captain in the 57th Regiment in 1825. Later that year he was appointed as commandant of the penal settlement of MORETON BAY (which was still known by that name, although it had been moved to the site of Brisbane early in 1825). Arriving there in May 1826, he immediately began a vigorous programme of public works and farming. He also quickly acquired a reputation for strict discipline; the harshness of his rule was evidenced by the large number of convicts who attempted to escape during his years at the settlement. On the other hand, on a number of occasions he interceded on behalf of convicts whom he thought to have been illegally sentenced or to have been unreasonably denied tickets of leave. He took part in a

number of exploration expeditions, including those which discovered LOGAN RIVER and Albert River and reached the headwaters of the RICHMOND RIVER. On a final expedition to the upper reaches of the Brisbane he was killed by Aborigines. Of his buildings, two survive, namely his commissariat store, which forms the lower floor of the State Stores in William Street, Brisbane, and a mill in Wickham Terrace, Brisbane, which was designed to be worked either as a treadmill or a windmill and which later became the State Observatory.
Further reading: Bateson, C. *Patrick Logan: Tyrant of Brisbane.* Ure Smith, Sydney, 1966.

Logan River QLD Located in the SE of the State, the Logan River rises in the McPHERSON RANGE near Mt Lindesay and Mt Barney, and flows for over 1 100km in a general NE then E course to an estuary at the S end of MORETON BAY. Maroon Dam on Burnett Creek, an upper tributary of the Logan, is an earth-and-rockfill structure completed in 1974 with an embankment height of 46m and a capacity of 38 400ML. The dam is a storage reservoir which regulates the river flow and provides irrigation water to an area of some 4000ha of dairylands and farms growing lucerne, maize and vegetables; also, the dam controls river flooding, supplies water for urban centres in the BEAUDESERT Shire and provides a venue for recreation and aquatic sports. The river takes its name from Captain Patrick LOGAN, the commandant of the Moreton Bay penal settlement in the 1820s.

logrunners *see* babblers, etc.

'The Valley' by Sydney Long

Art Gallery of S.A.

Long, Sydney (1871-1955) Artist. Born in GOULBURN in NSW, Long was one of the many talented people who was taught by Julian ASHTON. As a painter, Long is remembered for his works which depicted an Austra-

lian bush populated by fawns and nymphs. He was influenced by such English publications as *Yellow Book* and the *Studio.* At the time of his early work in the 1890s, Long gained publicity for his work *By Tranquil Waters,* which showed male nudes placed in a recognisably Australian landscape. The purchase of the work by the National Gallery of New South Wales in 1894 was criticised by a Member of the State Legislative Assembly who said it was an immoral work that should not have been purchased with public money. In 1910 Long moved to the UK and there lost interest in art nouveau. After his return to Australia in 1925, he established himself as a graphic artist and his landscape etchings were much in demand during the 1930s.

long toms *see* fishes, bony; fishes, freshwater

Longford TAS (population 2 207 in 1981) A small town in the N MIDLANDS, Longford is situated on the South ESK RIVER, some 20km SW of LAUNCESTON. It is the commercial and service centre for a productive agricultural and pastoral region (municipal population 5 830). The area was originally known as Norfolk Plains because of the large number of settlers from NORFOLK ISLAND who were granted land there in 1813. The Longford district, lying in the rain shadow of the GREAT WESTERN TIERS, receives an average annual rainfall of about 635mm, and commonly experiences hot dry spells during the summer months. To overcome the problems created by these climatic conditions, the CRESSY-Longford irrigation scheme was established; it commenced operation in 1971, using water from the tailrace of the POATINA hydro-electricity power station (part of the GREAT LAKE scheme) conveyed by channels to farm properties. The irrigated lands lie W and SW of Longford; the total area of the constituted 'irrigation district' is 9 000ha, of which 4 500ha can be supplied by gravitation and 2 500ha by pumping. Longford has been classified as a historic town since there are many old colonial homes in the area, some erected by convict labour. The National Trust (TAS) has classified over 30 of these for preservation, including several churches, a flour mill, the toll house and many homes. One of the best-known homes is 'Brickendon', located 2km out of the town and built in 1824 by William Archer, whose descendants still occupy it.

Longreach QLD (population 2 917 in 1981) Located in the central W of the State on the Landsborough Highway, 1 203km by road NW of Brisbane and 696km W of ROCKHAMPTON, Longreach is the business and service town for an extensive sheep and cattle grazing region. At an elevation of 191m above sea level, it is situated on the Thomson River which joins the BARCOO RIVER and becomes COOPER'S CREEK. Almost on the Tropic of Capricorn (its latitude is 23°S), it experiences long hot summers and dry winters. The average annual rainfall is 442mm, falling

mainly in the summer months. It is a rail town on a line running W from Rockhampton to WINTON and then linking with HUGHENDEN. Once known as an unkempt and struggling Outback town, in recent decades it has become a modern centre with several fine public buildings, such as the civic centre. But the spirit of the Outback that developed the livestock industries and shaped colourful legends of pioneer characters remains. Perhaps the most famous of these legends concerns the bushranger Harry Redford (Captain Starlight) who in 1870 stole 1000 head of cattle from the area and drove them 2 400km across the arid interior to SA. Though subsequently arrested, he was acquitted in a quite sensational trial. The incident inspired the portrayal of the character of Captain Starlight in Rolf BOLDREWOOD's novel *Robbery Under Arms* (1882-83). It was at Longreach that Qantas Airways had its beginnings and the hangar that was used as the headquarters for the original operations is preserved at the town's airport. The hangar was also the factory where the nation's first aircraft was built.

Longstaff, Sir John (1862-1941) Artist. Born at Clunes VIC, he studied at the Melbourne National Gallery School and at Cormans in Paris. A handsome, urbane, gentle and uncomplicated personality, he attracted commissions, especially for portraits, both in Australia and the UK. Despite his sojourn in Paris, and his contact with avant-garde art, he remained, after a few flirtations with French Impressionism, a conservative painter. His most famous work is *Arrival of Burke, Wills and King at Cooper's Creek, Sunday Evening, 21st April, 1861,* which was commissioned by William Gilbert, a Melbourne surgeon, for the National Gallery of Victoria. After a period as a fashionable society portraitist in London, Longstaff became an official war artist with the Australian Imperial Force (AIF) before re-

'Lady in Grey' by John Longstaff

turning to Australia in 1919. He was knighted in 1928 and died in Melbourne.

Lonsdale, William (1800-64) Administrator of the PORT PHILLIP District (later the colony of VIC). He came to Sydney to 1831 as an army lieutenant and was promoted to captain three years later. In 1836, when Governor BOURKE opened the Port Phillip District to authorised settlement, Lonsdale was appointed as army commandant, police magistrate and Superintendent there. He confirmed the site of the settlement, which had been chosen by BATMAN and others in 1835 and which was later named Melbourne by Bourke, and began to organise the construction of public works. Following the appointment of LA TROBE as Superintendent in 1839, Lonsdale retained the position of police magistrate, and in later years filled various other public offices.

William Lonsdale

looking glass plant *see* weeds

Loranthaceae *see* parasitic plants

Lord Howe Island NSW (population 287 in 1981) Located in the SW Pacific Ocean, 702km NE of Sydney and about 580km E of PORT MACQUARIE, this island is included in the State territory of NSW. It has an area of 1 350ha and is about 11km long and about 3km at its widest point. It is claimed as the world's most southerly coral island and depends almost entirely on tourism for its existence, offering visitors an informal and relaxed vacation with opportunities for water skiing, fishing, skindiving, bushwalking, mountain climbing, cycling and other outdoor sports. Some of the tourist brochures state that it 'presents a picture of breathtaking beauty, with beaches of soft coral sand, gracefully swaying palms and dramatic, cloud-capped twin mountain peaks standing like massive sentinels over a storybook lagoon'. The twin peaks, located in the S of the island, are Mt Lidgbird (763m) and Mt Gower (866m) which rise sheer from the sea; the latter peak may be climbed on a day's walk, but the ascent of the former peak is a feat attempted by few islanders or visitors. The island is linked to Sydney by a regular air ser-

vice. It was discovered by Lieutenant Lidgbird Ball in HMS *Supply* in 1788 on a voyage to NORFOLK ISLAND, and was named after Admiral Howe of the British Navy.

lorikeets *see* parrots, etc.

Lostock Dam NSW Constructed on the Paterson River, a tributary of the HUNTER, with a storage capacity of 19 680ML, this dam is situated 58km NW of MAITLAND. Rainfall throughout the Hunter Valley is variable and periods of drought are not uncommon. One such exceptionally dry period occurred between 1964 and 1967, and this led to an investigation of the possibility of constructing a dam on the Paterson to store water for irrigation, stock and domestic purposes. The Lostock, completed in 1971, was built as the result of these investigations; it has been designed to regulate river flow and conserve water, so that an area of 4 700ha is provided with a reliable water supply, thereby stabilising rural production and giving opportunities for further irrigation development.
See also Glenbawn Dam

lotus bird *see* waders

louse *see* lice

Loveless, George (1797-1874) Leader of the group of transported farm labourers popularly known as the 'Tolpuddle Martyrs'. Born in the village of Tolpuddle in Dorset, he worked as a ploughman and won a reputation throughout the district as a Wesleyan preacher and a leader in efforts by agricultural labourers to persuade farmers to raise wages. Although these efforts did secure a general rate of 10 shillings a week around Dorchester, in Tolpuddle itself farmers refused to pay more than nine shillings, and later reduced this to seven shillings, with suggestions of a further reduction to six shillings. At this point, in 1833, Loveless took the lead in founding a Friendly Society of Agricultural Labourers in the village. Although such trade unions had been legal since the repeal of the Combination Acts in 1825, Loveless and his fellow organisers made the mistake of holding an initiation ceremony at which members took an oath of loyalty. As a result, six of them—Loveless and his brother James, Thomas Stanfield and his son John, James Brine and James Hammett—were charged under an almost forgotten statute of 1797 with administering unlawful oaths, and were sentenced at the Dorchester Assizes to transportation for seven years. The other five reached Sydney in August 1834, but George Loveless who had been delayed by illness was sent to TAS and arrived in Hobart in September. He was employed at first as a shepherd and stock keeper on the Domain farm at Newton and later was assigned to a settler near RICHMOND. Meanwhile, a campaign was being waged by liberals in England to have the six men released and in March 1836 Lord John Russell ordered that pardons be issued. Only Hammett returned to Tolpuddle; the others,

after staying in England for a few years, during which Loveless became an active Chartist, emigrated to Canada. George Loveless died on a farm near London, Ontario.
Further reading: Brooks, H. *Six Heroes in Chains.* Looker, Poole, England, 1929; Marlow, J. *The Tolpuddle Martyrs.* Deutsch, London, 1971.

The Hon D.A. Lowe

Lowe, Douglas Ackley (1942-) Premier of TAS. After leaving school in Hobart, he became apprenticed as an electrician and also became such an active member of the Australian Labor Party (ALP) that at the age of only 23, shortly after gaining his tradesman's certificate, he was appointed full-time secretary of the ALP in TAS. He was elected to the House of Assembly in 1969, the year in which Labor lost office for the first time in 35 years, and became a member of Cabinet when the party regained power three years later. In 1974 he became president of the TAS branch of the ALP and in 1977, when William Arthur Neilson retired to become Agent-General in London, he succeeded him as Premier. In November 1981, following dissension within the TAS branch of the ALP over proposed hydroelectricity development and its environmental impact, Lowe was replaced as leader of the party, and therefore as Premier, by Harold Holgate. He promptly resigned from the ALP, but continued to sit in the House of Assembly as an Independent.

Loxton SA (population 3 100 in 1981) This town on the S bank of the MURRAY RIVER, downstream from RENMARK, is located 248km by road and 279km by rail NE of Adelaide. At an elevation of 66m, it experiences a mild climate, with a low average rainfall of 294mm evenly spread throughout the year. The town is the service centre for a prosperous wine producing, fruit growing, wheat cultivating and sheep grazing area. The vineyards and orchards are within the adjacent Loxton Irrigation Area, supplied with water pumped from the Murray. Over 2 400ha of irrigated farmland was developed as a post-World War II settlement scheme; several problems of soil drainage have been experienced in the area. The town takes its name from a boundary rider (William Charles Loxton) on Bookpurnong station who lived on the river bank at the present town site from 1878 to 1882.

lucerne *see* Papilionaceae

lucerne flea *see* springtails

lung fish *see* Queensland lung fish

luth *see* tortoises, etc.

Lutheran Church In the 1981 census 199 000 Australians (about 1.4 per cent of the population) were defined as Lutherans. Over 62 000 of these were in SA (5.3 per cent of the population of SA) and over 45 000 were in QLD (2.5 per cent of the population of QLD).

The initial development of Lutheranism in Australia began after King Frederick William III of Prussia formed a union between the Lutheran Church and the Reformed (Calvinistic) Church in his dominions. This caused whole congregations to emigrate, a number choosing Australia as their new home, partly because of the help offered by George Fife ANGAS. The first Lutherans reached Adelaide in 1838 under the leadership of Pastor Augustus Kavel. Among later SA groups one under the leadership of Pastor Fritzsche, which arrived in 1841, was particularly important.

St. John's Lutheran Church, Tanunda

The migrants formed their own Church, which had no formal ties with that in Germany. In general, they were in agreement on basic Lutheran beliefs—such as 'justification by faith' and acceptance of various 'confessions' or statements of belief—which dated back to the time of Martin Luther himself, and they all followed the traditional practice of allowing laymen to take a prominent part in Church affairs. Nevertheless, a split between the followers of Pastors Kavel and Fritzsche in 1846 was followed by a series of divisions between

Lutheran congregations throughout Australia, culminating in the formation of two main organisations, the United Evangelical Lutheran Church of Australia and the Evangelical Lutheran Church in Australia. In 1966, however, these merged as the Lutheran Church of Australia. This has a General Synod, but congregations in the various States function autonomously and have their own district Synods.

Missionary work has featured prominently in Lutheran activities. There are several Lutheran missions among the Aborigines, that at HERMANNSBURG in the NT being perhaps the best known. In conjunction with overseas Lutheran bodies, the Lutheran Church of Australia has also been particularly active in New Guinea, Lutherans forming the largest Protestant denomination in the nation of Papua New Guinea.

Further reading: van Sommers, T. 'The Lutherans' in *Religions in Australia*. Rigby, Adelaide, 1966.

Lycopodiaceae *see* Microphyllyta

Lyne, Sir William John (1844-1913) Premier of NSW. Born in TAS, he moved to NSW in 1875 after acquiring land in the ALBURY district. He became Member for Hume in the NSW Legislative Assembly five years later, and was Premier from September 1899 until March 1901. Although Lyne had been a consistent opponent of the federation movement, he was offered the position of Australia's first Prime Minister by the first Governor-General of the Commonwealth, the Earl of Hopetoun, who felt such an offer befitted the Premier of the oldest and most populous of the Australian colonies. However, when invited to form a government he gained so little support that he had no option but to suggest to the Governor-General that Edmund BARTON be sent for instead. Elected to represent Hume in the first federal Parliament, he became Minister for Home Affairs in Barton's Cabinet, and was later Minister for Trade and Customs and then Treasurer under Alfred DEAKIN.

Further reading: la Nauze, J.A. *The Hopetoun Blunder*. Melbourne University Press, Melbourne, 1957.

Lyons, Joseph Aloysius (1879-1939) Premier of TAS and Prime Minister of Australia. Born at Circular Head TAS, he began work as a teacher at the age of 16, and soon became active in the Teachers' Federation and the Labor Party. Elected to the TAS House of Assembly in 1909, he was Premier from 1923 to 1928, but in 1929 left State politics and won a seat in the federal House of Representatives. His prestige and experience immediately won him a position in SCULLIN's Cabinet, but the events of 1930-31 brought him to a crisis of loyalty that ended in his leaving the Labor Party.

In June 1930 the Treasurer, Edward THEODORE, resigned, pending the outcome of legal action regarding an allegation of corruption. Lyons accepted the position of acting Trea-

Joseph Aloysius Lyons

surer, but he made no claim to financial expertise and in January 1931 Scullin felt compelled to reinstate Theodore. Lyons objected to this move, since Theodore's name had not yet been cleared; moreover, he could not agree with the inflationary policy which Theodore wished to use in an effort to deal with the Depression. In February he and another prominent member of the Cabinet, J.E. Fenton, joined the ranks of the Opposition, and in May they and several other Labor dissidents merged with the Liberals to found the United Australia Party (UAP). At the elections in December 1931 the new party, with Lyons as leader, won a convincing victory and he became Prime Minister.

He retained office until his death in April 1939—at the head of a UAP Ministry until November 1934, and thereafter with a UAP/Country Party coalition Ministry. Although conscientious, he was not a man of great intellectual or political talent; in the first few years of his prime ministership he tended to lean heavily on the advice of J.G. Latham, his Minister for External Affairs, and in later years he was somewhat overshadowed by his Attorney-General and eventual successor, Robert MENZIES. His wife, Dame Enid Lyons, was a Member of the House of Representatives from 1943 to 1951, being the first woman to be elected to that chamber. As Vice-President of the Executive Council from 1949 to 1951 she also became the first woman to attain Cabinet rank.

Further reading: Lyons, Dame Enid *So We Take Comfort*. Heinemann, London, 1965.

lyrebirds Found only in Australia, these BIRDS belong to the family Menuridae* and are the largest of the PASSERINE BIRDS. They differ from all other birds, except the SCRUB-BIRDS, in the primitive structure of the syrinx (sound box) and in the separate clavicles (collar bones) which are fused together in all other birds to form the furcula (wish bone). Lyrebirds are confined to dense woodland, usually in mountainous country, and feed on insects, worms and grubs scraped from leaf-mould and leaf-litter. Although they sometimes roost in trees, they rarely fly and are susceptible to introduced predators such as foxes and feral

*Species, genus or family is endemic to Australia (see Preface)

A painting of lyrebirds from John Gould

National Library of Australia

cats. They nest on the ground, on rock ledges or tree stumps or in thick vine canopies; the nests are platform-shaped, composed of sticks and moss with an untidy dome of grass and fibre.

The superb lyrebird, *Menura* * *superba* (body 80cm to 95cm long; tail 45cm to 60cm long), the more studied species, occurs from VIC to southern QLD. The male has a lyre-shaped tail which is spread over its head during its courtship display. The less ornamental tail of the female lacks the filamentous central feathers. Both sexes have long legs, strong claws and dark greyish-brown plumage. The males maintain large territories (1.6ha to 3.7ha in Sherbrooke Forest VIC); the females occupy smaller territories within those of the males but their feeding areas are richer. Each territory contains several nesting sites which are defended by the hens against other females. Within their territories, the males sing at various stations (their songs include a large proportion of mimicry of a variety of other birds, including kookaburras; *see* KING-FISHERS). There are also several mounds in each territory, usually built on ridges and used by the male for his courtship displays; apparently, the male mates with several females. Mating takes place in winter when other birds which the lyrebird mimics are not breeding, and the care of the young is entirely the hen's task. The Albert lyrebird, *M.* * *alberti* (80cm to 95cm; 45cm to 60cm), lives in south-eastern QLD, mainly to the N of the range of the superb lyrebird. Its plumage is reddish-brown, and the lyre-shaped tail feathers of the male are shorter than those of the superb lyrebird. The territorial and breeding habits are apparently similar to those of the superb lyrebird, but the male Albert lyrebird usually displays on fallen logs and not on specially prepared mounds.

M

Maatsuyker Islands TAS This group of small rocky islands, located some 20km off the S coast of the State, was discovered and named by the Dutch explorer Abel TASMAN in 1642. The largest island of the group is De Witt Is; others are Mewstone Is (the farthest S of the group) and Maatsuyker Is on which is located the southernmost Australian lighthouse. The islands are a nesting place for many sea birds.

macadamia nut This is the only cultivated food plant that Australia has provided from its flora. It is also known as the Queensland nut, the bauple nut (from Mt Bauple QLD) or the bopple nut. The genus *Macadamia* (family PROTEACEAE) contains at least four species in E Australia but only two, *M. integrifolia* and *M. tetraphylla*, are cultivated, with the first-mentioned the more important. Two other species produce nuts that contain poisonous cyanide-producing glycosides. However, they were eaten by Aborigines, after suitable treatment. The leaves are produced in whorls of three or four, depending upon the species, and the flowers are in racemes. The nuts or fruit are surrounded by a leathery wall which splits at maturity but the shell of the nut is extremely hard and cannot be cracked with ordinary nutcrackers. They can be eaten raw, baked or fried and are claimed by enthusiasts to be the best-tasting of all nuts. Macadamia nuts have been grown for many years in Hawaii where much work has been done on selective breeding, but they have been grown commercially only recently in Australia and the area devoted to them is still small.

Macalister River VIC Located in GIPPS-LAND, the headwaters of this river lie on the S slopes of the GREAT DIVIDING RANGE, SE of Mt Buller. The river flows for over 200km S then SE beyond SALE to join the THOMSON RIVER, which then joins the LATROBE RIVER and empties into LAKE WELLINGTON. The GLENMAGGIE DAM on the Macalister, with a capacity of 190 300ML, is the main storage for an irrigation system which provides water to farms in the vicinity of MAFFRA, Sale, Heyfield and Stratford. The Cowwarr Weir on Rainbow Creek, constructed in 1957, controls river flow and diverts water for irrigation and domestic and stock supplies in the Macalister scheme. The Macalister was named in 1840 after a member of the party which explored the region and discovered the river.

Macarthur, John (1767-1834) Military officer, pastoralist and entrepreneur. Commonly regarded as the founder of the Australian wool industry, he was born in Devonshire and was an ensign in the British Army until 1789 when he made a jump in rank to lieutenant by joining the NEW SOUTH WALES CORPS immediately on its formation. He reached Sydney with the second fleet in June 1790, and a year later was sent to PARRAMATTA. There in 1793 Major Francis GROSE, who was acting as Governor, made him a grant of 100 acres (about 40ha), on which he built Elizabeth Farm House, named after his wife. In the following year he received another grant of the same size, in recognition of the speed with which he had begun clearing the first. He was the most active officer in the Corps in farming, pastoral and trading activities.

As Governors Hunter, KING and BLIGH tried in turn to cut down the privileges of the officers, and especially to curb their trading activities, they found Macarthur their most formidable opponent. Domineering, arrogant and consumed by ambition, he was also remarkably vindictive, and devoted himself single-mindedly to bringing about the downfall of anyone who opposed him. As related in the entry on Bligh, it was the latter's act of arresting Macarthur that led to the Governor's deposition in the RUM REBELLION. By that time, however, Macarthur had ceased to be an officer of the Corps. In 1801 he fought a duel with William PATERSON, his commanding officer, and wounded him seriously. As a result, King sent him to England for court martial, but he managed to turn this apparent misfortune to advantage. Almost from the beginning of his farming activities at Parramatta, he had been experimenting with the breeding of sheep for fine wool, and from 1797, when he had obtained some Merinos, he had concentrated on that breed. By the time King sent him to England he was producing fleeces of about 2.5kg, which was very creditable by the standards of the day, and he was

John Macarthur

determined to enter the English market in a large way. He took specimens of wool with him, and made such an impression on influential people in England that he was allowed to resign his commission and returned to Sydney with a letter from the Colonial Secretary, Lord Camden, instructing King to grant him 10 000 acres (about 4000ha). He selected this land in the district known as the COWPASTURES and named it Camden Park. There today, near the town of CAMDEN, can be seen descendants of the sheep with which he helped to make wool Australia's first great export commodity.

In March 1809 Macarthur accompanied Major JOHNSTON to England, so that they could attempt to justify their parts in the rebellion against Bligh. He was not punished, apart from being informed that MACQUARIE, the new Governor, had been instructed to bring him to trial if he were found in the colony. In effect, he was exiled from NSW, and it was only in 1817 that he was informed that it would be safe for him to return there. In the meantime, his wife had managed his flocks while he made an intensive study of the London wool market. After returning from exile he played little part in public affairs, but served on the Legislative Council briefly in 1825 and from 1829 to 1832, and was regarded as the leader of the 'exclusive' faction. Perhaps his most important achievement in this part of his life was his success in helping to persuade John BIGGE that the economic future of the colony lay in the hands of men of capital, producing wool on very large properties and depending largely on convict labour.
Further reading: Ellis, M.H. *John Macarthur.* Angus & Robertson, Cremorne NSW, 1973.

McArthur River

McArthur River NT Located in the BARKLY TABLELAND region, with its headwaters in the dissected uplands of the plateau, the river flows in a general NE direction for about 250km across the scarp of the tableland to the swampy, crocodile-infested coastal plains and into the GULF OF CARPENTARIA. The upper tributaries of the McArthur system (Kilgour and Glyde Rivers, Spellesie and Lancewood Creeks) usually flow only during the wet season. The river basin is used for cattle grazing; three large properties covering most of the upper and middle basin are Balbirini (4 501km^2), McArthur River station (4 245km^2) and Spring Creek station (4 082km^2). In the 1870s, when the OVERLAND TELEGRAPH was being built, supplies were brought by ship to BORROLOOLA on the McArthur, some 80km from the gulf coast, and then taken overland to the construction sites.

Macartney, Charles George (1886-1958) Cricketer. Born in MAITLAND in NSW and developing initially as a slow left-arm bowler, the diminutive Macartney was to become one of the leading batsmen (right-handed) of his day, reaching his peak in the 1920s. He made his Test début at Sydney in 1907 as a bowler and subsequently toured England in 1909, on one occasion at Leeds taking 11 wickets for 85 runs. Following

World War I he concentrated on batting and in the 1921 and 1926 tours of England he delighted spectators with his adventurous and daring hard-hitting, unexpected in a man of such small stature. In 1921, in a match against Nottingham, he made the highest individual score ever made in one day's cricket, scoring 345 runs, including 47 fours and four sixes, in a little under four hours. When playing for Australia at Leeds in 1926, he became the second batsman ever to score a century before lunch (TRUMPER had been the first). His batting record in first-class cricket matches was 14 217 runs for an average of 47, and before his retirement from cricket in 1935 he had amassed 48 separate centuries. He was known affectionately as the 'Governor-General'.

McAuley, James Phillip (1917-76) Poet and literary critic. Born and educated in Sydney, he was a school teacher for a short period, joined the Army Directorate of Research in 1943, was a co-author of the ERN MALLEY HOAX in the following year and in 1946 established his reputation as a lyric poet with the publication of the anthology *Under Aldebaran* (1946). From 1946 to 1960 he lectured at the Australian School of Pacific Administration in Sydney and in 1961 went to the University of Tasmania as Professor of English. Noted for his traditionalist views in social and political matters as well as in literature, he was founding editor of the journal *Quadrant*. He is accepted as one of Australia's greatest lyric poets and also showed himself capable of more sustained work in the epic *Captain Quiros* (1964). His poetry is notable for the classical order and discipline of its verse forms, its logical construction and careful craftsmanship, its simplicity of style and the sensitive use of verbal music. His published works include the verse collections *Collected Poems, 1936-70* (1971) and *Music Late at Night: Poems 1970-3* (1976), and the works of criticism *The End of Modernity* (1959), *Personal Elements in Australian Poetry* (1970), *Romanticism and Utopianism* (1972), *Christopher Brennan* (1973) and *A Map of Australian Verse: The Twentieth Century* (1975). He was appointed a member of the Order of Australia in 1975.
Further reading: Smith, V.B. *James McAuley.* Lansdowne, Melbourne, 1965.

McCabe, Stanley Joseph (1910-68) Cricketer. He was born at GRENFELL in NSW, and early in his cricketing career it was thought that his greatest talent lay in medium-pace bowling; contrary to expectations, however, he developed into one of Australia's most prolific Test batsmen of all time. He first represented Australia in Test match cricket in 1930 during a Test against England, and during the following decade compiled some of the fastest scores ever recorded in cricketing history. In 1932 in a match against England he scored 187, 100 of which was made up of boundaries. In 1935 in Johannesburg, his score of 189 not out included a century in 91

minutes. In 1938 in a Test in England, he compiled the fastest double century ever recorded in Test cricket—scoring 232 runs in 230 minutes while eight partners could add only 58 runs. He represented Australia in 39 Tests, scoring an aggregate of 2 748 runs, averaging 48.21. His aggregate in first-class matches totalled 11 951, including 29 centuries, for an average of 49.38. Not content with being a powerful and stylish batsman, McCabe was also an excellent fieldsman and a useful bowler. On retiring from cricket in 1941, he operated a sports store in Sydney and later became a member of the Sydney Cricket Ground Trust. He fell to his death from a cliff in Mosman NSW.

McCall, J.P. *see* Dawson, Peter

McCrae, Hugh Raymond (1876-1958) Poet. Born and educated in Melbourne, he spent most of his life either in Sydney or in nearby CAMDEN, working as a magazine editor, a drama critic, an actor and a free-lance writer. His verse is marked by consistently high craftsmanship, vivid depiction of scenes, and an effective use of rhythm, verbal music and imagery; and although its scope of interest is rather narrow, it gained him recognition as one of the leading Australian lyric poets of his day. His published works include *Satyrs and Sunlight* (1909), *Colombine* (1920), *Idyllia* (1922), *Satyrs and Sunlight* (1928, an extension of the 1909 work), *Poems* (1939), *Forests of Pan* (1944), *Voice of the Forest* (1945) and *The Ship of Heaven* (1951).

A self-portrait in oils by Fred McCubbin

McCubbin, Frederick (1855-1917) Artist. Born in Melbourne, the son of a baker, McCubbin studied at the Melbourne National Gallery School and the Artisans' School of Design, Carlton. He drew much inspiration from the landscape surrounding Melbourne and is one of the most distinguished regional painters. He attended the painting camps which Tom ROBERTS had established, and associated with other painters from the HEIDELBERG SCHOOL, such as Charles CONDER and Arthur STREETON. A competent figure painter, McCubbin's Australian bush scenes portrayed tragic incidents and hard-working, stoical pioneers, infused with a romantic melancholy that appealed to the growing sense of national identity; his grey depictions of the Australian bush are in complete contrast to the bright colours and sunny atmosphere of Arthur Streeton's work. As depictions of social history, McCubbin's paintings were a deliberate attempt to create for Australia a tradition of historical subjects, an important element in European painting. Thus in 1889 he painted *Down on His Luck* (in the Art Gallery of Western Australia), in 1896 *The Wallaby Track* (in the Art Gallery of New South Wales) and in 1905 *The Pioneers*, a large three-panelled work (in the National Gallery of Victoria). He died in South Yarra, Melbourne.

McCulloch, Sir James (1819-93) Premier of VIC.

Born in Glasgow, he emigrated to VIC in 1853 and became prominent in Melbourne business circles and as a supporter of many local charities and public causes. After being nominated to the Legislative Council in 1854, he was elected to the first Legislative Assembly under responsible government two years later. As Premier from 1863 to 1868, he led VIC's first stable administration, and also became involved in that colony's most bitter constitutional conflict when, in 1865, he tried to force a tariff Bill through the Legislative Council by 'tacking' it to a normal Appropriation Bill. However, the Council rejected the joint Bill, and the government was able to survive only by borrowing from the London Chartered Bank, of which McCulloch was sole local director. Following the 1866 elections, in which he won an increased majority, the Council gave way and passed the tariff as a separate Bill. In the meantime, Governor Sir Charles DARLING had been dismissed for displaying partisanship in the matter, and the crisis was prolonged by attempts on the part of McCulloch's supporters to compensate the ex-Governor by voting £20 000 to his wife. It was only in 1868, when Darling was reappointed to the colonial service and given a pension, that these attempts were finally abandoned. McCulloch formed three more Ministries—in 1868-69, 1870-71 and 1875-77—and served as Agent-General for VIC in London from 1872 to 1874. He retired from politics in 1878, and thereafter devoted himself to various business interests, including the development of the export trade in frozen meat.

McCullough, Colleen (1937-)

Popular novelist. She was born in WELLINGTON, NSW, but grew up in Sydney. Besides working briefly as a journalist, librarian and teacher, she trained as a neurophysiologist at Royal Prince Alfred Hospital in the Sydney suburb of Camperdown, and later worked in that profession in the UK and the USA. In 1974, when she held the position of Research Associate in the Department of Neurology at the Yale School of Internal Medicine in New Haven, Connecticut, she published the novel *Tim*, which attracted little attention. However, her next work was *The Thorn Birds*, which deals with the fortunes of a family named Cleary, first in New Zealand, and then on a grazing property, Drogheda, in inland NSW. Even before it appeared in print it was assured

of massive sales, since the paperback rights had already been sold for a record sum. She has since published another highly successful novel, *An Indecent Obsession* (1981).

John Fairfax & Sons Ltd

Colleen McCullough

MacDonnell Ranges

NT Located in the S part of the Territory, extending in a general E-W alignment for some 200km on both sides of the Stuart Highway, these ranges consist of a series of parallel ridges reaching their highest elevation at Mt Zeil (1 510m) near the W end. The ranges form the upper catchment basins of the FINKE and TODD Rivers, and their headwater streams, flowing generally S, have cut across the ridges in numerous spectacular gaps: the best known of these are Simpson's Gap (11km W of ALICE SPRINGS) and STANDLEY CHASM (48km W), but there are many others such as Redbank, Ormiston, Serpentine and Ellery Gorges (on the upper tributaries of the Finke); to the E of Alice Springs are Emily and Jessie Gaps and Trephina and N'Dhala Gorges (on the Todd tributaries). Alice Springs is situated near Heavitree Gap, formed by the upper Todd; the Stuart Highway and the central Australian railway approach Alice Springs from the S through this gap. The ranges lie in the arid centre of the continent where rainfall is low and unreliable; the ridges rise stark and barren above the surrounding plain country, yet the gorges contain surprisingly dense vegetational growth because moisture is concentrated there; the most famous in this regard is PALM VALLEY on a tributary of the Finke, 143km by road SW of Alice Springs and 15km beyond HERMANNSBURG. The MacDonnell Ranges were discovered in 1860 by the explorer John McDouall STUART, who recorded in his diary that he gave them the name 'MacDonnell after his excellency the governor-in-chief of South Australia as a token of his kindness to me'.

McEwen, Sir John (1900-80)

Country Party politician, deputy Prime Minister and Prime Minister. Born at Chiltern VIC, he

served on the staff of the Commonwealth Crown Solicitor from 1916 to 1918. He then joined the Australian Imperial Force (AIF), but because of the ending of hostilities his enlistment was not confirmed, and he became a farmer. Elected to the House of Representatives in 1934, he occupied a number of Cabinet positions after 1937, became deputy leader of the Country Party (now NATIONAL PARTY OF AUSTRALIA) from 1943 to 1958, and leader of that party and deputy Prime Minister from 1958 until his retirement from Parliament in 1971. After the death of Prime Minister HOLT in December 1967 McEwen was caretaker Prime Minister for three weeks.

A man of great energy and determination, he came to wield an influence far in excess of what one would have expected from the strength of his party following. After Holt's death he showed the strength of his position by stating openly that he would not be willing to serve under Holt's heir-apparent in the Liberal Party, McMAHON; this meant that it would have been pointless for the Liberals to elect McMahon as their leader, and so John GORTON gained the position and became Prime Minister.

The period of McEwen's leadership was a time of difficulty for the Country Party, for the growth of the cities and of manufacturing was not matched by expansion in the primary sector of the economy, and so the traditional base of the party's support was being made comparatively weaker. McEwen understood this, and used his high personal standing to persuade his fellow members to support policies which would have wider national appeal. His critics would claim that in doing so he tended to encourage the protection of the manufacturing industries to an unhealthy degree.

McGregor, Ken (1929-)

Tennis player. Born in Adelaide, he was a first-class athlete who excelled at Australian Rules football; he turned his prowess to tennis after his father persuaded him that there was a bigger future in this sport than in football. He came into prominence in 1950 when he and Frank SEDGMAN won Australia's first post-war Davis Cup competition. With Sedgman he formed a formidable doubles combination, winning the Australian, French and Wimbledon doubles championships in 1951 and 1952. In 1952 he defeated his doubles partner to win his only Australian singles championship, and then turned professional. A dedicated and talented sportsman, on retirement from tennis he returned to Australian Rules where his considerable ability earned him State selection. Today he maintains his sporting interests as proprietor of a sports store and squash courts.

McIlwraith, Sir Thomas (1835-1900)

Premier of QLD. Born in Ayr, Scotland, he migrated to VIC in 1854, and after a short period as a miner became a railway surveyor and engineer. In the 1860s he acquired a number of pastoral properties in QLD, and later undertook banking and commercial ventures there. In 1870 he was elected to the QLD Legislative Assembly and from the late 1870s to the early 1890s he and his Liberal opponent, Sir Samuel GRIFFITH, dominated the QLD political scene. He was Premier from 1879 to 1883 and for several months in 1888 and 1893. His best-remembered act during his three terms as Premier was his attempt in 1883 to forestall German penetration of New Guinea by declaring the annexation of the SE part of the island, Papua, in the name of the Queen. This action was repudiated by the British government, but was influential both in leading to the declaration of a British protectorate in the following year and in aiding the cause of federation in Australia.

As a conservative and a defender of the use of Kanaka labour, McIlwraith drew his strongest support from the N and the coastal sugar towns. He represented QLD at the federal convention of 1891, but was not in favour of a strong federal government, and at the time of the final referendum in 1899 spoke against the Constitution Bill.
Further reading: Bernays, C.A. *Queensland Politics During Sixty Years, 1859-1919.* Govt Printer, Brisbane, 1919.

Macintyre River

Macintyre River NSW This tributary of the BARWON-DARLING system flows from the main watershed of the GREAT DIVIDING RANGE across the N slopes and plains region of the State. The numerous streams forming the headwaters rise on the granite W slopes of the N part of the NEW ENGLAND Plateau around GLEN INNES; this is an area of hilly country at an elevation of about 1000m above sea level where the average annual rainfall exceeds 800mm. On the Severn River, one of the main headwater tributaries, is Pindari Dam, which has a storage capacity of 37 500ML and is located 22km upstream from Ashford. It was completed in 1969 and provides irrigation water, as well as stock and domestic supplies, for farmlands and towns downstream in the Severn and Macintyre Valleys. From the headwater zone, the river flows in a general NW direction, is joined by the DUMARESQ RIVER and for 240km it forms the State border between NSW and QLD, where it is a slow and meandering stream crossing a wide stretch of open plain country and flowing in a general W direction. It receives the Weir River as a right-bank tributary, at which point it changes its name to the Barwon.

Mackay

Mackay QLD (population 35 361 in 1981) This city on the central E coast of the State is sometimes referred to as the 'sugar capital' of Australia. Located at the junction of the Bruce and Peak Downs Highways, 1 074km by road NNW of Brisbane, 360km from ROCKHAMPTON and 400km SE of TOWNSVILLE, it is on the estuary of the PIONEER RIVER about 5km upstream from its mouth, in a region of cane farms, beef cattle grazing properties, tropical fruit plantations and dairy farms. Lying N of the Tropic of Capricorn, at the latitude of 21°S, it experiences warm to hot conditions throughout the year; the average annual rain-

fall is 1 672mm, concentrated in the summer season; 70 per cent of the yearly total falls from December to March. The sugar harvesting and crushing season runs from mid-June to the end of December when the seven mills in the district process a third of the total Australian crop. The raw sugar is transported to a bulk terminal at Mackay Harbour, located 5km N of the river mouth; this artificial harbour, developed originally in 1939, also has facilities for handling bulk petroleum, molasses, fertilisers and frozen meat. At Hay Point, further S, a large bulk-export installation handles coal brought from the inland mines at PEAK DOWNS, GOONYELLA and Saraji fields. A small boat harbour within Mackay Harbour provides moorings for visiting craft and for the cruise boats which operate regular services to islands of the GREAT BARRIER REEF, such as the islands in the WHITSUNDAY PASSAGE. Along the coastline both N and S of Mackay are several beach resorts, such as Black's, Eimeo and Illawaong Beaches. The Eungella National Park, covering 49 610ha of rainforest and eucalypt woodland, is located 83km W of the city along the Pioneer Valley. Three mountain parks lie NW of Mackay: Mt Jukes National Park (85km NW, 229ha), Mt Blackwood (31km, 1 060ha) and Mt Mandurana (11km, 112ha). The Cape Hillsborough and Wedge Is Park, 728ha of rainforest, woodland and mangrove coastal lands, is 45km N of the city, and the islands of the Newry Group, of which Rabbit Is is the largest (348ha), comprise a national park located off the coast NW of Mackay.

McKay, Heather Pamela

McKay, Heather Pamela *née* Blundell (1941-) Squash player. Born at QUEANBEYAN in NSW, she was originally a hockey player who took up squash to maintain fitness. She rose to international status in both hockey and squash and dominated world squash for almost two decades. Her impressive list of victories includes the Australian Amateur championship 14 successive times (1960-73)—she became ineligible for this championship when she turned professional in 1974—the British Squash title, which was recognised as the world championship until 1976, 16 successive times (1962-77), and the inaugural women's world championship in 1976. From 1962 to 1979 she won every competition she entered—no other sportsman or woman, in any sport, has maintained a longer winning record. In 1967 and again in 1971 she also represented NSW and Australia in women's hockey. Her amazing ability on the squash court has been attributed to her desire for perfection, her natural co-ordination, constant practice and exercise and her extraordinary will to win. She has received two Sportsman of the Year awards, one in 1968 awarded by the Sportsmen's Association of Australia, and the other, also in 1968, awarded by the Australian Broadcasting Commission. In 1969 she was made an MBE for her services to sport, and in 1979 she was appointed an AO.

McKay, Hugh Victor

McKay, Hugh Victor (1865-1926) Inventor. The son of a farmer, he was born in Raywood VIC and had little formal education. As a youth he drove a RIDLEY-type stripper on his father's property, and conceived the idea of a harvesting machine that would perform all the operations of stripping, threshing and cleaning the grain. He and one of his brothers finished building such a machine in 1884 and he patented it in the following year. However, he had great difficulty in financing its commercial manufacture; it was not until 1891 that he opened McKay's Harvesting Machine Co. Ltd at BALLARAT, but from that point success came rapidly. In 1906 he moved to Braybrook (later called Sunshine), a little to the W of the Melbourne metropolitan area, and by the time he died his agricultural machinery factory there was the largest in the S hemisphere. Today it is owned by Massey-Ferguson Australia Ltd.

Indirectly, McKay played an important part in the early development of the Commonwealth system of industrial conciliation and arbitration. In 1906 legislation was passed under which the manufacturers of various products covered by tariff protection were required to obtain a declaration from the Commonwealth Arbitration Court that the wages paid to their employees were 'fair and reasonable'. If they failed to do so their products were to be subjected to excise duty, and so they would, in effect, lose the benefit of tariff protection. This 'new protection' legislation was finally declared invalid by the High Court, but in the meantime H.V. McKay & Co. had applied to the Arbitration Court, and Mr Justice HIGGINS, in hearing the case, had established the principles of the basic wage and of 'margins' for skill.
See also arbitration and conciliation, industrial
Further reading: Palmer, V. 'The industrialist: H.V. McKay' in *National Portraits.* Melbourne University Press, Melbourne, 1968.

One of H.V. McKay's first harvesting machines, 1885

McKell, Sir William John

McKell, Sir William John (1891-) Premier of NSW and Governor-General of Australia. Born at Pambula in southern NSW, he was taken by his family to Sydney at the age of seven. He left school at the age of 13 to become apprenticed to a boilermaker, and soon became active in the Boilermakers' Union and in the Labor Party; in 1917 he was elected to the Legislative Assembly as Member for Redfern. At this time the Labor Party had no

trained legal men among its parliamentarians in NSW, but McKell remedied this lack by studying for matriculation at night and later becoming qualified as a barrister. He held portfolios in a number of Labor Ministries between 1920 and 1932, including that of Minister for Justice (1925-27, 1931-32). In 1939 he became leader of the ALP and of the Opposition, led his party to victory in the elections of 1941, and held the positions of Premier and Treasurer from then until 1947, when he was appointed Governor-General. This was the first time that a person had gone straight to the latter position from an active role in party politics, and there was considerable criticism of the appointment. However, McKell filled the position with dignity and impartiality until his retirement in 1953. He was made a GCMG in 1951 and in 1956-57 was a member of the Malayan Constitutional Committee.
Further reading: Kelly, V. *A Man of the People.* Alpha Books, Sydney, 1970.

Mackellar, Dorothea (1885-1968) Poet.
Born and educated in Sydney, she travelled widely, published several volumes of verse, wrote one novel and was co-author of two others. However, she is remembered today almost entirely for her descriptive poem 'My Country', which was written after she had witnessed the breaking of a drought while staying on a property near MAITLAND. It was published in the London *Spectator* in 1908 and soon became Australia's best-known lyric.

Mackenzie, Stuart Alexander
(1937-) Sculler. Born in Sydney, Mackenzie first gave notice of his rowing ability when he won the silver medal in the single sculls at the 1956 Olympic Games. In the following years he was to rise to international status, renowned as much for his superior sculling skills as he was for his conduct during and after races. In 1957 he won the New Zealand, Belgian, English and European championships, as well as his first Diamond Sculls, the coveted event held annually at the Henley Royal Regatta. Rowing had always been considered a gentleman's sport, and oarsmen were expected to act as gentlemen both in dress and behaviour as well as sportsmanship. Mackenzie frequently angered rowing spectators when, in most of his races, he managed to break one or more of the unwritten laws of conduct and behaviour. On one occasion he won while wearing a sweat suit and a bowler hat; on another he stopped during a race to admire the scenery and still won; and on another he humiliated his opponents by winning the race and then rowing back up the course to row to the finish again alongside the boat which came second. Dedicated, self-reliant and single-minded, he went on to win the Diamond Sculls for a record six consecutive years, 1957-62; despite his behaviour, there is no doubt he was the dominant singles sculler of his time.

Mackenzie River QLD This major tributary of the FITZROY RIVER is formed by the confluence of the Nogoa and Comet Rivers, inland from ROCKHAMPTON. It flows first in a general NE direction, cuts across Expedition Range, is joined by the Isaac-Connors river system from the N, then flows generally SE to a point about 110km SW of Rockhampton where it joins the DAWSON RIVER and so forms the Fitzroy. There are two weirs on the Mackenzie which provide water supplies to coal-mining centres in the region and to some rural properties. From the Bedford Weir, NE of EMERALD and completed in 1968, water is pumped to the town of BLACKWATER and to the coal mines S of the town; from the Bingegang Weir, further downstream and NE of Bedford Weir, water is pumped through a pipeline 113km long to its Saraji coalfield. These pipelines have been designed so that supplies of stock water are made available to landholders along the route.

mackerels *see* fisheries; fishes, bony; fishes, poisonous and venomous

Mackerras, Sir Alan Charles
(1925-) Conductor. He was born in the US and his parents returned to Australia in 1927. After attending the New South Wales Conservatorium of Music he later went to study at the Prague Academy of Music. He was principal oboist with the Sydney Symphony Orchestra (1944-46), conducted at Sadler's Wells Opera (1948-54), was conductor of the BBC Concert Orchestra (1954-56) and was a free-lance conductor throughout Europe, America and Australia (1956-66). In 1966 he was appointed First Conductor of the Hamburg State Opera, a position he retained until 1969. In the following year he was appointed Musical Director of the English National Opera, a position he relinquished recently in order to fulfil his many operatic and symphonic engagements throughout the world.

In addition to lecturing and writing articles on topics such as orchestration and 18th-century performance practice, Sir Charles has arranged music very successfully for ballets, most notably *Pineapple Poll* and *The Lady and the Fool.* However, he is probably best known today for his deeply sympathetic interpretations of Czechoslovakian music, especially the operas of Janaček. He has made many recordings, which span a wide field in operas, symphonies and oratorios. Sir Charles has made several conducting visits to Australia—for the opening of the SYDNEY OPERA HOUSE in 1973, for an ABC engagement in 1978 and for the Australian Opera in 1979 when he conducted performances of a return season of Janaček's *Jenufa.* He was made a CBE in 1974 and a Knight Bachelor in 1979.

Macksville NSW (population 2 352 in
1981) This small country town is situated on the Nambucca River, 13km inland from the coastline and some 12km by road SW of NAMBUCCA HEADS. Sydney is 515km S by road along the Pacific Highway and 552km away along the main NORTH COAST railway line. Macksville is a service centre for a productive rural district where maize, vegetables and bananas are grown, and dairy farming and sawmilling are important.

Maclean NSW (population 2 589 in 1981)
This country town on the NORTH COAST of the State is located in the CLARENCE RIVER valley at the junction of the N and S arms of the river, downstream from GRAFTON, and 710km via the Pacific Highway NNE of Sydney. It is a small commercial and service centre for the adjacent rural district where dairy farming, banana and sugar cane growing, fishing and timber-getting are the main activities.

National Gallery of VIC

'Elizabeth Bay and Elizabeth Bay House', a watercolour (1839) by Conrad Martens

Macleay family A family noted for public
service and contributions to the biological sciences in Australia.
Alexander Macleay (1767-1848) was born in Scotland and appointed Colonial Secretary of NSW in 1825, arriving in Sydney in 1826. He was granted 138 acres (56ha) at Elizabeth Bay, Sydney, on which he built Elizabeth Bay House, and where he established a garden with many rare plants. After retirement as Colonial Secretary he became, in 1843, Speaker of the Legislative Council. One-time secretary of the Linnaean Society of London, and a Fellow of the Royal Society, Macleay brought with him to Australia his insect collection which is now part of the Macleay Collection of Sydney University. He studied Australian birds and became the first president of the Australian Museum. He died from injuries in a carriage accident.
William Sharp Macleay (1792-1865) was born in England and was the eldest son of Alexander Macleay. He served in Cuba and was involved there in the abolition of the slave trade, and then migrated to Sydney in 1839. He added to the Macleay Collection and carried out work on local marine animals. He knew and corresponded with many important scientists of the day, including DARWIN, HUXLEY and Cuvier.
Sir George Macleay (1809-91) was born in London, and was the third son of Alexander Macleay. He was an explorer and accompanied STURT on his second expedition and served the Australian Museum and the Botanic Gardens of Sydney.
Sir William John Macleay (1820-91) was born in Scotland and was a nephew of Alexander Macleay. He was a pastoralist and experimented in wine producing near WAGGA

WAGGA. He founded the Wagga *Express* and was a member of the Legislative Council from 1856 to 1874. Sir William inherited the Macleay Collection and widened it to include zoological specimens, collecting in the TORRES STRAIT and parts of New Guinea. He published a pioneering work on Australian fishes, and, realising the importance of typhoid and other diseases, strongly urged the appointment of a government bacteriologist. In 1890 he donated the Macleay Collection to Sydney University to which he also left £12 000 to found a Chair of Bacteriology. The university returned the money (being dissatisfied with the conditions) and it was given eventually to the Linnaean Society of New South Wales of which Sir William had been the first president (1874). The money was to be used by the society for bacteriological research. Sir William also left the society £6000 for general purposes, and £35 000 to establish four Linnaean Macleay scholarships, which still exist.

Macleay River

NSW Located on the mid-NORTH COAST of the State, this river has a broad valley extending some 400km from the Pacific coast to the E escarpments of the NEW ENGLAND Plateau. It is situated between the HASTINGS RIVER to the S and the Nambucca-Bowra-Bellinger Rivers to the N. The tributaries which form the source of the Macleay at the W end of the valley, such as the Mihi, Baker's and Rockvale Creeks and Oaky, Apsley and Chandler Rivers, as well as the Macleay itself, have their headwaters on the plateau uplands. They cascade over the escarpments in spectacular waterfalls (the Mihi, WOLLOMOMBI, Yarrowitch, Dangar and Chandler Falls), then flow through steep gorges before entering the broad valley downstream. On the Oaky River a dam has been built across the gorge, with a small hydro-electricity generation scheme which provides peak-load power. On the Serpentine River, another headwater stream, there is a trout hatchery run by the State's Inland Fisheries Branch.

The Pacific Highway crosses the valley in a N-S direction between 15km and 20km from the coastline. The main North Coast railway follows a similar route but, after crossing the Macleay at KEMPSEY, it is located further inland to the W of the highway. The dominant rural activity of the valley is dairying on the rich river flats, as well as lucerne growing, maize crops and beef cattle raising. On the steeper sloping hilly areas and in the ranges, timber-getting is a major industry. The average annual rainfall at Kempsey is 1 213mm, with January to March the period of highest rainfall. In wet years, especially when heavy rain falls in the upper catchment area, the lower valley is subject to flooding and, in the worst years, much damage is done to farmlands. The main town of the valley is Kempsey, located on the river about 40km upstream from the mouth. Along the coast there are several holiday and tourist centres. The Hat Head National Park (3 988ha) stretches along the coast E and NE of Kempsey.

See also Armidale

McMahon, Gregan

(1874-1941) Actor. Born in Sydney, McMahon studied law at Sydney University, where he acted with the Dramatic Society. On leaving university he was engaged by Robert Brough, with whom he toured Australia and abroad, and by 1905 he was also directing amateurs in his own group, the Gregan McMahon Players. He continued to work in both professional and amateur theatre throughout his career. In 1911 he founded the Melbourne Repertory Society to stage good contemporary works, particularly those by Bernard Shaw, and the company gained its own theatre, the Playhouse, in 1916. In the 1920s he worked with the WILLIAMSON 'Firm', and in 1921 established a Sydney Repertory Society. During the Depression the Gregan McMahon Players performed regularly in Melbourne and gained a high reputation. McMahon was made a CBE in 1938.
Further reading: West, J. *Theatre in Australia.* Cassell, Sydney, 1978.

Sir William McMahon

McMahon, Sir William

(1908-) Prime Minister. Born in Sydney, he graduated in law from the University of Sydney, practised as a solicitor, and served in the Australian Imperial Force (AIF) from 1940 to 1945, attaining the rank of major. After the war he travelled widely, gained an economics degree and in 1949 was elected to the House of Representatives. Between 1951 and 1969 he filled a wide variety of Cabinet positions, winning respect particularly as Treasurer (1966-69). He became deputy leader of the Liberal Party in 1966, and after the death of Prime Minister HOLT late in 1967 was widely expected to succeed him. However, Sir John McEWEN, leader of the Country Party, which was in coalition with the Liberals, believed that McMahon had used his influence to weaken the Country Party, and stated that he would not serve under him. McMahon therefore declined to contest the ballot for party leadership, and John GORTON gained the position and with it that of Prime Minister. Following Gorton's resignation in 1971, McMahon became Prime Minister. By this time, however, the Liberal Party was badly divided, and in the 1972 elections the Austra-lian Labor Party (ALP) won a majority in the House of Representatives. McMahon was not offered a Cabinet position after the return of the coalition to power in 1975, and resigned from Parliament in 1982.

McPherson Range

QLD/NSW The crest of this range forms the State border and is the watershed between the headwaters of the TWEED and RICHMOND Rivers in NSW and the LOGAN and Nerang river systems in QLD. The range is an offshoot from the GREAT DIVIDING RANGE and extends on a general E-W alignment for about 130km from SW of WARWICK to the Pacific coastal plain. Much of the area is rugged and deeply dissected, with numerous waterfalls and dense rainforest vegetation. It is a basalt-capped range with the highest peaks rising to over 1 200m (Mt Barney 1 350m, Mt Lindesay 1 239m). There is a railway tunnel through the range at Richmond Gap, and the Mt Lindesay Highway crosses the W section. There are several national parks in the range: LAMINGTON Park (20 200ha), which includes rugged stretches of rainforest and a wilderness area in the S recommended for experienced bushwalkers only; Mt Barney National Park (6 200hs), in the W of the range; and Mt Lindesay Park (242ha), along the State border.

Macquarie Harbour

TAS This large inlet on the rugged W coast of the State, into which the KING and GORDON Rivers drain, extends over 30km inland in a NW-SE direction. The town of STRAHAN, the former exporting centre for copper from MOUNT LYELL, is situated on a N bay of the harbour. The inlet is a large trough, formed by faulting and then sculptured by glacial ice, with an average width of 8km, but with a narrow entrance known as Hell's Gates because of the strong tidal rip.

Sea elephants and royal penguins at South End Rookery, Macquarie Island

Macquarie Island

This sub-Antarctic island lies between New Zealand and ANTARCTICA at latitude 54°40'S and longitude 159°E, about 1 900km SE of Melbourne. The island is a long narrow wedge of land, extending N-S for over 30km and with an average width of 5km. The highest point is 427m above sea level and along most of the coastline cliffs drop sharply to the sea or to narrow sandy beaches. There are several lakes in the high hills which cover the island. At the N end is a rocky plateau joined to the main island by a narrow isthmus, and on the E side of this is Buckle's Bay, the only anchorage on the island. Here in 1948 the Australian National Antarctic Research Expeditions (ANARE) established a meteorological and research station which has functioned continuously since then as one of Australia's Antarctic bases. The island, which is part of the State of TAS, abounds in bird and animal life during the mildly warm months of the brief summer. In September, the beginning of spring, elephant seals come ashore for the birth of their young and many species of birds—several varieties of albatross, cormorants, petrels, gulls and penguins—start to arrive for nesting. At Hurd Point, the SE tip of the island, is one of the world's largest penguin rookeries.

Macquarie, Lachlan (1762-1824)

Governor of NSW. Born in Scotland, on the island of Ulva, he joined the British Army in 1776 and served in North America during the War of Independence and then in India for most of the period from 1788 to 1807. In 1809 the 73rd Regiment, of which he was in command as a lieutenant-colonel, was assigned to duty in NSW as replacement for the NEW SOUTH WALES CORPS and Macquarie was appointed Lieutenant-Governor of the colony. However, before the regiment had left England, the Governor-designate, Brigadier General Miles Nightingall, gave up the appointment on the grounds of ill health, and Macquarie applied successfully for the vacancy. He was instructed on his arrival in NSW to reinstate the deposed Governor BLIGH in office for one day before he himself took command, but when he reached Sydney late in 1809 Bligh was in TAS, and so on New Year's Day 1810 he read his commission and assumed office.

NSW Govt Printer

Governor Macquarie

Perhaps Macquarie's greatest contribution to the colony's progress was his construction of roads, bridges and public buildings. Before the end of his first year in office he had had a turnpike road constructed to PARRAMATTA, and by the time he left the colony he had built over 500km of well-constructed roads. The

longest of these traversed the BLUE MOUN-TAINS, and was hardly completed before Macquarie travelled along it and selected the site of BATHURST, Australia's first town beyond the GREAT DIVIDING RANGE. Among the notable buildings surviving from his time are the NSW Parliament House, the building commonly known as the Mint Building in Macquarie Street, the old convict barracks facing Queen's Square, St James' Church in Queen's Square, the main portion of the Conservatorium of Music, St Matthew's Church and the courthouse at WINDSOR, St Luke's Church at Liverpool, and the former Liverpool Hospital, now a technical college. Another achievement of note was the equipping of the colony with its first large supply of currency, which he did by obtaining £10 000 worth of Spanish dollars and having a circular piece punched out of the centre of each. This disc, known as a 'dump', was given a value of 15 pence and the outer ring, or 'holey dollar', was valued at five shillings, the normal value of the whole dollar elsewhere. He also encouraged the founding of the BANK OF NEW SOUTH WALES in 1817.

Mark Howard

A notable building of Macquarie's time – St James' Church, Queen's Square, Sydney

The most controversial aspect of Macquarie's rule was his policy towards emancipists (ex-convicts). He believed that good conduct 'should lead a man back to that rank in society which he had forfeited, and do away, as far as the case will admit, of all retrospect of bad conduct'. Accordingly he appointed emancipists to public positions, defended the right of emancipist attorneys to practise in the courts, and invited several emancipists to Government House. Such actions were bitterly opposed and criticised by many prominent free settlers. In 1819, largely as a result of complaints regarding Macquarie's emancipist policy and his alleged autocratic behaviour, John BIGGE was sent to report on the colony's progress and prospects. His reports, published after Macquarie had resigned in 1821, criticised the latter on a number of matters and were deeply resented by him. Macquarie was forbidden to reply to

them publicly, but in a bitter letter to the Colonial Secretary, Lord Bathurst, he defended his policies and detailed the great progress made by the colony during his term of office. However, his place in history is secure. Although he misjudged the way in which the colony would develop by under-rating the contribution that wealthy free settlers would make, he equipped the colony for future progress and in his treatment of convicts and emancipists showed a sense of compassion unusual at the time.

Further reading: Barnard, M. *Macquarie's World.* Oxford University Press, Melbourne, 1962; Ellis, M.H. *Lachlan Macquarie, His Life, Adventures and Times.* Angus & Robertson, Cremorne NSW, 1973.

Macquarie River

NSW This inland stream rises on the W slopes of the GREAT DIVIDING RANGE S of BATHURST and flows generally NW across the slopes and plains region to the DARLING RIVER drainage system. It was discovered and named after Governor Lachlan MACQUARIE by the explorer George EVANS in 1813. The general direction of flow is SE to NW through Bathurst, WELLINGTON, DUBBO and Narromine, then N beyond WAR-REN where it merges into the vast swamps of the Macquarie Marshes; beyond these it joins the CASTLEREAGH RIVER which flows into the Darling upstream from Brewarrina. The head-water streams, which include the Fish, Camp-bell, TURON and Cudgegong, have their sources in the dissected uplands of the range where the average annual rainfall is about 1000mm. Downstream, the topography is un-dulating; sheep grazing and wheat growing are dominant, and as the river merges into the inland plains sheep grazing progressively replaces agriculture as the average annual rain-fall declines. The Mitchell Highway crosses the river at Bathurst, then again at Wellington and Dubbo. Near the confluence of the Cudgegong and Macquarie Rivers, 32km upstream from Wellington, is the BURRENDONG DAM, completed in 1967, which provides irrigation for crops and live-stock in the lower valley, and regulates the river's flow so as to prevent major flooding. The Macquarie Marshes (18 211ha), declared a sanctuary in 1955, form a permanent refuge and breeding ground for many species of native birds and play an important role in the ecology of inland NSW.

Maffra

VIC (population 3 822 in 1981) This town on the MACALISTER RIVER in E GIPPSLAND is located 229km by road from Melbourne and 20km NW of SALE. Situated on the alluvial flats of the river valley, at an elevation of 26m above sea level, it has a mild climate, with an average annual rainfall of 584mm, evenly spread throughout the year; October has the most rain (61mm average), July the least (36mm). The town is the com-mercial and service centre for a rich rural region of irrigated dairy farms and fodder crops, part of the Macalister River irrigation scheme. The first irrigation settlement in

Gippsland was started here in 1926. The name Maffra was given to the town by a veteran of the Peninsular Wars, after Mafra on the W coast of Portugal.

maggots *see* flies

Magnetic Island QLD Located across Cleveland Bay from TOWNSVILLE, this island of 64km² was discovered and named by James COOK in 1770 when he thought, incorrectly, that the variations he noted in readings on his ship's compass were caused by magnetic forces due to iron on the island. Water-taxis can be hired and passenger launches and a vehicular ferry operate regularly from Townsville to the island. It has long been a popular recreation and holiday area but is increasingly becoming a launch-commuter suburb of the city. Part of the island is a national park (2 533ha) which contains rugged granite hills with hoop pine and eucalypt forests.

magpie-lark *see* mudnest builders

magpies *see* butcherbirds, etc.

mahogany This name is applied to certain eucalypts valued for their timber: bastard mahogany or bangalay, *Eucalyptus botryoides* (which grows in VIC and NSW), red mahogany, *E. resinifera* (NSW and QLD), and swamp mahogany, *E. robusta* (NSW).
See also Myrtaceae

maidenhair tree *see* Gymnospermae

Main Range QLD This section of the GREAT DIVIDING RANGE in south-eastern QLD forms the watershed between streams flowing inland to the CONDAMINE RIVER system and those draining to the E coast. The range extends from near TOOWOOMBA for about 100km on a N-S alignment to the NSW/QLD border, thus dividing the DARLING DOWNS region from the LOCKYER VALLEY and the Brisbane River lowlands. It is separated from the BUNYA RANGE, another section of the Great Dividing Range lying to the N, by a gap E of Toowoomba. Further S in the Main Range is the historic mountain pass—Cunningham's Gap—located 45km by road NE of WARWICK, discovered by the explorer Allan CUNNINGHAM in 1828 and now forming the route through the range for the Cunningham Highway from Brisbane to GOONDIWINDI. To the E and SE of Warwick the Main Range is rugged and dissected with several peaks rising to over 1 200m; MOUNT SUPERBUS (1 380m), Mt Asplenium (1 284m), Mt Roberts (1 328m) and Mt Huntley (1 265m).

Maitland NSW (population 38 863 in 1981) This city is located on the HUNTER RIVER, 192km by rail N of Sydney and 32km inland by road from NEWCASTLE. It is situated on the New England Highway and is an important railway junction of the main line through the Hunter Valley to the N tablelands and the

High Street in Maitland, 1886

NORTH COAST rail route. It is the largest urban settlement in the Hunter Valley, apart from Newcastle, and is the commercial and service centre for the productive rural region of the lower valley. The city of Maitland incorporates a number of smaller townships such as Morpeth, 8km E, and Telarah, 2km W. Settlement of this section of the Hunter Valley began in the early decades of the 19th century; farming and grazing on the rich alluvial river flats, and timber-cutting, particularly of cedar in nearby areas, were the main activities. In the early 1820s, a village, originally called Wallis Plain, was established on the W side of Wallis Creek; this became West Maitland. A government township was laid out in 1829 on the E side of the creek and this developed into East Maitland. The two were joined together, along with some adjacent villages, to form the city of Maitland in 1944.

Dairying and beef production are among the main primary industries of the district; vegetable growing to supply the Newcastle market is important on the alluvial river flats; lucerne and millet growing are also significant in the rural economy. To the SW and W of Maitland are located some of the valley's fine wine producing vineyards. There is an abattoir and a large livestock saleyard in the city where regular auctions of cattle, horses and sheep are held. Secondary industries in the area include textile mills, pottery works, furniture making, timber milling and some engineering workshops. River gravel, blue metal for road making, and clay for brick making are quarried in the district. The GRETA-Maitland coal deposits are located in an area SW of the city and, since the late 19th century, coal mining has been important. Though the coal industry in recent years has experienced a decline, there are many small centres such as CESSNOCK, Bellbird, KURRI KURRI, Abermain and WESTON, which have a tradition as coal towns.

In recent decades, Maitland has developed increasingly as a residential centre for people who work in Newcastle and commute daily. The location of Maitland on the alluvial plain

of the Hunter River has made parts of the city, particularly the low-lying sections near the river, subject to flood inundation. To overcome this problem, a plan for the relocation of some residential areas which are affected by flooding was instituted in the 1970s and future residential building on the lower lands was prohibited.
Further reading: Historical Buildings of Maitland and District. Maitland City Council, Mercury Print, 1965; Daly, M.T. *The Growth of Newcastle's Influence, with Special Reference to Maitland, Greater Cessnock and Raymond Terrace.* Hunter Valley Research Foundation, Newcastle, 1966; White, U. & Farrelly, A. *Newcastle and Hunter Valley Sketchbook.* Rigby, Adelaide, 1969.

Maitland SA (population 1 085 in 1981) This small town is situated in the centre of YORKE PENINSULA, at an elevation of 186m above sea level, 172km by road NW of Adelaide. It is the commercial and service centre for a rich grain growing and sheep grazing region. The annual average rainfall is 509mm, with a concentration in the winter months.

maize *see* agriculture; Gramineae

Mallacoota VIC (population 725 in 1981) This coastal township in the E section of E GIPPSLAND is about 560km E of Melbourne, located on the W side of Mallacoota Inlet, the estuary of the Genoa River, 22km off the Princes Highway. It is an important abalone port and a popular tourist centre, noted for its scenic beauty and for fishing and other aquatic sports. The inlet was formed in recent geological times, about 6000 years ago, when the sea rose to its present level and drowned an old river valley. The Croajingolong National Park covers 86 000ha of sandy islands, wooded foreshores, ocean beaches, heathland and forested ranges on both sides of Mallacoota Inlet and along the coastal zone.

mallee *see* Myrtaceae; vegetation

Mallee region *see* Wimmera-Mallee

mallee fowl *see* mound birds

Malley, Ern *see* Ern Malley Hoax

Maltese in Australia The 1981 census revealed that 57 001 persons resident in Australia had been born in Malta. C.A. Price, a leading authority on multicultural affairs, in a study of the ethnic origins of the Australian population based on an eight-generation analysis, estimated the total Maltese component to be equivalent to 116 400 persons in 1978.

The first Maltese settler was Antonio Azzopardi, a chief officer and ship's engineer, who lived in PORT PHILLIP BAY in about 1838 and who for some time served on ships trading between Port Phillip, Sydney and New Zealand. There are records of contact between Maltese people and Australia long before that date—a ship of Maltese nationality arrived in Hobart in 1830. Among the earliest Maltese settlers were a group of fishermen, domestic servants and labourers who arrived in QLD in the 1850s. The first organised immigration from Malta was for contract workers on the QLD canefields in 1883. The majority of Maltese arrived after World War II and many live on the urban-rural fringes of Melbourne and Sydney where they engage in market gardening and poultry farming. Others have found work in the manufacturing and building industries while some have become businessmen or financiers.

The Maltese people are proud of their national heritage and identity. They have a distinct language which is derived from Arabic, and large, closely knit networks of kin relationships. Most Maltese are Roman Catholics and many organisations have been set up to support their religious interests. Other organisations, such as the Maltese Guilds in Sydney and Adelaide, offer a wide range of social activities, while sport and the interests of ex-servicemen and the youth have also been supported by various organisations. Publications in the Maltese language include the weekly *Maltese Herald* in Sydney and the fortnightly *Times of Malta* in Melbourne. *Further reading:* Price, C.A. *Australian Immigration, A Bibliography and Digest.* Australian National University Press, Canberra, 1981

mammals These warm-blooded (homoiothermic) VERTEBRATES, belonging to the class Mammalia, suckle their young and have hair at some stage during their lives—even whales (*see* DOLPHINS, etc.) and Mexican 'hairless' dogs. Their constant high temperature, usually about 36°C, allows them to be active even when the surrounding temperature is low, unlike cold-blooded REPTILES which become sluggish. Some small mammals, however, may have difficulty in thermo-regulating at low temperatures because of their high surface area to body volume ratio. In hibernating mammals the body temperature is usually several degrees lower than in active mammals.

Many characteristic features allow mammals

Platypus

to maintain a high metabolic rate, a constant temperature and an active life even when environmental conditions are unfavourable. Hair, for example, is an insulator, preventing heat loss at low temperatures or heat gain in very hot conditions. Mammals eat regularly, compared with reptiles which can starve for long periods, and mammalian teeth have evolved in a way that enables them to deal efficiently with their food. The teeth are differentiated in most mammals into incisors for cutting, canines for stabbing and cheek teeth (molars and premolars) for crushing and grinding. The teeth are in sockets along the edges of the bones of the jaw and are usually replaced only once, whereas those of reptiles are replaced throughout life. The breathing passage and the food passage are separated in the mouth by a secondary bony palate; this allows a mammal to process food in its mouth and breathe at the same time. Reptiles, on the other hand, must bolt their food quickly in order to breathe, all except the CROCODILE, which has a similar bony secondary palate and can swallow food underwater.

Mammals have complex brains and behaviour. In general they are more mobile than reptiles as their limbs are held below the body whilst those of most reptiles sprawl out to the side. In mammals, as in BIRDS and crocodiles, the heart has four chambers, an arrangement which allows the complete and efficient separation of the blood going to and from the lungs, and the blood circulating through other parts of the body. The ribs are confined to the thoracic region, and the thorax is closed off behind by the muscular diaphragm, allowing more efficient and regular breathing.

It is not always possible to be sure when studying a FOSSIL if the animal was warm-blooded when alive, or if it suckled its young; often the fossil consists of only the skull. Technically, therefore, mammals are differentiated from reptiles by the way in which the lower jaw articulates with the skull. In mammals the jaw consists of a single bone, and two of the small bones that are found in the lower jaw of the reptiles have become two of the small bones that transmit vibrations in the ear of mammals.

The first mammals appeared during the Triassic period, about 195 million to 225 million years ago. They evolved from the synapsid or mammal-like reptiles which reached their peak before the flourishing of the dinosaurs. These have been found only recently in Australia. The first mammals, therefore, arose before the dinosaurs and for millions of years the two kinds of animals co-existed.

The living mammals are only a remnant of this class. There are about 4000 species extant (about 66 per cent of them RODENTS) whereas there are about 6000 reptiles, 10 000 birds and 20 000 FISHES. Strahan (*see below*) lists 252 species in Australia (about 5.75 per cent of the world's mammals on about five per cent of its land area). This list includes the SEALS but excludes the whales, and introduced mammals apart from the DINGO.

Australia and New Guinea are unique in having representatives of all existing subclasses of mammals. Current opinion divides class Mammalia into subclass Prototheria, subclass Metatheria and subclass Eutheria. Nevertheless, the metatherian mammals (MARSUPIALS) and the EUTHERIAN MAMMALS (sometimes called placental mammals) are more closely related to each other than to the Prototheria (MONOTREME MAMMALS).

The monotremes (platypus and spiny anteater) are egg-laying mammals with many reptilian characteristics, found only in Australia, New Guinea and some of the adjacent islands. The marsupials produce young in a very undeveloped state and nourish them, usually within a pouch (marsupium). Eutherian mammals produce young that are far more advanced than those of the marsupials at birth. The foetus and embryo are nourished through a placenta (technically an allantoic placenta) which allows the passage of materials from the mother's blood stream to that of the young. All eutherians have a placenta but it is misleading to separate them as the placental mammals as there are placentas (though of a different kind) in some marsupials. The eggs of marsupials are yolky whereas those of the eutherians have very little yolk and are not, of course, laid. Other characteristics of the three subclasses are given in the entries on monotreme mammals, marsupials and eutherian mammals.

It was once thought, naturally enough, that these three groups represented stages in the evolution of mammals. Nothing is known of the evolution of monotremes, however, and they may have evolved within Australasia. The only known fossils resemble the existing monotremes, but these are very specialised mammals which give no hint of their relationships from their anatomy. The idea that the eutherians evolved from the marsupials fitted in nicely with the presence of the latter in Australia for it was argued that the marsupials reached the continent from the N before the eutherians had evolved, and were then cut off by the rising sea. Elsewhere, the argument continued, the marsupials were eradicated by the more efficient eutherians, apart from in the Americas. Modern research has shown, however, that the marsupials and the eutherians both appeared at about the same time, during the Cretaceous period which lasted from about 135 million to 65 million years ago. There is some evidence, from the distribution of fossils, that the marsupials arose in the Americas and the eutherians arose in Europe, though fossils of both are found in both areas. This is consistent with the belief of many biologists that the marsupials were well placed to spread through GONDWANALAND from what is now South America to Australia before the supercontinent broke up but before they could reach, for example, New Zealand. The eutherian mammals, on the other hand, were unable to reach Australia through Gondwanaland but reached the continent later by 'island-hopping' from South-East Asia. Only small mammals such as rodents, flying mammals such as BATS and unusual mammals such as man could cross the water barriers along this route. Marsupial fossils, though common in Europe and the Americas, have never been found in Asia. This is consistent, of course, with the belief that marsupials never existed there, and that they entered Australasia by a S route. If marsupial fossils are eventually found in Antarctica this would be further evidence to support the Gondwanaland theory but Antarctica, with its covering of ice and snow, is a

difficult land for the palaeontologist.
See also continental drift
Further reading: Colbert, E.H. *Evolution of the Vertebrates.* (2nd edn) Wiley, New York, 1969 and *Wandering Lands and Animals.* Hutchinson, London, 1974; Matthews, L.H. *The Life of Mammals.* (2 vols) Universe Books, New York, 1970; Ride, W.D.L. *A Guide to the Native Mammals of Australia.* Oxford University Press, Melbourne, 1970; Keast, A., Erk, F.C. & Glass, B. (eds) *Evolutionary Mammals and Southern Continents.* New York State University Press, Albany, 1972; Cox, C.B., Healey, I.N. & Moore, P.D. *Biogeography.* (2nd edn) Blackwell, Oxford, 1976; Webb, J.E., Wallwork, J.A. & Elgood, J.H. *Guide to Living Mammals.* Macmillan, London, 1977; Archer, M. *Mammals in Australia.* The Australian Museum, Sydney, 1981; Woods, A. *Australian Invaders* (in press); Strahan, R. (ed.) *The Australian Museum Complete Book of Australian Mammals.* Angus & Robertson, Sydney, 1983.

mandarin *see* fishes, bony

Mandurah WA (population 10 978 in 1981) Located 76km by road S of Perth, straddled across the tidal estuary of Peel Inlet where three rivers (the Murray, Serpentine and HARVEY) flow into the sea, this town dates from 1829 when Thomas PEEL made an unsuccessful attempt to establish a settlement in the area. It is a small service centre, a fishing town and a holiday resort which attracts many visitors in the summer months when abundant sunshine and dry weather make it an attractive recreation area, especially for sailing and other aquatic sports. It has an annual rainfall of 897mm, concentrated mainly in the winter period with the highest falls in June (199mm average) and July (176mm). The town takes its name from an Aboriginal word meaning 'a trading place'.

mange *see* mites; parasites, animal

mangel-wurzel *see* Chenopodiaceae

mangroves *see* vegetation

Manjimup WA (population 4 150 in 1981) This timber town and service centre in the hardwood forests of the far SW of the State is 319km by rail and 309km by road SSE of Perth, 134km SE of BUNBURY and 37km S of BRIDGETOWN. Though the main focus of the town's activities is concerned with the karri forests of the region, there is some dairying, orcharding and potato growing in the adjacent rural areas. At an elevation of 280m above sea level, the town has an average annual rainfall of 1 055mm, falling mainly in the winter months (June and July both average over 180mm). The town's name comes from an Aboriginal name meaning 'rushes near a water hole'.

Mann, Leonard (1895-) Author and poet. Born and educated in Melbourne, where

Leonard Mann

he graduated in law from Melbourne University, Mann served in the Australian Imperial Force (AIF) in World War I. His publications include three volumes of poetry and five novels, but his reputation rests mainly on one of the latter, *Flesh in Armour* (1932), which is generally accepted as the best Australian work of literature based on experiences in World War I. Its loosely constructed plot deals with the experiences of a platoon, and in particular three of its members, on active service in France and on leave in England. Written in a casual style, it gives a convincing picture of the attitudes and behaviour of rank-and-file members of the first AIF.

mannikins *see* grass finches

Manning River NSW This river on the mid-NORTH COAST has a valley which stretches over 220km from the GREAT DIVIDING RANGE to the Pacific coastline. The headwater tributaries have their sources in the BARRINGTON TOPS area, the MOUNT ROYAL RANGE and the dissected scarplands of the NEW ENGLAND Plateau. Among the tributaries which make up the Manning River system are the Barnard (from the W), the Barrington (from the SW), the Myall (from the NW) and the Nowendoc, Cooplacuripa and Rowley's Rivers (from the N). The main towns in the valley are TAREE, WINGHAM and GLOUCESTER. The most important rural activity in the valley is dairying, which is concentrated on the river flats and the lower parts of adjacent hill land. Associated with the grazing of dairy cattle, fodder crops are grown (maize, sorghum, lucerne and oats), pigs are raised, and beef cattle are produced. In the upland parts of the valley, timber-getting is a major pursuit and sawmills dotted throughout the hills give ample evidence of the importance of this industry. The rainfall is variable, with dry spells at times and heavy rains at others, so that both floods and droughts are experienced. The Pacific Highway crosses the lower part of the valley on a general N-S route, while the main N railway line passes through Gloucester, Wingham and Taree in a general E-W direction. Downstream from Taree, the land consists mainly of the delta of the river, with coastal sand dunes and beaches along the ocean shore. Several well-known tourist centres are located in this coastal zone, such as Harrington, Old Bar and Halliday's Point. The Crowdy Bay National Park (5 736ha) is also located in this coastal belt, N of the river estuary, between the Pacific Highway and the coast, about 25km NE of Taree. Access to the park is gained either from the highway at Moorlands or from the N via Laurieton. Within the park there are varied landscape features including forest, heath and swamp areas; a series of low sand dunes running parallel to the coast and extending inland for some distance give evidence of past shorelines. The heathland attracts large numbers of honey-eaters and ground dwellers such as quail, as well as hawks and falcons which come from nearby forests to feed; many species of reptiles are also found including tortoises, snakes and lizards; the animal population in the park ranges from the tiny marsupial mice, native rats and possums, to large macropods such as red-necked wallabies and grey kangaroos.

Mannix, Daniel (1864-1963)

Roman Catholic Archbishop of Melbourne. Born in Ireland, he came to Australia in 1913 as assistant to Archbishop T.J. Carr of Melbourne, whom he succeeded in 1917. He was a man of commanding presence and strong personality with outstanding gifts of oratory, and for many years was the best-known Roman Catholic churchman in Australia. He promoted the growth of the Church's school system, assisted in the foundation of Newman College in Melbourne University, established Corpus Christi seminary at Werribee VIC and constantly denounced the lack of government aid to Church schools.

His political and social views involved him in a great deal of public controversy. He was outspoken on behalf of Irish independence, sympathised with the Easter rebels of 1916, and fought vigorously against conscription in the campaigns of 1916 and 1917. In 1920, after he had made public appearances in New York with Eamon de Valera, leader of the Irish republican movement, the ship on which he was crossing the Atlantic was intercepted by British destroyers, and he was forbidden to visit Ireland, Liverpool or Glasgow.

Mannix was prominent in encouraging Roman Catholic lay activity, and took a close interest in the National Secretariat of Catholic Action, founded in 1937. He was also a leading supporter of the Catholic Social Movement, the activities of which included fighting Communist influence in trade unions through industrial groups within the Australian Labor Party (ALP). Dr Herbert EVATT's attack in 1954 on the methods used by members of 'the

Courtesy of A.I.S. Canberra
Archbishop Mannix

Movement' was followed by bitter controversy within the ALP, culminating in the formation of the Democratic Labor Party, of which Dr Mannix remained a supporter until his death. *Further reading:* Brennan, N. *Dr Mannix.* Rigby, Adelaide, 1964.

Mannum SA (population 1 984 in 1981)

This town and former river port on the lower MURRAY RIVER is located 83km by road E of Adelaide. It is the service centre for a productive dairying region on the irrigated alluvial flats of the Murray and is a popular tourist and holiday area, with boating, swimming, fishing and other aquatic sports. It is the starting point of the 84km-long pipeline, completed in 1954, which carries water from the river across the MOUNT LOFTY RANGES to metropolitan Adelaide. The town had its beginnings in the early 1850s when Captain Randell, one of the pioneer steamer navigators on the Murray, built a home there. It developed as an important river trading centre and the paddle-wheeler *Marion* is now moored at the river bank as a floating museum.

man-o'-war birds see sea birds

Mansfield VIC (population 1 920 in 1981)

This small country town is located at the junction of the Midland and Maroondah Highways, 175km by road and 211km by rail NE of Melbourne. It is a service and commercial centre for a large farming and grazing district, as well as the gateway to the MOUNT BULLER ski resort, to EILDON RESERVOIR and to the scenic lands of the upper GOULBURN RIVER valley. It was named after the town of Mansfield in Nottinghamshire, England.

mantids

These predatory exopterygote INSECTS belonging to the order Mantodea are found in most of the warmer parts of the world; there are about 130 species in Australia. Mantids, with their cryptically coloured and shaped bodies, and fore-legs which snap shut round their prey like a closing penknife, are beautifully adapted to preying on other insects. Their peculiar stance while waiting in ambush—the head is raised and the fore-legs are outstretched as if in prayer—is responsible for their common name, praying mantis or mantid. The head, with its large eyes, and the first segment of the thorax are very mobile, enabling a mantid to follow the movements of potential prey without moving the rest of the body. Mantids have biting and chewing mouthparts. In all Australian species the females have very small wings, or no wings at all, whereas the males are usually fully winged. The eggs are laid in large cocoon-like capsules (ootheca), composed of solidified froth and resembling those of their close relatives, the COCKROACHES.

There are two families in Australia, the Amorphoscelidae and the Mantidae. The former contains small species which live on tree bark, whilst the latter, a much larger family, contains about 100 small to large species, often green in colour, with representatives in all parts of Australia.

Mantodea *see* mantids

manucode *see* birds of paradise

manufacturing

For many years after their foundation, the British colonies which became the Commonwealth of Australia depended for their prosperity on the export of primary products, manufactured goods being mostly imported. Today the value of Australia's manufactured products is about twice that of all primary industries, including mining. However, for several years large sections of the manufacturing industry have been facing grave problems, and there is general agreement that a large degree of restructuring of the secondary sector of the economy is needed; but the extent of this restructuring and how to achieve it are still matters for debate. The nature of current problems will be more easily understood if one begins by considering the historical circumstances under which manufacturing developed in Australia.

The early colonial period Almost as soon as the first British settlers landed, blacksmiths' forges were set up and within a short time small industrial establishments, such as brick works and lime kilns, had been started. The colonists took it for granted that their main task was to become self-sufficient in food, and that most manufactured goods would be imported. During the following half-century or more Australia remained very ill-equipped for manufacturing, lacking capital, skilled labour and a large population; by 1848 there were in all colonies combined only about 2000 people working in establishments officially classed as factories. Most factories, such as brick works, flour mills, tanneries, breweries and soap works, were engaged in treating local products.

From the gold rushes to federation At first, the gold rushes of the 1850s caused a setback for manufacturing, for they caused a labour shortage and provided increased wealth for buying imports. In time, however, they stimulated secondary industry. Firstly, they led to a population increase which in turn widened the opportunities for 'economies of scale' in local manufacturing. Secondly, the diggers included many skilled workers who, as the alluvial gold began to run out, provided manufacturers with a pool of experienced labour. Also, more capital for investment became available, and some of this was directed to manufacturing.

Between 1851 and 1861 the non-Aboriginal population of Australia increased nearly three-fold, and during the following 30 years there was another threefold increase, which was accompanied by great expansions in wool production and agriculture and by many new mineral discoveries. This led to increased opportunities for local manufacturers, and by 1890 there were in Australia over 11 000 establishments classified as factories, with a total workforce of 133 000, engaged mostly in processing local products. However, a significant number were turning out metal goods and machinery. Some of these factories had grown from blacksmiths' shops, where it was comparatively easy to move from repairing agricultural machinery to making it; others, such as the harvester works of H.V. McKay & Co. (see Hugh Victor MCKAY) in VIC developed from the work of local inventors. Others again were connected with the booming building industry, a notable example being the works of the Danks Co. in Melbourne, the leading manufacturer of plumbing equipment. Two important characteristics of manufacturing as a whole were that most factories were quite small, with fewer than 20 employees each, and that they produced almost entirely for the domestic market. The great distance between Australia and the sources of manufactured imports provided a certain degree of natural protection; on the other hand, it was difficult to export manufactured goods because potential markets were also mostly far away.

Manufacturing was heavily concentrated in VIC and NSW, and its development was accompanied by a great deal of controversy on the issue of free trade versus protection. VIC, for a variety of reasons, used tariffs from 1866 onwards to protect her industries, while NSW kept to free trade. However, it cannot be said that VIC gained a decisive advantage in manufacturing, for in 1889 the two colonies were approximately equal with regard to the number of factory workers and the value of factory output. But the VIC experience meant that when federation came the Commonwealth would adopt at least a mildly protectionist policy, since otherwise some of the nation's manufacturing enterprises would be unable to survive.

From federation to World War II The abolition of interstate tariffs at the time of federation and the imposition, not long afterwards, of a Commonwealth tariff on imported manufactures favoured the growth of secondary industries. With these advantages, as well as the benefits of a general recovery after

The Nomad aircraft, built by the Government Aircraft Factories in Melbourne, is an outstanding example of Australian success in manufacturing for export

the economic depression of the 1890s and a renewal of assisted immigration schemes, manufacturing expanded again, so that factory employment increased from 198 000 in 1901 to 312 000 in 1911.

World War I had important effects on Australian attitudes towards secondary industries, for the difficulty of importing many manufactured goods convinced the nation's leaders that a certain degree of industrial self-sufficiency was necessary for defence reasons—a belief which has affected government policies ever since. Although the manufacturing industry did not increase dramatically, the range of goods produced was significantly greater by 1918. A major cause of this increase was the opening of the NEWCASTLE steelworks in 1915, which not only gave Australian manufacturers ample supplies of good, cheap, locally produced iron and steel, but soon gave rise to a wide range of ancillary industries. The enterprise was successful from the outset, and by 1919 production of pig iron had reached over 330 000 tonnes a year, compared with a maximum capacity of a little over 200 000 tonnes in 1915 and a total Australian output of 48 000 tonnes in 1913.

Important developments took place in the smelting of metals. Before 1914 most of Australia's lead, zinc and copper concentrates had been sold to German firms, so after the outbreak of hostilities the Commonwealth government took the logical step of encouraging metal smelting and processing in Australia. In 1915 the main BROKEN HILL companies set up Broken Hill Associated Smelters to treat their ores at PORT PIRIE in SA, and shortly after the end of the war the Electrolytic Zinc Co. of Australia Ltd opened a plant for refining zinc concentrates electrolytically at RISDON COVE near Hobart. Government intervention also led to the development of the motor vehicle manufacturing industry in Australia. Because of war needs, imports of motor vehicles failed to keep up with demand. Although Australia was not in a position to

manufacture complete vehicles herself, the government felt she was able to manufacture car bodies and in 1917 it decreed that two out of every three chassis imported should be without bodies. By 1939 most cars sold in Australia were assembled locally, and equipped not only with Australian-made bodies, but also with many other locally made components, such as springs, shock absorbers, radiators and axles. (For further effects of government decrees see TRANSPORT.)

In the meantime the desirability of protection for Australian manufacturing had been generally accepted and the setting up of the Tariff Board (now the INDUSTRIES ASSISTANCE COMMISSION) in 1921 marked an attempt to put such protection on a better planned basis. The general picture during the following 20 years was one of moderate growth during the 1920s, a temporary decline during the Depression of the early 1930s, and, with the aid of import restrictions and the advantages of a depreciated currency, of very considerable growth during the late 1930s. By 1940-41 employment in factories had risen to 650 000.

World War II and after The effects of World War II on manufacturing were far greater than those of the 1914-18 war. Firstly, interruptions to overseas supplies, and therefore the incentive for Australia to manufacture goods for herself, were greater. Secondly, the war in Europe gave Australia opportunities to supply goods to British territories E of Suez, while the war with Japan made her a very important source of supply for Allied forces in the South-West Pacific Area. Industrial activity was therefore expanded to include a wide range of munitions, aircraft, ships, scientific equipment, and new types of machinery and metal manufactures. Finally, the fact that Australia came under direct attack reinforced the existing belief that national security depended to an important extent on industrial strength.

During the first few years of peace there were shortages of labour and materials, but the period from about 1948 to 1972 was marked by a great influx of overseas capital, by an immigration programme of unprecedented size, which provided both skilled labour and a larger domestic market, and by government policies aimed at full employment and rapid economic growth. Industrial protection continued, not only by means of tariffs but up to 1960 by import restrictions also. Under such favourable conditions established industries underwent further expansion and others, such as oil refining and the petrochemical and electronic industries, mushroomed. Perhaps most impressive of all was the motor vehicle industry—it produced nearly 500 000 vehicles of predominantly Australian content per year and it stimulated the growth of a wide range of other industries. By 1972-73 manufacturing was contributing over 26 per cent of the Gross Domestic Product, was absorbing 34 per cent of direct investment from overseas and 20 per cent of all private investment, and was employing 24 per cent of the workforce. It had also become more export-orientated; while still catering mainly for the domestic market, it was providing about 20 per cent of national exports, compared with six per cent in 1963-64. Nevertheless, even by that year signs of strain were becoming apparent.

Recent and current problems The symptoms of an ailing Australian manufacturing industry are clear. Firstly, the level of employment has declined—not merely in the percentage of the workforce engaged in manufacturing, but in the actual number of people employed. An employment peak was reached early in 1974, and by 1978 the total number employed in manufacturing had fallen by more than 200 000, particularly in the textiles, clothing and footwear industries. In late 1982, as the recession affecting nearly all industrialised nations deepened, a further fall began, including a marked decline in the iron and steel industry. Secondly, factory production has fallen and has been subject to marked fluctuations. Thirdly, profitability of the manufacturing sector has declined. And finally, this whole process of instability has occurred in spite of the maintenance of a high level of tariff protection, as well as the reimposition of quantitative import controls so as to preserve for local industry an agreed portion of the market in motor cars, textiles, clothing and footwear. In 1978 the Industries Assistance Commission calculated that the average level of tariff protection for Australian secondary industry was almost twice as high as that of manufacturing nations such as the USA, the UK and Japan, and nearly three times as high as that of France, West Germany, Italy and Sweden. Not only has this level of protection failed to stop the decline, but economists are freely forecasting that a major part of Australia's manufacturing industry may not survive until the end of the century. Only by the adoption of new approaches and a considerable amount of restructuring, they claim, can the secondary sector of the economy be enabled to contribute effectively to national prosperity.

Causes of current problems In estimating causes, a major difficulty is to decide the relative weights to be given to external factors which have affected the economies of the whole industrialised world, to internal causes peculiar to Australia, and to regional changes in E and South-East Asia. The external factors include problems of the international monetary system, the great increases in oil prices since 1973 and the related slowing down of economic growth in the world's major manufacturing and trading nations. With regard to internal causes, some blame the 25 per cent cut in tariffs made by the WHITLAM government in 1973, while others defend this as necessary therapy. An obvious cause is the fact that in the mid-1970s Australia's inflation rate was higher than those of her main trading partners, and many commentators therefore place a share of the blame on wage increases, particularly the 'wages explosion' of 1973-74. The *White Paper on Manufacturing Industry* (May 1977) states that between 1970 and 1975 minimum hourly rates in Australian manufacturing rose by 120 per cent, compared with 63 per cent in West Germany and 43 per cent in the USA, and therefore claims that 'these figures are at the heart of the major decline in competitiveness which we have witnessed in recent years.' On the other hand, the government of the late 1970s was criticised for adding to industry's troubles by trying to depress real wage levels and so dampening consumer demand. Another common argument is that the emergence of the minerals and energy sector as a major earner of foreign exchange and a focus for foreign investment capital has indirectly weakened the position of manufacturing. Criticism has also been directed at the payroll tax levied by State governments, which at a time of high wages has put an extra burden on industry and has prompted some manufacturers to substitute capital for labour.

The question remains, however, whether, apart from such temporary causes, there are basic long-term weaknesses. On this point the report of a government advisory committee—the Jackson Committee—which was issued in 1975, under the title *Policies for the Development of Manufacturing Industry: A Green paper*, states:

> In part, manufacturing's problems are manifestations of the world economic crisis in which all countries, including Australia, are enmeshed. But in Australian manufacturing there is a deep-seated and long-standing malaise. That malaise has sharpened the impact on industry of the recent economic crisis. When it passes, the malaise of manufacturing will still be there.

A common diagnosis of this malaise is that Australian manufacturers have concentrated too heavily on import-substitution, instead of looking for opportunities to specialise in areas where Australia has advantages and could therefore export successfully. They have been encouraged to do this, it is claimed, because the use of protection without discrimination has lessened the spirit of self-reliant efficiency, and has removed the incentive for industrialists to adapt to change in the national and world economic environment.

One such change, of great political as well as economic importance, has been the growth of manufacturing in a number of the relatively undeveloped nations of E and South-East Asia, particularly Hong Kong, Taiwan, South Korea, Singapore, Malaysia and—to a lesser extent—Thailand, the Philippines and Indonesia. Most of them have concentrated on labour-intensive industries such as textiles, clothing and footwear, where their abundance of low-cost labour gives them a great comparative advantage. Their hopes of raising their people's living standards depends to a very large extend on gaining access for their manufactures to richer nations such as Australia and they are therefore critical of Australia's protection of her high-cost, labour-intensive industries. It is likely that they will begin to place much more emphasis on manufactures of capital- and innovation-intensive types, thereby challenging Australian industry over a wider range of products.

Other sources of weakness in Australian industry are considered to be inadequate investment and therefore a low introduction rate of technology, poor management training and poor labour relations—the latter including not only frequent industrial disputes but high absenteeism and labour turnover. Finally, a frequent charge is that the apparent lack of long-term government planning has hampered decisiveness and initiative among industrialists.

Possibilities for the future There is a wide measure of agreement on the need for restructuring the secondary sector of the economy. General opinion is that protection must be put on a more stable and predictable basis; that in the case of some labour-intensive industries it must eventually be scaled down; that there must be more concentration on industries where Australia has technological advantages and can hope to win export markets; and that in all areas of manufacturing Australian firms must be prepared to innovate. Employment in some import-competing industries will almost inevitably contract even further and improved access will be given to certain manufactures from Australia's Asian neighbours. However, continued economic growth in Asia should provide many opportunities for Australians to win export markets and to enter into partnership arrangements with Asians. It is expected that there will be a trend towards a higher degree of processing of Australian minerals before they are exported, especially since Australia's rich energy resources give her an advantage in this field.

Sunrise industries Increasing attention has been paid recently to the concept of 'sunrise' industries. This term refers to high technology industries (most of them in manufacturing) which might act as wealth generators and compensate for the decline in traditional areas of manufacturing. The HAWKE government has undertaken to identify and encourage such industries, and its Minister for Science and Technology, Mr Barry Jones, has been a prolific writer and speaker on the subject. The 1983 Science and Technology Policy of the Australian Labor Party stated that areas which seem likely to have good prospects of success include: biotechnology, personal computers, computer software, custom-made computer chips, scientific instrumentation, medical technologies, lasers, communication technologies, industrial ceramics, solar technology, shape memory alloys, nuclear fusion as an energy source, robots, hydrogen generation and storage, various intermediate technology projects and biomass. In May 1983 the final report of the High Technology Financing Committee of the Australian Academy of Technological Sciences recommended that the government act urgently to aid the development of high technology industries, by encouraging the creation of private investment companies to provide management guidance and equity capital for eligible businesses—not only in manufacturing, but in other sections of the economy also—which have high growth potential.

See also economic history; iron and steel industry; motor vehicle industry.

Further reading: The following are publications of the Australian Government Publishing Service, Canberra: *Australian Manufacturing Council Reports.* (annually); *Industries Assistance Commission Reports.* (annually); *Policies for Development of Manufacturing Industry:* A Green Paper, 1975; *White Paper on Manufacturing Industry,* 1977; *Study Group on Structural Adjustment Report,* 1978. Other publications: Wawn, B.R. "Restructuring the Manufacturing Sector", in *Current Affairs Bulletin,* vol. 57, no. 1, June 1980; Jones, B.O. *Sleepers, Wake.* Oxford University Press, Melbourne, 1982; Australian Academy of Technological Sciences. *Developing High Technology Enterprises for Australia.* The Academy, Parkville, Vic., 1983.

maple, Queensland *see* crow's ash

Marble Bar WA (population 357 in 1981) Reputed to be the hottest place in Australia, Marble Bar claims a record of 160 consecutive days with temperatures over 37.8°C (100°F) and some of the highest recorded maximum temperatures in Australia. This town is on the Great Northern Highway, 1486km NNE of Perth and 193km SE of PORT HEDLAND; it is situated on the Coongan River, a S tributary of the DE GREY RIVER in the PILBARA region. Marble Bar was established as a gold-mining centre in the 1890s and was named after a rock-bar of jasper that crosses the river bed W of the town. At an elevation of 173m above sea level, it receives an average annual rainfall of 334mm, concentrated in the summer months. Gold ore is still crushed at the State Battery (2km out of town), a tin-separating plant is operated by Pilbara Tin Pty Ltd, and the Old Comet Gold Mine (11km to the S) is reminiscent of the boom days. The government

offices built in 1895 have been classified for preservation by the National Trust (WA).

Marchantia *see* Hepatophyta

mardo *see* native cats, etc.

marlins *see* fishes, bony

Marree SA This small township is located SE of LAKE EYRE where the BIRDSVILLE TRACK meets the central Australian railway. It was the main centre for camel caravans crossing the desert areas of the inland and attained importance as the railhead for cattle mobs driven down the Track from south-western QLD. The name Marree comes from an Aboriginal word meaning 'opossum place'. The region is typically arid, with an average annual rainfall of only 155mm.

Mareeba QLD (population 6 309 in 1981) The major urban centre on the ATHERTON TABLELAND, Mareeba is situated in the valley of the BARRON RIVER, at an elevation of 335m above sea level, and is noted for the production of tobacco. It is located on the Kennedy Highway, 64km by road WSW of CAIRNS, and has an average annual rainfall of 928mm which occurs mainly during the summer months, with a marked dry season from April to October. The area receives irrigation water by gravitational channels from the Tinaroo Falls Dam on the upper Barron. As well as tobacco, the district produces maize, vegetables, peanuts and timber.

Maria Island TAS Located off the SE coast, and originally a penal settlement (1825-32 and 1842-50), this island is now a national park (9 672ha). It was sighted by Abel TASMAN in 1642 and was named in honour of the wife of Anthony VAN DIEMEN, the Governor-in-Chief of the Dutch East India Co. in Batavia. In 1825, Lieutenant-Governor ARTHUR selected the N end of the island as a second convict settlement, to relieve pressure on MACQUARIE HARBOUR. It was named Darlington in honour of the Governor of NSW and has been well preserved. In the 1880s there was an attempt to develop wine making, fruit growing, fishing, sawmilling and a cement industry; these flourished until 1895 but then declined. Again in the 1920s there was an attempt to develop the island; a cement industry was established, but it closed in 1930, after which livestock grazing was the sole activity until Maria Is was acquired as a national park in 1972. It is planned to restore the historic landmarks and to develop it as a wildlife sanctuary. The island consists of two parts joined by a narrow sandy isthmus; in the N is Mt Maria, the highest point, rising to 709m.

marigold *see* Compositae

marine worms *see* annelids

Maroochydore QLD (combined population of Maroochydore and MOOLOOLABA 17 460 in 1981) This holiday resort on the SUNSHINE COAST, at the mouth of the Maroochy River, is situated 11km E of the Bruce Highway, some 20km N of CALOUNDRA and 114km by road N of Brisbane. The S parts of the town merge with the neighbouring beach resort, Mooloolaba. The district offers much to the tourist and holiday-maker. The town name comes from Aboriginal words meaning 'home of the black swan'.

Marsden, Samuel (1765-1838) Clergyman, missionary and farmer. He was born in Yorkshire, won a reputation in early manhood as a lay preacher, and was assisted to study for the priesthood by the Elland Society, an evangelical group within the Church of England. He came to NSW in 1794 as assistant to the Rev. Richard Johnson, and was appointed to PARRAMATTA, where, apart from travels abroad, he lived for the rest of his life. In religious activities he is best remembered for promotion of missionary work in New Zealand, which he visited seven times in addition to encouraging the work of the Church Missionary Society there. He was horrified at the moral tone of NSW, soon despaired of reforming the convicts and failed in attempts to convert the Aborigines. In fact he is remembered in NSW less for his work as a clergyman than for the severity of the punishments which he ordered as a magistrate, for his work in farming and sheep breeding and for his disputes with Governor MACQUARIE and others.

Reverend Samuel Marsden

An enthusiastic farmer almost from the time of his arrival, he wrote an excellent report on the colony's agriculture in 1798, followed this up with other reports to Sir Joseph BANKS and Governor KING, and was described by the latter as 'the best practical farmer in the country'. He obtained land both by grants and by purchase, and by 1805 possessed about 700ha and over 1 000 sheep. In sheep breeding he concentrated on large-framed breeds such as Suffolks, and was concerned mainly with the production of heavier carcases. However, in time he began to pay more attention to the production of fine wool. In 1808, during a visit to England, he had wool from his flocks made into a suit, and so impressed George III that he was given some Merinos from the royal stud. While his contribution to the wool industry was not nearly so great as John MAC-ARTHUR's it was nevertheless considerable.

He was a firm supporter of Governor BLIGH, but clashed repeatedly with Macquarie, of whose emancipist policy he disapproved. Two particularly notable quarrels arose from his indignant refusal to serve on the board of trustees for the turnpike road to Parramatta in company with two prominent ex-convicts, Andrew Thompson and Simeon Lord, and from his refusal to read from his pulpit a proclamation against food speculators. He was one of the chief complainants against Macquarie, and gave hostile witness against him during the inquiry by John BIGGE. He later clashed also with Governors BRISBANE and DARLING.
Further reading: Johnstone, S.M. *Samuel Marsden.* Angus & Robertson, Sydney, 1932; Yarwood, A.T. *Samuel Marsden.* Oxford University press, Melbourne, 1968.

Marsh, Graham (1944-) Golfer.
Born at KALGOORLIE in WA, Marsh might well have become a cricketer like his brother Rodney (wicket-keeper for Australia) had it not been for a broken arm. To strengthen his arm in preparation for a return to cricket, he took up golf. He decided to give up his teaching job in Perth in 1968 to become a professional golfer and in 1973 became the first golfer to win more than $100 000 in a year without playing one game on the American circuit. He concentrated most of his efforts on the Asian circuit and in 1976 won seven tournaments, four of them in Japan, where he was held in the highest esteem. In 1977, he won the World Match Play championship, had his first success on the lucrative American circuit, winning the Heritage Classic, continued his domination of the Asian circuit, and back home was voted Australian Sportsman of the Year. His extraordinary success in Japan continued throughout the late 1970s and in 1981 he scored his 20th Japanese victory with a win in the Sapporo Open. Although successful internationally it was not until the 1982 South Australian Open that he won a professional tournament in Australia. In the same year he won the Australian Masters, the Mitsubishi Galant (Japan), the Dunhill Queensland Open and the PEA championship, and he was made an MBE for his services to sport.

Marsh, Rodney William (1947-)
Cricketer. Born in WA, he first played for that State in 1968, and in his first match (against the West Indies) scored 110 not out. His first Test series was in the 1970-71 season. An aggressive left-handed batsman, noted particularly for his merciless square-cutting of short balls, he had by the end of the 1982-83 season scored 3 558 runs in 92 Tests, including three centuries, at an average of 26.75 per innings.

Rodney Marsh

However his fame rests mainly on his performance as a wicketkeeper. Although solidly-built, he has been noted for remarkable agility, and by the end of the 1982-83 season had been responsible for 334 dismissals (322 catches and 12 stumpings) in Test matches, these figures marking a record among players of all countries.

Marshall, Alan (1902-1984) Author.
Born at Noorat VIC, Marshall was crippled by polio as a child. Although he worked for some years as a factory accountant and then as an army education lecturer, he was a free-lance writer for most of his life. His works include one novel, *How Beautiful Are Thy Feet* (1949), which was set in the time of the Depression; three autobiographical works, namely *I Can Jump Puddles* (1955), *This Is The Grass* (1962) and *In Mine Own Heart* (1963); a book of Aboriginal myths, *People of the Dreamtime* (1952); and collections of short stories such as *Tell Us About the Turkey, Joe* (1946), *Hammers Over the Anvil* (1975) and *The Complete Short Stories of Alan Marshall* (1977). He is one of the most widely read of Australian authors, both in Australia and overseas, with his books appearing in about 20 countries and *I Can Jump Puddles* in particular having been widely translated. He was made an OBE in 1972.
Further reading: Marks, H. *I Can Jump Oceans: The World of Alan Marshall.* Nelson, West Melbourne, 1976.

Marshall, Alan John 'Jock' (1911-67)
Zoologist and author. Despite the loss of an arm in a shooting accident when a boy, Marshall served as a captain in the Australian Army Intelligence Service, leading a task force behind Japanese lines in New Guinea. He later became Foundation Professor of Zoology at Monash University. He wrote several books on zoological and other topics, including *Journey Among Men* (1962), written in co-

operation with the artist Russell DRYSDALE. He was prominent in conservation activities.

marsupial mice *see* marsupials; native cats, etc.

marsupial mole Belonging to the order Polyprotodonta (family Notoryctidae), the marsupial mole, *Notoryctes typhlops*, is the most remarkable of all MARSUPIALS in that, as a result of convergent evolution, it bears a striking resemblance to the placental mole of Europe and Africa. The head and body measure 14cm long, and the short, horny, ringed tail 2.5cm. The hind-foot has five toes with claws on three, whilst the fore-foot is spade-like with five toes. The muzzle is pointed and has a horny shield on the upper surface. There are no eyes, and the ears are visible externally only as small openings. The iridescent fur varies from yellowish-white to golden orange.

Marsupial moles are apparently rare animals (or it may be that they are just difficult to find). They occur in sandridge desert regions. Their food consists mainly of ants, beetle larvae and other insects.

Marsupial mole, *Notoryctes typhlops*

marsupials This group of MAMMALS, belonging to the subclass Metatheria, is now confined to Australasia and the Americas. In Australia and New Guinea they are the dominant mammals, though there are almost as many species of EUTHERIAN MAMMALS (RODENTS, BATS, DINGO) in Australia as marsupials. Authors vary in their estimates of the number of Australian marsupials but Strahan (*see below*) lists 130 species.

Marsupials give birth to very undeveloped young which they then suckle, usually within a pouch (marsupium). The young are firmly (though not immovably) attached to the teats till they reach a stage roughly equivalent to that of eutherian mammals at birth. Then they leave the pouch and teat, returning to them to feed at intervals. The egg is yolky compared with that of a eutherian mammal. In most marsupials the embryo makes little intimate contact with the walls of the uterus, and the yolk sac of the embryo absorbs fluids from the uterine wall. In NATIVE CATS (*Dasyurus* species) there is a placenta-like connection between the yolk sac and the wall, and in BANDICOOTS (*Perameles* species) a more complex placenta is formed. It is therefore misleading to separate the eutherian mammals as placental mammals though this is commonly done.

A quokka on Rottnest Island, WA

The gestation period is not necessarily short. It is no more than 38 days in even the largest KANGAROOS but in the marsupial mouse (*Antechinus* species) it is 25 to 31 days which is longer than that of a similarly sized shrew—the ecological eutherian equivalent of the marsupial mouse. In some marsupials an embryo will stop developing and remain quiescent in the uterus until some stimulus brings about the resumption of development. This is called a diapause. It was first studied among marsupials in the quokka, *Setonix brachyurus*, a small wallaby. While the quokka is nursing one offspring in the pouch, a small embryo is held in the uterus. This results from a mating in the summer immediately after the pouch young has been born. When the pouch young is removed so that the mother is no longer being suckled, the embryo will resume development, but the proportion that do so is reduced with time. Only a small proportion result in a birth if the pouch young remains in the pouch till August, the usual time at which it leaves. But the diapausing embryo will quickly replace any pouch young that is lost soon after it enters the pouch. This may occur, for example, because of a drought. With this arrangement the quokka, which is a seasonal breeder, does not have to wait till the following summer before she can reproduce again. In the red kangaroo, *Macropus rufus,* which breeds throughout the year, many females carry a diapausing embryo for the 230 days that the pouch young is suckling within the pouch. About 30 days before the pouch young is due to vacate the pouch the embryo resumes development, and is born soon after its older sibling leaves the pouch for good. The mother usually mates again shortly after the birth. In this way the red kangaroo, which lives in an arid environment with frequent food shortages, ensures that there is a regular supply of young. It is possible, therefore, that a female can have three young in three stages of development: a diapausing embryo, a suckling pouch young, and an occasionally suckling young at heel. Embryonic diapause is known to occur in some other kangaroos and wallabies, and some POSSUMS.

Newly born marsupials are very small (brush-tailed possum, *Trichosurus vulpecula*, 0.2g, mother about 1.5kg; red kangaroo, 1.5g, mother about 50kg) with well-developed forelimbs but underdeveloped hind-limbs. The skin is naked. After birth the young marsupial ('joey' in the case of a kangaroo) crawls through the mother's hair to the teat, without any help, and attaches itself firmly to suckle.

Kangaroo and joey

The structure of the reproductive organs of marsupials differs from those of other mammals and, indeed, is the only true criterion of the marsupial as not all marsupials have pouches, and as some other mammals do have a form of pouch. In the female there are two vaginas which join at the cloaca (the common opening of the gut and the reproductive tract) and two uteri (wombs). In the eutherians there is only one vagina and one uterus. In the male marsupial the tubules which lead from the testes to the penis do not loop round the ureters (the tubules which carry urine from the kidneys), as they do in eutherians. Furthermore, the scrotum of male marsupials is placed in front of the penis. Strangely, the young marsupial is not born through either of the vaginas; a passage opens between them as a birth canal, and heals again later, except in kangaroos where it becomes a permanent feature.

All living marsupials have two small bones, the epipubic bones (vestigal in the TASMANIAN WOLF, *Thylacinus cynocephalus*), projecting forwards from the pelvis. These help to support the pouch though they are found in both sexes, and also in MONOTREME MAMMALS. Their skulls differ from eutherian skulls in various ways; the most easily recognisable of which is the in-turned angular process on the jaw just below the point where the jaw articulates. They also differ in their dentition for marsupials are descended from mammals that had more teeth (50) than do eutherians (44 teeth). The difference lies in the incisor teeth which in eutherian mammals are never more than six in the upper jaw, and six in the lower one. Furthermore, marsupials do not have milk teeth followed by permanent teeth, apart from one cheek tooth in each jaw which is shed in early life.

Classification The marsupials are classified partly on the basis of their teeth, and partly on the structure of their feet. In the polyprotodont marsupials (for example, the native cats) there are three or more incisor teeth on each side of the two jaws; in diprotodont marsupials (for example, kangaroos and WOMBATS) there are six incisors in the upper jaw, but only two, which both point forwards, in the lower jaw. In syndactylous marsupials, toes two and three of the hind-foot are bound together as one, up to the claws—the resulting double claw is often used as a comb for grooming. In didactylous marsupials these toes are separate.

The classification of living marsupials varies from author to author. The following is the one used by Strahan (*see below*):

Subclass Metatheria or Marsupialia
  Order Polyprotodonta
    Suborder Didelphimorphia (opossums) All American Didactylous
    Suborder Dasyuromorphia. Didactylous
      Family Dasyuridae (native cats) Australasia (40)
      Family Thylacinidae (Tasmanian wolf) TAS (1)
      Family Myrmecobiidae (numbat) Australia (1)
    Suborder Notoryctemorphia. Didactylous
      Family Notoryctidae (MARSUPIAL MOLE) Australia (1)
    Suborder Peramelomorphia. Syndactylous
    Superfamily Perameloidea
      Family Peramelidae (bandicoots) Australasia (9)
      Family Thylacomyidae (bilbies) Australia (2)
  Order Diprotodonta All Australasian. All syndactylous
    Superfamily Vombatoidea
      Family Phascolarctidae (koala) (1)
      Family Vombatidae (wombats) (3)
    Superfamily Phalangeroidea
      Family Petauridae (large gliders and ringtail possums) (11)
      Family Phalangeridae (brushtail possums and cuscuses) (6)
      Family Burramyidae (pygmy possums and feathertail gliders) (6)
    Superfamily Tarsipedoidea
      Family Tarsipedidae (honey-possum) (1)
    Superfamily Macropodoidea
      Family Potoroidae (bettongs, potoroos and rat-kangaroos) (9)
      Family Macropodidae (remaining kangaroos and wallabies) (39)

(Numbers in brackets refer to number of species listed by Strahan.)

Origin of the Australasian marsupials The marsupials arose in North America during the Cretaceous period (*see* mammals). They spread into South America but disappeared in North America till the comparatively recent invasion across the Isthmus of Panama. They also spread into Europe. There are two opposing opinions about their entry into the Australian region. One holds that they entered from Asia by 'island hopping', the other that they entered through GONDWANALAND. The fossil record of marsupials in Australia is poor, stretching back only to the late Oligocene period 30 million years ago, and most of the fossils that have been found are quite closely related to modern forms. The nature of the first Australian marsupials can only be guessed at, but they probably resembled the didelphid opossums of America, carnivorous mammals that have changed little since the origin of the marsupials. Whatever they were like, they arrived in a country with no other mammals, except possibly MONOTREMES. They were consequently able to evolve in many directions to fill all the empty niches. Thus there are now kangaroos and wallabies which fill a role similar to that of antelope and cattle in other continents, the thylacine resembling the predatory wolf or dog, the Tasmanian devil playing the part of the badger or wolverine, and the marsupial mole resembling the eutherian moles so closely that they are easily confused. There is no Australasian aquatic marsupial though it is possible that one has existed in the past, without leaving any trace.

There were once many more kinds of marsupials than there are now. Some of these extinct marsupials were much larger than any living. *Diprotodon*, which was a wombat-like animal about the size of a bullock, survived till about 11 000 years ago. At about the same time there was a large, carnivorous marsupial lion, *Thylacoleo*, and browsing (as opposed to grazing) kangaroos reaching a height of 3m. The extinct wombat, *Phascolanus*, was about the size of a pig. Two alternative explanations are given for the disappearance of these large marsupials (and for the similar disappearance of large eutherians elsewhere). One is that there was some climatic change with which the animals could not cope. The other explanation is that they were destroyed by early man, using fire, traps and weapons, as he spread into new areas (the so-called Pleistocene Overkill).

Marsupials as mammals In the past many biologists have regarded marsupials as less efficient animals than eutherians. This view has recently been attacked by Dawson (*see below*) and others who point out the nicety with which the kangaroos, for example, are adapted to their arid, hot environment. The regulation of body temperature is extremely efficient though it was once believed that kangaroos were poor thermo-regulators because of their generally lower temperatures and lower basal metabolism. Similarly, they are extremely efficient in regulating and conserving water. Finally, a bounding kangaroo uses energy more efficiently than a galloping eutherian. Marsupials should not be regarded as primitive mammals but simply as different mammals.

Further reading: Ride, W.D.L. *A Guide to the Native Mammals of Australia.* Oxford University Press, Melbourne, 1970; Tyndale-Biscoe, H. *Life of Marsupials.* Arnold, London, 1973; Dawson, T.J. 'Kangaroos' in *Scientific American.* (vol 237, no 2, August 1977); Sharman, G.B. 'Marsupials' in *Encyclopaedia of the Animal World.* (vol 13) Bay Books, Sydney,

1977; Strahan, R. (ed.) *The Australian Museum Complete Book of Australian Mammals.* Angus & Robertson, Sydney, 1983.

Martens, Conrad (1801-78) Artist. He was born in the UK into an artistic family—both his brothers, Henry and J.W. Martens, were painters. His teacher was Copley Fielding. In 1832 he joined Captain Fitzroy on the survey vessel *Beagle* as Charles DARWIN's artist, replacing Augustus Earle, who was suffering from ill health. On conclusion of his contract Martens emigrated to Sydney in 1835 and settled in The Rocks as an art teacher. He became Assistant Parliamentary Librarian in 1863, a position which supplemented the irregular income he received from painting and which he held until his death. Martens produced oil paintings of Sydney Harbour and its environs in a style similar to the work of Claude Lorraine and Turner. His watercolours are generally considered to have greater merit and are of considerable historical value. Although he did work in and around the DARLING DOWNS, he preferred painting scenes of Sydney, and these also provided the basis for a series of lithographic views which he produced at irregular intervals in order to meet his financial commitments.

Martin, Sir James (1820-86) Premier and Chief Justice of NSW. Born in County Cork, Ireland, he was brought to NSW in 1821, when his father obtained a position as horse trainer to Governor BRISBANE. In 1836 he became a journalist on the staff of the *Australian*, and two years later published *The Australian Sketch-Book.* However, he decided that the law was the best means by which one of his lowly birth could rise to wealth and social prominence; he was admitted as a solicitor in 1845, was called to the Bar in 1856 and became a QC in 1857.

Elected to the Legislative Council in 1848, Martin was a member of the committee which drew up the constitution of NSW, and in 1856 was elected to the first Legislative Assembly. In many respects he proved conservative in politics, opposing the granting of manhood suffrage, the Land Acts of 1861 and the abolition of grants to religious organisations, but he was a firm supporter of PARKES' Public Schools Act of 1866. He was Attorney-General in two of COWPER's Ministries, and was Premier of NSW in 1863-65, 1866-68 and 1870-72. An assertive, self-willed and outspoken man, proud of his success and impatient with opponents, he aroused strong feelings of antagonism among many of his fellow politicians. In 1873 he was appointed Chief Justice, and filled that position with distinction until his death. Martin Place (now Martin Plaza) in Sydney was named after him. *Further reading:* Grainger, E. *Martin of Martin Place.* Alpha Books, Sydney, 1970.

martins *see* swallows, etc.

Mary Kathleen QLD (population 830 in 1981), A uranium-mining centre where ore

was extracted by open cut methods and where yellowcake was produced between 1958 and 1982, it is located in the NW of the State, in the Selwyn Range, on the Barkly Highway midway between MOUNT ISA and CLONCURRY, 1783km by road NW of Brisbane. The surrounding area is rough range country with an average annual rainfall of less than 500mm, concentrated in the summer months; a long dry season is experienced each year and droughts are not uncommon. The ore body was discovered in 1954 and named after the wife of one of the discoverers, Norman McConachy. The town was developed as a planned settlement, specially designed to accommodate the mine workers and their families, with modern facilities and with reticulated water supplied from a dam built on the nearby Corella River, a tributary of the FLINDERS RIVER. Mining at Mary Kathleen commenced in 1958, though activities were suspended in 1963, mainly because of excess uranium on world markets, and the mine was then placed on a care and maintenance basis. Commercial production re-commenced in 1976 and 359 tonnes of uranium were produced in that year, when it comprised Australia's only source of uranium. In the late 1970s the output expanded and by 1980, when the NARBALEK mine in NT commenced production, Mary Kathleen produced 708 tonnes of uranium, accounting for 45 per cent of Australia's total output. However, in September 1982, mining of the ore body ceased, the treatment plant produced its last yellowcake, and in early 1983 the operations were completely wound down, the equipment and everything else on the site was sold, thus bringing to an end the somewhat checkered 24-year career of this uranium mining venture, jointly owned by Conzinc Riotinto of Australia and the Australian Atomic Energy Commission.

Mary River QLD This is a perennial E coastal stream situated in the SE of the State, with its headwaters located in the Jimna and Conondale Ranges that lie inland from the SUNSHINE COAST, W of NAMBOUR. The stream flows in a general N course for over 320km to a swampy estuary on the Great Sandy Strait, W of FRASER ISLAND and about 40km downstream from the city of MARYBOROUGH. Rainfall over the basin is high: GYMPIE, located in the middle reaches, has an average annual rainfall of 1 161mm, and Maryborough 1 200mm. Though the rain occurs in all months, there is a marked summer maximum and hence this is the season when floods can occur. Much of the steeply sloping headwater country is forested and in the 19th century cedar logs were floated down the river. Forestry is still important in these upland parts, while on the alluvial flats of the valley there is intensive farming of sugar cane, tropical fruits and dairy pastures. Borumba Dam, located on the headwaters at the S of the catchment, completed in 1964 and with a capacity of 42 600ML, regulates the flow of the main stream, provides water for crop and pasture irrigation on the river flats, supplies the city of Gympie and provides flood protection for low-lying areas which were formerly inundated in times of high river.

Maryborough QLD (population 20 111 in 1981) A city, port and industrial centre, Maryborough is situated on the MARY RIVER about 40km upstream from its estuary on Great Sandy Strait. It is a city of tree-lined streets and parks, located on the Bruce Highway, 274km N of Brisbane, 92km N of GYMPIE and 119km by road SSE of BUNDABERG. It is a major commercial and service centre for a rich rural hinterland which produces sugar cane, citrus fruit, pineapples, dairy products and honey. Timber is also an important industry and there is a major reafforestation development at Tuan Creek, 24km SE of the city. It is also a fish marketing centre, claimed as second in importance in the State after Brisbane. Located at a latitude of 26°S, the city experiences warm to hot conditions throughout the year, with an average annual rainfall of 1 200mm which occurs all year round with a concentration in the summer season; February is the wettest month (181mm average), August the driest (41mm). As early as the 1860s Maryborough began to develop industrially and now has several timber mills, a flour mill, a milk factory, a foundry, an abattoir and a sugar mill. The Ululah Lagoon, adjacent to the city golf links, is a scenic bird sanctuary for black swans, geese, duck and snipe. Teddington Weir on Tinana Creek, 15km S, is the source of the city's water supply and is a popular recreation and picnic area. In 1863 coal was discovered in the Burrum area, about 30km NW of Maryborough, and the mines now supply the Howard power station. To the NE of the city, 34km away, is the Port of Maryborough, where ferries leave for the trip to FRASER ISLAND and where deep-sea vessels berth at Urangan. The coastal belt N of the city, facing HERVEY BAY, comprises a line of beach resorts for year-round aquatic recreation. Two national parks are located in the Hervey Bay area: Woodgate (5 498ha) on the N side of the Burrum River estuary and Burrum (1 618ha) on the S. The National Trust (QLD) has listed several buildings in the city for preservation, including the adult education centre and high school, some homes and the courthouse.

Maryborough VIC (population 7 858 in 1981) This city is located in the central uplands of the State on the Pyrenees Highway, 166km by road NW of Melbourne and 48km W of CASTLEMAINE. It is a rail centre, 187km (via Castlemaine) from Melbourne, with lines linking it to BALLARAT in the S, ARARAT in the W, Castlemaine in the E and the MURRAY RIVER (via the Mallee region) in the N and NW. At an elevation of 254m above sea level, it has an average annual rainfall of 526mm, spread throughout the year, but with a winter-spring maximum; June is the wettest month (57mm average), January the driest (29mm). It started as a gold-mining town in the 1850s, when it had a population of 30 000, and was originally called Simsons after two brothers who were grazing settlers. It was renamed Maryborough after the Irish town, became a borough in 1857 and was proclaimed a city in 1961. It is a business and service centre for a mixed farming and pastoral region. Among its secondary industries are a woollen mill, engineering workshops and dairy processing works. The National Trust (VIC) classified several buildings in the city including the courthouse, the town hall, the post office, the scout hall, the band rotunda, the Chinese funeral ovens (a relic of the mining days) and the fire station bell tower. A great attraction is the annual Highland Gathering held on New Year's Day.

Maryvale VIC This township in the LATROBE RIVER valley, located E of YALLOURN, 10km N of MORWELL and 8km W of TRARALGON off the Princes Highway, is the site of a large paper and pulp mill which utilises timber from the eucalypt forests in the adjacent areas of GIPPSLAND together with softwoods imported from pine growing regions in SE Australia. The town took its name from a property settled in the 1840s which was probably named after the squatter's wife.

Mathinna TAS This small township located on the upper reaches of the South ESK RIVER, in the NE of the State, was a major gold-mining centre from the 1880s until the early part of this century, and is now an area of extensive forestry development. It was named after an Aboriginal girl found wandering in the bush who was later 'adopted' by the then Governor of TAS, Sir John FRANKLIN.

Maurice, Furnley (1881-1942) Poet. This was the pen-name used by Frank Wilmot. Born and educated in Melbourne, he worked as a bookseller and publishing manager. His first notable volume of poetry was *Unconditioned Songs* (1913), which was published anonymously. Other include *To God: From the Weary Nations* (1917), *Eyes of Vigilance* (1920), *Arrows of Longing* (1921) and *Melbourne Odes* (1934). His poems reveal him as both a lover of nature and a social reformer. They are uneven in quality, many of them needing in particular to be more firmly structured. Nevertheless, the best of them entitle him to be considered as one of the leading Australian poets of his time.

Mawson This meteorological station and research base (latitude 67°36'S) located on MacRobertson Land, ANTARCTICA, is operated by the Australian National Antarctic Research Expeditions (ANARE). It was established in 1954 as Australia's first permanent research station on the Antarctic continent and was named in honour of Sir Douglas MAWSON.

Mawson, Sir Douglas (1882-1958) Scientist and Antarctic explorer. He was born in Yorkshire, but when he was four years old his family came to Sydney, where he was educated, graduating from the University of Sydney in mining engineering in 1902. In 1905 he was appointed as a lecturer at the University of Adelaide, where he later became Professor of Geology. Although his teaching, administrative and research activities in this position were of great merit, he is chiefly remembered for exploration and scientific discoveries in ANTARCTICA.

His achievements in Antarctica began in 1907, when, as a member of Shackleton's expedition, he took part in the first ascent of Mt Erebus and the first journey to the magnetic South Pole. In 1911 he was appointed as leader of the Australian Antarctic expedition. Late in 1912, with B.E.S. Ninnis and X. Mertz, he set out to explore the area W of the magnetic South Pole, but had a series of disasters. Ninnis and Mertz died about 62km from the main base, and Mawson's journey back to the base was perhaps the greatest feat of endurance in the history of Antarctic exploration.

His final work in Antarctica was in 1929-31 as leader of the British, Australian and New Zealand Antarctic Research Expedition (BANZARE). The present chief base of the Australian National Antarctic Research Expeditions (ANARE), on MacRobertson Land, is named MAWSON.
Further reading: Taylor, T.G. *Douglas Mawson.* Oxford University Press, Melbourne, 1962; Mawson, Sir Douglas *The Home of the Blizzard.* (new edn) Rigby, Adelaide, 1969.

May, Phillip William 'Phil' (1864-1903) Black and white artist. Born near Leeds, England, he had drawings accepted by the *Yorkshire Post* at the age of 14, and after further success in London, was engaged in 1885 by the Sydney BULLETIN. His drawings for that journal over the following nine years provide a humorous and often satirical commentary on national events and attitudes, and established him as one of the most notable black and white artists in Australian history. Returning to London, he contributed to a number of periodicals there, including *Punch.* Of the many collections of his drawings, perhaps those which give the best overall impression of his talents are: *The Phil May Album* (1899), *Phil May in Australia* and *The Phil May Folio* (1904) and *Humorists of the Pencil, Phil May* (1908).

mayflies These exopterygote INSECTS belong to the order Ephemeroptera, which contains about 124 Australian species in five families; most species belong to the families Baetidae and Leptophlebiidae. The nymphs live in freshwater and the adults are rarely found far from water sources such as pools and rivers. The nymphal stages may last for one or two years but the adults rarely live for more than a day or two, a characteristic which is reflected in the name of the order—'short-lived wings'.

The adults have two pairs of roughly triangular membranous wings and the fore-wings are much larger than the hind-wings. The flight is fluttering and in the cooler parts of Australia there are swarming flights for mating, usually above the water in which the fertilised female lays her eggs. The abdomen carries two, sometimes three, segmented 'tails'. The wings cannot be folded back over the abdomen when the insect is at rest. Mayflies are unique in that there are two winged stages: the dull coloured winged subimago (the 'dun' of game fishermen) and the complete imago which emerges from it about one day after the insect leaves the water ('spinner'). The nymphs also have three long 'tails' but also possess a series of gills on the front abdominal segments. Various species are found in a wide range of waters but each species is adapted to its particular habitat: some cling to stones in rapid streams, some are roughly shrimp-shaped and others burrow into organically rich silt. Most feed on organic debris, diatoms and algae but a few are carnivores. The adults do not feed and their mouthparts are vestigial.

Nymphs and adults are important food for many kinds of freshwater fish, and the artificial flies of trout fishermen are often modelled on duns and spinners.

Meale, Richard Graham (1932-)

Composer. Meale emerged as one of the leading figures in the new wave of Australian composers which appeared in the 1960s. His output is relatively small, and it is typical of him that frequent reassessment of his own works has resulted in his rejection of many of his earlier compositions. In the early 1960s, studies at the Institute of Ethnomusicology at the University of California in Los Angeles brought him into direct contact with Asian music, and as a result Indonesian and Japanese music were to play a creative role in his own stylistic development; this is apparent in such works as *Clouds Now and Then* (1969), *Images* (*Nagauta*) (1966) and *Soon It Will Die* (1969). His major symphonic work, *Nocturnes* (1967), for solo vibraphone, harp, celeste and orchestra, has been followed by chamber-proportioned works including *Interiors/Exteriors* (1970) for two pianos and three percussion, *Incredible Floridas* (*Homage to Arthur Rimbaud*) (1971) for flute, clarinet, violin, cello, piano and percussion, *Evocations* (1974) for oboe and chamber orchestra, and *String Quartet* (1975), *Viridan* (1979) and a second *String Quartet* (1980). He further distinguished himself in the 1960s through his Australian Broadcasting Commission (ABC) programmes on new and non-Western music, his encouragement of new composers through his International Society for Contemporary Music (ISCM) concerns and his own performances as a pianist of contemporary works. Since 1969 he has been resident in Adelaide. He was appointed MBE in 1971 for his contribution to music.
Further reading: Wood, E. 'Richard Meale' in *Australian Composition in the Twentieth Century*. Callaway, F. & Tunley, D. (eds) Oxford University Press, Melbourne, 1978.

measures *see* weights, etc.

Mecoptera *see* scorpion flies

Medibank, Medicare *see* social services

medics *see* Papilionaceae; weeds

Meekatharra WA (population 989 in 1981)

This small inland town on the Great Northern Highway is situated 762km NNE of PERTH and 538km by road NE of GERALDTON. It was established as a gold and copper mining centre in the 1890s and there are many abandoned mines in the district as evidence of its past importance. At an elevation of 517m above sea level, it experiences hot summer conditions, with January being the hottest month (over 36°C average), and a low average annual rainfall of 209mm. It is the rail terminus of a line from Geraldton through Mt Magnet (a distance of 545km), though now the trains carry only freight. Also, it is a centre for the FLYING DOCTOR SERVICE and a business town for a large sheep and cattle grazing area.

Megaloptera *see* alder flies

megapodes *see* mound birds

Melba, Dame Nellie (Helen Porter Mitchell) (1861-1931)

Soprano. Born in Burnley near Melbourne, she was one of the most famous operatic sopranos of all time. Her parents were musical but it was Pietro Cecchi, an Italian tenor and her teacher from 1879, who first urged her to make a career in singing. Early in 1882, however, after her mother's death, she accompanied her father to MACKAY in QLD where she met Charles Frederick Nesbitt Armstrong, manager of a sugar plantation. They were married in 1882 and a son was born in 1883. The marriage foundered and she returned to Melbourne when her son was three months old. Here she resumed her lessons with Cecchi and made her first concert appearances. When her father was appointed Victorian Commissioner to the Indian and Colonial Exhibition in London, she sailed with him, in March 1886, intent on an operatic career.

Disappointed by not being able to find a suitable teacher in London, she went to Paris where she auditioned for the famous singing teacher, Madame Mathilde Marchesi, and was accepted. She sang for the first time as 'Madame Melba' (an Italian-sounding adaptation of the name of her home city) in December 1886, and made a triumphant operatic début in *Rigoletto* in Brussels in October 1887. She was acclaimed in Paris as Ophelia in *Hamlet* and in London as Juliet in *Romeo and Juliet* in 1889. This was the beginning of her long and close association with Covent Garden, where she sang for many years in every season. She was equally successful on the Continent, from Milan to St Petersburg, as well as in the USA. She toured Australia in 1902-1903 and divided her time between Europe and Australia from 1909. She brought the Melba-Williamson Opera Company to Australia in 1911, and the proceeds from one of her Melbourne appear-

Dame Nellie Melba

Courtesy of A.I.S. Canberra

ances in 1913 provided the University's Conservatorium of Music with its Melba Hall.

W.J. Henderson, the critic of the New York *Sun*, who heard Melba at the peak of her career, has left some of the most revealing descriptions of her voice:

Its beauty, its power, its clarion quality differed from the fluty notes of Patti. It was not a better voice, but a different one. It had splendour. The tones glowed with a star-like brilliance. They flamed with a white flame. Her voice was of the full range needed for the coloratura and light lyric roles. It extended from B flat below the clef to the high F. The scale was beautifully equalised throughout and there was not the slightest change in the quality from bottom to top. All the tones were forward; there was never even a suspicion of throatiness. The full, flowing and facile emission of the tones has never been surpassed

As revealed on the early sound recordings, her trill, in its purity and evenness, has undoubtedly remained unsurpassed. Her dramatic interpretative powers in various roles seem to have been superficial, but she conquered rather by the brilliance and fluency of her ornamentation and the sensuous spell of her voice.

Throughout her long singing career, her voice retained this sensuous purity, and she could claim over 25 operas in her repertory. She made her final Covent Garden appearance in June 1926. She was an extraordinarily strong-willed and imperious personality, and much has been written about her in this respect. She died in Sydney and was buried at Lilydale, near Melbourne.
Further reading: Hetherington, J. *Melba: A Biography*. Cheshire, Melbourne, 1967.

Melbourne VIC (population 2 578 527 in 1981) The State capital and second-largest urban centre in Australia, Melbourne is located on the N shore of PORT PHILLIP BAY. The central business district of the city is located on the N bank of the YARRA RIVER about 6km from its estuary. The city was named in 1837 by the Governor of NSW, Sir Richard BOURKE, after the then British Prime Minister, William Lamb, Lord Melbourne.

History Port Phillip Bay was discovered by Lieutenant John MURRAY in 1802 when he brought his sailing ship, the *Lady Nelson*, into the inlet and landed near the present site of Sorrento. Later in the same year, Matthew FLINDERS explored the bay and reported favourably on the surrounding countryside. In 1803 David COLLINS, with a party of British settlers and convicts, landed on the E shore of the bay, again near the site of Sorrento, but their attempt to establish a township was unsuccessful and was abandoned a few months later. It was not until the 1830s that the roots of permanent settlement were established. In 1835, John BATMAN, a pastoralist from LAUN- CESTON in TAS, landed at Indented Head at the SW of the bay and arranged a 'treaty' with the Aborigines to 'purchase' about 240 000ha of land. Later in the same year, a second group of settlers from Launceston, led by John Pascoe Fawkner, established a camp on the Yarra. Both Batman and Fawkner were illegal squatters and Governor Bourke, whilst warn- ing the settlers of their trespass, realised he could not reverse the tide of settlement. He did, however, cancel Batman's 'purchase' and in 1836 sent William LONSDALE to the settle- ment as resident magistrate, with surveyors to lay out a town plan and arrange land sales. The design of the original street plan, made by Richard Hoddle in 1837, determined the pattern of the city core as it stands today. He laid out a grid of four long wide streets and eight shorter cross-streets on the N side of the Yarra River; the long streets, on a NE-SW axis, parallel to the river, were named Flinders (nearest the river, in honour of Matthew Flinders), Collins (after David Collins), Bourke (after the Colony's governor) and Lonsdale (after the resident magistrate).

Growth and expansion The initial develop- ment of the city was fairly slow. Some suburbs, such as St Kilda and Brighton, were started in the 1840s, but the separation of VIC from the colony of NSW in 1850 and the discovery of gold in 1851 brought a spate of fortune-seekers and gave a spurt to the town's growth. Though mining declined in subsequent decades and many miners left VIC for other gold-rush centres, Melbourne's expansion continued. From 1860 to 1890 it experienced a period of remarkable growth based partly on pastoral and agricultural development in the State (particularly wheat growing in the WIMMERA), and partly on the development of secondary industry in the city. Urban growth spread over the gently undulating plain N and E of the bay, guided by the location of rail routes and the tramway system. By 1891 the city con- tained over 490 000 people, but the economic

An oil painting of Spring Street in Melbourne by Charles Conder

depression of the 1890s reduced the pace of the city's growth and it was not until the first decade of this century that its population passed the half-million mark. The pattern of urban expansion continued to follow the main transport routes; the plains to the W and SW proved less attractive for residential develop- ment, partly because of their rocky nature and shallow soils, but also because noxious indus- tries had been established there. The more attractive undulating terrain to the E of the city was increasingly settled and this basic pattern of urban spread has remained largely unchanged, with residential development to the DANDENONG RANGES and down the MORNINGTON PENINSULA. By World War II, the city's population was over one million and in the 1960s it exceeded two million. By the 1981 census it accounted for 68 per cent of the State's population (*see* Table 1).

Climate Melbourne experiences a mild cli- mate with a warm to hot summer season and cool winter conditions. During summer there are sometimes several consecutive hot days when the maximum daily temperature reaches about 30°C; the hottest month is January (26.5°C average maximum), while the coldest month is July (6.2°C average minimum). The

Table 1

URBAN GROWTH OF MELBOURNE IN THE TWENTIETH CENTURY

Year	Population	% of State population
1901	494 129	41.1
1911	588 971	44.8
1921	766 465	50.1
1933	922 048	50.7
1954	1 524 111	62.1
1961	1 911 895	65.2
1971	2 394 117	68.4
1976	2 479 225	68.0
1981	2 578 527	65.3

Source: Australian Bureau of Statistics, Canberra.

city has an average annual rainfall of 658mm, spread evenly throughout all seasons; October is the wettest month (67mm average), January the driest (48mm).

City functions Metropolitan Melbourne re- flects the impressive and complex array of functions that are typical of large modern cities. It is the commercial, financial, legal, professional, cultural and administrative focus or the State. The compact and orderly central business district—a reflection of Hoddle's original plan—contains the city's major commercial, financial and administrative functions. The marked vertical growth of this zone in recent decades has given it a skyline dominated by rectangular silhouettes. Retail commerce is concentrated in an area bounded by Queen, Lonsdale, Exhibition and Collins Streets, with Bourke Street the centre of this activity. Insurance companies, banks and other offices tend to be clustered to the immediate W, where the head offices of some of Australia's largest companies and financial institutions are located. The core of government administration is centred on Spring Street and nearby Treasury Place.

The port of Melbourne begins immediately SW of the central business district, with only the railway yards and some waterfront industry acting as a buffer between the two. The port is essentially estuarine and requires continuous dredging. There are three main parts of the port; the wharves and docks of the Yarra, the piers at Williamstown, and the piers (Princes and Station) on the bay. Facilities are highly mechanised, with many wharves designed to handle particular kinds of cargoes.

The city contains a wide range of secondary industries. Early development of manufacturing was associated with essential light industries, such as food processing and clothing. Until the 1950s Melbourne had to rely heavily on supplies of black coal from NSW for power production and hence heavy industry, as it developed, was located near the port. However, with the rapid development of the brown coal deposits of the LATROBE RIVER valley in GIPPSLAND, the city has become largely independent of outside power resources and secondary industry has become more dispersed. In the inner suburbs, the heavier industries are located in South Melbourne, Port Melbourne and Altona. Fisherman's Bend, just W of Port Melbourne, has been a notable development on reclaimed swamp land since the 1930s and is now one of Australia's major centres of automobile manufacture and aircraft assembly. Other inner suburbs, such as Carlton, Fitzroy and Collingwood, produce a range of light industrial products. Many other suburbs, such as Footscray, Sunshine, Coburg and Preston, have varied industrial enterprises and in some outer suburbs large plants have been established, such as the Ford Motor Co. at Broadmeadow, and General Motors-Holden and the Heinz canned food organisation at Dandenong.

Melbourne offers a wide array of social, educational and recreational amenities. It has two cathedrals, three universities (Melbourne, Monash and Latrobe), many colleges, museums and theatres, as well as numerous parks, gardens and some of Australia's finest sporting facilities, including Flemington racecourse, the Melbourne Cricket Ground and Olympic Park. The autumn Moomba festival, with varied entertainment to suit all tastes, has become and annual feature of the city's life. The recently completed Victorian Arts Centre has

Robert Irving

The Melbourne Exhibition building erected in 1878

become the focus of performing arts.
Further reading: Wilson, M.G.A. *Port Phillip Bay.* Longmans, Melbourne, 1965; Shaw, J.H. & Emery, J.S. *Cities and Industries.* Jacaranda, Brisbane, 1968; Carroll, B. *Toorak and South Yarra.* (1973), *River Yarra.* (1973), *Melbourne Churches and Schools.* (1974), *Hawthorn and Kew.* (1975), *Richmond and East Melbourne.* (1977), all published by Rigby, Adelaide; Burt, J. & Carroll, B. *Victoria.* Rigby, Adelaide, 1977.

Meldrum, (Duncan) Max (1875-1955)
Artist. Born in Scotland, Meldrum arrived in Australia with his family when he was 14. He showed an early interest in painting and attended the National Gallery School, Melbourne. In 1899 he won the Travelling Art Scholarship and went to France, where he rejected both the academic school training and the modern art movement. He was greatly influenced by the tonal painting of Velàquez, Manet, Corot and Whistler, from which he designed his own colour theory. Meldrum returned to Australia in 1913, and established an art school in Melbourne. His theories were enthusiastically embraced and propagated by many. During the inter-war period, his influence was considerable, helped by his strong personality and an ability to put across his ideas on art with great fervour. His influence was later challenged by the arrival of such modernists as FRATER, BELL and SHORE. As a Trustee of the National Gallery, he spoke dogmatically against the acquisition by the Gallery of any work that showed the influence of the post-Impressionists or their followers.

Melton VIC (population 18 056 in 1981)
This country town is on the Western Highway and on the railway route to BALLARAT, 38km by rail WNW of Melbourne and 14km by road E of BACCHUS MARSH. It is a commercial and

service centre for a productive agricultural and pastoral district, dominated by grain growing and fat lamb raising. The area was developed in the 1840s and was named after Melton, a famous hunting district in Leicestershire, England.

Melville Island NT (population 554 in 1981)
This Aboriginal reserve is located off the NW coast of the Territory; the ARAFURA SEA washes its N shores, VAN DIEMEN GULF lies to the SE and it is separated from BATHURST ISLAND to the W by the narrow Apsley Strait and from the COBOURG PENINSULA to the E by the Dundas Strait. The N coast is deeply indented by long inlets such as Shark, Snake, Lethbridge and Brenton Bays. The island extends some 120km E-W, with a maximum N-S width of 70km, and covers an area of 5 698km^2. It was noted by the Dutch explorer Abel TASMAN in 1644 and the NW tip bears the name Cape Van Diemen. Phillip King, son of Governor KING, charted and named the island in 1818 in honour of the British First Lord of the Admiralty. In 1824, after finding PORT ESSINGTON unsuitable for a settlement site, Captain James Bremer established a convict post on Apsley Strait which he called Fort Dundas, but this was abandoned in 1829. It is now the site of a Roman Catholic mission, Garden Point. There is a government Aboriginal settlement at Milikapiti on Snake Bay where a timber-getting and sawmilling industry has been developed. The island experiences a two-cycle tropical climate typical of these N parts, with an average annual rainfall at Snake Bay of 1 594mm concentrated in the wet season (November to March) and a markedly dry period for the other months.

Menindee NSW (population 455 in 1981)
This small town on the DARLING RIVER, 1 150km W of Sydney, is situated at the junction of the Barrier and Silver City Highways. It is on the Indian-Pacific transcontinental railway route, 1 007km W of Sydney by rail and 118km E of BROKEN HILL. The name Menindee comes from the Aboriginal word meaning 'the yolk of an egg'. Located in the arid inland plains region of the State, at an elevation of 61m above sea level, it has an average annual rainfall of only 229mm. During the heyday of river transport in the 19th century, it was a port for paddle-wheel steamers hauling barges loaded with supplies on the up-river trip and with wool bales on the return journey. A pipeline 110km long, completed in 1952, carries water to Broken Hill from the Darling. A major water conservation scheme has been developed in this region for the storage and distribution of the Darling's waters. The scheme has utilised a series of natural lakes, formerly often only saltpans in dry times, which lie to the W of the river. The Kinchega National Park (44 005ha), dedicated in 1967, includes the two largest lakes (Menindee and Cawindilla) and contains large populations of emus, kangaroos and water birds.

Menzies, Sir Robert Gordon (1894-1978) Prime Minister. He has been quoted as saying that he regarded politics as one of the highest pursuits open to a man of talent, and he applied himself to it with such success that he dominated the Australian political scene for more than two decades and became Australia's longest-serving Prime Minister.

Born in the small town of Jeparit VIC, he graduated in law from Melbourne University and in 1918 entered on an outstandingly successful career at the Bar. Between 1928 and 1934 he was a member of the VIC Parliament, first in the Legislative Council and then in the Legislative Assembly, and at various times during these years held Cabinet positions. He then entered the federal Parliament as a Member of the House of Representatives for Kooyong, was immediately appointed Attorney-General and Minister for Industry, and in 1936 became deputy leader of the United Australia Party (UAP). In March 1939 he resigned from the Cabinet in protest at the abandonment of plans for a national insurance scheme, but in the following month Joseph LYONS died, and shortly afterwards Menzies succeeded him as leader of the UAP and Prime Minister. However, at this stage of his career he was notably lacking in patience in dealing with colleagues, and antagonised many members of the coalition parties. Dr Earle PAGE, leader of the Country Party, had conceived such a dislike for him that he refused to serve under him, and it was not until the following year that the coalition was re-formed. Then, as the military situation deteriorated in Europe, many government members became dissatisfied with Menzies' leadership of Australia's war effort, and in August 1941 he resigned, the position of Prime Minister passing to Sir Arthur FADDEN and then in October to John CURTIN of the Australian Labor Party (ALP).

Courtesy of A.I.S. Canberra

Sir Robert Menzies

At this stage many presumed that Menzies' political career was over, but in 1944 he founded a new Liberal Party as a successor to the demoralised UAP, capitalised on Labor's errors in the post-war years, led his party to victory in 1949 and retained the position of Prime Minister until his retirement 17 years

later. It is often pointed out that his success was aided by good fortune—by weakness in the leadership of the ALP, by the split in its ranks that led to the formation of the DEMOCRATIC LABOR PARTY, by generally favourable economic circumstances, and by an electoral distribution which told against Labor in the closely run elections of 1954 and 1961. Nevertheless, the success of the coalition parties was obviously due in very large measures to his leadership. A superb political tactician and a gifted speaker, he was merciless in exposing every weakness of the Opposition and masterly in presenting his own party's case. His critics argue that while he controlled the course of politics, he did not use this control to change the course of Australian history with any notable reforms. His defenders claim in reply that he gave the nation what it most needed, namely stability; they point, too, to such processes of gradual change as the expansion of social services and the growth of tertiary education during his period in office. In foreign policy it can be claimed that he showed too little interest in Asia, tended to excuse the white minority regimes in southern Africa, backed American policy too uncritically and erred in backing Britain during the Suez Canal crisis of 1956. His defenders, besides disputing these points, claim that by strengthening American-Australian friendship, while at the same time trying to preserve traditional links with Britain, he succeeded in the main aim of foreign policy—the strengthening of national security.

He was made a Knight of the Thistle in 1963, and after retirement succeeded Sir Winston Churchill as Lord Warden of the Cinque Ports. He was Chancellor of Melbourne University from 1967 to 1972. His publications include two volumes of memoirs, *Afternoon Light* (1967) and *The Measure of the Years* (1970).

Merimbula NSW (population 2 899 in 1981) A coastal resort centre and small service town in the SE of the State, it is located on the Princes Highway, 468km by road S of Sydney, about 30km SSE of BEGA, and 26km N of EDEN. It is one of the most popular resorts on the far S coast, especially for visitors from VIC and southern NSW. There are fine surfing beaches along the coast and the nearby lakes provide opportunities for sailing and other aquatic sports. The Merimbula airport is the base for aircraft spotting tuna off the coast. The old school house, built in 1874, has been listed by the National Trust (NSW) and is used as a local museum. The old wharf, though no longer in use, is of historic interest as it is one of the few remaining steamship wharves on the S coast; it is also a popular fishing spot.

Merredin WA (population 3 520 in 1981) Known as the 'heart of the wheat belt', Merredin is a major wheat and rail centre located on the Great Eastern Highway and on the railway line from Perth to KALGOORLIE, 286km ENE of Perth. At an elevation of

315km above sea level, it receives an average annual rainfall of 327mm, concentrated mainly in the winter months (June average 55mm, July 54mm) and dry summer conditions with January being the driest month (11mm). Its name came from the Aboriginal word for the huge, bare, granite rock in the region.

merrin *see* kangaroos, etc.

Mersey River TAS Located in the central-N of the State, this river rises in the lakes region of the CENTRAL PLATEAU and flows N across the GREAT WESTERN TIERS to its estuary on BASS STRAIT. The highest of its headwater tributaries have their source along the E side of the CRADLE MOUNTAIN-LAKE ST CLAIR National park near MOUNT OSSA (1 617m elevation) where there are numerous lakes of glacial origin. The course of the river is then in a general N direction, across the plateau region, where the altitude is over 1000m, thence in a deep gorge through the scarplands of the plateau, after which it changes to a W-E flow before finally turning again to a S-N direction as it nears the sea. Its 160km-long course thus descends from the central highlands to the N coastal plains, and this steep drop has been utilised in the Mersey-FORTH hydro-electricity scheme. This power development, begun in 1963 and completed in 1973, consists of seven power stations utilising the waters of the Mersey and Forth catchments. The highest point in the scheme is at Lake Mackenzie on the Fisher River, a tributary of the Mersey, at an elevation of 1 121m; a dam here, with a 14m-high wall, raises the level of Lake Mackenzie and water from the lake is taken by canal, tunnel and pipeline to the Fisher power station, which has an installed capacity of 43 200kW. On the upper Mersey, Rowallan Dam, completed in 1968, forms Lake Rowallan, the principal storage of the scheme, at an altitude of 488m; the rock-fill dam wall is 43m high and was the first to be constructed in this scheme. Water released from this dam is used for hydro-electricity development at Rowallan power station, which has an installed capacity of 10 450kW. About 1km below the junction of the Fisher and Mersey Rivers, Parangana Dam, with its 53m-high wall, diverts the flow of the Mersey W to the Forth River, where it is utilised in a series of five power stations in the Forth Valley.

Messenger, Herbert Henry 'Dally' (1883-1959) Footballer. Born in Sydney, he played first grade Rugby Union and represented NSW against QLD. By 1907 he was hailed as the finest Rugby player in Australia, a fast and elusive centre-three-quarter and an accurate and formidable goal kicker. Messenger was one of the first players to leave Rugby Union for the new professional code of Rugby League, which had started in 1907. He became the idol of the spectators; where Messenger went the crowds followed. After the first professional games played in Sydney against the New Zealand touring side, the New Zealand team invited him to join them on their tour of England. He captained Australia on the first professional tour of England in 1908-1909. His freakish tries and goal-kicking skills became legendary and in 1911 he set a season's point-scoring record of 270, a record which stood until 1935. Variously described as unorthodox, inspired, aggressive, brilliant and unpredictable, he died at GUNNEDAH in NSW.

messmate Several species of *Eucalyptus* (family MYRTACEAE) are called messmates, possibly because they usually grow in association with other species of the genus. The broad-leaved messmate or messmate stringybark, *E. obliqua*, has reddish-brown, stringy bark and broad, long lanceolate leaves. It is found in SA, NSW, VIC and TAS.

meteorites From time to time pieces of rock in orbit around the sun come close to the earth and are pulled down by the earth's gravity; if the fragment is large enough, it will survive the heat of entry into the earth's atmosphere and reach the surface, the impact often producing a large crater. Such a rock is then called a meteorite. Australia possesses one of the world's largest meteorite craters—the Wolf Creek crater discovered in 1947 in the KIMBERLEYS of north-western WA. It is 850m in diameter and the outer wall stands 30m above the surrounding plain.

The S parts of Australia are littered with other mementoes of the fall of rocks from outer space. These are small pieces of glassy material called tektites, which are believed to have been formed by the melting of rock materials under the tremendous heat produced as a meteorite falls. Recent research suggests that the meteorite responsible for the SA tektites fell about 700 000 years ago in ANTARCTICA.

Methodist Church
When the colony of NSW was founded, the Methodist Church in Britain had not yet broken away completely from the Church of England. It had originated with John and Charles Wesley, Anglican clergymen who at first intended to bring about a religious revival within the Church of England rather than to found a new Church. Followers of the Wesleys were evangelical in spirit, stressed belief in justification by faith and reliance on the Scriptures as the sole Christian authority, held revivalist meetings to spread their message and tended to favour spontaneous prayer during divine worship rather than adherence to any set form. Although Conferences of Methodists were held from 1784, the year 1795 is commonly regarded as the date when the Methodist Church became a totally separate entity in Britain.

Historical development in Australia The first clergyman in the colony of NSW, the Rev. Richard JOHNSON, was a member of the evangelical wing of the Church of England, and some authorities consider that he could be regarded as a Methodist. However, the first Australian clergyman who had been ordained a Methodist was the Rev. Samuel Leigh, who was sent to Sydney by the Wesleyan Missionary Society of London in 1815 and set up a church in the township of Castlereagh two years later. The close links that still existed between Methodism and Anglicanism at that time are shown by the fact that he frequently preached in Anglican churches, was very friendly with the Rev. Samuel MARSDEN and was sent briefly as a missionary to New Zealand by the latter. In 1821, after a visit to England, Leigh returned with the Rev. William Horton, who became the first Methodist minister in Hobart.

Courtesy of A.I.S. Canberra

Old Methodist church in the aboriginal settlement at Hermannsburg NT

From about 1840 onwards Methodism developed strongly, especially in the agricultural districts around Sydney, where there was a notable Methodist revival in the early 1840s, and in SA. In the latter the first colonists had included many Methodists, and services were conducted by laymen almost from the time of the first landing. The first minister, the Rev. William Longbottom, arrived by chance in 1837—he was shipwrecked on the SA coast on his way to WA—and decided to stay. At a later period an influx of Cornish miners to towns such as MOONTA and KADINA helped to make the proportion of Methodists in the population of the colony higher than anywhere else in Australia.

For many years Australia was regarded as a mission field, but following a visit by the Rev. Robert Young, and his recommendation that the Australian Church be given autonomy, the first Australian Conference was held in Sydney in 1855. In the meantime, various groups had seceded from the main body of the Methodist Church in Britain, and some of these gained adherents in Australia. Most notable were the Primitive Methodist Church and the Bible Christians, both of which became established first in SA in 1840 and 1850 respectively, and then spread to other parts of Australia, especially to mining centres. Other groups were the Methodist Connexion and the United Methodist Free Churches. However, from the 1880s onwards there was a movement for union between the various branches of Methodism in Australia, and by the early years of the 20th century this had almost been achieved in all States.

Mission and Social work From the time the Methodist Church was founded, Methodists were vigorous in missionary work at home and abroad. In keeping with this tradition, the Australian Church supplied missionaries to Tonga, Fiji, Samoa, the Solomon Islands, Papua, New Guinea and India. It founded a number of missions among Aborigines, and in the sparsely populated areas of Australia established several Inland Missions. It also paid attention to a widening range of social problems. Its Central Missions in the capital cities, the first of which dates from 1884, devoted themselves to social works as well as evangelism, and the Church mainained many other institutions for people in need. The Lifeline service, begun by the Rev. Alan Walker in 1963, enabled people in distress to telephone a central bureau for advice and comfort.

Church unity The increase in non-British immigration after 1945 tended to reduce the Methodist proportion of the population. The pre-war figure was about 10 per cent; in the census of 1976 the figure was 7.3 per cent. However, by the mid-1970s the movement for union between Methodists, Presbyterians and Congregationalists had developed strongly, support being strongest of all among the Methodists, and when the UNITING CHURCH IN AUSTRALIA was formed in 1977, the Methodist Church of Australia became part of it.

Further reading: Shapley, W.F. *Origins and Growth of Methodism in South Australia.* Methodist Centenary Committee, Adelaide, 1935; van Sommers, T. 'Methodists' in *Religions in Australia.* Rigby, Adelaide, 1966.

metric system *see* weights, etc.

Mewton-Wood, Noel (1922-53) Pianist. He was born in Melbourne and, after studying at the Melbourne Conservatorium, went to London at the age of 14 to study at the Royal Academy of Music. Later he went to Italy and was a student of Artur Schnabel. He made his concert début in London in 1940 in a concert at Queen's Hall conducted by Sir Thomas Beecham. His playing was highly praised and the great English conductor Sir Henry Wood once wrote: 'He reminds me of all the greatest pianists of the past, including Rubinstein, Liszt and Busoni.' Mewton-Wood won very great admiration for his performance of both classical and modern works and for his grasp of the widely differing styles of such composers as Schumann, Brahms, Stravinsky and Tippett.

mice *see* animals, introduced; rodents

mice, marsupial *see* marsupials; native cats, etc.

Micky Mouse plant *see* weeds

Microphyllyta This is a family of primitive, spore-bearing (sporophytic) plants which possess true stems, leaves and roots and in which the main plant body is diploid. This group was well represented in the flora of the Devonian period, but today only four genera exist, three of which (*Lycopodium, Selaginella* and *Isoetes*) are present in the Australian flora. The living and fossil members of this family can be divided into two series depending on whether or not they bear a minute tongue-like leaf outgrowth (a ligule) at the base of their leaves; of the extant Australian genera only *Lycopodium* lacks ligules.

The genus *Lycopodium*, which contains species commonly known as club mosses or ground pines, grows on other plants (epiphytic) or on the ground and occurs in both temperate and tropical environments. The spore-cases (sporangia) of *Lycopodium* are borne on the upper surface of the leaves, often as a dense cone-like structure (strobilus) from which these plants get their common names. The spores resulting from the process whereby the number of chromosomes in the nucleus is halved (meiosis) may develop into a minute free-living haploid gamete-bearing (gametophytic) plant which produces mobile sperm or ova and lives either on decaying organic matter (SAPROPHYTIC), or by photosynthesis. A new diploid plant develops after fertilisation has taken place.

Selanginella, a living representative of an ancient group of primitive vascular plants

In the genus *Selaginella* the leaves (sporophylls) are localised in strobili which differentiate into megasporophylls and microsporophylls. In the former only a few large spores mature and after germination produce ova; while in the latter many smaller spores are produced and yield sperm after germination. In many cases development of the haploid generation takes place largely before the spores are shed from their sporangia. In this genus all plants in the gametophytic stage are saprophytic. *Selaginella* species are diverse in habitat requirements; some are tropical and require moist conditions, whilst others live in environments subject to periodic desiccation. The latter group contains the resurrection plant, *S. hierochuntica*, of the south-western USA. Of the approximately 600 species in this genus, only nine are native to Australia, although a number of delicate, almost prostrate, exotic species are prized for fernhouses and the introduced *S. kraussiana* is a common glasshouse weed.

The genus *Isoetes* contains about 60 species commonly known as quillworts. These plants produce a small tuft of rush-like leaves, and occupy cool, aquatic or marshy habitats. Their life cycle is similar to that of *Selaginella*, but the spores do not begin to develop into gametophytes until they have been shed from their sporangia.

See also Appendix 5, Flower Structure and Glossary of Botanical Terms
Further reading: see Appendix 6, A Bibliography for Plants.

Middleback Ranges

Middleback Ranges SA These hills comprise the E section of the GAWLER RANGES, located some 50km inland from the NW shore of SPENCER GULF; they are famed for large deposits of high-grade haematite iron ore, which provided Australia's major source of ore until recent developments in WA. The iron ore has been mined by open-cut bench-type workings from hills in the ranges since the early years of this century. Iron Knob, located 54km NW of WHYALLA, was the first area mined and the ore was used as a smelting flux at PORT PIRIE. But the expansion of Australia's iron and steel industry, first at NEWCASTLE and later at PORT KEMBLA, led to increased mining at the Middleback Ranges. Iron Knob was quarried to become a worn-down hillock and although there is still high-grade ore under the Knob, the main focus is now at IRON MONARCH to the S. Other ore bearing hills within the ranges are Iron Baron and Iron Prince.

Open-cut mining of iron ore in the Middleback Ranges SA

midges *see* flies

Midland WA This railway and industrial centre, formerly called Midland Junction, located 16km NE of Perth city centre, is now a suburb of metropolitan Perth. The town was originally established by the British Midland Railway Co. (after which it was named) in return for land grants in WA. It became the rail junction of the KALGOORLIE line and it now has a variety of industrial enterprises, including railway workshops and abattoirs. The National Trust (WA) has classified 'Woodbridge', built in 1855 in Midland, for preservation for its architectural and historic importance.

Midlands TAS This lowland region in the E part of the State, stretching from LAUNCESTON in the N to Hobart in the S, is bounded by the CENTRAL PLATEAU on the W and the BEN LOMOND highland area and the coastal range on the E. Thus in its N section it includes the TAMAR RIVER estuary, which drains into BASS STRAIT, and the lower valleys of the streams draining into the Tamar (North ESK, Nile, Ben Lomond, South Esk and Macquarie). Further S it includes the valleys of the Coal, the Jordan and the lower DERWENT

Rivers. The Midlands Highway, 202km long, crosses the region in a general N-S direction, linking Hobart and Launceston.

Mildura VIC (population 15 762 in 1981) The city of Mildura, centre of a productive irrigation area known as SUNRAYSIA, is located on the S bank of the MURRAY RIVER at the junction of the Calder and Sturt Highways, 560km by road NW of Melbourne, in the Mallee region. The area was settled by graziers in the 1840s, but it was the development of irrigation in 1887 by the Canadian CHAFFEY BROTHERS, utilising water pumped from the Murray, that established it as a commercial and service centre for the area. It became a shire in 1890, a borough in 1920 and was proclaimed a city in 1934. In the latter decades of the 19th century when paddle-steamers were the main form of transport, Mildura was an important river port and nowadays tourists can savour the atmosphere of that time by taking a river cruise on a paddle-wheeler. The city took its name from two Aboriginal words: *dura* (or *cura*) meaning 'a fly', and *mil* meaning 'the eye', the combination of which indicated a place where sore eyes caused by the numerous flies were prevalent. The area has a mild climate and is noted for its abundant winter sunshine which attracts many tourists. The average annual rainfall is only 294mm, evenly spread throughout the year; August is the wettest month (29mm average), January the driest (19mm). Because of the low rainfall, those areas beyond the limits of the irrigation system are occupied by large sheep grazing properties. The irrigated lands are noted for the production of vine and citrus fruits, and there are canning and processing factories, fruit packing works and wineries. Tourist attractions in the city include the Arts Centre which comprises a theatre, an art gallery and a folk museum established in 'Rio Vista', the home of the irrigation pioneer William Chaffey, built in 1889; the Workingmen's Club, reputed to have the longest bar in the world; the statue of Chaffey in Deakin Avenue; and the display of the Chaffey pump tractor and other agricultural machinery. Within the district there are also numerous tourist attractions; Kings Billabong, 8km E of the city, which abounds with pelicans, swans, herons, ducks and storks; Hattah-Kulkyne National Park (48 000ha), which is located 70km S of Mildura and includes stretches of Hattah lake with red gums along the shore and a prolific bird life, as well as stretches of dry mallee country; Lock Is and Mildura Weir on the Murray, with its koala sanctuary, and several wineries, fruit packing and processing plants, which can be inspected by visitors.
Further reading; Hill, E. *Water into Gold.* Robertson & Mullins, Melbourne, 1940.

Miller, Godfrey Clive (1893-1964) Artist. Born in Wellington, New Zealand, Miller served with the cavalry in World War I, including a stint at Gallipoli, and after completing his architectural qualifications in Dunedin he began work in Suva, Fiji. Encouraged by A.H. O'Keefe, a Dunedin painter, he began to paint, and after a tour of Asia, he studied at the Slade School, London, from 1929 to 1931. He lived for a few years in Melbourne and settled finally in Sydney in 1939. In 1945 he began teaching at the East Sydney Technical College. A recluse by nature, his paintings were not shown to the public for many years. The first exhibition of his work, when he was 59, caused a great stir, and he shot to the forefront of contemporary Australian art overnight. His paintings were frequently reworked and tinkered with, but he is remembered for those paintings where a grid of lines fragments the object he paints and breaks the colours into a mosaic of low-keyed colours. This fragmentation was intended to express the fact, well known to physicists, that matter, although apparently stable to the eye, is constantly changing.

Miller, Keith Ross (1919-   ) Cricketer. Born in Sunshine VIC Miller was a highly individual and talented though sometimes erratic cricketer and is still considered one of the finest all-rounders Australia has produced. He was a fast bowler, sending down swift and at times fierce deliveries from a short run—in 55 Tests he took 170 wickets for an average of 22.97. He was also a powerful batsman who could spectacularly and quickly put runs on the scoreboard—in the same 55 Tests he scored 2 958 runs, including seven centuries, for an average of 36.97. With his flamboyant personality and his love of attacking the ball when batting, Miller became well liked by crowds everywhere, delighting them with his fiery cricket. When not bowling or batting, he was noted as an excellent slip fielder. When Miller played his last Test in 1956, he had missed only two Tests in post-war cricket. In the 1970s he became a cricket commentator on television.

millet *see* agriculture; Gramineae

Millicent SA (population 5 255 in 1981) This rural service town in the far SE of the State is 406km by road and 538km by rail SE of Adelaide, on the Princes Highway 51km NW of MOUNT GAMBIER. The town site is on a sandy ridge in the midst of former swamp lands where drainage schemes were started in the 1860s. The expansion of forestry and the development of land settlement in recent decades has led to the town's growth. It was named after Millicent Short, the daughter of the first Bishop of Adelaide and the wife of George Glen, the owner of the grazing station where the town now stands.

millipedes These ARTHROPODS constitute the class Diplopoda. Millipedes were formerly grouped with CENTIPEDES as myriapods, but biologists no longer believe that the two groups are closely related. They differ from the centipedes in having cylindrical bodies composed of segments (somites) some of which apparently carry two pairs of legs. These segments are, however, composed of

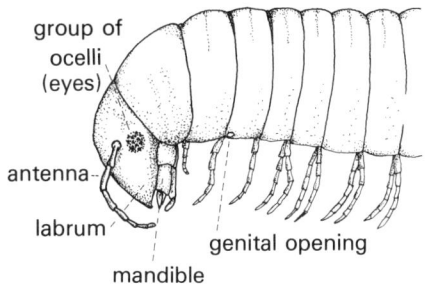

group of ocelli (eyes)

antenna

labrum

mandible

genital opening

Head and first few trunk segments of a millipede

two true segments fused together. The genital opening is placed between the second and third pairs of legs whereas in the centipedes it is at the end of the body. Millipedes feed on living or dead plant material (centipedes are carnivores) and some are occasionally pests. Many of them have glands on some of the segments from which oozes or spurts out an offensive liquid. None of the Australian species is dangerous but some large, tropical species in other countries have blinded chickens which were attacking them.

There are two distinct subclasses. The small subclass Pselaphognatha consists of millipedes with a soft skin (cuticle) which carries rows and tufts of scale-like bristles. The trunk has 11 to 13 body segments; each of the first four carries a single pair of legs and there are, in all, 13 to 17 pairs. Four species have been found in Australia in QLD, SA and south-western Australia.

A pill millipede

The subclass Chilognatha is composed of longer millipedes with tough cuticles which are often strengthened with lime. The first trunk segment (the collum) is limbless. The pill millipedes (order Glomerida), of which there are about 22 species in Australia belonging mainly to the genus *Cyliosoma*, have relatively short bodies with 17 to 23 pairs of legs and can roll up into a tight ball when alarmed. The remaining Australian millipedes in this subclass (about 130 species in more than 60 genera) have longer bodies, sometimes with more than 40 somites but, unlike some tropical species, few of them are more than about 4cm in length.

Mills, Martin (1893-1972) Novelist. This was the pen-name used by Martin à Beckett BOYD for three of his novels, one of which, *The Montfords* (1928), is perhaps the most

notable of all his works. It deals with the fortunes of a family who arrived in Australia in the 1840s and their descendants up to the time of World War I.

Mimosaceae This family of dicotyledonous flowering plants is particularly common in Australia, with *Acacia* (the wattles) being the most abundant genus. (Other genera found in Australia include *Neptunia*, *Abarema* and *Albizia*.)

The members of this family vary in size from prostrate shrubs to tall forest trees. They have alternate leaves which are usually compound with compound leaflets (bipinnate), or reduced to the extent that the leaf blade has been lost and the leaf stalk (petiole) has become flattened to serve as a leaf (phyllode). The petiole often contains one or more secretory cells (glands) on its surface, and may or may not have stipules. The flowers are usually small and arranged in spikes, racemes or heads. The tubular calyx has four to five divisions which meet without overlapping (valvate) and there is a corresponding number of valvate petals which are regularly arranged and are either free or joined at the base. The numerous stamens are free or joined in a tube and the superior ovary contains one cavity (loculus). The fruit is an edible pod (legume) and the seeds often bear a brightly coloured additional covering (an aril).

Wattles, with their cream or yellow fluffy spikes or globular heads, are present in almost all Australian plant communities. They are divided into two large groups, those with bipinnate leaves and those with phyllodes. It is supposed that phyllode evolution is related to long dry seasons, or generally arid conditions. The phyllodes may be large and flat or very reduced, often producing sharply pointed thorn-like foliage. Flowering times are specific for each species, but throughout the year there are always some in flower, which, combined with their rapid growth, makes them a very popular subject for cultivation. Popular species include the grey feather-foliaged Cootamundra wattle, *Acacia baileyana*; the dark green bushy Sydney wattle, *A. longifolia*, which is salt-spray tolerant; the grey-green bushy Queensland wattle, *A. podalyriifolia*; and the brilliantly flowered golden wattle, *A. pycnantha*. Two closed forest species which are often cultivated, or retained as shade trees on farms are blackwood, *A. melanoxylon*, which also produces choice timber, and the cedar wattle, *A. elata*.

Acacia species play an important role in Australian plant communities. Firstly, because their root nodules contain nitrogen-fixing bacteria, on dying they increase the total amount of nitrogen available to other plants. Secondly, they have hard-skinned seeds which do not germinate immediately after being shed from the plants, but remain dormant in the soil, often for decades. When the plant community is burnt, the heat breaks the dormancy of these seeds which then germinate rapidly, and form a soil-stabilising, nitrogen-enriching cover under which the more delicate and slower growing seedlings can become established. These *Acacia* species continue to grow extremely rapidly, and take up the plant nutrients in the ash before they are washed out of the area, which is particularly important in Australia where there are extensive areas of poor soil. As most *Acacia* species are more short-lived than most of the other members of the communities in which they occur, these nutrients are gradually returned to the soil as the *Acacia* species die and decay. *Acacia* species are also important as early colonisers of disturbed ground; they fulfill this role both after natural disturbances, such as the formation of new sand dunes, and after cleared and ploughed agricultural land has been abandoned. Brigalow, *A. harpophylla*, has such a capacity for recolonisation, both vegetatively and from seed, that it is regarded as something of a weed in extensive areas of dry N Australia where attempts are being made to establish improved pasture.

See also Appendix 5, Flower Structure and Glossary of Botanical Terms

Further reading: see Appendix 6, A Bibliography for Plants.

minerals and mining The mineral industry in Australia has been an important factor in the social and economic growth of the country. For example, the GOLD discoveries of the 1850s were responsible for the first major wave of immigration, for the settlement of inland areas, for the extension of roads, railways and communications and also for the handsome public buildings to be found in many cities and townships.

Australia's mineral wealth has been slow to unfold itself to the world because of a combination of adverse factors such as the size of the country, the relatively small population, the difficult climate in the interior, the large extent of mineral provinces, the distances of deposits from suitable port facilities and the remoteness of Australia from suitable international markets. While most of the surface deposits have now been discovered, only a superficial geological survey has been made of the whole country. Consequently, it is impossible to predict what mineral wealth lies below the barren surfaces of the Australian deserts. The knowledgeable prospector who was, until recently, the principal agent in mineral discovery, has now been replaced by the larger mining companies with their specialised mineral surveys.

The growth of the mineral industry has been outstanding. The ex-mine value of mineral production rose from $362 million in 1960 to over $7 400 million in 1980, and the export income increased from $125 million to over $6 800 million during the same period. In 1980 there were over 1 440 mining and quarrying establishments operating in Australia, employing over 73 400 persons, 46 per cent of them in metal mining.

Self-sufficiency Out of 38 principal mineral commodities, Australia is totally self-sufficient in at least 24; but in another dozen mineral commodities, she has a self-sufficiency of less than 60 per cent. Details are listed in Table 1. The

Table 1

SELF-SUFFICIENCY IN PRINCIPAL AUSTRALIAN MINERALS (1981)

Totally self-sufficient	Self-sufficiency less than 60%
Asbestos chrysotile	Asbestos – other types
Barite	Bentonite
Bauxite – aluminium	Chromite
Cadmium	Diamonds
Coal – black and brown	Diatomite
Copper	Fluorspar
Gold	Graphite
Gypsum	Magnesite
Ilmenite	Mercury
Iron ore	Mica
Lead	Phosphate rock and potassium products
Manganese ore	Sillimanite and kyanite
Nickel	Sulphur
Petroleum	
Rutile concentrate	Manufactured materials:
Salt	Ferrochrome and ferrosilicon
Silver	
Talc	
Tin	
Tungsten concentrate	
Zinc	
Zircon	
Manufactured materials:	
Cement	

Source: *Australian Mineral Industry Annual Review.* (1980) Australian Govt Publishing Service, Canberra.

country's future insufficiency in mineral products will be related to five or six principal minerals—PETROLEUM, sulphur, phosphate, potassium and certain forms of asbestos.

Mineral processing Since the late 1960s it has been recognised that there would be economic benefit if more mineral processing could be achieved in Australia. Indexes, showing the quantities of minerals processed as a percentage figure, were introduced as a means of indicating the level of processing domestically. Table 2 shows the production processing indexes (the percentage of mine production which is processed in Australia) and the export processing indexes (the percentage of total exports which are exported in processed form) for a variety of minerals. The indexes assume that the commodities are processed in the year in which they are produced or exported. In many cases the indexes are high, reaching almost 100 per cent for nickel and lead. Conversely, other metals such as pig iron and ferromanganese are expensive to produce and are exported mainly in the form of ore or in a semi-processed state, resulting in a low index.

Industrial disputes Industrial dispute statistics now refer only to disputes involving a stoppage of work of 10 man-days or more. In COAL mining the number of disputes annually in the late 1970s ranged between 240 and 290, involving between 48 000 and 107 000 workers and averaging two to nine days lost per worker. In other mining, the number of disputes was between 190 and 350 per year, involving 30 000 to 50 000 workers and averaging 2.8 to 5.4 days lost per worker. The difference in the performance of the two groups portrays the more concentrated distribution of coal mines

and the smaller number of mines, whereas the other category of the mining industry is widely scattered, isolated and employs more people.

Royalties The basis for assessing royalties in mining operations differs from State to State and can also vary within a particular State. As an example, the famous LEAD and ZINC mining field at BROKEN HILL in NSW is assessed differently to other mining areas in that State. Royalties can be paid on sand and gravel mined from Crown land; they are received from minerals, principally petroleum, and from offshore operations; and they can include lease rents and fees from mineral lands which may or may not include Aboriginal Benefits Trust Fund royalties. The pattern of payment of royalties in Australia has changed since 1970, with the result that they increased from less than $40 million to over $370 million in 1979-80.

Training mining engineers The senior management of the Australian metal mining industry is staffed almost entirely by Australians, but in the coal mining industry there is a greater spread of nationalities in the middle and senior managerial positions.

Four universities and several colleges of advanced education conduct undergraduate courses in mining engineering, covering a wide range of subjects including science, engineering science and engineering applications. Substantial technical support from mechanical, electrical, civil, chemical and metallurgical engineering is provided to the operational mining department on almost every reasonably sized metal mine, and scientific support is provided from a broad range of basic scientists.

Table 2

AUSTRALIAN MINE PRODUCTION OF URANIUM OXIDE 1977-80
(tonnes of U_3O_8, with tonnes of U in brackets)

Mining and Treatment Site	1977	1978	1979	1980
Mary Kathleen QLD	420 (356t U)	608 (516t U)	832 (760t U)	834.5 (708t U)
Narbalek NT	—	—	—	1 006 (853t U)
TOTAL	420 (356t U)	608 (516t U)	832 (760t U)	1 840.5 (1 561t U)

Source: *Australian Mineral Industry Annual Review.* (various issues) Australian Govt Publishing Service, Canberra.

Pattern of mineral trade Australia's trade in minerals has maintained a fixed pattern for at least a decade, indicating a traditional and regular export of the same type of primary mineral commodities during that period. All the principal components of this pattern are derived from Australian resources by domestic mining. However, exceptions which have also maintained a static pattern include the re-export of minerals such as industrial diamonds, graphite, mica and the platinum group of metals. This indicates either a national shortage of such minerals or a restriction on their export for commercial or strategic reasons.

Australia, once an important gold producing country, does not now include the value of gold shipments as part of its mineral exports, a policy adopted by many other countries. The implications of this are that the gold mining industry in Australia is not adequately recognised for its current significant contribution to the international balance of payments and that gold is now considered by Australians to be a superfluous component of the mining industry.

National mineral policy In the past, the influence of gold had a remarkable effect on the Australian mineral policy. Legislation was designed with the gold prospector and the small gold mining company in mind and even today this can be discerned beneath the amendments and additions which have built up over the years. The value of mine output in Australia reached a peak of $56 million in 1907 and did not touch this level again until 1937; this was due partly to ignorance of Australia's geology and of the techniques of resource evaluation. In 1939 the mineral industry was in such a depressed state that the country was in no condition to fight a war. During World War II, mine development in all sections of the industry ceased and only production operations were maintained. The Broken Hill lead-zinc mines made a splendid contribution to the war effort by exporting their products straight to North America.

The Australian mineral industry experienced a wave of expansion and progress in the 1960s and early 1970s, based on a foundation built up in the immediate pre- and post-war years. However, mineral policy has become a matter of considerable debate between mining companies and the State or federal departments;

the mining companies favour a dynamic and flexible policy, believing that the present static or fixed type of policy will not permit the mineral industry to adjust quickly enough to external changes. The increased voicing of opinions on how to cope with the problems of the mining industry has led to a distortion of many of the issues which would form part of the National Mineral Policy. The essential requirement of a mineral policy should be the national development of mineral resources within the country and should include factors such as resource evaluation, conservation, self-sufficiency, labour, community service, environmental conditions and integration of domestic and overseas markets. The major areas of government influence within the policy would include mining legislation and royalties, technical and community services, financial assistance, taxation and controls on trade, investment and production.

Energy minerals and energy policy The world is approaching an energy crisis and the policies adopted in the 1980s will determine the scope of social relationships which man will be able to enjoy in the year 2000 and beyond. The overall growth rate of energy consumption in Australia is forecast as 6.5 per cent per annum for the period up to 1990. Beyond that, it is possible only to predict and not to forecast with any degree of accuracy. The total primary energy needs of Australia will be met from the following sources: black

and brown coals, oil and gas, hydro-electric and wind power, URANIUM, power alcohol, manufactured gases and solar heat.

Despite the fact that the balanced supply of energy from the many sources available will be achieved only by a partnership between government and private industry the comprehensive policy promulgated by the federal government may never be possible as it does not have sovereign powers with respect to energy. In 1972 the Australian government established a Department of Minerals and Energy which included the following institutions: Bureau of Mineral Resources, Geology and Geophysics; Fuel Branch; Australian Atomic Energy Commission; Australian Atomic Energy Safety Review Committee; Joint Coal Board; National Coal Research Advisory Committee; Snowy Mts Hydro-Electricity Authority; Snowy Mts Council; Division of National Mapping; National Mapping Council; Australian Minerals Council; and the Pipeline Authority. The Department of Minerals and Energy has emphasised that the aim is to have an integrated and co-ordinated national fuel and energy policy and, within the limits imposed by Australian circumstances has worked towards the implementation of this expressed policy. However, the federal Parliament is not free to establish an integrated fuel and energy policy until the various State governments wish, collectively, to establish greater concord with it.

The best prospects for the discovery of increased reserves of petroleum and natural gas are on the continental shelf off northern WA. Pending the establishment of suitable Commonwealth legislation, these areas have been claimed by the WA government. The long-range programme conceived by the Commonwealth Department provides for a trans-continental national gas pipeline which will link up the WA fields with other deposits of oil and natural gas at Mereenie, PALM VALLEY and GIDGEALPA, and transport fuel to the SE States. Such a project could be a significant feature in the Commonwealth government's ability to secure agreements from those States which would benefit from a reliable source of cheap

Virginia Coy's claim, NT, 1879

National Library of Australia

energy. With respect to coal mining, the State governments remain firmly in control of the mining leases and of the safety regulations. The main coal exporting companies still engage in initial negotiations for the sale of coal even though the Australian government has intervened on several occasions, claiming higher contract prices for coal exported.

The economic and strategic importance of uranium has been recognised since 1946. The earliest exploration for uranium took place in 1942 at Radium Hill and in 1943 at Mt Painter in the FLINDERS RANGES, both in SA. Neither the grade nor the reserves of these deposits was outstanding, and higher grade, much larger deposits were to be discovered elsewhere in Australia within the following two decades. The discovery of these high grade uranium deposits led people to believe that Australia possessed a high percentage of the world's uranium resources, resulting in some national resistance to the exploitation of the deposits (*see* URANIUM).
Further reading: Sindon, A.J. *The Natural Resources of Australia, Prospects and Problems for Development.* Angus & Robertson (in assoc. with ANZAAS), Sydney, 1972; Warren, K. *Mineral Resources.* Penguin, 1973; Bureau of Mineral Resources, Geology and Geophysics *Australian Mineral Industry Annual Review.* Australian Govt Publishing Service, Canberra, 1974 and later editions; US Bureau of Mines *Mineral Facts and Problems, Bulletin 667.* US Department of the Interior, 1975; Corbett, A.H. *Energy for Australia.* Penguin, 1976.

miners *see* honeyeaters

mining *see* minerals, etc.

mint bushes *see* Christmas bush

Minton, Yvonne (1938-) Mezzo-soprano. Born in Sydney, Yvonne Minton won many vocal competitions before leaving for overseas study in 1961. Later that year, she won the Kathleen Ferrier Prize for the best contralto in the International Vocalist Competition at 's-Hertogenbosch in Holland. She made her major operatic début in England in the world premiere of Nicholas Maw's *One Man Show*, and this led to guest engagements with the Royal Opera, Covent Garden. She joined the Royal Opera permanently in 1965. Yvonne Minton made her American début singing Octavian at the Lyric Opera in Chicago, a role for which she has become deservedly famous and in which she appears in Solti's recording of *Der Rosenkavalier*. She has worked frequently in concert performances with Pierre Boulez, and in addition to all her operatic singing, maintains a busy concert schedule. She returned to sing Octavian in the Australian Opera's 1972 season, and is in constant demand in the opera houses of Europe, Britain and America for her glorious voice and her superbly intelligent performances.

mistletoe *see* parasitic plants

mistletoe bird *see* flowerpeckers

Mitchell River QLD Located in the far N of the State, this river rises on the W side of the GREAT DIVIDING RANGE, only about 50km NW of CAIRNS, and flows in a general W then NW course for some 550km across CAPE YORK to a mud-fringed estuary on the E shore of the GULF OF CARPENTARIA. Some of its S tributaries, such as the Lynd and Walsh Rivers, rise in the ATHERTON TABLELAND. The main N tributary is the PALMER RIVER. The whole of the catchment basin is a region of high rainfall (above 1000mm yearly), but it is concentrated in the summer months with a dry season of at least five months between April and October. Hence, the Mitchell experiences flood conditions in the wet season and ceases to flow during the dry season. The area is scrub country, mainly devoted to beef cattle raising, with much of the alluvial flats inundated by flood waters for several months. The river winds across the lowlands in countless meander loops, with numerous BILLABONGS, and it divides to form many ANABRANCHES, such as the Nassan River which has a separate mouth on the Gulf. An Anglican mission station is located on the Aboriginal reserve on the coastal plain, S of the river.

Mitchell River VIC Formed by the confluence of the Dargo and Wonnangatta Rivers which rise in the Dargo High Plains near MOUNT HOTHAM, the Mitchell flows for over 250km on a S then SE course across the coastal plain of GIPPSLAND through BAIRNSDALE to LAKE KING where it forms a long silt jetty jutting into the NW section of the lake. The Glenaladale National Park (183ha), lying W of the river, includes some areas of luxuriant sub-tropical vegetation inhabited by lyrebirds, parrots and bowerbirds; part of the park was severely damaged by fire in 1965, but substantial natural regeneration has taken place since then. The river was named in 1840 by the explorer Angus McMillan in honour of the Surveyor-General Sir Thomas MITCHELL.

Mitchell, Dame Roma Flinders (1913-) Jurist. Born and educated in Adelaide, she was admitted to the Bar in 1934, subsequently specialising in matrionial cases and lecturing in family law at the University of Adelaide. In 1965 she became the first woman QC in Australian history, and three years later was appointed a Justice of the Supreme Court of SA, again being the first woman to obtain such a position anywhere in Australia.

Mitchell, Sir Thomas Livingstone (1792-1855) Surveyor and explorer. He was born in Scotland, joined the British Army in 1811, and served in the Peninsular War. In 1827 he came to NSW as deputy Surveyor-General, and in the following year became Surveyor-General, a position he held until his death.

His fame as an explorer rests on four expeditions. Those of 1831, 1835 and 1836 completed

Sir Thomas Mitchell

the work of STURT and confirmed his conclusions about the W rivers. The aim of the last expedition in 1845-46 was to find a route from the settled districts of NSW to PORT ESSINGTON in the far N. Although Mitchell came nowhere near attaining his objective, he did useful work in exploring parts of what is now central QLD, and in discovering the BARCOO RIVER.

Mitchell's explorations have tended to overshadow his other achievements. His work in surveying, constructing and repairing roads and bridges during a period of expansion was of great merit. His literary output, too, was impressive, and included two works of a military nature, journals of his expeditions, a book on the cultivation of vines and olive trees, a translation of the Portuguese classic epic poem, *Os Lusiadas* by Camoes, and a geography of Australia.
See also exploration by land
Further reading: Cumpston, J.H.L. *Thomas Mitchell, Surveyor-General and Explorer.* Oxford University Press, London, 1954; Gardiner, L. *Thomas Mitchell.* Oxford University Press, Melbourne, 1962.

mites Together with TICKS, mites form the largest subclass (or order, according to some authorities), Acari, of the class Arachnida (ARACHNIDS). There are about 2000 known genera, containing about 20 000 species in the world but it is believed there are many more in existence. Only about 2000 species have been recorded from Australia but the true number probably lies between 30 000 and 40 000. Mites are difficult to identify and study and thus, despite their economic importance, they have attracted relatively few research workers.

Mites are small, some of them so tiny that they cannot be seen with the naked eye. They occur in varied habitats: in brackish water, in freshwater, on plants, and as PARASITES on and in animals, but they are particularly abundant in moist soils where they are the commonest animals. One species, *Nanorchestes antarcticus*, lives within a few hundred miles of the South Pole. Some mites transmit serious diseases of man and other animals. Many species are scavengers, others are predators and many feed on living plants.

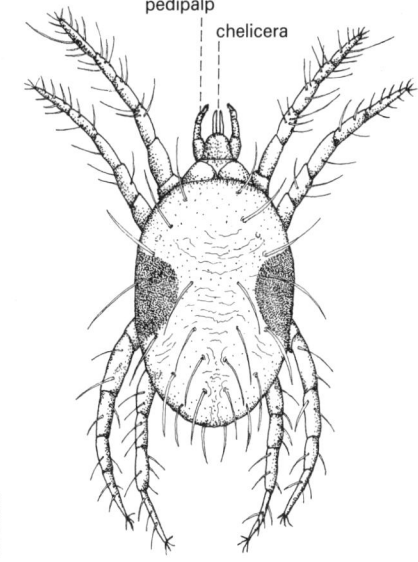

A red spider mite, *Tetranychus* species

Adult mites usually have eight legs, but some species have fewer. Most show no sign of external segmentation, and the body is not divided neatly into a cephalothorax and abdomen as it is in most arachnids. The chelicerae and the feelers (pedipalps) are contained in an anterior region (the gnathosoma), which articulates with the rest of the body (the idiosoma). The chelicerae may be pincer-like (chelate) or modified as piercing organs (stylets) and there may be a furrow across the idiosoma, between the second and third legs. The cuticle is either soft, or consists of hard plates. Mites respire by breathing tubes (tracheae), or simply through the body surface (integument).

The life cycle usually consists of six stages: egg, six-legged (hexapod) larva, protonymph, deutonymph, tritonymph and adult. In some species the deutonymph is a special resistant stage (the hypopus) which differs from the other stages both in appearance and behaviour.

Acarologists are not in total agreement as to the classification of mites and ticks. One system gives this group a subclass rank with seven orders. This scheme is followed in the main.

Notostigmata This is a small order, unknown, so far in Australia.

Tetrastigmata This order contains one genus of predatory mites, *Holothyrus* (2mm to 7mm), known only from Australia, New Guinea, the Seychelles, Mauritius and Sri Lanka. Little is known of these predatory mites.

Metastigmata The ticks.

Mesostigmata This is a large order, and contains small mites, almost all of which are less than 2mm in length. They resemble tiny ticks. Commonly found in soil, members of this order can withdraw their mouthparts into a cavity in the idiosoma. They include the uropodines—mites with weak mouthparts that

are believed to feed only upon fungi and spores—and the gamasids. Many gamasids are important predators and *Macrocheles muscaedomesticae* has been proposed as a BIOLOGICAL CONTROL agent for flies in farmyard manure.

Cryptostigmata The cryptostigmatic mites, also known as oribatid mites or beetle mites, are easily recognisable denizens of soil and leaf-litter (up to 100 000 per square metre), but some are also aquatic. They are cosmopolitan mites, looking superficially like tiny beetles; they range in size from about 0.2mm to 1.5mm, and have strong body plates. They feed on algae, fungi and decaying plant material.

Astigmata This order contains acarid mites, tiny (0.2mm to 1.5mm) thin-skinned species which respire through their integument. Many are free-living forms feeding on fungi, dead organic matter, or stored products, while some are parasites.

The free-living astigmatids include the following: the house-dust mite, *Dermatophagoides pteronyssinus*, a common cause of allergic conditions; *Carpoglyphus lactis*, a cosmopolitan mite of dried fruit, honeycombs and wine corks; the house mite, *Glycyphagus domesticus*, which is found in almost all kinds of organic material, as long as it is reasonably damp (wheat, flour, rush furniture, upholstered chairs, sugar, cheese, bee frames, tobacco and mascara); the cheese mite, *Tyrophagus* (*Tyrolichus*) *casei*, found in a range of habitats from cheeses to insect collections; and the cereal mite, *Acarus siro*. Many of these mites have been implicated in attacks of dermatitis and asthma. The free-living astigmatid mites have the idiosoma clearly divided into two parts by a furrow. The front four legs point forwards, and the hind four backwards.

The parasitic astigmatids include the notorious scabies itch mite, *Sarcoptes scabiei* (*see* parasites, human).

Psoroptic mange of sheep, once present in Australia, is caused by the astigmatid *Psoroptes ovis*, and is often fatal. Related species attack horses, cattle and goats. A common ear mite, *Otodectes cynotis*, found in dogs and sometimes in cats, feeds by puncturing the skin, causing intense irritation and sometimes deafness as the ear is filled with wax, blood and detritus. The poultry depluming mite, *Cnemidocoptes gallinae*, burrows into the skin at the base of the feathers and the birds often pull the feathers out. The poultry scaly-leg mite, *Cn. mutans*, causes a scaly thickening of the legs, and sometimes of the comb, of poultry, turkeys and pheasants.

Prostigmata (or Trombidiformes) This order contains a mixed group of mites, ranging in size from about 0.1mm to about 1.5mm. There are four large groups: Tarsonemini, Eleutherengona, Parasitengona and Tetrapodili.

1. Tarsonemini. Many of these mites parasitise insects. *Acarapis woodi* lives inside the tracheae of honey bees and sucks their blood through the tracheal wall; infested bees cannot fly and leave the hive to die. This disorder is acariasis, or Isle of Wight disease, and it

has been reported recently in Australia. Orthoptera (including locusts) and Hymenoptera are attacked in a similar way by the *Locustacarus* species. The grain itch mite, *Pyemotes herfsi*, is an ectoparasite of the larvae of some beetles and Hymenoptera, and of the larvae and pupae of moths and often occurs in infested stored products such as hay. Sometimes the fertilised females try to feed on workers who handle foodstuffs or hay causing a painful but transitory dermatitis. This species sometimes attacks the furniture beetle, *Anobium punctatum*. Some tarsonemids are plant parasites, and many of them cause malformations of the host plants. *Tarsonemus ananas* attacks pineapples in QLD by transmitting a fungal disease.

2. Eleutherengona. These mites are either free-living throughout their life, or are completely parasitic. The most notable parasites belong to the family Demodicidae and include the common follicle mite, *Demodex folliculorum*, which probably occurs in almost every living human, except young babies. It lives in sebaceous glands and at the roots of the eyelashes and can be found easily by squeezing out the contents of a blackhead, placing them in a drop of xylene to dissolve the fatty matter, and examining them under a microscope. It is an unusually shaped mite with a long, striated idiosoma which gives it a worm-like appearance. The length is about 0.4mm or less. Fortunately, considering its ubiquity, it rarely causes any harm but sometimes a rash of tiny red spots may appear. *D. canis*, however, causes severe mange in dogs.

The Eleutherengona group also contains some of the most important parasitic mites of plants, several of which have been introduced into Australia. They include the red-spider mites (genera *Metatetranychus*, *Bryobia*, *Panonychus*, etc.) of the family Tetranychidae which attack a great variety of crops including fruit trees and hops. These mites suck plant sap from the leaves causing a silvering or a bronzing, and often premature leaf fall. Some of them spin threads of silk under which they feed. The family Eupodidae contains the harmful, introduced red-legged earth mite, *Halotydeus destructor*, and the blue oat mite, *Penthaleus major*, which are both winter pests of pasture plants. The group also contains, however, several families of predatory mites, some of which have been used for the biological control of red-spider mites in various parts of the world, including Australia.

3. Parasitengona. These mites differ from the last group in that the larvae are parasites, but the adults are free-living. The larvae of the family Trombiculidae are known as chiggers, many of which attack mammals, including man and domestic animals, in the larval stage. Often they spread Rickettsial diseases such as scrub typhus, a disease which incapacitated more Allied soldiers than did the Japanese during World War II. Many of the members of the genus *Trombicula* cause an itch by their bites, but a vector of scrub typhus; *Leptotrombidium deliense*, occurs in N Australia where it sometimes transmits the disease. The

eggs are laid in or on the soil and the newly hatched, bright-red larva climbs vegetation and clings to a passing host. Other Parasitengona larvae attack insects; these include the water mites, some of which parasitise, for example, mosquito larvae. The adult water mites are often brightly coloured in blues and reds.

4. Tetrapodili. This last group of mites is difficult to fit into the classificatory scheme but is probably best placed here. They are microscopic plant parasites which often cause galling in their hosts. The cuticle is grooved so that the mite appears to be segmented, and there are only two pairs of legs (sometimes less). This group includes the citrus rust mites, such as *Phyllocoptruta oleivora* and *Tegolophus australis,* which produce brown discoloration of oranges and silvering of lemon skins; the citrus bud mite, *Eriophyes (Aceria) sheldoni,* responsible for distortion of citrus shoots and fruits; and the grape leaf blister mite, *Colomerus (E.) vitis,* a cosmopolitan pest which produces blisters on vine leaves.

Further reading: see under parasites. *Also* Williams, W.D. *Australian Freshwater Life.* (2nd edn) Macmillan, Melbourne, 1980; Hassan, E. *Major Insect and Mite Pest* (sic) *of Australian Crops.* Ento Press, Gatton QLD, 1977; Hely, P.C., Pasfield, G. and Gellatley, J.G. *Insect Pests of Fruit and Vegetables in NSW.* Inkata Press, Melbourne, 1982.

Blisters on a grape vine leaf caused by the grape leaf blister mite, *Eriophyes vitis*

mitre shells *see* gastropods

Mittagong NSW (population 4 266 in 1981) This town on the SOUTHERN TABLELANDS is located 125km SW of Sydney on the Hume Highway. It is a small service centre for the surrounding dairying and market gardening region. Its claim to historic fame is that it was the site of the first iron smelting industry in Australia; the building of a blast furnace was commenced in 1848 and for the following 30 years smelting was carried on intermittently. This infant industry was based on local raw materials: coal outcropped in the nearby valleys of the Nattai River, ironstone occurred in patches in the vicinity and limestone was

available at nearby Marulan. The industry had a chequered history and, because it was small, costly to operate and relatively inefficient, it finally expired in 1877.
See also iron and steel industry

Mitta Mitta River VIC This upper tributary of the MURRAY RIVER rises in the GREAT DIVIDING RANGE to the E and SE of the BOGONG HIGH PLAINS and flows for some 280km in a general NNW direction to join the Murray at HUME DAM. Some of the headwaters of the catchment basin are snow-covered in winter and the Alpine Road crosses the river at OMEO. The annual rainfall varies over different sections of the valley. The Omeo Highway, which links the Princes Highway at BAIRNSDALE with the Murray Valley Highway near TALLANGATTA, winds along the Mitta Mitta River valley through heavily timbered country in the uplands and rich pastoral and agricultural areas on the river plains. The construction of the DARTMOUTH DAM, across a gorge on the upper river, was started in 1972 as part of the Murray River water conservation scheme; it drains a catchment area of 3 613m^2 and with a storage capacity of 3 700 000ML is the largest reservoir in VIC. The name Mitta Mitta comes from an Aboriginal phrase and has several meanings: 'little waters', 'thunder' and 'where reeds grow'.

Mockridge, Russell (1928-58) Cyclist. Born in GEELONG in VIC, Mockridge was one of Australia's greatest cyclists. He first gave notice of his extraordinary ability in the 1950 Empire Games where he won gold medals in the 1000m time trial and the 1000m sprint. On the strength of his successes in 1950, he was selected for the 1952 Olympic Games. However, he was dropped from the team when he refused to sign an Olympic Federation bond stating that he would not turn professional for two years after the Games (a bond which all athletes of the time were asked to sign). Following the raising of an £800 bond by the people of Geelong, and his signing of a 12-month amateur bond, Mockridge was reinstated in the team and more than justified his selection with brilliant wins in the 1000m time trial, setting a new Olympic record, and the 2000m tandem event with Lionel Cox. During his amateur career, he won the Paris Amateur Grand Prix and caused a sensation shortly afterwards by beating all the world's top professional riders in the Open Grand Prix. Although a talented all-round cyclist, early in his career he had been reluctant to enter road races because of poor eyesight. However, after becoming professional he turned to road racing at which he was outstandingly successful, winning the Australian Professional Road Cycling championship three times in succession, 1956-58. Just before a trip to Europe he was killed when struck by a bus during a road race. The nation mourned the death of its favourite cyclist and 10 000 people attended his funeral.

Moe VIC (combined population of Moe and YALLOURN 18 158 in 1981) This town in the LATROBE RIVER valley, on the Princes Highway, 135km by road ESE of Melbourne, is adjacent to Yallourn on the S side of the river. It is a business and service centre for the nearby dairying and foresting regions, and in recent decades has increasingly become part of the planned urban growth associated with the mining and power generation developments on the open-cut coalfields of the valley. The town takes its name from an Aboriginal word meaning 'a swamp'. The GIPPSLAND Folk Museum, located on a 3ha site at the W entrance to the town, depicts the settlement and development of the region and includes a reconstructed pioneer street with homes, shops and buildings typical of the early days. It was officially opened in 1973 and is a popular tourist attraction.

Molle Islands QLD The coral-fringed islands of North, South and Mid-Molle are in the inner section of the GREAT BARRIER REEF, located NE of PROSERPINE between the WHITSUNDAY PASSAGE and the mainland coast. South Molle Is has been extensively developed as a tourist resort and can be reached by launch from Shute Harbour, by helicopter from Proserpine, or by air-launch from MACKAY via the Whitsunday airstrip.

molluscs The Mollusca is one of the largest of the invertebrate phyla, containing more than 80 000 known living species, and about 30 000 fossil species. In Australia and her adjacent waters there are about 400 land and freshwater molluscs, and about 10 000 marine species. The phylum contains SLUGS AND SNAILS and other members of the class Gastropoda (GASTROPODS); the coat-of-mail shells or CHITONS; the BIVALVE MOLLUSCS; the octopuses, squids and other members of the class Cephalopoda (CEPHALOPODS); and the TUSK SHELLS which form the class Scaphopoda.

Despite their apparent great diversity a common body plan can be discerned though some of the structures listed below are reduced or absent in some forms. The body consists of a head, often carrying tentacles, a visceral hump containing most of the internal organs, and a foot. The visceral hump is usually covered by a shell which consists of one unit (most gastropods), two units (bivalves) or several (chitons), but in some forms the shell may be absent. A fold of skin (the mantle) extends down from the visceral hump, enclosing a space (the mantle cavity) between it and the rest of the body. The gills and the anus are situated within this cavity. In some species the current of water propelled by the gills carries in food particles which are filtered out by the animal, but many molluscs feed by means of a horny, file-like structure (a radula) which is used for scraping off food particles and drawing them into the mouth. As the radula is worn down it is replaced by growth from behind. This simple arrangement is best seen in the chitons, commonly found in rock pools. The head of these animals is, however, greatly reduced. It

Mainland tiger snake, *Notechis scutatus*

Carpet snake, *Morelia variegata*

Red-bellied black snake, *Pseudechis porphyriacus*

Sea-snake, *Hydrophis* species

Taipan, *Oxyuranus scutellatus*

Tasmanian cave spider, *Hickmania troglodytes*

Wolf spider, Lycosid species

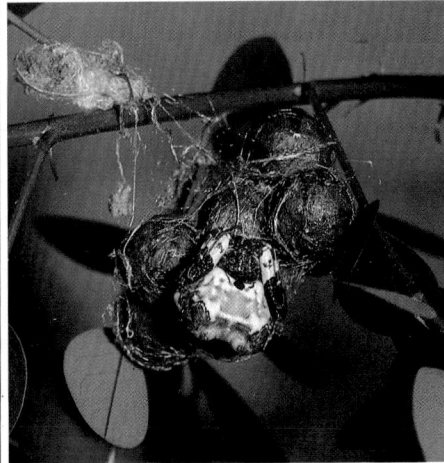

Red-back spider, *Latrodectus mactans hasselti*

Net-casting spider, *Dinopis subrufa*

Bird-dropping spider, *Celaenia excavata* with egg sacs

See also SNAKES and SPIDERS

Frilled Lizard, *Chlamydosaurus kingii* (see LIZARDS)

Black flying fox, *Pteropus alecto* (see BATS)

Mountain or Thornyl devil, *Moloch horridus* (see LIZARDS)

Platypus, *Ornithorhynchus anatinus*
(see MONOTREME MAMMALS)

Corroboree frog, *Pseudophryne corroboree* (see FROGS)

Snake-neck tortoise, *Chelodina longicollis* (see TORTOISES

Two common skinks: (above) shingle back,
Trachydosaurus rugosus; (below) eastern
blue-tongued, *Tiliqua scincoides* (see LIZARDS)

Australian water rat, *Hydromys chrysogaster*
(see RODENTS)

Spinifix hopping mouse, *Notomys alexis* (see RODENTS)

Doughboy scallop, *Chlamys asperrimus*

is more difficult to see the design in gastropods for during their development these usually undergo torsion. The visceral hump is twisted round so that the anus opens near the mouth.

Some molluscs are herbivores whilst others are carnivores; very few are parasites. Some move as slowly as the proverbial snail but the octopuses and the squids are swift predators. The group provides man with many food species such as oysters and mussels, and with a few pests, especially slugs, snails and oyster borers. Many terrestrial and aquatic snails are alternative hosts for parasitic FLATWORMS of man and other animals, and they are an important source of food for many different kinds of animals. The molluscs are the only source of PEARLS.

Further reading: Allan, J. *Australian Shells.* Georgian House, Melbourne, 1950; Morton, J.E. *Molluscs.* (5th edn) Hutchinson, London, 1979; Williams, W.D. *Australian Freshwater Life.* (2nd edn) Macmillan, Melbourne, 1980; Wright, C.A. *Flukes and Snails.* George Allen & Unwin, London, 1971; Coleman, N. *What Shell is That?* Paul Hamlyn, Sydney, 1975; Dakin, W.J., Bennett, I. & Pope, E. *Australian Seashores.* (6th edn) Angus & Robertson, Sydney, 1976; Child, J. *Australian Sea Shells.* (5th edn) Periwinkle Books, Dee Why West NSW, 1977.

mollymawks *see* sea birds

Molonglo River NSW/ACT This rather minor tributary of the MURRUMBIDGEE RIVER is located in the SOUTHERN TABLELANDS. From its source in the E part of the tablelands it flows NW, is joined by a tributary, the Queanbeyan River, then flows in a WNW direction across the ACT to its confluence with the Murrumbidgee near the NW border between the ACT and NSW. In

some sections of its course it flows through narrow gorges where it cuts across rocky ridges, while in other parts it has broad valleys with alluvial flats. The stream has assumed importance because Canberra is located in one of these broad valleys in its middle course. The Scrivener Dam, completed in 1963, was built across the Molonglo to form Lake Burley Griffin.

Molvig, Jon (1923-70) Artist. Born in NEWCASTLE in NSW, he served with the army in the Pacific, 1942-46, and became interested in painting. He studied at the East Sydney Technical College, 1947-49, and then travelled to the UK and the Continent. On his return in 1953 he settled in Brisbane and spent most of his life there. Molvig was an important figure in the 1950s and 1960s when Australia, in the face of public opposition, was trying to come to grips with contemporary art trends in the USA and Europe. While some art critics see Molvig as an eclectic painter, whose changes of style seemed inconsistent, others consider that the energy of his work and his intuitive use of colour produced some powerful works and some of the best portraits in Australian art history. He was an erratic but enthusiastic worker. One of his best works, *Ballad of a Dead Stockman,* can be seen in the Art Gallery of New South Wales.

Monaro NSW This region in the SE of the State comprises the S part of the SOUTHERN TABLELANDS, stretching from QUEANBEYAN to the VIC border. It is a plateau formation, part of the GREAT DIVIDING RANGE, with rugged hilly areas which in parts are deeply dissected by river valleys. On the E it drops by steep scarps to the narrow S coastal plain and the roads leading down these scarps (Macquarie Pass, Clyde Mt, Araluen Valley and Brown

Mt) are well known to motorists for their steep gradients and winding routes; on the W it merges into the SW slopes region. The headwaters of the MURRUMBIDGEE and the SNOWY Rivers are located in the SW of the area, and several coastal streams (SHOALHAVEN, Clyde, Moruya, Tuross and Towamba) rise here and flow to the Pacific. The main towns are Queanbeyan in the N, COOMA in the centre, and Bombala in the S. The Monaro Highway traverses the region from N to S, and the Snowy Mts Highway links the coastal belt to the inland slopes. The main Southern Tablelands railway extends S from GOULBURN through Queanbeyan and Cooma.

The general elevation of the plateau is about 800m, but there is considerable variation in the landforms with the highest peaks of the ranges rising to over 1 800m. On the surface of the plateau there are many lines of hills, roughly parallel and with a general N-S alignment (for example, Tinderry Range E of Queanbeyan, the Bimberi Range W of Canberra and the Monaro Range W of Cooma). Between these hills are river valleys, also with a N-S trend, sometimes narrow gorges, at other times broad plains, and with gaps through the ranges where the rivers cut across them. Grazing is the main rural industry of the Monaro; the better pastures are generally used for sheep, with beef cattle in the rougher wooded areas and dairying along some river flats. Timber-getting is important in many parts of the tablelands and, in some areas the distillation of *Eucalyptus* oil from leaves of native trees is a subsidiary activity. In the mid-SW of the plateau is the KOSCIUSKO National

A stock route on the Monaro plateau

Park, a famed winter ski resort and a summer trout fishing and bushwalking area. Here, too, are the major constructions of the SNOWY MOUNTAINS SCHEME.

Further reading: Wilson, J.L.J. (ed) 'Southern Tablelands—NSW' in *Current Affairs Bulletin.* (vol 15, no 10, 1955); Shaw, J.H. *The Face of Our Earth.* Shakespeare Head Press, Sydney, 1961; Hancock, W.K. *Discovering Monaro.* Cambridge University Press, London, 1972; Ruhen, O. *Southern Highlands Sketchbook.* Rigby, Adelaide, 1974.

Monash, Sir John (1865-1931) Engineer and soldier. Of Jewish descent, Monash was born in Melbourne and graduated in engineering from Melbourne University in 1891. Having joined the University Rifles as a student, he continued as a part-time officer in the militia and by 1913 had reached the rank of colonel. He joined the Australian Imperial Force (AIF) shortly after the outbreak of the war in 1914, commanded a brigade at GALLIPOLI, and then served with distinction in France. In March 1918 he was placed in command of the Australian Corps and further enhanced his reputation by his brilliant planning and leadership in the closing battles of the war. He was made a KCB in 1918 and a GCMG in 1919, and received honours also from the French, Belgian and US governments.

In 1920 he was made general manager and in the following year chairman of the State Electricity Commission of VIC. In these positions he played the major role in the establishment of brown-coal mining operations in the LATROBE RIVER valley for electricity generation and the making of briquettes. He received many honours, including a number of honorary degrees, and became president of the Zionist Federation of Australia in 1928. VIC's second university is named after him.
Further reading: Monash, Sir John *The Australian Victories in France in 1918.* Angus & Robertson, Sydney, 1936; Hetherington, J. *John Monash.* Oxford University Press, Melbourne, 1962; Edwards, C. *John Monash.* State Electricity Commission of VIC, Melbourne, 1970.

Courtesy of A.I.S. Canberra

Sir John Monash

Moncrieff, Gladys (1892-1976) Singer. She was born at BUNDABERG in QLD, the daughter of a musician and a singer. As a girl she toured QLD with her parents' picture show, singing to lantern slides. In her late teens she performed at the Empire Theatre, Brisbane, and in suburban vaudeville; in 1911 she was engaged by Hugh Ward of the J.C. WILLIAMSON 'Firm', from then on appearing

in Gilbert and Sullivan and other musical comedies. Her first leading role was in 1918 in *Katinka*, followed in 1921 by *The Maid of the Mountains*, with which she became identified. She left Australia for London in 1926 and appeared in *The Blue Mazurka* in 1926, returning to Australia in 1928 to appear in *Rio Rita*, in which she toured for the following two years. In 1933 she appeared in the Australian musical *Collit's Inn*, and thereafter in many musicals and operettas such as *The Merry Widow* and *Viktoria and Her Hussar*. Greatly loved by Australian audiences, she was affectionately dubbed 'our Glad'. She conducted her farewell tour in 1959, and in retirement moved to Surfers Paradise QLD, where she died.
Further reading: Moncrieff, G. *My Life of Song.* Rigby, Adelaide, 1971; West, J. *Theatre in Australia.* Cassell, Sydney, 1978.

monitors *see* lizards

monotreme mammals The smallest of the three surviving subclasses of MAMMALS, Prototheria, consists of only one order, Monotremata. Monotremes are distinctive, primitive, egg-laying mammals; only two types are known, spiny anteaters (or echidnas) and the platypus. The platypus is restricted to Australia but spiny anteaters occur in both Australia and New Guinea.

Monotremes share a number of features with REPTILES: both lay eggs with shells and large yolks; monotremes have the combined urino-genital and anal openings common in all reptiles; and the structure of some parts of a monotreme's skeleton, such as the shoulder girdle, is reptile-like. However, monotremes

are classed as mammals because they possess the typical hair and mammary glands. The latter have no teats but open into a pair of longitudinal grooves into which the milk oozes. The young are protected in a temporary pouch (marsupium). Male platypuses are unique in that they posses a venom gland and a spine on the hind-foot; the use of these features is disputed.

Unfortunately, the only fossils of monotremes found so far (all in Australia) resemble the living species. Because monotremes are very specialised animals—one living on land and feeding on insects, the other leading an aquatic existence and feeding on aquatic invertebrates—the fossils give no clues as to the relationships and ancestry of these animals. Furthermore, the adults do not have teeth which are an important guide to mammal relationships as they are often the only fossil remains.

There are two existing genera of spiny anteaters (family Tachyglossidae), each containing one species. *Tachyglossus aculeatus* (usually about 40cm long) is a common but secretive animal that occurs throughout Australia, including TAS, and New Guinea. The other genus, *Zaglossus*, has left fossils in Australia but is now restricted to New Guinea and some of the islands.

T. aculeatus has long spines (up to 6cm) on the back and the short tail and much of the face, but the limbs and underparts have only bristles and coarse hairs. The spines make it difficult for the animal to scratch its skin but the second digit of the hind-foot is very long and is used for grooming. The colour varies from light brown to black. The snout is long and beak-like and carries the two nostrils and a

An echidna, *Tachyglossus aculeatus*, at the Sir Colin McKenzie Wild Life Sanctuary in Healesville

tiny mouth at the end. The sense of sight is believed to be poor, but spiny anteaters have acute hearing, a very sensitive snout and, probably, a sense of smell. The limbs have very strong claws well adapted for digging; when disturbed, the animal virtually sinks into the ground—not head-first like most burrowing mammals. Once partly buried it is almost impossible to dislodge. Curiously, the fore-feet of spiny anteaters are partly webbed although they are completely terrestrial.

Spiny anteaters feed on insects. Termites form an important part of the diet where they are abundant but in many areas true ants form the bulk of the food. The insects are collected with the help of a long, extensile tongue.

Spiny anteaters usually lay a single egg which, some authorities believe, is deposited directly into the pouch. After hatching, the young is suckled in the pouch until it begins to develop spines when, not surprisingly, it is removed and placed in a den.

The platypus, *Ornithorhynchus anatinus* (45cm to 61cm), the only member of the family Ornithorhynchidae, is confined to E Australia, from COOKTOWN in QLD to SA and TAS, although it has been introduced on to KANGAROO ISLAND. Formerly, it was a diurnal creature, but in attempting to escape hunters who captured it for its pelt the platypus has become more nocturnal in its habits.

The most striking feature of this animal is the hairless, beak-like muzzle which is covered with thin, extremely sensitive skin. The rest of the body is covered with short dense fur which resists water. The eyes lie in a groove on the top of the head and look almost directly upwards, whilst the ear openings, which lack external parts, are at the end of the grooves, behind the eyes. The nostrils are on the snout, near the front and centre. When the platypus swims underwater it keeps its eyes closed tightly and so eats only those items of food—mainly small invertebrates—that it touches with its beak. The feet are webbed to aid swimming, and the tail is flattened and resembles that of the beaver.

The platypus nuzzles food from the mud at the bottom of creeks and stores large quantities in a pair of cheek pouches behind the beak. It prefers deep pools in which to live, preferably with steep banks and reeds. Within the banks it constructs tunnels which follow erratic courses and can be between 6m and 15m long; the entrance to the tunnel is a low archway. The nesting burrows of the females have blind cul-de-sacs and a larger nesting chamber lined with grass and leaves. Breeding occurs in the spring when the female lays one to three leathery eggs which stick together. There is probably a period of about a fortnight between mating and egg-laying, and incubation lasts about 10 days. During this time the entrance to the tunnel is blocked.

Both types of monotremes are still reasonably common and are now protected by law in Australia. However, some platypuses still drown in fish traps, as they can stay submerged for only a few minutes.

Further reading: Wood Jones, F. *The Mammals of South Australia.* (parts I-III) Govt Printer, Adelaide, 1923-25; Burrel, H. *The Platypus.* Angus & Robertson, Sydney, 1927; Griffiths, M.E. *Echidnas.* Pergamon Press, Oxford, 1968; Ride, W.D.L. *A Guide to the Native Mammals of Australia.* Oxford University Press, Melbourne, 1970; Augee, M.L. (ed) *Monotreme Biology.* The Royal Zoological Society of New South Wales, Mosman NSW, 1978; Grant, T. & Fanning, D. *The Platypus.* NSW University Press, Sydney, 1984.

Montague Island NSW Located off the S coast of the State, E of NAROOMA township, about 290km S of Sydney, this island is a wildlife sanctuary. It is a granite outcrop which was formerly quarried to provide stone for some of Sydney's major buildings, such as the General Post Office. The waters in the vicinity of the island are noted for deep-sea game fishing. On his voyage along the E coast in 1770, Captain COOK sighted the island and named the S point Cape Dromedary, thinking it to be part of the mainland. The name of the island was originally spelt 'Montagu', after George Montagu Dunk, Earl of Halifax. However, the final 'e' was added in general use and 'Montague' became the officially accepted and approved spelling.

Monte Bello Islands WA This group of low-lying uninhabited coral and limestone islands, partly mangrove-fringed, are located N of BARROW ISLAND off the NW coast of the State. The four main islands are North West, Trimouille, South East and Hermite. This group was named after the Duke of Montebello by the French explorer Nicholas BAUDIN on his 1801-1802 voyage. In 1952, the islands were the site of the first British atomic explosion.

Mooloolaba QLD (combined population of Mooloolaba and MAROOCHYDORE 17 460 in 1981) This holiday resort on the SUNSHINE COAST, near the mouth of the Mooloola River, is located 13km by road off the Bruce Highway, 16km N of CALOUNDRA and 116km by road N of Brisbane. The N fringes of the town merge into the S section of the coastal resort of Maroochydore. The district is a popular tourist centre, with facilities for boating, swimming, surfing, fishing and other aquatic sports. The town name comes from Aboriginal words meaning 'place of snapper fish'.

Moomba SA This natural gas field is located in the arid NE of the State, in the basin of COOPER'S CREEK, near the borders of QLD, NSW and SA. It was discovered in 1966 and, together with the gas from the nearby GIDGEALPA field; gas from Moomba is taken by a 780km-long pipeline to Adelaide. In 1974, the construction of a 1300km-long pipeline was commerced from these fields to Sydney; it was completed and came into operation in 1976.

Moonbi Range NSW Located NE of TAMWORTH, this range forms the SW scarp of the NEW ENGLAND Plateau. The sharp rise up the range is well known to motorists journeying N on the New England Highway from Tamworth to ARMIDALE.

Moonie QLD Located in the SE of the State at the junction of the Moonie and Leichhardt Highways, 331km by road W of Brisbane, 97km N of GOONDIWINDI and 116km SW of DALBY, Moonie was the site of Australia's first commercial oil strike and thus has a special place in the nation's history of petroleum exploration. It is situated in the N part of a geological formation known as the Surat Basin and it was here, in December 1961, that the first well struck oil. After 16 more wells had been drilled (14 of which found oil), a 306km-long pipeline to Brisbane was constructed in 1963. This was the first major hydrocarbon pipeline in Australia. Oil production from Moonie commenced in 1964 at a rate of 5 000 barrels per day and by 1966 it had increased to 9 000 barrels per day. A small oilfield at Alton, 88km SW of Moonie, was discovered in 1964 and a further one at Bennet, 64km N. By mid-1978 the Moonie field had produced about 19 million barrels of crude oil and its production rate was then about 950 barrels per day; it was considered that further drilling would probably offer reasonable prospects for the discovery of more small oil pools in the five to 10 million barrel range. Though these would be small compared to the BASS STRAIT fields, the cost of onshore exploitation at Moonie would be much cheaper than the offshore Bass Strait developments.

Moonta SA (population 1 924 in 1981) This small town in the NW of the YORKE PENINSULA is 167km by road NW of Adelaide. The region was settled in the 1830s as a pastoral district for sheep farmers seeking additional grazing land beyond the limited areas around Adelaide, but it was the discovery of copper in 1860 that led to the boom growth of the town. By 1875 it had a population of about 12 000 and, apart from Adelaide, was the biggest town in SA. Rich mines in the Moonta-KADINA-WALLAROO triangle attracted miners mainly from Cornwall in England and this gave rise to the 'Cousin Jack and Jenny' image of the region. The copper mines flourished until 1923 when low world prices and competition from new fields overseas caused the closing of the mines and the decline of 'Little Cornwall'. Nowadays Moonta is a quiet country town and a service centre for a productive rural district, particularly noted for barley growing; Moonta Bay, 3km W on the SPENCER GULF coast, once the seaport for the copper mines, is now a seaside holiday resort. However, in Moonta a breath of history still lingers in the air, with disused slag heaps, smelting works, mining installations and old cottages representing the 63 years of copper mining. The National Trust (SA) has classified and recorded many buildings in the town for preservation, dating from the 1860s and

Premier's Dept SA

The railway station at Moonta

1870s, including several churches, houses, banking premises, the post office, the town hall, the Masonic Temple and the railway station. The name Moonta comes from the Aboriginal word meaning 'dense impenetrable scrub'.

Moora WA (population 1 677 in 1981) This country town on the railway route between Perth and GERALDTON, 174km N of Perth by rail, is located between the NW Coastal Highway and the Great Northern Highway, 36km by road NNW of NEW NORCIA. It is a business and service centre for the surrounding sheep grazing and wheat farming region.

Moore, George (1923-) Jockey. Moore served his apprenticeship in Brisbane and became one of Australia's top jockeys in the post-World War II period. His highly successful record includes riding five winners at one meeting on five occasions and four winners at one meeting on 18 occasions. At the 1969 Randwick Easter Carnival, Moore won 15 of the 29 races run during the four-day event. His consistent success made him widely popular among punters, some of whom bet on every single horse he rode—a $10 bet placed on every horse he rode from 1956 (when he returned to racing following a three-year suspension) to April 1970 would have brought a profit of $1 831. During this period he rode 3 403 races for 1 040 wins, 620 seconds and 447 thirds. Also successful overseas, where his wins included the English Derby, the French Derby and the American San Diego Handicap, he finally retired after the 1972-73 season when he did not renew his jockey's licence. A highly skilled horseman with a deep understanding of horses, he was offered a training position in Hong Kong following his retirement and he quickly established himself there as a leading trainer.

Moorehead, Alan McCrae (1910-83) Author. Born in Melbourne, he lived abroad for many years and achieved great popular success with a number of books which combine the study of historical episodes or movements with contemporary observations of their geographical settings. These include *Gallipoli* (1956), *The White Nile* (1960), *The Blue Nile* (1962), *Cooper's Creek* (1963), which deals with the exploring expedition of BURKE and Wills, and *The Fatal Impact* (1966), which describes the effects of European penetration on the peoples of the Pacific. Other works by Moorehead include *Montgomery, A Biography* (1946) and *The Desert War: The North African Campaign, 1940-3* (1968).

moorhens see rails, etc.

Mooroopna VIC A town in the central N of the State, located just 3km across the GOULBURN RIVER from SHEPPARTON, it is on the Midland Highway, 68km W of BENALLA and 188km by road NNE of Melbourne. It is situated in the midst of the irrigated farmlands of the Goulburn Valley and, in many ways, is a satellite town of Shepparton; the combined population of the Shepparton-Mooroopna urban centre was 28 369 in 1981. At an elevation of 113m above sea level, and with an average yearly rainfall of 509mm, the rural activities of the district include fruit growing, dairying, fat lamb raising, vegetable growing and cattle grazing. There is a fruit and juice canning factory in the town.

Mootwingee NSW This small settlement is in the Bynguano Range in the arid far W of the State, beyond the DARLING RIVER, about 130km NE, of BROKEN HILL, between the Barrier and Silver City Highways. It has been proclaimed a historic site because of the wealth of Aboriginal relics in the area such as camp sites, tools and implements, stone arrangements, rock carvings and paintings. The region is one of low and unreliable rainfall where streams flow intermittently, but within the range there are semi-permanent water holes which were probably the reason why it was an important Aboriginal gathering place for ceremonies and rituals.

Moraceae see figs

Moranbah QLD (population 4 362 in 1981) This company mining town is located 13km off the Peak Downs Highway, 96km by road NE of Clermont and about 1 090km N of Brisbane. It is situated in the Isaacs River valley, a tributary of the MACKENZIE-FITZROY

Snake Cave at Mootwingee historic site

river system, inland from MACKAY. Most of the town has been built since 1969 by the two companies (Utah and Mitsubishi) involved in the development of the GOONYELLA (NNW of Moranbah) and PEAK DOWNS (SSE) coal mines.

Morant, Harry Harbord 'Breaker' (1865-1902) Horseman and minor balladist. Born in Devon, England, he came to QLD in about 1884, possibly as a result of a dispute over gambling debts, and moved to NSW in the 1890s. Because of his skill at horse breaking he became known as 'The Breaker', and used this as a pen-name when contributing ballads and other verse to the *Bulletin*. He went to the Boer War, was promoted to lieutenant, and then joined an irregular force, the Bushveldt Carbineers. In August 1901 a friend, Captain Hunt, was killed and his body mutilated by Boer guerillas. In reprisal, Boer prisoners were shot, and Morant, together with Captain P.J. Handcock and G.R. Wilton, was convicted of their murder. Wilton's sentence was commuted, but Morant and Handcock were executed by firing squad. In Australia there was a widespread belief that they had been cynically used as scapegoats by the British command. The incident has recently received great publicity through the film *Breaker Morant* (1980).
Further reading: Wilton, G.R. *Scapegoats of Empire: The Bushveldt Carbineers.* D.W. Paterson, Melbourne, 1907; Carnegie, M. & Shields, F. *In Search of Breaker Morant, Balladist and Bushveldt Carbineer.* H.H. Stephenson, Armadale VIC, 1979.

morays *see* fishes, bony

Moree NSW (population 10 455 in 1981) This town is located at the junction of the Newell and Gwydir Highways, on the GWYDIR RIVER, at an elevation of 209m above sea level, 670km by road NW of Sydney. It is a railway town on a branch line 97km N from NARRABRI, with a junction line SE to INVERELL. The name Moree comes from an Aboriginal word meaning 'a long spring' or 'a water hole'. The town has an annual rainfall of only 578mm and long dry spells are not uncommon. It is a service centre for the N part of the wheat and sheep lands of the NW slopes. The best-known tourist attraction is the artesian baths, with water at a temperature of 43°C from a bore over 900m deep. Bathing in these waters benefits people suffering from nervous, rheumatic and arthritic complaints. An overseas telecommunications station, with a huge parabolic dish antenna, is located 10km NW of Moree.

morel *see* fungi

Moreton Bay QLD This is a shallow coastal inlet in the SE of the State, located E and NE of Brisbane, into which the Brisbane River drains. The LOGAN RIVER has its estuary at the S of the bay and smaller streams, such as the Caboolture and Pine Rivers, drain into the

NW section. The mainland coast along the W border of Moreton Bay consists of a series of curved beaches — DECEPTION — Bramble, Waterloo, Raby and Redland Bays—separated by headlands. At the NW of the bay is BRIBIE ISLAND, with Pumicestone Channel between the island and the mainland; on the E limits of the bay are Moreton and North STRADBROKE Islands, which provide shelter from easterly storms; there are several smaller islands—such as Mud, St Helena, Peel and Green—within the bay. The first British settlement in QLD was at REDCLIFFE on the mid-W shore of Moreton Bay in 1824.

Moreton Bay chestnut *see* bean, black

Morgan SA (population 378 in 1981) This small township is situated on the MURRAY RIVER where the stream makes a sharp change in direction to flow generally S to its mouth. Located 166km NE of Adelaide, it is a rail terminus and was, until early this century, a river port. It is the starting point for the 360km-long water pipeline supplying WHYALLA, completed in 1944 and later extended to supply WOOMERA. The town was named in honour of Sir William Morgan, a parliamentarian of the 19th century.

Mornington Peninsula VIC Often called Melbourne's summer playground, the peninsula is located between PORT PHILLIP BAY and WESTERN PORT BAY. It is a tract of hilly country, extending some 50km on its NE-SW axis and is about 25km wide. The coastline varies from the sheltered swimming and boating waters of Port Phillip to exposed reefs, sandstone headlands and extensive sand dunes along the BASS STRAIT shore. It has long been a holiday and recreation area; a string of resort centres stretch 26km along the Nepean Highway from Dromana to Portsea and many of them have large permanent populations; the residents of some are daily commuters to the city. In addition, industrial growth along the shores of Westernport has resulted in the peninsula becoming increasingly important as a residential area. Hilly country, dominated by the high ridge from Arthur's Seat to Cape Schanck, occupies most of the S half of the peninsula. Farming is important over large areas, with fruit and vegetables being grown on the rich soils near Red Hill and Somerville. The township of Mornington on the W coast, 51km by road from Melbourne is a favourite spot for picnics throughout the year, with rural countryside, rocky headlands and sandy foreshores nearby.
Mt Martha (159m above sea level) in Mt Martha Park (53ha) provides panoramic views of Port Phillip Heads and, on clear days, vistas of the OTWAY RANGES across the bay. At McRae is the first homestead built on the peninsula (1844-45), restored by the National Trust (VIC) in 1971. Sorrento and Portsea are fashionable weekend resorts, but noted for their treacherous surfs. The danger of surfing at these beaches was highlighted in 1967 when the then Prime Minister of Australia, Harold

HOLT, disappeared whilst bathing in these waters.
At Stony Point on the E coast of the peninsula is HMAS *Cerebus*, more commonly known as Flinders Naval Base. The Cape Schanck Coastal Park (1 075ha), located on the SW shore facing Bass Strait, includes all the surf beaches between London Bridge and Cape Schanck, such as Portsea, Sorrento and Rye, and the National Parks Service of VIC has undertaken some major re-vegetation schemes along this coast to stabilise eroding sand dunes. The Nepean State Park (1 050ha) extends from Arthur's Seat to the coast near Cape Schanck and is noted for scenic grazing land and natural bush country.

Mort, Thomas Sutcliffe (1816-78) Pioneer merchant and industrialist. Born in Bolton, England, he arrived in Sydney in 1838, and five years later set up Mort and Co., which soon became Australia's largest wool-selling agency. He later became involved in mining, shale oil production, railway construction and dairying; also in shipbuilding and the construction of locomotives at Morts Dock, Balmain. He was largely responsible for the beginning of an export trade in frozen meat, but died before the first cargo left Australia in 1879.

Morwell VIC (population 16 488 in 1981) Located in the LATROBE RIVER valley on the Princes Highway, 150km ESE of Melbourne and 12km SE of YALLOURN, Morwell is one of the mining, industrial and power generating centres on the vast coalfields (brown coal) of the valley. It is situated E of the Morwell River, a S tributary of the Latrobe, and was originally a small service town for the dairying lands nearby. The development of the coalfields since the 1920s has seen its transformation into a busy mining and manufacturing town. The Morwell open-cut mine lies S of the town and adjacent to it is the power station and briquette factory. Some of the electricity generated here is used to operate the briquette plant but most of it is fed into the State supply network. The Hazelwood power station, the largest in VIC, is located S of Morwell; its eight chimneys, 137m high, dominate the skyline and its eight generators, each of 200MW capacity, are supplied with coal from the Morwell mine by a high-speed conveyor system up to 2.5km long. Cooling water for the

Dredgers at the Morwell open-cut mine in Latrobe Valley VIC

Courtesy of A.I.S. Canberra

Hazelwood station is stored in a pondage nearby, covering an area of 500ha, which not only provides a source of constantly circulating water for the generating plant, but also is used as a recreation area for swimming and boating. The Morwell National Park (140ha), located about 20km S of the town via CHURCHILL, includes rugged forest country, noted for the rare butterfly orchid. The town was named in 1888 after the Aboriginal word for a 'woolly possum'.

morwong *see* fisheries; fishes, bony

Moses, Jack (1860-1945) Moses was a writer of bush ballads and stories about the Australian bush. Born in Sydney, he was a commercial traveller for wines and his work took him into the rural regions where he became widely known for his readiness to recite his verse and to recount his stories of country life. The most famous of his ballads is 'Nine Miles from Gundagai', which tells the tale of the teamster and his dog that sat on the tuckerbox. It is commemorated by a statue on the Hume Highway near GUNDAGAI in the SW slopes region of NSW.

mosquitoes These FLIES (order Diptera) belong to the family Culicidae which contains about 230 known species in Australia, including about three introduced species. Adult mosquitoes may be distinguished from most other superficially similar flies by their long mouthparts and by the scales on the veins and posterior edge of their wings. Some genera also have scales on the body and the males of many species have bushy, feathery antennae.

The adult females of most species are notorious bloodsuckers but the males feed, if at all, on nectar and honeydew. The females usually need a blood meal for the development of their eggs and they are fairly specific in their choice of prey; most feed on man, but some will attack birds, reptiles or frogs. A few species of the tribe Toxorhynchitini (large insects with metallic colouring) do not suck blood but feed on flowers; the larvae are predators on aquatic insects, including other mosquito larvae. The adults of the *Malaya* species are even more unusual in that they obtain their food from ants, which feed them willingly.

All mosquito larvae are aquatic, most feeding on small particles in the water. They have to come to the surface to breathe which they do through respiratory openings (spiracles) near the end of the abdomen. An exception is the larva of the genus *Mansonia* which pierces the stems of water plants below the surface to extract oxygen from the tissues.

The various species of mosquitoes specialise in their larval habitats. The species called container breeders, such as *Aedes aegypti* and *A. notoscriptus*, breed in small accumulations of water, often temporary in nature. An adaptation to this environment is that the eggs must be dried for a time before they will hatch; this ensures that they hatch only when their pool or container refills. Thus, these species are

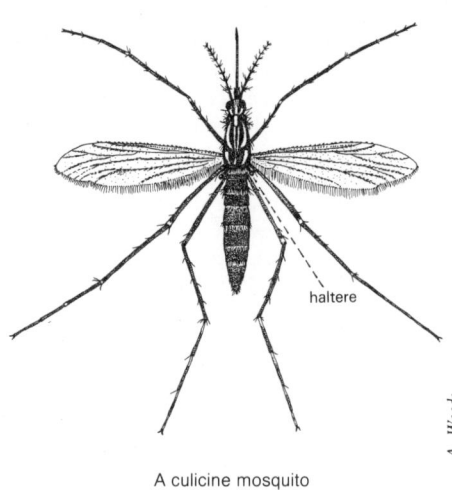

A culicine mosquito

easily carried from one part of the world to another in the water containers aboard ships. Most mosquitoes breed in freshwater but *Culex pipiens* prefers polluted water (and is therefore common in the cities and towns of underdeveloped countries) while *A. vigilax* breeds in brackish swamps and *A. australis* in extremely salty pools on the seashore.

The three most important genera in Australia are *Culex*, *Aedes* and *Anopheles*. The adult *Anopheles* species lack scales on the abdomen, and rest with the body at an angle to the surface; the body and proboscis are in a straight line. *Aedes* and *Culex* adults rest parallel to the surface, with the proboscis at an angle. Both have scales on the abdomen but whereas the *Culex* adults are generally brown in colour, the *Aedes* adults are usually grey to black with white markings. *Anopheles* larvae feed at the water surface from which they hang with their bodies parallel to the surface whereas *Aedes* and *Culex* larvae hang down at an angle of 45° from the surface of the water. Generally speaking, *C. p. fatigans*, one of the commonest representatives of the genus, feeds at night, often coming indoors. *Aedes* species can attack during the day or night, also often coming indoors, while *Anopheles* are night and dusk feeders.

The females of many species of mosquitoes are important carriers of diseases. Human malaria is spread by various *Anopheles* species, but avian malaria is transmitted by *Culex* species. However, the *Culex* species are more important as the carriers of filariasis. In Australia the yellow fever mosquito, *Aedes aegypti*, transmits dengue fever; in Africa and South America it transmits yellow fever. *C. annulirostris* carries Murray Valley encephalitis (MVE) whilst other arboviruses are passed on by various species. Some *Anopheles*, *Aedes* and *Culex* species can carry the heartworm of dogs, *Dirofilaria immitis*. MYXOMATOSIS is carried on the mouthparts of several mosquitoes, and species with predatory larvae have been used in BIOLOGICAL CONTROL experiments against other mosquitoes but with little success.

See also diseases, human

moss animalcules *see* ectoprocts

mosses *see* Bryophyta

mosses, sea *see* ectoprocts

Moss Vale NSW (population 4 414 in 1981) This town on the SOUTHERN TABLELANDS, at an elevation of 673m above sea level and 138km by road SW of Sydney, is situated on the Illawarra Highway connecting the tablelands to the S coast. It is a station on the main Sydney-Melbourne railway (143km by train from Sydney) and is connected by a spur line to WOLLONGONG on the coast. Limestone, quarried locally, is transported on this railway to the PORT KEMBLA steel works. Moss Vale experiences mild climatic conditions, with an average annual rainfall of 990mm, spread evenly throughout the year. The surrounding rural region produces wool, fat lambs, fodder crops and vegetables. Because of its elevation, mild climate and attractive scenery in the dissected parts of the plateau, it has long been a popular holiday area, especially for summer vacation.

moths *see* butterflies, etc.

motor sport The term motor sport embraces a variety of competitions all of which centre on the motor car. These competitions range from economy runs, in which competitors drive their cars gently and sedately as they try to coax more mileage from less fuel, to Grand Prix racing in which competitors push their cars to the extremes of performance in an effort to be first past the finishing line. Of all these forms of racing, road racing on specially prepared circuits is the most popular and some 80 meetings, 16 of which have international status, are held annually on the 14 circuits throughout Australia. With more than 2 000 licensed racing drivers competing at these meetings Australia rates in the top eight racing nations of the world.

History Since the introduction of the motor car into Australia in the late 19th century, owners have always been eager to prove the superiority of their vehicles. Races were held on beaches and along country roads until 1904 when track racing came into vogue, the first meeting being held on the grass horse-racing circuit at Sandown Park VIC. With the increase in the number of cars imported into Australia following World War I, special circuits were built. An autodrome (a circuit with banked corners) was built in Apsendale VIC, followed shortly by saucer-shaped concrete tracks with steep banks at Maroubra NSW and at Melbourne's Motordrome. These circuits were short-lived for, although they created some exciting racing, there were several fatalities.

At about this time a group of enthusiasts from the Victorian Light Car Club were searching for a venue for road racing, a branch of the sport popular in Europe at that time. They had little luck in their search on the mainland as local residents disapproved of the

An international race at Lakeside circuit near Brisbane

Courtesy of A.I.S. Canberra

idea. They finally chose a site on PHILLIP ISLAND (SE of Melbourne) which had the right requisites for road racing—long stretches of road and sharp corners—albeit dusty and gravel strewn. In March 1928 the first Australian Grand Prix took place on Phillip Is, with competing cars ranging from roadsters to Grand Prix Bugattis. This inaugural Grand Prix was won by an Englishman, Captain Arthur Waite, in a supercharged Brooklands model Austin Seven. A silver model of the car he drove later became the Grand Prix trophy. In 1937, it was decided that the national Grand Prix should not be restricted to one circuit and since then the race has been staged at various circuits throughout the country. The Grand Prix did not return to Phillip Is until 1978, in its golden anniversary year.

Although the Australian Grand Prix has consistently attracted drivers of international status, it has never counted towards a world championship.

The best-attended touring car event is the Hardie Ferodo 1000 held annually in October at the Mt Panorama circuit, BATHURST in NSW. It is the only car race now held at Mt Panorama following a decision by the Racing Car Drivers Club in 1973 to concentrate their Bathurst efforts on the Hardie Ferodo each year and let the motor-cycle racers have it for the rest of the year. The race is a gruelling test of men and machines, attracting top Australian and international competitors and ranking on the international calendar. Often in the Hardie Ferodo it is a matter of which car can hold together longest, as witnessed in 1976 when an Englishman, John Fitzpatrick, nursed his stricken Torana round the last 15 laps just managing to coast over the finishing line first with no brakes, a broken rear axle, a malfunctioning gearbox and no clutch.

Internationally, Australia has produced some

outstanding drivers. Jack BRABHAM won the world championship in 1959, 1960 and 1966 and Alan Jones won it in 1980.

Rallies Another popular form of motor sport is the rally. A rally may be a test of navigational skill, a test of driver skill and stamina or a test of car endurance. Rallies may range from a Sunday event, staged by a social club with participants driving their cars on major roads amidst other normal Sunday traffic, to long-distance events (for example, from London to Sydney) during which participants may have to guide their cars over OUTBACK roads which in reality are rough tracks barely distinguishable from the surrounding countryside. Considerable interest was aroused in this branch of the sport during the 1950s by the Redex Round Australia trials, staged by the Australian Sporting Car Club. The Mobil and Ampol oil companies supported the trials until 1958 when escalating organisational costs caused the two companies to withdraw their support and the event was discontinued. Big rallies are now relatively rare. The Southern Cross International Rally, which attracted many overseas and Australian teams for a number of years, was discontinued from 1980.

motor vehicles *see* transport

motor vehicle industry Until 1917 practically all motor vehicles in Australia were fully imported. In that year, however, the federal government paved the way for the development of a local manufacturing industry by decreeing that in future two out of every three chassis imported should be without bodies.
Foundation of the industry Of the body-building companies which were founded as a result of this step, the most successful was Holden's Motor-Body Builders, whose factory in the Adelaide suburb of Woodville, founded

in 1923, became the largest body-building plant in the British Empire. The existence of such plants encouraged overseas manufacturers to begin vehicle assembly in Australia. Ford did so at GEELONG and other locations in 1925-26, and in 1931 its Australian subsidiary merged with the Holden organisation to form General Motors-Holden's Ltd. In 1939 Chrysler began assembly in Adelaide. By that date not only were most cars sold in Australia assembled locally, but many components such as springs, radiators, shock absorbers and axles, were of Australian manufacture.
Development of full manufacturing Shortly after the end of World War II the federal government invited the motor industry to submit proposals for making complete vehicles locally. The first to respond was General Motors-Holden's, which expanded its plants at Woodville and Fishermen's Bend, Melbourne, and early in 1949 began production of its Holden car, which by 1958 was coming off the assembly lines at the rate of nearly 500 a day. Meanwhile Ford and Chrysler had increased the Australian content of their vehicles and a number of British firms were assembling cars with increased local content. In 1960, 97% of the domestic market was held by Australian producers, some of whom were also achieving profitable exports. The British Motor Corporation (which had been formed by a merger of Austin and Morris in 1952, and was later to become British Leyland Motor Corporation) and Germany's Volkswagen had become strongly established, they and the three American companies between them dominating the market. In truck manufacture International Harvester, with its main plant at DANDENONG, on the outskirts of Melbourne, had also become a major producer.
Methods of protection Initially the growing industry was protected by means of import restrictions, but in 1960 a 35% tariff was imposed instead. Then in 1964, largely in order to foster the manufacture of vehicle components in Australia, the government introduced a plan whereby a manufacturer who produced a model with a specified percentage of local content (rising in stages, and finally reaching 95%) would be permitted to import the remaining components duty-free. There has since been a succession of such plans, the plan current in the early 1980s being based on 85% local content.

The industry since 1970 In spite of such protective measures, the industry has ceased to prosper. In the words of a 1980 draft report of the INDUSTRIES ASSISTANCE COMMISSION: 'The local industry has not fared well recently. Sales and production have been stagnant; price competitiveness of both vehicles and components has been generally poor; profitability has not been good and employment has been declining.'

By 1969 there was a move among buyers towards small cars, and the local industry was under a strong threat from Japanese imports, which were well placed to meet this new trend in buyer preference. Volkswagen's share of the passenger car market had by this time sunk to less than 3%, and soon afterwards it ceased manufacturing in Australia. The remaining producers, faced with a stagnant market because of the general economic recession, as well as with Japanese competition, produced a greater range of models than before, and so became even less able to achieve economies of scale.

An IAC report of 1974 declared that there were more producers and more plants than the size of the market called for, and recommended a rationalisation of the industry through gradual abandonment of the local content plan and the eventual reduction of the tariff to 25%. Successive governments, however, have shrunk from applying such measures because of the unemployment which might result. Steps taken since that time include the establishment of a standard 85% local content plan, the imposition of import restrictions in order to ensure 80% of the market to domestic manufacturers, and lifting of the tariff to 57.5%. Early in 1982 an export facilitation plan was introduced, with the aim of encouraging manufacturers to concentrate on the capital-intensive, high technology aspects of the industry. It allows companies to reduce their local content — initially by 5%, and at a later stage by 7.5% — if they export Australian-made components equal in value to the extra components imported. Under this arrangement General Motors-Holden's proceeded with the building of a new engine plant, two-thirds of the production of which is exported for use by other GM subsidiaries in its international 'J-car'.

In the meantime the number of major producers has returned to five. Leyland ceased manufacturing in 1974, but Nissan (Datsun) and Toyota began production under the 85% local content plan in 1976, and Mitsubishi bought out the major share in Chrysler Australia in 1980. Toyota operates through Australian Motor Industries, ownership of which is shared equally between it and Australian investors; the other four major producers are fully-owned subsidiaries of overseas companies. The main assemblers outside the local content plan are Leyland, Renault and Volvo. Production and assembly for the whole industry are heavily concentrated in Melbourne and Adelaide. Annual sales of new vehicles in the 1980s has been around 450 000 for passenger vehicles and 600 000 for all motor vehicles (excluding motor cycles, for which there is no local manufacturing industry). It is generally agreed that this does not provide a large enough market for five main producers to operate efficiently and profitably. However, in view of levels of unemployment throughout Australia in 1984, all proposals for rationalising the industry, and especially proposals for lessening its level of protection, must be regarded as being extremely controversial.
See also transport

motorboat racing Australia's mild climate has made participation in motorboat racing popular. There are many stretches of water large enough to accommodate the boats and races are held on rivers and lakes

Scene from the 1972 BP Ocean Classic

throughout Australia. Larger boats compete in ocean races, the most important of which is the annual BP Ocean Classic from Sydney to NEWCASTLE and back. There are two main groups of racing boats, inboard and outboard (depending on whether the motor is attached to the inside or the outside of the boat's hull), and these two groups are divided into several classes depending on the size of the boat and the power of the motor. The Australasian Power Boat Association formed in 1962-63 controls the standards and activities of the 192 affiliated clubs in Australia and New Zealand. Australia is also a member of the world governing body, the Union of International Motor Boating.

In the setting of water speed records, Ken Warby has been outstanding. In November 1977, in the jet-powered *Spirit of Australia,* which he had designed and built himself, he set an unlimited world record of 464.44 kmh (288.6 mph) on Blowering Dam, near Tumut NSW. In October 1979, also in *Spirit of Australia* on Blowering Dam, he set a new record of 511.11 kmh (317.597 mph).

motorcycle racing Since the late 1960s motorcycles have become a popular mode of transport for young people. Paradoxically, the huge increase in the numbers of motorcycles on public roads has not been matched by a heightened interest in the sport of motorcycle racing although there has been a marginal increase in the numbers of spectators at selected meetings such as the BATHURST Easter meeting.

Much of the historical data on early motorcycle competitions is no longer extant but the information that has survived points to early similarities between motor car and motorcycle racing. Enthusiasts took part in similar events such as Reliability Trials and marathon events.

In 1905 a Sydney to Melbourne Reliability Trial was held in which both motorcycles and cars were entered. Because of the dangers inherent in such road racing events, motorcycle riders later opted for straight-line races over a defined course. Today, motorcycle road races are held on public roads, which are closed during the races, or on specially prepared circuits, the best known of which is the Mt Panorama circuit in Bathurst NSW where racing events were first held in 1938. The Bathurst Easter meeting at Mt Panorama is listed as an international event and regularly attracts world-class competitors.

Another form of motorcycle racing—dirt-track or speedway racing—is of Australian origin. In dirt-track racing, riders compete in races on an oval dirt track, skidding round the corners with one steel-plated shoe sliding along the dirt to maintain balance. First staged as part of an agricultural show at MAITLAND in NSW in the 1920s, dirt-track racing soon spread throughout Australia and to Britain where it was to become a major sporting attraction. The most successful Australian rider was Lionel Van Praag, 'the Flying Dutchman', who in 1936 won the world's first dirt-track championship which was held in London before 75 000 spectators.

mound birds Also called megapodes, these BIRDS belong to the Megapodiidae, which consists of 13 species related to the domestic fowl and restricted to Australia and neighbouring islands, parts of Polynesia and New Guinea. They use the heat of the sun or of decaying vegetation to incubate their eggs. The large mounds of vegetation built as incubators by the three Australian species were taken to be Aboriginal graves by some early explorers. Mound birds lay between 12 and 30 eggs, but because a single egg can weigh up to

VIC Govt Tourist Bureau

Mallee fowl, *Leipoa ocellata*

15 per cent of the female's body weight, several days may elapse between layings. It is usually the male's responsibility to keep the temperature constant in the mound by adding or removing vegetation, but neither he nor the female take care of the fledglings, which lead an independent existence as soon as they have struggled from the mound.

The scrubfowl, *Megapodius freycinet* (*reinwardt*), is about as big as a farmyard hen; it is brown above, grey below and has a small crest. Its mounds are about 1.5m high and 3m wide, but they are extended each year. The scrubfowl is a coastal rainforest species of N Australia; abroad it ranges from the Philippines to Polynesia. The diet consists of berries, roots, seeds and insects.

The brush turkey, *Alectura* lathami* (70cm), is a terrestrial, woodland species which occurs in NE Australia but was formerly more widespread. It is turkey-like, with black plumage, and its bare neck and bare vulturine head are bright red. The mounds, composed of rotting vegetation, are usually about 1m high and 3m wide.

The mallee fowl, *Leipoa* ocellata* (60cm). Is a ground-dwelling species which feeds on plant material and insects. There are bold brown and grey mottlings on the back and a black patch on the breast. The male constructs and tends the pyramid-shaped mounds of soil and vegetation and apparently tests the temperature with his tongue; the female lays 20 or more pinkish eggs over a long period. The Pulletop fauna reserve near GRIFFITH in NSW, where Frith (*see below*) carried out most of the original research on the mallee fowl, has been set aside as a sanctuary for this species. *Further reading;* Frith, H.J. *The Mallee Fowl.* Angus & Robertson, Sydney, 1967; Rowley, I. *Bird Life.* Collins, Sydney, 1974; von Frisch, K. *Animal Architecture.* Hutchinson, London, 1975.

Mount Anne TAS This peak in the S of the State, rising to 1 425m above sea level, is located at the headwaters of the HUON RIVER and forms part of the watershed between the Huon and its main N tributary, the Weld River. Mt Anne and Mt Eliza (1 288m), to the S, both lie E of LAKE PEDDER in rugged wilderness country which was glaciated during

*Species, genus or family is endemic to Australia (see Preface)

the Great Ice Age and both are included within the Southwest National Park.

Mount Barker SA (population 4 190 in 1981) A farming centre in the MOUNT LOFTY RANGES, it is located 35km SE of Adelaide, at an elevation of 330m. A peak of the same name, lying E of the town, rises to an elevation of 517m. The area experiences a mild climate with an average annual rainfall of 781mm concentrated mainly in the winter months. Rural activities include dairying, orcharding and fodder crop cultivation. The peak was named by the explorer Charles STURT to commemorate one of his party, Captain Collet Barker, who was killed by Aborigines at the mouth of the MURRAY RIVER in 1831.

Mount Barker WA (population 1 519 in 1981) This small inland town in the far S of the State is 48km N of ALBANY and 357km SE of Perth. At an elevation of 254m above sea level, it is located on the Albany Highway adjacent to the NW end of the PORONGORUP RANGE. A hill to the SW of the town (also called Mt Barker) provides a panoramic view of the farming, grazing and orcharding lands of the area. The town has an average annual rainfall of 756mm, concentrated in the winter months (June and July both have averages over 100mm), with a dry summer season. Sheep grazing and wheat growing, together with apple orcharding and, more recently, wine-grape growing, are the main rural activities.

Mount Bartle Frere QLD The highest mountain in QLD, it is located in the NE of the State between CAIRNS and INNISFAIL in the S of the BELLENDEN KER RANGE. It is a twin-peaked granite formation reaching an elevation of 1 657m above sea level, and is included within the Bellenden Ker National Park. The mountain was named in 1873 by the explorer and pastoralist, George Dalrymple, after Sir Henry Bartle Edmund Frere, president of the Royal Geographical Society.

Mount Baw Baw VIC This winter skiing centre is located E of Melbourne, within the GREAT DIVIDING RANGE near the headwaters of the YARRA, THOMSON and LATROBE Rivers. Reaching a height of 1 564m above sea level, it is the closest major snow resort to Melbourne, 179km (via Dandenong and Novjee) or 163km (via Lilydale and Powelltown) by road. Mt Baw Baw is a popular skiing area for day-trippers from Melbourne; in winter, the road is closed for about the last 5km below the ski village and a bus and ski-lift take visitors the remaining distance.

Mount Beauty VIC (population 1 509 in 1981) This model town with broad tree-lined streets and modern amenities was established in 1947 by the State Electricity Commission for the building of the Kiewa hydro-electricity scheme. Situated 346km by road NE of Melbourne in the upper section of the picturesque KIEWA RIVER valley, at the foot of the Victorian Alps, nestling below MOUNT BOGONG, it has

become a service centre and a tourist town. At an elevation of 365m above sea level, it experiences mild summer conditions and cool winters, with snow on the adjacent highlands; the average annual precipitation is 1 280mm, with August the month of highest falls (160mm average) and January the lowest (62mm). The area was originally a cattle mustering centre for the annual summer drives of the herds to feed on the lush grazing pastures of the BOGONG HIGH PLAINS. Beef and dairy cattle are still important in the region, together with timber-getting, pig farming and tobacco growing. It is an area of striking scenic beauty, attracting tourists in summer for trout fishing, bushwalking and horse riding; the FALLS CREEK snowfields, 32km away, are a popular winter resort. The regional headquarters of the State Electricity Commission are located in the town and the nearby Kiewa hydro-electricity scheme can be inspected by visitors.

Mount Bischoff TAS Located in the rugged NW region of the State, near the headwaters of the ARTHUR RIVER and the N tributaries of the PIEMAN RIVER, and rising to a height of 792m, it was the site of one of the world's largest tin deposits in the 1880s. The town of WARATAH (population 342 in 1981), the settlement for the mining operations, was once a flourishing centre and when the mining industry reached its peak in the early 1900s the township boasted four hotels and a population of about 6000. Tin was mined at Mt Bischoff and treated at the site until 1935; the mine was re-opened during World War II when tin was in short supply, but the end of the war saw the end of the mining. The name Bischoff was given in 1843 in honour of the chairman of the Van Diemen's Land Co.

Mount Bogong VIC The State's highest peak (1 986m), Mt Bogong is situated in the Victorian Alps, between the Omeo Highway and the Kiewa Valley Highway, E of MOUNT BEAUTY township and about 80km SSE of WODONGA. The small town of Bogong, built by the State Electricity Commission during the construction of the Kiewa hydro-electricity scheme, lies SW of the mountain on the KIEWA RIVER, 14km SE of Mt Beauty. At a height of 732m above sea level, the town receives a high rainfall of 1 538mm. The mountain and the township are included in the BOGONG HIGH PLAINS area.

Mount Buffalo VIC This has long been one of VIC's most popular tourist areas with its spectacular scenery of cliffs and waterfalls, the colourful wild flowers in spring, skiing in winter, and bushwalking, horse riding and camping in summer. Located near the town of BRIGHT, about 330km by road NE of Melbourne, the Mt Buffalo area was first reserved as a national park in 1898, was enlarged in 1908 and now covers 31 000ha, consisting of a plateau area with massive, steep-sided granite tors rising above the plateau surface. The highest of these is The Horn (commonly called Mt Buffalo) at the S end of the park, rising to 1 720m; others rise to over 1 500m, including Bald Hill (1 530m) and Mt McLeod (1540m). The plateau is drained by numerous streams, with gorge sections and waterfalls where they descend over the plateau scarps, forming the headwaters of tributaries of the OVENS RIVER. The Mt Buffalo Chalet at an elevation of 1 372m, near the NE border of the park, is a popular resort in both winter and summer. The mountain was so named by the explorers Hamilton HUME and William Hovell during their expedition from Sydney to PORT PHILLIP BAY in 1824, because it looked like a buffalo when viewed from a distance.

VIC Govt Travel Authority

Mount Buffalo

Mount Buller
VIC This is VIC's largest and busiest ski resort, located on the N side of the GREAT DIVIDING RANGE, E of the EILDON RESERVOIR, 237km by road NE of Melbourne and 43km E of MANSFIELD. The mountain rises to 1 804m above sea level, and the area forms the headwaters of the Broken River, a tributary of the OVENS. It is a resort especially popular with day trippers from Melbourne and boasts 14 ski-tows and 130 club lodges.

Mount Conner
NT Located in the S part of the Territory about 55km N of the SA/NT border and 90km ESE of AYERS ROCK, this mountain rises sharply from the desert plain N of the MUSGRAVE RANGES to an elevation of 855m above sea level. It is a flat-topped rocky outcrop bounded by 120m-high cliffs and situated in the S part of Curtin Springs pastoral station.

Mount Donna Buang
VIC This winter resort centre is one of Melbourne's main snow playgrounds, since it is only 95km by road ENE of the city. The approach road in winter is via WARBURTON, which is 18km from the mountain; during summer, the road via HEALESVILLE is also open. There is a sealed road to the summit and during winter it is kept clear of snow, so that visitors can drive right to the top, where there is parking available for about 200 vehicles. There are two toboggan runs at the summit and some sections which, though not steep enough for tobogganing, are ideal for novice skiing.

Mount Elephant
VIC Located in the WESTERN DISTRICT, NW of LAKE CORANGA-

MITE, some 40km by road N of CAMPERDOWN and about 14km W of Lismore township, it is the highest (394m above sea level) of the ancient volcanic cones which rise above the basalt plateau of the region.

Mount Feathertop
VIC The second-highest peak in the State (1 922m), it is a winter skiing centre in the Victorian Alps of the GREAT DIVIDING RANGE, located SE of BRIGHT near the headwaters of the OVENS and KIEWA Rivers and to the W of the BOGONG HIGH PLAINS. It is a flat basalt-capped mountain, rising above the tree-line, with lush alpine meadows and vivid wild flowers in spring and summer.

Mount Field
TAS This mountain consists of two peaks, Mt Field East (1 270m) and Mt Field West (1 434m), lying near the E and W borders, respectively, of the Mt Field National Park (16 257ha) in the S-central part of the State, 82km NW of Hobart. The park lies in the SW part of the DERWENT RIVER basin, between two of its major S tributaries, the Styx and the Florentine. The region contains a variety of landscapes from dense forests on the lower slopes to alpine moorlands in the higher parts, glaciated valleys and moraine-dammed lakes (for example, Lakes Fenton, Nicholls, Seal, Webster and Dobson), steep-sided gorges and cascading waterfalls (such as Russell Falls, over 40m high, and Horseshoe and Lady Barron Falls). Some of the best skiing areas in TAS are provided by the slopes of Mt Mawson, 183m above Lake Dobson, and by other snowfields in the national park from July to October.

Mount Gambier
SA (population 19 830 in 1981) This is the third-largest city in the State (after Adelaide and WHYALLA) and is located 456km by road and 490km by rail SE of Adelaide. At a height of 65m above sea level, it experiences a mild climate, with an average annual rainfall of 712mm concentrated in the winter season with the highest falls in July (101mm average). Adjacent to the town, rising to an elevation of 190m, is the extinct volcanic cone of Mt Gambier, containing BLUE LAKE within its crater. This peak was first sighted by Lieutenant James GRANT in 1800 during his explorations of the coastline, and named by him in honour of Admiral Lord Gambier, a British naval commander. Grant named Mt Schank, a smaller volcanic cone to the S, after another British admiral. On the summit of Mt Gambier, the Centenary Tower was erected to commemorate Grant's sighting. The town was initially established in 1854 as a private settlement on a pastoral property and was originally called Gambiertown. A district council was formed in 1863 and the township became a municipality in 1876 with a population of 2 500. Just prior to World War II the population reached 6 000 and in subsequent decades the city has experienced rapid growth with the development of a range of commercial and industrial enterprises: wood processing based on the pine forests of the region, concrete

Browne and Valley Lakes, Mount Gambier

Dennis's, Dept SA (rotated)

pipe works, a woollen yarn factory, and the processing of dairy products. It is the major service centre for the SE of the State and an important tourist resort. The National Trust (SA) has listed 28 sites in the city for preservation, including several churches, banks, hotels and cottages, the post office, the town hall and an old mill.
Further reading: Hill, L. *Mount Gambier Sketchbook*. Rigby, Adelaide, 1976.

Mount Garnet
QLD (population 558 in 1981) This is a tin mining township in the NE of the State, on the Kennedy Highway near the headwaters of the HERBERT RIVER, to the SW of the ATHERTON TABLELAND, and 140km by road inland from INNISFAIL. It was once a copper mining and smelting centre, but today alluvial tin deposits are mined by two dredging companies.

Mount Goldsworthy
WA (population 923 in 1981) Goldsworthy was the first mining town in the NW of the State to be built, in the boom period of the 1960s, solely for iron-ore workers. The town is located in the PILBARA region, 117km NE of PORT HEDLAND, just off the North West Coastal Highway, about 1 800km N of Perth. The nearby mountain was named in 1879 by Alexander Forrest in honour of the Colonial Secretary of the time, R.J. Goldsworthy. Production of ore began in 1966 and the mountain peak, originally 132m high, has been transformed by open-cut mining into a deep pit.

Mount Hann
WA This is the highest point of the KIMBERLEYS in the far N of the State, and it forms part of the watershed between the DRYSDALE RIVER flowing N to Napier-Broome Bay, the Charnley River draining S and W to Collier Bay, the Princess Regent River flowing NW to Hanover Bay, and the Hann River, a headwater tributary of the FITZROY RIVER. The mountain rises to over 240m above the main sandstone plateau block of the Kimberleys making its total height 854m above sea level.

Mount Hotham
VIC This winter ski resort and summer-time camping and bush-walking area is located in the Victorian Alps of the GREAT DIVIDING RANGE, some 367km NE of Melbourne, 55km by road SE of BRIGHT and 58km WNW along the Alpine Road from OMEO. It is a flat basalt-capped

mountain, 1 861m above sea level and is the source of the headwater tributaries of the KIEWA and OVENS Rivers (both flowing N to the MURRAY RIVER) and the Dargo River (a tributary of the MITCHELL RIVER). The Hotham alpine village, at a height of 1 747m, with a hotel, chalets, chairlifts and numerous club lodges, is claimed as Australia's highest ski village.

Mount Isa QLD (population 23 679 in 1981) The 'copper city' in the NW of the State, Mt Isa is located in the Selwyn Range and on the LEICHHARDT RIVER, about 200km E of the NT/QLD border on the Barkly Highway. At a height of 339m above sea level, it lies 1 845km by road NW of Brisbane, in harsh remote country which experiences a long dry season in the cooler months of the year. It has an average annual rainfall of only 429mm, concentrated in the summer season. The mineral wealth of the Mt Isa region was first discovered in 1923 when a prospector, John Miles, found ores bearing lead and silver. Although it has experienced varying fortunes as a mining town since that time and has been threatened by closure, the vast deposits located in recent decades have made it one of the nation's great mining centres. The underground mining operations produced about 70 per cent of Australia's copper during the 1970s, as well as large amounts of lead, zinc and silver. The ores are railed to TOWNSVILLE (a journey of about 970km) where they are refined for export.

The provision of adequate water supplies for both the community and the mining enterprises has always been a problem in such an arid environment; it is not uncommon, with the consistently high temperatures, for evaporation from surface storages to exceed the natural replenishment by rainfall. The first dam was built in 1929 on Rifle Creek; a further dam on the Leichhardt River was constructed in 1957, with a storage capacity of 107 000ML. This dam, called Lake Moondarra, located 19km N of the city, still supplies part of the urban and industrial needs and is also a popular area for recreation and aquatic sports. But the increasing demand for water in the 1960s led to the construction of Julius Dam, with a capacity of 127 000ML, at the junction of the Paroo and Leichhardt Rivers, located 70km NE of the city. Because of its isolation in an arid area, most food is brought great distances to Mt Isa: milk supplies come from the ATHERTON TABLELAND and beer from CAIRNS or even from Melbourne.

Mount Keira NSW Located WNW of the city of WOLLONGONG, this mountain reaches a height of 467m above sea level and is part of the E scarp of the SOUTHERN TABLELANDS. The scarp rises sharply from the narrow coastal plain of the ILLAWARRA region. Other distinctive parts of the escarpment are Mt Nebo (250m high) and Mt Kembla (534m). Below the sandstone of the scarp, there are important coal seams and Mt Keira was the

site of the first mine developed in the region in the late 1840s. It was also the site of Australia's worst mining disaster when 95 men perished in a mine explosion in 1902.

Mount Lofty Ranges SA This range of hills, with Mt Lofty as the highest peak (727m), extends on a N-S alignment for some 320km S from the PETERBOROUGH Gap, then SW to the FLEURIEU PENINSULA, generally parallel to and inland from the E coast of ST VINCENT GULF. The range is flanked by two important plains—that to the E is the plain of the lower MURRAY RIVER, and on the W is the coastal lowlands of the Adelaide Plain. Numerous streams which rise in the ranges, such as the Light, Gawler, Onkaparinga and Marne Rivers, form N-S valleys in the hills, then cut across the ridges to flow E or W to the plains. The general elevation of the ranges is 450m and the region is part of the 'Shatter Belt' of SA which includes a number of faults, horst-blocks and sunklands. The range is really a S extension of the FLINDERS RANGES and is divided by the BAROSSA VALLEY into N and S sections. The higher parts of the ranges have been deeply dissected by river erosion giving a ruggedly picturesque landscape where many areas have been proclaimed as conservation and recreation parks. The lower undulating hilly tracts are intensively farmed for vegetables, vines, pears and cherries; there is also flower growing, dairying and fodder crop cultivation. The S parts of the ranges are especially significant to the metropolitan population of Adelaide for the hills supply large quantities of food to the city, provide storage points for water supply reservoirs, and contain many attractive sites for recreation reserves and holiday resorts. On the summit of Mt Lofty there is an obelisk dedicated to the explorer Matthew FLINDERS who sighted and named the peak in 1802.

Mount Lyell TAS This mining centre is located in the rugged W coast ranges, 6km E of QUEENSTOWN and 250km from Hobart on the Lyell Highway. Gold was first found here in 1881 on the flank of Mt Owen, but the subsequent discovery of vast deposits of copper ores led to the growth of Queenstown as a booming mining centre in the latter decades of the 19th century. Copper is still the major product, with gold and silver as subsidiary by-products. The Mt Lyell Mining Co. operates the mine which literally determines the destiny of Queenstown inhabitants. The landscape around Mt Lyell, as around Queenstown, is particularly bizarre in that it is largely denuded of vegetation owing to the early mining and smelting operations. The copper refining processes for treating the ore were pioneered here, but the amount of timber required for firing the smelters as well as for mining the ores led to extensive logging. Fumes from the refining operations killed the mountain vegetation, and the heavy rainfall in the region resulted in severe soil erosion. Regeneration schemes are being undertaken, but many of the hills remain stark and barren. The mining products were

formerly taken by rack-and-pinion railway from Mt Lyell to STRAHAN on MACQUARIE HARBOUR on the W coast, but this line has now been dismantled and the copper is transported by road along the Lyell Highway to Hobart.

Mount Macedon VIC A peak in the GREAT DIVIDING RANGE, 1 013m above sea level, Mt Macedon is located 63km NNW of Melbourne, NE of the small town of Macedon (population 1 057 in 1981) on the Calder Highway. It is an ancient volcanic peak rising steeply from the surrounding country and was discovered and named by the explorer Major Thomas MITCHELL in 1836 when he ascended the summit and saw the developing settlement at PORT PHILLIP BAY. He selected the name to honour Alexander the Great of Macedonia. The 'Ash Wednesday' bushfires of February, 1983, caused extensive property damage and claimed several lives in the Mt Macedon region.

Mount Morgan QLD Located 38km SW of ROCKHAMPTON, this mountain no longer exists because the original rocky summit has been mined for gold, silver and copper since 1882; it is now an extensive excavation, claimed as the largest open-cut mine in the country. The town of Mt Morgan (population 2 974 in 1981), situated on the Dee River (which drains into the Don River and thence into the DAWSON RIVER), at an elevation of 240m above sea level, is essentially a mining centre which is adjacent to the gaping crater with its bench-terraces where mechanised methods are used to extract gold and copper. The open-cut excavation is about 230m deep and because of the brilliant colours down the mine face, it is a popular tourist attraction. Visitors are welcome to inspect the mining operations and the town's historical museum where a display of relics and records recalls the days of the 'Golden Mount' when the town boasted a population of 15 000 and had 16 hotels. There are many historic buildings in the town and the National Trust (QLD) has listed several for preservation, including the courthouse and police station, two bridges over the Dee River, the railway station, two hotels (the Queensland National and the Grand), the School of Arts and the Chinese shrine. The town takes its name from the Morgan brothers who started mining here in 1882.

Mount Newman WA (population 5 466 in 1981) A new mining town in the PILBARA region, Mt Newman was established in 1967 to exploit the vast iron ore reserves at Mt Whaleback, 6.5km to the S. The town is located just W of the Great Northern Highway, 1 184km NNE of Perth and 485km SSE of PORT HEDLAND. It is a town with modern amenities which has experienced rapid growth; by 1971 it had a population of 3 906. At a height of 546m above sea level, it has an arid climate with a low average annual rainfall of 317mm, concentrated mainly in the summer months.

The iron ore, mined by open-cut methods, is railed 420km to Port Hedland for export.

Mount Olga NT This mountain is the highest of a group of monoliths usually called the Olgas, lying 32km W of AYERS ROCK and some 460km by road SW of ALICE SPRINGS. It rises to 546m above the surrounding plains and to 1 072m above sea level. The group of rounded monoliths has a circumference of 22km and all are composed of conglomerate, red in colour, although they can appear to have a wide range of hues depending on the hour of the day and the weather conditions. They rise sheer from the plains with deep chasms between the giant domes. Although the climate is arid, with low and irregular rainfall, moisture is retained in these gorges (the largest is called Valley of the Winds) and lush vegetation of ghost gums and wild flowers flourish. The Olgas have the Aboriginal name Katatjuta and, together with Ayers Rock, they are important in the myths and ritual life of the Aboriginal people of the region. The whole area is included within a national park covering 132 538ha. Though somewhat less accessible than Ayers Rock, the Olgas are a popular tourist site. The mountain was named by the explorer Ernest GILES in 1872, in honour of a German Queen of the time.

Mount Olympus TAS Located in the central W highlands of the State, some 180km NW of Hobart, it rises immediately to the SW of LAKE ST CLAIR, its summit reaching 1 447m above sea level. It is a flat-topped mountain, capped by igneous rock (dolerite of Jurassic Age), bounded by steep cliffs and towering 700m above the lake. The whole area bears evidence of a landscape affected by the glacial erosion of the Great Ice Age, with sheer-sided valleys, truncated spurs and moraine-dammed lakes. The mountain lies in the SE section of the CRADLE MOUNTAIN-LAKE ST CLAIR National Park and the bushwalking track through the park skirts the foot of Mt Olympus for 18km along the lake shore. There are numerous other peaks in the vicinity rising to over 1 300m (such as Mt Byron to the NW 1 378m, Mt Hugel to the SW 1 397m and Mt Gould to the NNW 1 491m). Road access to the area is off the Lyell Highway along a branch road from the town of Derwent Bridge, but the road ends at Cynthia Bay on the SE shore of Lake St Clair and walking tracks from there circle Mt Olympus.

Mount Ossa TAS The highest mountain in the State (1 617m), Mt Ossa is located in the E-central part of the CRADLE MOUNTAIN-LAKE ST CLAIR National Park, in wilderness country W of the upper MERSEY RIVER. The area contains a number of peaks rising to over 1 400m (such as Mt Pelion East 1 433m, Mt Thetis 1 471m, Mt Massif 1 470m and Mt Pelion West 1 554m) and the steep-sided valleys, truncated spurs, moraine deposits and moraine-dammed lakes are all evidence of the glaciation which took place here during the Great Ice Age.

Mount Royal Range NSW This mountain range forms part of the divide between the HUNTER and MANNING Rivers. It is a branch of the GREAT DIVIDING RANGE, extending from Ben Hall's Gap at its NW extremity and making a curving arc which first trends NW to SE, then more directly N to S, around the headwaters of the upper Hunter River and its tributaries. The range stretches over a distance of about 80km and reaches its highest point of 1 586m above sea level in the section known as the BARRINGTON TOPS. The lake formed by GLENBAWN DAM on the Hunter River extends into the foothills of the range.

Mount Stromlo see astronomy

Mount Superbus QLD The highest point in south-eastern QLD, at an elevation of 1 380m above sea level, this mountain is located in the MAIN RANGE, E of WARWICK, where the upper tributaries of the CONDAMINE RIVER have their headwaters. The peak is situated where the Main Range and the McPHERSON RANGE meet, near the NSW/QLD border.

Mount Tom Price WA (population 3 540 in 1981) This new mining town in the HAMERSLEY RANGE was started in 1967 to exploit the vast iron ore resources by open-cut methods. The town is located in the isolated, arid, rugged country of the PILBARA region midway between the North West Coastal Highway and the Great Northern Highway, some 300km S of PORT HEDLAND and 116km SW of WITTENOOM. The mining operations are highly mechanised and the crushed ore is transported 294km by rail to the coastal port of DAMPIER, on a line specially built as part of the developmental project. The town was named in honour of Thomas Price, vice-president of the American company involved in the venture.

Mount Wellington TAS Located only 20km by road from Hobart's central business district a visit to the top of this mountain, 1 271m above sea level, provides a panoramic view of the city. When the author Anthony Trollope visited Hobart in 1871 he wrote that Mt Wellington was 'just enough of a mountain to give excitement to ladies and gentlemen in middle life'. It does provide spectacular panoramic views of the city and the lower DERWENT RIVER: in winter, when it is often snow-capped, it forms a scenic backdrop to the suburban expanse of the city. It was named after the Duke of Wellington in commemoration of the Battle of Waterloo. The first white man to climb the mountain is thought to have been Dr George BASS who was with Matthew FLINDERS' party in 1798. The lower section of the road up the mountain was constructed by convict labour in 1888 and it was not until 1937 that the road to the summit was completed. The transmitters of Hobart's television stations are located at the top of the mountain. The Mt Wellington Reserve

(1 175ha), controlled by the Hobart-City Council, is traversed by numerous walking tracks.

mountain ash Topped only by the redwood of California (a conifer), the mountain ash, *Eucalyptus regnans* (family MYRTACEAE), is the world's tallest broad-leafed tree. The tallest accurately measured example, felled at COLAC in VIC in 1890, was 105.46m, but there are reports of a fallen, broken specimen 132m long which may have been 152m tall when living; this would make it longer than any known redwood specimen. Most mountain ashes, however, are between 53m and 75m tall. They grow in VIC and southern TAS, often in pure stands, at altitudes from 150m to 900m. The bark is rough and fibrous to about 15m, and smooth and grey above. The timber is used for construction work and paper pulp.

mountain devil see honeysuckle; lizards; Proteaceae

Moura QLD (population 2 871 in 1981) A town on the Dawson Highway, Moura is located 654km by road NW of Brisbane, 66km W of BILOELA and 171km inland along the highway from GLADSTONE. Situated in the DAWSON RIVER valley, where livestock grazing is the main rural occupation, together with dairying and wheat and cotton growing, it has since the early 1960s become an important open-cut coal mining centre.

Mudgee NSW (population 6 013 in 1981) This town in the central W region of the State, 275km by road NW of Sydney, is located on the Cudgegong River, a headwater tributary of the MACQUARIE RIVER, at an elevation of 468m above sea level, lying W of the main watershed on the GREAT DIVIDING RANGE. It is a rail centre on a branch line from the main W railway (308km by train from Sydney) and the focus of a rural region with a wide range of produce—fine wool, beef cattle, wheat, dairy products, maize, wine grapes, lucerne, honey and vegetables. The town has an average annual rainfall of 667mm, evenly spread throughout the year, and experiences warm to hot summer months and cool frosty winters. The town's name comes from the Aboriginal word meaning either 'contented' or 'a bird's nest'.

The area around Mudgee was explored in the 1820s, it was proclaimed a village in 1836 and became a municipality in 1860. In the gold-rush days Mudgee was a boom town with many diggings in the district. It is still important for mineral mining, mainly shale, pottery clays and marble. It has a number of sawmills, wineries, honey processing works and a grain mill. A feature of the 1960s and 1970s was the expansion of the wine-grape industry in the district. Though wine was produced as long ago as the 1850s, it was in the 1960s that many vineyards were planted and production increased considerably.

Downstream from Mudgee is the BURRENDONG DAM, a major water reservoir located at the junction of the Cudgegong and Macquarie Rivers. The upper reaches of the lake formed by this dam, only about 15km from the town, provide a recreation area for local residents and an attractive summer tourist site. There are many fine buildings of historic and architectural interest in the town, and the National Trust (NSW) has listed and classified many for preservation, including St Mary's Catholic Church (built 1857), St John's Anglican Church (1860), the courthouse (1861), the Mechanics' Institute (1861), the police station (about 1860) and the post office (1860).

mudlark *see* mudnest builders

mudnest builders These PASSERINE BIRDS belong to the family Grallinidae, which consists of four species, one in New Guinea and three in Australia. The Australian species —the apostlebird, *Struthidea* cinerea* (33cm long), the white-winged chough, *Corcorax* melanorhamphos* (45cm), and the mudlark, *Grallina cyanoleuca** (25cm to 28cm)—all build bowl-shaped nests of mud and grass, which are placed on branches and often used for several successive years.

Apostlebirds and white-winged choughs are both highly social BIRDS, doing everything in small groups (nesting, rearing young and roosting); the group consists of eight to 20 birds, traditionally but not always 12 in the case of the apostlebirds. The apostlebird has a grey, spotted body, brown wings and a black tail. It feeds on insects and seeds in the woodlands and open forests of inland E Australia. The white-winged chough is a black, CROW-like bird with a large white patch on each wing, red eyes and a long, down-curved bill. It is found in south-eastern SA, VIC, NSW and most of central and southern QLD, in forest and woodland where it feeds on small animals, insects and seeds both on the ground and in trees.

The mudlark, also called the magpie-lark or the peewee, is a boldly patterned black and white bird which often attacks reflections in windows. It is common in open timber of various kinds, including suburban parks, throughout the mainland, but always near a supply of mud. Although omnivorous, it feeds mainly on insects.

mulga *see* Mimosaceae; vegetation

mulgara *see* native cats, etc.

mullet, land *see* lizards

Mullewa WA (population 918 in 1981) This small inland township is located 98km by road ENE of GERALDTON on the NORTHAM-Geraldton railway line and 510km by rail N of Perth. It is a wheat town, near the NW extremity of the WA wheat belt. At a height of 282m above sea level, it has a low average annual rainfall of 337mm, concentrated mainly in the winter months. The Catholic Church of Our Lady of Mt Carmel, built in 1927, has been classified by the National Trust (WA) for preservation.

*Species, genus or family is endemic to Australia (see Preface)

mulloway *see* fishes, bony

Mullumbimby NSW (population 2 234 in 1981) This country town on the NORTH COAST, between BYRON BAY and MURWILLUMBAH, is situated on the Brunswick River, 847km via the Pacific Highway N of Sydney. The surrounding area is a popular holiday and tourist resort. The rural district produces beef cattle and pigs, bananas and pineapples, avocados and other tropical fruits, timber and dairy produce. The town's name comes from an Aboriginal word meaning 'a small round hill'.

mundarda *see* possums, etc.

Mundaring Reservoir WA Located on the Helena River, a tributary of the SWAN RIVER, 42km E of Perth in the DARLING RANGE, this reservoir is the main storage point for the GOLDFIELDS WATER SUPPLY scheme. The construction of the weir across the river was begun in 1898 and completed in 1902 with a wall 30.5m high and a capacity of 21 000ML. From the reservoir, a 554km-long pipeline to KALGOORLIE was completed in 1903. In 1951 the height of the weir was increased to 40.2m and this enlarged the reservoir capacity to over 70 000ML. At the weir site there is a historic museum commemorating the gold discoveries in WA, the subsequent building of the pipeline, and the engineer, Charles O'CONNOR, responsible for the planning and design of the water supply scheme.

Mundaring Reservoir, the main storage of the Goldfields Water Supply scheme

munning *see* kangaroos, etc.

Munro, David Hugh 'Darby' (1913-66) Jockey. Born at Glenhuntly VIC, Darby rode his first winner at Sydney's Warwick Farm racecourse at the age of 14 and went on to win every major race in Australia. He was continually plagued with a weight problem which restricted his choice of mounts and kept him from winning a jockey's premiership, although he had some outstandingly successful periods, including seven consecutive wins in 1938 and nine wins at the 1940 Autumn meeting at Randwick. In addition to his three Melbourne Cup successes, he won three Sydney Cups, five AJC Derbys, five Victoria Derbys, two Doncaster Handicaps and two Epsom Handicaps. Skilful and audacious on a racehorse, and acclaimed as the greatest jockey of his time, Munro retired in 1955, after which he had some success as a trainer.

Murchison River WA Located in the central-NW of the State, with headwater tributaries in the Robinson Ranges, the river flows for more than 700km first W then S, and in a series of vast loops W again, to the Indian Ocean coast at Gartheaume Bay, about 130km NNW of GERALDTON. Since the river traverses regions of low rainfall, its flow is sporadic with some sections merely a series of pools, prior to the arrival of the winter rains. The KALBARRI National Park covers 186 076ha near the mouth of the Murchison and includes the spectacular 80km-long river gorge of renowned scenic beauty.

Rupert Murdoch

Murdoch, (Keith) Rupert (1931-) Newspaper publisher, Chairman of News Corporation Ltd. Son of the newspaper magnate Sir Keith Murdoch, he was educated at Geelong Grammar School and the University of Oxford. In 1952 he inherited a substantial holding in News Ltd., publisher of the struggling Adelaide *News*, but not in his father's main power base, the Herald and Weekly Times group. He soon made the *News* highly profitable, and has since acquired controlling interests in very many Australian and overseas newspapers, in television and radio stations, and in other areas of printing and publishing, with interests too in energy resources and other sections of the economy. His newspapers, far too numerous to list here, include, in Australia, the *Australian* and the Sydney *Daily Mirror* and *Daily Telegraph*; in the UK, *The Times* group, the *News of the World* and the *Sun*; and in the USA the New York *Post*, the *Star* (national weekly), the San Antonio *Express-News* and the Chicago *Sun-Times*. His television interests include Channel 10 in Sydney and Melbourne, and in the UK, London Weekend Television.

Murdoch, Sir Walter Logie Forbes (1874-1970) Essayist. Born in Scotland, he came with his parents to VIC in 1884, graduated from Melbourne University and in 1903 became an English lecturer there. He also became a regular contributor to the Melbourne *Herald*, and in 1911 resigned from his academic position to work as a full-time journalist. However, in the following year he accepted the position of Professor of English at the newly founded University of Western Australia, retaining that Chair until his retirement in 1939. He was Chancellor of the University from 1943 to 1947.

In 1923 he published the short but stimulating *Alfred Deakin—A Sketch*, but is remembered mainly for essays, most of which were first published in newspapers, mainly the Melbourne *Herald* and the Perth *West Australian*. In these little sermons', as he himself once called them, he commented with whimsical humour on many aspects of literature and life, with an easy, graceful style which won him a very wide audience. Collections of his essays include *Speaking Personally* (1930), which ran through many editions, *Saturday Mornings* (19317, *Moreover* (1932), *The Wild Planet* (1934), *Lucid Intervals* (1936), *The Spur of the Moment* (1939) and *Collected Essays* (1938). WA's second university is named after him.

murex *see* gastropods

Murgon QLD (population 2 327 in 1981) A town in the southern section of the BURNETT RIVER valley, located on the Bunya Highway, 267km by road NW of Brisbane, 45km NNE of KINGAROY, and about 100km inland (via the Bruce and Wide Bay Highways) from GYMPIE. It is called the 'Hub of the South Burnett', as it is the main service centre for a productive rural hinterland where the farming activities include grain growing, dairying, beef cattle grazing and fodder crop cultivation. Nearby is the Cherbourg Aboriginal community where the residents produce toy koalas, boomerangs and other artifacts for the tourist trade. White settlement of the Murgon district dates from 1843; the town name was taken from the local Aboriginal word for a lily pond.

Murray Basin *see* artesian water

Murray Bridge SA (population 8 664 in 1981) A town on the lower MURRAY RIVER, it is 77km by road and 97km by rail ESE of Adelaide, where the main Melbourne-Adelaide rail and road routes cross the river. At a height of 26m above sea level, it experiences a mild climate with an average annual rainfall of 341mm, concentrated mainly in the winter months. The town was known originally as Edwards Crossing, but the name was changed when the road bridge over the Murray was constructed in 1879. It was a river port until the early part of this century, when road and rail transport eclipsed river trade.

Murray Islands QLD This group of islands is in the GREAT BARRIER REEF, about 185km NE of CAPE YORK, 120km SE of the Papua New Guinea coastline, and near the E end of TORRES STRAIT. The three islands,

The paddle wheeler, 'Liba Liba' moored on the Murray river at Renmark

Maer (or Murray) to the N, Dowar in the centre and Wyer to the S, are coral-fringed; they form the most NE extent of QLD State territory.

Murray, John (1775- ?) Navigator. Murray arrived in Sydney in 1800 as master's mate on HMS *Porpoise*, and in the following year, as acting-lieutenant in command of the *Lady Nelson*, was sent to explore the S coast from WESTERN PORT BAY to Cape Otway. In the course of this voyage, in February 1802, he entered PORT PHILLIP BAY, which he named Port King, but which Governor KING later gave its present name. He also explored KING ISLAND. He returned to England in 1803.

Murray River Australia's principal river, some 2 600km long, the Murray rises in a section of the GREAT DIVIDING RANGE, Pilot Range (lying S of KOSCIUSKO), in rugged country over 1 800m above sea level, where the rainfall exceeds 1 300mm annually and where winter snow blankets the higher sections of the catchment area. In this headwater region the main tributaries, which have their source in the SNOWY MOUNTAINS, are the Geehi and Tooma Rivers. The course of the upper Murray forms a large arc as far as the HUME DAM, located 16km upstream from ALBURY just below the confluence with the MITTA MITTA RIVER (a left-bank tributary in VIC). The headwater basin above Albury consists of hilly dissected country, often with steep-sided gorges, rugged and heavily timbered. The Murray Valley Highway traverses this area, following the river course, linking with the Alpine Way which gives access to the highlands.

Below Albury, the Murray enters its plain tract where it meanders for over 2000km on a general W course across the inland plains of this SE section of the continent. Here it receives major tributaries from the VIC side, such as the KIEWA, OVENS, GOULBURN and CAMPASPE Rivers, and on the NSW side has many long ANABRANCHES, such as the EDWARDS and WAKOOL Rivers and Billabong Creek. The terrain slopes gradually W and the general elevation decreases inland: Albury is 163m above sea level, ECHUCA 96m and SWAN HILL 70m. The amount of rainfall received declines as the Murray flows through the plains into the semi-arid areas.

From Swan Hill to below MILDURA, the Murray continues through gently undulating semi-arid mallee country. Annual rainfall averages are low (Mildura 294mm) and there are extensive areas of sand ridges and numerous shallow depressions occupied by temporary lakes. In this section it receives the MURRUMBIDGEE-LACHLAN and the DARLING tributaries from the N side. Beyond Mildura, although the surrounding countryside is still a vast plain tract, the Murray is entrenched in a gorge-like valley, cut in limestone sediments, averaging 10km in width and in places bounded by steep cliffs over 30m high. The river meanders within this broad valley where there are many BILLABONGS and swampy areas. The gorge feature extends into SA beyond RENMARK, where it narrows to less than 2km in width and continues through WAIKERIE, MORGAN (where the river changes direction sharply to a N-S course), MANNUM and MURRAY BRIDGE. The Murray enters LAKE ALEXANDRINA some 77km from the sea.

For over 2000km the Murray forms the State border between NSW and VIC and for the final 320km of its course it lies in SA. Thus all three States have a vital interest in its waters, especially as large sections of the country through which it flows are semi-arid. The river was discovered by HUME and Hovell in 1824, charted by STURT in his epic journey of 1829-30 and, following the settlement by pastoralists in subsequent decades, early interest in the Murray focussed on navigation. From the 1850s paddle-wheel steamers provided the main form of transport for river settlements, but by the early years of the 20th century the river traffic had virtually ceased. It is interesting to note that there has been some revival of it in recent years to provide river trips for tourists.

Irrigation alongside the Murray river

In the 1880s, the problem of the division of the Murray waters amongst the States on an equitable basis began to assume importance, and it was realised that an interstate agreement for the conservation and use of these waters was essential. In these early days there was considerable conflict between navigation and irrigation interests. However, an overall plan was agreed to in 1915 and the River Murray Commission was established in 1917 to organise the construction works, consisting of large storage points on the upper Murray (Hume Dam) and at Lake Victoria near the SA border, together with 26 locks and weirs on the Murray and nine on the Murrumbidgee. In 1934, this agreement was varied to provide for the construction of the YARRAWONGA WEIR and of five barrages linking the islands at the mouth so as to prevent of saltwater from the sea entering the lakes and lower river in SA; also, these amendments to the scheme reduced the number of locks and weirs on the Murray to 13 (mainly because the locks had been included originally to provide for navigation but this was no longer significant). The design and building of these structures was undertaken in the 1920s and 1930s with the result that the waters of the Murray were regulated, the flow of the river was stabilised and water was available for irrigation. In the plain tract between Albury and Swan Hill the main system of irrigation is gravitational, by diversion from the Yarrawonga and TORRUM-BARRY Weirs (the latter located downstream from Echuca) into main canals and then by channels to farms. The weirs further downstream in the gorge section maintain the river height and so permit irrigation by pumping (for example, Mildura in VIC, Renmark in SA). A serious problem on irrigated land along

the Murray Valley has emerged in recent years; this is the increasing salinity (that is, salt content) of the river waters, and hence of the waters available for irrigation, whereby the top soils of some farming properties have become too saline for crop or pasture or orchard cultivation. Many investigations have been undertaken on various aspects of this problem, and some methods to combat it, particularly deep drainage systems to remove excess water, have been employed in certain areas.

Further reading: Eaton, J.H.O. *A Short History of the River Murray Works.* River Murray Commission, Govt Printer, Adelaide, 1945; *Report of the Murray Valley Resources Survey Committee on Resources and Development of the Murray Valley.* (2 vols) Department of National Development, Canberra, 1947; Macdonald Holmes, J. *The Murray Valley.* Angus & Robertson, Sydney, 1948; Rutherford, J. *The Southern Murray Basin.* Longmans, Melbourne, 1961.

Murrumbidgee irrigation areas

NSW The early development of irrigation along the MURRUMBIDGEE RIVER valley is linked with Sir Samuel McCaughey who, in 1899, on his North Yanco estate established a successful irrigation system which became the prototype of many later schemes. Using a series of pumps, a canal and ditches, he irrigated 16 000ha and grew lucerne and fodder crops on land previously considered useless. In 1906, largely owing to McCaughey's experiments, the State government passed the Barren Jack and Murrumbidgee Canals Construction Act which provided for the construction of BURRINJUCK DAM on the upper river, Berembed Diversion Weir (386km downstream) and a comprehensive irrigation scheme centred at Yanco. The scheme was designed

with Burrinjuck as the main storage reservoir; water released from here, as required for irrigation, would flow down the river to Berembed, where the weir would divert it into the Main Canal, and thence by smaller channels by flow of gravity to farm properties. Construction of Burrinjuck commenced in 1907. Water was first supplied for irrigation in 1912 and after World War I considerable expansion took place with the settlement of ex-servicemen on irrigation farms. By 1924, some 48 000ha were occupied and the towns of LEETON and GRIFFITH, designed by the noted architect Walter Burley GRIFFIN, were established. In these early days there was considerable scepticism about the ultimate success of the scheme and financial inducements were offered to encourage settlers. But, in spite of these doubts, the scheme flourished with intensive production of citrus and stone fruits, grapes, rice, wheat, wool, fat lambs, vegetables and beef cattle. Today, the Main Canal (155km long) has a maximum flow capacity of 4 900ML per day and supplies irrigation water to some 2 570 farms in the Yanco and Mirrool irrigation areas.

In addition, water is provided for livestock and some minor pasture irrigation in the Benerembah, Tabbita and Wah Wah irrigation districts. The construction of the Blowering Dam on the Tumut River, as part of the SNOWY MOUNTAINS SCHEME, led to the development of an additional irrigation area called Coleambally in the 1960s. This is situated S of the Murrumbidgee River, opposite the Yanco and Mirrool areas; the Gogeldrie Weir, 112km downstream from the Berembed Weir, diverts water from the river into the Coleambally Canal.

Murrumbidgee River NSW This inland river in the SW of the State drains into

The Murrumbidgee river near Hay in the Riverina region NSW

the MURRAY-DARLING system. It rises in the SNOWY MOUNTAINS N of Kiandra, flows on a general SE course, then makes a giant loop to flow N across the ACT, changes direction again and moves generally W for the rest of its course across the slopes and inland plains to join the Murray. Near its headwaters is Tantangara Dam, one of the structures of the SNOWY MOUNTAINS SCHEME. Among the upper tributaries are the Queanbeyan, Umaralla, Cotter, Yass and Goodradigbee Rivers which rise in the hills and ranges of the SOUTHERN TABLELANDS and flow generally N, forming the catchment of the BURRINJUCK DAM. Beyond this dam, the Murrumbidgee receives the Tumut River (on which the Blowering Dam has been built as part of the Snowy Scheme) as a left-bank tributary and flows through GUNDAGAI and WAGGA WAGGA, but before reaching NARRANDERA part of its waters are diverted by Berembed Weir into the main canal of the MURRUMBIDGEE IRRIGATION AREAS. Downstream from Narrandera is Gogeldrie Weir which diverts water for the Coleambally irrigation scheme. Thence the river flows W past Darlington Point and HAY, beyond which there are three weirs (Maude, Redbank and Balranald, to raise river level and stabilise flow) and finally in a SW direction past BALRANALD to join the Murray.

Thus, over its 2 170km meandering course, the Murrumbidgee, with its many BILLABONGS and ANABRANCHES, flows from the tablelands where the yearly rainfall is over 1 500mm into the lower rainfall area of the W slopes (Gundagai 716mm, Wagga 570mm) and then across the inland plains where the countryside becomes increasingly arid (Narrandera 441mm, Hay 360mm, Balranald 317mm). The Monaro Highway follows part of the upper valley on a N-S route, the Hume Highway crosses the N and E sections of the valley passing through YASS and Gundagai, the Sturt Highway follows the general W course of the river through Wagga, Narrandera and Hay, and the Olympic Way traverses the mid-E parts on a general N-S route through Wagga.

The name Murrumbidgee comes from the Aboriginal word meaning 'big water'. The upper reaches of the river were discovered by British explorers in the early 1820s; HUME and Hovell crossed it in 1824 on their trek through the interior, and Charles STURT explored the major part of it in 1829-30. Pastoral settlers followed with their bullock carts and herds of sheep and cattle. In 1858 the first paddlewheel steamer reached Wagga and during subsequent decades river transport was used to bring supplies to settlers and take rural produce out of the region. But the paddlewheelers were never a reliable form of transport, mainly because of river level variations and navigation problems, and after the 1880s road and rail haulage progressively took over.

Murrumburrah NSW (combined population of Murrumburrah and HARDEN 2 070 in 1981) A twin town to Harden, Murrumburrah is located in the SW slopes region, 357km by road SW of Sydney. It is a major railway junction on the main S route to VIC, between YASS and COOTAMUNDRA, with link lines to YOUNG and on to COWRA. Settlement of the district began in the 1830s soon after the discovery of the Yass Plains by the explorer Hamilton HUME. Local attractions include the Harden-Murrumburrah Historical Museum, a pottery and handcrafts centre, and the Barwang vineyard to the N of town. The name Murrumburrah comes from an Aboriginal phrase meaning 'two canoes on the way to the ceremonial initiation ground'.

Murwillumbah NSW (population 7 806 in 1981) This town on the TWEED RIVER in the NORTH COAST region is located 30km upstream from the river mouth. It is situated on the Pacific Highway, 886km by road N of Sydney, and is the rail terminus of a branch line from the main N railway; the train journey from Sydney is 935km, with the branch junction at CASINO, then passing through LISMORE and BYRON BAY. The town's name is an Aboriginal word and has a number of translations: the most commonly accepted one means 'place of many possums', but others include 'a good camping ground' and 'a place where many people are encamped'.

Murwillumbah in the Tweed valley, North Coast NSW.

The town is the commercial and business focus of the Tweed Valley and is surrounded by densely settled, rich farming and grazing lands. The highland areas are important for timber production, with sawmills dotted in the ranges, and many of the steeply sloping hills are devoted to banana plantations and beef cattle raising; on the river flats are lush dairy pastures, cane farms, fodder crops, rows of bushy pineapple plants and vegetable plots. The town contains a number of secondary industries including factories processing dairy products, timber mills and, at Condong (5km downstream), a sugar mill. The average annual rainfall at Condong is 1 722mm, with summer months receiving the highest falls. River flooding is not uncommon and the swirling muddy waters inundate the main streets of the town, sometimes to the height of shop awnings. The rugged McPHERSON RANGE, lying to the NW, forms a scenic backdrop to the valley. Mt Warning (1 157m high), 16km SW of the town, is a volcanic plug majestically dominating the landscape.
See also Gold Coast

museums By definition of the International Council of Museums' Statutes 1974, a museum is a non-profit-making, permanent institution, in the service of society and its development, and open to the public; which acquires, conserves, researches, communicates and exhibits for the purposes of study, education and enjoyment, material evidence of man and his environment. Within this definition come all museums and art galleries, botanic and zoological gardens, monuments and sites, nature reserves, science centres and planetaria.

In the capital cities of each Australian State, large government-funded museums have been established, the first in SYDNEY around the 1820's (now the Royal Botanic Gardens and The Australian Museum) and in the other States later in the 19th Century. These were in the main museums of natural history; museums of art; and in two cities (Sydney and MELBOURNE) museums of applied science, with their fields of study concentrated mainly on the Australian and Indo-Pacific regions. Federal museums in CANBERRA and DARWIN were established in the 20th Century, e.g. The Australian War Memorial, Australian National Gallery, Northern Territory Museum and Art Gallery and, still under construction in 1984, Museum of Australia. The growth of these federal and state museums is evidenced by new buildings (e.g. the QLD Museum in the new cultural complex), the restoration of old buildings added to the existing complex (e.g. the Powerhouse for the Museum of Applied Arts and Sciences in Sydney), or extensions to present buildings. Employing a wide range of professional staff and housing vast collections in their respective fields, all of these museums have grown to international standing in the major aspects of their work.

Outside the capital cities, there are a number of art museums particularly in VIC with large collections and active programmes (*see* below). Established mainly in the post World War II period, there are also many smaller museums, mainly historical in nature, and operating with a few exceptions on mostly volunteer staff. Organised by local community associations, with assistance in some cases from local Government and grants provided by the various State or Federal Ministries for the Arts, these museums have made a valuable contribution to our heritage through their collections of historical items from their districts.

Museums of transport have been developed in most States, many of them by enthusiastic private collectors or local societies; these include museums of trains or trams, cars and trucks, horse-drawn vehicles, ships and shipping, aircraft. The Western Australian Museum has a unique collection of Dutch ships wrecked off their coast during the 17th and 18th centuries.

The post-war period has also seen the rise of the so-called 'open air' museums where a town, farm or industry is re-created either by restoring old buildings, re-erecting original buildings from the locality on the museum site or creating facsimilies of them, with associated activities relevant to the period. Old Sydney Town in NSW, Sovereign Hill Gold Mining Village in VIC or Birdwood Mill Museum in SA are examples of

1913 Kangaroo First Commonwealth issue; 1913 ld engraved issue; 1935 Silver Jubille issue; 1932 6d Kookaburra, 1/- Lyrebird

1980 Waltzing Matilda strip

1959-64 Animals and Flowers Definitive issue

1959-64 Animals and Flowers Definitive issue

1978-80 Bird series

See also POSTAGE STAMPS

Note: Stamp reproductions have been defaced in accordance with Australia Post conditions

1978-80 Bird Series

20c AUSTRALIA — Little Grebe

AUSTRALIA 20c — Eastern Yellow Robin

AUSTRALIA 22c — White Tailed Kingfisher

AUSTRALIA 25c — Spur-wing Plover

AUSTRALIA 28c — Rainbow Bird

AUSTRALIA 30c — Pied Oystercatcher

1978-80 Bird series

AUSTRALIA 35c — Regent Bower Bird

40c AUSTRALIA — Lovely Wren

AUSTRALIA 45c — Masked Woodswallow

AUSTRALIA 50c — Flame Robin

AUSTRALIA 55c — Lotus-bird

AUSTRALIA 60c — King Parrot

1981-83 Animals, Reptiles and Amphibians series

Lace Monitor — AUSTRALIA 1c

Corroboree Frog — AUSTRALIA 3c

Eastern Snake-necked Tortoise — AUSTRALIA 15c

Blue Mountains Tree Frog — AUSTRALIA 27c

Smooth Knob-tailed Gecko — AUSTRALIA 40c

1981-83 Animals, Reptiles and Amphibians series

Yellow-faced Whip Snake — AUSTRALIA 65c

Crucifix Toad — AUSTRALIA 70c

Eastern Water Dragon — 75c AUSTRALIA

Centralian Blue-tongued Lizard — AUSTRALIA 85c

Freshwater Crocodile — 90c AUSTRALIA

1981-83 Animals, Reptiles and Amphibians series

Australia 5c — Queensland Hairy-nosed Wombat Endangered Species

Australia 24c — Thylacine (Tasmanian Tiger) Endangered Species

Australia 25c — Greater Bilby Endangered Species

Australia 30c — Bridled Nail-tailed Wallaby Endangered Species

Australia 50c — Leadbeater's Possum Endangered Species

Australia 55c — Stick-nest Rat Endangered Species

1983 Butterflies series

Australia 4c — Regent Skipper

Australia 10c — Cairns Birdwing

Australia 20c — Macleay's Swallow Tail

Australia 27c — Ulysses

Australia 30c — Chlorinda Hairstreak

Australia 80c — Amaryllis Azure

Australia $1 — Sword-Grass Brown

See also POSTAGE STAMPS

Note: Stamp reproductions have been defaced in accordance with Australia Post conditions

this kind of museum. Highly specialised museums, e.g. of minerals, shells, toys, mostly in private ownership but open to the public are also fairly widespread.

The relatively new field of industrial archaeology is making an impact with the restoration of buildings (potteries, pumping stations, gold working, etc) and the establishment of collections from the sites. Another development is the Aboriginal 'Keeping Place' museums, where sacred objects can be kept safely away from the uninitiated, but yet withdrawn for important ceremonies.

A museum's collections of whatever kind may be acquired by personal collecting, purchase, gift, bequest or exchange. As well as the objects themselves, it may include associated documents of various kinds, maps and photographs, newspapers and record books. Modern museums in Australia, as elsewhere, tend to specialise in one particular field compared with the encyclopedic collections of last century.

Any object acquired by a museum is numbered and registered in some form, either a card catalogue, accessions book or, increasingly in the larger museums, in some form of computer retrieval system. Recording the vital details of each object is essential if it is to be of use in future research or exhibition programmes. Objects once acquired must be adequately stored to prevent deterioration, either within the Museum or in off-site storage areas, e.g. at The Australian War Memorial's store at Mitchell. In recent years, trained conservators have been appointed to the staffs of the larger museums to advise on optimum environmental conditions for the storage of collections and to conserve and restore individual items which are felt to be of vital importance to the nation's heritage or are intended for inclusion in an exhibition.

In most modern exhibitions, the emphasis has moved from stress on individual objects to a topical approach, where the object is accompanied by other illustrative materials such as graphics, models or reconstructions of scenes to present a broader concept. There is also more stress on visitor involvement, where the ability to touch or manipulate the exhibit is encouraged, e.g. at Questacon, the experimental science centre in Canberra. Mention should also be made of the increase in recent years of the 'block-buster' exhibition, the large and important travelling exhibit usually promoted from overseas, which is strongly promoted and attracts thousands of visitors, e.g. 'Dinosaurs from China', 'Columbian Gold'. As well, travelling exhibitions in mobile vans or Museum Trains are being produced by some State museums in Australia as part of their extension services to rural areas.

Related to the exhibitions are the education programmes devised for various sectors of the community — school classes, family groups, tertiary students, the handicapped. A new professional element, the Education Officer, has been added to the museum staff. These Officers, often assisted by trained volunteers, provide lesson programmes, weekend and holiday activities, lectures, films, field studies, loan services, training courses and other services suited to the needs of each individual group.

Museums in Australia are aware of the needs of their visitors through surveys and evaluation studies and are endeavouring to make museums more interesting and enjoyable for their increasing numbers of visitors.

art museums More commonly called 'galleries' in Australia, public art museums were for a long time almost anomalies within the Australian scene. There were no princely collections to house and exhibit, the list of well-endowed patrons were alarmingly few and ill-informed, while public funding was miserly and cautious. Those that did have some idea what a gallery should be, saw it as performing a link with the cultural heritage of Europe. Its collection was gathered together for a role which was a blend of moral and educational purposes — to improve the lives of those who came to inspect it. For practical reasons, ARCHITECTURE was better places than PAINTING to implant a traditional imagery, and Australian cities and towns were soon able to point to some quite creditable structures that showed a knowledge of Palladium principles, Greek restraint, Gothic imagination and Palazzo self assurance.

Galleries in Australia nearly all began in the same way — not with a collection, but with a group of amateurs, diletante and artists, who having set up an art society, which organised exhibitions, art classes and commenced lobbying local or state governments for the major proportion of the money needed to erect a building. It was such a committee structure which planned the Tasmanian Museum and Art Gallery in 1838, eventually built in 1863. Similar committees were responsible for the founding of the National Gallery of VIC in 1861, the Art Gallery of NSW in 1874, the National Gallery of SA in 1879, the Ballarat Art Gallery in 1884, and both the QLD Art Gallery and the Art Gallery of WA in 1895.

Once a building was erected, or the first stage of one completed, public authorities regarded their principal activity over. The funding of the collections which, quite rightly, was seen as an unlimited, constant and timeless charge against the public purse, was seen as being primarily the responsibility of the gallery administration. Some galleries were lucky in this respect, but very few. The luckiest was Melbourne, where the 1904 Alfred Felton bequest enabled the State collection to gain some depths which was denied to other institutions.

A combination of lack of money and informed knowledge on the part of the committees entrusted with the collection of paintings and SCULPTURES, meant that Australia's public collections were undisciplined, filled with the mixture of a Victorian understanding of the history of art. Believing that the proper study of art was the study of the past, galleries were soon filled with plaster casts of Graeco-Roman statuary, facsimiles of old masters, or recent purchases from the Royal Academy, London.

It was not long before the collecting policies of the various galleries faced an elemental crisis. Did these institutions owe their primary obligation to the viewing public, or did they owe something to contemporary, creative Australian artists? The debate was pretty one-sided. The trustee system was overloaded by moneyed men, usually of a mercantile background, who relished their role as arbiters of taste, and who would fight for decades to keep their position of privilege. For them, the only proper art was that of previous centuries, preferably later than Raphael and Michelangelo, and work which was acceptable to London society. The result was that the public galleries took a long time to systematically collect Australian work. The redoubtable Julian ASHTON at the National Gallery of NSW in the late seventies and early eighties, attempted to persuade his fellow trustees to support indigenous painting, and beginning with the purchase of STREETON'S, 'Still glides the stream', was marginally successful. But overall, Australian painters found that to win acceptance from Australian galleries, they had first to go to England, and there attempt to win London respectability. It was an uphill battle, as BUNNY, FOX and others found out. There were exceptions — HEYSEN of SA springs to mind — but they were very much in the minority.

By the end of World War II, events began to overtake the trustee system. The influences of contemporary art in Europe, as well as the achievements of the French impressionists and post impressionists, were becoming overwhelming. The conservative forces were increasingly embattled. Representing the two sides were the directors of the National Gallery of VIC and the National Gallery of NSW. At the former, the director was the courageous, forthright reactionary, James MacDonald, who in the 1940s was confident enough to dismiss French Impressionists painters, who by then were either dead or very old. At the other side, was Hal Missingham, the director at Sydney, who combined a passion for the work of contemporary Australians with an amiable larrikinism.

By the 1960s, the public art galleries were becoming much more professionally based, and much more liberal in their approach to purchases. The influence of the Museum of Modern Art in New York inspired a new generation of gallery employees and supporters; a new breed of people were beginning to inhabit the offices of public galleries — the professional director and curator.

At the same time as the old, established galleries were being changed, a host of new regional galleries began to appear on the scene, especially in VIC, where a network of small, well built and well run institutions began to proliferate. Such a development could only have occurred with public support, and with an increasing community interest in the visual arts. By the seventies, the revolution was complete, and the galleries of Australia had entered upon the next step in their evolution. Professionally trained personnel were employed in all major institutions, and in most regional ones. A series of large international exhibitions came to the country, such as Modern Masters, the Chinese Exhibition and Old Master Paintings. Contemporary art, other than Australian was being collected by several institutions. Public appreciation and support for the galleries reached a level of participation which would have been unthinkable a generation previously. Regional galleries, with professional standards of preservation and display, were to be found from Rockhampton in the east to FREMANTLE in the west.

The final coping stone to all this development was the opening of the National Gallery of Australia at Canberra in 1982. Its genesis began with Prime Minister Fisher's suggestion in 1911 that the nation should collect paintings of 'notable Australians', a brief which was subsequently altered to include other Australian works. In the seventies its budget was massively increased, its collecting policy greatly expanded, curatorial departments were planned and a building was under construction. Its present position owes everything to the generations that made such an institution possible.

Musgrave Ranges SA/NT Located in the far NW of SA, and extending across the State border into the NT, these ranges have an E-W extent of some 150km and a N-S width of 15km. The highest point is Mt Woodroffe (1 513m) in the E part of the ranges; several other peaks rise to above 1 100m, such as Mt Morris (1 254m), Mt Woodward (1 224m) and Mt Everard (1 173m). Most of the range country lies within Aboriginal reserves, on either side of the SA/NT border, and so entry for non-Aboriginals is prohibited without a special permit. The ranges form the SW rim of the vast LAKE AMADEUS basin and streams rising in the N slopes of the Musgraves drain towards this depression, though rarely reach it except in times of heavy rain. The drainage pattern of streams from the S and SE, such as the Alberga River, is towards LAKE EYRE, although these also are not perennial and seldom reach the lake. The average annual rainfall at Ernabella station, near the E end of the ranges at a height of 676m above sea level, is only 240mm and this is unpredictable and quite variable from year to year.

mushrooms *see* agriculture; fungi

music This article provides an outline of the history of music in Australia.
Aboriginal music Tribal music of the Australian Aborigines had existed for thousands of years in Australia prior to the arrival of Europeans. The early white settlers failed to understand or assess the sacred, semi-sacred and secular music of the Aborigines they encountered, although in the earlier half of the 19th century a few composers did try to come to terms with this music by attempting to assimilate it into western-style songs and choral works. Little further interest was taken until the appearance of John ANTILL's ballet score *Corroboree* in the 1940s, while more recently George DREYFUS has written a *Sextet for Didjeridu and Wind Quintet*. However, the rhythmic complexity of much Australian Aboriginal music is such that it does not blend readily with western musical styles. The DIDJERIDU, the best-known Australian Aboriginal musical instrument, was traditionally used only in the far N of the continent, including ARNHEM LAND. Other instruments, mainly percussion, vary from area to area; as in nearly all tribal societies, instrumental music has no existence by itself, but is used to support singing and dancing. Music is an essential ingredient in the lives of tribal Aborigines, playing a vital part in their ceremonies. Ethnomusicological study of Australian Aboriginal music is relatively recent and as yet small-scaled, the chief work being undertaken by the Music Department of Monash University VIC, by Alice Moyle at the Institute of Aboriginal Studies in Canberra and by Catherine Ellis in Adelaide SA.

Early classical and traditional music As white settlement began in Australia with the transportation of convicts from the UK, it was inevitable that the early settlers were as divided musically as they were socially. For the administrators, army and navy officers and the few free settlers who accompanied them, music provided a solace in the midst of the hardships of establishing the new colony. This music included parlour songs, often of a sentimental kind, and music for the recently established piano, an instrument which quickly found great popularity even in the most remote parts of the country. Dance music was also required for occasions such as official celebrations at Government House, and church music was written as the various religious communities established themselves. All the music tended to be a continuation of the traditions which had been left behind in the UK and Europe. Music recalled home; hence 'Home, Sweet Home' by Sir Henry Bishop was very popular in colonial Australia, not only with the early settlers who longed for their eventual return to Europe, but also with the later 'currency' or Australian-born residents, who had no such longings.

By contrast, the much larger body of convicts, and the sailors and soldiers who accompanied them, brought with them a large repertoire of traditional songs, mainly from England, Ireland and Scotland. The first named piece of music known to have been performed on Australian soil, on 9 February 1788, was *The Rogue's March*, played at the drumming out of a sailor who had been caught in the tents of the women convicts. The regimental and navy bands provided most of the instrumental resources for the early settlers, playing for military, naval, church and civic occasions. They also played in the early theatres, such as Barnett LEVEY's Theatre Royal during the 1830s.

Little of the religious and ethical idealism which characterised much of the early music-making in North America was to be found in early Australian music. Very few of the early convict songs, many of them undoubtedly treasonable, have survived; 'Jim Jones' is one of the exceptions. Early traditional songs had such themes as the plight of convicts (for example, 'Moreton Bay') and the defiance of bushrangers (for example, 'The Death of Ben Hall'). Many of them set new words to older tunes—the tune of 'Moreton Bay' belongs to an Irish ballad, 'Youghal Harbour'. The gold rushes brought a new genre of songs; like their counterparts in the USA, they were often topical parodies set to well-known tunes and many were the work of professional entertainers such as Charles Thatcher. Another category of traditional songs was concerned with pastoral Australia and has bred a vast number of songs about the exploits of overlanders, stockriders, shearers and squatters. The best-known Australian Outback song is 'WALTZING MATILDA'. Traditional songs of the UK, some still retaining their original words, have been collected, and Australia's long dependence on overseas shipping inevitably encouraged the adaptation or invention of sea shanties such as 'Bound for South Australia'. In keeping with the male-dominated frontier society, humorous and boasting songs such as 'The Old Bark Hut', are also prominent, while songs about women and love which are so prominent in European traditional songs, hardly feature at all.

The NSW Conservatorium of Music in Sydney, originally designed as the stables for Government House

Choral societies and growth of musical institutions In 19th-century Australian society, as in the UK, choral societies, rather than orchestras, were the centre of musical organisation and concert performances. The *liedertafel* or song club of the German-speaking settlers, such as in SA, was a variant of this. Works such as Handel's *Messiah* were a staple part of the choral repertoire. In many instances the choral societies, with their preference for biblical oratorios and other works with religious texts, seemed to align themselves with such institutions as the schools of arts and the mechanics' institutes, which worked for the betterment of the working classes—in this case, through music.

Although not holding the prominent position they were to achieve in the 20th century as the centre of concert life, orchestras, both semi-professional and amateur, were cultivated in 19th-century Australia. The series of concerts organised by Frederick H. Cowan for the Melbourne Exhibition of 1888 are a good example of this. Notable orchestral enterprises pre-dating the formation of the Australian Broadcasting Commission (now AUSTRALIAN BROADCASTING CORPORATION, ABC), and with it the policy of employing and managing orchestras, include the orchestra established by Professor G.W.L. Marshall-Hall in Melbourne around the turn of the century; the orchestra founded by the Belgian conductor, Henri Verbrugghen, after he took up his appointment as first director of the NSW State Conservatorium of Music in 1915; and the orchestra based at Melbourne University, with which the young Bernard HEINZE built on the work of Marshall-Hall.

With the ABC came the establishment of professional orchestras in each State capital. In addition to its many different series of subscription concerts and recitals, the ABC's broadcasting of these concerts and its many studio broadcasts and recordings have made it the principal employer of Australian instrumentalists, as well as the principal supplier of live and broadcast concert-hall music. Only a handful of other professional orchestras exist. These include the two orchestras attached to the Australian Opera and the Australian Ballet, a professional theatre orchestra in Brisbane and the ABC National Training Orchestra, which, as its name suggests, acts as a transitional medium for young musicians preparing for an orchestral career. On the amateur scene, however, there has been a resurgence of good amateur orchestras, a movement which is particularly in evidence in the larger cities.

In the field of chamber music, Richard Goldner's formation of MUSICA VIVA AUSTRALIA proved a momentous act which established a highly respected entrepreneurial organisation (see below).

A wide spectrum of other musical societies and institutions also flourish, catering for everything from folk music to musicology (the scientific study of music). Prominent among these are the various types of music libraries and repositories, ranging from the music and sound-archives section of the National Library of Australia in Canberra to the recently established Australia Music Centre in The Rocks area of Sydney. The setting up of FM radio stations which are devoted entirely to music broadcasting has been another welcome addition. The recent development of the activities of the Musicological Society of Australia, through both the national body and the State chapters, shows the need for more widespread intellectual discussion of all aspects of music from both inside and outside Australia.

Nationalism and internationalism The idea of patriotic flag-waving in music has been prominent from earliest times. In 1826 bandmaster Kavanagh of the 3rd Regiment offered a song (now lost) entitled 'The Trumpet Sounds Australia's Fame', while Isaac Nathan's 'Star of the South' (1840s), Frederick Ellard's 'Crimea, Alma, Inkerman, Balaclava' (1850s) and John Burn's federation song with chorus, 'The Star of Australia' (1899), are representative of the patriotic songs which appeared whenever a major civic or State event seemed to warrant pieces of this nature. The fact that Australia has no one universally accepted national anthem is perhaps indicative of wider social implications regarding Australians' sense of a national identity.

A more serious and fundamental attempt at defining an Australian identity in music was made by Percy GRAINGER, who was in several respects perhaps the most original composer in Australia. Since World War II many composers have been influenced by the more international musical trends. However, it is interesting to observe that many Australian composers have chosen to return from overseas to work in their own country and that many of them believe to some extent in an Australian identity in music.

Music education In Australia music education has largely been of a haphazard nature. From the arrival of some of the earliest music teachers, such as William Vincent Wallace, John Phillip DEANE and Isaac Nathan, private teaching has accounted for the greater part of instrumental and singing training. Included in this is the contribution made by Roman Catholic Orders of nuns, many of whom brought music, particularly piano teaching, into the remote areas of the country. The influence of British institutions of musical education was felt strongly in the first half of the 20th century. Travelling examiners from the royal schools of music and Trinity College made yearly pilgrimages to Australia to examine young students through a system of graded music examinations, a system which was later adopted and is still pursued by the Australian Music Examinations Board (AMEB).

Specially trained music teachers are now a generally accepted part of secondary school education, while most primary and kindergarten music teaching is undertaken by class teachers. Recent pilot work carried out in Sydney's less affluent outer W suburbs in a modified Kodaly music education programme is just one of the many successful experiments being undertaken by highly trained music teachers throughout the country. Music education at a tertiary level includes many different courses and types of musical training within universities, conservatoria, colleges of advanced education and teacher training colleges. The chief parent musical education body in the country is the Australian Society for Music Education (ASME), but many other organisations exist to help cater for the particular educational requirements of different groups.

See also country music, jazz, pop music; musical composition and composers; opera; piano and pianists; singers and singing

Further reading: Manifold, J.S. (ed) The Penguin Australian Song Book. Penguin, Melbourne, 1964 and Who Wrote The Ballads? Australian Book Society, Sydney, 1964; Covell, R. Australia's Music: Themes of a New Society. Sun Books, Melbourne, 1967 and Music in Australia: Needs and Prospects. (2 vols) Unisearch, Sydney, 1970; Meredith, J. & Anderson, H. Folk Songs of Australia. Ure Smith, Sydney, 1968; Serle, G. From Deserts the Prophets Come: The Creative Spirit in Australia 1788-1972. Heinemann, Melbourne, 1973; Directory of Australian Music Organisations. Australia Music Centre, Sydney, 1978.

Musica Viva Australia The largest and most active chamber music organisation in the world, it was founded in Sydney by Richard Goldner shortly after World War II. Goldner's original aim was to form and maintain a professional chamber ensemble for the achievement of high musical standards and simultaneously to cultivate a wide audience for chamber music.

The society had to suspend activities from 1952 to 1955 because of the lack of any official subsidy or substantial private endowments, but thereafter began its primary operation of bringing to Australia a succession of distinguished ensembles of international calibre. While there is still no resident permanent ensemble, entrepreneurial activity has become Musica Viva's main function. Through its own management and in association with other music organisations it now presents concerts in all Australian capital cities and in 40 other centres throughout Australia. In 1982 it managed over 750 concerts both within Australia and overseas. Musica Viva's activities also include the promotion of Australian ensembles through concerts and tours within the country and overseas. Some of the international tours are managed in association with the Department of Foreign Affairs and the Music Board of the AUSTRALIA COUNCIL. It has also championed the commissioning and performance of new chamber works by Australian composers.

The organisation is based in Sydney with branches in all States to promote activities on a State and district level. Musica Viva has won a high reputation for its development and skilful economic management while continuing to use a comparatively small staff. It receives financial assistance from the Music Board of the Australia Council and the various State governments.

musical composition and composers Most visiting or resident musical composers in 19th-century Australia tended to continue the Victorian traditions of England by writing music for civic, State and church requirements. It was only with the music of Leipzig-trained Alfred HILL that Australian music achieved a new level of technical professionalism, while the works of Percy GRAINGER in the first half of the 20th century are among the outstanding contributions made to Australian music. For the most part, however, the geographical and cultural isolation which Australia experienced during the first half of the 20th century adversely affected composition and resulted in composers such as Arthur BENJAMIN having to leave the country permanently. At best, composers who stayed in Australia had to be content with composing only in their spare time, for no composers survived as professionals during this period. The work of composers such as John ANTILL, Clive Douglas and Robert Hughes is typical of the time, while the rare and individual talent of Dorian Le Gallienne in Melbourne stands as something of an exception to this general picture.

With the increase in communications after World War II, including the importation of contemporary styles of music via sound recordings, a new generation of composers, able to travel more readily overseas and to pursue their own musical interests, emerged in the 1960s. This was an exciting time, especially in Sydney, where, thanks to the activities of the local branch of the International Society for Contemporary Music (ICSM), new music by these composers was frequently performed, and, just as importantly, was discussed and written about by critics and academics such as Roger COVELL and Donald PEART. Outstanding among these composers were Peter SCULTHORPE, George DREYFUS, Colin Brumby, Richard MEALE, Felix WERDER, Nigel BUTTERLEY and Larry Sitsky. Many other composers had chosen to study and work abroad, and these included Margaret Sutherland, Peggy GLANVILLE-HICKS, David Lumsdaine, Don BANKS, Malcolm WILLIAMSON and Keith Humble. A number of these composers have since decided to return to work permanently in their home country. Other more conservative composers continued their professional work at home during the 1950s, 1960s and 1970s, and these included Raymond Hanson, James Penberthy and Eric Gross.

Younger composers Since the excitement created by the new compositional activity of the 1960s, an impressive though small group of younger composers has emerged. Many of these, such as Anne Boyd, Alison Bauld, Barry Conyngham, Ross Edwards and Ian Cugley, were pupils of the composers of the 1960s. Many of them are also intensely interested in the continuing debate concerning an Australian musical expression, which has in no way diminished the resources, Western and non-Western, which these younger composers feel free to draw upon for the development of their individual musical languages. Music threatre works on Australian themes by Alison Bauld (for example, *In a Dead Brown Land*) and Barry Conyngham (for example, *Edward John Eyre*) illustrate this very well, while Vincent Plush has used traditional Australian music in some compositions. However, it would be false to convey the impression that all recent Australian composition is moving towards a nationalistic form of expression. The variety of styles and expression among the younger composers, allied with the breadth of resources employed in musical and sound generation, augur well for musical composition in Australia.

Further reading: Covell, R. *Australia's Music: Themes of a New Society.* Sun Books, Melbourne, 1967; Murdoch, J. *Australia's Contemporary Composers.* Macmillan, Melbourne, 1972; Callaway, F. & Tunley, D. (eds) *Australian Composition in the Twentieth Century.* Oxford University Press, Melbourne, 1978.

Muslims in Australia

The 1981 census revealed that 76 792 persons resident in Australia were identified as Muslims.

Muslims (or Moslems) are people from various countries who are united by their faith in Islam, one of the world's strongest religions. Islam is an Arabic word meaning 'surrender' or 'submission' and the core of this religion is the belief that a man should surrender himself to God and obey the commandments of God as revealed through the archangel Gabriel to the prophet Muhammad who was born in the Arabian city of Mecca in AD 570. These laws were compiled before Muhammad's death and were published immediately after his death in the book called the *Quran* (or *Koran*).

The first Muslims who came to Australia (during the 1850s) were from Karachi in Pakistan (then part of India). These Afghan Muslims played a very important part in the early explorations of inland Australia as camel drivers and later they provided the only means of transport in Outback regions. The Afghan Muslims were proud of their religious faith and strict in its practices. They erected their own mosques, usually humble structures of corrugated iron with a small minaret; the first was built in Adelaide in 1898, the second in Perth in 1906 and the third in Brisbane in 1910. However, the children of these early Muslims merged into the Australian society because there was no provision for the teaching of the Islamic traditions in the Australian educational system.

Most Muslims in Australia today are migrants since World War II who have come from various European, Mediterranean, Middle Eastern and Asian countries such as Cyprus, Egypt, Turkey, Yugoslavia, Lebanon, Iran, Iraq, Jordan, Syria, India, Pakistan and South-East Asia. In addition to permanent migrants, many Muslim students come to study at Australian universities, particularly for postgraduate studies, from various Asian countries such as Malaysia, Pakistan, Indonesia, India and Bangladesh.

In April 1976, the Muslims held a conference in Brisbane at which representatives from all parts of Australia met and accepted a new formula and structure for the work of Islam in Australia—a three-tier confederation consisting of: 35 local Islamic societies which would function as independent organisations to provide services for their members; nine State Islamic Councils formed from the local Islamic societies; and the Australian Federation of Islamic Councils formed from the State Islamic Councils. All preparation, planning and implementation of projects, programmes and activities are now co-ordinated through this structure. Twenty-five mosques and Islamic centres have been built and the Australian Federation of Islamic Councils is now recruiting qualified Islamic teachers and Imams to organise and teach Muslim children and adults, set up libraries, carry-out preaching work and organise Muslim youth activities and social welfare work among migrant Muslims. Most Muslims in Australia do not have the financial resources to carry out their work without help from their more affluent compatriots in the wider Islamic world. However, efforts are being made to adopt programmes which will make them financially self-sufficient. The Australian Federation of Islamic Councils has embarked on investment projects and certain income-generating services to raise funds for the activities of the Muslim community.

The first major impact of the organised Muslims in Australia came in August 1979 when Christian and Muslim leaders participated in a joint conference in Melbourne on the theme 'Islam and Christianity'. The conference organiser was Father L.P. Fitzgerald, Master of Mannix College and the Australian representative for the Dominican Secretariat for Islamic Affairs. Although there have been many misunderstandings between Muslims and Christians, the conference noted that there are many doctrinal affinities between the two and expressed the wish that Muslims and Christians should co-operate to provide a more effective bulwark against atheism, materialism and indifference.

See also Indian sub-continent, settlers from

mussels *see* bivalve molluscs

Muswellbrook NSW (population 8 549 in 1981) A town on the upper HUNTER RIVER 289km by rail NNW of Sydney and some 170km inland by road from NEWCASTLE, Muswellbrook is situated on the New England Highway and is a railway town on the main line to the N tablelands. Dairying is the dominant rural activity of the district, along with cattle grazing, fodder crop cultivation and some sheep raising. The town is an important coal mining centre, with both open-cut and tunnel mines. In the late 1970s at Liddel, 16km SE of Muswellbrook on the New England Highway, a major electricity power station was completed; coal is supplied locally from the Liddel State Mine for the steam-power to drive the turbine generators of this station which require up to five million tonnes per year. The GLENBAWN DAM on the upper Hunter, completed in 1957, provides an assured water supply for Muswellbrook.

Liddel thermal power station near Muswellbrook

mutton *see* sheep, etc.

mutton bird *see* sea birds

myall This is the name used for various species of wattle (*Acacia*), belonging to the family MIMOSACEAE, and applied particularly to *A. pendula* which grows in the drier parts of NSW and QLD. The foliage consists of silver-grey, flattened stalks which resemble leaves (phyllodes) and which droop in the fashion of the weeping willows of Europe. Livestock eat the foliage during droughts and the Aborigines used the timber for boomerangs.

Myall Lake NSW This lake on the lower NORTH COAST, about 236km N of Sydney, is one of a series of lagoons, lying E of the Pacific Highway, which are connected by the Myall River to PORT STEPHENS. Some of these lakes, together with the strip of land lying between them and the sea, have been designated as a national park in order to preserve the natural vegetation, the bird and animal life, and some unique sand dunes NE of the lake. The park covers an area of more than 27 526ha and contains a diversity of scenery—spectacular headlands and long expanses of beach on the coast, heathland clothed in colourful wild flowers in the spring, stands of paper bark trees fringing the lagoons, and tall red-gum forests on some of the sand dunes. The lakes, which cover an area of over 10 000ha, are the breeding grounds for prawns and many species of fish, and provide a habitat for numerous water birds including black swans, ducks and cranes. The wildlife population of the park includes kangaroos, red-necked wallabies, spiny anteaters, bandicoots, possums, gliders and marsupial mice. There are several access routes to the park—from the S via the town of Bulahdelah, and from the Pacific Highway along Lakes Way to the N section of the park.

mycorrhiza see saprophytic plants

myna, Indian see animals, introduced; starlings

Myrtaceae This is a very large family of dicotyledonous flowering plants containing about 80 genera and 3000 species that are widely distributed throughout the tropics, with centres of concentration in Australia and tropical America.

Members of the Myrtaceae are evergreen shrubs, mallees or trees. Their simple leaves, oppositely or alternately arranged, are dotted with pellucid (transparent) oil-glands which may be obscure and are usually aromatic; the total absence of stipules is another common feature. The flowers are axillary and either solitary in cymes or umbels, or terminal in spikes, racemes or panicles. The floral tube is attached congenitally (adnate) to the ovary and this is often continued above the ovary summit. There are four or five sepals and a corresponding number of petals which are free (except in the *Eucalyptus* and *Acmena* species) above the floral tube. The stamens, which may number five or more, are free or united into five bundles opposite the petals. The inferior ovary consists of many cavities (locular) which each contain one or more ovulus. The style is simple and the stigma usually capitate. The fruit can take the form of a capsule, a nut, a berry or a schizocarp.

Eucalyptus Amongst the large number of Myrtaceae genera in Australia *Eucalyptus* is the most prominent, constituting about 95 per cent of the forest and woodland trees and providing the distinctive character of the Australian landscape. Although widely planted in the Mediterranean region, South America and California, this genus occurs naturally only in Australia, New Guinea, Timor, the Celebes and the Philippines. The genus has a wide range: from semi-arid sand plains of central Australia to the tree-line in the SNOWY MTS; also, in terms of numbers of species, the only genus which rivals it is *Acacia* (family MIMOSCEAE); *Acacia* species are more numerous in drier regions, and some extend into closed forests (rainforests) beyond the limits of eucalypt occurrence. Few *Acacia* species can equal eucalypts in size, and where they occur together, *Acacia* species generally form the understorey.

Eucalypts may be reduced in size if grown under harsh conditions, such as in shallow soils on exposed sites or near the tree-line. However, in deep, fertile, well-watered soils they form the tallest hardwoods in the world, growing to more than 100m high. The crowns of tall species vary in form from those which are slender-branched and feathery to those which are heavy, stubby-branched and round. Within the natural range in which each species occurs there is also considerable variation in form, depending on local environmental conditions. Eucalypts are easily recognisable because their petals and sepals are fused to form a small cup (calyptra) which is shed when the flower opens. Eucalypt flowers have many stamens, which are followed by a more or less persistent woody fruit, the gum nut, which assumes a number of diverse and interesting forms, depending on the species.

Eucalypts can be described according to their form, or their bark type. The latter groupings have some taxonomic validity, whereas the former tend to reflect environmental conditions. Forest form eucalypts have clean columnar trunks with small crowns, which occupy from a quarter to a third of the total height of the tree, and generally occur on sites with good soil and a plentiful water supply, in communities such as tall open forest. Woodland eucalypts are more stocky, with heavy branches low on the trunk, the canopy extending from half to two-thirds of the total tree height; such trees occur often on poorer, drier soils than the forest trees. Mallee eucalypts are multi-stemmed from the ground, with an underground stem (lignotuber) which is capable of regenerating from dormant buds after destruction of the crown. Such mallees occur in tall shrubland and open scrub, often on very poor soils or in arid situations. Shrubby eucalypts intergrade with mallees but generally have crowns extending to ground level, whereas mallees have a distinct crown stratum.

Bark types give rise to a number of common names, such as gums, bloodwoods and stringy-barks. Gums have a smooth bark, in shades of cream, white–olive, grey and pink, which is shed annually in ribbons or plates; bloodwoods have a persistent bark in plates or scales, often distinctively coloured where the new bark shows in the fissures; stringybarks have a long, fibrous persistent bark generally in shades of brown and grey; peppermint barks are distinguished from stringybarks by being less fibrous, and many have highly aromatic leaves; box barks are similar to peppermint barks but the leaves lack the aroma of the latter; ironbarks have hard, dark, deeply furrowed bark; and ashes are distinguished by the rough, fibrous bark on the trunk, and have smooth bark on the upper trunk and limbs.

A large number of *Eucalyptus* species are grown either commercially for their timber (used in construction work and paper making) or as garden ornamentals and shelter belts. They are popular in both cases because of their very rapid growth and because they are particularly suited to the Australian climate, although care must be taken to plant species from either the local or a similar environment. Their horticultural value is increased by the beauty of the foliage, bark and flowers of some species, as well as the natural variation within some species which has allowed selection of superior strains. Many eucalypts, particularly box barks, have excellent honey flowers, and the characteristic aromatic oils of the foliage have also formed the basis of a minor industry.

Other genera A variety of other Myrtaceae genera are found in a wide range of Australian plant communities, and many have also found their way into gardens, especially in recent years. In areas which are particularly water-logged, PAPERBARKS (*Melaleuca* species), and bottle brushes (*Callistemon* species), are common, although both also occur in well-drained habitats. Many species of *Melaleuca* form small trees of compact form with neat crowns in many shades of green and trunks covered with large curling sheets of supple white bark. *M. ericifolia* and *M. quinquenervia* are both important components of dune system vegetation, tolerating some salt, and of waterlogged soils, forming dense low closed forests; both species form excellent landscape subjects and, with the bracelet honey myrtle, *M. armillaris*, are widely planted also on drier sites. Many other *Melaleuca* shrub species are cultivated also, including *M. coccinea* (with red flowers), *M. glaberrima* (with pink flowers) and *M. pulchella* (with mauve flowers). *Callistemon* species (with their brushes of brightly coloured lemon, pink, scarlet and crimson flowers) are also widely cultivated, and selected strains of species such as *C. viminalis* form very handsome shrubs. *Kunzea* species, including the widely cultivated *K. baxteri*, also have bottle brush flowers.

Tea trees (*Leptospermum* species), with their distinctive flat, five-petalled flowers, vary from tall shrubs, such as the white-flowered, grey-leaved coastal tea tree, *L. laevigatum*, to dainty bushes, such as the pink-flowered peach blossom tea tree, *L. squarrosum*. Hybrid tea trees ranging from single pinks to double reds were amongst the earliest cultivars to be developed from the Australian flora. *Leptospermum* species are widespread in the understorey of woodland, and as part of the canopy of heath.

Amongst the tree-forming genera of the Myrtaceae, turpentine, *Syncarpia glomulifera*, forms a handsome tall tree rather like a coarse stringybark in appearance, but with the fruits fused into a compound head. The species of *Angophora*, with opposite adult leaves (*Eucalyptus* adult leaves are usually alternate) and heavy gnarled angular branches give a distinctive touch to the woodlands and open forests of the central coast of E Australia. The rusty apple, *A. costata*, which in summer has a smooth salmon pink bark and masses of creamy white flowers, is a rapid grower of outstanding beauty both in the garden and in the wild.

From moist, sheltered habitats, such as deep gullies and closed forests, a number of fleshy-fruited species, such as the lilly pilly, *Acmena smithii*, and brush cherry (*Syzygium* species), have been introduced into Australian gardens, their dense, dark green, glossy leaves contrasting vividly with the sparse, predominantly grey-brown and green canopies of many eucalypt species. Widely planted as street trees, the brush box, *Tristania conferta*, and the water gum, *T. laurina*, do not reach the heights here that they would if they were in the forest.

See also Appendix 5, Flower Structure and Glossary of Botanical Terms

Further reading: see Appendix 6, A Bibliography for Plants.

myrtle In Australia this name is given particularly to members of the myrtle family, MYRTACEAE. However, it is applied also to other plants, an example being the myrtle beech, *Nothofagus cunninghami*, a member of the beech family, Fagaceae.

myrtles, honey *see* paperbarks

Myrtleford VIC (population 2 815 in 1981) A country town in the NE of the State, Myrtleford is located on the OVENS RIVER, 286km by rail NE of Melbourne. At an elevation of 223m above sea level, it is on the Ovens Highway, 46km by road SE of WANGARATTA, 30km NW of BRIGHT, and 28km SSE of BEECHWORTH. It receives an average annual rainfall of 903mm, with the main falls in the winter months. The surrounding district is noted for the production of tobacco and hops, and is important also for dairying and beef cattle grazing. A tobacco and hops festival is held annually in autumn. Streams in the area offer excellent trout fishing and Lake Buffalo, 21km S of the town, created by a 29m-high dam wall across Buffalo Creek (a tributary of the Ovens) and completed in 1965, is a popular picnic and boating spot. The town stands in the foothills of the MOUNT BUFFALO uplands, an area of picturesque scenery. Squatters reached the region in the late 1830s and gold was discovered in 1853. The name Myrtleford was given to the town because of the profusion of myrtle trees.

Myxomatosis A virus disease affecting RABBITS, this was first described in laboratory stocks of the European rabbit in Montevideo in 1896. There were further outbreaks among European rabbits in the Americas and as these were almost invariably rapidly fatal it was

realised that the European rabbit was an 'accidental' and peculiarly susceptible victim of a disease that normally attacked some local animal. In 1942 Aragão in Brazil, discovered that the true hosts of the virus were native American rabbits which are more closely related to the European hare than to the European rabbit. Myxomatosis is an extremely mild disease in American rabbits, the usual symptom being a small swelling at the site of the bite of the MOSQUITOES which carry the disease. However, in European rabbits large tumours form in the connective tissues of the skin, especially round the eyes and mouth, and after a few days the eyes are completely and permanently closed.

In 1919 Aragão had suggested that myxomatosis could be used for the BIOLOGICAL CONTROL of rabbits but the Commonwealth Institute of Science and Industry, the predecessor of the COMMONWEALTH SCIENTIFIC AND INDUSTRIAL RESEARCH ORGANIZATION (CSIRO), opposed its introduction. The final agreement to try the virus in the field was largely as a result of the lobbying of Dame Jean Macnamara, a well-known specialist and research worker on poliomyelitis. Trials were carried out from 1936 to 1943 in semi-arid areas near PETERBOROUGH in SA and on the E side of SPENCER GULF. The importance of insect vectors in the transmission of the disease was not known at the time, otherwise more suitable testing areas would have been tried. The experiments were unsuccessful and interest waned until the CSIRO and the government of VIC began co-operative trials at Gunbower on the MURRAY RIVER in 1950. A little later the trials were extended to ALBURY. The virus seemed to have disappeared after a few weeks, despite the successful infection of at least 77 animals in the first few days, but some time later it reappeared at one of the test sites, and within nine weeks it had spread to cover an area of over one million square kilometres. The virus spread rapidly throughout Australia and it has been estimated that the value of the additional agricultural produce in the first year after the introduction of the disease was worth $100 million. At about the same time the disease, illegally or accidentally introduced, spread through Britain but the patterns of the outbreaks were different. This was because in Australia the main vectors (carriers) were mosquitoes, while in Britain the vectors were rabbit FLEAS, *Psilopsyllus cuniculi*. There was also some spread by direct contact.

The disease was so virulent in Australia that any strains which killed slowly, or which did not kill at all, were soon selected. The first attenuated virus strains were detected in the field the year after introduction. Strains of the virus can be divided into five grades with some subdivisions. Grade I virus kills 99 per cent or more of the affected animals. By 1958-59 no Grade I strains could be found and most were Grade III. By 1963-64 even Grade II strains were scarce, while Grade IV was common. Rabbit fleas, which, it was believed from their life cycle, would not select attenuated strains so quickly, were introduced, and the CSIRO

also began research on other possible insect vectors of the disease. The outbreaks changed from a series of summer epizootics (animal 'epidemics'), spread mainly by mosquitoes, to one of winter epizootics. However, the rabbit population started to grow again; although rabbits have not achieved their former numbers, in a sense Australia missed a golden opportunity to eradicate the rabbit from large areas. During the drought of the early 1980s, mosquitoes virtually disappeared in many areas, and rabbits further increased. If the remnants of the populations had been wiped out by such methods as trapping and warren destruction at the height of the outbreak, many areas probably would have remained free. The distribution of rabbit fleas has continued in the 1980s and will, it is hoped, increase the incidence of the disease.

N

Nabarlek NT This URANIUM mining site is located E of OENPELLI, N of the Spencer Range, in the W part of the ARNHEM LAND Aboriginal Reserve. It was one of the four main uranium mining centres (together with Ranger, Jabiluka and Koongarra) included in the Ranger Uranium Environmental Inquiry in the 1970s and, as a result of the reports of this inquiry, it was decided that the development of Nabarlek could proceed, subject to satisfactory compliance with environmental impact procedures and (since it was located in an Aboriginal reserve) with the agreement of the Aboriginal people. In 1977 the environmental impact statement for Nabarlek was published and in 1978 an agreement was reached between the mining company (Queensland Mines Ltd) and the Northern Land Council on behalf of the traditional Aboriginal owners. Between May and October 1979, the entire ore body at Nabarlek was mined and the 606 000 tonnes of ore (estimated to contain 12 000 tonnes of U_3O_8) was stockpiled to await future treatment, as the mill was then not completed. The treatment plant commenced operation in mid-1980 and produced 1 006 tonnes of U_3O_8 making up 55 per cent of Australia's total uranium production in that year.

Nagle, Kelvin David George 'Kel' (1920-) Golfer. Born in Sydney, Nagle turned from carpentry to golf when he took a job as assistant professional at Sydney's Pymble Golf Club in 1936. Service in the armed forces during World War II prevented him from playing in a golf tournament until he was 26, but from that time onwards he made his presence felt throughout the golfing world. High points of his career have been wins in the Centenary British Open (1960) and in the Open championships of Australia, Canada, France, Hong Kong, New Zealand and Switzerland. Forsaking power and length for accuracy early in his career, his masterly control of the ball led to his selection as Australian representative in the Canada Cup (now the World Cup) nine times; he won the championship in 1954 and 1959, partnered by Peter THOMSON. Until David GRAHAM won the event in 1981 no other Australian golfer had been closer to winning the highly prestigious US Open—in 1965 he tied for first place with Gary Player but subsequently lost the play-off. As a senior golfer he continued his worldwide successes with wins in the World Seniors (1971, 1975) and the British Seniors (1973, 1975), and teamed up with Peter Thomson to be runner-up in the Legends of Golf tournament in 1977 and 1981. Personable and friendly and held in high esteem by golfers throughout the world, Nagle is one of the few Australians to have been consistently successful on the highly competitive international golfing circuits.

Namatjira, Albert (1902-59) Artist.

Born at HERMANNSBURG, Namatjira was an Arunta Aboriginal who was taught European water-colour technique by Rex Battarbee and became an art teacher at the FINKE RIVER Aboriginal Mission School. In 1938, after an exhibition of his water-colours sold out in Melbourne, his work became very popular throughout Australia. Namatjira's water-colours were attractive to those who enjoyed realistic landscapes of the Australian interior, interpreted by an Aboriginal handling European technique with apparent skill. He was arrested for distributing some of his wealth amongst the Arunta in the form of alcohol. His sentence was commuted in 1958, but he died in ALICE SPRINGS in the following year.

Albert Namatjira

Courtesy of A.I.S. Canberra

Nambour QLD (population 7 965 in 1981)

Located on the Bruce Highway, in the SE of the State, Nambour is 111km by road N of Brisbane, 92km S of GYMPIE and about 16km inland from the coast on the narrow plain belt which rises steeply to the Blackall Range. The town, often called the unofficial capital of the SUNSHINE COAST, is a commercial and service centre for a productive sugar cane and tropical fruit growing region. Forestry is important in the upland areas and there are timber mills in the town and district. At an elevation of 31m above sea level, Nambour experiences a mild climate throughout the year, with a high average annual rainfall of 1 873mm. Though the rain comes in all seasons, January has the highest rainfall (308mm average) and September the lowest (45mm). Some well-known beach resorts are located along the coast adjacent to Nambour: Caloundra to the SE, Maroochydore to the E, and NOOSA HEADS to the NE. At Sunshine Plantation, 16km S, where the big pineapple replica stands 15m high, visitors can go on a narrow-gauge train ride through the pineapple and tropical fruit areas and see an audio-visual display explaining the industry. The Suncoast dairy, 6km N of the town, gives visitors an opportunity to see the operations of the dairy industry. At Buderim, about 20km SE, on a rich red soil plateau between the Blackall Range and the coast, there are farms growing avocados, citrus fruits, strawberries and ginger, and in the town itself is Australia's only ginger factory.

Nambucca Heads NSW (population 4 053 in 1981) This popular holiday resort on the NORTH COAST is situated at the mouth of the Nambucca River, 529km by road N of Sydney on the Pacific Highway and 12km by road NE of MACKSVILLE. The surrounding rural district is noted for dairying, fruit growing, vegetable cultivation and timber-getting. The name Nambucca comes from an Aboriginal word meaning 'entrance to the sea' or 'crooked river'.

Namoi River NSW This major headwater tributary of the BARWON RIVER rises in the SW part of the NEW ENGLAND Plateau. It has a total length from its source to the Barwon junction at WALGETT of 847km, and with its tributaries drains an area of 43 000km². The name Namoi comes from the Aboriginal word *ngnamai* (or *nygamai*) which is applied to a species of *Acacia* tree. Settlement of the valley dates back to the years immediately following the exploration by Sir Thomas MITCHELL in 1831. It developed first as a sheep grazing region, but now it has a wide range of pastoral and agriculture products—wheat, wool, fat stock, lucerne and other fodder crops. The completion of the KEEPIT DAM on the Namoi in 1960 has led to the development of a major cotton growing industry downstream from NARRABRI around WEE WAA. The Oxley Highway traverses the valley on an E-W route from TAMWORTH to COONABARABRAN, crossing the river at GUNNEDAH. The Newell Highway crosses the valley from Coonabara-

Irrigation channel carrying water to cotton farms in the Namoi valley

J.H. Shaw

bran in the S to Narrabri on the river, thence N to MOREE. A branch railway from the main N tablelands line passes along the valley through Gunnedah, Narrabri, Wee Waa and on to Walgett.

nannygai *see* fishes, bony

Naracoorte SA (population 4 758 in 1981) This rural service centre in the SE of the State is 348km by road and 386km by rail SE of Adelaide, about 23km W of the VIC/SA border. At an elevation of 58m above sea level, it experiences a mild climate, with an average annual rainfall of 586mm falling mainly in winter. It is one of the oldest towns in the SE, founded as a private settlement by William McIntosh in 1848 and purchased by the government in 1855. The National Trust (SA) has listed for preservation more than a dozen buildings in the town including the old flour mill, the old district council chambers, the public school, two churches and several cottages. The surrounding rural areas are important for forestry, wheat growing, dairying and livestock grazing. The town's name is derived from the Aboriginal word *narra-coorta* meaning 'a large pool or water hole'. Limestone caves, 13km S of the town, contain one of the most important deposits of extinct marsupial remains in the world.

narcissus *see* Liliaceae

nardoo *see* Pteridophyta

Narooma NSW (population 2 758 in 1981) A small town and tourist resort on the S coast of the State, 353km by road from Sydney, on the Princes Highway, Narooma is located at the mouth of the Wagonga River, between Moruya and BEGA. It is a popular holiday centre, with swimming, surfing, boating and other aquatic sports, and the adjacent coastal waters are well known for big-game fishing. The natural coastal feature called the Glass House Rocks lies 2km S of the main Narooma surfing beach, and 8km offshore is the wildlife sanctuary of MONTAGUE ISLAND. As well as tourism, the district is noted for oyster farming and for timber-getting. The historical village of Central Tilba is located 15km S of Narooma on the Princes Highway; established in 1894, little has been altered since then and hence the village retains some unique features; it has been classified by the National Trust (NSW)

as an 'unusual mountain village' which should be preserved as part of the national heritage. The name Narooma comes from an Aboriginal word meaning 'blue water'. The town site, surveyed in the 1880s, was named Noorooma, and this spelling was officially changed to Narooma in 1972.

Narrabri NSW (population 7 290 in 1981) This town is in the NW of the State where the Newell Highway crosses an ANABRANCH of the NAMOI RIVER, 572km by road NW of Sydney. It is on a branch rail line, off the main N tablelands route, from the Werris Creek junction to WALGETT. From Narrabri, a further branch rail goes N to MOREE. At an elevation of 662m above sea level, it experiences hot summers and mild winters. The average annual rainfall is 662mm, with a concentration in the five spring and summer months between November and March: all of these months receive an average rainfall of 60mm, with January and February above 70mm. About 26km E of the town lies the majestic Nandewar Range, with the rugged mountain scenery of the Mt Kaputar National Park, ·which covers 35 050ha and contains numerous old volcanic peaks over 1 200m high. Mt Kaputar itself (1 509m) is a striking remnant.

Narrabri is becoming known internationally as a research centre in astronomy; at Culgoora, 29km W of the town, is the COMMONWEALTH SCIENTIFIC AND INDUSTRIAL RESEARCH ORGANIZATION (CSIRO) radio heliograph used to explore solar terrestrial relationships such as the origin and effects of sun spots and solar flares. It is a unique instrument consisting of 96 radio telescope aerials arranged at equal intervals around the perimeter of a circle 3km in diameter. The Stellar Intensity Interferometer at the solar observatory is used to measure the angular diameter and temperature of stars. There is a wheat research station 10km N of the town and a cotton research station at Myall Vale 25km NW along the WEE WAA road. The name Narrabri comes from an Aboriginal word meaning 'forked sticks'.

Narrandera NSW (population 5 013 in 1981) A town in the RIVERINA region of the State, 584km by road SW of Sydney, near the junction of the Sturt and Newell Highways, Narrandera is located on the MURRUMBIDGEE RIVER and on the main canal leading from the

The old Star Hotel at Narrandera, now a youth hostel

NSW Dept of Tourism

river to the irrigation areas. It is a rail junction town (580km by train from Sydney) with lines E from JUNEE, W to LEETON and HAY, and SW to Tocumwal. At an elevation of 176m above sea level, it receives an average annual rainfall of only 441mm, spread uniformly through all seasons, but irrigation water has added stability and prosperity to the rural economy. The area is noted for its high quality Merino and Border Leicester sheep, for wool, mutton, beef, pigs and poultry, as well as citrus and stone fruits, vegetables, lucerne, maize, oats and barley. The town contains a stock-feed factory, a flour mill, sawmills, and concrete-pipe and building-stone works. At the Inland Fisheries Research Station, 6km SE of the town, important research on fish species of inland rivers is carried out. The NSW Forestry Commission has a nursery for tree seedlings 2km SE of the town. There is a 71ha nature reserve (3km out of town on the N bank of the river) which is a koala regeneration centre. The Berembed Weir, originally constructed in 1910 and located 40km SE of the town, diverts water from the river into the main irrigation canal. The name Narrandera comes from an Aboriginal word meaning 'place of the goanna' or 'place of blue-tongued lizards'. The town is one of the oldest settlements in the Riverina (proclaimed a village in 1863) and the National Trust (NSW) has listed numerous buildings for preservation: the courthouse, the police station, the CBC bank, several hotels (Star, Narrandera, Royal Mail), the railway station, the ANZ bank, Richards 'The Big Store', and St Thomas Anglican Church.

Narrogin WA (population 4 969 in 1981) Located on the Great Southern Highway 189km by road SE of Perth, it is the commercial and service centre of a productive agricultural and pastoral region. It is a rail junction on the Great Southern Railway, 233km via YORK from Perth, at an elevation of 340m above sea level on the inland plateau, where sheep grazing and wheat growing are the main rural activities. It has an average annual rainfall of 507mm, concentrated mainly in the winter months (June and July, the wettest months, 94mm and 91mm respectively), with a dry period during summer. The town receives its water supply by a 129km-long pipeline from the Wellington Dam on the Collie River.

Narromine NSW (population 2 994 in 1981) A small town in the NW plains region of the State, on the Mitchell Highway, 452km by road NW of Sydney and 40km W of DUBBO. It is also on the railway branch line from Dubbo which goes to NYNGAN and thence on to BOURKE. Situated on the MACQUARIE RIVER at an elevation of 240m above sea level, it is a service and commercial centre for a productive rural region, where irrigation water from BURRENDONG DAM is used for the production of citrus fruits, sorghum, maize, soya-beans and tomatoes. There is a co-operative citrus packing works and a juice production factory

in the town. There are many sheep grazing properties and several horse studs in the district. The town is the administrative centre for the Narromine Shire which, at the census of 1981, had a population of 6 356. Numerous buildings in the town·have been listed by the National Trust (NSW) and the Burraway Street group, which includes three hotels and several shops, has been classified by the Trust for preservation.

National Anthem As a British colony, Australia originally took Britain's national anthem, *God Save the Queen/King*, as the official song to be sung or played on ceremonial occasions as a sign of patriotism. However, with the passing of the colonial era and increased feelings of nationalism in Australian society, there were proposals, and sometimes quite strong advocacy, that Australia should have its own separate and distinctly Australian anthem to replace *God Save the Queen*. Many tunes and lyrics were composed, politicians and political parties became involved, some quests for a suitable anthem were held, and numerous songs were considered such as *Song of Australia*, *Advance Australia Fair* and *Waltzing Matilda*. In 1974, the Whitlam Labour government conducted an opinion poll to find which to these three songs the Australian people preferred. The results showed a majority in favour of *Advance Australia Fair* and so it was decided that it would become the anthem, except on regal and vice-regal occasions, when both it and *God Save the Queen* would be played. But, with the dismissal of the Labour government in 1975 and the subsequent election of the Fraser Liberal govennment, *God Save the Queen* was reinstated as the sole anthem to be played on regal and vice-regal occasions. A further poll was held on the matter in 1977 when people were asked to indicate their preferences between four alternatives: the three songs in the previous poll and *God Save the Queen*. Over 40% of the voters preferred *Advance Australia Fair*, while less than 20% voted for *God Save the Queen*. In late 1983, the official position was that the tune of *Advance Australia Fair* (but not the words) was the National Song and could be played on official occasions, provided there was no regal or vice-regal person present, but that on regal and vice-regal occasions *God Save the Queen* must be played.

National Country Party of Australia *see* National Party of Australia

National Film Library *see* film

National Film Theatre of Australia *see* film

national parks and reserves Areas of land or ocean set aside by governments for the CONSERVATION of flora, fauna, vegetation, scenic beauty and sites of historical or scientific interest are often called national parks but

Table 1

AREAS OF NATIONAL PARKS AND OTHER TYPES OF RESERVES IN AUSTRALIAN STATES AND TERRITORIES AS AT JUNE 1982 ('000ha)

State/ Territory	National Parks	Fauna or Game Reserves	Nature or Scenic Reserves	Conservation Reserves	Others	Total	% of State/Terr. Area
NSW	2 551	—	469	—	—	3 020	3.8
NT	1 227[4]	—	13	3	—	1 243	0.9
QLD	3 245	26	—	—	79	3 350[2]	1.9
SA	551	19	3	3 884	—	4 457	4.5
TAS	865	11	29	33[1]	18	956	14.1
VIC	686	99	—	—	306	1 091[5]	4.8
WA	4 364	—	9 667	—	3	14 034	5.6
ACT	—	—	61	—	1	62	25.6
TOTAL	13 489	155	10 242	3 920	407	28 213	3.7[3]

Notes:
1. A further 833 845ha are reserved as Conservation areas in TAS but since other uses are permitted they are not included in the figures here.
2. In addition in QLD there are 4 693 224ha of Marine National Parks.
3. This figure is a percentage of the total land area of Australia.
4. Includes 191 659ha of Aboriginal National Parks in NT.
5. A further 4 000ha in VIC are reserved for nature conservation.
Source: *Nature Conservation Reserves in Australia* (1982) (ed M. D. Hinchey), Occasional Paper No. 7, Australian National Parks and Wildlife Service, Canberra, 1982.

usage differs from country to country. In some, the term 'national park' is restricted to large areas considered to be of national importance and in which public recreation is an important activity, while smaller areas may be designated as 'fauna reserves' or something similar; in others, these smaller areas may be included within the national park category. The dedication of the land of the public also varies considerably from government to government. The land may be dedicated by an Act of Parliament (or its equivalent) so that the use of the reserve for any other purpose can be sanctioned only by another Act, but often the 'ownership' of the land by the public is less secure. In some cases (e.g. Uluru, Kakadu) some or all of the land is owned by Aborigines who lease it to the appropriate government.

The areas in Australia set aside for conservation (*see* Table 1) make up about four per cent of the land area of the continent. This falls far short of the goal of five per cent or more which has been set by the UN for each country in the world. However, the percentage increased greatly in Australia in the 1970s and there are prospects for further large increases.

The degree of conservation varies greatly from one national park to another (the term 'national park' is used in its widest sense from now on). At the one extreme there are certain areas, often small, to which the general public has no access; at the other extreme are the large public parks with good access roads, camping facilities and, often, motels. There may even be some commercial exploitation and, in game reserves in some States, licences may be granted for shooting certain introduced game animals and waterfowl.

The various parks of the States are mainly under the control of the State governments (even when called national parks), while those of the Territories are under federal control. Included in the national parks are the Aboriginal reserves to which non-Aborigines are not admitted except by special permission.

The first national park in the world was established in 1872 at Yellowstone, Wyoming, USA. In the same year the small parkland in Perth known as Kings Park was dedicated to the public. In 1879 the national park (now the Royal National Park) just S of Sydney was created; it was the first park in the world to be called a national park. TAS, however, had passed laws in 1863 to protect areas of scenic beauty. Other early national parks in Australia were: Fern Tree Gully in VIC, 1882; Belair National Park, now a recreation park, in SA, 1891 (the only one in SA till 1956); Ku-ring-gai in NSW, 1894; WILSON'S PROMONTORY in VIC, 1908; and TAMBORINE MOUNTAIN and parts of the BUNYA RANGE (as reserves) in QLD, 1908.

Conservation of fauna and flora Animals and plants are more often driven to extinction by the destruction of their habitats than by direct attack. The key to the successful conservation of a species is the preservation of as much of its natural habitat as possible. This is best done by setting aside areas as parks and reserves which, ideally, should contain large samples of the major habitats of the country, from alpine to wetland and marine. Individual parks should be large enough to maintain viable populations of the species to be preserved. This area may be surprisingly small, as with the noisy scrub-bird in its reserve at Two People's Bay WA, but several thousand hectares may be needed for some populations of marsupials (*see* FORESTRY).

It may be very difficult to conserve certain migratory and nomadic species by setting aside national parks. Many blossom-feeding birds, for example, range widely following the opening blossoms, and a single park, or even a group of parks and reserves, may not be able to provide them with food throughout the year. Similarly, many waterfowl which may live successfully for years in an inland park may be forced to search for coastal wetlands during droughts. Unfortunately, there are too few

such wetlands left in the more populated parts of Australia.

A park, once set aside, cannot be left to its own devices; however large it may be, it has definite boundaries and it will be influenced by developments outside those boundaries. Before European settlement any populations of animals or plants that disappeared from an area would often be restored, in time, by immigrants from outside but parks are 'islands' in which such natural recolonisation may not occur. The biologists in charge of a reserve must therefore manage it, perhaps even culling some species when their populations grow too large. No Australian park authority has yet been faced with the problems that confront certain African rangers who have to shoot large numbers of elephants to prevent destruction of their habitat, but a similar problem could arise with some large marsupials, especially if predators such as the dingo are eradicated. The authorities must also destroy alien animals, such as feral cats and goats, and introduced weed plants. The activities of the public must be controlled, for in some habitats trail-bikes, four-wheel-drive vehicles and even walking boots can damage the delicate vegetation cover enough to initiate an erosion gully.

Despite the recent surge in dedications of parks, Australia has by no means provided areas representing all the various habitats. In 1977 it was estimated that only about one half of the approximately 900 identified plant communities in Australia are represented in parks, though the percentages are higher in SA and TAS.

Conservation of historical sites These present the authorities with different problems such as the preservation of rock paintings which were formerly renewed by the Aborigines from time to time, and the protection of sites from vandalism. This is particularly difficult where the sites are in remote areas and where supervision is therefore spasmodic.

New South Wales There are more than 50 national parks in the State, covering a total area of over 2.5 million hectares and including a wide variety of landscapes, from coastal areas to highland regions and semi-arid inland country. KOSCIUSKO National Park (629 708ha), which includes Australia's highest mountain peak, is the largest. It includes extensive winter snowfields, glacial lakes, alpine moors and forest lands and extends about 160km from the VIC border N to the ACT.

Angourie National Park, North Coast NSW

NSW Dept of Tourism

Within 150km of Sydney, there are several large national parks. The Royal National Park (15 017ha) lies to the S of the city and includes forested sandstone plateau areas, dissected by steep valleys, as well as coastal cliffs and beaches; it is a popular picnic area for Sydney residents. To the N of the city is Ku-ring-gai Chase National Park (14 712ha) with similar sandstone plateau landscapes and deep gorges, overlooking inlets where the HAWKESBURY RIVER merges into BROKEN BAY. Also in the lower Hawkesbury region is Dharug National Park (14 230ha) and the Brisbane Water National Park (8 294ha). In the BLUE MOUNTAINS to the W of Sydney are the Blue Mts National Park (208 756ha) and Kanangra Boyd National Park (68 039ha), where numerous waterfalls cascade over the steep sandstone valley walls, and where there are spectacular vistas at numerous vantage points.

Of the many coastal parks in NSW, MYALL LAKES National Park (27 526ha), located N of NEWCASTLE, with access from the Pacific Highway via the township of Tea Gardens, is considered by many people as the most attractive. It includes tranquil expanses of water fringed with paperbark trees, stretches of sand dunes—some of which still support tall red gum forests—and sandy beaches along the coastline. The WARRUMBUNGLE National Park (19 456ha) in the inland NW of the State near COONABARABRAN offers spectacular scenery resulting from ancient volcanic plugs and spires towering above the surrounding plains. NEW ENGLAND National Park (23 554ha), located E of ARMIDALE, off the road from the New England Plateau to GRAFTON, is noted for its precipitous gorges along the plateau scarp, deep rainforest-clad valleys where only experienced bushwalkers should venture, and superb panoramic vistas over the dissected escarpment and the coastal area. BARRINGTON TOPS National Park (16 325ha), 96km NW of NEWCASTLE, is a basalt-capped plateau, much dissected by river valleys, with rugged terrain, scenic waterfalls, Antarctic beech rainforests draped with moss, abundant bird life, grasslands and sub-alpine woodlands on the plateau tops.

Northern Territory Within the NT the total area of national parks exceeds 1.2 million ha, which includes over 191,000ha of Aboriginal National Parks. The most famous national park is Uluru (132 538ha), located SW of ALICE SPRINGS, where the massive tors rise sheer from the surrounding plain; Uluru includes AYERS ROCK and MOUNT OLGA.

The KAKADU national park, located in the ALLIGATOR RIVERS region, about 200km E of Darwin, includes an outstanding collection of Aboriginal rock art.

In the MACDONNELL RANGES there are several national parks which include the spectacular gorges carved by streams cutting across the ranges. The largest is Ormiston Gorge National Park (4 655ha), 132km W of Alice Springs. Others are the Ellery Creek Big Hole (1 766ha), 93km from Alice Springs; Serpentine Gorge National Park (518ha),

105km from Alice Springs; and Redbank Gorge National Park (1 295ha), 161km from Alice Springs. A unique though small area (16ha) is the Henbury Meteorite Craters National Park, located W of the Stuart Highway, S of Alice Springs and just S of the FINKE RIVER: it includes 13 craters (the largest is 183m wide and 6m above ground), formed when a meteorite hit the earth about 4 700 years ago. The Finke Gorge National Park, WSW of Alice Springs and 19km S of HERMANNSBURG, includes PALM VALLEY which is noted for the unique occurrence of tall cabbage palms in the gorge.

Visitors to parks in the NT are advised to check road conditions with the Territory Parks and Wildlife Commission, as extensive flooding can occur, especially in the wet season (summer months), making road travel hazardous.

Queensland There are over 280 national parks in the State, covering more than 3.2 million hectares, representing 1.9 per cent of QLD. The major parks are mentioned here.

Eungella National Park (49 691ha), located 83km W of MACKAY via the Pioneer Valley, contains a large area of tropical rainforest, some grassy eucalypt woodland, areas of exceptional fern growth, rugged range country with prominent peaks and deep gorges. Most of the park is inaccessible except to experienced bushwalkers, but there is a walking track, a camping area and picnic facilities to allow visitors access to some of the vegetation types and points of interest. LAMINGTON National Park (20 200ha) is located in the range country along the QLD/NSW border, about 100km S of Brisbane and inland from the GOLD COAST; it includes areas of rainforest, eucalypt forest and heathland, with panoramic views and spectacular waterfalls. There are numerous picnic facilities and walking tracks, and two resort centres. The wilderness areas in the S are recommended only for experienced bushwalkers. The Chillagoe Caves area, located about 140km inland from CAIRNS, beyond the ATHERTON TABLELAND and MAREEBA, includes nine small national parks, with sheer limestone outcrops and numerous spectacular caves. Regular guided tours are available through three of these caves. CARNARVON National Park (160 000ha), in the headwater country of the FITZROY RIVER, SW of EMERALD and about 400km inland from the ROCKHAMPTON coast, contains stretches of rugged sandstone gorge country, with basalt-capped uplands, many Aboriginal carvings and paintings, and a varied animal and plant life. There are several walking paths within the Carnarvon Creek gorge, but there are no tracks out of the gorge to the plateau country, which is largely a wilderness area. In wet weather, the access road into the park can become impassable and visitors are advised to bring several days' food supply in case they are stranded within the park area. Bunya Mts National Park (11 700ha), on the GREAT DIVIDING RANGE, between KINGAROY and DALBY, has a variety of vegetation types, including rainforest areas with bunya

Freshwater Creek in the Cooloola National Park QLD

and hoop pine, and grassy stretches known locally as 'the Balds'. There are extensive picnic and camping facilities, and numerous walking tracks. Elevations reach 1000m and the weather may be quite cold even in the summer months. BELLENDEN KER National Park (31 000ha), on the E slopes of the range between INNISFAIL and CAIRNS, contains QLD's highest mountain, MOUNT BARTLE FRERE (1 657m). There are several spectacular waterfalls, dense upland rainforests, and numerous mammals, birds and reptiles endemic to QLD. The GLASSHOUSE MOUNTAIN area, located 70km N of Brisbane, adjacent to the Bruce Highway and at the S approach to the SUNSHINE COAST, includes four national parks around the volcanic stumps which rise spectacularly to elevations over 500m above the surrounding countryside.

There are also some very large national parks in remote areas of QLD such as Lakefield National Park (528 000ha) NW of COOKTOWN; Jardine River National Park (235 000ha) in the N of CAPE YORK; Staaten National Park (467 000ha) inland from the E shore of the GULF OF CARPENTARIA; and SIMPSON DESERT National Park (505 000ha) adjacent to POEPPEL'S CORNER at the NT/SA/QLD border. Within the GREAT BARRIER REEF, and in the channel between the main reef and the E coast of the State, there are many small national parks on islands such as HERON, LINDEMAN, GREEN, MAGNETIC, DUNK and LIZARD.

South Australia The total area of the nine national parks in SA is 551 000ha. These parks include a variety of environments from coastal locations to inland desert areas. Some of the best-known parks are mentioned here.

FLINDERS RANGES National Park (78 426ha), the largest in the State, is located in the N section of the ranges, N of HAWKER and E of

LAKE TORRENS. It was established in 1945, though part of it had been a forest reserve since 1921 and WILPENA POUND was proclaimed a national pleasure resort in 1945. It contains a wide variety of wildlife, some spectacularly colourful mountain scenery, and in recent years has become a tourist mecca. COORONG National Park (37 186ha), along the SE coast of the State, stretches from Younghusband Peninsula at the MURRAY RIVER mouth for 106km, and includes the narrow strip of coastal sand dunes, the elongated lagoon lying behind the dunes and a strip of land across the lagoon to the Princes Highway. It is noted for its unique beach and dune vegetation and for its prolific bird life. The Coorong game reserves (6 840ha) divide the national park into two sections.

Flinders Chase National Park (59 003ha), established in 1919, occupies the W end of KANGAROO ISLAND. Much of the park is wilderness country, but there are roads into and walking tracks through some sections, which provide opportunities for visitors to see the granite boulder formations and a variety of native animals and birds, including the seal colonies in some of the coastal bays. Lincoln National Park (17 083ha), on the SE tip of EYRE PENINSULA, S of PORT LINCOLN, was established in 1941. The park is noted for its scenic coastal cliffs, stretches of sandhills, limestone ridges, animal life (including grey kangaroos) and land and sea birds. It is well provided with access roads and walking tracks. Mt Remarkable National Park (8 648ha), the smallest in SA, located in the S of the Flinders Ranges, N of PORT PIRIE and SE of PORT AUGUSTA, is a rugged and densely forested area, with spectacular mountain scenery dissected by sheer gorges.

In addition to national parks, SA has a large area of over 3.8 million hectares set aside in conservation parks. There are more than 160 of these parkland areas, ranging in size from a few hectares to over 250 000ha; perhaps the best known is Cleland (790ha), set in the wooded foothills of the MOUNT LOFTY RANGES overlooking Adelaide.

Tasmania With more than 865 000ha of national parks, TAS has a higher proportion of its area (14.1 per cent) than any other State set aside as national parklands. The relatively small size of TAS, combined with the road network of the State, makes most of the parks readily accessible from the major cities, but the climatic conditions, particularly the unpredictable cold weather that occurs in the highlands, makes summer the season of choice to visit the parks. The main national parks are mentioned here.

CRADLE MOUNTAIN-LAKE ST CLAIR National Park (126 205ha), established in 1922 in the W central highlands, is accessible from either the N (95km from DEVONPORT) or the S (via the Lyell Highway). It is an area of rugged mountain scenery, containing some of TAS's highest peaks (Cradle Mt, MOUNT OSSA, Barn Bluff and Mt Pelion West), numerous lakes, deep gorges and several waterfalls, glaciated land-

Coorong National Park SA

scapes and alpine moorland. The principal walking route, called the Overland Track, extends from Cradle Valley (in the N) to Lake St Clair, a distance of 85km. FRENCHMANS CAP National Park (13 000ha), in the W highlands, off the Lyell Highway, 40km E of QUEENSTOWN, is in a region of rugged, glaciated, mountainous country; much of the park is a wilderness area, recommended only for experienced bushwalkers. The massive white quartz peak of Frenchmans Cap, with a 300m face on the E side, is the principal feature of the park. BEN LOMOND National Park (16 526ha), located in the NE uplands of the State, 45km SE of LAUNCESTON, is a high plateau region, with steep bordering scarps, and is the principal skiing area of TAS.

MOUNT FIELD National Park (16 257ha), established in 1916, is in the S highlands, 75km W of Hobart; it includes glaciated mountainous country, several lakes, dense eucalypt forest at lower levels and alpine moorland in the more elevated parts. It is a popular ski resort. Freycinet National Park (10 010ha) on the E coast off the Tasman Highway includes FREYCINET PENINSULA, with several seaside resorts, scenic coastal vistas, many sea birds and massive red granite peaks. It was established in 1916. MARIA ISLAND National Park (9 672ha), located off the E coast from Orford, is accessible by boat or aeroplane from Triabunna and is noted for its wildlife (including Forester kangaroos and Bennett's wallabies) and for the ruins of a penal settlement. Southwest National Park (403 240ha), the largest in TAS, established in 1968, is a rugged wilderness region in the SW of the State, recommended for only the hardy bushwalker. Within the park are many landscape features, such as ARTHUR RANGE, FEDERATION PEAK, MOUNT ANNE and LAKE PEDDER. PORT ARTHUR and TASMAN PENINSULA, a historic and scenic area in the SE of the State, is the most popular tourist attraction in TAS. As well as the famous convict ruins of the Port Arthur penal settlement, the region includes a number of scenic and historic attractions such as EAGLEHAWK NECK, the Tessellated Pavement, Tasman's Arch and numerous coastal cliffs, sheltered bays and caverns.

Victoria There are over 25 national parks in VIC, varying in size from less than 100ha to over 100 000ha, and covering a total area of more than 685 000ha. Among the smallest are the Organ Pipes National Park (85ha), located

26km from Melbourne on the Calder Highway, and Fern Tree Gully (459ha) in the DANDENONG RANGES, 35km E of Melbourne. The largest is Wyperfield National Park (100 000ha) in the sandy mallee country of the NW. Port Campbell National Park (700ha), 250km SW of Melbourne, along the S coast between Princetown and Port Campbell, S of the Great Ocean Road, is famed for its coastal formations, such as London Bridge and the Twelve Apostles. Wilson's Promontory National Park (49 000ha), the southernmost part of the Australian mainland, is accessible from the South Gippsland Highway. With its beaches, granite headlands and a variety of animals, plants and bird life, it is one of the State's most popular parks in the summer holiday season.

MOUNT BUFFALO National Park (31 000ha), 330km NE of Melbourne, is a winter ski resort and summer-time bushwalking and horse riding area. The rugged plateau features spectacular granite formations, mountain streams and waterfalls, and a variety of native plant and bird life. The Lakes National Park (2 380ha), in E GIPPSLAND, 330km ESE of Melbourne, along the E coast of the State, is noted for its diverse flora, prolific aquatic bird life and abundant native animals, such as kangaroos, wallabies and possums.

Western Australia There are more than 50 national parks in WA, with a total area of almost 4.4 million hectares, ranging in size from 33ha to over 590 000ha. YANCHEP National Park (2 799ha), located on the coastal plain 51km N of Perth, is noted for limestone caves, the spring-time display of wild flowers, a colony of koala bears (established in 1938), water birds on Loch McNess and a variety of recreation facilities including picnic areas, a golf course, a swimming pool, boating on the loch, launch trips and sporting ovals. STIRLING RANGE National Park (115 671ha) in the SW of the State, 65km N of ALBANY, includes the entire Stirling Range mountain system where the highest peaks rise to over 1000m above sea level. The features of the park include the rugged peaks, the scenic panoramas, a profusion of wild flowers in spring, abundant bird life, native animals and varied vegetation. There are several roads through the park and numerous walking tracks. PORONGORUP National Park (2 401ha), also in the SW, 37km N of Albany, is a granite range rising to 650m above sea level, with steep-sided round-topped

Thurra river in E Gippsland, part of the Captain James Cook National Park VIC

peaks, balancing rocks, luxuriant karri forests and colourful displays of wild flowers. There are access roads into and through the park, and several walking trails. HAMERSLEY RANGE National Park (590 176ha) is the largest in the State, located in the mid-N between the FORTESCUE and ASHBURTON Rivers. Established in 1969, it includes rugged range country, with steep gorges and sheer cliffs, as well as abundant wild flowers, bird life and native animals.

In the KIMBERLEYS there are several parks covering range and gorge country; the best known of these is Geike Gorge National Park (3 136ha) on the FITZROY RIVER (20km NE of Fitzroy Crossing), often claimed as one of the most unforgettable sights in Australia. It consists of a steep-sided gorge about 10km long, with cliffs over 100m high, cut by the river through a fossilised coral reef. There is a camping area in the park and boat trips are available through the gorge. Walpole-Nornalup National Park (18 116ha), on the S coast, 121km W of Albany and 117km SE of MANJIMUP, contains tall karri forests, fine coastal scenery and the broad expanse of Walpole and Nornalup Inlets. It is one of WA's oldest parks, established in 1910, expanded in 1924 and again in 1977. JOHN FORREST National Park (1 578ha), located on the crest of the DARLING RANGE, 26km E of Perth, is noted for the display of wild flowers from July to October. Also within the park there are waterfalls, Glen Brook and Mahogany Creek Dams, vantage points with views over Perth and the coastal plains, picnic areas, a swimming pool and numerous walking tracks.

Further reading: Webb, L.J. *et al* (eds) *The Last of the Lands—Conservation in Australia.* Jacaranda, Milton QLD, 1969; Morcombe, M. *Australia's National Parks.* Summit Books, Sydney, 1978; Raymond, R. *Discover Australia's National Parks.* Ure Smith, Sydney, 1978.

Nationalist Party *see* political history

National Party of Australia

The existence of the National Party of Australia illustrates the conflict between country and city interests because this political party, unlike any other, caters specifically for rural interests and until the QLD state election in 1983 held no metropolitan city seats. It alleges that national progress can be achieved only by support for agriculture, primary industries and the country towns because the country is the backbone of Australia.

Origin and organisation After World War I wheat farmers used their Farmers and Settlers Associations to help organise the Progressive Party to ensure the election of parliamentarians who would help preserve the compulsory wheat marketing system introduced as a wartime emergency measure. This marketing system had given the wheat farmers a predictable price for their wheat and they did not want to see it abolished. The wheat farmers were soon supported in their political campaign by graziers concerned about high rising

CONTROLLING THE TRAFFIC
"W.J. McWilliams, M.P., leader of the Country party, consisting of 12 members, said that his party would hold the balance of power in the Federal Parliament."

Cartoon of 1923 illustrating the effect on federal politics of the newly-formed Country Party

tariffs, dairy farmers unhappy about price fixing, and returned servicemen and others who were simply disillusioned with the then existing Nationalist and Labor parties. In 1920 the name was changed from Progressive Party to the Australian Country Party; in 1975 it was changed to National Country Party of Australia and in 1982 it was changed again to National Party of Australia.

This political party has never had an organisation for the whole of Australia. It has had an arrangement for a federal organisation and separate State organisations and the name adopted by each State organisation has emphasised the autonomous nature of that political party in the total organisation. The federal organisation has less control over its State parties than either the Liberal or Labor parties and has little control over the policies formulated by the National parliamentarians. The tradition is for the parliamentary leader to have the greatest power and influence in all party decisions.

The unique relationship which exists in the overall picture of this party is illustrated in the varying names adopted. The position at the beginning of 1983 was as follows: the term 'National Party of Australia' was adopted for use in federal electorates; in four States the title was National Party of Australia—NSW, National Party of Australia—VIC, National Party of Australia—QLD, National Party of Australia—SA; in WA it was called National Country Party and in the NT it was called NT Country Liberal Party; there was no organisation in TAS.

Splits and mergers In the early 1940s the VIC Country Party left the Australian Country Party and federal and State Country Party candidates competed against each other. At the beginning of the 1980s the State candidates were known as members of the National Party and the federal candidates were known as the National Country Party of Australia, but they

did not compete against each other.

In TAS the Country Party was first represented in Parliament in 1922 but it was absorbed and ceased to exist as an independent party.

In SA the Country Party fused with the Liberal Federation in 1932 and became known as the Liberal Country League. In the mid-1970s there was a revival under the name of National Country Party of Australia and it had one representative in the State House of Assembly. In 1982 the name was changed to National Party of Australia—SA.

In WA in 1978 a split occurred in the State party, and those members who remained in coalition with the Liberals retained the name National Country Party of Australia while those refusing to join the coalition adopted the name of National Party.

Policy and performance The National Party of Australia is very vocal in its support for private enterprise and in its condemnation of socialism—it is even more anti-Communist than the Liberal Party. Nevertheless, it advocates and has gained government intervention to provide assistance to the rural sector in the form of subsidies, bounties, marketing assistance, irrigation, roads, country schools and country hospitals, telecommunications and port facilities. It has also been able to get special advantages for the country in special taxation concessions for primary producers.

The strength of the National Party has stemmed mainly from its role as a partner in coalition governments and its grip on portfolios of significance to the rural community. In the federal government and in State governments in NSW and WA it has coalesced with the main non-Labor party. In VIC it has not maintained the close association with the major non-Labor party that has been usual elsewhere, and from 1935 to 1943 actually held office with Labor support. In QLD it has reached its position of greatest power, and from 1957 held office as the senior partner in a coalition with the Liberal Party until Oct 1983 when it was able to form a government on its own. In SA and TAS it has had no real existence. A NT government was legally established on 1 July 1978 and since then the NT Country Liberal Party has been in office there.

See also Appendix 2, Government of Australia; political history; political parties
Further reading: Ellis, U. *A History of the Australian Country Party.* Cheshire, Melbourne, 1963; Gruen, F.H. 'Rural Australia' in Davies, A.F. & Encel, S. (eds) *Australian Society.* Cheshire, Melbourne, 1971; Heatley, A. *Northern Territory!* Australian Journal of Public Administration (vol 40, no 1, March 1981).

National Trust The National Trust is a nationwide CONSERVATION organisation founded at the end of World War II and later incorporated by Acts of Parliament in each State. Briefly stated, its objects are: to acquire, protect and preserve, for the benefit of the public, lands and buildings of beauty or of national, historic, scientific, architectural or cultural interest; to safeguard natural features and scenic landscape, and conserve wildlife; and to encourage and promote public appreciation, knowledge and enjoyment of these things.

The first National Trust had been set up in England in 1895 by people concerned at the destruction of historic buildings and landscape. William Morris' words still motivate National Trust philosophies in Britain, the USA and Australia. He wrote: 'Old buildings do not belong to us only; they belonged to our forefathers and they will belong to our descendants unless we play them false. They are not in any sense our property to do as we like with them. We are only trustees for those who come after us.'

Many people are surprised to learn that the Trust does not have any statutory powers; on the contrary, it advocates the protection of the nation's heritage by legislative process. The branches of the National Trust in each State have participated in the formation of National Parks and Wildlife Services, and have been involved in the preparation of State legislation to safeguard historic places and in the drafting of federal legislation such as the Australian Heritage Commission Act (*see* HERITAGE CONSERVATION LEGISLATION).

Because it is a community organisation (there are about 62 000 subscribing members throughout Australia), the Trust works mostly through an extensive network of volunteers and scores of small, expert committees. The range of committee work is suggested by a short list of some of their names: Landscape Conservation, Historic Buildings, Urban Conservation, Industrial Archaeology and Cemeteries. In each State there is a director and a small technical and administrative staff.

The role of the National Trust as an 'advocate of the cultural environment' may be summarised by referring to three of the most important ways in which its objects are achieved. The first is by producing and updating registers of historic places. For NSW, for instance, the register is a volume of some 175 pages, backed up by a detailed and comprehensive survey and assessment file, summarising research in primary and secondary documents, building styles and history. The criteria for inclusion in a register are based firmly on heritage qualities.

Secondly, the Trust provides educational and advisory services. There is an extensive publishing programme of books, reports and pamphlets, and Trust staff participate in many school and university programmes. Panels advise members and the public about architecture, landscape, legal matters and antiques.

Thirdly, the Trust acquires, maintains and opens to the public a number of significant properties. They include great houses such as 'Rippon Lea', in Melbourne, tiny structures such as the A.J. Small Lookout at Bilgola Head in Sydney, complete natural environments such as MONTAGUE ISLAND, and man-made landscapes such as Everglades at Leura.

The National Trust continues to grow as public awareness of the cultural heritage increases. Its work complements that of the government conservation organisations and is achieved without regard to political pressures.

native cats and their allies Belonging to the order Polyprotodonta, these carnivorous MARSUPIALS are contained in a large superfamily Dasyuroidea. This group may be divided into four families: 1. native cats, the Tasmanian devil and the marsupial mice (family Dasyuridae) 2. the banded anteater or numbat (family Myrmecobiidae) 3. the TASMANIAN WOLF (family Thylacinidae) and 4. the MARSUPIAL MOLE (family Notoryctidae). The toes on the feet of the dasyuroids are completely separate, unlike those of KANGAROOS, BANDICOOTS and POSSUMS, and there are three pairs of incisors on the lower jaw. Some of the smaller members could be confused with RODENTS for the pouch in this group is often not well developed, but the males can be distinguished from those of the placental MAMMALS by the fact that the scrotum is in front of the penis, and in both sexes the faces are sharper and the incisor teeth are quite different from those of rodents. In habits at least, the marsupial mice more closely resemble the shrew of Europe and Asia than the mice of those areas.

Native cats The four species in Australia belong to the genus *Dasyurus*. They are white-spotted animals with muzzles that are far more pointed than those of a true cat. Their legs are short and the body is lean. Native cats are agile, active animals and excellent climbers. They have been greatly reduced in numbers because of their predation on poultry, as well as by the destruction of their habitats.

The tiger cat or spotted-tail quoll, *D. maculatus* (head and body 64cm; tail 48cm), is the largest species, and feeds mainly on birds and small mammals in rainforest and sclerophyll forest. It ranges from eastern QLD to SA but is commonest in TAS. The upperparts are dark brown, the underparts pale yellow and the white spots occur on both the body and the tail. It shelters in piles of stones and hollow logs. The eastern native cat or quoll, *D. viverrinus* (43cm; 28cm), of SE Australia, differs from the tiger cat in the absence of spots on the tail (though this is white-tipped) and in having four toes, not five, on the hind-foot. It lives in dry sclerophyll forest in the E and S parts of VIC, eastern NSW, south-eastern SA and TAS; till at least 1962 it could still be found in Vaucluse, a coastal suburb of Sydney. The quoll is less inclined to hunt in trees than are other native cats. The similarly sized western native cat or chuditch, *D. geoffroii*, also has an unspotted tail but usually has five toes on the hind-foot. It is found at various places W of the GREAT DIVIDING RANGE and in SW WA in forests, woodlands and possibly more arid habitats as well. The satanellus or northern native quoll, *D. (Satanellus) hallucatus* (28cm; 22cm), has five hind-toes and an unspotted tail. It is a N species, living in forests, woodlands and rocky outcrops to as far S as GYMPIE in QLD.

Tasmanian devil The Tasmanian devil, *Sarcophilus harrisii* (65cm; 26cm), is a black and white (sometimes all black) carnivore that fills in TAS a niche that is occupied by wolverines in Eurasia. It is a very powerful animal with a short, broad muzzle and strong jaws that probably feeds more on carrion than on the prey it catches. When fighting or menacing an enemy it makes a most impressive noise. Cave remains show that it once occurred commonly on the mainland though now restricted to sclerophyll forests with rocks in TAS.

Marsupial mice This term is used very loosely, for although some resemble mice, others are much larger than a mouse or have fatter or more furry tails. Several genera, including some large ones, are included here.

The members of the genus *Antechinus* and some related genera are the marsupials that are most commonly known as marsupial mice. The body and head together usually have a length of about 10cm to 13cm; the tail is about two-thirds the length of the body and is not tufted. The yellow-footed antechinus or mardo, *A. flavipes*, lives in rain or sclerophyll forest along the E mainland coasts and in south-western WA. It nests under logs or in sandstone outcrops, and often builds a nest of gum leaves in the roofs of caves. The head and the front part of the body are dark, grizzled greyish-brown, the hind-parts browner, and the upper surfaces of the feet are yellow or off-white. It is usually a solitary, agile, climbing hunter which feeds on invertebrates and mice. The related species are the brown antechinus, *A. stuartii*, found in rainforest to woodland and sandstone-cave country in E Australia, and the fawn antechinus, *A. bellus*, found in tropical savanna woodland in the NT.

A. godmani, the Atherton antechinus, is an often misidentified species from mountain rainforest in north-eastern QLD. It is larger than the yellow-footed species but otherwise similar externally.

The little red antechinus, *A. rosamondae*, occurs in the PILBARA region of WA. The males have only one mating season and die soon after. Its fur is rough and brown to coppery-brown in colour. It is found in *Spinifex* grassland.

The dusky or Swainson's antechinus, *A. swainsonii*, is a rainforest and wet sclerophyll forest species found in eastern NSW, VIC, southern SA and TAS. It is also found in alpine woodland and heaths—where there is dense vegetation and deep litter. It is dark in colour and has short ears and very long fore-claws. A solitary, nocturnal, insect-eating animal, it is common in VIC and TAS. A related form is the swamp antechinus, *A. minimus*, found in tussock grassland and coastal habitats of VIC, SA and TAS. It is greyish-brown above and, like the dusky species, has long fore-claws.

The cinnamon antechinus, *A. leo*, is a recently described species (1980) known so far only from a small area in NE Cape York where it appears to be common. It was formerly confused with *A. flavipes* but does not have the light eye ring of that species.

The animal formerly known as *A. macdonnellensis*, the fat-tailed antechinus, has been moved to another genus, but the population of the far north of WA has been recognised as a new species (1982) which, as yet, has been given no scientific name. The Ninbing antechinus, as it is called, is a small, light greyish-brown species with long hairs on the base of the tail. The fat-tailed antechinus, now *Pseudantechinus macdonnellensis* is similar, but with a fat, tapering tail without the long hairs. It occurs in a roughly rectangular area from the coast of WA to the Gulf of Carpentaria coastline in QLD.

The dibbler, *Parantechinus apicalis* (14.5cm; 10.5-11.5cm), is found in sclerophyll woodland, scrubs and heath, inland, but not far from the coast, in SW WA. The animal had not been captured in the wild since 1881 (and not often before then) till 1976 when it was found at Cheyne Beach, near ALBANY. It is a brown marsupial with white freckles and a white eye-ring. There are long hairs on the tail, especially near the base. The dibbler is an agile climber. The sandstone antechinus, *P. bilarni* (6cm to 10cm; 8cm to 11cm) lives in quartz-sandstone country on part of the ARNHEM LAND escarpment.

The genus *Phascogale* contains two species, the wambenger, tuan or brush-tailed phascogale, *P. tapoatafa* (23cm; 20cm), and the smaller red-tailed wambenger, *P. calura*. The tuan is a bluish-grey animal with the terminal half of the tail clothed in long, black hairs which it fluffs out, especially when excited. The snout is pointed and the ears are large and pointed. It is a solitary animal that spends most of its active life hunting in trees at night for insects and small vertebrates such as birds and mice. Its habitats vary from rain to sclerophyll forest in parts of WA, QLD, the NT, SA, southern VIC and eastern NSW. The red-tailed wambenger is more reddish in colour (especially at the base of the tail) though the brush is black. It is found in sclerophyll woodland in inland SW WA, the NT, SA, north-western VIC and south-western NSW, but its habitats are threatened.

The genus *Dasyuroides* contains the kowari or Byrne's marsupial mouse, *D. byrnei* (16.5cm; 12cm), a reddish-grey and white animal with a black brush. It resembles the tuan but has only four hind-toes. It is a burrowing carnivore in desert grassland or steppe in the Centre.

The genus *Dasycercus* contains the mulgara or crest-tailed marsupial mouse, *D. cristicauda* (12.5cm to 22cm; 7.5cm to 17cm). The tail has a short black crest and is thick at the base; the ears are short and round. It is a burrowing carnivore of stony and *Spinifex* desert of the Centre. The food consists of insects and rodents and other small vertebrates which apparently supply it with all its water needs. It is a social animal.

The genus *Planigale* contains some of the smallest marsupials. The long-tailed planigale, *P. ingrami* (6.4cm; 5.7cm) is the smallest. It is a savanna woodland and grassland species found in the E and N parts of QLD, the NT, the Kimberleys. It lives under grass tussocks and in ground crevices, and feeds on insects, especially Orthoptera. The upperparts are greyish-brown and the underparts lighter. The other species are similar though slightly larger. The narrow-nosed planigale, *P. tenuirostris*, is found in N central NSW, S central QLD and NE SA and its head is less triangular in shape.

The common planigale, *P. maculata* (till recently included in *Antechinus* despite its possession of a pouch) is larger than the last two species. It is common in various habitats in eastern coastal Australia from central NSW to the tip of Cape York, and at the 'Top End' of the NT. It is a ferocious creature which tackles insects larger than itself. The paucident planigale, *P. gilesi*, is a predator from the arid centre which differs from the other planigales in possessing fewer teeth.

The dunnarts or narrow-footed marsupial mice (*Sminthopsis* species) are distinguished from all other similar animals by the narrowness of the hind-foot which does not exceed 3mm. They are normally divided into two groups, the thin-tailed and the fat-tailed marsupial mice (the latter have fat tails only after good seasons).

There are six species of thin-tailed dunnarts. The common dunnart, *S. murina* (9cm; 9cm) is a grizzled, mouse-grey animal, lighter below, with a pointed snout and big eyes and ears. It is a largely solitary, terrestrial insectivore which lives in forest, woodland and heath with largest populations on land that has been burned during the previous 2 to 4 years. It occurs in most of NSW and VIC, south SA and south-west WA. Recently it was separated from the very similar Ooldea dunnart, *S. ooldea* which lives in arid habitats in the Centre, though the ranges overlap. In captivity its tail will fatten. The white-footed dunnart, *S. leucopus*, uses a variety of habitats in southernmost NSW and VIC, and in TAS. The red-cheeked dunnart, *S. virginiae*, now includes several groups formerly thought to be separate species; it occurs in northern WA, the NW of the NT and in NE Cape York and in New Guinea, most often in open savannah. The attractive long-tailed dunnart, *S. longicaudata* is unmistakable—the tail is more than twice as long as the head and body together. Unfortunately few specimens are known but it appears to occur in rugged, rocky habitats in the arid zone from the Centre to central coast region of WA. One population occurs in the GIBSON DESERT nature reserve. The sandhill dunnart, *S. psammophila*, the largest dunnart (9-11.4cm; 11.4-13cm), is even more elusive; one specimen caught in 1894 near LAKE AMADEUS, and five in 1969 on the EYRE PENINSULA. At both places it appeared to live in low sandridge country.

There are five or six species of fat-tailed dunnarts. The fat-tailed dunnart, *S. crassicaudata* (8.9cm; 5.1cm) is an inland species in NSW and extends to the coast in VIC and SA; it also occurs in southern WA. It is found in woodlands, heaths, grasslands and stony places. The muzzle is pointed, the ears are large and oval, the head and body are grey and the belly is white. It burrows in sandhills and cracked earth. The other species are the larapinta or stripe-faced dunnart, *S. macroura*, found in the deserts, savanna woodlands and grasslands from central Australia to W WA; the white-tailed dunnart, *S. granulipes*, found in various habitats in south-western WA; and the hairy-footed dunnart, *S. hirtipes*, which lives in the Western Desert. The Julia Creek dunnart, *S. douglasi*, is known from only four specimens collected in QLD between 1931 and 1972. Little is known of the Carpentaria dunnart, *S. butleri*, from the Kimberley region of WA and, formerly at least, from Cape York; it is probably common where it does occur.

The genus *Antechinomys* contains the wuhl-wuhl and the kultarr, long-legged carnivores which were once thought to hop like kangaroos and were therefore called jerboa-like marsupials. Ride and Marlow (*see below*) have shown, however, that they gallop, landing on the fore-feet. The wuhl-wuhl, *A. laniger spenceri* (10cm; 13cm) occurs in WA, north-western SA and the NT in woodlands, tree steppe and deserts. The long tail carries a distinct tuft, the snout is pointed and the ears are long and oval. The general colour is sandy brown, with white below. This solitary species burrows beneath *Spinifex* grass, saltbush and so on. The kultarr, *A. laniger laniger*, a little smaller and darker in colour, is found in inland NSW, northern VIC and southern QLD.

Before 1975 it was thought that the planigales were the smallest marsupials but the members of a genus first described in that year are probably even smaller, though they are not as small as the smallest eutherian mammal, the Etruscan shrew (3.6cm to 5.2cm; 2.4cm to 2.9cm). Two species of the genus, *Ningaui*, are known but there are probably more. They resemble dunnarts but have relatively broader hind feet. The Wongai ningaui, *N. ridei*

(5.7cm to 7.1cm; 5.9cm to 7.1cm), and some related undescribed forms are common over much of inland Australia where they live on insects. The Pilbara ningaui, *N. timealeyi* (4.6cm to 5.7cm; 5.9cm to 7.9cm) is a bristly-furred predator from grassland in the Hamersley Plateau, WA. Small specimens of this animal weigh no more than two grams.

Numbat or banded anteater The numbat or banded anteater, *Myrmecobius fasciatus* (25cm; 18cm), is an unmistakeable slender marsupial with a pointed muzzle and short, erect ears. The body is reddish brown but the rump, which carries about six white cross bars, is much darker. There is a black stripe through the eye and the long, bushy tail is yellowish. The toes (four hind, five fore) are strongly clawed and very effective in digging out termites which the animal detects by smell. The tongue is extremely long (as in all mammals that have evolved as ant or termite eaters). Unlike most marsupials, the numbat is active during the day. It shelters in hollow logs. It was once more common than it is now; it formerly ranged from SW WA to SW NSW, but now occurs only in a small area of SW WA.
Further reading: Ride, W.D.L. *A Guide to the Native Mammals of Australia.* Oxford University Press, Melbourne, 1970; Marlow, B. *Marsupials of Australia.* Jacaranda Press, Brisbane, 1972; Archer, M. (ed) *Carnivorous Marsupials.* (vols 1 & 2) The Royal Zoological Society of New South Wales, Sydney, 1982; Strahan, R. (ed.) *The Australian Museum Complete Book of Australian Mammals.* Angus & Robertson, Sydney, 1983.

native cherry *see* parasitic plants

native companion *see* cranes

native currant *see* parasitic plants

native plants *see* flora; vegetation; and individual family entries such as Cyperaceae; Epacridaceae; Gramineae; Mimosaceae; Myrtaceae; Orchidaceae; Papilionaceae; Restionaceae; Rutaceae

native rose This name is given to a small, pink-flowered, highly scented shrub, *Boronia serrulata.* Found in NSW, it belongs to the worldwide family RUTACEAE.

native trout *see* fishes, freshwater

native-hens *see* rails, etc.

naturalisation *see* citizenship

Nauru Island This small island (2 130ha) in the central Pacific Ocean, just S of the equator, is noted for its phosphate deposits. Since 1968 it has been an independent republic. Before World War I, it was a German territory but then became an Australian Mandated Territory and there was an agreement between the governments of Britain, Australia and

New Zealand whereby an organisation was established (called the British Phosphate Commissioners) to extract the phosphate deposits. During World War II, the island was occupied by Japanese forces and, following the war, the Nauruan people were concerned about the territorial status of the island and sought independence. After this was achieved in 1968, the Nauru Phosphate Corporation was established (1970) as a government-owned enterprise. Whilst phosphate mining has brought a considerable degree of affluence to the Nauruan people, it is estimated that the deposits will be exhausted by the end of this century and hence the government is seeking alternative activities and investments to ensure economic viability.

nautilus, pearly *see* cephalopods

Navy, Royal Australian *see* defence

needle bush *see* weeds

Neilson, John Shaw (1872-1942) Poet. Born in PENOLA in SA he moved to NHILL in VIC in 1889. He had only a few years of schooling and began work at an early age, first on his father's farm and then in many forms of bush work and other manual occupations. He began publishing poems in newspapers in 1890, and after having some printed in the *Bulletin* in 1896 received a great deal of encouragement and advice from A.G. STEPHENS, editor of that journal's Red Page. He was an emotional mystic and most of his poems were lyrics of sensitive delicacy based on the contemplation of natural beauty. Although the range of his work is narrow, he must be ranked among the best of Australian lyric poets, the quality of his poetry being all the more remarkable because of his lack of education, his isolation from the mainstream of intellectual life, and the fact

that failing eyesight from the age of about 30 curtailed his reading and forced him to dictate his poems. The bulk of his published work is to be found in *Collected Poems* (1934), *Beauty Imposes* (1938) and *Unpublished Poems* (1947). *Further reading:* Anderson, H.M. *John Shaw Neilson.* Rigby, Adelaide, 1972.

Nelson Bay NSW (population 7 930 in 1981) A town and holiday resort on the SE shore of PORT STEPHENS, Nelson Bay is some 220km by road from Sydney and 50km by road NE of NEWCASTLE. It is the main urban centre on Port Stephens and has developed rapidly in recent years; many holiday homes have been constructed in the area by Newcastle residents.

Nematoda *see* roundworms

Nematomorpha *see* hairworms

Nemertea *see* ribbon worms

Nepean River NSW Though a relatively short stream, with a N-S extent of only about 100km, it is significant because, together with its tributaries, the Nepean provides the catchment for Sydney's water supply. It rises in the SOUTHERN TABLELANDS near MITTAGONG, 40km inland from WOLLONGONG. It flows in a general N direction past Picton, CAMDEN and PENRITH; though its course meanders, often in broad loops, the general trend is parallel to the E coast of the State. The Nepean Dam is located on the upper section of the river, and three other dams (Avon, Cordeaux and Cataract) are on headwater tributaries, all providing reservoirs for the metropolitan supply. On the WARRAGAMBA RIVER, which joins the Nepean lower downstream from the SW and has the Wollondilly, Cox and Nattai as feeder streams, there is another major reservoir. Along parts of its course, the Nepean flows in a broad shal-

A picnic boat race on the Nepean river

A. Healy

low valley trough, while in other parts, where it cuts across plateau areas, it is entrenched in sheer gorges often over 180m deep. The river stretch near Penrith, where the stream is broad and there are long straight sections, is famed for rowing regattas. The Grose River, a W tributary flowing from the BLUE MOUNTAINS and well known to bushwalkers for its corridor canyon, joins the Nepean near RICHMOND. Downstream from this junction, the river changes name and becomes the HAWKESBURY. *See also* Windsor

Nerli, Marchese Girolamo Pieri Ballati

(1863-1926) Artist. Born in Siena, Italy, Nerli arrived in Melbourne in 1885, having trained at the Art School in Florence. He moved to Sydney, where he joined forces with Charles CONDER and Julian ASHTON in preaching the doctrine that landscape painting should be done on the site, rather than in the studio. His free brush work and his fascination for scenes containing water reflections show some knowledge of French Impressionism, and influenced Charles Conder considerably. Nerli later moved to New Zealand where he taught art and, for three years, was the director of the Dunedin Art Gallery. He married in 1898 and returned to Italy, where he settled at Nervi, near Genoa, and established himself as a popular painter.

netball

Known as women's BASKETBALL until 1970, netball is one of the more popular women's sports in Australia. The game resembles basketball in that the aim in both sports is to throw a ball through rings placed at both ends of the court, but there are significant differences in the rules, the number of players, the size and markings of the court and the weight of the ball.

The sport first became popular in the 1920s, a popularity which led to the formation, in 1926, of the All-Australian Women's Basketball Association (the All-Australia Netball Association since 1970), and since that time each State has fielded a team in annual interstate tournaments. Australia has an excellent record in the world championships which are held every four years, with wins in the first championship in 1963, second place in 1967 and first again in the 1971 and 1975 championships. In 1979 Australia shared first place in the world championships with Trinidad and New Zealand and in 1983 was outright first.

nettles and nettle trees

Nettles belong to the Urticaceae, a widespread tropical and temperate family. Certain genera contain plants with stinging hairs upon the leaves. Among them are *Urtica* which includes in Australia the introduced small nettle, *U. urens*, and the scrub nettle, *U. incisa*, which, though a forest herb, is often a weed of waste places. The giant nettle tree of NSW and QLD, *Dendrocnide (Laportea) excelsa*, can reach a height of 45m; it must be treated with respect.

Neuroptera *see* antlions, etc.

New Australia

This was the name given to a utopian socialist settlement founded by Australians in Paraguay in 1893. Its members abandoned socialism in 1897.
See also Lane, William

Deeply dissected country in the E of the New England plateau

New England

NSW This plateau in the N part of the State is one section of the GREAT DIVIDING RANGE of E Australia. It extends S from the QLD border for about 320km, lying some 60km inland from the NORTH COAST and averaging 130km in width. It forms the main watershed between rivers flowing E to the Pacific (RICHMOND, CLARENCE and MACLEAY) and those flowing generally W to join the DARLING system (MACINTYRE, GWYDIR and NAMOI). The E rivers are comparatively short but flow swiftly and may carry large volumes of flood water when there is heavy rain on the plateau and coastal areas; they have their headwaters on the plateau and plunge over the escarpment—forming spectacular waterfalls (for example, WOLLOMOMBI, Dangar, Ebor, Mihi, Chandler)—into sheer gorges before entering wider valleys on the North Coast. In contrast, the W rivers are longer, with more gentle gradients since they flow across the inland slopes and plains; though they can flood in times of heavy rain, they usually flow as slow meandering streams. The general elevation of the plateau is about 900m above sea level, though there is some variation in height (ARMIDALE 995m, GLEN INNES 1 073m, TENTERFIELD 863m), and there are peaks which rise well above the plateau surface, such as Round Mt (1 610m) situated near Wollomombi E of Armidale, Chandler's Peak (1 565m) E of Guyra, and Capoompeta (1 555m) and Bajimba (1 525m) both NE of Deepwater. Though the plateau is the watershed divide between E and W flowing rivers, there are no sharp ridges nor does the divide form a distinct landscape feature, for the country consists of gently undulating topography with the more elevated hills standing out as remnants of harder rock. Because of its elevation, the region has a climate of mild to warm summers and cold winters with frequent frosts and occasional light snow in the higher parts. The central parts of the plateau receive an annual average rainfall of about 800mm but along the E escarpment much higher rainfalls, exceeding 2000mm yearly, are experienced.

The settlement of New England followed upon the explorations of John OXLEY in 1818; by the 1830s, squatters with sheep flocks had moved into the area. The discovery of gold in the region in the 1850s and again in the 1880s and the location of profitable tin ores in the 1870s brought a boom period which affected rural land use. Many of the sheep properties were subdivided into small farms and crop growing, particularly of wheat and other cereals, became prominent. But the long severe winters were unsuitable for grain crops and when the mining boom was over, grazing again became the major activity, as it is today. Sheep are the main livestock, though cattle in recent years have become increasingly important. Orcharding is important in some areas around Armidale, URALLA and Tenterfield; maize is grown mainly in the N section around Tenterfield and Glen Innes; dairying is practised on river flats near the towns and is especially important at DORRIGO; vegetables are grown on some pockets of volcanic soils; timber-getting is a significant industry in the heavily forested N and NE sections. Mining is still carried on in parts of the region (for example, tin at Emmaville) and fossicking for gem stones, especially sapphires, is a leisure-time pursuit for some residents and visitors. The University of New England is located at Armidale. The New England National Park (23 554ha) lies 70km E of Armidale; the Apsley Gorge National Park (6 630ha) SE of Walcha includes some scenic waterfall and gorge country; the Bald Rock Park (2 104ha) 29km N of Tenterfield includes the large granite dome called Bald Rock which rises to 1 277m above sea level.
Further reading: Voisey, A.H. *The Building of New England.* University of New England, Armidale, 1955; Thorpe, E. *The New England Plateau.* Longmans, Melbourne, 1957; *New England Essays: Studies of Environment in Northern New South Wales.* University of New England, Armidale, 1963; Walker, R. *Old New England: A History of the Northern Tablelands, 1880-1900.* Sydney University Press, Sydney, 1966; Lea, D.A.M. *et al Atlas of New England.* University of New England, Armidale, 1977.

New Guard

This vigilante-type organisation was formed in Sydney in 1931 under the leadership of a solicitor and ex-army officer named Eric Campbell. Its stated objectives included such generalities as loyalty to the throne, support for the British Empire and the suppression of disloyal elements in government, industry and society, and its members were expected to support the police in the event of a breakdown in law and order. More specifically, it was aimed at combating Communism, and since its members considered J.T. LANG an encourager of 'Reds', it was strongly opposed to his policies and influence. On the other hand, Lang and his supporters likened the New Guard to Fascist and other paramilitary organisations in Europe, but although it was organised on military lines and its members used the Fascist salute, it proved to be but a pale shadow of extremist groups in many other countries. Its members were involved in minor clashes with Communists and Lang supporters at political meetings, but its most newsworthy exploit occurred at the opening of the SYDNEY HARBOUR BRIDGE when a member named de Groot, mounted on horseback, managed to slash the ribbon with his sword before Premier Lang had a chance to cut it. In 1932 its leadership claimed to have 100 000 followers, but at the very most this could be taken only as referring to people who felt a general sympathy for its opposition to Communism and Lang. Support for the New Guard began to dwindle after Lang's dismissal and electoral defeat in 1932, and by 1935 it had apparently faded away. *Further reading:* Campbell, E. *The Rallying Point: My Story of the New Guard.* Melbourne University Press, Melbourne, 1975.

New Guinea *see* Papua New Guinea

New Holland This was the name given by the Dutch to the parts of the Australian mainland which they discovered. *See also* discovery

New Norcia WA Located on the Great Northern Highway, some 130km NE of Perth and about 85km inland from the Indian Ocean coastline on the upper reaches of the Moore River, this small settlement is a Benedictine monastery established by Spanish monks in 1846 to undertake missionary work among the Aboriginal population. It is named after the birthplace of St Benedict in Italy. Secondary boarding school facilities provide for students from a wide area and there is a museum annex to the monastery containing treasures brought from Spain.

New Norfolk TAS (population 6 243 in 1981) Located 38km NW of Hobart on the Lyell Highway, this town is situated on the DERWENT RIVER upstream from the State capital. It owes its beginnings and its name to the displaced settlers from the abandoned NORFOLK ISLAND settlement who were granted land in the Derwent Valley in 1808. It is now a thriving business centre, the unofficial 'capital' of the valley, the service centre for a rich rural district of hop farms and apple orchards and the residential centre for the BOYER newsprint mills located 6km downstream. Among the many historic buildings in New Norfolk is St Matthew's Anglican Church, the oldest existing church building in TAS. It has been classified for preservation by the National Trust (TAS), as have several other buildings of architectural and historical importance such as the Bush Inn, Willow Court and Hall Green. The Old Colony Inn, built in 1835, is a popular tourist feature.

New South Wales (NSW) The State of NSW has an area of 801 428km², the fourth-largest State of the nation, occupying about 10 per cent of the area of Australia. The E boundary, along the coastline of the S Pacific Ocean, extends for some 1 900km from Point Danger in the N to CAPE HOWE in the S. The W boundary is defined by the 141st meridian of E longitude. On the N, the 29th parallel of S latitude forms the major part of the boundary, but the E section of this boundary follows the MACINTYRE and DUMARESQ Rivers and thence along the crest of the ranges (including the McPHERSON RANGE) to the coast. The S State boundary is defined by the S bank of the MURRAY RIVER to its source in the GREAT DIVIDING RANGE, and thence by a direct line to Cape Howe on the coast.

Landform features The State can be conveniently divided into four main natural landform regions: the coastal districts, the highland belt (the tablelands), the W slopes and the W plains.

St. Benedict's Residence for Boys in New Norcia built at the turn of the century

The coastal valleys and plains, adjacent to the S Pacific Ocean, vary considerably in width: on the NORTH COAST the average width is about 80km, while on the S coast the plain is generally narrower, averaging about 30km wide although in some places it is less than 1km. The valley of the HUNTER RIVER, in the mid-coastal section, is the widest part of the coastal region, extending for about 240km inland.

The tablelands are part of the Great Dividing Range and consist of a series of plateaus and hilly ranges which form the watershed between rivers draining E into the Pacific and those draining inland into the Murray-DARLING system. This region varies in width from 50km to 160km, and in elevation from an average of 750m in the N, to the highest point, Mt KOSCIUSKO (2 228m) in the S section. These various parts of the highland belt are known by different names: in the N is the NEW ENGLAND region; the central part comprises the BLUE MOUNTAINS, while the MONARO region and the SOUTHERN TABLELANDS form the S part. There are many individual peaks, prominent bluffs, upland hilly tracts and areas of quite rugged terrain within the tablelands region; although referred to as mountains or ranges, they are not true mountains compared with the great ranges in other continents of the world. The SNOWY MOUNTAINS, in the far S of the region, are probably the best-known of these because of their popularity for winter skiing and because of the vast hydro-electricity scheme which has been constructed there. The E scarplands of the tablelands are clearly marked and quite sheer in many areas; there are numerous spectacular waterfalls and gorges where the streams plunge from the uplands to the coastal plains.

The W slopes, lying between the highlands and the W plains, consist of undulating and hilly country, rugged in parts, but sloping gradually and decreasing in elevation towards the W. This region includes the RIVERINA and the upper courses of the inland rivers of the State, such as the NAMOI, CASTLEREAGH, BOGAN, MACQUARIE, LACHLAN and MURRUMBIDGEE, which drain into the Murray-Darling system. The W plains, covering almost two-thirds of the State's area, consist of a vast tract of level or gently undulating country, broken only by hilly outcrops (such as the Barrier Range in the SW near BROKEN HILL and the WARRUMBUNGLE and Nandewar Ranges in the NE) which rise starkly from the broad plains. The region is traversed diagonally from NE to SW by the Darling River and is drained by its numerous tributaries which have their headwaters in the tablelands; these streams flow across the slopes, follow meandering courses which are often intermittent and form many BILLABONGS and ANABRANCHES in their lower reaches on the plains. When heavy rains occur in the headwater catchment areas, these streams break their banks and inundate wide expanses of the countryside. Such flooding in wet seasons can remain for long periods and create serious transport problems.

Windmills pumping bore water is a common sight in the Western plains of NSW

J.H. Shaw

Climate In general, the climatic conditions throughout the State are mild and equable, although very high summer temperatures are experienced (particularly in the far W and NW) and some markedly low winter temperatures occur on the Southern Tablelands. Along the coastal belt the range between the average winter and summer temperatures is only about 10°C (at LISMORE on the North Coast the range is 10.3°C, at Sydney it is 8.7°C and at NOWRA on the S coast it is 8.8°C). On the highlands the range between the average winter and summer months is somewhat greater (ARMIDALE in the New England region has a range of 12.7°C, at BATHURST it is 13.1°C, and at GOULBURN on the Southern Tablelands it is 12.6°C). In the far W of the State the range between average winter and summer conditions is even greater (BOURKE has a range of 15.4°C and Broken Hill 13.9°C). Most of the State is subject to the influence of frosts during five or more months of the year and the extent and severity of these varies according to elevation and to distance from the coastline. Occasional light snowfalls can occur in many areas of the State, but heavy falls are a regular feature in only the highest parts of the Southern Tablelands.

The rainfall varies markedly in different parts of the State. Generally, the coastal regions have higher yearly totals and the amount received declines progressively inland. The average annual rainfall along the coastal stretch varies from 750mm to 1 500mm; on the tablelands it ranges from 700mm to 1000mm, in the slopes region from 500mm to 700mm, and in the W plains from as low as 180mm up to about 400mm. This decreasing rainfall with increasing distance from the coast is well illustrated by the figures for Lismore (1 341mm average), Armidale (815mm), YOUNG (690mm) and Bourke (347mm). Just over 35 per cent of the whole area of the State receives less than 350mm rainfall yearly, while only nine per cent of the state receives more than 1000mm annually. It is not uncommon for different parts of the State to experience lengthy periods of drought, but for the whole area to suffer dry conditions at the same time is most unusual. In the N and NE sections of the State the seasonal occurrence of rain shows a summer maximum; in the SW of the State there is a winter maximum; in the central and SE sections the rainfall is distributed fairly uniformly throughout the year.

Population At the 1981 census, NSW had a population of 5 237 068, making it the largest State in terms of population and accounting for about 35.1 per cent of Australia's people. About 55 per cent of the State's population live within the urban metropolis of Sydney, and the three largest urban centres (Sydney, WOLLONGONG and NEWCASTLE) account for about 64 per cent of the total State population. The population at each census this century is shown in Table 1. NSW had reached its first million of population by 1887, about 100 years after the foundation of the colony; by 1919 it had passed the two-million mark, by 1947 three million, by 1962 four million and in 1978 it had over five million people. The rate of growth in the first decade of this century was somewhat slow, owing to the commercial and industrial stagnation in the 1890s and the consequent almost total suspension of assisted immigration. As economic conditions improved, the rate of population growth accelerated and between the censuses of 1911 and 1921, despite the effects of World War I, the average annual rate of increase in population was 2.46 per cent, the highest for any intercensal period this century. The years 1921-33 commenced with

Table 1

POPULATION GROWTH OF NEW SOUTH WALES IN THE TWENTIETH CENTURY

Year	Population	Average growth rate (%)
1901	1 355 355	1.86*
1911	1 646 734	1.97
1921	2 100 371	2.46
1933	2 600 847	1.76
1947	2 984 838	0.99
1954	3 423 529	1.98
1961	3 917 013	1.94
1966	4 237 901	1.58
1971	4 601 180	1.66
1976	4 914 300	1.36
1981†	5 237 068	1.31

Note: * indicates the growth rate from 1891 to 1901; † the 1981 figure is the Estimated Resident Population (Preliminary).
Source: Australian Bureau of Statistics, Canberra.

a recession, followed by a period of steady progress and a revival of immigration until 1928, and then ended in years of severe depression and substantial emigration. The period 1933-47 was marked by a gradual recovery from the Depression, followed by World War II, a lower rate of natural increase and reduced immigration; the average yearly rate of growth (0.99 per cent) during this period was the lowest of any period in this century. The years between World War II and 1961 showed a high rate of natural increase in population and considerable growth from immigration. Since 1961 there have been lower growth rates, reflecting reduced rates of natural increase and immigration.

History: Founding and early years NSW was officially founded by Governor Arthur

PHILLIP on 26 January 1788. Most historians agree that the main reason for its foundation was the British government's need to dispose of convicts. At the time transportation overseas was a common criminal punishment but because the American colonies, to which most transported convicts had been sent formerly, had become independent, a new penal settlement was needed. In 1786 Lord Sydney, the Home Secretary, announced that it would be at BOTANY BAY, in the land which COOK had named New South Wales. In his first statement on the matter Lord Sydney mentioned no other reasons for establishing a settlement there; nevertheless, some historians, most notably Geoffrey Blainey in *The Tyranny of Distance* (1975) and other writings, have argued that the commercial and strategic advantages of having a colony in the South Seas must have had a decisive influence on the British government's decision.

Phillip soon decided that Botany Bay was unsuitable, and moved to a bay, which he named SYDNEY COVE, in nearby PORT JACKSON. The difficulties which he met there are described in his biography.

By 1793 Britain was at war with France, and for some years little thought was given to the affairs of her distant penal colony. This is illustrated by the fact that the second Governor, John HUNTER, did not reach Sydney until September 1795, nearly three years after Phillip's departure. In the meantime Major GROSE and Captain PATERSON, officers of the NEW SOUTH WALES CORPS, the regiment which had replaced the original garrison of marines, had in turn carried on the administration. Both men were generous in making land grants to their fellow officers and in assigning convict servants to them, and by the time Hunter arrived officers had become the colony's chief farmers. They had also come to dominate its trade, including that in 'rum', as the colonists termed all alcoholic spirits. Governors Hunter, KING (1800-1805) and BLIGH (1805-1808) struggled to curb the officers' privileges, but with little success, and in January 1808, in the incident commonly known as the RUM REBELLION, Bligh was deposed by the commanding officer of the Corps, Major George JOHNSTON. For nearly two years the colony was again administered by officers of the Corps—first Johnston, then Lieutenant Joseph Foveaux and finally Paterson.

Not only did the colony have a troubled history during its first 20 years, but its growth in population and wealth was disappointing. When Bligh's successor, Colonel Lachlan MACQUARIE, arrived at the end of 1809 the total population was still only about 11 000, of whom the great majority were convicts, ex-convicts or the descendants of convicts.

A new view of the colony The arrival of Macquarie brought an end to disputes between Governors and the colony's military forces, for he brought his own regiment with him and the New South Wales Corps was disbanded early in 1810. (The entry on Macquarie describes his work in developing the colony, his policy

George Street, Sydney, 1892

ance. In 1883 the major silver-lead-zinc field of Broken Hill was discovered, while the discovery of the main MAITLAND coal seam five years later confirmed the position of NSW as Australia's leading coal producer and also helped the development of manufacturing.

Between the gold rushes and federation, NSW developed her manufacturing industries with about the same degree of success as VIC, in spite of the fact that she pursued a free-trade policy, whereas VIC adopted a policy of tariff protection (*see* ECONOMIC HISTORY).

From 1914 to the present The growth of Australian manufacturing during World War I was strengthened in NSW by the opening of the BROKEN HILL PROPRIETARY COMPANY LIMITED's (BHP) iron and steel works at Newcastle in 1915. The State already possessed Australia's only large iron works, that of G. & A. Hoskins at LITHGOW, but the BHP enterprise was on a larger scale. NSW remained Australia's only producer of iron and steel until the opening by BHP of a blast furnace at WHYALLA in SA in 1941.

Sheep country in the SW slopes of NSW

During the period of economic development since the end of World War II, NSW has remained Australia's greatest centre of manufacturing, although the increase of manufacturing in the outlying States has lessened her comparative advantage. Although increases in the output of iron and steel have been particularly striking, the building of integrated iron and steel works by BHP in SA and WA has lessened the prominence of NSW in this area of industry. In primary industry, NSW has remained the leading producer of wool and wheat, although in some years she has been surpassed in wheat production by WA.
Further reading: Flanagan, R. *History of New South Wales.* Sampson Low, London, 1862; Lang, J.D. *An Historical and Statistical Account of New South Wales.* (4th edn) Sampson Low, London, 1875.

New South Wales Corps This army regiment was recruited in 1789 to replace the three companies of marines who had been sent on the FIRST FLEET as the garrison of the colony of NSW. Since Major Ross, the commander of the marines, had disagreed with Governor PHILLIP regarding his men's responsibilities, and in particular had refused to allow the officers to sit as jurors, the officers of the Corps were made specifically liable for jury and magisterial service.

of trying to prevent discrimination against ex-convicts, and the increase in population and wealth that took place during his term of office.) By the time Macquarie left Australia a new view of the colony's future was emerging.

Macquarie continued the policy of giving land grants to ex-convicts and encouraging them to engage in agriculture. He thought that the future of the colony depended largely on the work of such small farmers. Many of the richer free settlers, however, believed that NSW was most likely to become prosperous through the activities of men of capital, owning large properties and concentrating on the production of wool. This view impressed John BIGGE, the commissioner sent in 1819 to report on the state of the colony and its future prospects, and was gradually accepted by the authorities in Britain; this meant that although NSW remained a penal settlement, there was more emphasis on free settlement and an increasing willingness to allow the colonists to take part in the work of the government.

The pastoral age 1821-51 During this period there was rapid development. The exploration of practically the whole of SE Australia was completed, and in the wake of the explorers came the wool-growers, whose success in providing the colony with its first reliable source of export income led to the period becoming known as the pastoral age. A tragic aspect of this expansion, however, was its effect on the Aborigines. European settlement disrupted their way of life, and when they clashed with the settlers they had no hope of winning. The spread of the pastoral industry in SE Australia finally led to the near-extinction of the Aborigines there.

Convicts continued to be sent during most of this period, but their usefulness to the colony was now seen in a different light, with more stress on the provision of cheap labour for the pastoral industry. At the same time, however, the number of free settlers arriving from Britain increased greatly, and from 1832 onwards included many working-class people taking advantage of the assisted passage scheme that began in that year or the 'bounty' system of sponsored immigration that started in 1835. This growth of a free population added to the pressures which caused the abolition of transportation to the mainland of NSW in 1840 and to the whole of E Australia in 1852. It also swelled the demand for self-government. In the meantime the colony's area had changed, first being increased by the moving of its border W in 1825, and then being decreased by the setting up of the separate colonies of TAS, SA and VIC.

From the gold rushes to World War I The two most important features of the 1850s were the attainment of internal self-government and the gold rushes (*see* POLITICAL HISTORY and GOLD DISCOVERIES respectively.) The gold discoveries benefited VIC more than NSW so that by the 1860s the former had become the most populous of the Australian colonies and Melbourne had become larger than Sydney. Nevertheless, by the end of the century the mother colony had regained the lead, mainly because it has greater land resources than VIC. Until the 1890s land development was mainly for pastoral purposes, and made NSW the dominant Australian wool producer. After the 1980s, as drought hit the pastoralists, the wheat and dairying industries expanded rapidly. Largely because of the work of William FARRER in producing rust-resistant varieties, wheat production increased tenfold between 1891 and 1914. Mining was also of considerable import-

The first detachments of the new force, under Captain Nicholas Nepean, arrived on the transports *Surprize, Scarborough* and *Neptune* in June 1790, and the remainder, including the commanding officer, Major Francis GROSE, in February 1792. In December 1792 Governor Phillip left the colony and Grose, who held a commission as Lieutenant-Governor, administered the affairs of the colony until he sailed for England two years later. The next most senior officer, Captain William PATERSON, took over the administration until the arrival of Governor HUNTER in September 1795. In this period the officers were able to establish themselves as the colony's chief farmers and traders; their success in farming was partly because of the generosity of their successive commanding officers in granting them land and supplying them with assigned convicts supported at government expense, and partly a result of their general skill and initiative. As for trade, they had the great advantage of being able to obtain advances against their salaries in the form of bills drawn on the British Treasury in London, or paymaster's bills on regimental funds in London. The colony contained practically no money, and merchant captains preferred the officers' bills to the local promissory notes and store receipts which most inhabitants had to use for currency. Consequently, the officers were able for a time to secure a near monopoly of incoming trade and to sell with very high profit margins.

In internal trade, too, the officers could use their position of authority and superior financial standing to obstruct the humbler settlers' access to the commissary, or government store, and so were in a position to buy such farmers' produce cheaply. The efforts of Governors HUNTER, KING and BLIGH to curb the officers' trading activities were only partly successful, and helped to lead to Bligh's deposition in January 1808 in the so-called RUM REBELLION. This incident, although it placed officers of the Corps in full control of the colony for the following two years, led inevitably to its recall. When Governor MACQUARIE came to the colony in 1809 he brought his own regiment, the 73rd, with him. Some men of the Corps, which thereafter became known simply as the 102nd Regiment, took the opportunity of enlisting in the 73rd, and the rest returned to England in 1810.

Further reading: Evatt, H.V. *Rum Rebellion*. Angus & Robertson, Cremorne NSW, 1975.

New Zealand; Economic Relations
Closer Economic Relations with Australia (CER), a trade agreement which came into force on 1 January 1983, means a gradual phasing out of import/export controls for trade between New Zealand and Australia.

Newcastle
Newcastle NSW A major city and important port located at the mouth of the HUNTER RIVER, Newcastle is 168km by rail and 172km by road N of Sydney. The population within the city boundaries in 1981 was 135 194 but the total population of the urban area, including the city and adjoining suburbs, was 258 956, making it the second-largest urban centre in NSW and the sixth-largest in Australia. The central business district of the city and the main residential areas are situated on the S shore of the Hunter River estuary; on the N shore there is little development, apart from the suburb of Stockton. The suburbs extend W along the lower Hunter Valley, SW and S over the adjacent hill lands to LAKE MACQUARIE, and E to coastal beaches such as Merewether, Redhead and Dudley. The city is the commercial, general business and service focus for the Hunter Valley region, as well as an important industrial and shipping centre.

The site of Newcastle was discovered in 1797, nine years after the first settlement at Sydney, when Lieutenant John Shortland, commanding a whaleboat in pursuit of runaway convicts, entered the sheltered river estuary, which he named the Hunter. He explored the environs and made a further discovery of a coal seam, which can be seen today in the cliffside. In 1804 the area was made a convict settlement, to which the most serious offenders were sent to serve their sentences. The settlement was originally called King's Town, but the name was changed to Newcastle by Governor KING in 1804 and the surrounding district was called Northumberland after the city of Newcastle upon Tyne and the county of Northumberland in England. Convict labour was used to cut cedar timber, to mine coal and to quarry limestone. Overseas trade in coal began early, and by 1814 Newcastle was sending more than 150 tonnes yearly to India, payment being made in Bengal rum. At first, the coal mining was located near the coast and there were mines in areas now occupied by the city and its suburbs. However, as these became partially exhausted and as more profitable coal seams were discovered inland around MAITLAND and CESSNOCK, the centre of the mining industry moved about 30km W. Improvements to the estuarine harbour also began early, with the start of construction in 1818 of a breakwater on the S headland, which eventually joined Nobby's Is to the mainland; the lighthouse on this headland was erected as a navigational aid in 1858. An event of considerable importance to the growth and development of the district in the 19th century was the formation in 1824 of the Australian Agricultural Co. which was primarily interested in rural activities but also prominent in the development of the coalfields. In 1859 Newcastle was proclaimed a municipality, and in 1885 a city. Before 1889, Newcastle's chief means of communication was by sea, but in that year, with the completion of the bridge across the HAWKESBURY RIVER, a rail link with Sydney was established. By 1891, the city's population had risen to 50 000.

A further event which stimulated the rate of Newcastle's progress was the decision by the BROKEN HILL PROPRIETARY COMPANY LIMITED (BHP) in 1913 to establish its iron and steel works at Port Waratah on the S bank of the lower Hunter River, some 5km WNW of the city. Over subsequent decades the growth of the BHP steel industry complex has highlighted the city's development. Allied industries include those producing wire and wire netting, galvanised iron, axles, nails, wire rope and various engineering products, as well as the NSW State Dockyard for building, refitting and repair of ships. In more recent years, Newcastle's industry has become more diversified and now includes the manufacture of textiles, wood fibre boards, electrical equipment, fertilisers and many other products. Newcastle ranks as the second-busiest port in Australia. It has wharfage accommodation for general cargo and special facilities for handling coal, wheat, bulk oil and livestock cargoes. The port is the clearing point for coal produced by the northern NSW coalfields, and other exports include iron and steel goods, wool,

No 2 Bloom Mill at Newcastle steelworks

wheat, timber, butter and frozen meat. The city contains a university, a cathedral, a modern cultural centre, an art gallery opened in 1976 and a College of Advanced Education (formerly called the Newcastle Teachers College). It includes a wide range of professional services and civic amenities, and although the heavy industries seem to dominate the atmosphere of the city, the nearby coastal beaches and the Lake Macquarie area to the S provide important leisure-time recreation facilities.

See also iron and steel industry

Further reading: Daly, M.T. *The Growth of Newcastle and its Suburbs.* Hunter Valley Research Foundation, Newcastle, 1966; White, U. & Farrelly, A. *Newcastle and Hunter Valley Sketchbook.* Rigby, Adelaide, 1969; *Hunter 2000: Conservation of Lands and Buildings of Natural, Historical, Scenic or Recreational Value in the Hunter Region.* The National Trust of Australia (NSW), Sydney, 1972.

Newcastle Waters NT This small town is on the Stuart Highway 741km SE of Darwin and 121km S of DALY WATERS, at an elevation of 210m. It is in the arid interior region of the Territory; the average annual rainfall is only 494mm, concentrated mainly in the four-month wet season (December to March), and there are long drought spells. The explorer John McDouall STUART named the site in 1872 after the British Secretary of State for the Colonies. It is a livestock mustering centre and a staging post on the highway for road transport.

John Newcombe

Newcombe, John David (1944-) Tennis player. Born in Sydney, Newcombe burst on to the world stage of tennis when the bitter split between amateur and professional tennis was about to heal (tennis tournaments have been open to amateurs and professionals since 1968) and was to become the leading amateur in the world in 1967 and the leading player in the world in 1970. A talented and determined player with a fierce serve, he won

Wimbledon and the US singles championship in 1967. Many cynics felt that the top players in amateur tennis would be also-rans once professional players were allowed to enter world tennis tournaments. Newcombe was to prove them wrong by winning Wimbledon again in 1970 and 1971, to become the first Australian to win three Wimbledon titles, and by winning the US title again in 1973. Also wily and cunning as a doubles player, he won the Wimbledon doubles title in 1965, 1966, 1968, 1969, 1970 and 1974, the US doubles title in 1967 and the Australian doubles title in 1965, 1967, 1971 and 1973, usually partnered by the left-handed Tony ROCHE. Affectionately known as 'Newk' by friends, colleagues and followers of tennis, since retiring from tournament tennis he has concentrated on teaching at one of the 12 tennis camps with which he is associated in the US and in Australia.

Newman *see* Mount Newman WA

newspapers In spite of its relatively small population, Australia is among the leading newspaper-reading nations in the world. In 1982 the combined circulation of the country's metropolitan daily newspapers and the main national daily was more than four million and that of Sunday newspapers nearly three million. Although more than 500 newspapers are published in Australia, circulation is dominated by the metropolitan dailies. The only national general newspaper is the *Australian*, which is printed simultaneously in a number of State capitals. The *Australian Financial Review* is also national in its circulation but, as its name indicates, it is a specialist business and financial publication. The weekly *National Times*, although sometimes referred to as a national newspaper, is more properly described as a journal of topical comment. The most time-honoured of Australian magazines, the BULLETIN, also concentrates on topical comment.

In general the political standpoint of the Press is conservative. The only Labor daily in Australia is the BROKEN HILL *Barrier Daily Truth*, which is subsidised by the trade unions of that town, but, as a country newspaper, has a limited circulation. However, the main newspapers do not necessarily oppose the Australian Labor Party (ALP) on all occasions. Moreover, the extent to which the Press influences voting behaviour is a matter for debate.

There are many suburban newspapers—more than 50 in Sydney alone—and most of them are free, depending on advertisements for their revenue. Country newspapers also exist in great numbers considering the size of the population; in NSW alone there are about 140 of them. However, very few provincial cities have newspapers which rival those of the capital cities, even in their own districts. The main exception is the LAUNCESTON *Examiner*, which dominates northern TAS and has a circulation about two-thirds that of the Hobart *Mercury*. In this case, however, it must be realised that TAS is the only State in which the population of the main provincial city is

comparable with that of the capital.

Since the 1940s a considerable number of non-English newspapers and magazines have appeared in Australia, most of them weeklies or monthlies. Those in Italian and Greek are particularly widely read, two of the best-known being *Il Globo* (Melbourne) and *La Fiamma* (Sydney).

Freedom of the Press In Australia freedom of the Press is not defined by statute, but rests on common law. Since the days of Governor DARLING there have been few attempts by governments, apart from wartime censorship, to control what newspapers publish. Concern is widely felt, however, at the tendency for newspaper ownership to become concentrated in the hands of a few companies, especially as these same companies are engaged in magazine publishing and have extensive control of radio and television companies. At present three organisations—the Herald and Weekly Times group, John Fairfax and Sons Ltd and the News Ltd group—control between them almost the whole of the metropolitan Press, the *Canberra Times, Australian, Australian Financial Review, National Times* and a number of country papers. Critics of this trend claim that it is undesirable for so few proprietors to exercise such wide control over the presentation of information to the public.

Journalists' and proprietors' associations The majority of Australian journalists, as well as photographers and artists working for newspapers and many employees of radio and television news services, belong to the Australian Journalists' Association (AJA). The main associations of newspaper proprietors and managers are the Australian Newspapers Council, the Australian Provincial Press Association (a federal organisation for the Country Press Associations in the various States) and the Regional Dailies of Australia Ltd. In conjunction with the AJA, these three bodies in 1976 set up the AUSTRALIAN PRESS COUNCIL.

Metropolitan newspapers The main newspapers of the State capitals have retained their dominance because of the original development of Australia as six separate colonies, the federal nature of government today, the concentration of population in the capital cities and the great distances between these cities. Each of these newspapers carries a large amount of local and State news which no national paper could match. One result of the fragmentation of readership between them is that they do not support large numbers of overseas staff or even interstate staff. They therefore rely fairly heavily on news services. Australian Associated Press, which works in conjunction with Reuter's in some parts of the world, supplies much of their overseas news; Australian United Press Ltd distributes interstate news, particularly to the provincial and country Press but also to some extent to metropolitan papers.

The main metropolitan papers at present are as follows. Sydney has the morning *Daily Telegraph* and *Sydney Morning Herald*, the evening *Daily Mirror* and *Sun*, and the Sunday *Sun-Herald* and *Sunday Telegraph*. Melbourne has the morning *Age* and *Sun News-Pictorial*, the evening *Herald* and the weekly *Sunday Observer, Melbourne Sunday Press* and *Truth*. Of these in 1983 the *Sun News-Pictorial* had the highest circulation (594 000) among morning dailies throughout Australia and the *Herald* the largest circulation (357 000) among evening dailies. The smaller capitals have fewer papers than Sydney and Melbourne. Brisbane has the morning *Courier-Mail* and *Daily Sun*, the evening *Telegraph* and the weekend *Sunday Mail* and *Sunday Sun;* Adelaide has the morning *Advertiser*, evening *News* and the weekend *Sunday Mail;* Perth has the morning *West Australian*, the evening *Daily News* and the weekend *Sunday Independent, Weekend News, Western Mail* and *Sunday Times;* and Hobart has the morning *Mercury*, the weekend *Saturday Evening Mercury* and the weekly *Tasmanian Mail*.

Among these papers the distinction between the 'quality' and 'popular' Press is not as clear-cut as in some other countries. In general, however, the morning papers tend to give more attention to serious news and carry more special articles of intellectual worth, while evening and weekend papers concentrate more on sensational news items, on sport and on comic strips.

Early history in NSW and TAS When Australia was first colonised, newspapers were a comparatively new phenomenon in Britain and their publication was hampered by such official devices as the imposition of heavy stamp duties and the passing of licensing regulations which enabled the government to close them down if it wished. Moreover, the law regarding libel was not yet well defined, and any strong criticism of the government was liable to bring prosecution for criminal or seditious libel.

In a penal colony the government was likely to be even more sensitive to criticism, and when one considers also how small the population of NSW was for many years, it is not surprising to find that an independent Press was slow to emerge. The first paper to appear was the weekly *Sydney Gazette and New South Wales Advertiser*, in March 1803. It was printed on a government press with government ink and paper by George Howe, who before being transported for shoplifting, had worked on *The Times* in London. Until 1826 it carried the words 'Published by Authority' at its masthead, and as a semi-official publication dependent on government support it naturally avoided all political discussion. After Howe's death in 1821 it was edited by his son Robert, who also succeeded his father in the salaried post of Government Printer.

The first completely independent newspaper, the *Australian*, appeared in 1824. Its proprietors, William WENTWORTH and Robert Wardell, did not ask Governor BRISBANE for permission to publish, and from the beginning their paper was critical of the government, and advocated such reforms as the establishment of an elected Assembly and the introduction of trial by jury. In May 1826 the *Monitor* (*Sydney Monitor* from August 1828) appeared; under

National Library of Australia

Sketch showing the printing of the Melbourne Age early in its history

the editorship of E.S. Hall it began criticising the government and established interests even more trenchantly than the *Australian*.

Governor Brisbane took a tolerant attitude towards these papers. However, his successor, DARLING, was stung by their criticism, particularly in the case of two soldiers, Sudds and Thompson, who, after being convicted of stealing, were publicly discharged from their regiment loaded with chains and iron collars. Sudds died a few days later, and both papers accused Darling of behaving both illegally and with great cruelty in the matter. The Governor tried to curb such criticism by passing two pieces of legislation, the first introducing a newspaper licensing system and the second imposing a prohibitively high stamp duty of fourpence a copy. The Chief Justice, Sir Francis FORBES, refused to certify that these measures were consistent with the laws of England, and so under the provisions of the New South Wales Judicature Act of 1823 neither went into operation. However, both newspapers continued to be harassed by other means, including prosecutions for seditious and criminal libel; at one time the editors of both papers were writing their editorials in PARRAMATTA gaol. Following the appointment of Governor BOURKE in 1831 freedom of the Press became accepted. In the year of Bourke's appointment the *Sydney Herald* was launched as a weekly. It became a daily in 1840, was renamed the *Sydney Morning Herald* in 1842 and came under the control of the Fairfax family in 1853. It proved to be too strong a competitor for the earlier papers, all of which went out of business during the 1840s.

In TAS the first two newspapers were the short-lived *Derwent Star and Van Diemen's Land Intelligencer* (1810) and *Van Diemen's Land Gazette and General Advertiser* (1814). The more important *Hobart Town Gazette and*

Southern Reporter, founded in 1816 by Andrew BENT, the Government Printer, functioned at first both as an official gazette and as a general newspaper. In 1825 its official function was taken over by the new government-owned *Van Diemen's Land Gazette*, edited by G.T. Howe and James Ross; Ross also published the unofficial *Hobart Town Courier* from 1827. In the meantime Bent continued publication of his paper, at first under its original title and then as the *Colonial Times*.

As in NSW the authorities used various means to shackle the Press in TAS in this period. In 1825 a successful libel action resulted in a term of imprisonment for Bent. Two years later the Legislative Council passed an Act providing for the licensing of newspapers, which Chief Justice Sir John Pedder, unlike Sir Francis Forbes in a similar situation in NSW, certified as being consistent with the laws of England. However, it was later disallowed by the British government.

Early history in the other colonies In VIC the first papers, both appearing in 1838, were the *Port Phillip Gazette* and J.P. Fawkner's *Melbourne Advertiser*. The latter appeared only briefly, but was revived in the following year as the daily *Port Phillip Patriot and Melbourne Advertiser*. The year 1840 saw the birth of the *Port Phillip Herald*, which developed into the present-day *Herald*. It became the *Melbourne Morning Herald* in 1849, and appeared under its present title, as an evening daily, in 1869. Among morning newspapers, the *Age* appeared in 1854, and two years later was bought by Ebenezer Syme. David, Ebenezer's brother became a partner, and from 1859, when Ebenezer's health failed, was in full control. Perhaps no newspaper proprietor in Australian history has had such a strong influence on public opinion regarding important issues. In particular he led the campaign against the retention of property qualifications for Members of the Legislative Assembly, and was a leading advocate of tariff protection.

In SA the first newspaper was the *South Australian Gazette and Colonial Register*, the first issue of which was printed in London in June 1836 before the first settlers had even reached the colony, and the second in Adelaide a year later. It published all government announcements until 1839, when the *Government Gazette* was launched. The general news section then continued as the *Register*, became the *Register News-Pictorial* in 1929, and two years later was taken over by the *Advertiser* which had been founded as the *South Australian Advertiser* in 1858.

Brisbane's first paper was the *Moreton Bay Courier* (1846), which became the *Brisbane Courier* in 1864 and the modern *Courier-Mail* in 1933. Many other papers appeared briefly either while QLD was part of NSW or fairly soon after separation. However, the sole survivor among them is the *Telegraph*, founded in 1872.

In Perth the first paper to be printed was the *Fremantle Observer, Perth Gazette and Western Australian Journal*, which appeared briefly in 1831. Two years later Charles Macfaull, using

Montage illustrating the printing of newspapers in SA in the 1880s

a government press leased to him on condition that he did government printing also, began publication of the *Perth Gazette and Western Australian Journal*, which after a change of title to *Perth Gazette and Independent Journal of Politics and News* in the 1840s continued until 1864. It then amalgamated with the *Western Australian Times*, which had been founded in the previous year and developed into the present-day *West Australian*.

Further reading: Holden, W.S. *Australia Goes to Press.* Wayne State University Press, Detroit, 1961; Mayer, H. *The Press in Australia.* Lansdowne, Melbourne, 1964; Walker, R.B. *The Newspaper Press in New South Wales, 1803-1920.* Sydney University Press, Sydney, 1976; *Press, Radio and TV Guide.* (annually) Country Press Ltd, Sydney; *Australian Advertising Rate and Data Service: Newspapers.* (monthly) Thomson Publications, Chippendale, NSW.

newts *see* amphibians

Nhill VIC (population 2 067 in 1981) A small country town in the WIMMERA district of western VIC, Nhill is situated on the Western Highway, 65km from the SA border, 377km by road 400km by rail NW of Melbourne. It is a service centre for a rich farming and grazing region which produces wool, wheat, oats, barley and dairy products. The name Nhill comes from an Aboriginal word with several meanings: 'place of spirits', 'red clay' and 'mist over the water'.

Nhulunbuy NT (population 4 138 in 1981) This company town was built in the 1970s as the residential centre for workers and their families employed at the bauxite mine and the ore treatment plant on GOVE PENIN-

SULA, located at the NE extremity of the ARNHEM LAND Aboriginal Reserve, more than 600km due E of DARWIN. The site of the town is at the foot of Mount Saunders, overlooking a lake lying S of Cape Wirrawawoi on the NE coastal region of the peninsula. The town experiences a tropical two-season climate, typical of the N parts of the NT, with an average annual rainfall of some 1 360mm, concentrated in the summer months, with a markedly dry season in the cooler period of the year.

Nicholls, Sir Douglas Ralph (1906-) Governor of SA. Born in the RIVERINA district of NSW, he received little formal education as a child, but in adult life studied to become a minister of the Church of Christ, and became pastor of the Churches of Christ Aborigines Mission in the Melbourne suburb of Fitzroy. Earlier he had become well known as a professional runner and an Australian Rules footballer, playing for Fitzroy in the Victorian Football League and winning a place in the VIC team. In 1976 he was appointed Governor of SA, becoming the first Aboriginal to fill a vice-regal position, but in the following year he resigned because of ill health. He was director of the Aborigines Advancement League from 1969 to 1974 and was made OBE in 1968 and knighted in 1972.

Nicholson, John (1954-) Cyclist. Born in Melbourne, Nicholson concentrated on one aspect of cycle racing—sprinting—at which he was to become world champion. His first Australian amateur senior title came when he won the 1000m sprint in 1970, a title he regained in 1972. Before turning professional in 1974, he represented Australia in Commonwealth and Olympic Games, winning gold medals in the

1000m sprint at the 1970 and 1974 Commonwealth Games and a silver medal in the 1972 Olympic Games. He competed for the world professional sprint title in 1974 and came second but took the title in 1975 and defended it successfully in the following year. The years 1975 and 1976 were good years for Nicholson for he won the Australian professional sprint title in both years in addition to his world titles. In 1978, tragedy hit when he broke his hip in a fall while racing at Coburg Velodrome, Melbourne. He was told that he might never race again and that he would be out of action for at least six months before he could begin to walk again. An indication of Nicholson's courage and dedication to cycling is that before he had fully recovered from the accident, he had freinds assist him on to his bicycle so that he could recommence training, but he was not able to attain competitive success again.

nickel The uses of this metal range over a wide field, but more than 90 per cent of the total production is used in the manufacture of nickel alloys, where strength and resistance to corrosion are required. Nickel research in the USA is directed almost entirely towards physical metallurgy; that is, developing nickel alloys and new uses for the metal. Nickel will find extensive application to the desalination of sea water with the increased use of atomic energy. Other uses of nickel are as a catalyst and in the manufacture of batteries, dyes, pigments and insecticides.

Extraction Nickel deposits fall into three categories—nickel-copper sulphides, nickel silicates and nickel laterites. The principal ores are chalcopyrite, pentlandite and pyrrhotite. After concentration the nickel ore is roasted and then smelted with silica, coke and limestone to form a mixture of nickel and copper sulphides together with a little iron. The iron and most of the sulphur are oxidised and removed and the copper and nickel separated. The crude nickel oxide is then refined. The by-products and co-products of nickel are copper, the platinum metals, cobalt, silver and gold. Primary nickel is marketed in the form of cathodes, powder, briquettes, pellets, ingots and shot or as an oxide sinter or ferro-nickel.

Production Prior to 1870, production of nickel was limited to small deposits in such countries as Japan, Greece, Germany, Italy, Scandinavia and the USA. Silicate ore was discovered in New Caledonia in 1864 and this was the world's principal source of nickel from 1875 to 1905, after which Canada became the leading producer. In 1966, a large nickel deposit was discovered in WA, now the nation's main area of nickel mining.

Australia, the fourth-largest producer after Canada, the USSR and New Caledonia, had a mine production of 74 323 tonnes in 1980 which represented 9.7 per cent of the world's total. The principal nickel mining centres are in the KALGOORLIE area of WA; a lateritic deposit is mined near Greenvale, inland from TOWNSVILLE in QLD. There is a smelter at Kalgoorlie, and refineries at KWINANA in WA and Yabulu, 24km N of Townsville. As shown in Table 1, Australian nickel production rose rapidly in the early and mid-1970s.

The industry World reserves of nickel are estimated at nearly 60 million tonnes, but as the estimates are based on incomplete information they are probably low, with the actual figure probably twice this.

Further reading: see under minerals and mining.

nightjars *see* frogmouths, etc.

nightshade *see* Solanaceae; weeds

Niland, D'Arcy Francis (1917-66) Author and journalist. Born in GLEN INNES in NSW, he was named after the boxer, Les DARCY. He wrote a number of plays, more than 500 short stories, many radio and television scripts and, with his wife Ruth PARK, a joint autobiography, *The Drums Go Bang* (1956). However, he is best remembered for his novels, most of which achieved considerable popular success and which include *The Big Smoke* (1951), *The Shiralee* (1955), *Call Me When the Cross Turns Over* (1957) and *Dead Men Running* (1969).

Nineteen Counties Historically, this term is used to refer to the 19 counties around Sydney, extending about 200km to 300km N, S and W. In 1829, in an effort to keep settlement concentrated, Governor DARLING declared them to be the only area legally open to settlement. Many SQUATTERS, however, ignored this restriction.

See also land settlement and tenure

Ninety Mile Beach VIC Located along the E coast of the State, from near Yarram to beyond LAKES ENTRANCE, this is an uninterrupted stretch of sand ridge and dune beachfront over 140km long on BASS STRAIT. It has been built up in recent geological times by the accumulation of sea-transported sand. In the mid E section of the beach, LAKE REEVE (one of the GIPPSLAND lakes) forms a long lagoon behind the sand ridge. An artificial channel has been cut through the dunes at Lakes Entrance to provide an outlet for the lakes. The Gippsland Lakes Coastal Park (15 500ha) includes a section of Lake Reeve and the beach

along the coast where sparse vegetation holds the sand dunes in fragile balance against the forces of wind erosion.

Noble, Montague Alfred 'Monty' (1873-1940) Cricketer. Born in Sydney, Noble is remembered as one of Australia's greatest all-round cricketers—a steady, even-tempered batsman noted for his brilliant defence and a medium-pace bowler capable of consistently bowling a perfect length. For example, in a match against the English county side of Sussex in 1905, he scored 267 runs (in the good time of five hours) and took six wickets for 39. Of the 42 Tests he played for Australia, he captained the side for 15 of them and proved himself one of Australia's most successful captains. He was determined to win and his determination was ably supported by attributes of cool resourcefulness and steadiness at all times, even when the odds were against him. In his Test matches against England, he scored a total of 1 905 runs for an average of 30.72 and took 115 wickets for an average of 24.78 runs. After his retirement from competitive cricket, Noble became well known as a cricketing broadcaster and commentator and as an author of books on cricket. He was also a trustee of the Sydney Cricket Ground where a stand is named after him.

noddies *see* sea birds

Nolan, Sir Sidney Robert (1917-) Artist. Born in Melbourne, Nolan became fascinated by contemporary art movements in Europe although he had no systematic art training. After seeing the *Herald* exhibition of French and Modern Art in Melbourne's town hall in 1939, he researched the work of Picasso, Klee and Schwitters, and became attracted to the work of the recently arrived Danila VASSILIEFF. However, while the art of the N hemisphere stimulated his art, it never controlled it. His patrons, the newspaper *Sunday* and John Reed of Melbourne, saw to his material needs (which they did for many artists) until recognition came his way.

Nolan's work has usually been in the form of a series of paintings around a particular theme. The Dimboola and WIMMERA paintings, from 1942, depicted Australian landscape and presented the public with the uncompromising quality of much of Australian country life. After World War II he painted the St Kilda series, which was influenced by his childhood memories of the park there. In 1947 he painted the Ned KELLY series; it was this series that projected Nolan onto the English art scene through Lord Kenneth Clark who, during his visit to Australia, was urged to see Nolan's work by Professor Joseph Burke of Melbourne University. This was followed by the Outback QLD series of 1948, the Mrs Fraser series and the Convict Gracefell series. In 1949-50, Nolan completed a new series, which depicted central Australian landscapes and had been inspired by a trans-continental flight to Darwin. He later painted a series of brutal scenes of death by starvation and heat. From 1954 until 1957, his works were inspired by southern Italy and the island of Hydra; in 1960, an exhibition was held of his Leda and the Swan series in London, an event which established him as an internationally known painter. In the mid-1950s, Nolan began using polyvinyl acetate which, like water-colours, needs fast application, cannot be retouched, and whose transparent qualities can be used for dramatic effects, as in the Leda and the Swan series. He has used this technique in subsequent work, such as his GALLIPOLI series which was inspired by the death of his brother in the war, and also in the

'The Trial' by Sidney Nolan 1946-47. (Synthetic polymer paint on composition board)

Australian National Gallery

large number of works he did as the result of his visit to central Africa. He was made a CBE in 1963, knighted in 1981 and made an OM in 1983.

noolbenger *see* possums, etc.

Noosa Heads QLD (combined population of Noosa and TEWANTIN 9 965 in 1981) The furthest N of the beach resorts on the SUNSHINE COAST in the SE of the State, it is located on the S side of the Noosa River estuary, some 150km by road N of Brisbane and 24km E of the Bruce Highway. It is a popular holiday and recreation centre, with the Noosa River National Park to the E covering 469ha of coastal heathland and forest. The township of Noosaville, about 6km inland from Noosa Heads, on the S bank of the Noosa River, has several tourist attractions including the House of Shells, Tall Ships (a collection of ship models, with a display showing the craft of model-making), the *Laguna Belle* (a paddle-steamer restaurant) and cruises on the river and nearby lakes.

Sunshine beach from Noosa QLD

Norfolk Island Located in the SW Pacific Ocean, about 1 670km NE of Sydney and 1000km NW of Auckland (NZ), it is a small hilly island extending some 8km E-W and 5km N-S and covering an area of 36km². It was discovered by James COOK in 1774 and was settled from Sydney in 1788 as a penal colony. It remained as a convict settlement until 1814, and was so used again in 1825-56; many of the buildings erected during these times have been restored and are now popular tourist attractions. During the convict period the island was the scene of some inhuman brutalities and experiments in prisoner rehabilitation. In 1856 it became a Crown colony and some descendants of the mutineers from HMS *Bounty* were brought there from Pitcairn Is. In 1897 it became a NSW dependency and in 1914 it was proclaimed an Australian territory. Until 1979 it was governed through a resident administrator with an advisory council, but in that year a step was taken towards the establishment of representative government on the island when a nine-member Legislative Assembly was elected by residents. Many attempts have been made to develop farming, but most have been unsuccessful and tourism is now the major industry. There is no income tax payable by residents on income earned on the island.

Normanton QLD (population 926 in 1981) A small township in the GULF COUNTRY, it is located on the Norman River about 90km upstream from its mouth. It is the administrative headquarters for the Carpentaria Shire and a service centre for a vast cattle grazing region, with a climate typical of the tropical N: high temperatures throughout the year and an annual rainfall of 932mm which occurs in the summer months, with a long dry season for much of the year. In the latter decades of the 19th century Normanton was a boom town when cattle shipments were made from the river mouth. The recent development of KARUMBA as a fishing port at the mouth has again led to attempts to revive the cattle export trade. A unique railway with steel sleepers to foil the termites links Normanton to Croydon, about 158km inland.

Miner drilling blast holes in the quartz at Central Norseman Gold Corp Regent mines

Norseman WA (population 1 895 in 1981) An inland mining town located on the Eyre Highway junction, Norseman is 206km N by road of ESPERANCE and 186km ESE of COOLGARDIE. It is linked by rail to towns both N and S, and the rail journey via KALGOORLIE to Perth is 849km. The town has been the scene of continuous mining since gold was first discovered there in 1892. It is still a gold-mining centre, but is also important for nickel and for pyrites as a source of sulphur for the manufacture of superphosphate fertiliser. Huge mine tailing dumps dominate the townscape. It is in a semi-arid region of low rainfall (279mm average) and the town water supply comes by pipeline, as an extension from the GOLDFIELDS WATER SUPPLY scheme, from the MUNDARING RESERVOIR.

North Coast NSW Extending from the QLD border to S of the MANNING RIVER valley, this region, stretching some 580km N-S, consists of a series of fertile river valleys separated by hilly divides. The rivers rise in the E scarplands of the GREAT DIVIDING RANGE, or in the ranges branching from it, and flow generally E to the Pacific Ocean. The northernmost of these river valleys is the TWEED, with the RICHMOND and CLARENCE the next two rivers coming S, followed by the MACLEAY, HASTINGS and Manning Rivers with some minor streams and creeks draining small sections of the coastal belt. Routes in this area, such as the Pacific Highway or the main N railway line, pass alternately through the lush green river flats of the valleys and the rugged forested hill lands of the dividing

watersheds. To the W of the coastal zone, the scarps of the NEW ENGLAND Plateau rise abruptly, so that a journey, such as along the Bruxner, Gwydir or Oxley Highways, from the coast to the tablelands involves a steep and winding climb. In their upper reaches, some of the coastal rivers such as the Clarence and the Macleay have cut deep gorges into the scarp of the tablelands. At the furthest end of these gorges are magnificent waterfalls (for example, WOLLOMOMBI, Mihi, Chandler, Ebor, Dangar, Apsley and Yarrowitch Falls) where the streams and their upper tributaries plunge from the plateau surface into the sheer-walled gorges. The hilly divides which separate the valleys are really dissected spurs jutting out from the tablelands. In some parts of the coast, these spurs reach almost to the sea (for example, at COFFS HARBOUR); the plateau scarp comes to within 5km of the coast and thus gives a broad belt of hill land with very little coastal plain.

The climate of this coastal region is subtropical, with no really cold season, a few mildly cool months in winter, and hot humid summer days. Rainfall varies from as low as about 760mm to over 1 700mm yearly, with places on the coast (for example, BYRON BAY has an average annual rainfall of 1 667mm) receiving greater amounts than places inland in the valleys (for example, CASINO has 1 107mm average yearly). However, along the scarplands heavy rainfall is experienced. Tropical cyclones often move down from the QLD coast or in from the adjacent sea, bringing torrential rains to the coast in summer months. When heavy rain occurs over the catchment areas of any of the coastal rivers, serious flooding can occur on the farming lands of the river flats, as well as in the towns. Floods are an ever-present menace to places such as LISMORE, GRAFTON, KEMPSEY and MURWILLUMBAH. Strange as it may seem, droughts are also experienced along the coast, because of the high variability of the rain from year to year.

The most important rural activity of the North Coast is dairying, combined with fodder crop cultivation, such as maize and sorghum, to supplement the pasture grasses. Dairy farms vary in size from about 20ha on river flats to 120ha where there is hilly land in the farm area. Mechanical milking is almost universal on the farms, and many other operations concerned with pasture and crop production are done mechanically. About half the milk produced on the North Coast is separated on the farms and the cream goes to local factories for butter making. Cheese is made at some places, such as TAREE and Lismore, but it is a relatively minor product. Some farms deliver whole milk to the towns and cities in their area for local consumption; others supply whole milk to factories producing ice cream, powdered or condensed milk. Pigs are raised on many dairy farms, feeding on the skim milk, together with corn or some cereal meal. Sugar cane growing is a major rural activity in the three N valleys (Tweed, Richmond and Clarence) and in each there is a mill for crushing the cane and producing raw sugar. Where farms include hilly land, beef cattle are often

NSW Dept of Tourism

Ellenborough Falls, North Coast NSW

grazed. Timber-getting in the forested uplands is an important element of the economy. Banana farming is found at Coffs Harbour and in the three N valleys, and pineapples are grown on some parts of the coast. In each of the coastal river valleys there is one main town or city (for example, Murwillumbah in the Tweed, Taree in the Manning), with many minor urban centres. Lismore is the largest city on the coast, with a population of 24 035 in 1981.

See also Ballina; Port Macquarie
Further reading: Shaw, J.H. *The Face of Our Earth.* Shakespeare Head, Sydney, 1958; *Clarence Valley Development—Problems of Water Utilisation, Communications and Population.* University of New England, Clarence Regional Office, Grafton, 1959; *Farm Problems on the North Coast.* University of New England, Clarence Regional Office, Grafton, 1960; Devery, J. *The North Coast of New South Wales.* Longmans, Melbourne, 1963; Shaw, J.H. & Kirkwood, F.G. *Landscape Studies.* Longmans, Melbourne, 1969.

North West Cape WA Jutting out into the Indian Ocean in the NW of the State, this 96km-long peninsula forms the W shore of Exmouth Gulf. Much of the cape is comprised of sand dunes, though the Cape Range National park, covering 50 581ha in the central and W parts of the peninsula, includes a hilly ridge with some spectacular gorge scenery, caves, Aboriginal paintings and carvings. The new town of EXMOUTH and the US naval communications station which it serves are located in the N part of the cape. The township of Learmonth, in the SE of the cape, was a military and air base during World War II and is now important as a prawn processing centre. Wildlife is abundant on the cape, particularly kangaroos and emus. Deep-sea and game fishing are popular both in the gulf and along the coastal waters. Though the naval communica-

tions base is a restricted area, other parts of the cape, especially the national park, provide scenic attractions for visitors.

North West Shelf WA This part of the sea floor, located off the PILBARA coast in the NW of the State, has proved to be a massive natural gas field. As early as 1964, geophysical surveys had indicated that the rock structures in these offshore regions were promising prospects for oil or gas. Although a number of dry wells were initially drilled, gas was first discovered in 1971 at the southern end of the Shelf in the North Rankin and Goodwyn structures (and later in the Angel field), located in the Indian Ocean about 170km from DAMPIER, between BARROW ISLAND and the area offshore from PORT HEDLAND. Subsequent drilling confirmed that these fields could form the basis of a major gas development, and planning for this project proceeded. Also, further to the NE, in the section of the Shelf lying offshore between BROOME and WYNDHAM, other submarine drilling operations produced large gas flows at Scotts Reef field in the Browse Basin. In 1980, the joint venture companies involved in the development project announced their intention to proceed with the scheme: the most expensive single developmental project in Australia's history, estimated then to cost $11 000 million. The basic plan was to extract the gas from the offshore fields and pipe it to a treatment plant on the Pilbara coast; this involved the construction of two offshore platforms (the first scheduled to be in production by 1984, the second by 1986), a submarine pipeline 135km long from the platforms to Withnell Bay on Burrup Peninsula, 10km N of Dampier, a processing plant and storage facilities at the shore terminal, and construction by the WA State Energy Commission of a 1500km-long onshore pipeline from Withnell Bay to Perth.

Northam WA (population 6 791 in 1981) One of WA's pioneer country towns, Northam is located in the AVON VALLEY, 98km by road NE of Perth. It is a business and service centre for a productive sheep and wheat farming region and a major railway focus, with lines E to KALGOORLIE, S to ALBANY and NW to GERALDTON. A weir across the Avon River has provided a sanctuary for many species of birds and for a collection of rare white swans for which the town is renowned. At an elevation of 149m above sea level, the area experiences a mild climate with hot summers and cool winters; the town has an average annual rainfall of 435mm, concentrated mainly in the winter months. Several buildings in the town and district have been listed for preservation by the National Trust (WA), including 'Morby Cottage' (c1838), St John's Church (1890) and 'Glen Avon' at Katrine (c1860).

Northam, Sir William Herbert (1905-) Yachtsman. Born in Torquay, England, it was not until he reached his mid-40s

that Northam became interested in sailing and yet he became the first Australian to win an Olympic gold medal for sailing. He started sailing in ocean racing yachts with his first boat, *Saskia*, in which he won the 1955 Sayonara Cup, then one of the most prestigious racing events in Australia. His next boat was *Caprice of Huon*, with which he also had considerable success. After a time he tired of ocean racing, sold *Caprice of Huon* and was instrumental in the building of *Gretel*, the 1962 challenger for the America's Cup, serving on the management committee of the *Gretel* syndicate. In 1963 he started building *Barranjoey*, a 5.5m boat which he intended entering in the 1964 Olympic trials. He entered the trials, won the right to represent Australia and took his crew of Pod O'Donnell and Dick Sargeant to the Tokyo Olympics where he became the oldest competitor from any nation ever to win a gold medal and the first Australian to win a yachting gold medal. Competitors sailing against him found that beneath his jokes and ready smile, he possessed a steely success-orientated determination and a fierce will to win. He was knighted in 1976.

Northampton WA (population 750 in 1981) Located 51km N of GERALDTON on the North West Coastal Highway 176km NNW of Perth, this small township is a business and service centre for a productive wheat growing and sheep grazing region. It was established in 1848 as a lead and copper mining town.

Northern Territory (NT) The Northern Territory has an area of 1 346 200km², comprising 17.5 per cent of the area of Australia. It has a coastline of some 6 200km on the Timor Sea, the ARAFURA SEA and the GULF OF CARPENTARIA. The S boundary with SA is defined by the 26th parallel of S latitude, the W boundary with WA is the meridian of 129°E longitude, and the E boundary with QLD is the 138°E meridian.
Landform features There are three main natural landform regions: the N coastal plains and plateaus, the central basins, and the S ranges and valleys.
   The N section consists of a low flat coastline of sandy beaches and mud-flats, thickly fringed with mangrove swamps, intersected by numerous rivers (such as the DALY, ADELAIDE, ALLIGATOR, VICTORIA and ROPER) and indented by bays and inlets. There are many offshore islands: BATHURST ISLAND, MELVILLE ISLAND, CROKER ISLAND, ELCHO ISLAND, the WESSEL ISLANDS, GROOTE EYLANDT and the Sir Edward Pellew Group. Inland from the coast there are low, but much dissected plateau areas: the BARKLY TABLELAND lying S of the GULF COUNTRY, ARNHEM LAND occupying the NE part of the NT, and the rugged land in the NW which forms the catchment basins for rivers draining to the Timor Sea.
   The central section of the NT consists of a vast belt of semi-arid country which becomes increasingly dry to the S and merges into the TANAMI DESERT on the W. It is a region of low elevation, broken by bare ridges and ranges,

with intermittent streams flowing only in wet seasons and shallow depressions which occasionally contain water. The Stuart Highway from Darwin through TENNANT CREEK to ALICE SPRINGS crosses this stretch of the arid inland on a N-S route.

The S part of the NT, commonly known as the CENTRE, includes a series of ranges, such as the MACDONNELL, MUSGRAVE, Petermann and James Ranges, with broad basins (for example, the LAKE AMADEUS basin) between them, and giant rock formations rising sheer above the surrounding countryside (such as AYERS ROCK, MOUNT OLGA and MOUNT CONNER). In the SE of this region is the SIMPSON DESERT. The FINKE RIVER drains SE from the MacDonnell Ranges towards LAKE EYRE in SA; other streams, such as the TODD RIVER, peter out in the desert.

Climate With the exception of a S strip about 300km wide, the whole of the NT lies in the tropics and hence experiences warm to hot conditions throughout the year. Rainfall decreases inland, varying from over 1 500mm in the humid coastal areas of the N to less than 250mm in the arid inland regions. Darwin has an average annual rainfall of 1 813mm, Tennant Creek receives 312mm and Alice Springs only 246mm. The NT has a two-season climate: a hot wet summer of up to five months and a warm markedly dry winter season. Darwin receives almost 90 per cent of its total yearly rainfall in the five months from November to March. This concentration of rain in the summer months, when onshore monsoonal winds often bring torrential downpours, is a characteristic feature of the NT, but the length of the wet season and the amount of rain which falls can vary greatly from year to year and from place to place.

Population The total population of the NT at the 1981 census was 124 500 (estimated resident population). The two major urban centres are Darwin (population 56 482 in 1981) and Alice Springs (18 395); the only other towns with over 3000 people are Nhulunbuy (4 138, the residential centre for the GOVE PENINSULA bauxite mining operations), KATHERINE (3 737) and Tennant Creek (3 118). Of the NT's total population, two-thirds are urban dwellers.

History The NT has presented the Commonwealth government with problems of great importance and difficulty. Firstly, although it is thinly inhabited, the task of developing it is complicated by its harsh climate and its distance from the more highly developed parts of the continent. Secondly, the composition of its population, which is nearly 30 per cent Aboriginal, presents the government with formidable challenges in eliminating racial discrimination and raising the status of Aborigines. Finally, the presence in the NT of most of Australia's deposits of uranium ore, in areas where the Aborigines claim traditional ownership of the land, has presented the government with the need to make major policy decisions.

Economic development from 1824 to 1945 The first British settlements in the NT were

A ceremony to mark the NT Centenary of Exploration 1960-1960

Courtesy of A.I.S. Canberra

made at Melville Is in 1824 and PORT ESSINGTON in 1838, but both were soon abandoned. Even after QLD became a separate colony, and the NT was therefore cut off from the main part of NSW, it remained for a few years officially part of the latter. Then, after the explorer John McDouall STUART had crossed the continent from Adelaide to the N coast, SA became interested in it, and in 1863 took over the administration. In 1869 the town of Palmerston (renamed Darwin in 1911) was established, and in 1872 the OVERLAND TELEGRAPH was completed between it and Adelaide.

In 1901 the Commonwealth government began negotiating the transfer of the NT from SA administration, but this was not completed until 1911. Economic development during the whole period of SA control had been extremely slow. A railway had been built from Darwin to PINE CREEK, and gold discoveries had been made at the latter town and other places. Rural industries, however, had failed to flourish, cattle raising being the only one of importance. The non-Aboriginal population in 1911 was only 3 310. Under Commonwealth administration development remained slow for a long time. However, with the extension of the railway S to Katherine, by 1939 the number of cattle had doubled, to reach about one million, and during the 1930s, defence and air transport installations brought an increase to Darwin's population. World War II brought about a great deal of construction. Two major sealed highways were built—the Stuart Highway, linking the railhead at Alice Springs with Darwin, and the Barkly Highway, running from MOUNT ISA in QLD to the Stuart Highway near Tennant Creek. The entry of Japan into the war caused a further increase in defence installations, and by early 1943 there were about 100 000 members of the armed

forces in the NT, their presence stimulating food production and service industries.

Economic development since 1945 Development has been more rapid since the war. Measures such as the building of 'beef roads' put the cattle industry on a more viable economic footing from the early 1960s until the slump of 1974. Mining has expanded greatly as the result of the discovery of uranium ore at RUM JUNGLE in 1948, of very large deposits of bauxite at Gove in 1951 and of lesser mineral deposits elsewhere. Recently, very large deposits of high-grade uranium ore have been found in the Ranger, Jabiluka, OENPELLI and NABARLEK locations in the Alligator Rivers area. Development of these deposits, however, was delayed pending the issuing of the two reports of the Fox inquiry in 1976 and 1977 into the mining and export of uranium. Further delays have occurred because of the need for public discussion in view of opposition by the Australian Labor Party, trade unions and environmentalists, and by the need for the mining companies and the government to negotiate with the Northern Land Council, a statutory body representing 16 000 Aborigines in 33 communities and groups who are the traditional owners of land needed for mining. The general development of the NT suffered a setback in December 1974 when a cyclone destroyed most of Darwin. However, the city has now been rebuilt.

Political development Before the Commonwealth took control, the people of the NT had taken part in SA elections and from 1901, as part of the electorate of Grey, had participated in federal elections. The transfer to the Commonwealth therefore brought a decrease in the political rights of the inhabitants of the NT, for the Territory had no legislature of its own and was not represented in the Commonwealth

Parliament. In 1922, however, they were given the right to elect one Member to the House of Representatives, and in 1974 the right to elect two Senators. In the meantime a Legislative Council had been set up in 1947, consisting of the Administrator, seven official Members and six elected Members. It was empowered to enact ordinances for 'the peace, order and good government of the Territory'. Such measures, however, were subject to the assent of the Administrator, while regulations regarding Crown lands and Aborigines were subject to 'the signification of the Governor-General's pleasure'—in other words, to approval by the Commonwealth government. In later years the Legislative Council was enlarged and the proportion of elected members increased, and in 1974 it was replaced by a fully elected Legislative Assembly. During the 1975 election campaign Prime Minister FRASER committed the Liberal and National Country Parties to a policy of full Statehood for the NT and, as a step towards this, it was given wide powers of self-government in 1978.

Norway, Neville Shute *see* Shute, Neville

Nothofagus *see* beech, southern; flora; fossils

Nowra NSW (combined population of Nowra and BOMADERRY 17 885 in 1981) A town in the ILLWARRA region of the S coast, located on the S bank of the SHOALHAVEN RIVER about 13km from its mouth, Nowra is 8m above sea level and 161km by road from Sydney on the Princes Highway. The town of Bomaderry, on the N bank of the river opposite Nowra, is the rail terminus of the S coast line, 153km from Sydney. Nowra receives an average rainfall of 1 153mm (February, the highest, 153mm average); summers are pleasantly warm, with hot days in January and February, and winters are mild. The district is noted for its dairying and there is a milk processing factory at Bomaderry. Vegetable growing on the plains and timber-getting in the adjacent hills are important. There is a large paper mill in the town and other small secondary industries such as agricultural machinery manufacturing and rubber products works. The Royal Australian Navy's Fleet Air Arm Base (HMAS *Albatross*) is located about 10km from Nowra. Along the nearby coast, there are many holiday resorts such as Greenwell Point, Crookhaven Heads, Culburra and Currarong. The Morton National Park (112 460ha), lying W of Nowra, includes the gorges and waterfalls, such as Belmore and Fitzroy, of the upper Shoalhaven. The town's name comes from the Aboriginal word meaning 'a black cockatoo'.

nudibranchs *see* gastropods

Nullagine WA A small inland township on the great Northern Highway 1 374km N of Perth and about 120km SE of MARBLE BAR,

Nullagine is situated on Nullagine Creek, a S tributary of the DE GREY RIVER in the PILBARA region. Founded as a gold-mining town in 1888, it still depends on mining (gold and antimony) in the area. At an elevation of 377m, it experiences very hot summer conditions (average maximum temperatures reach over 40°C in December and January) and an average annual rainfall of 326mm, concentrated in the summer months (January, the highest, 74mm average).

Nullarbor Plain SA/WA Extending from the SW part of SA for about 725km E-W into WA, and from the GREAT AUSTRALIAN BIGHT N for about 400km, it is called a plain, though in fact it is a limestone plateau with cliffs bordering the Bight shoreline, rising gently inland to elevations of about 180m. The precise land boundaries of the Nullarbor are ill-defined, but it probably covers an area of over 270 000km^2. It is a region of low rainfall—Cook SA, on the transcontinental railway, has an annual average of 165mm and EUCLA in WA, on the Eyre Highway near the SA border, receives 254mm. There is little surface water and there are no streams on the plain because most of the rainfall drains through the porous limestone, forming sink holes, tunnels and caverns. Apart from small hamlets on the transcontinental railway (160km inland) and along the Eyre Highway (near the coast), there are only scattered sheep stations on the margins of the plain. One section of the transcontinental railway across the plain extends for 478km in a straight route and is claimed as the longest stretch of straight railway line in the world. The name Nullarbor was given to the region by E. Alfred Delisser in 1866, derived from the Latin *nullus arbor* meaning 'no tree'.

A rail town on the Nullarbor Plain WA

numbat *see* native cats, etc.

numbfish *see* sharks, etc.

Numurkah VIC (population 2 713 in 1981) This country town is in the GOULBURN RIVER valley region of the N-central part of the State, 215km by rail N of Melbourne. Located N of SHEPPARTON on the Goulburn Valley Highway, it is 108m above sea level and receives an average annual rainfall of 453mm. The surrounding rural district is noted for dairying, fruit growing and livestock grazing; much of the land is irrigated and intensively developed. The area was occupied by squatters in the 1830s and opened for closer settlement in the

1880s; in recent decades the subdivision of large grazing holdings into smaller dairying and orcharding blocks has brought significant growth to the town. The name Numurkah comes from an Aboriginal word meaning 'war shield'.

Nuriootpa SA (population 2 851 in 1981) One of the main towns of the BAROSSA VALLEY, 72km by road from ADELAIDE, it is located in the N part of the North Para River valley. At an elevation of 274m, it experiences mild winter conditions, warm dry summers, and an average annual rainfall of 506mm concentrated mainly in winter. The climate is ideal for grape growing, and wine production is the main rural industry. The surrounding areas also produce vegetables, pigs, poultry, sheep and fruit. The name of the town comes from an Aboriginal word meaning literally 'the neck country', derived from a legend concerning the neck of a mythical being.

nut grass *see* Cyperaceae; weeds

Nuyts Archipelago SA This group of about 30 islands and rocky isles is located in the GREAT AUSTRALIAN BIGHT, SW of Denial and Smoky Bays; the largest of the group is St Peter's Is, 15km offshore from CEDUNA; the islands furthermost from the coast are called the Isles of St Francis. The group was named by Matthew FLINDERS in 1802 to honour the Dutch explorer Peiter Nuijts who sailed along this coast in 1627.

Nyngan NSW (population 2 485 in 1981) This small town is situated on the BOGAN RIVER at the junction of the Mitchell and Barrier Highways in the W plains region of the State, some 580km by road NW of Sydney. It is a railway junction (622km from Sydney) with one line extending NW to BOURKE and the other W to COBAR. At an elevation of 174m above sea level, it has an average annual rainfall of 425mm, with highest falls in the summer season. It experiences high summer temperatures and warm sunny winters, though the winter evenings can be crisply cool. The town is a service centre to a large rural district where livestock grazing and wheat farming dominate; the district boasts numerous sheep and cattle studs. To the N and E of Nyngan are a series of creeks, really large ANABRANCHES, which connect the Bogan to the MACQUARIE RIVER, and it is these creeks which indirectly provide the water supply for the mining town of Cobar, 32km W of Nyngan; water is diverted from the Macquarie River to storage areas in the Bogan near Nyngan by a 68km-long canal, then pumped along a pipeline to Cobar.

O

oak, swamp, forest and river *see* Casuarin-aceae

oak, silky *see* silky oak

Oakey QLD (population 2 857 in 1981) A small country town in the DARLING DOWNS region, on the Warrego Highway, Oakey is 29km NW of TOOWOOMBA, 83km SE of DALBY, and 160km W of Brisbane. At an elevation of 402m above sea level, it is located in a rural district where dairying, grain farming and livestock grazing are the principal primary industries. The area was first settled in the 1840s, but the town developed only when the railway arrived in the late 1860s. The town has a claim to horse racing fame, for the race-horse Bernborough, regarded as one of the best-bred horses in Australia, was raised locally and a statue of the horse now stands in the town.

Oatlands TAS (population 545 in 1981; municipal population 2 100) A small service town on the Midland Highway, 84km N of Hobart, on the shores of Lake Dulverton, it is listed as one of TAS's historic towns. Governor MACQUARIE named the site in 1821 because it reminded him of his native Scotland and the grain which grew there. It became a military base and a staging post between Hobart and LAUNCESTON. Much of the town's development took place in the 1830s and it is said that almost every resident lives in a historic building. The National Trust (TAS) has classified and listed many of these for pre-servation because of their architectural and historical importance.

Old Mill, Oatlands TAS

oats *see* agriculture; Gramineae

O'Brien, John *see* Hartigan, Patrick Joseph

O'Brien, Justin Maurice (1917-) Artist. Born in Hurstville NSW, O'Brien studied and taught painting in Sydney. He became a prisoner in Athens whilst serving with the Australian Army Medical Corps, and his imprisonment there and at Torun in Poland gave him the time to continue his art, which reflected a recently awakened interest in Byzantine religious subjects. On his return to Sydney as a repatriated POW in 1944, an exhibition of his POW work caused an immediate stir. To a country attuned to religious art of a decadent and sentimental variety, O'Brien's work had an astringent and timeless quality that appealed to many. His work shows a great concern for line, rather than modelling, while his rich colours and elongated figures are reminiscent of the paintings of Siena in the 15th century.

Ocean Grove VIC (combined population of Ocean Grove and BARWON HEADS 6 776 in 1981) This popular seaside holiday resort is on the E side of the BARWON RIVER estuary, 93km by road SW of Melbourne. Its twin town, on the opposite side of the river mouth, is Barwon Heads. Ocean Grove was founded as a Methodist settlement in 1887 and was given the same name as a similar settlement in New Jersey, USA. One of the main resort centres for Melbourne and GEELONG, it includes more than 3km of surf beach and opportunities for swimming, fishing and boating in the estuarine waters. In recent decades it has experienced rapid urban and commercial development.

O'Connor, Charles Yelverton (1843-1902) Engineer. At Victoria Quay, FREMANTLE, stands a life-size bronze statue of O'Connor, overlooking his first major engineering achievement—the start of Freman-tle Harbour. Born in Gravelmouth, County Meath in Ireland, he migrated in 1865 to New Zealand where he worked as a civil engineer until 1891 when he came to WA as Engineer-in-Chief of Public Works and Manager of Railways. To plan and construct a suitable harbour for the colony was his first major undertaking. He proposed the SWAN RIVER mouth as the site for this development and, though there was considerable opposition to his scheme, it was accepted and the work on Fremantle Harbour project started in 1892. Also in the early 1890s he was responsible for several railway developments—the rebuilding of the line through the DARLING RANGE and the extension of the route to SOUTHERN CROSS —but perhaps his most important project was the GOLDFIELDS WATER SUPPLY scheme, which included the building of MUNDARING RESERVOIR on the Helena River and the con-struction of pipelines to COOLGARDIE and KALGOORLIE. This proposal also met with much criticism and, although it stands as a tribute to his vision, O'Connor was not destined to see it completed. The strong opposition affected his health and he com-mitted suicide in 1902.

O'Connor, Raymond James (1926-) Premier of WA. He was born in Perth, served in Bougainville and New Britain during World War II, and in 1956 stood unsuccessfully as an independent candidate for election to the Legislative Assembly of WA. Shortly afterwards he joined the Liberal Party and gained election to the Legislative Assembly in 1959. He joined the Cabinet of Sir David BRAND in 1965, became deputy Premier to Sir Charles COURT in 1980, and when the latter resigned from Parliament in January 1982, succeeded him as Premier. Following the Labour victory of February 1983, he was suc-ceeded as Premier by Brian BURKE.

octopus *see* cephalopods

Odonata *see* damselflies, etc.

O'Dowd, Bernard Patrick (1866-1953) Poet. Born in Beaufort VIC, he graduated in arts and law from Melbourne University, became an assistant librarian in the Supreme Court library, and was later appointed Parliamentary Draftsman for VIC. As he explained in *Poetry Militant: An Austra-lian Plea for Poetry of Purpose* (1909), he believed that poetry needed to have social purpose and to deal with 'the real questions' of the era in which the poet lives. Accordingly, he used his own verse to develop his radical social and political views. While his early work is considered by some to be crude in style, his later poems are more lyrical in tone, and *The Bush* (1912) in particular was one of the most popular poems of its time. His published volumes of poetry include *Dawnward?* (1903), *The Silent Land and Other Verses* (1906), *The Bush* and *Selected Poems* (1928).
Further reading: Anderson, H.M. *The Poet Militant: Bernard O'Dowd.* Hill of Content, Melbourne, 1969.

Courtesy of A.I.S. Canberra
Class in progress at Oenpelli Primary School NT

Oenpelli NT (population 452 in 1981) This Anglican mission station is located near the East ALLIGATOR RIVER in the NW of ARNHEM LAND in a lowland area, only 7m above sea level, just W of the escarpment of the Spencer Range. The mission has fostered the development of tropical fruit and vegetable growing, cattle raising and buffalo hunting. Since the settlement lies within the Arnhem Land Aboriginal Reserve, it is closed to non-Aborigines unless they have special permission to enter. The climate is typical of the N regions, with a high annual rainfall of 1 360mm, but with distinct wet and dry seasons. The paintings by the Aborigines of this area, mainly by the Gunwinggu tribe, both on bark and in rock caves and shelters, are among the most distinctive in Australia; they illustrate tribal beliefs about how their people originated, they depict scenes from the myths and legends of the tribe and they tell the stories of spirit ancestors.

Ogilvie, William Henry (1869-1963) Poet. Born in Scotland, he came to Australia in 1889 and worked as a drover, horse breaker and general station hand. He wrote a number of bush ballads, romantic in style, most of which were first published in the *Bulletin*. The ballads later appeared in book form as *Fair Girls and Grey Horses* (1899) and *Hearts of Gold* (1903) and proved to be extremely popular. Ogilvie returned to Scotland in 1901, and later published many more volumes of verse and prose. Most of these were on Scottish themes, but he did write some poems with Australian themes, publishing them in 1916 under the title *The Australian and Other Verses*.

oil *see* minerals, etc.; petroleum, etc.

oil seeds *see* agriculture

old man's whiskers *see* Cyperaceae

Oliphant, Sir Mark (Marcus Laurence Elwin) (1901-) Physicist and Governor of SA. Born and educated in Adelaide, Sir Mark became a research student in 1927 at Cavendish Laboratory, Cambridge University which was then the centre of research in the new field of nuclear physics—the study of the structure of the atom. The director of the Cavendish was the New Zealand-born Nobel Prize winner, Ernest Rutherford, who had a profound influence on Oliphant. Together they discovered the nature of the nuclear reactions involving hydrogen, reactions that provide the energy of the sun.

In 1937 Oliphant became Professor of Physics at the University of Birmingham and while there was involved in two projects of great significance to the war effort—the development of microwave radar and moves to harness the destructive power of nuclear fission. During the later years of World War II, he took up residence in the USA as a member of the Manhattan Project team that produced the atomic bomb. He was opposed to the use of the bomb against civilian targets and after the war became associated with the Pugwash Movement, a group of scientists formed by Bertrand Russell to warn of the dangers of the nuclear arms race.

Oliphant was one of a number of prominent Australian academics living in Britain who guided the Australian government in the founding of the Australian National University. The group included FLOREY and Hancock but only Oliphant was prepared to take up a post at the new university, becoming foundation director of the Research School of Physical Sciences, a post which he held from 1950 to 1963. He was also very prominent in moves that led to the establishment of the Australian Academy of Science and was its first president. In 1959 he was made a KBE; he was appointed Governor of SA in 1971 (and remained in this post until 1976), and was made a Companion of the Order of Australia in 1977.

Olsen, John (1928-) Artist. Born in NEWCASTLE in NSW, Olsen studied at Julian ASHTON's Sydney Art School. His strong criticism of artistic standards in Sydney was shown in his involvement with the anti-ARCHIBALD PRIZE demonstration at the Art Gallery of New South Wales in 1953. Paul Haefliger, a Sydney art critic, recognised Olsen's talent and helped raise money to send him to Europe where, amongst other things, he worked on engravings with S.W. Hayter at Atelier 17 in Paris. On his return to Australia he exhibited with the 'Sydney Nine' exhibition of 1961 and made his mark as one of the more creative and stimulating painters of Sydney.

Olsen's works are readily identifiable by the spidery and seemingly irrational scrawl which alternately jerks and flows on a background of changing colour densities and tones. Olsen believes that the act of creation is the result of many experiences at many levels; it cannot be achieved by a slavish application of rules but rather from a free-wheeling experience that draws from both the objective and subjective world, hence combining several different levels of experience. This attitude towards painting has been greatly influenced by his teacher, John PASSMORE.

Olympic Games The man largely responsible for the revival of the modern era of Olympic Games was Baron Pierre de Coubertin. Although not a sportsman himself, his desire to revive the Olympics was inspired by two things: the camaraderie he witnessed in sporting groups and the excavation in the late 1880s of the original ancient Olympic site. He felt that bringing together the athletes of the world would engender peace and brotherhood, and to forward this aim he invited representatives of national sporting organisations to an athletic congress in 1894 where he put forward his proposal of holding a trial Games. The proposal was eventually accepted and the first Games of the modern era took place in Athens in 1896. Since that time the Games have been held every fourth year with the exception of the years during the two world wars.

Australia is one of only three countries to have taken part in every Olympic Games since 1896—the other two are the UK and Greece—and at only one Games since that time, that of 1904, did Australia fail to win a medal.

Outstandingly successful on the basis of population, Australian successes reached a peak at the Melbourne Olympics in 1956 when Australians won 13 gold medals, eight silver and 13 bronze to be placed third overall, behind the USSR and the USA.

With regard to the 1980 Moscow Olympics, the Australian government requested that the Australian Olympic Federation not send a team to Moscow. When pressed as to whether the request was a directive not to go, the government replied that it could not so direct in a democracy. The Federation therefore ignored the request and prepared to send a team, while the government exerted considerable pressure on sporting groups and individuals not to go. The equestrian team, the men's hockey team and the yachting team withdrew, as did a few individuals from other sports. The eventual representation was by 176 members in 15 sports.
See also Appendix 8, Australian Medallists in Olympic Games

Ombudsman The SA government established the first office of Ombudsman in 1972 and since then the VIC, NSW and TAS governments have established similar offices. In QLD and WA there is a Parliamentary Commissioner for Administrative Investigations who performs similar functions. The federal government appointed Professor Jack Richardson as its first Ombudsman, and he took up office on 1 July 1977.

The federal Ombudsman is an official appointed by the Crown under the Ombudsman Act to investigate, informally and in private, complaints about actions of government departments and certain prescribed government authorities. The executive powers of the government have greatly extended in scope and direction and, as no administration is perfect, it is inevitable that mistakes are made. Any member of the public, a company, an organisation or an association may complain to the Ombudsman about an action relating to a matter of administration which may involve a decision or recommendation made by the administration; or it may involve failure or refusal to take any action or to make a decision or recommendation.

The Ombudsman has the right to examine files and other records held by a department or authority relating to a complaint. He may also enter government premises, take evidence on oath, and recommend remedies, where appropriate, to the department, authority or Minister concerned. If he is not satisfied that adequate remedial action is taken as a result he may report directly to the Prime Minister and the Parliament.

Omeo VIC (population 272 in 1981) This small township is located on the headwaters of the MITTA MITTA RIVER where the Alpine Road meets the Omeo Highway, at an elevation of 649m above sea level, near the section of the GREAT DIVIDING RANGE called Bowen Mts. Situated amidst picturesque highland scenery, it began as a goldfields town in the 1850s and is now the centre of a rich grazing district. The name Omeo comes from an Aboriginal word meaning 'mountains'.

Onslow WA (population 594 in 1981) A small township on the NW coast, Onslow is some 20km NE of the ASHBURTON RIVER estuary, 80km W of the North West Coastal Highway and 1 360km by road N of Perth. The original town site was proclaimed in 1883 and it developed as a port and service town for sheep raising and gold mining in the Ashburton region and for pearling luggers. During World War II it was a submarine refuelling base for the US Navy. It is now the depot for sea cargo services to the commercial oil field on BARROW ISLAND.

Oodnadatta SA Located in the arid mid-N of the State, on the PORT AUGUSTA-ALICE SPRINGS railway line, NW of LAKE EYRE, this small settlement was the railhead of the central Australia railway until 1929 when the line was extended to Alice Springs. At an elevation of 113m above sea level, the township has an average annual rainfall of only 155mm, though this is highly variable from year to year. The name Oodnadatta comes from the Aboriginal word meaning 'the yellow flower of the mulga tree'.

opals Australia, the world's major producer of opals, supplies more than 90 per cent of these gem stones to the world market. The main centres of production are LIGHTNING RIDGE in NSW, and COOBER PEDY and ANDAMOOKA in SA; less important centres are White Cliffs in the far NW of NSW (a major producer in former times), the WINTON, QUILPIE and CUNNAMULLA districts in QLD, and near KALGOORLIE in WA. Even though they are located in the desolate arid interior of the continent, the opal mining areas have become popular tourist attractions where visitors can try their luck at fossicking and perhaps purchase stones from the local miners.
Further reading: Colahan, J. *Australian Opal Safari.* Rigby, Adelaide, 1973. O'Leary, B.A. *A Field Guide to Australian Opals.* Rigby, Adelaide, 1977.

opera Since the earliest period of white settlement Australians have displayed conspicuous skill in performing opera and equally conspicuous relish in witnessing it. According to COVELL, Australian performers seem to be able to tap a source of emotionalism nearer to the surface than most of their British counterparts, and as political or cultural colonials, they have had the constant incentive of having to prove themselves in the major European and American scenes of operatic activity. The large number of talented Australian SINGERS in opera has often been the subject of comment. It has been attributed to such factors as Australia's warm climate, Australian nasal habits of speech and the national liking for the demonstration of sporting ability.

This particular approach to opera was fostered in the aria competitions of the early eisteddfods, and to this day has continued to generate excitement in the respective aria competitions sponsored by the Sydney *Sun* newspaper, the Melbourne *Sun-Pictorial* and by the Shell Oil Co. in Canberra. The now legendary Mobil Quest, also sponsored by an oil company, used radio between 1949 and 1957 to broadcast these competitions to a wide listening audience and gave financial assistance

Looking for opals at Lightning Ridge NSW

to prize winners to enable them to travel and study abroad.
Singers and conductors On the whole, Australians have preferred their opera singers to make their reputation elsewhere before returning to receive the applause of their fellow countrymen. This has also been related to an earlier lack of continuous permanent employment for opera singers in the country; the popularity of the soprano Marilyn Richardson, who has worked almost entirely in Australia, proves an exception in current times.

The careers of Dame Nellie MELBA and Dame Joan SUTHERLAND are the most conspicuous examples of Australian singers who have attained international fame through study and achievement overseas. Other prominent Australian singers of the 19th and 20th centuries include Marie Burgess (Madame Carandini), Mrs Wallace-Bushelle (sister of the composer William Vincent Wallace), Eliza WINSTANLEY, Amy Sherwin ('the Tasmanian Nightingale'), Frances Alda, Florence AUSTRAL, John BROWNLEE, Marjorie LAWRENCE, Joan HAMMOND, Elsie Morison, Marie Collier, June BRONHILL, Yvonne MINTON and Donald SMITH. Two sopranos who distinguished themselves particularly in the lighter forms of opera and operetta were Nellie STEWART and Gladys MONCRIEFF.

Australian operatic conductors of distinction include such immigrants as Alberto Zelman (who arrived with a touring opera company in 1871), Gustav Slapoffski and the former Vienna Boys' Choir member, Georg Tintner. Australian-born conductors include Joseph Post, Denis Vaughan and Charles MACKERRAS.
Performance Accepting the contemporary English description of opera as a drama in spoken dialogue with plenty of songs, operatic performance in Australia dates back to at least 1796, when *The Poor Soldier* (words by John O'Keefe, music by William Shield) was performed in Sydney. Ballad operas were also popular in the early decades of the 19th century, and at least seven operas (including Sir Henry Bishop's production of Mozart's *The Marriage of Figaro*) were performed at Barnett LEVEY's Theatre Royal in Sydney in 1833. In the 1840s the Italian opera began to dominate, with performances of Rossini's *The Barber of Seville* (1843) and Rossini's *Cenerentola* (Cinderella) in 1846. Contemporary records also confirm the performance of Weber's *Der Freischütz* at the Royal Victoria Theatre in Pitt Street in 1845.

Prominent promoters at this time included George COPPIN, who organised a Melbourne opera season in 1856, and William Saurin Lyster, who arrived with his own company in 1861 and spent most of the following 20 years bringing to Australians works by Rossini, Donizetti, Bellini, Meyerbeer, Verdi, Wagner and many other composers. It would seem these companies attained quite high singing standards. Often Lyster presented the newest works of Verdi and others within a few years of their first performances in Europe.

Other promoters also continued to organise opera seasons throughout the latter half of the 19th century. These included Martin Simonsen and his wife Fannie (from 1887 to 1895), Annis Montague and Charles Turner (early 1880s) and George Musgrove (first season in Sydney in 1881). One Australian-based promoter, Luscombe Searelle, took his company to South Africa in 1889, performing at the Johannesburg goldfields and transporting from Australia a prefabricated iron theatre. James WILLIAMSON, an American actor-turned manager, presented his first performance of Gilbert and Sullivan light opera in 1879. In 1893 he and George Musgrove staged an ambitious season which included the then new operas of *Cavalleria Rusticana* and *Pagliacci*. The Melba-Williamson touring company of 1911 was succeeded by a series of successful imported touring companies which continued under Williamson's name long after his death, and which ended with the Sutherland-Williamson company of 1965. Another remarkable instance of entrepreneurial adventure in Australian opera was the visit in 1912, and again in 1913, of a company organised by an Irish promoter, Thomas Quinlan. This company visited Australia in the course of two world tours with 200 singers, chorus and orchestra. There were more than 3000 costumes and 300 tons of scenery, and the repertoire included Offenbach's *Tales of Hoffmann*, Wagner's *Tristan and Isolde*, Debussy's *The Prodigal Son*, Puccini's *Manon Lescaut* and *The Girl of the Golden West* and Wagner's *The Mastersingers* and *The Ring of the Nibelung*.

Growth of Australian-based opera The 1930s were a bad time for theatre in general and, because of opera's expense, for opera in particular. The Depression, the first boom of sound-track films and the imposition of a crippling entertainment tax combined to dampen theatrical enterprise, with the notable exception of the company brought in by Sir Benjamin Fuller in 1934-35 to celebrate Melbourne's centenary. Nevertheless, the drop in operatic traffic from overseas seems to have stimulated what can now be seen as the beginnings of permanent resident opera on a nationally and locally subsidised basis. In 1935 Gertrude Johnson, an experienced Australian soprano who had sung regularly at Covent Garden, set up the National Theatre Movement. A comparable enterprise began in Sydney in 1951 at the instigation of Clarice Lorenz, and it eventually became known as the National Opera of Australia.

The growth of operatic activity was stimulated in 1956 when the Australian Elizabethan Theatre Trust formed a national touring company which was able to call on the orchestral resources of the ABC. The formation of an independently governed Australian Opera in 1970 with increased government and private support inaugurated an era in which it came to be regarded as a national institution which was as worthy of support as museums or art galleries. Since the opening of SYDNEY OPERA HOUSE in 1973, the Australian Opera has made its home there, while continuing to tour other States. The healthy element of rivalry

Scene from Wagner's 'The Mastersingers' at Sydney Opera House

between the States and the inability of the Australian Opera to travel throughout the whole country encouraged the formation and support of regional opera companies in SA, VIC, QLD and WA. These companies, along with other active university and conservatoire-based companies, such as the University of New South Wales Opera, have led to a greater variety in Australia's operatic life and to the ability to present lesser known works without the financial considerations imposed on a large national company. Most important, they have also pioneered works by Australian composers (*see* MUSICAL COMPOSITION, etc.), many of whom have shown a marked talent and preference for operatic composition.

Further reading: Covell, R. *Australia's Music: Themes of a New Society*. Sun Books, Melbourne, 1967; Mackenzie, B. & Mackenzie, F. *Singers of Australia: From Melba to Sutherland*. Lansdowne, Melbourne, 1967; Cargher, J. *Opera and Ballet in Australia*. Cassell, Sydney, 1977; Love, H. *The Golden Age of Australian Opera: W.S. Lyster and his Companies, 1861-1880*. Currency Press, Sydney, 1981.

Opera House *see* Sydney Opera House

Opperman, Sir Hubert Ferdinand (1904-) Cyclist and politician. Born in ROCHESTER in VIC, he excelled in all types of road cycling events and was to dominate distance and endurance racing throughout the 1920s and 1930s. He won the Australian Road championship in 1924, 1926, 1927 and 1929, during which time he also achieved international fame by scoring brilliant wins in a variety of events of Europe. In 1928 he won the French Bol D'Or and was named Athlete of the Year by a Paris newspaper. He won the Paris-Brest-Paris event in 1931 and captained the Australian team in the Tour de France from 1928 to 1931. In 1934 he won the English Bidlake Memorial Prize. Possessed of fierce and courageous determination, he set a number of endurance records, including the world unpaced track record of 489 miles, the world unpaced road record of 505¾ miles, the world motor-paced record for 24 hours of 860 miles and the motor-paced record for 1000 miles which took him 28 hours and 55 minutes of continuous cycling. He became a Member of the House of Representatives in 1949 for

the seat of CORIO in VIC and held that seat until 1967. In the period 1960-63 he was Minister for Shipping and Transport, and from 1963 to 1966 he held the Immigration portfolio. On retirement from politics he was appointed Australian High Commissioner in Malta, a position he held from 1967 to 1972. He received his knighthood in 1968.

Orange NSW (population 27 625 in 1981) A city in the central W region of the State, Orange is located on the Mitchell Highway and on the main W railway, 262km by road and 323km by rail W of Sydney. At an elevation of 868m above sea level, it is situated in gently undulating hill land; Mt Canobolas, an extinct volcanic dome 1 396m above sea level, is about 14km SE of Orange. The city experiences an invigorating climate, with warm to hot summer conditions and cool to cold winters in which it is not uncommon for snow to fall on Mt Canobolas and even occasionally on Orange itself. The average annual rainfall is 876mm, spread fairly uniformly throughout the year, with June the month of lowest rainfall, and the three summer months, December to February, the period of highest rainfall. It is a busy commercial centre serving a rich rural district producing sheep, cattle, pigs, potatoes, fruit (especially apples and cherries), wheat, oats, vegetables and dairy produce. It is an important stock-selling centre and has a wide variety of secondary industries—woollen mills, abattoirs, timber mills, an ice cream factory, engineering workshops and brick and tile works. There is a co-operative cool-store for fruit, though recent trends in the orcharding industry have been for owners to install their own cool-stores on their properties, as well as to develop irrigation for their orchards from dams and boreholes. There is a base hospital in the city, a psychiatric hospital at Bloomfield some 4km S, an agricultural college and a wide variety of sporting and recreation facilities.

Orange was named by Surveyor-General Thomas MITCHELL in the 1820s after the Prince of Orange (later the King of Holland) with whom Mitchell had served in the Peninsular War in Spain. It was gazetted as a township in 1846 and became a busy centre in the gold-rush days of the 1850s when gold was found at several places in the district (Ophir 26km NE, Lucknow 10km SE). In 1877 the railway from Sydney reached Orange, in 1885 it was proclaimed a town and in 1946 it became a city. In the 1970s, plans were made for the BATHURST-Orange area to be developed as a major inland urban centre with a population of 300 000. Among the tourist attractions of the area are the Banjo PATERSON Memorial obelisk, 3km NE of the city, marking the birthplace of the famous poet; Mt Canobolas Park, 14km SE, a sanctuary for native flora and fauna; Dewcrisp orchard, 4km W, where visitors can inspect the orchard operations; the cherry blossom festival held annually in October; and the Ophir goldfields where the historic mine tunnels can be visited and where visitors can try their luck fossicking

Winter snowfall in the Central Tablelands Orange district

for alluvial gold. A large number of buildings in Orange have been listed by the National Trust (NSW) for preservation, and among those classified as especially important are St Joseph's Catholic Church, the Anglican Church, the public school and residence, the courthouse, the post office, Cook Park and Duntry League Country Club.

Oraparinna SA A barytes-mining centre on the E edge of the N FLINDERS RANGES, Oraparinna is over 450km N of Adelaide. It is the headquarters of the Flinders Ranges National Park. The name Oraparinna is an Aboriginal word meaning 'a creek with tea trees'. Copper, phosphate and asbestos were formerly mined in the area and visitors can inspect the old workings.

Orban, Desiderius (1884-) Artist. Born in Gyor, Hungary, Orban was one of a number of European artists who came to Australia in the 1930s. An early interest in art, nurtured by his mother, led him to study in Paris on completion of his military service. He joined 'The Eights', a group of Hungarian artists who had worked in Paris. Their first exhibition in Budapest introduced Hungary to the work of artists influenced by the Cubists and the Fauvists, as well as by Matisse, Picasso and Cézanne. In 1931 he founded the Arts-Crafts Academy, which became the most important art school in Budapest. Orban migrated in 1939 to Australia, where he became well known as a teacher, artist and lecturer. Retrospective exhibitions were held at NEWCASTLE Regional Art Gallery in 1969 and at the Art Gallery of New South Wales in 1975; also in 1975, Orban was made an OBE. In 1982, the Hungarian government honoured Orban by making him a Member of the Order of the Hungarian Flag. In early 1983, at the age of 98, though his vision was somewhat impaired, he was still painting. Orban has always believed strongly in the need for the artist to listen to his creative imagination, and to avoid hiding behind rules and traditions. His own work shows a fascination for structure and form, and is expressed in richly coloured low tones.

Orbost VIC (population 2 586 in 1981) This small rural service centre is located in E GIPPSLAND on the SNOWY RIVER, 16km upstream from its mouth, 380km E of Melbourne on the Princes Highway and 64km by road E of

LAKES ENTRANCE. At an elevation of 45m above sea level, situated on the alluvial coastal plain, it experiences a mild climate with warm to hot summers and cool winters. The average annual rainfall is 839mm, spread throughout the year. Dairying, fodder crop cultivation, market gardening and timber-getting are important in the surrounding rural regions. Orbost is the terminus of the Gippsland railway, 372km from Melbourne.

Orchidaceae This very large family of monocotyledonous flowering plants contains about 700 genera and 17 500 species. Genera of orchids are equally well represented worldwide in both tropical and temperate zones, but the number of actual species present in the tropics is far larger than in temperate zones. Orchids are amongst the most prized of horticultural plants: selected cultivars and hybrids of many species are grown in hot-houses all over the world, and easily cultivated specimens of genera such as *Cymbidium* are included in every orchid enthusiast's collection. The popularity of orchids can probably be attributed to their diverse flower form and colour, their exotic and fragile appearance, and to the length of life of the cut flowers. While some species have delicate scents, this is lacking in most of the popularly cultivated types.

Spider orchid, *Caladenis* species

Orchids are herbaceous perennial herbs which are rooted in the soil (terrestrial) or grow on fallen wood or trees (epiphytic); although most species are free-living, some terrestrial species obtain their food from dead or decaying plants (SAPROPHYTIC). Terrestrial and saprophytic species have fleshy root-like underground stems (rhizomes) or tubers. Some epiphytes have creeping rhizomes with fibrous roots; the roots have a spongy covering (velamen) which absorbs water from the air. Other epiphytic species have erect stems and no rhizomes; the region between the nodes on the stem is often swollen and bulb-like and is known as a pseudobulb. The leaves are alternate or basal and are sometimes reduced to scales. The flowers of all species have three sepals and three petals. The petals alternate with the sepals; one petal, often called the lip (labellum) and normally the lowest part of the flower, is generally different in shape, size and colour from the other two. In the developing bud the lip is the uppermost petal but as the flower grows it twists through 180°. The centre of the flower contains a club-like structure (column) which has been formed by the

fusion of the stigma, the style and the stamen (most orchids have only one stamen). The stigma is usually concave and consists of three lobes which are fused; the upper margin of the stigma forms a platform-like appendage (rostellum). The ovary is inferior; the ovules develop on the ridges inside the ovary. The seed pod contains numerous minute seeds.

Flowers may be spotted, striped or of two contrasting colours, with the speals and lateral petals of one colour and the labellum of another colour. Flower colours include clear yellows, cream, white, all shades of pink, green, dark—almost black—reds and also unusual clear blues.

Pink fingers orchid, *Caladenia carnea*

Most orchids are pollinated by insects or birds; several species of orchids have evolved a very close relationship with a single species of insect whereby the flower is so similar to the female insect that the male tries to mate with it. The pollen grains at the top of the stamen (anther) are grouped into waxy clumps (pollinia). The bodies of insects or birds pick up the sticky liquid which covers the rostellum; the pollinia then stick to the insect or bird and are carried from flower to flower.

The terrestrial orchids of the heaths, woodlands and open forests of temperate Australia have delighted generations of bush lovers, and their varied flower shapes have given rise to a wealth of most descriptive names. These dainty species include the spider orchid (*Caladenia* species), the rabbit orchid, *C. menziesii*, the cow orchid, *Cryptostylis subulata*, the duck orchid (*Caleana* species), the donkey orchid, *Diurus longifolia*, the nanny goat orchid, *D. laevis*, the beard orchid (*Calochilus* species), the sun orchid (*Thelymitra* species), the greenhood orchid (*Pterostylis* species), the leek orchid (*Prasophyllum* species), the gnat orchid (*Acianthus* species) and the helmet orchid (*Corybas* species). The stout leafless spikes of the pink hyacinth orchid, *Dipodium punctatum*, and the brown potato orchid, *Gastrodia sesamoides*, are also found in this region.

Epiphytic orchids are abundant in the tropical region, though a few species also occur in the closed forests of the temperate region. The largest Australian genus is *Dendrobium*, though many other genera, including *Liparis, Papillilabium, Sarcochilus* and *Bulbophyllum*, are also present. Whilst some epiphytic species are large-leaved and showy, others are so tiny that a lens is necessary to view the flowers. Foliage varies from a broad-leaved tuft, such as that displayed by the rock orchid, *Dendrobium speciosum*, to the thick short tongue-like leaves of *D. linguiforme* or the almost leafless masses of bead-like pseudobulbs of *Bulbophyllum minutissmum*.

See also Angiospermae; Appendix 5, Flower Structure and Glossary of Botanical Terms
Further reading: see Appendix 6, A Bibliography for Plants.

Ord River WA Located in the far N of the State, it rises in the E KIMBERLEYS, and flows first E then generally N to the E arm of Cambridge Gulf. Some tributaries, such as the Denham and Bow Rivers, have their source in the Durack Range; others rise in the Carr-Boyd Range; and some from the E, such as the Behn and Negri, rise in the NT near the NT/WA border. The whole catchment basin covers an area of more than 41 000km². The region experiences a tropical climate with a distinct wet season which usually commences in November or December, but can start as early as October or as late as January. The wettest months are January, February and March when tropical rainstorms and occasional cyclonic storms occur. During the wet season these storms can lead to major flooding, particularly on the alluvial flats of the lower stream. There is a marked dry season of at least six months between April and November. Rainfall inland is lower than that in areas nearer the coast; HALL'S CREEK, located on a headwater tributary, has an average annual rainfall of 469mm, while KUNUNURRA, on the downstream flood plain, receives 787mm.

The potential of the Ord Valley for irrigated agriculture was first recognised in the 1930s, and in the 1940s a research station was established to carry out experiments on the alluvial soils of the flood plain. Also, surveys were made of suitable dam sites and studies undertaken of farming possibilities. From these came the Ord River irrigation project, comprising a major storage dam, a diversion dam, an irrigation area and a new township. Work on the scheme commenced in 1960; by 1963 the diversion dam, built at Bandicoot Bar (a natural quartzite sill in the river bed), was completed, the township of Kununurra had been established to the E of the lower river (106km by road SE of WYNDHAM), and the first 30 irrigated farms had been allocated. The construction of the major storage dam, located where the Ord enters the Carr-Boyd Range (about 160km SE of Wyndham and 48km upstream from the diversion dam), commenced in 1969 and was officially opened in 1972. It is called the Ord River dam and its principal function is to hold a large quantity of water in storage and release it in a controlled manner to keep the Kununurra diversion dam full. The water body created by the Ord River dam, called Lake Argyle, has a volume of

Lake Argyle with the Ord Dam, middle right

5 658 000ML, covers a surface area of over 740km² and is the largest man-made lake in Australia.

Despite the availability of irrigation water and the agricultural trials conducted at the Kimberley research station, the scheme has been beset by numerous difficulties. It was at first thought that cotton would be the main crop, but insect pests were a major problem and, although aerial spraying was tried, cotton growing proved unsuccessful. Other problems that have been encountered are that the soils in the irrigation area require heavy applications of nitrogen and phosphate fertilisers, and careful farm management is needed, particularly in relation to the time of planting, irrigating, fertiliser application and harvesting, to produce good yields. Rice, oil seeds and grain sorghum have been grown, and some irrigated pastures for cattle fattening have been developed. A further problem which any form of commercial agriculture faces is the remoteness of the area and great distances to markets.

The discovery of diamonds in 1979 at Smoke Creek, a tributary of the Ord which drains into the SW corner of Lake Argyle, may be an important factor in the future development of the region. The field has proved to be a major strike, claimed as the world's biggest (based on 'grades'—the number of carats of diamonds for each tonne of kimberlite rock), and in late 1981 it was regarded as sufficiently important to arouse considerable speculation about the impact the field could have on world diamond trade.

By early 1983, Argyle Diamond Mines (the joint venture company), had extracted 800 000 carats of diamonds, with the largest stone being an eight carat diamond classified as gem quality; both the size of the field and its high grades (up to 26.5 carats to the tonne) had by then been confirmed and plans were being made so as to produce between 20 and 25 million carats of diamonds a year.

Further reading: Ord Irrigation Project. Public Works Department, Perth, 1973; *Water Supplies and Irrigation*. Public Works Department, Perth, 1975.

Order of St John This voluntary charitable organisation is strongly established in Australia. It derives its title from the medieval Order of St John which maintained hospitals for pilgrims and also included knights who fought against the Turks. The medieval badge, featuring an eight-pointed star, was derived from that of the Italian city-state of Amalfi, merchants from which founded a famous hospice in Jerusalem in the year 1050. When the modern English Order was founded as a charitable organisation in 1831, it added two lions and two unicorns to the medieval badge. The Franco-Prussian War of 1870 made the Order's leaders aware of the need for trained first-aid workers, and so in 1877-78 it set up the St John Ambulance Association to teach first-aid and the St John Ambulance Brigade for those who had completed such training. At about the same time it established a hospital in Jerusalem. In 1888 Queen Victoria granted it a Charter, making it a British Royal Order of Chivalry.

The Order became established in Australia in the 1880s. Since 1949 it has been under the control of its own central governing body, the Priory. The Governor-General is the Prior, and the Governor of each State a deputy Prior. Its work is carried out under the direction of State Councils through the St John Ambulance Association, the St John Ambulance Brigade and the Hospitallers. The Association is the recognised authority for teaching first-aid to the general public and industry, and for issuing first-aid certificates. The Brigade consists of several thousand voluntary workers, including girls and boys, who put their first-aid training to practical use by serving at public gatherings. They are intended also to provide a reserve for the medical services of the Defence Force and for service at times of natural disaster. The Hospitallers assist in financing the Order's famous opthalmic hospital in Jerusalem.

orienteering This sport was introduced into Australia in 1969 and is gaining a reputation as an enjoyable way of keeping fit for the individual or for the whole family. Orienteering involves finding the way around a defined course with the aid of a compass and map, in as short a time as possible. To make sure each runner completes the prescribed course, there are a number of control points around the course marked with flags. Each control point has a pair of punch pliers which competitors must use to mark their score cards. As each punch puts a unique stamp on to the score cards, officials can tell if a competitor has toured the complete course. The governing body for the sport is the Orienteering Federation of Australia, which in late 1977 organised Australia's first international orienteering carnival at BALLARAT in VIC, attracting competitors from 10 countries. With an increasing emphasis being placed on exercise and physical fitness throughout Australia, orienteering seems assured of a successful and popular future.

orioles and figbirds These PASSERINE BIRDS belong to an Old World and Australian family, Oriolidae. Their flight is usually undulating and their diet consists of insects and fruit, especially figs. There are three Australian species, two orioles and one figbird.

Southern figbird, *Sphecotheres rieilloti*

The orioles are yellow or yellowish-green; both species are rather drab compared with some exotic species. The olive-backed oriole, *Oriolus sagittatus* (25cm to 28cm long), has streaked underparts, while the yellow oriole. *O. flavocinctus* (25cm to 28cm), is plain below, The former lives in woodlands in north-eastern WA, the NT, QLD, eastern NSW, VIC and south-eastern SA, and often flies high above the trees; the yellow oriole is found in wet forests and mangroves in N Australia. Both species have melodious songs.

Male figbirds, *Sphecotheres viridis* (28cm), are far more attractive than the females. While the female is mainly brown, the male has a black head, a greenish back, a black and white tail, patches of red skin on the face and a yellow or green belly. They live in forests, woodlands

Yellow oriole, *Oriolus flavocinctus*

and orchards, in the far N, and in SE QLD and eastern NSW.

Orthodox Churches In the census returns of 1981, the religious category 'Orthodox' included over 421 000 people, or about 2.9 per cent of the Australian population. A heavy majority of them were in NSW and VIC, with strong concentrations in certain suburban areas of Sydney and Melbourne. The total number showed a great increase over the preceding two or three decades, mainly because of immigration from Greece, and to a lesser extent from parts of E Europe.

The classification 'Orthodox' covers members of a number of Churches which, although they operate independently, share common beliefs, forms of worship and organisational features. All hold in particular respect the Archbishop of Constantinople (Istanbul), who has the title of 'Ecumenical Patriarch'. However, his actual authority does not extend beyond his own patriarchate, or province, of the Greek Orthodox Church, except for certain areas, including Australia, where that area's Church is considered to be in a 'mission' situation. All Orthodox Churches trace their origin back to the split in 1054 between the E and W branches of Christianity; the split was based partly on questions of belief, especially as regards the nature of the Trinity, but also on regional differences of outlook and the refusal of E Christians to accept the claims to supremacy of the Pope, or Bishop of Rome.

In Australia the vast majority of Orthodox Christians belong to the Greek Orthodox Church, and most of the remainder to the Russian Orthodox Church. However, there are also adherents of other Churches, including the Antiochan, Bulgarian, Romanian, Serbian, Syrian and Ukrainian, as well as small groups of Armenians and others who are accustomed to calling themselves Orthodox, but have not been in communion with the main body of Orthodoxy for many centuries. In 1979 the Greek, Serbian, Romanian, Russian and Antiochan Orthodox Churches formed a Standing Conference of Canonical Orthodox Churches in Australia.

The Greek Orthodox Church The first Greek Orthodox church was built in Sydney in 1898 and the first in Melbourne in 1900. Growth remained slow until the beginning of large-scale Greek immigration after World War II. In 1959 Australia and New Zealand were made an archdiocese (the area under the direction of an Archbishop), but New Zealand was detached from it in 1970. In 1983 there were under the authority of the Archdiocese 101 churches and monasteries and over 100 priests. The hierarchy included the Primate, Archbishop Stylianos and assistant Bishops in Melbourne and Adelaide. The Archdiocese was still under the jurisdiction of the Patriarchate of Constantinople. However, because of controversy over matters of Church organisation, some Greek Orthodox communities and their churches have formed the Independent (Autocephalic) Archdiocese of Australia, and do not acknowledge the authority of the official Archdiocese.

See also Greeks in Australia
Further reading: Eastern Orthodoxy in Australia. Australian Council of Churches, Sydney, 1966; van Sommers, T. 'The Orthodox Churches' in *Religions in Australia.* Rigby, Adelaide, 1966.

Orthoptera *see* crickets, etc.

O'Shanassy, Sir John (1818-83) Premier of VIC. Born in County Tipperary, Ireland, he emigrated to the PORT PHILLIP BAY district in 1839, and after farming for a short time at WESTERN PORT BAY opened a drapery business in Melbourne. He became prominent in the movement for the separation of the Port Phillip District from NSW and as an opponent of transportation; when the colony of VIC was formed in 1851 he was elected to the Legislative Council. During the troubles leading up to the EUREKA STOCKADE rebellion he showed sympathy for the miners and was a member of a committee which in 1853 recommended the modification of the licence fee which was the root cause of disaffection on the goldfields. He was also a member of the committee which drew up the Constitution of VIC and on the advent of responsible government in 1856 was elected to the Legislative Assembly. During the confused power struggles that preceded the formation of fairly stable political groupings, he was Premier on three occasions—for seven weeks in 1857 and for longer periods in 1858-59 and 1861-63. He served in the Legislative Council from 1868 to 1874, returned to the Lower House in 1877 and retired only shortly before his death.

Patricia O'Shane

O'Shane, Patricia (1941-) Barrister and public administrator. Born at Mossman,

QLD, she was educated in CAIRNS and at the Brisbane Teachers' College, becoming the first Aboriginal woman teacher in QLD. She later studied Law at the University of Sydney, graduating LLB, and in 1978 became the first Aboriginal barrister in Australian history. In 1981 she was appointed Departmental Head of the NSW Ministry of Aboriginal Affairs, being both the first woman and the first Aboriginal to become head of a ministerial department anywhere in Australia.

osprey *see* birds of prey

ostrich *see* animals, introduced

Otway Ranges VIC Located SW of GEELONG, between Great Ocean Road and the Princes Highway, these ranges have a NE-SW alignment, generally parallel to the coast, extending from N of Lorne SW beyond Apollo Bay to the rugged cliffs of Cape Otway. They consist of an upfaulted block of sandstones and other sedimentary rocks, with Mt Saline (582m elevation) the highest point. The two largest streams which rise in the ranges are the Gellibrand River flowing generally SW, and the BARWON RIVER which flows NE, then E, beyond Geelong. Several small streams (St George, Cumberland, Wye, Kennett and Parker Rivers) drain the steep SE slopes of the ranges to estuaries on BASS STRAIT. The region is one of high rainfall: Cape Otway has an average annual rainfall of 887mm, Lorne receives 873mm and the Gellibrand forestry station averages 1 045mm. Much of the higher and more steeply sloping sections of the ranges are heavily forested and sawmilling is important; the lower slopes and the stream flats are occupied by dairy and potato growing farms. The cape was named by Lieutenant James GRANT in 1800 to honour his naval friend Captain William Albany Ottway.

Ouse River TAS A tributary of the DERWENT RIVER, the Ouse rises in the lakes region of the CENTRAL PLATEAU and flows in a general S direction for about 110km, to join the Derwent near the small township of Ouse at the junction of the Lyell and Tarraleah Highways, 89km NW of Hobart. The river is diverted twice to provide supplementary water for the vast hydro-electricity generation systems in the highlands of the State. The first diversion is to GREAT LAKE, whence it flows via the SHANNON RIVER to WADDAMANNA power station and back again into the Ouse River. The second diversion is to LAKE ECHO by the 13km-long Monpeelyata Canal, from which it is used to augment supplies to the TUNGATINAH power station.

Outback This is a common term for the thinly inhabited inland areas of Australia.

Ovens River VIC An upper tributary of the MURRAY RIVER, it rises near MOUNT HOTHAM in the GREAT DIVIDING RANGE, and flows some 230km in a general NW direction through BRIGHT, MYRTLEFORD and WANGARATTA to join the Murray upstream from YARRAWONGA. Two main tributaries are the Buffalo and King Rivers, both from the S; the Buffalo Dam (capacity 24 050ML) has been constructed across the former, and the William Hovell Dam (12 300ML) on the upper section of the latter. Water from these storage points is used lower downstream for irrigating high-value crops, especially hops and tobacco, as well as pastures and fodder crops. The upper parts of the Ovens River basin are snow-covered in winter and MOUNT BUFFALO, MOUNT FEATHERTOP and Mt Hotham are popular ski resorts. Much of the adjacent hill country is heavily timbered and there are logging centres throughout the valley. The annual rainfall varies from over 1 500mm in the headwater highlands, to 1 300mm in the vicinity of Bright, about 900mm at Myrtleford and 640mm at Wangaratta. The Hume Highway cuts across the lower valley, the Ovens Highway extends from Wangaratta upstream to Bright, and the Alpine Road leads from Bright across the headwaters and the divide to OMEO. The Alpine Road is subject to heavy snow from June to October and, though it is snow-ploughed and normally kept open for vehicles, chains have to be attached; occasional blizzard conditions can make access impossible. The Ovens region was opened up by gold miners in the 1850s and dredge mining continued into the early decades of this century, but it is now the pastoral, agricultual and timber industries which form the basis of the valley economy. The river was named by the explorers HUME and Hovell in 1824 after Major Ovens, private secretary to Governor BRISBANE.

overlanders In colonial times this name was applied to drovers who took stock overland from settled districts to areas which were only just being opened up. Examples are J. Hawdon and J. Gardiner, who took stock from the settled parts of NSW to the newly settled PORT PHILLIP District in the late 1830s, and members of the DURACK FAMILY, who in the 1880s took several thousand cattle from western QLD to the KIMBERLEYS district of WA.

overland telegraph SA/NT The erection of this overhead telegraphic line, connecting Adelaide to Darwin, was commenced in 1870 and completed in 1872. It was an event of considerable importance for it provided the first direct link for Australian cities with countries overseas. The building of the line was a quite outstanding achievement as it crossed the vast arid interior of the continent through which, only a decade earlier, the explorer John MacDouall STUART had made his epic journey. The construction of the telegraph line, which followed the route taken by Stuart, was the vision of Charles Todd, then the Postmaster-General of SA. He supervised the organisation of the project and had to overcome major transport problems, as well as facing the difficulties of the wet seasons. Camels were used to supply the central section of the line and ships brought materials and supplies for the construction of the N section. The telegraph line was connected to a submarine cable between Darwin and Java, laid in 1871, and so provided a vital communication link with world centres.

owls These BIRDS belong to the order Strigiformes, which is divided into two families—the barn owls (Tytonidae) and the true owls (Strigidae). Almost all owls are nocturnal birds of prey, feeding on insects and small mammals such as rodents and small birds. Their soft plumage, usually a cryptic brown and grey, allows them to fly almost without a sound. The size of the eyes enables the owl to see well in a very dim light; they are placed at the front so that they can see only forwards unless the owl turns its large head, which it can do to a remarkable degree. The beak is short and hooked and often largely concealed by facial feathers. The outer toe can be turned backwards but is usually kept pointing sideways.

Masked owl, *Tyto novaehollandiae*

Barn owls are widespread birds with a large facial disc which is usually heart-shaped and surrounded by dark margins; their call is a loud screech. The barn owl, *Tyto alba* (33cm to 36cm long), probably has a wider natural distribution than any other land bird in the world; it is found throughout Australia, being particularly common in open woodlands. The masked owl, *T. novaehollandiae* (38cm to 40cm), is very similar in its habits and appearance to the barn owl but has more feathers on the legs. It is an uncommon species which inhabits woodlands and savannas, but is absent from the Centre. A rare species is the sooty owl, *T. tenebricosa* (33cm to 40cm), a dark brownish-grey bird found in scattered forests in E Australia. Perhaps the rarest member of this family is the grass owl, *T.*

longimembris (33cm to 36cm). It occurs in the grasslands of SE and NE Australia, but is common overseas.

True owls can be distinguished from barn owls by their more hawk-like faces and their less obvious facial masks. The boobook owl, *Ninox novaeseelandiae* (30cm to 35cm), takes its name from its well-known call. It is a brown bird with boldly streaked underparts, dark patches around the eyes and often with white spots on the back. Boobooks are found throughout Australia wherever there are trees suitable for nesting and roosting. Less widespread is the barking owl, *N. connivens* (40cm to 45cm), which has a dog-like bark but is also known to scream. It is boldly marked below and has very large, striking yellow eyes; it is found in N and E Australia and in the extreme SW, but not in TAS. The rufous owl, *N. rufa* (43cm to 50cm), a rare species, has white bars on the abdomen and a dark area around the eyes. It lives in wet forests in mid-coastal and north-eastern QLD, E CAPE YORK, the N part of the NT and north-eastern WA. The largest owl in Australia is the powerful owl, *N. strenua** (60cm), an uncommon species with dark brown underparts. Found in forests and deep gullies in SE Australia (but not in TAS), it feeds on birds and medium-sized animals, such as possums.

National Library of Australia

John Oxley

Oxley, John Joseph William Molesworth
(1785-1828) Surveyor and explorer. Born in Yorkshire, he joined the British Navy in 1799, came to Sydney in 1802 and in 1812 was appointed Surveyor-General of NSW. In 1817 he attempted to trace the course of the LACHLAN RIVER, but before he had proceeded very far he found that it entered a vast area of swamps which he was unable to penetrate. In the following year he led an expedition along the MACQUARIE RIVER, only to find that it too became lost in reed-beds. He then struck E, reaching the sea at PORT MACQUARIE. Besides his work in land surveying and exploration, he made several coastal surveys, the most important being in 1823,

when Governor BRISBANE sent him N of Sydney to find a site for a new penal settlement. On this voyage he discovered the TWEED RIVER and explored MORETON BAY, where he met three shipwrecked sailors who showed him the river which he named the Brisbane. His discoveries led to the foundation of a settlement at Moreton Bay in 1824.

In politics Oxley was one of the strongest opponents of Governor MACQUARIE's emancipist policy, and was for a short time in 1824-25 a member of the colony's first Legislative Council. He was active in the development of banking, learned societies and the colony's first library, became the owner of large properties near CAMDEN, and was a pioneer settler in the BOWRAL district.
See also exploration by land
Further reading: Dunlop, E. *John Oxley.* Oxford University Press, Melbourne, 1960.

oyster borers *see* gastropods

oystercatchers *see* waders

oyster culture Oysters and their culture are discussed briefly under BIVALVE MOLLUSCS. Almost all the leases are in NSW, mostly at PORT STEPHENS, on the GEORGES, HAWKESBURY and MANNING Rivers and in Wallis Lake (*see* MYALL LAKES). A few leases are situated in southern QLD. The oysters are marketed in bags, each bag containing about 100 dozen. About 10 000 tonnes (live weight) are produced each year. Oyster leases are particularly susceptible to pollution: pollution by organic matter which may introduce harmful bacteria or viruses and pollution by oil from a spill from a tanker which can kill many young oysters.

oysters *see* bivalve molluscs; fisheries

oyster wafer *see* flatworms

P

pademelons *see* kangaroos, etc.

Page, Sir Earle Christmas Grafton
(1880-1961) Medical practitioner, politician and Prime Minister. Born at GRAFTON in NSW, he graduated in medicine from the University of Sydney and in 1903 began a practice in his native town. In 1916-17 he served as a senior medical officer in the Australian Imperial Force (AIF), and two years later disposed of his medical practice and won a

seat in the House of Representatives. In 1921 he became leader of the newly formed COUNTRY PARTY. In 1923, when, William HUGHES was replaced by Stanley BRUCE as leader of the Nationalist Party and Prime Minister, the Country Party entered into a coalition with the Nationalists and Page became deputy Prime Minister and Treasurer, positions which he continued to hold until the Labor victory of 1929.

When the Country Party entered into coalition with the UNITED AUSTRALIA PARTY (UAP) in 1934 he again became deputy Prime Minister, and after the death of Joseph LYONS in 1939 was Prime Minister for 19 days until the election of Robert MENZIES as UAP leader. Page disliked Menzies as heartily as he had Hughes, and at this stage refused to serve under him, a stand which led to his replacement as leader of the Country Party later in the year and to the re-forming of a coalition in 1940. He held portfolios under Menzies in 1940-41 and 1949-56 and remained in the House of Representatives until the year of his death. He was the first Chancellor of the University of New England and was active in the movement for a new State in the New England district of NSW.
Further reading: Page, Sir Earle *Truant Surgeon: The Inside Story of Forty Years of Australian Political Life.* Angus & Robertson, Sydney, 1963.

painted snipe *see* waders

painting and painters This article deals with painting and painters in Australia since the arrival of the First Fleet. The earliest painters were the topographical artists who worked with the expeditions sent out from the convict settlement at Sydney to survey the surrounding land and its flora and fauna. In 1792 the first professional artist, Thomas WATLING, arrived in Australia, transported for forgery. The first artist who came as a free settler and who tried to live by his art was Conrad MARTENS.

Between 1830 and 1870, there were very few artists of note working in Australia. They painted in the European tradition and the standard of their work was generally low. During the gold-rush period of the 1850s all of them gravitated to VIC where the newly acquired wealth created some patronage, albeit erratic. Among them was Eugene VON GUERARD, whose work experienced some popularity on the goldfields, and Louis BUVELOT.

During the 1880s, the first national school of painting began to establish itself. Led by Tom ROBERTS and known as the HEIDELBERG SCHOOL, it was mildly influenced by French Impressionism, but more so by Whistler's tonal Impressionism. The School's inspiration was thus more English than French and it resulted in Australian subjects, bathed in Australian light and rich in Australian colours. Silver greys and dark greens gave way to bright blues and golds, and crags in mist and streams in torrent gave way to gum trees and rocky outcrops.

*Species, genus or family is endemic to Australia (see Preface)

The collapse of the land boom in VIC in the 1890s drove many artists, including Arthur STREETON, to Sydney where Julian ASHTON was promoting Australian artists with such enthusiasm that Sydney became as attractive as Melbourne as a place where artists could live and sell their work. However, despite the early international flavour of the Heidelberg School, Australian painting began to become very insular. The creation of amateur art societies during the affluent days preceding the economic depression of the 1890s and the paternalism of the trustee system operating in the State galleries combined to act as inhibiting factors upon the acceptance of recent art trends from Britain and the Continent.

This growing insularity from modern developments in art was enhanced by the Royal Academy, in London. The Academy, then in steady decline in artistic creativity after the days of Constable, Turner and Reynolds, had an awesome reputation and its contempt for Expressionism, post-Impressionism and Cubism ensured that few Australian painters would be tempted to stray from the traditional path.

Julian Ashton

Australian painting at this time became generally associated with either mannered portraits, such as those done by George LAMBERT, or landscapes of gum trees, blue skies and white sheep. The most capable and well-known executors of this style were Hans HEYSEN, Arthur Streeton and Elioth GRUNER. The few artists who did not paint in this style, such as Rupert BUNNY, John RUSSELL, Charles CONDER and E. Phillips FOX, were either ignored or had left Australia in disgust. Public and private patronage had become very conservative, and of new developments overseas were ignored or dismissed.

However, beneath this dominant belief in conservative representation, small currents of discontent were growing. In Sydney a group of artists including Roland WAKELIN, Grace Cossington SMITH and Roy DE MAISTRE began attending Dattilo Rubbo's classes and were stimulated by his ideas and attitudes. During World War I Smith, de Maistre and

Wakelin began to explore the works of Gauguin, Cézanne and Van Gogh, and their paintings, together with that of Margaret PRESTON, began slowly to change public opinion. In the 1930s, the lessons of Cubism and its aftermath, Futurism, began to arouse interest and a second wave of modernism, led by such painters as Frank Hinder, Rah FIZELLE and Grace CROWLEY, began to influence conventional painting.

'The Mother' oil on canvas painting by George Lambert, 1906

In Melbourne, the reaction in the 1930s and 1940s to the prevailing conservatism was far stronger than in Sydney. Led by George BELL, a convert to recent developments in European painting, and assisted by Arnold SHORE, William FRATER and the writer Adrian Lawlor, the Melbourne scene erupted. The

conservatives, led by the Attorney-General, Robert MENZIES, attempted to discipline the art world by establishing an Australian Royal Academy, but the avant-garde retorted by forming the Contemporary Art Society; and feelings were further roused by the arrival, in 1939, of the *Herald* Exhibition of French and British Modern Art, held in the Melbourne town hall.

During and after World War II, Melbourne painting became political and much of it was concerned with social change. Complacency and political conservatism were as much the enemy as literal representation of the Australian countryside in blues and golds. Albert TUCKER, Sidney NOLAN, Danila VASSILIEFF, John PERCEVAL, Arthur BOYD and Jose BERGNER produced images that many conservative critics found upsetting.

After World War II Sydney painting continued to develop in accordance with its tradition of respect for the past and for good workmanship. William DOBELL became the best-known Sydney artist, his portraits showing a rhythm and richness of colour and texture that owed much to his respect for great painters of the past. Lloyd REES found the calmness of the Italian Renaissance landscape in Sydney's sandstone country and BATHURST's rolling hills. Russell DRYSDALE had a love of Renaissance perspectives and a classical concern for form. John PASSMORE analysed form and atmosphere in the classical tradition that had fascinated Rembrandt and Cézanne.

During the 1950s Sydney moved into abstract painting, led by Ralph BALSON. The earlier interest of many Sydney artists in Cubist and post-Cubist developments provided a launching pad for those who now emerged. For example, John OLSEN's abstracts were influ-

'The Artist's Camp' oil painting by Tom Roberts

enced by the earlier works of William Rose. Other Sydney artists who moved into abstract painting included Eric Smith, John Coburn, Thomas Gleghorn, Frank Hodgkinson, Stanislaus Rapotec, Leonard Hessing, Margo Lewers, Ian FAIRWEATHER and Carl Plate. By the 1960s the abstract painters had developed a crusading zeal and this had an effect upon Melbourne where artists were interested mainly in figurative work, and some had grave doubts about the authenticity of the mass conversion to abstract work then sweeping the world. The late 1950s in Sydney saw the beginning of texture painting, led by Elwyn Lynn, and the emergence of a group of assemblage artists, known as the Annandale Imitation Realists, who rebelled against much of Australian art and life by creating works made from the flotsam and jetsam of consumer society. In the 1970s sculpture, which had never been prominent in Australian art, began to attract young and experimental artists, but there were few developments in the field of painting apart from some lingering interest in 'pop' art.

The patronage of painters changed dramatically after World War II. The previous situation, whereby only a minority could attract patronage, changed and an increasing number of painters began to experience the pleasure of having their work purchased. The émigrés from Hitler's Europe increased the numbers aware of the purchasing opportunities available, while some, such as Sali HERMAN and Desiderius ORBAN, promoted the importance of painting to an ever-increasing audience by means of lecture programmes. Dealer galleries, led by Rudy Komon of Paddington, inaugurated an aggressive programme of enlisting artists who could supply work, drumming up potential clients and nurturing collectors. Post-war overseas travel increased the level of public sophistication, and the trustees of State galleries began to increase the scope and quantity of paintings purchased by Australia. In the 1960s regional galleries began to be established and their exhibitions led to an increasing awareness amongst the public of Australian painters. In the 1970s the assistance to painters through the Visual Arts Board of the Australia Council and the increasing number of exhibitions being toured through the Art Gallery Directors' Council helped to increase public recognition of Australian art.

Pakenham VIC (combined population of Pakenham, Pakenham East and Pakenham South 2 671 in 1981) This township is located on the Princes Highway and on the railway route to GIPPSLAND, 58km by rail SE of Melbourne. There is also a larger town at Pakenham East and one at Pakenham South (about 12km off the highway). The main rural activities in the adjacent areas are dairying and beef cattle grazing, with some production of apples for cider making. The town was named after General Pakenham who served in the Crimean War.

Pakistan, settlers from see Indian subcontinent, settlers from

Palm Group QLD An island group in Halifax Bay, it is located E of INGHAM, SE of HINCHINBROOK ISLAND and NNW of TOWNSVILLE, in the channel between the GREAT BARRIER REEF and the central-E coast of the State. The largest of the group is Great Palm Is, a hilly and forested island with its highest point, Mt Bentley, reaching some 550m above sea level. Other islands in the group are Pelorus, Orpheus, Curacoa and Havannah. Orpheus Is, with a fringing coral reef and thick forest cover, has been developed as a tourist resort and can be reached by launch from either Townsville or Dungeness.

Palm Valley NT The Palm River is a tributary of the FINKE RIVER and is located some 143km SSW of ALICE SPRINGS in the Krichauff Ranges, S of the MACDONNELL RANGES. The gorge-valley of this stream, with steep red sandstone cliffs, is similar to many gorges in the region and, because of the concentration of moisture within the confines of the valley, it contains lush vegetation which contrasts markedly with the arid landscapes of the area. The occurrence of a rare palm, *Livistona mariae*, has given the valley its name. A flora and fauna reserve, covering 458km², includes the valley and the Finke River gorge. Access to the reserve is by road from Alice Springs, W along the Larapinta Drive for 128km to HERMANNSBURG, and then S for 15km to Palm Valley. In 1965, large reserves of natural gas were discovered in the rock structures beneath the valley and cost feasibility studies were made for transporting the gas by pipeline to alternative consumption centres. In the early 1980s, after agreement had been reached with the Aboriginal owners of the land, construction of a 145km-long pipeline to Alice Springs commenced to supply gas for the town's power generation plant; it was completed and came into operation in 1983.

Palmae This monocotyledonous family of flowering plants contains some 250 genera and over 2000 species primarily of tropical occurrence but with its extreme N limit in the Mediterranean region. Although some genera are extremely rich in species—the largest, *Calamus*, containing 250 species—many contain few species, and about 75 are monotypic. Each tropical area, including individual islands, tends to have its own group of genera which are not found elsewhere.

The palms are most unusual monocotyledons in that they develop trunks and reach considerable heights (up to 30m); few other monocotyledons do so, because the group as a whole lacks the ability to develop true secondary thickening or wood, though a few other genera (for example, *Cordyline* in the family Agavaceae, *Xanthorrhoea* and *Kingia* in the family Xanthorrhoeaceae) also form trunks without wood.

Members of the Palmae have large pleated leaves which are divided pinnately (the shape of a feather) or palmately (in the shape of a fan). The base of the leaves encloses or embraces the stem. The flowers are regular,

Blackboys, *Xanthorrhoea*

VIC Govt Travel Authority

usually unisexual and grow in large clusters; when young they are enclosed in a sheath-like bract. Each flower consists of two whorls, each whorl containing three perianth segments and usually three stamens. The ovary is superior and has between one and three locules. The fruit occurs as a berry or a drupe.

Australian palms are generally found in northern closed forests or around streams in drier but warm habitats. The most familiar examples are the bangalow palm, *Archontophoenix cunninghamiana*, and the cabbage tree palm, *Livistona australis*. The latter was once common behind the sandy inlets around PORT JACKSON, but was quickly destroyed by the first European settlers who felled it and used the leaves for thatching. One of the most curious occurrences of palms is that of *Livistona* species in the MACDONNELL RANGES, where local topographical features enable a suitably moist environment to develop in an otherwise semi-arid region. A notable feature of the banks of most rivers in N Australia is the occurrence of large groups of pandanus palms. Despite their common name, however, *Pandanus* species do not belong to the Palmae but to the family Pandanaceae.

The family contains two extremely important food plants: the date palm, *Phoenix dactylefera*, the fruit of which has been a staple for many N African societies in the past and is now also a valuable export; and the coconut palm, *Cocus nucifera*.

See also Angiospermae; Appendix 5, Flower Structure and Glossary of Botanical Terms
Further reading: see Appendix 6, A Bibliography for Plants.

Palmer, (Edward) Vance (1885-1959) Author. Born in BUNDABERG in QLD, he worked as a journalist in Brisbane and London and as a tutor and bookkeeper in various parts of QLD, and served in the army in World War I. A man of versatile literary talent, he wrote plays, poetry, works of literary criticism and short stories and was active in theatrical circles, particularly in the 1920s. However, his reputation rests mainly on his novels, which include *The Outpost* (1924), which was rewritten as *The Hurricane* (1935), *The Man Hamilton* (1928), *Men are Human* (1930), *The Passage* (1930), *Daybreak* (1932), *The Swayne*

Family (1934), *Legend for Sanderson* (1937), *Cyclone* (1947) and a trilogy consisting of *Golconda* (1948), *Seedtime* (1957) and *The Big Fellow* (1959). In these novels he used simple, well-constructed plots for the psychological analysis of ordinary people, generally in rural settings—mining towns and small coastal settlements—rather than in cities.

See also literature

Further reading: Heseltine, H. *Vance Palmer*. Queensland University Press, St Lucia QLD, 1970.

Palmer, Janet Gertrude 'Nettie' *née* Higgins (1885-1964) Author. Born in BENDIGO in VIC, she was educated at the Presbyterian Ladies' College, Melbourne—the school which provided the setting for Henry Handel RICHARDSON's novel, *The Getting of Wisdom* (1910)—and at Melbourne University. She lived for some years in London, Paris and Berlin, and by the time she married Vance PALMER in 1914 had begun to attract favourable attention as a writer of simple, musical, lyrical poems. Her published works include *The South Wind* (verse, 1914) and *Shadowy Paths* (verse, 1915), *Modern Australian Literature* (1924), *Talking It Over* (essays, 1932), *Henry Bournes Higgins: A Memoir* (1931), *Henry Handel Richardson: A Study* (1950) and *Fourteen Years* (extracts from her journals, 1948). She was the first writer to popularise the works of Henry Handel Richardson in Australia.

Palmer River QLD The main tributary of the MITCHELL RIVER, located in the far N of the State, it rises on the W slopes of the GREAT DIVIDING RANGE, NW of CAIRNS, and flows in a generally W direction across CAPE YORK peninsula. It joins the Mitchell as a right-bank tributary about 160km from its mouth on the GULF OF CARPENTARIA. It was the scene of a gold rush in the 1870s, but now only ghost towns, such as Maytown, remain as evidence of those mining times.

palms *see* Palmae

pampas lily-of-the-valley *see* Solanaceae

Pandanaceae *see* Palmae

Pandanus *see* Palmae

paperbarks These trees and shrubs belong to the genus *Melaleuca* (family MYRTACEAE), which occurs throughout Australia. The bark is often spongy and papery and is easily peeled from the tree. Many species are found in coastal swamps and lagoons in the area N of Sydney. Members of this genus are sometimes called tea trees or honey myrtles.

Papilionaceae This very large family of dicotyledonous flowering plants contains 300 genera and 5 500 species of cosmopolitan distribution, mainly in temperate regions. Many of these plants are economically important,

such as peas (*Pisum* species), beans (*Phaseolus* and *Vicia* species), soybeans (*Glycine* species), groundnuts (*Arachis* species), lentils (*Lens* species), clover (*Trifolium* species), lucerne (*Medicago* species) and ornamental plants such as *Wisteria* and sweet peas (*Lathyrus* species).

The members of the family Papilionaceae may be herbs, shrubs, climbers or trees. The leaves are usually alternately arranged and are simple or compound; they often consist of three leaflets (for example, in clover) or are modified with twining tendrils (for example, the sweet pea). In nearly all species the flowers, which are in spikes, racemes or heads, have five butterfly-like petals; the uppermost one (the standard) is usually enlarged and colourful and surrounds the two lateral ones (the wings), while the two basal ones are joined to form a boat-shaped structure (keel) which envelops the stamens and ovary. There are usually 10 stamens; in some species the stamens are all free, but in most species they are all joined to form a tubular structure, or nine are joined and one is free. The sepals (usually five) are fused at the base, forming a cup around the base of the rest of the flower. The ovary is superior, simple, and has a single cavity (loculi), and the number of seeds ranges from one to many. The fruit is either a legume (pod) or a lomentum (pod which breaks when mature into one-seeded parts).

A. Woods
Common aotus, *Aotus ericoides villosa*

A very large number of species is present in Australia, occurring in almost all types of plant communities. Herbaceous species of the genera *Trifolium, Medicago, Vicia, Lotus* and *Lupinus* are widespread in open grassy habitats. Only one species (of the genus *Lotus*) is a native Australian plant; the rest have been introduced either as improved pasture species (for example, *Trifolium*) or have accompanied European pasture introductions as WEEDS (for example, *Medicago* and *Vicia*).

Shrubby species are abundant in heath, wood-

land, open forest and scrubs. Amongst these species are members of the genera *Dillwynia, Pultenaea, Aotus, Phyllota* and *Daviesia*, which are often called eggs-and-bacon, because all contain some species in which the flowers are partly yellowish-orange and partly brownish-red. Other shrubs found in these habitats include species of *Hovea* (blue flowers) and *Mirbelia* (purple flowers). Whilst most species prefer well-drained soil, and many tolerate semi-arid conditions, an interesting leafless shrub, *Viminaria juncea*, grows only in waterlogged sites such as sedgeland.

Climbing or trailing plants include some of Australia's most attractive ground-cover or fast-growing plants, such as the coral pea, *Hardenbergia violacea*, which has violet-blue flowers and is a favoured ground cover, and different species of *Kennedia*, which have flower colours ranging from black and gold to bright red. The large shrubs and small trees of the Papilionaceae are fairly rare in Australia; many, such as the tree lucerne, *Chamaecytisus prolifer*, gorse, *Ulex europaeus*, and the coral tree, *Erythrina indica*, are introduced species which have become naturalised in Australian plant communities or are agricultural weeds or pasture species.

Amongst pasture species, clovers, particularly white or dutch clover, *T. repens*, are widely used as improved pasture species in cool to warm temperate Australia. Lucerne, *M. sativa*, is also widely grown both for browsing pasture, ensilage and haymaking. In sub-tropical and tropical Australia a large number of legumes have been introduced which are able to combine with the tall tropical grasses (GRAMINEAE) to form improved pasture. These include centro, *Centrosema pubesceus*, from South America; *Desmodium* species from Central America and the West Indies; glycine, *Glycine wightii*, from the Old World tropics; siratro, *Macroptilium atropurpureum*, from Central and South America; stylo, *Stylosanthes guyanensis*, from Latin America; and Townsville stylo, *S. humilis*, from South America.

Like the members of the MIMOSACEAE, with which this family and another closely related one (Caesalpinaceae) is often combined (into the Leguminosae), the Papilionaceae has the ability to fix atmospheric nitrogen through bacteria which live symbiotically with the plant in root nodules. Also like the members of the Mimosaceae, many Papilionaceae have hard seeds which do not germinate as soon as they are shed, even if conditions are favourable. This last capacity, combined with long-lasting viability, enables the seed to lie dormant in the soil for many years, often delaying germination until after a fire has passed, the heat stimulating germination. Subsequent growth is often very rapid because of the plant's ability to fix its own nitrogen, which enables it to make use of all the nutrients in the ash left by the fire. Many Papilionaceae shrubs are quite short-lived, or do not grow well once the mature vegetation has re-established itself, a fact which underlies the common observation that 'the flowers are better after a fire'. *Acacia* species and

Papilionaceae may be best considered to play the same role in natural Australian ecosystems as weeds do in man-made ecosystems; indeed, many weeds are members of the Papilionaceae. *See also* Appendix 5, Flower Structure and Glossary of Botanical Terms; environment *Further reading: see* Appendix 6, A Bibliography for Plants.

Papua New Guinea

Before gaining independence in September 1975, this nation was an Australian external territory, known as the Territory of Papua and New Guinea. Because of this former association and also its geographical proximity, it has close links with Australia and receives more aid from Australia than does any other developing nation.

Establishment of Australian control Australian interest in New Guinea became strong in the early 1880s, largely because of rumours that Germany had territorial ambitions there. In 1884, following strong representations by the Australian colonies, the British government proclaimed a protectorate over the SE part of the island, Papua, whereupon Germany did likewise in the NE and adjacent smaller islands. In 1888 the British protectorate was formally annexed as a colony, the administration being entrusted to QLD. After federation, the British government agreed that Papua should become a federal territory as soon as the Commonwealth Parliament had passed laws for it. Such laws were provided by the Papua Act of 1905, and in the following year Commonwealth officials took control. In 1907 Hubert Murray (who was later knighted) was appointed acting Administrator, and in 1908 was made Lieutenant-Governor. During his long period in office, which lasted until 1940, nearly the whole of Papua was explored and brought under administrative control. However, economic progress was slow, little was done to involve the indigenous people in the work of government, and education was left almost entirely to religious missions.

In the meantime, Australia had extended her control to include the whole E half of New Guinea. Following the outbreak of war in 1914, Australian forces had quickly occupied German New Guinea, and in 1919 this territory was made a mandate of the League of Nations, with Australia as the administering power. Its administration was kept separate from that of Papua, but followed broadly similar policies. During the following two decades economic progress, although slow, was somewhat faster than in Papua, being aided by the discovery of gold at Wau and Bulolo and by better opportunities for the development of export crops.

World War II and its aftermath Within a few months of the outbreak of war in the Pacific, the Japanese had occupied the most important centres in New Guinea. They planned also to occupy Port Moresby, the administrative capital of Papua, but were prevented from doing so by the defeat of an invasion fleet in the Battle of the Coral Sea, by the Australian repulse of a landing at Milne

Hoisting the British flag at Port Moresby 1884

National Library of Australia

Bay in the SE corner of the territory, and finally by the defeat of a force which they had sent over the Owen Stanley Range along the route which became known as the Kokoda Trail. Australian and American troops then captured the N coast bases of Buna and Gona, and during the remainder of the war Australian forces re-established Allied control over other N areas.

Both territories had been placed under a military administration at the outbreak of war, and when peace returned a joint administration was continued, on the grounds of efficiency and economy. United administration was made permanent by the Papua and New Guinea Act of 1949-50, which provided for one Administrator, one Supreme Court and one Public Service for the combined territory. Meanwhile, in 1946 a Trusteeship Agreement had been concluded, making the former League of Nations mandate a Trust Territory of the UN.

Development Before World War II it had seemed that in a country as undeveloped as New Guinea colonial control might well last almost indefinitely. However, the post-war decline of colonialism throughout the world gradually dispelled this view, and the pace of economic, educational and political development quickened, particularly from about 1960. In education up to that date the main effort had been put into primary schooling, but as it became clear that independence might have to come within a few decades rather than generations, more stress was placed on higher education and developments included the opening of a university in Port Moresby in 1970. In economic development there was increased encouragement for the indigenous people to involve themselves in business enterprises and in the growing of export crops. Efforts to locate and develop mineral deposits were also increased, the most successful result being the starting of production from one of the world's largest copper deposits, on the

island of Bougainville. Underlying the whole process of economic development was a rapidly increasing flow of aid from the Australian government.

Progress to independence In the 1950s the main way in which indigenous people became involved in the work of government was through the setting up of local government councils. It is true that in 1949 a Legislative Council was introduced, but a majority of its members were officials.

In 1960 the Legislative Council was enlarged, and its composition changed to include many more indigenous people as well as more elected members. However, criticism from the UN continued to mount, and in 1964 a far more sweeping step was taken. The Legislative Council was replaced by a House of Assembly consisting of 10 officials, 10 elected European members and 44 other members elected irrespective of race; elections were held on the basis of full adult franchise. In 1968 a second House of Assembly was elected, without any seats being reserved for Europeans, and during its four-year term some of the members began to undertake the responsibilities of Ministers. When a third House of Assembly was elected in 1972, Michael Somare became Chief Minister, and at the coming of independence he was appointed Prime Minister.

Australia has maintained close ties with independent Papua New Guinea. In 1978 agreement was reached on maritime boundaries between the two nations—a matter which has been complicated by the fact that all 17 inhabited islands of TORRES STRAIT had been under QLD jurisdiction since 1879, although some of them are very close to the Papuan coast. A treaty signed in December 1978 settled sea bed and fishing jurisdiction as well as sovereignty over the Torres Strait islands, and also set a protected zone in which Papua New Guineans and Torres Strait islanders are guaranteed access to traditional fishing grounds, regardless of the jurisdiction in which they fall. Australia recognised Papua New Guinean sovereignty over three islands, while Papua New Guinea recognised Australian sovereignty over the rest.

Further reading: Hastings, P. *New Guinea: Problems and Prospects.* Cheshire, Melbourne, 1969; Hudson, W. J. (ed) *Australia and Papua New Guinea.* Sydney University Press, Sydney, 1971; Griffin, James, *Papua New Guinea: A Political History.* Heinemann, Richmond, VIC, 1979.

papyrus *see* Cyperaceae

Paraburdoo WA (population 2 357 in 1981) A company town in the PILBARA region, 390km by rail SE of DAMPIER and 98km S of MOUNT TOM PRICE, it was built in 1970 as a residential centre for the miners and their families and as a service town for the iron ore mining operations nearby. The town's name is derived from the Aboriginal name of a creek in the vicinity. The ore is transported by rail from Paraburdoo via Mt Tom Price to the coastal ports of Dampier, where it is made into pellets prior to export.

parachuting This is not a sport which is practised by a large number of Australians because of the expense involved and because the risks attached to it attract only the stout-hearted. The sport started to develop in 1958 and championships for men began in 1960 and for women in 1962. The championships are divided into three sections: Style, in which a competitor must perform six manoeuvres before opening the parachute; Accuracy, with the jumper aiming to land on a disc 10cm in diameter; and Relative-jumping, with a team of jumpers creating formations while free-falling.

parakeelyas Belonging to the genus *Calandrinia* (family Portulaceae), these are perennial or annual succulent plants which grow in arid areas. The genus is also represented in the Americas, from British Columbia to Chile. The purple, red, pink or white flowers are carried in loose racemes and close quickly in dull weather. Parakeelyas are an important food and moisture supply for travelling stock. Aborigines used the leaves as food and made flour from the seeds.

paramecium *see* protozoons

parasites A parasite is an organism that lives at the expense of another organism, living for all or part of its life in intimate association with the host. An endoparasite feeds within the tissues of the host, an ectoparasite on (or at least in connection with) the surface of the host. There are probably more parasitic species than non-parasitic species of organisms and thus virtually all organisms (in Australia and elsewhere) harbour one or more kinds of parasites.

It is not in the interest of the parasite to kill or even damage the host greatly as this would lessen the chances of the parasite's sur-

viving. When a parasitic species consistently kills a host species it is usually an indication that the association is relatively recent (*see*, for example, MYXOMATOSIS virus and European RABBITS in Australia).

Many insects (such as some FLIES and ANTS, BEES AND WASPS) are endoparasites or ectoparasites of other insects but as these kill their hosts, usually before they can become adults, many biologists prefer to think of the association as extended predation, and to call the parasites parasitoids. A few insects are true parasites (for example, bot flies).

The structure and the life cycles of many parasites are greatly modified when compared with those of their free-living relatives. Often two or more hosts are obligatory (for example, the human malaria parasites require *Anopheles* MOSQUITOES and man; and the HYDATID CYST TAPEWORM requires either dogs and sheep or dingoes and wallabies). In many parasites there is sexual and asexual reproduction, the latter to build up numbers rapidly to increase the probability that some will survive and find a new host. An animal that transfers a parasite to another kind of organism is called a vector.

Parasitic plants Relatively few plants are parasitic; some Australian examples are discussed in the entry on PARASITIC PLANTS.

Parasitic animals Most phyla contain at least some parasites or parasitoids; some phyla or classes are entirely parasitic. The most important phyla are Protozoa (PROTOZOONS), Platyhelminthes (FLATWORMS), Nematoda (ROUNDWORMS) and Arthropoda (ARTHROPODS). Parasitic protozoons almost always infest animals but parasitic platyhelminths attack only animals. The Nematoda contains

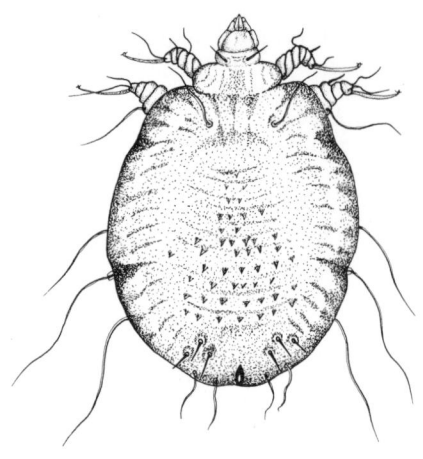

Adult scabies mite

many species parasitic on other animals and many which live in the tissues of plants. The Crustacea (CRUSTACEANS) contains many fish parasites.

Parasitic micro-organisms Parasitic micro-organisms (such as some bacteria, FUNGI and viruses) are often distinguished as pathogens, at least when they cause disease. In general, parasitic fungi attack plants though some cause diseases in, for example, man (athlete's foot) and fishes. Some bacteria attack plants but most pathogenic species infect animals. Virus diseases affect animals, plants and other micro-organisms.

See also diseases, livestock; diseases, plant; parasites, livestock

Further reading: Lapage, G. *Animals Parasitic in Man.* Penguin Books, Harmondsworth, 1957; Schmidt, G.D. & Roberts, L.S. *Founda-*

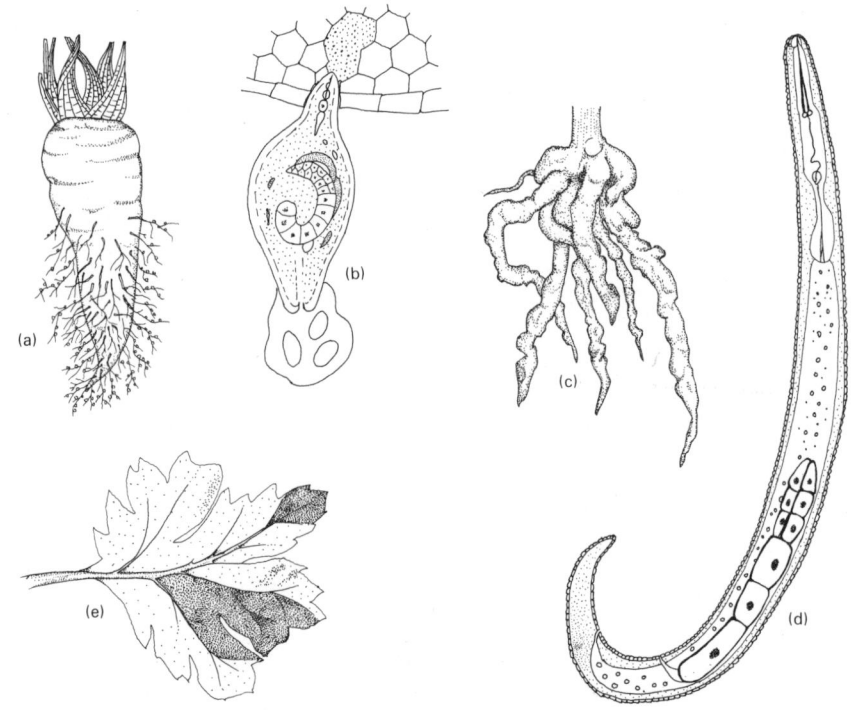

Some plant parasitic nematodes and the damage caused by them: (a) beet, with proliferation of roots caused by beet root eelworm; (b) adult female beet root eelworm protruding from root (greatly enlarged); (c) plant roots damaged by root knot eelworms; (d) typical soil-dwelling nematode; (e) damage caused by a *Chrysanthemum* leaf eelworm

tions of Parasitology. C.V. Mosby Co., St Louis, 1977.

parasites, human

This article is restricted to animal ectoparasites of man in Australia; internal PARASITES are discussed in the entry on DISEASES, HUMAN. Several ectoparasites are more or less cosmopolitan and were introduced by Europeans or Aborigines (or both) at various times. Some parasites of domestic animals also attack man from time to time and he is sometimes infested by native species.

Lice (order Phthiraptera) LICE are true ectoparasites which die within a few hours if removed from their hosts. Two species are specific to man: the body and head louse, *Pediculus humanus*, and the crab or pubic louse, *Phthirus pubis*.

P. humanus has two interfertile forms but interbreeding is probably very rare in nature for one, *P. h. capitis*, is restricted to the head hair and the other, *P. h. humanus*, occurs only on the body. Body lice are a little larger than head lice (female body lice 3.8mm; female head lice 3.2mm). Body lice can spread two important diseases: louse-borne typhus which has occurred in Australia, and louse-borne relapsing fever which has not. Head lice can transmit the diseases experimentally but do not appear ever to do so naturally. (Recently, this species has been regarded as being two separate species, namely *P. capitis* and *P. humanus*, though many authorities still treat it as one.)

Body lice are relatively uncommon in Australia, the commonest victims being elderly, unhygienic people. Head lice are far more common, especially among young people, even when they keep themselves scrupulously clean. Girls are more prone to attack than boys, and it seems that this is not merely a result of different hair lengths. The lice are often transferred when children place their heads close together, or try on each other's hats and scarves. Treatment is carried out now simply by the application of various insecticides, and there is no longer any need for the victim to shave or closely crop the scalp. All members of a family should undergo the treatment.

Crab lice live where the hairs are relatively widely separated, that is in the pubic region, in the armpits and, rarely, on the eye lashes. Transmission is usually during sexual contact but the lice may be passed on with infested linen and towels. The crab louse differs in shape from the body louse, its large claws giving it a superficial resemblance to a crustacean. It is not known to transmit any diseases but its bite, like that of head lice, is irritating.

The scabies mite (subclass Acari) These MITES were thought during the Middle Ages to be an early stage of the louse but they were classified as mites by Dr Thomas Mouffet, the 'father of English entomology' (and the reputed grandfather of 'Little Miss Muffet'). The scabies mite, *Sarcoptes scabiei*, attacks

foxes, several domestic mammals and a species of wombat as well as man but the races of the mite do not apparently transfer successfully from host to host. The female lays her eggs in burrows in the skin; the burrows may eventually reach a length of 5cm. The larvae and nymphs shelter in hair follicles and small burrows. The life cycle, from egg laying to egg laying, takes about two weeks. Victims who have never been attacked before develop a hypersensitivity about a month after infestation. This causes an intolerable itch, and often a severe rash. The rash, however, appears on parts of the body which are remote from the sites of infestation; the infested areas are commonly on the webs between the fingers. Small vesicles may appear near the sites of infestation and on other parts of the body.

Patients who have been infested previously may react quickly to a new infestation but often the symptoms do not persist. The mites are most likely to be transmitted in crowded families, especially when beds are shared, but they can be passed on by more casual contacts. The disease is quite common among Aborigines in some parts of N Australia but also occurs sporadically in most parts of the country.

Various native mites (larval stages of trombiculids) sometimes infest man in Australia and can cause severe itching. Some species transmit the dangerous scrub typhus in parts of N Australia.

The bed bug The bed bug, *Cimex lectularis* (order Hemiptera), is an introduced species, probably sub-tropical in origin. These BUGS are extremely flattened and hide in crevices such as cracks in furniture or behind wallpaper. They also lay their eggs in such places. They emerge at night to feed on their victims. They can detect the presence of the prey by its warmth but only from a distance of a few centimetres. The adults can survive for about a year without feeding if the temperature is low and the relative humidity is about 90 per cent. With the general improvements in building and furniture making techniques bed bugs are now much less common than they were 30 years ago but they are still found in crowded inner suburbs.

Fleas (order Siphonaptera) Man is attacked in Australia by several species of FLEAS, including the human flea, *Pulex irritans*, the cat flea, *Ctenocephalides felis*, and the dog flea, *Ct. canis*; he is more likely to be attacked by the cat and dog fleas, both of which are common. Other species which sometimes attack man are the rare tropical rat flea, *Xenopsylla cheopis* (the chief vector of plague), and the European poultry flea, *Ceratophyllus gallinae*.

Ticks (order Metastigmata) The most dangerous of the TICKS which attack man in Australia is the native paralysis tick, *Ixodes holocyclus*. These are often 'collected' in the bush or in overgrown gardens in E Australia, especially after a damp period. They can usually be removed safely by placing the points of a partly open pair of scissors beneath the 'shoulders' of a tick and levering the animal

out. Fine forceps may be used but great care must be taken to avoid squeezing saliva into the victim, or leaving the mouthparts behind. Any malaise resulting from tick infestation, especially if the ticks were there for more than an hour or so, calls for medical attention. There have been a few fatalities among children as a result of paralysis tick infestations.

Further reading: see under parasites; parasites, livestock; fleas; mites; lice; ticks.

parasites, livestock

Livestock (including domestic animals such as cats and dogs) in Australia are parasitised by several hundred different species of parasitic animals. Often these can result in the death of an animal, or, at least, greatly reduce its productivity. The most important PARASITES are ROUNDWORMS (phylum Nematoda), FLUKES and TAPEWORMS (phylum Platyhelminthes), and some PROTOZOONS and ARTHROPODS. Most of these parasites were originally introduced into Australia with the animals themselves. The first stock to reach the country, however, had to undergo a long sea journey during which acute diseases would quickly kill the animals; consequently, only those parasites which caused chronic diseases, or had little effect on their hosts, arrived in the early days of European settlement. During the 19th century, however, some parasites were brought with animals from the then Dutch East Indies when military establishments were set up on the N coasts of Australia. In recent years strict quarantine has reduced the rate of entry of diseases and parasites of livestock and other animals. The following sections deal with a few of the more important animal parasites in Australia.

Endoparasites

1. Roundworms. Many nematodes attack sheep. They include the barber's pole worm, *Haemonchus contortus* (13mm to 40mm long), so-called because of the spiralling red stripe on the white body. Sheep become infested when they eat grass contaminated with droppings containing the larval worms. Between 500 and 1000 individuals will severely affect the sheep; they live within the stomach linings. Anaemia and swollen, fluid-filled jaws (bottle-jaw) are common symptoms. Tiny black scour or hair worms of sheep (*Trichostrongylus* and *Cooperia* species) live in the small intestine. The larvae are swallowed by the sheep, as with the barber's pole worm. Older sheep develop an immunity to an infestation but lambs are very

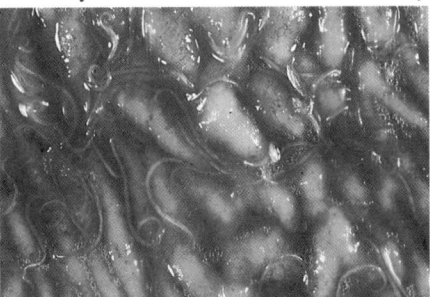

Hookworm, *Bunostomum* species

Whipworm, *Trichuris* species

susceptible. Some nematodes enter the body through the skin and reach the intestine through the blood stream. These include the hookworm (*Bunostomum* species) and the intestinal threadworm, *Strongyloides papillosus*. The nodule worm, *Oesophagostomum columbianum*, the ends of which curl like a shepherd's crook, forms nodules on the wall of the large intestine.

Among the nematodes infesting dogs and cats there are some which can attack man, though they cannot complete their life cycle in the normal way and wander in the tissues in search of a suitable resting place. When the nematode wanders just below the skin the condition is called cutaneous larva migrans but sometimes the nematodes can attack deeper organs, often with serious consequences, especially in children. This form of the disease is called visceral larva migrans and can result in blindness, liver damage or even death. The nematode species involved include *Toxascaris leonina* of cats and *Toxocara canis* of dogs.

2. Flukes and tapeworms. The most important fluke parasite of sheep and cattle in Australia is the LIVER FLUKE. It can sometimes infest man, not as a result of his eating infested sheep but usually by eating wild watercress.

The most serious tapeworm parasite is the HYDATID CYST TAPEWORM of dogs which sometimes attacks man in the larval stage. The beef tapeworm, *Taenia sagatina*, another species which can be transmitted to man, is fairly common. In 1967 about 0.2 per cent of the almost one million cattle slaughtered at VIC export abattoirs showed signs of infestation while at a Sydney abattoir the percentage condemnation of carcases varied from 0.01 to 0.9. Fortunately, human infestations are usually harmless and the victim is often unaware of the presence of the tapeworm. Pork tapeworm, *T. solium*, a potentially dangerous parasite when it attacks man, is very rare in Australia.

3. Protozoons. The most important disease in Australia caused by protozoons is tick fever of cattle (protozoons are endoparasites; TICKS are ectoparasites). The disease is caused by three species (though not all are present in a single case), *Babesia argentina*, *B. bigemina* and *Anaplasma marginale*. The tick which is the vector of the disease is *Boophilus microplus*, which was probably brought to Australia in 1872 on Brahman cattle from Jakarta. The disease first broke out at GLENCOE, near Darwin, in 1880.

The tick now infests at least 1 300 000km² in N Australia, an area which carries about 30 per cent of the country's beef cattle. Some beasts have been found to carry as many as 20 000 of the ticks in various stages but European breeds are far more susceptible than are Zebu and Zebu-crosses.

The fever in the cattle is caused by the rapid asexual reproductions of the parasitic protozoons in the red blood cells. The urine is often stained red by free haemoglobin. Some animals die but those that recover are apparently immune for the rest of their lives. The disease is usually mild in calves which rarely show the red water symptoms. Outbreaks are thus most severe when the ticks and the disease first enter a new area. Strict quarantine is used to prevent the further spread of the tick, which cannot travel far except on an animal's back. Unfortunately, it can also infest horses, sheep, kangaroos, wallabies and dogs though it cannot complete its life cycle on the last three.

Ectoparasites
1. Ticks. The most important ectoparasite in Australia is the cattle tick, which has been discussed above.
2. Fleas. FLEAS are ectoparasites which feed on the blood of birds and mammals.
3. Flies. Apart from the cattle tick the most important ectoparasites in Australia are the sheep BLOWFLIES. There are also several bloodsucking FLIES which visit animals for blood meals, sometimes infecting them with diseases such as ephemeral fever of cattle, but which are not parasitic in that they do not live permanently on the animal's surface. They include the small BUFFALO FLY, *Siphona irritans*, which lives only in the wetter parts of N Australia. It breeds in fresh cattle and buffalo dung and thus may be eventually controlled by introduced dung beetles (*see* BIOLOGICAL CONTROL). Another bloodsucking species is the sheep ked or 'tick', *Melophagus ovinus*, a greatly modified wingless fly which lives its entire life in the fleece of sheep, sucking blood and spoiling the wool.
4. Lice. In Australia domestic animals can be infested by several species of LICE. The approximate number of species are as follows: cattle—five sucking lice, one biting; horses—two biting species, one sucking species; pigs—one sucking louse; sheep—one biting species, two sucking species; dogs—two biting, one sucking; cats—one biting species. There are also many species infesting poultry. Particular species generally infest specific parts of the body. Louse infestations irritate the sheep and can reduce the quality of the wool. The largest louse attacking domestic animals is found on the pig. The adult female of this sucking louse, *Haematopinus suis*, is about 5mm long (most louse species are 2mm long or less); this species may act as a carrier of swine pox fever.

5. Mites. Many MITES attack Australian livestock. The most important species are mentioned here.

The itch mite of sheep, *Psorergates ovis*, is a microscopically small species first discovered

Mistletoe (*Amyema* species) on Eucalypt

in NSW in 1940. It has since been found throughout the continent and also in South Africa and New Zealand. Generally, only isolated animals in a flock are affected; their fleece is ragged as in sheep infested with lice. The mites live entirely in the superficial layers of the skin. The disease sheep scab or psoroptic mange, caused by *Psoroptes ovis*, first came to Australia in 1788 and eventually became one of the most serious diseases in the country, but it was eradicated by 1896.

Several domestic animals suffer, like man, from the scabies mite, *Sarcoptes scabiei*, though in the animals it causes a mange. This species also attacks foxes and wombats. The forms of the scabies mite found on different host species appear identical though they cannot persist for more than a generation or two on a strange host. Some species of mites attack the ears of their victims. Among these is *Otodectes cynotis*, which causes odectic mange, a common sickness of dogs in Australia, and sometimes also of cats.

Among other manges afflicting dogs the most serious is the demodectic type caused by *Demodex canis*, which has an elongated, worm-like body, about 0.25mm to 0.36mm in length. This species lives within sebaceous glands and hair follicles even in healthy animals but sometimes the numbers increase dramatically causing a dermatitis which is often followed by secondary infections by bacteria. The resulting disease is called red mange; it may be fatal, especially when young dogs are afflicted. The skin often has a characteristic mousy smell.

Various species of mites attack poultry. Feather mites which live in or on the feathers are usually unimportant, but the depluming mite, *Knemidocoptes gallinae*, and the scaly leg mite, *Kn. mutans*, which may cause grotesque swellings of the bare parts of the body, can be serious.

See also diseases, livestock; grazing industry
Further reading: see under parasites. *Also* Roberts, F.H.S. *Insects Affecting Livestock.* Angus & Robertson, Sydney, 1952; Hungerford, T.C. *Diseases of Livestock.* (8th end) McGraw-Hill, Sydney, 1975.

parasitic plants Australia has three main families of flowering plants which are PARASITES: the Loranthaceae (mistletoes), the Santalaceae and the Cassythaceae (dodders). Although each of these families is taxonomically separate, the parasitic members show a number of common vegetative characteristics which are related to their mode of life. Many species are leafless or almost so, and have specialised organs which attach them to the living host plant from which they obtain food, salts and manufactured food. Most species are green in some part (leaves or stems) and are able to carry out limited photosynthesis for themselves.

The Loranthaceae contains a number of shrubs which are generally parasitic on the branches of the host, though the species of the genera *Atkinsonia* and *Nuytsia* are root parasites. The host trees for both *Amyema* and *Muellerina* are largely eucalypts, although *A. gaudichandii* is parasitic on *Melaleuca* (paperbark) and *A. quandang* on *Acacia*. At most times of the year the mistletoe is difficult to distinguish from the host, but under drought conditions the parasite generally remains leafy and healthy while the host loses most of its leaves, the parasite competing successfully for water taken up by the host. Other parasitic genera in this family include *Amylotheca, Lysiana, Dendrophthoe, Viscum* and *Nothothixos*; the last-mentioned is a parasite on other parasitic Loranthaceae. The most curious genus, *Korthalsella*, which forms tufts of articulated upright branches, is a parasite of closed forest species such as SASSAFRAS, *Doryphora sassafras*, and lily pilly, *Acmena smithii*.

Members of the Santalaceae are generally root parasites, and many are almost leafless. The best-known examples are the native cherry, *Exocarpos cupressiformis*, and the native currant, *Leptomeria acida*, which are widespread in woodland and open forests and thought to be parasitic on *Eucalyptus* roots. Other Australian parasitic genera include *Santalum* and *Choretrum*.

The Cassythaceae is represented by a single genus, *Cassytha*, known as devil's twine or dodder; the latter name is also applied to a parasitic member of the family Convolvulaceae, *Cuscuta australis*. Species of *Cassytha* are all twining parasites with no leaves; the stems are attached to the host by small sucker 'feet' (haustoria) through which the parasite gains nutriment. *Cassytha* species are not host specific, but smother and kill groups of adjacent shrubs regardless of species.
See also Appendix 5, Flower Structure and Glossary of Botanical Terms
Further reading: see Appendix 6, A Bibliography for Plants.

pardalotes *see* flowerpeckers

Park, Ruth Author and journalist. Born in New Zealand, she worked as a journalist in Auckland, and in 1942 moved to Sydney, where she married a fellow journalist and author, D'Arcy NILAND. She has written many children's books and scripts for radio, films and television, but has attained her greatest success with her novels, especially *Harp in the South* (1947), which gives a sentimental but realistic picture of life in a slum suburb of Sydney. It was a notable popular success and was translated into 11 languages. Her other novels include *Poor Man's Orange* (1948), *The Witch's Thorn* (1951), *A Power of Roses* (1953), *Pink Flannel* (1955), *One-a-Pecker, Two-a-Pecker* (1958) and *The Good Looking Women* (1961). She and her husband wrote a joint autobiography, *The Drums Go Bang* (1956).

Parkes NSW (population 9 047 in 1981) A town in the central W slopes region of the State, it is located on the Newell Highway 367km by road W of Sydney. It is an important railway focus (446km by rail from Sydney) on the main W line (the 'Indian-Pacific' route), with a branch line S to FORBES. At an elevation of 316m above sea level, situated in the area of rolling hills between the headwaters of the BOGAN RIVER and tributaries of the LACHLAN RIVER, it experiences hot summers and mild winters, with an annual average rainfall of 569mm, spread uniformly throughout the year. The town serves as the business and market centre for a rich rural district producing wheat, wool, fat lambs, cattle and pigs. The early settlement of the area was by squatters but the town really owes its birth to the discovery of gold in 1862 at the locality known as the 'Golden Bar', NE of the town. Other mines in the boom years were 'The Pioneer', 'No Mistake' and a rich alluvial lead mine called 'The Bushman' which gave the town its original name. Later, in 1873, the name was changed to Parkes to honour Sir Henry PARKES and the main street was called Clarinda Street to commemorate Lady Parkes. It was proclaimed a municipality in 1883 and the railway from Sydney reached the town in 1893. Among the tourist attractions are the Henry Parkes Historical Museum, a motor museum of vintage cars, the Pioneer Park Museum containing agricultural machinery from the early days to the present time and a school and a church dating from the days when the horse and buggy were used. The courthouse group of buildings in the town has been classified by the National Trust (NSW) for preservation. A CSIRO radio telescope, an impressive structure with a movable saucer-shaped aerial system 65m in diameter, is located 18km N of Parkes.

Parkes, Sir Henry (1815-96) Premier of NSW. The son of a tenant farmer, he was born in Warwickshire, England, began work at the age of eight in a rope-making establishment and later served an apprenticeship as an ivory turner. Although he had little formal education, he read widely and contributed writings in prose and verse to the *Chartist*. He and his first wife, Clarinda, came to Sydney in 1839 as assisted immigrants, and he worked in various capacities, including those of farm labourer and customs officer, before setting up his own ivory and bone turning business. He became actively engaged in politics in the late 1840s, was prominent in the anti-transportation movement, and from 1850 to 1858 published a newspaper, the *Empire*, first as a weekly and then as a daily. He was elected to the Legislative Council in 1854 and to the new Legislative Assembly in 1856, and during the following 40 years came to dominate the political scene in NSW. He became leader of the free trade faction, and was Premier for five terms, totalling 12 years. He was appointed KCMG in 1877 and GCMG in 1888.

Parkes' most notable achievements were in promoting immigration, in education and in

Radiotelescope at Parkes NSW

O. Munn

the movement for federation. He was responsible for the Public Schools Act of 1866, which unified the administration of education under a Council of Education, and for the Public Instruction Act of 1880, which ended State aid for denominational schools, placed public education under a Ministry and provided for the setting up of State high schools. With regard to federation, at an intercolonial conference in 1880-81 he suggested the formation of a federal council, but failed to win sufficient support and dropped the proposal. However, when such a body was set up in 1885, he opposed participation by NSW on the grounds that the council had insufficient power, and would prove an obstacle in the path of true federation. In 1889, in a speech at the northern NSW town of TENTERFIELD, he called for the framing of a constitution providing for a federal Parliament with full power over matters of importance to Australia as a whole. Having thus launched the federation movement, he was unable to play a very important part in carrying it through. When the convention of 1891 had produced a constitution, he sensed that there was strong opposition to it in NSW and delayed introducing it into Parliament. He was not given another opportunity. In October he went out of office, being replaced by George Dibbs, an opponent of federation; in the same month Parkes was replaced by George REID as leader of the free trade faction. In the elections of 1895 he failed to retain his seat.

Sir Henry Parkes

Parkes was impressive in bearing and as an orator, and he had immense energy, political guile and skill in public administration. However, his personality was marred by extreme vanity and spitefulness towards opponents. He was also inept at managing his personal finances. He lived in an almost continuous state of financial crisis and died in poverty. His publications included six volumes of verse, none of it highly regarded, and a number of prose works, including the autobio-

graphical *Fifty Years in the Making of Australian History* (1892).

Further reading: Lyne, C.E. *Life of Sir Henry Parkes.* Angus & Robertson, Sydney, 1896; Martin, A.W. 'Sir Henry Parkes and Public Education in New South Wales' in French, E.L. (ed) *Melbourne Studies in Education 1960-61.* Melbourne University Press, Melbourne, 1962 and *Henry Parkes.* Oxford University Press, Melbourne, 1964.

Parramatta NSW (population 130 935 in 1981) A residential, commercial and industrial city, 24km W of SYDNEY COVE, it is now included within the greater metropolitan Sydney area, forming a major suburban satellite centre. It is situated at the head of the Parramatta River, which is the W extension of PORT JACKSON and which, at Parramatta, is little more than a small creek.

The city is rich in history. A few months after the establishment of the first British settlement in 1788, Governor Arthur PHILLIP himself explored the site in the search for better farming land than that around Sydney Cove. The alluvial flats of the Parramatta River and the adjacent gently undulating hilly land offered good agricultural possibilities. A settlement was established in November 1788 and in the following year was yielding crops. It was initially called Rose Hill after a British Treasury official, but this was changed a few years later to Parramatta, an Aboriginal word meaning 'head of the waters'. Plans for the town were drawn in 1790 by William Dawes; the first wine produced in Australia came from a vineyard planted near Parramatta in 1791; in the following year, the first land grant in the colony was made to James RUSE who established an experimental farm at Parramatta; and by 1793 a ferry was operating to

Sydney and a road by 1794. The building of the town proceeded in those early years with several government institutions such as convict barracks and a school for orphans. Some historic buildings still survive. Among these the best known are Elizabeth Farm House built by John MACARTHUR in 1793; St John's Church, begun in 1797 and opened in 1803, when it was described as 'the best public building in the colony'; and the old Government House (1799-1816). The National Trust (NSW) has placed many buildings in Parramatta on its classified list, thereby indicating that the Trust considers that these are 'essential to the heritage of Australia and must be conserved'.

Further reading: Jervis, J. *The Cradle City of Australia: A History of Parramatta, 1788-1961.* Council of the City of Parramatta, 1961; Proudfoot, H. *Old Government House—The Building and Its Landscape.* Angus & Robertson, Sydney, 1971; Emanuel, C. & van Sommers, T. *Parramatta Sketchbook.* Rigby, Adelaide, 1977; *National Trust Register.* The National Trust of Australia (NSW), Sydney, 1978.

parrots, cockatoos and lorikeets These colourful BIRDS belong to the family Psittacidae, which contains 328 species of parrots, 55 of which occur in Australia (48 are endemic). The Australian species may be divided into 'true' parrots, cockatoos and lorikeets. All species have short, massive beaks with the upper mandible down-curved and pointed; the beak is often used for climbing. The legs and neck are short, and the zygodactylous feet (two toes pointing forwards, two backwards) are able to hold food. Most species are vegetarian, and lay eggs in tree hollows or termite nests. Many parrots are easily tamed

Old Government House, Parramatta NSW

and are often kept as pets or in aviaries; part of their attraction is their ability to 'talk' and their apparent intelligence. They have suffered greatly from being smuggled out of Australia to overseas collectors who are willing to pay high prices for these protected and often rare birds. The parrots described below are mostly the common species, taken from the main genera.

The true parrots usually have long tails and spend a great deal of their time feeding on the ground; two species in this group are completely terrestrial. The genus *Electus* is represented by the red-sided parrot, *E. roratus* (33cm long). This species is unusual in that the female is more brightly coloured than the male. The male is green with a patch of red and a yellow and black bill, whereas the female is red with blue on the breast and a black bill. Found in the rainforest of CAPE YORK, it feeds on fruits, seeds and nectar.

The genus *Opopsitta (Psittaculirostris)* contains Australia's smallest parrot, the fig parrot, *O. diopthalma* (13cm to 18cm), which has a short tail. This species is mainly green, with some blue and red, and it frequents fruit-bearing trees, especially native figs, in northern NSW and parts of QLD.

The genus *Polytelis* * consists of three fairly rare species whose numbers have been depleted because of their popularity with overseas collectors. The superb parrot, *P.* * swainsonii* (35cm to 40cm), is pale green with yellow markings on the head and throat and a red band on the chest (the yellow and red is absent in the female). Restricted to woodland areas near watercourses in SE Australia, it feeds mainly on seeds and nectar. The regent parrot, *P.* * anthopeplus* (38cm), (male bright yellow, female dull olive-green) is found in the area around the junction of SA, NSW and VIC borders, and in south-western WA where it sometimes is regarded as a pest by wheat farmers. The Alexandra parrot, *P.* * alexandrae* (38cm to 46cm), a nomadic species found in central Australia, is violet and green with a rose-pink throat.

There are seven species in the genus *Neophema* *; these long-tailed birds are mainly green and yellow in colour, measure between 20cm and 23cm long, and favour dry habitats. The Bourke parrot, *N.* * bourkii*, is blue-grey above and rose-pink below. Found in central Australia, it is a partly nocturnal bird which spends much of its time on the ground searching for seeds from grasses and *Acacia* trees. A common species of the sand dunes and rocky coasts of southern Australia is the rock parrot, *N.* * petrophila*. Its plumage is blue, yellow and olive green, and its diet consists mainly of the seeds of ground plants. The nesting site is usually a hole in a cliff face or beneath a rock. The rarer orange-bellied parrot, *N.* * chrysogaster*, may be a geographical variant of the rock parrot; it has similar habits but a more E distribution. A common and gregarious member of this genus is the elegant parrot, *N.* * elegans*, a blue, yellow and greenish-yellow species which lives in forest clearings and open woodlands in

southern SA and south-western WA.

The unique genus *Pezoporus* * consists of two rare species which may be related to the kakapo parrot of New Zealand. The ground parrot, *P.* * wallicus* (body 33cm to 36cm; tail 20cm), is a grass-green bird with blotches and bars of yellow and black. A ground-dwelling species of wet coastal heath and rough ground in SE Australia and TAS, it is active at dusk, dawn and during the night, when it may fly. It feeds on seeds, and scratches a hollow in the sand in which to lay its eggs. Because of European settlement and introduced predators, the night parrot, *P.* * occidentalis* (33cm to 36cm), is probably extinct. It is (or was) similar to the ground parrot but the tail is much shorter and the nests are made in porcupine grass and possibly in caves. Its distribution is given as parts of central Australia.

The very familiar budgerigar, *Melopsittacus* * undulatus* (body 18cm; tail 10cm), is an abundant species in wooded savanna in most of Australia. It scarcely needs description, but it should be noted that wild budgerigars are green with black bars on the back and a bright yellow face. During periods of drought, these seed-eating birds die in their thousands near drying water holes.

The parrots known as rosellas belong to the genus *Platycercus* * and take their name from Rose Hill ('rosehillers'), a former name of PARRAMATTA. They have short, rounded wings which give them a characteristic undulating flight; their plumage patterns and colours vary, but all have a scalloped or marbled pattern on the back. There are probably seven species in this genus, though it is difficult to determine the exact number of species because some may be simply geographical variants. Perhaps the best-known species is the crimson rosella, *P.* * elegans* (33cm to 36cm). The head and underparts are crimson, there is a violet patch below the eye, the rump and tail are purple, the back is mottled and the wings are blue. This handsome bird lives in woodlands and forests in the SE and near CAIRNS in QLD, feeding on seeds, flowers, honey and insects.

The genus *Psephotus* * contains seven species; all have long, broad, tapering tails but, unlike the rosellas, none have face patches or mottled backs. One species, the paradise parrot, *P.* * pulcherrimus* (28cm to 30cm), is apparently extinct. A common species is the blue-bonnet parrot, *P.* * haematogaster* (28cm to 30cm), found in inland SE Australia, in open country with scattered trees for nesting. It has a bright blue face and is golden yellow on the shoulders; the rest of the plumage varies according to the locality. Another common species, the mulga parrot, *P.* * varius* (28cm to 30cm), is mainly green, with some red and yellow on the belly, a small red cap and a yellow patch on the wing. This widespread species frequents dry to arid savanna country and spends much of its time on the ground, searching for seeds. The golden-shouldered parrot, *P.* * chrysopterygius* (body 25cm; tail 15cm), is mainly bluish-green below with yellow shoulders, mainly brown wings and a

red rump. Found in savanna woodland in Cape York, it is among those parrot species which nest in termite mounds; its nests are kept clean by a scavenging moth which is not known in any other habitat.

Most cockatoos are large birds with erectile crests and short, square tails; they usually feed on the ground. The palm cockatoo, *Probosciger aterrimus* (60cm), an all-black bird with a very long crest, is really a New Guinea species with a bridgehead on the tip of Cape York. As the name suggests, it favours the seeds of the pandanus palm, but it also eats fruit, leaves and flowers.

The genus *Calyptorhynchus* * contains four species of cockatoos; all are mainly black, with a coloured band on the centre of the tail. They feed on fruit, honey, tree seeds and grubs. The white-tailed cockatoo, *C.* * baudinii* (51cm to 56cm), frequents forests and sandplains in SW Australia. The red-tailed cockatoo, *C.* * banksii (C.* * magnificus)* (60cm), which has a distinct, rather fluffy crest, and the yellow-tailed cockatoo, *C.* * funereus* (60cm to 65cm), frequent forests and woodlands; the former is scattered throughout the mainland, while the latter occurs in SE Australia. The glossy cockatoo, *C.* * lathami* (45cm to 50cm), has no crest; the male has a red band on the tail, whereas the female's tail is red with black bars. This species is found in forests and woodlands with casuarina trees in SE Australia, but not in TAS.

One of the most distinctive cockatoos is the male gang-gang cockatoo, *Callocephalon* * fimbriatum* (30cm to 33cm). Mostly black, it has a bright red head with a forward-curving crest. It lives in the mountains of SE Australia, feeding on seeds and insects procured mostly in trees. Another unmistakeable cockatoo is the galah, *Eolophus* * (Cacatua) roseicapilla* (35cm), found in open country throughout Australia but rare in TAS. Its wings, crest and back are light grey, while most of the rest of the body is deep pink. Galahs often fly in large flocks, making a very colourful spectacle. They feed on seeds, roots and cereals, sometimes damaging crops.

The white cockatoos and corellas belong to the genus *Cacatua*; four species are represented in Australia. A noisy species is the sulphur-crested cockatoo, *C. galerita* (40cm to 43cm), a white bird with a long yellow crest, which is often kept as a household pet. It is found in the forests of most States, feeding on various seeds, roots, cereals and insects. A species which is becoming rarer is the Major Mitchell cockatoo, *C. leadbeateri* * (38cm to 41cm), a pinkish-white bird with a red, yellow and white crest. It lives in timbered areas in the arid parts of Australia and feeds on seeds, roots and cereals. The little corella, *C. sanguinea* (35cm to 38cm), an almost endemic species, and the long-billed corella, *C. tenuirostris* * (38cm), are both white birds with indistinct, pinkish crests; they can be distinguished by the shape of their beaks, the upper mandible in the latter species being much longer. While the common little corella is extending its range on the mainland as it bene-

Species, genus or family is endemic to Australia (see Preface)

fits from agriculture, the long-billed species of SE and SW is now rare, and becoming rarer.

The cockatiel, *Nymphicus* hollandicus* (25cm to 28cm) is a slim, grey bird with a crest and a long tail; the male has a yellow face and crest and a reddish ear patch, while the face of the female is browner. Cockatiels are nomadic, flock-forming birds with a swift, erratic flight. They live in open woodlands and savanna in dry parts of the mainland, feeding mainly on seeds.

Lorikeets are tree-dwelling parrots with brush-like tongues for collecting nectar. They fly swiftly, usually in flocks. The lorikeets belonging to the genus *Trichoglossus* are green-backed birds with a red or yellow collar and some red on the underwing. The rainbow lorikeet, *T. moluccanus** (25cm to 30cm), is a red-breasted, blue-headed bird with a pale greenish-yellow collar, a red beak and blue bars on the belly. Found in forests, woods and gardens in N, E and SE Australia, these beautiful birds often form large flocks and travel long distances in search of fruit and blossom-laden trees. The similar red-collared lorikeet, *T. rubritorquis* (25cm to 30cm), lives in the NT and northern WA. The scaly-breasted lorikeet, *T. chlorolepidotus** (20cm), of E Australia (but not TAS) has yellow scallops on the breast and a scalloped collar. This nomadic bird feeds on nectar.

The varied lorikeet, *Psitteuteles versicolor** (18cm to 20cm), is a mainly green bird with a red cap and black underwings. Usually seen in flocks, it frequents flowering gum trees in northern WA, the NT and QLD.

The lorikeets of the genus *Glossopsitta** have short, pointed tails and some red on the face. A mainly green species is the musk lorikeet, *G.* concinna* (23cm), which is distinguished by a broad red band which runs from the forehead, to the neck, cutting through the eye. This nomadic bird is found in wooded country in E Australia, south-eastern SA and TAS, feeding on nectar and fruit, and often causing damage in orchards. The purple-crowned lorikeet, *G.* porphyrocephala* (15cm to 18cm), has pale blue underparts and red under the wings. It frequents blossom-bearing and fruit trees in SE and SW Australia (but not TAS). The little lorikeet, *G.* pusilla* (15cm to 18cm), also feeds on fruit and nectar, often travelling a considerable distance to find fruit and blossom-bearing trees. This species is mainly green, with a distinct red mask and a black bill. It occurs in E Australia and south-eastern SA.

Further Reading: Harman, I. *Australian Parrots in Bush and Aviary.* David & Charles, Newton Abbot, 1981; Law, R. *Lories and Lorikeets: The Brush-tongued Parrots.* Inkata Press, Melbourne, 1978; Robinson, L. *Australian Parrots in Colour.* Rigby, Adelaide, 1970.

parsley *see* Umbelliferae

parsnip *see* Umbelliferae

*Species, genus or family is endemic to Australia (see Preface)

passerine birds More than half of all known BIRDS are termed passerine, and they belong to the largest order (Passeriformes) of the class Aves. Passerines are perching birds or song birds, and include such familiar forms as sparrows, thrushes, currawongs and ravens. They are differentiated from all other orders (collectively known as non-passerine) by certain technical details of the skull. In general, passerines are small birds with a complete set of wing quills and with the first toe directed backwards and the other three forwards; the feet are never webbed. Most passerines hop, but a few, such as starlings, walk or run. The young are always naked and helpless when they hatch.

In Australia there are about 344 species (246 endemic) of passerine birds (46 per cent), divided into *c.*34 families. The classification of these species has proved a difficult task. In many families, similar forms replace each other in different parts of the continent; another difficulty is that many species have been named after birds of similar appearance in Europe, and consequently 'wrens' and 'thrushes' appear in several families. No attempt is made in this encyclopedia to mention all species. The names used as headings can be taken only as a rough guide to the species discussed in the family concerned.

passion fruit This is the common name given to species of the genus *Passiflora* (family Passifloraceae); various species, native and introduced, occur in Australia. The commercial passion fruit is an introduced species, *P. edulis.* The native passion fruit of NSW and QLD, *P. herbetiana*, is a climbing plant, like all members of the genus; it has dark green, lobed leaves and the flowers are green or reddish.

Passmore, John Richard (1904-) Artist. Born in Sydney, Passmore studied at Julian ASHTON's Sydney Art School. He went to Europe in 1933 and his return 17 years later brought to Sydney a new approach to art for he was the only Australian painter at the time who had seen the original works of Picasso and Cézanne. The influence of his experience in Europe can be seen in his work and in the works of his art students in Sydney, particularly OLSEN. His paintings showed an attempt to analyse the form and shifting viewpoints—geographical and historical—of a particular object or scene. The Sydney Harbour in particular, and the sea in general, dominated his works. The trend in painting in Sydney changed in 1956 when Passmore, along with friends and pupils, exhibited in a show entitled 'Direction I'; the show launched abstract painting in Sydney and this movement was to dominate the art scene there for nearly 20 years.

patents, trade marks and designs Section 52 (xviii) of the federal Constitution gives the Commonwealth Parliament power to legislate with regard to 'COPYRIGHT, patents of inventions and designs, and trade marks'.

However, the States continued to grant patents until the Commonwealth Patents Act 1903 came into operation.

At present, the granting of patents is governed by the Patents Act 1952-73, which is administered by the Commissioner of Patents. Registration of the users of trade marks and their assignment with or without the goodwill of the business concerned is provided for under the Trade Marks Act 1955-73. Registration of designs is covered by the Designs Act 1906-73. The Commissioner of Patents is also Registrar of Trade Marks and Registrar of Designs. Information regarding all three matters, including a list of patent attorneys, is available from the Patent Trade Marks and Design Office in each capital city. Free pamphlets issued by the Office include *Questions and Answers about Patents, How to Apply for a Patent* and similar ones dealing with trade marks and with designs.

Andrew Barton ('Banjo') Paterson

Paterson, Andrew Barton 'Banjo' (1864-1941) Poet. Born near ORANGE in NSW, he grew up on a station near YASS, was educated in Sydney and qualified as a solicitor. After some years he left legal work for journalism and from 1899 to 1900 was a war correspondent in South Africa. He then worked as an editor for a time, was a pastoralist in the MONARO district of NSW and in World War I was an ambulance driver in France and, later, Remount Officer for the Australian Imperial Force (AIF) in Egypt. His publications include an anthology entitled *The Old Bush Songs* (1905) and three works of fiction. However, it is as a poet, particularly as a writer of bush ballads, that he is remembered; ballads such as his 'The Man from Snowy River' and 'Clancy of the Overflow' are perhaps the best-known poems in Australian literature. His ballads deal mainly with station life—in areas fairly close to settlement, not in the far Outback—and with the world of the drover. He avoids the grimmer aspects of such life, concentrating on the exciting and humorous. Yet within these limits he gives a realistic picture, and reflects faithfully the feelings which Australians of his time had for the country. His published works of poetry include *The Man From Snowy River and Other*

Commonwealth of Australia

New South Wales

Victoria

South Australia

Western Australia

Queensland

Tasmania

Northern Territory

See also FLAGS

Commonwealth of Australia

New South Wales

Victoria

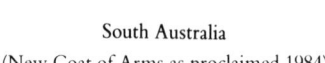

South Australia
(New Coat of Arms as proclaimed 1984)

Western Australia

Queensland
(As modernised with supporters 1977)

Tasmania

Northern Territory

City of Canberra

See also FLAGS

Verses (1895), which went through many editions, *Rio Grande's Last Race and Other Verses* (1902), *Saltbush Bill JP and Other Verses* (1917), *The Collected Verse of A.B. Paterson* (1921) and *The Animals That Noah Forgot* (1933).
Further reading: Semmler, C.W. *A.B. Paterson.* Oxford University Press, Melbourne, 1967 and *The Banjo of the Bush.* (2nd edn) Queensland University Press, St Lucia QLD, 1974.

Paterson, William (1755-1810) Lieutenant-Governor of NSW. Born in Montrose, Scotland, he developed in boyhood a very strong interest in science, particularly in botany. In early manhood he travelled extensively in the interior of South Africa, subsequently publishing a narrative of his journeys, which was dedicated to Sir Joseph BANKS. For most of the rest of his life he corresponded with Banks and sent him botanical specimens. He joined the British Army in 1781 and came to NSW as a lieutenant of the NEW SOUTH WALES CORPS in 1791. After Major GROSE had left the colony in December 1794 Paterson filled the post of administrator until the arrival of Governor HUNTER nine months later. In 1801 he explored the HUNTER RIVER and in the same year was appointed Lieutenant-Governor of NSW by Governor KING. Three years later he was sent to found a settlement at PORT DALRYMPLE in TAS. He first settled at York Town and in 1806 established another settlement, further up the TAMAR RIVER, which became known as LAUNCESTON, named after Governor King's birthplace in Cornwall. When he heard of the rebellion against BLIGH he decided to return to Sydney, but delayed his departure from TAS, using various pretexts, and did not leave until January 1809. On arrival in Sydney he took charge of the colony, remaining in command until the arrival of Governor MACQUARIE. He refused to reinstate Bligh, insisting that both Bligh and Major JOHNSTON, who had deposed him, should go to England so that the affair could be judged by the authorities there; Bligh, however, after being allowed to board the *Porpoise*, sailed to TAS. Paterson himself sailed for England with Johnston and most of the New South Wales Corps in May 1810, but died on the voyage.

It seems clear that he was more deeply interested in science than in his administrative duties. He was elected a member of the Royal Society in 1798 while on leave in England. His botanical specimens are preserved at the Natural History Museum, South Kensington, London.

Paterson's curse *see* weeds

paua shell *see* gastropods

pauropods The Pauropoda is a cosmopolitan class (about 400 species) of soil-dwelling ARTHROPODS which lack a common name. Resembling MILLIPEDES, they are minute (0.5mm to 2mm long), white, soft-bodied animals with 12 trunk segments, nine of which

carry legs, and are the only arthropods which have branched antennae. They appear to be general scavengers in the soil.

Peacock, Andrew Sharp (1938-) Federal parliamentary leader of the LIBERAL PARTY OF AUSTRALIA. Educated in Melbourne, he graduated LLB from Melbourne University and practised as a solicitor before winning the federal seat of Kooyong, which had previously been held by Sir Robert MENZIES, in a by-election in 1966. Even before this he had won prominence in the Liberal Party, having become president of its VIC branch at the age of 26. He became a Minister in 1969, and in later years held a variety of portfolios, most notably that for Foreign Affairs from 1976 to 1981. However, he then clashed with Prime Minister FRASER, resigned from Cabinet, and in 1982 made an unsuccessful bid for the party leadership. After the Labor victory in the general election of March 1983 and the resignation of Fraser from party leadership, Peacock was elected to succeed him. A fluent speaker, skilful in media presentation, he is regarded as being more moderate in style and more pragmatic in outlook than his predecessor.

Peak Downs QLD The Peak Downs Highway in the central E part of the State links Clermont to MACKAY on a NE-SW route of about 280km, passing across the Drummond, Denham, Kerlong and Connors Ranges. On part of its inland section, the highway skirts the watershed divide between the S tributaries of the Suttor River (which drains into the BURDEKIN) and the headwaters of Isaacs River (which drains into the MACKENZIE). The region of the 'downs' country, lying NE of Clermont, is an area of rolling countryside,

with a number of distinctive volcanic outcrops rising above the general terrain, where many townships and station properties have the name 'downs', (for example, Cumberland Downs, Olive Downs, Logan Downs, Leichhardt Downs). The Peak Downs settlement, located 24km SE of the highway and 120km by road NE of Clermont, was started in the late 1940s by a British company which cleared the light scrub country for crop growing, mainly of sorghum. Though the project was not very successful, it led to a diversification of rural activities. Open-cut coal mining is important at Peak Downs and at Saraji, 24km S.

peanuts *see* agriculture

peanut worms These sedentary marine worms belong to the phylum Sipunculida, which contains about 250 species. The species *Phascolosoma noduliferum* is common on Australian rocky shores, usually in sand or gravel beneath stones. Like most members of the phylum, the body is cylindrical. The front end of the body (the introvert) can be turned inside the rest. The mouth is at the front end and is surrounded by tentacles. The worm passes sand and gravel through its gut, extracting organic matter for food.

Pearce, Henry Robert 'Bobby' (1905-1976) Sculler. He was born in London and later emigrated to Australia. He started his career at the age of six and was to become the greatest sculler the world has known. His first sculling win came in a race for youths under 16 which he won when he was six years and three months old. He won his first Australian amateur championship in 1927, and in 1928 he was the natural selection to represent Aus-

Aerial view of open-cut mining at Peak Downs QLD

Courtesy of A.I.S. Canberra

tralia in sculling at the Amsterdam Olympic Games. He celebrated his selection by winning Australia's first Olympic gold medal for rowing when he won the single sculls, a success he repeated in the 1932 Los Angeles Games. In 1931, he won the most prestigious of amateur sculling events—the Henley Diamond Sculls—one of only four Australians to do so. A superbly fit and outstandingly talented sculler, so confident was he of his ability that on occasions he trained with and coached his opponents before races. He turned professional in 1933 and in the same year won the world professional sculling title. On his retirement in 1948 he held the distinction of being the only sculling champion never to have lost a race either as an amateur or as a professional. He died in Toronto, Canada, shortly before the Montreal Olympic Games.

Pearl, Cyril Alston (1906-) Journalist and author. Born in WA, he was educated in Sydney and worked there as a journalist, becoming editor of the *Sunday Telegraph* (1939-49), the magazine *A.M.* (1949-54) and the *Sunday Mirror* (1960-61). His published works are mainly in the fields of Australian history and biography, and include *Our Yesterdays* (1954), which contains an outstanding selection of Australian historical photographs, *Wild Men of Sydney* (1959), *Morrison of Peking* (1967), *Brilliant Dan Deniehy* (1972), *The Three Lives of Gavan Duffy* (1979) and *The Dunera Scandal* (1983). Other works include *The Girl with the Swansdown Seat* (1955), which deals with sexual morals in Victorian England, *Dublin in Bloomtime* (1969) and a number of lighter books such as the witty and satirical *So You Want to be an Australian* (1959).

pearls and pearling Pearling in Australia began in the 1850s, in northern WA. Regular pearling in E waters began with Captain Banner's voyage in the *Julia Percy* to the Warrior Reefs, N of THURSDAY ISLAND, in 1868. The pearlers were in search of mother-of-pearl from oysters and trochus shells. At first, Aborigines were employed as divers but when this was forbidden they were replaced by Indonesian and Timorese divers. Later, Japanese divers and skippers became prominent in the industry.

Nickol Bay, near DAMPIER in WA, was the first pearling port but by the 1890s BROOME in WA and Thursday Is had become the most important ports, with Darwin playing a smaller part. Thursday Is was, at one time, the largest pearling port that has ever existed. In 1904 there were 403 pearling luggers in WA, mainly in Broome, 378 in Thursday Is and about 50 in Darwin. As the shells became scarcer in shallow waters the divers had to move into deeper seas. The industry became extremely dangerous—accidents were frequent and many pearlers were killed during cyclones—and this led to a slow decline in pearling. Although there was a small revival in pearling during and after World War II artificial substitutes for mother-of-pearl

robbed the pearlers of many of their traditional markets.

Nowadays, traditional methods have been replaced by a technique developed in Japan to produce cultured pearls. Most of the firms in the pearl culturing industry are joint Japanese and Australian enterprises. In Australia young gold-lip pearl shell oysters, *Pinctada maxima*, and the black-lip species, *P. margaritifera* (see BIVALVE MOLLUSCS), are collected for pearl culture. In Japan a smaller species is used. The Australian species produces a pearl of about 18mm in diameter in two to three years, whereas in Japan the process takes about twice as long. A nucleus, usually made from an American freshwater mussel, is placed under a mantle graft on the foot of the oyster which is then placed in a wire cage floating from a wooden raft. Periodically, the oyster is examined by X-rays to see if the pearl has 'taken'. When the pearls are gathered, the mother-of-pearl is also extracted for export.

The largest pearl found in Australia is the drop-shaped 'Star of the West' (Broome, 1917). It weighed 6.48g and was sold in London for £6000. The largest pearl in the world is probably the 'Pearl of Laotze', taken from a giant clam at Palawan in the Philippines in 1934. It weighs 6 378g and is 14cm in diameter and 24cm long. It was valued at US$4 080 000 in 1971.

pearlwort *see* Caryophyllaceae

pearly nautilus *see* cephalopods

Peart, Donald (1909-) Musician. Born in Wiltshire, England, Donald Peart was educated at Queen's College, Oxford, and at the Royal College of Music, where he also became a professor, before taking up his appointment as Foundation Professor of Music at the University of Sydney in 1947. Among his wide interests and activities in furthering many facets of music, he is highly regarded for his work in fostering Australian MUSICAL COMPOSITION and performance, and for encouraging contemporary and avant-garde music in Australia. He was responsible for re-founding the International Society for Contemporary Music (ISCM) in Sydney in 1956 and founded the Musicological Society of Australia in 1963.

peas *see* agriculture; Papilionaceae

peat moss *see* Bryophyta

Peel, Thomas (1793-1865) Colonial promoter and pioneer. Born in Lancashire, he was a relative of Sir Robert Peel and the son of the owner of a large textile manufacturing business. When James STIRLING recommended the founding of a colony in WA Peel organised a group of prospective investors. Most of them withdrew when the government announced the terms on which it would grant land, but Peel retained his interest. Traditionally he has been credited with investing £50 000 in the colony,

but it appears that this was done in partnership with the wealthy ex-convict, Solomon Levy, who provided the finance, while Peel acted as working manager and had the partnership's land registered in his name. From the outset, his life in the colony was marked by misfortune. He had been promised first choice of 250 000 acres of prime land on condition that his first settlers reached Perth by 1 November 1829, but they arrived six weeks later and he was obliged to take land of lesser quality. In all, more than 500 settlers were brought out by the partnership. However, the general difficulties besetting the colony, as well as particular misfortunes such as the late delivery of stores and stock and Peel's being for a time incapacitated by a gunshot wound in his right hand, made it impossible for him to employ the settlers effectively. Many left his service and he became embroiled in a series of lawsuits, some of his labourers suing him for wages promised but not paid, and he suing them for the return of passage money. After Levy's death in 1833, he devoted himself mainly to attempts to develop his personal land grant in the PINJARRA district. Although he failed to attain prosperity in the colony, he remained there until his death.
Further reading: Hasluck, A. *Thomas Peel of Swan River.* Oxford University Press, Melbourne, 1965.

peewee *see* mudnest builders

pelican *see* sea birds

Pemberton WA (population 871 in 1981) A small township in the hardwood forests of the far SW of the State, Pemberton is 352km by rail and 342km by road SSE of Perth, 167km by rail from BUNBURY and 33km SW of MANJIMUP. Though the main activities of the town focus on the karri forests of the region, there is some local potato growing, dairying and hop farming. At an elevation of 171m above sea level, it receives an average annual rainfall of 1 255mm, concentrated mainly in the winter months.

Penguin TAS (population 2 616 in 1981) This small service town on the N coastal plain is 17km E of BURNIE and 31km W of DEVONPORT along the Bass Highway. The town was named at the time of settlement, in the 1860s, because of the numbers of fairy penguin rookeries, still found today along the coast. It started as a timber town and is still important for milling, as well as for potato production, vegetable growing and dairying. A prominent landscape feature which provides spectacular panoramic views of the area is Mt Montgomery (471m) located some 5km inland, forming the N extent of the Dial Range. Small quantities of iron ore (ilmenite) are mined at Ironcliffe Road and used in cement and pigment production.

penguins These well-known, flightless, marine birds belong to the family Spheniscidae. Nine of the world's 18 species have

Moulting Adelie penguins photographed in Antarctica during the Mawson Expedition 1911-13

National Library of Australia

been recorded from Australia; most are rare and only the little or fairy penguin, *Eudyptula minor* (38cm to 43cm long), is a resident breeder. Found in temperate seas from WA to southern QLD, it is a shiny bluish-grey bird with white underparts and a short, white tail. It breeds on many S islands; the white eggs are laid in burrows or in hollows under bushes and ledges. Two other species are common: the rockhopper penguin, *Eudyptes chrysocome* (60cm), found in the S seas as far N as FRE-MANTLE and mid-NSW, and the thick-billed penguin, *E. pachyrhynchus* (60cm), found further S, particularly near TAS. Both species have drooping yellow plumes which extend from the edge of the crown but do not meet on the forehead; the flippers of the former species have narrow white margins front and rear, while those of the latter have a white margin on the rear only. All species feed on fish and squid.

Rockhopper penguin, *Eudyptes chrysocome*

G. W. Johnstone (N.P.I.A.W.)

pennyworts *see* Umbelliferae

Penola SA (population 1 205 in 1981) A country town in the SE corner of the State, Penola is 434km by rail SE of Adelaide. It is located 51km N of MOUNT GAMBIER and 51km S of NARACOORTE in a region where large pine plantations provide timber for sawmilling, the town's principal industry. There is also some dairying, livestock grazing and fruit growing in the district. The name of the town comes from an Aboriginal word meaning 'swamp'.

Penrith NSW (population 108 717 in 1981) A city located 55km W of Sydney on the NEPEAN RIVER and named after Penrith in Cumberland, England, it was founded in 1815 at a river crossing on the road leading from Sydney across the BLUE MOUNTAINS. In 1871 it was proclaimed a municipality. It is on the main W railway which was electrified as far as Penrith in 1955. The surrounding district is important for primary produce for the metro-politan market; rural activities include poultry farming, orcharding, cattle raising and pig breeding. River gravel is quarried on the Nepean in the area. Penrith was proclaimed a city in 1959 and currently forms the W fringe of the Sydney metropolis. It has experienced rapid growth in recent decades, increasing in population from about 12 500 in 1961, to over 60 000 in 1971 and over 108 000 in 1981. Many of the residents are daily commuters to the inner suburbs and central business area of Sydney. Manufacturing industry has developed in the region, with factories producing cloth-ing, electronic goods, furniture, engineering and chemical products. The stretch of the Nepean near Penrith is the venue for many aquatic sports, the best known of which is the rowing regatta held annually between the public schools of Sydney.

pens, sea *see* coelenterates

Penton, Brian Con (1904-51) Journalist and novelist. Born and educated in Brisbane, he worked as a reporter mainly on the *Sydney Morning Herald*, the London *Daily Express* and the Sydney *Daily Telegraph*. He became editor of the last-mentioned paper in 1941, and became notable for his frank editorials on controversial issues and for his opposition to wartime political censorship. His novels, *Landtakers* (1934) and *Inheritors* (1936), deal with the fortunes of an immigrant, who estab-lished himself as a pastoralist in QLD in the mid-19th century, and of his descendants. They stress the primitive conditions and the more brutal aspects of life in the bush.

peppermint barks *see* Myrtaceae

Perceval, John (1923-) Artist. Born at Bruce Rock WA, Perceval had little art train-ing. He had no desire to make good this deficiency on the grounds that an academic training could stultify his imagination and destroy the spontaneity of his Expressionist style. In this respect he was like other Mel-bourne contemporaries, Sidney NOLAN and Albert TUCKER. John Reed, the Melbourne patron of the avant-garde in poetry and paint-ing, first reproduced the work of Perceval in 1943 in the publication *Angry Penguins*. Perceval's friendship with the artist Arthur BOYD (he was to marry Boyd's sister) mutually influenced their work. After World War II, he abandoned painting and worked for 10 years helping to establish the Boyd pottery works at Murrumbee VIC, where his ceramic sculp-tures won him high praise. In 1956 he returned to painting, and produced work which evoked an Australian landscape full of joyous life, vitality and rich colour, and which contrasted sharply with the works of such con-temporaries as Sidney Nolan and Russell DRYSDALE who depicted the Australian bush-land in harsh, almost inhuman terms.

perches *see* fisheries; fishes, bony; fishes, freshwater

perentie *see* lizards

peripatids These small, velvety-skinned animals, commonly referred to as Peripatus (the genus to which many belong), have been likened to slugs with legs. They have simi-larities with both the ANNELIDS and the ARTHROPODS and are sometimes included in the phylum Arthropoda though they are more often placed in a phylum of their own, the Onychophora. There are only about 70 species still living but very similar animals lived in the Cambrian period; there are probably at least five or six Australian species in three genera. Most species produce living young, but some lay eggs. Peripatids are among the oldest inhabitants of Australia.

When first discovered in 1825 peripatids were thought to be MOLLUSCS, despite the legs. The Australian species range in length from about 1cm to 5cm. The head carries a pair of ringed antennae and a pair of oral nipples (papillae) flanking the mouth, which is furnished with mandibles. There are 14 or more pairs of unjointed but ringed legs, each with a pair of claws. Like arthropods, peripatids possess tracheae for breathing, and the main body cavity is filled with blood. They move by muscular contractions of the body in the fashion of an earthworm though the body is held above the substrate by the legs.

Peripatids are mainly carnivorous animals living in damp places such as the inside of decaying logs. The food consists of woodlice, other invertebrates and insects, especially termites.

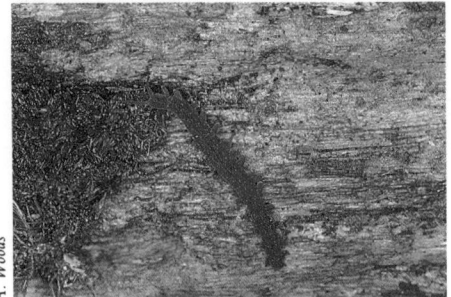

Peripatus

The Australian species have been little studied; the egg-laying genus *Ooperipatus* has been found in QLD, NSW, VIC and TAS. The live-bearing *Peripatoides orientalis* occurs in NSW and the allied *P. gilesi* in WA. A species has been reported from a height of 1 700m on KOSKIUSKO, and another species from the arid Centre of the continent.

periwinkles *see* gastropods

Charles Perkins

Perkins, Charles Nelson (1936-)
Aboriginal leader. Of Arunta descent, he was born at Alice Springs and educated there and at the Le Fevre Boys' Technical School in Adelaide. After beginning work as an apprentice fitter and turner, he became a professional soccer player, winning a place in the Everton team in England. He returned to SA in 1960,

but later moved to Sydney, where he attended university and in 1973 graduated BA, the first Aboriginal to do so. In the meantime he had joined the federal Department of Aboriginal Affairs, rising to become Deputy Director (1979-81). In 1981 he was appointed chairman of the Aboriginal Development Commission, an independent all-Aboriginal body set up in 1980 to assist Aboriginal and Torres Strait Islander groups and individuals to acquire land, engage in business enterprises, obtain finance and receive training. In March 1983, he was appointed Permanent Head of the federal Department of Aboriginal Affairs. He has been a candid and, at times, controversial spokesman for Aborigines, and has taken part in the work of a great many organisations and movements concerned with Aboriginal welfare.

Perth TAS (population 1 229 in 1981) A small country town on the Midland Highway, Perth is 18km S of LAUNCESTON and 8km by road NE of LONGFORD. It is a minor service centre, located in a productive agricultural and pastoral district. The site for the township was selected by Governor Lachlan MACQUARIE in 1821; it was proclaimed a township and parish in 1836, and named after the town Perth in Scotland. There are several historical buildings of interest in the town, including the Eskleigh Home (built in 1870, with outbuildings built in 1835, now classified by the National Trust of TAS), the Baptist and Methodist Churches, the Walter Bottell Inn and the Old Crown Inn.

Perth WA (population 809 035 in 1981) The capital city and largest urban centre of WESTERN AUSTRALIA, located on the banks of the SWAN RIVER in the SW of the State, it is the fifth-largest city in Australia. The city is situated where the Swan broadens into two shallow basins—Perth Water and Melville Water—and the suburbs extend from the Indian Ocean coastline inland to the foothills of the DARLING RANGE.

History The Swan River estuary was discovered in 1677 by the Dutch explorer Willem de Vlamingh, who named the river after the black swans he saw there. The first white settlement in WA was made near ALBANY in 1826 and it was not until 1829 that Lieutenant (later Sir) James STIRLING landed on the S side of the Swan River estuary, proclaimed the colony and selected a site for the establishment of a town. At the end of the first year of settlement, the population of Perth numbered 850. Although progress was slow in the early years, by 1833 a Legislative Council had been appointed, a civil court established and the first newspaper published. The original Causeway Birdge across the Swan was completed in 1841 and by 1856 Perth was formally constituted as a city. By 1867 the population had increased to 5 224, when the foundation stone of the present town hall was laid. The late 1880s and 1890s, however, brought a new era of explosive growth to the city with the gold discoveries, first in the N in the KIMBERLEYS (1885), Yilgarn (1887), PILBARA

Table 1

URBAN GROWTH OF PERTH IN THE TWENTIETH CENTURY

Year	Population	% of State population
1901	36 274	19.7
1911	106 792	37.9
1921	154 873	46.5
1933	207 469	47.3
1954	348 647	54.5
1961	420 133	57.0
1971	641 800	62.3
1976	731 275	64.0
1981	809 035	62.3

Source: Australian Bureau of Statistics, Canberra.

(1888) and MURCHISON (1889) and then, to the E, COOLGARDIE (1892) and KALGOORLIE (1893). The city grew rapidly in response to the gold boom and by the turn of the century, the population had reached over 35 000.

City site Perth lies on the coastal plain between the Darling Range to the E and a belt of limestone and sand dunes along the Indian Ocean coast to the W. Its suburbs spread on both sides of the Swan, E to beyond MIDLAND, and SE towards Armadale; there is almost continuous urban development downstream for 17km to the port of FREMANTLE (now included in metropolitan Perth). The central business district of the city consists of an elongated rectangle, with a grid street pattern, located on the N side of Perth Water between the river bank and the railway, with St George's Terrace as the main business and civic focus and Hay Street and Murray Street the retail shopping centres. The Causeway Bridge crosses the Swan, using Heirisson Is, at the E end of the inner city, and the Narrows Bridge crosses the river at the strait between Perth and Melville Waters. Perth is a city of parks and gardens, several of them (Stirling Gardens, Supreme Court Gardens and Queen's Gardens) within or adjacent to the inner city; King's Park (403ha) is a vast reserve of natural bushland and gardens with walking trails, lakes, lookouts and picnic areas, providing a fine recreation area just downstream from the central city zone. The Swan Water, separating the downtown area from the S suburbs, gives the city an aquatic sporting facility of outstanding beauty. Freeways now link Perth to Fremantle, KWINANA and the N suburbs.

Climate Perth experiences a mild climate throughout the year, with warm to hot days in summer and rather cool conditions in winter. The average monthly temperature in February, the hottest month, is 31.4°C, while in July, the coldest month, the average is 17.6°C. The average annual rainfall is 837mm, falling mainly in the winter (June, the wettest month, 194mm average), with a dry season in summer (January, the driest month, 6mm average).

Population During this century Perth has grown from a town of 36 274 in 1901 to 731 275 in 1976 and 809 035 in 1981, when it accounted for 62.3 per cent of the State's total population. The statistics of its population at

Winthrop Hall, University of Western Australia

various censuses over 75 years are set out in Table 1.

Industry As well as being the major commercial, financial and service centre of the State, Perth is also an industrial city. Manufacturing is still found in the older industrial areas of Subiaco-Jolimont and Bassendean-Midland, but in recent times the Welshpool-Kewdale area to the E and the Osborne area to the NW have expanded considerably. Kwinana, S of Fremantle, has become the State's major industrial area.

City features The city offers much to the resident and to the tourist—scenic beauty, sporting activities, cultural events, historic sites, art galleries and elegant architecture. It is the terminus of the trans-Australian railway, the State focus of main highways, and an international and national airport centre. There are two universities in Perth: the University of Western Australia, located on Matilda Bay in the subury of Nedlands, and Murdoch University, established in 1975, S of the river. The Perth Entertainment Centre, situated in the main city block, has seating for 8000 people, and is the venue for a variety of events, from concerts to tennis championships. A large number of buildings in the city—many dating from the 1850s—have been listed for preservation by the National Trust (WA); these include several buildings in St George's Terrace, such as Government House, St Andrew's Church, the Palace Tavern and the Old Perth Boys' School.
See also Rottnest Island; Swanland
Further reading: Ward, K. *Perth Sketchbook.* Rigby, Adelaide, 1976 and *Swan River Sketchbook.* Rigby, Adelaide, 1978; Stannage, C.T., *The People of Perth.* Carroll's for Perth City Council, Perth, 1979.

pest control Pests are organisms which harm man or his property. The damage may be caused directly—by a caterpillar eating a crop, for example—or indirectly—by MOSQUITOES transmitting malaria or WEEDS robbing a wheat plant of light, water and nutrients. Pest control is usually thought of as the direct destruction of the pest but the true aim should be the lessening or avoidance of the damage that it causes. Broadly speaking, the methods of control can be divided into chemical control and alternative methods. Chemical control has blossomed since World War II with the discovery and marketing of many potent pesticides such as DDT and its allies, the organo-

phosphate insecticides, the 'hormones' and other selective weed-killers (2,4-D, MCPA and so on) and the organic fungicides. Most of these chemicals have been selective in the sense that they are much more poisonous to the target organisms—insect pests, broad-leafed weeds and so on—than to vertebrate animals and crop plants. They have the advantage that they can be applied quickly and easily to the crop when the pest appears, or to protect the crop when the pest is likely to appear. Usually the costs of application are far less than the financial benefits achieved.

Unfortunately, chemical control can have harmful side effects. DDT and its related compounds, the so-called chlorinated hydrocarbon insecticides, are very stable chemically, and have affinity for fats and oils. They can be transported in various ways far from the site of application and, in certain circumstances, can enter an ecological food chain. Because of their affinity for fats they become more and more concentrated along the chain with the final links, the predatory animals, amassing very large concentrations indeed. This may cause sickness or even death. In some areas the egg shells of BIRDS OF PREY such as peregrine falcons have been thinned, causing the failure of many broods. Less stable compounds such as the organophosphates (such as malathion) do not enter food chains in this way and do not persist in the environment for more than a few weeks but they are more expensive than the chlorinated hydrocarbons.

When first used, such chemicals are very effective against their target organisms but most pest populations contain a few individuals that are resistant to their effects. This resistance, when of the inheritable form, spreads quickly in the population when the

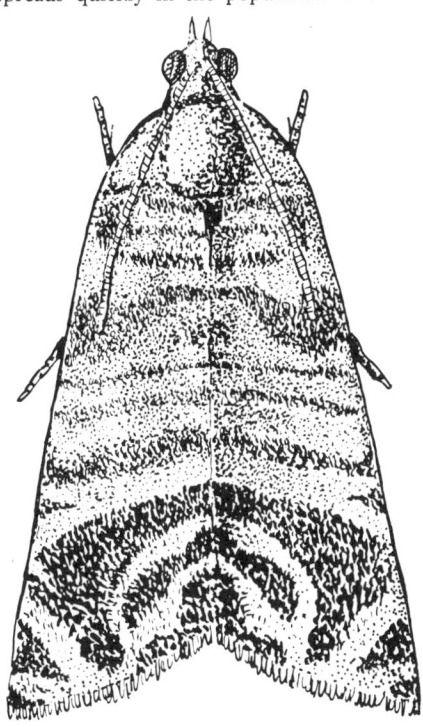

Codling moth, *Cydia pomonella*

Spraying fruit trees with an organophosphate insecticide. Note protective clothing

pesticidal pressure is maintained generation after generation. Intolerable levels of resistance appear in some pest populations after only a few generations, and the chemical has to be phased out. For example, many populations of the HOUSE FLY and COCKROACHES in Australia and elsewhere can withstand doses of DDT that are hundreds of times greater than those needed to kill their ancestors a few years ago. The rapid development of resistance to various insecticides among *Heliothis* caterpillars has made the growing of cotton very difficult in the NAMOI RIVER valley and some other parts of Australia, and impossible on the ORD RIVER.

A further difficulty is that most pesticides cannot distinguish between a pest and a related but beneficial organism. While they kill pests they will also kill the predators or PARASITES of those pests so that when the residues of the pesticide have disappeared the surviving pest individuals can multiply rapidly, unchecked by their natural enemies. Red-spider MITES were relatively unimportant animals a century ago. When DDT was used against pests sharing the same host plants as the spider mites (which are unharmed by DDT), the predators of the mites were destroyed. Freed from these restraints the spider mites developed into the most serious pests of some plants, particularly deciduous fruit trees. Fortunately, they can be controlled by organophosphate compounds though resistance to these has appeared in some regions.

Finally, there is the possible danger to human health of some of the compounds. Here, a distinction must be made between acute poisoning resulting from the ingestion of a large dose of the pesticide—almost always the result of gross carelessness or attempted suicide—and chronic effects resulting from long exposures. Virtually everyone contains some DDT or its derivatives in his or her body

Production testing, Goodwyn gas field

Bass Strait Offshore Oil and Gas

Map labels:
147°E
NSW
VIC
○ Offshore wells
— Pipelines
DANDENONG: gas and fuel terminal, distribution station
MELBOURNE
LONGFORD: gas processing and oil treatment plant
38°S
GEELONG. distribution station
CRIB POINT: oil tank farm, liquids jetty, fractionation plant
FRANKSTON
MORNINGTON
TUNA
MARLIN
FLOUNDER
SNAPPER
HALIBUT
BARRACOUTA
FORTESCUE
COBIA
MACKEREL
COBIA 2
WEST KINGFISH
KINGFISH A
KINGFISH B
BASS STRAIT
Wilson's Promontory
BASS STRAIT
0 20 40 60 80 100km

fat. While no one has so far shown that DDT in the body is good for people, there appears to be no link, according to the World Health Organization, between DDT at the levels found in the general public and any known disease. Negative evidence is, however, unsatisfactory evidence, and does not demonstrate that DDT (and other compounds) will never cause any illness. Until recently the common weedkillers have been regarded as virtually harmless to human beings but since 1978 there has been controversy about the possible teratogenic effects of 2,4,5-T preparations which can contain minute quantities of the dangerous compound dioxin.

At present, chemical pesticides are indispensable to man if he is to produce enough food to feed the world and to contain diseases such as malaria. There is, however, a revival of interest in other methods which do not use chemical pesticides. Some of these are simply traditional practices, such as cultivation to destroy weeds, which fell out of favour because they were more labour-demanding than chemical control. A very valuable approach is to use varieties of animals and plants that are resistant to the pests. Zebu-type cattle and hybrids are more resistant to cattle tick in QLD than are European cattle, and many plants are being developed that can withstand attack by certain nematodes, insects or diseases. Varieties of lucerne, for example, are being developed which can be grown in the presence of the spotted alfalfa aphid and the blue-green aphid which became widely established in Australia in 1978. Unfortunately, selective breeding is a slow process and it takes many years after the definition of a problem before a resistant variety can be found. Even then resistance may break down after a few years; this has happened regularly with wheat varieties resistant to rusts. New methods of genetic engineering will probably accelerate breeding methods.

Classical BIOLOGICAL CONTROL consists of introducing natural enemies of the pest—parasites, pathogens or predators—into its environment.

Alternative methods of control are not without side-effects but they are generally less serious than those caused by the misuse of chemicals. However, at present, alternative methods are not comprehensive enough to allow the chemical pesticides to be abandoned completely. Methods are, however, being developed which allow the integration of chemicals with other methods so that the chemicals interfere as little as possible with other control agents. The successful application of integrated control methods depends upon a thorough knowledge of the biology of the pest species present, and a good understanding of the whole ecosystem concerned. Integrated control in fruit crops and in cotton cultivation are examples of successful applications of the methods in Australia.

Further reading: Woods, A. *Pest Control: A Survey.* McGraw-Hill, UK, 1974; Gunn, D.L. & Stevens, J.G.R. (eds) *Pesticides and Human Welfare.* Oxford University Press, Oxford, 1976; Senate Standing Committee on Science and the Environment. *Pesticides and the Health of Australian Vietnam Veterans: First Report.* Australian Government Publishing Service, Canberra, 1982.

Peterborough SA (population 2 575 in 1981) This small town is located at the S end of the FLINDERS RANGES and the N end of the MOUNT LOFTY RANGES, 254km by road N of Adelaide. It is a rail junction where narrow, broad and standard gauges converge; lines radiate N to BROKEN HILL, S to Adelaide, NW to QUORN and SW to PORT PIRIE, and the Indian Pacific railway service calls regularly at Peterborough. The town was originally called Petersburg, after a local settler Peter Doeeke, but was changed during World War I.

petrels *see* sea birds

petroleum and natural gas The main use of petroleum is in the production of liquid fuels: gasoline and diesel for automobiles, aircraft and trains; kerosene for jet aircraft and heating; light and heavy oils for lubrication, heating and trains; and residual fuel oils for static and marine boilers. Other

Table 1

AUSTRALIAN PRODUCTION OF CRUDE OIL AND NATURAL GAS 1970-81 ($\times$ '000m³)

Year	VIC	QLD	SA	WA	TOTAL
Crude oil					
1970	7 488	216	—	2 652	10 356
1973	20 206	109	—	2 306	22 621
1978	23 343	64	—	1 780	25 187
1979	23 815	76	—	1 477	25 368
1980	20 508	83	—	1 648	22 239
1981	21 349	81	46	1 365	22 842
Natural gas					
1970	625 491	214 195	651 326	11 489	1 502 501
1973	1 794 800	375 173	1 196 236	883 034	4 249 246
1978	3 461 135	280 656	2 750 858	827 619	7 320 268
1979	4 020 826	296 522	3 207 296	856 792	8 381 436
1980	4 547 774	319 908	3 816 346	883 376	9 567 404
1981*	5 702 000	358 000	4 346 000	863 000	11 268 000

Note : *statistics for 1981 are rounded to nearest million m³
(note : totals may not always agree with sums of figures due to rounding)
Source : *Australian Mineral Industry Annual Review* (1970-81) Australian Govt Publishing Service, Canberra.

Table 2

ESTIMATED RECOVERABLE RESERVES OF PETROLEUM IN AUSTRALIA (as at December 1981)

	INITIAL RESERVES				CURRENT RESERVES			
	Hydrocarbon Liquids ($\times 10^6 m^3$)			Natural (Sales) Gas ($\times 10^9 m^3$)	Hydrocarbon Liquids ($\times 10^6 m^3$)			Natural (Sales) Gas ($\times 10^9 m^3$)
		Natural Gas Liquids				Natural Gas Liquids		
BASINS AND FIELDS	Crude Oil	Condensate	Liquefied Petroleum Gas (LPG)		Crude Oil	Condensate	Liquefied Petroleum Gas (LPG)	
Bowen-Surat Moonie, Alton, Bennett, Trinidad, Conloi, Cabawin, Kincora, Boxleigh, Silver Springs, Thomby Creek, Roma area producing gas fields	4.30	0.25	—	5.08	0.77	0.16	—	1.95
Gippsland Barracouta, Halibut, Kingfish, Mackerel, Marlin, Tuna, Snapper, Cobia, W Kingfish, S Mackerel, Fortescue, Flounder	465.80	34.40	88.70	220.40	235.80	28.90	62.10	184.30
Cooper & Eromanga Big Lake, Darlingie, Moomba, Gidgealpa, Brolga, Brumby, Burke, Della, Dullingari, Epsilon, Fly Lake, Merrimelia, Mudrangie, Moorari, Roseneath, Strzelecki, Tirrawarra, Toolachee, Namur Kidman, Munkarie, Ashby, Dullingarie North, Marabooka and Cuttapirrie	8.10	9.10	16.24	119.30	8.10	8.43	14.98	95.31
Perth Dongara, Mondarra, Yardarino, Woodada and Mt Horner	1.33	0.10	—	15.98	1.24	0.06	—	7.82
Carnarvon & Canning Barrow Is, North Rankin and Blina	40.65	20.79	25.09	216.46	11.98	20.74	25.05	213.76
TOTAL	520.18	64.64	130.03	577.22	257.89	58.29	102.13	503.14

Source: Bureau of Mineral Resrouces, Canberra.

products include synthetic rubbers, explosives, waxes, medicinal products, detergents, grease and asphalt. Natural gas, often found together with crude oil, is used predominantly for heating and as a feed for the manufacture of synthetic hydrocarbon chemicals.

It is generally agreed that the source material of petroleum is organic, composed of the accumulation of plant and animal remains buried under thick sequences of younger sediments.

History The first exploratory oil well in Australia was drilled in 1892 in the COORONG region of SA where a black bitumen-like substance, which coated the ground, was found to yield oil. This well proved to be dry as did others drilled in the 1890s in SA. The first discovery of importance was made at ROMA in QLD in 1900 when gas was found whilst drilling for ARTESIAN WATER, and several wells, drilled in the first decade of this century, gave good gas flows. In 1906, gas from a bore lit Roma for 10 nights, but the flow failed. The search for oil continued throughout the 1920s and 1930s but with limited success; Roma again came to prominence in 1927 when a well yielded gas and

oil, and a small amount of oil was found at the LAKES ENTRANCE area of E GIPPSLAND in VIC. After World War II the tempo of oil exploration increased with the first commercial oil field found at ROUGH RANGE near EXMOUTH GULF in WA at a depth of 1 219m. In 1961 the MOONIE oil field in QLD was discovered; in 1963 an oil and gas strike was made at Roma and the GIDGEALPA gas field in SA was discovered; in 1964 the Mereeni gas and oil field in the NT, the Dongara gas field and the BARROW ISLAND oil field in WA and the Alton oil field in QLD were located. But up until this time no really major strike had been made; in 1965, however, two large gas fields, Barracouta and Marlin, were found, followed by the discovery of two oil fields, Halibut and Kingfish, in 1967. These BASS STRAIT fields have continued to dominate the Australian petroleum scene, though numerous other strikes of oil and gas have been made throughout the country.

Production Although the Australian production of 22 million cubic metres of crude oil in 1980 represents less than one per cent of the total world output, it provides 70 per cent of the nation's domestic petroleum requirements.

The production statistics, shown in Table 1, indicate the rapid growth of the industry, with the output more than doubling between 1970 and 1980. This marked expansion was due to the development of the Bass Strait oil deposits in VIC where the Barracouta, Halibut, Mackerel, Tuna and Kingfish platforms and the Cobia sub-sea well accounted for 92 per cent of the 1980 Australian total. The Barrow Is field in WA (Carnarvon Basin) is another significant producer; the remaining small fraction of the nation's output is obtained from the Moonie, Alton and Bennett fields in QLD (Surat Basin).

The production of natural gas has shown an even greater growth rate, rising from 1.5 billion cubic metres in 1970 to 9.5 billion cubic metres in 1980. VIC accounted for over 47 per cent of the 1980 total, followed by SA, WA and QLD, in that order.

The VIC gas fields are located offshore in the Bass Strait; the gas is conveyed from the production platforms by pipeline to a processing plant at Longford on the Gippsland coast and thence by a 172km-long pipeline to Melbourne and on to GEELONG. The SA gas fields, located at MOOMBA and Gidgealpa in the COOPER'S CREEK basin, are linked to Adelaide by a 783km-long pipeline and to Sydney by a 1300km-long pipeline. In WA natural gas is piped 411km to Perth from near Dongara at the N end of the Perth basin. However, an offshore gas field of vast proportions was discovered in the NORTH WEST SHELF region, off the PILBARA coast of WA in the 1970s, and in the early 1980s development of this field was proceeding. In QLD, the main gas fields in the Roma region are connected to Brisbane by a pipeline 414km long.

Petrov enquiry On 3 April 1954, Vladimir Michailovich Petrov, the Third Secretary at the Soviet Embassy in Canberra, asked the Australian government for political asylum, and not long afterwards his wife, after being freed dramatically from armed Soviet guards at Darwin airport, did likewise. Petrov's revelation that he had been in charge of Soviet non-military espionage in Australia led to the appointment of a Royal Commission, which reported that Soviet espionage had indeed been carried out, but that the only Australians who had knowingly assisted it were members of the Communist Party.

Although the Commission's findings were not particularly dramatic, the case had important political effects. The USSR, alleging that Petrov had stolen Embassy funds, demanded that he be handed over as a criminal and, when this request was refused, broke off diplomatic relations with Australia. In domestic politics the affair must have told against the Australian Labor Party (ALP) in the elections of May 1954, and had further damaging effects on that party when its leader, Dr Herbert EVATT, obtained permission to appear before the Commission as counsel for members of his staff, two of whom had been named in one of the documents handed over by Petrov. Evatt claimed that this document had been fabricated as part of a plot to discredit the ALP, but the Commissioners dismissed this claim as being unsupported by the evidence, and finally withdrew permission for him to appear before them. The whole affair caused deep divisions of opinion in ALP ranks, and helped to bring about a split in 1955, which in turn led to the formation of the DEMOCRATIC LABOR PARTY and helped to keep the ALP out of office in the federal sphere for another 17 years.
Further reading: Bialoguski, M. *The Petrov Story.* Heinemann, London, 1955; Stubbs, J. & Whitlam, N. *A Nest of Traitors.* Jacaranda, Milton QLD, 1974. Thwaites, M. *Truth Will Out: ASID and the Petrovs.* Collins, Sydney, 1980.

petty spurge *see* Euphorbiaceae

Petunia *see* Solanaceae

phalangids *see* harvestmen; spiders

phalaropes *see* waders

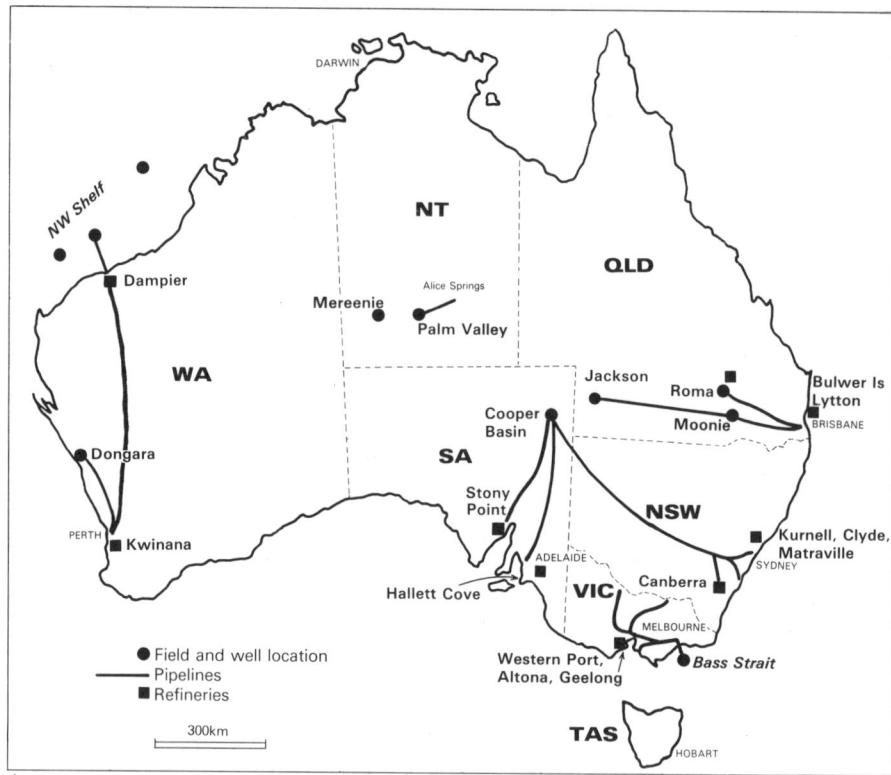

Petroleum and natural gas map

phascogale *see* native cats, etc.

Phasmatodea *see* stick insects

pheasants and quails These game BIRDS belong to the almost cosmopolitan family Phasianidae, which contains 165 species; in Australia there are seven species, of which four are introduced.

The three native species are the stubble quail, *Coturnix pectoralis**, (15cm to 18cm long), the brown quail, *C. ypsilophorus, (C. australis)* (15cm to 20cm), and the king quail, *C. chinensis* (15cm to 18cm). These species resemble BUTTON QUAILS in appearance and habits, but have a small, distinct hind-toe.

The stubble quail has grey upperparts and black-streaked underparts; the male has a cinnamon-buff throat, the female a white one. The colour of the plumage camouflages these birds as they feed gregariously on grass seeds and insects in grasslands, on swamp margins and among cereal crops.

King quail, *Coturnix chinensis*

The brown quail, which is also found in New Guinea and adjacent islands, is brownish above and barred black below; the upperparts of the female are thickly blotched with black. This species is fairly common in grassy areas near swamps.

The king quail is more brightly coloured than the other two species, and the sexes are very different in appearance. The male has a black and white throat, a bluish-grey breast, a chestnut belly and blackish upperparts; the female is duller and has black barred underparts. The king quail frequents the wet grasslands of N, E and SE Australia; its status is uncertain, but it may be fairly common.

The introduced California quail, *Lophortyx californicus* (24cm), a mainly greyish-brown bird, is easily distinguished by its size and its forward-curving crest. It is wild on KING ISLAND and in parts of coastal VIC.

The ring-necked pheasant, *Phasianus colchicus* (60cm to 1m), has been introduced many times as a game bird and for breeding for the table. It is mainly red and brown with a red facial skin; the male has a glossy dark green head and a white collar. This species has a number of wild colonies, including those on ROTTNEST ISLAND, on King Is, in WA, near Adelaide and in southern TAS. There is a feral population of the domestic fowl (*Gallus* species; 40cm to 51cm) on North West Is in the CAPRICORN GROUP. It has reverted to the black-breasted form of the wild species and apparently lives without freshwater. The peafowl (peacock), *Pavo cristatus* (body 75cm; tail 1m), is also feral on Rottnest Is.

*Species, genus or family is endemic to Australia (see Preface)

Philesiaceae *see* Liliaceae

Phillip, Arthur (1738-1814) Governor of NSW. He was born in London, the son of a language teacher who had migrated there from Frankfurt. In 1755, having completed his apprenticeship in the mercantile marine, he joined the Royal Navy as a midshipman, saw active service during the Seven Years' War, and after the conclusion of hostilities was retired on half-pay. He engaged in farming until 1774, when, with the permission of the Admiralty, he joined the Portuguese Navy. Four years later, when Britain and France were again at war, he returned to the Royal Navy, attained the rank of post-captain in 1781, and in 1784 was retired again on half-pay. Two years later Lord Sydney, the Home Secretary, chose him as Governor of the proposed penal settlement in NSW, probably on the recommendation of his neighbour, Sir George Rose, Secretary to the Treasury.

National Library of Australia

Governor Arthur Phillip by Henry Raeburn, after Francis Wheatley

Phillip supervised the preparation of the FIRST FLEET in close detail, but was not given the opportunity to precede it to NSW to make preparations there for the arrival of the convicts. He reached BOTANY BAY in January 1788, with 11 ships carrying over 700 convicts and three companies of marines, who, together with a few dependents, some servants and several civil officials, numbered about 300. He was immediately faced with unforeseen difficulties. Judging Botany Bay unsuitable because of the exposed anchorage, poor soil and lack of fresh water, he moved his charges to SYDNEY COVE in nearby PORT JACKSON, where on 26 January he proclaimed the foundation of the colony. He quickly established the first government farm at FARM COVE, but work there was hampered by the unfamiliar climatic conditions and vegetation, the refusal of Major Ross to allow his marines to act as supervisors of the convicts at their work, the unwillingness to work of most of the convicts and the lack of skilled farmers among them.

The settlement had been provided with supplies for two years, but it was soon evident that this would not be enough, and Phillip promptly appealed to England for further supplies and for the sending of free settlers and convicts with useful skills. While waiting for a response he took vigorous measures to conserve and supplement existing supplies of food. He explored in search of better land, and when he found it at Rose Hill (PARRAMATTA) he made that the main centre of farming. Some convicts were sent to NORFOLK ISLAND, which was reputed to be very fertile. The *Sirius*, the larger of the two ships remaining in the colony, was sent to Cape Town for food—a mission which involved the circumnavigation of the globe. Finally, early in 1790, rations were drastically reduced for convicts and non-convicts alike. Nevertheless, food supplies had run perilously low by the time the second fleet arrived in June 1790. It brought supplies and an army regiment, the NEW SOUTH WALES CORPS, which was to replace the marines, but it and later ships also brought many more convicts, large numbers of them in bad health. Consequently, the colony was not free of the danger of starvation until almost the time Phillip sailed for England, in December 1792. By that time nearly 200 ex-convicts and ex-marines had been settled on the land and a total area of more than 700ha was under cultivation.

Phillip had displayed remarkable courage and determination in the face of hardships and obstacles. He had also made an attempt to establish friendly relations with the Aborigines and to arrive at just verdicts when conflict occurred between them and the convicts. However, he lacked understanding of Aboriginal culture and of the effects of European settlement on it. Phillip resigned the governorship on the grounds of ill health, although by 1796 he had recovered sufficiently to resume duty in the navy. He was promoted to Rear-Admiral in 1799, retired in 1805, and shortly before his death was promoted to Admiral. There is a memorial to him in Bath Abbey and portraits of him in the Mitchell and Dixson Galleries, Sydney.

Further reading: Mackaness, G. *Admiral Arthur Phillip*. Angus & Roberston, Sydney, 1937; Anon. *The Voyage of Governor Phillip to Botany Bay*. John Stockdale, London, 1789 (reprinted Georgian House, Melbourne, 1950); Barnard Eldershaw, M. *Phillip of Australia*. Angus & Robertson, London, 1977.

Phillip Island VIC (population of Phillip Is Shire 3 070 in 1981) Located at the SE of WESTERN PORT BAY, the island is a popular recreation and holiday resort which can be reached by road (122km SE of Melbourne) over a bridge at San Remo (16km W of WONTHAGGI), by sea from Stony Point on the E side of MORNINGTON PENINSULA (by hydrofoil or ferry) or by air from Melbourne International, Essendon or Moorabbin airports. The island stretches E-W for about 20km and varies in N-S extent, with its widest part over

12km. Tourist attractions include the famed evening parade of fairy penguins at Summerland Beach on the SW coast, koalas (especially in the Owen Roberts reserve), the motor-racing circuit, the seal colony beyond the Nobbies (off the SW tip of the island), the Kingston Gardens zoo, the remains of the wreck of the sailing ship *Speke* and muttonbird rookeries in the SW. The scenery varies from undulating pasture lands and sheltered bays to surfing beaches and rocky headlands, with opportunities for sailing, fishing and water skiing. The S coast, facing BASS STRAIT, has several stretches of sandy beaches and numerous cliffs and headlands such as Cape Wollamai (with the island's highest point, reaching 109m), the Gap, Red Cliff Heads and Phelan Bluff. The N coast is more sheltered and is the site of the main urban settlements: Cowes (population 1 536 in 1981) is the largest; other small townships are Newhaven in the SE across the bridge from San Remo, Rhyll to the NE and Ventor on the NW coast. The island was discovered by the explorer George BASS in 1798, but it was not until 1826 that it was officially made a British possession when a settlement was established at Rhyll so as to warn off French explorers who might have intended to occupy it. This first settlement was abandoned three years later and it remained largely unoccupied until the 1860s. Originally the island was called Snapper Is, then Grant Is; it was later named after the first governor of NSW, Arthur PHILLIP.

Phthiraptera *see* lice

piano and pianists For many early settlers in Australia the piano embodied the essence of the civilisation they were leaving behind them in Europe, and particularly in the UK. Visitors to Australia in the late 19th century frequently remarked on the number to be found, even in romote parts of the country. The instrument became an emblem of gentility, a sacred object beyond the reach of pioneering improvisation. Because of this, countless families endured considerable sacrifices to bring pianos across thousands of miles of ocean in unsuitable ships to Australia and thence across great distances of land in bullock drays.

The earliest references to piano playing in Australia were in the 1790s when Surgeon Worgan landed a piano and when, not long afterwards, Elizabeth Macarthur announced to a friend that she was making satisfactory progress in playing 'God Save the King' and *Foot's Minuet*. The earliest performances of an advanced nature appear to have been provided by some visiting English composer-pianists, including Charles Horsley and Charles Packer. Soloists of considerable eminence who have toured Australia include Arabella Goddard, Paderewski, Teresa Carreño, Backhaus and Schnabel. Some outstanding visiting pianists settled in Australia; these include Isadore Goodman and Alexander Sverjensky. Australian pianists still feel the need to study and work overseas in order to measure themselves against international standards. In the 19th century, this need was even greater, as Australia's geographical isolation was greater. Frederick Ellard, son of a music-seller in George Street, Sydney, and himself a composer as well as a pianist, was among those who left to further their studies overseas. He left Australia in the 1840s and returned about 10 years later, ready to communicate his hard-earned fluency and experience. As early as the 1870s and 1880s Australia was beginning to produce some prodigy pianists, of which two outstanding examples were Ernest HUTCHESON, who eventually became president of the Juilliard School of Music in New York, and Elsie Hall from TOOWOOMBA, who was already making an impact in London by the time she was 12 and winning the approval of Bernard Shaw. Other pianists, such as Arthur BENJAMIN, contributed much through their teaching, Benjamin's finest pupil at the Royal College of Music in London being Benjamin Britten.

The greatest Australian pianist, and perhaps the leading figure in Australian composition, is Percy GRAINGER. He too was a prodigy, and a leading artist of the age of the reproducing piano. The piano rolls he made in that period are still highly prized. He enjoyed for a while the life of the touring wonder-pianist, was a friend of Grieg and the most trusted interpreter of Grieg's piano concerto, and pioneered the work of new composers, such as Debussy. He thus had all the right credentials for an imposing career in the concert hall and his playing was as full of character as his original compositions and arrangements for keyboard.

This tradition of pianistic virtuosity has been furthered by many other Australians, including Eileen JOYCE, Noel MEWTON-WOOD, another Melbourne-born pianist who enjoyed a remarkable though short career overseas before his untimely death at the age of 31. Roger WOODWARD has earned an impressive international reputation, and his extraordinary talent, intellectual stature and force of personality have combined to offer a special example in the history of Australian musical development.
Further reading: Covell, R. *Australia's Music: Themes of a New Society.* Sun Books, Melbourne, 1967.

Pichi Richi Pass SA Located NE of PORT AUGUSTA and SW of QUORN, it is a gorge, 16km long, through a W section of the S FLINDERS RANGES. It provides a natural corridor from the coastal plains at the N end of SPENCER GULF, through the ranges, to WILLOCHRA BASIN. It was used by the pioneer settlers as a transport route and the original narrow-gauge central Australian railway, now replaced by a standard-gauge line located further W, went through the pass. The Pichi Richi Railway Preservation Society has restored a section of the old narrow-gauge line through the pass; it operates steam trains as a

Premier's Dept SA
Pichi Richi railway, Flinders Ranges SA

tourist attraction and the public can subscribe to this project by purchasing railway sleepers for one dollar each at the Quorn tourist office. The name Pichi Richi comes from the Aboriginal word for a local bush which possesses narcotic properties when chewed.

Picton NSW (population 1 817 in 1981) A small town located on the Hume Highway and on the main south-western railway route, it is 80km by road and 82km by rail SW of Sydney, and 20km S of CAMDEN. Situated in hilly country at an elevation of 168m above sea level, it is a commercial and service centre for a productive rural district. It receives an average annual rainfall of 806mm, spread fairly uniformly throughout the year, but with

somewhat higher falls in the summer months. First settled by Europeans in the 1820s, it was originally called Stonequarry, but was later named Picton in honour of General Sir Thomas Picton, a hero at the Battle of Waterloo. Several buildings in the town have been listed by the National Trust (NSW) and the Jarvisfield group, which includes 'Jarvisfield' (now the Picton Golf Club, built in 1864) and the former Razorback Inn (1830s), has been classified for preservation as an essential part of the cultural heritage of the nation.

Pieman River TAS The headwater tributaries of this system rise in the rugged terrain of the CRADLE MOUNTAIN-LAKE ST CLAIR National Park, located in the NW mountain region of the State. Two tributaries, the Mackintosh and the Murchison, join E of ROSEBERY to form the Pieman which then flows in a general W direction to Hardwick Bay on the NW coast. Over its course of 105km, the river drains a catchment area of 3 900km^2 of steep mountains and thick rainforests, where the average annual rainfall is over 2 800mm. A major hyro-electricity power station has been planned for this river basin, consisting of four dams and three power stations. Construction of the scheme commenced in 1973 and is due for completion in 1986.

pig industry Pig production is a relatively small industry in Australia. The pig population reached a peak of 3 259 000 in 1972-73; it was 2 420 000 in 1980-81. Until 1964 pig population figures showed a pattern of two years expansion followed by a rapid fall in numbers, but between 1964 and 1973 there was a continuous increase in the size of the population. The number of pigs slaughtered (4 665 700) and the production of pig meat (236 500 tonnes) also were at a peak in 1972-73 (*see* Table 1).

The increase in pig numbers between 1964 and 1973 was stimulated by a rising demand for pork, partly because of high beef prices, and by the ready availability of wheat grain for pig

Table 1

PIG NUMBERS AND PIG MEAT PRODUCTION IN AUSTRALIA 1951-81

Year	Pig numbers* ('000)	Pigs slaughtered ('000)	Pig meat production (tonnes)
1951-52	1 022	1 488	—
1961-62	1 615	1 219	—
1968-69	2 253	3 310	—
1970-71	2 590	3 764	179.5
1972-73	3 259	4 666	236.5
1974-75	2 197	3 299	171.8
1975-76	2 173	3 376	179.1
1979-80	2 520	3 913	220.0
1980-81	2 427	4 240	234.1

Note: * numbers at 31 March.
Source: Australian Bureau of Statistics, Canberra.

feed. While the population of pigs increased, the number of farm holdings which carried pigs fell from 50 851 in 1956 to 19 279 in 1980. As a result, the average size of herds increased from 23 in 1956 to 91 in 1976. In 1980 there were 223 herds with more than 1000 sows in the herd (*see* Table 2).

Approximately half of the pig meat is consumed as pork with the remainder being processed into ham, bacon and small goods. Consumption in Australia is low compared with the USA and Western Europe, although it rose from approximately 6kg per person in 1952-53 to between 13.5kg and 16.4kg per person in the first half of the 1970s. Recently the industry has introduced the concept of the superporker which involves production of heavier, leaner carcases and new methods of cutting up carcases. It is expected that vigorous promotion of these cuts may raise the production and consumption of pork relative to bacon and ham. A very small quantity of pig meat is exported, mainly to Japan. The peak level of exports was 20 400 tonnes, in 1972-73, but by the early 1980s this had fallen to between 2 100 to 2 500 tonnes each year.

There is considerable variation between piggeries in terms of the intensity of management applied to the pigs. In some small units there is a minimum level of management with rudimentary structures provided for shelter and the pigs being fed on grain and food scraps. Skim-milk also may be fed but has declined in importance as a result of the move to the sale of whole milk from dairy farms. It is not longer permissible to feed pigs with swill from catering establishments, such as restaurants, because of the danger of spreading foot and mouth disease organisms which may be present in some imported foodstuffs. In modern piggeries, particularly in the large units, the animals are housed in buildings in which the temperature is controlled and are fed specially formulated rations. Genetic principles are applied in the selection of breeding stock and there is close attention to the prevention and control of disease. Many large units are controlled by companies which also are involved in the production of broiler chickens and the manufacture of feeds.

pigeons *see* doves, etc.

pigface This is the common name given to a group of prostrate perennials with thick, fleshy angular leaves, found mainly on the coast in many parts of Australia. Belonging to the genus *Carpobrotus* (family Aizoaceae), they are better known to gardeners as *Mesembryanthemum*, the genus in which they were placed formerly. A common species in NSW and QLD is angular pigface, *C. glaucescens*; its leaves are triangular in section and its flowers are large and reddish-purple. The leaves and fruit are edible, though saline.

pigs *see* animals, introduced; pig industry

Piguenit, William Charles (1836-1914) Artist. Born in Hobart of English parents, Piguenit worked for 42 years with the Tasmanian Survey Department, before retiring in 1872 to paint full-time. He was a lover of romantic and sublime landscapes—mountains in mist, grandiose plains or dramatic cloud effects. His paintings have historic interest as part of the development of Australian art, though they may be considered colourless and technically unimaginative. He was outspokenly conservative and he resigned from the Art Society of New South Wales, itself a conservative body, because of its then mild interest in French Impressionism.

pike *see* fishes, bony

Pilbara WA The Pilbara region is a statistical division in the N of the State, covering over 444 000km², extending E-W from the Indian Ocean coastline to the NT border, and from the Tropic of Capricorn N to the KIMBERLEYS. The E and central sections include vast stretches of the GREAT SANDY DESERT and the W section is crossed by the DE GREY and FORTESCUE Rivers. It is a region of low and variable rainfall, containing some of the most inhospitably arid areas of the continent, as well as some strikingly spectacular gorge and range scenery, sparsely settled with sheep grazing properties and rich in mineral ores. Within this region are great iron ore deposits, developed since the 1960s, at centres such as MOUNT NEWMAN, MOUNT TOM PRICE, MOUNT GOLDSWORTHY and ROBE RIVER. Other minerals in the area include tin, lead, nickel and manganese; oil and natural gas are located off-shore. Recent discoveries of large natural gas reserves near the NORTH WEST CAPE have led to proposals for the development of the Pilbara as a major industrial area. Two large national parks are located in the Pilbara: HAMERSLEY RANGE National Park

Pilbara landscape WA

(590 176ha) and Chichester National Park (150 609ha).

pilchard *see* fishes, bony

pilot bird *see* warblers, etc.

pin worms *see* roundworms

pine *see* forestry; Gymnospermae

Pine Creek NT (population 214 in 1981) A small township located on the Stuart Highway and on the N Australian railway, Pine Creek is 246km by road SE of Darwin at an elevation of 189m. In the 1870s it was a boom gold-mining town, but with the decline of mining, it became a virtual ghost town. In 1967 the Frances Creek iron-ore mine (about 25km N) began operations and a spur rail line was constructed to transport the ore. Pine Creek experiences a climate typical of the N regions, with an average annual rainfall of 1 128mm, concentrated in the summer months, and a long dry season from April to October.

Pinjarra WA (population 1 336 in 1981) This small town is located 87km S of Perth, on the coastal plain, where the South-Western Highway and the railway from Perth to BUNBURY cross the MURRAY RIVER, E of Peel Inlet

Playford Club Hotel, Pine Creek, 1891

Aluminium refinery at Pinjarra WA

WA Dept of Tourism

and about 20km SE of MANDURAH. It is a service centre to a fertile rural area where dairying, orcharding and market gardening are the main farming activities. It was here that, in 1834, the so-called Battle of Pinjarra took place; this was a punitive military expedition undertaken after a soldier had been killed by Aborigines. A plant for the treatment of bauxite, mined in the DARLING RANGE, was established in 1972.

pinks *see* Caryophyllaceae

Pioneer River QLD Located in the central E coastal region of the State, it rises in the Eungella National Park and flows for some 80km in an E direction to an estuary on the Coral Sea coast. About 5km upstream from its mouth is the city of MACKAY. The Eungella National Park is an upland area covering 49 691ha; much of it is rugged and inaccessible except to experienced bushwalkers, and it contains large sections of rainforest, prominent peaks, rocky gorges and dense fern growth. Along the lower reaches of the Pioneer Valley, between the Clarke and O'Connor Ranges, is a rich alluvial plain which is intensively cultivated with cane farms, tropical fruit growing, beef cattle properties and dairy farms.

pipi *see* bivalve molluscs

pipistrelle *see* bats, etc.

pipits and wagtails These terrestrial PASSERINE BIRDS, which run and walk, belong to the family Motacillidae. They are slim, long-tailed birds with slender, pointed bills and they feed on seeds and insects. Of the 48 species in the world, only four are represented in Australia (the willie wagtail belongs to a separate family; *see* FLYCATCHERS).

The pipit, *Anthus novaeseelandiae* (16cm long), is common throughout Australia, especially in the S. It is a brown bird with blackish streaks and is well camouflaged in the sparsely vegetated open habitats that it favours.

The three wagtails are rare, non-breeding vagrants from the N hemisphere.

pitcher plant *see* saprophytic plants

pittas These PASSERINE BIRDS belong to the family Pittidae which is represented in central Africa, South-East Asia, New Guinea and Australia. They are plump, short-tailed, brightly coloured BIRDS which feed in rainforests and mangroves on ground insects and other invertebrates.

The most common species in Australia is the noisy pitta, *Pitta versicolor* (20cm to 25cm long), which ranges from CAPE YORK to northern NSW. This elusive bird has a dark

Kim White (N.P.I.A.W.)

Noisy pitta, *Pitta versicolor*

brown crown, a black face, green and blue wings and a red rump. It is very similar to the rainbow pitta, *P. iris* * (15cm to 18cm), a black-breasted species of the N coastal areas of WA and the NT. The rainbow pitta is an uncommon species, as is the red-bellied pitta, *P. erythrogaster* (18cm), which has a broad blue band on its black breast; this species occurs in E Cape York to which it may sometimes migrate from New Guinea.

The rainbow pitta is sedentary but the other species are, to some extent, migratory.

pituri *see* Solanaceae

placental mammals *see* eutherian mammals

plain turkey *see* bustard

planarians *see* flatworms

planigales *see* native cats, etc.

plankton These are small aquatic organisms which have such limited powers of locomotion that they are carried virtually passively by the currents, although many perform regular vertical migrations during the course of the day and night. They are divided into phytoplankton (plants) and zooplankton (animals).

The phytoplankton consists of unicellular and filamentous ALGAE and serves as food for animals of the zooplankton and large organisms. It is found only in those levels of the sea or lakes in which there is enough light for photosynthesis. It is richest in polar regions (where the water is more viscous than in the tropics), above the continental shelves and where upwellings of bottom water bring nutrients to the surface.

The zooplankton contains the eggs, larvae and adults of many animals that are permanent members of the plankton (for example, the predatory ARROW WORMS); the eggs and larval stages of many animals, such as FISHES, whose juvenile and adult stages are active swimmers and thus members of the nekton; and the eggs and larvae of animals, mainly invertebrates, which later settle on the bottom or on surfaces as sessile or slowly moving organisms. The development of planktonic larval stages in such organisms ensures that the species are dispersed and do not become overcrowded but, of course, very few of the larvae reach maturity.

Plankton occurs in fresh, brackish and salt waters. In the seas most individuals (larvae or adults) of the zooplankton belong to the ANNELIDS and other WORMS, the arrow worms, the CRUSTACEANS, the MOLLUSCS, the ECHINODERMS and the fishes.

Phytoplankton ('the pastures of the sea') and the zooplankton are supremely important lower levels in the food webs of the seas and inland waters. For example, whalebone whales (*see* DOLPHINS, etc.) live almost entirely on KRILL.

Further reading: Hardy, Sir Alister *The Open*

*Species, genus or family is endemic to Australia (see Preface)

Sea; Its Natural History: The World of Plankton. Collins, London, 1956; Russel, F.S. & Yonge, C.M. *The Seas.* (4th edn) Frederick Warne & Co., London, 1975.

plant-hoppers *see* bugs

plants, native *see* flora; vegetation; and individual family entries such as Cyperaceae; Epacridaceae; Gramineae; Mimosaceae; Myrtaceae; Orchidaceae; Papilionaceae; Restionaceae; Rutaceae

Platyhelminthes *see* flatworms

platypus *see* monotreme mammals

Playford, Sir Thomas (1896-1981) Premier of SA. The grandson of a former Premier also named Thomas Playford, he was born at Norton's Summit SA and entered the House of Assembly in 1933. In 1938 he became Commissioner for Crown Lands and Minister for Irrigation, and later in the same year became Premier, retaining office until 1965. During these 27 years he continued with the policy of encouraging secondary industry which had first been suggested by Auditor-General J.W. Wainwright in 1935 and had been pursued by Playford's predeces-

Sir Thomas Playford

sor, R.L. Butler. This policy led to a marked diversification in the economy of the State, a rapid growth of population, an even greater concentration of population than before in Adelaide and its immediate surroundings, and, ironically, a tilting of the balance of electoral support away from his party, the Liberal and Country League, and towards the Australian Labor Party. For some years he retained office only by virtue of an electoral distribution which favoured country voters heavily, but finally, in 1965, Labor gained an electoral victory. Playford's term of office had set a record for Australia and for the Commonwealth of Nations. He retired from politics in 1967.

Plecoptera *see* stoneflies

plovers *see* waders

plum, wild *see* apple

Poatina TAS This small village was built to house the construction workers on the hydro-electric power development which forms a major part of the GREAT LAKE scheme; it is located 56km by road SE of LAUNCESTON, at the NE edge of the GREAT WESTERN TIERS which form the boundary scarp of the CENTRAL PLATEAU. The name Poatina (Aboriginal for 'cavern') is more importantly associated with the underground power station, the State's largest, with an installed capacity of 300 000k W, commissioned in 1964. From the NE corner of Great Lake water flows via a 7km-long tunnel through the Tiers and then by a hillside penstock and down a 150m-deep shaft to the underground Poatina station. Additional water for this scheme has been provided by damming ARTHURS LAKE, from which water is pumped into Great Lake, thereby augmenting the Poatina supply.

Poeppel's Corner This is the point where the borders of SA, QLD and the NT meet; it is located in the arid lands of the SIMPSON DESERT and was named after a SA surveyor, Augustus John Poeppel, who marked the spot in 1883 (and corrected it the following year) with a large coolabah-tree stump.

poinsettia *see* Euphorbiaceae

pointer *see* sharks, etc.

Polding, John Bede (1794-1877) Bishop of the Roman Catholic Church. He was born in Liverpool, joined the Benedictine Order in 1811 and was ordained in 1819. In 1833, when the Roman Catholic Church in Australia was attached to the see of Mauritius, William Ullathorne was sent as Vicar-General and recommended that it be separated. The recommendation was accepted and Polding was chosen as Australia's first Roman Catholic bishop. However, the setting up of a hierarchy with titles duplicating those of Anglican bishops would have provoked controversy, and so he was consecrated as Titular Bishop of Hiero-Caesarea and Vicar-Apostolic of NEW HOLLAND and VAN DIEMEN'S LAND. He arrived in Sydney in 1835 and in the following year consecrated St Mary's Church as his cathedral. Almost immediately after his arrival he began an intensive mission to convicts, as well as applying himself vigorously to the task of Church organisation and travelling widely throughout his huge diocese. In 1842 he was made Archbishop of Sydney and Metropolitan of Australia, a title which he was allowed to retain in spite of a vigorous protest from the Anglican bishop, William BROUGHTON.

He won general respect for his zeal, sincerity and humanity, but in some ways misjudged the ways in which the Roman Catholic Church needed to develop in Australia. In particular, his ambition to keep his archdiocese under the care of the Benedictine Order was unrealistic and caused considerable friction within the Roman Catholic community. His order had no prospect of recruiting the number of priests required. Moreover, its members in Australia were recruited predominantly from England, and since members of their faith in Australia were of Irish origin, it was inevitable that in time a high proportion of the clergy and hierarchy would also be Irish. Nevertheless, the Church developed strongly during his long term of office. By the time he died there were 12 Roman Catholic dioceses in Australia.

Further reading: Suttor, T.L.L. *Hierarchy and Democracy in Australia 1788-1870.* Melbourne University Press, Melbourne, 1965; Leavey, M. *John Bede Polding.* Oxford University Press, Melbourne, 1971. O'Donoghue, F., *The Bishop of Botany Bay: the life of John Bede Polding, Australia's First Archbishop.* Angus & Robertson, London, 1982.

Poles in Australia The 1981 census revealed that 33 031 persons resident in Australia had been born in Poland. C.A. Price, a leading authority on multicultural affairs, in a study of the ethnic origin of the Australian population based on an eight-generation analysis, estimated the total Polish component to be equivalent to 134 700 persons in 1978.

The fact that only 6 573 persons of Polish birth were living in Australia in 1947 indicates the large-scale immigration of Polish refugees following World War II.

Early links between Poland and Australia. One of the earliest Poles to visit Australia for a period of four years was Count Paul Edmund STRZELECKI. Between 1839 and 1843 he explored the AUSTRALIAN ALPS, GIPPSLAND (which he named) and parts of TAS. He named Australia's highest peak MT. KOSCIUSKO after a Polish patriot, General Tadeusz Kosciuszko. His own name has survived in the Strzelecki Peaks on FLINDERS ISLAND; the STRZELECKI RANGES in GIPPSLAND, VIC, and the Strzelecki Creek in SA.

Other Polish visitors in the early days of colonisation included G.J. Broinowski, the author of *Birds in Australia*, (1890) and two other students of natural history—W. Blandowski and J. Lhotsky.

In the 1850s many Poles migrated to Australia to join the rush to the gold-fields and some of them were involved in the EUREKA STOCKADE. Later migrants during the nineteenth century settled on KANGAROO ISLAND, SA and the Upper Dawson Valley, QLD at Cracow.

Immigration from Poland in the twentieth century The census figures listed below indicate that the number of Australians who had been born in Poland increased slowly between 1921 and 1947 but escalated after that date, reaching a peak in 1966 and then started to decline until by 1981 it was only slightly over half of the 1966 figure. The steady decrease in the figures listed is explained by the fact that a higher proportion of the refugees were elderly people than in most other ethnic groups coming to Australia in the postwar period.

Year	Number	Year	Number	Year	Number
1921	1 780	1954	56 594	1971	59 700
1933	3 239	1961	60 049	1976	56 051
1947	6 573	1966	61 641	1981	33 031

The migrants coming to Australia after World War II represented a large proportion of the labour force employed to build the SNOWY MOUNTAINS Hydro-Electric Scheme and other large-scale public works.

Most Poles came to Australia as refugees and they settled in the large urban centres of NSW and VIC but there were smaller communities in ADELAIDE, PERTH, BRISBANE, HOBART, CANBERRA, QUEANBEYAN and in the industrial cities of GEELONG, WOLLONGONG and NEWCASTLE. The residential distribution was influenced by the religious beliefs of the migrants. More than 90% were of the Roman Catholic faith and were widely dispersed in the community. The remaining Poles comprised Jews, and followers of Orthodox and Lutheran faith. The Jewish Poles settled close to Jewish institutions in Australia, while those following Orthodox and Lutheran faiths settled mainly in Adelaide.

Polish periodicals published in Australia include the weekly *Wiadomosci Polskie* (Sydney), *Tygodnik Polski* (Melbourne) and *Naza Droga* (Adelaide).

Notable Polish-born Australians include: Professor Jerzy Zubrzycki, CBE, MBE, Foundation Professor of Sociology, Australian National University; Professor Antoni Emil Karbowiak, University of New South Wales; Rev. Friedrich Wilhem Albrecht, MBE, Superintendent of the Finke River Mission from 1926-1971, and an authority on the aboriginals of Central Australia; Peter Stephen Wilenski, Chairman of the Australian Public Service Board and formerly Foundation Professor of Management, Australian Graduate School of Management, University of NSW; Josef Stanislaw Ostoja-Kotkowski, a multiaward winning artist and sculptor and Mrs. Wiska Listwan, OBE, President of the Cornucopia Committee (a charity group in Sydney), who has pioneered the celebrity-importing style of fund-raising.

Police-Citizens Boys' Clubs The history of these clubs in NSW began in 1937 when the first was opened in the inner Sydney district of Woolloomooloo. Its popularity very soon led to the foundation of several others, and in 1938 the Federation of New South Wales Police-Citizens Boys' Clubs was formed and incorporated under the Companies Act. By June 1982 there were 50 clubs functioning. They provide a wide range of sporting, cultural and educational activities and more than half of them have bands, including brass, pipe, woodwind and brass, banjo-ukelele, modern swing combinations and drum corps. Organised inter-club competitions in judo, boxing, wrestling, weight-lifting, fencing, table tennis and gymnastics are held regularly. The Federation is controlled by a Council of Management, and each club is administered by a committee of citizens and police, chaired by the local Officer-in-Charge of Police and with a member of the Police Service as Secretary-Supervisor. Members must be between the ages of eight and 21. Girls are now admitted as associate members; the 1982 membership included over 25 000 girls and over 175 000 boys. The government assists financially in the building and equipping of new clubs, but the cost of maintaining clubs is the responsibility of the local branches.

political history This article deals with the history of government and politics in three main sections, namely: the evolution of parliamentary government in the six colonies which are now the States of the Commonwealth of Australia; the federation movement; and the story of political parties and policies in the federal sphere since the Commonwealth came into existence in 1901.

THE EVOLUTION OF PARLIAMENTARY GOVERNMENT

Obstacles to self-government By the 18th century most British colonies of settlement had a considerable measure of self-government. Thus the 13 colonies that became the USA had elected assemblies, with wide powers over internal legislation and taxation, long before gaining independence. Such institutions were slow to develop in Australia, for three basic reasons. First, the initial settlement was undertaken by the British government for its own purposes, not by free men who expected to enjoy at least the degree of participation in government which existed in the mother country. Secondly, NSW and VAN DIEMEN'S LAND began as penal settlements, in which firm control by the executive was considered essential. Finally, when free settlers began to arrive they came, for many years, only in small numbers, and it was assumed that a fairly large population was needed for free institutions to flourish.

Powers of the early Governors In keeping with the nature of NSW as a penal colony, the early Governors were commissioned to exercise a wide range of legislative and executive powers. They made regulations and prescribed penalties to enforce them, imposed taxes and controlled public funds, made grants of land and controlled the assignment of convicts. Their decisions were subject to approval by the Crown, which in practice meant the member of the British Cabinet responsible for the colonies (at first the Home Secretary and later the Secretary for War and the Colonies). Within the colony, however, there were no political institutions to limit a Governor's powers.

Progress to responsible government As shown in Table 1, this took place in three main stages. First, the Governor was given a small Legislative Council to assist him in making regulations. It included a number of important officials, and a few non-officials appointed by the Governor. In NSW such a body was set up by the New South Wales Judicature Act of 1823, following a considerable growth in the free population during Governor MACQUARIE's term of office, complaints against various autocratic acts of Macquarie, and calls by William WENTWORTH and others for the granting of free institutions. Usually, the number of Members in a Legislative Council was increased after a few years, and these Members were given the power to override the Governor's decision by a majority vote. This was done in NSW in 1828.

The second stage consisted of a further enlargement of the Legislative Council, with provision for two-thirds of the Members to be elected. This step was taken in NSW by the Constitution Act of 1842, following a massive increase in free immigration during the 1830s and the abolition of transportation to the mainland of NSW in 1840. The Council was given considerable power over local finance, but the Governor was left with wide powers, including the right to appoint and dismiss the heads of government departments, and control over Crown lands and the proceeds from their sale.

The final stage involved the acceptance of a locally framed constitution providing for a Parliament of two Houses. In 1852 NSW, VIC, SA and TAS (then still known officially as Van Diemen's Land) were invited to draw

Table 1

THE DEVELOPMENT OF PARLIAMENTARY GOVERNMENT

	NSW	VIC	QLD	SA	WA	TAS
The colony is founded	1788	1851	1859	1836	1829	1825
A small nominated Legislative Council is set up	1823	—	—	1842	1832	1825
A larger Legislative Council is set up, two-thirds of the members being elected	1843	1851	—	1851	1870	1851
A Parliament of two Houses first meets, and a Premier and Cabinet, responsible to the Lower House, are appointed	1856	1855	1859	1856	1890	1856

Note: the dates given are those when the bodies referred to first met. In most cases the legislation authorising them was passed a year or two earlier.

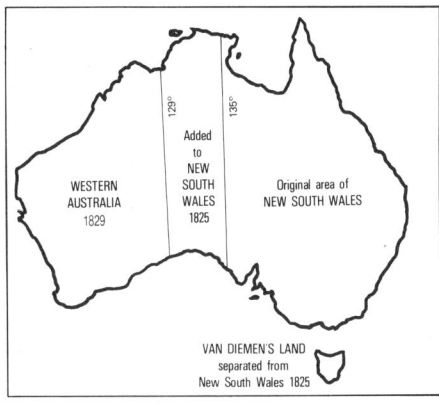

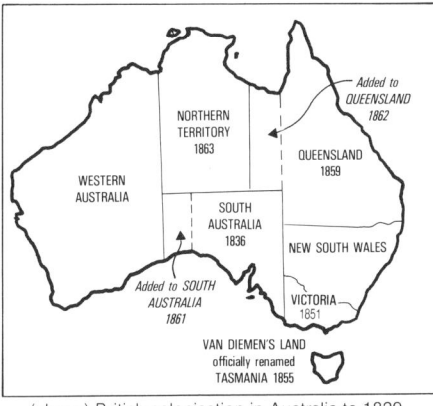

(above) British colonisation in Australia to 1829
(below) New colonies and boundary changes after
1829

up constitutions; at the same time the complete abolition of transportation to E Australia was announced. The constitutions submitted by NSW, VIC and TAS were approved in 1855 and that for SA in 1856. All provided for bicameral (two-chamber) Parliaments, the Upper House of each being called the Legislative Council and the Lower House the Legislative Assembly in NSW and VIC and the House of Assembly in the other two colonies. Each Lower House was elected—by manhood suffrage in SA and on a franchise based on moderate property qualifications in the other colonies. In NSW Members of the Legislative Council were nominated by the Governor; in the other colonies they were elected, but the franchise was based on high property qualifications, with educational or professional status as an alternative in some cases. In each colony executive power was in the hands of a Premier and Cabinet, who had to hold the support of the Lower House. Similar constitutions were approved for QLD when it became a separate colony in 1859 and for WA in 1890. Although in theory the Governors still had the right to summon and dismiss Ministers and to refuse consent to legislation (as they do today), in practice the colonies had attained internal self-government.

Some subsequent changes The main parliamentary reforms advocated in Britain by the Chartists were attained relatively quickly in Australia. For example, manhood suffrage was practised in Lower House elections in all six colonies by 1900 and female suffrage by 1908,

the corresponding dates in Britain being 1918 and 1928. The secret ballot was in use by 1859 in all of the five colonies that were self-governing, whereas in Britain it was not adopted until 1872. Change came more slowly, however, for the Legislative Councils. In 1922 that of QLD was abolished, and in 1934 that of NSW was reformed (*see* GOVERNMENT OF AUSTRALIA). In the other States the franchise remained restricted in Upper House elections until recently, full adult suffrage being introduced only in 1950 in VIC, 1964 in WA, 1968 in TAS and 1973 in SA.

THE FEDERATION MOVEMENT
Early suggestions and attempts From the late 1840s, when plans were being made to separate VIC from NSW, various proposals for federation were put forward, New Zealand being included in some cases. However, the idea attracted little support until the 1880s, by which time Australian nationalism was stronger and communication between the colonies easier. Moreover, political leaders were becoming aware of the difficulty of handling common problems such as defence, foreign affairs and immigration without some kind of central government.

In 1883 a meeting of Premiers adopted a resolution calling for a 'Federal Council of Australasia'. Two years later such a body was set up, but it was merely a consultative body, containing representatives of the Parliaments of the Australian colonies and New Zealand. It made recommendations to those Parliaments but had no legislative or executive powers. Membership was not compulsory, and NSW, the richest and most populous colony, did not send representatives to any of the Council's meetings. In 1889 Sir Henry PARKES, Premier of NSW, launched a campaign for the framing of a constitution providing for a federal Parliament with power to legislate on matters of importance affecting Australia as a whole. This led to a convention in 1891 which was attended by delegates from the Parliaments of the Australian colonies and New Zealand. When the resulting constitution was debated

in the NSW Parliament it met with such strong opposition that it was not put to a vote. The governments of the other colonies, lacking a strong lead from NSW, did not proceed to introduce a Constitution Bill in their Parliaments.

Grounds of opposition Opposition in NSW sprang from a general feeling that it would suffer in any sharing of power with the others, from rivalry with VIC, from uncertainty about the location of the federal capital, and from the realisation that the federation would need to be at least moderately protectionist, whereas popular feeling in NSW favoured free trade. There was also strong opposition in the older-settled districts of WA—largely because of their geographical isolation—and in southern QLD—where economic competition from NSW was feared.

The achievement of federation In 1897-98 a second convention was held, delegates coming from all colonies except QLD. In 1898 the resulting constitution was put to a referendum in NSW, VIC, SA and TAS, and accepted in all of these colonies except NSW. The constitution was then amended at a Premiers' conference, and submitted to another referendum in all colonies except WA. It was accepted in all five colonies, and was submitted to the British government; after it had been amended in a few more particulars a Bill providing for federation was passed by the Imperial Parliament. In the meantime, the constitution had been accepted by referendum in WA, so that when the Commonwealth came into being on 1 January 1901, it included as States all six former colonies.

FEDERAL PARTIES AND POLICIES
SINCE FEDERATION
The formative period, 1901-14 During the early years of federation, Australian politicians concentrated on establishing the organs of the Commonwealth government, legislating for a 'white Australia', and establishing defence forces and policies for the new nation. In all these matters the parties were in substantial

Opening of the first federal parliament by the Duke of York, 9th May 1901. Oil painting by Tom Roberts

Australasian Federation Conference, Melbourne 1890. This meeting of two delegates from the Parliament of each Australian colony and from New Zealand led to the holding of the first Federal Convention the following year

Courtesy of A.I.S. Canberra

agreement. More controversial areas of legislation were industrial arbitration and social services. By 1909 the political parties had regrouped into a Liberal-versus-Labour alignment, which has been the main basis of party rivalry ever since.

In the first Commonwealth Parliament there were three important groups. In the House of Representatives the protectionists numbered 32, the free-traders 27 and members of the Labor Party 16. The two larger groups lacked organisation; many of the members were only loosely attached to one or the other of them. Labor, however, insisted on strict party discipline; its candidates at elections had to pledge support for the party's objectives, which included social services, industrial arbitration, the nationalisation of monopolies, increased land taxes and the prevention of non-European immigration. Since the protectionists, with some notable exceptions, tended to be more liberal than the free-traders, Labor gave them its general support for the first few years.

Edmund Barton, the protectionist leader and first Prime Minister, concentrated on establishing the various Public Service departments, setting up the High Court, providing for the exclusion of non-European immigrants by the Immigration Restriction Act and arranging for the repatriation of Pacific islanders—known as KANAKAS—by means of the Pacific Islands Labourers Act. Alfred Deakin, who succeeded Barton in 1903, placed the emphasis on social legislation. With Labor support he established the Commonwealth Court of Conciliation and Arbitration, introduced Commonwealth age and invalid pensions, and passed the Defence Acts of 1903

and 1904 which provided for volunteer enlistment in time of peace, but allowed for military conscription for home defence in time of war.

By this time the distinction between protectionists and free-traders was fairly insignificant; most of the former believed in only a moderate level of tariff protection, while the latter realised that complete free trade was impracticable. Meanwhile, Labor was gathering strength, and members of both non-Labor parties feared what George REID delighted in calling 'the socialist tiger'. In 1909, therefore, the two parties joined to form the Fusion Party (later called the LIBERAL PARTY) but this did not prevent Labor from gaining a majority in both Houses in the elections of 1910. During the following three years the Labor administration, with Andrew FISHER as Prime Minister, extended age pensions, introduced maternity allowances, founded the Commonwealth Bank and introduced a land tax. It also passed a Defence Act, similar to one introduced by Deakin, providing for compulsory military training, for a part-time militia in addition to the regular army, for a military academy at Duntroon, and for a naval academy at JERVIS BAY. It proceeded with Deakin's plans for an Australian Navy, taking delivery of the first ships in 1913.

In the elections of 1913 the Liberals, under Joseph COOK, won a majority in the House of Representatives. However, Labor still controlled the Senate, and so in 1914 Cook used the provisions of Section 57 of the Constitution to obtain a double dissolution (that is, recommended to the Governor-General that an election be held for the whole of the Senate, as well as for the House of Representatives).

His move miscarried, for Labor won a majority in both chambers. Fisher was again Prime Minister; when he retired in 1915 he was replaced by William Morris HUGHES.

Nationalist Party dominance, 1917-29 In 1916 there occurred the first of the three great splits within the AUSTRALIAN LABOR PARTY (ALP). The attempt by Hughes to introduce CONSCRIPTION led to the expulsion from the party of himself and 24 other federal parliamentarians, who then joined the Liberals in forming the Nationalist Party. Hughes remained Prime Minister and in 1917 and 1919 led the Nationalists to electoral victories. However, the elections of 1922 gave Nationalists and Labor an equal number of seats in the House of Representatives, with the newly formed COUNTRY PARTY holding the balance of power. Strong antipathy between Hughes and the Country Party led to his replacement in 1923 by Stanley BRUCE, with the Country Party leader, Earle PAGE, as his deputy. The Bruce-Page coalition remained in power until 1929.

From the Depression to post-war reconstruction, 1929-49 During the period of Nationalist/Country Party ascendancy the ALP had adopted a specific socialist aim—'socialisation of industry, production, distribution and exchange'. However, when it returned to office under James SCULLIN, its electoral programme included the expansion of social services and public works, but not the nationalisation of any particular industries. The political effects of its attempts to cope with the Depression (*see* ECONOMIC HISTORY) were another split in the party and its banishment to the Opposition benches for another lengthy period. The split arose from disagreement between Scullin and J.T. LANG, Premier of NSW, which culminated in March 1931 in the expulsion of the whole NSW branch and the formation of a new federal Labor Party in that State. About the same time Joseph LYONS and other right-wing federal Labor members joined with the Nationalists in the third anti-Labor 'fusion' of the century, to form the UNITED AUSTRALIA PARTY (UAP). In November Lang's supporters in the House of Representatives voted against the government and brought about its downfall. The UAP won the subsequent elections and Lyons became Prime Minister. He remained in office at the head of a UAP Cabinet until 1934, and then with a UAP/Country Party coalition Cabinet until his death in 1939.

There followed a period of dissension within the coalition. Following Lyons' death Page was Prime Minister for three weeks, until the newly elected UAP leader, Robert MENZIES, took over. However, it was a year before the Country Party agreed to form a coalition under Menzies' leadership, and as the military situation in Europe deteriorated during 1940 both coalition parties began to criticise his leadership of Australia's war effort. In August 1941 he resigned, being replaced as Prime Minister by Arthur FADDEN, Page's successor as Country Party leader. However, in October

'The Blue Mountain Road', watercolour 1839, by Conrad Martens, in the National Gallery of Victoria

'Yarra Flats', watercolour 1871, by Louis Buvelot, in the National Gallery of Victoria

'Mills Plains', oil on canvas 1836, by John Glover, in the Tasmanian Museum and Art Gallery

'Mount Wellington from New Town Bay Tasmania', oil painting 1872, by William Piguenit, in the National Gallery of Victoria

'Departure of the Orient', oil on canvas 1888, by Charles Conder, in the Art Gallery of New South Wales

'The Breakaway', oil on canvas 1890-91, by Tom Roberts, in the Art Gallery of South Australia

See also separate entries and PAINTING AND PAINTERS

'Droving Into the Light' oil on canvas 1921, by Hans Heysen, in the Art Gallery of Western Australia

'Wimmera Landscape', oil on canvas, by Arthur Boyd in the National Gallery of Victoria

'Fires On' Lapstone Tunnel, oil on canvas 1891, by Sir Arthur Streeton, in the Art Gallery of New South Wales

'Farm Cove' or 'The Fruit Seller at Farm Cove', oil on canvas 1915 by Roland Wakelin, in the Australian National Gallery

See also separate entries and PAINTING AND PAINTERS

two independents in the House of Representatives, on whose votes the government depended for a majority, withdrew their support, and John CURTIN, the Labor leader, was asked by the Governor-General to form a government.

The ALP won a landslide victory in the elections of 1943, and Curtin remained Prime Minister until his death in July 1945. Three of his actions and policies marked the beginning of important long-term trends. The first was his quick recognition after the Japanese attack on Pearl Harbour that Australia's security now rested on help from the USA rather than from Britain. The second was the introduction of uniform tax in 1942 which has made it impracticable for any State to reintroduce its own income tax, thereby giving the federal government more financial dominance over the States than any other development since federation. The third was his government's insistence that the needs of the war should not prevent Labor's implementation of its welfare policies; this marked the beginning of the continuing Commonwealth dominance in social services.

Although Labor won the 1946 elections under the leadership of Curtin's successor, Ben CHIFLEY, the new Liberal Party, formed by Menzies from the remnants of the UAP, polled strongly. During the following three years the Opposition parties skilfully exploited public resentment against the continuance of wartime controls, especially petrol rationing, and against attempts to nationalise domestic airlines and the private trading banks (both declared unconstitutional by the High Court). The 1949 elections saw the beginning of a 23-year period of government by a Liberal/Country Party coalition.

From 1949 to the present One factor in the success of the coalition between 1949 and 1972 was Menzies' outstanding political ability. A superb debater and tactician, he was adept at persuading electors that Labor was not strongly enough opposed to Communism, that its economic policies were irresponsible, and that its parliamentarians were too strongly under the control of the party's federal conference. Undoubtedly, Menzies owed a lot to fortune. First, the economic boom of the 1950s and 1960s naturally gave an advantage to the parties in power. Secondly, the spread of Communism in Asia and the entry into Australia of many migrants who had suffered under Communism swelled electoral support for his claim that Labor was insufficiently anti-Communist. Thirdly, in 1955 another major split occurred in the ALP, leading to the foundation of a breakaway Anti-Communist Labor Party, later renamed the DEMOCRATIC LABOR PARTY (DLP). Although the DLP remained a minor party, it achieved sufficient electoral support, especially in VIC, to play an important role in keeping the ALP out of office.

Labor regained office under Gough WHITLAM in 1972 on a programme which included the recognition of the People's Republic of China, the abolition of the National Service

Courtesy of A.I.S. Canberra

The first federal ministry (taken late in its term of office). Standing l to r: Senator J.G. Drake, Postmaster General; Senator R.E. O'Connor, Vice-President of the Executive Council; Sir P.P. Fysh, Honorary Minister; G.G. Kingston, Trade and Customs; Sir John Forrest, Defence. Seated l to r: Sir W.J. Lyne, Home Affairs; Edmund Barton, Prime Minister and Minister for External Affairs; Lord Tennyson, Governor General; A. Deakin, Attorney General; Sir George Turner, Treasurer. Not present: N. Lewis, Honorary Minister

Act, increased attention to education, urban problems and Aboriginal affairs, and the introduction of a new health scheme. However, the opposition parties retained control of the Senate, which during the following two years blocked a number of Bills passed by the House of Representatives. In 1974, when the Senate blocked a supply Bill, Whitlam secured a dissolution of both Houses. He won the subsequent election in May but was still without a majority in the Senate. During the following 18 months the economy deteriorated further, and late in 1975 there occurred a constitutional crisis unprecedented in Australian history. As inflation and unemployment increased, it was evident that the Opposition was likely to attempt to use the Senate majority to block supply and so force the government to yet another election. Finally the senate passed a motion that consideration of two Appropriation Bills should be deferred until the government had agreed to hold an election, but Mr Whitlam refused to take this course. On 11 November the Governor-General, Sir John KERR, broke the deadlock by dismissing the Labor government, appointing the Liberal leader, Malcolm FRASER, as caretaker Prime Minister, and dissolving both Houses of Parliament. This action brought an element of almost unprecedented bitterness into Australian politics. In the election of December 1975, Labor was decisively defeated, winning only 36 seats out of 127 in the House of Representatives and 27 out of 64 in the Senate. In December 1977, when Fraser secured an early election for the House of Representatives and half of the Senate, the coalition won another sweeping

victory. In October 1980 it again defeated Labor; however, its majority in the House of Representatives was cut heavily and it failed to maintain an absolute majority in the Senate. A striking feature of these two general elections was the measure of success achieved by a new party, the AUSTRALIAN DEMOCRATS. Founded by D. Chipp, a former Liberal Minister, it has shown no prospects of winning seats in the House of Representatives. However, in 1977 two of its candidates for the Senate (including Chipp) were elected, and in 1980 it increased its representation there to five, thus attaining the 'balance of power' between the government and Labor. Its success illustrates the fact that the electorate is now more volatile than formerly, with more potential 'swinging' voters who feel critical, at least in some respects, of both the coalition parties and Labor. This trend was confirmed in the election of March 1983, when the ALP gained a convincing victory in the House of Representatives, but the Australian Democrats again won five seats in the Senate, and continued to hold the balance of power there.

See also Cabinet government; political parties; See Appendix 2: Government in Australia.
Further reading: Deakin, A. *The Federal Story: The Inner History of the Federal Cause.* (2nd edn) Melbourne University Press, Melbourne, 1965; Lumb, R.D. *The Constitutions of the Australian States* (2nd edn) Queensland University Press, Brisbane, 1965; la Nauze, J.A. *The Making of the Australian Constitution.* Melbourne University Press, Melbourne, 1972; Alexander, F. *Australia Since Federation.* (3rd edn) Nelson, West Melbourne, 1976; Quick, J. & Garran, R.R. *The Annotated Con-*

stitution of the Australian Commonwealth.
Legal Books, Sydney, 1976.

political parties In Australia, as
elsewhere, the development of parliamentary
government has been accompanied by the
growth of political parties. These are private,
voluntary organisations, composed of people
who are in general agreement regarding the
policies which they think governments should
follow. They try to have such policies adopted
by selecting candidates to represent the party
at elections and by supporting them with
publicity and other forms of help. Most of the
organisational work of the party is carried out
by voluntary workers although all but the very
smallest parties have a nucleus of paid
workers. In return for being selected and
helped, the candidate is expected to support
the party's policy during the election
campaign and in Parliament if elected. The
various Australian parties differ somewhat in
the strictness with which they enforce this
requirement. The basic aim of each party is to
have sufficient candidates elected to gain
control of the government. Smaller parties,
however, realise that, for the time being at
least, they must be content with the secondary
aim of getting enough members elected to
form a coalition government with a large
party, or perhaps to hold the balance of power
between the larger parties.

**Political parties and parliamentary gov-
ernment** Political parties are essential for
government in Australia to work, because
Parliament needs a government and an Opposition. If there are only two political parties
then the one with the majority of Members in
the Lower House forms the government. If
there are more than two, then it may be necessary for two or more parties to form a coalition
government in order to have a majority. The
leader of the government and the leader of the
Opposition are paid salaries which are
financed from funds provided for the
operation of Parliament. Political parties are
also essential for the operation of CABINET
GOVERNMENT because they supply a stable
majority of Members within the House of
Representatives from whom Ministers can be
selected.

Table 1

**SEATS HELD BY AUSTRALIAN
POLITICAL PARTIES IN HOUSE OF
REPRESENTATIVES AND SENATE
FOLLOWING 1983 GENERAL ELECTION**

	Lower House	Upper House
Australian Democrats	0	5
Australian Labor Party	75	30
Liberal Party of Aust.	33	24
National Party of Aust.	17	4
Independents	0	1
TOTAL	125	64

Size of political parties In the 1980s
membership of all political parties in Australia
was estimated to be about four per cent of the
electorate, which compares with approximately 12 per cent in Britain. The lower
percentage in Australia is probably the result
of compulsory voting which has reduced the
need to recruit large numbers of members for
each party.

Political parties at present A considerable
number of political parties has been founded
during this century, but since 1910 only three
have proved to be durable in the Parliaments—
Labor, Liberal and National. The DEMOCRA-
TIC LABOR PARTY had members elected to the
Senate for nearly a decade, the Australian
Democrats have also had members elected to
the Senate since 1977, and the Communist
Party has existed outside the Parliaments since
the 1920s. At the 1983 federal elections the
major political parties endorsing candidates
for election were: AUSTRALIAN LABOR PARTY,
LIBERAL PARTY and NATIONAL PARTY OF
AUSTRALIA. The minor parties endorsing
candidates included: Advance Victoria, Aus-
tralia, Australia First Movement, Australian
Christian, Australian Democrats, Australian
Independent, Australian Republicans, Call to
Australia, Christian Voice, Communist Party
of Australia, Conservative Nationalist, Country
Liberal, Deadly Serious Party of Australia,
Democratic Labor, Engineered Australia Plan,
Green Party of Australia, Independent British
Conservative, National Country, National
Humanitarian, National Party of Western Aus-
tralia, National South West Coalition, New Aus-
tralian, Party to Expose the Petrov Conspiracy,
Peace on Earth, Pensioner Party of Australia,
Progress, Proud to be an Australian, Social
Democrats, Socialist Labour League, Socialist
Party of Australia, Socialist Workers, The
Integrity Team, True Independents and the
White Australia Movement; there were also a
number of ungrouped candidates.

As a result of the 1983 election the parties
were represented in the federal Parliament as
shown in Table 1. The leader of the government (Australian Labor Party) was Robert
James Lee ('Bob') HAWKE, and after the
election Andrew Sharp PEACOCK became
leader of the Liberal Party and leader of the
Opposition in Parliament.

**Policies and programmes of political
parties** Most political parties prepare a
printed document known as a platform which
sets out their ideology and the policies and
programmes which they would like to have
adopted. These platforms are usually altered
before elections in order to bring them up to
date with current events and circumstances.
Most parties will supply a copy of their
platform to anyone interested.

Political parties and the future Political
parties in Australia have been developed in a
society with an English-speaking population
whose ancestors came from Great Britain.
However, since 1947 Australia has become a
multi-cultural population and it has been
predicted that ethnic politics will become

important in the 1980s. The influence of
ethnic migrant communities could alter the
pattern of political parties in Australia in the
future.
Further reading: Loveday, P., Martin, A.W., &
Parker, R.S. (eds) *The Emergence of the Australian Party System.* Hale & Iremonger, Sydney,
1977; Emy, H.V. *The Politics of Australian
Democracy.* Macmillan, South Melbourne,
1974; Forell, C.R. *How We are Governed.*
Cheshire, Melbourne, 1978.

polo This is a ball game played from horseback. The aim of the four-man mounted team
is to hit or guide the ball with a polo stick
through the goal posts situated at both ends of
the playing field. As the game is played at a
fast pace and is particularly exacting on the
stamina and wind of the horses (called polo
ponies) the game is divided into six periods
(chukkas) and the horses are changed and
rested between chukkas.

It is thought that polo was introduced into
Australia from India by British Army officers
in the mid-1870s. Until the 1940s the game
was confined mainly to country areas, but
since World War II polo matches have been
included as part of the entertainment in the
annual Royal Agricultural Shows in Sydney
and Melbourne. Tours by top-ranking
Argentinian teams (1964, 1968 and 1972),
teams from the USA (1976 and 1981) and
from England (1977 and 1980) and overseas
tours by Australian teams (such as the tour to
California and Texas in 1982 and to India and
Pakistan in 1983) have vastly improved the
standard of play, and Australia ranks among
the top polo-playing countries in the world
today.

Pontville TAS (population 908 in 1981) A
small town on the Midland Highway, 27km N
of Hobart, it is the seat of local government for
the Brighton municipality. It is listed as a historic
town, dating from the 1830s and noted for its
freestone buildings.

poplars *see* forestry

population The total population of
Australia, as derived from the preliminary
counts of the 1981 census, was 14 544 488.
However, this figure was subsequently
adjusted to account for under-enumeration
and for other things such as people who were
temporarily overseas at the time of the census,
giving an estimated resident population (preliminary) of 14 926 786. The distribution of
this population between the States and Territories (*see* Table 1) shows that NSW is the
largest (with over 35 per cent of the total
population), TAS the smallest and the two
Territories, ACT and the NT, smaller than
any of the States.

The population statistics of the capital cities
in each State (*see* entries on capital cities)
indicate the dominance of these cities: for

Table 1

POPULATION IN STATES AND TERRITORIES AT THE 1981 CENSUS (to the nearest thousand)

State Territory	Population* ('000s)	% of total population
NSW	5 237	35.1
VIC	3 949	26.5
QLD	2 345	15.7
SA	1 319	8.8
WA	1 299	8.7
TAS	427	2.9
ACT	227	1.5
NT	123	0.8
TOTAL	14 926	100.0

Note: * adjusted for under-enumeration; † the 1981 figures are Estimated Resident Population (Preliminary).
Source: Australian Bureau of Statistics, Canberra.

example, in SA, Adelaide accounts for 69 per cent of the State's population; in VIC, Melbourne accounts for 65 per cent; Perth has 62 per cent of WA's population; and Sydney contains 55 per cent of the NSW population. Melbourne and Sydney together account for over a third (36.5 per cent) of Australia's total population.

The growth of Australia's population during this century is shown in Table 2. At the turn of the century, the total population was under four million; by the 1921 census, it had exceeded five million; in the 1950s, it was over eight million; by 1971 almost 13 million; and by 1981 it was was nearly 15 million.

Table 2

AUSTRALIA'S POPULATION GROWTH IN THE TWENTIETH CENTURY

Census year*	Population (millions)
1901	3.77
1911	4.46
1921	5.44
1933	6.63
1947	7.58
1954	8.99
1961	10.51
1971†	12.94
1976†	13.92
1981††	14.93

Note: * prior to 1971 the statistics do not include full-blood Aborigines; † the 1971 and 1976 figures are adjusted for under-enumeration; †† the 1981 figure is the Estimated Resident Population (Preliminary).
Source: Australian Bureau of Statistics, Canberra.

pop music Australia has never been short of musical talent and many excellent performers have come to the fore during the rock era. However, overseas success has continually proved elusive, and although the situation is changing rapidly, it is interesting to look back at the many attempts which have been made over the years.

The average Australian tends to interpret overseas as meaning Britain and America. Even though large numbers of records by Australian performers are sold in many other countries around the world, most people back home fail to see these achievements as significant.

Possibly this emphasis on British and American success stems from Australia's historical connections with those two countries, particularly Britain. Countless promising careers were brought to a halt during the fifties and sixties by a lemming-like determination to make it in England.

Admittedly, there was some incentive with Slim Dusty, Rolf HARRIS, Frank Ifield and the Seekers occasionally appearing on the British charts from 1959 to 1964, but three of these were country and novelty performances, while the Seekers were a folk group. When it came to rock-'n'roll, there was a strong attitude in Britain that anything the colonials could do, the mother country could do better.

The Easybeats moved to Britain and made the Top 10 in 1966 with 'Friday on my Mind' which also reached the US Top 20 the following year, but they were unable to capitalize on that success and faded from the scene soon after. Over the next three or four years, many of Australia's top performers made the pilgrimage with high hopes which were soon dashed.

The exception to the rule was the Bee Gees who had lived in Australia for ten years after migrating from England in 1957. Returning to England, they signed with Robert Stigwood, an Australian who had set up in management in Britain. 'New York Mining Disaster, 1941' went on to be a hit in both the UK and US.

Why were the Bee Gees so successful when others failed? The difference lay primarily in management. Most Australian performers went to England without either contacts or a specific contract. Frequently, the trip had been the prize in a contest such as Hoadleys National Battle of the Sounds, but when the groups arrived they were on their own without any experience in dealing with hard-nosed record company bosses.

Daddy Cool were the first to break out of the traditional rut when they focussed on America in 1971. Their first tour was not terribly successful, but it proved that breaking into the US market might not be impossible. The same year, Olivia Newton-John, who had won a trip to England as a talent quest prize in 1965, made the US charts with 'If Not For You'. Three years later, she won two Grammy awards for 'I Honestly Love You' which had been written by Peter Allen, who had gone to America to work with Judy Garland in 1962. He has since become a star performer in his own right.

However, Olivia's songs had been recorded in England. It wasn't until 1975 that an Australian-recorded single by an Australian made it to the US charts, when John Paul Young's 'Yesterday's Hero' reached the top 50.

This success seemed to spark something of a mass exodus. Brian Cadd went to live in the US. Colleen Hewett left to record the album 'M'Lady'. The following year, Sherbet's 'Howzat' made the Top 10 in the UK and charted in Thailand, South Africa and Europe, and Skyhooks made their first US tour.

Glenn Wheatley, formerly of the Masters Apprentices had two years working with Capital records in Los Angeles, learning the intricacies of the US record business, before he returned to Australia in 1974 to begin preparations for launching Little River Band whose debut album in the US sold 200,000 copies in 1976. The following year, 'Help Is On Its Way' made the the US Top 20 and the band toured extensively in the US, Holland, Britain and Japan.

Meanwhile, Air Supply, the band which was to make history three years later, was embarking on its first US tour as support act for Rod Stewart. Back in England, AC/DC had signed with Atlantic records.

1978 saw LRB scoring their highest US chart position yet when 'Reminiscing' made number three, and also became a hit in Spain, France and South America. John Paul Young's 'Standing in the Rain' charted in the US, Italy, South Africa, Holland, Germany, France and other countries. When he toured South Africa, JPY was greeted with hysteria reminiscent of sixties beatlemania. 'Love is in the Air' finally saw JPY on the US Top 40 and into the Top 10 in the UK, Scandanavia, France, Italy and other countries. AC/DC who had already developed a large British following, began to advance on the US and Jon English's 'Hollywood Seven' gained airplay in Europe.

Little River Band scored another first in 1979 when they were awarded a platinum record for sales of 500,000 by the 'Sleeper Catcher' LP, and a further gold award for sales of 100,000 in Canada.

1980 saw a virtual avalanche of Australian successes which continues to flow today. Split Enz made the US Top 50 with 'True Colours'. AC/DC shot to number 1 in the UK with 'Back in Black' which also reached the US Top 20. The television series, 'Against the Wind', featuring Jon English, was screened in Europe and the theme song, 'Six Ribbons', sung by English, topped several charts. The following year, he toured Europe with great success. But, the big excitement in music circles came from Air Supply who scored three US Top 10 hits and had 'All Out of Love' as the first Australian single to reach number 1 on the US chart.

The overseas success stories continue. Among the artists who have acquired contracts for overseas release are Rose Tattoo, Mondo Rock, Icehouse, Cold Chisel, Split Enz, James Freud and Rick Springfield.

The most successful Australian records generally seem to have been in the novelty style, such as Slim Dusty's 'Pub With No Beer' and Rolf Harris's 'Tie Me Kangaroo Down, Sport', and Lucky Starr's 'I've Been Everywhere'.

Another novelty song came on the scene in 1981. Joe Dolce's 'Shaddup You Face' is the best-selling single in Australia's history, as well as topping the UK and several European charts and making an appearance on the US chart.

porbeagle *see* sharks, etc.

'porcupine' *see* monotreme mammals

porgies *see* fishes, bony

Porifera *see* sponges

Porongorup Range WA Located about 40km N of ALBANY and just E of MOUNT BARKER in the far S of the State, this small granitic range rises sharply from the plains and is over 600m high. The range has a general NW-SE alignment, with karri forests on the lower slopes and brilliant displays of native flowering plants in spring-time between the stark granite boulders of the tops. The Porongorup National Park, (2 401ha) includes more than 20 peaks over 600m high (Nancy's Peak 652m, Devil's Slide 670m), which give striking panoramic views of the STIRLING RANGE to the N and Albany to the S.

Port Adelaide SA Located on an estuarine inlet on the E shore of ST VINCENT GULF, 24km by road NW of Adelaide and now part of the metropolitan area, it is the major port of SA. When Colonel William LIGHT designed Adelaide city in the 1830s, he planned for a canal to link the city to Port Adelaide, but the canal was never built and his planned route is now occupied by a wide highway connecting the city to its port. The facilities at the port include a container terminal and modern facilities at the Outer Harbour for ocean-going passenger vessels. The harbour is sheltered by a long sand spit, on a N-S alignment, with the main channel (dredged to 8m depth) between the spit and Torrens Is.
Further reading: Halls, C. *Port Adelaide Sketchbook.* Rigby, Adelaide, 1973.

Port Alma QLD It is the port for ROCKHAMPTON, located on the S shore of the FITZROY RIVER estuary, 34km S of Rockhampton city. It was developed in the 1880s to handle the export of agricultural, pastoral and mineral products from the Fitzroy region. It is a well-sheltered deep-water port which handles wool, wheat, meat and mineral exports; there is a terminal for the import of petroleum products and an oil refinery. At Bajool, 26km inland from the port, there is a salt works, with vast brine ponds which attract many sea birds.

Port Arthur TAS An inlet on the S coast of TASMAN PENINSULA, Port Arthur is 114km by road from Hobart via the Arthur Highway. Between 1830 and 1877, the W coast of the inlet was the main convict penal settlement of VAN DIEMEN'S LAND, claimed by some writers to be a prison of considerable notoriety and brutality. Escape from this prison was made particularly difficult because the narrow isthmus of EAGLEHAWK NECK, which links the peninsular to the main coast, was established as a military guard post, with hounds tethered

Port Adelaide

at close intervals across the narrow stretch of land. The penal settlement is now in ruins and is a popular tourist site. The main buildings of interest are the church, the 'model' prison where the 'silent system' of punishment was employed, the penitentiary, the guard house and magazine, the hospital and several cottages.

Port Augusta SA (population 15 254 in 1981) Located at the head of SPENCER GULF, it is a major transport centre, 310km by road (via the PORT PIRIE bypass) NNW of Adelaide. It was established in 1854 as a port serving the pastoral and agricultural settlements in the Outback regions of the State. It is an important rail junction where the central Australian railway goes N to ALICE SPRINGS, the transcontinental railway (the Indian-Pacific route) goes W to WA, and a line SW links it with WHYALLA. It is also a main focus of road routes—the Princes Highway from the SE, the Stuart Highway to the NW and the Eyre Highway to the SW and W. The city is an important electricity generation centre, using coal from LEIGH CREEK. It experiences a mild climate with an annual average rainfall of 256mm, evenly spread throughout the year. The National Trust of SA has classified several buildings in the town for preservation including the courthouse (1884), the gaol (1884), the institute (1875), the town hall (1866) and the water works building (1869). Inland from the Spencer Gulf coast, E of Port Augusta, is the S part of the FLINDERS RANGES; Mt Brown (961m), a peak on the W edge of the ranges, located 19km E of Port

Architectural relics of the convict settlement at Port Arthur TAS

J.H. Shaw

Aerial view of Port Augusta

Augusta, was sighted and named by the explorer Matthew FLINDERS in 1802.
Further reading: Branson, V.M. *Port Augusta Sketchbook.* Rigby, Adelaide, 1977.

Port Dalrymple

TAS Located on BASS STRAIT, this coastal inlet is the lower port of the TAMAR RIVER estuary, some 50km downstream from LAUNCESTON. The history of the Tamar dates from 1798 when the explorers BASS and FLINDERS named the river Port Dalrymple, and the name was used for the first settlement established in 1804 by Colonel William PATERSON, near the present site of GEORGE TOWN on the E shore of the port.

Port Davey

TAS A deep inlet on the SW coast in rugged wilderness country, it was glaciated during the Great Ice Age, making it a fiord formation. It consists of two main branches at right-angles: the Old River, which rises in ARTHUR RANGE and drains into the E-W branch; and the Davey River, which has its main source in the Frankland Range (SW of LAKE PEDDER) and drains into the N-S branch of the port. There is no settlement at the port.

Port Essington

NT An inlet on the N coast of COBOURG PENINSULA, extending inland for 40km, it is bounded at its W entrance by Vashon Heads and by Smith Point to the E. It was discovered and charted by Phillip King, son of Governor KING, in 1819, and as a result of his recommendations it was the site of early attempts to establish white settlements. In 1824 the first of these was made but lack of fresh water forced the party to move to MELVILLE ISLAND after a few days; in 1838 a settlement named Victoria was established on the SW shore of the port but, although it lasted 11 years, it too was abandoned. This settlement was the point reached by Ludwig LEICHHARDT in 1845 after his overland journey from MORETON BAY in QLD. Nowadays, only the ruins of Victoria remain, for the hopes that it would become a major tropical port for N Australia were never realised and were finally eclipsed by the selection in 1869 of the site of Darwin, about 180km to the SW. Cobourg Peninsula is now a wildlife sanctuary and a flora and fauna reserve.

Port Fairy

VIC (population 2 276 in 1981) A coastal town, a major fishing port and a rail terminus on the Pacific Highway, it is 291km by road and 300km by rail WSW of Melbourne, 27km W of WARRNAMBOOL and 64km E of PORTLAND. Situated on the W side of the Moyne River estuary, with surfing beaches along the adjacent coast, it is a popular holiday centre in the summer months. In the early 19th century sealing ships used it as an operating base and it took its name from one of these, *The Fairy*, which is claimed to have sheltered there in the 1820s. The settlement was originally known as Belfast, but the borough of Port Fairy was officially created in 1887. During the 1880s the port was second only to Sydney in volume of trade. It has many historic buildings and the National Trust (VIC) has classified over 30 of these (and recorded another 18) for preservation, including the lighthouse group (1859), the former customs house (1860-61), the courthouse (1860), the powder magazine (1860), the Methodist church (1855), St Andrews Presbyterian Church (1854), several hotels and numerous cottages.

Port Hedland

WA (population 12 948 in 1981) Claimed as WA's fastest-growing town, the iron ore boom of the PILBARA region has brought remarkable growth to this port town in recent decades. Located over 1 720km by road N of Perth along the Great Northern Highway, near its junction with the NW Coastal Highway, the town is situated on an island in a shallow bay, linked to the mainland by a causeway. It was named after Captain Peter Hedland who discovered the bay in 1829. The first sheep station in the region was started in 1864 alongside the nearby DE GREY RIVER and some of the descendants of the early pioneer pastoralists still work on the original properties. In the 1870s, pearls were found along the coast and the port became the base for the luggers. The town grew with gold and manganese discoveries and it was linked by rail to MARBLE BAR, but as the minerals petered out, Port Hedland languished and in 1946 the population numbered only 150.

In the 1950s there was a spurt of development, again based on mining in the region, but the major growth started in the 1960s with the discovery of rich iron ore deposits; by 1971 the population had reached 9 229 and by 1981 over 12 000. The harbour has been deepened by dredging, long jetties have been constructed to accommodate the ore vessels, and separate loading facilities have been built on Finucane Is. Railways link Port Hedland to the ore fields at MOUNT NEWMAN (420km) and MOUNT GOLDSWORTHY (114km). Another important export industry developed in recent times near Port Hedland, is salt production. The town experiences very hot summer conditions (its latitude is 20°S) with the three months, December to February, having average maximum temperatures over 36°C. The average annual rainfall is 307mm, concentrated in the summer months (February, the wettest, 92mm average).

Port Jackson

The port on which Sydney, the capital city of NSW, is located, it includes Sydney Harbour and Middle Harbour; the W extension of the port is named Parramatta River and a branch extending NW is the Lane Cove River. Many parts of the port foreshores are dominated by steep sandstone cliffs, alternating with small coves, some of which are public reserves and provide swimming beaches such as Nielson Park, Balmoral and Parsley Bay. The entrance to the port, about 1.5km wide, is flanked by two sheer sandstone headlands. When James COOK explored the E coast of Australia in 1770, he noted these

Loading iron ore at Port Hedland WA

SBS Productions

headlands and named the inlet Port Jackson, but did not enter it. However, it was at SYDNEY COVE, within the port, that Governor PHILLIP established the first white settlement on the continent in 1788. Here is how Phillip described the port:

> We got into Port Jackson early in the afternoon, and had the satisfaction of finding the finest harbour in the world, in which a thousand sail of the line may ride in the most perfect security . . . the different coves were examined with all possible expedition. I fixed on the one that had the best spring of water, and in which the ships can anchor so close to the shore that at a very small expense quays may be made at which the largest ships may unload. This cove, which I honoured with the name of Sydney, is about a quarter of a mile across at its entrance, and half a mile in length . . . this harbour is, in extent and security, very superior to any other that I have ever seen—containing a considerable number of coves, formed by narrow necks of land, mostly rocks, covered with timber, and the face of the country, when viewed from the harbour, is the same, with few exceptions.

The fine features of the harbour, noted so accurately by Phillip, are due to its mode of formation in geological time; it is a drowned river valley, called a ria harbour, with deep water and many sheltered bays which provide anchorage for passenger and cargo vessels. The main city ferry and hydrofoil terminal is located at Circular Quay on Sydney Cove. On the W side of this cove is the Overseas Passenger Terminal, and on the E is Bennelong Point where the SYDNEY OPERA HOUSE stands. The SYDNEY HARBOUR BRIDGE joins Dawes Point on the S shore of the harbour to Milsons Point on the N.

In 1975, Sydney Harbour National Park was

proclaimed over all State-owned foreshore lands (such as Nielson Park, Bradley's Head, Ashton Park, Grotto Point and Dobroyd Point) and two small islands within the port (Shark and Clarke Islands). This move was taken in order to preserve the foreshores and headlands of the harbour as public recreation areas and to prevent any residential, commercial or industrial development of these lands. Additional lands, owned by the Commonwealth government, were later added to the national park.

Further reading: Hurley, F. *Sydney—A Camera Study.* (revd edn) Angus & Robertson, Sydney, 1961; Shaw, J.H. *The Face of Our Earth.* Shakespeare Head, Sydney, 1958; White, U. & Sriber, C. *Sydney Harbour Sketchbook.* Rigby, Adelaide, 1968; Baglin, D. & Mullins, B. *Sydney.* Rigby Adelaide, 1976; Gillett, R. & Mellior-Phelps, M. *Century of Ships in Sydney Harbour.* Rigby, Adelaide, 1980. Stephenson, P.R. & Kennedy, B. *The History and Description of Sydney Harbour.* Reed, Sydney, 1980.

Port Kembla NSW An important industrial centre and port in the ILLAWARRA region of the S coast, 90km from Sydney, 6km S of central WOLLONGONG, it is now incorporated within the city of Wollongong. It is located E of the Princes Highway and is a railway terminus linked to the main S coast line, to a branch line from collieries (Mt Kembla and Kemira) situated in the scarplands to the W, and to the line which ascends the scarp and reaches MOSS VALE on the tablelands. The name Kembla comes from an Aboriginal word meaning 'abundant game' or 'plenty of wildfowl'. From the 1880s, the port was a coal shipping centre and in the early decades of the 20th century manufacturing industries, such as copper smelting and fabrication, fertiliser production and silica firebrick making, developed in the region. But an important event in the growth of Port Kembla was the construction of a major iron and steel plant there in 1928 by the Australian Iron and Steel Co.; in the years following World War II, further expansion of this enterprise made it into the largest integrated steelworks of the nation, employing a staff of about 20 000, and producing a wide range of rolled steel products as well as pig iron and ingot steel. The development of the port facilities has been associated with this industrial growth: the artifical harbour has been progressively improved (for example, by dredging and breakwater construction) and in the 1950s an 'inner harbour' was constructed by utilising a swampy tidal area known as Tom Thumb Lagoon.
See also iron and steel industry

Port Latta TAS A township on the NW coast, Port Latta is 31km E of SMITHTON and 39km W of WYNYARD along the Bass Highway. It is a man-made port, the site of the administrative offices, the pelletising plant and the offshore loading facilities and is the N end

of the 85km-long pipeline carrying a slurry of crushed iron ore from the SAVAGE RIVER mines. At Port Latta the ore is pelletised, moved by conveyor along the huge jetty, and loaded into bulk carriers for export to Japan.

Port Lincoln SA (population 10 675 in 1981) Located at the SE tip of EYRE PENINSULA, 663km by road from Adelaide, it is the major port, the chief service centre and the largest town of the peninsula. Situated on Boston Bay, a fine harbour claimed to be three times the area of Sydney Harbour, it has a large grain silo complex with three jetties where ocean-going vessels berth to load wheat, barley, frozen meat, fish and wool, or to offload phosphate rock for the town's fertiliser factory. Australia's largest tuna fleet is based at the port and the Tunarama festival, held in January each year, celebrates the opening of the tuna fishing season. The town is a year-round seaside resort, enjoying a mild climate, with an average annual rainfall of 486mm concentrated in the winter months (June and July, the highest, 74mm and 78mm respectively). The port was named by the explorer Matthew FLINDERS 1802 after his native county, Lincolnshire, in England. The first settlement was made in 1838 and the early history of the area included some grim encounters between settlers and Aborigines. Lack of surface water and the difficulties of overland transport retarded development and it was not until the 20th century that the town began to prosper as a port and a major business centre of the region. In 1921 it was proclaimed a municipality. The Lincoln National Park (17 083ha), dedicated in 1962, lies SE of Port Lincoln, occupying the SE tip of Eyre Peninsula.
Further reading: Baillie, P. *Port Lincoln Sketchbook.* Rigby, Adelaide, 1972.

Port Macquarie NSW (population 19 572 in 1981) A town on the mid-N coast of the State, at the mouth of the HASTINGS RIVER, it is 419km by road N of Sydney, and 10km E of the Pacific Highway. It is a town of some historic note, dating from quite early times of British settlement in Australia. In 1818 John OXLEY, then Surveyor-General in the colony, discovered the Hastings River and its estuary, which he named after Governor MACQUARIE. In 1821 a penal settlement was

Port Kembla steelworks (1979)

Surfing beach south of Port Macquarie NSW

established at the port, which was then the northernmost point of settlement. On a hill overlooking the town St Thomas' Anglican Church was built in 1824; it still stands today, with its old box pews and its tablets, and has been classified by the National Trust (NSW) for preservation because of its historic value. By 1830, the penal settlement was abolished and the area was made available for settlers to occupy and farm the land of the valley. A historical museum in the town gives visitors the opportunity to view some aspects of the early pioneering days.

The town is now a popular tourist and holiday centre. It experiences a mild climate throughout the year and has fine coastal beaches nearby for surfing; good fishing can be found in the area and large stretches of water are available for aquatic sports. Other resort centres in the district are Blackman's Point to the N and Lake Cathie to the S, with the scenic Comboyne Plateau inland to the WSW.

Port Phillip Association *see* Batman, John

Port Phillip Bay VIC This is an enclosed basin, with Melbourne and its port area situated on its N shore, GEELONG to the SW on CORIO BAY, the MORNINGTON PENINSULA forming the SE and S shorelines and the Bellarine Peninsula located at the SW; it has a narrow S entrance (about 1 100m wide, called the Rip) between Point Lonsdale on the W and Point Nepean on the E, where a rapid tidal race is experienced. The E and SE shorelines have long been recreation resorts, but in recent years have increasingly become commuter residential areas (such as Mornington, Rosebud, Sorrento and Dromana) for city workers. The YARRA RIVER drains into Hobsons Bay, via a dredged estuary, at the N section of Port Phillip Bay, and the Werribee River has its estuary on the NW shore. The

first ship to enter the bay was a sailing vessel under the command of Lieutenant John MURRAY in 1802. He landed near the present site of Sorrento and named the bay Port King after Governor KING. It was later changed to Port Phillip, in honour of Governor Arthur PHILLIP, the colony's first Governor.
Further reading: Austin, K.A. *Port Phillip Bay Sketchbook.* Rigby, Adelaide, 1970; Kerr, C.G. *Port Phillip Bay.* Rigby, Adelaide, 1979.

Port Pirie SA (population 14 695 in 1981) The largest urban centre in the mid-N of SA, located on the shores of the Port Pirie River, a tidal inlet off the NE coast of SPENCER GULF, it is 228km by road NNW of Adelaide. The city owes its importance to a variety of factors. It is a road and rail focus for routes to the FLINDERS RANGES, to PORT AUGUSTA and beyond to ALICE SPRINGS, and via the trans-continental railway to Perth. It is also a major industrial centre, the site of the Broken Hill Association Smelters where lead and zinc ores from BROKEN HILL are treated at one of the world's largest smelting and refining plants. It is a major port, second in SA to Adelaide, for the shipment of these mineral products and for the export of grain crops from the rural hinterland. It is a business and service centre of a productive farming and grazing region. The average annual rainfall is 343mm, concentrated in the winter months (June, the highest, 41mm). The name of the city comes from the schooner *John Pirie*, the first vessel to navigate the river channel in 1854; the schooner's anchor is on display in the city's Memorial Park.

Port Stanvac SA An oil refinery, established in 1963, it is 32km SSW of Adelaide city, to the S of Hallet Cove on the E shore of ST VINCENT GULF. It is a deep-water port where installations have been provided for the berthing of tankers and the bulk handling of oil.

Port Stephens NSW A coastal inlet, it is some 35km N of NEWCASTLE on the central coast of the State. It is a long inlet, extending about 25km inland, and is the estuary of the Karuah River. Geologically, it is a drowned valley which provides a sheltered harbour with many coves within the main inlet. Though the entrance is partly closed off from the sea by sand bars, it would seem to have many features ideal for development as a major port. Several proposals have been made for such development, but none has so far been adopted.

The port was sighted and named by Captain COOK on his journey along the E coast in 1770, but he did not enter it. In 1812, Governor MACQUARIE explored the inlet in a search for a settlement site to the N of Newcastle. Although he reported favourably on it as a harbour he did not proceed with the establishment of a township. The area did, however, become a centre for cedar-cutting in the early part of the 19th century and vessels loaded timber for shipment overseas. In the

Premier's Dept SA

Port Pirie grain silos

early part of the 20th century, a recommendation was made that the navy establish a submarine base at the port, but the idea was abandoned. Then in 1928 a further suggestion was made to develop it as a port with an oil refinery, but this too was not adopted. It thus remained, until the late 1960s, a quiet fishing, prawning and oyster-culture centre, with a modest influx of tourists in summer months. During the 1970s it became a more popular holiday area, especially for residents of Newcastle and the lower HUNTER RIVER valley. Nelson Bay, near the S headland of the

inlet, is the main town (population 7 930 in 1981) and there are a number of small village resorts such as Karuah, Soldiers Point, Tanilba Bay, Lemon Tree Passage and Tea Gardens dotted around the foreshores of the estuary. The Port Stephens lighthouse, built in 1862, and the keeper's house asociated with it, have been classified by the National Trust (NSW) for preservation as historically and architecturally important buildings.

Porter, Hal (1911-) Author. Born in Melbourne, he grew up in the GIPPSLAND town of BAIRNSDALE and from 1927 to 1951 taught in schools in a number of States and in Japan. He has published several volumes of poems and short stories, three plays, a biography, a book of travel and the novels *A Handful of Pennies* (1958), *The Tilted Cross* (1961) and *The Right Thing* (1971). Many consider his best writing to be in the three autobiographical works *The Watcher on the Cast-Iron Balcony* (1963), *The Paper Chase* (1966) and *The Extra* (1975).
Further reading: Lord, M. *Hal Porter.* Oxford University Press, Melbourne, 1974.

Portland VIC (population 9 353 in 1981) A town on the W shore of Portland Bay, with a deep-sea harbour and modern port facilities, it is the only significant sea port between GEELONG and Adelaide. It is 364km by road WSW of Melbourne on the Princes Highway and 403km by rail from the metropolitan capital. The history of the town dates from 1834 when the HENTY brothers landed there and established the first white settlement in VIC, though the bay had been discovered and named by Lieutenant James GRANT in 1800

NSW Dept of Tourism

Shoal Bay, Port Stephens NSW

after the Duke of Portland. It became a whaling port and Whalers Point, just S of the lighthouse, was used by whale-spotters from the late 1830s to the 1860s.

The modern harbour developments, involving the construction of two breakwaters to form an area of 100ha of sheltered water, were opened in 1960, thereby markedly increasing the trade of the port. Petroleum products are the main imports, while wool, wheat and frozen meat are the major exports. The town's secondary industries include fertiliser manufacture and meat and dairy processing. CAPE NELSON, State Park (210ha) lies S of the town and Mt Richmond National Park (1 707ha), lying 32km to the W, is renowned for its wild flowers, especially the native orchids. The National Trust (VIC) has classified more than 30 buildings in Portland (and recorded over another 30) for preservation, including numerous homes from the late 1850s, the courthouse (c1852), the customs house (c1850), the ANZ Bank (c1863), the London Guest House (1843), the town hall (c1863) and a wool store (1855).
Further reading: Vaughan, B. *Portland Sketchbook.* Rigby, Adelaide, 1975.

ports Australia's principal seaports, listed in order of the total deadweight tonnage of overseas ships entering in the year 1981-82, are as follows. Tonnage (in thousands) is indicated after each.

Melbourne VIC	34 046
Dampier WA	33 580
Port Hedland WA	33 288
Sydney NSW	30 881
Fremantle WA	24 460
Newcastle NSW	20 996
Hay Point QLD	20 288
Brisbane QLD	20 229
Gladstone QLD	15 398
Port Walcott WA	15 277
Botany Bay NSW	14 595
Port Kembla NSW	10 901
Port Adelaide SA	9 656

Portuguese man-of-war *see* coelenterates

possums and gliders Belonging to the order Diprotodonta and divided into four families—Phalangeridae, Petauridae, Burramyidae and Tarsipedidae—these animals form the most successful group of Australian MARSUPIALS after the KANGAROOS AND WALLABIES of the family Macropodidae. They are not closely related to the American opossum, despite the name. All have diprotodont dentition (one pair of incisors in lower jaw, pointing forwards) and on the hind-foot the second and third toes are joined together (syndactyly). The five-toed fore-foot is, however, more hand-like than those of the kangaroos and BANDICOOTS. The pouch opens forwards. Possums and gliders are arboreal in habit, and several are completely vegetarian. Many are abundant but as they are nocturnal animals they are not often seen.

Phalangeridae This family contains the largest possums and the cuscuses. The commonest is the cat-sized brush-tailed possum or silver grey, *Trichosurus vulpecula* (head and body 35 to 55cm long; tail 25 to 40cm long), which is found in most parts of Australia in suitable habitats. The moderately prehensile tail is bushy, but naked below to give a better grip, and has a pink, naked tip. The tail, the large, oval ears and the conspicuous pink nose differentiate this species from other possums. The colour varies from area to area but typically the head and body are silver grey and the belly yellowish. It feeds on buds, shoots, leaves and fruit and has thrived since European settlers introduced exotic shrubs, trees and fruit. Normally, it nests in hollow branches of trees but it will readily occupy the roofs of houses where its noisy courtships and urination can be a nuisance. It has also become a great pest in New Zealand's forests. Its natural habitat is dry sclerophyll woodland and open forest. This species is often hunted because of its abundance and its damage to forestry. The skins are used as trimmings, for example, in clothes manufacture, and also as shuttle-linings in the manufacture of nylon and rayon.

The genus *Trichosurus* contains two other species. The northern brush possum, *T. arnhemensis* (42cm; 27cm), a grey animal, smaller and more slender than the brush-tailed possum, is found in the KIMBERLEYS, the northern NT and BARROW ISLAND. The mountain brush possum, *T. caninus* (50cm; 40cm), which has short ears, occurs in forests in the mountains of south-eastern QLD, NSW and VIC. The genus *Wyulda* contains the scaly-tailed possum, *W. squamicaudata* (40cm; 30cm), probably a rare possum, from the Kimberleys. The base of the tail is covered with fur but the remainder has rasp-like scales.

Cuscuses are distinctive possums from CAPE YORK (there are several species in New Guinea). They have very round heads with very short ears, protruding yellow eyes and long, prehensile tails which are naked on the distal half. Cuscuses live in rainforest trees and rarely descend to the ground. The spotted cuscus, *Phalanger maculatus* (40cm; 37cm), is often covered with blotches but may be plain. The general colour is often very pale grey. The grey cuscus, *P. orientalis*, (37cm; 30cm), is unspotted, darker in colour, and has a dark dorsal stripe.

Petauridae This family contains about 11 species, including the ringtails and most of the gliders. Ringtails usually live in thicker woodland than brush-tailed possums. They take their common name from the curling of the prehensile tails. Unlike the brush-tails they make nests or dreys of twigs and leaves high in trees. They are placed in three genera.

The common ringtail, *Pseudocheirus perigrinus* (32cm; 32cm), is a common E species ranging from Cape York to south-eastern SA. The TAS and SW Australian forms are sometimes regarded as separate species. The head is short, the muzzle pointed and the short, round ears have a patch of white behind them. The rest of the head is reddish-grey, as is the upper body. The belly is greyish-white and the legs reddish. The white-tipped tail tapers, and is naked below. This species lives in a range of woodlands from rainforest to sclerophyll, especially near water. The mongan or Herbert River ringtail, *P. herbertensis* (35cm; 36cm), of north-eastern QLD rainforest, is dark brown; the toolah or green or striped ringtail, *P. archeri* (36cm; 32cm), is a golden-green possum with two stripes down its back and is also found in north-eastern QLD. The brushy-tailed lemuroid ringtail, *Hemibelideus lemuroides* (36cm; 35cm), lives in dense rainforest near CAIRNS. Its tail is bushy, unlike those of all other ringtails. The rock ringtail or wogoit, *Pseudocheires dahli* (35cm; 23cm), of ARNHEM LAND and the Kimberleys, has a

Spotted cuscus, *Phalanger maculatus*

short, thick tail which is possibly not prehensile.

Gliding, according to Ride (*see below*) seems to have arisen three times in the possums. Their flying membrane is an extension of the skin on the side of the body which is spread out when the animal stretches its limbs. In most gliders the skin stretches from the hand to the ankle, but in the greater glider, *Petaurodies volans* (40cm; 52cm), it reaches only the elbow. Gliders climb to the tree tops and then glide down to the base of another tree. There are four species of gliders in this family.

The greater glider is a long, bushy-tailed animal, black in colour with a white belly. The head is short and the muzzle pointed. There are also grey and pure white varieties. It occurs in sclerophyll forest and tall woodland from eastern QLD (ROCKAMPTON) to the DANDENONG RANGES. It is often abundant. The food consists of leaves and shoots of eucalypts. Greater gliders have been found to cover a distance of about 54m, descending at an angle of about 40°. Some biologists have estimated the flight distance as up to 74m. During the flight this glider is silent. They are usually solitary or in pairs.

The fluffy or yellow-bellied glider, *Petaurus australis* (28cm; 43cm), is noisier in flight. It lives in sclerophyll forest, mainly in mountains, from BUNDABERG to PORTLAND, but has also been recorded near Cairns. It is relatively uncommon. The upperparts are dark, and the belly cream to orange. It glides further than the greater glider (up to 100m) but the flight is shallower. Yellow-bellied gliders feed mainly on nectar, blossoms and sap from manna gums, *Eucalyptus viminalis*. Sugar gliders, *P. breviceps* (17cm; 19cm), are squirrel-like, grey animals with a black stripe on the centre of the face, extending on to the back. They feed on insects, buds and blossoms in sclerophyll forest and woodland from the Kimberleys through eastern NSW to south-eastern SA. Sugar gliders have been introduced into TAS. The very similar, but slightly larger squirrel glider, *P. norfolcensis* (18cm to 23cm; 22cm to 30cm), lives in similar habitats, but extending further inland, in eastern VIC, eastern NSW and eastern QLD.

Leadbeater's possum or the fairy possum, *Gymnobelideus leadbeateri* (16cm; 17cm), was thought to be extinct till rediscovered in 1961 in VIC. It ranges over about 1000km² in southern VIC, and may have a still wider range. It is a small brownish-grey species with a long, dark dorsal stripe and a bushy tail. Its whole appearance is squirrel-like. This nocturnal animal lives in wet sclerophyll forest where it probably feeds on nectar and insects.

The striking, noisy and smelly striped possum, *Dactylopsila trivirgata* (26cm; 33cm), of Cape York is a squirrel-like possum, pale yellow or white in colour with black stripes down the midline and the flanks. The fourth toe on the hand is very long and is used as a probe to extract insects from wood which it detects by drumming with its toes. This method of extracting insects with a long toe resembles the behaviour of the aye-aye, a lemur-relative of Madagascar. It occurs in open woodland and rainforest, but is uncommon.

Burramyidae One of the gliders belongs to this family. The pigmy or feather-tail glider, *Acrobates pygmaeus* (7cm; 7.5cm), is a tiny, mouse-like creature whose tail has a row of stiff bristles on each side, giving it a feather-like appearance. The colour is greyish-brown above and white on the belly. Unlike the other gliders this species is social, feeding on insects and on the nectar and blossoms in small groups. It ranges from eastern QLD to south-eastern SA, living in sclerophyll forest and woodland; though not often seen, it is common.

The rest of the family are mouse-sized species apart from burramys or the mountain pigmy possum, *Burramys parvus* (one specimen 10cm, 15cm; a second 23.5cm, 14cm), which is about as large as a rat. Burramys was known only as a fossil till August 1966 when a specimen was found in a ski-hut on MOUNT HOTHAM at an altitude of 1 770m. Several other specimens have been trapped since then, on Mt Hotham, on MOUNT BEAUTY and in KOSCIUSKO National Park, at similar altitudes.

The other pigmy possums belong to the genus *Cercartetus*; it now seems that there are four species, all very much alike. They are mouse-sized and mouse-like, apart from their teeth, pouch and syndactyl hind-feet. Little is known of their biology but they appear to live largely on insects. The mundarda or western pigmy possum, *C. concinnus* (14cm to 20cm total length), is found in S SA, W VIC and SW WA in dry sclerophyll forests with undergrowth and in heaths. The eastern pigmy possum, *C. nanus* (15cm to 21.5cm total length) lives in wet and dry sclerophyll forest in south-eastern SA, eastern NSW, VIC and TAS. The little or Tasmanian pigmy possum, *C. lepidus* (15cm total length), occurs in sclerophyll forest in SA and on KANGAROO ISLAND as well as in TAS. The long-tailed pigmy possum, *C. caudatus* (11cm; 13.5cm), is known only from TOWNSVILLE to COOKTOWN

Pygmy possum, *Cercartetus* species

Courtesy of A.I.S. Canberra

in QLD though it also lives in New Guinea. It frequents rainforest.

Tarsipedidae The honey possum or noolbenger, *Tarsipes rostratus* (6.8cm; 8.3cm), is restricted to tree and shrub heaths in SW Australia. The noolbenger is highly specialised for feeding on nectar and pollen from native shrubs. The muzzle is very long and pointed so that the mouth is tube-like. The tongue is brushed at the tip like those of the typical HONEYEATER birds. It is probable that any insects found in the blossoms are also eaten. The head and body are grey and the belly is yellow white. The back carries three longitudinal, black stripes and the long, tapering tail is prehensile. These fairly common animals are usually solitary or in pairs, but being nocturnal they are not often seen. They are not closely related to other possums. *Further reading: see under* kangaroos, etc. *Also* Russel, R. *Spotlight on Possums*. University of Queensland Press, Brisbane, 1980.

postage stamps The first printed postage stamps of the six Australian colonies were issued in the following years: NSW 1850, VIC 1851, TAS 1853, WA 1854, SA 1855 and QLD 1860. For some years previously, however, NSW had issued letter sheets with impressed stamps. Section 52 (v) of the federal Constitution gave the Commonwealth power with regard to 'postal, telegraphic, telephonic and other like services', and from 1901 the issuing of postage stamps became the responsibility of the federal Postmaster-General's Department, which assumed control of the State Post and Telegraphic Departments. Since 1975 it has been the responsibility of the Australian Postal Commission (trading as Australia Post). A recent trend has been the issuing of First Day Covers and stamp packs on a very wide range of themes. Examples include ships of the Antarctic (covers being postmarked at the Antarctic station of the collector's choice), Australian folklore, the opening of the new High Court building in Canberra and of the Tarcoola-ALICE SPRINGS railway, as well as more traditional subjects such as Australian animals and birds. Information regarding all such collector's items can be obtained from any post office, from Philatelic Sales Centres in the capital cities, and in the pages of the official periodical *Australian Stamp Bulletin*.
Further reading: Hornadge, B. (ed) *Stamp News*. (monthly).

G.B. Baker (N.P.I.A.W.)
Feather-tailed glider, *Acrobates pygmaeus*

postal and telecommunications services Prior to 1975 postal and telecommunications services were under the control of the Postmaster-General's Department. On 1 July of that year, however, they became the responsibility of two new statutory authorities. The Australian Telecommunications Commission (trading under the name Telecom) is entrusted with responsibility for the planning, establishing, maintaining and operating of telecommunications services within Australia, and for providing, at the request of the Australian government, technical assistance outside Australia with regard to such services in other countries. The Australian Postal Commission (trading under the name Australia Post) is entrusted with managing and improving postal services, while avoiding the financial losses of previous years. The Postal Services Act of 1975 sets specific financial objectives for postal services.

The residual functions of the former Postmaster-General's Department have been taken over by the new Department of Communications; this authority has also taken over, from the former Department of the Media, responsibility for policy matters concerned with BROADCASTING. The Department's main function is therefore to provide advice to the Minister on policy regarding postal, telegraphic, telephone, broadcasting and similar services. Telecommunications services between Australia and other countries, external territories and ships at sea remain the responsibility of the Overseas Telecommunications Commission (Australia) which was established in 1946.

potatoes *see* Solanaceae, agriculture

potoroos *see* kangaroos, etc.

poultry industry The commercial poultry industry is located in all States, usually near the capital cities and large provincial towns. In addition, substantial quantities of eggs and poultry meat are produced by rural and urban dwellers, primarily for their own use, though small quantities may be sold privately.

Commercial egg production is controlled through the imposition of hen quotas which are enforced by State governments. The object of the national quota is to bring production closely into line with domestic demand and to prevent large surpluses. Production and marketing of eggs are controlled by Egg Marketing Boards in the different States. The main export product is egg pulp and Japan is the only important market. Exports of shell eggs are made to Papua New Guinea but they represent a very small proportion of total exports. The total annual value of exports of eggs and egg products ranged from $8 million to $13 million in the late 1970s and early 1980s.

The peak production of eggs on commercial farms was 209 million dozen in 1971-72; this fell to between 180 million and 200 million dozen in the remainder of the 1970s. The number of registered poultry farms declined from 16 891 in 1965-66, to 7 115 in 1972-72 and 2 700 in 1980-81. However, over the same period the average flock size rose from 562 hens to 1 716 hens to 3 684 hens. In 1972 all State governments agreed to implement statutory measures to control production, with provision for an annual review of quotas.

In the poultry meat industry the main product is chicken meat, produced from broiler chickens. Small quantities of meat are produced from turkeys, ducks and pheasants. The industry experienced a spectacular increase in production in the 1960s and 1970s, and by 1980 poultry meat was as important as beef in the Australian diet. Between 1965-66 and 1980-81 production rose from 68 878 tonnes to 207 161 tonnes and the per capita consumption rose from approximately 6kg to approximately 15kg. In 1980-81, 221.7 million chickens were slaughtered at an average carcase weight of 1.32kg. Exports of poultry meat are small with the main markets being Papua New Guinea and the Pacific islands.

In the broiler chicken industry there are a few very large integrated companies which breed, hatch and grow the chickens, produce the feed, and slaughter, process and market the meat. Associated with these companies are contract growers who raise chickens from one day old to seven or eight weeks old at which point they are slaughtered. The broiler chicken industry is the most technically advanced of the meat producing industries. Scientific principles and methods are applied in the production of breeding stock and feeding, housing and disease control. The fact that the industry is mainly run by large companies who handle at stages from breeding to marketing helps to continuing technical development.

Praed, Mrs Campbell *née* Murray-Prior (1851-1935) Novelist. Rosa Caroline Praed wrote under the name of Mrs Campbell Praed. Born in QLD, she went with her husband to England in 1876 and returned to Australia only once for a brief visit. She wrote more than 40 novels (three were written in collaboration with Justin McCarthy); about half of her novels refer at least in part to Australia, and the later ones reflect her growing preoccupation with psychic matters and her belief in reincarnation. Those with Australian settings include *An Australian Heroine* (1880), *The Romance of a Station* (1889), *Outlaw and Lawmaker* (1893), *Mrs Tregaskiss* (1895), *The Maid of the River* (1905) and *Lady Bridget in the Never Never Land* (1915).

pratincoles and coursers These BIRDS belong to the Old World and Australasian family Glareolidae; only two species occur in Australia. The Australian pratincole or courser, *Stiltia* * *isabella* (20cm long), is a dry plains bird of the inland and near-coastal areas of most of Australia, apart from the SE,

Australian pratincole, *Stiltia isabella*

the SW and TAS, and may also breed in New Guinea. Cinnamon-brown above and chestnut below, it has a black streak through the eye, a sharp brown bill, a white patch on the rump, long pointed wings and a square tail. It runs rapidly, catching insects on the ground, and when in flight adopts a bobbing, zigzag motion. The eggs are laid on a bare patch of ground within a circle of pebbles or sticks.

The Oriental pratincole, *Glareola pratincola* (20cm), is a common, non-breeding visitor from N Asia to the dry plains in NW Australia. It is mainly dark in colour, with a black oval on the throat surrounding a pale area; it has a deeply forked tail, and catches insects on the wing, its flight resembling that of SWALLOWS.

prawn fisheries Prawns have long been caught in Australian waters but until the 1960s when overseas markets became important, it was a small-scale industry. Prawning was restricted to estuaries and lagoons until 1948 when prawns were found in large numbers at sea near NEWCASTLE. Though deep-sea prawns had been reported earlier by, for example, the *Endeavour* (see FISHERIES), little notice was given to the finds by the professionals. After the Newcastle finds, however, more and more prawning grounds were discovered, culminating in the discovery of the rich grounds in the GULF OF CARPENTARIA.

Nearly all the species of commercial prawns belong to the family Penaeidae (see CRUSTACEANS). Much of the work on the biology of the commercial species was carried out by Professor Dakin of Sydney University. The important Australian species are listed below.

1. The king prawn, *Penaeus plebejus*, of SE Australia. This species can reach a length of 30cm and in life is flesh-coloured, with a blue tail fan. The cuticle is smooth.

2. The western king prawn or blue-leg king prawn, *P. latisulcatus*. This is an important species in WA; it also occurs in the Gulf of Carpentaria. It is closely related to the king prawn.

3. The common tiger prawn, *P. esculentus*, found round the Australian coast, has vertical brown stripes on a light, sometimes greenish, background, and its length can reach about

Table 1

VALUE AND QUANTITY OF
CRUSTACEANS AND PRAWNS
CAUGHT IN 1977-78
(in $'000 and tonnes liveweight)

State	Lobsters	Crabs	Prawns
	Value	Value	Value
NSW	863	663	8 845
VIC	1 573	7	172
QLD	238	1 187	30 020
SA	7 307	6	7 062
WA	49 294	132	15 369
TAS	5 019	—	—
NT	36	24	8 100
TOTAL	15 036	1 887	54 199
	Quantity	Quantity	Quantity
NSW	155	225	2 430
VIC	307	6	33
QLD	126	481	8 428
SA	1 912	4	2 234
WA	10 536	125	3 531
TAS	1 192	—	—
NT	21	11	2 165
TOTAL	3 713	727	15 290

Source: *Australian Fisheries*. (March 1979)

25cm. It is fished commercially from north QLD to the Gulf, traditionally at night. Other tiger prawns are also fished; these include the giant tiger or panda, *P. monodon*, which measures up to 33cm, and is dark grey or dark blue, with white bands.

4. The banana prawn, *P. merguensis*. This species forms vast swarms at certain times when moving to the spawning grounds. They are often fished in large numbers in the Gulf of Carpentaria and in EXMOUTH GULF from about March to June, July or August. In the Gulf of Carpentaria the trawlers are based at KARUMBA, WEIPA and THURSDAY ISLAND, and the prawns are also fished by Russian and Japanese vessels. The banana prawn is light coloured with small, darker spots, and with yellowish legs and tail fan; it reaches a length of about 25cm.

5. The greasyback prawn, *Metapenaeus mastersii*, and its relatives. These are smaller prawns, reaching a length of about 15cm, which are used almost entirely on the local markets. The school prawn, *M. macleayi*, is a related species fished in NSW. It feeds in estuaries and moves out to sea where it forms large shoals between December and May.

Most prawn fishing now takes place in N waters where about 150 trawlers, attended by refrigerated carrier ships, fish in the Gulf each year. The statistics for prawns and certain other crustaceans for 1977-78 are shown in Table 1.

prawns *see* crustaceans; prawn fisheries

praying mantid or mantis *see* mantids

preferential voting Also known as the alternative-ballot system, this is a method of electing representatives to Parliament or local government councils. In the preferential system the voter has to place a number against every candidate's name, to indicate his order of preference. Failure to number all candidates makes the vote invalid. A candidate with an absolute majority of first preferences wins, but if there is no absolute majority the candidate with the lowest number of first preferences is eliminated and his second preferences are distributed among the relevant remaining candidates. If a clear majority is still not obtained the preferences of the second-last candidate are distributed. The procedure continues until one candidate has half of the valid votes plus one. The advantage of this system is that it allows the voter a greater choice of candidates because it stops voters from automatically discounting support for minority political parties as wasted votes, as happens with 'first-past-the-post' systems; it also ensures that a winning candidate will have a majority of the total votes cast. The disadvantages of the system are that supporters of a minority political party can determine an election result by allotting their second preference votes to one of the major political parties and have an influence far exceeding their true electoral representation. Also, people wishing to protest or who simply do not care about the result of an election often cast a DONKEY VOTE. Thus a political party may be elected as the government on the basis of the second preference votes cast by a minority of party supporters, or even by the unthinking filling in of preferences by electors. Another disadvantage is that the preferential system of voting does not ensure that the party which gains a majority of votes will gain an absolute majority of seats. QLD introduced optional preferential voting in 1892, and continued it until 1942. From 1942 to 1962 QLD operated elections on the 'first-past-the-post' system and since 1962 has had the compulsory preferential voting system. Both WA and VIC legislated for compulsory preferential voting in 1911. The federal government adopted preferential voting in 1919, NSW in 1926 and SA in 1936. NSW changed to optional preferential voting in 1979; in 1983 the federal government considered changing to optional. TAS does not use the preferential voting system for its State elections, but of course must use this system for federal elections.
Further reading: Emy, H.V. *The Politics of Australian Democracy.* Macmillan, Melbourne, 1974; Rydon, J. 'Political power' in Gibb, D.M. & Hannan, A.W. (eds) *Debate and Decision.* Heinemann Educational Australia, VIC, 1975; Solomon, D. *Australia's Government and Parliament.* Thomas Nelson (Australia) Ltd, Melbourne, 1976.

Prell, Charles Ernest (1865-1946) Nurseryman. Born in VIC, Prell studied pasture improvement and introduced the combination 'sub. and super.' (that is, subterranean clover with superphosphate).
See also agriculture

Premiers' Conference This is an annual meeting of the Prime Minister and the Premiers of the States held mainly to discuss the size and method of allocation of Commonwealth grants to the States.

Presbyterian Church In the census of 1976, 6.6 per cent of Australians were classified as Presbyterian in religion, making this denomination the fourth-largest, very slightly behind the Methodists, but considerably smaller than Anglicans and Roman Catholics. In VIC, where Presbyterianism had been particularly strong since the time of the gold rushes, it accounted for 8.3 per cent of the population. Since the time of that census, however, many Presbyterian congregations have joined with Methodists and Congregationalists to form the UNITING CHURCH IN AUSTRALIA. In the 1981 census 637 000 people, or 4.4 per cent of the population, were identified as Presbyterians.

Historical development The term 'Presbyterian' first came into use in Scotland and England, the name 'Reformed Churches' being most generally applied on the Continent to groups with similar beliefs and practices. Presbyterianism arose under the influence of the reformer John Calvin, of whom the Scot, John Knox, was a disciple. The actual name refers not to matters of belief but to a type of organisation which Presbyterians believe to be based on that of the early Christian Church; the essence of this organisation is that the government of the Church is undertaken in meetings of lay elders and ministers, but without overriding control by prelates or bishops.

Since Presbyterianism was strongest in Scotland, where it became the Established Church, it was brought to Australia mainly by Scottish settlers. Relatively few convicts were sent from Scotland, but Scottish free settlers arrived in the very early years of colonisation. In 1809 some of the latter built a church in the township of Ebenezer on the HAWKESBURY RIVER; this is now the oldest church building in Australia. For some years, services there and

Presbyterian church in Scone NSW

National Library of Australia

in other locations were conducted by laymen. In 1822 the first Presbyterian clergyman, the Rev. Archibald Alexander, reached Australia and established himself in Hobart. In the following year John Dunmore LANG reached Sydney, and soon afterwards established Scots Church. During the following several decades the growth of Presbyterianism was strongly influenced by Lang—not only through his spiritual ministry, but also through his recruitment of ministers and encouragement of immigration from Scotland.

As in Scotland, Presbyterianism in Australia was subject to many divisions and secession movements. In Scotland these were based mainly on relations between Church and State and aspects of Church government, rather than on questions of doctrine; the greatest split was the 'Great Disruption' of 1843, when a large number of ministers broke away from the Established Church of Scotland to form the Free Church of Scotland. Some years later a number of other secession presbyteries (district councils) and churches joined to form the United Presbyterian Church. Although the causes of the various splits did not apply fully in Australia, nevertheless Presbyterianism there was subject to divisions similar to those in Scotland, with John Dunmore Lang's quarrelsome nature adding fuel to the fires of dissension, particularly in NSW.

The pattern of division was, in fact, most complicated in NSW, where by the mid-1850s there were four main divisions of Presbyterianism, but by 1865 all but a few Free Churches had united as the Presbyterian Church of NSW. In VIC, where the first official Presbyterian minister, the Rev. James Forbes, was appointed in 1838, splits occurred almost immediately, but had been virtually healed by 1851. Divisions in other colonies were overcome at various times up to the 1890s, although to this day a small number of Free Churches have remained independent. In 1901 the main State Churches entered into a federal union as the Presbyterian Church of Australia. Its General Assembly was given supreme authority in a number of matters, including doctrine, worship, mission and theological education, but the State Assemblies retained considerably autonomy.

Presbyterians and Church union Not long after its formation, the General Assembly became involved in discussions about a possible union with Methodists and Congregationalists. However, in the course of negotiations at various times during the following 70 years or so, it became evident that support for union was less strong among Presbyterians than among members of the other two denominations. Even when a formal 'Basis for Union' was approved by the General Assembly in 1974, there was still considerable opposition, especially in NSW. When the Uniting Church in Australia was formed in 1977, a substantial minority of congregations elected to remain in the separate Presbyterian Church of Australia.

Further reading: Ross, C.S. *The Scottish*

St. Andrew's Church, Singleton NSW

Church in Victoria, 1851-1901. Hutchinson, Melbourne, 1901; van Sommers, T. *Religions in Australia.* Rigby, Adelaide, 1966.

Press Council, Australian *see* Australian Press Council

Preston, Margaret Rose (1875-1963) Artist. Born in Adelaide, she studied at the Adelaide School of Design and the Gallery School in Melbourne, and then visited Munich and Paris. She returned to Europe again in 1910 and stayed there until 1918; after this period her paintings showed the use of strong colour, a growing sense of design and an increasing abstraction of form. She became known as one of the moderns in Sydney, and was a member of the Contemporary Group established in 1926 by Thea Proctor and George LAMBERT. Her strong sense of design and her popular paintings of native flowers during the 1920s attracted many patrons and during the late 1920s and the 1930s her work was in great demand. She worked not only in oils but also in woodcuts, linocuts, silk-screens and monotype; she was a passionate promoter of Australian nationalism and frequently used Aboriginal motifs and native plants as subjects for her works.

Prichard, Katharine Susannah (1883-1969) Author. Born in Fiji, she was educated in Melbourne and began publishing articles and short stories in periodicals while working as a governess in the GIPPSLAND district of VIC and in western NSW. Between 1915 and 1950 she wrote more than a dozen novels, of which the best-known are *Working Bullocks* (1926), which is set in the timber country of WA, *Coonardoo* (1929), which deals with the culture clash between Aborigines and white settlers on cattle stations in WA, *Haxby's Circus* (1930) and a trilogy set in the KALGOORLIE-COOLGARDIE goldfields, namely

The Roaring Nineties (1946), *Golden Miles* (1948) and *Winged Seeds* (1950). She also published an autobiography entitled *Child of the Hurricane* (1963), two volumes of verse, a play and a collection of short stories, *Potch and Colour* (1944). She was a foundation and life-long member of the Communist Party of Australia, and her writings make clear her sympathy for those whom she considered to be downtrodden or victimised.

Further reading: Darke-Brockman, H. *Katharine Susannah Prichard.* Oxford University Press, Melbourne, 1967.

prickly pears These cacti belong to the genus *Opuntia*; several species were introduced into Australia at various times and for various reasons. Captain PHILLIP, for example, brought the tree pear for breeding the cochineal insects, the source of the red dyestuff. Prickly pears have segmented stalks, usually with sharp spines, and range in size from shrubs to tree-like forms. They grow easily and quickly from fragments. Various species became serious pests in Australia till they were largely controlled by the *Cactoblastis* moth and other insects (*see* BIOLOGICAL CONTROL; WEEDS). With one possible African exception, all cacti are native to the Americas.

Prime Minister of Australia The term 'Prime Minister' is copied from Great Britain and dates from the 18th century in that country. When George I became King in 1714, he decided not to attend Cabinet meetings which he could not understand—he came from the German state of Hanover and could not speak English. However, he did need supplies of money, and so he appointed the Treasurer as his principal adviser to keep him informed of Cabinet decisions and to arrange the supply of money for the King. Sir Robert Walpole was Britain's first Prime Minister and Treasurer, 1721-42. The first

Prime Minister of Australia was Sir Edmund BARTON, 1901-1903. In 1983 the Prime Minister was Robert HAWKE.

The Prime Minister is head of the government but not Head of State. In Great Britain the Head of State is the ruling monarch; in Australia the ruling monarch is represented by the Governor-General.

See also Cabinet government

prions *see* sea birds

privet *see* weeds

proboscis worms *see* ribbon worms

proportional representation Proportional representation is a system of voting which is based on the use of a quota principle to determine who should be elected. This system makes use of the multi-member constituency and the single transferable vote; it is usual for each electorate to return between three and seven members. The quota of votes a candidate must receive in order to be elected depends on the relationship of the estimated number of valid votes for the electorate and the number of seats to be filled. Each voter marks his preferences opposite the names of the candidates in accordance with the number of seats to be filled (*see* PREFERENTIAL VOTING). If no candidate achieves the quota, then the candidate with the lowest number of first preferences is eliminated, and the second preferences on his ballot papers are distributed. This procedure is repeated until the required number of candidates is elected. Systems of proportional voting are used in Australia for the federal Senate, the TAS House of Assembly (for which a method known as the Hare-Clark system is used) the Legislative Councils of NSW and SA, and most local government councils. In Senate elections each State is a single constituency; each State has 10 Senators, five being returned at each normal general election. In TAS there are five House of Assembly constituencies, each returning seven members. In elections for the Legislative Councils of NSW and SA, the whole State forms a single electorate.

It is claimed that the use of the system of proportional representation enables each political party to be represented in Parliament more or less according to the total number of votes it gains at the election.

Proserpine QLD (population 3 058 in 1981) A sugar milling centre and service town situated on the Proserpine River in the central E coastal region of the State, Proserpine is 1 203km NNW of Brisbane along the Bruce Highway, 124km NW of MACKAY and 66km SE of BOWEN. At an elevation of only 13m above sea level, the town has a tropical climate with an average annual rainfall of 1 803mm, concentrated in the summer months; January is the wettest (397mm average), August the driest (35mm). The surrounding rural area is dominated by sugar and banana farms and beef cattle properties. Along the adjacent

coastline there are several holiday resorts: Cannonvale, Airlie Beach and Shute Harbour. The town has a number of tourist attractions: a folk museum, an aquarium for tropical fish and a wildlife sanctuary (with crocodiles, cassowaries and a reptile house); from Shute Harbour there are launch cruises to island resorts in the WHITSUNDAY PASSAGE and CUMBERLAND ISLANDS; and flights by aeroplane or helicopter are available to HAYMAN ISLAND and to view the outer reef of the GREAT BARRIER REEF.

Proteaceae This is a large family of flowering plants which reaches its greatest species diversity in Australia and South Africa, though it is also present in South and Central America, South-East Asia and India. It contains 61 genera and approximately 1 400 species, about two-thirds of these species occurring in Australia. The type genus is *Protea* which is native to South Africa. Some Australian genera are *Banksia, Grevillea, Hakea, Lomatia, Lambertia* (mountain devil), *Isopogon* (drum sticks), *Persoonia* (geebung), *Petrophile* (cone sticks), *Telopea* (waratah) and *Xylomelum* (woody pear).

The plants of the Proteaceae are trees or shrubs, usually with hard, coriaceous leaves. The leaves are simple and smooth-margined or much-lobed and are arranged alternately. The bisexual flowers are regular or irregular and consist of four perianth segments in a single whorl: when young these segments are joined but separate later, often as a tube slit on one side. The four stamens are opposite and attached to the perianth segments, and the anthers are often sessile. Flowers may be a spike or a raceme or solitary, and are often arranged in showy clusters. The ovary is superior and contains one locule. The single-seeded fruit occurs as an achene, a drupe or a follicle.

Members of the Proteaceae occur in a wide

range of plant communities, from closed forest to open heath. Closed forest species include the magnificent fire wheel tree, *Stenocarpus sinuatus*, but the greatest wealth of species occurs in drier communities such as woodlands and heaths, though some species also occur in swampy habitats (for example, *Banksia robur, Agastachys odorata* and *Symphionema paludosus*) *Banksia* species, in which the flowers are aggregated into dense spikes, have long-persisting woody cones as fruit and vary from prostrate shrubs to small trees; many species, especially of WA origin, are now in cultivation. *Grevillea* species, which are generally shrubby, are also widely cultivated. Hybrids and selected cultivars of superior form, richness of flowering and ease of cultivation have established *Grevillea* species as garden favourites; the flowers of these species display a very wide range of colours, from greens, browns and gold to pink, red, lilac and grey. The SILKY OAK, *G. robusta*, a large tree member of the genus, is also popular in cultivation as well as for producing timber of great beauty. The New South Wales waratah, *Telopea speciossisima*, is also widely cultivated for its magnificent scarlet blossom. Many members of the South African genus *Protea* are cultivated most successfully in southern Australia, the beauty of the living flowers being equalled if not excelled by that of the dried flowers.

The dry fruits of many Australian Proteaceae are very diverse in form, from the cones of the *Banksia* species to the 'devil faces' of *Lambertia formosa*. These fruits fulfill a very important function in relationship to forest fire. By persisting, seed intact, often for many years on the plant, a ready supply of seed is available after a forest fire, the heat of which opens the follicles to release the seed after the fire has passed. Many Proteaceae also have a further method of ensuring regeneration after a fire: they have a lignotuber, which is a rather

Woody fruits of cone sticks (*Petrophile*) opened by fire

T.M. Howard

swollen stem section, covered with dormant buds just below the soil surface, from which new shoots can arise after the crown has been destroyed by fire or by other means.

See also Appendix 5, Flower Structure and Glossary of Botanical Terms

Further reading: see Appendix 6, A Bibliography for Plants.

protozoons A subkingdom and phylum of the animal kingdom, the Protozoa contains all those animals which consist of a single cell. Some of the organisms included here are green and photosynthetic at times, and are therefore also plants. For this reason the Protozoa and single-celled plants are often grouped in a separate kingdom, the Protista. It is impossible to say how many species occur in Australia but possibly most of the world's 30 000 or more species are represented in the region or its seas. Many are marine or freshwater species but some occur in the soil and several are PARASITES of man or other animals. Nearly all species are microscopically small. The phylum is usually divided into four classes which are discussed briefly below.

Mastigophora These small animals move around in water by means of relatively long whip-like structures (flagella). They engulf small particles of food into the cytoplasm where it is digested. Many have a pigmented eye-spot which is sensitive to light, and some are photosynthetic. Most are free-living in freshwater or saltwater but some are parasitic. The group includes, for example, the trypanosomes which causes African sleeping sickness and Chaga's disease in South and Central America. A related species is a blood parasite in rats, and occurs in Australia, but the symptoms are mild.

Sarcodina These protozoons move by means of extensions (pseudopodia) of the body. The class includes the well-known naked amoeba but many (the protozoons known as Foraminifera and Radiolaria) have minute coats of silica or calcium carbonate which are often of intricate shape. Their dead bodies help to build chalk and other rocks. Most members of the class are free-living, often marine, but one is the cause of amoebic dysentery, a very severe disease.

Sporozoa This is a large group of parasitic protozoons with extremely complex life histories which often involve two different kinds of hosts. The *Babesia* species, for example, which are the cause of tick fever of cattle in QLD and elsewhere, alternate between cattle and ticks, while the various species of the genus *Plasmodium* that cause malaria in man and other primates are spread by *Anopheles* mosquitoes. Certain other sporozoons cause the disease coccidiosis of poultry, rabbits and other animals.

Ciliophora or Ciliata This is a large class of about 6000 species, all of which carry, for at least part of their lives, minute hair-like appendages (cilia) which are used for locomotion and to create currents of water carrying food particles. Most species, such as the familiar slipper animalcules (*Paramecium*

species) which occur in pond water, have a constant, usually asymmetrical shape. *Vorticella* species are also extremely common pond inhabitants; these tulip-shaped animals attach themselves to plants by a long stalk and have a ring of cilia round the mouth for food collection.

See also diseases and epidemics, human; diseases, livestock

Further reading: Baker, J.R. *Parasitic Protozoa.* Hutchinson, London, 1969; Williams, W.D. *Australian Freshwater Life.* (2nd edn) Macmillan, Melbourne, 1980.

proturans This is a small class of the phylum Arthropoda (ARTHROPODS). It was formerly regarded as an order of the INSECTS. There are about 30 species of these delicate, pale, six-legged arthropods known in Australia. They live in damp soil or leaf-litter, but as they are less than 2mm long they are rarely seen, and very little is known about them. They can be distinguished from insects by the absence of eyes and antennae, and from the DIPLURANS by the absence of forceps (cerci) on the abdomen.

pseudoscorpions These tiny animals belong to the order Pseudoscorpiones, of the class Arachnida (ARACHNIDS). They are also called false SCORPIONS and book scorpions, and are best described as being small scorpions without a post-abdomen or terminal sting. The pedipalps are large-larger, indeed, than the walking legs. The chelicerae are relatively small. There are four, two or no eyes. A peculiar feature of the animals is their ability to produce silk from small glands on the chelicerae. The silk is used to spin a cocoon for the eggs.

Pseudoscorpions are secretive predators that live in such places as leaf-litter, under bark and in compost. Sometimes they are found clinging to flies, chafer beetles or other insects which they use for transport to new breeding sites—a phenomenon known as phoresy. There are probably more than 100 Australian species but they have been little studied and are difficult to identify.

Further reading: see under scorpions.

Psocoptera *see* booklice

Pteridophyta The Pteridophyta or ferns are vascular, seedless plants in which the main plant body is diploid and the most prominent organ is the leaf, with branching veins, giving it a feather-like appearance (pteridophyte means feather-plant). There are probably about 15 000 species of ferns in the world. With their origin in the Devonian period, ferns have remained successful to the present, with a great diversity of habitat and growth form. At one extreme are the erect-stemmed, large-leaved tree ferns which grow in closed forests (such as *Cyathea* and *Dicksonia* species), at the other are tiny aquatic organisms (such as *Salivinia* and *Azolla* species). A very large group of intermediate size includes the familiar cultivated varieties, and the natives of shady ravines and woodlands, in

Nardoo, *Marsilea drummondii*, an unusual aquatic fern used by Aborigines as food

both temperate and tropical communities.

As a group, ferns thrive best in moist, shady environments although a few (for example, *Cheilanthes* species) inhabit rock fissures in bright sunlight where they are subject to periodic desiccation. Most ferns are perennials, and some, such as bracken (*Pteridium* species), have remarkable powers of vegetative reproduction which enables them to occupy habitats well beyond their sexually reproductive range. Survival from year to year and asexual reproduction takes place by means of fleshy underground stems (rhizomes); the portions of the leaves above the soil die at the end of each growing season and a new set of leaves, already developed near the rhizome apex during this growing season, is elevated the following spring.

In most ferns, the leaves have a unique arrangement in the bud, known as the circinate vernation, which results in coiling of the leaf and gives rise to the common descriptive term 'fiddle head'. Fern leaves may be simple, or compound with the leaflets attached to a rhachis, a prolongation of the petiole. Stems are mostly prostrate, either on the surface or under the soil, except for tree ferns; roots originate amongst the leaf bases.

At maturity, ferns become spore-bearing (sporophytic) whereby clusters of spore-cases (sporangia) develop on the lower surface of the fronds. Each group of sporangia (sorus) is usually covered by a flap of tissue (the indusium). The arrangement of the sori is generally specific to each genus of ferns. The numerous spores arise by meiosis, the process whereby the number of chromosomes in the nucleus is halved. After shedding, the spores germinate and develop into tiny, heart-shaped, green, haploid, gamete-bearing (gametophytic) plants; fern gametophytes are known as prothalli. They produce ova and motile sperm and, after fertilisation, new fern plants are

Groundferns (foreground), tree ferns and cabbage tree palm in middle distance

produced but usually only one succeeds in developing from each prothallus.

The diverse Australian fern flora can be roughly divided into three main categories: tree ferns: ground ferns; and ferns which grow on other plants (epiphytes). Amongst the epiphytes are delicate closed forest dwellers: filmy ferns such as those of the genera *Hymenophyllum* and *Mecodium;* robust tufts such as the bird's nest fern, *Asplenium australasicum*; and the elkhorns and staghorns of the genus *Platycerium* which have two types of fronds—vegetative bracket-like humus collectors and long antler-like reproductive fronds. Three tree fern genera, *Todea, Cyathea* and *Dicksonia*, are found in Australia; the latter two genera contain members which form substantial slender trees, and are popular in cultivation. The trunks of these ferns are capable of producing roots at any position, so that cut sections containing the frond apex grow readily when planted. The ground ferns are extremely diverse, and vary from the simple pinnate clumps of fishbone ferns (*Blechnum* species) to the delicate compoundly divided fronds of the *Athyrium, Adiantum* and *Lastreopsis* species.

Many fern species have been introduced as indoor or garden plants and some of these have become naturalised aliens. In natural communities, especially near large urban centres, some species such as the Boston fern (*Nephrolepis* species) have become WEEDS. Amongst the aquatic Australian ferns is the nardoo (*Marsilea* species), the capsules of which are part of the traditional Aboriginal diet. This plant also has unusual fronds with four terminal leaflets.

See also Appendix 5, Flower Structure and Glossary of Botanical Terms
Further reading: see Appendix 6, A Bibliography for Plants.

Public Lending Right This is the recognised right of authors and publishers, and in certain cases of editors, illustrators and translators, to receive payment for the use of their books in public lending libraries. A scheme for making such payments to Australian authors, publishers and others as mentioned above, funded by the Commonwealth government, first came into operation in 1975. For some years it was administered by a standing committee of the AUSTRALIA COUNCIL. In October 1980, however, responsibility was transferred to a Public Lending Right Committee appointed by the Minister for Home Affairs. This committee includes representatives of the interests of Australian authors, publishers and librarians, together with nominees of the Literature Board of the Australia Council, the National Library, the Attorney-General's Department and the Bureau of Statistics.'

public service administration

When Governor PHILLIP stepped ashore at BOTANY BAY in 1788 he was answerable to the British Colonial Secretary for the administration of the settlement. He delegated the details of the administration to the military. A Judge Advocate was appointed to handle judicial work and as the settlement expanded into a colony, a Colonial Secretary was appointed to cope with correspondence. Thus the basis for a public service organisation was laid. When a Legislative Council was set up to assist the Governor, a Colonial Treasurer was appointed and later an Auditor-General. Each colony developed its own system of administration and when granted self-government it inherited the British system whereby public servants come under the control of Ministers of the Crown who in turn are responsible to the local Parliament. Parliaments enact legislation which the public service must administer.

Public service administration since Federation Australia has a federal, a Northern Territory, and six separate State public services. Each State also organises a system of local government under the control of a Minister for Local Government. Many services provided involve more than one department and co-ordination is provided by the Department of the Prime Minister and Cabinet (federal) or Premier (State), Treasury, and Public Service Board. There are many functions where each level of government has some responsibility (for example, health, when the federal level controls Medicare, the States control hospitals and local government provides health inspectors). Co-ordination between each level of public service administration is achieved by over a hundred intergovernmental committees of senior officers who meet several times a year to confer and make plans.

Public service administration is monitored by the Auditor-General, Solicitor-General, the OMBUDSMAN and ASIO.

Structure of departments The traditional form of government administration is that of a department under the control of a Minister

responsible to Parliament. Each department will have a permanent head with the title of Secretary, Under-Secretary or Director-General and he acts as chief official adviser to the Minister as well as general manager of the department. Below this senior official will be a hierarchy built up of divisions or branches.

Statutory Authorities Statutory Authorities are created by a special statute as an alternative to the traditional form of government department which can be created or abolished by the government of the day. Australia has many boards and commissions which are Statutory Authorities and some have the legal status of corporate bodies. Examples are the Reserve Bank of Australia, Trans Australia Airlines, CSIRO and State Electricity Commissions.

Recruitment to the public services By the time of federation, open competition had been accepted as the main way of entering the service and this meant entry from school at the base grade. However, modifications have been made over the years with preference being given to ex-servicemen after World Wars I and II and the provision of trainee-cadetships whereby candidates were selected from school and sent to a university as full-time students, subject to a bond to serve in the public service for a stated period after graduation. Traineeships were offered in the fields of agriculture, architecture, engineering and education. With the expansion of government services and activities after World War II and particularly the introduction of social services, it was necessary to recruit graduates directly from the universities as well as providing cadet-traineeships. Although there have been some appointments to higher positions from outside the service, these appointments have been exceptional and the public services have operated as a career service with preference for promotion to higher positions being given to employees already in the service on the basis of a combination of merit and seniority.

Employment of women Until the late 1960s only single women could gain permanent employment in the public services but since then the marriage bar has been removed and the principle of equal pay has been progressively introduced. The opportunity for women to gain promotion to the higher levels of government administration greatly increased in SA, VIC, NSW and TAS when anti-discrimination legislation was passed in 1977-78 and policies of affirmative action were adopted to bring about equal employment opportunities for women and minority groups. In the federal service women accounted for 28.4 per cent of the permanent staff in June 1972 and 36.2 per cent in June 1982. Over the same period the number of women in the Second Division rose from nil to 2.1 per cent.

Recent issues in public administration In the late 1950s and throughout the 1960s public concern was expressed about the growing power of executive government and the role of public servants in the determination of, and administration of government policy. The 1970s began a revival of parliamentary power with attempts to compel governments to explain what they were doing in many areas of policy and why they were doing it. Parliamentary committees were established for various purposes including an examination of departmental estimates and six investigations were carried out into the functions, responsibilities, accountability and effectiveness of public administration. These included the Bland Board of Inquiry in VIC (1973–1975); the Corbett Committee SA (1973–1975; a ministerial inquiry into the machinery of government NSW (1974); a Royal Commission on Australian Government chaired by Dr H.C. COOMBS (1974–1976); Administrative Review Committee chaired by Sir Henry Bland to inquire further into the federal public service (1976) and a Review of the NSW Public Service carried out by Professor Peter Wilenski (1977).

By 1983 Australia was in the vanguard of reforms to promote public service accountability through non-parliamentary review of administrative decisions and actions. The federal government had established by statute a comprehensive range of appointed officials, tribunals and councils which included: the OMBUDSMAN, an Administrative Appeals Tribunal, provision for simplified judicial review of ministerial decisions, creation of the Administrative Review Council, extension of the functions of the Auditor-General to include efficiency auditing, creation of the Australian Law Reform Commission which was required to examine administrative practices with a view to law reform, and in 1982 the Freedom of Information Act was passed. After its election in March, 1983 a Labor Task Force continued to operate (it had been established while Labor was in Opposition) and this may mean that public service reform will be constantly under review.

See also Cabinet government; government of Australia; quango and Ombudsman.

Further reading: Wiltshire, K. *An Introduction to Australian Public Administration.* Cassell Australia, North Melbourne, 1975; Wilenski, P. *Directions for Change—Review of New South Wales Government Administration.* NSW Gov. Printer, 1977; Smith, R.F.I. & Weller, P. *Public Service Inquiries in Australia.* University of Queensland Press, St Lucia QLD, 1978; Spann, R.N. *Government Administration in Australia.* George Allen & Unwin Australia Pty Ltd, North Sydney NSW, 1979. J.R. Nethercote (Editor), *Parliament and Bureaucracy* Hale & Iremonger, Sydney, 1982.

puff balls *see* fungi

Pugh, Clifton Ernest (1924–) Artist. Born in Melbourne, Pugh was in New Guinea during World War II and, after being invalided out, studied at the National Gallery School and then in 1951 settled at Cottle's Bridge outside Melbourne. In 1954 he crossed the NULLARBOR PLAIN, an experience which confirmed his obsession with nature and which is depicted in his illustrated book *Death of a Wombat* (1972). His work as a portraitist was influenced by William DARGIE and among his many portraits is one of Gough WHITLAM, now in Parliament House, Canberra.

pullers *see* fishes, bony

purple top *see* weeds

pyrethrum *see* Compositae

pythons *see* snakes

Qantas *see* transport

quails *see* pheasants, etc.; buttonquails, etc.

quail-thrushes *see* babblers, etc.

quandongs There are three species of quandongs in Australia; two belong to the family Santalaceae, the third to the family Elaeocarpaceae. The sweet quandong, *Santalum acuminatum*, is a small tree or shrub (1m to 4m tall) which grows in mallee and other dry, temperate areas. The flowers are inconspicuous and green; the edible fruits are pendulous and globular (2cm to 3cm in diameter) and are green at first but waxy-red later. When ripe they fall to the ground and rattle when shaken. They were used by European settlers for jams and jellies, and by the Aborigines. The bitter quandong, *S. murrayanum,* found in all mainland States, has inedible fruits. The blue quandong, *Elaeocarpus grandis*, also called the blue fig or the bracelet tree, is a very tall rainforest species which grows in northern NSW and QLD. The flowers are lily-like and the edible fruit is bright blue. The leaves, when they are ready to fall, turn bright red.

quango This word was coined by Alan Pifer of the Carnegie Corporation of New York and Tony Baker of Essex University in England to refer to *quasi-non-governmental (or semi-private) organisations*. An Australian example of the original quango would be the AUSTRALIAN RED CROSS or the Royal Australian Institute of Public Administration, which are subsidised or otherwise assisted to carry out certain functions for the government. However, during the 1979 UK general election the word 'quango' was applied to all government agencies when Mrs. Thatcher planned a 'slaughter of Britain's quangos' as a remedy for big government, and in the same year Australian Senator Peter Rae insisted that quangos will overrun the world if we don't stop them. Thus by the 1980s, in spite of academic protest, the word 'quango' became associated with big government and big-business public corporations like QANTAS,

TAA, the Wheat Board and the Commonwealth Banking Corporation all of which are presented as a threat to private enterprise and evidence of big government. This widening of the term's meaning was so successful that the 1982 Annual Conference of the Royal Australian Institute of Public Administration held in Melbourne, chose as its general topic a discussion of quangos.

Further reading: Australian Journal of Public Administration, vol. XLII, No. 1, March, 1983.

Queanbeyan NSW (population 19 375 in 1981) A city on the SOUTHERN TABLELANDS, Queanbeyan is 320km by road SW of Sydney and 16km ESE of Canberra. It is situated on the Queanbeyan River, a small headwater stream which joins the MOLONGLO RIVER near the city and thence flows into the MURRUMBIDGEE RIVER. The proximity of Queanbeyan and Canberra has had an influence on both urban centres. In the early days of Canberra's development, Queanbeyan was important as a shopping centre for residents of the national capital; many Canberra employees lived in Queanbeyan and commuted daily by bus; recreation facilities, not available in one centre, were found in the other; when Canberra was growing rapidly and accommodation was not available for the influx of people, many of them resided in Queanbeyan; and some industry developed in Queanbeyan to provide building and construction materials for Canberra's expansion. The city is a commercial and market centre for pastoral and farming communities in the middle section of the Southern Tablelands. Sheep and cattle grazing are important rural activities of the region, as well as crops such as wheat, maize, oats, potatoes and lucerne on stream flats. A tourist attraction is the Molonglo (Mills Cross) radio telescope located near Hoskinstown, 24km SE of Queanbeyan. Queanbeyan is an Aboriginal word meaning 'clear water'.

Queenscliff VIC (population 3 420 in 1981) This town is a popular and rather fashionable seaside resort on the S shore of Bellarine Peninsula, which forms the W headland of the PORT PHILLIP BAY entrance. It is located 109km by rail SW of Melbourne via GEELONG and, as well as being a holiday resort, it is an important commercial fishing centre. The Port Phillip pilot service, which guides ships through the entrance channels of the bay, is located in Queenscliff. During summer months a regular passenger ferry service operates between Queenscliff and Sorrento, on MORNINGTON PENINSULA. The town dates back to the 1830s when it was a fishing village; formerly known as Shortland Bluff, it was subsequently named in honour of Queen Victoria.

Queensland (QLD) The State of QLD has an area of 1 272 200km^2 and is the second-largest State after WA, occupying 22.5 per cent of the total area of Australia. It has a coastline of 7 400km along the Pacific Ocean and the GULF OF CARPENTARIA. The greatest distance N-S is 2 100km and E-W 1 450km. The area N of the Tropic of Capricorn is 934 000km², 54 per cent of the whole State. The boundary on the S is formed mainly by the 29th parallel of latitude, but the E section of this boundary follows the MACINTYRE and DUMARESQ Rivers and thence along the crest of the range (including the McPHERSON RANGE) to Point Danger on the coast. The W boundary is marked mainly by the 138°E meridian of longitude, but in the SW corner of the State, where it adjoins SA and the NT, the boundary is along the 26°S line of latitude and along the 141°E line of longitude. Where QLD, the NT and SA meet is called POEPPEL'S CORNER, and the point where QLD and SA meet, at the intersection of the 26th parallel and the 141st meridian, is called Haddon Corner.

Table 1

POPULATION GROWTH OF QUEENSLAND IN THE TWENTIETH CENTURY

Year	Population*
1901	498 129
1911	605 813
1921	755 972
1933	947 534
1947	1 106 415
1954	1 318 259
1961	1 518 828
1971	1 827 065
1976	2 037 197
1981†	2 345 335

Note: * prior to 1966, full-blood Aborigines were not included; † the 1981 figure is the Estimated Resident Population (Preliminary).
Source: Australian Bureau of Statistics, Canberra.

Landform features The State can be divided into five natural landform regions: the E highlands, the W plains, the uplands of the NW, the E coastal plains, and the offshore islands and reefs.

The E highlands, comprising the N part of the GREAT DIVIDING RANGE, stretch from CAPE YORK to the S border of the State. This belt of uplands, running generally parallel to the E coast with a NNW to SSE trend, forms the watershed between rivers flowing to the E coast (such as the TULLY, HERBERT, BURDEKIN, FITZROY and MARY) and those flowing inland to the Gulf of Carpentaria (for example, the MITCHELL and GILBERT) or to the MURRAY-DARLING river system (for example, the BALONNE and CONDAMINE) or to inland lakes, such as LAKE EYRE, in the arid interior of the continent (for example, the BARCOO RIVER and COOPER'S CREEK). The highest mountain in the belt is MOUNT BARTLE FRERE (1 657m). However, not all of the highland area is mountainous; many parts consist of plateaus and high plains, often deeply dissected by gorges, especially along the E scarplands, where rivers have carved sheer canyons with scenic waterfalls. On the W inland side, the highlands descend more

Little Mulgrave river, Atherton Tablelands QLD

gradually into hilly country and then merge into the broad plains. Different names are used for various sections of the highlands—the Richardson and Gieke Ranges are in the far N, the ATHERTON TABLELAND (or Plateau) is further S, and the BUNYA, CARNARVON and MAIN Ranges are in the SE.

The W plains cover about two-thirds of the State, occupying most of the inland regions. Long rivers with gentle gradients, mostly intermittent, flow across the plains in meandering courses with many ANABRANCHES, often losing themselves in the dry interior. In times of high rainfall, these streams flood and cover the plains in vast sheets of slow-moving water which may linger for many months. Only in exceptionally wet years do the DIAMANTINA RIVER and Cooper's Creek reach Lake Eyre. There are many temporary lakes in shallow depressions on the plains and the name CHANNEL COUNTRY, given to the region in the far SW of the State aptly indicates the nature of the terrain. Also in this far SW area wind-blown sand forms longitudinal dunes on the E margin of the SIMPSON DESERT.

The uplands of the NW resemble parts of the E highlands, both being composed of old folded rocks which have given rise to rugged country in which there are some major mineral deposits (for example, at MOUNT ISA). Beyond the main uplands is the BARKLY TABLELAND which extends into the NT.

The E coastal plains along the Pacific seaboard, consisting of the lower sections of river valleys, narrow stretches of plain land and long sandy beaches, vary considerably in width. In some parts, the hilly sections of the coastal ranges or offshoots of the highlands reach right down to the coast, while in other parts the coastal zone extends for over 200km inland. Much of this plains region is productive farming and grazing land, especially for sugar cane and tropical fruit growing, fodder-crop cultivation, dairying and beef cattle raising. Also in this region are many of the major urban centres of the State, such as Brisbane, ROCKHAMPTON, CAIRNS, MACKAY, BUNDABERG, TOWNSVILLE and the GOLD COAST.

The offshore islands and coral reefs along the E coast, together with the GREAT BARRIER REEF, comprise a unique region. The reef is the largest coral formation of this type in the world and many resorts, such as HAYMAN, LINDEMAN, LIZARD and BRAMPTON Islands, have been developed to cater for the tourist trade.

Climate The climatic conditions vary throughout the State from tropical and sub-tropical in the N and E, to semi-arid in the central W and arid in the far SW corner. High daytime temperatures are a normal feature in the period from October to March and temperatures exceeding 40°C are often experienced in inland areas, but living conditions are not as uncomfortable as these temperatures may indicate because they are accompanied by low humidity. In the coastal regions, sea breezes moderate the summer temperatures to some extent, but on the tropical coast, N of Rockhampton, the humid conditions are enervating. Daytime temperatures during winter are quite mild, frosts are rare except at high altitudes and, with clear skies and general lack of cloud, the climatic conditions are almost ideal; they have played a significant part in making many coastal sections of the State attractive winter tourist resorts.

Annual rainfall varies from as low as 150mm in the arid SW of the State to about 4000mm in parts of the sugar lands of the NE coast. The region around INNISFAIL. (average annual rainfall in the town 3 644mm) is the wettest area in Australia. Every part of QLD receives more rain in summer than in winter. The concentration of rain in the summer months is more pronounced in the N and W where there is a long dry season during the cooler period of the year. Along the E coast, both the tropical and sub-tropical regions receive their main rains in summer, but there is not such a marked dry season in winter. A distinctive feature of the rainfall pattern over the State is the high variability both from year to year and from place

Queen Mary's Falls QLD

to place within a single year. This is caused by the unreliable nature of the cyclones and the tropical depressions which with accompanying thunderstorms bring a large part of the spring and early summer rains. Tropical cyclones are a feature of northern QLD, especially along the NE coast. On average, three cyclones occur each summer; they develop over the adjacent tropical oceans and bring heavy rains and high winds, often over 110km an hour, which frequently cause considerable damage to crops and farmlands in rural areas and to houses and other structures in urban centres.

Population At the 1981 census, QLD had a population of 2 345 335 (*see* Table 1), making it the third-largest State, in terms of population, after NSW and VIC. About 40 per cent of the State's population live within the metropolitan capital of Brisbane; there are four cities with over 50 000 people—Gold Coast (135 437), Townsville (86 112), TOOWOOMBA (63 401) and Rockhampton (50 146)—and five others with over 20 000 people (Cairns, Bundaberg, Mackay, Mt Isa and MARYBOROUGH). Of these 10 largest urban centres, only two (Toowoomba and Mt Isa) are beyond the E coastal belt, indicating a feature of the population distribution within the State, namely that it is concentrated mainly in the E coastal areas, especially in the SE.

History Until 1859 the area now comprising the State of QLD was part of NSW, and its first settlement, like that of NSW, was founded in order to provide a suitable place for the disposal of convicts.

From first settlement to separation, 1824-59 John BIGGE, who was sent in 1819 to report on the progress of the colony of NSW, came to believe that the system of transportation was not achieving its aim of providing a deterrent to crime and a means of reforming the convicts. Included in the recommendations he made for a more effective system was the establishment of new penal settlements some distance from Sydney, for the more hardened criminals. In 1823, in accordance with this recommendation, Governor BRISBANE sent John OXLEY northward by sea to look for a suitable site. At MORETON BAY Oxley discovered and named

Brisbane river at City Reach

the Brisbane River, and praised the district around it so warmly that in the following year the Governor sent him back there with a party of convicts and soldiers to found a settlement. On 24 September Oxley landed his charges at the site of modern REDCLIFFE, under the command of Lieutenant Henry Miller, but early in 1825 they moved up the river to the site of modern Brisbane. For the following 15 years it remained a penal settlement and obtained a reputation for the severity with which its inmates were treated, especially under Patrick LOGAN, who was Commandant from 1826 to 1830. In 1839, however, most of the convicts were withdrawn and three years later the Moreton Bay district was opened to free settlement. Meanwhile, in 1827 the explorer Allan CUNNINGHAM had discovered the DARLING DOWNS and in 1840 the first squatters settled there, near the site of modern WARWICK.

Until 1859 the population grew very slowly, and was confined almost entirely to the More-

ton Bay area and the Darling Downs. In 1851 Moreton Bay was granted a member in the Legislative Council of NSW, but as in the case of the PORT PHILLIP District a decade earlier, distance from Sydney led to the growth of a separatist movement. Its leaders hoped that the boundary with NSW would be placed as far S as the CLARENCE RIVER, but when the colony of QLD was finally created in 1859 it was with its present S border. It was granted a Parliament with a Legislative Assembly elected by manhood suffrage and a Legislative Council nominated by the Governor. The population in 1859 was only 23 500.

From separation to federation Development progressed more rapidly after separation, and by 1870 the population was 115 000. Economic progress at this stage was heavily dependent on the pastoral industry. The climate of central QLD favoured cattle rather than sheep and there was a greater concentration of cattle here than in the other colonies. Progress in agriculture was comparatively disappointing. In wheat production particularly, QLD lagged behind the other colonies because plant varieties suitable for the Darling Downs were not developed until the 1940s. For a while cotton showed promise, but production declined after the end of the American Civil War and the resumption of exports from the USA to Britain.

Two industries of major importance in attracting population to central and northern QLD were gold mining and sugar cane growing; they also generated controversy regarding non-European immigration. The chief gold discoveries were at GYMPIE (1867), CHARTERS TOWERS (1872), the PALMER RIVER (1873) and MOUNT MORGAN (1882). In the 1870s Chinese dominated the N fields, especially Palmer River, where in 1877 they numbered 17 000; their presence caused the colonial governments to move towards a common policy of

Cooloola National Park QLD

Cattle mustering

Dept. of Primary Industry QLD

exclusion. However, within several years most of them had left QLD as the surface gold had been worked out. On the other hand, the presence of Pacific islanders in the canefields raised more complex and long-lasting problems (*see* KANAKAS).

In the 1890s QLD was deeply divided on the issue of federation. Support was strongest in the N, where isolation from the main population centres of Australia and the proximity to German New Guinea gave force to the 'unity is strength' argument. Moreover, federation was supported by many sugar planters, for while it seemed certain that a federal government would prohibit Kanaka labour, it was expected also to provide protection for the sugar industry. Many people in southern QLD, on the other hand, feared economic competition from NSW. The outcome was that after Sir Samuel GRIFFITH, an ardent federationist, had retired from politics in 1893 to become Chief Justice, support for federation languished. QLD did not send representatives to the convention of 1897-98, nor did she participate in the first referendum. She did hold a referendum in 1899, but only after the four S colonies had voted to form a federation. Even then, although an affirmative majority was recorded for QLD as a whole, negative majorities in every Brisbane electorate and a number of other electorates in the S reflected the regional division of opinion that still existed when the colony became a State of the Commonwealth.

Development since federation Until recently QLD's economy was still heavily dependent on the rural sector. The percentage of the workforce employed in primary industry, excluding mining, remained close to 30 per cent, well above the Australian average, until the 1930s. Then it fell, but the census of 1954 showed a figure of 20 per cent compared with one of 13 per cent for the nation as a

whole. Within the rural sector the leading growth industry, until recently, was sugar. However, from the 1950s the wheat industry began at last to become firmly established, as plant varieties suitable for the Darling Downs were developed. As the leading cattle State, QLD also benefited from the boom in beef exports in the 1960s and early 1970s. Until recently, manufacturing grew slowly, and was concentrated heavily on goods needed by primary producers, on the processing of food, and on building materials. In 1954 it accounted for 22 per cent of the workforce, compared with 27 per cent for Australia as a whole, these figures reflecting the fact that QLD has always been on the fringe of industrial development. NSW and VIC have had the advantage, not only of a more central situation, but also of having gained large populations and considerable manufacturing capacity earlier than QLD. Therefore they have been, in most respects, more attractive areas for investment.

Since 1960 the scene has changed. Manufacturing has increased in importance, but the most striking developments have been in mining. For more than half a century mining had undergone a general decline as old fields were worked out without any important new finds being made, apart from the silver-lead-zinc deposits at Mt Isa in 1923 and later the copper deposits in the same field. More recently, however, the exploitation of massive deposits of bauxite at WEIPA and of coal in the BOWEN RIVER basin, has transformed the economic picture. Mining has attracted great amounts of investment capital, and has caused the growth of associated enterprises, such as the giant alumina plant and aluminium smelter at Gladstone.

In government, QLD has been exceptional as the only State to adopt a single chamber parliamentary system, the Legislative Council

having been abolished in 1922. In party politics, QLD is noted for the early growth of the Labor Party, its almost total dominance of State politics for many years, and its virtual eclipse since the late 1950s. From 1908 to 1957 Labor was out of office for a total of only seven years. In 1957, however, the split which occurred in the S States two years earlier spread to QLD, with the result that Labor lost office and has not regained it since. From 1957 until 1983 QLD was governed by a coalition of the Country (later NATIONAL) and LIBERAL Parties. The Liberals then left the coalition, but following its success in the October 1983 election, the National Party under Mr. BJELKE-PETERSEN was able to continue in government without the need for a coalition. *Further reading:* Bernays, C.A. *Queensland Politics During Sixty Years.* Govt. Printer, Brisbane, 1919 and *Queensland: Our Seventh Political Decade.* Angus & Robertson, Sydney, 1930; Fitzgerald, R. *From the Dreaming to 1915: A History of Queensland,* University of QLD Press, 1982; Johnston, W.R. *The Call of the Land: A History of Queensland to the Present Day.* Jacaranda, St. Lucia, 1982.

Queensland halibut *see* fishes, bony

Queensland kauri *see* Gymnospermae

Queensland lace bark *see* Sterculiaceae

Queensland lung fish This primitive, air-breathing fish belongs to the order Dipnoi (class Osteichthyes, subclass Sarcopterygii). This order (*see* FISHES, BONY) was once widespread throughout the world but is now represented only by the Queensland lung fish, *Neoceratodus forsteri*; the African lung fishes (*Proropterus* species) of the Congo River region; and the South American lung fish, *Lepidosiren paradoxa*, of the Amazon River basin. The fossil record of lung fish can be traced back to the Devonian and Triassic periods.

The Queensland lung fish is native to the MARY and BURNETT Rivers of QLD, hence it is sometimes called the Burnett River salmon, but it has been introduced into other waters (for example, the Brisbane River in 1895 and 1896, as a result of which it now occurs in the Enoggera Reservoir and in parts of the Stanley River). The body is covered with large, overlapping scales and is long (up to 1.5m) and heavy, with a rather pointed tail furnished with a continuous fin from the dorsal to the anal regions. The eyes are small, and the cockscomb-teeth are adapted to crushing. The fins are flipper-like, and the fish often supports itself on the anterior ones. It breathes largely by means of gills but it has a single lung, attached by a tube to the alimentary canal, through which it can gulp air at the surface should the water be particularly foul. However, it is less of an air-breathing fish than its African and American cousins. It is mainly carnivorous, feeding on worms, crustaceans and snails, but it also eats some plant food. The eggs are laid from August to October in shallow water and are attached to water plants. Lung fish are delicious eating but are totally protected now although they do not seem to be in any great danger.

Further reading: Lake, J.S. *Freshwater Fishes and Rivers of Australia.* Nelson, Melbourne, 1971.

Queensland maple *see* crow's ash; forestry

Queensland walnut *see* forestry

Queenstown

TAS (population 3 714 in 1981) A mining town in the W coast ranges, Queenstown is located on the Lyell Highway near its junction with the Murchison Highway, 256km W of Hobart. At an elevation of 129m above sea level, the town is situated in rugged country N of the KING RIVER and NE of MACQUARIE HARBOUR. It is in a region of heavy rainfall, receiving an average of 2 450mm yearly. Rain occurs in copious amounts throughout the year. Winters are cold and windy, with frequent frosts and sleet; summers are somewhat milder, and in January and February there are often hot days when the maximum daily temperature rises to over 22°C. The region would even now probably be uninhabited were it not for its vast mineral wealth. The MOUNT LYELL Mining Co. is entirely responsible for the existence of Queenstown and most of the inhabitants are connected directly or indirectly with the company. The discovery in 1881 of alluvial gold at Mt Lyell, 6km from Queenstown, and the subsequent finds of silver and copper ores led to a mushroom growth of the town in the latter part of the 19th century, when it is claimed to have had 14 hotels; today only five remain, but the town still retains much of the atmosphere of the old mining days. It is literally carved out of the mountains which rise up on all sides and which are largely denuded of vegetation. The deforestation of the area resulted from the extensive cutting and logging of trees needed for mining and for stoking the smelters in the early days; the fumes from the smelting operations further contributed to the process, and the heavy rainfall of the area caused severe soil erosion. By 1900 the district was bare of vegetation. Since then there has been a slow natural regeneration, now being greatly assisted by the mining company and local authorities.

Quick, Sir John

(1852-1932) Politician and author. His family migrated from Cornwall to the BENDIGO goldfields in 1854. After working as a journalist and graduating in law, he was elected Member of the Legislative Assembly for Bendigo in 1880 and during the following decade became one of the most influential figures in the federation movement. At a conference of pro-federation organisations of COROWA in 1893 he suggested that the delegates to a second national convention should be elected by popular vote, and that the proposed constitution should then be put to the people of each colony in a referendum. The

Queenstown TAS showing denuded hills in the background

adoption of this plan did a great deal to arouse interest in the federation movement and to bring it to a successful conclusion. Sir John was a member of the 1897-98 convention, Member of the House of Representatives for Bendigo from 1901 to 1913, and deputy president of the Commonwealth Arbitration Court from 1922 to 1930. His publications include *The Annotated Constitution of the Australian Commonwealth* (with Sir Robert GARRAN, 1901), *The Judicial Power of the Commonwealth* (with Littleton E. Groom, 1904) and *The Legislative Powers of the Commonwealth and the States of Australia* (1919).

quillworts *see* Microphyllyta

Quilpie

QLD (population of 694 in 1981) Located in the SW of the State, 983km by road W of Brisbane and 217km W of CHARLEVILLE, Quilpie is called the gateway to the CHANNEL COUNTRY. It is a small township in a region of sparse population; Quilpie Shire, with an area of 67 842km² contained only 1 420 people in the 1981 census. Although it is situated in the vast arid interior of the continent, the township is an important service and collecting centre for the Outback properties where sheep and cattle are grazed.

Quirindi

NSW (population 2 851 in 1981) A country town on the railway route to the NEW ENGLAND region, 393km by rail N of Sydney, Quirindi is located SW of TAMWORTH in the Liverpool Plains area. At an elevation of 390m above sea level, it receives an average annual rainfall of 680mm spread evenly throughout the year. The town is a service centre for a rich rural hinterland, which produces wool, wheat, lucerne and vegetables, beef and dairy cattle, pigs and poultry. The town takes its name from the language of the

original Aboriginal inhabitants of the area, but could have been derived from either of two words, one of which means 'waters fall together' and the other 'dead tree on a mountain top'. The Surveyor-General, Thomas MITCHELL, called it Cuerindie.

Quist, Adrian Karl

(1913-) Tennis player. Born in Medindie SA, Quist was coaxed into playing serious tennis when he was 13 by English cricketer Patsy Hendren and was to become one of the best doubles players Australia has ever produced. Although a talented singles player—VIC singles champion in 1935, 1936 and 1938, NSW singles champion in 1935 and 1947, and Australian singles champion in 1936, 1940 and 1948—it was as a doubles player that he reigned supreme. In 1936 and 1937 he won his first two Australian doubles titles with Don Turnbull and followed this with eight straight victories with John Bromwich, to make the record an unequalled 10 successive wins. A cunning and fast all-court player, his career stretched throughout the 1930s and 1940s—in 1935 he won his first Wimbledon doubles title with Jack CRAWFORD and 15 years later he won the title again, this time with John Bromwich. He also won the French doubles in 1935 and the US doubles in 1939. Quist and Bromwich formed a combination which is regarded as one of the greatest doubles combinations in the history of tennis.

quokka *see* kangaroos, etc.; marsupials

quoll *see* native cats, etc.

Quorn

SA (population 1 049 in 1981) This small service town is located 337km by road and 347km by rail NNW of Adelaide and 40km NE of PORT AUGUSTA, inland from the head of SPENCER GULF. It is the treatment

National Library of Australia

Quorn railway station 1928

centre for the barytes mined at ORAPARINNA in the FLINDERS RANGES. The original central Australian railway line passed through Quorn, but the town was bypassed when the standard-gauge line was constructed in 1956. During the period of great northward wheat expansion in SA (1860-85), the town was a flourishing centre with flour mills and machinery works, but the decline of wheat growing owing to drought conditions brought a corresponding decline in its importance. The town still retains an old pioneering atmosphere and several buildings have been listed for preservation by the National Trust (SA) including the railway station, four hotels, 'Kanyaka' homestead ruins, the town hall and the mill museum.

R

rabbits The European rabbit, *Oryctolagus cuniculus*, which originated in the Mediterranean area, is the most noxious animal pest introduced into Australia by Europeans.

Five rabbits arrived with the FIRST FLEET, but these, like the many others which followed during the early days of the colony, were domestic rabbits. Some undoubtedly escaped but did not become pests. The rabbits which later became such a scourge were all probably descendants from 24 wild English rabbits brought to GEELONG by Thomas Austin who released them for sport on his estate at Barwon Park in 1859. They bred successfully at Geelong and started to spread to the surrounding countryside. The NULLARBOR PLAIN served as a barrier to the spreading rabbits for a time, but they reached Fowlers Bay SA in about 1891. In 1901 they were widespread in the COOLGARDIE goldfields and were found as far S as ESPERANCE. The stable distribution today covers suitable habitats throughout NSW, VIC and most of SA (but not KANGAROO ISLAND), the S two-thirds of WA, S inland QLD and the NE two-thirds of TAS. There are isolated populations further N and the front once reached the GULF OF CARPENTARIA.

It has been estimated that seven rabbits eat as much as one sheep and, of course, breed much more quickly. The severity of the damage depends upon the habitat and the weather. Land in good condition can be regenerated, but land under stress may be permanently damaged by high infestations. The selective feeding of rabbits leads to the disappearance of some plant species, such as the nitrogen-rich legumes, and their replacement by low-value plants, such as thistles. Rabbits also eat young trees in forest nurseries, prevent the regeneration of forests and compete with some native mammals; the disappearance over much of its range of the rabbit-eared BANDICOOT has been partly blamed upon the rabbit.

Studies by the COMMONWEALTH SCIENTIFIC AND INDUSTRIAL RESEARCH ORGANIZATION (CSIRO) have shown that under suitable climatic conditions, females produce from four to six litters a year with an average litter size of 5.7; whilst under sub-alpine conditions (for example, in the Snowy Plains NSW) about two litters are produced annually, each containing four to five young. Furthermore, the animals in the milder area mature more quickly, so that under the most favourable climatic conditions populations can increase 14 times in a generation time of 19 months.

Early methods of control included trapping, shooting and poisoning. By 1869 canned rabbits were being exported to Britain and later the introduction of the freezing of meat for export by Thomas MORT led to the shipping of carcases as well. In 1896 VIC alone exported 1 300 000 dead rabbits to London, and by the 1920s the total Australian figure had risen to an annual average of nine million. From 1874 rabbit fur replaced beaver as a material for hat making. Rabbits were a lucrative business for some people and so extermination attempts were not as wholehearted as they might have been. Attempts were made to stop the further spread of rabbits by erecting barrier fences in their path but often these were completed only after the rabbits had already passed and they were often damaged later or covered with drifting sand so that they no longer proved an obstacle.

The greatest setback to the rabbit in Australia came with the introduction of the MYXOMATOSIS virus. The virus has, however, lost much of its original potency and the rabbit populations have recovered to some extent. CSIRO scientists are trying to find ways of increasing the effects of myxomatosis (for example, by using rabbit fleas as vectors) and, in addition, they are carrying out basic research on the rabbit's biology, physiology, behaviour and ecology in Australia, searching for some new means of control. The CSIRO is also continuing its search for other BIOLOGICAL CONTROL agents and is experimenting with various promising FLUKES and TAPEWORMS. Today, control is carried out by shooting, poisoning, fumigation and warren destruction.

Further reading: Rolls, E.C. *They All Ran Wild*. Angus & Robertson, Sydney, 1969.

radio *see* broadcasting

radio astronomy *see* astronomy

Radio Australia *see* Australian Broadcasting Corporation.

Rafferty, Chips (1909-71) Film actor and producer. Born in BROKEN HILL, NSW, his real name was John William Pilbeam Goffage. His portrayal of the outback-bushman image in Australian films made the name Chips Rafferty well known throughout the nation from the 1940s. Among the films in which he acted were *Forty Thousand Horseman* (1940), *Rats of Tobruk* (1944), *The Overlanders* (1946) and *Kangaroo* (1952). He was also an advocate for the Australian film industry, formed a production company, and was involved in the production of a number of films including *The Phantom Stockman* (1953), *King of the Coral Sea* (1954), *They're a Weird Mob* (1965) and *Wake in Fright* (1970).

Raffles Bay NT A coastal inlet on the N shore of COBOURG PENINSULA, lying E of PORT ESSINGTON, Raffles Bay was the site of an early settlement in the Territory. During the 1820s it was feared that both the Dutch and the French were going to gain a foothold in N Australia and so the British launched a number of expeditions to establish settlements there. The first of these was at MELVILLE ISLAND in 1824 and the second, under the command of Captain James STIRLING, was made at Raffles Bay in 1827. The settlement was called Fort Wellington; the settlers, faced with such problems as the tropical climatic conditions, the remoteness, and difficulties in getting supplies, abandoned Fort Wellington in 1829.

ragwort *see* Compositae

D. Greig (N.P.I.A.W.)

Tasmanian native-hen, *Gallinula mortierii*

rails, crakes, moorhens and their allies These BIRDS belong to the family Rallidae and are generally referred to as rallids. There are 16 Australian rallids, of which three are uncommon; the most common rallids are described below.

Rails and crakes are secretive birds which lurk in thick vegetation and are more often heard than seen. Although most species are reluctant to fly, many do make long-distance flights; thus oceanic islands have often been colonised by rallids which sometimes subsequently lose their power of flight (for example, the weka of New Zealand). The general appearance is that of a domestic hen, but rails have long beaks whereas crakes' beaks are shorter and thicker.

H & J Beste (N.P.I.A.W.)

Red-necked rail, *Rallina tricolor*

Many crakes are slender, enabling them to move easily through thick vegetation.

The banded rail, *Rallus philippensis* (30cm long), is a swift-footed brown bird, with black and white bars on the breast and a chestnut patch on the throat. There is a chestnut streak through the eye, and a white one above it. This species ranges from India to the SW Pacific, living in aquatic habitats along coasts and on islands; in Australia it is widely distributed. The nests are shallow scrapes in the ground, lined with grass. Two other common rails—the red-necked species, *Rallina tricolor* (30cm), and the chestnut species, *Eulabeornis castaneoventris* (40cm)—are found in the mangroves and wet forests of N and NE Australia. The former, predominantly blackish-brown with a reddish-brown head and chest, nests in a hole in the ground, lined with dead leaves. The latter, which is chestnut below and brownish-green above with a grey head, builds flat nests of sticks in mangrove trees.

A widespread species among the crakes is the marsh crake, *Porzana pusilla* (15cm), known in Europe as Baillon's crake. Found in thick swamp vegetation in coastal and near-coastal areas throughout the continent, particularly in the S and in TAS, it has a pale grey breast and throat, brown wings and a dark grey, barred belly. This species flits quickly from one tussock to another, flicking its tail constantly. The similar spotted crake, *P. fluminea** (18cm), is also more common in the S and frequents the shores of lakes and brackish waters. Its saucer-shaped nests of grasses are placed in shallow water, in clumps of vegetation. The white-browed crake, *P. cinerea* (18cm), of the N coastal swamps and mangroves, has white underparts and mottled dark brown upperparts. It often wanders among the branches of trees, climbing with ease.

Moorhens, native-hens, the bush-hen, the swamphen and the coot are aquatic birds which also resemble the domestic hen in appearance. In all species, the bill is extended to form a bony shield on the face, hence the expression 'as bald as a coot'.

The Tasmanian native-hen, *Gallinula mortierii (Tribornyx mortieri)* (45cm), is a flightless, highly socialised 'oversized moorhen' much studied by CSIRO biologists. Greenbilled, with olive and brown plumage and a white patch on the wings, it can run at 50km an hour. It feeds on green plants and is regarded as a pest by TAS graziers because it competes with livestock and fouls pasture. This species is replaced on the mainland by the common black-tailed native-hen, *G. (T.) ventralis** (35cm), a bird which invaded the streets of Adelaide and Perth in the early days of settlement. Unlike the TAS species, the black-tailed species is a nomadic bird which can fly well. It is bantam-like, with a strong bill, brown plumage and white spots on the flanks.

The dusky moorhen, *G. tenebrosa* (35cm), is common on inland waters, including ponds in city parks. This shy bird is dark and plump with a red frontal shield, and it constantly flicks its tail. Also common in city parks, as well as on the margins of lakes and creeks, is the widespread Old World swamphen or purple gallinule, *G. (Porphyrio) porphyrio* (45cm), a large black bird with a purple sheen. It has a massive red bill, a red frontal crest, and strong, long, red legs.

Belonging to a separate subfamily is the coot, *Fulica atra* (38cm), a widespread Old World water bird. It is dark, with a conspicuous white frontal shield, and is common on open waters throughout Australia. It is an expert swimmer and diver; when swimming, the head jerks back and forth constantly.

Further reading: (for the Tasmanian native-hen) Rowley, I. *Bird Life*. Collins, Sydney, 1974.

Railton TAS (population 857 in 1981) This small town is located on the N plains, 23km S of DEVONPORT and W of the lower MERSEY RIVER. It is a service centre for the rich farming lands of the adjacent district noted for dairying, orcharding and the production of fat lambs, potatoes, vegetables and fodder crops, but it is best known as the home of the Goliath Portland Cement Co., one of TAS's major industries, based on limestone quarried near the town.

railways *see* transport

rain making In much of Australia, rainfall is inadequate to support rural industry. Even in established pastoral or grain growing areas rainfall can be highly variable and unreliable. It is not surprising, therefore, that the technology of 'rain making' has been studied extensively in Australia.

The first rain making experiments were conducted just after World War II by the COMMONWEALTH SCIENTIFIC AND INDUSTRIAL RESEARCH ORGANIZATION (CSIRO) Division of Radiophysics. During the war this division had been engaged in research on radar and had discovered that falling rain could produce an echo on a radar set. This led to the scientific study of the processes that convert water droplets in clouds into falling rain, and to attempts to speed up this process by seeding suitable clouds with particles of 'dry ice' (frozen carbon dioxide) dropped from an aircraft. More recently crystals of silver iodide have been used.

For rain making to be of economic importance, it must be demonstrated to work over large areas and not simply in isolated clouds. The natural variability of rainfall in time and space makes such proof difficult to obtain and the results over the past 30 years have not always been consistent. Rain making is also limited by the availability of suitable clouds. A number of large carefully planned experiments have been carried out and, in some of these, increases in rainfall of 20 per cent have been observed, the increased rainfall being evident over large areas. There is only one chance in 50 that the extra rain would have fallen without human help.

rainbow bird These brightly coloured birds belong to the group known as bee-eaters (family Meropidae), which are related to KINGFISHERS. The rainbow bird, *Merops ornatus* (20cm long), the only Australian bee-eater, is a typical example of this group. It is a slim bird with a long, down-curved bill and long central feathers in its tail. The back is mainly applegreen, the throat yellow, the nape buff, the rump light blue and the underparts greenish or light blue; there is a black band through the eye and a black patch on the breast.

Rainbow birds prefer open areas, spending winter in N Australia, or on islands N of the continent, and flying to southern Australia for the summer. They feed on insects, particularly bees and wasps; they breed only in Australia, in tunnels excavated in sandy soils.

*Species, genus or family is endemic to Australia (see Preface)

Rainbow bird, *Merops ornatus*

Ramsay, Hugh (1877-1906) Artist. Born in Glasgow, Ramsay arrived in Australia as a babe in arms. He studied at the National Gallery School, Melbourne, and in 1900 travelled to Europe with his friend, George LAMBERT, to study at Colarossi's in Paris. He admired and was influenced by the works of Manet and Velásquez. His compositions show a great subtlety in their use of light and in the control of mass and space. His spartan living conditions in Paris affected his health, and he contracted tuberculosis; this forced him to return to Australia in 1902. He died in Melbourne after four years of great painting activity.

rats, black and sewer see animals, introduced

ravens see crows, etc.

Rawlinson Range WA This is a hilly range in the mid-E arid region of the State, at the SE of the GIBSON DESERT, near the WA/NT border, with peaks rising to 250m above the surrounding landscape and reaching heights of over 1 200m above sea level. It is a W extension of the crystalline MUSGRAVE and Petermann Ranges of SA and the NT into WA, forming a great arc with a general SE-NW trend. The range is an area of low and unreliable rainfall. The Giles meteorological station in the range, at a height of 580m, has an average annual rainfall of only 246mm; the two months of highest rainfall are January (30mm average) and February (57mm). Summer temperatures are very high, with monthly maxima around 40°C.

Raymond Terrace NSW (population 7 548 in 1981) This country town is located on the lower HUNTER RIVER, 26km N of NEWCASTLE and 193km by road N of Sydney. At a height of 12m above sea level, it receives an average annual rainfall of 1 160mm. It is the administrative headquarters of the PORT STEPHENS Shire council, as well as a service and business centre for a rich farming and dairying district. There are numerous industrial enterprises in the area, including a fibreboard plant and a rayon factory. This area of the Hunter Valley was settled in the early

decades of the 19th century; the village was gazetted in 1837 and during the 1840s became a thriving river port.

rays see fishes, poisonous and venomous; sharks, etc.

Receveur, Louis (?-1788) A French Franciscan and naturalist. Receveur served as chaplain and naturalist on the *Astrolabe* under LA PEROUSE. He died on 17 February 1788 at BOTANY BAY and is buried near the monument to his Commander who disappeared after sailing from Australia. There is an unfounded belief that the land on which the grave and monument are situated belongs to France.

Recherche Archipelago WA This is a group of more than 100 small islands off the ESPERANCE section of the S coast of the State, scattered E-W over a distance of some 200km. Among the largest are Mondrain Is, Middle Is, North Twin Peak Is and Sandy Hook Is. The archipelago was named in 1792 by the French explorer Bruni d'Entrecasteaux after one of his ships.

Red Cliffs VIC (population 2 409 in 1981) This small country town is located in the NW of the State, on the Calder Highway, 16km S of MILDURA, and 544km by road NW of Melbourne. It is the service centre for a productive district of vineyards and citrus orchards, supplied with irrigation water by a pumping system from the nearby MURRAY RIVER. A large fruit packing shed and a major winery are landmarks of the area. The town and the irrigation district were established after World War I as a settlement scheme for ex-servicemen, and given the name Red Cliffs because of the nature of the Murray River cliffs.

Red Cross Society, Australian see Australian Red Cross Society

Redcliffe QLD (population 43 820 in 1981) A rapidly expanding city located on a peninsula facing the N section of MORETON BAY, Redcliffe is 32km by road NNE of Brisbane. It is linked by a causeway across Bramble Bay to the main road through Sandgate to Brisbane and a bridge duplicating this crossing was completed in 1980, as part of the Hornibrook Highway. The good road connections to Brisbane have been a major factor in developing Redcliffe as a commuter suburb. The peninsula has a 19km-long coastline of beaches and headlands where there are good facilities for swimming, fishing and boating. The explorer John OXLEY selected the peninsula in 1824 as the site for the first settlement on Moreton Bay, but the settlement was moved shortly afterwards to the present site of Brisbane.

Redfern, William (?1774-1833) Pioneer surgeon. While there is some uncertainty about the date and place of Redfern's birth, it is known that he grew up in Wiltshire and that in 1797, after passing the examinations of the

London Company of Surgeons, he was commissioned as a surgeon's mate in the British Navy. A few months later his ship was involved in the mutiny at The Nore, and Redfern was charged with encouraging the mutineers by advising them to 'be more united among themselves'. A court martial sentenced him to death, but this was commuted to transportation for life, and after four years in prison in England he arrived in Sydney in December 1801. He was immediately appointed as an assistant surgeon at NORFOLK ISLAND, where Lieutenant-Governor Foveaux soon gave him a conditional pardon; in 1803 Governor KING converted this into a free pardon. Redfern returned to Sydney in 1808; he was given a position there as assistant surgeon and later took charge of the Sydney Hospital when it was completed in 1816. Also, he established an extensive private practice; he was personal physician to Governors BLIGH and MACQUARIE, and became a close friend of the latter and his family. In 1814 he issued a report on health conditions on convict ships which led to the implementation of a number of improvements; it is regarded as the first important public health report in Australian history.

In 1821 he went to England with Edward Eagar to present a petition to the King from leading emancipists, and two years later had the gratification of seeing some of the petitioners' wishes met by the provisions of the New South Wales Judicature Act. On returning to NSW he gave up his medical practice and devoted himself to farming near Minto, attending to his property in the area which is now the Sydney suburb of Redfern, and to various charitable and other community activities. He is reported to have had a somewhat brusque manner, and certainly reacted angrily whenever aspersions were cast on his background, a notable example of this being his public horsewhipping of the publisher, Robert Howe, for attacking him in the *Sydney Gazette*. *Further reading:* Ford, Sir Edward *The Life and Work of William Redfern*. Australian Medical Publishing Co., Sydney, 1953.

redthroat see warblers

Reed, Joseph (1823-90) Architect. It has been said that Melbourne is Joseph Reed's city, for the great number of large and important 19th-century buildings he designed transformed what was a little pioneer town into one of the most attractive cities in Australia.

Reed was a Cornishman who arrived in Melbourne during the gold rush in 1853. He designed the town hall in GEELONG in the same year and in 1854 he won the competition for the design of the Victorian Public Library. Thereafter his commissions read like a catalogue of almost every important building in Melbourne: among them were Melbourne University buildings including Ormond College and Wilson Hall; 10 banks, several churches, the town hall, the weather bureau, the trades hall and the Exhibition building. In 1863 Reed visited Europe where he was captivated by the brick architecture in Lombardy.

The influence is evident in some of his subsequent polychrome brick buildings, notably the Independent Church in Collins Street, and the Sargood mansion 'Rippon Lea' at Elsternwick, now a National Trust building.

Reed's designs covered a wide range of architectural styles. Wilson Hall was Gothic, while Ormond College was Scottish Baronial. His town halls were Classical: asymmetrical Italianate for Melbourne town hall, symmetrical Palladian for Geelong town hall. The Independent Church was Romanesque in appearance. The architectural practice which Reed established has continued uninterrupted under various changes of name since Reed took Frederick Barnes into partnership in 1862. It is now known as Bates, Smart and McCutcheon, and is the oldest and one of the largest practices in Australia.
Further reading: Freeland, J.M. *Architecture in Australia—A History.* Penguin Books, Ringwood, 1972.

reeds *see* Gramineae

Rees, Lloyd Frederic (1895-) Artist. Born in Brisbane, Rees studied at the Brisbane Technical College and the Chelsea Polytechnic, London. After working as a draughts-man in Brisbane, he moved to Sydney where he worked as an illustrator with the commerical art firm of Smith and Julius, a great meeting place for artists at that time. He toured Europe in the 1920s and was particularly affected by the Tuscan landscape in Italy. After returning to Australia, he began to paint landscapes, especially of the Sydney sandstone country, the area around BATHURST and ORANGE, and the S coast region of Gerringong and Mt Saddleback. From 1927 to 1934, Rees concentrated on drawing, before returning again to painting. His detailed drawing technique and the influence of the Tuscan landscape and its colours resulted in landscape paintings that emphasised the geological age of Australia, with its bared stone outlines and its timelessness. Rees was granted an honorary doctorate for his services to art by the University of Sydney in 1970, and appointed a CMG in 1978.

referendum *see* government of Australia

Reiby, Mary (1777–1855) Convict and pioneer businesswoman. She was born in Lancashire, England, and at the age of 13 was sentenced to seven years' transportation for stealing a horse. Arriving in Sydney in 1792, she worked as a nursemaid in the household of Major Francis GROSE until 1794, when she married Thomas Reiby, a former officer of the East India Company who had become a farmer and trader. In 1811 both Reiby and his partner Edward Wills died, leaving Mary in control of extensive interests in shipping, trading, warehousing, farming and other areas of business—and also with seven children to support. She coped with the situation very capably, becoming Australia's first notable businesswoman. She was also very active in charitable causes and community activities, and was on friendly terms with Governor MACQUARIE.

Reid, Sir George Houston (1845-1918) Premier of NSW and Prime Minister. Born near Paisley, Scotland, he was brought by his parents to Melbourne in 1852 and to Sydney in 1856. He worked as a clerk for many years, first in a merchant's office and then in the Colonial Treasury; he also studied law and was called to the Bar in 1879. In the following year he was elected to the NSW Legislative Assembly, succeeded PARKES as leader of the free trade party in 1891, and from 1894 to 1899 was Premier.

At first he opposed federation on the grounds of free trade, believing that a federal government would have to be at least moderately protectionist, and claiming that NSW would then be in the position, as he put it, of 'a sober man forced to keep house with five drunkards'. However, he soon came to see that federation was inevitable, and concentrated on trying to ensure that the federal contract contained terms as favourable to NSW as possible. His resultant manoeuvrings at the time of the 1898 referendum caused the *Bulletin* to dub him 'Yes-No Reid'.

QLD Art Gallery

A pen and ink drawing of the Treasury Buildings by Lloyd Rees about 1920

Courtesy of AIS Canberra

Sir George Reid

Elected to the first House of Representatives, he became leader of the free trade party and of the Opposition, and as an arch-opponent of Labor became well known for his warnings about the dangers to be expected from the 'socialist tiger'. In August 1904 he seized the chance to form a coalition of free traders and protectionists and, by forcing John WATSON's Labor administration from office, became Prime Minister. However, by July 1905 Alfred DEAKIN was in a position, with protectionist and Labor backing, to force Reid from office. During the following few years Reid began to realise that there was little future for him in Australian politics, and in 1910 he resigned from Parliament to become the first Australian High Commissioner in London. He retained that position until 1916 when he became a Member of the House of Commons for two years. A man of extremely portly build, he was throughout his public career a cartoonist's delight, and was also famous as a master of witty repartee.

Further reading: Reid, Sir George H. *My Reminiscences.* Cassell, London, 1917.

religion This entry is confined to a general discussion of religion in Australia, in particular the balance between the various denominations. Any denomination which includes more than one per cent of the Australian population is treated in more detail in a separate entry.

The general situation The 1981 census results show that 76.38 per cent of Australia's population are Christians, the largest denominations being ANGLICAN or Church of England (26.14 per cent), ROMAN CATHOLIC or Catholic (25.98 per cent), UNITING CHURCH IN AUSTRALIA (4.89 per cent) and PRESBYTERIANS (4.38 per cent). Although all congregations of the METHODIST Church became officially part of the Uniting Church in 1977, nevertheless 3.37 per cent of the Australian population gave their religion as Methodist in the 1981 census.

Only 1.36 per cent (mainly Hebrew and MUSLIM) were classified as non-Christian, but 10.81 per cent stated that they had no religion, and 10.94 per cent did not answer the question on religion.

Historical trends In general, the pattern of religious affiliation has reflected trends in immigration. Since most settlers after 1788 have come from Europe, the great majority of Australians have always professed themselves to be Christians, their particular affiliations being decided largely by their national origins. Moreover, until fairly recently immigration was predominantly from the British Isles, and hence people's religion tended to be based on ethnic origin within Britain and Ireland. Thus most adherents of the Church of England, the Roman Catholic Church and the Presbyterian Church were of English, Irish and Scottish origin respectively. Of the other denominations, the Methodists, BAPTISTS, Quakers (Friends), CONGREGATIONALISTS and SALVATION ARMY members were predominantly of English or Welsh origin, while most LUTHERANS were of German origin.

In contrast to the USA, where such sects as the Church of Christ and the SEVENTH DAY ADVENTISTS were founded, no new Christian sects have been founded in Australia. Indeed, the members of existing Churches have made few innovations even in forms of worship, in methods of training the clergy or in Church organisation. For many years they tended to draw their clergy from the country of main origin.

Immigration patterns have also contributed to certain variations in the pattern of religious adherence in different parts of Australia. An example of this can be seen in SA, which attracted fewer Irish immigrants than the other colonies, but which received a fairly large number of Germans; as a result the proportion of Roman Catholics there is lower than the national average and that of Lutherans is higher. However, the unusually high proportion of Uniting Church members and Methodists (15.2 per cent) and the low proportion of Presbyterians (1.7 per cent) are harder to explain. In TAS, which received a high proportion of its settlers from England and has not been affected by post-1945 immigration as strongly as the mainland colonies, the proportion of Anglicans (36.1 per cent) is the highest of any State, and that of Roman Catholics (18.7 per cent) the lowest. Yet another regional variation, namely that Roman Catholics form an unusually high proportion of the population of the ACT, would appear to be a result of the tendency of Roman Catholics to obtain employment in the Public Service.

Since 1945, for the first time in Australia's history more settlers have come from the continent of Europe than from Britain. This trend has contributed to a fall in the proportion of Anglicans, Methodists and Presbyterians and a rise in that of Roman Catholics and members of ORTHODOX CHURCHES. Among Roman Catholics the proportion of people of Irish origin is now lower than before, and that of Italians higher.

During the last few decades, in Australia as in many other countries, there has been a growing ecumenical spirit among the different Christian denominations. This has been shown in the development of the AUSTRALIAN COUNCIL OF CHURCHES, the foundation of the Uniting Church in Australia, wider dialogue between the Roman Catholic Church and other denominations, and a general increase in interdenominational understanding and co-operation. There has also been increased communication between Christian and non-Christian communities—as, for example, in 1979, when Christian and Muslim leaders participated in a conference in Melbourne with the theme that together they could provide a more effective bulwark against atheism, materialism and indifference.

Another historical trend to be noted is that from the late nineteenth century, and especially during recent decades, there has been an increasing realisation among non-Aborigines of the depth and complexity of Aboriginal religious beliefs, and of the ways in which such beliefs have affected every aspect of the Aborigines' life, including their relationship with the land.

Growth of smaller sects During recent years there has also been a considerable growth of smaller sects. Old-established groups such as Jehovah's Witnesses and the Mormons (Church of Latter Day Saints) have increased their membership, and many sects which were completely or relatively unknown a few decades ago have appeared. The latter include Scientology, the Hare Krishna Movement, the Children of God, the Ananda Marga, the Unification Church, and Transcendental Meditation groups. Reliable figures for the membership of most of these are lacking. However it seems clear that they have gained followers mainly from the comparatively young (17-27 years), and mainly also in the capital cities. Reasons commonly given for their growth include a widespread feeling of disillusionment with modern society and its materialist values, a feeling of alienation caused by such events and trends as the Vietnam War, the nuclear arms race and degradation of the environment, the absence of effective religious education from the lives of many young people and a susceptibility to charismatic leadership.

Further reading: van Sommers, T. *Religions in Australia.* Rigby, Adelaide, 1966; Moll, H. *Religion in Australia: A Sociological Investigation.* Nelson, Melbourne, 1971; 'The Sects', in *Current Affairs Bulletin,* vol. 58 no. 4, Sept. 1981.

remoras *see* fishes, bony

Rene, Roy 'Mo' (1892-1954) Comedian. Born Harry van der Sluys—or Sluice—in Adelaide, 'Mo' was the son of a cigar maker. He sang as 'Master Roy' and appeared in pantomime at the Theatre Royal, and at the Adelaide Tivoli; while in his teens he moved to Melbourne and appeared at the Gaiety, and on the suburban vaudeville circuit in 'nigger-minstrel' parts, from which his characteristic black-and-white make-up of later years was derived. In 1916 he teamed up with Nat Phillips, who became 'Stiffy' in the famous 'Stiffy and Mo' comedy partnership which lasted until the late 1920s. 'Mo' appeared in vaudeville at the Ful-

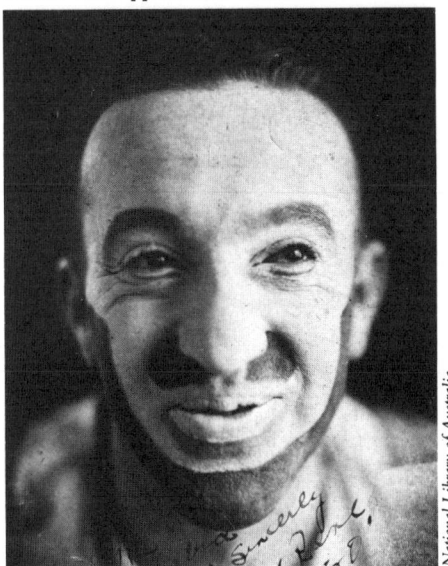

Roy Rene 'Mo'

lers Theatre and later the Tivoli throughout the Depression, entertaining audiences with his earthy and often outrageous humour and his famous catch-phrase, 'Strike me lucky!' In the 1940s, with the radio series 'McCackie Mansions', he took up a career in broadcasting which continued till after 1950. His last stage appearance was in *Hellzapoppin* in 1949-50. *Further reading*: Rene, R. *Mo's Memoirs*. Reed & Harris, Melbourne, 1945; West, J. *Theatre in Australia*. Cassell, Sydney, 1978.

Renison Bell TAS This tin-mining township is situated on the Murchison Highway in the rugged W coast ranges, 42km by road N of QUEENSTOWN, 11km W of ROSEBERY and 17km NE of ZEEHAN. Although ores have been mined in this area since the early days of this century, further major discoveries of rich fields in the 1960s led to the reopening of the Renison tin mine and the establishment in the town of a concentrating mill for processing the ores. This new development has had a major impact not only on Renison Bell but also on nearby Zeehan.

Renmark SA (population 3 475 in 1981) A town and irrigation area on the MURRAY RIVER, Renmark is located just W of the VIC border, 254km by road and 344km by rail NE of Adelaide. At a height of 20m above sea level, the town has a mild semi-arid climate with a low average annual rainfall of 263mm evenly spread throughout the year. It is the service centre and the site of processing works for a productive rural region of vineyards and orchards. The town takes its name from an Aboriginal word meaning 'red mud' and was first recorded in 1830 when the explorer Charles STURT heard the word applied to the broad bend of the river. Renmark was the site of the first irrigation development in SA, started by the Canadian CHAFFEY BROTHERS

in 1887, using water pumped from the Murray. The irrigation area now covers over 7000ha and produces grapes (for wines and dried fruits), citrus and stone fruits. The industries of the town include fruit packing, canning, wine making and distilling. Renmark was a river port until the early part of this century and the paddle-wheel steamer *Industry* is moored permanently at the river bank as a floating museum and a reminder of the days when the river boats were the main means of transport. The town is a popular tourist centre, with boating, fishing, aquatic sports, river cruises and a wide variety of recreational facilities available for visitors.

Renner, Ingo (1941-) Glider pilot. Born in Bremen, West Germany, Renner had his earliest experience with gliders when, as a child of eight, he built his first model glider. He experienced his first glider flight with an instructor at the age of 13, and the exhilaration and freedom of the sport irrevocably addicted him to gliding. He came to Australia in 1967 and worked as a ship builder in Brisbane but returned to Germany three years later. He was soon persuaded to return to Australia to teach at the gliding school in Tocumwal NSW. He then decided to live in a caravan permanently parked near the Tocumwal aerodrome, which allowed him to spend up to seven hours a day in the air. The practice paid off and during the period 1973-78 Renner won six consecutive Australian National 15m championships. In the 1976 World Gliding championship in Finland, Renner won the Standard Class title and thereby became the first Australian to win a world gliding title. His prize was a PIK 20 glider, the first glider he had ever owned. He defeated five top American glider pilots in 1977 to win the Smirnoff Sailplane Derby, from the W coast to the E coast of the USA, the longest gliding race in the world. Modest

and unassuming, Renner is dedicated to physical fitness which, coupled with a deep knowledge of aerodynamics and a detailed understanding of meteorological conditions, has kept him at the top of Australian gliding. In 1983 he held 11 national titles.

repatriation benefits The provision of repatriation (veterans') benefits is the responsibility of the Repatriation Commission, which has a central office in Canberra and a branch office in each State capital. Its chairman is also secretary of the Department of Veterans' Affairs (formerly the Department of Repatriation), which provides the administrative machinery for the Commission's work. There is a wide range of benefits, of which the largest are: disability and dependants' pensions, service pensions and allowances, medical treatment for veterans with respect to injuries or illnesses caused or aggravated by their service, and medical treatment for the widows and dependants of deceased veterans whose deaths were service-related. Benefits are provided with respect to the two world wars, the South African war of 1899-1902, operations in Korea, Malaya and certain operational areas of the British Commonwealth Far East Strategic Reserve or the Special Overseas Forces, and, in certain circumstances, the Regular Defence Forces.

reptiles These cold-blooded VERTEBRATES make up the large class Reptilia; they evolved from the AMPHIBIANS during the Carboniferous period more than 280 million years ago, and are ancestral to BIRDS and MAMMALS. Their main advance over amphibians was in the development of a shelled egg with an amnion ('a private pond') which could develop on dry land. Reptiles were thus able to colonise land environments without having to return to water to reproduce. They differ further from amphibians in various skeletal details and by having a scaly skin; and they differ from mammals in not suckling their young, in being hairless and, again, in various skeletal details. Reptiles were once more numerous than they are now. During the Cretaceous and Jurassic periods they were the dominant animals (dinosaurs) on land, but there were also aquatic and aerial forms.

The primary classification of reptiles is based on the structure of the skull and in particular upon the openings in the skull wall.
1. Subclass Anapsida. This contains the order Chelonia (TORTOISES AND TURTLES) and two extinct orders containing the stem reptiles and the aquatic mesosaurs.
2. Subclass Synapsida. This is an extinct subclass containing the mammal-like reptiles, some of which were the ancestors of the mammals.
3. Subclass Euryapsida. This is an extinct subclass of mainly aquatic reptiles such as the plesiosaurs and ichthyosaurs.
4. Subclass Diapsida. This is a successful subclass of ruling reptiles which contained the extinct dinosaurs and their allies. The three surviving orders are: order Crocodilia (CROCO-

Premier's Dept S.A

Paddle steamer 'Industry' moored on the Murray river at Renmark SA

Saltwater crocodile, *Crocodylus porosis*

DILES), order Rhynchocephalia (which contains only the 'living fossil', the tuatara of New Zealand) and the order Squamata (SNAKES and LIZARDS).

All surviving orders of reptiles, apart from the Rhynchocephalia, are well represented in Australia. There are about 6000 species in the world and about 530 species have been described in Australia, but, no doubt, many more await discovery. Many of the Australian species and genera are endemic but there is only one Australasian endemic family, the Pygopodidae, a group of legless lizards. Unfortunately, many Australian reptiles (particularly lizards) have no common names.

reserves *see* national parks, etc.

Restionaceae

This monocotyledonous family of flowering plants is distributed mostly in the S hemisphere, especially in south Africa and Australia. All members are perennial herbs, tough and wiry or rush-like with creeping or tufted rhizomes. Members are easily recognisable by their banded stems; the darker bands are the leaves which are reduced to sheaths around the stem and are split on one side. Most species have separate male and female plants (dioecious). The flowers are small, each subtended by an empty bract (a glume) and arranged in spikelets in a lax inflorescence; the perianth has six segments or fewer, arranged in two whorls. There are one or a few female flowers in a spikelet. Male flowers usually have three stamens opposite the inner perianth segments. The fruit is a nut or a capsule.

The members of this family, which are generally overlooked by the casual observer, are widespread and abundant in a number of Australian plant communities, notably sedgelands (swamps), heaths and some woodlands. All are well adapted to surviving forest fires because of their underground rhizomes, which simply shoot again after the crowns have been destroyed. Because of this quality they are among the first plants to appear after a fire, and one of the longest to persist under a high fire frequency. Many species also appear to be restricted to, but widespread throughout, specific communities, which combined with their long persistence makes them good indicator species for interpreting recent changes in natural vegetation. Several species of these ground cover plants have potential as cultivated plants, particularly for areas of water-

logged or damp ground. Three such species are *Lepyrodia scariosa, Restio fastigiatus* and *Leptocarpus tenax*, all of which give a pale brown, greyish-green to reddish-brown permanent wheatfield-like effect. *R. tetraphyllus*, which often grows to 1m high, in feathery pale green clumps, has great potential as an accent or foliage plant.

See also Angiospermae; Appendix 5, Flower Structure and Glossary of Botanical Terms
Further reading: see Appendix 6, A Bibliography for Plants.

resurrection plant *see* Microphyllyta

Returned Services League of Australia

(RSL) With over 260 000 members in nearly 2000 sub-branches, this organisation is by far the largest and most influential Australian ex-service association. Moreover, it contains a far higher percentage of ex-servicemen than equivalent overseas bodies such as the American Legion and the British Legion.

History During World War I, returned soldiers' associations were formed in all six States. In 1916 those in VIC, QLD, SA and TAS came together to form the Returned Sailors' and Soldiers' Imperial League of Australia. Similar organisations in NSW and WA joined in 1917 and 1918. The League's fundamental aim was to protect the interests of returning servicemen with regard to such matters as pensions, health services and employment. From the beginning it did valuable work in making ex-servicemen aware of their rights, in lobbying for repatriation benefits and in persuading all State governments except that of QLD to legislate in favour of preference for ex-servicemen in employment.

In 1918 it was recognised by the Commonwealth government as the official spokesman for ex-servicemen, and since 1940 has been allowed direct access to Cabinet sub-committees concerned with repatriation matters. Its title was changed to the Returned Sailors', Soldiers' and Airmen's Imperial League of Australia in 1940 and to its present form in 1965. In the meantime its membership had been progressively extended to include servicemen from wars after that of 1914-18. For many years it was open only to those with service in the defence forces or the merchant navy in an actual theatre of war. However, by 1981 the League's national headquarters had recommended that membership be extended to all who had spent a minimum of six months in one of the armed services, and all branches adopted such a policy.

Organisation and activities The RSL has a federal form of organisation. State branches, which have considerable autonomy, elect delegates every two years to a National Congress, and there is a National Executive, with headquarters in Canberra. Local bodies within each State are known as sub-branches.

The RSL carries out a great deal of welfare work among ex-servicemen and women, and conducts a number of youth clubs. It receives financial support for its welfare work from the

RSL social clubs, which draw a high proportion of their membership from RSL ranks but are not controlled by it. Besides concerning itself directly with the interests of ex-servicemen and women, the RSL has devoted itself to promoting various causes which it sees as being closely connected with the security of Australia. It expresses views and exerts its influence on matters of defence planning and policy, foreign policy, internal security and immigration. Thus for many years it voiced strong opposition to the relaxation of Australia's restrictive immigration policy, and it has been outspoken in its opposition to Communism and to any internal or external policies which it has judged to favour the spread of Communist influence. In such matters it has tended to be strongly conservative, and has been criticised in some quarters for going beyond its fundamental objectives by intervening in political issues.
Further reading: Kristianson, G.L. *The Politics of Patriotism.* Australian National University Press, Canberra, 1966; *Directory of Ex-Service Organisations.* (annually, 1971-) Australian Govt. Publishing Service, Canberra.

Rhododendron *see* Epacridaceae

ribbon worms

Comprising the small phylum Nemertea, these are smooth, somewhat flattened, primitive worms whose most remarkable feature is the long, narrow, hollow tube (proboscis) which is normally stored in a pocket in the head. When the animal attacks prey, the proboscis is shot out with great rapidity, turning inside-out in the process. It coils round the prey and may inject venom. This appendage has given rise to the alternative common name, proboscis worm.

Most nemerteans are marine. One freshwater species, *Prostoma graecense*, has been found in QLD but it was probably introduced. There are several terrestrial nemerteans, belonging to the genus *Geonemertes*, which are to be found under bark, in leaf-litter and in similar damp places. Although they are believed to have evolved from marine nemerteans rather than freshwater ones, they range from sea level to 1 500m. One species, *G. dendyi*, has been introduced into European glass-houses from SW Australia. Many nemerteans are brightly coloured—for example, the vivid orange seashore species, *Gorgonorhynchus repens*, which has a highly branched proboscis.
Further reading: Gibson, R. *Nemerteans.* Hutchinson, London, 1972.

rice *see* agriculture; Gramineae

Richardson, Henry Handel

(1870-1946) Novelist. This was the pen-name of Ethel Florence Lindesay Robertson, the daughter of an Irishman who migrated to VIC in the early 1850s, lived for a time in BALLA-RAT, practised medicine in Melbourne and died in 1879 after several years of mental illness. Educated at the Presbyterian Ladies' College, Melbourne and at the Leipzig Conservatory, in 1895 she married John George

Robertson, whom she had met in Leipzig and who later became first Professor of German Literature at the University of London. Abandoning her original hope of becoming a concert pianist, she turned to literature and in 1908 published *Maurice Guest*, a novel based on her life in Leipzig. Two years later she published *The Getting of Wisdom*, based on her school-days in Melbourne. She then began work on a trilogy, under the general title of *The Fortunes of Richard Mahony*, which was to a large extent based on the career of her father. The three volumes, *Australia Felix*, *The Way Home* and *Ultima Thule* appeared between 1917 and 1929, and it was only after publication of the last that the power of the whole work was appreciated by the critics. The acclaim which she then received placed her firmly in the front rank of Australian novelists. Her later writings included a volume of short stories, *The End of Childhood* (1934), and a novel based on the life of Cosima Lizst, *The Young Cosima* (1939).
Further reading: Kramer, L. *Henry Handel Richardson.* Oxford University Press, Melbourne, 1967; Elliott, W.D. *Henry Handel Richardson.* Angus & Robertson, London, 1977.

Richea *see* Epacridaceae

Richmond NSW (combined population of Richmond, North Richmond and WINDSOR 17 952 in 1981) This town is situated in the HAWKESBURY RIVER district 64km NW of Sydney. This section of the Hawkesbury was settled as farming land during the last decade of the 18th century and the area still produces vegetables and citrus fruits for the Sydney metropolitan market. Richmond was one of five towns established in this region by Governor Lachland MACQUARIE after he inspected the farming settlements in 1810. He appreciated the problems which the farmers faced when the river flooded and the lower areas were inundated, as still occasionally happens accordingly; his five towns (Windsor, Richmond, Pitt Town, Castlereagh and Wilberforce) were sited on higher ground to provide storage places for crops and a retreat for settlers during floods. Richmond is situated within a semi-circular loop of the Hawkesbury River, 22m above sea level on a terrace ridge beyond the alluvial river flats. Some of the residents of the town are now daily commuters to Sydney, while others are employed in local food processing and textile factories, offices and shops; an agricultural college is located on the S fringe of the town and an air force base to the NE.

Richmond TAS (population 587 in 1981) This small historic town is located some 28km by road NE of Hobart. Shortly after Lieutenant BOWEN established his first settlement in TAS in 1803, he explored the Richmond district and found coal there; the area became known as the Coal River district and this name for the river is still retained. A freestone bridge across it, built in 1823, is claimed as the oldest

Richmond stone arch bridge, TAS

extant bridge in Australia. Many buildings in the town have been classified by the National Trust (TAS) for preservation, including several hotels (Richmond Arms, Star and Garter), churches (St Luke's, St John's and the Congregational), municipal buildings (the courthouse and the town hall), and numerous cottages and colonial houses dating from the 1820s and 1830s. The surrounding rural district is rich farming and grazing country, particularly noted for fat lamb production.
Further reading: Woodberry, J. *Historic Richmond Sketchbook.* Rigby, Adelaide, 1977.

Richmond River NSW A river on the NORTH COAST, the Richmond is located between CLARENCE RIVER valley to the S and the TWEED RIVER valley to the N. It rises in the McPHERSON RANGE on the QLD border and flows first in a S direction, then E past CASINO, to reach the sea at BALLINA, thus covering a course of some 260km. Much of the upland headwater country, where the river and its tributaries rise, is rugged, heavily forested and is important for timber-getting and sawmilling. Lower downstream, the valley widens and the broad alluvial plains provide good grazing and farming land, producing beef and dairy cattle and crops of maize, sorghum, bananas and sugar cane. There is a sugar mill at Broadwater on the lower section of the river. The largest city of the North Coast region, LISMORE is situated on the river, 28km by road inland from the estuary. Other urban centres are Casino, Ballina and Kyogle. The Pacific Highway skirts the E section of the Richmond Valley on a general N-S route, while the Bruxner Highway crosses it from Ballina in the E, through Lismore and Casino, up the escarpment of the NEW ENGLAND Plateau to TENTERFIELD. The main N railway comes to Casino (805km by rail from Sydney), where there is a junction, with a branch line going E through Lismore and the main line N passing through Kyogle.

High rainfalls occur along the coast but the amount received declines inland—Broadwater has an annual average of 1 459mm, Lismore 1 349mm and Casino 1 107mm. Summer and early autumn are the times of highest rainfall, when flooding of the lowlands and some urban centres can occur. On Iron Pot Creek, one of the headwater tributaries, at a site 32km W of Kyogle, is the Toonumber Dam, completed in 1971; although it has a comparatively small storage capacity (11 000ML) it is important in stabilising the flow and conserving the waters of the Richmond. The coastal zone is a popular tourist region, with good surfing beaches and opportunities for fishing and aquatic sports.

Pineapple farming in the lower Richmond Valley NSW

Among the better-known resort centres are Evan's Head, Ballina, Lennox Head and BYRON BAY. The Broadwater National Park (3 062ha) stretches 7km along the coastal dunes and beaches N of Evan's Head. The Tucki Tucki nature reserve, 16km S of Lismore, is a natural habitat for koala bears. In 1958, residents of the Tucki district, alarmed at the decline in koala food trees, formed a committee dedicated to preserving the much depleted local koala population. Along a basalt-ridge in the area, they planted areas of suitable trees, including the forest red gum, and in 1963 4ha of this planted area became the nature reserve, where the bears are being studied, as part of an overall programme to conserve koalas in NSW.

Ridley, John

Ridley, John (1806-87) Pioneer miller and inventor. Ridley was born near Sunderland in the County of Durham, England. In 1839 he emigrated with his wife and two children to SA, where he set himself up as a miller. In the summer of 1842-43 there was a particularly good harvest, but a scarcity of labourers to reap it, a situation which moved the Corn Exchange Committee to offer a reward for the best harvesting machine submitted to it. The contest was won by Ridley, who entered a stripping machine, in which combs caught the ears while revolving beaters knocked them into a box. This machine proved so popular that by the 1860s there were said to be over 30 000 of its type throughout Australia.

Claims were made that Ridley's design had actually been invented by another SA settler, John Wrathall Bull, but Ridley maintained that he had based it on a description in *An Encyclopaedia of Agriculture*, by J.C. Loudon, of a machine said to have been used by the ancient Gauls. In any case, even if Bull conceived the basic idea first, Ridley was certainly the first to apply it to a working machine. He made practically no profit from it and refused to patent it, regarding it as his gift to the colony where he had grown wealthy from his mill, from shares in the BURRA copper mine and from dealings in property. In 1853 he returned to England, where during the remaining years of his life he devoted himself mainly to matters of religion.
Further reading: Ridley, A.E. *A Backward Glance: The Story of John Ridley.* J. Clarke & Co., London, 1904.

riflebirds see birds of paradise

ringer This is a colloquial name for the fastest shearer in a shearing shed.

ringtails see possums, etc.

Risdon Cove

Risdon Cove TAS Located on the E shore of the DERWENT RIVER, 8km upstream from Hobart, Risdon Cove was the site of the first British settlement in VAN DIEMEN'S LAND in 1803. It was subsequently abandoned when the settlement was moved downstream and across the river to Sullivan's Cove (now the location of Hobart's port facilities) on the W shore. Today, Risdon Cove is a wooded area, while Risdon Vale is an E suburb of Hobart, inland from the river foreshores. Across the Derwent from the cove is the Electrolytic Zinc Co.'s giant Risdon industrial complex at GLENORCHY.

Riverina

Riverina NSW This name is used for a region located in the SW of the State, bounded on the N and NW by the LACHLAN RIVER and on the S by the MURRAY RIVER. The E boundary is rather ill-defined, but traditionally the E limits of the Riverina are in a stretch of countryside broadly set by a N-S zone linking CONDOBOLIN, TEMORA, JUNEE, WAGGA WAGGA and ALBURY. The MURRUMBIDGEE RIVER flows in a general E-W direction across the central part of the region. The landforms in the E section consist of gently rolling hills which rise to a general height of between 200m and 300m above sea level (Junee 301m, Temora 292m and Condobolin 199m); further W these merge into the broad sweeping SW plains of the State with the elevation progressively decreasing (Wagga 186m, GRIFFITH 128m, HAY 94m and BALRANALD 61m). A similar pattern is evident in the rainfall from E to W across the region: higher annual rainfall averages occur in the E (Junee 533mm, Temora 523mm and Wagga 570mm); these decline towards the W (Griffith 411mm, Hay 360mm and Balranald 317mm). The rural land use is a reflection of this changing physical environment: in the E, wheat growing dominates but moving W, sheep grazing becomes increasingly important until, in the far W of the region, wool production is the basis of the economy. However, this simple

Sheep grazing lands of the Riverina NSW

pattern of rural change from E to W has been much modified by the use of irrigation; the MURRUMBIDGEE IRRIGATION AREAS in the central Riverina are the most extensive development, producing citrus, wine-grapes and other fruits, fat lambs, rice and other cereal crops. There are many other irrigation districts in the region providing water for livestock and domestic use.

The two largest urban centres in the Riverina are Wagga Wagga and Albury; other important commercial and service centres are Griffith, DENILIQUIN, LEETON, NARRANDERA, Temora, Junee, Condobolin and Hay. The Hume Highway on a SW-NE route skirts to E edge of the region; the Olympic Way and the Newell and Cobb Highways cross it on N-S routes; and the Lachlan Valley Way and the Mid-Western, Sturt and Riverina Highways traverse it on E-W routes. A network of railways from the NSW system serves the region and the VIC railway extends across the Murray at ECHUCA with two lines reaching Deniliquin and Balranald (306km and 438km respectively from Melbourne).

Rivett, Sir Albert Cherbury David

Rivett, Sir Albert Cherbury David (1885-1961) Science administrator. David Rivett was a son of a Congregationalist minister who had a large family and slender means. A series of scholarships paid for his education, culminating in a Rhodes Scholarship to Oxford. Rivett soon established a sound reputation as a chemist and lecturer and in 1924 he was appointed to the Chair of Chemistry at the University of Melbourne. In 1927 he was asked by the Prime Minister, Stanley BRUCE, to become the first executive officer of the fledgling Council for Scientific and Industrial Research. The rest of his working life was dedicated to building up what later became the COMMONWEALTH SCIENTIFIC AND INDUSTRIAL RESEARCH ORGANIZATION (CSIRO), one of the world's great scientific institutions.

Although Rivett's association with the CSIRO ended in 1949, it remains in many ways his creation. He fought to establish the most favourable conditions for scientific research, free from bureaucratic interference. Having found the best man to do a particular piece of work, he gave him whatever help was needed and then left him to complete the task, firmly believing that such a course brought forth the best results in the shortest time. In his later years Rivett was involved in the

Ridley's stripper

founding of the Australian National University and the Australian Academy of Science. In an obituary in the science journal *Nature* a former colleague said that Rivett 'had contributed perhaps more than any other to the present healthy state of Australian science'.

roads *see* transport

Robe SA (population 590 in 1981) A small township on the SE coast of the State, Robe is 340km by road SE of Adelaide. It was an important port for wool shipment in the latter half of the 19th century, but its trading activities were eclipsed by the development of road and rail transport. It is now a quiet seaside resort with a historical atmosphere and many buildings dating from its heyday; the National Trust (SA) has listed 14 of these buildings. The town was named after Frederick Holt Robe, the fourth Governor of SA.

Robe River WA This small stream in the NW of the State drains into the Indian Ocean between the FORTESCUE RIVER to the N and the ASHBURTON RIVER to the S. A major iron ore mining centre is located upstream in the Mt Enid area, where the small settlement of Pannawonica, 48km E of the Coastal Highway, is the headquarters of the mining operations. The ore is transported by rail to Cape Lambert where there is a pelletising plant and facilities for export loading.

Roberts, Thomas William (1856-1931) Artist. Born in Dorchester, England, Roberts arrived in Melbourne, at the age of 13, with his widowed mother. He attended the National Gallery School, Melbourne, and worked as a photographic assistant in Stewart's Studio, Bourke Street, saving enough money for his journey to Britain in 1881. He studied at the Royal Academy School, London, one of the first painters to go to the UK for this purpose. On his return in 1885 he established artists' camps at Box Hill, Melbourne; the camps lasted until 1888. Later he joined other artists at camps near Eaglemont, overlooking the YARRA (*see* HEIDELBURG SCHOOL), and between 1891 and 1896 helped established another one on Little Sirius Cove, Sydney. He returned periodically to Europe until World War I, during which he served with the RAMC at Wandsworth. He died at Kallista, near Melbourne.

Roberts' work falls into three categories—landscape, portraiture and figure painting. His portraiture after 1891 gained him a wide reputation, and included a commission of £2000 for the immense canvas, painted between 1901 and 1903, of the opening of the first federal Parliament. However, he is remembered mainly for his figure paintings which illustrated scenes of rural life. These paintings reflected the search for a national identity, the disillusionment with urban life during the 1890s and the suffering during times of economic depression. His notable works include *The Bullock Team* (c1893), in the Manly Art Gallery, *Bailed Up* (1895), in the Art Gallery of New South Wales, *The Breakaway* (1890-91), in the Art Gallery of South Australia, *Shearing the Rams* (1890), in the National Gallery of Victoria and *The Splitters* (c1886) in the BALLARAT Fine Art Gallery. His belief that Australia should develop a national school of painting, and that it should be based on a fresh appraisal of nature, was pursued with such tenacity that he was given the nickname of 'Bulldog'.

Robertson, George (1860-1933) Bookseller and publisher. Born in England, he was apprenticed to a bookseller in his youth, but then emigrated, first to New Zealand and in 1882 to Sydney. In 1886 he and D.M. Angus set up in partnership as booksellers, and two years later became publishers also. Angus died in 1900, but nevertheless when the business became a public company in 1907 the name Angus and Robertson Ltd. was used. For many years it was the only important publisher of Australian books, and performed most valuable service in the encouragement of Australian literature.

Robertson, Sir John (1816-91) Land reformer and Premier of NSW. Born near London, he came to Sydney with his parents in 1820. From 1833 to 1835 he travelled in Europe and South America, and on his return joined his father on a property in the HUNTER VALLEY. He later acquired other holdings, including the licence to a grazing property of about 8000ha on the Liverpool Plains. He welcomed Governor BOURKE's move of 1836, which allowed squatters to retain the use of their runs by paying an annual licence fee. However, in spite of the fact that he owned a lot of land, he took a moderate position during the subsequent controversies regarding security of land tenure.

In politics he was a radical, opposed to State aid for religion and supporting adult male suffrage, the secret ballot and equal electorates. Elected to the Legislative Assembly of NSW in 1856, he was Premier five times between 1860 and 1886. His most famous piece of legislation was the Crown Lands Alienation Act of 1861, which was designed to encourage agriculture by giving intending farmers the opportunity to buy sections of the pastoral leases which occupied most of the fertile land in the colony. It permitted the purchase, at £1 an acre, of up to 320 acres (about 130ha) of Crown lands, even if the particular land chosen had not been officially surveyed. Parts of pastoral leases on which improvements had been made were, however, excluded. Initially, the selector paid a quarter of the price; if after three years he had occupied and improved the property, he could obtain freehold title by paying the balance. A second piece of land legislation in the same year, the Occupancy Act, reduced the length of squatters' leases to a maximum of five years, whereas formerly they had been 14 years in unsettled areas and seven years in 'intermediate' areas, where most of the potential agricultural land was. These Acts, although an ambitious attempt to solve the problem of 'unlocking the land', were not very successful for the squatters were ingenious in finding ways to evade them.

Towards the end of his life, Robertson was a strong opponent of federation, partly because of his belief in free trade, but largely through a general fear that the less populous colonies would gain advantage at the expense of NSW, and would even 'filch from us . . . our most valuable territory, which they have ever been eagerly straining to obtain'.

See also land settlement, etc.
Further reading: Baker, D.W.A. 'The origins of Robertson's Land Acts' in *Historical Studies of Australia and New Zealand*. (vol 8, May 1958).

robins In Britain and the USA the name 'robin' is given to red-breasted birds belonging to the family Turdidae, which contains the THRUSHES. In Australia, there are two species of scrub robins which are placed in this family, but neither species has a brightly coloured breast. The 16 other species of robins represented in Australia are placed in the family Muscicapidae (*see* FLYCATCHERS).

Robinson, George Augustus (1788-1866) Protector of Aborigines. Born in London, he worked in early manhood as a bricklayer, and in 1824 emigrated to TAS where, after he had established himself successfully as a builder, his wife and five children joined him. As an active member of the Methodist community he engaged in charitable work among seamen, and from his observations of Aborigines on the waterfront developed a general interest in Aboriginal welfare. In 1829 he accepted a position as a Conciliator of Aborigines. By that time relations between European settlers and the Aborigines had deteriorated to the point where the complete extermination of the latter seemed imminent. Robinson believed that the only hope of preventing this lay in persuading the remaining members of the race to place themselves under government protection. For several years he travelled around TAS, including unexplored country on the W coast, visiting every remaining group. By early 1835 all the survivors—only about 200—had surrendered. At Robinson's suggestion they were subsequently sent to FLINDERS ISLAND in BASS STRAIT, but they failed to prosper there, and in 1876 the last full-blooded member of their race in TAS died. Meanwhile, Robinson had been appointed in 1839 to the position of Chief Protector of Aborigines in the PORT PHILLIP District, but his work there brought no notable success and in 1849 the position was abolished.

Further reading: Plomley, N.J.B. (ed) *Friendly Mission*. Tasmanian Historical Research Association, Hobart, 1966.

Roche, Tony (1945-) Tennis player. He was born in the country town of Tarcutta NSW. A left-handed player of considerable ability, he suffered from a painfully recurrent elbow injury. He rose to international status with wins in the German and French Opens in 1966, and after losses to LAVER in the final of the first Open Wimbledon in 1968 and in the final of the US singles title in 1969, he was clearly heir apparent to Laver's position of number one in the world. During the same period he formed a formidable doubles combination with right-handed NEWCOMBE to win the Wimbledon doubles title in 1965, 1968, 1969 and 1970. But by 1970, when he lost the US singles final to ROSEWALL, tennis elbow began to interfere with his game. He was appointed MBE in 1981.

Rochester VIC (population 2 396 in 1981) This is a small country town located on the Northern Highway, about 30km S of ECHUCA, 65km by road NE of BENDIGO, and 179km by road from Melbourne. It is also on the N rail route to Echuca (which is linked with the NSW railway system), 223km by rail N of Melbourne. The town is situated on the CAMPASPE RIVER, and is a service centre for a rich irrigation district nearby, concentrating on intensive dairying; there is a large milk processing factory in the town. It was originally called Rowechester, after Dr Rowe, one of the pioneer squatters in the district, but in the 1860s this was altered to Rochester, after the English town of that name, because Lands Office officials thought the previous name had been a misspelling.

Rockhampton QLD (population 50 146 in 1981) A major commercial city on the central QLD coast, Rockhampton is located on the FITZROY RIVER about 60km from its mouth. It is on the Bruce Highway, 678km by road NNW of Brisbane and 135km NW of GLADSTONE, with the Capricorn Highway leading W to EMERALD and BARCALDINE, and the Burnett Highway running SW through MOUNT MORGAN and BILOELA. The city is situated on the alluvial flats of the Fitzroy

Valley, at an elevation of only 8m above sea level, between the Berserker Range to the E and N (with Mt Arthur, 607m high, providing a panoramic vista) and the Athelstone Range to the SW. The city was founded in 1855 as a river crossing to serve the pastoral holding Gracemere settled by the Archer brothers, 9km SW of the crossing. The discovery of gold in 1858 at Cannoona, 37km N, brought a rush of fortune-seekers, who used the village site as their staging camp. The PEAK DOWNS mining rush of 1861, the construction of the railway in 1867 across the GREAT DIVIDING RANGE to the W grazing land, and the Mt Morgan gold strike in 1882 all contributed to the growth of the town. It is now the focal point of a productive hinterland of coal and copper mines, cattle and sheep grazing properties, wheat, sorghum and cotton farms, forested hills and timber industries, dairy farms and pineapple plantations. Two of Australia's largest meat processing and exporting factories are located at Rockhampton, as well as two flour mills, a butter factory, a railway workshop, a cotton ginnery and a fruit canning works. The city has a typical tropical climate with warm to hot conditions throughout the year; the average annual rainfall is 858mm, concentrated in the summer months; February is the wettest (179mm average), September is the driest (23mm). PORT ALMA, Rockhampton's harbour, located 34km S of the city on the S side of the Fitzroy estuary, exports rural and mineral produce from the hinterland.

The city is located on the Tropic of Capricorn; a 14m spire at the junction of the Bruce and Capricorn Highways marks the location of the tropic. The Rainbow Fountain in the city's Central Square is a unique attraction, especially at night. A barrage, located 2km upstream from the Fitzroy River bridge, holds freshwater for urban and industrial use, prevents the infusion of tidal saltwater upstream, and provides a venue for aquatic sports. In the

rugged Berserker Range, about 26km N, there are limestone caves, open for inspection. The National Trust (QLD) has listed many buildings in the city for preservation because of their historic and architectural importance; among these are the old School of Arts, the railway roundhouse, St Joseph's Cathedral and several other churches, the post office, the Supreme Court, the Masonic Club, the customs house, several hotels and cottages.

rockhopper *see* penguins

Rockingham WA (population 24 932 in 1981) A satellite town SW of Perth, it is situated on Mangles Bay in COCKBURN SOUND about 40km from the city centre. In the 1840s it was a timber port, named after a ship which had been wrecked in the bay in the 1830s. It is planned to make it one of WA's major ports with facilities for handling the flow of trade associated with the industrial development of the E Rockingham and KWINANA areas.

Rocklands Dam VIC Situated on the GLENELG RIVER in the GRAMPIANS, 14km E of Balmoral township, this reservoir has a capacity of 335 500ML, drains a catchment area of 1 458km², has a wall with a maximum height of 28m, and is the main storage point for the WIMMERA-MALLEE domestic and livestock water supply scheme. The dam was completed in 1953 and took its name from one of the early grazing properties in the area. The construction, and its role in the water scheme, was the first example in VIC of a S-flowing stream being dammed and diverted N via a tunnel.

Rocky Cape TAS This headland on the BASS STRAIT coastline, between SMITHTON and WYNYARD, is included within the Rocky Cape National Park which covers 3 050ha of coastal heath and woodland between the Bass Highway and the N coast. The twin peaks at Rocky Cape, named by George BASS and Matthew FLINDERS in 1798, form a dominant feature of the coastline. The national park includes some of the best Aboriginal archeological sites in TAS and is noted for its array of wild flowers in spring and summer. Wombats, wallabies, possums and echidnas inhabit the park.

rodents Belonging to the family Muridae (order Rodentia), these numerous and cosmopolitan EUTHERIAN MAMMALS (placental mammals) are widely distributed throughout Australia. Many are known from only a few specimens so there is some doubt as to the exact number of existing species in Australia and their classification. Strahan (*see* below) lists 58, including 3 introduced species.

Rodents are gnawing animals with a pair of constantly growing incisors in the upper and lower jaws; these teeth are often yellow in colour. There are no canine teeth. Most rodents are herbivores or scavengers though some will take animal prey when they can. In this article the measurements which appear in parentheses will refer firstly to the combined

Rockhampton Post Office

head and body length and secondly to the tail length.

Australian rodents are divided into four groups; the bush-rats which belong to the cosmopolitan genus *Rattus* (this genus also contains the introduced brown rats and the ship or black rats); the mosaic-tailed rats which are based mainly in New Guinea; the so-called old endemics; and the water rats. The old endemics are peculiar to Australia, having no close relatives elsewhere apart from some that have migrated to New Guinea. They are descendants of the first rodents that colonised Australia.

Superficially, many of the native rodents resemble marsupial mice and other MARSUPIALS of the NATIVE CAT family but they can be distinguished easily by their characteristic teeth, and by the absence of a pouch in the females. However, it is very difficult to distinguish many rodents from each other without first examining the skull and teeth. The relative dimensions of the parts of the body and the disposition of the teats in the females also aid identification. The teats are found on the chest (pectoral), near the armpits, and in the groin (inguinal).

Bush-rats Strahan recognises seven species of the native genus *Rattus*. The southern bush-rat, *R. fuscipes* (11cm to 19cm; tail the same or a little shorter), includes the forms previously called *R. fuscipes*, *R. assimilis* and *R. greyi*. It is a shy, nocturnal, fluffy, brown-furred rat which lives in burrows during the day. Its normal habitat is in damp, dense vegetation in which it makes tunnel-like runways; it occurs mainly in coastal Australia from north-eastern QLD to SA, and in south-western WA. Its food consists of seeds, green plants, fungi and some insects.

The swamp rat, *R. lutreolus*, is about as large as the southern bush-rat, but the tail is much shorter than the rest of the body. The fur is dark brownish-black, and the feet are black. It is most commonly found at the edge of swamps and waterways where it feeds on plant materials, carrion and the eggs and nestlings of water birds. It occurs in coastal SA, VIC, NSW and QLD, and in TAS.

The long-haired or plague rat, *R. vilosissimus*, is well known for its periodic population explosions. The outbreaks begin in central QLD every five to seven years, and spread into the Centre. This short-tailed species has a head and body length of about 14cm to 22cm. The fur is grey with many longer black hairs. It is widespread in the rainy season but restricted to well-watered areas at other times of the year.

The introduced ship rat or black rat, *R. rattus* (16.5cm to 20.5cm; 18.5cm to 24.5cm), is often found in the wild far from human habitation.

Mosaic-tailed rats Most rats and mice have regular rings of scales around their tails but the mosaic-tailed rats have a distinctive arrangement of their own. There are probably five species in Australia. The giant white-tailed rat, *Uromys caudimaculatus*, is about

Giant white-tailed rat, *Uromys caudimaculatus*

60cm in total length, while the *Melomys* species are only about 23cm. The latter are sometimes pests of sugar cane fields and coconut plantations and are mostly confined to north-eastern QLD.

Old endemics As these rodents have been in Australia the longest they have a very wide distribution. Females belonging to this group drag their suckling young around with them, clinging to the teats.

Species of tree-rat include the golden-backed tree-rat, *Mesembriomys macrurus* (22cm; about 30cm), which is said to be still reasonably common in savanna woodland in north-western WA. It also occurs in tropical closed forest, and will go onto beaches to eat oysters. It takes its name from the golden-brown stripe which runs down its back from the head to the rump. The sides and underparts are brownish-grey and white. The long tail is bushy with a white tip. The rabbit-sized, black-footed tree-rat, *M. gouldii* (25cm to 31cm; 33cm to 41cm), is also found in savanna woodland in the far N.

There are two members of the genus *Conilurus*, the brush-tailed rabbit-rat or tree-rat, *C. penicillatus* (15cm to 20cm; 18cm to 22cm), and the white-footed rabbit-rat or tree-rat, *C. albipes* (23cm to 26cm; 22cm to 24cm). They are solidly built rats with broad, blunt heads and black-tipped tails. The first still exists in the NT but the latter is probably extinct. Tree-rats are agile climbers which often seek refuge in trees but which come to ground to feed.

There were two species of stick-nest or house-building rats on the Australian mainland before the arrival of Europeans, but, possibly as a result of the predation by introduced foxes and cats, they have since disappeared. They were the greater stick-nest rat, *Leporillus conditor* (19cm to 26cm; 14cm to 18cm), and the lesser stick-nest rat or tilliken, *L. apicalis* (17cm to 20cm; 22cm to 24cm). A population of the larger species still exists on

Franklin Is in the NUYTS ARCHIPELAGO. Stick-nest rats were found mainly in the interior, especially on the NULLARBOR PLAIN, where they built nests, often communally, of interwoven twigs which they presumably used as a day-time shelter from the heat; sometimes these were built over rabbit burrows.

The Australian hopping-mice are long-tailed, long-legged mice which leap along like miniature kangaroos. Strahan recognises nine living species, all belonging to the genus *Notomys*. They do not need to drink water but can obtain enough moisture from dry seeds by a process of metabolic breakdown. They conserve water by producing a very concentrated urine and by sheltering during the day in burrows where the temperature is low and the humidity high. Mitchell's hopping mouse, *N. mitchelli* (10cm to 12.5cm; about 15cm), is one of the more widespread species, occurring in sclerophyll woodlands, tree and shrub heaths and grasslands in western NSW, north-western VIC, SA and WA. The colour is greyish or yellowish-brown and the tail is tufted. The spinifex hopping-mouse or dargarwarra, *N. alexis*, of desert complexes, dunes and grasslands in the Centre, is almost as large as *N. mitchelli*. It is sandy-brown and lives in simple burrows up to 1.5m deep with two to six entrance shafts.

The genus *Zyzomys* contains three species of rock-rats which live, as their name suggests, among rocky outcrops in the Centre and the N. Their tails are thick and strongly ringed but easily break off, like those of some lizards. The common rock-rat, *Z. argurus* (9cm to 14cm; tail the same), is about as large as a small ship rat. The fine fur is yellowish-brown above and paler below. This species occurs in the PILBARA region and the Kimberleys of WA, in the NT and in northern QLD. The large rock-rat, *Z. woodwardii* (14cm to 16cm; 11.5cm to 12cm), found in the Kimberleys and in ARNHEM LAND, is larger than a ship rat and has a stocky build; it resembles a guinea-pig. The central or MacDonnell Range rock-rat, *Z. pedunculatus* (11cm to 14cm; tail the same), is a brown, soft-furred species with a tail well covered with hair. It is commonly found in the NT.

The broad-toothed rat, *Mastacomys fuscus* (14.5cm to 17.5cm; 10cm to 13cm), is an alpine species that was once widespread but which now survives in only a few hilly areas in NSW, TAS and VIC. These rats live in wet, boggy places which are often covered by snow during winter; the animals then tunnel beneath the snow. Their diet consists largely of tough grasses and this may account for the well-developed form of the molar teeth.

There are about 22 other species of old endemics that do not show marked specialisations. In general they belong to the genera *Pseudomys* or *Leggadina* and are similar in appearance to the domestic house-mouse, *Mus musculus*, although they are not, of course, closely related. They range in size from that of a small house-mouse to that of a small rat, and they are generally grouped together as the 'native mice'. In most cases very little is known about their biology or their status. Most live in undeveloped regions such as the arid interior, the coastal islands and the W coastal sand heaths.

Water-rats The two Australian species of this group belong to the separate subfamily Hydromyinae. In all there are 10 genera; the genus *Hydromys* (three species) occurs in Australia, New Guinea and New Britain, the genus *Xeromys* (a single and very rare species) is endemic to northern QLD and Arnhem Land, and the other eight genera are confined to New Guinea.

The Australian water-rat, *H. chrysogaster* (23cm to 35cm; tail about the same), is found in Australia, New Guinea and the Aru and Kei Islands. It differs from the other rodents in many ways. Apart from the platypus it is the only Australian non-marine mammal that is well adapted for an aquatic life for it has webs on the hind-feet and a thick, soft fur for which it is still hunted in some States. It is entirely flesh-eating, and lives on fish, freshwater crayfish (yabbies in NSW), mussels and some land animals. It opens mussels by leaving them in the sun's heat until the muscles relax. Water-rats are still common and may be found by freshwater rivers and creeks throughout Australia. On some islands (for example, in BASS STRAIT) they frequent the seashore. Their colouring varies from black in the SW, to golden brown and orange or grey and white in the SE.

Further reading: Ride, W.D.L. *A Guide to the Native Mammals of Australia.* Oxford University Press, Melbourne, 1970; Frith, H.J. *Wildlife Conservation.* Angus & Robertson, Sydney, 1973; Troughton, E. *Furred Animals of Australia.* (9th edn, abridged) Angus & Robertson, Sydney, 1973; Tyler, M.J. (ed) *The Status of Endangered Australasian Wildlife.* Royal Zoological Society of South Australia, Adelaide, 1978; Watts, C.H.S. & Aslin, A.J. *The Rodents of Australia.* Angus & Robertson,

Sydney, 1981; Strahan, R. (ed) *The Australian Museum Complete Book of Australian Mammals.* Angus & Robertson, Sydney, 1983.

rodeos *see* roughriding

Roebourne WA (population 1 688 in 1981) A town in the PILBARA region, on the North-Western Highway 1 591km from Perth and 58km E of DAMPIER, Roebourne is situated on the Harding River, some 13km inland from the Indian Ocean coast. It was settled in 1864 as a service township for the vast pastoral areas of the region and was named after John Septimus Roe, WA's first Surveyor-General. In the 1870s and 1880s it was the centre for the copper and gold miners of the Pilbara, but it declined when a railway was built to its rival, PORT HEDLAND, in 1912. A tramway once connected Roebourne to the port of Cossack, a former pearling centre and now a ghost town, 13km away on the coast. Situated on the coastal plain, at an elevation of 12m, Roebourne experiences a tropical climate, with very high summer temperatures and an average annual rainfall of only 321mm, with a dry period in the spring and early summer. The National Trust (WA) has listed three buildings in the town for preservation: the courthouse (1887), the Anglican church (1895) and the police station (formerly the gaol, 1887).

rollers *see* dollarbird

Roma QLD (population 5 706 in 1981) Located near the junction of the Warrego and Carnarvon Highways, 493km WNW of Brisbane, and on the railway line to CHARLEVILLE, Roma is in a livestock grazing region where there is also some viticulture and wine-making. Situated on Bungil Creek, a tributary

of the BALONNE RIVER, at an elevation of 300m above sea level, it has an average annual rainfall of 593mm, concentrated mainly in the summer. Roma is probably best known for its association with Australia's early search for oil and natural gas. It was here in 1900, when a bore was being drilled for ARTESIAN WATER, that the first discovery of natural gas was made. Though this and several other early strikes proved disappointing, and some speculators lost heavily on their investments, a mini-refinery to process the 'wet' gas was built in 1928. In 1961 Australia's first commercial natural gas project was inaugurated at Roma and in 1969 a 438km-long pipeline was completed to carry the gas to Brisbane; several other gas fields in the region are now connected to this pipeline system.

Roman Catholic Church The Roman Catholic Church has more professed adherents in Australia than any other denomination except for the ANGLICAN CHURCH OF AUSTRALIA. Its members usually refer to themselves as Catholics rather than Roman Catholics, and the census of 1981 showed that 26 per cent of the population were identified under one or the other of these titles.

Historical development In the early years of British settlement the authorities were not favourably disposed towards the Roman Catholic Church, especially as most of its members in Australia were Irish, including many transported for rebellion against English rule. The CASTLE HILL RISING of 1804, which was instigated mainly by Irish convicts, strengthened the official distrust of this Church.

The first priests to reach NSW were Fathers James Dixon, Peter O'Neill and James Harold, all transported in 1800-1801 for alleged complicity in the Irish rebellion of

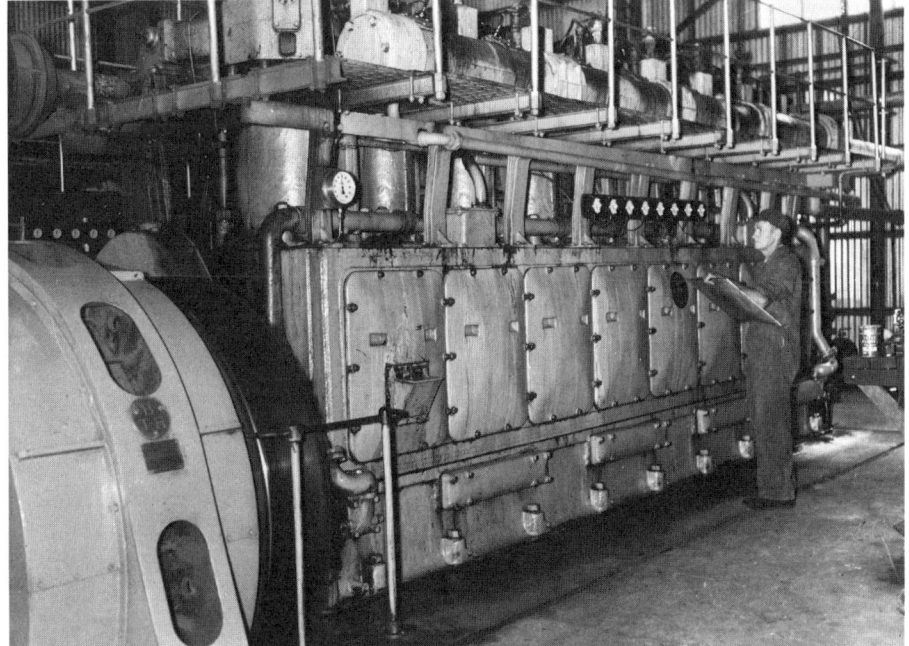

Engine in the Roma Power House run on natural gas

QLD Govt Tourist Bureau

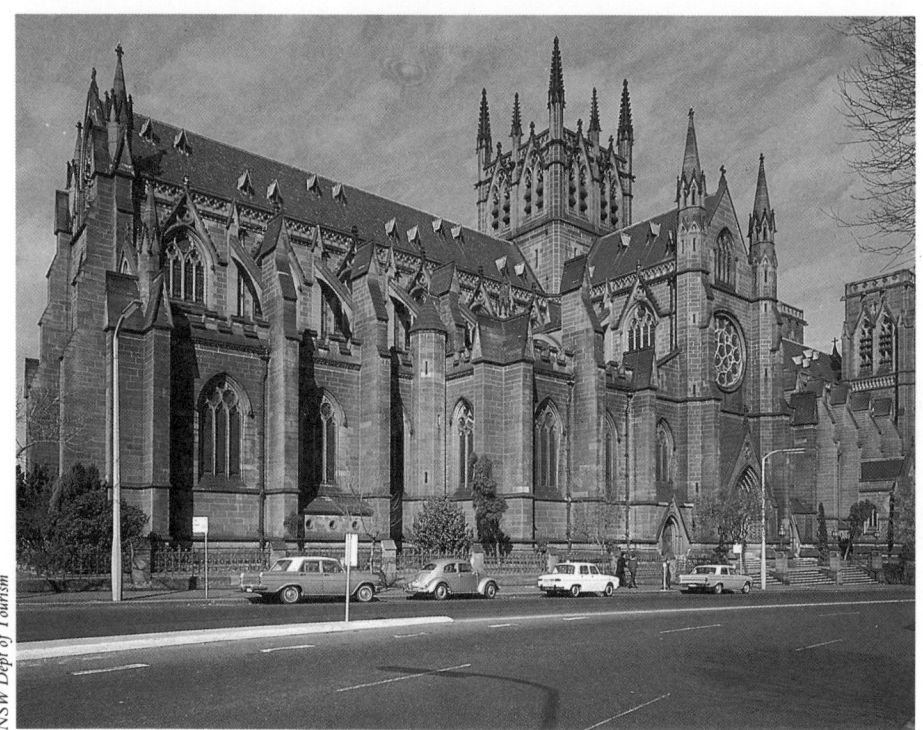

NSW Dept of Tourism

St Mary's Cathedral, Sydney NSW

1798. In 1803 they were given permission to hold religious services, but this right was withdrawn in the following year. In 1817 Father Jeremiah O'Flynn arrived without official approval, and was sent back in 1818 by Governor MACQUARIE. Nevertheless, by that time the official attitude was in favour of Roman Catholics in the colony being allowed to have their own clergy. In 1820 Fathers John Joseph Therry and Phillip Conolly arrived, with the approval of the Colonial Office. Macquarie welcomed them, and later laid the foundation stone of Father Therry's first church, on the site of the present St Mary's Cathedral in Sydney. The new spirit of tolerance was aided by the passing of the Catholic Emancipation Act in Britain in 1829 and by the appointment as Governor of Sir Richard BOURKE, who was of Irish birth and sympathetic to the Roman Catholic Church. By his Church Act of 1836 Bourke provided State aid for all of the main religious denominations—a practice which was continued until 1862 in NSW, and was also applied for various periods in the other colonies.

In the meantime in 1833 W.B. Ullathorne had been appointed as Vicar Apostolic of the Church in Australia, and two years later he had been succeeded by John POLDING, who had the status of a Bishop. In 1842 Polding was given the title of Archbishop of Sydney and Metropolitan of Australia. By the time of his death in 1877 there were 12 Roman Catholic dioceses (areas under the leadership of bishops) in Australia.

Ullathorne and Polding were both Englishmen and members of the Benedictine Order. For some years Polding hoped that English Benedictines would continue to provide clergy

for Australia. Others, however, argued that since most adherents of the Church in Australia were of Irish origin, the only way to keep the faith strong among them was to provide a predominantly Irish clergy. In the 1860s this view was accepted by the Vatican, and for the following half-century or more most Bishops appointed to Australia and most priests recruited for service there were Irish by birth and training. It was not until the 1930s that Australian-born Bishops were first appointed.

From the 1870s until quite recently, an important political question for Roman Catholics was that of State aid for denominational schools. Church leaders denounced the

abolition of such aid at the time when 'free, compulsory and secular' systems of education were introduced, and even without State support continued to maintain a system of primary and secondary schools, to which the great majority of Roman Catholic children went. This imposed a great financial burden on the Church, which was not lightened until government began to revert to policies of State aid in the 1960s (*see* EDUCATION).

Immigration since World War II has caused an increase in the proportion of Roman Catholics in the population, and has also altered the ethnic composition of Church membership. For the first time in Australia's history the majority of Roman Catholic immigrants have come from countries other than Ireland. Although Italians have predominated, the ethnic variety among the newcomers is indicated by the fact that the Mass is now celebrated in Australia in over 20 different languages.

The Church today Today the Church has in Australia 30 ecclesiastical 'territories'. Of these, seven are archdioceses (areas under the direction of Archbishops) and 23 (including the 'national' diocese of St Maron's of Sydney for members of the Maronite rite) are dioceses. There are about 2 400 diocesan priests, with another 1 400 priests being members of religious institutes. The work of the most important Church general welfare organisation, the St Vincent de Paul Society, is carried on mostly by laymen. In general, the place of laymen within the Church has been deeply influenced by the concept of Catholic Action, which was put forward on a worldwide basis in the 1930s to involve laymen in opposition to Communism, in the application of the Church's ideals of social justice, and in charitable and missionary work. An important organisation which has been associated with the Church, although not under its direct control or sponsorship, is the

Holy Trinity Church, New Norcia WA

National Civic Council. It is a successor to the Catholic Social Movement, which was formed in the early 1940s with the specific aim of opposing Communist leadership in trade unions. Charges by the Labor leader, Dr Herbert EVATT, that members of 'the Movement' were interfering unduly in the internal affairs of the Australian Labor Party led in 1955 to the split in that party which culminated in the formation of the DEMOCRATIC LABOR PARTY.

As with other denominations, during the 20th century the Roman Catholic Church has widened greatly the range of its charitable and welfare activities and has become deeply involved in matters pertaining to social justice. It has also continued to maintain a comprehensive system of schools, which provide education for most Roman Catholic children. However, whereas in the past these schools were staffed almost entirely by nuns, brothers and priests, in recent years the religious teaching orders have not been able to maintain this situation, and lay teachers now comprise a high proportion of most school staffs. Moreover, the increasing costs of education and the resumption of State aid for non-government schools have brought about a situation in which most of the cost of the Roman Catholic school system is now met from public funds.
See also religion
Further reading: Fogarty, R. *Catholic Education in Australia, 1806-1950.* (2 vols) Melbourne University Press, Melbourne, 1959; Murtagh, J.G. *Australia: The Catholic Chapter.* (2nd edn) Angus & Robertson, Sydney, 1959; O'Farrell, P. *The Catholic Church in Australia: A Short History, 1788-1967.* Nelson, Melbourne, 1968; *The Catholic Church and Community in Australia.* Nelson, Melbourne, 1977.

Roper River NT With its headwaters in the highland country SE of KATHERINE, the Roper flows for some 400km into Limmen Bight at the SW end of the GULF OF CARPENTARIA. Its lower course forms part of the S boundary of the ARNHEM LAND Aboriginal Reserve. The main tributaries from the S are Birdum Creek (which rises near DALY WATERS), and the Strangways and Hodgson Rivers; those from the N are Flying Fox Creek and the Wilton and Phelp Rivers (all rising in the Arnhem Land highlands). The Stuart Highway and the N Australian railway follow the upper Roper Valley for about 80km, and from Mataranka the Roper Highway leads E to Roper Bar police station 194km away. The river, like all those in the tropical N of the Territory, experiences a high-water flow in the wet summer months, during which time it can spread over vast areas of the adjacent lowlands. The two main settlements are Roper Bar and Ngukurr mission station (population 391 in 1981). There is a prawn fishing base on the S side of the lower estuary. The average annual rainfall at the mission station is 731mm, relatively low for these N parts, owing to its location in the rain-shadow of the highlands.

rorqual *see* dolphins, etc.

Rose, Lionel Edmond (1948-) Boxer. He was born in the country town of WARRAGUL in VIC. An Australian Aboriginal who was brought up in a one-room shanty, Rose was to become only the second Australian boxer ever to have won a world title and he was to fight the richest fight ever staged in Australia. Progressing rapidly up the amateur ladder, he was narrowly beaten in 1964 by a 21-year-old for the Australian Bantamweight title and thereby lost a chance to represent Australia at the Tokyo Olympics. In the same year he turned professional, and during the following two years he lost only two of 20 bouts, culminating on 28 October 1966 with a win over Noel Kunde for the Australian Bantamweight title. In February 1969 his defeat of Fighting Harada in Tokyo for the World Bantamweight title started a revival of interest in boxing in Australia. Rose fought two successful defences of his world title, against Takao Sakurai in 1968 and against Alan Rudkin in 1969, and for this latter fight the purse was $92 000—the largest purse ever fought for in Australia. Rose received $80 000 for his win. On 22 August 1969 he lost his world title to Ruben Olivares. He tried, unsuccessfully, for a comeback in 1975. In 1968 he was made an MBE for services to sport.

Lionel Rose with his world bantamweight trophy

Rose, (Iain) Murray (1939-) Swimmer. Born in the UK, Rose came to Australia in 1941, had his first swimming lessons at the age of five, and by the mid-1950s was the star of Australian men's swimming. In the 1956 Olympic Games held in Melbourne, in which Australia had its best Olympic Games in history, Rose was the outstanding performer of the swimming team, winning three gold medals—the 400m freestyle (setting a new Olympic record), the 1500m freestyle and as a member of the victorious 4 × 200m relay team. At the trials for the 1956

Olympics, he became the first swimmer in history to break 18 minutes for the 1500m distance. He went to America in 1957 to study and returned in 1960 to train for the 1960 Olympics, in which he retained his 400m title and won the silver medal in the 1500m. In the 1962 Commonwealth Games he won two individual and two relay gold medals but he was debarred from the 1964 Tokyo Olympics by the Australian Swimming Union because he was not available when the Olympic trials were being held—he was in America at the time completing his studies. Determined and aggressive as a competitor, Rose felt that swimming was not an end in itself, but a means of preparing a person to meet the bigger challenges of life.

rose, native *see* native rose

Rosebery TAS (population 2 675 in 1981) A mining town in the W coast ranges, Rosebery is situated on the Murchison Highway, 125km S of BURNIE and 55km by road N of QUEENSTOWN in the catchment basin of the PIEMAN RIVER. The discovery of gold in 1893 led to the establishment of the town, named after Lord Rosebery, then Prime Minister of Britain. Although some gold is still obtained, zinc and lead are the basis of the mining activities. Rosebery is very much a 'company town', owing its existence to the Electrolytic Zinc Co. (EZ), which operates a number of mines in the district. From the Hercules mine, near Williamsford, 7km from Rosebery, the ore is carried by an aerial ropeway called 'The Buckets' to the EZ treatment plant. The zinc ore is taken by road to Risdon (N of Hobart) for refining, and the lead is transported by rail to Burnie for export. A popular tourist attraction at Rosebery is a visit to the EZ.

rosellas *see* parrots, etc.

Rosewall, Kenneth Robert (1934-) Tennis player. Born in Sydney, Rosewall is an all-time great of tennis. He was near the top of world tennis for a quarter of a century, from 1953, when he was the youngest person ever to win the Australian and French singles titles, to 1978, when he was ranked number 15 in the world. The year 1953 was also a big one for Rosewall because he teamed up with Lew HOAD to form the 'tennis twins' combination which retained the Davis Cup for Australia for the fourth successive year. Lost in the limbo of professional tennis during his best years (1957-67), he re-emerged when professionals became eligible to enter tournaments for national titles in 1968 to win again championships he had been winning 14 years or more previously. For example, he won the French singles title in 1953 and again in 1968, the US singles title in 1956 and again in 1970 and the Australian singles title in 1955 and again in 1971. In his 40th year, in 1974, he fought through to the finals of both the Wimbledon singles and the US singles titles at a time when prize-money was escalating, the resulting competition for the money and the prestige fierce, and the big tournaments such as these two dominated by strong, superbly fit young players in their early 20s. Possessed of an insatiable will to win and a determination to maintain peak physical fitness, Rosewall has set a record for longevity at the top of world tennis that is unlikely to be bettered.

rosewood *see* forestry

The arch stones of this road bridge in Ross TAS were carved by Daniel Herbert, a convict stoneman

Ross

Ross TAS (population 550 in 1981) Listed as one of TAS's historic towns, this small settlement is located 121km N of Hobart along the Midland Highway, 10km S of CAMPBELL TOWN, and 81km by road S of LAUNCESTON. It is in the MIDLANDS region, at a height of 76m above sea level, on the Macquarie River, a tributary of the South ESK RIVER. Selected as one of the early sites for a town in TAS, it was named by Governor MACQUARIE in 1921 in honour of his close friend in Scotland, H.M. Buchanan, whose family seat was Ross. It became an important military centre, livestock market and coach change on the road between Hobart and Launceston. It is now a small business centre for the sheep and beef cattle grazing properties of the rural district. It has many historic buildings and retains an atmosphere of English charm. The Ross Bridge, built by convict labour and opened in 1836, is a well-known feature with unique carvings. It has been classified by the National Trust (TAS), together with over 20 buildings including churches, inns, the council chambers, the post office, the cemetery and several homes.

Rotary clubs

Rotary clubs These are associations of business and professional men, whose worldwide organisation, Rotary International, now covers nearly 18 000 clubs with a membership of over 800 000 in more than 150 countries. Their general objective is to foster the ideals of service, and in particular to encourage acquaintance as an opportunity for service, high ethical standards in business and the professions, the application of the ideal of service in each member's personal, business and community life, and the advancement of international understanding, peace and goodwill.

The first Rotary club was founded in Chicago in 1905, and the first Australian clubs were formed in Sydney and Melbourne in 1921. Today in Oceania (or the 'down under' area) there are 1 179 clubs—944 in Australia and

Papua New Guinea and 235 in New Zealand and the Pacific Islands. Membership in the whole area is about 49 000, including over 37 000 in Australia and Papua New Guinea. As in other countries, membership of Australian clubs is based on the general principle that there should be only one member from each field of occupational interest. Members raise funds for, and devote their time to, a wide range of charitable and community causes. Through the Rotary Foundation they also provide awards for sending young men and women overseas.

Since 1968 many Rotary clubs have also sponsored Rotoract clubs. These are service clubs for young adults (ages 18 to 28), each of which is expected to work on at least three major service projects annually—one to serve the community, another to promote international understanding and a third to stimulate high ethical standards in business and the professions.

Further reading: Hunt, H. *The Story of Rotary in Australia, 1921-71.* Regional Rotary Institute, Melbourne, 1971.

rotifers

rotifers These aquatic, mainly freshwater, multicellular animals form the small phylum Rotifera; they are no larger than the PROTOZOONS that normally share their habitat. They are called rotifers or wheel animalcules because the circular arrangement of tiny hair-like structures (cilia) around the mouth often resembles a rotating wheel as the cilia beat in a stream of food. Rotifers often temporarily attach themselves by their tails to water plants or pieces of debris as they feed. Like many other tiny, aquatic animals, almost all of the 1 500 species in the world are cosmopolitan. Rotifers are favourite objects with amateur microscopists.

Further reading: Williams, W.D. *Australian Freshwater Life.* Sun Books, Melbourne, 1968.

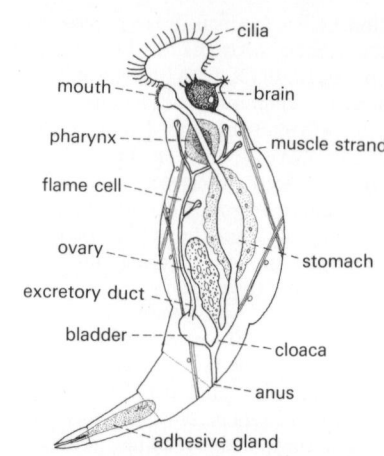

Section through a rotifer, showing some of the internal organs

Rottnest Island

Rottnest Island WA A small island located about 20km NW of FREMANTLE and 32km W of Perth off the Indian Ocean coastline it is composed of limestone, partly covered by sand, with numerous bays and beaches and several saltwater lakes (such as Lake Baghdad and Herschell Lake). It extends E-W for about 11km and N-S for about 5km at its widest point. It is a popular tourist and holiday resort, connected to the mainland by air and boat services. The main settlement is Thompson Bay in the NE. The island was named by the Dutch explorer Willem de Vlamingh in 1696 because of the prevalence on the island of what he thought were rats' nests, but these in fact were made by small wallabies, called quokkas, which still exist there (*see* KANGAROOS AND WALLABIES). The island was first settled by farmers in the 1830s; later it became a prison, mainly for Aborigines, and during World War II it was a military camp.

Rottnest Island WA

Rough Range WA Located near the S end of Exmouth Gulf in the NW of the State, Rough Range was the site of Australia's first discovery of flowing oil. In 1953 West Australian Petroleum Ltd (WAPET) struck oil at a depth of 1219m and caused a wave of excitement and optimism to sweep the nation. However, as a commercial prospect, Rough Range proved a disappointment, as further drilling showed it to be a small field, not worth developing.

A roughrider hangs on grimly

roughriding In the sport of roughriding, horse riders compete with each other in showing their mastery over a wildly bucking horse.

The sport was not run on an organised basis until the 1880s. One of the earliest recorded events was in 1888, when the National Agricultural Society of VIC ran a roughriding competition which was won by Gus Powell. Travelling rodeo shows spread the increasing popularity of roughriding throughout most of Australia; in 1927 a Western carnival held in Adelaide attracted an estimated 50 000 people. The late 1920s—and the 1930s were the hey-days of rodeo. Following the success in 1934 in Melbourne of a Wild West Show which featured top Australian riders as well as a number of visiting cowboys, The Royal Agricultural Society of NSW planned an international rodeo for its 1938 show.

During the 1940s and 1950s interest in rodeo diminished because of the drift of population from country to city and the readily available, alternative forms of entertainment, particularly television, in country areas. In the late 1970s, however, the sport experienced a revival and a major rodeo in MOUNT ISA in 1977 attracted 30 000 people and in September 1978 riders from the USA, Canada, New Zealand and Australia competed in the World Rodeo Titles at the Sydney Showground for prize-money totalling $60 000. In 1980 a competition between Canadian and Australian roughriders was held in conjunction with the Royal Agricul-

tural Show in Sydney and in 1982 a team representing the Australian Bushmen's Carnival Association competed in the North American Rodeo Commission's championships in Denver, Colorado, coming sixth overall.

Of the 200 rodeos and bushmen's carnivals held throughout Australia annually, about 120 are controlled by the Australian Rough-Riders Association. This organisation has 13 000 members and its headquarters are in WARWICK. About a third of these rodeos are accredited as championship points award events, enabling riders to win points toward the annual Australian championship.

Further reading: Ridgway, J. & Lowden, J. *Rodeo at Lang Lang.* Lowden Publishing Co., Kilmore, VIC, 1976.

roundworms This is the common name given to the primitive WORMS comprising the phylum Nematoda, though many nematodes are also known by other common names, such as eelworm and heartworm. Nematodes have a thick, elastic cuticle, and body muscles so arranged that most can wriggle only in one plane, characteristically throwing the body into 'S' shapes. The majority of nematodes are microscopically small; the largest—for example, the human roundworm (*Ascaris* species)—are only a few centimetres long.

Nematodes occur virtually everywhere, from the deepest seas to the sparse soil on the tops of mountains. Many are parasites of plants and animals. One species occurs commonly in natural vinegars; another is said to occur only in sodden beer mats in German beer gardens.

Many species are parasites of livestock (*see* PARASITES, LIVESTOCK) and are of great economic concern to graziers in Australia. One species, the dog heartworm, *Dirofilaria immitis*, is becoming more dangerous in the S of Australia. It has long been so in the N. Several species attack man. Adult filaria worms, for example, block the lymphatic

system, causing gross enlargements of parts of the body (elephantiasis or filariasis). The larval nematodes, which are transmitted by mosquitoes, live in the blood. They are important in Polynesia and in South-East Asia, and the disease has occurred in N. Australia. Pin worms are common in Australian school children, especially when young. The females emerge from the anus at night to lay eggs and the itching is so severe that the child may scratch himself, get eggs on the fingers and later swallow them (and thus re-infest himself).

Hookworms, which cause a severe debilitating disease, are common in the N, especially among Aboriginal children. The infective larvae enter the body through the skin, especially that of the feet. Great efforts are being made to eradicate them in the QLD Aboriginal settlements where the incidence dropped from over 60 per cent in 1960 to less than one per cent in 1970.

Many nematodes are severe plant parasites. The cyst-forming eelworms form cysts on the roots of attacked plants. The cysts are the swollen, dead bodies of the adult females and contain eggs which hatch slowly over a number of years. The cereal-attacking species, *Heterodera avenae*, has long been established in Australia. Rootknot eelworms (*Meloidogyne* species) cause swellings, which contain the ripe, swollen bodies of females, on the roots of a wide range of plants.

Most nematodes are free-living, often in the soil where they feed on organic matter but sometimes attack roots. There they are sometimes attacked by fungi which 'lassoo' them (actually surround them with contracting rings) and extract the body fluids.

See also diseases and epidemics, human; diseases, plant

Further reading: Southey, J.F. (ed) *Plant Nematology: Ministry of Agriculture, Fisheries and Food (Gt. Brit.) Technical Bulletin 7.*

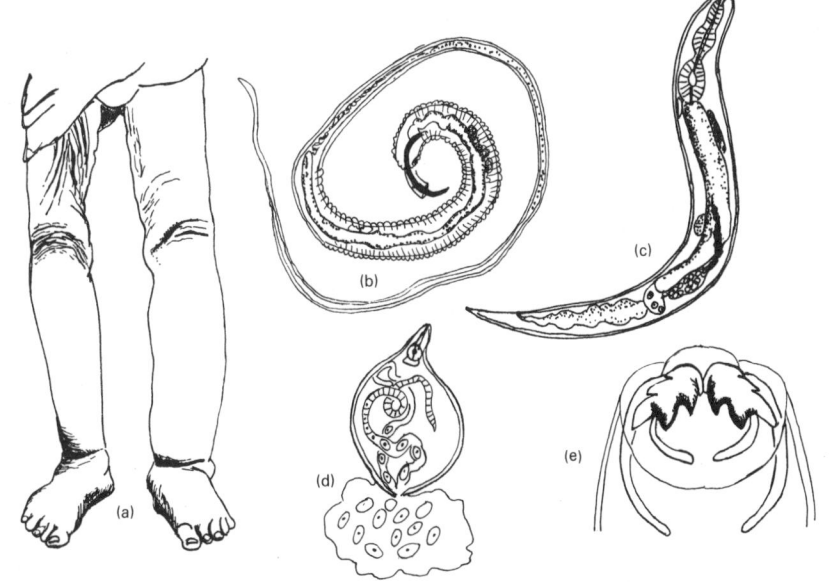

A. Woods

(a) Elephantiasis, a disease caused by roundworms; (b) whipworm; (c) typical soil nematode; (d) female root-knot eelworm and egg-sac; (e) mouth and jaws of a hookworm of dogs

HMSO, London, 1965; Crofton, H.D. *Nematodes*. Hutchinson, London, 1966; Moodie, P.M. *Aboriginal Health*. Australian National University Press, Canberra, 1973.

rowing This sport has had a long and proud history in Australia marked by a prominent period in the latter half of the 19th century and the beginning of the 20th century when it was the nation's major sporting attraction. When Edward Trickett returned from England with the world professional sculling championship in 1876, for example, 25 000 Australians and several brass bands turned out at Circular Quay, Sydney, to welcome him home. And in 1889 when Henry SEARLE died only three months after capturing the world championship, he was accorded a hero's funeral, the funeral cortege proceeding initially through the streets of Melbourne, then by train to Sydney for another procession and finally to his home town of GRAFTON for yet another procession. Even in 1925, an estimated 150 000 turned out to watch the start of the annual Henley-on-YARRA regatta in Melbourne. But since World War II, even though Australia has continued to produce world-class champions, interest has diminished.

History Although the first recorded rowing event was held in Sydney Harbour, in 1818, the sport developed far more rapidly in VIC. By 1869 VIC could boast 10 rowing clubs, whereas the first club in NSW was not founded until 1870. Each colony was eager to pit the skills of their rowers against competitors from other colonies. This led to the start of inter-colonial racing for fours in 1863, for single sculls in 1868, and for eights in 1878. These races were mostly between crews from VIC and NSW, but in 1885 TAS and QLD joined the battle for supremacy in the eights. SA had been willing to race since 1881, but

because of differences over the definition of an amateur—SA included manual labourers in its crews whereas other States excluded manual labourers from holding amateur status—did not compete until 1899. WA had competed for the first time two years earlier.

Sculling The highlight of 19th century rowing was the world championship sculling win by Edward Trickett in 1876. This win is thought to be the first world championship win by an Australian in any sport. Trickett was the first of a long line of world champion Australian scullers. Bill Beach, Peter Kemp, Henry Searle, James Stanbury, George and Charles Towns and Jim Paddon kept the world championship in Australia for most of the late 1800s and early 1900s, but it was Bobby PEARCE who was to excite everyone's imagination. Merv Wood kept up the fine sculling tradition set by Pearce by winning the gold medal at the 1948 Olympics and silver medal in 1952. Then came Stuart MACKENZIE, the silver medallist in the 1956 Olympics, who created more adverse publicity both for himself and for Australia than any previous Australian sculler.

Eights In the eights, traditionally the glamour event in any regatta, Australia has a less illustrious history than in the single sculls. The first international event in which Australia participated was the 1912 Olympics in Stockholm. On the way to the Games the crew won the Grand Challenge Cup at Henley, but failed to fill a place at the Games. The best finish to date in the Olympics was in 1968 when Australia won the silver medal, failing by less than a second to take the gold.

King's Cup Nationally there is fierce competition for the annual King's Cup, an interstate race for eights. The first King's Cup was actually an international race held at Henley in 1919 with the trophy a handsome cup donated by King George V. A crew drawn from the Australian Infantry Forces serving in Europe

at the time won the race for Australia, and brought the cup back with them. In the following year the custodians of the Cup, the Australian War Museum Committee, refused to part with it when the race was again due. Representatives of the winning crew petitioned King George to make the Cup a trophy to be competed for annually among the States of Australia. The King finally acquiesced and the first race was held in 1922, SA winning the inaugural event.

Royal Australian Air Force see defence

Royal Australian Navy see defence

Royal Flying Doctor Service see Flying Doctor Service

Roycroft family
In the world of show-jumping and eventing in Australia, the name of Roycroft has long been synonymous with skilful and competitive horsemanship. William Roycroft and his three sons, Wayne, Barry and Clarke, are well-known and respected riders both in Australia and internationally, and all have represented Australia in Olympic Games equestrian events.

James William Roycroft 'Bill' (1914–) born in VIC and like many other farmers' children of his time he rode his horse to and from school every day. At the age of 15 he competed in his first adult competition and his successes since that time have put him among the top Three Day Event competitors in the world. His first major international success was in 1960 when he was a member of the winning Australian team in the Three Day Trials at the Rome Olympic Games. For Australia to win the event, Roycroft had to ride in the show-jumping event, but on the previous day, in a fall sustained in the cross-country event, he had cracked a collar-bone. With grim determination he rode in the event and Australia won its first ever team gold medal. He captained the Australian equestrian team to the following four Olympics, making him the only Australian to represent his country at five Olympic Games. In 1968 and 1976 his team won bronze medals in the Three Day Trials. In 1969 he was made an OBE for his services to equestrian sport.

Barry Thomas Roycroft (1944-) was born in VIC, and has ridden all his life. Trained by his father, he became a notable show-jumper, competing in his first adult show-jumping competition in 1961 at the Royal Easter Show, Sydney. He has had wins in the VIC Show Jumping championships and placings in the Australian championships. One of his best performances was in 1968 at the Royal Melbourne Show, where he became the first Australian to clear seven feet in the puissance. He represented Australia in show-jumping in the 1976 Olympic Games.

Wayne William Roycroft (1946-) was born in VIC, and became familiar with horses from an early age, riding to and from school and belonging to a pony club. After his intro-

The Australian Light weight Eights crew preparing for the 1979 World Championship

Courtesy of A.I.S. Canberra

duction into adult competition when he was 11 years old, he competed widely in show-jumping and horse trials, culminating with a win in the Australian Show Jumping championships in 1968. Wayne was a member of the Olympic Games teams which won bronze medals in the 1968 and 1976 Olympics in the Three Day Trials.

RSL *see* Returned Services League of Australia

rubber *see* Euphorbiaceae

Rudd, Steele (1868-1935) Author. This was the pen-name under which Arthur Hoey Davis wrote his humorous literary sketches and novels. He was born near TOOWOOMBA in QLD, worked at various jobs in the bush after leaving school at the age of 11, joined the QLD Public Service in 1886, and from 1903 onwards devoted himself to writing. He began publishing sketches in the *Bulletin* in 1895, and in 1899 a number of these were issued in book form as *On Our Selection*. This proved to be immensely popular, and later provided material for a play, a number of films and many radio and television programmes. It was followed by many more volumes, of which *Our New Selection* (1902) and *Back at Our Selection* (1906) were probably the most popular. His stories present an exaggerated humorous picture of the life of small farmers, and were based to some extent on characters and situations in real life, but his 'slapstick' style takes them far beyond the limits of realism. Although his work is considered to lack literary merit, his characters Dad, Dave and Mabel could be considered part of Australian folklore.
Further reading: Drayton, E. *The Life and Times of Steele Rudd*. Lansdowne Press, Melbourne, 1976.

ruff *see* fishes, bony

Rugby There are two forms of Rugby played in Australia—Rugby Union, the amateur game, and Rugby League, the professional game. There are a number of differences between the two codes, the main one being the number of players per side—Rugby Union has 15 players whereas Rugby League has 13.
Rugby Union Rugby takes its name from Rugby School, England, where the game originated in 1823. During the following 50 years Rugby became widely popular and in 1872 21 London teams decided to combine and form the Rugby Union, a purely amateur organisation responsible for laying down rules and bringing uniformity to the game.

Rugby Union was first played in Australia in 1864 at the University of Sydney NSW. Teams of students were formed to play against each other and also to play against crews of visiting British warships. In the developing stages of Rugby Union, when there was no uniformity, with clubs playing to their own rules and no referees, games tended to be rough and disorderly. To help clarify rules and to make the game more orderly, the Southern Rugby

Rugby league football game

NSW Dept of Tourism

Union was formed in 1874, only two years after the formation of the English Union. The Southern Rugby Union followed the rules laid down by the English Union which, though far from perfect, afforded uniform guidelines. It was not until 1890 that referees were given controlling powers.

The first inter-colonial match was held in 1882 between NSW and QLD, with NSW the victors by 28 points to two. The first international match took place in 1888 when a British team visited Australia and convincingly defeated all-comers. Australia performed much better on the first tour to England in 1908-1909, winning 25 games, losing five and drawing two. It was on this tour that the name Wallabies was first used, and since that time the national Rugby Union side has been called the Wallabies. By the early 1900s Rugby Union had become the most important football code in NSW, drawing crowds of 15 000 and more to weekly club matches. In 1907 a Test match against the New Zealand All Blacks attracted 52 000 people to the Sydney Cricket Ground. The same year signalled the beginnings of the decline of Rugby Union with the formation of a professional Rugby code, Rugby League. There had been growing dissatisfaction among players over expenses and their amateur status; to a small breakaway group, consisting of players concerned that they received no compensation for injuries incurred during play, the new professional Rugby League offered a more secure future. These few players formed the foundation of the League. Rugby Union declined rapidly and by the end of World War I only schoolboy Rugby Union was played.

By 1925 Rugby Union was on the rise again but it has never achieved the same level of popularity it held in the early 1900s. International matches, however, often draw very large crowds, and the code is still a very popular school sport. *See also* Appendix 12.
Rugby League In 1907 professional Rugby was being seriously considered in Australia. Matters were brought to a head when a member of the Sydney Rugby Club, Alex Burdon, broke a collar-bone while on tour and was unable to work for 10 weeks, during which time he received no salary and was also obliged to pay his own medical expenses so as not to infringe his amateur status. The injustice of Burdon's situation was discussed among sportsmen at Victor TRUMPER's store. (Trumper was a noted Australian cricketer and his store was a popular meeting place for sportsmen.) At this meeting was James J. Giltinan, a strong supporter of the sport who had been advocating reforms in the Union prior to the meeting. He suggested that an Australian Rugby League be formed from the dissatisfied Rugby Union players and that a meeting be arranged to form a professional game with rules to provide compensation for players.

The first professional matches were played in 1907 between New Zealand's first professional side, which had stopped over in Australia on its way to England, and a team of Australians gathered together with some difficulty. Public feeling was very much against the breakaways and players were reluctant to change to professionalism. Three matches were played under Union rules as no one in Australia or New Zealand at the time knew the professional game as it was being played in England—professional Rugby started in the N of England in 1895. New Zealand won all three matches. The New Zealand team were impressed with the performance of 'Dally' MESSENGER and he accepted an invitation to play for their team on the English tour. The profits from the Australia-New Zealand matches were put towards the formation of the NSW Rugby League. By 1908 the League had assembled eight teams but the hostility and resentment of the Press and the public kept spectators to a minimum at these early League Club competitions. The year 1908 also saw the formation of Rugby League in QLD and shortly thereafter a representative team from QLD visited NSW. Representative football between the two States has been played ever since. Although Rugby League is played in other States of Australia, it is in NSW and QLD that the game has the most popular following.

The first Australian Rugby League tour of England took place in 1908-1909. The team could afford only one-way tickets and optimistically assumed that gate money earned in England would pay their way back to Australia. But unemployment was widespread in England at the time and many League supporters could not afford to pay the admission price to watch the matches. By keeping expenses to a minimum, including on occasions travelling all night to save on hotel bills, the cost of the return tickets was barely covered and the English Northern Union (the professional body) gave each Australian player 10 shillings pocket money for the trip home. At the time the Australian Rugby League side (the Kangaroos) was touring England, the Rugby Union side (the Wallabies) was also touring there. On the return to Australia of both sides, 14 of the Wallaby team changed over from Union to the League. This mass defection led to the decline of Rugby Union and put Rugby League into the ascendancy, with spectators following the outstanding players.

Rugby League continued to grow and prosper with occasional changes being made to the game to make it faster and to make teams more evenly matched, therefore causing more excitement for spectators. Some of the earliest changes made were the elimination of two forwards, reducing a team to 13 players instead of Union's 15, and the replacement of line-outs with scrums.

In NSW there are two controlling bodies for the sport—the New South Wales Rugby League which controls the city competition and the Country Rugby League which controls the game in the country areas of NSW and is affiliated with the New South Wales Rugby League. There are annual contests between country and city teams. In QLD, the Queensland Rugby League administers the game throughout the State. Rugby League is now characterised by rich Sydney clubs attracting players from QLD, NSW country areas and the amateur Union code. The game is so popular, particularly in Sydney, that it has become common for companies to use players to advertise their products and to pay clubs to display prominently the company name on players' jerseys.

International Rugby League During the last few decades Australia has dominated international Rugby League. Between 1954 and 1977 she won the World Cup and similar championship competitions between the world's leading Rugby League countries on

five occasions out of the eight times they were held. Between 1978 and 1983 no such multi-team contests were held, but there were many Test series with other individual countries and Australia lost only one of these. *See also* Appendix 13.

Rum Jungle NT Located 105km by road S of Darwin, W of the Stuart Highway, Rum Jungle was the site of the first large uranium mine in Australia. Discovered in 1949, a township and a processing plant were established, but mining ceased in 1964 when the mine and equipment were sold. The township of BATCHELOR (population 308 in 1981), 6km SE, was built to house the mine workers. Deposits of other ores (silver-lead and copper) have been found in the area and these may lead to future mining developments. The name Rum Jungle is claimed to date from gold-rush days of the 1870s.

Rum Rebellion This name was commonly given to the incident in which Governor BLIGH was deposed by Major George JOHNSTON, commanding officer of the NEW SOUTH WALES CORPS, on 26 January 1808.
Background to the rebellion The background lay in the efforts by Governors HUNTER, KING and Bligh to break down the position of economic privilege attained by the officers of the colony's military force, the New South Wales Corps, including attempts to prevent them from trading in alcoholic spirits. Bligh stirred up even greater hostility among the officers than Hunter and King had done, partly because he was more successful than they had been, but also on account of his uncontrollable temper, immoderate language and general lack of skill in handling people. The man who led the opposition to the governor's policies was John MACARTHUR, who had been an officer of the Corps but had resigned his commission and was devoting himself to farming and commercial activities, particularly to the production of fine wool from Merino sheep.

A series of quarrels between Bligh and Macarthur culminated in a dispute regarding the trading vessel *Parramatta*, of which Macarthur was part-owner and on which a convict had, without the knowledge of the owners escaped to Tahiti. It was customary for shipowners to enter into a bond of £900 to guarantee that they would not assist convicts to escape, and in this case a board consisting of Bligh, Judge-Advocate Richard Atkins and Robert CAMPBELL decided that the bond should be forfeited. Macarthur retaliated by announcing that he had abandoned the ship, and after several days the crew, running out of food, came ashore, thus breaking port regulations. Macarthur was charged with causing this offence, but when served with a warrant refused to submit to arrest and spoke with great contempt of the Governor. Shortly afterwards he was arrested on a second warrant, but granted bail. On 25 January 1808, he appeared before a court consisting of Atkins and six military officers, charged with 'inciting the people to hatred and

contempt of the government, and certain high misdemeanours'. As soon as the court opened, Macarthur demanded that Atkins step down from the bench, claiming that he owed Macarthur money and that a suit was pending between them, that he had been Macarthur's inveterate enemy for years, and that he was a swindler. The six officers, who had dined with Macarthur until late the previous evening, sided with him, but Atkins refused to step down, and the court broke up in confusion. On the following morning Macarthur was arrested on an escape warrant and Bligh sent notes to the six officers of the court stating that they were charged with certain crimes, and must appear before him on the following day.
The rebellion and its aftermath On the afternoon of 26 January Major Johnston came to Sydney from his farm at Annandale and quickly decided to support the officers of the court. He released Macarthur, who then drew up a petition, finally signed by about 150 citizens, claiming that the colony was in a state where 'every man's Property, Liberty and Life is endangered' and urging Johnston'to place Governor Bligh under an arrest and assume Command of the Colony'. Johnston sent a letter to Bligh asking him to resign his authority and submit to arrest; when Bligh refused, soldiers were sent to Government House to carry out the arrest. It was alleged that the Governor was found hiding under a bed, but if this was so it could hardly have been on account of cowardice, for he had on a number of occasions given proof of great physical courage. He claimed that he had hoped to evade his captors and to escape to the HAWKESBURY, where the small farmers, who appreciated his efforts in reducing the officers' privileges, would have supported him.

The sequel to the affair is explained in the biographical entries on Bligh, Johnston and Macarthur. Here it shall be noted simply that after Governor MACQUARIE had taken command at the beginning of 1810, Johnston was court martialled in England and found guilty of mutiny, but was punished only by being dismissed from the Army. Macarthur was forced to remain in England from 1810 to 1817. Bligh was exonerated of conduct justifying his deposition and was later promoted to Vice-Admiral, but was never again placed in a position of active command.
Further reading: Mackaness, G. *The Life of Vice-Admiral William Bligh.* (new edn) Angus & Robertson, Sydney, 1951; Evatt, H.V. *Rum Rebellion.* Angus & Robertson, Cremorne NSW, 1975.

Ruse, James (1760-1837) Pioneer farmer. Born in Launceston, Cornwall, he became a farmer but in 1782 was sentenced to transportation for seven years for breaking and entering. The first five years of his sentence were spent mainly in prison hulks, and then he was sent to NSW on the FIRST FLEET. His sentence expired in July 1789 and a few months later Governor PHILLIP, impressed both by his skill as a farmer and his good behaviour, provided him with land on which a hut had been built,

Courtesy of A.I.S. Canberra

Experiment Farm Cottage in Ruse St, Parramatta, built in 1799, is the second oldest building in Australia

and with farm implements and supplies, promising that if he worked well he would be given a grant of 30 acres (about 12ha). Although he had no plough at this stage, and therefore had to cultivate his land with hoe and spade, Ruse worked so successfully that in February 1791 he announced that he could maintain himself. In 1790 he had married a convict woman, Elizabeth Perry, and he continued to draw rations for her and their child until December 1791, but then announced that he needed no more assistance at all from the government. He received a title to his farm in February 1792, this being the first land grant made in the colony. Since Phillip had regarded the whole project as an experiment, undertaken 'in order to know in what time a man might be able to support himself', Ruse's land became known as Experiment Farm. In 1793 he sold it to Surgeon John Harris, who built a residence on it which still stands, and is known as Experiment Farm Cottage. Situated in Ruse Street, PARRAMATTA, it has been restored by the National Trust and is open for inspection by the public. After leaving Experiment Farm, Ruse farmed in the HAWKESBURY RIVER district and near Bankstown. His tombstone, in the churchyard of St John's, CAMPBELLTOWN, bears the inscription:

My Mother Reread Me Tenderley
With Me She Took Much Paines
And When I Arrived In This Coelney
I sowed The Forst Grain And Now
With My Hevenly Father I hope
For Ever To Remain.

Further reading: Tolchard, C. *The Humble Adventurer: The Life and Times of James Ruse.* Lansdowne Press, Melbourne, 1965.

Russell, John Peter (1858-1930) Artist.

Born in Darlinghurst, Sydney, the son of a foundry owner (P.N. Russell & Co.), Russell had a very comfortable upbringing and the assurance of a regular income to follow a career of his choice. That choice was painting. In 1881 he began his studies at the Slade School of Art, London, which he left periodically to go to the Continent. He was introduced to French Impressionism by his Slade teacher, the émigré . Alphonse Legros, and while studying at Comon's Atelier in Paris, he met Van Gogh, with whom a friendship was established. After his marriage to one of Rodin's models, Marianna Matiocco, he built a house at Belle-Île, off the coast of Brittany, in 1887. Here he offered hospitality to many artists, including Monet, whose Belle-Île series were painted whilst there. After the death of Marianna, Russell began to lose his enthusiasm for painting. He left Brittany and lived in italy, Britain and New Zealand before returning to Australia in 1921. He died in Randwick, Sydney; at the time of his death his early oil paintings and later water-colours were unknown to the Australian public, partly because of his self-imposed obscurity.

rusty apple *see* Myrtaceae

Rutaceae This is a dicotyledonous family

of temperate and sub-tropical flowering plants, containing about 100 genera and distributed largely throughout the S hemisphere but being particularly well developed in Australia and Africa. An important genus introduced into Australia includes species of *Citrus*, cultivated commercially in NSW and VIC.

Members of the Rutaceae are shrubs or trees with simple or compound leaves which are oppositely or alternately arranged and dotted with translucent (pellucid) oil glands which impart a strong aroma to the bruised foliage. This latter characteristic is shared by many members of the family MYRTACEAE from which the family Rutaceae may be distinguished by never having woody persistent fruits and by the often unpleasant odours emitted by the foliage in comparison with the

sharp fresh odours of the Myrtaceae. The flowers are regular and bisexual, with four or five sepals which are free or joined at the base or form a cup, and there are an equal number of petals which are also usually free. The stamens either equal the number of the petals, or double them, but are rarely more numerous; they are usually free. The superior ovary is surrounded by a disc and has four to five cavities (locules) with one to two seeds in each loculus; the style is usually simple. The fruit is usually an explosive capsule, a berry, or a capsule which splits at maturity into dry segments.

The genera belonging to this family include some of Australia's loveliest flowering shrubs, prized for their range of flower colour and in some cases for their scent. The *Boronia* genus is outstanding in both respects, with the popular brown species, *B. megastigma*, being among Australia's most prized horticultural introductions in many parts of the world. Delicate shades of pink and rose are contributed by *B. pinnata* and *B. heterophylla* respectively, whilst the Sydney rock rose, *B. serrulata*, forms a small compact shrub with closely pressed rhomboidal leaves and a penetrating fresh lemon scent. Genera such as *Eriostemon* and *Crowea* are prized for their prolific production of starry pink spring flowers. The genus *Correa* includes the salt-tolerant *C. alba*, with silver-grey foliage and white star flowers, and *C. reflexa*, with drooping red bell-shaped flowers. Most of these shrub species, and members of the genera *Phebalium* and *Zieria*, occur in heath and woodland. Closed forest species include a number of broad-leaved small trees, including the genera *Euodia*, *Acronychia* and *Geijera*.

See also Angiospermae; Appendix 5, Flower Structure and Glossary of Botanical Terms
Further reading: see Appendix 6, A Bibliography for Plants.

Rutherglen VIC (population 1 454 in

1981) Situated on the Murray Valley Highway, at an elevation of 167m above sea level, 275km by road and 272km by rail NE of Melbourne, 49km W of WODONGA and 10Km S of the MURRAY RIVER, Rutherglen's prosperity once depended on gold mining, but today it is one of VIC's main vine growing centres. Several of the wineries can be inspected by visitors, including Seppelts, located in the town. A wine festival is held biennially in March. Lake Moodemere, 8km W of the town, is a popular aquatic recreation area; there is an agricultural research station 7km SE of Rutherglen. The town was named in the 1860s after Rutherglen in Scotland.

rye *see* agriculture; Gramineae

S

sailing and yachting Strictly speaking, the terms "sailing" and "yachting" should not be regarded as synonymous. The former should be applied only to keel craft, and not to dinghy sailing craft with centreboards. However the national controlling body, the Australian Yachting Federation, refers to all sail racing under its auspices as "yachting". The sport has become increasingly popular since 1945, and today more than 100 000 people are members of clubs affiliated with the Federation. Many others, who sail for pleasure only, are not included in this figure.

The sport of sailing began in Australia among the crews of visiting ships. The crews of merchantmen, naval vessels, whalers and sealers that regularly called into Australian ports often found recreation in racing one another in the ships' long boats, and they were occasionally joined by settlers. The first recorded regatta in Australia was held on the DERWENT RIVER in TAS in 1827, organised by naval officers. Sydney's first regatta was held four months later, the entrants being manned by officers and crews from two visiting naval vessels. Some privately owned vessels also competed. The year 1827 was an important one in the history of Australian sailing, as it also saw the launching of the first Australian-built yacht designed purely for pleasure sailing. Robert Campbell, a wealthy ship owner, built the craft and named it *The Model*. Until that time yachts had been designed primarily for warfare, transport or for catching whales and seals. It was not until some 28 years later that the first permanent yacht club came into existence. This was the Victoria Yacht Club, formed in 1856 and later renamed the Royal Yacht Club of Victoria. A Sydney club was formed shortly afterwards in 1862. Named the Royal Sydney Yacht Squadron it was the first yachting club outside Britain to bear the royal designation. Yacht squadrons and clubs developed in other States and now most bays and harbours near the major population centres have at least one club.

Sailing vessels fall into distinct categories according to size and design. There is the elite group of keel craft designed principally for offshore racing. There is a second group which includes keel craft designed for inshore racing and pleasure cruising. The third group is the lightweight group and includes centreboard craft small enough to be towed behind a vehicle to an appropriate launching site. Several new classes of sailing craft have been designed by Australians, the most famous being the 18-footers. Eighteen-footer racing is unique in sailing in that it is commercially sponsored with sponsors' names and logos featured prominently on the sails, and crews competing for money prizes as well as trophies. The world championships during the late 1970s and early 1980s were dominated by the boat *Color 7*, sponsored by the Sydney television station ATN Channel 7. Recent years have seen the development of what could be considered a fourth group, including 'surf cats' (light catamarans which can be launched from ocean beaches) and sailboards (which are essentially surfboards fitted with centreboards and free-standing rigs).

Sydney to Hobart Yacht Race This is an annual ocean race with competing boats leaving Sydney on Boxing Day. Until 1945, although ocean races were a regular feature of the Australian yachting scene, there were no annual races. In 1945, an English naval captain, John Illingsworth, suggested to a group of Sydney yachtsmen that a race to Hobart would be more exciting than a Christmas cruise. As a result nine starters set off for Hobart, and Illingsworth, skippering the small boat *Rani*, won line honours and also on handicap. Since then the race has been an annual event and has become the principal ocean race in Australia. Every second year the Sydney–Hobart race forms the final event in the international four-race Southern Cross Cup competition. *See also* Appendix 15.

Admiral's Cup Every two years, the yachting nations of the world each select a team of three yachts to travel to England to contest a series of races. The team which amasses the most points in the series is awarded the Admiral's Cup, which has come to be recognised as the symbol of yachting supremacy. Australia first entered the event in 1965 and took overall second place behind the English team. On Australia's second attempt, in 1967, the yachts *Balandra*, *Mercedes III* and *Caprice of Huon* surprised the world when they won the Cup by a record margin. Australia came in second in 1969 and 1973, and won the Cup again in 1979.

Olympic Games Australian yachtsmen

Australia II in trials off Port Phillip Bay

entered the Olympics for the first time in 1948 but it was not until the 1956 Games that a yachting medal was won. The first gold medal was won in 1964 in the 5.5m class when Bill NORTHAM, then 60 years old, skippered *Barrenjoey* to success. Two gold medals were won at Munich in 1972 with Dave Forbes winning in the Star class and John Cuneo winning in the Dragon class.

Level rating competition Level rating racing was instigated by John Peytel of France in 1965. Yachts of similar size but without handicaps race against one another, allowing yachts to experiment with sail area and hull shape as long as they conform to the 27.5-foot rating, a rating designated One Ton. With the success of this original class, others soon developed—Half Ton, Quarter Ton, Three-Quarter Ton and Two Ton. The level rating system provides exciting racing with all yachts within a class theoretically capable of the same speed. Syd Fischer of Sydney was the first Australian to win an international level rating competition when he won the One Ton Cup in 1971 with the yacht *Stormy Petrel*. The Half Ton class has proved very popular in Australia and the 1975 world championship was won by an Australian crew skippered by Tom Stephenson in *Foxy Lady*.

America's Cup Among the most coveted of all yachting prizes is the America's Cup, an international event for 12m yachts. In 1962 Australia became the fourth nation to challenge the USA for this prestigious trophy, retained by the USA since the inception of the race; the Australian entry was *Gretel*, which was defeated by the American defender *Weatherly* four races to one. Challenges in 1967 (*Dame Pattie*), 1970 (*Gretel II*), 1974 (*Southern Cross*), 1977 (*Australia*) and 1980 (*Australia*) were also unsuccessful. However in 1983, *Australia II*, entered by a syndicate headed by Alan BOND, was victorious.

Women's sailing The first world women's sailing championships were held in England in 1977 and the Australian Yachting Federation sent an official team to compete. The single-handed Laser class was won by Lyndal Coxon, from Sydney; she won the event again in 1978. Another Australian, Vanessa Dudley, was fifth behind Coxon in 1977 and second in 1978, having won in 1974 the Junior World Championship Moth title in Japan. *See also* HARDY, J.G.

Further reading: Ross, B. *The Sailing Australians*. Rigby, Adelaide, 1973; d'Alpuget, L. *Yachting in Australia—Yesterday, Today, Tomorrow*. Hutchinson, Sydney, 1980.

St Arnaud VIC (population 2 720 in 1981) This country town is located in the WIMMERA district, on the Sunraysia Highway and on the railway line to MILDURA, 225km by rail NW of Melbourne. At an elevation of 239m above sea level, it has an average annual rainfall of 504mm and is the service and business centre for a productive farming and grazing district. The town has a range of secondary industries including a flour mill, a stock feed factory, a brick works and a farm machinery plant.

Teddington Reservoir, 26km S of the town, is a popular picnic spot where there is trout fishing. In the 1850s, the town became an important gold mining centre and was named after Marshall Jaques Leroy de St Arnaud, who commanded French troops in the Crimean War.

St George QLD (population 2 204 in 1981) Located on the BALONNE RIVER, at the junction of the Moonie, Carnarvon and Balonne Highways, 523km by road W of Brisbane in the SE of the State, it is a commercial and service town for an irrigation area growing cotton, grain and fruits, and raising sheep. At an elevation of 201m above sea level, to the W of the DARLING DOWNS, it has an average annual rainfall of 510mm, falling mainly in the summer, with a dry period in winter and spring. The Beadmore Dam, located at the confluence of the Balonne and Maranoa Rivers about 20km upstream from St George, was completed in 1972 and has a storage capacity of 101 000ML. It is the main reservoir for the St George irrigation area and along with two weirs (Moolabah and Buckingham) controls river flow and provides a regulated supply for the irrigated lands. The town takes its name from the fact that the explorer Sir Thomas MITCHELL crossed the Balonne near the present town site on St George's Day (23 April) in 1846.

St John Ambulance *see* Order of St John

St John's wort A troublesome perennial WEED, St John's wort, *Hypericum perforatum* (family Hypericaceae), was first introduced from Europe into the OVENS RIVER valley as a medicinal plant. The yellow flowers have a starry appearance. The leaves are dotted with glands containing hypericin; the hypericin sensitises to strong sunlight light-coloured livestock which eat the plant. St John's wort occurs in VIC, SA and NSW, and is partly controlled by leaf beetles.
See also biological control

St Vincent Gulf SA A shallow triangular-shaped coastal inlet, extending 145km N-S and 60km wide at its S entrance, it is located between YORKE PENINSULA on the W and the coastal plains adjacent to the MOUNT LOFTY RANGES on the E. The gulf was formed in relatively recent geological times when the region was fractured by a series of faults and a crustal block between two of these fault lines subsided. The inlet was named by the explorer Matthew FLINDERS in 1802 in honour of a British Admiral, the Earl St Vincent.

salamanders *see* amphibians

Sale VIC (population 12 968 in 1981) Located at the junction of the Princes and South Gippsland Highways 214km by road E of Melbourne, on the THOMSON RIVER W of LAKE WELLINGTON, it is the administrative centre for the BASS STRAIT oil and gas fields.

At an elevation of only 5m above sea level, situated on the alluvial flats of the lake-studded coastal plain on the S edge of the MACALISTER RIVER irrigation area, it experiences a mild climate with warm to hot summers and cool winters. The average annual rainfall is 629mm, spread throughout the year. Originally called Flooding Creek, the city was named Sale in 1853 after a British Army general, Sir Henry Sale, who was killed in India. It became a borough in 1863, a town in 1924 and a city in 1950; in recent years it has experienced rapid growth because of the offshore oil and gas developments. Lake Guthridge, near the city centre, is an attractive garden area and wildlife sanctuary.

salmon *see* fisheries; fishes, bony; fishes, freshwater

salps *see* sea squirts, etc.

saltbush *see* Chenopodiaceae

Salvation Army In 1865 William Booth, a former Methodist preacher, opened his Christian Mission in the East End of London, providing help for the desperately poor by such means as the setting up of 'soup kitchens' and night shelters, and striving to bring about a religious revival by means of street marches and meetings featuring the singing of hymns to the accompaniment of band music. Although he did not at first intend to set up a new Church, by 1878 his followers had become organised as the Salvation Army. In 1881 the first corps of this organisation was set up in Adelaide. A year later Major and Mrs James Barker were sent to extend the movement, and by 1891 there were Army corps in all the Australian colonies and New Zealand.

From 1895 to 1901 Herbert Booth (the youngest son of William Booth) was Commandant in Australia. He brought about a great extension of welfare work and founded a training college in Melbourne, but was accused by some of tending to neglect the spiritual side of the Army's activities. In 1909 New Zealand was separated from the Australian Command, and in 1921 a division was made between the Eastern Command (QLD and NSW) and Southern Command (the other four States).

In the 1981 census some 71 000 Australians were identified as belonging to the Salvation Army. However, the welfare work of the Army has continued to be greater in scale than this figure alone would indicate. Traditional activities, such as general family welfare, the maintenance of hostels for the destitute, children's homes and convalescent homes are still important, but new social needs have led the Army, like other religious denominations, into areas such as the running of alcohol and drug rehabilitation centres and 'senior citizens' housing projects.

salvation Jane *see* biological control; weeds

samphire *see* Chenopodiaceae

sand dollars *see* sea urchins

sand snail *see* gastropods

sand spurry *see* Caryopyllaceae

sandalwoods These small trees belong to the genus *Santalum* (family Santalaceae). They have a light timber, with a fragrant odour, which yields an oil and is used for carving and for making incense. One example is the fragrant sandalwood, *S. spicatum*, of SA and WA. Sandalwoods are root parasites, at least when young.
See also parasitic plants

sand-hoppers *see* crustaceans

sandpipers *see* waders

Santa Gertrudis *see* beef cattle industry

Santalaceae *see* parasitic plants

Santamaria, Bartholomew Augustine (1915-) Leading Roman Catholic layman, writer and publicist. Born in Brunswick, Melbourne, he graduated in arts (1934) and law (1935) from the University of Melbourne, and subsequently took the MA degree from the same university. He has occupied several prominent positions, including: secretary of the National Catholic Rural Movement (1939-61); assistant director (1937-47) then director (1947-54) of Catholic Action; president of the Catholic Social Movement (1943-57); and, since 1957, president of the National Civic Council. He was one of the leading figures involved in the split within the AUSTRALIAN LABOR PARTY which led to the foundation of the DEMOCRATIC LABOR PARTY. His publications include: *The Price of Freedom* (1964), *Point of View* (1969), *The Defence of Australia* (1970), *Philosophies in Collision* (1973), *Archbishop Mannix: His Contribution to the Art of Public Leadership in Australia* (1978) and *Against the Tide* (1981).

Santry, Michel Santry (1934-) Artist, sculptor and designer. Born in Sydney, his artistic ability was developed under the guidance of both his artist-parents, as well as by intermittent studies at East Sydney Technical College. In the 1950s and early 1960s he worked as an architectural draughtsman, television designer and scenic artist for stage shows. Since 1957 he has completed over 200 artistic commissions, which take the form of sculptures, murals, mosaics, tapestries, stained glass, kinetic works and fountains, located in art centres, public buildings, a university, churches and shopping centres. Among the best known and most outstanding of these are: the stainless steel sculpture suspended over the stairs in the Barbican Arts Centre, London; the main curtain, in black mirrored stainless steel, at the Royal Shakespeare Theatre, London; a coloured stainless steel relief mural in the Landeszentralbank Head Office, Hamburg; and a suspended sculpture of brass, polished steel and acrylic plates, entitled 'Arcturus', in the entrance foyer to the Melbourne Concert Hall of the Victorian Arts Centre.

saprophytic plants The term 'saprophytic' is applied to plants which are entirely or partly dependent on dead or decaying matter for their food. Those that depend entirely on dead organic material possess no chlorophyll themselves; species that require only a few nutrients derived from dead organic matter manufacture their basic requirements through photosynthesis.

Saprophytic Australian plants come from a number of families, including ORCHIDACEAE.

Some orchids, such as the potato orchid (*Gastrodia* species) and the hyacinth orchid (*Dipodium* species), develop leafless flowering stalks annually and are dependent entirely on organic matter in the soil for food; many orchids which grow on other plants (epiphytic) must live in association with a fungus on the roots (mycorrhiza) in order to survive. Some plants, such as sundews (*Drosera* species) and the pitcher plant, *Cephalotus follicularis*, are dependent on insects, trapped by sticky hairs or pit traps, as a source of nitrogen which is generally of low availability in the swampy soils which they frequent. The trapped insects are digested by enzymes secreted by the plants, and the raw materials are then absorbed.

Michel Santry standing under his gold and brushed stainless steel octahedron-shaped sculpture suspended from the skylight in the foyer of the Barbican Centre, London

Many plants, while not saprophytic or parasitic, live under natural conditions in a close association with mycorrhizal fungi which enable them to absorb water and salts more efficiently (for example, *Eucalyptus*, family MYRTACEAE) or harbour nitrogen-fixing bacteria in special nodules on their roots (for example, species in the families MIMOSACEAE, and PAPILIONACEAE). These plants can be grown without their accompanying organisms, as can sundews without insects, provided an adequate range of nutrients is easily available to the roots.
Further reading: see Appendix 6, A Bibliography for Plants.

Sarina QLD (population 2 815 in 1981) A town in the central coastal region of the State, Sarina is 1037km by road N of Brisbane, and 36km S of MACKAY on the Bruce Highway. It is situated on Plane Creek, about 6km upstream from the estuary on Sarina Inlet. Sugar cane growing is the principal farming activity of the region; there is a sugar mill nearby and a distillery producing industrial alcohol. There are several beach resorts along the adjacent coastal stretch. To the NE of the town is Hay Point, the coal-export loading complex, serving the extensive mining developments located inland at GOONYELLA and PEAK DOWNS.

sarsaparilla *see* Liliaceae

sassafras This is the name of an American tree and is applied to several Australian trees including *Doryophora sassafras* (family Monimiaceae), a widespread rainforest tree of E Australia. All parts of the tree are aromatic. Oliver's sassafras, *Cinnamomum oliveri* (family Lauraceae), is related to the introduced camphor laurel, *C. camphora*, from China and Japan.
See also parasitic plants

satanellus *see* native cats, etc.

satinay *see* forestry

satinwood *see* Christmas bush

Savage River TAS This is the name of a tributary of the PIEMAN RIVER and of a township (population 1 141 in 1981) in the rugged NW region of the State, located on a branch road off the Waratah Highway 115km by road SW of BURNIE. The township houses workers on the Savage River iron ore project. Extensive deposits of iron ore were discovered in the area many years ago but only recently has an economical method of extracting and treating the ore been devised. The project has been financed by a consortium of American, Japanese and Australian interests, and the operation is unique in that the ore is formed into a slurry and pumped through an 85km-long pipeline to PORT LATTA on the NW coast. Here the ore is pelletised for bulk shipment overseas. So vast is the extent of the ore deposits in this area that plans are

being pursued to establish an integrated steel industry in co-operation with the State government. The township is located at an elevation of 352m above sea level, and has a high average annual rainfall of 1997mm; winter is the season of highest falls (July average, 259mm), yet even in summer months considerable falls occur (January 92mm and February, the lowest, 83mm).

Savery, Henry (1791-1842) Novelist. Born in England, he was transported for forgery and reached Hobart in 1825. His *Quintus Servinton* (1830-31) is of historical significance as it was the first novel to be written and published in Australia. He is also generally credited with the writing of *The Hermit in Van Diemen's Land* (1829), which is a collection of descriptive and narrative articles written originally for the *Colonial Times*; however, there has been some argument about the authorship of this work. Savery was convicted of a fresh offence in 1840, and died in the penal settlement of PORT ARTHUR two years later.

sawfish *see* sharks, etc.

sawflies *see* ants, etc.

Sawtell NSW (population 5 963 in 1981) A small town and holiday resort on the NORTH COAST of the State, 576km N of Sydney, and 10km by road S of COFFS HARBOUR, it is a station on the North Coast railway route. It is a popular year-round holiday centre, with fishing, swimming, boating and other aquatic sports. The town and coastal region has grown rapidly in recent decades. The town was named after one of the early landholders, Oswald Sawtell.

scabies mite *see* parasites, human

scale insects *see* bugs

scale worms *see* annelids

scallops *see* bivalve molluscs

scaly-foots *see* lizards

Scaphopoda *see* tusk shells

schools of the air *see* Education of children in remote areas *under* education

Scone NSW (population 3 950 in 1981) A country town located in the upper HUNTER RIVER valley, it is some 300km N of Sydney on the New England Highway, and 130km by road inland from NEWCASTLE. It is on the railway route through the Hunter Valley to the N tablelands. At an elevation of 201m above sea level, it receives an average yearly rainfall of 1134mm. The town is a service and livestock selling centre for a rich rural district, raising beef and dairy cattle, sheep and pigs; there are several thoroughbred horse and

cattle studs in the area. The GLENBAWN DAM on the Hunter is located 14km SE of Scone. The town was named by a Scottish pioneer settler after Scone in Scotland.

scorpion flies These INSECTS belong to the endopterygote order, Mecoptera. There are about 24 species in Australia, and the individuals of some species are very common. Usually found in damp habitats, scorpion flies are rather fragile, long-legged insects with two pairs of net-veined wings. The head is long (in extreme cases it has a horse-like appearance) and carries large, compound eyes and long, filiform, many-segmented antennae (short in a few species). The common name is derived from the fact that the males of certain groups have a swollen tip to the abdomen. The larvae resemble the caterpillars of moths (*see* BUTTERFLIES, etc.) but they have compound eyes. The larvae pupate in an earthen cell below the surface of the soil.

The larvae are carnivores which feed on other insects, as do the adult males. The males catch prey while on the wing or on vegetation but the females apparently do not take living prey. Both adult sexes also feed on nectar.

There are two suborders, Protomecoptera and Eumecoptera. The former is represented in Australia by only two specimens of *Austromerope poultoni* found in the WA. The suborder Eumecoptera is represented by four families in Australia. The commonest Australian scorpion flies belong to the family Bittacidae (six species in Australia, belonging to the genus *Harpobittacus*); some are found in moist areas and the others in dry habitats. They have a wing span of about 50mm. The family Panorpidae, which is essentially a family of the N hemisphere, is represented by the peculiar, wingless *Apteropanorpa tasmanica* which has been collected on snow in TAS.

scorpions The oldest known terrestrial ARTHROPODS (dating back to the Silurian period), scorpions form the order Scorpiones of the class Arachnida (ARACHNIDS). They are nocturnal predators which hide during the day under stones and litter. Although they are found in the warmer regions of the world, they are not restricted to hot arid areas; many species are found in humid habitats. There are about 600 species in the world, and about 30 in Australia.

The scorpion's body is long and consists of a cephalothorax covered with a carapace, and an abdomen distinctly divided into two sections—the wider pre-abdomen and the narrower post-abdomen which terminates in the sting. There is a pair of large eyes in the centre of the carapace, and a number of smaller eyes along the anterior lateral edges. The chelicerae are small, three-sectioned pincers. The pedipalps are very large and each consists of six parts, the last two of which form huge pincers. There are four pairs of walking legs. The second abdominal segment carries a pair of sensory organs (pectens). These comb-like organs are possibly temperature sensors.

Scorpions, like SPIDERS, breathe through lungbooks.

Many scorpions are very venomous, but the Australian species, are not thought to be dangerous though the stings are painful. They should not be confused with PSEUDO-SCORPIONS, which are much smaller and lack the sting. Scorpions are justly renowned for their elaborate courtship dances. They produce living young.

There appear to be three families represented in Australia: Buthidae, Scorpionidae and Bothriuridae. The Buthidae contains a commonly encountered species, the small marbled scorpion, *Lychas marmoreus*, which is 2.5cm to 5cm long and has relatively small pedipalps; this species occurs throughout Australia. Species of *Urodacus* (Scorpionidae) of N and W Australia can reach a length of 12cm.
Further reading: Savory, T. *Arachnida.* (2nd edn) Academic Press, London & New York, 1977.

Scott, Thomas Hobbes (1783-1860)
Anglican Archdeacon of NSW. Born near Oxford, England, he served as a Vice-Consul at Bordeaux and later attended the University of Oxford. In 1819 he came to NSW as secretary to his brother-in-law, John BIGGE, who had been appointed as a commissioner to report on the state of the colony and its future prospects. On his return to England Scott was ordained, in 1822. Two years later he was asked to make recommendations regarding the provision of churches and schools in NSW, and in the same year was appointed to the newly created position of Archdeacon of the colony.

Scott believed that the Church of England should control education, and had recommended that a seventh of the Crown lands in the colony should be put in trust to support the Church and schools. Such an arrangement was put into effect in 1826, with the establishment of the Church and School Corporation. This step naturally aroused opposition, as did his conservative political views. He became involved in many disputes and lawsuits, and was bitterly attacked in the columns of the colony's two independent newspapers, the *Australian* and the *Monitor*.

Scott returned to England in 1829, being succeeded by William Grant BROUGHTON. He had shown himself a tireless administrator and had succeeded in doubling the number of children in the colony's schools. However, his attempt to 'establish' the Church of England and to give it control of education soon ended in failure. The Church and School Corporation was suspended in 1829 and abolished in 1833, and the Church Act of 1836 provided State aid for the Roman Catholic, Presbyterian and Wesleyan Churches as well as for the Church of England.
Further reading: Border, Rev. J.T.R. *Church and State in Australia, 1788-1872.* Society for the Propagation of Christian Knowledge, London, 1962.

Scottish Martyrs
This title was popularly applied to five men—Thomas Muir, Thomas Fyshe Palmer, William Skirving, Joseph Gerrald and Maurice Margarot—who were transported to Australia in the 1790s. All were members of societies advocating parliamentary reform. However, the occurrence of the French Revolution and Britain's subsequent involvement in war against France had produced in the Tory government of Britain a strong reaction against all proposals for political or social reform in Britain. All were sentenced to transportation on charges of sedition in 1793-94. In the case of Palmer, a clergyman, the charge was based on his having transcribed and circulated a pamphlet deemed to be seditious, for which he received a sentence of seven years. The others received sentences of 14 years each on charges arising out of their participation in a convention of delegates from reform societies, held in Edinburgh.

Of the five, Margarot stands out as being of less worthy character than the others, and seems to have been moved more by jealousy of the ruling classes than by sincere attachment to democratic ideals. The other four appear to have been men of great sincerity and high character. Muir, Skirving, Palmer and Margarot arrived in NSW in October 1794 and were given freedom there on condition that they did not engage in political activity. Gerrald, who was in poor health, was kept in Newgate Gaol for nearly a year after being sentenced. He did not reach NSW until November 1795, and he and Skirving died in the following year. Muir escaped in 1796 on an American ship and died in Paris three years later. Palmer served his full sentence and left NSW; he died on the island of Guam in 1802. Margarot alone returned to Britain, where he died in 1815. There is a monument to these five men on Calton Hill, Edinburgh.
Further reading: Clune, F. *The Scottish Martyrs.* Angus & Robertson, Sydney, 1969.

Scottsdale
TAS (population of the town 2 002 in 1981; and of the municipality 4 320). This township is the commercial hub of the NE region, serving some of the richest agricultural and forestry country of the State. Located 70km NE of LAUNCESTON on the Tasman Highway, at an elevation of 190m above sea level, it has an average annual rainfall of 1167mm; July and August are the wettest months while February and March are the driest. It was named after James Scott, the government surveyor who in 1855 explored the then unknown NE hinterland.

scouring rushes *see* Arthrophyta

Scout Association of Australia
The scouting movement, founded in England in 1907 according to the ideas of Lord Baden-Powell, is well established in Australia. Of the approximately 100 national Scout Associations in the world, very few have a membership exceeding that of the Scout Association of Australia, which (excluding adult leaders) was over 120 000 in 1982.

As in other countries, the movement provides a programme for training boys and young men (and, at its senior levels, girls and young women) for responsible citizenship; the programme is based on a group system, a graded series of tests and proficiency badges, and open-air activities. Under the guidance of adults, members are encouraged to become increasingly self-governing in the successive age groups. The Association co-operates with the GIRL GUIDES' ASSOCIATION OF AUSTRALIA, but is separate from it in constitution, organisation and finances.

The Association's administrative hierarchy consists of five levels—national, branch (State or Territory), area, district and group. Each local group may contain a Cub Pack (age eight to 10), a Scout Troop (10½ to 14), a Venturer Unit (14 to 17) and a Rover Crew (17 to 24), but need not necessarily have all of these. Groups may be sponsored by bodies such as churches, universities, colleges, schools, hospitals, and the Armed Forces. Such groups are known as 'Sponsored Groups' in contrast to 'Open Groups'. A notable recent development has been the admission of girls and young women to Venturer Units and Rover Crews. All persons in positions of adult leadership in uniformed sections of the Associations are appointed by Warrant. At the group level they are known as Leaders or Assistant Leaders (Group Leader, Cub Leader, Assistant Cub Leader and so on). The general term 'Scouter' is applied to all adult leaders.

screw worm fly *see* biological control; parasites, livestock

scrub, open and closed *see* vegetation

scrub-birds
The family Atrichornithidae* consists of two species of primitive PASSERINE BIRDS known as scrub-birds; both species of these BIRDS are shy insect eaters that live in dense undergrowth. Because of anatomical similarities, it is believed that scrub-birds are related to LYREBIRDS.

The rufous scrub-bird, *Atrichornis* * *rufescens* (body 16cm long; tail 7.5cm long), has a broad, tapering tail, long legs and long toes. The plumage has a silky sheen and is reddish-brown with fine bars; there are two black streaks along the breast and abdomen, and the breast of the male is partly black. Like lyrebirds, rufous scrub-birds have a fine song and are adept at mimicking the calls of other birds. Development is destroying their habitat and they are now confined to thickets in rainforest in the QLD/NSW border area.

The noisy scrub-bird, *A.* * *clamosus* (23cm; 10cm), is also an endangered species; as far as is known, it survives as a single population (estimated at about 500 in 1973) in coastal rushes and dense gullies at Two Peoples Bay in south-western WA. It is a blackish-brown bird, with some white on the chin and, as the name suggests, it has a loud clear, rich song

Species, genus or family is endemic to Australia (see Preface)

which includes much mimicking of other species. It was first described in 1842, and thereafter was seen by only three naturalists (in the latter half of the 19th century) until the discovery of the Two Peoples Bay population in 1961.
Further reading: Frith, H.J. *Wildlife Conservation.* Angus & Robertson, Sydney, 1973.

scrub fowl *see* mound birds

scrub robins *see* thrushes, etc.

scrubwrens *see* warblers, etc.

James Henry Scullin

Scullin, James Henry (1876-1953) Prime Minister. Born in Trewalla VIC, he worked as a grocer, an Australian Workers' Union organiser and a journalist; he joined the Labor Party in 1903, and in 1910 entered federal politics as a Member of the House of Representatives (MHR) for the country electorate of Corangamite. Defeated in the election of 1913, he was elected MHR in 1922 for the Melbourne suburban seat of Yarra, became a deputy leader of the Australian Labor Party (ALP) in 1927 and leader in the following year. Following the ALP victory in the 1929 elections, he became Prime Minister, but had hardly taken office when the full weight of the worldwide Depression was felt in Australia. Although a competent man, of obvious sincerity and integrity, he lacked the qualities of decisiveness and political toughness which might have brought at least moderate success in dealing with such a situation. Nevertheless, it must be recognised that circumstances were very much against him. He was committed by his party's election programme to an extension of social services and public works, and could hardly have switched almost immediately to the policy of financial restraint that he was finally forced to accept in the form of the Premiers' Plan. On the other hand, his inclination to follow the inflationary approach advocated by his Treasurer, Edward

THEODORE, was rendered impossible by the opposition of the Commonwealth Bank Board and the fact that, without a Senate majority, Labor could not pass legislation to increase its power over the Board. He was further hampered by the divisions within his party which finally led to a three-way split (*see* POLITICAL HISTORY). After Labor's defeat in the elections of December 1931 he retained his leadership until 1935, when he resigned because of ill health. However, he remained a Member of Parliament until 1949.
Further reading: Makin, N.J.O. *Federal Labor Leaders.* Union Printing, Sydney, 1961; Robertson, J., *J.H. Scullin—A Political Biography.* University of WA Press, Nedlands, WA, 1974.

sculpture At a time of confusion and disagreement in the Australian visual arts, the terms of reference of sculpture are broad and flexible and prone to constant examination and revision. Indeed some art professionals feel that traditional sculptural values are becoming obsolete in relation to much of today's three-dimensional work, while others consider this freedom of approach permits sculpture to be regenerative and self-renewing. While some sculptors search for ways to make statements in keeping with the current fashion for art which expresses intensely personal values, other three-dimensional artists feel that what has been traditionally accepted as sculpture, i.e., permanent objects, has nothing new to say. They consider that their three-dimensional work—private, transitory, refuting accepted sculptural notions and expectations—is the only legitimate form of three-dimensional expression.

The 'new' three-dimensional expression in Australia evolved from both international and local post-modernism and conceptual art during the 1970s, together with the investigation of the properties of art by such systems as semiotics, structuralism and post structuralism. An equally potent influence was the 1976 Biennale of Sydney, known officially as 'Recent International Forms in Art' and familiarly as the 'sculpture' Biennale. This provided an international and Australian display of three-dimensional work and process art which challenged the orthodox definition of sculpture and reconstituted it to include such forms as video art, body art, earthworks, installations and performance art which hitherto defied categorization. The major concern of artists represented was to make a strong personal statement; the medium they chose arose from that intent.

While the language of object sculpture remains formal and coherent, understandable to most, the language of the new work is personal and idiosyncratic, speaking only to a select few. Artists who continue to work in this mode are Mike Parr, John Lethbridge, Robert Owen, Adrian Hall, Bridgette Macarthur and Lorraine Hepburn. Yet while there is no current prescription for sculpture, there is a movement among object-makers to return to more traditional styles. There is a revival of interest in the figure, and in public sculpture which stands

for civic and patriotic aspiration. There is a renewed interest in techniques such as carving and in natural materials such as wood and stone.

Nevertheless the strongest element of Australian work at present appears to be constructed metal sculpture, which has survived despite changes in style by many of its practitioners during the 1970s, and has received continued support despite the radical broadening of the sculptural definition over the past ten years. A leading sculptor in this field is Michel SANTRY; also Ron Robertson-Swann in his personal interpretation of the ideas of internationally renowned English sculptor Anthony Caro, and Ian McKay in large-scale outdoor welded metal works.

Partly because of the influence of the early exponents of constructed sculpture, in their role as teachers, the 'movement' has remained self-renewing well into the 1980s and today the approach of the young sculptors, whose work is far from mere regurgitation of that of their mentors, refutes any accusations of lack of ideas ascribed to it by some of the more avant-garde three-dimensional artists. Although it recognizes common sculptural concerns, the work of these younger artists reveals intensely personal sculptural values and decisiveness of notion, exemplified particularly well in the elegant grey compositional essays by Michael LeGrand, the theatrically expressive work of Ken Lamb, and the brooding introspective withheld steel statements of Kevin Norton.

Unlike Australian painters, Australian sculptors have not had a lasting physical relationship with the Australian landscape. Indeed, as they remained free from parochialism, and consistently international in outlook, three-dimensional rather than two-dimensional art has been the leader of new art movements and new ways of looking at art during the twentieth century. Yet although Australian sculpture does not feel the need to be aggressively Australian, the air of machismo of some large-scale welded metal work may indicate a trait in the Australian character.

A 'sculpturefest' held every three years in the country town of MILDURA gives Australian sculptors the opportunity to experiment with local materials, sticks, stones and soil, which shape works into ecological statements coming to grips with the primordial nature of the Australian landscape in the manner of the paintings of Sidney NOLAN. Yet the personal and private nature of these works, their temporary nature and the problems of removal prevent them from being art which is easily shared.

At a time when Australian painters appear to be ever more involved in the internationally based New Expressionism, working themselves into a painterly frenzy and lashing out on canvas to make a confusion of comments to a hostile world, Australian sculptors and three-dimensional artists are making highly articulate statements in a variety of ways. The past ten years have seen the development of support for Australian sculpture in the form of opportunity for representation in large-scale art events such as the Biennales of Sydney and Australian Perspecta; a large-scale commercial gallery at Glebe in Sydney, devoted exclusively to the representation of three-dimensional work, which opened in 1982; general interest in three-dimensional work by commercial galleries, numerous creative commissions and sculpture prizes, and flourishing sculpture departments in many art schools. All these factors add up to the fact that, in the early 1980s, three-dimensional art is the Australian art world's most exciting growth industry.

Sculthorpe, Peter Joshua (1929-)

Composer. Sculthorpe has probably done more than any other composer in Australia to actively promote the idea of the uniqueness of the Australian composer and of the real possibility of developing a music which is truly and recognisably Australian. He was born in LAUNCESTON in TAS and was one of the many composers to receive his early musical training at the Melbourne University Conservatorium. He has been a Reader in music at the University of Sydney since 1965, and as a teacher of composition there has had a great influence on younger composers. He is undoubtedly one of Australia's most successful and widely known composers, both in his own country and overseas. Music and painting were pursued with equal enthusiasm during his childhood; his large output of paintings of the Australian landscape has close affinities with the internationally successful Australian landscape painters of the 1960s and 1970s.

Sculthorpe is perhaps best known for his *Sun Music* series which evokes the differing and often harsh aspects of the sun in the Australian environment. His music is eminently approachable, at times highly evocative, at other times almost richly Romantic. He favours slower moving, sometimes almost melancholy, textures, as in such works as *Irkanda IV* and his *Sixth String Quartet*. Although influenced by the music of Asia and in particular that of Bali, Sculthorpe's music does express something that is, perhaps by its very repetitive nature, uniquely Australian. Despite his large-scale music theatre work, *Rites of Passage*, which received its premiere from the Australian Opera in Sydney Opera House in 1974, most of Sculthorpe's work is on a smaller scale. Much of his music has been recorded on disc, and it is characteristic of his following in Australia that the celebration of his 50th birthday in 1979 should have been marked by a musical tribute of both his own works and works specially composed for him on that occasion by many other Australian composers.

Further reading: Hannan, M. 'Peter Sculthorpe'

in Callaway, F. & Tunley, D. (eds) *Australian Composition in the Twentieth Century*. Oxford University Press, Melbourne, 1978.

sea anemones *see* coelenterates

sea birds Most of the many species of BIRDS which are associated with the sea are contained in four orders: Procellariiformes, which includes albatrosses, mollymawks, petrels, shearwaters and prions; Pelecaniformes, which contains the pelican, the DARTER, CORMORANTS, frigate birds, gannets and boobies; Charadriiformes, to which the WADERS and the gull-like birds belong; and Sphenisciformes, which consists of the PENGUINS.

Procellariiformes The common features of all members of this order is that they have tubular nostrils which lie above or alongside the beak. Most species are non-breeding visitors. A few never come to land except to breed; they usually nest in burrows or among rocks.

The family Diomedeidae contains 15 species of albatrosses and mollymawks, nine of which occur in sub-Antarctic and Australian temperate waters. They measure between 75cm and 1.3m long and are black and white, with white underparts, broad beaks, short tails and very long wings. They are justly renowned for keeping aloft for several days at a stretch, often in the wake of ships, by soaring on the winds. Two species—the wandering albatross, *Diomedea exulans* (1.3m long), and the royal albatross, *D. epomophora* (1.3m), have the greatest wingspan of all birds (up to 4m). Five species are fairly common in Australian waters: the wandering albatross, the black-browed albatross, *D. melanophris* (1m; wingspan 2.25m to 2.75m), the yellow-nosed albatross, *D. chlororhyncos* (81cm; wingspan 2m to 2.5m), the grey-headed albatross, *D. chrysostoma* (75cm; wingspan 2m to 2.5m), and the white-capped albatross, *D. cauta* (1m; wingspan 2.5m to 2.75m). All but the last mentioned are non-breeding visitors; the white-capped species, which extends to New Zealand, nests on islands around TAS. Mollymawk is the name given to some of the smaller, darker species, such as the sooty albatross, *Phoebetria fusca* (75cm; wingspan 2m to 2.5m), a rare straggler.

The family Procellariidae contains petrels, shearwaters and prions, all species in which the nostrils are enclosed in a single tube. Completely adapted to the sea, these birds are clumsy and vulnerable on land. Of the 36 representatives in Australian waters, most are rare, non-breeding visitors. A fairly common species, particularly in the wake of storms, is the southern giant petrel, *Macronectes giganteus* (1m; wingspan 2m to 2.5m), also called nellie or stinker, which is completely dark or completely white. It occurs in the S seas, whereas the rarer northern giant petrel, *M. halli* (80cm; wingspan 2m), a dark brown or dark grey bird, occurs in the SE seas. A common non-breeding visitor from the sub-

Composer Peter Sculthorpe at his home in Sydney

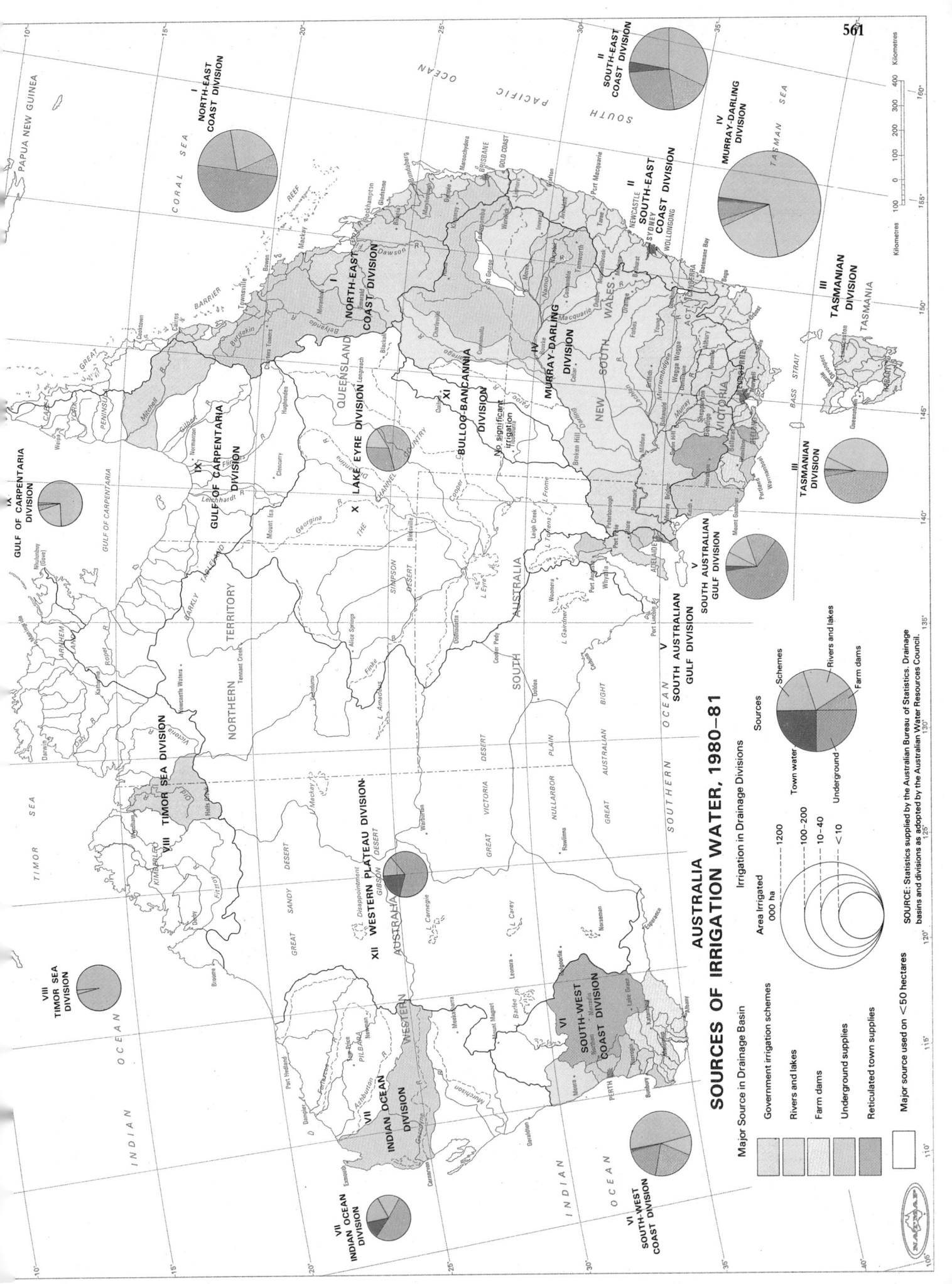

561

AUSTRALIA
SOURCES OF IRRIGATION WATER, 1980–81

Irrigation in Drainage Divisions

Major Source in Drainage Basin

Government irrigation schemes

Rivers and lakes

Farm dams

Underground supplies

Reticulated town supplies

Major source used on <50 hectares

Sources

Schemes

Rivers and lakes

Town water

Farm dams

Underground

Area Irrigated
000 ha

1200

100–200

10–40

<10

SOURCE: Statistics supplied by the Australian Bureau of Statistics. Drainage basins and divisions as adopted by the Australian Water Resources Council.

I NORTH-EAST COAST DIVISION

II SOUTH-EAST COAST DIVISION

III TASMANIAN DIVISION

IV MURRAY-DARLING DIVISION

V SOUTH AUSTRALIAN GULF DIVISION

VI SOUTH-WEST COAST DIVISION

VII INDIAN OCEAN DIVISION

VIII TIMOR SEA DIVISION

IX GULF OF CARPENTARIA DIVISION

X LAKE EYRE DIVISION

XI BULLOO-BANCANNIA DIVISION

No significant irrigation

XII WESTERN PLATEAU DIVISION

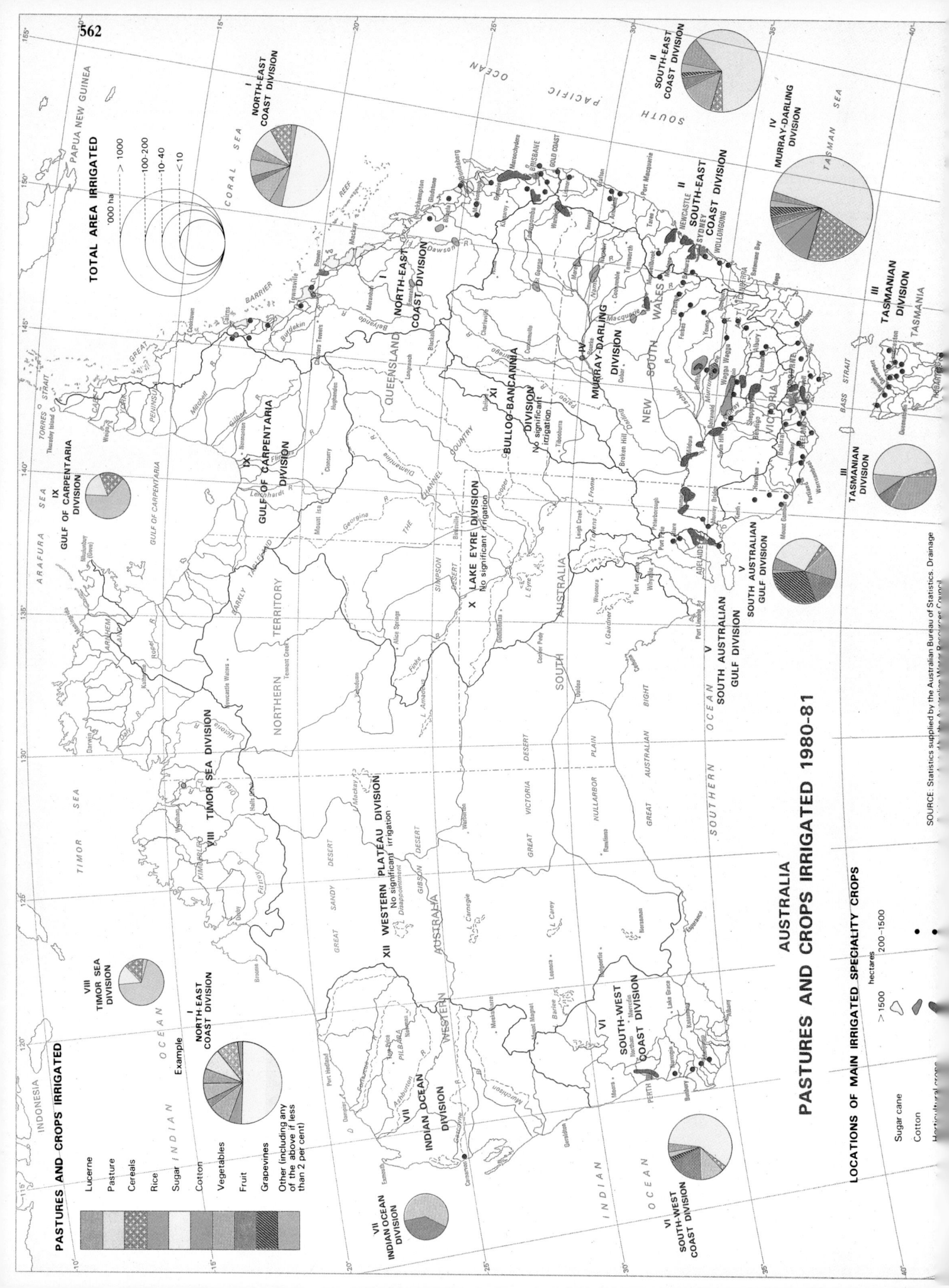

Gould's petrel, *Pterodroma leucoptera*

Antarctic is the cape petrel, *Daption capense* (40cm; wingspan 1m), a pied, black-headed species which patters along the water surface while feeding.

The genus *Pterodroma* contains the gadfly petrels—short-billed, broad-tailed birds which are either completely dark or dark above and white below. Of the 11 species known from Australian waters, only two breed there: the great-winged petrel, *P. macroptera* (40cm), a blackish species which nests on islands off WA, and the Gould petrel, *P. leucoptera* (30cm), a black-capped, grey bird which nests on Cabbage Tree Is off PORT STEPHENS.

The small petrels whose dead bodies are often washed up on the shore are known as prions, or whalebirds, and belong to the genus *Pachyptila*. Prions fly swiftly and erratically just above the water surface. They are about 30cm long and dove-grey in colour with a black 'M' marking on the back and wings, and a black-tipped tail. Of the six species known from Australia only one, the fairy prion, *P. turtur* (25cm to 28cm), nests on Australian islands.

Shearwaters belong to the genus *Puffinus* but should not confused with the puffins of the N hemisphere. Most shearwaters make long-distance migrations and, as the name suggests, they often flutter and glide just above the surface of the ocean. Of the eight species known from Australian waters, five breed there: the fleshy-footed shearwater, *P. carneipes* (48cm), which breeds on islands off southern WA; the short-tailed shearwater or mutton bird, *P. tenuirostris** (40cm to 43cm), which breeds on the SW, S and SE coasts of Australia; the wedge-tailed shearwater, *P. pacificus* (40cm to 46cm), which breeds on coastal islands off WA; the sooty shearwater, *P. griseus* (46cm to 51cm), which breeds on the SE coast; and the little shearwater, *P. assimilis* (25cm to 30cm), which breeds on the mid-WA

and southern QLD coasts. The Tasmanian mutton bird may be Australia's commonest bird and is the only wild bird exploited commercially—for flesh and oil. Mutton birds migrate from their nesting grounds in late April or early May each year, following a figure-of-eight course around the Pacific and returning always in the last week of September; egg-laying always begins on about 20 November and finishes on about 1 December.

The family Hydrobatidae contains the storm-petrels, closely related to but smaller (less than 25cm) than petrels of the family Procellariidae. Also known as Mother Carey's chickens, seven species occur in Australian waters but only one, the white-faced storm-

petrel, *Pelagodroma marina*, nests there. Two other species are common: the widely distributed Wilson storm-petrel, *Oceanites oceanicus* (15cm), a black bird with white on the tail and a grey band on the wing, and the similar black-bellied storm-petrel, *Fregetta tropica* (20cm), of the S seas.

The diving petrels of the family Pelecanio-didae are very small, with short legs and necks. They have a whirring flight, and often bounce on the waves; they also 'fly' underwater, like penguins. Of the four species in the world, two occur in Australian waters; one, the Georgian petrel, *Pelecanoides georgicus* (20cm), is a rare straggler, while the other, the diving petrel, *P. urinatrix* (20cm), is common and breeds on islands off VIC and TAS.

Pelecaniformes The members of this fish-eating order are recognised by the webbing of all four toes; the first toe (the hind-toe of most birds) is turned forward. Also they possess throat pouches. A typical example is the pelican, *Pelicanus conspicillatus** (1.75cm to 2m), the only pelican species found in Australian waters. Widely distributed in suitable habitats, this black and white bird is often seen fishing in the shallows, lowering its hooked bill and expanded pouch into the water to catch fish and crustaceans; it rarely dives for food. It feeds in marine and fresh water, particularly in large lakes and estuaries, and flies and swims well but on land has an ungainly, waddling gait. Pelicans breed in colonies.

The two Australian species of frigate birds, or man-o'-war birds, of the family Fregatidae, are medium-sized, piratical birds which force other birds to disgorge their food. They are black, with long thin wings, long hooked bills and long forked tails; the males have a large red pouch of inflatable skin on the throat. The lesser frigate bird, *Fregata ariel* (body 75cm; tail 30cm), is a common breeding species in

Silver gull, *Larus novaehollandiae*

Species, genus or family is endemic to Australia (see Preface)

tropical Australian seas; the greater frigate bird, *F. minor* (1m), is an uncommon non-breeding visitor.

The family Phaethontidae contains the tropic or bosun birds, mainly white birds with two long central tail feathers; they fly high and are greatly attracted to ships. Of the two Australian species, one, the white-tailed tropic bird, *Phaethon lepturus* (body 40cm; tail streamers 25cm) is a rare visitor, while the other, the red-tailed tropic bird, *P. rubricanda* (body 45cm; tail streamers 30cm), is a common breeding species which nests on Raine Is QLD and near CAPE NATURALISTE WA.

The gannets and boobies of the family Sulidae plunge from great heights for food and have strong, torpedo-shaped bodies and strong conical beaks. The gannet, *Morus serrator* (1m), mainly white with black tips on the wings and tail, breeds in large colonies called gannetries and usually feeds in flocks in temperate and subtropical waters. Boobies are white and black, or mainly brown. Three species nest on various tropical Australian islands; the red-footed booby, *Sula sula* (75cm); the masked booby, *S. dactylatra* (76cm to 86cm); and the brown booby, *S. leucogaster* (75cm).

Charadriiformes The gull-like birds of this order are divided into two families. The family Stercorariidae contains the skuas, piratical birds which rob other species of their food. They have long central tail feathers and white patches on the flight feathers. All four species are dark-plumaged except the great skua, *Stercorarius skua* (60cm), an Antarctic species which has light and dark phases. The great skua, the Arctic skua, *S. parasiticus* (40cm), and the pomarine skua, *S. pomarinus* (50cm), are regular non-breeding visitors.

The family Laridae contains the gulls, noddies and terns. Gulls are white birds with grey or black on the wings and back, thick hooked bills and rounded tails. Their roughly made nests of a variety of materials are built on the ground or among rocks. Of the three species which occur in Australian waters two are common: the silver gull, *Larus novaehollandiae* (38cm), a grey-backed scavenger in many S towns, which has black-tipped wings and scarlet eyes and legs; and the Pacific gull, *L. pacificus** (60cm), a black-backed omnivorous species of the S coasts.

Noddies are mainly black in colouring, with wedge-shaped tails, and they feed on fish and squid in tropical seas. Three species are very common: the common noddy, *Anous stolidus* (38cm), a sooty-black bird with a white forehead; the lesser noddy, *A. tenuirostris* (28cm to 30cm), similar to the common noddy but with a square or slightly forked tail; and the white-capped noddy, *A. minutus* (28cm to 30cm).

The 16 Australian species of terns, of the genus *Sterna*, look like large white, black-capped SWALLOWS which flutter above the water and then dive down for prey. Five are uncommon or rare, and some species, such as the whiskered tern, *S. hybrida* (25cm), are

*Species, genus or family is endemic to Australia (see Preface)

mainly inland-water species. One of the commonest species is the sooty tern, *S. fuscata* (45cm), of N Australian waters; it is black above and white below, with a deeply forked tail, and it feeds mainly on squid.

Further reading: Serventy, D.L., Serventy, V. & Warham, J. *The Handbook of Australian Sea Birds.* Reed, Sydney, 1971.

sea biscuits *see* sea urchins

sea cows
Also known as sirens, these EUTHERIAN MAMMALS belong to the order Sirenia; sightings of sea cows may have been the basis for stories of mermaids. These mammals have massive, crudely streamlined bodies with thick grey skins and almost no hair. They have paddle-like fore-limbs but no hind-limbs, and push themselves along with their horizontal tail flukes; the pelvis is vestigial. They feed on vegetation such as green algae and marine grasses in shallow waters and estuaries. Members of this order include: the dugong, *Dugong australis*, the only surviving member of the family Dugongidae, found in the tropical Indian Ocean, the Red Sea and the W Pacific, and reaching the N Australian coast, though fossil remains have been found as far S as Sydney; the manatees of the family Trichechidae, found on both sides of the tropical Atlantic; and the huge Steller's sea cow, *Hydrodamalis gigas* (up to 7.5m long), which formerly lived in the Bering Sea but was exterminated by sealers and whalers within 50 years of its discovery in 1741.

In the dugong, the teeth consist of a single incisor on each side of the upper jaw, no canines, and four to six tall, cement-covered cheek teeth. The cheek teeth are replaced from behind as they wear out and this is one of the reasons why dugongs are believed to be more closely related to elephants and hyraxes than to any other mammals. Further evidence of this relationship is the position of the teats,

which are between the paddles, and the retention of the testes within the body. The normal length of a dugong is about 3m but some reach 5m. The dugong was once a common species over most of its range but, being an inoffensive animal that feeds in herds in the shallows, it was greatly exploited by sealers and whalers. The dugong has recently been given complete protection in Australian waters though Aborigines are still allowed to kill it in QLD for food. There were once huge herds of dugongs in MORETON BAY in QLD but now the only regions in which they are fairly common are in far NW Australia and the TORRES STRAIT.

Further reading: Carrington, R. *Mermaids and Mastodons.* Chatto & Windus, London, 1957; Marshall, A.J. (ed) *The Great Extermination.* Panther Books, London, 1968, Marsh, H. (ed.), *The Dugong: Proceedings of a Seminar/ Workshop ... at James Cook University.* Townsville, 1981.

sea cucumbers
These marine invertebrates form the class Holothuroidea (phylum Echinodermata; *see* ECHINODERMS) which contains about 500 species. Many are sausage-shaped, with the long axis from the mouth to the anus, but some are almost spherical and others are long and worm-like. Their sizes range from about 2.5cm to more than 1m. Many small and medium-sized species occur in Australian waters.

Sea cucumbers are basically radially symmetrical but they have become, to some extent, bilaterally symmetrical as well. Thus, the body is divided, as in the SEA URCHINS, into five ambulacral areas and five interambulacral areas, all of which run from the mouth region to the anus, but three ambulacral areas and their two enclosed interambulacral areas have become a 'sole' on which the animal lies. This ventral surface differs from the dorsal surface (consisting of

Dugong, *Dugong australis*

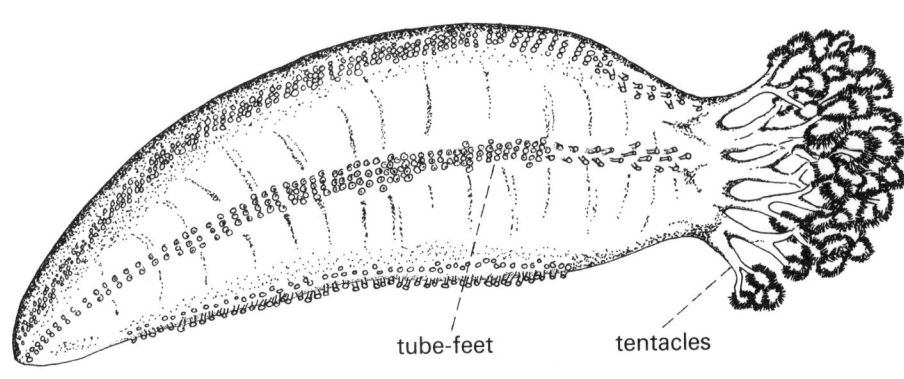

tube-feet   tentacles

A typical sea cucumber

the other three interambulacral areas and the two ambulacral areas) in various ways. In many species, for example, the tube feet on the sole have better-developed suckers than do those on the upper surface.

There are tentacles around the mouth of sea cucumbers but no arms. The thick, tough skin has many microscopic calcareous spicules, representing the skeleton, embedded in it. The interior is taken up by a well-developed alimentary canal. Unlike most echinoderms, sea cucumbers have a pair of branched structures (respiratory trees) which stem from the cloacal part of the gut. These fill with water carrying oxygen, then empty slowly. The animal thus respires through its cloaca. Attached to the bases of the respiratory trees are the defensive organs known as Cuvierian tubules; when the sea cucumber is attacked by a predator the sticky tubules are shot out through the anus and swell rapidly, enveloping the attacker while the prey escapes.

Sea cucumbers have remarkable powers of regeneration. When roughly handled they will shoot out a large part of their viscera but after some time these are completely regenerated. Sea cucumbers feed on particles they collect on their tentacles which are highly modified tube feet. In some species these are large and much branched, and collect plankton and detritus from the water; when they are sufficiently covered the tentacles are put into the mouth and wiped clean. In many other species the tentacles are quite short and the animal collects its food by burrowing through mud or sand.

There are more than 150 species of sea cucumbers in Australian waters. The larger ones are found in tropical areas and many of these were formerly collected each year by Macassans who came down from the Indonesian islands to collect and smoke the animals on N coasts. The dried, smoked animals were taken back to Indonesia for export to China. The culinary species are known as bêche-de-mer or trepang.

Sea cucumbers may be found at all depths of the sea. *Holothuria* species are common on sandy patches in coral reefs; *H. edelis* is a common, deep red species about 20cm long and about 2cm in diameter. *Stichopus chloronatus*, another coral reef species, is dark green in colour and is one of the sea cucumbers that often harbours a mess-mate fish, a species of *Carapus*, in its body cavity (*see* FISHES, BONY). *Leptosynpata dolabrifera* is an Australian example of a group of sea cucumbers, the Apoda, in which there are no tube feet. It is a burrowing species with a transparent skin. *Further reading: see under* sea stars. For details on the Macassans and trepanging *see* Mulvaney, D.J. *The Prehistory of Australia.* (2nd edn) Penguin Books, Harmondsworth, 1975.

sea dragons *see* fishes, bony

sea gooseberries *see* ctenophores

sea hares *see* gastropods

sea horses *see* fishes, bony

sea lilies and feather stars These marine invertebrates form the oldest and most primitive still-living class, Crinoidea, of the phylum Echinodermata (ECHINODERMS). Fossil sea lilies are among the oldest of all fossils. Sea lilies are stalked animals which are attached to the sea bed; there are about 80 species still in existence. Feather stars (comatulids) are free-swimming; there are about 550 species, mainly in the Indo-Pacific.

A feather star

The sea lilies differ from other echinoderms in having the mouth on the upper surface. The stalk is attached to the underside (calyx) which is cup-like. The stalk is jointed and often has small, jointed appendages (cirri) arranged as whorls on each joint; in the feather stars the cirri are used to cling to rocks or to rest on soft sand and silt. The upper surface wall is more or less membranous, whereas the calyx is composed of the hard ossicles of the skeleton. The mouth opens in the centre of the membrane, and the anus is situated near to it. There are five ambulacral grooves (*see* SEA URCHINS) radiating from the mouth to the five bases of the arms. In most sea lilies the arms branch almost immediately into two so that the animal appears to have 10 arms; in the feather stars the arms branch many times. The arms also have side branches (pinnules) which give them a feathery appearance, and the ambulacral grooves extend along the arms and into each of the pinnules. There are tube feet, in groups of three, in the grooves on the pinnules and there are also single tube feet near the mouth. The tube feet are used only for feeding. Particles of food fall on to the outstretched arms and are moved into the ambulacral grooves by the tube feet. Here the particles are trapped in mucus which is moved towards the mouth by minute hairs (flagella).

Sea lilies occur in deeper waters but feather stars, such as *Ptilometra australis*, are often found in shallow water. *P. australis* is found at a depth of a few metres along the E coasts of Australia and at times is common enough to clog the nets of fishermen. *Further reading: see under* sea stars.

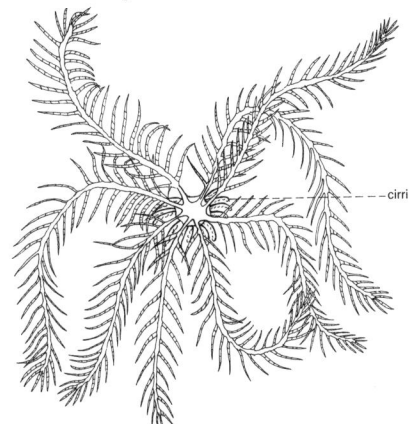

cirri

Cross section of a feather star

sea mice *see* annelids

sea mosses *see* ectoprocts

sea moths *see* fishes, bony

sea parsley *see* Umbelliferae

sea pens *see* coelenterates

sea pike *see* fishes, bony

sea slugs *see* gastropods

sea snakes *see* snakes

sea spiders A small group of marine animals which superficially resemble spiders, sea spiders belong to the class Pycnogonida of the phylum Arthropoda (ARTHROPODS). They have four to five pairs of usually long, spindly legs. The head carries a pair of chelicerae, somewhat similar to those of ARACHNIDS, a pair of palps and a pair of ovigerous legs which are used to carry the eggs. This is, however, the duty of the male and the ovigerous legs may be absent in the females. There are four eyes in the neck region. The abdomen behind the last pair of legs is extremely short.

Sea spiders occur in all oceans and are quite common though not often seen unless deliberately looked for among hydroids, corals and so forth. Most are only a few millimetres long though some deep-sea species can have a body length of more than 5cm and a leg span of 60cm. They are carnivores which feed on sessile animals.

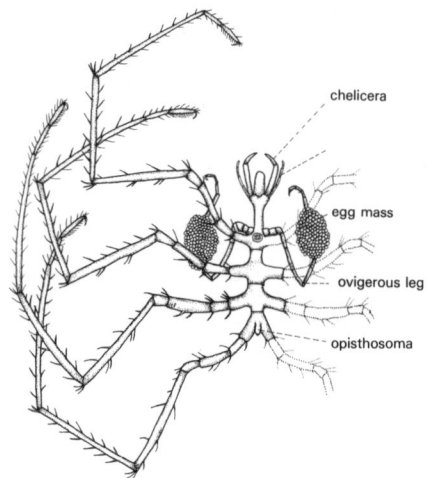

A sea spider, *Nymphon rubrum*

sea squirts and their allies Although these marine animals are CHORDATES and thus more closely related to the VERTEBRATES than to any other group of animals, they do not have backbones. Belonging to the subphylum Urochordata, their relationship to the vertebrates is shown by the presence of a notochord in the tadpole-like larvae which is lost in most adult urochordates. They are divided into three classes: Ascidacea, Larvacea and Thaliacea.

Ascidacea This is the most familiar of the three classes, being found on most of the world's seashores; they are well represented in Australia (about 100 species). An ascidian is a sessile animal with a thick, tough coat (test) surrounding the body. Two siphons, an incurrent and an excurrent, project from the top of the body. Water passes through the incurrent siphon into the mouth and pharynx. The latter has a ciliated groove (the endostyle) on one surface which produces mucus in which food particles carried by the water are trapped. The mucus and food then pass down into the stomach. The pharynx is large and

Two speciments of cunjevoi, their tests covered with fragments of shell and grit

bag-shaped, and its walls are pierced by many slits (the pharyngeal slits); the water passes through the slits and oxygen is extracted and carbon dioxide is released. The water then passes out of the atrium through the exhalent siphon.

The central nervous system in the adult consists of a single elongated, solid ganglion (compare with the hollow, complex central nervous system of the vertebrates). In the larva it is, however, more complex and hollow. Like most of the urochordates ascidians are hermaphrodite.

The transparent, tiny (1mm to 5mm long) larva has a tail that is four or five times as long as the trunk. Within the tail there is an elongated notochord which serves as a strengthening rod and a dorsal, hollow nerve chord. The front of this, inside the head, swells out a little to form the brain. When it is fully grown the larva attaches to a solid support by means of three adhesive nipple-like protuberances (papillae), and transforms to the adult. Many zoologists believe that the vertebrates arose when a population of ascidian larvae (or animals similar to them) did not pass into the sessile stage, but became sexually mature while still free-living.

The individuals of colonial ascidians are much smaller than the solitary species. Each has its own intake siphon but several share an exhalant one. Often the whole colony is an encrustation dotted with stars which are the openings of siphons; sometimes, however, this pattern is absent and the colony is not then easily distinguished from a sponge.

A typical ascidian found along southern Australian coasts is cunjevoi, *Pyura praeputialis*, a large, simple, non-colonial species

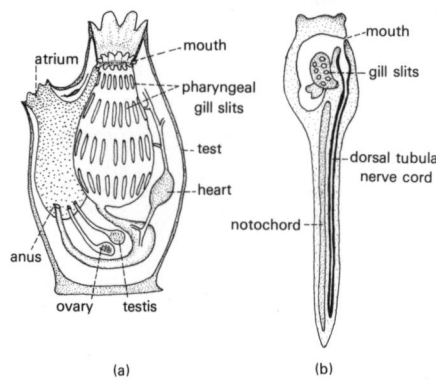

A typical ascidian: (a) adult (b) larva

whose red inner flesh is often used as bait; it occupies the lowest zone of the littoral species on many rocky seashores and may often be seen at extreme low tide. Common in both hemispheres, usually as a fouling organism on boats and harbour works, is *Cionia intestinalis*. The cylindrical, contractile body, with prominent siphons, is between 7.5cm and 12cm long.

Species of sea tulips are common on Australian coasts. They are reddish ascidians, easily recognised by their long stalks which are used for attachment to submerged rocks and wharf piles. *Pyura (Boltenia) gibbosa* and *P. (B.) pachydermatina* are found on, for example, the coast of NSW.

Larvacea Members of this class are more likely to be found in the sea than on the shore. The adults have retained the larval form, and are solitary and free-swimming, usually in the open ocean. The test is only temporary and gelatinous. The nervous system is well developed, there are only two pharyngeal clefts, and the atrium is absent. These animals never reproduce by budding.

Thaliacea Also more common in the sea than on the seashore, the members of this class are colonial animals which, although they multiply from a stalk or stolon, are free-floating like jellyfish. The adults are tail-less and the test is permanent. The individuals are barrel-shaped. *Thalia* species are sometimes washed up on Australian shores. *Pyrosoma* species form long, ribbon-shaped colonies which are brightly luminescent when agitated.

Further reading: Hardy, Sir Alister *The Open Sea; The World of Plankton.* Collins, London, 1956; Dakin, W.J., Bennett, I. & Pope, E. *Australian Seashores.* (6th edn) Angus & Robertson, Sydney, 1976.

sea stars Often called star fish although they are not related to fishes, these ECHINODERMS belong to the class Asteroidea. The body consists of a central disc with radiating arms. The gradual merging of the arms with the central disc distinguishes them from the much more active BRITTLE STARS in which the arms start abruptly from the disc. Furthermore, in the sea stars there are extensions of the gut into the arms whereas in brittle stars the arms are almost solid. Most sea stars have five arms but some, such as the large *Coscinasterias calamaria*, may have from seven to 11. The arms may be longer than the disc is wide, or shorter. The mouth is on the under (oral) surface, and the anus and sieve plate on the upper (aboral) surface. The skin has minute, beating hair-like structures (flagella) which carry away debris that falls on the animal; it is also covered with spines. The endoskeleton is a lattice work of rods, crosses and units of other shapes. A groove runs down each arm on the oral surface to the mouth; it is bordered with spines and from it arise two series of the tube feet.

Sea stars are bottom-living, carnivorous animals which feed on such animals as snails, crustaceans and annelids and on dead animals. Some wrap themselves around bivalve mol-

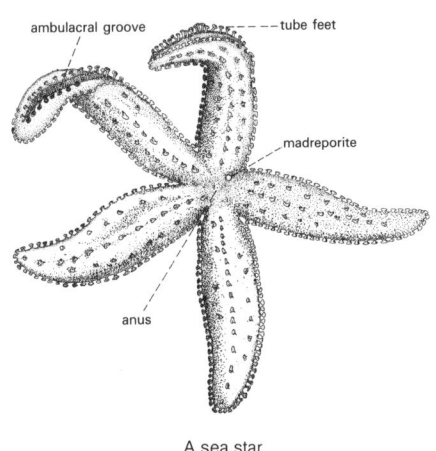

A sea star

luscs, gradually opening the shells by suction of hundreds of tube feet working in relays. When the two shells are slightly parted the sea star extrudes its stomach and inserts it inside the mollusc to digest the soft parts. A few sea stars feed on small particles which are carried along the arm grooves to the mouth with the aid of flagella.

There are many species in Australian coastal waters. *Patiriella exigua* is a very common species in rock pools along most of the coasts. The arms are so short that the animal is a pentagon with slightly concave edges. The colour is variable but is usually a pastel blue, green, red or orange. This species is usually found in the higher rock pools. In the pools near low water the closely related *P. calcar* is commoner. This has eight arms, and they are a little longer than those of *P. exigua. P. gunnii* is a hexagonal species.

C. calamaria, a large sea star that can reach a diameter of 25cm, belongs to a group of sea stars which possess pedicellaria. These are tiny organs on the aboral surface with jaws that work like pincers; they are used to rid the sea star of small attacking organisms, such as parasites, and to pick up and drop debris overboard. (In SEA URCHINS the pedicellaria are stalked.) *C. calamaria* is a species that reproduces by division so the number of arms is variable, and very often they are of unequal length. The smaller arms are the ones that are being regenerated. It is a colourful sea star, especially under a lens, with blotches of pale blue and green. It is mainly a temperate species, found at lower tide levels, usually on rocky shores.

The sea star, *Coscinasterias* (below) and an unidentified species above

Corwn of thorns starfish (*Acanthaster-planci*) feeding on coral

The most notorious sea star is the crown of thorns, *Acanthaster planci*, which occurs on reefs throughout the Indo-Pacific. It is sometimes more than 40cm in diameter when fully grown, and is armed with long, sharp spines which cause severe pain and numbness for some hours, possibly resulting from a venom. This species has destroyed large areas of coral reef by grazing on the corals. It has 13 to 17 arms.

Further reading: Bennett, I. *The Fringe of the Sea.* Rigby, Adelaide, 1966; Dakin, W.J., Bennett, I. & Pope, E. *Australian Seashores.* (6th edn) Angus & Robertson, Sydney, 1976.

sea tulips *see* sea quirts etc.

sea urchins There are many species of these marine invertebrates in Australian seas; they form the class Echinoidea of the phylum Echninodermata (ECHINODERMS). The body is usually more or less spherical, and covered with spines though there are some flattened forms (sand dollars, sea biscuits and heart urchins). In the more or less spherical forms—the regular urchins—the skeleton (test) is made of interlocking plates which are divided into five ambulacral zones and five interambulacral zones alternating with them. The zones run longitudinally and each consists of two rows of plates. The ambulacral plates have holes that allow the tube feet to protrude. Both kinds of zone are studded with small bosses on which the socketed spines move. These tests are commonly found on the seashore with the calcareous plates exposed, and the spines missing. Between the spines are numerous stalked pedicellariae (*see* SEA STARS). The spines are often venomous, with venom sacs surrounding the sharp tips; they are brittle and snap off easily in the skin of anyone who handles a sea urchin. The test of a living sea urchin is covered by a skin. The spines and tube feet are used to move the animal along.

The sea urchin rests on its mouth with the anus and the sieve plate of the water vascular system at the 'North Pole'. In the opening of the mouth the tips of five teeth may be seen. The urchin uses these for grazing on algae on rocks. The teeth form part of a structure of plates and muscles which surrounds the pharynx and which was first described by Aristotle; because of its shape the feeding apparatus is called Aristotle's lantern. The

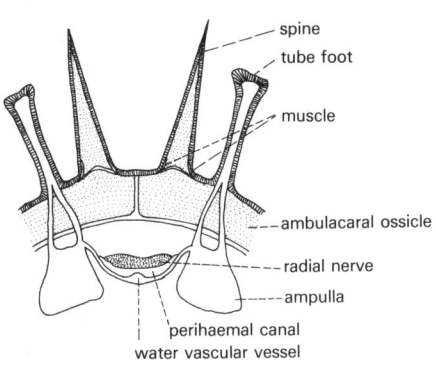

Section through test of a sea urchin

teeth grow continuously to make up for the wear and tear at the grazing end.

The flattened sea urchins burrow in the sand and show several modifications for this kind of life. They are bilaterally symmetrical, and they have small spines. Many regular urchins burrow into rock or coral, especially when they are living in areas exposed to the waves. Sometimes they grow as they burrow so that the entrance hole becomes too small to serve as an exit. Many species living between the tides use debris, held above them by the tube feet, as sunshades.

The slate-pencil urchin, *Phyllacanthus parvispinus*, is an unusual species because the spines are rounded, and, as the common name suggests, resemble old-fashioned slate pencils. This and similar species occur in QLD, NSW and SW Australia, usually in slightly deeper waters than those frequented by seashore collectors. Sea urchins of the family Centrechinidae have, in contrast, very long needle-like spines and are often large with a purple, red or black body, though the spines may be iridescent. The commonest species of temperate Australia is probably the rock-boring sea urchin, *Heliocidaris erythrogramma*. It varies in colour from olive green to purple. Small specimens are often found under stones rather than in burrows. The spines are about 2.5cm long and round in cross-section throughout. The heart urchin, *Echinocardium cordatum*, is common in estuarine sands of NSW, and also occurs in Europe.

Further reading: see under sea stars.

sea walnuts *see* ctenophores

seablite *see* Chenopodiaceae

sealing The killing of SEALS for their skins and for oil began in Australia in the late 18th century; these products were the first Australian exports. The first large-scale operations were on the BASS STRAIT islands where the animals were clubbed or stabbed to death, but by 1806 they were becoming so scarce that the sealers turned to other grounds along the S coasts. Eventually, those based in NSW began working the coasts of New Zealand and S islands of the Pacific. MACQUARIE ISLAND became an important sealing centre but by about 1830 large-scale sealing had more or less ended. The trade attracted ships from Britain, North America, Mauritius and Australia and there were often clashes between the crews of various ships. Seals are now protected in Australian waters though they may be culled, under licence, when they interfere seriously with commercial fishing. The elephant seal has, however, been driven from the region and its nearest station is now on Macquarie Is.

seals The seals form an order, Pinnipedia, of aquatic (almost always marine) placental MAMMALS, related to the Carnivora. Though well adapted to the water they return to the land or to permanent ice to breed. They feed on fish, squid, molluscs and penguins. Unlike the whales they have four limbs with the feet fully webbed. Their teeth are differentiated in the normal mammalian way into incisors, canines and cheek teeth, but the cheek teeth are generally conical. The fore-limbs act as flippers when the seal swims, while the hind-limbs face backwards and push the animal along.

There are three families. One, the Odobenidae, contains one species, the walrus, which is found only in the N hemisphere. The other two families are found in both hemispheres. The family Otariidae, the sea lions, are the seals that can scramble around rocks or over circus rings because the hind-feet can be turned beneath the body on land. The family Phocidae contains the true seals; these species cannot turn their feet forward and are thus much more clumsy on shore. Sea lions have a small external ear which the phocids lack. Both kinds have a small tail which is absent in the walrus. Male sea lions have an external scrotum but in the phocids the testes remain within the abdomen. Sea lions feed mainly on small fish, phocids on various foods depending upon the species; these diets include fish, squid, shellfish, macroplankton and penguins. There are six genera of sea lions (with a total of 12 species) and 13 genera of phocids (18 species).

Three species of sea lions are regularly found in Australian waters; all three breed on the mainland or adjacent islands. One phocid, the elephant seal, *Mirounga leonina*, formerly bred on KING ISLAND but was wiped out in the early 19th century. It is now only a regular visitor to TAS and sometimes to the mainland.

Otariidae The Australian sea lion or white-naped hair seal, *Neophoca cinerea* (1.5m to 2.4 long; the males much larger than the females) breeds on islands from HOUTMAN ABROLHOS to KANGAROO ISLAND and on the mainland at Point Labatt SA. This species is an example of the hair seals, so called because the adults lose the soft under-fur that makes the pelts of fur seals so attractive to hunters. Adult male Australian sea lions have a white or yellowish mane at the nape of the neck. The face is dog-like. The general colour is brown but, as with all seals, the colour appears to be darker when the animal is wet; the limbs are greyer. The

Australian sea-lions at Seal Bay SA

females are often called clapmatches (or klap-matches), a derivative of a Dutch word for a seaman's cap. The Australian sea lion is a shore-loving species which spends much of its time on land. It breeds once a year, from October to December, the female producing one pup. The old bull has a small harem of females which he guards till after birth and mating.

The Australian fur seal, *Arctocephalus pusillus* (males 2.2m; females up to 1.5m), now ranges from southern NSW to PHILLIP ISLAND and WESTERN PORT BAY, on islands and rocks. It is also found on TAS islands and one colony has been discovered on the TAS mainland. The muzzle is short and pointed, and not dog-like. The males (wigs) are a little larger than the females, and bulkier around the shoulders. The females are also often called clapmatches. The colour, when dry, is brown dorsally and very dark brown ventrally; the under-fur is chestnut in colour. Wet animals appear to be almost black. It is a more sea-going animal than the hair seal. The wigs begin to come ashore in November and fight for territories. The females arrive a few weeks later, and the pups are all born by about mid-January when the males return to the sea after mating with the members of their large harems.

The Australian fur seal was once much more widely distributed but sealing began in 1798 (it was, at first, a much more important industry than whaling) and signs of a decline in population began by 1806. The last sealing at Kangaroo Is was in about 1880 and on the RECHERCHE ARCHIPELAGO in 1920. All Australian seals are now protected by law though individuals may be killed, with official permission, when they interfere too much with fishing. The largest rookery is now on

Seal Rocks, Western Port Bay, where the population is estimated at 5 000. There are other colonies which may be as large on other VIC islands, and the total population is probably between 20 000 and 25 000.

The New Zealand fur seal, *A. forsteri*, is a little smaller than the Australian fur seal but otherwise similar. It has rookeries off the coasts of SA and WA, from the Recherche Archipelago to Kangaroo Is.

Phocidae The elephant seal is the only phocid that has bred within Australian waters, at least in historic times. It is a widespread species with a circumpolar distribution, sometimes occurring even on the Antarctic mainland. There are large colonies on South Georgia Is, MACQUARIE ISLAND, Kerguelen Is and the Falklands. Bulls are about 4m long and four tonnes in weight. The cows are 3m long and weigh about one tonne. The bull has a trunk-like proboscis which can be inflated during the breeding season so that it becomes 60cm or more long. It is almost certainly used as a resounding chamber to amplify the bull's roar. Bulls are light grey to brown, with lighter underparts, while females and

Bull sea elephant

immatures are a uniform grey. Unlike other seals, elephant seals have few teeth and only the canines appear to be of much use. The nails are also reduced, and completely missing from the hind-feet. They feed on squid, cuttlefish, fishes and even sharks, all of which they can take at considerable depths.

Bulls normally come ashore for mating in September and fight fiercely for territories, often inflicting deep cuts and scratches on their opponents with their long canines. A few weeks later the females arrive and are claimed by the dominant bulls (beachmasters). A harem usually contains 10 to 20 females, but may reach as many as 50. The females pup about a week after coming ashore and mate again soon afterwards. The 1m-long pups suckle for about three weeks, fast for another three, moult and are then ready to take to the sea. Only about 50 per cent of the pups survive to adulthood.

Other phocids sometimes stray into Australian waters. The nomadic, predatory leopard seal, *Hydrurga leptonyx* (2m to 3.4m) has been seen several times in the Sydney region. The crabeater seal, *Lobodon carcinophagus* (2.7m), a krill-eating species, has also been seen on the coasts of NSW, and TAS.
Further reading: King, J.E. *Seals of the World.* British Museum (Natural History), London, 1964; Ride, W.D.L. *A Guide to the Native Mammals of Australia.* Oxford University Press, Melbourne, 1970; Martin, R.M. *Mammals of the Oceans.* Hutchinson, Richmond VIC, 1977. Strahan R. (ed.) *The Australian Museum Complete Book of Australian Mammals.* Angus & Robertson, Sydney, 1983.

Searle, Henry Ernest (1866-89) Professional sculler.

Born in GRAFTON in NSW, he started his successful career in light skiffs but it was not until he changed to outriggers that he began to win important races. In 1888 he moved to Sydney and after several wins there he won the first major championship of his career, defeating Peter Kemp to win the 1888 world championship. In the same year he went to England to race against William O'Connor, the North American champion; the match took place on the Thames, with Searle an easy winner. On his return journey to Australia, he contracted typhoid and died in Melbourne. At that time rowing was extremely popular, and Searle's death, cutting short a brilliant and promising career, was mourned by thousands throughout the country. He was accorded a hero's funeral, the funeral cortege proceeding first through the streets of Melbourne, then by train to Sydney for another procession and finally to his home town of Grafton for yet another procession, before being buried at MACLEAN in NSW.

SEATO see South-East Asia Treaty Organisation

seaweed see algae

sedges see Cyperaceae

Sedgman, Francis Arthur (1927-)
Tennis player. Born in the Melbourne suburb of Mont Albert, Sedgman was spotted by Harry HOPMAN when he was 12 and invited to join an after-school coaching class and by 1952 was the world's leading amateur. Although his formative teenage years were disrupted by World War II, his tireless work both in the gymnasium and on the tennis court paid off and earned him his first State title, the Victorian Junior title, in 1945. In 1948 he won the Wimbledon doubles with John Bromwich, having travelled to the tournament at his own expense because he had missed selection for the Australian overseas touring team. During the following four years he was at the forefront of a drive which took Australia to world supremacy in tennis. In each of those four years he played in the Australian Davis Cup team, losing only three of the 29 matches he played. In 1951 and 1952 he swept into world prominence by winning the Australian, French and Wimbledon doubles titles partnered by Ken McGREGOR. He won the US singles title in the same two years (to become the first Australian to win this championship), and then won the coveted Wimbledon singles title in 1952. In the following year he turned professional. A powerful server with an aggressive game, he was one of the first exponents of the 'power game' in Australian tennis.

Seidler, Harry (1923-) Architect.
Born in Vienna, Harry Seidler went to Canada to study architecture at the University of Manitoba, and graduated in 1944. A scholarship won there took him to Harvard University for a Master's degree under the direction of Walter Gropius, and he worked with Marcel Breuer in New York and Oscar Niemeyer in Rio de Janeiro before coming to Australia in 1948. The influence of all three men is evident in Seidler's work.

The effect of his first Australian building—a small house at Turramurra, a Sydney suburb, completed in 1950—was far reaching. It was a highly sophisticated, box-like form on thin metal columns and blades of stonework, and it introduced the International style into Australia. His subsequent buildings, often criticised for being inappropriate to the Australian climate, were nevertheless consistently well built, disciplined and uncomprisingly modern. They included large blocks of home units at Blues Point and Diamond Bay, and Housing Commission flats at Rosebery in Sydney. With the completion of the Australia Square development in Sydney in 1967, Seidler accomplished not only the tallest, fastest and best-organised skyscraper project, but the first example of a comprehensive development in an amalgamation of a large number of separately owned sites. This notable achievement was virtually repeated at the MLC complex in Martin Place, Sydney, and its office tower is the highest occupied structure in Australia.

Seidler has used other systems of building: the Government Stores Building at Alexandria has an enormous space-frame roof covering a vast floor area; the ski lodge at Thredbo which was built in 1962 has an obliquely aligned exposed timber frame which resembles the shape and growth of the snow gums among which it stands. Seidler's designs have won many awards and have been widely published. For outstanding achievement in architectural design and for the promotion of architecture and the profession, he was awarded the Gold Medal of the Royal Australian Institute of Architects in 1976.
Further reading: Blake, P. *Architecture for the New World: The Work of Harry Seidler.* Horwitz, Sydney, 1978.

Selaginellaceae see Microphyllyta

Senate see government of Australia

sergeant Baker see fishes, bony

sergeant-majors see fishes, bony

Service/Tertiary and quaternary industries
These include all those which provide a service but do not provide a good, for example advertising, communication, domestic service, entertainment, finance, import and export services, information, power, professional services, public services, tourist and travel services, transport and distribution, wholesale and retail traders. Building and construction which re-arranges building materials and components into buildings and structures is difficult to classify. In Australia it has been customary to list it under tertiary because it does not produce a portable good, but some countries list it under the manufacturing sector.

Major entries dealing with particular service industries in this encyclopedia are: BANKING, BROADCASTING, DEFENCE, EDUCATION. ELECTRICITY, NEWSPAPERS, SOCIAL SERVICES and TRANSPORT.

The accompanying table shows that in 1910 primary industry in Australia employed 25.5% of all persons employed, manufacturing 18.4% and services 48.7%. Since then the output has increased in both the primary and manufacturing sectors but the proportion of persons employed has decreased because increased productivity has resulted from mechanisation and improved technology. In contrast in the service industries the number of services has increased and the proportion of persons employed has also increased. The 1981 census figures reveal 6% for primary, 17.7% for manufacturing and 67% for services.

Growth areas in the service industries are to be found in three broad sections. First in advertising, retailing, real estate, finance, insurance, business services and the professions as a result of higher levels of private consumption and higher levels of private investment. Secondly, the services provided by the government increased following the

EMPLOYMENT IN INDUSTRY SECTORS 1910–1981

Industry	Percentage of working population									
	1910	1921	1933	1947	1954	1961	1966	1971	1976	1981
Primary	25.5	21.9	20.9	16.8	13.4	10.9	9.4	7.4	7.0	6.0
Mining	7.4	2.9	2.6	1.9	1.7	1.3	1.2	1.4	1.3	1.4
Manufacturing	18.4	22.3	23.0	27.9	29.9	29.2	29.2	23.2	19.7	17.7
Services/Teritary & Quaternary	48.7	52.9	53.5	53.4	55.0	56.6	58.5	63.9	65.2	67.0
Others—not stated						2.0	1.7	4.1	6.8	7.9

100%

adoption of policies providing welfare and social security for the disadvantaged, and the adoption of policies based on the teaching of J.M. Keynes in the late 1930s that governments should engage in economic management to combat fluctuations in economic activity. The third area of growth is that embracing communications and the handling of information. This area has become known as the quaternary sector.

Quaternary sector The twentieth century has experienced an explosion of knowledge and Australian society as a whole has become hungry for information, but in particular, government, business and industries cannot function without information being made available to them. This has led to industries evolving to research, process and store information. People employed in the quaternary sector have jobs which involve the processing of symbols such as words, images and figures and symbolic objects such as money, cheques and title deeds.

Further reading: Wilson, R.K. and Wilson, G. 'The Service Industries in Australia' in *Current Affairs Bulletin* (vol. 57, no. 4 September, 1980).

Seventh-Day Adventist Church This Christian denomination originated in the USA in the 1850s, under the leadership of William Miller. Its name rose from its members' belief in the imminent Advent, or Second Coming, of Jesus Christ, and from the fact that they celebrate the seventh day (Saturday) as the Sabbath. They practise baptism by immersion of believers old enough to make a confession of faith, believe in the full inspiration of Holy Scripture, and lay great stress on health rules. They avoid alcohol, tobacco and drugs, and recommend vegetarianism as the ideal diet. Adventist health-food factories produce such foods as whole-grain cereal products, vegetable extracts, dried fruits, peanut butter and other nut preparations. The Church is very active in the fields of health services and foreign missions.

A small group of Adventist ministers arrived in Melbourne in 1885, and founded a church there in the following year. By 1900 there were 39 churches in various parts of Australia. In the meantime a missionary training centre, Avondale College, had been opened at Cooranbong, NSW, 145km N of Sydney. Today it is recognised as a College of Advanced Education and offers courses leading to awards in education and theology. In 1902 a printing works and health-food factory were built at Warburton, VIC, and in the following year a sanatarium and medical training centre (now the Sydney Adventist Hospital) were opened at the Sydney suburb of Wahroonga. In the 1981 census only 47 474 people were identified as Seventh-Day Adventists; nevertheless, because of the Church's varied activities, it must be considered to have exerted an influence out of proportion to the number of its members.

Seymour VIC (population 6 492 in 1981) A major commercial and service town on the GOULBURN RIVER at the intersection of the Hume and Goulburn Valley Highways, Seymour is 98km N of Melbourne and 84km S of SHEPPARTON. At an elevation of 142m above sea level, it has an average annual rainfall of 596mm, which occurs throughout the year, with a concentration in winter. The original settlement was made in 1843 as a river crossing point and named after Lord Seymour, a British Cabinet Minister. It developed as a transport junction, on main highways and on the interstate (Melbourne-Sydney) rail route, 99km by train from Melbourne. Lake Nagambie, formed by the Goulburn Weir, about 27km N of Seymour, is a popular aquatic playground. Mitchelton, a commercial vineyard and tourist complex on the banks of the Goulburn, about 20km W of Seymour, was opened in 1974 to show visitors the art of wine making, with opportunities to inspect the cellars and sample the produce.

Shannon River TAS This stream joins the GREAT LAKE to the OUSE RIVER in the CENTRAL PLATEAU region of the State; it flows from the S extremity of the Great Lake and its course lies to the W of the Lakes Highway, flowing in a general N-S direction. It was the site of one of the earliest developments of hydro-electricity in TAS; this was at WADDAMANNA, where a small plant produced power for Hobart in 1916. Later, the generating capacity was increased and another plant was built at Shannon in 1934. These stations have now largely been superseded (Shannon now disused, Waddamanna used only for peak consumption) by major developments to the NE of the Great Lake.

Shark Bay WA A large shallow coastal inlet located some 900km NNW of Perth between GERALDTON and CARNARVON, it was named by the explorer William DAMPIER in 1699. The inlet has two main sections divided by Peron Peninsula: the W section is named Denham Sound (with Henri Freycinet Estuary at its S end); the E part of the bay is named Hamelin Pool at its SE end. The W and SW extent of the bay is marked by an arc of elongated islands: Bernier Is at the N, Dorre Is in the centre and DIRK HARTOG ISLAND at the S. Formerly a pearling area, the bay is now a major fishing centre, claimed as one of the best fish breeding grounds of the nation, with abundant mackerel, snapper, groper, kingfish and tuna. It is renowned for game fishing (not only for sharks, but also sail-fish and marlin) and for prawns and lobsters. DENHAM, on the W side of Peron Peninsula, has freezing and export processing works for handling the products. The average rainfall at Hamelin Pool is only 210mm, indicating the arid nature of the region.

See also: stromatolites

sharks and rays There are about 200 species of sharks in the world, and about 350 species of rays and their allies, belonging to the class Chondrichthyes, the second-largest class of FISHES. (There are also about 25 species of ghost sharks or chimaeras which are treated here as a separate class, Holocephali.) The class Chondrichthyes (sometimes called elasmobranchs) is subdivided into the superorder Selachoidei (the sharks and their allies) and the superorder Batoidei (the rays). It is difficult to say how many occur in Australian waters; one estimate is about 90 species of sharks and over 50 species of rays, but some are small or rarely seen. Some of the commonest species and all those species that are dangerous or potentially dangerous to man in Australian waters are mentioned below.

The most characteristic feature of this class is the skeleton, which is always composed of cartilage or gristle; sometimes this is partly calcified but there is never true bone. Sharks have the typical shape of fast-swimming fishes; rays and their allies can be regarded as sharks that have taken to a bottom-living mode of life. The body is flattened and the pectoral fins are completely joined to the head and body. The skin is covered by enamel-coated dermal denticles ('skin teeth'). The teeth within the mouth are modified denticles which are replaced as they are worn away or lost. The gill openings (five to seven pairs) are open slits which are not covered by a bony plate as they are in bony fishes; many sharks and all rays have another opening (the spiracle) behind the eye, which allows them to breathe even when half buried, belly down. There are paired pectoral and pelvic fins, the latter with claspers in the male because fertilisation is internal. There can be up to two dorsal fins above the spine and sometimes an anal fin below the body. The fins are more fleshy than they are in the bony fish. Internally, the gut

Sawfish, *Pristis* species

has a distinctive spiral valve, and there is no swim bladder to help the fish to maintain its position in the water. Sharks must swim continuously to maintain their height above the bottom but the body weight is lessened by the large amounts of oil in the liver. The young may be produced as eggs or born as miniature versions of their parents.

The sharks include the largest living VERTE-BRATES, after the whales. The largest, a plankton feeder, is called the whale shark. Most sharks and rays, however, are scavengers and carnivores and many of the sharks will attack man, often with fatal results.

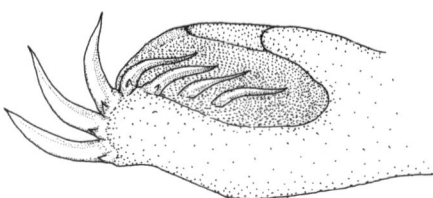

Section through the jaw of a sand shark showing teeth

Selachnoidei A typical shark has a stream-lined body, a ventral mouth well armed with teeth, and a snout or rostrum above the mouth. Some, however, are intermediate in shape between the typical sharks and the rays. Representatives of six orders are found in the Australian region.

1. Order Hexanchiformes. This order contains the ancient seven-gilled sharks, two species of which are found in southern Australian waters. They have seven pairs of gill slits and a single dorsal fin. The one-finned shark, *Heptranchus dakini* (up to 1m long), a green-eyed species with a long, tapering snout, has jagged teeth in the upper jaw and comb-like teeth in the lower jaw. The seven-gilled or ground shark, *Notorhynchus cepedianus* (up to 3m), common in shallow waters on some S coasts, has a broad, blunt head with only one median, jagged tooth at the front of the upper jaw and comb-like teeth in the lower jaw. Sandy-coloured with black and white spots, this species is potentially dangerous.

2. Order Heterodontiformes. This order contains the horn or Port Jackson sharks; very similar animals flourished in the Carboniferous period 200 million years ago. They are coastal Pacific, bottom-dwelling, blunt-headed fish characterised by a spine on the front edge of each of the two dorsal fins and by the anal fin. They have a pavement of flattened teeth with which they grind up sea urchins, molluscs and crustaceans. They lay their eggs in cases with spiral flanges and often with long tendrils which anchor them to weed and stones. The Port Jackson shark, *Heterodontus portusjacksoni* (about 1.4m), a light brown species with dark marks on the face and shoulders, ranges from WA to southern QLD along the S coasts at depths of up to about 170m. The crested Port Jackson shark, *H. galeatus*, a more N species (QLD, NSW), has distinct crests above the eye. Both species are harmless to man, though the spines can introduce a painful venom into the body.

3. Order Lamniformes. This order contains the true sharks and is represented by 10 (or nine according to some authorities) families in Australian seas.

The family Sphyrnidae contains the unmis-takeable hammer-head sharks, one of which, *Sphyrna lewini* (up to 5m), is recorded from all States. It is a pelagic species which sometimes comes into shallow water. The head has lateral extensions with eyes on the tips. It is suggested that this widened head acts as a hydrofoil which helps the shark to swim pre-cisely at slow speeds. It feeds on large fish and

Shark boat in Lakes Entrance VIC

is dangerous to man. It is a viviparous species.

The family Orectolabidae contains the carpet sharks, slow, brightly-coloured, bottom-dwelling species with fringes or tentacles on the lips and head. The best-known species is probably the spotted wobbegong, *Orectolobus maculatus* (up to 3m), found in reef caves in shallow water from WA through TAS to southern QLD. Inoffensive unless provoked, it has a flattened body which is light brown and covered with light-edged eye spots and bars.

The family Hemiscyllidae contains the cat-sharks, which resemble the carpet sharks but lack the mouth and head fringes. These usually long and slender harmless sharks have two dorsal fins, both behind the pectoral fin, and lay eggs in purses.

The family Alopiidae contains the thresher shark, *Alopias caudatus* (up to 5m), which cannot be confused with any other shark for the upper lobe of the tail fin is longer than the head and body together. It beats the water with its tail to drive fish into compact schools upon which it can easily prey. Considered to be harmless to man because of the smallness of the teeth, its body is bluish-grey or greenish above and white below.

The family Cetorhinidae contains the basking shark, *Cetorhinus maximus* (occasionally up to 12m), which despite its size is quite harmless. It has a ventral mouth and feeds on plankton which it strains from the water with its long gill-rakers. It frequently basks on the surface of the open sea.

The family Rhincodontidae contains the larger whale shark, *Rhincodon typus* (up to 14m), a rather hump-backed shark with a terminal mouth and long gill slits. Plankton is extracted from the water by the long gill-rakers.

The family Isuridae (the porbeagle family) contains two dangerous Australian sharks. The sharks of this family are large, viviparous fish that swim at the surface of the open sea in all oceans. The strong, torpedo-shaped body has a distinct keel on each side of the tail stalk. In the white pointer, *Carcharodon carcharias* (up to 7.5m), also known as the white death or the great white shark, the teeth are large triangles with serrated edges and can number 200. The colour is grey to greyish-blue above and white below. It is a cosmopolitan tropical and temperate species which rarely attacks people near the shore. The blue pointer or mako, *Isurus glaucus* (up to about 4m), is a favourite fish of game fisherman because of its fighting qualities. The teeth are long and awl-shaped and can be extended to grapple prey. These dark blue and white sharks have long pointed snouts and long gill slits.

The family Triakidae contains the whiskery or smooth dog sharks. A common example is the widespread harmless gummy shark (so called from its flattened teeth) or sweet william (from its smell), *Mustelus antarcticus* (1m). It is a long, thin species, grey with white spots and easily recognised by its flattened pavement of teeth. It feeds on invertebrates and is itself eaten as flake.

Port Jackson shark, *Heterodontus portusjacksoni*

Neville Coleman

The family Carchariidae contains the grey nurse shark, *Carcharias arenarius* (up to 5m), which has a reputation of being a fierce man-killer, although this is disputed by many biologists and seamen. It is recognised by its long, awl-like, fearsome-looking teeth which have spiny processes at the base, by its long tail fin and short pectoral fins, and by the position of its gill slits which are well forward of the pectoral fin. It is grey or brown above and white below. In the 1850s this species was caught by rod and line commercially to provide oil for lamps for Sydney. It is now one of the commonest sharks in aquaria.

The family Carcharhinidae contains the typical sharks, including several man-killers as well as many harmless species. In this family the first dorsal fin is well in front of the pectoral fins, and the last gill slit is usually just over the base of the pectoral fin. The wide-spread tope or school shark, *Galeorhinus australis* (about 1.8m), is white and grey or brown, with a long, pointed snout and a wide lobe on the upper tail fin. It is an important species commercially, and has been overfished in some areas. It is harmless to man, although it often robs anglers of their catch. The tiger shark, *Galeocerda cuvieri* (up to about 5m), is a bluish-grey and whitish-grey shark with distinct dark bars. The tail fin has a narrow upper lobe, the gill slits are small and the teeth are cockscomb-shaped with strong serrations. This robust, dangerous species occurs in estuaries and in open seas off WA, SA, NSW, QLD and NT and is a common scavenger in harbours. In 1935 a specimen in the Coogee Aquarium NSW disgorged a tattooed arm which led to a murder investigation—the so-called 'Shark Arm Case'.

The family Carcharhinidae also contains the whalers, of which there are several species in Australian waters. The bronze whaler, *Carcharhinus obscurus* (up to 3m) which has a distinctive bronze colouring, and the black

whaler, *C. macrurus* (4m), brownish or dark grey above, are probably responsible for most of the shark attacks on the E coasts. The black whaler is often confused with the grey nurse shark. The northern whaler, *C. stevensi* (about 4m), an E sub-tropical species, is also considered to be dangerous. The blue whaler or great blue shark, *Prionace glauca* (3m), ranges from southern QLD to WA, and must also be considered potentially dangerous. It is bright blue above and white below. Several species of the whalers penetrate estuaries and rivers and often travel well into freshwater reaches.

4. Order Squaliformes. This order contains the dogfishes, small and harmless sharks which have two dorsal fins but no anal fins. In one family, the Squalidae, there is a spine on each dorsal fin. A few live in shallow waters but most are found further from the land. One of the more unusual squalids is the prickly dogfish, *Oxynotus bruniensis* (60cm), which has a triangular cross-section (flattened below) and a very spiny skin. The dorsal fins are large and tall. It occurs in S seas.

5. Order Pristiophoriformes. This order contains the saw sharks, deep-water, shark-like fish with long flattened snouts armed with projecting teeth on each side. Found in southern Australian waters, they are distinguished from the larger sawfish (*see below*) by the feelers on each side of the snout, and by the lateral position of the gill slits.

6. Order Squatiniformes. This order contains the angel sharks, which are intermediate in shape between the rays and the typical sharks. They have flattened bodies and wide pectoral fins but the gill slits are lateral and there are two dorsal fins. The angel shark or monk fish, *Squatina australis* (1.5m), a sandy-coloured species with white and grey spots, lives at moderate depths in S seas.

Batoidei Rays and their allies are flattened fish with the pectoral fins joined to the head and body. The gill slits are ventral, but the spiracle, which is much larger than in sharks, is dorsal. When half buried in sand rays inspire through the spiracle and pass water out through the gill slits (sharks take in water through the mouth). There are five orders represented in Australian waters.

1. Order Pristiformes. Known as sawfish, the rays of this order are very similar to the saw sharks but the gill slits are ventral and there are no feelers on the snout. They are also larger than their shark relatives. Most are tropical species but the green sawfish, *Pristis zijsron* (up to 7.3m; saw about 2m), is found as far S as NSW and is common in muddy estuaries where it feeds on fish. Although mainly a marine species it also is common in freshwater; it has been found 240km from the sea in the GILBERT and Walsh Rivers in northern QLD.

2. Order Myliobatiformes. This order contains the stingrays and eagle rays. These rays have, at the most, a single small dorsal fin, and there is usually a spine or barb near the base of the tail.

The members of the family Ulophoridae, known as stingarees, have a small, leaf-like tail fin. Most are less than 1m long, with a short, barbed, venomous spine, a relatively short tail and pavement-like teeth for crushing invertebrates. There are several species belonging to the genus *Urolophorus*, the commonest probably being the common stingaree, *U. testaceus* (76cm), which is common in shallow water (to 130m) on sandy flats from southern QLD to SA.

The family Myliobatidae, the eagle rays, have long, whip-like tails, somewhat pointed 'wings' and elevated eyes so that they can look sideways; they often leap clear of the water. The eagle ray, *Myliobatus australis* (width of 'wing' about 1m; tail about twice the length of the disc), is greenish with blue spots and cross bands. It is found in all Australian States though the family, as a whole, is tropical. The spotted eagle ray, *Aetobatus narinari* (width 3m; very long tail), is white spotted and occurs off QLD and NSW. Both species eat molluscs and are sometimes pests of oyster leases.

The family Dasyatidae contains the largest stingrays, which have whip-like tails and a long, barbed, venomous spine. The largest is the smooth stingray, *Dasyatis brevicaudata* (width about 2m; length about 4m). It ranges from WA to NSW and TAS, and has killed humans. This species so impressed Captain COOK in May 1770 that he initially gave the name Stingray Harbour to BOTANY BAY.

The family Mobulidae contains the devil rays, which resemble the eagle rays but are at once recognised by the horns which protrude from the disc. These immense fishes often leap from the water to crash back with a great splash, possibly in an attempt to rid themselves of sucker fish. The devil ray, *Manta birostris* (width up to 7m), is found in all tropical oceans where it swims near the surface, gathering plankton and small fishes. It can weigh up to two tonnes. Despite its size it is regarded as harmless to man. It does not possess a tail barb. The ox-ray, *Mobula diabolus*, is a little smaller and feeds on small fishes.

3. Order Rajiformes. This order contains the skates, which are rays with short, blunt-ending tails and two dorsal fins. They have no stinging spines but the males of some species have thorns on the back and near the edges of the fins. There is no tail fin. The females lay eggs in horny purses (mermaid's purses). Most skates are deep-water fishes but the Melbourne skate, *Raja whitleyi* (about 1.5m long) of the family Rajidae, is also found in shallower water off SA, VIC and NSW.

4. Order Rhinobatiformes. This order contains the shovelnose rays and fiddlers, many species of which have a body which resembles that of a guitar or fiddle. The tail is relatively short and thick, and carries a tail fin and two dorsal fins. The snouts of the shovelnose group are generally pointed, and those of the fiddlers are more rounded. They have pavement teeth for crushing invertebrates and produce living young.

5. Order Torpediniformes. This small order contains the electric rays; they have electric organs and can turn on the voltage at will, for attack or defence. The electrical organs are masses of modified muscle and are found on each side of the body disc, between the eyes and the margin of the disc, and extending to the last gill slit. The voltage is believed to range from eight volts to about 220 volts but it falls off with repeated use. There is a record of shock being detected right along a line of 12 people standing hand in hand. The numbfish, *Hypnos monopterygium* (up to 60cm), has two dorsal fins, a well-developed tail fin and the body is an almost round disc. Brown above and yellowish below, it is found on the sand-flats of estuaries of S coasts, from WA to southern QLD.

Class Holocephali: ghost sharks or chimaeras This small group of strange cartilaginous fish is very ancient, the first known fossil being 180 million years old. In many ways they resemble the elasmobranchs, but there is only one gill slit, covered with a flap, and the males have extra claspers on the head. The skin is smooth and silvery.

The spookfish, *Hydrolagus ogilbyi* (85cm) is a large-headed, large-eyed fish with a long, pointed tail, a long posterior dorsal fin, a spiked anterior dorsal fin and no tail fin. It is silvery on the back and yellowish below, but the fins are dark. It is found in the GREAT AUSTRALIAN BIGHT, BASS STRAIT and off NSW. The ghost or elephant shark, *Callorhynchus milii* (1.1m), of the family Collorhynchidae, is a silvery, slightly luminescent fish with some darker patches. The tail is shark-like, and there are two dorsal fins. This species ranges from WA to TAS and NSW and is quite common.

Further reading: see under fishes.

sheep and wool Sheep were brought to Australia by the first European settlers in 1788 but numbers remained small in the early years of the colony. Traditionally, Australia has had the largest sheep population in the world, but in 1981 there were more sheep in the USSR (141.6 million) than in Australia (134.4 million). Within Australia, the dominant sheep State is NSW (46.1 million in 1981) followed by WA (30.8 million), VIC (25.5 million), SA (17 million), QLD (10.6 million) and TAS (4.4 million).

The principal products of the sheep industry are wool, meat, sheepskins and live sheep. Less important by-products are offal, tallow, lanoline and endocrine glands for use in the pharmaceutical industry. Wool annually contributes between 75 and 85 per cent of the gross value of production from the sheep industry.

Approximately 75 per cent of the sheep are Merinos, seven per cent are Corriedales and Polwarths, 15 per cent are cross-breeds and comebacks (cross-breeds with over half Merino breeding in the cross), and the remainder belong to several breeds which originated in the UK. The Merino is derived from sheep which were abundant in Spain in the 18th century and which were brought to Australia from South Africa, Germany, the UK and the USA throughout the 19th century. Renowned for wool production rather than for meat production, the breed is divided into several strains, including the fine-wools, medium Peppins, medium non-Peppins and strong-wools (or South Australians). Within each strain there may be several types; for example, in the strong-wools there are the Bungaree and Collinsville types. Fine-wools are nearest in appearance and production to the sheep imported originally; the other strains have resulted from efforts to develop sheep better adapted to Australian conditions. Fine-wools and medium Peppins are found on the tablelands of NSW, the W districts of VIC and in TAS; medium Peppins are also found on the slopes and plains of NSW, QLD, VIC and WA. The medium non-Peppin strain is mostly restricted to the central slopes and plains in NSW. The strong-wools were developed for semi-arid and arid areas and are now abundant in these regions in NSW, SA and WA.

The Corriedale and Polwarth breeds were developed from the Merino in Australasia in an attempt to combine the wool production of the Merino with the meat-producing characteristics of some British breeds, such as the Lincoln. Corriedale and Polwarths are popular in localised regions in southern NSW, VIC and TAS and have been successfully exported—there are now more Corriedales in South America than in Australia.

Value of production The total contribution of the sheep industry through wool, sheepskins and sheep meats generally exceeds 20 per cent of the gross value of rural production, making it the largest single rural industry (see Table 1).

There are differences among the strains in the amount of wool produced, the diameter of the wool fibres and in the liveweight of the sheep. Average wool production and liveweight are lowest in the fine strains, intermediate in

Table 1

RELATIVE CONTRIBUTION OF RURAL PRODUCTS TO GROSS VALUE OF RURAL PRODUCTION IN AUSTRALIA IN SELECTED YEARS

Product	Proportion of gross value of production (%)						
	Average for 1936-77 to 1938-39	1949-50	1959-60	1969-70	1979-80	1980-81	1981-82
Wool and sheepskins	23.7	36.7	29.5	19.4	14.9	14.5	14.1
Sheep meats	11.3	5.5	7.8	5.7	5.2	6.0	4.7
Beef meats	12.5	7.1	14.2	15.6	20.4	17.8	15.0
Whole milk	6.6	10.6	12.7	10.9	5.8	7.2	7.9
Wheat for grain	12.4	18.8	10.4	14.4	21.4	14.6	21.0
Other	33.5	21.3	25.4	34.0	33.3	39.9	37.3
TOTAL	100.0	100.0	100.0	100.0	100.0	100.0	100.0
Gross value of rural production ($m)*	417	1 579	2 646	3 790	11 720	11 525	12 670

Note: * figures rounded off to nearest thousand.
Source: Australian Bureau of Statistics and Bureau of Agricultural Economics, Canberra. Quarterly Review of the Rural Economy (vol 5, no 3, Nov 1983) Australian Govt Publishing Service, Canberra.

Table 2

CONTRIBUTION OF PASTORAL COMMODITIES TO AUSTRALIAN RURAL EXPORTS

Average for 3 years ending:	Total value of rural exports $m	Wool, sheep meats & live sheep %	Beef & veal %	Dairy Products %	Wheat %
1938-39	231	51.1	4.0	10.8	18.6
1950-51	1 265	64.9	1.0	5.4	15.5
1962-63	1 560	51.3	7.6	5.1	17.3
1967-68	1 899	46.0	10.4	5.6	18.2
1970-71	2 028	41.1	13.2	4.9	17.8
1973-74	3 082	37.0	18.0	4.6	13.9
1976-77	4 415	29.1	10.8	4.3	22.2
1979-80	6 589	28.3	17.6	3.5	20.4
1980-81	7 489	28.6	16.5	3.5	21.2

Source: Australian Bureau of Statistics and Bureau of Agricultural Economics, Canberra.

Table 3

VALUE OF TOTAL EXPORTS AND RURAL EXPORTS AND THE CONTRIBUTION OF THE SHEEP INDUSTRY TO RURAL EXPORTS AND TOTAL EXPORTS IN AUSTRALIA IN SELECTED YEARS

Period	Total exports	Exports of rural products	Exports of wool, live sheep & sheep meats		
			Value	As % of exports of rural products	As % of total exports
	$m	$m	$m	%	%
1938-39	271	231	118	51.1	43.5
1950-51	1 410	1 265	821	64.9	58.2
1959-60	1 816	1 451	837	57.7	46.1
1969-70	3 960	2 108	906	43.0	22.9
1970-71	4 204	2 105	667	31.7	15.9
1973-74	6 663	3 509	1 327	37.8	19.9
1974-75	8 490	3 863	895	23.2	10.5
1976-77	11 399	5 123	1 806	35.2	15.8
1979-80	18 634	8 550	2 126	24.9	11.4
1980-81	18 409	8 170	2 400	29.4	13.0
1981-82	19 036	7 850	2 324	29.6	12.2

Source: Bureau of Agricultural Economics, Canberra.

the medium and highest in the strong strains. Fibre diameter varies from 19 micrometres in the fine to 26 micrometres in the strong, although within a strain there can be considerable variation in diameter due primarily to variation in the nutrition of the sheep.

Value of exports The sheep industry is the largest single contributor to the value of rural exports (see Table 2). The value of wool and skins exported accounts for the main share of the industry's contribution, with the value of sheep meats usually accounting for less than five per cent of the annual total value of rural exports (see Table 3).

Wool The Merino breed, the breeds derived from the Merino (Corriedale and Polwarth) and the crosses with the Merino produce fine apparel wool which is used in the manufacture of materials for clothing, fine curtains, upholstery and blankets. Over the five years to 1980, Australia had only 14 per cent of the world's sheep but produced 26 per cent of the world's wool, about 55 per cent of the world's Merino wool and about half of the total volume of wool sold in the international market.

In the manufacture of apparel wool, finer wools are more valuable than coarser wools. In 1980-81, 75.4 per cent of the wool sold at auction in Australia was 24 micrometres or finer in average diameter, while only 5.5 per cent was 30 micrometres or greater. Most of the wool is exported without being processed, as greasy wool or as wool on sheepskins. In the 1970s these exports contributed between 20 and 30 per cent of the annual value of rural exports (eight to 12 per cent of the value of total exports). In the 1960s and 1970s Japan was the major importer of wool from Australia, followed by the USSR, France, Italy and the Federal Republic of Germany. Australia exports wool to more than 20 countries.

Most of the wool is sold at public auction. In the 1970s substantial changes occurred in the

VIC Dept of Agriculture

British breed sheep

J.P. Kennedy

Merino sheep in a semi-arid environment

Courtesy of A.I.S. Canberra

Stud sheep at the saleyards

Courtesy of the Wool Board

Mechanical sheep shearing

Premier's Dept QLD

P.R. McMahon

(above) Typical sheep farming homestead in QLD
(below) Angora goats are bred for their highly-prized mohair

methods of preparing and presenting wool for sale. These changes involved the adoption of a method of classifying wool in the shearing shed known as objective clip preparation, pre-sale measurement of wool and sale-by-sample. In objective clip preparation the wool is sorted into categories according to the apparent diameter, length and colour of fibres. Fleeces with distinct defects are kept separate. Pre-sale measurement takes place in the storage depots which are operated by selling brokers who handle the wool for the producers; samples of wool are measured to determine the content of clean wool, the degree of contamination with vegetable matter and the average diameter of the fibres. For sale-by-sample the data obtained in these measurements are made available to potential buyers along with a sample of the wool.

Since 1974 the Australian Wool Corporation has operated a reserve price scheme in the wool auction. The Corporation recommends minimum prices for all wool categories and purchases at auctions those offerings which do not reach the minimum price. The Corporation maintains stocks of wool in Australia and in selected locations overseas, and sells from the stocks when the opportunity occurs.

Sheep meat This is classified as either lamb or mutton. Lamb is the meat of sheep which have not grown a permanent incisor teeth and generally are less than 15 months old. Almost all the lamb is consumed on the domestic market, while nearly half of the mutton produced is exported, principally to Japan, the Middle East and the UK. During the 1970s a substantial trade in live sheep developed between Australia and Singapore and the Middle East—approximately 5.8 million were exported in 1981-82. The total value of exports of lamb, mutton and live sheep reached a peak of $456 million in 1980-81 (5.3 per cent of the value of all rural exports), and in 1981-82 was $401 million.

Consumption of sheep meat in Australia averaged 19.4kg per capita between 1977 and 1981. This is similar to the level of consumption in New Zealand but more than twice the level in Greece, the UK and the Republic of Ireland which have the next highest levels of consumption.

Most of the mutton produced in Australia is derived from wool-producing flocks of Merinos, Corriedales or Polwarths by the slaughter of wethers (castrated males) and ewes at the end of their reproductive life (known as cast-for-age ewes).

Production of lamb is based on the cross-breeding of British breed rams and Merino ewes ('first cross' lambs) and the cross-breeding of British breed rams and crossbred ewes ('second cross' lambs). The production of second cross lambs is usually the concern of specialist prime lamb producers located in areas where there is relatively reliable rainfall, or irrigation, which permits the establishment of highly productive pastures with a long growing season. Lamb is also produced by the slaughterings of Merino lambs, first cross female lambs and progeny of Corriedale and

Australian Dorset horn sheep are one of the major sires for the fat lamb trade

Polwarth breeds.

Approximately 75 per cent of the lamb is produced in NSW and VIC, with NSW being the more important State. The domestic market is the main consumer of lamb in all States but there is some variation between States in the volume and percentage of production available for export. WA, SA and VIC tend to depend on the export market to a much greater extent that NSW.

Sheep and lambs destined for slaughter are sold in various ways, including public auction in saleyards in capital cities and large regional centres, private negotiation between buyer and seller on the farm, consignment to an abattoir for slaughter and subsequent sale of carcases on behalf of the producer, and purchase by a central marketing authority. Research is being conducted to develop and implement a system for classification of carcases.

Systems of production The systems of production in operation in Australia can be classified according to the main source of

income as: wool production; prime lamb production; breeding rams; and breeding crossbred ewes. More than one system may operate on the same property.

Wool production is the most common system. The sheep involved are almost invariably Merinos, the exceptions being Corriedales, Polwarths and comebacks. Most wool-producing flocks are also breeding flocks so income may be obtained from the sale of wethers and ewes (for slaughter or breeding).

Prime lamb producing flocks usually consist of crossbred ewes and British breed rams. Normally, the ewes are bought-in and all lambs are sold for slaughter. Wool production from the ewes is also a source of income.

The majority of ram breeding flocks are registered studs: that is, the sheep are registered in a stud book which is maintained by a breed society. However, some rams are bred in large commercial flocks and in co-operatives. Usually, a stud is run in conjunction with a

Table 4

AVERAGE WEIGHT OF FLEECE SHORN FROM SHEEP AND LAMBS (INCLUDING CRUTCHINGS)
(kilograms per head)

Average for 5 years ending:	NSW	VIC	QLD	SA	WA	TAS	Australia
1930	3.74	3.83	3.45	3.94	3.24	3.10	3.66
1940	3.72	3.16	3.48	3.97	3.38	2.97	3.56
1950	3.82	3.57	3.85	4.48	3.57	3.01	3.80
1960	3.93	3.91	4.44	4.80	4.16	3.56	4.05
1970	4.03	3.81	4.26	5.02	4.19	3.85	4.15
1980	4.23	3.89	4.42	5.06	4.33	4.00	4.30
Average for the years:							
1970-71	4.08	4.01	4.39	4.90	4.07	3.99	4.18
1975-76	4.10	3.81	4.48	4.87	4.47	4.13	4.27
1979-80	4.27	4.01	4.58	5.20	4.20	4.00	4.33
1980-81	4.10	3.97	4.07	5.07	4.36	3.91	4.25

Source: *Wool Production and Utilisation*. (various issues), Australian Bureau of Statistics, Canberra.

commercial flock on the same property.

Flocks which breed crossbred ewes supply these to prime lamb producing flocks. Commonly, cast-for-age Merino ewes are mated to Border Leicester rams. The wether progeny are sold for slaughter while the ewes are sold when they are seven to 12 months old.

Wool production per sheep The amount of wool produced by a sheep each year is influenced by such factors as nutrition, health, age, heredity and reproduction. Average annual production per sheep in Australia varies from year to year principally because of variation in nutrition (*see* Table 4).

While the average wool production of New Zealand sheep is greater than Australian sheep, New Zealand sheep produce coarser and less valuable wool. In all the other countries the sheep produce less wool, on average, than in Australia. Within Australia the regions of lowest wool production are in the semi-arid areas of QLD and WA; the highest wool weights are produced in semi-arid areas of southern Australia, probably because the sheep here are the South Australian strain of Merino which has the genetic potential to produce high rates of wool growth.

Sheep shearing takes place throughout the year, with a concentration in August, September and October. However, in QLD, May to July is the most popular quarter for shearing, while in SA and TAS most of the sheep are shorn between August and January. Most sheep are shorn by professional shearers, employed either by a shearing contractor or directly by the wool growers. Sheep are shorn with mechanical shears driven by electric or fuel-powered motors. As soon as the fleece is shorn it is spread out on a table to be skirted. This involves removal of wool which is coloured, stained, soiled with mud or faeces or heavily contaminated with dust, burrs and seeds and small pieces of skin which may have been removed during the shearing. The fleece

wool is then classed and pressed into bales weighing up to 200kg, branded to identify the grower and transported to a central storage depot, where it is sampled and arranged into sale lots.

Reproduction The reproduction rate of a flock is usually measured according to the percentage of lambs marked in relation to the number of ewes joined. Lamb marking usually occurs when the lambs are between two and eight weeks old and involves removal of the tail, castration of males (except in ram breeding flocks) and placement of an identifying mark in the ear. The number of ewes joined is the number of ewes which are placed with rams for mating. The reproduction rates (lambing percentage) is influenced by nutrition, health, climate, age and heredity and varies from year to year in a flock and in the country; in Australia it is considerably below the genetic potential of the sheep because of poor nutrition and harsh climate. The lowest lambing percentages are in the N semi-arid areas of the continent; the highest are in TAS

Courtesy of A.I.S. Canberra

VIC Dept of Agriculture

(above) Merino ram (below) Merino ewe

and the coastal high rainfall regions of southern Australia where improved pastures provide good levels of nutrition and cross-breeding enhances reproductive performance.

Lambing is not confined to a particular season in Australia. A survey by the Bureau of Agricultural Economics revealed that in 1972-73, 32.4 per cent of lambs were born in autumn, 40.7 per cent in winter, 16.8 per cent in spring, 1.5 per cent in summer and 8.6 per cent were born in a combination of seasons. The time of lambing tends to be regulated according to climatic conditions and to the seasonal variation in lamb prices. The spread of lambing is possible because the Merino has a long breeding season. There is considerable experimental evidence, however, which shows that the peak of fertility and fecundity occurs in the autumn. The gestation period in sheep is approximately five months; their highest nutritional requirements are during late pregnancy and lactation so this period should coincide with the season when pasture availability is highest. Newborn lambs are likely to die if the weather is cold, wet and windy, or very hot, and consequently producers attempt to avoid lambing when these conditions are probable. In some cases where lambing occurs during adverse weather, shelter is provided in sheds or by shelter belts of trees or shrubs.

Rams The ratio of rams to ewes at joining varies considerably between flocks and regions. For Australia as a whole the ratio was estimated to be approximately 1.25:100 in 1969-70. Most of the rams in use are bred in studs and sold to producers. In the Merino breed there is a hierarchical three-tiered structure of studs—'parent', 'daughter' and 'general' studs. Parent studs supply rams to daughter and general studs. The daughter studs purchase rams only from their parent stud or from another daughter stud of the same parent stud; the arrangement of a parent stud and its daughters is called a 'family group'. General studs purchase rams from more than one family group. Some large commercial flocks breed rams for their own use rather than relying entirely on purchase from studs; in recent years some co-operative ram breeding flocks have developed whereby sheep breeders contribute their best ewes to a central flock which breeds rams and supplies them to contributing flocks.

The large studs usually engage a sheep classer who examines young rams and recommends which ones should be culled, retained as sires for the stud or be sold. Experiments have shown that clean wool production per head is a fairly highly heritable characteristic in Merinos, and the scientific recommendation is that heavy emphasis should be placed on selecting rams which produce high weights of clean wool of an acceptable fibre diameter. To assist breeders, fleece measurement laboratories are provided by Departments of Agriculture, the University of New South Wales and the Australian Wool Testing Authority. Breeders weigh the fleeces and remove small samples of wool which are used to measure yield of clean wool and fibre dia-

(above) Corriedale ram (below) Corriedale ewe and lamb

meter. Some breeders now use these facilities to obtain objective data to assist them in ram selection and also provide the data to potential purchasers of rams.

Health There are many infectious organisms, parasites, nutritional disorders and toxicities of plants which produce disease in sheep. Ill health may cause mortality, reduce wool production, affect wool quality and depress growth and reproduction rates. Substantial costs may be incurred in preventing and controlling disease. For example, the Bureau of Agricultural Economics estimated that the costs of controlling sheep BLOWFLY and internal parasites were $28 million and $51 million in 1969 and 1970 respectively.

Blowfly strike is the infestation of the skin of living sheep by the larvae (maggots) of blowflies, of which the primary green blowfly,

Lucilia cuprina, is the main species involved in Australia. The most common area to be struck is the crutch; soiling with urine and faeces is a major predisposing factor to crutch strike of Merino sheep. Urine soiling can be reduced and subsequent blowfly strike effectively controlled by mulesing and correct tail docking. Mulesing involves the excision of a boomerang-shaped strip of wooled skin from each buttock and, in some cases, the removal of skin from over the base of the tail and the dorsal surface of the tail. Faecal soiling can be reduced by treatment of sheep to control internal parasitism and by nutritional management. Outbreaks of blowfly strike on the body can be severe but are generally restricted to periods of prolonged heavy rainfall in the warm months of the year. Young sheep are most severely affected and invariably develop fleece rot, a

Southern fiddler ray, *Trygonorhina fasciata guanerius* (*see* SHARKS AND RAYS)

Tiger shark, *Galeocerda cuvieri* (*see* SHARKS AND RAYS)

Ornate wobbegong, *Orectolobus ornatus* (*see* SHARKS AND RAYS)

Spotted wobbegong, *Orectolobus maculatus* (*see* SHARKS AND RAYS)

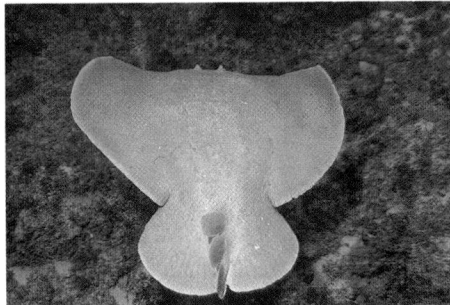

Electric ray or numbfish, *Hypnos monopterygium* (*see* SHARKS AND RAYS)

A toado, *Sphoeroides hamiltoni* (*see* FISHES POISONOUS)

A stingray, *Urolophus testaceus* (*see* FISHES POISONOUS)

Bottle brush tree, *Callistemon* species (*see* MYRTACEAE)

Black kangaroo paw, *Anigosanthos* species (*see* HAEMODORACEAE)

Sturt's desert pea,*Clianthus formosus* (*see* PAPILIONACEAE)

Banksia species (*see* PROTEACEAE)

Drum sticks, *Isopogon* species (*see* PROTEACEAE)

Grevillea species (*see* PROTEACEAE)

Burrawong, *Macrozamia* species (*see* GYMNOSPERMAE)

Wool samples arranged in sale lots in the 1970's

Courtesy of the Wool Board

condition which follows a mild dermatitis brought about by continued wetting of the skin. The treatment of body strike depends mainly on introducing insecticides onto the wool, but insecticidal resistance in blowflies has reduced the efficacy of this treatment.

The important internal parasites of sheep are ROUNDWORMS (nematodes) and LIVER FLUKES. Female roundworms in the sheep's digestive tract lay eggs which are passed out in the faeces, hatch and develop into larvae; these are picked up by sheep eating infected pasture. Internal parasites can be controlled by drenching the sheep with drugs which kill worms and by management procedures which restrict the intake of larvae. The life cycle of liver flukes involves two hosts, sheep and snails. Control involves elimination of snails, by killing them or by draining areas where they live, and drenching sheep.

Infectious organisms cause a wide variety of diseases in sheep; many of the diseases can be prevented by appropriate vaccination. Nutritional disorders in sheep may be due to inadequacy of nutrients, such as a deficiency or imbalance in the diet of minerals and vitamins, or an excess of compounds in the diet. An example of the latter is the reproductive disorder known as clover disease which is due to excessive intake of phyto-oestrogens which are present in some cultivars of subterranean clover.

See also disease, livestock; grazing industry
Further reading: Alexander, G. & Williams, O. *The Pastoral Industries of Australia.* Sydney University Press, Sydney, 1973; Bureau of Agricultural Economics *Rural Industry in Australia.* Australian Govt Publishing Service, Canberra, 1975; *Sheep Production Guide.* Graziers' Association of NSW, Sydney, 1976.

Sheffield Shield *see* cricket

shellfish *see* molluscs

shells *see* bivalve molluscs; gastropods

shells, coat-of-mail *see* chitons

she-oak *see* Casuarinaceae

Shepparton VIC (population 28 369 in 1981). Located on the E bank of the lower GOULBURN RIVER in central northern VIC, at the intersection of the Goulburn Valley and Midland Highways, 182km N of Melbourne, it is the regional business, administrative and service focus of a large tract of irrigated farmlands. At an elevation of 113m above sea level, it is the centre of an extensive area of alluvial plain country producing vegetables, dairy products, fat lambs, beef cattle and fruits, and experiences high summer temperatures and cool, frosty conditions in winter. It receives an average annual rainfall of 509mm, spread throughout the year, but with the highest rainfall in winter. The city began as a crossing point on the Goulburn River in the early 1850s; it was called McGuire's Punt originally, but in 1855 was named after one of the pioneer settlers, Sherbourne Sheppard. It became a shire centre in 1884, a separate borough in 1927 and a city in 1949.

The city has a variety of secondary industries, some based on the rural produce of the region, such as a milk and butter processing factory, fruit canneries and a soup factory; others include a major textile mill (producing worsted yarns, synthetic fibres and knitting wools), a metal-fabrication factory, engineering workshops and brick works. Six kilometres N of the city is the shortwave station Radio Australia, and 32km E of the city on the lower slopes of Mt Major is Dookie Agricultural College, established in 1886 as a centre for training and research; both are open to visitors.

Shepparton boasts a modern civic centre, completed in 1965, which includes the town hall, an art gallery, a theatre and the municipal offices. Victoria Park, with its scenic 20ha lake, provides an attractive entrance to the city from the S. In 1973 the city council started a unique venture on a 24ha site, 4km N of the city, by establishing an International Village which depicts the customs and traditions of about 30 nations; the village is located on an island, surrounded by a man-made waterway on which boats transport visitors from one 'country' to another. WARANGA RESERVOIR, an important storage basin in the Goulburn Valley irrigation scheme, lies some 20km SW of the city.

shipping *see* transport

shipworm *see* bivalve molluscs

Shoalhaven River NSW A coastal river, it rises in the SOUTHERN TABLELANDS (about 40km inland from Moruya), flows in a general S-N direction between ridges in open plateau country to the W of BRAIDWOOD, until it reaches the Bungonia area (E of GOULBURN). Here it enters a precipitous gorge and makes a sharp turn to flow E, then descends into a broad open valley, flowing across the coastal plain to its delta at NOWRA and thence to the sea. In the upland parts of the Shoalhaven River basin the country is dominated by sheep and cattle grazing, with some fodder crop cultivation along stream flats. Much of the middle section of the basin consists of rugged, timbered land included in the Morton National Park (112 460ha) which contains spectacular gorge country and several major waterfalls (such as Belmore and Fitzroy Falls) where tributaries plunge over the plateau scarps. In the lower reaches on the coastal plains, the flats are used mainly for dairying, fodder crops and vegetable growing. The Princes Highway crosses the lower part of the valley at Nowra, 13km from the mouth and 161km by road S of Sydney.

Irrigation canal near Shepparton VIC

J.H. Shaw

shooting The first organised civilian shooting club in Australia was the Sydney Rifle Club, formed in 1842. In 1860 a New South Wales Rifle Association was formed, and this was followed by the setting up of similar organisations in the other colonies. In 1888 the first national body was formed, and after a number of name changes this became the National Rifle Association of Australia. For small-bore shooting the main organising body became the Australian Small Bore Rifle Association.

The main full-bore rifle shooting competition in each State has long been the Queen's (formerly King's) Prize, and since 1972 a national Queen's Prize contest has been held at Canberra. A Commonwealth of Nations Queen's Prize is also awarded annually at Bisley, England, and this has been won four times by Australians: by Walter Addison of SA (1907), Percy Pavey of VIC (1948), Ross Graham of VIC (1978) and Geoff Ayling of TAS (1981). Until the 1970s, rifle shooting was strictly a male domain, but since then the sport has been thrown open to women, who have shown great skill at it. Thus Libby Felton won the WA Queen's Prize and the QLD Rifle Championship (corresponding to the earlier Queen's Prize), in 1974 and was runner-up at Bisley two years later; and Helen Griffiths won the QLD Rifle Championship in 1979.

Clay-target shooting, which involves firing at clay discs catapulted into the air to resemble birds in flight, developed strongly in Australia from the 1920s, and by the late 1970s there were about 130 clubs with 5 000 members. Trapshooting, involving the shooting of live birds on their release from cages, was for a time a popular sport, but by 1956 had been banned in all States.

Pistol shooting also became organised comparatively recently, the first competitions being launched in SA and TAS in 1947. It developed strongly from that time, under the encouragement of a noted marksman, Lionel Bibby, and in 1956 the Amateur Pistol Shooting Union of Australia was formed, so that Australia could organise entrants for the pistol shooting events at the Melbourne Olympics. Today the activities of this body, and of the organising bodies of other sections of the sport, such as those mentioned above and also the Australian Clay Target Association and the Field and Game Federation of Australia, are co-ordinated through the Australian Shooting Association.

Shore, Arnold Joseph Victor (1897-1963)

Artist. Born in Melbourne, Shore studied at the National Gallery School and with Max MELDRUM. This conventional training led at first to conventional work, but on seeing reproductions of the work of such post-Impressionists as Van Gogh, Shore changed his techniques. With George BELL he started an art school in 1932 to teach painting of a more modern tone, and joined William FRATER in promoting a more progressive approach to painting.

shoveler *see* ducks, etc.

shovel-headed garden worm *see* flatworms

show-jumping and eventing Until the advent of the car, the horse was the basic means of transport throughout Australia. While the car quickly replaced the horse in city areas, in rural areas the horse remained the mainstay of transport, and even now it is not uncommon for country children to ride their horses to school, often over long distances. It is no surprise therefore that Australia's best horsemen and women have come from families living in the rural areas of Australia. Some riders, such as Bill ROYCROFT and Laurie Morgan, developed their childhood habits of riding to school across country with abundant natural obstacles, such as fences, creeks and fallen trees, into specialised skills which brought them international successes.

Australian riders suffer from a major disadvantage in that they are isolated from Europe and the Americas, which are the major centres for equestrian sports. This isolation is disadvantageous for two reasons. Firstly, it is expensive for Australians and their horses to travel overseas and for the same reason overseas competitors rarely visit Australia. Secondly, exacting quarantine regulations make bringing a horse into Australia or even returning to Australia with an Australian horse an expensive, time-consuming task. Despite these difficulties, Australian riders have an enviable international reputation which has been growing, particularly since

1960. In that year, Laurie Morgan, then 45, won the individual gold medal in the Three Day Event at the Rome Olympics. Another Australian, Neil Lavis, won the silver medal in the same event. Disregarding a cracked collarbone caused by a fall in the cross-country event, Bill Roycroft rode in the show-jumping event to help Australia capture the team gold medal. Successes since then include: 1968 Olympic Games in Mexico City bronze medal for team event; 1976 Olympic Games at Montreal bronze medal for team event; 1978 King George V Gold Cup won by Jeff McVean on *Claret* in London; 1979 F.E.I. International Trophy won by Greg Eurell on *Johnny Mac*; 1981 Champion Jumper Stakes at the Horse of the Year Show won by Chris Smith on *Sanskrit*; 1982 F.E.I. International Trophy won by Guy Greighton on *Mikneil*.

shrikes, cuckoo- *see* cuckoo-shrikes, etc.

shrike-tits *see* thickheads

shrimps *see* crustaceans

shrubland *see* vegetation

shrubtit *see* warblers, etc.

Shute, Neville (1899-1960)

Novelist. This was the pen-name used by Neville Shute Norway. Born in London, he qualified as an air pilot, but until his departure from the UK worked mainly as an aeronautical engineer and designer. Critical of post-war controls and welfare state measures in Britain, he settled in Australia with his family in 1950 and farmed

Show jumper in action

at Langwarrin VIC. His novels were marked by a lively narrative style and achieved great popular success. They include: *The Pied Piper* (1942); *A Town Like Alice* (1950), which tells the story of an English girl who, as a refugee from the Japanese in Malaya, met and married an Australian soldier and later used an inheritance to equip a northern QLD township with the amenities which she had seen in ALICE SPRINGS; *In the Wet* (1953), a story in which the Queen leaves a degenerate Britain to live in Australia; and *On the Beach* (1957), which pictures Australia as the last refuge from the slowly spreading radioactivity resulting from a nuclear war.

Siding Spring Mountain

NSW A volcanic peak in the WARRUMBUNGLE RANGE, about 600km *NW* of Sydney and 24km *W* of COONABARABRAN, it is the site of an astronomical observatory, built in the late 1960s and officially opened by Prince Charles in 1973. The observatory is a joint British and Australian enterprise in which the main telescope, like all modern telescopes, is a large reflector dish; it has a diameter of 3.75m and, at the time of its installation, was the second-largest in the world. At the observatory there is an exhibition, called 'Exploring the Universe', which visitors can view.

silky oak

Belonging to the family PROTEACEAE, the silky oak, *Grevillea robusta*, is a tall tree with large inflorescences of golden flowers, and with light-green, soft, much dissected leaves. It grows in QLD and NSW.

silver

This metal was used for jewellery and ornaments as far back as the 4th century BC and is noted in the earliest records of man in the Mediterranean areas and Asia Minor. The Roman Empire adopted silver as the basis of its monetary system, using gold and bronze in the higher and lower value coinage respectively. In the 16th and 17th centuries, Spanish explorers exploited silver ores in Mexico, Peru and Bolivia, the last named becoming the principal producer until the 18th century.

Production Silver ore, mainly as argentite (Ag_2S), accounts for only about 25 per cent of the world's production of the metal, the bulk being obtained as a by-product of the lead-zinc

Siding Spring Mountain observatory near Coonabarabran NSW

NSW Dept of Tourism

mining industry, with a little from copper and nickel operations. The photographic industry supplies silver-bearing waste as a secondary silver.

In 1980, Australia produced 766 816kg of silver, making it the world's sixth-largest mine producer with 6.6 per cent of the total. QLD (in particular MOUNT ISA) accounted for over half of this figure with BROKEN HILL in NSW, ROSEBERRY in TAS, KALGOORLIE in WA and TENNANT CREEK in the NT accounting for most of the remainder. The production, by States, for the period 1970-80 is shown in Table 1. The co-products and by-products from silver mining are restricted to copper, lead and zinc, with lesser amounts of antimony, gold, fluorine and uranium.

The photographic industry consumes almost 30 per cent of the world's silver; other principal uses of the material are in the electric, electronic and chemical industries and as silverware and jewellery. Silver solders and brazing alloys are used in refrigerator and air-conditioning manufacture and other uses have been established in medicine and dentistry. The use of silver in coinage is declining.

The industry The structure of the industry in Australia is such that six or seven companies produce the bulk of the silver. The economic factors associated with silver production interlock closely with the production and economics of other metals. The forecast is of an annual growth rate of two per cent to a demand of 22 million kilograms of primary silver in the year 2000. The world reserves of silver are difficult to assess accurately. It is assumed that about 66 per cent of the estimated resources occur in lead-zinc deposits or in association with copper. The recoverable reserves are estimated at 200 million kilograms with a possibility of three times that quantity being ultimately available.
Further reading: see under minerals and mining.

silver-biddies *see* fishes, bony

silvereyes

Also known as white-eyes or zosterops, these PASSERINE BIRDS belong to the family Zosteropidae, which contains 80 species, four of which occur in Australia. In appearance and habits these BIRDS resemble FLOWERPECKERS and HONEYEATERS, but are distinguishable by the conspicuous ring of white feathers around the eyes. Their plumage is dull greenish-yellow, with patches of grey and white, and their bills are pointed and slightly down-curved. They use their brush-tipped tongues to extract honey and fruit juices; this diet is supplemented by insects, usually caught on the ground, and seeds. Their cup-shaped nests are built in bushes or small trees.

Table 1

MINE PRODUCTION OF SILVER IN AUSTRALIA 1970-80
(in kilograms)

State	1970	1973	1978	1979	1980
QLD	407 438	326 575	417 377	456 734	405 490
NSW	339 290	296 320	309 936	296 451	301 494
TAS	53 296	76 903	86 192	76 662	57 160
SA	31	1 473	—	10	6
WA	3 241	2 261	1 678	1 819	1 850
NT	5 148	3 882	341	534	816
TOTAL	808 444	707 414	812 524	832 210	766 816

Source: *Australian Mineral Industry Annual Review* (1970-80) Australian Govt Publishing Service, Canberra.

Courtesy of A.I.S. Canberra

The eastern silvereye, *Zosterops lateralis*

Three species frequent the coastal heathland and woodland areas of Australia: the western silvereye, *Zosterops gouldi** (12cm long), of W and SW Australia; the eastern silvereye, *Z. lateralis* (12cm), of E and SE Australia; and the pale silvereye, *Z. chloris* (10cm), recorded on the islands off north-eastern QLD. The yellow silvereye, *Z. lutea** (10cm), of N and NW Australia, is more often seen in mangrove areas.

silverfish *see* bristletails

Simpson Desert This vast arid area lies in the SE of the NT and extends into south-western QLD and the NE of SA, covering an area of about 78 000km². It is a region of low and irregular rainfall, at most times completely devoid of surface water, but a number of streams, such as TODD RIVER, flow seasonally from the E MACDONNELL RANGES into the desert fringes and peter out. Much of the area is covered by long parallel sand dunes about 500m apart and up to 60m high; in other parts there are large clay pans which are usually dry, but in an occasional wet period they contain expanses of shallow water and attract large numbers of water birds. The SA section of the desert lies N of LAKE EYRE, W of the BIRDS-VILLE TRACK, and E of the central Australian railway line. The Simpson Desert Conservation Park in SA, established in 1967, covers an area of 692 680ha, and in QLD the Simpson Desert National Park is 505 000ha. The explorer Charles STURT was the first white man to enter the desert (in 1845), but it remained largely unexplored until this century. An aerial survey of it was made by C.T. Madigan in 1929 and he named it in honour of A.A. Simpson, then president of the Royal Geographical Society of Australasia (SA branch). Madigan first crossed the desert by camel in 1939.

Further reading: Madigan, C.T. *Crossing the Dead Heart.* Georgian House, Melbourne, 1946.

singers and singing Judged by international operatic standards Australia has produced a high proportion of outstanding singers. Various theories have been advanced to account for this phenomenon, and include the warmly attractive climate, good diet, the desire of Australians to prove themselves in international competition and the beneficial results to singing of nasal habits of speech. The climatic and other parallels between Australia and Italy, also famous for its singers, have often been remarked on. The list of Australian singers who have distinguished themselves both at home and abroad is very long, and includes Nellie MELBA, John BROWNLEE, Peter DAWSON, Florence AUSTRAL, Marjorie LAWRENCE, Harold WILLIAMS, Joan HAMMOND, June BRONHILL, Donald SMITH, Yvonne MINTON and Joan SUTHERLAND.

Only recently has Australia been able to claim a stable national OPERA company. In the past, Australians have been very happy for their opera singers to go to Europe for training and experience and, having won fame there, to welcome them back in triumph. Since the establishment of the Australian Opera in 1970 more singers have been willing to return to work in their own country, and thus enrich the local music scene. However, young singers still find it essential to further their training overseas, and understandably many establish their reputations entirely abroad.

Certain factors have assisted aspiring singers in their desire to study overseas. Among these were the now legendary 'Mobile Quest', a weekly radio programme sponsored by an oil company from 1949 to 1957. Coming at a time when Australians were still dependent on radio as an important source of entertainment,

this programme appealed to the deep-seated interest of Australians in contests by presenting the best vocal talent in the country in the form of an aria competition. Other aria competitions have also had a long record of success, and among these the Sydney and Melbourne *Sun Aria* competitions (both sponsored by newspapers) and the *Shell Aria* competition in Canberra continue to attract singers through generous prize-money and assistance towards overseas study.

Australia's conspicuous singing talent has not been confined to operatic singing. The choral traditions of the 19th century, the primary sources of music making at that time, did much to foster singing talent at an amateur level. Eisteddfods served a similar function, especially in those areas settled by the Welsh and Cornish, which included such mining areas as the goldfields of BALLARAT and the coalfields of NEWCASTLE The singing traditions of the very large proportion of Irish settlers and the highly developed choral traditions of the smaller German settlements have also played a significant role in the history of singing in Australia.

Singers of operetta and related theatre have long been popular in the country, and many Australian singers in the field of light entertainment, such as Gladys MONCRIEFF and Olivia Newton-John, have achieved fame nationally and internationally.

Further reading: Mackenzie, B. & Mackenzie, F. *Singers of Australia: From Melba to Sutherland.* Lansdowne, Melbourne, 1967.

Vineyards in the Pokolbin district near Singleton NSW

Singleton NSW (population 9 572 in 1981) A town on the HUNTER RIVER, Singleton is 239km by rail NNW of Sydney and 79km inland by road from NEWCASTLE. It is situated on the New England Highway and is a railway town on the main line through the Hunter Valley to the N tablelands. The surrounding rural areas, for which it functions as the local commercial and service centre, are dominated by dairying, together with cattle grazing, fodder crop cultivation and sheep raising. There are a number of stud farms, with many fine homesteads, on the rich grazing lands surrounding the town. Vineyards in the district produce table wines for which the Hunter Valley is renowned. As in other urban settlements located on the Hunter River, the low-lying sections of the town are subject to flooding. There are several interesting old buildings in the town and the National Trust (NSW) has classified a number of these for preservation as part of the cultural heritage, including the courthouse, the Club House Hotel, 'Ewbank', the showground pavilions and rotunda, and All Saints Anglican Church. At Liddel on the New England Highway, 32km N of Singleton, there is a major electricity power station. An assured water supply for Singleton has been provided by the GLENBAWN DAM on the upper Hunter, completed in 1957.

See also Maitland; Muswellbrook

Siphonaptera *see* fleas

sittellas These PASSERINE BIRDS belong to the family Neosittidae, an Australian and New Guinea family. The five Australian species, all measuring 10cm to 12cm long, are endemic, and one or other occurs in almost every part of Australia, except TAS, in open forests and woodlands. Sittellas are small, dumpy BIRDS which find their food in the bark of trees and, unlike other Australian birds, they can run up *and down* tree trunks and branches.

The orange-winged sittella, *Neositta chrysoptera**, of SE Australia, has streaked underparts, a dark head and an orange patch on the wings. In the similar white-headed species, *N. leucocephala**, of eastern NSW and southeastern QLD, and the striated species, *N. striata**, of CAPE YORK, the underparts are more heavily streaked with black; the former has a completely white head, while the latter has a black crown and white patch on the wings. The ranges of the black-capped sittella, *N. pileata**, which occurs throughout most of southern Australia, and the white-winged sittella, *N. leucoptera**, of N Australia, overlap in the S parts of the NT. Both species have black caps, more extensive in the female, and plain white underparts.

skates *see* sharks, etc.

skeleton weed *see* Compositae; weeds

skiing This sport is possible in only three Australian States—NSW, VIC and TAS—and although the area of skiable snow within these States covers an area larger than the total area of Switzerland, the popular resorts are far removed from the major population centres. Apart from Hobart and Canberra, which are both small in terms of population, there is no capital city within 160km of a developed ski resort. Because of the long distances and the

Cross country skiing

Courtesy of A.I.S. Canberra

fact that skiing is an expensive sport—the combined cost of accommodation, equipment, special clothing and chair-lift or tow-bar tickets put it beyond many budgets—it is not accessible to many Australians. An estimated 250 000 skiers visit the winter slopes annually.
History Australia was the first country in the world to form a ski club and the first to organise competitive skiing as a sport. During the winters in the gold-rush town of Kiandra NSW, the only successful mode of travelling was on skis, which had probably been introduced into Australia by Norwegian gold miners during the 1850s. Young people of the time quickly saw the possibilities for fun and enjoyment in this novel form of travel and the sport became popular in the early 1860s. A natural growth of this newly discovered entertainment was competitive racing. By the end of the decade cross-country ski races were an established annual event at Kiandra and to organise these races the Kiandra Snow-shoe Club was formed in 1870, the first of its kind in the world. From these localised beginnings the development over the following 80 years was slow and sporadic. To cater for the handful of enthusiasts who regularly visited the snowfields, the Hotel Kosciusko in the Australian Alps was built in 1909, followed in 1910 by the Chalet on MOUNT BUFFALO in VIC. The new European sport of downhill racing reached Australia in the late 1920s, and rope tows were installed at Charlotte Pass and on Mt Buffalo in about 1938.

In the 1950s a number of factors contributed to the rapid development of skiing. Firstly, the post-war immigration programme resulted in the arrival in Australia of increasing numbers of Europeans and, in particular, Scandinavians to whom skiing was second nature. Secondly, with the construction of sealed roads resulting from work carried out by the Snowy Mts Authority in NSW and by the State Electricity

Commission and the Forestry Commission in VIC new areas with better snow cover and more challenging slopes were made accessible, such as Thredbo and Perisher Valley in NSW and MOUNT BULLER and FALLS CREEK in VIC. It was in these latter areas that the major development of the 1960s and 1970s took place and skiing is now a boom sport, the only complaints being that the season is too short (from early June to early October) and that the sport is so popular that during the peak periods the snowfields are too crowded. In very recent years there has also been a resurgence of interest in cross-country skiing.
International competition Having competed in the Olympics since 1952, Australia is gradually building a worthwhile reputation in skiing. The outstanding skier to date has been Malcolm Milne who for three years at the end of the 1960s was rated in the world's top five. In 1970 he astounded Europe by winning a major race on the Alpine circuit at Val d'Isere in the French Alps. In 1983 the leading Australian skier was Steven Lee who was among the top 20 world skiers in down-hill racing events.
Further reading: Plociennik, H. *Australia's Snowfields.* Paul Hamlyn, Sydney, 1976.

skin-diving This is the generic term Australians use for both diving with an air tank (scuba-diving) and diving with a snorkel but no air tank (skin-diving). Australia has a lengthy coastline liberally sprinkled with islands, reefs and rocky outcrops which form fertile breeding grounds for a great variety of aquatic life. It is this variety which lures the skin-diver, either as a spearfisherman out to bag a meal or as an underwater explorer fascinated by the ever-changing underwater scenery.

In the 1920s skin-divers were still a curiosity but in the following two decades, with literature on the sport becoming more readily available, a greater interest was shown by Australians. After World War II, with the advent of Self-Contained Underwater Breathing Apparatus (scuba) allowing skin-divers to dive to greater depths and to continue breathing under water for prolonged periods, a greater number of people were eager to try skin-diving. Since the 1960s world-renowned Australian underwater photographers such as Ben and Eva Cropp and Ron and Valerie Taylor have also brought favourable publicity to the sport with their award-winning films and photographs of sea life. Competitions in skin-diving were tried in the 1960s but people who enjoy skin-diving in Australia prefer to keep the sport on a pleasurable, recreational basis rather than approaching it as a competitive sport.

skinks *see* lizards

skipjacks *see* fishes, bony

skuas *see* sea birds

slaters *see* crustaceans

Slessor, Kenneth Adolf (1901-71) Poet and journalist. Born in ORANGE in NSW, he worked from 1920 as a journalist in Sydney and Melbourne, was editor-in-chief of the Sydney *Smith's Weekly* from 1927 to 1939, and editor of the literary journal *Southerly* from 1956 to 1961. During World War II he was an official war correspondent, covering the Battle of Britain and campaigns in the Middle East and New Guinea. In the 1920s he was a member of the group known as the Bohemians, led by Norman LINDSAY and Hugh McCRAE, and the poems in his first published volume, *Earth-visitors* (1926), show the influence of both of these men, but in later work he developed his own outlook and style, and established himself as perhaps the most notable Australian poet of his time. His published works include *Five Visions of Captain Cook* (in *Trio: A Book of Poems* by K. Slessor, K. Matthews and C. Simpson, 1931), *Five Bells: XX Poems* (1939), *One Hundred Poems, 1919-1939* (1944), and *Poems* (1957). The most recent selection of his work is *Selected Poems* (1975).
Further reading: Burns, G. *Kenneth Slessor.* (new edn) Oxford University Press, Melbourne, 1975. Stewart, D. *A Man of Sydney— An Appreciation of Kenneth Slessor.* Nelson, Melbourne, 1977.

Slim, Sir William Joseph, First Viscount of Yarralumla (1891-1970), Field Marshal and Governor-General of Australia. Born in Bristol, England he was commissioned in the British Army in 1914 and during World War I served in GALLIPOLI, France and Mesopotamia. He then served in the Indian Army, and during World War II commanded Indian troops in the Sudan, Eritrea, Syria and Persia before being transferred to Burma as Com-

mander of the 14th Army. Following his outstanding success against the Japanese in Burma he was made Commander of Allied Land Forces in South-East Asia (1945-46), Commandant of the Imperial Defence College (1946-47) and Chief of the Imperial General Staff (1948-52). He served as Governor-General of Australia from 1953 to 1959.

slugs and snails This article deals with the terrestrial and freshwater GASTROPODS of Australia. Most of these MOLLUSCS belong to the pulmonate, air-breathing group (subclass Pulmonata) of the Gastropoda. Snails have an obvious external shell into which the body can usually be withdrawn completely; slugs have no external shell or, at the most, a very small one.

Native terrestrial snails Australia has a large native snail fauna and there are also many introduced species. There are probably several hundred native species of snails, but many of them are so small (about 1mm across) that they are undescribed and difficult to identify. Only a few of the native species and their families are discussed here. Various kinds of snails are found in all kinds of terrestrial habitats, from the arid interior to coastal rainforests. When conditions are dry, however, they are concealed in damp places or under the surface of the soil. Few are found in suburban gardens for they have been displaced by introduced species such as *Helix aspersa*, the common garden snail of Europe. Most snails are herbivores but a few are carnivorous. Although most of the land snails are pulmonates a very few species belong to the subclass Prosobranchia. These are most easily recognised by the presence of an operculum which is not found in the pulmonates. Most are very small and occur in coastal N Australia.

Allan's land snail, *Pedinogyra allanae*

The family Hedleyellidae contains the so-called Australian native snail or giant panda, *Hedlyella falconeri*, which resembles a giant garden snail. The shell is a glossy brownish-red yellow with some dark blotches and bands. It can reach 10cm in height and diameter, and is found in mountain rainforest from QLD to near the HUNTER RIVER in NSW. There are

several related though smaller species in similar habitats in SE Australia.

Many Australian snails were once placed in the genus *Helix*, the genus to which the introduced garden snail belongs. They have been separated and placed into several other families, the most important of which is the Hadridae. A typical example is Fraser's snail, *Sphaerospira fraseri*, which is reddish-yellow with many spiralling chestnut bands, though some specimens are darker. The shell is about 5cm across and 5cm tall. It ranges from southern QLD to northern NSW. Some snails from this family live in the arid regions of central Australia.

In Australia, the family Papuinidae is largely confined to northern QLD. The snails are small and delicate; most of them climb on the trunks, branches and leaves of trees.

The family Chloritidae is also composed of small snails, but their shells are circular and flattened. They are yellow to reddish-brown but the distinguishing feature of many of them is the clothing of short or long hairs. They range from NSW to QLD. A few closely related species in NW Australia and the NT are similar but hairless.

The family Xanthomelonidae contains the melon snails (*Xanthomelon* species) which have globular, glossy shells.

The family Paryphantidae contains the chief native carnivorous snails of Australia, some of which attack the introduced garden snail. *Strangesta capillacea*, an example from NSW, occurs commonly in the Sydney region, usually in the bush but sometimes in suburban gardens. The thin, flat, almost circular shell is about 2.5cm in diameter and is horn yellow, reddish or chestnut.

The families Notoridae and Charopidae contain most of the tiny land snails of Australia (1mm to less than 2.5cm in diameter). Notorids are the larger, ranging from about 1cm to 2.5cm in diameter. The shells are rather glassy and the snails are found only in the warmer parts of Australia. Charopids, also called endodonts, are rarely more than 8mm in diameter and have glassy delicate shells. They are found throughout the Pacific region but are commonest in the S parts of Australia.

The family Bothriembryontidae contains the buliminoid snail; SW Australia is almost the only place in the world where these are found. Four species reach SA and one occurs in the arid regions of central Australia. There is a related Tasmanian form. The shells are long and oval, and fairly smooth. They range in length from 1.2cm to 5cm, and vary greatly in colour. Most buliminoid snails are found on trees and shrubs in native forests.

The family Succineidae contains the amber shells, which are often confused with water snails (*see below*) for they live in damp places, usually near to ponds and creeks. Some cluster under the bark of eucalypts. Their small, delicate shells are right-handed (whereas those of water snails can be either left- or right-handed), the spires are short and the body whorls are swollen.

Common melon snail, *Xanthomelon padrystylum*

Chrysalis snails, which belong to several families, are small, soil-living snails which resemble the chrysalids of moths (*see* BUTTER-FLIES, etc.) in their shape. Most of them are only 1mm to 2mm long.

The family Helicarionidae contains the glass or slug-like snails. These pulmonates range from TAS to QLD and have long bodies similar to those of slugs but they carry a simple, delicate, glossy shell on their backs and, unlike most slugs, the tail is squared off at the end. The Sydney glass snail, *Vercularion freycinetti*, quite common in the Sydney region, has a green shell which is about 1.2cm across. The animal itself is orange-grey with an orange-red edging to the foot.

Introduced terrestrial snails The most conspicuous snails in Australia are the introduced species for they have virtually displaced all the native species from suburban gardens and banished them to the bush. The introduced European garden snail is so common and familiar that it needs no description. It is closely related to the culinary snail or *escargot* of Europe and is, in fact, perfectly edible. It is a classic 'tramp' species and is now found in all continents apart from Antarctica; in Australia it is commoner in the S than in the N.

The sand-dune snail, *Theba pisana*, is a European species that has become a pest in California and South Africa, and sometimes reaches plague numbers in SA. It seems to infest only ground frequented by man.

The pointed snail, *Cochlicella acuta*, is often found in bush. It is a European species with an elongated shell about 2.6cm long. It is well established in all the S States.

Several carnivorous species have become established. An interesting example is the garlic snail, *Oxychilus alliarius*, which has a flat, glossy, semi-transparent shell about 5mm wide and 2.5mm tall. It smells like garlic when confined in a tube. It is still uncommon in

Australia, and prefers dark, shady spots. It was formerly confused with the similar, but larger, cellar snail, *O. cellarius*, which is established in SE Australia.

The giant African snail, *Achatina fulica*, has not yet colonised Australia though there is a great danger that it will do so. An infestation was found at CAIRNS in 1977 but it was destroyed. Juveniles have been found in containers landed at Sydney. The snails weigh more than 500g; they not only eat plants, they also flatten them. The snail has been taken by man to many Asian and Pacific countries and it was widely spread by Japanese soldiers during World War II as an emergency food supply. It is common in New Guinea and Indonesia.

Terrestrial slugs Most slugs have either no shell or a small one inside their tissues. They are nocturnal scavengers and omnivores, and some attack plants. The day is usually spent within the soil. The front third of the body carries a shield (the mantle). This has a respiratory opening on the right side. Usually there are two pairs of tentacles, the first with eyes at the tip.

Common native slug, *Tribonophorus graeffei*

There are very few native slugs in Australia. The most familiar is *Tribonophorus graeffei* which can reach a length of 15cm. Usually it is

hunched up into a circular shape about 5cm across. It has only one pair of tentacles—the first. The colour varies but there is always a pink band round the body and a reddish triangle surrounding the breathing pore.

The commonest introduced species is probably the yellow slug, *Lehmannia (Limacus) flava*. The mucus produced by the foot as it moves is iridescent. When fully stretched it is about 10cm long. It feeds on decaying matter which it often seeks indoors. Other introduced species include the grey slug, *L. maximus*, up to 23cm long, an omnivore; the very destructive field slug, *Agriolimax agrestis*, about 3cm long, a species which produces copious slime when irritated; and the jet slug, *Milax gagetes*, an often completely black species, about 5cm long, which also destroys plants.

Water snails This section covers some of the snails found in inland waters in Australia. They are not all freshwater species for many of Australia's lakes are extremely saline. One family often has representatives in water three times saltier than the sea. In general, the water snails are herbivores but some are omnivorous. They are not common in polluted or acid waters. Though they do little damage by themselves water snails are important as intermediate hosts of flukes parasitic in man and other animals (*see* DISEASES AND EPIDEMICS, HUMAN; DISEASES, LIVESTOCK).

There are 10 important families found in inland waters and four families that are mainly marine. The purely inland forms belong to the subclasses Prosobranchia and Pulmonata.

1. Prosobranchia. All these snails have an operculum. The family Thiaridae contains the marsh or black snails, found mainly in E and N Australia. The shells are spiral and turret-shaped and often many centimetres long.

The family Truncatellidae consists of the salt-lake water snails. There are probably two Australian genera, *Coxiella* and *Coxiellada*. They apparently occur only in saline lakes and they are usually dark in colour and less than 1.3cm long.

The family Bythiniidae contains the Australian gabba, *Gabbia australis*, a little river snail about 6mm long; it is brown in colour but often has black encrustations.

The family Hydrobiidae contains several genera, most of which are found in SE Australia and particularly in TAS. Some of these snails live in brackish water. They are small, with dark shells which are only about 3mm long.

The family Viviparidae contains 10 known species of river snails which are found throughout hot countries in freshwater streams. Most Australian species occur in N and central Australia.

2. Pulmonata. This subclass includes the family Ferrissiidae, the most easily recognised freshwater univalves for they resemble small limpets. Common in TAS, SE and SW Australia, most of them are 6mm or less in width. They are usually found on submerged plants.

The family Planorbidae formerly contained only snails with flattened shells but it has been widened to include the family Bulinidae which have spired shells. The flattened species are usually small, 6mm or less in diameter. This family and the family Limnaeidae (*see below*) contain most of the species involved in the transmission of flukes, and in the condition called bather's itch.

The members of the family Limnaeidae have right-handed shells and belong to one genus, *Lymnaea*, which can be divided into two groups. Those in the first group have globular shells which are 2.5cm or more in length. The main species, possibly the only native species, in this group is *L. lessoni* but the large European *L. stagnalis* has been introduced. The second group consists of species less than 1.7cm in length. There is probably only one native species, *L. tomentosa*, which is widespread in E Australia and is the chief carrier of liver fluke in Australia. Cattle and sheep are also affected by the trematode fluke (*Paramphistomum* species) which has carriers among snails belonging to the genera *Bulinus*, *Galba* and *Planorbis*.

Further reading: see under gastropods; molluscs. *Also* Ellis, A.E. *British Snails.* Oxford University Press, Oxford, 1926; Runham, N.W. & Hunter, P.J. *Terrestrial Slugs.* Hutchinson, London, 1970; Wright, C.A. *Flukes and Snails.* George Allen & Unwin, London, 1971; Smith, B.J. & Kershaw, R.C. *Field-Guide to the Non-Marine Molluscs of South-Eastern Australia.* Australian National University Press, Canberra, 1979.

Smart, Jeffrey (1921-) Artist. Born in Adelaide, Smart studied at the School of Arts and Crafts in Adelaide, and at the Academie Montmartre and La Grande Chaumiere in Paris. He taught at the King's School and East Sydney Technical College. In the 1960s he went to live in Italy. Since the 1950s the themes and style of his work have been fairly consistent; he uses rich colours and many of his pictures give a sense of pervading silence. His favourite subject is the city which is portrayed as a technologically impressive but lonely and insensitive place.

Smith brothers Sir Keith (1890-1955) and Sir Ross (1892-1922) Aviators. Both were born in Adelaide and educated there and in Scotland. In World War I Keith was rejected from entry into the Australian Imperial Force (AIF) on grounds of health, but succeeded in joining the Royal Flying Corps. Ross joined the AIF, but in October 1916 entered the newly formed Australian Flying Corps; at the end of the war he was Australia's most highly decorated airman, having been awarded the Air Force Cross, the Military Cross with bar and the Distinguished Flying Cross with two bars. After the war he piloted a Handley Page bomber from Cairo to Calcutta. Shortly afterwards the Prime Minister of Australia, William HUGHES, announced the offer of a prize of £10 000 for the first flight from England to Australia, provided that it was made before the end of 1919 by an Australian crew, in a British-built machine, and was performed in

The Smith brothers' *Vickers Vimy* just after landing at Darwin. The two aviators are to the right of centre and Sergeants Bennett and Shiers to the left of centre

an overall time of not more than 30 days. Ross Smith, on returning to England from India, applied to Vickers for an aeroplane in which to compete for this prize, and, on the strength of his wartime record and his experience on the Cairo-Calcutta flight, was provided with a Vickers Vimy. For crew he chose his brother Keith as navigator and assistant pilot, and Sergeants J.M. Bennett and W.H. Shiers, who had accompanied him to India, as mechanics. They left England on 12 November 1919 and reached Darwin in a little under 28 days.

Soon afterwards Sir Ross planned to circumnavigate the world in a Vickers Viking amphibian, but during a test flight in England in 1922 his aeroplane crashed, and he and Bennett were killed. In the following year Sir Keith joined the staff of Vickers, becoming the company's first Australian representative. He subsequently became chairman of directors of a number of companies, including Vickers-Armstrong (Aust.) Pty Ltd, and a director of several others. The aeroplane in which the two brothers won fame has been preserved, with other mementoes of the flight, at Adelaide Airport in a museum built under the provisions of Sir Keith's will.

Further reading: Price, A. *The Skies Remember: The Story of Ross and Keith Smith.* Angus & Robertson, Sydney, 1969.

Smith family This voluntary welfare organisation, which operates throughout NSW and the ACT, is the largest body of its kind in Australia. It began in 1922 when five Sydney businessmen, alarmed at the extent of poverty in Sydney, donated packages of toys, puzzles, games and sweets to a Home for Boys in the suburb of Carlingford. When the matron asked whom she should thank for the gifts, one of the donors replied, 'Just call us Smiths, matron. We are members of a very big

family.' This principle of anonymity has continued ever since, the names of members, donors and those receiving aid being kept confidential. Forms of material help include donations of food, clothing, furniture and household goods; financial assistance is given for such purposes as redeeming grocery orders, paying back rents, housing bonds, gas, electrcity and other household bills. Qualified welfare workers give advice and guidance, and aid is sometimes arranged in legal matters. The organisation is run by an honorary Board of Directors and the staff include paid employees and a large number of voluntary helpers.

Smith, Donald (1922-) Tenor. Born in BUNDABERG in QLD, Don Smith has won recognition and a great following among Australians during a career which has, unlike the careers of most Australian singers, been pursued almost entirely in his native country. After World War II he began singing frequently on the local radio station and then moved to Brisbane. In 1951 the visiting Italian Grand Opera Company invited him to sing with the company on its Australian tour. He joined the national company in 1958, singing with great success in *Peter Grimes*, *The Barber of Seville*, *Fidelio* and *Rigoletto*. From 1963 to 1968 he worked with Sadler's Wells Opera Company and the Royal Opera, Covent Garden, and in 1969 he appeared as guest artist with Mexico City Opera. Since returning to Australia his principal roles with the Australian Opera include those of Gustavus (*A Masked Ball*), Pinkerton (*Madama Butterfly*), Calaf (*Turandot*), Don Alvaro (*The Force of Destiny*), Canio (*Pagliacci*), Turridu (*Cavalleria Rusticana*), Luigi (*Il Tabarro*), Radames (*Aida*), Dick Johnson (*The Girl of the Golden West*), Cavaradossi (*Tosca*), the Duke (*Rigoletto*), Don Jose

(*Carmen*) and Erik (*The Flying Dutchman*).

Smith, Sir Elliot Grafton (1871-1937)

Anatomist and anthropologist. Born in NSW, he worked in Cambridge on the brain and its evolution, and in 1900 was appointed Professor of Anatomy in Cairo where he became an authority on ancient Egyptians. Later he was a professor at Manchester and at University College, London. He visited China to study the remains of Peking Man. Smith was a keen supporter of the Diffusionist School which held that culture spread outwards from centres of civilisation, the chief of which, in his opinion, was Egypt.

Smith, Grace Cossington (1892-)

Artist. Born in Sydney, she became a pupil of Dattilo Rubbo, an Italian who ran an art school in Bligh Street, Sydney, and who encouraged experimentation. Among his pupils was Norah Simpson, a young Australian who whilst in England had seen the work of the post-Impressionists, such as Ven Gogh and Gauguin, and had brought back a series of colour prints. The post-Impressionist use of colour had a great influence on Cossington Smith; she wrote that 'my chief interest has always been colour ... it has to shine' and that 'my aim always has been to express form in colour.' She applied the paint with a loaded brush, giving her work a robustness and vivacity that attracted much attention in the art world in Australia. In 1928 she held her first one-person show, but because of her retiring nature she allowed the other Australian post-Impressionists, Roy DE MAISTRE and Roland WAKELIN, to dominate the movement in Sydney. The still lifes and interiors she painted in the 1950s and 1960s are vibrant with light and vitality.

Smith, Maria Ann (1801-70)

Maria Smith was the 'Granny Smith' in whose garden at Eastwood, Sydney, the first apple tree of that variety grew. The seed had been taken from rotting TAS apples bought in the market.

Smith, Thomas John (1920-)

Horse trainer. Born in the NSW country town of Goolgowi, Smith was introduced to racing as an apprentice jockey and was to become Australia's most successful trainer. Graduating from riding to training in the early 1940s, the first horse he trained was an ex-buckjumper named Bragger. It took him three years to shape the unruly and unpredictable Bragger into a winning racehorse and the 13 races Smith won with him helped establish his reputation as a skilful trainer. In the 1960s and 1970s he was the dominant figure on the Australian racing scene having won every major race on the racing calendar and establishing a number of Australian, Commonwealth and world training records. In the 1962-63 season for the first time he trained more than 100 winners, a feat he repeated in every season from 1966-67 to 1980-81; in 1973-74 he established a Commonwealth re-

cord by training 185 winners in one season; his total of 23 Derby wins is a world record; and at the end of the 1980-81 season he won the Sydney Trainers Premiership for a record 29th time in succession. At the Randwick Easter Carnival in 1969 his horses won 14 of the 29 races, and in every season since 1973-74 his horses have won in excess of $1 million, his best season being 1979-80 when they won $2 750 000. A colourful and extroverted figure with a penchant for fashionable hats and brightly patterned bow ties, Smith is a dedicated and knowledgeable trainer whose skill with, and understanding of, thoroughbreds have made him the most successful trainer in Australia's history.

Smithton

TAS (population 3 378 in 1981) A rural service centre in the NW coastal region of the State on the Duck River, Smithton is 86km W of BURNIE and 136km from DEVONPORT along the Bass Highway. At an elevation of only 9m above sea level, located on the coastal plain adjoining BASS STRAIT, it experience a mild climate with an average annual rainfall of 1103mm; the rain comes mostly in winter. The economy of the town is based on dairy farming, timber-getting, vegetable growing, pig raising and fishing. There is a large dolomite deposit in the district; the town has a modern butter and casein factory, several sawmills, a vegetable processing plant and a bacon factory. Circular Head, a peninsula to the NE, was the first settlement in the region and was named by George BASS and Matthew FLINDERS in 1798.

snail, elephant *see* gastropods

snail, sand *see* gastropods

snails *see* slugs, etc.

snake-bird *see* darter

snakes These carnivorous REPTILES belong to the suborder Serpentes (order Squamata) and are easily distinguished from all other animals except some legless LIZARDS. The differences are discussed in the entry on lizards; briefly, the main difference is that the lower jaw of a snake is loosely attached to the skull by elastic ligaments so that the jaw can be disarticulated when the snake has to swallow prey wider than itself. Many snakes are venomous but few are aggressive towards man unless provoked. Apparently unprovoked attacks by a snake usually result when the victim unwittingly stands between the snake and its escape route (for further details and for first aid treatment *see* ANIMALS, VENOMOUS).

Snakes are covered with scales; on the belly the scales are usually large and broad. When the snake moves it throws its body into a series of curves, and the large ventral scales give it the necessary purchase on the ground so that it can push itself along. A series of waves, resulting from the expansion and contraction of muscles attached to the vertebrae, is translated into the forward motion of the snake.

Snakes do not have movable eyelids; the eyes are covered by a transparent scale (the brille) which is also found in some lizards. The long, forked tongue fits into a basal sheath, as in the goannas among the lizards. At the front of the palate there is a pair of sensory sacs, each with a channel to the interior of the mouth (Jacobson's organ); the tongue flickers in and out of the mouth, and when drawn in the two tips are inserted into the two sacs, depositing there any particles that the tongue has collected. Snakes have no external ears and there is strong evidence that they are deaf though they are sensitive to vibrations transmitted through the ground.

There are between 2 300 and 2 400 species of snakes in the world. About 110 species, in five families, occur in Australia: Typhlopidae (22 species); Boidae (10 species); Acrochoridae (two species); Colubridae (11 species); and Elapidae (65 species). There are, in addition, several sea-snakes in Australian waters.

Typhlopidae Known as worm snakes, the members of this family are harmless, subterranean, non-venomous snakes which live on small worms and insects, especially termites. They are also called blind snakes because the eyes are little more than black spots beneath the cuticle. The body, which does not taper markedly towards the tail, is covered with thick, smooth, overlapping scales which are uniform in size around the body. The lower jaw is able to move independently of the upper jaw to some extent but not as much as in the typical snakes. The mouth is small, ventral and some distance from the snout. The teeth are small and there are no fangs.

Although the family has representatives in most of the warmer parts of the world, these snakes are rarely seen since they are usually within their burrows; they may emerge and move on the surface after rain. All the Australian species belong to the genus *Typhlina*, and it is difficult to distinguish between the various species. Examples are found in all parts of Australia (apart from TAS).

Boidae This family contains the pythons and the boa constrictors. All Australian members belong to the python group (Pythoninae) which differ from the boas (Boinae) in various details in the skull and teeth and in the production of living young by the boas. In general, the two groups do not occur in the same localities. Boas and pythons kill their prey by constriction but do not crush their victims to death—when the victim breathes out the snake tightens his coils a little more till, eventually, the victim suffocates.

Pythons possess a pair of cloacal spurs, flanking the vent; these are the vestiges of the hind-limbs and are larger in the males than in the females. These bulky, largely nocturnal snakes move slowly and feed mainly on warm-blooded animals but will also take reptiles. They stay coiled round their eggs till they hatch. There are four genera in Australia. The genus *Aspidites* contains the black-headed python, *A. melanocephalus* (1.5m; about 2.5m), of the N third of Australia. The body is brown with darker bars but the head, throat and neck are shiny, jet black. It is found in many habitats except the most arid, hunting at night for small mammals, terrestrial birds and reptiles. The colour of the woma, *A. ramsayi* (1.5m; 2.7m), varies; this species of the dry interior has, like *A. melanocephalus*, a small head not distinctly separated from the neck.

The only member of the genus *Chondropython* is *C. viridis* (1.2m; 2m), the green python, which in Australia is confined to the rainforest in the NE of CAPE YORK. The adults are emerald green with some light blue bars; the juveniles are bright yellow, gold or orange. This arboreal species lives on small mammals and birds.

The genus *Liasis* is found in Australia, New Guinea and Indonesia. Australia's largest snake, the amethystine or scrub python, *L. amethystinus* (3.5m; 8.5m), is found in E Cape York in a variety of habitats, including scrub on coral cays. The head is large and broader than the slim body and neck. The upperparts are light brown with darker zig-zag markings while the underparts are light. This apparently bad-tempered snake can give a serious bite and eats warm-blooded animals, particularly poultry, up to the size of a small wallaby. Children's python, *L. childreni* (75cm; 1.5m), found in many habitats from desert to rainforest in the N half of Australia and as far S as WILCANNIA in NSW, is a stout-bodied python with a distinctly separate head, light brown above with darker patches, and white below. It eats small vertebrates. The water python, *L. fuscus* (2m; 3m), found near water (in which it takes refuge) from north-eastern WA to Cape York and north-eastern QLD, is an iridescent snake, dark above and yellow below apart from the tail underside which is dark. The head is long and only slightly marked off from the long, powerful body. It feeds on various vertebrates. The olive python, *L. olivaceus* (2.5m; 4m); a N species ranging from W Cape York to central western WA, is olive to olive-brown above and cream coloured below and has a long head which is distinct from the neck. Found mainly in rocky areas but also in monsoon forest or savanna, its main food consists of warm-blooded vertebrates.

The genus *Morelia* contains carpet and diamond pythons, the most widespread of the Australian pythons, occurring throughout the mainland (apart from some parts of the SE) in a wide variety of habitats. There are two distinct forms, usually regarded as subspecies, but they hybridise in the N rivers region of NSW to give forms with yet more patterns. The diamond python, *M. spilotes spilotes*, (2m; 4m), is jet-black above with yellow spots forming diamonds and rosettes, and cream to yellow below with some black marks. It is found on the E coast of NSW and inland to the GREAT DIVIDING RANGE. The carpet python, *M. s. variegata* (2m; 4m), is more variable in colour but is often brown above with yellow, black or dark brown irregular markings, and

cream or yellow and black-checked below. Both subspecies have a robust body and a large, distinct head. They feed on various vertebrates and are often arboreal. In country districts householders (and often publicans) keep them in outhouses to control rats.

Acrochordidae The two species in this family, commonly known as wart snakes, range from South-East Asia to the coastal districts of N Australia. They are completely aquatic. The scales carry warts which give the skin the feel of a file or rasp, and which make the skins attractive to manufacturers of fancy leather goods. The little file snake, *Acrochordus granulatus* (60cm; 1.2m), a grey to almost black species, is an estuarine and marine species which feeds in the intertidal zone on crustaceans and fish. The Javan file snake, *A javanicus* (1.5m; 2.5m), is usually found in freshwater and feeds on fish. Both species produce living young. Neither is venomous.

Colubridae Although this family of generally harmless land snakes and back-fanged aquatic snakes contains about two-thirds of all species of snakes, only 10 occur in Australia, mostly in the N.

There are two subfamilies in Australia: Colubrinae (solid-toothed non-venomous snakes and venomous rear-fanged snakes) and Homalopsinae (venomous, rear-fanged, oriental water snakes). The fangs of the venomous snakes have a groove to convey the venom. None of the Australian colubrids is dangerous to man, largely because the snake cannot deliver an efficient bite, and because of the nature of the venom. Australian colubrids can be distinguished from other Australian snakes by many features, including an almost cylindrical tail and a single row of enlarged ventral scales.

1. Colubrinae. The keelback or freshwater snake, *Amphiesma mairii* (50cm; 1m), a northern species, is a solid-toothed, non-venomous snake that is always found near water and swamps; it feeds on frogs and lays eggs. The colour is variable: the back is grey to reddish or black, and the underparts cream, green, brown or salmon. The scales are keeled.

The brown tree snake, *Boiga irregularis* (1.4m; 2m), which has a similar distribution though it is found S of Sydney, is a venomous rear-fanged snake not regarded as dangerous to man, but aggressive if provoked. The colour and pattern vary with the locality. This nocturnal, egg-laying arboreal species forages on the ground for small vertebrates and eggs. There are two species of green tree snakes in Australia, both with slender bodies and whip-like tails—the northern tree snake, *Dendrelaphis calligaster* (80cm; 1.2m), found in E Cape York, some Torres Strait islands and New Guinea, and the common tree snake, *D. punctulatus* (1.2m; 2m), which ranges from north-eastern WA to southern NSW in coastal regions. These solid-toothed, diurnal species are green and yellow in the S but can be entirely golden or yellow in the N. Although they are arboreal, they will also forage on the ground and live beneath rocks and ledges,

sometimes in small groups. These egg-laying snakes live mainly on small, cold-blooded vertebrates; they can swim well and sometimes eat fish.

The genus *Stegonotus* has one Australian representative—the slaty-grey snake, *S. cucullatus* (average length 1.3m) a N nocturnal snake which often comes indoors.

2. Homalopsinae. Found in mangroves and fresh, coastal and estuarine waters, this subfamily includes the bockadam, *Cerberus rhynchops* (60cm; 1.6m), which ranges from South-East Asia to the coastal fringe of N Australia from north-eastern WA to Cape York. It has small, beady, upward-pointing eyes and is light grey to brown above and white to salmon or yellow below. The head is broad and there is a dark streak through the eye. This species feeds on small fish and crustaceans and it produces living young.

The other members of the subfamily also have small eyes and are all aquatic. The spotted snake, *Enhydris punctata* (30cm; 50cm), has a distribution similar to that of the bockadam though it does not reach Cape York. Macleay's water snake, *E. polylepis*, (60cm; 80cm), is also a N species. The white-bellied mangrove snake, *Fordonia leucobalia* (60cm; 1m), with a distribution similar to that of the bockadam though it extends to NE Cape York, is glossy black above and white below. *Myron richardsonii* (40cm; 60cm), is also a mangrove species of the far N.

Elapidae The two chief families of venomous land snakes are the Viperidae (vipers and rattlesnakes, not represented in Australia) and the Elapidae. Besides the Australian species (which total about 65) discussed below, the Elapidae includes the cobras, mambas and kraits of the Old World, and the coral snakes of the Americas. Apart from the venom apparatus, the elapids do not differ greatly from the colubrids from which they are probably an evolutionary offshoot. The relatively short fangs situated at the front of the jaw each contain a venom canal which opens near the tip. The venoms of the Australian species are mainly neurotoxic (though some contain other components as well). Every part of Australia has at least one resident species of elapid, and all those which cause possibly fatal or very serious bites are mentioned here.

Among the Australian elapids there are some that lay eggs, some that produce living young which emerge shortly before birth from eggs that have developed within the females, and some that produce living young that have been nourished by a well-developed placenta.

The genus *Acanthophis* contains two highly dangerous death adders, the common death adder, *A. antarcticus* (40cm; 1m), and the desert death adder, *A. pyrrhus* (up to 75cm). The former occurs in the coastal areas of Australia, except the extreme S and TAS; the latter is found in the arid regions of all States apart from VIC. These stocky snakes have a broad head which is distinct from the body and a curved spine on the relatively short, tapering tail. The tail is used as a lure for mice and other prey, and not as a sting, contrary to

Tiger snake, *Notechis* pecies

an old belief. The common death adder is usually grey to reddish above, with darker cross bands, and the underparts light with dark blotches. The desert death adder is brick-red above, with bands and cream below, and the scales are rougher than those of the common species. These aggressive nocturnal snakes have a rapid strike and often lie in wait, partly covered with litter, for prey. Before the production of a specific antivenene half the bites from common death adders ended fatally. Both species are ovoviviparous (producing living young from eggs hatched within the body.

The genus *Austrelaps* contains one species (possibly two), the copperhead, *A. superbus* (1.3m; 1.7m), a large-eyed snake with round pupils, confined to SE Australia and TAS. The head is narrow and the body thickset. The colour varies greatly but is usually dark above and yellow or dull grey below. The lips appear to be striped. A timid snake of swamps, river banks and creeks in coastal ranges, this species often occurs in large numbers; though its venom is extremely toxic bites are rare. Copperheads are ovoviviparous and feed mainly on frogs and other cold-blooded vertebrates.

The genus *Cacophis* contains three small, secretive species found along parts of the E coast. All are less than 1m long and all have a white or yellow band encircling, or partly encircling, the head. These nocturnal snakes strike viciously but rarely actually bite and are probably not dangerous.

The genus *Demansia* contains the whip snakes, elongated, swift diurnal species; large whip snakes can deliver a serious bite. The black whip snake, *D. atra* (1m), ranges from southern QLD along the coasts to north-eastern WA. *D. olivacea* (60cm), is found in north-western QLD, northern NT and northern WA. The yellow-faced whip snake,

D. psammophis, (80cm), which occurs throughout Australia apart from the tropical N (though it does occur in Cape York), TAS and the extreme SW and SE, has a distinct head, a yellow border to the eye and a black mark below the eye; olive brown to grey above, sometimes with reddish brown marks, and greyish-blue or green below, this egg-laying species favours sandy areas and sandstone country, living under large stones, sometimes in groups, and feeding on small reptiles and frogs. The collared whip snake, *D. torquata* (50cm), is a little known species from western NT, northern NSW and most of QLD.

The genus *Denisonia* contains four small to large, nocturnal species with representatives in most parts of Australia except TAS. One, the ornamental snake, *D. maculata* (50cm), a robust snake found in the ROCKHAMPTON and CHARTERS TOWERS areas of QLD, is potentially dangerous. Its tail is short and tapering, and its general colour is black to brownish-cream flecked black dorsally, and light ventrally, with black spots. The bite of the related De Vis' banded snake, *D. devisii* (50cm), is said to be very painful. It resembles the ornamental species but has irregular cross bands, dark in colour, along most of the body. Found in inland central QLD and northern NSW, it lives in litter, beneath logs and so on, as does the ornamental snake.

The genus *Echiopsis* contains *E. curta* (40cm; 60cm), the bardick, a species of the extreme S, from SW Australia to north-western VIC and south-western NSW. This adder-like snake has smooth scales, variable in colour. Its venom rapidly paralyses mice but its toxicity to man is unknown. Its biology is little known.

The genus *Hemiaspis* contains two E species. The black-bellied swamp snake, *H. signata* (about 50cm), a coastal species from northern QLD to S of Sydney, can bite painfully though not dangerously. Found both in dry

places and (more often) in marshy areas, it is generally active during the day or at dusk but is also nocturnal during warm periods. It is ovoviviparous and feeds on skinks and frogs.

The genus *Hoplocephalus*, confined to the mainland of E Australia, contains species which can all climb well. The pale-headed snake, *H. bitorquatus* (50cm), which ranges along the coasts from Cape York to just N of Sydney, is light brown or grey above with a broad, light band on the nape of the neck. This ovoviviparous snake of wet to dry woodlands feeds on skinks and delivers a painful though probably not dangerous bite. The broad-headed snake, *H. bungaroides* (60cm), found only on the HAWKESBURY sandstones in the Sydney region, has a venom which produces acute but not fatal symptoms. Jet-black above with irregular bands of yellow scales and a broad head, it has been confused with a young diamond python. Stephen's banded snake, *H. stephensi* (45cm), a coastal species from GOSFORD in NSW to southern QLD, in wet forests and rainforest, is brown or yellow above, with irregular, broad cross bands. The bands are sometimes missing or become longitudinal stripes. The head is black with a lighter patch on each side. The venom is painful and a bite requires treatment. All three species are nocturnal, ovoviviparous snakes.

The genus *Notechis* contains two species (and several subspecies) of the highly venomous tiger snakes. Found in southern Australia in a wide range of habitats, often close to centres of population, they have been responsible for many of the fatal cases of snake bite. The exact classification of the tiger snakes is still obscure; the one used here follows Cogger (*see below*). The black tiger snake, *N. ater* (1.5cm), occurs in south-western WA, southern SA, KANGAROO ISLAND and TAS and adjacent islands; *N. a. ater* in the FLINDERS RANGES; *N. a. humphreysi* on BASS STRAIT islands and TAS; *N. a. niger* on Kangaroo Is and the nearby islands; *N. a. occidentalis* in south-western WA; and *N. a. serventyi* on Chappel Is in the Bass Strait. All these snakes have black to very dark brown heads and bodies and grey underparts; there may be faint cross bands (more common in juveniles). Usually diurnal but also abroad on warm nights, they feed on frogs and small mammals, on mutton bird chicks on the islands and, on KING ISLAND, on each other. The eastern or mainland tiger snake, *N. scutatus* (1.2m), a SE species, can be found in varied habitats from rainforest to open floodplains. Often olive, brown, reddish or dark brown above, usually with narrow, yellowish cross bands, and light below, this diurnal species feeds mainly on frogs.

The genus *Oxyuranus* contains Australia's second most venomous and dangerous snake, the taipan, *O. scutellatus scutellatus* (2m; 3.35m). Before the production of a specific antivenene in 1955 taipan bites were almost always fatal but, fortunately, they were rare because of the snake's distribution and retiring and non-aggressive disposition. One 'milking' yields about 120mg of dried venom (tiger snakes, 35mg); a well-grown taipan carries enough venom to kill about 23 500 mice (tiger snakes 8 800). The head is large and long, and distinctly marked off from the slender neck. The cylindrical body tapers towards the tail and is so flexible and comparatively light that a taipan can bite even when held at arm's length by the tail. The back varies from light brown to dark brown or almost black, while the underparts are yellow with orange spots. There is some doubt about the taipan's distribution. Cogger gives it as mainly northern NT and possibly the KIMBERLEY Division of WA; Gow and Swanson (*see below*) say it extends from the GULF OF CARPENTARIA inland to near the NT/SA border and probably western NSW. (The doubts about the distribution may have arisen because of the existence of another snake which, until 1975, was confused with the taipan—the fierce or giant brown snake, *Parademansia* (*Oxyuranus*) *microlepidota* (2m; 2.5m) from arid parts of E central Australia. A recent milking of one specimen yielded enough venom to kill a quarter of a million mice, thus qualifying this as the most venomous land snake in the world.) Mainly diurnal, though it also forages on warm nights, most of the taipan's diet consists of small mammals. An egg-laying species, it frequents many habitats from savanna to tropical wet sclerophyll forest and is often found in sugar cane fields.

The genus *Pseudechis* contains one of Australia's most widespread elapids, the mulga or king brown snake, *P. australis* (2m). Ranging from tropical forests to deserts, this venomous and dangerous species feeds on small mammals, snakes and lizards, and frogs. It is coppery to olive brown above, but the scales often have black edges which produce a network pattern; the underparts are cream or salmon pink, often with orange patches. It is thought to be ovoviviparous. Collett's snake, *P. colletti* (1.5m), found in central QLD, is a related species of which little is known but which is possibly dangerous. The red-bellied black snake, *P. porphyriacus* (1.5m; 2.5m), is possibly the most commonly encountered venomous snake along the E coast (from Cape York to eastern SA) especially near streams, swamps and lagoons. This small-headed snake is glossy, purplish-black above and red or orange below. An ovoviviparous species, it feeds upon cold-blooded vertebrates, including fish, and small mammals and reptiles. The venom is largely harmorrhagic (attacking the walls of the blood vessels) and while the injury is local the pain is severe and the bite needs medical attention. The blue-bellied or spotted black snake, *P. guttatus* (1.5m), lives in many kinds of habitats in north-eastern NSW and south-eastern QLD. The colour of this diurnal snake is variable, some lacking the cream spots on the dorsal surfaces; the bite is a little more serious than that of the red-bellied black snake.

The genus *Pseudonaja* contains several highly venomous species. The dugite, *P. affinis* (1.5m), one of Australia's most venomous snakes, is found in a narrow coastal strip of south-western WA. Small-headed and

Carpet snake

with a slender body, it is olive above, often with numerous black specks, and dark below. The speckled brown snake, *P. guttata* (50cm; 80cm), of central QLD and NT, has a venom whose toxicity is unknown and could be dangerous; the upperparts are fawn to bright orange, with specks that appear when the snake moves, and the belly light with orange blotches. The western brown snake, *P. nuchalis* (1.5m), a deadly snake which lives in a variety of habitats ranging W from central QLD to the coasts (absent from the E coasts, Cape York, most of VIC, southern SA and TAS) is a swift-moving diurnal snake; it is very variable in colour but is usually light brown to almost black above with a 'V' or 'W'-shaped mark on the neck and a few dark cross bands, and cream, grey, yellow or orange below. The eastern brown snake, *P. textilis* (1.5m) ranges over the rest of the continent (not TAS) but overlaps in the W with *P. nuchalis*. Grey, brown or almost black above and light below with orange, grey or brown spots, it hides in rabbit burrows, stone piles, slabs or rocks and so on; it is found in a wide range of habitats though it seems to prefer drier ones. It is a nervous, aggressive species which, if it gets a grip, chews its very dangerous venom into the wound. There are several other brown snakes in this genus, all of which should be regarded as potentially dangerous.

The genus *Simoselaps* contains six attractive, small, nocturnal burrowing snakes which are not dangerous to man; all are 60cm or less in length, and all have a black bar through the eyes and most have another behind the head.

The genus *Suta* contains the myall or curl snake, *S. suta* (40cm; 60cm). Found in arid regions, living under logs or in crevices or debris, this nocturnal species feeds on small lizards and frogs. The large, flat head is distinct from the flattened body and the

upperparts are brown, the head and nape darker and the belly white or cream. It is called the curl snake because of its characteristic defensive posture—curled tensely, like a spring. Though it is not dangerous, the bite is painful.

The genus *Tropidechis* contains the rough-scaled snake, *T. carinatus* (75cm), a potentially very dangerous snake found in central Cape York, southern QLD and northern NSW. It is dark above, with bands, and light below, and is easily recognised by the strong keels on the body scales. An aggressive nocturnal species of wet forests and rainforests, it feeds on small vertebrates and has caused at least one adult death. It is easily mistaken for the harmless keelback or freshwater snake, *Amphiesma mairii*.

The genus *Unechis* is closely related to the genera *Denisonia* and *Suta*, and is represented in most parts of Australia except the NW. The six species (all 40cm or less) appear to be secretive and nocturnal, offering little threat to man.

The genus *Vermicella* contains two species which are readily recognised. The bandy-bandy, *V. annulata* (40cm), a black and white banded species with the bands more or less encircling the body, is a nocturnal, burrowing snake which probably lives entirely on blind worms. When provoked it holds parts of its body, in loops, above the ground. This egg-laying species is found in N central WA, northern VIC and most of the rest of the mainland States. The very similar northern bandy-bandy *V. multifasciata*, is found in north-western NT and extreme north-eastern WA.

Sea-snakes The true sea-snakes (family Hydrophilidae) are considered separately because, like most marine animals of Australian waters, their distribution is often uncertain. The family is believed to be closely related to the Elapidae but there are certain adaptations for a marine life, such as nostrils that can be closed by valves and vertically compressed, paddle-like tails. The genus *Laticauda* contains the only egg-laying species, but these are, in fact, largely terrestrial, going to sea to feed. *Laticauda* sea-snakes have overlapping scales, unlike the smooth scales of other species of sea-snakes. Mainly nocturnal, they are most likely to be encountered on NW coasts, E of the Torres Straits. The two species, *L. colubrina* (about 1m) and *L. laticauda* (about 80cm) are bluish-grey or blue above, with numerous cross bands; they are inoffensive but should be treated with respect.

Many, if not all, sea-snakes are extremely venomous though the bite is not painful. A victim may not realise that he has been bitten before the general symptoms begin to be manifested. No fatalities appear to have occurred in Australia but they are common in South-East Asia, especially among fisherman. As most records of sea-snakes are from N coastal waters, a bite would be dangerous because of the difficulty in obtaining medical aid. Cogger lists 32 species in 12 genera which are resident in, or often seen in, Australian waters. All hydrophilid snakes are Pacific and Indo-Pacific animals; none is known from the Atlantic Ocean.

The species with the widest distribution, both in the world and in Australian waters, is the yellow-bellied sea-snake, *Pelamis platurus* (70cm), which often comes as far S as Sydney and Perth and has been recorded from TAS. This pelagic, fish-eating snake is black above and pale (often yellow) below; the tail is yellow with black spots and bars, the general pattern resembling interlocked fingers.
Further reading: Parker, H.W. *Natural History of Snakes.* British Museum (Natural History), London, 1965; Worrell, E. *Dangerous Snakes of Australia and New Guinea.* Angus & Robertson, Sydney, 1966 and *Reptiles of Australia.* (2nd edn) Angus & Robertson, Sydney, 1970; Morris, D. & Morris, R. *Men and Snakes.* Sphere Books, London, 1968; Stackhouse, J. *Australia's Venomous Wildlife.* Hamlyn, Sydney, 1970; Cogger, H.G. *Reptiles and Amphibians of Australia.* A.H. & A.W. Reed, Sydney, 1975; Gow, G.F. & Swanson, S. *Snakes and Lizards of Australia.* Angus & Robertson, Sydney, 1977; Caras, R. *Dangerous to Man.* Penguin Books, Harmondsworth, 1978; Sutherland, S.K. *Venomous Creatures of Australia: A Field Guide with Notes on First Aid.* Oxford University Press, Melbourne, 1981.

snappers *see* fisheries; fishes, bony

snipes *see* waders

snowberries *see* Epacridaceae

Snowy Mountains NSW This relatively small range, which is part of the GREAT DIVIDING RANGE of E Australia and located in the SW section of the MONARO region, has attained prominence because of several unique features. It contains the highest land of the continent, with KOSCIUSKO (2230m above sea level) the highest peak; within the range there are several other peaks (Mt Twynam, Mt Townsend and Carruthers Peak) which stand as residuals above the plateau surface. During the Great Ice Age, this area was covered by glacial ice, and the landscape features bear evidence of this (for example, the valley cross-sections, moraine deposits, and moraine-dammed lakes). The higher parts of the range extend above the tree-line (about 1800m elevation) and in summer are carpeted with a dense covering of alpine grasses, low shrubs and flowering plants. These alpine meadows were once used for summer grazing of sheep and cattle but this annual migration of herds from the lower-lying regions into the high-lands is no longer permitted because of the hazards of soil erosion. In the winter the range is snow-clad and is a major skiing attraction for those seeking cross-country treks in remote areas away from the popular resorts in the lower valleys of the region such as Perisher Valley and Thredbo Valley. Another reason why this range has become almost a household name in Australia is the development of the vast hydro-electricity SNOWY MOUNTAINS SCHEME. The range forms the watershed between upper tributaries of the MURRAY RIVER and the headwaters of the SNOWY RIVER; the W side of the range, drained by the Murray, is steep and ruggedly dissected; the E side, where the Snowy rises, is more gently sloping country. The Kosciusko National Park, covering 629 708ha, includes the range and the river headwaters. The Alpine Way provides a scenic journey from JINDABYNE, along the Thredbo Valley, around the S end of the range and across the Geehi Valley to the Murray Valley Highway. The streams in the national park are popular for summer trout fishing and the park provides many opportunities for bushwalkers.

Courtesy of A.I.S. Canberra
Chairlift in the Perisher Valley skifields NSW

Snowy Mountains Hydroelectric Authority
Tumut 2 underground power station

Snowy Mountains Scheme Completed in 1972, this scheme is one of the greatest civil engineering projects undertaken in Australia. It is a hydro-electricity and irrigation complex comprising seven power stations, 16 dams, 80km of aqueducts and 145km of tunnels; it is located in the SE part of NSW, between the ACT and the VIC border, where the MURRAY, MURRUMBIDGEE and SNOWY RIVERS have their headwaters in the SW section of the MONARO region of the SOUTHERN TABLELANDS. The total cost of the scheme was $800 million. It has a total generating capacity of 3 740 000kW and each year it provides an additional 2 361 600ML of water for irrigation along the Murray and Murrumbidgee Valleys. The basic outline of the scheme is that the waters of the Snowy River and its tributary, the EUCUMBENE, are impounded in storage reservoirs in their upper reaches; this water is then diverted inland by long tunnels driven W through the Snowy Mts to the Murray and Murrumbidgee Rivers; travelling through these tunnels, and down the shafts associated with them, the water falls some 760m, generating large amounts of electricity as it passes through the power stations.

The earliest proposals for utilising the water of the Snowy River to supplement the flows of inland rivers for rural production date from the 1880s when heavy losses were caused by lengthy droughts. However, when the drought abated and better seasons returned, the proposals to divert the Snowy were quietly shelved. During the following half century several investigations were made and a number of proposals suggested both for developing the hydro-electricity potential and for diverting the Snowy inland for irrigation use. It was not until 1949 that, after further investigation and consultation between the Commonwealth government and the VIC and NSW governments, the Snowy Mts Hydro-electric Power Act was passed by the Commonwealth government, by which the Snowy Mts Hydro-electric Authority was established with the responsibility to design and construct the scheme, and William Hudson (later Sir) was appointed Commissioner. Broadly, the scheme as finally constructed falls into two sections: the Snowy-Murray development and the Snowy-Tumut development. Both these

Table 1

SNOWY MOUNTAINS SCHEME POWER STATIONS AND STORAGE RESERVOIRS

Main Storages	Capacity (ML)	Power Stations	Installed Capacity (MW)
Eucumbene	4 800 000	Tumut (T3)	1 500
Blowering	1 630 000	Murray (M1)	950
Talbingo	950 000	Murray (M2)	550
Jindabyne	690 000	Tumut (T1)	320
Tantangara	254 000	Tumut (T2)	280
Tumut	52 800	Blowering (B)	80
Jounama	43 800	Guthega (G)	60
Tooma	28 100		
Khancoban	21 500		
Geehi	21 000		

Source: Publications of the Snowy Mountains Authority.

are connected by tunnels to the main regulating storage, Lake Eucumbene. (See Table 1).

Snowy-Murray development This involves the diversion of the Snowy River through a tunnel system to the Geehi River, and thence to the Swampy Plain River, a tributary of the Murray. In passing through the tunnel system, the diverted water falls some 820m and generates hydro-electricity at Murray 1 and Murray 2 power stations. Additional power is generated in Guthega station which uses water from the upper Snowy River. An essential part of this development is the two-way-flow Eucumbene-Snowy tunnel whereby excess water from the Snowy can be diverted for storage in Lake Eucumbene, and low flows in the Snowy and Geehi can be supplemented by drawing stored water from Lake Eucumbene back through the same tunnel and delivering it to The Murray power stations. Additional water for this part of the scheme is pumped from lake Jindabyne into the tunnel system.

Snowy-Tumut development This N part of the scheme provides for the diversion of the Eucumbene, upper Murrumbidgee and Tooma Rivers to the Tumut River, and for the generation of electricity at four power stations (T1, T2, T3 and Blowering). The Eucumbene-Tumut tunnel is also a two-way-flow system which normally diverts water from Lake Eucumbene to the Tumut Pond Reservoir but, during periods of high flow in the Tumut and Tooma Rivers, excess water can be sent in the reverse direction.

Snowy River NSW/VIC As a result of Banjo PATERSON's poem 'The Man from Snowy River', this stream has become part of Australian folklore. It rises in the SNOWY MOUNTAINS near KOSCIUSKO above the tree-line, then flows through rugged heavily timbered gorge country, making an almost circular loop before flowing S across the NSW/VIC border, thence through E GIPPSLAND in VIC to reach the sea beyond ORBOST. Its headwaters are snow-clad in winter, being part of the Kosciusko National Park, with numerous popular skiing resorts. The main

tributaries in NSW are the EUCUMBENE, Thredbo, Maclaughlin and Bombala Rivers, while the Buchan River is the main VIC tributary. Two major storages of the SNOWY MOUNTAINS SCHEME, Lakes Eucumbene and Jindabyne, are in the upper section of the river basin. Towns located in the NSW catchment are Bombala, JINDABYNE, Adaminaby and Delegate. In the VIC section of the valley, grazing of beef cattle and sheep dominate the upper parts, which dairying and fodder crop cultivation in the lower reaches.

Snuggery SA A small township in the far SE of the State, Snuggery is 11km SE of MILLICENT and 40km NW of MOUNT GAMBIER on the Princes Highway. It is located amidst extensive pine plantations which provide the timber for a cellulose and paper making plant.

soapwort see Caryophyllaceae

soccer Because of the worldwide popularit of soccer as a spectator sport, administrator and players have always had high hopes for th game in Australia, but it was not until th 1970s that these began to be realised. Tw events in the 1970s put soccer on a more soli foundation in Australia and set it on a cours which could in time threaten the dominar positions of the rival football codes o AUSTRALIAN RULES and RUGBY League. Th first event was in 1974, when Australi reached the finals of the World Cup. I successfully negotiating the hard-fought elim nation rounds which preceded the finals th Australian team (the Socceroos) brough soccer to the favourable attention of mos Australians and gave Australian soccer a new prestige. This prestige was enhanced i 1977—soccer went national, thanks to a thre year sponsorship by Philips Industries of national league to be fought out between team from NSW, VIC, QLD, SA and the ACT.

History Soccer was brought to Australia b J.W. Fletcher, an English schoolmaster. I 1880 he and a friend, J.A. Todd, convened meeting 'to consider and promote the intro duction of the English Association game int NSW'. They founded the Wanderers' Clu which played its first match in 1880 agains The King's School at PARRAMATTA. By th turn of the century the new sport was bein played throughout Australia. While the mor aggressive body-contact sport of Rugby Union and the more spectacular Australian Rule attracted the spectators, soccer tended t attract the players. By 1906 in NSW alon there were 100 registered clubs, but th standard of play was low and did not begin t improve until well after World War II whe an influx of migrants from Europe, wher

Australian soccer team at the World Cup elimination match in Sydney 1973

soccer has wide popular appeal, considerably stimulated the game throughout most of Australia.

Soccer is now firmly established in Australia, and is particularly strong at junior level. The Australian Soccer Federation has calculated that over 190 000 young people play soccer in junior competitions, not including school teams.

World Cup The World Cup is a four-yearly event in which Australia first competed in 1965 and again in 1969, but on both occasions failed to get through the elimination rounds. In 1973, Australia burst into world prominence by winning, in the elimination rounds, the right to represent the South Pacific Zone at Munich where the final 16 teams were to play off for the Cup. Although the Socceroos failed to win a match at Munich, in winning through to the finals they gained for Australian soccer both at home and abroad more favourable publicity than it had received since its introduction in 1880.

National league In 1977 for the first time a premiership played on a national basis was instituted for a three-year trial. It was called the Philips Soccer League of Australia in deference to Philips Industries who agreed to meet the massive travelling costs involved in such a venture. In its first year 14 teams from NSW, VIC, QLD, SA and the ACT contested a spirited competition which was won finally by the NSW team of Easts-Hakoah. Following the initial success of the league, both in terms of standard of play and spectator sport, the numbers of teams was increased to 16 and in 1980 Philips Industries renewed their sponsorship for a further three years.
Further reading: Warren, J. & Dettre, A. *Soccer in Australia.* Paul Hamlyn, Sydney, 1974.

Socialist Party of Australia *see* Communism in Australia

Socialist Workers' Party *see* Communism in Australia

social services The term 'social services' is used in a variety of ways. In its broadest sense it can be taken to cover all measures which have as their aim the improvement of human welfare. The following discussion deals with social services in a narrower sense, referring mainly to income security measures by which governments make direct or indirect payments to people in particular need.

Attitudes before 1900 In Australia as elsewhere most social services are of comparatively recent origin, the concept of the 'welfare state' having been developed only during the 20th century in line with the general increase in the range of responsibilities undertaken by governments. In early colonial times the provision of help for people in need, such as the sick, the poor, the homeless, the aged and orphans, was left mainly to voluntary organisations which were generally associated with the Churches. An early example is the Society for the Promotion of Christian Knowledge

and Benevolence, which was founded in 1813 and five years later was reconstituted as the Benevolent Society of New South Wales. Aided by government grants, it became the chief relief agency in the colony.

In one important respect the situation with regard to relief from poverty was different from that in the UK. In the latter, people in distress were likely to have close ties with their local communities, and so have some prospect of obtaining private help; and if public help was necessary, it was given by the local authorities. In Australia, however, central government was established before local government and, in the circumstances of a penal colony, had from the beginning assumed wide responsibilities. So, although the general belief at the time was that the provision of social welfare measures by the state would tend to undermine people's self-reliance, there was greater pressure on governments to help the unfortunate than was the case in the UK.

The compromise reached was that welfare measures should be carried out mainly by government-subsidised agencies. By the late 19th century, however, the disadvantages of such a system were becoming more and more apparent. Governments had come to feel the need to co-ordinate the work of the voluntary agencies and to exercise some supervision over the way in which public money was being spent. Thus in 1866 in NSW a Public Insitutions Inspection Bill was passed and an Inspector of Public Charities was appointed, with power to inspect all institutions which were aided from public revenue. In the same colony in 1873-74 a Royal Commission on Public Charities held a thorough inquiry into methods of improving public welfare. Such steps as these were signs of gradual change in attitude. Governments were moving very slowly towards the idea of public responsibility for a comprehensive welfare programme. This in turn led to a shift of emphasis in social services from the voluntary organisations to State governments, and then from the latter to the federal government.

From federation to World War II The growing belief that governments should guarantee a minimum standard of welfare to certain disadvantaged groups found expression in the introduction of old age pensions in NSW and VIC in 1900, just before federation. QLD followed suit in 1908, but in the following year the Commonwealth government began a similar scheme which superseded those of the States. In 1910 the Commonwealth also introduced invalid pensions, and in 1912 maternity allowances, but then followed a period of nearly 30 years during which there was no major nationwide extension of social services. One reason for this pause was that the only social service powers specifically allocated to the Commonwealth in the Australian Constitution were with regard to invalid and old age pensions. Even more important was the fact that the cost of extending social services further was considerable, and to finance them from normal government

revenue seemed to be impossible. On a number of occasions inquiries were held into the possibility of introducing a contributory national insurance scheme, but the costs of this also seemed to be prohibitively high, and although a National Insurance Act was passed in 1938, it was never put into operation.

In the meantime the States had continued to give assistance to voluntary organisations and had taken some new initiatives. NSW had begun a limited scheme of child endowment, NSW and VIC had introduced widows' pensions, and all States had taken steps in unemployment relief. In 1923 QLD had introduced a scheme of unemployment insurance, and during the Depression all States set up food relief systems and other forms of assistance for the unemployed, these being continued to some extent until the Commonwealth introduced unemployment benefits in 1944.

Expansion during and after World War II The Labor government which came into power in 1941 was committed to a comprehensive social security programme, and since it also aimed at the redistribution of income, it favoured the financing of social services from taxation revenue rather than through a contributory insurance scheme. The previous MENZIES government had introduced child endowment in 1941, and Labor followed this up with widows' pensions in 1942, funeral benefits for invalid and old age pensioners in 1943 and sickness and unemployment benefits in 1944. To finance these benefits it designated part of income tax as a social services contribution, which was paid into a special national welfare fund; this arrangement was later abandoned, and social services are now paid from general taxation revenue.

The authority of the Commonwealth to legislate in these matters was put beyond doubt by the passing of a referendum in 1946, giving it power to legislate on 'the provision of maternity allowances, widows' pensions, child endowment, unemployment, pharmaceutical, sickness and hospital benefits, medical and dental services (but not so as to authorise any form of civil conscription), benefits to students and family allowances'.

Since 1945 the most important area of concern in social security has been that of HEALTH. The Menzies government which came into office in 1949 recognised the need for health welfare services, but wished to introduce them on at least a partly contributory basis. During the 1950s it therefore set up a system of voluntary insurance, by which those who joined private health funds had a portion of their hospital and medical expenses paid by the government, in addition to the portion paid by the funds out of their own resources. Special provisions were made for pensioners and the chronically ill. Criticism of this scheme, and its replacement by the universal health insurance scheme known as Medibank, are mentioned below. The trend away from the direct payment of money by the government to persons in need has been shown also by a renewed tendency to subsidise voluntary welfare bodies, instances of this being seen with regard to the provision of housing for the aged and various forms of help for the disabled. Another way in which governments have helped to attain welfare aims indirectly is by granting exemptions from taxes and other government charges. This has encouraged the growth of private superannuation schemes and has had some effect in lessening the need for direct social security payments. Examples of concessions in government charges at federal, State and local levels can be seen in the concessions given to pensioners with regard to telephone rentals, fares on public transport, and municipal or shire council rates. In spite of these trends, however, direct spending on social security services has continued to increase, and has tended to become a higher proportion of the federal budget.

Medibank and Medicare In the closing years of the long period of Liberal/Country Party government from 1949 to 1972, the national health scheme came under strong criticism, particularly on the grounds that many people were not members of health funds and were therefore not insured against health costs. The Australian Labor Party (ALP), proposed the introduction of a universal health insurance scheme, known as Medibank, which would be financed partly by a levy on income. During the WHITLAM government's term of office from 1972 to 1975 the Opposition parties used their Senate majority, first to delay the main Medibank legislation, and then to defeat the proposal for a levy on incomes. Hence, when the scheme was at last introduced in 1975, it was financed entirely from consolidated revenue. It made available free standard-ward hospital treatment and payment of the major portion (basically 85 per cent) of scheduled medical fees. It also encouraged doctors to bulk-bill Medibank for their services, at 85 per cent of scheduled fees, and if they did so the patient paid no charge. If people desired extra coverage—for the services of a doctor of their own choice in intermediate or private accommodation in hospital, or for part of the cost of dental, optical and pharmaceutical services—they could obtain it by insuring with private health funds.

The FRASER government which took office in December 1975 introduced a series of changes which gradually dismembered the Medibank scheme. From September 1981 Commonwealth benefits were restricted to those who had taken out insurance with a health society, and to certain disadvantaged categories including the unemployed, pensioners, newly arrived migrants and refugees, and low-income earners. The Labor government which took office in March 1983 acted quickly to set up a new universal health insurance scheme. Known as Medicare, it came into operation in February 1984. It gives the same basic cover as Medibank did, but is financed by means of a 1% levy on taxable incomes. As before, people are free to gain extra cover by insuring with private health funds.

Pensions This section concerns the types of pensions payable. Rates are not given, as these are subject to various allowances, and are indexed, being increased in accordance with rises in the CONSUMER PRICE INDEX each May and November.

An age (formerly called old age) pension may be paid to a man over 65 or a woman over 60. An invalid pension may be paid to a person aged 16 or more who is unable to earn a living because of permanent disability, or who is permanently blind. A widow's pension or a supporting parent's benefit may be paid to a person who on his or her own is bringing up a child or supporting a student. A widow's pension may also be paid to a woman of 50 or more if she is a widow, even though she is not bringing up children; to a woman of similar age who is a divorcee; to a woman who has been deserted by her husband for six months or more; to a woman whose husband is in a mental hospital; to a woman whose husband has been in prison for six months or more; or to a woman who was the dependant of a man for at least three years prior to his death. There is also provision for the payment of a temporary widow's pension in special cases not covered by the circumstances mentioned above.

Benefits Besides the supporting parent's benefit and the widow's pension, the two main disability benefits are for unemployment and sickness. However, a special benefit may be paid to people who are unable to provide for themselves or their families without assistance, but do not qualify for benefits or pensions so far mentioned. Unemployment benefit may be paid to unemployed men aged from 16 to 64 and to unemployed women aged 16 to 59 who are willing and able to work, have registered with the Commonwealth Employment Service, and have taken reasonable steps to obtain work. Sickness benefit, payable to a person whose sickness has caused loss of income through temporary inability to work, operates on conditions and rates parallel to those of unemployment benefit.

Other assistance The other main form of assistance paid to individuals directly is family allowance, payable to people bringing up children or supporting a full-time student up to the age of 25. Payment on account of a student is subject to a test on the student's income. Assistance is also given to guardians of a child whose parents are both dead, or one dead and the other a long-term inmate of a prison or mental hospital; to the parents or guardians of severely mentally or physically handicapped children under the age of 16 years and living in the family home; and to medically certified handicapped people in sheltered employment.

Assistance to organisations Assistance programmes for physically or mentally handicapped persons provide subsidies towards the cost of purchasing, constructing or renting premises for use as training centres, active therapy centres, sheltered workshops or residential accommodation. Subsidies may also be paid for equipping and maintaining such centres and for ancillary recreational, rehabilitation and holiday facilities. Under the Homeless Persons Assistance Act, assistance is available to approved non-profit organisations and local government bodies which provide temporary accommodation, meals and personal services for homeless men and women. Subsidies may also be paid to organisations providing accommodation for the aged or disabled people, or which provide special care for the very old or frail or disabled in hostel-type institutions; to organisations which provide meals for aged and invalid people in their own homes; for the cost of keeping patients in nursing homes; and for integrated childhood services—pre-school, family, before and after school and vacation care.

The above forms of assistance are all provided by the Commonwealth government. State governments also provide many welfare services through assistance to organisations; these vary from State to State. Details can be obtained from each State Welfare Department, as can details of assistance available for individuals in need who are not covered by Commonwealth social services.

softball Although softball originated in the USA in 1900, it was not played in Australia until the early 1940s. During World War II, it was introduced to Australians by American nurses who played it for recreation. Since that time the sport has experienced considerable growth and now boasts 150 000 registered players throughout the country. Softball and BASEBALL have many similarities but softball is played on a smaller area which may explain the popularity of the game with women who are the main supporters and players of the game in Australia. The Australian Softball Federation was formed in 1949 with a four-State membership and since then WA, TAS and the ACT have also joined and now enter teams in the annual national championships. In 1978 the Federation accepted an application made by the NT to enter a team, bringing the total number of teams to eight. After the annual national championships, an Australian team is chosen to compete in the World Series, in which Australia has a good record including a win in the final over the USA in 1965.

Solanaceae This dicotyledonous family of flowering plants contains about 85 genera and over 2 000 species, many of great importance as a source of food and drugs (such as species of potatoes, tomatoes, tobacco and nightshade). Solanaceae is cosmopolitan, but is best-developed in tropical southern America and the West Indies.

Members of this family may be herbs, shrubs, trees or woody climbers. The leaves are alternately arranged and there are no stipules. The conspicuous flowers are bisexual and solitary or in clusters; they have five fused petals and may be regular or slightly irregular. The corolla is rounded or tubular in shape and usually

Blackberry nightshade, *Solanum nigrum*

consists of five lobes. There are usually five stamens which alternate with the corolla lobes. The ovary is simple and superior; it contains two cavities (locules), though sometimes it develops a further two by the growth of internal cavity walls. The fruit is either a berry or a capsule, often containing many seeds.

Some of the most important plants in this family are the potato, *Solanum tuberosum*, the eggplant, *S. melongena*, the tomato, *Lycopersicum esculentum*, the tree tomato, *Cyphomandra betacea*, the Cape gooseberry, *Physalis peruviana*, chillies and cayenne pepper (*Capsicum* species), and tobacco, *Nicotiana tabacum*. Many species are highly poisonous but yield alkaloids of medicinal value; these include jimsonweed, *Datura stramonium* and deadly nightshade, *Atropa belladonna*. Among the Australian species which yield alkaloids are pituri, *Duboisia hopwoodii*, used by the Aborigines of central QLD as chewing tobacco, and *D. leichhardtii*, the leaves from which are used in the preparation of atropine. The best-known drug plant in this family is mandrake, *Mandragora officinarum*, a perennial herb from the Mediterranean region which has been known as a powerful painkiller for over 2 000 years; it has become surrounded by a host of legends, including the assertion that it emits a shriek when pulled from the ground.

Many members of the Solanaceae are ornamental garden plants; these include species of *Petunia, Nicotiana, Solanum, Schizanthus* and *Cestrum*. A number of native Australian Solaneceae colonise bare ground and, since the advent of European farming methods, have become WEEDS. These include several species of *Solanum*, such as the kangaroo apple, *S. laciniatum*, Narrawa burr, *S. cinereum*, and apple of Sodom, *S. sodomaeum*. Introduced species which have become weeds include pampas lily-of-the-valley, *Salpichroa origanifolia*, African box thorn, *Lycium ferocissimum*, and apple of Peru, *Nicandra physalodes*.

See also Angiospermae; Appendix 5; Flower Structure and Glossary of Botanical Terms
Further reading: see Appendix 6, A Bibliography for Plants.

Solander, Daniel Carl (1736-82)

Botanist. Solander qualified as a doctor of medicine in Sweden and first went to England in 1760 where he taught English botanists the Linnaean system of plant classification. He aided Sir Joseph BANKS as a naturalist on Captain COOK's *Endeavour* voyage (1768-71). He worked in Iceland in 1772, and later became a curator at the British Museum. Cape Solander on BOTANY BAY was named after him.

soles *see* fishes, bony

songlarks *see* warblers

Sorell TAS (combined population of Sorell and Midway Point 5 150 in 1981) This town is located 27km NE of Hobart at the junction of the Arthur and Tasman Highways. It is the service centre for a productive rural district important for fat lamb raising. It was founded in 1821 by Lieutenant-Governor SORELL who, it is claimed, considered moving the capital of the colony there from Hobart. Until 1866, when a causeway was built across coastal inlets thereby providing a direct link to Hobart, it remained a somewhat isolated settlement, even though it was then significant as a wheat producing district. The two causeways over the Pitt Water, both about 1.5km long, link Sorell to Midway Point. In recent times, there has been considerable resort development in the area along Frederick Henry Bay.

Sorell, William (1775-1848) Lieutenant-

Governor of TAS. Probably born in the West Indies, Sorell joined the army as an ensign in 1790, and served in the West Indies, South Africa and other places before resigning from military service in 1813. Appointed Lieutenant-Governor of TAS (still officially known then as VAN DIEMEN'S LAND) in 1816, he arrived in the colony in April 1817, and very soon began to justify the reputation of an able administrator which he had won in the army. He replaced the haphazard methods of his predecessor, Thomas DAVEY, with sound administrative procedures, built convict barracks and other public buildings, and systematised the use of rewards and punishments for convicts by opening the special penal settlement at MACQUARIE HARBOUR for hardened offenders, while providing for the granting of tickets of leave as a reward for good behaviour. He also had some success in quelling bushranging. During his term of office the Bank of Van Diemen's Land was founded and both the wool and wheat industries prospered to the point where a profitable export trade developed. Sorell encouraged all of these developments and was held in general esteem. He left TAS in June 1824, being succeeded by George ARTHUR.
Further reading: Giblin, R.W. *The Early History of Tasmania.* (vol 2) Melbourne University Press, Melbourne, 1939.

sorghum *see* agriculture

South Australia (SA) The State of SA

has an area of 984 375km², occupying about 12.8 per cent of the total area of Australia. It has a coastline of some 3700km on the GREAT AUSTRALIAN BIGHT, on the two inlets of SPENCER GULF and ST VINCENT GULF, and along the curving coast of the COORONG to the VIC border. The N boundary with the NT and QLD is defined by the 26th parallel of S latitude and the W boundary with WA is the meridian of 129°E longitude. The E boundary, separating SA from the three E States, is somewhat unusual for it has a 'dog-leg' junction at the MURRAY RIVER where NSW, VIC and SA meet. Although it was originally fixed as the 141st meridian of E longitude, when SA was proclaimed as a separate colony in the 1830s the section of the boundary line dividing VIC from SA was incorrectly marked when surveys were made in the 1840s. This was partly due to the inadequacy of surveying instruments available at the time. The line was marked at the 140°58'E longitude, about 3.6km E of where it should have been, and although this led to litigation between the States and an appeal to the Privy Council, the surveyed boundary remained. Hence the SA boundary with NSW and QLD is on the 141st meridian, the SA/VIC boundary is W of this meridian and the two parts do not meet at the same point on the Murray.
Landform features The State can be divided into four main landform regions: the W area, the LAKE EYRE basin, the MURRAY RIVER basin, and the central region of highlands, coastal plains and gulfs.

The W half of the State consists of a low plateau at an elevation of between 150m and 300m, fringed to the S by the low undulating

Premier's Dept S.A.

Bunyeroo valley in the Flinders Ranges SA

country of the NULLARBOR PLAIN extending to the shores of the Great Australian Bight. The whole area is an arid and semi-arid region of low rainfall and sparse population, with vast expanses covered by sandhills and extensive dune formations. In the NW section, where there is a large Aboriginal reserve, several ranges rise above the general plateau level. The main one is the MUSGRAVE RANGE, which extends across the State border into the NT; it has several peaks over 1100m elevation and includes Mt Woodroffe (1513m), the State's highest mountain. Other ranges in this area are the Everard, Birksgate, RAWLINSON, and Mann Ranges. The E part of this range country forms the headwaters of numerous intermittent streams which drain towards Lake Eyre. In the central section of the W region is the GREAT VICTORIA DESERT with the WOOMERA rocket range to the E. This is barren forbidding country with sandhills, salt-pans and shallow depressions which, though often marked on maps as lakes, seldom contain water. The S section of this region consists of the limestone Nullarbor Plain where the transcontinental railway line and the EYRE HIGHWAY link the E parts of the continent to WA.

The Lake Eyre basin in the central-N of the State includes a series of vast shallow depressions, which become lakes only after occasional heavy rains. The largest of these, Lake Eyre, is a region of internal drainage fed by a series of intermittent streams including the FINKE and DIAMANTINA Rivers and COPPER'S CREEK.

The Murray River basin in the SE of the State adjoining VIC consists of the valley of the river, the surrounding mallee lands and the far SE corner where MOUNT GAMBIER, MILLICENT, NARACOORTE and BORDERTOWN are the main centres. The section of the

Murray in SA extends for some 640km from the State border to LAKE ALEXANDRINA and thence, via the barrages across its mouth, to the sea at ENCOUNTER BAY. Along a coastal stretch of this SE region are the Coorong and the Ninety Mile Beach. In the Mt Gambier area there is a series of recently active volcanoes; the cone of Mt Gambier itself, with its picturesque crater lakes, is the largest; volcanic ash has made the surrounding area a rich agricultural and pastoral district.

In the central S region of the State lie the MOUNT LOFTY RANGES and the FLINDERS RANGES (which comprise the highland belt), EYRE PENINSULA and YORKE PENINSULA, and the two broad inlets, Spencer Gulf and St Vincent Gulf. This region is commonly called the 'shatter belt', for in quite recent geological times it has been fractured by faults and subjected to tectonic movements. In these movements, some blocks of the crust were elevated to form horsts, others were thrust downward to become sunken areas, and some were tilted as well as moved upward. The main horst blocks are Eyre and Yorke Peninsulas and the Mt Lofty and Flinders Ranges; the 'sunklands' are now occupied by the two gulfs. This area still occasionally experiences mild earth tremors due to crustal movement along the fault lines. Along the N side of the Eyre Peninsula triangle are the comparatively low hills of the GAWLER RANGES, while to the W of WHYALLA are the MIDDLEBACK RANGES, noted for their iron ore deposits. The Mt Lofty Ranges, with Mt Lofty as the highest peak (727m), extend N-S between St Vincent Gulf and the Murray River. KANGAROO ISLAND, the largest island off the SA coast, is structurally part of the Mt Lofty highlands, separated from the mainland by INVESTIGATOR STRAIT. The Flinders Ranges are a N

extension of the Mt Lofty Ranges, stretching for over 400km on a N-S alignment; they consist of ancient sedimentary rocks, much folded, faulted and uplifted, with many precipitous gorges and unique basins such as WILPENA POUND. An extension from the Flinders Ranges, N of PETERBOROUGH, stretches via the Olary Ridges to the Barrier Range and BROKEN HILL in NSW. In the far N, the Flinders Ranges divide, with one spur circling the N end of LAKE TORRENS and the other ending N of LAKE FROME.

Climate SA is the driest of the Australian States with over 80 per cent of its area receiving an average annual rainfall of less than 250mm and only about one per cent of the area receiving above 750mm. The wettest part of the State is the Mt Lofty Ranges area, immediately E of Adelaide, where the annual total exceeds 1200mm. The SE section of SA has a Mediterranean-type climate, with hot and dry summer conditions, and cool wet winters; concentration of rain in the period from April to September is a distinct feature of the climate. In the interior of the State, where semi-arid and arid conditions prevail, the rainfall is quite erratic, often with long dry spells. Snowfalls are infrequent in SA and are mainly confined to the Mt Lofty and S Flinders Ranges.

Population The total population of SA at the 1981 census was 1 319 327 (estimated resident population), making it the fourth-largest State in the nation, accounting for just under nine per cent of Australia's population. About 67 per cent of SA's people live within metropolitan Adelaide (882 520 in 1981); other major urban centres are Whyalla (29 962), Mt Gambier (19 830), PORT PIRIE (14 695), PORT AUGUSTA (15 254) and PORT LINCOLN (10 675). Of the whole State population, some 85 per cent are urban dwellers.

The growth of SA's population during the 20th century is shown in Table 1. During the early decades of the century, growth was

Table 1

POPULATION GROWTH OF SOUTH AUSTRALIA IN THE TWENTIETH CENTURY

Year*	Population†
1901	358 346
1911	408 558
1921	495 160
1933	580 949
1947	646 073
1954	797 094
1961	971 487
1971	1 185 300
1976	1 261 600
1981††	1 319 327

Note: * the 1971 and 1976 figures are adjusted for under-enumeration; † prior to 1966 full-blood Aborigines were not included; †† the 1981 figure is the Estimated Resident Population (Preliminary).
Source: Australian Bureau of Statistics, Canberra.

relatively slow and by 1921 the total State population was under half a million. The years following World War II saw greater growth and by early 1963 the population of the State was over one million. The urban dominance of Adelaide showed an increase in the 1960s; at the 1961 census Adelaide accounted for 60 per cent of the State's population, at the 1966 census for 66 per cent, and at the censuses of 1971 and 1976 for 69 per cent; at the 1981 census it was 67 per cent.

History Of all the Australian colonies, SA was the only one whose foundation was inspired by a systematic theory of colonisation (*see* Edward Gibbon WAKEFIELD). The key doctrine of Wakefield's theory was that land should be sold at a 'sufficient' price—sufficient, that is, to allow only a minority of settlers to purchase it. Wakefield argued that this arrangement would attract men of capital, but would ensure that others worked for wages. Thus land, labour and capital would be kept in balance, especially if the proceeds of land sales were to be used to bring more immigrants.

Foundation and early difficulties When these ideas were first published there was great interest in theories of colonisation. Wakefield attracted many disciples, and when in 1830 news reached Britain of Charles STURT's journey down the Murray, some of them conceived the idea of applying Wakefield's principles to a new colony in southern Australia. The South Australian Land Co. was formed, with the idea of founding a chartered colony, but the Colonial Office was not in favour of such a course. The cause was then taken up by the South Australian Association, which in 1834 secured the passage of the South Australian Act. This provided for an awkward mixture of a Crown colony and a chartered colony. In general matters its Governor was to be under the control of the Colonial Office, but land sales and immigration were to follow Wakefield's general principles and were to be managed by a Board of Commissioners, one member of which was to reside in the colony. Land was to be sold at not less than 12 shillings an acre, an assisted immigration scheme being funded from the proceeds. No convicts were to be transported to the colony.

Before the first settlers could be sent, the Commissioners were required to sell land orders worth £35 000, a task which might have taken a very long time had not the South Australian Co., founded by George Fife ANGAS, made large purchases. The positions of Governor, Resident Commissioner and Surveyor-General were filled respectively by Captain John HINDMARSH, J.H. Fisher and William LIGHT. Unfortunately, the work of these men was made unnecessarily hard by lack of preliminary planning. The first of the company's settlers were allowed to sail before Light and his team of surveyors had even left England. In July 1836 the settlers landed on Kangaroo Is, but when Light joined them a month later he chose the plain below Mt

Lofty, on the E shore of St Vincent Gulf, as the site of the colony's main town, Adelaide. By the time Hindmarsh had arrived and had proclaimed the colony on 28 December, more than 300 settlers were waiting for their land, but the number of surveyors was too small for the work facing them, and the first country sections were not ready for occupation until May 1838. Meanwhile, many settlers had been engaging in speculation in land and land orders.

In 1838 Hindmarsh and Fisher, who had been in disagreement on many matters, were recalled, and George GAWLER was appointed as both Governor and Resident Commissioner. By the time he arrived in October the colony had a population of 5 000, but farming had hardly begun. He tried to cope with the situation by speeding up land surveys and by an ambitious programme of public works, but in doing so grossly exceeded authorised expenditure, bridging the gap with bills drawn on the Commissioners. By late 1840 it was evident that the colony was bankrupt, and in May 1841 Gawler was replaced by George GREY.

Prosperity and self-government, 1841-56 On the appointment of Grey the Board of Commissioners was abolished and SA was made an ordinary Crown colony. During the following 10 years a number of factors combined to bring it prosperity. Grey followed a policy of rigid economy, and the British government finally gave the colony the opportunity to make a fresh start by paying its debts of £225 000. Copper was discovered at KAPUNDA in 1842 and BURRA in 1844. Aided by the invention of Australia's first harvesting machine, John RIDLEY's stripper, the colony's wheat farmers flourished. A demographic point worth noting is that the colony attracted many German settlers.

The gold rushes at first appeared to be a threat to the colony's newly won prosperity,

for no gold was found there, and many of its citizens went to the VIC fields. However, the Bullion Act of 1852 brought some indirect profit from the rushes for it provided for a higher price for gold in Adelaide than on the diggings, thereby diverting some of the flow of gold to SA, and in particular making it worthwhile for South Australians who had found gold to send it home to be invested in property. The rushes also provided an expanded market for SA wheat. As in the E colonies, the gold rush also saw the advent of responsible government. In 1842 a nominated Legislative Council had been set up, and in 1850 it was enlarged to 24 members, of whom 16 were to be elected. In 1856 a constitution was approved which provided for a Parliament consisting of a House of Assembly, elected by secret ballot on the basis of adult male suffrage, and a Legislative Council elected on a very restricted franchise based on property qualifications.

From self-government to federation SA continued to be heavily dependent on rural industries. She was not as well placed as NSW and VIC for manufacturing, and her mineral sources were limited. Although she possessed the largest deposits of high grade iron ore yet discovered in Australia these were little used until the BROKEN HILL PROPRIETARY COMPANY LIMITED (BHP) opened its Newcastle iron works in 1915; and the deposits of copper found at MOONTA and WALLAROO in the 1860s did not compare in value with the mineral resources already found, or soon to be found, in most other colonies. However, the discovery of one of the world's major silver-lead-zinc deposits at Broken Hill brought indirect benefits, for although that town is in NSW, most of its commerce was from the beginning with nearby SA and its output was exported mainly through Port Pirie.

Within the rural sector wheat growing pre-

Parliament House Adelaide

Port Pirie SA

dominated and SA remained Australia's leading producer until overtaken by VIC late in the 19th century. In 1887 the foundation of an irrigation scheme by the CHAFFEY BROTHERS at RENMARK marked the beginning of the Murray River fruit industry, while Germans in the BAROSSA VALLEY and elsewhere made SA the leading colony in wine production. In politics, SA became, in 1894, the first Australian colony to give women the vote.

Developments since federation SA entered the Commonwealth with certain economic disadvantages. As already noted, she had limited mineral resources. She also had only a very small proportion of well-watered land, and efforts to develop what resources she did possess had burdened her citizens with a public debt twice as high per head as was the case in NSW and VIC. Efforts to encourage manufacturing by moderately protectionist tariffs had produced some results, but the abolition of interstate tariffs after federation soon caused a loss of manufacturing enterprise to NSW and VIC. This lack of manufacturing became an increasing disadvantage with the steady drift of population to Adelaide, which by 1929 contained about 55 per cent of the population.

A turning point was reached in 1935 when the Auditor-General, J.W. Wainwright, put forward a plan for attracting secondary industry by such incentives as the reduction of company tax and the provision of improved credit facilities. This plan was adopted by the Premier, R. Butler, and continued vigorously by his successor, Sir Thomas PLAYFORD. Highlights in the drive for industrialisation have included the provision of cheap, conveniently situated land, the effective provision of workers' houses by the Housing Trust, the use of LEIGH CREEK sub-bituminous coal to lessen dependence on higher-grade NSW coal, the construction of a ship-building yard and an iron and steelworks at Whyalla, the conversion of munitions works at Salisbury into a centre for long-range weapons development, the establishment of a rocket range at Woomera, the concentration in Adelaide of a large part of the nation's motor car and domestic appliance manufacturing industry, and the use for industrial and domestic purposes of natural gas from the GIDGEALPA-MOOMBA field in the far N of the State. Developments in primary

industries have included the reclamation of large areas of formerly barren land by the use of trace elements and the establishment of large pine plantations to compensate for the State's lack of forest resources.

In politics, SA has been notable among mainland States for the relative weakness of the Country Party (now the NATIONAL PARTY). After being linked for many years with the LIBERAL PARTY as the National Country League, it is now organised as a separate party, but in 1983 held only one seat in the House of Assembly. Another feature is that the fortunes of the AUSTRALIAN LABOR PARTY have fluctuated strongly. Although a Labor administration came into office as early as 1905, the predominance of primary industry told against the party and, as the population became concentrated in Adelaide, Labor was given a handicap by the growing discrepancy between rural and metropolitan electorates in terms of population size. However, the growth of secondary industries during the Playford era and the electoral redistribution of 1970 removed these disadvantages and since that date SA has tended to be a Labor stronghold. *Further reading:* Price, A.G. *Founders and Pioneers of South Australia.* F.W. Preece & Sons, Adelaide, 1929 and *The Foundation and Settlement of South Australia, 1828-45.* Libraries Board of South Australia, Adelaide, 1973; Pike, D. *Paradise of Dissent.* Longmans Green, London, 1957; Berekmeri, S. *South Australia.* Robert Hale, London, 1972.

South-East Asia Treaty Organization

The South-East Asia Collective Defence Treaty, usually referred to as SEATO after the South-East Asia Treaty Organization set up under it, was signed in Manila in September 1954 by representatives of Australia, France, New Zealand, Pakistan, the Philippines, Thailand, the UK and the USA, and was approved by the Australian Parliament in February 1955. It was an obvious reaction to the spread of Communism in Asia, most immediately in North Vietnam, and to the fear that it might spread further throughout South-East Asia. Its primary aim was indicated in Article IV (1), which reads as follows:

> Each Party recognises that aggression by means of an armed attack in the Treaty Area against any of the Parties or against any State or Territory which the Parties by unanimous agreement may hereafter designate, would endanger its own peace and safety, and agrees that it will in that event act to meet the common danger in accordance with its constitutional processes . . .

In a protocol, the USA reserved its obligation to cases of 'Communist aggression', and in a further protocol the 'designated' states were named as Laos, Cambodia and South Vietnam. Subsequently, an organisation was set up to co-ordinate military defence planning against possible Communist aggression and to provide economic aid to Asian members, especially in

fields that affected their ability to resist Communist external aggression or internal subversion.

The treaty attracted considerable criticism within Australia, especially from the Australian Labor Party (ALP) which, while it did not oppose Australia's signing it, was doubtful of its value. Among the misgivings expressed at various times were: that the members' obligations were stated too vaguely; that 'Communist aggression' would be hard to define, and might be confused with nationalist independence movements; that there were too few Asian members; and that the interest in Asia of two important members, the UK and France, was on the wane. On the other hand, defenders of the treaty have argued that its very existence may have acted as a deterrent to further acts of open aggression such as that committed by North Korea in 1950.

Faith in the continued usefulness of the Organization waned in the early 1970s, as Communist regimes took control of South Vietnam, Laos and Cambodia. Pakistan withdrew in 1972 and France ceased paying her financial contribution in mid-1974. In the meantime, in September 1973, the Organization's military activities were drastically reduced, although it continued to support internal security and development programmes in Thailand and the Philippines. In September 1975 the Ministerial Council announced that the Organization would be completely phased out over two years. It was finally disbanded in June 1977. *Further reading:* Watt, Sir Alan *The Evolution of Australian Foreign Policy, 1938-1965.* Cambridge University Press, London, 1967.

southern beech *see* beech, southern

Southern Cross *see* astronomy

Southern Cross WA (population 798 in 1981) A small township on the Great Eastern Highway and on the PERTH-KALGOORLIE railway, Southern Cross is 405km ENE of Perth and 252km by rail WSW of Kalgoorlie. It was named after the famous constellation, which the gold prospectors used as a direction guide when they discovered the Yilgarn field in 1888. The town was originally designed in grand style, with broad streets named after heavenly constellations, but as the gold gave out, it declined. It is now a service centre for a wheat growing and sheep grazing region of relatively low rainfall. The town's water supply comes via a pipeline from MUNDARING RESERVOIR which is part of the GOLDFIELDS WATER SUPPLY scheme.

Southern Tablelands NSW A highland region in the SE part of the State, it is a section of the GREAT DIVIDING RANGE lying S of the BLUE MOUNTAINS and extending S to the NSW/VIC border. It varies in elevation from about 600m in the N to over 2100m in the KOSCIUSKO area. It is a plateau formation, with extensive stretches of gently undulating country, interrupted by lines of hills, with considerable gorge and valley dissection. The S part of the tablelands is called the MONARO region, with the SNOWY MOUNTAINS to the far SW. The ACT and the nation's capital city, CANBERRA, lie within the tablelands.

The E boundary of the plateau is clearly defined by a steep scarp which descends to the narrow plains of the S coast and the ILLAWARRA region. On its W side, the boundary of the plateau is less clear and the tablelands gradually merge into the hilly dissected country of the SW slopes region. The tablelands form the watershed divide and the headwater catchment zone of streams draining E to the Pacific coastline, such as the SHOAL-HAVEN, Clyde and Moruya Rivers, and those draining W, such as the MURRUMBIDGEE, LACHLAN and MURRAY. In most places, however, the watershed is rather indistinct and consists only of hills and ridges rising slightly above the general plateau level. The principal towns of the tablelands are GOULBURN in the N, QUEANBEYAN and Canberra in the central part, and COOMA in the S. The Hume Highway crosses the N section of the region, the Monaro Highway crosses the N section of the region, the Monaro Highway traverses it on a general N-S route, and the Snowy Mts Highway links the S coastal belt to the tablelands.

Like the rest of the Great Dividing Range, the Southern Tablelands were created by gentle uplift in fairly recent geological times. But the amount of uplift was not uniform over the whole plateau; also, numerous fault lines developed and a number of rifts and horsts were formed. Minor earth tremors are not uncommon over the tablelands and these are related to the instability of the earth's crust in the region and the faulting in the past. On some parts of the plateau, there are areas of internal drainage where waters of former streams have been blocked by faulting and earth movement. The best-known and largest

of these is LAKE GEORGE, adjacent to the highway between Goulburn and Canberra.

There is a pronounced similarity in vegetation over the whole tablelands. Eucalypts of many species dominate and form a light forest over most of the region. In the highest parts, around the Kosciusko area, altitude strongly affects the vegetation. Trees become stunted and twisted as elevation increases, and at about 1950m the tree-line is reached. Above this level, stunted shrubs, grasses and flowering plants carpet the ground in the summer months. During winter, it is covered with deep snow. Timber-getting is an important industry in many parts of the tablelands and in some areas eucalyptus oil is distilled from the leaves of certain species. Much of the forest on the more gently sloping parts of the region has been cleared for livestock grazing. The plateau is not rich farming country; there are small pockets of fertile land and limited areas which are good for cultivation; it is generally more suited to grazing than to agriculture. Sheep grazing, with beef cattle in the rougher country, and dairying and fodder crop cultivation along some river flats, are the main rural industries.

soybean see Papilionaceae

Spanish-speaking people in Australia In 1978 the then Commissioner for Community Relations, A.J. Grassby, estimated that there were 150 000 Spanish-speaking people in Australia who had migrated from 30 different countries in Europe, South and Central America, Africa and Asia. The Commissioner also claimed that Spanish-speaking children formed the seventh-largest group in Australian primary schools and the tenth-largest in Australian secondary schools. Spanish-speaking people have very diverse cultural backgrounds and the only thing they have in common is the Spanish language.

History of migration The gold rushes of the 1850s brought many fortune hunters of Hispanic background to Australia but this did not result in a permanent local community. Also in the 19th century the Benedictine monks of NEW NORCIA established a settlement N of Perth. Before 1914 a few hundred Basques settled permanently in northern QLD and in the 1920s a few Catalans came to Australia. The official immigration figures of 1947 indicate that there were less than 3 000 Spanish-speaking people in Australia. The majority of the Hispanic migrants came to Australia between 1959 and 1961; there was a smaller influx in the 1960s and 1970s.

Spanish heritage in Australia Spanish is offered as a subject in universities in NSW, VIC and SA. Spanish and Latin American restaurants have been established, a Spanish Club has been set up in Sydney and Spanish programmes are presented on ethnic radio.

sparrowhawk see birds of prey

sparrows see animals, introduced; weaverbirds

Spears, Robert (1893-1950) Cyclist. Born in DUBBO in NSW, Spears' cycling career spanned two decades, from 1910 to 1930, during which he won international acclaim and became the idol of European and American cycling fans. He never raced as an amateur, entering and winning his first professional race at Narromine NSW in 1910. A versatile cyclist, participating in events ranging from sprints to six-day events, it was after he moved to the USA that his international status began to grow. In 1916 he won the US sprint championship and by 1918 was the all-round cycling champion of the US. In the same year he made his début in Europe where he became so popular that on one occasion when he was prevented by a train accident from appearing in a race in Milan, the spectators became so enraged by his non-appearance that they burned to the ground a grandstand capable of seating 40 000. In the early 1920s he was at his peak: he won the world sprint title in 1920 and 24 grand prix in Europe and was acclaimed as the greatest rider the world had known. Spears was affectionately known as 'Long Bob' on account of his height and unusually long legs—the long legs caused a slight problem in that all his machines had to be made specially for him. His popularity was such that he commanded £80 a ride and in one three-year period netted £40 000 in prize-money. Coupled with revenue from advertising and appearance fees, this made him a wealthy man and he retired in 1930, after which he returned to Sydney where he remained actively associated with cycling. Spears died in the city he loved best and where he had been most popular, Paris.

HQ of the Snowy Mountain Authority in Cooma, a principal town in the Southern Tablelands

Spence, Catherine Helen (1825-1910)

Novelist and social reformer. Born in Melrose, Scotland, she was brought to Adelaide at the age of 14, and later worked as a governess, a teacher and, from the age of 25, as a journalist. Her novels *Clara Morrison* (1854), *Tender and True* (1856), *Mr Hogarth's Will* (1865) and *The Author's Daughter* (1868) give a more realistic picture of Australian life than was the case with most writing of the period. Throughout her adult life she was active as an advocate of political and social reform, particularly proportional representation and women's suffrage.

Spencer Gulf

SA A shallow triangular-shaped coastal inlet, 85km wide at its S entrance and extending 320km N-S, it is located between EYRE and YORKE Peninsulas. The gulf was formed in relatively recent geological times by subsidence of the land between fault fractures. The explorer Matthew FLINDERS discovered and named the inlet in 1802 to honour Earl Spencer, the chairman of the British Board of Admiralty.

Spencer, Sir Walter Baldwin (1860-1929)

Biologist and anthropologist. Born in Britain, he studied and wrote on the Aborigines of N Australia. He died during an anthropological expedition to Tierra del Fuego.

Spender, Sir Percy Claude (1897-)

Statesman, diplomat and jurist. Born and educated in Sydney, he served in the Australian Imperial Force (AIF) in World War I and the Australian Military Forces (AMF) in World War II. After being called to the NSW Bar in 1923 and becoming a KC 12 years later, he entered politics as Member for Warringah in 1937 and retained this seat until 1951. He held a number of portfolios during the periods 1939-41 and 1949-51, but is remembered chiefly for his achievements as Minister for External Affairs in 1949-51. A chairman of the Australian delegation to the Colombo Conference in 1950, he played a major role in the launching of the COLOMBO PLAN, which was in fact known initially as the Spender Plan. He was also vice-president of the General Assembly of the UN in 1950-51, vice-president of the Japanese peace treaty conference in 1951, and Australian representative at the ANZUS PACT negotiations in the same year. In later years he was Australian Ambassador to the USA (1951-58), a Justice of the International Court (1958-64) and President of the International Court of Justice, the Hague (1964-67).
Further reading: Spender, P.C. *Exercises in Diplomacy: The Anzus Pact and the Colombo Plan.* Sydney University Press, Sydney, 1969.

Sphagnum *see* Bryophyta

spiders

These terrestrial invertebrates make up the order Araneae of the class Arachnida (ARACHNIDS). More than 30 000 species have

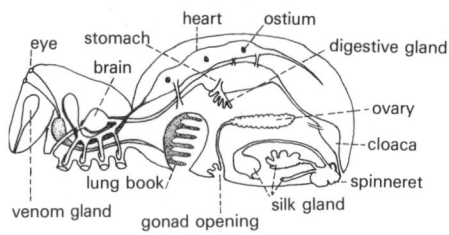
Body of a spider showing some internal organs

been described but this is only a small proportion of all the spiders in the world. Similarly, there are more than 1 400 known species in Australia but there are also many undescribed ones.

The body of a spider is divided into two distinct parts: the fused head and thorax or cephalothorax (prosoma) and the abdomen (opisthosoma). The prosoma has four pairs of clawed walking legs, two pedipalps which in the males carry a swollen end that is used for inserting sperm into the female, and a pair of chelicerae (fangs). The prosoma and the opisthosoma are joined by a narrow waist through which runs the gut and the nerve cord. There is no external sign of segmentation in the abdomen except in one small suborder that is not represented in Australia. On the underside of the abdomen the lung-books are visible as light coloured patches near the waist. The tip of the abdomen carries the usually joined finger-like structures (spinnerets) from which silk issues. The number of spinnerets varies from one pair to four. Silk is commonly produced by spiders but not all use it to make webs. Funnel-web spiders, for example, use it to make a retreat, and hunting spiders of various kinds use it to form a lifeline up which they run if they fall.

The eyes (usually eight, sometimes six) are simple and their exact position is important in spider identification; the so-called diurnal eyes are dark in colour and the nocturnal ones are pearly white. Most spiders have venom sacs in the prosoma and venom canals leading to the tip of the chelicerae, but only a few species (for example, the Sydney funnel-web spider and the red-back spider) can kill an adult human. (For first aid treatment, *see* ANIMALS VENOMOUS.)

There are four suborders of spiders, three of which are represented in Australia: Mygalomorphae, Hypochilomorphae and Araneomorphae.

Mygalomorphae This suborder consists of the trapdoor and funnel-web group of spiders. They are medium to large, all very much alike in appearance and usually dark in colour. From above, the bases of the large chelicerae are prominent; the chelicerae strike downwards so that the spider has to rear up on its two back pairs of legs in order to strike effectively. The venom glands are housed within the chelicerae. Mygalomorphs are long-lived spiders and have long, leg-like pedipalps, four lung books and one to three pairs of spinnerets. There are about 140 species of mygalomorph spiders in Australia and although the

families also occur in other countries, several genera and many species are endemic; several species are exceedingly dangerous.

The families Barychelidae and Theraphosidae are characterised by dense tufts of hair surrounding the claws which enable the spiders to climb out of glass jars with ease. The Barychelidae (five Australian genera, three endemic) are velvety and dark, the opisthosoma is sometimes mottled and some males are bright red on the underparts of the thorax. Barychelids are usually large and have two or four spinnerets (but the last joint of the lateral spinnerets is short and rounded); the three rows of eyes are set on a low hump. The family is represented in all parts of Australia, except the SE; in tropical and arid areas these spiders construct burrows with trapdoors. *Idiommata* is a widespread genus of about five species, all believed to be very venomous; they live in silk-lined burrows about 20cm deep which are closed by saucer-shaped lids.

The family Theraphosidae, distinguished from the barychelids by the long terminal segments on the lateral pair of the two pairs of spinnerets, are called bird-eating spiders in the Americas; some Australian species sometimes kill and eat birds, including small chickens. There are four Australian genera. *Selencosmia* (about six species) contains the tropical barking spider, *S. crassipes*, which has sound-producing rods and hairs on the chelicerae and maxillae (lobes on the bases of the pedipalps). The rubbing together of these is said to produce a noise. The spiders of this family do not make trapdoors to the burrows but there may be loose sheets of silk round the opening which is often concealed.

The Dipluridae is a large family of rather long-legged spiders, with four or six spinnerets; the last segments of the lateral spinnerets are long and pointed. There are three subfamilies. The Hexathelinae, which have six spinnerets, are small, rare and restricted to mountainous parts of E Australia and TAS; the Macrothelinae contains the infamous funnel-web spiders (*Atrax* species) and have four spinnerets and only one row of teeth on the paired tarsal claws; the Diplurinae have two rows of teeth on the tarsal claws.

Atrax is an E genus, ranging from QLD to TAS and VIC with separate populations near Adelaide and on the EYRE PENINSULA. All *Atrax* species should be regarded as potential killers but so far only one, the Sydney funnel-web, *A. robustus*, extremely common in some parts of the Sydney area, has caused human fatalities.

Although most bites do not result in envenomation, every bite merits immediate hospital attention. *A. robustus* (female up to about 3.4cm long; male 2.5cm) has a shiny, usually black prosoma, a duller, dark brown opisthosoma and reddish-brown underparts. The male has relatively long legs and, when mature at least, a spine on each of the second legs which is used during mating to keep the female's chelicerae apart. The spinnerets are easily seen from above. Some authorities say

Sydney funnelweb spider, *Atrax robustus*

A. Woods

the species is restricted to within a radius of 160km from Sydney though others state that it extends into north-eastern VIC. Though *A. robustus* bites are sometimes fatal to human beings, monkeys and young mice, they appear to be comparatively harmless to most other animals. The material that is toxic to man and monkeys is Atraxotoxin; the venom of male spiders contains much more Atraxotoxin than does that of the females, and all human fatalities have been caused, as far as is known, by males. In warm periods during the summer the males wander in search of females, and sometimes take refuge during the day in houses; they attack readily if they appear to be threatened. The northern-rivers or tree funnel-web spider, *A. formidabilis*, a larger but similar species, is found in northern NSW and southern QLD. Unlike *A. robustus* which always nests at ground level, the N species sometimes makes its nest in a tree-hole some distance above the ground. Funnel-web nests never have trapdoors but usually have a funnel or sleeve of white silk extending from the opening; the Sydney species builds retreats into sandstone crevices and rockeries, to the bases of trees or plants, or under rubbish, very often in the gardens of certain suburbs.

The Diplurinae spiders' burrows are silk-lined and have no funnels extending from the opening, although a few rare species build trapdoors.

The family Ctenizidae, with at least 18 Australian genera, contains species with a row of stout spines (a rastellum) on the basal segment of the chelicerae. This enables them to dig in hard soil which defeats other mygalo-morphs. There are four spinnerets, the lateral ones having short, rounded terminal segments. There are three tarsal claws. The burrows are usually sealed with close-fitting doors composed of silk or of silk and earth particles. The ctenizids are the species to which the name 'trapdoor spiders' is most accurately applied.

This family contains the genus *Missulena*, several species of which are widespread. Often called mouse spiders, they are dark squat species. The males (considerably smaller than the females) often have red chelicerae. Seen in profile, the back of the bulbous head is almost vertical. A few bites have been recorded but they have not had serious consequences. The vertical silk-lined burrow is closed with a double door, and there is a side burrow which is used as a brood chamber and has a door of its own. Mouse spiders feed on snails and insects caught near the burrow.

Other genera in the family Ctenizidae include *Arbanitis*, *Dyarcyops*, *Blakistonia* and *Idiosoma*. The Adelaide trapdoor spider, *B. aurea*, a golden brown transversely striped species, closes its tunnels with a concave plug of silk and soil. *Idiosoma* species occur in south-western WA and are brown or black.

The family Migidae has only a few Austra-lian species. They construct burrows with a door but they have no rastellum. The last segment of the lateral spinneret is short and rounded. The legs are spiny. *Migas nitens* and *Heteromigas dovei* are small species, occurring only in TAS.

Hypochilomorphae These spiders have four lung-books, like the mygalomorphs, but chelicerae which cross at the tip, as in the Araneomorphae. There are two families in Australia, the Hickmaniidae (or Hypochilidae), restricted to TAS, and the Gradungulidae, known so far only from QLD and NSW.

The Hickmaniidae are represented only in TAS, North America, China and Chile. The single Australian species is the Tasmanian cave spider, *Hickmania troglodytes* (female about 1.9cm; male about 1.3cm), which occurs throughout TAS, not only in caves but wherever it finds a dark cavity large enough to contain its horizontal sheet web. The legs of the female are long and thin, the first pair being about 7.5cm long. The web is large; one in a cave at Mole Creek was 1.22m × 0.6m. The spider runs along the undersurface of the sheet. The Tasmanian cave species is one of the cribellate spiders; these spiders have a small sieve-like plate (cribellum) just in front

Trapdoor spider, *Idiommata species*

Courtesy of A.I.S. Canberra

of the spinnerets which produces fine silk threads; the silk threads are combed out by a comb of bristles (calamistrum) on the fourth leg, giving the silk a characteristic hackled appearance.

The family Gradungulidae, unknown till its first representative was discovered in New Zealand in 1955, has since been found in E Australia. Generally, they are hunting spiders which do not build a snare, and, consequently, usually do not have a cribellum. The vagrant hunting spider (*Gradungula* species), a cryptically coloured small species which resembles a wolf spider (*see below*), lives on the leaf litter in *Nothofagus* forest.

Araneomorphae There are at least 1 300 species of Australian 'ordinary' spiders, divided into about 30 families. Only the most important of these are discussed here. All have two lung-books apart from some very small species which respire through the cuticle. The tips of the chelicerae cross. The families are distinguished by such features as eye number, tarsal claw number (two or three), presence or absence of a calamistrum and cribellum, number of tracheal openings or spiracles, and the use to which the silk is put (for example, as snares or life-lines). Four common families are cribellate: Oecobiidae, Dinopidae, Dictynidae and Uloboridae.

The name Oecobiidae means 'house-dweller' and the only species found in Australia, *Oecobius annulipes* (2mm), is a cosmopolitan spider, usually associated with buildings. It is a light-coloured, dark-mottled species with ringed legs; the legs bend back characteristically at the ends. The tiny, flat webs are built on projections on walls, at the corners of doors and so on.

The family Dinopidae contains the ogre-faced spiders or net-casting spiders. There are eight eyes; one pair, extremely large and pointing forwards, do indeed give the spider an ogre-like expression. The body, particularly the opisthosoma, is elongated and the legs are long. During the day the spider hides in vegetation, with legs one and two held together as one and with legs three and four pressed to the body, so that it resembles a small stick. It spins a small, rectangular web of hackled silk which it holds at the corners with the front two pairs of legs. Hanging upside down from a few threads of silk it waits till a passing insect comes near enough and then lunges forward, enveloping the prey in the outstretched net.

The family Dictynidae contains a few species which can give human beings a serious bite. The web consists of units of two parallel strands criss-crossed by woolly silk from the cribellum. These units often fan out from a central tube or point but the basic pattern is often obscured by the addition of extra layers of webbing. The black house spiders (*Ixeuticus* species), which can give a serious bite, commonly build their webs in and around crevices in houses, outhouses, shearing sheds and under verandahs.

The family Uloboridae contains species which make orb-webs, an attainment developed independently of the true orb-web spiders of the family Araneidae. The web is usually built horizontally, and the spider rests below. *Uloborus* species occur throughout Australia, and *U. geniculatus*, often found in and near houses, is a cosmopolitan species.

The family Pholcidae consists of several genera of spiders which lack the cribellum and calamistrum and in which the chelicerae are fused at the base. The familiar daddy-long-legs spider, *Pholcus phalangioides*, a cosmopolitan yellowish species which is almost invariably associated with remote dark corners in houses, has a cylindrical opisthosoma and long, ringed but spineless legs. The web is a messy tangle of threads, sometimes in the form of an horizontal sheet. The spiders live within the web and the adult female carries her bundle of eggs which is almost naked apart from a few retaining threads.

The family Sicariidae (also lacking a cribellum and calamistrum) consists of the spitting spiders. There are three species in Australia: the common *Scytodes thoracica* and two scarce endemic species in the same genus. The spitting spider is yellowish with darker markings and a lyre-shaped patch on the high, swollen carapace. The spider stalks its prey slowly and when near enough sprays it with a gummy material which binds it to the surface.

The members of the family Dysderidae (also lacking a cribellum and calamistrum) have a pair of large openings (spiracles) to the trachea behind the lung-books. This family contains the introduced *Dysdera crocata* (female 1.2cm to 1.4cm; male smaller), which occurs in SE Australia and TAS. It is a vagrant (that is, a hunter which does not make a snare) spider which lives on woodlice in damp places, often in gardens. It avoids habitats with ants. The very large chelicerae, the legs and the prosoma are bright reddish-brown and the opisthosoma is cream-coloured. It has caused severe sickness in human beings in Australia.

The family Oonopidae also lacks a cribellum and calamistrum and is the most closely related family to the Dysderidae. It contains a number of small, six-eyed spiders which live under stones and in leaf-litter.

None of the families mentioned hereafter are cribellate and all have a single tracheal opening which is often difficult to see. One group has two tarsal claws with a tuft of hairs representing the third claw, the other group has three claws and no claw tufts.

The Salticidae is a familiar family in the two-clawed group. The front of the head is square; two of the eight eyes point forward. These usually small hunting spiders have short, strong legs and an unmistakable alert air, and are commonly known as jumping spiders as they stalk their prey and leap at it from a short distance, grasping it with the front pair of legs; some even leap at flying insects. There are over 60 genera in Australia; in temperate regions they are often drab coloured but some of the tropical species are brightly patterned. *Myrmarachne*, a genus of E and central Australia, consists of about nine species that mimic, and often prey on, ants. The genus *Saits* contains a number of small but brightly coloured species (peacock or rainbow spiders) in QLD, NSW, VIC and WA. There are movable flaps on the opisthosoma which may serve as wings for planing when the spiders leap.

The family Selenopidae, also a two-clawed group with eyes in two rows, is represented in Australia only by the widespread *Selenops australiensis*, a small flattened spider found under stones, bark and so on. All the legs turn to the front.

The family Sparassidae contains two-clawed spiders which have been given such names as huntsmen spiders, triantelopes, giant crab spiders or tarantulas. They are large flattened spiders with crab-like (laterigrade) legs and dense scopulae (tufts of hairs on the legs). The eye arrangement is two rows of four. Some species often come indoors, scuttling sideways or forwards across walls and ceilings. Their appearance is alarming but they are not aggressive to human beings though the bite of one of the commonest genera, *Olios* (25 species), can be painful.

The family Thomisidae, the crab or flower spider, is a large two-clawed group which contains generally small spiders with at least the two front pairs of legs laterigrade; there are no scopulae, and sometimes the claw tufts are absent. Usually found in bush and forest, but rarely near houses, they may hunt on bark or between stones, or lie in wait in flowers and on leaves. The colour varies from drab browns to white or green, sometimes with orange or red markings. Thomisids do not make snares but ambush their prey.

The family Clubionidae contains mainly small two-clawed spiders which often live within silken tubes inside rolled-up leaves, either among leaves or down on the ground in litter. They resemble some of the Gnaphosidae (*see below*) but differ in that the foremost

Leaf-rolling spider, *Phonognatha wagneri*

A Woods

spinnerets almost touch. Of the 19 genera in this family, the most important are *Clubiona, Miturga, Supunna* and *Chiracanthium*. The last genus contains several species of which *C. mordax* (about 1cm) is known to be dangerously venomous and of which others are thought to be so. *C. mordax*, a widespread, fragile, buff-coloured species, is more or less cylindrical, with strong chelicerae and long, spindly legs. Its transparent tubes, from which it emerges at night to hunt, are sometimes seen in the corners of buildings. *Miturga* species (about 1.7cm) are greyish-brown spiders with two dark brown stripes on the sides of the carapace and four lines of spots, white or yellow in colour, on the undersurface of the opisthosoma. There is some evidence that some of these spiders can bite severely, producing necrotic sores.

The two-clawed spiders of the family Gnaphosidae (or Drassidae) have two widely separated anterior spinnerets. There are about 16 Australian genera in two distinct groups. The spiders of the first group are so flattened that they appear to have been squashed. The genus *Hemicloea* (about 18 species) is typical; these mainly medium-sized, shiny, brown or black spiders have strongly laterigrade legs and a relatively hairless body, and they live under bark or in cracks in flat stones. *Rebilus* spiders are similar but are reddish-brown, smaller and a little more hairy. A typical genus of the second group is *Lampona*, which contains small to medium-sized, dark spiders with cylindrical bodies, often with a white tip to the abdomen; these species emerge from leaf-litter and stones to hunt at night, often indoors, and some can bite severely.

The family Theridiidae contains the three-clawed, comb-footed spiders, so called because of the ventral row of serrated bristles on the fourth tarsus; this is used to play out sticky silk when enveloping prey, but it may be difficult to see. A typical web is a tangle of threads with tighter threads running from the centre to a nearby surface. The taut threads have sticky droplets near their bases. If an insect catches against one of these it breaks off, with the insect attached. The spider then crawls out of the tangle or its retreat to envelop its prey in silk. The prey is consumed inside the tangle web. Such a web is built by the red-back spider, *Latrodectus mactans hasselti*, a species now believed by many experts to be the same as the black widow of America and the katipo ('night biter') of New Zealand. The adult female has long, spindly legs and is velvety black in colour, with red marks on the back of the globular opisthosoma, and an hour-glass red mark on the underside. Sometimes the dorsal marks are orange, pink or light grey. The much smaller males are creamy brown with red or orange marks and juveniles are cream with black spots, becoming darker with successive moults. The webs are made in such locations as buildings, rubbish, old cans, machinery and tyres, but are always partly attached to the ground. The red-back spider is not aggressive

Female red-back spider, *Latrodectus mactans hasselti*

and is only likely to bite when accidentally squeezed or when defending the egg cocoons. An effective antivenene is readily available. The male is thought to be non-venomous. The webs of the grey house spider, *Achaearanea* (*Theridion*) *tepidariorum*, a cosmopolitan widespread species originating in some unidentified warm region, are common in houses throughout Australia, usually in corners of rooms or at the junction of walls and ceilings. Mating takes place throughout the year. The male is a little smaller than the female; both are light coloured with dark speckles and dark rings round the legs. The family Theridiidae also contains numerous native species of the largest spider genus, *Theridion*, and the dew drop spider, *Argyrodes antipodianus*, a small black species with a silver, black-streaked upper opisthosoma.

The family Argiopidae contains the true orb-web spinners whose webs need little description. The most familiar are the garden spiders of the genus *Eriophora* (up to 2.4cm; many species), which have a hunched appearance and coarse hairs on the body and legs. The web is vertical with a central hole, and is often remade every evening. St Andrew's cross spiders (*Argiope* species) make unmistakable orb-webs with two broad bands of silk in an 'X' shape, crossing at the centre (stabilamentum). The spider rests on the stabilamentum with its legs stretched along the arms. The females often make transverse bands of red, yellow and black on the abdomen. Many of the spiders of the family Argiopidae have bizarre shapes. The genus *Cyclosa* contains spiders with long abdomens, broad at the front, attenuated behind, and three terminal lobes. The genus *Gasteracantha* (about seven species) contains the shiny spiders which often occur near swamps and ponds; they carry pointed 'spines' along the lateral and posterior edges. The genus *Tetragnatha* is unmistakable; these spiders have extremely long front legs and very large chelicerae furnished with strong teeth and long fangs. They make small orb-webs and often rest on reeds with the legs outstretched so that they are difficult to detect. The family Argiopidae also contains the golden orb weavers (*Nephila* species) which make the most spectacular of all webs. The

webs are strong enough to trap birds and are built in high, windy places; they are permanent and usually occupied by the owner. These species (females 2.5cm or more) have a mat of short silvery hairs on the body. Also in this family are the leaf-rolling spiders, easily recognised by their web and their retreat, and commonly found in gardens. An example is *Phonognatha wagneri*, found in E Australia, which makes an incomplete orb in which is suspended a rolled-up leaf or sometimes a snail shell in which the spider hides.

Other members of the Argiopidae do not make a web of any kind. The genus *Celaenia* (about seven species) found mostly in SE Australia and TAS, is composed of spiders which lie in wait with the front legs outstretched, ready to catch passing moths. The death's head, orchard or bird-dropping spider, *C. excavata*, is of such a colour and shape when hunched up that it resembles a bird dropping. Spiders of the genus *Dicrostichus* dangle a long thread of silk with a sticky droplet at the end; when a suitable moth approaches the thread is twirled round rapidly and, with luck, catches the prey. The magnificent spider, *D. magnificus* (1cm), has a cream coloured, salmon-spotted opisthosoma with a fine brown network and two yellow humps. The hairy imperial spider, *D. furcatus*, is similar but dull brown and with a hairy opisthosoma.

The Linyphiidae is a large family of small spiders which are difficult to identify. In the subfamily Linyphiinae there are many species with long legs and globular opisthosoma which make bell-tent webs. The subfamily Erigoninae consists of minute spiders whose tiny webs (diameter 2cm to 3cm) on foliage or under logs and stones are made conspicuous by dew. These spiders are often responsible for gossamer which covers the vegetation after they have dispersed.

The Lycosidae is a family of familiar spiders commonly known as wolf spiders. The front of the prosoma is high, and the eyes are arranged in three rows. The body is coloured with contrasting patterns of blacks, greys, browns and yellows. Many are vagrant hunters but some use a permanent burrow or other retreat. Lycosids generally live in swampy places, some are found on the seashore and several live in gardens. The widespread genus *Lycosa* contains the spider responsible for outbreaks of tarantulism in S Italy.

The members of the family Pisauridae resemble the lycosids but their eyes are in two rows of four. They often run on the surface of swamps after prey. The large, widespread spiders of the genus *Dolomodes* frequently run across the surface of water and submerge to catch small fish or insects. They are often called nursery web spiders because they make a special shelter for their egg cocoons by binding leaves together; they remain in attendance until the young hatch.

The family Agelenidae contains the cobweb spiders. They make sheet webs with a tubular retreat at one side. One genus of four species, *Desis*, includes a marine spider, *D. marina*, which lives in silk-lined crevices in rocks and corals between the tides, and hunts at low tide. In form agelenids resemble wolf spiders but they have their eyes in two rows of four. The best-known species is probably the cosmopolitan *Tegenaria domestica*.

In 1974 a representative of a family of spiders previously unknown in Australia, the Loxoscelidae, was discovered in Adelaide. The fiddleback or brown recluse spider, *Loxosceles rufescens*, in now thought to have been present in Australia for at least 40 years. It belongs to a family of toxic spiders whose bites produce large ulcers at the site, and sometimes also fatal kidney damage.

Further reading: Bristowe, W.S. *The World of Spiders.* Collins, London, 1958; Hadlington, B. *Know your Australian Spiders and Ticks.* Huntsmen Press, Peakhurst NSW, 1962; Child, J. *Australian Spiders.* Periwinkle Press, Gladesville NSW, 1965; Main, B.Y. *Spiders of Australia.* Jacaranda Press, Brisbane, 1967 and *Spiders.* Collins, Sydney, 1976; Clyne, D. *A Guide to Australian Spiders.* Nelson, Melbourne, 1969; Mascord, R. *Australian Spiders in Colour.* A.H. & A.W. Reed, Sydney, 1981; Sutherland, S.K. *Venomous Creatures of Australia: A Field Guide with Notes on First Aid.* Oxford University Press, Melbourne, 1981.

spinach *see* Chenopodiaceae

spinebills *see* honeyeaters

spinefeet *see* fishes, bony

Spinifex This is the name of a genus of creeping, maritime grasses. Hairy Spinifex, *S. hirsutus*, is common on sandy beaches in S and E Australia where it effectively binds the sand. The name is also applied, incorrectly, to drought resistant, tussock-forming grasses of the genus *Triodia* (about 30 species) which cover vast areas of interior Australia; these grasses are rich in resins which were used as gums for hafting tools by the Aborigines, and their leaves are rolled, rigid and spiky. *T. irritans* is best known as porcupine grass.

spinifexbird *see* warblers

spiny anteaters *see* monotreme mammals

spiny-headed worms These primitive, parasitic, worm-shaped animals belong to the phylum Acanthocephala. There are about 500 species, some of which occur in Australia, ranging in size from less than 10mm to over 500mm. Their common name is derived from the fact that the snout (proboscis) is covered with hooks. The proboscis and the neck can be withdrawn into the trunk. The young stages are parasites in crustaceans and insects, the adults in the guts of vertebrates, especially fishes, birds and carnivorous mammals.

Spirula *see* cephalopods

spitfire grubs *see* ants, etc.

Spofforth, Frederick Robert (1853-1926) Cricketer. Born in the Sydney suburb of Balmain, he was attracted to cricket as a boy and concentrated initially on fast under-arm bowling, but changed to fast over-arm after watching G. Tarrant of the 1864 English touring side. Nicknamed 'the Demon' and described as being as 'irresistible as an avalanche' he became one of Australia's finest bowlers. Spofforth's greatest asset was control, and his ability to consistently and accurately bowl a good length, varying the pace and amount of break of the ball at will, wreaked havoc among the English sides of the time. In Melbourne in 1879 against Lord Harris' English side he became the first Test bowler to take a hat trick (three wickets with three consecutive balls). He holds the record for taking the most wickets in a Test (14 for 90 runs against England in 1882). Of all Australian bowlers who have taken more than 75 Test wickets, only one has bettered Spofforth's achievement—94 wickets at an average of 18.41. The London *Home News* of 1878 wrote: 'His delivery is quite appalling; the balls thunder in like cannon shot.'

sponges These multicellular animals are contained in the phylum Porifera. Sponges, which are all aquatic and nearly entirely marine, are little more than colonies of cells for there is little integration between the various cells, and no nervous system. The simplest kind of sponge consists of a cylinder with a large opening through which water passes out of the animal. The water, which carries food particles, is brought into the cylinder through porocytes in the body wall. These are simply cells with a hole right through them through which the water passes. The currents of water are created by innumerable cells (choanocytes) inside the cylinder. Each is equipped with a long, hair-like structure (flagellum) to move the water. The base of the flagellum is surrounded by a collar of cytoplasm in which food particles are trapped before being absorbed and digested in the body of the cell. The outside of the body is covered, except where the incurrent pores pierce the surface, by flat, pavement cells. A network of horny fibres (as in the familiar bath sponge), or of interlocking spicules of silica or calcium carbonate, act as a kind of internal skeleton to give support to the body. More complex sponges differ mainly in the subdivision of the internal space which is divided into complicated canals. When some sponges are broken up into their constituent cells, by passing them through a very fine mesh of fabric, they will re-assemble themselves as complete sponges. This underlines the comparative simplicity of their structure and organisation. They were recognised as animals only in the 18th century.

There are at least 12 freshwater species in Australia, all of which encrust underwater logs, stones and so on. They may reach a

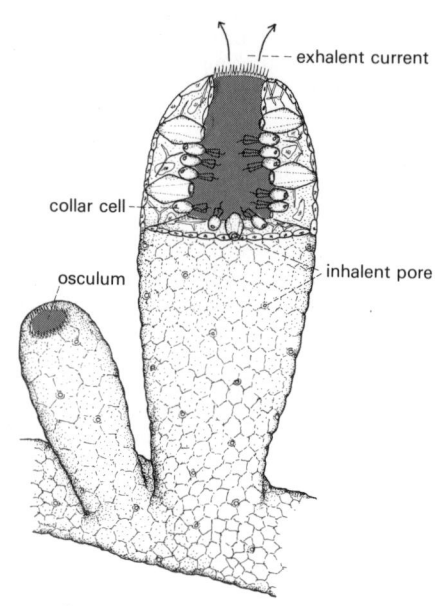

Sponge cut away to show internal organs

diameter of about 1m, but are rarely more than 3cm thick.

Marine sponges are far more numerous, and range from the seashore to the depths of the ocean. Species of *Scypha* are small, grey or white cup-shaped sponges with a limy skeleton found on jetty piles below low-water mark. Most of the common shore sponges of southern Australia, however, have skeletons of silica; among them are the heliotrope-coloured encrusted species of *Haliclona*. Another encrusting species, possibly belonging to the genus *Halichondria*, has been likened to a piece of bread covered with green mould.

Several seashore sponges will be found to have other kinds of animals, such as sea anemones (phylum Coelenterata; *see* COELENTERATES) and BIVALVE MOLLUSCS, living within them.

Further reading: Dakin, W.J., Bennett, I. & Pope, E. *Australian Seashores.* (6th edn) Angus & Robertson, Sydney, 1976; Williams, W.D. *Australian Freshwater Life.* (2nd edn) Macmillan, Melbourne, 1980.

spookfish *see* sharks, etc.

spoonbills *see* ibises, etc.

springtails These small ARTHROPODS (2mm to 10mm long) were formerly classed with the INSECTS but are now placed in a separate class, Collembola, of their own. There is one order, divided into two sub-orders; about 215 species are known in Australia. Springtails have antennae and three pairs of legs. Many species have a fork on the tail which fits on to an appendage nearer the front of the body. When the fork is suddenly released the animal springs several times its own length.

Most species live on the soil, in leaf-litter and in decaying plant material. Some may be found on the surface of water, even on the surface of seashore rock pools, and one or two species may be seen congregated on the surface of snow. Springtails feed mainly on algae, fungi, lichens and decaying organic matter but some attack living plants. The introduced lucerne flea, *Sminthurus viridis*, is so called because of its shape and jumping ability and because it is a serious pest of lucerne and other leguminous crops in southern Australia.

spruce *see* Gymnospermae

spurges *see* Euphorbiaceae

spurry, corn *see* Caryophyllaceae

squash It is claimed that Australia has more squash clubs and women squash players than any other nation. However, the game receives very little publicity in Australia and the world champion squash players that Australia has produced are virtually unknown in their home country.

The first squash court to be built in Australia was in a Sydney gymnasium in 1919. A boom in the sport occurred after World War II on the return of many servicemen and women who had learnt to play the game in recreation centres overseas. Since that time, the sport has continued to grow. There are squash courts in most city suburbs and in the larger country towns, and many sporting and recreation clubs also have courts. Australia was the first country to introduce public courts, the first of which opened in Melbourne in 1935.

Heather MCKAY is the best woman player Australia has produced, winning the British Open title from 1962 to 1977. Since then it has been won by other Australians: Sue Newman (1978), Barbara Wall (1979), and Vicki Cardwell (1980-82). The Australian women's team won the world championship in 1981 and 1983. Australia has also excelled in men's squash, the two top players being Ken HISCOE and

Heather McKay in action

Geoff HUNT. In 1982 the junior men's team came second in the world championship, Chris Dittmar being individual runner-up.

squatters This term was applied originally to settlers who occupied Crown lands illegally in order to graze sheep. This practice became very common in the 1820s and 1830s.

Origins of the squatting movement The movement developed as the result of a clash between economic opportunity and official land policy. Following the breeding experiments of John MACARTHUR and Samuel MARSDEN, wool had provided NSW with its first reliable export commodity, and by the 1820s the wool industry was expanding rapidly. In that same decade, however, the government had begun to phase out free land grants, and in 1831 decreed that Crown lands should thereafter be disposed of only by public auction, with a minimum price of five shillings an acre. This figure was raised to 12 shillings in 1839 and to £1 in 1842. In the meantime, official policy had turned in favour of keeping settlement concentrated, and in 1829 Governor DARLING had decreed that settlement was to be limited to the NINETEEN COUNTIES, which comprised an area extending about 200km from Sydney. The squatters ignored the land and settlement regulations and would simply travel inland until they came to suitable unoccupied land.

The squatters' living conditions and grazing methods The squatters' lives were marked by hardship and dangers. Their property and their lives were threatened by drought, bushfires and in some cases by hostile Aborigines. Their flocks were sometimes ravaged by dingoes. Until they gained security of tenure they had no incentive to build elaborate residences, and in any case the expense of establishing their flocks and the high costs of transporting goods from the settled districts forced most of them to live very frugal lives for many years. Their first

An exploring party of squatters in search of a 'run'

houses were slab huts with bark roofs and earth floors, and usually contained very little furniture.

Their grazing methods involved the use of large areas of comparatively unimproved land. The 'runs' were not fenced, but the boundaries might be marked roughly by axe-cuts on trees or a plough furrow. The sheep were divided into flocks of a few hundred, each flock being followed throughout the day by a shepherd. In the evening he brought his charges to a fold made of hurdles (portable fences) and put them in charge of a hut-keeper, who was responsible for them during the night.

Legalisation of the squatters' position In the early 1830s the authorities in Britain, under the influence of Edward Gibbon WAKEFIELD's ideas, continued their efforts to keep settlement concentrated. Governor BOURKE, who took office in 1831, was instructed to suppress the squatting movement. Even by the time of his arrival, however, half the colony's sheep were beyond the official boundaries, and by 1835 the squatters were nearing the MURRAY RIVER in the S and spreading over the NEW ENGLAND Plateau to the N. Bourke soon realised that the colony's prosperity depended largely on wool produced by the squatters. Moreover, as he pointed out in his despatches, most of them were respectable people, ex-officers and younger sons of well-to-do English families, possessed of initiative and some capital—just the type of settler the colony needed; they were too independent, as well as too numerous, to be driven off their land. He wrote in a despatch of 1836 that 'not all the armies of England ... could drive back our herds within the Nineteen Countries.'

Bourke's point of view prevailed, and in 1836 he was allowed to introduce a licensing system, by which a squatter was allowed to retain the use of his run on the payment of an annual fee of £10 a year. However, there was no guarantee that his licence would be

National Library of Australia

A squatter's first home (a somewhat idealised contemporary presentation)

renewed the following year, and if it was not, he gained no compensation for the improvements he had made to the land. For the following decade, therefore, the squatters aimed at gaining greater security of tenure by means of long-term leases, with provisions for them to buy at least part of their runs at a low price. They came close to gaining all their demands through the Orders-in-Council of 1847, which allowed for long leases except in settled districts and allowed leaseholders to buy all or part of their runs at a fixed price of £1 an acre (*see* LAND TENURE). The result was to give a relatively small number of men control of most of the good grazing land in E Australia. Once the squatters' position had been legalised, the name began to lose its unfavourable connotation, and to be applied to any grazier who owned or leased a large amount of land. *Further reading:* Kiddle, M. *Men of Yesterday.* Melbourne University Press, Melbourne, 1961; Roberts, S.H. *The Squatting Age in Australia, 1835-47.* (2nd edn) Melbourne University Press, Melbourne, 1964; Gilbert, P.F. *Squatters and Immigrants.* Jacaranda, Milton QLD, 1970.

squids *see* cephalopods

Sri Lanka, settlers from *see* Indian subcontinent, settlers from

staghorns *see* Pteridophyta

Standley Chasm NT Located 48km W of ALICE SPRINGS, this spectacular natural gorge, only 4m wide with sheer walls reaching up to about 80m high, is a cleft in the MACDONNELL RANGES. Here is how the author, Ernestine HILL, in her book *The Territory* (1951), described the pioneer teacher after whom the chasm is named: 'A magnificent natural monument commemorates Mrs Ida Standley, first school teacher of central Australia. With no more than half a dozen

white children in school at Alice Springs, Mrs Standley gathered the half-castes out of the blacks' camps, taught them to read and write, the girls to sew and cook ... Rambling the ranges they discovered the most spectacular gap in the MacDonnells, where a javelin of bright sun splits the red crags ... So it was named for a woman of infinite kindness—Standley's Chasm.'

Stanley TAS (population 603 in 1981) A small town on the W part of the BASS STRAIT coast, it is 78km by road W of BURNIE. Historically, Stanley is one of the most interesting towns of the NW coast for it was here that the VAN DIEMEN'S LAND Co. established its headquarters and built 'Highfield' in 1835. Many of the old buildings of the early days have been restored and are popular tourist attractions. A former Prime Minister of Australia, Joseph LYONS, was born in the town. A striking scenic feature is The Nut, a rock outcrop 150m high which dominates the coastal landscape.

Stanthorpe QLD (population 3 966 in 1981) Located in the GRANITE BELT on the New England Highway, 219km by road SW of Brisbane and 58km S of WARWICK, it is the business and service centre for an orcharding and vine growing region. At an elevation of 792km above sea level, adjacent to the spectacular ranges forming the NSW/QLD border, it has an average annual rainfall of 760mm concentrated mostly in the summer months; January is the wettest (97mm average), August the driest (45mm). The town dates from the 1870s, when it was a focal point of a tin mining area and was known as Stannum. Wine production is an important industry of the region and several wineries are open for inspection by visitors. The Apple and Grape Harvest festival is held biennially in March when the fruit trees and vines are laden. The Girraween National Park (11 300ha), S of the

town, is noted for its massive granite tors, balancing rocks and mountain peaks; among these features are those bearing such names as the Eye of the Needle, the Sphinx, the Brothers and the Aztec Temple; Mt Norman (1267m elevation) is the highest point. The Storm King Dam, SE of Stanthorpe on the upper Severn River, is a popular recreation and aquatic sports area.

starfish *see* sea stars

starlings These PASSERINE BIRDS belong to the large family Sturnidae; there are three species in Australia, two of which are introduced. The native species is the shining starling, *Aplonis metallica* (25cm long), a breeding visitor to north-eastern QLD. Its plumage is glossy black (white-breasted when young), and it has red eyes and a long tail. The diet consists of insects and fruits, particularly nutmegs. Shining starlings breed in large colonies; the nests are suspended from the branches of tall trees and are domed structures composed of tendrils.

The European starling, *Sturnus vulgaris* (20cm), is a familiar, self-assertive bird with iridescent black, often spotted, plumage. Introduced into VIC in the 1850s and 1860s to control insect pests it has since become so abundant in some parts of SE Australia that it in turn is now considered a pest because it attacks fruit and seeds and because it competes with many native species for nesting sites. Its white eggs are laid in an untidy collection of grass and feathers in tree hollows or the crevices of buildings.

The Indian myna, *Acridotheres tristis* (24cm), an omnivorous bird like its European relative is chocolate brown, with a yellow bill and face patch, and a white patch on the wing, conspicuous in flight. The eggs are blue, and the

(above) the Indian myna, *Acridotheres tristis* (below) European starling, *Sturnus vulgaris*

E. Hosking (N.P.I.A.W.)

The shining starling, *Aplonis metallica*

nests resemble those of the European starling. The Indian myna was one of the first animals to be used for BIOLOGICAL CONTROL, having been introduced into Mauritius in the 18th century to control locusts. Introduced into VIC in 1863 and 1872 to control grasshoppers and cane-beetles, it is now common in many urban areas of E Australia, where it scavenges for food in streets and rubbish tips.
See also animals, introduced

starwort *see* Caryophyllaceae

Statute of Westminster
This was an Act of the British Parliament (1931) by which the complete independence of Australia and other self-governing countries of the Empire was formally recognised.
See also foreign relations

Stawell
VIC (population 6 160 in 1981) Situated N of the GREAT DIVIDING RANGE and at the N end of the GRAMPIANS, at an elevation of 232m above sea level, in the WIMMERA region in the central-W of the State, it is a commercial and service centre for a productive wheat growing and sheep grazing region. It is located on the Western Highway, 235km by road NW of Melbourne, 31km NW of ARARAT and 66km SE of HORSHAM; it is also on the main interstate (Melbourne-Adelaide) railway line, 241km from Melbourne. It receives an average annual rainfall of 533mm, which falls throughout the year, but with a concentration in winter and spring. Gold was discovered in the district in the 1850s and with the development of rich quartz reefs the population grew to 30 000 by 1857. The settlement was officially proclaimed in 1858 and named after the then Attorney-General, William Foster Stawell. It became a shire centre in 1864, a borough in 1869 and a town in 1957. Grape growing for wines is an important local rural industry and there are several wineries at Great Western, 13km SE of the town on the Western Highway. Stawell is well known for its annual professional foot-race, the Stawell Easter Gift. The National Trust (VIC) has listed several buildings in the town for preservation including the old police

residence (1869), 'Ledcourt' homestead, the old powder magazine, the post office (1874-75), the former courthouse and the shire hall (1865).

Stead, Christina Ellen
(1902-83) Novelist. Born and educated in Sydney, she worked as a teacher and office worker before going to London in 1928. She then found employment in financial houses in Paris and elsewhere, and married William Blake, a broker with strong literary interest. After living in the USA for many years she returned to Australia in 1974. Her novels and short stories, which are notable for their effective satire and rich imagery, have won her an international reputation. Those which are set wholly or mainly in Australia include some of the stories in *The Salzburg Tales* (1934) and the novels *Seven Poor Men of Sydney* (1934) and *For Love Alone* (1944). Of her other novels the best-known are probably *Houses of All Nations* (1938) and *The Man Who Loved Children* (1941).

steel *see* iron, etc.

Stephen, Sir Ninian
(1923-) Governor-General. Born near Oxford, in England, he came to Australia at the age of 16, served in the Second AIF in the Pacific in World War II, and then completed his legal studies at Melbourne University. After being called to the Victorian Bar in 1951 he became a QC in 1967, a Judge of the Victorian Supreme Court in 1970 and a Justice of the High Court of Australia in 1972. In January 1982 it was announced that Sir Ninian would succeed Sir Zelman COWEN as Governor-General in the following July. Both before and after his appointment he has expressed the view that the conventions underlying the Constitution and the reserve powers of the Crown should be coded and written into the Constitution.

Stephens, Alfred George
(1865-1933) Editor, publisher and literary critic. Born in TOOWOOMBA in QLD he worked as a journalist in various parts of that colony before obtaining a position as sub-editor on the Sydney *Bulletin* in 1894. As editor of that journal's literary section, which he named the Red Page in 1896, he played a vital part in the development of Australian literature. Every notable Australian writer of the time had work published on the Red Page, and since Stephens was also in charge of the *Bulletin's* book publishing division for some years, he was able to help many of them to have their writings published in book form. After leaving the *Bulletin* in 1906 he worked at free-lance editing, literary criticism and lecturing. In 1899 he had published five numbers of a literary magazine called the *Bookfellow*. He revived this as a weekly for a time in 1907, and brought it out again, with some interruptions, between 1911 and 1925. Although he was adept in perceiving and encouraging talent in

others, his own creative writing, which included one work of fiction, several small volumes of poetry and some short plays, was undistinguished. However, his publications *The Red Pagan* (1904), *Victor Daley: A Biographical and Critical Notice* (1905), *Henry Kendall: A Critical Review* (1928) and *Chris Brennan: A Monograph* (1933) form a useful body of literary criticism.

Sterculiaceae
This dicotyledonous family of flowering plants contains about 50 genera of tropical and sub-tropical distribution. Sometimes referred to as the cocoa or chocolate family, it is best developed in Africa, but also well developed in Australia.

The members of the Sterculiaceae are trees, shrubs or herbs. The leaves are alternate, usually simple, and are often covered with star-shaped hairs; stipules may be present. The flowers are often unisexual and are solitary or in clusters; they have three to five sepals and either five often minute petals or none at all. The whorl sepals which form the outer covering of the flower when in bud (calyx) are tubular and either lobed or joined at the base. There are between five and 15 stamens, either separate or partly joined. The ovary is superior and contains between three and five cavities (locules). The fruit is dry and usually is a follicle or a splitting capsule.

The best-known Australian genus is *Brachychiton*, which contains three widespread and extensively cultivated species. The Illawarra flame, *B. acerifolium*, and the Queensland lace bark, *B. discolor*, are both natives of closed forest, while the kurrajong, *B. populneum*, occurs as an occasional tree on dry, rocky sites in E Australia and towards the W into semi-arid environments. The foliage of the kurrajong is sometimes cut for cattle fodder in drought times. Less familiar in cultivation is *B. bidwillii*, which has scarlet bell-shaped flowers, and the bottle tree, *B. rupestre*, which develops girths of up to 10m. Amongst the shrubby genera represented in Australia are *Lasiopetalum*, *Seringia* and *Rulingia*, all components of heath, woodland and open forest; a number of species have been brought into cultivation in recent years.
See also Angiospermae; Appendix 5, Flower Structure and Glossary of Botanical Terms
Further reading: see Appendix 6, A Bibliography for Plants.

Stewart, Douglas Alexander
(1913-) Poet and literary critic. Born in New Zealand, he worked as a journalist there and in Sydney, and from 1939 to 1961 was literary editor of the *Bulletin*. His versatility is shown by the list of his published works. These include two highly regarded volumes of literary criticism, *The Flesh and the Spirit* (1947) and *The Broad Stream* (1975); a collection of short stories; a volume of reminiscences, *Norman Lindsay: A Personal Memoir* (1975); several volumes of verse, including *Collected Poems, 1936-67* (1967); and the verse plays *The Fire on the Snow* (1941), which deals with

Scott's Antarctic expedition and is written for the radio, *Ned Kelly* (1943) and *The Shipwreck* (1946). His poetic style is light, fresh and strongly individualistic, showing no clear signs of influence by other writers.
Further reading: Keesing, N. *Douglas Stewart.* Lansdowne, Melbourne, 1965; Semmler, C.W. *Douglas Stewart.* Twayne, New York, 1974.

Stewart, Nellie (1858-1931) Actress. One of the best-loved stars of the Australian stage, Nellie Stewart came from a theatrical family—her grandmother was Theodosia Yates who performed in Hobart in the 1840s, and her mother was the actress Mrs Guerin. She played her first role in 1864 at a benefit performance for Charles John Kean (an English actor who toured Australia, America and Jamaica in 1863-66), and as a child appeared in pantomimes and toured in an entertainment, *Rainbow Revels*, written for the Stewart family by Garnet Walch. In 1880 George COPPIN engaged her to play in *Sinbad* at the Theatre Royal, Melbourne, and set her on the road to stardom. After a brief early marriage she lived with George Musgrove of the J.C. WILLIAMSON 'Firm', who helped direct her career in England and the USA as well as in Australia. She performed chiefly in operetta and pantomime, her most notable roles being in *Cinderella* and *Sweet Nell of Old Drury*, with which she became identified and which she revived twice in the 1920s when she was nearly 70. In later years she gave acting classes, and wrote her autobiography. Her last performance was in 1931 in the balcony scene from *Romeo and Juliet*.
Further reading: Skill, M. *Sweet Nell of Old Sydney.* Urania Publishing Co., Sydney, 1974; West, J. *Theatre in Australia.* Cassell, Sydney, 1978.

stick insects These large to very large plant-eating INSECTS belong to the exopterygote order Phasmatodea; about 130 species are known from Australia. Stick insects or phasmids mimic their surroundings superbly. Most species are similar in colour and texture to the twigs on which they feed. Their slow movements and the peculiar distorted positions that they assume add to the deception. When disturbed many species go into a cataleptic state, the limbs and body retaining for a long period any position that they are placed in. This ruse saves many from predation. Some insects have flat outgrowths from the body and legs which give the animals a close resemblance to leaves; two such species are found in the N of Australia, though many occur in New Guinea.

The body of a stick insect is long and narrow, as are the three similar pairs of legs. Most species lack wings but in species in which wings do occur they are usually large and functional in the male, and small and virtually useless in the female. The fore-wings are short, thickened tegmina which do not cover more than the base of the folded hind-wings.

The antennae vary in length from very short to very long. The mouthparts are of the typical biting and chewing form. The two sexes often differ markedly, not only in the absence or presence of wings, but also in the shape of the body. The female short-winged species, *Extatosoma tiaratum*, for example, has a much heavier body than the male and is far spinier than the fully-winged male.

Reproduction is often parthenogenetic but this does not appear to be obligatory in Australian species. Most species drop their eggs, which often resemble the seeds of plants, onto the soil below the trees and bushes on which the adults feed. The nymphs resemble the adults. Some species can reach high population densities and, like LOCUSTS, some of these show phase differences. At low densities, for example, the nymphs of *Didymuria violescens*, a common pest of eucalypts, are green; at high densities the insects have patterns of black and yellow. This is presumably a warning colouration.

stilts *see* waders

stingaree *see* fishes, poisonous and venomous; sharks, etc.

stingers *see* coelenterates

Stirling, Sir James (1791-1865) Governor. He was born in Lanarkshire, Scotland, joined the British Navy at the age of 12 and saw active service in European and American waters. In 1826 he was given command of the SUCCESS, with instructions to deliver currency to Sydney, then to sail to MELVILLE ISLAND in the NT and transport its garrison to RAFFLES BAY on the mainland. However, in Sydney he obtained permission to survey the SW coast

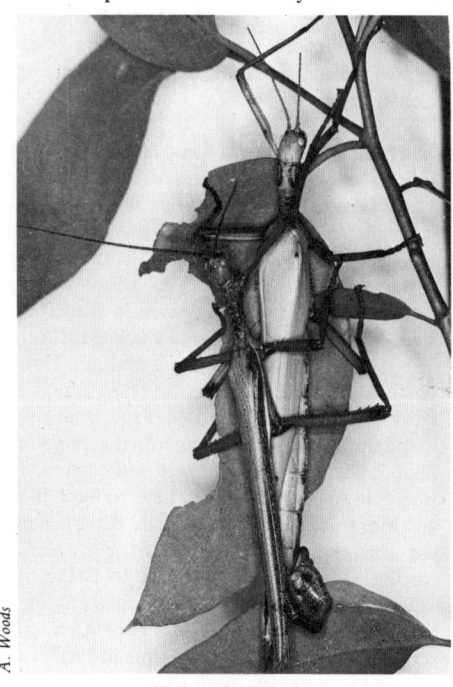
Mating stick insects

A. Woods

Sir James Stirling

before going to Melville Is and was so impressed by the land along the SWAN RIVER that he recommended the founding of a settlement there. When in 1829 his recommendation bore fruit he was made Lieutenant-Govenor of WA, the position being raised to that of a full governorship in 1832. The early difficulties of the colony must be blamed partly on his over-enthusiastic appraisal of the land beside the Swan, and he has been criticised too for slowness in realising the colony's deficiencies after its foundation. However, he must be given credit for patience in listening to the settlers' complaints, and for his efforts to obtain from the British government further assistance for the colony. In dealing with the Aborigines, unfortunately, he was content to rely on the kind of 'pacification' policy that was dominant in NSW, punishing severely those Aborigines who attacked the white man or interfered with his possessions. He personally led the punitive PINJARRA expedition against the Aborigines of the Murray River district. He left the colony in 1839, resumed his naval career and rose to the rank of Admiral.
Further reading: Crowley, F.K. *Australia's Western Third.* Heinemann, Melbourne, 1970; Mills, R.C. *The Colonisation of Australia, 1829-1842.* Sydney University Press, Sydney, 1974.

Stirling Range WA Rising abruptly and spectacularly from the surrounding countryside, about 80km N of ALBANY in the S part of the State, this range extends about 80km on an E-W alignment lying E of the Great Southern Highway and NE of MOUNT BARKER. The highest peak is Bluff Knoll (1073m) in the E section of the range. Four other peaks reach over 1000m: Ellen Peak (1012m), Pyungoorup Peak (1060m), Coyanarup Peak (1046m) and Tollbrunup Peak (1052m). The panoramic views from these and other peaks provide striking vistas of the adjacent landscape. Because of the height of the range and its close proximity to the S coast, the climate differs from that of the surrounding area and this has produced a great variety of wild flowers,

National Parks Authority WA

Stirling Range National Park

particularly on the rocky tops. The Stirling Range National Park (115 671ha) includes the whole range system; there are roads through the park and walking tracks provide access to most of the peaks. The range was named in 1835 in honour of Captain James STIRLING, the first Governor of WA.

Stivens, Dallas George 'Dal' (1911-) Author and journalist. Born in BLAYNEY in NSW, he was educated in Sydney, became a journalist on the Sydney *Daily Telegraph* and during World War II was in the Army Education Service. After the war he worked as a public servant and then as a free-lance writer in Sydney and London. He has concentrated on short stories, being at his best in humorous writing, particularly in bush 'tall stories'. Collections of his stories include *The Tramp* (1936), *The Courtship of Uncle Henry* (1946), *The Gambling Ghost* (1953), *Ironbark Bill* (1955) and *The Scholarly Mouse* (1957). He has been a particularly active member of the Australian Society of Authors, of which he was foundation president.

stoneflies These small to medium-sized INSECTS form the exopterygote order Plecopters; they have aquatic nymphs and are generally found near streams. There are about 84 species in Australia confined, as far as is known, to cool temperate regions. Australian stoneflies appear to be closely allied to those of New Zealand and South America. Their nymphs are important as food of freshwater fish, especially trout.

The adults are soft-bodied, dull-coloured, inconspicuous insects with two pairs of sparsely veined wings, long, many-segmented antennae and a pair of short, segmented tails (cerci). The wings are loosely coupled together in flight, and wrapped round the body when at rest. The adults have biting mouthparts and may feed on algae near the streams that they frequent. The nymphs resemble the adults apart from their lack of wings. They breathe either through gills (round the anus, on the mouthparts or on the thorax) or through the soft body cuticle. The food consists of small aquatic plants. There may be as many as 30 instars before the nymphs reach the adult stage.

storks *see* jabiru

Storm Bay TAS This broad coastal inlet in the SE of the State lies between BRUNY ISLAND and TASMAN PENINSULA. The DERWENT RIVER, upon which Hobart is located, flows into Storm Bay. It was named by the Dutch explorer Abel TASMAN in 1642 when stormy conditions prevented his ships from anchoring there.

storm-petrels *see* sea birds

Stow, (Julian) Randolph (1935-) Author. Although he has published a considerable quantity of verse, including the collections *Act One* (1957) and *A Counterfeit Silence: Selected Poems* (1969), his literary reputation rests mainly on his novels, *In a Haunted Land* (1965), *The Bystander* (1957), *To the Islands* (1958), *Tourmaline* (1963), a children's book *The Merry-Go-Round in the Sea* (1965), *Midnite* (1967) and *Visitants* (1979). Set mainly in the GERALDTON district of WA, where he was born, or in the far N of that State, these novels are particularly notable for the author's ability to link the qualities of the landscapes in those regions with the emotions of his characters. This is done most successfully in *To the Islands*, in which the disillusioned manager of an Aboriginal mission journeys deep into the wilderness to regain peace of mind.

Stradbroke Island QLD Two low sandy islands lying SE of MORETON BAY have the name Stradbroke because, until a storm in 1896 cut a channel between them, they formed a single island. Both are long sand spits, on a NNE-WSW axis; the N one is the larger (about 40km long and 10km wide). Mineral sands have been commercially exploited and there are several holiday centres. The Blue Lake National Park (445ha) is a freshwater lake surrounded by eucalypt woodland on the N island; access to this park is by vehicular ferry from Redland Bay or Cleveland.

Strahan TAS (population 402 in 1981) Situated on MACQUARIE HARBOUR, it is the port town of the W coast, 297km by road W of Hobart via the Lyell Highway and 41km from QUEENSTOWN. Formerly, it was the exporting centre for copper mined at MOUNT LYELL; the copper was transported by a rack-and-pinion railway down the steep mountain slopes to the port, but the rail line has been dismantled and the copper is now taken by road to Hobart. Several buildings in the town stand as memorials to Strahan's former importance as a shipping centre, and have been listed for preservation by the National Trust (TAS): the Union Steamship Co.'s building (built in 1899 and now the council chambers), the customs house and the railway station (1897). The town is located in the high rainfall region of the W part of the State, receiving an annual average of 1696mm. Fishing and forestry are the main industries of the district.

Strathalbyn SA (population 1 756 in 1981) This country town is located on the Angus River, 82km by rail SE of Adelaide. At an elevation of 67m above sea level, it has an average annual rainfall of 495mm, with a distinct concentration in winter months. It is a service centre to a rural farming and grazing district, with some wine-grape cultivation at nearby Langhornes Creek. The town was named by early Scottish settlers; *strath* is Gaelic for 'a broad valley', and 'Albyn' is a variation of the name 'Albion' from the Albion Iron and Steel Mills in Glasgow.

Strathbogie Ranges VIC Located E of 'EYMOUR, between the upper GOULBURN RIVER and its tributary the Broken River, NW of the EILDON RESERVOIR, these ranges consist of a rugged, dissected and forested plateau area, with Mt Wombat (860m) the highest point. It was one of the areas where the KELLY gang of bushrangers roamed in the 1870s.

Streaky Bay SA (population 985 in 1981) A coastal inlet and a town on the W coast of EYRE PENINSULA, Streaky Bay is 748km by road from Adelaide. The town is located on the Flinders Highway, 296km NW of PORT LINCOLN, on a site discovered by the explorer Matthew FLINDERS in 1802 and so named by him because of the streaky discoloration in the waters of the bay. The region had in fact been visited much earlier, in 1627, by the Dutch navigator Pieter Nuijts. At an elevation of 13m above sea level, the town has an average annual rainfall of 378mm, concentrated mainly in the winter season. The main industries of the area are fishing, wheat growing and sheep grazing. The bay is considered to be the only safe all-weather anchorage along the extensive stretch of the S coast of the continent between Port Lincoln and KING GEORGE SOUND in WA.

Streeton, Sir Arthur Ernest (1867-1943) Artist. Born at Mt Duneed VIC, he studied at the Melbourne National Gallery School while working as a lithographic apprentice. As a painter, his work gave respectability to the Australian landscape as a legitimate art subject, while his introduction of light tones and bright colours became an Australian convention for many decades. His fine painting, *Fires On (Lapstone Tunnel)* (1891, now in the Art Gallery of New South Wales), illustrates much of Streeton's technique—blue skies, bright light, and agile, square brush strokes laying down chunky forms in light tones. Streeton met Tom ROBERTS and Frederick McCUBBIN at Mentone, PORT PHILLIP BAY, in 1886, and as a result joined them and Charles CONDER at painting camps in and around Eaglemont. Following the purchase in 1890 by the Art Gallery of New South Wales of his *Still Glides the Stream*—the first Australian artist to be represented in a public collection—Streeton moved to Sydney, and with Roberts established artists' camps on Little Sirius Cove, Mosman, in 1891. During the depression of the 1890s these camps became popular meeting places for artists.

From the mid-1890s, Streeton moved away from shoreline subjects and began to paint scenes of the BLUE MOUNTAINS and the HAWKESBURY. *The Purple Noon's Transparent Might* (1896; now in the National Gallery of Victoria) is the most well-known painting of this period and it established Streeton's reputation in Australia. He lived in England for some years after 1898, but failed to gain the reputation he desired. He served with a medical unit in World War I before becoming a war artist. Although his work deteriorated after about 1910, his position as the 'grand old man' of Australian painting had been firmly established and he was knighted in 1937. He died at Olinda VIC.

strepsipterans These endopterygote INSECTS are probably descended from the Coleoptera (BEETLES); they are so little known by the layman that they have not acquired a common name. There are 94 species in Australia. The males range in size from about 1.5mm to 4mm and are dark, winged insects; their hind-wings are relatively very large but their fore-wings are reduced to tiny structures resembling elytra. The eyes are relatively large and in appearance resemble berries. The adult females are wingless and rather shapeless, and are often completely parasitic. The hosts are chiefly Hemiptera (BUGS) and Hymenoptera (ANTS, BEES AND WASPS). The female does not lay eggs but releases many (often more than a thousand) first-stage larvae that have developed within her. Those that parasitise homopterans (order Hemiptera) burrow through the cuticle of any nymph that they can find. The hymenopteran parasites cling to an adult to be carried back to the nest where they parasitise larvae. A parasitised host is said to be stylopised and, if a female, it often develops male characteristics as a result of the infestation.

There are five families of strepsipterans in Australia, the most primitive of which, the Mengeidae, has non-parasitic adult females. The larvae of both sexes are, however, parasitic. The largest family, the Stylopidae, contains species that parasitise bees and wasps.

Strickland, Shirley (1925-) Athlete. Born in Guildford WA, she concentrated her racing efforts on sprint and hurdle events, and became the first Australian athlete to win medals in three consecutive Olympic Games. In the 1948 Olympics she won three medals, a silver in the 4 × 100m relay, and bronzes in the 100m sprint and the 80m hurdle event. In the 1952 Games she won the 80m hurdle event in world record time, becoming the first woman hurdler to break 11 seconds in this event, and in the 1956 Olympics she won the same event again, breaking her own world record. In 1952 she won the bronze medal in the 100m sprint and in 1956 she was a member of the winning Australian relay team, bringing her Olympic medal tally to seven, more than any other Australian woman athlete before or since. After her retirement from competitive running she remained active in athletics as a coach in Perth.

stringybarks *see* Myrtaceae

stromatolites Stromatolites are large, layered mounds of blue-green ALGAE and silt. Living examples have been discovered only recently, in the West Indies and, in profusion, at SHARK BAY, WA. Fossil stromatolites, however, go back almost to the beginning of the fossil record. Blue-green algae were among the first organisms to exist, and the stromatolites at Shark Bay give us a glimpse of life on earth near to its beginning. The high salinity in those parts of the bay where they occur prevents marine invertebrates from grazing them away but, unfortunately, these unique 'living fossils' are threatened by development.

Strutt, William (1825-1915) Artist. Born in Devon, Strutt was trained by his father, a painter of miniatures, and later studied in Paris. The clean lines and flowing forms of his drawings show the influence of the fashionable neo-classical techniques of the Paris schools. He emigrated to Australia in 1851 and went to the BALLARAT goldfields. His eye condition, the reason for his move to Australia, improved, and he began painting again. He showed a preference for depicting historical events in Australian rural life. *Black Thursday* (now in the State Library of Victoria), a large work depicting the terrible bushfires of 1851 and painted after he returned to London, is one of his most impressive works. He returned to the UK in 1862 and developed an interest in religious paintings.

Strzelecki, Sir Paul Edmund de (1797-1873) Explorer and scientist. Born near Poznan, in Prussian-annexed Poland, he lived for some years in England and then travelled widely in the Americas, the Pacific and New Zealand before coming to Sydney in 1839. During the following years he travelled extensively in NSW and TAS, studying geology and mineralogy. On a journey of exploration in 1840 he discovered and ascended a peak in the SNOWY MOUNTAINS which he named after the Polish patriot Kosciuszko. It has been claimed that it was not Australia's highest peak, now known as KOSCIUSKO, which Strzelecki ascended, but the nearby Mt Townsend. In 1845, two years after leaving Australia, he published the highly regarded scientific work, *Physical Description of New South Wales and Van Diemen's Land*.

Strzelecki Ranges VIC A stretch of rugged dissected upland country in W GIPPSLAND, situated between the Princes and South Gippsland Highways, SE of Melbourne, the ranges were named in honour of the Polish explorer, Sir Paul Edmund de STRZELECKI. Located E of WESTERN PORT BAY, they stretch for about 100km on an E-W axis from S of WARRAGUL to SE of TRARALGON. Originally, the area was heavily timbered but much of it has been cleared for farming and grazing, particularly dairying, and the forested parts are mainly in the more elevated areas to guard against soil erosion. The general elevation of the ranges is about 300m, but the highest sections, such as near Balook in the E, reach to over 650m. The annual rainfall is high (usually over 1000mm) and is spread throughout all seasons. The Grand Ridge Road follows the crest of the ranges for 132km from the Warragul-KORUMBURRA Road (the junction is 8km N of Strzelecki township) to the YARRAM-Traralgon Road near Carrajung. The scenery along this winding route varies from steep pastures dotted with farms and pine hedges to pockets of the dense rainforest which once clothed the ranges.

stump-jump plough *see* Technological improvements *under* agriculture

Stuart, John McDouall (1815-66) Explorer. Born in Scotland, he emigrated to SA in 1839 and quickly won a reputation as a surveyor and draughtsman. He developed a strong interest in the exploration of the interior, and in 1844-45 was a member of Charles STURT's expedition to the SIMPSON DESERT. In 1858 the SA government, hoping

John McDouall Stuart

that fertile land might yet be found in central Australia, offered a reward of £2000 for the first crossing of the continent from S to N, and Stuart became determined to win it. In that same year he made a long journey in the country W of LAKE TORRENS and in 1860, with only two companions, made his first attempt to cross the continent—a feat which he finally achieved on the third attempt in 1862 (*see* EXPLORATION BY LAND).

His expeditions form an interesting contrast with the one undertaken by BURKE and Wills. With far less equipment and manpower at his disposal than Burke had, Stuart crossed the continent by a longer and more difficult route, without loss of life, and with far more important results. As a result of his exploration the government of SA was moved in 1863 to ask that the administration of the NT be entrusted to it, a request which the British authorities were only too glad to grant. DARWIN, first known as Palmerston, was established as the NT's main town, and in 1872 the OVERLAND TELEGRAPH was built from there to Adelaide, approximately along the route of Stuart's expeditions.
Further reading: Webster, M.S. *John McDouall Stuart.* Melbourne University Press, Melbourne, 1958; Mudie, I. *The Heroic Journey of John McDouall Stuart.* Angus & Robertson, Sydney, 1968; Hardman, W. (ed) *The Journal of John McDouall Stuart.* (2nd edn) Libraries Board of South Australia, Adelaide, 1975.

Sturt, Charles (1795-1869) Explorer.
Perhaps the best-known of Australia's inland explorers, he was born in India, educated at Harrow, and entered the British Army as an ensign in 1813. After serving in the later stages of the Peninsular War, in Canada against the Americans in the war of 1812, in the army of occupation in France and on garrison duty in Ireland, he came to Sydney with the rank of captain in 1827. During the following few years he made two major journeys of exploration and effectively cleared up the mystery of the inland rivers of SE Australia. On the first, in 1828, he followed the MACQUARIE RIVER

until it ran dry, and discovered the DARLING RIVER. In 1829-30 he went by boat down the MURRUMBIDGEE and MURRAY Rivers to the sea, noting on the way the entry of what he presumed was the Darling into the Murray. He concluded correctly that all the inland rivers formed part of the Murray-Darling system.

Sturt later settled in Adelaide, where he held various positions in the SA public service, but without gaining the promotion which he felt that he deserved. It was from Adelaide that he set out in 1844 on his last great expedition, the aim of which was to reach the centre of the continent. Finally defeated by the great sand ridges of the SIMPSON DESERT, he returned to Adelaide with his health shattered. He went back to England in 1853. To the end of his life he felt that his achievements had not received

Charles Sturt

NSW Govt Printer

due official recognition, his disappointments including failure to achieve the position of Governor of SA, VIC or QLD. Although it was finally decided to nominate him KCMG, he died before this honour could be conferred. Sturt was certainly one of Australia's outstanding explorers. Not only were his journeys arduous and of great practical importance, but all were marked by detailed observation of the country and its resources. His house in the Adelaide suburb of Grange is preserved as a national monument.
See also exploration by land
Further reading: Sturt, C. *Two Expeditions into the Interior of Southern Australia.* Smith Elder, London, 1833 (reprinted Public Library of South Australia, Adelaide, 1963) and *Narrative of an Expedition into Central Australia.* (2 vols) T. & W. Boone, London, 1849 (reprinted Libraries Board of South Australia, Adelaide, 1965). Beale, E. *Sturt: the Chipped Idol.* Sydney University Press, 1979.

Sturt's Stony Desert SA This arid area in the NE of the State is crossed by the BIRDS-VILLE TRACK and lies between COOPER'S CREEK and the Warburton River, which both flow intermittently to LAKE EYRE. It is a

region of low and erratic rainfall, covered by sand dunes, clay pans and GIBBERS (hence the name 'stony'). The desert was first crossed by the explorer Charles STURT in 1845, who found it a particularly desolate region with no sign of the inland sea he had hoped to discover.

sugar cane *see* agriculture

Sulman Competition This is an annual
competition endowed by the family of the late Sir John Sulman, and arranged by the Trustees of the Art Gallery of New South Wales. The two categories, which alternate each year, are genre painting (figure composition representing some aspect of everyday life) and subject painting (in which the theme is idealised or dramatised and derived from history, poetry, mythology or religion). The competition was established in 1936.

sunbirds The only representative of the
largely African family of PASSERINE BIRDS, Nectariniidae, which reaches Australia is the yellow-breasted sunbird, *Nectarinia jugularis* (12cm long). These birds have a slender, down-curved bill (2cm long) and a tubular tongue which enables them to extract nectar from flowers, where they also catch insects; they are often seen hovering, like a humming-bird, near flowering trees and shrubs. The plumage is greenish above and bright yellow below, and the male has an iridescent black throat. The yellow-breasted sunbird has colonised mangroves and the edges of rain-forests in north-eastern QLD, and appears to be extending its range southwards. The nests,

F. Park (N.P.I.A.W.)

Yellow-breasted sunbird, *Nectarinia jugularis*

suspended from bushes, trees and buildings, are long, oval-shaped structures with a tail-piece and a hooded side entrance, made of bark, grasses and dead leaves, lined with fine grasses and bound with cobweb.

Sunbury VIC (population 11 083 in 1981)
A town on the Melbourne-BENDIGO railway route, Sunbury is 38km by rail NW of Melbourne and 54km SE of KYNETON. At an elevation of 214m above sea level, it is set in a farming and grazing district which was originally settled in the 1830s. In the 1850s, when

the gold rush to Bendigo began, the nucleus of the town developed at Jackson Creek crossing. It was called after Sunbury-on-Thames in Middlesex, England.

sundews *see* saprophytic plants

sundowner This term was applied to any tramp or SWAGMAN in the Outback who arrived at a homestead not long before sundown, too late to do any work but in time for a meal.

sunflower *see* Compositae

Sunraysia VIC This is the name applied to the irrigation area on the MURRAY RIVER in north-western VIC, famous for its abundant summer sunshine and for the production of vine and citrus fruits. The main urban centre in the area is MILDURA (population 15 762 in 1981); smaller ones are RED CLIFFS (2 409), Merbein (1 735) and Irymple (726).

Sunshine Coast QLD One of QLD's premier holiday areas, the Sunshine Coast is located in the SE of the State stretching from Caloundra (99km N of Brisbane by road) to NOOSA HEADS (150km from Brisbane) with NAMBOUR as the largest urban centre. It is part of the sub-tropical coastal plain, drained by a number of short streams which flow in general W-E courses (such as the Mooloobah and Marrochy Rivers), rising in the Blackall Range and with estuaries along the Pacific Ocean coast. The lowlands are intensively used for the production of sugar cane, tropical fruits and dairy products. The coastal strip consists of a series of surfing beaches, headlands and river estuaries which provide varied scenery and opportunities for fishing and aquatic sports. Though the rainfall is high in the area (Nambour average annual rainfall 1873mm), the abundant sunshine throughout much of the year makes it a popular holiday and tourist area.

surfboard riding The art of standing on a short length of fibreglass and guiding it to shore on the biggest wave available is a relatively new sport in Australia. Popularised in the late 1950s with the advent of smaller, lighter and more manoeuvrable surfboards, surfboard riding proved most attractive to the teenage generations of the 1960s and 1970s and now boasts some 400 000 adherents.
History Surfboard riding has a lengthy history in its country of origin, Hawaii, stretching back at least to 1778 when Captain COOK visited the islands and was amazed at the skill of the islanders in skimming across the water 'on the summit of the largest surge'. However, the sport did not reach Australia until the 20th century. In 1905 an Hawaiian surfboard was sent to C.D. Paterson of Sydney, but in those days the boards were large, heavy and cumbersome. In 1915 Duke Kahanamoku of Hawaii came to Sydney to participate in the NSW swimming championships. During his

Enjoying the winter sunshine at Maroochydore, Sunshine Coast QLD

stay he demonstrated surfboard riding with a new, lighter board and the sport quickly gained a popular following. In 1956 the Malibu board, an even lighter board made of styrene foam coated with fibreglass, was demonstrated by a team of Hawaiian surfers. Since then, surfboard riding has climbed to the heights of popularity that it now enjoys.

Not long after the 1956 Hawaiian team's visit, Australians started to make a name for themselves in international competitions. Bob Pike won the Peru International championship in 1962. In 1963 Bernard 'Midget' Farrelly won the Makaha International surf competition. In 1964 the official world championship was established, and was won by Australians twice in the first three years—by Farrelly in 1964 and by Robert 'Nat' Young in 1966. In more recent years Australians have tended to dominate the scene, the world championship having been won by Peter Townend in 1976, Wayne 'Rabbit' Bartholomew in 1978, and by

Peter Townend balances down the face of a big one

March past at an Australian surf championship

Mark Richards in 1975 and in every year from 1979 to 1983.

surf lifesaving Swimming in the surf has always carried with it potential dangers. Waves may prove more powerful than their size and shape suggest, a sandbank may suddenly collapse, or a rip or strong current may develop unexpectedly. Any of these events can be frightening to the inexperienced swimmer who in the ensuing panic to swim back to shore may get into difficulties. It is at such times that surf lifesavers risk their own lives to save the lives of those in danger. The lifesavers not only risk their lives—a number have been drowned performing rescues—but they receive no payment for their services. In fact they pay annual subscriptions to be members of a surf club. The services rendered by the 14 000 lifesavers throughout the country make Australia's beaches among the safest in the world.

History Until the early 1900s, Australians were barred from surfing by restrictive laws which made bathing in the sea within view of other members of the public (that is, near dwellings, bridges and streets) illegal between 6 a.m. and 8 p.m. One of those prosecuted for illegal bathing was the rector of St Mary's in Waverley, and a group was formed to help the clergyman in his legal battle. This same group formed the Bondi Surf Bathers' Life Saving Club in 1906, the first such organisation in the world. Initially a variety of rescue methods were tried; most of them were introduced by Lyster Ormsby, the first captain of the Bondi Club. One of the earliest techniques was the human chain, with would-be rescuers interlocking hands. Life-lines anchored on the beach and attached to floating life-buoys were also tried but found to be ineffective. In 1906 the method which was to prove the most lastingly successful was first displayed. This was the line-and-reel method whereby the rescuer, wearing a harness attached by line to the reel,

swims out to the victim and the pair are assisted back to the beach by other members of the lifesaving team who reel in the line.

In 1907 the Mayors of Waverley, Randwick and Manly and members of several surf clubs formed the New South Wales Surf Bathers' Association. Within three years a lifesaving drill had been formulated, and examinations had been established for prospective members of lifesaving clubs. The outbreak of World War I seriously depleted the numbers of lifesavers as most club members enlisted. However, the movement had been firmly established and, after the war, membership began to increase once again. In 1922 the Surf Life Saving Association of Australia was formed and by 1930 84 beaches in NSW, QLD, WA and TAS were patrolled by surf lifesaving clubs. There are now some 230 surf lifesaving clubs around Australia with more than 14 000 active members and some 16 000 other members.

Surf carnivals To improve and streamline methods, efficiency contests between clubs were introduced in the early 1900s and so surf carnivals were born. The first surf carnival was held in Sydney at Manly beach with displays and competitions in lifesaving, swimming and surfing. One of the main attractions at the carnival was the appearance of a surf boat specially designed for Australian conditions by Walter Biddell. The boat, which held a crew of three, was of the catamaran-type and was the forerunner of the more versatile single-hulled five-man boat which was to feature in spectacular races at later carnivals. As the carnivals became more popular, surf racing, belt races and boat races came to be included in the carnival programmes (surf racing in 1914 and the others in 1919). A new event was introduced into surf carnivals in 1966—the Iron Man championship. When the starter's gun is fired, contestants are required to swim, paddle a board, handle a surf-ski and sprint along the

beach—a gruelling multiple event with the winner obviously deserving the title of Iron Man.

Surfers Paradise QLD *see* Gold Coast

Sutherland, Dame Joan (1926-) Soprano and *prima donna*. Joan Sutherland was born in Sydney. Encouraged by her mother, an outstanding amateur mezzo-soprano, she won a scholarship in 1946 to study singing under John and Aida Dickens. In 1949 she won the *Sun* Aria contest and in the following year the Mobil Quest, a nation-wide commercial radio programme which encouraged and brought into the limelight young vocal talent. After a farewell recital in the Sydney town hall on 20 April 1951 she went to the Royal College of Music in London where she studied with Clive Carey, who in his young days had been associated with Dame Nellie MELBA and Jean de Reszke. She was given a contract with Covent Garden in 1952 and made her début there that year as the First Lady in *The Magic Flute*. Shortly afterwards she appeared in the role of Clothilde on the occasion of Maria Callas's London début in *Norma*.

In 1954 Joan Sutherland married Richard BONYNGE, a fellow Australian who was studying piano in London. Bonynge gradually assumed the conducting of all his wife's operatic appearances, and to his knowledge she fully attributes her success both in the selection of appropriate operatic roles from the 18th and 19th centuries, and in the writing of embellishments and cadenzas suitable to both the musical style and her vocal capabilities. She made her North American début in 1958 in Canada, and at the same time was building a reputation for her performances in operas by Handel such as *Alcina*, *Rodelinda* and *Samson*. In 1959 she won undisputed recognition as a great *prima donna* for her performance at

Dame Joan Sutherland

Courtesy of A.I.S. Canberra

Covent Garden in the title role of *Lucia di Lammermoor*. During the following two years she sang in Milan, Genoa, Venice, Palermo, Vienna, Cologne and Paris, where she was acclaimed as having one of the greatest voices of the century. In recognition of these achievements she was made a CBE in 1961.

The following years saw a number of revivals of 18th- and 19th-century operas in which Sutherland triumphed in the high coloratura roles. In 1965 she returned to sing in Australia with the Sutherland-Williamson International Grand Opera Company and since 1974 has sung with the Australian Opera each year as guest artist. She was further honoured with the awards of AC in 1975 and DBE in 1979. She has made more complete operatic recordings than any other singer in history and now lives alternately in Europe and Australia while continuing to fulfil her demanding international career.

swagman This is the traditional name used for tramps travelling country roads with their few belongings rolled up in a bundle or 'swag'.

swallows and martins These gregarious PASSERINE BIRDS belong to the family Hirundinidae, which contains 75 species, five of which occur in Australia. There is no real difference between them except that martins have shallower forked tails than swallows. These BIRDS are similar in appearance and feeding habits (catching insects during long periods of flight) to the unrelated SWIFTS and WOODSWALLOWS, but their wings are shorter than those of swifts and do not have the rather bat-like appearance of woodswallows' wings.

Many swallows are migratory, leaving an area in winter when the weather is cold and the insect prey scarce, but the white-backed swallow, *Cheramoeca* leucosternum* (15cm long), can withstand cold periods by becoming torpid and remaining in deep nesting tunnels, excavated in soft sand banks and lined with bark, leaves and grass. It is a black bird with white on the crown, throat and back and a deeply forked tail, and is found in open country throughout most of the mainland.

The welcome swallow, *Hirundo neoxena** (15cm), black above and white below with a reddish throat, is found throughout Australia except in forests and deserts. It is sedentary in the W but migratory in the E, breeding in the S and migrating N in winter. The similar barn swallow, *H. rustica* (15cm), is a rare vagrant from the N hemisphere.

Although both the species of martins are endemic, the tree martin, *Petrochelidon nigricans** (13cm), migrates to New Guinea. It is a black and white, almost square-tailed bird with some red on the forehead. Very common in open woodlands throughout Australia, it breeds in the S. The fairy martin, *P. ariel** (12cm), is similar in appearance (but has a brown head), habitat and distribution.

swamp *see* vegetation

swamphen *see* rails, etc.

*Species, genus or family is endemic to Australia (see Preface)

Swan Hill VIC (population 8 398 in 1981) Located on the S bank of the MURRAY RIVER, in the NW of the State on the Murray Valley Highway, 340km by road and 345km by rail from Melbourne, it is a commercial and service centre of a productive irrigation district. At an elevation of 70m above sea level, it experiences hot summer conditions and sunny frosty winters, with an average annual rainfall of 345mm, spread throughout the year. The area was named by the explorer Sir Thomas MITCHELL in 1836 when he camped on a sandy rise by the river and was disturbed at night by the calls of black swans on the nearby lagoon. The area where he camped is now the site of a Pioneer Settlement, a re-creation of life in the early days which includes such attractions as the veteran paddle-steamer *Gem*. The town started in 1846 as a river crossing point and by 1863 it could boast 11 houses, three stores and two inns. It developed as a river port in the days of the paddle-wheelers and visitors can take a cruise on the river aboard the paddle-steamer *Pyap*. Swan Hill became a shire in 1871, a borough (separated from the shire) in 1939 and was proclaimed a city in 1965. The surrounding rural district produces wool, wheat and dairy cattle; the intensively developed irrigation farms grow fruits, vines and vegetables and raise fat lambs on improved pastures. The industries of the city include fruit packing, vegetable canning and processing of dairy products. The paddle-steamers *Gems* and *Pyap* have been classified by the National Trust (VIC), as well as the homestead 'Tyntynder' built in the late 1840s. The city also has a military museum and a museum housing vintage cars.

Swan River WA This is the river upon which Perth and FREMANTLE are located, in the SW corner of the State. The upper section is called the AVON RIVER and the lower section (about 70km), the Swan. This anomaly came about because the two parts of the one river were discovered independently and their common identity was not realised until 1834. The headwaters of the river system lie to the E of the DARLING RANGE, where tributaries such as the Dale (from the S), the Mortlock (from the E) and the North Mortlock (from the N) drain into the Avon. Further downstream, the Toodyay and Brockman Rivers are right-bank tributaries, while the Cannin and Helena Rivers join the Swan from the SE. Where the river cuts across the Darling Scarp, there are gorges and numerous rapids. On the river flats of the coastal plain above Perth, the valley is intensively used for orchards and vineyards. Where the river passes through the city, widens to form two shallow tidal basins (Perth and Melville Waters) which provide a picturesque setting for the metropolis and good facilities for aquatic recreation. The estuary narrows in its final section at Fremantle where it reaches the Indian Ocean. The John Forrest National Park (1578ha), situated at the top of the Darling Range escarpment, about 27km E of Perth, is famous for its spring-time display

of wild flowers; the Glen Brook Dam on Jane Brook is located within the park.

The Swan River was discovered in 1697 by the Dutch explorer, William de Vlamingh, who first saw there the black swans from which the river took its name. The first Englishman to explore the river was James STIRLING, in 1827. He recommended that a colony be established on the river and in 1829 the first white settlement on the Swan was made, with Stirling as the Lieutenant-Governor.

Further reading: Ward, K. *Swan River Sketchbook.* Rigby, Adelaide, 1978.

Swanland WA The SW corner of WA is often referred to as Swanland. This region includes not only Perth and the port cities of FREMANTLE and ALBANY, but also COLLIE, the only source of coal in WA, KWINANA, a major industrial centre, and large stretches of good forest country and all the best agricultural and pastoral land of the State. It experiences a mild climate: summers are warm to hot and markedly dry, winters are cool and wet. The average annual rainfall varies from over 1200mm on the far S coast of the region to less than 300mm in the inland parts to the E and N. Three-quarters of the rain falls in the winter months, between May and October, when evaporation is low, so its efficiency for crop production is high. The rain is very reliable in terms of both the amount which falls and the time of occurrence. The landscape of the region is dominated by an extensive plateau, consisting of undulating and hilly country between 150m and 450m elevation, bounded on its W margin by the DARLING RANGE (highest point, Mt Cook, 583m), with narrow coastal plains along the Indian and Southern Oceans. The main streams, which rise on the plateau, and cut across the ranges to the W coast, are the AVON-SWAN system, the HARVEY and the Collie, while those flowing to the S coast include the BLACKWOOD, the Warren, the Frankland, the King and the Kaglan. The STIRLING RANGE, N of Albany in the SE of the

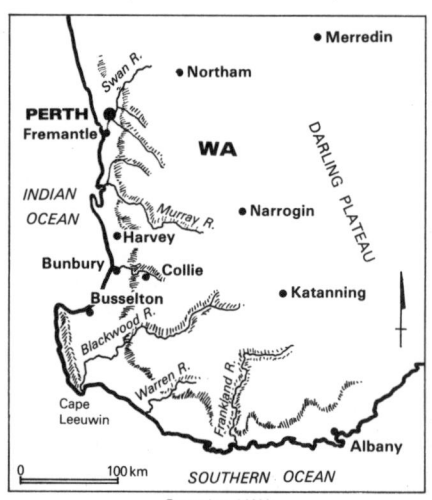

Swanland WA

region, includes peaks rising to over 1000m above sea level.

The first white settlement in Swanland was near Albany. It started as a military establishment in 1826 and became a centre for a sheep grazing district and later a coaling station for ships sailing between Sydney and London. Settlements were established on the Swan River in 1829 and at BUNBURY in 1830. Development was slow until the last decades of the 19th century when timber industries, fruit growing and mining brought rapid progress and led to the extension of the railway lines to places such as Collie, BUSSELTON and BRIDGETOWN. Later development of wheat growing, dairying, beef cattle and sheep grazing and the growth of secondary industries brought further progress to the rural economy. The MUNDARING RESERVOIR was built in 1902 on the Helena River, a tributary of the Swan, as the storage point for the GOLDFIELDS WATER SUPPLY scheme. Along the narrow coastal plain between Bunbury and MANDURAH, WA's first irrigation project was established. This consisted of a series of dams—Harvey Dam was the first (1916) and others include the Wellington Dam on the Collie River (1933), Samson's Brook Dam (1940), Stirling Dam on the Harvey (1948), and Waroona Dam (1966)—to store water for release during the dry summer season for irrigating pastures, fodder crops, orchards and market gardens on the alluvial flats of the plains.

Further reading: Wilson, J.L.J. (ed) 'South-Western Australia' in *Current Affairs Bulletin.* (vol 14, no 10, 1954); Shaw, J.H. & Kirkwood, F.G. *From Jungles to Snowlands.* Shakespeare Head Press, Sydney, 1958; Gentilli, J. *The South-West.* Longmans, Melbourne, 1960.

swans *see* ducks, etc.

sweet briar *see* weeds

sweet lips *see* fishes, bony

sweet peas *see* Papilionaceae

sweet William *see* sharks, etc.

swifts Of the 76 species of swifts in the world, five occur in Australia. Belonging to the family Apodidae, swifts are perhaps the most aerial of all birds—some species are able to mate and 'rest' in flight. Though not closely related, they resemble SWALLOWS but are swifter and have longer and narrower wings which form a sickle-shape in flight. Like swallows, they catch insects on the wing.

The only resident species is the grey swiftlet, *Collocalia spodiopygia* (11.5cm long), found in coastal NE and E Australia. Blackish-brown above and brownish-grey below, with a pale grey rump and glossy black wings, this bird breeds in caves in which, like bats, it can fly safely in complete darkness using echolocation. Its white eggs are laid in bracket-shaped nests attached to the walls and roofs of caves and composed of saliva and vegetable material. In the case of the Asian edible nest swiftlet, the nest is made entirely of saliva, and is the principal ingredient of birds' nest soup. The uniform swiftlet, *C. vanikorensis* (11.5cm), which is similar to the resident species but has a brownish-grey rump, and the glossy swiftlet, *C. esculenta* (9cm), a white-bellied species with glossy blue-green upperparts, are non-breeding visitors which migrate from New Guinea to the tip of CAPE YORK.

Common throughout Australia is the fork-tailed swift, *Apus pacificus* (length 18cm; wingspan 40cm), a predominantly black species with a white rump and a white throat. The spine-tailed swift, *Chaetura caudacutus* (20cm), common throughout the E half of Australia, is brownish-black with a light grey patch on the centre of the back; it takes its common name from the short spines which extend from its square tail. Both these species are non-breeding visitors from the N hemisphere.

swimming and diving In the international sporting world Australia is probably best known for its swimmers and tennis players. Many more Olympic medals have been won by Australia in swimming events than in any other sport. However, the position as the leading swimming nation in the world which Australia held after the 1956 Melbourne Olympics was relinquished in the late 1970s to the USA and the newly emergent East Germans. Diving is becoming increasingly popular in Australia and steps have been taken recently to remove this sport from the shadow of swimming.

Swimming Australia first gained worldwide recognition as a leader in swimming with the introduction of the Australian crawl. There is some dispute as to who developed this stroke. Some say it was London-born Frederick Cavill (*see* CAVILL FAMILY), who emigrated to Australia in 1879 and built a floating swimming bath in Sydney, while others give the honour to Alick Wickham of the Solomon Islands who came to Australia at the age of 10 in 1898. Yet another school of thought believes that Cavill saw Wickham 'crawling' through the water and adopted the stoke in his training programme.

Freddy Lane won the first Olympic swimming gold medal for Australia in Paris in 1900 in the 200m event. He also won a gold medal in the obstacle race (an event which has not appeared in an Olympic Games since that time). In the 1904–1905 swimming season Barney Bede Kieran won every Australian title from 220 yards to one mile; shortly afterwards, competing in England, he broke eight world records. F.E. (later Sir Frank) BEAUREPAIRE represented Australia in the 1908, 1920 and 1924 Olympic Games, winning a bronze medal on each occasion plus a silver medal in 1908. Andrew Murray 'Boy' CHARLTON set his first world record in 1923 at the age of 15 for the 880 yards freestyle and in the 1924 Paris Olympics he won a gold medal in the 1500m freestyle.

Among the early women swimmers was Annette KELLERMAN, at one time world record holder for the mile but probably better remembered for the scandal she caused by wearing one-piece swimming costumes considered too revealing at the time. The first Olympic Games in which women competed were held in 1912 in Stockholm, where Fanny DURACK became the first Australian woman to win an Olympic gold medal when she won the 100m freestyle event.

The period between 1924 and 1956 proved a lean time for Australian swimmers. Only two Olympic gold medals were won, both in the 200m breast-stroke event, in 1932 and in 1952. Australia began to improve in swimming in the early 1950s. For four years before the 1956 Melbourne Olympics, Professor Frank Cotton of Sydney University compiled a mass of information about training methods used overseas and, with the help of Forbes Carlile, a completely different approach to the training of athletes was introduced. There followed a gruelling training programme which certainly paid dividends, for the 1956 Olympic Games were the best ever for Australia and especially for Australian swimmers. In the men's 100m freestyle Jon HENRICKS, John Devitt and Gary Chapman came in first, second and third, and in the women's 100m freestyle Dawn FRASER, Lorraine CRAPP and Faith Leech finished first, second and third. Murray ROSE won two gold medals, in the 400m and 1500m freestyle events, and David Thiele and John Monckton came in first and second in the 100m backstroke. Australia won the men's 4 × 200m relay and the women's 4 × 100m relay. Lorraine Crapp and Dawn Fraser finished first and second in the 400m freestyle. Australia was very firmly on top of the swimming world.

Since the Melbourne Olympics, Australia has continued to produce many brilliant swimmers, those of the period shortly after 1956 including Kevin Berry, Murray Garretty, Terry Gathercole, John and Ilsa KONRADS, Ian O'Brien and Bob Windle and those of later years Shane GOULD, Lyn McClements, Beverley Whitfield, Gail Neal, Brad Cooper, Karen Moras, Sonya Gray, Jenny Turrall, Mike WENDEN, Michelle Ford, Stephen Holland, Tracey WICKHAM, Lisa Curry, Lisa Forrest, Neil Brooks and Max Metzker. However, in overall national performance Australia has been clearly surpassed by the USA and East Germany. Australian swimmers won five gold medals at the Rome Olympics (1960), four at Tokyo (1964), only two at Mexico (1968), six—including three by Shane GOULD—at Munich (1972), none at Montreal (1976), and two at Moscow (1980). Australia has tended to dominate swimming at the Commonwealth Games, winning 13 gold medals at the 1982 Brisbane Games.

Training methods have changed dramatically over the years and the success of these changes is evident. It now includes swimming at least five miles a day, weight-lifting, floor exercises and strict diets, whereas Fanny Durack, star of the early 1900s, said she rarely trained more than a 'mile or two' a week.

Diving Previously affiliated with the Amateur Swimming Association, the Australian Amateur Diving Association was formed in 1978. The growth in popularity of this sport has been strongest in NSW. In the late 1970s there were no indoor diving pools but now many States are building indoor diving pools to cater for the increased demand. Evidence of the growing popularity of the sport was the 1978 NSW State championships which attracted 83 competitors.

Australian divers have not been outstanding in international competition, their only Olympic gold medal being that won by R.C. Eve in the men's plain high tower dive at Paris in 1924. In Commonwealth Games 12 gold medals have been won, including 4 in men's events by Don Wagstaff (two at Kingston in 1966 and two at Edinburgh in 1970). At the Brisbane Games Jenny Donnet and Valerie Beddoe won gold medals, while Stephen Foley won two silver medals.

See also Appendix 8 and Appendix 9.

Archibald fountain in Hyde Park, Sydney

Sydney (population 2 874 415 in 1981) Capital of the State of NEW SOUTH WALES, located on the SE coast of the continent midway between the N and S borders of the State, Sydney is the largest city in Australia, the site of the first white settlement, and the main port of the nation. The city takes its name from Lord Sydney, the British Home Secretary from 1784 to 1789, who was mainly responsible for the establishment of a convict settlement in Australia in 1788.

Settlement In his explorations of the E coast of Australia in 1770, James COOK examined BOTANY BAY and gave such a glowing report of it that when Captain Arthur PHILLIP came to establish a penal colony in 1788, his fleet sailed into Botany Bay. Phillip quickly realised that it was not an ideal place for a settlement and moved to another coastal inlet, 9km N, now called PORT JACKSON. On 26 January 1788, in a small bay on the S side of the port, he hoisted the British flag, fired a salute and named the bay SYDNEY COVE. This cove, though now much changed, is part of the Circular Quay section of the inner city of Sydney. Each year, 26 January is celebrated as AUSTRALIA DAY and is a public holiday. Phillip chose the port as the location for the colony for very sound and practical reasons. He realised that it was an excellent harbour with many small coves and bays and with deep water close to the shoreline where ships could shelter safely from winds and high seas. These features of the harbour have been significant in making Sydney a commercial and trading city. Furthermore, adjacent to Phillip's settlement site, there was a supply of good quality fresh water from the Tank Stream, and he thought that the surrounding land would be suitable for farming. Though the soils proved poor for crops and the Tank Stream now runs in a storm water drain beneath the

streets of the city, the main business core has developed in this area.

Population From this colonial convict settlement, Sydney has grown into a major metropolis containing almost 20 per cent of the population of Australia and about 55 per cent of the State's population at the 1981 census. The growth of Sydney during the 20th century is shown in Table 1.

Climate Sydney experiences warm to hot summer conditions in December, January and February, when the mean monthly temperatures are above 21°C. Some very hot summer days occur when the daily maximum temperature rises to over 42°C. A common feature, on such summer days, is the occurrence in the late afternoon or early evening of a gusty cool wind from the S, known locally as the 'southerly buster', which brings welcome relief from the hot conditions. Winters are mild to cool; July is the coolest month with the mean monthly temperature below 12°C. Occasional winter frosts and some sleet may occur, but snow is an almost unknown phenomenon. The average annual rainfall is just over 1200mm, evenly spread throughout the year. Thunderstorms with heavy downpours are a feature of the summer months.

Landscape The contrast which Phillip had noted between Botany Bay and Port Jackson is directly related to the landforms of the region. Botany Bay lies within the Sydney Plain, while Port Jackson is mostly within the adjoining plateau area. The Sydney Plain, also called the Cumberland Plain because it is in the County of Cumberland, consists of a gently undulating tract of lowland with average elevation between 30m and 60m, and some hills rising to about 90m. The plain extends W to PENRITH on the NEPEAN RIVER, and from WINDSOR in the N to beyond CAMDEN in the S. There are alluvial flats along parts of the rivers and sandy stret-

ches on some of the low-lying coastal areas.

Surrounding this plain on three sides is a belt of plateau country, capped by HAWKESBURY sandstone which gives unique landscape features to the region. The area N of Sydney is called the Hornsby Plateau, to the S the Woronora Plateau, and to the W the BLUE MOUNTAINS Plateau which rises to over 1000m. These plateaus have been considerably dissected by stream erosion and so consist of remnant ridges cut by deep gorges, providing many attractive and challenging sites for bushwalkers and rock climbers. Settlement is sparse on these plateaus and is confined to ridgetops where level land makes transport and building rather easier. Port Jackson lies on the Hornsby Plateau and hence the harbour foreshores are almost everywhere bounded by steep sandstone cliffs. The E section of the port is commonly called Sydney Harbour. The unique features of the harbour are the result of events in the

Table 1

URBAN GROWTH OF SYDNEY IN THE TWENTIETH CENTURY

Year	Population (millions)	% of State total
1901	0.48	35.5
1911	0.69	42.1
1921	1.03	49.0
1933	1.33	51.1
1947	1.65	55.0
1954	1.86	54.4
1961	2.18	55.7
1966	2.45	57.8
1971	2.73	59.4
1976	2.77	56.4
1981	2.87	54.9

Source: Australian Bureau of Statistics, Canberra.

geological past when the area consisted of a network of deep, steep-sided river valleys. This was prior to the last Great Ice Age, and when the ice melted as the earth warmed up, the sea level rose by about 60m, the valley network was flooded and the harbour was formed with its sheer cliffs, deep water, numerous minor bays and many small rocky islands, such as Shark, Clarke, Goat, Cockatoo and Pinchgut (Fort Denison). Along much of the coastline around Sydney, the steep cliffs alternate with sandy crescents to give an abundance of surfing beaches, such as Bondi, Coogee, Manly, Curl Curl and Deewhy, for which the city is renowned.

City core The central business district of the city, covering about 2.5km², is located on the S shore of the harbour, extending from Sydney Cove (Circular Quay) for about 2.5km to Central Railway; it is bounded on the W by Darling Harbour, and on the E by a stretch of parkland including the Botanic Gardens, the Domain and Hyde Park. The street pattern within this core is a rectangular grid with the N-S streets parallel to the course of the old Tank Stream, following tracks made by the early settlers. Many of these streets, laid out in an era before the motor car, now carry only one-way traffic to permit more rapid movement and reduce vehicle congestion. Public transport in the inner city is provided by buses and a two-track electric railway loop, partially underground, linking Circular Quay to the Central Railway station. The electric tramway system of the city and suburbs was abandoned in 1961 and replaced by bus transport.

The city core functions as a centre of administrative, financial and professional offices, and of retail and wholesale trading. As in most large cities of the world, particular activities are localised in specific areas. For example, the retail shopping zone occupies a rectangle in the centre of the core; banking, insurance and financial houses, characterised by tall office buildings, are found mainly further N; the State Parliament house and government offices are concentrated mainly along Macquarie and adjacent streets; around Phillip Street and Queens Square the legal profession and the law courts are clustered; and one side of Macquarie Street is dominated by the medical and dental professions. Since World War II much of the inner city has been rebuilt with high-rise office blocks and shopping complexes. Also, over the same period, many business firms have moved their premises away from the inner city, especially across the harbour to the N suburbs extending from North Sydney to Chatswood.

Some examples of early colonial architecture still stand in the city. St James' Church and the Conservatorium of Music (originally the stables of Government House) are two examples of buildings designed by the convict architect Francis GREENWAY. The Sydney town hall, the General Post Office and the Queen Victoria Building stand as monuments of Victorian times. Martin Place was converted, in 1974, to a pedestrian plaza and this

has reinforced its role as the city's focus for ceremonies and outdoor performances of many types. Undoubtedly, the best-known modern building is the SYDNEY OPERA HOUSE, opened in 1973.

The suburbs The built-up area of Sydney extends over 100km in a N-S direction from Palm Beach in the N to Cronulla in the S; inland from the coast the suburbs extend over 60km to the W where the urban settlement merges into rural land. The overall pattern of the metropolis can be likened to one half of a vast spider's web, with the city core as its focus, surrounded by suburban zones, and tentacles of settlement extending beyond this along transport routes.

Until the 1880s, when the population was about 225 000, the city was strikingly compact, extending S over the Cumberland Plain towards Botany Bay. During the remainder of the 19th century, the inner suburban arc from

Paddington and Darlinghurst through Surry Hills, Redfern, Glebe, Ultimo and Pyrmont became densely packed with long rows of terrace-houses, many of which still remain. Parts of this old inner urban zone have now become heavily industrialised, but others, such as Paddington, have developed into fashionable residential areas and there has been much restoration of terrace-houses.

The extension of tentacle railway lines and electric tramways in the early decades of the 20th century encouraged the spread of urban settlement, particularly to the W, SW and NW where suburbs such as Marrickville, Bankstown, Canterbury, Five Dock, Drummoyne and Gladesville started to develop as bungalow-type residential areas. Also, many harbour-side suburbs depending on ferry transport grew in this period. The opening of the SYDNEY HARBOUR BRIDGE in 1932 established direct road and rail access to areas N of the harbour and

Circular Quay, Sydney, in the 1950's

NSW Dept of Tourism

this led to rapid growth along the railway line from North Sydney to Hornsby, with the development of some select suburbs such as Pymble, Killara and Wahroonga.

The decades since World War II have seen the continued growth of Sydney, as the population statistics show. Urban spread has pushed the spider's web pattern outward in all directions. There has also been upward expansion of the city, as blocks of high-rise home units have been built in most suburbs. In some of the older inner suburbs, such as Redfern, there has been extensive slum clearance and the replacement of the terraces with apartment blocks. This rapid urban growth has required much planning, not only for the residential development itself, but for the facilities and amenities needed by the suburban population. The 1951 Cumberland County Plan, which incorporated the concept of a green belt zone surrounding the city, was largely eclipsed by the speed of post-war developments. In 1968 the Sydney Region Outline Plan proposed a series of satellite towns, such as Camden and CAMPBELLTOWN in the S and Blacktown, Mt Druitt and Penrith in the W; the implementation of plans for these developments commenced in the 1970s.

Further reading: Barlow, M.H. *Urban Geography—Sydney.* Angus & Robertson, Sydney, 1967; Clarke, A.N. *Historic Sydney and New South Wales.* The Central Press, Sydney, 1968; Shaw, J.H. & Kirkwood, F.G. *Landscape Studies.* Longman Australia, Melbourne, 1969; Taylor, G. *Sydneyside Scenery and How It Came About.* Angus & Robertson, Sydney, 1970; Conolly, G.K. *Urban Landscapes in Sydney.* Longman Australia, Melbourne, 1971; Baglin, D. & Mullins, B. *Sydney.* Rigby, Adelaide, 1976; Park R. *The Companion Guide to Sydney.* Collins, Sydney, 1973.

Sydney Cove NSW This small bay lying between Dawes Point on the W and Bennelong Point on the E is part of the S shore of Sydney Harbour and was the site of the first British settlement in Australia. Though the cove still bears the name given to it by Governor Arthur PHILLIP, the shoreline has been much changed and extended by reclamation. The inner section of the cove, called Circular Quay, is now dominated by ferry wharves for harbour passenger transport. the W shore is occupied by the offices of the Maritime Services Board, the Overseas Passenger Terminal and wharves for police, customs and navigation launches. Beyond these waterfront features of the W shore of the cove lies the historic area of the Rocks where many homes and buildings dating back to the earliest days of settlement can be found. The Rocks area is currently being redeveloped and the plans include some parklands, the restoration of many of the old buildings and the preservation of some of the old terrace houses to keep it as a residential area on the fringe of the city core, yet retaining the flavour of bygone days in Sydney. Among the significant architectural features of the

Rocks are Holy Trinity Church (more commonly known as the Garrison Church), the Observatory, the Agar Steps and the sandstone building which was originally a military hospital, then for over a century was occupied by Fort Street High School and since 1974 has been the headquarters of the National Trust in NSW. Along the E shore of Sydney Cove there are some wharves, but the dominant feature here is the SYDNEY OPERA HOUSE on the tip of Bennelong Point.

See also Port Jackson; Sydney Harbour Bridge
Further reading: White, U. & Ruhen, O. *The Rocks Sydney.* Rigby, Adelaide, 1966; Emanuel, C. & Ruhen, O. *Historic Buildings of Sydney Sketchbook.* Rigby, Adelaide, 1972; Emanuel, C. *The Historic Rocks Area of Sydney.* Rigby, Adelaide, 1974; Emanuel, C. & van Sommers, T. *Sydney Sketchbook.* Rigby, Adelaide, 1974.

Sydney Harbour Bridge This arch bridge connects the central business district of Sydney to the N suburbs of the city, joining Dawes Point on the S side of the harbour to Milsons Point on the N shore. When it was completed in 1932, it was the largest of its type in the world; it is still among the largest single-arch bridges. The maximum height of the arch above mean high tide water is 135m. The length of the span is 503m, while the total length of the bridge, including approaches, is almost 3.9km. The grey granite pylons stand 87m high. The bridge was designed by a British firm, Dorman Long of Middlesborough; the supervising engineer was Dr J.J.C. Bradfield whose name has been given to a major highway which crosses the bridge. It took nine years to build and at the official opening, on 19 March 1932, the proceedings were disrupted when an officer of the NEW GUARD cut the ceremonial ribbon before the Premier of NSW, J.T. LANG, could do so. The bridge carries an eight-lane roadway (which originally

included tramways), a pedestrian pathway and dual railway tracks.
See also Port Jackson; Sydney Cove
Further reading: Dupain, M. & Tanner, H. *Building the Sydney Harbour Bridge—The Photography of Henri Mallard.* Sun Books, Melbourne, 1976; Emanuel, C. & van Sommers, T. *Sydney Harbour Sketchbook.* Rigby, Adelaide, 1976.

Sydney Opera House Regarded as one of the greatest architectural and engineering achievements of the 20th century because of its unique design, the Sydney Opera House was the centre of controversy from its conception by the NSW State government in 1954 to its completion in 1972. The Opera House stands on Bennelong Point, which itself is steeped in history, being associated with the arrival of the FIRST FLEET in 1788. From 1819 until 1902 it was used as a fortress; it was then converted into a tram depot, which remained until construction of the Opera House began in 1959.

When the government announced in 1955 that an international competition would be held to find a design for an opera house, worldwide interest was aroused. On 29 January 1957 the first prize was awarded to a Danish architect, Joern UTZON, who submitted his sketches without ever having visited Australia, basing his drawings on photographs of Sydney Harbour and the site. Almost immediately after construction began, doubts arose as to the feasibility of building the roof sections (or shells) as originally planned. After much controversy the system of constructing the roof was modified and in the process the shape of the roof was slightly altered. In 1967 the last roof section was lowered into place.

Meanwhile, in 1965, a new government had come into office and early in 1966, following disagreement with government officials and

Sydney Harbour Bridge

engineers over methods of construction, Utzon resigned as architect. Some months later he was replaced by a panel of Sydney architects consisting of Peter Hall, David Littlemore and Lionel Todd. On the advice of the panel much of the interior of the building was redesigned, the major change being that the smaller hall was to become the Opera Theatre and the larger auditorium, to be known as the Concert Hall, would henceforth be the permanent home of the Sydney Symphony Orchestra. This arrangement of the functions of the two main halls engendered further controversy among a public already dissatisfied over rising costs and concerned that the building would be used solely for operas and classical performances. However, it had always been intended that the Opera House would be available for all forms of entertainment. Thus, while full-scale productions of opera and ballet are held in the Opera Theatre, the Concert Hall is available for performances of every form of music—symphony concerts, chamber recitals, pop, jazz, and folk concerts, as well as solo performances. Besides the Concert Hall and the Opera Theatre, the complex houses a Drama Theatre, Music Room, Exhibition Hall, Recording Hall and two restaurants, as well as rehearsal rooms and a dining room for artists and staff.

The cost of constructing this unque building was astronomical. From an original estimate of $7 million, costs soared until the final figure was in excess of $100 million. This was financed mainly by profits from NSW State Lotteries; other sources of revenue were the government and public appeals. The Opera House is so highly regarded throughout the world that a picture of it as one of the world's greatest engineering feats was included in a space probe, the contents of which were designed to portray the earth, its people and its technology to any would-be interceptor from another world.

Sydney rock rose see Rutaceae

symphylids Symphyla is the name given to a class of small, CENTIPEDE-like ARTHROPODS which lack a common name. Symphylids are from 2mm to 10mm long; the trunk consists of 12 segments which carry legs though there are from 15 to 22 plates along the back. The 13th segment, the one adjoining the segment carrying the anus, has a pair of spinnerets which are thought to be modified legs. The genital opening is on the third trunk segment whereas that of centipedes is at the end of the body. The antennae are well developed. The larvae, on hatching, have about six pairs of legs; the rest are added as the animals grow. Moulting continues throughout life. Symphylids live in soil and leaf-litter. Some are pests of crops; various species in QLD for example, may prevent the establishment of pineapples.

Sydney Opera House at night

T

table tennis Considered more as a novelty or lunch-time interlude rather than a serious sport, the indoor game of table tennis has never enjoyed the spectator appeal or player interest of outdoor ball games in Australia. Recently, however, public interest in the game has been stimulated by television coverage of the annual Wills International tournament. The skills exhibited by top-class players in tournaments such as the Wills convinced many that table tennis can be played as a serious competitive sport and this has led to increased popularity.

From the time table tennis was first played in Australia during the latter half of the 19th century—it was then known as ping pong—SA pioneered the organisation of the game. The first championships were held in that State in 1898, and SA was the first to form a State Association, in 1923. QLD followed in the same year, VIC in 1925 and NSW in 1930. In 1933 the Australian Board of Control was formed by these four States (later to become the Australian Table Tennis Association in 1937 after affiliation with the International Table Tennis Federation) and the first Australian championships were held in Melbourne with only men competing. Women's championships were not held until 1936. Since 1940, when the first representative side to leave the country competed in the Pan Pacific tournament in Japan, Australia has been gaining an eviable international reputation, enhanced in visits to China in 1971 and visits by China in 1972, Czechoslovakia in 1973, Japan in 1974 and France in 1975. Australia now competes regularly in the British Commonwealth and world championships.

Tailem Bend SA (population 1 677 in 1981) This town is on the lower MURRAY RIVER, downstream from MURRAY BRIDGE on Dukes Highway, 101km by road and 120km by rail SE of Adelaide. At an elevation of 21m above sea level, it experiences a mild climate, with an average annual rainfall of 387mm, spread throughout the year but with a winter maximum. It is also a service centre for productive dairying lands, irrigated from the Murray, on the reclaimed flood plains. The town is a main railway focus where the branch line to the Mallee region meets the main line to Adelaide. The name is probably derived from an Aboriginal word *thelim* which refers to the bend in the river, but another explanation is that it comes from the phrase 'tail em', referring to the days when lambs were tailed there in large numbers.

tailor see fishes, bony

taipan see snakes

Tallangatta VIC (population 953 in 1981) On the S shore of the lake formed by the HUME DAM, at the confluence of the MITTA MITTA and MURRAY Rivers, this small township was relocated in 1956 when the capacity of the reservoir was enlarged. The old township, 7km E, is almost totally submerged. The new town, with a village green bordered by commercial buildings, is 343km NE of Melbourne, at the junction of the Omeo and Murray Valley Highways, 47km SE of WODONGA. Its lakeside location made Tallangatta a popular summer tourist and holiday centre, with opportunities for boating, swimming, fishing and water skiing. The adjacent rural areas are occupied by dairy farms, cattle grazing properties and softwood timber plantations. The town's name comes from an Aboriginal word meaning either 'many kurrajong trees' or 'belonging to water'.

tallow wood This is a large eucalypt, *Eucalyptus microcorys* (family MYRTACEAE) which produces a greasy, yellow or light brown timber, excellent for flooring. It is common in the coastal areas of northern NSW and southern QLD and sometimes occurs in rainforest.

Tamar River TAS The North and South ESK RIVERS, located in the central-N of the State, join at LAUNCESTON and become the Tamar River, which flows in a SE-NW direction some 65km to BASS STRAIT. The explorers George BASS and Matthew FLINDERS explored the Tamar estuary in 1789 and called it PORT DALRYMPLE; the seaward section of the Tamar still bears this name. The East and West Tamar Highways traverse the two sides of the estuary downstream from Launceston. On the E shore of the lower estuary is the industrial port of BELL BAY. On the W bank, 5km from Launceston, is the Trevallyn hydro-electric power station, which uses water from the South Esk, supplemented from the GREAT LAKE scheme after the waters have generated power at the POATINA station. The alluvial flats and river terraces adjoining the Tamar are productive rural areas noted for apple and pear orchards, fodder crop growing, dairying, fat lamb raising, vegetable cultivation and beef cattle grazing.

Tambo River VIC Located in GIPPSLAND, it rises in the Bowen Mts (part of the GREAT DIVIDING RANGE) NE of OMEO and flows S for 200km from the highlands, across the coastal plains, to drain into LAKE KING, where it has formed a long silt jetty on the NE shore of the lake. Much of the alluvial flats of the valley is intensively farmed (maize crops and improved pastures). The name Tambo comes from an Aboriginal word meaning 'fish'.

Tamborine Mountain QLD An upland resort area in the SE of the State, it is 75km S of Brisbane and 45km inland from the GOLD COAST, between the Pacific and Mt Lindesay Highways. It is a basalt-capped region of red soils, rising to an elevation of 650m above sea level, with productive farming and grazing lands. There are several small national parks in the area such as Cedar Creek (230ha), Joalah (36ha), Witches Falls (131ha) and Palm Grove (118ha) which preserve areas of rainforest vegetation and contain scenic waterfalls.

Tamworth NSW (population 29 656 in 1981) The largest city in northern NSW it is

View of Tamworth NSW

located on the New England Highway, 451km by road N of Sydney. The Oxley Highway from COONABARABRAN and GUNNEDAH in the W joins the New England Highway at Tamworth. The city is also a main station on the N tablelands railway, 455km by rail N of Sydney with a branch line to Manilla and Barraba. It is situated on the Peel River, a tributary of the NAMOI RIVER, at an elevation of 995m above sea level. It is the headquarters of the East-West Airlines and has regular air services to Sydney and Brisbane. It is a major business and commercial centre, servicing a rich rural district producing wool, wheat, fat stock, pigs, poultry, eggs, dairy products, fruit, honey and vegetables. The alluvial flats of the Peel and other streams in the area grow fine crops of lucerne. There are livestock studs in the district breeding high-quality cattle, sheep and horses. The city has a range of secondary industries including timber mills, steel-fabrication works, a large flour mill, engineering workshops, an abattoir, a stockfeed factory, an egg-pulp plant, and factories making furniture, fibrous plaster, cement pipes and tiles. The climate experienced in the city is one of warm to hot summers, with some very hot and dry days, and mildly cool winter months with frosts a common feature. The average annual rainfall is 673mm, distributed throughout the year, but with slightly more rain in the summer period. January is the month of highest rainfall (81mm average), April and May the lowest (both 42mm).

The explorations of John OXLEY in the N parts of the State in 1818 opened the way for the settlement of this area by squatters. In 1830, the Australian Agricultural Company was granted two large areas of land (one of which was called the Goonoo Goonoo property) covering 145 000ha along the S bank of the Peel river. As the district was settled, the

nucleus of an urban centre developed and the town was gazetted in 1850. It was named after a town in Staffordshire, England; the river was named after Sir Robert Peel (British Prime Minister 1842-45). Tamworth became a municipality in 1876 and in 1946 was proclaimed a city. It is often referred to as the 'city of light', as it was the first town in Australia to have electric street lighting (1888). A considerable number of buildings in the city have been listed by the National Trust (NSW) for preservation, including Woolpack Inn (built in 1859), the Mechanics Institute (1866), Calala House (1877), the Post Office (1886), the Retreat Theatre (formerly the Headmaster's Residence, 1857) and the Lands Office (1889). The city has a folk museum, containing Aboriginal artifacts, early agricultural machinery and the first aeroplane built in NSW; also, there are several art and craft centres. The Australasian Country Music Awards festival held annually in the city attracts many visitors. Among the educational institutions, the Farrer Memorial Agricultural High School is a unique secondary school in that it has a specialised rural orientation. An agricultural research station adjacent to the city is concerned with investigations related to farming and grazing in the district. In the upper reaches of Peel River, gold mining has been important in the past, at centres such as Nundle and Hanging Rock, SE from Tamworth, and some people still enjoy amateur fossicking there. The Dungowan Dam, 60km SE, in the hills of the GREAT DIVIDING RANGE, has a storage capacity of 600 000ML and is the source of the city's water supply. The KEEPIT DAM on the Namoi River, 56km NW of Tamworth, was built primarily to control the river flow and to conserve water for irrigation and has become a popular spot for picnics, swimming, yachting and water skiing.

Tanami Desert NT Located in the mid-W part of the Territory, S of the VICTORIA RIVER basin and W of TENNANT CREEK, between the Stuart Highway and the WA/NT border, it is an arid desolate region of sand hills and rocky outcrops. The small settlement of Tanami, now abandoned, was the site of a gold rush in the early part of this century. The former Tanami Wildlife Sanctuary, covering more than 3.75 million ha, extended over large tracts of the desert country; in the early 1980s, control of the sanctuary was transferred to the traditional Aboriginal owners of the land.

tandans *see* fishes, freshwater

Tangney, Dame Dorothy Margaret (1911-) Politician. Born in Perth, she graduated BA, DipEd from the University of WA and became a teacher with the Education Department of WA. In 1943 she became the first woman to be elected to the Senate, where she continued to sit until retirement in 1968. She played an active part in the work of the Senate, being a member of many of its committees, and was also a member of a number of overseas parliamentary delegations, and of the federal executive of the AUSTRALIAN LABOUR PARTY. She was created DBE in the year of her retirement.

Tanunda SA (population 2 621 in 1981) This small town in the S section of the BAROSSA VALLEY is 71km by road from Adelaide. It is an important centre of the grape growing industry and retains much of the German atmosphere it had when it was settled in the 1840s. The town's name comes from an Aboriginal word meaning 'many birds upon a creek'.

tapeworms Belonging to the class Cestoda of the phylum Platyhelminthes, tapeworms are FLATWORMS that are highly modified for parasitism (*see* PARASITES). There are two subclasses. The Cestodaria is composed of worms in which the body is not divided into segments; they are parasites of fishes. The more important subclass, Eucestoda, contains the tapeworms whose body (strobila) is divided into a number of segments (proglottids), each of which contains a set of male and female sex organs. Although the proglottids are, in some ways, separate individuals, they are connected by two nerve cords, two excretory canals and muscles. There is no gut as tapeworms absorb their food from the host's gut contents through their skins. The proglottids bud off at the neck region from the head (scolex) which has hooks, suckers or other structures to help it to cling to the tissues of the host. Most tapeworms need two or more different kinds of host animal during their life cycle. The adult is almost always found in a vertebrate. They live within its gut, often for many years. Sometimes they persist without producing obvious symptoms.

Some larval cestodes are more or less restricted to aquatic hosts, though the adults may infest terrestrial vertebrates. The first larval host is a crustacean (often a copepod), and the second and third hosts are amphibians or fish. In the case of the fish tapeworm, *Diphyllobothrium latum*, the eggs hatch in water to produce a free-swimming larva (the coracidium), which may be swallowed by a freshwater copepod. If the copepod is eaten by a fish it may pass down a fish food-chain. When an infested fish is eaten by one of various kinds of mammals the plerocercoid larva develops into the adult tapeworm (3m to 9m long) within the gut.

Man becomes infested if and when he eats affected raw fish. The fish tapeworm is the largest tapeworm found in man and can live for about 20 years. It is often carried to new countries by immigrants, but its spread can be stopped by cooking fish properly and by preventing sewage from contaminating freshwaters from which food fish are taken. The victim usually suffers from stomach pains, loss of weight and anaemia resulting from the tapeworm's heavy demands for vitamin B_{12}.

The tapeworms that infest terrestrial invertebrates and vertebrates have a different life cycle for they lack the free-living coracidium stage. Instead, the egg contains a six-hooked onchosphere larva, as it is called. When swallowed by an invertebrate (usually an insect, wood louse or centipede), this develops into a cysticercoid larva which contains a fully formed scolex. Vertebrates become infested when they eat one of the invertebrates. Often, however, the invertebrate host has been dropped and replaced by an intermediate vertebrate host. In at least one common species, the dwarf tapeworm, *Hymenolepis nana*, there is only one host in the cycle—man—who swallows the onchosphere. This species, which is only 7mm to 100mm long, often occurs in very large numbers in any one host individual and was one of the commonest worms infesting Aboriginals in Australia.

The beef tapeworm, *Taenia sagatina*, uses man as the host in which the adults live, the larval stages occurring in cattle. The cattle become infested when they eat fodder contaminated with eggs from human faeces. Victims are often unaware that they are parasitised though the tapeworm may be several metres long. The pork tapeworm, *T. solium*, is fortunately much rarer for it is potentially far more dangerous as the larval stage can infest man, sometimes inside the brain.

The most serious tapeworm in Australia is an introduced species, the HYDATID CYST TAPEWORM, *Echinococcus granulosus*, the adults of which occur in dogs and dingos. The larval stage, which is a large fluid-filled bag producing new individuals asexually, is found in sheep, wallabies and man, often in vital organs.

The COMMONWEALTH SCIENTIFIC AND INDUSTRIAL RESEARCH ORGANIZATION (CSIRO) has conducted experiments on the possibility of using certain tapeworms and FLUKES as BIOLOGICAL CONTROL agents for the rabbit.
Further reading: Lapage, G. *Animals Parasitic in Man*. Penguin Books, Harmondsworth, 1957; Moodie, P.M. *Aboriginal Health*, Australian National University Press, Canberra, 1973.

tardigrades *see* water bears

Taree NSW (population 14 696 in 1981) A town located on the MANNING RIVER in the mid-NORTH COAST region, about 20km inland, it is situated on the Pacific Highway 336km by

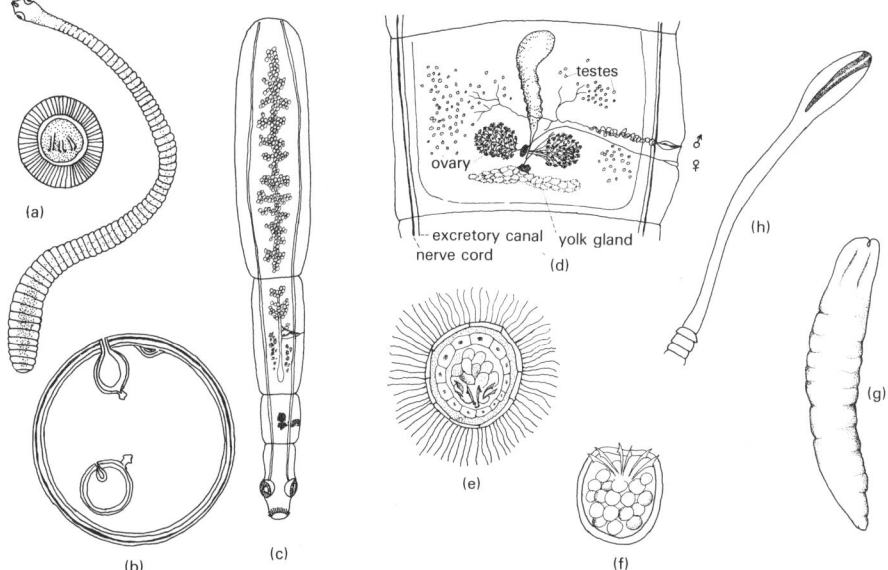

Some tapeworms which attack man and animals : (a) dwarf tapeworm with egg; (b) section through hydatid cyst showing daughter cysts; (c) hydatid cyst tapeworm from a dog; (d) section through segment of typical tapeworm; (e,f,g) developmental stages of a fish tapeworm – (e) coracidium; (f) embryo; (g) pleroceroid; (h) bothrium and first three segments of a fish tapeworm

road N of Sydney, and on the main North Coast railway line, 379km by rail N of Sydney. It is the largest urban centre in the Manning Valley and functions as the commercial and service focus for the rural regions. Dairying is the main farming activity on the rich river flats in the area; fodder crop cultivation, beef cattle grazing and pig raising also contribute to the local economy. Taree experiences a mild climate throughout the year, with an average annual rainfall of 1 178mm and a concentration of rain in the summer and early autumn months. Downstream from the town, the land comprises alluvial silt deposits forming a delta zone which, though fertile for farming, is subject to flooding in times of high river. Also, the lower parts of the town experience floods when the headwater tributaries have heavy rainstorms and the main stream breaks its banks. The adjacent coastal zone is a popular tourist area, particularly at the resorts of Old Bar, Harrington and Halliday's Point. On the waters of the Manning River motorboat racing, water skiing and sailing events attract a large following. There are several good surfing beaches along the nearby coast and anglers can do well at many fishing spots both on the coast and the river. Taree was founded in 1854 as a 'private town' and was originally designed to serve as a port for the shipping of rural produce from the Manning Valley. However, it has never been developed as a port.

tarpon *see* fishes, bony

Tarraleah TAS A small village in the CEN-TRAL PLATEAU region of the State, it is 123km NW of Hobart just off the Tarraleah Highway, in the Nive River valley, a tributary of the DERWENT RIVER. It provides accommodation for the workers of Tarraleah and TUN-GATINAH hydro-electric power stations, which are part of the generation scheme of the upper Derwent Valley. This section of the power system uses water from LAKE KING WIL-LIAM (an artificial lake formed by the construction of Clark Dam), which is first used for power generation at Butlers Gorge station at the foot of the dam; then the water is conveyed 22.5km by canals and steel pipes to Tarraleah power station in the Nive Gorge where it passes through the turbines of the generating station. Commissioned in 1938, the station has an installed capacity of 90 000kW. The name Tarraleah comes from a TAS Aboriginal word meaning 'a forester kangaroo'.

Tasman, Abel Janszoon (*c.* 1603-59) Navigator. Born in Groningen, Holland, he went to the East Indies as a seaman in 1633. He won rapid promotion in the service of the East India Co., made voyages to Japan and other parts of the N Pacific and to Sumatra. He is remembered mainly for his discovery of TAS and New Zealand in 1642 and for his voyage along the N coast of Australia in 1644 (*see* DISCOVERY). The first of these voyages showed that if there was an enormous Great

Abel Janszoon Tasman

South Land, it was not in the region of Australia, and his second demonstrated that the parts of N and W Australia discovered by the Dutch were all part of one continent. Important as his discoveries were, his failure to find opportunities for trade tended to deter the Dutch from further exploration in and around Australia. *Further reading:* Heeres, J.E. (ed) *Abel Janszoon Tasman's Journal of His Discovery of Van Diemen's Land and New Zealand in 1642.* F. Muller, Amsterdam, 1898.

Tasman Peninsula TAS Located on the SE coast, lying E of STORM BAY and covering an area of some 500km², this peninsula has a heavily indented coastline with numerous inlets (Norfolk Bay to the N, Wedge Bay to the W, Maingon Bay on the S and Foresque bay on the E) and many rocky headlands (Cape Pillar on the SE coast, Cape Raoul on the S, Green Head at the NW tip and Cape Hauy along the E coast). Steep cliffs, rocky stacks and blow-holes along the coast provide some unique scenic features. The narrow isthmus of EAGLEHAWK NECK joins it to Forestier Peninsula. Sheep grazing and fruit growing are found in the N and central parts of the peninsula, and there are extensive State forests in the E. PORT ARTHUR, which contains the ruins of a 19th-century penal convict settlement, is a popular tourist site located in the S section. Nubeena, a small town on the W side, serves

as the commercial and administrative centre and is the focus of rural and fishing activities. Taranna, 11km N of Port Arthur, is the headquarters of the forestry service.

Tasmania (TAS) The smallest State of Australia, TAS consists of a group of islands located S of the SE corner of the continent. The major island is Tasmania and the largest of the lesser islands are KING, FLINDERS and BRUNY Islands. MACQUARIE ISLAND, a sub-Antarctic island in the Southern Ocean, is part of the State also. BASS STRAIT, approximately 240km wide, separates TAS from the mainland and thus forms the N boundary, while the boundary to the E is the Tasman Sea and that to the W and SW is the Southern Ocean. The total area of the State, calculated by point digitising (*see* AREA), is 67 800km², making up 0.88 per cent of the total area of Australia. From N to S, TAS extends about 296km and from E to W about 315km.

Landform features The island consists of a series of plateau blocks, an E-central valley and a small N coastal lowland. The plateau blocks are a continuation of the GREAT DIVIDING RANGE of the mainland, interrupted and detached from the E highlands of the continental mass by Bass Strait. TAS is dominated by high country; it has the largest proportion of its area in highlands of any State of Australia. These highlands, though strictly plateaus in

Table 1

POPULATION GROWTH OF TASMANIA 1820-1981

Year	Population
1820	5 400
1850	68 870
1900	172 900
1920	209 425
1940	240 191
1960	343 910
1976	407 400
1981*	427 308

Note: * the 1981 figure is the Estimated Resident Population (Preliminary).
Source: Australian Bureau of Statistics, Canberra.

terms of their structure and formation, are usually referred to as mountains. A distinctive feature of the countryside is not so much the height of the uplands—only six peaks reach over 1500m—but rather the frequency with which the uplands occur. The highest peak is MOUNT OSSA (1617m), located 16km NW of LAKE ST CLAIR, just W of the CENTRAL PLATEAU region; in the same area are Mt Pelion West (1554m), Barn Bluff (1559m) and CRADLE MOUNTAIN (1545m). In the NE of the State is the BEN LOMOND highland region, with Legges Tor (1573m) and Stacks Bluff (1527m) the highest points. Deep gorges, carved into the highland areas, make some of the country exceedingly rugged and the SW part of the State is so wild and inaccessible that it is one of the least-known parts of the nation. The plateaus are mostly bounded by steep escarpments, called tiers (such as GREAT WESTERN TIERS), and these enhance the impression of a mountainous country.

During the last Great Ice Age, many of the highland areas of TAS were glaciated and the evidence of this is strikingly portrayed in the landscape. The glaciers carved out deep steep-sided valleys, leaving boulders and moraine scree when they later melted and retreated. Many of the valleys were blocked by these deposits and lakes were formed, such as Lake St Clair and LAKE PEDDER, while in other parts the glacial ice gouged out basins which are now occupied by lakes such as ARTHURS LAKE, GREAT LAKE and LAKE SORELL. The highlands are sparsely populated but their scenic grandeur attracts many summer visitors and there are several winter ski resorts. The mountains have aided the State's development in several ways: some areas (including ROSEBERY, QUEENSTOWN, MOUNT BISCHOFF and SAVAGE RIVER) have yielded valuable minerals; other parts have good forest resources which have led to the development of the lumbering industry and to the establishment of paper pulp mills; there are many steeply graded streams, particularly where they plunge over the plateau scarps into gorges, and innumerable natural lake storages, often enlarged by dam construction, which have been harnessed for the generation of hydro-electricity which in turn has aided the development of manufacturing. It is, however, in the lowlands of the State where agriculture and pastoral industries flourish, where secondary industries have developed and where towns and cities have grown. The valleys of the DERWENT (with Hobart on the estuary), the HUON and the TAMAR-ESK system, together with the N coastal plains, are the most important areas economically.

Climate Since no point within the State lies more than 115km from the coast and because the island is located between latitudes 40°S and 44°S, it experiences a temperate maritime type of climate. Summers are generally warm and winters cool, with extremes of temperature experienced only occasionally. The climatic pattern is similar to that of many parts of W Europe and this is one of the reasons why TAS is often said to be like England. It lies in the path of the 'roaring forties', a W stream of polar maritime air; these W winds reach their greatest strength and persistence during the winter months and, combined with the mountainous terrain in the W half of the State, give a marked variation in the climate, especially the rainfall, from W to E. Over much of the W highlands, the annual rainfall exceeds 2000mm and the wettest parts receive more than 3500mm; Queenstown has an average of 2450mm and ZEEHAN 2444mm. The central lowlands of the State, lying in a rain-shadow region, receive much lower rainfall; the driest parts of the MIDLANDS average less than 500mm per year. NEW NORFOLK receives 549mm and Hobart 662mm. In the NE part of the State, the annual rainfall varies from 550mm on the coast to 1300mm in the highlands. Snow can be experienced in the mountains at any time of the year, but the heaviest falls occur in late winter and early spring, and patches of snow often remain on the peaks until December.

Although most of TAS has relatively high rainfall, droughts are sometimes experienced, but they are usually less severe and of shorter duration than in other parts of the continent. Floods are not uncommon; the South Esk system is the most seriously affected, since many of its streams rise in the highlands, where the rainfall is high, and then flow across flat country. The Derwent River has experienced extensive flooding, but the construction of four dams across the river since 1960 for hydro-electricity generation has provided greater control of the river discharge.

Population The total population of TAS at the 1981 census (estimated resident population) was 427 308, making it the smallest State of Australia, with 2.86 per cent of the nation's people. Metropolitan Hobart, with a population of 128 603, accounted for almost a third (30.1 per cent) of the State in 1981 and, with LAUNCESTON (the second-largest city, 64 555), made up 45 per cent of the State's population. The growth of the State population since 1820 is shown in Table 1. It was not until 1870 that the population exceeded 100 000; after 1910 it passed the 200 000 mark, in the 1940s it reached a quarter-million, and in the 1970s it exceeded 400 000.

History Known officially as VAN DIEMEN'S LAND until 1855, TAS received its first British settlers as a result of the fear of French occupation of the mainland. Disturbed by the presence of the explorer Nicholas BAUDIN in Australian waters, Governor KING proclaimed in 1803 that: 'It being expedient to establish His Majesty's right to Van Dieman's (sic) Land, His Excellency has been pleased to direct Lieutenant John Bowen ... to form an establishment on that island.'

From first settlement to 1825 With 48 other settlers, including 35 convicts, John BOWEN landed in September 1803 at RISDON COVE on the Derwent, naming the little settlement Hobart. In the following February David COLLINS also reached the Derwent, having abandoned his short-lived settlement at PORT PHILLIP BAY. His party landed at Sullivan's

Ruins of the penal settlement at Port Arthur TAS

J.H. Shaw

Cove, where it was later joined by Bowen's party. Collins used the name Hobart Town for the settlement, and this remained the official name until 1881, when it reverted to Hobart. Later in 1804 King sent Lieutenant-Colonel William PATERSON to found a settlement at PORT DALRYMPLE in the N of the island, and two years later Paterson relocated this settlement at the present site of Launceston. Although his rank was only that of Superintendent, while Collins was a Lieutenant-Governor, Paterson was not subject to orders from the latter. Separate commands for the two settlements were maintained until 1812, when the whole island was placed under the jurisdiction of the Lieutenant-Governor in Hobart.

For the first several years the two settlements struggled to survive. It was some years before they became self-sufficient in food and, in the meantime, extra supplies had to be sent from Sydney, or from England via Sydney. Complaints about delays in the sending of food and other necessities were common. Progress remained slow under Lieutenant-Governor DAVEY (1813-17), but speeded up under William SORELL (1817-24). As on the mainland, the export of wool became the basis of prosperity; wheat, potatoes and hops were exported to the mainland, and whaling and sealing brought in considerable revenue. When John BIGGE visited the island in 1820 he was impressed by what he saw and recommended that it be made a separate colony; this was done five years later.

In the meantime, a large part of the island had been explored. In February 1807 Lieutenant Thomas Laycock and four others travelled from Port Dalrymple to Hobart, and in October a surveyor, Charles Grimes, crossed the island approximately along the route of the modern Midland Highway. In 1817 John

Lake Pedder, SW TAS

Dept of Tourism TAS

Beaumont reached the Great Lake, and in 1819-20 led an expedition up the E coast to St Patrick's Head and thence to Port Dalrymple.

From separation to responsible government, 1825-55 Separation was proclaimed during the term of office of Lieutenant-Governor George ARTHUR (1824-36), who was provided with a nominated Legislative Council of from five to seven members to assist him in making regulations and raising revenue. In 1828, as in NSW, the Legislative Council was increased to 15 members, all nominated.

Arthur faced serious problems in three main areas: the penal system, bushranging and relations between settlers and Aborigines. He reorganised the penal system in an effort to make it a more effective instrument of reformation, and had great success in suppressing bushranging, but his attempts to deal with the Aborigines led to tragedy. Having decided on a policy of segregation, he tried to round up the surviving Aborigines in 1830, in a drive involving 3 000 men. Although this was a failure, its aim was later achieved by less dramatic methods. George ROBINSON and others persuaded the Aborigines to place themselves under government protection, and they were sent finally to Flinders Is in Bass Strait. There, however, they failed to thrive and in 1876 the last full-blooded Aboriginal of those who had inhabited TAS died.

In economic development the colony was hampered by a shortage of land compared with the mainland, and by the 1830s this was leading many settlers to consider settlement on the opposite shore of Bass Strait. People such as the HENTY FAMILY, John BATMAN and John Pascoe FAWKNER settled there without official authorisation, and after Governor BOURKE opened up the Port Phillip District to official settlement many more Tasmanians crossed the Strait. One effect of this exodus was a short-lived land boom in TAS, but this collapsed in 1841 and was followed by about five years of economic depression. By that time too the Colony was receiving less income from whaling and sealing for by 1830 there were few seals left in Bass Strait, and whaling flourished only a little longer. In 1836 there were nine whaling stations near Hobart, but during the following few years the numbers of whales in the vicinity of TAS declined sharply.

In the meantime, almost the whole island had been explored. A good deal of exploration resulted from the granting of over 100 000ha in the NW to the Van Diemen's Land Co. in 1825. Agents of the company penetrated unexplored areas in their search for good land,

Courtesy of A.I.S. Canberra

Aerial view of Hobart

Queenstown TAS

and even after farming activities had started they continued to explore. The most notable of them was Henry Hellyer, who went SE from Circular Head to St Valentine's Peak and then W to the ARTHUR RIVER. The rounding up of the surviving Aborigines also involved some important exploration, most notably the journey by George Robinson from Hobart to PORT DAVEY and thence up the W coast to Circular Head in 1831. In the following year W.S. Sharland reached Lake St Clair, as did Surveyor-General George Frankland in 1835; Frankland later went from Hobart via Lake Pedder to the Port Davey plains. After the 1830s only minor tasks of exploration remained to be done.

When transportation to the mainland of NSW was abolished in 1840, matters connected with the convict system began to dominate the politics of TAS. Previously, free settlers had benefited from the labour of assigned servants, but now many convicts were sent on probation, providing more direct competition with free labour. At the same time, the total number of convicts sent to TAS increased greatly, and as the cost of police and gaols had to be met from colonial revenues it became very difficult to balance the budget. In 1845, as a protest against this situation, six members of the Legislative Council resigned, and were widely hailed as the 'Patriotic Six'. Demands for the abolition of transportation and for an extension of self-government became stronger, and the 1850s brought success for both campaigns. The Australian Colonies Government Act of 1850 provided for a new Legislative Council of 24 members, 16 of whom were to be elected, and in the elections of 1851 all elective seats were won by members of the Anti-Transportation League. In the following year the ending of transportation to the whole of E Australia was announced and at the same time the TAS Legislative Council, like those of NSW, VIC

and SA, was invited to draw up a constitution. This received the royal assent in 1855. It provided for a Parliament containing a House of Assembly, elected on the basis of moderate property qualifications, and a Legislative Council, the franchise for which was based on higher property qualifications. The first elections under this constitution took place in 1856. In the meantime, later in 1855, the name of the colony had been changed officially from Van Diemen's Land to TAS.

From responsible government to 1914 The pattern of development of TAS after 1856 differed in some respects from that of Australia as a whole. A great exodus of population to the VIC goldfields was followed from about 1858 by an economic depression, which was marked by a decline in exports, continued emigration to the mainland and high levels of unemployment. The government found it difficult to meet the costs of welfare measures and the political scene was marked by instability, eight Ministries holding office during the first 13 years of responsible government. The

Mt Lyell TAS

tendency to urbanisation was not as strong as on the mainland, and it may have been partly as a consequence of this that politics tended to be dominated by conservative groups, and parliamentary reforms came later than on the mainland. Trade unionism was weak until the growth of mining in the 1890s and a TAS Labor Party was not founded until 1903. The vote was not extended to all adult males until 1900, nor to women until 1903. In 1906 the Hare Clark system of proportional representation (see PROPORTIONAL REPRESENTATION was adopted for the State Parliament, and has been maintained ever since.

In the 1870s and 1880s there was an economic recovery, based to a large extent on a mining boom. Tin was discovered at Mt Bischoff in 1871, gold at Beaconsfield in 1877, silver and lead at Zeehan in 1882, and gold, silver and copper at MOUNT LYELL at various times during the 1870s and 1880s. After 1888 fruit growing expanded as refrigerated shipping opened up the British market. While TAS had missed out on part of the 'long boom' enjoyed by the other E colonies from the 1860s to the 1880s, the development of mining and fruit growing helped to save her from the worst effects of the depression of the 1890s.

From 1914 to the present The economic development of TAS was perhaps affected less by World War I than that of Australia as a whole. It was also less affected by the boom of the 1920s, but on the other hand suffered a little less than most other States during the Depression. TAS's dependence on primary industry was largely responsible for these divergences from the general picture. Since the mid-1930s there has been a considerable expansion of secondary industries, based on the provision of cheap hydro-electric power; however, the proportion of workers engaged in manufacturing is still below the national average. Moreover, in recent decades TAS's rate of general economic and population growth has lagged.

In State politics the AUSTRALIAN LABOR PARTY (ALP), although it was late in becoming established, has dominated the scene in recent decades. However, TAS voters have tended to distinguish between State and federal issues, and in Commonwealth elections have 'swung' quite strongly. Thus Labor held power in the State Parliament from 1972 to 1982, but in elections for the federal House of Representatives, results varied from Labor winning all five TAS seats in 1972 and 1974 to the LIBERAL PARTY winning all five in 1975, 1977, 1980 and 1983. Finally, it is worth noting that in spite of the importance of the rural vote, the NATIONAL PARTY has never become established in TAS.

In recent years, proposals for the construction of hydro-electricity schemes in the SW wilderness region of TAS have been particularly divisive issues. The LAKE PEDDER development aroused much controversy in the 1970s, and in the early 1980s the proposal for a hydro-electricity scheme on the lower GORDON RIVER met with strong opposition from some community groups. In an attempt to resolve the

Courtesy of A.I.S. Canberra

Gordon power station TAS

issue, and to seek public reaction to the scheme, a referendum was held in 1981; voters were given the choice of the 'Gordon-below-Franklin' scheme, which would flood not only the lower Gordon but also its picturesque tributary the Franklin, and the 'Gordon-above-Olga' scheme, which would not affect the Franklin (favoured by the government). The desire of the Premier, Douglas LOWE, to add a third option, rejecting both schemes, led to his replacement by Harold Holgate and his resignation from the ALP. However, although a narrow majority of those voting chose the 'Gordon-below-Franklin' option, about 40 per cent cast informal votes, the vast majority of these writing 'no dams' across their ballot papers. Early in 1982 the government announced that it would accept the majority opinion and begin work on the 'Gordon-below-Franklin' scheme. The Liberal government of R.T. GRAY, which won office in May of that year was also pledged to build the dam, in spite of vigorous opposition by environmentalist groups. However in 1983 the Labor federal government of R.J. HAWKE was successful in passing legislation to prevent the scheme proceeding, and in defeating a High Court appeal by TAS and QLD against the legislation.

Further reading: West, J. *The History of Tasmania.* Henry Dowling, Launceston, 1852; Fenton, J. *A History of Tasmania.* J. Walch & Sons, Hobart, 1884; Giblin, R.W. *The Early*

History of Tasmania. (vol 1) Methuen, London, 1928 and *The Early History of Tasmania.* (vol 2) Melbourne University Press, Melbourne, 1939.

Tasmanian devil *see* native cats, etc.

Tasmanian wolf Belonging to the family Thylacinidae (order Polyprotodonta), the Tasmanian wolf, *Thylacinus cyanocephalus,* also known as the thylacine, may still exist in the remote parts of TAS (if it exists, it is Australia's largest carnivorous MARSUPIAL). The head and body of this dog-like animal measure 1.1m, and the thick-based tail 53cm. The muzzle is long and narrow but the powerful jaws can be opened to a very wide gape. The hind-legs are relatively long when compared with those of a dog but despite old accounts there is no evidence that it moves like a kangaroo. The general colour is olive brown and there are about 16 dark brown transverse stripes on the hind-quarters and lower back.

Thylacines were formerly widespread on the mainland and in New Guinea: a skeleton found in a cave on the NULLARBOR PLAIN in 1963 was only a little over 3 000 years old. It is possible that the thylacine (and the Tasmanian devil) were displaced from the mainland by the DINGO brought by the Aborigines; the dingo did not reach TAS. When Europeans colonised TAS thylacines were common in open woodlands in the NE, but because the animal attacked domestic livestock a bounty was placed on it by the Van Diemen's Land Co. in 1836. In 1888 the government introduced a bounty for the whole of the island and between 1888 and 1909 paid for 2 184 dead animals. After 1910 no animals were killed for the bounty, the numbers having fallen sharply after 1901; none have been killed in the wild since 1930 and the last zoo specimen died in Hobart shortly before World War II. In 1957, however, apparent thylacine tracks were discovered on the island, and since then apparent hair and dung specimens have been found. A thylacine lair has been reported and also several sheep killed in the thylacine manner—the offal eaten, and the jugular vein severed for the blood. There are also reported sightings, the most recent one being made in 1977 by two policemen in a patrol car on a country road.

Further reading: Guiler, E.R. 'The thylacine' in McMichael, D.F. (ed) *A Treasury of Australian Wildlife.* Ure Smith, Sydney, 1968; Frith, H.J. *Wildlife Conservation.* Angus & Robertson, Sydney, 1973; Archer, M. (ed) *Carnivorous Marsupials.* (vols 1 & 2) The Royal Zoological Society of New South Wales, Sydney (in press).

Tatura VIC (population 2 694 in 1981) A country town in the GOULBURN RIVER valley region in the central-N of the State, it is 177km by road N of Melbourne, 3km S of the Midland Highway and 20km by road WSW of SHEPPARTON. At an elevation of 114m above sea level, it has an average yearly rainfall of

506mm and is the centre of a productive irrigation area where dairying, fruit growing and the cultivation of tomatoes are the major rural activities. The town has a number of secondary industries concerned with the processing of rural produce, such as a butter factory, a tomato processing factory and an abattoir, as well as a textile factory and an engineering workshop. The town name comes from an Aboriginal word meaning a 'small lagoon'.

Taxation Among the powers given to the Commonwealth by the federal Constitution is that of taxation, but only with regard to customs and excise is it made an exclusive power. In other fields the Constitution leaves taxation as a power shared between Commonwealth and States. For some years after federation the Commonwealth confined itself to customs and excise, and the amount of tax revenue raised by it was small compared with that raised by the States. However, that situation has long since been reversed, and today the greater part of the States' revenue comes from Commonwealth grants.

Among the historical developments which have caused this change there have been: a small number of constitutional amendments, most importantly that of 1946, which gave the Commonwealth wide powers with regard to social services; the effects of the two world wars, which involved massive Commonwealth expenditure; a general increase in the scope and magnitude of central government responsibilities; and the action of the Commonwealth in introducing uniform income tax legislation in 1942, which virtually excluded the States from this important field.

Commonwealth taxation today In recent years the Commonwealth has raised over half of its total tax revenue from personal income tax. Other important sources of revenue are customs duties, excise (including the increasingly important crude-oil levy, designed to raise the price of Australian-produced petroleum to 'world parity'), income tax on companies and sales tax. Minor taxes (totalling only a few per cent of total tax revenue) include withholding tax, payroll tax, departure tax and stamp duties.

Income tax Australia relies more heavily than most countries on income tax on individuals. Many critics have claimed that a more even 'tax mix' would be preferable.

The monopoly of income tax—the major 'growth tax'—by the Commonwealth has also been widely criticised on the grounds that it has reduced the States to a position of subservience. However, under the 'new federalism' arrangements introduced by the FRASER government, agreed minimum percentages of income tax receipts are now paid to the States and to local government bodies. Whether the States are better off under the new arrangement is a matter of public debate.

States taxes Besides general purpose assistance, the States receive from the Commonwealth many special purpose grants—that is,

'Black Mountain, Canberra' oil painting 1944 by Roland Wakelin, in the National Gallery of Victoria

'Near the Docks' oil painting 1949 by Sali Herman, in the Art Gallery of New South Wales

See PAINTING AND PAINTERS

'The Rabbiters' oil on canvas by Russell Drysdale, in the National Gallery of Victoria

'Day of Winter', oil painting 1959 by Clifton Pugh, in the National Gallery of Victoria

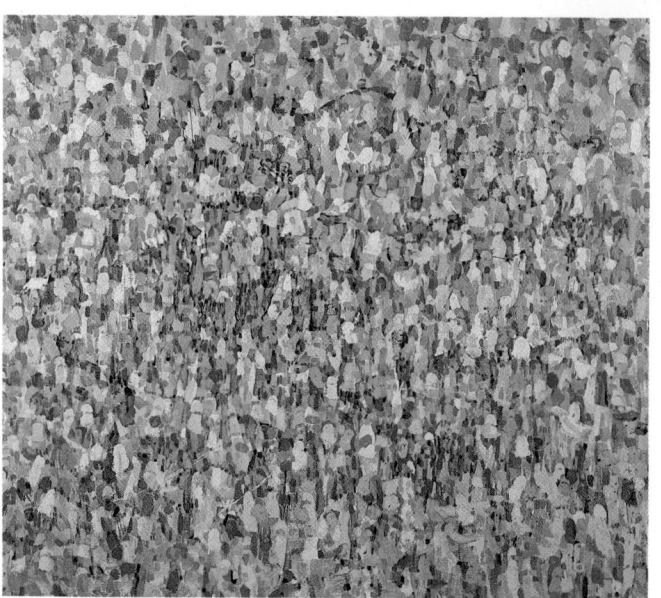

'Non-Objective Abstract' oil painting 1958 by Ralph Balson, in the National Gallery of Victoria

See PAINTING AND PAINTERS

money granted on condition that it is spent in certain ways. The States' own taxes are confined mainly to payroll tax, stamp duties, probate duties and various forms of licence fees. There is little variation from State to State.

Taylor, Jeannie *see* Gunn, Mrs Aeneas

Taylor, Thomas Griffith (1880-1963)
Geographer. Born at Walthamstow, England, he arrived in Sydney in 1893 and was educated at Sydney Grammar School, the University of Sydney (where he graduated in engineering and science) and at Cambridge University. Between 1910 and 1913 he was the senior geologist with Scott's Antarctic expedition. In 1920 he was appointed Associate Professor of Geography at the University of Sydney and held this post until 1929, during which time he became an outspoken and controversial scientist and author. He founded the Geographical Society of New South Wales in 1928 and the Society has a Griffith Taylor Memorial Lecture biennially in his honour. Between 1928 and 1934 he was the Senior Professor of Geography at the University of Chicago, and in the period 1935-51 he was Foundation Professor of Geography at the University of Toronto. On his retirement in 1951, he returned to Australia; he was elected a Fellow of the Australian Academy in 1954, became the foundation president of the Institute of Australian Geographers in 1959, and was awarded the Medal of the Royal Society of New South Wales in 1961.

tea trees *see* paperbarks

teak, Australian *see* crow's ash

teals *see* ducks, etc.

tektites *see* meteorites

telephone services *see* postal and telecommunication services

television *see* broadcasting

Temora NSW (population 4 350 in 1981)
This town is in the SW slopes region, 449km by road WSW of Sydney, in gently undulating hill country where the slopes merge into the great W plain. It is a rail town (486km from Sydney) on a branch line from COOTAMUNDRA on the main S route, and is a junction for lines W to GRIFFITH and NW to LAKE CARGELLIGO. At an elevation of 292m above sea level, the town experiences hot summer conditions, cool and often frosty winters and an average annual rainfall of 523mm, uniformly distributed throughout the year. It is a business and service centre for an important wheat growing district and is a bulk wheat storage terminal with large silos. The district was first settled by pastoralists in the 1840s and became a booming area when gold was discovered in the 1880s. An interesting rock and mineral museum in the town recalls the mining days. The

town took the name of one of the early properties which included the present town site, but its origin is uncertain. The post office, three banks (ANZ, NSW and CBC) and the Railway Hotel have been listed by the National Trust (NSW) for preservation as part of the nation's cultural heritage.

Tennant Creek NT (population 3 118 in 1981)
A major mining town on the Stuart Highway, it is 506km by road N of ALICE SPRINGS and 25km S of 'Three Corners' where the Barkly and Stuart Highways meet. At an elevation of 375m, it lies in arid country which receives an average annual rainfall of only 312mm and can experience long drought periods. In 1862, when John McDouall STUART was attempting to cross the continent from S to N, he came to a small creek and named it after an associate, John Tennant of PORT LINCOLN. A decade later, with the completion of the OVERLAND TELEGRAPH line, a telegraph station was built near the creek and some cattle stations were established in the area. The present town is not located at the original creek site, but is 11km S because, it is claimed, a wagon carrying building materials for the construction of a hotel became bogged there in an unusually heavy downpour of rain, and so it was there that the hotel was built and this became the nucleus of the town. Gold was discovered in the area in the 1920s, but the richest find was in 1934 at the mine called Nobles Nob. The town became a boom mining camp and by 1935 there were 140 leases being worked by prospectors. Another mining boom, based primarily on copper but also on gold and silver, occurred in the 1950s and the prosperity of this boom brought modern amenities to the town. The Peko mine, E of the highway, was the first, in 1955; then followed the Orlando mine, NW of the town (mainly gold with some copper and silver), the Juno mine in the SE (gold, bismuth, copper and silver), the Warrego mine to the NW (started in 1972) and the Gecko mine further to the NW (1974). A smelter to treat the ores was completed in 1973: the treated ores are transported by road to the Alice Springs railhead.

Tennant, Kylie (Mrs L.C. Rodd) (1912-)
Author. Born in the Sydney suburb of Manly, she was worked in a variety of occupations, partly in order to gather material for her writing. Her works include the play *Tether a Dragon* (1951), children's books, such as *All the Proud Tribesmen* (1960), a short history of Australia, *Australia: Her Story* (1953) and the political biography *Evatt: Politics and Justice* (1970). However, her reputation rests mainly on her novels, which are based on extensive personal involvement in, and first-hand knowledge of, the settings, and exhibit a particular sympathy for the vagabond, fringe-dwelling elements in society. They include *Tiburon* (1935), which deals with the fringe dwellers of a country town during the Depression; *The Battlers* (1941), which is concerned with itin-

erant bush workers; *Lost Haven* (1946); *Foveaux* (1939), which is set in a decayed inner Sydney suburb; *Ride on Stranger* (1943); *Time Enough Later* (1943); and *The Honey Flow* (1956).
Further reading: Dick, M. *The Novels of Kylie Tennant*. Rigby, Adelaide, 1966.

tennis In a few sports Australia has consistently produced world-class players. Tennis is one such sport and Australians have regularly won such symbols of world supremacy as the Davis Cup and the Wimbledon championship. Such a world dominance is not gained without a firm basis, which in Australia is found in school competitions, club tennis and the increasingly popular social game.
History Tennis may be played on any surface, but the traditional surface is grass and this form of tennis is called lawn tennis. Lawn tennis was first introduced into Australia in the 1870s. In 1869 in London a new sport called Sphairistike had been demonstrated. With such a difficult name, it was felt that the sport would not find ready acceptance and as it was a type of tennis and had been demonstrated on a grassed area, it was renamed lawn tennis. The sport caught on rapidly in England where the first championship was held in 1877 at Wimbledon, a name which has been associated with tennis ever since. In about 1874 this new sport was introduced into Australia where it was also readily accepted, and by 1878 the Melbourne Cricket Club (MCC) had organised club tennis. The MCC, in keeping with its vigorous and innovative approach to cricket administration, was also responsible in 1880 for the first tennis tournament which was to develop later into the Victorian championships. NSW was a decade behind VIC in introducing organised tennis and it was not until 1890 that the New South Wales Lawn Tennis Association (NSW LTA) was formed. An indication of how readily tennis was accepted was that within 12 months the NSW LTA had registered 23 teams.
The first Australian championship was held in Melbourne in 1905 and in the same year Australia in conjunction with New Zealand challenged for the Davis Cup, which since its inception in 1900 had been restricted to matches played between Britain and the USA. This first challenge was unsuccessful, but a similar challenge in 1907 brought the Davis Cup for the first time to Australia, signalling the entry of a new force into international tennis.
International competition Internationally, Australia has an enviable reputation. Since 1905, when the first great Australian tennis player, Norman BROOKES, reached the finals at Wimbledon, Australians have consistently won international tennis honours. In 1907 Brookes again returned to England where he scooped the pool, winning the Wimbledon singles, doubles and mixed doubles and, partnered by Anthony Wilding of New Zealand, winning the Davis Cup for Australasia.

N.Z. Herald

Margaret Court

LAVER, John NEWCOMBE and Ken Rosewall were dominant.

Tennis in Australia is both a participatory sport and a spectator sport. Televised tournaments are still popular with viewers but the major development is in the establishment of new courts and the sales of new equipment. As quickly as older-style courts are repaired with all-weather surfaces or new courts built they are booked up for some time ahead by social players. *See also* Cawley, E.; Court, M.; Crawford, J.; Fraser, N.; Emerson, R.; McGregor, K.; Quist, A.; Roche, A.; Sedgman, F.

tenpin bowling The forerunner of tenpin bowling, ninepin bowling, originated in Germany and spread to the USA in the 1800s. The game was immediately popular and with the increase in interest came an increase in gambling, with criminal elements rigging matches to enrich themselves. This led to a ban on bowling at ninepins but the devotees of the game found a loophole in the wording of the ban and outwitted it by adding another pin and calling the game tenpin bowling. Although it is thought that ninepin bowling was played in Australia by German settlers in the 1850s, it was not until 1960 that the first commercial bowling centres were opened. In 1962 the Australian Tenpin Bowling Congress was formed and the first annual Australian championships were held.

During the early 1960s, bowling centres were erected in major cities and towns throughout the country to cater for the rapidly growing demand, but by the mid-1960s this demand had already begun to wane and by the late 1960s some bowling centres had to close through lack of public support. In 1978 Australia's leading bowlers formed themselves into a player's union, the National Open Bowlers' Association. In international competition, Australia's outstanding performer has been Jeanette Baker, winner of the World Tenpin Bowling Cup in 1982 and 1983. She is the only woman to have won the Cup in successive years. A growing professionalism, increased sponsorship and wide television coverage have given the sport a new appeal but, although amateur interest is steadily growing, it is unlikely that the excitement and interest generated by the sport's introduction will be repeated.

Tenterfield NSW (population 3 402 in 1981) A town in the N part of the NEW ENGLAND Plateau, it is situated at the junction of the New England, Mt Lindesay and Bruxner Highways, 757km by road N of Sydney. The N tableland train terminates at Tenterfield, 774km by rail from Sydney; formerly this line continued to Wallangarra on the State border, but the service has been discontinued due to lack of rail traffic. At an elevation of 863m above sea level, Tenterfield is just W of the main watershed between streams flowing E to the Pacific (the headwater tributaries of the CLARENCE RIVER)

From this first international victory, Australia went from strength to strength, culminating in the two decades from 1950 to 1970 when Australia was the dominant force on the world tennis scene. It was during this period, in 1954, that a world record crowd of 25 578 turned out at White City in Sydney to watch two 20-year-olds, Lew HOAD and Ken ROSEWALL, defend the Davis Cup they had won for Australia the previous year. Such was the excitement engendered by this pair that more than 9 000 applications for seats had to be returned. This period, between 1950 and 1970, was the era of Harry HOPMAN. As non-playing captain coach of the Davis Cup team he guided Australia to an unequalled 15 successes during this period. It is a tribute to Hopman's coaching skills that players who

were winning the Davis Cup for Australia were also winning the major international singles championships. During this 20-year period the prestigious US singles title was won by Australians on eight occasions and the Wimbledon title on nine occasions.

The Davis Cup was the symbol of tennis supremacy until 1968, when Open tennis was introduced; both amateurs and professionals became eligible for all tournaments and the emphasis was on individual rather than team effort. Since that time tennis competitions between countries have declined in popularity and now there is only marginal interest in the Davis Cup. Moreover, among the top professionals, Australians have been far less prominent in recent years than in the early days of Open tennis, when players such as Rod

and those flowing N and W to the inland drainage system of the continent. The town experiences warm summer conditions, but the winters are severe, with frosts and light snow common. The average annual rainfall is 847mm, spread throughout the year but with a concentration in the summer period from December through February. The rural districts surrounding the town are used mainly for grazing of beef cattle and sheep, with some dairying on nearby alluvial flats and timber-getting in the forested hill lands. The town has meat works, sawmills, a butter factory and some small engineering workshops. The National Trust (NSW) has listed a number of homes and other buildings in the town and has classified 'Ayrdrie', a homestead located 2km from the town on the road to CASINO, for preservation as an essential part of the cultural heritage. Tenterfield is sometimes referred to as 'the birthplace of Australian federation', for it was there, in 1889, that Sir Henry PARKES, then Premier of NSW, made an important speech advocating the federation of the States. The Bald Rock National Park (2104ha), located 29km N of Tenterfield between the Mt Lindesay Highway and the State border, includes the impressive granite dome of Bald Rock which rises 22m above the surrounding countryside and reaches a height of 1277m above sea level. The park contains a variety of fauna—grey kangaroos, wombats, tiger cats, wallabies and several species of possums.

teraglin see fishes, bony

Terang VIC (population 2 111 in 1981) A small country town in the WESTERN DISTRICT of the State on the Princes Highway, it is 22km by road W of CAMPERDOWN, 47km NE of WARRNAMBOOL and 217km by road WSW of Melbourne. It is also on the railway route to Warrnambool and HAMILTON, 221km by rail from Melbourne. It is in the centre of a productive farming and grazing region, where there is dairying, wool growing, fat lamb production and beef cattle raising. Within the adjacent district there are four butter factories and creameries, as well as a large powdered-milk factory. The town has an average yearly rainfall of 786mm, concentrated in the winter and spring months; August is the wettest (93mm average), January the driest (38mm). A distinctive landscape feature of the district is Mt Noorat, an extinct volcano about 10km to the NW. The town dates from the 1850s and several buildings in the area have been classified by the National Trust (VIC), including 'Eeyeuk' (a homestead 9km N of the town), 'Marida Yallock' (which dates from 1841) and Thomson Memorial Church (1893). The name Terang comes from an Aboriginal word meaning 'a twig with leaves'.

termites These exopterygote INSECTS form the order Isoptera, which contains about 246 species (about 51 undescribed, and at least three introduced) in Australia. Termites are extremely destructive of living or structural

wood and of some crops (see PEST CONTROL). All termites are social insects among which individuals help in the rearing of siblings. Because the organisation of the colonies is similar to that of ANTS, BEES AND WASPS (order Hymenoptera), termites are often called 'white ants' though they are more closely related to COCKROACHES (order Blattodea), as their structure reveals.

In advanced termite species there are four distinct castes which usually consist of both sexes. The four castes are: primary reproductives (the king and queen which found the colony); supplementary reproductives (neoteinics); soldiers; and workers. It is believed that every fertilised egg is potentially capable of developing into any caste; the fate of any individual is controlled by various factors such as type of feeding, presence or absence of chemical messengers (pheromones) in the colony, and the relative numbers of the different castes at the time. These factors work through the agency of hormones within the developing termite.

Only the adult primary reproductives have wings but these are shed soon after the nuptial swarming flight, leaving short, triangular bases. A colony normally contains only one king and queen but these remain fertile for several years. When they die they are replaced by one or more pairs of supplementary reproductives. These do not become winged though they have rounded wing buds.

Soldiers have well-sclerotised heads which are often larger than the rest of the body. In primitive genera there may be compound eyes. In many termites soldiers have large mandibles for colony defence and in some species the head is so shaped that it can block a hole in the nest wall, or even a gallery. Some species have nasute soldiers which spray a liquid over attackers; this quickly hardens, immobilising the enemy.

The workers are the commonest individuals in most colonies. They are blind and the cuticle is soft. A colony also contains large numbers of nymphs which may carry out some of the work.

Termite nests There is a large range of types of nests. Some species live within cavities excavated in damp or dry wood—their food. Subterranean termites build their nests underground or within a log or tree stump and construct underground tunnels or above-ground galleries to their food. Most termites die if exposed to the open air and sunlight. Mound-building termites build termitaria ('ant-hills') which are often complex in structure. The outer part is made from very hard clay or earth; the core is made of a softer, woody material and contains galleries, brood chambers and the royal cell. Galleries and tunnels run from the mound to food sources; some may reach a length of 100m. Most termitaria are small but those of the grass-eating *Nasutitermes triodiae*, of N Australia, may be 7m tall. The termitaria of *Amitermes meridionalis*, a species also found in the N, are wedge-shaped with the broad faces to E and W so that the midday sun falls only on the narrow edge. Within termitaria in

Termite damage to a neglected stack of wood

general the humidity is very high, and the temperature variations are damped in relation to those outside. Two species of *Microcertotermes* often build clay-covered nests on telegraph poles and tree tunks, while two *Nasutitermes* species make their of carton-like material (a mixture of chewed wood and faeces) on trees.
Life cycle A colony is founded by a king and queen. At the beginning of the nuptial flight winged termites swarm from the colony. Often the swarming of a particular species is synchronised over a wide area, thus ensuring at least some cross-fertilisation. The winged termites land, shed their wings and form pairs. The male follows the queen in tandem till a suitable site is found. After sealing themselves within a small chamber the pair mate. The first small brood is tended by the male and female but later the work is taken over by advanced nymphs and workers. Some primitive species also form new colonies by emigration.
Termitophiles Termite nests usually contain an assortment of other animals, mainly insects and other ARTHROPODS. Some are scavengers, some feed on eggs and young termites, and some receive food from their hosts in return for various attractive substances.
Australian termites Five families are represented in Australia. The family Mastotermitidae, elsewhere found only as fossils, contains the single species *Mastotermes darwiniensis* of the NT. This is the most primitive of termites and its structure clearly shows its kinship with cockroaches. The subterranean colonies can contain millions of individuals. The species can be very destructive to unprotected buildings. The family Kalotermitidae contains the dry-wood termites, primitive species which live in small colonies within wood. There are no workers, and the tasks of the colony are performed by advanced nymphs. This is also true of the damp-wood termites, family Termopsidae, whose colonies always occur in wood, usually in standing trees or fallen logs.

The two remaining families have true workers. The family Rhinotermitidae contains the widespread genus *Coptotermes* among which are found the most destructive Australian termites. The soldiers discharge a drop of milky fluid from the frontal gland when disturbed; they are not, however, nasute soldiers and, in fact, possess large mandibles. All live in subterranean nests, sometimes with clay-covered mounds above, and feed on wood. The largest family of termites in

Australia is the Termitidae. Abroad, the family contains species which cultivate fungi within the nests for food but the Australian representatives all feed on wood or grass. Subterranean nests, mounds and tree nests are constructed by various members of the family, with a least one species, *Incolitermes pumilis*, building its nest within the nests of *Coptotermes* species. The soldiers may be nasute or provided with mandibles, depending upon the species.

It is estimated that Australian termites cause several million dollars' worth of damage annually to timber in buildings, as well as to standing timber. In vulnerable areas buildings may be protected by building them on a concrete raft. Baffle plates built into the brickwork can also give some protection to timber, but these can be by-passed by the covered runways of some species. The accurate identification of the attacking species is essential in termite control.
Further reading: Harris, W.V. *Termites, their Recognition and Control.* Longmans, London, 1961; Howse, P.E. *Termites.* Hutchinson, London, 1970; Hadlington, P.W. & Cooney, N.G. *A Guide to Pest Control in Australia.* (3rd edn) New South Wales University Press, Sydney, 1979.

terns *see* sea birds

Terrigal NSW Terrigal and the adjoining town, WAMBERAL, are situated on the beach zone of the central coast region; both are increasingly becoming retirement centres and during the summer months they are popular holiday resorts for Sydney people. Terrigal is some 96km by road from Sydney, 12km by road E of GOSFORD and 14km S of The ENTRANCE. On the coast S of Terrigal is a well-known rocky headland called The Skillion; climbers who scale it are rewarded with superb coastal panoramas. The name Terrigal comes from an Aboriginal word meaning 'place of little birds'.

tertiary industries *see* service/tertiary and quaternary industries

Tewantin QLD (combined population of Tewantin and NOOSA HEADS 9 965 in 1981) A tourist centre on the SUNSHINE COAST, 167km by road N of Brisbane, Tewantin is situated in a picturesque setting on the Noosa River, upstream from Noosa Heads, with Mt Tinbeerwah and the State forest as a backdrop to the W of the town. It is a popular holiday resort which offers visitors opportunities for swimming, fishing, boating, other aquatic sports and launch trips on the adjacent lakes. The town has an average annual rainfall of 1709mm, concentrated in the summer months (February and March, the two wettest months, 233mm and 241mm respectively), with a somewhat drier period in the spring (August, the driest month, 53mm). The surrounding district produces sugar cane, pineapples, timber, dairy produce and beef cattle.

theatre Theatre made an early start in Australia. In the year after the arrival of the FIRST FLEET, to celebrate George III's birthday on 4 June 1789, a group of convicts and officers staged Farquhar's *The Recruiting Officer* in a hut decorated with candles and coloured paper. A specially written prologue and epilogue commented on the novel circumstances of a stage performance in NSW.
Early theatre in NSW In 1796 Robert Sidaway set up a playhouse, possibly in Bligh Street, which the better-behaved prisoners were allowed to attend; the admission 'fee' was meat or flour to the value of one shilling. The theatre was closed in 1798 on the Governor's orders because of the rowdy behaviour of its audiences. Another playhouse was in business in 1800, but records of dramatic performances during the early 19th century are scanty. Convict settlements at NORFOLK ISLAND and PARRAMATTA continued to produce plays, and there are records of performances in Sydney Gaol in 1826 and of a convict group which flourished at Emu Plains until it was disbanded in 1830.

The credit for establishing professional theatre in Sydney belongs to a Sydney merchant named Barnett LEVEY, who in 1829 began offering 'At Home' concerts in the Assembly Rooms of his Royal Hotel, part of an odd complex of buildings known as the Colchester Warehouse in George Street. These evenings consisted of songs and sketches, many by Levey himself, but his repeated requests for a theatre licence met with the steadfast refusal of the authorities. Not until the arrival of Governor BOURKE in 1832 was Levey granted his licence, and professional theatre was born in Australia on 26 December 1832, in the Assembly Room of the Theatre Royal, with performances of *Black Ey'd Susan* and *Monsieur Tonson*. The Theatre Royal itself was opened in 1833. A rather disorganised company operated until 1838, the year in which the larger Royal Victoria Theatre was opened in Pitt Street. Established by Joseph Wyatt, its company included Conrad Knowles, Frances Nesbitt and Eliza WINSTANLEY. A tent theatre, the Olympic, was opened by Signor Delle Casse in 1842, and Joseph Simmons' Royal City Theatre opened in 1843, lasting only a few weeks against the Royal Victoria's competition.
Early theatre in the other colonies In Hobart in the 1830s Samson Cameron conducted entertainments at the Freemasons Tavern, and John Phillip DEANE presented plays in his Argyle Rooms. In 1837 Hobart too gained a Royal Victoria theatre, today the Theatre Royal, Australia's oldest playhouse still in use. The first performance in Adelaide was in 1838, in the Adelaide Tavern in Franklin Street (the connection between theatre and public houses in the early years has often been commented on). In 1839 Samson Cameron arrived in Adelaide to open yet another Royal Victoria Theatre, and two years later the Queen's Theatre was open by John Lazar. Melbourne had to wait until 1841 for its first theatre, the Pavilion, a rickety and not alto-

gether waterproof structure alongside the Eagle Tavern in Bourke Street. Melbourne theatre received a great boost from the goldfields, where music-hall style entertainments flourished, and a number of ambitious but short-lived legitimate theatres were opened. Diggers were noted for their rowdy behaviour and extravagant appreciation of visiting performers in tossing notes and even nuggets onto the stage. One of the most colourful of goldfields entertainers was Lola Montez, who bewitched and outraged audiences with her notorious 'spider dance'.

Theatre in Australia survived the advent of cinema and the disruption of World War I, and its glamour and diversity remained largely unchanged until the 1930s. The Williamson Firm still concentrated on musical theatre, a number of young Australian stars rising through its ranks to become internationally known, among them Cyril Ritchard, Madge Elliott and Gladys MONCRIEFF. A new generation of vaudeville artists grew up, the greatest being 'Mo' (Roy RENE) whose name is usually linked with that of his partner 'Stiffy', Nat Phillips. Jim Gerald (famous for his pantomime 'dames'), George Wallace, Queenie Paul and Mike Connors, and Edgley and Dawe with their Midnight Frolics, kept vaudeville alive during the Depression of the 1930s, making it one of the few kinds of theatre to survive the austerity.
Serious drama Serious drama was a good deal less robust, and was found mainly in small theatre groups founded by dedicated actors and directors. Gregan McMAHON established his Melbourne Repertory Society in 1911, and continued to present quality drama, his Gregan McMahon Players performing throughout the Depression. Alan WILKIE toured Australia with productions of Shakespeare after World War I, and later John Alden presented Shakespeare with the backing of the Williamson Firm. In the late 1930s and early 1940s the Minerva Theatre in Sydney, under Kathleen Robinson, staged contemporary classics as well as light entertainment pieces. But the presentation of classics and serious new drama was almost exclusively taken up by the 'little theatres' which sprang up from the 1930s onwards—groups such as Carrie Tennant's Community Theatre and Doris Fitton's Independent Theatre, both in Sydney, the Little Theatre (St Martin's) in Melbourne, and the New Theatres in several capitals. Many of these groups worked in converted halls, with semi-professional casts and low budgets; but good drama—and the works of Australian playwrights—were kept alive for more than a generation by groups of this kind.

However, these theatres gave little scope for professional careers to talented young actors and actresses already adversely affected by the commercial policy of importing leading players from England and America. Consequently, there was an exodus of performers after World War II, Peter Finch, Judith Anderson, Leo McKern, Robert HELPMANN, Barry HUMPHERIES and many others found the local theatre scene too limiting and became firmly established overseas, returning occasionally for touring seasons. Until well into the 1950s Australian theatre still largely depended on tours by overseas celebrities or its own noted expatriates for sophisticated and fully professional drama.

The first entrepreneurs With professional theatre now firmly established in the major colonies, the stage was set for Australia's first entrepreneur, George Selth COPPIN. Coppin's right to the title 'father of the Australian theatre' has been disputed, but he certainly established the practice of bringing overseas celebrities to Australia for extended tours, a practice which dominated Australian theatre for the following century. Though this gave Australians opportunities to see the best of international theatre, it also tended to overshadow the local artists and to confirm the view that 'the best' always came from abroad. In the early days, however, many of Coppin's imported stars became strongly identified with Australia, among them the Irish tragedian G.V. Brooke, who was in partnership with Coppin for a time. The English couple Charles Kean and Ellen Tree, Robert Heir and his wife Fanny Cathcart, Barry Sullivan, Walter Montgomery, Edwin Booth and Madame Celeste all visited Australia, and a regular touring circuit of Australia and New Zealand developed.

In 1874 Coppin engaged a performer whose influence on Australian theatre was longlasting. James Cassius WILLIAMSON and his wife Maggie Moore came with a play, *Struck Oil*, which took Australia by storm. Williamson returned to Australia and in 1882 founded the 'Triumvirate' (with George Musgrove and Arthur Garner) which evolved into the management known simply as 'the Firm' and which had a near-monopoly of commercial entertainment. Williamson continued to import overseas stars and companies for extended tours, and also presented the latest musical and comedy successes from London and New York, a policy which changed little over the hundred years of the Firm's management.

The late 19th century saw the golden years of Australian theatre, in spite of the slump in the 1890s. The great artists of the European stage visited Australia. Madame Ristori toured in *Marie Stuart* in 1875, and the legendary Sarah Bernhardt came in 1891, the same year which saw Janet Achurch in Ibsen's new play, *A Doll's House*. Overseas stars such as Grattan Riggs, Mrs Brown Potter, Kyrle Bellew, Wilson Barrett and John F. Sheridan also toured Australia, while some visiting actor-managers made it 'home' for a time. Robert Brough and the younger Dion Boucicault founded the stylish Brough-Boucicault Company in the late 1880s, one of its chief performers being George Titheradge. The Shakespearean George Rignold, Alfred DAMPIER, Bland Holt and George DARRELL staged melodramas, and musical theatre flourished, one of its brightest stars being Nellie STEWART. The 1890s also saw the rise of variety theatre. Many of the great artists of English

music-hall entertainment visited Australia, including Fred Leslie, Marie Lloyd and the Australian-born Florrie Forde. Pantomime flourished, with charming 'principal boys' such as Ada Reeve and Florence Young and the Williamson pantomimes were said to have cost as much as all the rest of the year's shows put together. Drama companies and musical and variety acts, such as the Lynch Family Bellringers, toured widely, taking theatre to remote towns throughout Australia.

The principle of theatre subsidy In 1954 the Elizabethan Theatre Trust was established to act as an entrepreneurial body and to foster professional theatre. The principle of subsidy changed the face of Australian theatre over the following decade. The Trust established its own company, the Trust Players, in 1959, and brought home noted expatriates Juditch Anderson, to play in *Medea*, and Leo Mckern, to play the title role in Douglas STEWART's *Ned Kelly*; it also staged a number of new Australian plays. During the 1960s the 'little theatres' which had for so long staged the classics and good new drama were to a great extent replaced by major subsidised companies in each capital city. These companies are generally regarded as 'State companies' and include the Melbourne Theatre Company, the Tasmanian Theatre Company, the South Australian Theatre Company, the Queensland Theatre Company, the Playhouse in Perth and a new Sydney company to replace the former Old Tote Theatre Company. These theatres are now the backbone of the profession in Australia, staging the classics and new overseas and local works, and affording employment to actors and actresses who a generation earlier would have become expatriates.

Each capital city has its share of smaller, more experimental theatres, many of which are also subsidised. The Nimrod Theatre in Sydney has a high reputation for its sophisticated performances of new Australian works and of

original interpretations of Shakespeare. The Pram Factory in Melbourne, another theatre which has fostered Australian playwrights, has operated on a collective basis and has developed a rough but energetic ensemble style based on vaudeville and popular theatre tradition. Semi-professional and amateur groups such as the New Theatre in Sydney and La Boite in Brisbane achieve high standards, and contribute to the great diversity of theatrical fare in Australia today. The Williamson Firm virtually ceased operations in 1976, but a reformed company continues to present the best of musical theatre in the larger capitals.

Recently, there has been a sudden boom in theatre restaurants, most of them providing revue-style or music-hall entertainments. Until its closure in 1980, the Music Hall at Neutral Bay in Sydney had a high reputation for its staging of 'hiss the villain' melodramas updated to contemporary tastes.

Training and funding The National Institute of Dramatic Art (NIDA), based at the University of New South Wales, provides training for young actors, directors, technicians and designers, and similar courses are held at the Victoria College of the Arts in Melbourne. The Theatre Board of the AUSTRALIA COUNCIL (the funding body for the arts in Australia) allots subsidies to the major companies, but also allocates funds for individual performers, designers or directors who need to further their experience in Australia or abroad, and for special projects in community theatre or experimental ventures which might not be able to pay their own way.

For most of its history, theatre in Australia has been a pale reflection of British theatre, and the focus for Australians has tended to be the West End and the major English companies. Now, nearly a century and a half since professional theatre was established in Sydney, it seems that has changed. With subsidy has come a firmly established theatrical profession,

Nimrod Theatre, Surry Hills Sydney

J.H. Shaw

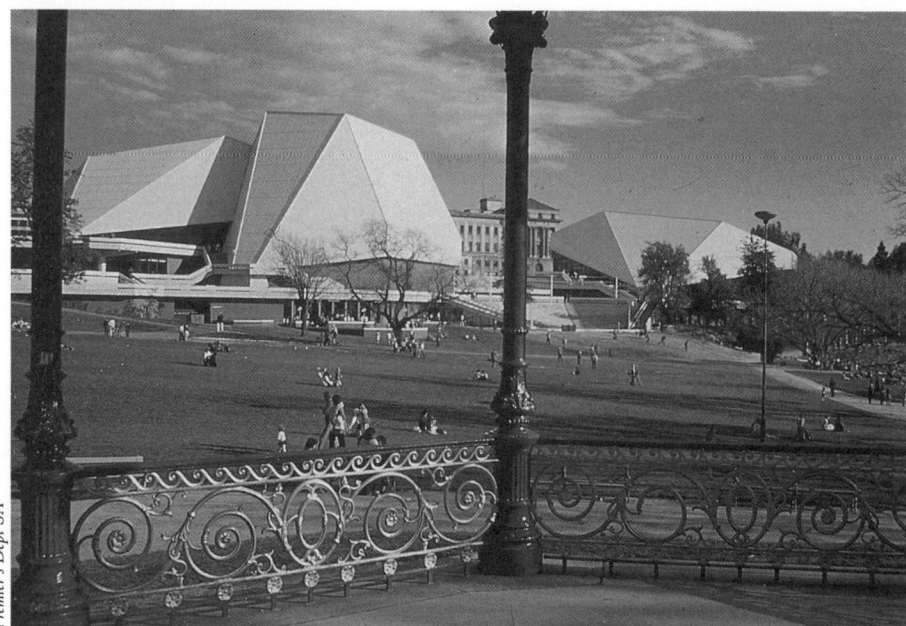

Premier's Dept S.A.

Looking across Elder Park to the Festival Centre, Adelaide

and a new group of talented local playwrights, actors and directors who believe that Australian theatre is not just a branch of the British theatre, but must be based on its own plays and performers and have its roots in Australia. *See also* drama

Further reading: McGuire, P., Arnott, B. & McGuire, F.M. *The Australian Theatre.* Oxford University Press, Melbourne, 1948; Bagot, A. *Coppin the Great: Father of the Australian Theatre.* Melbourne University Press, Melbourne, 1965; Porter, H. *Stars of Australian Stage and Screen.* Rigby, Adelaide, 1965; Allen, J. *Entertainment Arts in Australia.* Paul Hamlyn, Sydney, 1968; Irvin, E. *Theatre Comes to Australia.* University of Queensland Press, Brisbane, 1971; Dicker, I. *James Cassius Williamson.* Elizabeth Tudor Press, Sydney, 1974; West J. *Theatre in Australia.* Cassell, Sydney, 1978.

The Entrance NSW *see* Entrance.

Theodore, Edward Granville 'Red Ted' (1884-1950)

Politician. Born at PORT ADELAIDE, he worked as a miner in WA and at BROKEN HILL and as a prospector in northern QLD before entering the QLD Legislative Assembly in 1909. During the following 16 years he occupied various positions in Labor ministries, and was Premier from 1919 to 1925, after which he retired from State politics to contest a federal seat. In 1927 he entered the House of Representatives as Member for Dalley NSW. He immediately became deputy leader of the Australian Labor Party (ALP) and therefore of the Opposition, and after the ALP victory of 1929 was appointed Treasurer in James SCULLIN's Cabinet.

To deal with the Depression which swept over the nation almost as soon as Labor had gained office, Theodore advocated an inflationary approach which bore similarities to the theory of J.M. Keynes. Three obstacles, however, prevented him from having any chance of putting his ideas into practice. Firstly, bitter enmity developed between him and J.T. LANG, Labor Premier of NSW. Secondly, the government lacked sufficient power over the Commonwealth Bank Board to gain financial backing for his plan, and since it did not have a majority in the Senate could not legislate to increase its power. Thirdly, a QLD Royal Commission, appointed to examine allegations that as Premier of QLD Theodore had used his position to gain financial advantage with regard to a mine at Mungana, reported against him. In June 1930 he resigned as Treasurer pending the result of a legal action arising from the Mungana affair. The action was resolved in his favour in September 1931, but in the meantime Scullin had reappointed him Treasurer—an action which helped to antagonise Lang on the one hand and two conservative members of the federal Cabinet, Joseph LYONS and J.E. Fenton, on the other, and so contributed to a three-way split in Labor's ranks. Theodore was defeated in the election of December 1931, and thereafter devoted himself to business interests, including a very profitable gold-mining venture in Fiji. He was employed by the Commonwealth government from 1942 to 1944 as director of the Allied Works Council.

Further reading: Young, I. *Theodore, His Life and Times.* Alpha, Sydney, 1971.

thickheads

This term is applied to whistlers, some species of THRUSHES, shrike-tits and the bellbird, all PASSERINE BIRDS which belong to the family Pachycephalidae. Although they are thought to be closely related to FLYCATCHERS, these BIRDS are more likely to feed on grubs and caterpillars than on flying insects. A typical thickhead is a well-built bird with a relatively thick head; because some species have hooked bills they are called shrike-thrushes or shrike-tits, but they are not related to the thrushes, shrikes or tits of Europe.

Of the 20 Australian species (15 endemic), nine belong the genus *Pachycephala.* Known as whistlers, but originally called thickheads, these species have loud, clear whistles. The most widespread species is the rufous whistler, *P. rufiventris* (16cm long), which frequents woodlands, forests and gardens throughout the mainland. The male is dark grey above and cinnamon-brown below, with a black band on the face and throat (absent in the female). The common golden whistler, *P. pectoralis** (16cm), is a fairly inactive bird which feeds in tree foliage in forests and woodlands in SW, SE and E Australia and TAS. The male has a black head, a white throat and bright yellow underparts; the female is brownish-grey above and buff below. Similar in appearance and habits is the mangrove golden whistler, *P. melanura** (15cm), an uncommon species which occurs only in the N coastal mangroves. Other common whistlers are the olive species, *P. olivacea** (18cm to 20cm), found in the forests and thickets of TAS and coastal SE Australia; the brown whistler, *P. simplex* (14cm), which occurs in the coastal forests of the NT; and the grey whistler, *P. griseiceps* (14cm), of CAPE YORK.

The genus *Colluricincla* contains seven species of Australian (shrike-) thrushes, plump, grey or brown birds which resemble the song thrush in general appearance but lack the spotted breast. Their songs are loud and attractive and their diet consists of insects and small animals. Three very similar species are the grey thrush, *C. harmonica** (23cm), of E and SE Australia, the brown thrush, *C. brunnea** (23cm), of N Australia, and the western thrush, *C. rufiventris** (23cm), found in SA and the southern parts of WA and the NT.

The three populations of shrike-tits (genus *Falcunculus**) may be separate species or all members of one species. One population is in the E, one in the N and one in the W. All measuring 17cm to 19cm long, these birds have yellow underparts, greyish or yellowish wings, a black face with two white bands and a distinct black crest; the powerful, notched bills are well suited to pulling bark off trees in search of insects.

The crested bellbird, *Oreoica gutturalis** (20cm), is a widespread, common bird on the mainland, living in dry woodlands and arid areas. The male has a black crest; the black continues as a streak downwards through the eye and behind the white face; the wings and tail are light brown, and the rest of the body is grey. The female lacks the black and white facial pattern. Bellbirds have a wide range of ventriloquial calls, including the well-known bell-like call.

Thistle Island SA

This is the largest of a group of islands located off the SE tip of EYRE PENINSULA, at the SW of SPENCER GULF and E of Cape Catastrophe. This island and seven others in the vicinity were named by the explorer Matthew FLINDERS in 1802 after the eight members of the crew of the *Investigator* who were drowned here when their cutter overturned. The other seven islands are Grindal, Hopkins, Lewis, Little, Smith, Taylor and Williams.

thistles *see* Compositae; weeds

Thompson, John Ashburton (1848-1915) Physician. Born in England, he migrated for health reasons in 1878, first to New Zealand, then to Australia. In 1883 he studied dengue fever in QLD and in 1884 became a public medical officer in Sydney. He founded what was, in effect if not in name, the department of public health. He was largely responsible for the drafting of pure food laws throughout Australia, ensuring that they were uniform enough to facilitate the movement of food through the country. He became an expert on leprosy and during the plague outbreak in Sydney in 1900 (*see* DISEASES, HUMAN) he confirmed the hypothesis put forward by a French scientist, P.L.G. Simond, that the bacillus was transmitted from rats to humans by fleas.

Thomson, Peter William (1929-) Golfer. Born in Melbourne, he first played golf, at the age of 12 on a nine-hole course opposite his childhood home, with just one club—an old two iron given to him by his grandfather. Within three years he was that course's Club champion and within six years the VIC champion. In 1951, his first year as a professional, Thomson went to England where he finished sixth in his first British Open, a championship he was later to dominate. While in England he set a new British record of 62 for 18 holes of competitive golf. He won his first Australian Open at the age of 21. Without doubt a golfer of exceptional ability, he went on to win the British Open five times (a feat bettered only by the father of modern golf, Harry Vardon), the Australian Open three times, and at various times throughout his career the Open championships of New Zealand, Hong Kong, Philippines, India, Italy and Spain. Thomson owed much of his success to his calm temperament and his ability to produce match-winning shots in the final rounds of major golf tournaments. Although he still plays competitive golf, since 1964 his energies have been spent less on winning golf and more on administering golf in his position as president of the Professional Golfers' Association of Australia.

Thomson River VIC Located in GIPPSLAND, it rises near MOUNT BAW BAW about 120km E of Melbourne and flows for some 210km S and E beyond SALE to join the LATROBE RIVER. Macalister River is a N tributary. The waters of the upper Thomson have been diverted and are carried by a 19km-long tunnel to the upper YARRA RIVER to augment Melbourne's water supply. The river was named by the explorer STRZELECKI in 1840 in honour of Sir Edward Deas Thomson, the NSW Colonial Secretary at that time.

Species, genus or family is endemic to Australia (see Preface)

thorn apple *see* Solanaceae; weeds

thornbills *see* warblers

threadfins *see* fishes, bony

thrips These INSECTS belong to the exopterygote order Thysanoptera, which contains about 400 known species in Australia, several of which are introduced. Almost all thrips are tiny insects with elongated bodies. The ends of the feet carry protrusible bladders. The mouthparts are exceptional in that they are asymmetrical; they are used for rasping and piercing. The wings, when present, consist of two pairs of strap-like structures with long fringes.

There are two suborders, the Tubulifera and the Terebrantia. In the former the end of the abdomen is tubular whereas in the latter it is either rounded or conical. The Tubulifera tend to be larger, darker and less likely to fly than the Terebrantia. Many are found under bark, in leaf-litter and so on, and they are often gregarious. Some attack plants and a few are gall formers; some thrips are predators of other insects. The Terebrantia are more associated with flowers and grasses and some are serious pests. The endemic *Thrips imaginis* feeds on many imported and native flowers; the cosmopolitan *T. tabaci* is a common pest of cotton, tobacco and onions. The gladiolus thrips, *Taeniothrips simplex*, is responsible for the frequently seen silvering of the foliage which results from air leaking into the lesions caused by the thrip.

thrushes and scrub robins The names 'thrush' and 'robin' are applied to many species of BIRDS (*see* BABBLERS; THICKHEADS; FLYCATCHERS); the true thrushes and the scrub robins are PASSERINE BIRDS, a group of five species which belong to the family Turdidae.

The ground thrush, *Zoothera dauma* (25cm to 28cm long), brown above and white below with the rounded black tips of the feathers giving an overall scalloped effect, is common in south-eastern QLD, SE Australia and TAS. It frequents forests, thickets and gullies, feeding on insects and other small animals. Its relatively infrequent song—a flute-like whistle and a melodious warble—is not as striking as the rich, clear songs of the introduced song thrush, *Turdus philomelos* (23cm), and the introduced blackbird, *T. merula* (25cm). The song thrush, brown above and spotted black on pale buff below, is found in the vicinity of Melbourne, while the blackbird (male all black, female brown) is found near Adelaide and Sydney and in VIC and TAS; both species live mainly on the ground, but sing high up in trees.

The two species of scrub robins found in Australia are terrestrial birds which feed on insects and snails. The uncommon southern scrub robin, *Drymodes brunneopygia** (20cm), a brown bird with a white eye-ring and two white bars on the shoulders, lives in mallee and scrubby sand plains in SW Australia, south-eastern SA, north-western VIC and south-western NSW. It hops about on the ground, seldom flying. The more common northern scrub robin, *D. superciliaris* (19cm to 20cm), which lives in forest clearings and margins in CAPE YORK, has a reddish-brown back and a white face with a vertical black band through the eye.

Thunderbolt, Captain *see* Ward, Frederick

Thursday Island QLD (population 2 283 in 1981) Located NW of CAPE YORK in TORRES STRAIT, the island is the administrative headquarters for the islands of the region, as well as for the GULF OF CARPENTARIA and Cape York. It is a small island (just over 3km²)

Ground thrush, *Zoothera dauma*

R.B. Legge (N.P.I.A.W.)

with a central hill (115m above sea level) surrounded by a coastal plain. Two adjacent islands (Prince of Wales and Horn) are much larger; the airstrip is on Horn Is and passengers are taken by launch to Thursday Is. For many years the island was famed for its pearl divers and trochus fishermen; this activity has declined but there has been some development of a cultured pearl industry. A freezing plant processes fish, prawns and other marine products. The island is the base for pilots who navigate ships through the dangerous waters of Torres Strait. It is uncertain who named Thursday Is; it may have been Lieutenant Phillip Parker King, who surveyed the area in 1819, or James COOK. Within Torres Strait there are also islands called Sunday, Tuesday, Wednesday and Friday.

thylacine *see* Tasmanian wolf

Thysanoptera *see* thrips

Thysanura *see* bristletails

ticks The seven hundred or so species of ticks in the world form one group, Metastigmata (regarded by some as a suborder, by others as an order), of the subclass Acari, which also includes the MITES. Although these PARASITES are closely related to the mites they are usually considered separately because of their relatively large size. They parasitise all kinds of vertebrates, except fish. Their mouthparts are adapted for boring into the flesh and sucking blood or other fluids. The body is oval and has a leathery cuticle. The 'head' (capitulum) can be withdrawn into a cavity in the body. The capitulum carries the hypostome, a projecting, paired structure with backwardly pointing teeth for anchorage. The pedipalps flank the hypostome; the chelicerae, in sheaths, lie below the hypostome and each ends in a toothed pincer.

Ticks are divided into two groups: the ixodid or hard ticks and the argasid or soft ticks. The ixodid ticks have a dorsal plate (scutum) on the upper surface of the body, relatively large in the males but smaller in the females. It may be coloured or ornamented in various ways. The argasid ticks lack this plate.

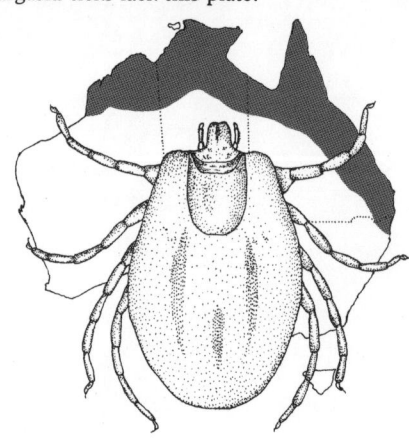

Distribution of the cattle tick in Australia

There are four stages in the life cycle: egg, six-legged larva, nymph and adult. Argasid ticks have several nymphal stages. The eggs are laid on soil and vegetation. The larva or seed tick climbs on vegetation and fastens onto any suitable passing host. When fully fed it moults to the nymphal stage. After feeding this too moults and becomes the adult. The female engorges till she is large and ripe, then drops off to lay her eggs. The males do not increase greatly in size.

Argasid ticks usually lurk in the nests, lairs and dens of their hosts, feeding when these are present. Ixodid ticks may be one-host, two-host or three-host ticks. One-host ticks complete their life cycle, from larva to engorged adult, on the one individual. The larva and nymph of the two-host tick feed on one host; then the engorged nymph falls, moults to the adult stage and finds another host, often another species, on which to feed. Three-host ticks spend the larval, nymphal and adult stages on separate hosts which may be of different species. Ticks are damaging because heavy infestations rob the hosts of large quantities of blood. Many of them also transmit serious diseases (*see* DISEASES AND EPIDEMICS, HUMAN; DISEASES, LIVESTOCK). Host specificity is not strict, though ticks that live on cold-blooded vertebrates do not attack warm-blooded ones, and *vice versa*.

Over 70 species are known in Australia of which at least four are introduced. There are two genera of argasid ticks and six (two introduced) of ixodid ticks.

The genus *Argas* contains 10 argasid species, and the genus *Ornithodoros* three. The body of the *Argas* species has a flattened margin so that it appears to be sharp-edged. These species parasitise birds and bats. *A. persicus*, a cosmopolitan pest of poultry, can transmit fowl tick fever and fowl plague. *Ornithodoros* ticks, which do not have a narrow margin to the body, sometimes attack man, causing severe reactions such as temporary blindness. Abroad, several species transmit Rickettsial relapsing fevers. The kangaroo tick, *O. gurneyi*, attacks macropods; it normally hides in caves or under shade trees frequented by its hosts and can live for several months without feeding.

The introduced genus *Boophilus* contains one-host ixodid species. These species lack the 'pie-crust' sculpturing (festoons) that is characteristic of many ixodid ticks. Several species are important because of the direct damage they do to cattle by sucking their blood, and also by transmitting serious diseases (*see* PARASITES, LIVESTOCK).

The ixodids of the widespread genus *Ixodes* lack eyes and festoons. At least three species attack livestock in Australia. The best known is the paralysis or scrub tick, *I. holocyclus*, of E Australia. This is a three-host species which often uses native mammals, such as bandicoots, as larval and nymphal hosts. The adults attack native mammals, all kinds of livestock, dogs and, sometimes, human beings. The saliva, which is injected by the feeding tick, attacks the nervous system and causes weakness after prolonged feeding. If neglected paralysis may occur, usually starting in the lower limbs but, in extreme cases, eventually attacking the respiratory centre, sometimes causing death. This is quite common in dogs, though an antitoxin is available. There are a few recorded cases of human fatalities.

Amblyomma is a genus of ixodid ticks with eyes and festoons. *A. triguttatum* is a common ectoparasite of kangaroos and it sometimes also attacks livestock and dogs.
Further reading: see under mites. *Also* Roberts, F.H.S. *Insects Affecting Livestock*. Angus & Robertson, Sydney, 1952; *Cattle Tick in Australia: Cattle Tick Control Commission Enquiry —Report 1973*. Australian Govt Publishing Service, Canberra, 1975.

tiger cat *see* native cats, etc.

tilliken *see* rodents

timber Timber-getting was one of the earliest European activities in Australia and many settlements were originally founded as the bases of timber cutters. CEDAR was one of the first of the valuable trees to be exploited and is now comparatively rare. Trees in both native forests and plantations are usually felled by chain saws or felling machinery though wood chopping using axes remains a popular competitive sport in Australia. Machines are also widely used for hauling the timber, sawn to suitable lengths, from the forest to the loading sites, and also to load them onto timber jinkers to be taken to the sawmills.

There are about 860 log sawmilling establishments in Australia, employing almost 14 000 people. About 80 more establishments, with about 6 000 employees, are concerned with the manufacture of plywoods and similar boards. The plywood industry makes use of imported timbers as well as native-grown trees. Australia also imports about a quarter of its sawn timber needs though it is hoped that the country will be self-sufficient by the end of the century or shortly afterwards. In 1978-79 the industry produced 3 110 000m³ of undressed sawn timber (46 per cent of which was coniferous), 3 800 000 tonnes of woodchips, 11 419 000m² of plywood, 564 000m³ of resin-bonded particle board, 671 544 tonnes of wood pulp and 1 271 138 tonnes of paper and allied products. The following list includes some of the main timber trees of Australia with notes on their uses.
Hardwoods ASH, alpine, *Eucalyptus gigantea*. Coarse-textured, straight-grained plain-figured wood; used for general building and pulping, cabinet making and sporting goods.
Ash, mountain, *E. regnans*. Similar to alpine ash.
BEAN, BLACK, *Castanospermum australe*. Straight-grained timber with dark brown to almost black heartwood with prominent figuring; used as a decorative wood and in high-class cabinet work.
Beech, MYRTLE, *Nothofagus cunninghamii*. White to reddish-brown timber; used for interior work and furniture making.

Timber mill in eastern New England

Dundas blackbutt, *Eucalyptus dundasi*

Bangalow, *Eucalyptus botryoides*

BLACKBUTT, *E. pilularis*. Widely used for general building construction.

BLACKWOOD, *Acacia melanoxylon*. Golden to reddish-brown timber; valued for cabinet work and furniture making.

CEDAR, red, *Cedrela toona*. Highly prized timber for interior work.

Coachwood, *Ceratopetalum apetalum*. Light brown to pinkish fine-textured wood; used for general interior work.

Gum, river red, *E. camaldulensis*. Reddish, very hard, durable wood; used for heavy construction (such as wharf and bridge building and sleepers).

Gum, spotted, *E. maculata*. Light to greyish-brown; valuable for heavy framing, and for tool handles and similar work.

Ironbark, grey, *E. paniculata*. Used for heavy construction work.

Jarrah, *E. marginata*. One of the most widely used and versatile timbers, especially in WA; reddish-brown in colour.

Karri, *E. diversicola*. A timber resembling jarrah though lighter in colour; used for heavy construction work.

MAHOGANY, red, *E. resinifera*. A timber similar in appearance to jarrah; used in building construction, though not in contact with the soil.

MAHOGANY, rose, *Dysoxylum fraseranum*. Pink to reddish-brown and heavy; used in cabinet making.

MAPLE, Queensland, *Flindersia brayleyana*. A beautifully figured pink to pinkish-brown timber; highly valued for decorative interior work and veneers.

OAK, SILKY, *Cardwellia sublimis*. Silky-textured, pink to reddish-brown timber; used for cabinet work, parquet flooring and veneers.

SATINAY, *Syncarpis hillii*. Also known as Frazer Island turpentine, red to reddish-brown timber; used in furniture, handles, general building and plywood.

TALLOW WOOD, *E. microcorys*. Heavy yellowish-brown to brown timber; used for heavy construction work, flooring, weather boards and so on.

TURPENTINE *Syncarpia laurifolia*. Red to reddish-brown timber which, when dressed, is sometimes called luster; used for heavy construction work.

WALNUT, Queensland, *Endiandra palmerstoni*. Variegated, well-figured wood; used for decorative panelling, furniture and cabinet making, and veneers; has high electrical resistance.

Softwoods Kauri, Queensland, *Agathis robusta*. Used for internal construction, furniture and musical instruments.

PINE, celery top, *Phyllocladus asplenifolius*. Used for joinery, indoors and outdoors, and for doors, flooring and chemical containers.

PINE, cypress, white, *Callitris glauca*. Valuable timber for building construction where termites and other borers are a threat.

PINE, hoop, *Auracaria cunninghami*. Light-coloured timber; used for general interior work.

PINE, huon, *Dacrydium franklinii*. A favourite wood for ship building but the species, which is very slow growing, is thought to be in some danger of extinction.

PINE, King William, *Athrotaxis selaginoides*. Used for internal joinery and boat building.

PINE, radiata, *Pinus radiata*. Introduced softwood for general carpentry and joinery.

See also forestry

Further reading: Walton, J.A. *Woodwork in Theory and Practice*. Australasian Publishing Co., Sydney, 1970.

time zones There are three time zones in Australia:

1. Eastern Australian Time, 10 hours ahead of Greenwich Time, based on the 150°E meridian of longitude, which is the time for QLD, NSW, ACT, VIC and TAS;

2. South Australian Time, nine and a half hours ahead of Greenwich Time, based on the 142°30'E meridian of longitude, used in SA, NT and at BROKEN HILL in the far W of NSW;

3. Western Australian Time, eight hours ahead of Greenwich Time, based on the 120°E meridian, used in WA.

However, summer time in some States is varied from these standard zone times, because of DAYLIGHT SAVING. This is a system whereby clocks are put forward by one hour during summer months. The origin of the Australian time zones goes back to the 1890s when the various colonial governments in the States decided to standardise their time according to Greenwich Time, so that the times adopted were based upon meridians of longitude, each 15° of longitude being equal to one hour of time. It was agreed that the E States (QLD, NSW, VIC and TAS) would base their time on the 150°E meridian (10 hours ahead of Greenwich), that SA and NT would base their time on the 135°E meridian (nine hours ahead of Greenwich) and WA time would be based on the 120°E line. Following this agreement, SA decided in 1898 to change its time base to the 142°30'E meridian, and since the NT was then under the administration of SA, this became the time line of the Territory.

tin Australia has produced tin in commercial quantities since the 1870s. The first mining operations near INVERELL in north-western NSW commenced in 1871. In the following year, mining of the extensive tin deposits at MOUNT BISCHOFF in north-western TAS started, followed by RENISON BELL and Storeys Creek in TAS, STANTHORPE and Herberton in QLD, Greenbushes in WA, and Tingha, Deepwater, TENTERFIELD and Emmaville in the NEW ENGLAND region of northern NSW. Australia became one of the world's leading producers of tin in the 1870s and in some years was the largest producer. Though the profitability of tin mining has fluctuated with varying world prices, Australia ranked fifth in mine production of tin in 1980 (after Malaysia, Thailand, Indonesia and Bolivia). During the 1970s, the average Australian level of tin concentrate production was about 10 000 tonnes; the year of highest production was 1979 with 12 571 tonnes (see Table 1).

Table 1

AUSTRALIAN PRODUCTION OF TIN-IN-CONCENTRATES 1972-81 (tonnes)

Year	Production
1972	11 997
1973	10 801
1974	10 481
1975	9 577
1976	10 611
1977	10 634
1978	11 864
1979	12 571
1980	11 588
1981	12 267

Source: *Australian Mineral Industry Review*. (1970-81) Australian Govt Publishing Service, Canberra.

TAS accounted for 53.8 per cent of total Australian production of tin concentrates in 1980 (see Table 2). The other two major producing States are NSW and QLD, which accounted for 18.6 per cent and 24.0 per cent respectively of tin concentrates in 1980. In TAS the two main producers are Renison Bell (11km W of ROSEBERY in north-western TAS) and the Mt Cleveland Mine at Luina (21km E of SAVAGE RIVER, also in the NW); smaller production sites in TAS are Aberfoyle and Storeys Creek,

on the Slopes of BEN LOMOND in north-eastern TAS. The principal production centre in NSW in Ardlethan, located W of TEMORA in the RIVERINA region; smaller amounts of alluvial tin are mined at Emmaville. In QLD, the Herberton district, located SW of ATHERTON near the headwaters of the HERBERT RIVER, and the adjacent MAREEBA district are the main sources of tin. WA's tin production comes from Greenbushes, located SE of BUNBURY, and Moolyella in the PILBARA region of the NW.

tjuringa This is the name given to a stone, worked into an oval, circular or pear shape and often decorated with spiral designs, circles, lines or tracks of birds and mammals incised on the surface. The manufacture is prehistoric in all areas except central Australia. The stones were often rubbed with red ochre or charcoal and are extremely sacred objects to their Aboriginal owners; they often represented the home of the owner's spirit or his totem animal. Some tribes made wooden tjuringas; these were sometimes also used as BULLROARERS.

toadoes see fishes, bony; fishes, poisonous and venomous

toads see frogs, etc.

toadstools see fungi

tobacco see agriculture; Solanaceae

tobies see fishes, bony

Tobruk see War in the Middle East *under* World War II

Todd, Sir Charles (1826-1910) Astronomer, electrical engineer and meteorologist. Born in London, he worked at the Royal Observatory, Greenwich, and at the Cambridge University observatory before being appointed observer and superintendent of telegraphs in SA in 1855. In 1970 he was also appointed postmaster-general of SA. His work

Table 2

AUSTRALIAN PRODUCTION OF TIN (CONTENT OF TIN-IN-CONCENTRATES)

State	Tin Content	%
QLD	2 697	22.1
NSW	1 883	15.4
VIC	—	—
TAS	7 023	57.4
WA	553	4.5
NT	77	0.6
TOTAL	12 233*	100.0

Note: * in 1981, there were 34 tonnes of tin in tin-copper concentrates, giving a total for that year of 12 267 tonnes. Source: *Australian Mineral Industry Annual Review*. 1981 Australian Govt Publishing Service, Canberra.

included the equipping of the Adelaide observatory, the setting up of a network of meteorological stations, and the design and construction of a number of telegraph lines, including the SA sections of the lines connecting Adelaide with Melbourne and Perth. However, his fame rests above all on the construction of the overland line from Adelaide to Palmerston (later named DARWIN), which he designed and supervised, and which brought him international recognition. He was appointed CMG (1872) and KCMG (1893), and received numerous other honours, including election as a Fellow of the Royal Astronomical Society and a Fellow of the Royal Society. The TODD RIVER is named after him, and ALICE SPRINGS after his wife.

Todd River NT The river upon which ALICE SPRINGS is located, it rises in the MACDONNELL RANGES and follows a general SE course over 300km (flowing only in wet years), petering out in the SIMPSON DESERT in the SE corner of the Territory. The river and its upper tributaries have cut deep gorges where they cross the ridges of the MacDonnells; the best-known of these in Simpson's Gap (22km W of Alice Springs), but several others, equally spectacular, lie in the E section of the MacDonnell Ranges, such as Emily Gap and Trephina Gorge. The sandy bed of the Todd at Alice Springs, though occasionally a torrent, is usually dry and is the scene of a rather hilarious 'boat' race, called the Henley-on-Todd Regatta, held annually in late August or early September, when the crews run with their fully rigged but bottomless boats through the soft sandy river bed. The Todd River was named after Sir Charles Heavitree Todd, the Postmaster General of SA in the early 1870s when the OVERLAND TELEGRAPH was constructed.

Tolpuddle Martyrs see Loveless, George

tomatoes see Solanaceae

tommy ruff see fishes, bony

Tom Price WA see Mount Tom Price

tongue worms These parasitic animals belong to a small phylum, Pentostomida, which is related to the ARTHROPODS. Known from Asia, Europe and Australia and the Arctic, they live in the lungs and nasal passages of carnivorous vertebrates, usually tropical reptiles such as snakes, lizards and crocodiles, but in some cases in mammals and birds.

The body is between 2cm and 13cm in length. There are four leg-like protuberances at the front of the body, bearing claws, and a fifth swelling with the mouth. The body has a thick, chitinous cuticle. The larval stage, which occurs in intermediate hosts such as rabbits, is an oval animal with a short tail and four stumpy, clawed legs. When the intermediate host is eaten the larvae enter the predator's stomach. They reach the lungs by passing along the alimentary canal.

The species that attacks mammals (especially dogs), *Linguatula serrata*, sometimes infests man, especially in the Middle East and Asia. The commonest species which attacks man, however, is *Armillifer armillatus*, found in Africa, South-East Asia and China.

toolache *see* kangaroos, etc.

Toowoomba QLD (population 63 401 in 1981) Often called the 'Garden City' of the State, situated on the crest of the GREAT DIVIDING RANGE at an elevation of 610m above sea level, about 130km by road W of Brisbane, it is the gateway to the rich and scenic DARLING DOWNS. It is the major commercial and industrial centre of the Downs, located on the Warrego Highway, 91km W of IPSWICH, 84km SE of DALBY and 84km N of WARWICK. Due to its elevation, the city experiences a mountain coolness in the summer months, whilst winter months can be mild but frosty. The average annual rainfall is 955mm, concentrated mainly in summer, with a drier period in winter and spring; January and February are the two months of highest rainfall (140mm and 121mm respectively) and August and September the two lowest (42mm and 48mm respectively). As well as being the principal commercial city for the productive farming and grazing lands of the Downs, Toowoomba has a wide range of secondary industries: dairy processing, flour milling, food canning, engineering and brewing.

There are numerous tourist attractions in the city; these include the Lionel Lindsay Gallery, the COBB & CO. Museum, the Steele RUDD Memorial where the author A.H. Davis (whose pen-name was Steele Rudd) was born in 1868, St Matthew's Church, which has some interesting records of pioneering days, and numerous parks and gardens. A special motor drive, known as the Blue Arrow Route, directed by signposts for 52km through the city and along the escarpment of the range, provides visitors with a tour of the scenic, architectural and historic highlights of the city. It includes the lookout at Mt Kynoch (710m elevation) which gives panoramic views across the city to the range, Mt Lofty (715m) which provides a vista of the Downs, and Picnic Point (704m), a massive tor on the crest of the range. The National Trust (QLD) has listed several buildings in the city for preservation including Bull's Head Inn, the post office and a number of homes. The municipal quarry, an extinct volcanic cone, is a unique tourist attraction, especially to those interested in geology. Each September the city blossoms into a festive mood for the annual carnival of flowers. The city's name comes from an Aboriginal word which has several possible meanings: 'the swamp', 'the native melon which grew by the swamp' or 'underground water'. The original settlement was known as The Swamp, but this was not popular with some of the early residents and the name Toowoomba was officially adopted in 1858.

Further reading: Hinchcliffe, B. *Toowoomba Sketchbook*. Rigby, Adelaide, 1977.

tope *see* sharks, etc.

top-shells *see* gastropods

torpedo *see* sharks, etc.

Torquay VIC (population 2 879 in 1981) This seaside holiday resort is located on the BASS STRAIT coastline, 23km by road S of GEELONG. It is situated on the Great Ocean Road and is a popular tourist centre where there are fine surfing beaches and rugged scenic coastlines. It was named after Torquay in Devonshire, England.

Torrens River SA Rising in the MOUNT LOFTY RANGES, NE of Adelaide near Mt Pleasant, it flows for some 65km first in a SW direction, then W through Adelaide city to ST VINCENT GULF. On the upper reaches, in a gorge section of the stream course, dams have been constructed to provide part of Adelaide's water supply. Where the river passes through the city between N and S Adelaide, it has been dammed to form LAKE TORRENS, used for aquatic sports. In 1937 the mouth of the river was diverted and an artificial outlet to the sea was created between Henley and West Beaches on the gulf coast. The river was named in honour of Colonel Robert Richard Torrens, chairman of the Colonisation Commissioners for SA.

Torrens, Sir Robert Richard (1814-84) Land titles reformer. He was born in Cork, Ireland. His father, after whom the TORRENS RIVER and LAKE TORRENS in SA are named, was prominent in the moves leading to the foundation of that colony, and was chairman of the Colonisation Committee that planned the first settlement. Robert Torrens emigrated to SA in 1840, and became Collector of Customs in Adelaide. At that time there were moves in England and Australia to simplify the cumbersome traditional systems of land titles. He developed an absorbing interest in this movement, and devised a system in which only one title deed is needed to prove ownership, and all necessary information for transfer of land is contained in easily accessible form in a public register. Elected to the colony's first House of Assembly in 1857, he promptly incorporated his system in a Bill which was passed in the following year as the Real Property Act. In the meantime he had been Premier briefly in 1857, but in 1858 resigned his seat to become head of the Land Titles Department. In that position he supervised the implementation of the Act and publicised its merits so successfully that by the time he returned to England in 1863 his system had been adopted in all colonies except WA, where it was adopted in 1874. He was a member of the House of Commons from 1868 to 1874, but did not gain an opportunity to have legislation on land titles reform introduced there.

Today, however, his system or ones similar to it are common throughout the world.
Further reading: Kerr, D. *The Principles of the Australian Land Title (Torrens) System*. Law Book Company, Sydney, 1927.

Torres, Luis Vaez de Spanish navigator. Very little is known about his life apart from the voyage which in 1606 brought him very close to Australia. In December 1605 he sailed from Callao, Peru, as captain of the *San Pedrico*, one of the ships in an expedition commanded by Pedro Fernandez de Quiros. By that time the Spaniards had done a considerable amount of exploration fairly close to Australia. In 1545 they had named New Guinea, and their explorer Mendana, sailing like De Quiros from Peru, and also like him searching for the fabled Great South Land, had discovered the Solomons in 1568 and the Marquesas and Santa Cruz Islands in 1595. De Quiros, who had been with Mendana on the latter voyage, hoped to return to the Santa Cruz Islands, then discover the Great South Land and convert its inhabitants to Christianity.

De Quiros failed in his first objective, arriving instead at the New Hebrides, where one island impressed him so much by its size that he named it Austrialia del Espiritu Santo (meaning 'Southern Land of the Holy Spirit', but containing in its first word a play on the word 'Austria', in reference to the fact that Philip III of Spain was from the royal house of Austria). Not long afterwards he became separated from the rest of the expedition, consisting of Torres' ship and the launch *Tres Reyes*, and sailed to Mexico. The reason for his departure is uncertain, but may have been due to a state of mutiny or near-mutiny among his crew. Torres decided to continue with the work of the expedition, and sailed SW, but when he was about midway between the New Hebrides and the E coast of Australia he abandoned the search for the Great South Land and turned N towards Manila. He then came to the S coast of New Guinea, failed to make his way around the E tip of that island, and went W through the passage now known as TORRES STRAIT, to the Moluccas and thence to the Philippines.

There has been considerable argument as to whether Torres saw the Australian coast. The surviving sources of information about his voyage seem to indicate that he kept fairly close to the New Guinea shore. It is most unlikely that he saw even the tip of CAPE YORK, and if he did see it he must surely have taken it for yet another island among the many to the S of his route.
Further reading: Clark, C.M.H. *A History of Australia*. (vol 1) Melbourne University Press, Melbourne, 1962; Wood, G.A. *The Discovery of Australia*. (revd by Beaglehole, J.C.) Macmillan, South Melbourne, 1969.

Torres Strait QLD Lying between CAPE YORK and PAPUA NEW GUINEA, this strait links the Coral Sea on the E to the ARAFURA SEA on the W. The main shipping channel through the strait, called Prince of Wales Channel, is located between Goode and Banks Islands; because of the treacherous tidal flow and the presence of numerous coral reefs and shifting sand bars, ships sailing through these waters must take on an official pilot from THURSDAY ISLAND. The strait takes its name from the Spanish explorer Luis Vaez de TORRES, who passed through it in 1606 and thereby established that New Guinea and Australia were separate.

tortoises and turtles Belonging to the order Chelonia (or Testudines) these REPTILES have characteristic shells from which the limbs, head and tail protrude. This is the only surviving order from the subclass which contained the original or stem reptiles; there are about 210 surviving species. The usage of the common names 'turtles' and 'tortoises' varies from country to country, but in Australia turtles are usually the marine forms while the tortoises are freshwater chelonians that also come on land. In Europe 'tortoise' is often used for land dwellers such as the Grecian tortoise, a popular pet.

Typically, the chelonian shell consists of an inner layer of thick, bony plates and an outer layer of thin, horny scales (scutes). The scutes are comparable to the scales of other reptiles. There is no correspondence between the position and number of bony plates and scutes. The lower part of the shell (that is, the part below the body) is called the plastron; the part above is the carapace. The bones of the carapace are arranged in five rows and are attached to the vertebrae and ribs. The limb girdles are therefore modified and lie inside the ribs. The stout limbs have five digits each but in the marine turtles they are paddle-shaped. Chelonians have a horny beak but no living species has teeth—the sharp ridges at the edges of the jaws are used for feeding.

There are two suborders. The suborder Cryptodira contains the sea turtles and most other living chelonians. In this group the neck is bent and folded vertically when the head is withdrawn. The only Australian representatives are the marine turtles, apart from one recently discovered freshwater species. The suborder Pleurodira is restricted to Australasia, sub-Saharan Africa, and South America, which may indicate a GONDWANALAND origin. Sometimes called side-neck turtles because the neck is folded sideways when the animal withdraws it into the shell, these web-footed chelonians are largely carnivorous but also eat some plant material such as fruit. The animal food includes molluscs, insects and crustaceans, but very little fish. Conversely, many animals prey on tortoises, but mainly when they are very small.

The eggs are laid in holes scooped in the sand, above water level, and the incubation time varies markedly from species to species (three to six months in short-necked tortoises but up to two years in long-necked tortoises; *see below*). Often the eggs are laid in such

situations that rain is necessary to soften the ground before the hatchlings can emerge.

In SE Australia tortoises often hibernate, but this may not happen in SW Australia. Hibernation can take place either on land, with the tortoises just covered with soil and debris, or in the water, where, apparently, the tortoise respires through its excretory passage (cloaca). In very hot weather, it may aestivate; it drinks as much water as possible, then retreats to a damp spot and burrows in, or retires to the mud at the bottom of its pond or creek. Tortoises are usually active early in the morning or late in the afternoon. During the day they often emerge from the water to sunbathe, dropping into the water when disturbed. Water is essential for all Australian chelonians; many that are sold as pets perish because they are kept in a pondless garden; normally they try to escape to search for water.

Freshwater chelonians The number of freshwater chelonian species in Australia is probably about 15. All but one are pleurodires. 1. Suborder Cryptodira. One freshwater chelonian of Australia belongs to this group: the pitted-shelled turtle or pig-nosed turtle, *Carettochelys insculpta*, the only member of the family Carettocheylidae. It was thought to be restricted to New Guinea until a specimen was discovered in 1969 in the DALY RIVER in the NT. It is now known to occur in several coastal rivers of the NT and may be even more widely distributed in N Australia. It is the only freshwater chelonian with flippers. The carapace is not horny but is covered with a delicate skin which is grooved over the bony plates beneath. The maximum length of an adult is probably about 70cm. The turtle is grey, olive grey or greyish-brown above, and the underparts are light coloured. Pignosed turtles feed on snails, small fish and fruit (figs and pandanus) that fall into the water. They live in freshwater, in estuarine reaches and sometimes in isolated billabongs.

2. Suborder Pleurodira. All the remaining freshwater chelonians of Australia belong to four genera of the family Chelidae, which is restricted to Australia, New Guinea and South America. The limbs are typically reptilian—jointed, with ankle joints and four or five claws. The feet are webbed and most species have sensory barbels near the mouth.

The genus *Chelodina* contains about six known species in Australia. When fully extended from the shell, the neck and head are, together, about as long as the body, hence their common name—long-necked or snake-necked tortoises. Most parts of Australia, apart from TAS and the arid regions, have representatives of the genus. The common snake-neck tortoise, *C. longicollis* (shell length 25cm), ranges from Adelaide along the E coastal regions to CAPE YORK. The colour varies, but in adults is usually dark above and white or cream below; the sutures between the horny plates of the carapace's lower edges and the plastron are black, though sometimes the hatchlings have an orange or red plastron. It lives in still waters, swamps, and slow-moving rivers, feeding on small fish, crustaceans, molluscs and tadpoles. The broad-shelled river tortoise, *C. expansa* (50cm), occurs in the MURRAY-DARLING system, and in parts of south-eastern QLD. The oblong tortoise, *C. oblonga* (40cm), of south-western WA, easily recognised by the shape of its shell, has an excessively long neck which is not completely covered when withdrawn. The flat-shelled tortoise, *C. steindachneri* (20cm), is also a WA species which ranges from the DE GREY RIVER to the Irwin River. Little is known of its biology and it is strictly protected. The two N species are the New Guinea snake-neck tortoise, *C. novaeguineae* (30cm), of Cape York, which is very similar to *C. longicollis*, and the northern snake-necked tortoise, *C. rugosa* (40cm), which ranges from the KIMBERLEYS to Cape York.

Long-necked tortoise

Courtesy of A.I.S. Canberra

Flat-backed turtle

The genus *Elseya* contains two species of tortoises with moderately long necks (extended head and neck much shorter than shell length). The snapping tortoise, *E. dentata* (35cm) which ranges from the Kimberleys to W Cape York, can give a severe bite. The neck has many small tubercles and adults have a horny casque on the head; macrocephaly (enlarged head) often occurs in old specimens. Brown above, sometimes with darker blotches, and yellow on the plastron, this species lives in larger rivers and oxbow lakes, feeding on molluscs, crustaceans, fish and some fruit. The saw-shelled tortoise, *E. latisternum* (20cm), could be confused in some areas with the snapping tortoise for it is variable throughout its range (from Cape York to northern NSW). The back edge of the carapace is serrated except when worn, as in old specimens, and the tubercles on the upper neck are pointed; macrocephaly never occurs.

The genus *Emydura* is closely related to the *Elseya* species but lacks the horny casque, except when very old. Krefft's river tortoise, *E. kreffti* (25cm), is found in the larger rivers and billabongs in the E and NE parts of QLD. It is a pale brown, olive brown or almost black above and has a yellow or bluish-green stripe running backwards from the eyes. The Murray-River short-necked tortoise or Macquarie tortoise, *E. macquaria* (30cm), which ranges from southernmost QLD to SA, has a yellow stripe on the chin but no line behind the eye, though some juveniles may have a yellow spot there; the carapace varies from light to dark brown or olive green. The similar Brisbane tortoise, *E. signata* (20cm), ranges from extreme south-eastern QLD to northern NSW, in coastal rivers. There are two or three other *Emydura* species in the N

but the classification of the genus is in doubt.

Australia's smallest chelonian, the western swamp tortoise, *Pseudemydura umbrina* (15cm), a species with a squarish shell, is restricted to a few swamps at Bullsbrook on the SWAN coastal plain, near Perth. The area is now a reserve. This species was first described in 1839 and not seen again till 1954. The waterholes in which it lives often dry up for six months at a time. The head has a casque, and there are large, conical tubercles on the short neck.

Marine chelonians Six species of marine turtles are recorded from Australian shores and adjacent seas. The one marine turtle that is not recorded is Kemp's ridley, *Lepidochelys kempi*, an Atlantic species. The flatback, *Chelonia depressa* (1.2m), is confined to Australian waters. The other five species are widely spread in warm and temperate waters. All seven species, apart from the leathery turtle, *Dermochelys coriacea* (3m), belong to the family Cheloniidae in which the shell is bony and covered with plates and sometimes also with a thin skin. The feet are paddle-like but have one or more claws.

The loggerhead turtle, *Caretta caretta* (1.5cm), is distinguished by the five costal shields (the row of shields on the carapace between the central row, called vertebrals, and the outer row, called marginals) on each side, by the non-overlapping of the scutes of the carapace in adults and by the lack of a noticeable beak. Dark brown above and light coloured below, it has a heart-shaped shell and a large head which is very broad posteriorly. This species occurs quite commonly on the coasts of the N half of Australia, and sometimes ventures into cooler waters. It nests at many places on the mainland, laying about 50 eggs (which look like ping-pong balls) at any time of

the year, but mainly from October to May. The eggs and hatchlings are taken by many predators. The turtles are carnivores which appear to feed mainly in deeper waters.

The two species of *Chelonia* have four costal shields and lack a beak. The flatback turtle has a flat carapace. It is grey, pale greyish-green or olive above, and in the adults, covered with a thin skin. The plastron and the skin below are creamy yellow, a colour which extends to the sides of the neck and the face. Common in coastal waters on N Australia, but less common on the GREAT BARRIER REEF, it breeds throughout its range, laying about 50 large eggs in holes on the shore. The widespread green turtle, *C. mydas* (about 1m), which is greener in colour, occurs on the coasts of the N half of Australia, and breeds throughout its range, laying about 100 relatively small eggs. Young green turtles are carnivorous, but the adults are believed to be herbivores. Green turtles are traditionally the chief ingredient of turtle soup.

The hawksbill turtle, *Eretmochelys imbricata* (1m), has four costal shields, strongly overlapping scutes in adults, and a distinct parrot-like beak formed by the upper jaw. Though it is common along the tropical coast of N Australia, the hawksbill has rarely been recorded breeding there. Common on coral reefs, this species is a carnivore which also feeds on algae. It is the source of commercial tortoiseshell and is also used to make turtle soup.

The leathery turtle or luth is the only member of the family Dermochelyidae. It is the most wide ranging of the turtles, and often moves into temperate waters. It is resident, for example, to almost as far S as the NSW/VIC border, and has been recorded all round the coast. Instead of the usual turtle shell, it has a leathery skin with many small, polygonal bones embedded in it, forming a mosaic; some of the larger bones are arranged in rows dorsally and ventrally, producing a number of high keels. Breeding in Australia is very rare but luths do nest at times near Limpus on the central coast of QLD. They have been seen feeding on jellyfish and bluebottles. The luth is probably the most seriously threatened of the marine turtles and the world numbers are very low.

Attempts have been made to establish turtle farming as an industry for N Australian Aboriginals and Torres Strait Islanders.

Further reading: Goode, J. *Freshwater Tortoises of Australia and New Guinea* (in the family Chelidae). Lansdowne Press, Melbourne, 1967; Worrell, E. *Reptiles of Australia* (2nd edn) Angus & Robertson, Sydney, 1970; Bustard, R. *Australian Sea Turtles.* Collins, London & Sydney, 1972 (also issued with the title *Sea Turtles*) and *Kay's Turtles.* Collins, London & Sydney, 1973; Cogger, H.G. *Reptiles and Amphibians of Australia.* A.H. & A.W. Reed, Sydney, 1975; Cann, J. *Tortoises of Australia.* Angus & Robertson, Sydney, 1978.

Torrumbarry Weir VIC Located on the MURRAY RIVER 32km downstream from ECHUCA, it is a lock-and-weir structure, completed in 1923 by the VIC government. It was the first construction undertaken by VIC as part of the River Murray Agreement made between the Commonwealth and three States (NSW, VIC and SA) for the conservation and utilisation of the Murray waters. The weir controls river flow, raises the level of the waters and so permits the diversion of water into channels for irrigating crops and pastures by gravity flow on the riverine plains further downstream. Since the weir was planned at a time when it was still thought that the Murray would become a major 'highway' of river traffic, a lock was included in the design of the structure so as to permit boats to be raised and lowered on their journeys along the river.

totalizators These are betting machines which allow punters at racing, trotting and greyhound meetings to wager on the outcome of each race. The totalizator, or tote as it is more commonly called, automatically registers all wagers placed and continuously displays the odds of each starter. All wagers are pooled, a commission deducted from the total and the remaining distributed to winning punters after each race. Introduced into Australia at Sydney's Randwick racecourse in 1917 by George Alfred (later Sir George) Julius, the totalizator achieved slow but steady acceptance throughout Australia. It is now in operation at every horse racing, trotting and greyhound meeting, although the modern computer-based totalizator is a far cry from the 'wheels, ropes and pulleys' contrivance which the Australian Jockey Club bought for use at Randwick in 1917.

As well as win (first place only) and place (first, second or third) betting, there is a wide variety of combinations a punter can try to select. Some of the more popular combinations are quinella (first and second in the one race) and double (two winners). However, the most popular combination is the trifecta (first, second and third in the one race), mainly because of the large payouts which may exceed $10 000 for a $1 investment, the record (up to March 1983) being $348 894 for a winning trifecta at a Melbourne horse race on 26 February 1983.

Totalizator Agency Boards In all States legalised off-course betting is organised by State government controlled Totalizator Agency Boards (TABs). Introduced in the early 1960s in an effort to eradicate illegal off-course betting (better known as SP or Starting Price betting) and to channel part of the GAMBLING dollar in the form of taxes into the State coffers, the TABs have been highly successful and are now multi-million-dollar agencies. An indication of the size and extent of these agencies can be gauged by the statistics of one State TAB. The NSW TAB in the 1982-83 financial year employed 4 538 people (including casual and part time) to handle over $1220 million which was invested by punters. The TAB is obliged to distribute part of its

Torrumbarry Weir on the Murray river

Courtesy of A.I.S. Canberra

profits to racing clubs.

Towns, Robert (1794-1873) Merchant, shipowner and farmer. Born in Northumberland, England, he went to sea in his youth and between 1827 and 1842 visited Australia a number of times in command of merchant vessels. In 1833 he married a half-sister of William Charles WENTWORTH, and 10 years later settled in Sydney, where he became prominent as a merchant and shipowner and was at various times president of the Bank of New South Wales and of the Sydney Chamber of Commerce. His trading ventures extended to many parts of the Pacific, and to India and England.

In the 1860s he acquired land on the DARLING DOWNS, at MORETON BAY and in northern QLD, and in 1863 recruited a large number of KANAKAS to work on his cotton plantations near Brisbane, a step which was later copied by most sugar growers in QLD and northern NSW. About that time he became interested in the benefits to be gained by the opening of a new port in the N of QLD, and in 1865 established trading and farming ventures at Cleveland Bay, where TOWNSVILLE, now QLD's third-largest city, was named after him.

Townsville QLD (population 86 112 in 1981) The third-largest city in the State (after BRISBANE and the GOLD COAST), its rapid growth in recent years is indicated by a population increase of more than 10 000 in the five years from 1971 to 1976 and of over 7 000 in the period 1976-81. The city is located on the shore of Cleveland Bay at the mouth of Ross Creek, 1 486km by road NNW of Brisbane, on the NE coast of the State. At a latitude of 19°S, it boasts year-round tropical warmth and an average of eight hours sunshine per day. It has a high yearly rainfall of 1204mm, concentrated mainly in the

summer months, with a drier period from April to November; in the four months from December to March it receives 80 per cent of its total annual rainfall. It is an important transport centre, located on the Bruce Highway with the Flinders Highway going W into the interior; it is also a rail junction of the coastal route and a line extending SW and W to CHARTERS TOWERS, HUGHENDEN, CLONCURRY and MOUNT ISA. It is a major commercial, industrial and service centre, with a railway locomotive workshop, mineral refining plants, a meat processing plant and freezing works, a cement factory and a variety of smaller industrial enterprises. The port handles meat, sugar, timber, fertilisers, bulk oil, minerals and concentrates, and has facilities for container ships. The city is also an important educational centre with a range of schools, a College of Advanced Education (formerly the Townsville Teachers' College), the James Cook University (opened in 1970) and, at Turtle Bay, the Australian Institute of Marine Science Research. There is a major Army barracks and a RAAF base. The city skyline is dominated by Mt Cuthering, commonly called Castle Hill, which rises 285m above the city, with a scenic lookout on top which provides panoramic views of the surrounding country. MAGNETIC ISLAND, 40 minutes by launch across Cleveland Bay, is a popular tourist resort; within easy access of the city is the GREAT BARRIER REEF which can be visited by launch or viewed on an air tour. There are several national parks in the region: Bowling Green Bay National Park (55 300ha), which includes Mt Elliott, some 30km SE of the city, with rugged mountain scenery and rainforest, Mt Burrumbush with its granite outcrop, and Cape Cleveland with the granite cape, mangrove forest and salt pans; the Crystal Creek–Mt Spec National Park (7 224ha) which lies

The main street, Townsville QLD

85km NW of the city; and the national park which covers 2553ha of Magnetic Is.

Townsville began in 1864 when Robert TOWNS, a merchant and pioneer cotton grower, selected it as a suitable site for a port. A wharf, wool store and meat works were established in the early days of the settlement. It was originally called Castletown but in 1866 was renamed after its founder. The mineral discoveries of the 1870s, the railway development in subsequent decades, and the improvement of the harbour by breakwater construction and dredging all assisted in the city's growth. The National Trust (QLD) has listed more than 20 buildings for preservation including Bishops Lodge, the old institute of tropical medicine, the post office, Magnetic House, the courthouse and several hotels and banks.

trade marks and designs see patents, etc.

trade unions Australia is commonly regarded as having one of the strongest trade union movements in the world. In 1983 it had more than 300 registered unions, whose combined membership of nearly three million comprised over 55 per cent of the total workforce. In general, the organisation, methods and political affiliation of the unions have a strong resemblance to those in Britain.

Early history During the 1830s and 1840s various associations of skilled workers were formed in Australian cities. Some were temporary associations which were formed to meet particular crises; others bore more resemblance to benefit societies than to modern trade unions, collecting dues from members to pay unemployment, sickness and funeral benefits. Those which tried to secure higher wages and better working conditions were hampered by

such legislation as the Masters and Servants Acts of 1828 and 1840 in NSW, which prescribed prison sentences for the breaking of agreements by employees, the leaving of employment without notice and acts of conspiracy aimed at altering wages or hours.

The true beginning of trade unionism in Australia was in the gold-rush era. At that time unions were still confined to the skilled trades and tended to concentrate on hours and conditions, the achievement of an eight-hour day (in a six-day working week) being the main objective of many of them. This was achieved in 1853 by the Operative Stonemasons' Society in Sydney, and by a number of building unions in 1856 in Melbourne where, on 21 April 1856, the victory was celebrated by Australia's first Eight-Hour Day procession. Such annual celebrations consolidated the trade union movement by leading to the formation of a Labor Council in each colony and to the building of Trades Halls.

Small craft unions, confined mainly to the capital cities, remained common for a few decades after the gold rushes, but their struc-

ture became increasingly affected by the foundation of unions among miners and pastoral workers and of large inter-colonial unions which aimed at recruiting all workers in particular industries. The organisation of a nationwide trade union movement was fostered by inter-colonial conferences, the first of which was held in Sydney in 1879.

The 1880s and 1890s These decades were marked by stronger inter-colonial organisation, by the growth of large industrial unions, by the influence of socialist ideas, and by a series of defeats which played a part in turning unionists' attention towards political action and industrial arbitration. Discussions at inter-colonial conferences—in Melbourne (1884), Sydney (1885), Adelaide (1886), Brisbane (1888), Hobart (1889) and BALLARAT (1891)—indicated a growth of socialist opinions; there was a strengthening of the feeling that there was a basic clash of interests between labour and capital, and that the workers needed to organise themselves against employers.

Development of unionism among miners and shearers was especially important. The first mining union had been the HUNTER RIVER Coal Miners' Association (1861), followed by unions, such as the BENDIGO Miners' Union (1872), formed on the goldfields. In 1882 several miners' unions joined to form the Amalgamated Miners' Association (AMA), with W.G. Spence as secretary. In 1886 Spence left the AMA to become secretary of the newly formed Australian Shearers' Union (ASU) which began in VIC and quickly spread to NSW and SA. The significance of these two unions was that they were inter-colonial; that they were not based on the capital cities and that they aimed at being industrial, not craft, organisations which included semi-skilled and unskilled workers. The modern Miners' Federation is derived from the AMA and the Australian Workers' Union from the ASU. These miners' and shearers' organisations displayed greater militancy than earlier unions. Shearers, as seasonal itinerant workers, had been subjected to what they considered unfair practices, such as being forced to buy their rations at station stores, and the unions tried to eliminate such practices by having a standard form of contract, backed up by full union membership among shearers. The employers, in an attempt to preserve the right to bargain

Table 1

WORKING DAYS LOST ANNUALLY PER THOUSAND EMPLOYEES IN THE WORKFORCE 1975-81

Year	All causes	All causes, excluding those not involving employer/employee relationships*
1975	717	676
1976	773	344
1977	336	323
1978	434	387
1979	788	594
1980	650	592
1981	800	794

Note: * for example, inter-union or intra-union disputes, political protests, etc.
Source: *Yearbook Australia 1983*. Australian Bureau of Statistics, Canberra.

State Library of NSW

Police escorting non-union carters in Melbourne during the maritime strike, 1890

with each employee or group of employees without union 'interference', formed such associations as the Pastoralists' Union, the Employers' Union and the Chamber of Manufactures.

Although strikes became more frequent, the unions did use other means to secure their aims, such as political lobbying and, from 1874 onwards, occasionally sponsoring parliamentary candidates. By the late 1880s, however, there was a growing belief that a union-backed political party was needed. At the same time, the idea that State systems of industrial arbitration might provide protection for workers was also growing in popularity. The inter-colonial conference of 1889 passed a resolution that 'every effort should be made to obtain direct representation of Labour in Parliament' and another calling for the setting up of boards of conciliation and arbitration.

The strikes of the 1890s A major trial of strength between unions and employers was hastened by the economic depression of the 1890s, which made employers even less likely to grant concessions. When the clash came it began with an unlikely group—ships' officers. In 1889 the Melbourne branch of the Maritime Officers' Association joined other maritime unions in affiliating with the Trades Hall. Shipowners objected to this, saying it would undermine discipline, and a strike began which soon widened to include other maritime unions, coal miners, shearers and carters. However, the depression ensured that abundant 'free labour' was available, and after two months all the unionists involved had to go back to work on whatever terms they could obtain. A strike by miners in BROKEN HILL in 1892 and another by shearers in 1894 were also defeated.

These failures, accompanied by the jailing of many union leaders on charges of riotous behaviour and by the use of troops and police to protect non-union labour, provided the final

arguments in favour of political action, and produced at least a cautious acceptance of industrial arbitration. Labor Electoral Leagues began to be set up, leading to the foundation of a national Labor Party, officially entitled AUSTRALIAN LABOR PARTY (ALP) from 1918 onwards. The creation of schemes of industrial conciliation and arbitration became official Labor policy (*see* ARBITRATION, etc.).

From 1900 to 1939 The economic recovery in the early 1900s was accompanied by a renewed growth of unionism. The registration of unions with arbitration bodies, and attempts to have preference for unionists included in awards, gave workers strong incentives to join, and between 1901 and 1914 membership increased fivefold to about half a million. The foundation of the Commonwealth Court of Conciliation and Arbitration in 1904 also gave local unions a motive for federating in order to gain national awards. Nevertheless, arbitration was opposed by many militant unionists, who saw it as a form of collaboration with capitalism. Syndicalist ideas, including the replacement of craft unions by large industrial unions and the reliance on industrial rather than political action, were promoted by organisations such as the Industrial Workers of the World, the Victorian Socialist Party and the Socialist Labor Party, but failed to win majority support.

Australia's participation in World War I was supported by union leaders and the Labor Party, but the fall in real wages that occurred during the war years, charges of 'war profiteering' and the conscription controversy caused a great deal of industrial unrest. Notable strikes included those on the Melbourne waterfront and in the Broken Hill Mines in 1916, and one which began in the NSW railway workshops in 1917 and spread to other industries until it involved over 70 000 workers in NSW alone. Disillusionment with the failure of this strike led to the formation of the One Big Union

Movement, which its founders saw as the prelude to the founding of a socialist state but which failed because it lacked the support of the leaders of the established unions. The wartime wave of strikes continued into 1920 and 1921, including the 'Big Strike' in Broken Hill from May 1919 to November 1920 which resulted in revolutionary changes in health provisions in the mines. Two significant developments in the 1920s were the adoption in 1921 of a formal socialist policy of nationalisation and worker control of industries, with centralised control by a Supreme Economic Council, and the founding of the AUSTRALIAN COUNCIL OF TRADE UNIONS (ACTU) in 1927. The Depression of the 1930s opened with one of the most bitter strikes in Australian history —about 10 000 NSW miners held out for 16 months against a 20 per cent cut in award wages announced by colliery owners in February 1929. As the Depression deepened, however, the unions could do little to resist the lowering of wages. Membership fell sharply between 1929 and 1933, but recovered as economic conditions improved.

Since 1939 Although a special congress of the ACTU in 1940 passed a resolution supporting the war effort, relations between the unions and the MENZIES government were strained. After the ALP had gained office in 1941 there was closer co-operation between unions and government. Union representatives were included in government advisory bodies and in production committees in munitions factories. Although strikes still occurred, many were 'wild-cat' strikes, called by local militants, not by the union leadership.

During and after the war Communists gained office in a number of key unions, and their activities led to conflict with the CHIFLEY government and, indirectly, to a split in the ALP. In 1949 Communist-led coal miners went on strike, but the Labor governments of the Commonwealth and NSW combined to oppose them. The funds of the Miners' Federation and of other unions assisting the strikers were frozen, several union officials were jailed for contempt of the Arbitration Court, and the army was used to mine open-cut coal. At about the same time the ALP gave support to 'industrial groups' which were organised in unions to fight against Communist leadership. The activities of these groups led to a split in the ALP in 1955 (*see* POLITICAL HISTORY).

Among the trends since the 1950s have been an increase in the influence of the ACTU, the use of collective bargaining outside the arbitration system, an increased use of bans and partial stoppages as distinct from outright strikes, an increased incidence of stoppages in essential service industries, and a tendency for unions to widen their activities beyond those concerned solely with wages and working conditions. The extension of union activities has included the use of direct action on environmental and political issues (for example 'green bans' on various property development projects, imposed particularly by the NSW branch of the Builders' Labourers' Federation

Continuous coal miner and operator underground at a mine near Wollongong (*see* COAL)

Open-cut coal mine near Singleton NSW (*see* COAL)

Open-cut tin mine at Ardlethan NSW (*see* TIN)

Assembling solar heating panels at Beasley's, Adelaide (*see* MANUFACTURING)

Opal field at Coober Pedy SA where many of the dwellings are underground

Engine assembly line at General Motors/Holden, Fishermen's Bend VIC (*see* MOTOR VEHICLE INDUSTRY)

Trawling near Portland VIC (*see* FISHERIES)

Timber mill in the Northern Tablelands region NSW (*see* FORESTRY)

Road haulage units for transporting manganese ore (*see* MINING)

Iron ore mine in the Middleback Ranges (*see* IRON ORE)

Blasting at Iron Monarch mine SA

Loading iron ore at Mt Newman WA (*see* IRON ORE)

Iron ore blending plant

Teeming steel into ingot moulds

Blast furnace casting

Tapping a furnace at Whylla SA (*see* IRON AND STEEL)

Sample taking at a steelmaking furnace

Transferring molten iron to charging ladle at a steelmaking furnace

Iron stripping

Red hot skelp coiled on strip reel at the steelworks (*see* IRON AND STEEL)

Loading wire for export at Newcastle (*see* IRON AND STEEL)

and also the undertaking of various business ventures such as the ACTU's involvement in retail stores, service stations, a tourist agency, housing projects and superannuation schemes.

Unions today Although the Australian trade union movement may appear highly fragmented—there are over 300 unions—about two-thirds of all unionists belong to the 30 largest unions, and the true picture therefore is of a fairly small number of large unions and a multitude of small ones. Wide differences exist with regard to organisation and range of membership. Most of the large unions are federated, with members in at least two States. Many, such as the Amalgamated Society of Carpenters and Joiners and the Operative Painters and Decorators Union of Australia, are craft unions, while others, such as the Printing Industry Employees' Union and the Australian Glass Workers' Union, are industrial organisations. However, even in an industry covered by one of the latter type of unions, some manual workers belong to craft unions, while office workers belong to 'white collar' unions such as the Federated Clerks' Union of Australia. Others again, such as the Australian Workers' Union and the Federated Miscellaneous Workers' Union, are general unions, with members in a wide range of industries and occupations.

Organisation The variation in the size and complexity of trade unions is reflected in their structure. Nevertheless, certain general features stand out. A large federal union can be divided into four levels—the work-place, district, State and federal levels. State unions generally have the same type of structure, without the federal level, while a small local union may have only the work-place and district levels.

At the work-place level—a particular office, factory or other industrial establishment—union members elect a committee, and perhaps, in a large work-place, a 'shop steward' or union representative for each section. The committee promotes membership and attends to local issues. At the district level (or local branch, or sub-branch, level) officers are elected at an annual meeting, and general meetings are usually held monthly. If the union covers several occupations, but is not spread over a very large geographical area, sub-branches may be on an occupational, not a district, basis.

At the State level each sub-branch sends delegates to an annual conference, where State policies and submissions regarding federal policies are worked out. A smaller body, generally called a council, meets more frequently to deal with matters arising between annual conferences. An executive body, which typically consists of a president, secretary, treasurer and one or two vice-presidents, meets more frequently still. At least the president and vice-presidents will be elected, often by a postal ballot of members. In some unions the division into branches is on a regional, but not a State, basis.

At the federal level delegates from the State or regional branches form a council, which may meet only annually. It is the highest policy-making body of the union. Between its meetings an executive made up mainly of full-time salaried officials carries on the work of the union. However, there is a very great variation between unions with regard to the strength of their federal organisation. In many federal unions some of the members work under State awards, and if these form the majority, then officials of the State branches do most of the essential work. In such cases the federal organisation may be weak and the State branches practically autonomous.

There are also various forms of inter-union organisation. In some work-places there are committees with representatives of all the unions which have members there. The same arrangement sometimes applies on an industry basis at State or federal level. There may also be co-operation between State unions of similar type, as in the case of the Australian Teachers' Federation, a consultative body linking the various teachers' unions in the States. Inter-union organisations which are not confined to one industry or vocation include the Labor Councils (known in some cases as Trades and Labor Councils or Trades Hall Councils). There are more than one of these in each State, but those in the metropolitan cities are naturally the most important. On a national scale the ACTU co-ordinates the activities of unions to some extent.

Objectives In Australia, as in other democracies, the primary aims of trade unions are to improve the economic conditions of their members and to maintain their security of employment. In pursuing the first of these, Australian unions have shown little interest in organising pension schemes and other mutual benefit services, but have concentrated heavily on raising wages and on shortening the standard working week. In recent years unions have also increased their efforts to influence governments on such matters as price control and taxation, on the grounds that policies in these areas affect workers' real disposable incomes.

With regard to security of employment, Australian employees can in general be legally dismissed providing they are given a period of notice. Unions have traditionally tried to obtain legislation in favour of preference for unionists in employment. An earlier aim, that of compulsory unionism, aroused considerable public opposition, and in 1957 the ACTU dropped it from its policy, in favour of preference for unionists. A third objective, the improvement of working conditions, is still important, but less so than in the past, when such matters as poor health and safety provisions in mines were high on the lists of complaints among the unionists concerned.

Political objectives, in the sense of securing legislation favourable to unionists, have always been important, and are responsible for the fact that most unions are affiliated with the ALP. However, action on issues not specifically concerned with the economic welfare of unionists has become increasingly common. Examples are watersiders' attempts to aid Indonesian nationalists by refusing to load Dutch ships in the late 1940s, and opposition to government policy on the mining and export of uranium in recent years. An objective which has received considerable attention in some other countries—worker participation in industrial decision-making—has not been stressed in Australia.

Methods Because of the existence of both State and Commonwealth conciliation and arbitration tribunals, the basic method by which trade unions pursue their aims is through the submission of claims to these bodies. Collective bargaining with single employers or with employers' organisations is therefore not of such dominant importance as in many other countries. However, during the 1950s there was a strong tendency to practise collective bargaining in order to obtain 'over-award' payments (that is, payments over and above awards made by industrial tribunals).

The ultimate weapon in the hands of unionists is, of course, the strike. In interpreting strike statistics (*see* Table 1) one should keep in mind that strikes tend to be concentrated in certain industries. Traditionally, these have included mining, shipping, stevedoring, building, the metal industries and transport. In recent years, however, strikes by workers in publicly owned service industries, particularly postal services and power supply, and in oil refineries, have been prominent. In such strikes, while the number of workers actually on strike may be quite small, the effects in causing others to be 'stood down' and in disrupting industry generally may be great. There has also been a tendency for aggrieved workers to apply various types of work bans instead of outright strikes, or to use 'rolling strike' techniques, in which groups of workers strike for short periods only, one group at a time. Finally, it should be noted that the use of violence has been comparatively rare in Australian strikes. When it has occurred (for instance, during the great strikes of the 1890s, on the Melbourne waterfront in 1928, and during the coal miners' strike of 1929-30) it has generally arisen from the use of non-union labour in order to break the strike—a step which employers are most unlikely to take under present conditions.

Further reading: Matthews, P. & Ford, G. *Australian Trade Unions.* Sun, Melbourne, 1968; Fitzpatrick, B. *A Short History of the Australian Labor Movement.* (2nd edn) Macmillan, South Melbourne, 1969; Martin, R.M. *Trade Unions in Australia.* Penguin, Ringwood VIC, 1975.

Trafalgar VIC (population 2 109 in 1981) A small town in western GIPPSLAND, on the Princes Highway between WARRAGUL and MORWELL, 126km by road ESE of Melbourne. At an elevation of 68m above sea level, it is on the railway route through Gippsland, 120km by rail from Melbourne, and is the administrative centre for Narracan Shire; it is a minor service and business centre for a productive dairying and mixed farming region. The town was founded in the 1860s and was named after the famed naval battle at which the British fleet defeated the French off Cape Trafalgar in 1805.

transport Australia is a large, thinly populated country, far from its main trading partners and from the lands which have supplied most of its settlers, and transport has therefore been a very important factor in its economic development.

ROAD TRANSPORT
Early roads For many years, NSW's roads were little more than strips of cleared land, unpaved and badly surveyed, and it was only after 1810 that worthwhile improvements were made. Governor MACQUARIE's decision to put the construction and maintenance of main roads on a toll system was first applied to PARRAMATTA Road, and by 1822, the year after Macquarie's return to Britain, the colony had about 480km of well-paved roads. Meanwhile, road making methods in Britain were being transformed by the work of Telford and Macadam, and, mainly after Sir Thomas MITCHELL's appointment as Surveyor-General of NSW in 1827, these new methods were applied in Australia. However, the development of the pastoral industry in the 1830s and 1840s and the gold rushes of the 1850s resulted in such a rapid increase in population that the authorities were unable to extend the road system quickly enough for the increased demand, and could not even maintain the condition of existing roads. The advent of the railway made matters worse, for governments tended to give priority to railway building for inland transport, and to concentrate on low-cost roads leading to rail centres.

Better roads began to be built with the coming of the motor car and by the 1920s each State had set up a central main roads authority. During World War II defence considerations led to a great deal of construction, a notable example being the transformation of 960km of the Stuart Highway, linking the railheads of ALICE SPRINGS and LARRIMAH in the NT, from little better than a bush track to a modern fully sealed highway.

Roads today A notable feature of road development since the war has been the increased role of the Commonwealth, which has made specific grants for roads designated as 'strategic' and for others which have been seen as important on economic grounds, such as the 'beef roads' for the transport of cattle in N Australia. The Commonwealth government has also made general grants to the States for roads, and in recent years it has provided more than a third of total road building costs. (*See* Table 1).

The general pattern of administration now is for the main roads in each State (including certain city traffic arteries) to be the responsibility of a government department, such as the New South Wales Department of Main Roads, or of

A typical coach, QLD 1873. (Painting attributed to Joseph Clarke)

a statutory body, such as the Victorian Country Roads Board. Roads considered to be wholly or almost wholly of local importance are built and maintained by local government authorities. Apart from Commonwealth grants, State road authorities rely on such sources of finance as motor vehicle taxation, drivers' licence fees, loan funds and levies on local government bodies. The building of expressways (on a few of which a toll must be paid) has increased in recent years. However, they are not as extensive as in most developed nations.

Road vehicles in colonial times In the early days bullock teams—able to cover about 16km a day—provided the main means for moving heavy goods over long distances. At first the most common vehicles were two-wheeled drays, which could negotiate the rough tracks better than the four-wheeled waggons which became common later. As roads improved, faster horse-drawn carts and coaches came into more general use. The great coaching era came with the gold rushes, when the need for inland transport increased greatly. During the 1850s and 1860s coaches provided the basic passenger transport in the Australian countryside, COBB & CO. being by far the largest of the companies involved. After 1870, however, railways gradually drove coaches out of business.

A bullock team and wagon about 1900

Table 1

ROADS OPEN TO GENERAL TRAFFIC ON 30 JUNE 1981
(in kilometres)

	NSW	VIC	QLD	SA	WA†	TAS	NT	ACT†	Australia
Bitumen or concrete	70 277	63 196	47 562	20 586	32 593	7 808	5 598	1 865	249 485
Gravel or other improved surface	66 616	48 197	34 381	81 536	39 214	13 952	4 123	327	565 437
Formed or cleared only	52 280	46 682	78 938		86 914	729	11 626	42	
TOTAL	189 183	158 075	160 981	102 122	158 721	22 489	21 347	2 234	815 142

Note: * 1878 figures;† 1980 figures (later figures not available).
Source: *Yearbook Australia* 1982-83. Australian Bureau of Statistics, Canberra.

Table 2

MOTOR VEHICLES ON REGISTER ON 30 JUNE 1982*
(in thousands)

Type of vehicle	NSW	VIC	QLD	SA	WA	TAS	NT	ACT	Australia
Motor cars and station wagons	2 114.6	1 731.2	997.7	579.2	555.6	190.0	32.4	93.1	6 293.8
Utilities, panel vans, trucks and buses	538.1	366.3	343.4	128.9	197.4	50.8	22.0	14.5	1 661.4
Motor cycles	131.4	74.3	98.4	36.6	36.1	5.8	3.8	4.4	390.8
TOTAL	2 784.1	2 171.8	1 439.5	744.4	789.1	246.6	58.2	112.0	8 346.0

Note: excluding tractors, plant and equipment, caravans and trailers.
Source: *Motor Vehicle Registrations Australia* (October 1983) Australian Bureau of Statistics, Canberra.

Motor vehicles During the 1890s quite a few cars were imported and a number of enthusiasts built their own machines. The first motor vehicle to run in Australia was probably that of Charles Highland, of Annandale, Sydney, who in 1894 fitted a Daimler engine onto a three-wheeled carriage. The first entirely Australian-made car was probably that built by two Victorians, Tarrant and Lewis, in 1899. Because Australian-made vehicles were more expensive than imported models, most of the cars were English or American. By 1917 there were about 45 000 motor vehicles in Australia (nine for every thousand of the population). Since then Australia has become one of the most car-conscious nations in the world, as one would expect in view of its generally high standard of living, the great distances between its towns and cities, and the fact that so many of its people live in the sprawling suburbs of very large cities.

In freight transport, Australia's comparative lack of canals and navigable rivers, and the difficulty of servicing the scattered population fully by rail, has brought about greater dependence on motor vehicles. Not only have they largely taken over local delivery, but since the 1940s, they have provided strong competition for the railways even in long distance transport, except for bulk cargoes such as wheat and minerals.

The number of various types of motor vehicles in June 1982 is shown in Table 2. The total number represents more than one motor vehicle for every two people in the Australian population.

Motor vehicle manufacture A motor car manufacturing industry began shortly after World War I, when body building companies, notably Holden's Motorbody Builders, of Adelaide, began to flourish. From the mid-1920s onwards overseas companies began to set up assembly plants in Australia, with the three American giants, Ford, General Motors and Chrysler between them dominating the field. In 1931 General Motors Australia Pty Ltd merged with the Holden organisation to form General Motors-Holden's Ltd. The lack of a complete motor building industry was felt severely during World War II when enormous numbers of motor vehicles had to be imported for war purposes. After the war the Commonwealth government invited the motor industry to submit proposals for making complete motor vehicles in Australia, the first company to respond being General Motors-Holden's, which began the manufacture of its Holden car in January 1949 (at the rate of 10 a day). Other overseas companies, including Ford, Chrysler, the British Motor Corporation (later Leyland) and Volkswagen, responded by increasing the

Cable trams were once widely used in Melbourne and Sydney

Public Transport Commission NSW

local content of their Australian-assembled vehicles, until most motor cars and many other vehicles sold in Australia consisted mainly of Australian-made components.

Up to the mid-1960s, the Australian car industry was generally regarded as being very successful. Then Japanese cars began to enter the market in considerable numbers, some being fully imported but an increasing proportion being locally assembled and containing some Australian components. It soon appeared that the number of local assemblers and manufacturers was too large for the market. Volkswagen and Leyland ceased the local manufacture of cars and Chrysler's profitability declined, while Japanese firms, most notably Nissan and Toyota, increased their activities and share of the market. In 1983 General Motors-Holden's and Ford were still the two largest manufacturers, but the Japanese Mitsubishi Corporation and Mitsubishi Motors Corporation had purchased Chrysler Australia. Local manufacturing survived only with the benefit of tariffs and import quotas.

Tram, trolley-bus and bus services From 1879 steam trams were used in a number of Australian cities, but after 1898 were gradually replaced by electric trams, these becoming the chief form of public transport in city streets for many years. Cable trams were also used in Sydney and Melbourne, while some cities made a limited use of electric trolley-buses. Neither of these types of vehicles is in use in Australia today. Motor buses have replaced electric trams in all cities except for several lines in Melbourne and one in Adelaide. Government bus services operate in all State capitals and a number of provincial cities. In such cities private bus services generally operate only as 'feeder services' taking passengers to railway stations or government bus routes.

RAILWAYS

History Construction of the first railway line, from Sydney to Parramatta Junction, began in 1850, but progress was slow and the first line to open was that from Melbourne to Port Melbourne in 1854. These lines, and a number of others, were begun by companies, but because it was very difficult to make railways show a profit in a country as sparsely populated as Australia the colonial governments soon took over nearly all the lines. The governments realised that railways would open up the new country, and so Australia's railway systems increased rapidly, from 40km in 1860 to 5888km in 1880, to 20 792km in 1900, and to 43 198km in 1954. The most recently constructed lines are the Eastern Suburbs (mainly underground) line in Sydney, opened in 1979, and the Melbourne underground, which became fully operational in 1984.

Unfortunately, a major engineering blunder was made in the early years. The first line in NSW was planned for standard gauge of 4 feet 8½ inches (1435mm), but subsequently the company concerned engaged an Irish engineer who persuaded the company to change to 5 feet 3 inches (1600mm). VIC and SA also

The Melbourne Express (Sydney-Albury) about 1900

Public Transport Commission NSW

adopted that gauge. The Irishman, however, was replaced by a Scot who insisted on changing back to standard gauge, which exasperated the S colonies; they had already ordered rolling stock for 5 feet 3 inch rails, and continued with that gauge. The confusion worsened when a cheaper 3 feet 6 inches (1067mm) gauge was adopted in QLD, WA, TAS and the N part of SA. When the Commonwealth government built the Trans-Australian line, linking the WA and SA lines, it made it of standard gauge. As a result, a traveller from Brisbane to Perth encountered five breaks of gauge. In comparatively recent years the gauge situation has been greatly improved. There are still three gauges in use, but extra standard gauge lines have been built from Brisbane to the NSW border, from PORT AUGUSTA, Adelaide and BROKEN HILL to PORT PIRIE, from ALBURY to Melbourne, from KALGOORLIE to Perth, and from the trans-continental line to ALICE SPRINGS. Thus all mainland State capitals are now connected to the standard gauge network.

Role of the Commonwealth government The Commonwealth government entered the field of railway ownership when it took over the administration of the NT from SA in 1911, thus acquiring the Darwin-PINE CREEK line. This was later extended to Birdum but during World War II Larrimah became the effective railhead. Other lines acquired or built by the Commonwealth were the Port Augusta-OODNADATTA line (acquired from SA, later extended to Alice Springs but replaced in 1980 by a new Tarcoola-Alice Springs line), the Trans-Australian line (from Kalgoorlie to Port Augusta, later extended to Port Pirie), the Port Augusta-WHYALLA line, and the ACT line (from QUEANBEYAN to Canberra). A further development of great importance took place on 1 July 1975, when Commonwealth and State legislation was passed to transfer the Tasmanian Government Railways (which now have no passenger services) and the non-

A train on the Indian Pacific route, Sydney to Perth

metropolitan lines of South Australian Railways to the control of the Commonwealth. The Australian National Railways Commission was set up to control the transferred systems and those of the former Commonwealth Railways.

Non-government railways These include many short lines operating in mines, industrial estates and harbour precincts. More important, however, are company lines which take iron ore from inland mines to ports. Although the total length of these is very short compared to that of government lines, they transport a greater weight of freight.

SHIPPING

The importance of steamships For many years after 1788 one of the great barriers to the rapid settlement of Australia was the arduousness of the slow passage by sailing ship required to reach it. This changed with the coming of steamships, which lessened the horrors of the voyage and so attracted migrants and brought Australia's primary exports much closer, in terms of sailing time, to their markets. The first steamship to reach Australia was the *Sophia Jane*, a 260-tonne paddle-steamer which arrived in PORT JACKSON in 1831. Like all streamships of the time, she relied on sails as well as steam. In the same year the first Australian-built steamer, the *William the Fourth*, began a service from Sydney to NEWCASTLE, and during the 1830s a number of steam ferries came into service in Sydney Harbour. In 1852 the P & O Co. began the first regular steam mail service from England with the vessels *Chusan* and *Australia*. In the same year the sailing clipper *Marco Polo* sailed from Liverpool to Melbourne in 68 days—a week faster than either the *Chusan* or *Australia*. It was not until the 1870s, when their engines became more reliable, that steamships began seriously to challenge sailing ships on the England-Australia run.

In the coastal trade steamships were an important factor in developing some districts, such as the NORTH COAST of NSW. However the linking of the coastal towns to Sydney by rail has eliminated most of their coastal sea trade. Today steamships are used mainly to move bulky cargoes, such as iron ore, from YAMPI SOUND and Whyalla.

Inland transport For some time steamships played a fairly important part in inland transport. Paddle-steamers began operating on the MURRAY and DARLING Rivers in 1853, not long after the SA government had offered £2000 each to the owners of the first two steamships to navigate the Murray from GOOLWA to the junction with the Darling. In 1853 two vessels succeeded in doing this. One, the 20-tonne *Mary Ann*, was not large enough to qualify for one of the prizes. Built at MANNUM, it ascended the Murray as far as Moama (on the NSW bank opposite ECHUCA). The other was the 70-tonne *Lady Augusta*, which sailed from Sydney, over the sand bar at the mouth of the Murray, and up the river to SWAN HILL. Until the advent of the railways, paddle-steamers were widely used to carry various cargoes, particularly wool, and towns such as Echuca and WILCANNIA (normally the limits of navigation on the Murray and the Darling respectively) became busy ports.

Ferry services For many years ferries were an important form of transport in all the present State capitals except Adelaide—the only one not on a navigable river or estuary. They are still of moderate importance in Sydney, but play a negligible role elsewhere. In Sydney, ferries propelled by sails and oars began operating from 1789, and steam ferries from 1831. The opening of the Harbour Bridge in 1932, the development of other forms of public transport, and the popularity of private motor cars affected ferry traffic adversely, and the two main companies operating them, Sydney Ferries Ltd. and the Port Jackson and Manly Steamship Co., were taken over by the NSW government in 1951 and 1974 respectively. Today ferries on Sydney Harbour still carry about 16 million passengers a year, but this is only about 9% the number of bus passengers and 7% the number of train passengers in the metropolitan area.

Melbourne had a service from Sandridge (Port Melbourne) to Williamstown from 1840 to 1914, and for some years there was also a daily service to Geelong. In Brisbane ferries were essential for crossing from one bank of the river to the other until the first bridge was built in 1865, and in 1846 the steamer *Experiment* began a Brisbane-IPSWICH service. In WA ferries were the main form of transport from Perth to Fremantle in the very early colonial period, and in 1854 the first steam ferry, the *Pioneer*, appeared on the Swan River. In Hobart a service from the city to Kangaroo Point (modern Bellerive) began in 1816, and the first steamship, the *Surprise* arrived in 1832. The importance of ferries was greatly reduced after the opening of a pontoon bridge across the Derwent in 1942.

Shipping today In 1980-81 Australia's most important PORTS, measured by the deadweight tonnage of shipping entering, were, in order, DAMPIER, Melbourne, PORT HEDLAND, Sydney, FREMANTLE, Newcastle, Brisbane, Hay Point and Port Walcott. The list reflects the importance of mineral exports; two of the first three ports named are engaged almost entirely in exporting iron ore, and for three of the others minerals form the bulk of the cargo handled.

Control of shipping The Commonwealth has power to legislate with regard to trade and commerce with other countries and between the States. This includes navigation and shipping. This power is exercised mainly through the Navigation Act, which provides a wide-ranging set of controls over ships and their crews, passengers and cargoes. The Commonwealth government has also established the Australian Shipping Commission (originally Australian Coastal Shipping Commission) to maintain, establish and operate interstate, overseas and territorial shipping services. It operates the Australian National Line fleet, which in 1983 numbered 33 vessels, and also operates specialised terminals at a number of ports. The Australian Shipbuilding Board, another Commonwealth body, gives the Minister advice regarding that industry. Government assistance to the industry is decided in the light of recommendations from this Board and of inquiries by the INDUSTRIES ASSISTANCE COMMISSION (formerly the Tariff Board).

AVIATION

History Because of the long distances between the main centres of population in Australia, and between Australia and other countries, aviation has played a very important part in the country's history. The work of Lawrence HARGRAVE on the study of wing structure led to his attempt to fly in 1894 when he was lifted to a height of about 5m by four box kites fixed together. The first powered flight in Australia was made in 1910 by J.R. Duigan of VIC in a machine which he had built himself, and in which by the end of that year he was covering distances up to about 200m. In 1912 W.E. Hart, in an imported Bristol machine, flew from PENRITH to Parramatta and then on to Sydney, attaining a height of about 2000m at one stage, and in 1914 a French pilot in a Bleriot machine flew from Melbourne to Sydney in two days.

Meanwhile, a start had been made with military aviation. In 1911 the Commonwealth government had advertised for 'two competent mechanists and aviators'. The successful applicants arrived from England in 1913, and in the following August the Point Cook flying school received its first four student pilots. Early in World War I many Australians became pilots in the Royal Flying Corps, and in 1916 the government formed the Australian Flying Corps, which by 1918 had four squadrons engaged in the front line and four more training in England.

The foundations of civil aviation At the end of the war, with vastly improved planes and many experienced pilots available, the prospects for commercial aviation seemed favourable, but obstacles still existed in the form of lack of airfields, navigational aids and fuelling facilities. Public interest in aviation received great impetus when, in March 1919, Prime Minister HUGHES announced his government's offer of a prize of £10 000 for the first successful flight from England to Australia. The prize was won by Ross and Keith SMITH, and in December 1920 the government gave further encouragement to the development of aviation by the passing of an Air Navigation Act, which provided for such matters as the registration, inspection and licensing of aircraft and the examining and licensing of pilots and mechanics. The government's action in subsidising air mail services was also influential, and during the 1920s a number of aviation companies were founded. These included QANTAS (QLD and NT Air Services), which began flying in 1921 and in its first year of flying carried 1 100 passengers, so impressing the civil aviation authorities that it was given a contract to carry passengers and

Courtesy of A.I.S. Canberra

John Duigan's first Australian built powered aeroplane, 1910

mail between CHARLEVILLE and CLONCURRY. In later years it built up many other services within QLD, and in 1934, in partnership with Imperial Airways, founded Qantas Empire Airways, which in the following year began flying the Australia-Singapore section of a regular service between England and Australia.

In 1930, Australian National Airways, founded by Charles KINGSFORD SMITH and C.T.P. Ulm, began Sydney-Brisbane and Melbourne-Sydney services. In the following year it opened a Melbourne-Hobart service, but soon afterwards had to suspend all scheduled services because of the economic depression.

During the 1920s and 1930s the growth of commercial aviation throughout the world was aided by the making of record-breaking flights by a number of Australians, including the Smith brothers, Sir Charles KINGSFORD-SMITH and Bert HINKLER. Another event of great importance was the 1934 MacRobertson Air Race from England to Australia, held to celebrate the centenary of the founding of Melbourne and won by two English pilots.

Further developments By the late 1930s the main Australian airline was the second Australian National Airways (ANA), founded by Victor and Ivan Holyman. It greatly increased domestic aviation by importing the Douglas DC2 in 1936 and the DC3 in 1937; these aircraft were far in advance of any previously used. Since World War II, air travel in Australia, as elsewhere, has really boomed. In the year 1945-46 the number of passengers carried on internal routes was 522 157; by the early 1980s the figure was over 11 million. The post-war period also saw the entry of the Commonwealth government into the field of airline ownership. In 1945 the CHIFLEY administration introduced legislation to nationalise airlines, only to have it declared unconstitutional by the High Court. The government thereupon set up the Australian National Airlines Commission, which launched Trans-Australia Airlines (TAA) in 1946. At first TAA was assisted by being given the carriage of air mail wherever possible, but the Liberal/Country Party government which replaced Labor in 1949 varied this arrangement so that ANA gained a share of this revenue. In 1957 ANA was purchased by the ANSETT organisation, which combined it with its own smaller airline.

Meanwhile in 1947 the shares in Qantas Empire Airways held by British Overseas Airways Corporation (the successor to Imperial Airways) passed to the Commonwealth government. Later in the same year the Commonwealth purchased the remaining Qantas shares, thus becoming the sole owner. Thus by 1957 the present pattern had been set, with Australia's one overseas airline being government-owned, and with most domestic passenger traffic shared between one government-owned and one large independent airline.

Internal services Control of air transport is exercised by the Commonwealth Department of Aviation. With regard to interstate services, successive governments since 1952 have followed a 'two airlines policy', as a result of which the majority of scheduled services with passenger and all-freight aircraft are provided by Ansett Airlines and TAA. The basis of the policy is to ensure that these two airlines maintain fleets of comparable size and quality, with both providing equal capacities on all principal routes. Ansett Airlines and TAA also fly non-competitive interstate routes while several smaller airlines operate mainly within certain States. These include Skywest

(WA) and East-West Airlines (NSW)—control of which passed to Skywest in 1983. Others are subsidiaries of Ansett Airlines. There are many regular flights by charter firms with small single and twin-engined aircraft on routes which are not flown by the major carriers. These are officially classified as commuter services, not airline services. Other general aviation activities, including charter work and private flying, have increased rapidly; the total hours flown in general aviation is about five times as great as the total hours flown by airline aircraft.

International air services Australia has air service agreements or arrangements with approximately 30 countries, by which Qantas is granted rights to operate services from Australia to and through the countries in question, and designated airlines of these countries are granted traffic rights in Australia. In the early, 1980s passenger movements into and out of Australia were about two million a year each way, nearly half being in Qantas aircraft.

Airports and facilities There are about 450 airports and airfields throughout Australia, about a fifth being owned by the Commonwealth government and the others by local authorities or private interests. Over 400 navigational aids are in service and over 140 airports and airfields are equipped with nightlanding facilities.

Further reading: Brogden, S. *The History of Australian Aviation.* Hawthorn Press, Melbourne, 1960; Williams, P.J. & Serle, R. *Ships in Australian Waters.* Angus & Robertson, Sydney, 1968; Testro, R. *A Pictorial History of Australian Railways.* Lansdowne, Melbourne, 1971; Stubbs, P. *The Australian Motor Industry: A Study in Protection and Growth.* Cheshire, Melbourne, 1972; Colwell, M. *Ships and Seafarers in Australian Waters.* Lansdowne, Melbourne, 1973; Smith, P.A. *Romance of Australian Railways.* Rigby, Adelaide, 1976.

Traralgon VIC (population 18 059 in 1981) A city in GIPPSLAND, it is located S of the LATROBE RIVER on the Princes Highway 164km by road ESE of Melbourne, 15km NE of MORWELL and 48km W of SALE. It is a commercial and service centre for the productive dairying lands of the mid-valley, but has been influenced by, and grown with, the development of the vast brown-coal deposits of the region. It has also shared in the industrial expansion based on mining and power generation, and has a number of light industries. It is the terminus of the electrified railway line from Melbourne (a rail journey of 158km) and is a rail junction of a loop route NE through Heyfield and of the route through Sale into E Gippsland. The area was settled in the 1840s and the name Traralgon, coming from an Aboriginal word meaning 'river of little fishes', was given to the shire in 1879. It became a borough, separated from the shire, in 1961, and was proclaimed a city in 1964.

tree ferns *see* Pteridophyta

tree tomato *see* Solanaceae

treecreepers Belonging to the Climacteridae, an Australian and New Guinea family of PASSERINE BIRDS, these birds are probably unrelated to treecreepers of other parts of the world despite their similar behaviour. There are seven endemic species in Australia, all belonging to the genus *Climacteris*. They climb spirally up a trunk of a tree in small hops, pausing occasionally to probe for insects, and then fly down to another tree to repeat the process; they also feed on the ground or on fallen tree trunks. Treecreepers are usually brown or greyish with, in some cases, a streaked belly. A paler patch is visible on the wing when they fly. Representatives occur in most parts of Australia other than TAS. The white-browed treecreeper, *C. affinis**, for example, is fairly common in MULGA and MALLEE, and in patches of woodland, in coastal areas of E Australia from southern QLD to VIC, and the black treecreeper, *C. melanota**, lives in forests and woodland in CAPE YORK. The habitats of the various species vary from mulga to rainforest.

tree-hoppers *see* bugs

trematodes *see* flukes

trepang *see* sea cucumbers

trevallies *see* fishes, bony

Trichoptera *see* caddis flies

trigger plants These herbs belong to the genus *Stylidium* (family Stylidaceae), which is represented in Australia and other countries; there are about 110 endemic species in Australia. The leaves are grass-like and the pink, white or red flowers occur in racemes or panicles. When the base of the curved style is touched by an insect it springs up across the flower, showering the insect with pollen; then it slowly bends down again below the petals, and the process is repeated until the flower is fertilised.

trillers *see* cuckoo-shrikes, etc.

trilobites These are among the commonest of FOSSILS in Australia and overseas. They form a subphylum, the Trilobitomorpha, of the phylum Arthropoda (ARTHROPODS). They were abundant during the Cambrian and Ordovician periods and disappeared at the end of the Palaeozoic era. Over 3 900 separate species are known in the world and at least 450 species from Cambrian rocks alone have been found in Australia.

Trilobites had flattened, more or less oval bodies. The cuticle of the upper surface was far thicker than that of the lower surface which carried the appendages; consequently most fossils consist only of the upperparts. Most species were from 3cm to 10cm long but a few were smaller than 1mm and some were 60cm or more long. The body consisted of three

Female white-browed treecreeper, *Climacteris affinis*

R.W. Fidler (N.P.I.A.W.)

parts: head region (cephalon), thorax and pygidium. Each of these was divided into three regions (lobes)—hence the name—by two longitudinal furrows. On each side of the upper lip (labrum), the head carried an antenna. The head also bore a pair of compound eyes. The segments behind the head carried biramous limbs.

Most trilobites lived on the bottom of the sea where they crawled over sand and mud but some were burrowers, and a few could swim. The smallest species formed part of the PLANKTON. The larval stages of some trilobites are known as fossils. The relationship of the trilobites with the other arthropods is a matter of argument but many zoologists believe them to be closely related to the CRUSTACEANS.

tritons *see* gastropods

tropic birds *see* sea birds

trotting This is a popular horse racing sport throughout Australia. At trotting meetings, usually held at night, horses driven by drivers in lightweight sulkies race against each other and a night's racing programme most often consists of one trotting event and seven or eight pacing events. Trotting is a natural gait for a horse, with diagonally opposite legs moving simultaneously. Pacing on the other hand is an unnatural gait, with legs on the same side of the horse's body moving simultaneously. A horse has to be taught to pace and to do this he is hobbled—legs on the same side of the body are loosely strapped together and the horse wears these hobbles when he races. The skill in training both trotters and pacers is to train the horse to go as fast as possible without 'breaking'—that is, without breaking into a gallop. Pacing races predominate in Australia with the preparation of pacers for racing being less difficult than the preparation of trotters.

History The beginnings of trotting in Australia are similar to the sport's beginnings in other parts of the world. Owners were proud of their horses' ability to trot and would display this ability in improvised races, sometimes upsetting the normal flow of traffic and alarming pedestrians by racing along major roads. From these picnic race beginnings trotting became increasingly popular and with the appearance of specially designed light gig outfits in the early 1900s, the sport began in earnest. Night trotting was introduced in some States in the early 1900s (WA 1914, SA 1920), but the Gaming and Betting Laws in force at that time forbad betting after sunset and, as the laying of wagers was such a large part of the sport, it was not until the repeal of such laws (after World War II in most States) that night trotting began to flourish. From that time on the sport experienced an enormous boost with much larger attendances and increased financial turnover. Two events in the 1960s and 1970s further enhanced trotting's position as a sporting attraction. The first of these was the advent of government-controlled off-course betting throughout Australia during the 1960s through the TOTALIZATOR Agency Board (TAB). This enabled fans to bet legally on trotting events without attending the race track. As part of the TAB profits are channelled back into trotting, clubs have been able to provide improved facilities for spectators and increase prize-money. The second event was the introduction in 1977 of the trifecta, a form of betting in which the punter has to correctly select the first, second and third place-getters in order. As the odds against selecting first, second and third in order are quite large, this form of betting has resulted in some huge dividends.

Inter-Dominion Trotting also has a large following in New Zealand and there is a constant flow of horses and drivers between Australia and New Zealand. The Inter-Dominion

*Species, genus or family is endemic to Australia (see Preface)

NSW Dept of Tourism

Race meeting at Muswellbrook

championship is the most important annual event of the trotting calendar and is held in turn in the Australian States and in New Zealand. It involves a number of heats and a final, the elimination of horses being decided according to a system of points awarded for placings in the heats.

Tracks The major tracks in Australia are Harold Park NSW (named in 1929 in honour of Childe Harold, a famous sire); Moonee Valley VIC; Globe Derby Park SA; Gloucester Park WA; and Albion Park QLD. The national body for trotting is the Australian Trotting Council, formed in 1973 to establish uniform rules, handicapping systems and to decide on feature events.

Drivers and horses The most successful driver up until 1983 was Kevin Newman who in April 1977 drove his 1000th winner and who has won the Harold Park drivers' premiership a record nine times. Although not as successful as Newman in terms of winners, Perc Hall enjoyed a lengthy and popular career as a driver, retiring at the end of the 1976-77 season at the age of 65, having driven more than 500 winners. In the late 1970s and early 1980s outstanding horses have included Pure Steel, Paleface Adios and Hondo Grattan. Hondo Grattan, winner of many races at Harold Park, was twice judged as NSW Harness Horse of the Year, and was the first horse to win two successive Inter-Dominion championships. Paleface Adios moved into the limelight on the retirement of his arch rival, Hondo Grattan. He won an average of one race in every two starts and became the first three-year-old in Australia or New Zealand to break the two-minute mile. Towards the end of the 1970s another pacer, Pure Steel, began amassing record stake winnings and in

1979 became the first Australian pacer to have won more than $500 000.

trout *see* fishes, freshwater

trout, native *see* fishes, freshwater

truffles *see* fungi

Truganini (1803-76) Tasmanian Aboriginal. The daughter of Mungana, a leading member of the BRUNY ISLAND tribe, she helped George ROBINSON to gather the remaining Tasmanian Aborigines between 1830 and 1835, so that they could be placed under government protection. When Robinson went to PORT PHILLIP in 1838 as Chief Protector of Aborigines, she accompanied him, but later rejoined the survivors among the groups gathered by him in Tasmania. They had been sent to FLINDERS ISLAND, but in 1856 were moved to Oyster Bay, on the west coast of Tasmania. By 1873 all but she had died, making her the last known full-blooded member of her race. She spent the few remaining years of her life in Hobart. Her skeleton was kept for many years in the Hobart Museum, but in 1976 it was cremated and the ashes spread over the waters of the D'ENTRECASTEAUX CHANNEL, not far from her birthplace.

Trumper, Victor Thomas (1877-1915) Cricketer. Born in Sydney, Trumper learned to bat on Moore Park, a spacious recreational area then on the outskirts of the city. A stylish and outstanding batsman, he came to be so highly regarded throughout the cricketing world that on his premature death from Bright's disease during World War I the

English newspaper billboards forgot the war to announce 'Death of a Great Cricketer'. Variously described as lifting batsmanship 'from prose into poetry', as satisfying 'the ultimate criterion of style—minimum of effort, maximum of effect', and possessed of 'unsurpassed brilliance', Trumper was to go down in cricketing history not so much for what he scored but for how he scored. His first century against England, in 1899, was labelled a 'classic and unfinished cricketing symphony of 135 runs'. Trumper played for Australia from 1899 to 1912, and although many batsmen since have bettered his top Test score of 214, bettered his Test average of 39.06 and scored more Test centuries than his eight, he is regarded as one of the finest batsmen the world has known.

trypanosomes *see* protozoons

tuan *see* native cats, etc.

tubeworms *see* annelids

Tucker, Albert (1914-) Artist. Born in Melbourne, Tucker was a self-taught painter who believed that training killed vitality and spontaneity. His early work showed a close affinity to German Expressionism, with its hard contrasts, sharp colours and loose paint work. A strong social comment on what he saw as the moral degradation of city life increasingly pervaded his work; his *Images of Modern Evil* turned familiar Melbourne scenes into surreal nightmares of disgust and despair. This vision alienated him from many, and in 1947 he went to Japan and eventually to Europe and the USA. In Europe his painting took on a more abstract form and tended to depict the loneliness of explorers, the Outback and bushrangers. In 1960, Tucker returned to Australia, where he found an increasing enthusiasm for his paintings and a greater acceptance of his vision.

Tuckwell, Barry (1931-) Musician. Born in Melbourne, Tuckwell studied at the NSW Conservatorium of Music before taking up appointments as horn player in both the Sydney and Melbourne Symphony Orchestras. He later played with the Scottish National Orchestra and the Bournemouth Symphony Orchestra before joining the London Symphony Orchestra, with which he worked from 1955 to 1968. Since then he has become famous as a horn soloist and virtuoso, but is also well known for his work as a chamber musician and conductor and has made numerous recordings. He lives in London.

Tuggerah Lakes NSW A series of three inter-connected lakes, the Tuggerah Lakes are on the central coast, approximately midway between Sydney and NEWCASTLE. The individual lakes are, from S to N, Tuggerah, Budgewoi and Munmorah, stretching N-S over a distance of some 35km. The lakes are really a series of lagoons formed by the accumulation of sand barriers, deposited along the seashore as sand bars and dunes, which have

NSW Dept of Tourism

The Entrance, Tuggerah Lakes

blocked the estuaries of former coastal streams. A narrow channel through the sand dunes at The ENTRANCE links the lakes with the sea. The area is a popular tourist resort and many Sydney residents have holiday cottages in the lakeside towns such as BUDGEWOI, Toukley, Long Jetty, The Entrance and Gorokan, or at the coastal centres such as Toowoon Bay, Soldiers Beach and Norahville. The main commercial centre of the district is WYONG. A large thermal power station for electricity generation, forming part of the State's inter-connected power system, is located near Munmorah Lake and utilises water from the lake for cooling the generating equipment.

tulips *see* Liliaceae

tulipwood A timber tree of coastal northern NSW and QLD, tulipwood, *Harpulia pendula* (family Sapindaceae) is often grown as a street tree, especially in QLD. The flowers are in-conspicuous but the fruit is bright orange and splits to reveal two black seeds.

Tully QLD (population 2 728 in 1981) A small town in the far N coastal region of the State, on the Bruce Highway, 1 587km by road NNW of Brisbane (highway routes), 96km N of INGHAM, and 52km S of INNISFAIL. Situated at the foot of Mt Tyson (674m), in the plains of the TULLY RIVER valley, the town lays claim to being the wettest place in Australia, with an average rainfall of 4 267mm; though rain occurs in all months of the year, the summer season is the period of greatest concentration. The town is a service and commercial centre for a productive rural hinterland where sugar cane dominates the economy; the district also produces bananas, timber and beef cattle. The Hull River

National Park, located SE of Tully, covers 1 080ha of typical coastal plains country, including some stretches of rain forest with fan palms.

Tully River QLD A perennial stream in the NE of the State, rising in the Cardwell Range, SW of INNISFAIL, it flows for over 110km to an estuary on Rockingham Bay, SE of TULLY town. The basin is in a region of high rainfall (annual average over the catchment area is 2500mm), concentrated mainly in the summer months. Tully Falls, 30m high, where the river descends from the uplands into Kareeya Gorge, were once among the most spectacular in Australia, but water has now been diverted above the falls for hydro-electric power generation. Koombooloomba Dam on the headwaters provides the storage for the power scheme, which is QLD's largest hydro-electricity generation site. The dam was completed in 1961 and in 1965 it was enlarged to a capacity of 201 000ML with a 52m-high wall.

Tumut NSW (population of the town 5 816 in 1981; of the shire 11 399). A town in the S western slopes region of the State, on the Snowy Mts Highway, it is 459km by road SW of Sydney. At an elevation of 274m above sea level, it is situated on the Tumut River, a tributary of the MURRUMBIDGEE RIVER. It is a rail centre on a branch line off the main S route from COOTAMUNDRA through GUNDA-GAI, a distance of 531km from Sydney, in the midst of picturesque rural countryside of sheep and cattle properties, dairy farms, orchards, lucerne flats and pine forests. It is an important timber milling town, with several sawmills and a pine-board factory; broom millet is grown in the area and there is a broom factory; also, there is a fruit cannery and a marble factory where visitors can see local marble being cut and polished. The town experiences warm summers and cold frosty winters; it has an average rainfall of 895mm, with the highest falls in the cooler months and lower amounts in summer. The name Tumut comes from an Aboriginal word meaning 'a camping place by the river'. The rivers of the district are well known for trout fishing and there is a trout hatchery 16km S. Upstream from Tumut are two of the major storage dams of the SNOWY MOUNTAINS SCHEME (Blowering and Talbingo Reservoirs) and two

NSW Dept of Tourism

Beef cattle grazing in the Tumut district

power stations (Tumut 1 and Tumut 3), one being 365m below ground level. The lakes formed by the dams are popular summer attractions for fishing, sailing and other aquatic sports. Several buildings in the town have been listed by the National Trust (NSW) for preservation, including All Saints Anglican Church (built 1875-82), St Mary's Catholic Church (1877), the Oriental Hotel (c 1876), CBC Bank (1889) and Rural Bank (1891).

tuna *see* fisheries; fishes, bony

Tuncurry NSW (combined population of Tuncurry and FORSTER 9 260 in 1981). A coastal holiday resort near Forster on the mid-NORTH COAST of the State, it is 333km by road NNE of Sydney, lying E of the Pacific Highway and SSE of TAREE. Tuncurry and Forster are located on opposite sides of the entrance to Wallis Lake, the former on the N headland, the latter on the S. Fishing, oyster farming, boat building and dairying are the main local industries. The area is a popular vacation resort which provides the visitor with opportunities for swimming, surfing, boating and other aquatic sports.

Tungatinah TAS A dam and power station on the Nive River, a tributary of the DERWENT RIVER, it is located in the CENTRAL PLATEAU region of the State, some 120km NW of Hobart. It is the largest of the hydro-electricity generation stations of the Derwent system, with an installed capacity of 125 MW, and receives its water from three adjoining catchments on the plateau between the GREAT LAKE and LAKE ST CLAIR: the principal catchment is drained by the Nive River; the others are the Clarence River (to the W) and LAKE ECHO (to the E) which have been diverted to augment supplies to Tungatinah. Lake Echo provides the main storage for the scheme.

tunnies *see* fishes, bony

turban shells *see* gastropods

turkey, brush *see* mound birds

turkey, plain *see* bustard

Turner, Charles Thomas Biass (1862-1944) Cricketer. Born at BATHURST in NSW, Turner's failure to make the cricket team of his local school did not deter him from practising bowling after dispatching the early morning coaches for COBB & CO. for whom he worked on leaving school. Turner, later nick-named 'the Terror', first encountered English cricketers in 1881 when he played for a local Bathurst side against an England eleven; he captured 17 wickets for 69 runs including all 10 for 36 in the second innings. Relying on accuracy and change of pace, in 1887-88 he became the first and only bowler to amass 100 wickets in an Australian season. In the 1888 tour of England Turner captured 314 of the 663 wickets to fall to the Australians for an

Tumut 3 power station and pressure lines

average of 11, including 9 for 15, 8 for 13 and 9 for 37. In 17 Test matches against England he took 101 wickets for an average of 16, including five or more wickets in an innings 11 times. A courageous and tireless mainstay of the Australian attack of the time, he was the first of the great medium-pacers, and one of the best bowlers of all time on a helpful wicket.

Turner, Ethyl Sibyl (Mrs H.R. Curlewis) (1872-1958) Author. Born in England, she was brought to Australia as a girl and grew up in Sydney. Her writings include short stories and about 30 novels, written for and about girls. Although some of her work has been criticised for indulging in excessive sentimentality or melodrama, in general she gives a credible picture of children's behaviour, and many consider some of her novels to be the best of their kind written in Australia. The first of them, *Seven Little Australians* (1894), has been the most widely read and is said to have sold over a million copies.

turnstone *see* waders

Turon River NSW One of the headwater tributaries of the MACQUARIE RIVER, it rises W of the GREAT DIVIDING RANGE near the town of Portland, and flows generally NW to the inland drainage system, joining the Macquarie 80km NW of BATHURST. It flows through mixed farming country which is dissected and hilly and which reaches over 900m above sea level in the upper sections of the basin. The area has historic connections with the early settlement of Australia for it was the centre of a major gold-mining boom following Edward HARGRAVES' discovery near Bathurst in 1851.

Thousands of diggers flocked to the Turon Valley fields, especially Sofala and HILL END. The boom was short-lived, although profitable for some, and the mining settlements became ghost towns. In recent years, Hill End has been declared an official historic site; many of the buildings have been restored and it is a popular tourist attraction.

turpentine *see* forestry; Myrtaceae

turtles *see* tortoises, etc.

tusk shells This is the common name given to a small class (Scaphopoda) of MOLLUSCS in which the shell is shaped like an elephant's tusk or trumpet and is open at both ends. There are about 200 burrowing, marine species in the world with a few in Australian waters. Most species live in fairly deep water. Scaphopods feed on microscopic organisms from the sea water or the sand in which they burrow, carried in by water currents. There are no gills and oxygen is absorbed through the large mantle surface. The head is rudimentary but is furnished with a radula. The elephant tusk shell, *Dentalium elephantium* (about 7.5cm long) has been found near Darwin. Some smaller species are found in S waters.

Tweed River NSW The Tweed, 80km long, occupies the most northerly and one of the smallest valleys on the NORTH COAST of the State. It has been described as 'an Eden to delight any eye', for packed within the compact valley, bathed by copious rain and abundant sub-tropical sunshine, there are rugged and densely forested ranges, timber mills dotted through the hills, banana plantations on the steep slopes, productive sugar cane farms, lush green dairy pastures, vegetable plots and groves of pineapple plants; along the coast, there are fishing fleets and inviting stretches of surf and sand. The upper reaches of the river consist of three main streams, called 'arms'; the N and middle arms rise in the McPHERSON RANGE which forms part of the State border between NSW and QLD; the S arm has its source in the Nightcap Range which forms part of the valley watershed to the SW. The main town in the mid-valley is MURWILLUM-BAH. Tweed Heads, at the river mouth, is a seaside resort centre which, with COOLAN-GATTA (across the river in the adjoining State), forms part of the city of the GOLD COAST. The Tweed Shire at the 1981 census had a population of 40 058, which indicates the density of rural settlement in the lower valley. Rainfall is high throughout the region; at Condong sugar mill, downstream from Murwillumbah, the average annual rainfall is 1 722mm, with the period January to March receiving the highest rainfall. Floods are experienced in times of heavy rainfall and these inundate the low-lying farmlands and the river towns. The Pacific Highway traverses the valley in a 'V'-shaped route from the SE to Murwillumbah, thence in a NE direction following the general trend of the river to the coast. A branch railway off the main N line (from CASINO through LISMORE and BYRON BAY) terminates at Murwillumbah.

A dominant landscape feature, visible from most parts of the valley, is the jagged peak of Mt Warning (1157m above sea level), located 16km SW of Murwillumbah. It is a volcanic plug, the remnant of a large volcano of the geological past. This peak was sighted and named by James COOK on his voyage along the E coast in 1770. The Mt Warning National Park covers an area of 2138ha around the peak and includes stretches of lush sub-tropical rainforest on the lower slopes forming a canopy which almost completely excludes the sunlight;

Old buildings at Boydtown NSW

in this dense vegetation, bushwalkers are advised to keep to the formed tracks as it is easy, even for experienced bushmen, to become lost; on the higher slopes of the park the rainforest is more open and mosses, ferns and orchids are common. Lyrebirds, brush turkeys, wallabies, white possums and gliders inhabit the park. The coastal zone of the valley is a popular tourist region, with good surfing beaches and opportunities for swimming, fishing and other water sports. Murwillumbah is the venue for the Banana Festival which each year attracts many visitors.

Twofold Bay NSW On the S coast, some 490km by road from Sydney, this bay consists of several curved beaches between rocky headlands, with the town of EDEN on its N section.

In the 1840s, the bay was the site of a visionary enterprise, undertaken by Benjamin BOYD, aimed at establishing Boydtown as a major port-city. The venture was unsuccessful and today the only remnants of it are a tower (which was planned as a lighthouse to guide ships into the port and which has been listed by the National Trust for preservation as part of the nation's cultural heritage), a church now in ruins, and the Sea Horse Inn (built in 1843, once the rendezvous of whalers, now a tourist hotel). Much of the area of this ghost town is now included in the Ben Boyd National Park. The bay was once the centre of a major whaling industry; fishing is still an important activity. In 1968, a woodchip mill was established on a S headland of the bay, amid much publicity and considerable resistance from conservationists, to process logs from nearby forests for export to Japan.

two-up This game, which is illegal except in certain licensed casinos, originated from pitch-and-toss. Two pennies are placed on a small wooden bat, called a kip, and then tossed in the air with a flick of the wrist to set the pennies spinning. The person tossing is called the spinner and he tries to spin the pennies so that they both fall heads up. Others participating in the game, the players, wager that he will fail and that the pennies will fall tails up. If the pennies fall showing one head and one tail, the toss is called a no-throw and the pennies are spun again. The players form a circle and place their bets in front of them. If the spinner 'head 'em'—that is, the pennies fall heads up—he collects these bets. If they fall tails up, the spinner pays the players. This is the game at its simplest, but when it is played in large 'schools' there are frequently side wagers between players on how many heads or tails will be thrown in succession and on other possible combinations.

Barges carrying sugar cane to the Codong Mill in the Tweed valley NSW

Popular among servicemen, two-up experienced two peaks of popularity following the two world wars when it was often played by returned servicemen at re-union gatherings. Although the popularity of the game has decreased, due in part to the ready availability of other, legal, forms of gambling, two-up still enjoys a resurgence each year on 25 April (Anzac Day). On this day, following the ceremonial march and the traditional re-union at the local hotel or club, returned servicemen frequently gather to play two-up.

U

Ulladulla NSW (population 6 016 in 1981). A holiday resort and fishing port on the S coast, 9m above sea level, it is located on the Princes Highway 229km by road S of Sydney. It is the operating centre of a fishing fleet which provides fresh fish to the Sydney market. Dairying and timber-cutting are important in the district. The town has an average annual rainfall of 1266mm, June being the month of highest rainfall. Several of the coastal areas nearby, such as Mollymook, Lake Conjola and Lake Burrill, have developed as retirement and tourist centres. The town's name comes from the Aboriginal word meaning 'a safe harbour'. The lighthouse on the coast, built in 1889, has been listed by the National Trust (NSW) for preservation.

Ulverston TAS (population 9 413 in 1981). Located in the N central coastal region of the State at the mouth of the Lever River, Ulverston is 21km W of DEVONPORT and 18km E of BURNIE on the Bass Highway. It is a commercial and service centre for a productive rural region noted for potatoes, vegetables, cereals, dairying, beef cattle and fodder crops. In recent years industrial development has advanced in the town with the accent on timber industries and frozen and canned vegetable production. It is a popular holiday and tourist resort, with extensive beaches and good fishing nearby, and is increasingly becoming a retirement centre. The town has placed considerable emphasis on the development of tourism and attracts many summer visitors; it is also a convenient starting point for tours along the FORTH RIVER and into the CRADLE MOUNTAIN-LAKE ST CLAIR National Park.

Umbelliferae This is a large family (sometimes called the parsley family) of dicotyledonous flowering plants with about 125 genera and 2 900 species; although these species are cosmpolitan, they are most abundant in the temperate regions of the N hemisphere.

Members of the Umbelliferae are herbs (usually aromatic) or shrubs. In most species the leaves are compound and alternately arranged or, often, basal. In herbaceous species the leaf stalk (petiole) is often expanded into a sheathing base but basal leaf appendages (stipules) are usually absent. The flowers are usually bisexual and regular and in most species are arranged in single or compound flat-topped clusters (umbels), often subtended by whorls of bracts. There are five small sepals (though these are sometimes absent), and five petals, often bent inwards; the five stamens alternate with the petals. The inferior ovary contains two cavities (locules), each with one ovule. The two styles are free and swollen at the base into a nectar secreting disc. The fruits are schizocarps (that is, they split when mature into carpels); the carpels usually have longitudinal ridges and linear oil channels (vittae).

This family contains a number of economically important food plants, as well as some poisonous members, including hemlock, *Conium maculatum*. Roots are eaten of carrots, *Daucus carota*, and parsnip, *Pastinaca sativa*, leaves and stems of celery, *Apium dulce*, angelica, *Angelica archangelica*, parsley, *Petroselinum crispum*, and fennel, *Foeniculum vulgare*, and seeds used for flavouring include caraway, *Carum carvi*, coriander, *Coriandrum sativum*, and dill, *Peucedanum graveolens*.

The family is well represented in Australia by both herbaceous and woody species, as well as by introduced WEEDS. Pennyworts (*Hydrocotyle* species) form a dense creeping cover in many woodlands and forests, whilst the sea parsley, *Apium prostratum*, is common near brackish water, and *Trachymene* species occur either in heaths or in highland grasslands. Native and introduced species of *Eryngium* have rigid, prickly bracts; some are cultivated as ornamental plants. The most striking native herbaceous Umbelliferae is the flannel flower, *Actinotus helianthi*, though a number of less conspicuous species of *Actinotus* occur in coastal heaths or highland peat soils. Amongst the shrubby native species are a number of species of *Platysace* including a dainty, spreading, white-flowered shrub, *P. linearifolia*, which is worthy of cultivation, and *Xanthosia* species which are inconspicuous components of heath and open forest.

See also Angiospermae; Appendix 5, Flower Structure and Glossary of Botanical Terms
Further reading: see Appendix 6, A Bibliography for Plants.

umbrella tree A rainforest tree, *Schefflera (Brassaia) actinophylla* (family Araliaceae), of northern NSW and QLD, the umbrella tree is often grown as an ornamental in temperate areas; it can also be grown successfully as an indoor plant. The divided leaves are large and palmate, and have long leaf stalks arranged on the stem like the ribs of an umbrella. The leaflets are large and leathery. The red flowers, which attract nectar-loving birds, are borne on long stalks. Umbrella trees often have several stems and sometimes begin life as epiphytes (growing on other plants).

United Australia Party *see* political history

Uniting Church in Australia Suggestions for union between Congregationalists, Methodists and Presbyterians in Australia have a history dating back to the early years of this century but little progress was made until the 1950s, when a Joint Commission on Church Union was appointed. Its report was issued in 1964 and after considerable discussion and revision was presented for consideration by the three Churches in 1971. Approval was given for this 'Basis of Union' by the Assembly of the Congregational Church of Australia in 1974, and by the General Conference of the METHODIST CHURCH of Australasia and the General Assembly of the PRESBYTERIAN CHURCH of Australia in the following year. Even at this stage there was some opposition, especially among sections of the Presbyterian Church. However, legal challenges in the Supreme Court of NSW and the High Court of Australia proved unsuccessful and the Uniting Church in Australia was inaugurated in June 1977. Some Congregational and a considerable number of Presbyterian congregations elected not to join it, but all Methodist churches, under their national constitution, were bound by the decision of their General Conference.

Under the terms of the 'Basis of Union', the Uniting Church recognised and accepted as ministers 'all who have held such office in any of the uniting Churches, and who, being in good standing in any of those Churches at the time of union, adhere to the Basis of Union'. Under similar conditions it accepted as elders or leaders those holding the office of elder, deacon or leader in any of the three Churches. It is governed by a system of interrelated councils, all of which include lay people, namely: councils of the various congregations; Parish Councils, each governing a group of congregations recognised as a parish (although a large congregation may be recognised as a parish on its own); Presbyteries or councils having oversight of all parishes within a district or region; Synods, operating at regional or State level; and an Assembly which is responsible for the Church's belief and worship and for its life and mission at the national level, and maintains programmes through its Council of Mission, Council of Christian Education, Council for Ministerial Education and other councils, committees and work groups.

In the 1981 census, 712 000 people, or 4.9 per cent of the population, were identified as belonging to the Uniting Church. However, in view of the fact that 490 000 people were still identified as Methodist or Wesleyan, it seems that many members of the Uniting Church,

---

Courtesy of A.I.S. Canberra

Ranger uranium mine, Jabiru NT

either nominal or active, have continued to use the names of the separate uniting Churches for purposes of census identification.

Further reading: Pearson, K. *Understanding the Uniting Church in Australia.* Joint Board of Christian Education, Melbourne, 1977.

universities: *see* Appendix 4, Higher Educational Institutions; education

Upfield, Arthur William (1888-1964) Author. Born in England, he came to Australia in 1911, landing in Adelaide but subsequently adopting a wandering life and working in a variety of bush occupations. He wrote more than 30 detective novels, which were internationally successful, achieving their best sales in the USA. They were unusual in that their plots were set in the Australian bush and most of them—beginning with *Bareekee* (1929)—featured Detective-Inspector Napoleon Bonaparte ('Bony'), a half-caste Aboriginal noted for his unconventional methods.

Uralla NSW (population 2 090 in 1981) A small township in the NEW ENGLAND region of the State, 555km by rail and 544km by road NW of Sydney, some 20km SW of ARMIDALE and 93km NE of TAMWORTH. It is situated on the New England Highway, and on the tablelands rail route, at an elevation of 1 017m above sea level. It receives an average annual rainfall of 808mm, spread throughout all months of the year, but with a spring and summer concentration; January is the wettest month, with an average of 105mm. The town is a small service and business centre for a productive grazing and orcharding region, noted for fine wool production. European settlement of the Uralla district started in the early 1830s; one of the oldest grazing properties in New England, 'Gostwyck', located 11km SE of Uralla, bears the name of an early settler, Edward Gostwyck Cory. Just S of the town, beside the highway, is 'Thunderbolt's Rock', claimed as the lookout site and hiding place of the famed 'gentleman' bushranger Thunderbolt (Frederick Ward); he was shot nearby in 1870 by a police constable and was buried in Uralla cemetery. Several buildings in the town have been listed by the National Trust (NSW), including the Courthouse, Post Offfice (built in 1885), Masonic Hall (1884), Literary Institute (1886), flour mill (1870) and Oddfellows hall (1888).

uranium First discovered in the oxide form in 1789 by a German chemist, elemental uranium was not isolated until some 50 years later. Its radioactive properties were noted by Becquerel in 1896. The main ores of uranium are pitchblende, uraninite, carnotite, autunite and torbernite. The first mining of uranium was concerned with the production of radium; however, after 1946 weapons and power generation became important when the limited potential life of fossil fuels was realised, and now most uranium is used for weapons, propulsion and power stations. It is also used for research in industry and medicine and in the chemical, glass and ceramic industries, and small quantities of depleted uranium are used in specialised non-energy applications.

Production World production of uranium in 1980 was 44 078 tonnes of which Australia produced 1 561 tonnes, making it the eighth-largest producer. The total output, until 1980, was from the MARY KATHLEEN mine in QLD. In 1980 the treatment plant at NABARLEK mine site in the NT commenced production, adding significantly to Australia's total output. In the early 1980s, several other uranium mining ven-

tures were in various stages of development (including the Ranger, Jabiluka and Koongarra sites in the NT, the Yeelirrie, Lake Way and Manyingee sites in WA, and Olympic Dam in central SA).

The industry In its early stages, the structure of the uranium mining industry in Australia was very simple — there was only one mine, at Mary Kathleen, with an operational treatment plant. However, developments in the 1970s changed that simple pattern and the matter of uranium mining became a subject of considerable controversy, involving both political and environmental considerations, as well as land rights negotiations, where prospective mining sites were located on traditional Aboriginal lands.

Following the reports of the Ranger Uranium Environmental Inquiry, the government decided in 1977 that further mining and export of uranium should proceed on a carefully regulated and controlled basis. Strategically, a supply of uranium is important for national security purposes and for future energy requirements. Australia has a significant percentage of the world's proven low-cost uranium reserves and currently consumes only a small quantity of the annual production.

See Table 2 Page 421.

Urunga NSW (population 2 045 in 1981) A small town and seaside resort on the NORTH COAST, at the mouth of the Bellinger River, 563km by road NNE of Sydney, about 20km N of NAMBUCCA HEADS and 30km S of COFFS HARBOUR. At an elevation of 6m above sea level, it is on the coastal railway route, 581km by rail from Sydney. Formerly a timber-milling town, Urunga is now a popular tourist resort which experiences a summertime influx of visitors. The town name comes from an Aboriginal word meaning 'long white beach'.

John Fairfax & Sons Ltd

Jorn (Joern) Utzon

Utzon, Jørn (Joern) (1918–) Danish architect, designer of the SYDNEY OPERA HOUSE. Born in Copenhagen, he graduated from the Copenhagen Royal Academy of Fine Arts, winning the gold medal for architecture. During the following years he worked as an architect in Denmark, and travelled extensively in many countries of Europe, as well as USA and Mexico. He won the competition organised by the NSW State Government in 1955 for the design of a cultural centre, which became known as the Opera House, at Bennelong Point, Sydney. He was awarded the first prize of $10,000 in this world-wide competition and was given a contract to supervise the construction. Utzon's innovative design received much international acclaim, including the Gold Medal of the Royal Australian Institute of Architects; however, almost from the beginning of the project in 1959, there were problems, particularly about the sail-like structure of the roof. Utzon clashed with some local people and with a few politicians; construction costs rose rapidly, the problems increased, and the clashes intensified, and finally in 1966 he resigned. He was replaced by a panel of local architects and, on their advice, modifications were made to the design, and construction was completed in 1973. Utzon subsequently became a professor of architecture at the University of Hawaii, and now lives in Spain. His latest completed project is the Parliament House Complex at Kuwait.

V

van Diemen, Anthony (1593-1645) Dutch colonial administrator. He first came to the Dutch East Indies as a soldier, and in 1616 landed from the *Mauritius*, on which Willem JANSZ was officer in charge of the cargo on the coast of WA. In later years he rose rapidly in the service of the East India Co., and was Governor-General of the Indies from 1636 to 1645. He became interested in clearing up the mystery of the fabled Great South Land and was responsible for sending Abel TASMAN on two important voyages (*see* DISCOVERY). Tasman gave the name Van Diemen's Land to the part of TAS which he discovered, this title being later applied to the British colony there and retained officially until 1855. After van Diemen's death a despatch from Holland expressed disapproval of the expenditure of so much money on voyages which had brought the company no profit. Not surprisingly therefore, later Governors-General did not continue van Diemen's policy of exploration.

Van Diemen Gulf NT Located in the NW of the Territory, between the mainland and MELVILLE ISLAND, with COBOURG PENINSULA along its N fringe, it was discovered and named by the Dutch explorer Abel TASMAN in 1644. Dundas Strait at the NW of the Gulf and Clarence Strait at the SW separate the mainland from Melville Is. The East and South ALLIGATOR RIVERS and the Mary River drain into the gulf with swampy crocodile-infested estuaries along the mangrove-fringed S coast.

Van Diemen's Land The Dutch explorer Abel TASMAN gave this name to the section of TAS which he discovered in 1642, in honour of Anthony VAN DIEMEN, Governor of the Netherlands East Indies. The name was not officially changed to TAS until the granting of responsible government in 1855.

van Praagh, Dame Margaret 'Peggy' (1910-) Ballet dancer, teacher, Artistic Director. Born in London where she enjoyed considerable success as a Principal Dancer, Ballet Mistress and Assistant Artistic Director, Dame Peggy was to become the founding and longest-serving Artistic Director of The Australian Ballet. After studying ballet and modern dance in London she became Principal Dancer of Tudor's London Ballet in 1938, a position she held until 1940 when she joined Sadler's Wells (later the Royal) Ballet. With Sadler's Wells she first showed artistic potential, rising to the position of Ballet Mistress and later to that of Assistant Artistic Director for the period 1952-55. Her first major visit to Australia was in 1960 when she toured as Artistic Director of the Borovansky Ballet. She returned in 1962 to take up the position of founding Artistic Director of The Australian Ballet, a position she was to hold until 1974 (jointly with Sir Robert HELPMANN, 1965-74) when she was forced to retire due to ill health following a third hip operation. With characteristic determination she surmounted her physical difficulties to return for a one-year period as Artistic Director in 1978. In addition to her creative talents, Dame Peggy was noted for her ability to shrewdly compromise between satisfying the wishes of the traditionally conservative Australian ballet audiences and deepening and expending the creative base of a young and vigorous ballet company through the performance of innovative and experimental ballets.

Vassilieff, Danila (1899-1957) Artist. Born in Russia, he served with the White Russian armies and later worked on railway construction work in NT. He had some art training in Rio de Janiero and did itinerant painting in the West Indies and Europe. He returned to Australia in 1937 and with Josl BERGNER became a strong influence upon the Melbourne modern painters. His enthusiasm for child art was carried into his work, and the resultant direct images in his lively style were important in forming the Expressionist attitudes among the young painters of Melbourne's 'angry decade', the 1940s. Vassilieff began carving in stone in 1951.

veal *see* beef cattle industry

vegetables *see* agriculture; Chenopodiaceae; Compositae; Euphorbiaceae; Gramineae; Papilionaceae; Solanaceae; Umbelliferae

vegetation The vegetation of Australia shows a general correlation with the major climatic zones of the continent. In the N, summer rainfall predominates, in the S, winter rainfall. Rainfall is more reliable and more evenly distributed throughout the year on the E coast and a marked gradient in reliability and amount received occurs from the high rainfall areas of the S, E and N coastal regions to the arid interior and W coast. The general pattern of vegetation reflecting climatic changes is locally modified by changes in topography, geology, drainage and soils.

Several attempts have been made to classify Australian plant communities, and many of the names used, such as 'rainforest', 'heath' and 'wet sclerophyll forest', have gained considerable public acceptance and understanding. No classification of something so variable as vegetation can ever be entirely satisfactory, but the most recent and satisfactory classification to be devised (as part of the 1967-72 International Biological Programme) has reduced the host of possible parameters to be used to two. Table 1 is based on these two parameters (zonations). Vegetation consists of growing plants — the natural vegetation, parks, gardens, agricultural land and waste ground, but only natural vegetation is considered here. Families are given for species only when those families are described elsewhere in this encyclopedia.

It is obvious to everyone that both the types and groupings of plants vary from place to place. Individual assemblages of plants growing naturally together, in balance with one another, the ENVIRONMENT and their FAUNA, are generally termed plant communities; communities may not always be made up of the same plant species at different places, but they retain a common element in terms of their structure. A plant community of dense short shrubs is obviously different from one of lofty trees, and each type is easily recognisable. Although short shrubby communities may consist of a single layer (stratum) of plants this is not usually true of taller communities, where it may be possible to recognise many strata—tall tree, short tree, tall or short shrub and ground cover—though only a selection of these strata is present in any one community. Because the tallest stratum is in the best position to catch the sun (to use in photosynthesis) and is the most obvious, it has been called the 'dominant' stratum, and upon its life form (tree, shrub, herb) and its average height and cover the primary structural forms of Australian vegetation can be defined. The apparently arbitrary subdivisions into height classes shown in Table 1 represent some fairly well-defined aggregations of height classes. The same is true of the projective foliage cover, where the percentage of cover is measured as a two-dimensional projection of the crowns of the upper-storey over a flat land surface.

Table 1

STRUCTURAL FORMS OF VEGETATION IN AUSTRALIA

Life form and height of tallest stratum*	Projective foilage cover of tallest stratum*			
	Dense (70–100%)	Mid dense (30–70%)	Sparse (10–30%)	Very sparse† (<10%)
Trees†† 30m	Tall closed forest*	Tall open forest	Tall woodland§	Tall open woodland§
Trees†† 10–30m	Closed forest*	Open forest	Woodland	Open woodland§
Trees†† 5–10m	Low closed forest*	Low open forest	Low woodland	Low open woodland
Shrubs†† 2–8m	Closed scrub	Open scrub	Tall shrubland	Tall open shrubland
Shrubs†† 0–2m	Closed heath	Open heath	Low shrubland	Low open shrubland§
Hummock grasses 0–2m	—	—	Hummock grassland	Open hummock grassland§
Herbs (incl. moss, ferns, hemicryptophytes, geophytes, therophytes, hydrophytes, helophytes)	Closed herbland ¶	Herbland ¶	Open herbland ¶	—
	Closed tussock grassland	Tussock grassland	Open tussock grassland	—
	Closed grassland	Grassland	Open grassland	—
	Closed herbfield	Herbfield	Open herbfield	—
	Closed sedgeland	Sedgeland	Open sedgeland	—
	Closed fernland	Fernland	Open fernland§	—
	Closed mossland	Mossland	Open mossland§	—

Note: * isolated trees (emergents) may project from the canopy of some communities (Richards, Tansley, and Watt, *Imp. for Inst. Pap.* no 19, 1939, 6) — in some closed forests, emergent *Araucaria, Acacia,* or *Eucalyptus* species may be so frequent that the resultant structural form may be classified better as an open forest; † some ecologists prefer to ignore scattered trees and shrubs, equivalent to emergents in a predominantly grassland, heath, or shrubland formation; †† a tree is defined as a woody plant more than 5m tall, usually with a single stem, and a shrub is a woody plant less than 8m tall, frequently with many stems arising at or near the base (slightly modified from Beadle and Costin *Proc. Linn. Soc. N.S.W.* 77, 1952, 61); § these formations are rare in Australia; ¶ appropriate names for the community will depend on the nature of the dominant herb.

Mountain ash, *Eucalyptus regnans*

Mangroves, *Avicennia marina*, lining a tidal estuary

Some terms, such as 'rainforest' and 'mallee', are conspicuously absent from Table 1; other familiar ones, such as 'woodland' and 'forest', are strictly redefined as belonging to particular cover/height categories and not used in the looser sense of much plant geography literature.

Within each plant formation defined on a structural basis many alliances can be recognised, using specific dominant plant names, or adding other community characteristics to the names. For example, woodland can be described as grassy, shrubby or layered depending on the type of plants or strata of plants present in the under-storey. Vegetation descriptions are here confined to the major plant formations shown in Table 1.

Closed forest Table 1 shows three divisions: tall closed forest, low closed forest and closed forest. Closed forest corresponds with that commonly called rainforest, but on strict structural definition many mangrove communities might also be so defined (these are, however, considered under 'Vegetation of extreme habitats' *below*). All closed forests possess dense canopies in the upper stratum, so that little light penetrates to the lower strata. The upper stratum varies from 5m to 40m, sometimes with a few taller trees. Closed forests are found in well-watered areas along the E coast from CAPE YORK to TAS.

Communities with a smaller range of species and often less structurally complex are found in coastal regions of the NT where rainfall, though high, is markedly seasonal.

Two distinct species assemblages divide the closed forests of Australia into two: those of the N have a strong floristic affinity (*see* FLORA) with the Malaysian Region, whilst those of the S have affinities with New Zealand and South America. The two assemblages overlap in distribution, in that the northern closed forest extends from Cape York to WILSON'S PROMONTORY, becoming poorer in species and restricted to an increasingly smaller range of elevation from N to S; in the S it is restricted to sites at or near sea level on

Wilson's Promontory. The southern closed forest is developed only in TAS, from sea level to the tree-line, but throughout E Australia and New Guinea it replaces the northern closed forest at the latter's upper altitudinal limit.

Closed forests are all self-perpetuating: that is, they contain at any one time a wide distribution of girth and age classes, from seedlings to saplings, to poles, mature and over-mature trees. Long-established closed forests, however, show a preponderance of the larger size classes, as the mature to over-mature portions of the individual tree's life is disproportionately long in comparison to the pre-mature stages.

1. Northern closed forest. Characteristic of tropical areas, these forest alliances possess an evergreen upper stratum varying in height from 15m to 40m, from which taller (emergent) evergreen or semi-deciduous trees may arise. The tree species making up one acre (0.4ha) of northern closed forest may belong to many families and may number up to 100. Most trees possess large leaves (over 45cm^2). Leaves are always present; plank buttresses, vascular epiphytes and palms (family PALMAE) are characteristic. Northern closed forests of sub-tropical to warm temperate alliances, as well as having fewer species in the southern regions, have generally shorter trees than tropical forests. Leaves are smaller and though palms and lianas are usually present, emergents, vascular epiphytes and plank buttresses are increasingly rare.

2. Southern closed forest. In contrast to the extreme diversity of the flora of the northern closed forests, southern closed forests are usually dominated in the upper stratum by a single species, generally of *Nothofagus* (*see* BEECH, SOUTHERN). Occasionally species of *Podocarpus* (family GYMNOSPERMAE), *Dacrydium* (family Gymnospermae), *Athrotaxis* or *Atherosperma* may also be present. Robust lianas, palms and plank buttresses are never present, but the under-storey is generally dominated by a layer of ground and tree ferns (phylum PTERIDOPHYTA). Epiphytic mosses (phylum BRYOPHYTA), liverworts (phylum HEPATOPHYTA) and LICHENS are extremely well represented.

Open forest Australian open forests are usually dominated by evergreen *Eucalyptus* trees (family MYRTACEAE) with a foliage cover of between 30 and 70 per cent. Trees are usually of forest form with clean, straight trunks and with crowns occupying less than a half of the total tree height. Open forests are found in the higher rainfall areas of both the tropical and temperate regions, and very considerably in both height and complexity.

1. Tall open forest. This community was formerly called 'wet sclerophyll' forest. Exceptionally tall *Eucalyptus* trees, often over 60m in height, are characteristic in the wetter parts of VIC, TAS, NSW and QLD. Slightly shorter forests occur in the SW corner of WA. Much light penetrates the canopy which, owing to the dropping nature of the

Eucalyptus leaves, usually has a projective canopy cover nearer to 30 than to 70 per cent. A dense under-storey of small trees or tall shrubs is thus able to develop; tree ferns are often prominent in the under-storey and grasses (family GRAMINEAE), ground ferns and herbs often develop as a dense ground cover. Forest fires are damaging to eucalypts, but where fires are rare they can regenerate successfully, and produce forests of trees of similar age and girth.

2. Open forest. Within the open forest community a number of under-storey types may develop. The first, an assemblage of small hard-leafed shrubs (up to 2m tall) is common on the very infertile soils S of the Tropic of Capricorn. The second, on more fertile soils S of the Tropic of Capricorn, is dominated by herbs—mainly grasses, sedges (family CYPERACEAE) and broad-leafed herbs. Intermediate soils may exhibit an intermingling of these two extremes. To the N of the Tropic of Capricorn open forests generally have a distinctly layered under-storey, with a distinct stratum of short trees and tall shrubs, and a ground stratum of tropical grasses and herbs, often over 1m in height. Open forests are subject to frequent fires but because the eucalypts in these communities are better able to regenerate, such forests may contain a very wide range of girths the larger sizes having many healed scars and other signs of past fires.

3. Low open forest. These communities are found in areas less favourable to open forests; they are similar in terms of structure and species, but have a lower overall height (5m to 10m). Because of drought, waterlogging or lower sub-alpine temperatures, such sites generally provide a shorter growing season. In other sites different dominant species may occur, such as snow gum, *E. pauciflora*, in sub-alpine VIC and NSW.

Woodland Australian woodlands are usually dominated by evergreen *Eucalyptus* trees, or occasionally by *Callitris* (family CUPRESSACEAE), *Casuarina* (family CASUARINACEAE), *Melaleuca* (family Myrtraceae) or *Acacia* trees (family MIMOSACEAE). The trees are usually of woodland form, with short heavily branched boles and with the crown depth exceeding half the total tree height. This community is the most familiar of all Australian plant communities, occurring in a broad arc on the drier inland side of the open forest areas from the KIMBERLEYS, across the NT, on the inland side of the GREAT DIVIDING RANGE in QLD, NSW and VIC, in small areas in SA and on the E coast of TAS. The height, form and density of trees varies within this range, taller, denser forest form trees occurring on moister sites and shorter, sparser woodland form trees occupying the driest sites. Tree species can withstand frequent fires, and the range of girth sizes in any one stand may be very wide, though considerably broken up in frequency of occurrence, reflecting past fire history.

Open woodland Occurring at the driest limit of grassy woodlands or on deep sandy soils in the higher rainfall areas of E Australia, these

communities are characterised by scattered low trees (under 10m) which grow in clumps or singly. The under-stories consist of hummock grasses (*Triodia* species) in QLD and the NT, or of tussock grasses (such as *Lomandra* and *Danthonia* species) in the rain shadow of the MOUNT LOFTY RANGES in SA, or of dense small hard-leafed shrubs in E Australia.

Closed scrub This community is dominated by shrubs (2m to 8m tall) with a very dense canopy. Although not widespread in Australia, closed shrubs often form an important part of coastal dune and swamp complexes, with species of *Melaleuca* and *Leptospermum* (family Myrtaceae) as the dominant stratum. Owing to the heavy canopy cover, very few plants are able to develop in the under-storey, though members of the family Cyperaceae are often present as scattered tussocks.

Open scrub This is a very important community over wide areas of southern Australia within the 250mm-500mm annual rainfall zone. Open scrub is dominated by multi-stemmed shrubs (2m to 8m tall) with a projective foliage cover of between 30 and 70 per cent; these shrubs are characterised by the formation of large woody underground structures (lignotubers) from which several stems arise. The mallee eucalypts fall into this category; many are characteristic of calcareous or sandy infertile soils. Frequent fires occur in these communities, but recovery from dormant buds on the lignotuber rapidly restores the mature characteristics of the community. A number of subdivisions can be made on the basis of the dominant under-storey type.

In grassy open scrub tussocks of species such as *Danthonia* and *Stipa* (family Graminaea) dominate the under-storey. This community merges with grassy woodland and is characteristic of soils with heavy calcareous subsoils. On deep sandy soils towards the drier limits of open scrubs *Triodia* grass hummocks become common in the under-storey. Open scrubs with a dense under-storey of small hard-leafed shrubs merge with shrubby woodland at the wetter limits of the community. The community is common on calcareous soils developed on former coastal dunes. On sandy soils underlain by heavy clays the shrubby under-storey is much more sparse. Towards the drier limits of the open scrub semi-succulent shrubs become important in, and eventually dominate, the under-storey.

Tall shrubland This community is dominated by multi-stemmed sparse (10 to 30 per cent cover) shrubs (2m to 8m tall), and occurs in the semi-arid regions of Australia, with an annual rainfall often less than 250mm. Mulga, *Acacia aneura*, is the most extensive shrub making up the upper-storey, but species of *Cassia* (family Caesalpinaceae), *Eremophila* (family Myoporaceae) and *Acacia* may dominate tall shrublands on rocky hillsides in semi-arid Australia. A low shrub under-storey may be present, either of small hard or semi-succulent leafed shrubs.

Tall open shrubland Very open stands of mulga may fit within this category, and in N

Australia the pindan, *Acacia holosericea*, which occurs S of the Kimberleys, is a good example. In southern Australia the mallee heath, chiefly on sandy soils, with scattered mallee eucalypts and a dense under-storey of small hard-leafed shrubs, is the most familiar example.

Low shrubland This community is dominated by shrubs from the CHENOPODIACEAE, with semi-succulent, often hairy leaves. Plants are generally separated from one another by a distance equal to or greater than the diameter of the shrubs. After rain these open spaces are occupied by a wealth of ephemerals, particularly COMPOSITAE, Gramineae and PAPILIONACEAE. This community covers a large area of the arid zone of southern Australia, such as the NULLARBOR PLAIN, where trees are absent or rare. More frequently it is interspersed by communities of low woodland or tall shrubland. The chenopodiaceous shrubs form a valuable fodder reserve for sheep in times of drought, though extensive areas have been destroyed by over-grazing. Salt marshes found near tidal inlets and around central Australian salt plains are also covered with low shrubland.

Closed and open heath These communities consist of evergreen small hard-leafed shrubs (0.2m to 2m tall). Spacing of shrubs varies from dense to mid-dense to sparse at the drier limits of the heath community. Annual herbs and grasses are rare, though members of the Cyperaceae and RESTIONACEAE may be common. Many dicotyledonous families are co-dominant, including Casuarinaceae, PROTEACEAE, Papilionaceae, Mimosaceae, Myrtaceae and EPACRIDACEAE. Fires are frequent, but the vegetation rapidly returns to its former appearance through recovery from lignotubers, rhizomes or seeds.

Heath communities are confined to very infertile soils in the higher rainfall regions of the E and S parts of Australia, and often merge into open forests, woodlands and shrublands as an under-storey. The effective growing season of this community is restricted by both severe waterlogging and drought. The heath community occurs in two distinct areas: sub-alpine and coastal. Coastal heaths occur along the sandy coastal plains from Cape York to TAS to the SW of WA. Sub-alpine heaths are found on peaty soils accumulated in wide valleys of high elevation in NSW, VIC and TAS.

Closed grassland This community is dominated by members of the Gramineae, either of tussock-like, rhizomatous or densely spaced individual grass plants. Herbs are often abundant. Such communities are characteristic of the extensive flood-plains along the major rivers draining the N coast of Australia on heavy black soils which are alternately flooded and dry and cracked. Other closed grassland communities occur in sub-alpine areas of SE Australia.

Closed herbfield This sub-alpine community is dominated by herbs, or herbs and grasses, forming a continuous cover. *Sphagnum* (phylum Bryophyta) bogs may be common in wet hollows within the community.

Tussock grassland Tussock grassland or tussock sedgeland is dominated by separate compact tussocks of perennial grasses, rushes, sedges or *Lomandra* species. A herbaceous ground layer is frequently present. Across the N of Australia (within the 380mm-711mm annual rainfall zone) an open tussock grassland dominated by Mitchell grass (*Astrebla* species) occupies large tracts of rolling plains with a cracking calcareous clay soil. On the heavy cracking basaltic clay soils of western VIC small tussocks of kangaroo grass (*Themeda australis*) and wallaby grass (*Danthonia* species) are dominant, though little now remains of the original vegetation. In both areas herbs are prominant between the tussocks except in dry seasons or drought years. In the N portion of the Mt Lofty Ranges (within a 508mm-635mm rainfall zone) *Lomandra* and *Danthonia* species form a tussock grassland rich in herbs. Cold winter temperatures and shallow soils may inhibit the establishment of tree seedlings in this area.

Hummock grassland This distinctive Australian plant community is dominated by large perennial hump-like tussocks of *Triodia* and *Plectrachne* species (family Gramineae). Individual hummocks may be 1m across, and as they grow outward the centre dies, producing rings or broken crescents of hummocks. Between the well-spaced hummocks (10 to 30 per cent cover) the ground is generally bare, except for a brief flush of ephemerals following rains. Hummock grassland is monotonous and uniform over extensive arid areas of skeletal and deep sandy soils of the N half of Australia (within a 127mm-355mm annual rainfall zone); a few examples are found also in the S half of the continent.

Vegetation of extreme habitats Although it is possible to classify the individual elements of community assemblages of extreme habitats, such as salt marshes, bogs and dunes, the interrelationships are so often seral (in successive stages) or controlled by variations in one overriding environmental parameter that each complex is best dealt with as a whole.

1. Mangrove vegetation. Mangrove vegetation establishes itself on muddy (or sandy) areas subject to tidal influence. Some trees are rarely immersed but many are flooded twice daily. The various species common on these waterlogged saline habitats possess 'breathing roots' (pneumatophores). The stands consist of a tree layer only, ranging from closed forest to woodland. Around N Australian coasts a zonation of mangrove species occurs from seaward to landward, in this order: *Avicennia* species and *Sonnertia* species: *Bruguiera* species; *Ceriops* species; the *Avicennia* again. S of the NSW/QLD border, stands of mangroves are more restricted in species: *Avicennia* species and *Aegiceras* species extend S to Sydney, with *Avicennia* alone occurring in isolated pockets of the VIC, SA and WA shoreline. In the S part of the Australian mainland mangrove communities are often bordered on the landward side by low shrublands of salt tolerant plants.

2. Coastal dune vegetation. Low coastal dune systems are present intermittently along the Australian coastline. Most of these dunes were formed during the retreat of the sea from a past higher level to the present level; however, the most seaward dune is still exposed to periodic destruction and renewal and a distinct succession of plant communities is seen in the building of this dune. In the S half of the continent, scattered plants of *Cakile maritima*, *Atriplex cinerea* (family Chenopodiacea) or *Festucca littoralis* (family Gramineae) colonise the seaward fringe of the dune. Behind these, long creeping rhizomes of *Spinifex hirsutus* (family Gramineae) bind the sand and enable species such as *Scirpus nodosus* (family Cyperaceae), *Lepidosperma gladiatum* (family Cyperaceae) and *Hibbertia volubilis* to become established. As dunes become more stable shrubs such as *Acacia longifolia*, *Olearia axillaris* (family Compositae), *Leucopogon* species (family Epacridaceae) and *Correa alba* (family RUTACEAE) can grow. Behind these shrubs, species become taller and denser, and may grade into woodlands of *Eucalyptus*, *Casuarina*, *Acacia* or *Banksia* (family Proteaceae) or to a dune swale complex of dry wet heath and swamp. Dune succession is not as clearly defined in N Australia, though *Spinifex longifolius* and *Ipomoea pes-caprae* (family Convolvulaceae) are the main colonisers on the seaward dunes.

See also Appendix 5, Flower Structure and Glossary of Botanical Terms.
Further reading: See Appendix 6, A Bibliography for Plants.

Venus's girdle *see* ctenophores

Verge, John (*c.*1781-1861) Architect. During the 1830s, when Sydney was being transformed and when a flood of free settlers, expanding trade and the opening-up of inland pastoral enterprises gave new impetus to the growth of architecture, John Verge produced some of the finest buildings ever designed in Australia. He was born in Hampshire, England, and in 1826 had to retire from a successful building practice in London because of ill health. He came to Australia in 1828 seeking a healthier life, and began farming on a grant near DUNGOG in NSW. By 1831, however, he had built a house in Sydney and was already entering the architectural world again, gathering about him many prominent colonial clients. He became the most prolific architect of his period, being responsible for nearly a hundred distinguished buildings. Many of them remain today: his Elizabeth Bay House, designed for Colonial Secretary Alexander MACLEAY, has recently been restored and its oval stair hall is perhaps the most spectacular colonial room in Australia.

Verge's work has been described as the high-water mark of the Regency style; he also used Greek forms (as at the Vineyard, Rydalmere, near PARRAMATTA, a large house built in 1835 for Hannibal Macarthur and now demolished), and Gothic forms (the Church of St Mary the Virgin, Denham Court, Ingleburn, SW of Sydney, built 1836), and dabbled in Chinese designs and in what he called the Russian style. Among Verge's many surviving houses are 'Rockwall' and 'Tusculum' at Pott's Point, 'Tempe House' at Tempe, an inner suburb of Sydney (now St Magdalene's Retreat) and 'Lyndhurst' at Glebe, overlooking Sydney Harbour, W of Sydney. All have now been altered. He designed many early Sydney terraces, including the famous Lyons Terrace in Liverpool Street, but the only Verge terrace still standing is at 39-41 Lower Fort Street in the Rocks, Sydney. His masterpiece is Camden Park House, Camden NSW, the most important colonial country house in Australia; Verge designed and supervised it between 1831 and 1835 for John MACARTHUR. It is a well-preserved building in a beautiful parkland setting.

Further reading: Broadbent, J. *The Golden Decade of Australian Architecture.* Dave Ell Press, Sydney, 1978.

vertebrates Animals with backbones are called vertebrates and include such familiar organisms as FISHES, AMPHIBIANS, REPTILES, BIRDS and MAMMALS. They form a subphylum of the phylum Chordata (CHORDATES). According to one commonly used classification, the Chordata is divided into the subphylum Urochordata or Tunicata (SEA SQUIRTS AND THEIR ALLIES), the subphylum Acrania or Cephalochordata (LANCELETS) and the subphylum Craniata or Vertebrata (vertebrates).

All chordates have the following characteristics at some stage in their life: a stiffening rod (notochord) running dorsally for at least part of the length; a nervous system with the main trunk (the central nervous system) placed dorsally; and gill pouches in the pharynx. The notochord is not the vertebral column though in the vertebrates it is replaced, during the development, by the vertebral column. Gill slits or pouches develop in all embryonic vertebrates though, of course, many adult vertebrates do not have gills. Vertebrates have the above characteristics of chordates but they also have the backbone or vertebral column (not necessarily made of bone; it is cartilaginous in sharks) which encloses the dorsal nerve cord. The front part of the central nervous system, the brain, is enclosed in a skull—hence the alternative name, craniates.

The classification of the vertebrates is as follows:

Subphylum Craniata or Vertebrata
 Superclass Agnatha (vertebrates with a skull but without jaws and limbs) LAMPREYS AND HAGFISHES
 Superclass Gnathostomata (vertebrates with jaws, skull and paired limbs, the last secondarily absent in some forms such as snakes)
  Class Chondrichthyes SHARKS AND RAYS

Class Holocephali	Ghost sharks (*see under* sharks and rays)
Class Osteichthyes	True fishes or bony fishes (see FISHES, BONY)
Class Amphibia	Amphibians
Class Reptilia	Reptiles
Class Aves	Birds
Class Mammalia	Mammals

The classes Aves, Mammalia and Reptilia are often known collectively as the amniote vertebrates because of the way in which the embryonic membranes are formed; together with the class Amphibia they are also sometimes referred to as the tetrapods. The sharks and rays, the ghost sharks, the bony fishes and the lampreys and hagfishes are often referred to collectively as the fishes (pisces) though they are extremely diverse. There are, in addition, several extinct, fish-like classes of vertebrates.

Victor Harbour SA (population 4 522 in 1981) This town is on the S coast of FLEURIEU PENINSULA, overlooking ENCOUNTER BAY, 84km by road S of Adelaide. It was once a whaling and sealing port but is now a business and service centre for a productive rural hinterland, and an important holiday and tourist centre. It was named by Captain Richard Crozier, who surveyed the harbour in 1837, after his vessel HMS *Victor*. A causeway links the town to Granite Is, an early whaling station.

Further reading: Branson, V.M. *Victor Harbour Sketchbook.* Rigby, Adelaide, 1975.

Victoria (VIC) The State of VIC has an area of 227600km² and is the second-smallest of the States of Australia, occupying only about three per cent of the nation's total area. The boundaries of the State consist of the coastline along the S and SE, the MURRAY RIVER between VIC and NSW, a straight line boundary from the source of the Murray to CAPE HOWE on the E coast, and a straight vertical line as the border between VIC and SA extending from the coast to the Murray. But the delineation of these boundaries was not as simple as this statement may imply. Their origins go back to a series of Imperial Acts which defined the borders between different colonies and to the subsequent determination of the precise location of these borders.
1. The SA/VIC border. The first British colony established in Australia was NSW and it originally included all of the E part of the continent as far inland as the 150°E longitude. However, when the Province of SA was established in the 1830s, its E boundary (now SA/VIC border) was fixed as 'the One hundred and forty-first Degree of East Longitude'. In the 1840s, surveys were carried out to mark the precise location of this meridian of longitude on the ground but, owing to a number of problems and the inadequacies of instruments then available, the boundary was marked at 140° 58'E longitude (approximately 3.6km W

Table 1

POPULATION GROWTH OF VICTORIA IN THE TWENTIETH CENTURY

Year	Population
1901	1 201 070
1911	1 315 551
1921	1 531 280
1933	1 820 261
1954	2 452 341
1961	2 930 113
1971	3 502 351
1976	3 646 981*
1981†	3 948 555

Note: * after the census in 1976, an official estimate, taking into account 'under-enumeration', was stated as 3 746 000; † the 1981 figure was the Estimated Resident Population (Preliminary). Source: Australian Bureau of Statistics, Canberra.

of where it should have been). This led to some litigation and an appeal to the Privy Council, but the surveyed boundary remained, which means that the SA/VIC boundary is on the 140° 58'E meridian of longitude and the SA/NSW boundary is on the 141°E meridian, and at the Murray River there is therefore a 'dog-leg' junction of the three State borders.
2. The Murray River. In 1842, the PORT PHILLIP District of the colony of NSW was defined in an Imperial Act which set the N boundary as 'a straight line drawn from Cape Howe to the nearest Source of the River Murray, and thence the Course of that River to the Eastern Boundary of the Province of South Australia'. Thus, when VIC became a separate colony in 1851, the Murray River became the border, but the question arose as to which colony had jurisdiction over the waters of the river. The position was clarified by an Imperial Act of 1855 which decreed that the river course was within NSW and that the border was therefore along the left bank.
3. Cape Howe to the Murray. The delineation of this straight line section involved a decision as to where the 'source' of the Murray was located and what precise point on Cape Howe was to be the boundary. Fortunately, this was determined by survey, without legal battles, and the line was marked by 1872.
4. Offshore boundaries. The Imperial Act which separated VIC from NSW did not define the S seaward boundary of the new colony. However, the N boundary of VAN DIEMEN'S LAND (TAS) had been defined in 1825 as the line of latitude 39° 12'S. This lies about 7km S of WILSON'S PROMONTORY and is generally accepted as the S limit of VIC's State territory.

Landform features Part of the GREAT DIVIDING RANGE of E Australia forms a belt of highland country extending E-W across the central section of the State. The highlands are widest and highest in the NE and far E of the State, and taper towards the W to the GRAMPIANS and the Dundas Tableland. The highland belt divides the N plains and the WIMMERA-MALLEE region in the NW from the coastal plains and hill lands of the S rim of the State, and forms the watershed between streams which are tributaries of the Murray River (KIEWA, MITTA MITTA, OVENS, GOULBURN, LODDON and CAMPASPE Rivers) and those which drain to estuaries on the S coast (SNOWY, TAMBO, MITCHELL, MACALISTER-THOMSON-LATROBE, YARRA, Hopkins, Eumeralla and GLENELG Rivers). A broad low pass to the N of Melbourne, the Kilmore Gap, provides an easy route across the highland belt and divides the highlands into E and W sections.

The E uplands consist of rugged, deeply dissected and forested country, with the highest points reaching to over 1 900m (MOUNT BOGONG 1 986m, MOUNT FEATHERTOP 1 922m); there are large areas of plateau-like landscape, called 'high plains', with gently undulating topography at elevations of about 1 300m, such as the BOGONG HIGH PLAINS and the Dargo high plains. Above about 1000m elevation, the E highlands are snow-capped during the winter months; but even the highest areas are free of snow in summer. Numerous ski resorts have been developed such as FALLS CREEK, MOUNT HOTHAM, MOUNT BUFFALO and MOUNT BULLER. The W section of the highlands, in contrast with the E section, is lower in elevation and consists of more gently sloping hilly country at an average height of 600m. There are extensive areas of relatively flat landscape with broad river valleys and occasional resistant masses of igneous rock, such as MOUNT MACEDON (1 013m), rising above the general level. A distinctive feature of the W highlands is the volcanic activity of the recent geological past, when lava flows covered much of the landscape. The Grampians, consisting of a series of resistant sandstone ridges, is the most rugged part of this region; the highest peak, Mt William (1 167m), has a spectacular E escarpment and a broad summit area.

A further feature due to recent volcanic activity is the volcanic plain of the WESTERN DISTRICT of the State. Covering an area of 2300km², this region extends from the Grampians S to WARRNAMBOOL and COLAC, composed of vast basalt lava flows, with volcanic cones, such as MOUNT ELEPHANT (394m elevation), rising sharply from the plains. The S uplands of VIC include the OTWAY RANGES, MORNINGTON PENINSULA and the rugged highlands to the SW of the GIPPSLAND plains.

Climate The average annual rainfall over the State varies from 250mm in the driest parts of the Mallee to 2600mm in the E parts of the highlands. The N riverine plains receive between 300mm and 600mm annually, while the plains of central Gippsland receive between 500mm and 700mm. Rain normally occurs throughout the year, but with higher falls in winter in all areas except E Gippsland. Dry spells and extended periods of drought are fairly common, particularly in the N and NW parts of the State. Winter snow is a regular feature on the highlands, though the heaviest falls are normally in sparsely populated areas. The length of the snow season in the alpine regions varies from three to five months.

Summer temperatures in VIC are high, except for the upper alpine regions of the highlands. The average maximum temperatures in summer range from below 20°C on the coastal plains to over 32°C in the Mallee region of the NW. January and February are the hottest months and bushfires are a hazard during the summer season. July is the month of lowest temperatures when much of the highland areas have maximum temperatures below 10°C and the more elevated sections experience even colder conditions. The lower-lying parts of the State have milder winter conditions; in July the average maximum along the coastal zone is 13°C and in the Mallee is 16°C.

Population The total population of the State, recorded at the 1981 census, was 3 948 555, making it the second-largest State in the nation, accounting for 26.5 per cent of Australia's population. About 65 per cent of VIC's people live within metropolitan Melbourne, and, together with the next three largest urban centres—GEELONG (125 269), BALLARAT (62 640) and BENDIGO (52 739)—make up 71 per cent of the State's total population. Other major urban centres with over 20 000 people are SHEPPARTON (28 369) and WARRNAMBOOL (21 415), while there are several with more than 10 000 people, such as MOE-YALLOURN, WANGARATTA, MORWELL, TRARALGON, MILDURA, SALE and HORSHAM. The growth of VIC's population during the 20th century is shown in Table 1. At the 1901 census 41 per cent of the population lived in Melbourne, by 1933 54 per cent were Melbourne residents, by 1954 Melbourne accounted for 62 per cent of the State's population and at the 1981 census the figure was 65 per cent. Since the early 1970s, the rate of natural increase has declined and there has been a lower level of immigration compared to the 1950s and 1960s.

History As in the case of TAS, the first two settlements in the area now known as Victoria were made because of fears that the French might settle in southern Australia.

First settlement In 1803 David COLLINS was sent with a party of 455 settlers, including 299 convicts, to Port Phillip Bay, but it appears that from the beginning he did not have his heart in the project. After landing at an unpromising site near modern Sorrento, he made a cursory examination of the rest of the district, informed Governor KING that it was unsuitable for settlement, and after a few months obtained permission to move his charges to TAS. The journey of HUME and Hovell overland to CORIO BAY in 1824, and another 'French scare' soon afterwards, revived interest in the area and in 1826 a party of soldiers and convicts was sent to WESTERN PORT BAY. The site chosen was not impressive, fear of the French soon faded, and the settlement was abandoned in 1828. Interest in the area remained high, particularly in TAS,

'Collins Street, Town of Melbourne, NSW, 1839', a watercolour by H. Knight

National Library of Australia

where by the 1830s most of the good farming land had been occupied, but official policy by that time had turned towards concentrating mainland settlement in the NINETEEN COUNTIES. Petitions for land by John BATMAN and the HENTY FAMILY were rejected; nevertheless, the Hentys settled without authorisation at Portland Bay in 1834, and parties organised by Batman and John Pascoe FAWKNER did likewise at Port Phillip Bay in the following year.

A year after Batman's first visit there were 177 settlers at Port Phillip Bay, with 26 000 sheep. Meanwhile, Governor BOURKE had declared that a 'treaty' made by Batman with the local Aborigines had no legal standing, and that all the settlers were trespassing on Crown lands. However, he knew that it was impossible to prevent 'squatting' and persuaded the Colonial Office to allow the district to be opened up for settlement. In September 1836 Captain William LONSDALE was sent as police magistrate and administrator, and three surveyors began preparations for land sales. Lonsdale confirmed the location of the town centre, at the place where Fawkner's followers had established themselves, and when Bourke visited the settlement in March 1839 he named it Melbourne, after the then British Prime Minister. In the same year Lonsdale was replaced by Charles Joseph LA TROBE, who remained in command for 15 years, with the title of Superintendent until 1851 and then as Lieutenant-Governor.

Moves for separation and against transportation During the 1840s the main political issues were concerned with transportation and the demand for separation from NSW. Because the Port Phillip District was founded by free settlers shortly before the 1840 decision to abandon transportation to the mainland of NSW, it was spared the main impact of the convict system. However, in the late 1840s convicts were again sent to the colony either on conditional pardons or on tickets of leave. In the Port Phillip District, as elsewhere, public opinion was sharply divided on the question, with some employers favouring the full resumption of transportation but most people being opposed to the sending of convicts under any conditions. When in 1849 the transport *Randolph* reached Port Phillip the public outcry was such that La Trobe sent it on to Sydney.

Agitation for separation developed strongly from the very beginning. In various aspects of public administration Port Phillip had its own local branches—its own land office, customs and police establishments and a branch of the Supreme Court—but it was claimed that officials in Sydney did not understand local problems, and that an unjustifiably large share of the tax money collected in the district was spent elsewhere. When in 1842 NSW gained a new Legislative Council, six of the elective seats were reserved for the Port Phillip District, but the transport difficulties between Melbourne and Sydney were so great that the southerners regarded their representation as ineffective. This point of view was emphasised in the 1848 elections by the facetious election of the British Colonial Secretary, Earl Grey, as the representative for Melbourne. A petition announcing his election and repeating the demand for separation was sent to London, and was probably influential in causing the British government to make provision, in the Australian Colonies' Government Act of 1850, for the creation of the colony of VIC in the following year. The new colony had a Legislative Council of 30 members, 10 nominated by the Governor and the others elected, which exercised control over all revenue except that from the sale of Crown lands.

From separation to federation, 1851-1901
In 1852 the Legislative Council (and those of the other three E colonies) was invited to draw up a constitution, which was accepted by the Imperial Parliament in 1855. It provided for a Parliament consisting of a Legislative Council and a Legislative Assembly, elected on a franchise based on high property or educational qualifications in the case of the former and much lower property or income qualifications in the case of the latter.

The effects of the gold rushes of the 1850s (*see* GOLD DISCOVERIES; ECONOMIC HISTORY; EUREKA STOCKADE; IMMIGRATION RESTRICTION) were felt with particular force in VIC. This is shown by the fact that within a decade of its foundation, VIC had become the most populous of the Australian colonies and Melbourne had become Australia's largest city. The independent character of so many gold-rush immigrants and their demands for reform must be considered a cause of the democratic electoral changes which took place after the granting of responsible government. In 1856 the secret ballot was introduced, in 1857 adult male suffrage was established in elections for the Legislative Assembly and

Princess Bridge and central city area of Melbourne from the River Yarra

property qualifications for members were abolished, in 1859 the term of the Assembly was reduced from five years to three, and in 1870 payment for Members of Parliament was begun. However, the Legislative Council remained a very conservative and exclusive body until 1881 when, after clashes between the two Houses, its franchise was widened to include more than half of the adult male population, and property qualifications for Members were significantly lowered.

In the mining industry, the number of men working reached a peak in 1858, by which time most of the easily won alluvial gold had been extracted. The number of miners then declined sharply, with an increased proportion of those remaining being employed by companies engaged in deep-reef mining. The need to find employment for ex-miners added strength to the protectionist movement, which had been begun by farmers in the Geelong district and by 1859 had led to the founding of the Tariff League of Victoria. In 1860 David Syme, the new proprietor of the *Age* newspaper, joined the movement, and in 1866 a moderately protectionist tariff was passed. In 1877 Graham BERRY pushed through a more highly protectionist tariff. The effects of these measures, however, are difficult to judge, for while manufacturing increased greatly, the statistics available do not prove decisively that VIC's protectionist policy was notably more successful than that of free trade in NSW in diverting labour to industry.

In the rural sector of the economy, the balance between various industries changed markedly in the period after the gold rushes. Although the pastoral industry expanded, it did not do so as strongly as elsewhere. In 1851 VIC had more sheep than any other Australian

colony, but during the following 40 years she was relegated to third place, behind NSW and QLD. On the other hand, in the same period she displaced SA as premier wheat producer, and in the 1880s she began Australia's first large irrigation project, at Mildura.

The boom of the 1880s was particularly strong in VIC, and the subsequent depression correspondingly severe. During the boom the colony attracted a high proportion of the inflow of migrants and investment capital into Australia. Melbourne was the scene of feverish construction activity and of intense speculation in land and houses. The collapse of the building boom between 1889 and 1891, accompanied by falls in wheat and wool prices, brought insolvencies, failures of land banks and then of banks of issue, and severe unemployment. For more than 20 years the number of emigrants exceeded that of immigrants, so that NSW forged ahead of VIC in population and Sydney regained its position as Australia's largest city.

Development since federation Recovery from the depression was slow. In the first decade of this century there was a short-lived revival in gold mining, some recovery in wheat and wool, and a considerable growth of the dairy industry. Employment in manufacturing nearly doubled between 1901 and 1911, and was given further encouragement by the difficulty of obtaining imported manufactures during World War I. From 1902 a succession of Ministries had followed a more ambitious public works programme than that of any other State; this included the development of Australia's best road system, extensive irrigation works, railway and tramway construction and a beginning, in 1918, of large-scale development of the Latrobe Valley brown-coal deposits for electricity generation and other purposes. The trend towards urbanisation and industrialisation continued—by 1929 the value of manufacturing output was about three times that of pastoral and agricultural combined, and Melbourne contained 56 per cent of the State's population. Because of her dependence on manufacturing, VIC was afflicted with unemployment even higher than that for Australia as a whole during the depression of the 1930s. There was, however, a strong revival of gold mining and from 1934 manufacturing recovered. Notable features of economic development since then have been the continuing expansion of brown-coal production, the concentration of motor car manufacturing and assembling plants in Melbourne and Geelong, and the discovery of a major oil and gas field in BASS STRAIT.

VIC Govt Travel Authority

Sheep grazing property in VIC

In federal politics VIC has been the most important power base of the LIBERAL PARTY, providing from the time of Sir Robert MENZIES onwards a high proportion of its parliamentary leadership. In State politics the AUSTRALIAN LABOR PARTY (ALP) has been comparatively weak, but on the other hand there has been a high degree of antagonism between the Liberal and Country (now NATIONAL) Parties. From the 1920s to the 1950s the Country Party had considerable success, owing to an electoral distribution which favoured country electorates and to the party's willingness to accept Labor support to keep it in office. The longest period of Country Party power was from 1935 to 1945, during which time it held office almost continuously under Sir Albert DUNSTAN. However, since the electoral redistribution in 1954, it has been far less important. The favouring of rural electorates obviously told against Labor, which did not achieve a full term in office until 1929-32. The redistribution of 1954 removed its electoral handicap, but the split in the party's ranks in the following year, culminating in the formation of the DEMOCRATIC LABOR PARTY (DLP), was particularly wide in VIC. DLP success in VIC, its main power base, was a major factor in keeping the ALP out of power there and in

the federal sphere for many years. However, Labor gained office, under John CAIN, in 1982.
Further reading: Bonwick, J. *Port Phillip Settlement.* Sampson Low, London, 1883; Turner, H.G. *A History of the Colony of Victoria.* Longmans Greens, London, 1904; Eggleston, F.W. *State Socialism in Victoria.* P.S. King & Son, London, 1932; Doyle, E.A. (ed) *The Story of the Century 1851-1951.* Specialty Press, Melbourne, 1951.

Victoria River NT Located in the NW of the Territory, with its headwaters in upland country about 100km SW of Wave Hill and 120km E of the WA/NT border, it flows for some 650km N and then NW to Queen's Channel on JOSEPH BONAPARTE GULF. The upper catchment basin receives low rainfall (for example, Cattle Creek on Wave Hill station has an annual average of 402mm), concentrated in the summer months (December to March), and so most of the headwater tributaries, such as Camfield, Giles and Gordon Creeks, flow only seasonally. In the middle section of the basin, the rainfall is higher (Victoria River Downs station has an annual average of 597mm), and along the coastal zone over 1 200mm are received annually. The main tributaries are the Wickham and Baines from the S, and the Angalarri from the N.
The valley is occupied by some 20 cattle stations: Wave Hill, the largest, covers 12 580km²; Victoria River Downs, the second-largest, is 12 359km²; others are Coolibah (N of the lower river, 10 269km²), Auvergne (SW of the lower river, stretching to the WA border, 10 230km²), Humbert River (on the upper Wickham, 5631km²), Delamere (5289km²) and Montejinni (3149km²). Most of the properties are held under leasehold by big pastoral companies. The cattle are sent overland to QLD for fattening or are slaughtered at meat works at Darwin, KATHERINE and Montejinni. Transport has always been a problem for the grazing industry in these remote parts, but the development of roads in recent years, such as the Victoria and Buchanan Highways linking the valley to Katherine, has increased the use of large 'road-trains' for cattle movement. The Victoria River was discovered in 1839 by John WICKHAM, commander of HMS *Beagle*, who travelled 145km upstream from the mouth and named it in honour of Queen Victoria. The upper reaches of the valley were traced by Sir Augustus GREGORY in 1855-56, and in the 1880s the region was occupied by pastoralists, some of whom had made journeys of over 3000km from NSW and QLD with their herds.

Vietnam War Not long after the end of World War II, France became involved in a Communist-led revolt in Vietnam, which then formed part of French Indo-China. This conflict ended with an agreement, reached at an international conference in Geneva in 1954, by which the forces opposed to the French

withdrew to the N of the 17th parallel, while the French and their supporters retired to the S of that line. The conference also issued a recommendation that elections should be held in 1956 to reunite the country. By that date the French had withdrawn the last of their forces and both sections of the country were independent. However, the S government did not consider itself bound by the recommendation regarding joint elections, and so Vietnam remained divided into the Communist-ruled Democratic Republic of Vietnam (North Vietnam, with Hanoi as its capital) and the non-Communist, American-aided, Republic of Vietnam (South Vietnam, with Saigon as its capital). By the late 1950s, Communist guerrillas (known as Vietcong) were again active in South Vietnam, and the USA began increasing its aid to the Saigon government. By 1964 American ground forces were being sent.

The Liberal/Country Party government of Australia supported American involvement, and from 1962 to 1972 Australian servicemen also participated in the war. The government's attitude was consistent with its general foreign and defence policies; it was based particularly on general concern regarding the spread of Communism in Asia, a belief that Australia could best be made safe by a policy of 'forward defence', the realisation that if Australia was ever again under threat of attack her survival was likely to depend once more on American help, and on a desire for the USA to maintain a strong presence in South-East Asia. Moreover, the Australian government accepted the American view that the activities of the National Liberation Front (NLF), the guerrillas' political organisation, were masterminded by North Vietnam, and were part of a Chinese-guided drive that might in time engulf the whole of South-East Asia. In 1962 Australia sent military advisers to South Vietnam, and in 1965 backed these up with the 1st Battalion, Royal Australian Regiment. In the following year Australia's commitment was raised to two battalions, forming the First Australian Task Force. This was based in Phuoc Tuy province, SE of Saigon, and was raised to a strength of three battalions in 1967. For several years it was engaged not only in restraining guerrilla activity and in action against units of the NLF/North Vietnam army main force, but in aid and welfare work of many kinds. Australia also contributed four destroyers (*Perth, Hobart, Brisbane* and *Vendetta*) to the war, and three squadrons of the RAAF.

Meanwhile, in Australia strong opposition to American and Australian involvement in the war had been mounted by the Australian Labor Party (ALP) and many other organisations and individuals. Such opposition rested on three main claims: firstly, that the war was not in the main one of aggression by North Vietnam, and that American and Australian intervention was both unwise and unjustified; secondly, that the doctrine of 'forward defence' was faulty; and thirdly, that it was wrong to commit conscripts to such a war. The conscripts were enlisted under the provisions of the National Service Act, but not for short courses of training simply to build up a trained reserve, as had been the practice between 1951 and 1959. From 1965 all 20-year-old men were obliged to register for national service, and from their ranks some were selected by a type of lottery, based on their dates of birth. Subject to health and other checks, these were required to serve a two-year term in the Australian Regular Army (ARA), including active service abroad if required. Service in the part-time citizen forces was allowed as an alternative. From 1966 national servicemen were included in the forces sent to Vietnam.

Even at the end of 1966 it appeared that the government had strong majority support for its Vietnam policy, for in the elections of November it won an easy victory, after a campaign in which the war had featured as the main issue. During the following six years, however, as the horrors of the war became widely publicised and the number of American troops was increased to over 500 000 without victory being secured, opposition became more widespread, and anti-war demonstrations more frequent and vigorous, in Australia as in the USA. Following the election of Richard Nixon as President of the USA in 1969, however, the number of Americans in Vietnam was reduced. Australia also reduced its commitment. By 1972 all of its combat forces had been withdrawn, and after the ALP victory that December all remaining military advisers were promptly recalled also. In the following year a cease-fire came into operation and the last American troops were withdrawn. Subsequently, the cease-fire arrangements broke down and fighting was resumed. However, neither the USA, nor Australia, nor any of the other nations which had formerly provided armed help for the Saigon government, intervened again, and by 1975 the whole of Vietnam was under Communist rule. Australian casualties in the war had included 423 killed and 2 398 wounded, nearly half of each category being national servicemen.

Further reading: *Australian Outlook.* (Special Vietnam issue, vol 23, April 1969); Albinski, H.S. *Politics and Foreign Policy in Australia: The Impact of Vietnam and Conscription.* Duke University Press, Durham, North Carolina, 1970; Odgers, G. *Mission Vietnam: Royal Australian Air Force Operations, 1964-1972.* Australian Govt Publishing Service, Canberra, 1974.

Vietnamese refugees in Australia The exodus of refugees from Vietnam since 1975 has posed a new social, economic and humanitarian problem for Australia, and resulted in the unauthorised arrival of the BOAT PEOPLE in Darwin. Although no comprehensive studies have been made as to why people left Vietnam or even what kinds of people left, it is reasonable to assume that expropriation of private property, the forced relocation of

English language class for Vietnamese refugees at The Springvale immigrant settlement centre

people and the economic hardships experienced as a result of successive natural disasters affected a broad range of people that included farmers, fishermen, tradesmen and businessmen. Refugees also feared that they would be subjected to political, economic, racial and religious persecution if they remained in Vietnam; ethnic Chinese in particular were affected by such measures as the nationalisation of assets and redeployment in new economic zones in Vietnam since the end of the VIETNAM WAR in April 1975. Hostilities in the late 1970s between Vietnam and the People's Republic of China worsened the position of this group.

Between April 1975 and June 1983 Australia accepted 78 020 refugees from Vietnam and elsewhere in Indo-China. These refugees are racially and culturally very different from most Australians, and not long ago would not have been acceptable as settlers under any circumstances. Many novel and interesting ideas for refugee settlement schemes have been proffered by the Australian community and a number have been successfully developed.
See also immigration

volcanoes *see* geology

volute shells *see* gastropods

von Guerard, Eugene (1812-1901) Artist. Born in Vienna, the son of a court painter, von Guerard arrived in Australia in 1852. Until 1881, when he returned to Europe, he did a series of sketches of the BALLARAT goldfields and a number of extremely detailed Victorian landscapes in a highly finished style. His colour was influenced by his European training, rather than by

his observation of Australia, and he showed a meticulous attention to detail. He became curator of the National Gallery and the principal of its Art School in 1870. He died in Britain.

von Mueller, Baron Sir Ferdinand Jakob Heinrich (1825-96) Botanist and explorer. Born at Rostock in Germany, von Mueller is regarded by many as the father of Australian botany. He migrated to Australia in 1847 and was appointed Government Botanist of VIC. He explored many regions, including the GRAMPIANS, WILSON'S PROMONTORY, GIPPSLAND, MOUNT BUFFALO and MOUNT BULLER. During an exploration of the SNOWY RIVER and the MURRAY RIVER, a journey of about 6 500km, he collected about 1 500 species of plants. In 1855 he joined Sir Augustus GREGORY's N Australian expedition. He was the director of the Melbourne Botanical Gardens from 1857 to 1873 and amassed a plant collection of 350 000 specimens. On the discredit side, he introduced various plants including (possibly) *Paspalum* grass and watercress, some of which became weeds; he also promoted the growing of brambles to provide florists with suitable foliage for making wreaths. The King of Wurtemburg made von Mueller a hereditary baron for his services to botany in 1869 and he was appointed KCMG by Queen Victoria in 1879. He published several hundred papers and books on Australian plants, some entirely in Latin.
Further reading: Moyal, A. M. (ed) *Scientists in Nineteenth Century Australia: A Documentary History.* Cassel Australia, Stanmore NSW, 1976; Kynaston, E. *A Man on Edge.* Allen Lane, Ringwood VIC, 1981.

von Nida, Norman Guy (1914-)
Golfer. Born in Sydney, he was one of a family of seven children. Introduced to golf at the age of 11—caddying to earn himself some pocket money—von Nida was to develop into one of Australia's greatest golfers. In 1932, at the age of 18, he won his first major amateur title, the QLD Amateur championship, and turned professional one week later. His dedication to practice and determination to win led to a long string of professional titles and domination of the Australian circuit from 1935 to 1955. The most prestigious title in Australia is the Australian Open, and from 1949 to 1955 von Nida dominated this tournament as no other golfer had done, winning three times (1950, 1952 and 1953) and being runner-up four times (1949, 1951, 1954 and 1955). On touring Britain he won the coveted Vardon Trophy in 1947 and the Dunlop Masters in 1948. Throughout his golfing career, he was a controversial figure, his hasty temper leading to arguments with golf officials, fellow players and photographers, but he always remained popular with the spectators who consistently followed 'The Von' and admired his outstanding golfing talents. He has always been willing to help young professionals with their game and their mental approach to tournament play, and players such as Bruce DEVLIN, Peter THOMSON and even the great South African golfer Gary Player have benefited from his expert advice. Von Nida was admired and respected all over the world, but particularly in Australia where his dynamic personality and golfing talent have done much for golf.

voting *see* elections

Waddamanna TAS A power station and small village, Waddamanna lies 26km S of GREAT LAKE in the CENTRAL PLATEAU region of the State, between the Marlborough and Lake Highways, 120km NW of Hobart. It was the site of one of the earliest hydro-electricity generating stations in TAS. In 1911 a company built a small dam at the outlet from Great Lake to control the flow of water to Waddamanna, where it was intended to generate power; in 1914 the assets of the company were purchased by the State government and by 1916 equipment was installed and power generated for ore smelting, domestic lighting and tramway operation in Hobart. Later the scheme was enlarged and a second power station built, but Waddamanna is now used only for peak power generation, as it has largely been superseded by major power developments NE of Great Lake.

waders These BIRDS belong to the order Charadriiformes, which is divided into eight families. Most waders are long-legged, long-beaked birds which frequent seashores and tidal flats, probing the mud or overturning stones in search of small animals. Many are famous for the manner in which they defend their young; some distract intruders by fluttering away slowly, feigning a broken limb, while others may dive-bomb the intruder. Most Australian species are summer immigrants in non-breeding plumage from the N hemisphere. This entry deals mainly with the resident species.

The pan-tropical family Jacanidae contains seven species of long-legged, long-toed birds which live and nest on floating vegetation, feeding on water insects and plant material. The Australian representative, the jacana or lotus bird, *Irediparra gallinacea* (length 23cm; legs 10cm; hind and middle toes each 7.5cm), is a black, white and brown bird with a red comb. Also called lilytrotters from their habit of walking on water lilies in quiet inland waters, jacanas feed on water insects and vegetation. When in flight the legs trail behind the body. The jacana occurs in a wide coastal band from north-eastern WA to central NSW.

The family Rostratulidae contains only two species, one in South America and the other, the painted snipe, *Rostratula benghalensis* (25cm long), in Europe and Australia. A furtive, quiet bird, the painted snipe has a thin bill (5cm long), a broad white ring around the eye and white underparts: the more richly coloured female has greenish shoulders and a dark chestnut head, neck and breast, while the male has a greyish head and a greyish-brown back. The flight is rather clumsy, with the legs dangling, and when walking or standing the head is held low and slightly retracted. Found in all States except the NT, painted snipes feed on aquatic insects and plant material in the shallows of inland swamps and marshes.

The family Haematopodidae contains the oystercatchers, dark birds with long, chisel-like beaks and medium-length red legs. The sooty oystercatcher, *Haematopus fuliginosus** (45cm), a completely black species which favours rocky shores, may be a black form of the more common pied oystercatcher, *H. ostralegus* (45cm), found throughout Australia on beaches and mud-flats. Both species feed on marine animals in the intertidal zone but, despite their name, they probably only rarely eat oysters.

The family Charadriidae contains the plovers and dotterels; in this family, the beak is shorter than the head. The three 'lapwing' plovers belonging to the genus *Vanellus*, all of which breed in Australia, are about 35cm long and have yellow or red wattles on the face. These birds have an erratic flight and are often nomadic. The masked plover, *V. miles*, found in moist grasslands, swamps and estuaries in N Australia, and the spurwing plover, *V. novaehollandiae**, found in similar habitats in E and SE Australia (both species have recently colonised south-western WA), may be identical. There is a spur on the wing, used for offensive and defensive purposes; the wings are brown, the wattles yellow, the underparts white and the head black and white, the black being more extensive in the spurwing. Both species feed on insects, small animals and vegetable matter. The banded plover, *V. tricolor** is similar except that the wattles are red and the black on the head extends to form a band on the breast.

The genus *Charadrius* contains about 24 species known as plovers or sand plovers elsewhere but called dotterels in Australia and New Zealand. Of the 10 species in Australia, two are extremely rare and four are endemic. Most are about 25cm long, brownish-grey

Spurwing plover, *Vanellus miles*

E. Carthew (N.P.I.A.W.)

Species, genus or family is endemic to Australia (see Preface)

above and white below; in some cases there are striking black markings on the head, neck and breast. They are found mainly on sea-shores, feeding on insects and small animals; four are common non-breeding visitors, while the remainder usually lay their eggs in shallow depressions in the sand.

The three species contained in the genus *Pluvialis* are non-breeding summer visitors from the Arctic regions. Found throughout Australia, mainly in coastal areas, are two common species—the grey plover, *P. squatarola* (25cm to 28cm), mostly white below with dappled upperparts and white speckles on the greyish-brown face and breast, and the eastern golden plover, *P. dominica* (23cm to 25cm), similar but with a yellowish breast.

The Australian dotterel, *Peltohyas australis** (20cm), stands apart from the rest of the family. A fairly common bird near water in the arid and semi-arid areas of central Australia, it has a chestnut and brown belly, a black breast, a white forehead and a black band on the crown of the head and the face. It is a terrestrial bird, sometimes solitary and sometimes in small groups.

Of the 70 members of the family Scolopacidae, 31 occur in Australia; all are non-breeding visitors from the N hemisphere and most are greyish in colour. This family includes sandpipers, curlews, whimbrels, snipes, tattlers, knots, godwits and the turnstone. In all species the bill is longer, often much longer, than the head length; while most have straight bills, some, such as the whimbrel, *Numenius phaeopus* (40cm to 45cm), and the eastern curlew, *N. madagascariensis* (50cm to 65cm), have down-curved bills and others, such as the greenshank, *Tringa nebularia* (33cm), have up-curved ones. The species with the longest bill (7.5cm) is the Japanese snipe, *Gallinago hardwickii* (30cm to 33cm), a boldly patterned black and buff bird with a reddish tail which frequents the marshes and moist woodlands of the E half of Australia.

The family Phalaropodidae contains three species, two of which are rare visitors to Australia—the red-necked phalarope, *Phalaropus lobatus* (23cm), and the Wilson phalarope, *P. tricolor* (23cm). These species have two unusual features: firstly, their dense undercoat of breast and belly feathers enables them to sit very high on the water; and, secondly, the appearance and behaviour of the sexes are reversed whereby the females are more brightly coloured and the males undertake the usual female duties.

The avocets and stilts of the family Recurvirostridae are unmistakeable waders. Avocets are inland-water and seashore birds with long, upturned bills, chestnut-brown heads and black and white bodies. Despite their long legs, they sometimes swim and up-end like ducks to reach their prey—small aquatic animals and insects. The Australian species, *Recurvirostra novaehollandiae** (length 45cm; bill 9cm), is fairly common in all States but does not occur in the NT and is extinct in New Zealand. Stilts frequent coastal and inland waters, feeding mainly on insects, brine shrimps and snails. Their legs are relatively longer (hence the name) than those of any other bird, apart from flamingoes. The two species found in Australia are the pied stilt, *Himantopus himantopus* (38cm), a cosmopolitan bird, and the banded stilt, *Cladorhynchus** leucocephalus* (38cm), black and white with a chestnut patch on the breast.

The species known as stone curlews—large-eyed nocturnal birds which resemble the BUSTARD—belong to the family Burhinidae. The two Australian species have stout, dagger-like bills. The bush curlew, *Burhinus magnirostris** (length 56cm; tail 18cm), a streaked, greyish-brown bird with a white face, frequents open woodlands and plains throughout Australia, feeding on insects. The beach curlew, *Esacus magnirostris* (55cm), plain greyish-brown above and below with a boldly pied facial pattern, is found mainly on tropical coasts, feeding on crustaceans, small animals and insects.

Wagga Wagga NSW (population 36 832 in 1981) A city in the RIVERINA region on the MURRUMBIDGEE RIVER, it is 488km by road SW of Sydney, on the Sturt Highway. It is a station on the main Sydney-Melbourne railway route, 518km from Sydney and is a main airways centre with services linking it to capital cities. At an elevation of 186m above sea level, it experiences hot summer conditions, cool frosty winters and an average annual rainfall of about 570mm uniformly distributed throughout the year. The city name is usually abbreviated to a single 'Wagga', an Aboriginal word for which there are several explanations, the most usually accepted being 'many crows', but others are 'a sick or dying man reeling with exhaustion', 'to dance', 'to slide', or 'to grind'. The city is a regional focus for an extensive rural district producing wheat, sheep, beef cattle, lucerne, oats and other crops. It is also an important educational centre with an agricultural college, a College of Advanced Education (formerly the Teachers' College), a regional technical college, along with several State and private secondary and primary schools. There is an agricultural research institute 9km N of the city and it was here that William FARRER worked for some years and developed valuable varieties of wheat. There is a wide range of secondary industries in the city including flour mills, cheese and butter factories, an abattoir, milk processing works, an iron foundry, engineering workshops, a bacon processing factory, rubber goods works and a terrazzo making plant.

Though some early settlement by pastoralists took place in this region in the 1820s, it was after the exploratory journey of Charles STURT in 1829-30 that a SW movement of settlers from the GUNDAGAI district into the river frontage land near Wagga took place. A village nucleus developed at a crossing point on the Murrumbidgee and this was officially recognised by the proclamation of the town in 1849. In these early days the ravages of floods were felt both on the rural properties and in the town, especially the lower-lying N parts of the settlement. Bullock waggons were the main form of transport in these times, but in the late 1850s river transport commenced and for several decades it proved valuable; however, it was eclipsed by more reliable and efficient road and rail haulage. In 1870 Wagga was proclaimed a borough and in the late 1870s the railway reached, then crossed, the Murrumbidgee with the construction of a rail bridge. As the district became more closely settled, the town grew, its service functions expanded and in 1946 it became a city. The National Trust (NSW) has listed several buildings in Wagga for preservation—a number of churches, two public schools, the council chambers, the railway station, the courthouse, the post office, the ANZ and CBC (now National Australia) Banks, and the offices of the lands department and the shire. Tourist attractions include the soil conservation research centre, Forest Hill RAAF station, the botanic gardens and the zoo, Kapooka Army camp (10km S of the city), Lake Albert (6km S) for aquatic sports, murray cod hatcheries (8km E) where various river fish are bred for sale to farmers and fishing clubs, and the Wallacetown Museum (20km N) with a collection of firearms dating from the 1840s.

Further reading: Shaw, J.H. *The Urban Evolution of Wagga Wagga.* University of New England, Armidale, 1960; Swan, K. *A History of Wagga Wagga.* Hogein, Sydney, 1970.

Wagin WA (population 1 488 in 1981) This small inland town is located 229km SE of Perth on the Great Southern Highway, 51km S of NARROGIN and 55km N of KATANNING. It is a rail junction on the Perth-ALBANY line, with branch routes E to towns in the wheat belt and W to COLLIE and BUNBURY. At an elevation of 256m above sea level and with an average annual rainfall of 433mm, it is a service and commercial centre to a grain growing, fodder crop and livestock grazing region. The town name comes from an Aboriginal word meaning 'the place where emus drink'.

wagtail, willie *see* flycatchers, etc.

wagtails *see* pipits, etc.

wahoo *see* fishes, bony

Waikerie SA (population 1 629 in 1981) A town and irrigation area on the MURRAY RIVER, downstream from LOXTON, it is located 173km by road and 288km by rail NE of Adelaide. At an elevation of 31m above sea level, the town experiences a mild climate, with a low rainfall of 247mm evenly spread throughout the year. It is the service centre for a prosperous region of vineyards and orchards where the lush green irrigated lands stand in stark contrast to the semi-arid mallee scrub landscape of the surrounding countryside. The area was settled in pastoral holdings in

Species, genus or family is endemic to Australia (see Preface)

J.H. Shaw

Irrigated citrus orchards at Waikerie on the Murray river SA

1880, but the installation of pumping facilities for lifting water from the Murray in the early part of this century led to the establishment of the irrigation area in 1908. The name Waikerie comes from an Aboriginal word which has two interpretations: the first means 'white grubs' (which are found in abundance in mallee tree roots) and the second, more commonly accepted, means 'wings' or 'anything that flies' or 'a place where wildfowl settle'.

Wakefield, Edward Gibbon (1796-1862)

Political theorist. As the author of a theory of systematic colonisation, he had a strong influence on British colonial policy in Australia and elsewhere, and promoted colonisation in Australia and New Zealand. It was while serving a sentence in Newgate Gaol for abducting a 15-year-old schoolgirl heiress that he developed a strong interest in colonisation. The essentials of his theory were first put forward in *A Letter From Sydney* (1829), which was written in Newgate but was expressed so persuasively that it was commonly assumed to have been the work of an inhabitant of NSW. This work was followed by a large number of pamphlets, articles, letters and short books, and by the longer *A View of the Art of Colonization* (1849). His essential argument rested on the assertion that while land was usually available in abundance in new colonies for settlement, capital and labour were scarce. This imbalance resulted from the mistake of making land too easy to obtain, with the consequence that very few men were willing to work as labourers. This in turn deterred men of capital from investing in colonial property, or prevented them from prospering if they did so, because they could not obtain enough labour to work their land and enable them to earn a good return on their capital. In some

colonies this difficulty had been partly overcome by the use of slaves or convicts, but Wakefield disapproved of this, being interested only in promoting colonies based on free labour and free institutions.

The way to promote economic growth in such colonies, he believed, was to dispose of all Crown land by selling it at a fairly high price, so that only men of considerable capital could buy it, while others would work as labourers. When asked what price should be charged, he answered that it would vary according to many circumstances, but stressed that it should be a 'sufficient' price—sufficient, that is, to achieve its object of balancing the supply of land, labour and capital. On the other hand, he did not envisage it as being so high that the poorer settlers would necessarily remain labourers all their lives. In time, the

National Library of Australia

Edward Gibbon Wakefield

industrious and thrifty among them would be able to buy land, but by that time more labourers would have arrived. If the price of land was kept 'sufficient', the supply of labour should never fail; and this could be made even more certain if the proceeds of land sales were used to fund an immigration scheme.

Wakefield publicised his scheme vigorously and won many disciples, some of whom were responsible for the passing of the South Australia Act in 1834. However, the colony of SA was founded only on a partial application of his principles, and even before the first colonists had arrived there he had disassociated himself from the project. Nevertheless, the difficulties which the colony met during its early years could be considered to have uncovered flaws in his theory, founded as it was on speculation unbacked by practical experience. In the meantime, his theory had been influential in bringing about in 1831 the ending of land grants throughout Australia in favour of sale of Crown lands by auction, and a general trend in official policy towards keeping settlement concentrated.

After the foundation of SA, Wakefield went to Canada as an adviser to Lord Durham, and is considered to have had considerable influence on the latter's *Report on the Affairs of British North America* (1840) which, by recommending internal self-government for colonies, proved to be one of the most important documents in the history of British colonial policy. He also founded the New Zealand Association, which was responsible for sending settlers to New Zealand from 1839 onwards. He lived from 1841 to 1844 in Canada, where he was a member of the General Assembly and wielded considerable influence as a government adviser. In 1853 he emigrated to New Zealand, where he was elected to the first General Assembly, and where he spent the rest of his life.

Further reading: Bloomfield, P. *Edward Gibbon Wakefield, Builder of the British Commonwealth.* Longman, London, 1961; Phillip, J. *A Great View of Things: Edward Gibbon Wakefield.* Nelson, Melbourne, 1971.

Wakelin, Roland Shakespeare (1887–1971)

Artist. Born in the Wairarapa, New Zealand, he studied painting at the Wellington Technical College, where he was influenced by D. K. Richmond. He arrived in Sydney in 1912, and attended the art classes given by Dattilo Rubbo, whose progressive attitude towards painting appealed to him. Through Nora Simpson, a fellow pupil, Wakelin was introduced to the work of Cézanne; he was also influenced by the work of Emmanuel Phillips FOX. Wakelin's major work, *Fruit Seller at Farm Cove* (1915), now in the National Gallery of Australia in Canberra, showed the direction he was to take. He joined forces with Grace Cossington SMITH and Roy DE MAISTRE, but the work of these three painters aroused considerable antagonism at Royal Art Society Exhibitions. In 1919, Wakelin and de Maistre exhibited a collection of works which attempted to depict a relationship between the theory and harmony of music and the tones of the artist's palette. A visit to Europe in 1922 and contact with works by Van Gogh, Renoir and Manet further inspired Wakelin and by 1926 he had created a considerable reputation for himself. In that year, he was invited by George LAMBERT to exhibit with other progressive artists in the Grosvenor Galleries. This formed the basis of the Contemporary Art Society (*see* PAINTINGS AND PAINTERS). Later in life, Wakelin's work became more subdued.

Wakool River NSW An ANABRANCH of the EDWARDS RIVER, in the central MURRAY RIVER valley, it leaves the Edwards about 10km W of DENILIQUIN, meanders for some 145km through semi-arid plain country, and rejoins the Edwards above its confluence with the Murray River. The VIC railway system, extending across the Murray at ECHUCA, crosses the Wakool River near the town of Wakool (318km N of Melbourne) and goes on to its terminus at BALRANALD. Since this region experiences low rainfall (annual average about 400mm) and droughts are not uncommon, irrigation has been used to provide stability in the rural economy. In the 1930s a diversion weir was built on the Edwards River (called Stevens Weir after the then State Premier), about 25km downstream from Deniliquin, to provide for livestock watering and pasture irrigation. In 1935 water was first made available to properties in the Wakool Irrigation District, located between the Wakool and Edwards Rivers. Rice growing was started in this District in 1942 and has now become a major farming activity on heavy soils suited to its cultivation.
Further reading: Shaw, J.H. 'Land use in Deniliquin region' in *The Australian Geographer.* (vol V1, no 2, March 1953).

Walgett NSW (population 2 157 in 1981) This town is located near the junction of the BARWON and NAMOI Rivers, 697km NW of Sydney on the Castlereagh Highway. It is the terminus of a railway line which branches off the main N tablelands route at Werris Creek and passes along the Namoi Valley through GUNNEDAH and NARRABRI. The town is 736km from Sydney by rail, at an elevation of 133m above sea level and is an important cattle railhead for an extensive area in the NW of the State. The name Walgett comes from the Aboriginal word meaning 'meeting of the waters' or 'a river crossing' or 'a long water hole'. The town receives an average rainfall of only 474mm, but the rainfall is highly variable and droughts are not uncommon. The opal-mining town LIGHTNING RIDGE lies 74km N of Walgett along the Castlereagh Highway, and other opal fields are located at Grawin and Glengarry about 70km NW of Walgett. Narran Lake, some 80km WNW of Walgett, is a haven for many aquatic birds, with kangaroos, emus, wild pigs, duck and quail common in the area.

Kath Walker

Walker, Kathleen Jean Mary (1920-   ) Poet. Born on STRADBROKE ISLAND, off the QLD coast, Kath Walker is considered the most notable Aboriginal poet in Australia. She began work as a domestic servant at the age of 13, served as a telephonist in the Australian Women's Army Service during World War II, and later trained as a stenographer. Her two volumes of verse, *We Are Going* (1964) and *The Dawn Is at Hand* (1966), the collection of poems, short stories and speeches, *My People* (1970), the collection of reminiscences and Aboriginal stories, *Stradbroke Dreamtime* (1972), and the children's story, *Father Sky and Mother Earth* (1982), have won a wide audience, and have been favourably reviewed in Australia and Britain for their sincerity, depth of feeling and simplicity and clarity of style. Most of her writing deals with the Aboriginal people—with their culture and history, with their treatment by settlers and with their reactions to their present situation. Her anger against racial discrimination finds its strongest expression in the first of her volumes.

wallabies *see* kangaroos, etc.

Wallace's line *see* fauna

Wallaroo SA (population 2 043 in 1981) A small town on the SPENCER GULF coast of the YORKE PENINSULA, it is 159km NW of Adelaide. It is one of SA's principal outports and is a bulk handling centre for grain and fertiliser; grain silos dominate the town's skyline and large overseas vessels berth at the deep-sea jetty. There are two fertiliser plants in the town for the processing of phosphate rock. The beaches and sporting facilities attract many tourists and holiday-makers in the summer months. In 1860, the discovery of rich copper ores near Wallaroo, as well as around MOONTA and KADINA, led to a boom growth of the town and the immigration of many Cornish miners to the region. Wallaroo was developed as the main smelting centre. Though the mines were closed in 1923, many relics of the copper era remain and every two years in May a Cornish Festival is held in the three towns, recalling the heyday of 'Little Cornwall'. The National Trust (SA) has designated numerous buildings in Wallaroo as part of the nation's historical and cultural heritage; among these are the courthouse, the railway station, a chimney stack, the public school, the customs house, miners' cottages, the Methodist church and a pumping station associated with the Wallaroo mines.

wallaroos *see* kangaroos, etc.

walnuts, sea *see* ctenophores

Waltzing Matilda This is the title of the best-known and best-loved Australian OUTBACK song and a close contender for recognition as a truly national song. The most generally accepted story of how the song came to be written attributes the tune to Miss Christine Macpherson, who picked out the tune, imperfectly remembered from a band performance at the WARRNAMBOOL races in VIC, for Banjo PATERSON in central western QLD in 1895. This tune, to which Paterson adapted his words, seems to have been in turn adapted from a Scottish song, 'Thou Bonnie Wood of Craigielea', *see also* National Anthem. *Further reading:* Manifold, J.S. *Who Wrote The Ballads?* Australian Book Society, Sydney, 1964.

wambenger *see* native cats, etc.

Wamberal NSW This holiday resort on the central coast, adjacent to TERRIGAL, is located 11km E of GOSFORD. The surfing beaches and lagoons nearby attract many visitors to the area and in summer it experiences a tourist influx. In recent times, there has been considerable land subdivision and rapid urban development, making it increasingly a retirement area and a permanent residential settlement.

wandering Jew *see* weeds

Wangaratta VIC (population 16 202 in 1981) A city located at the confluence of the OVENS and King Rivers, and at the junction of the Hume and Ovens Highways, 235km by road NE of Melbourne and 72km SW of ALBURY, it is a major regional service centre. At an elevation of 150m above sea level, it experiences a mild climate with hot summer conditions and cool winters. The average annual rainfall is 650mm, concentrated mainly in winter; June is the wettest month (72mm average), January the driest (38mm). The surrounding rural regions are noted for hops, tobacco, wine-grapes, timber and dairy products. There are numerous industrial enterprises in the city including textile mills, factories producing building materials, dairy processing works and sawmills. The Warby Ranges lie to the W of the City and at Glenrowan Gap, where the Hume Highway and the rail route pass across the ranges, 16km SW of the city, is the small town of GLENROWAN where the bushranger Ned KELLY made his last stand.

There are several well-known vineyards in the area such as Taminick (20km SW on Lake Mokoan) and Milawa (16km SE). The district was settled by squatters in the 1830s and its name was taken from an Aboriginal word meaning 'a nesting place of cormorants'. It became a borough in 1863 and was proclaimed a city in 1959. Several buildings have been listed by the National Trust (VIC) for preservation, including St Patrick's Catholic Church

View of Wangi Wangi NSW

and the shire hall. Lake Mokoan, one of the storage basins of the GOULBURN Valley irrigation scheme which receives water diverted from Hollands Creek and the Broken River, is a popular recreation area for sailing, water skiing, fish and picnics.

Wangi Wangi NSW (combined population of Wangi Wangi and Rathmines, 5km N, 5 107 in 1981) This small town and resort centre is located on the W shores of LAKE MACQUARIE, 40km by road SW of NEWCASTLE. The town name, which is usually reduced to a single 'Wangi', comes from an Aboriginal word probably meaning 'big water'. Situated near the township and towering 76m over the surrounding lakeside landscape are the chimney stacks of the Wangi electricity power station. This is a thermal generating plant, using coal locally mined in the lower HUNTER RIVER valley. The famed Australian artist, Sir William DOBELL, lived near Wangi for many years and painted a number of landscapes of the area; one of his best-known paintings is entitled *Wangi Boy*.

Wanneroo WA (population 6 745 in 1981) A satellite town N of Perth, it is located 24km by road from the city centre. It is situated in part of the rural-urban fringe of the city, with orcharding, poultry farming, viticulture, market gardening and timber-getting in the environs. However, recent housing and urban development has transformed much of the rural scene into residential areas, partly as dormitory suburbs for commuters who work in the metropolitan city.

Waranga Reservoir One of the storage basins of the GOULBURN RIVER irrigation schemes, originally constructed in 1905 and enlarged in 1926, with a capacity of 411 200ML, it is the third-largest reservoir in VIC, located about 20km SW of SHEPPARTON

and just NE of Rushworth town. It receives its water supply by a major canal from the Goulburn Weir and releases it for use on irrigated farms in the W parts of the irrigation district. There are two public access points to the reservoir (each with facilities for picnics), one near the northernmost point, the other from the SW, 5km from Rushworth. The name Waranga comes from an Aboriginal word meaning 'to sing'.

Waratah TAS (population 342 in 1981) A small town in the rugged NW region, near the headwaters of the ARTHUR RIVER and the upper tributaries of the PIEMAN RIVER, at an elevation of 624m above sea level, it is 8km W of the junction of the Waratah and Murchison Highways. it was the residential township for workers at the MOUNT BISCHOFF tin mine from the 1870s to 1945. In the heyday of mining, in the early 1900s, the town boasted four hotels and a population of about 6000. As the tin mining operations declined, so too did the town, but in recent years it has experienced a revival due to the mining developments at SAVAGE RIVER and other sites in the district. The town has a high rainfall (average annual 2 201mm), with the highest rainfall in winter.

waratah *see* Proteaceae

warblers and their allies These PASSERINE BIRDS belong to the cosmopolitan family Sylviidae, which contains 52 Australian species (in 16 genera) of which 43 are endemic. Generally, warblers are small, dull-brown BIRDS with thin pointed bills. As their name suggests, most have melodious songs, which are often useful for identification. Their food consists of insects, and most species build domed nests.

The genus *Acrocephalus* contains the reed warbler, *A. australis* (16cm to 17cm long), a

J. Purnell, (N.P.I.A.W.)

Mangrove warbler, *Gerygone levigaster*

dark brown bird with lighter underparts and a small crest. Occurring throughout Australia, it tends to conceal itself in thick vegetation in wet places but reveals its whereabouts by its loud, attractive song.

The genus *Cisticola* contains two very similar species of fantailed warblers—the golden cisticola, *C. exilis* (10cm), which frequents thick vegetation in coastal areas, and the streaked cisticola, *C. juncidis* (10cm), which is restricted to the flood plain margins near BURKETOWN and ROCKHAMPTON in QLD. Both species have streaky brown plumage; the former has a golden crown and is less heavily streaked than the latter.

The two species of grassbirds found in Australia belong to the genus *Megalurus*. The little grassbird, *M. gramineus*★ (14cm), of E and SW Australia, and the uncommon tawny grassbird, *M. timoriensis* (19cm), of coastal N and E Australia, are brown, black-streaked, white-breasted birds which frequent swamp vegetation. The little grassbird is distinguished by its smaller size and streaked crown.

The genus *Cinclorhamphus*★ contains two species of songlarks—the rufous songlark, *C.*★ *mathewsi* (15cm to 18cm), and the brown songlark, *C.*★ *cruralis* (18cm to 25cm). Widespread in grassland and savanna areas, these brown mainly terrestrial birds lack the white margin on the tail typical of the bushlark and the PIPIT. They are best distinguished by their song—the rufous species has a musical trill while the brown songlark utters a harsh, grating call.

Some authorities put the remaining warblers in the family Acanthizidae, regarding the above-mentioned species as Old World warblers and those described below as Australian warblers.

The spinifexbird, *Eremiornis*★ *carteri* (15cm), is a reddish-brown, white-breasted warbler with a long drooping tail; it lives in spinifex grass in arid parts of NW and central Australia

and north-western QLD.

The three bristlebirds—the eastern species, *Dasyornis*★ *brachypterus* (21cm to 22cm), the western species, *D.*★ *longirostris* (18cm), and the rufous bristlebird, *D.* ★ *broadbenti* (23cm to 25cm)—take their name from the conspicuous bristles around the beak. These rare, predominantly dark brown birds live in dense vegetation in restricted coastal regions in S and SE Australia; some authorities place them in the same family as the FAIRY-WRENS.

The fairy warblers belong to the genus *Gerygone*; of the 18 species in Australia and New Guinea, nine occur in Australia. They are small birds, with white on the tail and above the eye, and most live among foliage, particularly in the wetter areas of N and E Australia. Five species are endemic: the fairy warbler, *G. flavida*★ (10cm), dull green above and yellow below; the dusky warbler, *G. tenebrosa*★ (11cm to 12cm), face and upperparts light brown, underparts white to buff; the mangrove warbler, *G. levigaster*★ (10cm), greyish-brown upperparts, white underparts, and white spots on the tip of the tail; the white-tailed warbler, *G. fusca*★ (10cm), a white and olive brown species which ranges to the centre of the continent; and the brown warbler, *G. mouki*★ (9cm), a greyish-brown and white bird with a violet-grey face.

The weebill, *Smicornis brevirostris*★ (8cm to 9cm), so called because of its very short beak, is a brownish bird with a yellowish face and yellowish underparts. Found throughout the mainland in dry forests and semi-arid regions where there is plentiful leaf cover, this active bird builds cup-shaped nests (often domed) of leaves and buds. The thornbills of the genus *Acanthiza* resemble the weebill, but have longer beaks. Found in the drier regions of southern Australia, they were once called tits because, like the European tomtits and bluetits, they tend to move around in small flocks, working an area for insects. All 12

species found in Australia are endemic. Most species nest in low bushes; the pear-shaped nests have a hooded side entrance and are made of grass and bark and sometimes decorated with blossom.

The three species of whitefaces, of the genus *Aphelocephala*★, are similar to the thornbill, but they are more dumpy and have a distinctive, vertical, white face band. Their dome-shaped nests are large, untidy structures of twigs placed almost anywhere. The most widespread is the southern whiteface, *A.*★ *leucopsis* (10cm), dark greyish-brown above and white below, which frequents woodland, savanna and arid scrub areas throughout the S half of the mainland.

The scrubwrens, the heathwrens and the scrubtit make up the genus *Sericornis*, which probably contains about 10 species. Slimmer and usually slightly larger than warblers and thornbills, they are predominantly brown, sometimes with yellow underparts; some species have white eyebrows or white bars on the shoulders. They search for insects on or near the ground in dense undergrowth, mostly in damper areas, with various species replacing each other in different parts of the country. All species build dome-shaped nests, with a side entrance, and place them on or near the ground.

Three species which are closely related to the *Sericornis* group are the fernwren, *Oreoscopus*★ *gutturalis* (14cm), a long-billed, mostly dark bronze-brown bird with a white chin which lives in rainforest undergrowth in north-eastern QLD; the redthroat, *Pyrrholaemus*★ *brunneus* (12cm), a brown bird found in arid southern Australia; and the striated fieldwren, *Calamanthus*★ *fuliginosus* (12cm), which has blackish-brown streaks above and below and occurs in southern Australia in treeless country, from moist heaths to stony plains.

The speckled warbler, *Chthonicola*★ *sagittata* (11cm to 12cm), is a bird of timberland areas in SE Australia. It has streaked plumage, a white face and a white-speckled crown. The hooded grass and bark nests are placed in a depression in the ground. The unique rock warbler, *Origma*★ *solitaria* (14cm), a white-throated, dark brown bird which frequents rocky gullies near water in the HAWKESBURY RIVER sandstone area near Sydney, attaches its globular nests of grass and fibres to overhanging rocks or the roofs of caves. The pilot bird, *Pycnoptilus*★ *floccosus* (16cm to 17cm), an uncommon dark brown bird with a white belly, frequents the forest floors of the SE corner of Australia. It gained the name pilot bird because of is often seen in the company of the superb LYREBIRD, but this may be only because it feeds in a similar way in similar places. Its domed nests of bark have a side entrance and are placed on the ground.

Warburton

Warburton VIC (population 2 009 in 1981) A small resort town on the upper YARRA RIVER, 76km by road ENE of Melbourne (via the Maroondah and Warburton highways), and about 40km SE of HEALSVILLE. Located

*Species, genus or family is endemic to Australia (see Preface)

amidst scenic hill country on the lower slopes of the GREAT DIVIDING RANGE, with Mt Bride and Mt Tugwell near the town, and MT DONNA BUANG 18km to the N, it has long been a vacation and convention centre for city people. Horse riding, canoeing and bush-walking are popular recreational activities, with winter skiing in the nearby mountain area. The town was named after Charles Warburton Carr, a police magistrate and warden who was prominent in the early days of European settlement.

Warburton Range

WA A hilly range in the mid-E arid region of the State, with peaks reaching over 700m above sea level, it forms the boundary between the GIBSON DESERT to the N and the GREAT VICTORIA DESERT to the S. The range has a general E-W trend along the 26°S parallel of latitude and is, geologically, a W continuation of the crystalline MUSGRAVE RANGES of the NT. The records of the meteorological station in the range, at an elevation of 364m above sea level, indicate the arid nature of the climate: the average annual rainfall is only 213mm, with the two wettest months being January (26mm average) and February (28mm).

Ward, Frederick

'Captain Thunderbolt' (1835-70) Bushranger. Born at WINDSOR in NSW, he worked as a youth in various jobs concerned with horses—as stockman. groom and horse breaker. His first criminal conviction was for horse stealing, in 1846. Sentenced to 10 years' imprisonment, he gained a ticket of leave after serving about half of this term, but before long was given an extended sentence for another horse stealing offence. This time he proved a less patient prisoner and in 1863 escaped from the penal establishment on Cockatoo Is in Sydney Harbour by swimming to the mainland. Taking to the bush he carried out robberies at first in the BOURKE district, but from 1864 concentrated on NEW ENGLAND and the HUNTER RIVER valley. He operated sometimes with a small gang but more often alone; he concentrated on holding up mail coaches and, by avoiding violence, won a reputation as a 'gentleman bushranger'. In May 1870 a police constable named Walker cornered Ward at the edge of a lagoon near Uralla, shot his horse from under him and then, while struggling with Ward in the water, shot him also. Thunderbolt Rock, in the same district, was one of Ward's lookouts. He was buried in Uralla.
Further reading: Macdonald, Rev. J.M. *Thunderbolt, an Australian Story.* Hurst & Blackett, London, 1894; Walker, R.B. 'Captain Thunderbolt, Bushranger' in *Journal of the Royal Australian Historical Society.* (vol 43, 1957).

Wardell, William Wilkinson

(1823-99) Architect. After training as an engineer, Wardell, a Londoner, was encouraged in the study of Gothic architecture by Augustus Pugin (one of the leading exponents of the Gothic Revival) and the Rev. J.H. Newman (later Cardinal) who became his friends. He was converted to Roman Catholicism, began an architectural practice in London, and built some 30 churches before contracting tuberculosis. He was advised to seek a healthier climate and sailed for Melbourne in 1858.

By 1861 he was Inspector-General of Public Works for VIC, with the right of private practice, and had already begun work on St Patrick's Cathedral, in the city of Melbourne, which is one of the most splendid examples of the Gothic Revival style in Australia. At the same time he designed, without charge, the Anglican Church of St John at Toorak, thereby angering private architects who did not have the sustenance of a civil servant's salary. St John's is one of the finest parish church designs. An indication of Wardell's widening reputation was that at the same time he was designing St John's College at the University of Sydney, the two new cathedrals dedicated to St Mary in Sydney and Hobart, and VIC's new Government House, his first essay into the Renaissance style.

Dismissed with many others by the VIC government in 1878, Wardell went to Europe and developed an enthusiasm for Italian architecture. Upon his return he settled in Sydney, and the remainder of his professional life was spent designing buildings with an Italianate flavour, such as the recently restored New South Wales Club in Blight Street, Sydney, with its attractive Roman facade. The English, Scottish and Australian Bank in Collins Street, Melbourne, commenced in 1883, is an example of Venetian design. Its extraordinarily ornate banking chamber, framed in iron, with columns cast at Mort's Engineering Works in Sydney and finely wrought decoration featuring Australian ferns, flowers and fruit, is one of the finest 19th-century buildings in Australia.

Further reading: Nairn, B. (ed) *Australian Dictionary of Biography.* (vol 6) Melbourne University Press, Melbourne, 1976.

Warracknabeal

VIC (population 2 735 in 1981) A country town in the WIMMERA region, at the junction of the Henty and Borung Highways, it is situated on Yarriambiak Creek, a tributary of the Wimmera River. It is on one of the tentacle railway lines of western VIC and is 349km by rail from Melbourne. At an elevation of 113m above sea level, it has an average annual rainfall of only 490mm. The surrounding rural region produces wool, wheat and fat lambs. It is usually accepted that the town's name originates from an Aboriginal word meaning 'gum trees around a hollow' or 'flooded red gum trees', although Mrs G.H. Warrack of Edinburgh, Scotland, claimed in 1932 that the town derived its name from her family and that *nabeal* was a Gaelic word meaning 'a ravine'.

Warragamba River

NSW A section of the NEPEAN-HAWKESBURY river system is called Warragamba. One of the headwater streams of this system, the WOLLONDILLY, which rises in the N part of the SOUTHERN TABLELANDS, is joined by the Cox River from the BLUE MOUNTAINS. Downstream from this junction to the point where it enters the Nepean, it is called Warragamba. Though all these streams are sections of the Nepean-Hawkesbury river system, the various parts of the river were given different names because they were discovered at different times in the early days of British exploration; it was only later realised that they were, in fact, parts of the one system. The section called the Warragamba is some 22km long and flows in a narrow steep-sided gorge bounded by sandstone cliffs and cutting through the sedimentary rocks of the Blue Mountains region. The

Warragamba Dam, a major source for Sydney's water supply

J.H. Shaw

Warragamba Dam wall, built across the gorge, is 116m high. The waters impounded by the dam (over two million ML) form the main reservoir for Sydney's water supply; they extend upstream in the gorge and into the valleys of the Cox and Wollondilly; the reservoir is named Lake Burragorang, an Aboriginal name meaning 'a tribe which lives in a valley where there is plenty of game'.

Warragul VIC (population 7 715 in 1981) A market and service town in the dairying and agricultural lands of W GIPPSLAND, Warragul is 129km by road ESE of Melbourne on the Princes Highway and 45km W of MORWELL. At an elevation of 116m above sea level, near the headwaters of tributaries of the LATROBE RIVER, it has a mild climate with a high average annual rainfall of 1 051mm; this rain occurs throughout the year, though the highest rainfall is in late winter and spring. The town is situated in an area of basaltic rocks which have produced particularly fertile soils suitable for cultivation and intensive grazing. It is an important commercial centre, with some light industries such as clothing, dairy processing and rope making. The historical museum and the annual arts festival are among the tourist attractions of the town. The name Warragul comes from an Aboriginal word meaning 'wild'.

Warren NSW (population 2 153 in 1981) A small country town in the NW plains region of the State, Warren is on the Oxley Highway, 19km off the Mitchell Highway, 75km by road SE of NYNGAN, 77km W of GILGANDRA, and 526km NW of Sydney. It is situated on the MACQUARIE RIVER, downstream from DUBBO, at an elevation of 198m above sea level and has an average annual rainfall of 598mm; October is the wettest month (98mm average), May is the driest (28mm). It is in the midst of a rich pastoral district, where there are several Merino studs. In recent times, irrigation water from BURRENDONG DAM has converted the previously unproductive black soil into farming land suitable for the cultivation of cotton, grain, sorghum and fodder crops. Birds are a feature of the Warren area and vast numbers of many species are to be found in Macquarie Marshes, 112km to the N. Warren's showground-racecourse complex is considered one of the best in inland NSW. The name Warren comes from an Aboriginal word meaning 'strong', 'substantial' or 'well-built'.

warrigal *see* dingo

Warrnambool VIC (population 21 415 in 1981) A picturesque and progressive city, it is located on the Princes Highway, 264km WSW of Melbourne, between PORTLAND and CAMPERDOWN, on the rugged W coast near the estuary of the Hopkins River. It lies on the S fringe of the WESTERN DISTRICT and is often called the capital of this rich dairying and vegetable growing region. It experiences a

Crater Bluff, Warrumbungle Range NSW

mild climate throughout the year, with an average annual rainfall of 726mm, concentrated in winter and spring. This climatic pattern, combined with fertile volcanic soils, has made the district a productive farming and grazing region, for which the city is the commercial and service centre. A number of large secondary industries play an important part in the district's economy including woollen mills, a garment factory and a dairy processing works, as well as small enterprises such as timber mills, a plastics factory and engineering workshops. There are numerous tourist attractions in the city: Albert Park (58ha), with its sporting facilities; Lady Bay Beach, for swimming and surfing; the nearby Hopkins River (for about 20km upstream to Hopkins Falls), for boating and fishing; an aquarium and marine museum; a reptile park (3km NE of the city); and Flagstaff Hill Maritime Village, a reminder of the city and port as it was in former days.

The name Warrnambool, given to the township in 1847, was taken from an Aboriginal word which has several possible meanings: 'place of plenty', 'a grassy watercourse' or 'running swamps'. The township became a municipality in 1855, a borough in 1863, a town in 1883 and a city in 1918. Several buildings have been listed by the National Trust (VIC) for preservation, including the lighthouse keeper's quarters and store (1859), the former National Bank, the post office, the art gallery (formerly the ANZ Bank), the Masonic temple and the district hospital (1854). SE of the city, along the Great Ocean Road, is Port Campbell National Park (700ha), known widely for its coastal scenery, along a 30km stretch, where the flat coastal plains terminate in a series of vertical cliffs, caverns, archways, and special features are

London Bridge, The Blowhole, Lochard Gorge and the Twelve Apostles.

Warrumbungle Range NSW This strikingly scenic range rises abruptly from the NW plain of the State, forming a N arc around the town of COONABARABRAN, some 580km by road NW of Sydney. It consists of a cluster of ancient volcanic peaks, formed by the hardening of lava inside the volcanoes and the subsequent erosion and removal of the outer cone, thus leaving the volcanic plugs jutting abruptly above the surrounding countryside. Among the peaks in the range are Belongery Spire, the Breadknife, the Needle and Crater Bluff. Mt Exmouth (or Wombelong), the highest peak, reaches 1 228m above sea level. The Warrumbungle National Park (19 456ha), 24km W of Connabarabran, includes spectacular scenery and is a popular bushwalking and rock climbing area. The name Warrumbungle comes from the Aboriginal word meaning 'short (or small) mountains'. The CASTLEREAGH RIVER rises on the S slopes of the range, and some headwater tributaries of the NAMOI RIVER rise to the N and NE.

Warung, Price (1855-1911) Journalist and short-story writer. This was the pen-name used by William Astley. Born in Liverpool, England, he was brought to Australia at the age of four, was educated in Melbourne and worked as a journalist in VIC, TAS and NSW. Early in his career he became interested in the history of the convict period and most of the stories which he contributed to the *Bulletin* and other journals were set in this period; many, indeed, were based on particular incidents involving convicts and referred to in historical documents. As might be expected, he tended to dwell on the dramatic and gruesome aspects of the convict system; however, his stories gave a vivid picture of some of the harsher aspects of life in early colonial times. Published collections of his stories include *Tales of the Convict System* (1892), *Tales of the Early Days* (1894), *Tales of the Old Regime and the Bullet of the Fated Ten* (1897), *Tales of the Isle of Death, Norfolk Island* (1898) and *Half-Crown Bob and Tales of the Riverine* (1898).

QLD Govt Tourist Bureau

Leslie Dam near Warwick QLD

Warwick QLD (population 8 853 in 1981) Often referred to as the 'Rose city', it is renowned for its picturesque rural countryside, its mild climate and its attractive parklands and gardens. It is located at the junction of the New England and Cunningham Highways, 161km SW of Brisbane, 84km S of TOOWOOMBA and 58km N of STANTHORPE in the S part of the DARLING DOWNS. Situated on the CONDAMINE RIVER at an elevation of 480m above sea level, it is the main commercial and service centre for a rich dairying, beef cattle and wheat growing region. It has an average annual rainfall of 644mm, concentrated mainly in the summer months, with a period of lower rainfall in winter and spring. The Leslie Dam on Sandy Creek, a tributary of the Condamine, lies 13km W of the city; it was completed in 1965, with a storage capacity of 107 310ML, a wall height of 24m and a crest length of 399m; it augments the city's water supply and provides water for the cultivation of irrigated crops such as cotton, lucerne, maize, pastures, sorghum and wheat along the flats of the Condamine Valley. The dam is also used as a recreation and aquatic sports area, and a regatta is held annually over the Queen's Birthday weekend in June. The Queen Mary Falls National Park (78ha), 44km SE of Warwick and 10km E of Killarney in the headwaters region of the Condamine, includes several waterfalls, rainforest in the gullies and stretches of tall open eucalypt woodland. The Cunningham's Gap park along the Cunningham Highway 50km NE of Warwick is part of the Main Range section of the Scenic Rim Nation Park which covers 10 500ha and includes stretches of rainforest and eucalypt forest. Connolly Dam at Silverwood, 19km S, is another popular picnic and recreation spot, and the 'Cherribah' mountain resort is a well-known holiday centre. Warwick is also noted for its annual rodeo and festival, held in

QLD Govt Tourist Bureau

Queen Mary Falls near Warwick QLD

October, and for the Rock-Swap Festival, held at Easter.

wasps *see* ants, etc

water bears Known also as bear animalcules, these minute, aquatic animals form the phylum Tardigrada. Most live in water films on damp moss, but some are freshwater animals and a few are marine. They range in size from about 0.5mm to 1mm. The body is short and more or less cylindrical, and carries four pairs of sturdy legs with claws; it is covered with a thin cuticle which is sometimes divided into plates. The body apparently does not contain chitin. Most water bears feed on the contents of plant cells, which are punctured by mouth stylets. Like many other minute aquatic animals, they can withstand desiccation and cold temperatures. When in this resistant stage they can be blown for long distances by the wind, and this accounts for the cosmopolitan distribution of some species; for example, an Australian species, *Macrobiotus hufelandi*, also occurs in Europe.

water boatmen *see* bugs

water fleas *see* crustaceans

water hyacinth This very beautiful but extremely noxious water plant, *Eichhornia crassipes* (family Pontederiaceae) came from South America and has spread to many of the warmer parts of the world. The flowers, which in appearance resemble those of a hyacinth, are blue with yellow markings. The fleshy leaves are round and are carried on spongy swollen stalks. The plant reproduces vegetatively by means of stolons and the floating mass can quickly block a waterway and reduce the water to a stinking slime. The water hyacinth occurs in NSW, VIC, QLD, TAS and SA. Considered to be a WEED, its BIOLOGICAL CONTROL is being investigated. *See also* Appendix 5, Flower Structure and Glossary of Botanical Terms

water polo This sport was first played in Australia in the late 19th century; with the establishment of the NSW Amateur Swimming Association in 1892, it became one of the activities of swimming clubs. Interstate competitions began in 1922 and the first Australian Water Polo championships were conducted in 1948 with teams from VIC, NSW and QLD competing. In the same year a water polo team represented Australia for the first time at the Olympic Games. Since 1965 a concerted effort has been made to elevate Australian water polo to world-class standard. To gain experience against top national sides, European tours were organised in 1965 and 1967 and teams were sent to the world championships in 1973 and 1975 and to each Olympic Games. On a European tour in 1978, Australia defeated Holland, the 1976 Olympic bronze medallists—the first time an Australian team had beaten a European country in international competition. The influx of migrants from Europe since World War II from Europe has helped spread interest in the game and lift the standard of play. Water polo is now so popular that, including school teams, there are more teams in Sydney than in any other city in the world. However, due in part to a lack of publicity, the sport does not attract large crowds.

water scorpions *see* bugs

water skiing Australians tend to excel at water sports and water skiing is no exception. It was probably introduced into the country in 1936 when Carl Atkinson water skied across Sydney Harbour much to the surprise of onlookers who had never seen water skiing before. The police were more concerned than surprised and, fearing for the safety of water traffic, banned Atkinson from making any repeat performances. Reg Johnston is also credited with introducing Australians to the sport: in the 1930s he was inspired to make himself some skis and try out the sport after seeing an American film on water skiing. However, the sport did not begin to develop until the 1950s when a buoyant economy coupled with cheaper boats provided a wider range of Australians with the means to afford water skiing. The sport is widely popular and on weekends and holidays most stretches of accessible calm water are criss-crossed with the lines of white foam left in the wake of speeding skiers.

A. Woods

Water hyacinth, *Eichhornia crassipes*

Competitive water skiing Water skiing championships are held in three sections: slalom, jump and tricks. In the slalom event competitors weave between buoys anchored at fixed intervals in the water and are awarded points depending on the speed of the towing boat and the length of the tow rope. In the jump, skiers are towed at speed up a ramp from which they launch themselves through the air, the winner being the skier who jumps the furthest. In the tricks section, competitors perform a variety of acrobatic manoeuvres, such as a 360° turn while being towed, and are awarded points depending on the difficulty of the trick and the skill of its execution. Australia has produced some oustandingly successful competitors, such as Bruce Cockburn. By 1977, in his eight years of competition in the Australian water skiing championships, Cockburn won the tricks eight times, the jump five times, the slalom twice and was overall points-score champion eight times. In 1969 he became the only Australian to win a world championship when he won the tricks section. Distance racing is another form of competitive water skiing and, in 1977, Robbie Woods (nicknamed 'the Bionic Kangaroo' by American skiers) became the youngest skier ever to win the US national title after winning 26 out of the 27 qualifying races. Barefoot water skiing is fast growing in popularity as a competitive event; Australians won all gold medals at the first world barefoot ski championships held on the MOLONGLO RIVER in Canberra in 1978. The Australians followed up this success by winning the teams event in the 1980 and 1982 world championships. Outstanding individual performances were by Brett Wing, who won the men's overall title on all three occasions, and by Kim Lampard, who won the women's overall title in 1980 and 1982.

Watling, Thomas (1762-) Artist. The proprietor of and teacher in a drawing academy in Dumfries, Watling was transported in 1792 for forging Bank of Scotland notes. He thus became the first artist to arrive in the colony. He recorded the animal and bird life of the convict settlement, and in 1794 he produced the first oil painting in Australia, *A Direct North General View of Sydney Cove*, now in the Dixson Galleries, Sydney. Watling received a conditional pardon in 1796. His place and date of death are unknown.

Watson, John Christian (1867-1941) First Labor Prime Minister of Australia. Born in Chile, he was taken by his parents to New Zealand as a child and came to Sydney in 1886. He worked as a compositor, and by 1893 had become president of the Sydney Trades and Labour Council and of the NSW branch of the Australian Labour Federation (ALF), the precursor of the AUSTRALIAN LABOR PARTY (ALP). In the following year he presided at the ALF conference which framed the 'solidarity pledge', by which Labor members have been required ever since to support caucus decisions. He was a member of

the NSW Legislative Assembly from 1894 to 1901, was then elected to the federal House of Representatives and became the first leader of the federal parliamentary Labor Party. He showed himself to be a clear speaker and a skilful political tactician, and in 1904 succeeded in reversing the roles of Labor and DEAKIN's protectionist party by becoming Prime Minister with protectionist support. After four months, however, when the House of Representatives rejected his proposal that provision be made for preference to unionists in the legislation setting up the Commonwealth Court of Conciliation and Arbitration, his Ministry fell. He was replaced as party leader by Andrew FISHER in 1907 and resigned from Parliament in 1910, but remained a member of the party until expelled for his support of conscription in 1916. He was subsequently director of a number of companies and was president of the National Roads and Motorists Association for many years.

wattles *see* Mimosaceae

wattlebirds *see* honeyeaters

Wauchope NSW (population 3 644 in 1981) A small country town in the mid-NORTH COAST region of the State, it is situated on the HASTINGS RIVER, inland from PORT MACQUARIE, 432km by road N of Sydney. At an elevation of only 9m above sea level, the town is the commercial and service centre of the Hastings Valley region. The district is noted for dairying, beef cattle grazing, lucerne growing, maize cultivation and timber-getting in the densely forested rugged ranges to the W. The town has an average annual rainfall of 1 282mm, with the greatest concentration in the summer season. There are several timber mills in the town, as well as plywood and veneer works.

wax flowers These shrubs belong to the genus *Eriostemon* (family RUTACEAE); the genus is represented in all States. The large flowers have waxy petals; they are usually star-shaped but some are cup-like. Several species are cultivated as ornamentals. An example of an Australian species is the native daphne, *E. myoporoides*, found in the E parts of the continent.

Wayatinah TAS A dam and power station at the confluence of the DERWENT and Nive Rivers, it is 8km S of the Tarraleah Highway and 120km NW of Hobart. These structures form part of the extensive hydro-electricity generating system of the upper Derwent Valley in the CENTRAL PLATEAU region of the State. Upstream from Wayatinah is the Butlers Gorge power station which utilises water released from LAKE KING WILLIAM through the Clark Dam outlets; after generating power at Butlers Gorge, this water, augmented by supplies brought by canal and pipeline from adjacent catchments, is utilised at three other generating stations (TARRALEAH, TUNGA-

TINAH and LIAPOOTAH) before it passes to Wayatinah station. Downstream on the main Derwent is the CATAGUNYA Dam and power station where the water is again used for hydro-electricity generation. The Wayatinah station, commissioned in 1957, has an installed capacity of 38 250kW. The name is taken from an Aboriginal word meaning 'a brook or creek'.

weather and climate Although a large proportion of Australia experiences unfavourable climatic conditions—more than half the interior is arid or semi-arid and the N coastline is a region of tropical heat and humidity—the SE and SW portions enjoy a pleasant, temperate climate and the settled regions in general have a uniformity of climate and weather hardly matched elsewhere in the world. This uniformity is due to the moderating influence of the oceans that surround the continent and to the lack of extensive areas of high mountains. Australia extends in latitude over 35°, from the near tropics to the 'roaring forties', but compared with land masses of similar size and position N of the equator has relatively little variation in climate; a few population centres experience extreme weather conditions, such as blizzards, tornadoes, intense heat or torrential rainfall.

Weather versus climate Weather refers to shifts in rainfall, winds, temperature and cloudiness from day to day and week to week, while climate is bound up with averages of these elements over years and decades. Weather is variable in time and space, fluctuating between extremes, though for the most part remaining close to long term averages which vary with the season of the year. Climate is not variable, although climatic averages are subject to drift and change over centuries and millennia.

The main factor shaping climate and weather in Australia is the position of the continent in relation to the circulation patterns within the atmosphere of the earth. The atmosphere can be likened to a huge engine, driven by the heat of the sun and transferring masses of hot and cold air by means of winds. The tilt of the earth combined with the yearly movement of the earth around the sun causes the sun to move N and S in the sky throughout the years. It is furthest N in June; in March and September, at the equinoxes, it stands over the equator at noon; and it reaches its greatest distance S in December, standing over the Tropic of Capricorn on midsummer day. The surface of the earth immediately beneath the sun receives the most heat. Here the air expands and rises, creating a zone of low pressure called the equatorial trough. In the summer of the N hemisphere the trough lies to the N of the equator; in the summer of the S hemisphere it lies across the N part of Australia.

Air which has risen from the trough flows toward the poles and cools. Some of it descends in a belt about 30° or 35° away from the trough, creating a zone of high pressure, known as the sub-tropical anti-cyclones or the

Table 1

COMPARATIVE CLIMATIC DATA FOR AUSTRALIAN CITIES

	Hobart	Melbourne	Canberra	Adelaide	Sydney	Perth	Brisbane	Darwin
Mean annual rainfall (mm)	622	658	639	533	1 216	883	1 146	1 813
Mean January rainfall (mm)	45	48	61	20	100	8	166	404
Mean July rainfall (mm)	54	49	38	66	107	174	57	1
Mean daily hours of sunshine	5.9	5.7	7.2	6.9	6.7	7.9	7.5	8.5
Annual number of cloudfree days	22	48	83	83	85	108	98	121
Annual number of rainy days	162	148	110	120	139	119	123	111
Mean daily max temp—January (°C)	21.8	26.5	27.5	28.5	25.7	30.3	28.9	31.9
Mean daily min temp—July (°C)	4.5	6.2	-0.3	7.9	8.3	9.2	9.8	20.2
Number of thunder days	5	13	20	15	25	13	34	71
Hottest day on record	4.1.1976	13.1.1939	1.2.1968	12.1.1939	14.1.1939	8.2.1933	26.1.1940	17.10.1892
(°C) max temp	40.8	45.6	42.2	47.6	45.3	44.6	43.2	40.5
Wettest day on record	15.9.1959	20.1.1963	21.10.1959	7.2.1925	28.2.1942	10.6.1920	21.1.1887	7.1.1897
(mm) rainfall	156	108	105	141	281	99	465	296

horse-latitudes. In summer the high pressure zone is centred on the 40th parallel and so lies mostly S of Australia; in winter it is located close to the 30th parallel and thus covers most of the continent. This annual movement of the pressure systems has a profound influence on the weather of the whole continent.

To complete the cycle there is a steady flow of air at the surface from the high pressure zone back towards the equatorial trough. The rotation of the earth bends these winds so that they appear to blow from the SE, and consequently they are known as the south-east trade winds. They blow steadily over most of the N regions during the winter. In summer, when the trough lies over N Australia, the far N coasts become subject to trade winds blowing down from the NW towards the trough. These trade winds are heavy with moisture drawn from the warm tropical seas and their arrival marks the start of the monsoon season, better known as 'the Wet'. Between December and March, the region between CAPE YORK and PORT HEDLAND receives almost all its annual rainfall, while in winter, owing to the dry SE trade winds blowing overland, there is almost a drought. Summer is also the season for tropical cyclones along N shores. These emanate from the equatorial trough and bring much of the summer rainfall, particularly along the far N coast of QLD, where the presence of mountains close to the shore helps to extract rain from these disturbances—the stretch from TOWNSVILLE to COOKTOWN is the wettest part of the continent, with annual falls usually above 2500mm (TULLY receives over 4200mm).

Seasonal movement of weather systems
In general, weather systems in the N move from E to W, under the influence of the SE trade winds; further S the trend is from W to E. The boundary between the two zones is formed by the belt of anti-cyclones. S of this belt, in the region of the 'roaring forties', the rotation of the earth causes a steady wind to blow from the W; this wind carries a series of intense low pressure cells, called depressions or cyclones, which are able to generate rain and strong winds. In summer, when the anti-cyclone belt lies across the GREAT AUSTRALIAN BIGHT and the SE of the continent, the lows

are forced far S. As winter advances, the anti-cyclone belt retreats N, allowing the lows to strike the S coasts. As a result, SW Australia, the coast of SA and the W parts of VIC and TAS are areas of winter rainfall, in contrast to the summer rain in the far N. The mountainous regions of western TAS are very wet, Lake Margaret having an annual rainfall of over 3600mm.

The S Ocean lows interact with the anti-cyclone belt, breaking it up into a series of migrating highs, separated by low pressure troughs which often bring a shift in wind and weather. These cross the continent at intervals of about five days, though this is variable. In the SE of the continent and on the E side of TAS, rainfall is largely uniform throughout the year, due to the combined influence of the westerlies and winds off the Tasman. On the SE coast, spring is often the driest season; rainfall is highest between the ocean and the GREAT DIVIDING RANGE.

Rainfall Australia is the driest continent, excluding Antarctica, and no continent has less runoff from its rivers. Much of the country is arid, with sandy and stony deserts receiving less than 250mm a year. The driest area is around the salt lakes of SA where annual falls of less than 100mm are common. There are many reasons for this dryness. The interior is far from the ocean and lacks the mountain ranges needed to extract moisture from winds. In WA, where the arid zone reaches the coast, a cold current reduces the amount of moisture in onshore winds. More importantly, much of Australia lies in the belt of anti-cyclones, which are responsible for many of the world's deserts. In an anti-cyclone, cold dry air is descending from the upper levels of the atmosphere, producing mostly fine clear weather and an outward flow of winds from the centre. Moisture-laden winds are usually unable to penetrate and bring rain.

The reliability of rainfall is of vital importance to agriculture. The regions of most reliable rain lie in the SW of WA, western TAS and in the S and W parts of VIC. Here the influence of persistent westerlies ensures that there is little variation in the annual rainfall. At the other extreme, a zone

stretching from around Birdsville QLD across to the WA coast shows great variability, a fact made more serious by the low annual rainfall. As an example, Whim Creek near the coast of WA received only 4mm of rain in 1924, while the rare occurrence of a tropical cyclone in the region has caused falls of more than 700mm in a single day.

The rainfall records for Australia have all been set along the NE coast of QLD. The record maximum for a single day is 910mm (at Crohamhurst, February 1893); for a single month 3000mm (at Crohamhurst, February 1893); and for a single year 7900mm (at Tully, 1950). For comparison, the world record for a day is 1170mm (at Baguio, the Philippines); for a month, 9300mm (at Cherrapunji, India); and for a year, 26500mm (at Cherrapunji).

Snow Since most of Australia lies in the mid-latitudes and lacks high mountains, only two areas have regular snow falls—the AUSTRALIAN ALPS, above 1500mm altitude, and the TAS highlands, above 1200m. During winter, when very cold air from the polar oceans enters Australia, snow can fall along the Great Dividing Range as far N as the NEW ENGLAND area and even into southern QLD.

Hail Hailstones are produced when small frozen raindrops are blown violently up and down inside thunderclouds; water freezes on the surface of the stone, causing it to grow in size until it is heavy enough to fall against the updraft. Hail most commonly occurs in the passage of cold fronts through the SE of the continent during the winter and early spring. Violent summer thunderstorms can also create hailstones, often of large size (up to 25cm in circumference); damage to fruit crops from large hailstones is common.

Frosts When the temperature of the air in contact with the ground falls below -1°C, water in the tissues of plants freezes, causing damage which may result in the death of the plant. Normally, water vapour in the air freezes at the same time, producing a covering of ice on the ground. If the air is very dry, a visible frost may not form although damage will still be done to plants. This condition is known as black frost. Frosts are more common in winter, in S latitudes and at high altitude. They are also more plentiful during cold outbreaks and in times of clear weather during the passage of an anti-cyclone. Frosts are unknown along the N coast from CARNARVON to BUNDABERG but occur six days out of seven in highland regions.

Thunderstorms Thunder and lightning occur together since thunder is the result of the rapid expansion of air caused by the heat of the lightning stroke. Lightning is electrical sparking on a gigantic scale resulting from the build-up of electrical charges in clouds, this in turn being caused by violent updrafts during the passage of a cold front or as the consequence of the heat of a summer day. Thunderstorms are commonest in the hot humid conditions in the far N of the continent, where thunder is heard on more than 60 days a year. The uplift of air crossing a mountain range can also cause thunderstorms; they occur on more than 40 days a year in areas of the Great Dividing Range in VIC, NSW and QLD.

Floods Despite the construction of control dams and levee banks, heavy rain still results in destructive floods along many Australian rivers. Coastal rivers in NSW and QLD flood most commonly in summer; rivers in the S part of the continent, including the MURRUM-BIDGEE-MURRAY system, flood in winter. Heavy summer monsoon rains in inland QLD drain S through the usually dry river beds of the CHANNEL COUNTRY and empty into the region of the great salt lakes, sometimes inundating for a brief time many thousands of square kilometres and often causing a spectacular though short-lived flowering of desert plants.

Drought The regions most prone to drought are those which combine low annual rainfall with high variability from year to year. TAS, southern VIC and the SW tip of the continent have the lowest incidence of drought; incidence is highest around Birdsville, in central WA and along the coast from ONSLOW to Port Hedland.

Hot areas and cold areas The most consistently hot regions lie in the N, particularly in inland areas away from the cooling effects of sea breezes. In western QLD and inland from the NW coast of WA shade temperatures rise to above 38°C (100°F) on most days in January. In the summer of 1923-24, MARBLE BAR in north-western WA experienced over 38°C on 160 consecutive days. The highest shade temperature on record, 53.1°C (127.5°F), was reached on 16 January 1889 at CLONCURRY in QLD. For a capital city, the record is held by Adelaide with a top temperature of 47.6°C (117.7°F) on 12 January 1939.

The month with the highest mean temperature varies from December in the far N (November in Darwin) to February in TAS. In the N, the build-up of monsoon cloud cools the latter part of summer, while in the S the time taken to warm the ocean delays the peak temperature until late summer. July is the coldest month throughout the continent, with the lowest temperatures occurring consistently in the far S and in the mountain regions. The lowest temperature on record is -22.2°C (-8°F)

at Charlotte Pass in the Australian Alps on 14 June 1945 and 22 July 1947. Of the capitals, Hobart has the lowest annual mean temperature, though the coldest day in a capital city, -2.8°C (27°F), was in Melbourne on 21 July 1869. For comparison, the world temperature extremes are 58.9°C (138°F) at Azizia in Tunisia and -88.3°C (-190.9°F) at Vostock in Antarctica.

Winds Australia is not a particularly windy continent. In most centres mean daily wind speeds are between 10kph and 20kph, though daily means approaching 40kph and gusts of well over 100kph do occur. Three of the main seasonal wind changes have been noted above: the spread of westerlies over the S regions with the advance of winter; the simultaneous contraction N along the E coast of the influence of the SE trade winds; and the onset in late spring of the NW monsoon along the far N Coast. A second set of seasonal changes relates to the movement of the belt of anti-cyclones. For example, in Sydney during winter the track of a typical high lies to the N of the city; since winds blow anti-clockwise around a high, the steady E movement of the high results in Sydney experiencing a regular cycle of winds spread over a week or more, commencing with SW winds which swing W and then NW. In summer, anti-cyclones pass generally to the S of the city and the cycle begins with S winds, swinging in turn SE, E, NE and N. Thus dry westerlies tend to prevail in winter and more humid winds from the E in summer. Similar considerations apply to other parts of the country.

The daily cycle of winds is most obvious in summer along the coast, where the land heats up more quickly than the nearby ocean as the day advances. Hot air over the land rises, cooler air from over the ocean flows into replace it and a sea breeze is established; at night the reverse occurs and a land breeze is established. The land breeze is commonly weaker than the sea breeze. The cooling effect of the sea breeze causes temperatures on a sunny summer day to be noticeably lower along the coast than at a point a short distance inland.

Past climate The climate of the inhabited parts of Australia has not always been as benign as it is now. Only 15 000 years ago, Australia was emerging from the last Great Ice Age, which had lasted for 100 000 years. At the height of this glacial period, average temperatures over Australia were lowered by up to 10°C. (As a comparison, the mean temperatures of Hobart and Brisbane today differ by about 8°C.) The lower temperatures meant less evaporation from the surrounding oceans and as a result the climate was also much drier then, with many places receiving only half their current rainfall. About 5000km² of the TAS highlands were covered with glaciers, as were parts of the SNOWY MOUNTAINS. None of these glaciers remain today. During the coldest time of the glacial, about 20 000 years ago, so much water became locked up in the polar ice-caps that sea levels were up to 120m lower than today. Dry land stretched from

New Guinea to TAS.

There have been many glacials over the past million years and on average the warm periods between them have lasted little more than 10 000 years. This would suggest that the present inter-glacial may soon by coming to an end. However, although the present climate is a little cooler and drier than it was during the warmest period of the inter-glacial about 5000 years ago, there is no clear evidence that the world is about to enter a new ice age, which would in any case take many centuries to arrive.

A changing climate? There is increasing evidence that Australia's climate does fluctuate, growing warmer and cooler, wetter and drier over periods of several decades. These conclusions are still tentative, because records are incomplete over much of the continent and no records go back much more than a century. According to some research, temperatures over SE Australia seem to have had a small but significant rise of a few tenths of a degree since the 1940s, and the rise of temperatures in capital cities has been even higher. Over much of E Australia there is evidence that summers are wetter and winters are drier than they were 60 years ago. These trends are probably due to natural forces not yet fully understood, and they tend to reverse themselves after a few decades. Of more concern is the possibility that human activities are now beginning to affect the climate in ways that may not be reversible. The small rise in temperature detected at several places in the S hemisphere has been attributed by some scientists to the steadily rising levels of carbon dioxide in the atmosphere, resulting from the worldwide increase in the burning of fossil fuels. On a smaller scale, the spread of cities alters the local climate, rising the mean temperature, strengthening the sea breeze and sometimes changing rainfall distribution.

Weather recording The value of reliable weather information to an economy based on rural industries has long been recognised. Regular meteorological observations began in 1822 with the establishment of PARRAMATTA Observatory by Governor BRISBANE. Other colonies did likewise over the following half century. Daily weather maps showing the location of the main weather systems were first produced in NSW in the 1870s. The opening of the OVERLAND TELEGRAPH in 1872 provided a chain of observing stations through the empty heart of the continent and facilitated the spread of weather data. In several colonies, amateur observers were encouraged to provide readings of rainfall and temperature to supplement the official observations.

The provision of meteorological services was one of the tasks transferred to the Commonwealth government at federation and the Bureau of Meteorology came into operation in 1908. The Bureau is now responsible for the collection and analysis of weather data from hundreds of stations across the continent, including automatic stations located off the NW and NE coasts. Data is also gathered in Antarctica. A great deal of use is made of high-speed computers to process the information, but weather prediction is still very dependent on the skill and experience of trained forecasters. In addition to regional and capital city forecasts, issued several times a day and covering 24- or 48-hour periods, specialised forecasts are provided for the benefit of shipping and airlines, commerce and industry. Advance warning is given of conditions likely to lead to floods, bushfires, hail, frosts and strong winds. These, if acted upon, can save millions of dollars annually in rural industries alone by giving farmers enough time to take protective action. A significant step forward in Australian meteorology was taken in 1977 with the inauguration of a ground station able to receive cloud pictures and other data from a geostationary weather satellite operated by Japan and positioned over Irian Jaya (the W section of New Guinea). This satellite provides a continuous watch over the evolving weather patterns around Australia. It is of particular value during the tropical cyclone season.

Australia has been active in the affairs of the World Meteorological Organisation (WMO) since the late 19th century and occupies a key role in the work of the WMO. Melbourne is the location of one of the three World Weather Watch Centres set up by the WMO for the international exchange of data. The other centres are in Moscow and Washington. With over 100 other countries, Australia is currently involved in the Global Atmospheric Research Programme (GARP). This vast international scientific effort will run for 10 years, with the aim of filling in the large gaps in man's knowledge about weather patterns, so enabling the limit of reliability of forecasts to be extended from the current four days to 10 or more. One of Australia's contributions to the programme will be the release into the S oceans of automated drifting buoys able to gather weather data in regions far from land-based stations and to relay that data by satellite.

weaverbirds These birds belong to the family Ploceidae which is represented in Australia by two introduced species—the house sparrow, *Passer domesticus* (15cm), and the tree sparrow, *P. montanus* (15cm). Both species are predominantly brown with grey underparts; the tree sparrow is distinguished by a chestnut cap and a black patch on each cheek. Found in the SE, the common house sparrow is a bold, gregarious bird which is unpopular in urban areas because of the mess its nest makes and which is generally regarded as a pest in rural areas because it attacks fruit and seedlings. The tree sparrow is more sparingly distributed, occurring only in parts of VIC and southern NSW. It does not chatter as cheerfully as the house sparrow, nor is it so bold.

According to Slater (*see below*), there are two other introduced species of this family represented in Australia—the grenadier weaver or red bishop bird, *Euplectes orix* (12cm to 14cm), naturalised on parts of the MURRAY RIVER in SA, and the white-winged whydah, *Coliuspas-*

ser albonotatus (15cm to 17cm), found near Sydney.
See also animals, introduced
Further reading: Slater, P. *A Field Guide to Australian Birds: Passerines.* Rigby, Adelaide, 1974.

web-spinners These mainly tropical INSECTS belong to the little-known order Embioptera, which is related to the orders Isoptera (TERMITES) and Dermaptera (EARWIGS). There are about 65 species in Australia, belonging to three families. They are small or medium-sized insects with long, narrow bodies. Females are always completely wingless but the males of some species have two pairs of rather similar wings, with the hind-wings a little smaller than the fore-wings.

Web-spinners live in colonies within tubes of silk which they spin from unique glands on the basal segments of the tarsi of the front legs. While many kinds of immature insects can spin silk it is only among the Embioptera that this ability is retained by the adults. The galleries, which the web-spinners construct by rotating the body as they release the silk, serve as runways to their food (which includes lichens, dead leaves and pieces of bark) and as retreats from predators. Web-spinners are considered to be gregarious rather than social insects for though they live in colonies there is no caste system or division of labour.

wedgebill *see* babblers, etc.

Wee Waa NSW (population 1 904 in 1981) A small town on the NAMOI RIVER in the NW of the State, Wee Waa is 42km W of NARRABRI, on the branch railway line which passes along the Namoi Valley to WALGETT. It is 599km by rail N from Sydney, at an elevation of 191m above sea level, and is the centre of an important cotton growing region which has developed since the early 1960s when irriga-

tion water became available from the KEEPIT DAM. There is a cotton research station 26km E of the town which is concerned with the development of cotton production and with environmental impact studies of this intensive system of irrigated farming. The cotton is machine-picked and ginned during the period from April until early July and this is a popular time for visitors. There are several cotton gins in the town. The name Wee Waa is Aboriginal for 'fire thrown away'.

weebill *see* warblers, etc.

weeds The term 'weed' has no validity as a scientific concept and is applied to plants which, from the human point of view, grow where they are not wanted. For example, in timber storage yards or on industrial sites any plant at all may be considered as a weed, whereas in cultivated fields any plant which competes with the food crop for soil moisture and nutrient is a weed; in a garden, consideration of aesthetics may override all others, though competition with desired plants, particularly annuals or seedlings, may also be important in deciding whether a plant should be considered a weed. Also, what to one person is a weed is to another a useful plant, an illustration of this being *Echium lycopsis*; to the grazier it is a weed which he calls Paterson's Curse, but to the apiarist it is an outstanding honey flower which in some states is called Salvation Jane.

Origin of Australian weeds Plants generally considered by the gardener, the farmer and the conservationist as weeds have varied origins. Some native plants (particularly of the families GRAMINEAE, COMPOSITAE, MIMOSACEAE and PAPILIONACEAE) which existed as part of a balanced ecosystem (*see* ENVIRONMENT) before the arrival of Europeans often played the part of colonisers following natural

Bales of cotton at Wee Waa NSW

J.H. Shaw

A. Woods

Cape weed, *Arctotheca calendula*, common on
pastures and waste land

Tickseed, *Coreopsis lanceolata*, a common roadside
weed in the Sydney region

disturbance (such as fire and landslides), occupying the bare ground rapidly, growing, flowering and seeding in a short period and then almost disappearing above ground, to wait as dormant seeds until the next disturbance. Thus they were much favoured by the widespread clearing of land after the arrival of Europeans, and those which had life cycles which fitted the periodicity of agricultural pursuits were therefore in a prime position to become weeds.

The early seed imported into Australia to establish food crops was not assessed for purity as is imported seed today, with the result that the first crops sown also produced the first crop of imported weed seeds, often long-standing companions of each particular crop, and selected through thousands of years of agriculture to exploit fully the crop situation. In this way a great many common European herbs became a feature of the Australian landscape, not only in cultivated fields, but also escaping to roadsides and waste places; thus when the soils of native plant communities are cleared they often produce not only their own native soil stored seed but also European weed seedlings as a first crop.

In addition to accidental introductions many plants which are now weeds were introduced

as garden plants, and escaped. Excellent examples are the PRICKLY PEARS (*Opuntia* species) and privet (*Ligustrum* species). In many cases the introduced species came from Britain, having been introduced into that country from all over the world; their full aggressiveness was not realised until they were returned to climatic conditions more like their natural habitat than an English garden. At the same time, most of these indirect introductions had shed their natural predator and competitor species so that there was nothing to hold them in check when released into a new and congenial environment. South African plants have been particularly successful in Australia, notably Cape ivy, *Senecio mikanoides*, African box thorn, *Lycium ferocissimum*, Cape weed, *Arctotheca calendula*, and boneseed, *Chrysan themoides monolifera*. Boneseed was introduced into NSW both as a garden plant and to help to stabilise rebuilt sand dunes after mining for mineral sands, but has since become a serious weed of coastal dunes in NSW and VIC and has crossed to TAS in recent years.

New weeds are still introduced from time to time, both as horticultural introductions and accidentally. Fumigation of cargo containers does not necessarily destroy seeds accidentally

included with the imports, and should conditions be suitable at the point of unloading a nuclear community of new weeds, from which seeds disperse quickly to all suitable habitats, soon becomes established. Accidental introductions also occur through the thoughtlessness of individual travellers who (despite laws to the contrary) often bring back from other countries small amounts of some attractive plant to grow in their gardens. New weeds can also be introduced by natural means—for instance, as 'passengers' on migratory birds. Extensive alterations of the local environment (such as the ORD RIVER scheme) may attract migratory birds from South-East Asia, and these birds bring seeds which they have eaten or picked up at their last resting place.

Weed dispersal Existing or potential weed species must have efficient mechanisms for seed dispersal if they are to succeed in occupying available niches as fast as possible. These mechanisms are common also to many nonweed species, and include: very light seed which is wind-dispersed over long distances—for example, dandelions (*Taraxacum* and *Hypochoeris* species) and many other species of the family Compositae; efficient methods of attaching themselves (with hooks, barbs, burrs, etc.) to the coats or feathers of animals or birds—for example, thistles (family Compositae) and many species of the family Graminae; and the ability to survive the digestive processes inside animals—for example, blackberries, briar roses and privet.

Seeds of weeds colonising disturbed ground must also be able to survive in the ground for a long periods when conditions are unsuitable for growth; to achieve this weed seeds are generally produced very abundantly, have a high longevity, and require the stimulus of disturbance to germinate. Peas (family Papilionaceae) and wattles (family Mimosaceae) fulfill all these conditions most efficiently, with generally large, abundant, long-lived, hard-coated seeds, but many families which have much smaller seeds, such as Compositae, Graminae, SOLANACEAE and EUPHORBIACEAE, produce even larger seed crops and survive equally efficiently.

Weed control Weed control, especially of widespread vigorous species which pose a threat to agriculture, is one of the preoccupations of the COMMONWEALTH SCIENTIFIC AND INDUSTRIAL RESEARCH ORGANIZATION (CSIRO) in Australia. There have been notable successes in the control of skeleton weed, *Chondrilla juncea*, which threatened wheat growing, and of prickly pears. Methods used to eradicate weeds range from hand removal to regular cultivation, heavy mulching, BIOLOGICAL CONTROL and chemical control (spraying). No one solution suits all weeds in all situations, but by far the most long-lasting results are obtained from the biological approach, in which natural diseases or predators are introduced to reduce a plant population to a size where it no longer poses a weed problem. Methods of management also vary, depending on the situation in which the weed is growing—agricultural control methods such as 'total kill' are quite unsuited to weed problems in native vegetation where only the weeds are to be eradicated. This latter problem has led to the development of a series of ecologically based techniques of hand weeding and mulching known as the Bradley Method, after its developer Miss J. Bradley. Whilst labour intensive, this method gives hope to all those who wish to preserve the small enclosures of natural vegetation left within the boundaries of Australia's large cities for the enjoyment and refreshment of future generations of Australians.
See also pest control
Further reading: see Appendix 6, A Bibliography for Plants.

weevers *see* fishes, bony

weevils *see* beetles

weights and measures The imperial system of weights (ounces, pounds, etc.) and measures (inches, feet, yards, etc.) was used in Australia until recently. Following the introduction of decimal currency in 1966, a programme of gradual conversion to metric weights and measures was developed and implemented under the direction of the Metric Conversion Board

set up by the Commonwealth government. By 1981 the conversion was effectively achieved, although there was still some retention of the use of imperial units because, for example, a considerable quantity of machinery from pre-metric times was still in use, and tools such as spanners were still available in imperial units as well as metric.

The bauxite processing plant and loading facilities at Weipa

Weipa QLD (population 2 433 in 1981) This is a bauxite mining town on the NW coast of CAPE YORK Peninsula. The explorer Matthew FLINDERS noted the red cliffs of this area in 1802 and as early as 1902 they were identified as bauxite, but it was not until 1955 that their size and economic significance were recognised. The vast deposits along 160km of the coastline rank as the largest known economic source of bauxite (the raw material for making aluminium) in the world. The Comalco company built the town as the residential centre for workers at the mines, the processing plant and the port. A railway, 19km long, brings the ore from the mining site to the port; some of the bauxite is shipped to GLADSTONE for refining and the remainder is exported overseas. Weipa is linked to CAIRNS by an air service.

Wellington NSW (population 5 280 in 1981) A country town in the central-W region of the State, it is located at the junction of the MACQUARIE and Bell Rivers, on the Mitchell Highway, 362km by road NW of Sydney and 50km SE of DUBBO. The area was discovered in 1817 by the explorer John OXLEY, who named it after the Duke of Wellington. It was established as a convict settlement in 1823, became a squatting area, and in 1846 was gazetted as a township. Situated at an elevation of 303m above sea level, the town has an average annual rainfall of 614mm, spread fairly evenly throughout all seasons. The rural produce of the district includes wheat, wool, fat lambs and beef cattle, with lucerne and vegetables along the alluvial flats of the rivers. The BURRENDONG DAM, on the Macquarie River, some 30km SE of the town, is an aquatic sports centre for tourists and local residents. The Wellington Caves, located 8km S of the town, are an important tourist attraction: they are limestone caves, of considerable scientific interest as the remains of many prehistoric animals have been found in them, including those of the diprotodon (giant wombat); they also contain what is claimed to be the world's largest stalagmite, measuring over 15m high and 30m around its base.

Wenden, Mike (1949-) Swimmer. Born in Sydney, Wenden took up swimming in 1963 when he was unable to play football because of a broken leg. He became a world-class swimmer, particularly in 100m and 200m events. His début in international competition was the 1966 Commonwealth Games in Kingston, Jamaica, where he won the 100m freestyle event. At the Mexico City Olympics he won gold medals in the 100m and 200m freestyle events (he was the only Australian male swimmer to win golds at Mexico City), a silver in the 4 x 200m relay and a bronze in the 4 x 100m relay. At the 1970 and 1974

Wellington Museum, Orana region NSW

Commonwealth Games he successfully defended his 100m title, and on retirement from competitive swimming in 1974 his medal tally included two gold, two silver and one bronze for Commonwealth Games events. In the 1969 New Year's Honours list he was made an MBE for his services to the sport of swimming.

Wentworth, D'Arcy (*c.* 1762-1827) Pioneer public servant and medical practitioner. Born near Portadown in County Down, Ireland, he served an apprenticeship there as a surgeon and apothecary and in 1785 went to London to gain further medical experience. For the following few years he seems to have led a double life, mixing in high social circles, but being tried twice for highway robbery, and being referred to publicly as 'the well-known highwayman'. On one occasion the charge against him was dismissed for lack of evidence, and on the other he was acquitted. Shortly after the second case, he sailed for Sydney as assistant surgeon on the *Neptune*. During the voyage he formed an association with a convict girl, Catherine Crowley, with whom he later lived until her death in 1800. Although he did not marry her, he acknowledged and supported their three sons, one of whom was William Charles WENTWORTH.

D'Arcy Wentworth arrived in Sydney in June 1790, and soon afterwards was sent to NORFOLK ISLAND as a surgeon. Back in Sydney in 1796, he was appointed assistant surgeon there. After a second period on Norfolk Is in 1799 he became surgeon at PARRAMATTA and from 1809 to 1819 was principal surgeon of the colony. He also filled a number of other public positions, including, under Governor MACQUARIE, those of police magistrate, superintendent of police and treasurer of the police fund. He was one of the three contractors responsible for building the original Sydney Hospital (the 'Rum Hospital') in Macquarie Street, and was one of the founders of the BANK OF NEW SOUTH WALES.

Wentworth Falls NSW (combined population of Wentworth Falls and KATOOMBA 13 942 in 1981) A town in the BLUE MOUNTAINS region, on the Western Highway and on the railway route through the mountains, it is located between Leura and LAWSON, about 100km by road from Sydney. It is a popular holiday resort, though it is increasingly becoming a dormitory town for commuters who work in Sydney or in some of the centres, such as PENRITH, to the W of Sydney. At an elevation of 884m above sea level, it receives an average annual rainfall of 1 374mm, concentrated mainly in the spring and summer months. The town was originally named Weatherboard, but subsequently was changed to honour one of the famed pioneer trio, William Charles WENTWORTH, who made the first crossing of the Blue Mts in 1813. The area adjacent to the town is famed for its scenic splendour, with vantage points giving spectacular views of the Jamison and

Wentworth Falls NSW

Burragorang Valleys, as well as steep gorges and numerous waterfalls.

Wentworth, William Charles (1790-1872) Explorer and statesman. The son of D'Arcy WENTWORTH and Catherine Crowley, he was born on NORFOLK ISLAND, or on a ship en route to it, came to Sydney in 1796, and in 1803 was sent to school in England. Returning in 1810, he won fame three years later, with William LAWSON and Gregory BLAXLAND, in finding a route across the BLUE MOUNTAINS. In 1816 he went again to England, studied law, and in 1819 published *A Statistical, Historical and Political Description of the Colony of New South Wales*, in which he made a vigorous plea for the granting of parliamentary government. He also attended Cambridge University for a short time, and wrote the poem 'Australasia'. He came back to Sydney in 1824, and in the same year, with Robert Wardell, founded Australia's first independent newspaper, the *Australian*. Two years later this journal's criticism goaded

William Charles Wentworth

Governor DARLING into determined but unsuccessful attempts to curtail the freedom of the Press. Meanwhile, Wentworth had become the undisputed leader of the emancipist faction—that is, of those who opposed all forms of discrimination against ex-convicts—and the colony's chief advocate of representative government and trial by jury. The passing of the Constitution act of 1842, which marked an important step on the road to self-government, must be credited largely to his efforts.

Up to the late 1830s, Wentworth appeared to be the champion of the common people, including emancipists, against the conservative landed classes, including the 'exclusives', who opposed the granting of full civil rights to ex-convicts. From that time, however, he tended to become identified with the conservative faction. This was partly because he had himself become a very large landowner, and because his policies had changed; for instance, he dropped his support for manhood suffrage in favour of a franchise based on property qualifications, and he became an advocate of continued transportation. Another factor to be considered is that the 1830s and 1840s brought into the colony a flood of free settlers, including Chartists and other advocates of parliamentary reform, whose views made Wentworth, once thought radical, appear conservative. Wentworth was still a leader in the movement for responsible government, but the gap between him and public opinion was illustrated when, as chairman of the committee of the Legislative Council which drew up a parliamentary constitution for NSW in 1853, he suggested that the Upper House should consist of the members of a colonial peerage. Following an amendment, which substituted a nominated Upper House for Wentworth's 'bunyip aristocracy' (as a wit had called his proposed peers), he was sent to England to see the Constitution Bill through the Imperial Parliament. Following its adoption, he remained in England for most of the rest of his life. His Sydney residence, Vaucluse House, has been preserved, with additions made after his time, and is open to the public.
Further reading: Melbourne, A.C.V. *William Charles Wentworth.* Discovery Press, Penrith NSW, 1972.

Werder, Felix (1922-) Composer.
Werder was born in Berlin and has lived in Melbourne since his arrival in Australia as a political prisoner in 1941. An extremely prolific composer, his works have been influenced by those of Hindemith, Schoenberg and Bartok and by the tradition of the Jewish liturgical modes, combined with the inheritance of German late Romanticism (*see* Covell *below*). Some of his chamber and larger works have been performed and recorded by organisations such as MUSICA VIVA AUSTRALIA and the Australian Broadcasting Commission (ABC) and in 1974 the Australian Opera performed one of his operas, *The Affair*, in the new Sydney Opera House. However, these performances represent a very small fraction

of Werder's total output.
See also musical composition and composers
Further reading: Covell, R. *Australia's Music: Themes of a New Society.* Sun Books, Melbourne, 1967; Radic, M. 'Felix Werder' in Callaway, F. & Tunley, D. (eds) *Australian Composition in the Twentieth Century.* Oxford University Press, Melbourne, 1978.

Werris Creek NSW (population 1 924 in
WA has an area of 2 525 500km², the largest it is 20km NNW of QUIRINDI, 40km SW of TAMWORTH, and 415km by road NW of Sydney. It is a railway town on the main N tablelands route and is the junction point for the line to GUNNEDAH, NARRABRI and the NW plains towns, as well as for the line W to Binnaway and thence to DUBBO. The principal activities in the town focus on the railway workshops and the marshalling yards. Sheep grazing and wheat growing are the main rural industries in the surrounding district, with some beef cattle grazing, fodder crop growing and mixed farming.

Wessel Islands NT This name is given
to a chain of islands in the ARAFURA SEA extending about 140km on a SW-NE alignment off Point Napier in the NE part of the ARNHEM LAND Aboriginal Reserve. The islands are included within the reserve and so are closed to non-Aboriginals except with special permission. The largest of the group, Marchimbar Is, is a long (over 50km) and narrow island, containing bauxite deposits, located to the NE of the chain. ELCHO ISLAND lies near the SW end of the Wessel group.

West, Morris Langlo (1916-)
Novelist. Born in the Melbourne suburb of St Kilda, he taught as a member of the Christian Brothers from 1934 to 1940, but left the order before taking final vows. He then joined the Australian Imperial Force (AIF), was later secretary to William HUGHES for a short time,

and worked in various capacities in radio. After writing several novels of little note, one under the name Julian Morris and others as Michael East, he attracted international attention with the documentary *Children of the Sun* (1957), which gives a vivid picture of life in the slums of Naples. This was followed by a string of novels, nearly all best-sellers, including *The Devil's Advocate* (1959), *Daughter of Silence* (1961), *The Shoes of the Fisherman* (1963), *The Ambassador* (1965), *The Tower of Babel* (1968), *Summer of the Red Wolf* (1971) *Harlequin* (1974), *The Navigator* (1976), *Proteus* (1979) *Clowns of God* (1981) and *The World Is Made of Glass* (1983). None of these has an Australian theme or setting; on the contrary, West has concentrated on themes of international interest, and has set a number of his novels in Italy, where he has lived for a considerable part of the time since 1955. He deals particularly with personal problems involving moral dilemmas, and has also chosen a number of themes that have been of major importance in international affairs at the time of writing; *The Ambassador*, for instance, refers to the Vietnam War and *The Tower of Babel* deals with the Arab-Israeli conflict.

West Wyalong NSW (population 3 778
in 1981) This country town in the central-W region of the State is located on the Mid-Western Highway, S of CONDOBOLIN, SW of FORBES and E of GRENFELL. It is also on a branch railway line from TEMORA and is 554km by rail W of Sydney. The surrounding rural region is noted for grain growing, livestock grazing, and timber-getting. At an elevation of 253m above sea level it receives an average annual rainfall of 480mm, spread evenly throughout the year. The original township of Wyalong is located 5km to the E; it was superseded in importance in the 1890s when a rich gold-bearing lode was discovered near West Wyalong, causing a mass migration to the new site which has remained the main

Morris West

Courtesy of A.I.S Canberra

commercial centre although the gold mines have long since been worked out and abandoned.

Westbury

Westbury TAS (population 1 161 in 1981) This small country town is situated on the Bass Highway, 16km E of DELORAINE and 34km by road WSW of LAUNCESTON. Settlement of the district began in the early 1820s and in 1828 an extensive townsite was surveyed, in the expectation that it would grow into a major urban centre. Though it did not grow as anticipated, there are many historical buildings in the town which have been classified by the National Trust (TAS), including Fitzpatrick's Inn (build in 1833, as the town's first hotel), Holy Trinity Roman Catholic Church (built in 1869), the White House (built in the 1840s), St Andrew's Church, the Methodist church, Leith House and Surgeon's Home (1832). The town is also noted for its village green, laid out in the original survey plan and used nowadays in traditional fashion for such events as fetes and displays. The surrounding district is productive farming, grazing and forestry country.

Western Australia

Western Australia (WA) The State of WA has an area of 2 525500km², the largest State of the nation, occupying almost a third of the total area of Australia. It also has the longest coastline of any State, 12 500km on the Timor Sea in the far NW, the Indian Ocean on the W, with the Southern Ocean and the GREAT AUSTRALIAN BIGHT along its S shores. The E boundary of the State, separating it from SA and the N T, is the 129th meridian of E longitude extending from the coast in JOSEPH BONAPARTE GULF in the N to Wilson Bluff on the Bight coastline. The State extends a distance of about 2400km in a N-S direction, from latitude 13°44' to beyond the 35th parallel of latitude, and E-W it stretches some 1600km at its widest. Just over a third of the area lies within the tropics.

Landform features The State can be divided into two major landform regions: the great plateau and the coastal plains.

1. The great plateau. This is the dominant feature, occupying more than 90 per cent of the State's area. The highest parts of the plateau, in the KIMBERLEYS of the NW, are about 1200m above sea level, but the general elevation is between 300m and 450m. Although there is considerable variation in the plateau level, the changes are mostly so gradual that it has a gently undulating surface. There are, however, hills and ranges which rise above the general plateau level such as the HAMERSELY RANGE in the PILBARA region of the NW, the RAWLINSON RANGE and WARBURTON RANGE in the E central part of the State, and the STIRLING RANGE in the far S. The DARLING RANGE, located inland from the SW coast, is part of the plateau scarpland where it descends to the coastal plain. Much of the great plateau is composed of ancient rocks of the pre-Cambrian shield, formed more than 500 million years ago and containing many minerals of economic importance. There are also some major sedimentary basins of younger geological age such as Joseph Bonaparte Gulf in the far N which extends into the NT, the CARNARVON Basin where the BOUGH RANGE oil strike was made in 1953, the Canning Basin of the W Kimberleys region, and the EUCLA Basin in the SE of the State where the limestone formations of the NULL-ARBOR PLAIN occur. The inland parts of the plateau include vast stretches of arid country, such as the GIBSON DESERT, the GREAT SANDY DESERT, where there are innumerable salt pans and ephemeral lakes of internal drainage, extensive sand and stony areas, sections with long dune formations and many stream channels which only occasionally contain water.

2. The coastal plains. These are generally narrow, rarely exceeding 20km in width, yet parts of the plains, especially in the SW of the State, are among the major areas of economic development. Along some sections of the coastline, such as the stretch of the Kimberley coast between King Sound and Joseph Bonaparte Gulf, the plateau reaches right to the coast, with bordering cliffs and numerous offshore islands. The main areas of coastal plains are on the W of SWANLAND, at King Sound, near PORT HEDLAND and around EXMOUTH GULF. In the W and NW of the State, there are several major rivers: ORD, FITZROY, FORTESCUE, ASHBURTON, GASCOYNE and MURCHISON; they rise in the plateau interior, have a marked seasonal flow because of the summer concentration of rainfall, with courses of several hundred kilometres, and descend over the plateau scarp, usually in gorge sections to estuaries on the Indian Ocean coast. In the SW, the rivers are generally shorter, such as the SWAN and HARVEY, but have been used in some important water conservation schemes.

Climate Because of the large size and the latitudinal extent of WA there is considerable variation in the climatic patterns in different parts of the State. These differences can be grouped into three main zones, N, central and SW. In the N parts, the climate is typically sub-tropical monsoonal, with high temperatures throughout the year; rainfall is concentrated in the summer months and there is a markedly dry period during the cooler months of the year. In the central zone of the State and extending to the SE there are large tracts of arid and semi-arid country, with low, erratic and unreliable rainfall. The SW section experiences a Mediterranean-type climate, with warm and dry summer conditions and cool, wet winters.

The two wettest areas of the State are in the far N on the Kimberley coast where the average annual rainfall exceeds 1000mm, and in the far SW of Swanland where the annual total is over 1200mm. The climatic contrast between these two regions is quite distinct, especially in the seasonal occurrence of the rainfall; in the Kimberleys, over 90 per cent of the total annual rainfall comes in the four summer months from December to March, while in Swanland there is a concentration of rain in winter, with over 70 per cent of the annual rainfall occurring in the five months from May to September.

The coldest month throughout the whole State is July; January is the hottest month in areas S of the tropic, but in the N parts December is hottest. The most consistently hot place is WYNDHAM, but MARBLE BAR, where the monthly average exceeds 37.8°C (100°F) for the five months from November to March, has the highest average maximum of any place in Australia. Long spells of hot weather are frequent in the N and not uncommon even in S parts. Coastal areas usually experience sea breezes in the summer afternoons or early evenings which bring relief from high temperatures. The sea breezes which affect Perth are known as the 'Fremantle Doctor'. Frosts are widespread during winter over the S parts and sometimes spread into the tropics. Snow occasionally falls in S districts, but only in one area, the Stirling Range, is it a regular feature and even there the falls are light and remain only a short time.

Population Although WA comprises almost a third of the total area of Australia, it contains only 8.7 per cent of the population. At the census of 1981 the State had a population of 1 299 094 (estimated resident population), making it the second-smallest State. About 62 per cent of WA's population live within the metropolitan capital of Perth; there are three other cities with over 19 000 people: BUNBURY (21 749), GERALDTON (20 895) and KALGOORLIE-BOULDER (19 848). Of the State's total population 83 per cent are urban dwellers. The growth of the State since 1901 is shown in Table 1. By the 1911 census, WA exceeded the quarter-million mark, by the 1947 census the population was over half a million and in the 1971 census it had reached over one million.

Table 1

POPULATION GROWTH OF WESTERN AUSTRALIA IN THE TWENTIETH CENTURY

Year*	Population
1901	184 124
1911	282 114
1921	332 732
1933	438 852
1947	502 480
1954	639 771
1961	736 629
1971†	1 043 100
1976†	1 169 800
1981††	1 299 094

Note: * prior to 1971 the statistics do not include full-blood Aborigines; † the 1971 and 1976 figures are adjusted for under-enumeration; †† the 1981 figure is Estimated Resident Population (Preliminary).
Source: Australian Bureau of Statistics, Canberra.

History As in TAS and VIC, the first British settlement established in WA was the result of fears that the French might colonise parts of southern Australia. These fears led Governor DARLING to establish settlements at WESTERN PORT BAY and KING GEORGE SOUND in 1826.

The former, in the area which later became VIC, was abandoned after two years, but the latter, which developed into the WA town of ALBANY, became permanent.

From first settlement to 1850 The King George Sound settlement was founded by Major Edmund LOCKYER with a party of 44 soldiers and convicts, and because at that time NSW extended W only to longitude 129°E, one of Lockyer's first acts was to proclaim British possession of the W part of the continent. At this stage the British government had no intention of setting up a separate colony in WA, but it soon came under pressure to do so. The leading spirit in this move was Captain (later Sir) James STIRLING, who in 1827 explored the land around the Swan River and recommended settlement there. He publicised his views widely and suggested that private enterprise might undertake the venture, whereupon a group of wealthy men, led by Thomas PEEL, offered to form a company which would take 10 000 settlers to the Swan, at no public expense, in return for a grant of four million acres. Late in 1828 a modification of this scheme was accepted. The government agreed to found the colony of WA under Stirling as Governor, and to grant to each settler 40 acres (16ha) of land for each three pounds he invested in the colony, full ownership being dependent upon further investment of the same amount within three years. Captain Charles FREMANTLE was sent ahead to proclaim formal possession, which he did on 2 May 1829. On 1 June the first settlers were landed on Garden Is, near the mouth of the river, and on 18 June the colony was proclaimed. At this stage the settlement at Albany was left under separate command, but two years later it was placed under Stirling's control.

The colony ran into serious difficulties from the very start. As in other parts of Australia, needless trouble was caused by failure to select the exact site of the township and to survey land ready for occupancy before the arrival of settlers. Then, when the site of Perth had been selected, it was found that the amount of fertile land was less than had been expected. Moreover, since there was no limit to the area which each settler might take up, according to his investment, settlement became very scattered; and since land was easy to acquire there was a general shortage of labourers. Finally, clashes with the Aborigines were more serious than in the early stage of settlement elsewhere, culminating in the so-called Battle of PINJARRA. The upshot of all these troubles was that, although the population reached 4000 before the end of 1830, many settlers despaired of the colony's future and moved to NSW and TAS. When Stirling left in 1839 the population was down to a little over 2000, and in 1850 it was still under 6000.

The convict period and after, 1850–80 Two associated factors were widely blamed, especially by followers of Edward Gibbon WAKEFIELD, for WA's economic troubles. The first was the lavish way in which land had been granted. By the 1840s, however,

'Swan River, Preparing to Encamp for the Night, 35 miles up, 1827' (Stirling's expedition) by Frederick Garling

Art Gallery of WA

this no longer applied, for in 1832 the system of selling Crown lands at auction with a minimum price of five shillings an acre had been introduced, and by 1843 the minimum had risen to £1 an acre. However, the other factor, shortage of labour, still applied, and produced a pro-transportation movement. In view of the opposition to transportation elsewhere, the British government was willing to accept the opportunity to send convicts to WA and between 1850 and 1868 nearly 10 000—all males—arrived.

The economic benefits of this influx were considerable. Convict labour was used to equip the colony with essential public works, their mere numbers increased the demand for foodstuffs and other goods, and government expenditure on them stimulated the economy.

Between 1850 and 1870 the population increased fourfold, external trade sixfold and the area under crops sevenfold. Nevertheless, transportation came under increasing criticism because of the high proportion of convicts and ex-convicts in the population, the imbalance between the sexes which it caused, and the delay in progress towards self-government which it involved. The ending of transportation brought the hoped-for advance towards self-government. In 1832 Governor Stirling had set up a nominated Legislative Council on the NSW model of 1823, and in 1870 this was replaced by one of 18 members, of whom 12 were elected. Other developments during the 1870s included the linking of WA to the E colonies OVERLAND TELEGRAPH in 1877, a great increase in wool exports, and strong

The Round House at Fremantle, originally designed as a gaol and probably WA's oldest surviving building.

WA Dept of Tourism

development of the pearling industry on the NW coast.

From 1880 to federation The years 1880-90 saw a turn for the better in a number of ways. The discovery of gold in the Kimberley, Pilbara and Yilgarn districts from 1885 caused minor rushes and gave hope of better finds, the population increased by more than half to 46 000, and in 1890 responsible government was granted. Then in the 1890s came the large-scale economic development for which the colony had waited so long. The discovery of the COOLGARDIE-Kalgoorlie goldfield in 1892-93 was the main factor in increasing the population to 180 000 by 1900. Since most of the gold had to be extracted by deep-shaft mining there was an inflow of investment capital. Moreover, rural industries expanded to meet the needs of the increased population. Thus WA experienced a boom at a time when the E colonies were undergoing an economic depression.

The federation movement produced a sharp division of opinion along regional lines. On the goldfields, pro-federation feeling was strong, but in most of the older-established districts there was strong opposition. The anti-federation attitude of the government caused the growth of a separatist movement on the goldfields, and it was only after the British Secretary of State for the Colonies had made references to this that a federation referendum was held in July 1900, just in time for the majority affirmative vote to bring WA into the Commonwealth of Australia as a foundation member.

From federation to 1945 After 1903 gold mining began to decline. At the same time the phasing out of the State's customs duties, which had given it some measure of protection against imports from the E, made it even harder than before for manufacturing to develop. For another 50 years WA was to depend very heavily on her primary industries, particularly wheat. The present wheat belt began to be opened up extensively for settlement after federation, the process being facilitated by the fact that most of the land had not been already occupied by pastoralists, and so the problem of 'unlocking the land' did not exist to the same extent as in most of the other colonies. By 1929 WA had become one of the leading wheat-producing States.

In politics, the Australian Labor Party (ALP) developed strength early, first attaining office in 1904. As in other States it was split by the conscription issue in 1916, but it did not split during the Depression. Consequently, it was stronger in WA than in most other States during the post-Depression period, holding office from 1933 to 1947. A notable feature of politics during the whole period was the occasional expression of strong anti-federation feeling, caused by the effects of the common national tariff, resentment at the power of the Commonwealth government, and a sense of being neglected by faraway politicians in Melbourne or Canberra. Thus in 1906 both Houses of Parliament voted in favour of a resolution suggesting the possibility of seces-

A gold escort in Coolgardie 1894

National Library of Australia

sion, and in a referendum in 1933 the voters supported secession by a two-to-one margin.

Some developments since 1945 Since 1945 the rate of population growth has been greater than that of Australia as a whole, giving an increase of 103 per cent between the censuses of 1947 and 1976, compared with a national increase of 84 per cent. In the same period, the economy became much more diversified. The agricultural and pastoral industries have continued to expand, a notable feature being the improvement of large areas of formerly barren land by the application of trace elements to the soil. However, the ambitious Ord River water conservation and irrigation scheme, undertaken by the State and Commonwealth governments together, has so far produced disappointing returns. In secondary industry, the mid-1950s proved to be a turning point, with the opening of a large oil refinery at KWINANA and the construction in the same area of a steel-rolling mill which has since been extended into an integrated iron and steel works. These have given impetus to many other industrial developments. The recent development of mining has been even more striking. In the early 1960s bauxite was discovered in the Darling Range, in 1966 the export of iron ore from the Pilbara began, in 1967 nickel production got under way at KAMBALDA, and petroleum production began at BARROW ISLAND, and in 1971 natural gas was first piped from Dongara to Perth. From being the most dependent of all the States on primary industry as late as the mid-1950s, WA has achieved a much better balance between rural, extractive and secondary industries. The prospect of natural gas and oil production offshore from the NORTH WEST CAPE gives promise of further economic growth and

View of Perth from King's Park

WA Dept of Tourism

diversification in the fairly near future.

In politics, the balance between the ALP and the combined LIBERAL PARTY and COUNTRY (now NATIONAL) PARTY has been fairly even for most of the post-war period. In recent years, however, it has fluctuated strongly. After 1974 Labor suffered a disastrous decline, especially in federal elections, but in 1983 won substantial majorities in both the State and federal spheres.

Further reading: Uren, M. *Land Looking West.* Oxford University Press, London, 1948; Crowley, F.K. & de Garis, B.K. *A Short History of Western Australia* (2nd edn) Macmillan, South Melbourne, 1969; Crowley, F.K. *Australia's Western Third.* Heinemann, Melbourne, 1970. Stannage, C.T. (ed.), *A New History of Western Australia.* University of WA Press, Nedlands, WA, 1981.

Western Australian Film Corporation *see* film

Western District

VIC This name is applied to the SW corner of the State, extending W from PORT PHILLIP BAY to the SA border, and from the S coast N to the GRAMPIANS. The main urban centres in the region are WARRNAMBOOL, HAMILTON, PORTLAND, COLAC and CAMPERDOWN. The OTWAY RANGES lie in the SE, but other parts of the district consist of extensive plains rising in the N towards the GREAT DIVIDING RANGE and the Grampians. The drainage pattern thus comprises streams which have a general N-to-S course and drain to estuaries on the S coast: the GLENELG RIVER and its tributary the Wannon in the W; the Eumeralla, Hopkins (and its tributary Mt Emu Creek) and Gellibrand Rivers in the centre and the E. Much of the E section of the district was the scene of volcanic activity in the recent geological past;

lava flows covered some areas, while extinct cones, many now filled by lakes, were left as unique landscape features (for example, Tower Hill at Koroit, Mt Leura at Camperdown). The largest natural lake in VIC, LAKE CORANGAMITE, is located N of the Princes Highway between Colac and Camperdown. The earliest permanent white settlement was made in this district at Portland by members of the HENTY FAMILY in 1834. The explorer Thomas MITCHELL reached the area in 1836 and was so impressed by its fertility that he called it 'Australia Felix'. Following his journey came squatters, some of whom established prosperous grazing properties and built stately mansions. The Western District is still a rich farming and livestock grazing region, with sheep, dairy and beef cattle, wheat, oats, vegetables (particularly potatoes and onions near Warrnambool and Colac) and extensive forestry areas of softwood pines and indigenous species.

Further reading: Kiddle, M. *Men of Yesterday: A Social History of the Western District of Victoria, 1834-90.* Melbourne University Press, Melbourne, 1961; McKinley, B. *Western District Sketchbook.* Rigby, Adelaide, 1971.

Westpac Banking Corporation *see* Bank of New South Wales

Western Port Bay

VIC A coastal inlet, commonly called Westernport, it is located SE of Melbourne, bounded by MORNINGTON PENINSULA on the W and by the plains adjoining the STRZELECKI RANGES on the E. The N shoreline is fringed by sandy and mudflat stretches, while PHILLIP ISLAND occupies much of the inlet at the S, with the entrance channel between this island and West Head on Mornington Peninsula. The bay is about 25km E-W in its central section, and French Is (218km²), used as a gaol, occupies much of the

central area of the bay. Considerable industrial development has taken place on the W shore, with an oil refinery at CRIB POINT. At Stony Point, on the W shore, is the RAN training centre, established in 1920, and known officially as HMAS *Cerebus* but more commonly called Flinders. The Bass Highway runs along the E shore and the South Gippsland Highway skirts the N shoreline. The bay was discovered and named by the explorer George BASS in 1798, because of its 'relative situation in relation to every other known harbour on the coast'.

Weston

NSW (combined population of Weston and KURRI KURRI 12 794 in 1981) A town on the lower HUNTER RIVER valley coalfields, it is 182km by road N of Sydney, adjacent to Kurri Kurri, 18km SW of MAITLAND and 11km by road E of CESSNOCK. Coal mining commenced in the early years of this century and has remained an important activity of the region; there is also dairying, orcharding, fodder crop cultivation and timber-getting in the adjacent rural areas.

wet sclerophyll forest *see* vegetation

whalebirds *see* sea birds

whalers *see* sharks, etc.

whales *see* dolphins, etc.

whaling

Along with SEALING, whaling was one of the first, if not the first, industries of Australia. It finished in 1979 when the last whaling station, at Cheynes Beach near ALBANY in WA (opened in 1952), closed down. In 1977, 508 male and 116 female sperm whales (*see* DOLPHINS, etc.) were taken, yielding 23 586 barrels of sperm oil, worth

Whaling in Twofold Bay NSW in the 1840s

State Library of NSW

$2 268 000, and $647 000 worth of by-products such as meat, meal and solubles.

Whale hunting began in the 1790s and the first whaling station was established in 1806, in TAS. It was not till 1833 that wool surpassed whale products in value as exports. At the beginning of the 19th century much of the whaling was carried out in bays and estuaries where the southern right whales came to calve. These whales provided whale bone for such items as corsets and umbrella ribs, but little oil. By 1841 there were 35 whaling stations in TAS alone, engaged in bay whaling, and many more on the mainland. The whalers also worked on the coasts of New Zealand from about 1830.

Deep-sea whaling was carried out with Sydney as a base and with Australian, American and British ships taking part. The main species hunted was the sperm whale which provided oil for lamps and spermaceti for candles. After 1850 the demand for the oil fell because of the use of mineral oils and the introduction of gas for domestic purposes. For a time, baleen whales were hunted instead, to supply the soap and margarine manufacturers, but sperm whales became important again as the baleen whale population declined. Whalers in TWOFOLD BAY NSW were often accompanied by schools of killer whales which, no doubt, had discovered that they could pick up many scraps. There are accounts of the killer whales driving the right whales for the hunters to catch, but these are probably exaggerated.

Norwegian whalers began operations at JERVIS BAY in NSW in 1912, but whaling declined between 1929 and 1935. In 1935 foreign ships began hunting, taking 7000 whales in three years. There was another peak in 1949 when humpback whales were discovered migrating along the W and E coasts. In 1949 the Australian government began coastal whaling from a shore station near CARNARVON in WA, but sold its interests to private enterprise in 1956. Eventually the hunting of humpback whales was banned and by 1963 only one of the five shore stations that had existed in the 1950s survived. Depletion in whale stocks and the strong opposition of conservation groups both in Australia and overseas led to the closing of the last station in 1979.

Australia was a founder member of the International Whaling Commission which attempts to control the hunting of whales by setting quotas and regulations on minimum sizes, and by banning the killing of certain species. However, there are some countries, such as the USSR and Japan, which do not subscribe to the Commission's regulations.

wheat *see* agriculture

wheel animalcules *see* rotifers

whelks *see* gastropods

whimbrel *see* waders

whipbirds *see* babblers, etc.

whisk fern *see* Psilophyta

whistlers *see* thickheads

'white-ants' *see* termites

White Australia Policy

This name has been commonly applied to the policy of preventing the entry into Australia, for purposes of permanent settlement, of people of non-European racial origin. However, the term was never officially used. An account of the development of such a policy, and of its modification and final abandonment in recent years, is given in the entry on IMMIGRATION RESTRICTION.

Courtesy of A.I.S. Canberra

Patrick White

White, Patrick Victor Martindale

(1912-) Author, and the first Australian to receive the Nobel Prize for literature. Born in London of Australian parents, he was educated first at MOSS VALE NSW and then at Cheltenham College, England. From 1929 he worked for a time as a JACKEROO, then returned to England to study at King's College, Cambridge, and during World War II served as an intelligence officer with the Royal Air Force. He returned to Australia permanently in 1948, and since then has lived first at Castle Hill, on the suburban fringe of Sydney, and then at Centennial Park, close to the city. His publications include *The Ploughman and Other Poems* (1935), the two volumes of short stories, *The Burnt Ones* (1964) and *The Cockatoos* (1974) and a number of plays, including *The Ham Funeral* (1961),

Courtesy of A.I.S. Canberra

Wheat harvesting in WA

Season at Sarsaparilla (1962), *A Cheery Soul* (1963), *Night on Bald Mountain* (1964), *Big Toys* (1977), *The Night the Prowler* (screenplay 1978), *Signal Driver* (1982) and *Netherwood* (1982). However, his reputation rests mainly on his novels, which include *Happy Valley* (1939), *The Tree of Man* (1955), *Voss* (1957), *Riders in the Chariot* (1961), *The Solid Mandala* (1966), *The Vivisector* (1970), *The Eye of the Storm* (1973), *A Fringe of Leaves* (1976) and *The Twyborn Affair* (1979). His autobiographical *Flaws in the Glass*, which he describes as a self portrait, appeared in 1981. He received the Nobel Prize in 1973, and used the prize-money to endow a literary award for distinguished Australian authors.
See also literature
Further reading: Dutton, G. *Patrick White* (2nd edn) Lansdowne, Melbourne, 1962; Dyce, J. *Patrick White as Playwright*. Queensland University Press, St Lucia QLD, 1974; Walsh, W. *Patrick White's Fiction*. Allen & Unwin, Sydney, 1977.

whitebait *see* fishes, freshwater

white death *see* sharks, etc.

white-eyes *see* silvereyes

whitefaces *see* warblers, etc.

whiteflies *see* bugs

Whiteley, Brett

(1939-) Artist. Born in Sydney, Whiteley showed early promise and a masterly control of line. After studying at Julian ASHTON's he went to Italy (where he won an Italian Travelling Scholarship) and subsequently to London. Acclaimed in 1961-63 for his exhibitions in the Whitechapel and Marlborough Galleries, London, his works were purchased by the Tate Gallery and by the Victoria and Albert Museum. Since then, Whiteley has become Australia's most international painter since Sidney NOLAN, exhibiting in various North American and European venues and having work purchased by several overseas galleries. Whiteley's earlier work showed an intense interest in the erotic and the nude, such as the Christie series and a series on nudes in the bath. Many of his later works were drawings and graphics which explored the animal world and which had been influenced originally by his visits to London Zoo. His landscapes, especially his large canvasses depicting Sydney Harbour, frequently have an underlying fleshy sexual quality that is joyful and sensual in its approach.

whitings *see* fisheries; fishes, bony

Whitlam, (Edward) Gough

(1916-) Prime Minister. The son of a Commonwealth Crown Solicitor, he was born in Melbourne but educated in Canberra and Sydney. He graduated BA from the University of Sydney in 1938, served in the Royal Australian Air Force (RAAF) from 1941 to 1945, then completed a

Edward Gough Whitlam

law degree and was called to the Bar in 1947. In the meantime, he had joined the Australian Labor Party (ALP) and in 1952 was elected to the House of Representatives as Member for the Sydney suburban seat of Werriwa. He was elected deputy leader of the ALP in 1960 and leader seven years later. During his first five years as leader he played a major role in changing the party structure so that the federal conference and executive included more parliamentarians, in restoring the party's public image, and in framing a platform which appealed to middle-class and 'swinging' voters. There is no doubt that his leadership was a major factor in the revival of Labor in the federal sphere, to the point where it gained office in 1972.

As Prime Minister he carried out a sweeping programme of change. In the area of foreign affairs and defence, Australia recognised the government of the People's Republic of China and supported its admission to the UN, withdrew all military advisers from South Vietnam, and repealed the National Service Act, under which conscripts had been sent to fight in Vietnam. In domestic affairs there was a considerable expansion in government expenditure, especially in areas such as education, Aboriginal affairs and urban and regional planning, and a new health insurance scheme, Medibank, was introduced.

The story of Labor's three years in office under Whitlam—of its survival of an electoral challenge in May 1974, its dismissal from office and its subsequent electoral defeat in 1975—is told in the entries on POLITICAL HISTORY and Sir John KERR. The quality of Whitlam's performance during these years is a matter for debate. There is no doubt of his skill as a speaker, his enormous capacity for work, and the qualities of imagination which enabled him to direct attention to issues of national importance which many people felt had been previously neglected. His defenders claim that he used these gifts to introduce a

new and much needed spirit of social reform into Australian politics; they see his downfall as the result of unfavourable economic circumstances largely beyond his control, and of unjustifiable breaking of political conventions by the Opposition and the Governor-General. On the other hand, his critics see him as suffering from arrogance, impatience and a lack of interest in economic matters; they claim that his impetuosity in expanding government expenditure and his government's benevolent attitude to wage increases contributed substantially to the nation's economic problems. He resigned from the leadership of the ALP after its defeat in the election of December 1977, and from Parliament in 1978. In 1983 he was appointed Australian ambassador to UNESCO. *Further reading:* Oakes, L. *Whitlam, PM: A Biography.* Angus & Robertson, Sydney, 1973.

Whitsunday Passage QLD When James COOK sailed the *Endeavour* through this 32km-long passage in 1770 he wrote: 'This passage I have named Whit Sunday's Passage as it was discovered on the day the Church commemorates the Festival.' This tropical waterway, which is only about 3km wide at its narrowest point, is located off the NE coast of QLD. To the E of the passage lies the Whitsunday group of islands, most of which are included in a national park; the largest of this group are Whitsunday Is (10 930ha) and Hook Is (5 180ha) and one of the best-known is HAYMAN ISLAND. To the W of the passage are coastal islands, such as Long Is, North and South MOLLE ISLANDS and DAYDREAM ISLAND, lying offshore from the Conway Range National Park coastline. At the S of the passage are the CUMBERLAND ISLANDS which include Shaw Is and LINDEMAN ISLAND. Several of the islands around the passage have been developed as tourist resorts, providing opportunities for aquatic pastimes such as fishing and coral-viewing, and visits to the outer section of the GREAT BARRIER REEF.

Blast furnace operation, Whyalla SA

whydah *see* weaverbirds

Whyalla SA (population 29 962 in 1981) The second-largest city in SA, located on the NW shore of SPENCER GULF, 386km by road NW of Adelaide, it is a major port and industrial centre. The part of the gulf coast where the city is now located was explored by Matthew FLINDERS in 1802; he called the site Hummock Hill and this name was still used in 1900 when a jetty was built there for shipping iron ore (from Iron Knob, 54km NW of the city) across the gulf for use as a smelter flux at PORT PIRIE. The only other industry in the vicinity at that time was a vast sheep grazing property and there was little development until 1911 when the BROKEN HILL PROPRIETARY COMPANY LIMITED (BHP) decided to

Whitsunday Passage QLD with Lindeman Is in the foregound

expand the ore shipping facilities to supply the NEWCASTLE (NSW) steelworks. The name Hummock Hill was retained until 1920, when it became Whyalla, an Aboriginal word meaning 'deep water place'. The growth of the town was relatively slow and in 1938 it had a population of only 1 400. However, the decisions by BHP in 1939 to dredge a deep-water harbour, build a blast furnace and establish Australia's biggest shipyard greatly influenced the progress of the town. A further step in its development came in 1958 when BHP announced that it would build an integrated steelworks, and by 1961, when it was proclaimed a city, the population was 13 700. The city is located in a region of low rainfall (average annual rainfall 273mm) and water supply was a problem from its earliest days; in 1943, a 374km-long pipeline was constructed to bring water from the Murray River for homes, gardens and irrigated farms. The Whyalla Conservation Park, located NNW of the city, with an area of 1 011ha, was established in 1971.

Wickham WA (population 2 387 in 1981) A company town and port, it was established in 1971 by Cliffs Robe River Iron Ore Associates as the export point from Cape Lambert of the iron ore mined in the ROBE RIVER region. Located 1754km by road N of Perth and 10km off the North Western Coastal Highway from ROEBOURNE, it was named in honour of John WICKHAM, who as hydrographic surveyor for the British Admiralty charted the NW coastline of WA from the sloop *Beagle* in 1840.

Wickham, John Clements (1789-1864) Marine surveyor and first Government Resident at MORETON BAY. He was born in Leith, Scotland, joined the British Navy as a midshipman in 1812, and in 1831 was appointed first lieutenant on the *Beagle*. This famous survey vessel, with the scientist Charles DARWIN on board, reached Australia in January 1836. In the following year Wickham became commander, and between that time and 1841, when he left the Navy because of ill health, he carried out valuable survey work on the NW coast. He returned to NSW in 1842, and in November was appointed police magistrate at Moreton Bay. In 1857 his rank was raised to that of Government Resident, a position which he kept until the creation of the separate colony of QLD in 1859. He returned to England in the following year, having declined suggestions that he should pursue a political career in QLD. Wickham Terrace in Brisbane and WICKHAM in WA are named after him.

Wickham, Tracey (1962-) Swimmer. Born in Brisbane, her first success in international swimming was in 1978 when she started breaking world records. The first record to go was the 1500m freestyle which she broke in a solo swim in Brisbane in February 1978. In the Australian championships three weeks later she broke the world 800m record. She represented Australia at the 1978 Commonwealth Games at Edmonton and won

the gold medal for the 800m, in which she broke her own world record, and also the gold medal in the 400m freestyle event. Later in the same year, at the world championships, she won not only the 800m event, but also the 400m, breaking the world record, her fourth world-record-breaking swim in 1978. She received a tumultuous reception on returning to Australia and shortly afterwards received the 1978 Australian Broadcasting Commission (ABC) Sportsman of the Year Award. In February 1979, she slashed eight seconds off her own 1500m world record. She was made an MBE in the 1979 New Year's Honours list in recognition of her outstanding swimming performances. At the Brisbane Commonwealth Games of 1982 she again won the 400m and 800m freestyle events.

Wilcannia NSW (population 984 in 1981) This small service town is on the W bank of the DARLING RIVER, 980km by road WNW of Sydney, on the Barrier Highway 20km from its junction with the Cobb Highway. Located in the dry inland plains region of the State, at an elevation of 76m above sea level, it has an average annual rainfall of only 252mm, with long drought spells a common feature of the climate. It is the commercial and service centre for a vast pastoral district, the headquarters of the Central Darling Shire and a depot town for several transport companies. During the 19th century it was an important river port for the paddle-wheel steamers on the Darling. The name Wilcannia comes from an Aboriginal word meaning 'a gap through which water flows'.

Wild, John Paul (1923-) Radio astronomer. Born in England, Wild settled in Australia after wartime experience as a naval radar

Science Communication Unit CSIRO

Dr J. Paul Wild, Chairman of CSIRO

officer. He joined the Division of Radiophysics of the COMMONWEALTH SCIENTIFIC AND INDUSTRIAL RESEARCH ORGANIZATION (CSIRO), then emerging as a centre of research in the new field of radio astronomy. Wild quickly developed new methods of detecting and analysing radio waves from the sun. This work established his international reputation as a radio astronomer and led to major new insights into processes taking place on the sun that have profound effects on earth. In the early 1960s he designed a revolutionary instrument to take pictures of the sun using radio waves rather than visible light. Built at Culgoora NSW, this 'radioheliograph' is still the only instrument of its kind. Adapting these techniques to a different purpose, Wild led a team which developed INTERSCAN, a new type of radio landing-aid for aircraft. In 1978, he and his colleagues scored a major triumph when the International Civil Aviation Organisation adopted Interscan for worldwide implementation over the next few decades. During his years with the CSIRO Wild rose through the ranks to become chief of the Division of Radiophysics in 1970 and chairman of the CSIRO in 1978.

wild duck *see* animals, introduced

wild plum *see* apple

Wilkes This is a research station in ANTARCTICA on Vincennes Bay at latitude 66°17'S. It was established in 1957 (the International Geophysical year) by America. It was transferred to Australia in 1959, but was replaced in 1969 by more modern installations at the nearby CASEY station.

Wilkie, Allan (?1889-1970) Actor and theatre manager. Born in Scotland, Wilkie came to Australia in 1915, his first job being with Nellie STEWART's New Zealand tour of *Sweet Nell of Old Drury*. In 1916 he played Shylock in George Marlow's Grand Shakespearean Company at the Princess Theatre, Melbourne, with Frediswynde Hunter Watts (who became his wife) as Portia. From 1916 to the late 1920s Wilkie's company toured Australia, presenting Shakespeare and occasionally other classics, with economical staging but elegant costumes and fine acting. In 1926 a fire at GEELONG destroyed the company's wardrobe and scenery, but an appeal raised £4000, and the company reopened for its regular Christmas season at the Hobart Theatre Royal in 1927. When the Depression struck, Wilkie, who had been made a CBE for services to theatre in 1925, left for Canada and later returned to Scotland.
Further reading: West, J. *Theatre in Australia.* Cassell, Sydney, 1978.

Wilkinson, Leslie (1882-1973) Architect. Wilkinson had a distinguished academic career in England and had travelled extensively in Europe before arriving in Australia in 1918 to become the first Professor of Architecture in

Robert Irving

Wilkinson's house, 'Greenway', Vaucluse, Sydney NSW

Australia, at the University of Sydney. The similarity of Sydney's climate to that of the Mediterranean and the continuity in Australia of the British tradition in design became the basis of Wilkinson's architectural philosophies. He built his own house at Vaucluse in Sydney and called it 'Greenway' in honour of Francis GREENWAY, whose work he greatly respected. The house, like many of Wilkinson's subsequent designs, was given a Georgian-Mediterranean character, with simple forms and good proportions, a courtyard for wind protection, ample verandahs, outdoor rooms and a garden integrated with the house by means of pergolas and screens. White became his favoured colour and his early students nicknamed him 'Whitewash' Wilkinson.

Wilkinson's work included university master-plans and buildings in Sydney (Departments of Botany and Physics, 1926), in WA and in TAS, as well as halls, banks, schools, churches and many houses. Two of his buildings, St Michael's Church at Vaucluse and Wiston Gardens at Double Bay, won the coveted Sulman Award. His last house, designed when he was 87 years old, was the Coote House, Vaucluse.

Wilkinson's influence upon Australian architecture has been profound, not only because of his buildings but also because of his 30 years of teaching at the University of Sydney and because his was an important voice in professional and community activites. He received the highest architectural honour when, in 1960, he was awarded the Gold Medal of the Royal Australian Institute of Architects. In 1961 the NSW Chapter of the Institute established a special award for meritorious domestic architecture and named it the Wilkinson Award.

Further reading: Freeland, J.M. *The Making of a Profession.* Angus & Robertson, Sydney, 1971.

Williams, Frederick Roland
(1927-82) Artist. Born in Richmond VIC, Williams studied at the Melbourne National Gallery School, Chelsea Art School and the Central School of Arts and Crafts, London. His early achievements were in etching, where his economy of line and tone won him acclaim. Later he turned to Australian landscape painting. With its high horizons, simple images and subtle but rich range of colours, Williams' landscape painting evokes the emptiness and stillness of the Outback in a vivid and controlled manner.

Williams, Harold (1893-1976) Baritone.
Born in Sydney, Williams was to enjoy a career in opera, oratorio and as a recording artist which spanned several decades and which established him as an outstanding figure in British musical life. It was while in England serving with the Australian forces during World War I that he was encouraged to undertake serious singing studies in London. This he did and he soon graduated to recitals and opera and oratorio performances. This was followed by appearances with the British National Opera Company, and at Covent Garden he sang the title role in *Boris Godounov* and Mephistopheles in *Faust*. With the English Opera Company he sang a score of important roles both in London and on tour. He also often sang at Promenade concerts, and was regarded as one of the outstanding soloists to appear during Toscanini's season at the Queen's Hall, notably in Beethoven's *Ninth Symphony*. He was looked upon as one of the leading British baritones of his day and his Columbia recordings of *Elijah* with Sir Malcolm Sargent and of *Messiah* with Sir Thomas Beecham were widely acclaimed in both the USA and Britain. He returned to live in Australia after World War II and joined the staff of the NSW State Conservatorium of Music in 1952 as Professor of Singing. Here he furthered the musical education of young Australian singers, among them Raymond Nilsson, Neil Easton and Margreta Elkins, all of whom were to enjoy prominent careers in London.

Williamson, David Keith (1942-)
Playwright. Born in Melbourne, he graduated in mechanical engineering from Monash University, and lectured in thermodynamics and psychology at Swinburne College, Melbourne. His first full-length play was *Stork*, staged at La Mama, Melbourne, in 1970 and filmed in 1971. *The Removalists*, first performed at La Mama in 1971, won for Nimrod Theatre in Sydney in 1972 the British George Devine Award for new plays and in the same year *Don's Party* enjoyed a spectacular success after a season at the Jane Street Theatre in Sydney. His later plays include *Fugglers Three* (1972), *What If You Died Tomorrow* (1973), *The Department* (1975), *A Handful of Friends* (1976) and *The Club* (1977). Several of his plays have been staged in London, and *The Club* was staged in New York in 1978. He has also written a number of film scripts, including *Petersen* and *Eliza Fraser*. He lives in Sydney.
Further reading: Rees, L. *A History of Australian Drama.* (vol 2) Angus & Robertson, Sydney, 1978; Fitzpatrick, P. *After the Doll.* Edward Arnold, Melbourne, 1979.

Williamson, James Cassius (1845-1913)
Actor and entrepreneur. Born in Pennsylvania, the son of a doctor, he became interested in theatre as a boy, and gained early experience in a provincial company and in New York and San Francisco. He married his stage partner, Maggie Moore, in 1873, the year in which George COPPIN offered the couple an engagement in Australia. They appeared in a play about Dutch immigrant life in the US, *Struck Oil*, in 1874, and enjoyed a spectacular success. In 1879 they returned to settle in Australia, and Williamson soon became the country's leading entrepreneur. In 1882 he, George Musgrove and Arthur Garner established their famous 'Triumvirate', which lasted for nine years, with theatres in Melbourne, Sydney and Adelaide. The Triumvirate, also known as 'the Firm', disbanded in the 1890s, leaving Williamson in sole control from 1900 onwards. He imported excellent light entertainment from overseas and gave Australian entertainers some opportunity to perform, but he had little sympathy with the native melodrama popular in his day, and is credited with saying that 'Australians don't want Australian.' In 1912 he travelled to America and Europe, and when he died in Paris, theatres throughout Australia were 'dark' for a night in memory of the man whose company was to dominate Australian theatre until the 1970s. The name J.C. Williamson has remained in use in Australian theatrical circles, even though the original company went out of existence in 1982.
Further reading: West, J. *Theatre in Australia.* Cassell, Sydney, 1978.

Williamson, Malcolm Benjamin Graham Christopher (1931-) Composer.

Born in Sydney, he was educated at Barker College and the New South Wales State Conservatorium of Music. In 1953 he left Sydney for London, where he established permanent residence. He has performed both as a pianist and an organist in Britain, and in 1974 became a Fellow of Creative Arts at the Australian National University in Canberra. In the following year he was appointed Master of the Queen's Musick, thereby becoming the first Australian to hold this long-established position. He was appointed CBE in 1976. Williamson's prodigious output includes symphonic, instrumental and choral music, and following the success of his first opera, *Our Man in Havana* (1963), Williamson turned his musical attentions more and more to the stage. Here, as in his concert works, his style appeals to a wide range of musical interests, from large-scale traditional opera such as *Our Man in Havana*, *The Violins of Saint-Jacques* and *Lucky Peter's Journey*, and the more chamber-type operas such as *English Eccentrics* and *The Growing Castle*, to works for children such as *Julius Caesar Jones* and *The Happy Prince*. He has also written works for non-professional performers (including children) such as *The Red Sea* and *Dunstan and the Devil*. *Further reading:* Chatterton, B. 'Malcolm Williamson' in Callaway, F. & Tunley, D. (eds) *Australian Composition in the Twentieth Century*. Oxford University Press, Melbourne, 1978.

willie wagtail see flycatchers, etc.

Willochra Basin SA

Located in the S FLINDERS RANGES, NE of PORT AUGUSTA, beyond PICHI RICHI PASS, it is an extensive basin in semi-arid country of low and unreliable rainfall, commonly called the Willochra Plains. It has a general N-S alignment where the Willochra Creek and its tributaries, though usually dry, can experience flash floods. The basin extends for some 100km N-S, about 30km E-W and drains to LAKE TORRENS. The original narrow-gauge central Australian railway line crossed the basin from QUORN to HAWKER, but the standard-gauge line, constructed in 1956, passes to the W. The name Willochra comes from a local Aboriginal word meaning 'green bushes'.

Wilmot, Frank Leslie Thompson see Maurice, Furnley

Wilpena Pound SA

Located within the FLINDERS RANGES National Park, some 430km N of Adelaide and 50km NE of HAWKER, this vast natural amphitheatre, surrounded by a jagged rim of quartzite, takes its name from an Aboriginal word meaning 'bent fingers' (thought to refer to the resemblance of the Pound to a cupped hand). It is one of the major tourist attractions within the N Flinders Ranges and a modern motel situated just outside the NE rim of the Pound, together with a camping and caravan park, provide facilities for visitors. St Marys Peak, rising to 1 189m, the highest peak in the ranges, is located at the NE of the Pound. The climate of the Wilpena area is semi-arid with an average rainfall of about 300mm, but within the Pound higher rainfall is experienced owing to the elevation (Wilpena Chalet receives an average of 391mm). Long hot summers and cool winters are experienced; on rare occasions snowfalls have been recorded on the surrounding peaks. The Pound is of profound significance in the Aboriginal mythology of the Flinders Ranges, the walls representing large mythical snakes, with St Marys Peak as the giant snake's head. There are Aboriginal carvings and paintings at Arkaroo Rock at the SE of the Pound.

Wilson's Promontory VIC

The most S point of mainland Australia, it consists of ancient granite hills with the highest peak, Mt Latrobe, rising to 754m above sea level. The promontory is triangular-shaped, extending N-S some 40km and 15km E-W in its middle section, with a coastline of about 130km. In the relatively recent geological past, it was probably an island and is now connected to the mainland by a low sand spit, lying between Waratah Bay on the W and CORNER INLET on the NE. At the lighthouse on the S tip, the granite cliffs fall sheer to the sea. Off the coast there are numerous islands: Shellback Is, Norman Is, the Glennie Islands and the Anser Islands off the W coast, Wattle Is off the S coast, Rabbit Is off the NE, and Granite and Benison Islands off the NW. Since 1905 part of the promontory has been a national park, now covering 49 000ha, including many of the offshore islands. Aborigines knew the area as Wammon and gathered shellfish around its shores; heaps of shells in middens bear testimony to this practice. The first European to sight the promontory was George BASS in 1798 and it was named after a London merchant, Thomas Wilson, a friend of Matthew FLINDERS. In the early 1800s, sealers and whalers operated in the area, as the name Sealers Cove, on the E shore, recalls. Later, it was the site of timber-getting, tin mining, grazing and, during World War II, commando training. The terrain varies from forests on the hilly uplands, to luxuriant fern gullies, open heathland, salt marshes, sandy beaches and rugged headlands. Access to the national park is from the South Gippsland Highway, turning S at Meeniyan or Foster, with a road to Tidal River, 32km inside the park boundary.

Wiluna WA (population 221 in 1981)

A small inland township in the mid-N of the State, Wiluna is 945km by road NE of Perth and 183km E of MEEKATHARRA off the Great Northern Highway. At an elevation of 518m above sea level, it is in a semi-arid area with an average annual rainfall of 240mm, concentrated mainly in the summer and autumn months. Formerly it was a gold-mining town and railway terminus, but now it is a declining service centre for a large pastoral area. The Canning stock route from the KIMBERLEYS formerly terminated at Wiluna railhead.

Wimmera-Mallee VIC

The Wimmera and the Mallee are two adjacent regions in the NW corner of the State, extending W from the LODDON RIVER to the SA border, and from the GRAMPIANS N to the MURRAY RIVER, covering an area of over 66 000km², with a population in 1981 of about 128 000 (Wimmera statistical division, 54 960; Northern Mallee statistical division, 72 910). The Wimmera includes the city of HORSHAM, the town of STAWELL and numerous smaller urban settlements such as Dimboola, Donald, and Birchip. The Mallee region includes the cities of MILDURA and SWAN HILL, and urban centres such as KERANG, Merbein, RED CLIFFS, Ouyen and Wycheproof.

The rainfall over these two regions varies from the S where yearly totals exceed 500mm (Horsham 533mm), to the N semi-arid sections where less than 300mm are received (Mildura

Irrigation channel, Wimmera-Mallee VIC

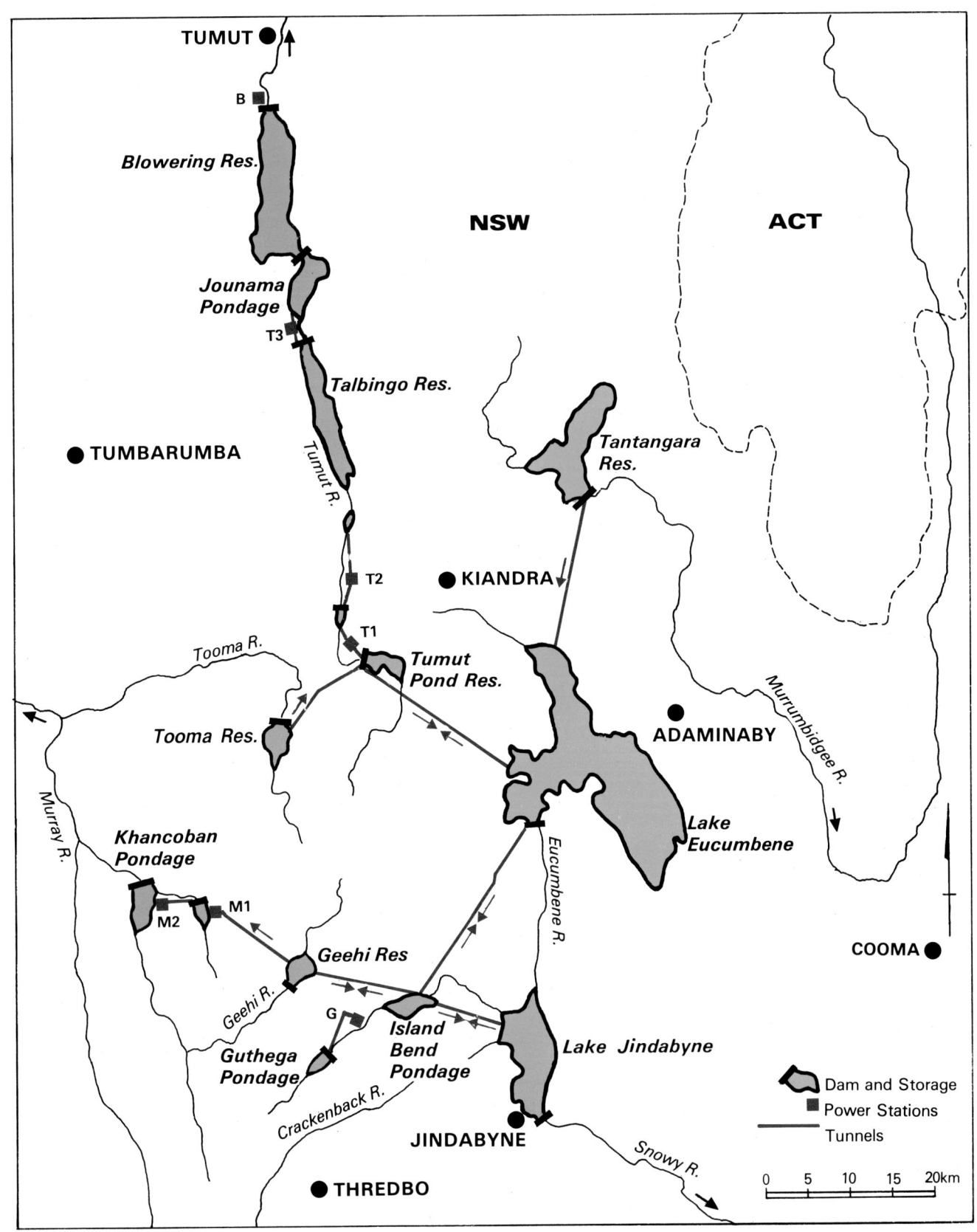

The Snowy Mountains Hydro-electric scheme (*see* SNOWY MOUNTAINS SCHEME)

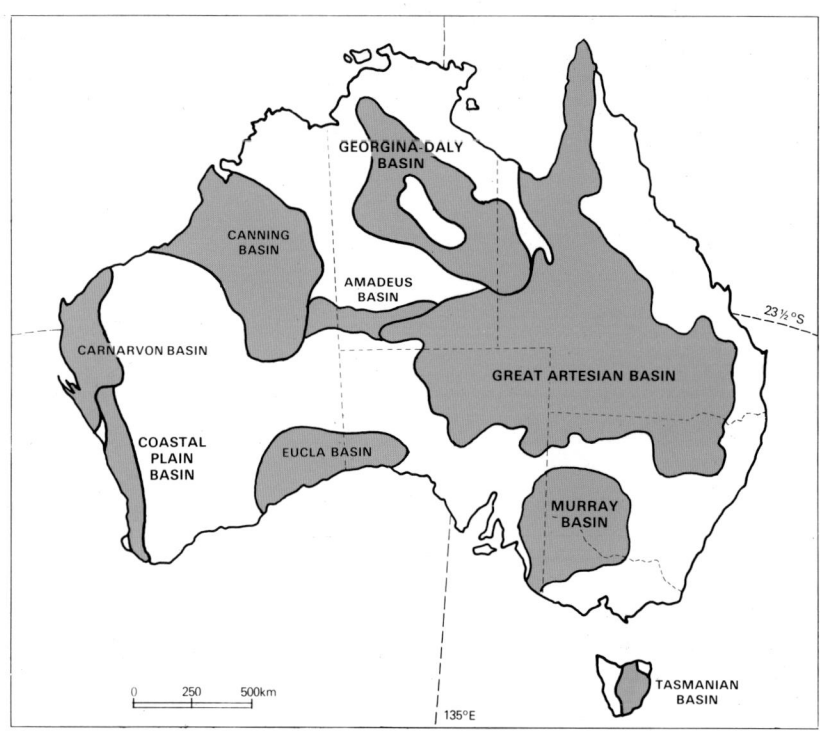

Main artesian basins (*see* ARTESIAN WATER)

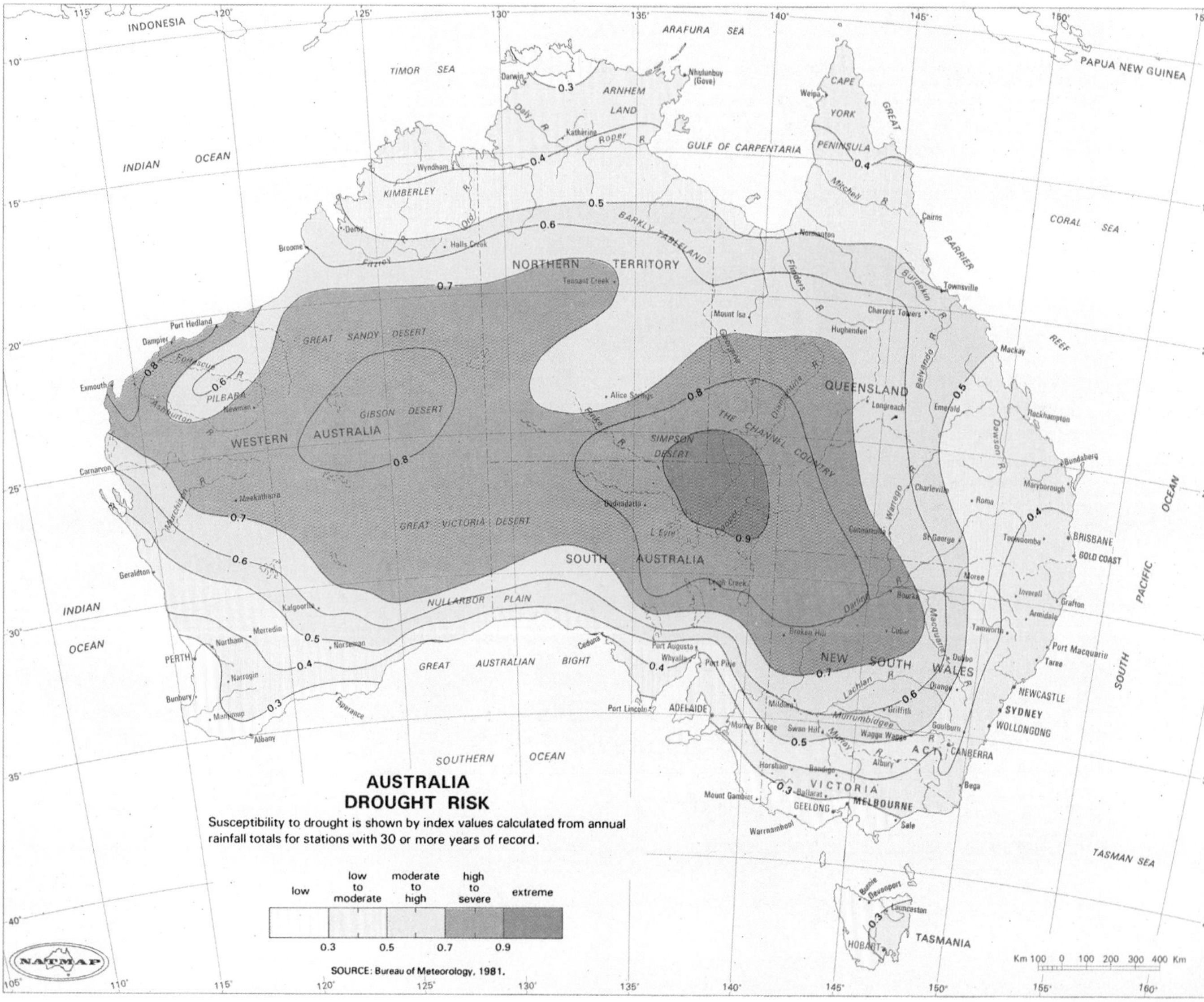

AUSTRALIA
DROUGHT RISK

Susceptibility to drought is shown by index values calculated from annual
rainfall totals for stations with 30 or more years of record.

low	low to moderate	moderate to high	high to severe	extreme

0.3   0.5   0.7   0.9

SOURCE: Bureau of Meteorology, 1981.

Km 100 0 100 200 300 400 Km

294mm and Merbein 275mm). The Wimmera River rises in the Grampians and flows N to LAKE HINDMARSH and LAKE ALBACUTYA, in an area of internal drainage. The better-watered S parts of the area are good farming and grazing lands, but the more arid sections have proved hazardous for crop farming. In the N, along the Murray, the SUNRAYSIA region is a productive irrigation area. The dry conditions over vast stretches have meant that water conservation and a reliable supply have been essential for development. The Wimmera-Mallee domestic and livestock water scheme has provided this. The Grampians form the catchment area for the scheme which provides 49 towns with reticulated water supplies; 6900 farms and 2800ha of irrigated land are supplied through 14 600km of channels; some of the earthen channels are being replaced by pipelines so as to reduce losses by seepage and evaporation. The largest reservoir in the scheme is ROCKLANDS DAM, completed in 1953, on the headwater of the GLENELG RIVER, but the earliest structure, Wartook Reservoir, was built in 1887; others date from the early decades of this century (for example, Lake Lonsdale 1903, Fyans Lake 1916, Pine Lake 1928) and Lake Bellfield, which has a capacity of 78 540ML, was completed in 1966. The 10 main storages of the scheme are interconnected and serve a complex system of canals and distributory channels. Wyperfield National Park, the largest national park in VIC, covering about 100 000ha, lies in the Mallee country, NW of Hopetoun and N of LAKE ALBACUTYA. The names Wimmera and Mallee both come from Aboriginal words; the former comes from *woomera* meaning 'a throwing stick' and the latter means 'scrub or thicket'.

Windsor

NSW (combined population of Windsor-RICHMOND 15 490 in 1981) A town on the HAWKESBURY RIVER 56km NW of Sydney, it is located in a district which was one of the first rural settlement regions in Australia. At the 1981 census Windsor was included in the Hawkesbury Shire (population 36 759 in 1981). As early as 1794, crops were being grown on the alluvial river flats for the colony's food supply. It is still important as a citrus fruit and vegetable growing area for the Sydney urban market. The early historic settlements along the Hawkesbury experienced a problem that continues to the present day—river flooding and inundation of the lowland farms. It was this problem which Governor MACQUARIE attempted to solve when he made a tour of inspection of the district in 1810; he decided to establish five townships on high ground where harvested crops could be stored in flood time and to which the settlers could retreat in safety. One of these townships in the area, previously known as Green Hills, was named Windsor after the English town on the Thames. A town plan was designed in the traditions of the 18th century, with a grid street pattern, a market square and provision for public buildings such as a school and a church. Windsor can thus claim to be the third-oldest

Restaurant in a colonial house on the Windsor Road

town in Australia, after Sydney and PARRA-MATTA. This early planning is still evident in the layout of the town and a number of examples of colonial buildings, some designed by the convict architect Francis GREENWAY, still stand. Among these are St Matthew's Church and its rectory, the courthouse, the Macquarie Arms Hotel, the Doctor's House and the Toll House. These and many others have been classified by the National Trust (NSW) as being of such historical and architectural significance that they must be preserved as part of the national heritage. Modern Windsor bears the stamp of Macquarie's influence, though it now contains some manufacturing industry (plastics, food processing); many of its residents are daily commuters to Sydney.

Grape picking

See also Nepean River
Further reading: Bladen, F.M. *Historical Records of New South Wales.* (vol 8) Govt Printer, Sydney, 1901; Clarke, A.N. *Historic Sydney and New South Wales.* The Central Press, Sydney, 1968; Bowd, D.G. *Macquarie Country—A History of the Hawkesbury.* Cheshire, Melbourne, 1969; Emanuel, C. & Thompson, P. *Windsor Sketchbook.* Rigby, Adelaide, 1975.

Wine industry

Captain Arthur PHILLIP planted the first grape vines, ceremoniously, at FARM COVE, Sydney, in 1788 and in time they provided the first Australian wine, which was judged to be 'tolerable'. Phillip later planted a second vineyard at Rose Hill (PARRAMATTA) where the conditions were more suitable for wine production. Eventually, in response to appeals for expert help, the British government sent out two French prisoners of war, in the belief apparently that because they were French they would know about wine production. In 1822 Gregory BLAXLAND sent the first Australian wine (about 1400 litres) to England, where it won a silver medal. A little later, John MACARTHUR began producing wine at CAMDEN PARK and PENRITH; by 1827 his yield was about 90 000 litres a year. None of these early sites however were ideal for wine production. The first grower who chose a suitable site was James Busby who first arrived in Australia to take up a teaching position in 1824. He returned to Europe in 1830 where he studied vine growing and wine making and then, with the encouragement of the British government, returned with 20 000 cuttings which he planted in the HUNTER RIVER valley. He is generally regarded as the true founder of Australian viticulture. Grapes were also planted in VIC at PORTLAND (1834) and near Lilydale (1838), and for a time VIC was the leading wine making State. Vineyards were established at Glenelg SA in 1838, and in the 1850s several German families moved into the BAROSSA VALLEY to which they brought their traditional skills, including those of wine making. Vineyards were first planted in WA in 1804, on the SWAN RIVER, and in QLD at ROMA in 1866.

Australian wines differ from those of Europe in that there is little emphasis upon the vintage year, for the wines are reasonably consistent from year to year, largely because of the warm, dry summers. Most vine growing areas in Australia have rainfalls of 250mm to 380mm in the winter, when the plants are dormant, and hot dry summers in which the fruit ripens well and escapes most diseases. The worst scourge has been phylloxera, a root-feeding insect related to the APHIDS and American in origin, which attacked vineyards in Europe and Australia at the end of the 19th century. It was overcome by the use of American root-stocks which had a resistance to the pest. It was particularly serious in NSW and VIC but did not reach the vines in SA. The grapes are also attacked by mildews and black spot, all of which are controlled or prevented from attacking the vines by fungicides. With Australia's wide range of climates and soils it has been possible to grow more than 50 varieties of grapes. The chief varieties are shown in Table 1.

Table 1

Australian Tourist Commission

Vintage Queens at the Barossa Valley Wine Festival

The industry consists of several large wine making companies, co-operatives and individual growers. Some of the large companies possess little land of their own but buy their

grapes in bulk from various growers, often using produce from several parts of the country in the production of one wine. They are geared to large-scale production with modern equipment and have excellent research and quality control facilities. Co-operatives produce wine from grapes from their own district but lack the large-scale production facilities of the large companies. Individual wine-makers produce excellent table wines under their own names but in smaller quantities.

Wine was comparatively neglected in Australia till the 1950s but since then its local sales have been steadily increasing. Recently there have been increases in white wine sales at the expense of the reds. Formerly, fortified wines were more popular than the table wines; the change in taste is due, partly at least, to the immigration of many Europeans since World War II. Despite the increasing popularity of wine, viticulture has proved unprofitable in some areas in recent years. In 1976-77 the yield per bearing hectare ranged from 18.2 tonnes (red wine grapes) and 20.9 tonnes (whites) in the MIA to 1.1 tonnes (reds) and one tonne (whites) in the Hunter River valley.

Major wine industry areas

1. Hunter Valley NSW. About 4000ha, near Pokolbin and MUSWELLBROOK. Rainfall 635mm to 760mm, including summer and autumn rains. Red and white table wines in

GRAPE VARIETIES IN 1979

Variety	Area (ha)*		Production (t freshweight)		
	Bearing	Total	Winemaking	Drying	Table
Red wine grapes:					
Cabernet Sauvignon	3 792	4 228	24 609	62	24 671
Grenache	5 606	5 731	52 267	645	52 912
Mataro	1 730	1 782	12 523	164	12 687
Shiraz	9 337	9 608	71 644	800	72 444
Other red wine grapes	1 840	2 093	12 877	2 437	15 314
TOTAL	22 305	23 442	173 920	4 108	178 028
White wine grapes:					
Doradillo	2 083	2 148	35 544	422	35 966
Palomino, Pedro Ximenez	2 712	2 773	35 657	25	35 682
Rhine Riesling	2 960	3 831	23 107	10	23 117
Clare Riesling	1 059	1 137	13 946	—	13 946
Semillon	2 537	2 804	29 205	32	29 237
Trevviano	1 597	1 808	20 366	48	20 414
Other white wine grapes	2 460	3 393	18 427	1 210	19 637
TOTAL	15 408	17 894	176 252	1 747	177 999
Multipurpose grapes:					
Currant	1 967	2 042	218	16 960	17 178
Muscat Gordo Blanco	3 998	4 445	60 090	7 630	67 720
Sultana	18 262	18 599	49 731	199 836	249 567
Waltham Cross	1 571	1 663	2 809	11 877	14 686
TOTAL	25 798	26 749	112 848	236 303	349 151
Other grapes:					
Muscat Hamburgh and Frontignan	546	589	1 917	1 234	3 151
Purple Cornichon, etc.	286	326	366	1 561	1 927
TOTAL	832	914	2 283	2 795	5 078
TOTAL GRAPES	64 342	68 999	465 303	244 953	710 256

Note: * excludes QLD and TAS.
Source: _Year Book Australia._ (no 65, 1981). Australian Bureau of Statistics, Canberra.

NSW Dept of Tourism

A vineyard at Pokolbin in the Hunter river region NSW

particular.

2. Murrumbidgee Valley NSW. About 5000ha in production near Griffith, under irrigation. Table and fortified wines.

3. MUDGEE NSW. Higher altitude than the Hunter, therefore later harvest.

4. Adelaide metropolitan area. Area of vineyards decreasing with the spread of the city but many wines still produced. Table and fortified wines.

5. McLaren Vale-Morphett Vale SA. Vineyards on deep sands, loams and heavy loams, often with high proportion of lime. Shiraz grows well here. Rainfall 530mm to 635mm. Mainly red table wines and port.

6. Coonawarra SA. Australia's southernmost vine growing area. Area about 2044ha, but increasing. Cool climate with rainfall about 635mm, soils reds and blacks over limestone, with plenty of subterranean water. High quality clarets.

7. Langhorne Creek SA. A dry area (about 360mm rainfall) but flood irrigation from the Bremer River produces heavy yields on the alluvial soils. Dessert wines and dry reds.

8. Barossa Valley SA. Vines grow both within the valley and on the adjacent hills. Rainfall varies with altitude from 510mm to 760mm. Fortified wines, brandies and light table wines.

9. Clare-Leasingham-Watervale SA. Hilly country between 305m and 610m high. Rainfall about 610mm, soils heavy loams with calcareous subsoils. Red and white table wines, and sherries.

10. Murray Valley SA. All the vineyards lie between WAILERIE and RENMARK and are irrigated because the rainfall is only about 200mm to 250mm. Sands and sandy loams, often with clay or calcareous subsoils. Formerly produced mainly sweet fortified wines and brandy but table wines are becoming more important.

Australian Tourist Commission

Coopering

11. Rutherglen VIC and Corowa NSW. These neighbouring areas were badly affected by phylloxera and have never completely recovered from the set-back. Rainfall about 580mm. Frontignac and Brown Muscat dessert wines, sherries and dry reds. Nearby Milawa, WANGARATTA and GLENROWAN produce red and white table wines.

12. Great Western VIC. Near STAWELL, on the GREAT DIVIDING RANGE, at about 305m above sea level. Rainfall about 503mm, soils light and of low fertility. Sparkling wines and red and white table wines.

13. GOULBURN RIVER valley VIC. A cool region with a rainfall of about 580mm. Red and white table wines.

14. MILDURA VIC. The vineyards of this area are irrigated from the Murray. Independent growers producing a wide range of grapes on the red sand soils. Other vineyards on the Murray are found at Boga, Robinvale and SWAN HILL.

15. Swan Valley WA. A region with deep alluvial soils, rainfall about 890mm and long hot summers. Full-bodied table and dessert wines.

16. Roma QLD. This district now produces mainly grapes for the table.

Marketing, promotion and research The industry is represented by the Australian Wine Board, the Australian Wine and Brandy Producers' Association (representing wine and brandy makers) and the Federal Grapegrowers Council (for the growers). The Wine Board is concerned with marketing at home and abroad. Only a small proportion of the wine is marketed overseas, the chief customer now being Canada. Formerly, there were substantial sales in Britain, mainly of fortified wines sold under the brand name 'Emu'. Some European wines and brandies are imported. Research on wine making and on grape growing is carried out by the CSIRO, the universities and many of the larger wine making companies.

Further reading: Murphy, D.F. *The Australian Wine Guide.* Sun Books, Melbourne, 1966; *Reference Paper: Wine, 1978.* Australian Information Service, Australian Govt Publishing Service, Canberra, 1978; 'The Australian Grape and Wine Industry' in *Quarterly Review of the Rural Economy* (vol 1, August 1979).

Table 2

PRODUCTION, CONSUMPTION AND EXPORTS OF AUSTRALIAN WINES (in millions litres)

Year	Production	Exports Quantity	Value ($m)	Australian consumption per head
1973-74	361.2	6.5	5.3	12.3
1974-75	356.2	6.2	5.5	13.0
1975-76	383.1	5.0	5.4	13.7
1976-77	339.6	4.7	5.4	14.3
1977-78	335.1	5.3	6.3	16.5
1979-80*	414.2	6.1	8.4	17.4

Note: * provisional.
Source: *Year Book Australia*. (no 65, 1981). Australian Bureau of Statistics, Canberra, 1979.

Wingham NSW (population 3 937 in 1981) A small country town in the lower NORTH COAST region of the State, it is situated on the MANNING RIVER, upstream from TAREE, 354km by road N of Sydney. It is the oldest settlement on the Manning River and was laid out as a township in 1843. The surrounding district is important for dairying, timber-getting and beef cattle grazing, as well as for some fine bush scenery. A pocket of dense scrubland, known as The Brush, quite near the centre of the town, has been preserved as a sample of the original brush vegetation, containing orchids, ferns and sub-tropical flowering plants, particularly red and purple bougainvillea. Between September and May each year, thousands of migratory flying foxes make The Brush their home. In Wingham Park a giant log, 13m long and with a girth over 4.5m, symbolises the role of the timber industry in the development of the Manning Valley.

Winstanley, Eliza (1818-82) Actress. Born in England, she came to Australia with her family at the age of 15. Her father became a scene painter at Barnett LEVEY's Theatre Royal in Sydney, where she made her début as Juliet in 1834. She soon became a favourite with Sydney audiences, playing at the Royal Victoria, Olympic and City Theatres. She married Henry O'Flaherty, a musician and playwright at the Royal Victoria, in 1841. In 1846 she went to England, where she performed at Manchester and in 1850 joined Charles Kean's company at the Princess's Theatre, London, appearing there for the following eight years, and later at the Lyceum Theatre. Apart from her work in the theatre, she published novels and became editor of a subsidiary of *Bow Bells* magazine. She returned to Australia in 1880.
Further reading: Irvin, E. *Theatre Comes to Australia.* University of Queensland Press, St Lucia, 1971.

Winston Churchill Memorial Trust This was set up in 1965, when a nationwide appeal in Australia raised over $4 million as a trust fund for providing study fellowships in memory of Britain's great wartime leader. About 50 fellowships, most of them for study projects of 14 weeks or less, are granted each year. Recipients are chosen from the following seven categories of interests: academic and professional subjects, education, public service, primary industry, secondary industry and commerce, community service and the arts.

Winton QLD (population 1 259 in 1981) Located on a tributary of the DIAMANTINA RIVER in the central N of the State, it is a rail and road focus for an extensive semi-arid grazing region. At an elevation of 187m above sea level, it is on the Landsborough Highway 1383km NW of Brisbane, 180km NW of LONGREACH and 338km SE of CLONCURRY. The average annual rainfall of 407mm is too low for crop cultivation and the wide plains are dominated by sheep and cattle properties. The rainfall occurs mostly in summer. The town water supply (and much of the water for livestock) comes from artesian bores, some over 1.2km deep. The Winton area was settled by graziers in the 1870s and the town developed as a service and collection point for rural produce. It is still one of the largest trucking centres for cattle in QLD and is the terminus of the 'beef road' from Boulia, 370km to the W. It is connected to ROCKHAMPTON and TOWNSVILLE by rail. Opals have been mined at several locations in the district since the 1890s and though the fields (such as Opalton, 125km SSW of Winton) have been abandoned as commercial mines, fossickers still try their luck there. It was at Dagworth station in 1895 that 'Banjo' PATERSON wrote WALTZING MATILDA, taking his theme from an incident which occurred at Combo waterhole in the Diamantina River. The first registered office of Qantas Airlines, formed in 1920, was in the town, and the first board meeting was held at the Winton Club in 1921.

wireworm *see* beetles

Wisteria *see* Papilionaceae

Wittenoom WA (population 247 in 1981) A small town and asbestos mining centre in the middle section of the FORTESCUE RIVER valley, on the N edge of the HAMERSLEY RANGE, Wittenoom is 181km W of the Great Northern Highway and 1464km N of Perth via this highway. At an elevation of 460m above sea level, it experiences very hot summer conditions and a low annual rainfall of 394mm. The existence of asbestos in the area had been known since the early decades of this century, but it was not until 1937 that mining began. The town was built in 1947 to provide homes and facilities for the mine workers, but low asbestos prices and high costs forced the closure of the mine in 1966. It seemed, however, that the town had a future in tourism, owing to the strikingly spectacular gorge scenery of the area, but it was decided in 1978 that the town should be abandoned because of the health hazards created by the asbestos.

wobbegong *see* sharks, etc.

Wodonga VIC (population 18 144 in 1981) Plans were made in the 1970s between the Australian and VIC governments for the twin towns of ALBURY and Wodonga, on opposite banks of the MURRAY RIVER, to be developed jointly as a major inland growth centre with an ultimate population of 300 000; at the census of 1981 the combined population was 53 251. The town is located 303km by road NE of Melbourne at the Hume and Murray Valley Highway junction, and on the standard-gauge interstate railway line 301km by rail from Melbourne. It grew from a river crossing and in pre-federation days was a customs collection point for livestock and goods passing into VIC from NSW. It is a commercial and service centre for a productive rural region on the river flats and adjacent hill lands and has a number of secondary industries, including sawmills, concrete works and a fertiliser factory. It receives an annual rainfall of 713mm, concentrated mainly in winter. Squatters settled the area in the 1830s and called it Wodonga, the Aboriginal name for an edible nut. When the township was surveyed in 1852 the name was changed to Belvoir, but in 1869 it reverted to the original name.

Wollomombi Falls NSW This is a spectacular waterfall in the E part of the NEW ENGLAND region, 39km E of ARMIDALE, where the Wollomombi River, an upper tributary of the MACLEAY RIVER, plunges from the plateau surface into a steep and narrow gorge. The falls, claimed to be the highest in Australia and the second-highest in the S hemisphere, have an initial sheer drop of 335m and a total descent to the gorge base of over 450m.

Wollondilly River NSW This river is an upper tributary of the NEPEAN-HAWKESBURY river system. The headwaters of the Wollondilly are in the SOUTHERN TABLELANDS, from where it flows in a general N direction, joined by its main tributaries, the Mulwaree, Wingecarribee and Nattai. Further downstream it receives the Cox River as a tributary from the BLUE MOUNTAINS and beyond this junction changes its name to become the WARRAGAMBA. This, in turn, joins the Nepean River which, further downstream, changes name to the Hawkesbury. This series of name changes (Wollondilly to Warragamba to Nepean to Hawkesbury) along the course of the river system often creates some confusion; it came about because different sections of the river were discovered at different times and were given separate names. The Aboriginal word *wollondilly* means 'water trickling over rocks'.

Wollongong NSW A major city on the narrow plain of the ILLAWARRA region of the S coast, it is located on the Princes Highway some 82km by road S of Sydney. The main S coast railway line passes through the city (83km by rail from Sydney) and a spur line connects it to MOSS VALE on the SOUTHERN TABLELAND. The Illawarra Highway, on a general E-W route, ascends the scarp of the tablelands via the Macquarie Pass to Moss Vale, and thence links the Princes and Hume Highways. The City of Wollongong (first proclaimed in 1942, the boundaries were extended in 1947) covers an area over 700km^2 stretching from N of Helensburg to the shores of Lake Illawarra; it includes a number of smaller urban centres such as Stanwell Park, Coalcliff, Austinmer, Thirrourl, Bulli, Woonona and the industrial centre of PORT KEMBLA. The population of the city at the 1981 census was 169 343, but the total population of the urban centre was 208 601.

Wollongong, on the Illawara coastal plain

The coastal plains on which the city is situated are narrow in the N where the cliff-scarp of the tableland reaches to the coast, but the plain widens progressively to the S and at Lake Illawarra is some 15km broad. A series of alternating headlands and beaches along the coast provide good surfing and scenic attractions. From vantage points on the scarp, such as Sublime Point above Austinmer, Mt Kembla (534km above sea level) and MOUNT KEIRA (467m), there are spectacular panoramic views of the whole region. Wollongong experiences a moderate climate, with warm to hot summer conditions and mild winters; the average annual rainfall is 1275mm, with the summer months having the highest falls (January 267mm, February 207mm) and the driest periods in July (24mm) and September (23mm). The central business district of the city is a major commercial and service focus for the rapidly developing industrial area of Port Kembla, as well as for the smaller urban centres of the region. There is a wide range of educational institutions in the city including a large technical college, an Institute of Education (formerly the Teachers College), the University of Wollongong (formerly a college of the University of New South Wales), and numerous State and independent secondary and primary schools.

The history of the district dates back to the voyage of James COOK, who in 1770 sighted this coastal stretch and attempted a landing, but was turned back by the heavy surf, and so continued his journey N to make the first landing in BOTANY BAY. Following the establishment of the first settlement in 1788, George BASS and Matthew FLINDERS in their tiny craft *Tom Thumb* explored the coast in 1796 and landed at Lake Illawarra. A year later a party of shipwrecked sailors passed through the area and reported finding coal; Bass returned to the area, aided by two of the shipwreck survivors, and discovered a coal seam at Coalcliff as well as other seams nearby. However, it was not until 60 years later that the first successful coal mine was opened (Mt Keira in 1857) and not until 1878 that Coalcliff mine was started. In the meantime, pastoral settlement of the Illawarra district had commenced and cedar cutting in the nearby forested areas proved lucrative. Wollongong Harbour was used in the early days of the 19th century for shipping the cedar, and later, for coal shipment, but as a port for large shipping it has long been superseded by Port Kembla.

The harbour is now used mainly by trawlers, commercial fishing boats and pleasure craft, and the fish market and boat harbour are popular tourist attractions.

The development of Wollongong has been linked with coal mining and the steel industry. There is a series of coal mines extending along the scarplands W of the city; geologically these coal seams are part of the same structure as the NEWCASTLE and LITHGOW coal measures. They outcrop in the escarpment and are worked mainly by adits driven horizontally into the cliff face. The quality and abundance of the coal was a prime reason for the development of the huge iron and steel industries at Port Kembla, and this in turn has led to the establishment of other manufacturing industries and to the expansion of the city.

The name Wollongong comes from the Aboriginal word which has several meanings: 'five islands', 'hard ground near the water' and 'see, the monster comes!' (the latter supposed to be an exclamation of fear uttered by the Aborigines when they first saw a sailing ship). There are many tourist attractions in the city and district: Bald Hill Lookout at Stanwell Park, with a monument to Lawrence HARGRAVE, the aviation pioneer, now a favourite spot for hang-gliding; Mt Kembla village, 15km from Wollongong, the site of a mine disaster in 1902 and now preserved as a village of yesteryear; the Port Kembla steelworks, the largest in the S hemisphere; the 200-year-old figtree located 6km S of the city; the Illawarra Historical Museum and the shell art display; various vantage points for scenic views (Bulli Pass Scenic Reserve, Mt Keira Lookout, Golden View Lookout); five dams which form part of the Sydney and Illawarra water supply system (Avon, Cordeaux, Cataract, Nepean and Woronora), located inland from Wol-

longong in the plateau uplands; the historic lighthouse at Belmore Basin (built in 1868) which has been listed for preservation by the National Trust (NSW); and other buildings listed by the Trust, including the courthouse (built in 1885) and St Michael's Cathedral (1858).

Further reading: Mathieson, R.S. *Illawarra and the South Coast Region.* Longmans, Melbourne, 1960; *Wollongong and Environs.* NRMA Touring Department, Sydney, 1976.

woma *see* snakes

wombat berry *see* Liliaceae

wombats These MARSUPIALS belong to the family Vombatidae (order Diprotodonta) which contains four species, distantly related to the POSSUMS and the KOALA. They are large, somewhat bear-like, thickset, short-legged animals with broad, blunt heads and very small tails. They are powerful burrowing vegetarians which feed nocturnally on tree roots, bark and grasses. They can reach a length of about 1.2m and a weight of about 39kg. Their habit of burrowing makes them unpopular with landowners, especially when the digging damages fences, and this has led to the killing of many of them, particularly the hairy-nosed wombat of the plains. Wombats are easily kept in captivity but, unfortunately, breeding in such conditions is rarely successful.

Forest wombats There appears to be only one species, namely the common wombat, *Vombatus ursinus* (head and body, 99cm; tail, *c.* 2.5cm), of south-eastern QLD, eastern NSW, southern VIC, south-eastern SA, TAS and the BASS STRAIT islands. It lives mainly in wet or dry sclerophyll forests and

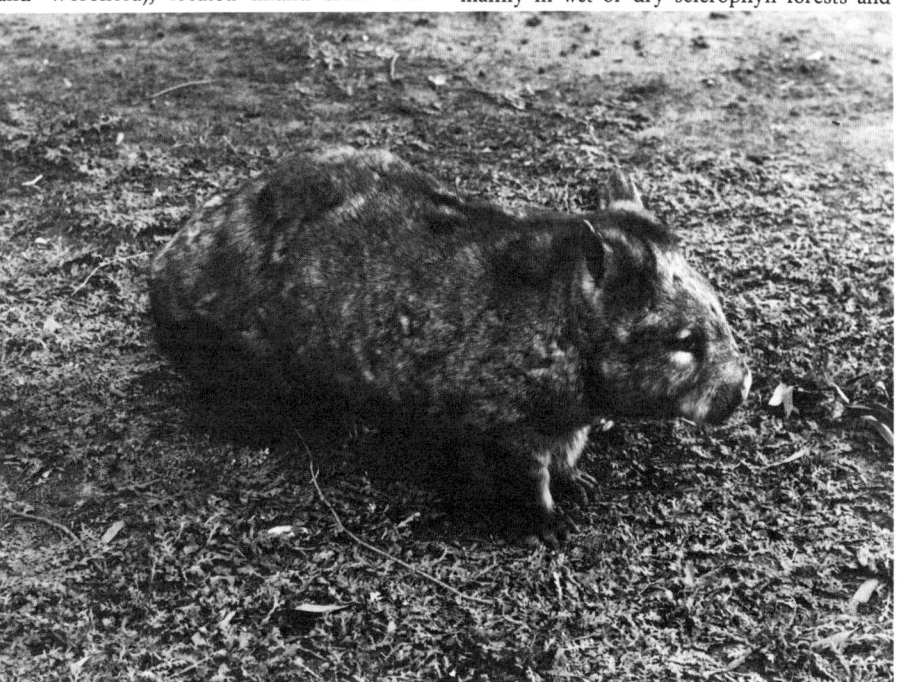

Hairy-nosed wombat, *Lasiorhinus latifrons*

woodlands, especially in rocky areas. The coarse hair is brown or black, the snout is naked, the ears are short and the pouch, as in all wombats, opens backwards.

Plains wombats After some disagreement in the past it now seems that there are two species of plains or hairy-nosed wombats. Both have hairy snouts and softer fur than the common wombat, and live in more open, arid habitats. The southern hairy-nosed wombat, *Lasiorhinus latifrons* (77cm to 93cm; 2.5cm to 6cm), has greyish fur, with white hair on the snout. It lives in semi-arid areas (200mm to 500mm annual rainfall) in southern SA and south-eastern WA. The northern hairy-nosed wombat, *L. krefftii* (*c.* 1m; *c.* 5cm), is greatly endangered; it probably survives in Epping Forest in central QLD and formerly occurred at places in southern QLD and northern NSW. It lives in flat, sandy country with grass or forest. It is a grey-brown animal, or grey with mottlings of browns and blacks but can be distinguished with certainty from its southern relative by certain skull measurements.

Further reading: see under kangaroos.

women in Australia Any discussion of the place of women in Australia must take into account the fact that, firstly, since the arrival of the first Europeans, Australia has always had a class-divided society. Secondly, every woman is influenced by her own personal circumstances and consideration of her needs, rights, responsibilities and power is affected by whether one is considering her as a citizen, a worker, a mother, a daughter, a student, a divorcee, a single parent, a member of a political party or civic club and so on. Furthermore, because the interdependence of society as a whole is very complex, altering the way it functions in one area can distort other areas. For all these reasons, claims that reforms have benefited women, or that proposed reforms would benefit women, must be qualified to mean 'some women'. Indeed, particular benefits for some women may cause disadvantages for other women. However, it is evident that, in Australia as in many other countries, there has been a trend in recent times for the range of choice in life-style for women to become much wider, particularly for women with outstanding skills; for the unskilled, for many migrants, and for members of disadvantaged groups in general, marked change has not been so evident.

This article is concerned with changes in the social structure which have affected women, and with trends in women's movements from 1788 onwards but particularly in recent years.

Aboriginal women In 1788 and for some decades thereafter, the vast majority of women in Australia were Aborigines. The effects of European settlement on Aboriginal society as a whole (*see* ABORIGINES) were particularly disastrous for women. The fact that men greatly outnumbered women in white society helped to increase the frequency of interracial sexual relationships which led to many Aboriginal women becoming isolated from their

Mary Nye, convict woman

Queen Victoria Museum & Art Gallery

tribal groups without becoming accepted in the British social system. They gave birth to a mixed-race population which was often exploited by the settlers as cheap labour. This process began in the Sydney region in the earliest years of British settlement and gradually spread throughout the continent, reaching its greatest dimensions in N Australia, where the Aborigines were more numerous than in the S, where the disproportion between the sexes in white society was great, and where the opportunities for exploiting cheap Aboriginal labour were more numerous than in more closely settled areas.

Convict women Among the white population, until about 1800 a majority of women were convicts and as such were to some extent outcasts from society. People in authority and wealthy free settlers tended to regard them as uniformly dissolute, not only because they had committed offences against society, but also because they were from the 'lower orders', and because most of them were single women separated from their families. The historical evidence shows, however, that such generalisations were unjustified, for their social backgrounds varied considerably and they had been convicted for a great range of offences, many of which would now be regarded as petty. Moreover, only a small proportion of them

were later convicted for crimes within the colonies. A number of factors helped most of them to attain in colonial society positions of greater security than they had enjoyed in Britain. Employment was easy to obtain, and so were husbands in a society where at first men greatly outnumbered women. The majority seem to have settled down within a few years of arrival into more or less the traditional pattern of family life, either through legal marriage or common law marriage. Some acquired husbands who became the wealthiest men in the colony, and a few married men of social or political importance.

Patriarchal social structure It is equally hard to generalise about those women who came as free settlers during the early colonial period, for they included groups as diverse as the wives of men of capital, the free wives of convicts or ex-convicts coming to rejoin their husbands and, from the 1830s, large numbers of young single women who came under assisted migration schemes. In general, however, these women inherited from Britain a patriarchal social structure similar to that operating in most western countries in the 19th century. The theoretical basis for this social structure was the sexual vulnerability of women, and under it women were afforded protection by a father, brother or husband who was held morally and/or legally responsible for his daughter, sister or wife. The rules were rigid, with no provision for deviation. Some women enjoyed happy personal relationships within the family and were unaware of the bondage of family duties and of allegations that they were exploited; other women derived spiritual power from their religious beliefs and commitment and did not recognise a need to be liberated. However, any woman who was not happy with her protector and wished to find some alternative life-style was faced with some form of discrimination and social injustice. On marriage a husband was given legal control of his wife's property and if a woman left her husband she would probably lose her right to maintenance and her right to her separate estate which may have arisen from settlement, gifts, or her own earnings. The 1881 New South Wales Matrimonial Causes Amendment Act made it possible for a wife to sue for divorce on the single ground of her husband's adultery. In 1892 the grounds for divorce were extended to include drunkenness, cruelty and desertion, and mothers could gain custody of children. It was not until 1893, with the passing of the Married Women's Property (Amendment) Act, that a married woman was given legal rights over her separate property. Even so, divorce laws which favoured the husband prevailed until the federal government passed the Family Law Act of 1975. Women who were deserted by their husbands, widows, orphans and others without a male protector had to depend on support from family or friends or to live outside the supports provided by the patriarchal system, as did the mixed-race Aboriginal women, women convicts and prostitutes. The numbers of these outcasts from the system were added to from time to time; for example, they were joined by the descendants of KANAKAS.

Social reforms which provided financial assistance to the women outside the patriarchal system and to women in general did not pose any threat to, or alter the operation of, the system. Nor did the introduction of government welfare services for women and children. Maternity allowances introduced by the FISHER government in 1912 were paid as a social support to the family; Child Endowment (now called Family Allowances) introduced in 1941 by the MENZIES Liberal/Country Party government was also seen as support for all families. In the same year the federal government introduced pensions for widows (although some State governments had paid widows' pensions previously). Australian widows' pensions are subject to very complex conditions, because as well as being means-tested they are paid under certain circumstances to all of the following: civilian widows, divorcees, wives deserted by their husbands for more than six months, wives with husbands in mental hospitals, wives whose husbands have been in prison for six months or more, women who were *de facto* wives for a period of three years before the death of the *de facto* husband, and unmarried mothers. Benefits to widows of servicemen are paid without

means tests. The Henderson Commission of Inquiry into Poverty in Australia (1975) reported that pensions for single mothers, deserted wives and widows were not sufficient to keep them above the poverty line in cases where there was little or no other source of income.

The modification of the patriarchal system was a slow process and was not the result of social reforms; nor did it occur because of political activity by women. In fact, it followed from events which could not have been foreseen. The two world wars introduced women to work outside the home in occupations vacated by men who joined the defence forces. Also, during WORLD WAR II, women joined the defence forces. Under the terms of benefits for ex-servicemen and women, women were given training for higher education after the war if they had served in one of the defence services. This started a trend for more and more women gaining tertiary education and seeking employment in professions in competition with men. Methods of contraception became more reliable and women were able to engage in family planning. By the time the 'pill' had been invented as the most reliable form of contraception the patriarchal system had already been modified and with the 'pill' its theoretical basis was no longer applicable. Women began to experiment with alternative life-styles, such as permissive temporary relationships, communal living and unmarried motherhood. However, the Report of the Royal Commission on Human Relationships published in November 1977 stated that an increased popularity of marriage had been discovered in its investigations. It also claimed that although the rate of divorce was increasing 75 per cent of divorcees remarry.

While the evolution of the family structure in Australian has been progressing from a rigid patriarchal one to one of a more flexible partnership, some migrants who have arrived in Australia have re-established a rigid patriarchal system in their communities. Many migrants believe that Australian society has become too permissive, that women still need parental control, and that a father or brother should chaperon young women until they are married. This belief was reinforced by the findings of the Royal Commission on Human Relationships, which drew attention to the fact that there were at least 60 000 abortions performed each year in Australia, and that young single women aged 15-24 were a dominant group having abortions. The Commission investigated the pressures exerted on girls and boys to engage in sexual relations and, although it did not recommend a return to the patriarchal system, it did suggest that moral and religious beliefs may help both boys and girls in withstanding such pressures and recommended that the risks of early intercourse should be made known to all girls.

Women's movements and political activity A complete and comprehensive history of women's movements has not yet been written but from the information so far

Catherine Helen Spence, pioneer fighter for women's rights

researched it seems that among the earliest women's movements were those which drew attention to the fact that women had different needs from men because they were different in nature and morality and in their duties to society. Because women did not have formal citizenship in Australia, they campaigned for an extension of citizenship rights to women and the right to vote in elections. Women were enfranchised in SA in 1894 (the first time women were given the vote in any English-speaking country), in WA in 1899, in NSW in 1902, in QLD in 1905, in VIC in 1908 and for federal elections in 1902. The campaign which achieved this privilege was supported by church groups including the Women's Christian Temperance Union. Their policy stressed women's moral role in the community and opposed the sale of alcohol. In NSW the campaign was started when Dora Montefiore was faced with the reality of the social position of a widow. She discovered on the death of her husband that she had no legal right to the guardianship of her children and she was granted such guardianship only because her husband had failed to appoint a guardian in his will. Had he done so, she discovered, she would have had no legal claim to her children. Horrified at this discovery, she invited Rose Scott, Margaret Windeyer, Mrs Wolstenhome and others to her Darlinghurst Road home in Sydney in 1891 and the Womanhood Suffrage League was founded. When the vote was granted to women in NSW in 1902 the difficulties associated with uniting women on more than a temporary basis or on a single issue became evident. The original organisation was replaced by three different organisations: the Women's Political Educational League, which tried to ensure that the best use was made of the vote and which lasted until 1910, its founder and leader, Rose Scott, believing that women betrayed their sex by joining political parties and should gain reforms through influence rather than by getting women

SA Archives

elected to Parliament; the Women's Progressive Association, which was linked with the AUSTRALIAN LABOR PARTY (ALP) and which continued to press for reforms until the 1920s; and the Women's Liberal League, renamed the Women's Reform League in 1911. Similar organisations sprang up in all States.

The policies adopted by early women's movements envisaged a society which would be more moral and compassionate, and the energies of women in these movements were expended in trying to gain protection for women and children in employment, to gain support and protection for women and children through social welfare and to achieve equality and justice before the law.

With the emergence of political parties, women's movements formed wings to each political party and submitted resolutions which were considered in the overall party policy formulation. However, there were many feminist organisations which remained outside the formal political party structure; they would isolate issues of importance to women and then search across party lines for support (a technique adopted by the Women's Electoral Lobby in 1972). Attempts to field candidates in an election were rare but not unknown: for example, in NSW the Women's Party nominated candidates for the State general elections in 1920 and 1932. However, when the feminist organisations expanded their policies to cover wider issues they became discredited. The Women's Liberal League in NSW and the QLD Women's Electoral League launched an attack against socialism and the women associated with the ALP and the Communist Party counterattacked. During the Depression Jessie Street emerged as a champion of feminism but she became identified with the causes of Communism. Later in the 1940s Adela Pankhurst Walsh founded the Women's Guild of Empire which was exposed as an extreme right-wing organisation. Gradually, all feminist organisations lost their non-aligned image and became suspect in the minds of non-committed women in the community. Women's movements were also handicapped because the issues which concerned women and their welfare were only one factor in the overall picture of how Australian society worked. This became particularly obvious during the Depression; problems associated with unemployment of women were part of a total economic problem and because the breadwinner in the family was assumed to be the male, married women were refused employment in many fields. The divisions between women on broad political, social and economic issues were widened rather than narrowed as time progressed because there was no overall philosophical basis for their ideas.

A movement started in the USA in the 1960s, the Women's Liberation movement, provided a new approach to women's movements. It attracted young, activist, middle-class, well-educated women, and aimed to obtain equality between the sexes in work and pay, an education system which did not inculcate traditional attitudes towards woman's role in society, the provision of free child-care facilities and legislation for abortion on demand. Two organisations in Australia—the Women's Electoral Lobby and the Women's Media Action Group—were particularly active in spreading the ideas and philosophy of this movement. The Women's Electoral Lobby was very active in lobbying for support across party lines during the 1972 federal general election; a Labor government was returned (the first in 23 years) and during its term of office it introduced a number of reforms which favoured the women in Australia, and which made it easier for them to enter the workforce. In 1972 the government intervened in the Equal Pay Case; and in 1973-74 it provided $75 million for pre-school education and child care, introduced basic maternity leave provisions for women in the Australian public service and appointed a Women's Adviser to the Prime Minister on policy issues such as child care, education, employment, Aboriginal women and migrant women.

Women's movements in Australia are indebted to international bodies which formulated a coherent policy in the field of discrimination. The International Women's Suffrage Alliance and the UN Status of Women Commission have provided basic policies copied in Australia. During 1975, declared as the International Women's Year by the UN, women's movements in Australia became very vocal. The Whitlam Labor government participated in the conference held in Mexico in 1975 and sponsored many activities including the National 'Women and Politics' Conference in Canberra.

In 1978 the Fraser coalition government established the National Women's Advisory Council (NWAC) to give women a consultative voice at federal government level and to advise the government through the Office of Women's Affairs. Active feminists were appointed to the first NWAC (1978-80). The Council produced comprehensive and detailed reports including 'More than a Token Gesture', 'An Equal Voice' and 'My Child was born Disabled'.

In 1977-78 State governments in SA, VIC, NSW and TAS passed anti-discrimination legislation on the grounds of sex and marital status and adopted policies of affirmative action to bring about equal employment opportunities for women and minority groups in society.

Although the above reforms were welcomed by many feminist groups, by the late 1970s concern was beginning to spread with regard to some of them. For example, provisions of the Family Law Act 1975, some recommendations made by the Royal Commission on Human Relationships 1977, some government legislation, some policies of the more radical women's movements and the policies of the NWAC were all seen by some groups of women as a threat to the family as a unit in society. Conflict between radical and conservative lobby groups became pronounced at regional, State and national meetings organised by the NWAC to mark the mid-point of the UN Decade for Women and to discuss an Australian National Plan of Action for the rest of the decade. Eventually, the concern of the conservatives was consolidated in March 1980 when 250 delegates representing women's organisations with a nationwide membership attended the Women for the Family and Society Conference at Macquarie University in North Ryde NSW. The Conference passed a number of resolutions which were sent as petitions to the Prime Minister of Australia and the Premier in each State. In general, these resolutions asked that the family be protected by legislation and that all legislation passed by governments in Australia be carefully scrutinised from the viewpoint of its impact on the normal family unit in society.

There were two marked reactions to this division between women's lobby groups. In August 1980 the government changed the membership of the NWAC. The conservative lobby groups were now represented on the Council through the appointment of the NSW President of the Women's Action Alliance. This organisation is closely linked with the other conservative groups—Women Who Want to be Women, The Festival of Light, the National Civic Council, Women and the Family and the Right to Life Association. The government also appointed women who were active members of the Liberal Party or the National Party (then the National Country Party). Although some feminists were also reappointed to the Council they had lost the complete control of it and the NWAC lost its claim to have no political bias.

The second reaction to the division between women's lobby groups was seen in the behaviour of women standing for election at the 1980 federal elections, and the fact that the major political parties did not respond to the Women's Electoral Lobby campaign which listed among important issues the increase and indexation of family allowance, and the recognition of child care expenses as an income tax deduction. A record number of 74 women stood for the House of Representatives and 34 for the Senate but women candidates in winnable seats tended to avoid controversial feminist issues in their campaign. Throughout 1983 the conflict between conservative and radical groups of women continued and appears to be irreconcilable. In December, Dr. Anne Summers became head of the Office for Status of Women in the Prime Minister's Department. The function of this office is to monitor all government policies for their impact on women, to set up a national data base on women and undertake a national research programme with information supplied by the women members of the Labor Caucus and from a new body to be set up to replace the National Women's Advisory Council. Dr. Summers was previously a university lecturer in politics, then a political correspondent and had also been an active radical feminist.

At the end of 1983 there appeared to have been only marginal improvement in the work opportunities and rewards for those women

who seek to find financial independence and personal fulfilment in a paid occupation. It is true that between 1972 when the equal pay principle was fully established and 1982, the average female earnings as a proportion of the average male earnings increased from 65% to 78%. Nevertheless the 1981 census figures show clearly that the majority of women still work in low pay, low status occupations.
Further reading: Mayer, H. (ed.) *Labor to Power—Australia's 1972 election.* Angus & Robertson, Sydney, 1973. (Contains 7 essays on the Women's Electoral Lobby); Summers, A. *Damned Whores and God's Police.* Penguin, Ringwood, VIC, 1975; Royal Commission on Human Relationships. Final Report, vol. 1, Commonwealth Government Printer, Canberra, 1977; Mackinolty, J. and Radi, H. (eds.) *In Pursuit of Justice.* Hale & Iremonger, Sydney, 1979; Bettison, M. & Summers, A. *Her Story—Australian Women in Print.* Hale and Iremonger, Sydney, 1980; Daniels, K. & Murnane, M. *Uphill all the Way—a Documentary History of Women in Australia.* University of Queensland Press, St. Lucia, QLD, 1980; Connors, L. "The Politics of the National Women's Advisory Council" in *Politics* (vol. 16, no 2, November, 1981); Hargreaves, K. *Women at Work.* Penguin, Ringwood, VIC. 1982; Grimshaw, P. & Strahan. L. (eds.) *The Half-Open Door.* Hale & Iremonger, Sydney, 1982; Lofthouse, A. *Who's Who of Women in Australia.* Methuen, N. Ryde, NSW, 1982.

Wonthaggi VIC (population 4 796 in 1981) Located on the Bass Highway, 129km by road SE of Melbourne and SE of WESTERN PORT BAY, this small industrial town was formerly a coal mining centre. The town was developed as a residential and service centre for the mine which was opened in 1910. Its seams of black coal made the VIC railways independent of imports from NSW and coal production continued there until 1968. The closure of the mine came about because of a number of factors: the thin and faulted seams made mining difficult, there was increasing competition from the brown coal of the LATROBE VALLEY, and increasing numbers of diesel locomotives reduced the demand by the railways for coal. The fertile Bass Valley and Glenalvie dairying districts adjoin the town and provide numerous scenic drives. The average annual rainfall of 928mm, concentrated in winter and spring, makes the areas suitable for intensive livestock grazing. At an elevation of 40m above sea level, the town is located 8km inland from the seaside resort of Cape Paterson. The name Wonthaggi comes from an Aboriginal word meaning 'to pull along'.

wood worm *see* beetles

wood-chopping This is a uniquely Australian sport (also called axemanship) in which axemen compete against one another in chopping through logs. During the 1800s, as the practice of felling and cutting timber swelled

to an industry, professional timber-getters competed against each other in felling trees. These individual contests in time gave rise to organised competitions at country shows and carnivals. The long-term success of these competitions was virtually ensured by the close finish in the earliest contest on record. In 1874, in TAS, Joe Smith and Jack Biggs met in a tree-felling match in which the trees measured 120cm in diameter. Smith was the winner, but only just—Biggs' tree began to fall as Smith's hit the ground. Since World War II wood-chopping events have been a regular feature of the large agricultural shows which are held annually in most major cities throughout Australia.

Wood-chopping competitions are arranged in three classes: underhand, standing block and tree felling. In underhand events the axeman stands on a short log, chopping between his feet. In standing block events the axeman stands on the ground and chops sideways into a vertical log. In tree felling events the axeman has to chop through a vertical log at a point about 4m from the ground—to do this he has to climb the log, and as he climbs he chops wedges in the log to support the footboards on which he stands. Most events are handicap events, with axemen starting at different times, and close finishes are common, providing exciting entertainment for spectators.

woodland *see* vegetation

woodlice *see* crustaceans

woodswallows These PASSERINE BIRDS belong to a small family, Artamidae, which is represented in the Oriental and Australian regions; there are six Australian species. Woodswallows are not closely related to SWALLOWS, although both hawk for insects.

Dusky woodswallow, *Artamus cyanopterus*

They are more robust BIRDS than true swallows, but have long wings; the bill is blue with a black tip and, like HONEYEATERS, the tongue is brush-tipped. Woodswallows of one kind or another inhabit most parts of Australia, feeding on insects but sometimes supplementing their diet with nectar or by scavenging at rubbish dumps. They cluster together in roosts, especially in cold weather.

The dusky woodswallow, *Artamus cyanopterus** (18'cm long), a dark greyish-brown species with a shallow-forked tail, is found in forests and woodlands throughout Australia where the rainfall exceeds about 500mm a year; it is replaced by the similar black-faced woodswallow, *A. cinereus* (18cm), in savanna woodlands where the rainfall is lower. The widespread masked woodswallow, *A. personatus** (18cm to 20cm), a small, light-coloured species with a mask-like black patch on the face, is often seen in woodland areas in the company of the white-browed woodswallow, *A. superciliosus** (18cm to 20cm), which has reddish-brown underparts, a black face and throat and a white band above the eye. The white-breasted woodswallow, *A. leucorhynchus* (17cm), a fairly widespread species which favours well-timbered areas, is almost a house-

Wood-chopping

*Species, genus or family is endemic to Australia (see Preface)

hold bird in the urban areas of north-eastern QLD; it is a graceful bird, brown and grey above and white on its breast and rump. The little woodswallow, *A. minor** (12cm), is darkly coloured, and frequents forests and savanna woodlands, particularly in N Australia.

Woodward, Roger (1944-) Pianist.
With his abundant musicality and pianistic virtuosity in interpreting both the classical piano repertory and that of the avant-garde, Woodward has already become something of a legend. His international career has been studded with awards, and as well as touring the USA and playing with all the leading E and W European conductors and orchestras, he has made many recordings for EMI/HMV, Decca, Polydor, Polskie Nagranie and RCA. He is also well known for his collaborations with composers, including Iannis Xenakis, Pierre Boulez, Jean Barraqué, Toru Takemitsu, Karlheinz Stockhausen, Sylvano Bussotti, Luciano Berio, John Cage, Morton Feldman, Krzysztof Penderecki, Witold Lutoslawski and Richard MEALE. Many of these composers have written works especially for him. He now lives in London and makes regular performing visits to Australia.

woodwasps *see* ants, etc.

woody pear *see* Proteaceae

wool *see* sheep, etc.

Woolgoolga NSW (population 2 079 in 1981) A small resort centre in the mid-NORTH COAST region of the State, located on the Pacific Highway 618km by road from Sydney, 26km N of COFFS HARBOUR and 59km SE of GRAFTON. It is a popular holiday resort, with both surfing on the coast and swimming in the adjacent lagoon, along with fishing and other aquatic sports. At an elevation of only 31m above sea level, it has an average annual rainfall of 1768mm; rain occurs in all months, but there is a concentration in the period from January to April. There is a Sikh temple in the town, where the local Indian community members worship.

woolly bears *see* beetles

woolybutt These eucalypts (family MYRTACEAE) are so called because of the character of the bark. Species of woolybutt include *Eucalyptus miniata*, a timber tree of N Australia, and *E. longifolia* (also called peppermint) of VIC and NSW.

Woomera SA (population 1 800 in 1981) A town just off the Stuart Highway and the transcontinental railway, W of LAKE TORRENS and about 175km NW of PORT AUGUSTA, Woomera was established in 1947 to house workers at the rocket testing range. At an elevation of 165m above sea level, the town and the range are in the arid regions where the

HMAS *Sydney*

yearly rainfall is only 190mm and where scorchingly high summer temperatures are commonly experienced. The Stuart Highway passes through the Woomera Prohibited Area and travellers are not allowed to deviate from the highway in this area unless they have a special permit. An American space-tracking station was located at Island Lagoon 22km S of the town for about 10 years, closing operations at the end of 1972. The Joint Defence Space Communications Station, jointly operated by the Australian and US Departments of Defence, is located 17km S of Woomera. A wide range of launch vehicles, pilotless aircraft and missiles have been tested on the Woomera rocket range, including a series of satellite launcher vehicles for the European Launcher Development Organisation (ELDO), missiles such as Malkara and Ikara, and Jindivik, a pilotless aircraft. Australia's first satellite (WRESAT) was launched from the range in 1967. The UK atomic weapon test sites near Maralinga and at Emu are located in the Woomera Prohibited Area.

woomera This is the name of a stick used by Aborigines to throw spears. One end notches into the butt of the spear and the other end is held in the hand. It effectually makes

the user's arm longer, giving him greater leverage and giving the spear greater velocity. Some Aborigines hafted a stone *tula* chisel on to the hand-held part of the woomera, converting it into a multi-purpose tool.

World War 1 When Britain because of her commitment to protect Belgium, was forced to declare war on Germany in August 1914, a general election campaign was in progress in Australia. Both the main parties, however, expressed strong support for the mother country. The outgoing Liberal Cabinet, under Prime Minister Joseph COOK, accepted the British declaration as binding on Australia, and offered to provide an expeditionary force of 20 000 men, as well as putting the Australian Navy under the command of the Admiralty. Andrew FISHER, the Labor leader, pledged Australian support 'to the last man and the last shilling'. Recruiting of a volunteer force, the AUSTRALIAN IMPERIAL FORCE (AIF), for overseas service was begun almost immediately. At first the British authorities assumed that its brigades would be incorporated in British divisions, but the Inspector-General of the Australian Army, Brigadier-General W.T. Bridges, insisted that it be organised in all-Australian divisions.

Capture of German possesions in the South Pacific
Australia's first combat task was to capture Germany's colonies in the South Pacific, this being regarded as urgent because the enemy had constructed a network of powerful radio stations in New Guinea, the Carolines, Nauru and Samoa, and these could be used to direct the activities of naval vessels preying on Allied shipping.

Within a few days of the outbreak of the war, the Australian government had begun to organise a task force, known as the Australian Naval and Military Expeditionary Force, for this purpose. On 13 September, after naval shelling

Australians on the way to take up a front line position in the Ypres Sector in Belgium on October 25th 1917. The ruins of Ypres can be seen in the background

*Species, genus or family is endemic to Australia (see Preface)

and some land fighting, it captured Rabaul, the capital of German New Guinea, and a few days later accepted the surrender of the German forces in the area. In the meantime New Zealand forces had taken German Samoa, and during the next few months all German possesions in the Pacific south of the Equator had been occupied. Australian casualties had been only five dead and four wounded. A very serious loss at this time, however, was that of the submarine *AEI*, which had gone on patrol near New Guinea in September, and had failed to return. German possessions north of the Equator, including the Caroline, Mariana and Marshall Islands, were occupied by the Japanese — a step which caused misgivings in Australia, for although Japan had been allied to Britain since 1902, there was widespread fear that she might follow an expansionary policy in the Pacific. As it turned out, these fears were not realised until World War II, when the former German possessions provided important bases for Japan's forces during her southward drive.

The Cocos Islands naval engagement The fact that German raiders were at large in the early stage of the war caused great concern. In the Pacific the cruisers *Scharnhorst* and *Gneisnau* might have caused immense damage had it not been for the presence of Australian ships, and in particular of the battle cruiser *Australia*, which was sent cruising in Samoan waters in October and November. Eventually the two German vessels left the Pacific and were destroyed by British forces at the Battle of the Falkland Islands. However it was not long before an Australian-German naval action was fought elsewhere.

In November the first troops of the AIF, together with New Zealanders, embarked from ALBANY, the troopships being escorted by the Australian cruisers *Sydney* and *Melbourne* the British cruiser *Minotaur* and Japanese battle cruiser *Ibuki*. As it crossed the Indian Ocean, word was received by radio that the German cruiser *Emden* had appeared off the Cocos Islands, and the *Sydney* was despatched to deal with her. The *Emden* had been spectacularly successful as a raider, having sunk or captured 27 Allied ships, shelled the port of Madras, and thoroughly disorganised shipping in the Indian Ocean. At the Cocos Islands she sent a landing party to put the radio and telegraph stations out of action and cut the cable to PERTH. Then the *Sydney* — heavier, faster and with 6-inch guns against her antagonist's 4.1-inch ones, appeared. However the Germans put up a brave and skilful resistance and scored hits on the *Sydney*. Only after a two-hour battle was the *Emden* reduced to a battered hulk on the beach of Keeling Island.

The Middle East Apart from the above actions, all hostilities involving Australian forces took place in the Middle East and Europe. The expeditionary force which left Australia in November 1914 consisted of the 1st division of the AIF (or the Australian Division, as it was simply called at first), a Light Horse Brigade, an engineers unit and a field ambulance unit. It was expected to proceed through the Suez Canal to Britain for final training, and to serve

Men of the Australian Light Horse in the Sinai Desert

Australian War Memorial

in Europe. However by the time the troops reached the Red Sea it had become clear that there were insufficient camps in Britain for them or for the New Zealanders, so they disembarked in Egypt, where the two nations' forces were formed into the Australian and New Zealand Army Corps, under the command of an Englishman, General William Birdwood. Meanwhile Turkey had joined the war on the side of the Central Powers, and in February 1915 men of the Corps (now known, from the initial letters of its title, as *Anzacs*) helped to repulse a Turkish attack on the Suez Canal. Then, on 25 April 1915, as related in the entry on GALLIPOLI, they landed at Anzac Cove, as part of the ambitious Allied attempt to force a way through the Dardanelles, capture the Turkish capital, Constantinople (Istanbul), make it possible for Britain and France to provide aid to Russia, and perhaps even force Turkey out of the war. However, after eight months of heroic efforts, the Gallipoli campaign had to be judged a failure, and the troops were evacuated. Total casualties among the British, Australian, New Zealand, Indian and French forces engaged had been over 33 000 killed and 78 000 wounded, about one-quarter being Australian.

Early in 1916 the Australian infantry from Gallipoli, together with new units which had arrived during the campaign, were sent to Britain, to prepare for service on the Western Front. The Light Horse, however, including those who had fought on foot at Gallipoli, remained in the Middle East. There were by this time three brigades of Light Horse, which were combined with the New Zealand Mounted Rifles Brigade to form the Anzac Mounted Division, under the command of an Australian, Major-General H. G. Chauvel. An Imperial Camel Corps was also formed, initially with two battalions, one being composed of men selected from each Australian infantry brigade, and the other of English and Scottish territorials. A third battalion, composed of Australians and New Zealanders, and a fourth, composed of Australians only, had been added by the end of 1916. Early in 1917 an Imperial Mounted Division, with one British brigade and two of Australian Light Horse, was also formed, and a few months

later it was renamed the Australian Mounted Division. The Camel Corps and the two mounted divisions formed the Desert Mounted Corps. Under the command of Major-General Chauvel, this Corps was to play a major role in the conquest of Sinai and Palestine, and in forcing Turkey to seek peace.

The Sinai, Palestine and Syria It was not long before the Australian Light Horse was again in action. In August 1916 the Turks launched a major attack against Romani, west of the Suez Canal, but were repulsed by Australian, New Zealand and British troops. The Anzacs then took part in a general British advance across the Egyptian border into Palestine, and in two unsuccessful attempts to capture Gaza. After this the British commander, General Sir Archibald Murray, was replaced by General Sir E. H. M. Allenby, and Chauvel was placed in command of the Desert Mounted Corps. At the time of Allenby's appointment the British government had decided to strengthen its forces in Egypt. The army's infantry and artillery strength was increased, a railway and water pipeline were pushed forward into the Sinai, and in October 1917, after some months of reorganisation, Allenby launched an offensive.

The first major objective was the ancient city of Beersheba. While British infantry advanced towards it, the Desert Mounted Corps under Chauvel was sent deep into the desert to sweep around and attack it from the east and north. This manoeuvre was completed with a three-kilometre cavalry charge by the 4th Light Horse Brigade, under shrapnel, against Turkish trenches. This led to the fall of the town and to a general advance. On 8 December the Turks withdrew from Jerusalem, and on 19 February the Anzac Mounted Division took part in the capture of Jericho.

The advance along the Jordan Valley was made against strong Turkish and German resistance, and it was late September before the Anzac Mounted Division and infantry forces captured Amman. Chauvel's cavalry then advanced rapidly, bypassed Damascus to cut off the enemy's retreat, and on 1 October the 5th Light Horse Brigade rode into that city. This practically ended the campaign, with the capture in the final stages of about 75 000 prisoners, including 31 000 by the Anzac Mounted Division alone. Turkey signed an armistice on 30 October, Australian forces having played a major role in forcing her from the war.

The Western Front By the time of the Gallipoli evacuation large infantry reinforcements had reached Egypt. It was decided therefore to form two new divisions, the 2nd and 4th. While the Light Horse remained in Egypt, all three infantry divisions were despatched to Britain for service in France. Meanwhile the 3rd Division had been sent to Britain direct from Australia, and the 5th Division arrived soon afterward. By July 1916 there were more than 90 000 Australians on the Western Front, and another 90 000 were training in England.

In April AIF troops entered a quiet sector of the Front near Armentières. On 1 July the British commander, General Sir Douglas Haig, launched an offensive on the Somme, but on that first day his forces suffered some 60 000 casualties, and the Australians were soon called on for support. On 19 July the 5th Division went into attack at Fromelles, in order to divert German troops from the Somme, but the operation was ill-planned, and within two days the Australians had suffered 5 500 casualties. Later in the month 1 Anzac Corps (1st, 2nd and 4th Divisions) went into action around Pozieres, and in five weeks of desperate fighting suffered 23 000 casualties.

During the following two years the AIF continued to be involved in many of the most hard-fought battles of the war. In 1917, these included action at Bapaume and Bullecourt in March-May, at Messines in June, and in the Battle of Menin Road, at Polygon Wood and around Passchendaele during the Ypres offensive of September-October.

At the beginning of 1918 the five Australian divisions were formed into the Australian Corps, under General Birdwood, with No. 3 Squadron, Australian Flying Corps as its air unit. In March the Germans launched a major offensive on the Arras- St. Quentin sector, the aim being to reach Amiens and so separate the British and French armies and force the British to retreat to the sea. The AIF was heavily engaged in repelling this offensive, perhaps its outstanding exploit being the recapture of the village of Villers Bretonneux, from where the advancing Germans had been able to see Amiens Cathedral. Shortly after this, on 31 March 1918, Lieutenant-General John MONASH, replaced Birdwood as commander of the Australian Corps, with Brigadier-General T. A. BLAMEY as chief of staff.

In the closing battles of the war the Australians were again in the thick of the action. The Allied offensive of August 1918 opened with a vital breakthrough by the Australians and Canadians south of the Somme, and helped to make 8 August, in the words of the German commander, Ludendorff, 'the black day of the German Army'.

At the end of August Monash launched a successful attack on Mont St. Quentin, and in mid-September the AIF, with American forces, advanced against the central portion of the Germans' last main line of defence, the Hindenburg Line, which they penetrated on 5 October. By this time the Australian Corps had been in action for over six months, and casualties had been such that most of its brigades had been reduced from four to three. The whole Corps was withdrawn to rest, and by the time it was ready to go into action again the Armistice of 11 November was signed and the war was at an end.

Naval and air operations The importance of Australia's having acquired its own navy was demonstrated, as we have already mentioned, by the rapid capture of German possessions in the Pacific, by the deterrent effect which the presence of the *Australia* had on potential German raiders there, and by the *Sydney*'s destruction of the *Emden*. During the remainder of the war, ships of the Royal Australian Navy served at various times in the Mediterranean, in the West Indies, on the China station and in British and Australian waters. The only major losses were the two submarines *AE1* (as mentioned above) and *AE2*. The latter penetrated the Dardanelles on the day of the Gallipoli landing, and entered the Sea of Marmara; but on 30 April 1915 was so badly damaged by Turkish gunfire that her crew had to sink her and surrender.

Important work was done also by the Royal Australian Naval Brigade, which was responsible for such matters as patrolling harbours, minesweeping, defending docks and radio stations, and providing gunners and signalmen for armed merchant ships. Although its operations were mainly on the home front, one detachment from it assisted in the capture of German possessions in the Pacific, and another served at Gallipoli and in Egypt.

The war also brought about the birth of an Australian air force. Shortly before the outbreak of hostilities a flying school had been set up at Point Cook, VIC, and in April 1915 four pilots and a large number of mechanics and other support staff were sent from it to Iraq. Although known as the Australian Flying Corps, they formed part of the AIF.

Later, many members of the AIF (including Charles KINGSFORD SMITH) were allowed to transfer to the Royal Flying Corps, and other Australians (such as 'Bert' HINKLER) were allowed into it straight from civilian life. However in September 1915 the British government suggested that the Dominions might care to raise their own aviation units, and by March 1917 Australia had formed and sent overseas four squadrons of the Australian Flying Corps (predecessor of the Royal Australian Air Force). No.1 Squadron, which absorbed the survivors of the unit sent earlier to Iraq, remained in the Middle East and played an extremely important part in Allenby's Palestine campaign. For a time it was equipped with BE2cs (pathetically inadequate) and RE8s (its replacement, but in some ways worse) both being inferior to the German planes opposing them. Nevertheless the Australians held their own. Their work in helping to maintain British control of the skies during the preparations for Allenby's offensive of October 1917 was particularly important, as it denied the enemy knowledge of British prepa-

rations, and contributed greatly to the element of surprise which was vital to the full success of the opening attacks. Early in 1918 the squadron received Bristol fighters, and was able to perform even more effectively. Throughout the campaign it received many recruits, both as pilots and as ground staff, from the AIF.

The other three squadrons fought on the Western Front. No 3 Squadron, which reached France first, in September 1917, was an observation squadron equipped with RE8s., and from early 1918 was attached to the Australian Corps. It was men from this squadron who recovered and buried the body of Manfred von Richtofen, the 'Red Baron'. Squadrons 2 and 4 were scouting (fighter) squadrons. The former, flying first DH5s and later SE5as, arrived a fortnight after 3, and 4, flying Sopwith Camels, arrived in December. The SE5s and Camels were the best of the WW1 British fighters in regular use, but for different reasons. The Camel, with 1294 aircraft downed to its credit, was the most succesful aircraft of the war. It could outmanoeuvre *any* other aircraft but was equally hard to fly, as it was tail-heavy, and was subject to a gyroscopic effect. The result was death for inexperienced pilots, but in the hands of an expert the Camel was outstanding. The SE5a got its reputation from overall performance, tractability, and as a superb gun platform. It was effective in the hands of novice and expert alike.

The performance of the pilots matched their machines. No 2 Squadron, flying 'circus' formation from April 1918 formed the spearhead of the 80th Wing's bombing raids along with No. 4. Their British commander wrote 'They were the finest material as an attacking force in the air.'

The home front In Australia itself, the war had far-reaching economic effects including government involvement in the marketing of many products; for example, agreements were made with the British government for the disposal of wool, meat and dairy exports, and a wheat marketing board was set up. Metal exports posed a particularly difficult problem, since before the war German companies had purchased large quantities of ore concentrates. The government therefore encouraged the smelting of ores in Australia. In 1915 BROKEN HILL mining companies set up Broken Hill Associated Smelters, which opened a lead smelter at PORT PIRIE, and by the end of the war preparations for the refining of zinc at RISDON COVE, near Hobart, by the Electrolytic Zinc Co. of Australia Ltd were nearly complete. There was also considerable development in manufacturing, this being facilitated by the entry of the BROKEN HILL PROPRIETARY COMPANY LIMITED into the iron and steel industry with the opening of the NEWCASTLE works in 1915.

The most contentious political question was that of CONSCRIPTION. William HUGHES leader of the Australian Labor Party (ALP) and Prime Minister since 1915, became convinced that conscription for overseas service was necessary. A proposal to this effect was put to the people in a referendum in October 1916, but was defeated. The issue split the ALP. Hughes and a number of his supporters were expelled from the party, but by joining with the Liberal opposition to form the Nationalist Party Hughes was able to retain office as Prime Minister. Although the general elections of May 1917 resulted in a Nationalist victory, a proposal for conscription was defeated in a second referendum in December. Throughout the war, therefore, Australian forces serving overseas consisted entirely of volunteers. A total of 416 000 enlisted in the armed forces, of whom 329 000 served overseas and 60 000 died on active service.

Further reading: Bean, C.E.W. (ed) *The Official History of Australia in the War of 1914–1918.* (12 vols) Australian War Memorial, Canberra, 1921–43; Bean, C.E.W. *Anzac to Amiens.* Australian War Memorial, Canberra, 1946; Laffin, J. *Anzacs at War.* Abelard-Schuman, London, 1965; Gammage, B. *The Broken Years.* Australian National University Press, Canberra, 1974.

World War II

World War II When Britain declared war on Germany in 1939, Prime Minister MENZIES took the view that, although Australia was an independent nation, because of its allegiance to the Crown it too was bound by the decision. Australia therefore made no separate declaration of war. Whether Menzies was right or wrong, there was no doubt that public feeling was solidly behind Britain. However, the atmosphere was different from that of 1914 in one respect: Japan was already at war in China, and the fear that she might look for other conquests while the European powers were engaged elsewhere was stronger than it had been during WORLD WAR I. Therefore, no immediate decision was taken with regard to sending an expeditionary force overseas. On 15 September the government announced that it would recruit 20 000 men for service either in Australia or overseas, and would also call up the militia to receive one month's training. Lieut.-General Thomas BLAMEY was placed in command of the new force, the bulk of the new recruits were formed into the 6th Division, and on 28 November the decision to send a force overseas was announced. The first units embarked for Palestine on 9 January 1940, and so a second Australian Expeditionary Force was following in the footsteps of the first AIF of 1914. In the meantime conscription for home service in the militia had been introduced on 1 January 1940. Also, as explained in detail in a later section of this entry, plans had been launched to expand the Royal Australian Air Force, Australia had agreed to join the Empire Air Training Scheme, and No. 10 Squadron of the RAAF had been offered for service in Britain.

War in the Middle East As in World War I, the AIF's first battles were fought in the Middle East. At the beginning of the war there seemed to be no prospect of hostilities breaking out there, and it was intended that the Australian 6th Division, and the 7th Division which arrived not long after it, would complete their training in Palestine, and then join the British Expeditionary Force in France. However the entry of Italy into the war in June 1940 transformed the situaton. The Middle East was now a theatre of war, and Britain's control over the

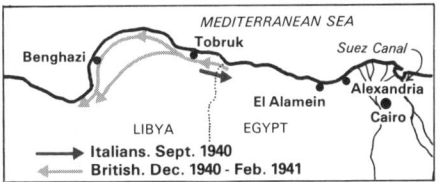

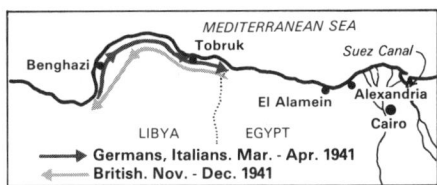

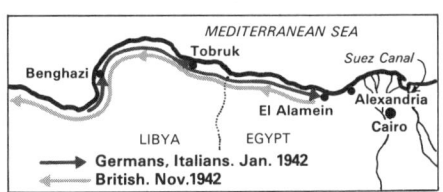

The North African campaign, in which Australians figured prominently from December 1940 to November 1942

Suez Canal was in danger.

In September 1940 five Italian divisions under Marshal Graziani advanced into Egypt. British forces under General Wavell counter-attacked and, by the end of the first week in December, had pushed the Italians back to the border. Mussolini ordered the commandant of Bardia to 'stand at whatever cost' but on 5 January it surrendered to the newly-arrived Australian 6th Division. The Australians then played a major role in the advance to Benghazi, which troops of the 6th Division entered on 6th February. A few days later the British 7th Armoured Division had reached El Agheila, where the advance was halted.

Greece, Crete and Libya At this point it appeared possible that Wavell's forces might soon overrun the whole of Libya. However a new commitment was now judged to be necessary. Since 1940 the Creeks had been battling successfully against Italian invading forces, but

it seemed likely that the Germans would intervene. Wavell was ordered to send whatever forces he could possibly spare to Greece. At first he planned to include both the 6th and 7th Australian Divisions, but when the Germans launched an invasion of both Greece and Yugoslavia on 6 April 1941, only part of the 6th Division had crossed the Mediterranean; the 7th was then kept in Libya, to meet a new threat in that area, namely an Axis counter-offensive led by General Rommel, whose Afrika Corps had been sent to bolster the Italian forces.

The force sent to Greece, though it fought bravely, was unable to withstand the numerically superior German invaders, and by 25 April re-embarkation had begun, 48 000 of the 62 000 men landed being successfully withdrawn during the next several days. The Australians had lost over 800 killed or wounded, and over 2 000 of them were taken prisoner. In the meantime the King and government of Greece had taken refuge on the island of Crete, and many of the British troops, including a large part of the Australian 6th Division, had been landed there also. On 20 May the Germans launched an invasion with parachute and glider-borne troops — by far the largest such operation so far attempted. A week later the British government decided to evacuate Crete, but among the troops left behind as prisoners were over 3 000 Australians.

It was then feared that the Germans might follow up their success by invading Syria and Lebanon, which were held by French troops of the Vichy government (which had made peace with Germany). Wavell was therefore given yet another task — to occupy these territories. On 8 June 1941 he launched an invasion with a force which included the 21st and 25th Brigades of the Australian 7th Division as well as British, Indian and Free French units. Despite strong resistance by the Vichy forces, their commander was forced to accept an armistice on 12 July.

From Tobruk to El Alamein Not surprisingly, the sending of troops to Greece had made

Sir Thomas Blamey inspecting Australian troops who defeated the Japanese in New Guinea

Australian War Memorial

Members of 'C' Company of 2/13 Battalion on a daytime patrol in the Tobruk area

it impossible for Wavell's weakened army in Libya to maintain its position. Late in March Rommel began an advance which finally took him past the Egyptian border. However as the retreating Allied troops neared the fortified town of Tobruk, it was decided that it could and must be held. The Australian 18th Brigade was already there, with a British artillery regiment. These were now joined by the 9th Division, which had replaced the 6th when the latter was withdrawn for service in Greece, and by other British and Australian units, the whole force being placed under the command of an Australian, Major-General L.J. Morshead. The siege of the town began on 11 April, but despite all that Rommel could do, the defenders held out for 242 days, being then relieved by British forces again advancing from Egypt. By that time, however, only one Australian battalion was left at Tobruk, the other units having been withdrawn by sea from August onwards, and replaced with British and Polish troops. Also in October 1941 General Morshead had been succeeded by Major-General Scobie, of the British 70th Division.

Following the relief of Tobruk, Rommel was driven back deep into Libya, but in January he advanced once more. On this occasion Tobruk was not held, and the German-Italian army advanced as far as El Alamein, only about 120 kilometres from Alexandria. By this time, war had broken out in the Pacific, and the Australian 6th and 7th Divisions had been withdrawn from the Middle East for the defence of their homeland. However the 9th remained long enough to participate in the Battle of El Alamein (November 1942), which opened the way for the final defeat of all German and Italian forces in North Africa. Then it too returned to Australia.

War against Japan By mid-1941 it had

become evident that war with Japan was becoming more likely and since Singapore was accepted as the main bulwark against any Japanese advance S, Australian forces were sent to Malaya. The Japanese attack on Pearl Harbour in December brought a fundamental change, not only in the pattern of Australia's war effort, but also in her general FOREIGN RELATIONS and DEFENCE policies. Prime Minister John CURTIN, in a New Year's Day message to the nation, stressed Australia's new dependence on America, saying:

'Without inhibitions of any kind I make it

quite clear that Australia looks to America, free of any pangs as to our traditional links of kinship with the United Kingdom. We know that Australia can go and Britain can still hold on. We are, therefore, determined that Australia shall not go and we shall exert all our energies towards the shaping of a plan, with the United States as its keystone, which will give our country some confidence of being able to hold out until the tide of battle swings against the enemy.'

In March 1942, when General Douglas MacArthur came to Australia from the Philippines, Curtin nominated him as Supreme Commander, Allied Forces in the South-West Pacific. Meanwhile, Australian forces had already suffered heavy losses at the hands of the Japanese.

From Pearl Harbour to Midway Almost simultaneously with their attack on Pearl Harbour, the Japanese landed troops on the coast of southern Thailand and north-eastern Malaya, and two days later, on 10 December 1941, they sank the British capital ships *Prince of Wales* and *Repulse*, which had been sent to Singapore only a short time before. It soon became evident that the invincibility of Singapore, in which Australians had been taught to believe, was a myth. They had been told that no enemy could advance along the Malayan peninsula and attack the great base in force from the landward side, but it was now clear that the naval base was of little use against the Japanese, and that the defence of Malaya depended on land forces, including the 8th Division of the AIF, under Major-General H. Gordon BENNETT.

By the time Australian troops were brought into action, most of the peninsula had been lost, and Bennett's essential task was to try to hold the southern State of Johore. On 14 January his men successfully ambushed the advancing

Australian War Memorial

Men of the famous 'bush artillery', 2/17 Battalion manning a captured Italian field gun at Tobruk

At this stage the Japanese planned to safeguard their far-flung conquests by capturing Port Moresby, and various Pacific islands, including the key American base at Midway. However their strategic defeat in the air-sea Battle of the CORAL SEA (7–8 May), in which Australian land-based aircraft, as well as HMAS *Australia* and *Hobart*, participated, saved Port Moresby; and the decisive victory of the Americans near Midway (3–6 June) marked the virtual end of Japanese expansion in the Pacific.

The Pacific war after Midway After the Battle of Midway, General MacArthur was directed to drive the Japanese from New Britain, New Ireland and the parts of New Guinea which they had occupied.

However at about the same time the enemy, having failed to reach Port Moresby by sea, decided to take it by land. In July 1942, from a base at Buna, on the north coast of Papua, they advanced over the Owen Stanley Range by way of the little-used Kokoda Trail. The Australian 25th Brigade fell back along this narrow track, which passes through some of the most difficult terrain in the world, winding through dense jungle, ascending precipitous mountain ridges and plunging down to swift-flowing streams crossed by log bridges; and the Japanese reached Ioribaiwa, only about 50 kilometres by air from Port Moresby, before being checked. In the meantime they had attacked from another direction, by landing troops at Milne Bay, on the eastern tip of Papua, on 25 August. By 6 September, however, the Australian defenders, including units of the militia as well as the AIF, had won a convincing victory, this being the first time in the war that the Japanese had been defeated on land. Then, on 23 September, the Australians began to advance along the Kokoda Trail. With both AIF and militia participating, they drove the enemy back over the range, and by late

The maximum extent of Japanese advance

Japanese at Gemas, inflicting heavy casualties, but were then forced to retreat, and by 31 January all of them had been withdrawn to Singapore. The causeway to the mainland was then blown up, and Singapore had indeed become an island fortress.

On the night of 8–9 February, the Japanese made large-scale landings, mainly in the north-west of the island, where Australian troops were stationed. Aided by their control of the sea and air, they forced the defenders back towards the heavily-bombed city, and on 15 February the British commander, General Percival, surrendered. Among the 130 000 prisoners taken by the Japanese were more than 15 000 Australians. Australian casualties during the campaign had been 1789 dead or missing and 1306 wounded.

Four days after the surrender of Singapore, the Japanese made a heavy air raid on Darwin. On 19 February they landed in Timor, but in the Portuguese part of the island failed to force the surrender of the 2/2nd Australian Independent Company, which kept up resistance from the hills. By 28 February they were pouring ashore in Java, where about 3000 Australians, who had been landed at Batavia (Djakarta) not long before, fought desperately before being ordered to surrender. Early in March landings were made on the north coast of the New Guinea mainland (Rabaul and New Ireland having been seized from their Australian defenders earlier in the war).

Meanwhile the 1 Australian Corps (6th and

7th Divisions) had been returning from the Middle East, the intention being that it should disembark in Java and Sumatra. However this had become impracticable, and Prime Minister Curtin insisted that the Corps return to Australia, despite pressure from Churchill and Roosevelt that it be diverted to Burma.

Native stretcher bearers carrying a wounded Australian along the Kokoda Trail

The Kokoda Trail

January they and the Americans had captured the coastal bases of Buna, Gona and Sanananda. Australian casualties to this stage in Papua and New Guinea were 2165 dead and 3533 wounded.

Throughout the remainder of the war, Australians were engaged in fighting the Japanese in other parts of New Guinea — in the Wau-Salamaua-Nassau Bay area, at Lae and the Huon Peninsula, in the Markham and Ramu Valleys, in the Aitape-Wewak area, at Madang, and elsewhere. In November 1944 the 5th Division landed in New Britain, and by March the powerful Japanese forces there had been contained in the Gazelle Peninsula. Australian forces also fought in Bougainville (Solomon Islands), and towards the end of the war made a number of landings in Borneo and nearby islands.

The Royal Australian Navy When war broke out the Royal Australian navy included the 8-inch gun cruisers *Australia* and *Canberra*, the 6-inch gun cruisers *Adelaide*, *Hobart*, *Perth* and *Sydney*, the destroyers *Stuart*, *Vampire*, *Vendetta*, *Voyager* and *Waterhen*, and two sloops. Within a short time these were joined by several liners which had been converted to armed merchant cruisers. Early in the war the destroyers were sent to the Mediterranean, where they were soon after joined by *Sydney*. Then, after the entry of Italy into the war and the surrender of France, the *Australia* joined the British Home Fleet. In December 1940, *Perth* replaced *Sydney* in the Mediterranean. All of these vessels saw action on a number of occasions, *Sydney* in particular winning attention for sinking the Italian cruiser *Bartolomeo Colleoni*. In June 1941 *Waterhen* was sunk by enemy air attack, and in November the sloop *Parramatta* was torpedoed and sank.

After Pearl Harbour, the RAN's operations were naturally concentrated in waters closer to Australia, and the great amount of action in which they participated can be judged by their losses. In April 1942 the destroyer *Vampire* was sunk during action against a Japanese force which had entered the Bay of Bengal. In August 1942 the cruisers *Australia*, *Canberra* and *Hobart* formed part of the naval support force for American landings on Guadalcanal and Tulagi in the Solomon Islands, and *Canberra* was among the four Allied cruisers sunk by a Japanese cruiser force. Other losses and achieve-

ments included the sinking of a Japanese submarine by the destroyer *Arunta;* the participation of the corvette *Deloraine* and the minesweepers *Katoomba* and *Lithgow* in the sinking of a Japanese submarine off Darwin in January 1942; the loss of the destroyer *Nestor* in the Mediterranean in July 1942; the sinking of *Perth* in Sunda Strait in February 1942, and of the sloop *Yarra* south of Java soon afterwards; the loss of the destroyer *Voyager*, which ran aground on Timor in September, and of the corvette *Armidale* off Timor in December; and heavy damage to *Australia* on two occasions in the Philippines, the second incident putting her out of action for the remainder of the war. A particularly tragic loss was that of the cruiser *Sydney*, which in November 1941, SW of CARNARVON, WA, approached the disguised German raider *Kormoran*, was fired on at close range, and later sank with the loss of her entire crew.

The Royal Australian Air Force The RAAF was the first of Australia's armed services to provide help for Britain in the opening stage of the war. Within a few weeks of the beginning of hostilities the government offered Britain No. 10 Squadron, which had been sent to take delivery of Sunderland flying boats. It joined RAF Coastal Command soon afterwards, being later joined by another Sunderland squadron, No. 461. Meanwhile, early in October 1939 an Empire Air Training Scheme had been launched, with the purpose of training, for the whole British Commonwealth and Empire, 50 000 airmen each year. Australia agreed to join the scheme, with a quota of 10 000 pilots, navigators and gunners a year for service with the Royal Air Force. As a result, great numbers of Australians served in RAF units, but a number of RAAF squadrons were also formed for service in the European theatre.

After the entry of Italy into the war, Australia quickly supplied air units as well as ground

forces for the Middle East theatre, the first RAAF unit to arrive being No. 3 Squadron. Several other squadrons soon joined it, and hence when war broke out in the Pacific, most of Australia's airmen and planes were abroad. At home there were only 13 squadrons, six being equipped with Wirraway aircraft, which were quite inadequate for coping with their Japanese adversaries. Among the most courageous actions of the war was that of No. 24 Squadron's Wirraway pilots against the Japanese air attack on Rabaul in January 1942.

Early in 1942 American squadrons were sent to reinforce the RAAF, and the latter's own strength was rapidly increased, a notable step being the formation of three squadrons equipped with Kittyhawk fighters, the first of which, No. 75, was in action before the end of March. Early in 1943, too, No. 1 RAF Spitfire Wing arrived from Britain. With rapidly expanding strength, members of the RAAF served with distinction in many parts of the South-West Pacific. At the end of the war, of the 154 000 Australians serving in the RAAF, 137 000 were in that area.

Women's services The women's services played a very important part in the war effort. Women enlisted in great numbers, undertook a wider variety of roles than in earlier wars, and were exposed to even greater dangers. Enlistments in the Women's Royal Australian Naval Service, the Australian Women's Army Service, the Women's Auxiliary Australian Air Force, the RAN Nursing Service, the Australian Army Nursing Service and the RAAF Nursing Service reached a combined total of over 63 000.

Of the nursing services, the RAN Nursing Service was by far the smallest, its members serving in Australia and New Guinea. Members of the Australian Army Nursing Service served overseas in the United Kingdom, throughout the Middle East, in Ceylon (Sri Lanka), in Malaya, New Guinea and several other parts

Nurses relaxing in northern Australia

Australian War Memorial

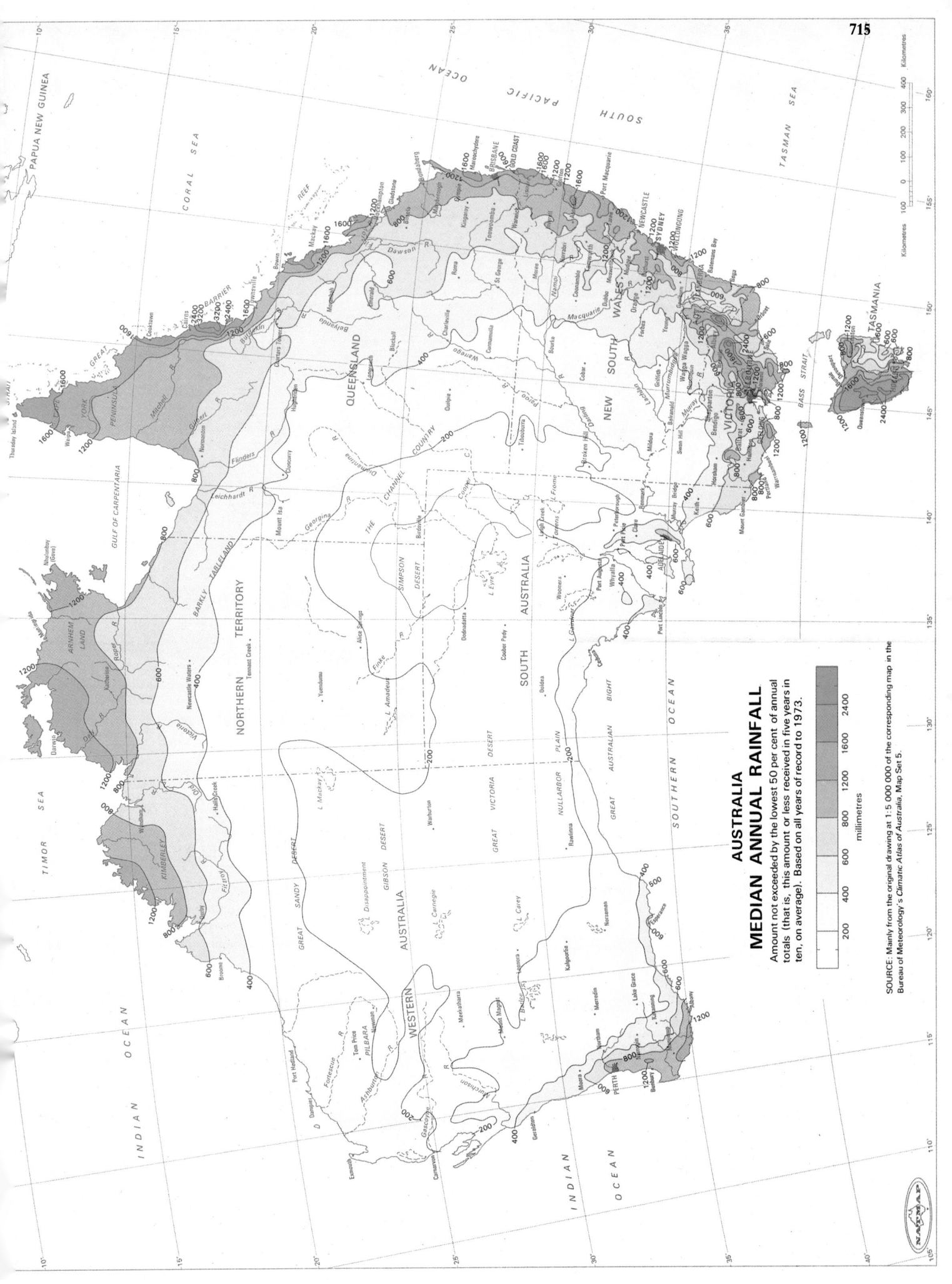

AUSTRALIA
MEDIAN ANNUAL RAINFALL

Amount not exceeded by the lowest 50 per cent of annual totals (that is, this amount or less received in five years in ten, on average). Based on all years of record to 1973.

millimetres

| 200 | 400 | 600 | 800 | 1200 | 1600 | 2400 |

SOURCE: Mainly from the original drawing at 1:5 000 000 of the corresponding map in the Bureau of Meteorology's *Climatic Atlas of Australia*, Map Set 5.

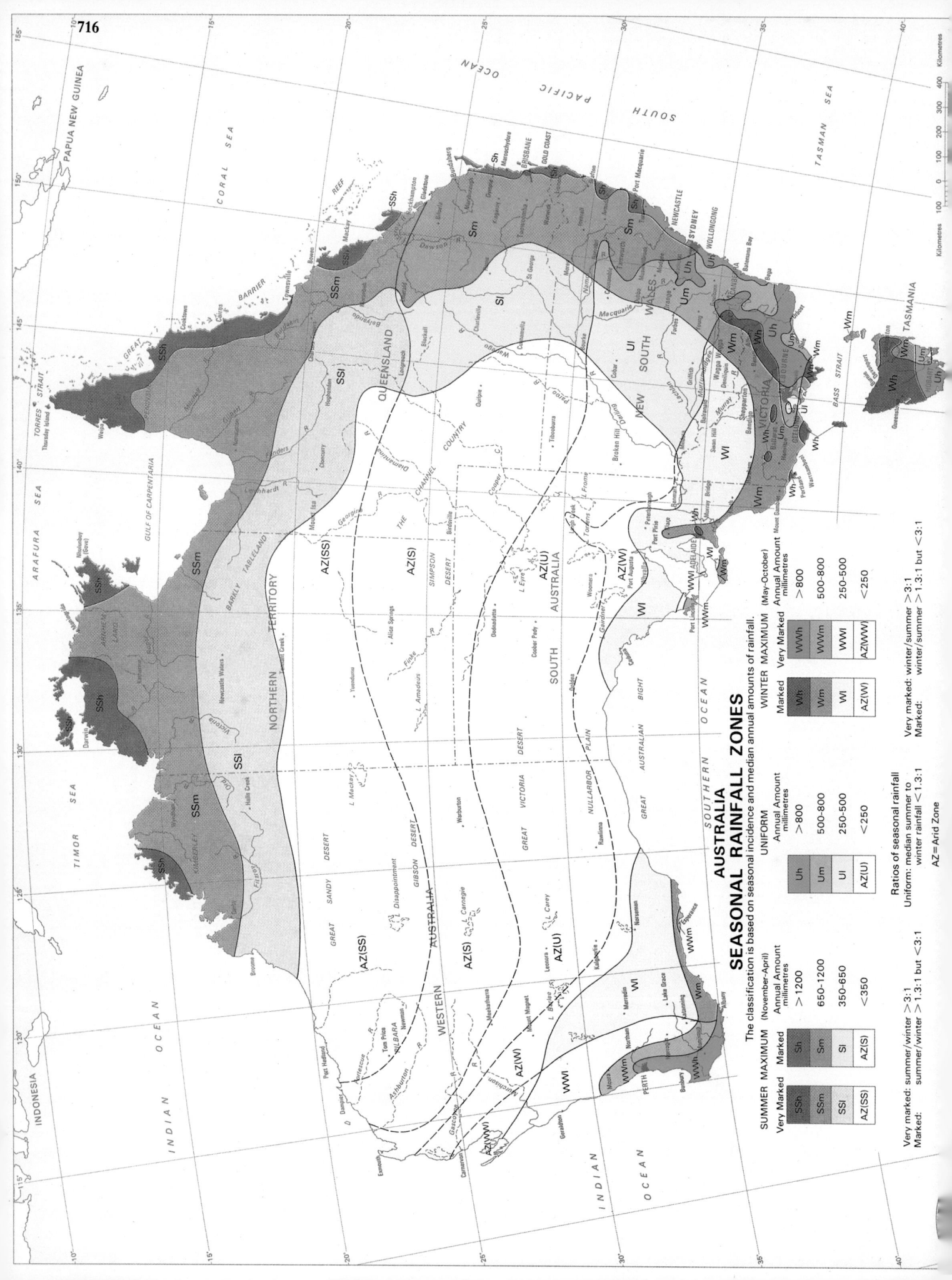

The Australian War Memorial, Canberra

J.H. Shaw

of the South-West Pacific, and later in Japan. Of the 126 who served in Malaya 41 died in captivity, were executed, or were lost at sea. The RAAF Nursing Service was comparatively small, with a maximum strength of about 600, but its members served in a number of operational areas as well as in Australia.

Casualties and prisoners of war The Australian armed forces were much larger than in World War 1, and served in more widely scattered theatres of war. Total enlistments were 926 000 men and 63 100 women. The number who were killed in action or died while prisoners of war was 33 552 (Army 21 136, RAN 1854, RAAF 10 562). Over 8600 became prisoners of Germany or Italy, and over 22 200 were captured by the Japanese. By the end of the war 7964 of the latter had been killed, had died of disease, or had been drowned at sea.

The home front The war produced no political issue as divisive as that of CONSCRIPTION in 1916–17. The Defence Act allowed the use of conscripted members of the militia anywhere in Australia and the territories, including Papua and New Guinea. When fighting moved further N, Curtin was able to secure, without splitting his party, an amendment allowing them to be used in a wide zone of the South-West Pacific stretching as far N as the equator. The effects on civilian life in World War II were much greater than in World War I. The government was given power to direct manpower into essential work and to eliminate forms of production that were not necessary for the war effort. Meat, butter, sugar, tea, clothing and petrol were rationed. The manufacturing sector of the economy underwent great expansion, production of munitions, aeroplanes and ships being backed up by growth in the chemical, electrical, metallurgical and machine tool industries and in many aspects of engineering. Politically, the clearest effect was a change in the balance of power between the Commonwealth and the

States. Particularly important was the introduction of uniform income tax by the Commonwealth, a step which has excluded the States from this important field of taxation to this day. The Commonwealth also became predominant as a dispenser of social services, its power in this area being confirmed by referendum in 1946.

Further reading: Long, G. (ed) *Australia in the War of 1939–1945.* (22 vols) Australian War Memorial, Canberra, 1952–70; Long, G. *The Six Years War: A Concise History of Australia in the 1939–1945 War.* Australian War Memorial, Canberra, 1973.

worms The name 'worm' is applied to so many different kinds of animals—from certain snakes to some very primitive invertebrates—that it now has little zoological meaning. It is used for any animal that is limbless (or apparently so) and is long and thin. The word 'worm' is even used for certain insect larvae; for example, the caterpillars of certain geometrid moths are called inchworms. Zoologists prefer to restrict the term to the 'true' worm phylum, the Annelida (ANNELIDS), which contains the segmented species such as the earthworms. The various kinds of other worms discussed in this encyclopedia include ACORN WORMS, ARROW WORMS, blind worms (*see* SNAKES), FLATWORMS (which include TAPEWORMS), PEANUT WORMS, RIBBON WORMS and ROUNDWORMS (which include hookworms and eelworms).

woylie *see* kangaroos, etc.

Woy Woy NSW This small service town and tourist centre is 72km N of Sydney and 8km S of GOSFORD, on the W shore of the BRISBANE WATER. It is the focus for a number of smaller settlements located along the Brisbane Water foreshores such as Davistown,

Killcare, Saratoga and Ettalong, to which it is connected by bus and ferry services. The name Woy Woy is Aboriginal, meaning 'deep water' or 'much water'. The district is a major holiday and recreation area, particularly for Sydney residents, many of whom own cottages there. It is also important as a retirement area and some of the local people work in Sydney and commute either by road or rail.
See also Broken Bay

The Rt Hon Neville Wran

Wran, Neville (1926–) Premier of NSW. Born and educated in Sydney, he graduated in law from the University of Sydney, practised for some years as a solicitor, and in 1957 was called to the Bar, where he specialised in industrial law. He also took an active part in the affairs of the Australian Labor Party (ALP), and in 1967 became a member of the State executive. He entered Parliament as a Member of the Legislative Council in 1970, but resigned in 1973 and won a seat in the Legislative Assembly. Not long afterwards he was elected Labor parliamentary leader, and after his party had won a closely fought election in May 1976 he became Premier. In 1978, 1981 and 1984 he again led his party to victory in NSW, and in 1980 also became federal president of the ALP.

wrasses *see* fishes, bony

wrens The name 'wren' is given to several different kinds of birds which are small in size and usually have a jaunty tail, but which are unrelated to the true wren of Europe. Emuwrens and grasswrens are discussed under FAIRY-WRENS; scrubwrens, heathwrens, fernwrens and fieldwrens are discussed under WARBLERS.

wrestling This sport has enjoyed popularity in varying degrees in Australia since the arrival of the First Fleet. Bouts were arranged amongst convicts and soldiers, and miners in the gold rushes found it entertaining to pit their strength against each other. The enthusiasm engendered by these amateur bouts led enterprising entrepreneurs to arrange professional matches and in the 1880s professional wrestling began. Spectator interest increased with the arrival of professional wrestlers from other countries. One such new arrival was world champion 'Strangler' Tom Cannon who defeated local star William Miller. Miller was considered at that time to be best all-round athlete in the world with expertise in fencing, weight-lifting, gymnastics and boxing as well as wrestling. Professional wrestling in Australia since World War II and more particularly since the introduction of television has become more of an entertainment than a sport with gimmicks and showmanship taking priority over wrestling skill. Nevertheless, the more exacting amateur wrestling has always had its devotees, such as Dick Garrard, who, in addition to a silver medal at the 1948 Olympics, won gold medals in the 1934, 1938 and 1950 Commonwealth Games and lost only nine contests in his career of 525.

Wright, Judith Arundel (Mrs J. McKinney) (1915-) Poet. A fifth-generation Australian on her father's side, she was born in ARMIDALE in the NEW ENGLAND district of NSW and was educated there and at the University of Sydney. Her reputation as one of Australia's leading contemporary poets was established with her first volume, *The Moving Image* (1946), which revealed in particular her power of evoking the spirit of Australian landscapes and suggesting the quality of the life led by their inhabitants. Later volumes include *Woman to Man* (1949), *The Gateway* (1953), *The Two Fires* (1955), *Birds* (1962), *Collected Poems, 1942-70* (1971), *Fourth Quarter (1976) and Journeys* (1982). She has been an active participant in conservation movements; *Because I Was Invited* (1975) contains essays and the text of addresses and lectures on both poetry and the conservation of Australian resources, and *The Coral Battleground* (1977) deals with conservation problems concerning the GREAT BARRIER REEF.
See also literature
Further reading: Hope, A.D. *Judith Wright*. Oxford University Press, Melbourne, 1975; Thompson, A.K. (ed) *Critical Essays on Judith Wright*. Jacaranda, Brisbane, 1968.

wuhl-wuhl *see* native cats, etc.

Wundowie WA (population 720 in 1981) This small town is located in the DARLING RANGE about 70km NE of Perth on the rail line to NORTHAM, 50km beyond MIDLAND junction. It was the site of the first blast furnace developed in WA in 1948 and of a wood distillation and charcoal manufacturing plant, using eucalypt hardwood from the adjacent forests. The iron smelting industry was initially based on locally mined iron ore

(limonite) but was subsequently replaced by haematite ore from KOOLYANOBBING.

wurrung *see* kangaroos, etc.

Wyangala Dam NSW This storage reservoir is on the LACHLAN RIVER, 48km upstream from COWRA, in the central W slopes region of the State. It was completed in 1936, but subsequent observations revealed that it could be subjected to high stress conditions, so an enlarged dam was constructed in 1971; a rock-fill embankment with a rolled earth-filled core was built immediately downstream of the original wall. It has a storage capacity of 1 220 000ML, collecting run-off from a catchment area of 8290km². The water provides irrigation for farmlands downstream, as well as livestock and town supplies along the Lachlan. The lake formed by the dam provides important recreation facilities for local residents and visitors; there is a caravan park on the waterfront and a country club, with opportunities for fishing, swimming, camping, boating and water skiing.

Wyndham WA (population 1 509 in 1981) Located on the W arm of Cambridge Gulf about 145km from the WA/NT border, in the far N of the State, 943km by road NE of DERBY and over 3400km along the Great Northern Highway from Perth, it is the State's most northerly port. It was founded in the 1880s as the outlet for the E KIMBERLEYS region goldfields and is still the exporting centre for beef and other rural produce from the ORD RIVER valley. It is linked by a 98km-long bitumen road to KUNUNURRA, the urban centre of the Ord irrigation scheme. Like most towns on the NW coast, it experiences a big tidal range (as much as 10m between high and low tides) and vessels need careful pilotage in the gulf channel. The climate is tropical, with hot conditions throughout the year; it has an average annual rainfall of 693mm, concentrated in summer (January average of 194mm, February 166mm), with a markedly dry season from May to October.

Wynne Prize In terms of the bequest of Richard Wynne of Mt Wilson, the Trustees of the Art Gallery of New South Wales award an annual prize of $1 000 for the best painting of an Australian landscape, or the best figure sculpture by an Australian artist. The prize was established in 1897.

Wynyard TAS (population 4 582 in 1981) Located in a prosperous farming district in the NW coastal region of the State, at the mouth of the Inglis River, it is 16km W of BURNIE and 65km from DEVONPORT along the Bass Highway. At an elevation of 16m above sea level on the N coastal plain, it experiences a mild climate with an average annual rainfall of 1040mm, concentrated mainly in the winter months. The town is a business and service centre for the surrounding rural region where dairy farming, vegetable and potato cultiva-

tion, beef cattle raising, fat lamb production, grain cropping (wheat, oats, barley), fishing and forestry are important. There is a large butter, bacon and cheese factory and a vegetable canning plant in the town.

Wyong NSW (population 3 902 in 1981) This town is 106km by road N of Sydney and 65km S of NEWCASTLE, on the main northern railway line and the Pacific Highway. It is a service centre for a rural district where dairying, citrus fruit growing, poultry farming and timber milling are important. It is situated on the Wyong River, a short stream which drains into TUGGERAH LAKES, lying to the E between the Pacific Highway and the coastline. The name Wyong comes from an Aboriginal word meaning 'a spring' or 'a place of running water'.

XYZ

yabbies *see* crustaceans

yachting *see* sailing

yallara *see* bandicoots

Yallourn VIC (population of Yallourn and MOE 18 158 in 1981) Located on the S bank of the LATROBE RIVER, 143km by road ESE of Melbourne and 38km E of WARRAGUL, it was one of the main mining centres on the vast open-cut brown coalfields of the Latrobe Valley. The first attempt to win coal from the Yallourn field was made in 1889, at an open-cut site N of the Latrobe River (now Yallourn North), but the major development of the area was started in the 1920s when the Victorian State Electricity Commission commenced operations there. A power station was established, a briquette factory (to produce compressed blocks, suitable as fuel, from the brown coal) was built and the Yallourn township started. The coalfields had several favourable features: the deposits extended over vast areas of the valley, the seams were thick (over 60m average), and the overburden covering the coal was relatively shallow (average about 12m). This enabled highly mechanised open-cut methods to be used in the mining operations. Yallourn was planned as a garden town, with a central square, numerous parks, recreation facilities and modern amenities. However, it was situated on part of the coal deposits and by the 1970s it became necessary to move the town so that the coal beneath it could be mined. The name Yallourn was derived from two Aboriginal words: *yalleen* meaning 'brown' and *lourn* meaning 'fuel'.

Yamba NSW (population 2 528 in 1981) A resort town in the NORTH COAST region of the State, located on the southern headland at the mouth of the CLARENCE RIVER, 13km E of the Pacific Highway, 738km by road from Sydney and some 70km NE of GRAFTON. At an elevation of only 29m above sea level, it has an average rainfall of 1 447mm, spread throughout all months of the year, but with a somewhat drier period in the springtime. It is a popular summer holiday centre, with surfing, fishing and other aquatic sports. The Yuraygir National Park is located along the coastal plain, S of Yamba; it covers 13 055ha of sand dunes, woodlands, swampy areas, forested stretches and rocky headlands, with a wide variety of bird life including emus, brolgas and pelicans.

Yampi Sound WA A stretch of coastal water, dotted with many islands, it is located between Collier Bay and King Sound, and is bounded by the BUCCANEER ARCHIPELAGO on its seaward side and the coastline of the W KIMBERLEYS region, in the far NW of the State. Two of the islands in Yampi Sound, COCKATOO and KOOLAN, have large, high-quality iron ore deposits, owned and mined by the BROKEN HILL PROPRIETARY COMPANY LIMITED. Like most coastal areas of the NW, the Sound experiences a big tidal range (as much as 10m between high and low tides) with a rapid tidal race, which creates hazardous conditions for shipping. The name Yampi comes from an Aboriginal word meaning 'fresh water'.

Yanchep WA (population 486 in 1981) A small township located on Loch McNess, it is 52km NNW of Perth on the limestone coastal plain and about 4km inland from the Indian Ocean coast. The Yanchep National Park (2799ha) contains many caves (the Crystal and Yonderup are the best known; guided tours are conducted for visitors), a colony of koala bears (established in 1938), facilities for swimming, boating and sailing, and superb spring-time displays of wild flowers. Black swans, ducks and other water birds are abundant on the lake. An area of 141ha of the park has been developed to provide a variety of recreational amenities (such as sporting ovals and barbecue sites) and a modern marina was constructed as the operating base where preparations were made for the 1974 America's Cup Challenge. Being so close to Perth, this area provides a fine amenity for the metropolitan population.

Yarra River VIC The headwaters of the Yarra are located near MOUNT BAW BAW in the GREAT DIVIDING RANGE, about 120km NE of Melbourne, in an area which is also the source of the GOULBURN and THOMSON Rivers. It flows for some 250km on a general W and SW course and passes through Melbourne to a dredged estuary on PORT PHILLIP BAY. Since the early days of settlement the Yarra has been important for the city's water supply and the upper reaches of the river still provide part of the metropolitan requirements. As the city has grown it has been necessary to undertake flood control and reclamation schemes in the meandering sections of the lower stream. Along the course of the Yarra there is much countryside of scenic beauty and the valley is a popular area for day trips from the city. The largest urban centres along the river are HEALESVILLE (population 4 526 in 1981) and WARBURTON (2 009). The name Yarra comes from an Aboriginal word meaning 'running water'.
Further reading: Carroll, B. *River Yarra Sketchbook*. Rigby, Adelaide, 1973.

Yarram VIC (population 2 085 in 1981) A small country town in GIPPSLAND, it is located on the Tarra River, 74km SSW of SALE along the south Gippsland Highway, 62km SSE of TRARALGON and 222km by road SE of Melbourne. It is also a railway terminus of the line through KORUMBURRA and LEONGATHA, 220km by rail from Melbourne. It is a service centre for the surrounding farming and forestry district, as well as the touring centre from which trips start to CORNER INLET and the NINETY MILE BEACH. Two national parks are located in the Yarram region: Bulga National Park (80ha) set aside as a park in 1904, is noted for its giant mountain ash trees and its fine tree ferns; Tarra Valley National Park (140ha) is also noted for its luxuriant vegetation, as well as for a waterfall on the upper reaches of Tarra River and for koalas. The name Yarram comes from an Aboriginal word meaning 'waterfalls', 'plenty of water' or 'water always flowing'.

Yarrawonga VIC (population 3 442 in 1981) This small country town is on the MURRAY RIVER and on the Murray Valley Highway, 47km W of RUTHERGLEN, 56km by road NW of WANGARATTA, and 261km by road NNE of Melbourne. The twin town in NSW on the N side of the Murray is Mulwala (the name comes from the Aboriginal word for rain), and the VIC railway system extends across the border into NSW beyond Mulwala into the RIVERINA region. Yarrawonga is 260km by rail from Melbourne and is in the centre of a grazing, fruit growing, dairying and wheat farming region. Nearby is Lake Mulwala, formed from the waters of the Murray impounded by YARRAWONGA WEIR; the lake covers an area of 6075ha, with a shoreline of 43km, and provides facilities for swimming, boating and fishing. The name Yarrawonga comes from an Aboriginal term meaning 'cormorant's nesting place'.

Yarrawonga Weir VIC Located on the MURRAY RIVER, some 210km downstream from ALBURY, this structure regulates river flow and raises the water level so that it can be diverted from the main stream into irrigation canals in both NSW and VIC. The weir, built as part of the scheme to conserve and control the Murray water, is near the town of YARRAWONGA and its twin town Mulwala.

Yass NSW (population 4 283 in 1981) A small town 299km by road SW of Sydney, near the junction of the Hume and Barton Highways, it is situated on the Yass River, a headwater tributary of the MURRUMBIDGEE RIVER, upstream from the BURRINJUCK DAM. The main S railway passes through Yass Junction, the railhead of the town, a journey of 315km from Sydney. At an elevation of 506m above sea level, it experiences warm summers and cool frosty winters, with an average annual rainfall of 637mm spread uniformly throughout the year. In the 1830s, following the explorations of HUME and Hovell in 1824 (Hamilton Hume is buried in Yass cemetery), the area was settled by pastoralists. The town was gazetted in 1837 and became a municipality in 1873. It is now the centre of a rich grazing region, with several sheep and cattle studs and many properties noted for fine Merino wool. The name Yass comes from an Aboriginal word meaning 'running water'. Some 50km SW of the town, on the W shore of Lake Burrinjuck, is a recreation reserve with a caravan park and other accommodation facilities for visitors, set in picturesque bushland and providing opportunities for boating, fishing, swimming, water skiing and bushwalking. Many buildings in Yass have been listed for preservation by the National Trust (NSW) and several others, such as the courthouse, ANZ Bank, the post office, Rural Bank, St Clement's Anglican Church and some historic cottages have been classified as essential to the heritage of the nation.

Yeppoon QLD (population 6 447 in 1981) A country town and seaside resort on the CAPRICORN COAST, it is 723km by road NNW of Brisbane and 40km NE of ROCKHAMPTON. Situated on Keppel Bay, it is the largest coastal resort in the region, with superb beaches and scenic coastal panoramas. Pineapple farms fringe the landward side of the town.

Yirrkala NT (population 543 in 1981) An Aboriginal community, it is located on GOVE PENINSULA, at the NE extremity of ARNHEM LAND, where a Methodist mission was established in 1953. In the 1970s the Yirrkala people were involved in the controversy over land rights and the development of the bauxite deposits on the peninsula. Also, in response to the increasing importance placed on self-management among Aboriginal communities in recent times, the control of the mission was transferred in 1976 to the Yirrkala people.

York WA (population 1 136 in 1981) Located on the AVON RIVER, 96km E of Perth, it is one of the earliest rural settlements in WA. At an elevation of 173m above sea level, it experiences a mild climate, with an average annual rainfall of 454mm, concentrated in winter, with a dry summer season. The pioneering atmosphere of yester-year still pervades the town and more than 30 buildings have been listed for preservation by the National Trust (WA), including several

National Library of Australia

Sketch of York, WA, by W.S. Hatton, 1857

colonial homes, churches, hotels, the town hall, the post office, the courthouse and the old gaol.

Yorke Peninsula

Yorke Peninsula SA This boot-shaped peninsula lies between ST VINCENT GULF to the E and SPENCER GULF to the W, with INVESTIGATOR STRAIT to the S separating the peninsula from KANGAROO ISLAND. It extends 180km from the apex of St Vincent Gulf to Cape Spencer at its SW tip, and averages 40km wide. Like many of the landscape features of this region, it was discovered by the explorer Matthew FLINDERS in 1802 and named after Charles Philip Yorke, then First Lord of the British Admiralty. The French explorer Nicholas BAUDIN visited the peninsula shortly after Flinders; the first white inhabitants were sealers and it was not until the 1840s that settlers took up land there and laid the foundations of the cereal crop farming which still remains an important feature of the rural scene. From 1860 to the early decades of the 20th century, copper was mined in the N parts of the peninsula near KADINA, MOONTA and WALLAROO. At the SW tip of the peninsula is the Innes National Park, dedicated in 1970 and covering 9 142ha of undulating sand dunes, salt lakes, clay pans and spectacular coastal cliffs. The rediscovery of the rare mallee-whipbird in 1965 was one of the main reasons for dedication of the park; the wreck of the Norwegian iron barque *Ethel*, driven ashore in 1904 after striking a reef, lies at the foot of the cliffs near Reef Head.

Young

Young NSW (population 6 906 in 1981) A town in the SW slopes region of the State, it is located at the junction of the Henry Lawson Way and the Olympic Way, 390km by road WSW of Sydney. It is on a link railway between the main S route and the main W line, and can be reached either via Harden (a train journey of 440km from Sydney) or via

BLAYNEY (417km). It is situated in rolling hill land at an elevation of 432m above sea level, near the source of a number of streams which drain into the LACHLAN RIVER. It experiences a climate typical of inland towns, with warm to hot summer conditions and mildly cool winters, and receives an average annual rainfall of 657mm, evenly spread throughout the year. The town is a commercial and service centre for a fertile grazing, farming and orcharding district producing wheat, wool, fat lambs, lucerne and cherries. Like many towns of the Lachlan Valley, it was a gold-mining centre in the 1860s, originally called Lambing Flat, and was the site of the anti-Chinese LAMBING FLAT RIOTS in the gold-rush days. It

Young High School, NSW

NSW Dept of Tourism

was renamed in honour of Sir John Young, Governor of NSW in the 1860s. The Lambing Flat Historical Folk Museum provides visitors with glimpses of the past, and Chinaman's Dam, 3km SE of the town, a popular picnic and swimming spot, was Young's first water supply and was used by Chinese diggers for sluicing gold. The National Trust (NSW) has listed several buildings in the town for preservation, including the high school assembly hall (built 1884-86), the technical college (formerly a gaol, built 1876), the public school (1883) and the railway station (1885).

Young Men's Christian Association

Young Men's Christian Association Founded in London in 1844, the YMCA(commonly referred to by its members as 'the Y') aims at developing the physical fitness and mental well-being of its members and others participating in its programmes, at fostering their self-confidence and self-respect, and at aiding their growth as responsible family members and citizens. These aims are the basis of its motto, 'Spirit, Mind and Body'. From London it soon spread throughout the UK and to other countries, and quickly established a reputation as a pioneer in physical education. Particular sports which it popularised are volleyball and basketball.

The first YMCA in Australia was founded in Adelaide in 1850, and by 1854 there were others in Sydney, Melbourne and Hobart. There are now 29 YMCAs throughout Australia, with over 300 000 people participating in their programmes. Normally, about a third of all participants are enrolled members, each of whom is either a member of a Christian Church or has subscribed to a statement of Christian faith. The Australian YMCA, which is a member of the World Alliance of YMCAs, is organised on a federal basis. Its National Council includes a National

Convention which meets every four years and a National Board which meets at least six times a year. Operating units of the National Council include State Councils, a Youth College and Youth Trust for leadership training and development, a Defence Forces Committee to organise Defence Force welfare work and a World Work Committee to deal with aid for overseas projects. Since the 1950s the programmes of the various Associations have been expanded to include women and girls, this practice being formally affirmed in a new statement of objectives adopted in 1971.

Young Women's Christian Association

This international organisation, which has members in more than 80 countries, has 39 associations and groups in Australia, with State Councils in the five mainland States and a national headquarters in Melbourne. Membership is about 12 000, with approximately 60 000 girls and women participating in YWCA activities.

The movement began in England in 1855, when two separate groups using the name YWCA were founded by women who were worried about the effects of the industrial revolution and the Crimean War on the lives of young women and girls. The two groups combined in 1877 and in 1894 similar organisations in a number of countries formed the World YWCA. In Australia the first YWCA was formed in GEELONG in VIC in 1872. It lapsed for some years, but from 1880 others were formed, and in 1907 a National Association of Australasia was established. As in other countries, the YWCA in Australia has provided recreational and skill-learning activities for its members and others, has conducted classes in physical, health and cultural education, and has run hostels and employment agencies. Since World War II its work among migrants has expanded greatly and in recent years it has paid increasing attention to helping women who are socially isolated in the suburbs of large cities. Community work also includes mother/child play-groups, involvement with senior citizens, and Mailbag Clubs to provide activities for women in the Outback. In physical activities there has been an increased emphasis on non-competitive forms, such as yoga and fitness programmes.

Yugoslavs in Australia

The 1981 census revealed that 149 335 persons resident in Australia had been born in Yugoslavia. C.A. Price, a leading authority on multicultural affairs, in a study of the ethnic origins of the Australian population based on an eight-generation analysis, estimated the total Yugoslav component to be equivalent to 221 200 persons in 1978. The Term 'Yugoslav' covers a mosaic of peoples, combining six major and 18 minor ethnic groups, and independent figures for all the ethnic groups are not available. Migration from territories now included in the nation of Yugoslavia commenced more than a century ago and one of the oldest Yugoslav cultural centres in Australia is located at BROKEN HILL. Since

World War II Yugoslav-born persons have migrated to all States and to the two Territories in Australia but the largest numbers are to be found in NSW and VIC.

Although the State of Yugoslavia was founded as recently as 1918, the people born in this new territory have been under foreign domination for nearly six centuries and the discord among the peoples labelled collectively as Yugoslav has been transplanted to every country where they have settled. Although serious conflict between different folk communities in Australia has been kept to a minimum, there have been a few clashes between groups who support royalism for their country of origin, groups who are dedicated to an independent political arrangement for their particular ethnic group in their homeland and groups who support the present federal structure of Yugoslavia.

Attempts to lessen latent conflict have been made by Jovanaka Noussair (née Secanski), who established the Yugoslav-Australian Association at Newtown, Sydney, in 1974. This organisation set up the Information-Welfare Centre which aims to meet the settlement needs of all newly arrived Yugoslav immigrants, catering for all ethnic groups among them. It has also established a number of ethnic schools run on a non-profit basis which provide Saturday classes to teach languages and cultural background to the children of Yugoslav-born persons. At present, the schools teach Serbo-Croat, Croat-Serbian, Macedonian and Slovenian. A number of Yugoslav newspapers are now published in Australia and ethnic radio broadcasts which are now being made in every State include programmes for Yugoslav-born people.

Notable Yugoslavs in Australia These include Senator Misha Lajovic; Jack Tripovitch, Leader of the Opposition in the VIC Legislative Council; Ralph Sarich, 1972 Inventor of the Year, who designed an orbital car engine; Dr Nikola Chuchkovich, an expert on the psychological problems of immigrants; Etela Piha, opera singer; the Most Rev. Matthew Beovich, Archbishop of Adelaide; Fabian Lovokovic, Hon. Secretary of the Croation Central Council of Australia; and Dr Vasil Tulevski, a leading figure in the Yugoslav-Macedonian community.

Further reading: Price, C.A. *Australian Immigration, A Bibliography and Digest.* Australian National University Press, Canberra, 1981.

Zebu

see beef cattle industry; dairy cattle industry

Zeehan

TAS (population 1 750 in 1981) A former boom mining town in the rugged W coast ranges, at an elevation of 172m above sea level, it is located 38km by road NW of QUEENSTOWN, 28km SW of ROSEBERY, and 155km via the Waratah Highway from BURNIE. The history of Zeehan dates back to 1642 when the Dutch explorer, Abel TASMAN, sighted a mountain peak which he named Mt Zeehan, after one of his ships; the peak is located 5km S of the present town. Zeehan

developed in the 1880s when silver-lead ores were discovered and over the following three decades it became a boom town, boasting 26 hotels and a population of over 8 000 in the early years of this century. It proved to be a rich mining field, but the ores were soon exhausted and the town declined. Recently, it has experienced a revival with new mining development at RENISON BELL, 17km NE. Many of Zeehan's buildings of the boom period still stand as historic reminders of the rich mining days, including the Grand Hotel (1899) and the School of Mines (1894, now the West Coast Pioneers' Memorial Museum). Zeehan has a high annual rainfall (2444mm average) the highest month being July (265mm) and the lowest February (114mm).

zinc

This versatile metal, essential to modern living, was first identified and named 'zinken' in the 16th century. However, brass, made by adding zinc ore to copper ore prior to smelting, was in common use long before that time; brass bracelets dating back to 500 BC have been found on the island of Rhodes. The art of zinc smelting, developed by the Indians and Chinese, was introduced to England in 1739, and once it became established in Europe and America, the metallurgy of zinc improved rapidly. The major end uses of zinc are in the domestic, transport and construction fields, where it is used for galvanising, brass and bronze products, castings and rolled zinc. Zinc oxide, used extensively in the rubber, paint, ceramic and chemical industries, is also contained in animal and plant nutrients. In terms of annual consumption, zinc stands third amongst the non-ferrous metals of the world, surpassed only by copper and aluminium.

Extraction The commercial introduction of froth flotation methods of extracting zinc minerals from run-of-mine ore is an important recent development now in general use. After flotation, the sulphide concentrate is roasted to form zinc oxide which is then either distilled at temperatures of up to 1300°C or dissolved in dilute sulphuric acid and electrolysed. Both methods can produce zinc of exceptional purity. By-products and co-products include gold, silver, copper, lead fluorspar and manganese with cadmium, gallium, germanium, indium and thallium recovered from gases, flue dusts and residues from smelting operations.

Production The recoverable reserves of zinc in the world are approximately 120 million tonnes but total possible reserves are probably twice that amount. Australia's reserves at present amount to 15 million tonnes of zinc. The Australian mine production of zinc in 1980 contained 495 312 tonnes of metal, making it the fourth-largest producer (7.4 per cent of world production) after Canada, the USSR and Peru. Zinc is a co-product of LEAD mining and thus it is produced at MOUNT ISA in QLD, BROKEN HILL in NSW and ROSEBERY in TAS. The production statistics for the various States are shown in Table 1. Smelting is carried out at Mt Isa and PORT PIRIE in SA; the largest domestic refinery is located near RISDON COVE in TAS, while a

Table 1

MINE PRODUCTION OF ZINC IN AUSTRALIA 1970-81

State	1970	1978	1979	1980	1981
QLD	114 203	127 980	128 647	113 634	124 302
NSW	325 507	267 925	325 281	327 404	306 610
TAS	46 895	77 388	75 229	54 274	74 413
SA	76	—	—	—	—
NT	526	—	—	—	—
TOTAL	487 207	473 293	529 157	496 312	518 297*

Source: *Australian Mineral Industry Annual Review.* (1970-80) Australian Govt Publishing Service, Canberra.
* note: WA produced 12 972 tonnes of zinc in 1981

Perth Zoo

Australian Tourist Commission

smaller one operates at Cockle Creek in NSW.

Australia is the second-largest exporter of zinc, accounting for 14 per cent of the total world exports.

The industry The structure of the Australian lead-zinc industry, which has a similar pattern to that developed in the USA, consists of six or seven large mining companies with substantial equities in smelters and refineries.

Further reading: see under minerals and mining.

Zinnia *see* Compositae

zosterops *see* silvereyes

zoos The major zoological gardens, or zoos, in Australia are in SYDNEY, MELBOURNE, ADELAIDE, PERTH, and DUBBO, NSW. There are also many smaller privately owned collections of animals such as a reptile farm at GOSFORD, NSW (partly a tourist attraction, and partly a source of venoms for the production of antivenenes by the Commonwealth Serum Laboratories) and the Lion Park at the Warragamba Dam, NSW.

The functions of modern zoos are education, conservation, scientific research and entertainment. In Australia they also had another purpose in the 19th century—namely as a means of holding and breeding animals that were to be naturalised in Australia. This was the aim of the various ACCLIMATIZATION SOCIETIES which later developed into the zoological societies of today; the state zoological societies are still closely associated with their respective zoos.

The first important zoo in Sydney was in Moore Park and was used to hold animals for acclimatization though later it was also opened to the public and included native animals. In 1912 work began on establishing the Taronga Zoo Park, with the control vested in a trust, on a site overlooking Sydney Harbour. The site, which occupies about 32ha, is hilly and is probably one of the most attractive in the world. The zoo was officially opened in 1916. In 1973 the control passed to a statutory body, the Zoological Parks Board of NSW. Since then the amenities for the animals have been greatly improved and the changes are being continued. In June, 1983, the zoo held about 4170 specimens of vertebrates, with representatives of 721 species and subspecies. It has been particularly successful in the breeding of

Giraffes at Western Plains Zoo, Dubbo NSW

R. Palozzi, Australian Tourist Commission

birds and rare reptiles, it has a larger collection of the perenially popular chimpanzees than any other zoo in the world and holds, together with other conservation-worthy species, Sumatran tigers and Père David's deer. As is to be expected it surpasses all overseas zoos in its holdings of native animals, and one particular attractive feature is the reversed daylight house where animals can be seen about their nocturnal business at a time that

suits the tourist. Behind the scenes are extensive quarantine, veterinary, food storage and other essential facilities. The zoo is largely self-supporting (the public are invited to sponsor individual animals for a year at a time) but the NSW Government provides teachers for the education section. The Western Plains Zoo at Dubbo is an open-range zoo in which the barriers between the animals and the visitors are skilfully concealed, and where the

Cheetah at Western Plains Zoo, Dubbo NSW

H. Millen, Australian Tourist Commission

animals have large paddocks in which to move freely. Its area is about 280ha and in 1983 there were about 680 specimens, consisting of 56 species and subspecies.

There was a private zoo in Melbourne in 1853. The Royal Park Zoo, now the Melbourne Zoological Gardens, was founded in 1861. Among its earlier exhibits were some of the camels from the ill-fated Burke and Wills expedition. It is near to the Yarra river, and close to the botanical gardens. The Adelaide zoo was founded in 1878 and now occupies an 8 hectare site near the centre of the city. The zoo in Perth was opened in 1898 and occupies an 8 ha site near the centre of the the city. Among its more remarkable exhibits are Sumatran orang-utans and several species of gibbons. The former zoo in Hobart has the melancholy distinction of the being the place where the last known specimen of the TASMANIAN WOLF died. There are two small public zoos in BURNIE and LAUNCESTON. In QLD the Lone Pine Koala Sanctuary, 11km from Brisbane, is noteworthy.

At the end of the 19th century Australia's zoos were unusual in that the directors of three of them, Sydney, Melbourne and Perth, were brothers—the Le Souefs.

APPENDICES

APPENDIX I

AUSTRALIAN   CHRONOLOGY

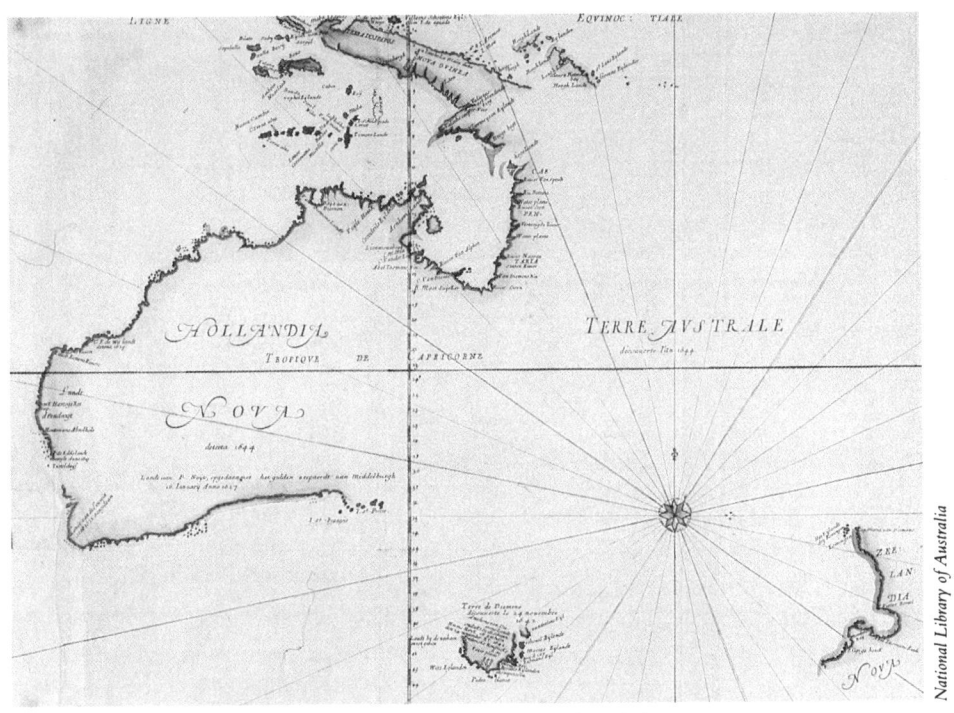

A French map of 1644 showing the extent of Dutch discoveries

At least 40000 Before Present: Arrival of first Aborigines.

1606 Willem JANSZ, in the Dutch ship *Duyfken*, discovers the W coast of CAPE YORK Peninsula. A Spaniard, Luis Vaez de TORRES, sails through TORRES STRAIT.

1616 Dirk HARTOG, in the *Eendracht*, lands on an island in SHARK BAY in WA.

1623 The captains of the *Pera* and *Arnhem* explore parts of the GULF OF CARPENTARIA and ARNHEM LAND.

1642 Abel Janszoon TASMAN discovers part of TAS, which he calls VAN DIEMEN'S LAND.

1644 Tasman charts most of the N coast.

1688 William DAMPIER visits the NW coast in the *Cygnet*.

1699 Dampier sails along parts of the W and N coasts in the *Roebuck*.

1770 Lieutenant James COOK, in the *Endeavour*, discovers the E coast, which he names New South Wales and claims in the name of King George III.

The Death of Cook, an oil painting by George Carter

1779 Joseph BANKS recommends BOTANY BAY as the best site for a penal settlement.

1786 Lord Sydney announces the decision to found a penal settlement at Botany Bay.

1788 The FIRST FLEET, under Governor PHILLIP, arrives at Botany Bay, but Phillip soon moves his settlers to SYDNEY COVE, in nearby PORT JACKSON, and on 26 January proclaims the

A painting by Thomas Baines depicting the raising of the British flag in Sydney Cove, 1788

foundation of the colony. In March NORFOLK ISLAND is settled and in November Rose Hill (PARRAMATTA) is made the chief farming site.

1790   The colony's food supply runs dangerously low, but is improved when ships arrive in June. The first detachment of the NEW SOUTH WALES CORPS arrives.

1792   In December Phillip leaves the colony, leaving Major Francis GROSE in command.

1793   The first free settlers reach New South Wales.

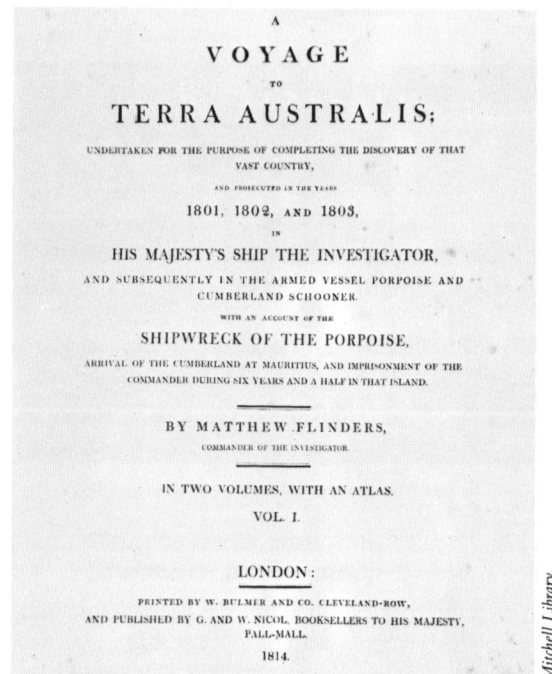

The title page of Flinders' *A Voyage to Terra Australis*

1794   Grose resigns, leaving Captain William PATERSON in charge as administrator.

1795   In September Captain John HUNTER takes office as Governor.

1798   George BASS sails from Sydney to WESTERN PORT BAY.

1799   Bass and Matthew FLINDERS complete the circumnavigation of TAS.

1800   Governor KING replaces Hunter.

1801   Settlement is begun at NEWCASTLE (only to be abandoned in the following year).

1802   PORT PHILLIP BAY is explored by Lieutenant John MURRAY. Matthew Flinders explores a large part of S coast.

Part of the front page of the Sydney *Gazette*, 10th August 1806

1803   Australia's first newspaper, the *Sydney Gazette and New South Wales Advertiser*, is published. Lieutenant BOWEN founds a settlement at RISDON COVE, on the DERWENT in TAS. Lieutenant-Governor David COLLINS founds a short-lived settlement at Port Phillip. Matthew Flinders completes the circumnavigation of Australia (begun in 1801).

1804 Lieutenant-Governor William Paterson founds a settlement at PORT DALRYMPLE, in northern TAS. Collins moves the Port Phillip settlement to TAS, and chooses the site of HOBART. Lord Camden, the British Home Secretary, is impressed by samples of wool produced by John MACARTHUR, and orders that he be granted over 4000ha of land.

1806 Governor BLIGH replaces King.

1808 On 26 January Bligh is deposed in the incident commonly referred to as the RUM REBELLION.

1810 Governor Lachlan MACQUARIE takes office. The New South Wales Corps is recalled.

William Charles Wentworth

George William Evans

1813 Gregory BLAXLAND, William LAWSON and William WENTWORTH find a route most of the way across the BLUE MOUNTAINS. George EVANS makes a complete crossing. Flinders' account of his exploration, recommends official use of name ''Australia''.

1815 A road is completed across the Blue Mts and the town of BATHURST founded.

The civic square at Bathurst with buildings constructed in convict days

1817 Australia's first bank, the BANK OF NEW SOUTH WALES, is founded.

1819 John Thomas BIGGE arrives as commissioner, to report on the state of the colony.

1821 Governor Macquarie resigns. A penal settlement is established at PORT MACQUARIE.

1822 A penal settlement is established at MACQUARIE HARBOUR in TAS.

1823 The New South Wales Judicature Act provides for the setting up of Supreme Courts and nominated Legislative councils at Sydney and Hobart.

A convict chain gang

1824 A penal settlement is established at MORETON BAY. The *Australian*, Australia's first independent newspaper, is published. Limited trial by jury in civil cases is introduced.

1825 TAS (officially known as Van Diemen's Land until 1855) is made a separate colony. The Moreton Bay settlement is moved to the site of Brisbane.

1826 Settlements are founded at Westernport in VIC (abandoned in 1828) and KING GEORGE SOUND (ALBANY) in WA.

1827 Allan CUNNINGHAM discovers the DARLING DOWNS in QLD.

1828 The NSW and TAS Legislative Council enlarged and given wider powers.

1828–30 Charles STURT, in two journeys, solves the mystery of the inland rivers, and makes clear the general pattern of the MURRAY-DARLING system.

1829 The colony of WA is founded.

1830 A penal settlement is founded at PORT ARTHUR in TAS.

1831 The Ripon Regulations prescribe sale by auction as the method for disposing of Crown lands, and so bring to an end the system of land grants.

1832 The first assisted IMMIGRATION scheme is launched.

1833 Trial by jury is extended to criminal cases in NSW.

1834 The South Australian Act provides for the setting up of a colony based partly on the ideas of Edward Gibbon WAKEFIELD. The HENTY brothers settle at PORTLAND BAY in VIC.

1835 Parties organised by John BATMAN and John Pascoe FAWKNER settle without authorisation at Port Phillip. John Bede POLDING, the first ROMAN CATHOLIC bishop in Australia, arrives in Sydney.

corporation, the first local government body in Australia, is founded.

1842 The NSW Legislative Council is enlarged to 36 members, 24 of whom are to be elected. SA is given a nominated Legislative Council. The Moreton Bay district is opened to free settlement. Copper is discovered at KAPUNDA in SA.

1845 Ludwig LEICHHARDT completes a journey, begun in the previous year, from the Darling Downs to PORT ESSINGTON, on the N coast.

Three survivors of Leichhardt's expedition to the NT in 1844-45

National Library of Australia

The proposed town of Adelaide 1836 by Colonel William Light

1836 The explorer, Major Thomas MITCHELL, crosses western VIC and meets the Hentys at Portland Bay. A licence system for SQUATTERS is introduced. The first settlers arrive in SA. The settlement at Port Phillip is officially recognised. William Grant BROUGHTON is installed as the first bishop of the CHURCH OF ENGLAND in Australia.

1837 Governor BOURKE visits the Port Phillip settlement and names it Melbourne.

1840 Transportation to the mainland of NSW is ended. The first squatters reach the DARLING DOWNS. The Adelaide Municipal

1846 Charles Sturt returns to Adelaide after an unsuccessful two-year attempt to reach the centre of the continent.

1848 Leichhardt sets out on an attempt to cross the continent from E to W, but is not seen by Europeans again.

1850 Transportation is begun to WA. The Australian Colonies Government Act provides for the Port Phillip District to become the colony of VIC, and for SA, TAS and VIC to have Legislative Councils in which two-thirds of the members are to be elected.

1851 VIC becomes a separate colony. GOLD DIS-

COVERIES in NSW, and much larger ones in VIC, cause a major rush.

Painting depicting a scene from the Gold Rush days

1852 The ending of transportation to the whole of E Australia is announced. The *Chusan*, first steamship to run a regular service to Australia, reaches Sydney.

1854 A revolt by miners at the EUREKA STOCKADE in BALLARAT, is crushed. Australia's first steam railway, from Melbourne to Port Melbourne, is opened.

Charles Sturt

1855 Responsible government is granted to NSW, VIC and TAS and the first VIC Parliament is elected. The Sydney-Parramatta railway is opened.

1856 Responsible government is granted to SA. The first Parliaments are elected in that colony, NSW and TAS. The first Eight-Hour Day procession is held by building workers in Melbourne.

The banner carried in the first Eight Hour Day procession in Melbourne in 1856

First NSW Government 1856

1858 Telegraph links Adelaide, Melbourne and Sydney.

1859 QLD becomes a separate colony, with responsible government.

1860 BURKE and Wills set out from Melbourne to cross the continent from S to N.

William John Wills, Burke's lieutenant

Young employees at Moonta mine where copper was discovered in 1861

1861 Burke, Wills and two other members of their expedition die on the return journey from the Gulf of Carpentaria. Copper is discovered at MOONTA and WALLAROO in SA. Anti-Chinese riots occur at Lambing Flat.

1862 John McDouall STUART, on a third attempt, succeeds in crossing the continent from Adelaide to the N coast.

1863 The NT is placed under the administration of SA.

1864 Sugar is produced commercially in QLD.

1866 Sir Henry PARKES' Public Schools Act is passed in NSW. VIC's first protective tariff is introduced.

1867 Gold is discovered at GYMPIE in QLD.

1868 Transportation to WA is ended.

1870 The last British troops are withdrawn from Australia. WA is granted partly elected Legislative Council.

1872 The OVERLAND TELEGRAPH from Darwin to Adelaide is completed. Gold is discovered at CHARTERS TOWERS in QLD.

1873 The first Factories Act is passed in VIC. Gold is discovered at the PALMER RIVER in QLD.

1876 The last full-blooded Tasmanian Aboriginal dies.

The first overland telegraph pole at Darwin

Telecom Australia

1877 Perth is linked to the E colonies by telegraph.

1880 Ned KELLY is hanged. Public telephone exchanges are opened in Sydney, Melbourne and Brisbane. The first cargo of refrigerated Australian meat reaches London.

Charters Towers Stock and Mining Exchange

1882 Gold is discovered at MOUNT MORGAN in QLD.

The first mine sunk at Broken Hill

1883 Silver is discovered at BROKEN HILL in NSW. Sydney and Melbourne are linked by rail.

McKay harvester

1884 Hugh Victor McKAY builds his first harvesting machine.

1885 The British Parliament legislates for the setting up of a Federal Council of Australasia.

1886 William FARRER begins his wheat-breeding experiments. The CHAFFEY BROTHERS agree to found an irrigation settlement at MILDURA in VIC.

1887 Adelaide and Melbourne are linked by rail.

1888 Mechanical shears prove their worth when the shearing at Dunlop station, NSW, is done

Hand-shearing sheep prior to 1888

entirely with them. The Melbourne land boom collapses. Sydney and Brisbane are linked by rail.

1889 Henry Parkes, in a speech at TENTERFIELD in NSW, calls for federation of the Australian colonies.

1890 The maritime strike, first of the great strikes of the 1890s, occurs. WA is granted responsible government.

1891 The first federal convention produces a draft constitution. The first colonial Labor Party is formed, in NSW. A severe economic depression affects the whole of E Australia.

1892 Gold is discovered at COOLGARDIE in WA. An industrial tribunal is set up in NSW.

1893 Gold is discovered at KALGOORLIE in WA. A socialist settlement, NEW AUSTRALIA, is founded by William LANE in Paraguay.

1894 SA becomes the first Australian colony to give the vote to women.

1896 Wages boards are established in VIC.

1898 The second federal convention, which began

Australian War Memorial

Troops in trenches during the Boer War

in the previous year, finishes the framing of a federal constitution. The constitution is accepted by referendum in SA, VIC and TAS, but does not gain sufficient votes in NSW.

1899 The constitution is accepted by referendum in all colonies except WA. Australian troops are sent to the BOER WAR.

1900 The Commonwealth of Australia Constitution Act is passed by the British Parliament and receives the royal assent. The constitution is accepted by referendum in WA.

already in Australia. The Australian flag is chosen.

1902 Women are enfranchised for federal elections. A Commonwealth tariff is introduced. William Farrer's wheat strain, 'Federation', becomes available.

1903 A bounty scheme for Australian sugar is introduced. The High Court of Australia is constituted. Alfred DEAKIN succeeds Barton as Prime Minister. A Defence Act authorises military conscription, but only for home DEFENCE.

Tasmanian Museum & Art Gallery

United Australia decorations on the Tasmanian Parliament 1901

1901 The Commonwealth of Australia comes into existence with Edmund BARTON as Prime Minister. The first federal Parliament is opened in Melbourne by the Duke of York (later King George V). The Immigration Restriction Act provides the means for the exclusion of non-European migrants. The Pacific Islands Labourers' Act provides for the ending of recruitment of KANAKA labour, and the repatriation of most of the Kanakas

1904 The Commonwealth Court of Conciliation and arbitration is established. The first federal Labor ministry, under John Christian WATSON, holds office for four months.

1906 British New Guinea, renamed PAPUA, becomes an Australian Territory.

1907 The first federal basic wage is established, in the Harvester Case.

1908 The Commonwealth Literary Fund is

Kanaka women working in the fields

John Oxley Library

established. The Commonwealth legislates to establish old-age and invalid pensions. The Yass-Canberra district is chosen for the Federal capital.

1909 Sir George REID is appointed first Australian High Commissioner in London. A two-party political system is brought about by the joining of free-traders and protectionists in the 'Fusion' (or LIBERAL) Party.

1910 Compulsory military training (first authorised in 1909) is extended. The first ships of the Australian Navy (the destroyers *Parramatta* and *Yarra*) arrive in Australia. For the first time one party (Labor) wins an absolute majority of seats in a federal election.

1911 The Royal Military College of Australia is founded at Duntroon. The administration of the NT passes to the Commonwealth.

1912 The Commonwealth Bank is opened. An American architect, Walter Burley GRIFFIN, wins a competition for the design of the federal capital.

Canberra Coat of Arms

Australian Tourist Commission

1913 The name 'Canberra' is chosen for the federal capital. The Royal Australian Naval College is founded.

1914 Britain's declaration of war automatically commits Australia to war also. The first double dissolution of the federal Parliament is followed by a Labor victory in an election for both Houses. The first contingent of the Australian Expeditionary Force sails for Egypt, and one of the escorting vessels, HMAS *Sydney*, sinks the German raider *Emden*. Meanwhile, Australian naval and military forces have occupied German New Guinea.

HMAS *Sydney* sinks the German raider *Emden*

Australian War Memorial

1915 The Royal Australian Naval College is moved from temporary quarters at GEELONG to JERVIS BAY. Troops of the Australian and New Zealand Army Corps land on the GALLIPOLI Peninsula, 25 April. The BROKEN HILL PROPRIETARY COMPANY's iron and steelworks is opened at Newcastle. William Lawrence Bragg becomes the first Australian-born winner of a Nobel Prize, sharing the prize for physics with his father, William Henry Bragg.

1916 The Returned Sailors' and Soldiers' Imperial League (now the RETURNED SERVICES LEAGUE OF AUSTRALIA) is founded. A pro-

Australian War Memorial

Anzac Cove, Gallipoli

posal for military conscription for overseas service is defeated in a referendum. William Morris HUGHES and many other pro-CONSCRIPTION parliamentarians are expelled from the AUSTRALIAN LABOR PARTY (ALP).

1917 Expelled Labor parliamentarians join the Liberals to form the Nationalist Party under the leadership of W.M. Hughes. The new party wins elections for the NSW and Commonwealth Parliaments. However, the proposal for military conscription is again defeated in a referendum. The transcontinental railway from PORT AUGUSTA in SA to Kalgoorlie in WA is completed.

1919 Australian representatives attend the Paris Peace Conference and Australia becomes a member of the League of Nations.

1920 The Communist Party of Australia is founded. Parliamentarians sponsored by various primary producers' organisations join together to form a federal Country Party.

1921 Former German New Guinea becomes a mandate of the League of Nations, with Australia as the administering nation.

1922 The QLD Legislative Council is abolished. Qantas (QLD and NT Aerial Service) begins its first regular service, between CHARLEVILLE and CLONCURRY in QLD.

1923 Silver and lead ores are discovered in MOUNT ISA in QLD. First broadcasting service in Australia begins.

1926 At an Imperial Conference the concept of the independence of Australia and other Dominions within the British Commonwealth of Nations is defined. The Council for Scientific and Industrial Research (later the COMMONWEALTH SCIENTIFIC AND INDUSTRIAL RESEARCH ORGANIZATION) is established.

1927 Seat of federal parliament moved from Melbourne to Canberra.

National Library of Australia

Joseph Lyons with his wife and family

1928 The Commonwealth-States agreement that borrowings be co-ordinated through the LOAN COUNCIL is approved by referendum.

1929 After 12 years of Nationalist or Nationalist/ Country Party government, the ALP returns to office under James SCULLIN.

1930 The full effects of the worldwide economic Depression are felt in Australia.

1931 The Premiers' Plan for dealing with the Depression is adopted. Wage rates are lowered and the Australian pound devalued. Sir Isaac ISSACS becomes the first Australian-born Governor-General. The ALP undergoes a three-way split. Joseph LYONS and others join with the Nationalists to form the United Australia Party while supporters of John LANG form a 'Lang Labor' group and help to bring the Scullin government down.

1932 In January a United Australia Party government under Joseph Lyons takes office. The SYDNEY HARBOUR BRIDGE is opened. The Governor of NSW, Sir Philip Game, dismisses Lang from the premiership. The AUSTRALIAN BROADCASTING COMMISSION (now CORPORATION) is established.

John Bradfield, designer of the Sydney Harbour Bridge, with his wife

John Fairfax & Sons Ltd

1933 A large section of ANTARCTICA is declared the Australian Antarctic Territory. In a referendum in WA a majority vote in favour of secession from the Commonwealth.

1935 The Broken Hill Proprietary Co. Ltd gains a monopoly of iron and steel making by taking over Australian Iron and Steel.

1939 The worst BUSHFIRES in Australian history cause the loss of 71 lives in VIC. The Commonwealth Court of Conciliation and Arbitration declares a 44-hour standard working week. Prime Minister MENZIES accepts Britain's declaration of war on Germany as binding on Australia also. Recruiting begins for the second AUSTRALIAN IMPERIAL FORCE (AIF) and conscrip-

tion for home defence is introduced. Australia participates in the Empire Air Training Scheme.

1940 The first units of the AIF sail for the Middle East. In December Australian troops engage in action in Libya. First Australian diplomat to a foreign country appointed (R.G. CASEY to USA).

Courtesy of A.I.S. Canberra

John Curtin and Ben Chifley

1941 Australian forces are engaged in North Africa, Greece, Crete and Syria. The 9th Division is involved in the siege of Tobruk. In October a Labor government takes office under John CURTIN. On 8 December Australia declares war on Japan.

Australian War Memorial

The Japanese bomb Darwin

1942 The Japanese capture Singapore; their prisoners include over 15 000 Australians. They bomb Darwin and other N towns and land in New Guinea. General Douglas MacArthur arrives in Australia. The Japanese lose the air-sea battles of the CORAL SEA and Midway and are driven back along the Kokoda in New Guinea. In Egypt the 9th Division takes part in the Battle of El Alamein. The Commonwealth government introduces widows' pensions and begins levying uniform income tax.

1943 Military conscription is extended to cover service in a large area of the South Pacific.

1944 Robert Menzies founds a new Liberal Party, as successor to the United Australia Party. Commonwealth unemployment and sickness benefits are introduced.

1945 Germany surrenders, and in the closing stage of the war against Japan Australian troops land in Borneo. Australia participates in the San Francisco Conference, and becomes a founding member of UNO. Howard FLOREY

wins the Nobel Prize for medicine. Japan surrenders after dropping of two atomic bombs.

1946 The Australian National University is established. The powers of the Commonwealth government regarding social services are extended by referendum. An Act to nationalise internal airlines having been declared invalid by the High Court, Trans-Australia Airlines is established. A missile-testing range is established at WOOMERA in SA.

1947 The NT Legislative Council is established. Qantas Empire Airways is nationalised. The Commonwealth Court of Conciliation and Arbitration introduces a 40-hour week.

1948 An Act passed in the previous year to nationalise private trading banks is declared invalid by the High Court. Production of the Holden car begins.

1949 The SNOWY MOUNTAINS SCHEME is begun. The Commonwealth government applies

United Nations

Dr H.V. Evatt signing the Charter of the United Nations on behalf of Australia, June 1945

legal penalties and uses troops to end a national coal strike. Uranium deposits are found at RUM JUNGLE in the NT. A Legislative Council is set up in the Territory of Papua and New Guinea. Liberal/Country Party government led by R.G. Menzies take office.

Snowy Mountains Authority

The Snowy Mountains scheme begins

1950 Australia is a prime mover in the launching of the COLOMBO PLAN. Australian forces are sent to the KOREAN WAR, and units of the RAAF are stationed in Malaya, where they help combat Communist insurgency.

1951 A Commonwealth-States conference on Aboriginal affairs agrees on a policy of assimilation.

1952 The ANZUS PACT is signed by Australia, New Zealand and the USA.

1953 The Australian Atomic Energy Commission is established.

1954 Australia signs the SOUTH-EAST ASIA TREATY ORGANISATION (SEATO) agreement. Uranium is discovered at MARY KATHLEEN in QLD. A Royal Commission enquires into the allegations by the former Soviet diplomat and espionage agent, Vladimir PETROV, who has been granted political asylum.

Australian Consolidated Press

Mrs Petrov escorted by two Russian agents in Sydney

1955 Disagreement over methods of combating COMMUNISM in TRADE UNIONS leads to a split in the ALP, and the formation of a rival Anti-Communist Labor Party (later DEMOCRATIC LABOR PARTY). Australian ground troops are sent to help combat Communist insurgency in Malaya.

1956 Television broadcasting begins. The OLYMPIC GAMES are held in Melbourne.

1957 Joern Utzon of Denmark wins a competition for the design of the SYDNEY OPERA HOUSE. The Australia-Japan Trade Agreement is signed.

Australian troops playing cricket during the Korean war

Television broadcasting in 1956

Australian Broadcasting Commission (John Pearson)

1958 A small nuclear reactor begins operation at Lucas Heights, near Sydney.

1959 Sir Macfarlane BURNET shares the Nobel Prize for medicine. The Federal Council for the Advancement of Aborigines is set up. A more liberal attitude towards the immigration of people of non-European racial origin is officially announced.

1960 Enormous deposits of iron ore are discovered in the PILBARA district of WA and ban on exports is abolished. The first ADELAIDE FESTIVAL OF ARTS is held.

1962 A standard-gauge rail link between Sydney and Melbourne is completed. Australian military advisers are sent to Vietnam. Right to vote given to all Aborigines.

1963 Sir John ECCLES shares the Nobel Prize for medicine. Large-scale mining of bauxite at WEIPA in QLD begins. The United States

Bauxite mining at Weipa in QLD

Naval Communications Station at NORTH WEST CAPE in WA, is founded.

1964 Elections are held for the Territory of Papua and New Guinea's first House of Assembly. Conscription for military service, based on election by ballot, is introduced.

1965 Australian combat troops are sent to participate in the VIETNAM WAR.

1966 After a continuous term of 17 years as Prime Minister, Sir Robert Menzies retires. A further liberalisation of policy with regard to non-European immigration spells the virtual end of the traditional policy of exclusion. Decimal currency is introduced.
Conscripted National Servicemen are included in troops sent to Vietnam.

£1 notes are destroyed after the introduction of decimal currency

1967 Bushfires in TAS claim 62 lives. A proposal to give the Commonwealth power to legislate with regard to Aborigines is carried by referendum. The Prime Minister, Harold HOLT, disappears while swimming.

1969 The Commonwealth Conciliation and Arbitration Commission accepts the principle of equal pay for women. Commercial production of petroleum and natural gas from the BASS STRAIT field begins.

1970 Mass demonstrations are organised, on a much greater scale than previously, against Australian participation in the Vietnam War. Voting age lowered to 18 for WA and SA State elections.

Neville Bonner and his wife

1971 Neville BONNER is elected a Senator for QLD, becoming the first Aboriginal member of the Commonwealth Parliament. Australia joins the Organisation for Economic Co-operation and Development (OECD). Australian combat troops are withdrawn from Vietnam. Singapore, Malaysia, the UK, Australia and New Zealand sign a defence agreement. The ALP adopts an immigration policy which includes avoidance of discrimination on the grounds of race.

The search for Harold Holt

Canberra Times

Gough Whitlam

1972 The ALP wins a federal election after being out of office since 1949; Gough WHITLAM becomes Prime Minister. Conscription for military service is abandoned. Australia recognises the People's Republic of China and takes steps towards the establishment of diplomatic relations with it.

1973 The voting age for federal and remaining state elections is lowered to 18. Patrick WHITE is awarded the Nobel Prize for literature. The Queen opens the Sydney Opera House.

1974 The NT and ACT are granted Legislative Assemblies. A double dissolution of the Commonwealth Parliament is held and Labor is returned to office. The first joint sitting of the Senate and the House of Representatives, to resolve a deadlock between them, is held. The NT and the ACT are given the right to elect two Senators each. On Christmas Day, the greater part of Darwin is destroyed by a cyclone.

1975 The Commonwealth Conciliation and Arbitration Commission adopts a system of wage indexation. Papua New Guinea becomes independent. The Medibank health insurance scheme is introduced. A constitutional crisis occurs when the Senate defers its decision on two Appropriation Bills; the Governor-General, Sir John KERR, dismisses the Whitlam government and appoints Malcolm FRASER as caretaker Prime Minister. In the subsequent election the Liberal and National Country parties win a landslide victory.

1976 Sir Douglas NICHOLLS is appointed Governor of SA, being the first Aboriginal to fill a vice-regal position. The first report of the Fox enquiry into uranium mining and export is released. Japan and Australia sign a Treaty of Friendship and Co-operation.

1977 The worst rail disaster in Australia's history occurs in the Sydney suburb of Granville. The ALP adopts a policy of opposition to the mining and export of uranium except for the filling of existing contracts, but the federal Government announces a policy of exporting uranium under certain conditions. The second report of the Fox enquiry is released. The government parties win another convincing victory in a federal election. Whitlam resigns the leadership of the ALP and William HAYDEN is elected as his successor. Australian Democrats party is founded.

1978 Australia and Papua New Guinea reach agreement on the boundary between them. Large numbers of refugees from Vietnam (BOAT PEOPLE) reach Darwin. The NT is granted extensive powers of self-government.

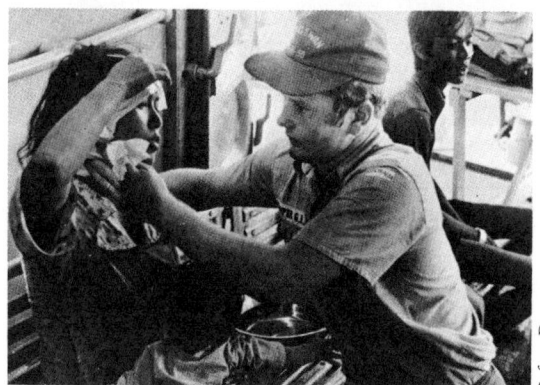

Defence Department

Vietnamese refugees receiving medical attention

1979 The problem of Vietnamese refugees intensifies. Australia, which by June has accepted about 32 000, agrees to take 14 000 more for the year 1979–80.

1980 The Australian government supports President Carter's call for a boycott of the Olympic Games in Moscow, because of the entry of Soviet troops in Afghanistan. Some individuals and contingents withdraw from the Australian team, but the majority compete at the Games.

1981 Australia is host to a general Commonwealth Heads of Government Meeting (CHOGM) in Melbourne.

1982 A Royal Australian Air Force Contingent is provided as part of the international supervisory force in the Sinai, following Israel's return of the last zone of that region to Egypt.

1983 Bushfires claim over 70 lives in VIC and SA; R.J. HAWKE replaces William HAYDEN as leader of the ALP, and after his party's victory in a general election, becomes Prime Minister. The Commonwealth legislates to prevent the building of a dam on the lower GORDON R., which would have flooded the FRANKLIN R., and wins a High Court appeal on the issue. The AUSTRALIAN BROAD- CASTING CORPORATION replaces the former Commission. By mid-year the total number of refugees from Indo-China accepted as settlers since April 1975 reaches over 78 000. Australia wins the America's Cup.

Bushfire victims

David Syme & Co Ltd

R.J. Hawke

Courtesy of A.I.S. Canberra

APPENDIX 2

GOVERNMENT OF AUSTRALIA

Courtesy of A.I.S. Canberra

House of Representatives in session

Australia was founded as a colony of Great Britain. As the population increased and spread over more and more of the country, Australia was divided into six separate and independent colonies. These colonies were united in 1901 as a federation of six States governed as a constitutional monarchy.

Listed below are the reigning monarchs from 1788 when the first colony was founded; Governors-General and Administrators who have represented the monarch since 1901; the number and duration of each federal Parliament; and a list of Prime Ministers and the political persuasion of each federal government since 1901.

For each of the six States, Governors, Lieutenant-Governors and Administrators, appointed by the British Parliament from the foundation of each colony to the granting of responsible government for each one, are listed. From the granting of responsible government the lists include the Governors representing the monarch, Premiers and the political persuasion of governments from the earliest date when it could be clearly determined.

Monarchs from 1788

George III	1760–1820
George IV	1820–30
William IV	1830–37
Victoria	1837–1901
Edward VII	1901–10
George V	1910–36
Edward VIII	1936
George VI	1936–52
Elizabeth II	1952–

FEDERAL

Governors-General and Administrators

Earl of Hopetoun	1 Jan 1901–	9 Jan 1903
Lord Tennyson (acting Governor-General)	17 Jul 1902–	9 Jan 1903
Lord Tennyson	9 Jan 1903–	21 Jan 1904
Lord Northcote	21 Jan 1904–	9 Sep 1908
Earl of Dudley	9 Sep 1908–	31 Jul 1911
Lord Chelmsford (Administrator)	21 Dec 1909–	27 Jan 1910
Lord Denman	31 Jul 1911–	18 May 1914
Sir Ronald C. Munro-Ferguson	18 May 1914–	6 Oct 1920
Lord Forster of Lepe	6 Oct 1920–	8 Oct 1925
Lord Stonehaven	8 Oct 1925–	22 Jan 1931
Lord Somers (Administrator)	3 Oct 1930–	22 Jan 1931
Sir Issac Alfred ISAACS	22 Jan 1931–	23 Jan 1936
Lord Gowrie	23 Jan 1936–	30 Jan 1945
Lord Huntingfield (Administrator)	29 Mar 1938–	24 Sep 1938

Major-General Sir Winston Dugan (Administrator)	5 Sep 1944– 30 Jan 1945
H.R.H. Duke of Gloucester	30 Jan 1945–11 Mar 1947
Major-General Sir Winston Dugan (Administrator)	19 Jan 1947–11 Mar 1947
Sir William John McKELL	11 Mar 1947– 8 May 1953
General Sir John Northcott (Administrator)	19 Jul 1951– 14 Dec 1951
Field Marshall Sir William J. SLIM	8 May 1953– 2 Feb 1960
General Sir John Northcott (Administrator)	30 Jul 1956– 22 Oct 1956
General Sir Reginald A. Dallas Brooks (Administrator)	8 Jan 1959– 16 Jan 1959
Viscount Dunrossil	2 Feb 1960– 3 Feb 1961
General Sir Reginald A. Dallas Brooks (Administrator)	4 Feb 1961– 3 Aug 1961
Viscount De L'Isle	3 Aug 1961– 22 Sep 1965
General Sir Reginald A. Dallas Brooks (Administrator)	5 Jun 1962– 3 Oct 1962 21 Nov 1962– 18 Dec 1962
Lieutenant-General Sir Eric Woodward (Administrator)	16 Jun 1964– 30 Aug 1964
Colonel Sir Henry Abel Smith (Administrator)	7 May 1965– 22 Sep 1965
Lord CASEY	22 Sep 1965– 30 Apr 1969
Lieutenant-General Sir Edric Bastyan (Administrator)	24 Apr 1967– 1 Jun 1967
Sir Paul HASLUCK	30 Apr 1969– 10 Jul 1974
Major-General Sir Rohan Delacombe (Administrator)	11 Feb 1971– 18 Feb 1971 12 Oct 1971– 19 Oct 1971 29 Jun 1972– 9 Aug 1972
Sir John KERR	11 Jun 1974– 7 Dec 1977
Sir Zelman COWEN	8 Dec 1977– 29 Jul 1982
Sir Ninian STEPHEN	29 Jul 1982–

Sir Isaac Isaacs

Courtesy of A.I.S. Canberra

Sir William McKell

Courtesy of A.I.S. Canberra

Sir Ninian Stephen

Courtesy of A.I.S. Canberra

Federal Parliaments of Australia

Listed below are the federal Parliaments since federation in 1901.

Parliament No:	Duration of Parliament Opening	Dissolution
First	9 May 1901	23 Nov 1903
Second	2 Mar 1904	5 Nov 1906
Third	20 Feb 1907	19 Feb 1910
Fourth	1 Jul 1910	23 Apr 1913
Fifth	9 Jul 1913	30 Jul 1914
Sixth	8 Oct 1914	26 Mar 1917
Seventh	14 Jun 1917	3 Nov 1919
Eighth	26 Feb 1920	6 Nov 1922
Ninth	28 Feb 1923	3 Oct 1925
Tenth	13 Jan 1926	9 Oct 1928
Eleventh	6 Feb 1929	16 Sep 1929
Twelfth	20 Nov 1929	27 Nov 1931
Thirteenth	17 Feb 1932	7 Aug 1934
Fourteenth	23 Oct 1934	21 Sep 1937
Fifteenth	30 Nov 1937	27 Aug 1940
Sixteenth	20 Nov 1940	7 Jul 1943
Seventeenth	23 Sep 1943	16 Aug 1946
Eighteenth	6 Nov 1946	31 Oct 1949
Nineteenth	22 Feb 1950	19 Mar 1951
Twentieth	12 Jun 1951	21 Apr 1954
Twenty-first	4 Aug 1954	4 Nov 1955
Twenty-second	15 Feb 1956	14 Oct 1958
Twenty-third	17 Feb 1959	2 Nov 1961
Twenty-fourth	20 Feb 1962	1 Nov 1963
Twenty-fifth	25 Feb 1964	31 Oct 1966
Twenty-sixth	21 Feb 1967	29 Sep 1969
Twenty-seventh	25 Nov 1969	2 Nov 1972
Twenty-eighth	27 Feb 1973	11 Apr 1974
Twenty-ninth	9 Jul 1974	11 Nov 1975
Thirtieth	17 Feb 1976	10 Nov 1977
Thirty-first	21 Feb 1978	19 Sep 1980
Thirty-second	25 Nov 1980	3 Feb 1983
Thirty-third	21 Apr 1983	

Federal government of Australia

Listed below are the Prime Ministers with date of appointment and the political persuasion of the government since 1901.

Prime Ministers	Date of appointment	Political persuasion of government
Sir Edmund BARTON	1 Jan 1901	Protectionist
Alfred DEAKIN	24 Sep 1903	Protectionist
John Christian WATSON	27 Apr 1904	Labor
Sir George Houston REID	18 Aug 1904	Free Trade/ Protectionist Coalition
Alfred Deakin	5 Jul 1905	Protectionist
Andrew FISHER	13 Nov 1908	Labor
Alfred Deakin	2 Jun 1909	Fusion of Free Traders, Protectionists and Tariff Reformers

Sir Edmund Barton

National Library of Australia

Alfred Deakin

National Library of Australia

Sir Earle Page

Australian News and Information Bureau

Andrew Fisher	29 Apr 1910	Labor
Sir Joseph COOK	24 Jun 1913	Liberal
Andrew Fisher	17 Sep 1914	Labor
William Morris HUGHES	27 Oct 1915	Labor
William Morris Hughes	14 Nov 1916	National Labour
William Morris Hughes	17 Feb 1917	Nationalist
Stanley Melbourne BRUCE	9 Feb 1923	Nationalist/ Country Coalition
James Henry SCULLIN	22 Oct 1929	Labor
Joseph Aloysius LYONS	6 Jan 1932	United Australia
Joseph Aloysius Lyons	7 Nov 1938	United Australia/ Country Coalition
Sir Earle PAGE	7 Apr 1939	Country/United Australia Coalition
Robert Gordon MENZIES	26 Apr 1939	United Australia
Robert Gordon Menzies	14 Mar 1940	United Australia/ Country Coalition
Arthur William FADDEN	29 Aug 1941	Country/United Australia Coalition
John Joseph CURTIN	7 Oct 1941	Labor
Francis Michael FORDE	6 Jul 1945	Labor
Joseph Benedict CHIFLEY	13 Jul 1945	Labor
Sir Robert Gordon Menzies	19 Dec 1949	Liberal/Country Coalition
Harold Edward HOLT	26 Jan 1966	Liberal/Country Coalition
Sir John McEWEN	19 Dec 1967	Liberal/Country Coalition
John Grey GORTON	10 Jan 1968	Liberal/Country Coalition
William McMAHON	10 Mar 1971	Liberal/Country Coalition
Edward Gough WHITLAM	5 Dec 1972	Labor
John Malcolm FRASER	11 Nov 1975	Caretaker Government
John Malcolm Fraser	22 Dec 1975	Liberal/Country (later National) Coalition
Robert James Lee HAWKE	11 Mar 1983	Labor

Courtesy of A.I.S. Canberra

Robert G. Menzies

John Grey Gorton

William McMahon

STATES

New South Wales

Part 1. A list of Governors, Lieutenant-Governors and Administrators from the foundation of the colony to the granting of responsible government 1788–1856.

Governors	Lieutenant-Governors and Administrators	Date of appointment
Captain Arthur PHILLIP		26 Jan 1788
	Major Francis GROSE	11 Dec 1792
	Captain William PATERSON	17 Dec 1794
Captain John HUNTER		11 Sep 1795
Captain Philip Gidley KING		28 Sep 1800
Captain William BLIGH		13 Aug 1806

During Governor Bligh's suspension the government was administered by the following members of the NEW SOUTH WALES CORPS:

Governors	Lieutenant-Governors and Administrators	Date of appointment
	Lieutenant-Colonel George JOHNSTON	26 Jan 1808
	Lieutenant-Colonel Joseph Foveaux	30 Jul 1808
	Colonel William Paterson	9 Jan 1809
Major-General Lachlan MACQUARIE		1 Jan 1810
Major-General Sir Thomas Makdougall BRISBANE		1 Dec 1821
	Colonel William Stewart	1 Dec 1825
Lieutenant-General Ralph DARLING		19 Dec 1825
	Colonel Patrick Lindesay	22 Oct 1831
Major-General Sir Richard BOURKE		3 Dec 1831
	Lieutenant-Colonel Kenneth Snodgrass	6 Dec 1837
Sir George GIPPS		24 Feb 1838
	Sir Maurice O'Connell	12 Jul 1846
Sir Charles Fitzroy		3 Aug 1846

Governor Macquarie

Part 2. A list of Governors from the granting of responsible government.

Governors	Date of appointment
Sir William Dension	20 Jan 1855
Sir John Young	16 May 1861
Earl of Belmore	8 Jan 1868
Sir Hercules Robinson	3 Jun 1872
Sir Augustus Loftus	4 Aug 1879
Lord Carrington	12 Dec 1885
Earl of Jersey	15 Jan 1891
Sir Robert Duff	29 May 1893
Viscount Hampden	21 Nov 1895
Earl Beauchamp	18 May 1899
Admiral Sir Harry Rawson	27 May 1902
Lord Chelmsford	28 May 1909
Sir Gerald Strickland	14 Mar 1913
Sir Walter Davidson	18 Feb 1918
Admiral Sir Dudley de Chair	28 Feb 1924
Air Vice-Marshal Sir Philip GAME	29 May 1930
Brigadier-General Sir Alexander Hore-Ruthven	21 Feb 1935
Admiral Sir David Anderson	6 Aug 1936
Lord Wakehurst	8 Apr 1937
General Sir John Northcott	1 Aug 1946
Lieutenant-General Sir Eric Woodward	1 Aug 1957
Sir Arthur Roden Cutler	20 Jan 1966
Air Marshal Sir James Rowland	20 Jan 1981

Courtesy of A.I.S. Canberra

Sir Roden Cutler

NSW Dept of Tourism

(left) Parliament House, Sydney. The central structure is one of the buildings of Governor Macquarie's 'Rum Hospital'

Part 3. A list of Premiers since responsible government with date of appointment and the political persuasion of the government since 1890.

Premiers	Date of appointment	Political persuasion
S.A. Donaldson	6 Jun 1856	—
C. COWPER	26 Aug 1856	—
H.W. Parker	3 Oct 1856	—
C. Cowper	7 Sep 1857	—
W. Forster	27 Oct 1859	—
J. ROBERTSON	9 Mar 1860	—
C. Cowper	10 Jan 1861	—
J. MARTIN	16 Oct 1863	—
C. Cowper	3 Feb 1865	—
J. Martin	22 Jan 1866	—
J. Robertson	27 Oct 1868	—
C. Cowper	13 Jan 1870	—
Sir James Martin	16 Dec 1870	—
H. PARKES	14 May 1872	—
J. Robertson	9 Feb 1875	—
H. Parkes	22 Mar 1877	—
Sir John Robertson	17 Aug 1877	—
J.S. Farnell	18 Dec 1877	—
Sir Henry Parkes	21 Dec 1878	—
A. Stuart	5 Jan 1883	—
G.R. Dibbs	7 Oct 1885	—
Sir John Robertson	22 Dec 1885	—
Sir Patrick Jennings	26 Feb 1886	—
Sir Henry Parkes	20 Jan 1887	—
G.R. Dibbs	17 Jan 1889	—
Sir Henry Parkes	8 Mar 1889	Free Trade
Sir George Dibbs	23 Oct 1891	Protectionist
G.H. REID	3 Aug 1894	Free Trade
Sir William LYNE	14 Sep 1899	Protectionist
J. See	28 Mar 1901	Protectionist
T. Waddell	15 Jun 1904	Protectionist
J.H. Carruthers	30 Aug 1904	Liberal-Reform
C.G. Wade	2 Oct 1907	Liberal-Reform

J.S.T. McGowen	21 Oct 1910	Labor
W.A. HOLMAN	30 Jun 1913	Labor
W.A. Holman	15 Nov 1916	Nationalist
J. Storey	13 Apr 1920	Labor
J. Dooley	10 Oct 1921	Labor
Sir George Fuller	20 Dec 1921	Nationalist/ Progressive Coalition
J. Dooley	20 Dec 1921	Labor
Sir George Fuller	13 Apr 1922	Nationalist/ Progressive Coalition
J.T. LANG	17 Jun 1925	Labor
T.R. Bavin	18 Oct 1927	Nationalist/ Country Coalition
J.T. Lang	4 Nov 1930	Labor
B.S.B. Stevens	16 May 1932	United Australia/ Country Coalition
A. Mair	5 Aug 1939	United Australia/ Country Coalition
W.J. McKELL	16 May 1941	Labor
J. McGirr	6 Feb 1947	Labor
J.J. CAHILL	3 Apr 1952	Labor
R.J. Heffron	28 Oct 1959	Labor
J.B. Renshaw	30 Apr 1964	Labor
Sir Robert ASKIN	13 May 1965	Liberal/Country Coalition
T.L. Lewis	3 Jan 1975	Liberal/Country Coalition
Sir Eric Willis	23 Jan 1976	Liberal/Country Coalition
N.K. WRAN	14 May 1976	Labor

Sir John Robertson

NSW Govt Printer

Victoria

Part 1. A list of Governors, Lieutenant-Governors and Administrators from the foundation of the colony to the granting of responsible government 1839–1855.

Governors	Lieutenant-Governors and Administrators	Date of appointment
	Charles Joseph LA TROBE	30 Sep 1839
	John Vesey Fitzgerald	6 May 1854
	Captain Sir Charles HOTHAM	22 Jun 1854

Part 2. A list of Governors from the granting of responsible government.

Governors	Date of appointment
Captain Sir Charles Hotham	22 May 1855
Sir Henry Barkly	26 Dec 1856
Sir Charles Darling	11 Sept 1863
Sir John Manners-Sutton	15 Aug 1866
Sir George Ferguson Bowen	30 Jul 1873
Marquess of Normanby	29 Apr 1879
Sir Henry Loch	15 Jul 1884
Earl of Hopetoun	28 Nov 1889
Lord Brassey	25 Oct 1895
Sir George Clarke	10 Dec 1901
Major-General Sir Reginald Talbot	25 Apr 1904
Sir Thomas Carmichael	27 Jul 1908
Sir John Fuller	24 May 1911
Sir Arthur Stanley	23 Feb 1914
Earl of Stradbroke	24 Feb 1921
Lord Somers	28 Jun 1926
Lord Huntingfield	14 May 1934
Major-General Sir Winston Dugan	17 Jul 1939
General Sir Reginald Dallas Brooks	18 Oct 1949
Major-General Sir Rohan Delacombe	8 May 1963
Sir Henry Winneke	3 Jun 1974
Rear Admiral Sir Brian Stewart Murray	1 Mar 1982

Part 3. A list of Premiers since responsible government with dates of appointment and the political persuasion of the government since 1886.

Premiers	Date of appointment	Political persuasion
W.C. Haines	28 Nov 1855	—
J. O'SHANASSY	11 Mar 1857	—
W.C. Haines	29 Apr 1857	—
J. O'Shanassy	10 Mar 1858	—
W. Nicholson	27 Oct 1859	—
R. Heales	26 Nov 1860	—
J. O'Shanassy	14 Nov 1861	—
J. McCULLOCH	27 Jun 1863	—
S. Sladen	6 May 1868	—
J. McCulloch	11 Jul 1868	—
J.A. MacPherson	20 Sep 1869	—
J. McCulloch	9 Apr 1870	—

Governor Hotham

Mansell Collection

Sir Henry Winneke

Courtesy of A.I.S. Canberra

Sir Brian Murray

Courtesy of A.I.S. Canberra

C.G. DUFFY	19 Jun 1871	—
J.G. Francis	10 Jun 1872	—
G.B. Kerferd	31 Jul 1874	—
G. BERRY	7 Aug 1875	—
Sir James McCulloch	20 Oct 1875	—
G. Berry	21 May 1877	—
J. Service	5 May 1880	—
G. Berry	3 Aug 1880	—
B. O'Loghlen	9 Jul 1881	—
J. Service	8 Mar 1883	—
D. Gillies	18 Feb 1886	Conservative/ Liberal Coalition
J. Munro	5 Nov 1890	National/Liberal Coalition
W. Shiels	16 Feb 1892	Liberal
J.B. Patterson	23 Jan 1893	Conservative
G. Turner	27 Sept 1894	Liberal
A. McLean	5 Dec 1899	Liberal
Sir George Turner	19 Nov 1900	Liberal
A.J. Peacock	12 Feb 1901	Liberal
W.H. Irvine	10 Jun 1902	Reform
T. Bent	16 Feb 1904	Reform
J. Murray	8 Jan 1909	Liberal
W.A. Watt	18 May 1912	Liberal
G.A. Elmslie	9 Dec 1913	Labor
W.A. Watt	22 Dec 1913	Liberal
Sir Alexander Peacock	18 Jun 1914	Liberal
J. Bowser	29 Nov 1917	National
H.S.W. Lawson	21 Mar 1918	National
H.S.W. Lawson	7 Sep 1923	National/ Country Coalition
H.S.W. Lawson	19 Mar 1924	National
Sir Alexander Peacock	28 Apr 1924	National
G.M. Prendergast	18 Jul 1924	Labor
J. Allan	18 Nov 1924	Country/ National Coalition
E.J. Hogan	20 May 1927	Labor
Sir William McPherson	22 Nov 1928	National
E.J. Hogan	12 Dec 1929	Labor
Sir Stanley Argyle	19 May 1932	United Australia/ Country Coalition
A.A. DUNSTAN	2 Apr 1935	Country
J. Cain	14 Sep 1943	Labor
A.A. Dunstan	18 Sep 1943	Country/United Australia Coalition
I. Macfarlan	2 Oct 1945	Liberal
J. Cain	21 Nov 1945	Labor
T.T. Hollway	20 Nov 1947	Liberal/Country Coalition
T.T. Hollway	3 Dec 1948	Liberal
J.G.B. McDonald	27 Jun 1950	Country
T.T. Hollway	28 Oct 1952	Electoral Reform
J.G.B. McDonald	31 Oct 1952	Country
J. Cain	17 Dec 1952	Labor
Sir Henry BOLTE	7 Jun 1955	Liberal and Country
R.J. Hamer	23 Aug 1972	Liberal
L.H.S. Thompson	5 Jun 1981	Liberal
J. CAIN	8 Apr 1982	Labor

The opening of a new parliamentary session

Mr John Cain

QLD State Public Relations Bureau

Queensland's Parliament House

Queensland

Part 1. A list of Governors from the date QLD was separated from NSW and granted responsible government as a separate colony.

Governors	Date of appointment
Sir George Ferguson BOWEN	10 Dec 1859
Colonel Samuel Wemsley Blackall	14 Aug 1868
Marquess of Normanby	12 Aug 1871
William Wellington Cairns	23 Jan 1875
Sir Arthur Edward Kennedy	20 Jul 1877
Sir Anthony Musgrave	6 Nov 1883
General Sir Henry Wylie Norman	1 May 1889
Lord Lamington	9 Apr 1896
Major-General Sir Herbert Chermside	24 Mar 1902
Lord Chelmsford	20 Nov 1905
Sir William Macgregor	2 Dec 1909
Major Sir Hamilton Goold-Adams	15 Mar 1915
Lieutenant-Colonel Sir Matthew Nathan	3 Dec 1920
Lieutenant-General Sir Thomas Goodwin	13 Jun 1927
Colonel Sir Leslie Orme Wilson	13 Jun 1932
Lieutenant-General Sir John Lavarack	1 Oct 1946
Colonel Sir Henry Abel Smith	18 Mar 1958
Sir Alan Mansfield	21 Mar 1966
Air Marshal Sir Colin Hannah	21 Mar 1972
Commodore Sir James Ramsay	22 Apr 1977

Part 2. A list of the Premiers since responsible government with date of appointment and the political persuasion of the government since 1911.

Premiers	Date of appointment	Political persuasion
R.G.W. Herbert	10 Dec 1859	—
A. Macalister	1 Feb 1866	—

Courtesy of A.I.S. Canberra

Sir Alan James Mansfield

Courtesy of A.I.S. Canberra

Sir James Ramsay

R.G.W. Herbert	20 Jul 1866	—
A. Macalister	7 Aug 1866	—
R.R. Mackenzie	15 Aug 1867	—
C. Lilley	25 Nov 1868	—
A.H. Palmer	3 May 1870	—
A. Macalister	8 Jan 1874	—
G. Thorn	5 Jun 1876	—
J. Douglas	8 Mar 1877	—
T. McILWRAITH	21 Jan 1879	—
S.W. GRIFFITH	13 Nov 1883	—
Sir Thomas McIlwraith	13 Jun 1888	—
B.D. Morehead	30 Nov 1888	—
Sir Samuel Griffith	12 Aug 1890	—
Sir Thomas McIlwraith	27 Mar 1893	—
H.M. Nelson	27 Oct 1893	—
T.J. Byrnes	13 Apr 1898	—
J.R. Dickson	1 Oct 1898	—
A. Dawson	1 Dec 1899	Labor
R. Philp	7 Dec 1899	—
A. Morgan	17 Sep 1903	—
W. Kidston	19 Jan 1906	—
R. Philp	19 Nov 1907	—
W. Kidston	18 Feb 1908	—
D.F. Denham	7 Feb 1911	Liberal
T.J. Ryan	1 Jun 1915	Labor
E.G. THEODORE	22 Oct 1919	Labor

Sydney Morning Herald

E.G. Theodore

W.N. Gillies	26 Feb 1925	Labor
W. McCormack	22 Oct 1925	Labor
A.E. Moore	21 May 1929	Country/ National/ Progressive Coalition
W. Forgan Smith	17 Jun 1932	Labor
F.A. Cooper	16 Sep 1942	Labor
E.M. Hanlon	7 Mar 1946	Labor
V.C. GAIR	17 Jan 1952	Labor
G.F.R. Nicklin	12 Aug 1957	Country/Liberal Coalition

J.C.A. Pizzey	17 Jan 1968	Country/Liberal Coalition
G.W.W. Chalk	1 Aug 1968	Country/Liberal Coalition
J. BJELKE- PETERSEN	8 Aug 1968	Country (later changed to National)/ Liberal Coalition, later National

South Australia

Part 1. A list of Governors and Administrators from the foundation of the colony to the granting of responsible government 1836-56. Until 1901, when the holder of the office was known as simply 'Governor', different titles were given to the holders of this office. Each of the first three Governors was styled 'Governor and Commander-in-Chief'; the following two holding the same office were called 'Lieutenant-Governor' and the title was later changed to 'Captain-General' and 'Governor-in-Chief', then back to 'Governor and Commander-in-Chief'. To avoid confusion, the first seven Governors of SA are listed under that title.

Governors	Administrators	Date of appointment
Captain John HINDMARSH		28 Dec 1836
	George Milner Stephen	16 Jul 1838
Lieutenant- Colonel George GAWLER		17 Oct 1838
Captain George GREY		15 May 1841

Alexander Turnbull Library

Sir George Edward Grey

Lieutenant-
Colonel
Frederick Holt
Robe   25 Oct 1845
Sir Henry
Edward Fox
Young   2 Aug 1848
Boyle Travers
Finniss   20 Dec 1854

Part 2. A list of Governors from the granting of responsible government.

Governors	Date of appointment
Sir Richard Graves MacDonnell	8 Jun 1855
Sir Dominick Daly	4 Mar 1862
Sir James Fergusson	16 Feb 1869
Sir Anthony Musgrave	9 Jun 1873
Sir William Drummond	2 Oct 1877
Sir William Robinson	19 Feb 1883
Earl of Kintore	11 Apr 1889
Sir Thomas Buxton	29 Oct 1895
Lord Tennyson	10 Apr 1899
Sir George Le Hunte	1 Jul 1903
Admiral Sir Day Bosanquet	29 Mar 1909
Lieutenant-Colonel Sir Henry Gawley	18 Apr 1914
Lieutenant-Colonel Sir William Weigall	9 Jun 1920
Lieutenant-General Sir George Bridges	4 Dec 1922
Lord Gowrie	14 May 1928
Major-General Sir Winston Dugan	28 Jul 1934
Sir Charles Barclay-Harvey	12 Aug 1939
Lieutenant-General Sir Charles Norrie	19 Dec 1944
Air Vice-Marshall Sir Robert George	23 Feb 1953
Lieutenant-General Sir Edric Bastyan	5 Apr 1961
Major-General Sir James Harrison	4 Dec 1968
Sir Mark OLIPHANT	1 Dec 1971
Sir Douglas NICHOLLS	1 Dec 1976
Rev. Sir Keith Seaman	1 Sep 1977
Lieutenant-General Sir Donald Dunstan	23 Apr 1982

Part 3. A list of the Premiers since responsible government with date of appointment and the political persuasion of the government since 1893.

Premiers	Date of appointment	Political persuasion
B.T. Finniss	24 Oct 1856	—
J. Baker	21 Aug 1857	—
R.R. TORRENS	1 Sep 1857	—
R.D. Hanson	30 Sep 1857	—
T. Reynolds	9 May 1860	—
G.M. Waterhouse	8 Oct 1861	—
F.S. Dutton	4 Jul 1863	—
H. Ayers	15 Jul 1863	—
A. Blyth	4 Aug 1864	—
F.S. Dutton	22 Mar 1865	—
H. Ayers	20 Sep 1865	—
J. Hart	23 Oct 1865	—
J.P. Boucaut	28 Mar 1866	—
H. Ayers	3 May 1867	—
J. Hart	24 Sep 1868	—
H. Ayers	13 Oct 1868	—
H.B.T. Strangways	3 Nov 1868	—
J. Hart	30 May 1870	—
A. Blyth	10 Nov 1871	—

Pastor Sir Douglas Nicholls

Courtesy of A.I.S. Canberra

Lt General Sir Donald Dunstan

Courtesy of A.I.S. Canberra

Sir H. Ayers	22 Jan 1972	—
A. Blyth	22 Jul 1873	—
J.P. Boucaut	3 Jun 1875	—
J. Colton	6 Jun 1876	—
J.P. Boucaut	26 Oct 1877	—
W. Morgan	27 Sep 1878	—
J.C. Bray	24 Jun 1881	—
J. Colton	16 Jun 1884	—
J.W. Downer	16 Jun 1885	—
T. Playford	11 Jun 1887	—
J.A. Cockburn	27 Jun 1889	
T. Playford	19 Aug 1890	—
F.W. Holder	21 Jun 1892	—
Sir John Downer	15 Oct 1892	—
C.C. KINGSTON	16 Jun 1893	Liberal
V.L. Solomon	1 Dec 1899	Conservative
F.W. Holder	8 Dec 1899	Liberal
J.G. Jenkins	15 May 1901	Liberal; Liberal/ Conservative Coalition
R. Butler	1 Mar 1905	Conservative
T. Price	26 Jul 1905	Labor/Liberal Coalition
A.H. Peake	5 Jun 1909	Liberal
J. Verran	3 Jun 1910	Labor
A.H. Peake	17 Feb 1912	Liberal
C. Vaughan	3 Apr 1915	Labor
A.H. Peake	14 Jul 1917	Liberal until 27 Aug 1917 thereafter Liberal/ National Coalition
H.N. Barwell	8 Apr 1920	Liberal
J. Gunn	16 Apr 1924	Labor
L.L. Hill	28 Aug 1926	Labor
R.L. Butler	8 Apr 1927	Liberal/ Country Coalition
L.L. Hill	17 Apr 1930	Labor
R.S. Richards	13 Feb 1933	Labor
R.L. Butler	18 Apr 1933	Liberal Country League
Sir Thomas PLAYFORD	5 Nov 1938	Liberal Country League
F.H. Walsh	10 Mar 1965	Labor
D.A. DUNSTAN	1 Jun 1967	Labor
R.S. Hall	17 Apr 1968	Liberal Country League
D.A. Dunstan	2 Jun 1970	Labor
J.D. Corcoran	15 Feb 1979	Labor
D. Tonkin	18 Sep 1979	Liberal
J.C. BANNON	10 Nov 1982	Labor

Premier's Dept SA

David Oliver Tonkin

Courtesy of A.I.S. Canberra

John Bannon

Western Australia

Part 1. A list of Governors, Lieutenant-Governors and Administrators from the foundation of the colony to the granting of responsible government 1828–90.

Governors	Lieutenant-Governors and Administrators	Date of appointment
	Captain James STIRLING	30 Dec 1828
Captain James Stirling		6 Feb 1832
	Captain Frederick Chidley Irwin	12 Aug 1832
	Captain Richard Daniell	14 Sep 1833
	Captain Picton Beete	11 May 1834
	Captain Richard Daniell	24 May 1834
Captain James Stirling		19 Aug 1834
John Hutt		3 Jan 1839
Lieutenant-Colonel Andrew Clarke		27 Jan 1846
Lieutenant-Colonel Frederick Irwin		12 Feb 1847
Captain Charles Fitzgerald		12 Aug 1848
Arthur Edward Kennedy		23 Jul 1855
	Lieutenant-Colonel John Bruce	20 Feb 1862
John Stephen Hampton		28 Feb 1862
	Lieutenant-Colonel John Bruce	2 Nov 1868
Frederick Weld		30 Sep 1869
	Lieutenant-Colonel E.D. Harvest	4 Jan 1875
William Cleaver Francis Robinson		11 Jan 1875
	Lieutenant-Colonel E.D. Harvest	7 Sep 1877
	Major-General Sir Harry St. George Ord	12 Nov 1877
Major-General Sir Harry St. George Ord		30 Jan 1878
Sir William Cleaver Francis Robinson		10 Apr 1880
	Henry Thomas Wrenfordsley	14 Feb 1883
Sir Frederick Napier Broome		2 Jun 1883

Part 2. A list of Governors from the granting of responsible government.

Governors	Date of appointment
Sir William Cleaver Francis Robinson	20 Oct 1890
Lieutenant-Colonel Sir Gerard Smith	23 Dec 1895
Captain Sir Arthur Lawley	1 May 1901
Admiral Sir Frederick George Denham Bedford	24 Mar 1903
Sir Gerald Strickland	31 May 1909
Major-General Sir Harry Barron	17 Mar 1913
Sir William Grey Ellison-Macartney	9 Apr 1917
Sir Francis Alexander Newdigate Newdegate	9 April 1920
Colonel Sir William Robert Campion	28 Oct 1924
Sir James Mitchell	5 Oct 1948
Lieutenant-General Sir Charles Henry Gairdner	6 Nov 1951
Major-General Sir Douglas Anthony Kendrew	25 Oct 1963
Air Commodore Hughie Idwal Edwards	7 Jan 1974
Air Chief Marshall Sir Wallace Kyle	24 Nov 1975

Courtesy of A.I.S. Canberra

Sir Wallace Kyle

Rear Admiral Sir Richard Trowbridge	25 Nov 1980

(March 1984, Professor Gordon Stanley Reid was Governor Designate and was expected to assume office in July 1984.

Part 3. A list of Premiers since responsible government with date of appointment and the political persuasion of the government since 1890.

Premiers	Date of appointment	Political persuasion
J. FORREST	29 Dec 1890	Protectionist or Conservative
G. Throssell	15 Feb 1901	Conservative
G. Leake	25 May 1901	Liberal
A.E. Morgans	21 Nov 1901	Conservative
G. Leake	23 Dec 1901	Liberal
W.H. James	1 Jul 1902	Liberal
H. Daglish	10 Aug 1904	Labor
C.H. Rason	25 Aug 1905	Liberal
N.J. Moore	7 May 1906	Liberal
F. Wilson	16 Sep 1910	Liberal
J. Scaddan	7 Oct 1911	Labor
F. Wilson	27 Jul 1916	Liberal
H.B. Lefroy	28 Jun 1917	National Coalition
H.P. Colebatch	17 Apr 1919	National Coalition
J. Mitchell	17 May 1919	National Coalition
P. Collier	16 Apr 1924	Labor
Sir James Mitchell	24 Apr 1930	National/ Country Coalition
P. Collier	24 Apr 1933	Labor
J.C. Willcock	20 Aug 1936	Labor
F.J.S. Wise	31 Jul 1945	Labor
D.R. McLarty	1 Apr 1947	Liberal/ Country Coalition
A.R.G. Hawke	23 Feb 1953	Labor
D. BRAND	2 Apr 1959	Liberal/ Country Coalition
J.T. Tonkin	3 Mar 1971	Labor
Sir Charles COURT	8 Apr 1974	Liberal/ Country Coalition
R.J. O'CONNOR	25 Jan 1982	Liberal/ National Country Coalition
B. BURKE	25 Feb 1983	Labor

Tasmania

Part 1. A list of Lieutenant-Governors and Administrators from the foundation of the colony to the granting of responsible government 1804–56.

Lieutenant-Governors	Administrators	Date of appointment
Colonel David COLLINS		16 Feb 1804
	Lieutenant Edward Lord and Captain John Murray	24 Mar 1810
	Major Andrew Geils	20 Feb 1812
Colonel Thomas DAVEY		4 Feb 1813

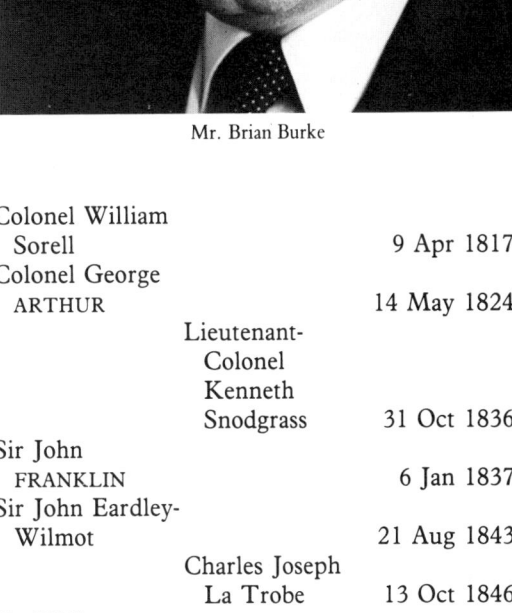

Mr. Brian Burke

Courtesy of A.I.S. Canberra

Colonel William Sorell		9 Apr 1817
Colonel George ARTHUR		14 May 1824
	Lieutenant-Colonel Kenneth Snodgrass	31 Oct 1836
Sir John FRANKLIN		6 Jan 1837
Sir John Eardley-Wilmot		21 Aug 1843
	Charles Joseph La Trobe	13 Oct 1846
Sir William Thomas Denison		26 Jan 1847

Part 2. A list of Governors from the granting of responsible government.

Governors	Date of appointment
Sir Henry Young	8 Jan 1855
Colonel Thomas Browne	16 Jun 1862
Charles Du Cane	15 Jan 1869
Frederick Aloysius Weld	13 Jan 1875
Major Sir George Strahan	7 Dec 1881
Sir Robert Hamilton	11 Mar 1887
Viscount Gormanston	8 Aug 1893
Captain Sir Arthur Havelock	8 Nov 1901
Sir Gerald Strickland	28 Oct 1904
Major-General Sir Harry Barron	29 Sep 1909
Sir William Grey Ellison-Macartney	4 Jun 1913
Sir Francis Alexander Newdigate Newdegate	6 Jul 1917
Sir William Allardyce	16 Apr 1920

Captain Sir James O'Grady	23 Dec 1924
Sir Ernest Clark	4 Aug 1933
Sir Hugh Binney	24 Dec 1945
Sir Ronald Cross	23 Aug 1951
Lord Rowallan	21 Oct 1959
Lieutenant-General Sir Charles Gairdner	24 Sep 1963
Lieutenant-General Sir Edric Bastyan	2 Dec 1968
Sir Stanley Burbury	5 Dec 1973
Sir James Plimsoll	1 Oct 1982

Part 3. A list of Premiers since responsible government with date of appointment and the political persuasion of the government since 1887.

Premiers	*Date of appointment*	*Political persuasion*
W.T.N. Champ	1 Nov 1856	—
T.G. Gregson	26 Feb 1857	—
W.P. Weston	25 Apr 1857	—
F. Smith	12 May 1857	—
W.P. Weston	1 Nov 1860	—
T.D. Chapman	2 Aug 1861	—
J. Whyte	20 Jan 1863	—
R. Dry	24 Nov 1866	—
J.M. Wilson	4 Aug 1869	—
F.M. Innes	4 Nov 1872	—
A. Kennerley	4 Aug 1873	—
T. Reibey	20 Jul 1876	—
P.O. Fysh	9 Aug 1877	—
W.R. Giblin	5 Mar 1878	—
W.L. Crowther	20 Dec 1878	—
W.R. Giblin	30 Oct 1879	—
A. Douglas	15 Aug 1884	—
J.W. Agnew	8 Mar 1886	—
P.O. Fysh	30 Mar 1887	Liberal
H. Dobson	17 Aug 1892	Conservative
E. Braddon	14 Apr 1894	Liberal
N.E. Lewis	12 Oct 1899	Conservative
W.B. Propsting	9 Apr 1903	Liberal Democrat
J.W. Evans	12 Jul 1904	Liberal
N.E. Lewis	19 Jun 1909	Liberal Fusion
J. Earle	20 Oct 1909	Labor
N.E. Lewis	27 Oct 1909	Liberal
A.E. Solomon	14 Jun 1912	Liberal
J. Earle	6 Apr 1914	Labor
W. Lee	15 Apr 1916	Liberal; Nationalist
J.B. Hayes	12 Aug 1922	Nationalist Country
W. Lee	14 Aug 1923	Nationalist
J.A. LYONS	25 Oct 1923	Labor
J.C. McPhee	15 Jun 1928	Nationalist
W. Lee	15 Mar 1934	Nationalist
A.G. Ogilvie	22 Jun 1934	Labor
E. Dwyer-Gray	11 Jun 1939	Labor
R. Cosgrove	18 Dec 1939	Labor
E. Brooker	19 Dec 1947	Labor
R. Cosgrove	25 Feb 1948	Labor
E.E. Reece	26 Aug 1958	Labor
W.A. Bethune	26 May 1969	Liberal/Centre

Sir Stanley Burbury

Courtesy of A.I.S. Canberra

Sir James Plimsoll

Courtesy of A.I.S. Canberra

Mr Robin Gray

Courtesy of A.I.S. Canberra

E.E. Reece	3 May 1972	Labor
W.A. Neilson	31 Mar 1975	Labor
D. LOWE	1 Dec 1977	Labor
H.N. Holgate	11 Nov 1981	Labor
R.T. GRAY	26 May 1982	Liberal

Northern Territory*

Part 1. A list of Government Residents from 1863, when the Northern Territory was annexed to the Colony of South Australia until 1 January, 1911.

Government Resident at Escape Cliffs	Date of appointment	Took office
B.T. Finniss	3 Mar 1864	
J.T. Manton (Acting)	4 Nov 1865	

Government Resident at Palmerston (renamed Darwin 1911)

G.W. Goyder	Nov 1868	5 Feb 1869
Dr J.S. Millner (Acting)	Dec 1869	22 Jan 1870
Capt. W. Bloomfield Douglas	22 Mar 1870	24 Jun 1870
Dr J.S. Millner (Acting)	10 Jun 1873	10 Jun 1873
G.B. Scott	17 Sep 1873	1 Nov 1873
E.W. Price	1 Jul 1876	1 Jul 1876
G.R. McMinn (Acting)	8 Mar 1883	8 Mar 1883
J. Langdon Parsons	19 Mar 1884	9 May 1884
J.G. Knight	15 Feb 1890	16 Jul 1890
Judge C.J. Dashwood		27 Apr 1892
Judge C.E. Herbert	1 Apr 1905	1 Apr 1905
Judge S.J. Mitchell	1 Apr 1910	1 Apr 1910

Part 2. A list of Administrators from 1 January, 1911 when the Northern Territory and adjacent islands were transferred to the control of the Federal Government.

Government Resident at Darwin	Date of appointment	Took office
Judge S.J. Mitchell (Acting)		1 Jan 1911
Dr J.A. Gilruth	13 Mar 1912	16 Apr 1912
H.E. Carey (Director)		1 Aug 1919
M.S.C. Smith (Acting)		1 Dec 1919
M.S.C. Smith (Deputy)		15 Jan 1921
F.C. Urquhart	17 Jan 1921	25 Apr 1921
E.C. Playford (Acting)		17 Jan 1926

Government Resident at Darwin for North Australia

R.H. Weddell		1 Feb 1927

Government Resident at Alice Springs for Central Australia

J.C. Cawood	15 Dec 1926	1 Mar 1927
V.G. Carrington (Acting)		11 Dec 1929

Administrator resident at Darwin for the Northern Territory

R.H. Weddell	12 Jun 1931
J.A. Carrodus (Acting)	15 Mar 1934
C.L.A. Abbott	29 Mar 1937

1942-1945 Military Administration at Darwin
(During this period C.L.A. Abbott was Administrator for the Northern Territory but resident at Alice Springs.)

L.H.A. Giles (Acting)	26 May 1946
A.R. Driver	1 Jul 1946
F.J.S. Wise	1 Jul 1951
J.C. Archer	1 Jul 1956
R.B. Nott	1 Apr 1961
R.L. Dean	1 Oct 1964
F.C. Chaney	3 Mar 1970
T.A. O'Brien (Acting)	1 Aug 1973
J.N. Nelson	10 Dec 1973
E.F. Dwyer (Acting)	17 Nov 1975
J.A. England	1 Jun 1976
Commodore E.E. Johnston	1 Jan 1981

Part 3. A list of Chief Ministers since the granting of self government on 1 July, 1978. Although 1 July, 1978 is recognised as the date on which self government of the Northern Territory commenced, some executive functions were transferred from the Federal Government to the Northern Territory Government prior to that date as from 1 January, 1977. During the interim period G.A. Letts, then P.A.E. Everingham, held the position of Majority Leader and Chief Secretary.

Chief Minister	Date of appointment	Political Persuasion
P.A.E. Everingham	30 Jun 1978	NT/Country Liberal

Paul Everingham

*Most of the information for the Northern Territory was kindly provided by Mr V.T. O'Brien and was prepared from South Australian, Northern Territory or Federal Government Gazettes for a minor Northern Territory History Award. Supplementary informations was supplied by officers of the Australian Archives. As far as we are aware this detailed information has not been published previously.

APPENDIX 3

AUSTRALIAN OF THE YEAR AWARDS

The Australian of the Year Award and the Young Australian of the Year Award are made to Australians who have made an outstanding contribution to the Australian achievement. The Awards are made by the National Australia Day Committee after seeking nominations from all levels of the Australian community and recognise two Australians who have given much to their country.

AUSTRALIAN OF THE YEAR

1960   Sir Macfarlane BURNET
1961   Miss Joan SUTHERLAND
1962   Mr Jock Sturrock
1963   Sir John ECCLES
1964   Miss Dawn FRASER
1965   Sir Robert HELPMANN
1966   Mr Jack BRABHAM
1967   'The Seekers'
1968   Mr Lionel ROSE
1969   Lord CASEY
1970   Cardinal Sir Norman Gilroy
1971   Mrs Evonne CAWLEY (Goolagong)
1972   Miss Shane GOULD
1973   Mr Patrick WHITE
1974   Sir Bernard HEINZE
1975   Professor John W. CORNFORTH
1976   Sir Edward Dunlop
1977   Mrs Raigh Roe
1978   Mr Galarrwuy Yunupingu
1979   Mr Harry Butler
1980   Professor Manning CLARK
1981   Sir John Crawford
1982   Sir Edward Williams
1983   Mr Robert de CASTELLA

YOUNG AUSTRALIAN OF THE YEAR

1979   Miss Julie Sochacki
1980   Mr Peter Hill
1981   Mr Paul Radley
1982   Mr Mark Ella
1983   Mr Michael Waldock

Robert Helpmann, dancer, choreographer, actor and producer

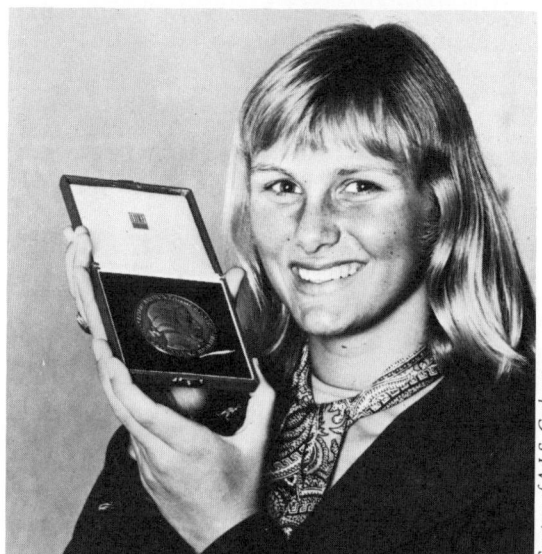

Swimmer Shane Gould

Sir Bernard Heinze conducting

Sir Edward Williams, Chairman of the XII Commonwealth Games Foundation

ART AWARDS

Archibald Prize

Awarded annually by the trustees of the Art Gallery of New South Wales for the best portrait submitted by an artist resident in Australia, preferably of a person prominent in art, letters, science or politics.

Year	Painter	Portrait of:
1921	W.B. McInnes	Desbrowe Annear
1922	W.B. McInnes	Prof. Harrison Moore
1923	W.B. McInnes	A Lady
1924	W.B. McInnes	Miss Collins
1925	John Longstaff	Maurice Moscovitch
1926	W.B. McInnes	Silk and Lace
1927	G.W. Lambert	Mrs Murdoch
1928	John Longstaff	Dr Alexander Leeper
1929	John Longstaff	W.A. Holman
1930	W.B. McInnes	Drum Major H. McClelland
1931	John Longstaff	Sir John Sulman
1932	E. Buckmaster	Sir William Irvine
1933	C. Wheeler	Ambrose Pratt
1934	Henry Hanke	Self Portrait
1935	John Longstaff	A.B. (Banjo) Paterson
1936	W.B. McInnes	Dr Julian Smith
1937	Normand Baker	Self Portrait
1938	Nora Heysen	Mine Elink Schuurman
1939	Max Meldrum	The Hon. G.J. Bell
1940	Max Meldrum	Dr J. Forbes McKenzie
1941	W. Dargie	Sir James Elder
1942	W. Dargie	Corporal Jim Gordon
1943	William Dobell	Joshua Smith
1944	Joshua Smith	The Hon. S. Rosevear
1945	W. Dargie	Lt-General Edmund Herring
1946	W. Dargie	L.C. Robson
1947	W. Dargie	Sir Marcus Clark
1948	William Dobell	Margaret Olley
1949	Arthur Murch	Bonar Dunlop
1950	W. Dargie	Sir Leslie McConnan
1951	Ivor Hele	Laurie Thomas
1952	W. Dargie	Essington Lewis
1953	Ivor Hele	Sir Henry Simpson Newland
1954	Ivor Hele	The Rt Hon. R.G. Menzies
1955	Ivor Hele	Robert Campbell
1956	W. Dargie	Albert Namatjira
1957	Ivor Hele	Self Portrait
1958	W. Pidgeon	Ray Walker
1959	William Dobell	Dr Edward McMahon
1960	Judy Cassab	Stanislaus Rapotec
1961	W. Pidgeon	Rabbi Dr I. Porush
1962	Louis Kahan	Patrick White
1963	J. Carrington Smith	Prof. James McAuley
1964	Not awarded	
1965	Clifton Pugh	R. A. Henderson
1966	Jon Molvig	Charles Blackman
1967	Judy Cassab	Margo Lewers
1968	W. Pidgeon	Lloyd Rees
1969	Ray Crooke	George Johnston
1970	Eric Smith	Gruzman—Architect
1971	Clifton Pugh	Sir John McEwen
1972	Clifton Pugh	The Hon. E. G. Whitlam
1973	Janet Dawson	Michael Boddy Reading
1974	Sam Fullbrook	Jockey Norman Stephens
1975	Kevin Connor	The Hon. Sir Frank Kitto
1976	Brett Whiteley	Self-Portrait in the Studio
1977	Kevin Connor	Robert Klippel
1978	Brett Whiteley	Art, Life and the Other Thing
1979	Wes Walters	Philip Adams
1980	Not awarded	
1981	Eric Smith	Rudy Komon
1982	Eric Smith	Peter Sculthorpe
1983	Nigel Thomson	Chandler Coventry

John McCaughey Memorial Art Prize

Awarded irregularly by the National Gallery of Victoria for a painting depicting an Australian scene or some aspect of Australian life.

Year	Artist	Painting:
1957	John Perceval	Gannets Diving
1958	Noel Counihan	After Work
1959	Sali Herman	Country Street Scene
1960	Kenneth de Silva	Come In Spinner
1961	Roger Kemp	Organized Forms
1965	Gill Jamieson	The Pigs
1966	Anthony Irving	Uncle John's 1919 Homecoming
1968	Michael Shannon	Early Morning, Melbourne
1972	Donald Laycock	Star Cycles
1975	John Firth-Smith	From Here
1979	Paul Tartos	Untitled Pink
	Ken Whisson	Flag for the City of Sydney
1981	Imants Tillers	The Modern Picture (Worlds in Collision)
1983	Craig Gough	Sandringham Series No.18
	Mandy Martin	Powerhouse 3

'Easter in My Room' by Maryanne Coutts

Commonwealth Banking Corp

'In Mockery of Christ' by Suzie Marston

Commonwealth Banking Corp

Blake Prize for Religious Art

Year   Artist

1951	Justin O'Brien	
1952	Frank Hinder	
1953	Michael Kmit	
1954	Charles Bannon	
1955	Donald Friend	
1956	Eric Smith	
1957	Elwyn Lynn	
1958	Eric Smith	
1959	Eric Smith	
1960	John Coburn	
1961	Stanislaus Rapotec	
1962	Eric Smith	
1963	Leonard French	
1964	Michael Kitching	
1965	Asher Bilu	
1966	Rodney Milgate	
1967	Desiderius Orban	
1968	Roger Kemp	
1969	Eric Smith	
1970	Eric Smith and Roger Kemp	
1971	Desiderius Orban	
1972	Joseph Szabo	
1973	Keith Looby	
1974	Stuart Maxwell and Ken Whisson	
1975	Rodney Milgate	
1976	David Voigt	
1977	John Coburn and Rodney Milgate	
1978	Noel Tunks	
1979	Ian Gentle and Alex Trompf	
1980	Leonard French	
1981	David Voigt	
1982	Maryanne Coutts and Suzie Marston	
1983	Geoffrey Harvey and Ann Taylor	

(a) 'The Offering' by Ann Taylor (natural materials)

(b) 'Sunday School Work Books' by Geoffrey Harvey (collage and mixed media)

APPENDIX 4

HIGHER EDUCATIONAL INSTITUTIONS 1984

Higher Educational Institutions 1984
A. Universities and University Colleges.
B. Colleges of Advanced Education (CAEs)and similar institutions.

The details given for each institution are:
its official title, followed by its enrolment in 1983.
Where the institution is essentially single-purpose, but the title does not make this clear, the type of education in which it specialises is also noted;
its location, unless the title makes this clear.

Courtesy of A.I.S. Canberra

Aerial view of Australian National University with Canberra city in the background

Australian Capital Territory
A. *Australian National University* (5 900) Canberra.
Royal Military College (483) Duntroon, 3km E of Canberra City. It is a Faculty of Military Studies of the University of New South Wales.
B. *Canberra College of Advanced Education* (5 900)
Canberra School of Art (299)
Canberra School of Music (750)
Signadou College of Education (330) Watson, a suburb of Canberra.

Northern Territory
B. *Darwin Community College* (940)

New South Wales
A. *Macquarie University* (11 000) 18km NW of the Sydney city centre.
New England, the University of (8 716) ARMIDALE.
New South Wales, the University of (18 416) Kensington, 7km from the Sydney city centre.

It also has a Faculty of Military Studies at the Royal Military College, Duntroon, in the ACT.
Newcastle, the University of (4 435) Shortland, about 12km W of the city centre.
Royal Australian Naval College (102) First year students at JERVIS BAY, NSW; later years at the University of NSW campus, Kensington.
Sydney, the University of (18 342)
Wollongong, the University of (4 500) Includes the former Wollongong Institute of Education.

J.H. Shaw

Australian Film and Television school in North Ryde, NSW

B. *Armidale College of Advanced Education* (1 600)
Australian College of Physical Education (99) Croydon, an inner W suburb of Sydney.
Australian Film and Television School (387) North Ryde, a Sydney suburb.
Avondale College (500) Cooranbong, 145km N of Sydney.
Catholic College of Education (1 500) Formed in 1982 by the amalgamation of the Catholic Teachers' College, St Mary College of Education and Polding College. Campuses in several suburbs of Sydney.
Cumberland College of Health Sciences (1 400) Lidcombe, a W suburb of Sydney.
Hawkesbury Agricultural College (1 000) RICHMOND, 50km NW of Sydney.
Kuring-gai College of Advanced Education (3 200) Lindfield, a N suburb of Sydney.
Macarthur Institute of Higher Education (1 300) Formerly the Milperra College of Advanced Education. Campuses at Milperra, a south-western Sydney suburb, and CAMPBELLTOWN.
Mitchell College of Advanced Education (5 000) BATHURST.

Moore Theological College (138) Newtown, an inner suburb of Sydney.

The National Institute of Dramatic Art (123) The grounds of the University of New South Wales.

Nepean College of Advanced Education (1 610) Kingswood and Westmead, W suburbs of Sydney.

New South Wales Department of Technical and Further Education (1 372) students in diploma or associate diploma courses at Technical Colleges throughout the State).

New South Wales Institute of Technology (8 488) Four main campuses in Sydney, the main one at Broadway, near the city centre.

New South Wales State Conservatorium of Music (510) Main location in central Sydney; branches in NEWCASTLE and WOLLONGONG, but the latter does not provide tertiary courses.

Newcastle College of Advanced Education (2700)

Northern Rivers College of Advanced Education (1 065) LISMORE.

Orange Agricultural College (445) 8km from the town of ORANGE.

Riverina College of Advanced Education (5 200) Since 1982 has incorporated the former GOULBURN CAE. Campuses in WAGGA WAGGA, ALBURY-WODONGA and Goulburn.

St John's College (30 in theology) Morpeth, near Newcastle.

St Paul's National Seminary (55 in theology) Kensington, an inner suburb of Sydney.

Sydney College of the Arts (688) Balmain, an inner Sydney suburb.

Sydney College of Advanced Education (4 679) mainly in teacher education and art) Formed in 1982 by the amalgamation of Alexander Mackie College, Guild Teachers' College, Nursery School Teachers' College, Sydney Kindergarten Teachers' College and Sydney Teachers' College. Campuses in several Sydney and surburban locations. Includes the City Art Institute.

Union Theological Institute (200) Hunters Hill and North Turramurra, suburbs of Sydney.

United Theological College (72) Enfield, a W suburb of Sydney.

Victoria

A. *Deakin University* (5 526) GEELONG.

Latrobe University (8 900) Bundoora, 15km N of Melbourne city centre.

Melbourne, the University of (15 850) In the N part of the city of Melbourne, with an affiliated college (The Royal Australian Air Force Academy) at Point Cook, 30km from the city.

Monash University (14 087) Clayton, a SE suburb of Melbourne.

Royal Australian Air Force Academy (146) *See* Melbourne, the University of.

B. *Ballarat College of Advance Education* (2 000)

Bendigo College of Advanced Education (1 945)

Chisholm Institute of Technology (5 900) Formed in 1982 by the amalgamation of the Caulfield Institute of Technology and the State College of Victoria, Frankston. Campuses in the Melbourne suburbs named above.

Footscray Institute of Technology (3 200) Footscray, a W suburb of Melbourne.

Gippsland Institute of Advanced Education (2 670) Near Morwell, in the LATROBE Valley.

Hawthorn Institute of Education (1 450 in technical teacher education) 8km E of Melbourne city centre.

Institute of Catholic Education (1 652) BALLARAT and the Melbourne suburbs of Ascot Vale and Oakleigh.

Lincoln Institute of Health Sciences (1 925) Central Melbourne.

Marcus Oldham Farm Management College (70) 8km W of Geelong.

Melbourne College of Advanced Education (4 555) Formed in 1983 by the amalgamation of the Melbourne State College and the Institute of Early Childhood Development. Campuses in the inner Melbourne suburbs of Carlton and Kew.

Phillip Institute of Technology (4 500) Formed in 1982 by the amalgamation of State College of Victoria at COBURG and Preston Institute of Technology.

Royal Melbourne Institute of Technology (11 028)

Swinburne Institute of Technology (5 650) Glenferrie, an inner suburb of Melbourne.

Victoria College (7 511) Formed in 1982 by the amalgamation of Prahran College of Advanced Education and the State Colleges of Victoria, Burwood, Rusden and Toorak. Campuses in several Melbourne suburbs.

Victoria College of Arts (550) Close to the Melbourne city centre.

Victorian College of Pharmacy, Ltd (400) Close to the Melbourne city centre.

Warnambool Institute of Advanced Education (1 653)

University of Queensland, Brisbane

Queensland

A. *Griffith University* (2 800) Nathan, 10km from Brisbane city centre.

James Cook University of North Queensland (3 050) TOWNSVILLE. Includes the Townsville College of Advanced Education.

Queensland, the University of (17 948) Main campus at St Lucia, 8km from the Brisbane city centre.

B. *Brisbane College of Advanced Education* (7 101) Formed in 1982 by the amalgamation of Brisbane Kindergarten Teachers' College, Kelvin Grove College of Advanced Education, Mt Gravatt College of Advanced Education and North Brisbane College of Advanced Education. Campuses in several Brisbane suburbs.
Capricornia Institute of Advanced Education (2 400) Near ROCKHAMPTON.
Darling Downs Institute of Advanced Education (4 500) TOOWOOMBA, 7km from city centre.
McCauley College (500 in teacher education) Dutton Park, suburb of Brisbane.
Mackay College of Technical and Further Education (16 in sugar technology).
Queensland Agricultural College (1 100) Near GATTON, 100km W of Brisbane.
Queensland College of Art (1 033) Seven Hills, 10km from Brisbane city centre.
Queensland Conservatorium of Music (284) Near the centre of Brisbane.
Queensland Institute of Technology (8 000) Brisbane.
Townsville College of Advanced Education (2 607).
Townsville College of Technical and Further Education (2 007).

South Australia

A. *Adelaide, the University of* (9 100)
Flinders University of South Australia (4 000) Bedford Park, 10km S of the Adelaide city centre.

B. *Roseworthy Agricultural College* (452) 50km N of Adelaide.
South Australian College of Advanced Education (10 450) Formed in 1982 by the amalgamation of Adelaide College of the Arts and Education, Hartley College of Advanced Education, Salisbury College of Advanced Education and Sturt College of Advanced Education. Campuses near Adelaide city centre and in several suburban locations.
South Australian Institute of Technology (6 800) Adelaide (one near city centre, one 12km N) and WHYALLA.

Western Australia

A. *Murdoch University* (3 250) 15km S of Perth city centre.
Western Australia, the University of (9 966) Crawley, 5km from Perth city centre.

B. *Western Australian College of Advanced Education* (6 195) Formed in 1982 by the amalgamation of Churchlands College of Advanced Education, Claremont Teachers' College, Mt Lawley College of Advanced Education and Nedlands College of Advanced Education. Campuses in several suburbs of Perth.
Western Australian Institute of Technology (11 930) Main Campus in the Perth Suburb of South Bentley, but the Institute includes the Muresk Agricultural College near NORTHAM, and the Western Australian School of Mines at KALGOORLIE.

Tasmania

A. *Tasmania, the University of* (5 200) Sandy Bay, a suburb of Hobart.

B. *Tasmania College of Advanced Education* (2 158) Newnham, a suburb of LAUNCESTON.
Australian Maritime College (576) Opened in 1981 at Beauty Point, 50km from Launceston.

Further reading: Directory of Higher Education Courses (yearly) Australian Govt Printing Service, Canberra.

AVERAGE MONTHLY
MAXIMUM TEMPERATURES

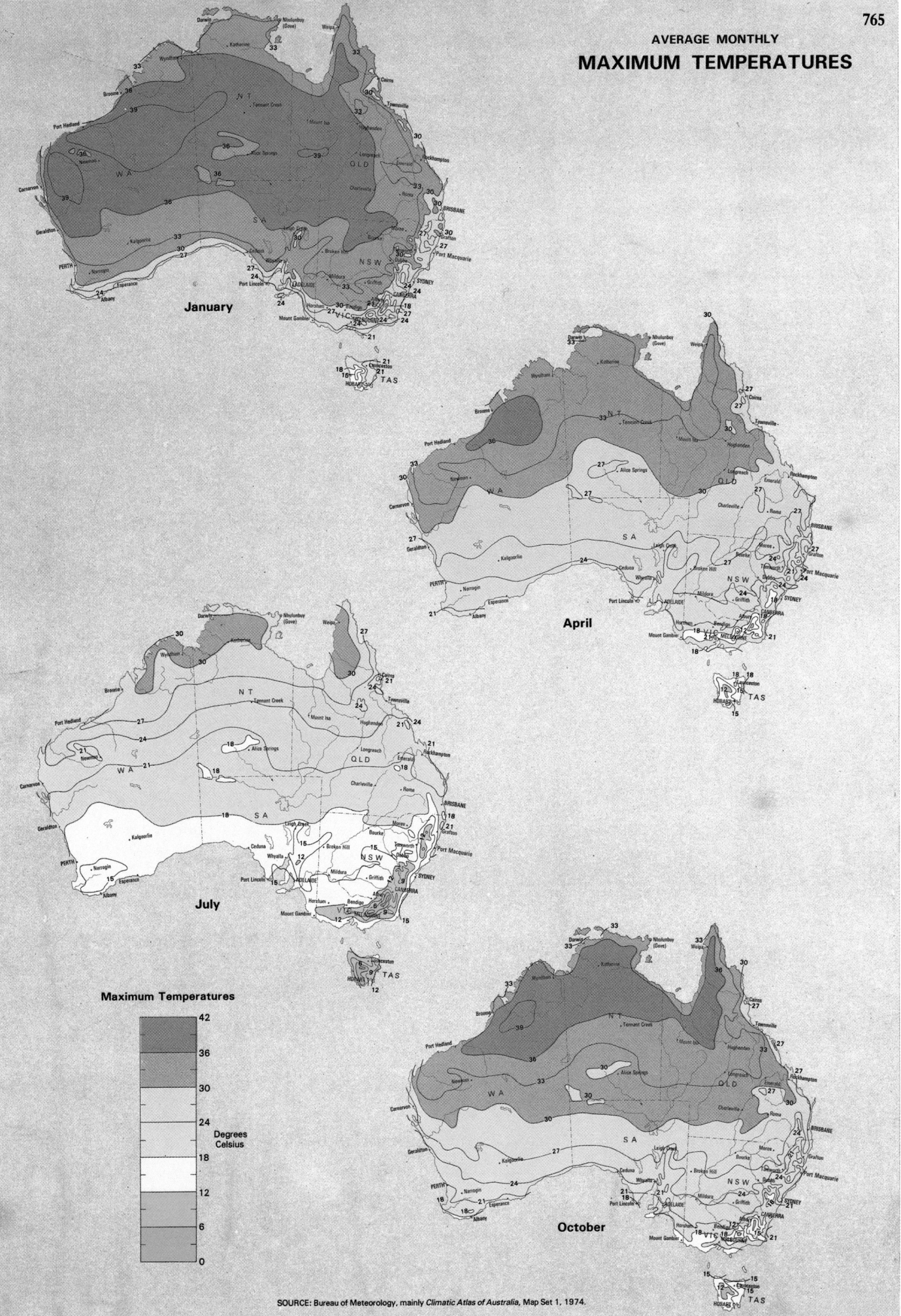

January

April

July

October

Maximum Temperatures

	42
	36
	30
	24
	Degrees
	Celsius
	18
	12
	6
	0

SOURCE: Bureau of Meteorology, mainly *Climatic Atlas of Australia*, Map Set 1, 1974.

January

April

July

October

Minimum Temperatures

	30
	24
	18
	12 Degrees
	Celsius
	6
	0
	-6

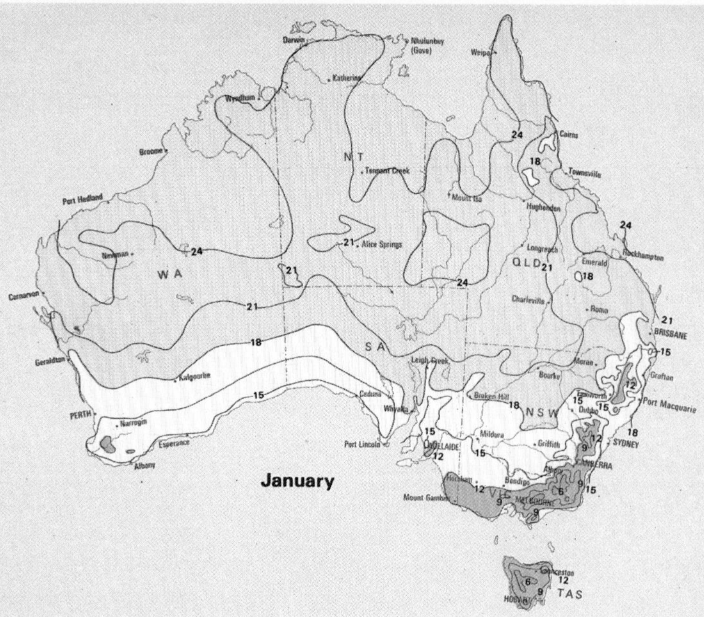

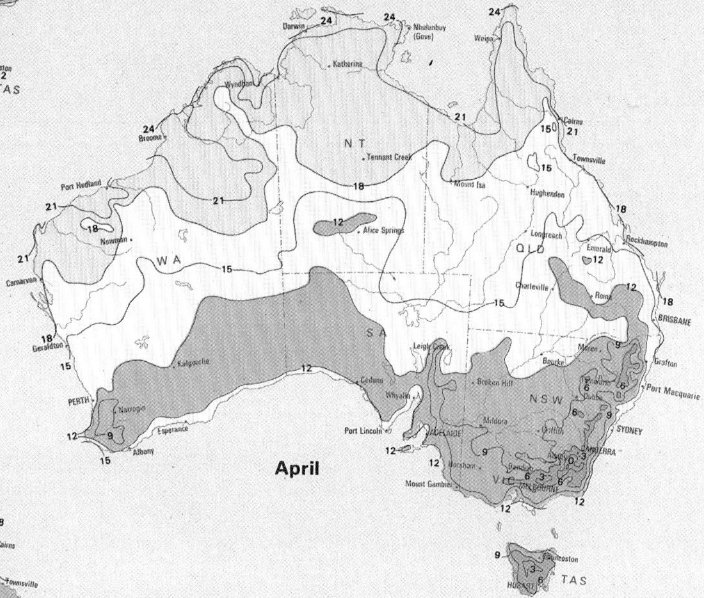

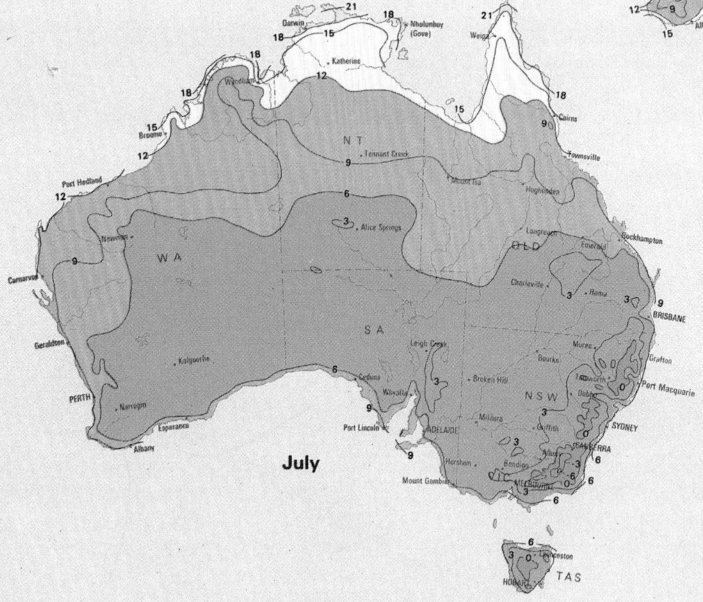

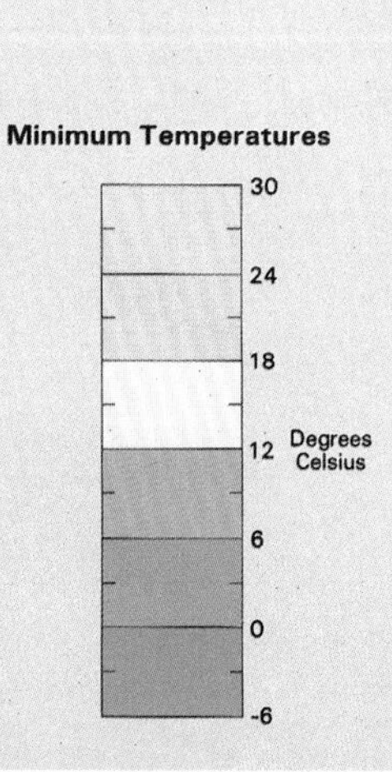

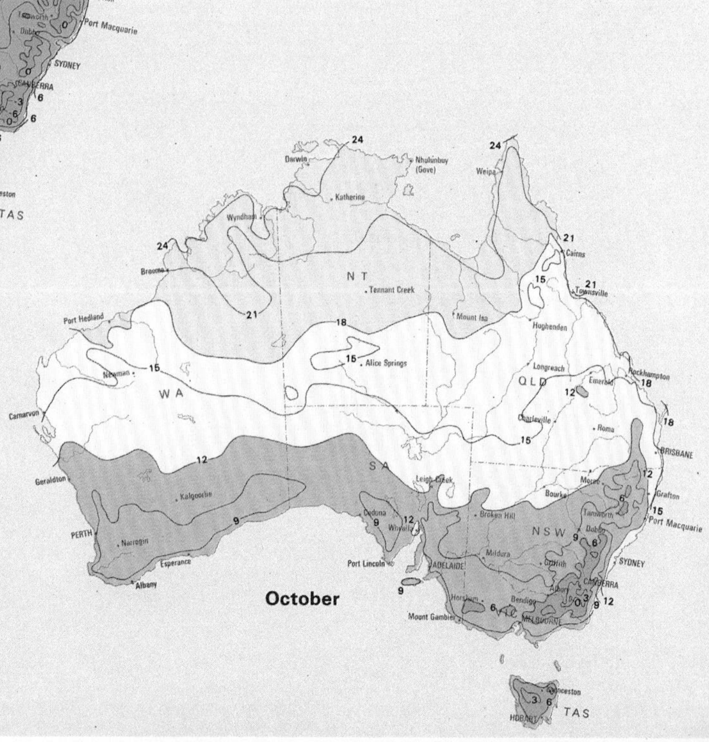

APPENDIX 5

FLOWER STRUCTURE AND GLOSSARY OF BOTANICAL TERMS

The angiosperm flower, which is described in the entry of ANGIOSPERMAE, is the principal structure on which the classification of flowering plants is constructed. To enable a proper understanding of the floral description given under each angiosperm family, some understanding of the specialised nomenclature employed to describe the arrange-ments and relationship of floral parts is provided in this appendix. To further assist in the under-standing of these articles, leaf structures, shapes and arrangements are also covered, and a glossary of botanical terms not explained in the diagrams below or in the botanical entries is given.

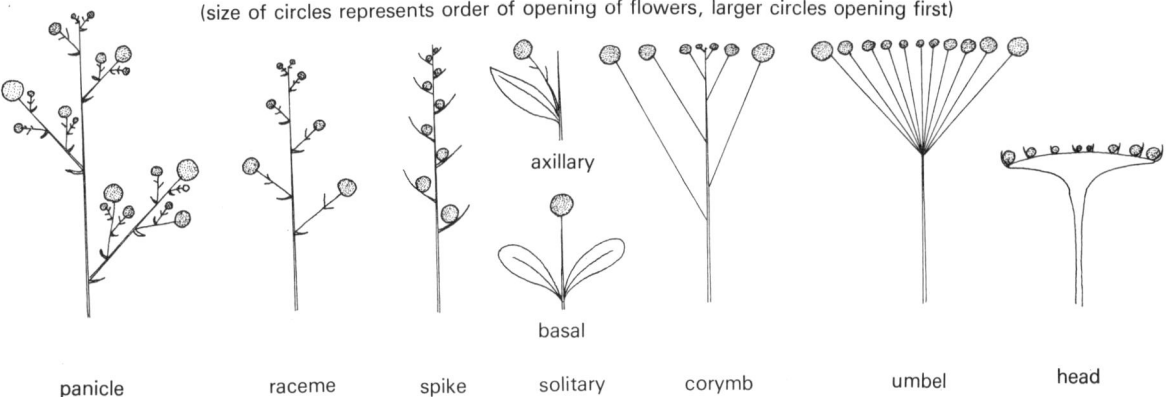

(size of circles represents order of opening of flowers, larger circles opening first)

axillary

basal

panicle   raceme   spike   solitary   corymb   umbel   head

Flower arrangement or inflorescence type

Glossary of Terms not covered in diagrams

achene	a simple dry fruit derived from a superior ovary, not splitting open at maturity
aril	an expansion of the stalk connecting the seed to the ovary wall which grows partly or entirely over the seed
berry	a simple fleshy fruit with no hard layer in the fruit wall; seeds usually numerous
bisexual	flowers which have both male and female parts in the same flower
bract	leaf-like structures or scale which sub-tend an inflorescence or flower
bracteole	a small bract situated on the pedicel below the flower but not subtending it
capsule	a dry simple fruit which opens at maturity by slits or pores, formed from two or more joined carpels

coriacious	leathery
dioecious	male and female flowers borne on separate plants
disc	a plate of tissue sometimes found between whorls of floral segments, or the dilated base of the style on the ovary in some UMBELLIFERAE fruits
drupe	a succulent, non-splitting fruit derived from a single carpel and having a stony layer in the fruit wall
epipetalous	stamens attached to the petals
follicle	a dry splitting fruit formed from one carpel and having one longitudinal opening at maturity
imbricate	with overlapping edges
irregular flower	a flower which has one or more of its segments dissimilar in shape from the others of the whorl

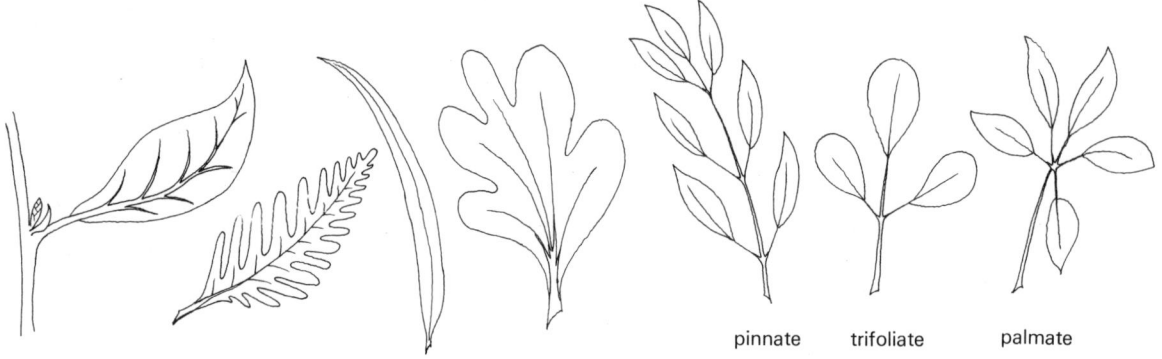

pinnate   trifoliate   palmate

Some simple leaves   ### Some compound leaves

legume   a dry splitting fruit formed from one carpel and having two longitudinal openings at maturity, or a member of one of the families PAPILIONACEAE, MIMOSACEASE or Caesalpinaceae

lodicule   one or two scales below the stamens and the ovary of a grass, regarded as reduced perianth

lomentum   a dry fruit derived from one carpel which breaks up transversely into one-seeded sections at maturity

mericarp   a single carpel unit formed by the splitting of a schizocarp

monoecious having separate male and female flowers both borne on the same plant

pappus   the appendages (hairs, scales, etc.) at the top of the fruit (cypsela) of members of the family COMPOSITAE

pedicel   the stalk of each single flower or of a spikelet of grass

peduncle   the stalk of an inflorescence or a solitary flower

perianth   the calyx and corolla collectively, especially when they are the same in appearance

polygamous having bisexual and unisexual flowers mixed together

regular flower   having a radially symmetrical perianth

rotate   having a regular corolla with petals spread flat like a wheel

schizocarp a dry fruit which at maturity breaks into individual carpels (mericarps)

spathe   a sheath-like bract around an inflorescence

staminode   a sterile stamen, often modified in shape

succulent   juicy or fleshy leaves and stems

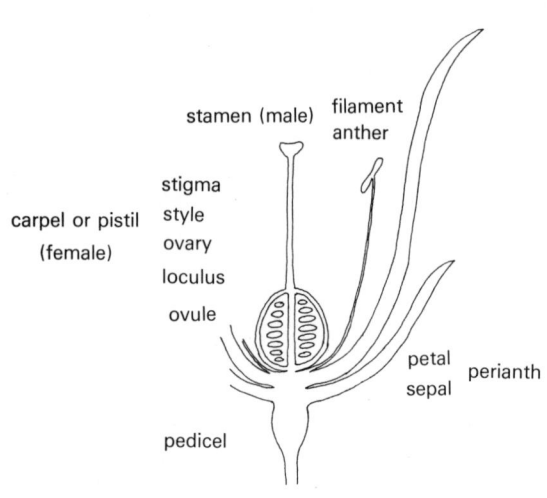

Parts of a flower

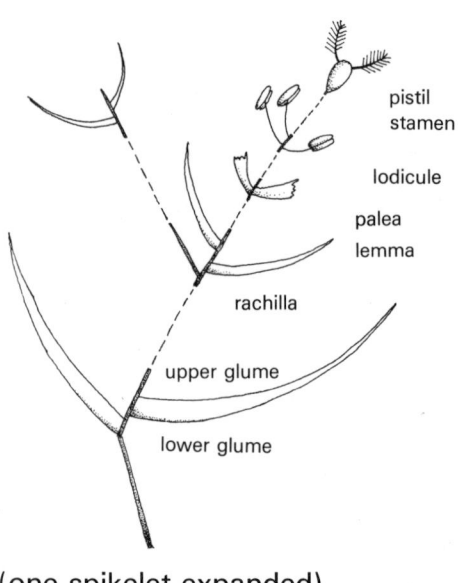

(one spikelet expanded)

The grass flower

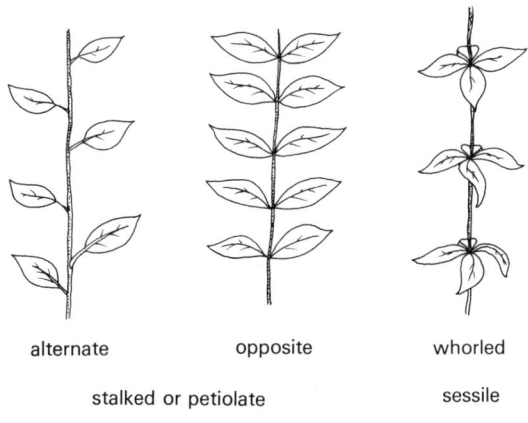

alternate   opposite   whorled

stalked or petiolate   sessile

Leaf arrangement

valvate   with edges touching, or opening by valves

See also Angiospermae; and individual plant families listed thereunder

Further reading: Porter, C.L. *Taxonomy of Flowering Plants.* (2nd edn) Freeman, San Francisco, 1959.

GLOSSARY OF SCIENTIFIC TERMS

This glossary contains mainly biological and geological terms; botanical terms will be found above although some which are used in both zoology and botany are included. Many zoological terms are explained in the body of the text but not in every article in which they occur. A term used in the article on BEETLES, for example, may not be defined there as it is applicable to all INSECTS. An examination of the article on insects will reveal its meaning. As far as possible, words defined in standard English dictionaries are not included unless they have a specialist meaning not to be found in such a reference book. Italic type within a definition refers to another entry in this glossary.

aboral surface	In ECHINODERMS, the surface opposite to that carrying the mouth. Usually the upper surface.
adductor	Of muscles: bringing two parts together.
aestivate	To spend the summer or a hot period in an inactive state. The summer-time equivalent of hibernation.
alginate	A product of brown ALGAE, used for various industrial and medicinal purposes.
ambulacral groove	A groove in the arms of ECHINODERMS in which the tube-feet are situated.
ammonoid	Referring to an ammonite, an early relative of octopuses and squids, with a coiled, external shell.
amnion	The membrane of the fluid-filled sac in which embroyonic reptiles, birds

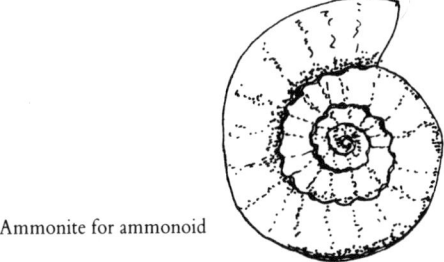

Ammonite for ammonoid

and mammals develop. Sometimes refers to the whole sac.

annulus	A ring of tissue round the stalk of certain mushrooms and similar FUNGI. Term sometimes used for a segment in an ANNELID.
antenna	The feeler on the head of an INSECT and related animals.
antivenene	A material produced by injecting venom into an animal, used to combat the effects of snake bites, spider bites

etc. in human beings and other animals.

apterygote Referring to INSECTS which do not possess wings, and which are descended from wingless ancestors; for example, SILVERFISH but not FLEAS.

arbovirus A virus attacking animals which is carried by and transmitted by, insects — for example, yellow fever, dengue fever and Murray Valley encephalitis.

ascomycete A member of one of the large subdivisions of the FUNGI.

asexual reproduction Reproduction which does not involve the fusion of male and female sex cells, for example, the splitting of an amoeba into two.

autochthonous Arising in the land itself: MONOTREMES, for example, are autochthonous to Australia and New Guinea since they are believed to have evolved there.

bilaterally symmetrical With a clear left side and a right side, one being more or less the mirror image of the other. In bilaterally symmetrical animals there is only one plane with such a symmetry. In radial symmetry there is more than one such plane.

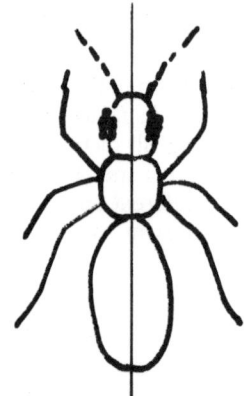

Bilateral symmetry

biomass The total mass of organisms in a particular place. The term may refer to a single species, to several species or to all species present.

biramous With two branches. Many of the limbs of CRUSTACEA are biramous while those of INSECTS are all uniramous.

bisexual Existing as two sexes — male and female.

brille The transparent covering, shaped like a watch-glass, over the eye of some reptiles (German: 'eye-glass').

byssus Fine threads (byssal threads) which some MOLLUSCS such as mussels use to attach themselves to the surface.

calamistrum A distinctive series of curved bristles on the dorsal surface of the fourth leg of certain SPIDERS: important in identification.

calyptron Lobe at the base of the wing of certain FLIESimportant in classification. Also calypter.

carapace i. Part of the 'shell' of a CRUSTACEAN, consisting of fused dorsal plates enclosing part of the head and thorax. ii. The shell of a TORTOISE or turtle.

cartilaginous Consisting of cartilage or 'gristle' as opposed to bone.

cephalothorax The head and thorax, as a unit, in ARACHNIDS and CRUSTACEA.

cercaria The fourth and final larval stage in the development of a typical FLUKE. It may be swallowed in this stage by a vertebrate host, or it may develop a resistant coat before being swallowed (metacercaria).

cere Soft swelling at the base of the upper beak of a bird. Conspicuous in the budgerigar.

chaeta A bristle of an ANNELID containing *chitin*.

chelate Pincer-like.

chelicera The fang of a SPIDER, or the corresponding *chelate* appendage of other ARACHNIDS. Often used to inject venom.

Chelicerae of a spider

chitin Horny substance consisting of very large molecules based on sugars, found in the *cuticle* of ARTHROPODS and some FUNGI, and in the *chaetae* of ANNELIDS.

Choanocyte

choanocyte Cell in the inner chamber of a SPONGE which is provided with a collar and a flagellum. The numerous choanocytes within a sponge keep the water circulating.

ciliated — Provided with cilia.

cilium — A minute hair-like filament on the surface of a cell. A *ciliated* cell or PROTOZOON is provided with many cilia whose concerted movements move the cell or fluid across its surface. A *flagellum* is similar, but larger, and a cell typically carries only one or two flagelli; (plural cilia).

clitellum — A 'saddle' on an ANNELID where the skin is thickened, and well provided with blood vessels and glands. It forms the slime tube which binds mating worms together and which forms the cocoon for eggs.

cloaca — A common opening for the excretory, reproductive and digestive systems of animals. It occurs, for example, in FISHES, AMPHIBIA, REPTILES, BIRDS MONOTREMES and MARSUPIALS but not in EUTHERIAN MAMMALS.

coelom — The body-cavity of most animals (though not COELENTERATES, SPONGES and PROTOZOA) between the outer wall and the internal organs. It resembles the *pseudocoelom* found in some animals but arises in the embryo in a different way.

commensal — A partner in *commensalism*.

commensalism — The living together of two or more organisms, sharing the same food ('at the same table') but not so dependent one upon the others that the association is parasitism (PARASITES) or *symbiosis*.

coracidium — A *ciliated* aquatic larva of the giant fish TAPEWORM or a related species, hatching from the egg.

corvid — A member of the CROW family.

cosmopolitan — In biology, occurring on virtually every major land mass, and often on many islands, though not usually in Anarctica. The house mouse is thus a cosmopolitan species.

coxa — The first or basal segment of the limb of an ARTHROPOD.

cribellum — A sieve-like plate, part of the spinning apparatus of certain SPIDERS.

crinoid — A SEA-LILY or feather-star.

cryptic — Aiding in making an organism inconspicuous — thus cryptic colour, pattern, behaviour.

cucurbit — A cucumber or related plant.

cultivar — A variety produced by and for cultivation.

cuticle — A layer of horny, non-cellular material serving as the outer layer of many animals and plants.

cypris larva — A larval stage in the development of BARNACLES and related animals. Its *carapace* consists of two sections (valves) closed by *adductor* muscles.

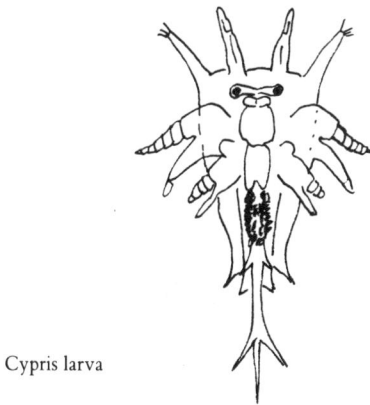

Cypris larva

cytoplasm — The protoplasm of a cell, excluding the *nucleus*.

demersal — Living near the bottom of the sea.

detritus — Material, organic and inorganic, produced by erosion by water.

deutonymph — The *instar* of a mite.

diapause — A slowing down of metabolism and development, usually in response to a seasonal change. Applies particularly to INSECTS.

dichotomy — A division into two.

diploid — With two complete sets of chromosomes, one derived from the female parent, the other from the male parent. Typically a diploid cell is formed by the fertilisation of one *haploid* sex-cell (the egg or ovum) by another, the sperm, or by the 'copycat' division of another diploid cell. Often symbolised as 2n.

diurnal — Active in the day time.

ecdysis — Moulting, especially in ARTHROPODS which, being encased in a rigid *exoskeleton*, must periodically moult their 'skin' if they are to grow. The stage between two ecdyses is an *instar*.

echolocation — The identification of an object, and determination of its position, by bouncing sounds off it. Commonly used by animals which fly in the dark, such as certain BATS and cave SWIFTS, and by some whales.

ecosystem — The system formed by all the organisms living in a particular place and those parts of their non-living environment which influence them. Material tends to cycle in an ecosystem, but energy passes through.

The dimensions are a matter of convenience: you can consider, for example, the ecosystem of a tree log, or the ecosystem of the Snowy Mountains.

ecotone — The transition zone between two *ecosystems* — for example, between a forest and a paddock.

ectoderm — One of the three fundamental layers of tissue in most embryonic animals, giving rise to nervous tissue and the skin among other tissues.

ectoparasite — A PARASITE which lives on the surface of its host, or at least in direct contact with it, whereas an *endoparasite* lives within the host.

elytron — The hard, shell-like fore-wing of a BEETLE (plural: elytra).

endemic — i. Disease: present in a region but not in an epidemic phase ii. Biogeography: of a species, native to, and restricted at present to, a particular region, though possibly introduced to another region by man.

endoderm — The innermost of the three basic tissue layers in most embryonic animals, giving rise to the gut.

endoparasite — A PARASITE living within the tissues, or in some body cavity, of its host.

endopterygote — An INSECT whose wings (when present) are not apparent in the developing young (the larva) but which form within the *pupa*. The larval stages do not resemble the adult or imago.

ephemeral — Lasting for only a short time.

eucaryotic organism — An organism whose cell or cells contain a *nucleus* enclosed in a membrane, organised chromosomes, and *mitochondria*. Most organisms are eucaryotic; bacteria and blue-green ALGAE are *procaryotic*.

evolution, convergent — The evolution of similar structures, patterns of behaviour and so on in unrelated organisms as a result of similar evolutionary pressures. Octopuses, which are predators with complex behaviours, have eyes similar to those of vertebrates, as a result of convergent evolution.

exopterygote — An INSECT whose wings (when present) develop externally as 'wing buds' which can be seen in the young or *nymph*. There is no *pupa* in the life cycle.

exoskeleton — An external skeleton, not surrounded by muscle and other tissues. The hard plates of an ARTHROPOD form its exoskeleton.

exotic — Not native.

fault — A fracture in rocks, along which movement has taken place, and displacement of strata.

femur — i. The thigh-bone of a VERTEBRATE. ii. The third, and usually the largest, segment of an ARTHROPOD's leg (plural, femora).

feral — Living and reproducing in the wild, without man's management, but descended from a domesticated species. Usually applied only to animals.

flagellum — A minute, hair-like filament on the surface of a cell, similar to, but larger than, a *cilium*.

gamete — An *haploid* sex-cell with nucleus and cytoplasm. The fertilisation of one kind by another produces a *zygote*.

ganglion — A concentration of nerve cells, consisting mainly of the bodies of the cells rather than their long fibres.

ganoid — Referring to a thick fish scale with a heavy layer of an enamel-like material (ganoine), or to a primitive fish with such scales (for example, sturgeons).

gaster — That part of a ANT, bee or wasp body behind the waist. The apparent abdomen which actually contains a thoracic segment.

gibber — A surface layer of small stones in certain Australian deserts. The term is restricted to Australia.

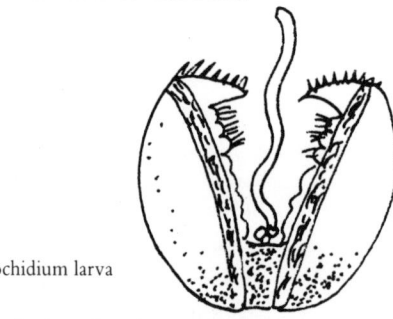

Glochidium larva

glochidium larva — A tiny developmental stage of some freshwater mussels which attaches itself to the surface of a fish and develops parasitically.

gnathosoma — The front part of the body of a mite, carrying the mouthparts.

gonad — Ovary or testis.

habit — Mode of growth, general appearance and so on of a plant.

haploid — Containing only a single set of chromosomes; cf diploid. Symbolised by n.

hermaphrodite — An individual animal which is of both sexes.

heterozygote An individual *diploid* organism which has different genes at a particular locus (position on a chromosome) on each of the two sister chromosomes; *cf. homozygote,*

hexapod An animal with six legs. Most of them are INSECTS.

homologous Referring to two structures which may or may not have the same function, but which have the same evolutionary origin. The wing of a bird, the arm of a man and the front leg of a dog are homologous; the wing of a fly and a bird are not.

homozygote An individual diploid organism which has identical genes at a particular locus (position on a chromosome) on each of the two sister chromosomes; *cf. heterozygote.*

horst An elevated area of land between two geological faults.

hydranth A polyp of a colonial COELENTERATE with mouth and tentacles.

hyperparasite A parasite parasitic on a parasite.

hyphae The individual threads or filaments of FUNGI.

hypopus An additional development stage in some MITES. It may be either a largely immobile form with very reduced legs, or a form with suckers well adapted to attaching to flying insects for dispersal.

idiosoma The body, other than the gnathosoma of MITES.

indigenous Native to a region as opposed to introduced or exotic.

inguinal In the groin region.

instar stage (larva, nymph) between two *ecdyses* or moults in the development of an ARTHROPOD.

integument A general term for the covering or coat of an organism.

inter-ambulacral Referring to the area between the *ambulacral grooves* in ECHINODERMS.

introduced Refers to an organism which as been brought, accidentally or intentionally, into a region by man and which (usually) has become established there.

invertebrate An animal without a backbone or vertebral column.

labellum The expanded tip of the *labium* in FLIES.

labium One of the mouth-parts of an INSECT — the lower 'lip'.

labrum One of the mouth-parts of an INSECT — the upper 'lip'.

larva A young, post-embryonic, stage in the lives of many kinds of animals, and usually quite different in appearance from the adult; for example, a caterpillar.

lateral line A series of sense-organs, sensitive to touch and vibrations, along the sides of a fish.

laterigrade Walking sideways like a crab. Usually applied to certain spiders.

lung book Or book-lung. The breathing structure in many ARACHNIDS, consisting of a chamber into which air can enter, into which protrudes many leaflets across the surfaces of which oxygen and carbon dioxide can pass.

mandible i. The lower jaw of VERTEBRATES composed of a single bone (MAMMALS) or more than one. ii. One of the first paired structures in the mouth-parts of INSECTS. Toothed in some insects, needle-like in some others, absent in yet others. iii. A similar structure in certain other ARTHROPODS.

mantle A soft fold of the integument, next to the shell when present, in MOLLUSCS.

maxilla i. The upper jaw, or part of it, in VERTEBRATES. ii. One of the paired appendages behind the mandibles in many ARTHROPODS.

medusa The jelly-fish stage in the life-cycle of many COELENTERATES. Usually dish-shaped with the mouth below, and floating in the water.

meiosis The division of a *diploid* cell to produce *haploid* daughter cells. A two-stage process resulting in four daughter cells. Important in the formation of *gametes.*

mesentery A fold of tissue in an animal holding internal organs in position.

metacercaria A *cerceria* that has developed a protective coat (encysted) while awaiting being eaten by a host.

metamere A body segment.

miracidium The first larval form of a FLUKE which, after hatching from the egg, must burrow into a water snail.

mito-chondrion A minute structure (organelle) within a cell in which energy is produced — the 'power-house' of the cell.

murine Referring to the house-mouse, the black rat and closely related RODENTS.

nasute Specialised soldier-TERMITE which can spray a secretion from the head to defend the colony.

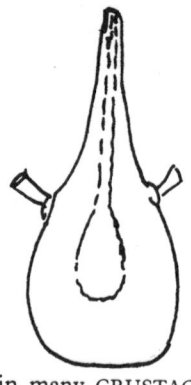

Nasute termite head
(gland dotted)

nauplius larva	A larval form in many CRUSTACEA with a rounded body, three pairs of appendages and a single eye.

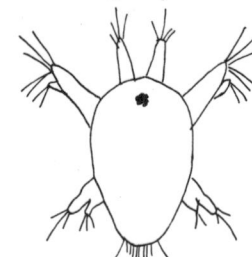

Nauplius larva

nephridium   A primitive and comparatively simple type of excretory organ in many *invertebrates* such as earthworms.

notochord   An elastic skeletal rod beneath the nerve cord in all chordate animals (adults or embryos). In adult VERTEBRATES it is more or less obliterated by the backbone when this develops.

nucleus   An important part of most cells. Bounded by a membrane, it contains the genetic material of the cell, and controls most of the functions of the cell.

nymph   An immature stage in the development of an *exopterygote* INSECT such as cockroach. Usually it resembles the adult but does not have fully grown wings.

ocellum   A simple (one-unit) eye in many ARTHROPODS.

omnivore   An animal which eats a wide variety of food-stuffs including plant and animal matter, e.g. *Homo sapiens*.

ootheca   The egg purse of a COCKROACH or MANTID.

operculum   A flap or lid sealing an aperture, for example in the shell of some snails.

opisthosoma   In some ARACHNIDS such as spiders, the hind part of the body, behind the *prosoma*. Opisthosoma = abdomen; *prosoma = cephalothorax*.

oral surface   In ECHINODERMS the surface carrying the mouth (*cf aboral surface*). In most cases the lower surface.

ossification   The process of being changed into bone.

ovigerous legs   Legs adapted for carrying developing eggs, in particular in the SEA SPIDERS.

oviparous   Reproducing by laying eggs.

ovipositor   Egg-laying apparatus.

ovoviviparous   Reproduction by producing eggs which have a definite shell, but which hatch within the body, for example, many SNAKES.

oxbow   A lake formed by the separation of a loop of a river.

palp   Feelers on the mouthparts of INSECTS (on the *maxilla* and the *labium*) and CRUSTACEA (*mandible*) or close to the mouth of polychaete ANNELIDS. Presumably usually concerned with the senses of taste and touch. Also palpus.

A paradodium with chaetae

parapodium   Paired, fleshy projections on the sides of polychaete ANNELIDS for propulsion or creating currents of water.

parthenogenesis   Reproduction from an egg (animals) or seed (plants) but without fertilisation. Common, for example, in the APHIDS.

pathogen   An organism or virus causing a disease in animals or plants, but usually restricted to micro-organisms.

pecten   Any comb-shaped structure but applied particularly to sense-organs on the undersurface of SCORPIONS, a sound-producing organ in some INSECTS and a blood-vessel structure in the eyes of birds.

pectoral girdle   That part of the skeleton to which the front limbs are attached. Thus pectoral fins in FISHES are the fins attached to the pectoral girdle.

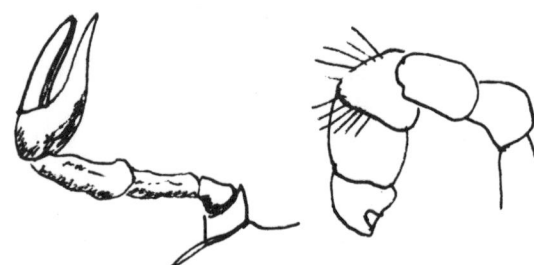

Pedipalps of a scorpion and a male spider

pedipalps   The second pair of appendages in the ARACHNIDS. Their form varies greatly from group to group: in SCORPIONS they are the large pincers, in SPIDERS the 'boxing gloves' which males use to introduce sperm.

pelagic   Organisms living in the open sea.

periostracum   The outermost layer of a MOLLUSC's shell, composed of a horny material. Usually missing from shells in collections.

peristomium   Those parts of an animal that surround its mouth, and especially the first segment of an earthworm.

photophores   A light-producing organ found in some FISHES and CRUSTACEA.

phylum   A major division of the Animal Kingdom. Animals in different phyla differ fundamentally in their basic body plans. Though a major division, some phyla contain very few animals (see PERIPATUS). The term has been replaced in botany by Division though it is still found in some books.

pinnate   Feather-like.

placenta   An organ which links a developing mammal with the uterus of its mother, through which the young mammal is nourished. The term placental mammals is sometimes applied to the EUTHERIAN MAMMALS though a placenta (but of a different structure) is found in some MARSUPIALS.

planula larva   A flat ciliated larva of a COELENTERATE which lacks a body cavity.

plastid   A minute body (organelle) inside a cell, often coloured. Some in plant cells are concerned with photosynthesis.

plastron   i. The ventral parts of the shell of a TORTOISE or turtle, the upper part of which is the *carapace*. ii. The thin silvery coat of air which some air-breathing aquatic INSECTS take with them when they dive.

pleurodire   A TORTOISE or turtle of the group to which all but one of the Australian land and freshwater species belong. Also known as side-neck turtles because of the way in which the neck is folded into the *carapace*.

polyp   The cylindrical form of a COELENTERATE. May be solitary or colonial and usually attached to the *substrate* or to its fellows at the base, and often with a mouth, surrounded by tentacles at the free end.

porocyte   A perforated cell in a SPONGE through which water flows into the inner chambers.

proboscis   A trunk-like projection on the head in some INSECTS, ANNELIDS, and NEMERTEANS. Also the trunk of an elephant; (plural, proboscises).

procaryotic organism   (Also prokaryotic). Primitive unicellular organisms (which may link to form chains) which lack true nuclei and nuclear membranes and *mitochondria*; the bacteria and blue-green ALGAE; *cf. eucaryotic organisms* (eukaryotic).

proglottis   One of the (usually) many segments of a TAPEWORM which bud off from the head or *scolex*; plural, proglottids or proglottides.

proleg   Short unjointed legs on the abdomen of larvae of BUTTERFLIES and MOTHS and some sawflies.

pronotum   The dorsal plate of the first thoracic segment of INSECTS.

prosoma   The front part (cephalothorax) of the body of an ARACHNID carrying the *chelicerae*, *pedipalps* and four pairs of walking legs.

prostomium   The part of the body in front of the mouth in ANNELIDS.

protonymph   Second instar of a MITE.

protoplasm   The living 'stuff' of cells.

pseudocoelom   The body cavity between the outer wall and the internal organs in ROUNDWORMS and some related animals. Similar to the *coelom* but formed embryologically in a different way.

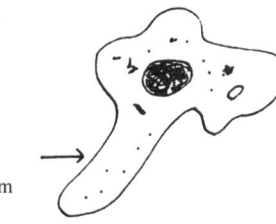

Pseudopodium

pseudopodium   Temporary extrusions of *protoplasm* in some PROTOZOA such as *Amoeba* for movement or to engulf food particles.

pulmonate   Referring to a GASTROPOD mollusc with a 'lung' for breathing air.

pupa   A usually immobile stage in *endopterygote* INSECTS, between the larval stages and the adult. During the pupal stage the body form is completely reorganised.

pygidium   1. The last or anal segment of an ANNELID. ii. In INSECTS the last dorsal segment of the abdomen.

quinones — Chemical compounds widely distributed in nature, particularly in INSECTS and in plants where they may function as feeding deterrents. They contain the benzene ring carrying two double-bonded oxygen atoms.

radially symmetrical — The body symmetry seen in ECHINODERMS and COELENTERATES; *cf. bilaterally symmetrical.*

Radial symmetry

radula — Rasp-like organ in the mouth of certain MOLLUSCS for scraping off particles from their food.

raptorial — Adapted for seizing prey, as the claws of a BIRD OF PREY or the fore-legs of a MANTID.

rastellum — A rake of strong spines on the base of the chelicera of certain SPIDERS which burrow in the soil.

redia — The third larval stage in the lives of certain FLUKES: a sac-like organism in which more rediae or *cercariae* develop.

rift valley — A long valley between *faults*.

rostrum — A pointed projection, for example, on the *carapace* of some crabs.

sacrum or *sacral vertebrae* — Strong, fused *vertebrae* attached to the pelvis.

saprophytic — Living on decomposing organic matter.

scarp — An abrupt slope, sometimes a cliff, formed sometimes as a result of *a fault* or by the erosion of inclined strata of rock.

scolex — The 'head' of a TAPEWORM from which the *proglottids* bud.

scopula — A small, dense, tuft of hairs.

scute — An external scale in REPTILES (especially CROCODILES), FISHES and INSECTS.

selection — The evolutionary process in which an advantageous, inheritable trait becomes general in the population because those individuals possessing it have a better chance of reproducing than those which do not. Selection may be natural, or, as in the breeding of new *cultivars* or varieties of animals, artificial.

septum — A partition between two cavities or two tissues.

sessile — i. In botany, attached directly without a stalk. ii. In zoology, fixed in one position, as is a BARNACLE.

setae — An alternative spelling of *chaetae*.

siliceous — Consisting of silicon dioxide (sand; quartz).

solanaceous — Related to the potato, tomato and nightshades.

somites — Segmentally arranged blocks of the embryonic tissue (mesoderm) in VERTEBRATES which gives rise to muscles, vertebrae and so on.

spat — Larval stages of oysters.

spermatozoa — Male sex cells; sperm.

sphenoid — A wedge-shaped bone in the base of the cranium in some mammals, including man.

spicule — Minute bodies, needle-like or with many points, of calcium carbonate or silica, forming a skeleton in SPONGES, and in some COELENTERATES, ECHINODERMS and PROTOZOA.

sporocyst — i. A stage in the production of spores in certain PROTOZOA when the spores are contained in an envelope before they are liberated. ii. A larval stage in the development of some FLUKES.

strobilation — i. Reproduction by the body segmenting into individuals, as in some TAPEWORMS and COELENTERATES. ii. A segmentation in the formation of cones in CONIFERS, etc.

stylets — A needle-like appendage, as in the mouthparts of MOSQUITOES.

subimago — A winged stage, unique to the MAYFLIES, which moults to the true adult stage or imago.

substrate — A loosely applied term for the material or surface on which an organism lives.

swale — Found in the expression 'swell and swale' (or swag and swell): undulating land, often associated with old glacial deposits.

symbiosis — The living together of two (or more) species to their mutual benefit; LICHENS, for example, are the result of a symbiosis between certain ALGAE and FUNGI.

syndactyle — With some of the digits of the fore or hind limb bound together as in KANGAROOS.

tarsus — i. the heel-bones of a VERTEBRATE. ii. The final few segments of the leg of an INSECT, SPIDER and so on.

tegmen   i. The thickened fore-wing of a CRICKET, LOCUST, COCKROACH and MANTID. ii. The leathery surround of the mouth in a *crinoid*; (plural, tegmina).

telson   A single terminal appendage on the end of the abdomen of ARTHROPODS' — the tail flap in many CRUSTACEA, the sting in a SCORPION, but absent in adult INSECTS.

teratogenic   Referring to an agent which produces birth abnormalities. The drug thalidomide, for example is teratogenic (a teratogen) and the herbicide Agent Orange is alleged to be.

tergum   A dorsal segmental plate in ARTHROPODS.

test   i. The tough coat of an animal such as a SEA-SQUIRT. ii. The tough coat of a seed.

tick, seed   A larval stage of a tick, about the size of a seed.

trachea   i. The wind-pipe in air-breathing vertebrates. ii. One of the breathing tubes which ramify in the body of an INSECT and some other ARTHROPODS. iii. Spiral or ringed vascular tissue in plants.

tracheoles   The finest branches of a *trachea* in animals.

tritonymph   The *instar* following the *deutonymph* in mites.

trochus   A GASTROPOD valued for its mother of pearl.

uniramous   Having no branches. Usually applied to unbranched limbs in ARTHROPODS.

unisexual   Distinctly male or female.

vacuole   A clear space in a cell.

valvate   Hinged only at the margin as in the shells of BIVALVE MOLLUSCS.

vector   An animal which transmits parasites or pathogens. *Anopheles* mosquitoes are vectors of malaria.

venation   The pattern of veins on an INSECT's wing or a leaf: important in identification and classification.

ventral   On, or near, the lower surface of an organism.

vertebra   An individual bone of the backbone.

vesicle   A small gas or fluid-filled cavity in an organism.

viscera   Internal organs often in the various body cavities of an animal: gut, liver, and so on.

viviparous   Bringing young forth alive rather than as an egg.

zygote   A fertilised egg but before it begins to divide (single cell, diploid).

APPENDIX 6

A BIBLIOGRAPHY FOR PLANTS

Australian Forestry & Timber Bureau *Forest Trees of Australia.* Government Printer, Canberra, 1957.

Baglin, D. & Mullins, B. *Australian Wattles.* Horwitz, Sydney, 1968.

Beadle, N.C.W. Evans, O.D. & Carolin, R.C. *Flora of the Sydney Region.* A.H. & A.W. Reed, Sydney, 1972.

Beadle, N.C.W. *Students' Flora of North Eastern New South Wales.* University of New England, Armidale, 1971 (Part 1) 1972 (Part 2) 1976 (Part 3).

Black, J.M. *Flora of South Australia.* (2nd edn) Government Printer, Adelaide, 1960 (Part 1) 1963 (Part 2) 1964 (Part 3) 1965 (Part 4) 1965 (Supplement).

Blake, S.T. & Roff, C. *The Honey Flora of South-Eastern Queensland.* Department of Agriculture and Stock, Brisbane, 1958.

Blomberry, A.M. *What Wildflower is That?* Paul Hamlyn, New South Wales, 1972.

Bold, H.C. *The Plant Kingdom.* (4th edn) Prentice Hall, New Jersey, 1977.

Burbridge, N.T. *The Gum Trees of the Australian Capital Territory.* Tottdell, Canberra, 1963.

Burbridge, N.T. & Gray, M. *Flora of the Australian Capital Territory.* Australian National University Press, Canberra, 1970.

Cady, L. & Rotherham, E.R. *Australian Native Orchids in Colour.* A.H. & A.W. Reed, Sydney, 1970.

Child, J. *Trees of the Sydney Region.* Cheshire-Lansdowne, Melbourne, 1968.

Chippendale, T.M. *Wildflowers of Central Australia.* Jacaranda, Brisbane, 1968.

Chippendale, T.M. & Chippendale, G. *Wildflowers of the Australian Capital Territory.* Jacaranda, Brisbane, 1972.

Clifford, H.T. *Eucalypts of the Brisbane Region.* Queensland Museum, Brisbane, 1972.

Clyne, D. *Australian Ground Orchids.* Periwinkle, Melbourne, 1970.

Clyne, D. *Australian Rock and Tree Orchids.* Periwinkle, Melbourne, 1972.

Crafts, A.S. *Modern Weed Control.* University of California Press, USA, 1975.

Cribb, A.B. & Cribb, J.W. *Wild Food in Australia.* Collins, Sydney, 1974.

Curtis, W.M. *The Students' Flora of Tasmania.* Government Printer, Tasmania, 1956 (Part 1) 1963 (Part 2) 1967 (Part 3).

Dallimore, W. & Jackson, A.B. *A Handbook of the Coniferae and Ginkgoaceae.* (4th edn, revd by Harrison, S.G.) Edward Arnold, 1966.

Debach, P. *Biological Control by Natural Enemies.* Cambridge University Press, New York, 1974.

Dockrill, A.W. *Australian Indigenous Orchids* (vol 1) The Society for Growing Australian Plants, Sydney, 1969.

Erickson, R. *Orchids of the West.* Paterson Brokensha, Perth, 1965.

Everest, S.L. *Poisonous Plants of Australia.* Angus & Robertson, Sydney, 1974.

Fairall, A.R. *West Australian Native Plants in Cultivation.* Pergamon, Australia, 1970.

Francis, W.D. *Australian Rain Forest Trees.* (3rd edn) Australian Government Printer, Canberra, 1970.

Gardner, C.A. *Wildflowers of Western Australia.* West Australian Newspapers Ltd, Perth, 1959.

Garnet, J.R. *The Wildflowers of Wilson's Promontory National Park.* Lothian, Melbourne, 1971.

Good, R. *The Geography of Flowering Plants* (3rd edn) Longman, London, 1964.

Grieve, B.J. & Blackall, W.E. *How to Know Western Australian Wildflowers.* University of Western Australian Press, Perth, 1954 (Part 1) 1956 (Part 2) 1965 (Part 3) 1975 (Part 4).

Harris, T.Y. *Alpine Plants of Australia.* Angus & Robertson, Sydney, 1970.

Hillier & Sons *Hilliers' Manual of Trees and Shrubs.* David & Charles, Newton Abbot, 1974.

Hosel, J. *Wildflowers of South-East Australia.* Lansdowne, Melbourne, 1969.

Hyde-Wyatt, B.H. & Morris, D. *Tasmanian Weed Handbook.* Tasmanian Department of Agriculture, Hobart, 1975.

Kelly, S. *Eucalypts.* Nelson, Melbourne, 1969 (vol 1) 1978 (vol 2).

Lazarides, M. *The Grasses of Central Australia.* Australian National University Press, Canberra, 1970.

Lord, E.E. *Shrubs and Trees for Australian Gardens.* (4th edn) Lothian, Australia, 1970.

Macoboy, S. *What Flower is That?* Paul Hamlyn, New South Wales, 1969.

Maiden, J.H. *The Useful Native Plants of Australia.* (facsimile edn) Compendium, Melbourne, 1975.

Meadly, G.R.W. *Weeds of Western Australia.* Department of Agriculture, Perth, 1965.

Millett, M. *Australian Eucalypts.* Lansdowne, Melbourne, 1969.

Morcombe, M. & Morcombe, I. *Wildflowers of Western Australia.* Lansdowne, Melbourne, 1970.

Morley, B.D. *Wild Flowers of the World.* Rainbird Reference Books, 1970.

Murray, K.G. (ed) *The Alpine Flowers of the Kosciusko State Park.* K.G. Murray Publishing Co., Sydney, 1962.

Oakman, H. *Colourful Trees for Australian Gardens.* Rigby, Adelaide, 1976.

Parsons, W.T. *Noxious Weeds of Victoria.* Inkata, Melbourne, 1973.

Perry, F. *Flowers of the World.* Paul Hamlyn, England, 1972.

Rose, J. *Herbs and Things.* Grosset & Dunlap, New York, 1972.

Saddler, M. & Gemmell, N. *Gum Trees in South Australia.* Investigator, Adelaide, 1969.

Scott, A.M., Stone, I.G. & Rosser, C. *The Mosses of Southern Australia.* Academic Press, London, 1976.

Specht, R.L. 'Vegetation' in Leeper, G.W. (ed) *The Australian Environment.* (4th edn) CSIRO & Melbourne University Press, Melbourne, 1970.

Specht, R.L. *The Vegetation of South Australia* (2nd edn) Government Printer, Adelaide, 1972.

Specht, R.L., Roe, E.M. & Boughton, V.W. 'Conservation of Major Plant Communities in Australia and Papua New Guinea' in *Australian Journal of Botany.* (Supplement No 7) CSIRO, Melbourne, 1974.

Swarbrick, J.T. *The Australian Weed Control Handbook.* (3rd edn) Plant Press, Toowoomba, 1976.

Tothill, J.C. & Hacker, J.P. *The Grasses of South East Queensland.* Queensland University Press, Brisbane, 1973.

Wakefield, N.A. *Ferns of Victoria and Tasmania.* Field Naturalists Club of Victoria, Melbourne, 1955.

Willis, J.H. *A Handbook to Plants in Victoria.* (vol 1) Melbourne University Press, Melbourne, 1962.

Willis, J.H., Fuhrer, B.A. & Rotherham, E.R. *Field Guide to the Flowers and Plants of Victoria.* A.H. & A.W. Reed, Melbourne, 1975.

Woods, A. *Pest Control: A Survey.* McGraw-Hill, UK, 1974.

Also: Pamphlets published by Department of Agriculture in each State and Territory.

APPENDIX 7

ANIMALS EXTINCT,
ENDANGERED OR VULNERABLE
SINCE 1788

The animals listed here as extinct may not yet be so as information is incomplete and records may be revised within the next few years. However, if they are not extinct they are certainly very rare, some of them not having been seen since the 19th century. In some cases recent intensive searches have failed to find the animals concerned. Some of the animals extinct before the arrival of the Europeans are referred to in the entry on FOSSILS.

Abbreviations: V, vulnerable; EN, endangered; EX, extinct; po. possibly; pr, probably. Dates, when given, are those of the last known reliable sighting or capture in the wild.

Marsupials

1. Macropodoidea (KANGAROOS AND WALLABIES).
Bettongia penicillata, brush-tail bettong, EN;
B. lesuer, burrowing bettong, V;
B. tropica, northern bettong, V;
Caloprymnus campestris, desert rat-kangaroo, prEX (1935);
Potorous longipes, long-footed potoroo, EN;
P. Platyops, broad-faced potoroo, prEX (1875);
Lagorchestes asomatus, central hare-wallaby, prEX (1931);
L. hirsutus, rufous hare-wallaby, V;
L. leporides, eastern hare-wallaby, prEx (1890);
Lagostrophus fasciatus, banded hare-wallaby, V;
Onychogalea fraenata, bridled nail-tail wallaby, EN;
O. lunata, crescent nail-tail wallaby, prEX (1956?);
Petrogale persephone, Proserpine rock wallaby, poV;
Macropus greyi, Toolache wallaby, prEX (1920s).

Numbat

2. Dasyuridae, Myrmecobiidae (NATIVE CATS AND THEIR ALLIES).
Parantechinus apicalis, dibbler, VpoEN;
Phascogale calura, red-tailed phascogale, poEND;
Sminthopsis douglasi, Julia Creek dunnart, poV;
S. psammophila, sandhill dunnart, poV;
Myrmecobius fasciatus, numbat, EN.

3. Thylacinidae (THYLACINE OR TASMANIAN WOLF).
Thylacinus cyanocephalus, Tasmanian wolf, prEX though many biologists believe that it may survive. Report in early 1984, for example, claimed that it can still be found in TAS.

4. Phalangeroidea (POSSUMS AND GLIDERS)
Gymnobelideus leadbeateri, Leadbeater's possum, EN;
Burramys parvus, mountain pygmy possum, V.

5. Vombatidae (WOMBATS)
Lasiorhinus barnardi, hairy-nosed wombat, EN.

6. Perameloidea (BANDICOOTS)
Chaeropus ecaudatus, pig-footed bandicoot, prEX (1920s, reported by Aborigines);
Perameles bougainville, western barred bandicoot, V;
P. eremiana, desert bandicoot, prEX (1931);
Macrotis lagotis, greater bilby, EN.

Pig-footed bandicoot

Eutherian Mammals (Terrestrial)

1. Chiroptera (BATS).

Macroderma gigas, ghost bat, V;
Rhinonycteris aurantius, orange horseshoe bat, V.

2. Rodentia (RODENTS)
Conilurus albipes, white-footed tree-rat, prEX (1875);
Leporillus apicalis, lesser stick-nest rat, prEX (1933);
L. conditor, greater stick-nest rat, V;
Notomys amplus, short-tailed hopping-mouse, prEX (only 2 specimens known, 1896);
N. aquilo, northern hopping-mouse, poV;
N. longicaudatus, long-tailed hopping-mouse, poEX (1901);
N. macrotis, big-eared hopping-mouse, prEX (2 specimens, 1850);
N. mordax, Darling-Downs hopping-mouse prEX (1 specimen, before 1846);
Pseudomys fieldi, Alice Springs mouse, prEX (1 specimen, 1895);
P. pillagensis, Pilliga mouse, poV;
P. praeconis, Shark Bay mouse, V;
P. oralis, Hastings River mouse, V;
P. shortridgei, heath mouse VpoEN;
Zyzomys pedunculatus, Central rock-rat, poV.

Birds (excluding endangered species on islands such as Norfolk, Christmas, and Lord Howe).
Pterodroma leucoptera leucoptera, Gould's petrel, EN;
Stictonetta naevosa, freckled duck, V;
Erythrotriochis radiatus, red goshawk, poV;
Pedionomus torquatus, plains-wanderer, EN;
Eupodotis australis, bustard, V;
Anous tenuirostris, lesser noddy, V;
Geopsittacus occidentalis, night parrot, rare, long thought extinct, recently sighted (1979);
Cyclopsitta diopthalmia coxeni, Coxen's fig parrot, EN sub-species;
Neophema chrysogaster, orange-bellied parrot, EN;
Pezoporus wallicus, ground parrot, EN;
Psephotus chrysopterygius, golden-shouldered parrot, this race of the species EN;
P. pulcherrimus, paradise parrot, prEX (1927);
Atrichornis clamosus, noisy scrub-bird, V;
A. rufescens, rufous scrub-bird, V;

Noisy scrub-bird

Malurus coronatus, purple-crowned fairy-wren, V;
Amytornis dorothaea, Carpentarian grass-wren, V;
Dasyornis longirostris, western bristlebird, EN;
D. brachypterus, eastern bristlebird, poV;
Pardolotus quadragintus, forty-spotted pardalote, V;
Dromaius novaehollandiae, subspecies of TAS, KANGAROO ISLAND and KING ISLAND, and possibly some on mainland, EX.

Paradise parrot

Other Vertebrates Little is known of the status of many other vertebrates. The following lists only EN and EX species.

Reptiles
Pseudemydura umbrina, western swamp tortoise, EN;
Aprasia parapulchella, legless lizard, EN;
Hoplocephalus bungaroides, broad-headed snake, EN;
Dermochelys coriacea, leathery turtle, EN.

Amphibians
Rheobatrachus silus, platypus frog, EN.

Fishes
Maccullochella macquariensis, Murray cod, trout cod, EN.
Source; Groves, R.H. and W.D.L. Ride (Editors), *Species at Risk; Research in Australia,* Australian Academy of Science, Canberra, 1982.

APPENDIX 8

AUSTRALIAN MEDALLISTS IN OLYMPIC GAMES

Russell Mockridge

1896 Athens

Athletics Men:	E.H. Flack	800m	Gold
	E.H. Flack	1500m	Gold

1900 Paris

Archery Men:	Mackintosh	Game Shooting	Gold
Athletics Men:	S. Rowley	60m	Bronze
	S. Rowley	100m	Bronze
	S. Rowley	200m	Bronze
Swimming Men:	F. Lane	200m Freestyle	Gold
	F. Lane	200m Obstacle Race	Gold

1904 St Louis, USA
No medals

1908 London

Boxing	R.L. BAKER	Middleweight	Silver
Rugby Football	Australian team		Gold
Swimming Men:	F.E. BEAUREPAIRE	400m Freestyle	Silver
	F.E. Beaurepaire	1500m Freestyle	Bronze

1912 Stockholm

Swimming Men:	C. Healy		
	H. Hardwick	800m Relay	Gold
	L. Boardman		
	M. Champion		
	C. Healy	100m Freestyle	Silver
	H. Hardwick	400m Freestyle	Bronze
	H. Hardwick	1500m Freestyle	Bronze
Swimming Women:	F. DURACK	100m Freestyle	Gold
	M. Wylie	100m Freestyle	Silver

1920 Antwerp

Athletics Men:	G.R. Parker	3000m Walk	Silver

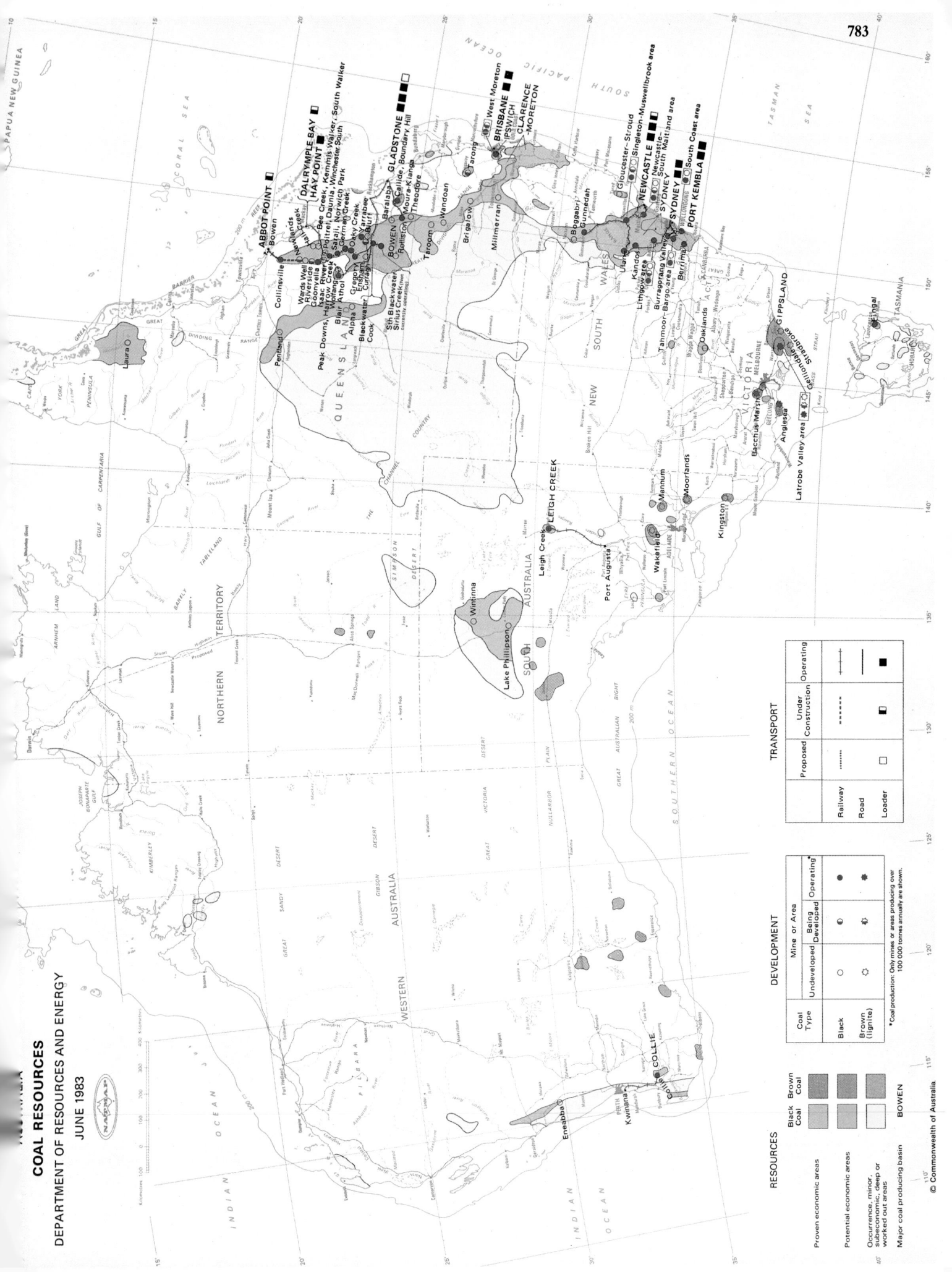

COAL RESOURCES

DEPARTMENT OF RESOURCES AND ENERGY

JUNE 1983

RESOURCES

	Black Coal	Brown Coal
Proven economic areas		
Potential economic areas		
Occurrence, minor, subeconomic, deep or worked out areas		
Major coal producing basin		BOWEN

DEVELOPMENT

Coal Type	Mine or Area		
	Undeveloped	Being Developed	Operating
Black	○	◑	●
Brown (lignite)	✿	✾	✸

*Coal production: Only mines or areas producing over 100 000 tonnes annually are shown.

TRANSPORT

	Proposed	Under Construction	Operating
Railway	·······	-------	—+—
Road	·······	-------	——
Loader	☐	◧	■

© Commonwealth of Australia

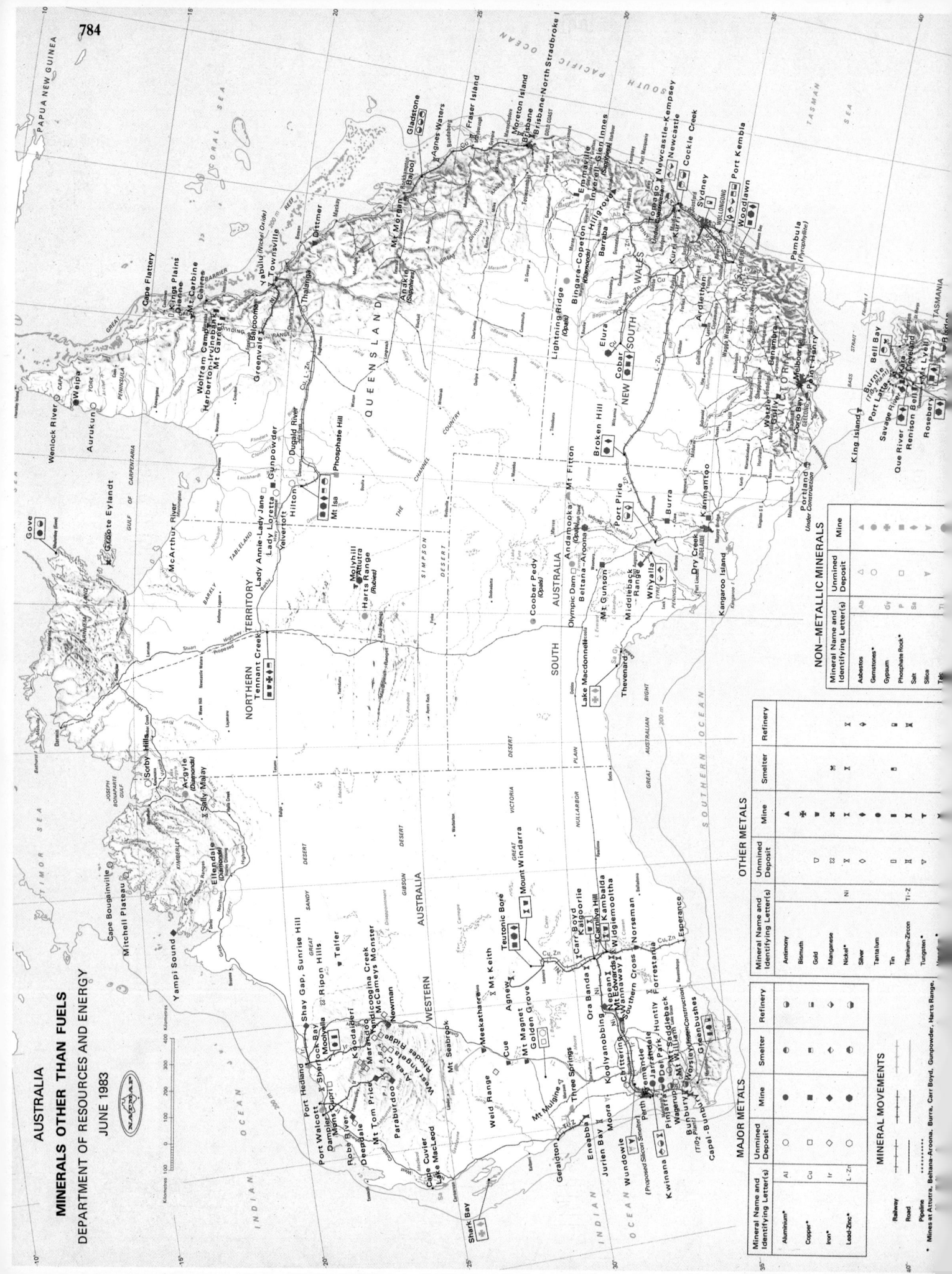

784

AUSTRALIA
MINERALS OTHER THAN FUELS
DEPARTMENT OF RESOURCES AND ENERGY
JUNE 1983

Swimming Men:	F.E. Beaurepaire		
	W. Herald	800m Relay	Silver
	I. Stedman		
	H. Hay		
	F.E. Beaurepaire	1500m Freestyle	Bronze

1924 Paris

Athletics Men:	A.W. Winter	Hop, Step and Jump	Gold
Diving Men:	R.C. Eve	Plain High Tower Dive	Gold
Swimming Men:	A. CHARLTON	1500m Freestyle	Gold
	F.E. Beaurepaire		
	A. Charlton	800m Relay	Silver
	M. Christie		
	E. Henry		
	A. Charlton	400m Freestyle	Bronze
	F.E. Beaurepaire	1500m Freestyle	Bronze

1928 Amsterdam

Cycling	E.L. Gray	1000m Time Trial	Bronze
Rowing	H.R. PEARCE	Single Sculls	Gold
Swimming Men:	A. Charlton	400m Freestyle	Silver
	A. Charlton	1500m Freestyle	Silver

1932 Los Angeles

Cycling	E.L. Gray	1000m Time Trial	Gold
Rowing	H.R. PEARCE	Single Sculls	Gold
Swimming Women:	C. Dennis	200m Breaststroke	Gold
	P. Mealing	100m Backstroke	Silver
Wrestling	E. Scarf	Light Heavyweight	Bronze

1936 Berlin

Athletics Men:	J. Metcalfe	Hop, Step and Jump	Bronze

1948 London

Athletics Men:	J. Winter	High Jump	Gold
	G. Avery	Hop, Step and Jump	Silver
	T.W. Bruce	Long Jump	Silver
Athletics Women:	S. STRICKLAND		
	J. Matson	400m Relay	Silver
	B. McKinnon		
	J. King		
	S. Strickland	100m	Bronze
	S. Strickland	80m Hurdles	Bronze
Rowing	M.T. Wood	Single Sculls	Gold
Swimming Men:	J. Marshall	1500m Freestyle	Silver
	J. Marshall	400m Freestyle	Bronze
Swimming Women:	N. Lyons	200m Breaststroke	Silver
	J.J. Davies	100m Backstroke	Bronze
Wrestling	R. Garrard	Welterweight	Silver
	J. Armstrong	Heavyweight	Bronze

1952 Helsinki

Athletics Women:	M. JACKSON	100m	Gold
	M. Jackson	200m	Gold
	S. Strickland	80m Hurdles	Gold
	S. Strickland	100m	Bronze
Cycling	R. MOCKRIDGE	1000m Time Trial	Gold
	R. Mockridge	2000m Tandem	Gold
	L. Cox		
	L. Cox	1000m Sprint	Silver
Rowing	M.T. Wood	Single Sculls	Silver
	Australian Crew	Eights	Bronze
Swimming Men:	J. Davies	200m Breaststroke	Gold
Weightlifting	V. Barberis	Lightweight	Bronze

1956 Melbourne

Athletics Men:	G. Gipson		
	L. Gregory	4×400m Relay	Silver
	D. Lean		
	K. Gosper		

	C. Porter	High Jump	Silver
	H. Hogan	100m	Bronze
	J. LANDY	1500m	Bronze
	A. Lawrence	10 000m	Bronze

Australian News & Information Bureau

John Landy

Athletics Women:	B. CUTHBERT	100m	Gold
	B. Cuthbert	200m	Gold
	S. Strickland	80m Hurdles	Gold
	S. Strickland		
	N. Crocker	4×100m Relay	Gold
	F. Mellor		
	B. Cuthbert		
	M. Mathews	100m	Bronze
	M. Mathews	200m	Bronze
	N. Thrower	80m Hurdles	Bronze
Boxing	K. Hogarth	Welterweight	Bronze
Canoeing	D. Green	10 000m Kayak Pairs	Bronze
	W. Brown		
Cycling	I. Browne	2000m Tandem	Gold
	A. Marchant		
	R. Ploog	1000m Sprint	Bronze
Rowing	S. McKENZIE	Single Sculls	Silver
	M. Riley	Double Sculls	Bronze
	M.T. Wood		
	Australian Crew	Eights	Bronze
Swimming Men:	J. HENRICKS	100m Freestyle	Gold
	M. Rose	400m Freestyle	Gold
	M. Rose	1500m Freestyle	Gold
	D. Thiele	100m Backstroke	Gold
	K. O'Halloran		
	J. Devitt	4×200m Relay	Gold
	M. Rose		
	J. Henricks		
	J. Devitt	100m Freestyle	Silver
	J. Monckton	100m Backstroke	Silver
	G. Chapman	100m Freestyle	Bronze
Swimming Women:	L. CRAPP	400m Freestyle	Gold
	D. FRASER	100m Freestyle	Gold

	D. Fraser		
	F. Leech	4×100m Relay	Gold
	S. Morgan		
	L. Crapp		
	L. Crapp	100m Freestyle	Silver
	D. Fraser	400m Freestyle	Silver
	F. Leech	100m Freestyle	Bronze
Yachting	R. Tasker	International 12m² Sharpie Class	Silver
	J. Sturrock	5.5 metre Class	Bronze

1960 Rome:

Athletics Men:	H. ELLIOTT	1500m	Gold
	N. Freeman	20km Walk	Silver
	D. Power	10 000m	Bronze
Athletics Women:	B. Jones	800m	Silver
Boxing	A. Madigan	Light Heavyweight	Bronze
	O. Taylor	Bantamweight	Bronze
Equestrian Sport	L. Morgan		
	N. Lavis	Three-day Event	Gold
	W. ROYCROFT		
	L. Morgan	Individual Event	Gold
	N. Lavis	Individual Event	Silver
Swimming Men:	J. Devitt	100m Freestyle	Gold
	J. KONRADS	1500m Freestyle	Gold
	M. Rose	400m Freestyle	Gold
	D. Thiele	100m Backstroke	Gold
	N. Hayes	200m Butterfly	Silver
	M. Rose	1500m Freestyle	Silver
	D. Thiele		
	T. Gathercole	4×100m Medley Relay	Silver
	N. Hayes		
	C. Shipton		
	J. Konrads	400m Freestyle	Bronze
	D. Dickson		
	J. Devitt	4×200m Relay	Bronze
	M. Rose		
	J. Konrads		
Swimming Women:	D. Fraser	100m Freestyle	Gold
	D. Fraser		
	I. Konrads	4×100m Relay	Silver
	L. Crapp		
	A. Colquhoun		
	M. Wilson		
	F. Lassig	4×100m Medley Relay	Silver
	J. Andrew		
	D. Fraser		
	J. Andrew	100m Butterfly	Bronze

1964 Tokyo

Athletics Men:	R.W. CLARKE	10 000m	Bronze
Athletics Women:	B. Cuthbert	400m	Gold
	M.M. Brown	High Jump	Silver
	J.F. Amoore	400m	Bronze
	M. Black	200m	Bronze
	P. Kilborn	80m Hurdles	Bronze
Hockey	Australian team		Bronze
Judo	T. Boronovskis	Open	Bronze
Swimming Men:	K.J. Berry	200m Butterfly	Gold
	I. O'Brien	200m Breaststroke	Gold
	R.G. Windle	1500m Freestyle	Gold
	A.F. Wood	400m Freestyle	Bronze
	A.F. Wood	1500m Freestyle	Bronze
	K.J. Berry		
	D.G. Dickson	4×100m Medley Relay	Bronze
	I. O'Brien		
	P.A. Reynolds		

	D.G. Dickson		
	P.J. Doak	4×100m Relay	Bronze
	J.S. Ryan		
	R.G. Windle		
Swimming Women:	D. Fraser	100m Freestyle	Gold
	L. Bell		
	D. Fraser	4×100m Relay	Silver
	J. Murphy		
	R. Thorn		
Yachting	W. NORTHAM	5.5 metre Class	Gold

Courtesy of A.I.S. Canberra

Bill Northam presented his gold medal winning yacht *Barrenjoey* to the Royal Prince Alfred Yacht Club in Sydney

1968 Mexico

Athletics Men:	R. Doubell	800m	Gold
	P. Norman	200m	Silver
Athletics Women:	M. Caird	80m Hurdles	Gold
	R. Boyle	200m	Silver
	P. Kilborn	80m Hurdles	Silver
	J. Lamy	200m	Bronze
Equestrian Sport	William Roycroft		
	Wayne ROYCROFT	Three-day Event	Bronze
	J. Scanlon		
	B. Cobcroft		
Hockey	Australian team		Silver

Australian News & Information Bureau

Olympic equestrian, Bill Roycroft

Australian News & Information Bureau

Middle distance runner, Ralph Doubell

Rowing	Australian crew	Eights	Silver
Swimming Men:	M. WENDEN	100m Freestyle	Gold
	M. Wenden	200m Freestyle	Gold
	G. Rogers		
	G. White	4×200m Relay	Silver
	R. Windle		
	M. Wenden		
	G. Brough	1500 Freestyle	Bronze
	G. Rogers		
	R. Cusack	4×100m Relay	Bronze
	R. Windle		
	M. Wenden		
Swimming Women:	L. McClements	100m Butterfly	Gold
	L. Watson		
	J. Playfair	4×100m Medley Relay	Silver
	L. McClements		
	J. Steinbeck		
	K. Moras	400m Freestyle	Bronze

1972 Munich

Athletics Women:	R. Boyle	100m	Silver
	R. Boyle	200m	Silver
Cycling	D. Clark	1000m Time Trial	Silver
	J. NICHOLSON	1000m Sprint	Silver
	C. Sefton	Road Race	Silver
Swimming Men:	B. Cooper	400m Freestyle	Gold
	G. Windeatt	1500m Freestyle	Silver
Swimming Women:	S. GOULD	200m Medley	Gold
	S. Gould	200m Freestyle	Gold
	S. Gould	400m Freestyle	Gold
	B. Whitfield	200m Breaststroke	Gold
	G. Neal	400m Medley	Gold
	S. Gould	800m Freestyle	Silver
	S. Gould	100m Freestyle	Bronze
	B. Whitfield	100m Breaststroke	Bronze
Yachting	J. Cuneo		
	T. Anderson	Dragon Class	Gold
	J. Shaw		
	D. Forbes		
	J. Anderson	Star Class	Gold

1976 Montreal

Equestrian Sport	William Roycroft		
	M. Bennett	Three-day Event	Bronze
	D. Pigott		
	Wayne Roycroft		
Hockey	Australian team		Silver
Swimming Men:	S. Holland	1500m Freestyle	Bronze
Yachting	J. Bertrand	Finn Class	Bronze
	I. Brown		
	I. Ruff	470 Class	Bronze

1980 Moscow

Athletics Men:	R. Mitchell	400m Sprint	Silver
Canoeing Men:	J. Sumegi	Single Kayak 500m	Silver
Swimming Men:	M. Kerry		
	M. Tonelli		
	P. Evans	4 x 100m Medley Relay	Gold
	N. Brooks		
	G. Brewer	200m Freestyle	Bronze
	P. Evans	100m Breaststroke	Bronze
	M. Kerry	200m Backstroke	Bronze
	M. Metzker	1500m Freestyle	Bronze
Swimming Women:	M. Ford	800m Freestyle	Gold
	M. Ford	200m Butterfly	Bronze

APPENDIX 9

AUSTRALIAN GOLD MEDALLISTS IN COMMONWEALTH GAMES

1911 Festival of Empire, London, England

Boxing	H. Hardwick	Heavyweight
Swimming Men:	H. Hardwick	100 yards Freestyle

1930 Hamilton, Canada

Rowing	H.R. Pearce	Single Sculls
Swimming Men:	N. Ryan	440 yards Freestyle
	N. Ryan	1500 yards Freestyle

1934 London, England

Athletics Men:	J. Metcalfe	Hop, Step and Jump
Boxing	L. Cook	Lightweight
Cycling	E. Duncan Gray	1000m Time Trial
Swimming Men:	N. Ryan	440 yards Freestyle
	N. Ryan	1500 yards Freestyle
Swimming Women:	C. Dennis	220 yards Breaststroke
Wrestling	R. Garrard	Lightweight
	J. Knight	Heavyweight

1938 Sydney, Australia

Athletics Men:	J. Metcalfe	Hop, Step and Jump
Athletics Women:	D. Norman	100 yards
	D. Norman	220 yards
	D. Norman	Long Jump
	J. Coleman	
	A. Wearne	440 yards relay (220, 110, 110)
	D. Norman	
	J. Coleman	
	D. Norman	660 yards Relay (220, 110, 220, 110)
	T. Peake	
	J. Woodland	
Boxing	W. Smith	Welterweight
Cycling	E. Duncan Gray	1000m Sprint
	R. Porter	1000m Time Trial
Rowing	W. Bradley	Double Sculls
	C. Pearce	
	H. Turner	Single Sculls
	H. Freeth	
	D. Fraser	
	S. Elder	Coxed Fours
	J. Fisher (Stroke)	
	W. Kerr (cox)	
Swimming Men:	P. Oliver	110 yards Backstroke
Swimming Women:	B. de Lacy	110 yards Freestyle
	D. Green	440 yards Freestyle
	P. Norton	110 yards Backstroke
Diving Men:	R. Masters	Springboard
Diving Women:	I. Donnett	Springboard
	L. Hook	Tower

Wrestling	R. Garrard	Lightweight
	J. Knight	Heavyweight
	E. Purcell	Bantamweight
	R. Purchase	Featherweight
	E. Scarf	Light-Heavyweight
	J. Trevaskis	Welterweight

1950 Auckland, New Zealand

Athletics Men:	E.W. Carr	440 yards
	P. Gardner	120 yards Hurdles
	B. Oliver	Hop, Step and Jump
	I. Reed	Discus
	J. Treloar	100 yards
	J. Treloar	220 yards
	J. Winter	High Jump
	W. de Gruchy	
	D. Johnson	4×110 yards Relay
	A. Gordon	
	J. Treloar	
	R. Price	
	G. Gedge	4×440 yards Relay
	J. Humphreys	
	E.W. Carr	
Athletics Women:	M. JACKSON	100 yards
	M. Jackson	220 yards
	C. McGibbon	Javelin
	S. STRICKLAND	80m Hurdles
	M. Jackson	
	S. Strickland	440 yards Relay (220, 110, 110)
	V. Johnston	
	S. Strickland	
	V. Johnston	660 yards Relay (220, 110, 220, 110)
	M. Jackson	
	A. Shanley	
Cycling	W. Heseltine	10 miles Track
	R. MOCKRIDGE	1000m Sprint
	R. Mockridge	1000m Time Trial
	H. Sutherland	100km Road Race
Fencing	A. Jay	
	I. Lund	Épée Team
	C. Stanmore	
Rowing	W. Lambert	
	J. Webster	Pair-oar
	M. Riley	
	M.T. Wood	Double Sculls
	M.T. Wood	Single Sculls
	Australian crew	Eight-oar
Swimming Men:	D. Agnew	440 yards Freestyle
	D. Hawkins	220 yards Breaststroke
Swimming Women:	J.J. Davies	110 yards Backstroke
	M. McQuade	110 yards Freestyle
	J.J. Davies	
	M. McQuade	4×110 yards Freestyle Relay
	D. Norton	
	D. Spencer	
	J.J. Davies	
	B. Lyons	330 yards Medley Relay
	M. McQuade	
Water Polo	Australian team	
Wrestling	J. Armstrong	Heavyweight
	R. Garrard	Lightweight
	B. Harris	Flyweight

1954 Vancouver, Canada

Athletics Men:	J. Achurch	Javelin
	K. Gosper	440 yards
	D. Lean	440 yards Hurdles
Athletics Women:	M. Jackson-Nelson	100 yards
	M. Jackson-Nelson	220 yards
	G. Wallace	
	N. Fogarty	4×110 yards Relay
	W. Cripps	
	M. Jackson-Nelson	
Cycling	L. Cox	10 miles Track
	R. Ploog	1000m Time Trial (tie)
Fencing	I. Lund	Épée
Rowing	M. Riley	
	M.T. Wood	Double Sculls
	G. Williamson	
	P. Evatt	Coxed Fours
	M. Wood	
	D. Anderson (stroke)	
	L. Roberts (cox)	
Swimming Men:	G. Chapman	440 yards Freestyle
	J. HENRICKS	110 yards Freestyle
	G. Chapman	
	R. Aubrey	4×220 yards Freestyle Relay
	D. Hawkins	
	J. Henricks	
	C. Weld	
	D. Hawkins	330 yards Medley Relay
	J. Henricks	
Swimming Women:	L. CRAPP	110 yards Freestyle
	L. Crapp	440 yards Freestyle
Diving Women:	B. McAulay	Tower
Weightlifting	V. Barberis	Lightweight
Wrestling	G. Jameson	Bantamweight

1958 Cardiff, Wales

Athletics Men:	H. ELLIOTT	880 yards
	H. Elliott	Mile
	D. Power	6 Miles
	D. Power	Marathon
	I. Tomlinson	Triple Jump
Athletics Women:	M. Mason	High Jump
	M. Mathews-Willard	100 yards
	M. Mathews-Willard	220 yards
	A. Pazera	Javelin
	N. Thrower	80m Hurdles
Boxing	A. Madigan	Light-Heavyweight
	W. Taylor	Featherweight
Cycling	I. Browne	10 miles Track
	R. Ploog	1000m Sprint
Rowing	S. MACKENZIE	Single Sculls
Swimming Men:	J. Devitt	110 yards Freestyle
	T. Gathercole	220 yards Breaststroke
	J. KONRADS	440 yards Freestyle
	J. Konrads	1650 yards Freestyle
	J. Monckton	110 yards Backstroke
	J. Konrads	
	B. Wilkinson	4×220 yards Freestyle Relay
	J. Devitt	
	G. Chapman	
	J. Monckton	
	T. Gathercole	4×110 yards Medley Relay
	B. Wilkinson	
	J. Devitt	

John Devitt

John Konrads and his sister, Ilsa

Swimming Women:

B. Bainbridge	110 yards Butterfly
D. FRASER	110 yards Freestyle
I. KONRADS	440 yards Freestyle
D. Fraser	
S. Morgan	4×110 yards Freestyle Relay
L. Crapp	
A. Colquhoun	
M. Santos	

Weightlifting — Mid-Heavyweight

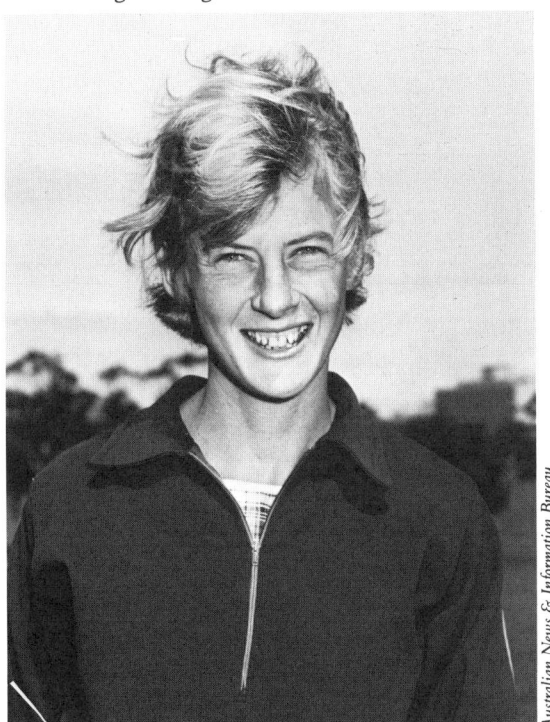

Betty Cuthbert

Kevin Berry

1962 Perth, Australia

Athletics Men:

T. Bickle	Pole Vault
P. Hobson	High Jump
A. Mitchell	Javelin
K. Roche	440 yards Hurdles
W. Selvey	Discus
I. Tomlinson	Triple Jump
T. Vincent	3000m Steeplechase

Athletics Women:

P. Kilborn	80m Hurdles
P. Kilborn	Long Jump
D. Willis	880 yards
R. Woodhouse	High Jump

	J. Bennet	
	G. Beasley	4×110 yards Relay
	B. Cox	
	B. CUTHBERT	
Boxing	J. Dynevor	Bantamweight
	A. Madigan	Light-Heavyweight
Cycling	D. Adams	10 miles Track
	P. Bartels	1000m Time Trial
	T. Harrison	1000m Sprint
	M. Langshaw	4000m Pursuit
Fencing	I. Lund	Epee
Rowing	Australian crew	Eight-oar
Swimming Men:	A. Alexander	440 yards Individual Medley
	K. Berry	110 yards Butterfly
	K. Berry	220 yards Butterfly
	J. Carroll	220 yards Backstroke
	I. O'Brien	110 yards Breaststroke
	I. O'Brien	220 yards Breaststroke
	M. ROSE	440 yards Freestyle
	M. Rose	1650 yards Freestyle
	P. Phelps	
	M. Rose	4×110 yards Freestyle Relay
	P. Doak	
	D. Dickson	
	M. Rose	
	A. Wood	4×220 yards Freestyle Relay
	A. Strahan	
	R. Windle	
	J. Carroll	
	I. O'Brien	4×110 yards Medley Relay
	K. Berry	
	D. Dickson	
Swimming Women:	D. Fraser	110 yards Freestyle
	D. Fraser	440 yards Freestyle
	L. Bell	
	R. Everuss	4×110 yards Freestyle Relay
	R. Thorn	
	D. Fraser	
	P. Sargeant	
	M. Ruygrok	4×110 yards Medley Relay
	L. McGill	
	D. Fraser	
Diving Women:	S. Knight	Tower
	S. Knight	Springboard
Weightlifting	A. Shannos	Heavyweight

1966 Kingston, Jamaica

Athletics Men:	T. Bickle	Pole Vault
	N. Clough	880 yards
	L. Peckham	High Jump
	K. Roche	440 yards Hurdles
Athletics Women:	M. Brown	High Jump
	D. Burge	100 yards
	D. Burge	220 yards
	P. Kilborn	80m Hurdles
	M. Parker	Javelin
	J. Pollock	440 yards
	J. Lamy	
	P. Kilborn	4×110 yards Relay
	J. Bennett	
	D. Burge	
Swimming Men:	R. Jackson	1650 yards Freestyle
	I. O'Brien	110 yards Breaststroke
	I. O'Brien	220 yards Breaststroke

	P. Reynolds	110 yards Backstroke
	P. Reynolds	220 yards Backstroke
	P. Reynolds	440 yards Individual Medley
	M. WENDEN	110 yards Freestyle
	R. Windle	440 yards Freestyle
	M. Wenden	
	J. Ryan	4×110 yards Freestyle Relay
	D. Dickson	
	R. Windle	
	M. Wenden	
	P. Reynolds	4×220 yards Freestyle Relay
	D. Dickson	
	R. Windle	
Swimming Women:	K. Wainwright	440 yards Freestyle
Weightlifting	G. Vakakis	Light-Heavyweight

Australian News & Information Bureau

Michael Wenden

1970 Edinburgh, Scotland

Athletics Men:	N. Freeman	20 mile Walk
	A. Manning	3000m Steeplechase
	P. May	Triple Jump
	L. Peckham	High Jump
	G. Smith	Decathlon
Athletics Women:	R. Boyle	100m
	R. Boyle	200m
	P. Kilborn	100m Hurdles
	P. Rivers	Javelin
	J. Lamy	
	P. Kilborn	4×100m Relay
	M. Hoffman	
	R. Boyle	
Cycling	G. Johnson	Tandem
	R. Jonker	
	J. Nicholson	1000m Sprint
Swimming Men:	M. Wenden	100m Freestyle
	M. Wenden	200m Freestyle
	G. White	400m Freestyle
	G. Windeatt	1500m Freestyle
	G. Rogers	
	W. Devenish	4×100m Freestyle Relay
	G. White	
	M. Wenden	
Swimming Women:	D. Langford	200m Individual Medley
	D. Langford	400m Individual Medley
	K. Moras	200m Freestyle
	K. Moras	400m Freestyle
	K. Moras	800m Freestyle

	M. Robinson	200m Butterfly
	L. Watson	100m Backstroke
	L. Watson	200m Backstroke
	B. Whitfield	100m Breaststroke
	B. Whitfield	200m Breaststroke
	D. Cain	
	L. Watson	4×100m Freestyle Relay
	J. Watts	
	D. Langford	
	L. Watson	
	B. Whitfield	4×100m Medley Relay
	A. Mabb	
	D. Langford	
Diving Men:	D. Wagstaff	Springboard
	D. Wagstaff	High Dive
Weightlifting	N. Ciancio	Light-Heavyweight
	R. Perry	Middleweight
	R. Rigby	Super-Heavyweight
	G. Vasiliades	Flyweight

1974 Christchurch, New Zealand

Athletics Men:	D. Baird	Pole Vault
	G. Windeyer	High Jump
	G. Lewis	
	L. D'Arcy	4×100m Relay
	A. Ratcliffe	
	G. Haskell	
Athletics Women:	R. Boyle	100m
	R. Boyle	200m
	C. Rendina	800m
	P. Rivers	Javelin
	J. Lamy	
	D. Robertson	4×100m Relay
	B. Boak	
	R. Boyle	
Cycling	J. NICHOLSON	1000m Sprint
	A. Paris	1000m Time Trial
	C. Sefton	114 mile Road Race
Shooting	Y. Gowland	Small-bore
Swimming Men:	S. Badger	200m Freestyle
	B. Cooper	200m Backstroke
	S. Holland	1500m Freestyle
	J. Kulasalu	400m Freestyle
	N. Rogers	100m Butterfly
	M. Tonelli	100m Backstroke
	M. Wenden	100m Freestyle
	J. Kulasalu	
	R. Nay	4×200m Freestyle Relay
	S. Badger	
	M. Wenden	
Swimming Women:	S. Gray	100m Freestyle
	S. Gray	200m Freestyle
	J. Turrall	400m Freestyle
	S. Yost	200m Butterfly
Diving Men:	D. Wagstaff	Springboard
	D. Wagstaff	Highboard
Weightlifting	M. Adams	Bantamweight
	N. Ciancio	Mid-Heavyweight
	G. Vasiliades	Featherweight

1978 Edmonton, Canada

Athletics Men:	P. Farmer	Hammer Throw
	R. Mitchell	400m
Athletics Women:	D. Boyd	200m

	K. Gibb	High Jump
	G. Mulhall	Shot Put
	J. Peckham	800m
Boxing	P. McElwaine	Middleweight
Cycling	P. Anderson	117 mile Road Race
	K. Tucker	1000m Sprint
	C. Fitzgerald	
	K. Nichols	4000m Teams Pursuit
	G. Sutton	
	S. Sutton	
Swimming Men:	R. McKeon	200m Freestyle
	R. McKeon	400m Freestyle
	M. Metzker	1500m Freestyle
	M. Morgan	100m Freestyle
	G. Patching	100m Backstroke
	M. Morgan	
	R. McKeon	4 × 200m Freestyle Relay
	M. Metzker	
	G. Brewer	
Swimming Women:	D. Forster	100m Backstroke
	M. Ford	200m Butterfly
	T. WICKHAM	400m Freestyle
	T. Wickham	800m Freestyle
Weightlifting	S. Castiglione	Middleweight
	R. Kabbas	Light-Heavyweight
	W. Stellios	Lightweight
Wrestling	Z. Kelevitz	Lightweight

1982 Brisbane, Australia

Athletics Men:	P. Bourke	800m
	G. Brown	400m Hurdles
	R. Boyd	Pole Vault
	G. Honey	Long Jump
	R. de Castella	Marathon
Athletics Women:	R. Boyle	400m
	S. Howland	Javelin
	G. Nunn	Heptathlon
	D. Flintoff	400m Hurdles
Cycling	M. Turtur	4000m Individual Pursuit
	G. West	
	M. Turtur	
	K. Nichols	Team Pursuit
	M. Grenda	
	K. Tucker	1000m Sprint
	K. Nichols	10 miles (16.09km)
Lawn Bowling	R. Dobbins	
	B. Sharp	
	D. Sherman	Men's fours
	K. Poole	
Shooting	A. Smith	Small-bore Rifle—Individual
	P. Adams	
	J. Tremelling	Free Pistol—Team
	P. Heuke	
	A. Taransky	Rapid Fire Pistol—Team
	J. Ellis	
	T. Rumbel	Olympic Trap—Team
	K. Affleck	
	G. Ayling	Full-bore Rifle—Team
	N. Ryan	
	A. Taransky	Centre Fire Pistol—Team
	P. Adams	
	G. Colbert	Air-Pistol—Team
Swimming Men:	N. Brooks	100m Freestyle
	M. Metzker	1500m Freestyle

	G. Fasala	
	G. Brewer	
	M. Delany	4×100m Freestyle Relay
	N. Brooks	
	D. Orbell	
	P. Evans	
	J. Sieben	4×100m Medley Relay
	N. Brooks	
	G. McGufficke	
	R. McKeon	
	P. Rowe	4×200m Freestyle Relay
	G. Brewer	
Swimming Women:	L. Forrest	100m Backstroke
	L. Curry	100m Butterfly
	L. Forrest	200m Backstroke
	M. Ford	200m Butterfly
	L. Curry	200m Medley
	T. Wickham	400m Freestyle
	L. Curry	400m Medley
	T. Wickham	800m Freestyle
Diving	J. Donnet	Springboard
	V. Beddoe	Tower
Weightlifting	N. Voukelatos	Fly weight
	R. Kabbas	Middle-heavy weight
	D. Lukin	Super-heavyweight

APPENDIX 10

MELBOURNE CUP WINNERS 1861–1983

Racehorse trainer, Bart Cummings, with a miniature of the Melbourne Cup presented to him after Think Big won the race in 1974

Courtesy of A.I.S. Canberra

1861 Archer	1885 Sheet Anchor	1909 Prince Foote
1862 Archer	1886 Arsenal	1910 Comedy King
1863 Banker	1887 Dunlop	1911 The Parisian
1864 Lantern	1888 Mentor	1912 Piastre
1865 Tory Boy	1889 Bravo	1913 Posinatus
1866 The Barb	1890 Carbine	1914 Kingsburgh
1867 Tim Whiffler	1891 Malvolio	1915 Patrobus
1868 Glencoe	1892 Glenloth	1916 Sasanof
1869 Warrior	1893 Tarcoola	1917 Westcourt
1870 Nimblefoot	1894 Patron	1918 Nightwatch
1871 The Pearl	1895 Auraria	1919 Artilleryman
1872 The Quack	1896 Newhaven	1920 Poitrel
1873 Don Juan	1897 Gaulus	1921 Sister Olive
1874 Haricot	1898 The Grafter	1922 King Ingoda
1875 Wollomai	1899 Merriwee	1923 Bitalli
1876 Briseis	1900 Clean Sweep	1924 Blackwood
1877 Chester	1901 Revenue	1925 Windbag
1878 Calamia	1902 The Victory	1926 Spearfelt
1879 Darriwell	1903 Lord Cardigan	1927 Trivalve
1880 Grand Flaneur	1904 Acrasia	1928 Statesman
1881 Zulu	1905 Blue Spec	1929 Nightmarch
1882 The Assyrian	1906 Poseidon	1930 Phar Lap
1883 Martini Henri	1907 Apologue	1931 White Nose
1884 Malua	1908 Lord Nolan	1932 Peter Pan

1933	Hall Mark
1934	Peter Pan
1935	Marabou
1936	Wotan
1937	The Trump
1938	Catalogue
1939	Rivette
1940	Old Rowley
1941	Skipton
1942	Colonus
1943	Dark Felt
1944	Sirius
1945	Rainbird
1946	Russia
1947	Hiraji
1948	Rimfire
1949	Foxzami
1950	Comic Court
1951	Delta
1952	Dalray
1953	Wodalla
1954	Rising Fast
1955	Toparoa
1956	Evening Peal
1957	Straight Draw
1958	Baystone
1959	Macdougal
1960	Hi Jinx
1961	Lord Fury
1962	Even Stevens
1963	Gatum Gatum
1964	Polo Prince
1965	Light Fingers
1966	Galilee
1967	Red Handed
1968	Rain Lover
1969	Rain Lover
1970	Baghdad Note
1971	Silver Knight
1972	Piping Lane
1973	Gala Supreme
1974	Think Big
1975	Think Big
1976	Van der Hum
1977	Gold and Black
1978	Arwon
1979	Hyperno
1980	Beldale Ball (USA)
1981	Just a Dash
1982	Gurner's Lane
1983	Kiwi

Australian News & Information Bureau

Hi Jinx leads Howsie and Ilumquh past the winning post in the 1960 Melbourne Cup

Courtesy of A.I.S. Canberra

Think Big wins the Melbourne Cup in 1975 for the second year in succession

Courtesy of A.I.S. Canberra

Gala Supreme wins the 1973 Melbourne Cup

Courtesy of A.I.S. Canberra

Hyperno was the winner of the 1979 Melbourne Cup

APPENDIX No. 11

ABC SPORTSMAN OF THE YEAR
WINNERS

Peter Thompson drives from the tee at the Royal Melbourne Golf Club

Herb Elliott winning an 880 yards event from Dr. Tony Blue in Brisbane

Year	Name	Field of Sport
1951	Frank SEDGMAN	Tennis
1952	Marjorie JACKSON	Athletics
1953	Jimmy CARRUTHERS	Boxing
1954	John LANDY	Athletics
1955	Peter THOMPSON	Golf
1956	Betty CUTHBERT	Athletics
1957	Stuart MACKENZIE	Sculler
1958	Herb ELLIOTT	Athletics
1959	Jack BRABHAM	Motor Racing
1960	Herb Elliott	Athletics
1961	Richie BENAUD	Cricket

Jack Brabham at the wheel of his Repco Brabham car at Warwich Farm racing circuit near Sydney

Richie Benaud

Australian News & Information Bureau

Dawn Fraser

Australian News & Information Bureau

Ron Clarke

1962	Dawn FRASER	Swimming		1973	Stephen Holland	Swimming
1963	Margaret Smith	Tennis		1974	Raelene BOYLE	Athletics
1964	Dawn Fraser	Swimming		1975	Bart CUMMINGS	Horse Trainer
1965	Ron CLARKE	Athletics		1976	Greg CHAPPELL	Cricket
1966	Jack Brabham	Motor Racing		1977	Graham MARSH	Golf
1967	Heather McKAY	Squash		1978	Tracey WICKHAM	Swimming
1968	Lionel ROSE	Boxing		1979	David GRAHAM	Golf
1969	Rod LAVER	Tennis		1980	Allan Jones	Motor Racing
1970	Margaret COURT (Smith)	Tennis		1981	Geoff HUNT	Squash
1971	Shane GOULD	Swimming		1982	Robert DE CASTELLA	Marathon
1972	Shane Gould	Swimming		1983	Robert de Castella	Marathon

Courtesy of A.I.S. Canberra

Lionel Rose

APPENDIX 12

AUSTRALIAN RULES FOOTBALL

Courtesy of A.I.S. Canberra

A high mark

Victorian Football League — VFL

Premiers

1897	Essendon	1926	Melbourne	1955	Melbourne
1898	Fitzroy	1927	Collingwood	1956	Melbourne
1899	Fitzroy	1928	Collingwood	1957	Melbourne
1900	Melbourne	1929	Collingwood	1958	Collingwood
1901	Essendon	1930	Collingwood	1959	Melbourne
1902	Collingwood	1931	Geelong	1960	Melbourne
1903	Collingwood	1932	Richmond	1961	Hawthorn
1904	Fitzroy	1933	S. Melbourne	1962	Essendon
1905	Fitzroy	1934	Richmond	1963	Geelong
1906	Carlton	1935	Collingwood	1964	Melbourne
1907	Carlton	1936	Collingwood	1965	Essendon
1908	Carlton	1937	Geelong	1966	St. Kilda
1909	S. Melbourne	1938	Carlton	1967	Richmond
1910	Collingwood	1939	Melbourne	1968	Carlton
1911	Essendon	1940	Melbourne	1969	Richmond
1912	Essendon	1941	Melbourne	1970	Carlton
1913	Fitzroy	1942	Essendon	1971	Hawthorn
1914	Carlton	1943	Richmond	1972	Carlton
1915	Carlton	1944	Fitzroy	1973	Richmond
1916	Fitzroy	1945	Carlton	1974	Richmond
1917	Collingwood	1946	Essendon	1975	N. Melbourne
1918	S. Melbourne	1947	Carlton	1976	Hawthorn
1919	Collingwood	1948	Melbourne	1977	N. Melbourne
1920	Richmond	1949	Essendon	1978	Hawthorn
1921	Richmond	1950	Essendon	1979	Carlton
1922	Fitzroy	1951	Geelong	1980	Richmond
1923	Essendon	1952	Geelong	1981	Carlton
1924	Essendon	1953	Collingwood	1982	Carlton
1925	Geelong	1954	Footscray	1983	Hawthorn

South Australian National Football League

Premiers

1878	Norwood	1931	N. Adelaide
1879	Norwood	1932	Sturt
1880	Norwood	1933	W. Torrens
1881	Norwood	1934	Glenelg
1882	Norwood	1935	S. Adelaide
1883	Norwood	1936	Pt. Adelaide
1884	Pt. Adelaide	1937	Pt. Adelaide
1885	S. Adelaide	1938	S. Adelaide
1886	Adelaide	1939	Pt. Adelaide
1887	Norwood	1940	Sturt
1888	Norwood	1941	Norwood
1889	Norwood	1942–44	No Competition
1890	Pt. Adelaide	1945	W. Torrens
1891	Norwood	1946	Norwood
1892	S. Adelaide	1947	W. Adelaide
1893	S. Adelaide	1948	Norwood
1894	Norwood	1949	N. Adelaide
1895	S. Adelaide	1950	Norwood
1896	S. Adelaide	1951	Pt. Adelaide
1897	Pt. Adelaide	1952	N. Adelaide
1898	S. Adelaide	1953	W. Torrens
1899	S. Adelaide	1954	Pt. Adelaide
1900	N. Adelaide	1955	Pt. Adelaide
1901	Norwood	1956	Pt. Adelaide
1902	N. Adelaide	1957	Pt. Adelaide
1903	Pt. Adelaide	1958	Pt. Adelaide
1904	Norwood	1959	Pt. Adelaide
1905	N. Adelaide	1960	N. Adelaide
1906	Pt. Adelaide	1961	W. Adelaide
1907	Norwood	1962	Pt. Adelaide
1908	W. Adelaide	1963	Pt. Adelaide
1909	W. Adelaide	1964	S. Adelaide
1910	Pt. Adelaide	1965	Pt. Adelaide
1911	W. Adelaide	1966	Sturt
1912	W. Adelaide	1967	Sturt
1913	Pt. Adelaide	1968	Sturt
1914	Pt. Adelaide	1969	Sturt
1915	Sturt	1970	Sturt
1916–18	No Competition	1971	N. Adelaide
1919	Sturt	1972	N. Adelaide
1920	N. Adelaide	1973	Glenelg
1921	Pt. Adelaide	1974	Sturt
1922	Norwood	1975	Norwood
1923	Norwood	1976	Sturt
1924	W. Torrens	1977	Pt. Adelaide
1925	Norwood	1978	Norwood
1926	Sturt	1979	Pt. Adelaide
1927	W. Adelaide	1980	Pt. Adelaide
1928	Pt. Adelaide	1981	Pt. Adelaide
1929	Norwood	1982	Norwood
1930	N. Adelaide	1983	W. Adelaide

Western Australian Football League

Premiers

1885	Fremantle	1935	W. Perth
1886	Unions	1936	E. Perth
1887	Fremantle	1937	E. Fremantle
1888	Fremantle	1938	Claremont
1889	Fremantle	1939	Claremont
1890	Fremantle	1940	Claremont
1891	Fremantle	1941	W. Perth
1892	Fremantle	1942	W. Perth
1893	Fremantle	1943	E. Fremantle
1894	Fremantle	1944	E. Perth
1895	Fremantle	1945	E. Fremantle
1896	Fremantle	1946	E. Fremantle
1897	W. Perth	1947	S. Fremantle
1898	Fremantle	1948	S. Fremantle
1899	W. Perth	1949	W. Perth
1900	E. Fremantle	1950	S. Fremantle
1901	W. Perth	1951	W. Perth
1902	E. Fremantle	1952	S. Fremantle
1903	E. Fremantle	1953	S. Fremantle
1904	E. Fremantle	1954	S. Fremantle
1905	W. Perth	1955	Perth
1906	E. Fremantle	1956	E. Perth
1907	Perth	1957	E. Fremantle
1908	E. Freemantle	1958	E. Perth
1909	E. Freemantle	1959	E. Perth
1910	E. Fremantle	1960	W. Perth
1911	E. Freemantle	1961	Swan District
1912	Subiaco	1962	Swan District
1913	Subiaco	1963	Swan District
1914	E. Fremantle	1964	Claremont
1915	Subiaco	1965	E. Fremantle
1916	S. Freemantle	1966	Perth
1917	S. Freemantle	1967	Perth
1918	E. Fremantle	1968	Perth
1919	E. Perth	1969	W. Perth
1920	E. Perth	1970	S. Fremantle
1921	E. Perth	1971	W. Perth
1922	E. Perth	1972	E. Perth
1923	E. Perth	1973	Subiaco
1924	Subiaco	1974	E. Fremantle
1925	E. Fremantle	1975	W. Perth
1926	E. Perth	1976	Perth
1927	E. Perth	1977	Perth
1928	E. Fremantle	1978	E. Perth
1929	E. Fremantle	1979	E. Fremantle
1930	E. Fremantle	1980	S. Fremantle
1931	E. Fremantle	1981	Claremont
1932	W. Perth	1982	Swan Districts
1933	E. Fremantle	1983	Swan Districts
1934	W. Perth		

Tasmanian Australian National Football League — TFL

Premiers

1945	N. Hobart	1965	Glenorchy
1946	Sandy Bay	1966	Hobart
1947	N. Hobart	1967	N. Hobart
1948	New Town	1968	New Norfolk
1949	New Town	1969	N. Hobart
1950	Hobart	1970	Clarence
1951	New Town	1971	Sandy Bay
1952	Sandy Bay	1972	Sandy Bay
1953	New Town	1973	Hobart
1954	Hobart	1974	N. Hobart
1955	New Town	1975	Glenorchy
1956	New Town	1976	Sandy Bay
1957	N. Hobart	1977	Sandy Bay
1958	Glenorchy	1978	Sandy Bay
1959	Hobart	1979	Clarence
1960	Hobart	1980	Hobart
1961	N. Hobart	1981	Clarence
1962	N. Hobart	1982	New Norfolk
1963	Hobart	1983	Glenorchy
1964	Sandy Bay		

Northern Tasmanian Football Association

Premiers

1945	Launceston	1965	Scottsdale
1946	N. Launceston	1966	City-South
1947	N. Launceston	1967	E. Launceston
1948	N. Launceston	1968	Scottsdale
1949	N. Launceston	1969	Launceston
1950	N. Launceston	1970	Scottsdale
1951	Launceston	1971	Scottsdale
1952	City	1972	City-South
1953	City	1973	Scottsdale
1954	City	1974	City-South
1955	Longford	1975	N. Launceston
1956	City	1976	Launceston
1957	Longford	1977	Scottsdale
1958	Longford	1978	N. Launceston
1959	City-South	1979	N. Launceston
1960	City-South	1980	N. Launceston
1961	N. Launceston	1981	N. Launceston
1962	City-South	1982	Scottsdale
1963	N. Launceston	1983	N. Launceston
1964	Scottsdale		

APPENDIX 13

CRICKET

TEST MATCHES
Australia v England

Year	Place	W—L—D	Aust. Captain
1876–77	Aus	1—1—0	D.W. GREGORY
1878–79	Aus	1—0—0	D.W. Gregory
1880	Eng	0—1—0	W.L. Murdoch
1881–82	Aus	2—0—2	W.L.Murdoch
1882	Eng	1—0—0	W.L. Murdoch
1882–83	Aus	2—2—0	W.L. Murdoch
1884	Eng	0—1—2	W.L. Murdoch
1884–85	Aus	2—3—0	W.L. Murdoch (1)
			T. Horan (2)
			H. Massie (1)
			J.McC. Blackham (1)
1886	Eng	0—3—0	H.J.H. Scott
1886–87	Aus	0—2—0	P.S. McDonnell
1887–88	Aus	0—1—0	P.S. McDonnell
1888	Eng	1—2—0	P.S. McDonnell
1890	Eng	0—2—0	W.L. Murdoch
1891–92	Aus	2—1—0	J.McC. Blackham
1893	Eng	0—1—2	J.McC. Blackham
1894–95	Aus	2—3—0	J.McC. Blackham (1)
			G. Giffen (4)
1896	Eng	1—2—0	G.H.S. Trott
1897–98	Aus	4—1—0	G.H.S. Trott
1899	Eng	1—0—4	J. Darling
1901–02	Aus	4—1—0	J. Darling (3)
			H. Trumble (2)
1902	Eng	2—1—2	J. Darling
1903–04	Aus	2—3—0	M.A. NOBLE
1905	Eng	0—2—3	J. Darling
1907–08	Aus	4—1—0	M.A. Noble
1909	Eng	2—1—2	M.A. Noble
1911–12	Aus	1—4—0	C. Hill
1912	Eng	0—1—2	S.E. GREGORY
1920–21	Aus	5—0—0	W.W. Armstrong
1921	Eng	3—0—2	W.W. Armstrong
1924–25	Aus	4—1—0	H.L. Collins
1926	Eng	0—1—4	H.L. Collins (3)
			W. Bardsley (2)
1928–29	Aus	1—4—0	J. Ryder
1930	Eng	2—1—2	W.M. Woodfull
1932–33	Aus	1—4—0	W.M. Woodfull
1934	Eng	2—1—2	W.M. Woodfull
1936–37	Aus	3—2—0	D.G. BRADMAN
1938	Eng	1—1—2	D.G. Bradman
1946–47	Aus	3—0—2	D.G. Bradman
1948	Eng	4—0—1	D.G. Bradman
1950–51	Aus	4—1—0	A.L. Hassett
1953	Eng	0—1—4	A.L. Hassett
1954–55	Aus	1—3—1	I.W. Johnson (4)
			A.R. Morris (1)
1956	Eng	1—2—2	I.W. Johnson
1958–59	Aus	4—0—1	R. BENAUD
1961	Eng	2—1—2	R. Benaud (4)
			R.N. Harvey (1)
1962–63	Aus	1—1—3	R. Benaud
1964	Eng	1—0—4	R.B. Simpson
1965–66	Aus	1—1—3	R.B. Simpson (3)
			B.C. Booth (2)
1968	Eng	1—1—3	W.M. Lawry (4)
			B.M. Jarman (1)
1970–71	Aus	0—2—4	W.M. Lawry (5)
			I.M. CHAPPELL (1)

In addition to the above six tests one was abandoned without a ball being bowled.

1972	Eng	2—2—1	I.M. Chappell
1974–75	Aus	4—1—1	I.M. Chappell
1975	Eng	1—0—3	I.M. Chappell
1977	Aus	1—0—0	G.S. CHAPPELL

Centenary Test Match to mark 100 years of Test Cricket between England and Australia held at Melbourne.

1977	Eng	0—3—2	G.S. Chappell
1978–79	Aus	1—5—0	G.N. Yallop
1979–80	Aus	3—0—0	G.S. Chappell
1980	Eng	0—0—1	G.S. Chappell

Centenary Test Match held at Lord's.

1981	Eng	1—3—2	K. Hughes
1982–83	Aus	2—1—2	G.S. Chappell

Australia v South Africa

Year	Place	W—L—D	Aust. Captain
1902–03	SA	2—0—1	J. Darling
1910–11	Aus	4—1—0	C. Hill
1912	Eng	2—0—1	S.E. Gregory
1921–22	SA	1—0—2	H.L. Collins
1931–32	Aus	5—0—0	W.M. Woodfull
1935–36	SA	4—0—1	V.Y. Richardson
1949–50	SA	4—0—1	A.L. Hassett
1952–53	Aus	2—2—1	A.L. Hassett
1957–58	SA	3—0—2	I.D. Craig
1963–64	Aus	1—1—3	R. Benaud (1)
			R.B. Simpson (4)
1966–67	SA	1—3—1	R.B. Simpson
1970	SA	0—4—0	W.M. Lawry

Australia v West Indies

Year	Place	W—L—D	Aust. Captain
1930–31	Aus	4—1—0	W.M. Woodfull
1951–52	Aus	4—1—0	A.L. Hassett (4)
			A.R. Morris (1)
1954	WI	3—0—2	I.W. Johnson
1960–61	Aus	2—1—1	R. Benaud

In addition to these four test matches, one test match was tied — the first tie in Test Cricket. Aus. scored 505 and 232; WI scored 453 and 284.

Year	Place	W—L—D	Aust. Captain
1964	WI	1—2—2	R.B. Simpson
1968–69	Aus	3—1—1	W.M. Lawry
1973	WI	2—0—3	I.M. Chappell
1975–76	Aus	5—1—0	G.S. Chappell
1977	WI	1—3—1	R.B. Simpson
1979–80	Aus	0—2—1	G.S. Chappell
1981–82	Aus	1—1—1	G.S. Chappell

Australia v New Zealand

Year	Place	W—L—D	Aust. Captain
1946	NZ	1—0—0	W.A. Brown
1973–74	Aus	2—0—1	I.M. Chappell
1974	NZ	1—1—1	I.M. Chappell
1977	NZ	1—0—1	G.S. Chappell
1980	Aus	2—0—1	G.S. Chappell
1982	NZ	1—1—1	G.S. Chappell

Australia v India

Year	Place	W—L—D	Aust. Captain
1947–48	Aus	4—0—1	D.G. Bradman
1956	India	2—0—1	I.W. Johnson(2)
			R.R. Lindwall (1)
1959–60	India	2—1—2	R. Benaud
1964	India	1—1—1	R.B. Simpson
1967–68	Aus	4—0—0	R.B. Simpson (2)
			W.M. Lawry (2)
1969	India	3—1—1	W.M. Lawry
1977–78	Aus	3—2—0	R.B. Simpson
1979	India	0—2—4	K. Hughes
1980–81	Aus	1—1—1	G.S. Chappell

Australia v Pakistan

Year	Place	W—L—D	Aust. Captain
1956	Pak	0—1—0	I.W. Johnson
1959	Pak	2—0—1	R. Benaud
1964	Pak	0—0—1	R.B. Simpson
1964	Aus	0—0—1	R.B. Simpson
1972–73	Aus	3—0—0	I.M. Chappell
1976–77	Aus	1—1—1	G.S. Chappell
1979	Aus	1—1—0	G.N. Yallop
1980	Pak	0—1—2	G.S. Chappell
1981	Aus	2—1—0	G.S. Chappell
1982–83	Pak	0—3—0	K. Hughes
1983–84	Aus	2—1—2	K. Hughes

Australia v Sri Lanka

Year	Place	W—L—D	Aust. Captain
1983	SL	1—0—0	G.S. Chappell

APPENDIX 14

RUGBY LEAGUE

Courtesy of A.I.S. Canberra

Sydney Rugby League Premiership game

Australia v Great Britain

Year	Place	W—L—D	Test Scores (Aus first)
1908–09	GB	0—2—1	22–22 5–15 5–6
1910	Aus	1—1—1	20–27 13–13 32–15
1911–12	GB	2—0—1	19–10 11–11 33–8
1914	Aus	1—2—0	5–33 12–7 6–14
1920	Aus	2—1—0	8–4 21–8 13–23
1921–22	GB	1—2—0	5–6 16–2 0–6
1924	Aus	1—2—0	3–22 3–5 21–11
1928	Aus	1—2—0	12–15 0–8 21–14
1929–30	GB	1—2—1	31–8 3–9 0–0 0–3
1932	Aus	1—2—0	6–8 15–6 13–18
1933	GB	0—3—0	0–4 5–7 16–19
1936	Aus	1—2—0	24–8 7–12 7–12
1937–38	GB	1—2—0	4–5 3–13 13–3
1946	Aus	0—2—1	8–8 5–14 7–20
1948–49	GB	0—3—0	21–23 7–16 9–23
1950	Aus	2—1—0	4–6 15–3 5–2
1952–53	GB	1—2—0	6–19 5–21 27–7
1954	Aus	2—1—0	37–12 21–38 20–16
1956–57	GB	1—2—0	10–21 22–9 0–19
1958	Aus	1—2—0	25–8 18–25 17–40
1959–60	GB	1—2—0	22–14 10–11 12–18
1962	Aus	1—2—0	12–31 10–17 18–17
1963	GB	2—1—0	28–2 50–12 5–16
1966	Aus	2—1—0	13–17 6–4 19–14
1967	GB	2—1—0	11–16 17–11 11–3
1970	Aus	1—2—0	37–15 7–28 17–21
1973	GB	2—1—0	11–21 14–6 15–5
1974	Aus	2—1—0	12–6 11–16 22–18
1978	GB	2—1—0	15–9 14–18 23–6
1979	Aus	3—0—0	35–0 24–16 28–2
1982	GB	3—0—0	40–4 27–6 32–8

Australia v New Zealand

Year	Place	W—L—D	Test Scores (Aus first)
1908	Aus	1—1—0	12–24 14–9
1909	Aus	2—1—0	11–19 10–5 25–5
1919	NZ	3—1—0	44–21 10–26 34–23 32–2
1935	NZ	2—1—0	14–22 29–8 31–8
1937	NZ	1—1—0	12–8 15–16
1948	Aus	1—1—0	19–21 13–4
1949	NZ	1—1—0	21–26 13–10
1952	Aus	1—2—0	25–13 25–49 9–19
1953	NZ	1—2—0	5–25 11–12 18–16
1956	Aus	3—0—0	12–9 8–2 31–14
1959	Aus	2—1—0	9–8 38–10 12–28
1961	NZ	1—1—0	10–12 10–8
1963	Aus	2—1—0	7–3 13–16 14–0
1965	NZ	1—1—0	13–8 5–7
1967	Aus	3—0—0	22–13 35–22 13–9
1969	NZ	1—1—0	20–10 14–18
1971	NZ	0—1—0	3–24
1972	Aus	2—0—0	36–11 31–7
1978	Aus	3—0—0	24–2 38–7 33–16
1980	NZ	2—0—0	27–6 15–6
1982	Aus	2—0—0	11–8 20–2
1983	NZ	1—0—0	16–4
1983	Aus	0—1—0	

Australia V France

Year	Place	W—L—D	Test Scores (Aus first)
1937-38	Fran.	2—0—0	36-6 16-11
1948-49	Fran.	2—0—0	29-10 10-0
1951	Aus	1—2—0	15-26 23-11 14-35
1952-53	Fran.	1—2—0	16-12 0-5 5-13
1955	Aus	1—2—0	20-8 28-29 5-8
1956-57	Fran.	3—0—0	15-8 10-6 25-21
1959-60	Fran.	3—0—0	20-19 17-2 16-8
1960	Aus	1—1—1	8-8 56-6 5-7
1963-64	Fran.	2—1—0	5-8 21-9 16-8
1964	Aus	3—0—0	20-6 27-2 35-9
1967-68	Fran.	0—2—1	7-7 3-10 13-16
1973	Fran.	2—0—0	21-9 14-3
1978	Fran.	0—2—0	10-13 10-11
1981	Aus	2—0—0	43-3 17-2
1982	Fran.	2—0—0	15-4 23-9

Australia v Papua New Guinea

Year	Place	W—L—D	Test Scores (Aus first)
1982	PNG	1—0—0	38-2

SYDNEY FIRST GRADE RUGBY LEAGUE PREMIERSHIP

Year	Club	Year	Club
1908	South Sydney	1946	Balmain
1909	South Sydney	1947	Balmain
1910	Newtown	1948	Western Suburbs
1911	Eastern Suburbs	1949	St George
1912	Eastern Suburbs	1950	South Sydney
1913	Eastern Suburbs	1951	South Sydney
1914	South Sydney	1952	Western Suburbs
1915	Balmain	1953	South Sydney
1916	Balmain	1954	South Sydney
1917	Balmain	1955	South Sydney
1918	South Sydney	1956	St George
1919	Balmain	1957	St George
1920	Balmain	1958	St George
1921	North Sydney	1959	St George
1922	North Sydney	1960	St George
1923	Eastern Suburbs	1961	St George
1924	Balmain	1962	St George
1925	South Sydney	1963	St George
1926	South Sydney	1964	St George
1927	South Sydney	1965	St George
1928	South Sydney	1966	St George
1929	South Sydney	1967	South Sydney
1930	Western Suburbs	1968	South Sydney
1931	South Sydney	1969	Balmain
1932	South Sydney	1970	South Sydney
1933	Newtown	1971	South Sydney
1934	Western Suburbs	1972	Manly-Warringah
1935	Eastern Suburbs	1973	Manly-Warringah
1936	Eastern Suburbs	1974	Eastern Suburbs
1937	Eastern Suburbs	1975	Eastern Suburbs
1938	Canterbury-Bankstown	1976	Manly-Warringah
1939	Balmain	1977	St George
1940	Eastern Suburbs	1978	Manly-Warringah
1941	St George	1979	St George
1942	Canterbury-Bankstown	1980	Canterbury-Bankstown
1943	Newtown	1981	Parramatta
1944	Balmain	1982	Parramatta
1945	Eastern Suburbs	1983	Parramatta

BRISBANE FIRST GRADE RUGBY LEAGUE PREMIERSHIP

Year	Club	Year	Club
1909	Valley	1947	Eastern Suburbs
1910	Ipswich	1948	Western Suburbs
1911	Valley-Toombul	1949	Southern Suburbs
1912	Natives	1950	Eastern Suburbs
1913	West End	1951	Southern Suburbs
1914	Valley	1952	Western Suburbs
1915	Valley	1953	Southern Suburbs
1916	Western Suburbs	1954	Western Suburbs
1917	Valley	1955	Valley
1918	Valley	1956	Brothers
1919	Valley	1957	Valley
1920	Western Suburbs	1958	Brothers
1921	Carlton	1959	Northern Suburbs
1922	Western Suburbs	1960	Northern Suburbs
1923	Coorparoo	1961	Northern Suburbs
1924	Valley	1962	Northern Suburbs
1925	Carlton	1963	Northern Suburbs
1926	Brothers	1964	Northern Suburbs
1927	Grammar	1965	Recliffe
1928	University	1966	Northern Suburbs
1929	University	1967	Brothers
1930	Carlton	1968	Brothers
1931	Valley	1969	Northern Suburbs
1932	Western Suburbs	1970	Valley
1933	Valley	1971	Valley
1934	Northern Suburbs	1972	Eastern Suburbs
1935	Brothers	1973	Valley
1936	Western Suburbs	1974	Valley
1937	Valley	1975	Western Suburbs
1938	Northern Suburbs	1976	Western Suburbs
1939	Brothers	1977	Eastern Suburbs
1940	Northern Suburbs	1978	Eastern Suburbs
1941	Valley	1979	Valley
1942	Brothers	1980	Northern Suburbs
1943	Brothers	1981	Southern Suburbs
1944	Valley	1982	Wynnum-Manly
1945	Southern Suburbs	1983	Eastern Suburbs
1946	Valley		

APPENDIX 15

RUGBY UNION

Australia v British Isles

Year	Place	W—L—D	Test Scores (Aus First)
1899	Aus	1—3—0	13-3 0-11 10-11 0-13
1904	Aus	0—3—0	0-17 3-17 0-16
1930	Aus	1—0—0	6-5
1950	Aus	0—2—0	6-19 3-24
1959	Aus	0—2—0	6-17 3-24
1966	Aus	0—2—0	8-11 0-31

Australia v England

Year	Place	W—L—D	Test Scores (Aus First)
1909	Eng	1—0—0	9-3
1948	Eng	1—0—0	11-0
1958	Eng	0—1—0	6-9
1963	Aus	1—0—0	18-9
1967	Eng	1—0—0	23-11
1973	Eng	0—1—0	3-20
1975	Aus	2—0—0	16-9 30-21
1976	Eng	0—1—0	6-23
1982	Eng	0—1—0	11-15

Australia v Scotland

Year	Place	W—L—D	Test Scores (Aus First)
1947	Scot	1—0—0	16-7
1958	Scot	0—1—0	8-12
1966	Scot	0—1—0	5-11
1968	Scot	0—1—0	3-9
1970	Aus	1—0—0	23-3
1975	Scot	0—1—0	3-10
1982	Aus	1—1—0	7-12 33-9

Australia v Ireland

Year	Place	W—L—D	Test Scores (Aus First)
1947	Ire	1—0—0	16-7
1958	Ire	0—1—0	6-9
1967	Ire	0—1—0	8-15
1967	Aus	0—1—0	5-11
1968	Ire	0—1—0	3-10
1976	Ire	1—0—0	20-10
1979	Aus	0—2—0	12-27 3-9
1981	Ire	1—0—0	16-12

Australia v Wales

Year	Place	W-L-D	Test Scores (Aus First)
1908	Wales	0—1—0	6-9
1947	Wales	0—1—0	0-6
1958	Wales	0—1—0	3-9
1966	Wales	1—0—0	14-11
1969	Aus	0—1—0	16-19
1973	Wales	0—1—0	0-24
1975	Wales	0—1—0	3-28
1978	Aus	2—0—0	18-8 19-17
1981	Wales	0—1—0	3-18

Australia v New Zealand

Year	Place	W-L-D	Test Scores (Aus First)
1903	Aus	0—1—0	3-22
1905	NZ	0—1—0	3-14
1907	Aus	0—2—1	6-26 5-14 5-5
1910	Aus	1—2—0	0-6 11-0 13-28
1913	NZ	1—2—0	5-30 13-25 16-5
1914	Aus	0—3—0	0-5 0-17 7-22
1929	Aus	3—0—0	9-8 17-9 15-13
1931	NZ	0—1—0	13-20
1932	Aus	1—2—0	22-17 3-21 13-21
1934	Aus	1—0—1	25-11 3-3
1936	NZ	0—2—0	6-11 13-38
1938	Aus	0—3—0	9-24 14-20 6-14
1946	NZ	0—2—0	8-31 10-14
1947	Aus	0—2—0	5-13 14-27
1949	NZ	2—0—0	11-6 16-9
1951	Aus	0—3—0	0-8 11-17 6-16
1952	NZ	1—1—0	14-9 8-15
1955	NZ	1—2—0	8-16 0-8 8-3
1957	Aus	0—2—0	11-25 9-22
1958	NZ	1—2—0	3-25 6-3 8-17
1962	Aus	0—2—1	6-20 5-14 9-9
1962	NZ	0—2—0	0-3 8-16
1964	NZ	1—2—0	9-14 3-18 20-5
1967	NZ	0—1—0	9-29
1968	Aus	0—2—0	11-27 18-19
1972	NZ	0—3—0	6-29 17-30 3-38
1974	Aus	0—2—1	6-11 16-16 6-16
1978	NZ	1—2—0	12-13 6-22 30-16
1979	Aus	1—0—0	12-6
1980	Aus	2—1—0	13-9 9-12 26-10
1982	NZ	1—2—0	16-23 19-16 18-33

Australia v South Africa

Year	Place	W-L-D	Test Scores (Aus First)
1933	SA	2—3—0	3-17 21-6 3-12 0-11 15-4
1937	Aus	0—2—0	5-9 17-21
1953	SA	1—3—0	3-25 18-14 8-18 9-22
1956	Aus	0—2—0	0-9 0-9
1961	SA	0—2—0	3-28 11-23
1963	SA	2—2—0	3-14 9-5 11-9 6-22
1965	Aus	2—0—0	18-11 12-8
1969	SA	0—4—0	11-30 9-16 3-11 8-19
1971	Aus	0—3—0	11-19 6-14 6-18

Australia v France

Year	Place	W—L—D	Test Scores (Aus First)
1948	Fran	0—1—0	6–13
1958	Fran	0—1—0	0–19
1961	Aus	0—1—0	8–15
1967	Fran	0—1—0	14–20
1968	Aus	1—0—0	11–10
1971	Fran	1—1—0	13–11 9–18
1972	Aus	0—1—1	14–14 15–16
1976	Fran	0—2—0	15–18 6–34
1981	Aus	2—0—0	17–15 24–14

Australia v Tonga

Year	Place	W-L-D	Test Scores (Aus First)
1973	Aus	1—1—0	30–12 11–16

Australia v Fiji

Year	Place	W-L-D	Test Scores (Aus First)
1952	Aus	1—1—0	15–9 15–17
1954	Aus	1—1—0	22–19 16–18
1961	Aus	2—0—1	24–6 20–14 3–3
1972	Fiji	1—0—0	21–19
1976	Aus	3—0—0	22–6 21–9 27–17
1980	Fiji	1—0—0	22–9

Australia v Japan

Year	Place	W-L-D	Test Scores (Aus First)
1975	Aus	2—0—0	37–7 50–25

SYDNEY FIRST GRADE RUGBY UNION PREMIERSHIP

Year	Winner	Year	Winner
1900	Glebe	1943	Manly
1901	Glebe and University	1944	Eastern Suburbs
		1945	University
1902	Western Suburbs	1946	Eastern Suburbs
1903	Eastern Suburbs	1947	Eastern Suburbs
1904	University	1948	Randwick
1905	South Sydney	1949	Gordon
1906	Glebe	1950	Manly
1907	Glebe	1951	University
1908	Newtown	1952	Gordon
1909	Glebe	1953	University
1910	Newtown	1954	University
1911	Newtown	1955	University
1912	Glebe	1956	Gordon
1913	Eastern Suburbs	1957	St George
1914	Glebe	1958	Gordon
1915–18	No competition	1959	Randwick
1919	University	1960	Northern Suburbs
1920	University	1961	University
1921	Eastern Suburbs	1962	University
1922	Manly	1963	Northern Suburbs
1923	University	1964	Northern Suburbs
1924	University	1965	Randwick
1925	Glebe and Balmain	1966	Randwick
		1967	Randwick
1926	University	1968	University
1927	University	1969	Eastern Suburbs
1928	University	1970	University
1929	Western Suburbs	1971	Randwick
1930	Randwick	1972	University
1931	Eastern Suburbs	1973	Randwick
1932	Manly	1974	Randwick
1933	Northern Suburbs	1975	Northern Suburbs
1934	Randwick	1976	Gordon
1935	Northern Suburbs	1977	Parramatta
1936	Drummoyne	1978	Randwick
1937	University	1979	Randwick
1938	Randwick	1980	Randwick
1939	University	1981	Randwick
1940	Randwick	1982	Randwick
1941	Eastern Suburbs	1983	Manly
1942	Manly		

BRISBANE FIRST GRADE RUGBY UNION PREMIERSHIP

Year	Winner	Year	Winner
1887	Ipswich Rangers	1947	University
1888	Union Harriers	1948	University
1889	Wallaroos	1949	Christian Brothers
1890	Wallaroos	1950	Christian Brothers
1891	Arfoma	1951	Christian Brothers
1892	Past & Present Grammar	1952	University
		1953	Christian Brothers
1893	Boomerangs	1954	University
1894	Boomerangs	1955	University
1895	City	1956	University
1896	City	1957	University
1897	City	1958	Southern Districts
1898	Past Grammar	1959	Christian Brothers
1899	Past Grammar	1960	University
1900	City	1961	GPS Old Boys
1901	North Brisbane	1962	University
1902	North Brisbane	1963	Teachers
1903	North Brisbane	1964	University
1904	North Brisbane tie with Valley	1965	University
		1966	Brothers
1905–14	no records kept	1967	University
1915	Brothers	1968	Brothers
1916–28	No competition	1969	University
1929	YMCA	1970	University
1930	University	1971	Brothers
1931	University	1972	GPS Old Boys
1932	University	1973	Brothers
1933	YMCA	1974	Brothers
1934	University	1975	Brothers
1935	Eagle Junction	1976	Teachers-North
1936	Eagle Junction	1977	Western Suburbs
1937	Eagle Junction	1978	Brothers
1938	Eagle Junction	1979	University
1939	YMCA	1980	Brothers
1940–45	No competition	1981	Brothers
1946	Christian Brothers Old Boys	1982	Brothers
		1983	Brothers

APPENDIX 16

SAILING/YACHTING

SYDNEY-HOBART RACE

The start of the 1979 Sydney-Hobart Yacht Race

Courtesy of A.I.S. Canberra

Year	Winner corrected time	Owner/ Charterer	Fastest Yacht	No. of starters
1945	Rani	Capt.J. Illingworth, RN	Rani	9
1946	Christina	J.R. Bull	Morna	19
1947	Westward	G.D. Gibson	Morna	28
1948	Westward	G.D. Gibson	Morna	18
1949	Trade Winds	M.E. Davey	Waltzing Matilda	15
1950	Nerida	C.P. Hazelgrove	Margaret Rintoul	16
1951	Struen Marie	T. Williamson	Margaret Rintoul	14
1952	Ingrid	J.S. Taylor	Nocturne	17
1953	Ripple	R.C. Hobson	Solveig	23
1954	Solveig	T. & M. Halvorsen	Kurrewa IV (formerly Morna)	17
1955	Moonbi	H.S. Evans	Even	17
1956	Solo	V. Meyer	Kurrewa IV	28
1957	Anitra V	T. & M. Halvorsen	Kurrewa IV	20
1958	Siandra	G.P. Newland	Solo	22
1959	Cherana	R.T. Williams	Solo	30
1960	Siandra	G.P. Newland	Kurrewa IV	32
1961	Rival	A. Burgin & N. Rundle	Astor	35
1962	Solo	V. Meyer	Ondine	42
1963	Freya	T. & M. Halvorsen	Astor	44
1964	Freya	T. & M. Halvorsen	Astor	37
1965	Freya	T. & M. Halvorsen	Stormvogel	49
1966	Cadence	H.S. Mason	Fidelis	44
1967	Rainbow 11	C. Bouzaid	Pen-Duick III	67
1968	Koomooloo	D. O'Neill	Ondine	67
1969	Morning Cloud	E. Heath	Crusade	79
1970	Pacha	R. Crichton-Brown	Buccaneer	61

1971	Pathfinder	B. Wilson	Kialoa II	76
1972	American Eagle	R.E. Turner	American Eagle	79
1973	Ceil III	W. Turnbull	Helsal	90
1974	Love & War	P. Kurts	Ondine	63
1975	Rampage	P. Packer	Kialoa	102
1976	Piccolo	J. Pickles	Ballyhoo	85
1977	Kialoa	J.B. Kilroy	Kialoa	131
1978	Love & War	P. Kurts	Apollo	97
1979	Screw Loose	R.J. Cummings	Bumblebee IV	147
1980	New Zealand	NZ Round the World Com.	New Zealand	102
1981	Zeus II	J.R. Dunstan	Vengeance	159
1982	Scallywag	R.E. Johnston	Condor of Bermuda	120
1983	Challenge	L.A. Abrahams	Condor of Bermuda	173

APPENDIX 17

DISASTERS

NATURAL AND MAN MADE

This Appendix lists the most important civilian disasters. Casualties and disasters relating to the defence forces are covered in entries on wars. However, the following wartime disasters are included because they occurred within Australia or very close to the coast: the first air raid on Darwin, in February 1942; the midget submarine attack on Sydney Harbour, in May 1942; and the sinking of the hospital ship *Centaur*, in February, 1943. The crash of an RAAF aircraft at Canberra in August 1940 is also listed, since it involved the death of civilians, including three Cabinet Ministers, and the collision of *HMAS Melbourne* and *HMAS Voyager* is included because of the intense public debate which it aroused.

Date	Type	Place	Details
1788–1799			
1788 Mar	Shipping	Vanikoro Island in the Pacific Ocean	*Astrolabe* and *Boussole,* ships of the French explorer, La Perouse, after leaving Botany Bay, were wrecked with no survivors.
1788 Oct 28	Shipping	Borneo	*Friendship,* one of the transports from the First Fleet, sank near Borneo on the way back to England.
1789	Epidemic	Sydney	In April the dead bodies of many Aborigines were found in coves around Port Jackson. The colony's surgeons noticed that the bodies were marked as if from smallpox. Phillip was puzzled, because he had observed no symptoms of smallpox on the First Fleet. Nevertheless it seemed certain that the Aborigines (for the first of countless times) had been struck by a disease introduced by Europeans.
1789–91	Drought	NSW	The colonists of NSW experienced their first period of drought.
1789	Shipping	Near Cape Town	*HMS Guardian,* which was bringing supplies to NSW, struck an iceberg. Many of those on board left in five of the ship's boats but only one boatload survived. With 63 still on board, the captain managed to sail the damaged ship to the coast of southern Africa at False Bay, but there it was blown ashore and wrecked. Meanwhile food supplies in the colony of NSW were running low.
1790 Mar 19	Shipping	Norfolk Island	*HMS Sirius,* former flagship of the First Fleet, and Phillip's main means of sending for food, was wrecked at Norfolk Island. The colony was then in danger of famine and the weekly ration for each person was reduced to 2 lbs pork, 2 lbs rice and 2½ lbs flour.
1790 June	Health	Sydney	The transports *Surprize, Scarborough* and *Neptune* reached Sydney. Of the 1026 convicts who had embarked on them, 267 had died. Of the survivors, 488 were too ill to work. Thirty tents were put up as a hospital for them.
1791	Caterpillar plague	Norfolk Island	Caterpillars destroyed the crop at Norfolk Island. Partly as a result of this, the whole colony was again in danger of famine.

Date	Type	Place	Details
1797 Feb 9	Shipping	Bass Strait	The merchant ship *Sydney Cove* was wrecked on Preservation Island. Of the crew, 17 set out in a longboat but were wrecked. However 3 managed to reach Sydney by land. The ships, *Eliza* and *Francis*, were sent to pick up other crew members but on the return voyage the *Eliza* disappeared.
1798–99	Drought	NSW	Severe crop failure.
1799 Mar	Flood	Hawkesbury River, NSW	Severe damage to property and crops, one man was drowned.

1800–1809

Date	Type	Place	Details
1803	Drought	NSW	Severe crop failure.
1803 Aug 17	Shipping	Wreck Reef, QLD	The *Porpoise*, on which Matthew Flinders was travelling to Britain, was wrecked. Flinders reached Sydney in a small boat and later returned with a rescue expedition and saved the other survivors.
1805 Mar 20	Shipping	Newcastle, NSW	The Australian-built schooner *Francis* was wrecked on Oyster Bank.
1806 Mar	Flood	Hawkesbury River, NSW	Five people were drowned in a record flood.
1806 Apr 22	Shipping	Newcastle, NSW	The schooner, *Governor King* was wrecked on Oyster Bank.
1806 Aug 25	Shipping	Tasman Sea	The whaler *Britannia* sank, but some of its crew reached Newcastle in two boats 14 days later.
1809	Flood	TAS and NSW	Both the Derwent and Hawkesbury Rivers overflowed.
1809	Drought	NSW	Beginning of an unusually severe drought.

1810–1819

Date	Type	Place	Details
1810–1811	Drought	NSW	Continuation of the drought which began in 1809.
1813	Drought	NSW	Beginning of a severe drought which lasted until 1815, and provided Blaxland, Lawson and Wentworth with an added incentive to cross the Blue Mountains and open up new pastures.
1814 May 20	Shipping	Sydney	The transport *Three Bees* caught fire and blew up in Sydney Cove. Shot from her guns landed in Bridge Street.
1816 Jan 19	Shipping	Newcastle, NSW	The schooner *Estramina* was wrecked on Oyster Bank.
1816 Sept 12	Shipping	Trial Bay, NSW	Simeon Lord's brig *Trial* which had been taken by convicts, was wrecked at Trial Bay. There were no survivors.
1819	Shipping	Bathurst Bay, QLD	The ship *Frederick* was wrecked near the entrance to the Bay with the loss of 28 lives.

1820–1829

Date	Type	Place	Details
1822 Jan	Fire	Sydney	A fire in the barracks situated on the site of modern Wynyard Park, was put out with the use of fire engines — small carts with hand-worked pumps. This was the first time such machines had been used in Australia.
1822 Oct 28	Shipping	D'Entrecasteaux Channel, TAS	The ship *Actaeon* was wrecked near Recherche Bay.
1824	Drought	NSW	A particularly poor harvest because of drought.
1826–29	Drought	NSW	A severe drought occurred, during which Lake George dried up, and the Darling River, which was discovered at this time by STURT ceased flowing.

1830–1839

Date	Type	Place	Details
1830 May	Flood	Perth	For the first time in WA, a serious flood was recorded.
1834 Aug 25	Shipping	Sydney Harbour	The *Edward Lombe* was wrecked on Middle Head as it entered the harbour. Of 19 people on board, 12 were lost.
1835 Apr 12	Shipping	D'Entrecasteaux Channel, TAS	The transport *George III* struck rocks and sank. Of 220 convicts aboard, 139 were lost, but only two of the crew.
1835 May 14	Shipping	King Island, TAS	There were only 15 survivors out of a total of 241 convicts, free settlers and crew when the transport *Neva* struck the Navarine Reef and sank.
1835 Jul 17	Shipping	D'Entrecasteaux Channel, TAS	The barque *Enchantress* sank with the loss of about 50 lives.
1835 Dec 13	Shipping	Wreck Bay, NSW	The transport *Neva* ran ashore and broke up completely, but only two people out of 250 on board were lost.

Date	Type	Place	Details
1836 May 21	Shipping	Swain Reefs, QLD	The adventures of Captain Fraser, his wife Eliza and the crew of the brig *Stirling Castle* have been the subject of much writing, and have been portrayed in the film *Eliza Fraser* (Tim Burstall, 1976). Contemporary accounts differ in some details, but the main events appear to have been as follows. After the shipwreck, which occurred about 200 kilometres off the Queensland coast between the latitudes of present day Rockhampton and Mackay, all 18 people aboard escaped in the pinnace and longboat. A few days later Mrs. Fraser gave birth to a child, who died. After three weeks in the boats they reached an island of the Bunker Group, near the site of modern Gladstone, but disagreement broke out regarding the course to be followed. The boatswain and six others mutinied, and made off in the longboat with the better part of the provisions, while the others reached Great Sandy Island (now called Fraser Island). Once again the party split, some of the seamen setting off to walk to Brisbane, while the Frasers and four crew members stayed with a group of Aborigines. The Aboriginal women made Mrs. Fraser their servant. Eventually three seamen reached Brisbane, and a rescue party set out, guided by a convict, John Graham, who had previously escaped and lived among the Aborigines, but had then given himself up. In the meantime Fraser and the first mate had died, but the second mate, two other seamen and Mrs. Fraser were rescued. Graham, who had shown great bravery in entering the camp of the Aborigines who were still holding Mrs Fraser captive, was given a ticket of leave and a reward of £10.
1837	Floods	SA	On several occasions during the year the settlers around Adelaide encountered floods — the first recorded in the colony.
1837–39	Drought	NSW	A particularly severe period of drought.
1838	Drought	WA	The first drought recorded in WA.
1839	Drought	SA	A drought was reported for the first time in SA.
1839 Dec	Flood	Melbourne	The settlers in Melbourne reported, for the first time, serious flooding on the Yarra and Saltwater (Maribyrnong) Rivers.
1839 Dec	Shipping	Preservation Island, TAS	The barque *Britomart* left Melbourne, but was never seen again. Later, however, part of her deckhouse and some of her papers were discovered in the possession of some of the inhabitants of Preservation Island in the Furneaux Group.

1840–1849

Date	Type	Place	Details
1841 Jan	Flood	Brisbane	For the first time, the colonists of the Moreton Bay District (later QLD) reported a major flood on the Brisbane River.
1843	Drought	Hobart	A severe drought affected the Hobart district.
1845	Shipping	Torres Strait	Probably in April, the cutter *America* was wrecked in Torres Strait, the crew of five being lost, but a woman named Barbara Thompson survived. She was cared for by Aborigines until October 1849, when HMS *Rattlesnake*, which had stopped for water, took her aboard.
1845 Aug 4	Shipping	King Island, TAS	In Australia's worst maritime disaster, the barque *Cataraqui*, bound for Melbourne, was driven ashore on King Island in the early hours of the morning. Of the 370 emigrant passengers and 46 crew, about 200 were still on the wreck at first light, and at nightfall about 70 were still lashed to the remaining section, but on the following day the wreck broke up completely. The survivors numbered only 9.
1847 Mar 4	Shipping	Amity Point, QLD	On a voyage from Brisbane to the northern rivers of NSW, the paddle steamer *Sovereign* was wrecked on Amity Point, at the northern end of North Stradbroke Island, with the loss of 46 lives. Ten people were rescued by the crew of the local pilot boat.
1848 Oct 27	Shipping	Bass Strait	The convict transport *Governor Phillip* was wrecked near Cape Barren Island in Bass Strait. However nearly all the convicts were saved, largely through the efforts of Lieutenant Griffiths, who died trying to rescue the last four of them as the ship sank.

Date	Type	Place	Details
1850–1859			
1851 Feb 6	Bushfire	VIC	On 'Black Thursday' (this being the first of many times when the word 'black' was applied to a day marked by bushfires), Victoria's worst fires up to that time reached their peak. The summer had been very hot and dry, and on 'Black Thursday' Melbourne was swept by clouds of dust and smoke, was ringed with fires in all landward directions, and by 11 am was sweltering in a temperature of 47 degrees Celsius. Meanwhile most districts of Victoria were undergoing similar trials. Fires spread from the Dandenongs and the Plenty Ranges northwards to the Murray River; westwards through the Western District and the Wimmera to the SA border; and along the whole coast from Cape Otway to Cape Schanck. Gippsland was the main area to suffer little from fires, but settlers in some localities there reported that smoke and dust from the west and north made the day almost as dark as night. The population of Victoria was at that time less than 100 000, and this doubtless explains why the number of deaths, namely 10, was less than in some severe bushfires of later times.
1852 Jun 25	Flood	Gundagai, NSW	The Murrumbidgee River swept away a large part of Gundagai and drowned 89 of the town's 250 people.
1852 Sep 3	Shipping	Rottnest Island, WA	The barque *Eglinton* was wrecked, but only 2 out of 51 on board drowned. The cargo included a valuable consignment of gold, which was recovered.
1853 May 15	Shipping	Gabo Island	*SS Monumental City*, the first screw steamship to cross the Pacific, was wrecked near Gabo Island, with the loss of 33 lives. Fifty-three people were saved by means of a lifeline rigged by an able seaman who had reached the shore in a boat. This wreck resulted in a lighthouse being built on Gabo Island.
1854	Drought	VIC	The first reference to drought in the colony.
1857 Jun 30	Shipping	Guichen Bay, SA	The Dutch barque *Koenig Willem II* was blown ashore, with the loss of 16 lives.
1857 Aug 20	Shipping	Sydney	In one of the best-known shipping disasters in Australian history, the *Dunbar*, with 121 people on board, was wrecked near South Head. The ship approached Sydney in the evening, with a gale blowing and very low visibility, but the captain, James Green, probably sighted Macquarie Light, and decided to sail through the Heads that night, instead of standing off until morning. However he missed the entrance, and the ship struck the rocks at the foot of the cliff known as the Gap, a little S of South Head. On the following morning pieces of wreckage were noticed and a search was made. Many bodies were found at and near the Gap, but the wreck had already broken up, and it was only when a mailbag was recovered that the *Dunbar* was identified. On the morning of 22 August weak cries were heard, and the sole survivor, a seaman named Johnson, who had been clinging to a ledge for 36 hours, was rescued. As a result of the disaster, a lighthouse was built on Inner South Head. The ship's anchor, which was recovered in 1910, is now displayed at the clifftop. In 1955 divers pinpointed the position of the wreck, and brought up more relics.
1857 Aug 24	Shipping	Off Cape Otway, VIC	The steamships *Champion* and *Ladybird* collided, the former sinking within a few minutes, with the loss of 32 lives.
1857 Oct 24	Shipping	Sydney	The clipper *Catherine Adamson* drifted on to Inner North Head in a gale, and sank with the loss of 21 lives.
1858	Drought	QLD	Drought conditions were reported, for the first time, from QLD (then still part of NSW).
1859 Aug 6	Shipping	Near Cape Northumberland, SA	The *SS Admella*, on her way from Port Adelaide to Melbourne, struck Carpenter's Rocks. Rescue attempts over 7 days saved the lives of 22 people, but 89 lives were lost.
1859 Sep 23	Shipping	Torres Strait	The *Sapphire*, carrying horses from Sydney to India, was wrecked near Raine Is. Although the crew of 18 reached Hammond Is., all but one were killed by islanders.

Date	Type	Place	Details
1860–1869			
1862 Jun	Shipping	Between Melbourne and New Zealand	The small paddle-steamer *Comet,* built for service on the Parramatta River, and quite unsuitable for ocean voyages, left Melbourne with gold prospectors bound for New Zealand, but was never heard of again.
1863	Floods	Eastern colonies	This was a year of floods at Hobart, TAS; in south-central VIC; in S-E QLD; and in NSW on the Macleay (where 10 people were drowned) and the Darling River.
1864	Fire	Brisbane	Fire destroyed 14 shops in Queen St. in April, and 50 old buildings between Queen, Albert, Elizabeth and George Sts. in December.
1864 Jun 2	Shipping	Seal Rocks, NSW	The steamship *Rainbow* sank with the loss of 7 out of the 16 on board.
1864–66	Drought	All mainland colonies	Severe droughts affected most of NSW and QLD; in VIC the north was worst hit; in SA the whole colony was affected, but the effects were most severe in the north, where stock losses were heavy; in WA wheat crops were badly affected, especially in 1864.
1865 Jun 29	Fire	Sydney	Fire completely destroyed St. Mary's Cathedral.
1866 Jul 12	Shipping	Newcastle, NSW	The paddle steamer *Cawarra* sank while trying to enter Newcastle harbour. Only one of the 63 on board survived.
1867 Mar 20	Shipping	Near Port Hacking, NSW	The schooner *Albion* sank, with the loss of 5 out of 7 on board.
1868 Jan 16	Shipping	Port Phillip Heads, VIC	All on board were saved when the 1287-ton ship *Light of the Age* was wrecked, but 6 men drowned during salvage operations.
1869 May 9	Shipping	Newcastle Bight, NSW	All on board (probably 7) died when the brig *Burnet* was wrecked.
1870–1879			
1874 Dec 23	Fire	Windsor, NSW	One person was killed and 45 houses destroyed in the main street.
1874 May 23	Shipping	Bass Strait	Only 9 out of 88 on board survived when the iron sailing ship *British Admiral* was wrecked on King Island.
1875 Feb 24	Shipping	Off Townsville, QLD	Only 24 of the 126 people on board were saved when the steamer *Gothenburg* ran on to a reef.
1875	Floods	NSW, QLD, TAS and SA	The areas mainly affected were the coast and tablelands of NSW, S-E QLD, the north of TAS and the Sturt and Para Rivers south of Adelaide.
1875 Dec 24	Cyclone	Exmouth Gulf, WA	Many vessels in the pearling fleet were damaged or destroyed, and 59 lives were lost.
1876 Sep 10	Shipping	Off Jervis Bay, NSW	*SS Dandenong* sank, but the barque *Albert William* picked up 41 of the 81 on board.
1876 Dec 1	Shipping	Near Cape Leeuwin, WA	When the *SS Georgette* was wrecked, 16-year-old Grace Bussel (after whose family the town of Busselton is named) rode 13km to the scene. A lifeboat crowded with women and children had capsized, but Grace rode her horse into the surf, saved a number of them, and continued rescuing others for 4 hours. She was awarded a medal by Royal Humane Society.
1878 Jan 14	Cyclone	Darwin, NT	Every building in the town was damaged.
1878 Jun 1	Railway	Emu Plains, NSW	A head-on collision between two trains caused the deaths of 5 people.
1878 Jan 1	Shipping	West of Cape Otway, VIC	The iron clipper *Loch Ard,* on her third voyage to Australia, struck rocks at the mouth of a narrow gorge (now named Loch Ard Gorge) in high cliffs. Of the 50 people on board, the only survivors were an apprentice, Tom Pearce, and a teen-age girl, Eva Carmichael, who had clung to a hen coop until pulled ashore by Pearce.
1880–1889			
1880–87	Epidemics	Several colonies	Epidemics of smallpox occurred in NSW (1880–81 and 1882–85; VIC (1882 and 1884–85); SA (1884); and TAS (1887).
1881 Aug 30	Railway	Jolimont, VIC	Four people were killed in a derailment.
1881 Oct	Shipping	South Coast, NSW	*SS Balclutha,* with 22 people aboard, disappeared during a gale, somewhere north of Gabo Island.
1882 Nov 11	Shipping	Sydney	While unloading in Neutral Bay, the collier *Austral* sank, with the loss of 5 lives. She was later refloated.
1882 Dec 2	Railway	Burnley, VIC	A head-on collision resulted in 7 deaths.

Date	Type	Place	Details
1882 Dec 12	Mining	Creswick, VIC	A flood in the Australasian gold mine (which has been restored and is now a tourist attraction) resulted in the deaths of 44 men. The toll would have been greater but for the bravery of Michael Carmody, who risked his life to warn 17 miners and lead them to safety.
1884–86	Drought	QLD, NSW, VIC and SA	This was a general period of drought, during which sheep and cattle numbers declined and crops were light. In 1885–86 the NSW wheat yield per acre was the lowest for 15 years, and in SA in 1885 it was the lowest on record.
1884 Jan 30	Cyclone	Bowen, QLD	Most houses in the town were unroofed.
1885 Jan 25	Railway	Near Cootamundra NSW	A derailment, caused by a flood, resulted in 7 deaths.
1886	Epidemic	Sydney	Outbreaks of typhoid occurred in the suburbs of Leichhardt and Balmain.
1886 Dec 7	Shipping	Off North Coast NSW	Thirty-six lives were lost when the steamship *Keilawarra* collided with the *Helen Nicol* and sank, between North and South Solitary Islands.
1886 Dec 24	Fire	Adelaide	The Academy of Music Theatre was burned down for the second time within 24 months, 2 firefighters being killed on this occasion.
1887 Mar 23	Mining	Bulli, NSW	This, the worst mining disaster in early Australian history, was found by a commission of enquiry to have been due to culpable negligence by management, but also to habitual carelessness by many miners. The mine entrance was on the side of a hill overlooking the town. Main drives, or 'headings' went horizontally into the hill, with smaller tunnels, or 'bords' branching out from them. The mine was notoriously gassy and members of the management had become lax regarding regulations; government inspectors had not been sufficiently diligent. The miners claimed that they were in danger of being sacked if they made too much fuss about the keeping of safety regulations; however many of them had developed the habit of taking the gauze screen which was designed to prevent the naked flame from igniting gas in the surrounding air, from their safety lamps; some also smoked at the coal face. A third potential cause of disaster at the particular time lay in the fact that a long strike had ended not long before, and more inexperienced men than usual were therefore working in the mine. On the night before the disaster gas had been ignited in one heading, without causing an explosion, but was not reported. Then, during the next afternoon, a massive explosion occurred in a bord about 1.5km along a heading. Its force was such that one miner, running towards the entrance, was blown through it, and landed (alive) about 100 metres away. Eighty-one men were killed.
1887 May 11	Railway	Windsor, VIC	Brake failure caused one train to run into another, causing the deaths of 7 people.
1887 Jun 21	Railway	Peat's Ferry NSW	Brake failure caused a train to get out of control, 6 people being killed when it collided with another.

1890–1899

Date	Type	Place	Details
1890 Feb 20	Shipping	Torres Strait	When the liner *Quetta* struck an uncharted rock (since named Quetta Rock), and sank within 3 minutes, 133 lives were lost. Fortunately other ships were quickly informed, and three which arrived at the scene were mainly responsible for the fact that there were 158 survivors.
1890	Floods	All colonies	Serious floods of this year included those in Brisbane, on the Darling River in NSW, and on the lower Murray River in SA, with general flooding also in the S-W of WA and in TAS.
1890 Oct 2	Fire	Sydney	Most of the buildings between Pitt Street, Castlereagh Street, Hosking Place and the present Martin Plaza were destroyed in a spectacular blaze.

Date	Type	Place	Details
1891 Sep 6	Shipping	Moonlight Head VIC	When the barque *Fiji* was wrecked at Moonlight Head, west of Cape Otway, 11 of the people on board, as well as one man engaged in rescue operations, were drowned. However 15 were rescued with the help of improvised rocket lifesaving apparatus.
1892 Apr 27	Railway	Tarana, NSW	A derailment caused 8 deaths.
1892 Jun 17	Fire	Sydney	The Theatre Royal — built on the site of the former Prince of Wales Theatre which had been burned down in 1860 and 1872 — was in its turn destroyed by fire.
1893 Feb	Flood	Brisbane	This was the first time that an Australian capital city had been struck by a really massive flood. Between late January and mid-February, three cyclones struck S-E QLD and the far north coast of NSW, bringing torrential rain. There was extensive flooding, but nowhere else was it comparable to that in Brisbane. By 5 February large areas of the central city and the riverside suburbs were under water, about 500 houses had been swept away, and debris had piled up against the Indooroopilly railway bridge and threatened its safety. During that day a loaded goods train was driven on to the bridge to keep it steady, but it soon became evident that this would be of no use, and the train was shunted back. Not long afterwards about half of the bridge was carried away, and on the following day the Victoria Bridge collapsed also. Meanwhile the gunboat *Paluma* and the 2000-ton steamship *Elamang* had been carried into the Botanic Gardens, where they were later left high and dry, and numerous smaller craft had been swept out to sea. After the first week of February the water level fell but on the 13th and 17th new peaks were reached, and the steamship *Lady Musgrave* was carried into New Farm Park, where she was deposited in the site of the present rose garden. They also floated the two vessels from the Botanic Gardens. The official death toll for the whole flood was 35, and it was claimed that nearly one-tenth of Brisbane's 90 000 people were left homeless. At one stage the water level at the Brisbane Post Office reached 31 ft 2 ins (about 9.5 m), which still stands as a record.
1894 Oct 31	Railway	Redfern, NSW	A head-on collision between a suburban and a country train caused 11 deaths.
1895 Aug 8	Shipping	Seal Rocks, NSW	The *SS Catterthun* was wrecked, with the loss of 31 lives.
1895–1903	Drought	All colonies	This was the longest and most severe period of drought in Australian history. It affected all six colonies, causing enormous stock losses and crop failures.
1895 Jul 18	Mining	Broken Hill, NSW	Nine men died in an accident at the South Broken Hill mine.
1896 Jan 26	Cyclone	Townsville, QLD	A cyclone caused damage from Townsville to Brisbane, but was most severe in Townsville, where 18 people died.
1896 Feb 13	Shipping	Brisbane	The *Pearl*, which was being used as a ferry during the reconstruction of the Victoria Bridge after the 1893 flood, fouled the anchor chains of the yacht *Lucinda* and sank. Twenty-eight bodies were recovered, but the death toll may have been higher.
1897 Jan 6	Cyclone	Darwin, NT	The town was struck by a cyclone more severe than any in its history except for Cyclone Tracy of 1974.
1897 Nov 21	Fire	Melbourne	A spectacular fire took place between Flinders Lane and Flinders, Elizabeth and Swanston Sts.
1897 Dec 31	Bushfire	TAS	A fire which spread from Mt. Wellington to other areas caused the deaths of at least 6 people.
1898 May	Shipping	Tasman Sea	The schooner *Adelaide*, with 7 on board left Newcastle but was never seen again.
1898 May 6	Shipping	Near Broken Bay, NSW	The paddle steamer *Maitland* was wrecked within sight of Barranjoey Lighthouse. The death toll was 27, but 35 people were saved after a seaman had swum ashore with a lifeline.
1899 Mar 4	Cyclone	Bathurst Bay, QLD	Cyclone Mahina proved to be the most destructive in terms of loss of life, in Australian history, sinking 55 vessels in the pearling fleet and killing over 300 people.

Date	Type	Place	Details
1900–1909			
1900	Epidemic	Sydney	Outbreaks of bubonic plague had occurred in parts of Asia and the Pacific during the previous year, and on 15 January a case was reported in Adelaide. However the epidemic which followed was centred in Sydney, where 103 people died from the plague during the year. Measures taken in order to minimise the spread of the disease included the removal of vast quantities of garbage from slum areas, and the killing of tens of thousands of rats.
1901 Feb 15	Railway	Sydenham, NSW	A train derailment caused 9 deaths.
1901 Mar 21	Shipping	Bass Strait	The *SS Federal*, en route from Port Kembla to Albany, WA, sank with the loss of 21 lives.
1901 Jul 10	Fire	Sydney	This was perhaps the most spectacular city fire in Sydney's history, and was one of the most tragic. It was first detected in the toy department of Sydney's largest store, Anthony Hordern and Sons'. Firemen's efforts to save the people in the store were hampered by the fact that their longest ladders could reach only a little more than halfway to the roof. Five of Anthony Hordern's employees died.
1902 Jul 31	Mining	Mt Kembla, NSW	The explosion in the Mt Kembla colliery on this day, killed 96, the greatest loss of life in any mining disaster in Australian history. Unlike the Bulli mine, where 81 men had died 15 years earlier, the Mt Kembla mine was regarded as being particularly safe — so much so that the miners did not normally use safety lamps. Early one afternoon there was an explosion so great that it caused a rockslide which covered the entrance to the main shaft and trapped more than 250 miners underground. Most managed to make their way to the surface, but the death toll was 96. A Royal Commission found that the tragedy had been caused by the naked flames of miners' lights igniting the gas, known as fire-damp, and by subsequent explosions of coal dust. It recommended that safety lamps be used in all south coast coal mines.
1903 Mar 9	Cyclone	Townsville, QLD	When Cyclone Leonta struck the town, 10 people died.
1903 May 26	Shipping	Off Point Stephens, NSW	*SS Oakland* was wrecked on Cabbage Tree Island, with the loss of 11 lives.
1906	Floods	Eastern States	The widespread floods of this year included those on the Fitzroy and Dawson Rivers in QLD, the inland rivers of NSW, the Campaspe, Glenelg, Wannon, Goulburn and Saltwater (Maribyrnong) Rivers in VIC, and the Murray River in SA.
1907 Jan 19	Cyclone & Shipping	Cooktown, QLD	A cyclone did great damage, and caused the ketch *Pilot* to sink off nearby Cape Flattery, with the loss of 6 lives.
1907 Apr 22	Shipping	Off Port Adelaide, SA	During the night, the barque *Norma*, which was at anchor, was rammed amidships by the *Ardencraig*, and sank with the loss of one crew member. A few hours later the *SS Jessie Darling* passed over the site, ripped her bottom open and settled on top of the *Norma*. The wreckage of both vessels was a danger to vessels approaching or leaving Port Adelaide until removed several years later.
1907 Sep 15	Fire	Murwillimbah, NSW	Fire destroyed 59 buildings in the business district.
1908 Apr 20	Railway	Sunshine, VIC	This, Victoria's worst rail disaster, occurred on Easter Monday, when many people were returning from holidays. A crowded train from Ballarat, running late, pulled up at Sunshine station, west of Melbourne. Moments later it was rammed from behind, at high speed, by another train, coming from Bendigo, which was not scheduled to stop at Sunshine. Damage to the Bendigo train was slight, but in the Ballarat train 44 people died and over 400 were injured, 72 of them seriously. The drivers of the two locomotives on the Bendigo train were later tried for manslaughter, the prosecution alleging that they had disregarded a warning signal. The leading driver, however, claimed that his brakes had failed, and both drivers were acquitted.

Date	Type	Place	Details
1910–1919			
1910 Jul 18	Railway	Richmond, VIC	Nine people died when a train hit a stationary locomotive.
1911–16	Drought	All States and NT	This was a period of general national drought, which varied, however, in duration from State to State. It was particularly long drawn-out in QLD, which suffered heavy cattle and sheep losses and had some poor cane harvests. The whole of NSW was drought-stricken by 1914, with the Riverina worst affected. In VIC conditions were worst in 1914, when the Murray stopped flowing below Swan Hill. SW and WA were hard hit from the beginning, with the amount of wheat harvested per acre dropping to the lowest figures ever recorded by 1914. In TAS the drought lasted from 1913 to 1915.
1911 Mar 24	Shipping	Cape Bowling Green, QLD	The SS Yongala, travelling from Brisbane to Townsville, sank in deep water with the loss of 120 lives during a cyclone. Although a wreck was located soon afterwards, it was not identified as being that of the Yongala until skin divers reached it in 1958.
1912 Mar 21	Shipping	Off Balla Balla, WA	The liner SS Koombana sank during a cyclone, with the loss of 149 lives, on her way from Port Hedland to Broome.
1912 Oct 12	Mining	Mt. Lyell, TAS	A fire in the North Lyle tin mine caused the death of 42 men by suffocation.
1914 Mar 16	Railway	Exeter, NSW	A rail collision at Exeter station caused the death of 14 people.
1914 Mar 27	Shipping	Cape Moreton, QLD	The SS Paul was wrecked, with the loss of 18 lives.
1914 Dec	Shipping	Southern Ocean	The Australian Fisheries Investigation steamship Endeavour sank while returning from Macquarie Island. All 24 on board were lost.
1916 Dec	Flood	Clermont, QLD	Floods, resulting from a cyclone, washed away most of the town, causing 62 deaths.
1916–17	Floods	All States	There was extensive flooding in QLD and TAS, and more localised floods in NSW, SA, VIC and
1918–20	Drought	All States & NT	A major national drought. VIC was the least affected State, only the northern and western districts suffering badly.
1918 Jan	Cyclone, Flood & Tidal Wave	Mackay, QLD	A violent cyclone sent a 3.5m tidal wave up the Pioneer River. When this met floodwaters rushing downstream, the town was flooded, with immense damage to property and the loss of 30 lives.
1918 Mar	Cyclone	Far North QLD	A particularly violent cyclone destroyed a large part of Innisfail, and caused damage also in Cairns, Ingham and Cardwell and on the Atherton Tableland. The death toll was 17.
1918 Sep 20	Shipping	Off Wollongong, NSW	The SS Undola sank with all hands. It was suspected that she may have hit a mine from the German raider Wolf.
1919-20	Epidemic	The whole of Australia	The virulent 'swine' or pneumonic influenza, which swept the whole world from about the end of World War I, and was thought to have killed more people than died in the war itself, reached Australia late in January 1919, and continued at epidemic levels until the following year. About half of the population was attacked, and in 1919 about 12 000 people died from the disease.
1920–1929			
1920 Sep	Shipwreck	Bass Strait	The barquentine Southern Cross, with 11 on board, disappeared on a voyage from Melbourne to TAS. Wreckage was found on King Island.
1920	Railway	NSW and WA	On Aug 3, a train shunted into the back of another at Hurstville, NSW, causing 5 deaths. On Nov 6, a timber train crashed at Wokalup, WA, causing 9 deaths.
1920–21	Bushfires	TAS	In 1920 the N-W suffered the worst bushfires since 1897, and in the following year the N-E met a similar fate.
1921 Jan 21	Cyclone	WA	A particularly extensive cyclone, over 1600 km in diameter, caused damage from Roebourne to Geraldton.
1921	Floods	Eastern and central Australia	Severe flooding in TAS, the N of SA, southern QLD, northern VIC, and on the Murrumbidgee and Murray Rivers.
1921 Jun	Shipping	Off NSW coast	On June 25 the small steamship Our Jack sank with the loss of 5 lives off the Manning River and on the very next day 30 out of 31 crew members drowned when the SS Fitzroy went down in a gale off Cape Hawke.

Date	Type	Place	Details
1921 Sep 19	Mining	Mt. Mulligan, QLD	A massive explosion at the Mt. Mulligan coal mine, 25 km from Chillagoe, killed 75 of the 76 men underground. The mine had been considered so free of firedamp that the miners used lamps with naked flames. However a commission of enquiry found that safety precautions in general had not been carried out well, and that explosives had been stored in the mine carelessly.
1921 Dec 6	Mining	Kalgoorlie, WA	Six died when a cage fell at the Golden Horseshoe mine.
1921–22	Epidemic	Brisbane & Sydney	An outbreak of plague, spread by rats from the *SS Wyreema*, caused 10 deaths in Sydney and 28 in Brisbane.
1923	Cyclone	Far N QLD	During the last week of March and the first week April, a cyclone struck the Torres Strait Islands, Cape York Peninsula and Groote Eylandt, and caused the *Douglas Mawson* to sink in the Gulf of Carpentaria with the loss of 20 lives.
1923 Sep 1	Mining	Cessnock, NSW	An explosion in the Bellbird colliery caused 20 deaths. Had it not occurred between shifts, the death toll could have been greater.
1924 Apr 26	Fire	Port Adelaide, SA	Three firemen were killed and 10 other people injured when petrol exploded during a fire on the *SS City of Singapore*.
1925	Flood	Murrumbidgee River, NSW	Floods on this river were among the worst ever. Great damage was done in Gundagai, Wagga Wagga and elsewhere.
1925 Jun 9	Railway	Traveston, QLD	When a train was derailed on a bridge, a carriage fell from the bridge and 10 people were killed.
1926 Feb	Bushfire	VIC	In this month fires spread throughout the State, but the worst were in the big timber country around Warburton, Powelltown and Noojee. The death toll was 31.
1926	Railway	VIC, NSW	Three railway accidents involving fatalities occurred in this year. On May 26 a collision at Caulfield, VIC caused 3 deaths. On Jan 10 the collapse of a bridge at Aberdeen, NSW, caused a train to overturn, with the loss of 5 lives. On September 13, a collision at Muralla, NSW, led to 27 deaths.
1927 Feb 19	Shipping	Off Terigal, NSW	The collier *Galava* foundered at night in fine weather, for reasons never satisfactorily explained, with the loss of 5 lives.
1927 Nov 3	Shipping	Sydney Harbour	On this day the wooden-hulled ferry *Greycliffe*, with about 100 people on board, was proceeding from Circular Quay to Watson's Bay. She was off Bradley's Head when the liner *Tahiti*, of nearly 8000 tons, hit her amidships, causing her to sink within two minutes. The death toll was not established exactly, but was certainly over 40. At the subsequent enquiry, Mr. Justice Campbell found that the *Tahiti* had been travelling at excessive speed, but that a change of course by the *Greycliffe* had also contributed to the accident.
1929	Air	N-W Australia	When Charles Kingsford Smith's *Southern Cross* was forced to land in the arid N-W, an air search was organised. Among those taking part were K. Anderson and R. Hitchcock, who were themselves forced to land with engine trouble. Not long afterwards *Southern Cross* was found, with its crew safe, but by the time Anderson and Hitchcock's plane was located both had died.
1929 Apr 4	Dam collapse	Derby, TAS	Following a cloudburst, a dam on the Cascade River gave way, and water poured into the town and down the shafts of a tin mine. The death toll was 14.
1930–1939			
1931	Floods	All States	Floods took place along the QLD coast in February; in NSW during most of the year, especially on the south coast and southern inland; in N and N-E VIC; in S of SA; along the Murray River; in N and E of TAS and S-W of WA.
1931 Feb 20	Mining	Wonthaggi, VIC	An explosion caused 4 deaths in the State coal mine.
1931 Mar 21	Air	Snowy Mountains	The disappearance of Australian National Airways' Avro Ten *Southern Cloud* with 8 on board during a flight from Sydney to Melbourne, was Australia's first, and perhaps most publicised, air mystery. In spite of intensive searching, no sign of the plane was found until 1958, when its wreckage was discovered in the Toolang Range, only 26 km away from the Sydney-Melbourne air route.

Date	Type	Place	Details
1932 Jul 10	Shipping	Apollo Bay, VIC	*SS Casino* was holed by her own anchor while berthing, and 9 lives were lost.
1933–36	Drought	TAS	A general period of drought, broken by winter rains in 1934.
1933 Jun 24	Shipping	Off Gabo Island, NSW	*SS Christina Fraser* disappeared with all 17 of her crew. Charles Kingsford Smith's *Southern Cross* took part in the search for her.
1934 Mar 11	Cyclone	Far N QLD	A cyclone, lasting for the following three days, sank many ships of the pearling fleet, and caused 75 deaths.
1934	Floods	All mainland States	There were floods in central QLD, especially around Charleville, along the QLD coast, in S-E NSW, around St. Vincent Gulf in SA and in the Fortescue, Grey and Central Coast divisions of WA. However, VIC suffered most, with severe flooding of the Yarra and in Gippsland, and the loss of 35 lives.
1934 Oct 19	Air	Off Wilson's Promontory, VIC	Holyman Airways' *Miss Hobart*, with 12 on board, disappeared during a Melbourne-Hobart flight.
1935 Mar 25	Cyclone	N-W Coast, WA	A cyclone lasting for the next 3 days sank 20 pearling vessels and caused 140 deaths.
1936–39	Drought	Mainland States	This was a period of general drought, reaching its peak at different times in various areas.
1936 Jan 1	Shipping	Bass Strait	*SS Paringa*, engaged in towing the tanker *Vincas* to Japan, sank in a gale with the loss of 31 lives.
1937 Feb 15	Mining	Wonthaggi, VIC	An explosion in the State coal mine caused 13 deaths. The toll would have been much higher but for the fact that a strike was in progress.
1937 Feb 16	Air	McPherson Range, QLD	The Airlines of Australia's Stinson A, *City of Brisbane*, crashed in dense rain forest, with 5 deaths. The disaster received great publicity because of the exploits of Bernard O'Reilly in locating the wreck and 2 survivors.
1937 Mar 11	Cyclone	Darwin, NT	A cyclone did great damage in and around Darwin, and killed 5 people.
1938 Feb 6	Surf	Bondi, NSW	A series of freak waves at Bondi Beach caused over 200 surfers to be swept out to sea. Mass rescue operations by lifesavers kept the death toll down to 5.
1938 Oct 25	Air	Mt Dandenong, VIC	Australian National Airways' DC2 *Kyeema* crashed in bad weather, 18 passengers and crew being killed.
1939 Jan	Bushfires,	VIC, NSW	Bushfires broke out in many parts of VIC early in this month — around Lorne and the Cape Otway region, in the Western District N of Portland, in parts of the Wimmera, and especially in the Great Dividing Range N-W of Melbourne. On 'Black Friday', February 13, those in the last-mentioned area reached their peak, destroying the town of Noojee and a number of sawmills, badly damaging other townships in the big timber country, and causing 71 deaths. Fires in southern NSW were also extensive, causing 6 deaths.

1940–1949

Date	Type	Place	Details
1940–45	Drought	Throughout Australia	The years 1936–45 were marked by a series of droughts, but the later part of the period was particularly disastrous, the two worst years being 1940 and 1944. In NSW, water restrictions were imposed in Sydney in 1940, and by early 1945 many rivers, including the Hunter, had ceased flowing. Elsewhere, Brisbane had water restrictions in 1940 and 1941 and Adelaide in 1945. In VIC the worst years were from 1943–45, and in 1944 the Murray River was at the lowest level ever recorded. Throughout Australia crop and stock losses were very heavy.
1940 Aug 13	Air	Canberra	An RAAF Lockheed Hudson crashed while coming in to land at Canberra with no survivors. Among the 10 dead were three Cabinet Ministers, namely Brigadier G.A. Street (Army), J.V. Fairbairn (Air) and Sir Henry Gullett (Vice-President of the Executive Council), as well as General Sir Cyril Brudenell White, Chief of the General Staff.
1940 Nov 26	Shipping	Port Phillip	*HMAS Goorangi*, an auxiliary minesweeper, was rammed by *MV Duntroon*, and sank with the loss of all 24 on board.

Date	Type	Place	Details
1942 Feb 19	Air raids	Darwin, NT	The first war attacks ever made on Australia (as distinct from its external territories) occurred when the Japanese launched two air raids on Darwin on this day. The first was aimed mainly at the wharfs and at ships in the harbour, but did great damage in the town also. The second concentrated on the RAAF base. Casualties were 243 killed and about 350 wounded — far greater than in any of the later raids on Darwin and other towns in N Australia. In the harbour the destroyer *USS Peary* was sunk by dive bombers, 7 other ships were either sunk directly or after catching fire, 3 were beached and 10 others were damaged. Those sunk after catching fire included the 5960-ton *Neptuna*, which was loaded with munitions, including a large number of depth charges, and which blew up spectacularly before going to the bottom. At a subsequent Commission of Enquiry it was established that a general alarm had not been given until the Japanese attackers were almost over the town, although warnings of the approach of many unidentified aircraft had been received from a coastwatcher on Melville Island nearly 40 minutes beforehand and from a priest at Bathurst Island Mission 20 minutes beforehand.
1942 Feb 20	Air	Belmont, QLD	The DH86A *Sydney* crashed with 9 dead.
1942 Apr 21	Air	Annaburoo Station, NT	A Lockheed 14 crashed, killing 12.
1942 May 31	Submarine attack	Sydney	On a number of occasions early in the Pacific war, the Japanese made use of two-man midget submarines, carried on the decks of large submarines until they were near their targets. On this occasion, five large submarines, three with midgets clamped to their decks, and at least one of the others carrying a very small spotter bi-plane, gathered some distance off Sydney Heads. In the early hours of May 30 a spotter plane was assembled and launched, and noted the presence in the harbour of the cruiser *USS Chicago* and a large number of other warships. On the evening of the following day the midget submarines set out. The first, No 14, became entangled in an anti-torpedo net and was detected, but its commander then blew it up. The second, referred to as Midget 'A' because its number was not ascertained, fired two torpedoes at *USS Chicago*. One torpedo passed underneath the cruiser, and blew up the former ferry *Kuttabul*, which was being used as quarters for naval ratings, 19 of whom were killed. The other torpedo failed to explode. Midget 'A' then made good her escape, but some time later the third submarine, No 21, which had been depth-charged near the Heads earlier in the action, penetrated the harbour defences. Hours of furious activity failed to find it, until late next morning it was discovered tangled in the anchor cable of a patrol boat, its officers having committed suicide.
1943 May 8	Railway	Near Wodonga, VIC	In Australia's worst level-crossing smash, 25 servicemen and servicewomen, travelling by bus, died.
1943 May 14	Shipping	Off Cape Moreton, QLD	The hospital ship *Centaur*, travelling to the war zone and with no patients on board, was torpedoed at night, and sank in a few minutes with the loss of 268 lives.
1944	Bushfires	VIC	Bushfires, mainly in Gippsland, caused 51 deaths. At one stage part of the brown coal seam at the Yallourn open-cut mine caught fire.
1944 Jan 20	Railway	Brooklyn, NSW	One of Australia's worst level-crossing accidents, involving a bus, caused 17 deaths.
1944 Jul 20	Air	Mount Kitchener, SA	A DH89 Rapide crashed, killing 7.
1945	Air	VIC, QLD, WA	Three notable air crashes occurred in this year: an Australian National Airlines' Stinson 2A-W *Tokana* near Redesdale, VIC, on January 31 (10 deaths); a Douglas DC3 at Horn Island, QLD, on May 5 (6 deaths) and of a DH86-A (formerly *Melbourne*) on June 24 at Geraldton, WA (10 killed).

Date	Type	Place	Details
1946 Mar 10	Air	Hobart	A Douglas DC3 crashed, killing 25.
1947	Railway	QLD	On May 5 QLD's worst rail accident occurred when 16 died in a derailment at Camp Mountain. On October 18 a head-on collision at Tamaree killed 8.
1947 Aug 7	Fire	Melbourne	A fire on the ship *Mahia* at Victoria Dock caused the death of 10 painters and dockers.
1948 Sep 2	Air	Quirindi, NSW	ANA's DC3 *Lutana* crashed, killing 13.
1948 Sep 28	Air	Lord Howe Island	The crash of a Consolidated Catalina flying boat killed 7.
1949	Cyclone	QLD	A week-long cyclone in late Feb and early Mar caused enormous damage between Rockhampton and Bundaberg and killed 4 people.
1949	Floods	Eastern Australia	This was a year of floods on the N and central coasts and inland rivers of NSW, in S and E VIC, and in inland QLD. Lake Eyre filled to a higher level than ever previously reported, and the waters of the Darling River spread to a width of over 80 km.
1949 Mar 10	Air	Coolangatta, QLD	The crash of a Queensland Airlines Lockheed Lodestar caused 21 deaths.
1949 Jul 2	Air	Guildford, WA	MacRobertson Miller Airlines' DC3 *Fitzroy* crashed, 18 dying.
1950–1959			
1950	Floods	NSW	At various times during this year coastal areas in NSW suffered from a combination of storms, floods and high seas. Several lives were lost during cyclonic conditions in January, but the worst month was June, when 26 died during severe flooding.
1950	Air	Near York, WA	ANA's DC4 *Amana* crashed, with the loss of 29 lives.
1951	Floods	QLD, NSW, VIC, WA	The areas most affected were the QLD tropical interior, the Richmond, Hunter, Nepean, Hawkesbury, Georges and Lachland Rivers in NSW, the Murray River, the Loddon and other W rivers in VIC, and the WA central coast.
1951	Bushfires	Throughout Australia	In SA fires raged in the Adelaide Hills in January, and 5 firefighters died. During the first few months of the year large areas were also burned out in central-western QLD and in the S-W of WA. In July a fire burned for 3 weeks around Newcastle Waters, NT. In TAS there were fires in a number of places, the worst being in the Huon district, where great quantities of marketable timber were destroyed. In the S of NSW fires which began in January were still burning at the end of the year, and finally claimed 6 lives.
1951 Feb 24	Railway	Horsham, VIC	In a collision between a bus and a train at a level crossing, 11 people died.
1952	Floods	NSW, VIC, TAS	The areas worst affected were several north coast rivers, and the Murrumbidgee, Lachlan and Macquarie Rivers in NSW; Gippsland and the Goulburn and Loddon Rivers in VIC, and the Derwent Valley in TAS.
1952	Bushfires	Vic	Widespread fire caused the loss of 10 lives during the first three months of the year.
1952 Mar 7	Railway	Berala, NSW	A suburban train crash caused the deaths of 10 people.
1952 Jun 7	Railway	Boronia, VIC	A collision between a bus and a train at a level-crossing caused 9 deaths.
1952 Sep 10	Shipping	Pacific Ocean	*MV Awahou* disappeared, with 12 on board, after leaving Sydney for Lord Howe Island.
1953 Dec 19	Railway	Sydenham, NSW	When a suburban train hit a stationary locomotive 5 people died.
1954 Feb	Floods	NSW, QLD, TAS	In QLD 10 died in floods at Rockhampton. In NSW at least 26 died, 22 of them in the Richmond River area. There was also flooding in E and S TAS.
1954 Oct 13	Mining	Collinsville, QLD	Seven men were asphyxiated by gas in the State coal mine.
1955 Jan 2	Bushfires	Adelaide	Fires in the Adelaide hills caused the deaths of 2 firefighters.
1955 Feb	Floods	NSW	There was serious flooding on the N-W inland rivers, but even worse troubles were experienced on the North Coast rivers, especially at Maitland, where the Hunter River reached a record height. Twenty-two people drowned, 11 of them in Maitland.
1955 Apr 10	Air	Forbes, NSW	An Auster crashed, killing 5.
1956 Jan	Floods	All States	Floods occurred in WA around Broome, throughout TAS, along the Murray River, throughout NSW, and on the Darling Downs, QLD.

Date	Type	Place	Details
1956 Mar	Cyclone	QLD	A cyclone caused great damage in Cairns and Townsville, and 4 people drowned in floods.
1956 Dec 1	Railway	Wallumbilla, QLD	Five were killed when a train hit stationary carriages.
1957 Jun 24	Air	Horn Island, QLD	A Lockheed Hudson crashed killing 6.
1957 Dec	Bushfires	Blue Mountains, NSW	Fire destroyed more than 150 houses and caused the deaths of 5 people.
1958 Apr 5	Bushfire	Wandilo district, SA	Eight firefighters died during this fire.
1958–59	Drought	Most mainland States	For all States except TAS and VIC, and for the NT, these years marked the beginning of a drought which lasted until 1968.

1960–1969

Date	Type	Place	Details
1960–68	Drought	Australia-wide	Except in S-E Australia, most of the continent had been suffering drought conditions from 1958 or 1959. In the 60s conditions worsened, and the S-E was afflicted also. Overall, the decade 1958–1968 must be ranked as a period of drought more widespread and disastrous for the nation as a whole than any since 1895–1902. In central Australia and the inland areas of NSW and QLD maximum severity was reached between 1964 and 1966. Most of VIC was comparatively untouched until 1965, but then suffered severely, especially in 1967. In TAS extremely dry conditions in 1966–67 led to disastrous bushfires around Hobart in 1967.
1960 Feb 20	Railway	Bogantungan, QLD	Seven people died when a bridge collapsed under a train.
1960 Apr	Floods	TAS	Hobart, the Derwent and Huon valleys and the southern midlands suffered their worst floods ever.
1960 Jun 10	Air	Mackay, QLD	Trans Australia Airlines (TAA) suffered its first fatal passengers accident when the Fokker Friendship *Abel Tasman* plunged into the sea after taking off from Mackay, 29 people perishing.
1961 Jan	Bushfires	S-W WA	Fires swept through enormous areas of jarrah forests, destroying the settlements of Holyoake and Nanga Brook and most of Dwellingup. Remarkably, no lives were lost.
1961 May 12	Air	Longreach, QLD	A Beech 95/55 crashed, 5 people being killed.
1961 Nov 30	Air	Botany Bay, NSW	A Vickers Viscount, owned by TAA but under charter to Ansett-ANA, crashed into the bay shortly after take-off, in bad weather, with 15 deaths.
1962	Bushfires	VIC	There were numerous fires early in the year. The worst, which spread from the Dandenongs, to within 20 km of the city centre, caused 8 deaths.
1963	Floods	NSW, QLD, NT, WA	There were severe floods on the inland rivers of NSW and QLD and around Darwin in the NT. In WA the town of Busselton was isolated by unprecedented floods. Meanwhile much of Australia was in the grip of drought.
1964 Feb 10	Shipping	Off Jervis Bay, NSW	The collision of the aircraft carrier *HMAS Melbourne* and the destroyer *HMAS Voyager*, which resulted in the death of 82 men from the latter, was Australia's worst peacetime disaster involving the armed services. During the exercises, the *Voyager* was ordered to change position, but in attempting to do so turned across *Melbourne's* path and was cut in two. At a subsequent Royal Commission it was found that the destroyer had caused the tragedy, but that it was impossible to identify the person or persons responsible. Qualified criticism was also expressed, however, of Captain Robertson and two other officers of the *Melbourne*. Shortly afterwards Captain Robertson was given a shore command and resigned from the Navy in protest. A number of prominent people, including MPs, were not satisfied with the Commission's finding, alleging that the captain of the *Voyager*, who had been killed, had been unfit to command because of a health condition which he had concealed, and that the criticism of Captain Robertson and his two officers had been unjustified. A second Royal Commission held in 1967, upheld these claims, and Captain Robertson was paid $60 000 tax free as an 'act of grace' in lieu of the superannuation rights which he had lost.

Date	Type	Place	Details
1965	Bushfires	NSW, VIC	Widespread bushfires in the early months caused 11 deaths.
1965 Nov 9	Mining	Bulli, NSW	A fire, caused by ignition of gas in a coal mine, caused 4 deaths.
1966	Air	SA, QLD, NT	Three notable aircraft crashes were a Cessna 175 near Canopus Homestead, SA on January 1, with 5 dead; an Ansett-ANA Vickers Viscount near Winton, QLD, on September 22, with 24 dead; and a Lockheed Hudson at Tennant Creek, NT. on September 24, with 6 dead.
1966 Aug 13	Fire	Melbourne	A fire in a men's hostel in the central city resulted in 30 deaths. This was Australia's most tragic building fire.
1966 Oct 21	Mining	Wyee, NSW	Collapse of a tunnel roof in a coal mine caused 5 deaths.
1966–67	Cyclones	QLD, NSW	Between November and March an unprecedented succession of cyclones struck the coast of QLD and N-NSW. These were followed in June by non-cyclonic storms. On QLD's Gold Coast the washing away of many waterfront buildings was prevented only by thousands of volunteers piling protective walls of sandbags.
1967 Feb 7	Bushfires	S-E TAS	During a period of only about 5 hours on this 'Black Tuesday' 54 people died and 1300 homes were destroyed in the Hobart area, and the death toll finally rose to 62. Heavy rains in the preceding winter and spring, followed by an unusually hot and dry summer had laid the ground for disaster, and by early February numerous fires were breaking out. They were considered to be reasonably under control until February 7, when gale force winds made it impossible to contain them, and they spread so fiercely that the smoke haze from them finally reached New Zealand.
1967 Dec 29	Air	Daly Waters, NT	Six died in the crash of a Cessna 206.
1968 Dec 31	Air	Near Port Hedland, WA	A McRobertson Miller Airlines Vickers Viscount crashed, killing 26.
1969 Jan 8	Bushfires	VIC	In widespread fires throughout VIC, 23 people died, most of them at Lara, near Geelong.
1969	Air	SA, VIC, NT	Light aircraft crashes during the year included: a Cessna 206 on February 8 at Kyancutta, SA (6 dead); a Cessna 210 near Mount Buangor, VIC on July 17 (5 dead); and a Cessna 402 at Gove, NT on December 22 (5 dead).
1969 Aug 25	Shipping	Off Smokey Cape, NSW	Only 5 out of the crew of 26 were rescued when the *MV Noongah* sank while taking a cargo of steel from Newcastle to Townsville.

1970–1979

Date	Type	Place	Details
1970 Jan	Cyclone	QLD	Thirteen lives were lost when Cyclone Ada struck the QLD coast and Barrier Reef holiday resorts.
1971 Jan 27	Air	Near Carnarvon, WA	Six were killed when a Piper PA23 crashed between Carnarvon and Jandakot, WA.
1971 Dec 4	Cyclone	QLD	Cyclone Althea caused great damage and loss of 3 lives in and around Townsville.
1972	Air	NT, NSW, SA	Crashes during this year included: a Beech 65/80 on January 20, near Alice Springs, NT (7 dead); a Cessna 310N on April 2 at Wilcurra Homestead, NSW (6 dead); and a Piper Navajo PA 31 on July 13 at Adelaide (8 dead).
1972 Jul 31	Mining	Box Flat, QLD	An underground explosion in the Box Flat coal mine, near Ipswich, killed 17 men.
1973 Mar 8	Fire	Brisbane, QLD	In one of Australia's most tragic building fires, 15 people died when the Whiskey A Go Go nightclub was deliberately set alight. Two men were jailed for the offence.
1973–74	Floods	All States and NT	Floods between July 1973 and June 1974 were among the most widespread in any 12-month period in Australian history. In WA the Transcontinental Railway was cut east of Kalgoorlie. In SA northern towns such as Oodnadatta, Maree, Moomba and Coober Pedy were isolated, the rail link to Alice Springs was cut and Lake Eyre filled. In January 1974 in Brisbane about 6700 homes were flooded and 12 people drowned, while many other QLD cities and towns suffered damage. In NSW there were floods on coastal rivers, particularly the Richmond and Bellinger. In TAS the St. Marys district was badly affected, and in VIC record heights were reached by the Ovens and Maribyrnong Rivers.

Date	Type	Place	Details
1974 Dec 25	Cyclone	Darwin, NT	The destruction of Darwin by Cyclone Tracy was the worst natural disaster, in terms of damage, in Australian history, and was among the worst in terms of lives lost. Fifty people died on land and 16 at sea, and more than half the houses in this city of 47 000 were damaged beyond repair. The cyclone had been moving across the Arafura Sea for several days, and at first was not expected to strike, or even pass very close to, Darwin. However during the 24 hours preceding the disaster it swung towards the S-E. It reached the city very late on Christmas Eve, and attained maximum force in the early hours of Christmas morning, registering a wind speed of 217 km/h at Darwin Airport before the gauge was broken. By the time day dawned, Darwin was cut off from the outside world, since radio transmitting towers had been blown down, telephone lines were cut, and even the defence forces' communications systems were out of action. It was the afternoon of Christmas Day before details of the disaster were known in Canberra. A rescue operation was then organised by Major-General Alan Stretton, director-general of the National Disasters Organisation. About 35 000 people were evacuated by air and sea, and the Darwin Reconstruction Commission was formed to plan rebuilding. By the end of 1977 the work of reconstruction was considered to be practically finished and the Commission went out of existence.
1974–75	Bushfires	NSW	Widespread fires in the W and others on the outskirts of Sydney caused great damage and the death of 3 people.
1975	Floods	All States	In February Maree and Oodnadatta in SA, were isolated by floods. In October and November floods occurred in TAS, in N and W Vic and along the Murray, Murrumbidgee and Lachlan. In December floods occurred in QLD, where the Condamine River reached its highest level of the twentieth century, and around Port Hedland, WA.
1975 Jan 5	Bridge collapse	Hobart	When the bulk carrier *Lake Illawarra*, loaded with zinc concentrates, hit a pier of the bridge spanning the Derwent, a large section of the roadway collapsed, killing 7 members of the ship's crew, and causing 5 motorists to die when their vehicles fell into the river. The bridge, opened only in 1964, had been designed with the possibility of such an accident in mind. However it had been presumed that only the piers at either side of the middle span would be in danger. These had therefore been protected with granite fenders, but the ship struck one of the minor piers. At the hearings of the subsequent Marine Court of Enquiry it was revealed that the *Lake Illawarra* had been affected by malfunctioning of its steering gear on the voyage from Port Pirie in SA. However the Court reported that the captain, whose record had previously been exemplary, had been guilty of careless navigation in this instance. It was October 1977 before the bridge had been repaired and reopened.
1975 Sep 21	Mining	Moura, QLD	A fire, caused by the explosion of methane gas, resulted in the deaths of 13 men at the Kianga coal mine.
1975 Dec 25	Fire	Sydney	A blaze in the Savoy Hotel, King's Cross, killed 15 people.
1977 Jan 18	Railway	Granville, NSW	This was by far the worst railway accident in Australia's history. Shortly after 8 a.m. a train, crowded with commuters from the Blue Mountains, left the tracks near Granville station, and hit the pylons supporting the four-lane Bold Street overpass. Nearly the whole roadway of the bridge, consisting of reinforced concrete, collapsed, crushing two of the train's carriages, and killing more than half of the people in them almost instantly. The final casualty list was 83 dead and 213 injured. The subsequent investigation by Judge J.H. Staunton exonerated the driver of the train, and attributed the tragedy to the poor condition of the railway tracks. His report was accompanied by an announcement by the Minister for Transport and Highways of a $200 million programme for the improvement of rail tracks throughout NSW.

Date	Type	Place	Details
1977	Bushfires	VIC, NSW	In February a widespread fire in the Western District of VIC caused the death of 5 people and up to 3 million sheep. In December a series of fires in the Blue Mountains, NSW, killed 2 people and caused enormous damage.
1978 Feb	Cyclone	WA	Five people died in the S-W of the State in storms associated with Cyclone Alby.
1978 Jul 10	Air	Essendon, VIC	When a Partavia P68B crashed, 6 occupants of a house near Essendon Airport were killed.
1979 Jul 24	Mining	Appin, NSW	An explosion of methane gas in a coal mine caused 14 deaths.

1980–1984

Date	Type	Place	Details
1980–83	Drought	NSW, VIC, QLD, SA	Although this period of drought was not as long as some earlier ones, at its height it was extremely severe. The first area to be seriously affected was the S-E of NSW, which had had a dry year in 1979. The area which was officially declared to be drought-affected spread steadily, until by mid-1982 conditions were critical over practically the whole of the eastern mainland States. Indeed, during a period of 6–7 months ending in November, large parts of NSW, VIC and SA had the lowest rainfall figures ever recorded for that part of the year. Dry conditions continued for a few months of 1983, but by mid-year the drought had broken.
1980	Bushfires	SA, VIC, NSW	This drought year saw many bushfires, most notably: in the Adelaide hills in February; in East Gippsland in October; and on the southern outskirts of Sydney (where 5 volunteer firemen died) in November.
1980 Feb 21	Air	Sydney Airport	Thirteen people died when a Beech Super King Air 200 crashed at take-off.
1981	Air	NSW, QLD	Air disasters included: a Cessna 210M missing near Barrington Tops, NSW, with 5 on board, on Aug 9; a Cessna 210 missing, with 5 on board, near Dungog, NSW, on Aug 9; and a Cessna 206 which crashed at Charleville, QLD, on Sep 21, with 7 dead.
1982	Air	QLD, VIC	Air disasters included: a Cessna 411A at Archerfield, QLD, on Jan 5; a Bell 206B Jet Ranger near Lang Lang, VIC, on Jan 7; and a Cessna 210-5, presumed lost at sea, N QLD, on Sept 30. Five lives were lost in each case.
1983	Bushfires	VIC, SA, NSW	Bushfires which were among the most tragic in Australian history occurred during the first few months of the year, when, after a severe drought, fire danger was at its highest. In January 3 fire-fighters died at Grays Point near Sydney, and 2 at Greendale, VIC. Then, in fires which ironically reached their height on Ash Wednesday, a total of 72 people died in the Dandenong Ranges and nearby, N-E of Melbourne, and in the Adelaide Hills.
1984 Mar	Cyclone	NT	More than 400 people were left homeless when Cyclone Cathy destroyed the town of Borroloola, on the Gulf of Carpentaria. Although it is thought to have caused the death of only one person, this cyclone was one of the fiercest on record, with wind gusts estimated at 280 km/h.

SUBJECT INDEX

To help you find the information you want on any specific topic, look up the subject in general, e.g., **ARTS, NATURAL HISTORY.** There you will find a list of entries in this encyclopedia which relate to that subject, together with the appropriate page number. Subject entries may also have sub-sections, e.g., **ARTS: Architecture, Ballet, Drama and Theatre, Film,** etc., under which you will find further entries relating to particular aspects of the subject.

To make it simpler to find the information, some entries are listed under more than one heading and, in the Natural History section, the strict biological classifications are not always adhered to.

Place-names (cities, towns, mountains, rivers, regions, districts) which do not appear in the index, are all listed alphabetically in the main text.

†indicates a major article on a subject, and a suitable starting point when following a particular line of research.

Numerals in *italic* type refer to colour illustrations and maps.

COMMUNICATIONS *see* **TRANSPORT
and COMMUNICATIONS**

CONVICTS *see* **HISTORY, Convicts and
Crime**

CONSTITUTION and LAW
see also **HISTORY; POLITICS and
POLITICIANS; SOCIETY**

DISASTERS
see also **HISTORY, Wars**

EDUCATION

Educationists

ELECTRICITY *see* **COMMERCE and
INDUSTRY; NATURAL
RESOURCES**

EXPLORATION

Explorers and Surveyors

sawfish *see* sharks, etc., 570
sea dragons *see* fishes, bony, 232
sea horses *see* fishes, bony, 232
sea moths *see* fishes, bony, 232
sea pike *see* fishes, bony, 232
sergeant Baker *see* fishes, bony, 232, *172*
sergeant-majors *see* fishes, bony, 232
†sharks and rays, 570, *579*
silver-biddies *see* fishes, bony, 232
skates *see* sharks, etc., 570
skipjacks *see* fishes, bony, 232
snappers *see* fisheries, 230; fishes, bony, 232
soles *see* fishes, bony, 232
spinefeet *see* fishes, bony, 232
spookfish *see* sharks, etc., 570
squids *see* cephalopods, 122
starfish *see* sea stars, 566
stingaree *see* fishes, poisonous and venomous, 243; sharks, etc., 570
sweet lips *see* fishes, bony, 232
sweet William *see* sharks, etc., 570
tailor *see* fishes, bony, 232
tandans *see* fishes, freshwater, 238
tarpon *see* fishes, bony, 232
teraglin *see* fishes, bony, 232
threadflies *see* fishes, bony, 232
toadoes *see* fishes, bony, 232; fishes, poisonous and venomous, 243, *579*
tobies *see* fishes, bony, 232
tommy ruff *see* fishes, bony, 232
tope *see* sharks, etc., 570
torpedo *see* sharks, etc., 570
trevallies *see* fishes, bony, 232
trout *see* fishes, freshwater, 238
trout, native *see* fishes, freshwater, 238
tuna *see* fisheries, 230; fishes, bony, 232
tunnies *see* fishes, bony, 232
wahoo *see* fishes, bony, 232
weevers *see* fishes, bony, 232
whalers *see* sharks, etc., 570
whitebait *see* fishes, bony, 232 ; fishes, freshwater, 238
white death *see* sharks, etc., 570
whitings *see* fisheries, 230; fishes, bony, 232
wobbegong *see* sharks, etc., 570, *579*
wrasses *see* fishes, bony, 232

Insects and their Allies
alder flies, 11
animals, venomous — arachnids, ants and bees, 20
antlions and lacewings, 24
ants, bees and wasps, 25
aphids, 27
arachnids, 28
arthropods, 37
back-swimmers *see* bugs, 100
bees *see* ants, etc., 25; bee-keeping, etc., 66
beetles, 66, *103*
biological control, 72
Blattodea *see* cockroaches, 132
blowflies, 82
booklice, 87
bristletails, 95
buffalo fly, 100
bugs, 100, *103*
butterflies and moths, 109, *104*
caddis flies, 111

centipedes, 121
chiggers *see* mites, 422
cicadas, 128
cluster flies *see* blowflies, 82
cockroaches, 132
Coleoptera *see* beetles, 66
cottony-cushion scale *see* biological control, 72
crickets and grasshoppers, 155, *103*
curl bug *see* beetles, 66
daddy-longlegs *see* harvestmen, 312; spiders, 602
damselflies and dragonflies, 166
Dermaptera *see* earwigs, 200
diplurans, 180
Diptera *see* flies, 246
dragonflies *see* damselflies, etc., 166, *103*
dun *see* mayflies, etc., 412
earwigs, 200
Embioptera *see* web-spinners, 683
Ephemeroptera *see* mayflies, 412
firebrat *see* bristletails, 95
fireflies *see* beetles, 66; flies, 246
fleas, 245
fleas, water *see* crustaceans, 157
flies, 246
froghoppers *see* bugs, 100
fungus gnats *see* flies, 246
glow worms *see* flies, 246
grass-grubs *see* butterflies, etc., 109
grasshoppers *see* crickets, etc., 155, *103*
greenfly *see* aphids, 27
grouse-locusts *see* crickets, etc., 155
harvestmen, 312
Hemiptera *see* bugs, 100
house fly, 327
Hymenoptera *see* ants, etc., 25
†insects, 337, *103*
†insects, introduced, 338
Isoptera *see* termites, 633
katydids *see* crickets, etc., 155
keds *see* flies, 246
lacewings *see* antlions, etc., 24
ladybirds *see* beetles, 66
lantern flies *see* bugs, 100
lawn scarab *see* beetles, 66
leaf-hoppers *see* bugs, 100
leaf insects *see* stick insects, 610
Lepidoptera *see* butterflies, etc., 109
lerps *see* bugs, 100
lice, 381
locusts, 391
louse *see* lice, 381
lucerne flea *see* springtails, 606
maggots *see* flies, 246
mantids, 405, *103*
Mantodea *see* mantids, 405
mayflies, 412
Mecoptera *see* scorpion flies, 557
Megaloptera *see* alder flies, 11
midges *see* flies, 246
millipedes, 419
mites, 422
mosquitoes, 432
moths *see* butterflies, etc., 109
Neuroptera *see* antlions, etc., 24
Odonata *see* damselflies, etc., 166
Orthoptera *see* crickets, etc., 155
pauropods, 495
peripatids, 497

phalangids *see* harvestmen, 312; spiders, 602
Phasmatodea *see* stick insects, 610
Phthiraptera *see* lice, 381
plant-hoppers *see* bugs, 100
Plecoptera *see* stoneflies, 611
praying mantid or mantis *see* mantids, 405, *103*
proturans, 526
pseudoscorpions, 526
Psocoptera *see* booklice, 87
sawflies *see* ants, etc., 25
scale insects *see* bugs, 100
scorpion flies, 557
scorpions, 557, *103*
silverfish *see* bristletails, 95
Siphonaptera *see* fleas, 245
spitfire grubs *see* ants, etc., 25
springtails, 606
stick insects, 610, *103*
stoneflies, 611
strepsipterans, 612
symphylids, 621
termites, 633
thrips, 637
Thysanoptera *see* thrips, 637
Thysanura *see* bristletails, 95
ticks, 638
tree-hoppers *see* bugs, 100
Trichoptera *see* caddis flies, 111
wasps *see* ants, etc., 25
water boatmen *see* bugs, 100
water scorpions *see* bugs, 100
web-spinners, 683
weevils *see* beetles, 66, *103*
'white-ants' *see* termites, 633
whiteflies *see* bugs, 100
wireworm *see* beetles, 66
woodwasps *see* ants, etc., 25
wood worm *see* beetles, 66
woolly bears *see* beetles, 66

Lizards and Reptiles
crocodiles, 155
dragons *see* lizards, 388, *426*
geckos *see* lizards, 388
goannas *see* lizards, 388
land mullet *see* lizards, 388
†lizards, 388
luth *see* tortoises, 642
monitors *see* lizards, 328
mountain devil *see* lizards, 388, *426*
mullet, land *see* lizards, 388
perentie *see* lizards, 388
†reptiles, 538, *426*
scaly-foots *see* lizards, 388
skinks *see* lizards, 388, *426*
tortoises and turtles, 642
turtles *see* tortoises, etc., 642, *426*

Mammals
ambergris *see* dolphins, etc., 190
†animals, introduced — mammals, 19
anteater, banded *see* native cats, etc., 457
anteater, spiny *see* monotreme mammals, 428
antechinus *see* native cats, etc., 457
baleen *see* dolphins, etc., 190
bandicoots, 53, *171*
bats, 61
bettongs *see* kangaroos, etc., 350

Hoad, L.A., 321
Hopman, H.C., 325
Laver, R.G., 372
McGregor, K., 397
Newcombe, J.D., 465
Quist, A.K., 532
Roche, T., 542
Rosewall, K.R., 547
Sedgman, F.A., 569
table tennis, 621
tennis, 631

SURVEYORS *see* **EXPLORATION,
Explorers and Surveyors**

TELEVISION *see* **RADIO and
TELEVISION**

**TRANSPORT and
COMMUNICATIONS**
see also **AVIATION**
aviation *see* transport, 650
Bradfield, J.J.C., 92
Cobb & Co., 131
Interscan, 339
overland telegraph, 480
Pichi Richi Pass, 504
postage stamps, 521, *443, 444*
postal and telecommunications services,
  522
Qantas *see* transport, 650
railways *see* transport, 650
roads *see* transport, 650
shipping *see* transport, 650
Sydney Harbour Bridge, 620
telephone services *see* postal and
  telecommunications services, 522
Todd, Sir C., 640
Torrumbarry Weir, 642
†transport, 650, *647*

TREES *see* **NATURAL HISTORY,
BOTANY**

VEGETATION *see* **NATURAL
HISTORY, BOTANY**

WEATHER *see* **GEOGRAPHY and
CLIMATE**

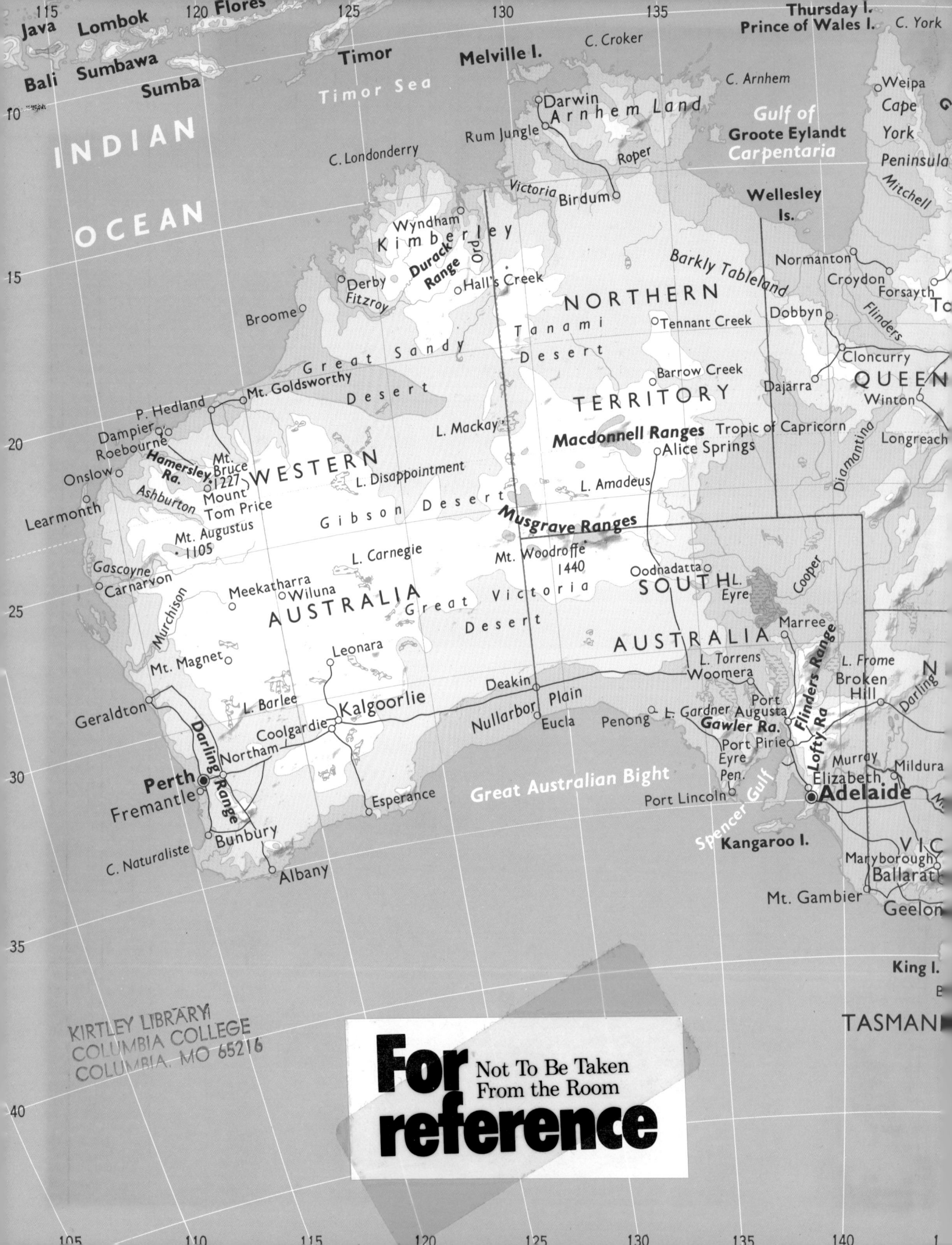

Latitude labels (left edge): 10, 15, 20, 25, 30, 35, 40

Longitude labels (top): 115, 120 Flores, 125, 130, 135

Map labels:

Java, Lombok, Flores, Thursday I., Prince of Wales I., C. York

Bali, Sumbawa, Timor, Melville I., C. Croker, C. Arnhem, Weipa

Sumba, Timor Sea, Darwin, Arnhem Land, Gulf of Groote Eylandt, Cape, York

INDIAN, Rum Jungle, Roper, Carpentaria, Peninsula, Mitchell

C. Londonderry, Victoria, Birdum, Wellesley Is., Normanton, Croydon, Forsayth

OCEAN, Wyndham, Kimberley, Durack Range, Hall's Creek, NORTHERN, Barkly Tableland, Dobbyn, Flinders, To

Derby, Fitzroy, Tanami, Desert, Tennant Creek, Cloncurry, QUEEN

Broome, Great Sandy, Barrow Creek, Dajarra, Winton

Mt. Goldsworthy, Desert, TERRITORY, Macdonnell Ranges, Tropic of Capricorn, Longreach

P. Hedland, L. Mackay, Alice Springs, Diamantina

Dampier, Roebourne, Hamersley Ra., Mt. Bruce (1227), WESTERN, L. Disappointment, L. Amadeus

Onslow, Ashburton, Mount Tom Price, Gibson Desert, Musgrave Ranges, SOUTH

Learmonth, Mt. Augustus ·1105, L. Carnegie, Mt. Woodroffe 1440, Oodnadatta, AUSTRALIA, Cooper

Gascoyne, Meekatharra, Wiluna, AUSTRALIA, Great Victoria, Eyre, Marree

Carnarvon, Murchison, Desert, L. Torrens, Woomera, Flinders Range, L. Frome, Broken Hill, N

Mt. Magnet, Leonara, SOUTH AUSTRALIA, Port Augusta, Lofty Ra., Darling

Geraldton, L. Barlee, Kalgoorlie, Deakin, Gawler Ra., Port Pirie, Murray, Mildura

Coolgardie, Northam, Nullarbor Plain, Eucla, Penong, Eyre Pen., Elizabeth, Adelaide

Perth, Fremantle, Darling Range, Esperance, Great Australian Bight, Port Lincoln, Spencer Gulf, VIC

Bunbury, C. Naturaliste, Albany, Kangaroo I., Maryborough, Ballarat, Geelon

Mt. Gambier, King I., TASMAN